Biography
Almanac

Related Titles from Gale

American Diaries. This two-volume work is a chronologically arranged annotated bibliography of published American diaries and journals written from 1491 to 1980. Entries include full bibliographic information and are extensively annotated, indicating such information as historic events, modes of travel, diary's emphasis, religious affiliation, personal names, background on the diarist, and more.

Biographical Dictionaries and Related Works. A reference guide to over 16,000 biographical dictionaries. Entries are arranged in three sections: Universal Biography, National or Area Biography, and Biography by Vocation with indexes by author, title, and subject.

Biography and Genealogy Master Index. A multi-volume compilation containing 3.25 million citations to biographical articles appearing in more than 350 contemporary who's whos and other works of collective biography, including historical as well as present-day men and women of note. Updated and expanded by annual supplements through 1986, the 1981 through 1985 supplements have been cumulated into a five-volume single alphabetically sequenced set.

Contemporary Newsmakers. Four quarterly issues furnish up-to-date biographical profiles on people in the news. Covering all fields, from business and international affairs to literature and the arts, the articles feature photographs of individuals along with biographical and career data. *Contemporary Newsmakers* is annually cumulated into a hardbound volume.

In Black and White. This work identifies over 15,000 notable blacks in America, Africa, and elsewhere and the magazines, books, and newspapers in which information about them may be found. Entries provide full name, birth and/or death dates, occupation, and a list of publications where more information may be found. Also available: interedition supplement providing new and updated entries for about 7,000 notable blacks.

Pseudonyms and Nicknames Dictionary. Uncovers over 50,000 pseudonyms and nicknames used by some 40,000 individuals. Included are historical as well as contemporary figures from all walks of life. Entries furnish original and assumed names, birth and/or death dates, nationality and occupation, and codes indicating sources of additional information.

ISSN 0738 0097

Biography Almanac

A comprehensive reference guide to more than 24,000 famous and infamous newsmakers from Biblical times to the present as found in over 550 readily available biographical sources

THIRD EDITION

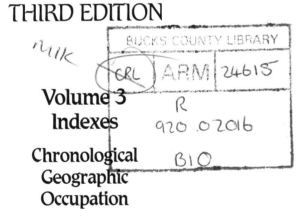

Volume 3
Indexes

Chronological
Geographic
Occupation

Susan L. Stetler, Editor

Gale Research Company • Book Tower
Detroit, Michigan 48226

Editor: Susan L. Stetler

Editorial Assistants: Michael Mengden and Alicia S. Robinson

Research Assistants: Evabelle MacKay and Elizabeth Rentenbach

External Production Supervisor: Mary Beth Trimper
External Senior Production Associate: Dorothy Kalleberg
External Production Assistants: Linda Davis and Darlene K. Maxey
Art Director: Arthur Chartow
Internal Production Supervisor: Laura Bryant
Internal Production Associate: Louise Gagne
Internal Senior Production Assistant: Sandra M. Rock

Editorial Data Systems Director: Dennis LaBeau
Editorial Data Systems and Programming Supervisor: Diane H. Belickas
Editorial Data Systems Program Design: Al Fernandez, Jr. and Barry Trute

Publisher: Frederick G. Ruffner
Editorial Director: Dedria Bryfonski
Associate Editorial Director: Ellen T. Crowley
Senior Editor, Research: Anne M. Brewer

Library of Congress Cataloging in Publication Data

Biography almanac. — 1st ed.- — Detroit, Mich.: Gale Research
   Co., c1981-

    v.; 21 cm.

   Irregular.
   Vols. for 1983-   issued in parts.
   Supplements issued between editions.
   Editor: 1981-   A. Brewer.
   ISSN 0738-0097 = Biography almanac.

   1. Biography—Periodicals. 2. Biography—Indexes—Periodicals. 3. Biography—Indexes.   I. Brewer, Annie M.   II. Gale Research Company.
CT104.B56   920'.02—dc19   83-641014
                                    AACR 2   MARC-S

Contents

Volume 1

Volume 2

Volume 3

Introduction

The third volume of *Biography Almanac* contains three indexes of interest to the researcher and trivia buff. New to this edition is the inclusion of an Occupation Index. The Occupation Index lists all *Biography Almanac* entrants by the occupation(s) found in the main entry in the Biographies Volumes. This allows the reader to see everyone with a similar occupation grouped together. For example, the presidents of the United States are given the occupation US President and appear alphabetically in the Occupation Index under that listing; likewise all of the hockey players are found under Hockey Player. Entrants with more than one occupation in their main entry can be under each of the occupations in the Occupation Index.

Actor
Brosnan, Pierce
Brown, Bryan
Caan, James
Hagman, Larry
Heston, Charlton
Hoffman, Dustin
Holden, William
Holloway, Stanley
Moore, Roger
Redford, Robert
Redgrave, Michael Scudamore, Sir
Reed, Oliver
Reed, Robert
Selleck, Tom
Sellers, Peter Richard Henry
Williams, Billy Dee
Williams, Robert
Willis, Bruce

Chronological Index and Geographic Index Updated, Expanded

The other indexes—Chronological Index and Geographic Index—were included in the second edition, but have been expanded and updated reflecting the new material contained in the Biographies Volumes.

The Chronological Index lists all *Biography Almanac* entrants who were born or died in a specific month on a specific day. The year of birth or death appears before the entrant's name in chronological order. For example, this index lists 69 people who were born on July 4 and 38 people who died on July 4.

July 4
b. 1918 Landers, Ann
b. 1918 Van Buren, Abigail
b. 1920 Garraty, John Arthur
b. 1924 Saint, Eva Marie
b. 1927 Simon, Neil
b. 1928 Boyd, Stephen
b. 1928 Lollobrigida, Gina
b. 1931 Hudson, Joseph Lowthian, Jr.
d. 1826 Adams, John
d. 1826 Jefferson, Thomas
d. 1831 Monroe, James
d. 1848 Chateaubriand, Francois Rene de

The Geographic Index enables the user to find everyone who was born or who died in a specific location. The index is divided into three general sections: the United States, Canada, and Foreign. The United States is further broken down by state and then by city within the state; Canada is broken down by province and city; and Foreign is in alphabetical order by country and city within the country. Below each city are the names of those people listed in *Biography Almanac* who were either born or who died in that location, followed by the birth or death date. Under New York, New York, for example Norman Rockwell is listed with his birthdate, Feb. 3, 1984, and Nelson Rockefeller is listed with his deathdate, Jan. 26, 1979. Rockwell also appears under Stockbridge, Massachusetts, with his deathdate and Rockefeller appears under Bar Harbor, Maine, with his birthdate.

MASSACHUSETTS
Stockbridge, Massachusetts
Bowker, R(ichard) R(ogers)
   d. Nov. 12, 1933
Field, Cyrus West b. Nov 30, 1819
French, Daniel Chester d. Oct 7, 1931
Hopkins, Mark b. Feb 4, 1802
Niebuhr, Reinhold d. Jun 1, 1971
Rockwell, Norman d. Nov 8, 1978
Sedgwick, Catherine Maria b. Dec 28, 1789

MAINE
Bar Harbor, Maine
Ralston, Esther b. 1902
Rockefeller, Nelson A(ldrich) b. Jul 9, 1908

The trivia buff will be interested in the names appearing in the Geographic Index under Woodland Hills, California. Most of them are deaths and all of the people who died there were actors and actresses. Further research reveals that the Motion Pictures Country Home, a retirement home for actors and actresses, is located in Woodland Hills. Also, the Dominican Republic has always been a hotbed for major league baseball players, and the names listed under the Dominican Republic in the Geographic Index confirm this.

Biography Almanac

Indexes

Chronological Index

b. 1932 Moore, Terry
b. 1936 Allen, Richard Vincent
b. 1940 Jahn, Helmut
b. 1940 Langella, Frank
b. 1943 Britz, Jerilyn
b. 1943 Novello, Don
b. 1955 Hoyt, Lamarr (Dewey Lamarr)
b. 1958 Silk, Dave
d. 379 Basil (the Great), Saint
d. 1730 Sewall, Samuel
d. 1732 Nicolini
d. 1782 Bach, Johann Christian
d. 1787 Middleton, Arthur
d. 1793 Guardi, Francesco
d. 1854 Place, Francis
d. 1858 Leslie, Eliza
d. 1881 Blanqui, Louis Auguste
d. 1894 Hertz, Heinrich Rudolph
d. 1896 Beach, Alfred Ely
d. 1901 Donnelly, Ignatius
d. 1904 Pabst, Frederick
d. 1923 Keeler, "Wee Willie" (William Henry)
d. 1934 Wassermann, Jakob
d. 1940 Tallmadge, Thomas Eddy
d. 1942 Hackett, Charles
d. 1944 Lutyens, Edwin Landseer, Sir
d. 1948 May, Edna
d. 1949 Campbell, Malcolm, Sir
d. 1953 Williams, "Hank" (Hiram)
d. 1954 Norwich, Alfred Duff Cooper, Viscount
d. 1956 Hague, Frank
d. 1958 Weston, Edward
d. 1960 Sullavan, Margaret
d. 1962 Fairless, Benjamin F
d. 1963 Kerr, Robert Samuel
d. 1963 Mead, George Houk
d. 1966 Auriol, Vincent
d. 1969 Fleming, Ian
d. 1969 MacLane, Barton
d. 1971 Ford, Arthur A
d. 1972 Chevalier, Maurice Auguste
d. 1974 Loeffler, Kenneth D
d. 1978 Ascoli, Max
d. 1978 Davis, Hal Charles
d. 1980 Deutsch, Adolph
d. 1980 Nenni, Pietro
d. 1981 Menuhin, Hephzibah
d. 1981 Michalowski, Kazimierz
d. 1982 Buono, Victor (Charles Victor)
d. 1982 Grahame, Margot
d. 1984 Korner, Alexis
d. 1986 Friedman, Max

January 2

b. 1647 Bacon, Nathaniel
b. 1727 Wolfe, James
b. 1752 Freneau, Philip Morin
b. 1803 Thurber, Charles
b. 1810 Miller, Alfred Jacob
b. 1830 Flagler, Henry Morrison

b. 1830 Kingsley, Henry
b. 1837 Balakirev, Mili Alekseyevich
b. 1857 Opper, Frederick Burr
b. 1857 Thomas, Martha Carey
b. 1865 Phelps, William Lyon
b. 1866 Murray, Gilbert (George Gilbert Aime)
b. 1870 Barlach, Ernst Heinrich
b. 1881 Varley, F(rederick) H(orseman)
b. 1886 Lawrence, Florence
b. 1889 Schipa, Tito
b. 1894 Nathan, Robert
b. 1894 Rodzinski, Artur
b. 1895 Bernadotte, Folke, Count
b. 1895 Leonidoff, Leon
b. 1901 Ralf, Torsten
b. 1904 Melton, James
b. 1904 Rand, Sally
b. 1905 Tippett, Michael Kemp, Sir
b. 1905 Zampa, Luigi
b. 1906 Campbell, E Simms
b. 1911 Glass, David Victor
b. 1916 Neumann, Robert Gerhard
b. 1917 Zorina, Vera
b. 1919 Hicks, Beatrice Alice
b. 1920 Asimov, Isaac
b. 1926 Bush-Brown, Albert
b. 1927 Evers, Jason
b. 1927 Marchetti, Gino
b. 1928 Rostenkowski, Daniel David
b. 1930 LaRosa, Julius
b. 1932 Little, (Flora) Jean
b. 1936 Miller, Roger Dean
b. 1939 Bakker, Jim (James Orsen)
b. 1947 Hill, Calvin
d. 1783 Bodmer, Johann Jakob
d. 1801 Lavater, Johann Casper
d. 1850 Peel, Robert, Sir
d. 1879 Cushing, Caleb
d. 1887 Newberry, John Stoughton
d. 1891 Kinglake, Alexander William
d. 1892 Meigs, Montgomery Cunningham
d. 1904 Longstreet, James
d. 1915 Goldmark, Karl
d. 1916 Lamar, Joseph Rucker
d. 1917 Tylor, Edward Bennett, Sir
d. 1924 Baring-Gould, Sabine
d. 1928 Fuller, Loie
d. 1928 Stevens, Emily A
d. 1940 Casey, Edward Pearce
d. 1952 Davidson, Jo
d. 1963 Carson, Jack
d. 1963 Powell, Dick
d. 1965 Hansberry, Lorraine
d. 1966 Millikan, Clark Blanchard
d. 1966 Wilkins, Ernest Hatch
d. 1969 Miller, Gilbert Heron
d. 1971 Knox, E(dmund) G(eorge) V(alpy)
d. 1972 Gilbreth, Lillian Moller
d. 1974 Bohlen, Charles Eustis
d. 1974 Cord, E(rret) L(obban)

d. 1974 Ritter, "Tex" (Woodward Maurice)
d. 1977 Garner, Erroll
d. 1981 Keener, Jefferson Ward
d. 1981 Lynch, David
d. 1981 Watts, Richard, Jr.
d. 1982 Hampton, Hope
d. 1982 Harman, Fred
d. 1983 Seiler, James, W
d. 1985 Cushman, Robert Everton, Jr.
d. 1986 Gaines, Clarence F
d. 1986 Gunn, Hartford Nelson, Jr.
d. 1986 Veeck, Bill (William Louis)

January 3
b. 106 BC Cicero, Marcus Tullius
b. 1698 Metastasio, Pietro
b. 1793 Mott, Lucretia Coffin
b. 1806 Sontag, Henriette
b. 1831 Fenn, George Manville
b. 1840 Damien, Father
b. 1840 Holt, Henry
b. 1867 Lytton, Henry Alfred, Sir
b. 1870 Richardson, Henry Handel, pseud.
b. 1875 Tchernichovski, Saul Gutmanovich
b. 1876 Pieck, Wilhelm
b. 1879 Coolidge, Grace Anne Goodhue
b. 1883 Adler, David
b. 1883 Attlee, Clement Richard Attlee, Earl
b. 1886 Fletcher, John Gould
b. 1888 Bridie, James, pseud.
b. 1888 Morrison of Lambeth, Herbert Stanley Morrison, Baron
b. 1892 Tolkien, J(ohn) R(onald) R(euel)
b. 1893 Seldes, Gilbert Vivian
b. 1897 Davies, Marion
b. 1898 Loder, John
b. 1898 Ryan, T(ubal) Claude
b. 1900 Arzner, Dorothy
b. 1900 Pitts, Zasu (Eliza Susan)
b. 1900 Russell, Donald Joseph
b. 1906 Morgan, William Wilson
b. 1907 Wong, Anna May (Lu Tsong)
b. 1908 Milland, Ray(mond Alton)
b. 1909 Borge, Victor
b. 1909 Crankshaw, Edward
b. 1911 Hazam, Lou(is J)
b. 1913 Chute, Beatrice Joy
b. 1914 Bodard, Lucien Albert
b. 1915 Dempsey, John Noel
b. 1915 Levine, Jack
b. 1916 Furness, Betty (Elizabeth Mary)
b. 1916 King, Warren Thomas
b. 1917 Straus, Roger W(illiams), Jr.
b. 1917 Walters, Vernon Anthony
b. 1918 Andrews, Maxine
b. 1919 White, Jesse
b. 1922 Travers, Bill
b. 1926 Anglund, Joan Walsh
b. 1926 Blumenthal, W Michael
b. 1932 Coleman, Dabney
b. 1932 Fenten, D X

b. 1934 Hills, Carla Anderson
b. 1936 Einhorn, Eddie (Edward Martin)
b. 1936 Rollin, Betty
b. 1936 Ruppee, Loret Miller
b. 1939 Hull, Bobby (Robert Martin)
b. 1944 Lacey, Robert
b. 1944 Principal, Victoria
b. 1945 Stills, Stephen
b. 1946 Jones, John Paul
d. 1543 Cabrillo, Juan Rodriguez
d. 1785 Galuppi, Baldassare
d. 1795 Wedgwood, Josiah
d. 1858 Rachel
d. 1875 Larousse, Pierre Athanase
d. 1882 Ainsworth, W(illiam) H(arrison)
d. 1894 Peabody, Elizabeth Palmer
d. 1895 Ives, James Merritt
d. 1912 Evans, Robley Dunglison
d. 1916 Dodge, Grenville Mellen
d. 1919 Duveneck, Frank
d. 1923 Hasek, Jaroslav
d. 1930 Briggs, Clare
d. 1933 Pickford, Jack
d. 1941 Bergson, Henri Louis
d. 1945 Cayce, Edgar
d. 1947 Reid, Ogden Mills
d. 1949 Aitken, Robert
d. 1950 Jannings, Emil
d. 1951 Howell, Albert S
d. 1956 Gretchaninov, Aleksandr Tikhonovich
d. 1959 Muir, Edwin
d. 1960 Everleigh, Ada
d. 1960 Sjostrom, Victor
d. 1960 Spry, Constance
d. 1965 Avery, Milton (Clark)
d. 1966 Higgins, Marguerite
d. 1967 Ruby, Jack
d. 1970 Aylward, Gladys
d. 1972 Wilson, Charles Edward
d. 1974 Daley, Arthur
d. 1975 Cross, Milton John
d. 1979 Hilton, Conrad Nicholson
d. 1980 Adamson, Joy Friederike Victoria Gessner
d. 1981 Alice (Mary Victoria Augusta Pauline)
d. 1982 Canham, Erwin Dain
d. 1983 Bond, George Foote

January 4
b. 1581 Ussher, James
b. 1679 Wolcott, Roger
b. 1710 Pergolesi, Giovanni Battista
b. 1785 Grimm, Jakob Ludwig Karl
b. 1790 Berryer, Pierre Antoine
b. 1809 Braille, Louis
b. 1813 Pitman, Isaac
b. 1831 Dutton, E(dward) P(ayson)
b. 1838 Tom Thumb, General
b. 1855 Brann, William Cowper
b. 1858 Glass, Carter

b. 1870 Pitt, Percy
b. 1874 Suk, Josef
b. 1877 Hartley, Marsden
b. 1878 Coppard, A(lfred) E(dgar)
b. 1878 John, Augustus Edwin
b. 1881 Lehmbruck, Wilhelm
b. 1881 Merola, Gaetano
b. 1883 Eastman, Max Forrester
b. 1884 DuBois, Guy Pene
b. 1887 Witte, Edwin Emil
b. 1894 Woody, Regina Llewellyn Jones
b. 1895 Grumman, Leroy Randle
b. 1896 Dirksen, Everett McKinley
b. 1901 Berger, Raoul
b. 1902 McCone, John A
b. 1905 Holloway, Sterling
b. 1908 Columbo, Russ
b. 1910 Crawford, James Strickland
b. 1910 Paul, Gabe (Gabriel)
b. 1912 Helmore, Tom
b. 1914 Wyman, Jane
b. 1920 Colby, William Egan
b. 1922 Battelle, Phyllis Marie
b. 1925 Lujack, John(ny)
b. 1929 Etzioni, Amitai Werner
b. 1929 Rush, Barbara
b. 1930 Shula, Don Francis
b. 1932 Saura Carlos (Atares Carlos)
b. 1935 Patterson, Floyd
b. 1937 Bumbry, Grace Ann Jaeckel
b. 1938 Cannon, Dyan
b. 1941 Reagan, Maureen
b. 1942 McLaughlin, John
b. 1943 Kearns, Doris H
b. 1951 Cochran, Barbara Ann
d. 1782 Gabriel, Ange-Jacques
d. 1789 Nelson, Thomas, Jr.
d. 1821 Seton, Elizabeth Ann Bayley, Saint
d. 1877 Vanderbilt, Cornelius
d. 1880 Feuerbach, Anselm
d. 1882 Draper, John William
d. 1891 Keene, Charles Samuel
d. 1905 Thomas, Theodore
d. 1908 Young, Charles Augustus
d. 1914 Mitchell, Silas Weir
d. 1920 Dodge, John Francis
d. 1920 Perez Galdos, Benito
d. 1931 Connor, Roger
d. 1942 Skinner, Otis
d. 1956 Damon, Ralph Shepard
d. 1957 Espinosa, Al
d. 1960 Camus, Albert
d. 1961 Fitzgerald, Barry
d. 1961 Schroedinger, Erwin
d. 1964 Dumke, Ralph
d. 1965 Eliot, T(homas) S(tearns)
d. 1967 Campbell, Donald Malcolm
d. 1967 Garden, Mary
d. 1969 Hilton, Daisy
d. 1969 Hilton, Violet

d. 1974 Starrett, Vincent (Charles Vincent Emerson)
d. 1975 Montana, Bob
d. 1976 Leventhal, Albert Rice
d. 1979 Bennett, Harry Herbert
d. 1981 Rabin, Yehuda L
d. 1982 Banning, Margaret Culkin
d. 1983 Rosenthal, Benjamin Stanley
d. 1984 Geschwind, Norman
d. 1986 Isherwood, Christopher William
d. 1986 Merkel, Una

January 5
b. Lange, Ted
b. 1779 Decatur, Stephen
b. 1855 Gillette, King Camp
b. 1864 Carver, George Washington
b. 1864 Hodge, Frederick Webb
b. 1869 Jones, Matilda Sissieretta Joyner
b. 1871 Converse, Frederick Shepherd
b. 1874 Erlanger, Joseph
b. 1875 Blackton, James Stuart
b. 1876 Adenauer, Konrad
b. 1877 Coffin, Henry Sloane
b. 1879 Norworth, Jack
b. 1880 Sachse, Leopold
b. 1882 Swope, Herbert Bayard
b. 1887 Hodges, Courtney
b. 1890 Kauff, Benny (Benjamin Michael)
b. 1895 Piccard, Jeannette Ridlon
b. 1897 Jessup, Philip Caryl
b. 1900 Tanguy, Yves
b. 1902 Gibbons, Stella Dorethea
b. 1906 Davison, William
b. 1907 Marsala, Joe
b. 1909 Aumont, Jean-Pierre
b. 1909 Kurnitz, Harry
b. 1913 Wilson, Kemmons
b. 1917 Wagner, Wieland Adolf Gottfried
b. 1918 Dixon, Jeane Pinckert
b. 1919 Gazzelloni, Severino
b. 1919 Ryder, Alfred
b. 1920 Michelangeli, Arturo Benedetti
b. 1920 Wingler, Hans Maria
b. 1921 Durrenmatt, Friedrich
b. 1921 Jean, Grand Duke of Luxembourg
b. 1923 Phillips, Sam
b. 1925 Opel, John Roberts
b. 1926 Schell, Maria Margarethe
b. 1926 Snodgrass, W(illiam) D(eWitt)
b. 1926 Williams, Hosea Lorenzo
b. 1928 Bhutto, Zulfikar Ali
b. 1928 Mondale, Walter Frederick
b. 1931 Ailey, Alvin
b. 1931 Brendel, Alfred
b. 1931 Davis, Walter
b. 1931 Duvall, Robert Selden
b. 1932 Layden, Frank (Francis Patrick)
b. 1932 Noll, Chuck (Charles H)
b. 1938 Agee, William McReynolds
b. 1938 Juan Carlos I
b. 1941 McKinley, Chuck (Charles Robert)

b. 1946 Keaton, Diane
b. 1947 Morris, "Mercury" (Eugene)
b. 1947 Switzer, Katherine Virginia
b. 1949 Brown, George
b. 1954 Martin, Pamela Sue
b. 1958 Kittle, Ron(ald Dale)
b. 1960 Kerr, Tim
d. 1066 Edward the Confessor
d. 1589 Catherine de Medici
d. 1796 Huntington, Samuel
d. 1867 Smith, Alexander
d. 1886 Lippincott, Joshua Ballinger
d. 1922 Shackleton, Ernest Henry, Sir
d. 1933 Coolidge, (John) Calvin
d. 1941 Johnson, Amy
d. 1943 Carver, George Washington
d. 1946 Joyce, William
d. 1948 Harrison, Mary Scott Lord
      Dimmick
d. 1954 Maranville, "Rabbit" (Walter
      James Vincent)
d. 1954 Scott, Walter
d. 1956 LaFarge, Christopher
d. 1956 Mistinguett
d. 1963 Hornsby, Rogers
d. 1969 Yablonski, Joseph
d. 1970 Born, Max
d. 1971 Liston, "Sonny" (Charles)
d. 1971 Shearer, Douglas
d. 1974 Brogan, Denis William, Sir
d. 1976 Costello, John Aloysius
d. 1977 Stevens, Onslow
d. 1979 Mingus, Charles
d. 1981 Martin, James, Sir
d. 1982 Conreid, Hans
d. 1982 Lembeck, Harvey

January 6
b. 1412 Joan of Arc
b. 1730 Chittenden, Thomas
b. 1799 Smith, Jedediah Strong
b. 1811 Sumner, Charles
b. 1822 Schliemann, Heinrich
b. 1832 Dore, Gustave (Paul Gustave)
b. 1838 Bruch, Max
b. 1842 King, Clarence
b. 1845 Lee-Hamilton, Eugene Jacob
b. 1850 Bernstein, Eduard
b. 1869 Wagner, Siegfried (Helferich)
b. 1872 Scriabin, Alexander Nicholaevich
b. 1874 Niblo, Fred
b. 1878 Sandburg, Carl August
b. 1879 Patterson, Joseph Medill
b. 1880 Mix, Tom
b. 1882 Pecora, Ferdinand
b. 1882 Rayburn, Sam(uel Taliaferro)
b. 1887 Kelly, George Edward
b. 1889 Craven, Thomas
b. 1896 Pritzker, Abram Nicholas
b. 1900 Hulme, Kathryn Cavarly
b. 1903 Abravanel, Maurice
b. 1903 Sullivan, Francis Loftus

b. 1907 Valentino, Francesco
b. 1908 DiSalle, Michael Vincent
b. 1910 Morris, Wright Marion
b. 1911 Adams, Joey
b. 1912 Manfred, Frederick Feikema
b. 1913 Brown, Tom (Thomas Edward)
b. 1913 Gierek, Edward
b. 1913 Young, Loretta Gretchen
b. 1914 Thomas, Danny
b. 1915 Lilly, John C
b. 1915 Watts, Alan Wilson
b. 1917 Jumblatt, Kamal Fouad
b. 1919 Cleaver, Vera Allen
b. 1920 Moon, Sung Myung
b. 1920 Wynn, Early
b. 1921 Harris, Louis
b. 1921 Middlecoff, Cary
b. 1923 Timerman, Jacobo
b. 1924 Kim Dae Jung
b. 1924 Scruggs, Earl
b. 1925 DeLorean, John Zachary
b. 1926 Branca, Ralph Theodore Joseph
b. 1926 Gavilan, Kid
b. 1928 Behn, Noel
b. 1929 Tayback, Vic
b. 1930 Keniston, Kenneth
b. 1931 Doctorow, E(dgar) L(aurence)
b. 1935 Capucine
b. 1939 Rose, Murray
b. 1944 Franklin, Bonnie Gail
b. 1945 Freeman, Seth
b. 1953 Young, Malcolm
b. 1957 Lopez, Nancy
b. 1959 Sledge, Kathy
d. 1542 Orley, Bernard van
d. 1725 Chikamatsu, Monzaemon
d. 1785 Salomon, Haym
d. 1793 Goldoni, Carlo
d. 1831 Kreutzer, Rodolphe
d. 1840 Burney, Fanny (Frances)
d. 1849 Coleridge, Hartley
d. 1855 Wood, Sarah Sayward Barrell
      Keating
d. 1882 Dana, Richard Henry, Jr.
d. 1884 Mendel, Gregor Johann
d. 1906 Krauss, Gabrielle
d. 1913 Schott, Anton
d. 1919 Roosevelt, Theodore
d. 1932 Rosenwald, Julius
d. 1939 Kelly, Walter C
d. 1942 Calve, Emma
d. 1942 Flannagan, John Bernard
d. 1943 Lowell, Abbott Lawrence
d. 1944 Tarbell, Ida Minerva
d. 1946 Summerville, "Slim" (George J)
d. 1949 Fleming, Victor
d. 1950 Brady, William Aloysius
d. 1959 Cohen, Octavus Roy
d. 1963 Vandercook, John Womack
d. 1963 Young, Stark
d. 1966 Lurcat, Jean Marie

d. 1970 Hynes, John B
d. 1972 Pully, B S
d. 1974 Siqueiros, David A
d. 1975 Wheeler, Burton Kendall
d. 1977 Gropper, William
d. 1978 Gordon, John F
d. 1978 MacArthur, John Donald
d. 1981 Cronin, A(rchibald) J(oseph)
d. 1981 Neal, Larry (Lawrence P)
d. 1981 Urey, Harold Clayton
d. 1982 Crawford, William Hulfish
d. 1984 Welch, Robert Henry Winborne, Jr.
d. 1985 Horrocks, Brian Gwynne, Sir

January 7

b. 1718 Putnam, Israel
b. 1745 Montgolfier, Jacques Etienne
b. 1768 Bonaparte, Joseph
b. 1800 Fillmore, Millard
b. 1829 Angell, James Burrill
b. 1830 Bierstadt, Albert
b. 1832 Talmadge, Thomas de Witt
b. 1844 Bernadette of Lourdes
b. 1858 Ben-Yehuda, Eliezer
b. 1863 Lloyd George of Dwyfor, David Lloyd George, Earl
b. 1867 Maginnis, Charles Donagh
b. 1871 Horder, Thomas Jeeves
b. 1873 Zukor, Adolph
b. 1879 McCann, Alfred Watterson
b. 1880 Rollins, Carl Purington
b. 1881 Gest, Morris
b. 1883 Cunningham, Andrew Browne, Viscount
b. 1884 Giovannitti, Arturo
b. 1893 Wayman, Dorothy
b. 1899 Poulenc, Francis
b. 1901 Brownlee, John
b. 1903 Hurston, Zora Neale
b. 1903 Pauley, Edwin Wendell
b. 1905 Dent, Alan Holmes
b. 1907 Zabaleta, Nicanor
b. 1908 Allen, "Red" (Henry James, Jr.)
b. 1908 Gibberd, Frederick
b. 1910 Faubus, Orval Eugene
b. 1911 Baker, Laura Nelson
b. 1911 McQueen, "Butterfly" (Thelma)
b. 1912 Addams, Charles Samuel
b. 1913 Mize, Johnny (John Robert)
b. 1916 Estes, E(lliott) M(arantette)
b. 1918 Lasky, Victor
b. 1919 Duncan, Robert
b. 1922 Gardenia, Vincent
b. 1923 Dark, Alvin Ralph
b. 1925 Durrell, Gerald Malcolm
b. 1926 Kirk, Claude Roy, Jr.
b. 1928 Blatty, William Peter
b. 1930 Kiker, Douglas
b. 1931 Mattingly, Mack Francis
b. 1933 Kneip, Richard
b. 1934 Murphy, (John) Reg(inald)

b. 1935 Kubasov, Valery Nikolaevich
b. 1936 Davies, Hunter
b. 1940 Berkow, Ira Harvey
b. 1945 Conigliaro, Tony (Anthony Richard)
b. 1947 Wenner, Jann
b. 1948 Loggins, Kenny (Kenneth Clarke)
b. 1956 Liut, Mike (Michael)
b. 1957 Janaszak, Steve
d. 1536 Catherine of Aragon
d. 1715 Fenelon, Francois de Salignac
d. 1830 Lawrence, Thomas, Sir
d. 1872 Fisk, Jim (James)
d. 1926 Mueller, Christian F
d. 1927 Stanton, Frank Lebby
d. 1931 Channing, Edward
d. 1932 Maginot, Andre
d. 1943 Crile, George Washington
d. 1943 Tesla, Nikola
d. 1944 Hoover, Lou Henry
d. 1950 Banks, Monty (Montague)
d. 1953 Johnson, Osa Helen Leighty
d. 1956 Tucker, Preston Thomas
d. 1958 Anglin, Margaret Mary
d. 1971 Kollmar, Richard
d. 1972 Berryman, John
d. 1975 Abercrombie, James Smither
d. 1977 Stuckey, Williamson
d. 1978 Flanner, Janet
d. 1982 Post, Wally (Walter Charles)
d. 1983 Coates, Edith
d. 1983 Hanks, Nancy
d. 1984 Case, Anna
d. 1984 Hunt, Jack Reed
d. 1984 Kastler, Alfred
d. 1985 Guarnieri, Johnny (John A)
d. 1985 Lyons, Eugene

January 8

b. 1735 Carroll, John
b. 1786 Biddle, Nicholas
b. 1792 Mason, Lowell
b. 1821 Longstreet, James
b. 1823 Wallace, Alfred Russell
b. 1824 Collins, Wilkie (William)
b. 1830 VonBulow, Hans Guido
b. 1836 Alma-Tadema, Lawrence, Sir
b. 1862 Doubleday, Frank Nelson
b. 1864 Johnson, (Byron) Ban(croft)
b. 1867 Balch, Emily G
b. 1869 Genthe, Arnold
b. 1870 Holmes, Burton
b. 1880 Kurt, Melanie
b. 1881 Neihardt, John Gneisenau
b. 1881 Piper, William Thomas
b. 1883 Hurley, Patrick Jay
b. 1885 Curtin, John
b. 1890 Clark, Bennett Champ
b. 1891 Kiplinger, W(illard) M(onroe)
b. 1891 Nijinska, Bronislava
b. 1892 O'Connor, Basil
b. 1893 Kindler, Hans

b. 1896 Weinberger, Jaromir
b. 1899 Adams, Sherman Llewellyn
b. 1901 Malenkov, Georgi Maximilianovich
b. 1902 Rogers, Carl Ransom
b. 1902 Smith, Kenneth Danforth
b. 1904 Arno, Peter
b. 1908 Frankau, Pamela
b. 1911 Watt, George Willard
b. 1912 Ferrer, Jose Vicente
b. 1914 Watson, Thomas John, Jr.
b. 1917 Taylor, Peter
b. 1922 Simon, Abbey
b. 1923 Storch, Larry
b. 1923 Tozzi, Giorgio
b. 1924 Moody, Ron
b. 1926 Geschwind, Norman
b. 1926 Mori, Hanae
b. 1928 Gorton, Slade
b. 1928 Vanocur, Sander
b. 1930 Sales, Soupy
b. 1931 Graham, Bill
b. 1933 Osgood, Charles
b. 1935 Presley, Elvis (Elvis Aaron)
b. 1937 Bassey, Shirley
b. 1939 Mimieux, Yvette Carmen M
b. 1941 Chapman, Graham
b. 1943 Murray, Charles Alan
b. 1946 Krieger, Robby
b. 1947 Bowie, David
b. 1953 Stastny, Marian
b. 1953 Sutter, (Howard) Bruce
b. 1955 Reno, Mike
d. 1337 Giotto di Bondone
d. 1642 Galileo
d. 1713 Corelli, Arcangelo
d. 1775 Baskerville, John
d. 1825 Whitney, Eli
d. 1890 McArthur, John
d. 1892 Rodgers, Christopher Raymond
Perry
d. 1896 Verlaine, Paul Marie
d. 1914 Buckner, Simon B
d. 1916 Rehan, Ada
d. 1919 O'Rourke, Jim (James Henry)
d. 1920 Powell, Maud
d. 1925 Bellows, George Wesley
d. 1929 Duke, Benjamin Newton
d. 1934 Bely, Andrey, pseud.
d. 1941 Baden-Powell, Robert Stephenson
Smyth Baden-Powell, Baron
d. 1948 Tauber, Richard
d. 1950 Schumpeter, Joseph Alois
d. 1952 Maury, Antonia Caetana De Paiua
Pereira
d. 1960 Haynes, George Edward
d. 1961 Rowe, "Schoolboy" (Lynwood
Thomas)
d. 1965 Onions, Charles Talbut
d. 1967 Heim, Jacques
d. 1968 Van Paassen, Pierre
d. 1972 Patchen, Kenneth

d. 1975 Gregson, John
d. 1975 Tucker, Richard
d. 1976 Chou En-Lai
d. 1978 Kiernan, Walter
d. 1978 Ross, Roy G
d. 1981 Beard, Matthew, Jr.
d. 1981 Jagendorf, Moritz
d. 1982 Shaw, Reta
d. 1983 McCall, Thomas Lawson
d. 1986 Fournier, Pierre

January 9
b. 1590 Vouet, Simon
b. 1674 Keiser, Reinhard
b. 1724 Backus, Isaac
b. 1728 Warton, Thomas
b. 1837 Chesebrough, Robert Augustus
b. 1856 Reese, Lizette Woodworth
b. 1857 Fuller, Henry Blake
b. 1859 Catt, Carrie Chapman
b. 1867 Urlus, Jacques
b. 1870 Strauss, Joseph Baermann
b. 1873 Bialik, Chaim Nachman
b. 1878 Watson, John Broadus
b. 1881 Abercrombie, Lascelles
b. 1881 Papini, Giovanni
b. 1886 Brooks, Walter R(ollin)
b. 1886 Holt, Ivan Lee
b. 1886 Rosenthal, Ida Cohen
b. 1890 Capek, Karel
b. 1894 Goldberg, Ben Zion
b. 1894 Markel, Lester
b. 1898 Fields, Gracie
b. 1900 Halliburton, Richard
b. 1901 Young, "Chic" (Murat Bernard)
b. 1902 Bing, Rudolf(Franz Josef), Sir
b. 1903 Banky, Vilma
b. 1904 Balanchine, George
b. 1908 Beauvoir, Simone de
b. 1908 Trefflich, Henry Herbert Frederick
b. 1910 Hitch, Charles Johnston
b. 1913 Donahue, Woolworth
b. 1913 Nixon, Richard Milhous
b. 1915 Mikkelsen, Henning Dahl
b. 1916 Holland, Jerome Heartwell
b. 1916 Pease, James
b. 1917 Louise, Anita
b. 1918 Chaikin, Sol Chick
b. 1922 Toure, Ahmed Sekou
b. 1925 Lamas, Fernando
b. 1925 Van Cleef, Lee
b. 1928 Krantz, Judith
b. 1929 Friel, Brian
b. 1929 Matheson, Scott Milne
b. 1930 Sloane, Dennis
b. 1934 Starr, Bart (Bryan B)
b. 1935 Denver, Bob
b. 1938 Woods, Stuart
b. 1941 Baez, Joan
b. 1941 York, Susannah
b. 1944 Page, Jimmy (James Patrick)
b. 1945 Biondi, Frank J, Jr,

b. 1950 Stein, James R
b. 1951 Gayle, Crystal
b. 1958 McClanahan, Rob
d. 1324 Marco Polo
d. 1868 Hopkins, John Henry
d. 1872 Halleck, Henry
d. 1873 Napoleon III
d. 1876 Howe, Samuel Gridley
d. 1878 Victor Emmanuel II
d. 1893 Judson, Egbert Putnam
d. 1904 Gordon, John Brown
d. 1908 Busch, Wilhelm
d. 1923 Mansfield, Katherine
d. 1930 Bok, Edward William
d. 1936 Gilbert, John
d. 1938 Gruelle, Johnny (John Barton)
d. 1942 Curtis, Heber Doust
d. 1943 Collingwood, Robin George
d. 1947 Mannheim, Karl
d. 1951 Nethersole, Olga
d. 1954 Braniff, Thomas Elmer
d. 1961 Balch, Emily G
d. 1966 Foerster, Friedrich Wilhelm
d. 1967 Frank, Waldo
d. 1971 Flick, Elmer Harrison
d. 1972 Shawn, Ted (Edwin Meyers)
d. 1976 Granger, Lester
d. 1976 Taylor, Phoebe Atwood
d. 1979 Nervi, Pier Luigi
d. 1982 Musso, Vido
d. 1984 Gibberd, Frederick
d. 1985 Mayer, Robert
d. 1986 Chase, Lucia
d. 1986 Powolny, Frank

January 10
b. 1769 Ney, Michel de la Moskova, Prince
b. 1804 Ames, Oakes
b. 1820 Drew, Louisa Lane
b. 1834 Acton, John Emerich Edward Dalberg-Acton, Baron
b. 1835 Wright, Harry (William Henry)
b. 1859 U'Ren, William Simon
b. 1860 Roberts, Charles George Douglas, Sir
b. 1873 Christy, Howard Chandler
b. 1880 Bayes, Nora
b. 1882 Sills, Milton
b. 1883 Bushman, Francis X(avier)
b. 1885 Gifford, Walter Sherman
b. 1887 Jeffers, (John) Robinson
b. 1889 Held, John, Jr.
b. 1892 Malone, Dumas
b. 1895 Davis, Meyer
b. 1898 Blodgett, Katherine Burr
b. 1903 Hepworth, Barbara
b. 1903 Roos, Frank John, Jr.
b. 1904 Bolger, Ray
b. 1904 Burck, Jacob
b. 1907 Shenker, Morris Abraham
b. 1908 Henreid, Paul

b. 1908 Lee, Bernard
b. 1910 Martinon, Jean
b. 1910 Ulanova, Galina
b. 1911 Kirkpatrick, Ralph
b. 1913 Husak, Gustav
b. 1913 Shehu, Mehmet
b. 1915 Dixon, Dean
b. 1918 Chung, Arthur
b. 1921 Ward, Rodger
b. 1924 Chillida, Eduard
b. 1927 MacKenzie, Gisele
b. 1927 Ray, Johnnie (John Alvin)
b. 1928 Brooks, Donald Marc
b. 1928 Levine, Philip
b. 1929 Charlip, Remy
b. 1931 Galella, Ron
b. 1931 Sanders, Marlene
b. 1935 Milnes, Sherrill Eustace
b. 1936 Crane, Daniel B
b. 1938 Mahovlich, Frank (Francis William)
b. 1938 McCovey, Willie Lee
b. 1939 Horowitz, David Joel
b. 1939 Mineo, Sal
b. 1939 Toomey, Bill (William)
b. 1941 Caputo, Philip Joseph
b. 1943 Annaud, Jean-Jacques
b. 1943 Croce, Jim
b. 1944 Sinatra, Frank, Jr. (Francis Albert)
b. 1945 Stewart, Rod(erick David)
b. 1947 Morris, James Peppler
b. 1948 Fagen, Donald
b. 1949 Browne, Walter Shawn
b. 1949 Foreman, George
b. 1952 Benatar, Pat
b. 1963 Leveille, Normand
d. 1645 Laud, William
d. 1778 Linnaeus, Carolus
d. 1785 Stiegel, Henry William
d. 1862 Colt, Samuel
d. 1880 Leslie, Frank, pseud.
d. 1883 Mudd, Samuel Alexander
d. 1906 Harper, William Rainey
d. 1908 Spreckels, Claus
d. 1917 Cody, "Buffalo Bill" (William Frederick)
d. 1937 Eddy, Clarence
d. 1941 Lavery, John, Sir
d. 1941 Penner, Joe
d. 1946 Cullen, Countee
d. 1946 VonTilzer, Harry
d. 1950 Poole, Ernest
d. 1951 Lewis, Sinclair
d. 1957 Mistral, Gabriela
d. 1957 Wilder, Laura Elizabeth Ingalls
d. 1961 Hammett, (Samuel) Dashiell
d. 1967 Burchfield, Charles
d. 1968 Reuther, Roy
d. 1969 Brownlee, John
d. 1969 Lamburn, Richmal Crompton
d. 1970 Olson, Charles

d. 1971 Cacers, Ernest
d. 1971 Chanel, "Coco" (Gabrielle)
d. 1972 Goodman, Al(fred)
d. 1972 Gulbenkian, Nubar Sarkis
d. 1975 Chamberlain, Samuel
d. 1976 Howlin' Wolf
d. 1978 Braden, Spruille
d. 1978 Gillis, Don
d. 1980 Meany, George
d. 1981 Brodie, Fawn McKay
d. 1982 Lynde, Paul Edward
d. 1984 Souvanna, Phouma
d. 1986 Kraft, Joseph
d. 1986 Seifert, Jaroslav

January 11

b. 938 Scargill, Arthur
b. 1503 Parmigiano
b. 1757 Hamilton, Alexander
b. 1759 Lunardi, Vincenzo
b. 1801 Kirkland, Caroline Matilda
Stansbury
b. 1807 Cornell, Ezra
b. 1814 Paget, James, Sir
b. 1815 MacDonald, John Alexander
b. 1825 Taylor, Bayard
b. 1839 Simmons, Franklin
b. 1842 James, William
b. 1850 Arthur, Joseph Charles
b. 1856 Sinding, Christian
b. 1858 Selfridge, Harry Gordon
b. 1859 Curzon of Kedleston, George
Nathaniel Curzon, Marquis
b. 1865 Dixon, Thomas
b. 1868 Ruhlmann, Francois
b. 1870 Rice, Alice Caldwell Hegan
b. 1871 Eddy, Sherwood
b. 1873 Morrow, Dwight Whitney
b. 1875 Gliere, Reinhold Moritzovich
b. 1876 Flick, Elmer Harrison
b. 1884 Fitch, Aubrey
b. 1885 Paul, Alice
b. 1886 Zucco, George
b. 1888 Conklin, Chester
b. 1889 Bridges, Calvin Blackman
b. 1890 Blue, Monte
b. 1890 Carey, Max George
b. 1893 Pasero, Tancredi
b. 1894 Ballinger, Margaret (Violet
Margaret Livingstone)
b. 1895 Hammond, Laurens
b. 1897 DeVoto, Bernard Augustine
b. 1898 Pierrot, George Francis
b. 1899 LeGallienne, Eva
b. 1902 Lahey, Edwin A(loysius)
b. 1903 Paton, Alan Stewart
b. 1905 Lee, Manfred B(ennington)
b. 1907 Mendes-France, Pierre
b. 1909 Stander, Lionel
b. 1910 Bratteli, Trygve Martin
b. 1910 Solomon, Izler

b. 1912 Rowe, "Schoolboy" (Lynwood
Thomas)
b. 1919 McCurdy, Ed
b. 1921 Kreps, Juanita Morris
b. 1923 Ashley, Thomas William Ludlow
b. 1924 Guillemin, Roger
b. 1926 Tinker, Grant A
b. 1928 Wolper, David Lloyd
b. 1930 Stacey, Thomas Charles Gerard
b. 1930 Taylor, Rod(ney)
b. 1931 Rodgers, Mary
b. 1934 Rafshoon, Gerald Monroe
b. 1935 Mears, Walter R(obert)
b. 1936 Hesse, Eva
b. 1942 Clemons, Clarence
b. 1947 Calder-Marshall, Anna Lucia
b. 1952 Crenshaw, Ben Daniel
b. 1957 Dawkins, Darryl
b. 1963 Caulkins, Tracy
d. 1494 Ghirlandaio, Domenico
d. 1788 Grasse, Count Francois Joseph
Paul de
d. 1797 Lee, Francis Lightfoot
d. 1801 Cimarosa, Domenico
d. 1817 Dwight, Timothy
d. 1836 Molson, John
d. 1837 Field, John
d. 1837 Gerard, Francois
d. 1843 Key, Francis Scott
d. 1874 Borden, Gail
d. 1893 Butler, Benjamin Franklin
d. 1909 Wharton, Joseph
d. 1928 Hardy, Thomas
d. 1931 Straus, Nathan
d. 1935 Sembrich, Marcella
d. 1940 Mellor, Walter
d. 1941 Bridge, Frank
d. 1941 Lasker, Emanuel
d. 1942 Nast, Conde
d. 1943 Guiterman, Arthur
d. 1944 Christie, John Walter
d. 1944 Ciano (di Cortellazzo), Conte
Galeazzo
d. 1944 King, Charles
d. 1947 Tanguay, Eva
d. 1949 Doubleday, Nelson
d. 1949 Friesz, Othon
d. 1952 Lattre de Tassigny, Jean de
d. 1952 Pertile, Aureliano
d. 1954 Straus, Oskar
d. 1955 Graziani, Rodolfo
d. 1962 Adler, Elmer
d. 1966 Giacometti, Alberto
d. 1966 Shastri, Lal Badahur
d. 1968 Stabile, Mariano
d. 1970 March, Hal
d. 1975 Lorenz, Max
d. 1976 Schoonmaker, Frank Musselman
d. 1978 Leibowitz, Samuel Simon
d. 1979 Soo, Jack
d. 1980 Pym, Barbara Mary Crampton

d. 1981 MacDonald, Malcolm John
d. 1982 Horikoshi, Jiro
d. 1983 Podgorny, Nikolai Viktorovich
d. 1984 LaRue, Jack
d. 1984 Licavoli, Peter Joseph, Sr.

January 12
b. 1588 Winthrop, John
b. 1628 Perrault, Charles
b. 1729 Burke, Edmund
b. 1729 Spallanzani, Lazzaro
b. 1737 Hancock, John
b. 1746 Pestalozzi, Johann Heinrich
b. 1834 Marty, Martin
b. 1837 Jensen, Adolph
b. 1841 Henry, Edward Lamson
b. 1852 Joffre, Joseph Jacques Cesaire
b. 1854 Marquis, Albert Nelson
b. 1856 Sargent, John Singer
b. 1861 Baldwin, James Mark
b. 1864 Russell, Annie
b. 1864 Schoen-Rene, Anna
b. 1870 Richman, Charles
b. 1876 London, Jack (John Griffith)
b. 1876 Wolf-Ferrari, Ermanno
b. 1878 Kahles, Charles William
b. 1879 Harroun, Ray
b. 1884 Horst, Louis
b. 1885 Fuess, Claude Moore
b. 1887 Helburn, Theresa
b. 1890 Johnson, Mordecai Wyatt
b. 1893 Goering, Hermann Wilhelm
b. 1893 Rosenberg, Alfred
b. 1894 Carpentier, Georges
b. 1896 Wechsler, David
b. 1898 Watts, Richard, Jr.
b. 1899 Crisler, "Fritz" (Herbert Orin)
b. 1901 Johnson, Arno Hollock
b. 1901 Jooss, Kurt
b. 1902 Lewis, Joe E
b. 1907 Ritter, "Tex" (Woodward Maurice)
b. 1908 Delannoy, Jean
b. 1908 Limon, Jose Arcadio
b. 1908 Lowinsky, Edward Elias
b. 1908 Ludwig, Leopold
b. 1910 Kelly, "Patsy" (Sarah Veronica Rose)
b. 1911 Almond, Gabriel Abraham
b. 1912 Rainer, Luise
b. 1912 Young, "Trummy" (James Osborne)
b. 1913 Schachte, Henry Miner
b. 1914 Gurney, Edward John
b. 1915 Agronsky, Martin Zama
b. 1916 Botha, Pieter Willem
b. 1916 Wehrwein, Austin Carl
b. 1917 Hendl, Walter
b. 1918 Sullivan, Walter Seager, Jr.
b. 1920 Farmer, James
b. 1920 Uppman, Theodor
b. 1921 Highsmith, Patricia
b. 1926 Price, Ray

b. 1930 Horton, Tim (Miles Gilbert)
b. 1930 Yarborough, Glenn
b. 1935 Kreskin
b. 1936 Brannigan, Bill
b. 1939 Golden, William Lee
b. 1941 Howells, Anne Elizabeth
b. 1942 Dohrn, Bernadine Rae
b. 1948 Andrews, Anthony
b. 1950 Jones, Randy (Randall Leo)
b. 1951 Madlock, Bill (William Jr.)
b. 1951 Pearson, Drew
b. 1955 Alley, Kirstie
b. 1960 Wilkins, Dominique
d. 1829 Schlegel, Friedrich von (Karl Wilhelm Friedrich von)
d. 1838 Humphreys, Joshua
d. 1880 Arthur, Ellen Lewis Herndon
d. 1897 Pitman, Isaac
d. 1899 Walker, Hiram
d. 1927 Daly, Arnold
d. 1932 King, Grace Elizabeth
d. 1935 Daniels, Frank
d. 1947 Eigenmann, Rosa Smith
d. 1956 Langford, Sam
d. 1958 Willard, Frank Henry
d. 1960 Shute, Nevil
d. 1967 Holt, Ivan Lee
d. 1967 Smith, Holland McTeire
d. 1972 Colum, Padraic
d. 1976 Christie, Agatha Mary Clarissa Miller, Dame
d. 1977 Clouzot, Henri-George
d. 1978 Metcalf, Lee
d. 1978 Sheekman, Arthur
d. 1980 Ronne, Finn
d. 1981 Whitehead, Don(ald Ford)

January 13
b. 1784 Woodworth, Samuel
b. 1808 Chase, Salmon Portland
b. 1832 Alger, Horatio
b. 1867 Townsend, Francis Everett
b. 1878 Reid Dick, William, Sir
b. 1884 Hathaway, Sibyl Collings
b. 1884 Tucker, Sophie
b. 1885 Fuller, Alfred Carl
b. 1890 Davis, Elmer Holmes
b. 1898 Tagliabue, Carlo
b. 1899 DeRochemont, Louis
b. 1900 Straus, Jack Isidor
b. 1901 Guthrie, A(lfred) B(ertram), Jr.
b. 1902 Drummond, Roscoe (James Roscoe)
b. 1903 Francis, Kay
b. 1904 Addinsell, Richard
b. 1905 Messel, Oliver
b. 1908 Wheeler, Earle G
b. 1911 Mecom, John Whitfield
b. 1915 Stewart, Potter
b. 1919 Archerd, Army (Armand)
b. 1919 Stack, Robert
b. 1924 Petit, Roland

d. 1942 Fisher, Fred
d. 1943 Richards, Laura Elizabeth Howe
d. 1949 Howard, Willie
d. 1954 Carney, Don
d. 1955 Booth, Hubert Cecil
d. 1956 Kaye-Smith, Sheila
d. 1957 Bogart, Humphrey de Forest
d. 1959 Cole, George Douglas Howard
d. 1965 MacDonald, Jeanette
d. 1969 Sedran, Barney
d. 1970 Murphy, John Joseph
d. 1977 Eden, Anthony
d. 1977 Finch, Peter
d. 1978 Abrahams, Harold
d. 1978 Godel, Kurt
d. 1980 Ardrey, Robert
d. 1981 Lilienthal, David Eli
d. 1984 Haddad, Saad
d. 1986 Reed, Donna

January 15
b. 1622 Moliere, pseud.
b. 1716 Livingston, Philip
b. 1791 Grillparzer, Franz
b. 1809 Proudhon, Pierre Joseph
b. 1810 Foster, Abigail Kelley
b. 1822 Marchesi, Salvatore
b. 1825 Strakosch, Maurice
b. 1831 Niemann, Albert
b. 1841 Stanley, Frederick Arthur, Earl of Derby
b. 1844 Younger, Cole (Thomas Coleman)
b. 1845 Vogl, Heinrich
b. 1861 Bullard, Robert Lee
b. 1864 Johnston, Frances Benjamin
b. 1866 Soderblom, Nathan
b. 1872 Davis, John Staige
b. 1882 Burr, Henry
b. 1885 DeLaRoche, Mazo
b. 1886 Howe, Clarence Decatur
b. 1886 Newell, Edward Theodore
b. 1891 Mandelshtam, Osip Emilyevich
b. 1893 Novello, Ivor
b. 1897 Barr, Stringfellow
b. 1898 Fox, Uffa
b. 1899 Ace, Goodman
b. 1899 Whitaker, Rogers E(rnest) M(alcolm)
b. 1902 Saud (Ibn Abdul Aziz al Saud)
b. 1906 Onassis, Aristotle Socrates
b. 1908 Teller, Edward
b. 1909 Krupa, Gene
b. 1909 Siegmeister, Elie
b. 1911 Feuer, Cy
b. 1912 Debre, Michel Jean Pierre
b. 1913 Bridges, Lloyd (Lloyd Vernet II)
b. 1914 Trevor-Roper, Hugh Redwald
b. 1915 Borg, Veda Ann
b. 1915 Lomax, Alan
b. 1918 Byrd, Robert Carlyle
b. 1918 Figueiredo, Joao Baptista de Oliveira

b. 1918 Nasser, Gamal Abdel
b. 1920 Davies, Bob (Robert Edris)
b. 1920 O'Connor, John Joseph, Cardinal
b. 1921 Barker, Cliff
b. 1922 Marcinkus, Paul C
b. 1925 Slenczynska, Ruth
b. 1926 Berry, Chuck (Charles Edward Anderson)
b. 1926 MacLeish, Rod(erick)
b. 1927 Badura-Skoda, Paul
b. 1929 King, Martin Luther, Jr.
b. 1931 Hoving, Thomas Pearsall Field
b. 1933 Gaines, Ernest J
b. 1935 Goodman, Martin Wise
b. 1936 Conroy, Frank
b. 1937 O'Brien, Margaret (Angela Maxine)
b. 1943 Eizenstat, Stuart E
b. 1946 Tennant, Veronica
b. 1951 Charo
b. 1951 DiGregorio, Ernie
b. 1953 White, Randy Lee
d. 1783 Alexander, William
d. 1865 Everett, Edward
d. 1876 Johnson, Eliza McCardle
d. 1892 Rogers, Randolph
d. 1893 Kemble, Fanny (Frances Anne)
d. 1893 Smith, Horace
d. 1896 Brady, Mathew B
d. 1909 Reyer, (Louis) Ernest (Etienne)
d. 1915 Farmer, Fannie Merritt
d. 1919 Luxemburg, Rosa
d. 1948 Daniels, Josephus
d. 1949 Ponzi, Charles
d. 1950 Arnold, Henry Harley
d. 1951 Ironside, Henry Allan
d. 1951 Swinton, Ernest Dunlop, Sir
d. 1953 Knote, Heinrich
d. 1955 Tanguy, Yves
d. 1960 Smart, Jack Scott
d. 1964 Teagarden, Jack (Weldon John)
d. 1966 Balewa, Abubakar
d. 1968 Masterton, Bill (William)
d. 1970 Fischer, Louis
d. 1970 Piper, William Thomas
d. 1971 Dall, John
d. 1971 Shambaugh, Jessie Field
d. 1972 Ashford, Daisy
d. 1980 Fogarty, Anne
d. 1982 Jarman, John
d. 1982 Sender, Ramon Jose
d. 1982 Smith, "Red" (Walter Wellesley)
d. 1983 Lansky, Meyer
d. 1983 Lauder, Joseph H
d. 1983 Strudwick, Shepperd
d. 1983 Weaver, "Doodles" (Winstead Sheffield Glendening Dixon)
d. 1986 Crowley, Jim (James)

January 16
b. 1725 Piccini, Nicola
b. 1749 Alfieri, Vittorio

b. 1815 Halleck, Henry
b. 1864 Bacon, Frank
b. 1872 Craig, Gordon (Edward Henry Gordon)
b. 1873 Collins, James Joseph (Jimmy)
b. 1874 Service, Robert William
b. 1878 Carey, Harry
b. 1882 Wilson, Margaret
b. 1884 Decker, Alonzo G
b. 1890 Ackerman, Carl William
b. 1893 Bordoni, Irene
b. 1894 Chamberlin, (B) Guy
b. 1894 Mills, Irving
b. 1895 Weyerhaeuser, Frederick Edward
b. 1901 Batista y Zaldivar, Fulgencio
b. 1901 Riding, Laura
b. 1906 Wynyard, Diana
b. 1907 Knox, Alexander
b. 1909 Merman, Ethel
b. 1911 Dean, "Dizzy" (Jay Hanna)
b. 1911 Frei, Eduardo (Montalva Eduardo)
b. 1914 Wagner, Roger
b. 1916 Rothschild, Edmund Leopold de
b. 1917 Hartley, Fred Lloyd
b. 1918 Silliphant, Stirling Dale
b. 1920 Reid, Elliott
b. 1923 Hecht, Anthony Evan
b. 1927 Jurado, Katy
b. 1928 Kennedy, William
b. 1928 Kitt, Eartha Mae
b. 1929 Lowenstein, Allard Kenneth
b. 1929 Scavullo, Francesco
b. 1930 Podhoretz, Norman
b. 1932 Berry, Jim
b. 1932 Fossey, Dian
b. 1933 Lorengar, Pilar
b. 1934 Horne, Marilyn
b. 1935 Foyt, A(nthony) J(oseph, Jr.)
b. 1936 White, Michael Simon
b. 1944 Milsap, Ronnie
b. 1948 Carpenter, John
b. 1950 Allen, Debbie
b. 1960 Sade
d. 1794 Gibbon, Edward
d. 1865 Proudhon, Pierre Joseph
d. 1878 Bowles, Samuel, II
d. 1886 Ponchielli, Amilcare
d. 1891 Delibes, Leo
d. 1901 Barbier, Jules
d. 1901 Bocklin, Arnold
d. 1906 Field, Marshall
d. 1915 Williams, Gus
d. 1917 Dewey, George
d. 1920 DeKoven, (Henry Louis) Reginald
d. 1935 Barker, "Ma" (Arizona Donnie Clark)
d. 1935 Barker, Fred
d. 1936 Fish, Albert
d. 1936 Russell, Annie
d. 1938 Pickering, William Henry
d. 1942 Lombard, Carole

d. 1943 Kellogg, John Harvey
d. 1945 Patten, Gilbert
d. 1957 Toscanini, Arturo
d. 1962 Mestrovic, Ivan
d. 1962 Tawney, Richard Henry
d. 1962 Toffenetti, Dario Louis
d. 1966 Hodges, Courtney
d. 1968 Infeld, Leopold
d. 1968 Jones, Bob
d. 1969 Smith, Courtney Craig
d. 1970 Breger, Dave
d. 1972 Seville, David
d. 1974 Lovejoy, Clarence Earle
d. 1981 Lee, Bernard
d. 1985 Fitzgerald, Robert Stuart
d. 1985 Orkin, Ruth

January 17
b. 1600 Calderon de la Barca, Pedro
b. 1612 Fairfax, Thomas
b. 1706 Franklin, Benjamin
b. 1734 Gossec, Francois Joseph
b. 1759 Cuffe, Paul
b. 1761 Hall, James, Sir
b. 1771 Brown, Charles Brockden
b. 1796 Fairbanks, Thaddeus
b. 1800 Cushing, Caleb
b. 1837 Browning, Oscar
b. 1851 Frost, Arthur Burdett
b. 1853 Belmont, Alva Erskine Smith Vanderbilt
b. 1857 Kienzl, Wilhelm
b. 1860 Chekhov, Anton Pavlovich
b. 1863 Stanislavsky, Konstantin Sergeyevich
b. 1867 Laemmle, Carl, Sr.
b. 1876 Hague, Frank
b. 1883 Mackenzie, Compton (Edward Montague, Sir)
b. 1884 Beery, Noah
b. 1884 Sennett, Mack
b. 1885 Kern, Jerome David
b. 1886 Firbank, Ronald
b. 1886 Martin, Glenn Luther
b. 1892 Bennett, Harry Herbert
b. 1893 Scott, Evelyn
b. 1896 Davis, Loyal
b. 1899 Capone, Al(phonse)
b. 1899 Hutchins, Robert Maynard
b. 1899 Shute, Nevil
b. 1901 Asther, Nils
b. 1903 Hull, Warren
b. 1906 Glass, Hiram Bentley
b. 1907 Blasingame, Francis James Levi
b. 1910 Catlett, "Big Sid" (Sidney)
b. 1910 Rush, Kenneth
b. 1911 McCain, John Sidney, Jr.
b. 1911 Nickerson, Albert L
b. 1911 Stigler, George Joseph
b. 1912 Landis, Frederick
b. 1913 Musso, Vido
b. 1914 Stafford, William Edgar

b. 1915 Angott, Sammy (Samuel Engotti)
b. 1917 White, Betty
b. 1922 Echeverria Alvarez, Louis
b. 1922 Katzenbach, Nicholas de Belleville
b. 1925 Hanson, Duane Elwood
b. 1926 Minow, Newton Norman
b. 1926 Shearer, Moira
b. 1927 Dooley, Thomas Anthony
b. 1928 Sassoon, Vidal
b. 1931 Jones, James Earl
b. 1931 Zimmer, Don(ald William)
b. 1932 Aga Khan, Sadruddin, Prince
b. 1933 North, Sheree
b. 1934 Lewis, Shari
b. 1934 Schanberg, Sydney H
b. 1935 Thompson, Josiah
b. 1938 Bellairs, John
b. 1940 Keino, Kip (Hezekiah Kipchoge)
b. 1942 Ali, Muhammad
b. 1944 Frazier, Joe
b. 1948 Taylor, Mick
b. 1949 Kaufman, Andy
b. 1952 Porter, Darrell Ray
d. 1686 Dolci, Carlo
d. 1733 Byng, George Torrington, Viscount
d. 1833 Rush, William
d. 1846 Inman, Henry
d. 1861 Montez, Lola
d. 1869 Dargomijsky, Alexander
d. 1874 Chang and Eng
d. 1891 Bancroft, George
d. 1893 Hayes, Rutherford B(irchard)
d. 1910 Crapper, Thomas
d. 1911 Galton, Francis, Sir
d. 1922 Selden, George Baldwin
d. 1929 Goldberger, Joseph
d. 1932 Gore, Charles
d. 1933 Tiffany, Louis Comfort
d. 1946 Kalisch, Paul
d. 1953 Jaggar, Thomas Augustus
d. 1964 Allen, Arthur Augustus
d. 1964 White, T(erence) H(anbury)
d. 1964 Woodcock, Amos Walter Wright
d. 1966 Donehue, Vincent J
d. 1969 Duke, Vernon
d. 1972 Hudson, Rochelle
d. 1972 Smith, Betty
d. 1972 Spectorsky, Auguste Compte
d. 1973 Walker, Ralph Thomas
d. 1974 Seaton, Frederick Andrew
d. 1975 Rojas Pinilla, Gustavo
d. 1982 Shalamov, Varlam Tikhonovich
d. 1985 Rigby, Harry

January 18
b. 1689 Montesquieu, Charles Louis de
b. 1754 Martin y Soler, Vicente
b. 1779 Roget, Peter Mark
b. 1782 Webster, Daniel
b. 1811 Laboulage, Edouard Rose
b. 1835 Cui, Cesar Antonovich
b. 1840 Dobson, Henry Austin

b. 1841 Chabrier, (Alexis) Emmanuel
b. 1848 Graydon, James Weir
b. 1858 Williams, Daniel Hale
b. 1866 Mullgardt, Louis Christian
b. 1870 Nethersole, Olga
b. 1879 Giraud, Henri Honore
b. 1881 Strong, Austin
b. 1882 Milne, A(lan) A(lexander)
b. 1884 Ransome, Arthur Mitchell
b. 1886 Pevsner, Antoine
b. 1892 Hardy, Oliver
b. 1893 Guillen, Jorge
b. 1894 Berlin, Richard E
b. 1896 Ritola, Ville
b. 1899 Shands, Alfred Rives, Jr.
b. 1904 Grant, Cary
b. 1907 Ferencsik, Janos
b. 1908 Bronowski, Jacob
b. 1910 Boulding, Kenneth Ewart
b. 1912 Sansom, William
b. 1913 Kaye, Danny
b. 1918 Chaney, Norman
b. 1918 Roudebush, Richard Lowell
b. 1922 Moore, Constance
b. 1931 Lear, Evelyn
b. 1932 Schmidt, Joe (Joseph Paul)
b. 1933 Boorman, John
b. 1933 Dolby, Ray Milton
b. 1938 Flood, Curt(is Charles)
b. 1938 Wildmon, Donald Ellis
b. 1941 Goldsboro, Bobby
b. 1950 Villeneuve, Gilles
b. 1953 Hudson, Brett Stuart Patrick
b. 1961 Messier, Mark Douglas
d. 1859 Vail, Alfred Lewis
d. 1862 Tyler, John
d. 1873 Lytton, Edward George Earle
Lytton Bulwer-Lytton, 1st Baron Lytton
d. 1878 Becquerel, Antoine-Cesar
d. 1886 Tichatschek, Joseph
d. 1887 Upchurch, John Jorden
d. 1908 Stedman, Edmund Clarence
d. 1912 Winkelmann, Hermann
d. 1918 Materna, Amalia
d. 1919 Astor, William Waldorf Astor,
Viscount
d. 1923 Reid, Wallace Eugene
d. 1927 Low, Juliette Gordon
d. 1929 Loeb, Sophia Irene Simon
d. 1936 Kipling, Rudyard
d. 1939 Schultze, Carl Edward
d. 1951 Holt, Jack (Charles John)
d. 1955 Duesenberg, August S
d. 1957 Wolff, Fritz
d. 1961 Dooley, Thomas Anthony
d. 1961 Lumumba, Patrice Emergy
d. 1963 Gaitskell, Hugh Todd Naylor
d. 1967 Nesbit, Evelyn
d. 1967 Ross, Barney
d. 1968 Hilbert, Egon
d. 1968 Vandenberg, Arthur Hendrick, Jr.

d. 1968 Wheeler, Bert
d. 1970 McKay, David O
d. 1971 Calvert, Catherine
d. 1971 Finlay, Virgil
d. 1972 Burtin, Will
d. 1972 France, Harry Clinton
d. 1973 Stevens, S(tanley) S(mith)
d. 1976 August, Jan
d. 1977 Bijedic, Dzemal
d. 1977 Gilmore, Gary Mark
d. 1977 Printemps, Yvonne
d. 1977 Zuckmayer, Carl
d. 1978 Betz, Carl
d. 1978 Greenwood, Charlotte
d. 1980 Beaton, Cecil Walter Hardy, Sir
d. 1980 Britton, Barbara
d. 1983 Illia, Arturo Umberto
d. 1984 Kerr, Malcolm (Hooper)
d. 1985 Stoll, George
d. 1985 Wolfenden, John Frederick, Sir

January 19
b. 1736 Watt, James
b. 1782 Auber, Daniel Francois Esprit
b. 1798 Comte, Auguste
b. 1803 Whitman, Sarah Helen Power
b. 1807 Lee, Robert E(dward)
b. 1809 Poe, Edgar Allan
b. 1813 Bessemer, Henry, Sir
b. 1814 Perrin, Emile Cesare
b. 1839 Cezanne, Paul
b. 1842 Ladd, George Trumbull
b. 1848 Keith, Minor Cooper
b. 1850 Birrell, Augustine
b. 1858 Brieux, Eugene
b. 1873 Dupree, Minnie
b. 1884 Wolff, Albert Louis
b. 1886 Davenport, Harry George Bryant
b. 1887 Woollcott, Alexander Humphreys
b. 1889 Taeuber-Arp, Sophie
b. 1900 Christians, Mady
b. 1903 Nyiregyhazi, Ervin
b. 1904 Blough, Roger Miles
b. 1905 Hobby, Oveta Culp
b. 1906 Ross, Lanny
b. 1909 Hotter, Hans
b. 1909 Pudney, John Sleigh
b. 1915 Ruder, Melvin
b. 1917 Nicolson, Nigel
b. 1917 Raitt, John Emmet
b. 1918 Cleveland, James Harlan
b. 1918 Johnson, John Harold
b. 1919 Eberle, Ray
b. 1919 Park, Choong-Hoon
b. 1919 Salinger, J(erome) D(avid)
b. 1920 Perez de Cuellar, Javier
b. 1922 Madison, Guy
b. 1923 Moyes, Patricia
b. 1923 Stapleton, Jean
b. 1924 Revel, Jean Francois
b. 1925 Bawden, Nina Mary Mabey
b. 1926 Weaver, Fritz William

b. 1930 Dickerson, Nancy Hanschman
b. 1931 MacNeil, Robert Breckenridge
       Ware
b. 1932 Lester, Richard
b. 1932 MacBeth, George Mann
b. 1935 Hedren, "Tippi" (Natalie Kay)
b. 1936 Rahman, Ziaur
b. 1939 Everly, Phil
b. 1942 Crawford, Michael Patrick
b. 1943 Joplin, Janis
b. 1944 Fabares, Shelley (Michelle Marie)
b. 1946 Parton, Dolly Rebecca
b. 1947 Compton, Ann
b. 1949 Palmer, Robert
b. 1950 Matlack, Jon(athan Trumpbour)
b. 1953 Arnaz, Desi(derio Alberto, IV), Jr.
b. 1954 Bichler, Joyce
b. 1957 Anderson, O(ttis) J(erome)
d. 1576 Sachs, Hans
d. 1729 Congreve, William
d. 1833 Herold, Louis Joseph Ferdinand
d. 1848 D'Israeli, Isaac
d. 1931 McCann, Alfred Watterson
d. 1934 Fisher, Harrison
d. 1940 Borah, William E
d. 1943 O'Connell, Hugh
d. 1948 Sobol, Louis
d. 1952 Howard, "Curly" (Jerry)
d. 1953 Schnering, Otto
d. 1954 Greenstreet, Sydney Hughes
d. 1965 Pate, Maurice
d. 1968 Harroun, Ray
d. 1972 Chapman, John (Arthur)
d. 1972 Rabin, Michael
d. 1973 Crawford, Jack (John Shea)
d. 1975 Benton, Thomas Hart
d. 1980 Douglas, William Orville
d. 1980 Goldman, Richard Franko
d. 1981 Evans, Clifford
d. 1982 Plumb, Charles
d. 1982 Zaturenska, Marya
d. 1983 Carson, Robert
d. 1983 Costa, Don
d. 1984 Bentley, Max (Maxwell Herbert
       Lloyd)

January 20
b. 1562 Rinuccini, Ottavio
b. 1707 Frederick Louis
b. 1732 Lee, Richard Henry
b. 1804 Sue, Eugene Joseph Marie
b. 1806 Willis, Nathaniel Parker
b. 1814 Wilmot, David
b. 1856 Blatch, Harriot Eaton Stanton
b. 1864 Taylor, Charles Alonzo
b. 1866 Cunha, Euclides da
b. 1866 LeGallienne, Richard
b. 1876 Hofmann, Josef
b. 1877 Saint Denis, Ruth
b. 1878 Currie, Finlay
b. 1883 Wrather, William Embry
b. 1884 Merritt, Abraham

b. 1886 Young, James Webb
b. 1889 Toffenetti, Dario Louis
b. 1890 Owsley, Frank Lawrence
b. 1894 Gray, Harold
b. 1894 Piston, Walter
b. 1896 Burns, George
b. 1899 Tcherepnin, Alexander
b. 1900 Clive, Colin
b. 1903 Ames, Leon
b. 1904 Cordon, Norman
b. 1904 Danilova, Alexandra
b. 1906 McNeill, Robert Edward, Jr.
b. 1910 Adamson, Joy Friederike Victoria
Gessner
b. 1910 Johnson, Josephine Winslow
b. 1912 Briggs, Walter Owen, Jr.
b. 1914 Plomley, Roy
b. 1914 Watt, Douglas (Benjamin)
b. 1915 Graves, Harold Nathan
b. 1915 Marek, Kurt W
b. 1916 Stone, Paula
b. 1919 Cooper, Lester Irving
b. 1920 Fellini, Federico
b. 1920 Landau, Ely A
b. 1922 Anthony, Ray
b. 1925 Bloustein, Edward J
b. 1926 Neal, Patricia
b. 1930 Aldrin, Edwin E(ugene), Jr.
b. 1932 Carr, Martin
b. 1934 Johnson, Arte
b. 1937 Provine, Dorothy Michele
b. 1940 Jenkins, Carol Elizabeth Heiss
b. 1945 Rothenberg, Susan
b. 1948 Shcharansky, Anatoly Borisovich
b. 1949 Stanley, Paul
b. 1955 Kennedy, Bill (William Patrick)
b. 1956 Naber, John
b. 1958 Lamas, Lorenzo
b. 1962 Humphries, Stefan
b. 1964 Guillen, Ozzie (Oswaldo Jose)
d. 1745 Charles VII
d. 1779 Garrick, David
d. 1837 Soane, John, Sir
d. 1867 Willis, Nathaniel Parker
d. 1875 Millet, Jean Francois
d. 1881 Sothern, Edward Askew
d. 1900 Blackmore, Richard Doddridge
d. 1900 Ruskin, John
d. 1930 Cobb, Will D
d. 1936 George V
d. 1944 Cattell, James McKeen
d. 1947 Gibson, Josh(ua)
d. 1947 Volstead, Andrew J
d. 1957 Connolly, James B
d. 1958 Lambert, Ward L
d. 1962 Jeffers, (John) Robinson
d. 1965 Altrock, Nick (Nicholas)
d. 1965 Freed, Alan
d. 1968 Beatty, Alfred Chester, Sir
d. 1968 Stacton, David Derek
d. 1970 Humphrey, George Magoffin

d. 1971 Anderson, Gilbert M
d. 1972 Casadesus, Jean
d. 1974 Blunden, Edmund Charles
d. 1975 Summersby, Kay
d. 1978 Highet, Gilbert Arthur
d. 1982 Baxter, Frank Condie
d. 1984 Weissmuller, Johnny

January 21
b. 1738 Allen, Ethan
b. 1743 Fitch, John
b. 1813 Fremont, John Charles
b. 1815 Wells, Horace
b. 1821 Breckinridge, John Cabell
b. 1824 Jackson, "Stonewall" (Thomas
Jonathan)
b. 1845 Mallinckrodt, Edward
b. 1855 Browning, John Moses
b. 1867 Weygand, Maxime
b. 1878 Garrod, Hethcote William
b. 1883 Hackett, Francis
b. 1884 Baldwin, Roger Nash
b. 1885 Nobile, Umberto
b. 1887 Koehler, Wolfgang
b. 1887 Kohler, Wolfgang
b. 1891 Elman, Mischa
b. 1893 Barnaby, Ralph S
b. 1895 Balenciaga, Cristobal
b. 1900 Naish, J(oseph) Carrol
b. 1902 Duffy, Ben (Bernard Cornelius)
b. 1904 Blackmur, Richard Palmer
b. 1904 Crawford, John Edmund
b. 1905 Dior, Christian
b. 1906 Moiseyev, Igor Alexandrovich
b. 1915 Sefton, William
b. 1918 Janigro, Antonio
b. 1919 Falkenburg, Jinx (Eugenia Lincoln)
b. 1920 Barrow, Errol Walton
b. 1921 Clark, Barney Bailey
b. 1922 Scofield, Paul
b. 1923 Savalas, "Telly" (Aristoteles)
b. 1925 Hill, Benny (Benjamin)
b. 1926 Mikva, Abner Joseph
b. 1926 Reeves, Steve
b. 1928 Bignone, Reynaldo Benito Antonio
b. 1933 Wrigley, William
b. 1938 Wolfman Jack
b. 1940 Nicklaus, Jack
b. 1941 Domingo, Placido
b. 1941 Havens, Richie
b. 1942 Davis, Mac
b. 1944 Abbott, Jack (Rufus Jack Henry)
b. 1950 Ocean, Billy
b. 1952 Johnson, "Billy White Shoes"
(William Arthur)
b. 1955 Fleming, Peter
b. 1957 Benson, Robby
d. 1609 Scaliger, Joseph Justus
d. 1793 Louis XVI
d. 1795 Wallis, Samuel
d. 1796 Burns, Robert
d. 1815 Claudius, Matthias

d. 1851 Lortzing, Gustav Albert
d. 1872 Grillparzer, Franz
d. 1892 Adams, John Couch
d. 1901 Gray, Elisha
d. 1914 Ginn, Edwin
d. 1914 Smith, Donald Alexander
d. 1924 Lenin, Nikolai
d. 1926 Golgi, Camillo
d. 1928 Goethals, George Washington
d. 1931 Kahles, Charles William
d. 1932 Strachey, (Giles) Lytton
d. 1933 Moore, George Augustus
d. 1938 Melies, Georges
d. 1948 Wolf-Ferrari, Ermanno
d. 1949 Cawthorn, Joseph
d. 1950 Orwell, George, pseud.
d. 1951 Cossart, Ernest
d. 1954 Chambers, Edmund Kerchever, Sir
d. 1958 Bowers, Claude Gernade
d. 1959 DeMille, Cecil B(lount)
d. 1959 Switzer, Carl
d. 1961 Cone, Russell Glenn
d. 1962 Cockrell, Ewing
d. 1964 Schildkraut, Joseph
d. 1967 Sheridan, Ann
d. 1971 Russell, Richard Brevard, Jr.
d. 1972 Chandos, Oliver Lyttelton
d. 1973 Szabolcsi, Bence
d. 1974 Strauss, Lewis Lichtenstein
d. 1975 Bosley, Harold A
d. 1978 Utley, Freda
d. 1981 Douglass, Lathrop
d. 1981 Joslyn, Allyn Morgan
d. 1981 Strong, James Matthew
d. 1981 Stronge, (Charles) Norman
   (Lockhart), Sir
d. 1982 Irish, Edward Simmons (Ned)
d. 1984 Wilson, Jackie

January 22
b. 1440 Ivan III
b. 1561 Bacon, Francis, Sir
b. 1690 Lancret, Nicolas
b. 1729 Lessing, Gotthold Ephraim
b. 1775 Ampere, Andre Marie
b. 1775 Garcia, Manuel del Popolo
   Vincente, I
b. 1788 Byron, George Gordon Noel
   Byron, Baron
b. 1788 Schopenhauer, Arthur
b. 1797 Harper, John
b. 1802 Upjohn, Richard
b. 1837 Moran, Thomas
b. 1848 Laffan, William Mackay
b. 1849 Strindberg, August (Johan August)
b. 1850 Brookings, Robert Somers
b. 1853 Gore, Charles
b. 1858 Webb, Beatrice Potter
b. 1862 Fuller, Loie
b. 1866 Barton, George
b. 1874 Harkness, Edward Stephen
b. 1875 Griffith, D(avid Lewelyn) W(ark)

b. 1877 Schacht, Hjalmar Horace Greeley
b. 1878 Collier, Constance
b. 1879 Picabia, Francis
b. 1885 Doherty, Robert Ernest
b. 1887 Olds, Irving S
b. 1889 Baumeister, Willi
b. 1890 Vinson, Frederick Moore
b. 1891 Alexander, Franz Gabriel
b. 1892 Dassault, Marcel
b. 1893 Oursler, (Charles) Fulton
b. 1893 Veidt, Conrad
b. 1894 Morgan, Charles Langbridge
b. 1894 Ponselle, Rosa
b. 1895 Alley, Norman William
b. 1902 Fendler, Edvard
b. 1903 Jacobs, Al(bert T)
b. 1903 Sutton, Margaret Beebe
b. 1906 Cox, Gardner
b. 1906 Howard, Robert Ervin
b. 1906 Levy, Julien
b. 1908 Landau, Lev Davidovich
b. 1909 Sothern, Ann
b. 1909 Thant, U
b. 1911 Danco, Suzanne
b. 1911 Powell, Gordon G
b. 1916 Teichmann, Howard Miles
b. 1918 Lach, Elmer James
b. 1920 Kristol, Irving
b. 1920 Stavropoulos, George Peter
b. 1920 Volkov, Leon
b. 1920 Warfield, William Caesar
b. 1924 Johnson, "J J" (James Louis)
b. 1928 Bayh, Birch Evans, Jr.
b. 1931 Rayner, Claire Berenice
b. 1932 Laurie, Piper
b. 1934 Bixby, Bill
b. 1934 Kerr, Graham
b. 1935 Cooke, Sam
b. 1935 DuPont, Pierre Samuel, IV
b. 1937 Pastora (Gomez), Eden
b. 1937 Wambaugh, Joseph Aloysius, Jr.
b. 1938 Beard, Peter Hill
b. 1940 Hurt, John
b. 1945 Cristofer, Michael
b. 1945 Harris, William
b. 1946 Savard, Serge A
b. 1949 Perry, Steve
b. 1955 Hayes, Lester
b. 1957 Bossy, Mike (Michael)
b. 1958 White, Charles Raymond
b. 1959 Blair, Linda Denise
d. 1796 Morris, Lewis
d. 1832 Pitcher, Molly
d. 1840 Blumenbach, Johann Friedrich
d. 1861 Velluti, Giovanni Battista
d. 1870 Prentice, George Denison
d. 1892 Bradley, Joseph P
d. 1901 Victoria
d. 1919 Larsson, Carl (Olof)
d. 1922 Bryce, James Bryce, Viscount
d. 1927 Rhodes, James Ford

d. 1930 Mather, Stephen Tyng
d. 1945 Symons, Arthur
d. 1950 Hale, Alan
d. 1956 Greene, Ward
d. 1957 Perry, Ralph Barton
d. 1964 Blitzstein, Marc
d. 1965 Stuhldreher, Harry A
d. 1966 Marshall, Herbert
d. 1967 Buckley, Charles Anthony
d. 1968 Arbuzov, Aleksandr
d. 1968 Dargan, Olive Tilford
d. 1968 Kahanamoku, Duke
d. 1970 Folsom, Frank M
d. 1971 Guggenheim, Harry Frank
d. 1973 Johnson, Lyndon Baines
d. 1974 Volkov, Leon
d. 1978 Wengenroth, Stow
d. 1982 Farber, Edward Rolke
d. 1982 Frei, Eduardo (Montalva Eduardo)
d. 1983 Madden, Donald
d. 1986 Clinchy, Everett Ross

January 23
b. 1598 Mansart, Francois
b. 1692 Caslon, William
b. 1730 Hewes, Joseph
b. 1783 Stendhal
b. 1818 Boutwell, George Sewell
b. 1832 Manet, Edouard
b. 1841 Coquelin, Benoit Constant
b. 1869 Croly, Herbert David
b. 1880 Poole, Ernest
b. 1884 McManus, George
b. 1887 Wenrich, Percy
b. 1890 Rosing, Vladimir
b. 1893 Pangborn, Franklin
b. 1896 Charlotte Aldegonde E M
     Wilhelmine
b. 1898 Eisenstein, Sergei Mikhailovich
b. 1898 Utley, Freda
b. 1899 Denning, Alfred Thompson
b. 1899 Kane, Joseph Nathan
b. 1901 Wirtz, Arthur M
b. 1902 Klopfer, Donald Simon
b. 1903 Galamian, Ivan
b. 1903 Scott, Randolph
b. 1904 Zukofsky, Louis
b. 1905 Zacharias, Jerrold R(einarch)
b. 1906 Steele, Bob
b. 1907 Duryea, Dan
b. 1907 Yukawa, Hideki
b. 1910 Reinhardt, Django (Jean Baptiste)
b. 1911 Eifert, Virginia Snider
b. 1916 Duncan, David Douglas
b. 1919 Kovacs, Ernie
b. 1922 Golub, Leon Albert
b. 1923 Logan, John
b. 1924 Lautenberg, Frank R
b. 1925 Arnold, Danny
b. 1928 Moreau, Jeanne
b. 1929 Clarkson, Ewan
b. 1930 Pogue, William R(eid)

b. 1931 Chun Doo Hwan
b. 1933 Rivera, Chita
b. 1936 Golonka, Arlene
b. 1937 Zylis-Gara, Teresa
b. 1943 Gerard, Gil
b. 1944 Hauer, Rutger
b. 1950 Cunningham, Bill
b. 1950 Federici, Daniel Paul
b. 1950 Simmons, Pat(rick)
b. 1953 Haden, Pat(rick Capper)
b. 1953 Zander, Robin
b. 1957 Caroline, Princess
b. 1958 Christoff, Steve
b. 1963 Olajuwon, Akeem Abdul Ajibola
d. 1516 Ferdinand V
d. 1622 Baffin, William
d. 1750 Muratori, Ludovico
d. 1766 Caslon, William
d. 1789 Cleland, John
d. 1795 Sullivan, John
d. 1800 Rutledge, Edward
d. 1806 Pitt, William
d. 1810 Hoppner, John
d. 1828 Randolph, Mary
d. 1858 Lablache, Luigi
d. 1866 Peacock, Thomas Love
d. 1875 Kingsley, Charles
d. 1879 Jensen, Adolph
d. 1883 Beard, George Miller
d. 1883 Dore, Gustave (Paul Gustave)
d. 1893 Brooks, Phillips
d. 1893 Lamar, Lucius Q C
d. 1908 MacDowell, Edward Alexander
d. 1922 Nikisch, Arthur
d. 1924 Morrice, James Wilson
d. 1931 Pavlova, Anna
d. 1931 Rubens, Alma
d. 1943 Rice, Cale Young
d. 1943 Woollcott, Alexander Humphreys
d. 1944 Munch, Edvard
d. 1945 Moltke, Helmuth James, graf von
d. 1947 Bonnard, Pierre
d. 1956 Evans, Billy (William George)
d. 1956 Korda, Alexander, Sir
d. 1960 Suckow, Ruth
d. 1961 Lawrie, Lee
d. 1964 Horst, Louis
d. 1973 Ory, "Kid" (Edward)
d. 1974 Mueller, "Heinie" (Clarence
     Franklin)
d. 1976 Robeson, Paul Leroy
d. 1976 Thomas, James William Tudor
d. 1978 Kath, Terry
d. 1980 Buttrick, George Arthur
d. 1980 Shapero, Nate S
d. 1980 Williams, Paul R(evere)
d. 1981 Barber, Samuel
d. 1982 Sillman, Leonard
d. 1983 Bane, Frank B
d. 1985 Beard, James Andrews

d. 1986 Beuys, Joseph
d. 1986 Leser, Tina
January 24
b. 76 Hadrian
b. 1670 Congreve, William
b. 1705 Farinelli
b. 1712 Frederick the Great
b. 1732 Beaumarchais, Pierre Augustin
    Caron de
b. 1749 Fox, Charles James
b. 1776 Hoffmann, Ernst Theodor
    Amadeus
b. 1811 Barnard, Henry
b. 1820 Raymond, Henry Jarvis
b. 1828 Cohn, Ferdinand Julius
b. 1850 Murfree, Mary Noailles
b. 1860 Kroger, Bernard Henry
b. 1862 Wharton, Edith
b. 1867 Mayo, Katherine
b. 1871 Jaggar, Thomas Augustus
b. 1883 Winwood, Estelle
b. 1885 Biddle, George
b. 1888 Baum, Vicki
b. 1896 King, Henry
b. 1899 Vandenberg, Hoyt Sanford
b. 1901 Romm, Mikhail
b. 1902 Kiernan, Walter
b. 1903 DeWohl, Louis
b. 1907 Couve de Murville, (Jacques)
    Maurice
b. 1908 Ford, Alexander
b. 1908 Sandys, Duncan
b. 1909 Cassandre, A(dolphe) M(ouron)
b. 1909 Kagel, Sam
b. 1909 Todd, Ann
b. 1911 Mathieson, Muir
b. 1913 Dello Joio, Norman Joseph
b. 1915 Goodson, Mark
b. 1915 Motherwell, Robert Burns
b. 1916 Haas, Walter A(braham), Jr.
b. 1917 Borgnine, Ernest
b. 1918 Roberts, Oral
b. 1920 Cable, Mary
b. 1920 Saddler, Donald
b. 1921 Connolly, Sybil
b. 1923 Rama Rau, Santha
b. 1924 Hill, Herbert
b. 1925 Tallchief, Maria
b. 1927 Burns, Jerry (Jerome Monahan)
b. 1927 Hawkins, Paula Fickes
b. 1928 Morris, Desmond
b. 1932 Nouwen, Henri J M
b. 1933 Beatty, Roger
b. 1934 Goldberg, Leonard
b. 1935 Rompollo, Dominic
b. 1936 Kershaw, Doug(las James)
b. 1937 Clark, Monte
b. 1939 Stevens, Ray
b. 1941 Diamond, Neil
b. 1947 Bradley, Bill (William)
b. 1947 Chinaglia, Giorgio

b. 1949 Belushi, John
b. 1960 Kinski, Nastassja
b. 1968 Retton, Mary Lou
d. 41 Caligula
d. 1813 Clymer, George
d. 1828 Lamb, Caroline Ponsonby, Lady
d. 1848 Wells, Horace
d. 1851 Spontini, Gasparo
d. 1883 Flotow, Friedrich von, Baron
d. 1895 Churchill, Randolph Henry
    Spencer, Lord
d. 1911 Philips, David Graham
d. 1930 Felton, Rebecca Ann Latimer
d. 1930 Sammarco, Mario
d. 1938 Barlach, Ernst Heinrich
d. 1950 Montana, "Bull" (Louis)
d. 1960 Ford, Russ(ell William)
d. 1961 Gilbert, A(lfred) C(arleton)
d. 1963 Harbach, Otto Abels
d. 1965 Churchill, Winston Leonard
    Spencer, Sir
d. 1972 Austin, Gene
d. 1972 Cowan, Jerome
d. 1973 Naish, J(oseph) Carrol
d. 1973 Weintal, Edward
d. 1975 Fine, Larry
d. 1977 Lilly, Eli
d. 1977 Shor, "Toots" (Bernard)
d. 1980 Poe, James
d. 1982 Ovando Candia, Alfredo
d. 1983 Cukor, George Dewey
d. 1983 Erickson, Eric
d. 1984 Kroc, Ray(mond) Albert
d. 1984 Reeves, Rosser
d. 1986 Hubbard, L(afayette) Ron(ald)
d. 1986 MacRae, Gordon

January 25
b. 1627 Boyle, Robert
b. 1759 Burns, Robert
b. 1783 Colgate, William
b. 1812 Page, Charles Grafton
b. 1813 Sims, James Marion
b. 1825 Pickett, George Edward
b. 1854 Shaw, Mary
b. 1860 Curtis, Charles
b. 1861 Bobbs, William Conrad
b. 1866 Scotti, Antonio
b. 1871 Park, Maud May Wood
b. 1874 Johnson, Hewlett
b. 1874 Maugham, William Somerset
b. 1876 Leonard, William Ellery
b. 1878 Alexanderson, Ernst Frederik
    Werner
b. 1881 Ludwig, Emil
b. 1882 Woolf, Virginia (Adeline Virginia
    Stephen)
b. 1884 Kilenyi, Edward, Sr.
b. 1886 Furtwangler, Wilhelm
b. 1891 Bullitt, William C
b. 1895 Mills, Florence
b. 1899 Spaak, Paul-Henri

b. 1901 Wilder, Robert Ingersoll
b. 1906 Dunnock, Mildred
b. 1914 Flora, James Royer
b. 1915 Deiss, Joseph Jay
b. 1917 Prigogine, Ilya
b. 1918 Harwell, Ernie
b. 1919 Newman, Edwin Harold
b. 1923 Galamison, Milton Arthur
b. 1923 Rinkoff, Barbara Jean
b. 1925 Maneloveg, Herbert Donald
b. 1928 Shevardnadze, Eduard
     Amvrosiyevich
b. 1929 Golson, Benny
b. 1930 Shuster, Alvin
b. 1933 Aquino, Corazon Cojuangco
b. 1934 Allen, Elizabeth
b. 1935 Eanes, Antonio Ramalho
b. 1936 Hyland, Diana
b. 1936 Jones, Dean
b. 1941 Baker, "Buddy" (Elzie Wylie, Jr.)
b. 1950 Cotten, Michael
b. 1951 Prefontaine, Steve Roland
b. 1954 Finch, Rick (Richard)
d. 1640 Burton, Robert
d. 1852 Bellinghausen, Fabian Gottlieb von
d. 1855 Nerval, Gerard de
d. 1906 Wheeler, Joseph
d. 1908 Ouida, pseud.
d. 1910 Faust, Lotta
d. 1920 Modigliani, Amedeo
d. 1921 Bonfanti, Marie
d. 1929 Underwood, Oscar Wilder
d. 1947 Capone, Al(phonse)
d. 1949 Marshall, Peter
d. 1952 Moran, Polly
d. 1953 Jacobs, Michael S
d. 1953 Pitkin, Walter Boughton
d. 1957 Tuthill, Harry J
d. 1960 Barrymore, Diana
d. 1967 Bastianini, Ettore
d. 1969 Castle, Irene Foote
d. 1972 Hayden, Carl Trumball
d. 1975 Kellems, Vivien
d. 1976 Henderson, Vivian Wilson
d. 1980 Harsh, George
d. 1981 Astaire, Adele
d. 1985 Smith, Paul Joseph

January 26
b. Bible, Frances Lillian
b. 1801 Quidor, John
b. 1826 Grant, Julia Dent
b. 1831 Dodge, Mary Elizabeth Mapes
b. 1832 Shiras, George, Jr.
b. 1842 Coppee, Francois Edouard Joachim
b. 2847 Clark, John Bates
b. 1861 Lowden, Frank O(rren)
b. 1871 Adams, Samuel Hopkins
b. 1872 Morgan, Julia
b. 1877 Dongen, Kees van
b. 1878 Gabrilowitsch, Ossip
b. 1880 MacArthur, Douglas

b. 1884 Andrews, Roy Chapman
b. 1884 Sapir, Edward
b. 1887 Mitscher, Marc A
b. 1891 Costello, Frank
b. 1902 Brent, Romney
b. 1904 Keys, Ancel Benjamin
b. 1905 Cousins, Margaret
b. 1905 Trapp, Maria Augusta von
b. 1907 Selye, "Hans" (Hugo Bruno)
b. 1908 Esmond, Jill
b. 1908 Grappelli, Stephane
b. 1912 Baird, Cora Eisenberg
b. 1912 Cannon, Howard Walter
b. 1912 Sheinwold, Alfred
b. 1913 Prince, William
b. 1913 Van Heusen, Jimmy (James)
b. 1914 DeManio, Jack
b. 1914 Robinson, Paul Minnich
b. 1915 Hopper, William
b. 1918 Ceausescu, Nicolae
b. 1918 Farmer, Philip Jose
b. 1921 Morita, Akio
b. 1923 Jeffreys, Anne
b. 1925 Leslie, Joan
b. 1925 Newman, Paul
b. 1925 Ryan, Claude
b. 1927 Redfield, William
b. 1928 Vadim, Roger
b. 1929 Feiffer, Jules Ralph
b. 1929 Kronhausen, Phyllis Carmen
b. 1930 Gumbleton, Thomas
b. 1932 Clements, George Harold
b. 1935 Uecker, Bob (Robert George)
b. 1939 Garfield, Brian Wynne
b. 1943 Hite, Robert Ernest, Jr.
b. 1944 Davis, Angela Yvonne
b. 1945 DuPre, Jacqueline
b. 1946 Hampton, Christopher James
b. 1946 Siskel, Eugene Karl
b. 1947 Dewaere, Patrick
b. 1950 Youngblood, (Herbert) Jack(son)
b. 1957 McCourt, Dale Allen
b. 1957 Van Halen, Eddie (Edward)
b. 1961 Gretzky, Wayne
b. 1963 Ridgeley, Andrew
d. 1823 Jenner, Edward
d. 1824 Gericault, Jean Louis Andre
     Theodore
d. 1839 Van Rensselaer, Stephen
d. 1860 Schroder-Devrient, Wilhelmine
d. 1885 Gordon, Charles George
d. 1891 Otto, Nikolaus August
d. 1893 Doubleday, Abner
d. 1932 Wrigley, William, Jr.
d. 1933 Belmont, Alva Erskine Smith
     Vanderbilt
d. 1935 Ippolitov-Ivanov, Mikhail
     Mikhailovich
d. 1936 Ittner, William Butts
d. 1945 Pendergast, Thomas J
d. 1945 Szabo, Violette Bushell

b. 1884 Piccard, Jean Felix
b. 1887 Rubinstein, Arthur
b. 1890 Fergusson, Harvey
b. 1891 Doak, Bill (William Leopold)
b. 1891 Sedran, Barney
b. 1892 Lubitsch, Ernst
b. 1893 Silver, Abba Hillel
b. 1897 Katayev, Valentin
b. 1900 Neel, Alice Hartley
b. 1900 Perkins, Milo Randolph
b. 1901 Barthe, Richmond
b. 1902 Barr, Alfred Hamilton, Jr.
b. 1911 Metcalf, Lee
b. 1911 Moss, Arnold
b. 1912 Pollock, Jackson
b. 1912 Wolfson, Louis Elwood
b. 1918 Yeend, Frances
b. 1929 Oldenburg, Claes Thure
b. 1932 O'Brien, Parry
b. 1933 Sontag, Susan
b. 1935 Pryor, Nicholas
b. 1936 Alda, Alan
b. 1943 Howard, Susan
b. 1946 Allen, Rick
b. 1946 Beck, John
b. 1948 Baryshnikov, Mikhail
b. 1950 Benton, Barbie
b. 1956 Schilling, Peter
b. 1957 Price, Nick
b. 1961 Williard, Daniel
d. 1547 Henry VIII
d. 1596 Drake, Francis, Sir
d. 1613 Bodley, Thomas, Sir
d. 1725 Peter the Great
d. 814 Charlemagne
d. 1829 Burke, William
d. 1859 Prescott, William Hickling
d. 1865 Romani, Felice
d. 1868 Head, Edmund Walker, Sir
d. 1903 Planquette, Jean(-Robert)
d. 1918 McCrae, John
d. 1926 Kohler, Kaufmann
d. 1930 Destinn, Emmy
d. 1933 Saintsbury, George Edward
  Bateman
d. 1933 Teasdale, Sara
d. 1939 Yeats, William Butler
d. 1947 Gagn, Reynaldo
d. 1960 Hurston, Zora Neale
d. 1963 Farrow, John Villiers
d. 1963 Piccard, Jean Felix
d. 1965 Weygand, Maxime
d. 1966 Quill, Mike (Michael J)
d. 1969 Herbst, Josephine Frey
d. 1969 Steinberg, Sigfrid Henry
d. 1975 Novotny, Antonin
d. 1977 Prinze, Freddie
d. 1981 Gerber, John
d. 1981 Gribble, Harry Wagstaff Graham
d. 1984 Dexter, Al
d. 1984 Dooley, Rae (Rachel Rice)

d. 1985 Saunders, Allen
d. 1986 Jarvis, Gregory
d. 1986 McAuliffe, Christa (Sharon Christa
  Corrigan)
d. 1986 McNair, Ronald
d. 1986 Onizuka, Ellison
d. 1986 Resnik, Judy (Judith)
d. 1986 Scobee, Dick (Francis Richard)
d. 1986 Smith, Michael John

January 29
b. 1688 Swedenborg, Emanuel
b. 1717 Amherst, Jeffrey
b. 1737 Paine, Thomas
b. 1754 Cleaveland, Moses
b. 1756 Lee, Henry
b. 1761 Gallatin, Albert (Abraham Alfonse
  Albert)
b. 1773 Mohs, Friedrich
b. 1835 Woolsey, Sarah Chauncey
b. 1843 McKinley, William
b. 1862 Delius, Frederick
b. 1866 Rolland, Romain
b. 1870 Bordeaux, Henry
b. 1872 Rothenstein, William, Sir
b. 1873 Palmer, Frederick
b. 1874 Davis, Owen
b. 1874 Rockefeller, John D(avison), Jr.
b. 1878 Akeley, Mary Lee Jobe
b. 1878 George, Walter Franklin
b. 1878 Oldfield, Barney (Berna Eli)
b. 1880 Fields, W C
b. 1895 Berle, Adolf Augustus, Jr.
b. 1898 Muller, Maria
b. 1901 DuMont, Allen Balcom
b. 1905 Delmar, Vina Croter
b. 1905 Newman, Barnett
b. 1907 Bernstein, Sid(ney Ralph)
b. 1909 Marshal, Alan
b. 1909 Masur, Harold Q
b. 1911 Eldridge, Roy
b. 1912 Griffiths, Martha Wright
b. 1913 Schneider, Nina
b. 1914 Prudden, Bonnie
b. 1916 Mature, Victor
b. 1918 Barber, Bernard
b. 1918 Forsythe, John
b. 1920 Allsop, Kenneth
b. 1920 Krantz, Hazel Newman
b. 1922 Richman, Milton
b. 1923 Chayefsky, "Paddy" (Sidney)
b. 1924 Nono, Luigi
b. 1925 Abrahams, Doris Cole
b. 1925 Crichton, Robert
b. 1929 Petri, Elio
b. 1931 Bricusse, Leslie
b. 1936 Harrison, Noel
b. 1939 Greer, Germaine
b. 1940 Diaz, Justino
b. 1942 Longet, Claudine Georgette
b. 1943 Quinn, Pat (John Brian Patrick)
b. 1943 Ross, Katharine

b. 1945 Caponi, Donna
b. 1945 Selleck, Tom
b. 1951 Jillian, Ann
b. 1954 Galbreath, Tony (Anthony)
b. 1958 Norton-Taylor, Judy
b. 1959 Foligno, Mike (Michael Anthony)
b. 1960 Louganis, Greg(ory Efthimios)
d. 1647 Meres, Francis
d. 1820 George III
d. 1829 Barras, Paul Francois Jean
Nicolas, Comte de
d. 1859 Thomas, Seth
d. 1888 Lear, Edward
d. 1899 Sisley, Alfred
d. 1901 Armour, Philip Danforth
d. 1923 Vedder, Elihu
d. 1930 Tappan, Eva March
d. 1935 Dellenbaugh, Frederick Samuel
d. 1940 Harkness, Edward Stephen
d. 1941 Metaxas, John(Ioannis)
d. 1944 White, William Allen
d. 1946 Hopkins, Harry Lloyd
d. 1951 Bridie, James, pseud.
d. 1956 Mencken, H(enry) L(ouis)
d. 1960 Harrell, Mack
d. 1962 Kreisler, Fritz
d. 1963 Frost, Robert Lee
d. 1964 Anderson, Mary
d. 1964 Ladd, Alan
d. 1968 Black, Frank J.
d. 1969 Boehm, Edward M
d. 1969 Dulles, Allen Welsh
d. 1970 Harris, Lauren
d. 1970 Liddell Hart, Basil Henry
d. 1974 Bates, H(erbert) E(rnest)
d. 1978 McCoy, Tim(othy John Fitzgerald)
d. 1979 Soby, James Thrall
d. 1980 Durante, Jimmy (James Francis)
d. 1981 Cole, "Cozy" (William Randolph)
d. 1981 Glassco, John Stinson
d. 1982 Namgyal, Palden Thondup
d. 1983 Ingersoll, Stuart H
d. 1984 Goodrich, Frances

January 30
b. 1720 Bellotto, Bernardo
b. 1750 Thomas, Isaiah
b. 1775 Landor, Walter Savage
b. 1792 Hopkins, John Henry
b. 1797 Sumner, Edwin V
b. 1841 Faure, Felix
b. 1841 Townsend, George Alfred
b. 1861 Loeffler, Charles Martin Tornov
b. 1862 Damrosch, Walter Johannes
b. 1866 Burgess, Gelett (Frank Gelett)
b. 1882 Roosevelt, Franklin Delano
b. 1885 Towers, John Henry
b. 1891 Beech, Walter Herschel
b. 1899 Theiler, Max
b. 1900 Hunt, Martita
b. 1902 Pevsner, Nikolaus Bernhard Leon,
Sir

b. 1903 Gassner, John Waldhorn
b. 1909 Alinsky, Saul David
b. 1911 Foyle, Christina
b. 1911 McDowell, Frank
b. 1911 Sanderson, Ivan Terence
b. 1912 Tuchman, Barbara Wertheim
b. 1914 Marlowe, Hugh
b. 1914 Wayne, David
b. 1915 Ireland, John
b. 1915 Profumo, John Dennis
b. 1917 Darion, Joseph
b. 1918 Opatashu, David
b. 1920 Anderson, Michael
b. 1923 Dropo, Walt
b. 1923 Martin, Dick
b. 1924 Alexander, Lloyd Chudley
b. 1925 Malone, Dorothy
b. 1927 Palme, (Sven) Olof (Joachim)
b. 1928 Leigh, Mitch
b. 1928 Meskill, Thomas J
b. 1928 Prince, Hal (Harold Smith)
b. 1929 Stevens, Morton
b. 1931 Hackman, Gene (Eugene Alden)
b. 1933 Brautigan, Richard
b. 1933 Rukeyser, Louis Richard
b. 1934 Markus, Robert
b. 1936 Grimes, Tammy Lee
b. 1937 Redgrave, Vanessa
b. 1937 Spassky, Boris Vasilyevich
b. 1943 Balin, Marty
b. 1943 Deane, Sandy
b. 1943 Johnson, Dave (David Allen)
b. 1944 Harrell, Lynn Morris
b. 1946 Beesley, H(orace) Brent
b. 1951 Collins, Phil
b. 1955 Cromwell, Nolan
b. 1955 Strange, Curtis
b. 1955 Thompson, Mychal
d. 1649 Charles I
d. 1652 LaTour, George Dumesnil de
d. 1797 Glover, John
d. 1806 Martin y Soler, Vicente
d. 1836 Ross, Betsy (Elizabeth Griscom)
d. 1838 Osceola Nickanochee
d. 1872 Chesney, Francis Rawdon
d. 1888 Gray, Asa
d. 1888 Howitt, Mary
d. 1889 Rudolf of Hapsburg
d. 1891 Kalakaua, David
d. 1909 Finley, Martha
d. 1916 Jacobs, Joseph
d. 1926 Doughty, Charles Montagu
d. 1926 LaMarr, Barbara
d. 1928 Fibiger, Johannes Andreas Grib
d. 1934 Doubleday, Frank Nelson
d. 1948 Gandhi, Mahatma
d. 1948 Pennock, Herb(ert Jefferis)
d. 1948 Wright, Orville
d. 1951 Porsche, Ferdinand
d. 1954 Anderson, John Murray
d. 1954 Wilson, Henry Braid

d. 1955 Lert, Ernst
d. 1963 Poulenc, Francis
d. 1979 Muir, Malcolm
d. 1980 Byrd, Henry
d. 1980 Dagover, Lil (Marta Maria Liletta)
d. 1980 Margolius, Sidney Senier
d. 1980 Papanin, Ivan D
d. 1981 Gopallawa, William
d. 1982 Holloway, Stanley
d. 1982 Hopkins, "Lightnin'" (Sam)
d. 1982 Lynd, Helen Merrell
d. 1983 Cunningham, Alan Gordon, Sir
d. 1983 Machlup, Fritz
d. 1983 Stevens, Robert Ten Broeck
d. 1984 Coxe, George Harmon
d. 1986 Erickson, Leif

January 31
b. 1734 Morris, Robert
b. 1735 Crevecoeur, Michel-Guillaume Jean de
b. 1752 Morris, Gouverneur
b. 1788 Romani, Felice
b. 1797 Schubert, Franz Peter
b. 1806 Harper, Fletcher
b. 1830 Blaine, James Gillespie
b. 1831 Wurlitzer, Rudolph
b. 1841 Stanley, Henry Morton, Sir
b. 1848 Straus, Nathan
b. 1851 Webb, William Seward
b. 1860 Huneker, James Gibbons
b. 1872 Hughes, Rupert
b. 1875 Grey, Zane
b. 1876 Spargo, John
b. 1881 Langmuir, Irving
b. 1885 Pavlova, Anna
b. 1892 Cantor, Eddie
b. 1894 Jones, Isham
b. 1896 Strauss, Lewis Lichtenstein
b. 1900 Humes, Harold Louis
b. 1900 Parsons, Betty Pierson
b. 1901 Fabian, Robert Honey
b. 1902 Myrdal, Alva Reimer
b. 1903 Bankhead, Tallulah Brockman
b. 1903 Cowles, Gardner
b. 1905 O'Hara, John Henry
b. 1908 Cantwell, Robert Emmett
b. 1914 Addonizio, Hugh Joseph
b. 1914 Walcott, "Jersey Joe"
b. 1915 Hackett, Bobby (Robert Leo)
b. 1915 Merton, Thomas
b. 1915 Moore, Garry
b. 1916 Parker, Frank
b. 1919 Robinson, Jackie (John Roosevelt)
b. 1920 Udall, Stewart Lee
b. 1920 Warnke, Paul Culliton
b. 1921 Agar, John
b. 1921 Lanza, Mario
b. 1923 Channing, Carol
b. 1923 Dru, Joanne
b. 1923 Mailer, Norman
b. 1925 Hooks, Benjamin Lawson

b. 1929 Simmons, Jean
b. 1931 Banks, Ernie (Ernest)
b. 1931 Carbine, Patricia Theresa
b. 1931 Chataway, Christopher John
b. 1931 Haworth, Mary Robbins
b. 1934 Franciscus, James Grover
b. 1937 Glass, Philip
b. 1937 Pleshette, Suzanne
b. 1938 Beatrix
b. 1938 Watt, James Gaius
b. 1940 Margolin, Stuart
b. 1944 Walter, Jessica
b. 1946 Kath, Terry
b. 1947 Ryan, Nolan (Lynn Nolan)
b. 1951 Casey, H(arry) W(ayne)
b. 1955 Ruzici, Virginia
b. 1957 Babashoff, Shirley
d. 1606 Fawkes, Guy
d. 1783 Majorano, Gaetano
d. 1788 Stuart, Charles Edward Louis Philip
d. 1795 Pemberton, John Clifford
d. 1854 Pellico, Silvio
d. 1866 Ruckert, Friedrich
d. 1891 Meissonier, Jean Louis Ernest
d. 1907 Eaton, Timothy
d. 1919 Goodwin, Nat C
d. 1922 Borglum, Solon Hannibal
d. 1925 Cable, George Washington
d. 1933 Galsworthy, John
d. 1934 Wellman, Walter
d. 1944 Giraudoux, Jean
d. 1945 Slovik, Eddie (Edward Donald)
d. 1947 Kling, John Gradwohl
d. 1951 Cochran, C(harles) B(lake)
d. 1954 Bates, Florence
d. 1955 Washington, "Buck" (Ford Lee)
d. 1956 Milne, A(lan) A(lexander)
d. 1961 Thompson, Dorothy
d. 1965 Cooper, Kent
d. 1966 Manship, Paul
d. 1968 Pillsbury, John Sargent
d. 1970 Bell, Herbert A
d. 1972 Barlow, Howard
d. 1972 Boyce, Westray Battle
d. 1972 Mahendra, Bir Bikram Shah Dev
d. 1973 Frisch, Ragnar
d. 1974 Goldwyn, Samuel
d. 1974 Pryor, Roger
d. 1976 Miranda, Ernesto
d. 1976 Wells, Linton
d. 1979 Pratt, Gerald Hillary
d. 1980 Crosby, Alexander L
d. 1981 Butterfield, Roger Place
d. 1982 Calder, Peter Ritchie
d. 1982 Turnbull, Agnes Sligh
d. 1984 Bricktop
d. 1986 Jessup, Philip Caryl

b. 1800 Gregg, William
b. 1803 Johnston, Albert S
b. 1811 Bacon, Delia Salter
b. 1825 Dalton, John Call
b. 1828 Meredith, George
b. 1859 Ellis, Havelock(Henry Havelock)
b. 1861 Guggenheim, Solomon Robert
b. 1864 Asquith, Emma Alice Margot
b. 1867 Saunders, Charles E
b. 1873 Neurath, Constantin Freiherr von
b. 1875 Kreisler, Fritz
b. 1877 Towne, Charles Hanson
b. 1882 Joyce, James Augustus Aloysius
b. 1883 McCulley, Johnston
b. 1883 Smith, Howard Worth
b. 1884 Sakall, S Z
b. 1886 Benet, William Rose
b. 1888 Lloyd, Frank
b. 1889 Lattre de Tassigny, Jean de
b. 1890 Correll, Charles J
b. 1891 Segni, Antonio
b. 1895 Halas, George Stanley
b. 1898 Brinton, Clarence Crane
b. 1899 Caudill, Rebecca
b. 1901 Heifetz, Jascha
b. 1901 Husch, Gerhard
b. 1901 Kahn, Louis I
b. 1902 Morris, Newbold
b. 1904 Gruber, Frank
b. 1905 Hayward, John Davy
b. 1905 Rand, Ayn
b. 1906 Gordon, Gale
b. 1908 Ferrell, Wes(ley Cheek)
b. 1908 Rossellini, Renzo
b. 1908 Tinney, Cal(vin Lawrence)
b. 1909 Albertson, Frank
b. 1909 Randhawa, Mohinder Singh
b. 1911 Bjoerling, Jussi
b. 1912 Lane, Burton
b. 1914 Apostoli, Fred B
b. 1914 Dedijer, Vladimir
b. 1915 Eban, Abba
b. 1919 Tucker, Forrest Meredith
b. 1921 Geist, Jacob
b. 1923 Dickey, James
b. 1923 Granville, Bonita
b. 1923 Schoendienst, "Red" (Albert Fred)
b. 1923 Smith, Liz (Mary Elizabeth)
b. 1924 Stitt, "Sonny" (Edward)
b. 1926 Fogarty, Anne
b. 1926 Giscard d'Estaing, Valery
b. 1927 Getz, Stan
b. 1927 Kaplow, Herbert E
b. 1928 Stritch, Elaine
b. 1931 Agt, Andries Antonius Maria van
b. 1931 Viorst, Judith (Stahl)
b. 1935 Wagner, Jane
b. 1936 LaFollette, Bronson Cutting
b. 1937 Buford, Don(ald Alvin)
b. 1937 Smothers, Tommy (Thomas Bolyn, III)

b. 1938 Estes, Simon Lamont
b. 1940 Arroyo, Martina
b. 1942 Diller, Barry Charles
b. 1942 Hopkins, Bo
b. 1942 Nash, Graham
b. 1947 Fawcett, Farrah Leni
b. 1948 Savitch, Jessica Beth
b. 1953 Brinkley, Christie
b. 1954 Tudor, John Thomas
b. 1963 Dahlin, Kjell
d. 1491 Schongauer, Martin
d. 1529 Castiglione, Baldassare, Conte
d. 1594 Palestrina, Giovanni
d. 1804 Walton, George
d. 1826 Brillat-Savarin, Jean Anthelme
d. 1884 Matteson, Tompkins Harrison
d. 1884 Phillips, Wendell
d. 1900 Wittenmyer, Annie Turner
d. 1904 Whitney, William Collins
d. 1907 Mendeleev, Dmitri
d. 1918 Sullivan, John L(awrence)
d. 1919 Leroux, Xavier
d. 1921 Mancinelli, Luigi
d. 1922 Taylor, William Desmond
d. 1936 Seaman, Owen, Sir
d. 1944 Guilbert, Yvette
d. 1948 Lamont, Thomas William
d. 1956 Burns, Bob
d. 1956 Grapewin, Charley (Charles)
d. 1957 Morgan, Julia
d. 1962 Budd, Ralph
d. 1963 Gaxton, William
d. 1965 Blackmur, Richard Palmer
d. 1967 Roos, Frank John, Jr.
d. 1967 Sevitzky, Fabien
d. 1968 Serafin, Tullio
d. 1969 Karloff, Boris
d. 1969 Martinelli, Giovanni
d. 1970 Russell, Bertrand Arthur William
d. 1971 Hellmann, Richard
d. 1972 Barney, Natalie Clifford
d. 1972 Landis, Jessie Royce
d. 1974 Lakatos, Imre
d. 1978 Barrie, Wendy
d. 1979 Douglas, Aaron
d. 1979 Vicious, Sid
d. 1981 Addonizio, Hugh Joseph
d. 1982 Stanford, Sally

Febuary 3

b. Bridges, James
b. 1757 Volney, (Constantin) Francois Chasseboeuf
b. 1807 Johnston, Joseph Eggleston
b. 1809 Mendelssohn, Felix
b. 1811 Greeley, Horace
b. 1820 Kane, Elisha Kent
b. 1821 Blackwell, Elizabeth
b. 1823 Baird, Spencer Fullerton
b. 1826 Bagehot, Walter
b. 1830 Salisbury, Robert Arthur Talbot, 3rd Marquess

Chronological Index

b. 1897 Erhard, Ludwig
b. 1898 Monroe, Marion
b. 1900 Impellitteri, Vincent R
b. 1901 Werth, Alexander
b. 1902 Lindbergh, Charles Augustus
b. 1904 Covarrubias, Miguel
b. 1904 Kantor, Mackinlay
b. 1905 Foy, Eddie, Jr.
b. 1906 Bonhoeffer, Dietrich
b. 1907 Spivakovsky, Tossy
b. 1909 Coote, Robert
b. 1910 Ellison, Virginia Howell
b. 1912 Leinsdorf, Erich
b. 1912 Nelson, Byron (John Byron, Jr.)
b. 1912 Richardson, Scovel
b. 1913 Parks, Rosa Lee
b. 1913 Stevenson, Janet
b. 1915 Evans, Ray
b. 1915 Talman, William
b. 1917 Yahya Khan, Agha Muhammad
b. 1918 Lupino, Ida
b. 1920 Beebe, Burdetta Faye
b. 1921 Friedan, Betty Naomi Goldstein
b. 1923 Bain, Conrad Stafford
b. 1925 Hoban, Russell
b. 1925 Wisdom, Norman
b. 1926 Tassell, Gustave
b. 1926 Welch, Ken
b. 1931 Peron, Isabel
b. 1932 Coover, Robert
b. 1935 Talvela, Martti Olavi
b. 1938 Riegle, Donald Wayne, Jr.
b. 1940 Bakke, Allan Paul
b. 1940 Broadhurst, Kent
b. 1943 Lee, Gary Earl
b. 1943 Miller, Cheryl
b. 1944 Davis, Andrew Frank
b. 1945 Brenner, David
b. 1947 Quayle, (James) Dan(forth)
b. 1948 Cooper, Alice
b. 1949 Beck, Michael
b. 1950 Franklin, Pamela
b. 1961 Savard, Denis
d. 1617 Elzevir, Louis
d. 1833 O'Keeffe, John
d. 1881 Carlyle, Thomas
d. 1894 Sax, Adolphe
d. 1909 Clarkson, John Gibson
d. 1928 Lorentz, Hendrick Antoon
d. 1939 Sapir, Edward
d. 1953 Williams, Ben Ames
d. 1959 O'Connor, Una
d. 1963 Weldon, John
d. 1964 Conroy, Frank
d. 1965 Girdler, Tom Mercer
d. 1966 Beebe, Lucius Morris
d. 1966 Grosvenor, Gilbert Hovey
d. 1968 Cassady, Neal
d. 1970 Bogan, Louise
d. 1975 Hill, Howard
d. 1975 Jordan, Louis

d. 1977 Dresser, Davis
d. 1978 Evans, Bergen Baldwin
d. 1980 Laye, Camara
d. 1980 Summerskill, Edith Clara, Baroness
d. 1983 Ameche, Jim
d. 1983 Carpenter, Karen Ann
d. 1984 Kaplan, Henry
d. 1985 Blackwell, Betsy Talbot
d. 1985 Wexley, John

Febuary 5
b. 1687 Geminiani, Francesco
b. 1723 Witherspoon, John
b. 1725 Otis, James
b. 1779 Pike, Zebulon Montgomery
b. 1788 Peel, Robert, Sir
b. 1810 Bull, Ole Bornemann
b. 1837 Moody, Dwight Lyman
b. 1840 Dunlop, John Boyd
b. 1840 Maxim, Hiram Stevens, Sir
b. 1848 Huysmans, Joris Karl
b. 1848 Mancinelli, Luigi
b. 1848 Starr, Belle Shirley
b. 1855 Merriam, Clinton Hart
b. 1871 Gardner, Mary Sewall
b. 1873 Elliott, Maxine
b. 1873 Heiser, Victor George
b. 1878 Citroen, Andre Gustave
b. 1882 Lattuada, Felice
b. 1888 Fraser, Bruce Austin, Sir
b. 1894 Morgan, Frederick
b. 1898 McGill, Ralph Emerson
b. 1900 Stevenson, Adlai Ewing, Jr.
b. 1901 Sheekman, Arthur
b. 1902 Kaper, Bronislau
b. 1903 Owings, Nathaniel Alexander
b. 1903 Payson, Joan Whitney
b. 1906 Carradine, John Richmond
b. 1907 Bender, Hans
b. 1907 Simon, Norton
b. 1907 White, William Smith
b. 1908 Gervasi, Frank
b. 1908 Hilton, Daisy
b. 1908 Hilton, Violet
b. 1914 Burroughs, William S(eward)
b. 1914 Hodgkin, Alan Lloyd
b. 1915 Hofstadter, Robert
b. 1915 Millar, Margaret Ellis
b. 1915 Sanderlin, George William
b. 1917 Edelmann, Otto
b. 1918 Holt, Tim
b. 1919 Buttons, Red
b. 1919 Papandreou, Andreas George
b. 1921 Adam, Ken
b. 1921 Pritchard, John Michael
b. 1926 Sulzberger, Arthur Ochs
b. 1928 Greeley, Andrew Moran
b. 1932 Kalb, Bernard
b. 1933 King, Claude
b. 1934 Aaron, Hank (Henry Louis)
b. 1934 Cherry, Don(ald Stewart)
b. 1937 Damon, Stuart

d. 1967 Morgenthau, Henry, Jr.
d. 1968 Berry, James Gomer
d. 1970 Karns, Roscoe
d. 1978 Cole, Charles Woolsey
d. 1981 Camerini, Mario
d. 1981 Frederika Louise
d. 1981 Montenegro, Hugo
d. 1982 Nicholson, Ben
d. 1984 Ernst, Jimmy
d. 1984 Guillen, Jorge
d. 1986 Yamasaki, Minoru

Febuary 7

b. 1478 More, Thomas, Sir
b. 1612 Killigrew, Thomas
b. 1688 Colden, Cadwallader
b. 1741 Fuseli, Henry
b. 1804 Deere, John
b. 1806 Hoffman, Charles Fenno
b. 1812 Dickens, Charles John Huffam
b. 1815 Beatty, Alfred Chester, Sir
b. 1834 Mendeleev, Dmitri
b. 1837 Murray, James Augustus Henry, Sir
b. 1859 Nevada, Emma
b. 1862 Maybeck, Bernard Ralph
b. 1863 Hope, Anthony
b. 1867 Wilder, Laura Elizabeth Ingalls
b. 1870 Adler, Alfred
b. 1874 Fuertes, Louis Agassiz
b. 1883 Blake, Eubie (James Hubert)
b. 1885 Lewis, Sinclair
b. 1889 Muzio, Claudia
b. 1892 Behrens, Earl Charles
b. 1895 Van Paassen, Pierre
b. 1896 Paludan, Jacob (Stig Henning Jacob Puggard)
b. 1897 Porter, Quincy
b. 1904 Dorne, Albert
b. 1904 Nugent, Edward
b. 1905 Von Euler, Ulf
b. 1908 Crabbe, "Buster" (Larry)
b. 1919 Iwama, Kazuo
b. 1919 Mahoney, Jock
b. 1920 Bracken, Eddie (Edward Vincent)
b. 1920 Brand, Oscar
b. 1920 Wang, An
b. 1923 Brasselle, Keefe
b. 1923 Harewood, George Henry Hubert Lascelles, Earl
b. 1924 Bryan, Dora
b. 1926 Feoktistov, Konstantin Petrovich
b. 1930 Bar-Ilian, David Jacob
b. 1932 Talese, Gay
b. 1932 Worden, Alfred Merrill
b. 1937 Jay, Peter
b. 1938 Thomopoulos, Anthony Denis
b. 1939 Reed, John Shepard
b. 1947 Lonsberry, Ross (David Ross)
b. 1953 Quisenberry, Dan(iel Raymond)
b. 1955 Benirschke, Rolf Joachim
b. 1957 Garcia, Damaso Domingo

b. 1962 McCrory, Milton
b. 1964 Woodhead, Cynthia
d. 1728 Iberville, Pierre Le Moyne, sieur d'
d. 1779 Boyce, William
d. 1799 Ch'ien Lung
d. 1823 Radcliffe, Ann
d. 1854 Fitzpatrick, Thomas
d. 1887 Borodin, Alexander Profirevich
d. 1936 Heggie, O P
d. 1937 Root, Elihu
d. 1938 Firestone, Harvey Samuel
d. 1948 McKenzie, "Red" (William)
d. 1949 Dimitrov, Georgi
d. 1952 Epstein, Philip G
d. 1954 Nelson, "Battling"
d. 1959 Lajoie, Nap(oleon)
d. 1959 Malan, Daniel F
d. 1960 Henderson, Leon
d. 1963 Pleasants, Henry
d. 1968 Poling, Daniel A
d. 1974 McGraw, Donald Cushing
d. 1975 Stein, Clarence S
d. 1979 Giles, Warren Crandall
d. 1979 Mengele, Josef
d. 1980 Ballinger, Margaret (Violet Margaret Livingstone)
d. 1982 Robinson, M(aurice) R(ichard)
d. 1985 Jacobs, Walter L

Febuary 8

b. 1559 Casaubon, Isaac
b. 1577 Burton, Robert
b. 1700 Bernoulli, David
b. 1804 Lander, Richard Lemon
b. 1819 Ruskin, John
b. 1820 Sherman, William Tecumseh
b. 1828 Verne, Jules
b. 1851 Chopin, Kate
b. 1878 Buber, Martin
b. 1880 Faust, Lotta
b. 1883 Schumpeter, Joseph Alois
b. 1888 Evans, Edith Mary Booth, Dame
b. 1890 Menjou, Adolphe Jean
b. 1892 Ruggles, Charles
b. 1894 Bishop, Billy (William Avery)
b. 1894 Vidor, King Wallis
b. 1895 Samuel, Maurice
b. 1900 Kredel, Fritz
b. 1902 Talbot, Lyle
b. 1903 Rahman, Abdul, Prince
b. 1906 Balsam, Artur
b. 1906 Carlson, Chester
b. 1906 Roth, Henry
b. 1907 Cole, Charles Woolsey
b. 1907 Middleton, Ray
b. 1908 McCormick, Myron
b. 1911 Bishop, Elizabeth
b. 1915 Jenkins, Newell
b. 1915 Lustig, Alvin
b. 1918 Field, Betty
b. 1919 Morrow, Buddy

b. 1920 Turner, "Lana" (Julia Jean
      Mildred Frances)
b. 1922 Glanzman, Louis S
b. 1925 Lemmon, Jack (John Uhler, III)
b. 1926 Cassady, Neal
b. 1930 Rey, Alejandro
b. 1931 Dean, James
b. 1932 Williams, John Towner
b. 1938 Ameling, Elly
b. 1938 Stewart, Andrew
b. 1941 Rush, Tom
b. 1942 Klein, Robert
b. 1942 Nolte, Nick
b. 1948 Light, Judith
b. 1949 Adams, Brooke
b. 1956 Johnson, Marques Kevin
b. 1958 Miller, Barry
b. 1968 Coleman, Gary
d. 1587 Mary, Queen of Scots
d. 1877 Wilkes, Charles
d. 1880 Sykes, George
d. 1887 Courtright, Jim (Timothy Isaiah)
d. 1903 Glaisher, James
d. 1909 Mendes, Catulle (Abraham Catulle)
d. 1920 Dehmel, Richard
d. 1921 Kropotkin, Peter Alekseyevich,
      Prince
d. 1926 Bateson, William
d. 1935 Evans, Charles
d. 1936 Curtis, Charles
d. 1941 Van Devanter, Willis
d. 1943 Casey, Dan(iel Maurice)
d. 1944 Cavalieri, Lina
d. 1949 Leoni, Franco
d. 1951 Thyssen, Fritz
d. 1956 Mack, Connie
d. 1957 Von Neumann, John
d. 1959 Berger, Meyer
d. 1959 Donovan, William Joseph
d. 1960 Austin, John Langshaw
d. 1967 Gollancz, Victor, Sir
d. 1972 Chinard, Gilbert
d. 1973 Coates, Robert Myron
d. 1974 Zwicky, Fritz
d. 1975 Green, Martyn
d. 1975 Robinson, Robert
d. 1979 Catlin, George Edward Gordon,
      Sir
d. 1979 Starch, Daniel
d. 1982 Whitney, John Hay
d. 1984 Aries, Philippe
d. 1985 Jaffe, Sam(uel Anderson)

Febuary 9
b. 1739 Bartram, William
b. 1741 Gretry, Andre Ernest Modeste
b. 1773 Harrison, William Henry
b. 1814 Tilden, Samuel Jones
b. 1822 Parton, James
b. 1826 Bowles, Samuel, II
b. 1826 Logan, John Alexander
b. 1840 Sampson, William T

b. 1865 Campbell, Mrs. Patrick
b. 1866 Ade, George
b. 1874 Lowell, Amy
b. 1883 Carter, John Garnet
b. 1885 Berg, Alban
b. 1889 Bamberger, Julian Maas
b. 1891 Colman, Ronald
b. 1891 Nenni, Pietro
b. 1892 Wood, Peggy
b. 1895 Vargas, Alberto
b. 1896 Parks, Floyd Lavinius
b. 1899 Donlevy, Brian
b. 1899 Langer, Walter C
b. 1899 Miller, Max
b. 1902 Harman, Fred
b. 1909 Angel, Heather
b. 1909 Miranda, Carmen
b. 1909 Rusk, Dean (David Dean)
b. 1909 Wilson, John N
b. 1910 Monod, Jacques
b. 1911 Snively, William Daniel, Jr.
b. 1912 Moorer, Thomas H(inman)
b. 1914 Lee, Gypsy Rose
b. 1914 Tubb, Ernie (Ernest)
b. 1914 Veeck, Bill (William Louis)
b. 1923 Behan, Brendan
b. 1923 Grayson, Kathryn
b. 1926 FitzGerald, Garret
b. 1928 Frazetta, Frank
b. 1928 Mudd, Roger Harrison
b. 1934 Ziegler, John Augustus, Jr.
b. 1939 Suzman, Janet
b. 1941 King, Carole
b. 1944 Walker, Alice
b. 1945 Bergey, Bill
b. 1945 Farrow, Mia Villiers
b. 1946 Webb, James H(enry)
b. 1951 Thomas, Dennis
b. 1956 Ford, Phil Jackson
d. 1567 Darnley, Henry Stuart, Lord
d. 1881 Dostoyevsky, Fyodor Mikhailovich
d. 1891 Jongkind, Johan Barthold
d. 1901 Harvey, Frederick Henry
d. 1906 Dunbar, Paul Laurence
d. 1921 Huneker, James Gibbons
d. 1925 Kerr, Alexander H
d. 1925 Lowell, Amy
d. 1931 Converse, Marquis M
d. 1934 Freshfield, Douglas William
d. 1937 Quiroga, Horacio
d. 1940 Dodd, William Edward
d. 1951 Duchin, Eddie
d. 1952 Douglas, Norman
d. 1961 Tydings, Millard Evelyn
d. 1963 Kassem, Abdul Karim
d. 1964 Chotzinoff, Samuel
d. 1966 Tucker, Sophie
d. 1969 Hayes, "Gabby" (George Francis)
d. 1969 Lescaze, William
d. 1972 Craig, May
d. 1976 Faith, Percy

d. 1977 Ilyushin, Sergei Vladimirovich
d. 1978 King, Warren Thomas
d. 1979 Gabor, Dennis
d. 1979 Tate, Allen (John Orley)
d. 1981 Anderson, Jack Zuinglius
d. 1981 Haley, Bill (William John Clifford, Jr.)
d. 1981 Thompson, Cecil
d. 1984 Andropov, Yuri Vladimirovich
d. 1984 Polk, Ralph Lane
d. 1986 Menard, H William
d. 1986 Pritzker, Abram Nicholas

Febuary 10
b. 1775 Lamb, Charles
b. 1821 Blair, Francis Preston
b. 1824 Plimsoll, Samuel
b. 1844 Barrett, William, Sir
b. 1846 Remsen, Ira
b. 1858 McDougall, Walt(er)
b. 1864 Roller, Alfred
b. 1868 White, William Allen
b. 1869 Cortissoz, Royal
b. 1870 Bonci, Alessandro
b. 1872 Hartford, John Augustine
b. 1878 Farnol, Jeffery
b. 1884 Evans, Billy (William George)
b. 1887 Sawyer, Charles
b. 1887 Ungaretti, Giuseppe
b. 1892 Hale, Alan
b. 1893 Durante, Jimmy (James Francis)
b. 1893 Tilden, Bill (William Tatem, Jr.)
b. 1894 MacMillan, Harold
b. 1894 Pennock, Herb(ert Jefferis)
b. 1897 Enders, John Franklin
b. 1898 Anderson, Judith, Dame
b. 1898 Brecht, Bertolt Eugene Friedrich
b. 1900 Sunay, Cevdet
b. 1902 Adler, Stella
b. 1902 Brattain, Walter Houser
b. 1902 Webb, "Chick" (William)
b. 1905 Brown, Walter Augustine
b. 1905 Chaney, Lon, Jr. (Creighton)
b. 1905 Livingston, J(oseph) A(rnold)
b. 1906 Farrow, John Villiers
b. 1906 Rhodes, Erik
b. 1910 Cebotari, Maria
b. 1910 Grenfell, Joyce Irene
b. 1913 Smith, Merriman
b. 1914 Adler, Larry (Lawrence Cecil)
b. 1920 Comfort, Alexander
b. 1922 Patterson, Neva
b. 1923 Henderson, Vivian Wilson
b. 1923 Siepi, Cesare
b. 1927 Lind, Jakov
b. 1927 Price, Leontyne
b. 1927 Weidenbaum, Murray Lew
b. 1930 Goldsmith, Jerry
b. 1930 Wagner, Robert John, Jr.
b. 1933 Schickel, Richard
b. 1939 Kolb, Barbara Anne
b. 1940 Flack, Roberta

b. 1940 Toomey, Mary Rand
b. 1944 Allen, Peter Woolnough
b. 1944 Lappe, Francis Moore
b. 1946 Donovan
b. 1950 Spitz, Mark Andrew
b. 1955 Norman, Greg
b. 1956 Beller, Kathleen
b. 1959 O'Grady, Sean
d. 1755 Montesquieu, Charles Louis de
d. 1837 Pushkin, Aleksandr Sergeyevich
d. 1857 Thompson, David
d. 1862 Siddal, Elizabeth Eleanor
d. 1868 Brewster, David, Sir
d. 1876 Johnson, Reverdy
d. 1878 Bernard, Claude
d. 1880 Cremieux, Isaac-Adolphe
d. 1899 Lampman, Archibald
d. 1912 Lister, Joseph
d. 1923 Roentgen, Wilhelm Konrad
d. 1924 Visscher, William Lightfoot
d. 1928 Little Tich
d. 1932 Wallace, Edgar
d. 1938 Whiting, Richard Armstrong
d. 1942 Henderson, Lawrence Joseph
d. 1942 Rice, Alice Caldwell Hegan
d. 1948 Eisenstein, Sergei Mikhailovich
d. 1949 Abe, Isao
d. 1955 McDonald, Harl
d. 1956 Trenchard, Hugh Montague, First Viscount
d. 1960 Cape, Herbert Jonathan
d. 1960 Stepinac, Alojzije, Cardinal
d. 1963 Taylor, John Henry
d. 1966 Dillon, William A
d. 1966 Rose, Billy
d. 1976 Kern, Harold G
d. 1981 Levy, Julien
d. 1981 Rebbot, Olivier
d. 1981 Shirley-Smith, Hubert
d. 1983 Franz, Eduard
d. 1986 Aherne, Brian de Lacy
d. 1986 Satherly, Arthur Edward

Febuary 11
b. 1766 Dunlap, William
b. 1800 Talbot, William Henry Fox
b. 1802 Child, Lydia Maria
b. 1812 Stephens, Alexander Hamilton
b. 1839 Gibbs, Josiah Willard
b. 1847 Edison, Thomas Alva
b. 1863 Fitzgerald, John Francis
b. 1883 Klenau, Paul von
b. 1887 Hanfstaengl, Ernst Franz Sedgwick
b. 1887 Hewitt, Henry Kent
b. 1888 Persinger, Louis
b. 1889 Mills, John
b. 1890 Pasternak, Boris Leonidovich
b. 1897 Darden, Colgate Whitehead
b. 1898 Szilard, Leo
b. 1900 Hitchcock, Tommy (Thomas, Jr.)
b. 1901 Hulman, Tony (Anton), Jr.
b. 1902 McBride, Floyd Mickey

b. 1916 Alioto, Joseph Lawrence
b. 1917 DiMaggio, Dom(inic Paul)
b. 1917 Scherman, Thomas K
b. 1923 Dugan, Alan
b. 1923 Zeffirelli, Franco
b. 1926 Garagiola, Joe (Joseph Henry)
b. 1926 Mitchell, Joan
b. 1926 Van Doren, Charles Lincoln
b. 1930 Specter, Arlen
b. 1934 Howard, Anthony
b. 1934 Russell, Bill (William Felton)
b. 1935 Manzarek, Ray
b. 1936 Baker, Joe Don
b. 1938 Blume, Judy Sussman
b. 1939 Hancock, John D
b. 1944 Pasarell, Charlie
b. 1945 Adams, Maud
b. 1945 DeYoung, Cliff
b. 1948 Kurzweil, Ray(mond)
b. 1949 Knight, Stan
b. 1950 Hackett, Steve
b. 1953 MacCorkindale, Simon
b. 1959 Nance, Larry Donnell
d. 1538 Altdorfer, Albrecht
d. 1554 Grey, Jane, Lady
d. 1728 Steffani, Agostino
d. 1763 Marivaux, Pierre Carlet de
d. 1804 Kant, Immanuel
d. 1834 Schleiermacher, Friedrich Ernst Daniel
d. 1841 Cooper, Astley Paston, Sir
d. 1871 Cary, Alice
d. 1886 Caldecott, Randolph
d. 1894 VonBulow, Hans Guido
d. 1896 Thomas, (Charles Louis) Ambroise
d. 1897 Martin, Homer Dodge
d. 1915 Crosby, Fanny (Frances Jane)
d. 1916 Trowbridge, John Townsend
d. 1929 Langtry, Lillie
d. 1942 Wood, Grant
d. 1947 Lewin, Kurt
d. 1947 Toler, Sidney
d. 1949 Levinsky, "Battling"
d. 1955 Moore, Tom
d. 1955 Sakall, S Z
d. 1959 Antheil, George
d. 1960 Clark, Bobby
d. 1962 Darling, Jay Norwood
d. 1967 Spanier, "Muggsy" (Francis Joseph)
d. 1971 Glueck, Nelson
d. 1971 Penney, J(ames) C(ash)
d. 1973 Maritain, Jacques
d. 1976 Mineo, Sal
d. 1978 Engelman, Wilfred
d. 1978 Taylor, Sydney Brenner
d. 1979 Renoir, Jean
d. 1980 Berger, Samuel David
d. 1980 Rukeyser, Muriel
d. 1981 Dixon, Jean
d. 1981 Fraser, Bruce Austin, Sir

d. 1982 Jory, Victor
d. 1983 Blake, Eubie (James Hubert)
d. 1985 Colasanto, Nicholas
d. 1985 Cortazar, Julio
d. 1985 Lengyel, Emil
d. 1986 Lazare, Kaplan
d. 1986 Stone, Sidney

Febuary 13
b. 1728 Hunter, John
b. 1754 Talleyrand-Perigord, Charles Maurice de
b. 1778 Sor, Fernando
b. 1815 Stoltz, Rosine
b. 1831 Rawlins, John A
b. 1835 Ahmad, Mirza Ghulam Hazat
b. 1849 Churchill, Randolph Henry Spencer, Lord
b. 1861 Curran, Charles Courtney
b. 1870 Godowsky, Leopold
b. 1873 Chaliapin, Feodor Ivanovitch
b. 1877 Smith, (Robert) Sidney
b. 1879 Naidu, Sarojini
b. 1881 Farjeon, Eleanor
b. 1885 Truman, Bess
b. 1888 Papandreou, George
b. 1891 Paul, Elliot Harold
b. 1892 Jackson, Robert Houghwout
b. 1892 Wood, Grant
b. 1895 Wilder, Joseph
b. 1901 Gibbon, Lewis Grassic, pseud.
b. 1901 Kuznetsov, Vasili Vasilievich
b. 1903 Simenon, Georges
b. 1904 Manone, "Wingy" (Joseph)
b. 1905 McKelway, St. Clair
b. 1908 Frederick, Pauline
b. 1908 Hayton, Lennie (Leonard George)
b. 1910 Cowles, Fleur Fenton
b. 1910 Shockley, William (Bradford)
b. 1911 Muir, Jean
b. 1913 Agostini, Peter
b. 1915 Bettger, Lyle
b. 1918 Berg, Patty (Patricia Jane)
b. 1918 Smith, Oliver
b. 1919 Edwards, Joan
b. 1919 Ford, "Tennessee Ernie" (Ernest J)
b. 1919 Robinson, Eddie
b. 1920 Farrell, Eileen
b. 1921 Warner, Rawleigh, Jr.
b. 1922 Pym, Francis Leslie
b. 1923 Abdnor, James S
b. 1923 Bilandic, Michael Anthony
b. 1923 Chapin, Schuyler Garrison
b. 1923 Shafran, Daniel
b. 1923 Yeager, Chuck (Charles Elwood)
b. 1924 Stevens, Leslie
b. 1928 Fried, Gerald
b. 1929 Torrijos Herrera, Omar
b. 1931 Klarsfeld, Beate
b. 1932 Bergerac, Michel C
b. 1933 Ungaro, Emanuel Matteotti
b. 1934 Segal, George

b. 1938 Reed, Oliver (Robert Oliver)
b. 1941 Rhodes, Samuel
b. 1943 Lynley, Carol
b. 1944 Channing, Stockard
b. 1944 Tork, Peter
d. 1728 Mather, Cotton
d. 1818 Clark, George Rogers
d. 1882 Garnet, Henry Highland
d. 1883 Wagner, Richard
d. 1888 Lamy, Jean Baptist
d. 1891 Porter, David Dixon
d. 1913 Major, Charles
d. 1914 Bertillon, Alphonse
d. 1926 Holt, Henry
d. 1927 Adams, Brooks
d. 1938 McIntyre, Oscar Odd
d. 1945 Szold, Henrietta
d. 1946 Neilson, William A
d. 1950 Sabatini, Rafael
d. 1951 Douglas, Lloyd Cassel
d. 1952 Einstein, Alfred
d. 1952 Tey, Josephine, pseud.
d. 1954 Allen, Frederick Lewis
d. 1954 Perry, Bliss
d. 1958 Rouault, Georges
d. 1963 Reynolds, Robert Rice
d. 1966 Stephen, John
d. 1968 Marsh, Mae
d. 1968 Pizzetti, Ildebrando
d. 1974 Arndt, Adolf
d. 1974 Golenpaul, Dan
d. 1975 Van Dusen, Henry Pitney
d. 1976 Pons, Lily
d. 1980 Janssen, David
d. 1980 Monroney, Mike (Aimer Stillwell)
d. 1981 Kaufman, Joseph William
d. 1985 Harris, Joseph Pratt
d. 1985 Jacobs, Al(bert T)

Febuary 14
b. 1404 Alberti, Leon Battista
b. 1483 Babur
b. 1602 Cavalli, Francesco
b. 1612 Butler, Samuel
b. 1760 Allen, Richard
b. 1768 Krylov, Ivan Andreyevich
b. 1813 Dargomijsky, Alexander
b. 1817 Douglass, Frederick
b. 1819 Sholes, Christopher Latham
b. 1823 Powell, William Henry
b. 1838 Ginn, Edwin
b. 1856 Harris, Frank
b. 1859 Ferris, George Washington Gale
b. 1860 Lillie, Gordon William
b. 1864 Zangwill, Israel
b. 1865 Anderson, Carl Thomas
b. 1872 Grove, Frederick Philip
b. 1882 Nathan, George Jean
b. 1884 Lange, Hans
b. 1889 Auerbach-Levy, William
b. 1894 Benny, Jack
b. 1898 Zwicky, Fritz

b. 1902 Erwin, Stuart
b. 1905 Ritter, Thelma
b. 1910 Dragonette, Jessica
b. 1910 Longden, Johnny
b. 1911 Kolff, Willem Johan
b. 1911 Porter, Bernard H
b. 1913 Allen, Mel
b. 1913 Hayes, "Woody" (Wayne Woodrow)
b. 1913 Hoffa, Jimmy (James Riddle)
b. 1913 Pike, James Albert
b. 1915 Austin, John Paul
b. 1917 Hauptman, Herbert Aaron
b. 1921 Downs, Hugh
b. 1922 Kaufman, Murray
b. 1925 Lawrence, Elliot
b. 1931 Geoffrion, Bernie (Bernard)
b. 1932 Morrow, Vic
b. 1932 Schroeder, William
b. 1933 Cook, Michael
b. 1933 Crosby, Joan Carew
b. 1934 Henderson, Florence
b. 1935 Wright, Mickey
b. 1938 Chamberlin, Lee
b. 1941 Tsongas, Paul Efthemios
b. 1943 Andersen, Eric
b. 1944 Bernstein, Carl
b. 1944 Parker, Alan William
b. 1944 Peterson, Ronnie
b. 1946 Hines, Gregory Oliver
b. 1950 Dent, Phil
d. 1571 Cellini, Benvenuto
d. 1779 Cook, James, Captain
d. 1780 Blackstone, William, Sir
d. 1864 Dyce, William
d. 1870 Harper, Joseph Wesley
d. 1884 Roosevelt, Alice Lee
d. 1885 Hotchkiss, Benjamin Berkeley
d. 1891 Sherman, William Tecumseh
d. 1923 Link, Theodore Carl
d. 1925 Bausch, John Jacob
d. 1945 Rothenstein, William, Sir
d. 1948 Brown, Mordecai Peter Centennial
d. 1958 Pankhurst, Christabel, Dame
d. 1958 Twelvetrees, Helen
d. 1959 Dodds, "Baby" (Warren)
d. 1959 Irwin, Wallace
d. 1963 Shannon, Fred Albert
d. 1965 Inghelbrecht, Desire
d. 1967 Rumann, Sig(fried)
d. 1969 Genovese, Vito
d. 1975 Huxley, Julian Sorell, Sir
d. 1975 Wodehouse, P(elham) G(renville)
d. 1978 Rattner, Abraham
d. 1979 Dubs, Adolph
d. 1979 Tunnard, Christopher
d. 1982 Jackson, "Hurricane" (Thomas)
d. 1984 Mili, Gjon
d. 1985 Spigelgass, Leonard
d. 1986 Wilder, Clinton

Febuary 15

b. 1564 Galileo
b. 1571 Praetorius, Michael
b. 1710 Louis XV
b. 1726 Clark, Abraham
b. 1748 Bentham, Jeremy
b. 1760 Lesueur, Jean-Francois
b. 1797 Steinway, Henry Engelhard
b. 1803 Sutter, John Augustus
b. 1809 McCormick, Cyrus Hall
b. 1812 Tiffany, Charles Lewis
b. 1817 Daubigny, Charles Francois
b. 1820 Anthony, Susan Brownell
b. 1829 Mitchell, Silas Weir
b. 1834 Haeckel, Ernst Heinrich
b. 1835 Dabney, Virginius
b. 1842 Quad, M, pseud.
b. 1845 Root, Elihu
b. 1858 Pickering, William Henry
b. 1861 Mackinder, Halford John, Sir
b. 1861 Whitehead, Alfred North
b. 1874 Shackleton, Ernest Henry, Sir
b. 1880 Davidson, J Brownlee
b. 1880 Hergesheimer, Joseph
b. 1882 Barrymore, John
b. 1883 Rohmer, Sax, pseud.
b. 1884 Gilbert, A(lfred) C(arleton)
b. 1884 Piccaver, Alfred
b. 1887 Bateman, Henry Mayo
b. 1890 Ley, Robert
b. 1892 Forrestal, James Vincent
b. 1893 Baxter, James Phinney, III
b. 1893 Donaldson, Walter
b. 1897 Blaik, "Red" (Earl Henry)
b. 1899 Auric, Georges
b. 1899 Josephson, Matthew
b. 1899 Keppard, Freddie
b. 1899 Sondergaard, Gale
b. 1900 Thomas, Charles Allen
b. 1901 Bracken, Brendan Rendall, Viscount
b. 1901 Humphreys, Christmas (Travers Christmas)
b. 1905 Arlen, Harold
b. 1907 Romero, Cesar
b. 1910 Aitken, Max (John William Maxwell)
b. 1910 Naylor, Bob
b. 1911 Woodcock, Leonard Freel
b. 1914 Boggs, Hale (Thomas Hale)
b. 1914 McCarthy, Kevin
b. 1915 Jordan, Taft
b. 1916 Ballantine, Ian
b. 1916 Seton-Watson, Hugh (George Hugh Nicholas)
b. 1922 Anderson, John Bayard
b. 1922 Kahn, Herman
b. 1927 Dunlop, Frank
b. 1927 Korman, Harvey Herschel
b. 1929 Hill, Graham (Norman Graham)
b. 1929 Schlesinger, James Rodney

b. 1930 Moore, Sara Jane
b. 1931 Bloom, Claire
b. 1933 Adolfo
b. 1935 Block, John Rusling
b. 1935 Brownmiller, Susan
b. 1935 Chaffee, Roger Bruce
b. 1947 Hamer, Rusty
b. 1948 Berenson, Marisa
b. 1948 Cey, Ron(ald Charles)
b. 1949 Anderson, Ken(neth Allan)
b. 1951 Manchester, Melissa Toni
b. 1951 Seymour, Jane
b. 1953 Adams, Tony (Anthony Patrick)
b. 1957 Stevens, Greer
d. 1479 Antonello da Messina
d. 1621 Praetorius, Michael
d. 1713 Shaftesbury, Anthony Ashley Cooper, Earl
d. 1781 Lessing, Gotthold Ephraim
d. 1820 Ellery, William
d. 1857 Glinka, Mikhail Ivanovich
d. 1865 Wiseman, Nicholas Patrick Stephen
d. 1885 Damrosch, Leopold
d. 1888 Locke, David Ross
d. 1904 Hanna, Mark (Marcus Alonzo)
d. 1905 Wallace, Lewis
d. 1918 Castle, Vernon
d. 1925 DeYoung, Michel Harry
d. 1928 Oxford and Asquith, Henry Herbert Asquith, Earl
d. 1929 Stone, Melville Elijah
d. 1931 Leitzel, Lillian
d. 1955 Maginnis, Charles Donagh
d. 1965 Cole, Nat "King" (Nathaniel Adams)
d. 1967 Bullitt, William C
d. 1967 Duryea, J(ames) Frank
d. 1969 Russell, "Pee Wee" (Charles Ellsworth)
d. 1970 Dowding, Hugh C T, Baron
d. 1972 Snow, Edgar Parks
d. 1973 Cox, Wally (Wallace Maynard)
d. 1973 Holt, Tim
d. 1978 Chase, Ilka
d. 1981 Bloomfield, Mike (Michael)
d. 1982 Dietrich, Noah
d. 1982 Enoch, Kurt
d. 1984 Merman, Ethel

Febuary 16

b. 1497 Melanchthon, Philip Schwarzerd
b. 1774 Rode, Jacques Pierre Joseph
b. 1812 Wilson, Henry
b. 1821 Barth, Heinrich
b. 1822 Galton, Francis, Sir
b. 1838 Adams, Henry Brooks
b. 1840 Watterson, Henry
b. 1848 DeVries, Hugo
b. 1852 Russell, Charles Taze
b. 1860 Fels, Samuel Simeon
b. 1864 Harvey, George Brinton M
b. 1866 Hamilton, Billy (William Robert)

b. 1918 Vallone, Raf(faele)
b. 1923 Clausen, A(lden) W(inship)
b. 1924 Truman, Margaret (Mary
Margaret)
b. 1925 Holbrook, Hal (Harold Rowe, Jr.)
b. 1926 Kohlmeier, Louis Martin, Jr.
b. 1928 Jones, Tom
b. 1929 Plante, Jacques (Joseph Jacques
Omer)
b. 1929 Potok, Chaim
b. 1931 Craig, Roger Lee
b. 1934 Bates, Alan Arthur
b. 1936 Bartholomew, Reginald
b. 1936 Brown, Jim (James Nathaniel)
b. 1938 Henry, Martha
b. 1942 Newton, Huey P
b. 1947 Buckley, Tim
b. 1959 Lomax, Neil Vincent
b. 1963 Jordon, Michael Jeffery
d. 1600 Bruno, Giordano
d. 1652 Allegri, Gregorio
d. 1673 Moliere, pseud.
d. 1796 Macpherson, James
d. 1827 Pestalozzi, Johann Heinrich
d. 1830 Rutgers, Henry
d. 1856 Heine, Heinrich
d. 1875 Argelander, Friedrich Wilhelm
August
d. 1876 Bushnell, Horace
d. 1876 Cushman, Charlotte Saunders
d. 1877 Mosenthal, Salomon Hermann von
d. 1890 Sholes, Christopher Latham
d. 1901 Nevin, Ethelbert Woodbridge
d. 1907 Olcott, Henry Steel
d. 1909 Geronimo
d. 1913 Miller, Joaquin, pseud.
d. 1919 Laurier, Wilfrid, Sir
d. 1925 Valleria, Alwina
d. 1934 Albert I
d. 1943 Keogan, George
d. 1961 Naldi, Nita
d. 1962 Walter, Bruno
d. 1963 Lockridge, Frances Louise
d. 1966 Hofmann, Hans
d. 1966 Sloan, Alfred Pritchard, Jr.
d. 1968 Mennen, William Gerhard
d. 1968 Wolfit, Donald, Sir
d. 1970 Agnon, S(hmuel) Y(osef)
d. 1970 Newman, Alfred
d. 1971 Berle, Adolf Augustus, Jr.
d. 1971 Mays, David John
d. 1974 Cole, Jack
d. 1977 Howe, Quincy
d. 1980 Sutherland, Graham Vivian
d. 1981 Garnett, David
d. 1982 Chylak, Nester
d. 1982 Monk, Thelonius Sphere
d. 1982 Strasberg, Lee
d. 1983 Pasero, Tancredi
d. 1984 Stuart, Jesse Hilton
d. 1986 Krishnamurti, Jiddu

d. 1986 Ruffing, "Red" (Charles Herbert)
d. 1986 Stewart, Paul

Febuary 18
b. 1516 Mary I
b. 1609 Clarendon, Edward Hyde, Earl
b. 1626 Redi, Francesco
b. 1745 Volta, Alessandro
b. 1775 Girtin, Thomas
b. 1792 Gorham, Jabez
b. 1795 Peabody, George
b. 1805 Goldsborough, Louis M
b. 1823 Cropsey, Jasper Francis
b. 1832 Chanute, Octave
b. 1838 Mach, Ernst
b. 1848 Tiffany, Louis Comfort
b. 1853 Belmont, August, Jr.
b. 1853 Fenollosa, Ernest Francisco
b. 1858 Sembrich, Marcella
b. 1859 Aleichem, Shalom, pseud.
b. 1862 Schwab, Charles Michael
b. 1878 Ames, Blanche
b. 1884 Laidler, Harry Wellington
b. 1884 McIntyre, Oscar Odd
b. 1888 Sheil, Bernard James, Archbishop
b. 1890 Arnold, Edward
b. 1892 Willkie, Wendell Lewis
b. 1894 Segovia, Andres
b. 1894 Williams, Paul R(evere)
b. 1895 Gipp, George
b. 1896 Breton, Andre
b. 1896 Harris, Joseph Pratt
b. 1896 Mitropoulos, Dimitri
b. 1898 Hadden, Briton
b. 1898 Munoz Marin, Luis
b. 1901 Berlenbach, Paul
b. 1903 Podgorny, Nikolai Viktorovich
b. 1907 DeWolfe, Billy
b. 1909 Stegner, Wallace Earle
b. 1913 Clark, Dane
b. 1915 Calvert, Phyllis
b. 1915 Gordon, Joe (Joseph Lowell)
b. 1918 Saint-Subber, Arnold
b. 1919 Hoveyda, Amir Abbas
b. 1920 Cullen, Bill (William Lawrence)
b. 1920 Palance, Jack
b. 1921 Faulkner, Brian
b. 1922 Brown, Helen Gurley
b. 1925 Kennedy, George
b. 1926 Gorr, Rita
b. 1927 Warner, John William
b. 1929 Deighton, Len (Leonard Cyril)
b. 1930 Wilson, Gahan
b. 1931 Hart, John(ny Lewis)
b. 1931 Morrison, Toni
b. 1932 Forman, Milos
b. 1932 Michals, Duane Steven
b. 1933 Novak, Kim (Marilyn)
b. 1933 Ono, Yoko
b. 1933 Ure, Mary
b. 1934 Ceccato, Aldo
b. 1935 Richardson, Jack

Chronological Index

d. 1985 Gorkin, Jess
d. 1985 Julesberg, Elizabeth Rider Montgomery
d. 1985 Lopez Bravo, Gregorio
d. 1985 Sutton, Carol
d. 1986 Eastland, James Oliver

Febuary 20
b. 1770 Holderlin, Johann C F
b. 1772 Chauncey, Isaac
b. 1791 Czerny, Karl
b. 1816 Rimmer, William
b. 1820 Vieuxtemps, Henri
b. 1829 Jefferson, Joseph
b. 1833 Crittenton, Charles Nelson
b. 1844 Slocum, Joshua
b. 1860 Howell, William H(enry)
b. 1863 Pissaro, Lucien
b. 1872 Trumbull, Charles Gallaudet
b. 1874 Bottomley, Gordon
b. 1874 Garden, Mary
b. 1886 Freuchen, Peter
b. 1887 Ebert, Carl (Anton Charles)
b. 1887 Massey, Vincent
b. 1888 Rambert, Dame Marie
b. 1892 Rice, "Sam" (Edgar Charles)
b. 1893 Crouse, Russel
b. 1897 Albright, Ivan Le Lorraine
b. 1897 Albright, Malvin Marr
b. 1898 Ferrari, Enzo
b. 1899 Whitney, C(ornelius) V(anderbilt)
b. 1901 Dubos, Rene Jules
b. 1901 Naguib, Mohammed
b. 1902 Adams, Ansel Easton
b. 1904 Brownell, Herbert, Jr.
b. 1904 Kosygin, Aleksei Nikolaevich
b. 1906 Fletcher, Bramwell
b. 1908 Kingsbury-Smith, Joseph
b. 1909 Alvary, Lorenzo
b. 1911 Grahame, Margot
b. 1912 Boulle, Pierre Francois Marie-Louis
b. 1912 Humphrey, Muriel Fay Buck
b. 1913 Conner, Nadine
b. 1913 Henrich, Tommy (Thomas David)
b. 1914 Daly, John Charles, Jr.
b. 1914 MacKellar, William
b. 1916 Slavenska, Mia
b. 1916 Tripp, Paul
b. 1918 Hesse, Don
b. 1923 Burnham, Forbes (Linden Forbes Sampson)
b. 1924 Fraser, Donald Mackay
b. 1924 Poitier, Sidney
b. 1924 Unser, Bobby
b. 1924 Vanderbilt, Gloria Morgan
b. 1925 Altman, Robert B
b. 1926 Matheson, Richard Burton
b. 1927 Cohn, Roy Marcus
b. 1928 Face, Roy (Elroy Leon)
b. 1930 Minguy, Claude
b. 1931 Blake, Amanda

b. 1932 Sidaris, Andy
b. 1933 Christian, Mary Blount
b. 1937 Wilson, Nancy
b. 1941 Sainte-Marie, "Buffy" (Beverly)
b. 1942 Esposito, Phil(ip)
b. 1942 McConnell, Mitch
b. 1946 Duncan, Sandy
b. 1947 Strauss, Peter
b. 1949 O'Neill, Jennifer
b. 1951 Albert, Edward
b. 1954 Hearst, Patty (Patricia Campbell)
b. 1961 Lundquist, Steve
b. 1963 Barkley, Charles Wade
d. 1437 James I
d. 1677 Spinoza, Baruch (Benedictus de)
d. 1707 Aurangzeb
d. 1810 Hofer, Andreas
d. 1877 Goldsborough, Louis M
d. 1893 Beauregard, Pierre Gustav Toutant de
d. 1895 Douglass, Frederick
d. 1908 Marchesi, Salvatore
d. 1916 Sbriglia, Giovanni
d. 1920 Peary, Robert Edwin
d. 1941 Lanman, Charles Rockwell
d. 1951 Maude, Cyril
d. 1953 Randall, James Garfield
d. 1954 Duncan, Augustin
d. 1959 Housman, Laurence
d. 1960 Woolley, Charles Leonard, Sir
d. 1961 Gardner, Mary Sewall
d. 1961 Grainger, Percy Aldridge
d. 1963 Fricsay, Ferenc
d. 1966 Hunter, Dard
d. 1966 Nimitz, Chester William
d. 1968 Asquith, Anthony
d. 1969 Ansermet, Ernest Alexandre
d. 1972 Mayer, Maria Goeppert
d. 1972 Winchell, Walter
d. 1973 Szigeti, Joseph
d. 1974 Strauss, Robert
d. 1976 Aurell, Tage
d. 1976 Cassin, Rene
d. 1976 Kuhlman, Kathryn
d. 1980 Longworth, Alice Roosevelt
d. 1980 Rhine, J(oseph) B(anks)
d. 1980 Shippen, Katherine Binney
d. 1981 Gunzberg, Nicolas de, Baron
d. 1982 Cornell, Douglas B
d. 1982 Dubos, Rene Jules
d. 1982 Scholem, Gershom Gerhard
d. 1985 Kashdan, Isaac
d. 1985 Nash, Clarence
d. 1985 Wilcox, Francis (Orlando)

Febuary 21
b. McClanahan, (Eddi-)Rue
b. 1752 Rochester, Nathaniel
b. 1801 Newman, John Henry, Cardinal
b. 1815 Meissonier, Jean Louis Ernest
b. 1821 Scribner, Charles
b. 1836 Delibes, Leo

b. 1917 Leek, Sybil
b. 1918 Abel, Sid(ney Gerald)
b. 1918 Finley, Charlie (Charles Oscar)
b. 1923 Ogilvie, Richard Buell
b. 1925 Gorey, Edward St. John
b. 1926 Hunt, Nelson Bunker
b. 1927 Mitchell, Guy
b. 1929 Duren, Ryne (Rinold George)
b. 1929 Nixon, Marni
b. 1932 Kennedy, Edward Moore
b. 1934 Anderson, "Sparky" (George Lee)
b. 1936 Roth, Frank
b. 1938 Reed, Ishmael
b. 1943 Van Arsdale, Dick (Richard
   Albert)
b. 1943 Van Arsdale, Tom (Thomas)
b. 1948 Awtrey, Dennis
b. 1949 Lauda, Niki (Nikolaus-Andreas)
b. 1950 Erving, Julius Winfield
b. 1956 Alcott, Amy
b. 1959 Lloyd, Lewis Kevin
b. 1965 La Fontaine, Pat
d. 1512 Vespucci, Amerigo
d. 1680 Deshayes, Catherine
d. 1781 Taylor, George
d. 1797 Munchhausen, Hierony mus Karl
   Friedrich von, Baron
d. 1810 Brown, Charles Brockden
d. 1827 Peale, Charles Willson
d. 1845 Smith Sydney
d. 1875 Corot, Jean Baptiste Camille
d. 1875 Lyell, Charles, Sir
d. 1896 Nye, Edgar Wilson (Bill)
d. 1903 Wolf, Hugo
d. 1904 Stephen, Leslie, Sir
d. 1921 Anderson, Elizabeth Milbank
d. 1932 Gadski, Johanna
d. 1939 Machado, Antonio
d. 1942 Zweig, Stefan
d. 1945 Baker, Sara Josephine
d. 1945 Tolstoy, Alexey Nikolaevich
d. 1947 Thaw, Harry Kendall
d. 1955 Goddard, Calvin Hooker
d. 1956 Carnegie, Hattie
d. 1960 Borduas, Paul-Emile
d. 1961 DeCuevas, Marquis
d. 1965 Frankfurter, Felix
d. 1968 Arno, Peter
d. 1968 Lucas, Scott Wike
d. 1973 Bowen, Elizabeth Dorothea Cole
d. 1973 Paxinou, Katina
d. 1973 Rockefeller, Winthrop
d. 1976 Baddeley, Angela (Madeleine
   Angela Clinton)
d. 1976 Ballard, Florence
d. 1978 Borland, Hal
d. 1978 Lawrence, Josephine
d. 1978 McGinley, Phyllis
d. 1980 Kokoschka, Oskar
d. 1981 Padover, Saul Kussiel
d. 1981 Smith, Joe

d. 1984 David
d. 1985 Espriu, Salvador
d. 1985 Scourby, Alexander
d. 1985 Zimbalist, Efrem

Febuary 23
b. 1400 Gutenberg, Johannes
b. 1633 Pepys, Samuel
b. 1685 Handel, George Frederick
b. 1743 Rothschild, Mayer Amschel
b. 1787 Willard, Emma Hart
b. 1846 Horlick, William
b. 1857 Deland, Margaret Wade
b. 1861 Wilson, Henry Braid
b. 1868 DuBois, W(illiam) E(dward)
   B(urghardt)
b. 1880 Chapin, Roy Dikeman
b. 1882 Fischer, Anton Otto
b. 1883 Fleming, Victor
b. 1883 Jaspers, Karl
b. 1884 Funk, Casimir
b. 1892 Tabouis, Genevieve
b. 1899 Kastner, Erich
b. 1899 Taurog, Norman
b. 1901 Nichols, Ruth Rowland
b. 1903 Alexandrov, Grigori
b. 1904 Shirer, William L(awrence)
b. 1905 Victor, Sally Josephs
b. 1907 Karamanlis, Constantine
b. 1911 Allen, Walter Ernest
b. 1911 Williams, G Mennen
b. 1915 Weingarten, Violet
b. 1916 Wheeler, Elmer P
b. 1920 Netsch, Walter Andrew, Jr.
b. 1929 Howard, Elston Gene
b. 1930 Davis, Gerry
b. 1931 Wesselmann, Tom
b. 1933 Calhoun, Lee Q
b. 1938 Chase, Sylvia
b. 1938 Varsi, Diane
b. 1939 Fonda, Peter
b. 1943 Biletnikoff, Fred(erick)
b. 1944 Winter, Johnny (John Dawson,
   III)
b. 1948 Arnot, Robert Burns
b. 1949 Garneau, Marc
b. 1951 Dibbs, Eddie (Edward George)
b. 1951 Jones, "Too Tall" (Edward Lee)
d. 1482 DellaRobbia, Luca
d. 1507 Bellini, Gentile
d. 1792 Reynolds, Joshua, Sir
d. 1800 Warton, Joseph
d. 1821 Keats, John
d. 1848 Adams, John Quincy
d. 1855 Gauss, Karl Friedrich
d. 1900 Dowson, Ernest Christopher
d. 1911 Quanah
d. 1930 Normand, Mabel
d. 1931 Melba, Dame Nellie
d. 1934 Elgar, Edward William, Sir
d. 1944 Baekeland, Leo Hendrick
d. 1946 Yamashita, Tomoyuki

b. 1873 Caruso, Enrico
b. 1881 Foster, William Zebulon
b. 1883 Alice (Mary Victoria Augusta Pauline)
b. 1888 Dulles, John Foster
b. 1888 Ferguson, Homer
b. 1890 Hess, Myra
b. 1896 Farrar, John Chipman
b. 1896 McClellan, John Little
b. 1899 Boyer, Harold R
b. 1900 Harris, Jed
b. 1901 Marx, "Zeppo" (Herbert)
b. 1903 Clancy, "King" (Francis Michael)
b. 1904 Davis, Adelle
b. 1905 Carter, Katherine Jones
b. 1905 Miller, Perry Gilbert Eddy
b. 1907 Chase, Mary Coyle
b. 1908 Slaughter, Frank G
b. 1910 Fenwick, Millicent Hammond
b. 1912 Frobe, Gert
b. 1913 Backus, Jim (James Gilmore)
b. 1914 Bonham, Frank
b. 1915 Nunn, Harold F
b. 1917 Burgess, Anthony
b. 1917 Raymond, James C
b. 1918 Riggs, Bobby (Robert Larimore)
b. 1919 Bendick, Jeanne
b. 1919 Irvin, Monte (Monford Merrill)
b. 1920 Habib, Philip Charles
b. 1920 Justice, William Wayne
b. 1923 Glazer, Nathan
b. 1925 Kirk, Lisa
b. 1925 Zipprodt, Patricia
b. 1928 Gelbart, Larry
b. 1928 Stern, Richard Gustave
b. 1929 George, Christopher
b. 1932 Young, Faron
b. 1934 Lema, Tony (Anthony David)
b. 1937 Courtenay, Tom
b. 1937 Schieffer, Bob
b. 1938 Baker, Diane
b. 1939 Leonard, John
b. 1943 Harrison, George
b. 1951 Cedeno, Cesar
b. 1951 Hedberg, Anders
b. 1954 Brenley, Bob (Robert Earl)
b. 1957 Wood, Stuart
d. 1601 Devereaux, Robert
d. 1723 Wren, Christopher, Sir
d. 1796 Seabury, Samuel
d. 1799 Dawes, William
d. 1852 Moore, Thomas
d. 1864 Harrison, Anna Tuthill Symmes
d. 1899 Reuter, Paul Julius Von
d. 1914 Tenniel, John, Sir
d. 1922 Landru, Henri Desire
d. 1925 McCormick, Joseph Medill
d. 1934 McGraw, John Joseph
d. 1944 Boyd, James
d. 1944 McNary, Charles Linza
d. 1950 Lauder, Harry MacLennan, Sir

d. 1957 Moran, "Bugs" (George C)
d. 1964 Archipenko, Alexander Porfirievich
d. 1964 Burke, Johnny
d. 1964 Metalious, Grace de Repentigny
d. 1970 Rothko, Mark
d. 1974 Aldrich, Winthrop Williams
d. 1975 Muhammad, Elijah
d. 1977 McCulloch, Robert P
d. 1978 James, Daniel, Jr.
d. 1979 Focke, Heinrich
d. 1980 Hayden, Robert Earl
d. 1983 Cowles, John, Sr.
d. 1983 Williams, "Tennessee" (Thomas Lanier)
d. 1984 West, Jessamyn
d. 1985 Weatherwax, Rudd B
d. 1986 Lowe, Edwin S

Febuary 26
b. Bernhardt, Melvin
b. 1671 Shaftesbury, Anthony Ashley Cooper, Earl
b. 1786 Argo, Dominique Francois Jean
b. 1802 Hugo, Victor Marie
b. 1808 Daumier, Honore
b. 1817 Wallace, Horace Binney
b. 1832 Nicolay, John George
b. 1836 Vedder, Elihu
b. 1844 Lurton, Horace Harmon
b. 1846 Cody, "Buffalo Bill" (William Frederick)
b. 1849 McDowell, Katharine Sherwood Bonner
b. 1852 Kellogg, John Harvey
b. 1857 Coue, Emile
b. 1866 Dow, Herbert Henry
b. 1877 Dirks, Rudolph
b. 1878 Destinn, Emmy
b. 1878 Malevich, Kasimir Severinovich
b. 1879 Bridge, Frank
b. 1879 Luhan, Mabel Dodge
b. 1882 Kimmel, Husband Edward
b. 1887 Alexander, Grover Cleveland
b. 1890 Vought, Chance Milton
b. 1891 Baugh, Albert Croll
b. 1893 Frawley, William
b. 1893 Richards, Ivor Armstrong
b. 1894 Harmon, Ernest N
b. 1896 Carlson, Evans Fordyce
b. 1903 Natta, Giulio
b. 1906 Romano, Umberto
b. 1908 Avery, "Tex" (Frederick Bean)
b. 1908 Groth, John August
b. 1908 LeFleming, Christopher Kaye
b. 1909 Carroll, Madeleine
b. 1913 Barker, George Granville
b. 1914 Alda, Robert
b. 1914 Wilson, Malcolm
b. 1916 Gleason, Jackie
b. 1917 Taft, Robert Alphonso, Jr.
b. 1918 Bowen, Otis Ray
b. 1918 Sturgeon, Theodore Hamilton

d. 1706 Evelyn, John
d. 1710 Duluth, Daniel
d. 1795 Marion, Francis
d. 1830 Hicks, Elias
d. 1844 Biddle, Nicholas
d. 1887 Sill, Edward Rowland
d. 1905 Boutwell, George Sewell
d. 1906 Langley, Samuel Pierpont
d. 1919 Edmunds, George Franklin
d. 1929 Hadden, Briton
d. 1936 Pavlov, Ivan Petrovich
d. 1940 Graves, William Sidney
d. 1942 Berry, Martha McChesney
d. 1955 Friganza, Trixie
d. 1955 Howard, Tom
d. 1956 Peters, Brandon
d. 1959 Farrand, Beatrix Jones
d. 1969 Boles, John
d. 1969 Craven, Thomas
d. 1970 Bruce Lockhart, Robert Hamilton, Sir
d. 1970 Dionne, Marie
d. 1970 Lockhart, (Robert Hamilton) Bruce, (Sir)
d. 1972 Brady, Pat (Robert Patrick)
d. 1972 Heiser, Victor George
d. 1974 Fremont-Smith, Frank
d. 1977 Carr, John Dickson
d. 1977 Dahlberg, Edward
d. 1980 Tobias, George
d. 1984 Paton, Richard
d. 1985 Lodge, Henry Cabot, Jr.
d. 1985 Moncreiffe, Jain (Rupert Jain)
d. 1985 O'Malley, J Pat
d. 1986 Plante, Jacques (Joseph Jacques Omer)

Febuary 28
b. 1533 Montaigne, Michel Eyquem de
b. 1743 Hauy, Rene Just
b. 1783 Rossetti, Gabriele Pasquale Giuseppe
b. 1797 Lyon, Mary
b. 1820 Rachel
b. 1820 Tenniel, John, Sir
b. 1824 Blondin, Jean Francois Gravelet
b. 1860 Berger, Victor L
b. 1860 Kittredge, G(eorge) L(yman)
b. 1865 Grenfell, Wilfred Thomason, Sir
b. 1865 Symons, Arthur
b. 1871 Irving, Isabel
b. 1876 Carpenter, John Alden
b. 1877 Breuil, Henri Abbe
b. 1882 Farrar, Geraldine
b. 1887 Zorach, William
b. 1889 Dietrich, Noah
b. 1890 Nijinsky, Vaslav
b. 1893 Hecht, Ben
b. 1895 Novaes, Guiomar
b. 1896 Hench, Philip Showalter
b. 1898 Picon, Molly
b. 1901 Pauling, Linus Carl

b. 1905 Jones, Glyn
b. 1906 Siegel, "Bugsy" (Benjamin)
b. 1907 Caniff, Milt(on Arthur)
b. 1907 Cox, Herald Rea
b. 1908 Brown, Dee (Alexander)
b. 1909 Cromie, Robert Allen
b. 1909 LaBern, Arthur Joseph
b. 1909 Spender, Stephen
b. 1910 Falter, John
b. 1912 Walsh, Michael Patrick
b. 1913 Minnelli, Vincente
b. 1915 Frings, "Ketti"
b. 1915 Mostel, Zero (Samuel Joel)
b. 1917 Malcolm, George
b. 1918 Dinkeloo, John Gerard
b. 1919 Urquhart, Brian Edward
b. 1923 Durning, Charles
b. 1923 Obata, Gyo
b. 1924 Kraft, Chris(topher Columbus, Jr.)
b. 1925 Burke, James Edward
b. 1926 Stalina, Svetlana Alliluyeva
b. 1928 Ackerman, Bettye
b. 1928 Baker, Stanley, Sir
b. 1930 MacLeod, Gavin
b. 1931 Smith, Dean Edwards
b. 1933 Furie, Sidney J
b. 1939 Tune, Tommy (Thomas James)
b. 1940 Andretti, Mario Gabriel
b. 1940 Takada, Kenzo
b. 1941 Brock, Alice May
b. 1941 Sanders, Marty
b. 1942 Bonner, Frank
b. 1942 Phillips, Robin
b. 1942 South, Joe
b. 1945 Smith, "Bubba" (Charles Aaron)
b. 1945 Wynn, Tracy Keenan
b. 1947 Beacham, Stephanie
b. 1948 Peters, Bernadette
b. 1952 Manion, Eddie
b. 1953 Raines, Cristina
b. 1958 Pavelich, Mark
b. 1960 Stratten, Dorothy
d. 1626 Tourneur, Cyril
d. 1648 Christian IV
d. 1682 Stradella, Alessandro
d. 1781 Stockton, Richard
d. 1908 Lucca, Pauline
d. 1916 James, Henry
d. 1925 Ebert, Friedrich
d. 1941 Alfonso XIII
d. 1949 Towne, Charles Hanson
d. 1951 Armstrong, Harry
d. 1953 Sukenik, Eliazer Lipa
d. 1959 Anderson, Maxwell
d. 1960 Olivetti, Adriano
d. 1963 Prasad, Rajendra
d. 1963 Rixey, Eppa
d. 1964 Lesnevich, Gus
d. 1967 Howe, Mark De Wolfe
d. 1967 Luce, Henry Robinson
d. 1968 Hall, Juanita

b. 1942 Guber, Peter (Howard Peter)
b. 1945 Benedict, Dirk
b. 1945 Daltrey, Roger
b. 1953 Henderson, "Hollywood" (Thomas)
b. 1954 Bach, Catherine
b. 1954 Howard, Ron
d. 1620 Campion, Thomas
d. 1698 Redi, Francesco
d. 1869 Lamartine, Alphonse Marie Louis
   de Prat de
d. 1875 Corbiere, Tristan
d. 1894 Poole, William Frederick
d. 1906 Pereda, Jose Marie de
d. 1938 D'Annunzio, Gabriele
d. 1938 Harney, Benjamin Robertson
d. 1952 Azuela, Mariano
d. 1958 Balla, Giacomo
d. 1959 Booth, "Albie" (Albert James, Jr.)
d. 1962 Piccard, Auguste
d. 1964 Cordon, Norman
d. 1965 Beemer, Brace
d. 1966 Baillie, Hugh
d. 1969 Ames, Blanche
d. 1969 Kerr, Andrew
d. 1972 Babin, Victor
d. 1972 Golschmann, Vladimir
d. 1976 Martinon, Jean
d. 1978 Scott, Paul Mark
d. 1979 Costello, Dolores
d. 1980 Ashford, Emmett Littleton
d. 1980 Cooper, Wilhelmina Behmenburg
d. 1980 Niles, John Jacob
d. 1982 Spivak, Charlie
d. 1984 Coogan, Jackie (Jack Leslie)
d. 1985 List, Eugene
d. 1986 Towle, Katherine Amelia

March 2

b. 1760 Desmoulins, Camille
b. 1769 Clinton, DeWitt
b. 1779 Poinsett, Joel Roberts
b. 1793 Houston, Sam(uel)
b. 1813 Macfarren, George Alexander, Sir
b. 1819 Brannan, Samuel
b. 1824 Smetana, Bedrich
b. 1829 Schurz, Carl
b. 1836 Brown, Henry Billings
b. 1846 Roze, Marie
b. 1876 Pius XII, Pope
b. 1880 Kreuger, Ivar
b. 1890 DeKruif, Paul Henry
b. 1895 Aurell, Tage
b. 1895 Frisch, Ragnar
b. 1897 Schuster, Max Lincoln
b. 1900 Bee, Clair Francis
b. 1900 Weill, Kurt
b. 1902 Condon, Edward
b. 1902 Grigson, Geoffrey Edward Harvey
b. 1902 Monroney, Mike (Aimer Stillwell)
b. 1904 Dreyfuss, Henry
b. 1904 Seuss, Doctor, pseud.
b. 1905 Blitzstein, Marc

b. 1909 Ott, Mel(vin Thomas)
b. 1917 Arnaz, Desi
b. 1919 Jones, Jennifer
b. 1920 Ritt, Martin
b. 1921 Sattler, Helen Roney
b. 1923 Michel, Robert H(enry)
b. 1923 Watson, "Doc" (Arthel)
b. 1927 Brademas, John
b. 1930 Cullum, John
b. 1931 Gorbachev, Mikhail S
b. 1931 Wolfe, Tom (Thomas Kennerly,
   Jr.)
b. 1933 Dillon, Leo
b. 1934 Cosgrove, Gordon Dean
b. 1937 Crum, Denny Edwin
b. 1942 Firbank, Louis
b. 1942 Irving, John
b. 1944 Reed, Lou
b. 1949 Gallagher, Rory
b. 1950 Carpenter, Karen Ann
b. 1954 Johnson, Pete
b. 1958 Curren, Kevin
d. 1644 Frescobaldi, Girolamo
d. 1797 Walpole, Horace
d. 1797 Wilkes, John
d. 1854 Rubini, Giovanni-Battista
d. 1894 Early, Jubal Anderson
d. 1895 Morisot, Berthe
d. 1907 Manns, Augustus, Sir
d. 1921 Clark, "Champ" (James
   Beauchamp)
d. 1930 Lawrence, D(avid) H(erbert)
d. 1933 Walsh, Thomas James
d. 1938 Scripps, Robert Paine
d. 1939 Carter, Howard
d. 1942 Christian, Charlie (Charles)
d. 1945 Carr, Emily
d. 1947 Marston, William Moulton
d. 1948 Brill, Abraham Arden
d. 1949 Naidu, Sarojini
d. 1957 Maybeck, Bernard Ralph
d. 1958 Held, John, Jr.
d. 1959 Blore, Eric
d. 1960 Camnitz, Howie (Samuel Howard)
d. 1972 Feis, Herbert
d. 1972 Sack, Erna
d. 1974 Petrocelli, Anthony
d. 1977 Bothwell, Jean
d. 1977 Mowrer, Edgar Ansel
d. 1978 Begle, Edward G(riffith)
d. 1978 Pei, Mario Andrew
d. 1982 Dick, Philip K(indred)
d. 1985 Kelly, John Brenden, Jr.
d. 1986 Rudenko, Lyudmila

March 3

b. Williams, Darnell
b. 1606 Waller, Edmund
b. 1756 Godwin, William
b. 1802 Nourrit, Adolphe
b. 1803 Decamps, Alexandre Gabriel
b. 1818 Ingersoll, Simon

b. 1909 Helmsley, Harry Brakmann
b. 1910 Boothroyd, John Basil
b. 1912 Leitner, Ferdinand
b. 1913 Garfield, John
b. 1914 Cooper, Morton Cecil
b. 1916 Miller, Arjay Ray
b. 1916 Whiffen, Marcus
b. 1918 DuPont, Margaret Osborne
b. 1921 Greenwood, Joan
b. 1922 O'Driscoll, Martha
b. 1923 King, Francis Henry
b. 1924 O'Donnell, Kenneth
b. 1926 DeVos, Richard Martin
b. 1928 Sillitoe, Alan
b. 1929 Haitink, Bernard
b. 1931 Rivlin, Alice Mitchell
b. 1932 Makeba, Miriam
b. 1936 Clark, James
b. 1937 McNair, Barbara
b. 1939 Carner, Joanne Gunderson
b. 1939 Prentiss, Paula
b. 1941 Stargell, Willie (Wilver Dornel)
b. 1944 Brown, Judie
b. 1948 Squire, Chris
b. 1953 Lenz, Kay
b. 1961 Mancini, Ray
b. 1969 Bono, Chastity
d. 1825 Peale, Raphael
d. 1832 Champollion, Jean Francois
d. 1842 Forten, James
d. 1852 Gogol, Nikolai Vasilievich
d. 1858 Perry, Matthew Calbraith, Commodore
d. 1864 King, Thomas Starr
d. 1868 Chisholm, Jesse
d. 1883 Stephens, Alexander Hamilton
d. 1888 Alcott, Amos Bronson
d. 1901 Revels, Hiram R
d. 1903 Shorthouse, Joseph Henry
d. 1906 Schofield, John McAllister
d. 1916 Marc, Franz
d. 1922 Williams, Bert (Egbert Austin)
d. 1925 Moszkowski, Moritz
d. 1925 Ward, John Montgomery
d. 1940 Garland, Hamlin
d. 1944 Buchalter, "Lepke" (Louis)
d. 1946 Waldron, Charles D
d. 1948 Artaud, Antonin
d. 1948 Berdyaev, Nikolay A
d. 1949 Angell, James Rowland
d. 1952 Christy, Howard Chandler
d. 1957 Graham, Evarts Ambrose
d. 1960 Warren, Leonard
d. 1963 Olds, Irving S
d. 1963 Williams, William Carlos
d. 1974 Gottlieb, Adolph
d. 1982 Eden, Dorothy
d. 1986 Greenfield, Howard

March 5
b. Sikking, James B
b. 1133 Henry II

b. 1512 Mercator, Gerhardus
b. 1575 Oughtred, William
b. 1658 Cadillac, Antoine
b. 1696 Tiepolo, Giambattista (Giovanni Battista)
b. 1794 Grier, Robert Cooper
b. 1817 Layard, Austin Henry, Sir
b. 1824 Ives, James Merritt
b. 1824 Larcom, Lucy
b. 1836 Goodnight, Charles
b. 1853 Foote, Arthur William
b. 1853 Pyle, Howard
b. 1860 Thompson, Sam(uel Luther)
b. 1870 Norris, Frank(lin)
b. 1879 Beveridge, William Henry, Lord
b. 1882 VanAlstyne, Egbert Anson
b. 1887 Villa-Lobos, Heitor
b. 1891 Fitzpatrick, Daniel R
b. 1891 Johnson, "Chic" (Harold Ogden)
b. 1893 Sands, Dorothy
b. 1894 Daniell, Henry
b. 1897 Herbst, Josephine Frey
b. 1904 Rahner, Karl
b. 1907 Rosenbloom, Carroll D
b. 1908 Harrison, Rex (Reginald Carey)
b. 1918 Tobin, James
b. 1919 Boles, Paul Darcy
b. 1922 Pasolini, Pier Paolo
b. 1927 Cassidy, Jack
b. 1930 Crandall, Del(mar Wesley)
b. 1930 Maazel, Lorin
b. 1931 Cobb, Jerrie
b. 1931 Tuckwell, Barry Emmanuel
b. 1936 Stockwell, Dean
b. 1938 Wainwright, James
b. 1939 Fuller, Charles
b. 1940 Auletta, Robert
b. 1940 Eggar, Samantha
b. 1941 Sand, Paul
b. 1942 Gonzalez Marquez, Felipe
b. 1945 Matson, Randy (James Randel)
b. 1946 Bleier, "Rocky" (Robert Patrick)
b. 1946 Warren, Michael
b. 1947 Hodges, Eddie (Samuel Edward)
b. 1947 Tekulve, Kent(on Charles)
b. 1949 Gwilym, Mike
b. 1950 Fodor, Eugene Nicholas
b. 1958 Gibb, Andy
d. 1534 Correggio, Antonio Allegri da
d. 1770 Attucks, Crispus
d. 1778 Arne, Thomas Augustine
d. 1815 Mesmer, Franz Anton
d. 1827 Laplace, Pierre Simon, Marquis de
d. 1849 Lyon, Mary
d. 1876 Piave, Francesco Maria
d. 1923 Ayer, Francis Wayland
d. 1927 Remsen, Ira
d. 1930 Ladd-Franklin, Christine
d. 1940 Elliott, Maxine
d. 1941 Quidde, Ludwig
d. 1944 Jacob, Max

d. 1973 Buck, Pearl S(ydenstricker)
d. 1976 Rosenbloom, Maxie
d. 1978 MacLiammoir, Michael
d. 1981 Hightower, Florence Josephine
   Cole
d. 1982 Rand, Ayn
d. 1983 Berberian, Cathy
d. 1983 Maclean, Donald Duart
d. 1984 Niemoller, (Friedrich Gustav Emil)
   Martin
d. 1985 Sloane, Eric
d. 1985 Sour, Robert B(andler)
d. 1986 Caesar, Adolph
d. 1986 O'Keeffe, Georgia

March 7
b. 1671 MacGregor, Robert
b. 1707 Hopkins, Stephen
b. 1785 Manzoni, Alessandro (Antonio)
b. 1788 Becquerel, Antoine-Cesar
b. 1792 Herschel, John Frederick William,
   Sir
b. 1802 Landseer, Edwin Henry, Sir
b. 1822 Masse, Victor
b. 1838 Roe, Edward Payson
b. 1841 Nelson, William Rockhill
b. 1844 Comstock, Anthony
b. 1845 Palmer, Daniel David
b. 1849 Burbank, Luther
b. 1850 Clark, "Champ" (James
   Beauchamp)
b. 1850 Masaryk, Tomas Garrigue
b. 1866 Ernst, Paul
b. 1872 Mondrian, Piet(er Cornelis)
b. 1875 Ravel, Maurice Joseph
b. 1887 Parkhurst, Helen
b. 1889 Williams, Ben Ames
b. 1890 Danforth, David Charles
b. 1893 Avery, Milton (Clark)
b. 1902 Oenslager, Donald Mitchell
b. 1909 Magnani, Anna
b. 1914 DaCosta, Morton
b. 1914 Hauge, Gabriel
b. 1914 Sann, Paul
b. 1915 Chaban-Delmas, Jacques
b. 1927 Broderick, James Joseph
b. 1928 Elegant, Robert Sampson
b. 1930 Armstrong-Jones, Antony Charles
   Robert
b. 1930 Marlowe, Marion
b. 1935 DeVita, Vincent Theodore, Jr.
b. 1935 Donghia, Angelo R
b. 1938 Guthrie, Janet
b. 1940 Travanti, Daniel J(ohn)
b. 1941 Grimes, J William
b. 1941 Read, Piers Paul
b. 1943 White, Chris(topher Taylor)
b. 1945 Heard, John
b. 1946 Wolf, Peter
b. 1950 Harris, Franco
b. 1950 Richard, J(ames) R(odney)
b. 1952 Swann, Lynn Curtis

b. 1960 Lendl, Ivan
d. 161 Antoninus Pius
d. 1274 Aquinas, Thomas, Saint
d. 1827 Volta, Alessandro
d. 1883 Green, John Richard
d. 1902 Galvin, "Pud" (James Francis)
d. 1911 Fogazzaro, Antonio
d. 1932 Briand, Aristide
d. 1935 Duane, William
d. 1935 Tabor, Elizabeth Bonduel McCourt
   Doe
d. 1940 Finley, John Huston
d. 1940 Markham, Edwin
d. 1941 Eltinge, Julian
d. 1941 Sanborn, Pitts
d. 1942 Sarg, Tony (Anthony Frederick)
d. 1945 Dawson, Bertrand Edward
d. 1950 Korzybski, Alfred Habdank
d. 1952 Yogananda, Paramahansa
d. 1954 Hays, Will Harrison
d. 1957 Lewis, Wyndham
d. 1967 Compton, Wilson Martindale
d. 1967 Toklas, Alice B(abette)
d. 1971 Balaban, Barney
d. 1971 Smith, "Stevie" (Florence
   Margaret)
d. 1975 Blue, Ben
d. 1976 Patman, (John Williams) Wright
d. 1979 Novaes, Guiomar
d. 1980 Patterson, William Allan
d. 1981 Billington, Ray Allen
d. 1981 Crowther, Bosley (Francis Bosley)
d. 1981 Kondrashin, Kiril Petrovich
d. 1983 Black, William
d. 1983 Markevitch, Igor
d. 1984 Rotha, Paul
d. 1985 Woodruff, Robert Winship
d. 1986 Javits, Jacob Koppel

March 8
b. 1714 Bach, Carl Philipp Emanuel
b. 1783 Van Buren, Hannah Hoes
b. 1788 Hamilton, William, Sir
b. 1822 Johnston, Richard Malcolm
b. 1825 Barbier, Jules
b. 1836 Butler, Matthew Calbraith
b. 1839 Crafts, James Mason
b. 1840 Emin Pasha
b. 1841 Holmes, Oliver Wendell, Jr.
b. 1849 Winkelmann, Hermann
b. 1858 Leoncavallo, Ruggiero
b. 1859 Grahame, Kenneth
b. 1865 Goudy, Frederic William
b. 1867 Davenport, Homer Calvin
b. 1873 Held, Anna
b. 1878 Currie, Barton Wood
b. 1879 Hahn, Otto
b. 1883 Starch, Daniel
b. 1884 Lanza, Anthony Joseph
b. 1886 Kendall, Edward C(alvin)
b. 1888 Chase, Stuart
b. 1890 Fowler, Gene

b. 1923 Buckley, James Lane
b. 1923 Courreges, Andre
b. 1924 Gold, Herbert
b. 1925 Miller, G(eorge) William
b. 1927 Jensen, Jackie (Jack Eugene)
b. 1930 Schippers, Thomas
b. 1931 Hills, Roderick M
b. 1932 Smith, Keely
b. 1934 Gagarin, Yuri Alexseyevich
b. 1934 Van Patten, Joyce
b. 1936 Brown, Kenneth H
b. 1936 Gilley, Mickey Leroy
b. 1936 Ingels, Marty
b. 1939 Bricklin, Malcolm N
b. 1940 Julia, Raul
b. 1942 Campaneris, Bert (Dagoberto Blanco)
b. 1943 Fischer, Bobby (Robert James)
b. 1945 Trower, Robin
b. 1945 Van Devere, Trish
b. 1947 Kennerly, David Hume
b. 1948 Curtis, John Duffield, II
b. 1948 Fischl, Eric
b. 1950 North, Andy
b. 1954 Sands, Bobby (Robert Gerard)
b. 1957 Lewis, Chris .
b. 1971 Lewis, Emmanuel
d. 1633 Herbert, George
d. 1661 Mazarin, Jules, Cardinal
d. 1851 Oersted, Hans Christian
d. 1872 Krieghoff, Cornelius
d. 1873 Knight, Charles
d. 1878 Anderssen, Adolf (Karl Ernst Adolf)
d. 1893 Taine, Hippolyte Adolphe
d. 1895 Sacher-Masoch, Leopold von
d. 1907 Dowie, John Alexander
d. 1918 Wedekind, Frank
d. 1925 Metcalf, Willard L
d. 1927 Potthast, Edward Henry
d. 1928 Wanamaker, Rodman
d. 1930 Mercer, Henry Chapman
d. 1937 More, Paul Elmer
d. 1944 Brown, A Roy
d. 1947 Catt, Carrie Chapman
d. 1950 Evans, Timothy
d. 1955 Henson, Matthew Alexander
d. 1957 Horthy de Nagybanya, Nicholas
d. 1963 Melcher, Frederic Gershon
d. 1964 DePaolis, Alessio
d. 1965 Murphy, Jimmy (James Edward)
d. 1969 Brackett, Charles
d. 1969 Christaller, Walter
d. 1969 Crane, Richard O
d. 1969 Hawley, Cameron
d. 1971 Knaths, Karl (Otto Karl)
d. 1972 O'Connor, Basil
d. 1974 Sutherland, Earl Wilbur, Jr.
d. 1975 Dunninger, Joseph
d. 1977 Bolton, Frances Payne
d. 1981 Delbruck, Max

d. 1981 Judy, Steven
d. 1981 Von Wangenheim, Chris
d. 1982 Butler of Saffron Walden, Richard Austen, Baron
d. 1983 Emerson, Faye Margaret
d. 1985 Jenner, William Ezra

March 10
b. 1452 Ferdinand V
b. 1626 Malpighi, Marcello
b. 1730 Ross, George
b. 1749 DaPonte, Lorenzo
b. 1772 Schlegel, Friedrich von (Karl Wilhelm Friedrich von)
b. 1780 Trollope, Frances
b. 1788 Eichendorff, Joseph Karl Benedict
b. 1810 McCloskey, John
b. 1833 Alarcon, Pedro Antonio de
b. 1844 Sarasate, Pablo de
b. 1867 Wald, Lillian D
b. 1873 Wassermann, Jakob
b. 1880 Jacobs, Michael S
b. 1886 Laubenthal, Rudolf
b. 1886 Waller, Fred(erick)
b. 1888 Fitzgerald, Barry
b. 1888 Mayer, Oscar Gottfried
b. 1891 Wang Shih-chieh
b. 1892 Honegger, Arthur
b. 1892 Turner, Eva
b. 1897 Hoyt, Palmer (Edwin Palmer)
b. 1898 Bacharach, Bert(ram Mark)
b. 1900 Billingsley, Sherman
b. 1900 Brayman, Harold
b. 1903 Beiderbecke, "Bix" (Leon Bismark)
b. 1904 Fishback, Margaret
b. 1905 Masserman, Jules H(oman)
b. 1908 Wragge, Sidney
b. 1909 Galento, Tony (Anthony)
b. 1911 Anderson, Warner
b. 1915 Bertoia, Harry
b. 1915 Groves, Charles, Sir
b. 1917 Merrill, John Putnam
b. 1918 Broun, Heywood Hale
b. 1920 Kent, Jack (John Wellington)
b. 1922 Mason, Pamela Helen
b. 1928 Akins, Virgil
b. 1928 Ray, James Earl
b. 1928 Tennenbaum, Silvia
b. 1928 Tsai, Gerald, Jr.
b. 1934 Rechy, John Franklin
b. 1940 Rabe, David William
b. 1941 Torrence, Dean
b. 1943 Limbert, John William, Jr.
b. 1945 Houghton, Katharine
b. 1947 Greene, Bob (Robert Bernard, Jr.)
b. 1947 Scholz, Tom
b. 1948 Carr, Austin George
b. 1953 Gareau, Jacqueline
b. 1955 DeBarge, Bunny
b. 1956 Myricks, Larry
b. 1964 Edward
d. 1810 Cavendish, Henry

b. 1824 Prang, Louis
b. 1825 Manns, Augustus, Sir
b. 1831 Studebaker, Clement
b. 1832 Boycott, Charles Cunningham
b. 1832 Friedel, Charles
b. 1835 Newcomb, Simon
b. 1838 Perkin, William Henry, Sir
b. 1858 Ochs, Adolph Simon
b. 1863 D'Annunzio, Gabriele
b. 1868 Whitechurch, Victor Lorenzo
b. 1873 White, Stewart Edward
b. 1877 Adams, Annette Abbott
b. 1881 Tanner, Valno Alfred
b. 1888 Johnson, Hall
b. 1888 Knappertsbusch, Hans
b. 1894 Meyer, Joseph
b. 1900 Rojas Pinilla, Gustavo
b. 1902 Fenton, Leslie
b. 1908 Conley, Eugene
b. 1910 Ohira, Masayoshi
b. 1910 Stevens, Roger L
b. 1911 Diaz Ordaz, Gustavo
b. 1911 Moats, Alice-Leone
b. 1912 Brown, Les(ter Raymond)
b. 1912 Spyropoulos, Jannis
b. 1913 Mikhalkov, Sergei Vladimirovich
b. 1915 Mucha, Jiri
b. 1917 Withers, Googie
b. 1918 Gottschalk, Robert
b. 1920 DeKooning, Elaine Marie
        Catherine Fried
b. 1921 Agnelli, Giovanni
b. 1921 MacRae, Gordon
b. 1921 McCafferty, Don
b. 1922 Kerouac, Jack
b. 1922 Kirkland, Lane (Joseph Lane)
b. 1923 Schirra, Wally (Walter Marty, Jr.)
b. 1925 Delerue, Georges
b. 1926 Holmes, John Clennon
b. 1928 Albee, Edward Franklin, III
b. 1930 Law, Vernon Sanders
b. 1931 Thomas, Billy
b. 1932 Young, Andrew J
b. 1936 Cohen, Daniel
b. 1936 Dobyns, Lloyd Allen, Jr.
b. 1938 Panov, Valery
b. 1940 Jarreau, Al
b. 1941 Feldon, Barbara
b. 1942 Kantner, Paul
b. 1946 Minnelli, Liza
b. 1948 Mosely, Mark DeWayne
b. 1948 Taylor, James Vernon
b. 1956 Murphy, Dale Bryan
b. 1957 Allen, Leslie
b. 1957 Jackson, Marlon David
b. 1962 Strawbery, Darryl Eugene
d. 1471 Malory, Thomas, Sir
d. 1507 Borgia, Cesare
d. 1519 Borgia, Lucrezia
d. 1622 Bull, John
d. 1749 Magnasco, Alessandro Lissandrino

d. 1845 Lee, Jason
d. 1888 Bergh, Henry
d. 1902 Altgeld, John Peter
d. 1908 Amicis, Edmond de
d. 1914 Westinghouse, George
d. 1915 Witte, Sergei
d. 1924 Chardonnet, Louis Marie
d. 1925 Sun Yat-Sen
d. 1926 Scripps, Edward Wyllis
d. 1927 Rothwell, Walter Henry
d. 1929 Candler, Asa Griggs
d. 1932 Kreuger, Ivar
d. 1935 Pupin, Michael Idvorsky
d. 1937 Hubay, Jeno
d. 1937 Widor, Charles Marie Jean Albert
d. 1942 Bragg, William Henry, Sir
d. 1947 Churchill, Winston
d. 1950 Mann, Heinrich Ludwig
d. 1951 Bauer, Harold
d. 1955 Parker, Charlie (Charles
        Christopher)
d. 1957 Hull, Josephine
d. 1963 Oxnam, G(arfield) Bromley
d. 1966 Meriwether, Lee
d. 1967 Muller-Munk, Peter
d. 1971 Burns, David
d. 1973 Frisch, Frankie (Frank Francis)
d. 1980 Anson, Jay
d. 1980 Gero, Erno
d. 1981 Barnetson, William Denholm, Lord
d. 1985 Adams, "Tom" (John Michael
        Geoffrey Maningham)
d. 1985 Ormandy, Eugene

March 13
b. 1733 Priestley, Joseph
b. 1764 Grey, Charles
b. 1782 Wyss, Johann Rudolf
b. 1798 Fillmore, Abigail Powers
b. 1813 Delmonico, Lorenzo
b. 1855 Lowell, Percival
b. 1860 Wolf, Hugo
b. 1869 Menendez Pidal, Ramon
b. 1870 Glackens, William James
b. 1872 Keeler, "Wee Willie" (William
        Henry)
b. 1872 Villard, Oswald
b. 1884 Walpole, Hugh Seymour, Sir
b. 1886 Baker, Frank (John Franklin)
b. 1886 Untermeyer, Jean Starr
b. 1887 Gris, Juan
b. 1887 Vandegrift, Alexander Archer
b. 1890 Busch, Fritz
b. 1890 Idris I
b. 1892 Flanner, Janet
b. 1894 Braden, Spruille
b. 1898 Hathaway, Henry
b. 1899 Van Vleck, John Hasbrouck
b. 1902 Fix, Paul
b. 1908 Annenberg, Walter Hubert
b. 1908 Key, Valdimer Orlando, Jr.
b. 1908 Stewart, Paul

d. 1866 Sparks, Jared
d. 1878 Petroff, Ossip
d. 1883 Marx, Karl Heinrich
d. 1918 Garfield, Lucretia Rudolph
d. 1920 Sonzogno, Edoardo
d. 1925 Camp, Walter Chauncey
d. 1929 Smith, Clarence
d. 1932 Eastman, George
d. 1932 Turner, Frederick Jackson
d. 1936 Haldane, John Scott
d. 1951 Lewton, Val Ivan
d. 1952 Ferguson, Homer Lenoir
d. 1953 Gottwald, Klement
d. 1961 Marcosson, Isaac Frederick
d. 1965 Browning, Frederick A(rthur)
     M(ontague), Sir
d. 1967 Hobart, Alice Tisdale Nourse
d. 1968 Bache, Harold Leopold
d. 1968 Panofsky, Erwin
d. 1969 Shahn, Ben(jamin)
d. 1970 Perls, Frederick Salomon
d. 1973 Aiken, Howard Hathaway
d. 1973 Young, "Chic" (Murat Bernard)
d. 1975 Hayward, Susan
d. 1976 Berkeley, "Busby"
d. 1976 Dole, Charles Minot
d. 1980 Brosio, Manlio Giovanni
d. 1980 Dennison, Robert Lee
d. 1980 Lowenstein, Allard Kenneth
d. 1981 Perry, Eleanor Bayer

March 15
b. 1738 Beccaria, Cesare
b. 1767 Jackson, Andrew
b. 1830 Heyse, Paul Johann
b. 1838 Fletcher, Alice Cunningham
b. 1848 Kendal, Madge
b. 1848 Reichmann, Theodor
b. 1852 Gregory, Isabella Augusta Persse,
     Lady
b. 1854 Behring, Emil Adolph von
b. 1867 Johnson, Lionel Pigot
b. 1871 McIlwain, Charles Howard
b. 1874 Ickes, Harold LeClair
b. 1875 Irwin, Wallace
b. 1875 Shubert, Lee
b. 1879 Catto, Thomas Sivewright, Baron
b. 1883 Bernhard, Lucian
b. 1887 May, Marjorie Merriweather
b. 1887 Post, Marjorie Merriweather
b. 1891 Ray, Charles
b. 1893 Chandos, Oliver Lyttelton
b. 1904 Brent, George
b. 1904 O'Malley, J Pat
b. 1905 Webster, Margaret
b. 1907 McPartland, Jimmy (James
     Duigald)
b. 1907 Osborne, John Franklin
b. 1908 Baum, Kurt
b. 1911 Allen, Ivan, Jr.
b. 1912 Hopkins, "Lightnin'" (Sam)
b. 1913 Wasserman, Lew(is Robert)

b. 1914 Carey, MacDonald (Edward
     Macdonald)
b. 1915 Schoenbach, Sol Israel
b. 1915 Schoenbrun, David
b. 1916 James, Harry
b. 1917 Kirbo, Charles
b. 1918 Imlach, "Punch" (George)
b. 1919 Avakian, George
b. 1919 Gregson, John
b. 1921 Daly, Maureen Patricia
b. 1922 Brinsmead, Hesba Fay
b. 1923 Cony, Edward Roger
b. 1924 Sabu
b. 1926 Van Brocklin, Norm(an Mack)
b. 1927 Rosand, Aaron
b. 1931 Marchibroda, Ted (Theodore
     Joseph)
b. 1932 Bean, Alan L
b. 1933 DeBroca, Philippe Claude Alex
b. 1933 Taylor, Cecil Percival
b. 1935 Hirsch, Judd
b. 1940 Lesh, Phil
b. 1941 Love, Mike
b. 1942 Adelman, Sybil
b. 1944 Stone, Sly
b. 1946 Bonds, Bobby Lee
b. 1947 Cooder, Ry(land Peter)
b. 1955 Hatcher, Mickey (Michael Vaughn,
     Jr.)
b. 1955 Snider, Dee (Daniel Dee)
b. 1959 Baines, Harold Douglass
b. 1959 Teltscher, Eliot
b. 1961 Cummings, Terry (Robert Terrell)
b. 1964 Rockwell
d. 44 BC Julius Caesar
d. 1673 Rosa, Salvator
d. 1842 Cherubini, Maria Luigi
d. 1889 Bissell, Melville Reuben
d. 1898 Bessemer, Henry, Sir
d. 1905 Guggenheim, Meyer
d. 1915 Crane, Walter
d. 1925 Wassermann, August von
d. 1937 Lovecraft, H(oward) P(hillips)
d. 1942 Field, Rachel Lyman
d. 1959 Hines, Duncan
d. 1959 Young, Lester Willis
d. 1962 Compton, Arthur Holly
d. 1965 Phillips, Harry Irving
d. 1966 Saperstein, Abraham
d. 1968 Castelnuovo-Tedesco, Mario
d. 1974 Horne, Josh L
d. 1975 Onassis, Aristotle Socrates
d. 1975 Sheean, (James) Vincent
d. 1976 Mielziner, Jo
d. 1979 Britt, Steuart Henderson
d. 1981 Clair, Rene
d. 1982 Rickword, Edgell (John Edgell)
d. 1983 Sert, Jose Luis
d. 1983 West, Dame Rebecca, pseud.

March 16

b. 1739 Clymer, George
b. 1751 Madison, James
b. 1774 Flinders, Matthew
b. 1787 Ohm, Georg Simon
b. 1789 Chesney, Francis Rawdon
b. 1839 Sully-Prudhomme, Rene Francois Armand
b. 1866 Chambers, Edmund Kerchever, Sir
b. 1875 MacKaye, Percy Wallace
b. 1878 Walthall, Henry B
b. 1880 Stout, William Bushnell
b. 1885 Holloway, Emory
b. 1889 Janis, Elsie
b. 1892 Petrillo, James Caesar
b. 1897 Nagel, Conrad
b. 1899 Millis, Walter
b. 1900 Burns, Eveline Mabel
b. 1903 Mansfield, Michael Joseph
b. 1904 Myer, "Buddy" (Charles Solomon)
b. 1905 Woltman, Frederick Enos
b. 1906 Waner, Lloyd James
b. 1908 Rossen, Robert
b. 1909 Dean, Patrick Henry, Sir
b. 1911 La Tour du Pin, Patrice de
b. 1911 Mengele, Josef
b. 1912 Nixon, Patricia (Thelma Catherine Patricia Ryan)
b. 1912 Rosenthal, Jean
b. 1914 Mayer, Oscar Gottfried
b. 1914 Westmoreland, William Childs
b. 1920 Addison, John
b. 1920 McKern, Leo
b. 1924 Ludwig, Christa
b. 1926 Goodell, Charles Ellsworth
b. 1926 Lewis, Jerry
b. 1927 Braff, Ruby
b. 1927 Courtney, Clint(on Dawson)
b. 1927 Komarov, Vladimir
b. 1927 Moynihan, Daniel Patrick
b. 1932 Cunningham, R Walter
b. 1935 Berganza, Teresa
b. 1935 Park, Tongsun
b. 1937 Armstrong, William L
b. 1939 Sobieski, Carol
b. 1940 Bertolucci, Bernardo
b. 1942 Crozier, Roger Allan
b. 1949 Estrada, Erik (Henry Enrique)
b. 1951 Nelligan, Kate (Patricia Colleen)
b. 1952 Ford, Jack (John Gardner)
b. 1954 Stacy, Hollis
b. 1954 Wilson, Nancy
b. 1955 Huppert, Isabelle
b. 1957 Benoit, Joan
d. 1680 LaRochefoucauld, Francois, Duc de
d. 1736 Pergolesi, Giovanni Battista
d. 1838 Bowditch, Nathaniel
d. 1864 Surtees, Robert Smith
d. 1898 Beardsley, Aubrey Vincent
d. 1899 Medill, Joseph

d. 1903 Bean, Roy
d. 1909 Timken, Henry
d. 1917 Studebaker, John Mohler
d. 1932 Monro, Harold Edward
d. 1937 Hobson, Richmond Pearson
d. 1940 Barton, George
d. 1940 Lagerlof, Selma Ottiliana Lovisa
d. 1942 Zemlinsky, Alexander von
d. 1957 Brancusi, Constantin
d. 1963 Beveridge, William Henry, Lord
d. 1969 Brown, John Mason
d. 1970 Adamov, Arthur
d. 1970 Terrell, Tammi
d. 1971 Daniels, "Bebe" (Virginia)
d. 1971 Dewey, Thomas Edmund
d. 1972 Traynor, "Pie" (Harold Joseph)
d. 1974 Gerber, Daniel Frank
d. 1975 Mesta, Perle Skirvin
d. 1975 Walker, "T-Bone" (Aaron)
d. 1977 Jumblatt, Kamal Fouad
d. 1979 Massine, Leonide Fedorovich
d. 1979 Monnet, Jean (Omer Gabriel)
d. 1981 Blumenthal, Monica David
d. 1983 Godfrey, Arthur Michael
d. 1985 Sessions, Roger Huntington
d. 1985 Shore, Eddie
d. 1985 Stone, Louis

March 17

b. 1628 Girardon, Francois
b. 1764 Pinkney, William
b. 1777 Taney, Roger Brooke
b. 1787 Kean, Edmund
b. 1805 Garcia, Manuel Patricio Rodriguez, II
b. 1832 Conway, Moncure Daniel
b. 1834 Daimler, Gottlieb
b. 1843 Lawton, Henry Ware
b. 1846 Greenaway, Kate (Catherine)
b. 1848 Morris, Clara
b. 1850 Link, Theodore Carl
b. 1874 Wise, Stephen Samuel
b. 1877 Gardner, George
b. 1879 Grauman, Sid(ney Patrick)
b. 1884 Buck, Frank
b. 1885 Chaplin, Sydney Dryden
b. 1890 Clarke, Harry
b. 1893 Garrett, Eileen Jeanette Lyttle
b. 1894 Green, Paul Eliot
b. 1896 Lynd, Helen Merrell
b. 1899 Summerfield, Arthur Ellsworth
b. 1900 Howard, "Shemp" (Samuel)
b. 1901 Catledge, Turner
b. 1901 Newman, Alfred
b. 1902 Jones, Bobby (Robert Tyre)
b. 1903 Britain, Radie
b. 1903 Childs, Marquis William
b. 1904 Gross, Chaim
b. 1904 Hamilton, Patrick
b. 1906 O'Shea, Michael
b. 1907 Miki, Takeo
b. 1907 Pastore, John Orlando

b. 1909 Garry, Charles R
b. 1910 Rustin, Bayard
b. 1910 Werblin, "Sonny" (David
      Abraham)
b. 1911 Gilbreth, Frank Bunker, Jr.
b. 1913 Karpin, Fred Leon
b. 1914 Baugh, Sammy (Samuel Adrian)
b. 1915 McGee, Gale William
b. 1917 Brisson, Frederick
b. 1918 McCambridge, Mercedes
b. 1919 Cole, Nat "King" (Nathaniel
      Adams)
b. 1919 Reiser, Pete (Harold Patrick)
b. 1925 Rees, Ennis
b. 1930 Horn, Paul Joseph
b. 1930 Irwin, James Benson
b. 1933 Janifer, Laurence
b. 1933 Van Vooren, Monique
b. 1938 Nureyev, Rudolf
b. 1940 White, Mark Wells, Jr.
b. 1944 Sebastian, John
b. 1949 Duffy, Patrick
b. 1951 Russell, Kurt (Von Vogel)
b. 1953 Muncie, "Chuck" (Henry Vance)
b. 1954 Down, Lesley-Anne
b. 1954 Stocker, Wally
b. 1959 Ainge, Dan(iel Rae)
b. 1964 Lowe, Rob(ert Hepler)
d. 180 Marcus Aurelius Antoninus
d. 1584 Ivan IV
d. 1782 Bernoulli, David
d. 1853 Doppler, Christian Johann
d. 1862 Halevy, Jacques Francois
      Fromental
d. 1871 Chambers, Robert
d. 1885 Warner, Susan Bogert
d. 1919 Cox, Kenyon
d. 1940 Anderson, George Everett
d. 1952 Wenrich, Percy
d. 1956 Allen, Fred
d. 1956 Joliot-Curie, Irene
d. 1959 Ehmke, Howard Jonathan
d. 1962 Busoni, Rafaello
d. 1965 Reynolds, Quentin
d. 1965 Stagg, Amos Alonzo
d. 1968 Millis, Walter
d. 1969 Magnin, Grover Arnold
d. 1974 Kahn, Louis I
d. 1976 Visconti, Luchino
d. 1980 Bealer, Alex W(inkler III)
d. 1981 Dean, "Daffy" (Paul Dee)
d. 1981 Gray, Nicholas Stuart
d. 1983 Tromp, Solco Walle
d. 1986 Glubb, John Bagot, Sir

March 18
b. 1578 Elsheimer, Adam
b. 1782 Calhoun, John Caldwell
b. 1800 Lieber, Franz
b. 1800 Smithson, Harriet Constance
b. 1813 Lippincott, Joshua Ballinger
b. 1823 Seiss, Joseph Augustus

b. 1837 Cleveland, (Stephen) Grover
b. 1838 Cremer, William Randal, Sir
b. 1842 Mallarme, Stephane
b. 1844 Rimsky-Korsakov, Nikolai
      Andreevich
b. 1847 Canfield, James Hulme
b. 1851 Coghlan, Rose
b. 1858 Diesel, Rudolf Christian Karl
b. 1869 Chamberlain, Neville
b. 1875 Branch, Anna Hempstead
b. 1877 Cayce, Edgar
b. 1882 Malipiero, Gian Francesco
b. 1886 Horton, Edward Everett
b. 1886 Koffka, Kurt
b. 1891 Banning, Margaret Culkin
b. 1892 Clyde, Andy
b. 1892 Cochrane, Edward Lull
b. 1892 Coffin, Robert Peter Tristram
b. 1893 Owen, Wilfred
b. 1897 Jenkins, Ray Howard
b. 1900 Delaney, Jack
b. 1901 Hall, Manly Palmer
b. 1904 Conze, Edward
b. 1905 Donat, Robert
b. 1905 Parnis, Mollie
b. 1910 Tarnower, Herman
b. 1911 Burnette, Smiley (Lester Alvin)
b. 1912 Lawrence, Robert
b. 1913 Amerasinghe, Hamilton Shirley
b. 1913 Clement, Rene
b. 1913 Crawford, William Hulfish
b. 1915 Condon, Richard Thomas
b. 1923 Granatelli, Anthony Joseph
b. 1926 Graves, Peter
b. 1927 Kander, John
b. 1927 Plimpton, George
b. 1932 Updike, John Hoyer
b. 1938 Pride, Charley
b. 1941 Pickett, Wilson
b. 1944 Dobson, Kevin
b. 1946 Reagan, Michael
b. 1950 Dourif, Brad
b. 1952 Webster, Mike (Michael Lewis)
b. 1956 Stenmark, Ingemar
b. 1959 Cara, Irene
b. 1961 Warner, Curt
b. 1963 Williams, Vanessa
d. 1455 Angelico, Fra
d. 1740 Diver, Jenny
d. 1745 Walpole, Robert
d. 1768 Sterne, Laurence
d. 1882 Earp, Morgan
d. 1892 Van Depoele, Charles Joseph
d. 1899 Marsh, Othniel Charles
d. 1931 Johnson, (Byron) Ban(croft)
d. 1932 Olcott, Chauncey (Chancellor)
d. 1936 Venizelos, Eleutherios
d. 1945 Kalish, Max
d. 1947 Durant, William Crapo
d. 1956 Bromfield, Louis Brucker
d. 1956 Decker, Alonzo G

b. 1906 Beame, Abraham David
b. 1906 Nelson, Ozzie (Oswald George)
b. 1907 MacLennan, Hugh
b. 1908 Redgrave, Michael Scudamore, Sir
b. 1908 Stanton, Frank
b. 1909 Forbes, Kathryn, pseud.
b. 1914 Corey, Wendell
b. 1915 Kirchschlager, Rudolf
b. 1918 Barry, Jack
b. 1918 McPartland, Margaret Marian
b. 1920 Cleaver, William Joseph (Bill)
b. 1920 Hershey, Lenore
b. 1922 Goulding, Ray
b. 1922 Reiner, Carl
b. 1922 Young, Margaret Ann Buckner
b. 1925 Ehrlichman, John Daniel
b. 1928 Rogers, Fred McFeely
b. 1931 Linden, Hal
b. 1936 Owen, Tobias Chant
b. 1937 Reed, Jerry
b. 1939 Mulroney, Brian (Martin Brian)
b. 1941 Corrales, Pat(rick)
b. 1942 Schmidt, Benno Charles, Jr.
b. 1943 Witt, Paul Junger
b. 1948 Orr, Bobby (Robert Gordon)
b. 1950 Hurt, William
b. 1951 Palmer, Carl
b. 1954 Simmer, Charlie (Charles Robert)
b. 1961 Baker, Kathy
d. 1413 Henry IV
d. 1727 Newton, Isaac, Sir
d. 1730 Lecouvreur, Adrienne
d. 1751 Frederick Louis
d. 1799 Bard, John
d. 1809 Bateman, Mary
d. 1894 Kossuth, Lajos
d. 1903 Leland, Charles Godfrey
d. 1915 Adams, Charles Francis, Jr.
d. 1925 Curzon of Kedleston, George
Nathaniel Curzon, Marquis
d. 1929 Foch, Ferdinand
d. 1931 Comstock, John Henry
d. 1936 Cunninghame, Graham Robert
Boutine
d. 1942 Taylor, Charles Alonzo
d. 1943 Lowden, Frank O(rren)
d. 1945 Douglas, Alfred Bruce, Lord
d. 1946 Richardson, Henry Handel, pseud.
d. 1956 Stout, William Bushnell
d. 1957 Chase, Edna Woolman
d. 1964 Behan, Brendan
d. 1967 Morgan, Frederick
d. 1970 Hussey, Christopher Edward Clive
d. 1972 Maxwell, Marilyn
d. 1974 Clarke, Austin
d. 1974 Huntley, Chet (Chester Robert)
d. 1975 Schocken, Theodore
d. 1978 Brugnon, Jacques
d. 1981 Jaffee, Irving
d. 1982 Copeland, Jo
d. 1984 Coveleski, Stanley Anthony

March 21
b. 1274 Robert I
b. 1685 Bach, Johann Sebastian
b. 1713 Lewis, Francis
b. 1736 Ledoux, Claude Nicolas
b. 1763 Richter, Jean Paul F
b. 1768 Fourier, Jean Baptiste
b. 1806 Juarez, Benito Pablo
b. 1809 Gogol, Nikolai Vasilievich
b. 1821 Leslie, Frank, pseud.
b. 1839 Mussorgsky, Modest Petrovich
b. 1842 Rosa, Carl
b. 1859 Savage, Henry Wilson
b. 1865 Fisher, Herbert Albert Laurens
b. 1866 Maury, Antonia Caetana De Paiua
Pereira
b. 1867 Ziegfeld, Flo(renz)
b. 1869 Kahn, Albert
b. 1878 Amato, Pasquale
b. 1880 Hofmann, Hans
b. 1882 Anderson, Gilbert M
b. 1885 Pulitzer, Joseph, II
b. 1887 Mendelsohn, Eric
b. 1887 Van Dyke, W(oodbridge) S(trong)
b. 1888 Ball, Edward
b. 1898 Wyman, Willard Gordon
b. 1900 Kletzki, Paul
b. 1900 Leontovich, Eugenie
b. 1901 Weintal, Edward
b. 1903 Hellinger, Mark
b. 1905 Konetzni, Hilde
b. 1905 McGinley, Phyllis
b. 1906 Deutsch, Helen
b. 1906 Rockefeller, John D(avison), III
b. 1907 Sweet, John Howard
b. 1912 Bull, Peter
b. 1912 Tomlinson, Frank
b. 1914 Tortelier, Paul
b. 1916 Duke, Robin (Anthony Hare)
b. 1917 Barnetson, William Denholm, Lord
b. 1917 Yadin, Yigael
b. 1918 Lucey, Patrick Joseph
b. 1922 Casewit, Curtis
b. 1922 Nederlander, James Morton
b. 1923 Lindsey, Mort
b. 1924 Berman, Morton
b. 1925 Brook, Peter
b. 1925 Jones, Madison Percy, Jr.
b. 1927 Genscher, Hans-Dietrich
b. 1929 Bergman, Jules Verne
b. 1929 Coco, James
b. 1930 Fraser, John Malcolm
b. 1933 Heseltine, Michael Ray Dibdin
b. 1934 Freeman, Al, Jr.
b. 1934 Mehta, Ved Parkash
b. 1935 Davis, Mary L
b. 1936 Broadbent, Ed (John Edward)
b. 1937 Flores, Tom (Thomas Raymond)
b. 1939 Davis, Tommy (Thomas Herman,
Jr.)
b. 1939 Widdoes, Kathleen

d. 1978 Wheelock, John Hall
d. 1979 Lyon, Ben
d. 1981 Elliott, "Jumbo" (James Francis)
d. 1981 McCain, John Sidney, Jr.
d. 1982 Fitzgerald, Ed(ward)
d. 1982 Parker, "Buddy" (Raymond)
d. 1984 Webster, Paul Francois
d. 1986 Arnow, Harriette Louisa Simpson
d. 1986 Bricker, John William
d. 1986 Dinning, Max

March 23
b. 1430 Margaret of Anjou
b. 1699 Bartram, John
b. 1736 Saint Clair, Arthur
b. 1823 Colfax, Schuyler
b. 1854 Milner, Alfred
b. 1857 Farmer, Fannie Merritt
b. 1858 Chapais, Thomas, Sir
b. 1858 Quidde, Ludwig
b. 1865 Cawein, Madison Julius
b. 1865 Ford, Paul Leicester
b. 1874 Leyendecker, Joseph Christian
b. 1878 Schreker, Franz
b. 1880 Stauffer, Charles Albert
b. 1880 Wolheim, Louis
b. 1881 Martin du Gard, Roger
b. 1881 Staudinger, Hermann
b. 1883 Burt, Cyril Lodowic, Sir
b. 1884 Allen, Florence Ellinwood
b. 1887 Hillman, Sidney
b. 1892 Buttrick, George Arthur
b. 1895 Rudhyar, Dane
b. 1897 Farrar, Margaret Petherbridge
b. 1898 Dawn, Hazel
b. 1898 Grivas, George Theodorus
b. 1899 Adamic, Louis
b. 1900 Fromm, Erich
b. 1902 Dodge, Bertha S
b. 1902 Ober, Philip
b. 1906 Evans, Richard Louis
b. 1907 Bovet, Daniele
b. 1908 Crawford, Joan
b. 1910 Kurosawa, Akira
b. 1912 Cameron, Eleanor Francis
b. 1912 VonBraun, Wernher
b. 1913 Escobar, Sixto
b. 1917 Guarnieri, Johnny (John A)
b. 1921 Campbell, Donald Malcolm
b. 1921 Smyslov, Vasili Vasil'evich
b. 1926 Wright, Martha
b. 1927 Crespin, Regine
b. 1929 Bannister, Roger, Sir
b. 1933 Jenkins, Hayes Alan
b. 1935 Slavitt, David R
b. 1938 Breedlove, (Norman) Craig
b. 1938 Jackson, Maynard Holbrook, Jr.
b. 1951 Jaworski, Ron(ald Vincent)
b. 1952 Stevenson, Teofilo
b. 1953 Khan, Chaka
b. 1955 Malone, Moses Eugene
b. 1957 Plummer, Amanda

d. 1680 Fouquet, Nicolas
d. 1819 Kotzebue, August Friedrich
Ferdinand von
d. 1842 Stendhal
d. 1877 Unger, Caroline
d. 1888 Waite, Morrison Remick
d. 1890 Schenck, Robert Cumming
d. 1931 Schmedes, Erik
d. 1941 Rourke, Constance Mayfield
d. 1943 Schillinger, Joseph
d. 1946 Largo Caballero, Francisco
d. 1947 Rankin, Arthur
d. 1949 Hendrick, Burton Jesse
d. 1953 Dufy, Raoul
d. 1953 Prin, Alice
d. 1956 Dixon, Mort
d. 1960 Adams, Franklin P(ierce)
d. 1961 Mason, Max
d. 1964 Lanza, Anthony Joseph
d. 1965 Murray, Mae
d. 1968 O'Connor, Edwin Greene
d. 1969 Lismer, Arthur
d. 1970 Pyne, Joe
d. 1972 Balenciaga, Cristobal
d. 1973 Maynard, Ken
d. 1974 Molyneux, Edward H
d. 1980 Johnson, Gerald White
d. 1980 Okun, Arthur Melvin
d. 1981 Auchinleck, Claude, Sir
d. 1981 Hailwood, Mike (Stanley Michael
Bailey)
d. 1981 Lasker, Edward
d. 1982 Feingold, Benjamin Franklin
d. 1982 Greer, "Sonny" (William
Alexander)
d. 1982 Praz, Mario
d. 1983 Fitzgibbon, (Robert Louis)
Constantine
d. 1985 Harris, Patricia Roberts
d. 1985 Sims, "Zoot" (John Haley)

March 24
b. 1754 Barlow, Joel
b. 1755 King, Rufus
b. 1808 Malibran, Maria Felicita
b. 1820 Crosby, Fanny (Frances Jane)
b. 1821 Marchesi, Mathilde de Castrone
b. 1827 Wheeler, Candace Thurber
b. 1828 Gray, Horace
b. 1834 Morris, William
b. 1834 Powell, John Wesley
b. 1842 Krauss, Gabrielle
b. 1851 Bannerman, Francis
b. 1855 Mellon, Andrew William
b. 1858 Adamowski, Timothee
b. 1862 Benson, Frank Weston
b. 1872 Birch, Stephen
b. 1873 Coolidge, Dane
b. 1874 Einaudi, Luigi
b. 1874 Houdini, Harry
b. 1882 Marinuzzi, Gino
b. 1884 Debye, Peter Joseph William

b. 1927 Wasserburg, Gerald Joseph
b. 1928 Lovell, Jim (James A, Jr.)
b. 1929 Hicks, David Nightingale
b. 1931 Haigh, Kenneth
b. 1932 Gilliatt, Penelope Ann Douglas
b. 1932 Marriott, John Willard, Jr.
b. 1935 Steinem, Gloria
b. 1937 Monaghan, Tom
b. 1938 Axton, Hoyt Wayne
b. 1940 Bryant, Anita
b. 1942 Franklin, Aretha
b. 1942 Glaser, Paul Michael
b. 1947 John, Elton
b. 1948 Bedelia, Bonnie
b. 1949 Lowe, Nick
b. 1955 Mazzilli, Lee Louis
d. 1458 Santillana, Inigo Lopez de
Mendoza
d. 1712 Grew, Nehemiah
d. 1736 Vincennes, Francois Marie Bissot
d. 1794 Condorcet, Marie-Jean-Antoine
d. 1801 Novalis
d. 1809 Seward, Anna
d. 1818 Lee, Henry
d. 1857 Colgate, William
d. 1903 Byers, William Newton
d. 1914 Mistral, Frederic
d. 1918 Debussy, Claude Achille
d. 1919 Lehmbruck, Wilhelm
d. 1921 Burroughs, John
d. 1935 Zanelli, Renato
d. 1936 McCullough, Paul
d. 1937 Drinkwater, John
d. 1950 Buck, Frank
d. 1951 Catlett, "Big Sid" (Sidney)
d. 1951 Collins, Eddie (Edward
Trowbridge, Sr.)
d. 1956 Newton, Robert
d. 1965 Liuzzo, Viola
d. 1966 Hill, Virginia
d. 1966 Watson, Mark Skinner
d. 1969 Eastman, Max Forrester
d. 1969 Mowbray, Alan
d. 1973 Steichen, Edward Jean
d. 1975 Cooper, Joseph D
d. 1975 Faisal (Ibn Abdul-Aziz al Saud)
d. 1976 Albers, Josef
d. 1976 Montgomery of Alamein, Bernard
Law Montgomery, Viscount
d. 1977 Johnson, Nunnally
d. 1978 Hulbert, Jack
d. 1980 Barthes, Roland
d. 1980 Susskind, Walter
d. 1980 Wright, James Arlington
d. 1981 Douglas, Emmitt
d. 1981 Robitscher, Jonas Bondi, Jr.
d. 1982 Ace, Goodman
d. 1983 Gates, Thomas Sovereign, Jr.
d. 1985 Armstrong, Charles B

March 26
b. 1724 Laurens, Henry
b. 1773 Bowditch, Nathaniel
b. 1778 Ashley, William Henry
b. 1817 Haupt, Herman
b. 1820 Upchurch, John Jorden
b. 1838 Lecky, William Edward Hartpole
b. 1850 Bellamy, Edward
b. 1851 Bradley, Andrew Cecil
b. 1858 Delano, Jane Arminda
b. 1859 Housman, A(lfred) E(dward)
b. 1867 Woodbridge, Frederick James
Eugene
b. 1873 DuMaurier, Gerald Hubert, Sir
b. 1874 Frost, Robert Lee
b. 1874 Nast, Conde
b. 1875 Rhee, Syngman
b. 1876 Ammann, Othmar Hermann
b. 1880 Hines, Duncan
b. 1881 Kellogg, Howard
b. 1884 Backhaus, Wilhelm
b. 1892 Douglas, Paul Howard
b. 1893 Conant, James Bryant
b. 1893 Togliatti, Palmiro
b. 1895 Carney, Robert Bostwick
b. 1899 Ursuleac, Viorica
b. 1905 Cluytens, Andre
b. 1905 Frankl, Viktor E
b. 1907 Lasch, Robert
b. 1909 Campora, Hector Jose
b. 1909 Rafferty, "Chips"
b. 1911 Austin, John Langshaw
b. 1911 Williams, "Tennessee" (Thomas
Lanier)
b. 1916 Hayden, Sterling
b. 1916 Stokely, Alfred Jehu
b. 1919 Martin, Strother
b. 1922 Milliken, William G(rawn)
b. 1923 Elliott, Bob
b. 1925 Boulez, Pierre
b. 1926 Hinde, Thomas
b. 1930 Corso, Gregory
b. 1930 O'Connor, Sandra Day
b. 1931 Nimoy, Leonard
b. 1933 Deloria, Vine, Jr.
b. 1934 Arkin, Alan Wolf
b. 1934 Cappelletti, "Duke" (Gino)
b. 1936 Jofre, Eder
b. 1937 Embry, Wayne
b. 1937 Lee, James
b. 1939 Caan, James
b. 1942 Jong, Erica
b. 1943 Woodward, Bob (Robert Upshur)
b. 1944 Ross, Diana
b. 1948 Tyler, Steve
b. 1949 Lawrence, Vicki
b. 1950 Pendergrass, Teddy (Theodore D)
b. 1950 Short, Martin
b. 1954 Sliwa, Curtis
b. 1960 Allen, Marcus
b. 1962 Blab, Uwe Konstantine

March 28

b. 1475 Bartolommeo, Fra
b. 1592 Comenius, Johann Amos
b. 1652 Sewall, Samuel
b. 1660 George I
b. 1749 Laplace, Pierre Simon, Marquis de
b. 1793 Schoolcraft, Henry Rowe
b. 1800 Tamburini, Antonio
b. 1817 DeSanctis, Francesco
b. 1818 Hampton, Wade
b. 1836 Pabst, Frederick
b. 1862 Briand, Aristide
b. 1868 Hapgood, Norman
b. 1868 Jaegers, Albert
b. 1871 Mengelberg, Willem (Josef Willem)
b. 1873 Sedgwick, Anne Douglas
b. 1877 Laessle, Albert
b. 1878 Lehman, Herbert Henry
b. 1879 Westley, Helen
b. 1891 Whiteman, Paul
b. 1893 Skouras, Spyros Panagiotes
b. 1895 Herter, Christian Archibald
b. 1895 Kimball, Spencer Woolley
b. 1899 Busch, August Anheuser, Jr.
b. 1902 Ayme, Marcel
b. 1902 Perkins, Marlin (Richard Marlin)
b. 1902 Robson, Flora McKenzie, Dame
b. 1903 Serkin, Rudolph
b. 1905 Berman, Pandro Samuel
b. 1905 Perkins, (Richard) Marlin
b. 1907 Lazar, Irving Paul
b. 1909 Algren, Nelson
b. 1909 Warneke, Lon(nie)
b. 1910 O'Keefe, Dennis
b. 1914 Anhalt, Edward
b. 1914 Lovejoy, Frank
b. 1914 Muskie, Edmund Sixtus
b. 1915 Knauer, Virginia Harrington Wright
b. 1917 Meloy, Francis Edward, Jr.
b. 1918 Bailey, Pearl Mae
b. 1921 Goulding, Phil G
b. 1923 Jones, Thad(deus Joseph)
b. 1924 Bartholomew, Freddie (Frederick Llewellyn)
b. 1925 Richardson, S(tanley) D(ennis)
b. 1928 Brzezinski, Zbigniew Kazimierz
b. 1933 Murkowski, Frank Hughes
b. 1934 Ruddy, Al(bert Stotland)
b. 1937 Trotta, Liz (Elizabeth)
b. 1938 Stern, Leonard Norman
b. 1940 Loughery, Kevin Michael
b. 1942 Kinnock, Neil Gordon
b. 1942 Ramey, Samuel Edward
b. 1943 Ferrell, Conchata Galen
b. 1944 Barry, Rick (Richard Francis, III)
b. 1944 Howard, Ken(neth Joseph Jr.)
b. 1945 Brunhart, Hans
b. 1951 Kain, Karen Alexandria
d. 1621 Rinuccini, Ottavio
d. 1760 Woffington, Margaret

d. 1852 Braille, Louis
d. 1870 Thomas, George Henry
d. 1881 Mussorgsky, Modest Petrovich
d. 1886 Trench, Richard Chenevix
d. 1898 Seidl, Anton
d. 1910 Brewer, David Josiah
d. 1910 Colonne, Edouard
d. 1917 Ryder, Albert Pinkham
d. 1929 Bates, Katherine Lee
d. 1938 House, Edward Mandell
d. 1939 Goldsmith, Fred Ernest
d. 1941 Woolf, Virginia (Adeline Virginia Stephen)
d. 1943 Rachmaninoff, Sergei Vasilyevich
d. 1944 Leacock, Stephen Butler
d. 1947 Evers, John Joseph
d. 1953 Thorpe, Jim (James Francis)
d. 1954 Kiam, Omar
d. 1957 Morley, Christopher Darlington
d. 1958 Klein, Chuck (Charles Herbert)
d. 1961 Crosley, Powel, Jr.
d. 1962 Neyland, Robert Reese
d. 1963 Templeton, Alec
d. 1965 Dane, Clemence, pseud.
d. 1965 Seagrave, Gordon Stifler
d. 1968 Dreyer, Carl Theodore
d. 1969 Eisenhower, Dwight David
d. 1970 Gallo, Fortune
d. 1971 Fairchild, Sherman Mills
d. 1972 Paul-Boncour, Joseph
d. 1973 Kalatozov, Mikhail
d. 1973 Rosenthal, Ida Cohen
d. 1974 Fields, Dorothy
d. 1974 Rosay, Francoise
d. 1976 Arlen, Richard
d. 1978 Wragge, Sidney
d. 1979 Kelly, Emmett
d. 1980 Haymes, Dick (Richard)
d. 1980 Soria, Dario
d. 1981 Hollowood, Albert Bernard
d. 1982 Uris, Harold David
d. 1984 Dragon, Carmen
d. 1985 Chagall, Marc
d. 1986 Gilmore, Virginia

March 29

b. 1790 Tyler, John
b. 1819 Drake, Edwin Laurentine
b. 1819 Wise, Isaac Mayer
b. 1831 Barr, Amelia Edith Huddleston
b. 1853 Thomson, Elihu
b. 1859 Mayer, Oscar Ferdinand
b. 1865 Bonsal, Stephen
b. 1867 Salignac, Eustase Thomas
b. 1867 Young, "Cy" (Denton True)
b. 1868 Cawthorn, Joseph
b. 1869 Lutyens, Edwin Landseer, Sir
b. 1869 Neilson, William A
b. 1875 Hoover, Lou Henry
b. 1878 Von Tilzer, Albert
b. 1880 Lhevinne, Rosina L
b. 1881 Hood, Raymond Matthewson

b. 1883 Savage, Eugene Francis
b. 1885 Bolton, Frances Payne
b. 1888 Casey, James E
b. 1889 Lindsay, Howard
b. 1891 Baxter, Warner
b. 1892 Mindszenty, Jozsef, Cardinal
b. 1896 Kleberg, Robert Justus, Jr.
b. 1899 Beria, Lavrenti Pavlovich
b. 1900 Elton, Charles Sutherland
b. 1901 Montagu, Ewen (Edward Samuel)
b. 1906 Allred, Rulon Clark
b. 1906 Biggs, Edward George Power
b. 1906 Stevens, Onslow
b. 1908 O'Connell, Arthur
b. 1914 Foster, Phil
b. 1915 Handlin, Oscar
b. 1916 McCarthy, Eugene Joseph
b. 1917 Holmes, Tommy (Thomas Francis)
b. 1918 Walton, Sam Moore
b. 1919 Heckart, Eileen
b. 1920 Duerk, Alene B
b. 1921 Bogarde, Dirk
b. 1922 Fain, Ferris Roy
b. 1927 Vane, John Robert, Sir
b. 1936 Guest, Judith
b. 1937 Carter, Billy
b. 1942 Pressler, Larry
b. 1943 Idle, Eric
b. 1943 Vangelis
b. 1944 McLain, Denny (Dennis Dale)
b. 1945 Frazier, Walt
b. 1951 Cort, Bud
b. 1951 Ut, Huynh Cong
b. 1954 Quinlan, Karen Ann
b. 1955 Campbell, Earl Christian
b. 1956 Thomas, Kurt
d. 1772 Swedenborg, Emanuel
d. 1848 Astor, John Jacob
d. 1891 Seurat, Georges Pierre
d. 1903 Swift, Gustavus Franklin
d. 1909 Canfield, James Hulme
d. 1934 Kahn, Otto Hermann
d. 1937 Szymanowski, Karol
d. 1939 Machado y Morales, Gerardo
d. 1943 Gillmore, Frank
d. 1957 Cary, Joyce (Arthur Joyce Lunel)
d. 1958 Handy, W(illiam) C(hristopher)
d. 1969 Wyman, Willard Gordon
d. 1970 Brittain, Vera Mary
d. 1970 Strong, Anna Louise
d. 1972 Rank, J(oseph) Arthur
d. 1973 Cooper, Melville
d. 1975 Hibbs, Ben
d. 1978 Papashvily, George
d. 1980 Watt, George Willard
d. 1981 Tieri, Frank
d. 1981 Williams, Eric Eustace
d. 1982 Bloch, Raymond A
d. 1982 Deutsch, Helene R
d. 1982 Giauque, William F(rancis)
d. 1982 Hallstein, Walter

d. 1982 Orff, Carl
d. 1982 Twining, Nathan F(arragut)
d. 1983 Barrows, Marjorie (Ruth)
d. 1985 Terry, Luther Leonidas

March 30
b. 1135 Maimonides, Moses
b. 1727 Traetta, Tommaso
b. 1746 Goya y Lucientes, Francisco Jose
      de
b. 1820 Sewell, Anna
b. 1842 Fiske, John
b. 1844 Verlaine, Paul Marie
b. 1853 Van Gogh, Vincent Willem
b. 1858 Hopper, De Wolfe (William De
      Wolfe)
b. 1858 Hopper, DeWolf
b. 1872 Vassilenko, Sergei
b. 1876 Beers, Clifford Whittingham
b. 1880 O'Casey, Sean
b. 1882 Klein, Melanie
b. 1883 Davidson, Jo
b. 1888 Nilsson, Anna Q(uerentia)
b. 1892 Odlum, Floyd Bostwick
b. 1892 Panofsky, Erwin
b. 1895 Giono, Jean
b. 1896 Raphaelson, Samson
b. 1913 Helms, Richard McGarrah
b. 1913 Laine, Frankie
b. 1918 Evans, Bob (Robert L)
b. 1919 Bundy, McGeorge
b. 1920 Bey, Turhan
b. 1926 Chaplin, Sydney
b. 1930 Astin, John Allen
b. 1930 Jones, Robert C
b. 1930 Marshall, Peter
b. 1937 Beatty, Warren
b. 1940 Lucas, Jerry
b. 1943 Etchison, Dennis (William Dennis)
b. 1945 Clapton, Eric
b. 1948 Mangrum, Jim Dandy
d. 1764 Locatelli, Pietro
d. 1837 Constable, John
d. 1853 Fillmore, Abigail Powers
d. 1882 Griffiths, John Willis
d. 1912 May, Karl Friedrich
d. 1936 Fuller-Maitland, John Alexander
d. 1936 Supervia, Conchita
d. 1950 Blum, Leon
d. 1955 Pulitzer, Joseph, II
d. 1956 Bentley, Edmund Clerihew
d. 1965 Hench, Philip Showalter
d. 1966 Morris, Newbold
d. 1966 Parrish, Maxfield
d. 1967 Toomer, Jean
d. 1968 Scholl, William M
d. 1970 McCormick, Cyrus Hall
d. 1972 Heatter, Gabriel
d. 1974 Cottam, Clarence
d. 1979 Velasco Ibarra, Jose Maria
d. 1980 Mantovani, Annunzio
d. 1980 Thang, Ton Duc

d. 1981 Edwards, Sherman
d. 1981 Wallace, DeWitt
d. 1982 McHale, Tom
d. 1982 Richardson, Scovel
d. 1982 Thomas, Charles Allen
d. 1983 Peterson, Lorraine Collett
d. 1984 Barzini, Luigi Giorgio, Jr.
d. 1984 Rahner, Karl
d. 1985 Gerasimov, Innokentii Petrovich
d. 1985 Peary, Harold
d. 1985 Spanel, Abram N
d. 1986 Cagney, James (James Francis, Jr.)

March 31
b. 1596 Descartes, Rene
b. 1621 Marvell, Andrew
b. 1684 Durante, Francesco
b. 1732 Haydn, Franz Joseph
b. 1809 Fitzgerald, Edward
b. 1811 Bunsen, Robert Wilhelm Eberhard
b. 1824 Hunt, William Morris
b. 1835 LaFarge, John
b. 1844 Lang, Andrew
b. 1848 Astor, William Waldorf Astor, Viscount
b. 1870 Cox, James Middleton, Sr.
b. 1870 Ryan, Tommy
b. 1878 Johnson, Jack (John Arthur)
b. 1880 Birley, Oswald Hornby Joseph, Sir
b. 1882 Chukovsky, Korney Ivanovich
b. 1888 Rockwell, Willard F
b. 1890 Bragg, William Lawrence, Sir
b. 1890 Wright, Lloyd (Frank Lloyd, Jr.)
b. 1893 Krauss, Clemens
b. 1894 Ilyushin, Sergei Vladimirovich
b. 1895 Cherniavsky, Josef
b. 1895 Fisher, Vardis
b. 1895 McCloy, John Jay
b. 1896 Nolan, Jeannette Covert
b. 1899 White, Antonia
b. 1900 Henry William Frederick Albert
b. 1907 Quillan, Eddie
b. 1908 Kitchell, Iva
b. 1908 Norvo, "Red" (Kenneth)
b. 1911 Golden, William
b. 1911 Hamer, Robert
b. 1911 Liebow, Averill A(braham)
b. 1912 Lederer, William Julius
b. 1914 Paz, Octavio
b. 1915 Morgan, Henry
b. 1916 Mayer, Norman D
b. 1916 Oldenbourg, Zoe
b. 1916 Wood, John Howland, Jr.
b. 1918 Bolt, Tommy (Thomas)
b. 1922 Kiley, Richard
b. 1924 Ally, Carl Joseph
b. 1925 Buscaglia, Leo (Felice Leonardo)
b. 1926 Alfonsin Foulkes, Raul Ricardo
b. 1926 Fowles, John
b. 1927 Becker, Stephen David
b. 1927 Chavez, Cesar
b. 1927 Daniels, William

b. 1928 Frizzell, "Lefty" (William Orville)
b. 1928 Howe, Gordie (Gordon)
b. 1929 Claiborne, Liz (Elisabeth)
b. 1932 Jakes, John
b. 1932 Oshima, Nagrsa
b. 1934 Jones, Shirley
b. 1935 Alpert, Herb
b. 1935 Chamberlain, Richard
b. 1936 German, Bruce W
b. 1939 Horovitz, Israel
b. 1939 Schlondorff, Volker
b. 1940 Leahy, Patrick Joseph
b. 1943 Walken, Christopher
b. 1945 Kaplan, Gabe (Gabriel)
b. 1946 Perlman, Rhea
b. 1948 Ralphs, Mick
b. 1954 Brock, Tony
b. 1959 Young, Angus
b. 1961 Brown, Ron(ald James)
b. 1965 Barrasso, Tom (Thomas)
d. 1631 Donne, John
d. 1816 Asbury, Francis
d. 1816 Ducis, Jean Francois
d. 1840 Brummell, "Beau" (George Bryan)
d. 1850 Calhoun, John Caldwell
d. 1855 Bronte, Charlotte
d. 1903 Butterick, Ebenezer
d. 1913 Morgan, J(ohn) P(ierpont)
d. 1917 Behring, Emil Adolph von
d. 1931 Rockne, Knute Kenneth
d. 1945 Hawes, Harriet Ann Boyd
d. 1951 Forbes, Ralph
d. 1956 DePalma, Ralph
d. 1957 Lockhart, Gene (Eugene)
d. 1961 Faber, Geoffrey Cust, Sir
d. 1970 Price, Nancy (Lillian Nancy Bache)
d. 1970 Timoshenko, Semen Konstantinovich
d. 1976 Strand, Paul
d. 1976 Streeter, Edward
d. 1978 Best, Charles Herbert
d. 1980 Boussac, Marcel
d. 1980 Owens, Jesse (James Cleveland)
d. 1981 Bagnold, Enid
d. 1983 Stead, Christina Ellen
d. 1985 Deckers, Jeanine
d. 1986 Aldrich, Richard Stoddard
d. 1986 Ritz, Harry

APRIL

b. 1645 Mansart, Jules Hardouin
b. 1673 Nicolini
b. 1722 Warton, Joseph
b. 1875 Tobin, Daniel Joseph
b. 1915 Hemingway, Leicester
b. 1921 Daubeny, Peter Lauderdale, Sir
b. 1925 Shagari, Alhaji Shehu Usman Aliyu
b. 1939 Sparks, Fred
b. 1951 Carrack, Paul

b. 1840 Zola, Emile Edouard Charles
b. 1847 Steel, Flora Annie Webster
b. 1850 Laughlin, James Laurence
b. 1851 Walker, Emery, Sir
b. 1862 Butler, Nicholas Murray
b. 1869 Berryman, Clifford Kennedy
b. 1870 Jennings, Hugh(ey Ambrose)
b. 1875 Chrysler, Walter Percy
b. 1889 Cardus, Neville, Sir
b. 1891 Buchanan, Jack
b. 1891 Ernst, Max
b. 1891 Howes, Frank Stewart
b. 1902 Peugeot, Rodolphe
b. 1903 Hubbard, Orville Liscum
b. 1904 Chambers, Paul, Sir
b. 1905 Adler, Kurt Herbert
b. 1905 Lifar, Serge
b. 1907 Appling, Luke (Lucius Benjamin)
b. 1908 Ebsen, Buddy
b. 1909 Marsala, Marty
b. 1910 Selznick, Irene
b. 1912 Mills, Herbert
b. 1913 Blofeld, John
b. 1914 Guinness, Alec, Sir
b. 1920 Webb, Jack Randolph
b. 1924 Avila, Bobby (Roberto Francisco
        Gonzalez)
b. 1925 Fraser, George MacDonald
b. 1925 Owen, Lewis James
b. 1925 Shulman, Morton
b. 1926 Brabham, Jack (John Arthur)
b. 1926 Duffy, James E
b. 1927 Callaway, Howard Hollis
b. 1927 Tynan, Kenneth Peacock
b. 1928 Bernardin, Joseph Louis, Cardinal
b. 1928 Gam, Rita Elenore
b. 1935 Geyer, Georgie Anne
b. 1936 Owens, Rochelle
b. 1939 Gaye, Marvin (Marvin Pentz)
b. 1941 Russell, Leon
b. 1945 Sutton, Don(ald Howard)
b. 1948 Harris, Emmylou
b. 1954 Palillo, Ron
b. 1959 Goodell, Brian Stuart
d. 1787 Gage, Thomas
d. 1791 Mirabeau, Honore Gabriel Riquetti
d. 1865 Cobden, Richard
d. 1865 Hill, Ambrose Powell
d. 1872 Morse, Samuel Finley Breese
d. 1880 Wieniawski, Henri
d. 1898 Brann, William Cowper
d. 1900 Church, Frederick Edwin
d. 1922 Rorschach, Hermann
d. 1923 Jefferson, Thomas
d. 1932 Coghlan, Rose
d. 1935 Moten, Bennie
d. 1952 Lyot, Bernard Ferdinand
d. 1954 Heffelfinger, "Pudge" (William
        Walter)
d. 1954 Vandenberg, Hoyt Sanford
d. 1956 Pisis, Filippo de

d. 1957 Sparks, Ned
d. 1961 Riegger, Wallingford
d. 1966 Forester, Cecil Scott
d. 1967 Gassner, John Waldhorn
d. 1968 Landau, Lev Davidovich
d. 1972 Hodges, Gil(bert Raymond)
d. 1973 Horenstein, Jascha
d. 1974 Pompidou, Georges Jean Raymond
d. 1975 Cannon, Poppy
d. 1979 Rosenbloom, Carroll D
d. 1980 Reed, Stanley Forman
d. 1982 Bird, Junius Bouton
d. 1982 Coslow, Sam
d. 1985 Tebelak, John Michael
d. 1986 Paris, Jerry

April 3
b. 1593 Herbert, George
b. 1751 Lemoyne, Jean-Baptiste
b. 1778 Bretonneau, Pierre Fidele
b. 1783 Irving, Washington
b. 1793 Lardner, Dionysius
b. 1798 Wilkes, Charles
b. 1822 Hale, Edward Everett
b. 1823 Tweed, "Boss" (William Marcy)
b. 1837 Burroughs, John
b. 1838 Gambetta, Leon
b. 1861 DeKoven, (Henry Louis) Reginald
b. 1876 Anglin, Margaret Mary
b. 1881 Gasperi, Alcide de
b. 1885 Dwan, Allan
b. 1885 Fisher, "Bud" (Harry Conway)
b. 1888 Webb, Walter Prescott
b. 1893 Howard, Leslie
b. 1894 Wilson, "Dooley" (Arthur)
b. 1895 Castelnuovo-Tedesco, Mario
b. 1895 Confrey, "Zez" (Edward E)
b. 1895 Mischakoff, Mischa
b. 1896 Traglia, Luigi, Cardinal
b. 1897 Aalberg, John O
b. 1898 Ghelderode, Michel de
b. 1898 Jessel, George Albert
b. 1898 Luce, Henry Robinson
b. 1900 Brownwell, Samuel Miller
b. 1902 Gehlen, Reinhard
b. 1904 Wright, Russel
b. 1905 Halliday, Richard
b. 1906 Steegmuller, Francis
b. 1911 DiDonato, Pietro
b. 1911 Walsh, Stella
b. 1912 Eden, Dorothy
b. 1915 Cody, Iron Eyes
b. 1916 Caen, Herb
b. 1918 Ehrling, Sixten
b. 1919 Edwards, Sherman
b. 1923 Sterling, Jan
b. 1923 Wortman, Sterling
b. 1924 Brando, Marlon
b. 1924 Day, Doris
b. 1925 Benn, Tony (Anthony Wedgwood)
b. 1926 Grissom, Virgil Ivan
b. 1929 Khan, Fazlur Rahman

d. 1889 Remington, Eliphalet
d. 1900 Van Camp, Gilbert C
d. 1912 Funk, Isaac Kauffman
d. 1914 Weyerhaeuser, Frederick
d. 1917 Joplin, Scott
d. 1919 Crookes, William, Sir
d. 1932 Ostwald, Wilhelm
d. 1933 Custer, Elizabeth Bacon
d. 1943 Laparra, Raoul
d. 1949 Kent, Arthur Atwater
d. 1958 Stompanato, Johnny
d. 1959 Cleghorn, Sarah Norcliffe
d. 1961 Sachse, Leopold
d. 1963 Robards, Jason
d. 1967 Chamberlin, (B) Guy
d. 1968 King, Martin Luther, Jr.
d. 1969 Gallegos, Romulo
d. 1969 Welch, Herbert
d. 1972 Powell, Adam Clayton, Jr.
d. 1979 Bhutto, Zulfikar Ali
d. 1981 Jensen, Alfred Julio
d. 1983 Rapp, Danny
d. 1983 Swanson, Gloria May Josephine
d. 1984 Merrill, John Putnam

April 5
b. 1588 Hobbes, Thomas
b. 1649 Yale, Elihu
b. 1732 Fragonard, Jean Honore
b. 1732 Rittenhouse, David
b. 1761 Ludington, Sybil
b. 1784 Spohr, Louis Ludwig
b. 1798 Chickering, Jonas
b. 1824 Dobell, Sydney Thompson
b. 1825 Holmes, Mary Jane Hawes
b. 1827 Lister, Joseph
b. 1834 Stockton, Frank (Francis Richard)
b. 1837 Swinburne, Algernon Charles
b. 1856 Washington, Booker T(aliafero)
b. 1858 Burpee, W(ashington) Atlee
b. 1865 Filene, Lincoln
b. 1869 Roussel, Albert
b. 1871 Warner, "Pop" (Glenn Scobey)
b. 1874 Jones, Jesse Holman
b. 1883 Speicher, Eugene Edward
b. 1893 Burpee, David
b. 1893 DePaolis, Alessio
b. 1894 Bell, Lawrence Dale
b. 1898 Dehnert, Henry
b. 1899 Anderson, Elda Emma
b. 1899 Blalock, Alfred
b. 1900 Bayer, Herbert
b. 1900 Tracy, Spencer
b. 1901 Alexander, Hattie Elizabeth
b. 1901 Bowles, Chester Bliss
b. 1901 Douglas, Melvyn
b. 1901 Johnson, Raynor C(arey)
b. 1901 Julian, "Doggie" (Alvin T)
b. 1904 Eberhart, Richard
b. 1908 Carey, Ernestine Muller Gilbreth
b. 1908 Davis, Bette (Ruth Elizabeth)
b. 1908 Hemingway, Mary Welsh

b. 1908 Karajan, Herbert von
b. 1908 Ram, Jagjivan
b. 1913 Clave, Antoni
b. 1916 Peck, Gregory
b. 1917 Bloch, Robert Albert
b. 1920 Hailey, Arthur
b. 1921 Lewis, Robert Q
b. 1922 Storm, Gale
b. 1923 Thieu, Nguyen Van
b. 1924 Chew, Peter
b. 1926 Corman, Roger William
b. 1929 Claus, Hugo
b. 1930 Cheshire, Maxine
b. 1930 Costa, Mary
b. 1934 Gorshin, Frank John
b. 1941 Burdon, Eric
b. 1942 Moriarty, Michael
b. 1943 Gail, Max(well Trowbridge, Jr.)
b. 1949 Resnik, Judy (Judith)
b. 1950 Faltskog, Agnetha
b. 1952 Mayer, "Sandy" (Alex)
b. 1958 Kriek, Johann
d. 1621 Carver, John
d. 1684 Van Cortlandt, Oloff Stevenszen
d. 1765 Young, Edward
d. 1794 Danton, Georges Jacques
d. 1794 Desmoulins, Camille
d. 1906 Johnson, Eastman
d. 1921 Mifflin, George Harrison
d. 1923 Mallock, William Hurrell
d. 1928 Depew, Chauncey M
d. 1933 Biggers, Earl Derr
d. 1944 Winter, Alice Vivian Ames
d. 1946 Youmans, Vincent
d. 1961 Canby, Henry Seidel
d. 1964 MacArthur, Douglas
d. 1966 Gill, Amory Tingle
d. 1967 Elman, Mischa
d. 1967 Muller, Hermann Joseph
d. 1971 Mowrer, Paul Scott
d. 1972 Donahue, Woolworth
d. 1972 Donlevy, Brian
d. 1974 Crossman, Richard Howard
    Stafford
d. 1974 Vyvyan, Jennifer Brigit
d. 1975 Chiang Kai-Shek
d. 1976 Davis, Meyer
d. 1976 Hughes, Howard Robard
d. 1978 Tagliabue, Carlo
d. 1980 McCarty, Mary
d. 1981 Ethridge, Mark Foster
d. 1982 Fortas, Abe
d. 1982 Lawrenson, Helen Brown
d. 1984 Harris, Arthur Travers, Sir

April 6
b. Ratzenberger, John
b. 1745 Dawes, William
b. 1773 Mill, James
b. 1823 Medill, Joseph
b. 1826 Moreau, Gustave
b. 1852 Cole, Timothy

b. 1866 Steffens, Lincoln
b. 1867 Cassidy, Butch
b. 1870 Straus, Oskar
b. 1878 Eberle, Mary Abastenia St. Leger
b. 1879 Prouty, Jed
b. 1884 Huston, Walter
b. 1890 Fokker, Anthony Herman Gerard
b. 1890 Tydings, Millard Evelyn
b. 1892 Douglas, Donald Willis
b. 1892 Thomas, Lowell Jackson
b. 1895 Craig, Cleo F
b. 1895 Robin, Leo
b. 1897 Coates, Robert Myron
b. 1903 Cochrane, Mickey (Gordon
   Stanley)
b. 1903 Edgerton, Harold Eugene
b. 1903 Jackson, Charles Reginald
b. 1904 Kiesinger, Kurt Georg
b. 1907 Day, Chon
b. 1908 Lombardi, Ernie (Ernesto Natali)
b. 1913 Ruchlis, Hy(man)
b. 1914 Reeves, George
b. 1915 Lipton, Martha
b. 1918 Ovando Candia, Alfredo
b. 1924 Benzell, Mimi (Miriam Ruth)
b. 1926 Butterfield, Alexander Porter
b. 1926 Donegan, Dorothy
b. 1926 Paisley, Ian Richard Kyle
b. 1927 Mulligan, Gerry (Gerald Joseph)
b. 1928 Watson, James Dewey
b. 1929 Previn, Andre
b. 1930 Lansing, Joi
b. 1931 Dixon, Ivan
b. 1936 Thinnes, Roy
b. 1937 Haggard, Merle Ronald
b. 1937 Williams, Billy Dee
b. 1944 Phillips, Michelle Gillam
b. 1951 Blyleven, Bert (Rikalbert)
b. 1952 Larocque, Michel Raymond
b. 1953 Henner, Marilu
b. 1953 Lynn, Janet
d. 1199 Richard I
d. 1520 Raphael
d. 1528 Durer, Albrecht
d. 1590 Walsingham, Francis, Sir
d. 1614 Greco, El
d. 1637 Jonson, Ben(jamin)
d. 1641 Domenichino, Il
d. 1779 Traetta, Tommaso
d. 1862 Johnston, Albert S
d. 1864 Kirkland, Caroline Matilda
   Stansbury
d. 1907 Drummond, William Henry
d. 1912 Pascoli, Giovanni
d. 1923 Fletcher, Alice Cunningham
d. 1935 Robinson, Edwin Arlington
d. 1936 Breese, Edmund
d. 1936 Lavigne, "Kid" (George)
d. 1941 Burr, Henry
d. 1944 O'Neill, Rose Cecil
d. 1961 Bordet, Jules Jean Baptiste Vincent

d. 1963 Struve, Otto
d. 1966 Brunner, Emil
d. 1967 Connor, William Neil, Sir
d. 1970 Sheppard, Sam(uel)
d. 1970 Tenggren, Gustaf Adolf
d. 1971 Stravinsky, Igor Fedorovich
d. 1972 Lubke, Heinrich
d. 1974 Jackson, A(lexander) Y(oung)
d. 1976 Thompson, Ruth Plumly
d. 1978 Kelly, Stephen Eugene
d. 1978 Nabokov, Nicolas
d. 1980 Collier, John
d. 1984 Peers, William Raymond

April 7
b. 1613 Dou, Gerard
b. 1640 Hennepin, Louis
b. 1726 Burney, Charles
b. 1770 Wordsworth, William
b. 1772 Fourier, Francois Marie Charles
b. 1775 Lowell, Francis Cabot
b. 1780 Channing, William Ellery
b. 1781 Chantrey, Francis Legatt, Sir
b. 1786 King, William Rufus de Vane
b. 1792 Drexel, Francis Martin
b. 1794 Rubini, Giovanni-Battista
b. 1809 Glaisher, James
b. 1846 Tosti, Francesco Paola
b. 1847 Jacobsen, Jens Peter
b. 1856 Fuller-Maitland, John Alexander
b. 1859 Camp, Walter Chauncey
b. 1860 Kellogg, Will Keith
b. 1869 Fairchild, David Grandison
b. 1873 McGraw, John Joseph
b. 1884 Dodd, Charles Harold
b. 1884 Malinowski, Bronislaw
b. 1891 Eliot, Martha May
b. 1891 Low, David, Sir
b. 1893 Armstrong, Hamilton Fish
b. 1893 Castle, Irene Foote
b. 1893 Dulles, Allen Welsh
b. 1894 Brenan, Gerald (Edward Fitz-
   Gerald)
b. 1895 Flannagan, John Bernard
b. 1895 Wheeler, Bert
b. 1896 Fairchild, Sherman Mills
b. 1896 Leonard, Benny
b. 1897 Winchell, Walter
b. 1899 Casadesus, Robert
b. 1899 Mistral, Gabriela
b. 1901 Paton, Richard
b. 1907 Gordon-Walker of Leyton, Patrick
   Chrestien Gordon-Walker, Baron
b. 1907 Liebman, Joshua Loth
b. 1907 Shimkin, Leon
b. 1908 Faith, Percy
b. 1908 Fitzsimmons, Frank
b. 1909 Jones, Joseph John (Joe)
b. 1909 Snow, Dorothea Johnston
b. 1912 Lawrence, Jack
b. 1913 Vanik, Charles Albert
b. 1915 Holiday, Billie

b. 1917 Armstrong, R G
b. 1918 Doerr, Bobby (Robert Pershing)
b. 1920 Shankar, Ravi
b. 1928 Garner, James
b. 1928 Pakula, Alan Jay
b. 1931 Barthelme, Donald
b. 1931 Ellsberg, Daniel
b. 1933 Rogers, Wayne
b. 1935 Carter, Hodding (William
  Hodding, III)
b. 1935 Gregorian, Vartan
b. 1936 Cordes, Eugene Harold
b. 1936 Jones, Preston St. Vrain
b. 1938 Brown, Jerry (Edmund Gerald, Jr.)
b. 1939 Coppola, Francis Ford
b. 1939 Frost, David
b. 1943 Dryden, Spencer
b. 1946 Blankers-Koen, Fanny
b. 1949 Oates, John
b. 1954 Dorsett, Tony (Anthony Drew)
b. 1954 Gillies, Clark
d. 1626 Dowland, John
d. 1668 Davenant, William, Sir
d. 1803 Toussaint l'Ouverture, Pierre
  Dominique
d. 1823 Charles, Jacques-Alexandre-Cesar
d. 1836 Godwin, William
d. 1868 McGee, Thomas D'Arcy
d. 1891 Barnum, P(hineas) T(aylor)
d. 1931 Chadwick, George Whitefield
d. 1936 Miller, Marilyn
d. 1940 Adler, Cyrus
d. 1940 Faversham, William Alfred
d. 1947 Ford, Henry
d. 1950 Huston, Walter
d. 1954 Kurusu, Saburo
d. 1955 Bara, Theda
d. 1958 Paul, Elliot Harold
d. 1961 Bell, Vanessa
d. 1961 McGee, Molly
d. 1968 Clark, James
d. 1972 Blythe, Betty
d. 1972 Zaleski, August
d. 1973 Elisofon, Eliot
d. 1976 McBride, Mary Margaret
d. 1977 Daryush, Elizabeth Bridges
d. 1979 Hoveyda, Amir Abbas
d. 1979 Sawyer, Charles
d. 1980 Braly, Malcolm
d. 1980 Rosenberg, Jakob
d. 1981 Taurog, Norman
d. 1982 Benet, Brenda
d. 1984 Church, Frank
d. 1986 Moore, Don W

April 8
b. 1460 Ponce de Leon, Juan
b. 1692 Tartini, Giuseppe
b. 1726 Morris, Lewis
b. 1842 Custer, Elizabeth Bacon
b. 1850 Welch, William Henry
b. 1858 Keenan, Frank

b. 1859 Husserl, Edmund
b. 1869 Cushing, Harvey Williams
b. 1875 Albert I
b. 1879 Schauffler, Robert Haven
b. 1886 Barnes, Margaret Ayer
b. 1887 Connolly, Walter
b. 1888 Price, Florence Beatrice Smith
b. 1889 Boult, Adrian Cedric, Sir
b. 1892 Neutra, Richard Joseph
b. 1894 Pickford, Mary
b. 1896 Harburg, E(dgar) Y(ipsel)
b. 1897 Skidmore, Louis
b. 1898 Bowra, Maurice, Sir
b. 1898 Wilson, Hazel Hutchins
b. 1899 Meyerhoff, Joseph
b. 1902 Krips, Josef
b. 1905 Chase, Ilka
b. 1906 Jobin, Raoul
b. 1908 Whitehead, Don(ald Ford)
b. 1911 Calvin, Melvin
b. 1912 Henie, Sonja
b. 1914 Giroux, Robert
b. 1915 Higbe, Kirby (Walter Kirby)
b. 1918 Ford, Betty (Elizabeth Bloomer)
b. 1918 Swarthout, Glendon Fred
b. 1919 Smith, Ian Douglas
b. 1921 Bass, Alfie (Alfred)
b. 1922 Friendly, Ed
b. 1922 Green, Gerald
b. 1922 McRae, Carmen
b. 1923 Corelli, Franco
b. 1926 Greene, Shecky
b. 1926 Moltmann, Jurgen
b. 1927 Thomas, Jess
b. 1928 Porter, Eric
b. 1929 Berry, Walter
b. 1929 Brel, Jacques
b. 1930 Fenton, Thomas Trail
b. 1930 Reardon, John
b. 1932 Gavin, John
b. 1933 Ebb, Fred
b. 1937 Hersh, Seymour
b. 1940 Havlicek, John
b. 1940 Lennon, Peggy
b. 1943 Bennett, Michael
b. 1943 Hiller, John Frederick
b. 1954 Carter, Gary Edmund
b. 1954 Schneider, John
b. 1955 Bell, Ricky Lynn
b. 1963 Lennon, Julian (John Charles
  Julian)
d. 217 Caracalla, Marcus Aurelius
  Antonius
d. 1492 Medici, Lorenzo de
d. 1835 Humboldt, Wilhelm von
d. 1848 Donizetti, Gaetano
d. 1861 Otis, Elisha Graves
d. 1885 Moodie, Susanna
d. 1885 White, Richard Grant
d. 1917 Bateman, Kate Josephine
d. 1919 Woolworth, Frank Winfield

d. 1920 Griffes, Charles Tomlinson
d. 1926 Weir, John F(erguson)
d. 1931 Karlfeldt, Erik Axel
d. 1935 Ochs, Adolph Simon
d. 1937 Foote, Arthur William
d. 1938 Oliver, Joe (Joseph)
d. 1941 Prevost, Marcel
d. 1943 Sears, Richard Dudley
d. 1950 Nijinsky, Vaslav
d. 1954 Scheff, Frizi
d. 1958 Nathan, George Jean
d. 1978 Frick, Ford Christopher
d. 1979 Price, Garrett
d. 1980 Farb, Peter
d. 1981 Bradley, Omar Nelson
d. 1981 Russell, Edward Frederick
　　　 Langley, Baron of Liverpool
d. 1984 Kapitsa, Pyotr
d. 1985 Coots, J Fred

April 9
b. 1649 Monmouth, James Scott, Duke
b. 1798 Pasta, Giuditta Negri
b. 1806 Brunel, Isambard Kingdom
b. 1821 Baudelaire, Charles Pierre
b. 1830 Muybridge, Eadweard
b. 1835 Leopold II
b. 1863 Kitson, Henry Hudson
b. 1865 Ludendorff, Erich Friedrich
　　　 Wilhelm
b. 1865 Steinmetz, Charles Proteus
b. 1870 Lenin, Nikolai
b. 1872 Blum, Leon
b. 1875 Futrelle, Jacques
b. 1879 Meighan, Thomas
b. 1883 King, Frank
b. 1887 Adair, Frank E(arl)
b. 1888 Hurok, Sol
b. 1889 Zimbalist, Efrem
b. 1891 Szenkar, Eugen
b. 1891 Wiggins, Archibald Lee Manning
b. 1893 Burchfield, Charles
b. 1893 Fineman, Irving
b. 1893 Gollancz, Victor, Sir
b. 1894 Manville, Tommy (Thomas
　　　 Franklin, Jr.)
b. 1897 Anthony, Joseph
b. 1897 Gambling, John Bradley
b. 1898 Lambeau, "Curly" (Earl L)
b. 1898 Patzak, Julius
b. 1898 Robeson, Paul Leroy
b. 1899 McDonnell, James Smith
b. 1900 Green, Julien
b. 1900 Jenkins, Allen
b. 1901 Kotsching, Walter Maria
b. 1902 Cecil, Edward Christian David
　　　 Gascoyne
b. 1903 Pincus, Gregory
b. 1904 Bond, Ward
b. 1905 Fulbright, James William
b. 1906 Dorati, Antal
b. 1906 Gaitskell, Hugh Todd Naylor

b. 1908 Allan, Elizabeth
b. 1908 Krumgold, Joseph
b. 1908 Wilcox, Francis (Orlando)
b. 1909 Helpmann, Robert Murray, Sir
b. 1910 Ribicoff, Abraham Alexander
b. 1912 Borglum, James Lincoln
　　　 Delamothe
b. 1915 Wibberley, Leonard Patrick
　　　 O'Connor
b. 1916 Leonard, Bill (William Augustus,
　　　 II)
b. 1917 Hewes, Henry
b. 1919 Moncreiffe, Jain (Rupert Jain)
b. 1923 Levy, Leonard Williams
b. 1926 Hefner, Hugh Marston
b. 1928 Arizin, Paul
b. 1928 Lehrer, Tom (Thomas Andrew)
b. 1929 Learned, Michael
b. 1931 Hatfield, Richard
b. 1932 Krassner, Paul
b. 1932 Perkins, Carl
b. 1933 Belmondo, Jean-Paul
b. 1935 Schreiber, Avery
b. 1942 DeWilde, Brandon
b. 1954 Quaid, Dennis
b. 1957 Ballesteros, Seve(riano)
b. 1957 Macy, Kyle Robert
d. 1626 Bacon, Francis, Sir
d. 1778 Hesselius, John
d. 1841 Ladd, William
d. 1852 Payne, John Howard
d. 1872 Corning, Erastus
d. 1882 Rossetti, Dante Gabriel
d. 1889 Chevreul, Michel
d. 1899 Field, Stephen Johnson
d. 1905 Woolsey, Sarah Chauncey
d. 1909 Crawford, Francis Marion
d. 1917 Thomas, Edward
d. 1922 Manson, Patrick, Sir
d. 1926 Miller, Henry John
d. 1937 Paine, Albert Bigelow
d. 1940 Campbell, Mrs. Patrick
d. 1941 Witmark, Isidore
d. 1945 Bonhoeffer, Dietrich
d. 1945 Canaris, Wilhelm
d. 1956 Little, "Little Jack"
d. 1959 Wright, Frank Lloyd
d. 1961 Zog I
d. 1962 Lamb, Harold Albert
d. 1963 Jones, Joseph John (Joe)
d. 1963 Moiseiwitsch, Benno
d. 1964 Brendel, El(mer)
d. 1965 Minton, Sherman
d. 1970 Wright, Cobina
d. 1971 Harridge, Will(iam)
d. 1972 Byrnes, James Francis
d. 1973 Picasso, Pablo
d. 1976 Ochs, Phil(ip David)
d. 1977 Grant, Bruce
d. 1981 Scott, Austin W

d. 1982 Barrios, Francisco Javier
d. 1982 Pelletier, Wilfred

April 10
b. 1583 Grotius, Hugo
b. 1755 Hahnemann, (Christian Friedrich)
Samuel
b. 1778 Hazlitt, William
b. 1794 Perry, Matthew Calbraith,
Commodore
b. 1810 Day, Benjamin Henry
b. 1827 Wallace, Lewis
b. 1829 Booth, William
b. 1835 Villard, Henry
b. 1847 Pulitzer, Joseph
b. 1850 Davenport, Fanny Lily Gypsy
b. 1857 Levy-Bruhl, Lucien
b. 1862 Cross, Wilbur
b. 1864 D'Albert, Eugene
b. 1865 Miner, Jack (John Thomas)
b. 1867 Russell, George William
b. 1868 Arliss, George
b. 1872 Hirshfield, Morris
b. 1879 Hertz, John Daniel
b. 1881 Little, Edward Herman
b. 1882 Perkins, Frances
b. 1883 Gibran, Kahlil
b. 1885 Gimbel, Bernard Feustman
b. 1885 Spaeth, Sigmund Gottfried
b. 1887 Houssay, Bernardo Alberto
b. 1889 Murray, Mae
b. 1891 Assis Chateaubriand, Francisco de
b. 1891 McCoy, Tim(othy John Fitzgerald)
b. 1892 DeSabata, Victor
b. 1894 Nicholson, Ben
b. 1895 Russell, Edward Frederick
Langley, Baron of Liverpool
b. 1897 Youngs, Ross Middlebrook
b. 1898 Gregory, Horace Victor
b. 1903 Graf, Herbert
b. 1903 Luce, Clare Boothe
b. 1906 Darvas, Lili
b. 1906 Gates, Thomas Sovereign, Jr.
b. 1907 Murphy, Charles
b. 1908 Feather, Victor
b. 1909 Cannon, Jimmy (James J)
b. 1911 Schumann, Maurice
b. 1912 Hofheinz, Roy Mark
b. 1913 Heym, Stefan
b. 1915 DeButts, John Dulany
b. 1915 Morgan, Harry
b. 1921 Connors, "Chuck" (Kevin Joseph)
b. 1921 Wooley, Sheb
b. 1924 Noland, Kenneth Clifton
b. 1927 Brandon, Brumsic, Jr.
b. 1929 VonSydow, Max Carl Adolf
b. 1930 Blanton, (Leonard) Ray
b. 1931 Dozier, James Lee
b. 1931 Lary, Frank Strong
b. 1932 Rhodes, Hari
b. 1934 Halberstam, David
b. 1936 Madden, John

b. 1938 Meredith, Don (Joseph Donald)
b. 1941 Theroux, Paul Edward
b. 1948 Blount, Mel(vin Cornell)
b. 1951 Roth, Mark Stephan
d. 1585 Gregory XIII, Pope
d. 1644 Brewster, William
d. 1739 Turpin, Dick (Richard)
d. 1806 Gates, Horatio
d. 1858 Benton, Thomas Hart
d. 1876 Stewart, Alexander Turney
d. 1899 Tabor, Horace Austin Warner
d. 1909 Swinburne, Algernon Charles
d. 1915 Bitter, Karl Theodore Francis
d. 1919 Zapata, Emiliano
d. 1931 Gibran, Kahlil
d. 1933 Vandyke, Henry Jackson, Jr.
d. 1944 Day, Joseph Paul
d. 1945 Becker, Carl Lotus
d. 1945 Dickson, Gloria
d. 1947 Flagg, Ernest
d. 1954 Lumiere, Auguste Marie Louis
d. 1955 Teilhard de Chardin, Pierre
d. 1960 Benjamin, Arthur
d. 1966 Waugh, Evelyn Arthur St. John
d. 1969 Bentley, Alvin Morell
d. 1970 Piastro, Mishel
d. 1975 Evans, Walker
d. 1975 Main, Marjorie
d. 1976 Ortega, Santos
d. 1978 Nebel, "Long" John
d. 1980 Medford, Kay
d. 1980 White, Antonia
d. 1981 Ryan, Sylvester James
d. 1981 Thurman, Howard
d. 1983 Burton, Phillip
d. 1983 Wechsberg, Joseph
d. 1984 Middleton, Ray
d. 1985 Donghia, Angelo R
d. 1986 Creed, Linda
d. 1986 Crosby, James Morris

April 11
b. 1492 Marguerite d'Angouleme
b. 1755 Parkinson, James
b. 1770 Canning, George
b. 1794 Everett, Edward
b. 1819 Halle, Charles, Sir
b. 1821 Bergmann, Carl
b. 1825 Lassalle, Ferdinand
b. 1862 Campbell, William Wallace
b. 1862 Freeman, R(ichard) Austin
b. 1862 Hughes, Charles Evans
b. 1865 Ovington, Mary White
b. 1893 Acheson, Dean Gooderham
b. 1898 Holtz, Lou
b. 1901 Olivetti, Adriano
b. 1901 Wescott, Glenway
b. 1902 Reynolds, Quentin
b. 1905 Jozsef, Attila
b. 1908 Ancerl, Karel
b. 1908 Rosten, Leo Calvin
b. 1910 Clapp, Margaret Antoinette

d. 1938 Chaliapin, Feodor Ivanovitch
d. 1945 Roosevelt, Franklin Delano
d. 1959 Gleason, James
d. 1962 Pevsner, Antoine
d. 1965 Darnell, Linda
d. 1966 Allard, Sydney
d. 1970 Thorborg, Kerstin
d. 1972 Marek, Kurt W
d. 1973 Freed, Arthur
d. 1973 Senanayake, Dudley
d. 1974 Krock, Arthur
d. 1975 Baker, Josephine
d. 1976 Cooper, Miriam
d. 1976 Ford, Paul
d. 1976 Miller, William Ernest
d. 1976 Wolfgang, Myra K
d. 1977 Wrigley, Philip Knight
d. 1980 Tolbert, William Richard, Jr.
d. 1981 Guyer, Tennyson
d. 1981 Louis, Joe

April 13
b. 1519 Catherine de Medici
b. 1721 Hanson, John
b. 1732 North, Frederick North, Baron
b. 1743 Jefferson, Thomas
b. 1749 Bramah, Joseph
b. 1771 Trevithick, Richard
b. 1795 Harper, James
b. 1825 McGee, Thomas D'Arcy
b. 1852 Woolworth, Frank Winfield
b. 1854 Drummond, William Henry
b. 1854 Ely, Richard Theodore
b. 1859 Allen, Henry Tureman
b. 1860 Ensor, James
b. 1864 Marshall, Tully
b. 1873 Davis, John Williams
b. 1880 Leginska
b. 1881 Binswanger, Ludwig
b. 1892 Harris, Arthur Travers, Sir
b. 1892 Watson-Watt, Robert Alexander, Sir
b. 1896 Eaker, Ira Clarence
b. 1897 Braestrup, Carl Bjorn
b. 1899 Butts, Alfred Mosher
b. 1901 Dennison, Robert Lee
b. 1901 Lacan, Jacques Marie Emile
b. 1905 Agle, Nan Hayden
b. 1905 Padover, Saul Kussiel
b. 1906 Beckett, Samuel Barclay
b. 1906 Freeman, "Bud" (Lawrence)
b. 1907 Stassen, Harold Edward
b. 1909 Welty, Eudora
b. 1915 DeJong, Petrus
b. 1917 Anderson, Robert Orville
b. 1919 Keel, Howard
b. 1919 O'Hair, Madalyn Murray
b. 1921 Griese, Arnold
b. 1922 Braine, John
b. 1924 Donen, Stanley
b. 1925 Irving, Jules

b. 1929 McEwen, Terence Alexander (Terry)
b. 1930 Dillman, Bradford
b. 1931 Gurney, Dan
b. 1932 Letelier, Orlando
b. 1935 Waggoner, Lyle
b. 1937 Fox, Edward
b. 1937 Wilson, Lanford
b. 1941 Brown, Michael S
b. 1941 Price, Margaret Berenice
b. 1942 Conti, Bill
b. 1942 Parkhurst, Michael Hus
b. 1944 Casady, Jack
b. 1945 Dow, Tony
b. 1946 Green, Al
b. 1951 Bryson, Peabo (Robert Peabo)
b. 1951 Weinberg, Max M
b. 1963 Kasparov, Garry Kimovich
b. 1964 Saberhagen, Bret William
b. 1970 Schroder, Ricky
d. 1695 LaFontaine, Jean de
d. 1869 Rogers, Isaiah
d. 1886 Noyes, John Humphrey
d. 1890 Randall, Samuel J
d. 1894 Spitta, Philipp (Julius August Philipp)
d. 1906 Garnett, Richard
d. 1915 Nelson, William Rockhill
d. 1917 Brady, "Diamond Jim" (James Buchanan)
d. 1918 Kornilov, Lavr Georgyevich
d. 1936 Thurston, Howard
d. 1938 Grey Owl, pseud.
d. 1941 Cannon, Annie Jump
d. 1945 Cassirer, Ernst
d. 1959 Beinum, Eduard van
d. 1964 Harlan, Veit
d. 1966 Duhamel, Georges
d. 1970 Henry, William M
d. 1970 Smith, Merriman
d. 1973 Courboin, Charles
d. 1975 Bolton, Isabel
d. 1975 Parks, Larry
d. 1975 Tombalbaye, Nagarta Francois
d. 1981 Thomas, Gwyn
d. 1983 Humphreys, Christmas (Travers Christmas)
d. 1983 May, Morton David
d. 1984 Kirkpatrick, Ralph

April 14
b. 1629 Huygens, Christian
b. 1796 Bonneville, Benjamin
b. 1802 Bushnell, Horace
b. 1810 Morrill, Justin Smith
b. 1811 Fisher, Clara
b. 1820 Ballou, Maturin Murray
b. 1857 Kelley, Edgar Stillman
b. 1866 Sullivan, Anne
b. 1869 Van Heusen, John
b. 1879 Cabell, James Branch
b. 1885 Janney, Russell Dixon

b. 1951 Evans, Heloise Cruse
b. 1957 Ashford, Evelyn
d. 1632 Baltimore, George Calvert, Baron
d. 1764 Pompadour, Jeanne Antoinette
    Poisson
d. 1819 Evans, Oliver
d. 1844 Bulfinch, Charles
d. 1850 Tussaud, (Marie Gresholtz),
    Madame
d. 1865 Lincoln, Abraham
d. 1870 Willard, Emma Hart
d. 1888 Arnold, Matthew
d. 1889 Damien, Father
d. 1912 Futrelle, Jacques
d. 1912 Straus, Isidor
d. 1914 Townsend, George Alfred
d. 1919 Delano, Jane Arminda
d. 1925 Sargent, John Singer
d. 1927 LeRoux, Gaston
d. 1942 Johnson, Hugh S
d. 1944 Gentile, Giovanni
d. 1948 Rockefeller, Abby Aldrich
d. 1949 Beery, Wallace
d. 1952 Chernov, Viktor Mikhailovich
d. 1956 Nolde, Emil
d. 1958 Taylor, Estelle
d. 1971 Brodovitch, Alexey
d. 1972 Crowley, Leo T
d. 1975 Conte, Richard
d. 1976 Elazar, David
d. 1976 Smith, Gerald Lyman Kenneth
d. 1979 Caniglia, Maria
d. 1980 Bailey, Raymond
d. 1980 Sartre, Jean-Paul
d. 1982 Montor, Henry
d. 1983 Ten Boom, Corrie
d. 1984 Empson, William, Sir
d. 1986 Genet, Jean

April 16
b. 1728 Black, Joseph
b. 1786 Franklin, John
b. 1844 France, Anatole, pseud.
b. 1854 Coxey, Jacob Sechler
b. 1865 Hill, Grace Livingstone
b. 1867 Wright, Wilbur
b. 1871 Stephenson, Henry
b. 1871 Synge, John Millington
b. 1877 Turner, Thomas Wyatt
b. 1881 Halifax, Edward Frederick Lindley
b. 1889 Chaplin, Charlie
b. 1892 Jones, Howard Mumford
b. 1897 Cross, Milton John
b. 1897 Glubb, John Bagot, Sir
b. 1898 Dykstra, John
b. 1900 Adler, Polly
b. 1903 Pillsbury, Philip Winston
b. 1903 Waner, Paul Glee
b. 1904 Case, Clifford Philip
b. 1904 D'Orsay, Fifi
b. 1907 Seagram, Joseph William
b. 1911 Roueche, Berton

b. 1912 Williams, Garth Montgomery
b. 1913 Tremayne, Les
b. 1914 Hodiak, John
b. 1914 Jensen, Oliver Ormerod
b. 1918 Milligan, "Spike" (Terence Alan)
b. 1919 Cunningham, Merce
b. 1920 Nelson, Barry
b. 1921 Mollenhoff, Clark Raymond
b. 1921 Ustinov, Peter Alexander
b. 1922 Amis, Kingsley William
b. 1922 Tindemans, Leo(nard)
b. 1923 Moore, Arch Alfred, Jr.
b. 1924 Mancini, Henry
b. 1927 Ratzinger, Joseph, Cardinal
b. 1928 Sylbert, Richard
b. 1929 Adams, Edie
b. 1929 Hamilton, Roy
b. 1930 Mann, Herbie
b. 1933 Pappas, Ike
b. 1933 Wallis, Shani
b. 1934 Stigwood, Robert C
b. 1935 Vinton, Bobby (Stanley Robert)
b. 1939 Springfield, Dusty
b. 1940 Margrethe II
b. 1942 Lonborg, Jim (James Reynold)
b. 1947 Abdul-Jabbar, Kareem
b. 1949 Spooner, Bill
b. 1951 Bentley, John
d. 1446 Brunelleschi, Filippo
d. 1689 Behn, Aphra
d. 1788 Buffon, Georges Louis Leclerc
d. 1813 Kutuzov, Mikhail Ilarionovich
d. 1825 Fuseli, Henry
d. 1859 Tocqueville, Alexis, Comte de
d. 1864 Blanchard, Thomas
d. 1879 Bernadette of Lourdes
d. 1915 Aldrich, Nelson Wilmarth
d. 1916 Peck, George Wilbur
d. 1928 Statler, Ellsworth Milton
d. 1932 Geddes, Patrick, Sir
d. 1941 Danforth, William
d. 1956 Chaplin, Sydney Dryden
d. 1958 Black, Walter J
d. 1966 Gowers, Ernest Arthur, Sir
d. 1968 Bainter, Fay Okell
d. 1968 Ferber, Edna
d. 1970 Neutra, Richard Joseph
d. 1972 Kawabata, Yasunari
d. 1978 Clay, Lucius du Bignon
d. 1978 Lindner, Richard
d. 1978 Tsiranana, Philibert
d. 1978 Whitehead, (Walter) Edward
d. 1981 Debus, Sigurd Friedrich

April 17
b. 1622 Vaughan, Henry
b. 1741 Chase, Samuel
b. 1806 Simms, William Gilmore
b. 1820 Cartwright, Alexander Joy, Jr.
b. 1837 Morgan, J(ohn) P(ierpont)
b. 1842 Parkhurst, Charles Henry
b. 1849 Day, William Rufus

d. 1958 Gamelin, Maurice Gustave
d. 1960 Ruml, Beardsley
d. 1964 Hecht, Ben
d. 1968 Shipler, Guy Emery
d. 1971 Luboshutz, Pierre
d. 1973 Smith, Willie
d. 1974 Pagnol, Marcel Paul
d. 1982 Harnwell, Gaylord Probasco
d. 1982 Harrar, J(acob) George
d. 1984 Cole, Kenneth Stewart
d. 1984 Mahin, John Lee
d. 1985 Caton-Thompson, Gertrude
d. 1986 Bauer, Eddie
d. 1986 Dassault, Marcel

April 19
b. 1721 Sherman, Roger
b. 1772 Ricardo, David
b. 1831 Echegaray, Jose
b. 1832 Garfield, Lucretia Rudolph
b. 1836 Juilliard, Augustus D
b. 1858 Robson, May
b. 1868 Schillings, Max von
b. 1877 Evinrude, Ole
b. 1881 Shattuck, Arthur
b. 1886 Bandeira, Manuel (Filho Manuel)
b. 1891 Bacchelli, Riccardo
b. 1891 Rosay, Francoise
b. 1891 Wilcox, Herbert
b. 1892 Tailleferre, Germaine
b. 1897 Segal, Vivienne
b. 1899 Coghill, Nevill Henry Kendall
Aylmer
b. 1900 Hughes, Richard Arthur Warren
b. 1900 Michener, Roland
b. 1900 O'Brien, George
b. 1900 Talmadge, Constance
b. 1901 Summerskill, Edith Clara, Baroness
b. 1902 Latham, Jean Lee
b. 1903 Ness, Eliot
b. 1905 Swift, Kay
b. 1908 Keilberth, Joseph
b. 1910 Walters, "Bucky" (William Henry)
b. 1911 Williams, Ursula Moray
b. 1912 Seaborg, Glenn Theodore
b. 1918 Capa, Cornell
b. 1920 Fontaine, Frank
b. 1920 Mandel, Marvin
b. 1921 Navon, Yitzhak
b. 1927 Adams, Don
b. 1927 Kenneth
b. 1928 Korner, Alexis
b. 1930 O'Brian, Hugh
b. 1932 Botero (Angulo), Fernando
b. 1932 Mansfield, Jayne
b. 1933 Sargent, Dick
b. 1935 Moore, Dudley Stuart John
b. 1937 Donahue, Elinor
b. 1942 Price, Alan
b. 1947 Perahia, Murray
b. 1949 Picasso, Paloma
b. 1954 Carlyle, Randy

b. 1954 Francis, Trevor
b. 1956 Barker, Sue
b. 1962 Unser, Al, Jr.
d. 1560 Melanchthon, Philip Schwarzerd
d. 1588 Veronese, Paolo
d. 1813 Rush, Benjamin
d. 1824 Byron, George Gordon Noel
Byron, Baron
d. 1881 Disraeli, Benjamin
d. 1882 Darwin, Charles Robert
d. 1893 Symonds, John Addington
d. 1904 Isabella II
d. 1906 Curie, Pierre
d. 1914 Peirce, Charles Sanders
d. 1920 Mallinger, Mathilde
d. 1937 Parker, George Safford
d. 1944 Hitchcock, Tommy (Thomas, Jr.)
d. 1944 Noone, Jimmie
d. 1945 Fleming, John Ambrose
d. 1949 Wise, Stephen Samuel
d. 1962 Bliss, Robert Woods
d. 1963 Griswold, A Whitney
d. 1966 Tanner, Valno Alfred
d. 1967 Adenauer, Konrad
d. 1968 Bridges, Tommy (Thomas Jefferson
Davis)
d. 1973 Kelsen, Hans
d. 1973 Laszlo, Miklos
d. 1974 Ayub Khan, Mohammad
d. 1975 Schioetz, Aksel
d. 1978 Koch, John
d. 1979 Morton, Rogers Clark Ballard
d. 1983 Andrzejewski, Jerzy
d. 1986 Childress, Alvin

April 20
b. 121 Marcus Aurelius Antoninus
b. 1492 Aretino, Pietro
b. 1494 Agricola, Georgius
b. 1745 Pinel, Philippe
b. 1793 Laing, David
b. 1808 Napoleon III
b. 1826 Craik, Dinah Maria Mulock
b. 1850 French, Daniel Chester
b. 1860 Curtis, Charles Gordon
b. 1869 Chase, Mary Agnes
b. 1879 Poiret, Paul
b. 1882 Smith, Holland McTeire
b. 1883 Sloane, John
b. 1887 Lazzari, Virgilio
b. 1889 Hitler, Adolf
b. 1889 Kohler, Fred
b. 1890 Duplessis, Maurice le Noblet
b. 1892 Bancroft, Dave (David James)
b. 1893 Lloyd, Harold
b. 1893 Miro, Joan
b. 1893 Ratoff, Gregory
b. 1898 Firestone, Harvey Samuel, Jr.
b. 1899 Larsen, Roy Edward
b. 1900 Norell, Norman
b. 1902 Wolfit, Donald, Sir
b. 1904 Cabot, Bruce

b. 1905 Hochoy, Solomon, Sir
b. 1906 Marcus, Stanley
b. 1907 Soyer, Isaac
b. 1910 Wagner, Robert Ferdinand, Jr.
b. 1912 Chipperfield, Joseph Eugene
b. 1914 Hampton, Lionel
b. 1916 Lowery, Robert O
b. 1920 Stevens, John Paul
b. 1923 Puente, Tito
b. 1924 Foch, Nina
b. 1926 Verdugo, Elena
b. 1938 Cuthbert, Betty
b. 1939 Brundtland, Gro Harlem
b. 1941 O'Neal, Ryan
b. 1947 Tobias, Andrew
b. 1948 Potts, Nadia
b. 1949 Lange, Jessica
b. 1951 Vandross, Luther
b. 1959 Howard, Clint
b. 1961 Mattingly, Don(ald Arthur)
d. 1768 Canaletto, Antonio
d. 1769 Pontiac
d. 1812 Clinton, George
d. 1867 Bozeman, John M
d. 1899 Friedel, Charles
d. 1902 Stockton, Frank (Francis Richard)
d. 1903 Du Chaillu, Paul Belloni
d. 1908 Chadwick, Henry
d. 1912 Stoker, Bram
d. 1918 Braun, Karl Ferdinand
d. 1947 Patino, Simon Iturri
d. 1950 Deeping, (George) Warwick
d. 1959 Johnson, Edward
d. 1962 Whalen, Grover
d. 1968 Dirks, Rudolph
d. 1971 Hodges, Russ
d. 1973 Armstrong, Robert
d. 1974 Greer, Howard
d. 1974 Moorehead, Agnes
d. 1975 Clark, Sydney
d. 1976 Sansom, William
d. 1979 Dehnert, Henry
d. 1980 Kautner, Helmut
d. 1981 Denny-Brown, Derek Ernest
d. 1982 MacLeish, Archibald
d. 1984 Burnford, Sheila (Philip Cochrane Every)
d. 1985 Dutton, Ralph Stawell
d. 1986 Miller, Carl S

April 21
b. 1555 Carracci, Lodovico
b. 1729 Catherine the Great
b. 1782 Froebel, Friedrich Wilhelm August
b. 1816 Bronte, Charlotte
b. 1818 Billings, Josh, pseud.
b. 1828 Taine, Hippolyte Adolphe
b. 1836 Sonzogno, Edoardo
b. 1864 Weber, Max
b. 1870 Porter, Edwin
b. 1871 Blech, Leo
b. 1872 Bitzer, George William

b. 1882 Bridgman, Percy Williams
b. 1884 Frankau, Gilbert
b. 1884 Liebling, Estelle
b. 1887 McCarthy, Joe (Joseph Vincent)
b. 1889 Karrar, Paul
b. 1889 Prado Ugarteche, Manuel
b. 1893 Christaller, Walter
b. 1898 Owen, Steve (Stephen Joseph)
b. 1899 Day, James Wentworth
b. 1900 Fritzsche, Hans
b. 1905 Brown, Pat (Edmund Gerald)
b. 1907 Baker, Dorothy Dodds
b. 1909 May, Rollo
b. 1911 Warren, Leonard
b. 1912 Camus, Marcel
b. 1913 Parkinson, Norman
b. 1914 Gaines, Lee
b. 1914 Panama, Norman
b. 1916 Quinn, Anthony Rudolph Oaxaca
b. 1917 Lambert, J(ack) W(alter)
b. 1919 Cornell, Don
b. 1923 Mortimer, John Clifford
b. 1926 Elizabeth II
b. 1926 Leigh, Carolyn
b. 1927 Brustein, Robert Sanford
b. 1930 Mangano, Silvana
b. 1932 May, Elaine
b. 1932 Melnick, Daniel
b. 1934 Bailar, Benjamin Franklin
b. 1935 Grodin, Charles
b. 1935 Kean, Thomas Howard
b. 1941 Boren, David Lyle
b. 1942 Burford, Anne McGill Gorsuch
b. 1949 LuPone, Patti
b. 1950 Haywood, Spencer
b. 1951 Danza, Tony
b. 1960 Goulet, Michel
d. 1142 Abelard, Pierre
d. 1509 Henry VII
d. 1879 Dix, John Adams
d. 1900 Vogl, Heinrich
d. 1910 Twain, Mark, pseud.
d. 1914 Crockett, S(amuel) R(utherford)
d. 1916 Surratt, John Harrison
d. 1918 Richthofen, Manfred von, Baron
d. 1924 Corelli, Marie, pseud.
d. 1930 Bridges, Robert Seymour
d. 1933 Kilgour, Joseph
d. 1946 Keynes, John Maynard, Baron
d. 1952 Banks, Leslie
d. 1952 Cripps, Stafford, Sir
d. 1956 MacArthur, Charles
d. 1961 Melton, James
d. 1962 Page, Frederick Handley, Sir
d. 1965 Appleton, Edward Victor, Sir
d. 1969 Iturbi, Amparo
d. 1971 Duvalier, Francois
d. 1971 Eliot, George Fielding
d. 1971 Lowe, Edmund Dante
d. 1971 Parker, Cecil
d. 1977 Marx, "Gummo" (Milton)

d. 1978 Craig, Cleo F
d. 1978 Turner, Thomas Wyatt
d. 1980 Page, Joe (Joseph Francis)
d. 1981 Sauter, Eddie (Edward Ernest)
d. 1982 Shulsky, Sam
d. 1983 Slezak, Walter
d. 1984 Mercer, Mabel
d. 1985 Gernreich, Rudi
d. 1985 Hewitt, Foster (William Foster)
d. 1985 Mills, Irving

April 22
b. 1451 Isabella I
b. 1707 Fielding, Henry
b. 1711 Wheelock, Eleazar
b. 1722 Smart, Christopher
b. 1724 Kant, Immanuel
b. 1766 Stael-Holstein, Anne Louise
   Germaine (Necker), Baroness
b. 1792 Levy, Uriah Phillips
b. 1832 Morton, Julius Sterling
b. 1840 Redon, Odilon
b. 1860 Rehan, Ada
b. 1874 Glasgow, Ellen Anderson Gholson
b. 1876 Roelvaag, O(le) E(dvart)
b. 1876 Rolvaag, Ole Edvart
b. 1878 Gordon, Kitty
b. 1881 Kerensky, Alexander Fedorovitch
b. 1882 Brawley, Benjamin Griffith
b. 1887 Hall, James Norman
b. 1887 Wiese, Kurt
b. 1891 Gilpin, Laura
b. 1891 Sacco, Nicola
b. 1896 Ethridge, Mark Foster
b. 1899 Green, Martyn
b. 1902 Angoff, Charles
b. 1902 Vandercook, John Womack
b. 1903 Maxwell, Vera Huppe
b. 1904 Oppenheimer, J(ulius) Robert
b. 1908 Albert, Eddie
b. 1911 Atwater, Edith
b. 1912 Ferrier, Kathleen
b. 1914 DeHartog, Jan
b. 1914 Sisson, Charles Hubert
b. 1915 Barnes, Edward Larrabee
b. 1916 Menuhin, Yehudi
b. 1917 Chauvire, Yvette
b. 1918 Smith, William Jay
b. 1920 March, Hal
b. 1920 Winograd, Arthur
b. 1922 Diebenkorn, Richard
b. 1922 Mingus, Charles
b. 1924 Longley, James Bernard
b. 1924 Putch, William Henry
b. 1924 Weber, Robert Maxwell
b. 1925 Cole, George
b. 1925 MacNutt, Francis, Father
b. 1925 Spelling, Aaron
b. 1926 Rae, Charlotte
b. 1926 Stirling, James
b. 1931 Buchanan, John
b. 1932 Lane, Kenneth Jay

b. 1935 Cossotto, Fiorenza
b. 1937 Nicholson, Jack
b. 1938 Campbell, Glen Travis
b. 1939 Miller, Jason
b. 1945 Graham, Donald Edward
b. 1950 Frampton, Peter
b. 1953 Lysiak, Tom (Thomas James)
b. 1954 Bottoms, Joseph
b. 1959 McNeil, Freeman
b. 1960 Clampett, Bobby
b. 1961 Allen, Byron
d. 1821 Crome, John
d. 1827 Rowlandson, Thomas
d. 1833 Trevithick, Richard
d. 1875 Harper, John
d. 1892 Lalo, Edouard Victor Antoine
d. 1933 Royce, Frederick Henry, Sir
d. 1945 Kollwitz, Kathe Schmidt
d. 1946 Atwill, Lionel
d. 1946 Stone, Harlan Fiske
d. 1950 Houston, Charles Hamilton
d. 1957 Campbell, Roy
d. 1965 Dundee, Johnny
d. 1967 Conway, Tom
d. 1969 Humphries, Rolfe (George Rolfe)
d. 1970 Wank, Roland A
d. 1973 Burnett, Whit
d. 1978 Dean, Basil
d. 1978 Geer, Will
d. 1980 Froman, Jane
d. 1982 Grosvenor, Melville Bell
d. 1984 Adams, Ansel Easton
d. 1984 Marley, John
d. 1986 Agron, Salvador
d. 1986 Eliade, Mircea
d. 1986 Moores, Dick (Richard Arnold)

April 23
b. 1564 Shakespeare, William
b. 1728 Wallis, Samuel
b. 1731 Williams, William
b. 1775 Turner, Joseph Mallord William
b. 1791 Buchanan, James
b. 1813 Douglas, Stephen Arnold
b. 1813 Ozanam, Frederic
b. 1834 Depew, Chauncey M
b. 1844 Dole, Sanford Ballard
b. 1852 Markham, Edwin
b. 1853 Page, Thomas Nelson
b. 1858 Planck, Max Karl Ernst Ludwig
b. 1861 Allenby, Edmund Hynman
   Allenby, Viscount
b. 1867 Fibiger, Johannes Andreas Grib
b. 1880 Norden, Carl Lukas
b. 1882 Coates, Albert
b. 1886 Coveleski, Harry Frank
b. 1890 Murphy, Frank
b. 1891 Prokofiev, Sergei Sergeevich
b. 1893 Borzage, Frank
b. 1895 Noone, Jimmie
b. 1896 Kennedy, Margaret
b. 1897 Clay, Lucius du Bignon

b. 1954 Ferragamo, Vince
d. 1677 Parker, Thomas
d. 1779 Wheelock, Eleazar
d. 1791 Harrison, Benjamin
d. 1821 Frank, Johann Peter
d. 1846 Crescentini, Girolamo
d. 1854 Rossetti, Gabriele Pasquale
   Giuseppe
d. 1881 Fields, James T
d. 1907 Packer, Alfred G
d. 1933 Adler, Felix
d. 1936 Dunne, Finley Peter
d. 1938 Barnard, George Grey
d. 1941 Brush, George
d. 1942 Blackburn, "Jack" (Charles Henry)
d. 1942 Montgomery, Lucy Maud
d. 1947 Cather, Willa Sibert
d. 1956 Stephenson, Henry
d. 1960 Laue, Max Theodor Felix von
d. 1962 Hackett, Francis
d. 1964 Domagk, Gerhard
d. 1965 Dresser, Louise
d. 1965 Madden, Owen Victor
d. 1967 Komarov, Vladimir
d. 1968 Miles, Jackie
d. 1971 Hayton, Lennie (Leonard George)
d. 1973 Armstrong, Hamilton Fish
d. 1974 Abbott, "Bud" (William A)
d. 1974 Jonas, Franz
d. 1978 Nestingen, Ivan Arnold
d. 1980 Finletter, Thomas Knight
d. 1980 Semenenko, Serge
d. 1982 Ashbrook, John Milan
d. 1982 Ritola, Ville
d. 1985 Weinberg, Chester
d. 1986 Simpson, Wallis Warfield

April 25
b. 1215 Louis IX
b. 1599 Cromwell, Oliver
b. 1792 Keble, John
b. 1826 Deering, William
b. 1841 Lucca, Pauline
b. 1852 Cannon, James W
b. 1853 Stevens, John Frank
b. 1862 Grey of Fallodon, Edward
b. 1873 DeLaMare, Walter
b. 1873 Garis, Howard Roger
b. 1874 Marconi, Guglielmo
b. 1875 Nougues, Jean
b. 1880 Mellor, Walter
b. 1883 Ford, Russ(ell William)
b. 1891 Richardson, Sid
b. 1897 Pratt, Fletcher
b. 1900 Halpert, Edith Gregor
b. 1906 Brennan, William Joseph
b. 1907 Zinnemann, Fred
b. 1908 Murrow, Edward R(oscoe)
b. 1909 Pereira, William Leonard
b. 1910 Hirsch, Joseph
b. 1914 Lockridge, Ross Franklin, Jr.
b. 1914 Perez Jimenez, Marcos

b. 1918 Fitzgerald, Ella
b. 1918 Sirluck, Ernest
b. 1918 Varnay, Astrid
b. 1921 Appel, Karel Christian
b. 1923 King, Albert
b. 1923 Miller, Arnold Ray
b. 1925 Stacton, David Derek
b. 1928 Hayden, Melissa
b. 1928 Twombly, Cy
b. 1930 Mazursky, Paul
b. 1932 Lemon, "Meadowlark" (Meadow
   George, III)
b. 1933 Lukas, J Anthony
b. 1939 Lichfield, Patrick (Thomas Patrick
   John Anson, Earl)
b. 1940 Pacino, Al(fredo James)
b. 1945 Ulvaeus, Bjorn
b. 1946 Shire, Talia Rose Coppola
b. 1947 Cruyff, Johan
b. 1950 Scheja, Staffan
b. 1952 Tretyak, Vladislav
b. 1960 Schlicter, Art(hur E)
d. 1472 Alberti, Leon Battista
d. 1482 Margaret of Anjou
d. 1595 Tasso, Torquato
d. 1690 Teniers, David, the Younger
d. 1744 Celsius, Anders
d. 1800 Cowper, William
d. 1820 Volney, (Constantin) Francois
   Chasseboeuf
d. 1853 Beaumont, William
d. 1878 Sewell, Anna
d. 1919 Juilliard, Augustus D
d. 1920 Vail, Theodore Newton
d. 1928 Bennett, Floyd
d. 1928 Curel, Francois de
d. 1943 Nemirovich-Danchenko, Vladimir I
d. 1944 Herriman, George
d. 1945 Weatherford, Teddy
d. 1951 Wilson, Al
d. 1954 Hergesheimer, Joseph
d. 1955 Collier, Constance
d. 1955 Merriam, Frank Finley
d. 1958 Hickman, Herman Michael, Jr.
d. 1959 Mannes, David
d. 1960 Emerson, Hope
d. 1968 Davidson, Donald Grady
d. 1970 Louise, Anita
d. 1971 Soong, T V
d. 1972 Sanders, George
d. 1975 Duclos, Jacques
d. 1976 Brailowsky, Alexander
d. 1976 Brown, Ned (Edward Gerald)
d. 1976 Reed, Carol, Sir
d. 1982 Burnett, W(illiam) R(iley)
d. 1982 Butterfield, Lyman Henry
d. 1982 Cody, John Patrick
d. 1982 Johnson, Celia, Dame
d. 1982 Wilson, Don(ald Harlow)
d. 1983 Glenn, Carroll
d. 1985 Haydn, Richard

b. 1906 Maeght, Aime
b. 1909 Matlock, "Matty" (Julian Clifton)
b. 1910 Fischer, John
b. 1914 Cole, Jack
b. 1916 Slaughter, Enos Bradsher
b. 1918 Scali, John Alfred
b. 1920 Morgan, Edwin George
b. 1922 Klugman, Jack
b. 1925 Baron, Samuel
b. 1926 LaHaye, Tim
b. 1926 Paterson, Basil Alexander
b. 1927 King, Coretta Scott
b. 1931 Oistrakh, Igor Davidovich
b. 1932 Botha, Roelof Pik
b. 1932 Knox, Chuck (Charles Robert)
b. 1934 Aimee, Anouk
b. 1937 Dennis, Sandy
b. 1937 Jones, Phil(ip Howard)
b. 1938 Anthony, Earl
b. 1939 Carne, Judy
b. 1941 Blegen, Judith Eyer
b. 1947 Magnuson, Keith Arlen
b. 1950 Simmons, Calvin
b. 1951 Frehley, Ace
b. 1952 Gervin, George
b. 1959 Easton, Sheena
d. 1521 Magellan, Ferdinand
d. 1702 Bart, Jean
d. 1710 Betterton, Thomas
d. 1797 Babeuf, Francois Noel
d. 1813 Pike, Zebulon Montgomery
d. 1854 Pickering, William
d. 1882 Emerson, Ralph Waldo
d. 1886 Richardson, Henry Hobson
d. 1889 Barnard, Frederick Augustus
Porter
d. 1902 Morton, Julius Sterling
d. 1915 Scriabin, Alexander Nicholaevich
d. 1927 Beveridge, Albert Jeremiah
d. 1932 Crane, Hart
d. 1937 Schutzendorf, Gustav
d. 1938 Husserl, Edmund
d. 1948 Knudsen, William S
d. 1950 Cavanaugh, Hobart
d. 1954 Ralf, Torsten
d. 1961 DelRuth, Roy
d. 1965 Murrow, Edward R(oscoe)
d. 1972 Budenz, Louis Francis
d. 1972 Nkrumah, Kwame
d. 1981 Battles, Cliff(ord Franklin)
d. 1981 Roosevelt, John Aspinal
d. 1982 Tully, Tom
d. 1983 Catledge, Turner
d. 1986 Hynek, J(oseph) Allen
d. 1986 Love, Bessie

April 28
b. 1442 Edward IV
b. 1758 Monroe, James
b. 1817 Curtin, Andrew Gregg
b. 1840 Cox, Palmer
b. 1869 Goodhue, Bertram G

b. 1871 Homer, Louise
b. 1872 Esposito, Joseph
b. 1873 Bauer, Harold
b. 1874 Toler, Sidney
b. 1878 Barrymore, Lionel Blythe
b. 1889 Salazar, Antonio de Oliveira
b. 1892 Niles, John Jacob
b. 1896 Dunninger, Joseph
b. 1900 Gielgud, Val Henry
b. 1900 Thorez, Maurice
b. 1903 Fitts, Dudley
b. 1906 Bok, Bart J(an)
b. 1906 Godel, Kurt
b. 1906 Sacher, Paul
b. 1910 Borch, Fred J
b. 1910 Robinson, Francis Arthur
b. 1912 Sansom, Odette Marie Celine
b. 1913 Purdy, Ken(neth) William
b. 1917 Anderson, Robert Woodruff
b. 1919 Frasconi, Antonio
b. 1919 Muses, Charles Arthur
b. 1921 Evans, Rowland, Jr.
b. 1924 Kaunda, Kenneth David
b. 1926 Dearie, Blossom
b. 1926 Lee, Harper (Nelle Harper)
b. 1929 Bailey, Charles Waldo, II
b. 1930 Baker, James Addison, III
b. 1933 Faas, Horst
b. 1933 Jones, Carolyn
b. 1937 Hussain al Takriti, Saddam
b. 1938 Rosenfeld, Alvin Hirsch
b. 1938 Wilmerding, John
b. 1941 Ann-Margret
b. 1948 Strassman, Marcia
b. 1960 Browning, Tom (Thomas Leo)
d. 1676 Clarke, John
d. 1794 Estaing, Charles Henri Hector,
Comte d'
d. 1842 Bell, Charles
d. 1858 Muller, Johannes Peter
d. 1865 Cunard, Samuel, Sir
d. 1873 Manzoni, Alessandro (Antonio)
d. 1896 Treitschke, Heinrich Gotthard von
d. 1903 Gibbs, Josiah Willard
d. 1935 Mackenzie, Alexander, Sir
d. 1940 Tetrazzini, Luisa
d. 1943 Farnham, Sally James
d. 1944 Knox, Frank
d. 1945 Mussolini, Benito
d. 1946 Bartlett, Robert Abram
d. 1948 Breneman, Tom
d. 1950 Pope, Generoso
d. 1961 Connolly, Thomas Henry
d. 1967 Gibbs, William Francis
d. 1970 Begley, Ed(ward James)
d. 1972 Roessner, Elmer
d. 1976 Hughes, Richard Arthur Warren
d. 1976 Sperry, Armstrong W
d. 1981 Walker, Mickey
d. 1982 Corn, Ira George, Jr.
d. 1984 Ashton-Warner, Sylvia Constance

d. 1883 Manet, Edouard
d. 1889 Rosa, Carl
d. 1900 Jones, "Casey" (John Luther)
d. 1918 Princip, Gavrilo
d. 1934 Welch, William Henry
d. 1936 Housman, A(lfred) E(dward)
d. 1941 Porter, Edwin
d. 1942 Arthur, Joseph Charles
d. 1943 Webb, Beatrice Potter
d. 1944 Poiret, Paul
d. 1945 Braun, Eva
d. 1945 Hitler, Adolf
d. 1946 Hepbron, George
d. 1947 Wright, Almroth Edward, Sir
d. 1956 Barkley, Alben William
d. 1959 Nagai, Sokichi
d. 1960 Polacco, Giorgio
d. 1961 Fauset, Jessie Redmon
d. 1966 Farina, Richard
d. 1970 Johnson, Hall
d. 1970 Stevens, Inger
d. 1971 Roper, Elmo Burns, Jr.
d. 1972 Scala, Gia
d. 1977 Lewis, (Myrtle) Tillie
d. 1980 Kronenberger, Louis
d. 1980 Munoz Marin, Luis
d. 1981 Anderson, "Cat" (William Alonzo)
d. 1981 Bordes, Francois
d. 1982 Bangs, Lester
d. 1983 Balanchine, George
d. 1983 Waters, "Muddy"
d. 1985 Aitken, Max (John William Maxwell)
d. 1985 Sommers, Ben
d. 1986 Stevenson, Robert

April 31
b. 1901 Magee, Harry L

MAY

b. 1740 Pacchierotti, Gasparo
b. 1820 Surratt, Mary Eugenia Jenkins
b. 1867 Reymont, Wladyslaw Stanislaw
b. 1893 Pearlroth, Norbert
b. 1895 Chevallier, Gabriel
b. 1911 Galili, Israel
b. 1925 Ghorbal, Ashraf A.
b. 1925 Sheehan, William Edward, Jr.
b. 1946 Pisier, Marie-France
b. 1965 Bridges, Todd
d. 1540 Guicciardini, Francesco
d. 1607 Dyer, Edward, Sir
d. 1700 Jolliet, Louis
d. 1914 Pearce, Charles S
d. 1933 Whitechurch, Victor Lorenzo
d. 1943 Yamamoto, Isoroku
d. 1972 Bates, Ted (Theodore Lewis)
d. 1973 Balaban, Emanuel
d. 1974 Ochs, Adolph S, II
d. 1981 Wechsler, David
d. 1983 Kaper, Bronislau

May 1
b. 1672 Addison, Joseph
b. 1764 Latrobe, Benjamin Henry
b. 1769 Wellington, Arthur Wellesley, Duke
b. 1796 Booth, Junius Brutus
b. 1825 Inness, George
b. 1830 Jones, Mary Harris
b. 1839 Chardonnet, Louis Marie
b. 1845 Mifflin, George Harrison
b. 1848 Rhodes, James Ford
b. 1862 Prevost, Marcel
b. 1864 Jarvis, Anna
b. 1876 Swanson, Carl A
b. 1880 Lasker, Albert Davis
b. 1881 Teilhard de Chardin, Pierre
b. 1884 Quimby, Harriet
b. 1887 Cunningham, Alan Gordon, Sir
b. 1887 Wortman, Denys
b. 1892 Barlow, Howard
b. 1895 Sowerby, Leo
b. 1896 Clark, Mark Wayne
b. 1896 Collins, Joseph L
b. 1900 Caples, John
b. 1900 Roessner, Elmer
b. 1900 Silone, Ignazio
b. 1901 Gill, Amory Tingle
b. 1904 Valentina
b. 1905 Cagle, "Red" (Christian Keener)
b. 1906 Hobart, Rose
b. 1907 Roszak, Theodore
b. 1909 Smith, Kate (Kathryn Elizabeth)
b. 1910 Battles, Cliff(ord Franklin)
b. 1910 Hynek, J(oseph) Allen
b. 1910 Rockefeller, Mary French
b. 1912 Rockefeller, Winthrop
b. 1913 Susskind, Walter
b. 1916 Ford, Glenn
b. 1917 Beradino, John
b. 1917 Darrieux, Danielle
b. 1918 Paar, Jack
b. 1919 O'Herlihy, Dan
b. 1922 Goodman, Julian B
b. 1922 Mosel, Tad
b. 1923 Heller, Joseph
b. 1924 Kayibanda, Gregoire
b. 1924 Southern, Terry
b. 1925 Blair, Clay, Jr.
b. 1925 Carpenter, Scott (Malcolm Scott)
b. 1927 Bertini, Gary
b. 1927 Cordtz, Dan
b. 1929 Weaver, Thomas
b. 1930 Matson, Oliver G
b. 1939 Collins, Judy (Judith)
b. 1939 Robinson, Max C
b. 1940 Peretti, Elsa
b. 1945 Coolidge, Rita
b. 1954 Parker, Ray, Jr.
b. 1960 Cauthen, Steve
d. 1700 Dryden, John
d. 1873 Livingstone, David

d. 1889 Weir, Robert W
d. 1890 Brisbane, Albert
d. 1892 Lamperti, Francesco
d. 1901 Waterman, Lewis Edson
d. 1903 Arditi, Luigi
d. 1904 Dvorak, Anton
d. 1922 Cheney, John Vance
d. 1940 Brooke, L Leslie
d. 1952 Coulter, Ernest Kent
d. 1953 Shinn, Everett
d. 1957 Mitchell, Grant
d. 1964 Jones, "Spike" (Lindsay Armstrong)
d. 1968 Adams, Jack (John James)
d. 1968 Nicolson, Harold George, Sir
d. 1969 Logan, Ella
d. 1969 Rosenthal, Jean
d. 1971 Farrell, Glenda
d. 1973 Brill, Marty (Martin)
d. 1978 Khachaturian, Aram
d. 1978 Warner, Sylvia Townsend
d. 1981 Sneider, Vernon John
d. 1982 Fitzgerald, Albert J
d. 1982 Primrose, William
d. 1984 Barrett, John L
d. 1984 Jenkins, Gordon
d. 1985 Crossley, Archibald Maddock
d. 1985 Robins, Denise Naomi
d. 1986 Aulaire, Edgar Parin d'

May 2
b. 1660 Scarlatti, Alessandro
b. 1772 Novalis
b. 1779 Galt, John
b. 1810 Brewer, Ebenezer
b. 1851 Taylor, Graham
b. 1859 Jerome, Jerome Klapka
b. 1860 Herzl, Theodor
b. 1865 Fitch, (William) Clyde
b. 1866 Lazear, Jesse William
b. 1871 Duffy, Francis Patrick
b. 1879 Byrnes, James Francis
b. 1887 Castle, Vernon
b. 1887 Collins, Eddie (Edward Trowbridge, Sr.)
b. 1887 Griffis, Stanton
b. 1892 Richthofen, Manfred von, Baron
b. 1895 Bacon, Peggy
b. 1895 Hart, Lorenz Milton
b. 1895 Holman, Eugene
b. 1896 Van Doren, Dorothy Graffe
b. 1897 Coots, J Fred
b. 1902 Aherne, Brian de Lacy
b. 1903 Spock, Benjamin McLane
b. 1904 Crosby, "Bing" (Harry Lillis)
b. 1905 Armstrong, Charlotte
b. 1906 Halsman, Philippe
b. 1908 Bakewell, William
b. 1908 O'Brien-Moore, Erin
b. 1912 Springer, Axel Caesar
b. 1914 Woss, Kurt
b. 1920 Hutt, William Ian Dewitt

b. 1921 Ray, Satyajit
b. 1922 Rosenthal, Abraham Michael
b. 1923 Hillery, Patrick John
b. 1924 Bikel, Theodore Meir
b. 1925 Neville, John
b. 1927 Unger, Irwin
b. 1928 Falls, Joe
b. 1930 Slade, Bernard, pseud.
b. 1935 Faisal II
b. 1935 Hussein, Saddam
b. 1936 Rabin, Michael
b. 1946 Gore, Lesley
b. 1946 Henrit, Robert
b. 1949 Gatlin, Larry Wayne
b. 1953 Wilkes, Jamaal
d. 1519 Leonardo da Vinci
d. 1685 Ostade, Adriaen van
d. 1844 Beckford, William
d. 1857 Musset, Alfred de
d. 1864 Meyerbeer, Giacomo
d. 1912 Davenport, Homer Calvin
d. 1934 Procter, William Cooper
d. 1944 Leonard, William Ellery
d. 1955 Vollmer, Lula
d. 1957 McCarthy, Joe (Joseph Raymond)
d. 1960 Chessman, Caryl Whittier
d. 1963 Brooks, Van Wyck
d. 1964 Astor, Nancy Witcher (Langhorne) Astor, Viscountess
d. 1968 McLean, John Milton
d. 1969 Papen, Franz von
d. 1972 Hoover, J(ohn) Edgar
d. 1976 Bankhead, Dan(iel Robert)
d. 1977 Cole, Edward Nicholas
d. 1979 Natta, Giulio
d. 1980 Pal, George
d. 1981 Osborne, John Franklin
d. 1981 Robertson, Charles Sammis
d. 1982 Marlowe, Hugh
d. 1983 Van Brocklin, Norm(an Mack)
d. 1984 Barry, Jack
d. 1984 Clampett, Bob (Robert)
d. 1985 Bedells, Phyllis
d. 1985 Clinton, Larry
d. 1985 Eisenhower, Milton Stover

May 3
b. 1469 Machiavelli, Niccolo
b. 1761 Kotzebue, August Friedrich Ferdinand von
b. 1816 Meigs, Montgomery Cunningham
b. 1844 Carte, Richard d'Oyly
b. 1849 Bulow, Bernhard H M
b. 1849 Riis, Jacob August
b. 1853 Howe, Edgar Watson
b. 1856 Alvary, Max
b. 1859 Adams, Andy
b. 1860 Haldane, John Scott
b. 1879 Pollack, Egon
b. 1882 Dale, Chester
b. 1886 DuPre, Marcel
b. 1890 Fairless, Benjamin F

b. 1891 Rixey, Eppa
b. 1892 Bondi, Beulah
b. 1892 Thomson, George Paget
b. 1895 Mark, Herman F
b. 1897 Krishna Menon, V(engalil)
       K(rishnan)
b. 1898 Meir, Golda
b. 1899 MacMahon, Aline
b. 1900 Winwar, Frances (Francesca
       Vinciguerra)
b. 1901 Collier, John
b. 1902 Barbanell, Maurice
b. 1902 Kastler, Alfred
b. 1902 LaRue, Jack
b. 1902 Slezak, Walter
b. 1904 DeErdely, Francis (Ferenc)
b. 1906 Astor, Mary
b. 1906 Halsted, Anna Eleanor Roosevelt
b. 1907 Lee, Canada
b. 1907 Wilson, Earl
b. 1910 Corwin, Norman
b. 1910 Massey, D Curtis
b. 1911 Lawson, "Yank" (John R)
b. 1911 Margolius, Sidney Senier
b. 1912 Fox, Virgil Keel
b. 1912 Sarton, May
b. 1913 Blackwell, Earl
b. 1913 Inge, William
b. 1913 Kohut, Heinz
b. 1915 Comden, Betty
b. 1915 Lippold, Richard
b. 1916 Mathieu, Noel Jean
b. 1916 Paul, Oglesby
b. 1918 Simoneau, Leopold
b. 1919 Seeger, Pete(r)
b. 1920 Bankhead, Dan(iel Robert)
b. 1920 Lewis, John Aaron
b. 1920 Robinson, "Sugar" Ray
b. 1922 Svetlova, Marina
b. 1926 Davis, Ann Bradford
b. 1926 O'Horgan, Tom
b. 1927 Lazarus, Mell
b. 1928 Eckstein, George
b. 1934 Brown, James
b. 1935 Banner, James Morril, Jr.
b. 1936 Humperdinck, Engelbert
b. 1937 Valli, Frankie
b. 1938 Foreman, Carol Lee Tucker
b. 1943 Snepp, Frank Warren, III
b. 1946 Lopes, Davey (David Earl)
b. 1947 Henning, Doug(las James)
b. 1950 Hopkin, Mary
b. 1951 Cross, Christopher
b. 1951 Lane, Stewart F
d. 1763 Psalmanazar, George
d. 1839 Paer, Ferdinando
d. 1845 Hood, Thomas
d. 1856 Adam, Adolphe Charles
d. 1910 Ricketts, Howard T
d. 1914 Sickles, Daniel Edgar
d. 1916 MacDonagh, Thomas

d. 1916 Pearse, Padraic (Patrick Henry)
d. 1926 Straus, Oscar
d. 1927 Ball, Ernest
d. 1932 Fort, Charles Hoy
d. 1935 Manners, Charles
d. 1943 Andrews, Frank M(axwell)
d. 1945 Goebbels, Joseph (Paul Joseph)
d. 1954 Hooton, Earnest Albert
d. 1958 Cornelius, Henry
d. 1968 Hickok, Lorena A
d. 1972 Cabot, Bruce
d. 1974 Clapp, Margaret Antoinette
d. 1978 Downs, William Randall, Jr.
d. 1979 Angoff, Charles
d. 1979 O'Brien-Moore, Erin
d. 1980 Elliott, George Paul
d. 1982 Dantine, Helmut
d. 1982 Frazier, Brenda Diana Dudd
d. 1983 Skolsky, Sidney
d. 1984 Schneider, Alan
d. 1986 Alda, Robert

May 4
b. 1769 Lawrence, Thomas, Sir
b. 1770 Gerard, Francois
b. 1796 Mann, Horace
b. 1796 Prescott, William Hickling
b. 1806 Cooke, William Fothergil, Sir
b. 1820 Tyler, Julia Gardiner
b. 1825 Huxley, Thomas Henry
b. 1826 Church, Frederick Edwin
b. 1827 Speke, John Hanning
b. 1830 Mapleson, James Henry
b. 1851 Dewing, Thomas Wilmer
b. 1860 Reznicek, Emil von
b. 1864 Hovey, Richard
b. 1866 Corey, William Ellis
b. 1872 Wright, Harold Bell
b. 1874 Conrad, Frank
b. 1888 Malko, Nicolai
b. 1889 Spellman, Francis Joseph
b. 1890 Rosenfeld, Paul
b. 1896 Baxter, Frank Condie
b. 1896 Ochsner, (Edward William) Alton
b. 1902 Dexter, Al
b. 1902 Stone, W Clement
b. 1903 Adler, Luther (Lutha)
b. 1903 Layden, Elmer
b. 1904 Saito, Yoshishige
b. 1907 Kirstein, Lincoln Edward
b. 1909 DaSilva, Howard
b. 1914 Muller, Hilgard
b. 1918 Tanaka, Kakuei
b. 1919 Heloise
b. 1920 Schreiber, Hermann Otto Ludwig
b. 1922 Hambleton, Hugh George
b. 1925 Herrera Campins, Luis
b. 1928 Ferguson, Maynard
b. 1928 Mubarak, (Muhamed) Hosni
b. 1928 Rawls, Betsy (Elizabeth Earle)
b. 1929 Hepburn, Audrey
b. 1930 Peters, Roberta

b. 1860 Sherman, Frank Dempster
b. 1861 Tagore, Rabindranath, Sir
b. 1862 Underwood, Oscar Wilder
b. 1865 Christie, John Walter
b. 1868 LeRoux, Gaston
b. 1870 Giannini, Amadeo Peter
b. 1870 McCutcheon, John Tinney
b. 1875 Leahy, William Daniel
b. 1880 Ironside, William E
b. 1880 Kirchner, Ernst Ludwig
b. 1881 Martinez, Sierra Gregorio
b. 1886 Karfiol, Bernard
b. 1888 Celler, Emanuel
b. 1888 Stover, Russell
b. 1895 Valentino, Rudolph
b. 1897 Purtell, William Arthur
b. 1898 Gerber, Daniel Frank
b. 1899 Horenstein, Jascha
b. 1900 Mattingley, Garrett
b. 1902 Ophuls, Max
b. 1903 Golden, Harry Lewis
b. 1904 Mallowan, Max Edgar Lucien, Sir
b. 1905 Irish, Edward Simmons (Ned)
b. 1905 Martinson, Harry Edmund
b. 1905 Shor, "Toots" (Bernard)
b. 1906 Lattimore, Richmond Alexander
b. 1907 Ewbank, "Weeb" (Wilbur)
b. 1908 Hale, Nancy
b. 1911 Ballantrae, Lord
b. 1911 Glover, William H
b. 1913 Cavallaro, Carmen
b. 1913 Granger, Stewart
b. 1914 Jarrell, Randall
b. 1915 Welles, Orson (George Orson)
b. 1915 White, Theodore Harold
b. 1921 Wakefield, Dick (Richard Cummings)
b. 1924 Hunter, Ross
b. 1926 Piazza, Marguerite
b. 1928 Beers, Victor Gilbert
b. 1931 Mays, Willie Howard, Jr.
b. 1937 Terris, Susan
b. 1942 Maestro, Giulio
b. 1942 Stilwell, Richard Dale
b. 1945 Seger, Bob
b. 1950 Bond, Victoria
b. 1950 Hyatt, Joel
b. 1951 Doe, Samuel Kanyon
d. 1802 Lowell, John
d. 1826 Levasseur, Rosalie
d. 1840 Gallitzin, Demetrius Augustine
d. 1856 Hamilton, William, Sir
d. 1859 Humboldt, Alexander, Freiherr von
d. 1862 Thoreau, Henry David
d. 1870 Simpson, James Young, Sir
d. 1917 Stuart, Ruth McEnery
d. 1919 Baum, (Lyman) Frank
d. 1921 Fried, Alfred Hermann
d. 1930 Gilpin, Charles Sidney
d. 1943 Haines, Robert Terrel
d. 1947 Homer, Louise

d. 1949 Maeterlinck, Maurice
d. 1950 Pattee, Fred Lewis
d. 1950 Smedley, Agnes
d. 1952 Birley, Oswald Hornby Joseph, Sir
d. 1952 Montessori, Maria
d. 1954 Forbes, Bertie Charles
d. 1962 Grant, Gordon
d. 1962 Woolley, Monty (Edgar Montillion)
d. 1963 Weems, Ted (Wilfred Theodore)
d. 1973 MacMillan, Ernest Campbell, Sir
d. 1974 Crean, Robert
d. 1979 Ager, Milton
d. 1980 Levitt, Arthur, Jr.
d. 1981 Fitzsimmons, Frank
d. 1982 Littlejohn, Robert McGowan
d. 1983 Masters, John
d. 1983 Winding, Kai Chresten
d. 1985 Desjardins, Pete
d. 1985 Higbe, Kirby (Walter Kirby)

May 7

b. 1643 Van Cortlandt, Stephanus
b. 1774 Bainbridge, William
b. 1812 Browning, Robert
b. 1833 Brahms, Johannes
b. 1836 Cannon, Joseph Gurney
b. 1840 Tchaikovsky, Peter Ilyich
b. 1847 Rosebery, Archibald Philip Primrose, Earl
b. 1850 Seidl, Anton
b. 1883 Berry, James Gomer
b. 1885 Hayes, "Gabby" (George Francis)
b. 1892 MacLeish, Archibald
b. 1893 Atwood, Francis Clarke
b. 1901 Cooper, "Gary" (Frank James)
b. 1903 Zabolotskii, Nikolai Alekseevich
b. 1904 Lewton, Val Ivan
b. 1904 Walker, Harold Blake
b. 1905 Stoll, George
b. 1906 Corle, Edwin
b. 1909 Land, Edwin Herbert
b. 1913 Glazer, David
b. 1913 Powers, Anne
b. 1915 Elliot, Win (Irwin)
b. 1917 Rafferty, Max(well Lewis, Jr.)
b. 1919 Peron, Eva Duarte
b. 1920 Post, Elizabeth Lindley
b. 1921 Davies, Rodger Paul
b. 1921 Rebuffat, Gaston Louis Simon
b. 1922 McGavin, Darren
b. 1923 Baxter, Anne
b. 1923 Roche, John P
b. 1925 Kirk, Ruth Kratz
b. 1927 Jhabvala, Ruth Prawer
b. 1927 Soderstrom, Elisabeth Anna
b. 1928 Mitchelson, Marvin M(orris)
b. 1928 Siegel, Stanley E
b. 1928 Williams, Dick (Richard Hirschfield)
b. 1930 Fields, Totie
b. 1931 Brewer, Theresa

d. 1947 Selfridge, Harry Gordon
d. 1948 Gordon, Vera
d. 1949 Luden, William H
d. 1952 Kirby, Rollin
d. 1952 Robins, Elizabeth
d. 1954 Edwards, Alan
d. 1955 Park, Maud May Wood
d. 1957 Davidson, J Brownlee
d. 1958 Geddes, Norman Bel
d. 1964 Nomura, Kichisaburo
d. 1967 Andrews, LaVerne
d. 1967 Rice, Elmer
d. 1968 Wood, Craig Ralph
d. 1973 Vandegrift, Alexander Archer
d. 1974 May, Mortimer
d. 1975 Baker, George
d. 1975 Brundage, Avery
d. 1975 Slobodkin, Louis
d. 1976 Skaggs, M(arion) B
d. 1978 Rubicam, Raymond
d. 1981 Andrew, Prince of Russia
d. 1981 Lindsay, Margaret
d. 1982 Bogart, Neil
d. 1982 Villeneuve, Gilles
d. 1984 Wallace, Lila Bell Acheson
d. 1985 O'Brien, Edmond
d. 1985 Sturgeon, Theodore Hamilton

May 9

b. 1775 Brown, Jacob Jennings
b. 1800 Brown, John
b. 1801 Cousins, Samuel
b. 1813 Matteson, Tompkins Harrison
b. 1815 Blythe, David Gilmour
b. 1828 Cramp, Charles Henry
b. 1860 Barrie, James Matthew, Sir
b. 1865 Jordan, Elizabeth Garver
b. 1873 Cermak, Anton Joseph
b. 1874 Baylis, Lilian Mary
b. 1878 Gallo, Fortune
b. 1882 Kaiser, Henry John
b. 1883 Ortega y Gasset, Jose
b. 1886 Biddle, Francis Beverley
b. 1895 Barthelmess, Richard
b. 1896 Clarke, Austin
b. 1904 Bateson, Gregory
b. 1904 Wilson, Dorothy Clarke
b. 1906 Estes, Eleanor Ruth Rosenfeld
b. 1908 Sillman, Leonard
b. 1909 Hagerty, James Campbell
b. 1909 Hagerty, James Campbell
b. 1910 Woodhouse, Barbara Blackburn
b. 1911 Simeone, Harry
b. 1912 Armendariz, Pedro
b. 1914 Giulini, Carlo Maria
b. 1914 Kheel, Theodore Woodrow
b. 1914 Snow, Hank
b. 1918 Feld, Irvin
b. 1918 Freeman, Orville Lothrop
b. 1918 Wallace, Mike (Myron Leon)
b. 1920 Adams, Richard
b. 1921 Berrigan, Daniel J

b. 1923 Aaron, Chester Norman
b. 1925 Neville, Kris Ottman
b. 1928 Gonzales, "Pancho" (Richard Alonzo)
b. 1928 Scott, Barbara Ann
b. 1931 Brand, Vance DeVoe
b. 1936 Drinkwater, Terry
b. 1936 Finney, Albert
b. 1937 Jackson, Glenda
b. 1938 Simic, Charles
b. 1939 Boston, Ralph
b. 1940 Brooks, James L
b. 1942 Roe, Tommy
b. 1944 Furay, Richie
b. 1946 Bergen, Candice
b. 1948 Murphy, Calvin
b. 1949 Joel, Billy (William Martin)
b. 1954 Palligrosi, Tony
b. 1960 Gwynn, Tony (Anthony Keith)
b. 1965 Yzerman, Steve
d. 1657 Bradford, William
d. 1707 Buxtehude, Dietrich
d. 1791 Hopkinson, Francis
d. 1805 Schiller, Friedrich von (Johann Christoph Friedrich von)
d. 1850 Gay-Lussac, Joseph Louis
d. 1860 Goodrich, Samuel Griswold
d. 1860 James, George Payne Rainsford
d. 1864 Sedgwick, John
d. 1911 Higginson, Thomas Wentworth
d. 1914 Post, Charles William
d. 1919 Henry, Edward Lamson
d. 1931 Michelson, Albert Abraham
d. 1934 Morton, Joy
d. 1942 McNamee, Graham
d. 1945 Lalique, Rene
d. 1948 Allen, Viola Emily
d. 1952 Lee, Canada
d. 1957 Pinza, Ezio
d. 1958 Davies, Joseph Edward
d. 1958 Goodwin, Bill
d. 1963 Kuykendall, Ralph Simpson
d. 1968 Currie, Finlay
d. 1968 Dillon, George
d. 1968 Gray, Harold
d. 1968 Lorne, Marion
d. 1973 Brannigan, Owen
d. 1973 Leonard, Jack E
d. 1976 Kerner, Otto
d. 1976 Meinhof, Ulrike Marie
d. 1977 Jones, James
d. 1978 Moro, Aldo
d. 1979 Eaton, Cyrus Stephen
d. 1981 Algren, Nelson
d. 1981 Lincoln, Victoria Endicott
d. 1983 Hoffman, Anna Marie Lederer Rosenberg
d. 1983 Rosenberg, Anna Marie

May 10

b. 1760 Rouget de Lisle, Claude Joseph
b. 1770 Davout, Louis Nicholas

b. 1778 Ladd, William
b. 1789 Sparks, Jared
b. 1810 Shields, James
b. 1813 Blair, Montgomery
b. 1832 Grace, William Russell
b. 1837 Pinchback, Pinckney Benton Stewart
b. 1838 Bryce, James Bryce, Viscount
b. 1841 Bennett, James Gordon, Jr.
b. 1843 Kohler, Kaufmann
b. 1843 Perez Galdos, Benito
b. 1843 Williams, Edward Porter
b. 1850 Lipton, Thomas Johnstone, Sir
b. 1868 Barrow, Ed(ward Grant)
b. 1868 Hart, George Overbury
b. 1878 Stresemann, Gustav
b. 1886 Barth, Karl
b. 1886 Stapledon, Olaf (Wiliam Olaf)
b. 1888 Steiner, Max
b. 1890 Brown, Clarence
b. 1897 Allen of Hurtwood, Lady
b. 1897 Lowenfels, Walter
b. 1898 Durant, Ariel (Ida Ariel Ethel Kaufman)
b. 1899 Astaire, Fred
b. 1899 Tiomkin, Dimitri
b. 1902 Selznick, David O(liver)
b. 1908 Albert, Carl Bert
b. 1908 Barraclough, Geoffrey
b. 1909 Carter, "Mother" Maybelle
b. 1910 Berne, Eric Lennard
b. 1910 Demaret, Jimmy (James Newton B)
b. 1912 Viscardi, Henry, Jr
b. 1913 Gemmell, Alan
b. 1915 Dickens, Monica Enid
b. 1916 Babbitt, Milton Byron
b. 1918 Brazelton, T(homas) Berry
b. 1918 Margo
b. 1919 Bell, Daniel
b. 1919 Grasso, Ella
b. 1921 Walker, Nancy
b. 1923 Parseghian, Ara Raoul
b. 1925 Bechtel, Steve (Stephen Davison, Jr.)
b. 1932 Miles, Tichi Wilkerson
b. 1934 Jamison, Judith
b. 1935 Owens, Gary
b. 1937 Kopit, Arthur L
b. 1937 Press, Tamara
b. 1939 Darnton, Robert Choate
b. 1940 Dyer, Wayne
b. 1946 Blacque, Taurean
b. 1946 Mason, Dave
b. 1955 Chapman, Mark David
b. 1957 Mahre, Phil(lip)
b. 1957 Mahre, Steve(n)
d. 1696 LaBruyere, Jean de
d. 1774 Louis XV
d. 1807 Rochambeau, Jean Baptiste Donatien de Vimeur, Comte

d. 1818 Revere, Paul
d. 1860 Parker, Theodore
d. 1863 Jackson, "Stonewall" (Thomas Jonathan)
d. 1904 Stanley, Henry Morton, Sir
d. 1910 Cannizzaro, Stanislao
d. 1914 Nordica, Lillian
d. 1914 Schuch, Ernst von
d. 1918 Grass, John
d. 1920 Howells, William Dean
d. 1930 Stratemeyer, Edward L
d. 1933 Kurz, Selma
d. 1935 Witherspoon, Herbert
d. 1942 Weber, Joseph M
d. 1944 Michael, Moina Belle
d. 1950 Greene, Belle da Costa
d. 1955 Burns, Tommy
d. 1956 Mulford, Clarence Edward
d. 1956 Prouty, Jed
d. 1960 Schwartz, Maurice
d. 1963 Lipscomb, Eugene
d. 1964 Haney, Carol
d. 1964 Lebrun, Rico (Frederico)
d. 1968 Bloomingdale, Samuel
d. 1970 Reuther, Walter Philip
d. 1973 Green, Abel
d. 1977 Allred, Rulon Clark
d. 1979 Frankel, Charles
d. 1982 Sloane, Dennis
d. 1982 Weiss, Peter
d. 1986 Bernardi, Hershel
d. 1986 Tenzing, Norgay

May 11
b. 1720 Munchhausen, Hierony mus Karl Friedrich von, Baron
b. 1751 Earle, Ralph
b. 1752 Blumenbach, Johann Friedrich
b. 1766 D'Israeli, Isaac
b. 1811 Chang and Eng
b. 1811 LeVerrier, Urbain Jean Joseph
b. 1811 Scranton, George Whitfield
b. 1852 Fairbanks, Charles Warren
b. 1854 Mergenthaler, Ottmar
b. 1871 Schlesinger, Frank
b. 1880 Haynes, George Edward
b. 1881 Karman, Theodore Todor Von
b. 1881 Von Karman, Theodore
b. 1884 Gluck, Alma
b. 1885 Oliver, Joe (Joseph)
b. 1888 Berlin, Irving
b. 1889 Nash, Paul
b. 1891 Morgenthau, Henry, Jr.
b. 1892 Rutherford, Margaret
b. 1893 Gag, Wanda
b. 1893 Graham, Martha
b. 1894 Bunker, Ellsworth
b. 1895 Brugnon, Jacques
b. 1895 Still, William Grant
b. 1897 Gross, Robert Ellsworth
b. 1898 Billings, John Shaw
b. 1899 Ewing, Alfred Cyril

b. 1900 Cotton, Norris
b. 1902 Sayao, Bidu
b. 1903 Gehringer, Charlie (Charles Leonard)
b. 1904 Dali, Salvador
b. 1906 Higginbotham, "Jack" (Jay C)
b. 1907 Taylor, Kent
b. 1911 Silvers, Phil
b. 1912 Brooks, Foster Murrell
b. 1914 Severn, William Irving
b. 1914 Weaver, "Doodles" (Winstead Sheffield Glendening Dixon)
b. 1915 Philbrick, Herbert Arthur
b. 1918 Burnford, Sheila (Philip Cochrane Every)
b. 1918 Feynman, Richard Phillips
b. 1919 Hayes, John Michael
b. 1920 Pyle, Denver
b. 1922 Chylak, Nester
b. 1924 Garment, Leonard
b. 1924 Hewish, Antony
b. 1927 Sahl, Mort (Lyon)
b. 1928 Agam, Yaacov
b. 1930 Elkin, Stanley Lawrence
b. 1932 Valentino
b. 1938 McClure, Doug
b. 1941 Charney, Nicolas Herman
b. 1943 Greene, Nancy Catherine
b. 1946 Jarvik, Robert Koffler
b. 1947 Vonnegut, Mark
b. 1949 Martin, Jerry Lindsey
b. 1950 Nilsson, Ulf Gosta
b. 1950 Quaid, Randy
d. 1708 Mansart, Jules Hardouin
d. 1778 Pitt, William
d. 1779 Hart, John
d. 1831 Trumbull, John
d. 1849 Nicolai, Carl Otto
d. 1871 Herschel, John Frederick William, Sir
d. 1872 Read, Thomas Buchanan
d. 1896 Bunner, Henry Cuyler
d. 1916 Reger, Max
d. 1927 Colvin, Sidney, Sir
d. 1927 Gris, Juan
d. 1931 Cole, Timothy
d. 1934 Corey, William Ellis
d. 1935 Thompson, Edward Herbert
d. 1944 Bamberger, Louis
d. 1945 Commons, John Rogers
d. 1947 Goudy, Frederic William
d. 1954 Ives, Charles Edward
d. 1954 Lasser, Jacob Kay
d. 1954 Stover, Russell
d. 1956 Adams, Walter Sydney
d. 1958 Lelong, Lucien
d. 1960 Rockefeller, John D(avison), Jr.
d. 1962 Speicher, Eugene Edward
d. 1963 Gasser, Herbert Spencer
d. 1969 Fleishmann, Raoul H(erbert)
d. 1970 Hodges, Johnny

d. 1972 Trendle, George Washington
d. 1976 Aalto, Alvar Henrik (Hugo)
d. 1976 Kempe, Rudolf
d. 1978 Khaikin, Boris
d. 1979 Hutton, Barbara
d. 1981 Fuller, Hoyt William
d. 1981 Marley, Bob (Robert Nesta)
d. 1981 Whitaker, Rogers E(rnest) M(alcolm)
d. 1982 Burck, Jacob
d. 1985 Gould, Chester
d. 1986 Pollard, Fritz (Frederick D)

May 12
b. 1670 Augustus II
b. 1784 Knowles, James Sheridan
b. 1803 Liebig, Justus von
b. 1804 Baldwin, Robert
b. 1809 Giusti, Giuseppe
b. 1812 Lear, Edward
b. 1828 Rossetti, Dante Gabriel
b. 1829 Childs, George William
b. 1842 Massenet, Jules Emile Frederic
b. 1845 Faure, Gabriel Urbain
b. 1850 Lodge, Henry Cabot
b. 1855 Isham, Samuel
b. 1859 Nordica, Lillian
b. 1868 Shean, Al
b. 1873 MacDonald, J(ames) E(dward) H(ervey)
b. 1880 Ellsworth, Lincoln
b. 1883 Lert, Ernst
b. 1885 Sironi, Mario
b. 1888 Reik, Theodor
b. 1888 Stabile, Mariano
b. 1893 Black, Walter J
b. 1895 Giauque, William F(rancis)
b. 1895 Olsen, Harold G
b. 1900 Macy, George
b. 1901 Hinton, Christopher, Sir
b. 1902 Wylie, Philip Gordon
b. 1903 Hyde-White, Wilfrid
b. 1906 Ewing, William Maurice
b. 1906 Jones, "Gorilla" (William)
b. 1907 Charteris, Leslie
b. 1910 Ferrier, Henry Eliza
b. 1910 Jenkins, Gordon
b. 1912 Harshaw, Margaret
b. 1914 Smith, Howard K(ingsbury)
b. 1915 Engel, Lyle Kenyon
b. 1916 Simionato, Guilietta
b. 1918 Rosenberg, Julius
b. 1919 Townsend, Lynn Alfred
b. 1920 Murphy, Patrick Vincent
b. 1921 Beuys, Joseph
b. 1921 Mowat, Farley McGill
b. 1925 Berra, "Yogi" (Lawrence Peter)
b. 1925 Pierson, Frank R(omer)
b. 1925 Simon, John Ivan
b. 1926 Coleman, James Samuel
b. 1927 Crosby, James Morris
b. 1929 Bacharach, Burt

d. 1985 Behrens, Earl Charles
d. 1985 Diamond, Selma
d. 1985 Joy, Leatrice
d. 1986 Bohlem, Arndt von
d. 1986 Hearst, David W
d. 1986 O'Donnell, Peador

May 14
b. 1686 Fahrenheit, Gabriel Daniel
b. 1727 Gainsborough, Thomas
b. 1752 Dwight, Timothy
b. 1771 Owen, Robert
b. 1842 Sullivan, Arthur Seymour, Sir
b. 1843 Walker, Henry Oliver
b. 1853 Caine, Hall, Sir
b. 1867 Gillmore, Frank
b. 1870 Rogers, Bruce
b. 1873 Tcherepnin, Nicholas (Nicolai)
b. 1880 Forbes, Bertie Charles
b. 1881 Fulton, Maude
b. 1881 Walsh, Ed(ward Augustin)
b. 1883 Eltinge, Julian
b. 1885 Klemperer, Otto
b. 1894 Folsom, Frank M
b. 1895 Lehr, Lew
b. 1897 Bechet, Sidney
b. 1898 Singleton, "Zutty" (Arthur James)
b. 1899 Combs, Earle Bryan
b. 1900 Borland, Hal
b. 1902 Chidsey, Donald Barr
b. 1902 Dunbar, Helen Flanders
b. 1905 O'Callahan, Joseph Timothy
b. 1907 Ayub Khan, Mohammad
b. 1913 Doxiadis, Constantinos Apostolos
b. 1913 Jones, Clara Araminta Stanton
b. 1913 Terry, Walter
b. 1922 Clark, Robert Edward
b. 1922 Deacon, Richard
b. 1924 Babb, Howard Selden
b. 1925 Munsel, Patrice
b. 1929 Thompson, George Selden
b. 1929 Worsley, "Gump" (Lorne John)
b. 1932 Richards, Richard
b. 1934 Phillips, Sian
b. 1936 Darin, Bobby
b. 1937 Howser, Dick (Richard Dalton)
b. 1942 Perez, Tony (Atanasio Rigal)
b. 1943 Bruce, Jack
b. 1943 Urtain, Jose Manuel Ibar
b. 1944 Annis, Francesca
b. 1944 Lucas, George
b. 1945 Cornish, Gene
b. 1949 Laurel, Alicia Bay
b. 1951 Hubley, Season
b. 1952 Byrne, David
b. 1959 Vaive, Rick Claude
d. 1818 Lewis, Matthew Gregory
d. 1852 Adams, Louisa Catherine
d. 1897 Maretzek, Max
d. 1906 Schurz, Carl
d. 1912 Strindberg, August (Johan August)
d. 1918 Bennett, James Gordon, Jr.

d. 1919 Heinz, Henry John
d. 1925 Haggard, Henry Rider, Sir
d. 1931 Belasco, David
d. 1935 Frost, Edwin Brant
d. 1936 Allenby, Edmund Hynman
Allenby, Viscount
d. 1940 Goldman, Emma
d. 1953 Kuniyoshi, Yasuo
d. 1958 Dole, James
d. 1959 Bechet, Sidney
d. 1960 Bori, Lucrezia
d. 1965 Perkins, Frances
d. 1967 Gold, Michael
d. 1970 Burke, "Billie" (Mary William
Ethelberg Appleton)
d. 1975 Alexanderson, Ernst Frederik
Werner
d. 1977 Hutchins, Robert Maynard
d. 1978 Kipnis, Alexander
d. 1978 Lear, William Powell
d. 1978 Menzies, Robert Gordon, Sir
d. 1979 Rhys, Jean
d. 1979 Scherman, Thomas K
d. 1980 Ebert, Carl (Anton Charles)
d. 1980 Griffith, Hugh Emrys
d. 1982 Beaumont, Hugh
d. 1982 Rossellini, Renzo
d. 1983 Aleman, Miguel

May 15
b.   Haas, Karl
b. 1567 Monteverdi, Claudio
b. 1773 Metternich-Winneburg, Clemens
b. 1788 Gadsen, James
b. 1803 Lytton, Edward George Earle
Lytton Bulwer-Lytton, 1st Baron Lytton
b. 1819 Crittendon, Thomas L
b. 1820 Nightingale, Florence
b. 1845 Metchnikoff, Elie
b. 1852 Goldsmith, Fred Ernest
b. 1855 Bamberger, Louis
b. 1856 Baum, (Lyman) Frank
b. 1857 Fleming, Williamina Paton Stevens
b. 1859 Curie, Pierre
b. 1860 Wilson, Ellen Axson
b. 1862 Schnitzler, Arthur
b. 1863 Johnston, Annie Fellows
b. 1885 Daubert, Jake (Jacob Ellsworth)
b. 1887 Muir, Edwin
b. 1890 McNaughton, F(oye) F(isk)
b. 1894 Porter, Katherine Anne
b. 1898 Arletty
b. 1898 Skulnik, Menasha
b. 1900 Gordon, John F
b. 1901 Anderson, Dorothy Hansine
b. 1901 Spanel, Abram N
b. 1902 Daley, Richard Joseph
b. 1904 Fadiman, Clifton Paul
b. 1905 Cotten, Joseph
b. 1907 Appel, James Ziegler
b. 1907 Dodd, Thomas Joseph
b. 1909 Mason, James Neville

d. 1932 Dollar, Robert
d. 1938 Strauss, Joseph Baermann
d. 1942 Gest, Morris
d. 1942 Malinowski, Bronislaw
d. 1944 Ade, George
d. 1946 Tarkington, Booth
d. 1947 Hopkins, Fredrick, Sir
d. 1952 Johnston, Frances Benjamin
d. 1953 Reinhardt, Django (Jean Baptiste)
d. 1954 Krauss, Clemens
d. 1955 Agee, James Rufus
d. 1959 Cook, Joe
d. 1978 Steinberg, William (Hans Wilhelm)
d. 1979 Randolph, Asa Philip
d. 1984 Kaufman, Andy
d. 1984 Shaw, Irwin
d. 1985 Hamilton, Margaret
d. 1985 King, Wayne

May 17
b. 1741 Penn, John
b. 1749 Jenner, Edward
b. 1805 Surtees, Robert Smith
b. 1836 Steinitz, Wilhelm
b. 1860 Wheeler, Schuyler Skaats
b. 1865 Bennett, John
b. 1866 Satie, Erik
b. 1868 Dodge, Horace Elgin
b. 1873 Richardson, Dorothy Miller
b. 1875 Spingarn, Joel Elias
b. 1882 Lehman, Adele Lewisohn
b. 1889 Mackay, John Alexander
b. 1889 Reyes, Alfonso
b. 1890 James, Philip
b. 1893 Shields, Larry
b. 1895 Davis, James Curran
b. 1895 Derby, Jane (Jeanette Barr)
b. 1895 Hauser, Gayelord
b. 1896 Donnelly, Ruth
b. 1899 Webb, Del(bert Eugene)
b. 1900 Khomeini, Ayatollah Ruhollah
b. 1901 Egk, Werner
b. 1901 Lorenz, Max
b. 1901 Schonfield, Hugh
b. 1902 Cleva, Fausto
b. 1903 Bell, "Cool Papa" (James Thomas)
b. 1903 Norton, Elliott
b. 1904 Gabin, Jean
b. 1905 Patrick, John
b. 1906 Milanov, Zinka Kunc
b. 1907 McMahon, Horace
b. 1908 Prokosch, Frederic
b. 1908 Schorer, Mark
b. 1911 Kerr, Clark
b. 1911 O'Sullivan, Maureen
b. 1911 Rosenfeld, Henry J
b. 1912 Cox, Archibald
b. 1914 Alsop, Stewart Johonnot Oliver
b. 1916 Maugham, Robin (Robert Cecil Romer)
b. 1917 Creach, "Papa" (John)
b. 1918 Hunt, Jack Reed

b. 1918 Lubalin, Herbert Frederick
b. 1918 Nilsson, Birgit
b. 1919 Cassill, R(onald) V(erlin)
b. 1919 Miller, Merle
b. 1919 Sutton, Horace (Ashley)
b. 1920 Van Horne, Harriet
b. 1921 Brain, Dennis
b. 1921 Winship, Elizabeth
b. 1923 Mahoney, David Joseph, Jr.
b. 1923 Mennin, Peter
b. 1925 Luckenbach, Edgar Frederick, Jr.
b. 1931 Phelan, John Joseph
b. 1934 Morrall, Earl E
b. 1936 Hopper, Dennis
b. 1938 Bortoluzzi, Paolo
b. 1939 Purdy, Susan Gold
b. 1944 Winchester, Jesse (James Ridout)
b. 1950 Soltysik, Patricia Michelle
b. 1955 Winger, Debra
b. 1956 Leonard, "Sugar" Ray
d. 1510 Botticelli, Sandro
d. 1767 Wolcott, Roger
d. 1829 Jay, John
d. 1831 Rochester, Nathaniel
d. 1838 Talleyrand-Perigord, Charles Maurice de
d. 1839 Alison, Archibald
d. 1875 Breckinridge, John Cabell
d. 1883 Pinkham, Lydia Estes
d. 1886 Deere, John
d. 1924 Cummings, "Candy" (William Arthur)
d. 1929 Lehmann, Lilli
d. 1930 Croly, Herbert David
d. 1934 Gilbert, Cass
d. 1935 Dukas, Paul Abraham
d. 1948 Samaroff, Olga
d. 1962 Frazier, Edward Franklin
d. 1962 Muller, Harold P
d. 1964 Owen, Steve (Stephen Joseph)
d. 1969 Baer, "Bugs" (Arthur)
d. 1969 Olczewska, Maria
d. 1970 Balchin, Nigel Marlin
d. 1981 Piccard, Jeannette Ridlon
d. 1982 Walker, Frederick E
d. 1984 Sinclair, Gordon
d. 1985 Burrows, Abe (Abram S)

May 18
b. 1692 Butler, Joseph
b. 1810 Piave, Francesco Maria
b. 1814 Bakunin, Mikhail Aleksandrovich
b. 1815 Francis, James Bicheno
b. 1830 Goldmark, Karl
b. 1851 Peretz, Isaac Loeb
b. 1862 Daniels, Josephus
b. 1868 Nicholas II
b. 1872 Russell, Bertrand Arthur William
b. 1873 Silverman, Sime
b. 1883 Gropius, Walter Adolf
b. 1889 Midgeley, Thomas
b. 1891 Carnap, Rudolf

b. 1892 Pinza, Ezio
b. 1897 Capra, Frank
b. 1897 LaFollete, Philip Fox
b. 1897 Swerling, Jo
b. 1900 Keating, Kenneth B
b. 1902 Bein, Albert
b. 1902 Willson, Meredith
b. 1904 Javits, Jacob Koppel
b. 1906 Goldner, Orville
b. 1907 Curzon, Clifford Michael, Sir
b. 1907 Dohanos, Stevan
b. 1908 Tucker, Tommy
b. 1909 Gidal, Tim
b. 1910 Taylor, Phoebe Atwood
b. 1911 Gurie, Sigrid
b. 1911 Turner, Joe
b. 1912 Brooks, Richard
b. 1912 Como, Perry (Pierino Roland)
b. 1912 Crosby, John Campbell
b. 1912 Topping, Dan(iel Reid)
b. 1914 Balmain, Pierre Alexandre
b. 1917 Donald, James
b. 1918 Christoff, Boris
b. 1919 Fonteyn, Margot, Dame
b. 1919 Wurf, Jerry (Jerome)
b. 1920 John Paul II, Pope
b. 1921 Dennis, Patrick, pseud.
b. 1922 Macy, Bill
b. 1922 Winding, Kai Chresten
b. 1924 Edmonson, Munro Sterling
b. 1924 Francois, Samson
b. 1924 Justice, "Choo Choo" (Charles
Ronald)
b. 1924 Whitaker, Jack (John Francis)
b. 1930 Roberts, Pernell
b. 1930 Rudman, Warren Bruce
b. 1930 Seed, Jenny
b. 1931 Morse, Robert Alan
b. 1934 Hickman, Dwayne
b. 1937 Barth, Roland Sawyer
b. 1937 Robinson, Brooks Calbert, Jr.
b. 1945 Quarry, Jerry
b. 1946 Jackson, Reggie (Reginald
Martinez)
b. 1948 Bonsall, Joe
b. 1949 Wakeman, Rick
b. 1951 Sundburg, Jim (James Howard)
b. 1960 Kurri, Jarri
d. 1675 Marquette, Jacques, Pere
d. 1799 Beaumarchais, Pierre Augustin
Caron de
d. 1900 Grove, George, Sir
d. 1909 Meredith, George
d. 1910 Viardot-Garcia, Pauline
d. 1911 Mahler, Gustav
d. 1917 Pratt, Bela Lyon
d. 1922 Laveran, Alphonse
d. 1922 Raleigh, Walter Alexander, Sir
d. 1928 Haywood, "Big Bill" (William
Dudley)
d. 1929 Shaw, Mary

d. 1941 Ternina, Milka
d. 1949 Adams, James Truslow
d. 1951 Coxey, Jacob Sechler
d. 1954 Waller, Fred(erick)
d. 1955 Bethune, Mary McLeod
d. 1955 Pratella, Francesco Balilla
d. 1957 Rogers, Bruce
d. 1958 Davis, Elmer Holmes
d. 1960 Wurdemann, Audrey May
d. 1963 Davis, Ernie (Ernest R)
d. 1967 Clyde, Andy
d. 1969 Fitzpatrick, Daniel R
d. 1970 Sachs, Nelly
d. 1972 Edward VIII
d. 1973 Coste, Dieudonne
d. 1973 Rankin, Jeannette
d. 1974 Topping, Dan(iel Reid)
d. 1975 Anderson, Leroy
d. 1981 Rausch, James Stevens
d. 1981 Saroyan, William
d. 1983 Fielding, Temple Hornaday
d. 1986 Bubbles, John
d. 1986 Wilson, John Johnston

May 19

b. 1593 Jordaens, Jacob
b. 1762 Fichte, Johann Gottlieb
b. 1795 Hopkins, Johns
b. 1800 Brown, James
b. 1859 Melba, Dame Nellie
b. 1860 Orlando, Vittorio Emanuele
b. 1864 Akeley, Carl Ethan
b. 1877 Girdler, Tom Mercer
b. 1879 Astor, Nancy Witcher (Langhorne)
Astor, Viscountess
b. 1879 Bestor, Arthur Eugene
b. 1886 Schmitt, Bernadotte Everly
b. 1888 Simpson, William Hood
b. 1890 Ho Chi Minh
b. 1892 Foster, "Pops" (George Murphy)
b. 1893 VonSchmidt, Harold
b. 1894 Busse, Henry
b. 1895 Gray, Cecil
b. 1896 Alessandri, Jorge
b. 1896 Balcon, Michael Elias, Sir
b. 1896 Thorborg, Kerstin
b. 1901 Chandler, Dorothy Buffum
b. 1903 Chiang, Yee
b. 1903 Samuels, Ernest
b. 1904 Bushell, Anthony
b. 1904 Creighton, Thomas H(awk)
b. 1905 Copeland, Lammot du Pont
b. 1906 Schullian, Dorothy May
b. 1916 Bloom, Murray Teigh
b. 1923 Arbatov, Georgi
b. 1924 Wilson, Sandy (Alexander
Galbraith)
b. 1925 Malcolm X
b. 1926 Andrews, Mark N
b. 1928 Chapman, (Anthony) Colin (Bruce)
b. 1928 McDougald, Gil(bert James)
b. 1928 Pol Pot

b. 1928 Schayes, Dolph
b. 1929 Cox, Harvey Gallagher, Jr.
b. 1930 Hansberry, Lorraine
b. 1931 Tappy, Eric
b. 1932 Erdman, Paul E
b. 1934 Fitch, Bill (William C)
b. 1934 Lehrer, Jim (James Charles)
b. 1935 Hartman, David Downs
b. 1936 Jenrette, John Wilson, Jr.
b. 1939 Fox, James
b. 1939 Kwan, Nancy Kashen
b. 1939 Scobee, Dick (Francis Richard)
b. 1939 Young, Stephen
b. 1941 Ephron, Nora
b. 1945 Townshend, Peter Dennis Blandford
b. 1946 Rudd, Phil(lip)
b. 1947 Close, Glenn
b. 1949 Manning, Archie (Elisha Archie, III)
b. 1950 Caddell, Pat(rick Hayward)
b. 1952 Jones, Grace
b. 1954 Cerone, Rick (Richard Aldo)
b. 1956 Ford, Steven Meigs
b. 1956 Thompson, Jack
d. 1536 Boleyn, Anne
d. 1683 Killigrew, Thomas
d. 1777 Gwinnett, Button
d. 1795 Bartlett, Josiah
d. 1795 Boswell, James
d. 1825 Saint-Simon, Claude-Henri de Rouvroy
d. 1864 Hawthorne, Nathaniel
d. 1895 Marti, Jose
d. 1896 Field, Kate
d. 1898 Gladstone, William Ewart
d. 1901 Pretorius, Marthinus Wessel
d. 1917 Lockwood, Belva Ann Bennett
d. 1921 White, Edward Douglass
d. 1935 Lawrence, T(homas) E(dward)
d. 1941 Ridge, Lola
d. 1949 Heggen, Thomas Orls, Jr.
d. 1958 Colman, Ronald
d. 1959 Teschemacher, Marguerite
d. 1961 George, Grace
d. 1961 Howard, Joseph Edgar
d. 1963 Matzenauer, Margaret
d. 1968 Dehn, Adolf Arthur
d. 1969 Hawkins, "Bean" (Coleman)
d. 1970 Branner, Martin Michael
d. 1970 Schalk, Ray(mond William)
d. 1971 Nash, Ogden Frederick
d. 1981 O'Connell, Arthur
d. 1984 Betjeman, John, Sir
d. 1985 Lander, Toni
d. 1985 Martin, John

May 20
b. 1768 Madison, Dolly Payne Todd
b. 1799 Balzac, Honore de
b. 1806 Mill, John Stuart
b. 1808 Rice, Thomas Dartmouth

b. 1818 Fargo, William George
b. 1826 Palmer, Potter
b. 1851 Berliner, Emile
b. 1851 Lathrop, Rose Hawthorne
b. 1861 Smith, Christopher Columbus
b. 1880 Theodorescu, Ion N
b. 1882 Undset, Sigrid
b. 1890 Nevins, Allan
b. 1891 Browder, Earl Russell
b. 1892 Anslinger, Harry Jacob
b. 1892 Russell, Sydney Gordon, Sir
b. 1894 Saint Johns, Adela Rogers
b. 1899 Harlan, John Marshall
b. 1899 Taylor, Estelle
b. 1901 Euwe, Max (Machgielis)
b. 1901 Fleeson, Doris
b. 1904 Allingham, Margery
b. 1907 Mydans, Carl M
b. 1908 Stewart, Jimmy (James Maitland)
b. 1908 Whitehead, (Walter) Edward
b. 1909 Kunz, Erich
b. 1911 Field, Stanley
b. 1912 Drachler, Norman
b. 1913 Hewlett, William
b. 1915 Dayan, Moshe
b. 1916 Chadwick, William Owen
b. 1917 Lawson, Donald Elmer
b. 1918 Harlech, William David Ormsby-Gore, Baron
b. 1919 Gobel, George Leslie
b. 1920 Lee, Peggy
b. 1920 Menuhin, Hephzibah
b. 1922 Johnson, James Ralph
b. 1923 Fellows, Edith
b. 1923 Selvon, Samuel Dirkson
b. 1926 Hurst, George
b. 1927 Grant, "Bud" (Harold Peter)
b. 1928 Hedison, David (Albert David, Jr.)
b. 1930 McEachin, James Elton
b. 1931 Boyer, Ken(ton Lloyd)
b. 1935 Bessell, Ted
b. 1937 Hill, Dave
b. 1940 Mikita, Stan(ley)
b. 1940 Schell, Orville H
b. 1944 Cocker, "Joe" (Robert John)
b. 1946 Cher
b. 1946 Murcer, Bobby Ray
b. 1954 Henderson, Jimmy
b. 1958 Reagan, Ronald Prescott
d. 1506 Columbus, Christopher
d. 1690 Eliot, John
d. 1834 Lafayette, Marie Joseph Paul, Marquis
d. 1847 Lamb, Mary Ann
d. 1864 Clare, John
d. 1873 Cartier, Georges Etienne, Sir
d. 1896 Schumann, Clara Josephine Wieck
d. 1913 Flagler, Henry Morrison
d. 1935 Loeffler, Charles Martin Tornov
d. 1939 Carr, Joseph F

b. 1826 Langdell, Christopher Columbus
b. 1841 Mendes, Catulle (Abraham Catulle)
b. 1844 Cassatt, Mary
b. 1854 Schurman, Jacob Gould
b. 1859 Doyle, Arthur Conan, Sir
b. 1860 Einthoven, Willem
b. 1874 Malan, Daniel F
b. 1891 Sproul, Robert Gordon
b. 1894 Davis, Clyde Brion
b. 1895 Krishnamurti, Jiddu
b. 1900 Tolson, Clyde Anderson
b. 1902 Breuer, Marcel Lajos
b. 1903 Simmons, Al(oysius Harry)
b. 1906 Howe, Mark De Wolfe
b. 1907 Olivier, Laurence Kerr Olivier, Sir
b. 1908 Smith, Horton
b. 1912 Kadar, Janos
b. 1914 Packard, Vance Oakley
b. 1915 Baker, George
b. 1919 Boeynants, Paul Vanden
b. 1919 Pappas, Irene
b. 1921 Alexander, Donald Crichton
b. 1922 Crist, Judith Klein
b. 1923 Namgyal, Palden Thondup
b. 1924 Aznavour, Charles
b. 1925 King, James Ambros
b. 1927 Constantine, Michael
b. 1927 Martin, Quinn
b. 1928 Pickens, T(homas) Boone, (Jr.)
b. 1930 Marisol (Escobar)
b. 1934 Nero, Peter
b. 1934 Wills, Garry
b. 1938 Benjamin, Richard
b. 1938 Converse, Frank
b. 1938 Strasberg, Susan Elizabeth
b. 1940 Sarrazin, Michael
b. 1941 Winfield, Paul Edward
b. 1942 Brown, Roger
b. 1942 Parkins, Barbara
b. 1943 John, Tommy (Thomas Edward, Jr.)
b. 1943 Williams, Betty Smith
b. 1946 Best, George
b. 1950 Taupin, Bernie
d. 1849 Edgeworth, Maria
d. 1885 Hugo, Victor Marie
d. 1898 Bellamy, Edward
d. 1903 Reichmann, Theodor
d. 1910 Renard, Jules
d. 1911 Miller, Elizabeth Smith
d. 1923 Lopez-Portillo y Rojas, Jose
d. 1932 Gregory, Isabella Augusta Persse, Lady
d. 1934 Wesson, David
d. 1938 Glackens, William James
d. 1939 Toller, Ernst
d. 1943 Taft, Helen Herron
d. 1949 Forrestal, James Vincent
d. 1949 Pfitzner, Hans
d. 1954 Bender, "Chief" (Charles Albert)
d. 1955 Gallagher, Richard

d. 1965 Cooke, Samuel
d. 1967 Hughes, Langston (James Langston)
d. 1970 Krutch, Joseph Wood
d. 1972 Day-Lewis, Cecil
d. 1972 Rutherford, Margaret
d. 1975 Grove, "Lefty" (Robert Moses)
d. 1976 Bonavena, Oscar
d. 1976 Fitch, Aubrey
d. 1979 Jooss, Kurt
d. 1982 Sunay, Cevdet
d. 1984 Zaharias, George
d. 1986 Gabel, Martin

May 23

b. Fickett, Mary
b. 1707 Linnaeus, Carolus
b. 1734 Mesmer, Franz Anton
b. 1753 Viotti, Giovanni Battista
b. 1790 Dumont d'Urville, Jules Sebastian Cesar
b. 1799 Hood, Thomas
b. 1810 Fuller, Margaret
b. 1820 Eads, James Buchanan
b. 1821 White, Richard Grant
b. 1824 Burnside, Ambrose Everett
b. 1840 Appleby, John Francis
b. 1844 Abdu'l-Baha
b. 1846 Mansfield, Arabella
b. 1852 Chirol, Valentine, Sir
b. 1875 Sloan, Alfred Pritchard, Jr.
b. 1883 Fairbanks, Douglas
b. 1884 Pleasants, Henry
b. 1886 Gleason, James
b. 1888 Wheat, Zack (Zachariah Davis)
b. 1890 Marshall, Herbert
b. 1891 Lagerkvist, Par
b. 1893 Bodenheim, Maxwell
b. 1894 Thomas, James William Tudor
b. 1898 McHugh, Frank (Francis Curray)
b. 1900 Frank, Hans
b. 1903 O'Dell, Scott
b. 1906 Holman, Libby
b. 1908 Abramovitz, Max
b. 1908 Bardeen, John
b. 1910 Brown, Margaret Wise
b. 1910 Crothers, "Scatman" (Benjamin Sherman)
b. 1910 Shaw, Artie
b. 1912 Francaix, Jean
b. 1912 Goring, Marius
b. 1912 Payne, John
b. 1914 Lerman, Leo
b. 1914 Ward, Barbara Mary
b. 1918 Bate, Walter Jackson
b. 1919 Garrett, Betty
b. 1919 Kline, Franz Joseph
b. 1921 Blish, James Benjamin
b. 1921 O'Connell, Helen
b. 1923 Larrocha, Alicia de
b. 1928 Clooney, Rosemary
b. 1928 Davenport, Nigel

d. 1950 Wavell, Archibald Percival Wavell,
        Earl
d. 1952 Oursler, (Charles) Fulton
d. 1956 Kibbee, Guy
d. 1959 Dulles, John Foster
d. 1969 Green, Mitzi
d. 1970 Davison, Frank Dalby
d. 1971 Dodd, Thomas Joseph
d. 1974 Atwood, Angela
d. 1974 DeFreeze, Donald David
d. 1974 Ellington, "Duke" (Edward
        Kennedy)
d. 1974 Perry, Nancy Ling
d. 1974 Soltysik, Patricia Michelle
d. 1974 Wolfe, William Lawton
d. 1975 Howard, Moe
d. 1975 Lincoln, George A
d. 1977 Gordon, Lou
d. 1980 Gaunt, William
d. 1981 Jessel, George Albert
d. 1981 Lubalin, Herbert Frederick
d. 1981 Roldos Aguilera, Jamie

May 25
b. 1616 Dolci, Carlo
b. 1803 Emerson, Ralph Waldo
b. 1825 Wesson, Daniel Baird
b. 1847 Dowie, John Alexander
b. 1855 Pinero, Arthur Wing, Sir
b. 1860 Cattell, James McKeen
b. 1866 Schultze, Carl Edward
b. 1878 Robinson, Bill
b. 1879 Beaverbrook, William Maxwell
        Aitken, Baron
b. 1881 Bartok, Bela
b. 1884 Duranty, Walter
b. 1886 Murray, Philip
b. 1889 Sikorsky, Igor Ivanovich
b. 1891 Winterich, John Tracy
b. 1892 Tito
b. 1898 Cerf, Bennett Alfred
b. 1898 Tunney, "Gene" (James Joseph)
b. 1899 Artzybasheff, Boris Mikhailovich
b. 1905 Harsch, Joseph Close
b. 1907 Nu, U Thakin
b. 1908 Roethke, Theodore
b. 1911 Barnet, Will
b. 1913 Maclean, Donald Duart
b. 1916 Simms, Ginny (Virginia E)
b. 1917 Cochran, Steve
b. 1917 Cooper, Joseph D
b. 1917 Hesburgh, Theodore Martin
b. 1918 Akins, Claude
b. 1919 Sarnoff, Dorothy
b. 1921 David, Hal
b. 1922 Berlinguer, Enrico
b. 1923 Weitz, John
b. 1925 Crain, Jeanne
b. 1926 Davis, Miles Dewey
b. 1926 Kallen, Kitty
b. 1926 Sharman, Bill (William Walton)
b. 1927 Ludlum, Robert

b. 1929 Sills, Beverly
b. 1932 Bowen, Roger
b. 1932 Dunne, John Gregory
b. 1932 Jones, KC
b. 1934 Nessen, Ron(ald Harold)
b. 1936 Hall, Tom T
b. 1938 Thomas, Joyce Carol
b. 1939 McKellen, Ian Murray
b. 1943 Uggams, Leslie
b. 1947 Colter, Jessie
b. 1947 Valentine, Karen
b. 1955 Sellecca, Connie
d. 1681 Calderon de la Barca, Pedro
d. 1812 Malone, Edmund
d. 1883 Laboulage, Edouard Rose
d. 1917 DeReszke, Edouard
d. 1919 Walker, Sarah Breedlove
d. 1934 Holst, Gustav
d. 1937 Tanner, Henry Ossawa
d. 1939 Duveen, Joseph, Sir
d. 1942 Feuermann, Emanuel
d. 1953 Dulac, Edmund
d. 1954 Capa, Robert
d. 1963 Dryfoos, Orvil E
d. 1965 Grew, Joseph Clark
d. 1971 Conniff, Frank
d. 1979 Spenkelink, John Arthur
d. 1981 Ponselle, Rosa
d. 1983 Idris I
d. 1985 Hecht, Harold
d. 1985 Nathan, Robert
d. 1986 Canutt, Yakima (Enos Edward)

May 26
b. 1623 Petty, William, Sir
b. 673 Bede the Venerable
b. 1689 Montagu, Mary Wortley, Lady
b. 1764 Livingston, Edward
b. 1822 Goncourt, Edmond Louis Antoine
        Huot
b. 1837 Roebling, Washington Augustus
b. 1850 Lopez-Portillo y Rojas, Jose
b. 1865 Chambers, Robert W
b. 1872 Urban, Joseph Maria
b. 1876 Root, Jack
b. 1884 Winninger, Charles
b. 1885 DeCuevas, Marquis
b. 1886 Jolson, Al
b. 1890 Croft, Arthur C
b. 1893 Goossens, Eugene, Sir
b. 1894 Lukas, Paul
b. 1895 Hull, John Edwin
b. 1896 Munson, Gorham B(ert)
b. 1897 Talmadge, Norma
b. 1905 Guffey, Burnett
b. 1905 Uris, Harold David
b. 1906 Morini, Erica
b. 1907 Wayne, John
b. 1908 Morley, Robert
b. 1909 Anderson, Eugenie Moore
b. 1909 Busby, Matthew, Sir
b. 1909 Gucci, Aldo

d. 1840 Paganini, Niccolo
d. 1867 Bulfinch, Thomas
d. 1924 Herbert, Victor
d. 1937 Ives, Frederic Eugene
d. 1947 Carlson, Evans Fordyce
d. 1949 Ripley, Robert Leroy
d. 1953 Burkett, Jesse Cail
d. 1955 Ascari, Alberto
d. 1960 Flagg, James Montgomery
d. 1964 Collins, Ted
d. 1964 Nehru, Jawaharlal
d. 1969 Hunter, Jeffrey
d. 1970 Gimbel, Richard
d. 1971 Rafferty, "Chips"
d. 1974 Biossat, Bruce
d. 1974 Wiese, Kurt
d. 1976 McDevitt, Ruth
d. 1976 Teyte, Maggie, Dame
d. 1977 Bliven, Bruce
d. 1981 Wheeler, Roger Milton
d. 1986 Wrightsman, Charles Bierer

May 28
b. 1738 Guillotin, Joseph Ignace
b. 1759 Pitt, William
b. 1779 Moore, Thomas
b. 1807 Agassiz, Louis (Jean Louis Radolphe)
b. 1818 Beauregard, Pierre Gustav Toutant de
b. 1837 Pastor, Tony (Antonio)
b. 1853 Larsson, Carl (Olof)
b. 1857 Hilliard, Robert Cochran
b. 1871 Daly, Thomas Augustine
b. 1874 Cockrell, Ewing
b. 1877 Deeping, (George) Warwick
b. 1882 Hopwood, Avery
b. 1883 Zandonai, Riccardo
b. 1884 Benes, Eduard
b. 1886 Mayer, Arthur Loeb
b. 1888 Lambert, Ward L
b. 1888 Thorpe, Jim (James Francis)
b. 1896 Giles, Warren Crandall
b. 1897 Bolitho, Henry Hector
b. 1900 Ladnier, Tommy
b. 1900 Little, "Little Jack"
b. 1905 Kuter, Laurence S(herman)
b. 1906 Hills, Lee
b. 1906 Regan, Phil
b. 1907 Gilmore, Eddy Lanier King
b. 1908 Fleming, Ian Lancaster
b. 1910 Kempson, Rachel
b. 1910 Walker, "T-Bone" (Aaron)
b. 1911 Churchill, Randolph
b. 1912 White, Patrick Victor Martindale
b. 1915 McKay, Scott
b. 1916 Percy, Walker
b. 1917 Commoner, Barry
b. 1917 Sachs, Eddy (Edward Julius)
b. 1918 Birch, John
b. 1919 Swenson, May
b. 1925 Ecevit, Bulent

b. 1925 Fischer-Dieskau, Dietrich
b. 1925 Vickers, Martha
b. 1928 Rikhoff, Jean
b. 1928 Stein, Horst
b. 1929 Carson, Jeannie
b. 1930 Drake, Frank Donald
b. 1930 Seaga, Edward Phillip George
b. 1931 Birmingham, Stephen
b. 1931 Winkler, Irwin
b. 1934 Dionne Sisters
b. 1934 Dionne, Annette
b. 1934 Dionne, Cecile
b. 1934 Dionne, Emilie
b. 1934 Dionne, Marie
b. 1934 Dionne, Yvonne
b. 1935 Baker, Carroll
b. 1935 Rogers, Darryl D
b. 1938 West, Jerry
b. 1941 Howland, Beth
b. 1944 Knight, Gladys Maria
b. 1947 Locke, Sondra
b. 1955 Howe, Mark Steven
b. 1957 Gibson, Kirk Harold
d. 1805 Boccherini, Luigi
d. 1843 Webster, Noah
d. 1878 Russell, John, Lord
d. 1886 Bartlett, John Russell
d. 1886 Ostrovsky, Aleksandr
d. 1890 Nessler, Victor E
d. 1910 Balakirev, Mili Alekseyevich
d. 1910 Koch, Robert
d. 1933 Loeb, James
d. 1937 Adler, Alfred
d. 1940 Connolly, Walter
d. 1946 Glass, Carter
d. 1951 Mario, Queena
d. 1960 Zucco, George
d. 1968 Dongen, Kees van
d. 1970 Fawcett, Wilford Hamilton, Jr.
d. 1972 Irvin, Rea
d. 1973 Schmidt-Isserstedt, Hans
d. 1975 Charles, Ezzard
d. 1977 Cortez, Ricardo
d. 1979 Abercrombie, Michael
d. 1979 Little, Lou(is)
d. 1981 Williams, Mary Lou
d. 1981 Wyszynski, Stefan
d. 1983 Corning, Erastus, III
d. 1986 Aranason, H Harvard
d. 1986 Maclaughlin, Don
d. 1986 Tuttle, Lurene

May 29
b. 1630 Charles II
b. 1736 Henry, Patrick
b. 1826 Butterick, Ebenezer
b. 1828 Massey, Gerald
b. 1855 Bruce, David, Sir
b. 1860 Albeniz, Isaac Manuel Francisco
b. 1874 Chesterton, Gilbert Keith
b. 1880 Spengler, Oswald
b. 1883 Dafoe, Allan Roy

b. 1886 Khodasevich, Vladislav
b. 1889 Blackwell, Basil Henry, Sir
b. 1892 Brand, Max, pseud.
b. 1892 Faust, Frederick Schiller
b. 1893 Urey, Harold Clayton
b. 1894 VonSternberg, Josef
b. 1895 Grant, Jane
b. 1896 Youngdahl, Luther W
b. 1897 Korngold, Erich Wolfgang
b. 1898 Lillie, Beatrice
b. 1898 Rothermere, Esmond Cecil
   Harmsworth, Viscount
b. 1903 Hope, Bob (Leslie Townes)
b. 1906 White, T(erence) H(anbury)
b. 1910 Barolini, Antonio
b. 1912 Bresler, Jerry
b. 1912 Johnson, Pamela Hansford
b. 1913 Schneider, Richard Coy
b. 1913 Zale, Tony
b. 1915 Buketoff, Igor
b. 1915 Munchinger, Karl
b. 1917 Kennedy, John Fitzgerald
b. 1918 Shriner, Herb
b. 1922 Xenakis, Iannis
b. 1927 Toms, Carl
b. 1928 Rohatyn, Felix George
b. 1932 Ehrlich, Paul
b. 1939 Unser, Al
b. 1944 Berger, Helmut
b. 1944 Bishop, Maurice
b. 1948 Geary, Anthony
b. 1955 Hinckley, John Warnock, Jr.
b. 1963 Whelchel, Lisa
d. 1790 Putnam, Israel
d. 1814 Josephine
d. 1829 Davy, Humphrey, Sir
d. 1838 Milder-Hauptmann, Pauline Anna
d. 1866 Scott, Winfield
d. 1877 Harper, Fletcher
d. 1877 Motley, John L
d. 1892 Baha'u'llah
d. 1911 Gilbert, William Schwenck, Sir
d. 1914 Irving, Laurence Sidney
d. 1916 Hill, James Jerome
d. 1921 Thayer, Abbott Henderson
d. 1935 Suk, Josef
d. 1940 Anderson, Mary Antoinette
d. 1942 Barrymore, John
d. 1948 Whitty, May, Dame
d. 1950 Stoopnagle, Lemuel Q, Colonel
d. 1951 Brice, Fanny
d. 1953 Dean, "Man Mountain"
d. 1954 McCormick, Anne (Elizabeth)
   O'Hare
d. 1957 Whale, James
d. 1958 Jimenez, Juan Ramon
d. 1960 Pasternak, Boris Leonidovich
d. 1961 Gesell, Arnold
d. 1967 Pabst, Georg Wilhelm
d. 1970 Gunther, John
d. 1970 Hesse, Eva

d. 1972 Bernhard, Lucian
d. 1979 Pickford, Mary
d. 1979 Wood, John Howland, Jr.
d. 1980 Jaabari, Mohammed Ali, Sheik
d. 1981 Sun Yat-Sen, Chingling Soong,
   Madame
d. 1982 Schneider, "Romy"
d. 1984 Motley, Arthur Harrison
d. 1985 Plomley, Roy
d. 1986 Martin, John C

May 30
b. 1672 Peter the Great
b. 1794 Moscheles, Ignaz
b. 1810 Stephens, Ann Sophia
b. 1811 Belinsky, Vissarion
b. 1835 Austin, Alfred
b. 1846 Faberge, Peter Carl (Karl
   Gustavovich)
b. 1857 Peabody, Endicott
b. 1867 Davis, Arthur Vining
b. 1868 Dillingham, Charles Bancroft
b. 1874 Peabody, Josephine Preston
b. 1875 Gentile, Giovanni
b. 1879 Bell, Vanessa
b. 1882 Lewisohn, Ludwig
b. 1886 Eustis, Dorothy Leib Harrison
   Wood
b. 1887 Archipenko, Alexander Porfirievich
b. 1888 Farley, James A(loysius)
b. 1890 Langer, Lawrence
b. 1891 Bernie, Ben
b. 1893 Raisa, Rosa
b. 1896 Hawks, Howard Winchester
b. 1898 Farrington, Elizabeth Pruett
   (Mary)
b. 1899 Thalberg, Irving Grant
b. 1901 Felsenstein, Walter
b. 1901 Skinner, Cornelia Otis
b. 1901 Trumbauer, Frank(ie)
b. 1902 Fetchit, Stepin
b. 1903 Baldwin, William, Jr.
b. 1903 Conklin, Gladys Plemon
b. 1903 Cullen, Countee
b. 1904 Baldwin, Billy
b. 1908 Blanc, Mel(vin Jerome)
b. 1909 Frank, Jerome David
b. 1909 Goodman, Benny (Benjamin
   David)
b. 1909 Gray, Gordon
b. 1910 Metcalfe, Ralph H
b. 1912 Griffith, Hugh Emrys
b. 1912 Stein, Joseph
b. 1912 Symons, Julian Gustave
b. 1913 Erwin, "Pee Wee" (George)
b. 1915 Blair, Frank
b. 1915 Lang, Daniel
b. 1915 Manulis, Martin
b. 1920 London, George
b. 1922 Coit, Margaret Louise
b. 1923 Lydon, James (Jimmy)
b. 1925 Noffsinger, James P(hilip)

b. 1926 Jorgensen, Christine
b. 1927 Walker, Clint
b. 1928 Varda, Agnes
b. 1934 Leonov, Alexei Arkhipovich
b. 1936 Dullea, Keir
b. 1939 Pollard, Michael J
b. 1940 Sayers, Gale Eugene
b. 1942 Felske, John Frederick
b. 1944 MacRae, Meredith
b. 1946 Lightner, Candy
d. 1431 Joan of Arc
d. 1593 Marlowe, Christopher
d. 1640 Rubens, Peter Paul, Sir
d. 1744 Pope, Alexander
d. 1770 Boucher, Francois
d. 1778 Voltaire(, Francois Marie Arouet
   de)
d. 1885 Jacobsen, Jens Peter
d. 1911 Bradley, Milton
d. 1912 Wright, Wilbur
d. 1916 Mosby, John Singleton
d. 1918 Plekhanov, Georgi Valentinovich
d. 1930 Nansen, Fridtjof
d. 1936 Chaney, Norman
d. 1952 Lasker, Albert Davis
d. 1953 Wilson, "Dooley" (Arthur)
d. 1961 Trujillo (Molina), Rafael Leonidas
d. 1964 Sachs, Eddy (Edward Julius)
d. 1964 Szilard, Leo
d. 1967 Rains, Claude
d. 1969 Briscoe, Robert
d. 1971 DuPre, Marcel
d. 1975 Prefontaine, Steve Roland
d. 1976 Carey, Max George
d. 1976 Fuchida, Mitsuo
d. 1977 Desmond, Paul Breitenfeld
d. 1979 Martin, Fletcher
d. 1981 Rahman, Ziaur
d. 1983 Grubert, Carl Alfred
d. 1983 Guffey, Burnett
d. 1985 Jennings, Talbot
d. 1986 Ellis, Perry Edwin
d. 1986 Klopfer, Donald Simon

May 31
b. 1818 Andrew, John Albion
b. 1819 Whitman, Walt(er)
b. 1838 Sidgwick, Henry
b. 1866 Rebikov, Vladimir Ivanovich
b. 1871 Rusie, Amos William
b. 1872 Abbot, Charles Greeley
b. 1883 Alda, Frances
b. 1887 Leger, Alexis St. Leger (Marie-
   Rene Alexis St. Leger)
b. 1888 Holt, Jack (Charles John)
b. 1890 Townsend, William H(enry)
b. 1893 Coatsworth, Elizabeth Jane
b. 1894 Allen, Fred
b. 1895 Stewart, George Rippey
b. 1898 Peale, Norman Vincent
b. 1903 Russell, "Honey" (John)
b. 1905 Schneider, Herman

b. 1905 Thompson, Cecil
b. 1907 Alphand, Herve
b. 1908 Ameche, Don
b. 1908 Coates, Edith
b. 1909 Schmitt, Gladys
b. 1912 Deller, Alfred George
b. 1912 Jackson, Henry Martin
b. 1914 Valtman, Edmund Siegfried
b. 1914 Williams, Jay
b. 1919 Hartke, Vance
b. 1920 Williams, Edward Bennett
b. 1921 Valli, Alida
b. 1922 Elliott, Denholm
b. 1923 Kelly, Ellsworth
b. 1923 Rainier III, Prince
b. 1924 Harris, Patricia Roberts
b. 1925 Beck, Julian
b. 1928 Lateiner, Jacob
b. 1930 Eastwood, Clint
b. 1931 Jones, Reverend Jim (James)
b. 1932 Briggs, Fred
b. 1933 Sedelmaier, Joe (John Josef)
b. 1933 Verrett, Shirley
b. 1938 Hutton, Jim
b. 1938 Yarrow, Peter
b. 1939 Waite, Terry (Terence Hardy)
b. 1941 Paycheck, Johnny
b. 1943 Gless, Sharon
b. 1943 Namath, Joe (Joseph William)
b. 1943 Rowan, Ford
b. 1946 Fassbinder, Rainer Werner
b. 1949 Bonham, John Henry
b. 1950 Berenger, Tom (Thomas)
b. 1950 Harrison, Gregory
b. 1957 Craig, Jim (James)
b. 1965 Shields, Brooke
d. 1594 Tintoretto
d. 1740 Frederick William I
d. 1809 Haydn, Franz Joseph
d. 1832 Galois, Evariste
d. 1837 Grimaldi, Joseph
d. 1906 Davitt, Michael
d. 1908 Frechette, Louis-Honore
d. 1910 Blackwell, Elizabeth
d. 1934 Cody, Lew
d. 1953 Mildmay, Audrey
d. 1960 Funk, Walther
d. 1962 Eichmann, Adolf (Otto Adolf)
d. 1963 Hamilton, Edith
d. 1967 Strayhorn, Billy (William)
d. 1970 Sawchuk, Terry (Terrance Gordon)
d. 1970 Sheridan, Clare Consuelo
d. 1974 Davis, Adelle
d. 1976 Mitchell, Martha Elizabeth Beall
d. 1976 Monod, Jacques
d. 1977 Castle, William
d. 1977 Grauer, Ben(jamin Franklin)
d. 1978 Liebow, Averill A(braham)
d. 1978 Purtell, William Arthur
d. 1978 Wright, Lloyd (Frank Lloyd, Jr.)
d. 1981 Pella, Giuseppe

d. 1981 Ward, Barbara Mary
d. 1983 Dempsey, Jack (William Harrison)
d. 1985 Rebuffat, Gaston Louis Simon

JUNE

b. 1594 Poussin, Nicolas
b. 1652 Dampier, William
b. 1683 Young, Edward
b. 1812 Goncharov, Ivan A
b. 1829 Geronimo
b. 1879 Crofts, Freeman Willis
b. 1892 Madden, Owen Victor
b. 1898 Ferragamo, Salvatore
b. 1901 Romanov, Anastasia
b. 1902 Smith, Joe
b. 1910 Cockerell, Christopher
b. 1920 Tutuola, Amos
d. 1037 Avicenna (Ibn Sina)
d. 1329 Robert I
d. 1520 Montezuma II
d. 1592 Cavendish, Thomas
d. 1597 Barents, Willem
d. 1638 Minuit, Peter
d. 1697 Aubrey, John
d. 1848 Keokuk
d. 1937 Tukhachevski, Mikhail N
d. 1944 Douglas, Keith Castellain
d. 1947 Nimmons, George Croll
d. 1954 Locke, Alain Leroy
d. 1957 Lowry, Malcolm (Clarence Malcolm)
d. 1960 Pauker, Ana
d. 1961 Malko, Nicolai
d. 1977 Clark, Tom (Thomas Campbell)
d. 1977 VonBraun, Wernher
d. 1980 Dornberger, Walter Robert
d. 1985 Bush, Guy Terrell
d. 1985 Kamp, Irene Kittle
June 1
b. 1637 Marquette, Jacques, Pere
b. 1771 Paer, Ferdinando
b. 1780 Clausewitz, Karl von
b. 1801 Young, Brigham
b. 1804 Glinka, Mikhail Ivanovich
b. 1816 Monk, Maria
b. 1831 Hood, John Bell
b. 1833 Harlan, John Marshall
b. 1855 Angle, Edward Hartley
b. 1862 Patino, Simon Iturri
b. 1878 Masefield, John
b. 1880 Lahey, Frank Howard
b. 1881 Matzenauer, Margaret
b. 1882 Drinkwater, John
b. 1887 Brook, Clive (Clifford)
b. 1891 Onegin, Sigrid
b. 1895 Dulles, Eleanor Lansing
b. 1899 Janssen, Werner
b. 1901 Denny-Brown, Derek Ernest
b. 1901 Sukarno, Achmed
b. 1901 Van Druten, John William
b. 1902 Lindtberg, Leopold

b. 1905 Newton, Robert
b. 1907 Hecht, Harold
b. 1909 Rowe, James Henry, Jr.
b. 1910 Heatherton, Ray
b. 1917 McNellis, Maggi
b. 1918 Astor, Gavin
b. 1919 Whitehead, Edwin C
b. 1921 Riddle, Nelson
b. 1922 Caulfield, Joan
b. 1922 Spencer, William
b. 1924 Coffin, William Sloan
b. 1925 Hagopian, Louis Thomas
b. 1926 Burton, Phillip
b. 1926 Griffith, Andy (Andrew)
b. 1926 Monroe, Marilyn
b. 1926 Schweiker, Richard Schultz
b. 1934 Boone, "Pat" (Charles Eugene)
b. 1935 Ike, Reverend
b. 1936 Anderson, Douglas Dorland
b. 1937 McCullough, Colleen
b. 1939 Little, Cleavon Jake
b. 1940 Auberjonois, Rene Murat
b. 1941 Chance, (Wilmer) Dean
b. 1941 DeWaart, Edo
b. 1944 Powell, Robert
b. 1945 Oldfield, Brian
b. 1945 VonStade, Frederica
b. 1947 Wood, Ron(ald)
b. 1948 Sneva, Tom (Thomas Edsol)
b. 1949 Boothe, Powers
b. 1953 Berkowitz, David
b. 1961 Coffey, Paul
d. 1813 Lawrence, James
d. 1815 Gillray, James
d. 1823 Davout, Louis Nicholas
d. 1832 Sumter, Thomas
d. 1841 Wilkie, David
d. 1854 Judson, Emily Chubbock
d. 1868 Buchanan, James
d. 1872 Bennett, James Gordon
d. 1873 Howe, Joseph
d. 1879 Shields, James
d. 1898 Keene, Thomas Wallace
d. 1912 Burnham, Daniel H
d. 1925 Marshall, Thomas Riley
d. 1927 Borden, Lizzie Andrew
d. 1927 Bury, John Bagnell
d. 1940 Woodbridge, Frederick James Eugene
d. 1941 Dolly, Jenny
d. 1941 Walpole, Hugh Seymour, Sir
d. 1946 Antonescu, Ion
d. 1946 Slezak, Leo
d. 1952 Dewey, John
d. 1956 Jones, Jesse Holman
d. 1959 Rohmer, Sax, pseud.
d. 1960 Patrick, Lester B
d. 1963 Gougelman, Pierre
d. 1965 Funk, Wilfred John
d. 1965 Lambeau, "Curly" (Earl L)
d. 1967 Rudkin, Margaret Fogarty

d. 1968 Bynner, Harold Witter
d. 1968 Keller, Helen Adams
d. 1969 LeTourneau, Robert Gilmour
d. 1969 Tannenbaum, Frank
d. 1970 Ungaretti, Giuseppe
d. 1971 Murphy, Audie
d. 1971 Niebuhr, Reinhold
d. 1973 Firestone, Harvey Samuel, Jr.
d. 1973 Greaza, Walter N
d. 1973 Kornman, Mary
d. 1973 Parkhurst, Helen
d. 1979 Forssmann, Werner Theodor Otto
d. 1979 Mulhall, Jack
d. 1979 Partridge, Eric Honeywood
d. 1980 Marquard, "Rube" (Richard William)
d. 1980 Nielsen, Arthur C
d. 1981 Vinson, Carl
d. 1985 Greene, Richard
d. 1985 Price, Gwilym Alexander

June 2
b. 1732 Washington, Martha Dandridge Curtis
b. 1740 Sade, Marquis (Donatien Alphonse Francoise) de
b. 1743 Cagliostro, Alessandro, Conte di
b. 1773 Randolph, John
b. 1816 Aguilar, Grace
b. 1834 Stolz, Teresa
b. 1840 Hardy, Thomas
b. 1845 MacArthur, Arthur
b. 1857 Elgar, Edward William, Sir
b. 1857 Gjellerup, Karl Adolf
b. 1861 Taft, Helen Herron
b. 1863 Weingartner, Felix
b. 1864 Robinson, Wilbert
b. 1864 Webster, Ben(jamin)
b. 1869 Foerster, Friedrich Wilhelm
b. 1875 Mott, Charles Stewart
b. 1880 Gowers, Ernest Arthur, Sir
b. 1886 Whalen, Grover
b. 1890 Hopper, Hedda
b. 1891 Arnold, Thurman Wesley
b. 1893 Martin, John
b. 1897 Mueller, Reuben Herbert
b. 1899 Teale, Edwin Way
b. 1901 Andrews, Bert
b. 1902 Davis, Frederick C(lyde)
b. 1904 Weissmuller, Johnny
b. 1906 Catherall, Arthur
b. 1907 Lehmann, John Frederick
b. 1907 Todd, Mike (Michael)
b. 1908 Grauer, Ben(jamin Franklin)
b. 1913 Pym, Barbara Mary Crampton
b. 1915 Del Ray, Lester Ramon Alvarez
b. 1920 Schramm, Tex(as Edward)
b. 1921 Speight, Johnny
b. 1924 DeMott, Benjamin Haile
b. 1926 O'Shea, Milo
b. 1929 Barris, Chuck
b. 1930 Conrad, Charles, Jr.

b. 1937 Grooms, "Red" (Charles Roger)
b. 1937 Kellerman, Sally
b. 1939 Collier, Peter
b. 1939 Hamilton, William
b. 1940 Constantine XII
b. 1941 Keach, Stacy, Jr.
b. 1941 Nanne, Lou(is Vincent)
b. 1941 Watts, Charlie (Charles Robert)
b. 1944 Haid, Charles
b. 1944 Hamlisch, Marvin
b. 1944 Yepremian, Garo (Garabed S)
b. 1946 Roth, Richard Lynn
b. 1948 Innaurato, Albert
b. 1948 Mathers, Jerry
b. 1951 Robinson, Larry (Laurence Clark)
b. 1953 Canova, Diana
b. 1953 Stadler, Craig
b. 1956 Guerrero, Pedro
d. 1701 Scudery, Madeleine de
d. 1832 Garcia, Manuel del Popolo Vincente, I
d. 1882 Garibaldi, Guiseppe
d. 1894 Dabney, Virginius
d. 1910 Petipa, Marius
d. 1913 Austin, Alfred
d. 1928 Fortune, Timothy Thomas
d. 1930 Bolitho, William
d. 1941 Gehrig, Lou (Henry Louis)
d. 1942 Berigan, "Bunny" (Rowland Bernart)
d. 1943 Dafoe, Allan Roy
d. 1943 Howard, Leslie
d. 1943 Stevens, John Frank
d. 1951 Alain, pseud.
d. 1951 Erskine, John
d. 1956 Hersholt, Jean
d. 1961 DeWohl, Louis
d. 1961 Kaufman, George S(imon)
d. 1962 Sackville-West, Victoria Mary
d. 1967 Upjohn, Lawrence Northcote
d. 1969 Gorcey, Leo
d. 1970 McLaren, Bruce Leslie
d. 1974 Lunn, Arnold Henry Moore, Sir
d. 1977 Boyd, Stephen
d. 1979 Hutton, Jim
d. 1985 Brown, George Alfred

June 3
b. 39 Lucan
b. 1656 Tournefort, Joseph Pitton de
b. 1726 Hutton, James
b. 1804 Cobden, Richard
b. 1808 Davis, Jefferson
b. 1811 James, Henry
b. 1819 Ball, Thomas
b. 1819 Jongkind, Johan Barthold
b. 1844 Hobart, Garret Augustus
b. 1844 Liliencron, (Friedrich Adolf Axel) Detlev von
b. 1853 Petrie, (William Matthew) Flinders, Sir
b. 1864 Olds, Ranson E(li)

b. 1945 Waller, Gordon
b. 1946 Gregory, Bettina Louise
b. 1948 Post, Sandra
b. 1950 Golacinski, Alan Bruce
b. 1951 Stevenson, Parker
b. 1952 Weaver, Mike (Michael Dwayne)
b. 1961 DeBarge, El(dra)
b. 1965 Jaeger, Andrea
d. 1792 Burgoyne, John
d. 1798 Casanova (de Seingalt), Giovanni
       Giacomo
d. 1830 Sucre, Antonio J de
d. 1872 Moniuszko, Stanislaus
d. 1875 Morike, Eduard Friedrich
d. 1887 Wheeler, William Alrnon
d. 1912 Sangster, Margaret Elizabeth
d. 1913 Davison, Emily Wilding
d. 1918 Fairbanks, Charles Warren
d. 1925 Louys, Pierre
d. 1928 Chang Tso-Lin
d. 1939 Ladnier, Tommy
d. 1941 Wilhelm II
d. 1942 Heydrich, Reinhard
d. 1943 Roosevelt, Kermit
d. 1951 Koussevitzky, Serge Alexandrovich
d. 1962 Beebe, William (Charles William)
d. 1962 McCarthy, Clem
d. 1964 Warwick, Robert
d. 1968 Gish, Dorothy
d. 1970 McCracken, Branch
d. 1970 Schacht, Hjalmar Horace Greeley
d. 1970 Skulnik, Menasha
d. 1971 Lewis, Joe E
d. 1973 Bonnet, Georges
d. 1973 Bontemps, Arna Wendell
d. 1975 Leider, Frida
d. 1983 Tors, Ivan
d. 1985 North, John Ringling

June 5
b. 1718 Chippendale, Thomas
b. 1723 Smith, Adam
b. 1819 Adams, John Couch
b. 1826 Hallstrom, Ivar
b. 1874 Chesbro, "Happy Jack" (John
       Dwight)
b. 1877 Breck, John Henry
b. 1878 Villa, "Pancho" (Francisco)
b. 1879 Mayer, Robert
b. 1881 Wenner-Gren, Axel
b. 1882 Nelson, "Battling"
b. 1883 Keynes, John Maynard, Baron
b. 1886 Keaney, Frank
b. 1887 Benedict, Ruth Fulton
b. 1890 Kelly, Orie R
b. 1892 Compton-Burnett, Ivy, Dame
b. 1894 Thomson of Fleet, Roy Herbert
       Thomson, Baron
b. 1897 Chiang Mei-Ling
b. 1898 Boyd, William (Bill)
b. 1899 Garcia Lorca, Federico
b. 1900 Gabor, Dennis

b. 1908 Bickmore, Lee Smith
b. 1908 Randolph, Georgiana Ann
b. 1908 Rice, Craig
b. 1913 Marca-Relli, Conrad
b. 1914 Dunlop, John Thomas
b. 1915 Branley, Franklyn Mansfield
b. 1915 Kazin, Alfred
b. 1916 Rosen, Sidney
b. 1920 Ryan, Cornelius John
b. 1921 Bosin, Blackbear
b. 1924 Brissie, Lou (Leland Victor, Jr.)
b. 1925 Donovan, Art
b. 1929 Lansing, Robert
b. 1929 Richardson, Tony
b. 1931 Demy, Jacques
b. 1932 Brown, Christy
b. 1933 Helmond, Katherine
b. 1934 Michel, F Curtis
b. 1934 Moyers, Bill (William Don)
b. 1939 Clark, Joe (Charles Joseph)
b. 1939 Drabble, Margaret
b. 1944 Smith, Tommie
b. 1945 Carlos, John
b. 1947 Hare, David
b. 1949 Follett, Ken(neth Martin)
d. 1625 Gibbons, Orlando
d. 1816 Paisiello, Giovanni
d. 1826 Weber, Carl Maria von
d. 1863 Drexel, Francis Martin
d. 1900 Crane, Stephen
d. 1910 Henry, O, pseud.
d. 1916 Kitchener, Horatio Herbert
d. 1919 Coors, Adolph
d. 1920 Moore, Julia A Davis
d. 1944 Zandonai, Riccardo
d. 1945 Kaiser, Georg
d. 1946 Hormel, George Albert
d. 1946 Liggett, Louis Kroh
d. 1953 Farnum, William
d. 1953 Tilden, Bill (William Tatem, Jr.)
d. 1953 Young, Roland
d. 1963 Baziotes, William
d. 1965 Farjeon, Eleanor
d. 1970 Tufts, Sonny
d. 1978 Montoya, Joseph Manuel
d. 1984 Mohieddin, Faud

June 6
b. 1599 Velazquez, Diego Rodriguez de
       Silva
b. 1606 Corneille, Pierre
b. 1755 Hale, Nathan
b. 1756 Trumbull, John
b. 1771 Smith Sydney
b. 1799 Pushkin, Aleksandr Sergeyevich
b. 1804 Godey, Louis Antoine
b. 1820 Durrie, George Henry
b. 1850 Braun, Karl Ferdinand
b. 1860 Inge, William Ralph
b. 1868 Scott, Robert Falcon
b. 1875 Mann, Thomas
b. 1880 Cosgrave, William Thomas

b. 1907 Chalk, Oscar Roy
b. 1908 Goldovsky, Boris
b. 1908 Goodall, John Strickland
b. 1909 Rodino, Peter Wallace, Jr.
b. 1909 Tandy, Jessica
b. 1910 Annigoni, Pietro
b. 1913 Nash, N Richard
b. 1916 Darcy, Tom
b. 1917 Brooks, Gwendolyn
b. 1917 Cooke, David Coxe
b. 1919 Scherer, Ray(mond Lewis)
b. 1922 Graziano, Rocky
b. 1924 Gray, Dolores
b. 1928 Ivory, James
b. 1928 Strouse, Charles
b. 1929 Turner, John Napier
b. 1931 McKenna, Virginia
b. 1933 Karp, Lila
b. 1933 Score, Herb(ert Jude)
b. 1934 Blatchford, Joseph Hoffer
b. 1934 Entremont, Phillippe
b. 1934 Stewart, Wynn
b. 1937 Bernstein, Jay
b. 1940 Jones, Tom
b. 1941 Laredo, Jaime
b. 1943 Giovanni, Nikki
b. 1943 Osmond, Ken
b. 1946 Kreutzmann, Bill
b. 1947 Munson, Thurman Lee
b. 1955 Scarbury, Joey
b. 1958 Prince
d. 1394 Anne of Bohemia
d. 1826 Fraunhofer, Joseph von
d. 1859 Cox, David
d. 1884 Hoffman, Charles Fenno
d. 1886 Hoe, Richard March
d. 1893 Booth, Edwin Thomas
d. 1899 Daly, Augustin
d. 1910 Smith, Goldwin
d. 1914 Watts-Dunton, Theodore (Walter)
d. 1932 Paur, Emil
d. 1933 Curtis, Cyrus Hermann
     Kotszchmar
d. 1937 Harlow, Jean
d. 1954 Maverick, Maury
d. 1961 Barnard, Chester Irving
d. 1963 Pitts, Zasu (Eliza Susan)
d. 1964 Lewis, Meade Anderson Lux
d. 1965 Burgess, Thornton Waldo
d. 1965 Holliday, Judy
d. 1966 Arp, Hans
d. 1967 Parker, Dorothy Rothschild
d. 1968 Duryea, Dan
d. 1970 Forster, E(dward) M(organ)
d. 1971 Burnett, Leo
d. 1971 Rodale, Jerome Irving
d. 1972 Purdy, Ken(neth) William
d. 1975 Brent, Evelyn
d. 1976 Hackett, Bobby (Robert Leo)
d. 1978 Darken, Lawrence Stamper
d. 1978 Gordon, Joe (Joseph Lowell)

d. 1980 Bonelli, Richard
d. 1980 Guston, Philip
d. 1980 Miller, Henry
d. 1980 Spychalski, Marian
d. 1981 Gorman, Chester
d. 1982 Demara, Ferdinand Waldo, Jr.
d. 1986 Bickmore, Lee Smith

June 8
b. 1595 Parker, Thomas
b. 1683 Guarnieri, Giuseppe Antonio
b. 1783 Sully, Thomas
b. 1810 Schumann, Robert Alexander
b. 1813 Porter, David Dixon
b. 1814 Reade, Charles
b. 1829 Millais, John Everett, Sir
b. 1847 McKinley, Ida Saxton
b. 1863 Kraus, Ernst
b. 1869 Wright, Frank Lloyd
b. 1877 Wagner, Robert
b. 1887 Balaban, Barney
b. 1893 Scobie, Ronald Mackenzie
b. 1903 Yarborough, Ralph Webster
b. 1908 Redpath, James
b. 1910 Beck, C(harles) C(larence)
b. 1910 Campbell, John W
b. 1912 Kennedy, Walter
b. 1913 Diamand, Peter
b. 1913 Yourcenar, Marguerite, pseud.
b. 1916 Comencini, Luigi
b. 1916 Crick, Francis Harry Compton
b. 1917 Romney, Seymour Leonard
b. 1917 White, Byron Raymond
b. 1918 Esslin, Martin Julius
b. 1918 Preston, Robert
b. 1919 Fitzgibbon, (Robert Louis)
     Constantine
b. 1921 Campbell, Gordon Thomas
b. 1921 Smith, Alexis
b. 1921 Southall, Ivan Francis
b. 1921 Suharto, General
b. 1923 Boyd, Malcolm
b. 1923 Kirby, George
b. 1923 Rosenthal, Benjamin Stanley
b. 1924 Nofziger, Lyn (Franklyn Curran)
b. 1925 Bush, Barbara Pierce
b. 1925 Ennis, Del(mer)
b. 1925 Gaedel, Eddie (Edward Carl)
b. 1925 McNerney, Walter James
b. 1926 Neiman, LeRoy
b. 1926 Stiller, Jerry
b. 1927 Ross, Lillian
b. 1928 Kromm, Bobby (Robert)
b. 1930 Codron, Michael
b. 1930 Widerberg, Bo
b. 1932 Wynter, Dana
b. 1933 Rivers, Joan
b. 1934 Martin, Millicent
b. 1936 Darren, James
b. 1936 Wilson, Kenneth Geddes
b. 1937 McCandless, Bruce, II
b. 1939 Rukeyser, William Simon

June 10
b. 1819 Courbet, Gustave
b. 1832 Otto, Nikolaus August
b. 1833 Cushman, Pauline
b. 1835 Felton, Rebecca Ann Latimer
b. 1854 Curel, Francois de
b. 1857 Potthast, Edward Henry
b. 1862 Carter, Caroline Louise Dudley
b. 1862 Carter, Mrs. Leslie
b. 1863 Couperius, Louis (Marie Anne)
b. 1865 Cook, Frederick Albert
b. 1867 Meier-Graefe, Julius
b. 1880 Derain, Andre
b. 1881 Gruenberg, Sidonie Matsner
b. 1886 Hayakawa, Sessue (Kintaro)
b. 1887 Byrd, Harry Flood, Jr.
b. 1891 Dubin, Al
b. 1891 Levinsky, "Battling"
b. 1895 McDaniel, Hattie
b. 1897 Jagel, Frederick
b. 1898 Brokenshire, Norman
b. 1904 Loewe, Frederick
b. 1906 Crosby, Alexander L
b. 1907 Porter, Fairfield
b. 1910 Haydon, Julie
b. 1910 Howlin' Wolf
b. 1911 Rattigan, Terence Mervyn
b. 1912 Lesage, Jean
b. 1913 Cohen, Wilbur Joseph
b. 1913 Khrennikov, Tikhon Nikolaevich
b. 1915 Bellow, Saul
b. 1918 Morse, Barry
b. 1921 Philip, Prince
b. 1922 Garland, Judy
b. 1925 Costa, Don
b. 1925 Hentoff, Nat(han Irving)
b. 1926 Haver, June
b. 1926 Low, George M(ichael)
b. 1926 Middleton, Christopher
b. 1928 Sendak, Maurice Bernard
b. 1929 McDivitt, Jim (James Alton)
b. 1932 Johnston, J Bennett, Jr.
b. 1933 Bailey, F(rancis) Lee
b. 1933 Fairbanks, Chuck (Charles Leo)
b. 1936 Chesney, Marion
b. 1936 Freemantle, Brian Harry
b. 1943 Greenfield, Jeff
b. 1947 Singleton, Ken(neth Wayne)
b. 1950 Gianelli, John
b. 1951 Fouts, Dan(iel Francis)
b. 1953 Barrios, Francisco Javier
b. 1953 Ramirez, Raul
b. 1955 Stevens, Andrew
b. 1966 McKeon, Doug
d. 1798 Vancouver, George
d. 1836 Ampere, Andre Marie
d. 1858 Brown, Robert
d. 1865 Sigourney, Lydia Howard
d. 1899 Chausson, Ernest
d. 1909 Hale, Edward Everett
d. 1918 Boito, Arrigo

d. 1923 Loti, Pierre, pseud.
d. 1927 Woodhull, Victoria Claflin
d. 1930 Sperry, Elmer Ambrose
d. 1934 Delius, Frederick
d. 1937 Borden, Robert Laird, Sir
d. 1940 Garvey, Marcus Moziah
d. 1942 Lupino, Stanley
d. 1946 Johnson, Jack (John Arthur)
d. 1949 McCutcheon, John Tinney
d. 1949 Undset, Sigrid
d. 1956 Pratt, Fletcher
d. 1963 Root, Jack
d. 1966 Treece, Henry
d. 1967 Tracy, Spencer
d. 1971 Rennie, Michael
d. 1973 Inge, William
d. 1973 Kredel, Fritz
d. 1975 Hull, John Edwin
d. 1976 Zukor, Adolph
d. 1980 Sullivan, A(loysius) M(ichael)
d. 1982 Dali, Gala
d. 1982 Fassbinder, Rainer Werner
d. 1983 Reisenberg, Nadia
d. 1985 Armstrong, Jack Lawrence
d. 1986 Miller, Merle

June 11
b. 1561 Gongora y Argote, Don Luis de
b. 1572 Jonson, Ben(jamin)
b. 1741 Warren, Joseph
b. 1769 Royall, Anne Newport
b. 1776 Constable, John
b. 1857 Binet, Alfred
b. 1864 Strauss, Richard
b. 1876 Kroeber, Alfred Louis
b. 1879 Bresnaham, Roger Phillip
b. 1879 Pulitzer, Ralph
b. 1881 Kaplan, Mordecai
b. 1886 Gordon, Vera
b. 1886 Steinman, David Barnard
b. 1888 Akhmatova, Anna, pseud.
b. 1888 Vanzetti, Bartolomeo
b. 1892 Maney, Richard
b. 1895 Bulganin, Nikolai Aleksandrovich
b. 1899 Kawabata, Yasunari
b. 1900 Kresge, Stanley Sebastian
b. 1900 Spivak, Lawrence
b. 1903 Nevers, Ernie (Ernest A)
b. 1904 Smith, Clarence
b. 1907 Mellon, Paul
b. 1910 Coppola, Carmine
b. 1910 Cousteau, Jacques Yves
b. 1910 Geneen, Harold Sydney
b. 1911 Miles, Josephine
b. 1911 Nebel, "Long" John
b. 1912 Baziotes, William
b. 1912 Montgomery, Ruth Shick
b. 1913 Lombardi, Vince(nt Thomas)
b. 1913 Stevens, Rise
b. 1917 Gemmill, Henry
b. 1919 Todd, Richard
b. 1920 Howe, Irving

d. 1966 Hocking, William Ernest
d. 1966 Scherchen, Hermann
d. 1968 Read, Herbert, Sir
d. 1972 Alinsky, Saul David
d. 1972 Wilson, Edmund
d. 1975 Kober, Arthur
d. 1978 Cushman, Austin Thomas
d. 1980 Butlin, William Heygate Edmund,
   Sir
d. 1980 Stone, Milburn
d. 1982 Frisch, Karl von
d. 1982 Rambert, Dame Marie
d. 1983 Shearer, Norma
d. 1984 Ferencsik, Janos

June 13
b. 1752 Burney, Fanny (Frances)
b. 1786 Scott, Winfield
b. 1795 Arnold, Thomas
b. 1836 Saunders, William
b. 1843 Neuendorff, Adolf
b. 1854 Parsons, Charles Algernin, Sir
b. 1865 Yeats, William Butler
b. 1870 Bordet, Jules Jean Baptiste Vincent
b. 1875 Ferguson, Miriam Amanda
b. 1876 Franklin, Irene
b. 1879 Wood, Robert Elkington
b. 1880 Rose, Vincent
b. 1880 Stella, Joseph
b. 1881 Weber, Lois
b. 1884 Crohn, Burrill Bernard
b. 1884 Gilson, Etienne Henry
b. 1885 Igoe, "Hype" (Herbert A)
b. 1885 Schumann, Elisabeth
b. 1887 Frank, Bruno
b. 1892 Rathbone, Basil
b. 1894 Kanner, Leo
b. 1894 Lartique, Jacques-Henri
b. 1894 Van Doren, Mark
b. 1895 Wrightsman, Charles Bierer
b. 1897 Nurmi, Paavo
b. 1898 O'Neil, James F(rancis)
b. 1899 Chavez, Carlos
b. 1900 Hunter, Ian
b. 1901 Erlander, Tage Fritiof
b. 1903 Grange, "Red" (Harold Edward)
b. 1905 Colbert, Lester Lum
b. 1905 Turner, Roscoe Wilson
b. 1909 Nikolaidi, Elena
b. 1910 Christ-Janer, Albert
b. 1911 Alvarez, Luis Walter
b. 1911 Hays, Wayne Levere
b. 1912 Schoyer, (B) Preston
b. 1912 Taylor, Samuel (Albert)
b. 1913 Edwards, Ralph
b. 1913 Martin, David Stone
b. 1914 Franklin, Frederic
b. 1915 Budge, Don (John Donald)
b. 1916 Conway, Shirl
b. 1918 Joanis, John W
b. 1918 Johnson, Ben
b. 1920 Evans, Clifford

b. 1926 Lynde, Paul Edward
b. 1927 Ableman, Paul
b. 1934 Means, Marianne Hansen
b. 1935 Christo
b. 1937 Norton, Eleanor Holmes
b. 1943 McDowell, Malcolm
b. 1951 Thomas, Richard Earl
d. 323 BC Alexander the Great
d. 1939 Barker, "Doc" (Arthur)
d. 1946 Bowes, "Major" (Edward)
d. 1946 Guerin, Jules
d. 1952 Eames, Emma Hayden
d. 1953 Freeman, Douglas S
d. 1961 Jones, Benjamin Allyn
d. 1962 Goossens, Eugene, Sir
d. 1965 Buber, Martin
d. 1967 Ellington, Edward
d. 1969 Hunt, Martita
d. 1972 McPhatter, Clyde
d. 1973 Cott, Ted
d. 1974 Secunda, Sholom
d. 1976 Anda, Geza
d. 1976 Bolles, Don F
d. 1979 Hood, Darla Jean
d. 1980 Lampman, Evelyn Sibley
d. 1982 Griffin, Marvin (Samuel Marvin)
d. 1982 Khalid Ibn Abdul Aziz Al-Saud
d. 1982 Rafferty, Max(well Lewis, Jr.)
d. 1984 Owings, Nathaniel Alexander
d. 1986 Goodman, Benny (Benjamin
   David)
d. 1986 Greeley, Dana McLean

June 14
b. 1716 Harrison, Peter
b. 1730 Sacchini, Antonio
b. 1736 Coulomb, Charles Augustin de
b. 1805 Anderson, Robert
b. 1811 Stowe, Harriet (Elizabeth) Beecher
b. 1820 Bartlett, John
b. 1832 Mitchell, Margaret Julia
b. 1850 Kitchener, Horatio Herbert
b. 1855 LaFollette, Robert Marion
b. 1874 Bowes, "Major" (Edward)
b. 1884 McCormack, John
b. 1895 Adams, Jack (John James)
b. 1904 Bourke-White, Margaret
b. 1906 Lamb, Gil
b. 1907 Char, Rene (Emile)
b. 1908 Trotter, John Scott
b. 1909 Ives, Burl
b. 1910 Kempe, Rudolf
b. 1914 Peers, William Raymond
b. 1917 Rootes, William Edward Rootes,
   Baron
b. 1918 Aluko, Timothy Mofolorunso
b. 1918 McGuire, Dorothy
b. 1919 Wanamaker, Sam
b. 1922 Roche, Kevin (Eammon Kevin)
b. 1925 Salinger, Pierre Emil George
b. 1926 Newcombe, Don(ald)
b. 1928 Guevara, Che Ernesto

b. 1928 Udry, Janice May
b. 1929 Coleman, Cy
b. 1931 Gibbs, Marla Bradley
b. 1933 Kosinski, Jerzy Nikodem
b. 1934 Lehmann-Haupt, Christopher
b. 1935 Evans, Jerry
b. 1939 Andrews, Michael Alford
b. 1945 Argent, Rod(ney Terence)
b. 1952 Mekka, Eddie
b. 1955 Evans, Vince(nt Tobias)
b. 1958 Heiden, Eric
b. 1961 Boy George
d. 1594 Lassus, Orlandus de
d. 1800 Kleber, Jean Baptiste
d. 1801 Arnold, Benedict
d. 1825 L'Enfant, Pierre Charles
d. 1837 Leopardi, Giacomo
d. 1883 Fitzgerald, Edward
d. 1886 Mould, Jacob Wrey
d. 1886 Van Nostrand, David
d. 1908 Stanley, Frederick Arthur, Earl of
   Derby
d. 1909 Prang, Louis
d. 1914 Stevenson, Adlai Ewing
d. 1919 Alcock, John William, Sir
d. 1920 Weber, Max
d. 1926 Cassatt, Mary
d. 1927 Jerome, Jerome Klapka
d. 1928 Pankhurst, Emmeline Goulden
d. 1929 Keith, Minor Cooper
d. 1933 Pollack, Egon
d. 1936 Chesterton, Gilbert Keith
d. 1938 Campbell, William Wallace
d. 1939 Khodasevich, Vladislav
d. 1939 Pulitzer, Ralph
d. 1946 Baird, John Logie
d. 1946 Butterworth, Charles
d. 1948 Atherton, Gertrude Franklin
d. 1965 Kaltenborn, H(ans) V(on)
d. 1968 Quasimodo, Salvatore
d. 1971 Garcia, Carlos P
d. 1974 Perkoff, Stuart Z
d. 1977 Reed, Alan
d. 1978 Fabian, Robert Honey
d. 1978 Poulter, Thomas Charles
d. 1979 Shumlin, Herman Elliott
d. 1984 Pillsbury, Philip Winston
d. 1985 Johnson, Walter (Thomas Walter)
d. 1986 Borges, Jorge Luis
d. 1986 Lerner, Alan Jay
d. 1986 Perkins, (Richard) Marlin
d. 1986 Perkins, Marlin (Richard Marlin)

June 15
b. 1645 Godolphin, Sidney
b. 1767 Jackson, Rachel Donelson Robards
b. 1773 Benjamin, Asher
b. 1789 Henson, Josiah
b. 1815 Browne, "Phiz" (Hablot Knight)
b. 1835 Menken, Adah Isaacs
b. 1843 Grieg, Edvard Hagerup
b. 1847 Yost, Joseph Warren

b. 1856 Channing, Edward
b. 1861 Schumann-Heink, Ernestine Rossler
b. 1869 Witmark, Isidore
b. 1872 Gadski, Johanna
b. 1881 McFee, William
b. 1882 Antonescu, Ion
b. 1884 Friendly, Edwin Samson
b. 1884 Langdon, Harry
b. 1887 Hoffman, Malvina
b. 1888 D'Arcy, Martin Cyril
b. 1893 Weeks, Sinclair
b. 1894 Bennett, Robert Russell
b. 1895 Herrick, Elinore M
b. 1896 Jacobs, Walter L
b. 1900 Feingold, Benjamin Franklin
b. 1902 Erikson, Erik Homburger
b. 1902 Rudolf, Max
b. 1905 Justice, James Robertson
b. 1908 Anderson, Vernon Ellsworth
b. 1910 Rose, David
b. 1913 Huddleston, (Ernest Urban) Trevor
b. 1914 Andropov, Yuri Vladimirovich
b. 1914 Steinberg, Saul
b. 1916 Field, Marshall, IV
b. 1916 Simon, Herbert Alexander
b. 1917 Payne, Leon
b. 1921 Garner, Erroll
b. 1922 Udall, Mo(rris King)
b. 1923 Benarde, Melvin Albert
b. 1926 Fox, Carol
b. 1930 Pronovost, Marcel (Rene Marcel)
b. 1932 Cuomo, Mario Matthew
b. 1932 Roberts, Gene (Eugene Leslie, Jr.)
b. 1937 Jennings, Waylon
b. 1938 Williams, Billy Leo
b. 1943 Halliday, Johnny
b. 1945 Pagett, Nicola
b. 1954 Belushi, Jim (James)
b. 1954 Gibbs, Terri
b. 1956 Parrish, Lance Michael
b. 1958 Boggs, Wade Anthony
d. 1844 Campbell, Thomas
d. 1849 Polk, James K(nox)
d. 1888 Frederick III
d. 1889 Eminescu, Mihail
d. 1907 Jenney, William LeBaron
d. 1938 Kirchner, Ernst Ludwig
d. 1945 Rives, Amelie Louise
d. 1952 Gallatin, Albert Eugene
d. 1965 Cochran, Steve
d. 1965 Norden, Carl Lukas
d. 1968 Crawford, Sam(uel Earl)
d. 1968 Montgomery, Wes
d. 1970 Powdermaker, Hortense
d. 1977 Knorr, Nathan Homer
d. 1981 Dinkeloo, John Gerard
d. 1981 Rinehart, Frederick Roberts
d. 1981 Toynbee, Philip (Theodore Philip)
d. 1982 Pepper, Art(hur Edward)
d. 1984 Willson, Meredith

June 16
b. 1874 Meighen, Arthur
b. 1878 Torrence, Ernest
b. 1888 Clark, Bobby
b. 1889 Doubleday, Nelson
b. 1889 Hamlin, Talbot Faulkner
b. 1890 Laurel, Stan
b. 1892 Grossinger, Jennie
b. 1892 Rubicam, Raymond
b. 1895 Pitz, Henry Clarence
b. 1897 Masters, Kelly R
b. 1902 McClintock, Barbara
b. 1906 Munson, Ona
b. 1907 Pilkington, Francis M
b. 1909 Beilenson, Edna Rudolph
b. 1910 Albertson, Jack
b. 1910 Gesell, Gerhard Alden
b. 1910 Massey, Ilona
b. 1910 Velasco Alvarado, Juan
b. 1912 Powell, Enoch (John Enoch)
b. 1915 Rumor, Mariano
b. 1916 Luisetti, Angelo Enrico
b. 1917 Graham, Katharine Meyer
b. 1917 Penn, Irving
b. 1918 Elliott, George Paul
b. 1920 Griffin, John Howard
b. 1923 Colombo, Joseph Anthony
b. 1926 Rios Montt, Jose Efrain
b. 1928 Comissiona, Sergiu
b. 1930 Zsigmond, Vilmos
b. 1931 Hashimoto, Ken
b. 1935 Dine, Jim
b. 1937 Segal, Erich Wolf
b. 1938 Oates, Joyce Carol
b. 1940 Craddock, "Crash" (Billy)
b. 1940 Goldschmidt, Neil Edward
b. 1946 Sanderson, Derek Michael
b. 1946 Van Ark, Joan
b. 1946 Williams, Simon
b. 1948 Le Flore, Ron(ald)
b. 1951 Duran, Roberto
b. 1952 Vannelli, Gino
b. 1958 Griffith, Darrell Steven
b. 1962 Joyner, Wally (Wallace Keith)
d. 1464 Weyden, Rogier van der
d. 1722 Marlborough, John Churchill, Duke
d. 1752 Butler, Joseph
d. 1804 Hiller, Johann Adam
d. 1855 Gorrie, John
d. 1878 Long, Crawford Williamson
d. 1909 Albeniz, Isaac Manuel Francisco
d. 1929 Parrington, Vernon L(ouis)
d. 1934 Skelly, Hal
d. 1940 Heyward, (Edwin) DuBose
d. 1941 Franklin, Irene
d. 1943 Onegin, Sigrid
d. 1947 Huberman, Bronislaw
d. 1953 Bondfield, Margaret Grace
d. 1959 Reeves, George
d. 1966 Eifert, Virginia Snider

d. 1967 Denny, Reginald Leigh
d. 1969 Alexander of Tunis, Harold Rupert Leofric George Alexander, Earl
d. 1970 Piccolo, Brian
d. 1971 Reith, John Charles Walsham
d. 1973 Mann, Joseph
d. 1975 Courtney, Clint(on Dawson)
d. 1976 Meloy, Francis Edward, Jr.
d. 1978 Bernstein, Felicia Montealegre
d. 1981 Knight, John Shivley
d. 1982 Honeyman-Scott, James (Jimmy)
d. 1982 Kibbee, Robert Joseph
d. 1986 Norwich, Diana (Manners) Cooper, Viscountess

June 17
b. 1742 Hooper, William
b. 1743 Lowell, John
b. 1751 Humphreys, Joshua
b. 1818 Gounod, Charles Francois
b. 1832 Crookes, William, Sir
b. 1848 Maurel, Victor
b. 1860 Frohman, Charles
b. 1871 Johnson, James Weldon
b. 1873 Bloomingdale, Samuel
b. 1875 Mitchell, Grant
b. 1880 Van Vechten, Carl
b. 1881 Burns, Tommy
b. 1882 Herne, Chrystal Katharine
b. 1882 Stravinsky, Igor Fedorovich
b. 1883 Gordon, C Henry
b. 1893 Helck, Peter (Clarence Peter)
b. 1894 Bache, Harold Leopold
b. 1896 Lupino, Stanley
b. 1899 Fazenda, Louise
b. 1900 White, William Lindsay
b. 1902 Fain, Sammy
b. 1904 Bellamy, Ralph
b. 1907 Britt, Steuart Henderson
b. 1907 Eames, Charles
b. 1910 Foley, "Red" (Clyde Julian)
b. 1912 Gillis, Don
b. 1914 Hersey, John Richard
b. 1915 Goldman, Eric F
b. 1916 Atkinson, Ted
b. 1917 Martin, Dean
b. 1919 Brewster, Kingman, Jr.
b. 1920 Jacob, Francois
b. 1920 Reid, Beryl
b. 1921 Anderson, William Robert
b. 1921 Scott, Tony
b. 1922 Ross, David
b. 1923 Hirsch, "Crazylegs" (Elroy)
b. 1925 Fox, Sonny
b. 1929 Petrosian, Tigran Vartanovich
b. 1932 Murtha, John Patrick
b. 1937 Lupus, Peter
b. 1937 Maynard, Robert Clyve
b. 1946 Manilow, Barry
b. 1951 Piscopo, Joe (Joseph Charles)
b. 1955 Charboneau, Joe (Joseph)
d. 1696 John III, Sobieski

d. 1980 Fisher, Terence
d. 1981 Johnson, Pamela Hansford
d. 1981 Katona, George
d. 1982 Barnes, Djuna
d. 1982 Cheever, John
d. 1982 Hicks, Granville
d. 1982 Hillenkoetter, Roscoe H(enry)
d. 1982 Jurgens, Curt
d. 1983 Lewis, Robert Alvin
d. 1986 Smith, Frances Scott Fitzgerald
 Lanahan

June 19

b. Buttram, Pat
b. 1566 James I
b. 1623 Pascal, Blaise
b. 1854 Catalani, Alfredo
b. 1856 Hubbard, Elbert Green
b. 1863 Brady, William Aloysius
b. 1865 Whitty, May, Dame
b. 1869 Addison, Christopher, Viscount
b. 1872 Farrand, Beatrix Jones
b. 1877 Coburn, Charles Douville
b. 1880 Dwiggins, William Addison
b. 1881 Walker, Jimmy (James John)
b. 1882 Stein, Clarence S
b. 1887 Yurka, Blanche
b. 1888 Johnston, Frank H
b. 1890 Eberstadt, Ferdinand
b. 1894 Cicotte, Eddie (Edward V)
b. 1896 Simpson, Wallis Warfield
b. 1897 Hinshelwood, Cyril, Sir
b. 1897 Howard, Moe
b. 1898 Tharp, Louise Hall
b. 1899 Mellon, Richard King
b. 1900 Hobson, Laura Zametkin
b. 1902 Hoffman, Anna Marie Lederer
 Rosenberg
b. 1902 Lombardo, Guy Albert
b. 1903 Gehrig, Lou (Henry Louis)
b. 1905 Voskovec, George
b. 1906 Chain, Ernest Boris, Sir
b. 1908 Burdick, Quentin Northrop
b. 1908 Natwick, Mildred
b. 1910 Flory, Paul John
b. 1910 Fortas, Abe
b. 1912 Bomhard, Moritz
b. 1912 Gabel, Martin
b. 1914 Cranston, Alan MacGregor
b. 1918 Abram, Morris Berthold
b. 1919 Kael, Pauline
b. 1920 Jourdan, Louis
b. 1921 Howell, Thomas Heflin
b. 1921 Wrightson, Patricia
b. 1928 Marchand, Nancy
b. 1931 Lander, Toni
b. 1932 Pavan, Marisa
b. 1933 Angeli, Pier
b. 1935 DeVito, Tommy
b. 1936 Rowlands, Gena
b. 1942 Kasten, Robert W, Jr.
b. 1951 Wilson, Ann

b. 1954 Turner, Kathleen
b. 1959 DeBarge, Mark
d. 1786 Greene, Nathanael
d. 1794 Lee, Richard Henry
d. 1811 Chase, Samuel
d. 1867 Maximilian
d. 1914 Thomas, Brandon
d. 1937 Barrie, James Matthew, Sir
d. 1939 Abbott, Grace
d. 1940 Myers, Jerome
d. 1946 Sheaffer, Walter A
d. 1948 Roebuck, Alvah Curtis
d. 1952 Schlusnus, Heinrich
d. 1953 Rosenberg, Ethel Greenglass
d. 1953 Rosenberg, Julius
d. 1956 Watson, Thomas John, Sr.
d. 1962 Borzage, Frank
d. 1966 Wynn, Ed
d. 1971 Wood, Gar(field A)
d. 1974 Giancana, Salvatore (Sam)
d. 1977 Brooks, Geraldine
d. 1982 Lockridge, Richard
d. 1984 Krasner, Lee
d. 1985 Boulting, John
d. 1985 LeFleming, Christopher Kaye
d. 1985 Phillips, Marjorie Acker
d. 1986 Bias, Len

June 20

b. 1674 Rowe, Nicholas
b. 1819 Offenbach, Jacques
b. 1837 Brewer, David Josiah
b. 1858 Chesnutt, Charles Waddell
b. 1876 Ditmars, Raymond Lee
b. 1878 Morgan, Arthur
b. 1891 Costello, John Aloysius
b. 1894 Delacorte, George Thomas, Jr.
b. 1895 Price, Gwilym Alexander
b. 1896 Pelletier, Wilfred
b. 1899 Traubel, Helen
b. 1900 Levi, Julian Edwin
b. 1903 Croft-Cooke, Rupert
b. 1903 Vare, Glenna Collett
b. 1905 Hellman, Lillian
b. 1906 Burnshaw, Stanley
b. 1906 Jones, Robert Trent
b. 1909 Flynn, Errol
b. 1911 Patrick, Gail
b. 1913 Torrance, Jack
b. 1915 Lord, James Lawrence
b. 1915 Young, Terence
b. 1920 Paterson, Tom
b. 1921 Segura, "Pancho" (Francisco)
b. 1923 Gay, Peter Jack
b. 1924 Atkins, Chet (Chester B)
b. 1924 Murphy, Audie
b. 1929 Bronfman, Edgar Miles
b. 1930 Craig, Wendy
b. 1934 Podesta, Rossana
b. 1935 Dawson, Len (Leonard Ray)
b. 1942 Wilson, Brian Douglas
b. 1945 Murray, Anne

b. 1946 Watts, Andre
b. 1948 Sinatra, Christina
b. 1950 Longmuir, Alan
b. 1953 Lauper, Cyndi (Cynthia)
b. 1955 Anthony, Michael
b. 1959 Ogrodnick, John Alexander
d. 1836 Rouget de Lisle, Claude Joseph
d. 840 Louis I
d. 1870 Goncourt, Jules Alfred Huot de
d. 1876 Santa Anna, Antonio Lopez de
d. 1904 Seiss, Joseph Augustus
d. 1917 Crafts, James Mason
d. 1928 Mead, William Rutherford
d. 1940 Chase, Charley
d. 1940 Nevada, Emma
d. 1940 Reiss, Albert
d. 1945 Frank, Bruno
d. 1947 Siegel, "Bugsy" (Benjamin)
d. 1958 Alder, Kurt
d. 1958 Swope, Herbert Bayard
d. 1960 Kelly, John Brenden
d. 1965 Baruch, Bernard Mannes
d. 1969 Beall, Lester Thomas
d. 1969 Murchison, Clint(on Williams)
d. 1971 Ullman, James Ramsey
d. 1972 Johnson, Howard Deering
d. 1977 Cone, Fairfax Mastick
d. 1981 Erwin, "Pee Wee" (George)
d. 1984 Winwood, Estelle

June 21
b. 1639 Mather, Increase
b. 1774 Tompkins, Daniel D
b. 1805 Jackson, Charles Thomas
b. 1813 Aytoun, William Edmonstoune
b. 1832 Rainey, Joseph Hayne
b. 1850 Beard, Daniel Carter
b. 1855 Chausson, Ernest
b. 1859 Tanner, Henry Ossawa
b. 1880 Gesell, Arnold
b. 1882 Kent, Rockwell
b. 1884 Auchinleck, Claude, Sir
b. 1887 Ismay, Hastings Lionel, Baron
b. 1888 Upson, Ralph Hazlett
b. 1891 Nervi, Pier Luigi
b. 1891 Scherchen, Hermann
b. 1892 Niebuhr, Reinhold
b. 1892 Rosenberg, Hilding
b. 1895 Snyder, John Wesley
b. 1898 Peattie, Donald Culross
b. 1899 Gard, Wayne
b. 1900 Stickney, Dorothy
b. 1902 Foreman, Percy
b. 1902 Kesselring, Joseph
b. 1903 Costello, Helene
b. 1903 Hirschfeld, Al(bert)
b. 1903 Sjoberg, Alf
b. 1905 Sartre, Jean-Paul
b. 1906 Elting, Mary Letha
b. 1907 Prestopino, George
b. 1907 Shea, William Alfred
b. 1912 McCarthy, Mary

b. 1913 Mosconi, Willie (William Joseph)
b. 1916 Friedman, Herbert
b. 1918 Lopat, Ed(mund Walter)
b. 1919 Soleri, Paolo
b. 1920 Martin, James Slattin, Jr.
b. 1921 Emanuel, James A
b. 1921 Russell, Jane
b. 1922 Holliday, Judy
b. 1924 Bleiberg, Robert Marvin
b. 1925 Stapleton, Maureen
b. 1926 Ubell, Earl
b. 1927 Stokes, Carl Burton
b. 1928 Raskin, Judith
b. 1931 Grossman, Lawrence K
b. 1931 Heckler, Margaret Mary
b. 1932 Schifrin, Lalo Claudio
b. 1932 Strong, James Matthew
b. 1933 Kopell, Bernie (Bernard Morton)
b. 1935 Markham, Monte
b. 1935 Sagan, Francoise, pseud.
b. 1938 Ely, Ron
b. 1940 Cooke, Hope
b. 1940 Flaherty, Joe
b. 1940 Hartley, Mariette
b. 1941 Foat, Ginny
b. 1943 Serban, Andrei George
b. 1944 Davies, Ray(mond Douglas)
b. 1947 Baxter-Birney, Meredith
b. 1947 Gross, Michael
b. 1951 Lofgren, Nils
b. 1953 Bhutto, Benazir
b. 1956 Sutcliffe, Rick (Richard Lee)
b. 1982 William of Wales
d. 1529 Skelton, John
d. 1631 Smith, John
d. 1652 Jones, Inigo
d. 1852 Froebel, Friedrich Wilhelm August
d. 1874 Angstrom, Anders Jonas
d. 1877 Palmer, Nathaniel Brown
d. 1886 Home, Daniel Douglas
d. 1893 Stanford, Leland (Amasa Leland)
d. 1908 Rimsky-Korsakov, Nikolai Andreevich
d. 1926 Roze, Marie
d. 1934 Smith, Thorne
d. 1935 Roller, Alfred
d. 1940 Thompson, John Taliaferro
d. 1940 Vuillard, (Jean) Edouard
d. 1948 Brown, Alice
d. 1957 Farrere, Claude, pseud.
d. 1958 Ghormley, Robert Lee
d. 1967 List, Emanuel
d. 1968 Saint Denis, Ruth
d. 1969 Connolly, Maureen
d. 1970 Lucas, Jim Griffing
d. 1970 Sukarno, Achmed
d. 1971 Rose, Carl
d. 1973 Leahy, Frank
d. 1975 Oenslager, Donald Mitchell
d. 1978 Youngdahl, Luther W

d. 1985 Boiardi, Hector
d. 1985 Erlander, Tage Fritiof

June 22
b. 1748 Day, Thomas
b. 1763 Mehul, Etienne Nicolas
b. 1767 Humboldt, Wilhelm von
b. 1805 Mazzini, Giuseppe
b. 1837 Morphy, Paul Charles
b. 1844 Lothrop, Harriet Mulford Stone
b. 1846 Hawthorne, Julian
b. 1856 Haggard, Henry Rider, Sir
b. 1859 Damrosch, Frank Heino
b. 1861 Legler, Henry Eduard
b. 1871 McDougall, William
b. 1871 Raine, William MacLeod
b. 1882 Bercovici, Konrad
b. 1882 Scholl, William M
b. 1887 Huxley, Julian Sorell, Sir
b. 1888 Seeger, Alan
b. 1894 Eliot, George Fielding
b. 1894 Luboshutz, Pierre
b. 1898 Remarque, Erich Maria
b. 1902 Burns, David
b. 1903 Hubbell, Carl Owen
b. 1903 Sturtzel, Jane Levington
b. 1904 Wallmann, Margherita
b. 1906 Highet, Gilbert Arthur
b. 1906 Wilder, "Billy" (Samuel)
b. 1907 Lindbergh, Anne Spencer Morrow
b. 1908 Livingstone, Mary
b. 1909 Adler, "Buddy" (Maurice)
b. 1910 Dunham, Katherine
b. 1910 Pears, Peter, Sir
b. 1914 Lucas, Jim Griffing
b. 1915 Warmerdam, Cornelius
b. 1921 Champion, Gower
b. 1921 Papp, Joseph
b. 1922 Blass, Bill
b. 1928 Hermannsson, Steingrimur
b. 1928 Waite, Ralph
b. 1930 Bonatti, Walter
b. 1933 Feinstein, Dianne
b. 1934 Jordan, Don
b. 1937 Kristofferson, Kris
b. 1941 Bradley, Ed
b. 1943 Malcolm, Andrew H(ogarth)
b. 1944 Asher, Peter
b. 1947 Rawlings, Jerry John
b. 1948 Rundgren, Todd
b. 1949 Streep, Meryl (Mary Louise)
b. 1949 Wagner, Lindsay
b. 1954 Prinze, Freddie
d. 1527 Machiavelli, Niccolo
d. 1535 Fisher, John
d. 1864 McPherson, James Birdseye
d. 1874 Staunton, Howard
d. 1885 Mahdi, Mohammed Ahmed
d. 1896 Harris, Augustus, Sir
d. 1928 Frost, Arthur Burdett
d. 1950 Cowl, Jane
d. 1954 Compton, Karl Taylor

d. 1956 DeLaMare, Walter
d. 1965 Auslander, Joseph
d. 1965 Selznick, David O(liver)
d. 1968 Beckman, Johnny
d. 1969 Garland, Judy
d. 1974 Milhaud, Darius
d. 1975 Wahloo, Per
d. 1978 Krag, Jens Otto
d. 1981 Frankenstein, Alfred Victor
d. 1981 Harris, William Bliss
d. 1981 Lane, Lola
d. 1981 Linder, Harold Francis
d. 1983 Hinton, Christopher, Sir

June 23
b. 1625 Fell, John
b. 1685 Bernacchi, Antonio Maria
b. 1803 Lee, Jason
b. 1822 Darley, Felix Octavius Carr
b. 1832 Sbriglia, Giovanni
b. 1839 Mueller, Christian F
b. 1851 Eddy, Clarence
b. 1875 Milles, Carl
b. 1876 Cobb, Irvin Shrewsbury
b. 1890 Buckley, Charles Anthony
b. 1892 Butler, Paul
b. 1893 Davison, Frank Dalby
b. 1894 Edward VIII
b. 1894 Kinsey, Alfred Charles
b. 1894 Weiss, George Martin
b. 1896 Ferril, Thomas Hornsby
b. 1900 Noyes, Blanche Wilcox
b. 1900 Steelman, John R
b. 1903 Darling, Frank Fraser, Sir
b. 1904 Coon, Carleton Stevens
b. 1907 Willard, John Wesley
b. 1910 Anouilh, Jean Marie Lucienpierre
b. 1910 Little, (William) Lawson, Jr.
b. 1910 Morgan, Edward P
b. 1911 Ogilvy, David Mackenzie
b. 1913 Humes, Helen
b. 1913 Rogers, William Pierce
b. 1915 Price, Dennis
b. 1916 Worth, Irene
b. 1925 Blyden, Larry
b. 1925 Chennault, Anna Chan
b. 1927 Fosse, Bob
b. 1929 Carter, June
b. 1929 Lapidus, Ted
b. 1930 Dinitz, Simcha
b. 1930 Eisele, Donn Fulton
b. 1934 Torrey, Bill (William Arthur)
b. 1935 Ferre, Maurice Antonio
b. 1936 Bach, Richard David
b. 1940 Rudolph, Wilma Glodean
b. 1940 Trask, Diana
b. 1943 Levine, James
b. 1946 Shackelford, Ted
b. 1959 Gustafson, Karin
d. 1611 Hudson, Henry
d. 1832 Hall, James, Sir
d. 1836 Mill, James

d. 1868 Vassar, Matthew
d. 1895 Renwick, James
d. 1945 Lake, Simon
d. 1946 Hart, William Surrey
d. 1950 Fels, Samuel Simeon
d. 1955 Carter, Amon Giles
d. 1956 Gliere, Reinhold Moritzovich
d. 1965 Boland, Mary
d. 1967 Bamberger, Julian Maas
d. 1973 Holden, Fay
d. 1975 Priest, Ivy (Maude) Baker
d. 1976 Warneke, Lon(nie)
d. 1980 Gandhi, Sanjay
d. 1980 Still, Clyfford
d. 1983 Cervantes, Alfonso Juan
d. 1985 Kotsching, Walter Maria
d. 1985 McIlhenny, Walter S

June 24
b. 1450 Cabot, John
b. 1542 John of the Cross, Saint
b. 1747 O'Keeffe, John
b. 1763 Josephine
b. 1771 DuPont, Eleuthere Irenee
b. 1788 Blanchard, Thomas
b. 1813 Beecher, Henry Ward
b. 1831 Davis, Rebecca Blaine Harding
b. 1839 Swift, Gustavus Franklin
b. 1842 Bierce, Ambrose Gwinett
b. 1846 Schott, Anton
b. 1848 Adams, Brooks
b. 1856 Mercer, Henry Chapman
b. 1872 Crowninshield, Francis Welch
b. 1881 Randall, James Garfield
b. 1881 Tietjen, Heinz
b. 1883 Hess, Victor Francis
b. 1887 Watson, Mark Skinner
b. 1895 Dempsey, Jack (William Harrison)
b. 1897 Ludwig, Daniel Keith
b. 1899 George, Chief Dan
b. 1900 Austin, Gene
b. 1901 Partch, Harry
b. 1906 Fournier, Pierre
b. 1906 Harris, Phil
b. 1907 Schlumberger, Jean
b. 1907 Sheets, Millard Owen
b. 1909 Cavanna, Betty (Elizabeth Allen)
b. 1910 Kaufman, Irving R
b. 1911 Fangio, Juan Manuel
b. 1911 Sabato, Ernesto
b. 1912 Cousins, Norman
b. 1915 Hoyle, Fred
b. 1916 Ciardi, John Anthony
b. 1916 Hauberg, John Henry
b. 1919 Molinaro, Al
b. 1920 Ernst, Jimmy
b. 1923 Carter, Jack
b. 1927 Edwards, James Burrows
b. 1930 Chabrol, Claude
b. 1931 Casper, Billy (William Earl)
b. 1935 Hamill, "Pete" (William)
b. 1942 Fleetwood, Mick

b. 1942 Lee, Michele
b. 1944 Beck, Jeff
b. 1944 Wood, Chris
b. 1945 Blunstone, Colin
b. 1945 Stove, Betty
b. 1946 Onizuka, Ellison
b. 1949 Allen, Nancy
b. 1964 Suter, Gary
d. 79 AD Vespasian
d. 1637 Peiresc, Nicholas-Claude Fabri de
d. 1643 Hampden, John
d. 1803 Thornton, Matthew
d. 1860 Bonaparte, Jerome
d. 1877 Owen, Robert Dale
d. 1892 Ford, Bob (Robert Newton)
d. 1894 Healy, George Peter Alexander
d. 1908 Cleveland, (Stephen) Grover
d. 1909 Jewett, Sarah Orne
d. 1922 Rathenau, Walter
d. 1928 Blinn, Holbrook
d. 1930 Jewett, Henry
d. 1933 Jones, Matilda Sissieretta Joyner
d. 1946 Hare, James Henry
d. 1957 Bowes, Walter
d. 1959 Starkweather, Charles
d. 1964 Davis, Stuart
d. 1968 Alexander, Hattie Elizabeth
d. 1969 King, Frank
d. 1969 Ley, Willy
d. 1969 Pegler, Westbrook
d. 1972 Delderfield, Ronald Frederick
d. 1976 Cunningham, Imogen
d. 1980 Burpee, David
d. 1980 Kaufman, Boris
d. 1981 Albrand, Martha, pseud.
d. 1981 Ball, Edward
d. 1981 Butler, Paul
d. 1983 Miller, William E
d. 1983 Taft, Charles Phelps
d. 1984 Campbell, Clarence Sutherland

June 25
b. 1788 Pellico, Silvio
b. 1831 Miller, Olive Thorne
b. 1834 Potter, Henry Codman
b. 1852 Gaudi y Cornet, Antonio
b. 1860 Charpentier, Gustave
b. 1865 Henri, Robert
b. 1870 Childers, (Robert) Erskine
b. 1874 O'Neill, Rose Cecil
b. 1886 Arnold, Henry Harley
b. 1886 McIntyre, James Francis
b. 1887 Abbott, George Francis
b. 1893 Greenwood, Charlotte
b. 1894 Oberlith, Hermann Jules
b. 1894 Sturtzel, Howard Allison
b. 1898 Ascoli, Max
b. 1900 Chapman, John (Arthur)
b. 1900 Mountbatten of Burma, Louis
  Mountbatten, Earl
b. 1902 Rubloff, Arthur
b. 1903 Orwell, George, pseud.

b. 1903 Resnik, Muriel
b. 1903 Revere, Anne
b. 1903 Tracy, Arthur
b. 1904 Muller-Munk, Peter
b. 1906 Livesey, Roger
b. 1909 Fuchs, Daniel
b. 1911 Powers, Dudley
b. 1912 Cahill, William Thomas
b. 1912 Shapp, Milton J
b. 1915 Hayes, Peter Lind
b. 1916 Saxbe, William Bart
b. 1916 Toynbee, Philip (Theodore Philip)
b. 1921 Franca, Celia
b. 1923 Gilman, Dorothy
b. 1924 Lumet, Sidney
b. 1925 Briley, John Richard
b. 1925 Lockhart, June
b. 1927 Freedman, Gerald
b. 1928 Culliford, "Peyo" (Pierre)
b. 1929 Carle, Eric
b. 1933 Meredith, James Howard
b. 1937 Morgan, Marabel
b. 1942 Miller, James Clifford, III
b. 1942 Reed, Willis
b. 1942 Tremblay, Michel
b. 1945 Simon, Carly
b. 1946 Lanier, Allen
b. 1948 Walker, Jimmie (James Carter)
b. 1949 George, Phyllis
b. 1954 Lessard, Mario
b. 1963 Michael, George
d. 1634 Marston, John
d. 1767 Telemann, Georg Philipp
d. 1822 Hoffmann, Ernst Theodor
   Amadeus
d. 1830 George IV
d. 1830 McDowell, Ephraim
d. 1876 Cummins, George David
d. 1876 Custer, George Armstrong
d. 1879 Cooke, William Fothergil, Sir
d. 1889 Hayes, Lucy Webb
d. 1897 Oliphant, Margaret
d. 1898 Cohn, Ferdinand Julius
d. 1906 White, Stanford
d. 1912 Alma-Tadema, Lawrence, Sir
d. 1916 Eakins, Thomas
d. 1918 Beckley, Jake (Jacob Peter)
d. 1931 Saunders, William Laurence
d. 1937 Clive, Colin
d. 1947 Shaw, Albert
d. 1956 Arlen, Michael
d. 1956 King, Ernest Joseph
d. 1961 Ferguson, Miriam Amanda
d. 1969 Dix, Otto
d. 1971 Boyd-Orr, John Boyd Orr, Baron
d. 1971 Orr, John Boyd
d. 1972 Fleischer, Nat(haniel S)
d. 1972 McKenney, Ruth
d. 1975 Cowdry, Edmund Vincent
d. 1976 Mercer, Johnny
d. 1977 Kaufman, Sue

d. 1979 Halsman, Philippe
d. 1979 Hoyt, Palmer (Edwin Palmer)
d. 1980 Grattan, Clinton Hartley
d. 1983 Ginastera, Alberto
d. 1983 Monroe, Marion
d. 1984 Foucault, Michel

June 26
b. 1741 Langdon, John
b. 1742 Middleton, Arthur
b. 1812 Palmer, Frances Flora Bond
b. 1819 Doubleday, Abner
b. 1824 Kelvin, William Thomson, Baron
b. 1854 Borden, Robert Laird, Sir
b. 1865 Berenson, Bernard
b. 1875 Stracciari, Riccardo
b. 1881 Shambaugh, Jessie Field
b. 1885 Hempel, Frieda
b. 1891 Cohen, Octavus Roy
b. 1891 Howard, Sidney Coe
b. 1892 Buck, Pearl S(ydenstricker)
b. 1893 Broonzy, "Big Bill"
b. 1894 Eagels, Jeanne
b. 1894 Kapitsa, Pyotr
b. 1894 Lovejoy, Clarence Earle
b. 1898 Messerschmitt, Willy (Wilhelm)
b. 1899 Falkner, Murry Charles
b. 1900 Crooks, Richard Alexander
b. 1901 Symington, (William) Stuart
b. 1902 Brico, Antonia
b. 1902 Lear, William Powell
b. 1903 Herman, "Babe" (Floyd Caves)
b. 1904 Carroll, Gladys Hasty
b. 1904 Lorre, Peter
b. 1905 Ward, Lynd
b. 1906 Wolfenden, John Frederick, Sir
b. 1908 Knowland, William Fife
b. 1911 Levi, Edward Hirsch
b. 1912 Didrikson, "Babe" (Mildred)
b. 1914 Maltby, Richard E
b. 1914 Windgassen, Wolfgang Friedrich
   Hermann
b. 1915 Zolotow, Charlotte Shapiro
b. 1916 Dreier, Alex
b. 1916 Taddei, Giuseppe
b. 1919 Lasker, Joe
b. 1920 Farley, Walter
b. 1920 Hambro, Leonid
b. 1922 Parker, Eleanor
b. 1925 Brenner, Barbara Johnes
b. 1925 Burch, Robert Joseph
b. 1928 Druckman, Jacob Raphael
b. 1929 Glaser, Milton
b. 1931 Wilson, Colin Henry
b. 1933 Abbado, Claudio
b. 1934 Raab, Selwyn
b. 1934 Tunney, John Varick
b. 1936 Greer, Hal (Harold Everett)
b. 1939 Robb, Charles Spittal
b. 1940 Davis, Billy, Jr.
b. 1946 Bellwood, Pamela
d. 1541 Pizarro, Francisco

b. 1892 Campbell, Clifford, Sir
b. 1892 Gordon, Max
b. 1894 Forbes, Esther
b. 1894 Nicoll, (John Ramsay) Allardyce
b. 1901 Bruce, Ailsa Mellon
b. 1902 Dillinger, John Herbert
b. 1904 Rollini, Adrian
b. 1905 Binns, Joseph Patterson
b. 1905 Montagu, Ashley Montague Francis
b. 1906 Mayer, Maria Goeppert
b. 1907 Bull, Odd
b. 1909 Ambler, Eric
b. 1912 Celibidache, Sergiu
b. 1912 Coons, Albert Hewett
b. 1914 Arieti, Silvano
b. 1914 Flatt, Lester Raymond
b. 1914 Seymour, Dan
b. 1914 Trifa, Valerian
b. 1920 Hotchner, Aaron Edward
b. 1924 Dolci, Danilo
b. 1925 Klebe, Giselher
b. 1926 Booth, George
b. 1927 Evans, Harold Matthew
b. 1928 Brooks, Mel
b. 1934 Levin, Carl Milton
b. 1937 Luciano, Ron(ald Michael)
b. 1943 Johanson, Donald Carl
b. 1943 Laguna, Ismael
b. 1946 Radner, Gilda
b. 1948 Maravich, Pete
b. 1949 Baylor, Don Edward
b. 1959 Balukas, Jean
b. 1960 Elway, John Albert
b. 1969 Brisebois, Danielle
d. 1836 Madison, James
d. 1855 Raglan, Fitzroy James Henry Somerset, Baron
d. 1889 Mitchell, Maria
d. 1904 Emmett, Daniel Decatur
d. 1914 Franz Ferdinand
d. 1929 Carpenter, Edward
d. 1930 Schenck, Joe (Joseph T)
d. 1936 Berkman, Alexander
d. 1940 Balbo, Italo
d. 1941 Carle, Richard
d. 1946 Perry, Antoinette
d. 1955 Ljungberg, Gota
d. 1958 Noyes, Alfred
d. 1959 Shaver, Dorothy
d. 1962 Cochrane, Mickey (Gordon Stanley)
d. 1963 Baker, Frank (John Franklin)
d. 1965 Nichols, "Red" (Ernest Loring)
d. 1971 Binns, Archie Fred
d. 1971 Stangl, Franz Paul
d. 1974 Bush, Vannevar
d. 1975 Doxiadis, Constantinos Apostolos
d. 1975 Serling, Rod
d. 1975 Stevenson, Coke Robert
d. 1976 Baker, Stanley, Sir

d. 1978 DuPont, Clifford Walter
d. 1979 Cousteau, Philippe
d. 1979 Schulberg, Stuart
d. 1980 Douglas, Helen Mary Gahagan
d. 1980 Iturbi, Jose
d. 1981 Beheshti, Mohammad, Ayatollah
d. 1981 Fox, Terry (Terrance Stanley)
d. 1982 Mills, Harry
d. 1984 Astor, Gavin
d. 1984 Yadin, Yigael
d. 1985 Ward, Lynd

June 29
b. 1577 Rubens, Peter Paul, Sir
b. 1721 Kalb, Johann de
b. 1798 Leopardi, Giacomo
b. 1830 Ward, J(ohn) Q(uincy) A(dams)
b. 1835 Thaxter, Celia
b. 1852 McMaster, John Bach
b. 1858 Goethals, George Washington
b. 1861 Mayo, William James
b. 1863 Robinson, James Harvey
b. 1865 Borah, William E
b. 1868 Hale, George Ellery
b. 1874 Tetrazzini, Luisa
b. 1886 Cheney, Sheldon Warren
b. 1886 Schuman, Robert
b. 1886 Van Der Zee, James
b. 1900 Saint-Exupery, Antoine (Jean Baptiste Marie Roger) de
b. 1901 Eddy, Nelson
b. 1901 Inescort, Frieda
b. 1903 Voelker, John Donaldson
b. 1905 Gardner, Ed(ward Francis)
b. 1907 Davis, Joan
b. 1907 O'Dwyer, Paul
b. 1908 Anderson, Leroy
b. 1910 Loesser, Frank
b. 1911 Bernhard, Prince
b. 1911 Carter, Edward William
b. 1911 Herrmann, Bernard
b. 1912 Toland, John Willard
b. 1913 Meadows, Earle
b. 1914 Kubelik, Rafael
b. 1915 Trout, "Dizzy" (Paul Howard)
b. 1915 Warrick, Ruth
b. 1918 Lyng, Richard E
b. 1919 Pickens, "Slim"
b. 1920 Harryhausen, Ray
b. 1922 Vessey, John William, Jr.
b. 1924 Walford, Roy L(ee, Jr.)
b. 1928 Bannen, Ian
b. 1930 Evans, Bob (Robert)
b. 1930 Fallaci, Oriana
b. 1933 Sutton, Carol
b. 1936 Killebrew, Harmon Clayton
b. 1941 Carmichael, Stokely
b. 1943 Fass, Bob
b. 1944 Humphrey, Claude B
b. 1945 Little Eva
b. 1946 Furstenberg, Egon von
b. 1949 Dierdorf, Dan(iel Lee)

b. 1858 Metcalf, Willard L
b. 1858 Stephens, Alice Barber
b. 1861 Clarkson, John Gibson
b. 1872 Bleriot, Louis
b. 1873 Guy-Blanche, Alice
b. 1877 Davis, Benjamin Oliver
b. 1882 Glaspell, Susan Keating
b. 1890 Morgan, Frank
b. 1892 Cain, James Mallahan
b. 1892 Lurcat, Jean Marie
b. 1893 Parker, Daniel Francis
b. 1893 White, Walter Francis
b. 1897 Barry, Tom
b. 1897 Bickerman, Elias Joseph
b. 1898 Lyons, Eugene
b. 1899 Laughton, Charles
b. 1899 Tsatsos, Constantinos
b. 1900 Dorsey, Thomas Andrew
b. 1901 Phillips, Irna
b. 1902 Cohen, Myron
b. 1902 Sert, Jose Luis
b. 1902 Wyler, William
b. 1903 Emerson, Gladys Anderson
b. 1904 Calderone, Mary Steichen
b. 1906 Calder, Peter Ritchie
b. 1907 Bolotowsky, Ilya
b. 1907 Stern, Bill (William)
b. 1908 Ali, Ahmed
b. 1908 Lauder, Estee
b. 1909 Evans, Madge (Margherita)
b. 1911 Rey, Alvino
b. 1912 Matheson, Murray
b. 1912 Sherwood, Roberta
b. 1913 Sinclair, Jo, pseud.
b. 1915 Stafford, Jean
b. 1916 DeHavilland, Olivia
b. 1916 Shklovsky, Iosif Samvilovitch
b. 1921 Gherardi, Gherardo
b. 1921 Khama, Seretse M
b. 1922 Rampal, Jean-Pierre
b. 1925 Granger, Farley
b. 1926 Henze, Hans Werner
b. 1928 Denoff, Sam
b. 1931 Caron, Leslie Clare Margaret
b. 1934 Farr, Jamie
b. 1934 Marsh, Jean
b. 1934 Pollack, Sydney
b. 1935 Skorpen, Liespel Moak
b. 1936 Amos, Wally
b. 1940 Jones, Charles A, Jr.
b. 1941 Gilbert, Rod(rique Gabriel)
b. 1941 Quinn, Sally
b. 1941 Tharp, Twyla
b. 1942 Black, Karen
b. 1942 Bujold, Genevieve
b. 1945 Harry, Debbie (Deborah Ann)
b. 1946 Kovic, Ron
b. 1951 Anderson, Daryl
b. 1952 Aykroyd, Dan(iel Edward)
b. 1952 Shutt, Steve (Stephen John)
b. 1954 Hanauer, "Chip" (Lee Edward)

b. 1957 Patterson, Lorna
b. 1958 Lieberman, Nancy
b. 1960 King, Evelyn
b. 1961 Diana, Princess of Wales
b. 1961 Lewis, Carl (Frederick Carlton)
d. 1614 Casaubon, Isaac
d. 1860 Goodyear, Charles
d. 1884 Pinkerton, Allan
d. 1896 Stowe, Harriet (Elizabeth) Beecher
d. 1903 Henley, William Ernest
d. 1905 Hay, John Milton
d. 1906 Garcia, Manuel Patricio
       Rodriguez, II
d. 1912 Quimby, Harriet
d. 1925 Satie, Erik
d. 1925 Tryon, Dwight William
d. 1928 Hopwood, Avery
d. 1940 Turpin, Ben
d. 1942 Daudet, Leon
d. 1950 Saarinen, Eliel
d. 1952 Rosenbach, Abraham Simon Wolf
d. 1958 Laban, Rudolf von
d. 1963 Chautemps, Camille
d. 1964 Monteux, Pierre
d. 1964 Pound, Roscoe
d. 1965 Ruark, Robert Chester
d. 1965 Thornhill, Claude
d. 1971 Bragg, William Lawrence, Sir
d. 1973 Hammond, Laurens
d. 1974 Peron, Juan
d. 1980 Snow, C(harles) P(ercy), Sir
d. 1981 Breuer, Marcel Lajos
d. 1981 Daniel, Dan(iel)
d. 1981 Voskovec, George
d. 1983 Copeland, Lammot du Pont
d. 1983 Fuller, "Bucky" (Richard
       Buckminster)
d. 1983 Hoffman, Julius Jennings
d. 1985 Sterling, John Ewart Wallace
d. 1986 Wells, Edward

July 2
b. 1489 Cranmer, Thomas
b. 1714 Gluck, Christoph Wilibald
b. 1724 Klopstock, Friedrich Gottlieb
b. 1810 Toombs, Robert Augustus
b. 1836 Schnorr, Ludwig, von Carolsfeld
b. 1855 Barron, Clarence Walker
b. 1862 Bragg, William Henry, Sir
b. 1877 Hesse, Hermann
b. 1878 Wright, Henry
b. 1883 Kafka, Franz
b. 1888 Boyd, James
b. 1888 Waksman, Selman Abraham
b. 1892 Seyss-Inquart, Artur von
b. 1894 Kertesz, Andre
b. 1894 Treacher, Arthur
b. 1898 McAuliffe, Anthony Clement
b. 1900 Guthrie, Tyrone
b. 1903 Douglas-Home, Alexander
       Frederick
b. 1903 Harris, Harwell Hamilton

d. 1966 Taylor, (Joseph) Deems
d. 1969 Jones, Brian
d. 1970 Briggs, Walter Owen, Jr.
d. 1970 Keyes, Frances Parkinson
d. 1970 McGraw, Harold Whittlesey, Sr.
d. 1970 Newman, Barnett
d. 1971 Morrison, Jim (James Douglas)
d. 1972 Stark, Abe
d. 1973 Ancerl, Karel
d. 1973 Grable, Betty
d. 1976 Netanyahu, Yonatan
d. 1978 Breech, Ernest Robert
d. 1978 Daly, James
d. 1979 Van Slyke, Helen Lenore Vogt
d. 1981 Berman, Emile Zola
d. 1981 Martin, Ross
d. 1986 Bingham, Jonathan Brewster
d. 1986 Vallee, Rudy (Herbert Prior)

July 4

b. 1753 Blanchard, Francois
b. 1804 Hawthorne, Nathaniel
b. 1807 Garibaldi, Guiseppe
b. 1816 Walker, Hiram
b. 1819 Squibb, Edward Robinson
b. 1826 Foster, Stephen Collins
b. 1845 Barnardo, Thomas John
b. 1845 Lewis, Edmonia
b. 1847 Bailey, James Anthony
b. 1859 Welch, Mickey (Michael Francis)
b. 1862 Klimt, Gustav
b. 1863 Juch, Emma
b. 1867 Mather, Stephen Tyng
b. 1870 Moffatt, James
b. 1872 Coolidge, (John) Calvin
b. 1876 Farnum, William
b. 1876 Loeb, Sophia Irene Simon
b. 1879 Gaubert, Philippe
b. 1880 Rooney, Pat
b. 1883 Goldberg, Rube (Reuben Lucius)
b. 1884 Trendle, George Washington
b. 1885 Mayer, L(ouis) B(urt)
b. 1888 Armetta, Henry
b. 1889 Chotzinoff, Samuel
b. 1894 Carlson, "Doc" (Harold Clifford)
b. 1895 Caesar, Irving
b. 1899 Warren, Austin
b. 1900 Armstrong, Louis Daniel
b. 1900 Baddeley, Angela (Madeleine
    Angela Clinton)
b. 1901 Lawrence, Gertrude
b. 1902 Dwyer, Florence Price
b. 1902 Lansky, Meyer
b. 1902 Murphy, George Lloyd
b. 1903 Saperstein, Abraham
b. 1903 Trohan, Walter
b. 1904 Keane, Mary Nesta
b. 1905 Trilling, Lionel
b. 1907 Taubman, Howard (Hyman
    Howard)
b. 1908 Pennell, Joseph Stanley
b. 1910 Templeton, Alec

b. 1911 Miller, Mitch(ell William)
b. 1911 Moninari-Pradelli, Francesco
b. 1912 Graham, Virginia
b. 1916 Tokyo Rose
b. 1916 Toon, Malcolm
b. 1918 Landers, Ann
b. 1918 Van Buren, Abigail
b. 1919 Willis, Mary
b. 1920 Garraty, John Arthur
b. 1921 Debreu, Gerard
b. 1924 Saint, Eva Marie
b. 1927 Simon, (Marvin) Neil
b. 1928 Berberian, Cathy
b. 1928 Boyd, Stephen
b. 1928 Lollobrigida, Gina
b. 1929 Davis, Al(len)
b. 1929 Tanner, Chuck (Charles William,
    Jr.)
b. 1930 Steinbrenner, George Michael, III
b. 1931 Hudson, Joseph Lowthian, Jr.
b. 1934 Welland, Colin
b. 1938 Withers, Bill
b. 1941 Phelps, "Digger" (Richard)
b. 1942 Lanier, Hal (Harold Clifton)
b. 1943 Rivera, Geraldo
b. 1948 Arnoux, Rene Alexandre
b. 1948 Dale, Clamma Churita
b. 1955 Waite, John
b. 1962 Shriver, Pam(ela Howard)
b. 1977 Victoria Ingrid Alice Desiree
d. 1623 Byrd, William
d. 1627 Middleton, Thomas
d. 1761 Richardson, Samuel
d. 1826 Adams, John
d. 1826 Jefferson, Thomas
d. 1831 Monroe, James
d. 1848 Chateaubriand, Francois Rene de
d. 1857 Marcy, William Learned
d. 1880 Ripley, George
d. 1891 Hamlin, Hannibal
d. 1901 Fiske, John
d. 1910 Schiaparelli, Giovanni
d. 1916 Seeger, Alan
d. 1934 Bialik, Chaim Nachman
d. 1934 Curie, Marie
d. 1938 Lenglen, Suzanne
d. 1961 Celine, Louis-Ferdinand
d. 1961 Destouches, Louis-Ferdinand
d. 1962 Christie, John
d. 1963 Foyle, William Alfred
d. 1965 Bennett, Constance Campbell
d. 1969 Kelly, Orie R
d. 1970 Vanderbilt, Harold Stirling
d. 1971 Bowra, Maurice, Sir
d. 1971 Derleth, August
d. 1974 Heyer, Georgette
d. 1974 Husseini, Haj Amin
d. 1974 Webb, Del(bert Eugene)
d. 1975 Beatty, Morgan
d. 1979 Kroeber, Theodora Kracaw
d. 1980 Bateson, Gregory

d. 1981 Langer, Walter C
d. 1982 Guzman, Antonio
d. 1982 Sullivan, Daniel P
d. 1984 Hathaway, Starke R
d. 1985 DeQuay, Jan E
d. 1985 Visser T Hooft, Willem Adolf
d. 1986 Mack, Peter

July 5
b. 1709 Silhouette, Etienne de
b. 1755 Siddons, Sarah Kemble
b. 1756 Rush, William
b. 1781 Raffles, Thomas Stamford, Sir
b. 1794 Graham, Sylvester W
b. 1801 Farragut, David Glasgow
b. 1803 Borrow, George Henry
b. 1810 Barnum, P(hineas) T(aylor)
b. 1841 Whitney, William Collins
b. 1853 Rhodes, Cecil John
b. 1872 Herriot, Edouard
b. 1877 Landowska, Wanda
b. 1878 Gilman, Lawrence
b. 1878 Holbrooke, Josef
b. 1879 Davis, Dwight Filley
b. 1879 Jadlowker, Hermann
b. 1880 Kubelik, Jan
b. 1881 Landis, Walter Savage
b. 1888 Gasser, Herbert Spencer
b. 1889 Cocteau, Jean
b. 1890 Allen, Frederick Lewis
b. 1897 Regan, Theodore M, Jr.
b. 1897 Woldike, Mogens
b. 1898 Condie, Richard P
b. 1900 Achard, Marcel
b. 1900 Gaunt, William
b. 1902 Lodge, Henry Cabot, Jr.
b. 1903 Fischer, Irwin
b. 1904 Mayr, Ernst Walter
b. 1904 Stone, Milburn
b. 1908 Greeley, Dana McLean
b. 1909 Gromyko, Andrei Andreevich
b. 1911 Pompidou, Georges Jean Raymond
b. 1912 David, Mack
b. 1915 Paley, Barbara Cushing
b. 1918 Rochberg, George
b. 1921 Merrifield, R(obert) Bruce
b. 1923 McKay, John H
b. 1924 Starker, Janos
b. 1926 Jorge Blanco, Salvador
b. 1928 Maurey, Pierre
b. 1928 Oates, Warren
b. 1929 Carruthers, John(ny)
b. 1932 Backe, John David
b. 1932 Navasky, Victor Saul
b. 1937 Hayward, Brooke
b. 1937 Knight, Shirley
b. 1938 Goldwater, Barry Morris, Jr.
b. 1942 Feld, Eliot
b. 1944 Devine, Donald
b. 1944 Robertson, "Robbie" (Jaime)
b. 1946 Johnson, Pierre Marc
b. 1947 Kunz, George

b. 1948 Eisenhower, Julie Nixon
b. 1951 Gossage, "Goose" (Richard Michael)
b. 1951 Lewis, Huey
d. 1826 Raffles, Thomas Stamford, Sir
d. 1843 Macintosh, Charles
d. 1884 Masse, Victor
d. 1894 Layard, Austin Henry, Sir
d. 1899 Congreve, Richard
d. 1900 Barnard, Henry
d. 1908 Lie, Jonas (Laurite Idemil)
d. 1935 Herford, Oliver
d. 1937 Greenwood, Chester
d. 1945 Curtin, John
d. 1948 Bernanos, Georges
d. 1948 Landis, Carole
d. 1952 Skipworth, Alison
d. 1958 Crothers, Rachel
d. 1960 Partridge, Bellamy
d. 1962 Niebuhr, Helmut Richard
d. 1965 Rubirosa, Porfirio
d. 1966 Hevesy, George de
d. 1967 Barton, Bruce
d. 1969 Alexander, Ben (Nicholas Benton)
d. 1969 Backhaus, Wilhelm
d. 1969 Gropius, Walter Adolf
d. 1969 Mboya, Tom (Thomas Joseph)
d. 1969 McCarey, Leo
d. 1973 Hafey, "Chick" (Charles James)
d. 1974 Ransom, John Crowe
d. 1975 Dalla Rizza, Gilda
d. 1977 Gerhardi, William Alexander
d. 1981 Urrutia Lleo, Manuel
d. 1982 Jagel, Frederick
d. 1982 Mueller, Reuben Herbert
d. 1983 Dejongh, Peter
d. 1983 James, Harry
d. 1984 Bloom, Julius
d. 1986 Gemmell, Alan

July 6
b. 1747 Jones, John Paul
b. 1755 Flaxman, John
b. 1766 Wilson, Alexander
b. 1825 Rogers, Randolph
b. 1831 Gilman, Daniel Coit
b. 1832 Maximilian
b. 1858 Hobson, John Atkinson
b. 1859 Heidenstam, Carl Gustaf Verner von
b. 1866 Potter, Beatrix (Helen Beatrix)
b. 1876 Cobb, Will D
b. 1883 Morgan, Ralph
b. 1884 Dunoyer de Segonzac, Andre
b. 1884 Vanderbilt, Harold Stirling
b. 1888 Kellerman, Annette
b. 1891 O'Neill, Steve (Stephen Francis)
b. 1892 Yellen, Jack
b. 1895 Stuckgold, Grete Schmeidt
b. 1897 Damon, Ralph Shepard
b. 1899 Eberhart, Mignon Good
b. 1903 Theorell, (Axel) Hugh Teodor

b. 1913 Thomas, Gwyn
b. 1914 Abbas, Khwaja Ahmad
b. 1915 Andrews, LaVerne
b. 1917 Kirsten, Dorothy
b. 1918 Cabot, Sebastian
b. 1918 List, Eugene
b. 1921 Reagan, Nancy Davis
b. 1923 Jaruzelski, Wojciech Witold
b. 1925 Griffin, Merv(yn)
b. 1925 Haley, Bill (William John Clifford, Jr.)
b. 1925 O'Donnell, Cathy
b. 1927 Cabot, Susan
b. 1927 Leigh, Janet
b. 1927 Paulsen, Pat
b. 1930 Armstrong, George Edward
b. 1930 Skurzynski, Gloria
b. 1932 Reese, Della
b. 1935 Dalai Lama, the 14th Incarnate
b. 1935 Taylor, Arthur Robert
b. 1937 Ashkenazy, Vladimir Davidovich
b. 1937 Beatty, Ned
b. 1937 Head, Bessie
b. 1944 Forsyth, Rosemary
b. 1946 Dryer, Fred (John Frederick)
b. 1946 Stallone, Sylvester (Michael Sylvester)
b. 1946 Ward, Burt
b. 1946 Wyeth, Jamie (James Browning)
b. 1948 Park, Brad (Douglas Bradford)
b. 1952 Hack, Shelley
b. 1954 Randolph, Willie (William Larry, Jr.)
b. 1957 Duguay, Ron(ald)
b. 1957 Ford, Susan Elizabeth
b. 1968 Scarpelli, Glenn
d. 1415 Hus, Jan
d. 1533 Ariosto, Ludovico
d. 1535 More, Thomas, Sir
d. 1802 Morgan, Daniel
d. 1817 Savage, Edward
d. 1835 Marshall, John
d. 1851 Davenport, Thomas
d. 1893 Maupassant, Guy de (Henri Rene Albert Guy de)
d. 1906 Langdell, Christopher Columbus
d. 1916 Redon, Odilon
d. 1918 Mitchel, John Purroy
d. 1931 Acheson, Edward Goodrich
d. 1932 Grahame, Kenneth
d. 1942 Williard, Daniel
d. 1946 Lanvin, Jeanne
d. 1946 Pippin, Horace
d. 1951 Hall, James Norman
d. 1953 Ruffo, Titta
d. 1954 Pascal, Gabriel
d. 1959 Grosz, George Ehrenfried
d. 1960 Bevan, Aneurin
d. 1962 Faulkner, William
d. 1966 Jones, Sam(uel Pond)
d. 1969 Swarthout, Gladys

d. 1971 Armstrong, Louis Daniel
d. 1972 Athenagoras I
d. 1972 DeWilde, Brandon
d. 1973 Klemperer, Otto
d. 1978 Paley, Barbara Cushing
d. 1980 Patrick, Gail
d. 1981 Villa, Luz Corral de
d. 1982 Roa (y Garcia), Raul
d. 1986 Ram, Jagjivan

July 7

b.   Abercrombie, James Smither
b. 1843 Golgi, Camillo
b. 1860 Cahan, Abraham
b. 1860 Mahler, Gustav
b. 1863 Noyes, Frank B
b. 1867 Douglass, Andrew Ellicott
b. 1869 Atterbury, Grosvenor
b. 1876 Carle, Richard
b. 1883 Adams, Frank Ramsay
b. 1884 Feuchtwanger, Lion
b. 1887 Chagall, Marc
b. 1895 Hoffman, Julius Jennings
b. 1899 Cukor, George Dewey
b. 1901 DeSica, Vittorio
b. 1906 Hirschmann, Ira Arthur
b. 1906 Paige, "Satchel" (Leroy Robert)
b. 1907 Heinlein, Robert Anson
b. 1908 Arnow, Harriette Louisa Simpson
b. 1909 Apgar, Virginia
b. 1909 Herman, Billy (William Jennings)
b. 1910 Tunnard, Christopher
b. 1911 Menotti, Gian Carlo
b. 1914 Mayehoff, Eddie
b. 1915 Dominick, Peter Hoyt
b. 1915 Ford, Ruth Elizabeth
b. 1916 Robbie, Joe (Joseph)
b. 1917 O'Brien, Larry (Lawrence Francis)
b. 1918 Paulucci, Jeno Francisco
b. 1919 Kunstler, William Moses
b. 1920 Coleman, William T
b. 1920 Hechinger, Fred Michael
b. 1921 Charles, Ezzard
b. 1921 Wilder, Clinton
b. 1922 Cardin, Pierre
b. 1923 Ciulei, Liviu
b. 1924 Ford, Mary
b. 1926 Rushmore, Robert
b. 1927 Casadesus, Jean
b. 1927 Dixon, Alan John
b. 1927 Severinsen, "Doc" (Carl H)
b. 1928 Edwards, Vince
b. 1930 Jamal, Ahmad
b. 1939 Obraztsova, Elena
b. 1940 Starr, Ringo
b. 1944 Jacklin, Anthony
b. 1944 Steward, Emanuel
b. 1945 Rodford, Jim (James)
b. 1946 Spano, Joe
b. 1949 Duvall, Shelley
b. 1954 Dawson, Andre Nolan
b. 1954 O'Neill, Cherry Boone

d. 1984 Brassai
d. 1985 Cowles, Gardner
d. 1985 Foster, Phil
d. 1985 Hampson, Frank
d. 1985 Kuznets, Simon
d. 1986 Rickover, Hyman George

July 9
b. 1764 Radcliffe, Ann
b. 1766 Perkins, Jacob
b. 1775 Lewis, Matthew Gregory
b. 1811 Parton, Sara Payson Willis
b. 1819 Howe, Elias
b. 1828 Spreckels, Claus
b. 1858 Boas, Franz
b. 1878 Kaltenborn, H(ans) V(on)
b. 1879 Cassou, Jean
b. 1879 Respighi, Ottorino
b. 1887 Chapin, James Ormsbee
b. 1887 Morison, Samuel Eliot
b. 1888 Marks, Simon
b. 1894 Spencer, Percy Le Baron
b. 1894 Thompson, Dorothy
b. 1897 Lyons, Enid Muriel
b. 1897 Wedemeyer, Albert Coady
b. 1900 Schaefer, Rudolph Jay
b. 1901 Cartland, Barbara Hamilton
b. 1905 Campbell, Clarence Sutherland
b. 1907 Klutznick, Philip M
b. 1908 Brown, Paul
b. 1911 Peake, Mervyn Laurence
b. 1915 Diamond, David
b. 1916 Heath, Edward Richard George
b. 1919 Van Slyke, Helen Lenore Vogt
b. 1921 Jones, David Charles
b. 1924 Pennario, Leonard
b. 1926 Dale, Alan
b. 1927 Ames, Ed(mund Dantes)
b. 1928 Hall, Donald Joyce
b. 1929 Hassan II
b. 1929 Hazelwood, Lee
b. 1929 Post, Wally (Walter Charles)
b. 1932 Rumsfeld, Donald
b. 1933 Smith, Hedrick Laurence
b. 1934 Graves, Michael
b. 1936 Hampton, James
b. 1936 Jordan, June Meyer
b. 1937 Hockney, David
b. 1941 Aroldingen, Karin von
b. 1943 Edmiston, Mark Morton
b. 1946 Stone, George
b. 1947 Simpson, O(renthal) J(ames)
b. 1954 Sledge, Debbie
b. 1955 Wilson, Willie James
b. 1956 Hanks, Tom
d. 1747 Bononcini, Giovanni Battista
d. 1797 Burke, Edmund
d. 1828 Stuart, Gilbert Charles
d. 1843 Allston, Washington
d. 1850 Taylor, Zachary
d. 1856 Avogadro, Amedeo, Conte di
Quaregna

d. 1887 Merriam, Charles
d. 1923 Day, William Rufus
d. 1926 Lathrop, Rose Hawthorne
d. 1927 Drew, John
d. 1932 Gillette, King Camp
d. 1936 Wright, Henry
d. 1938 Cardozo, Benjamin Nathan
d. 1943 Beers, Clifford Whittingham
d. 1951 Heilmann, Harry Edwin
d. 1951 VanAlstyne, Egbert Anson
d. 1961 Marshal, Alan
d. 1968 Cadogan, Alexander George
　　　 Montague, Sir
d. 1968 Fisher, Vardis
d. 1970 Friendly, Edwin Samson
d. 1974 Brittain, Harry Ernest, Sir
d. 1974 Warren, Earl
d. 1976 Gingrich, Arnold
d. 1976 Yawkey, Thomas Austin
d. 1977 Eiseley, Loren Corey
d. 1977 Paul, Alice
d. 1979 Skinner, Cornelia Otis
d. 1979 Wilding, Michael
d. 1981 Levin, Meyer
d. 1982 Manone, "Wingy" (Joseph)
d. 1984 Hurd, Peter
d. 1984 Thompson, Randall
d. 1985 Charlotte Aldegonde E M
　　　 Wilhelmine

July 10
b. 1509 Calvin, John
b. 1723 Blackstone, William, Sir
b. 1792 Dallas, George Mifflin
b. 1792 Marryat, Frederick
b. 1802 Chambers, Robert
b. 1824 King, Richard
b. 1831 Pissarro, Camille Jacob
b. 1832 Arnold, Edwin
b. 1834 Whistler, James Abbott McNeill
b. 1835 Wieniawski, Henri
b. 1839 Busch, Adolphus
b. 1844 Materna, Amalia
b. 1852 Chalmers, William James
b. 1856 Tesla, Nikola
b. 1861 Paine, Albert Bigelow
b. 1867 Dunne, Finley Peter
b. 1871 Proust, Marcel
b. 1875 Bentley, Edmund Clerihew
b. 1875 Bethune, Mary McLeod
b. 1881 Richberg, Donald R(andall)
b. 1882 Hogg, Ima
b. 1884 Wood, Samuel Grosvenor
b. 1885 O'Hara, Mary
b. 1888 Chirico, Giorgio de
b. 1888 McNamee, Graham
b. 1889 Sissle, Noble
b. 1891 Tugwell, Rexford Guy
b. 1894 McHugh, Jimmy (James)
b. 1895 Goldmann, Nahum
b. 1895 Orff, Carl
b. 1896 Summerville, "Slim" (George J)

b. 1897 Brosio, Manilo Giovanni
b. 1897 Gilbert, John
b. 1897 Goodrich, Lloyd
b. 1899 Conkle, Ellsworth Prouty
b. 1900 Cole, Kenneth Stewart
b. 1902 Alder, Kurt
b. 1905 Gomez, Thomas
b. 1907 Stignani, Ebe
b. 1910 Bunting, Mary Ingraham
b. 1913 Welitsch, Ljuba
b. 1914 Shuster, Joe
b. 1915 Connolly, Mike
b. 1916 Provensen, Martin
b. 1917 Gabor, Magda
b. 1920 Brinkley, David McClure
b. 1921 Donnell, Jeff (Jean Marie)
b. 1921 La Motta, Jake (Jacob)
b. 1923 Hamner, Earl Henry, Jr.
b. 1923 Kerr, (Bridget) Jean Collins
b. 1923 Kerr, Jean
b. 1926 Banzer-Suarez, Hugo
b. 1926 Gwynne, Fred
b. 1928 Buffet, Bernard
b. 1931 Adams, Nick
b. 1933 Hatcher, Richard Gordon
b. 1933 Herman, Jerry
b. 1936 Boyer, Herbert Wayne
b. 1942 Millar, Jeff(rey) Lynn
b. 1943 Ashe, Arthur
b. 1945 Glass, Ron
b. 1945 Wade, Virginia
b. 1947 Guthrie, Arlo
b. 1960 Craig, Roger Timothy
d. 1099 Cid, El
d. 1686 Fell, John
d. 1863 Moore, Clement Clarke
d. 1884 Morphy, Paul Charles
d. 1886 Brown, Henry Kirke
d. 1889 Tyler, Julia Gardiner
d. 1931 Bates, William Horatio
d. 1933 Urban, Joseph Maria
d. 1940 Tovey, Donald Francis, Sir
d. 1941 Gaubert, Philippe
d. 1941 Morton, "Jelly Roll" (Joseph Ferdinand)
d. 1943 Schlesinger, Frank
d. 1944 Pissaro, Lucien
d. 1946 Hillman, Sidney
d. 1947 Rider-Kelsey, Corinne
d. 1949 Johnston, Frank H
d. 1953 Homer, Sidney
d. 1957 Asch, Sholem
d. 1965 Audiberti, Jacques
d. 1966 Hoffman, Malvina
d. 1968 Fitts, Dudley
d. 1970 Benediktsson, Bjarni
d. 1971 Bronfman, Samuel
d. 1972 Madeira, Jean
d. 1972 Weede, Robert
d. 1973 Brown, Dean

d. 1973 Warburg, Frederick Marcus
d. 1978 Rockefeller, John D(avison), III
d. 1979 Fiedler, Arthur
d. 1980 Krumgold, Joseph
d. 1982 Jeritza, Maria
d. 1983 Egk, Werner
d. 1985 Muller, Hilgard
d. 1986 Le Duan
d. 1986 Vlasic, Joseph

July 11
b. 1723 Marmontel, Jean Francois
b. 1754 Bowdler, Thomas
b. 1767 Adams, John Quincy
b. 1807 Tichatschek, Joseph
b. 1808 Reed, Henry Hope
b. 1811 Grove, William Robert, Sir
b. 1819 Warner, Susan Bogert
b. 1821 Feuillet, Octave
b. 1838 Wanamaker, John
b. 1846 Bloy, Leon Marie
b. 1854 Barrymore, Georgina Emma Drew
b. 1861 Norris, George William
b. 1876 Jacob, Max
b. 1880 Rankin, Jeannette
b. 1881 Bloch, Alexander
b. 1881 Kelland, Clarence Budington
b. 1890 O'Dwyer, William
b. 1890 Tedder, Arthur William Tedder, Baron
b. 1892 Mitchell, Thomas
b. 1894 Wanger, Walter
b. 1897 Connor, "Bull" (Theophilus Eugene)
b. 1899 Solomon, Samuel Joseph
b. 1899 White, E(lwyn) B(rooks)
b. 1904 Haworth, Leland John
b. 1906 Von Zell, Harry
b. 1907 Lea, Tom
b. 1910 Blane, Sally
b. 1912 Barry, Donald
b. 1913 Busia, Kofi A
b. 1916 Whitlam, Edward Gough
b. 1920 Brynner, Yul
b. 1922 TerHorst, Jerald Franklin
b. 1923 Barry, Daniel
b. 1925 Dobbs, Mattiwilda
b. 1925 Gedda, Nicolai
b. 1926 Buechner, Frederick
b. 1927 Maiman, Theodore
b. 1927 Somers, Brett
b. 1929 Prey, Hermann
b. 1931 Dalton, John Nichols
b. 1931 Hunter, Tab
b. 1934 Allison, Bob (William Robert)
b. 1944 Hudson, Lou
b. 1951 Pointer, Bonnie
b. 1952 Barber, Bill (William Charles)
b. 1953 Spinks, Leon
b. 1958 Lester, Mark
d. 1774 Johnson, William, Sir
d. 1804 Hamilton, Alexander

d. 1806 Smith, James
d. 1909 Newcomb, Simon
d. 1926 Bell, Gertrude Margaret
d. 1937 Gershwin, George
d. 1941 Evans, Arthur John, Sir
d. 1946 Nash, Paul
d. 1950 DeSylva, "Buddy" (George Gard)
d. 1952 Leonard, "Dutch" (Hubert Benjamin)
d. 1957 Aga Khan III
d. 1962 Hutton, Edward F
d. 1963 Kalmus, Herbert Thomas
d. 1964 Thorez, Maurice
d. 1965 Collins, Ray
d. 1966 Schwartz, Delmore
d. 1971 Campbell, John W
d. 1973 Ryan, Robert (Bushnell)
d. 1974 Lagerkvist, Par
d. 1975 Cordier, Andrew Wellington
d. 1975 Johnson, Crockett
d. 1976 Trotta, Maurice S
d. 1979 Crockett, James Underwood
d. 1983 MacDonald, Ross, pseud.

July 12
b. 100 BC Julius Caesar
b. 1730 Wedgwood, Josiah
b. 1813 Bernard, Claude
b. 1817 Thoreau, Henry David
b. 1824 Boudin, Eugene Louis
b. 1825 Stoddard, Richard Henry
b. 1840 Altman, Benjamin
b. 1842 Kellogg, Clara Louise
b. 1849 Osler, William, Sir
b. 1854 Eastman, George
b. 1878 Bloch, Claude Charles
b. 1879 Zuppke, Robert C
b. 1882 Browning, Tod
b. 1884 Modigliani, Amedeo
b. 1886 Bax, Clifford
b. 1886 Hersholt, Jean
b. 1889 Friedman, Max
b. 1892 Clarke, Gilmore David
b. 1893 Brain, Aubrey
b. 1894 Stromberg, Hunt
b. 1895 Flagstad, Kirsten
b. 1895 Hammerstein, Oscar, II
b. 1899 Fellig, Arthur
b. 1902 Julesberg, Elizabeth Rider Montgomery
b. 1904 Neruda, Pablo
b. 1908 Berle, Milton
b. 1909 Zim, Herbert Spencer
b. 1910 Faye, Joey
b. 1912 Bradley, Will
b. 1912 Deutsch, Karl Wolfgang
b. 1913 Oursler, William Charles
b. 1916 Curtis, Ken
b. 1916 Taylor, Sam
b. 1917 Wyeth, Andrew
b. 1919 Ralston, Vera
b. 1920 Andes, "Keith" (John Charles)

b. 1920 Berton, Pierre
b. 1922 Hatfield, Mark Odom
b. 1922 MacGregor, Clark
b. 1923 Fields, Freddie
b. 1923 Jenkins, Paul
b. 1925 Smith, Roger Bonham
b. 1926 Crosby, John
b. 1930 Pinsent, Gordon Edward
b. 1933 Westlake, Donald E(dwin)
b. 1934 Cliburn, Van (Harvey Lavan, Jr.)
b. 1937 Cosby, Bill
b. 1937 McFarlane, Robert Carl
b. 1941 Lahr, John
b. 1941 Parsons, Benny
b. 1942 Frawley, Dennis
b. 1942 Stoltzman, Richard Leslie
b. 1943 McVie, Christine Perfect
b. 1943 Silas, Paul
b. 1944 Nicholas, Denise
b. 1948 Egan, Walter Lindsay
b. 1948 Simmons, Richard
b. 1956 Soto, Mario Melvin
d. 1536 Erasmus, Desiderius
d. 1705 Oates, Titus
d. 1798 Fitch, John
d. 1814 Howe, William, Viscount
d. 1849 Madison, Dolly Payne Todd
d. 1851 Daguerre, Louis Jacques Mande
d. 1870 Dahlgren, John Adolph
d. 1888 Sibley, Hiram
d. 1892 Cartwright, Alexander Joy, Jr.
d. 1892 Field, Cyrus West
d. 1910 Rolls, Charles Stewart
d. 1916 Cohan, Josephine
d. 1929 Henri, Robert
d. 1931 Soderblom, Nathan
d. 1934 Evinrude, Ole
d. 1935 Dreyfus, Alfred
d. 1943 Loftus, Cissie
d. 1944 Compton, Betty
d. 1944 Roosevelt, Theodore, Jr.
d. 1946 Baker, Ray Stannard
d. 1950 Mendl, Lady Elsie de Wolfe
d. 1953 Rawlinson, Herbert
d. 1960 Adler, "Buddy" (Maurice)
d. 1961 DeLaRoche, Mazo
d. 1963 Grant, Harry Johnston
d. 1966 Suzuki, Daisetz Teitaro
d. 1973 Chaney, Lon, Jr. (Creighton)
d. 1975 Chapin, James Ormsbee
d. 1976 Howe, James Wong
d. 1976 Mack, Ted
d. 1978 Rothermere, Esmond Cecil Harmsworth, Viscount
d. 1978 Williams, Jay
d. 1979 Riperton, Minnie
d. 1981 Keeler, William
d. 1981 Little, Edward Herman
d. 1982 More, Kenneth Gilbert
d. 1983 Wood, Chris
d. 1985 Miller, Arnold Ray

b. 1918 Laurents, Arthur
b. 1919 Attwood, William
b. 1921 Garfield, Leon
b. 1923 Robertson, Dale
b. 1927 Chancellor, John William
b. 1928 Olaf, Pierre
b. 1928 Olson, Nancy
b. 1930 Bergen, Polly
b. 1931 Stephens, Robert
b. 1932 Grier, "Rosey" (Roosevelt)
b. 1933 Bourassa, Robert
b. 1933 Creighton, Fred(erick)
b. 1934 Elder, Lee
b. 1936 Overmyer, Robert F
b. 1938 Rubin, Jerry
b. 1938 Safdie, Moshe
b. 1940 Howatch, Susan
d. 1742 Bentley, Richard
d. 1779 Ross, George
d. 1816 Miranda, Francisco de
d. 1859 Borel d'Hauterive, Petrus
d. 1882 Ringo, John(ny)
d. 1887 Krupp, Alfred
d. 1904 Kruger, Paul (Stephanus Johannes Paulus)
d. 1907 Perkin, William Henry, Sir
d. 1918 Roosevelt, Quentin
d. 1934 Hawthorne, Julian
d. 1943 Bledsoe, Jules
d. 1954 Benavente y Martinez, Jacinto
d. 1958 Faisal II
d. 1963 Janney, Russell Dixon
d. 1965 Stevenson, Adlai Ewing, Jr.
d. 1967 Theodorescu, Ion N
d. 1970 Foster, Preston
d. 1970 Laidler, Harry Wellington
d. 1974 Hathaway, Sibyl Collings
d. 1974 Spaatz, Carl Andrew
d. 1975 Singleton, "Zutty" (Arthur James)
d. 1978 Messel, Oliver
d. 1982 Jensen, Jackie (Jack Eugene)
d. 1984 Delmar, Kenny
d. 1984 Schacht, Al(exander)
d. 1984 Tidyman, Ernest
d. 1986 Loewy, Raymond Fernand

July 15
b. 1573 Jones, Inigo
b. 1607 Rembrandt (Harmenszoon van Rijn)
b. 1779 Moore, Clement Clarke
b. 1796 Bulfinch, Thomas
b. 1808 Manning, Henry Edward
b. 1813 Healy, George Peter Alexander
b. 1850 Cabrini, Saint Frances Xavier
b. 1864 Tempest, Marie
b. 1865 Northcliffe, Alfred Charles William Harmsworth, Viscount
b. 1867 Charcot, Jean Baptiste Etienne Auguste
b. 1872 Hertz, Alfred
b. 1884 Myers, Garry Cleveland

b. 1889 Rambeau, Marjorie
b. 1893 Dieterle, William
b. 1900 Francis, Thomas, Jr.
b. 1902 Hackett, Raymond
b. 1903 Edmonds, Walter Dumaux
b. 1904 Kuh, Katherine
b. 1905 Fields, Dorothy
b. 1906 Armour, Richard Willard
b. 1908 Fisher, Max Martin
b. 1913 Innes, Hammond, pseud.
b. 1917 Conquest, Robert
b. 1918 Boehm, Eric Hartzell
b. 1918 Wanamaker, John Rodman
b. 1919 Murdoch, Iris (Jean Iris)
b. 1924 Denton, Jeremiah Andrew, Jr.
b. 1924 Phelps, Robert Eugene
b. 1925 Carey, Phil(ip)
b. 1926 Galtieri, Leopoldo Fortunato
b. 1927 Jellicoe, Ann
b. 1928 Benko, Paul Charles
b. 1931 Asencio, Diego Cortes
b. 1933 Bream, Julian
b. 1935 Karras, Alex(ander G)
b. 1935 Kercheval, Ken
b. 1935 Prescott, Peter Sherwin
b. 1936 Penner, Rudolph Gerhard
b. 1936 Voinovich, George Victor
b. 1939 Wayne, Patrick
b. 1944 Vincent, Jan-Michael
b. 1946 Ronstadt, Linda
b. 1952 Stallworth, John Lee
b. 1960 Aames, Willie
d. 1274 Bonaventure, Saint
d. 1609 Carracci, Annibale
d. 1782 Farinelli
d. 1828 Houdon, Jean Antoine
d. 1857 Czerny, Karl
d. 1859 Choate, Rufus
d. 1868 Morton, William Thomas Green
d. 1881 Billy the Kid
d. 1883 Tom Thumb, General
d. 1887 Andrews, Jane
d. 1912 Hudson, Joseph Lowthian
d. 1919 Fischer, Emil
d. 1924 Coryell, John Russell
d. 1927 Markievicz, Constance Georgine, Countess
d. 1929 Hofmannsthal, Hugo Hoffmann
d. 1930 Auer, Leopold
d. 1930 Barry, Leonora Marie Kearney
d. 1933 Babbitt, Irving
d. 1933 Keppard, Freddie
d. 1947 Donaldson, Walter
d. 1948 Chapais, Thomas, Sir
d. 1948 Pershing, John J(oseph)
d. 1951 Ovington, Mary White
d. 1957 Cox, James Middleton, Sr.
d. 1959 Bloch, Ernest
d. 1960 Tibbett, Lawrence Mervil
d. 1962 Maison, Rene
d. 1965 Shotwell, James Thomson

b. 1913 Wilson, Mitchell
b. 1915 Jarman, John
b. 1915 Rothstein, Arthur
b. 1916 Steber, Eleanor
b. 1917 Boudreau, Lou(is)
b. 1917 Diller, Phyllis
b. 1918 Manning, Irene
b. 1919 Cottrell, Alan Howard
b. 1920 Bell, Arthur Donald
b. 1920 Gould, Gordon
b. 1920 Monroe, Bill (William Blanc, Jr.)
b. 1920 Samaranch, Juan Antonio
b. 1921 Isaacs, Alick
b. 1922 Davie, Donald
b. 1923 Purdy, James
b. 1928 Dyer, Charles
b. 1928 Morello, Joseph A
b. 1933 Hines, Mimi
b. 1934 Sutherland, Donald
b. 1935 Carroll, Diahann
b. 1935 Civiletti, Benjamin R
b. 1935 Schickele, Peter
b. 1941 Bracey, John Henry, Jr.
b. 1941 Lamonica, Daryle Pat
b. 1942 Davis, Spencer
b. 1942 Garnett, Gale
b. 1951 Arnaz, Lucie Desiree
b. 1952 Hasselhof, David
b. 1952 Larson, Nicolette
b. 1952 Snow, Phoebe Laub
b. 1956 Trottier, Bryan John
d. 1790 Smith, Adam
d. 1793 Corday d'Armount, (Marie Anne) Charlotte
d. 1881 Bridger, James
d. 1887 Dix, Dorothea Lynde
d. 1903 Whistler, James Abbott McNeill
d. 1912 Poincare, Jules Henri
d. 1928 Obregon, Alvaro
d. 1935 Russell, George William
d. 1937 Pierne, Gabriel
d. 1946 Mihajlovic, Draza
d. 1947 Wallenberg, Raoul Gustav
d. 1949 Murphy, Frank
d. 1950 Booth, Evangeline Cory
d. 1953 Adams, Maude
d. 1959 Holiday, Billie
d. 1959 Munnings, Alfred James, Sir
d. 1961 Cobb, Ty(rus Raymond)
d. 1961 Reulbach, Ed(ward Marvin)
d. 1967 Coltrane, "Trane" (John William)
d. 1969 Lahey, Edwin A(loysius)
d. 1971 Edwards, Cliff
d. 1971 Nye, Gerald Prentice
d. 1973 Brown, Joe Evan
d. 1974 Dean, "Dizzy" (Jay Hanna)
d. 1975 Omlie, Phoebe Jane Fairgrave
d. 1980 Barry, Donald
d. 1980 Roskolenko, Harry
d. 1981 Barbanell, Maurice
d. 1984 Low, George M(ichael)

d. 1985 Langer, Suzanne K
d. 1985 Margo
d. 1985 Stewart, Wynn

July 18
b. 1635 Hooke, Robert
b. 1670 Bononcini, Giovanni Battista
b. 1811 Thackeray, William Makepeace
b. 1821 Viardot-Garcia, Pauline
b. 1843 Earp, Virgil W
b. 1845 Corbiere, Tristan
b. 1853 Lorentz, Hendrick Antoon
b. 1864 Huch, Ricarda (Octavia)
b. 1865 Housman, Laurence
b. 1870 Kornilov, Lavr Georgyevich
b. 1871 Balla, Giacomo
b. 1882 Hagedorn, Hermann
b. 1886 Buckner, Simon, Jr.
b. 1887 Quisling, Vidkun
b. 1888 Cowdry, Edmund Vincent
b. 1890 Wilson, Charles Erwin
b. 1891 Lockhart, Gene (Eugene)
b. 1891 McNutt, Paul Vories
b. 1893 Evans, Charles, Jr.
b. 1894 Dix, Richard
b. 1897 Spottswood, Stephen Gill
b. 1900 Marshall, S(amuel) L(yman) A(twood)
b. 1902 West, Jessamyn
b. 1903 Gruen, Victor
b. 1903 Wills, Chill
b. 1906 Hayakawa, S(amuel) I(chiye)
b. 1906 Odets, Clifford
b. 1908 Velez, Lupe
b. 1909 Wright, John Joseph
b. 1910 Baker, Elbert Hall, II
b. 1911 Cronyn, Hume
b. 1912 Levin, Harry Tuchman
b. 1912 Nelson, Harriet
b. 1912 Roy, Mike (Michael)
b. 1913 Rolvaag, Karl
b. 1913 Skelton, "Red" (Richard)
b. 1915 Sauer, William George
b. 1916 Armitage, Kenneth
b. 1916 Gray, Louis Patrick
b. 1918 Mandela, Nelson Rolihlahla
b. 1920 Redhead, Hugh McCulloch
b. 1921 Glenn, John Herschel, Jr.
b. 1922 Chayes, Abram J
b. 1926 Jennings, Elizabeth
b. 1926 Laurence, Margaret Jean
b. 1927 Masur, Kurt
b. 1929 Button, Dick (Richard Totten)
b. 1933 Evtushenko, Evgeniy Alexandrovich
b. 1934 Bond, Edward
b. 1935 Albright, Tenley Emma
b. 1939 Auger, Brian
b. 1939 Di Mucci, Dion
b. 1939 Thompson, Hunter S(tockton)
b. 1940 Torre, Joe (Joseph Paul)
b. 1941 Brolin, James
b. 1941 Reeves, Martha

b. 1943 Peete, Calvin
b. 1949 Bryson, Wally Carter
b. 1951 Lietzke, Bruce
d. 1100 Godfrey of Bouillon
d. 1609 Caravaggio, Michelangelo da
d. 1721 Watteau, Jean Antoine
d. 1792 Jones, John Paul
d. 1800 Rutledge, John
d. 1817 Austen, Jane
d. 1863 Shaw, Robert Gould
d. 1868 Leutze, Emanuel
d. 1872 Juarez, Benito Pablo
d. 1892 Cooke, Rose Terry
d. 1899 Alger, Horatio
d. 1916 Immelmann, Max
d. 1918 Douglas, Amanda Minnie
d. 1944 Rommel, Erwin Johannes Eugin
d. 1949 Novak, Vitezslav
d. 1950 Van Doren, Carl Clinton
d. 1954 Kelly, "Machine Gun" (George R)
d. 1958 DuBois, Guy Pene
d. 1962 Houdry, Eugene Jules
d. 1966 Heiden, Konrad
d. 1967 Castello Branco, Humberto
d. 1969 Armstrong, Charlotte
d. 1972 Fosdick, Raymond Blaine
d. 1972 Gentele, Goeran
d. 1973 Hawkins, Jack
d. 1983 Lichty, George
d. 1985 Hoffman, Robert C
d. 1985 Segal, Henry

July 19
b. 1698 Bodmer, Johann Jakob
b. 1802 Davenport, Thomas
b. 1814 Colt, Samuel
b. 1817 Bickerdyke, Mary Ann Ball
b. 1819 Keller, Gottfried
b. 1834 Degas, (Hilaire Germain) Edgar
b. 1846 Pickering, Edward Charles
b. 1847 Williams, Gus
b. 1860 Borden, Lizzie Andrew
b. 1865 Mayo, Charles Horace
b. 1876 Smith, Joseph Fielding
b. 1879 Mitchel, John Purroy
b. 1883 Fleischer, Max
b. 1885 Muir, Malcolm
b. 1893 Mayakovsky, Vladimir
b. 1896 Breeskin, Adelyn Dohme
b. 1896 Cronin, A(rchibald) J(oseph)
b. 1898 Marcuse, Herbert
b. 1900 Rosenberg, Anna Marie
b. 1901 Beals, Ralph Leon
b. 1901 Damita, Lily
b. 1903 Haskell, Arnold Lionel
b. 1905 Kentner, Louis Philip
b. 1905 Neel, (Louis) Boyd
b. 1905 Snow, Edgar Parks
b. 1913 Teagarden, Charles
b. 1916 Cavarretta, Phil(ip Joseph)
b. 1917 Scranton, William Warren
b. 1920 Medina, Patricia

b. 1921 Yalow, Rosalyn Sussman
b. 1922 McGovern, George Stanley
b. 1923 Hannum, Alex(ander Murray)
b. 1923 Hansen, Joseph
b. 1923 Rusher, William Allen
b. 1924 Hathaway, Stanley Knapp
b. 1924 Hingle, Pat (Martin Patterson)
b. 1926 Gallagher, Helen
b. 1927 Myrdal, Jan
b. 1930 Callahan, Daniel
b. 1935 Agee, Philip
b. 1938 Jordan, Richard
b. 1941 Carr, Vikki
b. 1943 Cole, Dennis
b. 1946 Nastase, Ilie
b. 1947 Leadon, Bernie
b. 1947 May, Brian
b. 1958 Hightower, Stephanie
b. 1959 Treas, Terri
d. 1374 Petrarch, Francesco
d. 1647 Hooker, Thomas
d. 1814 Flinders, Matthew
d. 1824 Iturbide, Augustin de
d. 1850 Fuller, Margaret
d. 1858 Porter, William Trotter
d. 1884 Sloan, Samuel
d. 1888 Roe, Edward Payson
d. 1892 Cook, Thomas
d. 1897 Boycott, Charles Cunningham
d. 1902 Acton, John Emerich Edward
    Dalberg-Acton, Baron
d. 1922 Goucher, John Franklin
d. 1923 Holabird, William
d. 1935 Sedgwick, Anne Douglas
d. 1944 Cook, Will Marion
d. 1957 Malaparte, Curzio
d. 1962 Davis, Clyde Brion
d. 1965 Gitlow, Benjamin
d. 1965 Rhee, Syngman
d. 1966 Akeley, Mary Lee Jobe
d. 1967 Shepard, Odell
d. 1969 Kopechne, Mary Jo
d. 1971 Myers, Garry Cleveland
d. 1972 Benson, Sally
d. 1974 Flynn, Joe (Joseph Anthony)
d. 1980 Morgenthau, Hans Joachim
d. 1985 Canaday, John (Edwin John)
d. 1985 Montagu, Ewen (Edward Samuel)

July 20
b. 1304 Petrarch, Francesco
b. 1661 Iberville, Pierre Le Moyne, sieur
    d'
b. 1820 Keene, Laura
b. 1838 Daly, Augustin
b. 1864 Karlfeldt, Erik Axel
b. 1869 Thurston, Howard
b. 1880 Keyserling, Hermann Alexander
b. 1888 McMurtrie, Douglas C
b. 1889 Reith, John Charles Walsham
b. 1890 Bara, Theda
b. 1890 Felton, Verna

b. 1890 George II
b. 1890 Morandi, Giorgio
b. 1891 Allyn, Stanley Charles
b. 1895 Corum, Martene Windsor
b. 1895 Moholy-Nagy, Laszlo
b. 1897 Reichstein, Tadeus
b. 1900 Arnold, Oren
b. 1901 Manush, "Heinie" (Henry Emmett)
b. 1907 Lincoln, George A
b. 1907 Simpson, Cedric Keith
b. 1909 Miller, William Mosley
b. 1914 Uhde, Hermann
b. 1919 Ford, Benson
b. 1919 Hillary, Edmund Percival, Sir
b. 1919 Stevens, K T
b. 1920 Richardson, Elliot Lee
b. 1924 Albright, Lola Jean
b. 1924 Berger, Thomas Louis
b. 1924 Sarkis, Elias
b. 1925 Fanon, Frantz
b. 1928 Haney, Paul Prichard
b. 1929 Ilitch, Mike
b. 1934 Howes, Sally Ann
b. 1936 Dole, Elizabeth Hanford
b. 1938 Mikulski, Barbara Ann
b. 1938 Rigg, Diana
b. 1939 Chicago, Judy
b. 1939 Wood, Natalie
b. 1940 Oliva, Tony (Antonio Pedro, Jr.)
b. 1944 Sheppard, T G
b. 1946 Carnes, Kim
b. 1947 Santana, Carlos (Devadip Carlos)
b. 1954 French, Jay Jay
b. 1956 Jausovec, Mima
b. 1960 Witt, Mike (Michael Arthur)
d. 1752 Pepusch, Johann Christoph (John)
d. 1891 Alarcon, Pedro Antonio de
d. 1902 Mackay, John William
d. 1912 Lang, Andrew
d. 1937 Marconi, Guglielmo
d. 1940 Maytag, Elmer Henry
d. 1941 Fields, Lew Maurice
d. 1944 Stauffenberg, Claus (Schenk Graf)
        Von
d. 1945 Valery, Paul Ambroise
d. 1951 Abdullah Ibn Hussein
d. 1953 Struther, Jan, pseud.
d. 1958 Pangborn, Franklin
d. 1959 Leahy, William Daniel
d. 1968 Hammond, Bray
d. 1969 Hamilton, Roy
d. 1970 Chace, Marian
d. 1970 MacLeod, Iain Norman
d. 1972 Flick, Friedrich
d. 1974 Jenkins, Allen
d. 1978 Brace, Gerald Warner
d. 1981 Kardiner, Abram
d. 1983 Reynolds, Frank
d. 1984 Fixx, James Fuller
d. 1985 Alexander, Leo
d. 1985 Johnson, Arno Hollock

July 21
b. 1664 Prior, Matthew
b. 1730 Adam, James
b. 1826 Loomis, Mahion
b. 1838 Muir, John
b. 1851 Bass, Sam
b. 1860 Olcott, Chauncey (Chancellor)
b. 1863 Smith, C Aubrey
b. 1864 Cleveland, Frances Folsom
b. 1873 Witherspoon, Herbert
b. 1881 Evers, John Joseph
b. 1885 Keyes, Frances Parkinson
b. 1893 Fallada, Hans, pseud.
b. 1894 Ulric, Lenore
b. 1895 Barnes, Leonard John
b. 1895 Maynard, Ken
b. 1896 Hickenlooper, Bourke B
b. 1899 Crane, Hart
b. 1899 Hemingway, Ernest Miller
b. 1905 Joslyn, Allyn Morgan
b. 1905 Kennedy, David M
b. 1905 Trilling, Diana Rubin
b. 1908 Jenner, William Ezra
b. 1911 McLuhan, (Herbert) Marshall
b. 1911 Polk, Ralph Lane
b. 1914 Aries, Philippe
b. 1920 Stern, Isaac
b. 1923 Wise, William H
b. 1924 Knotts, Don
b. 1924 Starr, Kay
b. 1924 Stone, Chuck (Charles Sumner)
b. 1926 Burke, Paul
b. 1926 Jewison, Norman
b. 1926 Premice, Josephine
b. 1926 Reisz, Karel
b. 1928 Keane, John B
b. 1930 Littler, Gene (Eugene Alex)
b. 1933 Gardner, John Champlin, Jr.
b. 1934 Miller, Jonathan
b. 1935 Stevens, Kaye (Catherine)
b. 1937 Frederickson, H Gray
b. 1938 Aspin, Leslie, Jr.
b. 1943 Herrmann, Edward
b. 1945 Lawson, Leigh
b. 1948 Stevens, Cat
b. 1952 Williams, Robin
d. 1865 Schnorr, Ludwig, von Carolsfeld
d. 1878 Bass, Sam
d. 1899 Ingersoll, Robert Green
d. 1908 Potter, Henry Codman
d. 1926 Roebling, Washington Augustus
d. 1928 Terry, Ellen Alicia, Dame
d. 1932 Bazin, Rene
d. 1938 Kroger, Bernard Henry
d. 1938 Wister, Owen
d. 1946 Rosenfeld, Paul
d. 1948 Glaspell, Susan Keating
d. 1954 Carter, John Garnet
d. 1957 Roberts, Kenneth
d. 1960 Hoffman, Al
d. 1962 Trevelyan, George Macaulay

b. 1883 Alanbrooke, Alan Francis Brooke, 1st Viscount
b. 1884 Warner, Albert
b. 1886 Madariaga (y Rojo), Salvador de
b. 1888 Chandler, Raymond Thornton
b. 1889 Bonnet, Georges
b. 1892 Haile Selassie I
b. 1893 Menninger, Karl Augustus
b. 1894 Stronge, (Charles) Norman (Lockhart), Sir
b. 1895 Poulson, Norris
b. 1895 Pringle, Aileen
b. 1895 Vidor, Florence
b. 1897 Cloete, Stuart
b. 1899 Chandler, Norman
b. 1899 Heinemann, Gustav Walter
b. 1901 Hibbs, Ben
b. 1902 Cowles, William Hutchinson, Jr.
b. 1907 Cunningham, Harry Blair
b. 1907 Huxley, Elspeth Josceline Grant
b. 1912 Miller, Carl S
b. 1913 Browne, Coral Edith
b. 1913 Foot, Michael
b. 1914 Foreman, Carl
b. 1915 Sardi, Vincent, Jr.
b. 1917 Arriola, Gus
b. 1917 Kreuger, Kurt
b. 1919 Reese, "Pee Wee" (Harold Henry)
b. 1925 DeHaven, Gloria
b. 1928 Fleisher, Leon
b. 1928 Selby, Hubert, Jr.
b. 1930 Landrieu, "Moon" (Maurice Edwin)
b. 1931 Troell, Jan
b. 1934 Convy, Bert
b. 1936 Drysdale, Don(ald Scott)
b. 1945 Danelli, Dino
b. 1947 Essex, David
d. 1757 Scarlatti, Domenico Girolamo
d. 1793 Sherman, Roger
d. 1845 Sublette, William L
d. 1875 Singer, Isaac Merrit
d. 1885 Grant, Ulysses S(impson)
d. 1914 Grimke, Charlotte Lottie Forten
d. 1916 Ramsay, William, Sir
d. 1923 Villa, "Pancho" (Francisco)
d. 1930 Curtiss, Glenn Hammond
d. 1933 Schillings, Max von
d. 1941 Kittredge, G(eorge) L(yman)
d. 1948 Griffith, D(avid Lewelyn) W(ark)
d. 1951 Flaherty, Robert Joseph
d. 1951 Petain, Henri Philippe
d. 1955 Hull, Cordell
d. 1957 Sterne, Maurice
d. 1962 Moore, Victor
d. 1966 Clift, Montgomery
d. 1969 Dell, Floyd
d. 1971 Heflin, Van Emmett Evan
d. 1971 Tubman, William Vacanarat Shadrach

d. 1973 Rickenbacker, Eddie (Edward Vernon)
d. 1980 Manning, Olivia
d. 1981 Owen, Guy, Jr.
d. 1982 Morrow, Vic
d. 1982 Parsons, Betty Pierson
d. 1983 Auric, Georges
d. 1983 Traube, Shepard
d. 1985 Kyser, "Kay" (James Kern)

July 24
b. 1783 Bolivar, Simon
b. 1796 Clayton, John Middleton
b. 1798 Dix, John Adams
b. 1802 Dumas, Alexandre
b. 1803 Adam, Adolphe Charles
b. 1803 Davis, Alexander Jackson
b. 1855 Gillette, William Hooker
b. 1857 Pontoppidan, Henrik
b. 1861 Renaud, Maurice
b. 1864 McCarthy, Tommy (Thomas Francis Michael)
b. 1864 Wedekind, Frank
b. 1867 Benson, Edward Frederic
b. 1876 Webster, Jean
b. 1878 Dunsany, Edward J M Plunkett, Baron
b. 1880 Bloch, Ernest
b. 1882 Thorndike, Lynn
b. 1892 Jones, Thomas Hudson
b. 1893 Aymar, Gordon Christian
b. 1898 Earhart, Amelia Mary
b. 1899 Loeb, Gerald Martin
b. 1900 Fitzgerald, Zelda
b. 1904 Killian, James Rhyne, Jr.
b. 1908 Williams, "Cootie" (Charles Melvin)
b. 1909 Curtis, Alan
b. 1910 Vera
b. 1911 Martinson, Joseph Bertram
b. 1911 Widgery, John Passmore, Baron
b. 1912 Wood, Guy B
b. 1913 Davis, Burke
b. 1914 Clark, Kenneth Bancroft
b. 1914 Silvera, Frank
b. 1916 Eberly, Bob
b. 1916 MacDonald, John Dann
b. 1917 Brickman, Morrie
b. 1920 Abzug, Bella Savitsky
b. 1920 Cohen, Alexander H
b. 1920 Ricci, Ruggiero
b. 1920 Ter-Arutunian, Rouben
b. 1921 DiStefano, Giuseppe
b. 1921 Taylor, Billy (William Edward)
b. 1922 Mathias, Charles McCurdy, Jr.
b. 1923 Weaver, William
b. 1924 Palevsky, Max
b. 1925 Addison, Adele
b. 1929 Yates, Peter
b. 1934 Ruckelshaus, William Doyle
b. 1935 Oliphant, Patrick Bruce
b. 1936 Buzzi, Ruth Ann

b. 1937 Sanders, Doug(las)
b. 1939 Bellamy, Walt
b. 1942 Sarandon, Chris
b. 1947 Serkin, Peter A
b. 1948 Hays, Robert
b. 1949 Trumka, Richard Louis
b. 1951 Carter, Lynda
b. 1957 O'Callahan, Jack
b. 1958 Carroll, Joe Barry
b. 1958 Grogan, Steve
d. 1862 Van Buren, Martin
d. 1865 Cotman, John S
d. 1894 Ingersoll, Simon
d. 1924 Cox, Palmer
d. 1948 Patterson, Eleanor Medill
d. 1952 Copeland, Charles Townsend
d. 1954 Terrell, Mary Church
d. 1957 Guitry, Sacha
d. 1966 Lema, Tony (Anthony David)
d. 1973 Saint Laurent, Louis Stephen
d. 1974 Carpenter, Leslie
d. 1974 Chadwick, James, Sir
d. 1974 Tyler, Parker
d. 1980 Sellers, Peter Richard Henry
d. 1981 Hauge, Gabriel
d. 1982 Lawler, Richard Harold
d. 1982 Markey, Lucille (Parker) Wright
d. 1986 Breeskin, Adelyn Dohme
d. 1986 Lipmann, Fritz Albert

July 25
b. Welch, Mitzie
b. 1654 Steffani, Agostino
b. 1750 Knox, Henry
b. 1775 Harrison, Anna Tuthill Symmes
b. 1799 Little, Charles Coffin
b. 1803 Maverick, Samuel Augustus
b. 1830 Bausch, John Jacob
b. 1844 Eakins, Thomas
b. 1848 Balfour, Arthur James Balfour, Earl
b. 1857 Sprague, Frank Julian
b. 1859 Belasco, David
b. 1870 Journet, Marcel
b. 1870 Parrish, Maxfield
b. 1870 Skipworth, Alison
b. 1878 Hasselmans, Louis
b. 1894 Brennan, Walter Andrew
b. 1896 Gale, Richard Nelson, Sir
b. 1898 Printemps, Yvonne
b. 1901 Wilson, John Johnston
b. 1902 Hoffer, Eric
b. 1902 Lee, Lila
b. 1905 Canetti, Elias
b. 1906 Hodges, Johnny
b. 1906 Wengenroth, Stow
b. 1913 Gilford, Jack
b. 1914 Strode, Woody
b. 1918 Amen, Irving
b. 1923 Francis, Sam
b. 1923 Gripe, Maria
b. 1924 Church, Frank

b. 1925 Newquist, Roy
b. 1925 Paris, Jerry
b. 1927 Dancer, Stanley
b. 1927 Decter, Midge
b. 1929 Farb, Peter
b. 1931 Forrester, Maureen
b. 1934 Calvo, Paul McDonald
b. 1935 Bullins, Ed
b. 1935 Khashoggi, Adnan
b. 1935 Robinson, John Alexander
b. 1935 Sherry, Larry (Lawrence)
b. 1937 Carmines, Al
b. 1941 Thurmond, Nate
b. 1943 Margolin, Janet
b. 1948 Goodman, Steve(n Benjamin)
b. 1954 Payton, Walter
b. 1978 Brown, Louise Joy
d. 1471 Thomas a Kempis
d. 1685 Monmouth, James Scott, Duke
d. 1794 Chenier, Marie-Andre de
d. 1834 Coleridge, Samuel Taylor
d. 1841 Rogers, Mary Cecilia
d. 1881 Clifford, Nathan
d. 1897 Packard, Elizabeth Parsons Ware
d. 1918 Rauschenbusch, Walter
d. 1930 Vought, Chance Milton
d. 1934 Dollfuss, Engelbert
d. 1937 Saunders, Charles E
d. 1945 Craig, Malin
d. 1951 Leyendecker, Joseph Christian
d. 1954 Raine, William MacLeod
d. 1958 Warner, Harry Morris
d. 1960 Defauw, Desire
d. 1964 Townsend, William H(enry)
d. 1964 Wolff, Mary Evaline
d. 1969 Gombrowicz, Witold
d. 1969 Moore, Douglas
d. 1972 Reventlow, Lance
d. 1980 Vysotsky, Vladimir Semyonovich
d. 1981 Widgery, John Passmore, Baron
d. 1982 Foster, Hal (Harold Rudolf)
d. 1982 Okada, Kenzo
d. 1984 Thornton, Willie Mae
d. 1986 Minnelli, Vincente

July 26
b. Wittop, Freddy
b. 1728 Gates, Horatio
b. 1739 Clinton, George
b. 1782 Field, John
b. 1796 Catlin, George
b. 1805 Brumidi, Constantino
b. 1846 Harper, William Rainey
b. 1850 Henry, Edward Richard, Sir
b. 1856 Shaw, George Bernard
b. 1858 Boole, Ella Alexander
b. 1858 House, Edward Mandell
b. 1866 Cilea, Francesco
b. 1874 Koussevitzky, Serge Alexandrovich
b. 1875 Jung, Carl Gustav
b. 1875 Machado, Antonio
b. 1876 Schelling, Ernest Henry

b. 1880 Lincoln, G(eorge) Gould
b. 1885 Maurois, Andre
b. 1886 Jannings, Emil
b. 1887 Boosey, Leslie Arthur
b. 1892 Jones, Sam(uel Pond)
b. 1892 Leonard, "Dutch" (Hubert Benjamin)
b. 1893 Grosz, George Ehrenfried
b. 1894 Huxley, Aldous Leonard
b. 1895 Graves, Robert Ranke
b. 1897 Butterworth, Charles
b. 1897 Gallico, Paul William
b. 1898 Gimbel, Richard
b. 1899 Walker, Danton MacIntyre
b. 1900 Mortimer, Charles Greenough
b. 1903 Kefauver, Estes
b. 1903 Voorhees, Donald
b. 1904 Link, Edwin Albert
b. 1904 Roark, Garland
b. 1906 Allen, Gracie Ethel Cecil Rosaline
b. 1908 Allende, Salvador
b. 1912 Vance, Vivian
b. 1914 Hawkins, Erskine Ramsey
b. 1918 Thompson, Frank, Jr.
b. 1919 Gilmore, Virginia
b. 1922 Edwards, Blake
b. 1922 Lord, Marjorie
b. 1923 Wilhelm, Hoyt (James Hoyt)
b. 1928 Cossiga, Francesco
b. 1928 Kubrick, Stanley
b. 1928 Lougheed, Peter
b. 1929 Lalonde, Marc
b. 1929 Shepherd, Jean Parker
b. 1929 Weissenberg, Alexis Sigismund
b. 1939 Haggerty, Sandra Clark
b. 1940 Kopechne, Mary Jo
b. 1943 Jagger, Mick (Michael Philip)
b. 1945 Martin, Kiel
b. 1950 George, Susan
b. 1951 Martin, Richard Lionel
b. 1954 Gerulaitis, Vitas
d. 1845 Benjamin, Asher
d. 1863 Crittenden, John Jordan
d. 1863 Houston, Sam(uel)
d. 1881 Borrow, George Henry
d. 1904 Rogers, John
d. 1915 Murray, James Augustus Henry, Sir
d. 1925 Bryan, William Jennings
d. 1926 Lincoln, Robert Todd
d. 1934 McCay, Winsor
d. 1939 Spingarn, Joel Elias
d. 1952 Peron, Eva Duarte
d. 1957 Tomasi di Lampedusa, Guiseppe
d. 1958 Rohde, Ruth Bryan Owen
d. 1965 Burdick, Eugene Leonard
d. 1967 Bitter, Francis
d. 1969 Walburn, Raymond
d. 1971 Arbus, Diane
d. 1973 White, William Lindsay
d. 1974 Byrnes, Eugene F

d. 1974 Stouffer, Vernon B
d. 1980 Hoskins, Allen Clayton
d. 1980 Richards, Stanley
d. 1980 Tynan, Kenneth Peacock
d. 1981 Ilg, Frances Lillian
d. 1981 Runkle, Janice
d. 1984 Gallup, George Horace
d. 1984 Gein, Ed
d. 1986 Harriman, W(illiam) Averell
d. 1986 Lyons, Ted (Theodore Amar)

July 27
b. 1768 Corday d'Armount, (Marie Anne) Charlotte
b. 1824 Dumas, Alexandre
b. 1835 Carducci, Giosue
b. 1844 Harrigan, Edward
b. 1867 Granados, Enrique
b. 1870 Belloc, Hilaire (Joseph Hilaire Pierre)
b. 1875 Fisher, Harrison
b. 1877 Dohnanyi, Erno von
b. 1878 Cline, Genevieve Rose
b. 1880 Tinker, Joe (Joseph Bert)
b. 1882 DeHavilland, Geoffrey
b. 1889 Bliven, Bruce
b. 1890 Lowry, Judith Ives
b. 1891 Thompson, Ruth Plumly
b. 1899 Houghton, Amory
b. 1899 McDonald, Harl
b. 1900 Haug, Hans
b. 1904 Christiansen, Arthur
b. 1904 Divine, Arthur Durham
b. 1904 Dolin, Anton, Sir
b. 1904 Rudenko, Lyudmila
b. 1906 Durocher, Leo Ernest
b. 1906 Wolff, Helen
b. 1908 Hamilton, Nancy
b. 1912 Markevitch, Igor
b. 1913 Corbett, Scott (Winfield Scott)
b. 1914 Horan, James David
b. 1914 White, Miles
b. 1915 DelMonaco, Mario
b. 1916 Ashmore, Harry Scott
b. 1916 Hardwick, Elizabeth
b. 1916 Wynn, Keenan
b. 1918 Rose, Leonard
b. 1919 Harman, Jeanne Perkins
b. 1922 Lear, Norman Milton
b. 1924 Baskin, Wade
b. 1924 Canby, Vincent
b. 1926 Cook, Marlow Webster
b. 1927 Peters, Brock
b. 1930 Williams, Shirley
b. 1931 Van Dyke, Jerry
b. 1932 Blair, David
b. 1936 Sapir, Richard
b. 1937 Galloway, Don
b. 1939 Costle, Douglas Michael
b. 1942 Gentry, Bobbie
b. 1943 Brown, Samuel W, Jr.
b. 1945 Muller, Bobby (Robert)

b. 1948 Fleming, Peggy Gale
b. 1948 Thomas, Betty
b. 1949 McGovern, Maureen Therese
b. 1952 Barnes, Marvin
b. 1953 Inatome, Rick
d. 1675 Turenne, Henri D'Auvergne,
    Vicomte
d. 1741 Vivaldi, Antonio
d. 1770 Dinwiddie, Robert
d. 1833 Bainbridge, William
d. 1841 Lermontov, Mikhail (Michael
    Jurevich)
d. 1844 Dalton, John
d. 1876 Channing, Walter
d. 1877 Nekrasov, Nikolay Alexeyevich
d. 1883 Blair, Montgomery
d. 1918 Kobbe, Gustav
d. 1924 Busoni, Ferruccio Benvenuto
d. 1929 Pictet, Raoul-Pierre
d. 1934 Lyautey, Louis Hubert Gonzalve
d. 1946 Stein, Gertrude
d. 1948 Tinker, Joe (Joseph Bert)
d. 1953 Gerould, Gordon Hall
d. 1958 Chennault, Claire Lee
d. 1962 Aldington, Richard
d. 1962 Konwitschny, Franz
d. 1963 Dauss, George August
d. 1964 Hagedorn, Hermann
d. 1969 Ford, Corey
d. 1970 Reid, Helen Rogers
d. 1970 Salazar, Antonio de Oliveira
d. 1970 Untermeyer, Jean Starr
d. 1971 Paumgartner, Bernhard
d. 1971 Weston, Edward F
d. 1972 Ellender, Allen Joseph
d. 1972 LaRose, Rose
d. 1975 Frizzell, "Lefty" (William Orville)
d. 1978 Ford, Benson
d. 1980 Pahlevi, Mohammed Riza
d. 1982 Seymour, Dan
d. 1984 Mason, James Neville
d. 1986 Lancaster, Osbert, Sir

July 28
b. Kelsey, Linda
b. 1746 Heyward, Thomas, Jr.
b. 1804 Feuerbach, Ludwig Andreas
b. 1811 Grisi, Guilia
b. 1859 Anderson, Mary Antoinette
b. 1859 Booth, Ballington
b. 1874 Cassirer, Ernst
b. 1874 Miller, Alice Duer
b. 1882 Pirelli, Alberto
b. 1887 Duchamp, Marcel
b. 1891 Gallagher, Richard
b. 1892 Brown, Joe Evan
b. 1896 LaMarr, Barbara
b. 1897 Martin, Kingsley
b. 1898 Gould, Charles Bruce
b. 1900 Maxon, Lou Russell
b. 1901 Vallee, Rudy (Herbert Prior)
b. 1902 Fearing, Kenneth Flexner

b. 1902 Rodgers, Richard
b. 1904 Lloyd, (John) Selwyn Brooke
b. 1907 Tupper, Earl Silas
b. 1908 Kerby, William Frederick
b. 1909 Lowry, Malcolm (Clarence
    Malcolm)
b. 1910 Goodwin, Bill
b. 1912 Wilding, Michael
b. 1913 Ryder, James Arthur
b. 1914 Dragon, Carmen
b. 1916 Brown, David
b. 1916 Cregar, Laird (Samuel)
b. 1922 Piccard, Jacques
b. 1927 Ashbery, John Lawrence
b. 1927 Carawan, Guy
b. 1929 Onassis, Jacqueline Lee Bouvier
    Kennedy
b. 1931 Hickman, Darryl
b. 1934 D'Amboise, Jacques
b. 1937 Duchin, Peter
b. 1938 Hughes, Robert Studley Forrest
b. 1939 Horner, Matina Souretis
b. 1941 Muti, Riccardo
b. 1943 Bradley, Bill (William Warren)
b. 1944 Bloomfield, Mike (Michael)
b. 1945 Davis, Jim (James Robert)
b. 1948 Engel, Georgia Bright
b. 1948 Struthers, Sally Anne
b. 1949 Blue, Vida Rochelle
b. 1951 Collins, Doug
b. 1958 Fox, Terry (Terrance Stanley)
d. 1540 Cromwell, Thomas
d. 1667 Cowley, Abraham
d. 1746 Zenger, John Peter
d. 1750 Bach, Johann Sebastian
d. 1794 Couthon, Georges
d. 1794 Robespierre, Maximilien Francois
    de
d. 1802 Sarti, Giuseppe
d. 1823 Cutler, Manasseh
d. 1836 Rothschild, Nathan Meyer
d. 1842 Brentano, Clemens Maria
d. 1844 Bonaparte, Joseph
d. 1852 Downing, Andrew Jackson
d. 1885 Montefiore, Moses Haim, Sir
d. 1903 Stoltz, Rosine
d. 1918 Treptow, Martin A
d. 1934 Dressler, Marie
d. 1939 Mayo, William James
d. 1939 Mercer, Beryl
d. 1942 Petrie, (William Matthew)
    Flinders, Sir
d. 1945 Asquith, Emma Alice Margot
d. 1952 McMahon, (James O') Brien
d. 1957 Abbott, Edith
d. 1967 Julian, "Doggie" (Alvin T)
d. 1968 Hahn, Otto
d. 1969 Loesser, Frank
d. 1970 Barbirolli, John, Sir
d. 1970 Caston, Saul
d. 1972 Traubel, Helen

d. 1973 Chase, Mary Ellen
d. 1974 McCafferty, Don
d. 1976 Feather, Victor
d. 1979 Irving, Jules
d. 1979 Seaton, George
d. 1981 Bloom, Harry
d. 1981 O'Neil, James F(rancis)
d. 1981 Pauley, Edwin Wendell
d. 1981 Wyler, William
d. 1982 Lucas, Nick
d. 1985 Audiard, Michel
d. 1986 Alcott, John

July 29
b. 1792 Drew, Daniel
b. 1796 Hunt, Walter
b. 1805 Powers, Hiram
b. 1805 Tocqueville, Alexis, Comte de
b. 1824 Johnson, Eastman
b. 1828 Pillsbury, John Sargent
b. 1832 Cesnola, Luigi Palma di
b. 1861 Roosevelt, Alice Lee
b. 1869 Tarkington, Booth
b. 1874 Woodsworth, James Shaver
b. 1876 Ouspenskaya, Maria
b. 1877 Beebe, William (Charles William)
b. 1878 Marquis, Don Robert Perry
b. 1883 Mussolini, Benito
b. 1884 Tietjens, Eunice
b. 1887 Romberg, Sigmund
b. 1889 Reuter, Ernst
b. 1890 Zuckerman, Ben
b. 1892 Powell, William
b. 1896 Catlin, George Edward Gordon, Sir
b. 1897 Shaver, Dorothy
b. 1898 Rabi, Isidor Isaac
b. 1900 Lattimore, Owen
b. 1900 Redman, Don
b. 1901 Bridges, Harry Renton
b. 1905 Hammarskjold, Dag
b. 1905 Kunitz, Stanley Jasspon
b. 1905 Todd, Thelma
b. 1907 Belli, Melvin Mouron
b. 1907 Butterfield, Roger Place
b. 1908 Kaiser, Edgar Fosburgh
b. 1909 Baker, Samm Sinclair
b. 1909 Crosby, Sumner McKnight
b. 1909 Himes, Chester Bomar
b. 1911 Iakovos, Archbishop
b. 1912 Corey, Irwin
b. 1914 Bich, Marcel
b. 1918 O'Connor, Edwin Greene
b. 1921 Marker, Chris
b. 1922 Popa, Vasko
b. 1923 Egan, Richard
b. 1924 Bochner, Lloyd
b. 1924 Ethridge, Mark Foster, Jr.
b. 1924 Horton, Robert
b. 1925 Lindsay, Ted (Robert Blake Theodore)
b. 1925 Theodorakis, Mikis

b. 1926 Carter, Don(ald Jones)
b. 1930 Perkoff, Stuart Z
b. 1930 Taylor, Paul
b. 1932 Kassebaum, Nancy Landon
b. 1933 Reuben, David
b. 1934 Fuller, Robert
b. 1938 Jennings, Peter Charles
b. 1941 Warner, David
b. 1952 Wedman, Scott Dean
b. 1953 Lee, Geddy
b. 1954 Adams, Alvan Leigh
b. 1956 Scialfa, Patty
b. 1956 Spinks, Michael
d. 1228 Langton, Stephen
d. 1833 Wilberforce, William
d. 1856 Schumann, Robert Alexander
d. 1890 Van Gogh, Vincent Willem
d. 1929 Fuller, Henry Blake
d. 1941 Leonard, Eddie
d. 1941 Stephenson, James
d. 1955 Reynolds, Richard S.
d. 1959 Peters, Frederick Emerson
d. 1960 Simon, Richard Leo
d. 1965 Graves, Alvin Cushman
d. 1966 Orr, Douglas William
d. 1973 Charriere, Henri
d. 1974 Elliot, Cass
d. 1974 Kastner, Erich
d. 1976 Cohen, "Mickey" (Meyer)
d. 1978 Nobile, Umberto
d. 1979 Marcuse, Herbert
d. 1981 Moses, Robert
d. 1981 Walsh, James Edward
d. 1982 Gale, Richard Nelson, Sir
d. 1982 Zworykin, Vladimir K(osma)
d. 1983 Bunuel, Luis
d. 1983 Crohn, Burrill Bernard
d. 1983 Massey, Raymond Hart
d. 1983 Niven, (James) David Graham
d. 1984 Waring, Fred Malcolm

July 30
b. 1511 Vasari, Giorgio
b. 1763 Rogers, Samuel
b. 1831 Blavatsky, Helena Petrovna
b. 1857 Veblen, Thorstein Bunde
b. 1863 Ford, Henry
b. 1867 Beck, Martin
b. 1880 McCormick, Robert Rutherford
b. 1889 Haldeman-Julius, Emanuel
b. 1889 Zworykin, Vladimir K(osma)
b. 1891 Stengel, "Casey" (Charles Dillon)
b. 1898 Moore, Henry
b. 1899 Binns, Archie Fred
b. 1899 Moore, Gerald
b. 1908 Suhl, Yuri
b. 1909 Parkinson, C(yril) Northcote
b. 1914 Killanin, Michael Morris, Lord
b. 1924 Gallen, Hugh J
b. 1924 Gass, William H
b. 1926 Bookspan, Martin
b. 1927 Johnson, Richard

b. 1930 Sowell, Thomas
b. 1931 Vohs, (Elinor) Joan
b. 1933 Byrnes, Edd
b. 1939 Bogdanovich, Peter
b. 1939 Smeal, Eleanor Marie Cutri
b. 1940 Schroeder, Patricia Scott
b. 1941 Anka, Paul
b. 1944 Rader, Doug(las L)
b. 1947 Atherton, William
b. 1947 Schwarzenegger, Arnold
b. 1955 Kenty, Hilmer
b. 1956 Larson, Reed David
b. 1957 Cartwright, Bill (James William)
b. 1958 Bush, Kate
b. 1958 Thompson, Daley (Francis Daley)
b. 1963 Mullin, Chris(topher Paul)
d. 1718 Penn, William
d. 1771 Gray, Thomas
d. 1784 Diderot, Denis
d. 1811 Hidalgo y Costilla, Miguel
d. 1849 Perkins, Jacob
d. 1875 Pickett, George Edward
d. 1894 Pater, Walter Horatio
d. 1898 Bismarck, Otto Edward Leopold
     von
d. 1918 Kilmer, Joyce (Alfred Joyce)
d. 1930 Schildkraut, Rudolph
d. 1941 Welch, Mickey (Michael Francis)
d. 1942 Blanton, Jimmy
d. 1944 Bausch, Edward
d. 1948 Breckinridge, Sophonisba Preston
d. 1955 Pogany, Willy
d. 1962 McCormick, Myron
d. 1963 Hurley, Patrick Jay
d. 1964 Engle, Clair
d. 1964 Landis, James McCauley
d. 1966 Craig, Gordon (Edward Henry
     Gordon)
d. 1970 Perlea, Jonel
d. 1970 Szell, George
d. 1973 Lee, Bruce
d. 1975 Blish, James Benjamin
d. 1975 Hoffa, Jimmy (James Riddle)
d. 1976 Bultmann, Rudolf
d. 1977 Holloway, Emory
d. 1983 Dietz, Howard M
d. 1983 Fontanne, Lynn
d. 1983 Plimpton, Francis Taylor Pearson
d. 1984 Renault, Gilbert (Leon Etienne
     Theodore)
d. 1986 Dalton, John Nichols

July 31
b. 1689 Richardson, Samuel
b. 1763 Kent, James
b. 1800 Wohler, Friedrich
b. 1803 Ericsson, John
b. 1816 Thomas, George Henry
b. 1822 Hewitt, Abram Stevens
b. 1835 Du Chaillu, Paul Belloni
b. 1837 Quantrill, William Clarke
b. 1848 Planquette, Jean(-Robert)

b. 1859 Smith, Theobald
b. 1860 Walcott, Mary Morris Vaux
b. 1867 Kresge, Sebastian Spering
b. 1869 Brasher, Rex
b. 1882 Ives, Herbert Eugene
b. 1899 Stevens, Robert Ten Broeck
b. 1900 Roper, Elmo Burns, Jr.
b. 1901 Dubuffet, Jean
b. 1904 Daley, Arthur
b. 1904 Dresser, Davis
b. 1911 Liberace, George J
b. 1912 Friedman, Milton
b. 1912 Kupcinet, Irv
b. 1915 Aptheker, Herbert
b. 1916 Todman, Bill (William Selden)
b. 1918 Rowen, Hobart
b. 1919 Conley, Renie
b. 1919 DelMar, Norman Rene
b. 1919 Gowdy, Curt
b. 1919 Morgenthau, Robert Morris
b. 1921 Young, Whitney Moore, Jr.
b. 1922 Axelson, Kenneth Strong
b. 1922 Bauer, Hank (Henry Albert)
b. 1923 Ertegun, Ahmet
b. 1925 Manner, Harold
b. 1926 Pollard, Jack
b. 1927 Nichols, Peter
b. 1929 Murray, Don(ald Patrick)
b. 1934 De Vorzon, Barry
b. 1939 Nuyen, France
b. 1943 Bennett, William John
b. 1943 Flannery, Susan
b. 1944 Chaplin, Geraldine
b. 1944 Lansing, Sherry Lee
b. 1946 Welch, Bob
b. 1951 Goolagong, Evonne
b. 1956 Maloney, Dave (David Wilfred)
b. 1957 Durham, Leon
b. 1962 Murray, Troy
d. 1556 Ignatius of Loyola, Saint
d. 1806 Lunardi, Vincenzo
d. 1854 Wilson, Samuel
d. 1867 Sedgwick, Catherine Maria
d. 1871 Cary, Phoebe
d. 1875 Johnson, Andrew
d. 1886 Liszt, Franz (Ferencz)
d. 1896 Hunt, Richard Morris
d. 1899 Brinton, Daniel Garrison
d. 1910 Carlisle, John Griffin
d. 1914 Jaures, Jean Leon
d. 1922 Murfree, Mary Noailles
d. 1937 Hires, Charles E
d. 1944 Lehand, "Missy" (Marguerite
     Alice)
d. 1944 Saint-Exupery, Antoine (Jean
     Baptiste Marie Roger) de
d. 1951 Haldeman-Julius, Emanuel
d. 1953 Taft, Robert A(lphonso)
d. 1957 Tchelitchew, Pavel
d. 1962 Britton, Edgar Clay
d. 1967 Kennedy, Margaret

d. 1970 Conzelman, Jimmy (James
    Gleason)
d. 1972 Spaak, Paul-Henri
d. 1978 Light, Enoch Henry
d. 1978 Widdemer, Margaret
d. 1980 Van, Bobby
d. 1981 Boni, Albert
d. 1981 Torrijos Herrera, Omar
d. 1982 Atwood, Francis Clarke
d. 1982 Chenoweth, Dean
d. 1984 Stern, Philip Van Doren
d. 1985 Blake, Eugene Carson
d. 1985 Blum, Stella
d. 1986 Ellin, Stanley
d. 1986 Wilson, Teddy (Theodore)

AUGUST

b. 1613 Taylor, Jeremy
b. 1635 Betterton, Thomas
b. 1870 Kuprin, Aleksandr Ivanovich
b. 1901 Boyce, Westray Battle
b. 1924 Ahidjo, Ahmadou
b. 1934 Sadat, Jihan Raouf
b. 1948 Steel, Danielle
d. 1574 Eustachio, Bartolomeo
d. 1625 Fletcher, John
d. 634 Abu Bakr
d. 1641 Heywood, Thomas
d. 1643 Hutchinson, Anne
d. 1682 Maitland, John
d. 1693 Blount, Charles
d. 1888 Pemberton, John Stith
d. 1903 Salisbury, Robert Arthur Talbot,
    3rd Marquess
d. 1927 Atget, Eugene (Jean-Eugene-
    Auguste)
d. 1950 Pavese, Cesare
d. 1966 Whitman, Charles Joseph
d. 1972 Roswaenge, Helge
d. 1975 Barger, Floyd
d. 1978 Lord, Mary Pillsbury

August 1
b. 10 BC Claudius I
b. 1744 Lamarck, Jean Baptiste Pierre
b. 1770 Clark, William
b. 1779 Key, Francis Scott
b. 1815 Dana, Richard Henry, Jr.
b. 1818 Mitchell, Maria
b. 1819 Melville, Herman
b. 1822 Grant, James
b. 1843 Lincoln, Robert Todd
b. 1848 Gailhard, Pierre
b. 1862 James, Montague Rhodes
b. 1864 Smith, Ellison DuRant
b. 1869 Hillquit, Morris
b. 1873 Hocking, William Ernest
b. 1878 Tanguay, Eva
b. 1881 Macaulay, Rose
b. 1885 Hevesy, George de
b. 1886 McLean, Evalyn Walsh
b. 1888 Whitney, Richard

b. 1891 Streeter, Edward
b. 1898 Stotz, Charles Morse
b. 1898 Ziff, William B
b. 1899 Dean, William Frishe
b. 1899 Steinberg, William (Hans Wilhelm)
b. 1902 Latzo, Pete
b. 1903 Horgan, Paul
b. 1909 Fawcett, Wilford Hamilton, Jr.
b. 1912 Jones, Henry
b. 1914 Mangrum, Lloyd
b. 1920 Cole, Maria
b. 1921 Kramer, Jack
b. 1922 Hill, Arthur
b. 1922 McColough, C(harles) Peter
b. 1923 Brown, Carter, pseud.
b. 1925 Bamberger, George Irvin
b. 1929 Stewart, Michael
b. 1930 Bart, Lionel
b. 1932 Kahane, Meir David
b. 1933 DeLuise, Dom
b. 1936 Saint Laurent, Yves Mathieu
b. 1937 D'Amato, Alfonse Marcello
b. 1937 Plotnik, Arthur
b. 1942 Garcia, Jerry (Jerome John)
b. 1942 Giannini, Giancarlo
b. 1947 Anderson, Rich
b. 1948 Branch, Cliff(ord)
b. 1951 Carroll, Jim
b. 1957 Peeters, Pete(r)
b. 1958 Vandeweghe, "Kiki" (Ernest
    Maurice)
b. 1959 Elliott, Joe
d. 1464 Medici, Cosimo de
d. 1714 Anne
d. 1743 Savage, Richard
d. 1866 Ross, John
d. 1903 Calamity Jane
d. 1911 Abbey, Edwin Austin
d. 1919 Hammerstein, Oscar
d. 1926 Zangwill, Israel
d. 1944 Quezon (y Molina), Manuel Luis
d. 1949 Moran, George
d. 1952 Brunler, Oscar
d. 1952 Higgins, Andrew J
d. 1961 Redman, Ben Ray
d. 1963 Roethke, Theodore
d. 1965 Howard, Eugene
d. 1965 Lynch, Joe
d. 1966 Gowdy, Hank (Henry Morgan)
d. 1966 Powell, Earl
d. 1970 Farmer, Frances
d. 1970 Fleeson, Doris
d. 1973 Malipiero, Gian Francesco
d. 1973 Ulbricht, Walter
d. 1977 Powers, Francis Gary
d. 1980 Depailler, Patrick
d. 1980 Martin, Strother
d. 1981 Chayefsky, "Paddy" (Sidney)
d. 1981 Lynch, Kevin
d. 1985 Walker, Joseph

b. 1910 Gunther, John
b. 1913 Gusberg, Saul Bernard
b. 1919 Wriston, Walter Bigelow
b. 1920 Hegan, Jim (James Edward)
b. 1920 James, P(hyllis) D(orothy)
b. 1921 Adler, Richard
b. 1921 Maxwell, Marilyn
b. 1922 Eisenhower, John Sheldon Doud
b. 1923 Hagen, Jean
b. 1923 Klein, Anne
b. 1924 Uris, Leon Marcus
b. 1925 Hargis, Billy James
b. 1926 Bennett, Tony
b. 1926 Murphy, John Michael
b. 1927 Scott, Gordon
b. 1930 Popov, Oleg Konstantinovich
b. 1931 Cord, Alex
b. 1933 Martinelli, Elsa
b. 1934 Savimbi, Jonas Malheiro
b. 1935 Lamm, Richard D
b. 1937 Habyarimana, Juvenal
b. 1937 Wakoski, Diane
b. 1940 Alworth, Lance Dwight
b. 1940 Sheen, Martin
b. 1950 Landis, John David
b. 1951 Dionne, Marcel
b. 1952 North, Jay
d. 1677 Borromini, Francesco
d. 1721 Gibbons, Grinling
d. 1792 Arkwright, Richard, Sir
d. 1875 Sue, Eugene Joseph Marie
d. 1881 Fargo, William George
d. 1888 Goodrich, Benjamin Franklin
d. 1891 Comstock, Elizabeth L
d. 1894 Inness, George
d. 1898 Gardner, Jean Louis Charles
d. 1907 Saint Gaudens, Augustus
d. 1916 Casement, Roger David
d. 1924 Conrad, Joseph
d. 1929 Berliner, Emile
d. 1929 Veblen, Thorstein Bunde
d. 1932 Brouthers, "Dan" (Dennis Joseph)
d. 1940 Jabotinsky, Vladimir Evgenevich
d. 1948 Ryan, Tommy
d. 1954 Aldrich, Bess Streeter
d. 1954 Colette, pseud.
d. 1962 Cromwell, Dean Bartlett
d. 1964 O'Connor, Flannery
d. 1966 Bruce, Lenny
d. 1968 Rokossovsky, Konstantin
d. 1971 Sloane, John
d. 1973 Condon, Eddie
d. 1976 Warner, Roger Sherman, Jr.
d. 1979 Ottaviani, Alfredo, Cardinal
d. 1982 Carritt, David Graham (Hugh David Graham)
d. 1983 Jones, Carolyn
d. 1986 Markham, Beryl

August 4
b. 1540 Scaliger, Joseph Justus
b. 1792 Irving, Edward

b. 1792 Shelley, Percy Bysshe
b. 1816 Sage, Russell
b. 1841 Hudson, William Henry
b. 1855 Mollenhauer, Emil
b. 1859 Hamsun, Knut Pederson
b. 1863 McAdie, Alexander George
b. 1867 Beckley, Jake (Jacob Peter)
b. 1870 Lauder, Harry MacLennan, Sir
b. 1873 Paul-Boncour, Joseph
b. 1875 Montemezzi, Italo
b. 1890 Luque, Dolf (Adolfo)
b. 1895 Anthony, Edward
b. 1897 Lyman, Abe
b. 1898 O'Connell, Hugh
b. 1900 Elizabeth, the Queen Mother
b. 1900 Illia, Arturo Umberto
b. 1904 Hobson, Harold
b. 1908 Kane, Helen
b. 1908 Lancaster, Osbert, Sir
b. 1909 Cunningham, Glenn Clarence
b. 1909 Faralla, Dana (Dorothy W)
b. 1910 Birnie, William Alfred Hart
b. 1910 Schuman, William Howard
b. 1912 Wallenberg, Raoul Gustav
b. 1913 Addy, Wesley
b. 1913 Hayden, Robert Earl
b. 1920 Dubs, Adolph
b. 1920 Thomas, Helen A
b. 1921 Richard, Maurice (Joseph Henri Maurice)
b. 1932 Tucci, Gabriella
b. 1934 Green, Dallas (George Dallas, Jr.)
b. 1938 Coburn, D(onald) L(ee)
b. 1942 Lange, David Russell
b. 1943 Cole, Tina
b. 1949 Riggins, John
b. 1952 Tabori, Kristoffer
b. 1953 Brand, Jack
b. 1956 Huntley, Joni
b. 1958 Decker, Mary
b. 1962 Clemens, Roger (William Roger)
d. 1265 Montfort, Simon de
d. 1639 Alarcon y Mendoza, Juan Ruiz de
d. 1741 Hamilton, Andrew
d. 1821 Floyd, William
d. 1834 Johnson, William
d. 1865 Aytoun, William Edmonstoune
d. 1875 Andersen, Hans Christian
d. 1886 Tilden, Samuel Jones
d. 1893 Bolton, Sarah Tittle Barrett
d. 1908 Howard, Bronson Crocker
d. 1922 Enver Pasha
d. 1929 Welsbach, Carl Auer von, Baron
d. 1930 Wagner, Siegfried (Helferich)
d. 1931 Williams, Daniel Hale
d. 1932 Oppenheim, James
d. 1938 White, Pearl
d. 1950 Coveleski, Harry Frank
d. 1957 George, Walter Franklin
d. 1976 Thomson of Fleet, Roy Herbert Thomson, Baron

b. 1906 Sterling, John Ewart Wallace
b. 1906 Strong, Ken
b. 1908 Jacobs, Helen Hull
b. 1908 Keener, Jefferson Ward
b. 1908 Lee, Will
b. 1909 Schnabel, Karl Ulrich
b. 1910 Crichton, Charles
b. 1911 Ball, Lucille
b. 1916 Cooney, Barbara
b. 1916 Hofstadter, Richard
b. 1917 Mitchum, Robert (Robert Charles Duran)
b. 1917 Tyne, George
b. 1918 Granz, Norman
b. 1919 Betz, Pauline
b. 1921 Raines, Ella
b. 1921 Reed, Betty Jane
b. 1922 Ford, Doug
b. 1922 Laingen, (Lowell) Bruce
b. 1922 Laker, Freddie (Frederick Alfred)
b. 1922 Lomax, Louis
b. 1922 Walker, Daniel
b. 1926 Finlay, Frank
b. 1926 Presser, Jackie
b. 1927 Warhol, Andy
b. 1930 Lincoln, Abbey
b. 1935 Benjamin, Adam, Jr.
b. 1938 Bonerz, Peter
b. 1943 Anderson, Michael, Jr.
b. 1945 Messersmith, Andy (John Alexander)
b. 1946 Lynch, Benny
b. 1957 Horner, Bob (James Robert)
b. 1958 DeBarge, Randy
d. 1660 Velazquez, Diego Rodriguez de Silva
d. 1891 Litolff, Henri Charles
d. 1893 Schirmer, Gustave
d. 1904 Hanslick, Eduard
d. 1914 Wilson, Ellen Axson
d. 1945 Johnson, Hiram W
d. 1946 Lazzeri, Tony (Anthony Michael)
d. 1954 Dionne, Emilie
d. 1954 Fairchild, David Grandison
d. 1955 Beecher, Janet
d. 1959 Sturges, Preston
d. 1960 Kemp, (Harry) Hibbard
d. 1964 Hardwicke, Cedric Webster, Sir
d. 1965 Carroll, Nancy
d. 1965 Sloane, Everett
d. 1967 Kiplinger, W(illard) M(onroe)
d. 1967 Weinberger, Jaromir
d. 1973 Batista y Zaldivar, Fulgencio
d. 1974 Ammons, "Jug" (Eugene)
d. 1974 Rounseville, Robert Field
d. 1975 Daubeny, Peter Lauderdale, Sir
d. 1976 Chu Te
d. 1976 Piatigorsky, Gregor
d. 1977 Bustamante, William Alexander
d. 1978 Hasselblad, Victor
d. 1978 Paul VI, Pope

d. 1978 Stone, Edward Durell
d. 1979 Kasznar, Kurt
d. 1980 Marini, Marino
d. 1981 Bliss, Ray C(harles)
d. 1981 Price, Byron
d. 1982 Clarke, Gilmore David
d. 1985 Burnham, Forbes (Linden Forbes Sampson)
d. 1986 Fernandez, Emilio
d. 1986 Schroeder, William

August 7
b. 1586 Andrae, Johann Valentin
b. 1726 Bowdoin, James
b. 1742 Greene, Nathanael
b. 1860 Moses, "Grandma" (Anna Mary Robertson)
b. 1867 Nolde, Emil
b. 1868 Bantock, Granville, Sir
b. 1876 Mata Hari
b. 1881 Darlan, Jean Francois
b. 1881 Enesco, Georges
b. 1883 Werrenrath, Reinald
b. 1886 Burke, "Billie" (Mary William Ethelberg Appleton)
b. 1887 McKechnie, Bill (William Boyd)
b. 1890 Flynn, Elizabeth Gurley
b. 1896 Bergen, John Joseph
b. 1901 Heiden, Konrad
b. 1903 Leakey, Louis Seymour Bazett
b. 1904 Bunche, Ralph Johnson
b. 1907 Dart, Justin Whitlock
b. 1911 Ray, Nicholas
b. 1912 Dorman, Maurice
b. 1919 Borg, Kim
b. 1921 Covington, Warren
b. 1925 Bryant, Felice
b. 1925 Weber, Carl
b. 1926 Freberg, Stan
b. 1926 Kaufman, Sue
b. 1927 Busbee, George Dekle
b. 1927 Edwards, Edwin Washington
b. 1928 Byars, Betsy
b. 1928 Randi, James
b. 1929 Larsen, Don(ald James)
b. 1929 Stapleton, Ruth Carter
b. 1937 Stern, Carl (Leonard)
b. 1938 Caldicott, Helen Broinowski
b. 1942 Comer, Anjanette
b. 1942 Keillor, Garrison (Gary Edward)
b. 1942 Thomas, B(illy) J(oe)
b. 1943 Cantrell, Lana
b. 1945 Page, Alan Cedric
b. 1949 Novi, Carlo
b. 1950 Crowell, Rodney
b. 1954 Kemp, Steve(n F)
b. 1958 Salazar, Alberto
d. 1657 Blake, Robert
d. 1817 DuPont de Nemours, Pierre Samuel
d. 1847 Rapp, George
d. 1848 Berzelius, Jons Jacob, Baron

d. 1893 Catalani, Alfredo
d. 1911 Allen, Elizabeth Ann Chase Akers
d. 1912 Hartmann, Franz
d. 1927 Wood, Leonard
d. 1929 Berger, Victor L
d. 1929 Medary, Milton B
d. 1931 Beiderbecke, "Bix" (Leon Bismark)
d. 1938 Stanislavsky, Konstantin
   Sergeyevich
d. 1941 Tagore, Rabindranath, Sir
d. 1957 Hardy, Oliver
d. 1960 Ferragamo, Salvatore
d. 1960 Firpo, Luis Angel
d. 1961 Buchman, Frank Nathan Daniel
d. 1961 Robinson, Claude Everett
d. 1965 Derby, Jane (Jeanette Barr)
d. 1969 Morgan, Russ
d. 1971 Evans, Orrin C
d. 1972 Lansing, Joi
d. 1973 Tunis, Edwin Burdett
d. 1974 Apgar, Virginia
d. 1979 Monsarrat, Nicholas John Turney
d. 1981 Arieti, Silvano
d. 1981 Noyes, David
d. 1984 Little Esther
d. 1984 Phillips, Esther

August 8
b.   Bellisario, Donald P
b. 1646 Kneller, Godfrey, Sir
b. 1694 Hutcheson, Francis
b. 1763 Bulfinch, Charles
b. 1779 Silliman, Benjamin
b. 1799 Palmer, Nathaniel Brown
b. 1819 Dana, Charles Anderson
b. 1822 Stoneman, George
b. 1825 Mould, Jacob Wrey
b. 1839 Miles, Nelson A
b. 1857 McIntyre, James
b. 1861 Bateson, William
b. 1861 Chaminade, Cecile
b. 1863 Bailey, Florence Augusta Merriam
b. 1875 Hamilton, Charles Harold St. John
b. 1879 Smith, Robert Holbrook
b. 1882 Samaroff, Olga
b. 1882 Stokowski, Olga Smaroff
b. 1884 Teasdale, Sara
b. 1886 Buck, Gene
b. 1886 Yon, Pietro Alessandro
b. 1896 Rawlings, Marjorie Kinnan
b. 1900 Young, Victor
b. 1901 Lawrence, Ernest Orlando
b. 1902 Dirac, Paul A M
b. 1905 Martini, Nino
b. 1906 Thon, William
b. 1907 Carter, Benny (Bennett Lester)
b. 1907 Stuart, Jesse Hilton
b. 1908 Goldberg, Arthur Joseph
b. 1909 Butterfield, Lyman Henry
b. 1910 Sidney, Sylvia
b. 1913 Stafford, Robert Theodore
b. 1915 Elliott, "Jumbo" (James Francis)

b. 1915 Shedd, Charlie W
b. 1919 DeLaurentiis, Dino
b. 1922 Gernreich, Rudi
b. 1923 Calhoun, Rory
b. 1923 Spaak, Fernand Paul Jules
b. 1923 Williams, Esther
b. 1926 Anderson, Richard Norman
b. 1926 Pierce, Webb
b. 1926 Switzer, Carl
b. 1927 Gadsby, Bill (William Alexander)
b. 1930 Mondale, Joan Adams
b. 1930 Talbot, Nita
b. 1932 Culver, John C
b. 1932 Tillis, Mel(vin)
b. 1933 Tex, Joe
b. 1936 Howard, Frank Oliver
b. 1937 Hoffman, Dustin
b. 1938 Stevens, Connie
b. 1942 Blanchard, James J
b. 1944 Depailler, Patrick
b. 1944 Weir, Peter
b. 1947 Dryden, Ken(neth Wayne)
b. 1947 Wilcox, Larry Dee
b. 1949 Sipe, Brian Winfield
b. 1950 Carradine, Keith Ian
b. 1953 Most, Donny
b. 1963 Lewis, Carol
d. 1553 Fracastoro, Gerolamo
d. 1827 Canning, George
d. 1856 Vestris, Lucia Elizabeth
d. 1898 Boudin, Eugene Louis
d. 1919 Haeckel, Ernst Heinrich
d. 1921 Ladd, George Trumbull
d. 1934 Robinson, Wilbert
d. 1940 Bonci, Alessandro
d. 1940 Coolidge, Dane
d. 1940 Dodds, Johnny
d. 1942 Genthe, Arnold
d. 1947 Denikin, Anton Ivanovich
d. 1948 Door, Rheta Childe
d. 1952 Weinman, Adolph A
d. 1955 Hartman, Grace
d. 1958 Bracken, Brendan Rendall,
   Viscount
d. 1959 Hinton, William Augustus
d. 1960 Walker, Danton MacIntyre
d. 1965 Jackson, Shirley
d. 1967 Magritte, Rene
d. 1973 Wiley, George A
d. 1975 Adderley, "Cannonball" (Julian
   Edwin)
d. 1978 Bakeless, John Edwin
d. 1979 McDonald, David John
d. 1980 Mercer, David
d. 1980 Yahya Khan, Agha Muhammad
d. 1981 McIlwee, Thomas
d. 1982 Braestrup, Carl Bjorn
d. 1983 Harger, Rolla
d. 1984 Khrushchev, Nina Petrovna
d. 1985 Brooks, Louise

August 9
- b. 1593 Walton, Izaak
- b. 1631 Dryden, John
- b. 1762 Randolph, Mary
- b. 1799 James, George Payne Rainsford
- b. 1812 Judson, Egbert Putnam
- b. 1819 Morton, William Thomas Green
- b. 1836 Gamble, James Norris
- b. 1875 Gagn, Reynaldo
- b. 1877 Young, Mahonri M
- b. 1880 Epstein, Jacob, Sir
- b. 1882 Guion, Connie Myers
- b. 1893 Bedells, Phyllis
- b. 1894 Starkie, Walter Fitzwilliam
- b. 1896 Massine, Leonide Fedorovich
- b. 1896 Piaget, Jean
- b. 1896 Sullivan, A(loysius) M(ichael)
- b. 1898 Hays, Brooks
- b. 1899 Kelly, Paul
- b. 1899 Pendleton, Nat
- b. 1901 Casadesus, Gaby Lhote
- b. 1901 Farrell, Charles
- b. 1902 Francescatti, Zino Rene
- b. 1902 Solomon
- b. 1905 Gaud, William Steen, Jr.
- b. 1905 Genn, Leo
- b. 1906 Wallace, Ed(ward Tatum)
- b. 1908 Landolfi, Tommaso
- b. 1913 Talmadge, Herman Eugene
- b. 1914 Fricsay, Ferenc
- b. 1918 Aldrich, Robert
- b. 1918 Cooper, Giles (Stannus)
- b. 1919 Houk, Ralph George
- b. 1920 Hoskins, Allen Clayton
- b. 1921 Exon, J(ohn) James, Jr.
- b. 1922 Larkin, Philip
- b. 1924 Quaison-Sackey, Alex(ander)
- b. 1927 Shaw, Robert
- b. 1928 Cousy, Bob (Robert Joseph)
- b. 1928 Johnson, Harold
- b. 1931 Jackson, "Hurricane" (Thomas)
- b. 1932 Halberstam, Michael Joseph
- b. 1937 Lewis, Jordan David
- b. 1938 Laver, Rod(ney George)
- b. 1940 Saint John, Jill
- b. 1942 Steinberg, David
- b. 1945 Norton, Ken(neth Howard)
- b. 1946 Kiick, Jim (James F)
- b. 1952 Cappelletti, John Raymond
- b. 1955 Ovett, Steve
- b. 1955 Williams, Doug(las Lee)
- b. 1956 Saucier, Kevin Andrew
- b. 1957 Griffith, Melanie
- b. 1959 Stastny, Anton
- b. 1963 Houston, Whitney
- d. 1848 Marryat, Frederick
- d. 1869 Little, Charles Coffin
- d. 1884 Elliott, Robert B
- d. 1892 Denver, James William
- d. 1911 Gates, John Warne
- d. 1919 Blakelock, Ralph Albert

- d. 1919 Leoncavallo, Ruggiero
- d. 1936 Steffens, Lincoln
- d. 1943 Soutine, Chaim
- d. 1949 Davenport, Harry George Bryant
- d. 1952 Farnol, Jeffery
- d. 1954 Marcantonio, Vito Anthony
- d. 1959 Epstein, Jacob, Sir
- d. 1961 Smith, Walter Bedell
- d. 1962 Hesse, Hermann
- d. 1965 Freeman, Joseph
- d. 1967 Orton, Joe (John Kingsley)
- d. 1967 Walbrook, Anton
- d. 1968 Stiedry, Fritz
- d. 1969 Powell, Cecil Frank
- d. 1969 Stratemeyer, George E
- d. 1969 Tate, Sharon
- d. 1973 Behrman, S(amuel) N(athaniel)
- d. 1973 Moberg, Vihelm
- d. 1973 Roxon, Lillian
- d. 1974 Luckenbach, Edgar Frederick, Jr.
- d. 1975 Shostakovich, Dmitri Dmitryevich
- d. 1976 Schmidt-Rottluf, Karl
- d. 1978 Cozzens, James Gould
- d. 1979 O'Malley, Walter Francis
- d. 1979 Zuckerman, Ben
- d. 1980 Cochran, Jacqueline
- d. 1980 Nugent, Elliott
- d. 1981 Feldman, Alvin Lindbergh
- d. 1984 Deacon, Richard

August 10
- b. 1729 Howe, William, Viscount
- b. 1753 Randolph, Edmund Jennings
- b. 1798 LaFeuer, Minard
- b. 1810 Cavour, Camillo Benso di
- b. 1821 Cooke, Jay
- b. 1823 Keene, Charles Samuel
- b. 1848 Harnett, William Michael
- b. 1848 Scott, Austin
- b. 1856 Doheny, Edward Lawrence
- b. 1861 Wright, Almroth Edward, Sir
- b. 1865 Glazunov, Alexander Constantinovich
- b. 1865 Morrice, James Wilson
- b. 1869 Binyon, Laurence
- b. 1874 Hoover, Herbert Clark
- b. 1877 Marshall, Frank James
- b. 1881 Bynner, Harold Witter
- b. 1887 Herbert, Hugh
- b. 1887 Thompson, Oscar
- b. 1887 Warner, Sam(uel Louis)
- b. 1890 Hart, Frances Noyes
- b. 1893 Moore, Douglas
- b. 1895 Richman, Harry
- b. 1895 Vertes, Marcel
- b. 1896 Sobol, Louis
- b. 1897 Nakian, Reuben
- b. 1900 Haley, Jack
- b. 1900 Porritt, Arthur Espie, Sir
- b. 1902 Siodmark, Curt
- b. 1904 Shearer, Norma
- b. 1908 Thornhill, Claude

b. 1910 Mohammed V
b. 1911 Chodorov, Jerome
b. 1911 Elkin, Benjamin
b. 1912 Amado, Jorge
b. 1914 Corey, Jeff
b. 1914 Malcuzynski, Witold
b. 1916 Beery, Noah, Jr.
b. 1918 Cobb, Arnett Cleophus
b. 1920 Holzman, William
b. 1923 Fleming, Rhonda
b. 1924 Hyer, Martha
b. 1928 Dean, Jimmy
b. 1928 Fisher, Eddie (Edwin Jack)
b. 1930 Goodman, George Jerome Waldo
b. 1933 Colavito, Rocky (Rocco Domenico)
b. 1938 Muldaur, Diana Charlton
b. 1940 Hatfield, Bobby
b. 1942 Johnson, Betsey
b. 1947 Anderson, Ian
b. 1948 Austin, Patti
b. 1950 Buse, Don
b. 1956 Fromholtz, Dianne
b. 1958 Dokes, Michael
b. 1959 Arquette, Rosanna
d. 1817 Lowell, Francis Cabot
d. 1838 Rodgers, John
d. 1861 Lyon, Nathaniel
d. 1867 Aldridge, Ira Frederick
d. 1868 Menken, Adah Isaacs
d. 1876 Lane, Edward William
d. 1906 Clarke, Rebecca Sophia
d. 1920 O'Neill, James
d. 1934 Kane, John
d. 1941 Howard, Cordelia
d. 1945 Goddard, Robert Hutchings
d. 1951 Bloor, "Mother" Ella Reeve
d. 1953 Burns, John Horne
d. 1960 Lloyd, Frank
d. 1961 Hilsberg, Alexander
d. 1961 Peterkin, Julia Mood
d. 1962 Husing, Ted
d. 1963 Kefauver, Estes
d. 1964 Fox, Fontaine Talbot, Jr.
d. 1966 Dressen, Charlie (Charles W)
d. 1970 Lapchick, Joseph Bohomiel
d. 1971 Ogg, Oscar
d. 1974 Massey, Ilona
d. 1979 Foran, Dick John Nicholas
d. 1979 Wright, John Joseph
d. 1981 Fisk, James Brown
d. 1984 Partch, Virgil Franklin, II
d. 1986 Engel, Lyle Kenyon

August 11
b. 1807 Atchison, David R
b. 1811 Benjamin, Judah Philip
b. 1823 Yonge, Charlotte Mary
b. 1833 Ingersoll, Robert Green
b. 1842 Elliott, Robert B
b. 1860 Melchers, Gari
b. 1862 Bond, Carrie Jacobs
b. 1865 Pinchot, Gifford

b. 1867 Bosworth, Hobart van Zandt
b. 1867 Weber, Joseph M
b. 1882 Graziani, Rodolfo
b. 1882 Kallen, Horace M
b. 1891 Broderick, Helen
b. 1892 MacDiarmid, Hugh, pseud.
b. 1897 Blyton, Enid Mary
b. 1897 Bogan, Louise
b. 1899 Hirshhorn, Joseph
b. 1900 Brogan, Denis William, Sir
b. 1900 Dunn, Alan
b. 1900 Mayes, Herbert Raymond
b. 1902 Nolan, Lloyd
b. 1902 Shoemaker, Vaughn Richard
b. 1903 Seagram, Joseph Edward Frowde
b. 1904 Woolley, Catherine (Jane Thayer)
b. 1907 Newsom, "Bobo" (Louis Norman)
b. 1908 Abel, I(orwith) W(ilbur)
b. 1911 Kittikachorn, Thanom
b. 1911 McCormick, Robert K
b. 1912 Harvey, Frank Laird
b. 1912 Parker, Jean
b. 1913 Crane, Nathalia Clara Ruth
b. 1913 Oliver, Edith
b. 1913 Wilson, Angus
b. 1916 Wind, Herbert Warren
b. 1917 Browne, Dik
b. 1920 Garrett, Ray, Jr.
b. 1921 Graff, Henry Franklin
b. 1921 Haley, Alex Palmer
b. 1922 Gallant, Mavis
b. 1922 Stuart, Lyle
b. 1925 Douglas, Mike
b. 1925 Rowan, Carl Thomas
b. 1926 Von Bulow, Claus
b. 1927 Dahl, Arlene
b. 1927 Leppard, Raymond John
b. 1932 Arrabal (Teran), Fernando
b. 1933 Berger, Terry
b. 1933 Falwell, Jerry
b. 1937 Massey, Anna
b. 1938 Kent, Allegra
b. 1941 Holtzman, Elizabeth
b. 1944 Coles, Joanna
b. 1944 Smith, Frederick Wallace
b. 1947 Brashler, William
b. 1949 Carmen, Eric
b. 1949 Charleson, Ian
b. 1955 Jackson, Joe
d. 1446 Nicholas of Cusa
d. 1486 William of Waynflete
d. 1494 Memling, Hans
d. 1778 Toplady, Augustus Montague
d. 1817 Pickens, Andrew
d. 1868 Stevens, Thaddeus
d. 1872 Mason, Lowell
d. 1875 Graham, William Alexander
d. 1881 Fillmore, Caroline Carmichael
    McIntosh
d. 1890 Newman, John Henry, Cardinal
d. 1914 Plancon, Pol-Henri

d. 1919 Carnegie, Andrew
d. 1930 Angle, Edward Hartley
d. 1937 Wharton, Edith
d. 1952 Martin, Riccardo
d. 1955 Seiberling, Frank Augustus
d. 1956 Pollock, Jackson
d. 1963 Seymour, Charles
d. 1964 Mannes, Leopold Damrosch
d. 1965 Lehman, Adele Lewisohn
d. 1972 Theiler, Max
d. 1973 Castle, Peggie
d. 1975 McAuliffe, Anthony Clement
d. 1976 May, Robert Lewis
d. 1977 Schorer, Mark
d. 1980 Robert, Paul
d. 1982 Drake, Tom
d. 1983 Wigg, George (Edward Cecil)
d. 1984 Knopf, Alfred Abraham
d. 1986 Jarvis, Howard Arnold
d. 1986 McKinley, Chuck (Charles Robert)

August 12
b. 1753 Bewick, Thomas
b. 1762 George IV
b. 1774 Southey, Robert
b. 1781 Mills, Robert
b. 1849 Thayer, Abbott Handerson
b. 1854 Thomas, Edith Matilda
b. 1856 Brady, "Diamond Jim" (James Buchanan)
b. 1859 Bacheller, Irving
b. 1859 Bates, Katherine Lee
b. 1862 Rosenwald, Julius
b. 1866 Benavente y Martinez, Jacinto
b. 1867 Hamilton, Edith
b. 1875 Panizza, Ettore
b. 1876 Rinehart, Mary Roberts
b. 1880 Mathewson, Christy (Christopher)
b. 1881 DeMille, Cecil B(lount)
b. 1882 Bellows, George Wesley
b. 1882 Bendix, Vincent
b. 1884 Swinnerton, Frank Arthur
b. 1885 Frederick, Pauline
b. 1887 Schroedinger, Erwin
b. 1888 Lorne, Marion
b. 1889 Sharp, Zerna A
b. 1890 Goodman, Al(fred)
b. 1892 Olczewska, Maria
b. 1892 Rea, Gardner
b. 1892 Schalk, Ray(mond William)
b. 1895 Lawler, Richard Harold
b. 1897 Struve, Otto
b. 1899 DeLeeuw, Adele Louise
b. 1903 Homolka, Oscar
b. 1905 Elting, Victor, Jr.
b. 1907 Sheares, Benjamin Henry
b. 1910 Ishak, Yusof bin
b. 1910 Sutermeister, Heinrich
b. 1911 Cantinflas
b. 1911 Downes, Edward Olin Davenport
b. 1911 Fuller, Samuel
b. 1912 Sullivan, Barry

b. 1913 Daniels, Draper
b. 1915 Wojciechowicz, Alexander
b. 1919 Aberle, John Wayne
b. 1919 Hutchinson, Fred(erick Charles)
b. 1919 Kidd, Michael
b. 1921 Monty, Gloria
b. 1921 Reynolds, Marjorie
b. 1923 Gannett, Ruth
b. 1925 Bumpers, Dale Leon
b. 1925 McWhirter, A(lan) Ross
b. 1925 McWhirter, Norris Dewar
b. 1926 Derek, John
b. 1927 Rostropovich, Mstislav Leopoldovich
b. 1927 Wagoner, Porter
b. 1929 Owens, "Buck" (Alvis E, Jr.)
b. 1931 Goldman, William
b. 1933 Jones, Parnelli (Rufus Parnell)
b. 1939 Hamilton, George
b. 1941 Feulner, Edwin John, Jr.
b. 1949 Knopfler, Mark
b. 1949 Ridgeway, Rick
b. 1950 Kleinfield, "Sonny" (Nathan Richard)
b. 1950 McGinnis, George
d. 1612 Gabrieli, Giovanni
d. 1633 Peri, Jacopo
d. 1715 Tate, Nahum
d. 1827 Blake, William
d. 1848 Stephenson, George
d. 1849 Gallatin, Albert (Abraham Alfonse Albert)
d. 1885 Jackson, Helen Maria Hunt Fiske
d. 1891 Lowell, James Russell
d. 1900 Steinitz, Wilhelm
d. 1914 Holland, John Philip
d. 1918 Held, Anna
d. 1928 Janacek, Leos
d. 1942 Amato, Pasquale
d. 1944 Kennedy, Joseph Patrick, Jr.
d. 1949 Shean, Al
d. 1955 Mann, Thomas
d. 1962 Holman, Eugene
d. 1964 Fleming, Ian Lancaster
d. 1967 Forbes, Esther
d. 1971 Cowles, William Hutchinson, Jr.
d. 1977 Lawson, John Howard
d. 1979 Karpis, Alvin
d. 1982 Charnley, John, Sir
d. 1982 Fonda, Henry Jaynes
d. 1982 Sanchez, Salvador

August 13
b. Walley, Deborah
b. 1422 Caxton, William
b. 1743 Lavoisier, Antoine Laurent
b. 1814 Angstrom, Anders Jonas
b. 1815 Phelps, Elizabeth Stuart
b. 1818 Stone, Lucy
b. 1820 Grove, George, Sir
b. 1823 Smith, Goldwin
b. 1849 Barry, Leonora Marie Kearney

b. 1925 Baker, Russell Wayne
b. 1926 Ghostley, Alice (Allyce)
b. 1926 Goscinny, Rene
b. 1926 Greco, Buddy (Armando)
b. 1928 Wertmuller, Lina von Eigg
b. 1930 Weaver, Earl Sidney
b. 1931 Raphael, Frederic Michael
b. 1935 Brodie, John Riley
b. 1940 Laffer, Arthur Betz
b. 1941 Crosby, David
b. 1941 Eyen, Tom
b. 1944 Smith, Robyn Caroline
b. 1945 Benet, Brenda
b. 1946 Saint James, Susan
b. 1952 Meyer, Debbie (Deborah)
b. 1954 Fidrych, Mark
b. 1959 Johnson, Earvin
d. 1856 Buckland, William
d. 1870 Farragut, David Glasgow
d. 1887 Jeffries, Richard
d. 1888 Crocker, Charles
d. 1891 Polk, Sarah Childress
d. 1922 Northcliffe, Alfred Charles William
       Harmsworth, Viscount
d. 1930 Mayakovsky, Vladimir
d. 1934 Hood, Raymond Matthewson
d. 1937 McNeile, Herman Cyril
d. 1938 Ronald, Landon, Sir
d. 1941 Kolbe, Maximilian
d. 1943 Kelley, Joe (Joseph James)
d. 1951 Hearst, William Randolph
d. 1953 Schorr, Friedrich
d. 1954 Eckener, Hugo
d. 1955 Kimball, Fiske
d. 1956 Brecht, Bertolt Eugene Friedrich
d. 1956 Neurath, Constantin Freiherr von
d. 1958 Beard, Mary Ritter
d. 1958 Broonzy, "Big Bill"
d. 1958 Joliot(-Curie), (Jean) Frederic
d. 1960 Clarke, Fred Clifford
d. 1961 Breuil, Henri Abbe
d. 1963 Odets, Clifford
d. 1966 Kreymborg, Alfred
d. 1967 Prado Ugarteche, Manuel
d. 1969 Gurie, Sigrid
d. 1969 Woolf, Leonard Sidney
d. 1971 Heard, Gerald (Henry FitzGerald)
d. 1972 Levant, Oscar
d. 1972 Romains, Jules
d. 1978 Venuti, Joe (Giuseppe)
d. 1980 Snider, Paul
d. 1980 Stratten, Dorothy
d. 1981 Bohm, Karl
d. 1981 Curran, Joseph Edwin
d. 1981 Herridge, Robert T
d. 1982 Magee, Patrick
d. 1982 Morton, Thruston Ballard
d. 1984 Priestley, J B (John Boynton)
d. 1985 Sondergaard, Gale
d. 1986 Haider, Michael Lawrence

August 15
b. Rose-Marie
b. 1432 Pulci, Luigi
b. 1688 Frederick William I
b. 1740 Claudius, Matthias
b. 1769 Napoleon I
b. 1771 Scott, Walter, Sir
b. 1785 DeQuincey, Thomas
b. 1803 Douglas, James, Sir
b. 1824 Chisum, John Simpson
b. 1824 Leland, Charles Godfrey
b. 1845 Crane, Walter
b. 1848 Pareto, Vilfredo
b. 1858 Calve, Emma
b. 1859 Comiskey, Charlie (Charles Albert)
b. 1860 Harding, Florence Kling De Wolfe
b. 1869 Michael, Moina Belle
b. 1875 Bartlett, Robert Abram
b. 1875 Coleridge-Taylor, Samuel
b. 1879 Barrymore, Ethel Mae Blythe
b. 1880 Shubert, Jacob J
b. 1883 Mestrovic, Ivan
b. 1885 Burton, Montague Maurice, Sir
b. 1887 Campbell, Walter Stanley
b. 1887 Ferber, Edna
b. 1888 Lawrence, T(homas) E(dward)
b. 1888 Spalding, Albert
b. 1889 Crowley, Leo T
b. 1890 Ibert, Jacques
b. 1893 Curtice, Harlow Herbert
b. 1896 Cori, Gerty Theresa
b. 1896 Glueck, Sheldon (Sol Sheldon)
b. 1898 Carter, Lillian
b. 1904 Baird, Bil (William Britton)
b. 1907 Trotta, Maurice S
b. 1908 Kerner, Otto
b. 1909 Winterhalter, Hugo
b. 1911 Van Dellen, Theodore Robert
b. 1912 Child, Julia McWilliams
b. 1912 Hiller, Wendy
b. 1914 Rand, Paul
b. 1915 Hasso, Signe Eleonora Cecilia
b. 1915 Turkle, Brinton Cassaday
b. 1917 Lynch, John
b. 1917 Romero y Galdamez, Oscar
       Arnulfo
b. 1919 Arundel, Honor Morfydd
b. 1919 Goheen, Robert Francis
b. 1919 Kiely, Benedict
b. 1921 Banner, Bob
b. 1921 Zabach, Florian
b. 1922 Baskin, Leonard
b. 1922 Foss, Lukas
b. 1924 Bolt, Robert
b. 1924 Schlafly, Phyllis Stewart
b. 1925 Connors, Mike
b. 1925 Peterson, Oscar (Emmauel)
b. 1927 Cranko, John
b. 1930 Mboya, Tom (Thomas Joseph)
b. 1931 Rule, Janice
b. 1935 Dale, Jim

d. 1980 Longley, James Bernard
d. 1983 Averill, Earl (Howard Earl)
d. 1983 Roy, Ross
d. 1986 Price, H(enry) Ryan

August 17
b. 1624 John III, Sobieski
b. 1699 Jussieu, Bernard de
b. 1779 Ritter, Karl
b. 1786 Crockett, Davy (David)
b. 1795 Drake, Joseph Rodman
b. 1800 Rogers, Isaiah
b. 1837 Grimke, Charlotte Lottie Forten
b. 1864 Bellincioni, Gemma
b. 1866 Marlowe, Julia
b. 1868 Porter, Gene Stratton
b. 1870 Hobson, Richmond Pearson
b. 1878 Gogarty, Oliver St. John
b. 1882 Kearns, Jack
b. 1885 Fleishmann, Raoul H(erbert)
b. 1887 Garvey, Marcus Moziah
b. 1888 Woolley, Monty (Edgar Montillion)
b. 1890 Hopkins, Harry Lloyd
b. 1891 Kardiner, Abram
b. 1892 West, Mae
b. 1896 Groves, Leslie Richard
b. 1896 Larkin, Oliver Waterman
b. 1898 Gero, Erno
b. 1899 Lewis, Janet
b. 1900 Howe, Quincy
b. 1901 MacDonald, Malcolm John
b. 1902 Aldrich, Richard Stoddard
b. 1903 Chasins, Abram
b. 1903 Sebastian, George
b. 1904 Harding, Ann
b. 1904 Whitney, John Hay
b. 1906 Bishop, Hazel
b. 1906 Caetano, Marcello
b. 1907 Peyrefitte, Roger
b. 1909 Clinton, Larry
b. 1909 McNally, Andrew, III
b. 1911 Botvinnik, Mikhail Moiseevich
b. 1913 York, Rudy (Rudolph Preston)
b. 1914 Downs, William Randall, Jr.
b. 1914 Roosevelt, Franklin Delano, Jr.
b. 1916 Toledano, Ralph de
b. 1918 Ankers, Evelyn
b. 1918 Brown, George Scratchley
b. 1918 Howe, Harold, II
b. 1921 O'Hara, Maureen
b. 1923 Rivers, Larry
b. 1924 Connell, Evan S, Jr.
b. 1925 Hawkes, John Clendennin Burne,
   Jr.
b. 1927 Cornfeld, Bernard
b. 1928 Rossant, James Stephan
b. 1929 Powers, Francis Gary
b. 1930 Bennett, Harve
b. 1930 Hughes, Ted
b. 1930 Warren, Gerald Lee
b. 1932 Naipaul, V(idiahar) S(urajprasad)
b. 1939 Sanders, Ed Parish

b. 1943 DeNiro, Robert
b. 1947 Talley, Gary
b. 1952 Piquet, Nelson
b. 1952 Vilas, Guillermo
b. 1958 Carlisle, Belinda
b. 1960 Penn, Sean
d. 1785 Trumbull, Jonathan
d. 1786 Frederick the Great
d. 1804 Heck, Barbara Ruckle
d. 1838 DaPonte, Lorenzo
d. 1850 San Martin, Jose de
d. 1878 Upjohn, Richard
d. 1880 Bull, Ole Bornemann
d. 1911 Reed, Myrtle
d. 1938 Lewisohn, Adolph
d. 1945 Marinuzzi, Gino
d. 1946 Pollock, Channing
d. 1954 Sarett, Lew R
d. 1955 Leger, Fernand
d. 1957 Langmuir, Irving
d. 1958 Brooks, Walter R(ollin)
d. 1959 Landowska, Wanda
d. 1963 Barthelmess, Richard
d. 1963 Gardner, Ed(ward Francis)
d. 1966 Spargo, John
d. 1969 Blaiberg, Philip
d. 1971 McMahon, Horace
d. 1973 Aiken, Conrad Potter
d. 1973 Radford, Arthur William
d. 1976 Redfield, William
d. 1979 Vance, Vivian
d. 1981 Keylor, Arthur W
d. 1983 Gershwin, Ira
d. 1985 Eden, Nicholas

August 18
b. 1587 Dare, Virginia
b. 1750 Salieri, Antonio
b. 1774 Lewis, Meriwether
b. 1792 Russell, John, Lord
b. 1803 Clifford, Nathan
b. 1807 Adams, Charles Francis, Sr.
b. 1834 Field, Marshall
b. 1838 Neumann, Angelo
b. 1838 Scaria, Emil
b. 1846 Evans, Robley Dunglison
b. 1854 Hyslop, James Hervey
b. 1873 Harbach, Otto Abels
b. 1875 Slezak, Leo
b. 1879 Edwards, Gus
b. 1880 Cleland, Thomas Maitland
b. 1888 Williams, J(ames) R(obert)
b. 1890 Clark, Sydney
b. 1890 Funk, Walther
b. 1890 Podoloff, Maurice
b. 1893 Davidson, Donald Grady
b. 1893 Grimes, Burleigh Arland
b. 1893 MacMillan, Ernest Campbell, Sir
b. 1896 Pickford, Jack
b. 1896 Warburg, James Paul
b. 1897 Mowbray, Alan
b. 1897 Rinehart, Stanley Marshall, Jr.

b. 1938 Goode, Wilson (Willie Wilson)
b. 1940 Baker, "Ginger" (Peter)
b. 1940 Nash, Johnny
b. 1942 Monk, Allan James
b. 1946 Clinton, Bill (William Jefferson)
b. 1947 Schwarz, Gerard
b. 1948 McRaney, Gerald
b. 1955 Nelson, Cindy
b. 1960 Darling, Ron(ald Maurice, Jr.)
d. 14 BC Augustus
d. 1457 Castagno, Andrea del
d. 1580 Palladio, Andrea
d. 1662 Pascal, Blaise
d. 1777 Herkimer, Nicholas
d. 1780 Kalb, Johann de
d. 1819 Watt, James
d. 1887 Baird, Spencer Fullerton
d. 1923 Pareto, Vilfredo
d. 1925 Lawson, Victor Fremont
d. 1929 Diaghilev, Sergei Pavlovich
d. 1936 Garcia Lorca, Federico
d. 1938 Frederick, Pauline
d. 1944 Wood, Henry Joseph, Sir
d. 1945 Bose, Subhas Chandra
d. 1954 Gasperi, Alcide de
d. 1967 Gernsback, Hugo
d. 1971 Melford, Austin (Alfred Austin)
d. 1974 Davies, Rodger Paul
d. 1975 Hogg, Ima
d. 1976 Sim, Alastair
d. 1977 Marx, "Groucho" (Julius)
d. 1977 Powers, John Robert
d. 1978 Mallowan, Max Edgar Lucien, Sir
d. 1982 Crisler, "Fritz" (Herbert Orin)
d. 1982 Davis, Loyal
d. 1985 Henderson, Robert W
d. 1986 Baddeley, Hermione Clinton

August 20
b. 1561 Peri, Jacopo
b. 1745 Asbury, Francis
b. 1778 O'Higgins, Bernardo
b. 1785 Perry, Oliver Hazard, Admiral
b. 1818 Bronte, Emily Jane
b. 1827 Decoster, Charles Theodore
b. 1833 Harrison, Benjamin
b. 1843 Nilsson, Christine
b. 1846 Mead, William Rutherford
b. 1860 Poincare, Raymond
b. 1869 Anderson, George Everett
b. 1879 Budd, Ralph
b. 1881 Guest, Edgar A(lbert)
b. 1884 Bultmann, Rudolf
b. 1885 Campana, Dino
b. 1886 Tillich, Paul Johannes
b. 1888 Thang, Ton Duc
b. 1890 Lovecraft, H(oward) P(hillips)
b. 1892 Aiken, George David
b. 1896 Gersten, Berta
b. 1898 Infeld, Leopold
b. 1898 Moberg, Vihelm
b. 1901 Quasimodo, Salvatore

b. 1903 Muto, Anthony
b. 1905 Naruse, Mikio
b. 1905 Schoonmaker, Frank Musselman
b. 1905 Teagarden, Jack (Weldon John)
b. 1906 Tuttle, Lurene
b. 1907 Fistoulari, Anatole
b. 1907 Reed, Alan
b. 1908 Davis, Kingsley
b. 1908 Lopez, Al(fonso Ramon)
b. 1910 Saarinen, Eero
b. 1913 Sperry, Roger Woolcott
b. 1916 Goldfinger, Nathaniel
b. 1917 Sanford, Terry
b. 1920 Kovel, Ralph Mallory
b. 1921 Susann, Jacqueline
b. 1922 Resnik, Regina
b. 1922 Rubinstein, S(amuel) Leonard
b. 1923 Granville, Joseph E(nsign)
b. 1923 Shattuck, Roger Whitney
b. 1926 Vickrey, Robert
b. 1933 Alexander, Sue
b. 1933 Mitchell, George John
b. 1936 Fracci, Carla
b. 1942 Hayes, Isaac
b. 1944 Gandhi, Rajiv Ratna
b. 1944 Nettles, Graig
b. 1946 Chung, Connie (Constance Yu-Hwa)
b. 1946 Fabius, Laurent
b. 1947 Pankow, James
b. 1948 Plant, Robert Anthony
b. 1951 Lynott, Phil(ip)
d. 1153 Bernard of Clairvaux, Saint
d. 1876 Palmer, Frances Flora Bond
d. 1879 Rimmer, William
d. 1886 Stephens, Ann Sophia
d. 1887 Laforgue, Jules
d. 1912 Booth, William
d. 1915 Ehrlich, Paul Ralph
d. 1928 Harvey, George Brinton M
d. 1946 Ragland, "Rags" (John Lee Morgan Beauregard)
d. 1946 Yost, Fielding Harris
d. 1952 Sadeh, Itzhak
d. 1953 Morrison, Cameron
d. 1957 Evans, Edward Ratcliffe Garth Russell
d. 1961 Bridgman, Percy Williams
d. 1972 Stark, Harold Raynsford
d. 1981 Cleaver, William Joseph (Bill)
d. 1981 Devine, Michael
d. 1982 Bloomingdale, Alfred S
d. 1986 Jones, Thad(deus Joseph)

August 21
b. 1725 Greuze, Jean-Baptiste
b. 1796 Durand, Asher Brown
b. 1811 Kelly, William
b. 1854 Munsey, Frank Andrew
b. 1872 Beardsley, Aubrey Vincent
b. 1887 Snow, Carmel White
b. 1890 Henry, William M

b. 1949 Nyad, Diana
b. 1963 DeBarge, James
b. 1964 Willander, Mats
d. 1485 Richard III
d. 1532 Warham, William
d. 1806 Fragonard, Jean Honore
d. 1818 Hastings, Warren
d. 1828 Gall, Franz Joseph
d. 1860 Decamps, Alexandre Gabriel
d. 1874 Dobell, Sydney Thompson
d. 1904 Chopin, Kate
d. 1922 Collins, Michael
d. 1922 Scalchi, Sofia
d. 1926 Eliot, Charles William
d. 1927 Fuertes, Louis Agassiz
d. 1939 Goldin, Horace
d. 1940 Lodge, Oliver Joseph, Sir
d. 1940 Walcott, Mary Morris Vaux
d. 1942 Fokine, Michel
d. 1942 Miller, Alice Duer
d. 1955 Downes, Olin (Edwin Olin)
d. 1957 Dent, Edward Joseph
d. 1958 Martin du Gard, Roger
d. 1960 Steinman, David Barnard
d. 1963 Morris, William Richard
d. 1963 Nuffield, William Richard Morris,
    Viscount
d. 1967 Pincus, Gregory
d. 1973 MacDonald-Wright, Stanton
d. 1974 Bronowski, Jacob
d. 1974 Wilder, Robert Ingersoll
d. 1976 Bachauer, Gina
d. 1976 Kubitschek (de Oliveira), Juscelino
d. 1978 Kenyatta, Jomo (Johnstone)
d. 1979 Farrell, James Thomas
d. 1980 McDonnell, James Smith
d. 1980 Stewart, George Rippey
d. 1982 Jacobsson, Ulla

August 23
b. 1754 Louis XVI
b. 1768 Cooper, Astley Paston, Sir
b. 1769 Cuvier, Georges, Baron
b. 1833 Burne-Jones, Edward
b. 1849 Henley, William Ernest
b. 1854 Moszkowski, Moritz
b. 1863 Rives, Amelie Louise
b. 1864 Venizelos, Eleutherios
b. 1867 Schwob, Marcel
b. 1869 Masters, Edgar Lee
b. 1883 Wainwright, Jonathan Mayhew
b. 1884 Cuppy, Will(iam Jacob)
b. 1884 Mills, Ogden Livingston
b. 1885 Tizard, Henry Thomas, Sir
b. 1887 Hansen, Alvin Harvey
b. 1889 Faber, Geoffrey Cust, Sir
b. 1890 Guggenheim, Harry Frank
b. 1894 Secunda, Sholom
b. 1898 Claude, Albert
b. 1898 Papashvily, George
b. 1900 Arvin, Newton
b. 1900 Krenek, Ernst

b. 1901 Bush, Guy Terrell
b. 1901 Cooper, John Sherman
b. 1903 Fuld, Stanley H
b. 1903 Millikan, Clark Blanchard
b. 1904 Primrose, William
b. 1905 Bushmiller, Ernie (Ernest Paul)
b. 1906 Ragland, "Rags" (John Lee
    Morgan Beauregard)
b. 1908 Adamov, Arthur
b. 1910 Cromley, Raymond Avolon
b. 1912 Kelly, Gene
b. 1913 Crosby, Bob (George Robert)
b. 1917 Williams, Tex
b. 1921 Brown, Charles Lee
b. 1922 Kell, George Clyde
b. 1926 Geertz, Clifford
b. 1927 Berger, Melvin H
b. 1927 Kaprow, Allan
b. 1928 Seldes, Marian
b. 1930 Miles, Vera
b. 1931 Kohn, William Roth
b. 1932 Boumedienne, Houari
b. 1932 Johnson, Howard Brennan
b. 1932 Russell, Mark
b. 1933 Fraser, Ian
b. 1933 Wilson, Pete
b. 1934 Eden, Barbara Jean
b. 1934 Jurgenson, "Sonny" (Christian
    Adolph, III)
b. 1935 Berger, Marilyn
b. 1940 Bill, Tony
b. 1940 Sanders, Richard Kinard
b. 1942 Barnett, Steve
b. 1942 McBride, Patricia
b. 1946 Moon, Keith
b. 1947 O'Hara, Jill
b. 1949 Springfield, Rick (Richard)
b. 1950 Long, Shelley
b. 1951 Hudson, Mark Jeffrey Anthony
b. 1951 Noor, Queen
b. 1957 Boddicker, Mike (Michael James)
d. 1723 Mather, Increase
d. 1806 Coulomb, Charles Augustin de
d. 1813 Wilson, Alexander
d. 1819 Perry, Oliver Hazard, Admiral
d. 1849 Hicks, Edward
d. 1863 Bartlett, John Sherren
d. 1902 Stolz, Teresa
d. 1926 Valentino, Rudolph
d. 1927 Sacco, Nicola
d. 1927 Vanzetti, Bartolomeo
d. 1933 Cahill, Marie
d. 1937 Roussel, Albert
d. 1939 Howard, Sidney Coe
d. 1959 Catto, Thomas Sivewright, Baron
d. 1959 Thayer, Tiffany Ellsworth
d. 1960 Hammerstein, Oscar, II
d. 1962 Gibson, "Hoot" (Edmund Richard)
d. 1963 Bottome, Phyllis, pseud.
d. 1963 Gray, Glen
d. 1966 Bushman, Francis X(avier)

d. 1968 Dale, Henry Hallett
d. 1968 Stromberg, Hunt
d. 1975 Brown, "Tarzan" (Ellison)
d. 1977 Cabot, Sebastian
d. 1977 Gabo, Naum Pevsner
d. 1982 Cavalcanti, Alberto
d. 1982 Moore, Stanford

August 24
b. 1591 Herrick, Robert
b. 1759 Wilberforce, William
b. 1784 Worcester, Joseph Emerson
b. 1795 Wallack, James William
b. 1810 Parker, Theodore
b. 1839 Napravnik, Eduard
b. 1847 McKim, Charles Follen
b. 1849 Comstock, John Henry
b. 1852 O'Rourke, Jim (James Henry)
b. 1856 Mottl, Felix
b. 1872 Beerbohm, Max (Sir Henry
Maximilian)
b. 1882 Pogany, Willy
b. 1884 Melford, Austin (Alfred Austin)
b. 1886 Gibbs, William Francis
b. 1887 Hooper, Harry Bartholomew
b. 1888 Jagendorf, Moritz
b. 1889 Gowdy, Hank (Henry Morgan)
b. 1890 Kahanamoku, Duke
b. 1890 Kendrick, Pearl Luella
b. 1894 Rhys, Jean
b. 1895 Cushing, Richard James, Cardinal
b. 1896 Baker, Phil
b. 1897 Rose, Fred
b. 1898 Cowley, Malcolm
b. 1898 Duffy, Clinton Truman
b. 1899 Borges, Jorge Luis
b. 1899 McManaway, James
b. 1900 Foster, Preston
b. 1902 Brandel, Fernand Paul
b. 1903 Sutherland, Graham Vivian
b. 1905 Stevens, Siaka Probyn
b. 1906 Kaufman, Boris
b. 1912 Kirby, Durward
b. 1913 Wilkinson, J(ohn) Burke
b. 1916 Dean, Alfred Lovill
b. 1917 Causley, Charles Stanley
b. 1917 James, Dennis
b. 1920 Colville, Alex (David Alexander)
b. 1922 Levesque, Rene
b. 1922 Zinn, Howard
b. 1923 Cater, Douglass
b. 1923 Jensen, Arthur Robert
b. 1924 Teicher, Louis
b. 1925 Hufstedler, Shirley (Ann) M(ount)
b. 1927 Shannon, William Vincent
b. 1928 Brooks, Angie Elizabeth
b. 1934 Baker, Kenny
b. 1938 Williams, Mason
b. 1942 Cleland, Max (Joseph Maxwell)
b. 1944 Capaldi, Jim
b. 1944 Jarvis, Gregory
b. 1951 Randisi, Robert Joseph

b. 1956 Cooney, Gerry (Gerald Arthur)
b. 1958 Guttenberg, Steve
b. 1960 Ripkin, Cal(vin Edwin, Jr.)
d. 79 Pliny the Elder
d. 1540 Parmigiano
d. 1680 Blood, Thomas
d. 1795 Philidor, Francois Andre Danican
d. 1918 Bates, Arlo
d. 1923 Wiggin, Kate Douglas
d. 1943 Weil, Simone
d. 1949 Dunne, John William
d. 1954 Vargas, Getulio Dornelles
d. 1956 Mizoguchi, Kenji
d. 1957 Knox, Ronald Arbuthnott
d. 1958 Blech, Leo
d. 1967 Kaiser, Henry John
d. 1971 Fergusson, Harvey
d. 1974 DeSeversky, Alexander Procofieff
d. 1975 Revson, Charles Haskell
d. 1978 Prima, Louis
d. 1981 Dean, William Frishe
d. 1982 Iwama, Kazuo
d. 1983 Nearing, Scott
d. 1985 Creston, Paul
d. 1985 Ryskind, Morrie

August 25
b. 1530 Ivan IV
b. 1744 Herder, Johann G von
b. 1819 Pinkerton, Allan
b. 1836 Harte, (Francis Bret)
b. 1850 Nye, Edgar Wilson (Bill)
b. 1861 Fawcett, George
b. 1862 Procter, William Cooper
b. 1873 Bates, Blanche Lyon
b. 1880 Cowen, Joshua Lionel
b. 1884 Auriol, Vincent
b. 1886 Stolz, Robert
b. 1889 Frank, Waldo
b. 1891 Gardner, Samuel
b. 1893 Dean, Henry Trendley
b. 1898 Dutton, Ralph Stawell
b. 1900 Kober, Arthur
b. 1900 Krebs, Hans Adolf, Sir
b. 1901 Engstrom, Elmer William
b. 1905 Bow, Clara Gordon
b. 1906 Panter-Downes, Mollie
b. 1908 Heindorf, Ray
b. 1909 Keeler, Ruby
b. 1912 Honecker, Erich
b. 1912 Key, Theodore
b. 1913 Kelly, Walt
b. 1913 Rostow, Eugene Victor
b. 1915 Trampler, Walter
b. 1917 DeFore, Don
b. 1917 Ferrer, Mel(chor Gaston)
b. 1918 Bernstein, Leonard
b. 1918 Greene, Richard
b. 1919 Wallace, George Corley
b. 1921 Moore, Brian
b. 1921 Oduber, Daniel
b. 1924 Hall, Monty

b. 1927 Gibson, Althea
b. 1930 Connery, Sean
b. 1931 Andrus, Cecil D(ale)
b. 1933 Skerritt, Tom (Thomas Roy)
b. 1938 Forsyth, Frederick
b. 1941 Bolt, Carol
b. 1941 Burden, Carter (Shirley Carter, Jr.)
b. 1943 Stemkowski, Pete(r David)
b. 1944 Black, Conrad
b. 1944 Demers, Jacques
b. 1946 Fingers, Rollie (Roland Glen)
b. 1947 Archer, Anne
b. 1949 Simmons, Gene
b. 1953 English, Doug (Lowell Douglas)
b. 1955 Bell, Earl
b. 1955 Costello, Elvis
d. 1270 Louis IX
d. 1770 Chatterton, Thomas
d. 1774 Jommelli, Niccolo
d. 1776 Hume, David
d. 1797 Chittenden, Thomas
d. 1822 Herschel, William
d. 1835 Rutledge, Ann
d. 1867 Faraday, Michael
d. 1868 Elliott, Charles Loring
d. 1895 Houghton, Henry Oscar
d. 1900 Nietzsche, Friedrich Wilhelm
d. 1904 Fantin-Latour, (Ignace) Henri
d. 1907 Coleridge, Mary Elizabeth
d. 1908 Becquerel, Antoine Henri
d. 1926 Moran, Thomas
d. 1936 Zinoviev, Grigori Evseevich
d. 1942 George Edward Alexander
       Edmund
d. 1945 Birch, John
d. 1948 Bottomley, Gordon
d. 1956 Kinsey, Alfred Charles
d. 1966 Tamiris, Helen
d. 1967 Muni, Paul
d. 1967 Rockwell, George Lincoln
d. 1969 Bruce, Ailsa Mellon
d. 1971 Lewis, Ted
d. 1973 Corcos, Lucille
d. 1975 Billings, John Shaw
d. 1977 Arvey, Jacob Meyer
d. 1979 Kenton, Stan(ley Newcomb)
d. 1980 Champion, Gower
d. 1981 Hulme, Kathryn Cavarly
d. 1983 Keller, Arthur C
d. 1984 Capote, Truman
d. 1984 Hoyt, Waite Charles
d. 1984 Varipapa, Andy
d. 1985 Smith, Samantha

August 26
b. 1676 Walpole, Robert
b. 1740 Montgolfier, Joseph Michel
b. 1745 Mackenzie, Henry
b. 1819 Albert, Prince
b. 1827 Wittenmyer, Annie Turner
b. 1833 Fawcett, Henry
b. 1838 Booth, John Wilkes

b. 1873 DeForest, Lee
b. 1874 Gale, Zona
b. 1875 Buchan, John, Sir
b. 1876 Couzens, James Joseph, Jr.
b. 1880 Apollinaire, Guillaume
b. 1880 Moeller, Philip
b. 1881 Irvin, Rea
b. 1882 Franck, James
b. 1884 Biggers, Earl Derr
b. 1885 Romains, Jules
b. 1886 Hunsaker, Jerome Clarke
b. 1890 Clark, Barrett H
b. 1895 Long, Earl Kemp
b. 1897 Roland, Ruth
b. 1898 Guggenheim, Peggy Marguerite
b. 1899 Tamayo, Rufino
b. 1901 Genaro, Frankie
b. 1901 Taylor, Maxwell Davenport
b. 1903 Dalrymple, Ian (Murray)
b. 1903 Miller, Caroline
b. 1903 Rushing, Jimmy
b. 1904 Isherwood, Christopher William
b. 1906 Bloom, Mickey (Milton)
b. 1906 Sabin, Albert Bruce
b. 1908 Wilbur, Cornelia Burwell
b. 1910 Wells, Edward
b. 1911 Lanin, Lester
b. 1911 Yablonky, Ben
b. 1914 Cortazar, Julio
b. 1916 Davis, Jim
b. 1916 Hill, Virginia
b. 1917 Smith, William French
b. 1918 Marshall, Robert J
b. 1919 Graham, Ronny
b. 1920 Parker, Brant (Julian)
b. 1921 Begelman, David
b. 1921 Bradlee, Ben(jamin Crowninshield)
b. 1922 Levine, Irving R
b. 1923 Sawallisch, Wolfgang
b. 1924 Graham, Gene
b. 1925 Clayton, Jan(e Byral)
b. 1925 Ragan, David
b. 1926 Gibbs, Georgia
b. 1932 Engle, Joe Henry
b. 1933 Chartoff, Robert
b. 1933 Wattenberg, Ben J
b. 1934 Heinsohn, Tommy
b. 1934 Leach, Will (Wilford Carson)
b. 1935 Ferraro, Geraldine Anne
b. 1943 Rosen, Sheldon
b. 1948 Simpson, Valerie
b. 1952 Rush, Billy
d. 1666 Hals, Frans
d. 1723 Leeuwenhoek, Anton van
d. 1795 Cagliostro, Alessandro, Conte di
d. 1850 Louis Phillippe
d. 1871 Scribner, Charles
d. 1894 Thaxter, Celia
d. 1908 Pastor, Tony (Antonio)
d. 1909 Fenn, George Manville
d. 1910 James, William

b. 1774 Seton, Elizabeth Ann Bayley, Saint
b. 1813 Very, Jones
b. 1828 Tolstoy, Leo Nikolayevich
b. 1831 Hayes, Lucy Webb
b. 1841 Weir, John F(erguson)
b. 1873 Saarinen, Eliel
b. 1879 Whipple, George H
b. 1886 Higgins, Andrew J
b. 1891 Chekhov, Michael
b. 1894 Bohm, Karl
b. 1896 O'Flaherty, Liam
b. 1899 Boyer, Charles
b. 1899 Grimm, Charlie (Charles John)
b. 1899 Howe, James Wong
b. 1903 Bettelheim, Bruno
b. 1903 Wagner-Regeny, Rudolf
b. 1906 Betjeman, John, Sir
b. 1907 Hart-Davis, Rupert (Charles Rupert)
b. 1907 Levene, Sam
b. 1908 Peterson, Roger Tory
b. 1910 Graves, Morris Cole
b. 1910 Koopmans, Tjalling (Charles)
b. 1911 Luns, Joseph Marie Antoine Hubert
b. 1913 Cudlipp, Hugh
b. 1913 Davies, Robertson
b. 1913 Irving, Robert Augustine
b. 1913 Tucker, Richard
b. 1916 Johnson, Van
b. 1917 Kirby, Jack
b. 1919 Hounsfield, Godfrey Newbold
b. 1921 Kulp, Nancy
b. 1922 Oakland, Simon
b. 1923 Henry, Pat
b. 1924 Ryan, Peggy (Margaret O'Rene)
b. 1925 O'Connor, Donald
b. 1925 Trifonov, Yuri Valentinovich
b. 1928 Stockhausen, Karlheinz
b. 1929 Roker, Roxie
b. 1930 Gazzara, Ben (Biago Anthony)
b. 1931 Shirley-Quirk, John Stanton
b. 1939 Mackin, Catherine Patricia
b. 1940 Cohen, William Sebastian
b. 1941 Plishka, Paul Peter
b. 1943 Piniella, Lou(is Victor)
b. 1946 Soul, David
b. 1948 Seraphine, Danny (Daniel)
b. 1950 Guidry, Ron(ald Ames)
b. 1958 Hamilton, Scott
d. 1645 Grotius, Hugo
d. 1818 DuSable, Jean Baptiste
d. 1859 Hunt, Leigh
d. 1861 Mackenzie, William Lyon
d. 1864 Lassalle, Ferdinand
d. 1880 Jackson, Charles Thomas
d. 1900 Sidgwick, Henry
d. 1903 Olmsted, Frederick Law
d. 1932 Nougues, Jean
d. 1937 Opper, Frederick Burr
d. 1947 Manolete

d. 1951 Walker, Robert
d. 1954 Burt, Maxwell Struthers
d. 1957 Randolph, Georgiana Ann
d. 1957 Rice, Craig
d. 1959 Martinu, Bohuslav
d. 1968 Henderson, Arthur
d. 1968 Mein, J Gordon
d. 1971 Leopold, Nathan Freudenthal
d. 1972 Gold, Harry
d. 1972 Leibowitz, Rene
d. 1978 Busia, Kofi A
d. 1978 Catton, Bruce
d. 1978 Mason, Francis van Wyck
d. 1978 Shaw, Robert
d. 1983 Clayton, Jan(e Byral)
d. 1984 Naguib, Mohammed
d. 1985 Gordon, Ruth

August 29

b. 1619 Colbert, Jean Baptiste
b. 1632 Locke, John
b. 1779 Berzelius, Jons Jacob, Baron
b. 1780 Ingres, Jean Auguste Dominique
b. 1780 Laffite, Jean
b. 1792 Finney, Charles Grandison
b. 1805 Maurice, Frederick Denison
b. 1809 Holmes, Oliver Wendell
b. 1811 Bergh, Henry
b. 1815 Carroll, Anna Ella
b. 1817 Leech, John
b. 1844 Carpenter, Edward
b. 1854 Jacobs, Joseph
b. 1855 Paur, Emil
b. 1862 Maeterlinck, Maurice
b. 1864 Dalton, Charles
b. 1876 Kettering, Charles Franklin
b. 1876 Muratore, Lucien
b. 1893 Fine, Sylvia
b. 1897 Roswaenge, Helge
b. 1897 Singmaster, Elsie
b. 1898 Sturges, Preston
b. 1899 Lemnitzer, Lyman Louis
b. 1900 Dollard, John
b. 1900 Kazee, Buell H(ilton)
b. 1904 Forssmann, Werner Theodor Otto
b. 1906 Gerold, Karl
b. 1907 Wechsberg, Joseph
b. 1909 Macready, George
b. 1909 Rennie, Michael
b. 1909 Walton, William Turner
b. 1911 Charnley, John, Sir
b. 1911 Conover, Harry
b. 1915 Bergman, Ingrid
b. 1915 Pritikin, Nathan
b. 1916 Montgomery, George
b. 1918 Crosland, Charles
b. 1920 Parker, Charlie (Charles Christopher)
b. 1923 Attenborough, Richard Samuel, Sir
b. 1924 Washington, Dinah
b. 1926 Lewenthal, Raymond
b. 1929 Gunn, Thom

b. 1834 Ponchielli, Amilcare
b. 1839 Denison, George Taylor
b. 1840 Verga, Giovanni
b. 1842 Jacobi, Mary Putnam
b. 1870 Montessori, Maria
b. 1874 Pierce, Edward Allen
b. 1875 Plank, Eddie (Edward Stewart)
b. 1879 Yoshihito
b. 1880 Wilhelmina
b. 1884 Cates, Clifton Bledsoe
b. 1885 Heyward, (Edwin) DuBose
b. 1885 Ohrbach, Nathan
b. 1897 March, Fredric
b. 1899 Riggs, Lynn
b. 1903 Godfrey, Arthur Michael
b. 1905 Meisner, Sanford
b. 1905 Schary, Dore
b. 1907 Hawkins, Gus (Augustus Freeman)
b. 1907 Magsaysay, Ramon
b. 1907 Shawn, William
b. 1908 Hinton, William Arthur
b. 1908 Saroyan, William
b. 1908 Sears, Robert Richardson
b. 1910 Baker, Charlotte
b. 1912 Vinay, Ramon
b. 1914 Basehart, Richard
b. 1916 Schorr, Daniel
b. 1917 Jordy, William H(enry)
b. 1918 Lerner, Alan Jay
b. 1921 Feeney, "Chub" (Charles Stoneham)
b. 1921 Pike, Otis
b. 1924 Hackett, Buddy
b. 1928 Coburn, James
b. 1930 Donovan, Raymond James
b. 1931 Beliveau, Jean Marc
b. 1933 Wagner, Robin
b. 1935 Cleaver, Eldridge
b. 1935 Robinson, Frank
b. 1936 Collins, Marva Deloise Nettles
b. 1937 Berlinger, Warren
b. 1939 Winter, Paul Theodore
b. 1942 Aoki, Isao
b. 1942 Valdez, Abelardo Lopez
b. 1945 Morrison, Van
b. 1945 Perlman, Itzhak
b. 1945 Shavers, Ernie
b. 1955 Moses, Edwin
b. 1956 Nilsson, Kent
b. 1957 Tilbrook, Glenn
d. 1688 Bunyan, John
d. 1797 Amherst, Jeffrey
d. 1811 Bougainville, Louis Antoine de
d. 1818 Saint Clair, Arthur
d. 1867 Baudelaire, Charles Pierre
d. 1892 Curtis, George William
d. 1897 Drew, Louisa Lane
d. 1905 Tamagno, Francesco
d. 1931 Caine, Hall, Sir
d. 1937 Wright, George
d. 1941 Tsvetayeva, Marina Ivanovna

d. 1946 Granville-Barker, Harley
d. 1946 Klenau, Paul von
d. 1948 Zhdanov, Andrei Alexandrovich
d. 1950 Nowicki, Matthew
d. 1951 Cahan, Abraham
d. 1952 Bourassa, Henri
d. 1955 Baumeister, Willi
d. 1956 MacKaye, Percy Wallace
d. 1963 Braque, Georges
d. 1966 Schmid, Eduard
d. 1967 Ehrenburg, Ilya Grigoryevich
d. 1968 O'Keefe, Dennis
d. 1969 Marciano, Rocky
d. 1973 Ford, John
d. 1976 Kazee, Buell H(ilton)
d. 1979 Rand, Sally
d. 1979 Seberg, Jean
d. 1981 Appel, James Ziegler
d. 1981 Hirshhorn, Joseph
d. 1985 Burnet, MacFarlane (Frank MacFarlane)
d. 1986 Coatsworth, Elizabeth Jane
d. 1986 Kekkonen, Urho Kaleva
d. 1986 Moore, Henry

SEPTEMBER

b. 1721 Randolph, Peyton
b. 1739 Rutledge, John
b. 1795 Mercadante, Saverio
b. 1822 Revels, Hiram R
b. 1824 Doyle, Richard
b. 1883 Zinoviev, Grigori Evseevich
b. 1888 Grey Owl, pseud.
b. 1890 Young, Clara Kimball
b. 1892 Piastro, Mishel
b. 1908 Graham, Sheilah
b. 1924 Moi, Daniel
d. 1570 Primaticcio, Francesco
d. 1655 Cyrano de Bergerac, Savinien de
d. 1828 Chaka
d. 1891 Goncharov, Ivan A
d. 1898 Crummell, Alexander
d. 1939 Rackham, Arthur
d. 1944 Gibson, Guy
d. 1983 Carr, Sabin
September 1
b. 1653 Pachelbel, Johann
b. 1748 Schikaneder, Johann Emanuel
b. 1791 Sigourney, Lydia Howard
b. 1804 Sand, George, pseud.
b. 1826 Beach, Alfred Ely
b. 1854 Humperdinck, Engelbert
b. 1858 Welsbach, Carl Auer von, Baron
b. 1864 Casement, Roger David
b. 1866 Corbett, James John
b. 1868 Bourassa, Henri
b. 1868 Hubbard, Kin (Frank McKinney)
b. 1873 Standing, Guy
b. 1875 Burroughs, Edgar Rice
b. 1886 Schoech, Othmar
b. 1891 Asbury, Herbert

b. 1892 Lamb, Harold Albert
b. 1892 Saltonstall, Leverett
b. 1893 Blythe, Betty
b. 1893 Kappel, Gertrude
b. 1893 Kuniyoshi, Yasuo
b. 1895 Schillinger, Joseph
b. 1898 Anthony, John J(ason)
b. 1898 Berger, Meyer
b. 1898 Hatlo, Jimmy
b. 1898 Miller, Marilyn
b. 1899 Arlen, Richard
b. 1900 Allen, William McPherson
b. 1900 Wilson, Don(ald Harlow)
b. 1904 Brown, Johnny Mack
b. 1906 Schioetz, Aksel
b. 1907 Balaguer, Joaquin
b. 1907 Emery, Anne
b. 1907 Reuther, Walter Philip
b. 1912 Giap, Vo Nguyen
b. 1920 Carpenter, Liz (Elizabeth
   Sutherland)
b. 1920 Farnsworth, Richard
b. 1922 Gassman, Vittorio
b. 1922 Laird, Melvin Robert
b. 1924 DeCarlo, Yvonne
b. 1924 Marciano, Rocky
b. 1925 Pepper, Art(hur Edward)
b. 1927 Bucher, Lloyd Mark
b. 1927 Rosovsky, Henry
b. 1928 Guy, Rosa Cuthbert
b. 1930 Blumenthal, Monica David
b. 1930 Holder, Geoffrey
b. 1933 Maharis, George
b. 1933 Twitty, Conway
b. 1935 Ozawa, Seiji
b. 1937 Douglas-Home, Charles
b. 1937 Geiberger, Al(len L)
b. 1937 O'Neal, Ron
b. 1939 Carty, Rico (Ricardo Adolfo
   Jacobo)
b. 1939 Tomlin, "Lily" (Mary Jean)
b. 1944 Slatkin, Leonard
b. 1946 Gibb, Barry
b. 1949 Maddox, Garry Lee
b. 1951 Cunningham, Mary Elizabeth
b. 1964 Bellows, Brian
d. 1556 Lotto, Lorenzo
d. 1557 Cartier, Jacques
d. 1715 Girardon, Francois
d. 1715 Louis XIV
d. 1729 Steele, Richard, Sir
d. 1838 Clark, William
d. 1912 Coleridge-Taylor, Samuel
d. 1937 Coubertin, Pierre de, Baron
d. 1940 Wald, Lillian D
d. 1943 Jacobs, William Wymark
d. 1944 Irving, Isabel
d. 1945 Craven, Frank
d. 1948 Beard, Charles Austin
d. 1951 McClung, Nellie Letitia Mooney
d. 1957 Brain, Dennis

d. 1959 Norworth, Jack
d. 1960 Jackson, "Aunt" Molly
d. 1960 Townsend, Francis Everett
d. 1961 Foster, William Zebulon
d. 1961 Saarinen, Eero
d. 1967 Sassoon, Siegfried
d. 1969 Pearson, Drew
d. 1970 Mauriac, Francois
d. 1971 Romanoff, Mike
d. 1972 Duffy, Ben (Bernard Cornelius)
d. 1973 Watkins, Arthur V(ivian)
d. 1977 Waters, Ethel
d. 1980 Evans, Bill (William John)
d. 1981 Harding, Ann
d. 1981 Speer, Albert
d. 1982 Curzon, Clifford Michael, Sir
d. 1982 Gomulka, Wladyslaw
d. 1983 Herzog, Arthur, Jr.
d. 1983 Jackson, Henry Martin
d. 1983 McDonald, Larry (Lawrence
   Patton)
d. 1985 Lewis, Saunders
d. 1985 Pitman, James (Isaac James)
d. 1986 Alessandri, Jorge

September 2
b. 1766 Forten, James
b. 1820 Hale, Lucretia Peabody
b. 1838 Liliuokalani, Lydia Kamekeha
b. 1839 George, Henry, Sr.
b. 1841 Ito, Hirobumi
b. 1850 Field, Eugene
b. 1850 Spalding, Albert Goodwill
b. 1852 Bourget, Paul (Charles Joseph)
b. 1853 Ostwald, Wilhelm
b. 1866 Johnson, Hiram W
b. 1887 Bruce Lockhart, Robert Hamilton,
   Sir
b. 1888 Schorr, Friedrich
b. 1892 Szigeti, Joseph
b. 1898 Archibald, Joe (Joseph Stopford)
b. 1899 Maury, Reuben
b. 1901 Rupp, Adolph F
b. 1902 Illingworth, Leslie Gilbert
b. 1902 Taylor, Henry Junior
b. 1904 Svanholm, Set
b. 1904 Trevino, Elizabeth Borton de
b. 1910 Dalrymple, Jean
b. 1911 Harrah, Bill (William Fisk)
b. 1912 Daiches, David
b. 1912 Xuan Thuy
b. 1914 Bearden, Romare Howard
b. 1914 Brown, George Alfred
b. 1917 Almeida, Laurindo
b. 1917 Amory, Cleveland
b. 1918 Drury, Allen Stuart
b. 1918 Fenelon, Fania
b. 1918 Mitchell, Martha Elizabeth Beall
b. 1923 Champion, Marge Celeste
b. 1928 Jackson, Margaret E
b. 1928 Stuart, Mel
b. 1933 Kerekou, Mathieu

b. 1936 Simpson, Alan Kooi
b. 1937 Ueberroth, Peter Victor
b. 1938 Mengers, Sue
b. 1940 Debray, Regis (Jules Regis)
b. 1943 Sather, Glen Cameron
b. 1943 Simon, Joe
b. 1948 Bradshaw, Terry Paxton
b. 1948 McAuliffe, Christa (Sharon Christa
  Corrigan)
b. 1951 Harmon, Mark
b. 1952 Connors, Jimmy (James Scott)
b. 1953 Danelo, Joe (Joseph Peter)
b. 1955 Purl, Linda
b. 1960 Dickerson, Eric Demetric
d. 1652 Ribera, Jusepe (Jose) de
d. 1765 Bouquet, Henry
d. 1793 Brown, William Hill
d. 1859 Bacon, Delia Salter
d. 1870 Maverick, Samuel Augustus
d. 1910 Rousseau, Henri
d. 1911 Harrigan, Edward
d. 1921 Dobson, Henry Austin
d. 1924 Shiras, George, Jr.
d. 1931 Schalk, Franz
d. 1934 Columbo, Russ
d. 1935 Bradley, Andrew Cecil
d. 1940 Gatti-Casazza, Giulio
d. 1943 Hartley, Marsden
d. 1953 Wainwright, Jonathan Mayhew
d. 1957 Freuchen, Peter
d. 1958 Palmer, Frederick
d. 1962 Blair, William Richards
d. 1969 Pike, James Albert
d. 1973 Tolkien, J(ohn) R(onald) R(euel)
d. 1974 Soyer, Moses
d. 1982 Schaefer, Rudolph Jay
d. 1985 Burns, Eveline Mabel

September 3
b. 1693 Locatelli, Pietro
b. 1728 Boulton, Matthew
b. 1735 Bach, Johann Christian
b. 1811 Noyes, John Humphrey
b. 1849 Jewett, Sarah Orne
b. 1856 Sullivan, Louis Henri
b. 1859 Jaures, Jean Leon
b. 1860 Filene, Edward Albert
b. 1861 Wrigley, William, Jr.
b. 1875 Porsche, Ferdinand
b. 1888 Rivers, Thomas Milton
b. 1894 Niebuhr, Helmut Richard
b. 1895 Houston, Charles Hamilton
b. 1898 Parker, Cecil
b. 1898 Spear, Roger Elliot
b. 1899 Benson, Ezra Taft
b. 1899 Burnet, MacFarlane (Frank
  MacFarlane)
b. 1900 Beinum, Eduard van
b. 1900 Benson, Sally
b. 1905 Anderson, Carl David
b. 1906 Powell, Lawrence Clark
b. 1907 Eiseley, Loren Corey

b. 1910 Maynor, Dorothy
b. 1912 Fisher, James Maxwell McConnell
b. 1913 Ladd, Alan
b. 1914 Ray, Dixy Lee
b. 1915 Carlisle, Kitty
b. 1916 Knight, Arthur
b. 1920 Higgins, Marguerite
b. 1921 Orkin, Ruth
b. 1923 Walker, Mort
b. 1925 Thompson, Hank
b. 1926 Flemming, Bill (William Norman)
b. 1926 Jackson, Anne
b. 1926 Lurie, Alison
b. 1926 Papas, Irene
b. 1927 Sidey, Hugh Swanson
b. 1928 Thorn, Gaston
b. 1931 Motta, John Richard
b. 1937 Brennan, Eileen Regina
b. 1938 Churchill, Caryl
b. 1939 Nicholas, Nicholas John, Jr.
b. 1942 Jardine, Al(lan)
b. 1943 Eichelberger, Dave
b. 1943 McCoo, Marilyn
b. 1943 Perrine, Valerie
b. 1965 Sheen, Charlie
d. 1634 Coke, Edward, Sir
d. 1658 Cromwell, Oliver
d. 1815 Murray, John
d. 1820 Latrobe, Benjamin Henry
d. 1857 McLoughlin, John
d. 1877 Thiers, Adolphe
d. 1881 Delmonico, Lorenzo
d. 1883 Turgenev, Ivan Sergeevich
d. 1924 Wagnalls, Adam Willis
d. 1939 Westermarck, Edward Alexander
d. 1942 James, Will(iam)
d. 1943 Moisseiff, Leon Solomon
d. 1943 Pallette, Eugene
d. 1944 Norris, George William
d. 1946 Rosenthal, Moriz
d. 1948 Benes, Eduard
d. 1957 Gannett, Frank Ernest
d. 1961 Gross, Robert Ellsworth
d. 1962 Cummings, E(dward) E(stlin)
d. 1963 MacNeice, Louis (Frederick Louis)
d. 1964 Hayes, Carlton Joseph Huntley
d. 1964 Holbrook, Stewart Hall
d. 1967 Dunn, James Howard
d. 1969 Ho Chi Minh
d. 1974 Partch, Harry
d. 1979 Capehart, Homer Earl
d. 1980 Renaldo, Duncan
d. 1981 Roszak, Theodore
d. 1981 Waugh, Alec (Alexander Raban)
d. 1982 Dannay, Frederic
d. 1984 Schwartz, Arthur
d. 1985 Jones, Jo(nathan)
d. 1985 Marks, Johnny (John David)

September 4
b. 518 BC? Pindar
b. 1768 Chateaubriand, Francois Rene de

b. 1802 Whitman, Marcus
b. 1803 Polk, Sarah Childress
b. 1804 Walter, Thomas Ustick
b. 1824 Bruckner, Anton
b. 1824 Cary, Phoebe
b. 1846 Burnham, Daniel H
b. 1848 Bowker, R(ichard) R(ogers)
b. 1862 Kerr, Alexander H
b. 1864 Ittner, William Butts
b. 1866 Lake, Simon
b. 1876 Kirby, Rollin
b. 1892 Milhaud, Darius
b. 1892 Smith, Pete
b. 1896 Artaud, Antonin
b. 1898 Ayres, Agnes
b. 1899 Kaminska, Ida
b. 1900 Love, George Hutchinson
b. 1902 McCabe, Mary O'Connell
b. 1904 Christian-Jaque
b. 1904 Gombrowicz, Witold
b. 1905 Renault, Mary, pseud.
b. 1906 Delbruck, Max
b. 1907 Griffin, Marvin (Samuel Marvin)
b. 1908 Dmytryk, Edward
b. 1908 Wright, Richard
b. 1910 Celebrezze, Anthony Joseph
b. 1912 Hoff, Sydney
b. 1912 Liberman, Alexander
b. 1913 Moore, Stanford
b. 1913 Savitt, Jan
b. 1913 Tange, Kenzo
b. 1916 Lowndes, Robert A(ugustine) W(ard)
b. 1917 Ford, Henry, II
b. 1918 Harvey, Paul
b. 1919 Morris, Howard
b. 1920 Claiborne, Craig
b. 1924 Aiken, Joan Delano
b. 1924 Kraft, Joseph
b. 1926 Illich, Ivan
b. 1926 Keough, Donald Raymond
b. 1926 Petersen, Donald Eugene
b. 1928 Rausch, James Stevens
b. 1928 York, Dick
b. 1929 Eagleton, Thomas Francis
b. 1931 Gaynor, Mitzi
b. 1934 Castellano, Richard
b. 1937 Fraser, Dawn
b. 1941 Harrelson, Ken(neth Smith)
b. 1944 Salt, Jennifer
b. 1949 Watson, Tom (Sturges)
b. 1950 White, Frank, Jr.
b. 1951 Reese, Don(ald Francis)
b. 1952 Romero Barcelo, Carlos
b. 1956 Gould, Shane
b. 1963 Vanbiesbrouck, John
d. 1846 Jouy, Victor (Joseph-Etienne) de
d. 1849 Monk, Maria
d. 1864 Long, Stephen H
d. 1902 Eggleston, Edward
d. 1907 Grieg, Edvard Hagerup

d. 1909 Fitch, (William) Clyde
d. 1913 Brown, Henry Billings
d. 1932 Bern, Paul
d. 1938 Hayes, Patrick J
d. 1944 Bianco, Margery Williams
d. 1951 Adamic, Louis
d. 1952 Sforza, Carlo
d. 1954 Laessle, Albert
d. 1963 Schuman, Robert
d. 1965 Schweitzer, Albert
d. 1970 Lombardi, Vince(nt Thomas)
d. 1971 Hickenlooper, Bourke B
d. 1973 Behn, Harry
d. 1974 Abrams, Creighton Williams
d. 1974 Achard, Marcel
d. 1977 Clark, Marion L
d. 1982 Tworkov, Jack
d. 1984 Kane, Harnett T(homas)
d. 1985 McCormick, Robert K
d. 1985 O'Brien, George
d. 1986 Greenberg, Hank (Henry Benjamin)

September 5
b. 1568 Campanella, Tommaso
b. 1745 Kutuzov, Mikhail Ilarionovich
b. 1774 Friedrich, Caspar David
b. 1791 Meyerbeer, Giacomo
b. 1804 Graham, William Alexander
b. 1807 Trench, Richard Chenevix
b. 1833 Hartford, George Huntington
b. 1835 Carlisle, John Griffin
b. 1847 James, Jesse Woodson
b. 1856 Watson, Thomas Edward
b. 1861 Raleigh, Walter Alexander, Sir
b. 1867 Beach, Mrs. H H A
b. 1875 Lajoie, Nap(oleon)
b. 1879 Rogers, Will(iam Penn Adair)
b. 1883 Petri, Angelo
b. 1885 Defauw, Desire
b. 1885 Wylie, Elinor Hoyt
b. 1891 Molyneux, Edward H
b. 1893 Rosenberg, Jakob
b. 1893 Sokolsky, George E
b. 1896 VonDoderer, Heimito
b. 1897 Carnovsky, Morris
b. 1897 Nielsen, Arthur C
b. 1898 Carlson, William Hugh
b. 1901 Bailey, Donald Coleman, Sir
b. 1901 Eldridge, Florence
b. 1902 Zanuck, Darryl Francis
b. 1904 Basso, Hamilton Joseph
b. 1905 Koestler, Arthur
b. 1905 Lewis, Meade Anderson Lux
b. 1907 Blough, Glenn Orlando
b. 1907 Douglass, Lathrop
b. 1912 Cage, John Milton, Jr.
b. 1913 Andrews, Wayne
b. 1916 Yerby, Frank Garvin
b. 1921 Valenti, Jack Joseph
b. 1927 Volcker, Paul Adolph
b. 1929 Newhart, Bob (George Robert)

b. 1929 Nikolayev, Andrian G
b. 1935 Erhard, Werner
b. 1935 Lawrence, Carol
b. 1936 Danforth, John Claggett
b. 1936 Kennedy, Joan Bennett
b. 1936 Kozol, Jonathan
b. 1936 Mazeroski, Bill (William Stanley)
b. 1937 Devane, William
b. 1937 Neal, Larry (Lawrence P)
b. 1938 Ferguson, John Bowie
b. 1939 Kilmer, Billy (William O)
b. 1942 Welch, Raquel
b. 1950 Guisewite, Cathy Lee
b. 1956 Denton, Steve
b. 1958 Maloney, Don(ald)
b. 1960 Gault, Willie
d. 1566 Suleiman I
d. 1569 Bruegel, Pieter, (The Elder)
d. 1857 Comte, Auguste
d. 1857 Duff, Mary Ann Dyke
d. 1877 Crazy Horse
d. 1894 Stoneman, George
d. 1898 Edmonds, Emma E
d. 1905 Virchow, Rudolf
d. 1912 MacArthur, Arthur
d. 1927 Loew, Marcus
d. 1933 Journet, Marcel
d. 1949 Minsky, Abraham Bennett
d. 1952 Robinson, Boardman
d. 1957 Parrish, Anne
d. 1960 Long, Earl Kemp
d. 1964 Flynn, Elizabeth Gurley
d. 1965 Sullivan, C(harles) Gardner
d. 1967 DeJong, David Cornel
d. 1969 White, Josh(ua Daniel)
d. 1970 Rindt, Jochen
d. 1972 Berger, David
d. 1972 Friedman, Ze'ev
d. 1972 Gutfreund, Yosef
d. 1972 Halfin, Eliezer
d. 1972 Romano, Joseph
d. 1972 Shapira, Amitzur
d. 1972 Shorr, Kehat
d. 1972 Slavin, Mark
d. 1972 Spitzer, Andre
d. 1972 Springer, Ya'acov
d. 1972 Weinberg, Moshe
d. 1974 Swinnerton, James Guilford
d. 1977 Batchelor, Clarence Daniel
d. 1977 Foley, Martha
d. 1979 Bolton, Guy Reginald
d. 1980 Loden, Barbara Ann
d. 1981 Maeght, Aime
d. 1982 Bader, Douglas Robert Steuart, Sir
d. 1982 Sebelius, Keith George
d. 1985 Morse, Philip McCord

September 6
b. 1711 Muhlenberg, Heinrich Melchior
b. 1757 Lafayette, Marie Joseph Paul,
    Marquis
b. 1766 Dalton, John

b. 1795 Wright, Frances (Fanny)
b. 1805 Greenough, Horatio
b. 1814 Cartier, Georges Etienne, Sir
b. 1819 Rosecrans, William Starke
b. 1857 Nuttall, Zelia Maria
b. 1860 Addams, Jane
b. 1873 Coffin, Howard Earle
b. 1875 Fuller, Ida
b. 1875 Train, Arthur Cheney
b. 1876 Robinson, Boardman
b. 1878 Canby, Henry Seidel
b. 1882 Marks, Charles
b. 1885 Kruger, Otto
b. 1888 Faber, "Red" (Urban Charles)
b. 1888 Kennedy, Joseph Patrick, Sr.
b. 1890 Chennault, Claire Lee
b. 1890 Weldon, John
b. 1891 Thomas, John Charles
b. 1892 Appleton, Edward Victor, Sir
b. 1893 Bricker, John William
b. 1895 Dornberger, Walter Robert
b. 1896 Praz, Mario
b. 1899 Rose, Billy
b. 1901 Jonsson, John Erik
b. 1902 Beatty, Morgan
b. 1903 Sananikone, Phoui
b. 1906 Rosenbloom, Maxie
b. 1908 Lavalle, Paul
b. 1908 Ziolkowski, Korczak
b. 1912 DiMaggio, Vince(nt Paul)
b. 1915 Strauss, Franz Josef
b. 1923 Peter II
b. 1924 Melcher, John
b. 1937 Worley, Jo Anne
b. 1938 Tower, Joan Peabody
b. 1939 Mark, Norman (Barry)
b. 1944 Kurtz, Swoosie
b. 1946 Boone, Ron
b. 1947 Curtin, Jane Therese
b. 1948 Smith, Claydes
d. 1683 Colbert, Jean Baptiste
d. 1782 Jefferson, Martha Wayles Skelton
d. 1869 Rawlins, John A
d. 1886 Godwin, Edward William
d. 1893 Fish, Hamilton
d. 1923 Dutton, E(dward) P(ayson)
d. 1937 Hadley, Henry Kimball
d. 1941 Kraus, Ernst
d. 1944 Tietjens, Eunice
d. 1950 Stapledon, Olaf (Wiliam Olaf)
d. 1952 Lawrence, Gertrude
d. 1956 Raymond, Alex(ander Gillespie)
d. 1959 Gwenn, Edmund
d. 1959 Kendall, Kay
d. 1960 Savo, Jimmy
d. 1966 Menninger, William C
d. 1966 Sanger, Margaret
d. 1966 Verwoerd, Hendrik F
d. 1971 Hawes, Elisabeth
d. 1974 Baclanova, Olga
d. 1974 Kruger, Otto

b. 1889 Taft, Robert A(lphonso)
b. 1896 Dietz, Howard M
b. 1897 Rodgers, Jimmie C
b. 1900 Pepper, Claude Denson
b. 1901 Verwoerd, Hendrik F
b. 1904 Cousins, Frank
b. 1905 Quill, Mike (Michael J)
b. 1905 Wilcoxon, Henry
b. 1907 Leonard, "Buck" (Walter Fenner)
b. 1908 Briggs, Austin Eugene
b. 1910 Barrault, Jean-Louis
b. 1911 Gibbons, Euell
b. 1914 Albrand, Martha, pseud.
b. 1914 Brooke, Hillary
b. 1918 Barton, Derek Harold Richard
b. 1919 Bowker, Albert Hosmer
b. 1921 Secombe, Harry
b. 1922 Caesar, Sid
b. 1922 Larouche, Lyndon H, Jr.
b. 1922 Pierce, Samuel Riley, Jr.
b. 1924 Ford, Wendell Hampton
b. 1924 Metalious, Grace de Repentigny
b. 1925 Darcel, Denise
b. 1925 Sellers, Peter Richard Henry
b. 1930 Ky, Nguyen Cao
b. 1931 Washam, Wisner McCamey
b. 1932 Cline, Patsy
b. 1933 Frayn, Michael
b. 1934 Davies, Peter Maxwell
b. 1937 Frum, Barbara
b. 1937 Lisi, Virna
b. 1938 Nunn, Sam(uel Augustus, Jr.)
b. 1941 Connelly, Christopher
b. 1945 Vachon, Rogie (Rogatien Rosarie)
b. 1946 Forsch, Ken(neth Roth)
b. 1946 McKernan, Ron
b. 1946 Mercury, Freddie
b. 1947 Beattie, Ann
b. 1947 Lavelle, Rita Marie
b. 1960 Casiraghi, Stefano
d. 1613 Gesualdo, Carlo
d. 1784 Lee, Ann
d. 1853 Ozanam, Frederic
d. 1869 Fessenden, William Pitt
d. 1879 Hunt, William Morris
d. 1894 Helmholtz, Herman Ludwig
   Ferdinand von
d. 1933 Chesebrough, Robert Augustus
d. 1933 Parkhurst, Charles Henry
d. 1935 Doheny, Edward Lawrence
d. 1937 Branch, Anna Hempstead
d. 1939 Gilman, Lawrence
d. 1945 Cret, Paul P(hilippe)
d. 1946 Eustis, Dorothy Leib Harrison
   Wood
d. 1949 Strauss, Richard
d. 1951 Sloan, John
d. 1953 Vinson, Frederick Moore
d. 1960 Pettiford, Oscar
d. 1964 Singer, Burns James Hyman
d. 1965 Cowen, Joshua Lionel

d. 1965 Dandridge, Dorothy
d. 1969 Collyer, "Bud" (Clayton)
d. 1969 David-Neel, Alexandra
d. 1969 Varley, F(rederick) H(orseman)
d. 1977 Mostel, Zero (Samuel Joel)
d. 1978 Torre-Nilsson, Leopoldo
d. 1980 Libby, Willard Frank
d. 1981 Wilkins, Roy
d. 1981 Yukawa, Hideki
d. 1982 Abdullah, Sheik Mohammad
d. 1985 Enders, John Franklin
d. 1986 Sweet, Blanche

September 9
b. 1585 Richelieu, Armand Jean du Plessis,
   Cardinal
b. 1711 Hutchinson, Thomas
b. 1754 Bligh, William, Captain
b. 1834 Shorthouse, Joseph Henry
b. 1850 Lawson, Victor Fremont
b. 1868 Austin, Mary Hunter
b. 1870 Pears, Charles
b. 1873 Reinhardt, Max
b. 1877 Agate, James Evershed
b. 1877 Chance, Frank Leroy
b. 1878 Crapsey, Adelaide
b. 1878 Osmena, Sergio
b. 1882 McCarthy, Clem
b. 1885 Sheridan, Clare Consuelo
b. 1886 Wheelock, John Hall
b. 1887 Landon, Alf(red Mossman)
b. 1887 Walburn, Raymond
b. 1890 Eccles, Marriner Stoddard
b. 1890 Lewin, Kurt
b. 1890 Sanders, "Colonel" (Harland
   David)
b. 1891 Marks, Percy
b. 1894 Freed, Arthur
b. 1898 Bridges, Styles
b. 1898 Frisch, Frankie (Frank Francis)
b. 1899 Brassai
b. 1899 Hamilton, Neil
b. 1899 Hoyt, Waite Charles
b. 1899 Nichols, Beverly
b. 1899 Smith, Cyrus Rowlett
b. 1900 Hilton, James
b. 1901 Hicks, Granville
b. 1903 Whitney, Phyllis Ayame
b. 1905 Levine, Joseph Edward
b. 1907 Edel, Leon (Joseph Leon)
b. 1908 Lorjou, Bernard Joseph Pierre
b. 1908 Pavese, Cesare
b. 1911 Goodman, Paul
b. 1911 Gorton, John Grey
b. 1917 Robbins, Frank
b. 1919 Jimmy the Greek
b. 1920 Aldridge, Michael
b. 1921 Prather, Richard Scott
b. 1923 Gajdusek, D(aniel) Carleton
b. 1924 Greer, Jane
b. 1925 Poirier, Richard
b. 1925 Robertson, Cliff

b. 1926 Duncan, Charles William, Jr.
b. 1928 Adderley, "Cannonball" (Julian Edwin)
b. 1928 LeWitt, Sol
b. 1932 Miles, Sylvia
b. 1934 Chandler, Don
b. 1935 Topol, Chaim
b. 1940 Smith, Dennis
b. 1941 Redding, Otis
b. 1946 Fried, Miriam
b. 1946 Preston, Billy (William Everett)
b. 1949 Curry, John Anthony
b. 1949 Theismann, Joe (Joseph Robert)
b. 1951 Keaton, Michael
b. 1951 Wopat, Tom
b. 1952 Cartwright, Angela
b. 1962 McNichol, Kristy
d. 1513 James IV
d. 1583 Gilbert, Humphrey, Sir
d. 1815 Copley, John Singleton
d. 1817 Cuffe, Paul
d. 1888 Savage, John
d. 1898 Mallarme, Stephane
d. 1901 Toulouse-Lautrec (Monfa), (Henri Marie Raymond de)
d. 1909 Harriman, Edward H
d. 1915 Spalding, Albert Goodwill
d. 1919 Mitchell, John
d. 1929 Quinn, Edmond T
d. 1933 Hart, George Overbury
d. 1934 Fry, Roger Eliot
d. 1939 Smith, Christopher Columbus
d. 1943 Andrews, Charles McLean
d. 1951 Gray, Cecil
d. 1956 Hughes, Rupert
d. 1960 Bjoerling, Jussi
d. 1962 Rooney, Pat
d. 1963 Fuess, Claude Moore
d. 1965 Staudinger, Hermann
d. 1975 McGiver, John
d. 1976 Mao Tse-Tung
d. 1977 O'Donnell, Kenneth
d. 1978 MacDiarmid, Hugh, pseud.
d. 1978 Warner, Jack Leonard
d. 1979 Larsen, Roy Edward
d. 1980 Clurman, Harold Edgar
d. 1980 Griffin, John Howard
d. 1981 Lacan, Jacques Marie Emile
d. 1985 Flory, Paul John
d. 1985 McNair, Malcolm Perrine

September 10
b. 1714 Jommelli, Niccolo
b. 1736 Braxton, Carter
b. 1753 Soane, John, Sir
b. 1771 Park, Mungo
b. 1787 Crittenden, John Jordan
b. 1828 Simmons, Zalmon G
b. 1836 Wheeler, Joseph
b. 1839 Funk, Isaac Kauffman
b. 1839 Peirce, Charles Sanders
b. 1870 Danforth, William H

b. 1873 Onions, Charles Talbut
b. 1874 Sullivan, Mark
b. 1885 Van Doren, Carl Clinton
b. 1886 Doolittle, Hilda
b. 1887 Gronchi, Giovanni
b. 1888 Fleming, Ian
b. 1890 Schiaparelli, (Elsa)
b. 1890 Werfel, Franz
b. 1890 Wheeler, Mortimer (Robert Eric Mortimer)
b. 1891 Burckhardt, Carl Jacob
b. 1892 Compton, Arthur Holly
b. 1895 Kelly, George Lange
b. 1896 Ryan, Sylvester James
b. 1898 Astaire, Adele
b. 1898 Love, Bessie
b. 1900 Stern, Philip Van Doren
b. 1902 Crowley, Jim (James)
b. 1903 Connolly, Cyril Vernon
b. 1906 Lyons, Leonard
b. 1907 Wray, Fay
b. 1908 Adams, Eve Bertrand
b. 1909 Brioni, Gaetano Savini, Marquis
b. 1909 Scott, Raymond
b. 1910 Reeves, Rosser
b. 1911 Grubert, Carl Alfred
b. 1912 Everson, William Oliver
b. 1914 Wise, Robert
b. 1915 O'Brien, Edmond
b. 1916 McCarten, John
b. 1916 Sebelius, Keith George
b. 1917 Gentele, Goeran
b. 1924 Kluszewski, Ted (Theodore Bernard)
b. 1925 Dennison, George
b. 1926 Fuller, Hoyt William
b. 1928 Sumac, Yma
b. 1929 Leonetti, Tommy
b. 1929 Palmer, Arnold Daniel
b. 1933 Khrunov, Evgeny
b. 1934 Anderson, Max (Maxie Leroy)
b. 1934 Kuralt, Charles Bishop
b. 1934 Maris, Roger Eugene
b. 1936 Lovesey, Peter Harmer
b. 1938 Lagerfeld, Karl
b. 1939 Mullavey, Greg
b. 1941 Gould, Stephen Jay
b. 1941 Hogwood, Christopher
b. 1944 Entwistle, John
b. 1945 Feliciano, Jose
b. 1947 Nelson, Larry Gene
b. 1948 Geeson, Judy
b. 1948 Lanier, Bob (Robert Jerry, Jr.)
b. 1948 Trudeau, Margaret Joan Sinclair
b. 1948 Waters, Charlie (Charles Tutan)
b. 1951 Danielson, Gary
b. 1951 Rogers, Bill (William Charles)
b. 1957 Burton, Kate (Katherine)
d. 1544 Marot, Clement
d. 1797 Godwin, Mary Wollstonecraft
d. 1827 Foscolo, (Niccolo) Ugo

d. 1842 Tyler, Letitia Christian
d. 1845 Story, Joseph
d. 1851 Gallaudet, Thomas Hopkins
d. 1922 Blunt, Wilfrid Scawen
d. 1935 Long, Huey Pierce
d. 1954 Derain, Andre
d. 1961 Carrillo, Leo
d. 1965 Divine, Father Major Jealous
d. 1965 Jordan, Bobby
d. 1971 Angeli, Pier
d. 1971 Darvi, Bella
d. 1972 Gersten, Berta
d. 1975 Sproul, Robert Gordon
d. 1975 Thomson, George Paget
d. 1976 Johnson, Mordecai Wyatt
d. 1976 Trumbo, Dalton
d. 1980 Kirkus, Virginia
d. 1983 Bloch, Felix
d. 1983 Lofts, Norah Robinson
d. 1983 Vorster, Balthazar Johannes (John)
d. 1984 Hunsaker, Jerome Clarke
d. 1985 Overstreet, Bonaro Wilkinson

September 11
b. 1524 Ronsard, Pierre de
b. 1611 Turenne, Henri D'Auvergne,
　　　　 Vicomte
b. 1700 Thomson, James
b. 1809 Price, Sterling
b. 1821 Beadle, Erastus Flavel
b. 1825 Hanslick, Eduard
b. 1829 Hill, Thomas
b. 1836 Ludlow, Fitz Hugh
b. 1854 Holabird, William
b. 1862 Byng, Julian Hedworth George,
　　　　 Viscount
b. 1862 Henry, O, pseud.
b. 1877 Jeans, James Hopwood, Sir
b. 1885 Lawrence, D(avid) H(erbert)
b. 1895 Bhave, Acharya Vinoba
b. 1895 Stillman, Irwin Maxwell
b. 1896 Kerr, Robert Samuel
b. 1901 Bates, Ted (Theodore Lewis)
b. 1909 Seymour, Anne Eckert
b. 1910 Schroder, Gerhard
b. 1913 Bryant, "Bear" (Paul William)
b. 1913 Lamarr, Hedy
b. 1917 Marcos, Ferdinand Edralin
b. 1917 Mitford, Jessica
b. 1918 Martin, Robert Bernard
b. 1921 Jobert, Michel
b. 1923 Drake, Betsy
b. 1923 Evers, Charles
b. 1923 Kotzky, Alex Sylvester
b. 1923 Schultz, Harry D
b. 1924 Landry, Tom (Thomas Wade)
b. 1925 Bergman, Alan
b. 1926 Richardson, Lee
b. 1926 Slote, Alfred
b. 1927 Schine, G(erard) David
b. 1928 Askew, Reubin O'Donovan
b. 1928 Kienzle, William X(avier)

b. 1931 Moffett, Ken(neth Elwood)
b. 1932 Packwood, Bob (Robert William)
b. 1935 Titov, Gherman Stepanovich
　　　　 (Herman)
b. 1936 Holliman, Earl
b. 1937 Crippen, Robert Laurel
b. 1940 DePalma, Brian Russell
b. 1940 Rhodes, Zandra
b. 1943 Falana, Lola
b. 1949 Liquori, Marty (Martin A)
d. 1823 Ricardo, David
d. 1851 Graham, Sylvester W
d. 1915 Van Horne, William Cornelius, Sir
d. 1940 Waugh, Frederick Judd
d. 1947 Bullard, Robert Lee
d. 1948 Jinnah, Mohammed Ali
d. 1949 Rabaud, Henri
d. 1950 Smuts, Jan Christian
d. 1953 Stone, Lewis
d. 1956 Bishop, Billy (William Avery)
d. 1958 Service, Robert William
d. 1959 Dinwiddie, John Ekin
d. 1959 Douglas, Paul
d. 1963 Low, David, Sir
d. 1966 Cantor, Charles
d. 1969 Payne, Leon
d. 1970 Morris, Chester
d. 1971 Blotta, Anthony
d. 1971 Khrushchev, Nikita Sergeyevich
d. 1972 Fleischer, Max
d. 1973 Allende, Salvador
d. 1974 Lenski, Lois
d. 1976 Carmer, Carl Lamson
d. 1978 Peterson, Ronnie
d. 1980 Sands, Dorothy
d. 1981 McHugh, Frank (Francis Curray)
d. 1982 Ryan, T(ubal) Claude
d. 1983 Heaton, Leonard
d. 1983 Wechsler, James Arthur

September 12
b. 1575 Hudson, Henry
b. 1806 Foote, Andrew Hull
b. 1812 Hoe, Richard March
b. 1818 Gatling, Richard Jordan
b. 1829 Feuerbach, Anselm
b. 1829 Warner, Charles Dudley
b. 1843 Leland, Henry Martyn
b. 1852 Oxford and Asquith, Henry
　　　　 Herbert Asquith, Earl
b. 1855 Sharp, William
b. 1880 Mencken, H(enry) L(ouis)
b. 1884 Groom, Bob (Robert)
b. 1888 Chevalier, Maurice Auguste
b. 1891 Sulzberger, Arthur Hays
b. 1892 Knopf, Alfred Abraham
b. 1893 Hershey, Lewis Blaine
b. 1894 Dovzhenko, Alexander
b. 1894 Gilbert, Billy
b. 1897 Gibson, Walter B(rown)
b. 1897 Joliot-Curie, Irene
b. 1898 Shahn, Ben(jamin)

b. 1901 Blue, Ben
b. 1902 Hamilton, Margaret
b. 1902 Kubitschek (de Oliveira), Juscelino
b. 1902 Zaturenska, Marya
b. 1907 MacNeice, Louis (Frederick Louis)
b. 1909 Chandler, "Spud" (Spurgeon Ferdinand)
b. 1909 Howard, Eddy
b. 1909 Kintner, Robert Edmonds
b. 1910 Engel, Lehman (Aaron Lehman)
b. 1910 Fields, Shep
b. 1912 Fath, Jacques
b. 1913 Owens, Jesse (James Cleveland)
b. 1913 Toyoda, Eiji
b. 1915 Kronhausen, Eberhard Wilhelm
b. 1916 Anderson, "Cat" (William Alonzo)
b. 1916 Bettenhausen, Tony (Melvin E)
b. 1917 Han, Suyin
b. 1920 Dailey, Irene
b. 1921 McGee, Frank
b. 1924 Morse, Ella Mae
b. 1925 Moore, Dick(ie)
b. 1931 Holm, Ian
b. 1931 Jones, George
b. 1934 Morton, Donald Lee
b. 1937 Chuvalo, George
b. 1938 Troyanos, Tatiana
b. 1940 Lolich, Mickey (Michael Stephen)
b. 1941 Gray, Linda
b. 1943 Muldaur, Maria
b. 1944 White, Barry
b. 1951 Fontana, Tom
b. 1952 Silver, Franelle
d. 1687 Alden, John
d. 1733 Couperin, Francois
d. 1739 Keiser, Reinhard
d. 1764 Rameau, Jean-Philippe
d. 1813 Randolph, Edmund Jennings
d. 1819 Blucher, Gebhard Leberecht von
d. 1860 Walker, William
d. 1860 Winebrenner, John
d. 1869 Roget, Peter Mark
d. 1870 Ludlow, Fitz Hugh
d. 1899 Vanderbilt, Cornelius
d. 1919 Andreyev, Leonid Nikolayevich
d. 1926 Maher, George Washington
d. 1939 Cowles, Henry Chandler
d. 1949 Burleigh, Harry Thacker
d. 1950 Clayton, Lou
d. 1953 Werrenrath, Reinald
d. 1966 Allen, Florence Ellinwood
d. 1969 Chamberlin, William Henry
d. 1971 Lin, Piao (Yu-Yung)
d. 1972 Boyd, William (Bill)
d. 1973 Post, Marjorie Merriweather
d. 1977 Biko, Steven
d. 1977 Godfrey, Isadore
d. 1977 Lowell, Robert Trail Spence, Jr.
d. 1981 Montale, Eugenio

September 13
b. 1722 Grasse, Count Francois Joseph Paul de
b. 1806 Drexel, Anthony J
b. 1813 MacMillan, Daniel
b. 1813 Sedgwick, John
b. 1819 Schumann, Clara Josephine Wieck
b. 1825 Rinehart, William H
b. 1844 Young, Ann Eliza Webb
b. 1851 Reed, Walter
b. 1853 Dellenbaugh, Frederick Samuel
b. 1853 Gram, Hans Christian Joachim
b. 1857 Hershey, Milton Snavely
b. 1860 Pershing, John J(oseph)
b. 1861 Waugh, Frederick Judd
b. 1863 Adler, Cyrus
b. 1874 Schoenberg, Arnold
b. 1876 Anderson, Sherwood
b. 1876 Marcosson, Isaac Frederick
b. 1880 Lasky, Jesse L
b. 1883 Lawes, Lewis Edward
b. 1886 Locke, Alain Leroy
b. 1886 Robinson, Robert
b. 1887 Roosevelt, Theodore, Jr.
b. 1894 Priestley, J B (John Boynton)
b. 1895 McDevitt, Ruth
b. 1898 Desormiere, Roger
b. 1900 Linder, Harold Francis
b. 1902 Hayward, Leland
b. 1904 George, Gladys
b. 1905 Colbert, Claudette
b. 1908 Devereux, George
b. 1909 Rhodes, James Allen
b. 1910 Berry, "Chu" (Leon)
b. 1912 Shaw, Reta
b. 1914 Feather, Leonard Geoffrey
b. 1915 Heiskell, Andrew
b. 1916 Dahl, Roald
b. 1917 Crook, William Grant
b. 1917 Haymes, Dick (Richard)
b. 1917 Ward, Robert Eugene
b. 1918 Charles, Ray
b. 1924 Brady, Scott
b. 1924 Jarre, Maurice
b. 1925 Torme, Mel(vin Howard)
b. 1926 Brimmer, Andrew Felton
b. 1926 Francis, Emile Percy
b. 1926 Sonnenfeldt, Helmut
b. 1926 Wharton, Clifton Reginald, Jr.
b. 1928 Indiana, Robert
b. 1929 Ghiaurov, Nicolai
b. 1931 Kennedy, Adrienne
b. 1932 Bain, Barbara
b. 1933 Murphy, Warren
b. 1934 Crystal, Lester M
b. 1937 Silverman, Fred
b. 1938 Martin, Judith
b. 1939 Speakes, Larry Melvin
b. 1944 Bisset, Jacqueline Fraser
b. 1944 Cetera, Peter
b. 1948 Carter, Nell

b. 1949 Dempsey, Rick (John Rikard)
b. 1954 Hurson, Martin
b. 1956 Sledge, Joni
d. 1506 Mantegna, Andrea
d. 1592 Montaigne, Michel Eyquem de
d. 1759 Wolfe, James
d. 1803 Barry, John
d. 1806 Fox, Charles James
d. 1832 Richard, Gabriel
d. 1867 Gregg, William
d. 1872 Feuerbach, Ludwig Andreas
d. 1881 Burnside, Ambrose Everett
d. 1894 Chabrier, (Alexis) Emmanuel
d. 1914 Saunders, William
d. 1917 Legler, Henry Eduard
d. 1925 Thomas, Edith Matilda
d. 1946 Hill, George Washington
d. 1950 Allgood, Sara
d. 1951 Szyk, Arthur
d. 1962 Duffy, Edmund
d. 1964 Honeywell, Mark Charles
d. 1969 Sheil, Bernard James, Archbishop
d. 1973 Field, Betty
d. 1977 Stokowski, Leopold
d. 1980 Abu Salma, pseud.
d. 1981 Humes, Helen
d. 1981 Loeb, William
d. 1982 Eldjarn, Kristjan
d. 1982 Hemingway, Leicester
d. 1982 Ober, Philip
d. 1982 Wallenberg, Marcus

September 14
b. 1486 Agrippa, Heinrich Cornelius
b. 1728 Warren, Mercy Otis
b. 1739 DuPont de Nemours, Pierre
Samuel
b. 1742 Wilson, James
b. 1760 Cherubini, Maria Luigi
b. 1769 Humboldt, Alexander, Freiherr von
b. 1816 Wood, James Rushmore
b. 1818 Congreve, Richard
b. 1846 Selden, George Baldwin
b. 1849 Pavlov, Ivan Petrovich
b. 1858 Hubay, Jeno
b. 1860 Garland, Hamlin
b. 1864 Cecil, Edgar Algernon Robert
b. 1867 Gibson, Charles Dana
b. 1869 Nichols, "Kid" (Charles Augustus)
b. 1873 Irwin, Will
b. 1880 Wilkins, Ernest Hatch
b. 1883 Sanger, Margaret
b. 1885 Gui, Vittorio
b. 1886 Masaryk, Jan Garrigue
b. 1887 Compton, Karl Taylor
b. 1887 Ketchel, Stanley
b. 1895 Lovett, Robert A(bercrombie)
b. 1896 Powers, John Robert
b. 1896 Sample, Paul Starrett
b. 1897 Rudkin, Margaret Fogarty
b. 1899 Wallis, Hal Brent
b. 1904 Germi, Pietro

b. 1908 Gaddis, Thomas (Eugene)
b. 1910 Hawkins, Jack
b. 1910 Liebermann, Rolf
b. 1912 Paulson, Donald Lowell
b. 1914 Armstrong, William Howard
b. 1914 Castellon, Frederico
b. 1914 Moore, Clayton
b. 1916 Bentley, Eric
b. 1917 Harris, Sydney J(ustin)
b. 1920 Klein, Lawrence Robert
b. 1920 Medford, Kay
b. 1921 Rudd, Hughes Day
b. 1923 Palmer, "Bud" (John S)
b. 1923 Rollins, Kenny
b. 1923 Rubin, Vitalii
b. 1926 Butor, Michel
b. 1927 Caidin, Martin
b. 1927 Szoka, Edmund Casimir
b. 1928 Shanker, Albert
b. 1929 Clark, Richard Clarence
b. 1929 Collins, Larry
b. 1931 Klima, Ivan
b. 1933 Caldwell, Zoe
b. 1933 Presnell, Harve
b. 1934 Millett, Kate
b. 1936 Samaras, Lucas
b. 1938 Williamson, Nicol
b. 1942 Floyd, Raymond
b. 1942 Lehman, John Francis, Jr.
b. 1944 Heatherton, Joey
b. 1959 Crosby, Mary Frances
d. 1321 Dante Alighieri
d. 1510 Catherine of Genoa, Saint
d. 1637 Vernier, Pierre
d. 1638 Harvard, John
d. 1743 Lancret, Nicolas
d. 1759 Montcalm, Louis Joseph de
d. 1788 Penn, John
d. 1836 Burr, Aaron
d. 1851 Cooper, James Fenimore
d. 1852 Wellington, Arthur Wellesley,
Duke
d. 1882 Pusey, Edward Bouverie
d. 1898 Burroughs, William Seward
d. 1901 McKinley, William
d. 1909 McKim, Charles Follen
d. 1911 Stolypin, Piotr Arkadevich
d. 1916 Royce, Josiah
d. 1927 Duncan, Isadora
d. 1935 Kendal, Madge
d. 1936 Gabrilowitsch, Ossip
d. 1936 Thalberg, Irving Grant
d. 1937 Masaryk, Tomas Garrigue
d. 1947 LeGallienne, Richard
d. 1951 Busch, Fritz
d. 1959 Adrian
d. 1959 Morris, Wayne
d. 1966 Berg, Gertrude
d. 1970 Carnap, Rudolf
d. 1972 Boyd, Louise Arner
d. 1979 Chain, Ernest Boris, Sir

b. 1899 Mueller, "Heinie" (Clarence Franklin)
b. 1899 Spewack, Samuel
b. 1911 Wald, Jerry (Jerome Irving)
b. 1913 Heckscher, August
b. 1914 Funt, Allen
b. 1914 Ready, William Bernard
b. 1915 Praeger, Frederick A
b. 1915 Walter, Cyril
b. 1919 Peter, Laurence Johnston
b. 1921 Brauer, Jerald Carl
b. 1923 Lee, Kuan Yew
b. 1923 Paige, Janis
b. 1924 Bacall, Lauren
b. 1924 Benton, Nelson (Joseph Nelson, Jr.)
b. 1925 Byrd, Charlie (Charles Lee)
b. 1925 Haughey, Charles James
b. 1925 King, B B (Riley B.)
b. 1926 Knowles, John
b. 1926 Schuller, Robert Harold
b. 1927 Bond, Tommy
b. 1927 Falk, Peter
b. 1930 Francis, Anne
b. 1930 Trabert, Tony (Marion Anthony)
b. 1934 Baylor, Elgin
b. 1934 Chakiris, George
b. 1935 Andre, Carl
b. 1935 Chaikin, Joseph
b. 1938 Benedictus, David
b. 1939 Breytenbach, Breyten
b. 1944 Henning, Linda Kaye
b. 1948 Casals, Rosemary
b. 1948 Jones, Kenny
b. 1949 Begley, Ed, Jr.
b. 1950 Classen, Willie
b. 1953 Pate, Jerry
b. 1955 Yount, Robin R
b. 1957 Hipple, Eric Ellsworth
b. 1959 Raines, Tim(othy)
d. 1672 Bradstreet, Anne
d. 1701 James II
d. 1736 Fahrenheit, Gabriel Daniel
d. 1847 Aguilar, Grace
d. 1869 Graham, Thomas
d. 1877 Coffin, Levi
d. 1903 Crowell, Luther Childs
d. 1932 Ross, Ronald, Sir
d. 1936 Charcot, Jean Baptiste Etienne Auguste
d. 1945 McCormack, John
d. 1948 Everleigh, Minna
d. 1951 Klem, Bill (William Joseph)
d. 1953 Corey, Lewis
d. 1956 Lugosi, Bela
d. 1964 Meiklejohn, Alexander
d. 1970 Garrett, Eileen Jeanette Lyttle
d. 1973 Licavoli, Thomas
d. 1974 Allen, Forest Clare
d. 1977 Bolan, Marc
d. 1977 Callas, Maria

d. 1977 Sheldon, William Herbert
d. 1980 Piaget, Jean

September 17
b. 1730 Steuben, Friedrich Wilhelm Ludolf Gerhard Augustin, Baron
b. 1730 VonSteuben, Friedrich Wilhelm
b. 1743 Condorcet, Marie-Jean-Antoine
b. 1801 Lane, Edward William
b. 1825 Lamar, Lucius Q C
b. 1854 Buick, David Dunbar
b. 1854 Ellsler, Effie
b. 1857 Tsiolkovsky, Konstantin Eduardovich
b. 1858 Vonnoh, Robert W
b. 1874 Turpin, Ben
b. 1880 Inghelbrecht, Desire
b. 1883 Williams, William Carlos
b. 1890 Heatter, Gabriel
b. 1892 Shapero, Nate S
b. 1900 Marriott, John Willard
b. 1900 Ostenso, Martha
b. 1901 Chichester, Francis Charles, Sir
b. 1902 Ralston, Esther
b. 1905 Colonna, Jerry
b. 1905 Costello, Dolores
b. 1906 Ashton, Frederick William, Sir
b. 1906 Jayewardene, Junius Richard
b. 1907 Burger, Warren Earl
b. 1907 Vinson, Helen
b. 1908 Creasey, John
b. 1909 Cole, Edward Nicholas
b. 1909 Enright, Elizabeth
b. 1916 Stewart, Mary (Florence Elinor)
b. 1916 Tsedenbal, Yumzahgin
b. 1918 Herzog, Chaim
b. 1922 Bourjaily, Vance
b. 1926 Henize, Karl Gordon
b. 1927 Blanda, George Frederick
b. 1927 Weiss, Ted
b. 1928 McDowall, Roddy (Roderick Andrew)
b. 1929 Crowley, Pat
b. 1929 Moss, Stirling Crauford
b. 1930 Mitchell, Edgar Dean
b. 1930 Stafford, Thomas P(atten)
b. 1931 Bancroft, Anne
b. 1933 Grassley, Charles Ernest
b. 1933 Loudon, Dorothy
b. 1934 Connolly, Maureen
b. 1935 Kesey, Ken
b. 1937 Cepeda, Orlando
b. 1938 Yarbrough, Lee Roy
b. 1939 Fey, Thomas Hossler
b. 1944 Messner, Reinhold
b. 1947 MacNelly, Jeff(rey Kenneth)
b. 1948 Ritter, John(athan Southworth)
b. 1950 Waybill, Fee
b. 1952 Solomon, Harold Charles
b. 1957 Kelser, Greg(ory)
b. 1960 Carter, Anthony
b. 1962 Rogers, Don(ald Lavert)

b. 1796 Coleridge, Hartley
b. 1802 Kossuth, Lajos
b. 1806 Dyce, William
b. 1829 Schirmer, Gustave
b. 1855 Klafsky, Katharina
b. 1867 Rackham, Arthur
b. 1879 Drum, Hugh A
b. 1879 Vance, Louis Joseph
b. 1879 Westheimer, Irvin Ferdinand
b. 1886 O'Sheel, Shaemas
b. 1887 Overman, Lynne
b. 1890 Truex, Ernest
b. 1894 Field, Rachel Lyman
b. 1897 Knight, George Wilson
b. 1898 Saragat, Giuseppe
b. 1899 Cortez, Ricardo
b. 1901 Pasternak, Joe (Joseph Vincent)
b. 1902 Leon, Henry Cecil
b. 1904 Evans, Bergen Baldwin
b. 1905 Hawley, Cameron
b. 1905 Jaworski, Leon
b. 1906 Freccia, Massimo
b. 1907 Powell, Lewis Franklin, Jr.
b. 1908 Waltari, Mika
b. 1909 Porsche, Ferdinand
b. 1910 Lasky, Jesse Louis, Jr.
b. 1910 Lindsay, Margaret
b. 1911 Golding, William Gerald
b. 1912 Daniel, Clifton, Jr.
b. 1914 Farmer, Frances
b. 1914 Morton, Rogers Clark Ballard
b. 1917 Greer, Michael
b. 1918 Kiplinger, Austin Huntington
b. 1919 Gumede, Josiah Zion
b. 1919 Thebom, Blanche
b. 1920 Angell, Roger
b. 1920 Leigh Guzman, Jorge Gustavo
b. 1921 Chapman, Christian Addison
b. 1922 Pep, Willie
b. 1922 Zatopek, Emil
b. 1926 Snider, "Duke" (Edwin Donald)
b. 1926 Wallace, Lurleen Burns
b. 1927 Brown, Harold
b. 1930 Harris, Rosemary
b. 1931 Benton, Brook
b. 1931 Danton, Ray(mond)
b. 1932 Royko, Mike
b. 1932 Wille, Lois Jean
b. 1933 McCallum, David
b. 1934 Epstein, Brian
b. 1935 Massi, Nick
b. 1936 Oerter, Al(fred A)
b. 1940 Medley, Bill
b. 1940 Tyson, Sylvia Fricker
b. 1940 Williams, Paul Hamilton
b. 1943 Morgan, Joe (Joseph Leonard)
b. 1944 Schenk, Ard
b. 1945 Blalock, Jane
b. 1945 Payne, Freda
b. 1947 Brown, Larry
b. 1947 Perry, Nancy Ling

b. 1948 Irons, Jeremy
b. 1949 Twiggy
b. 1951 Lunden, Joan
b. 1952 Rodgers, Nile
b. 1952 Stewart, David
b. 1961 Beaupre, Don(ald William)
d. 1668 Waller, Sir William
d. 1812 Rothschild, Mayer Amschel
d. 1860 Rice, Thomas Dartmouth
d. 1881 Garfield, James Abram
d. 1896 Marty, Martin
d. 1902 Masaoka, Tsunenori
d. 1905 Barnardo, Thomas John
d. 1916 Sherman, Frank Dempster
d. 1927 Barker, Herman
d. 1935 Tsiolkovsky, Konstantin
        Eduardovich
d. 1937 Loeb, William
d. 1946 Carr, Alexander
d. 1949 Cuppy, Will(iam Jacob)
d. 1950 Herne, Chrystal Katharine
d. 1954 Franklin, Miles, pseud.
d. 1955 Milles, Carl
d. 1957 Childe, Vere Gordon
d. 1965 Thomas, Elmer
d. 1967 Block, Martin
d. 1968 Carlson, Chester
d. 1968 Foley, "Red" (Clyde Julian)
d. 1969 Ingram, Rex
d. 1970 Danforth, David Charles
d. 1971 Albright, William Foxwell
d. 1972 Casadesus, Robert
d. 1973 Parsons, Gram
d. 1973 Wurster, William
d. 1978 Gilson, Etienne Henry
d. 1979 Birnie, William Alfred Hart
d. 1979 Jones, Preston St. Vrain
d. 1980 Gillott, Jacky
d. 1980 Lesser, Sol
d. 1985 Calvino, Italo
d. 1985 Straus, Jack Isidor

September 20
b. 1178 Emmet, Robert
b. 356 BC Alexander the Great
b. 1791 Aksakov, Sergei Timofeyevich
b. 1822 Miller, Elizabeth Smith
b. 1833 Locke, David Ross
b. 1869 Robey, George, Sir
b. 1872 Gamelin, Maurice Gustave
b. 1876 Ellis, Carleton
b. 1878 Sinclair, Upton Beall
b. 1879 Banning, Kendall
b. 1879 Cromwell, Dean Bartlett
b. 1879 Sjostrom, Victor
b. 1880 Pizzetti, Ildebrando
b. 1884 Perkins, Maxwell Evarts
b. 1885 Morton, "Jelly Roll" (Joseph
        Ferdinand)
b. 1886 Anderson, John Murray
b. 1886 Kenny, Sister Elizabeth
b. 1894 Collinge, Patricia

b. 1897 Barea, Arturo
b. 1897 Taft, Charles Phelps
b. 1898 Dressen, Charlie (Charles W)
b. 1898 Hoult, Norah
b. 1899 Nugent, Elliott
b. 1900 Castello Branco, Humberto
b. 1900 DeParis, Wilbur
b. 1900 Visser T Hooft, Willem Adolf
b. 1901 Edson, Gus
b. 1905 Bouche, Rene Robert
b. 1914 More, Kenneth Gilbert
b. 1917 Auerbach, "Red" (Arnold Jacob)
b. 1917 Rey, Fernando
b. 1922 Kapell, William
b. 1924 Galanos, James
b. 1924 Grant, Gogi
b. 1924 Meara, Anne
b. 1926 Bluhdorn, Charles G
b. 1927 Dankworth, John Philip William
b. 1927 Roberts, Rachel
b. 1928 Hall, Donald Andrew
b. 1928 Jennings, Gary
b. 1931 Palmer, Peter
b. 1934 Loren, Sophia
b. 1936 Church, Sam(uel Morgan, Jr.)
b. 1938 Lindstrom, Pia
b. 1951 Lafleur, Guy Damien
d. 1803 Emmet, Robert
d. 1852 Chase, Philander
d. 1860 Schopenhauer, Arthur
d. 1863 Grimm, Jakob Ludwig Karl
d. 1898 Fontane, Theodor
d. 1908 Sarasate, Pablo de
d. 1925 Bartlett, Paul Wayland
d. 1933 Besant, Annie Wood
d. 1946 Raimu
d. 1947 LaGuardia, Fiorello Henry
d. 1947 McCartan, Edward
d. 1949 Dix, Richard
d. 1951 Hartford, John Augustine
d. 1957 Sibelius, Jean
d. 1958 Wortman, Denys
d. 1960 Goodpasture, Ernest William
d. 1965 Holmes, Arthur
d. 1971 Seferiades, Giorgos Styljanou
d. 1972 Liebes, Dorothy Katherine Wright
d. 1973 Croce, Jim
d. 1975 Leger, Alexis St. Leger (Marie-
    Rene Alexis St. Leger)
d. 1975 Lopez, Vincent
d. 1976 Bloomgarden, Kermit
d. 1982 Hughes, Emmet John
d. 1984 Goodman, Steve(n Benjamin)

September 21
b. 1452 Savonarola, Girolamo
b. 1737 Hopkinson, Francis
b. 1756 McAdam, John Loudoun
b. 1788 Taylor, Margaret Smith
b. 1849 Gosse, Edmund William, Sir
b. 1853 Kamerlingh Onnes, Heike
b. 1855 Roosevelt, Sara Delano

b. 1859 Lohse, Otto
b. 1863 Bunny, John
b. 1863 Howell, Clark
b. 1866 Wells, H(erbert) G(eorge)
b. 1867 Stimson, Henry Lewis (Harry)
b. 1874 Holst, Gustav
b. 1884 Andrus, Ethel Percy
b. 1884 Price, Irving L
b. 1885 Webster, H(arold) T(ucker)
b. 1893 Willard, Frank Henry
b. 1896 Kelsey, Alice Geer
b. 1898 Tchelitchew, Pavel
b. 1902 Lane, Allen, Sir
b. 1903 Tucker, Preston Thomas
b. 1904 Hartung, Hans
b. 1906 Farago, Ladislas
b. 1906 Fitzgerald, Albert J
b. 1907 Bird, Junius Bouton
b. 1907 Bullard, Edward Crisp, Sir
b. 1907 Roskolenko, Harry
b. 1908 Corcos, Lucille
b. 1909 Nkrumah, Kwame
b. 1911 Engle, Clair
b. 1912 Jones, Chuck
b. 1912 MacGregor, Ian
b. 1914 Stewart, "Slam" (Leroy)
b. 1915 Chapin, Roy Dikeman
b. 1916 Giroud, Francoise
b. 1916 Kauffman, Ewing Marion
b. 1921 McHale, John Joseph
b. 1922 Hampton, Robert Edward
b. 1926 Glaser, Donald Arthur
b. 1927 Jensen, Virginia Allen
b. 1927 Sherman, Harry R
b. 1928 Ashbrook, John Milan
b. 1930 Addams, Dawn
b. 1931 Hagman, Larry
b. 1933 Alexander, Clifford L, Jr.
b. 1934 Cohen, Leonard
b. 1935 Gibson, Henry
b. 1938 Moe, Doug(las Edwin)
b. 1940 Kurtis, Bill Horton (William)
b. 1942 McDowell, Sam(uel Edward)
b. 1944 Flagg, Fannie (Frances Carlton)
b. 1944 Jordan, Hamilton (William
    Hamilton)
b. 1947 Felder, Don(ald William)
b. 1947 King, Stephen Edwin
b. 1947 Norman, Marsha Williams
b. 1949 Futter, Ellen Victoria
b. 1949 Gilmore, Artis
b. 1950 Murray, Bill
b. 1957 Moncrief, Sidney
b. 1971 David
d. 19 BC Virgil
d. 1558 Charles V
d. 1629 Coen, Jan Pieterszoon
d. 1798 Read, George
d. 1812 Schikaneder, Johann Emanuel
d. 1820 Drake, Joseph Rodman
d. 1832 Scott, Walter, Sir

d. 1862 Ross, James Clark, Sir
d. 1904 Joseph, Chief
d. 1908 Fenollosa, Ernest Francisco
d. 1915 Comstock, Anthony
d. 1924 Quad, M, pseud.
d. 1947 Carey, Harry
d. 1952 Burton, Montague Maurice, Sir
d. 1955 Brain, Aubrey
d. 1957 Haakon VII
d. 1957 Krupp von Bohlen und Halbach,
Bertha
d. 1959 Flexner, Abraham
d. 1961 Dickson, Earle Ensign
d. 1965 Larson, John Augustus
d. 1966 Reynaud, Paul
d. 1968 Jackson, Charles Reginald
d. 1971 Houssay, Bernardo Alberto
d. 1973 Plomer, William Charles Franklyn
d. 1973 Sands, Diana Patricia
d. 1974 Hull, Warren
d. 1974 Susann, Jacqueline
d. 1975 Ross, Ishbel
d. 1976 Letelier, Orlando
d. 1981 Hirsch, Joseph
d. 1985 Peel, Ronald Francis (Edward
Waite)

September 22
b.   Capero, Virginia
b. 1694 Chesterfield, Philip Dormer, Earl
b. 1791 Faraday, Michael
b. 1800 Locke, Richard Adams
b. 1829 Belknap, William Worth
b. 1862 Barres, Maurice
b. 1870 Pryor, Arthur W
b. 1872 Rothwell, Walter Henry
b. 1873 Day, Joseph Paul
b. 1878 Yoshida, Shigeru
b. 1882 Keitel, Wilhelm
b. 1885 VonStroheim, Erich
b. 1889 Dauss, George August
b. 1890 McCormick, Cyrus Hall
b. 1891 Flynn, Edward Joseph
b. 1892 Sullivan, Frank
b. 1894 Rethberg, Elizabeth
b. 1895 Deutsch, Babette
b. 1895 Janssen, Herbert
b. 1895 Meek, Samuel Williams
b. 1895 Muni, Paul
b. 1898 Wasson, R(obert) Gordon
b. 1899 Harlan, Veit
b. 1901 Alexander, Katherine
b. 1901 Huggins, Charles Brenton
b. 1902 Houseman, John
b. 1902 Jarvis, Howard Arnold
b. 1904 Valachi, Joe (Joseph M)
b. 1907 Strudwick, Shepperd
b. 1912 Martin, Graham Anderson
b. 1912 Vanderbilt, Alfred G
b. 1914 Scott, Martha Ellen
b. 1917 Hottelet, Richard C(urt)
b. 1920 Lemon, Bob (Robert Granville)

b. 1921 Szeryng, Henryk
b. 1922 Donehue, Vincent J
b. 1922 Yang, Chen Ning
b. 1923 Abse, Dannie
b. 1924 Middendorf, John William
b. 1927 Lasorda, Tom (Thomas Charles)
b. 1928 Stone, Richard Bernard (Dick)
b. 1930 James, Joni
b. 1930 Quint, Bert
b. 1932 Johansson, Ingemar
b. 1948 Phillips, Mark Anthony Peter
b. 1949 Carmichael, Harold
b. 1954 Belafonte-Harper, Shari
b. 1956 Boone, Debby (Deborah Ann)
b. 1957 Johnson, Mark
b. 1960 Babilonia, Tai Reina
b. 1960 Coleman, Vince(nt Maurice)
b. 1960 Jett, Joan
b. 1961 Baio, Scott Vincent
d. 1566 Agricola, Georgius
d. 1662 Biddle, John
d. 1776 Hale, Nathan
d. 1777 Bartram, John
d. 1851 Sherwood, Mary Martha
d. 1896 Klafsky, Katharina
d. 1905 Galli-Marie, Marie Celestine
d. 1914 Alain-Fournier, pseud.
d. 1933 Silverman, Sime
d. 1937 Roland, Ruth
d. 1942 Cram, Ralph Adams
d. 1945 Burke, Thomas
d. 1948 Bailey, Florence Augusta Merriam
d. 1949 Wood, Samuel Grosvenor
d. 1952 Webster, H(arold) T(ucker)
d. 1955 Kress, Samuel Henry
d. 1957 Gogarty, Oliver St. John
d. 1958 Rinehart, Mary Roberts
d. 1959 Ironside, William E
d. 1960 Klein, Melanie
d. 1961 Davies, Marion
d. 1965 Ammann, Othmar Hermann
d. 1968 Scott, Norman
d. 1969 Lopez Mateos, Adolfo
d. 1970 Francois, Samson
d. 1970 Hamilton, Alice
d. 1973 Dodd, Charles Harold
d. 1974 Brennan, Walter Andrew
d. 1976 Strode, Hudson
d. 1981 Warren, Harry
d. 1984 Mathieu, Noel Jean
d. 1985 Springer, Axel Caesar
d. 1985 Tabouis, Genevieve

September 23
b.   63 BC Augustus
b. 480 BC? Euripides
b. 1745 Sevier, John
b. 1800 McGuffey, William Holmes
b. 1829 Crook, George
b. 1838 Woodhull, Victoria Claflin
b. 1852 Halsted, William Stewart
b. 1861 Coleridge, Mary Elizabeth

b. 1931 Adams, "Tom" (John Michael Geoffrey Maningham)
b. 1931 Newley, Anthony
b. 1936 Henson, Jim (James Maury)
b. 1937 Leland, Timothy
b. 1938 Elvira, Pablo
b. 1939 Gillott, Jacky
b. 1942 Marsden, Gerry
b. 1942 McCartney, Linda
b. 1946 Greene, Joe (Joseph)
b. 1947 Zorn, Jim (John Eldon)
b. 1952 Kennedy, Joseph Patrick, III
d. 1541 Paracelsus, Philippus Aureolus
d. 1812 Bagration, Petr Ivanovich
d. 1813 Gretry, Andre Ernest Modeste
d. 1815 Sevier, John
d. 1834 Pedro I
d. 1920 Faberge, Peter Carl (Karl Gustavovich)
d. 1933 Liveright, Horace Brisbin
d. 1939 Gibbons, Floyd Phillips
d. 1939 Laemmle, Carl, Sr.
d. 1945 Argentinita
d. 1945 Geiger, Hans (Johannes Wilhelm)
d. 1948 William, Warren
d. 1961 Welles, Sumner
d. 1963 Chase, Mary Agnes
d. 1973 Neill, A(lexander) S(utherland)
d. 1974 Stone, Dorothy
d. 1975 Hunter, Ian
d. 1976 Brent, Romney
d. 1976 Douglas, Paul Howard
d. 1978 Bostock, Lyman Wesley
d. 1978 Etting, Ruth
d. 1981 Kelly, "Patsy" (Sarah Veronica Rose)
d. 1981 Ochsner, (Edward William) Alton
d. 1982 Churchill, Sarah
d. 1984 Hamilton, Neil
d. 1985 Mann, Paul

September 25
b. 1559 Borromini, Francesco
b. 1613 Perrault, Claude
b. 1683 Rameau, Jean-Philippe
b. 1711 Ch'ien Lung
b. 1793 Hemans, Felicia Dorothea Browne
b. 1807 Vail, Alfred Lewis
b. 1825 Mills, Darius Ogden
b. 1829 Rossetti, William Michael
b. 1832 Jenney, William LeBaron
b. 1843 Bissell, Melville Reuben
b. 1843 Chamberlin, Thomas Chrowder
b. 1866 Morgan, Thomas H
b. 1872 Cochran, C(harles) B(lake)
b. 1872 Sforza, Carlo
b. 1877 Calles, Plutarco
b. 1889 Cole, George Douglas Howard
b. 1890 Sackheim, Maxwell Byron
b. 1891 Britton, Edgar Clay
b. 1894 Briscoe, Robert
b. 1895 Lawson, John Howard

b. 1896 Pertini, Alessandro
b. 1897 Faulkner, William
b. 1898 Brackman, Robert
b. 1899 Buck, Paul Herman
b. 1899 Landis, James McCauley
b. 1902 Hoffman, Al
b. 1903 Rothko, Mark
b. 1905 Smith, "Red" (Walter Wellesley)
b. 1906 Shostakovich, Dmitri Dmitryevich
b. 1907 Bresson, Robert
b. 1907 Glendenning, Raymond Carl
b. 1908 Figueres Ferrer, Jose
b. 1909 Glasspole, Florizel Augustus
b. 1909 Woode, William Henri
b. 1911 Williams, Eric Eustace
b. 1912 Cooke, Jack Kent
b. 1914 Osborne, Leone Neal
b. 1915 Sperling, Godfrey, Jr.
b. 1918 Rizzuto, Phil(lip Francis)
b. 1921 Muldoon, Robert David, Sir
b. 1922 Bondarchuk, Sergei
b. 1926 Ray, Aldo
b. 1927 Davis, Colin
b. 1929 Barker, Ronnie
b. 1929 White, Kevin Hagan
b. 1931 Walters, Barbara
b. 1932 Gould, Glenn Herbert
b. 1932 Suarez Gonzales, Adolfo
b. 1933 Brown, Hubie (Hubert Jude)
b. 1933 Darling, Erik
b. 1933 Tyson, Ian
b. 1935 Sjowall, Maj
b. 1936 Prowse, Juliet
b. 1936 Trare, Moussa
b. 1942 Bonavena, Oscar
b. 1943 Walden, Robert
b. 1944 Douglas, Michael Kirk
b. 1946 Kendal, Felicity
b. 1947 Tiegs, Cheryl
b. 1949 Williams, Anson
b. 1951 McAdoo, Bob (Robert)
b. 1952 Hamill, Mark
b. 1952 Reeve, Christopher
b. 1961 Locklear, Heather
d. 1534 Clement VII
d. 1680 Butler, Samuel
d. 1849 Strauss, Johann, Sr.
d. 1870 Grier, Robert Cooper
d. 1871 Papineau, Louis-Joseph
d. 1877 LeVerrier, Urbain Jean Joseph
d. 1900 Lazear, Jesse William
d. 1900 Van Lew, Elizabeth
d. 1910 Mills, Darius Ogden
d. 1919 Freer, Charles Lang
d. 1920 Schiff, Jacob Henry
d. 1924 Crabtree, Lotta
d. 1928 Outcault, Richard Felton
d. 1929 Huggins, Miller James
d. 1933 Lardner, Ring(gold Wilmer)
d. 1936 Horlick, William
d. 1936 Sims, William Sowden

d. 1940 Clark, Marguerite
d. 1958 Watson, John Broadus
d. 1959 Broderick, Helen
d. 1960 Nichols, Ruth Rowland
d. 1960 Post, Emily Price
d. 1969 Reed, Peter Hugh
d. 1970 Fisher, James Maxwell McConnell
d. 1970 Liebling, Estelle
d. 1970 Remarque, Erich Maria
d. 1971 Black, Hugo LaFayette
d. 1975 Considine, Bob (Robert Bernard)
d. 1976 Faber, "Red" (Urban Charles)
d. 1980 Bonham, John Henry
d. 1980 Milestone, Lewis
d. 1982 Poulson, Norris
d. 1983 Leopold III
d. 1984 Pidgeon, Walter
d. 1985 Fishback, Margaret

September 26
b. Hurt, Mary Beth Supinger
b. 1774 Appleseed, Johnny
b. 1783 Taylor, Jane
b. 1791 Gericault, Jean Louis Andre
  Theodore
b. 1848 Walters, Henry
b. 1854 Bausch, Edward
b. 1862 Davies, Arthur Bowen
b. 1869 McCay, Winsor
b. 1874 Hine, Lewis Wickes
b. 1875 Gwenn, Edmund
b. 1876 Abbott, Edith
b. 1886 Hill, Archibald Vivian
b. 1887 Wallis, Barnes Neville, Sir
b. 1888 Dobie, J(ames) Frank
b. 1888 Eliot, T(homas) S(tearns)
b. 1889 Heidegger, Martin
b. 1891 Munch, Charles
b. 1892 Lynd, Robert Staughton
b. 1892 Tsvetayeva, Marina Ivanovna
b. 1893 Rosenstein, Nettie
b. 1895 Holden, Fay
b. 1895 Raft, George
b. 1897 Paul VI, Pope
b. 1897 Telva, Marion
b. 1898 Gershwin, George
b. 1898 Lockridge, Richard
b. 1901 Cook, Donald
b. 1902 Anastasia, Albert
b. 1907 Blunt, Anthony Frederick
b. 1908 Marlowe, Sylvia
b. 1914 LaLanne, Jack
b. 1917 Rico, Don(ato)
b. 1918 Morley, Eric Douglas
b. 1919 Britton, Barbara
b. 1924 Wincelberg, Shimon
b. 1925 Robbins, Marty
b. 1926 Coltrane, "Trane" (John William)
b. 1926 London, Julie
b. 1927 O'Neal, Patrick
b. 1928 Ray, Robert D
b. 1930 Wunderlich, Fritz

b. 1934 Mihajlov, Mihajlo
b. 1934 Morris, Greg
b. 1937 Weintraub, Jerry
b. 1939 Douglas, Donna
b. 1942 McCord, Kent
b. 1945 Ferry, Bryan
b. 1947 Allen, Lucius Oliver, Jr.
b. 1947 Anderson, Lynn
b. 1948 Newton-John, Olivia
b. 1962 Anderson, Melissa Sue
d. 1820 Boone, Daniel
d. 1826 Laing, Alexander Gordon
d. 1848 Bronte, Patrick Branwell
d. 1854 LaFeuer, Minard
d. 1868 Mobius, August Ferdinand
d. 1898 Davenport, Fanny Lily Gypsy
d. 1901 Nicolay, John George
d. 1904 Hearn, Lafcadio
d. 1918 Simmel, Georg
d. 1922 Watson, Thomas Edward
d. 1932 Davenport, Eva
d. 1935 Adams, Andy
d. 1936 Monroe, Harriet
d. 1937 Filene, Edward Albert
d. 1937 Smith, Bessie
d. 1938 Taylor, Graham
d. 1941 Walter, Eugene
d. 1947 Lofting, Hugh
d. 1951 Bryant, Lane
d. 1952 Parker, George Swinnerton
d. 1952 Santayana, George
d. 1957 Clark, Charles Badger
d. 1961 Eichelberger, Robert Lawrence
d. 1961 Wilson, Charles Erwin
d. 1963 Pennell, Joseph Stanley
d. 1966 Edson, Gus
d. 1966 Kane, Helen
d. 1971 Gipson, Lawrence Henry
d. 1972 Correll, Charles J
d. 1973 Bemis, Samuel Flagg
d. 1973 Magnani, Anna
d. 1974 McCarten, John
d. 1975 Paludan, Jacob (Stig Henning
  Jacob Puggard)
d. 1977 Lombardi, Ernie (Ernesto Natali)
d. 1977 Shankar, Uday
d. 1979 Cromwell, John
d. 1982 Bettis, Valerie
d. 1982 Kollsman, Paul
d. 1983 Stapleton, Ruth Carter
d. 1984 Manne, Shelly (Sheldon)

September 27
b. 1389 Medici, Cosimo de
b. 1627 Bossuet, Jacques Benigne
b. 1722 Adams, Samuel
b. 1772 Jefferson, Martha
b. 1783 Iturbide, Augustin de
b. 1792 Cruikshank, George
b. 1840 Mahan, Alfred Thayer
b. 1840 Nast, Thomas
b. 1842 Sherwin, Henry Alden

b. 1855 Morton, Joy
b. 1862 Botha, Louis
b. 1864 Dharmapala, Anagarika
b. 1874 Reed, Myrtle
b. 1875 Deledda, Grazia
b. 1877 Dole, James
b. 1879 Scott, Cyril (Meir)
b. 1884 Zirato, Bruno
b. 1886 Moley, Raymond
b. 1888 Dean, Basil
b. 1895 Arends, Leslie Cornelius
b. 1896 Ervin, Sam(uel James, Jr.)
b. 1898 Youmans, Vincent
b. 1900 Paddleford, Clementine Haskin
b. 1906 Empson, William, Sir
b. 1908 Chappell, William
b. 1914 Marshall, (Sarah) Catherine Wood
b. 1915 Marshall, Catherine
b. 1916 Fischetti, John
b. 1917 Auchincloss, Louis
b. 1918 Ryle, Martin, Sir
b. 1919 Percy, Charles Harting
b. 1920 Conrad, William
b. 1922 Jancso, Miklos
b. 1922 Penn, Arthur Heller
b. 1924 Powell, Earl
b. 1926 Meadows, Jayne Cotter
b. 1927 Gellis, Roberta Leah Jacobs
b. 1929 Harris, Leonard
b. 1929 Thompson, Sada Carolyn
b. 1930 Kipnis, Igor
b. 1933 Nolan, Kathy (Kathleen)
b. 1934 Howar, Barbara
b. 1934 Jarman, Claude, Jr.
b. 1934 Schaap, Dick (Richard J)
b. 1938 Farmer, Don
b. 1939 Whitworth, Kathy (Kathrynne Ann)
b. 1942 Weller, Michael
b. 1943 Bachman, Randy
b. 1945 Dichter, Mischa
b. 1947 Meat Loaf
b. 1949 Schmidt, Mike (Michael Jack)
b. 1953 Watts, Heather (Linda Heather)
b. 1954 Barrow, Keith E
b. 1958 Cassidy, Shaun Paul
d. 1660 Vincent de Paul, Saint
d. 1730 Eusden, Laurence
d. 1805 Moultrie, William
d. 1854 Reed, Henry Hope
d. 1870 Comstock, Henry Tompkins Paige
d. 1876 Bragg, Braxton
d. 1886 Cooke, John Esten
d. 1917 Degas, (Hilaire Germain) Edgar
d. 1919 Patti, Adelina Juana Maria
d. 1921 Humperdinck, Engelbert
d. 1944 McPherson, Aimee Semple
d. 1949 Adler, David
d. 1950 Knox, Rose Markward
d. 1950 Woodward, William E
d. 1953 Fritzsche, Hans

d. 1956 Didrikson, "Babe" (Mildred)
d. 1960 Pankhurst, (Estelle) Sylvia
d. 1961 Doolittle, Hilda
d. 1962 Giesler, Jerry (Harold Lee)
d. 1962 Skidmore, Louis
d. 1963 Christiansen, Arthur
d. 1964 Waln, Nora
d. 1965 Bow, Clara Gordon
d. 1971 Castellon, Frederico
d. 1976 Fishbein, Morris
d. 1977 Winslow, Ola Elizabeth
d. 1979 Fields, Gracie
d. 1980 Gelb, Lawrence
d. 1981 Montgomery, Robert Henry
d. 1982 Armour, Norman
d. 1982 Bowen, Billy
d. 1982 Romano, Umberto
d. 1983 Shear, Murray Jacob
d. 1984 Bunker, Ellsworth
d. 1985 Kertesz, Andre
d. 1985 Nolan, Lloyd

September 28
b. 1778 Douvillier, Suzanne Theodore Vaillande
b. 1789 Bright, Richard
b. 1803 Merimee, Prosper
b. 1820 Engels, Friedrich
b. 1834 Lamoureux, Charles
b. 1839 Willard, Frances E
b. 1840 Peck, George Wilbur
b. 1841 Clemenceau, Georges Eugene Benjamin
b. 1855 Brush, George
b. 1856 Thompson, Edward Herbert
b. 1856 Wiggin, Kate Douglas
b. 1863 MacMonnies, Fred W
b. 1866 Tschirky, Oscar
b. 1871 Badoglio, Pietro
b. 1880 Flanders, Ralph Edward
b. 1881 DeCordoba, Pedro
b. 1881 Sears, Eleonora Randolph
b. 1887 Brundage, Avery
b. 1888 McNeile, Herman Cyril
b. 1892 Rice, Elmer
b. 1893 Field, Marshall, III
b. 1894 Stark, Abe
b. 1895 Harrison, Wallace Kirkman
b. 1895 Petrie, Charles Alexander, Sir
b. 1897 Fraenkel, Heinrich
b. 1898 Carter, Boake
b. 1901 Paley, William Samuel
b. 1902 Okada, Kenzo
b. 1902 Sullivan, Ed(ward Vincent)
b. 1903 Billington, Ray Allen
b. 1905 Rivers, L(ucius) Mendel
b. 1905 Schmeling, Max(imilian)
b. 1906 Miller, Paul
b. 1908 Frondizi, Arturo
b. 1909 Capp, Al
b. 1910 Macapagal, Diosdado Pangan
b. 1911 Howe, Syd(ney Harris)

b. 1911 Vines, Ellsworth
b. 1913 Marble, Alice
b. 1913 Peters, Ellis, pseud.
b. 1915 Rosenberg, Ethel Greenglass
b. 1916 Finch, Peter
b. 1917 Davison, Frederic Ellis
b. 1917 Somes, Michael
b. 1919 Harmon, Tom (Thomas D)
b. 1922 Sedny, Jules
b. 1923 Windom, William
b. 1924 Mastroianni, Marcello
b. 1925 Stang, Arnold
b. 1928 Silver, Horace Ward Martin
   Tavares
b. 1934 Bardot, Brigitte
b. 1935 Crampton, Bruce Sidney
b. 1935 Gelmis, Joseph Stephen
b. 1935 Sears, Heather
b. 1938 King, Ben E
b. 1939 Luedtke, Kurt (Mamre)
b. 1950 Hofsiss, Jack Bernard
b. 1952 Kristel, Sylvia
b. 1962 Fuhr, Grant
d. 1776 Colden, Cadwallader
d. 1789 Day, Thomas
d. 1839 Dunlap, William
d. 1859 Ritter, Karl
d. 1891 Melville, Herman
d. 1895 Pasteur, Louis
d. 1914 Sears, Richard Warren
d. 1917 Hulme, Thomas Ernest
d. 1927 Einthoven, Willem
d. 1930 Guggenheim, Daniel
d. 1938 Conrad, Con
d. 1938 Duryea, Charles Edgar
d. 1946 Hoesslin, Franz von
d. 1953 Hubble, Edwin Powell
d. 1954 Lytell, Bert
d. 1956 Boeing, William Edward
d. 1956 Hodge, Frederick Webb
d. 1963 Raisa, Rosa
d. 1964 Brown, Nacio Herb
d. 1964 Marx, "Harpo" (Arthur)
d. 1966 Breton, Andre
d. 1966 Smith, Lillian
d. 1970 DosPassos, John
d. 1970 Nasser, Gamal Abdel
d. 1973 Auden, W(ystan) H(ugh)
d. 1974 Howes, Frank Stewart
d. 1976 Folsom, Marion Bayard
d. 1978 John Paul I, Pope
d. 1981 Betancourt, Romulo
d. 1985 Abbott, L(enwood) B(allard)

September 29
b. 1511 Servetus, Michael
b. 1547 Cervantes (Saavedra), Miguel(de)
b. 1703 Boucher, Francois
b. 1725 Clive, Robert
b. 1758 Nelson, Horatio Nelson, Viscount
b. 1759 Beckford, William
b. 1810 Gaskell, Elizabeth Cleghorn

b. 1831 Schofield, John McAllister
b. 1838 Richardson, Henry Hobson
b. 1849 Schwatka, Frederik
b. 1858 Mugnone, Leopoldo
b. 1864 Unamuno (y Jugo), Miguel de
b. 1871 Machado y Morales, Gerardo
b. 1872 Murchison, Kenneth MacKenzie
b. 1891 James, Marquis
b. 1895 Rhine, J(oseph) B(anks)
b. 1896 Gabor, Jolie
b. 1897 Agar, Herbert Sebastian
b. 1897 Queeny, Edgar Monsanto
b. 1898 Lysenko, Trofim Denisovich
b. 1899 Butlin, William Heygate Edmund,
   Sir
b. 1901 Fermi, Enrico
b. 1903 Aleman, Miguel
b. 1903 Harnwell, Gaylord Probasco
b. 1903 Neher, Fred
b. 1905 La Bara, Fidel
b. 1907 Autry, Gene (Orvon Gene)
b. 1908 Garson, Greer
b. 1910 Bruce, Virginia
b. 1910 Frankovich, Mike J
b. 1912 Antonioni, Michelangelo
b. 1913 Dixon, Paul Rand
b. 1913 Kramer, Stanley E
b. 1914 Condit, Carl Wilbur
b. 1915 Marshall, Brenda
b. 1916 Howard, Trevor Wallace
b. 1917 Luce, Charles (Franklin)
b. 1918 Wood, Woodrow Johnson
b. 1920 Butler, John
b. 1922 Scott, Lizabeth
b. 1923 Phillips, "Bum" (Oail Andrew)
b. 1925 Forrest, Steve
b. 1925 Tower, John Goodwin
b. 1927 McCloskey, Paul Norton, Jr.
b. 1927 Mertz, Barbara Louise Gross
b. 1930 Bonynge, Richard
b. 1931 Ekberg, Anita
b. 1932 Benton, Robert Douglass
b. 1932 Pfeiffer, Jane Cahill
b. 1933 Machel, Samora Moises
b. 1935 Lewis, Jerry Lee
b. 1936 Bennett, Hal
b. 1938 West, Adam
b. 1939 Linville, Larry Lavon
b. 1942 Kahn, Madeline Gail
b. 1942 McShane, Ian
b. 1942 Ponty, Jean-Luc
b. 1943 Walesa, Lech
b. 1948 Gumbel, Bryant Charles
b. 1956 Coe, Sebastian Newbold
b. 1960 Deer, Rob(ert George)
d. 1531 Sarto, Andrea del
d. 1825 Shays, Daniel
d. 1839 Mohs, Friedrich
d. 1867 Price, Sterling
d. 1902 Zola, Emile Edouard Charles
d. 1910 Davis, Rebecca Blaine Harding

d. 1910 Homer, Winslow
d. 1913 Diesel, Rudolf Christian Karl
d. 1931 Orpen, William
d. 1944 McMurtrie, Douglas C
d. 1945 Bartok, Bela
d. 1953 Reuter, Ernst
d. 1956 Somoza, Anastasio
d. 1959 Bairnsfather, Bruce
d. 1959 Richardson, Sid
d. 1966 Gimbel, Bernard Feustman
d. 1967 McCullers, Carson Smith
d. 1970 Horton, Edward Everett
d. 1970 Seldes, Gilbert Vivian
d. 1971 Moore, Roy W
d. 1974 Patrick, Van
d. 1975 Stengel, "Casey" (Charles Dillon)
d. 1977 Tcherepnin, Alexander
d. 1978 Obolensky, Serge
d. 1980 Abramson, Harold A(lexander)
d. 1982 Stratton, Monty Franklin Pierce
d. 1984 Porter, Hal

September 30

b. 1732 Necker, Jacques
b. 1788 Raglan, Fitzroy James Henry
    Somerset, Baron
b. 1857 Sudermann, Hermann
b. 1870 Lamont, Thomas William
b. 1875 Fisher, Fred
b. 1875 Voelker, Paul Frederick
b. 1882 Bancroft, George
b. 1882 Geiger, Hans (Johannes Wilhelm)
b. 1888 Poor, Henry Varnum
b. 1893 Sevitzky, Fabien
b. 1895 Milestone, Lewis
b. 1896 Forbes, Ralph
b. 1897 Dagover, Lil (Marta Maria Liletta)
b. 1897 Widdemer, Margaret
b. 1898 Adoree, Renee
b. 1898 Aulaire, Edgar Parin d'
b. 1905 Mott, Nevill Francis, Sir
b. 1905 Powell, Michael
b. 1906 Stewart, John Innes Mackintosh
b. 1907 Kramm, Joseph
b. 1912 Baker, Kenny (Kenneth Lawrence)
b. 1915 Clark, Peggy
b. 1915 Maddox, Lester Garfield
b. 1917 Park, Chung Hee
b. 1919 Neway, Patricia
b. 1921 Kerr, Deborah Jane
b. 1922 Pettiford, Oscar
b. 1922 Unruh, Jesse Marvin
b. 1924 Capote, Truman
b. 1926 Roberts, Robin Evan
b. 1927 Merwin, W(illiam) S(tanley)
b. 1927 Reiffel, Leonard
b. 1928 Fries, Charles W
b. 1928 Thomas, Piri
b. 1928 Wiesel, Elie(zer)
b. 1931 Dickinson, Angie
b. 1932 Podres, Johnny (John Joseph)
b. 1935 Corey, Jill

b. 1935 Mathis, Johnny (John Royce)
b. 1936 Haire, Bill
b. 1936 Sasser, Jim (James Ralph)
b. 1937 Ames, Nancy
b. 1937 Carpenter, William S, Jr.
b. 1939 Cariou, Len (Leonard)
b. 1942 Lyman, Frankie
b. 1943 Ogilvy, Ian
b. 1943 Powell, Jody (Joseph Lester)
b. 1946 Moussa, Ibrahim
b. 1947 Lenska, Rula
b. 1952 Wild, Jack
b. 1953 Allen, Deborah
b. 1954 Drew, John E
b. 1954 Rushen, Patrice
b. 1954 Williams, Barry
d. 1770 Whitefield, George
d. 1865 Wayland, Francis
d. 1897 Therese of Lisieux
d. 1943 Freeman, R(ichard) Austin
d. 1948 Roosevelt, Edith Kermit Carow
d. 1955 Chekhov, Michael
d. 1955 Dean, James
d. 1958 Singmaster, Elsie
d. 1959 Holmes, Taylor
d. 1960 Philby, Harold St. John Bridger
d. 1970 Westmore, Perc(ival)
d. 1976 Joseph, Richard
d. 1977 Ford, Mary
d. 1978 Bergen, Edgar John
d. 1981 Neel, (Louis) Boyd
d. 1982 George, Bill (William)
d. 1982 Janson, Horst Woldemar
d. 1983 Drummond, Roscoe (James
    Roscoe)
d. 1983 Martin, Freddy
d. 1983 Moorehead, Alan
d. 1984 Boylston, Helen Dore
d. 1985 Bayer, Herbert
d. 1985 MacInnes, Helen
d. 1985 Richter, Charles Francis
d. 1985 Signoret, Simone Henrietta
    Charlotte

OCTOBER

b. 1537 Grey, Jane, Lady
b. 1698 Logroscino, Nicola
b. 1807 LaFontaine, Louis H, Sir
b. 1861 Prendergast, Maurice Brazil
b. 1891 Konoye, Fumimaro, Prince
b. 1959 Ferguson, Sarah Margaret
b. 1960 Pahlevi, Riza Cyrus
d. 322 BC Demosthenes
d. 1527 Froben, Johann
d. 1629 Sandys, Edwin Sir
d. 1674 Herrick, Robert
d. 1676 Bacon, Nathaniel
d. 775 Mansur, (Abu Jafar Ibn
    Muhammad), Al
d. 1864 Anderson, William
d. 1932 Wovoka

b. 1904 Greene, Graham
b. 1904 Shastri, Lal Badahur
b. 1905 Seper, Franjo
b. 1906 Ley, Willy
b. 1909 Fielding, Lewis J
b. 1909 Hosking, Eric J
b. 1909 Raymond, Alex(ander Gillespie)
b. 1910 Carmichael, James Vinson
b. 1912 Knudsen, Semon Emil
b. 1921 Crispin, Edmund, pseud.
b. 1926 Farenthold, Frances T
b. 1926 Morris, Jan (James Humphrey)
b. 1927 Clarke, Shirley
b. 1928 Felker, Clay S
b. 1928 McFarland, "Spanky" (George Emmett)
b. 1928 Pannenberg, Wolfhart Ulrich
b. 1929 Gunn, Moses
b. 1932 Wills, Maury (Maurice Morning)
b. 1939 Reed, Rex
b. 1945 McLean, Don
b. 1946 Cox, Edward Finch
b. 1948 Karan, Donna Faske
b. 1950 Khambatta, Persis
b. 1950 Rutherford, Michael
b. 1951 Sting
b. 1960 Anderson, Glenn Chris
b. 1965 Casey, Dan(iel Maurice)
d. 1780 Andre, John
d. 1788 Lee, Charles
d. 1799 Iredell, James
d. 1803 Adams, Samuel
d. 1842 Channing, William Ellery
d. 1853 Argo, Dominique Francois Jean
d. 1872 Lieber, Franz
d. 1892 Renan, (Joseph) Ernest
d. 1909 Schley, Winfield Scott
d. 1920 Bruch, Max
d. 1927 Arrhenius, Svante August
d. 1928 Barron, Clarence Walker
d. 1931 Lipton, Thomas Johnstone, Sir
d. 1931 Nielsen, Carl August
d. 1933 Stribling, Young (William Lawrence)
d. 1943 Dett, Robert Nathaniel
d. 1950 Fitzgerald, John Francis
d. 1956 Bancroft, George
d. 1958 Magill, Hugh Stewart
d. 1958 Stopes, Marie Charlotte Carmichael
d. 1962 Lovejoy, Frank
d. 1969 Ar Buthnot, May Hill
d. 1970 Wilson, Edward Arthur
d. 1973 Hartman, Paul
d. 1973 Nurmi, Paavo
d. 1974 Shukshin, Vasilii Makarovich
d. 1981 Golden, Harry Lewis
d. 1981 Scott, Hazel Dorothy
d. 1985 Caudill, Rebecca
d. 1985 Hudson, Rock

October 3
b. 1771 Place, Francis
b. 1800 Bancroft, George
b. 1802 Ripley, George
b. 1803 Gorrie, John
b. 1829 Holly, James Theodore
b. 1844 Manson, Patrick, Sir
b. 1854 Gorgas, William Crawford
b. 1856 Fortune, Timothy Thomas
b. 1856 Hare, James Henry
b. 1870 Kraus, Felix von
b. 1872 Clarke, Fred Clifford
b. 1873 Horlick, Alexander James
b. 1877 Gildersleeve, Virginia Crocheron
b. 1879 Bigelow, Henry Bryant
b. 1880 Oland, Warner
b. 1882 Jackson, A(lexander) Y(oung)
b. 1886 Alain-Fournier, pseud.
b. 1890 Hull, Henry
b. 1890 Obolensky, Serge
b. 1891 Gannett, Lewis Stiles
b. 1894 Sharett, Moshe
b. 1897 Aragon, Louis Marie Antoine Alfred
b. 1898 McCarey, Leo
b. 1899 Berg, Gertrude
b. 1900 Wolfe, Thomas Clayton
b. 1902 Costa e Silva, Arthur da
b. 1908 Burke, Johnny
b. 1910 Hines, John Elbridge
b. 1911 Hordern, Michael
b. 1916 Herriot, James, pseud.
b. 1918 Cone, Molly Lamken
b. 1922 Bronson, Charles
b. 1923 Skrowaczewski, Stanislaw
b. 1925 Vidal, "Gore" (Eugene Luther)
b. 1925 Wein, George Theodore
b. 1928 Bruhn, Erik Belton Evers
b. 1929 Stern, Bert
b. 1930 Eden, Nicholas
b. 1931 Hall, Glenn Henry
b. 1933 Thompson, Thomas
b. 1935 Duke, Charles Moss, Jr.
b. 1936 Reich, Steve
b. 1938 Cochran, Eddie
b. 1940 Ferris, Barbara Gillian
b. 1940 Ratelle, (Joseph Gilbert Yvon) Jean
b. 1941 Checker, Chubby
b. 1941 Evans, Hiram W
b. 1943 Bingaman, Jeff
b. 1945 Saneev, Viktor
b. 1946 Dotson, Bob
b. 1947 Buckingham, Lindsey
b. 1950 Hensley, Pamela Gail
b. 1951 Winfield, Dave (David Mark)
b. 1959 Wagner, Jack Peter
d. 1226 Francis of Assisi, Saint
d. 1656 Standish, Miles
d. 1750 Mottley, John
d. 1838 Black Hawk

d. 1982 Gould, Glenn Herbert
d. 1982 Grumman, Leroy Randle
d. 1982 Terry, Walter

October 5
b. 1703 Edwards, Jonathan
b. 1712 Guardi, Francesco
b. 1713 Diderot, Denis
b. 1751 Iredell, James
b. 1824 Chadwick, Henry
b. 1829 Arthur, Chester Alan
b. 1840 Symonds, John Addington
b. 1848 O'Connor, Thomas Power
b. 1848 Trudeau, Edward Livingston
b. 1864 Lumiere, Louis Jean
b. 1869 Morrison, Cameron
b. 1879 Erskine, John
b. 1879 Rous, Peyton
b. 1882 Dresser, Louise
b. 1882 Goddard, Robert Hutchings
b. 1887 Cassin, Rene
b. 1890 Schmid, Eduard
b. 1893 Hibberd, Andrew Stuart
b. 1895 Smith, Walter Bedell
b. 1897 Loew, Arthur M
b. 1899 Bidault, Georges
b. 1899 Wallenberg, Marcus
b. 1902 Kroc, Ray(mond) Albert
b. 1905 Fodor, Eugene
b. 1906 Frankenstein, Alfred Victor
b. 1906 Jones, R William
b. 1907 Louis, Jean
b. 1908 Logan, Josh(ua Lockwood)
b. 1913 Fluckey, Eugene Bennett
b. 1918 Ludden, Allen Ellsworth
b. 1919 Pleasence, Donald
b. 1921 Tabbert, William
b. 1922 Keane, Bil
b. 1923 Berrigan, Philip Francis
b. 1923 Johns, Glynis
b. 1923 Lancaster, Bruce Morgan
b. 1924 Dana, Bill
b. 1924 Morton, Frederic
b. 1925 Morgan, Robert Burren
b. 1929 Gordon, Richard Francis, Jr.
b. 1930 Popovich, Pavel Romanovich
b. 1932 Burke, Yvonne Brathwaite Watson
b. 1933 Cilento, Diane
b. 1934 Taylor, Kenneth Douglas
b. 1936 Havel, Vaclav
b. 1937 Switzer, Barry
b. 1943 Miller, Steve
b. 1950 Conaway, Jeff
b. 1951 Allen, Karen
b. 1954 Geldof, Bob
b. 1957 Evert, Jeanne
b. 1965 Lemieux, Mario
d. 1787 Stone, Thomas
d. 1805 Cornwallis, Charles, Marquis
d. 1813 Tecumseh
d. 1885 Durant, Thomas Clark
d. 1892 Dalton, Gratton

d. 1892 Dalton, Robert
d. 1927 Warner, Sam(uel Louis)
d. 1931 Johnston, Annie Fellows
d. 1931 Morrow, Dwight Whitney
d. 1933 Adoree, Renee
d. 1934 Vigo, Jean
d. 1940 Booth, Ballington
d. 1941 Brandeis, Louis Dembitz
d. 1944 Maillol, Aristide
d. 1948 Cross, Wilbur
d. 1954 Charleston, Oscar McKinley
d. 1960 Kroeber, Alfred Louis
d. 1969 Fosdick, Harry Emerson
d. 1969 Hagen, Walter Charles
d. 1972 Dreyfuss, Henry
d. 1973 Blackmer, Sidney Alderman
d. 1973 Cott, Nate
d. 1974 Shazar, Zalman
d. 1974 Stignani, Ebe
d. 1975 Cantacuzene, Princess
d. 1977 Garber, Jan
d. 1981 Bullard, Dexter Means
d. 1981 Grahame, Gloria

October 6
b. 1573 Southampton, Henry Wriothesley, Earl
b. 1744 McGill, James
b. 1769 Brock, Isaac, Sir
b. 1773 Louis Phillippe
b. 1809 Griffiths, John Willis
b. 1820 Lind, Jenny (Johanna Maria)
b. 1844 Davis, Sam(uel)
b. 1846 Westinghouse, George
b. 1857 Dickman, Joseph Theodore
b. 1859 Seiberling, Frank Augustus
b. 1862 Beveridge, Albert Jeremiah
b. 1866 Fessenden, Reginald Aubrey
b. 1873 Sonneck, Oscar George Theodore
b. 1882 Szymanowski, Karol
b. 1887 Jeritza, Maria
b. 1887 LeCorbusier
b. 1889 Heard, Gerald (Henry FitzGerald)
b. 1893 Ager, Milton
b. 1894 McNair, Malcolm Perrine
b. 1895 Gordon, Caroline
b. 1895 Martineau, Jean
b. 1897 Cowan, Jerome
b. 1897 Dietz, David
b. 1902 Block, Joseph Leopold
b. 1902 Sharkey, Jack (Joseph Paul)
b. 1903 McMahon, (James O') Brien
b. 1905 Moody, Helen Wills
b. 1906 Gaynor, Janet
b. 1909 Carson, Robert
b. 1909 Lombard, Carole
b. 1911 Castle, Barbara Anne Betts
b. 1913 Dyer-Bennet, Richard
b. 1914 Heyerdahl, Thor
b. 1916 Ellin, Stanley
b. 1916 Sneider, Vernon John
b. 1921 Biro, Val

d. 1973 Price, Dennis
d. 1976 Lyons, Leonard
d. 1979 Lewis, Wilmarth Sheldon
d. 1983 Abell, George O(gden)

October 8
b. 1553 Thou, Jacques Auguste de
b. 1585 Schutz, Heinrich
b. 1609 Clarke, John
b. 1749 Levasseur, Rosalie
b. 1833 Stedman, Edmund Clarence
b. 1838 Hay, John Milton
b. 1846 Gary, Elbert H
b. 1857 Albee, Edward Franklin
b. 1861 Van Zandt, Marie
b. 1862 Sauer, Emil von
b. 1869 Duryea, J(ames) Frank
b. 1869 Hartmann, Sadakichi
b. 1872 Powys, John Cowper
b. 1873 Jarry, Alfred
b. 1878 Munnings, Alfred James, Sir
b. 1890 Hoffenstein, Samuel Goodman
b. 1890 Rickenbacker, Eddie (Edward Vernon)
b. 1895 Jones, "Biff" (Lawrence M)
b. 1895 Peron, Juan
b. 1896 Duvivier, Julien
b. 1897 Cisler, Walker Lee
b. 1897 Mamoulian, Rouben
b. 1897 Throckmorton, Cleon
b. 1900 Chermayeff, Serge
b. 1904 Taishoff, Sol Joseph
b. 1905 Levin, Meyer
b. 1908 Maltz, Albert
b. 1909 Harrell, Mack
b. 1909 Jaroszewicz, Piotr
b. 1910 Hall, Gus
b. 1912 Gardner, John William
b. 1913 Fielding, Temple Hornaday
b. 1913 Gilruth, Robert Rowe
b. 1913 Schumann, Walter
b. 1914 Schocken, Theodore
b. 1915 Vaughan, Bill (William Edward)
b. 1916 Matsunaga, Spark Masayuki
b. 1917 Lord, Walter
b. 1919 Ramsbotham, Peter, Sir
b. 1920 Herbert, Frank Patrick
b. 1922 Barnard, Christiaan Neethling
b. 1925 Magana, Alvaro (Alfredo)
b. 1925 Sinyavsky, Andrei
b. 1929 Dalis, Irene
b. 1929 Dohnanyi, Christoph von
b. 1931 Kerr, Malcolm (Hooper)
b. 1933 Korda, Michael Vincent
b. 1934 Brown, John Carter
b. 1936 Andrews, James Frederick
b. 1936 Barrett, Rona
b. 1937 Clodagh
b. 1940 Carradine, David
b. 1941 Jackson, Jesse Louis
b. 1941 Stevens, Shane
b. 1942 Tomasson, Helgi

b. 1943 Chase, "Chevy" (Cornelius Crane)
b. 1944 Browles, William Dodson, Jr.
b. 1946 Kucinich, Dennis John
b. 1948 Purcell, Sarah
b. 1950 Bell, "Kool" (Robert)
b. 1952 Adams, Cliff
b. 1956 Zimbalist, Stephanie
b. 1959 Eason, Tony (Charles Carroll, IV)
d. 1754 Fielding, Henry
d. 1793 Hancock, John
d. 1803 Alfieri, Vittorio
d. 1834 Boieldieu, Francois Adrien
d. 1837 Fourier, Francois Marie Charles
d. 1869 Pierce, Franklin
d. 1885 Perrin, Emile Cesare
d. 1895 Mahone, William
d. 1896 DuMaurier, George Louis P B
d. 1911 Binet, Alfred
d. 1914 Crapsey, Adelaide
d. 1941 Kahn, Gus
d. 1942 Ellsler, Effie
d. 1944 Willkie, Wendell Lewis
d. 1953 Bruce, Nigel
d. 1953 Ferrier, Kathleen
d. 1961 Hertz, John Daniel
d. 1963 Adams, Frank Ramsay
d. 1965 Costain, Thomas B
d. 1967 Attlee, Clement Richard Attlee, Earl
d. 1967 Guevara, Che Ernesto
d. 1967 Manville, Tommy (Thomas Franklin, Jr.)
d. 1974 Carney, Harry Howell
d. 1974 Hoffman, Paul Gray
d. 1975 Felsenstein, Walter
d. 1978 Gilliam, Jim (James William)
d. 1980 Dollard, John
d. 1980 Kendrick, Pearl Luella
d. 1981 Kohut, Heinz
d. 1982 Freud, Anna
d. 1982 Lamas, Fernando
d. 1983 Hackett, Joan
d. 1984 Brisson, Frederick
d. 1985 Bacchelli, Riccardo
d. 1985 Blough, Roger Miles
d. 1985 Welchman, Gordon

October 9
b. 1782 Cass, Lewis
b. 1822 Sykes, George
b. 1830 Hosmer, Harriet Goodhue
b. 1832 Allen, Elizabeth Ann Chase Akers
b. 1835 Saint-Saens, (Charles) Camille
b. 1839 Schley, Winfield Scott
b. 1848 Duveneck, Frank
b. 1852 Fischer, Emil
b. 1859 Dreyfus, Alfred
b. 1860 Wood, Leonard
b. 1863 Bok, Edward William
b. 1863 Bradford, Gamaliel
b. 1866 Loeb, William
b. 1873 Flesch, Karl

b. 1946 Vereen, Ben
b. 1952 Nystrom, Bob (Thor Robert)
b. 1953 Williams, Gus
b. 1955 Roth, David Lee
b. 1956 Navratilova, Martina
b. 1958 Tucker, Tanya
d. 1531 Zwingli, Huldreich
d. 1797 Braxton, Carter
d. 1836 Jefferson, Martha
d. 1857 Crawford, Thomas
d. 1872 Parton, Sara Payson Willis
d. 1872 Seward, William Henry
d. 1885 McCloskey, John
d. 1898 Puvis de Chavannes, Pierre Cecile
d. 1913 Busch, Adolphus
d. 1919 Genung, John Franklin
d. 1925 Duke, James Buchanan
d. 1944 Gottschalk, Ferdinand
d. 1948 Eaton, Mary
d. 1955 Stracciari, Riccardo
d. 1959 Ed, Carl Frank Ludwig
d. 1962 Allen, Vivian Beaumont
d. 1964 Cantor, Eddie
d. 1965 Uhde, Hermann
d. 1967 Keaney, Frank
d. 1970 Daladier, Edouard
d. 1970 Rapacki, Adam
d. 1971 Burt, Cyril Lodowic, Sir
d. 1971 Saerchinger, Cesar Victor Charles
d. 1976 Wallace, Ed(ward Tatum)
d. 1978 Metcalfe, Ralph H
d. 1979 Paray, Paul
d. 1980 Cheney, Sheldon Warren
d. 1980 Thomas, Billy
d. 1983 Debus, Kurt Heinrich
d. 1983 Richardson, Ralph David, Sir
d. 1984 Gaddis, Thomas (Eugene)
d. 1985 Brynner, Yul
d. 1985 Welles, Orson (George Orson)

October 11
b. 1809 Fowler, Orson Squire
b. 1835 Thomas, Theodore
b. 1844 Heinz, Henry John
b. 1860 Litvinne, Felia
b. 1863 Leroux, Xavier
b. 1871 Hawes, Harriet Ann Boyd
b. 1872 Stone, Harlan Fiske
b. 1881 Kelsen, Hans
b. 1881 Young, Stark
b. 1882 Dett, Robert Nathaniel
b. 1883 Stiedry, Fritz
b. 1884 Roosevelt, Eleanor
b. 1885 Mauriac, Francois
b. 1885 Sherman, Lowell
b. 1887 Hoppe, Willie (William F)
b. 1889 Lelong, Lucien
b. 1891 Ault, George Christian
b. 1891 Dickinson, Edwin W
b. 1892 Burgin, Richard
b. 1894 Lubke, Heinrich
b. 1894 Stoessel, Albert

b. 1895 Cann, Howard Goodsell
b. 1896 Firpo, Luis Angel
b. 1897 Auslander, Joseph
b. 1897 Twining, Nathan F(arragut)
b. 1899 Ewen, Frederic
b. 1900 Hartmann, Rudolph
b. 1900 Hubbard, Cal (Robert Calvin)
b. 1902 Ilg, Frances Lillian
b. 1902 Tully, Alice
b. 1903 Weatherford, Teddy
b. 1905 Alexander, Leo
b. 1906 Clark, "Dutch" (Earl)
b. 1906 Revson, Charles Haskell
b. 1908 Dodd, Robert Lee (Bobby)
b. 1908 Rolfe, "Red" (Robert Abial)
b. 1910 Alsop, Joseph Wright, Jr.
b. 1914 Day, J(ames) Edward
b. 1918 Bodsworth, Charles Frederick
b. 1918 Robbins, Jerome
b. 1919 Blakey, Art
b. 1925 Leonard, Elmore John, Jr.
b. 1926 Hyman, Earle
b. 1927 Tiffeau, Jacques Emile
b. 1930 Bufman, Zev
b. 1930 Payne, Sidney
b. 1930 Shevchenko, Arkady Nikolayevich
b. 1932 West, Dottie
b. 1935 Scheider, Roy Richard
b. 1936 Fullerton, (Charles) Gordon
b. 1937 Charlton, Robert
b. 1938 Leibman, Ron
b. 1939 Bueno, Maria Ester Audion
b. 1941 Shyer, Charles
b. 1946 Martins, Peter
b. 1948 Hall, Daryl
d. 1542 Wyatt, Thomas, Sir
d. 1779 Pulaski, Kazimierz
d. 1809 Lewis, Meriwether
d. 1889 Joule, James Prescott
d. 1896 Bruckner, Anton
d. 1915 Duniway, Abigail Jane Scott
d. 1915 Fabre, Jean Henri
d. 1918 Willard, Archibald MacNeal
d. 1919 Gjellerup, Karl Adolf
d. 1937 Mills, Ogden Livingston
d. 1937 Russell, Henry
d. 1950 Lord, Pauline
d. 1952 Conway, Jack
d. 1952 Kelly, "Shipwreck" (Alvin A)
d. 1953 Fraser, James Earle
d. 1958 Vlaminck, Maurice de
d. 1961 Marx, "Chico" (Leonard)
d. 1963 Piaf, Edith
d. 1964 Herrick, Elinore M
d. 1965 Lange, Dorothea Nutzhorn
d. 1967 Pendleton, Nat
d. 1968 White, George
d. 1970 Spitalny, Phil
d. 1971 Conklin, Chester
d. 1976 Boswell, Connee
d. 1977 Kantor, Mackinlay

b. 1920 Day, Laraine
b. 1921 Montand, Yves
b. 1921 Thomas, Bill
b. 1924 Gibbs, Terry
b. 1924 Russell, Nipsey
b. 1925 Bruce, Lenny
b. 1925 Gilroy, Frank D
b. 1925 Thatcher, Margaret Hilda Roberts
b. 1926 Herbert, John, pseud.
b. 1926 Lamb, Lawrence Edward
b. 1930 Geller, Bruce
b. 1931 Mathews, Eddie (Edwin Lee, Jr.)
b. 1938 McHenry, Donald Franchot
b. 1942 Garfunkel, Art(hur)
b. 1942 Tiffin, Pamela Kimberley
b. 1944 Lamm, Robert
b. 1946 Dalton, Lacy J
b. 1946 Wilson, Demond
b. 1949 Hagar, Sammy
b. 1951 Johnson, Beverly
b. 1958 Berliner, Ron
b. 1959 Osmond, Marie (Olive Marive)
d. 54 AD Claudius I
d. 1799 Paca, William
d. 1812 Brock, Isaac, Sir
d. 1815 Murat, Joachim
d. 1822 Canova, Antonio
d. 1869 Sainte-Beuve, Charles Augustin
d. 1882 Gobineau, Joseph Arthur, Comte de
d. 1886 Loomis, Mahion
d. 1890 Belknap, William Worth
d. 1905 Irving, Henry, Sir
d. 1908 Gilman, Daniel Coit
d. 1938 Segar, Elzie Crisler
d. 1939 Sterling, Ford
d. 1945 Hershey, Milton Snavely
d. 1946 Bannerman, Helen
d. 1947 Webb, Sidney James
d. 1956 Davis, Owen
d. 1961 Deren, Maya
d. 1966 Webb, Clifton
d. 1968 Bandeira, Manuel (Filho Manuel)
d. 1968 Benaderet, Bea
d. 1968 Unwin, Stanley, Sir
d. 1969 Crittenden, Christopher
d. 1973 Briggs, Austin Eugene
d. 1974 Kleberg, Robert Justus, Jr.
d. 1974 Rice, "Sam" (Edgar Charles)
d. 1974 Rubin, Reuven
d. 1974 Sullivan, Ed(ward Vincent)
d. 1980 Martin, Pete (Thornton)
d. 1981 Asther, Nils
d. 1981 Horan, James David
d. 1982 Sackler, Howard Oliver
d. 1984 Kelly, George Lange
d. 1984 Neel, Alice Hartley

October 14
b. 1633 James II
b. 1644 Penn, William
b. 1734 Lee, Francis Lightfoot

b. 1814 Lamy, Jean Baptist
b. 1816 Huntington, Daniel
b. 1847 O'Neill, James
b. 1857 Lamar, Joseph Rucker
b. 1863 Black, Winifred Sweet
b. 1867 Masaoka, Tsunenori
b. 1869 Duveen, Joseph, Sir
b. 1872 Hess, Sol
b. 1876 Ironside, Henry Allan
b. 1879 Franklin, Miles, pseud.
b. 1880 Bely, Andrey, pseud.
b. 1882 DeValera, Eamon
b. 1888 Mansfield, Katherine
b. 1888 Turnbull, Agnes Sligh
b. 1890 Conroy, Frank
b. 1890 Eisenhower, Dwight David
b. 1892 Welles, Sumner
b. 1893 Lenski, Lois
b. 1894 Cummings, E(dward) E(stlin)
b. 1894 Pate, Maurice
b. 1895 Baldwin, Horace
b. 1896 Gish, Lillian Diana
b. 1897 Liebes, Dorothy Katherine Wright
b. 1897 Warburg, Frederick Marcus
b. 1898 Wellman, Paul Iselin
b. 1901 Stuhldreher, Harry A
b. 1903 Cramer, Polly
b. 1906 Arendt, Hannah
b. 1907 Jones, Allan
b. 1907 McKenzie, "Red" (William)
b. 1910 Wooden, John Robert
b. 1911 Le Duc Tho
b. 1913 Casey, Hugh Thomas
b. 1914 Brecheen, Harry David
b. 1916 Koop, Charles Everett
b. 1917 Bibby, Thomas Geoffrey
b. 1920 Wolfington, Iggie
b. 1924 Kogan, Leonid Borisovich
b. 1928 Graffman, Gary
b. 1928 Moore, Roger George
b. 1930 Mobutu, Joseph-Desire
b. 1933 Webster, Donald Blake
b. 1936 Logan, Daniel
b. 1938 Dean, John Wesley
b. 1938 Montgomery, Melba
b. 1938 Pahlevi, Farah Diba
b. 1939 Lauren, Ralph
b. 1940 Richard, Cliff
b. 1943 Rentzel, Lance
b. 1943 Williams, Jimy (James Francis)
b. 1946 Sloan, Michael
b. 1949 Schultz, Dave (David William)
b. 1950 LLoyd, Robin
b. 1950 Young, Sheila
b. 1952 Anderson, Harry
b. 1953 Evigan, Greg(ory Ralph)
b. 1954 Aikens, Willie Mays
b. 1958 Daniel, Beth
b. 1958 Dolby, Thomas
b. 1959 Pero, A J
d. 1619 Daniel, Samuel

b. 1856 Wilde, Oscar Fingal O'Flahertie Wills
b. 1861 Bury, John Bagnell
b. 1877 Lawrie, Lee
b. 1881 Harridge, Will(iam)
b. 1882 Buttenheim, Edgar Joseph
b. 1886 Ben-Gurion, David
b. 1888 O'Neill, Eugene Gladstone
b. 1890 Strand, Paul
b. 1893 Carmer, Carl Lamson
b. 1898 Douglas, William Orville
b. 1900 Ardizzone, Edward Jeffrey Irving
b. 1900 Goslin, "Goose" (Leon Allen)
b. 1903 Washington, "Buck" (Ford Lee)
b. 1906 Brooks, Cleanth
b. 1908 Ardrey, Robert
b. 1908 Hoxha, Enver
b. 1912 Hansen, Clifford Peter
b. 1913 Pearce, Alice
b. 1915 Holdren, Judd Clifton
b. 1916 Winsor, Kathleen
b. 1921 Darnell, Linda
b. 1923 Hicks, Louise Day
b. 1923 Kaempfert, Bert
b. 1925 Evans, Daniel Jackson
b. 1925 Lansbury, Angela Brigid
b. 1927 Conrad, Michael
b. 1927 Grass, Gunter Wilhelm
b. 1929 VonHoffman, Nicholas
b. 1931 Colson, Charles Wendell
b. 1932 Lewis, Henry Jay
b. 1937 Anthony, Tony
b. 1940 DeBusschere, Dave (David Albert)
b. 1946 Somers, Suzanne
b. 1949 Weir, Bob (Robert Hall)
b. 1956 Belote, Melissa
d. 1523 Signorelli, Luca
d. 1553 Cranach, Lucas
d. 1555 Latimer, Hugh
d. 1621 Sweelinck, Jan Pieterszoon
d. 1628 Malherbe, Francois de
d. 1793 Hunter, John
d. 1793 Marie Antoinette
d. 1802 Strutt, Joseph
d. 1841 Barbaja, Domenica
d. 1928 Thompson, J(ames) Walter
d. 1933 Renaud, Maurice
d. 1937 Brunhoff, Jean de
d. 1946 Bantock, Granville, Sir
d. 1946 Frank, Hans
d. 1946 Frick, Wilhelm
d. 1946 Keitel, Wilhelm
d. 1946 Ribbentrop, Joachim von
d. 1946 Rosenberg, Alfred
d. 1946 Seyss-Inquart, Artur von
d. 1946 Streicher, Julius
d. 1951 Khan, Liaquat Ali
d. 1954 Crump, Edward Hull
d. 1959 Marshall, George Catlett
d. 1966 Wagner, Wieland Adolf Gottfried
d. 1972 Carroll, Leo G

d. 1973 Krupa, Gene
d. 1975 Gui, Vittorio
d. 1978 Rockwell, Willard F
d. 1981 Dayan, Moshe
d. 1981 Fairchild, Louis W
d. 1982 DelMonaco, Mario
d. 1982 Selye, "Hans" (Hugo Bruno)
d. 1983 Liberace, George J

October 17
b. 1727 Wilkes, John
b. 1729 Monsigny, Pierre-Alexandre
b. 1760 Saint-Simon, Claude-Henri de Rouvroy
b. 1781 Johnson, Richard Mentor
b. 1810 Mario, Giovanni Matteo
b. 1818 Van Lew, Elizabeth
b. 1846 Hudson, Joseph Lowthian
b. 1848 Cummings, "Candy" (William Arthur)
b. 1851 Ryan, Thomas Fortune
b. 1859 Hassam, Childe
b. 1864 Glyn, Elinor Sutherland
b. 1864 Lansing, Robert
b. 1867 Magonigle, Harold Van Buren
b. 1881 Chinard, Gilbert
b. 1883 Neill, A(lexander) S(utherland)
b. 1886 Goodpasture, Ernest William
b. 1893 Byington, Spring
b. 1895 Humphrey, Doris
b. 1901 Collins, Lee
b. 1903 Birdwell, Russell Juarez
b. 1903 Grechko, Andrei Antonovick
b. 1903 Ryan, Irene Noblete
b. 1903 West, Nathanael, pseud.
b. 1906 Cassidy, Harold Gomes
b. 1908 Arthur, Jean
b. 1908 Johnson, U(ral) Alexis
b. 1909 Cole, "Cozy" (William Randolph)
b. 1912 Belaunde-Terry, Fernando
b. 1912 John Paul I, Pope
b. 1914 Siegel, Jerry
b. 1915 Miller, Arthur
b. 1916 Marley, John
b. 1916 Partch, Virgil Franklin, II
b. 1917 Green, Elmer Ellsworth
b. 1917 Kahn, Alfred Edward
b. 1918 Hayworth, Rita
b. 1920 Abel, Elie
b. 1920 Clift, Montgomery
b. 1920 Kilbracken, John Raymond Godley
b. 1921 Brown, George Mackay
b. 1924 Coryell, Don(ald David)
b. 1926 Adams, Julie
b. 1926 Garland, Beverly
b. 1927 Bailey, Martin Jean
b. 1927 Boolootian, Richard Andrew
b. 1927 Poston, Tom
b. 1928 Bennett, Lerone, Jr.
b. 1928 Gilliam, Jim (James William)
b. 1930 Breslin, Jimmy
b. 1933 Anders, William Alison

b. 1938 Knievel, "Evel" (Robert Craig)
b. 1946 Seagren, Bob (Robert Lloyd)
b. 1947 McKean, Michael
b. 1948 Kidder, Margot
b. 1948 Wendt, George
b. 1949 Hudson, Bill (William Louis, II)
b. 1950 Rollins, Howard Ellsworth, Jr.
b. 1955 Bottoms, Sam
b. 1956 Morrow, Ken
b. 1957 Van Patten, Vince(nt)
d. 1586 Sidney, Philip, Sir
d. 1780 Bellotto, Bernardo
d. 1806 Dessalines, Jean J
d. 1837 Hummel, Johann Nepomuk
d. 1849 Chopin, Frederic Francois
d. 1868 Secord, Laura Ingersoll
d. 1879 Dana, Charles Anderson
d. 1887 Kirchhoff, Gustav Robert
d. 1891 Parton, James
d. 1893 Gounod, Charles Francois
d. 1896 Abbey, Henry Eugene
d. 1910 Howe, Julia Ward
d. 1910 Moody, William Vaughn
d. 1948 Cortissoz, Royal
d. 1972 Broda, "Turk" (Walter)
d. 1973 Balchen, Bernt
d. 1977 Balcon, Michael Elias, Sir
d. 1977 Chiang, Yee
d. 1977 Hubbard, Cal (Robert Calvin)
d. 1978 Dailey, Dan
d. 1978 Gronchi, Giovanni
d. 1979 Perelman, S(idney) J(oseph)
d. 1981 Guion, David Wendel Fentress
d. 1984 Garner, Peggy Ann
d. 1984 Hunter, Alberta
d. 1984 Michaux, Henri
d. 1984 Thill, Georges
d. 1985 Rosenstock, Joseph

October 18
b. 1595 Winslow, Edward
b. 1631 Wigglesworth, Michael
b. 1697 Canaletto, Antonio
b. 1706 Galuppi, Baldassare
b. 1714 Woffington, Margaret
b. 1740 Boswell, James
b. 1753 Cambaceres, Jean Jacques Regis de
b. 1777 Kleist, Heinrich von
b. 1785 Peacock, Thomas Love
b. 1799 Schonbein, Christian Friedrich
b. 1818 Ord, Edward Otho Cresap
b. 1831 Harrison, Frederic
b. 1831 Jackson, Helen Maria Hunt Fiske
b. 1844 Wiley, Harvey Washington
b. 1854 Andree, Salomon August
b. 1859 Bergson, Henri Louis
b. 1870 Suzuki, Daisetz Teitaro
b. 1875 Leonard, Eddie
b. 1875 Yarnell, Harry E
b. 1878 Adams, James Truslow
b. 1878 Artsybashev, Mikhail Petrovich
b. 1880 Jabotinsky, Vladimir Evgenevich

b. 1882 Burt, Maxwell Struthers
b. 1888 Waymack, W(illiam) W(esley)
b. 1892 Carroll, Leo G
b. 1895 Boles, John
b. 1895 DelRuth, Roy
b. 1896 Davis, Harold Lenoir
b. 1896 Holman, Nat
b. 1900 Lenya, Lotte
b. 1901 Mott, Ruth Rawlings
b. 1902 Hopkins, Miriam
b. 1904 Liebling, Abbot Joseph
b. 1905 Houphouet-Boigny, Felix
b. 1906 Kingsley, Sidney
b. 1912 Tsiranana, Philibert
b. 1914 Salt, Waldo
b. 1918 Troup, Bobby (Robert William)
b. 1919 Trudeau, Pierre Elliott
b. 1921 Helms, Jesse Alexander, Jr.
b. 1922 Stankiewicz, Richard Peter
b. 1924 Hodgson, Richard Sargeant
b. 1925 Mercouri, "Melina" (Maria Amalia)
b. 1927 Fanning, Katherine
b. 1927 Scott, George Campbell
b. 1929 Elkins, Hillard
b. 1930 Carlucci, Frank Charles, III
b. 1934 Stevens, Inger
b. 1935 Boyle, Peter
b. 1937 Dowler, Boyd
b. 1939 Ditka, Mike
b. 1939 Oswald, Lee Harvey
b. 1942 Horton, Willie (William Wattison)
b. 1944 Kurtz, Katherine
b. 1947 Nyro, Laura
b. 1948 Shange, Ntozake
b. 1951 Dawber, Pam
b. 1958 Hearns, Thomas (Tommy)
b. 1961 Marsalis, Wynton
b. 1961 Moran, Erin
d. 1678 Jordaens, Jacob
d. 1817 Mehul, Etienne Nicolas
d. 1865 Palmerston, Henry John Temple, Viscount
d. 1871 Babbage, Charles
d. 1878 Laing, David
d. 1893 Stone, Lucy
d. 1897 Worden, John Lorimer
d. 1901 Pillsbury, John Sargent
d. 1931 Edison, Thomas Alva
d. 1935 Lachaise, Gaston
d. 1945 Weyerhaeuser, Frederick Edward
d. 1948 Brauchitsch, Heinrich Alfred
d. 1953 D'Alvarez, Marguerite
d. 1955 Ortega y Gasset, Jose
d. 1956 Atterbury, Grosvenor
d. 1961 Darwin, Bernard Richard Meirion
d. 1966 Arden, Elizabeth
d. 1966 Kresge, Sebastian Spering
d. 1968 Tracy, Lee
d. 1973 Anderson, Margaret Carolyn
d. 1973 Kelly, Walt

d. 1977 Baader, Andreas
d. 1978 Mercader, Ramon
d. 1980 Teale, Edwin Way
d. 1981 Muncey, Bill (William)
d. 1981 Rubin, Vitalii
d. 1982 Mendes-France, Pierre
d. 1982 Truman, Bess
d. 1984 Hexum, Jon-Erik
d. 1985 Kent, Jack (John Wellington)

October 19
b. 1720 Woolman, John
b. 1741 Laclos, (Pierre) Choderlos de
b. 1748 Jefferson, Martha Wayles Skelton
b. 1784 Hunt, Leigh
b. 1784 McLoughlin, John
b. 1810 Clay, Cassius Marcellus
b. 1831 Hunter, Thomas
b. 1861 Burns, William John
b. 1862 Lumiere, Auguste Marie Louis
b. 1863 Finley, John Huston
b. 1868 Landes, Bertha Ethel
b. 1871 Cannon, Walter Bradford
b. 1876 Brown, Mordecai Peter Centennial
b. 1878 Sanborn, Pitts
b. 1885 Merrill, Charles Edward
b. 1889 Hurst, Fannie
b. 1889 Satherly, Arthur Edward
b. 1895 Mumford, Lewis
b. 1899 Asturias, Miguel Angel
b. 1899 Bauer, Eddie
b. 1901 Burke, Arleigh Albert
b. 1902 Grattan, Clinton Hartley
b. 1903 Giannini, Vittorio
b. 1908 Allen, Larry
b. 1909 Mott, William Penn, Jr.
b. 1910 Chandrasekhar, Subrahmanyan
b. 1914 Brazle, Al(pha Eugene)
b. 1916 Blum, Stella
b. 1916 Dausset, Jean (Baptiste Gabriel Joachim)
b. 1916 Gilels, Emil Grigorevich
b. 1918 Kirk, Russell
b. 1918 Strauss, Robert
b. 1921 Kalmbach, Herbert Warren
b. 1921 Power, Jules
b. 1922 Anderson, Jack Northman
b. 1924 Strougal, Lubomir
b. 1926 Wallant, Edward Lewis
b. 1931 LeCarre, John, pseud.
b. 1932 Reed, Robert
b. 1934 Gowon, Yakubu
b. 1935 Haynes, Lloyd (Samuel Lloyd)
b. 1937 Max, Peter
b. 1941 Ward, Simon
b. 1945 Lithgow, John Arthur
b. 1945 Riley, Jeannie C
b. 1949 Dickey, Lynn (Clifford Lynn)
b. 1960 Holliday, Jennifer Yvette
b. 1967 Carter, Amy
d. 1587 Medici, Francesco de
d. 1609 Arminius, Jacobus

d. 1745 Swift, Jonathan
d. 1790 Hall, Lyman
d. 1814 Warren, Mercy Otis
d. 1848 Guthrie, Samuel
d. 1875 Wheatstone, Charles, Sir
d. 1897 Pullman, George Mortimer
d. 1898 Frederic, Harold
d. 1899 Appleton, William Henry
d. 1909 Lombroso, Cesare
d. 1937 Rutherford, Ernest, Baron
d. 1945 Calles, Plutarco
d. 1945 Wyeth, N(ewell) C(onvers)
d. 1950 Doherty, Robert Ernest
d. 1950 Millay, Edna St. Vincent
d. 1952 Curtis, Edward Sheriff
d. 1954 Duffy, Hugh
d. 1955 Hodiak, John
d. 1956 Jones, Isham
d. 1961 Gunnison, Foster
d. 1961 Osmena, Sergio
d. 1970 Cardenas, Lazaro
d. 1971 Pirelli, Alberto
d. 1972 Drinker, Philip
d. 1972 Said bin Taimusr
d. 1975 Lord, Phillips H
d. 1976 Ford, Eleanor Clay
d. 1978 Young, Gig
d. 1980 Andrews, James Frederick
d. 1983 Bishop, Maurice

October 20
b. Christopher, William
b. 1632 Wren, Christopher, Sir
b. 1784 Palmerston, Henry John Temple, Viscount
b. 1822 Hughes, Thomas
b. 1825 Sickles, Daniel Edgar
b. 1854 Rimbaud, (Jean Nicolas) Arthur
b. 1859 Dewey, John
b. 1873 McClung, Nellie Letitia Mooney
b. 1874 Ives, Charles Edward
b. 1882 Lugosi, Bela
b. 1889 Dumont, Margaret
b. 1890 Minton, Sherman
b. 1891 Bemis, Samuel Flagg
b. 1891 Kenyatta, Jomo (Johnstone)
b. 1893 Chase, Charley
b. 1895 Ingram, Rex
b. 1895 Ryskind, Morrie
b. 1895 Wurster, William
b. 1897 Deutsch, Adolph
b. 1899 Brent, Evelyn
b. 1900 Morse, Wayne Lyman
b. 1904 Neagle, Anna, Dame
b. 1905 Dannay, Frederic
b. 1906 Johnson, Crockett
b. 1908 Francis, Arlene
b. 1913 Jones, "Grandpa" (Louis Marshall)
b. 1914 Davies, Leslie Purnell
b. 1917 Melville, Jean-Pierre
b. 1918 Ash, Roy Lawrence
b. 1919 Mathison, Richard Randolph

b. 1920 Jagan, Janet
b. 1922 Trethowan, Ian
b. 1923 Craft, Robert
b. 1925 Buchwald, Art(hur)
b. 1928 Brothers, Joyce Diane Bauer
b. 1930 Hall, David
b. 1931 Bratkowski, Zeke (Edmund R)
b. 1931 Caliguiri, Richard
b. 1931 Mantle, Mickey Charles
b. 1932 McClure, Michael
b. 1934 Dunn, Michael
b. 1935 Orbach Jerry
b. 1936 Seale, Bobby G
b. 1938 Marichal, Juan Antonio Sanchez
b. 1950 Curtis, Isaac
b. 1953 Hernandez, Keith
b. 1954 Selmon, Lee Roy
d. 1524 Linacre, Thomas
d. 1794 Adam, James
d. 1889 Babbitt, Benjamin Talbot
d. 1890 Burton, Richard Francis, Sir
d. 1900 Warner, Charles Dudley
d. 1906 Ewing, "Buck" (William)
d. 1913 Palmer, Daniel David
d. 1926 Debs, Eugene Victor
d. 1935 Greely, Adolphus Washington
d. 1935 Smith, (Robert) Sidney
d. 1936 Sullivan, Anne
d. 1937 Warburg, Felix Moritz
d. 1942 Robson, May
d. 1942 Stock, Frederick A
d. 1943 Bernie, Ben
d. 1949 Copeau, Jacques
d. 1950 Stimson, Henry Lewis (Harry)
d. 1955 Gulbenkian, Calouste S
d. 1956 Bell, Lawrence Dale
d. 1957 Buchanan, Jack
d. 1959 Krauss, Werner
d. 1962 Douglass, Andrew Ellicott
d. 1964 Hoover, Herbert Clark
d. 1966 Byrd, Harry Flood, Jr.
d. 1967 Yoshida, Shigeru
d. 1970 Lewis, Ted
d. 1972 Shapley, Harlow T
d. 1973 Chandler, Norman
d. 1974 Tabbert, William
d. 1977 Gaines, Steve
d. 1977 Van Zant, Ronnie (Ronald)
d. 1981 Chase, Mary Coyle
d. 1982 Ziolkowski, Korczak
d. 1983 Travis, Merle
d. 1984 Cori, Carl Ferdinand
d. 1984 Dirac, Paul A M

October 21
b. 1581 Domenichino, Il
b. 1651 Bart, Jean
b. 1672 Muratori, Ludovico
b. 1772 Coleridge, Samuel Taylor
b. 1790 Lamartine, Alphonse Marie Louis
de Prat de
b. 1808 Smith, Samuel Francis

b. 1813 Fillmore, Caroline Carmichael
McIntosh
b. 1833 Nobel, Alfred Bernhard
b. 1845 Carleton, Will
b. 1846 Amicis, Edmond de
b. 1855 Ball, Edmund B
b. 1869 Dodd, William Edward
b. 1870 Douglas, Alfred Bruce, Lord
b. 1876 Darling, Jay Norwood
b. 1884 Beecher, Janet
b. 1885 Wellesz, Egon
b. 1891 Burnett, Leo
b. 1891 Knaths, Karl (Otto Karl)
b. 1891 Shawn, Ted (Edwin Meyers)
b. 1892 Boni, Albert
b. 1892 Lopokova, Lydia Vasilievna
b. 1898 Walker, Stanley
b. 1899 Hussey, Christopher Edward Clive
b. 1901 Clark, Joseph Sill
b. 1908 Schneider, Alexander
b. 1911 Graves, Peter
b. 1911 Ussachevsky, Vladimir
b. 1912 Solti, Georg, Sir
b. 1914 Gardner, Martin
b. 1917 Gillespie, "Dizzy" (John Birks)
b. 1921 Arnold, Malcolm, Sir
b. 1921 Runcie, Robert Alexander K
b. 1927 Blucker, Robert Olof
b. 1928 Ford, "Whitey" (Edward Charles)
b. 1929 LeGuin, Ursula Kroeber
b. 1931 Royer, William Blackburn, Jr.
b. 1933 Brown, Georgia
b. 1936 Gray, Simon James Holliday
b. 1942 Bishop, Elvin
b. 1943 Piccolo, Brian
b. 1946 Loughname, Lee
b. 1951 Little, Sally
b. 1952 Davis, Patti
b. 1955 Faulkner, Eric
b. 1956 Fisher, Carrie Frances
b. 1971 Jagger, Jade
d. 1556 Aretino, Pietro
d. 1687 Waller, Edmund
d. 1805 Nelson, Horatio Nelson, Viscount
d. 1908 Norton, Charles Eliot
d. 1931 Schnitzler, Arthur
d. 1944 Brinkley, Nell
d. 1945 Armetta, Henry
d. 1956 Owsley, Frank Lawrence
d. 1965 McDonald, Marie
d. 1969 Kerouac, Jack
d. 1970 Rojankovsky, Feodor Stepanovich
d. 1970 Scopes, John Thomas
d. 1971 Bronson, Betty (Elizabeth Ada)
d. 1979 Hicks, Beatrice Alice
d. 1981 Dixon, Robert Ellington
d. 1984 Truffaut, Francois
d. 1985 White, Dan(iel James)

October 22
b. 1811 Liszt, Franz (Ferencz)
b. 1812 Clevenger, Shobal Vail

b. 1821 Huntington, Collis Potter
b. 1832 Damrosch, Leopold
b. 1834 Duniway, Abigail Jane Scott
b. 1843 Babcock, Stephen Moulton
b. 1859 Muck, Karl
b. 1880 Carr, Joseph F
b. 1881 Davisson, Clinton Joseph
b. 1882 Dulac, Edmund
b. 1882 Guggenheimer, Minnie
b. 1882 Wyeth, N(ewell) C(onvers)
b. 1884 Hill, George Washington
b. 1885 Martinelli, Giovanni
b. 1889 Balderston, John Lloyd
b. 1890 Welch, Joseph Nye
b. 1891 Chadwick, James, Sir
b. 1892 Rascoe, Burton
b. 1895 Beckman, Johnny
b. 1898 Rickword, Edgell (John Edgell)
b. 1899 Morris, William, Jr.
b. 1900 Stettinius, Edward R, Jr.
b. 1905 Bennett, Constance Campbell
b. 1907 Foxx, Jimmy (James Emory)
b. 1907 Wyeth, Henriette
b. 1908 Sutton, John
b. 1919 Lessing, Doris May
b. 1920 Green, Mitzi
b. 1920 Leary, Timothy Francis
b. 1921 Brassens, Georges
b. 1922 Chafee, John Hubbard
b. 1924 Levine, Albert Norman
b. 1925 Previn, Dory Langdon
b. 1925 Rauschenberg, Robert
b. 1931 Hanley, William
b. 1937 Ladd, Alan Walbridge, Jr.
b. 1938 Jacobi, Derek
b. 1938 Lloyd, Christopher
b. 1939 Roberts, Tony (David Anthony)
b. 1941 Wood, Wilbur Forrester
b. 1942 Funicello, Annette
b. 1943 Deneuve, Catherine
b. 1946 Brigati, Eddie
b. 1949 Goring, "Butch" (Robert Thomas)
b. 1952 Goldblum, Jeff
b. 1955 Anderson, Bonnie Marie
d. 1565 Grolier, Jean
d. 1775 Randolph, Peyton
d. 1806 Sheraton, Thomas
d. 1859 Spohr, Louis Ludwig
d. 1880 Child, Lydia Maria
d. 1906 Cezanne, Paul
d. 1917 Fitzsimmons, Bob (Robert Prometheus)
d. 1922 Abbott, Lyman
d. 1923 Maurel, Victor
d. 1926 Greb, Harry (Edward Henry)
d. 1927 Youngs, Ross Middlebrook
d. 1929 Chirol, Valentine, Sir
d. 1929 Hastings, Thomas
d. 1934 Floyd, "Pretty Boy" (Charles Arthur)

d. 1935 Carson, Edward Henry
d. 1936 Couzens, James Joseph, Jr.
d. 1937 Damrosch, Frank Heino
d. 1938 Irwin, May
d. 1944 Bennett, Richard
d. 1954 Kauffer, Edward McKnight
d. 1954 McManus, George
d. 1961 Schenck, Joseph M
d. 1962 Marcoux, Vanni
d. 1965 Tillich, Paul Johannes
d. 1966 Johnson, Hewlett
d. 1973 Casals, Pablo (Pau Carlos Salvador)
d. 1975 Toynbee, Arnold Joseph
d. 1978 Mikoyan, Anastas Ivanovich
d. 1979 Boulanger, Nadia Juliette
d. 1982 Jessup, Richard
d. 1983 Barrow, Keith E

October 23

b. 1698 Gabriel, Ange-Jacques
b. 1800 Lawrence, William Beach
b. 1801 Lortzing, Gustav Albert
b. 1805 Bartlett, John Russell
b. 1817 Denver, James William
b. 1817 Larousse, Pierre Athanase
b. 1823 Naudin, Emilio
b. 1835 Stevenson, Adlai Ewing
b. 1844 Bernhardt, Sarah
b. 1844 Bridges, Robert Seymour
b. 1844 Riel, Louis David
b. 1861 Converse, Marquis M
b. 1869 Heisman, John William
b. 1873 Coolidge, William David
b. 1876 Cret, Paul P(hilippe)
b. 1881 O'Connor, Una
b. 1885 Harris, Lauren
b. 1889 Saerchinger, Cesar Victor Charles
b. 1890 Baillie, Hugh
b. 1890 Littlejohn, Robert McGowan
b. 1895 Anderson, Clint(on Presba)
b. 1895 Maverick, Maury
b. 1899 Balchen, Bernt
b. 1899 Kimbrough, Emily
b. 1899 Tashman, Lilyan
b. 1904 Lincoln, Victoria Endicott
b. 1905 Bloch, Felix
b. 1906 Ederle, Gertrude Caroline
b. 1908 Oistrakh, David Fyodorovich
b. 1910 Fredericks, Carlton
b. 1913 Gorkin, Jess
b. 1916 Whittemore, Arthur Austin
b. 1918 Daly, James
b. 1918 Rudolph, Paul Marvin
b. 1920 Montana, Bob
b. 1920 Rizzo, Frank L
b. 1922 Gray, Coleen
b. 1922 Gray, Nicholas Stuart
b. 1923 Mardian, Robert Charles
b. 1923 Rorem, Ned
b. 1925 Carson, Johnny
b. 1927 Lamantia, Philip

b. 1929 Darvi, Bella
b. 1931 Bunning, Jim (James Paul David)
b. 1931 Clark, William P(atrick, Jr.)
b. 1931 Dors, Diana
b. 1932 Zimmerman, Paul
b. 1933 Moore, Jack
b. 1934 Rodriguez, "Chi-Chi" (Juan)
b. 1938 Heinz, (Henry) John, (III)
b. 1940 Pele
b. 1942 Crichton, (John) Michael
b. 1959 Yankovic, "Weird Al" (Alfred Matthew)
b. 1962 Flutie, Doug(las Richard)
d. 1823 Cartwright, Edmund
d. 1872 Gautier, Theophile (Pierre Jules Theophile)
d. 1893 Crittendon, Thomas L
d. 1925 Byrd, Richard Evelyn
d. 1927 Dickman, Joseph Theodore
d. 1935 Demuth, Charles
d. 1939 Grey, Zane
d. 1946 Seton, Ernest Thompson
d. 1950 Jolson, Al
d. 1952 Peters, Susan
d. 1957 Lyman, Abe
d. 1959 Golden, William
d. 1962 Telva, Marion
d. 1964 Mott, Frank Luther
d. 1965 Throckmorton, Cleon
d. 1972 Harriman, John Walter
d. 1977 Markel, Lester
d. 1978 Carter, "Mother" Maybelle
d. 1983 Savitch, Jessica Beth
d. 1984 Petrillo, James Caesar
d. 1984 Werner, Oskar
d. 1984 Whittemore, Arthur Austin

October 24
b. 1618 Aurangzeb
b. 1632 Leeuwenhoek, Anton van
b. 1784 Montefiore, Moses Haim, Sir
b. 1788 Hale, Sarah Josepha
b. 1808 Sartain, John
b. 1820 Fromentin, Eugene
b. 1830 Lockwood, Belva Ann Bennett
b. 1855 Sherman, James Schoolcraft
b. 1864 Leoni, Franco
b. 1868 David-Neel, Alexandra
b. 1871 Shrady, Henry M
b. 1879 Weston, Edward F
b. 1882 Thorndike, Sybil, Dame
b. 1890 Mainbocher
b. 1891 Trujillo (Molina), Rafael Leonidas
b. 1894 Lewis, Ted
b. 1899 Abbas, Ferhat
b. 1901 Eichenberg, Fritz
b. 1901 Gray, Gilda
b. 1904 Hart, Moss
b. 1909 McLean, John Milton
b. 1911 Kelley, Clarence Marion
b. 1912 Gellhorn, Peter
b. 1915 Gobbi, Tito

b. 1921 Jurinac, Sena
b. 1923 Day, Robin
b. 1923 Levertov, Denise
b. 1925 Berio, Luciano
b. 1926 Tittle, Y(elberton) A(braham)
b. 1927 Becaud, Gilbert
b. 1927 McNeil, Neil Venable
b. 1929 Brosnan, Jim (James Patrick)
b. 1930 Big Bopper, The
b. 1932 Dorfman, Dan
b. 1933 Bray, Charles William, III
b. 1933 Kray, Reggie (Reginald)
b. 1933 Kray, Ronnie (Ronald)
b. 1934 Walton, Tony
b. 1936 Hernandez-Colon, Rafael
b. 1936 Nelson, David
b. 1938 Watson, Jack Hearn, Jr.
b. 1940 Abraham, F Murray
b. 1941 Wyman, Bill (William George)
b. 1945 Ward, David S
b. 1947 Kline, Kevin
b. 1948 Griffin, Dale
b. 1949 White, Stan(ley Ray)
d. 1537 Seymour, Jane
d. 1601 Brahe, Tyge
d. 1842 O'Higgins, Bernardo
d. 1852 Webster, Daniel
d. 1911 Lewis, Ida
d. 1920 MacSwiney, Terence
d. 1926 Russell, Charles Marion
d. 1928 Davies, Arthur Bowen
d. 1935 Schultz, Dutch
d. 1944 Renault, Louis
d. 1945 Carmichael, Franklin
d. 1945 Quisling, Vidkun
d. 1946 Kline, Otis Adelbert
d. 1947 Digges, Dudley
d. 1948 Lehar, Franz
d. 1957 Dior, Christian
d. 1958 Moore, George Edward
d. 1963 Root, John Wellborn
d. 1970 Hofstadter, Richard
d. 1971 Ruggles, Carl
d. 1972 Robinson, Jackie (John Roosevelt)
d. 1972 Votipka, Thelma
d. 1972 Windsor, Claire
d. 1973 Brazle, Al(pha Eugene)
d. 1974 Oistrakh, David Fyodorovich
d. 1979 Belmont, Eleanor Robson
d. 1980 Aulaire, Ingri Mortenson d'
d. 1981 Head, Edith
d. 1981 Holm, John Cecil
d. 1984 King, Walter Woolf

October 25
b. 1767 Constant de Rebeque, (Henri) Benjamin
b. 1795 Kennedy, John Pendleton
b. 1800 Macaulay, Thomas Babington Macaulay, Baron
b. 1802 Bonington, Richard Parkes
b. 1811 Galois, Evariste

b. 1825 Strauss, Johann, Jr.
b. 1837 Harkness, Anna M Richardson
b. 1838 Bizet, Georges (Alexandre Cesar
Leopold)
b. 1864 Dodge, John Francis
b. 1864 Gretchaninov, Aleksandr
Tikhonovich
b. 1866 Patten, Gilbert
b. 1873 Willys, John North
b. 1874 Dawson, Geoffrey (George
Geoffrey)
b. 1881 Picasso, Pablo
b. 1884 Easton, Florence Gertrude
b. 1888 Byrd, Richard Evelyn
b. 1889 Bauer, Royal Daniel Michael
b. 1889 Gance, Abel
b. 1889 Wood, Joseph
b. 1890 Bennett, Floyd
b. 1891 Coughlin, Father (Charles Edward)
b. 1892 Dolly, Jenny
b. 1892 Dolly, Rosie
b. 1894 Phillips, Marjorie Acker
b. 1899 MacLiammoir, Michael
b. 1902 Commager, Henry Steele
b. 1902 Lang, Eddie
b. 1904 Gorky, Arshile
b. 1909 Draper, Paul
b. 1910 Lichine, David
b. 1912 Pearl, Minnie
b. 1913 Fletcher, Grant
b. 1914 Berryman, John
b. 1915 Cox, Constance
b. 1917 MacPhail, Lee (Leland Stanford,
Jr.)
b. 1921 Michael V
b. 1923 Thomson, Bobby (Robert Brown)
b. 1924 Brown, Bobby (Robert William)
b. 1924 Elliott, Osborn
b. 1926 Butcher, Willard C(arlisle)
b. 1926 McGuire, "Biff" (William J)
b. 1926 Vishnevskaya, Galina (Pavlovna)
b. 1927 Cook, Barbara
b. 1928 Franciosa, Anthony
b. 1928 Ross, Marion
b. 1930 Gray, Hanna
b. 1931 Girardot, Annie
b. 1933 Haley, Jack, Jr. (John J.)
b. 1935 Schweickart, Russell L
b. 1940 Knight, Bobby (Robert
Montgomery)
b. 1941 Tyler, Anne
b. 1942 Reddy, Helen
b. 1944 Anderson, Jon
b. 1948 Cowens, Dave (David William)
b. 1948 Issel, Dan
b. 1949 Houle, Rejean
b. 1950 Matuszak, John
b. 1951 Stemrick, Greg(ory Earl, Sr.)
b. 1952 Smalley, Roy Frederick, III
b. 1954 Eruzione, Mike
b. 1958 Ender, Kornelia

b. 1966 Clark, Wendel
d. 1180 John of Salisbury
d. 1400 Chaucer, Geoffrey
d. 1647 Torricelli, Evangelista
d. 1760 George II
d. 1806 Knox, Henry
d. 1877 Adams, Edwin
d. 1892 Harrison, Caroline Lavinia Scott
d. 1895 Halle, Charles, Sir
d. 1897 Sartain, John
d. 1900 Squibb, Edward Robinson
d. 1902 Norris, Frank(lin)
d. 1916 Chase, William Merritt
d. 1921 Masterson, "Bat" (William
Barclay)
d. 1934 Sprague, Frank Julian
d. 1938 Kuprin, Aleksandr Ivanovich
d. 1941 Delaunay, Robert
d. 1943 Hart, Frances Noyes
d. 1945 Ley, Robert
d. 1947 Ziegler, Edward
d. 1957 Dunsany, Edward J M Plunkett,
Baron
d. 1959 Cline, Genevieve Rose
d. 1960 Ferguson, Harry George
d. 1963 Desormiere, Roger
d. 1965 Knappertsbusch, Hans
d. 1971 Terry, Paul H
d. 1971 Wylie, Philip Gordon
d. 1972 Norell, Norman
d. 1974 Furtseva, Ekaterina Alexeyevna
d. 1974 Kroll, Leon
d. 1979 Darling, Frank Fraser, Sir
d. 1980 Dodds, Harold Willis
d. 1980 Fox, Virgil Keel
d. 1981 Dejean, Alain
d. 1981 Durant, Ariel (Ida Ariel Ethel
Kaufman)
d. 1981 Reiser, Pete (Harold Patrick)
d. 1983 Epperson, Frank W
d. 1984 Brautigan, Richard
d. 1985 Downey, Morton
d. 1985 Slotnick, Daniel Leonid

October 26
b. DeKnight, Jimmy
b. 1685 Scarlatti, Domenico Girolamo
b. 1803 Hansom, Joseph Aloysius
b. 1840 Keene, Thomas Wallace
b. 1854 Post, Charles William
b. 1861 Sears, Richard Dudley
b. 1863 Statler, Ellsworth Milton
b. 1874 Rockefeller, Abby Aldrich
b. 1876 Loftus, Cissie
b. 1877 Mason, Max
b. 1886 Starrett, Vincent (Charles Vincent
Emerson)
b. 1890 Eckstein, Gustav
b. 1894 Knight, John Shively
b. 1897 Lemnitz, Tiana
b. 1899 Johnson, "Judy" (William Julius)
b. 1901 Evergood, Philip Howard

d. 1975 Carpentier, Georges
d. 1975 Stout, Rex Todhunter
d. 1975 Wayman, Dorothy
d. 1977 Cain, James Mallahan
d. 1977 Hulman, Tony (Anton), Jr.
d. 1979 Coughlin, Father (Charles Edward)
d. 1980 La Marsh, Judy Verlyn
d. 1980 LaMarsh, Judy (Julia Verlyn)
d. 1983 Baldwin, Horace

October 28
b. 1728 Cook, James, Captain
b. 1759 Danton, Georges Jacques
b. 1798 Coffin, Levi
b. 1801 Inman, Henry
b. 1803 Unger, Caroline
b. 1808 Smith, Horace
b. 1844 Ezekiel, Moses Jacob
b. 1847 Thompson, J(ames) Walter
b. 1875 Grosvenor, Gilbert Hovey
b. 1880 Evans, Edward Ratcliffe Garth
   Russell
b. 1892 Johnson, "Dink" (Oliver)
b. 1894 Murphy, Robert Daniel
b. 1894 Wolff, Fritz
b. 1895 Chamberlain, Samuel
b. 1896 Hanson, Howard Harold
b. 1897 Speidel, Hans
b. 1902 Lanchester, Elsa
b. 1903 Chamberlain, John Rensselear
b. 1903 Waugh, Evelyn Arthur St. John
b. 1904 Dangerfield, George Bubb
b. 1907 Head, Edith
b. 1908 Oppenheimer, Harry Frederick
b. 1910 Bacon, Francis
b. 1910 Kamp, Irene Kittle
b. 1914 Salk, Jonas Edward
b. 1915 Soo, Jack
b. 1916 Harris, Willard Palmer (Bill)
b. 1917 Page, Joe (Joseph Francis)
b. 1920 Robitscher, Jonas Bondi, Jr.
b. 1920 Swados, Harvey
b. 1920 Turner, Claramae
b. 1926 Kuhn, Bowie Kent
b. 1927 Laine, Cleo
b. 1929 Ginzburg, Ralph
b. 1929 Goodman, Dody
b. 1929 Hollander, John
b. 1929 Plowright, Joan
b. 1930 Fifield, Elaine
b. 1930 Morton, Bruce Alexander
b. 1932 Kyprianou, Spyros
b. 1933 Parker, Suzy
b. 1936 Antes, Horst
b. 1936 Daniels, Charlie
b. 1937 Wilkens, Lenny (Leonard
   Randolph)
b. 1939 Alexander, Jane
b. 1945 Brett, Simon Anthony Lee
b. 1948 Hopkins, Telma Louise
b. 1949 Jenner, Bruce
b. 1952 Tcherkassky, Marianna Alexsavena

d. 1704 Locke, John
d. 1818 Adams, Abigail Smith
d. 1821 Pacchierotti, Gasparo
d. 1861 James, Edwin
d. 1874 Rinehart, William H
d. 1899 Mergenthaler, Ottmar
d. 1916 Abbe, Cleveland
d. 1929 Bulow, Bernhard H M
d. 1938 Kohler, Fred
d. 1939 Brady, Alice
d. 1944 White, Helen Magill
d. 1948 Dickey, Herbert Spencer
d. 1949 Gurdjieff, Georges Ivanovitch
d. 1951 Christians, Mady
d. 1954 Gorman, Herbert Sherman
d. 1959 Bauersfeld, Walther
d. 1963 Connally, Tom (Thomas Terry)
d. 1968 Meitner, Lise
d. 1969 Chukovsky, Korney Ivanovich
d. 1971 Foyle, Gilbert Samuel
d. 1973 Hussein, Taha
d. 1974 Jones, David
d. 1975 La Tour du Pin, Patrice de
d. 1980 Janney, Leon
d. 1983 Messmer, Otto

October 29
b. 1656 Halley, Edmund
b. 1682 Charlevoix, Pierre Francis Xavier
   de
b. 1745 Lee, Thomas Sim
b. 1815 Emmett, Daniel Decatur
b. 1831 Marsh, Othniel Charles
b. 1859 Ebbets, Charles H
b. 1873 Kelly, Walter C
b. 1879 Papen, Franz von
b. 1882 Giraudoux, Jean
b. 1883 Woodcock, Amos Walter Wright
b. 1885 Kidder, Alfred Vincent
b. 1890 Ottaviani, Alfredo, Cardinal
b. 1891 Brice, Fanny
b. 1895 Pearl, Jack
b. 1897 Goebbels, Joseph (Paul Joseph)
b. 1898 Emerson, Hope
b. 1900 Chapple, Stanley
b. 1901 Amfiteatrof, Daniele
b. 1901 Tamiroff, Akim
b. 1904 Westmore, Perc(ival)
b. 1905 Green, Henry
b. 1908 Ames, Louise Bates
b. 1910 Ayer, Alfred Jules
b. 1916 Gill, Jocelyn Ruth
b. 1916 Keogh, James
b. 1921 Mauldin, Bill (William Henry)
b. 1922 Hefti, Neal Paul
b. 1922 Messer, Alfred A
b. 1923 Djerassi, Carl
b. 1925 Brooks, Geraldine
b. 1925 Siegel, Larry
b. 1925 Sims, "Zoot" (John Haley)
b. 1926 Vickers, Jon
b. 1927 Sedgman, Frank (Francis Arthur)

b. 1932 Kitaj, R(onald) B(rooks)
b. 1936 Jayston, Michael
b. 1945 Moore, Melba
b. 1945 Simpson, Donald C
b. 1947 Dreyfuss, Richard Stephan
b. 1948 Jackson, Kate
b. 1948 Reynolds, Ricky
b. 1951 Barfield, Jesse Lee
b. 1953 Potvin, Denis Charles
b. 1961 Jackson, Randy (Steven Randall)
d. 1216 John, King of England
d. 1618 Raleigh, Walter, Sir
d. 1666 Shirley, James
d. 1783 Alembert, Jean le Rond d'
d. 1864 Leech, John
d. 1877 Forrest, Nathan Bedford
d. 1885 McClellan, George Brinton
d. 1892 Harnett, William Michael
d. 1897 George, Henry, Sr.
d. 1901 Czolgosz, Leon F
d. 1911 Pulitzer, Joseph
d. 1924 Burnett, Frances Eliza Hodgson
d. 1926 Webb, William Seward
d. 1932 Kitson, Theo Alice Ruggles
d. 1933 Luks, George Benjamin
d. 1947 Brach, Emil J
d. 1947 Cleveland, Frances Folsom
d. 1953 Kapell, William
d. 1953 Olsen, Harold G
d. 1956 Coffin, Robert Peter Tristram
d. 1957 Anastasia, Albert
d. 1957 Mayer, L(ouis) B(urt)
d. 1958 Akins, Zoe
d. 1961 McClintic, Guthrie
d. 1962 Resor, Stanley Burnett
d. 1963 Menjou, Adolphe Jean
d. 1965 McKechnie, Bill (William Boyd)
d. 1967 Duvivier, Julien
d. 1969 Douglas, Sholto (William Sholto)
d. 1971 Allman, Duane (Howard Duane)
d. 1975 Trotter, John Scott
d. 1982 Hall, Joyce Clyde
d. 1982 Thompson, Thomas
d. 1984 Bloom, Ursula
d. 1985 Allen, William McPherson
d. 1985 Douglas-Home, Charles

October 30
b. 1632 Vermeer, Jan
b. 1735 Adams, John
b. 1751 Sheridan, Richard Brinsley
b. 1762 Chenier, Marie-Andre de
b. 1807 Wadsworth, James Samuel
b. 1815 Comstock, Elizabeth L
b. 1815 Downing, Andrew Jackson
b. 1829 Conkling, Roscoe
b. 1829 Rogers, John
b. 1835 Patti, Carlotta
b. 1839 Sisley, Alfred
b. 1840 Sumner, William Graham
b. 1857 Atherton, Gertrude Franklin
b. 1867 Bonnard, Pierre

b. 1871 Valery, Paul Ambroise
b. 1873 Post, Emily Price
b. 1877 Rombauer, Irma von Starkloff
b. 1882 Halsey, William Frederick
b. 1883 Jones, Bob
b. 1884 Lea, Fanny Heaslip
b. 1885 Pound, Ezra Loomis
b. 1886 Akins, Zoe
b. 1888 Kirk, Alan Goodrich
b. 1891 Goddard, Calvin Hooker
b. 1894 Atlas, Charles
b. 1894 Heseltine, Phillip Arnold
b. 1895 Domagk, Gerhard
b. 1896 Dooley, Rae (Rachel Rice)
b. 1896 Gordon, Ruth
b. 1898 Terry, Bill (William Harold)
b. 1900 Granit, Ragnar Arthur
b. 1902 Overstreet, Bonaro Wilkinson
b. 1904 Foster, Joseph C
b. 1904 McElroy, Neil Hosler
b. 1904 Still, Clyfford
b. 1906 Smith, Paul Joseph
b. 1907 Leventhal, Albert Rice
b. 1908 Ustinov, Dmitri Fedorovich
b. 1912 Haynsworth, Clement Furman, Jr.
b. 1912 Parks, Gordon Alexander
        Buchanan
b. 1914 Laughlin, James, IV
b. 1914 Mohammed Zahir Shah
b. 1914 Montana, Patsy
b. 1915 Carnevale, Ben (Bernard L)
b. 1915 Friendly, Fred W
b. 1915 Hussey, Ruth Carol
b. 1917 Dobozy, Imre
b. 1922 Costa Mendez, Nicanor
b. 1923 Bernardi, Hershel
b. 1928 Flatt, Ernest O
b. 1928 Wigle, Ernest Douglas
b. 1932 Malle, Louis
b. 1933 Muhammad, Wallace D
b. 1934 Camp, Hamilton
b. 1936 Vermeil, Dick (Richard Albert)
b. 1937 Gautier, Dick
b. 1937 LeLouch, Claude
b. 1940 Fox, Charles
b. 1943 Slick, Grace Wing
b. 1945 Winkler, Henry Franklin
b. 1947 Schmidt, Tim(othy B)
b. 1949 Chones, Jim
b. 1950 Chenier, Phil(ip)
b. 1957 Mintz, Shlomo
b. 1958 Delaney, Joe Alton
b. 1960 Maradona, Diego
d. 1787 Galiani, Ferdinando
d. 1867 Andrew, John Albion
d. 1881 DeLong, George Washington
d. 1887 Walter, Thomas Ustick
d. 1893 Bodmer, Karl
d. 1903 Ozaki, Koyo, pseud.
d. 1910 Dunant, Jean Henri
d. 1912 Sherman, James Schoolcraft

d. 1923 Law, Andrew Bonar
d. 1928 Lansing, Robert
d. 1928 Sonneck, Oscar George Theodore
d. 1936 Taft, Lorado
d. 1937 Kraus, Felix von
d. 1950 Costello, Maurice
d. 1954 Shaw, Wilbur
d. 1958 Macaulay, Rose
d. 1961 Einaudi, Luigi
d. 1968 Kelton, Pert
d. 1968 Lane, Rose Wilder
d. 1968 Richter, Conrad Michael
d. 1969 Foster, "Pops" (George Murphy)
d. 1970 Martinson, Joseph Bertram
d. 1975 Kellerman, Annette
d. 1979 Mussolini, Rachele Guidi
d. 1979 Wallis, Barnes Neville, Sir
d. 1981 Brassens, Georges
d. 1983 Carter, Lillian
d. 1984 Engstrom, Elmer William
d. 1985 Grant, Kirby
d. 1985 Tanner, Marion

October 31

b. 1620 Evelyn, John
b. 1638 Hobbema, Meindert
b. 1740 Paca, William
b. 1795 Keats, John
b. 1821 Virchow, Rudolf
b. 1828 Hunt, Richard Morris
b. 1852 Freeman, Mary E Wilkins
b. 1860 Low, Juliette Gordon
b. 1860 Volstead, Andrew J
b. 1863 McAdoo, William Gibbs
b. 1864 Lang, William Cosmo Gordon,
    Baron
b. 1867 Delahanty, Edward James
b. 1867 Philips, David Graham
b. 1876 Barney, Natalie Clifford
b. 1880 Peterkin, Julia Mood
b. 1883 Allgood, Sara
b. 1886 Chiang Kai-Shek
b. 1888 Wilkins, George Hubert, Sir
b. 1893 Strode, Hudson
b. 1894 King, Charles
b. 1895 Liddell Hart, Basil Henry
b. 1896 Chace, Marian
b. 1899 Mandelstam, Nadezhda Yakovlevna
b. 1900 Waters, Ethel
b. 1902 Franz, Eduard
b. 1902 Shaw, Wilbur
b. 1905 Sour, Robert B(andler)
b. 1912 Evans, Dale
b. 1915 Wechsler, James Arthur
b. 1916 Barnett, Marvin Robert
b. 1918 Bell, Griffin Boyette
b. 1919 Sisco, Joseph John
b. 1920 Danielian, Leon
b. 1920 Francis, Dick
b. 1922 Geddes, Barbara Bel
b. 1922 Jacquet, Illinois

b. 1922 Norodom Sihanouk (Varman),
    Samdech Preah
b. 1927 Kahn, Roger
b. 1928 Sarris, Andrew
b. 1930 Collins, Mike (Michael)
b. 1931 Grant, Lee
b. 1931 Rather, Dan
b. 1934 Humes, James Calhoun
b. 1937 Landon, Michael
b. 1937 Paxton, Tom (Thomas R)
b. 1939 Dillon, Melinda
b. 1942 McNally, Dave (David Arthur)
b. 1942 Stiers, David Ogden
b. 1945 Keefe, Barrie Colin
b. 1947 Ballard, Russ(ell)
b. 1950 Candy, John
b. 1950 Goodfriend, Lynda
b. 1950 Pauley, (Margaret) Jane
b. 1955 Roberts, Xavier
b. 1965 Annabella
d. 1517 Bartolommeo, Fra
d. 1744 Leo, Leonardo
d. 1834 DuPont, Eleuthere Irenee
d. 1848 Kearny, Stephen Watts
d. 1879 Hooker, Joseph
d. 1887 Macfarren, George Alexander, Sir
d. 1916 Russell, Charles Taze
d. 1919 Wilcox, Ella Wheeler
d. 1926 Houdini, Harry
d. 1927 Long, John Luther
d. 1937 Faure, Elie
d. 1941 Berry, "Chu" (Leon)
d. 1943 Reinhardt, Max
d. 1944 Crosman, Henrietta
d. 1948 Landi, Elissa
d. 1949 Stettinius, Edward R, Jr.
d. 1950 Boettiger, John
d. 1956 Badoglio, Pietro
d. 1960 Avery, Sewell
d. 1960 Davis, Harold Lenoir
d. 1961 John, Augustus Edwin
d. 1961 Vertes, Marcel
d. 1963 Daniell, Henry
d. 1964 Toye, Francis
d. 1968 Novarro, Ramon
d. 1969 Pastor, Tony
d. 1970 Allyn, Stanley Charles
d. 1973 White, Paul Dudley
d. 1974 Myer, "Buddy" (Charles Solomon)
d. 1976 Wilder, Joseph
d. 1977 Colby, Carroll Burleigh
d. 1977 Smith, Chard Powers
d. 1981 Scherr, Max
d. 1983 Halas, George Stanley
d. 1983 Rashidov, Sharaf Rashidovich
d. 1984 Gandhi, Indira Priyadarshini
    Nehru

NOVEMBER

b. 1774 Bell, Charles
b. 1840 Galli-Marie, Marie Celestine

b. 1903 Jackson, Travis Calvin
b. 1905 Clark, Colin Grant
b. 1905 Dunn, James Howard
b. 1905 Keyserlingk, Robert Wendelin
b. 1906 Visconti, Luchino
b. 1909 Berigan, "Bunny" (Rowland
      Bernart)
b. 1911 Elytis, Odysseus
b. 1912 Conklin, Peggy (Margaret Eleanor)
b. 1913 Lancaster, Burt(on Stephen)
b. 1914 Guerard, Albert Joseph
b. 1914 Vander Meer, Johnny (John
      Samuel)
b. 1917 Rutherford, Ann
b. 1917 Wasserman, Dale
b. 1918 Adams, John Hanly
b. 1921 Schaefer, William Donald
b. 1923 Haughton, Billy
b. 1934 Rosewall, Ken
b. 1938 Buchanan, Patrick Joseph
b. 1939 Serra, Richard Anthony
b. 1941 Black, David, "Jay"
b. 1941 Stockton, Dave (David)
b. 1942 Hite, Shere
b. 1946 Paciorek, Tom (Thomas Marian)
b. 1958 McGee, Willie Dean
d. 1600 Hooker, Richard
d. 1879 Einhorn, David
d. 1887 Lind, Jenny (Johanna Maria)
d. 1892 Schwatka, Frederik
d. 1920 Guiney, Louise
d. 1926 Oakley, Annie
d. 1944 Midgeley, Thomas
d. 1950 Shaw, George Bernard
d. 1957 Young, Mahonri M
d. 1960 Mitropoulos, Dimitri
d. 1961 Thurber, James Grover
d. 1963 Ngo dinh Diem
d. 1966 Debye, Peter Joseph William
d. 1966 Hurt, Mississippi John
d. 1970 Cushing, Richard James, Cardinal
d. 1971 Vickers, Martha
d. 1975 Pasolini, Pier Paolo
d. 1976 Starkie, Walter Fitzwilliam
d. 1978 Gordon, Max
d. 1980 Sutton, Willie (William Francis)
d. 1982 Roloff, Lester
d. 1984 Barfield, Velma

November 3
b. 1560 Carracci, Annibale
b. 1782 Warrington, Lewis
b. 1793 Austin, Stephen Fuller
b. 1794 Bryant, William Cullen
b. 1801 Baedeker, Karl
b. 1801 Bellini, Vincenzo
b. 1816 Early, Jubal Anderson
b. 1830 Cooke, John Esten
b. 1831 Donnelly, Ignatius
b. 1834 Fleischmann, Charles Louis
b. 1841 Alden, Isabella Macdonald
b. 1845 White, Edward Douglass

b. 1858 Wellman, Walter
b. 1862 George, Henry, Jr.
b. 1879 Stefansson, Vihjalmur
b. 1880 Sterling, Ford
b. 1884 Martin, Joseph William, Jr.
b. 1887 Fleischer, Nat(haniel S)
b. 1892 Chao, Yuen Ren
b. 1895 Arvey, Jacob Meyer
b. 1896 Tenggren, Gustaf Adolf
b. 1901 Leopold III
b. 1901 Malraux, Andre
b. 1903 Boyd, Julian Parks
b. 1903 Evans, Walker
b. 1907 Haydn, Hiram Collins
b. 1908 Leone, Giovanni
b. 1908 Nagurski, "Bronko" (Bronislaw)
b. 1909 Reston, James Barrett
b. 1911 Turner, Joe
b. 1912 Donohue, Jack
b. 1912 Stroessner, Alfredo
b. 1913 Chapman, Leonard F, Jr.
b. 1914 Shamir, Yitzhak
b. 1917 O'Brien, Conor Cruise
b. 1918 Boullioun, E(rnest) H(erman, Jr.)
b. 1918 Feller, Bob (Robert William
      Andrew)
b. 1918 Long, Russell Billiu
b. 1919 Freed, Bert
b. 1927 Nordli, Odvar
b. 1927 Oakley, Don
b. 1930 Crane, Philip Miller
b. 1931 Lewis, Drew (Andrew Lindsay,
      Jr.)
b. 1931 Vitti, Monica
b. 1933 Barry, John
b. 1933 Berry, Ken
b. 1933 Dukakis, Michael Stanley
b. 1935 Brett, Jeremy
b. 1936 Emerson, Roy
b. 1937 Wayne, Paula
b. 1939 McNally, Terrence
b. 1942 Smith, Martin Cruz
b. 1944 Collin, Frank
b. 1948 Lulu
b. 1948 Shales, Tom (Thomas William)
b. 1949 Evans, Mike (Michael Jonas)
b. 1949 Holmes, Larry
b. 1954 Ant, Adam
b. 1955 Simms, Phil(ip)
b. 1956 Welch, Bob (Robert Lynn)
d. 1584 Borromeo, Charles, Saint
d. 1867 Persiani, Fanny
d. 1911 Colman, Norman Jay
d. 1917 Bloy, Leon Marie
d. 1940 Hine, Lewis Wickes
d. 1949 Desmond, William
d. 1949 Guggenheim, Solomon Robert
d. 1954 Matisse, Henri
d. 1956 Metzinger, Jean
d. 1957 Reich, Wilhelm
d. 1959 Cherniavsky, Josef

b. 1907 Browning, Alice Crolley
b. 1912 Rogers, Roy
b. 1912 Schafer, Natalie
b. 1913 Leigh, Vivien
b. 1913 McGiver, John
b. 1917 Auriol, Jacqueline Douet
b. 1919 Floren, Myron
b. 1926 Berger, John
b. 1927 Abernethy, Robert Gordon
b. 1930 Irving, Clifford Michael
b. 1930 Kennedy, Moorehead Cowell, Jr.
b. 1931 Turner, Ike
b. 1933 Edelman, Herb
b. 1933 Madden, Donald
b. 1934 Magruder, Jeb Stuart
b. 1940 Roldos Aguilera, Jamie
b. 1940 Sommer, Elke
b. 1942 Simon, Paul
b. 1943 Shepard, Sam
b. 1946 Parsons, Gram
b. 1947 Noone, Peter
b. 1952 Walton, Bill
b. 1957 Winslow, Kellen Boswell
b. 1958 Hexum, Jon-Erik
b. 1959 Adams, Bryan
b. 1963 O'Neal, Tatum
d. 1803 Laclos, (Pierre) Choderlos de
d. 1872 Sully, Thomas
d. 1874 Creighton, Edward
d. 1879 Maxwell, James Clerk
d. 1931 Roelvaag, O(le) E(dvart)
d. 1931 Rolvaag, Ole Edvart
d. 1933 Guinan, "Texas" (Mary Louise Cecilia)
d. 1938 Dewing, Thomas Wilmer
d. 1942 Cohan, George M(ichael)
d. 1944 Carrel, Alexis
d. 1946 Stella, Joseph
d. 1954 Page, "Hot Lips" (Oran Thaddeus)
d. 1955 Utrillo, Maurice
d. 1960 Bond, Ward
d. 1960 Horton, Johnny
d. 1960 Sennett, Mack
d. 1960 Waymack, W(illiam) W(esley)
d. 1961 Tobias, Channing Heggie
d. 1962 Garis, Howard Roger
d. 1971 Jones, "Toothpick" (Samuel)
d. 1972 Owen, (John) Reginald
d. 1975 Tatum, Edward Lawrie
d. 1975 Trilling, Lionel
d. 1977 Garst, Roswell
d. 1977 Goscinny, Rene
d. 1977 Lombardo, Guy Albert
d. 1979 Capp, Al
d. 1980 Lortz, Richard
d. 1980 Marshall, Laurence
d. 1982 Tati, Jacques
d. 1983 Benjamin, Curtis G
d. 1985 Kimball, Spencer Woolley

November 6
b. 1558 Kyd, Thomas
b. 1671 Cibber, Colley
b. 1771 Senefelder, Aloys
b. 1814 Sax, Adolphe
b. 1825 Gardner, Jean Louis Charles
b. 1833 Lie, Jonas (Laurite Idemil)
b. 1836 Lombroso, Cesare
b. 1841 Aldrich, Nelson Wilmarth
b. 1847 Meggendorfer, Lothar
b. 1848 Jeffries, Richard
b. 1851 Dow, Charles Henry
b. 1854 Sousa, John Philip
b. 1855 Kalisch, Paul
b. 1861 Naismith, James A
b. 1875 Dixon, Roland Burrage
b. 1877 Dillon, William A
b. 1882 Ince, Thomas H(arper)
b. 1882 Wallerstein, Lothar
b. 1883 Brophy, John
b. 1886 Kahn, Gus
b. 1887 Johnson, Walter Perry
b. 1890 Sherrill, Henry Knox
b. 1891 Buitoni, Giovanni
b. 1892 Olsen, Ole
b. 1892 Ross, Harold
b. 1893 Ford, Edsel Bryant
b. 1894 Harrison, Guy Fraser
b. 1901 Hall, Juanita
b. 1901 Katona, George
b. 1903 Rakosi, Carl
b. 1906 Lederer, Francis
b. 1907 Yost, Charles Woodruff
b. 1908 Canzoneri, Tony
b. 1908 Klassen, Elmer Theodore
b. 1910 Cohn, Arthur
b. 1911 Bosustow, Stephen
b. 1912 Brasch, Rudolph
b. 1912 Cakobau, Ratu George, Sir
b. 1912 Coleman, Lester L
b. 1914 Gerson, Noel Bertram
b. 1915 Oldfield, Maurice, Sir
b. 1916 Bushkin, Joe (Joseph)
b. 1916 Conniff, Ray
b. 1917 Rashidov, Sharaf Rashidovich
b. 1918 Scott, Ken
b. 1920 Rossi-Lemeni, Nicola
b. 1921 Jones, James
b. 1923 Griffin, Bob (Robert Paul)
b. 1930 McCormach, Mark Hume
b. 1931 Nichols, Mike
b. 1934 Anievas, Augustin
b. 1942 Shrimpton, Jean Rosemary
b. 1946 DeBartolo, Edward J, Jr.
b. 1946 Field, Sally Margaret
b. 1948 Frey, Glenn
b. 1949 Criss, Charlie (Charles W)
b. 1955 Shriver, Maria Owings
d. 1672 Schutz, Heinrich
d. 1790 Bowdoin, James
d. 1796 Catherine the Great

b. 1907 Hepburn, Katharine Houghton
b. 1908 Fowlie, Wallace
b. 1909 Erede, Alberto
b. 1910 Kane, Harnett T(homas)
b. 1910 Voit, Willard D
b. 1912 Dryfoos, Orvil E
b. 1912 Ronan, William J
b. 1913 Ambers, Lou
b. 1913 Strauss, Robert
b. 1916 Havoc, June
b. 1916 Weiss, Peter
b. 1918 Kirby, Robert Emory
b. 1918 Zapf, Hermann
b. 1921 Mirisch, Walter Mortimer
b. 1921 Saks, Gene
b. 1925 Flynn, Joe (Joseph Anthony)
b. 1927 Page, Patti
b. 1931 Safer, Morley
b. 1932 Bova, Ben(jamin William)
b. 1933 Rolle, Esther
b. 1935 Delon, Alain
b. 1936 Gibson, Edward George
b. 1948 Riperton, Minnie
b. 1949 Berger, Al
b. 1949 Raitt, Bonnie
b. 1952 Denny, John Allen
b. 1952 Hefner, Christie (Christine Ann)
b. 1954 Jones, Rickie Lee
b. 1961 Garrett, Leif
d. 1308 Duns Scotus, John
d. 1674 Milton, John
d. 1828 Bewick, Thomas
d. 1880 Drake, Edwin Laurentine
d. 1887 Holliday, "Doc" (John Henry)
d. 1890 Franck, Cesar Auguste
d. 1893 Parkman, Francis
d. 1894 Kelly, "King" (Michael Joseph)
d. 1901 Bickerdyke, Mary Ann Ball
d. 1908 Sardou, Victorien
d. 1917 Appleby, John Francis
d. 1928 Stiller, Mauritz
d. 1934 Baldwin, James Mark
d. 1948 Taggard, Genevieve
d. 1953 Bunin, Ivan Alekseevich
d. 1956 Field, Marshall, III
d. 1962 O'Brien, Willis Harold
d. 1965 Kilgallen, Dorothy
d. 1966 Baker, "Shorty" (Harold)
d. 1974 Hunter, "Ivory" Joe
d. 1976 Cramm, Gottfried von, Baron
d. 1977 Harris, "Bucky" (Stanley Raymond)
d. 1978 Rockwell, Norman
d. 1979 Ardizzone, Edward Jeffrey Irving
d. 1982 Politz, Alfred
d. 1983 Kaplan, Mordecai

November 9
b. 1731 Banneker, Benjamin
b. 1799 Mahan, Asa
b. 1801 Borden, Gail
b. 1802 Lovejoy, Elijah P

b. 1818 Turgenev, Ivan Sergeevich
b. 1825 Hill, Ambrose Powell
b. 1853 White, Stanford
b. 1859 Ippolitov-Ivanov, Mikhail Mikhailovich
b. 1861 Bache, Jules Sermon
b. 1865 Funston, Frederick
b. 1869 Dressler, Marie
b. 1873 Thyssen, Fritz
b. 1879 Holmes, John Haynes
b. 1881 Kalmus, Herbert Thomas
b. 1883 Oliver, Edna May
b. 1885 Pertile, Aureliano
b. 1886 Wynn, Ed
b. 1888 Monnet, Jean (Omer Gabriel)
b. 1889 Rains, Claude
b. 1899 Mezzrow, "Mezz" (Milton)
b. 1902 Asquith, Anthony
b. 1906 Spanier, "Muggsy" (Francis Joseph)
b. 1907 Stevenson, Edward A
b. 1908 Kilgore, Bernard
b. 1909 Drucker, Peter
b. 1913 Thompson, Kay
b. 1915 Shriver, (Robert) Sargent
b. 1917 Chadwick, Florence
b. 1918 Agnew, Spiro Theodore
b. 1919 Tavoulareas, William Peter
b. 1921 Drake, Stanley
b. 1921 Hines, Jerome
b. 1921 Paine, Thomas Otten
b. 1922 Dandridge, Dorothy
b. 1922 Lakatos, Imre
b. 1926 Leonard, Hugh, pseud.
b. 1928 Duke, Wayne
b. 1928 Sexton, Anne Harvey
b. 1931 Herzog, "Whitey" (Dorrel Norman Elvert)
b. 1931 Lipscomb, Eugene
b. 1932 Christy, Marian
b. 1934 Sagan, Carl Edward
b. 1935 Gibson, Bob (Robert)
b. 1936 Graham, Bob (Daniel Robert)
b. 1941 Gossett, D(aniel) Bruce
b. 1942 Weiskopf, Tom Daniel
b. 1948 Bouchard, Joe
b. 1952 Ferrigno, Lou
b. 1958 Higuera, Teddy (Teodoro Valenzuela)
d. 1802 Girtin, Thomas
d. 1819 Lee, Thomas Sim
d. 1856 Clayton, John Middleton
d. 1876 Tamburini, Antonio
d. 1911 Pyle, Howard
d. 1924 Lodge, Henry Cabot
d. 1926 Coffin, Charles Albert
d. 1930 Bliss, Tasker H
d. 1937 MacDonald, James Ramsay
d. 1940 Chamberlain, Neville
d. 1942 Curran, Charles Courtney
d. 1942 Oliver, Edna May

d. 1944 Marshall, Frank James
d. 1948 Kennedy, Edgar
d. 1951 Romberg, Sigmund
d. 1952 Weizmann, Chaim
d. 1953 Ibn-Saud
d. 1953 Thomas, Dylan Marlais
d. 1958 Fisher, Dorothy Frances Canfield
d. 1964 Cleland, Thomas Maitland
d. 1967 Bickford, Charles Ambrose
d. 1968 Corey, Wendell
d. 1970 Dawson, William L
d. 1970 DeGaulle, Charles Andre Joseph Marie
d. 1972 Berwind, Charles G
d. 1974 Wellesz, Egon
d. 1976 Halop, Billy
d. 1976 Lhevinne, Rosina L
d. 1980 Yung, Victor Sen
d. 1985 Rose, Helen Bronberg

November 10
b. 1483 Luther, Martin
b. 1493 Paracelsus, Philippus Aureolus
b. 1668 Couperin, Francois
b. 1683 George II
b. 1697 Hogarth, William
b. 1728 Goldsmith, Oliver
b. 1728 Herkimer, Nicholas
b. 1759 Schiller, Friedrich von (Johann Christoph Friedrich von)
b. 1802 Howe, Samuel Gridley
b. 1809 Einhorn, David
b. 1827 Terry, Alfred Howe
b. 1844 Thompson, John S D
b. 1847 Bridgman, Frederic Arthur
b. 1852 Vandyke, Henry Jackson, Jr.
b. 1856 Todd, Mabel Loomis
b. 1872 Moisseiff, Leon Solomon
b. 1873 Rabaud, Henri
b. 1874 Firestone, Idabelle Smith
b. 1874 MacMillan, Donald Baxter
b. 1879 Lindsay, (Nicholas) Vachel
b. 1879 Pearse, Padraic (Patrick Henry)
b. 1882 Dewey, Charles Schuveldt
b. 1883 Ficke, Arthur Davidson
b. 1887 Zweig, Arnold
b. 1893 Marquand, John Phillips
b. 1894 Normand, Mabel
b. 1895 Northrop, John Knudsen
b. 1899 Stowe, Leland
b. 1904 Geray, Steven
b. 1907 Bates, "Peg Leg" (Clayton)
b. 1907 Froman, Jane
b. 1907 Lawrence, Mildred Elwood
b. 1909 Marks, Johnny (John David)
b. 1911 Andrews, Harry
b. 1912 Tebbetts, "Birdie" (George Robert)
b. 1913 Shapiro, Karl Jay
b. 1916 May, (E William)
b. 1919 Fenneman, George
b. 1919 Tshombe, Moise
b. 1925 Burton, Richard

b. 1929 Bergman, Marilyn Keith
b. 1930 Pendleton, Clarence
b. 1930 Watt, Richard Martin
b. 1933 Evans, Ronald Ellwin
b. 1934 Cash, Norm(an Dalton)
b. 1935 Scott, Pippa (Phillippa)
b. 1940 Means, Russell Charles
b. 1944 Rice, Tim(othy Miles Bindon)
b. 1946 Stockman, David Allen
b. 1947 Gemayel, Bashir
b. 1948 Lake, Greg(ory)
b. 1949 Fargo, Donna
b. 1949 Reinking, Ann
b. 1955 Clark, Jack Anthony
b. 1959 Phillips, MacKenzie (Laura MacKenzie)
d. 1556 Chancellor, Richard
d. 1624 Southampton, Henry Wriothesley, Earl
d. 1779 Hewes, Joseph
d. 1789 Caswell, Richard
d. 1799 Black, Joseph
d. 1825 MacDonough, Thomas
d. 1843 Trumbull, John
d. 1875 Wilson, Henry
d. 1891 Rimbaud, (Jean Nicolas) Arthur
d. 1918 Apollinaire, Guillaume
d. 1938 Ataturk, Kemal
d. 1970 Torrance, Jack
d. 1971 Clark, Walter van Tilburg
d. 1971 Foster, Joseph C
d. 1977 Pudney, John Sleigh
d. 1981 Gance, Abel
d. 1982 Brezhnev, Leonid Ilyich
d. 1982 Petri, Elio
d. 1984 Bond, Sudie
d. 1985 MacDougall, Curtis Daniel

November 11
b. Moore, Demi
b. 1642 Boulle, Charles Andre
b. 1744 Adams, Abigail Smith
b. 1767 Romberg, Bernhard
b. 1771 Bichat, Marie Francois Xavier
b. 1771 McDowell, Ephraim
b. 1821 Dostoyevsky, Fyodor Mikhailovich
b. 1833 Borodin, Alexander Profirevich
b. 1836 Alden, Henry M
b. 1836 Aldrich, Thomas Bailey
b. 1846 Green, Anna Katharine
b. 1859 Insull, Samuel
b. 1863 Signac, Paul
b. 1864 Crile, George Washington
b. 1864 Fried, Alfred Hermann
b. 1868 Vuillard, (Jean) Edouard
b. 1872 Adams, Maude
b. 1872 Stock, Frederick A
b. 1882 Gustaf Adolf VI
b. 1883 Ansermet, Ernest Alexandre
b. 1885 Patton, George Smith, Jr.
b. 1887 Young, Roland
b. 1891 Ivogun, Maria

b. 1891 Maranville, "Rabbit" (Walter
    James Vincent)
b. 1892 Schacht, Al(exander)
b. 1893 Finletter, Thomas Knight
b. 1897 Allport, Gordon William
b. 1898 Clair, Rene
b. 1898 Eberle, Irmengarde
b. 1899 Green, Anne
b. 1899 O'Brien, Pat (William Joseph
    Patrick)
b. 1899 Traynor, "Pie" (Harold Joseph)
b. 1900 Scott, Hugh D, Jr.
b. 1901 Lindner, Richard
b. 1901 Mason, Francis van Wyck
b. 1904 Hiss, Alger
b. 1904 Penner, Joe
b. 1904 Spiegel, Sam
b. 1907 Barr, George
b. 1911 Knowles, Patric
b. 1911 Matta, Roberto Sebastian Antonio
    Echaurren
b. 1913 MacLeod, Iain Norman
b. 1913 Ryan, Robert (Bushnell)
b. 1914 Fast, Howard
b. 1915 Proxmire, William
b. 1918 Kaye, Stubby
b. 1920 Jenkins, Roy Harris
b. 1920 Tierney, Gene
b. 1921 Bell, Terrel Howard
b. 1922 Vonnegut, Kurt, Jr.
b. 1925 Winters, Jonathan
b. 1926 Fall, Bernard B
b. 1926 Lumley, Harry
b. 1927 Roose-Evans, James
b. 1928 Fuentes, Carlos
b. 1928 Zorinsky, Edward
b. 1934 Manson, Charles
b. 1935 Andersson, Bibi
b. 1936 Kohner, Susan
b. 1937 Celeste, Richard F
b. 1945 Alexander, Denise
b. 1945 Martell, Vincent
b. 1945 Ortega, Saavedra, Daniel
b. 1946 Metrinko, Michael John
b. 1947 Daugherty, Pat
b. 1950 Armstrong, Otis
b. 1951 Zoeller, "Fuzzy" (Frank Urban)
b. 1964 McKeon, Philip
d. 1750 Zeno, Apostolo
d. 1831 Turner, Nat
d. 1845 Brooks, Maria Gowen
d. 1855 Kierkegaard, Soren Aabye
d. 1869 Walker, Robert James
d. 1880 Kelly, Ned (Edward)
d. 1880 Mott, Lucretia Coffin
d. 1917 Liliuokalani, Lydia Kamekeha
d. 1936 Harding, Chester
d. 1938 Typhoid Mary
d. 1942 DeBeck, Billy
d. 1945 Kern, Jerome David
d. 1947 Lowndes, Marie Adelaide Belloc

d. 1948 Niblo, Fred
d. 1956 Young, Victor
d. 1958 Bazin, Andre
d. 1964 Piper, H(enry) Beam
d. 1969 Eberstadt, Ferdinand
d. 1971 Herbert, Alan Patrick, Sir
d. 1974 Ace, Jane Sherwood
d. 1975 Anderson, Clint(on Presba)
d. 1976 Calder, Alexander
d. 1978 Borgmann, "Benny" (Bernhard)
d. 1979 Tiomkin, Dimitri
d. 1980 Amalrik, Andrei Alekseyevich
d. 1984 King, Martin Luther, Sr.
d. 1984 Sheppard, Eugenia Benbow
d. 1985 Rothstein, Arthur

November 12
b. 1729 Bougainville, Louis Antoine de
b. 1730 Gabrielli, Catarina
b. 1746 Charles, Jacques-Alexandre-Cesar
b. 1751 Corbin, Margaret Cochran
b. 1790 Tyler, Letitia Christian
b. 1815 Stanton, Elizabeth Cady
b. 1817 Baha'u'llah
b. 1840 Rodin, Auguste (Francois Auguste
    Rene)
b. 1866 Collier, William, Sr.
b. 1866 Sun Yat-Sen
b. 1877 Austin, Warren R(obinson)
b. 1880 Stark, Harold Raynsford
b. 1886 Travers, Ben
b. 1888 Parrish, Anne
b. 1889 Wallace, DeWitt
b. 1891 Nicholson, Seth Barnes
b. 1891 Whiting, Richard Armstrong
b. 1903 Oakie, Jack
b. 1906 Dillon, George
b. 1906 Saidenberg, Daniel
b. 1908 Blackmun, Harry Andrew
b. 1910 Schenker, Tillie Abramson
b. 1911 Clayton, Buck
b. 1915 Barthes, Roland
b. 1917 Coors, Joseph
b. 1918 Stafford, Jo
b. 1919 Lefever, Ernest Warren
b. 1920 Quine, Richard
b. 1922 Hunter, Kim
b. 1926 Rysanek, Leonie
b. 1927 Secunda, (Holland) Arthur
b. 1928 Baker, Bobby (Robert Gene)
b. 1928 Muncey, Bill (William)
b. 1928 Sharmat, Marjorie Weinman
b. 1929 Kelly, Grace Patricia
b. 1931 Slotnick, Daniel Leonid
b. 1932 Forman, James Douglas
b. 1935 Briand, Rena
b. 1937 Balin, Ina
b. 1937 Fisher, Jules
b. 1937 Truly, Richard H
b. 1942 Powers, Stefanie
b. 1943 Hyland, Brian
b. 1943 Shawn, Wallace

b. 1944 Houston, Ken(neth Ray)
b. 1945 Young, Neil
b. 1947 Roeser, Donald
b. 1948 Harris, Cliff(ord Allen)
b. 1952 Bartkowski, Steve(n Joseph)
b. 1955 McKeown, Leslie
b. 1961 Comaneci, Nadia
d. 1035 Canute
d. 1554 Coronado, Francisco Vasquez de
d. 1595 Hawkins, John, Sir
d. 1671 Fairfax, Thomas
d. 1813 Crevecoeur, Michel-Guillaume Jean de
d. 1854 Kemble, Charles
d. 1865 Gaskell, Elizabeth Cleghorn
d. 1898 Fisher, Clara
d. 1900 Daly, Marcus
d. 1900 Villard, Henry
d. 1906 Shafter, William Rufus
d. 1908 Brooks, William Keith
d. 1926 Cannon, Joseph Gurney
d. 1933 Bowker, R(ichard) R(ogers)
d. 1937 Carter, Mrs. Leslie
d. 1939 Bethune, Norman
d. 1944 Kelley, Edgar Stillman
d. 1947 Moore, John Bassett
d. 1947 Orczy, Emmuska, Baroness
d. 1948 Giordano, Umberto
d. 1950 Marlowe, Julia
d. 1958 Curley, James Michael
d. 1963 Hodge, John Reed
d. 1964 Hutchinson, Fred(erick Charles)
d. 1965 Spaeth, Sigmund Gottfried
d. 1966 Porter, Quincy
d. 1969 Friedman, William
d. 1969 Scherman, Harry
d. 1972 Friml, Rudolf
d. 1975 Morgan, Arthur
d. 1975 Ross, David
d. 1976 Piston, Walter
d. 1981 Holden, William
d. 1984 Burman, Ben Lucien
d. 1984 Himes, Chester Bomar
d. 1985 Lindbergh, Pelle (Per-Eric)

November 13
b. 354 Augustine, Saint
b. 1785 Lamb, Caroline Ponsonby, Lady
b. 1787 Duveyrier, Anne Honore
b. 1792 Trelawny, Edward John
b. 1809 Dahlgren, John Adolph
b. 1814 Hooker, Joseph
b. 1831 Maxwell, James Clerk
b. 1833 Booth, Edwin Thomas
b. 1850 Evans, Charles
b. 1850 Stevenson, Robert Louis Balfour
b. 1853 Drew, John
b. 1854 Chadwick, George Whitefield
b. 1856 Brandeis, Louis Dembitz
b. 1866 Flexner, Abraham
b. 1872 Hupp, Louis Gorham
b. 1875 Kling, John Gradwohl

b. 1875 Swinnerton, James Guilford
b. 1882 Bartlett, Francis Alonzo
b. 1890 Richter, Conrad Michael
b. 1893 Beals, Carleton
b. 1893 Doisy, Edward Adelbert
b. 1893 Rubin, Reuven
b. 1894 Moten, Bennie
b. 1896 Beard, Myron Gould
b. 1900 Allison, Samuel King
b. 1900 King, Alexander
b. 1900 Miner, Worthington C
b. 1901 Sackville-West, Edward Charles
b. 1904 Caspary, Vera
b. 1906 Baddeley, Hermione Clinton
b. 1907 Buzzell, Eddie
b. 1908 Thibault, Conrad
b. 1908 Woodward, C(omer) Vann
b. 1910 Huie, William Bradford
b. 1913 Nol, Lon
b. 1913 Scourby, Alexander
b. 1914 Gibson, William
b. 1915 Benchley, Nathaniel Goddard
b. 1916 Ashford, Emmett Littleton
b. 1916 Elam, Jack
b. 1917 Sterling, Robert
b. 1920 Saxon, Charles David
b. 1922 Werner, Oskar
b. 1923 Christian, Linda
b. 1930 Harris, Fred Roy
b. 1932 Mulligan, Richard
b. 1933 Corri, Adrienne
b. 1934 Densen-Gerber, Judianne
b. 1934 Marshall, Garry Kent
b. 1938 Seberg, Jean
b. 1939 Higgins, George V
b. 1941 Rambo, Dack
b. 1949 Steen, Roger
b. 1950 Perreault, Gilbert
b. 1953 Tickner, Charlie
d. 1460 Henry the Navigator
d. 1619 Carracci, Lodovico
d. 1687 Gwyn, Nell (Eleanor)
d. 1849 Manning, Maria
d. 1868 Rossini, Gioacchino Antonio
d. 1883 Sims, James Marion
d. 1894 Stevenson, Robert Louis Balfour
d. 1903 Pissarro, Camille Jacob
d. 1907 Thompson, Francis Joseph
d. 1916 Lowell, Percival
d. 1916 Saki, pseud.
d. 1937 Carter, Caroline Louise Dudley
d. 1939 Weber, Lois
d. 1942 Crews, Laura Hope
d. 1942 Schoen-Rene, Anna
d. 1948 Bradford, Roark
d. 1949 Wallerstein, Lothar
d. 1951 Medtner, Nicholas
d. 1952 Brown, Margaret Wise
d. 1952 Egan, Richard B
d. 1953 Ives, Herbert Eugene
d. 1954 Fath, Jacques

d. 1955 DeVoto, Bernard Augustine
d. 1960 Hall, Josef Washington
d. 1961 Biddle, Anthony
d. 1963 Murray, Margaret Alice
d. 1967 Paddleford, Clementine Haskin
d. 1971 Bleeker, Sonia
d. 1972 Webster, Margaret
d. 1973 Lee, Lila
d. 1973 Lyons, James
d. 1974 DeSica, Vittorio
d. 1974 Silkwood, Karen
d. 1975 Sherriff, Robert Cedric
d. 1982 Deutsch, Babette
d. 1982 Kim, Duk Koo
d. 1983 Samples, "Junior" (Alvin)
d. 1985 Pereira, William Leonard

November 14
b. Yarmon, Betty
b. 1765 Fulton, Robert
b. 1774 Spontini, Gasparo
b. 1778 Hummel, Johann Nepomuk
b. 1797 Lyell, Charles, Sir
b. 1819 Rodgers, Christopher Raymond
Perry
b. 1828 McPherson, James Birdseye
b. 1838 Richards, William Trost
b. 1840 Monet, Claude
b. 1861 Turner, Frederick Jackson
b. 1863 Baekeland, Leo Hendrick
b. 1871 Coulter, Ernest Kent
b. 1871 Russell, Henry
b. 1881 Schenck, Nicholas Michael
b. 1885 Delaunay-Terk, Sonia
b. 1885 Rourke, Constance Mayfield
b. 1887 Paumgartner, Bernhard
b. 1889 Hussein, Taha
b. 1889 Nehru, Jawaharlal
b. 1890 Egan, Richard B
b. 1895 Lausche, Frank John
b. 1895 Lewis, Wilmarth Sheldon
b. 1896 Eisenhower, Mamie Geneva Doud
b. 1897 Curry, John Steuart
b. 1900 Copland, Aaron
b. 1902 Downey, Morton
b. 1904 Lord, Mary Pillsbury
b. 1904 Mannes, Marya
b. 1904 Ramsey, Arthur Michael
b. 1906 Brooks, Louise
b. 1907 Lindgren, Astrid
b. 1907 Steig, William
b. 1908 McCarthy, Joe (Joseph Raymond)
b. 1908 Salisbury, Harrison Evans
b. 1910 DeCamp, Rosemary
b. 1912 Hutton, Barbara
b. 1913 Smathers, George Armistead
b. 1914 Crozier, Eric
b. 1917 Field, Virginia (Margaret Cynthia
St. John)
b. 1918 Madeira, Jean
b. 1919 Desmond, Johnny
b. 1921 Keith, Brian

b. 1925 Medvedev, Zhores Aleksandrovich
b. 1927 Yepes, Narcisco
b. 1929 Stevenson, McLean
b. 1930 White, Ed(ward Higgins, II)
b. 1933 Haise, Fred W
b. 1935 Hussein (Ibn Talal)
b. 1942 Watson, Bryan Joseph
b. 1948 Charles
b. 1951 Bishop, Stephen
b. 1955 Hernandez, Willie (Guillermo
Villaneuva)
b. 1955 Sikma, Jack Wayne
d. 1716 Leibniz, Gottfried Wilhelm von
d. 1825 Richter, Jean Paul F
d. 1831 Hegel, Georg Wilhelm Friedrich
d. 1832 Carroll, Charles
d. 1901 Mapleson, James Henry
d. 1908 Tz'u Hsi
d. 1910 LaFarge, John
d. 1915 Washington, Booker T(aliafero)
d. 1916 George, Henry, Jr.
d. 1929 McGinnity, Joe (Joseph Jerome)
d. 1936 Howell, Clark
d. 1938 Gram, Hans Christian Joachim
d. 1944 Dallin, Cyrus
d. 1946 Falla, Manuel de
d. 1951 Benson, Frank Weston
d. 1954 Verrill, Alpheus Hyatt
d. 1955 Ayres, Ruby Mildred
d. 1955 Sherwood, Robert Emmet
d. 1955 Tobin, Daniel Joseph
d. 1956 Negrin, Juan
d. 1959 Cochrane, Edward Lull
d. 1960 Catlett, Walter
d. 1965 DeMarco, Tony
d. 1967 Kilgore, Bernard
d. 1968 Menendez Pidal, Ramon
d. 1972 Dies, Martin, Jr.
d. 1972 Litton, Charles
d. 1973 Schiaparelli, (Elsa)
d. 1974 Brown, Johnny Mack
d. 1975 Anslinger, Harry Jacob
d. 1980 Haskell, Arnold Lionel
d. 1983 Sheehan, Joseph Green
d. 1985 Koo, V(i) K(yuin) Wellington

November 15
b. 1708 Pitt, William
b. 1731 Cowper, William
b. 1738 Herschel, William
b. 1741 Lavater, Johann Casper
b. 1784 Bonaparte, Jerome
b. 1787 Cunard, Samuel, Sir
b. 1787 Leslie, Eliza
b. 1797 Weed, Thurlow
b. 1807 Petroff, Ossip
b. 1862 Hauptmann, Gerhart
b. 1873 Baker, Sara Josephine
b. 1875 Kurz, Selma
b. 1879 Cape, Herbert Jonathan
b. 1879 Stone, Lewis
b. 1881 Adams, Franklin P(ierce)

d. 1632 Gustavus Adolphus
d. 1806 Cleaveland, Moses
d. 1812 Walter, John
d. 1831 Clausewitz, Karl von
d. 1885 Riel, Louis David
d. 1895 Smith, Samuel Francis
d. 1902 Henty, George Alfred
d. 1909 Crittenton, Charles Nelson
d. 1928 Cecchetti, Enrico
d. 1936 Schumann-Heink, Ernestine Rossler
d. 1940 Beck, Martin
d. 1947 Carter, Boake
d. 1960 Gable, Clark
d. 1961 Rayburn, Sam(uel Taliaferro)
d. 1964 Peattie, Donald Culross
d. 1965 Blackstone, Harry
d. 1965 Cosgrave, William Thomas
d. 1965 DuMont, Allen Balcom
d. 1965 King, Alexander
d. 1969 Fenton, Carroll Lane
d. 1970 Lang, Harold
d. 1973 Watts, Alan Wilson
d. 1980 Aronson, Boris
d. 1982 Crosby, Sumner McKnight
d. 1984 Rose, Leonard
d. 1985 Sparkman, John Jackson

November 17
b. Michaels, Lorne
b. 1503 Bronzino II
b. 1749 Appert, Francois Nicolas
b. 1790 Mobius, August Ferdinand
b. 1793 Eastlake, Charles Lock
b. 1794 Grote, George
b. 1799 Peale, Titian Ramsay
b. 1815 Farnham, Eliza Wood Burhans
b. 1854 Lyautey, Louis Hubert Gonzalve
b. 1861 Lampman, Archibald
b. 1861 Nutting, Wallace
b. 1876 Lea, Homer
b. 1878 Abbott, Grace
b. 1879 Heggie, O P
b. 1887 Montgomery of Alamein, Bernard
   Law Montgomery, Viscount
b. 1891 Banting, Frederick Grant, Sir
b. 1899 Seidel, Toscha
b. 1901 Hallstein, Walter
b. 1901 Strasberg, Lee
b. 1903 Walters, Charles
b. 1904 Bernstein, Theodore Menline
b. 1904 Diederichs, Nicholaas
b. 1904 Hastie, William Henry
b. 1905 Auer, Mischa
b. 1906 Bronson, Betty (Elizabeth Ada)
b. 1906 Honda, Soichiro
b. 1907 Wimsatt, William Kurtz, Jr.
b. 1910 Wiley, William Bradford
b. 1912 Ackerman, Harry S
b. 1912 Rebozo, "Bebe" (Charles Gregory)
b. 1916 Silk, George
b. 1917 Lescoulie, Jack
b. 1919 Kay, Hershy

b. 1922 Schulberg, Stuart
b. 1923 Garcia, Mike (Edward Miguel)
b. 1924 Pereira, Aristides
b. 1925 Hudson, Rock
b. 1925 Mackerras, Charles, Sir (Alan
   Charles MacLaurin)
b. 1930 Amram, David Werner, III
b. 1930 Mathias, Bob (Robert Bruce)
b. 1937 Cook, Peter
b. 1939 Lightfoot, Gordon Meredith
b. 1939 Waugh, Auberon
b. 1942 Gaudio, Bob
b. 1942 Scorsese, Martin
b. 1944 Hutton, Lauren (Mary Laurence)
b. 1944 Seaver, Tom (George Thomas)
b. 1945 Hayes, Elvin Ernest
b. 1947 Vollbracht, Michaele J
b. 1950 Matthes, Roland
b. 1953 Martin, Dean Paul (Dino, Jr.)
d. 1558 Mary I
d. 1747 Lesage, Alain Rene
d. 1858 Owen, Robert
d. 1907 McClintock, Francis Leopold, Sir
d. 1913 Marchesi, Mathilde de Castrone
d. 1917 Rodin, Auguste (Francois Auguste
   Rene)
d. 1926 Akeley, Carl Ethan
d. 1941 Udet, Ernst
d. 1944 Peabody, Endicott
d. 1944 Smith, Ellison DuRant
d. 1947 Huch, Ricarda (Octavia)
d. 1955 Johnson, James Price
d. 1958 Cooper, Morton Cecil
d. 1959 Villa-Lobos, Heitor
d. 1961 Kauff, Benny (Benjamin Michael)
d. 1962 Davis, Arthur Vining
d. 1968 Peake, Mervyn Laurence
d. 1971 Cooper, Gladys, Dame
d. 1973 Mangrum, Lloyd
d. 1975 Bronk, Detlev Wulf
d. 1976 Block, Joseph Leopold
d. 1978 Dauphin, Claude Le Grand Maria
   Eugene
d. 1981 Eberly, Bob
d. 1981 Lang, Daniel
d. 1982 Donnelly, Ruth
d. 1985 Chase, Stuart
d. 1985 Nol, Lon

November 18
b. 1647 Bayle, Pierre
b. 1785 Wilkie, David
b. 1786 Weber, Carl Maria von
b. 1787 Daguerre, Louis Jacques Mande
b. 1810 Gray, Asa
b. 1826 Newberry, John Stoughton
b. 1836 Gilbert, William Schwenck, Sir
b. 1857 Knox, Rose Markward
b. 1860 Paderewski, Ignace Jan
b. 1862 Sunday, Billy (William Ashley)
b. 1868 Dehmel, Richard
b. 1870 Dix, Dorothy, pseud.

d. 1828 Schubert, Franz Peter
d. 1850 Johnson, Richard Mentor
d. 1867 Halleck, Fritz-Greene
d. 1868 Mount, William Sidney
d. 1873 Mallory, Stephen R
d. 1887 Lazarus, Emma
d. 1895 Vaux, Calvert
d. 1909 Laffan, William Mackay
d. 1915 Hill, Joe, pseud.
d. 1922 Bacon, Frank
d. 1924 Ince, Thomas H(arper)
d. 1949 Ensor, James
d. 1955 James, Marquis
d. 1956 Sullivan, Francis Loftus
d. 1960 Cooper, Emil
d. 1960 Gibbons, Tom
d. 1966 Connolly, Mike
d. 1967 Funk, Casimir
d. 1968 Norena, Eide
d. 1969 Sardi, Vincent, Sr.
d. 1971 Stern, Bill (William)
d. 1972 Ohrbach, Nathan
d. 1974 Brunis, George
d. 1978 Ryan, Leo Joseph
d. 1983 Kitchell, Iva
d. 1983 Leigh, Carolyn
d. 1984 Aiken, George David
d. 1985 Fetchit, Stepin
d. 1985 Joanis, John W

November 20

b. 1752 Chatterton, Thomas
b. 1773 Schuyler, Phillip John
b. 1837 Waterman, Lewis Edson
b. 1841 Laurier, Wilfrid, Sir
b. 1855 Royce, Josiah
b. 1858 Lagerlof, Selma Ottiliana Lovisa
b. 1862 Westermarck, Edward Alexander
b. 1866 Landis, Kenesaw Mountain
b. 1867 Hayes, Patrick J
b. 1869 Griffith, Clark Calvin
b. 1871 Guiterman, Arthur
b. 1873 Mason, Daniel Gregory
b. 1874 Curley, James Michael
b. 1875 Kalinin, Mikhail
b. 1878 Bowers, Claude Gernade
b. 1878 Gilpin, Charles Sidney
b. 1884 Thomas, Norman Mattoon
b. 1886 Frisch, Karl von
b. 1886 Hammond, Bray
b. 1887 Hooton, Earnest Albert
b. 1889 Hubble, Edwin Powell
b. 1891 Denny, Reginald Leigh
b. 1891 Murphy, Jimmy (James Edward)
b. 1894 Humphries, Rolfe (George Rolfe)
b. 1896 Armstrong, Robert
b. 1900 Gould, Chester
b. 1907 Clouzot, Henri-George
b. 1908 Cooke, (Alfred) Alistair
b. 1908 Romano, John
b. 1911 Hanfmann, George Maxim Anossov

b. 1914 Pucci, Emilio Marchese di Barsento
b. 1916 Canova, Judy
b. 1917 Locke, Bobbie
b. 1919 Keyes, Evelyn Louise
b. 1920 Thaxter, Phyllis
b. 1921 Garrison, Jim C
b. 1921 Newhouser, Harold (Hal)
b. 1923 Gordimer, Nadine
b. 1924 Allison, Fran(ces)
b. 1925 Christy, June
b. 1925 Kennedy, Robert Francis
b. 1925 Plisetskaya, Maya Mikhailovna
b. 1926 Ballard, Kaye
b. 1927 Parsons, Estelle
b. 1928 Cover, Franklin
b. 1929 Denenberg, Herbert S
b. 1932 Dawson, Richard
b. 1937 Linkletter, Jack
b. 1938 Smothers, Dick (Richard)
b. 1940 Einstein, Bob
b. 1942 Biden, Joseph Robinette, Jr.
b. 1942 Greenbaum, Norman
b. 1942 Monk, Meredith
b. 1945 Hamel, Veronica
b. 1945 Johnstone, Jay (John William, Jr.)
b. 1946 Allman, Duane (Howard Duane)
b. 1946 Cook, Greg(ory Lynn)
b. 1946 Woodruff, Judy Carline
b. 1947 Walsh, Joe (Joseph Fidler)
b. 1956 Gastineau, Mark (Marcus D)
d. 1591 Hatton, Christopher, Sir
d. 1692 Shadwell, Thomas
d. 1806 Backus, Isaac
d. 1888 Currier, Nathaniel
d. 1894 Rubinstein, Anton Gregorovitch
d. 1903 Horn, Tom
d. 1904 Cesnola, Luigi Palma di
d. 1910 Tolstoy, Leo Nikolayevich
d. 1925 Alexandra Caroline Mary Charlotte
d. 1925 Morris, Clara
d. 1933 Birrell, Augustine
d. 1935 Jellicoe, John
d. 1938 Hall, Edwin Herbert
d. 1940 Blatch, Harriot Eaton Stanton
d. 1950 Cilea, Francesco
d. 1952 Croce, Benedetto
d. 1954 Cessna, Clyde Vernon
d. 1957 Swope, Gerard
d. 1960 Rollins, Carl Purington
d. 1964 Howard, Roy Wilson
d. 1972 Grossinger, Jennie
d. 1973 Sherman, Allan
d. 1975 Franco, Francisco
d. 1976 Auchincloss, Hugh D
d. 1976 D'Arcy, Martin Cyril
d. 1976 Lysenko, Trofim Denisovich
d. 1978 Chirico, Giorgio de
d. 1981 Sheed, Frank (Francis Joseph)
d. 1982 Mackin, Catherine Patricia

b. 1894 Bayne, Beverly Pearl
b. 1895 Dehn, Adolf Arthur
b. 1895 Enoch, Kurt
b. 1896 Mays, David John
b. 1898 Blanding, Sarah Gibson
b. 1899 Berndt, Walter
b. 1899 Carmichael, Hoagy (Hoagland Howard)
b. 1900 Post, Wiley
b. 1901 Crane, Roy(ston Campbell)
b. 1902 Adonis, Joe
b. 1902 Feuermann, Emanuel
b. 1902 McDonald, David John
b. 1906 Patrick, Lee
b. 1910 Smith, Ethel
b. 1911 Cacers, Ernest
b. 1912 Duke, Doris
b. 1913 Berlitz, Charles L Frambach
b. 1913 Britten, (Edward) Benjamin
b. 1914 Townsend, Peter Wooldridge
b. 1917 Huxley, Andrew Fielding
b. 1918 Pell, Claiborne
b. 1918 Walston, Ray
b. 1921 Atherton, Alfred LeRoy, Jr.
b. 1921 Dangerfield, Rodney
b. 1923 Hiller, Arthur
b. 1923 Westwood, Jean Miles
b. 1924 Page, Geraldine
b. 1925 Schuller, Gunther
b. 1926 Burdette, Lew (Selva Lewis, Jr.)
b. 1930 Garriott, Owen
b. 1930 Hall, Peter Reginald Frederick, Sir
b. 1932 Vaughn, Robert
b. 1935 Callan, Michael
b. 1935 Protopopov, Ludmilla Evgenievna Belousova
b. 1940 Gilliam, Terry
b. 1941 Conti, Tom (Thomas Antonio)
b. 1941 Dante, Nicholas
b. 1942 Bluford, Guion Stewart, Jr.
b. 1942 Edwards, Harry (Jr.)
b. 1943 King, Billie Jean
b. 1947 Reynolds, Jack (John Sumner)
b. 1950 Bostock, Lyman Wesley
b. 1950 Luzinski, Greg(ory Michael)
b. 1958 Curtis, Jamie Lee
b. 1967 Becker, Boris
d. 1594 Frobisher, Martin
d. 1718 Blackbeard
d. 1774 Clive, Robert
d. 1783 Hanson, John
d. 1882 Weed, Thurlow
d. 1896 Ferris, George Washington Gale
d. 1900 Sullivan, Arthur Seymour, Sir
d. 1916 London, Jack (John Griffith)
d. 1921 Nilsson, Christine
d. 1932 Atkinson, William Walker
d. 1936 Graham, Ernest Robert
d. 1941 Koffka, Kurt
d. 1943 Hart, Lorenz Milton
d. 1943 Yon, Pietro Alessandro

d. 1944 Eddington, Arthur Stanley, Sir
d. 1953 Shields, Larry
d. 1954 Vishinskii, Andrei Yanuarevich
d. 1955 Howard, "Shemp" (Samuel)
d. 1959 Mallory, Molla
d. 1961 Gebert, Ernst
d. 1962 Coty, Rene
d. 1963 Huxley, Aldous Leonard
d. 1963 Kennedy, John Fitzgerald
d. 1963 Lewis, C(live) S(taples)
d. 1971 Confrey, "Zez" (Edward E)
d. 1972 Loper, Don
d. 1978 Traglia, Luigi, Cardinal
d. 1980 Leger, Jules
d. 1980 McCormack, John William
d. 1980 West, Mae
d. 1981 Krebs, Hans Adolf, Sir
d. 1981 Lightner, Theodore
d. 1982 Turkus, Burton B
d. 1983 Conrad, Michael
d. 1983 Wibberley, Leonard Patrick O'Connor

November 23

b. Landesberg, Steve
b. 1510 Tallis, Thomas
b. 1743 LaTour D'Auvergne, Theophile de
b. 1749 Rutledge, Edward
b. 1804 Pierce, Franklin
b. 1816 Duyckinck, Evert Augustus
b. 1834 Thomson, James
b. 1841 Croker, "Boss" (Richard)
b. 1846 Schuch, Ernst von
b. 1859 Billy the Kid
b. 1872 Ward, Fannie
b. 1876 Falla, Manuel de
b. 1878 King, Ernest Joseph
b. 1881 Enver Pasha
b. 1882 Reid, Helen Rogers
b. 1883 Orozco, Jose Clemente
b. 1884 Bolton, Guy Reginald
b. 1887 Karloff, Boris
b. 1889 Patch, Alexander M(c Carrell)
b. 1892 Erte
b. 1893 Marx, "Harpo" (Arthur)
b. 1893 Schram, Emil
b. 1894 Folsom, Marion Bayard
b. 1896 Gottwald, Klement
b. 1897 Etting, Ruth
b. 1897 Smith, Willie
b. 1898 Malinovsky, Rodion Y
b. 1902 Jory, Victor
b. 1907 Swanberg, William Andrew
b. 1913 Zolotow, Maurice
b. 1915 Dehner, John Forkum
b. 1924 Turnbull, Collin M(acmillan)
b. 1926 Duarte, Jose Napoleon
b. 1926 Hunter, Jeffrey
b. 1927 Chandler, Otis
b. 1928 Bock, Jerry (Jerrold Lewis)
b. 1930 Brock, Bill (William Emerson)
b. 1932 Toye, Clive Roy

d. 1961 Wenner-Gren, Axel
d. 1963 Ostenso, Martha
d. 1963 Oswald, Lee Harvey
d. 1963 Rosing, Vladimir
d. 1964 O'Dwyer, William
d. 1964 Schauffler, Robert Haven
d. 1972 Smallens, Alexander
d. 1976 Ward, Paul W
d. 1980 Agar, Herbert Sebastian
d. 1981 Thornton, Charles Bates
d. 1985 Turner, Joe

November 25
b. 1562 Vega (Carpio), Lope (Felix) de
b. 1729 Suvorov, Aleksandr V
b. 1752 Reichardt, Johann Friedrich
b. 1760 Babeuf, Francois Noel
b. 1775 Kemble, Charles
b. 1835 Carnegie, Andrew
b. 1842 Visscher, William Lightfoot
b. 1846 Nation, Carry A(melia Moore)
b. 1860 Perry, Bliss
b. 1862 Nevin, Ethelbert Woodbridge
b. 1874 Gans, Joe
b. 1874 Spence, Lewis (James Lewis
    Thomas Chalmers)
b. 1877 Granville-Barker, Harley
b. 1878 Kaiser, Georg
b. 1880 Woolf, Leonard Sidney
b. 1881 John XXIII, Pope
b. 1884 Cadogan, Alexander George
    Montague, Sir
b. 1887 Roberts, Roy Allison
b. 1893 Krutch, Joseph Wood
b. 1894 Stallings, Laurence
b. 1895 Kempff, (Wilhelm) Walter
    Friedrich
b. 1895 Mikoyan, Anastas Ivanovich
b. 1895 Santmyer, Helen Hooven
b. 1895 Svoboda, Ludvik
b. 1896 Thomson, Virgil Garnett
b. 1899 Burnett, W(illiam) R(iley)
b. 1900 Douglas, Helen Mary Gahagan
b. 1900 Schwartz, Arthur
b. 1902 Lapidus, Morris
b. 1902 Shore, Eddie
b. 1904 Landis, Jessie Royce
b. 1906 Jepson, Helen
b. 1911 Hogarth, Burne
b. 1912 Nikolais, Alwin
b. 1915 Pinochet Ugarte, Augusto
b. 1918 Opie, Peter Mason
b. 1919 Brodie, Steve
b. 1920 Montalban, Ricardo
b. 1922 Duggan, Maurice Noel
b. 1922 McCloskey, Robert James
b. 1923 Koivisto, Mauno Henrik
b. 1923 Wall, Art(hur Johnathan), Jr.
b. 1924 Desmond, Paul Breitenfeld
b. 1926 Drexler, Rosalyn
b. 1926 Schisgal, Murray
b. 1933 Crosby, Kathryn

b. 1939 Feldstein, Martin Stuart
b. 1940 Gibbs, Joe Jackson
b. 1945 Hagegard, Hakan
b. 1947 Larroquette, John
b. 1951 Dent, "Bucky" (Russell Earl)
b. 1960 Kennedy, John Fitzgerald, Jr.
b. 1963 Kosar, Bernie
b. 1966 Lattisaw, Stacy
d. 1560 Doria, Andrea
d. 1700 Van Cortlandt, Stephanus
d. 1748 Watts, Isaac
d. 1830 Rode, Jacques Pierre Joseph
d. 1841 Chantrey, Francis Legatt, Sir
d. 1885 Hendricks, Thomas Andrews
d. 1912 McLane, James Woods
d. 1928 Lummis, Charles Fletcher
d. 1937 Baylis, Lilian Mary
d. 1944 Landis, Kenesaw Mountain
d. 1946 Morgenthau, Henry
d. 1949 Robinson, Bill
d. 1954 Coffin, Henry Sloane
d. 1957 Kyne, Peter Bernard
d. 1957 Rivera, Diego
d. 1958 Kettering, Charles Franklin
d. 1962 Walker, Stanley
d. 1967 Zadkine, Ossip
d. 1968 Sinclair, Upton Beall
d. 1968 Siple, Paul Allman
d. 1970 Madison, Helene
d. 1970 Mishima, Yukio, pseud.
d. 1972 Coanda, Henri Marie
d. 1973 Harvey, Laurence
d. 1974 Lane, Rosemary
d. 1974 Thant, U
d. 1977 Carlson, Richard
d. 1979 Abrams, Harry Nathan
d. 1981 Albertson, Jack
d. 1982 Coote, Robert
d. 1982 Gray, Gordon
d. 1983 Baldwin, Billy
d. 1983 Baldwin, William, Jr.
d. 1983 Dolin, Anton, Sir
d. 1984 Goldman, Sylvan N
d. 1985 Podoloff, Maurice
d. 1985 Pusey, Merlo John

November 26
b. 1607 Harvard, John
b. 1726 Wolcott, Oliver, Sr.
b. 1761 Savage, Edward
b. 1807 Mount, William Sidney
b. 1827 White, Ellen Gould Harmon
b. 1830 Tabor, Horace Austin Warner
b. 1832 Walker, Mary Edwards
b. 1842 Kropotkin, Peter Alekseyevich,
    Prince
b. 1844 Benz, Karl Friedrich
b. 1857 Plekhanov, Georgi Valentinovich
b. 1858 Drexel, Mary Katherine
b. 1861 Fall, Albert Bacon
b. 1866 Duffy, Hugh
b. 1870 Knote, Heinrich

b. 1871 McIntyre, John Thomas
b. 1876 Carrier, Willis H
b. 1889 Phillips, Harry Irving
b. 1891 Nichols, Anne
b. 1892 Brackett, Charles
b. 1892 Guyon, Joe
b. 1893 Vaughan, Harry Hawkins
b. 1894 Papanin, Ivan D
b. 1894 Wiener, Norbert
b. 1900 Hauptmann, Bruno Richard
b. 1901 Grosvenor, Melville Bell
b. 1904 Flood, Daniel J
b. 1905 Williams, Emlyn (George Emlyn)
b. 1907 Dee, Frances
b. 1908 Spigelgass, Leonard
b. 1909 Gomez, "Lefty" (Vernon Louis)
b. 1910 Cusack, Cyril
b. 1911 Reshevsky, Samuel
b. 1912 Ionesco, Eugene
b. 1912 Sevareid, (Arnold) Eric
b. 1915 Wild, Earl
b. 1919 Pohl, Frederik
b. 1921 Gilot, Francoise
b. 1922 Schulz, Charles Monroe
b. 1924 Hoffman, Irwin
b. 1924 Segal, George
b. 1925 Hunt, Lois
b. 1925 Istomin, Eugene George
b. 1926 Butler, Michael
b. 1929 Saint John, Betta
b. 1933 Goulet, Robert
b. 1935 Pringle, Laurence
b. 1938 Goldsmith, Judith Ann Becker
b. 1938 Little, Rich(ard Caruthers)
b. 1938 Turner, Tina
b. 1942 Cole, Olivia
b. 1943 Paltrow, Bruce
b. 1943 Stenerud, Jan
b. 1946 McVie, John
b. 1947 Hebner, Richie (Richard Joseph)
b. 1948 Sargent, Ben
b. 1952 Turnbull, Wendy
b. 1981 Fiske, Jamie
d. 1504 Isabella I
d. 1836 McAdam, John Loudoun
d. 1857 Eichendorff, Joseph Karl Benedict
d. 1882 LeClear, Thomas
d. 1883 Truth, Sojourner
d. 1896 Patmore, Coventry Kersey Dighton
d. 1915 Burpee, W(ashington) Atlee
d. 1918 Bannerman, Francis
d. 1926 Browning, John Moses
d. 1930 Sverdrup, Otto
d. 1932 MacDonald, J(ames) E(dward) H(ervey)
d. 1940 Andresen, Ivar
d. 1940 Harmsworth, Harold Sidney
d. 1940 Rothermere, Harold Sidney Harmsworth
d. 1943 Roberts, Charles George Douglas, Sir

d. 1954 Doak, Bill (William Leopold)
d. 1954 Jones, Robert Edmond
d. 1956 Dorsey, Tommy (Thomas Francis)
d. 1961 Bridges, Styles
d. 1963 Galli-Curci, Amelita
d. 1967 Warner, Albert
d. 1968 Zweig, Arnold
d. 1970 Davis, Benjamin Oliver
d. 1971 Adonis, Joe
d. 1971 Day, Ned (Edward Gately)
d. 1971 Kempton, James Murray, Jr.
d. 1971 Kempton, Jean Goldschmidt
d. 1971 Young, Andrew
d. 1973 Haines, William
d. 1974 Connolly, Cyril Vernon
d. 1975 Pitz, Henry Clarence
d. 1980 Roberts, Rachel
d. 1981 Euwe, Max (Machgielis)
d. 1982 Harman, Hugh
d. 1984 Corena, Fernando
d. 1984 Lonergan, Bernard J F

November 27

b. 1701 Celsius, Anders
b. 1746 Livingston, Robert R
b. 1809 Kemble, Fanny (Frances Anne)
b. 1843 Vanderbilt, Cornelius
b. 1874 Beard, Charles Austin
b. 1874 Walter, Eugene
b. 1874 Weizmann, Chaim
b. 1878 Orpen, William
b. 1879 Genovese, Vito
b. 1884 DeCreeft, Jose
b. 1889 Hatch, Carl A
b. 1891 Salinas (y Serrano), Pedro
b. 1894 Matsushita, Konosuke
b. 1899 Abramson, Harold A(lexander)
b. 1900 Barzin, Leon Eugene
b. 1901 Husing, Ted
b. 1904 McNally, John Victor
b. 1906 Morton, (Henry) Digby
b. 1907 DeCamp, L(yon) Sprague
b. 1909 Agee, James Rufus
b. 1912 Merrick, David
b. 1914 Begle, Edward G(riffith)
b. 1915 Alessandro, Victor Nicholas
b. 1917 Smith, Bob
b. 1918 Beard, Dita Davis
b. 1921 Dubcek, Alexander
b. 1925 Boley, Forrest Irving
b. 1926 Thompson, Marshall
b. 1927 Rowling, Wallace Edward
b. 1927 Simon, William E(dward)
b. 1928 Klien, Walter
b. 1932 Aquino, Benigno Simeon, Jr.
b. 1932 Schecter, Jerrold
b. 1937 Sheehy, Gail Henion
b. 1939 Giusti, Dave (David John, Jr.)
b. 1940 Lee, Bruce
b. 1941 Rabbitt, Eddie (Edward Thomas)
b. 1942 Hendrix, Jimi (James Marshall)
b. 1944 DeVito, Danny Michael

b. 1944 Leland, "Mickey" (George
    Thomas)
b. 1957 Kennedy, Caroline Bouvier
d. 8 AD Horace
d. 1863 Davis, Sam(uel)
d. 1895 Dumas, Alexandre
d. 1901 Studebaker, Clement
d. 1922 Meynell, Alice
d. 1931 Bruce, David, Sir
d. 1934 Nelson, "Baby Face" (George)
d. 1948 Delaney, Jack
d. 1950 Braid, James
d. 1953 O'Neill, Eugene Gladstone
d. 1953 Powys, Theodore Francis
d. 1955 Honegger, Arthur
d. 1956 Kaempffert, Waldemar (Bernhard)
d. 1958 Rodzinski, Artur
d. 1959 Philipe, Gerard
d. 1960 Richberg, Donald R(andall)
d. 1971 Guyon, Joe
d. 1975 McWhirter, A(lan) Ross
d. 1976 Alessandro, Victor Nicholas
d. 1977 McClellan, John Little
d. 1978 Moscone, George Richard
d. 1979 Cavanagh, Jerry (Jerome Patrick)
d. 1981 Lenya, Lotte
d. 1982 Gordon, Steve
d. 1983 Furman, Roger
d. 1984 Duke, Robin (Anthony Hare)

November 28
b. 1628 Bunyan, John
b. 1632 Lully, Jean-Baptiste
b. 1729 Estaing, Charles Henri Hector,
    Comte d'
b. 1757 Blake, William
b. 1805 Stephens, John Lloyd
b. 1829 Rubinstein, Anton Gregorovitch
b. 1831 Mackay, John William
b. 1832 Stephen, Leslie, Sir
b. 1836 Martin, Homer Dodge
b. 1853 White, Helen Magill
b. 1865 Winter, Alice Vivian Ames
b. 1866 Bacon, Henry
b. 1866 Warfield, David
b. 1880 Blok, Aleksandr Aleksandrovich
b. 1881 Zweig, Stefan
b. 1889 Walker, Ralph Thomas
b. 1893 Downey, Fairfax Davis
b. 1894 Atkinson, (Justin) Brooks
b. 1894 Taggard, Genevieve
b. 1895 Iturbi, Jose
b. 1896 Black, Frank J.
b. 1900 Wigg, George (Edward Cecil)
b. 1901 Havighurst, Walter Edwin
b. 1901 Mountbatten, Edwina
b. 1902 Leclerc, Jacques-Philippe
b. 1904 Eastland, James Oliver
b. 1904 Mili, Gjon
b. 1904 Mitford, Nancy Freeman
b. 1907 Moravia, Alberto, pseud.
b. 1908 Levi-Strauss, Claude

b. 1909 Bampton, Rose Elizabeth
b. 1909 Bleeker, Sonia
b. 1912 Louis, Morris
b. 1916 Tregaskis, Richard William
b. 1918 L'Engle, Madeleine
b. 1924 Brutus, Dennis Vincent
b. 1925 Grahame, Gloria
b. 1926 Kops, Bernard
b. 1928 Costanza, "Midge" (Margaret)
b. 1928 Okun, Arthur Melvin
b. 1929 Gordy, Berry, Jr.
b. 1931 Ungerer, Tomi (Jean Thomas)
b. 1933 Lange, Hope Elise Ross
b. 1935 Stow, (Julian) Randolph
b. 1936 Hart, Gary Warren
b. 1942 Grogan, Emmett
b. 1942 Warfield, Paul Dryden
b. 1943 Newman, Randy
b. 1949 Godunov, Alexander (Boris
    Alexander)
b. 1952 Larrieu, Francie
b. 1955 Holladay, Terry Ann
b. 1958 Righetti, Dave (David Allan)
d. 1680 Bernini, Giovanni Lorenzo
d. 1694 Basho
d. 1698 Frontenac, Louis de
d. 1708 Tournefort, Joseph Pitton de
d. 1721 Cartouche, Louis Dominique
d. 1785 Whipple, William
d. 1794 Beccaria, Cesare
d. 1794 Steuben, Friedrich Wilhelm Ludolf
    Gerhard Augustin, Baron
d. 1794 VonSteuben, Friedrich Wilhelm
d. 1859 Irving, Washington
d. 1900 Skinner, Halcyon
d. 1921 Abdu'l-Baha
d. 1932 Van Rooy, Anton
d. 1933 Laughlin, James Laurence
d. 1938 McDougall, William
d. 1939 Naismith, James A
d. 1945 Davis, Dwight Filley
d. 1945 Fairfax, Beatrice, pseud.
d. 1947 Leclerc, Jacques-Philippe
d. 1954 Fermi, Enrico
d. 1959 DeErdely, Francis (Ferenc)
d. 1960 Wright, Richard
d. 1962 Wilhelmina
d. 1963 Silver, Abba Hillel
d. 1963 Wrather, William Embry
d. 1966 Giannini, Vittorio
d. 1968 Blyton, Enid Mary
d. 1972 Carmichael, James Vinson
d. 1972 Zirato, Bruno
d. 1976 Russell, Rosalind
d. 1979 Classen, Willie
d. 1979 Seagram, Joseph Edward Frowde
d. 1980 Ballantrae, Lord
d. 1980 Van Vleck, John Hasbrouck
d. 1981 Gimbel, Sophie Haas
d. 1984 Bell, Ricky Lynn
d. 1984 Speidel, Hans

b. 1923 Zimbalist, Efrem, Jr.
b. 1924 Chisholm, Shirley Anita St. Hill
b. 1924 Sherman, Allan
b. 1926 Schally, Andrew Victor
b. 1927 Crenna, Richard
b. 1928 Hall, Joe Beasman
b. 1928 Hecht, Chic
b. 1928 Scott, Norman
b. 1929 Clark, Dick (Richard Wagstaff)
b. 1929 Cooney, Joan Ganz
b. 1929 Wyman, Thomas Hunt
b. 1930 Liddy, G(eorge) Gordon
b. 1931 Walsh, Bill (William)
b. 1933 Procter, Barbara Gardner
b. 1935 Sachs, Samuel, II
b. 1936 Hoffman, Abbie (Abbott)
b. 1937 Guillaume, Robert
b. 1937 Stookey, (Noel) Paul
b. 1937 Threlkeld, Richard D
b. 1939 Keyworth, George Albert
b. 1940 Phillips, Kevin Price
b. 1943 Malick, Terence (Terry)
b. 1945 Lupu, Radu
b. 1947 Mamet, David
b. 1950 Westphal, Paul Douglas
b. 1952 Patinkin, Mandy
b. 1955 Idol, Billy
b. 1959 Hanika, Sylvia
b. 1962 Jackson, "Bo" (Vincent Edward)
d. 1603 Gilbert, William
d. 1654 Selden, John
d. 1694 Malpighi, Marcello
d. 1786 Galvez, Bernardo de
d. 1852 Booth, Junius Brutus
d. 1852 Phelps, Elizabeth Stuart
d. 1862 Knowles, James Sheridan
d. 1896 Steinway, Henry Engelhard
d. 1900 Wilde, Oscar Fingal O'Flahertie
    Wills
d. 1930 Jones, Mary Harris
d. 1931 Walters, Henry
d. 1932 Melchers, Gari
d. 1942 Jones, Buck
d. 1944 Fall, Albert Bacon
d. 1945 Ficke, Arthur Davidson
d. 1947 Lubitsch, Ernst
d. 1952 Kenny, Sister Elizabeth
d. 1953 Picabia, Francis
d. 1954 Furtwangler, Wilhelm
d. 1957 Gigli, Beniamino
d. 1963 Baker, Phil
d. 1963 Hatlo, Jimmy
d. 1964 Redman, Don
d. 1967 Kavanagh, Patrick
d. 1972 Mackenzie, Compton (Edward
    Montague, Sir)
d. 1972 McElroy, Neil Hosler
d. 1973 Yarnell, Bruce
d. 1975 Hill, Graham (Norman Graham)
d. 1975 Paul, Lester Warner
d. 1975 Pirandello, Fausto

d. 1977 Rattigan, Terence Mervyn
d. 1979 Gilpin, Laura
d. 1979 Grenfell, Joyce Irene
d. 1979 Kuter, Laurence S(herman)
d. 1979 Marx, "Zeppo" (Herbert)
d. 1982 Merrill, Henry Tindall
d. 1983 Llewellyn, Richard

DECEMBER

b. 1542 Mary, Queen of Scots
b. 1639 Racine, Jean Baptiste
b. 1841 Edmonds, Emma E
b. 1844 Coffin, Charles Albert
b. 1873 Mantle, (Robert) Burns
b. 1875 Wallace, Edgar
b. 1877 Nomura, Kichisaburo
b. 1899 Ulreich, Nura Woodson
b. 1915 Piaf, Edith
b. 1916 Ben Bella, Ahmed
b. 1948 Bangs, Lester
b. 1965 Witt, Katarina
d. 1556 Pontormo, Jacopo da
d. 1608 Dee, John
d. 1610 Elsheimer, Adam
d. 1957 Campbell, Walter Stanley
d. 1970 Stauffer, Charles Albert
d. 1972 Cornell, Joseph
d. 1973 O'Shea, Michael
d. 1978 Dent, Alan Holmes
d. 1978 Winston, Harry
d. 1980 Coulter, John William
d. 1985 Austin, John Paul
d. 1985 Grimes, Burleigh Arland
December 1
b. 1580 Peiresc, Nicholas-Claude Fabri de
b. 1729 Sarti, Giuseppe
b. 1765 Brown, William Hill
b. 1784 Castil-Blaze, Francois-Joseph
b. 1823 Reyer, (Louis) Ernest (Etienne)
b. 1826 Mahone, William
b. 1833 Andrews, Jane
b. 1844 Alexandra Caroline Mary Charlotte
b. 1847 Ladd-Franklin, Christine
b. 1847 Moore, Julia A Davis
b. 1863 Herford, Oliver
b. 1869 Sterling, George
b. 1872 Swope, Gerard
b. 1876 Clayton, Herbert
b. 1876 Creel, George
b. 1877 Beach, Rex Ellingwood
b. 1879 Bryant, Lane
b. 1884 Schmidt-Rottluf, Karl
b. 1885 Hunt, Frazier
b. 1886 Stout, Rex Todhunter
b. 1893 Toller, Ernst
b. 1896 Henderson, Ray
b. 1896 Shutta, Ethel
b. 1897 Ritchard, Cyril
b. 1899 Briggs, Ellis Ormsbee
b. 1899 Welch, Robert Henry Winborne,
    Jr.

b. 1901 Moore, Grace
b. 1902 Crittenden, Christopher
b. 1904 Boyle, Tony (William Anthony)
b. 1906 Sommers, Ben
b. 1910 Markova, Alicia
b. 1911 Alston, Walter Emmons
b. 1912 Yamasaki, Minoru
b. 1914 Martin, Mary
b. 1915 Johnston, Johnny
b. 1916 Stoutenburg, Adrien Pearl
b. 1917 Marion, "Slats" (Martin Whiteford)
b. 1919 Gilbert, Alfred Carlton, Jr.
b. 1920 Rohmer, Eric, pseud.
b. 1923 Turner, Stansfield
b. 1926 McLerie, Allyn Ann
b. 1927 Beard, Ralph
b. 1928 Michell, Keith
b. 1929 Doyle, David Fitzgerald
b. 1929 Shawn, Dick
b. 1931 Sovern, Michael I(ra)
b. 1933 Verdy, Violette
b. 1935 Allen, Woody
b. 1936 Rawls, Lou(is Allen)
b. 1939 Lennon, Dianne
b. 1939 Trevino, Lee Buck
b. 1940 Pryor, Richard Franklin Lennox Thomas
b. 1941 Wilson, Dennis
b. 1944 Bloom, Eric
b. 1945 Densmore, John
b. 1945 Midler, Bette
b. 1946 O'Sullivan, Gilbert
b. 1949 Brett, Jan Churchill
b. 1949 Foster, George Arthur
b. 1958 Tilton, Charlene
d. 1135 Henry I
d. 1455 Ghiberti, Lorenzo
d. 1701 Clarke, Jeremiah
d. 1797 Wolcott, Oliver, Sr.
d. 1914 Mahan, Alfred Thayer
d. 1920 Rebikov, Vladimir Ivanovich
d. 1935 Mayr, Richard
d. 1940 Richman, Charles
d. 1947 Crowley, Aleister (Edward Alexander)
d. 1948 Noyes, Frank B
d. 1952 Orlando, Vittorio Emanuele
d. 1954 Rose, Fred
d. 1958 Wilkins, George Hubert, Sir
d. 1964 Haldane, J(ohn) B(urdon) S(anderson)
d. 1970 Pool, David de Sola
d. 1972 Segni, Antonio
d. 1973 Ben-Gurion, David
d. 1974 Lincoln, G(eorge) Gould
d. 1974 Spottswood, Stephen Gill
d. 1975 Fox, "Nellie" (Jacob Nelson)
d. 1975 Halsted, Anna Eleanor Roosevelt
d. 1975 Kenny, Nick

d. 1975 Mayer, Edward Newton, Jr.
d. 1980 Irvin, Robert W

December 2
b. 1728 Galiani, Ferdinando
b. 1736 Montgomery, Richard
b. 1742 Scheele, Karl Wilhelm
b. 1760 Breckinridge, John
b. 1825 Pedro II
b. 1840 Cobden-Sanderson, Thomas James
b. 1859 Seurat, Georges Pierre
b. 1863 Ringling, Charles
b. 1866 Burleigh, Harry Thacker
b. 1868 Jammes, Francis
b. 1878 Candler, Charles Howard
b. 1883 Kazantzakis, Nikos
b. 1884 Draper, Ruth
b. 1889 Althouse, Paul Shearer
b. 1891 Dix, Otto
b. 1891 Merida, Carlos
b. 1893 Gaxton, William
b. 1895 William, Warren
b. 1896 Zhukov, Georgi Konstantinovich
b. 1897 Hoving, Walter
b. 1899 Adler, Peter Herman
b. 1899 Barbirolli, John, Sir
b. 1899 Benary-Isbert, Margot
b. 1904 Woods, Donald
b. 1906 Goldmark, Peter Carl
b. 1906 Harrar, J(acob) George
b. 1908 Gardner, Hy
b. 1910 Lynes, Joseph Russell, Jr.
b. 1910 Paige, Robert (John Arthur)
b. 1912 Sukman, Harry
b. 1914 Sauter, Eddie (Edward Ernest)
b. 1915 Green, Adolph
b. 1915 Hearst, Randolph Apperson
b. 1916 Bentley, John
b. 1916 Hearst, David W
b. 1916 Ventura, Charlie
b. 1917 Stone, Ezra (Chaim)
b. 1918 DeLugg, Milton
b. 1922 Diggs, Charles Coles, Jr.
b. 1924 Craig, William
b. 1924 Haig, Alexander Meigs, Jr.
b. 1924 Riklis, Mishulam
b. 1925 Harris, Julie
b. 1928 Demus, Joreg
b. 1931 Calder, Nigel David Ritchie
b. 1931 Meese, Edwin, III
b. 1935 Sample, Bill
b. 1938 Valerio, James Robert
b. 1940 Chapin, Dwight Lee
b. 1955 Christopher, Dennis
b. 1958 Gardner, Randy
b. 1960 Savage, Rick
d. 1594 Mercator, Gerhardus
d. 1812 Sacagawea
d. 1814 Sade, Marquis (Donatien Alphonse Francoise) de
d. 1859 Brown, John
d. 1863 Pierce, Jane Means

d. 1892 Gould, Jay (Jason)
d. 1893 Cushman, Pauline
d. 1894 Thompson, John S D
d. 1918 Rostand, Edmond Alexis
d. 1919 Frick, Henry Clay
d. 1921 Lincoln, Mary Johnson Bailey
d. 1931 Indy, Paul (Marie Theodore
     Vincent d')
d. 1933 Breasted, James Henry
d. 1935 Thomas, Martha Carey
d. 1937 Smith, Joe
d. 1939 Powys, Llewelyn
d. 1943 Dashwood, Elizabeth Monica
d. 1944 Lhevinne, Josef
d. 1944 Marinetti, Filippo Tommaso
d. 1949 Ammons, Albert C
d. 1950 Lipatti, Dinu
d. 1963 Sabu
d. 1964 York, Sergeant (Alvin Cullum)
d. 1966 Cooper, Giles (Stannus)
d. 1967 Spellman, Francis Joseph
d. 1968 Voroshilov, Kliment Efremovich
d. 1969 Potter, Stephen
d. 1972 Limon, Jose Arcadio
d. 1973 Haydn, Hiram Collins
d. 1975 Maserati, Ernesto
d. 1978 Dickinson, Edwin W
d. 1980 Gary, Romain
d. 1980 Gordon-Walker of Leyton, Patrick
     Chrestien Gordon-Walker, Baron
d. 1981 Harrison, Wallace Kirkman
d. 1981 Kay, Hershy
d. 1981 Oliver, James A(rthur)
d. 1982 Bugas, John Stephen
d. 1982 Feldman, Marty
d. 1982 Sackheim, Maxwell Byron
d. 1983 D'Orsay, Fifi
d. 1984 Hauser, Gayelord
d. 1984 Sukman, Harry
d. 1985 Larkin, Philip

December 3
b. 1478 Castiglione, Baldassare, Conte
b. 1755 Stuart, Gilbert Charles
b. 1795 Hill, Rowland, Sir
b. 1826 McClellan, George Brinton
b. 1838 Abbe, Cleveland
b. 1842 Pillsbury, Charles Alfred
b. 1842 Richards, Ellen Henrietta Swallow
b. 1845 Bradley, Henry
b. 1857 Conrad, Joseph
b. 1860 Moore, John Bassett
b. 1874 Lhevinne, Josef
b. 1879 Nagai, Sokichi
b. 1883 Webern, Anton von
b. 1884 Prasad, Rajendra
b. 1885 Lasker, Edward
b. 1889 Bern, Paul
b. 1892 Adler, Julius Ochs
b. 1895 Freud, Anna
b. 1897 Gropper, William
b. 1903 Holifield, Chet

b. 1907 McNeill, Don(ald Thomas)
b. 1908 Balchin, Nigel Marlin
b. 1912 Boswell, Connee
b. 1913 Lichine, Alexis
b. 1914 Parks, Larry
b. 1915 Hodgson, James Day
b. 1920 Canfield, Francis X(avier)
b. 1921 Doar, John
b. 1922 Nykvist, Sven Vilhem
b. 1923 Callas, Maria
b. 1923 Fears, Tom (Thomas Jesse)
b. 1923 Guarrera, Frank
b. 1924 Backus, John
b. 1926 Schoneberg, Sheldon Clyde
b. 1927 Curtin, Phyllis Smith
b. 1927 Husky, Ferlin
b. 1927 Wiggins, Charles Edward
b. 1930 Godard, Jean Luc
b. 1930 Williams, Andy
b. 1931 Martin, John
b. 1932 Morgan, Jaye P
b. 1934 Gorbatko, Viktor Vasiliyevich
b. 1937 Allison, Bobby (Robert Arthur)
b. 1940 Swift, Elizabeth Ann
b. 1945 Dean, Laura
b. 1949 Osbourne, "Ozzie" (John)
b. 1951 Brewer, Jim
b. 1951 Mears, Rick Ravon
b. 1952 Roland, Duane
b. 1956 Amati, Nicolo (Nicolaus)
b. 1956 Bochner, Hart
b. 1957 Jordan, Kathy (Kathryn)
b. 1960 Ramsey, Mike (Michael Allen)
d. 1592 Farnese, Alessandro
d. 1815 Carroll, John
d. 1854 Ritchie, Thomas
d. 1905 Bartlett, John
d. 1910 Eddy, Mary Baker Morse
d. 1926 Ringling, Charles
d. 1936 Ringling, John
d. 1937 Jozsef, Attila
d. 1940 Gordon, C Henry
d. 1941 Sinding, Christian
d. 1949 Barry, Philip
d. 1949 Ouspenskaya, Maria
d. 1963 Bentley, Elizabeth Terrill
d. 1978 Still, William Grant
d. 1981 Knott, Walter
d. 1983 Zablocki, Clement John

December 4
b. 34 Persius
b. 1584 Cotton, John
b. 1713 Gozzi, Gaspare
b. 1730 Moultrie, William
b. 1795 Carlyle, Thomas
b. 1835 Butler, Samuel
b. 1858 Greenwood, Chester
b. 1860 Hormel, George Albert
b. 1861 Russell, Lillian
b. 1865 Gulick, Luther Halsey
b. 1866 Kandinsky, Wassily

d. 1654 Sarasin, Jean Francois
d. 1758 Fasch, Johann Friedrich
d. 1784 Wheatley, Phillis
d. 1791 Mozart, Wolfgang Amadeus
d. 1870 Dumas, Alexandre
d. 1891 Pedro II
d. 1916 Richter, Hans
d. 1925 Reymont, Wladyslaw Stanislaw
d. 1926 Monet, Claude
d. 1931 Lindsay, (Nicholas) Vachel
d. 1940 Kubelik, Jan
d. 1945 Lang, William Cosmo Gordon, Baron
d. 1951 Jackson, Joe (Joseph Jefferson)
d. 1960 Teague, Walter Dorwin
d. 1962 Wallant, Edward Lewis
d. 1963 Lehman, Herbert Henry
d. 1965 Erlanger, Joseph
d. 1968 Clark, Fred
d. 1969 Dornier, Claude
d. 1973 Cannon, Jimmy (James J)
d. 1973 Watson-Watt, Robert Alexander, Sir
d. 1974 Germi, Pietro
d. 1974 Whitney, Richard
d. 1974 Wightman, Hazel Virginia Hotchkiss
d. 1975 Green, Constance Windsor McLaughlin
d. 1977 Gaud, William Steen, Jr.
d. 1978 Brown, George Scratchley
d. 1979 Delaunay-Terk, Sonia
d. 1980 Halberstam, Michael Joseph
d. 1980 McLean, Robert
d. 1983 Aldrich, Robert
d. 1983 Brown, Charlie
d. 1983 Morton, (Henry) Digby

December 6
b. 1732 Hastings, Warren
b. 1778 Gay-Lussac, Joseph Louis
b. 1794 Lablache, Luigi
b. 1803 Moodie, Susanna
b. 1804 Schroder-Devrient, Wilhelmine
b. 1806 DuPrez, Gilbert
b. 1833 Mosby, John Singleton
b. 1859 Sothern, Edward Hugh
b. 1863 Hall, Charles Martin
b. 1867 Bitter, Karl Theodore Francis
b. 1869 Lavigne, "Kid" (George)
b. 1872 Hart, William Surrey
b. 1876 Duesenberg, Frederick S
b. 1878 Braithwaite, William Stanley Beaumont
b. 1878 Pillsbury, John Sargent
b. 1883 Braniff, Thomas Elmer
b. 1884 Kroll, Leon
b. 1886 Kilmer, Joyce (Alfred Joyce)
b. 1887 Fontanne, Lynn
b. 1889 Lipman, Clara
b. 1889 Woodruff, Robert Winship
b. 1892 Sitwell, Osbert, Sir

b. 1893 Little, Lou(is)
b. 1893 Warner, Sylvia Townsend
b. 1896 Gershwin, Ira
b. 1898 Eisenstaedt, Alfred
b. 1898 Myrdal, Karl Gunnar
b. 1898 Shumlin, Herman Elliott
b. 1899 Conlan, "Jocko" (John Bertrand)
b. 1899 Mannes, Leopold Damrosch
b. 1904 Curie, Eve
b. 1904 Landi, Elissa
b. 1904 Thackrey, Russell I
b. 1905 Braddock, James J
b. 1905 DuPont, Clifford Walter
b. 1905 Yates, Elizabeth
b. 1906 Moorehead, Agnes
b. 1906 Spychalski, Marian
b. 1907 Ewen, David
b. 1908 Nelson, "Baby Face" (George)
b. 1909 Oboler, Arch
b. 1911 Berger, Samuel David
b. 1913 Holm, Eleanor
b. 1916 Eldjarn, Kristjan
b. 1920 Brubeck, Dave (David Warren)
b. 1920 Dimmock, Peter
b. 1921 Graham, Otto Everett
b. 1922 McGivern, William Peter
b. 1923 Bennett, John Charles
b. 1924 Cox, Wally (Wallace Maynard)
b. 1924 Foster, Susanna
b. 1927 Mink, Patsy Takemoto
b. 1932 King, Don(ald)
b. 1935 Epstein, Edward Jay
b. 1935 Mathews, Forrest David
b. 1935 Van, Bobby
b. 1940 Edlund, Richard
b. 1941 Perkins, (Walter) Ray
b. 1941 Speck, Richard Franklin
b. 1945 Bowa, Larry (Lawrence Robert)
b. 1948 Nickles, Donald Lee
b. 1948 Rosberg, Keke
b. 1953 Hulce, Thomas
b. 1953 Stones, Dwight
d. 345 Nicholas, Saint
d. 1718 Rowe, Nicholas
d. 1771 Morgagni, Giovanni Battista
d. 1777 Jussieu, Bernard de
d. 1779 Chardin, Jean Baptiste Simeon
d. 1867 Pacini, Giovanni
d. 1879 Bigelow, Erastus Brigham
d. 1882 Trollope, Anthony
d. 1889 Davis, Jefferson
d. 1892 Siemens, (Ernst) Werner von
d. 1902 Palmer, Alice Elvira Freeman
d. 1904 Blaikie, William
d. 1916 Tosti, Francesco Paola
d. 1924 Porter, Gene Stratton
d. 1939 Dalmores, Charles
d. 1942 Rusie, Amos William
d. 1948 Tough, Dave
d. 1949 Ledbetter, Huddie
d. 1951 Rothier, Leon

b. 1881 Colum, Padraic
b. 1885 Roberts, Kenneth
b. 1886 Rivera, Diego
b. 1888 Kimball, Fiske
b. 1889 Allen, Hervey (William Hervey)
b. 1890 Martinu, Bohuslav
b. 1894 Segar, Elzie Crisler
b. 1894 Thurber, James Grover
b. 1897 Tunis, Edwin Burdett
b. 1898 Burchard, John Ely
b. 1899 Qualen, John Mandt
b. 1899 Supervia, Conchita
b. 1900 Ingersoll, Ralph McAllister
b. 1901 Urrutia Lleo, Manuel
b. 1902 Jacoby, Oswald
b. 1903 Shera, Jesse Hauk
b. 1903 Simpson, Adele Smithline
b. 1904 Abrams, Harry Nathan
b. 1906 Llewellyn, Richard
b. 1908 Volpe, John Anthony
b. 1913 Schwartz, Delmore
b. 1914 Garrigue, Jean
b. 1917 Cantrick, Robert
b. 1920 DiCamerino, Roberta
b. 1920 Souzay, Gerard
b. 1921 Morgan, Terence
b. 1922 Freud, Lucian
b. 1922 Ritchie, Jean
b. 1925 Davis, Sammy, Jr.
b. 1928 Caldwell, John Charles
b. 1930 Crosby, Percy
b. 1930 Schell, Maximilian
b. 1932 Browning, James Louis
b. 1933 Wilson, "Flip" (Clerow)
b. 1937 MacArthur, James
b. 1938 Krause, Bernie (Bernard Leo)
b. 1939 Galway, James
b. 1941 Berenson, "Red" (Gordon Arthur)
b. 1943 Morrison, Jim (James Douglas)
b. 1946 Rubinstein, John
b. 1949 Gordon, Mary Catherine
b. 1953 Basinger, Kim
b. 1958 Rogers, George
b. 1959 Junior, E J (Ester James, III)
d. 1681 Ter Borch, Gerard
d. 1792 Laurens, Henry
d. 1830 Constant de Rebeque, (Henri) Benjamin
d. 1831 Hoban, James
d. 1853 Chickering, Jonas
d. 1859 DeQuincey, Thomas
d. 1885 Vanderbilt, William Henry
d. 1903 Spencer, Herbert
d. 1913 Simmons, Franklin
d. 1919 Weir, Julian Alden
d. 1939 Schelling, Ernest Henry
d. 1942 Kahn, Albert
d. 1944 Cregar, Laird (Samuel)
d. 1954 George, Gladys
d. 1958 Speaker, Tris(tram E)
d. 1964 Crosby, Percy

d. 1964 Marks, Simon
d. 1967 Mills, John
d. 1970 Poor, Henry Varnum
d. 1971 Widener, George D
d. 1977 Solomon, Samuel Joseph
d. 1978 Cantwell, Robert Emmett
d. 1978 Meir, Golda
d. 1980 Lennon, John Winston
d. 1982 Mayer, Norman D
d. 1982 Robbins, Marty
d. 1983 Holyoake, Keith Jacka, Sir
d. 1983 Pickens, "Slim"
d. 1984 Adler, Luther (Lutha)
d. 1985 Wambsganss, Bill (William Adolph)

December 9
b. 1561 Sandys, Edwin Sir
b. 1594 Gustavus Adolphus
b. 1608 Milton, John
b. 1848 Harris, Joel Chandler
b. 1864 Homer, Sidney
b. 1871 Kelley, Joe (Joseph James)
b. 1886 Birdseye, Clarence Frank
b. 1889 Kolehmainen, Hannes
b. 1893 Brett, George Platt, Jr.
b. 1895 Ibarruri, Dolores
b. 1897 Gingold, Hermione Ferdinanda
b. 1898 Kelly, Emmett
b. 1899 Adams, Leonie Fuller
b. 1902 Beebe, Lucius Morris
b. 1902 Butler of Saffron Walden, Richard Austen, Baron
b. 1904 Kronenberger, Louis
b. 1905 Trumbo, Dalton
b. 1906 Hopper, Grace Brewster Murray
b. 1906 Martin, Freddy
b. 1909 Fairbanks, Douglas, Jr.
b. 1911 Cobb, Lee J (Leo Jacob)
b. 1911 Crawford, Broderick
b. 1912 O'Neill, "Tip" (Thomas Philip)
b. 1914 Turnesa, Jim
b. 1915 Schwarzkopf, Elisabeth
b. 1916 Douglas, Kirk
b. 1921 Ellis, Harry Bearse
b. 1922 Foxx, Redd
b. 1925 Merrill, Dina
b. 1926 Dominguin, Luis Miguel
b. 1928 Van Patten, Dick
b. 1929 Cassavetes, John
b. 1929 Hawke, Bob (Robert James Lee)
b. 1930 Henry, Buck
b. 1930 Mejia Victores, Oscar Humberto
b. 1931 Hagan, Cliff(ord Oldham)
b. 1931 Reynolds, William
b. 1932 Byrd, Donald
b. 1932 Hartack, Billy (William, Jr.)
b. 1933 Moody, Orville
b. 1935 Bell, Steve (Stephen Scott)
b. 1941 Bridges, "Beau" (Lloyd Vernet, III)
b. 1942 Butkus, Dick (Richard J)

d. 1976 Lisagor, Peter Irvin
d. 1977 Rupp, Adolph F
d. 1979 Blodgett, Katherine Burr
d. 1979 Dvorak, Ann
d. 1979 Sheen, Fulton John, Bishop
d. 1980 Benedictos I
d. 1981 Kieran, John Francis
d. 1981 Marlowe, Sylvia
d. 1981 Wurf, Jerry (Jerome)
d. 1982 Gosden, Freeman Fisher
d. 1984 Teagarden, Charles

December 11
b. 1668 Zeno, Apostolo
b. 1781 Brewster, David, Sir
b. 1803 Berlioz, Louis Hector
b. 1810 Musset, Alfred de
b. 1822 Cummins, George David
b. 1843 Koch, Robert
b. 1854 Radbourn, "Old Hoss" (Charles Gardner)
b. 1863 Cannon, Annie Jump
b. 1867 Pratt, Bela Lyon
b. 1870 Weinman, Adolph A
b. 1874 Kraft, James Lewis
b. 1876 Comstock, Ada Louise
b. 1880 Carter, Amon Giles
b. 1882 Born, Max
b. 1882 LaGuardia, Fiorello Henry
b. 1886 McLaglen, Victor
b. 1889 Knott, Walter
b. 1892 Adams, Harriet Stratemeyer
b. 1892 Larson, John Augustus
b. 1894 Dowling, Eddie (Edward)
b. 1894 Lauri-Volpi, Giacoma
b. 1897 Van Dusen, Henry Pitney
b. 1901 Cabot, John Moors
b. 1903 Jensen, Alfred Julio
b. 1903 Mumford, Lawrence Quincy
b. 1904 Woolsey, Janette
b. 1905 Roland, Gilbert
b. 1908 Carter, Elliott Cook, Jr.
b. 1909 Seaton, Frederick Andrew
b. 1913 Marais, Jean
b. 1913 Ponti, Carlo
b. 1918 Solzhenitsyn, Aleksandr Isayevich
b. 1922 Westermann, H(orace) C(lifford)
b. 1923 Blair, Betsy
b. 1923 Turner, Morrie
b. 1924 Blanchard, "Doc" (Felix Anthony)
b. 1924 Windsor, Marie
b. 1925 Dalvit, Lewis David, Jr.
b. 1926 Barnet, Sylvan M, Jr.
b. 1926 Thornton, Willie Mae
b. 1930 Trintignant, Jean-Louis Xavier
b. 1931 Moreno, Rita
b. 1931 Rajneesh, Bhagwan Shree
b. 1931 Rothenberg, Jerome
b. 1939 Hayden, Tom (Thomas Emmett)
b. 1940 Gates, David
b. 1941 Baucus, Max Sieben
b. 1943 Kerry, John F

b. 1943 Mills, Donna
b. 1944 Lee, Brenda
b. 1945 Garr, Teri
b. 1946 George, Lynda Day
b. 1950 Onassis, Christina
b. 1952 Seidelman, Susan
b. 1953 Armstrong, Bess (Elizabeth Key)
b. 1954 Jackson, Jermaine La Jaune
b. 1962 Williams, Curtis
d. 1513 Pinturicchio
d. 1718 Charles XII
d. 1857 Castil-Blaze, Francois-Joseph
d. 1873 Beadle, William
d. 1880 Winchester, Oliver Fisher
d. 1883 Doyle, Richard
d. 1883 Mario, Giovanni Matteo
d. 1917 Bowell, Mackenzie, Sir
d. 1939 Walgreen, Charles Rudolph
d. 1941 Conrad, Frank
d. 1949 Berryman, Clifford Kennedy
d. 1951 Addison, Christopher, Viscount
d. 1953 Coates, Albert
d. 1955 Merrill, Frank Dow
d. 1959 Bottomley, Jim (James Leroy)
d. 1964 Cooke, Sam
d. 1964 Kilbride, Percy
d. 1967 Bigelow, Henry Bryant
d. 1967 DeSabata, Victor
d. 1968 Sulzberger, Arthur Hays
d. 1974 Hadley, Reed
d. 1980 Bergen, John Joseph
d. 1980 Lesage, Jean
d. 1980 Orwell, Sonia
d. 1981 Kaiser, Edgar Fosburgh
d. 1982 Miner, Worthington C
d. 1984 Ehricke, Krafft Arnold

December 12
b. 1745 Jay, John
b. 1747 Seward, Anna
b. 1786 Marcy, William Learned
b. 1805 Garrison, William Lloyd
b. 1805 Wells, Henry
b. 1821 Flaubert, Gustave
b. 1837 Green, John Richard
b. 1849 Vanderbilt, William Kissam
b. 1863 Munch, Edvard
b. 1864 Brisbane, Arthur
b. 1864 More, Paul Elmer
b. 1866 Parker, George Swinnerton
b. 1868 George, Stefan Anton
b. 1868 Milburn, Frank Pierce
b. 1871 Carr, Emily
b. 1873 Ridge, Lola
b. 1875 Rundstedt, Karl Rudolf Gerd von
b. 1878 Crothers, Rachel
b. 1879 Crews, Laura Hope
b. 1881 Warner, Harry Morris
b. 1883 Sterrett, Cliff
b. 1887 Jones, Robert Edmond
b. 1892 Wright, John Lloyd
b. 1893 Robinson, Edward G

b. 1933 Conway, "Tim" (Thomas Daniel)
b. 1934 Zanuck, Richard Darryl
b. 1935 Koren, Edward Benjamin
b. 1936 Aga Khan IV
b. 1941 Davidson, John
b. 1943 Jenkins, Ferguson Arthur
b. 1947 Garver, Kathy
b. 1953 Gainey, Bob (Robert Michael)
b. 1954 Anderson, John
b. 1959 Whitaker, Johnny
d. 1204 Maimonides, Moses
d. 1466 Donatello
d. 1784 Johnson, Samuel
d. 1843 Hull, Isaac
d. 1852 Wright, Frances (Fanny)
d. 1861 Albert, Prince
d. 1881 Quidor, John
d. 1924 Gompers, Samuel
d. 1932 Holland, William Jacob
d. 1945 Grese, Irma
d. 1959 Johnson, Charlie (Charles Wright)
d. 1960 Thomas, John Charles
d. 1961 Moses, "Grandma" (Anna Mary Robertson)
d. 1962 Sokolsky, George E
d. 1969 Spruance, Raymond Ames
d. 1972 Hartley, Leslie Poles
d. 1977 Petrie, Charles Alexander, Sir
d. 1978 Johnson, Herbert Fisk
d. 1981 Markham, "Pigmeat" (Dewey M)
d. 1983 Renault, Mary, pseud.
d. 1983 Schmemann, Alexander
d. 1985 Russell, Donald Joseph

December 14
b. 1503 Nostradamus
b. 1546 Brahe, Tyge
b. 1610 Teniers, David, the Younger
b. 1775 Chase, Philander
b. 1794 Corning, Erastus
b. 1824 Puvis de Chavannes, Pierre Cecile
b. 1847 Lassale, Jean
b. 1866 Fry, Roger Eliot
b. 1872 Doreste, Marion
b. 1882 Christie, John
b. 1884 Cowl, Jane
b. 1885 Pemberton, Brock
b. 1895 Eluard, Paul
b. 1895 George VI
b. 1896 Doolittle, James Harold
b. 1896 Howe, Edmund Perry
b. 1896 Markey, Lucille (Parker) Wright
b. 1897 Schuschnigg, Kurt von
b. 1897 Smith, Margaret Chase
b. 1897 Thill, Georges
b. 1898 Cowles, John, Sr.
b. 1901 Cochet, Henri
b. 1901 Michalowski, Kazimierz
b. 1901 Paul I
b. 1906 Soby, James Thrall
b. 1909 Tatum, Edward Lawrie

b. 1911 Jones, "Spike" (Lindsay Armstrong)
b. 1914 Amsterdam, Morey
b. 1914 Carstens, Karl Walter
b. 1914 Tureck, Rosalyn
b. 1915 Dailey, Dan
b. 1916 Priscilla of Boston
b. 1918 Aubrey, James Thomas, Jr.
b. 1919 Jackson, Shirley
b. 1920 Cary, Frank Taylor
b. 1923 McNair, Robert Evander
b. 1925 Jones, "Toothpick" (Samuel)
b. 1927 Feldman, Alvin Lindbergh
b. 1932 Lane, Abbe
b. 1932 Rich, Charlie (Charles Allan)
b. 1935 Remick, Lee
b. 1936 Bach, Bert Coates
b. 1938 Brand, Stewart
b. 1939 Davis, Ernie (Ernest R)
b. 1940 Schlussel, Mark Edward
b. 1942 Rosenberg, Sharon
b. 1946 Duke, Patty (Anna Marie)
b. 1946 Gandhi, Sanjay
b. 1946 Smith, Stan(ley Roger)
b. 1949 Buckner, Bill (William Joseph)
b. 1949 Williams, Cliff
b. 1954 Andersen, Ib Steen
d. 1591 John of the Cross, Saint
d. 1799 Washington, George
d. 1806 Breckinridge, John
d. 1861 Marschner, Heinrich
d. 1872 Kensett, John Frederick
d. 1902 Grant, Julia Dent
d. 1905 Haupt, Herman
d. 1944 Velez, Lupe
d. 1945 Baring, Maurice
d. 1947 Baldwin of Bewdley, Stanley Baldwin, Earl
d. 1947 Fyffe, Will
d. 1953 Rawlings, Marjorie Kinnan
d. 1959 Spencer, Stanley, Sir
d. 1960 Ratoff, Gregory
d. 1963 Washington, Dinah
d. 1964 Bendix, William
d. 1966 Felton, Verna
d. 1966 Whorf, Richard
d. 1968 Klose, Margarete
d. 1970 Slim, William Joseph
d. 1972 Berman, Eugene
d. 1974 Lippmann, Walter
d. 1975 Treacher, Arthur
d. 1977 Stulberg, Louis
d. 1978 Madariaga (y Rojo), Salvador de
d. 1980 Howard, Elston Gene
d. 1981 Benchley, Nathaniel Goddard
d. 1984 Aleixandre, Vicente
d. 1985 Maris, Roger Eugene

December 15
b. 1734 Romney, George
b. 1832 Eiffel, Alexandre Gustave
b. 1834 Young, Charles Augustus

d. 1863 Buford, John
d. 1890 Terry, Alfred Howe
d. 1897 Daudet, Alphonse Marie Leon
d. 1921 Saint-Saens, (Charles) Camille
d. 1922 Ben-Yehuda, Eliezer
d. 1928 Wylie, Elinor Hoyt
d. 1933 Chambers, Robert W
d. 1933 Vance, Louis Joseph
d. 1938 Murchison, Kenneth MacKenzie
d. 1940 Hamilton, Billy (William Robert)
d. 1947 Sodero, Cesare
d. 1951 Dix, Dorothy, pseud.
d. 1958 Corum, Martene Windsor
d. 1962 Dale, Chester
d. 1964 Davis, Phil
d. 1965 Maugham, William Somerset
d. 1965 Schipa, Tito
d. 1970 Lewis, Oscar
d. 1974 Pierce, Edward Allen
d. 1977 Schippers, Thomas
d. 1978 Buzhardt, J(oseph) Fred, Jr.
d. 1979 Chapman, Gilbert Whipple
d. 1980 Fisher, Welthy (Blakesley
    Honsinger)
d. 1980 Sanders, "Colonel" (Harland
    David)
d. 1981 Struss, Karl
d. 1982 Chapman, (Anthony) Colin (Bruce)
d. 1982 Hubbard, Orville Liscum
d. 1984 Prestopino, George

December 17
b. 1734 Floyd, William
b. 1749 Cimarosa, Domenico
b. 1760 Gannett, Deborah Sampson
b. 1760 Sampson, Deborah
b. 1778 Davy, Humphrey, Sir
b. 1797 Henry, Joseph
b. 1807 Whittier, John Greenleaf
b. 1824 King, Thomas Starr
b. 1830 Goncourt, Jules Alfred Huot de
b. 1853 Tree, Herbert Beerbohm
b. 1873 Ford, Ford Madox
b. 1873 Goldin, Horace
b. 1874 King, William Lyon Mackenzie
b. 1883 Raimu
b. 1884 Peirce, Waldo
b. 1884 Uttley, Alice Jane Taylor
b. 1894 Fiedler, Arthur
b. 1894 Kofoed, Jack (John C)
b. 1896 Biddle, Anthony
b. 1899 Paul, Lester Warner
b. 1900 Paxinou, Katina
b. 1903 Caldwell, Erskine Preston
b. 1904 Cadmus, Paul
b. 1904 Lonergan, Bernard J F
b. 1905 McLarnin, Jimmy
b. 1905 Verissimo, Erico Lopes
b. 1906 Martin, William McChesney, Jr.
b. 1908 Ashton-Warner, Sylvia Constance
b. 1908 Libby, Willard Frank
b. 1910 Oliver, Sy (Melvin James)

b. 1925 Tomkins, Calvin
b. 1927 Long, Richard
b. 1928 Beck, Marilyn (Mohr)
b. 1929 Safire, William L
b. 1930 Guccione, Bob (Robert Charles
    Joseph Edward Sabatini)
b. 1935 Costa, Victor Charles
b. 1936 Steele, Tommy
b. 1938 Snell, Peter George
b. 1940 Kendrick, Eddie
b. 1940 McIntyre, James Talmadge, Jr.
b. 1945 Cazenove, Christopher
b. 1948 Bonfanti, Jim Alexander
b. 1953 Livingston, Barry
b. 1962 Brown, Eddie Lee
d. 1737 Stradivari, Antonio
d. 1762 Geminiani, Francesco
d. 1830 Bolivar, Simon
d. 1870 Mercadante, Saverio
d. 1874 Cushing, William Barker
d. 1907 Kelvin, William Thomson, Baron
d. 1909 Leopold II
d. 1919 Renoir, (Pierre) Auguste
d. 1930 Heseltine, Phillip Arnold
d. 1935 Reese, Lizette Woodworth
d. 1944 Kandinsky, Wassily
d. 1946 Garnett, Constance
d. 1947 Spilsbury, Bernard Henry, Sir
d. 1955 McCoy, Horace
d. 1957 Sayers, Dorothy Leigh
d. 1959 Touchy, Roger
d. 1962 Mitchell, Thomas
d. 1964 Hess, Victor Francis
d. 1965 Ismay, Hastings Lionel, Baron
d. 1967 Holt, Harold Edward
d. 1969 Costa e Silva, Arthur da
d. 1971 Larkin, Oliver Waterman
d. 1973 Abbot, Charles Greeley
d. 1974 McCord, Andrew King
d. 1975 Sissle, Noble
d. 1975 Wimsatt, William Kurtz, Jr.
d. 1977 Marshall, S(amuel) L(yman)
    A(twood)
d. 1978 Frings, Joseph Richard
d. 1981 Shehu, Mehmet
d. 1982 Ferguson, Homer
d. 1982 Hoyt, Lawrence W
d. 1982 Kogan, Leonid Borisovich

December 18
b. 1779 Grimaldi, Joseph
b. 1792 Howitt, William
b. 1802 Prentice, George Denison
b. 1814 Bolton, Sarah Tittle Barrett
b. 1835 Abbott, Lyman
b. 1859 Thompson, Francis Joseph
b. 1861 MacDowell, Edward Alexander
b. 1862 Rosenthal, Moriz
b. 1863 Franz Ferdinand
b. 1870 Saki, pseud.
b. 1879 Klee, Paul
b. 1883 Teague, Walter Dorwin

d. 1851 Turner, Joseph Mallord William
d. 1878 Taylor, Bayard
d. 1883 DeSanctis, Francesco
d. 1899 Lawton, Henry Ware
d. 1921 Cannon, James W
d. 1932 Whitehill, Clarence Eugene
d. 1934 Dixon, Roland Burrage
d. 1947 Scott, Duncan Campbell
d. 1951 Capper, Arthur
d. 1953 Millikan, Robert Andrews
d. 1957 Van Druten, John William
d. 1968 Thomas, Norman Mattoon
d. 1977 Ross, Nellie Taylor
d. 1980 Campora, Hector Jose
d. 1980 Kosygin, Aleksei Nikolaevich
d. 1981 Frailberg, Selma
d. 1982 MacDonald, Dwight
d. 1983 Alexandrov, Grigori
d. 1984 Seton-Watson, Hugh (George
  Hugh Nicholas)

December 20
b. Callas, Charlie
b. 1579 Fletcher, John
b. 1629 Hooch, Pieter de
b. 1805 Graham, Thomas
b. 1824 Vaux, Calvert
b. 1833 Mudd, Samuel Alexander
b. 1849 Eminescu, Mihail
b. 1850 Anderson, Elizabeth Milbank
b. 1865 Mendl, Lady Elsie de Wolfe
b. 1867 Heffelfinger, "Pudge" (William
  Walter)
b. 1867 Lowes, John Livingston
b. 1868 Firestone, Harvey Samuel
b. 1868 Quinn, Edmond T
b. 1870 Cahill, Marie
b. 1871 Hadley, Henry Kimball
b. 1875 Grapewin, Charley (Charles)
b. 1875 Powys, Theodore Francis
b. 1876 Adams, Walter Sydney
b. 1877 Cooper, Emil
b. 1881 Rickey, Branch (Wesley Branch)
b. 1882 Tolstoy, Alexey Nikolaevich
b. 1884 Mennen, William Gerhard
b. 1886 Wightman, Hazel Virginia
  Hotchkiss
b. 1892 May, Mortimer
b. 1894 Menzies, Robert Gordon, Sir
b. 1895 Langer, Suzanne K
b. 1896 Browning, Frederick A(rthur)
  M(ontague), Sir
b. 1896 Hobbs, Leonard Sinclair
b. 1898 Votipka, Thelma
b. 1899 Ronne, Finn
b. 1899 Sparkman, John Jackson
b. 1900 Hartnett, "Gabby" (Charles Leo)
b. 1902 George Edward Alexander
  Edmund
b. 1902 Hook, Sidney
b. 1902 Lerner, Max
b. 1904 Dunne, Irene Marie

b. 1905 Dekker, Albert
b. 1907 Pratt, Lawrence Arthur
b. 1907 Webster, Paul Francois
b. 1910 Conacher, Charles, Sr.
b. 1911 Calisher, Hortense
b. 1914 Byrd, Harry Flood, Jr.
b. 1915 Mann, Paul
b. 1916 Smith, Courtney Craig
b. 1918 Totter, Audrey
b. 1919 Bettis, Valerie
b. 1920 Pitrone, Jean M
b. 1922 Hill, George Roy
b. 1924 La Marsh, Judy Verlyn
b. 1924 LaMarsh, Judy (Julia Verlyn)
b. 1926 Howe, (Richard Edward) Geoffrey,
  Sir
b. 1926 Lambsdorff, Otto
b. 1926 Levine, David
b. 1927 Burch, Dean
b. 1927 Simpson, Jim
b. 1928 Christiansen, Jack
b. 1932 Hillerman, John Benedict
b. 1933 Getty, Gordon Peter
b. 1934 Gorman, Leon Arthur
b. 1936 McDole, Carol
b. 1938 Harbison, John Harris
b. 1940 Goffstein, Marilyn
b. 1943 Tompkins, Angel
b. 1946 Geller, Uri
b. 1947 Criss, Peter
b. 1949 Cooper, Cecil
b. 1952 Agutter, Jenny
b. 1956 Baker, Blanche
d. 1866 Taylor, Ann
d. 1910 Neumann, Angelo
d. 1937 Ludendorff, Erich Friedrich
  Wilhelm
d. 1948 Smith, C Aubrey
d. 1953 Connelly, "One-Eyed" (James Leo)
d. 1953 Ziff, William B
d. 1954 Hilton, James
d. 1956 Risdon, Elizabeth
d. 1961 Hart, Moss
d. 1968 Brod, Max
d. 1968 Steinbeck, John Ernst
d. 1970 Schuster, Max Lincoln
d. 1971 Disney, Roy O
d. 1972 Hartnett, "Gabby" (Charles Leo)
d. 1972 Wright, John Lloyd
d. 1973 Darin, Bobby
d. 1976 Daley, Richard Joseph
d. 1980 Kintner, Robert Edmonds
d. 1981 Goodman, Martin Wise
d. 1982 Rubinstein, Arthur
d. 1983 Brandt, Bill (William)
d. 1983 Fenelon, Fania
d. 1984 Hill, Lester

December 21
b. 1118 A'Becket, Thomas
b. 1401 Masaccio
b. 1773 Brown, Robert

b. 1948 Garvey, Steve Patrick
b. 1949 Gibb, Maurice
b. 1949 Gibb, Robin
b. 1951 Grosvenor, Gerald Cavendish
b. 1951 Stephenson, Jan
b. 1954 Landreaux, Ken(neth Francis)
d. 1590 Pare, Ambroise
d. 1668 Daye, Stephen
d. 1767 Newbery, John
d. 1828 Jackson, Rachel Donelson Robards
d. 1867 Rousseau, (Pierre Etienne)
   Theodore
d. 1880 Eliot, George, pseud.
d. 1899 Moody, Dwight Lyman
d. 1902 Krafft-Ebing, Richard von
d. 1917 Cabrini, Saint Frances Xavier
d. 1921 Watterson, Henry
d. 1925 Munsey, Frank Andrew
d. 1935 Braslau, Sophie
d. 1939 Rainey, "Ma" (Gertrude)
d. 1940 West, Nathanael, pseud.
d. 1941 Mugnone, Leopoldo
d. 1943 Potter, Beatrix (Helen Beatrix)
d. 1944 Langdon, Harry
d. 1945 Neurath, Otto
d. 1945 Train, Arthur Cheney
d. 1948 Brian, Donald
d. 1950 Damrosch, Walter Johannes
d. 1957 Zuppke, Robert C
d. 1959 Gray, Gilda
d. 1968 Swing, Raymond Gram
d. 1969 VonSternberg, Josef
d. 1972 Wallington, Jimmy (James S.)
d. 1973 Phillips, Irna
d. 1974 Long, Richard
d. 1976 Wright, Russel
d. 1979 Zanuck, Darryl Francis
d. 1985 Condie, Richard P

December 23
b. Lucci, Susan
b. 1682 Gibbs, James
b. 1732 Arkwright, Richard, Sir
b. 1790 Champollion, Jean Francois
b. 1804 Sainte-Beuve, Charles Augustin
b. 1805 Smith, Joseph
b. 1815 Garnet, Henry Highland
b. 1850 Straus, Oscar
b. 1856 Duke, James Buchanan
b. 1858 Nemirovich-Danchenko, Vladimir I
b. 1860 Monroe, Harriet
b. 1867 Walker, Sarah Breedlove
b. 1872 Marin, John
b. 1875 Waldron, Charles D
b. 1881 Jimenez, Juan Ramon
b. 1885 Sardi, Vincent, Sr.
b. 1887 Blore, Eric
b. 1887 Cromwell, John
b. 1888 Rank, J(oseph) Arthur
b. 1889 Brunner, Emil
b. 1892 Greene, Ward
b. 1893 Douglas, Sholto (William Sholto)

b. 1896 Tomasi di Lampedusa, Guiseppe
b. 1900 Soglow, Otto
b. 1903 Kalatozov, Mikhail
b. 1907 Roosevelt, James
b. 1907 Ross, Barney
b. 1908 Karsh, Yousuf
b. 1911 Gregory, James
b. 1914 Coe, Frederick H
b. 1918 Greco, Jose
b. 1918 Schmidt, Helmut Heinrich
   Waldemar
b. 1919 Heggen, Thomas Orls, Jr.
b. 1921 Johnson, Robert Willard
b. 1922 Willingham, Calder Baynard, Jr.
b. 1923 Masursky, Harold
b. 1923 Okun, Milton
b. 1923 Stern, Leonard B
b. 1924 Devine, Dan(iel John)
b. 1924 Kalber, Floyd
b. 1924 Kurland, Bob
b. 1924 Roman, Ruth
b. 1925 Guardino, Harry
b. 1926 Bly, Robert Elwood
b. 1928 Jepsen, Roger William
b. 1929 Baker, Chet
b. 1929 Weber, Dick
b. 1933 Akihito, (Togusama)
b. 1935 Hornung, Paul Vernon
b. 1935 Little Esther
b. 1935 Phillips, Esther
b. 1936 Stacy, James
b. 1940 Graves, Nancy Stevenson
b. 1940 Kauokenen, Jorma
b. 1941 Hardin, Tim
b. 1947 Rodgers, Bill (William Henry)
b. 1948 Ham, Jack
b. 1949 Bender, Ariel
b. 1954 Teacher, Brian
d. 1631 Drayton, Michael
d. 1652 Cotton, John
d. 1795 Clinton, Henry, Sir
d. 1810 Queensberry, William Douglas,
   Duke
d. 1834 Malthus, Thomas Robert
d. 1872 Catlin, George
d. 1875 Saint Georges, Jules
d. 1884 Chisum, John Simpson
d. 1888 Oliphant, Laurence
d. 1889 Grady, Henry Woodfin
d. 1901 Croly, Jane Cunningham
d. 1923 Eiffel, Alexandre Gustave
d. 1939 Fokker, Anthony Herman Gerard
d. 1942 Cagle, "Red" (Christian Keener)
d. 1944 Gibson, Charles Dana
d. 1946 Davis, John Staige
d. 1948 Tojo, Hideki (Eiki)
d. 1953 Beria, Lavrenti Pavlovich
d. 1959 Halifax, Edward Frederick Lindley
d. 1966 VonDoderer, Heimito
d. 1970 Benzell, Mimi (Miriam Ruth)
d. 1970 Ruggles, Charles

b. 1878 Chevrolet, Louis Joseph
b. 1878 Schenck, Joseph M
b. 1879 George, Grace
b. 1881 Dill, John Greer, Sir
b. 1883 Utrillo, Maurice
b. 1885 Manship, Paul
b. 1886 Ory, "Kid" (Edward)
b. 1887 Hilton, Conrad Nicholson
b. 1888 Henderson, Robert W
b. 1888 Lawrence, David
b. 1888 Stravinsky, Vera de Bossett
b. 1889 Wallace, Lila Bell Acheson
b. 1892 West, Dame Rebecca, pseud.
b. 1893 Ripley, Robert Leroy
b. 1899 Bogart, Humphrey de Forest
b. 1899 Power, Donald Clinton
b. 1899 Soyer, Moses
b. 1899 Soyer, Raphael
b. 1900 MacLane, Barton
b. 1903 Bromberg, J. Edward
b. 1903 Cobleigh, Ira Underwood
b. 1903 Samstag, Nicholas
b. 1904 Swarthout, Gladys
b. 1906 Clifford, Clark McAdams
b. 1906 Grade, Lew, Sir
b. 1907 Calloway, Cab(ell)
b. 1907 Cruickshank, Andrew John
b. 1908 Crisp, Quentin, pseud.
b. 1908 Twelvetrees, Helen
b. 1909 Mazurki, Mike
b. 1910 Leiber, Fritz
b. 1911 Langley, Noel
b. 1913 Martin, Tony
b. 1914 Lewis, Oscar
b. 1914 Mabee, Carleton (Fred Carleton)
b. 1915 Rugolo, Pete
b. 1915 Wilson, Richard
b. 1917 Lowe, Jack Warren
b. 1918 Sadat, Anwar el
b. 1924 Serling, Rod
b. 1927 Fox, "Nellie" (Jacob Nelson)
b. 1931 Castaneda, Carlos
b. 1935 Little Richard
b. 1936 Hoge, James Fulton, Jr.
b. 1940 Spector, Phil(lip Harvey)
b. 1942 Durr, Francoise
b. 1945 Stabler, Ken(neth Michael)
b. 1946 Buffet, Jimmy
b. 1946 Csonka, Larry Richard
b. 1946 Sandy, Gary
b. 1948 Mandrell, Barbara Ann
b. 1949 Pastorini, Dan
b. 1949 Spacek, "Sissy" (Mary Elizabeth)
b. 1950 Rote, Kyle, Jr.
b. 1954 Lennox, Annie
b. 1957 Persinger, Gregory A
b. 1958 Henderson, Rickey Henley
d. 1635 Champlain, Samuel de
d. 1676 Cavendish, William, Duke of
    Newcastle
d. 1822 Pinkney, William

d. 1864 Wallack, James William
d. 1865 Barth, Heinrich
d. 1868 Yale, Linus
d. 1918 Miller, Olive Thorne
d. 1926 Yoshihito
d. 1935 Bourget, Paul (Charles Joseph)
d. 1936 Brisbane, Arthur
d. 1940 Ayres, Agnes
d. 1941 Bates, Blanche Lyon
d. 1946 Fields, W C
d. 1950 Torrence, Ridgley (Frederick
    Rridgley)
d. 1952 Moore, "Dinty" (James H)
d. 1953 Shubert, Lee
d. 1954 Ace, Johnny
d. 1956 Dwiggins, William Addison
d. 1957 Pathe, Charles
d. 1960 Garrod, Hethcote William
d. 1961 Brewster, Owen
d. 1961 Loewi, Otto
d. 1962 Austin, Warren R(obinson)
d. 1962 Davis, "Tobe" (Coller)
d. 1966 Nick the Greek
d. 1970 Wroth, Lawrence Councelman
d. 1972 Brown, Lawrence
d. 1973 Inonu, Ismet
d. 1974 Beard, Myron Gould
d. 1975 Burchard, John Ely
d. 1977 Chaplin, Charlie
d. 1978 Mortimer, Charles Greenough
d. 1979 Blondell, Joan
d. 1982 Bowling, Roger
d. 1982 Pearl, Jack
d. 1983 Miro, Joan

December 26
b. 1716 Gray, Thomas
b. 1738 Nelson, Thomas, Jr.
b. 1792 Babbage, Charles
b. 1819 Southworth, Emma Dorothy Eliza
    Nevitte
b. 1820 Boucicault, Dion
b. 1837 Bulkeley, Morgan
b. 1837 Dewey, George
b. 1853 Bazin, Rene
b. 1854 Tappan, Eva March
b. 1874 Angell, (Ralph) Norman, Sir
b. 1874 Rothier, Leon
b. 1891 Miller, Henry
b. 1893 Golschmann, Vladimir
b. 1893 Mao Tse-Tung
b. 1894 Toomer, Jean
b. 1902 Lytle, Andrew Nelson
b. 1903 Lazzeri, Tony (Anthony Michael)
b. 1904 Stribling, Young (William
    Lawrence)
b. 1905 Loeb, William
b. 1906 Cook, Elisha, Jr.
b. 1907 Gore, Albert Arnold
b. 1907 Stern, James
b. 1909 Wakeman, Frederic
b. 1914 Widmark, Richard

December 28
b. 1789 Sedgwick, Catherine Maria
b. 1816 Packard, Elizabeth Parsons Ware
b. 1823 Scott, Thomas
b. 1850 Tamagno, Francesco
b. 1856 Wilson, Woodrow (Thomas Woodrow)
b. 1869 Trumbauer, Horace
b. 1870 Hendrick, Burton Jesse
b. 1882 Eddington, Arthur Stanley, Sir
b. 1885 Allen, Arthur Augustus
b. 1888 Branner, Martin Michael
b. 1894 Broneer, Oscar Theodore
b. 1895 Brink, Carol Ryrie
b. 1896 Sessions, Roger Huntington
b. 1898 Franken, Rose
b. 1899 Murnau, Friedrich W
b. 1900 Lyons, Ted (Theodore Amar)
b. 1902 Adler, Mortimer Jerome
b. 1903 Von Neumann, John
b. 1905 Arquette, Cliff
b. 1905 Dean, Gordon Evans
b. 1905 Hines, "Fatha" (Earl Kenneth)
b. 1906 Bridges, Tommy (Thomas Jefferson Davis)
b. 1908 Ayres, Lew
b. 1908 Byrne, Brendan
b. 1911 Levenson, Sam(uel)
b. 1913 Jacobi, Lou
b. 1914 Bowman, Lee (Lucien Lee, Sr.)
b. 1917 Clarke, Ellis Emmanuel
b. 1922 Lee, Stan
b. 1925 Neff, Hildegarde
b. 1927 Babiuch, Edward
b. 1928 Lunn, Janet
b. 1929 Bieber, Owen Frederick
b. 1929 Sawchuk, Terry (Terrance Gordon)
b. 1931 Milner, Martin Sam
b. 1932 Haber, Joyce
b. 1932 Howell, Harry (Henry Vernon)
b. 1933 Portis, Charles
b. 1934 Smith, Maggie
b. 1938 Yarnell, Bruce
b. 1943 Peterson, David
b. 1945 Birendra Bir Bikram, Shah Dev
b. 1946 Green, Hubie (Hubert)
b. 1946 Winter, Edgar Holand
b. 1948 Prescott, Ken
b. 1950 Chilton, Alex
b. 1953 Clayderman, Richard
b. 1953 Pittman, Robert W
b. 1958 Scales, DeWayne Jay
b. 1959 Walls, Everson Collins
b. 1960 Bourque, Ray(mond Jean)
b. 1962 Lee, Keith Deywane
b. 1981 Carr, Elizabeth Jordan
d. 1706 Bayle, Pierre
d. 1734 MacGregor, Robert
d. 1859 Macaulay, Thomas Babington Macaulay, Baron
d. 1874 Smith, Gerrit

d. 1898 Morrill, Justin Smith
d. 1903 Gissing, George Robert
d. 1924 Spitteler, Karl Friedrich Georg
d. 1925 Esenin, Sergei Aleksandrovich
d. 1933 Vonnoh, Robert W
d. 1934 Sherman, Lowell
d. 1935 Day, Clarence Shepard, Jr.
d. 1937 Ravel, Maurice Joseph
d. 1938 Mandelshtam, Osip Emilyevich
d. 1941 Updike, Daniel Berkeley
d. 1945 Dreiser, Theodore
d. 1946 Bond, Carrie Jacobs
d. 1946 Hooker, Brian
d. 1947 Crowninshield, Francis Welch
d. 1949 Allen, Hervey (William Hervey)
d. 1949 Anderson, Ivie
d. 1951 Fairbank, Janet Ayer
d. 1956 Bennett, John
d. 1961 Wilson, Edith Bolling Galt
d. 1963 Hindemith, Paul
d. 1963 Liebling, Abbot Joseph
d. 1964 Sterrett, Cliff
d. 1965 Thorndike, Lynn
d. 1970 Rivers, L(ucius) Mendel
d. 1971 Steiner, Max
d. 1977 Heloise
d. 1981 Davis, James Curran
d. 1983 Demaret, Jimmy (James Newton B)
d. 1983 Wilson, Dennis
d. 1984 Peckinpah, (David) Sam(uel)

December 29
b. 1721 Pompadour, Jeanne Antoinette Poisson
b. 1766 Macintosh, Charles
b. 1800 Goodyear, Charles
b. 1808 Johnson, Andrew
b. 1809 Gladstone, William Ewart
b. 1848 Cheney, John Vance
b. 1859 Carranza, Venustiano
b. 1874 Honeywell, Mark Charles
b. 1876 Casals, Pablo (Pau Carlos Salvador)
b. 1876 DeLuca, Giuseppe
b. 1879 Mitchell, Billy (William)
b. 1881 Willard, Jess
b. 1891 Hall, Joyce Clyde
b. 1894 Hill, Lester
b. 1896 Siqueiros, David A
b. 1897 Mayer, Albert
b. 1898 Bledsoe, Jules
b. 1898 Cooke, Samuel
b. 1900 Corcoran, Thomas Gardiner
b. 1903 McCoy, Clyde
b. 1907 Weaver, Robert Clifton
b. 1912 Hicks, Peggy Glanville-
b. 1913 Werner, Pierre
b. 1915 Ruark, Robert Chester
b. 1917 Bradley, Tom (Thomas)
b. 1920 Lindfors, Viveca
b. 1932 Swenson, Inga

b. 1853 Bliss, Tasker H
b. 1855 Pascoli, Giovanni
b. 1857 Kelly, "King" (Michael Joseph)
b. 1860 Thompson, John Taliaferro
b. 1864 Ritchey, George Willis
b. 1866 Harding, Chester
b. 1869 Matisse, Henri
b. 1870 Connolly, Thomas Henry
b. 1878 Quiroga, Horacio
b. 1880 Marshall, George Catlett
b. 1882 Jones, Benjamin Allyn
b. 1884 Arden, Elizabeth
b. 1884 Reed, Stanley Forman
b. 1884 Viereck, George Sylvester
b. 1885 Hoesslin, Franz von
b. 1892 Robards, Jason
b. 1894 Negri, Pola
b. 1897 Orry-Kelly
b. 1899 Mearns, David Chambers
b. 1903 Lewyt, Alexander Milton
b. 1904 Milstein, Nathan
b. 1905 Mollet, Guy
b. 1905 Styne, Jule (Julius Kerwin Stein)
b. 1908 Kirby, John
b. 1908 Rothmuller, Marko A
b. 1908 Wiesenthal, Simon
b. 1909 Jones, Jonah
b. 1910 Kollmar, Richard
b. 1914 Brady, Pat (Robert Patrick)
b. 1916 Boller, Paul F, Jr.
b. 1916 Wierwille, Victor Paul
b. 1918 Hagg, Gunder
b. 1922 Bookout, John Frank, Jr.
b. 1922 McCracken, Joan
b. 1924 Allen, Rex E, Sr.
b. 1924 Brown, Pamela Beatrice
b. 1924 Kelley, Frank Joseph
b. 1925 Jones, Candy
b. 1927 Hanks, Nancy
b. 1928 McElhenny, Hugh
b. 1930 Odetta
b. 1936 Major, Clarence

b. 1937 Hopkins, Anthony
b. 1943 Denver, John
b. 1943 Kingsley, Ben
b. 1943 Miles, Sarah
b. 1944 Hackford, Taylor
b. 1946 Furstenberg, Diane Halfin von
b. 1946 Smith, Patti
b. 1947 Cummings, Burton
b. 1948 Matheson, Tim
b. 1948 Summer, Donna
b. 1951 Goytisolo, Fermin
d. 1719 Flamsteed, John
d. 1775 Montgomery, Richard
d. 1799 Marmontel, Jean Francois
d. 1864 Dallas, George Mifflin
d. 1877 Courbet, Gustave
d. 1882 Gambetta, Leon
d. 1891 Crowther, Samuel Adjai
d. 1900 Goodwin, Hannibal Williston
d. 1916 Rasputin, Grigori Efimovich
d. 1919 Van Zandt, Marie
d. 1936 Unamuno (y Jugo), Miguel de
d. 1941 Hess, Sol
d. 1944 Nash, George Frederick
d. 1951 Litvinov, Maxim
d. 1955 Lewisohn, Ludwig
d. 1959 Giovannitti, Arturo
d. 1960 Howe, Clarence Decatur
d. 1966 Persinger, Louis
d. 1969 Baccaloni, Salvatore
d. 1970 Reik, Theodor
d. 1971 Duel, Peter
d. 1971 Henderson, Ray
d. 1972 Clemente, Roberto Walker
d. 1976 Hayes, Roland
d. 1980 McLuhan, (Herbert) Marshall
d. 1980 Walsh, Raoul
d. 1981 Adair, Frank E(arl)
d. 1981 Seper, Franjo
d. 1985 Nelson, Rick (Eric Hilliard)
d. 1985 Spiegel, Sam

Geographic Index

Fort Payne, Alabama
Johnson, James Ralph b. May 20, 1922
Nelson, Larry Gene b. Sep 10, 1947
Ober, Philip b. Mar 23, 1902
Gadsden, Alabama
Cox, Jean b. Jan 14, 1922
Garland, Alabama
Shavers, Ernie b. Aug 31, 1945
Georgiana, Alabama
Williams, "Hank" (Hiram) b. Sep 15, 1923
Greensboro, Alabama
Hobson, Richmond Pearson
b. Aug 17, 1870
Grove Hill, Alabama
Mathews, Forrest David b. Dec 6, 1935
Harlan, Alabama
Black, Hugo LaFayette b. Feb 27, 1886
Hartford, Alabama
Wynn, Early b. Jan 6, 1920
Hartselle, Alabama
Huie, William Bradford b. Nov 13, 1910
Hueytown, Alabama
Allison, Bobby (Robert Arthur)
b. Dec 3, 1937
Huntsville, Alabama
Allen, Viola Emily b. Oct 27, 1867
Atkinson, (Justin) Brooks d. Jan 13, 1984
Bankhead, Tallulah Brockman
b. Jan 31, 1903
Sparkman, John Jackson d. Nov 16, 1985
Jasper, Alabama
Holliday, Polly Dean b. Jul 2, 1937
Leeds, Alabama
Barkley, Charles Wade b. Feb 20, 1963
Lexington, Alabama
Louis, Joe b. May 13, 1914
Linden, Alabama
Abernathy, Ralph David b. Mar 11, 1926
Lipscomb, Alabama
Hill, Virginia b. Aug 26, 1916
Marion, Alabama
King, Coretta Scott b. Apr 27, 1927
Mathews, Alabama
Rhodes, "Dusty" (James Lamar)
b. May 13, 1927
Mobile, Alabama
Aaron, Hank (Henry Louis)
b. Feb 5, 1934
Andrews, Mary Raymond Shipman b. 1860
Belmont, Alva Erskine Smith Vanderbilt
b. Jan 17, 1853
Campbell, William Edward March
b. Sep 18, 1893
Denton, Jeremiah Andrew, Jr.
b. Jul 15, 1924
Gorgas, William Crawford b. Oct 3, 1854
McCabe, Mary O'Connell b. Sep 4, 1902
McCovey, Willie Lee b. Jan 10, 1938
Paige, "Satchel" (Leroy Robert)
b. Jul 7, 1906
Reese, Don(ald Francis) b. Sep 4, 1951

Smith, Ozzie (Osborne Earl)
b. Dec 26, 1954
Williams, "Cootie" (Charles Melvin)
b. Jul 24, 1908
Monroeville, Alabama
Collins, Marva Deloise Nettles
b. Aug 31, 1936
Lee, Harper (Nelle Harper)
b. Apr 28, 1926
Montgomery, Alabama
Cater, Douglass b. Aug 24, 1923
Cole, Nat "King" (Nathaniel Adams)
b. Mar 17, 1919
Fitzgerald, Zelda b. Jul 24, 1900
Franklin, Mel(vin) b. Oct 12, 1942
Hill, Lester b. Dec 29, 1894
Hill, Lester d. Dec 20, 1984
Starr, Bart (Bryan B) b. Jan 9, 1934
Tennille, Toni b. May 8, 1943
Thornton, Willie Mae b. Dec 11, 1926
Wallace, Lurleen Burns d. May 7, 1968
Wilson, Willie James b. Jul 9, 1955
Montgomery County, Alabama
Owsley, Frank Lawrence b. Jan 20, 1890
Morgan County, Alabama
Jones, Dean b. Jan 25, 1936
Sparkman, John Jackson b. Dec 20, 1899
Moscow, Alabama
Bankhead, William Brockman
b. Apr 12, 1874
Mount Willing, Alabama
Moorer, Thomas H(inman) b. Feb 9, 1912
Northport, Alabama
Lary, Frank Strong b. Apr 10, 1931
Phoenix City, Alabama
Hawkins, Osie Penman, Jr.
b. Aug 16, 1913
Portersville, Alabama
Keener, Jefferson Ward b. Aug 6, 1908
Prattville, Alabama
Pickett, Wilson b. Mar 18, 1941
Ragland, Alabama
York, Rudy (Rudolph Preston)
b. Aug 17, 1913
Red Level, Alabama
Terry, Luther Leonidas b. Sep 15, 1911
Seale, Alabama
Smith, Holland McTeire b. Apr 20, 1882
Selma, Alabama
Bloch, Alexander b. Jul 11, 1881
Connor, "Bull" (Theophilus Eugene)
b. Jul 11, 1897
Gilmore, Eddy Lanier King
b. May 28, 1907
Liuzzo, Viola d. Mar 25, 1965
Shelby City, Alabama
Walthall, Henry B b. Mar 16, 1878
Siluria, Alabama
O'Donnell, Cathy b. Jul 6, 1925

Sylacauga, Alabama
Nabors, Jim (James Thurston)
b. Jun 12, 1932
Titus, Alabama
Sewell, Joe (Joseph Wheeler)
b. Oct 9, 1898
Troy, Alabama
Davenport, Willie b. Jun 8, 1943
Lewis, John Robert b. Feb 21, 1940
Rafferty, Max(well Lewis, Jr.)
d. Jun 13, 1982
Smith, Clarence b. Jun 11, 1904
Tuscaloosa, Alabama
Bryant, "Bear" (Paul William)
d. Jan 26, 1983
Foster, George Arthur b. Dec 1, 1949
Stallworth, John Lee b. Jul 15, 1952
Strode, Hudson d. Sep 22, 1976
Wallace, Lurleen Burns b. Sep 19, 1926
Washington, Dinah b. Aug 29, 1924
Young, Coleman A(lexander)
b. May 24, 1918
Tuscumbia, Alabama
Howell, Thomas Heflin b. Jun 19, 1921
Keller, Helen Adams b. Jun 27, 1880
Manush, "Heinie" (Henry Emmett)
b. Jul 20, 1901
Tuskegee, Alabama
Bridgman, Frederic Arthur
b. Nov 10, 1847
Carver, George Washington d. Jan 5, 1943
LaPread, Ronald b. 1948
Parks, Rosa Lee b. Feb 4, 1913
Richie, Lionel b. 1950
Washington, Booker T(aliafero)
d. Nov 14, 1915
Union Springs, Alabama
Blount, Winton Malcolm b. Feb 1, 1921
Clarke, John Henrik b. Jan 1, 1915
Kendrick, Eddie b. Dec 17, 1940
Vredenburgh, Alabama
Drew, John E b. Sep 30, 1954
Whistler, Alabama
Williams, Billy Leo b. Jun 15, 1938
Youngsboro, Alabama
Bullard, Robert Lee b. Jan 15, 1861

ALASKA

Boggs, Hale (Thomas Hale) d. Oct 1972
Roosevelt, Kermit d. Jun 4, 1943
Anchorage, Alaska
Bennett, John Charles d. May 4, 1980
Freuchen, Peter d. Sep 2, 1957
Simpson, Donald C b. Oct 29, 1945
Dawson City, Alaska
Jory, Victor b. Nov 23, 1902
Hackleburg, Alaska
James, Sonny b. Mar 1, 1929
Kvichak Bay, Alaska
DeLaurentiis, Federico d. 1981

Nome, Alaska
Murkowski, Frank Hughes
b. Mar 28, 1933
Point Barrow, Alaska
Post, Wiley d. Aug 15, 1935
Rogers, Will(iam Penn Adair)
d. Aug 15, 1935
Saint Paul Island, Alaska
Partch, Virgil Franklin, II b. Oct 17, 1916
Van Buren, Alaska
Adler, Cyrus b. Sep 13, 1863
Burns, Bob b. Aug 2, 1893

ARIZONA

Cochise b. 1815
Cochise d. Jun 9, 1874
Geronimo b. Jun 1829
Bisbee, Arizona
Frankovich, Mike J b. Sep 29, 1910
Cottonwood, Arizona
Fleming, Victor d. Jan 6, 1949
Flagstaff, Arizona
Devine, Andy b. Oct 7, 1905
Gill, Jocelyn Ruth b. Oct 29, 1916
Lowell, Percival d. Nov 13, 1916
Florence, Arizona
Arriola, Gus b. Jul 23, 1917
Mix, Tom d. Oct 12, 1940
Fort Huachuca, Arizona
Patch, Alexander M(c Carrell)
b. Nov 23, 1889
Glendale, Arizona
Robbins, Marty b. Sep 26, 1925
Globe, Arizona
Browning, James Louis b. Dec 8, 1932
Jacobs, Helen Hull b. Aug 6, 1908
Mesa, Arizona
Hayden, Carl Trumball d. Jan 25, 1972
Thiebaud, Wayne Morton b. Nov 15, 1920
Nogales, Arizona
Edmonson, Munro Sterling
b. May 18, 1924
McCoy, Tim(othy John Fitzgerald)
d. Jan 29, 1978
Mingus, Charles b. Apr 22, 1922
Phoenix, Arizona
Beard, Mary Ritter d. Aug 14, 1958
Bolles, Don F d. Jun 13, 1976
Boyer, Charles d. Aug 26, 1978
Brown, Kelly (Elford Cornelious Kelly
Kingman) d. Mar 13, 1981
Carter, Lynda b. Jul 24, 1951
Colter, Jessie b. May 25, 1947
Cooney, Joan Ganz b. Nov 30, 1929
Elam, Jack b. Nov 13, 1916
Fletcher, Arthur A b. Dec 22, 1924
Gilbreth, Lillian Moller d. Jan 2, 1972
Goldwater, Barry Morris b. Jan 1, 1909
Harman, Fred d. Jan 2, 1982
Humphrey, Elliott S d. Jun 6, 1981

King, Clarence d. Dec 24, 1901
King, Wayne d. May 16, 1985
Luce, Henry Robinson d. Feb 28, 1967
McFarland, Ernest William d. Jun 8, 1984
Miranda, Ernesto d. Jan 31, 1976
Moley, Raymond d. Feb 18, 1975
O'Connor, Basil d. Mar 9, 1972
Rausch, James Stevens d. May 18, 1981
Robb, Charles Spittal b. Jun 26, 1939
Spooner, Bill b. Apr 16, 1949
Vlasic, Joseph d. Jul 10, 1986
Welnick, Vince b. Feb 21, 1951
Wright, Frank Lloyd d. Apr 9, 1959
Wrigley, William, Jr. d. Jan 26, 1932

Prescott, Arizona
DeCamp, Rosemary b. Nov 14, 1910
Denny, John Allen b. Nov 8, 1952
Silas, Paul b. Jul 12, 1943
Willis, Mary b. Jul 4, 1919

Saint Johns, Arizona
Udall, Mo(rris King) b. Jun 15, 1922
Udall, Stewart Lee b. Jan 31, 1920

Scottsdale, Arizona
Astaire, Adele d. Jan 25, 1981
Bayne, Beverly Pearl d. Aug 18, 1982
Crabbe, "Buster" (Larry) d. Apr 23, 1983
Crane, Bob d. Jun 29, 1978
Davis, Loyal d. Aug 19, 1982
Grimm, Charlie (Charles John)
  d. Nov 15, 1983
Hynek, J(oseph) Allen d. Apr 27, 1986
Kelland, Clarence Budington
  d. Feb 18, 1964
Rubicam, Raymond d. May 8, 1978

Tempe, Arizona
Finch, Robert Hutchison b. Oct 9, 1925
Hayden, Carl Trumball b. Oct 2, 1877

Tombstone, Arizona
Earp, Morgan d. Mar 18, 1882

Tucson, Arizona
Alexander, Sue b. Aug 20, 1933
Ameche, Jim d. Feb 4, 1983
Apache Kid d. 1894
Bok, Bart J(an) d. Aug 5, 1983
Bordes, Francois d. Apr 30, 1981
Clinton, Larry d. May 2, 1985
DeConcini, Dennis Webster
  b. May 8, 1937
Donlon, Mary Honor d. Mar 5, 1977
Eden, Barbara Jean b. Aug 23, 1934
Freyse, William d. Mar 3, 1969
Gorin, Igor d. Mar 24, 1982
Kerr, Andrew d. Mar 1, 1969
Krutch, Joseph Wood d. May 22, 1970
Kuykendall, Ralph Simpson
  d. May 9, 1963
Licavoli, Peter Joseph, Sr. d. Jan 11, 1984
Owens, Jesse (James Cleveland)
  d. Mar 31, 1980
Pegler, Westbrook d. Jun 24, 1969

Rockefeller, John D(avison), Jr.
  d. May 11, 1960
Ronstadt, Linda b. Jul 15, 1946
Sanger, Margaret d. Sep 6, 1966
Sheil, Bernard James, Archbishop
  d. Sep 13, 1969
Smallens, Alexander d. Nov 24, 1972

Tuscon, Arizona
Douglass, Andrew Ellicott d. Oct 20, 1962
Lowden, Frank O(rren) d. Mar 20, 1943

Wilcox, Arizona
Allen, Rex E, Sr. b. Dec 31, 1924

Winslow, Arizona
Kleindienst, Richard Gordon
  b. Aug 5, 1923

Yavapai County, Arizona
Behn, Harry b. Sep 24, 1898

Yuma, Arizona
Chavez, Cesar b. Mar 31, 1927

ARKANSAS

Jones, Arthur A b. 1924

Arkansas City, Arkansas
Johnson, John Harold b. Jan 19, 1918

Black Oak, Arkansas
Mangrum, Jim Dandy b. Mar 30, 1948

Brinkley, Arkansas
Jordan, Louis b. Jul 8, 1908

Camden, Arkansas
Pryor, David Hampton b. Aug 29, 1934

Center Point, Arkansas
Shaver, Dorothy b. Jul 29, 1897

Charleston, Arkansas
Bumpers, Dale Leon b. Aug 12, 1925

Clifty, Arkansas
Vaughn, Joseph Floyd b. Mar 9, 1912

Combs, Arkansas
Faubus, Orval Eugene b. Jan 7, 1910

Crossett, Arkansas
Switzer, Barry b. Oct 5, 1937

De Witt, Arkansas
Holt, Ivan Lee b. Jan 9, 1886

Delight, Arkansas
Campbell, Glen Travis b. Apr 22, 1938

DeQueen, Arkansas
Bauer, Helen b. Aug 14, 1900

El Dorado, Arkansas
Brock, Lou(is Clark) b. Jun 18, 1939
Portis, Charles b. Dec 28, 1933
Rowe, "Schoolboy" (Lynwood Thomas)
  d. Jan 8, 1961

Eureka Springs, Arkansas
Castle, Irene Foote d. Jan 25, 1969
Chisum, John Simpson d. Dec 23, 1884

Fayetteville, Arkansas
Harris, Cliff(ord Allen) b. Nov 12, 1948
Stone, Edward Durell b. Mar 9, 1902

Forrest City, Arkansas
Green, Al b. Apr 13, 1946
Rich, Charlie (Charles Allan)
b. Dec 14, 1932
Fort Smith, Arkansas
Alexander, Katherine b. Sep 22, 1901
Bonneville, Benjamin d. Jun 12, 1878
Gravelly, Arkansas
Hunnicutt, Arthur b. Feb 17, 1911
Green Forest, Arkansas
Brown, Helen Gurley b. Feb 18, 1922
Harmony, Arkansas
Baskin, Wade b. Jul 27, 1924
Havana, Arkansas
Sain, Johnny (John Franklin)
b. Sep 15, 1918
Helena, Arkansas
Johnson, Alex(ander) b. Dec 7, 1942
Hope, Arkansas
Clinton, Bill (William Jefferson)
b. Aug 19, 1946
Dillon, Melinda b. Oct 31, 1939
Hot Springs, Arkansas
Blasingame, Francis James Levi
b. Jan 17, 1907
Ladd, Alan b. Sep 3, 1913
Lauck, Chester H d. Feb 21, 1980
Madden, Owen Victor d. Apr 24, 1965
Montana, Patsy b. Oct 30, 1914
Warneke, Lon(nie) d. Jun 23, 1976
Jenny Lind, Arkansas
Dodd, Mrs. John Bruce (Sonora Louise
Smart) b. 1882
Jonesboro, Arkansas
Daugherty, Pat b. Nov 11, 1947
Murphy, Ben(jamin Edward)
b. Mar 6, 1942
Snyder, John Wesley b. Jun 21, 1895
Kensett, Arkansas
Mills, Wilbur Daigh b. May 24, 1909
Kingsland, Arkansas
Bryant, "Bear" (Paul William)
b. Sep 11, 1913
Cash, Johnny b. Feb 26, 1932
Little Rock, Arkansas
Allen, Rick b. Jan 28, 1946
Anderson, Gilbert M b. Mar 21, 1882
Beatty, Morgan b. Sep 6, 1902
Bonner, Frank b. Feb 28, 1942
Boullioun, E(rnest) H(erman, Jr.)
b. Nov 3, 1918
Bridges, James b. Feb 3,
Cleaver, Eldridge b. Aug 31, 1935
Cooper, Morton Cecil d. Nov 17, 1958
Corn, Ira George, Jr. b. Aug 22, 1921
Dwyer, Cynthia b. 1931
Fletcher, John Gould b. Jan 3, 1886
Fletcher, John Gould d. May 20, 1950
Flippen, Jay C b. Mar 6, 1900
Foreman, Carol Lee Tucker
b. May 3, 1938

Gerard, Gil b. Jan 23, 1943
Graham, Fred Patterson b. Oct 6, 1931
Hays, Lee b. 1914
Hibbler, Al b. Aug 16, 1915
Humbard, Rex b. Aug 13, 1919
Knight, Stan b. Feb 12, 1949
Lawrence, Margaret d. Jun 9, 1929
Lawrence, Marjorie Florence
d. Jan 13, 1979
Liston, "Sonny" (Charles) b. May 8, 1932
MacArthur, Douglas b. Jan 26, 1880
McClellan, John Little d. Nov 27, 1977
Moncrief, Sidney b. Sep 21, 1957
Pendleton, Don b. Dec 12, 1927
Price, Florence Beatrice Smith
b. Apr 8, 1888
Robinson, Brooks Calbert, Jr.
b. May 18, 1937
Steenburgen, Mary b. 1953
Templeton, Fay b. Dec 25, 1865
Lucas, Arkansas
Dean, "Daffy" (Paul Dee) b. Aug 14, 1913
Dean, "Dizzy" (Jay Hanna)
b. Jan 16, 1911
Mammoth Spring, Arkansas
Harper, Tess b. 1950
Manilan, Arkansas
Reynolds, Ricky b. Oct 29, 1948
Marvell, Arkansas
Helm, Levon b. May 26, 1943
Mineola, Arkansas
Wakely, Jimmy b. Feb 16, 1914
Mineral Springs, Arkansas
Davis, Willie (William Henry)
b. Apr 15, 1940
Mount Ida, Arkansas
Warneke, Lon(nie) b. Mar 28, 1909
Mountain View, Arkansas
Powell, Dick b. Nov 24, 1904
North Little Rock, Arkansas
Blucker, Robert Olof b. Oct 21, 1927
Osceola, Arkansas
Wilson, Kemmons b. Jan 5, 1913
Pine Bluff, Arkansas
Alexander, Donald Crichton
b. May 22, 1921
Haynes, George Edward b. May 11, 1880
Mitchell, Martha Elizabeth Beall
b. Sep 2, 1918
Rison, Arkansas
Dedman, Robert H b. 1926
Russellville, Arkansas
Hays, Brooks b. Aug 9, 1898
Sheridan, Arkansas
McClellan, John Little b. Feb 25, 1896
Sparkman, Arkansas
Brown, Jim Ed (James Edward)
b. Apr 1, 1934
Springdale, Arkansas
Dean, "Daffy" (Paul Dee)
d. Mar 17, 1981

Swifton, Arkansas
Kell, George Clyde b. Aug 23, 1922
Texarkana, Arkansas
Rogers, Don(ald Lavert) b. Sep 17, 1962
Thornton, Arkansas
Steelman, John R b. Jun 23, 1900
Vanndale, Arkansas
Woodward, C(omer) Vann b. Nov 13, 1908
Waldo, Arkansas
Jackson, Travis Calvin b. Nov 2, 1903
West Helena, Arkansas
Warfield, William Caesar b. Jan 22, 1920
West Memphis, Arkansas
Lee, Keith Deywane b. Dec 28, 1962
Wynn, Arkansas
Boggs, Tom (Thomas) b. Jul 16, 1947

CALIFORNIA

Auger, Arleen b. 1943
Baskin, Burton d. 1967
Bennett, Harry Herbert d. Jan 4, 1979
Bergeron, Victor J b. 1903
Brittany, Morgan b. 1950
Crane, Richard O d. Mar 9, 1969
Fernald, John Bailey b. Nov 21, 1905
Halop, Billy d. Nov 9, 1976
Holling, Holling C(lancy) d. Sep 7, 1973
Lupus, Peter b. Jun 17, 1937
Martin, Dean Paul (Dino, Jr.)
    b. Nov 17, 1953
Morita, "Pat" (Noriyuki) b. 1932
Murnau, Friedrich W d. Mar 11, 1931
Reynolds, Quentin d. Mar 17, 1965
Seidel, Toscha d. Nov 15, 1962
Yarnell, Bruce d. Nov 30, 1973
Alameda, California
Doolittle, James Harold b. Dec 14, 1896
Erickson, Leif b. Oct 27, 1911
Heidt, Horace Murray b. May 21, 1901
Knowland, William Fife b. Jun 26, 1908
Lewis, Wilmarth Sheldon b. Nov 14, 1895
VonSchmidt, Harold b. May 19, 1893
Alcatraz, California
Barker, "Doc" (Arthur) d. Jun 13, 1939
Alhambra, California
Tiegs, Cheryl b. Sep 25, 1947
Vogel, Mitch b. 1956
Allegheny, California
Weber, Lois b. Jun 13, 1881
Alpha, California
Nevada, Emma b. Feb 7, 1859
Altadena, California
Branzell, Karin d. Dec 15, 1974
Grey, Zane d. Oct 23, 1939
LaMarr, Barbara d. Jan 30, 1926
Nixon, Marni b. Feb 22, 1929

Anaheim, California
Demara, Ferdinand Waldo, Jr.
    d. Jun 7, 1982
Wilson, Marie (Katherine Elizabeth)
    b. Aug 19, 1916
Antioch, California
Burke, Johnny b. Oct 3, 1908
Dragon, Carmen b. Jul 28, 1914
Marchetti, Gino b. Jan 2, 1927
Apple Valley, California
Buono, Victor (Charles Victor)
    d. Jan 1, 1982
Mangrum, Lloyd d. Nov 17, 1973
Sparks, Ned d. Apr 2, 1957
Thomas, John Charles d. Dec 13, 1960
Arcadia, California
Shipler, Guy Emery d. Apr 18, 1968
Arroyo Grande, California
Quimby, Harriet b. May 1, 1884
Atherton, California
Haider, Michael Lawrence d. Aug 14, 1986
Atwater, California
Hutchins, Will b. May 5, 1932
Avalon, California
Harrison, Gregory b. May 31, 1950
Azusa, California
Ritchey, George Willis d. Nov 4, 1945
Bakersfield, California
Engle, Clair b. Sep 21, 1911
Haggard, Merle Ronald b. Apr 6, 1937
Madison, Guy b. Jan 19, 1922
Nofziger, Lyn (Franklyn Curran)
    b. Jun 8, 1924
Shafter, William Rufus d. Nov 12, 1906
Tibbett, Lawrence Mervil b. Nov 16, 1896
Trevino, Elizabeth Borton de
    b. Sep 2, 1904
Baldwin Hills, California
Bubbles, John d. May 18, 1986
Beaumont, California
Bottel, Helen Alfea b. Mar 13, 1914
Bel Air, California
Kent, Arthur Atwater d. Apr 4, 1949
Mercer, Johnny d. Jun 25, 1976
Tate, Sharon d. Aug 9, 1969
Belvedere, California
Vance, Vivian d. Aug 17, 1979
Benicia, California
Mizner, Addison b. 1872
Berkeley, California
Anderson, Melissa Sue b. Sep 26, 1962
Cheney, Sheldon Warren b. Jun 29, 1886
Cheney, Sheldon Warren d. Oct 10, 1980
Chenier, Phil(ip) b. Oct 30, 1950
Compton, Arthur Holly d. Mar 15, 1962
Culp, Robert b. Aug 13, 1930
Davies, Rodger Paul b. May 7, 1921
Dean, William Frishe d. Aug 24, 1981
Evans, Herbert McLean d. Mar 6, 1971
Funikawa, Gyo b.
Gleason, Ralph Joseph d. Jun 3, 1975

Goulart, Ron(ald Joseph) b. Jan 13, 1933
Grassle, Karen Gene b. Feb 25,
Hafey, "Chick" (Charles James)
   b. Feb 12, 1903
Harris, Joseph Pratt d. Feb 13, 1985
Ivory, James b. Jun 7, 1928
Keith, William d. 1911
Kroeber, Theodora Kracaw d. Jul 4, 1979
LeGuin, Ursula Kroeber b. Oct 21, 1929
Lesh, Phil b. Mar 15, 1940
Martin, "Billy" (Alfred Manuel)
   b. May 16, 1928
Meiklejohn, Alexander d. Sep 16, 1964
Merriam, Clinton Hart d. Mar 19, 1942
Miles, Josephine d. May 12, 1985
Powdermaker, Hortense d. Jun 15, 1970
Scherr, Max d. Oct 31, 1981
Sproul, Robert Gordon d. Sep 10, 1975
Susskind, Walter d. Mar 25, 1980
Wilkes, Jamaal b. May 2, 1953

Berkley, California
Struve, Otto d. Apr 6, 1963

Beverly Hills, California
Adams, Nick d. Feb 5, 1968
Angeli, Pier d. Sep 10, 1971
Balderston, John Lloyd d. Mar 8, 1954
Barrymore, John Blythe Drew, Jr.
   b. Jun 4, 1932
Baxter, Warner d. May 7, 1951
Beery, Noah d. Apr 1, 1946
Beery, Wallace d. Apr 15, 1949
Bergen, Candice b. May 9, 1946
Bern, Paul d. Sep 4, 1932
Bernie, Ben d. Oct 20, 1943
Brice, Fanny d. May 29, 1951
Broderick, Helen d. Sep 25, 1959
Cantor, Eddie d. Oct 10, 1964
Castle, William d. May 31, 1977
Cawthorn, Joseph d. Jan 21, 1949
Chamberlain, Richard b. Mar 31, 1935
Chekhov, Michael d. Sep 30, 1955
Cody, Lew d. May 31, 1934
Collier, William, Sr. d. Jan 13, 1944
Connolly, Walter d. May 28, 1940
Craven, Frank d. Sep 1, 1945
Dall, John d. Jan 15, 1971
Dantine, Helmut d. May 3, 1982
Erwin, Stuart d. Dec 21, 1967
Farrow, John Villiers d. Jan 28, 1963
Fazenda, Louise d. Apr 17, 1962
Field, Rachel Lyman d. Mar 15, 1942
Fields, Joseph d. Mar 3, 1966
Fields, Lew Maurice d. Jul 20, 1941
Finch, Peter d. Jan 14, 1977
Fisher, Carrie Frances b. Oct 21, 1956
Foreman, Carl d. Jun 26, 1984
Frank, Bruno d. Jun 20, 1945
Gershwin, Ira d. Aug 17, 1983
Giesler, Jerry (Harold Lee)
   d. Sep 27, 1962
Gilbert, Bruce b. 1948

Gordon, Vera d. May 8, 1948
Grable, Betty d. Jul 3, 1973
Greenberg, Hank (Henry Benjamin)
   d. Sep 4, 1986
Gruenberg, Louis d. Jun 9, 1964
Hayward, Susan d. Mar 14, 1975
Hearst, William Randolph d. Aug 14, 1951
Hecht, Harold d. May 25, 1985
Hersholt, Jean d. Jun 2, 1956
Hitchcock, Alfred Joseph, Sir
   d. Apr 29, 1980
Hitchcock, Raymond d. Dec 24, 1929
Holt, Tim b. Feb 5, 1918
Hudson, Rock d. Oct 2, 1985
Huston, Walter d. Apr 7, 1950
Ince, Thomas H(arper) d. Nov 19, 1924
Iturbi, Amparo d. Apr 21, 1969
Jaffe, Sam d. Mar 24, 1984
Janis, Elsie d. Feb 26, 1956
Jones, Jack b. Jan 14, 1938
Kahn, Gus d. Oct 8, 1941
Kamen, Milt d. Feb 24, 1977
Kaper, Bronislau d. May 1983
King, Walter Woolf d. Oct 24, 1984
LaRocque, Rod d. Oct 15, 1969
Lasky, Jesse L d. Jan 13, 1958
Lawrence, Florence d. Dec 27, 1938
Levant, Oscar d. Aug 14, 1972
Lyman, Abe d. Oct 23, 1957
Lynde, Paul Edward d. Jan 10, 1982
Mann, Heinrich Ludwig d. Mar 12, 1950
Marshall, Herbert d. Jan 22, 1966
Maxwell, Marilyn d. Mar 20, 1972
McCoy, Horace d. Dec 17, 1955
McHugh, Jimmy (James) d. May 23, 1969
Menjou, Adolphe Jean d. Oct 29, 1963
Minnelli, Vincente d. Jul 25, 1986
Miranda, Carmen d. Aug 5, 1955
Mitchell, Thomas d. Dec 17, 1962
Morgan, Frank d. Sep 18, 1949
Murphy, Jimmy (James Edward)
   d. Mar 9, 1965
Newton, Robert d. Mar 25, 1956
Norworth, Jack d. Sep 1, 1959
Oldfield, Barney (Berna Eli)
   d. Oct 4, 1946
Pal, George d. May 2, 1980
Pauley, Edwin Wendell d. Jul 28, 1981
Powell, Eleanor d. Feb 11, 1982
Rachmaninoff, Sergei Vasilyevich
   d. Mar 28, 1943
Reed, Donna d. Jan 14, 1986
Reeves, George d. Jun 16, 1959
Renoir, Jean d. Feb 12, 1979
Robinson, Edward G d. Jan 26, 1973
Robson, May d. Oct 20, 1942
Rubinstein, John b. Dec 8, 1946
Russell, Rosalind d. Nov 28, 1976
Schenck, Joseph M d. Oct 22, 1961
Seaton, George d. Jul 28, 1979
Seville, David d. Jan 16, 1972

Siegel, "Bugsy" (Benjamin)
d. Jun 20, 1947
Smith, C Aubrey d. Dec 20, 1948
Stewart, Anita d. May 4, 1961
Toler, Sidney d. Feb 12, 1947
Tracy, Spencer d. Jun 10, 1967
Wald, Jerry (Jerome Irving)
d. Jul 13, 1962
Walker, Stuart Armstrong d. Mar 13, 1941
Walter, Bruno d. Feb 17, 1962
Webb, Clifton d. Oct 13, 1966
Webster, Paul Francois d. Mar 22, 1984
Werfel, Franz d. Aug 26, 1945
Whiting, Richard Armstrong
d. Feb 10, 1938
Whitty, May, Dame d. May 29, 1948
Wyler, William d. Jul 28, 1981
Wynn, Ed d. Jun 19, 1966

Big Sur, California
Flory, Paul John d. Sep 9, 1985

Blythe, California
Eason, Tony (Charles Carroll, IV)
b. Oct 8, 1959

Bolinas, California
Brautigan, Richard d. Oct 25, 1984

Borea, California
Hosmer, Craig (Chester Craig)
b. May 16, 1915

Brentwood, California
Andrews, LaVerne d. May 8, 1967
Brown, Joe Evan d. Jul 17, 1973
Carey, Harry d. Sep 21, 1947
Gleason, Lucille d. May 13, 1947
Nolan, Lloyd d. Sep 27, 1985
Schoenberg, Arnold d. Jul 13, 1951
Sloane, Everett d. Aug 6, 1965
Van Dyke, W(oodbridge) S(trong)
d. Feb 5, 1943

Brentwood Heights, California
Landis, Carole d. Jul 5, 1948

Buena Park, California
Knott, Walter d. Dec 3, 1981
Spenkelink, John Arthur b. 1949

Burbank, California
Arquette, Cliff d. Sep 23, 1974
Avery, "Tex" (Frederick Bean)
d. Aug 27, 1980
Bates, Florence d. Jan 31, 1954
Conreid, Hans d. Jan 5, 1982
Disney, Roy O d. Dec 20, 1971
Faylen, Frank d. Aug 2, 1985
Gold, Andrew b. Aug 2, 1951
Harmon, Mark b. Sep 2, 1951
Hayes, "Gabby" (George Francis)
d. Feb 9, 1969
Howard, Clint b. Apr 20, 1959
Jeffries, James Jackson d. Mar 3, 1953
Kanaly, Steve(n Francis) b. Mar 14, 1946
Loo, Richard d. Nov 20, 1983
Meiklejohn, William d. Apr 26, 1981
Moran, Erin b. Oct 18, 1961

Nash, Clarence d. Feb 20, 1985
Richman, Harry d. Nov 3, 1972
Ritter, John(athan Southworth)
b. Sep 17, 1948
Weaver, "Doodles" (Winstead Sheffield
Glendening Dixon) d. Jan 15, 1983

Calistoga, California
Hafey, "Chick" (Charles James)
d. Jul 5, 1973
Vermeil, Dick (Richard Albert)
b. Oct 30, 1936

Cambria, California
Papashvily, George d. Mar 29, 1978

Canoga Park, California
Hood, Darla Jean d. Jun 13, 1979

Capistrano Beach, California
Alter, Hobie (Hobart, Jr.) b. 1934

Carmel, California
Alinsky, Saul David d. Jun 12, 1972
Andrews, Roy Chapman d. Mar 11, 1960
Bonestell, Chesley d. Jun 11, 1986
Burgess, Gelett (Frank Gelett)
d. Sep 18, 1951
Farina, Richard d. Apr 30, 1966
Flavin, Martin Archer d. Dec 27, 1967
Hatlo, Jimmy d. Nov 30, 1963
Jeffers, (John) Robinson d. Jan 20, 1962
Rankin, Jeannette d. May 18, 1973
Remsen, Ira d. Mar 5, 1927
Sargent, Dick b. Apr 19, 1933
Steffens, Lincoln d. Aug 9, 1936
Van Niel, Cornelius B(ernardus)
d. Mar 10, 1985
Weston, Edward d. Jan 1, 1958

Castaic, California
Morrow, Vic d. Jul 23, 1982

Catalina Island, California
Wood, Natalie d. Nov 29, 1981

Cathedral City, California
Oakland, Simon d. Aug 29, 1983

Centerville, California
Moody, Helen Wills b. Oct 6, 1905

Chatsworth, California
Harman, Hugh d. Nov 26, 1982
Henry, William M d. Apr 13, 1970
Sabu d. Dec 2, 1963
Waters, Ethel d. Sep 1, 1977

Chico, California
Hayden, Russell b. Jun 12, 1912

Claremont, California
Davis, Glenn b. Dec 26, 1924
Mason, Max d. Mar 23, 1961
McFee, Henry Lee d. Mar 19, 1953
Suckow, Ruth d. Jan 23, 1960

Clinton, California
Craft, Ellen b. 1826

Coalinga, California
Stafford, Jo b. Nov 12, 1918

Compton, California
Conner, Nadine b. Feb 20, 1913

Concord, California
Brubeck, Dave (David Warren)
b. Dec 6, 1920
Corona, California
Grapewin, Charley (Charles)
d. Feb 2, 1956
Parks, Michael b. Apr 4, 1938
Corte Madera, California
McKernan, Ron d. Mar 8, 1973
Costa Mesa, California
Breedlove, (Norman) Craig
b. Mar 23, 1938
Nolan, Bob d. 1980
Covelo, California
Marks, Percy b. Sep 9, 1891
Covina, California
Clark, Jack Anthony b. Nov 10, 1955
Stafford, Jean b. Jul 1, 1915
Cressy, California
Suzuki, Pat (Chiyoko) b. Sep 23, 1931
Culver City, California
Bigard, Albany Barney Leon
d. Jun 27, 1980
Carter, Gary Edmund b. Apr 8, 1954
Chandler, Jeff d. Jun 17, 1961
Conway, Tom d. Apr 22, 1967
Korjus, Miliza d. Aug 26, 1980
Lennon, Janet b. Nov 15, 1946
Lowrey, "Peanuts" (Harry Lee)
b. Aug 27, 1918
Shearer, Douglas d. Jan 5, 1971
Verdon, Gwen (Gwyneth Evelyn)
b. Jan 13, 1925
Del Monte, California
Gilmore, Virginia b. Jul 26, 1919
Delano, California
Rambo, Dack b. Nov 13, 1941
Valente, Benita b.
Desert Hot Springs, California
Langley, Noel d. Nov 4, 1980
Dinuba, California
Turner, Claramae b. Oct 28, 1920
Dorris, California
Briles, Nelson Kelley b. Aug 5, 1943
Downey, California
Brasselle, Keefe d. Jul 7, 1981
Carpenter, Karen Ann d. Feb 4, 1983
Durango, California
Tully, Tom b. Aug 21, 1902
Eagleville, California
Vaughn, Joseph Floyd d. Aug 30, 1952
East Oakland, California
Pointer, Anita b. 1948
Pointer, Bonnie b. Jul 11, 1951
Pointer, June b. 1954
Pointer, Ruth b. 1946
El Cajon, California
Louganis, Greg(ory Efthimios)
b. Jan 29, 1960

El Centro, California
Cher b. May 20, 1946
Howard, Ken(neth Joseph Jr.)
b. Mar 28, 1944
West, Nathanael, pseud. d. Dec 22, 1940
El Cerrito, California
Einstein, Alfred d. Feb 13, 1952
El Monte, California
McDonald, "Country Joe" b. 1942
Wiggins, Charles Edward b. Dec 3, 1927
Encino, California
Abell, George O(gden) d. Oct 7, 1983
Breneman, Tom d. Apr 28, 1948
Carlson, Richard d. Nov 25, 1977
Carson, Jack d. Jan 2, 1963
Cowan, Jerome d. Jan 24, 1972
Hackett, Joan d. Oct 8, 1983
Horton, Edward Everett d. Sep 29, 1970
Marshall, Tully d. Mar 10, 1943
McGee, Molly d. Apr 7, 1961
Powers, Francis Gary d. Aug 1, 1977
Shaw, Reta d. Jan 8, 1982
Talman, William d. Aug 30, 1968
Tuttle, Lurene d. May 28, 1986
William, Warren d. Sep 24, 1948
Wills, Chill d. Dec 15, 1978
Zimbalist, Stephanie b. Oct 8, 1956
Escondido, California
Brannan, Samuel d. May 5, 1889
Hamilton, Neil d. Sep 24, 1984
Eureka, California
Cochran, Steve b. May 25, 1917
Swinnerton, James Guilford
b. Nov 13, 1875
Fallbrook, California
Costello, Dolores d. Mar 1, 1979
Truex, Ernest d. Jun 27, 1973
Fillmore, California
Clark, Monte b. Jan 24, 1937
Flintridge, California
Friganza, Trixie d. Feb 27, 1955
Fountain Valley, California
Satherly, Arthur Edward d. Feb 10, 1986
Fremont, California
Epperson, Frank W d. Oct 25, 1983
Fresno, California
Boolootian, Richard Andrew
b. Oct 17, 1927
Chance, Frank Leroy b. Sep 9, 1877
Connors, Mike b. Aug 15, 1925
Contino, Dick b. 1930
Flores, Tom (Thomas Raymond)
b. Mar 21, 1937
Kerkorian, Kirk b. Jun 6, 1917
Key, Theodore b. Aug 25, 1912
Lamonica, Daryle Pat b. Jul 17, 1941
Leonard, "Dutch" (Hubert Benjamin)
d. Jul 11, 1952
Menard, H William b. Dec 10, 1920
Peckinpah, (David) Sam(uel)
b. Feb 21, 1925

Peterson, Lorraine Collett d. Mar 30, 1983
Politi, Leo b. 1908
Saroyan, William b. Aug 31, 1908
Saroyan, William d. May 18, 1981
Seaver, Tom (George Thomas)
  b. Nov 17, 1944
Seville, David b. Jan 27, 1919
Webb, Del(bert Eugene) b. May 17, 1899
Fullerton, California
Forester, Cecil Scott d. Apr 2, 1966
Jones, Randy (Randall Leo)
  b. Jan 12, 1950
Nol, Lon d. Nov 17, 1985
Witt, Mike (Michael Arthur)
  b. Jul 20, 1960
Garden Grove, California
Trammell, Alan Stuart b. Feb 21, 1958
Gardena, California
Pepper, Art(hur Edward) b. Sep 1, 1925
Geyserville, California
Overstreet, Bonaro Wilkinson
  b. Oct 30, 1902
Gilroy, California
Anderson, Ivie b. 1904
Glen Ellen, California
London, Jack (John Griffith)
  d. Nov 22, 1916
Glendale, California
Armstrong, Charlotte d. Jul 18, 1969
Bosworth, Hobart van Zandt
  d. Dec 30, 1943
Dillon, Diane Claire Sorber
  b. Mar 13, 1933
Kornman, Mary d. Jun 1, 1973
Lhevinne, Rosina L d. Nov 9, 1976
Maybeck, Bernard Ralph d. Mar 2, 1957
McClure, Doug b. May 11, 1938
McGinnis, Scott b. Nov 19, 1958
Northrop, John Knudsen d. Feb 18, 1981
Peterson, Paul b. Sep 23, 1945
Powers, John Robert d. Aug 19, 1977
Smith, Gerald Lyman Kenneth
  d. Apr 15, 1976
Smith, Paul Joseph d. Jan 25, 1985
Stengel, "Casey" (Charles Dillon)
  d. Sep 29, 1975
Stumpf, Richard J b. Oct 15, 1926
Taylor, Charles Alonzo d. Mar 20, 1942
Glendora, California
Rand, Sally d. Aug 31, 1979
Goleta Valley, California
Guffey, Burnett d. May 30, 1983
Grass Valley, California
Royce, Josiah b. Nov 20, 1855
Greenbrae, California
Stanford, Sally d. Feb 2, 1982
Guerneville, California
Liebes, Dorothy Katherine Wright
  b. Oct 14, 1897

Hanford, California
Lord, Pauline b. 1890
Perry, Steve b. Jan 22, 1949
Hawthorne, California
Dryer, Fred (John Frederick)
  b. Jul 6, 1946
Saint John, Betta b. Nov 26, 1929
Wilson, Brian Douglas b. Jun 20, 1942
Wilson, Carl Dean b. Dec 21, 1946
Wilson, Dennis b. Dec 1, 1941
Hayward, California
Kolb, Claudia b. Dec 19, 1949
Healdsburg, California
Wightman, Hazel Virginia Hotchkiss
  b. Dec 20, 1886
Hemet, California
Nilsson, Anna Q(uerentia) d. Feb 11, 1974
Passarella, Art d. Oct 1981
Hermosa Beach, California
Marsh, Mae d. Feb 13, 1968
Hidden Hills, California
McDonald, Marie d. Oct 21, 1965
Hillsborough, California
Bergeron, Victor J d. Oct 11, 1984
Hollister, California
Anderson, Jack Zuinglius d. Feb 9, 1981
Hollywood, California
Adler, "Buddy" (Maurice) d. Jul 12, 1960
Adler, Polly d. Jun 9, 1962
Adrian d. Sep 14, 1959
Albertson, Jack d. Nov 25, 1981
Alexander, Ben (Nicholas Benton)
  d. Jul 5, 1969
Allen, Gracie Ethel Cecil Rosaline
  d. Aug 27, 1964
Arnaz, Lucie Desiree b. Jul 17, 1951
Atwill, Lionel d. Apr 22, 1946
Awtrey, Dennis b. Feb 22, 1948
Baer, Max d. Nov 21, 1959
Bainter, Fay Okell d. Apr 16, 1968
Baker, Diane b. Feb 25, 1938
Bakewell, William b. May 2, 1908
Barrymore, Ethel Mae Blythe
  d. Jun 18, 1959
Barrymore, John d. May 29, 1942
Baum, (Lyman) Frank d. May 6, 1919
Baum, Vicki d. Aug 29, 1960
Beavers, Louise d. Oct 26, 1962
Begley, Ed(ward James) d. Apr 28, 1970
Belushi, John d. Mar 5, 1982
Blackstone, Harry d. Nov 16, 1965
Bledsoe, Jules d. Jul 14, 1943
Blore, Eric d. Mar 2, 1959
Borg, Veda Ann d. Aug 16, 1973
Borzage, Frank d. Jun 19, 1962
Breen, Joseph Ignatius d. Dec 7, 1965
Brendel, El(mer) d. Apr 9, 1964
Bruce, Lenny d. Aug 3, 1966
Byington, Spring d. Sep 7, 1971
Cambridge, Godfrey d. Nov 29, 1976
Canova, Judy d. Aug 5, 1983

Cantor, Charles d. Sep 11, 1966
Carlisle, Belinda b. Aug 17, 1958
Carnes, Kim b. Jul 20, 1946
Carradine, David b. Oct 8, 1940
Carroll, Leo G d. Oct 16, 1972
Carter, Boake d. Nov 16, 1947
Castelnuovo-Tedesco, Mario
   d. Mar 15, 1968
Castle, Peggie d. Aug 11, 1973
Chase, Charley d. Jun 20, 1940
Clive, Colin d. Jun 25, 1937
Cole, Tina b. Aug 4, 1943
Collier, Peter b. Jun 2, 1939
Columbo, Russ d. Sep 2, 1934
Conklin, Chester d. Oct 11, 1971
Cooper, "Gary" (Frank James)
   d. May 13, 1961
Costello, Maurice d. Oct 30, 1950
Crawford, Christina b. Jun 11, 1939
Crawford, Sam(uel Earl) d. Jun 15, 1968
Cummings, Quinn b. Aug 13, 1967
Curtiz, Michael d. Apr 11, 1962
Dailey, Dan d. Oct 17, 1978
Dalmores, Charles d. Dec 6, 1939
Darby, Kim b. Jul 8, 1948
Darin, Bobby d. Dec 20, 1973
Davies, Marion d. Sep 22, 1961
DeForest, Lee d. Jun 30, 1961
Dekker, Albert d. May 5, 1968
DeMille, Cecil B(lount) d. Jan 21, 1959
Derek, John b. Aug 12, 1926
Dickson, Gloria d. Apr 10, 1945
Dolly, Jenny d. Jun 1, 1941
Douglas, Paul d. Sep 11, 1959
Dow, Tony b. Apr 13, 1945
Dreiser, Theodore d. Dec 28, 1945
Duel, Peter d. Dec 31, 1971
Eaton, Mary d. Oct 10, 1948
Edeson, Robert d. Mar 24, 1931
Edwards, Cliff d. Jul 17, 1971
Emerson, Hope d. Apr 25, 1960
Fitzgerald, F(rancis) Scott (Key)
   d. Dec 21, 1940
Flippen, Jay C d. Feb 3, 1971
Friml, Rudolf d. Nov 12, 1972
Gable, Clark d. Nov 16, 1960
Garr, Teri b. Dec 11, 1945
Garrett, Leif b. Nov 8, 1961
Gebert, Ernst d. Nov 22, 1961
Gershwin, George d. Jul 11, 1937
Gilbert, Billy d. Sep 23, 1971
Goulding, Edmund d. Dec 24, 1959
Grauman, Sid(ney Patrick) d. Mar 5, 1950
Gray, Gilda d. Dec 22, 1959
Green, Martyn d. Feb 8, 1975
Green, Paula b. Sep 18, 1927
Hackett, Raymond d. Jun 9, 1958
Haggerty, Dan b. Nov 19, 1941
Hale, Alan d. Jan 22, 1950
Hardin, Tim d. Dec 29, 1980
Hardy, Oliver d. Aug 7, 1957

Heflin, Van Emmett Evan d. Jul 23, 1971
Hellinger, Mark d. Dec 21, 1947
Herbert, Hugh d. Mar 13, 1951
Herriman, George d. Apr 25, 1944
Hershey, Barbara b. Feb 5, 1948
Hines, Jerome b. Nov 9, 1921
Hoffenstein, Samuel Goodman
   d. Oct 6, 1947
Holmes, Burton d. Jul 22, 1958
Holmes, Taylor d. Sep 30, 1959
Hopper, Hedda d. Feb 1, 1966
Howard, "Shemp" (Samuel)
   d. Nov 22, 1955
Howard, Moe d. May 24, 1975
Howe, James Wong d. Jul 12, 1976
Irene d. Nov 15, 1962
James, Will(iam) d. Sep 3, 1942
Jefferson, Thomas d. Apr 2, 1923
Jones, Isham d. Oct 19, 1956
Joplin, Janis d. Oct 3, 1970
Joyce, Alice d. Oct 9, 1955
Keaton, "Buster" (Joseph Francis)
   d. Feb 1, 1966
Kelly, "Patsy" (Sarah Veronica Rose)
   d. Sep 24, 1981
Kelly, Walt d. Oct 18, 1973
Kenton, Stan(ley Newcomb)
   d. Aug 25, 1979
Kilian, Victor d. Mar 11, 1979
Kirby, John d. 1952
Korngold, Erich Wolfgang
   d. Nov 29, 1957
Kovacs, Ernie d. Jan 13, 1962
Laemmle, Carl, Sr. d. Sep 24, 1939
Law, John Philip b. Sep 7, 1937
Lesser, Sol d. Sep 19, 1980
Lincoln, Elmo d. Jun 27, 1952
Little, "Little Jack" d. Apr 9, 1956
Lloyd, Harold d. Mar 8, 1971
Lorre, Peter d. Mar 24, 1964
Lugosi, Bela d. Sep 16, 1956
Marx, "Chico" (Leonard) d. Oct 11, 1961
Marx, "Harpo" (Arthur) d. Sep 28, 1964
McDaniel, Hattie d. Oct 26, 1952
McDevitt, Ruth d. May 27, 1976
McIntyre, Hal (Harold W) d. May 5, 1959
Monroe, Marilyn d. Aug 5, 1962
Montgomery, Elizabeth b. Apr 15, 1933
Mowbray, Alan d. Mar 25, 1969
Murray, Don(ald Patrick) b. Jul 31, 1929
Nazimova, Alla d. Jul 13, 1945
Nelson, Ozzie (Oswald George)
   d. Jun 3, 1975
Newman, Alfred d. Feb 17, 1970
Novarro, Ramon d. Oct 31, 1968
O'Brien, Willis Harold d. Nov 8, 1962
O'Connell, Hugh d. Jan 19, 1943
Oliver, Edna May d. Nov 9, 1942
Orry-Kelly d. Feb 26, 1964
Palmer, "Bud" (John S) b. Sep 14, 1923
Patrick, Gail d. Jul 6, 1980

Pitts, Zasu (Eliza Susan) d. Jun 7, 1963
Post, Marjorie Merriweather
  d. Sep 12, 1973
Powell, Dick d. Jan 2, 1963
Power, Tyrone (Frederick Tyrone Edmond)
  d. Dec 30, 1931
Powers, Stefanie b. Nov 12, 1942
Pyne, Joe d. Mar 23, 1970
Ragland, "Rags" (John Lee Morgan
  Beauregard) d. Aug 20, 1946
Rankin, Arthur d. Mar 23, 1947
Redman, Ben Ray d. Aug 1, 1961
Ross, Katharine b. Jan 29, 1943
Scheuer, Philip K(latz) d. Feb 18, 1985
Schumann-Heink, Ernestine Rossler
  d. Nov 16, 1936
Selznick, David O(liver) d. Jun 22, 1965
Sheridan, Ann d. Jan 21, 1967
Sherman, Lowell d. Dec 28, 1934
Shields, Larry d. Nov 22, 1953
Skolsky, Sidney d. May 3, 1983
Steiner, Max d. Dec 28, 1971
Stevens, Inger d. Apr 30, 1970
Stevens, K T b. Jul 20, 1919
Stockwell, Dean b. Mar 5, 1936
Stompanato, Johnny d. Apr 4, 1958
Sullivan, C(harles) Gardner d. Sep 5, 1965
Taylor, Estelle d. Apr 15, 1958
Taylor, William Desmond d. Feb 2, 1922
Thomas, Michael Tilson b. Dec 21, 1944
Tilden, Bill (William Tatem, Jr.)
  d. Jun 5, 1953
Tobias, George d. Feb 27, 1980
Turner, Joe d. Nov 24, 1985
Veidt, Conrad d. Apr 3, 1943
Verdugo, Elena b. Apr 20, 1926
VonSternberg, Josef d. Dec 22, 1969
Waldron, Charles D d. Mar 4, 1946
Wallace, Edgar d. Feb 10, 1932
Walter, Eugene d. Sep 26, 1941
Warner, Harry Morris d. Jul 25, 1958
Webster, Ben(jamin) d. Feb 26, 1947
West, Mae d. Nov 22, 1980
Whale, James d. May 29, 1957
Wood, Samuel Grosvenor d. Sep 22, 1949
Wright, Cobina d. Apr 9, 1970
Ziegfeld, Flo(renz) d. Jul 22, 1932
Zucco, George d. May 28, 1960

Hollywood Hills, California
Inge, William d. Jun 10, 1973
Oates, Warren d. Apr 3, 1982
Scala, Gia d. Apr 30, 1972
Wilson, Marie (Katherine Elizabeth)
  d. Nov 23, 1972

Holmby Hills, California
Lee, Dixie d. Nov 1, 1952
Livingstone, Mary d. Jun 30, 1983
Thornton, Charles Bates d. Nov 24, 1981

Huntington, California
Green, Mitzi d. May 24, 1969

Ignacio Valley, California
Walker, Joseph Reddeford d. Oct 27, 1876
Indio, California
Cochran, Jacqueline d. Aug 9, 1980
Van Druten, John William
  d. Dec 19, 1957
Inglewood, California
Bell, Ricky Lynn d. Nov 28, 1984
Blocker, Dan d. May 13, 1972
Childress, Alvin d. Apr 19, 1986
Lawrence, Vicki b. Mar 26, 1949
Lowrey, "Peanuts" (Harry Lee)
  d. Jul 2, 1986
O'Brien, Edmond d. May 8, 1985
Peckinpah, (David) Sam(uel)
  d. Dec 28, 1984
Sims, "Zoot" (John Haley) b. Oct 29, 1925
Irvine, California
Bailey, Raymond d. Apr 15, 1980
Colonius, Lillian b. Mar 19, 1911
Jonesboro, California
Rivers, Thomas Milton b. Sep 3, 1888
Joshua Tree, California
Parsons, Gram d. Sep 19, 1973
Julian, California
Rumann, Sig(fried) d. Feb 14, 1967
Kingsberg, California
Pickens, "Slim" b. Jun 29, 1919
La Costa, California
Ongais, Danny b. May 21, 1942
La Jolla, California
Baillie, Hugh d. Mar 1, 1966
Brink, Carol Ryrie d. Aug 15, 1981
Bullard, Edward Crisp, Sir d. Apr 3, 1980
Chandler, Raymond Thornton
  d. Mar 26, 1959
Cole, Kenneth Stewart d. Apr 18, 1984
Ehricke, Krafft Arnold d. Dec 11, 1984
Foster, Preston d. Jul 14, 1970
Galli-Curci, Amelita d. Nov 26, 1963
Gray, Harold d. May 9, 1968
Mayer, Maria Goeppert d. Feb 20, 1972
Menard, H William d. Feb 9, 1986
Miller, Max d. Dec 27, 1967
Naish, J(oseph) Carrol d. Jan 24, 1973
Peck, Gregory b. Apr 5, 1916
Robertson, Cliff b. Sep 9, 1925
Stone, Milburn d. Jun 12, 1980
Szilard, Leo d. May 30, 1964
Wright, Harold Bell d. May 24, 1944
La Mirada, California
Neff, Wallace b. 1895
La Quinta, California
Arzner, Dorothy d. Oct 1, 1979
Laguna Beach, California
Summerville, "Slim" (George J)
  d. Jan 6, 1946
Laguna Hills, California
Patrick, Lee d. Nov 21, 1982
Laguna Niguel, California
Armstrong, Jack Lawrence d. Jun 10, 1985

LaHabra, California
Coy, Harold b. Sep 24, 1902
LaJolla, California
Urey, Harold Clayton d. Jan 6, 1981
Lake Elsinore, California
Merrill, Henry Tindall d. Nov 30, 1982
LaMesa, California
Walton, Bill b. Nov 5, 1952
Lancaster, California
Stevens, George d. Mar 8, 1975
Lincoln, California
Clark, Fred b. Mar 9, 1914
Linden, California
Kuykendall, Ralph Simpson
b. Apr 12, 1885
Lodi, California
Aberle, John Wayne b. Aug 12, 1919
Cartwright, Bill (James William)
b. Jul 30, 1957
Lomita, California
Thorpe, Jim (James Francis)
d. Mar 28, 1953
Long Beach, California
Anderson, Jack Northman b. Oct 19, 1922
Andrus, Ethel Percy d. Jul 13, 1967
Bartlett, Jennifer Losch b. Mar 14, 1941
Britton, Barbara b. Sep 26, 1919
Costle, Douglas Michael b. Jul 27, 1939
Crane, Les b. 1934
Derek, Bo b. Nov 16, 1956
Garver, Kathy b. Dec 13, 1947
Gortner, (Hugh) Marjoe (Ross)
b. Jan 14, 1945
Hilton, James d. Dec 20, 1954
Jaeckel, Richard b. Oct 26, 1926
Jones, "Spike" (Lindsay Armstrong)
b. Dec 14, 1911
Kellerman, Sally b. Jun 2, 1937
King, Billie Jean b. Nov 22, 1943
Lynch, David b. Jan 2, 1981
Merriam, Frank Finley d. Apr 25, 1955
Monroe, Marion d. Jun 25, 1983
Okamura, Arthur b. Feb 24, 1932
Phillips, Michelle Gillam b. Apr 6, 1944
Ridgeway, Rick b. Aug 12, 1949
Rigby, Cathy b. Dec 12, 1952
Ryan, Peggy (Margaret O'Rene)
b. Aug 28, 1924
Saint James, Susan b. Aug 14, 1946
Sperling, Godfrey, Jr. b. Sep 25, 1915
Warmerdam, Cornelius b. Jun 22, 1915
Zerbe, Anthony b.
Los Angeles, California
Abbott, L(enwood) B(allard)
d. Sep 28, 1985
Abell, George O(gden) b. Mar 1, 1927
Ackerman, Forest J b. Nov 24, 1916
Ager, Milton d. May 6, 1979
Akins, Zoe d. Oct 29, 1958
Albert, Edward b. Feb 20, 1951
Alda, Robert d. May 3, 1986

Aldrich, Robert d. Dec 5, 1983
Alpert, Herb b. Mar 31, 1935
Anderson, Eddie d. Feb 28, 1977
Anderson, Ivie d. Dec 28, 1949
Arbuckle, "Fatty" (Roscoe Conkling)
d. Jun 29, 1933
Archer, Anne b. Aug 25, 1947
Armendariz, Pedro d. Jun 18, 1963
Arnaz, Desi(derio Alberto, IV), Jr.
b. Jan 19, 1953
Ash, Roy Lawrence b. Oct 20, 1918
Ashford, Emmett Littleton
b. Nov 13, 1916
Ashford, Emmett Littleton d. Mar 1, 1980
Astin, Mackenzie Alexander
b. May 12, 1973
Atkinson, William Walker d. Nov 22, 1932
Atwater, Edith d. Mar 19, 1986
Atwood, Angela d. May 24, 1974
Ayres, Agnes d. Dec 25, 1940
Babbitt, Bruce Edward b. Jun 27, 1938
Baby Leroy b. May 12, 1932
Baddeley, Hermione Clinton
d. Aug 19, 1986
Bainter, Fay Okell b. Dec 7, 1891
Baker, Belle d. Apr 29, 1957
Baker, George d. May 8, 1975
Bara, Theda d. Apr 7, 1955
Barnes, Billy b. Jan 27, 1927
Basehart, Richard d. Sep 17, 1984
Baxter-Birney, Meredith b. Jun 21, 1947
Bayes, Nora b. Jan 10, 1880
Beard, Matthew, Jr. b. Jan 1, 1925
Beard, Matthew, Jr. d. Jan 8, 1981
Beatty, Roger b. Jan 24, 1933
Benaderet, Bea d. Oct 13, 1968
Bendix, William d. Dec 14, 1964
Benet, Brenda b. Aug 14, 1945
Benet, Brenda d. Apr 7, 1982
Bennett, Richard d. Oct 22, 1944
Benny, Jack d. Dec 26, 1974
Beradino, John b. May 1, 1917
Beresford, Harry d. Oct 4, 1944
Berkeley, "Busby" b. Nov 29, 1895
Bernardi, Hershel d. May 10, 1986
Berry, Jan b. Apr 3, 1941
Betz, Carl d. Jan 18, 1978
Bitzer, George William d. Apr 29, 1944
Blackton, James Stuart d. Aug 13, 1941
Blanding, Don d. Jun 9, 1957
Blanton, Jimmy d. Jul 30, 1942
Blue, Ben d. Mar 7, 1975
Blythe, Betty b. Sep 1, 1893
Bogart, Humphrey de Forest
d. Jan 14, 1957
Bogart, Neil d. May 8, 1982
Bond, Carrie Jacobs d. Dec 28, 1946
Bond, Victoria b. May 6, 1950
Bonelli, Richard d. Jun 7, 1980
Bonham, Frank b. Feb 25, 1914
Bono, Chastity b. Mar 4, 1969

Bonoff, Karla b. Dec 27, 1952
Boone, Richard b. Jun 18, 1917
Bow, Clara Gordon d. Sep 27, 1965
Boyd, Stephen d. Jun 2, 1977
Braden, Spruille d. Jan 10, 1978
Brennan, Eileen Regina b. Sep 3, 1937
Brent, Evelyn d. Jun 7, 1975
Bridges, "Beau" (Lloyd Vernet, III)
    b. Dec 9, 1941
Bridges, Calvin Blackman d. Dec 27, 1938
Bridges, Jeff b. Dec 4, 1949
Brill, Marty (Martin) d. May 1, 1973
Brolin, James b. Jul 18, 1941
Brooks, Albert b. Jul 22, 1947
Brown, Judie b. Mar 4, 1944
Brown, Ron(ald James) b. Mar 31, 1961
Burden, Carter (Shirley Carter, Jr.)
    b. Aug 25, 1941
Burke, "Billie" (Mary William Ethelberg
    Appleton) d. May 14, 1970
Burke, Yvonne Brathwaite Watson
    b. Oct 5, 1932
Burnette, Smiley (Lester Alvin)
    d. Feb 16, 1967
Burroughs, Edgar Rice d. Mar 10, 1950
Buscaglia, Leo (Felice Leonardo)
    b. Mar 31, 1925
Butterworth, Charles d. Jun 14, 1946
Cadman, Charles Wakefield
    d. Dec 30, 1946
Caesar, Adolph d. Mar 6, 1986
Cage, John Milton, Jr. b. Sep 5, 1912
Calhoun, Rory b. Aug 8, 1923
Cannell, Stephen J b. Feb 5, 1943
Canutt, Yakima (Enos Edward)
    d. May 25, 1986
Capote, Truman d. Aug 25, 1984
Carawan, Guy b. Jul 28, 1927
Carr, Alexander d. Sep 19, 1946
Carradine, Robert Reed b. Mar 24, 1954
Carrillo, Leo b. Aug 6, 1880
Carson, Robert d. Jan 19, 1983
Carter, Caroline Louise Dudley
    d. Nov 13, 1937
Carter, Mrs. Leslie d. Nov 12, 1937
Cassidy, Shaun Paul b. Sep 27, 1958
Champion, Marge Celeste b. Sep 2, 1923
Chance, Frank Leroy d. Sep 15, 1924
Chandler, Norman d. Oct 20, 1973
Chandler, Otis b. Nov 23, 1927
Chaney, Lon (Alonso) d. Aug 26, 1930
Chaplin, Sydney b. Mar 30, 1926
Clayton, Jan(e Byral) d. Aug 28, 1983
Clyde, Andy d. May 18, 1967
Cobb, Lee J (Leo Jacob) d. Feb 11, 1976
Coe, Frederick H d. Apr 29, 1979
Cohen, "Mickey" (Meyer) d. Jul 29, 1976
Cohen, Octavus Roy d. Jan 6, 1959
Colasanto, Nicholas d. Feb 12, 1985
Cole, Charles Woolsey d. Feb 6, 1978
Cole, Jack d. Feb 17, 1974

Cole, Natalie (Stephanie Natalie Maria)
    b. Feb 6, 1949
Conrad, Michael d. Nov 22, 1983
Considine, Tim b. 1940
Constantine, Eddie b. 1917
Conte, Richard d. Apr 15, 1975
Cooder, Ry(land Peter) b. Mar 15, 1947
Coogan, Jackie (Jack Leslie)
    b. Oct 26, 1914
Cooke, Sam d. Dec 11, 1964
Coombs, Charles Ira b. Jun 27, 1914
Cooper, Jackie (John, Jr.) b. Sep 15, 1922
Corrales, Pat(rick) b. Mar 20, 1941
Costello, Chris b. Aug 15, 1947
Costello, Helene d. Jan 26, 1957
Costello, Lou d. Mar 3, 1959
Cox, Wally (Wallace Maynard)
    d. Feb 15, 1973
Cregar, Laird (Samuel) d. Dec 8, 1944
Crenna, Richard b. Nov 30, 1927
Cromwell, Dean Bartlett d. Aug 3, 1962
Crosby, Cathy Lee b. 1949
Crosby, David b. Aug 14, 1941
Crosby, Mary Frances b. Sep 14, 1959
Cukor, George Dewey d. Jan 24, 1983
Curtis, Edward Sheriff d. Oct 19, 1952
Dalton, Emmett d. Jul 13, 1937
Dart, Justin Whitlock d. Jan 26, 1984
Davenport, Harry George Bryant
    d. Aug 9, 1949
Davis, Edward Michael b. Nov 15, 1916
Davis, Patti b. Oct 21, 1952
Davis, Perscell b. 1958
De Patie, David H b. Dec 24, 1930
Deacon, Richard d. Aug 9, 1984
Dee, Frances b. Nov 26, 1907
DeErdely, Francis (Ferenc)
    d. Nov 28, 1959
DeFreeze, Donald David d. May 24, 1974
DeHaven, Gloria b. Jul 23, 1925
DeLavallade, Carmen b. Mar 6, 1931
DeLugg, Milton b. Dec 2, 1918
Densmore, John b. Dec 1, 1945
Desmond, Johnny d. Sep 6, 1985
Desmond, William d. Nov 3, 1949
DeWolfe, Billy d. Mar 5, 1974
DeYoung, Cliff b. Feb 12, 1945
Diamond, Selma d. May 13, 1985
Disney, Walt(er Elias) d. Dec 15, 1966
Dix, Richard d. Sep 20, 1949
Doerr, Bobby (Robert Pershing)
    b. Apr 7, 1918
Dolenz, Mickey b. Mar 8, 1945
Donohue, Jack d. Mar 27, 1984
Douglas, Lloyd Cassel d. Feb 13, 1951
Dumont, Margaret d. Mar 6, 1965
Dunne, Dominique d. Nov 4, 1982
Durant, Ariel (Ida Ariel Ethel Kaufman)
    d. Oct 25, 1981
Durant, Will(iam James) d. Nov 7, 1981
Duryea, Dan d. Jun 7, 1968

Earp, Wyatt Berry Stapp d. Jan 13, 1929
Eckstein, George b. May 3, 1928
Edwards, Alan d. May 8, 1954
Edwards, Gus d. Nov 7, 1945
Einstein, Bob b. Nov 20, 1940
Ellis, Dock Phillip, Jr. b. Mar 11, 1945
Ellsler, Effie d. Oct 8, 1942
Elman, Ziggy d. Jun 26, 1968
Epstein, Philip G d. Feb 7, 1952
Errol, Leon d. Oct 12, 1951
Faith, Percy d. Feb 9, 1976
Farnsworth, Richard b. Sep 1, 1920
Farnum, William d. Jun 5, 1953
Farrow, Mia Villiers b. Feb 9, 1945
Fears, Tom (Thomas Jesse) b. Dec 3, 1923
Feldman, Alvin Lindbergh d. Aug 9, 1981
Feuchtwanger, Lion d. Dec 21, 1958
Fields, Shep d. Feb 23, 1981
Fields, Stanley d. Apr 23, 1941
Fleischer, Max d. Sep 11, 1972
Fleming, Rhonda b. Aug 10, 1923
Flynn, Joe (Joseph Anthony)
    d. Jul 19, 1974
Fonda, Henry Jaynes d. Aug 12, 1982
Ford, Mary d. Sep 30, 1977
Foster, "Jodie" (Alicia Christian)
    b. Nov 19, 1962
Fowler, Gene d. Jul 2, 1960
Fraker, William A b. 1923
Francis, Genie b. May 26, 1962
Franz, Eduard d. Feb 10, 1983
Fratianne, Linda b. Aug 2, 1960
Frawley, William d. Mar 3, 1966
Frederick, Pauline d. Aug 19, 1938
Freed, Arthur d. Apr 12, 1973
Freeman, Seth b. Jan 6, 1945
Frings, "Ketti" d. Feb 11, 1981
Fuller, "Bucky" (Richard Buckminster)
    d. Jul 1, 1983
Fulton, Maude d. Nov 4, 1950
Gardner, John William b. Oct 8, 1912
Garland, Hamlin d. Mar 4, 1940
Garner, Erroll d. Jan 2, 1977
Garrett, Michael Lockett b. Apr 12, 1944
Gautier, Dick b. Oct 30, 1937
Gavin, John b. Apr 8, 1932
Gaye, Marvin (Marvin Pentz)
    d. Apr 1, 1984
Geer, Will d. Apr 22, 1978
George, Christopher d. Nov 29, 1983
George, Gladys d. Dec 8, 1954
Gernreich, Rudi d. Apr 21, 1985
Gesell, Gerhard Alden b. Jun 16, 1910
Getty, Gordon Peter b. Dec 20, 1933
Gilbert, John d. Jan 9, 1936
Gilbert, Melissa b. May 8, 1964
Gillette, King Camp d. Jul 9, 1932
Gilliam, Jim (James William)
    d. Oct 8, 1978
Gless, Sharon b. May 31, 1943
Goldsmith, Jerry b. Feb 10, 1930

Goldwater, Barry Morris, Jr.
    b. Jul 5, 1938
Goldwyn, Samuel d. Jan 31, 1974
Gonzales, "Pancho" (Richard Alonzo)
    b. May 9, 1928
Goodrich, Gail Charles b. Apr 23, 1943
Gordon, C Henry d. Dec 3, 1940
Gordon, Joe (Joseph Lowell)
    b. Feb 18, 1915
Gosden, Freeman Fisher d. Dec 10, 1982
Gottschalk, Robert d. 1982
Goyen, William d. Aug 29, 1983
Grahame, Gloria b. Nov 28, 1925
Granz, Norman b. Aug 6, 1918
Greenfield, Howard d. Mar 4, 1986
Greenstreet, Sydney Hughes
    d. Jan 19, 1954
Greenwood, Charlotte d. Jan 18, 1978
Greenwood, Lee b. Oct 27, 1942
Gregory, Cynthia Kathleen b. Jul 8, 1946
Grey, Virginia b. Mar 22, 1917
Griffith, D(avid Lewelyn) W(ark)
    d. Jul 23, 1948
Gwynn, Tony (Anthony Keith)
    b. May 9, 1960
Hadley, Reed d. Dec 11, 1974
Haldeman, H(arry) R(obert)
    b. Oct 27, 1926
Haley, Jack d. Jun 6, 1979
Haley, Jack, Jr. (John J.) b. Oct 25, 1933
Hampden, Walter d. Jun 11, 1955
Hannum, Alex(ander Murray)
    b. Jul 19, 1923
Harburg, E(dgar) Y(ipsel) d. Mar 5, 1981
Harlow, Jean d. Jun 7, 1937
Harryhausen, Ray b. Jun 29, 1920
Hartman, Paul d. Oct 2, 1973
Hathaway, Henry d. Feb 11, 1985
Haymes, Dick (Richard) d. Mar 28, 1980
Hayward, Brooke b. Jul 5, 1937
Head, Edith b. Oct 28, 1907
Head, Edith d. Oct 24, 1981
Healy, Ted d. Dec 21, 1937
Hearst, David W d. May 13, 1986
Heggie, O P d. Feb 7, 1936
Heindorf, Ray d. Feb 3, 1980
Henie, Sonja d. Oct 12, 1969
Hensley, Pamela Gail b. Oct 3, 1950
Herrmann, Bernard d. Dec 24, 1975
Hertz, John Daniel d. Oct 8, 1961
Hexum, Jon-Erik d. Oct 18, 1984
Hickman, Darryl b. Jul 28, 1931
Hickman, Dwayne b. May 18, 1934
Hillman, Chris b. Dec 4, 1942
Hills, Carla Anderson b. Jan 3, 1934
Hite, Robert Ernest, Jr. d. Apr 1981
Hoffman, Dustin b. Aug 8, 1937
Hofmann, Josef d. Feb 16, 1957
Holden, Fay d. Jun 23, 1973
Holdren, Judd Clifton d. Mar 11, 1974
Holt, Jack (Charles John) d. Jan 18, 1951

Hormel, George Albert d. Jun 5, 1946
Horton, Robert b. Jul 29, 1924
Hughes, Rupert d. Sep 9, 1956
Hutton, Barbara d. May 11, 1979
Hutton, Jim d. Jun 2, 1979
Huxley, Aldous Leonard d. Nov 22, 1963
Hyland, Diana d. Mar 27, 1977
Ingram, Rex d. Sep 19, 1969
Iturbi, Jose d. Jun 28, 1980
Janov, Arthur b. Aug 21, 1924
Jarvis, Howard Arnold d. Aug 11, 1986
Jenney, William LeBaron d. Jun 15, 1907
Jessel, George Albert d. May 24, 1981
Jillian, Ann b. Jan 29, 1951
Johnson, Bill (William D) b. 1961
Johnson, Martin Elmer d. Jan 13, 1937
Johnson, Nunnally d. Mar 25, 1977
Jones, "Spike" (Lindsay Armstrong)
    d. May 1, 1964
Jones, Carolyn d. Aug 3, 1983
Jones, Robert C b. Mar 30, 1930
Jordan, Bobby d. Sep 10, 1965
Jordan, Louis d. Feb 4, 1975
Kalmar, Bert d. Sep 18, 1947
Kalmus, Herbert Thomas d. Jul 11, 1963
Kamp, Irene Kittle d. Jun 1985
Karns, Roscoe d. Feb 6, 1970
Kashdan, Isaac d. Feb 20, 1985
Kassorla, Irene Chamie b. Aug 18, 1931
Kath, Terry d. Jan 23, 1978
Katt, William b. Feb 16, 1955
Kaufman, Andy d. May 16, 1984
Kaufman, Murray d. Feb 21, 1982
Kavner, Julie Deborah b. Sep 7, 1951
Keaton, Diane b. Jan 5, 1946
Kellaway, Cecil d. Feb 28, 1973
Kelly, Paul d. Nov 6, 1956
Kemp, Jack French b. Jul 13, 1935
Kennedy, Robert Francis d. Jun 6, 1968
Kert, Larry (Frederick Lawrence)
    b. Dec 5, 1930
Kilbride, Percy d. Dec 11, 1964
King, Cammie b. Aug 5, 1934
Kirk, Ruth Kratz b. May 7, 1925
Kirkwood, James b. Aug 22, 1930
Klein, Herbert George b. Apr 1, 1918
Kohler, Fred d. Oct 28, 1938
Kohner, Susan b. Nov 11, 1936
Kollsman, Paul d. Sep 26, 1982
Krasna, Norman d. Nov 1, 1984
Krieger, Robby b. Jan 8, 1946
Kurnitz, Harry d. Mar 18, 1968
Ladd, Alan Walbridge, Jr. b. Oct 22, 1937
Lahr, John b. Jul 12, 1941
Lamas, Fernando d. Oct 8, 1982
Lamas, Lorenzo b. Jan 20, 1958
Landreaux, Ken(neth Francis)
    b. Dec 22, 1954
Lang, Fritz d. Aug 2, 1976
Langdon, Harry d. Dec 22, 1944
Laughton, Charles d. Dec 15, 1962

Laurel, Alicia Bay b. May 14, 1949
Lawford, Peter d. Dec 24, 1984
Lea, Homer d. Nov 1, 1912
Lee, Gypsy Rose d. Apr 26, 1970
Lee, Michele b. Jun 24, 1942
Leginska d. Feb 26, 1970
Lembeck, Harvey d. Jan 5, 1982
Lennon, Dianne b. Dec 1, 1939
Lennon, Peggy b. Apr 8, 1940
Lenz, Kay b. Mar 4, 1953
Lewis, Henry Jay b. Oct 16, 1932
Libby, Willard Frank d. Sep 8, 1980
Lichine, David d. Jun 26, 1972
Lindley, Audra b. Sep 24, 1918
Lindsay, Margaret d. May 8, 1981
Little Esther d. Aug 7, 1984
Livingston, Barry b. Dec 17, 1953
Livingston, Stanley b. Nov 24, 1950
Locklear, Heather b. Sep 25, 1961
Long, Richard d. Dec 22, 1974
Love, Mike b. Mar 15, 1941
Lubitsch, Ernst d. Nov 30, 1947
Ludden, Allen Ellsworth d. Jun 9, 1981
Lundigan, William d. Dec 21, 1975
Lynn, Diana b. Oct 7, 1926
Lynn, Diana d. Dec 18, 1971
MacArthur, James b. Dec 8, 1937
Macready, George d. Jul 2, 1973
Maiman, Theodore b. Jul 11, 1927
Main, Marjorie d. Apr 10, 1975
Maltz, Albert d. Apr 26, 1985
Manne, Shelly (Sheldon) d. Sep 26, 1984
March, Fredric d. Apr 14, 1975
March, Hal d. Jan 11, 1970
Marion, Frances d. May 12, 1973
Marley, John d. Apr 22, 1984
Martin, Jennifer b. 1947
Martin, Quinn b. May 22, 1927
Marx, "Groucho" (Julius) d. Aug 19, 1977
Massey, Raymond Hart d. Jul 29, 1983
Matheson, Tim b. Dec 31, 1948
McAvoy, May d. Apr 26, 1984
McCallister, Lon b. Apr 17, 1923
McCarey, Leo b. Oct 3, 1898
McCord, Kent b. Sep 26, 1942
McCulloch, Robert P d. Feb 25, 1977
McDonough, Mary Elizabeth
    b. May 4, 1961
McElhenny, Hugh b. Dec 31, 1928
McIntyre, James Francis d. Jul 16, 1979
McNichol, Jimmy (James Vincent)
    b. Jul 2, 1961
McNichol, Kristy b. Sep 9, 1962
Meek, Donald d. Nov 18, 1946
Meiklejohn, William b. 1902
Merivale, Philip d. Mar 13, 1946
Meriwether, Lee b. May 27, 1935
Merkel, Una d. Jan 4, 1986
Miles, Jackie d. Apr 24, 1968
Miles, Tichi Wilkerson b. May 10, 1932
Milestone, Lewis d. Sep 25, 1980

Miller, Olive Thorne d. Dec 25, 1918
Mills, Harry d. Jun 28, 1982
Mimieux, Yvette Carmen M b. Jan 8, 1939
Mineo, Sal d. Feb 12, 1976
Minnelli, Liza b. Mar 12, 1946
Mitchell, Grant d. May 1, 1957
Monroe, Marilyn b. Jun 1, 1926
Montana, "Bull" (Louis) d. Jan 24, 1950
Moon, Warren b. Nov 18, 1956
Moore, Dick(ie) b. Sep 12, 1925
Moore, Terry b. Jan 1, 1932
Moran, Polly d. Jan 25, 1952
Morris, Wayne b. Feb 17, 1914
Morton, "Jelly Roll" (Joseph Ferdinand)
    d. Jul 10, 1941
Muir, John d. Dec 24, 1914
Murphy, Jack R b. May 26, 1937
Murray, Eddie Clarence b. Feb 24, 1956
Musso, Vido d. Jan 9, 1982
Nardini, Tom b. 1945
Nathan, Robert d. May 25, 1985
Newman, Randy b. Nov 28, 1943
Newmar, Julie b. Aug 16, 1935
Nicholson, Seth Barnes d. Jul 2, 1963
Nick the Greek d. Dec 25, 1966
Nin, Anais d. Oct 14, 1977
Noguchi, Isamu b. Nov 4, 1904
Nolan, Jeannette b. Dec 30, 1911
Noone, Jimmie d. Apr 19, 1944
North, Sheree b. Jan 17, 1933
Noyes, David d. Aug 7, 1981
O'Brien-Moore, Erin b. May 2, 1908
O'Brien-Moore, Erin d. May 3, 1979
O'Connell, Arthur d. May 19, 1981
O'Dell, Scott b. May 23, 1903
O'Donnell, Cathy d. Apr 11, 1970
O'Neal, Ryan b. Apr 20, 1941
O'Neal, Tatum b. Nov 5, 1963
Oakie, Jack d. Feb 23, 1978
Oberon, Merle d. Nov 23, 1979
Odets, Clifford d. Aug 14, 1963
Ornitz, Samuel d. Mar 11, 1957
Osmond, Ken b. Jun 7, 1943
Ouspenskaya, Maria d. Dec 3, 1949
Overgard, Bill b. Apr 30, 1926
Pallette, Eugene d. Sep 3, 1943
Palmer, Daniel David d. Oct 20, 1913
Palmer, Lilli d. Jan 27, 1986
Paris, Jerry d. Apr 2, 1986
Parker, Brant (Julian) b. Aug 26, 1920
Patterson, Melody b. 1947
Pearce, Alice d. Mar 3, 1966
Pepper, Art(hur Edward) d. Jun 15, 1982
Pereira, William Leonard d. Nov 13, 1985
Perry, Nancy Ling d. May 24, 1974
Peter II d. Nov 4, 1970
Phillips, Esther d. Aug 7, 1984
Piatigorsky, Gregor d. Aug 6, 1976
Porter, Gene Stratton d. Dec 6, 1924
Prang, Louis d. Jun 14, 1909
Prinze, Freddie d. Jan 28, 1977

Quarry, Jerry b. May 18, 1945
Raffin, Deborah b. Mar 13, 1953
Raisa, Rosa d. Sep 28, 1963
Raitt, Bonnie b. Nov 8, 1949
Ray, Charles d. Nov 23, 1943
Reagan, Maureen b. Jan 4, 1941
Reagan, Michael b. Mar 18, 1946
Reagan, Ronald Prescott b. May 20, 1958
Reed, Alan d. Jun 14, 1977
Reid, Wallace Eugene d. Jan 18, 1923
Reynolds, William b. Dec 9, 1931
Rice, Craig d. Aug 28, 1957
Riddle, Nelson d. Oct 6, 1985
Ride, Sally K b. May 26, 1951
Riggs, Bobby (Robert Larimore)
    b. Feb 25, 1918
Riperton, Minnie d. Jul 12, 1979
Roberts, Rachel d. Nov 26, 1980
Rogers, Darryl D b. May 28, 1935
Roland, Ruth d. Sep 22, 1937
Romanoff, Mike d. Sep 1, 1971
Root, Jack d. Jun 10, 1963
Rosing, Vladimir d. Nov 24, 1963
Ross, Joe E d. Aug 13, 1982
Rothwell, Walter Henry d. Mar 12, 1927
Roy, Mike (Michael) d. Jun 26, 1976
Rubens, Alma d. Jan 23, 1931
Rubin, Benny d. Jul 16, 1986
Ruggles, Charles b. Feb 8, 1892
Rushen, Patrice b. Sep 30, 1954
Russell, Gail d. Aug 26, 1961
Saint Denis, Ruth d. Jun 21, 1968
Saint John, Jill b. Aug 9, 1940
Saint Johns, Adela Rogers
    b. May 20, 1894
Sakall, S Z d. Feb 12, 1955
Sale, Charles Partlow d. Nov 7, 1936
Salt, Jennifer b. Sep 4, 1944
Sand, Paul b. Mar 5, 1941
Sandrich, Jay b. Feb 24, 1932
Schildkraut, Rudolph d. Jul 30, 1930
Schramm, Tex(as Edward) b. Jun 2, 1920
Schulberg, Stuart b. Nov 17, 1922
Scott, Pippa (Phillippa) b. Nov 10, 1935
Sebring, Jay d. Jul 8, 1969
Shapiro, Arnold b. Feb 1, 1941
Sherman, Allan d. Nov 20, 1973
Sherman, Harry R b. Sep 21, 1927
Sherry, Larry (Lawrence) b. Jul 25, 1935
Shyer, Charles b. Oct 11, 1941
Sikking, James B b. Mar 5,
Silverman, Sime d. Sep 22, 1933
Silvers, Phil d. Nov 1, 1985
Slatkin, Leonard b. Sep 1, 1944
Slezak, Erika b. Aug 5, 1946
Smalley, Roy Frederick, III
    b. Oct 25, 1952
Smith, Kent d. Apr 23, 1985
Smith, Pete d. 1979
Snider, "Duke" (Edwin Donald)
    b. Sep 19, 1926

Snider, Paul d. Aug 14, 1980
Soltysik, Patricia Michelle d. May 24, 1974
Soo, Jack d. Jan 11, 1979
Spigelgass, Leonard d. Feb 14, 1985
Stack, Robert b. Jan 13, 1919
Stacy, James b. Dec 23, 1936
Standing, Guy d. Feb 24, 1937
Stein, Jules Caesar d. Apr 29, 1981
Stephen, John d. Feb 13, 1966
Sterling, Ford d. Oct 13, 1939
Stevens, George, Jr. b. Apr 3, 1932
Stevens, Onslow b. Mar 29, 1906
Stevenson, Adlai Ewing, Jr. b. Feb 5, 1900
Stewart, Paul d. Feb 17, 1986
Still, William Grant d. Dec 3, 1978
Stone, Lewis d. Sep 11, 1953
Stone, Peter b. Feb 27, 1930
Stones, Dwight b. Dec 6, 1953
Stratten, Dorothy d. Aug 14, 1980
Strauss, Joseph Baermann d. May 16, 1938
Strawberry, Darryl Eugene
    b. Mar 12, 1962
Strode, Woody b. Jul 25, 1914
Stromberg, Hunt d. Aug 23, 1968
Tabori, Kristoffer b. Aug 4, 1952
Talmadge, Constance d. Nov 23, 1973
Tamblyn, Russ b. Dec 30, 1935
Tanen, Ned b. 1931
Tanguay, Eva d. Jan 11, 1947
Tatum, Art(hur) d. Nov 4, 1956
Thomas, Billy b. Mar 12, 1931
Thomas, Billy d. Oct 10, 1980
Thomas, Philip Michael b. May 26, 1949
Thompson, Thomas d. Oct 29, 1982
Thornton, Willie Mae d. Jul 25, 1984
Toch, Ernst d. Oct 1, 1961
Tokyo Rose b. Jul 4, 1916
Torrence, Dean b. Mar 10, 1941
Townsend, Francis Everett d. Sep 1, 1960
Trotter, John Scott d. Oct 29, 1975
Trumbo, Dalton d. Sep 10, 1976
Vallee, Rudy (Herbert Prior)
    d. Jul 3, 1986
Van, Bobby d. Jul 31, 1980
Vargas, Alberto d. Dec 30, 1983
Vera-Ellen d. Aug 30, 1981
Von Tilzer, Albert d. Oct 1, 1956
Wagner, Lindsay b. Jun 22, 1949
Wakely, Jimmy d. Sep 23, 1982
Walker, "T-Bone" (Aaron)
    d. Mar 16, 1975
Wallace, Amy b. Jul 3, 1955
Wallechinsky, David b. Feb 5, 1948
Walsh, Bill (William) b. Nov 30, 1931
Walsh, Raoul d. Dec 31, 1980
Ward, Burt b. Jul 6, 1946
Warner, Jack Leonard d. Sep 9, 1978
Warner, Sam(uel Louis) d. Oct 5, 1927
Warren, Earl b. Mar 19, 1891
Warren, Harry d. Sep 22, 1981
Warwick, Robert d. Jun 4, 1964

Watts, Heather (Linda Heather)
    b. Sep 27, 1953
Waxman, Franz d. Feb 24, 1967
Wayne, John d. Jun 11, 1979
Wayne, Patrick b. Jul 15, 1939
Weaver, "Doodles" (Winstead Sheffield
    Glendening Dixon) b. May 11, 1914
Webb, Jack Randolph d. Dec 23, 1982
Weber, Joseph M d. May 10, 1942
Weber, Lois d. Nov 13, 1939
Weber, Robert Maxwell b. Apr 22, 1924
Welch, Bob b. Jul 31, 1946
Welles, Orson (George Orson)
    d. Oct 10, 1985
Wellman, Paul Iselin d. Sep 17, 1966
Wellman, William Augustus
    d. Dec 9, 1975
Westermann, H(orace) C(lifford)
    b. Dec 11, 1922
Westover, Russell b. Aug 3, 1886
White, Charles Raymond b. Jan 22, 1958
White, George d. Oct 11, 1968
Willard, Frank Henry d. Jan 12, 1958
Willard, Jess d. Dec 15, 1968
Williams, Anson b. Sep 25, 1949
Williams, Esther b. Aug 8, 1923
Williams, Paul R(evere) b. Feb 18, 1894
Williams, Paul R(evere) d. Jan 23, 1980
Wilson, "Dooley" (Arthur)
    d. May 30, 1953
Winchell, Walter d. Feb 20, 1972
Windsor, Claire d. Oct 24, 1972
Winfield, Paul Edward b. May 22, 1941
Winwood, Estelle d. Jun 20, 1984
Wolfe, William Lawton d. May 24, 1974
Wolheim, Louis d. Feb 18, 1931
Wong, Anna May (Lu Tsong)
    b. Jan 3, 1907
Wynn, Tracy Keenan b. Feb 28, 1945
Yankovic, "Weird Al" (Alfred Matthew)
    b. Oct 23, 1959
Yarnell, Bruce b. Dec 28, 1938
Yogananda, Paramahansa d. Mar 7, 1952
Zanuck, Richard Darryl b. Dec 13, 1934
Zukor, Adolph d. Jun 10, 1976

Los Gatos, California
    MacDonald, Ross, pseud. b. Dec 13, 1915

Lucerne Valley, California
    Belbenoit, Rene Lucien d. Feb 26, 1959

Malibu, California
    Hutton, Timothy James b. Aug 16, 1960
    Jenkins, Gordon d. May 1, 1984
    Lebrun, Rico (Frederico) d. May 10, 1964
    Poe, James d. Jan 24, 1980
    Walters, Charles d. Aug 13, 1982

Malibu Beach, California
    Janssen, David d. Feb 13, 1980
    Woolsey, Robert d. Oct 1938

Mare Island, California
    Cochrane, Edward Lull b. Mar 18, 1892

Maricopa, California
Coleman, Lester L b. Nov 6, 1912
Marina del Rey, California
Gardner, Randy b. Dec 2, 1958
Wilson, Dennis d. Dec 28, 1983
Marino, California
Edwards, Ralph b. Jun 13, 1913
Martinez, California
DiMaggio, Vince(nt Paul) b. Sep 6, 1912
McGraw, "Tug" (Frank Edwin)
b. Aug 30, 1944
Marysville, California
Bacon, Frank b. Jan 16, 1864
Maywood, California
Messina, Jim b. Dec 5, 1947
Menlo Park, California
Behrens, Earl Charles d. May 13, 1985
Cowell, Henry Dixon b. Mar 11, 1897
Lewis, Clarence Irving d. Feb 3, 1964
Maslow, Abraham d. Jun 8, 1970
Nevins, Allan d. Mar 5, 1971
Poulter, Thomas Charles d. Jun 14, 1978
Merced, California
Leigh, Janet b. Jul 6, 1927
Mill Valley, California
Arden, Eve b. Apr 30, 1912
Hodges, Russ d. Apr 20, 1971
Watts, Alan Wilson d. Nov 16, 1973
Mission Hills, California
Weatherwax, Rudd B d. Feb 25, 1985
Modesto, California
Evans, Herbert McLean b. Sep 23, 1882
Gallo, Ernest b. 1910
Gallo, Julio b. 1911
Lucas, George b. May 14, 1944
Meyer, Joseph b. Mar 12, 1894
Pickens, "Slim" d. Dec 8, 1983
Presnell, Harve b. Sep 14, 1933
Spitz, Mark Andrew b. Feb 10, 1950
Monrovia, California
Baker, Kenny (Kenneth Lawrence)
b. Sep 30, 1912
Normand, Mabel d. Feb 23, 1930
Walthall, Henry B d. Jun 17, 1936
Montecito, California
Bayer, Herbert d. Sep 30, 1985
Dresser, Davis d. Feb 4, 1977
McLean, Robert d. Dec 5, 1980
Muni, Paul d. Aug 25, 1967
Rexroth, Kenneth d. Jun 6, 1982
Stone, Dorothy d. Sep 24, 1974
Monterey, California
Adams, Ansel Easton d. Apr 22, 1984
Berne, Eric Lennard d. Jul 15, 1970
Billings, Josh, pseud. d. Oct 14, 1885
Clampett, Bobby b. Apr 22, 1960
Crocker, Charles d. Aug 14, 1888
Espinosa, Al b. Mar 24, 1894
Hagar, Sammy b. Oct 13, 1949
Kennedy, Edgar b. Apr 26, 1890

Monterey Park, California
Mackie, Bob (Robert Gordon)
b. Mar 24, 1940
Napa, California
West, Jessamyn d. Feb 25, 1984
Nevada City, California
Marshall, Tully b. Apr 13, 1864
Newhall, California
Hart, William Surrey d. Jun 23, 1946
Partch, Virgil Franklin, II d. Aug 10, 1984
Williams, Tex d. Oct 11, 1985
Newport Beach, California
Aames, Willie b. Jul 15, 1960
DelRio, Dolores d. Apr 11, 1983
Martin, Freddy d. Sep 30, 1983
McLaglen, Victor d. Nov 7, 1959
Tully, Tom d. Apr 27, 1982
Voit, Willard D d. Feb 1980
North Hollywood, California
Arlen, Richard d. Mar 28, 1976
Barry, Donald d. Jul 17, 1980
Carle, Richard d. Jun 28, 1941
Felton, Verna d. Dec 14, 1966
Hauser, Gaylord d. Dec 2, 1984
Morgan, Vicki d. Jul 7, 1983
North, Jay b. Aug 3, 1952
Smithers, Jan b. Jul 3, 1949
Stone, Fred d. Mar 6, 1959
Yung, Victor Sen d. Nov 9, 1980
Northridge, California
Davis, Jim d. Apr 26, 1981
Harrison, Jenilee b. 1959
Norwalk, California
Anderson, "Cat" (William Alonzo)
d. Apr 30, 1981
Oakland, California
Anderson, Eddie b. Sep 18, 1905
Anderson, Jack Zuinglius b. 1904
Baer, Max, Jr. b. Dec 4, 1937
Bechtel, Steve (Stephen Davison, Jr.)
b. May 10, 1925
Budge, Don (John Donald)
b. Jun 13, 1915
Cashin, Bonnie b. 1915
Crabbe, "Buster" (Larry) b. Feb 7, 1908
Dellums, Ronald b. Nov 24, 1935
Duncan, Robert b. Jan 7, 1919
Fields, Debbi (Debra Jane Sivyer)
b. Sep 18, 1956
Giauque, William F(rancis)
d. Mar 29, 1982
Gilbreth, Lillian Moller b. May 24, 1878
Gorcey, Leo d. Jun 2, 1969
Gorman, Chester b. Mar 11, 1938
Hamill, Mark b. Sep 25, 1952
Hanks, Tom b. Jul 9, 1956
Hines, "Fatha" (Earl Kenneth)
d. Jul 22, 1983
Hobart, Alice Tisdale Nourse
d. Mar 14, 1967
Hoskins, Allen Clayton d. Jul 26, 1980

Howard, Sidney Coe b. Jun 26, 1891
Kingman, Dong M b. Apr 1, 1911
Knowland, William Fife d. Feb 23, 1974
Lange, Ted b. Jan 5,
Lema, Tony (Anthony David)
  b. Feb 25, 1934
Lombardi, Ernie (Ernesto Natali)
  b. Apr 6, 1908
McPherson, Aimee Semple d. Sep 27, 1944
Meese, Edwin, III b. Dec 2, 1931
Meyer, Russ b. 1922
Miller, Joaquin, pseud. d. Feb 17, 1913
Moore, Harry Thornton b. Aug 2, 1908
Moran, George d. Aug 1, 1949
Morris, Wayne d. Sep 14, 1959
Nachman, Gerald Weil b. Jan 13, 1938
O'Brien, Willis Harold b. 1886
Partch, Harry b. Jun 24, 1901
Powell, Teddy b. Mar 1, 1906
Rey, Alvino b. Jul 1, 1911
Roessner, Elmer b. May 1, 1900
Schmidt, Tim(othy B) b. Oct 30, 1947
Schorer, Mark d. Aug 11, 1977
Skaggs, M(arion) B d. May 8, 1976
Soo, Jack b. Oct 28, 1915
Stevens, George b. Dec 18, 1904
Tickner, Charlie b. Nov 13, 1953
Totheroh, Dan b. Jul 22, 1894
Turner, Morrie b. Dec 11, 1923
Van Fleet, Jo b. Dec 30, 1919
White, Miles b. Jul 27, 1914
Woolsey, Robert b. Aug 14, 1889

Ojai, California
Krishnamurti, Jiddu d. Feb 17, 1986
Linville, Larry Lavon b. Sep 29, 1939

Ontario, California
Crandall, Del(mar Wesley) b. Mar 5, 1930
Scarbury, Joey b. Jun 7, 1955
Yezierska, Anzia d. Nov 21, 1970

Orange, California
Deer, Rob(ert George) b. Sep 29, 1960
Devine, Andy d. Feb 18, 1977
Poulson, Norris d. Sep 25, 1982
Smith, Sammi b. Aug 5, 1943

Orange County, California
Warnes, Jennifer b. 1947

Oxnard, California
Birdwell, Russell Juarez d. Dec 15, 1977
Brennan, Walter Andrew d. Sep 22, 1974
Clark, William P(atrick, Jr.)
  b. Oct 23, 1931

Pacific Grove, California
Towle, Katherine Amelia d. Mar 1, 1986

Pacific Palisades, California
Bushman, Francis X(avier)
  d. Aug 23, 1966
Collier, John d. Apr 6, 1980
Conway, Jack d. Oct 11, 1952
Haydn, Richard d. Apr 25, 1985
Knight, Ted d. Aug 26, 1986

MacDonald-Wright, Stanton
  d. Aug 22, 1973
Mann, Klaus d. May 21, 1949
Margo d. Jul 17, 1985
Miller, Henry d. Jun 7, 1980
Nijinska, Bronislava d. Feb 21, 1972
Stephenson, James d. Jul 29, 1941
Vidor, Florence d. Nov 3, 1977

Pacoima, California
Valens, Richie b. May 13, 1941

Palermo, California
Murphy, "Turk" (Melvin) b. Dec 16, 1915

Palm Desert, California
Buchanan, Edgar d. 1979
Deutsch, Adolph d. Jan 1, 1980
Ford, John d. Aug 31, 1973
Howard, Eddy d. May 23, 1963
Hudson, Rochelle d. Jan 17, 1972
McGivern, William Peter d. Nov 18, 1982

Palm Springs, California
Alexander, Franz Gabriel d. Mar 8, 1964
Austin, Gene d. Jan 24, 1972
Berkeley, "Busby" d. Mar 14, 1976
Cramer, Polly d. May 13, 1981
Davis, Joan d. May 23, 1961
Demarest, William d. Dec 27, 1983
Dietrich, Noah d. Feb 15, 1982
Douglas, Donald Willis d. Feb 1, 1981
Freed, Alan d. Jan 20, 1965
Gaynor, Janet d. Sep 14, 1984
Goodwin, Bill d. May 9, 1958
Hart, Moss d. Dec 20, 1961
Hawks, Howard Winchester
  d. Dec 26, 1977
Hayden, Russell d. Jun 9, 1981
Hayton, Lennie (Leonard George)
  d. Apr 24, 1971
Hayward, Louis d. Feb 21, 1985
Hopper, William d. Mar 6, 1970
Ladd, Alan d. Jan 29, 1964
Marx, "Gummo" (Milton) d. Apr 21, 1977
Marx, "Zeppo" (Herbert) d. Nov 30, 1979
McDonald, David John d. Aug 8, 1979
Mills, Irving d. Apr 21, 1985
Montenegro, Hugo d. Feb 6, 1981
Motley, Arthur Harrison d. May 29, 1984
Powell, William d. Mar 5, 1984
Power, Thomas d. Dec 7, 1970
Rambeau, Marjorie d. Jul 7, 1970
Reiser, Pete (Harold Patrick)
  d. Oct 25, 1981
Rockefeller, Winthrop d. Feb 22, 1973
Rose, Helen Bronberg d. Nov 9, 1985
Swinnerton, James Guilford d. Sep 5, 1974
Tamiroff, Akim d. Sep 17, 1972
Tillstrom, Burr d. Dec 6, 1985
Wilson, Don(ald Harlow) d. Apr 25, 1982
Winninger, Charles d. Jan 1969
Young, Victor d. Nov 11, 1956
Zanuck, Darryl Francis d. Dec 22, 1979

Palo Alto, California
Alden, Isabella Macdonald d. Aug 5, 1930
Anson, Jay d. Mar 12, 1980
Begle, Edward G(riffith) d. Mar 2, 1978
Bliven, Bruce d. May 27, 1977
Buckingham, Lindsey b. Oct 3, 1947
Christiansen, Jack d. Jun 30, 1986
Cranston, Alan MacGregor
    b. Jun 19, 1914
Hamilton, William b. Jun 2, 1939
Kaplan, Henry d. Feb 4, 1984
Kreutzmann, Bill b. Jun 7, 1946
Larrieu, Francie b. Nov 28, 1952
Lawrence, Ernest Orlando d. Aug 27, 1958
Patchen, Kenneth d. Jan 8, 1972
Pitkin, Walter Boughton d. Jan 25, 1953
Polya, George d. Sep 7, 1985
Sears, Robert Richardson b. Aug 31, 1908
Stanford, Leland (Amasa Leland)
    d. Jun 21, 1893
Streithorst, Tom d. Feb 19, 1981
Veblen, Thorstein Bunde d. Aug 3, 1929
Warner, "Pop" (Glenn Scobey)
    d. Sep 7, 1954

Palos Verdes, California
Boyce, Christopher John b. 1953
Davis, Adelle d. May 31, 1974
Lee, Andrew Daulton b. 1952
Teltscher, Eliot b. Mar 15, 1959

Panorama City, California
Cameron, Kirk b. Oct 12, 1970
Middleton, Ray d. Apr 10, 1984

Pasadena, California
Adams, Walter Sydney d. May 11, 1956
Armour, Philip Danforth d. Jan 29, 1901
Beals, Ralph Leon b. Jul 19, 1901
Biggers, Earl Derr d. Apr 5, 1933
Bronson, Betty (Elizabeth Ada)
    d. Oct 21, 1971
Child, Julia McWilliams b. Aug 15, 1912
Cushman, Austin Thomas d. Jun 12, 1978
Davis, William Morris d. Feb 5, 1934
Delbruck, Max d. Mar 9, 1981
Dreyfuss, Henry d. Oct 5, 1972
Edmunds, George Franklin
    d. Feb 27, 1919
Engelmann, Robert A b. 1947
Field, Sally Margaret b. Nov 6, 1946
Fields, W C d. Dec 25, 1946
Fleming, Victor b. Feb 23, 1883
Freberg, Stan b. Aug 7, 1926
Frost, Arthur Burdett d. Jun 22, 1928
Garfield, Lucretia Rudolph
    d. Mar 14, 1918
Gleason, Lucille b. Feb 6, 1888
Hale, George Ellery d. Feb 21, 1938
Hamlin, Harry b. 1952
Harrah, Bill (William Fisk) b. Sep 2, 1911
Howland, Alfred Cornelius d. 1909
Husing, Ted d. Aug 10, 1962
Lightner, Candy b. May 30, 1946

Lilly, Doris b. Dec 26, 1926
Mardian, Robert Charles b. Oct 23, 1923
Matthiessen, Francis Otto b. Feb 19, 1902
McCrea, Joel b. Nov 5, 1905
Millikan, Clark Blanchard d. Jan 2, 1966
Morgan, Thomas H d. Dec 4, 1945
Nader, George b. Oct 9, 1921
Neff, Wallace d. Jun 8, 1982
Quinlan, Kathleen b. Nov 19, 1954
Richter, Charles Francis d. Sep 30, 1985
Silvera, Frank d. Jun 11, 1970
Smith, Stan(ley Roger) b. Dec 14, 1946
Sullivan, Kathleen b. 1954
Tokatyan, Armand d. Jun 12, 1960
Trumbull, Charles Gallaudet
    d. Jan 13, 1941
Turner, Frederick Jackson d. Mar 14, 1932
Walters, Charles b. Nov 17, 1903
Weyerhaeuser, Frederick d. Apr 4, 1914
Williams, J(ames) R(obert) d. Jun 18, 1957
Winter, Alice Vivian Ames d. Apr 5, 1944
Zwicky, Fritz d. Feb 8, 1974

Paso Robles, California
Dean, James d. Sep 30, 1955
Vidor, King Wallis d. Nov 1, 1982

Pearblossom, California
Voskovec, George d. Jul 1, 1981

Pebble Beach, California
Little, (William) Lawson, Jr.
    d. Feb 1, 1968
Spruance, Raymond Ames d. Dec 13, 1969

Phoenix, California
Nicks, "Stevie" (Stephanie)
    b. May 26, 1948

Placentia, California
Ten Boom, Corrie d. Apr 15, 1983

Placerville, California
Dunlop, John Thomas b. Jun 5, 1914

Plumas City, California
Marble, Alice b. Sep 28, 1913

Point Loma, California
Spalding, Albert Goodwill d. Sep 9, 1915

Pomona, California
Seagren, Bob (Robert Lloyd)
    b. Oct 17, 1946
Sheets, Millard Owen b. Jun 24, 1907

Poway, California
Creston, Paul d. Aug 24, 1985

Prattville, California
Adams, Annette Abbott b. Mar 12, 1877

Ramona, California
Martin, Ross d. Jul 3, 1981

Rancho Mirage, California
Carmichael, Hoagy (Hoagland Howard)
    d. Dec 27, 1981
Crawford, Broderick d. Apr 26, 1986
Foster, Phil d. Jul 8, 1985
Taurog, Norman d. Apr 7, 1981

Raymond, California
Hill, Thomas d. 1908

Red Bluff, California
Geiberger, Al(len L) b. Sep 1, 1937
Shaw, Robert Lawson b. Apr 30, 1916

Redlands, California
Harris, Harwell Hamilton b. Jul 2, 1903

Redondo Beach, California
Pierpoint, Robert Charles b. May 16, 1925
Rosecrans, William Starke d. Mar 11, 1898

Redwood City, California
Humphries, Rolfe (George Rolfe)
    d. Apr 22, 1969

Ripon, California
Anderson, Roy A(rnold) b. Dec 15, 1920

Riverside, California
Bonds, Bobby Lee b. Mar 15, 1946
Kerr, Alexander H d. Feb 9, 1925
Kistler, Darci b. 1964
Woodhead, Cynthia b. Feb 7, 1964

Rockport, California
Brinegar, Claude Stout b. Dec 16, 1926

Rodeo, California
Gomez, "Lefty" (Vernon Louis)
    b. Nov 26, 1909

Rolling Hills, California
Austin, Tracy Ann b. Dec 12, 1962

Sacramento, California
Adams, Annette Abbott d. Oct 26, 1956
Anderson, Mary Antoinette b. Jul 28, 1859
Benton, Barbie b. Jan 28, 1950
Bowa, Larry (Lawrence Robert)
    b. Dec 6, 1945
Caen, Herb b. Apr 3, 1916
Didion, Joan b. Dec 5, 1934
Elliott, Sam b. 1944
Everson, William Oliver b. Sep 10, 1912
Forsch, Bob (Robert Herbert)
    b. Jan 13, 1950
Forsch, Ken(neth Roth) b. Sep 8, 1946
George, Henry, Jr. b. Nov 3, 1862
Goodson, Mark b. Jan 24, 1915
Gordon, Joe (Joseph Lowell)
    d. Jun 7, 1978
Gorman, Chester d. Jun 7, 1981
Hathaway, Henry b. Mar 13, 1898
Johnson, Hiram W b. Sep 2, 1866
Lescoulie, Jack b. Nov 17, 1917
Lunden, Joan b. Sep 19, 1951
McNamara, John Francis b. Jun 4, 1932
Ringwald, Molly b. Feb 6, 1968
Rogers, Don(ald Lavert) d. Jun 27, 1986
Sanderson, Sybil b. Dec 7, 1865
Savitt, Jan d. Oct 4, 1948
Slenczynska, Ruth b. Jan 15, 1925
Warwick, Robert b. Oct 9, 1876

Sacremento, California
Collins, Ray b. Dec 10, 1889

Saint Helena, California
White, Ellen Gould Harmon
    d. Jul 16, 1915

Salinas, California
Felton, Verna b. Jul 20, 1890
Steinbeck, John Ernst b. Feb 27, 1902

San Bernardino, California
Hackman, Gene (Eugene Alden)
    b. Jan 30, 1931
Karns, Roscoe b. Sep 7, 1893
Kirk, Claude Roy, Jr. b. Jan 7, 1926
Knott, Walter b. Dec 11, 1889
Lemon, Bob (Robert Granville)
    b. Sep 22, 1920
McCloskey, Paul Norton, Jr.
    b. Sep 29, 1927
Stockton, Dave (David) b. Nov 2, 1941
Walker, Wesley Darcel b. May 26, 1955
Wayman, Dorothy b. Jan 7, 1893

San Bruno, California
McKernan, Ron b. Sep 8, 1946
Somers, Suzanne b. Oct 16, 1946

San Clemente, California
Chaney, Lon, Jr. (Creighton)
    d. Jul 12, 1973

San Diego, California
Allen, Marcus b. Mar 26, 1960
Armetta, Henry d. Oct 21, 1945
Bill, Tony b. Aug 23, 1940
Bishop, Stephen b. Nov 14, 1951
Buono, Victor (Charles Victor)
    b. Feb 3, 1938
Casper, Billy (William Earl)
    b. Jun 24, 1931
Chadwick, Florence b. Nov 9, 1917
Cheney, John Vance d. May 1, 1922
Clampett, Bob (Robert) b. May 8, 1913
Connolly, Maureen b. Sep 17, 1934
Danson, Ted (Edward Bridge, III)
    b. Dec 29, 1947
DeVarona, Donna b. 1947
Duvall, Robert Selden b. Jan 5, 1931
Eigenmann, Rosa Smith d. Jan 12, 1947
Fabray, Nanette b. Oct 27, 1920
Fitzsimmons, Frank d. May 6, 1981
Grady, Don b. Jun 8, 1944
Henry, Charlotte d. Apr 1980
Jaffee, Irving d. Mar 20, 1981
Jensen, Arthur Robert b. Aug 24, 1923
Kroc, Ray(mond) Albert d. Jan 24, 1984
Lansing, Robert b. Jun 5, 1929
Littler, Gene (Eugene Alex)
    b. Jul 21, 1930
Maddox, Gaynor b.
Nettles, Graig b. Aug 20, 1944
O'Brien, Margaret (Angela Maxine)
    b. Jan 15, 1937
Partch, Harry d. Sep 3, 1974
Pendleton, Nat d. Oct 11, 1967
Ritz, Harry d. Mar 31, 1986
Ryan, T(ubal) Claude d. Sep 11, 1982
Scripps, Robert Paine b. Oct 27, 1895
Sender, Ramon Jose d. Jan 15, 1982
Sipe, Brian Winfield b. Aug 8, 1949

Smith, Holland McTeire d. Jan 12, 1967
Stadler, Craig b. Jun 2, 1953
Teacher, Brian b. Dec 23, 1954
Tilton, Charlene b. Dec 1, 1958
Timken, Henry d. Mar 16, 1909
Van Dyke, W(oodbridge) S(trong)
  b. Mar 21, 1887
Walford, Roy L(ee, Jr.) b. Jun 29, 1924
Walker, Daniel b. Aug 6, 1922
Wilcox, Larry Dee b. Aug 8, 1947
Williams, Ted (Theodore Samuel)
  b. Aug 30, 1918
Wilson, Ann b. Jun 19, 1951
Wright, Mickey b. Feb 14, 1935

San Fernando, California
Arnold, Edward d. Apr 26, 1956
Burns, Bob d. Feb 2, 1956
Crum, Denny Edwin b. Mar 2, 1937

San Francisco, California
Adams, Ansel Easton b. Feb 20, 1902
Aitken, Robert b. May 8, 1878
Alioto, Joseph Lawrence b. Feb 12, 1916
Allen, Gracie Ethel Cecil Rosaline
  b. Jul 26, 1906
Alvarez, Luis Walter b. Jun 13, 1911
Alvarez, Walter Clement b. Jul 22, 1884
Alvarez, Walter Clement d. Jun 18, 1978
Andrus, Ethel Percy b. Sep 21, 1884
Anglim, Philip b. Feb 11, 1953
Anthony, John J(ason) d. Jul 16, 1970
Apostoli, Fred B d. Nov 29, 1973
Arzner, Dorothy b. Jan 3, 1900
Atherton, Gertrude Franklin
  b. Oct 30, 1857
Atherton, Gertrude Franklin
  d. Jun 14, 1948
Bailey, Raymond b. 1904
Bates, Blanche Lyon d. Dec 25, 1941
Bateson, Gregory d. Jul 4, 1980
Belasco, David b. Jul 25, 1859
Bixby, Bill b. Jan 22, 1934
Black, Winifred Sweet d. May 26, 1936
Blanc, Mel(vin Jerome) b. May 30, 1908
Blinn, Holbrook b. 1872
Bloomfield, Mike (Michael)
  d. Feb 15, 1981
Bonestell, Chesley b. 1888
Bonet, Lisa b. 1967
Born, Ernest Alexander b. 1898
Bowes, "Major" (Edward) b. Jun 14, 1874
Boyd, Louise Arner d. Sep 14, 1972
Brady, William Aloysius b. Jun 19, 1863
Brodie, John Riley b. Aug 14, 1935
Brown, Jerry (Edmund Gerald, Jr.)
  b. Apr 7, 1938
Brown, Nacio Herb d. Sep 28, 1964
Brown, Pat (Edmund Gerald)
  b. Apr 21, 1905
Burton, Phillip d. Apr 10, 1983
Camilli, Dolph (Adolph Louis)
  b. Apr 23, 1908

Campbell, William Wallace
  d. Jun 14, 1938
Casals, Rosemary b. Sep 16, 1948
Catlett, Walter b. Feb 4, 1889
Church, Sandra b. Jan 13, 1943
Cone, Fairfax Mastick b. Feb 21, 1903
Cook, Elisha, Jr. b. Dec 26, 1906
Cooke, Hope b. Jun 21, 1940
Corbett, James John b. Sep 1, 1866
Creel, George d. Oct 3, 1953
Crews, Laura Hope b. Dec 12, 1879
Crittenton, Charles Nelson
  d. Nov 16, 1909
Cronin, Joe (Joseph Edward)
  b. Oct 12, 1906
Cunningham, Imogen d. Jun 24, 1976
Cushman, Pauline d. Dec 2, 1893
Dahl-Wolfe, Louise b. 1895
De Cuir, John b. 1918
Desmond, Paul Breitenfeld
  b. Nov 25, 1924
Diller, Barry Charles b. Feb 2, 1942
Dillman, Bradford b. Apr 13, 1930
DiMaggio, Dom(inic Paul) b. Feb 12, 1917
DiMaggio, Joe (Joseph Paul)
  b. Nov 24, 1914
Dorgan, Thomas Aloysius b. Apr 29, 1877
Drew, John d. Jul 9, 1927
DuBay, William Bryan b. 1948
Dukes, David b. Jun 6, 1945
Duncan, Augustin b. Apr 12, 1873
Duncan, Isadora b. May 27, 1878
Dupree, Minnie b. Jan 19, 1873
Eastwood, Clint b. May 31, 1930
Egan, Richard b. Jul 29, 1923
Elder, Ruth d. Oct 9, 1977
Erlanger, Joseph b. Jan 5, 1874
Espinosa, Al d. Jan 4, 1957
Feingold, Benjamin Franklin
  d. Mar 23, 1982
Feinstein, Dianne b. Jun 22, 1933
Flavin, Martin Archer b. Nov 2, 1883
Fleisher, Leon b. Jul 23, 1928
Forbes, Kathryn, pseud. b. Mar 20, 1909
Forbes, Kathryn, pseud. d. May 15, 1966
Fossey, Dian b. Jan 16, 1932
Foster, "Pops" (George Murphy)
  d. Oct 30, 1969
Fouts, Dan(iel Francis) b. Jun 10, 1951
Frailberg, Selma d. Dec 19, 1981
Frankenstein, Alfred Victor
  d. Jun 22, 1981
Frost, Robert Lee b. Mar 26, 1874
Garcia, Jerry (Jerome John)
  b. Aug 1, 1942
Gaxton, William b. Dec 2, 1893
Geertz, Clifford b. Aug 23, 1926
Goldberg, Rube (Reuben Lucius)
  b. Jul 4, 1883
Goodwin, Bill b. Jul 28, 1910
Goulding, Phil G b. Mar 28, 1921

Grant, Gordon b. Jun 7, 1875
Haas, Walter A(braham), Jr.
  b. Jan 24, 1916
Haas, Walter A(braham), Sr. b. 1899
Haas, Walter A(braham), Sr.
  d. Dec 7, 1979
Haid, Charles b. Jun 2, 1944
Harding, Warren G(amaliel)
  d. Aug 2, 1923
Hartman, Paul b. Mar 1, 1904
Hawthorne, Julian d. Jul 14, 1934
Hayes, Peter Lind b. Jun 25, 1915
Hearst, Patty (Patricia Campbell)
  b. Feb 20, 1954
Hearst, William Randolph b. Apr 29, 1863
Heilmann, Harry Edwin b. Aug 3, 1894
Henry, William M b. Aug 21, 1890
Hernandez, Keith b. Oct 20, 1953
Hertz, Alfred d. Apr 17, 1942
Hoffer, Eric d. May 21, 1983
Holtz, Lou b. Apr 11, 1898
Hulme, Kathryn Cavarly b. Jan 6, 1900
Irvin, Rea b. Aug 26, 1881
Jackson, Helen Maria Hunt Fiske
  d. Aug 12, 1885
Jackson, Shirley b. Dec 14, 1919
Jacobs, Al(bert T) b. Jan 22, 1903
Jaffe, Sam(uel Anderson) b. 1924
Jagel, Frederick d. Jul 5, 1982
Jensen, Jackie (Jack Eugene)
  b. Mar 9, 1927
Jolson, Al d. Oct 23, 1950
Jones, KC b. May 25, 1932
Judson, Egbert Putnam d. Jan 9, 1893
Kagel, Sam b. Jan 24, 1909
Kaiser, Edgar Fosburgh d. Dec 11, 1981
Kalakaua, David d. Jan 30, 1891
Kantner, Paul b. Mar 12, 1942
Kapell, William d. Oct 29, 1953
Kelly, George Lange b. Sep 10, 1895
Kelly, George Lange d. Oct 13, 1984
Kennedy, Bill (William Patrick)
  b. Jan 20, 1955
Kilbride, Percy b. Jul 16, 1888
King, Thomas Starr d. Mar 4, 1864
King, Walter Woolf b. 1899
Kyne, Peter Bernard b. Oct 12, 1880
Kyne, Peter Bernard d. Nov 25, 1957
LaLanne, Jack b. Sep 26, 1914
Lamantia, Philip b. Oct 23, 1927
Lange, Dorothea Nutzhorn d. Oct 11, 1965
Lawson, John Howard d. Aug 12, 1977
Lazzeri, Tony (Anthony Michael)
  b. Dec 26, 1903
Lazzeri, Tony (Anthony Michael)
  d. Aug 6, 1946
Lee, Bruce b. Nov 27, 1940
Leroy, Mervyn b. Oct 15, 1900
Lewis, Huey b. Jul 5, 1951
Linkletter, Jack b. Nov 20, 1937
Loeb, Gerald Martin b. Jul 24, 1899

Loeb, Gerald Martin d. 1974
London, Jack (John Griffith)
  b. Jan 12, 1876
Lord, Marjorie b. Jul 26, 1922
Luisetti, Angelo Enrico b. Jun 16, 1916
Lyng, Richard E b. Jun 29, 1918
Magnin, Grover Arnold b. Dec 4, 1885
Magnin, Grover Arnold d. Mar 17, 1969
March, Hal b. Apr 22, 1920
Marion, Frances b. Nov 18, 1888
Martin, Tony b. Dec 25, 1913
Mather, Stephen Tyng b. Jul 4, 1867
Mathis, Johnny (John Royce)
  b. Sep 30, 1935
McCone, John A b. Jan 4, 1902
McDougald, Gil(bert James)
  b. May 19, 1928
McDowell, Irvin d. May 4, 1885
McGee, Willie Dean b. Nov 2, 1958
McKuen, Rod b. Apr 23, 1933
McNamara, Robert S(trange)
  b. Jun 9, 1916
Mendelsohn, Eric d. Sep 15, 1953
Menuhin, Hephzibah b. May 20, 1920
Menuhin, Jeremy b. 1951
Menuhin, Yaltah b.
Merola, Gaetano d. Aug 30, 1953
Miller, Johnny Laurence b. Apr 29, 1947
Mooney, Tom (Thomas J) d. Mar 6, 1942
Morgan, Julia b. Jan 26, 1872
Morgan, Julia d. Feb 2, 1957
Moscone, George Richard b. Nov 24, 1929
Moscone, George Richard d. Nov 27, 1978
Murray, Philip d. Oct 9, 1952
Nelson, Barry b. Apr 16, 1920
Nimitz, Chester William d. Feb 20, 1966
Nolan, Lloyd b. Aug 11, 1902
Norris, Frank(lin) d. Oct 25, 1902
Norris, Kathleen Thompson
  b. Jul 16, 1880
Norris, Kathleen Thompson
  d. Jun 18, 1960
Nuttall, Zelia Maria b. Sep 6, 1857
O'Brien, George b. Apr 19, 1900
Obata, Gyo b. Feb 28, 1923
Palmer, Nathaniel Brown d. Jun 21, 1877
Paris, Jerry b. Jul 25, 1925
Peers, William Raymond d. Apr 6, 1984
Petri, Angelo d. Oct 4, 1961
Pringle, Aileen b. Jul 23, 1895
Rambeau, Marjorie b. Jul 15, 1889
Rand, Ellen Gertrude Emmet
  b. Mar 4, 1875
Remenyi, Eduard d. May 15, 1898
Ricci, Ruggiero b. Jul 24, 1920
Roland, Ruth b. Aug 26, 1897
Rubens, Alma b. 1897
Russell, Donald Joseph d. Dec 13, 1985
Salinger, Pierre Emil George
  b. Jun 14, 1925
Sargeant, Winthrop b. Dec 10, 1903

Serra, Richard Anthony b. Nov 2, 1939
Sheila E b. Dec 12, 1959
Sherman, Lowell b. Oct 11, 1885
Shields, Alexander b.
Simmons, Calvin b. Apr 27, 1950
Simpson, O(renthal) J(ames) b. Jul 9, 1947
Smith, H(arry) Allen d. Feb 23, 1976
Smith, Robyn Caroline b. Aug 14, 1944
Snyder, Gary Sherman b. May 8, 1930
Soong, T V d. Apr 25, 1971
Spano, Joe b. Jul 7, 1946
Spreckels, Claus d. Jan 10, 1908
Sproul, Robert Gordon b. May 22, 1891
Steffens, Lincoln b. Apr 6, 1866
Stephenson, Henry d. Apr 24, 1956
Sterling, George d. Nov 18, 1926
Stewart, George Rippey d. Aug 22, 1980
Stilwell, Joseph Warren d. Oct 12, 1946
Stone, Irving b. Jul 14, 1903
Strong, Austin b. Jan 18, 1881
Templeton, Fay d. Oct 3, 1939
Thomas, George Henry d. Mar 28, 1870
Thurman, Howard d. Apr 10, 1981
Toklas, Alice B(abette) b. Apr 30, 1877
Tyrrell, Susan b. 1946
Van Doren, Dorothy Graffe
    b. May 2, 1896
Varsi, Diane b. Feb 23, 1938
Venturi, Ken(neth) b. May 15, 1931
Venuta, Benay b. Jan 27, 1911
Wagner, Robin b. Aug 31, 1933
Wanger, Walter b. Jul 11, 1894
Warfield, David b. Nov 28, 1866
Warner, Jack, Jr. b. Mar 27, 1916
Weinberger, Caspar Willard
    b. Aug 18, 1917
Weingarten, Violet b. Feb 23, 1915
Weir, Bob (Robert Hall) b. Oct 16, 1949
Weldon, Joan b. Aug 5, 1933
White, Dan(iel James) d. Oct 21, 1985
White, Stewart Edward d. Sep 18, 1946
Whitman, Stuart b. Feb 1, 1926
Wilson, Nancy b. Mar 16, 1954
Wood, Natalie b. Jul 20, 1939
Wummer, John d. Sep 6, 1977
Young, John Watts b. Sep 24, 1930
Yung, Victor Sen b. 1915
Zellerbach, William Joseph b. Sep 15, 1920
Zumwalt, Elmo Russell, Jr.
    b. Nov 24, 1920

San Fransico, California
Claire, Ina d. Feb 21, 1985

San Gabriel, California
Garcia, Mike (Edward Miguel)
    b. Nov 17, 1923
Howard, "Curly" (Jerry) d. Jan 19, 1952
Patton, George Smith, Jr. b. Nov 11, 1885
Plumb, Charles b. 1900

San Jose, California
Berry, Chuck (Charles Edward Anderson)
    b. Jan 15, 1926
Dalis, Irene b. Oct 8, 1929
Fleming, Peggy Gale b. Jul 27, 1948
Giannini, Amadeo Peter b. May 6, 1870
Granger, Farley b. Jul 1, 1925
Hewitt, Martin b. Feb 19, 1958
Lasky, Jesse L b. Sep 13, 1880
Lowe, Edmund Dante b. Mar 3, 1892
Marcum, John Arthur b. Aug 21, 1927
Pelkey, Edward d. 1983
Plunkett, Jim (James William, Jr.)
    b. Dec 5, 1947
Righetti, Dave (David Allan)
    b. Nov 28, 1958
Thomas, Debi b. 1968
Tupper, Earl Silas d. Oct 3, 1983
Uppman, Theodor b. Jan 12, 1920
San Juan Capistrano, California
O'Malley, J Pat d. Feb 27, 1985
San Leandro, California
Bridges, Lloyd (Lloyd Vernet II)
    b. Jan 15, 1913
San Luis Obispo, California
Hubbard, L(afayette) Ron(ald)
    d. Jan 24, 1986
Manley, Joan A Daniels b. Sep 23, 1932
San Marino, California
Baxter, Frank Condie d. Jan 20, 1982
Billington, Ray Allen d. Mar 7, 1981
Hubble, Edwin Powell d. Sep 28, 1953
Millikan, Robert Andrews d. Dec 19, 1953
San Mateo, California
Beebe, Lucius Morris d. Feb 4, 1966
Bostwick, Barry b. Feb 24, 1945
Carradine, Keith Ian b. Aug 8, 1950
Giannini, Amadeo Peter d. Jun 3, 1949
Griffin, Merv(yn) b. Jul 6, 1925
Logan, Ella d. May 1, 1969
Polk, Willis Jefferson d. 1924
Terry, Paul H b. Feb 19, 1887
San Miguel Island, California
Cabrillo, Juan Rodriguez d. Jan 3, 1543
San Pablo, California
Seeley, Blossom b. 1892
San Pedro, California
Armour, Richard Willard b. Jul 15, 1906
Johnson, Dennis W b. Sep 18, 1954
Towne, Robert (Burton) b. 1936
San Quentin, California
Chessman, Caryl Whittier d. May 2, 1960
Duffy, Clinton Truman b. Aug 24, 1898
Graham, Barbara d. Jun 3, 1955
Jackson, George d. Aug 21, 1971
San Rafael, California
Boyd, Louise Arner b. Sep 16, 1887
Dollar, Robert d. May 16, 1932
Nevers, Ernie (Ernest A) d. 1976
Westover, Russell d. Mar 6, 1966

Santa Ana, California
Ball, Ernest d. May 3, 1927
Curtis, Isaac b. Oct 20, 1950
Dick, Philip K(indred) d. Mar 2, 1982
Medley, Bill b. Sep 19, 1940
Prather, Richard Scott b. Sep 9, 1921
Raitt, John Emmet b. Jan 19, 1917
Stieb, Dave (David Andrew)
    b. Jul 22, 1957

Santa Barbara, California
Barrymore, Georgina Emma Drew
    d. Jul 2, 1893
Bottoms, Joseph b. Apr 22, 1954
Bottoms, Sam b. Oct 17, 1955
Bottoms, Timothy b. Aug 30, 1951
Brunler, Oscar d. Aug 1, 1952
Colman, Ronald d. May 19, 1958
Coulter, Ernest Kent d. May 1, 1952
Croly, Herbert David d. May 17, 1930
Cromwell, John d. Sep 26, 1979
Cunningham, Sam b. Aug 15, 1950
Dahlberg, Edward d. Feb 27, 1977
Dressler, Marie d. Jul 28, 1934
Drew, Richard G d. Dec 7, 1980
Geller, Bruce d. May 21, 1976
Gilmore, Virginia d. Mar 28, 1986
Hackford, Taylor b. Dec 31, 1944
Hagedorn, Hermann d. Jul 27, 1964
Hutchins, Robert Maynard
    d. May 14, 1977
Lane, Lola d. Jun 22, 1981
Lehmann, Lotte d. Aug 26, 1976
MacDonald, Ross, pseud. d. Jul 11, 1983
Monaghan, (James) Jay, (IV) d. 1981
Moran, Thomas d. Aug 25, 1926
Nordhoff, Charles Bernard d. Apr 11, 1947
Peattie, Donald Culross d. Nov 16, 1964
Pike, James Albert d. Sep 2, 1969
Post, Charles William d. May 9, 1914
Renaldo, Duncan d. Sep 3, 1980
Sills, Milton d. Sep 15, 1930
Stevenson, Robert d. Apr 30, 1986
Tugwell, Rexford Guy d. Jul 21, 1979
Turpin, Ben d. Jul 1, 1940

Santa Clara County, California
Hooper, Harry Bartholomew
    b. Aug 24, 1887

Santa Cruz, California
Garland, Beverly b. Oct 17, 1926
Hooper, Harry Bartholomew
    d. Dec 18, 1974
Josephson, Matthew d. Mar 13, 1978
Lombardi, Ernie (Ernesto Natali)
    d. Sep 26, 1977

Santa Maria, California
Lonborg, Jim (James Reynold)
    b. Apr 16, 1942
Williams, Jimy (James Francis)
    b. Oct 14, 1943

Santa Monica, California
Albertson, Frank d. Feb 29, 1964
Anderson, Warner d. Aug 26, 1976
Andrews, Edward d. Mar 8, 1985
Anger, Kenneth b. 1932
Armstrong, Robert d. Apr 20, 1973
Bailey, Jack d. Feb 1, 1980
Bancroft, George d. Oct 2, 1956
Black, Shirley Temple b. Apr 23, 1928
Blondell, Joan d. Dec 25, 1979
Bloomingdale, Alfred S d. Aug 20, 1982
Blumberg, Judy b. 1957
Brodie, Fawn McKay d. Jan 10, 1981
Browning, Tod d. Oct 6, 1962
Bruce, Nigel d. Oct 8, 1953
Buckley, Tim d. Jun 29, 1975
Burnett, W(illiam) R(iley) d. Apr 25, 1982
Carnap, Rudolf d. Sep 14, 1970
Carrillo, Leo d. Sep 10, 1961
Chaplin, Geraldine b. Jul 31, 1944
Clark, Fred d. Dec 5, 1968
Clayton, Lou d. Sep 12, 1950
Cole, Nat "King" (Nathaniel Adams)
    d. Feb 15, 1965
Collins, Ray d. Jul 11, 1965
Coogan, Jackie (Jack Leslie)
    d. Mar 1, 1984
Cowl, Jane d. Jun 22, 1950
Daniell, Henry d. Oct 31, 1963
Dern, Laura Elizabeth b. 1967
Donaldson, Walter d. Jul 15, 1947
Dragon, Carmen d. Mar 28, 1984
Duke, Vernon d. Jan 17, 1969
Dunn, James Howard d. Sep 3, 1967
Durante, Jimmy (James Francis)
    d. Jan 29, 1980
Ebert, Carl (Anton Charles)
    d. May 14, 1980
Erteszek, Jan d. Jun 27, 1986
Evans, Jerry b. Jun 14, 1935
Fabares, Shelley (Michelle Marie)
    b. Jan 19, 1944
Fairbanks, Douglas d. Dec 12, 1939
Fix, Paul d. Oct 14, 1983
Franklin, Bonnie Gail b. Jan 6, 1944
Gifford, Frank (Francis Newton)
    b. Aug 16, 1930
Gomez, Thomas d. Jun 18, 1971
Gray, Linda b. Sep 12, 1941
Griffith, Corinne d. Jul 13, 1979
Grofe, Ferde d. Apr 3, 1972
Gross, Robert Ellsworth d. Sep 3, 1961
Haines, William d. Nov 26, 1973
Harris, Roy Ellsworth d. Oct 1979
Hatch, Richard Lawrence b. May 21, 1946
Heard, Gerald (Henry FitzGerald)
    d. Aug 14, 1971
Hilton, Conrad Nicholson d. Jan 3, 1979
Holden, William d. Nov 12, 1981
Humes, Helen d. Sep 13, 1981

Isherwood, Christopher William
   d. Jan 4, 1986
Jenkins, Allen d. Jul 20, 1974
Jory, Victor d. Feb 12, 1982
Kasznar, Kurt d. Aug 6, 1979
Kellems, Vivien d. Jan 25, 1975
Kent, Allegra b. Aug 11, 1938
Lansing, Joi d. Aug 7, 1972
LaRue, Jack d. Jan 11, 1984
Laurel, Stan d. Feb 23, 1965
Lennon, Kathy b. Aug 22, 1942
Lloyd, Frank d. Aug 10, 1960
Lockhart, Gene (Eugene) d. Mar 31, 1957
Loper, Don d. Nov 22, 1972
MacLane, Barton d. Jan 1, 1969
Mahin, John Lee d. Apr 18, 1984
Mayer, L(ouis) B(urt) d. Oct 29, 1957
McCarey, Leo d. Jul 5, 1969
McManus, George d. Oct 22, 1954
Melchior, Lauritz d. Mar 18, 1973
Mercer, Beryl d. Jul 28, 1939
Mitchell, Millard d. Oct 12, 1953
Moore, Tom d. Feb 12, 1955
Nesbit, Evelyn d. Jan 18, 1967
Norton-Taylor, Judy b. Jan 29, 1958
O'Brien, Parry b. Jan 28, 1932
O'Brien, Pat (William Joseph Patrick)
   d. Oct 15, 1983
O'Keefe, Dennis d. Aug 31, 1968
Ober, Philip d. Sep 13, 1982
Olson, Johnny d. Oct 12, 1985
Overman, Lynne d. Feb 19, 1943
Pangborn, Franklin d. Jul 20, 1958
Pankhurst, Christabel, Dame
   d. Feb 14, 1958
Parsons, Louella Oettinger d. Dec 9, 1972
Penn, Sean b. Aug 17, 1960
Pickford, Mary d. May 29, 1979
Pidgeon, Walter d. Sep 25, 1984
Porter, Cole d. Oct 15, 1964
Priest, Ivy (Maude) Baker d. Jun 23, 1975
Quisenberry, Dan(iel Raymond)
   b. Feb 7, 1953
Redford, Robert b. Aug 18, 1937
Ring, Blanche d. Jan 13, 1961
Risdon, Elizabeth d. Dec 20, 1956
Ruggles, Charles d. Dec 23, 1970
Ryan, Irene Noblette d. Apr 26, 1973
Scott, Mike (Michael Warren)
   b. Apr 26, 1955
Segar, Elzie Crisler d. Oct 13, 1938
Shaughnessy, Clark Daniel
   d. May 15, 1970
Sheehan, Joseph Green d. Nov 14, 1983
Sheekman, Arthur d. Jan 12, 1978
Sherman, Bobby b. Jul 22, 1945
Struss, Karl d. Dec 16, 1981
Taylor, Robert d. Jun 8, 1969
Teena Marie b. 1957
Thalberg, Irving Grant d. Sep 14, 1936
Todd, Thelma d. Dec 18, 1935

Tracy, Lee d. Oct 18, 1968
Traubel, Helen d. Jul 28, 1972
Tufts, Sonny d. Jun 5, 1970
Tynan, Kenneth Peacock d. Jul 26, 1980
Walker, Robert d. Aug 28, 1951
Webb, Jack Randolph b. Apr 2, 1920
Whorf, Richard d. Dec 14, 1966
Wibberley, Leonard Patrick O'Connor
   d. Nov 22, 1983
Williams, Barry b. Sep 30, 1954
Willson, Meredith d. Jun 15, 1984
Wong, Anna May (Lu Tsong)
   d. Feb 3, 1961
Wood, Robert Dennis d. May 20, 1986
Wright, Lloyd (Frank Lloyd, Jr.)
   d. May 31, 1978

Santa Rosa, California
Burbank, Luther d. Apr 11, 1926
DeMornay, Rebecca b. 1962
Lichty, George d. Jul 18, 1983
London, Julie b. Sep 26, 1926
Perry, Nancy Ling b. Sep 19, 1947
Ripley, Robert Leroy b. Dec 25, 1893
Valentine, Karen b. May 25, 1947

Sausalito, California
Hayden, Sterling d. May 23, 1986
Oppenheimer, Frank F d. Feb 3, 1985
Spanier, "Muggsy" (Francis Joseph)
   d. Feb 12, 1967

Sepulveda, California
Switzer, Carl d. Jan 21, 1959

Shasta, California
Behrens, Earl Charles b. Feb 7, 1892

Sherman Oaks, California
Babilonia, Tai Reina b. Sep 22, 1960
DelRuth, Roy d. Apr 27, 1961
Dumke, Ralph d. Jan 4, 1964
Harding, Ann d. Sep 1, 1981
Marshack, Megan b. 1953
Miller, Cheryl b. Feb 4, 1943
Robards, Jason d. Apr 4, 1963

Sisson, California
Loos, Anita b. Apr 26, 1893

Solana Beach, California
Brent, George d. 1979

Sonoma, California
Arnold, Henry Harley d. Jan 15, 1950

Sonoma County, California
Kael, Pauline b. Jun 19, 1919

Sonora, California
Belli, Melvin Mouron b. Jul 29, 1907
Oxnam, G(arfield) Bromley
   b. Aug 14, 1891
Pastorini, Dan b. Dec 25, 1949

South Gate, California
Rozelle, "Pete" (Alvin Ray)
   b. Mar 1, 1926
Smith, Roger b. Dec 18, 1932

South Laguna, California
Boyd, William (Bill) d. Sep 12, 1972

South Pasadena, California
Anderson, Gilbert M d. Jan 20, 1971
DePalma, Ralph d. Mar 31, 1956
Rosenbloom, Maxie d. Mar 6, 1976
Squaw Valley, California
Erwin, Stuart b. Feb 14, 1902
Stanford, California
Halop, Florence d. Jun 29, 1986
Stockton, California
Baxley Barbara b. Jan 1, 1927
Beck, David b. 1894
Etchison, Dennis (William Dennis)
  b. Mar 30, 1943
Gianelli, John b. Jun 10, 1950
Goodell, Brian Stuart b. Apr 2, 1959
Kingston, Maxine Hong b. Oct 27, 1940
Lewis, (Myrtle) Tillie d. Apr 30, 1977
Montana, Bob b. Oct 23, 1920
Older, Fremont d. Mar 3, 1935
Stagg, Amos Alonzo d. Mar 17, 1965
Wurster, William b. Oct 20, 1895
Stovepipe Wells, California
Scott, Walter b. Jan 5, 1954
Studio City, California
Dragon, Daryl b. Aug 27, 1942
Parks, Larry d. Apr 13, 1975
Sunland, California
DeCordoba, Pedro d. Sep 17, 1950
Sunnyvale, California
Wozniak, Steven b. 1950
Taft, California
Bailey, Martin Jean b. Oct 17, 1927
Tarzana, California
Hodiak, John d. Oct 19, 1955
Temecula, California
Gardner, Erle Stanley d. Mar 11, 1970
Terra Bella, California
Baker, Dorothy Dodds d. Jun 18, 1968
Terra Ina, California
Gold, Michael d. May 14, 1967
Terra Linda, California
Bessie, Alvah d. Jul 21, 1985
Thousand Oaks, California
Martin, Strother d. Aug 1, 1980
Toluca Lake, California
King, Henry d. Jun 29, 1982
Torrance, California
Carlton, Larry Eugene b. 1948
Drake, Tom d. Aug 11, 1982
Ferragamo, Vince b. Apr 24, 1954
Hite, Robert Ernest, Jr. b. Jan 26, 1943
Lopez, Nancy b. Jan 6, 1957
O'Keefe, Walter d. Jun 26, 1983
Peary, Harold d. Mar 30, 1985
Wallace, Bobby (Roderick John)
  d. Nov 3, 1960
Westphal, Paul Douglas b. Nov 30, 1950
Torrence, California
Milland, Ray(mond Alton)
  d. Mar 10, 1986

Toulca Lake, California
Henning, Linda Kaye b. Sep 16, 1944
Towle, California
Towle, Katherine Amelia b. Apr 30, 1898
Tujunga, California
Adoree, Renee d. Oct 5, 1933
Tulare, California
Cromley, Raymond Avolon
  b. Aug 23, 1910
Mathias, Bob (Robert Bruce)
  b. Nov 17, 1930
Valencia, California
Powolny, Frank d. Jan 9, 1986
Vallejo, California
Buckner, Bill (William Joseph)
  b. Dec 14, 1949
Carney, Robert Bostwick b. Mar 26, 1895
Cone, Russell Glenn d. Jan 21, 1961
Van Nuys, California
Barrymore, Lionel Blythe d. Nov 15, 1954
Conrad, Con d. Sep 28, 1938
Crisp, Donald d. May 26, 1974
Drysdale, Don(ald Scott) b. Jul 23, 1936
Hartman, Grace d. Aug 8, 1955
Hunter, Jeffrey d. May 27, 1969
Lockwood, Gary b. Feb 21, 1937
Matzenauer, Margaret d. May 19, 1963
Peters, Jon b. 1945
Ryan, Tommy d. Aug 3, 1948
Saddler, Donald b. Jan 24, 1920
Stevens, Onslow d. Jan 5, 1977
Vickers, Martha d. Nov 2, 1971
Whitaker, Johnny b. Dec 13, 1959
Williams, Cindy b. Aug 22, 1948
Venice, California
Feld, Irvin d. Sep 6, 1984
Ventura, California
Carr, Sabin d. Sep 1983
Hutton, Ina Ray d. Feb 19, 1984
Vincent, Jan-Michael b. Jul 15, 1944
Visalia, California
Peters, Susan d. Oct 23, 1952
Vista, California
Patten, Gilbert d. Jan 16, 1945
Sasway, Benjamin H b. 1961
Walnut Creek, California
Duffy, Clinton Truman d. Oct 11, 1982
West Hollywood, California
Cassidy, Jack d. Dec 12, 1976
Dandridge, Dorothy d. Sep 8, 1965
West Los Angeles, California
Louise, Anita d. Apr 25, 1970
Weston, California
Alexander, Leo d. Jul 20, 1985
Westwood, California
Gardiner, Reginald d. Jul 7, 1980
McCarty, Mary d. Apr 5, 1980
White Rock, California
Wilson, John N b. Feb 9, 1909

Whittier, California
Babashoff, Shirley b. Jan 31, 1957
Patterson, Lorna b. Jul 1, 1957
Wakoski, Diane b. Aug 3, 1937
Yothers, Tina b. May 5, 1973

Woodland, California
Howard, Eddy b. Sep 12, 1909

Woodland Hills, California
Abbott, "Bud" (William A)
　d. Apr 24, 1974
Alley, Norman William d. Apr 1, 1981
Allgood, Sara d. Sep 13, 1950
Benson, Sally d. Jul 19, 1972
Blythe, Betty d. Apr 7, 1972
Brady, Scott d. Apr 17, 1985
Brown, Johnny Mack d. Nov 14, 1974
Bruce, Virginia d. Feb 24, 1982
Cabot, Bruce d. May 3, 1972
Catlett, Walter d. Nov 14, 1960
Cavanaugh, Hobart d. Apr 27, 1950
Cooper, Melville d. Mar 29, 1973
Corey, Wendell d. Nov 9, 1968
D'Orsay, Fifi d. Dec 2, 1983
Darwell, Jane d. Aug 13, 1967
Donlevy, Brian d. Apr 5, 1972
Dresser, Louise d. Apr 24, 1965
Dwan, Allan d. Dec 21, 1981
Fetchit, Stepin d. Nov 19, 1985
Fine, Larry d. Jan 24, 1975
Ford, Wallace d. Jun 11, 1966
Foy, Eddie, Jr. d. Jul 15, 1983
Frisco, Joe d. Feb 16, 1958
Garner, Peggy Ann d. Oct 17, 1984
Gibson, "Hoot" (Edmund Richard)
　d. Aug 23, 1962
Gleason, James d. Apr 12, 1959
Gwenn, Edmund d. Sep 6, 1959
Hagen, Jean d. 1977
Joslyn, Allyn Morgan d. Jan 21, 1981
Kennedy, Edgar d. Nov 9, 1948
Kennedy, Tom d. Oct 6, 1965
Kruger, Otto d. Sep 6, 1974
Lane, Rosemary d. Nov 25, 1974
Lowe, Edmund Dante d. Apr 21, 1971
Maynard, Ken d. Mar 23, 1973
Mulhall, Jack d. Jun 1, 1979
Murray, Mae d. Mar 23, 1965
Purviance, Edna d. Jan 13, 1958
Rawlinson, Herbert d. Jul 12, 1953
Robin, Leo d. Dec 29, 1984
Ruby, Harry d. Feb 23, 1974
Sennett, Mack d. Nov 5, 1960
Shearer, Norma d. Jun 12, 1983
Silverheels, Jay d. Mar 5, 1980
Sondergaard, Gale d. Aug 14, 1985
Von Zell, Harry d. Nov 21, 1981
Whalen, Michael d. Apr 14, 1974
Young, Clara Kimball d. Oct 15, 1960
Yount, Robin R b. Sep 16, 1955

Woodside, California
Sterling, John Ewart Wallace
　d. Jul 1, 1985
Yorba Linda, California
Nixon, Richard Milhous b. Jan 9, 1913
Yucaipa, California
Anton, Susan b. Oct 12, 1950
Yuma City, California
Hohman, Donald b. 1943

COLORADO

Barker, Lloyd d. 1949
Packer, Alfred G b. 1842
Reventlow, Lance d. Jul 25, 1972
Aspen, Colorado
Revere, Anne d. 1972
Ross, Harold b. Nov 6, 1892
Sabich, "Spider" (Vladimir)
　d. Mar 21, 1976
Atwood, Colorado
Shumlin, Herman Elliott b. Dec 6, 1898
Aurora, Colorado
Lowe, Jack Warren b. Dec 25, 1917
Bethune, Colorado
Pyle, Denver b. May 11, 1920
Boulder, Colorado
Burke, Arleigh Albert b. Oct 19, 1901
Carpenter, Scott (Malcolm Scott)
　b. May 1, 1925
Condon, Edward d. Mar 26, 1974
McDonald, Harl b. Jul 27, 1899
Shapley, Harlow T d. Oct 20, 1972
Tatum, Edward Lawrie b. Dec 14, 1909
Colorado Springs, Colorado
Andrews, Bert b. Jun 2, 1901
Byington, Spring b. Oct 17, 1893
Chaney, Lon (Alonso) b. Apr 1, 1883
Dingell, John David, Jr. b. Jul 8, 1926
Etting, Ruth d. Sep 24, 1978
Gilpin, Laura b. Apr 22, 1891
Gossage, "Goose" (Richard Michael)
　b. Jul 5, 1951
James, Daniel, Jr. d. Feb 25, 1978
Keys, Ancel Benjamin b. Jan 26, 1904
Lincoln, George A d. May 24, 1975
Lucas, Nick d. Jul 28, 1982
Moody, William Vaughn d. Oct 17, 1910
Morath, Max Edward b. Oct 1, 1926
Parrish, Anne b. Nov 12, 1888
Taber, Gladys Bagg b. Apr 12, 1899
Creede, Colorado
Elting, Mary Letha b. Jun 21, 1906
Ford, Bob (Robert Newton)
　d. Jun 24, 1892
Del Norte, Colorado
Graves, Alvin Cushman d. Jul 29, 1965
Denver, Colorado
Amaya, Victor b. Jul 2, 1954
Andrews, Bert d.
Bailey, Philip b. May 8, 1951

Barrett, William Edmund d. Sep 17, 1986
Beckwourth, James Pierson d. 1867
Bishop, Julie b. Aug 30, 1914
Bond, Ward b. Apr 9, 1904
Browning, John b. May 23, 1933
Carr, Gerald Paul b. Aug 22, 1932
Carroll, Joe Barry b. Jul 24, 1958
Chapman, John (Arthur) b. Jun 25, 1900
Chase, Mary Coyle b. Feb 25, 1907
Chase, Mary Coyle d. Oct 20, 1981
Cherrington, Ben Mark d. May 4, 1980
Cody, "Buffalo Bill" (William Frederick)
    d. Jan 10, 1917
Dalvit, Lewis David, Jr. b. Dec 11, 1925
Davidson, J Brownlee d. May 8, 1957
Davis, Marvin b. 1926
DeWilde, Brandon d. Jul 6, 1972
Drinkwater, Terry b. May 9, 1936
Eisenhower, John Sheldon Doud
    b. Aug 3, 1922
Fairbanks, Douglas b. May 23, 1883
Fodor, Eugene Nicholas b. Mar 5, 1950
Fowler, Gene b. Mar 8, 1890
Gaddis, Thomas (Eugene) b. Sep 14, 1908
Halliday, Richard b. Apr 3, 1905
Handler, Elliot b. 1916
Handler, Ruth b. Nov 4, 1916
Harris, William Bliss b. 1901
Hart, John b. Feb 1, 1932
Hingle, Pat (Martin Patterson)
    b. Jul 19, 1924
Hoyt, Palmer (Edwin Palmer)
    d. Jun 25, 1979
Hufstedler, Shirley (Ann) M(ount)
    b. Aug 24, 1925
Johnson, Robert Willard b. Dec 23, 1921
Kerry, John F b. Dec 11, 1943
Kroeber, Theodora Kracaw
    b. Mar 24, 1897
Lea, Homer b. Nov 17, 1876
Lustig, Alvin b. Feb 8, 1915
McArthur, Edwin Douglas b. Sep 24, 1907
McDonnell, James Smith b. Apr 9, 1899
McLean, Evalyn Walsh b. Aug 1, 1886
Morrison, Trudi Michelle b. 1950
Packer, Alfred G d. Apr 24, 1907
Perry, Antoinette b. Jun 27, 1888
Raine, William MacLeod d. Jul 25, 1954
Reed, Dean b. 1939
Robinson, Paul Minnich b. Jan 26, 1914
Roth, Richard Lynn b. Jun 2, 1946
Rush, Barbara b. Jan 4, 1929
Russell, Donald Joseph b. Jan 3, 1900
Simpson, Alan Kooi b. Sep 2, 1936
Stone, Fred b. Aug 19, 1873
Swigert, Jack (John Leonard, Jr.)
    b. Aug 30, 1931
Tabor, Horace Austin Warner
    d. Apr 10, 1899
Walker, Harold Blake b. May 7, 1904
Warner, Emily Howell b. 1940

Whiteman, Paul b. Mar 28, 1891
Youmans, Vincent d. Apr 5, 1946
Dillon, Colorado
    Markey, Enid b. Feb 22, 1886
Durango, Colorado
    Roosa, Stuart b. Aug 16, 1933
Fort Collins, Colorado
    White, Byron Raymond b. Jun 8, 1917
Fort Lyon, Colorado
    Carson, "Kit" (Christopher)
        d. May 23, 1868
Fowler, Colorado
    Clark, "Dutch" (Earl) b. Oct 11, 1906
Glenwood Springs, Colorado
    Holliday, "Doc" (John Henry)
        d. Nov 8, 1887
Golden, Colorado
    Coors, William K (Bill) b. 1916
Grand Junction, Colorado
    Brazle, Al(pha Eugene) d. Oct 24, 1973
Grand Valley, Colorado
    Libby, Willard Frank b. Dec 17, 1908
Greeley, Colorado
    Gipson, Lawrence Henry b. Dec 7, 1880
    Mack, Ted b. Feb 12, 1904
Green Mountain Falls, Colorado
    Brady, Pat (Robert Patrick)
        d. Feb 27, 1972
La Hunta, Colorado
    Kesey, Ken b. Sep 17, 1935
Lamar, Colorado
    Curtis, Ken b. Jul 12, 1916
Leadville, Colorado
    Sadler, Barry b. 1941
    Tabor, Elizabeth Bonduel McCourt Doe
        d. Mar 7, 1935
Longmont, Colorado
    Brand, Vance DeVoe b. May 9, 1931
Louisville, Colorado
    Jovanovich, William Iliya b. Feb 6, 1920
Manassa, Colorado
    Dempsey, Jack (William Harrison)
        b. Jun 24, 1895
Manitou Springs, Colorado
    Goodrich, Benjamin Franklin
        d. Aug 3, 1888
Middleton, Colorado
    Wriston, Walter Bigelow b. Aug 3, 1919
Montrose, Colorado
    Trumbo, Dalton b. Dec 9, 1905
Pagosa Springs, Colorado
    Harman, Hugh b. 1903
Palisade, Colorado
    Martin, Fletcher b. Apr 29, 1904
Pueblo, Colorado
    Packard, David b. Sep 7, 1912
Salida, Colorado
    Blane, Sally b. Jul 11, 1910
    Siegel, Morris J b. Nov 21, 1949
Steamboat Springs, Colorado
    McWilliams, Carey b. Dec 13, 1905

Georgetown, Connecticut
Aulaire, Edgar Parin d' d. May 1, 1986
Glastonbury, Connecticut
Disney, Doris Miles b. Dec 22, 1907
Welles, Gideon b. Jul 1, 1802
Greenwich, Connecticut
Allyn, Stanley Charles d. Oct 31, 1970
Blatch, Harriot Eaton Stanton
   d. Nov 20, 1940
Caldwell, Taylor (Janet Miriam Taylor)
   d. Aug 30, 1985
Close, Glenn b. May 19, 1947
Collyer, "Bud" (Clayton) d. Sep 8, 1969
Cooper, Wilhelmina Behmenburg
   d. Mar 1, 1980
Dole, Charles Minot d. Mar 14, 1976
Dorsey, Tommy (Thomas Francis)
   d. Nov 26, 1956
Douglass, Lathrop d. Jan 21, 1981
Fox, Fontaine Talbot, Jr. d. Aug 10, 1964
Hamill, Dorothy b. 1956
Hellmann, Richard d. Feb 2, 1971
Henderson, Ray d. Dec 31, 1971
Kennedy, Ethel Skakel b. Apr 11, 1928
Laeri, J(ohn) Howard d. Jun 27, 1986
McHugh, Frank (Francis Curray)
   d. Sep 11, 1981
McWilliams, Alden b. 1916
Meek, Samuel Williams d. Aug 15, 1981
Purl, Linda b. Sep 2, 1955
Stettinius, Edward R, Jr. d. Oct 31, 1949
Templeton, Alec d. Mar 28, 1963
Topping, Dan(iel Reid) b. May 18, 1912
Tunney, "Gene" (James Joseph)
   d. Nov 7, 1978
Warburg, James Paul d. Jun 3, 1969
Weiss, George Martin d. Aug 13, 1972
Winterhalter, Hugo d. Sep 17, 1973
Wortman, Sterling d. May 26, 1981
Griswold, Connecticut
Stanton, Henry Brewster b. 1805
Groton, Connecticut
Deane, Silas b. Dec 24, 1737
Kimmel, Husband Edward
   d. May 15, 1968
Seabury, Samuel b. Nov 30, 1729
Guilford, Connecticut
Clinchy, Everett Ross d. Jan 22, 1986
Halleck, Fritz-Greene b. Jul 8, 1790
Halleck, Fritz-Greene d. Nov 19, 1867
Kirkpatrick, Ralph d. Apr 13, 1984
Haddam, Connecticut
Field, Stephen Johnson b. Nov 4, 1816
Hadlyne, Connecticut
Hamilton, Alice d. Sep 22, 1970
Hamden, Connecticut
Angell, James Rowland d. Mar 4, 1949
Borgnine, Ernest b. Jan 24, 1917
Fitzgerald, Robert Stuart d. Jan 16, 1985
Wilder, Thornton Niven d. Dec 7, 1975

Hartford, Connecticut
Amara, Lucine b. Mar 1, 1927
Bacon, Delia Salter d. Sep 2, 1859
Barnard, Henry b. Jan 24, 1811
Barnard, Henry d. Jul 5, 1900
Begley, Ed(ward James) b. Mar 25, 1901
Birmingham, Stephen b. May 28, 1931
Buketoff, Igor b. May 29, 1915
Bulkeley, Morgan d. Nov 6, 1922
Bushnell, Horace d. Feb 17, 1876
Church, Frederick Edwin b. May 4, 1826
Collins, Larry b. Sep 14, 1929
Colt, Samuel b. Jul 19, 1814
Colt, Samuel d. Jan 10, 1862
Cooke, Rose Terry b. Feb 17, 1827
Corio, Ann b. 1914
Dillingham, Charles Bancroft
   b. May 30, 1868
Dockstader, Lew b. 1856
Dunne, John Gregory b. May 25, 1932
Durrie, George Henry b. Jun 6, 1820
Evans, Linda b. Nov 18, 1942
Fields, Totie b. May 7, 1930
Fiske, John b. Mar 30, 1842
Fitch, John b. Jan 21, 1743
Fuller, Alfred Carl d. Dec 4, 1973
Gallaudet, Thomas Hopkins
   d. Sep 10, 1851
Gill, Brendan b. Oct 4, 1914
Gillette, William Hooker b. Jul 24, 1855
Gillette, William Hooker d. Apr 29, 1937
Grasso, Ella d. Feb 5, 1981
Henderson, Robert W d. Aug 19, 1985
Hepburn, Katharine Houghton
   b. Nov 8, 1907
Hobbs, Leonard Sinclair d. Nov 1, 1977
Hooker, Thomas d. Jul 19, 1647
Houghton, Katharine b. Mar 10, 1945
Howe, Harold, II b. Aug 17, 1918
Kellin, Mike b. Apr 26, 1922
Kolb, Barbara Anne b. Feb 10, 1939
Lewis, Wilmarth Sheldon d. Oct 7, 1979
LeWitt, Sol b. Sep 9, 1928
McAuliffe, Dick (Richard John)
   b. Nov 29, 1939
McClintock, Barbara b. Jun 16, 1902
McCormick, Cyrus Hall d. Mar 30, 1970
Merrill, Gary Franklin b. Aug 2, 1915
Merrill, John Putnam b. Mar 10, 1917
Morgan, J(ohn) P(ierpont) b. Apr 17, 1837
Nelson, George H. b. 1908
O'Keefe, Walter b. Aug 18, 1900
O'Shea, Michael b. Mar 17, 1906
Olmsted, Frederick Law b. Apr 27, 1822
Purtell, William Arthur b. May 6, 1897
Purtell, William Arthur d. May 31, 1978
Rodgers, Bill (William Henry)
   b. Dec 23, 1947
Rome, Harold Jacob b. May 27, 1908
Saint Jacques, Raymond b. Mar 1, 1932
Sigourney, Lydia Howard d. Jun 10, 1865

Booth, "Albie" (Albert James, Jr.)
 b. Feb 1, 1908
Bouchet, Edward Alexander
 b. Sep 15, 1852
Broderick, James Joseph d. Nov 1, 1982
Camp, Walter Chauncey b. Apr 7, 1859
Capp, Al b. Sep 28, 1909
Carpenter, Karen Ann b. Mar 2, 1950
Carpenter, Richard Lynn b. Oct 15, 1946
Chamberlain, John Rensselear
 b. Oct 28, 1903
Coates, Robert Myron b. Apr 6, 1897
Comstock, Ada Louise d. Dec 12, 1973
Cook, Donald d. Oct 1, 1961
Cross, Wilbur d. Oct 5, 1948
Cushing, Harvey Williams d. Oct 7, 1939
Dana, James Dwight d. Apr 14, 1895
Dollard, John d. Oct 8, 1980
Durrie, George Henry d. Oct 15, 1863
Dwight, Timothy d. Jan 11, 1817
Ellsberg, Edward b. Nov 21, 1891
Evans, Walker d. Apr 10, 1975
Fischer, John d. Aug 18, 1978
Fischetti, John d. 1978
Foote, Andrew Hull b. Sep 12, 1806
Foote, Andrew Hull d. Jun 26, 1863
Gassner, John Waldhorn d. Apr 2, 1967
Gesell, Arnold d. May 29, 1961
Gibbs, Josiah Willard b. Feb 11, 1839
Gibbs, Josiah Willard d. Apr 28, 1903
Gilbert, Alfred Carlton, Jr. b. Dec 1, 1919
Goldsmith, Fred Ernest b. May 15, 1852
Goodyear, Charles b. Dec 29, 1800
Griswold, A Whitney d. Apr 19, 1963
Hall, Donald Andrew b. Sep 20, 1928
Harris, Louis b. Jan 6, 1921
Harrison, Peter d. Apr 30, 1775
Hemion, Dwight b. Mar 14, 1926
Hendrick, Burton Jesse b. Dec 28, 1870
Ingersoll, Ralph McAllister b. Dec 8, 1900
Jenkins, Newell b. Feb 8, 1915
Kellogg, Clara Louise d. May 13, 1916
Kiernan, Walter b. Jan 24, 1902
Koopmans, Tjalling (Charles)
 d. Feb 26, 1985
Lear, Norman Milton b. Jul 27, 1922
Levy, Julien d. Feb 10, 1981
Linton, Ralph d. Dec 24, 1953
Linton, William James d. Dec 29, 1897
Lothrop, Harriet Mulford Stone
 b. Jun 22, 1844
Malinowski, Bronislaw d. May 16, 1942
Marsh, Othniel Charles d. Mar 18, 1899
McCabe, Mary O'Connell d. Dec 24, 1975
McGuire, "Biff" (William J)
 b. Oct 25, 1926
McNerney, Walter James b. Jun 8, 1925
Morrow, Buddy b. Feb 8, 1919
Moses, Robert b. Dec 18, 1888
Murphy, George Lloyd b. Jul 4, 1902

Nevin, Ethelbert Woodbridge
 d. Feb 17, 1901
Newman, Alfred b. Mar 17, 1901
Palillo, Ron b. Apr 2, 1954
Peters, Frederick Emerson d. Jul 29, 1959
Phelps, William Lyon b. Jan 2, 1865
Phelps, William Lyon d. Aug 21, 1943
Phillips, Harry Irving b. Nov 26, 1889
Podoloff, Maurice d. Nov 25, 1985
Porter, Quincy b. Feb 7, 1897
Porter, Quincy d. Nov 12, 1966
Powell, Adam Clayton, Jr.
 b. Nov 29, 1908
Rudkin, Margaret Fogarty d. Jun 1, 1967
Sapir, Edward d. Feb 4, 1939
Seymour, Charles b. Jan 1, 1884
Sherman, Roger d. Jul 23, 1793
Silliman, Benjamin d. Nov 24, 1864
Sloan, Alfred Pritchard, Jr.
 b. May 23, 1875
Sobol, Louis b. Aug 10, 1896
Sperry, Armstrong W b. Nov 7, 1897
Spivak, Charlie b. Feb 17, 1906
Spock, Benjamin McLane b. May 2, 1903
Steegmuller, Francis b. Apr 3, 1906
Sullavan, Margaret d. Jan 1, 1960
Terry, Alfred Howe d. Dec 16, 1890
Theiler, Max d. Aug 11, 1972
Trotta, Liz (Elizabeth) b. Mar 28, 1937
Tunnard, Christopher d. Feb 14, 1979
Vare, Glenna Collett b. Jun 20, 1903
Verrill, Alpheus Hyatt b. Jul 23, 1871
Wallant, Edward Lewis b. Oct 19, 1926
Webster, Noah d. May 28, 1843
Weiss, George Martin b. Jun 23, 1894
Whitney, Eli d. Jan 8, 1825
Wimsatt, William Kurtz, Jr.
 d. Dec 17, 1975
Winchester, Oliver Fisher d. Dec 11, 1880

New London, Connecticut
Bolton, Isabel b. Aug 6, 1883
Brackman, Robert d. Jul 16, 1980
Branch, Anna Hempstead b. Mar 18, 1875
Branch, Anna Hempstead d. Sep 8, 1937
Branner, Martin Michael d. May 19, 1970
Carter, Jeff (Donnel Jeffrey)
 b. Aug 18, 1952
Chidsey, Donald Barr d. 1981
Ferguson, Elsie d. Nov 15, 1961
Hooker, Brian d. Dec 28, 1946
Mansfield, Richard d. Aug 30, 1907
O'Neill, James d. Aug 10, 1920
Pastor, Tony d. Oct 31, 1969
Prentice, George Denison b. Dec 18, 1802
Seabury, Samuel d. Feb 25, 1796
Shepard, Odell d. Jul 19, 1967

New Milford, Connecticut
Crohn, Burrill Bernard d. Jul 29, 1983
McFee, William d. Jul 2, 1966
Parkhurst, Helen d. Jun 1, 1973

Bushmiller, Ernie (Ernest Paul)
d. Aug 15, 1982
Dalton, Charles d. Jun 11, 1942
DeVinne, Theodore Low b. Dec 25, 1828
Dominick, Peter Hoyt b. Jul 7, 1915
Edson, Gus b. Sep 20, 1901
Edson, Gus d. Sep 26, 1966
Guptill, Arthur Leighton d. Feb 29, 1956
Hawkes, John Clendennin Burne, Jr.
b. Aug 17, 1925
Holman, Libby d. Jun 18, 1971
Kennedy, Walter b. Jun 8, 1912
Kennedy, Walter d. Jun 26, 1977
Lazar, Irving Paul b. Mar 28, 1907
Lloyd, Christopher b. Oct 22, 1938
Mili, Gjon d. Feb 14, 1984
Perkins, Maxwell Evarts d. Jun 17, 1947
Pinza, Ezio d. May 9, 1957
Robinson, Boardman d. Sep 5, 1952
Robinson, Jackie (John Roosevelt)
d. Oct 24, 1972
Simon, Richard Leo d. Jul 29, 1960
Smith, "Red" (Walter Wellesley)
d. Jan 15, 1982
Tinker, Grant A b. Jan 11, 1926
Valentine, Bobby (Robert John)
b. May 13, 1950
Vera b. Jul 24, 1910
Webster, H(arold) T(ucker)
d. Sep 22, 1952
Wood, Peggy d. Mar 18, 1978

Stanford, Connecticut
Blake, Eugene Carson d. Jul 31, 1985
Delmar, Kenny d. Jul 14, 1984

Stanwich, Connecticut
Ingersoll, Simon b. Mar 3, 1818

Sterling, Connecticut
Dow, Charles Henry b. Nov 6, 1851

Stonington, Connecticut
Akeley, Mary Lee Jobe d. Jul 19, 1966
Hart, John b. 1711
Palmer, Nathaniel Brown b. Aug 8, 1799

Stony Creek, Connecticut
Orr, Douglas William d. Jul 29, 1966

Stratford, Connecticut
Schoyer, (B) Preston d. Mar 13, 1978
Smith, Loring b. Nov 18, 1895

Suffield, Connecticut
Remington, Eliphalet b. Oct 27, 1793

Taconic, Connecticut
Schumpeter, Joseph Alois d. Jan 8, 1950

Terryville, Connecticut
Knight, Ted b. Dec 7, 1923

Torrington, Connecticut
Brown, John b. May 9, 1800
Eliot, George Fielding d. Apr 21, 1971
Van Doren, Carl Clinton d. Jul 18, 1950
Van Doren, Mark d. Dec 10, 1972

Trumbull, Connecticut
Boylston, Helen Dore d. Sep 30, 1984
Fish, Robert Lloyd d. Feb 24, 1981
Silliman, Benjamin b. Aug 8, 1779

Wallingford, Connecticut
Downey, Morton b. Nov 14, 1902
Hall, Lyman b. Apr 12, 1724

Warren, Connecticut
Finney, Charles Grandison
b. Aug 29, 1792
Lynd, Robert Staughton d. Nov 1, 1970

Washington, Connecticut
Beecher, Janet d. Aug 6, 1955

Waterbury, Connecticut
Bolger, William Frederick b. Mar 13, 1923
Chase, Lucia b. Mar 27, 1907
Connor, Roger b. Jul 1, 1857
Connor, Roger d. Jan 4, 1931
Crane, Bob b. Jul 13, 1928
Crosby, Sumner McKnight
d. Nov 16, 1982
Dixon, Jean b. Jul 14, 1894
Gabo, Naum Pevsner d. Aug 23, 1977
Hull, Warren a. Sep 21, 1974
Parker, Daniel Francis b. Jul 1, 1893
Parker, Daniel Francis d. May 20, 1967
Russell, Rosalind b. Jun 4, 1911
Schacht, Al(exander) d. Jul 14, 1984
Sirica, John Joseph b. Mar 19, 1904
Walker, Ralph Thomas b. Nov 28, 1889

Waterford, Connecticut
Enders, John Franklin d. Sep 8, 1985

Watertown, Connecticut
Hotchkiss, Benjamin Berkeley
b. Oct 1, 1826
Trumbull, John b. Apr 24, 1750

Weathersfield, Connecticut
Beadle, William d. Dec 11, 1873

West Cornwall, Connecticut
Skelly, Hal d. Jun 16, 1934

West Hartford, Connecticut
Bush-Brown, Albert b. Jan 2, 1926
Enders, John Franklin b. Feb 10, 1897
Naughton, David b. 1951
Stich-Randall, Teresa b. Dec 24, 1927
Webster, Noah b. Oct 16, 1758
Wilder, Joseph d. Oct 31, 1976

West Haven, Connecticut
Estes, Eleanor Ruth Rosenfeld
b. May 9, 1906
Ford, Doug b. Aug 6, 1922
Strong, Ken b. Aug 6, 1906

West Redding, Connecticut
Steichen, Edward Jean d. Mar 25, 1973

West Suffield, Connecticut
Graham, Sylvester W b. Jul 5, 1794

Weston, Connecticut
Helburn, Theresa d. Aug 18, 1959
Lawson, Robert d. May 26, 1957

Westport, Connecticut
Adams, James Truslow d. May 18, 1949
Chapman, John (Arthur) d. Jan 19, 1972
Egan, Richard B d. Nov 13, 1952
Fraser, James Earle d. Oct 11, 1953
Glackens, William James d. May 22, 1938
Glass, Montague (Marsden) d. Feb 3, 1934
Gramatky, Hardie d. Apr 29, 1979
Keller, Helen Adams d. Jun 1, 1968
Kipnis, Alexander d. May 14, 1978
Martin, Pamela Sue b. Jan 5, 1954
Raymond, Alex(ander Gillespie)
   d. Sep 6, 1956
VonSchmidt, Harold d. Jun 3, 1982
Wald, Lillian D d. Sep 1, 1940

Wethersfield, Connecticut
Andrews, Charles McLean b. Feb 22, 1863
Johnson, Betsey b. Aug 10, 1942

Willimantic, Connecticut
Dodd, Christopher John b. May 27, 1944
Farrell, Eileen b. Feb 13, 1920

Willington, Connecticut
Sparks, Jared b. May 10, 1789

Wilton, Connecticut
Aulaire, Ingri Mortenson d'
   d. Oct 24, 1980
Purdy, Ken(neth) William d. Jun 7, 1972

Windham, Connecticut
Huntington, Samuel b. Jul 3, 1731
Wheelock, Eleazar b. Apr 22, 1711

Windsor, Connecticut
Ladd-Franklin, Christine b. Dec 1, 1847
Sill, Edward Rowland b. Apr 29, 1841
Wolcott, Oliver, Sr. b. Nov 26, 1726
Wolcott, Roger b. Jan 4, 1679

Windsor Locks, Connecticut
Grasso, Ella b. May 10, 1919

Winsted, Connecticut
Brinton, Clarence Crane b. Feb 2, 1898
Nader, Ralph b. Feb 27, 1934

Wolcott, Connecticut
Alcott, Amos Bronson b. Nov 29, 1799
Thomas, Seth b. Aug 19, 1785

Woodbury, Connecticut
Anderson, Leroy d. May 18, 1975
Dalgleish, Alice d. Jun 11, 1979

DELAWARE

DuPont de Nemours, Pierre Samuel
   d. Aug 7, 1817

Christiana, Delaware
Copeland, Lammot du Pont
   b. May 19, 1905

Claymont, Delaware
Darley, Felix Octavius Carr
   d. Mar 27, 1888

Dagsborough, Delaware
Clayton, John Middleton b. Jul 24, 1796

Delaware County, Delaware
Canfield, James Hulme b. Mar 18, 1847
Humphreys, Joshua b. Jun 17, 1751

Dover, Delaware
Cannon, Annie Jump b. Dec 11, 1863
Clayton, John Middleton d. Nov 9, 1856
Rodney, Caesar b. Oct 7, 1728
Rodney, Caesar d. Jun 29, 1784
Sykes, George b. Oct 9, 1822

Georgetown, Delaware
Townsend, George Alfred b. Jan 30, 1841

Lewes, Delaware
Walter, James Willis b. 1922

Mount Cuba, Delaware
Copeland, Lammot du Pont d. Jul 1, 1983

New Castle, Delaware
Evans, Oliver b. 1755
Read, George d. Sep 21, 1798
Ross, George b. Mar 10, 1730

New Castle County, Delaware
MacDonough, Thomas b. Dec 31, 1783

Newport, Delaware
Green, Dallas (George Dallas, Jr.)
   b. Aug 4, 1934

Smyrna, Delaware
Cummins, George David b. Dec 11, 1822
Moore, John Bassett b. Dec 3, 1860

Wilmington, Delaware
Bertinelli, Valerie b. Apr 23, 1960
Canby, Henry Seidel b. Sep 6, 1878
Cooke, David Coxe b. Jun 7, 1917
DuPont, Pierre Samuel, III b. Jan 1, 1911
DuPont, Pierre Samuel, IV b. Jan 22, 1935
Frisch, Frankie (Frank Francis)
   d. Mar 12, 1973
Fuller, Edmund b. Mar 3, 1914
Heimlich, Henry J b. Feb 3, 1920
Hillyer, Robert d. Dec 24, 1961
Marquand, John Phillips b. Nov 10, 1893
Pyle, Howard b. Mar 5, 1853
Shands, Alfred Rives, Jr. d. 1981
Squibb, Edward Robinson b. Jul 4, 1819
Taylor, Estelle b. May 20, 1899
White, Randy Lee b. Jan 15, 1953
Widdoes, Kathleen b. Mar 21, 1939
Wyeth, Henriette b. Oct 22, 1907
Wyeth, Jamie (James Browning)
   b. Jul 6, 1946

DISTRICT OF COLUMBIA

Washington, District of Columbia
Abrams, Creighton Williams
   d. Sep 4, 1974
Abu Salma, pseud. d. Sep 13, 1980
Acheson, Edward Goodrich
   b. Mar 9, 1856
Adams, Charles Francis, Jr.
   d. Mar 20, 1915
Adams, Henry Brooks d. Mar 27, 1918
Adams, John Quincy d. Feb 23, 1848

Adams, Louisa Catherine d. May 14, 1852
Albee, Edward Franklin, III
  b. Mar 12, 1928
Allen, Robert Sharon d. Feb 23, 1981
Alsop, Stewart Johonnot Oliver
  d. May 26, 1974
Altrock, Nick (Nicholas) d. Jan 20, 1965
Ames, Nancy b. Sep 30, 1937
Anderson, Mary d. Jan 29, 1964
Auchincloss, Hugh D d. Nov 20, 1976
Bailey, Florence Augusta Merriam
  d. Sep 22, 1948
Bancroft, George d. Jan 17, 1891
Baylor, Elgin b. Sep 16, 1934
Beale, Betty b. 1912
Beattie, Ann b. Sep 8, 1947
Belknap, William Worth d. Oct 13, 1890
Belote, Melissa b. Oct 16, 1956
Benjamin, Adam, Jr. d. Sep 7, 1982
Bennett, John Charles b. Dec 6, 1923
Benton, Thomas Hart d. Apr 10, 1858
Berger, Samuel David d. Feb 12, 1980
Berliner, Emile d. Aug 3, 1929
Bernstein, Carl b. Feb 14, 1944
Berryman, Clifford Kennedy
  d. Dec 11, 1949
Biddle, Anthony d. Nov 13, 1961
Bing, Dave (David) b. Nov 29, 1943
Bingham, Hiram d. Jun 6, 1956
Biossat, Bruce d. May 27, 1974
Birney, David Edwin b. Apr 23, 1940
Blaine, James Gillespie d. Jan 27, 1893
Bliss, Tasker H d. Nov 9, 1930
Bloch, Claude Charles d. Oct 6, 1967
Bohlen, Charles Eustis d. Jan 2, 1974
Bonsal, Stephen d. Jun 8, 1951
Borah, William E d. Jan 19, 1940
Boren, David Lyle b. Apr 21, 1941
Bowes, Walter d. Jun 24, 1957
Boyce, Westray Battle d. Jan 31, 1972
Bradley, Joseph P d. Jan 22, 1892
Brandeis, Louis Dembitz d. Oct 5, 1941
Brandon, Brumsic, Jr. b. Apr 10, 1927
Brawley, Benjamin Griffith d. Feb 1, 1939
Brewer, David Josiah d. Mar 28, 1910
Brooke, Edward William b. Oct 26, 1919
Brookings, Robert Somers d. Nov 15, 1932
Brown, Blair b. 1948
Brown, George Scratchley d. Dec 5, 1978
Brown, Jacob Jennings d. Feb 24, 1828
Bruce, David Kirkpatrick Estes
  d. Dec 4, 1978
Brumidi, Constantino d. Feb 19, 1880
Buchanan, Angela Marie b. 1948
Buchanan, Patrick Joseph b. Nov 2, 1938
Buckley, Tim b. Feb 17, 1947
Buford, John d. Dec 16, 1863
Bundy, William Putnam b. Sep 24, 1917
Burke, "Billie" (Mary William Ethelberg
  Appleton) b. Aug 7, 1886
Butler, Benjamin Franklin d. Jan 11, 1893

Cabot, John Moors d. Feb 23, 1981
Callahan, Daniel b. Jul 19, 1930
Cantacuzene, Princess b. Jun 7, 1876
Cantacuzene, Princess d. Oct 5, 1975
Carpenter, Leslie d. Jul 24, 1974
Carr, Austin George b. Mar 10, 1948
Carroll, Anna Ella d. Feb 19, 1893
Casady, Jack b. Apr 13, 1944
Case, Clifford Philip d. Mar 5, 1982
Casey, Dan(iel Maurice) d. Feb 8, 1943
Chace, Marian d. Jul 20, 1970
Chase, Mary Agnes d. Sep 24, 1963
Chauncey, Isaac d. Jan 27, 1840
Chautemps, Camille d. Jul 1, 1963
Chretien, Henri d. Feb 6, 1956
Chung, Connie (Constance Yu-Hwa)
  b. Aug 20, 1946
Claire, Ina b. Oct 15, 1895
Clark, "Champ" (James Beauchamp)
  d. Mar 2, 1921
Clay, Henry d. Jun 29, 1852
Clinton, George d. Apr 20, 1812
Cobb, William Montague b. Oct 12, 1904
Cockrell, Ewing d. Jan 21, 1962
Cohen, Benjamin Victor d. Aug 15, 1983
Colby, Anita b. Aug 5, 1914
Connally, Tom (Thomas Terry)
  d. Oct 28, 1963
Considine, Bob (Robert Bernard)
  b. Nov 4, 1906
Cook, Will Marion b. Jan 27, 1869
Corcoran, Thomas Gardiner
  d. Dec 6, 1981
Corcoran, William Wilson d. Feb 24, 1888
Cordon, Norman b. Jan 20, 1904
Crawford, William Hulfish d. Jan 6, 1982
Curtis, Charles d. Feb 8, 1936
Cushing, William Barker d. Dec 17, 1874
Dahlgren, John Adolph d. Jul 12, 1870
Daniels, Josephus b. May 18, 1862
Dantley, Adrian Delano b. Feb 26, 1956
Davies, Joseph Edward d. May 9, 1958
Davis, Benjamin Oliver b. Jul 1, 1877
Davis, Benjamin Oliver, Jr.
  b. Dec 18, 1912
Davis, Dwight Filley d. Nov 28, 1945
Davis, Elmer Holmes d. May 18, 1958
Davison, Frederic Ellis b. Sep 28, 1917
Denver, James William d. Aug 9, 1892
Dewey, Charles Schuveldt d. Dec 26, 1980
Dewey, George d. Jan 16, 1917
Dill, John Greer, Sir d. Nov 4, 1944
Dirksen, Everett McKinley d. Sep 7, 1969
Donovan, William Joseph d. Feb 8, 1959
Douglas, Paul Howard d. Sep 24, 1976
Douglas, William Orville d. Jan 19, 1980
Drew, Charles Richard b. Jun 3, 1904
Drew, Charles Richard d. Apr 1, 1950
Dulles, Allen Welsh d. Jan 29, 1969
Dulles, John Foster b. Feb 25, 1888
Dulles, John Foster d. May 24, 1959

Eastman, Mary Henderson d. Feb 24, 1887
Eisenhower, Dwight David
  d. Mar 28, 1969
Eisenhower, Julie Nixon b. Jul 5, 1948
Eisenhower, Mamie Geneva Doud
  d. Nov 1, 1979
Ellington, "Duke" (Edward Kennedy)
  b. Apr 29, 1899
Ellington, Mercer b. Mar 11, 1919
Engel, Georgia Bright b. Jul 28, 1948
Engle, Clair d. Jul 30, 1964
Fairfax, Beatrice, pseud. b. 1878
Fanon, Frantz d. Dec 6, 1961
Fauntroy, Walter E b. Feb 6, 1933
Field, Stephen Johnson d. Apr 9, 1899
Fillmore, Abigail Powers d. Mar 30, 1853
Fish, Albert b. 1870
Fishback, Margaret b. Mar 10, 1904
Fitch, James Marston b. May 8, 1909
Fitzpatrick, Thomas d. Feb 7, 1854
Fleeson, Doris d. Aug 1, 1970
Fluckey, Eugene Bennett b. Oct 5, 1913
Fortas, Abe d. Apr 5, 1982
Frankfurter, Felix d. Feb 22, 1965
Frazier, Edward Franklin d. May 17, 1962
Friedman, William d. Nov 12, 1969
Friendly, Alfred d. Nov 7, 1983
Fryer, Robert b. Dec 18, 1920
Gaud, William Steen, Jr. d. Dec 5, 1977
Gaye, Marvin (Marvin Pentz)
  b. Apr 2, 1939
George, Jean Craighead b. Jul 2, 1919
Gerry, Elbridge d. Nov 23, 1814
Ghormley, Robert Lee d. Jun 21, 1958
Gibbons, Floyd Phillips b. Jul 16, 1887
Glass, Carter d. May 28, 1946
Goldberger, Joseph d. Jan 17, 1929
Goldman, Eric F b. Jun 17, 1915
Goldsborough, Louis M b. Feb 18, 1805
Goldsborough, Louis M d. Feb 20, 1877
Grant, Julia Dent d. Dec 14, 1902
Graves, Alvin Cushman b. Nov 4, 1909
Gray, Gordon d. Nov 25, 1982
Gray, Horace d. Sep 15, 1902
Greer, Jane b. Sep 9, 1924
Griffith, Clark Calvin d. Oct 27, 1955
Grimke, Charlotte Lottie Forten
  d. Jul 23, 1914
Grosvenor, Melville Bell b. Nov 26, 1901
Groves, Leslie Richard d. Jul 13, 1970
Grubert, Carl Alfred d. May 30, 1983
Guiteau, Charles Julius d. Jun 30, 1882
Halberstam, Michael Joseph
  d. Dec 5, 1980
Hale, Alan b. Feb 10, 1892
Hamilton, Edith d. May 31, 1963
Hanna, Mark (Marcus Alonzo)
  d. Feb 15, 1904
Harlan, John Marshall d. Oct 14, 1911
Harlan, John Marshall d. Dec 29, 1971
Harris, Patricia Roberts d. Mar 23, 1985

Harrison, Caroline Lavinia Scott
  d. Oct 25, 1892
Harrison, William Henry d. Apr 4, 1841
Hart, Philip Aloysius d. Dec 26, 1976
Hawes, Harriet Ann Boyd
  d. Mar 31, 1945
Hawn, Goldie Jean b. Nov 21, 1945
Hayes, Helen b. Oct 10, 1900
Heard, John b. Mar 7, 1945
Heaton, Leonard d. Sep 11, 1983
Henry, Joseph d. May 13, 1878
Herrmann, Edward b. Jul 21, 1943
Herter, Christian Archibald
  d. Dec 30, 1966
Hickman, Herman Michael, Jr.
  d. Apr 25, 1958
Higgins, Marguerite d. Jan 3, 1966
Hirshhorn, Joseph d. Aug 31, 1981
Hoban, James d. Dec 8, 1831
Hodge, John Reed d. Nov 12, 1963
Hokinson, Helen d. Nov 1, 1949
Holly, James Theodore b. Oct 3, 1829
Holmes, Oliver Wendell, Jr.
  d. Mar 6, 1935
Hooks, Robert b. Apr 18, 1937
Hoover, J(ohn) Edgar b. Jan 1, 1895
Hoover, J(ohn) Edgar d. May 2, 1972
Hopkins, Claude b. Aug 3, 1903
Houston, Charles Hamilton b. Sep 3, 1895
Houston, Charles Hamilton
  d. Apr 22, 1950
Huebner, Clarence R d. Sep 23, 1972
Hurt, William b. Mar 20, 1950
Ickes, Harold LeClair d. Feb 3, 1952
Jackson, Robert Houghwout
  d. Oct 9, 1954
Jefferson, Martha d. Oct 10, 1836
Johnson, Hugh S d. Apr 15, 1942
Johnson, Lynda Bird b. Mar 19, 1943
Johnson, Mordecai Wyatt d. Sep 10, 1976
Johnson, Walter Perry d. Dec 10, 1946
Johnston, Joseph Eggleston
  d. Feb 21, 1891
Jones, "Biff" (Lawrence M) b. Oct 8, 1895
Just, Ernest Everett d. Oct 27, 1941
Kaufman, Joseph William d. Feb 13, 1981
Kauokenen, Jorma b. Dec 23, 1940
Kennedy, Jayne b. Oct 27, 1951
Kerby, William Frederick b. Jul 28, 1908
Kerr, Robert Samuel d. Jan 1, 1963
Kintner, Robert Edmonds d. Dec 20, 1980
Kiplinger, Austin Huntington
  b. Sep 19, 1918
Knox, Frank d. Apr 28, 1944
Kraft, Joseph d. Jan 10, 1986
Krock, Arthur d. Apr 12, 1974
LaFollette, Bronson Cutting b. Feb 2, 1936
LaFollette, Robert Marion d. Jun 18, 1925
Lahey, Edwin A(loysius) d. Jul 17, 1969
Lamar, Joseph Rucker d. Jan 2, 1916
Lansing, Robert d. Oct 30, 1928

Lanston, Tolbert d. 1913
Lattimore, Owen b. Jul 29, 1900
Lattisaw, Stacy b. Nov 25, 1966
Learned, Michael b. Apr 9, 1929
Leonard, "Sugar" Ray b. May 17, 1956
Leonard, John b. Feb 25, 1939
Letelier, Orlando d. Sep 21, 1976
Leutze, Emanuel d. Jul 18, 1868
Lewis, Fulton, Jr. b. Apr 30, 1903
Lewis, Fulton, Jr. d. Aug 21, 1966
Lewis, John Llewellyn d. Jun 11, 1969
Liggett, Louis Kroh d. Jun 5, 1946
Limbert, John William, Jr.
    b. Mar 10, 1943
Lincoln, Abraham d. Apr 15, 1865
Lincoln, G(eorge) Gould b. Jul 26, 1880
Lincoln, G(eorge) Gould d. Dec 1, 1974
Littlejohn, Robert McGowan
    d. May 6, 1982
Lockwood, Belva Ann Bennett
    d. May 19, 1917
Logan, John Alexander d. Dec 26, 1886
Lombardi, Vince(nt Thomas)
    d. Sep 4, 1970
Longworth, Alice Roosevelt
    d. Feb 20, 1980
Louis, Morris d. Sep 7, 1962
Lucas, Jim Griffing d. Jun 21, 1970
MacArthur, Douglas d. Apr 5, 1964
Mack, Peter d. Jul 4, 1986
Mahan, Alfred Thayer d. Dec 1, 1914
Mahone, William d. Oct 8, 1895
Marriott, John Willard, Jr.
    b. Mar 25, 1932
Marshall, George Catlett d. Oct 16, 1959
Marshall, Peter d. Jan 25, 1949
Marshall, Thomas Riley d. Jun 1, 1925
Martin, James Slattin, Jr. b. Jun 21, 1920
Martin, Judith b. Sep 13, 1938
Mattingley, Garrett b. May 6, 1900
May, Marjorie Merriweather
    d. Oct 12, 1973
Mayer, Norman D d. Dec 8, 1982
McAdoo, William Gibbs d. Feb 1, 1941
McAuliffe, Anthony Clement
    b. Jul 2, 1898
McAuliffe, Anthony Clement
    d. Aug 11, 1975
McCormick, Joseph Medill d. Feb 25, 1925
McFarlane, Robert Carl b. Jul 12, 1937
McIlhenny, Walter S b. 1911
McKelway, St. Clair d. 1976
McLean, Evalyn Walsh d. Apr 26, 1947
McMahon, (James O') Brien
    d. Jul 28, 1952
McNamara, Margaret Craig d. Feb 3, 1981
McNamee, Graham b. Jul 10, 1888
Meany, George d. Jan 10, 1980
Mearns, David Chambers b. Dec 31, 1899
Meigs, Montgomery Cunningham
    d. Jan 2, 1892

Meloy, Francis Edward, Jr.
    b. Mar 28, 1917
Miles, Nelson A d. May 15, 1925
Miller, Linda Kay b. Sep 7, 1953
Mills, Florence b. Jan 25, 1895
Mills, Robert d. Mar 3, 1855
Montoya, Joseph Manuel d. Jun 5, 1978
Mosby, John Singleton d. May 30, 1916
Mudd, Roger Harrison b. Feb 9, 1928
Mumford, Lawrence Quincy
    d. Aug 15, 1982
Mundt, Karl Earl d. Aug 16, 1974
Nestingen, Ivan Arnold d. Apr 24, 1978
Newcomb, Simon d. Jul 11, 1909
Nicolay, John George d. Sep 26, 1901
Noor, Queen b. Aug 23, 1951
Norton, Eleanor Holmes b. Jun 13, 1937
Noyes, Blanche Wilcox d. 1981
Noyes, Frank B b. Jul 7, 1863
Noyes, Frank B d. Dec 1, 1948
Nye, Gerald Prentice d. Jul 17, 1971
Okun, Arthur Melvin d. Mar 23, 1980
Osborne, John Franklin d. May 2, 1981
Page, Charles Grafton d. May 5, 1868
Parks, Floyd Lavinius d. Mar 10, 1959
Pearson, Drew d. Sep 1, 1969
Peary, Robert Edwin d. Feb 20, 1920
Perkins, Osgood (James Ridley Osgood)
    d. Sep 23, 1937
Pershing, John J(oseph) d. Jul 15, 1948
Pfeiffer, Jane Cahill b. Sep 29, 1932
Phillips, Marjorie Acker d. Jun 19, 1985
Pinchback, Pinckney Benton Stewart
    d. Dec 21, 1921
Pinkney, William d. Dec 25, 1822
Pollock, Channing b. Mar 4, 1880
Porter, David Dixon d. Feb 13, 1891
Pusey, Merlo John d. Nov 25, 1985
Radford, Arthur William d. Aug 17, 1973
Randall, Dudley b. Jan 14, 1914
Randall, Samuel J d. Apr 13, 1890
Randolph, Mary d. Jan 23, 1828
Rawlings, Marjorie Kinnan b. Aug 8, 1896
Rawlins, John A d. Sep 6, 1869
Reed, Walter d. Nov 23, 1902
Reichelderfer, Francis Wylton
    d. Jan 26, 1983
Ritchie, Thomas d. Dec 3, 1854
Rivera, Chita b. Jan 23, 1933
Rodgers, Christopher Raymond Perry
    d. Jan 8, 1892
Rooney, John (James) d. Oct 26, 1975
Roosevelt, John Aspinal b. Mar 13, 1916
Roper, Daniel C d. Apr 11, 1943
Rose, Leonard b. Jul 27, 1918
Rosenthal, Benjamin Stanley
    d. Jan 4, 1983
Rosenthal, Joe (Joseph J) b. Oct 9, 1911
Ross, John d. Aug 1, 1866
Ross, Nellie Taylor d. Dec 19, 1977
Rowe, James Henry, Jr. d. Jun 17, 1984

Royall, Anne Newport d. Oct 1, 1854
Russell, Richard Brevard, Jr.
    d. Jan 21, 1971
Saint-Subber, Arnold b. Feb 18, 1918
Schenck, Robert Cumming
    d. Mar 23, 1890
Schmidt, Benno Charles, Jr.
    b. Mar 20, 1942
Schoolcraft, Henry Rowe d. Dec 10, 1864
Seaton, Frederick Andrew b. Dec 11, 1909
Seton-Watson, Hugh (George Hugh
    Nicholas) d. Dec 19, 1984
Shands, Alfred Rives, Jr. b. Jan 18, 1899
Shuster, Alvin b. Jan 25, 1930
Simpson, Jim b. Dec 20, 1927
Slaughter, Frank G b. Feb 25, 1908
Smith, Walter Bedell d. Aug 9, 1961
Solomon, Harold Charles b. Sep 17, 1952
Solomon, Samuel Joseph b. Jul 11, 1899
Sousa, John Philip b. Nov 6, 1854
Southworth, Emma Dorothy Eliza Nevitte
    b. Dec 26, 1819
Spaatz, Carl Andrew d. Jul 14, 1974
Spottswood, Stephen Gill d. Dec 1, 1974
Stanton, Edwin McMasters
    d. Dec 24, 1869
Stark, Harold Raynsford d. Aug 20, 1972
Stevens, Leslie b. Feb 13, 1924
Stevens, Thaddeus d. Aug 11, 1868
Stitt, "Sonny" (Edward) d. Jul 22, 1982
Stockton, Frank (Francis Richard)
    d. Apr 20, 1902
Stone, Harlan Fiske d. Apr 22, 1946
Sullivan, Daniel P b. 1912
Sumner, Charles d. Mar 11, 1874
Surratt, Mary Eugenia Jenkins
    d. Jul 7, 1865
Sutter, John Augustus d. Jun 18, 1880
Swift, Elizabeth Ann b. Dec 3, 1940
Swigert, Jack (John Leonard, Jr.)
    d. Dec 27, 1982
Swing, Raymond Gram d. Dec 22, 1968
Taft, Helen Herron d. May 22, 1943
Taft, William Howard d. Mar 8, 1930
Taishoff, Sol Joseph d. Aug 15, 1982
Tallmadge, Thomas Eddy b. Apr 24, 1876
Taylor, Zachary d. Jul 9, 1850
Thayer, George Chapman, Jr.
    d. Aug 13, 1973
Thayer, Mary Van Rensselaer
    d. Dec 12, 1983
Tolson, Clyde Anderson d. Apr 14, 1975
Toomer, Jean b. Dec 26, 1894
Tork, Peter b. Feb 13, 1944
Torresola, Griselio d. Nov 1, 1950
Towers, John Henry d. Apr 1, 1955
Train, Russell Errol b. Jun 4, 1920
Turner, Thomas Wyatt d. Apr 21, 1978
Tyler, Letitia Christian d. Sep 10, 1842
Utley, Freda d. Jan 21, 1978
Van Der Zee, James d. May 15, 1983

Van Slyke, Helen Lenore Vogt
    b. Jul 9, 1919
Vance, Louis Joseph b. Sep 19, 1879
Vandenberg, Hoyt Sanford d. Apr 2, 1954
Vinson, Frederick Moore d. Sep 8, 1953
Von Neumann, John d. Feb 8, 1957
Waite, Morrison Remick d. Mar 23, 1888
Walker, Robert James d. Nov 11, 1869
Wallop, Douglass (John Douglass, III)
    b. Mar 8, 1920
Ward, Lester Frank d. Apr 18, 1913
Warner, John William b. Feb 18, 1927
Warner, Roger Sherman, Jr.
    d. Aug 3, 1976
Warren, Earl d. Jul 9, 1974
Warrington, Lewis d. Oct 12, 1851
Watson, Thomas Edward d. Sep 26, 1922
Watterson, Henry b. Feb 16, 1840
Weaver, Robert Clifton b. Dec 29, 1907
Weaver, William b. Jul 24, 1923
Weintal, Edward d. Jan 24, 1973
Wells, Linton d. Jan 31, 1976
West, James Edward b. May 16, 1876
Wheeler, Burton Kendall d. Jan 6, 1975
Wheeler, Earle G b. Jan 13, 1908
White, Edward Douglass d. May 19, 1921
Wilcox, Francis (Orlando) d. Feb 20, 1985
Wiley, Harvey Washington d. Jun 30, 1930
Wilkes, Charles d. Feb 8, 1877
Wills, Maury (Maurice Morning)
    b. Oct 2, 1932
Wilson, Edith Bolling Galt
    d. Dec 28, 1961
Wilson, Ellen Axson d. Aug 6, 1914
Wilson, Henry d. Nov 10, 1875
Wilson, John Johnston b. Jul 25, 1901
Wilson, John Johnston d. May 18, 1986
Wilson, Woodrow (Thomas Woodrow)
    d. Feb 3, 1924
Wimsatt, William Kurtz, Jr.
    b. Nov 17, 1907
Worden, John Lorimer d. Oct 18, 1897
Wrather, William Embry d. Nov 28, 1963
Wright, Horatio Governeur d. Jul 2, 1899
Wurf, Jerry (Jerome) d. Dec 10, 1981
Yost, Charles Woodruff d. May 21, 1981
Youngdahl, Luther W d. Jun 21, 1978
Zablocki, Clement John d. Dec 3, 1983
Washinton, District of Columbia
Reynolds, Frank d. Jul 20, 1983

FLORIDA

Davis, Brad b. 1950
Lloyd, John Henry b. Apr 15, 1884
McClary, Thomas b. 1948
Orange, Walter b. 1947
Apalachicola, Florida
Gorrie, John d. Jun 16, 1855
Apopka, Florida
Anderson, John b. Dec 13, 1954

Arcadia, Florida
Dozier, James Lee b. Apr 10, 1931
Baker, Florida
Henderson, Leon b. Feb 22, 1906
Bal Harbour, Florida
Dewey, Thomas Edmund d. Mar 16, 1971
Stillman, Irwin Maxwell d. Aug 27, 1975
Boca Grande, Florida
Lamont, Thomas William d. Feb 2, 1948
Boca Raton, Florida
Curran, Joseph Edwin d. Aug 14, 1981
Wragge, Sidney d. Mar 28, 1978
Boynton Beach, Florida
Marshall, (Sarah) Catherine Wood
d. Mar 18, 1983
Marshall, Catherine d. Mar 18, 1983
McGraw, Donald Cushing d. Feb 7, 1974
Raymond, James C d. Oct 14, 1981
Bradenton, Florida
Doak, Bill (William Leopold)
d. Nov 26, 1954
Hutchinson, Fred(erick Charles)
d. Nov 12, 1964
McKechnie, Bill (William Boyd)
d. Oct 29, 1965
Broward, Florida
Humphries, Stefan b. Jan 20, 1962
Cape Canaveral, Florida
Chaffee, Roger Bruce d. Jan 27, 1967
Grissom, Virgil Ivan d. Jan 27, 1967
Jarvis, Gregory d. Jan 28, 1986
McAuliffe, Christa (Sharon Christa
Corrigan) d. Jan 28, 1986
McNair, Ronald d. Jan 28, 1986
Onizuka, Ellison d. Jan 28, 1986
Resnik, Judy (Judith) d. Jan 28, 1986
Scobee, Dick (Francis Richard)
d. Jan 28, 1986
Smith, Michael John d. Jan 28, 1986
White, Ed(ward Higgins, II)
d. Jan 27, 1967
Chiefland, Florida
Verrill, Alpheus Hyatt d. Nov 14, 1954
Chipley, Florida
Gilmore, Artis b. Sep 21, 1949
Clearwater, Florida
Battles, Cliff(ord Franklin) d. Apr 27, 1981
Cordiner, Ralph Jarron d. Dec 4, 1973
Merritt, Abraham d. Aug 30, 1943
Cocoa, Florida
Debus, Kurt Heinrich d. Oct 10, 1983
Coconut Grove, Florida
Deering, William d. Dec 9, 1913
Doubleday, Frank Nelson d. Jan 30, 1934
Fairchild, David Grandison d. Aug 6, 1954
Coral Gables, Florida
Auslander, Joseph d. Jun 22, 1965
Berliner, Ron b. Oct 13, 1958
Graham, Bob (Daniel Robert)
b. Nov 9, 1936
Kurtz, Katherine b. Oct 18, 1944

Crescent City, Florida
Randolph, Asa Philip b. Apr 15, 1889
Daytona Beach, Florida
Bethune, Mary McLeod d. May 18, 1955
Kiernan, Walter d. Jan 8, 1978
Lajoie, Nap(oleon) d. Feb 7, 1959
Thurman, Howard b. Nov 18, 1900
DeLand, Florida
Stetson, John Batterson d. Feb 18, 1906
Delray Beach, Florida
Johnson, Arno Hollock d. Jul 20, 1985
Little, Lou(is) d. May 28, 1979
Robertson, Charles Sammis d. May 2, 1981
Shriner, Herb d. Apr 23, 1970
Eatonville, Florida
Hurston, Zora Neale b. Jan 7, 1903
Fernandina, Florida
Merrill, Frank Dow d. Dec 11, 1955
Fort Lauderdale, Florida
Albright, Malvin Marr d. Sep 14, 1983
Evert, Chris(tine Marie) b. Dec 21, 1954
Evert, Jeanne b. Oct 5, 1957
Martin, Joseph William, Jr.
d. Mar 6, 1968
McNary, Charles Linza d. Feb 25, 1944
Fort Meyers, Florida
Stotz, Charles Morse d. Mar 5, 1985
Fort Pierce, Florida
Hurston, Zora Neale d. Jan 28, 1960
Ft. Lauderdale, Florida
Ortega, Santos d. Apr 10, 1976
Gainesville, Florida
Felder, Don(ald William) b. Sep 21, 1947
Henderson, Leon d. Feb 7, 1960
Petty, Tom b. 1953
Sarett, Lew R d. Aug 17, 1954
Wilder, Alec (Alexander Lafayette Chew)
d. Dec 24, 1980
Green Cove, Florida
Merrill, Charles Edward b. Oct 19, 1885
Green Cove Springs, Florida
Savage, Augusta Christine b. Feb 29, 1892
Hawthorne, Florida
Edwards, James Burrows b. Jun 24, 1927
Hialeah, Florida
Casey, H(arry) W(ayne) b. Jan 31, 1951
Rebbot, Olivier d. Feb 10, 1981
Smith, Ronnie b. 1952
Hobe Sound, Florida
Dominick, Peter Hoyt d. Mar 18, 1981
Hollywood, Florida
Basie, "Count" (William James, Jr.)
d. Apr 26, 1984
Homestead, Florida
Rollini, Adrian d. May 15, 1956
Homosassa Springs, Florida
Vance, Clarence Arthur d. Feb 16, 1961
Indian Creek Island, Florida
Binns, Joseph Patterson d. Nov 23, 1980

Jacksonville, Florida
Barnett, Marvin Robert b. Oct 31, 1916
Bonds, Gary U S b. Jun 6, 1939
Boone, "Pat" (Charles Eugene)
    b. Jun 1, 1934
Canova, Judy b. Nov 20, 1916
Carmichael, Harold b. Sep 22, 1949
Coleman, Vince(nt Maurice)
    b. Sep 22, 1960
Daniels, Billy b. 1914
Day, J(ames) Edward b. Oct 11, 1914
Dillon, George b. Nov 12, 1906
Johnson, Arno Hollock b. Jan 12, 1901
Johnson, James Weldon b. Jun 17, 1871
Sande, Earl d. Aug 18, 1968
Smith, Rex b. 1956
Walton, William Turner b. Aug 29, 1909
Watterson, Henry d. Dec 22, 1921
Yarbrough, Lee Roy d. Dec 7, 1984
Youngblood, (Herbert) Jack(son)
    b. Jan 26, 1950
Zacharias, Jerrold R(einarch)
    b. Jan 23, 1905

Jasper, Florida
Smith, Lillian b. Dec 12, 1897

Jay, Florida
Moore, Jackie Spencer b. Feb 19, 1939

Jensen Beach, Florida
Rinaldi, Kathy b. Mar 24, 1967

Juno Beach, Florida
Elliott, "Jumbo" (James Francis)
    d. Mar 22, 1981

Key West, Florida
Chapman, Leonard F, Jr. b. Nov 3, 1913
Fetchit, Stepin b. May 30, 1902

Lake Placid, Florida
Dewey, Melvil d. Dec 26, 1931

Lake Wales, Florida
Bok, Edward William d. Jan 9, 1930

Lakeland, Florida
Chiles, Lawton Mainor, Jr. b. Apr 3, 1930
Langford, Frances b. Apr 4, 1913

Largo, Florida
Sackheim, Maxwell Byron d. Dec 2, 1982

Live Oak, Florida
McNeill, Robert Edward, Jr.
    b. Jan 20, 1906

Longboat Key, Florida
Gorkin, Jess d. Feb 19, 1985

Manatee, Florida
Markham, Monte b. Jun 21, 1935

Marathon, Florida
Hawley, Cameron d. Mar 9, 1969
Lau, Charlie (Charles Richard)
    d. Mar 18, 1984

Marianna, Florida
Fortune, Timothy Thomas b. Oct 3, 1856
Goldsboro, Bobby b. Jan 18, 1941

Melbourne, Florida
Leek, Sybil d. Oct 26, 1982
Morrison, Jim (James Douglas)
    b. Dec 8, 1943

Miami, Florida
Allen, Hervey (William Hervey)
    d. Dec 28, 1949
Bauer, Harold d. Mar 12, 1951
Beckman, Johnny d. Jun 22, 1968
Bloch, Raymond A d. Mar 29, 1982
Brown, Eddie Lee b. Dec 17, 1962
Carlton, Steve(n Norman) b. Dec 22, 1944
Carney, Don d. Jan 14, 1954
Cermak, Anton Joseph d. Mar 6, 1933
Conrad, Frank d. Dec 11, 1941
Cox, James Middleton, Jr. d. Oct 27, 1974
Davis, Arthur Vining d. Nov 17, 1962
Dawson, Andre Nolan b. Jul 7, 1954
Desjardins, Pete d. May 6, 1985
Eddy, Nelson d. Mar 6, 1967
Ellis, Carleton d. Jan 13, 1941
Engel, Lyle Kenyon d. Aug 10, 1986
Evans, Billy (William George)
    d. Jan 23, 1956
Fitzsimmons, James E d. Mar 11, 1966
Ford, Arthur A d. Jan 1, 1971
Foxx, Jimmy (James Emory)
    d. Jul 21, 1967
Gordon, John Brown d. Jan 9, 1904
Grosvenor, Melville Bell d. Apr 22, 1982
Gustafson, Karin b. Jun 23, 1959
Harry, Debbie (Deborah Ann)
    b. Jul 1, 1945
Hemingway, Leicester d. Sep 13, 1982
Hoppe, Willie (William F) d. Feb 1, 1959
Howser, Dick (Richard Dalton)
    b. May 14, 1937
Jacobs, Walter L d. Feb 7, 1985
Johnson, Robert b. Mar 21, 1953
Kearns, Jack d. Jul 7, 1963
Klem, Bill (William Joseph)
    d. Sep 16, 1951
Kofoed, Jack (John C) d. Dec 27, 1979
Markey, Lucille (Parker) Wright
    d. Jul 24, 1982
Marley, Bob (Robert Nesta)
    d. May 11, 1981
Papanicolaou, George Nicholas
    d. Feb 19, 1962
Poitier, Sidney b. Feb 20, 1924
Powell, Adam Clayton, Jr. d. Apr 4, 1972
Roker, Roxie b. Aug 28, 1929
Rosenbloom, Carroll D d. Apr 2, 1979
Smith, Jerome b. Jun 18, 1953
Spear, Sammy d. Mar 11, 1975
Spitalny, Phil d. Oct 11, 1970
Sullivan, Daniel P d. Jul 4, 1982
Sutherland, Earl Wilbur, Jr.
    d. Mar 9, 1974
Topping, Dan(iel Reid) d. May 18, 1974
Vereen, Ben b. Oct 10, 1946

Walters, Lou d. 1977
Waters, Charlie (Charles Tutan)
  b. Sep 10, 1948
Wood, Gar(field A) d. Jun 19, 1971
Wurdemann, Audrey May
  d. May 18, 1960
Wylie, Philip Gordon d. Oct 25, 1971
Zwilich, Ellen Taaffe b. Apr 30, 1939

Miami Beach, Florida
Baldrige, Letitia Katherine b.
Blaisdell, George G d. 1978
Capone, Al(phonse) d. Jan 25, 1947
Carey, Max George d. May 30, 1976
Firestone, Harvey Samuel d. Feb 7, 1938
Gruelle, Johnny (John Barton)
  d. Jan 9, 1938
Hanks, Nancy b. Dec 31, 1927
Heatter, Gabriel d. Mar 30, 1972
Ingersoll, Ralph McAllister d. Mar 8, 1985
Kasdan, Lawrence Edward b. Jan 14, 1949
Lansky, Meyer d. Jan 15, 1983
Lewisohn, Ludwig d. Dec 31, 1955
Lopez, Vincent d. Sep 20, 1975
Machado y Morales, Gerardo
  d. Mar 29, 1939
May, Mortimer d. May 8, 1974
Schenck, Nicholas Michael d. Mar 3, 1969
Slobodkin, Louis d. May 8, 1975
Stover, Russell d. May 11, 1954
Thaw, Harry Kendall d. Feb 22, 1947
Vanderbilt, Cornelius, Jr. d. Jul 7, 1974
Warner, Albert d. Nov 26, 1967
Zevin, B(enjamin) D(avid) d. Dec 27, 1984

Naples, Florida
Arends, Leslie Cornelius d. Jul 16, 1985
Martin, John C d. May 29, 1986

New Smyrna, Florida
Blood, Ernest B d. Feb 5, 1955
Paine, Albert Bigelow d. Apr 9, 1937

Nokomis, Florida
Jessup, Richard d. Oct 22, 1982

North Miami, Florida
Lombardo, Carmen d. Apr 17, 1971

Ocala, Florida
Ashley, Elizabeth b. Aug 30, 1939
Johnson, Eddie b. Feb 24, 1955
O'Neal, Patrick b. Sep 26, 1927

Odessa, Florida
Politz, Alfred d. Nov 8, 1982

Oklawaha, Florida
Barker, "Ma" (Arizona Donnie Clark)
  d. Jan 16, 1935
Barker, Fred d. Jan 16, 1935

Orlando, Florida
Crane, Roy(ston Campbell) d. Jul 7, 1977
Dawkins, Darryl b. Jan 11, 1957
Duranty, Walter d. Oct 3, 1957
Ebsen, Buddy b. Apr 2, 1908
Garrett, George Palmer, Jr.
  b. Jun 11, 1929

Johnson, Dave (David Allen)
  b. Jan 30, 1943
McNeill, Robert Edward, Jr.
  d. May 4, 1981
Newsom, "Bobo" (Louis Norman)
  d. Dec 7, 1962
Roberts, Elizabeth Madox d. Mar 13, 1941
Shawn, Ted (Edwin Meyers)
  d. Jan 9, 1972
Tinker, Joe (Joseph Bert) d. Jul 27, 1948
West, Riff b. Apr 3, 1950

Ormond Beach, Florida
Boni, Albert d. Jul 31, 1981
Hunt, Jack Reed d. Jan 7, 1984
Kitchell, Iva d. Nov 19, 1983
Rockefeller, John D(avison)
  d. May 23, 1937

Pahokee, Florida
Tillis, Mel(vin) b. Aug 8, 1932

Palatka, Florida
Stilwell, Joseph Warren b. Mar 19, 1883

Palm Beach, Florida
Albee, Edward Franklin d. Mar 11, 1930
Bache, Jules Sermon d. Mar 24, 1944
Bishop, Billy (William Avery)
  d. Sep 11, 1956
Daniels, Frank d. Jan 12, 1935
DeMarco, Tony d. Nov 14, 1965
Dodge, Horace Elgin d. Dec 10, 1920
Donahue, Woolworth d. Apr 5, 1972
Downey, Morton d. Oct 25, 1985
Gambling, John Bradley d. Nov 21, 1974
Guggenheim, Meyer d. Mar 15, 1905
Jefferson, Joseph d. Apr 23, 1905
Kallen, Horace M d. Feb 16, 1974
Kennedy, David Anthony d. Apr 26, 1984
McKeen, John Elmer d. Feb 23, 1978
Mizner, Addison d. Feb 5, 1933
Pulitzer, Lilly b.
Reynolds, Burt b. Feb 11, 1936
Sawyer, Charles d. Apr 7, 1979
Sears, Eleonora Randolph d. Mar 26, 1968
Uris, Harold David d. Mar 28, 1982
Wood, Craig Ralph d. May 8, 1968

Panama City, Florida
Kelser, Greg(ory) b. Sep 17, 1957

Pembroke Pines, Florida
McHale, Tom d. Mar 30, 1982

Pensacola, Florida
Bouquet, Henry d. Sep 2, 1765
Butterfield, Alexander Porter
  b. Apr 6, 1926
Cochran, Jacqueline b. 1910
Dussault, Nancy b. Jun 30, 1936
Erickson, Leif d. Jan 30, 1986
James, Daniel, Jr. b. Feb 11, 1920
Kurtis, Bill Horton (William)
  b. Sep 21, 1940
Mallory, Stephen R d. Nov 19, 1873
Percy, Charles Harting b. Sep 27, 1919
Saucier, Kevin Andrew b. Aug 9, 1956

Flagler, Henry Morrison d. May 20, 1913
Fox, Virgil Keel d. Oct 25, 1980
Hodges, Gil(bert Raymond) d. Apr 2, 1972
Javits, Jacob Koppel d. Mar 7, 1986
MacArthur, John Donald d. Jan 6, 1978
Pillsbury, John Sargent d. Jan 31, 1968
Pomerantz, Fred P d. Feb 21, 1986
Ridder, Bernard Herman d. May 5, 1975
Summerfield, Arthur Ellsworth
     d. Apr 26, 1972
Winter Haven, Florida
Birdsong, Otis Lee b. Dec 9, 1955
Cleaver, William Joseph (Bill)
     d. Aug 20, 1981
Parsons, Gram b. Nov 5, 1946
Skidmore, Louis d. Sep 27, 1962
Stafford, Jim b. 1944
Winter Park, Florida
Churchill, Winston d. Mar 12, 1947
Feis, Herbert d. Mar 2, 1972
Gaines, Clarence F d. Jan 2, 1986
Homer, Louise d. May 6, 1947
Homer, Sidney d. Jul 10, 1953
King, Frank d. Jun 24, 1969
Pattee, Fred Lewis d. May 6, 1950
Russell, Annie d. Jan 16, 1936

GEORGIA

Bethune, Thomas Greene b. 1849
Bozeman, John M b. 1835
Daniels, Jeff b. 1955
Osceola Nickanochee b. 1804
Albany, Georgia
Charles, Ray b. Sep 23, 1930
Dawson, William L b. Apr 26, 1886
James, Harry b. Mar 15, 1916
Jones, Edward Vason b. Aug 3, 1909
Jones, Edward Vason d. Oct 1, 1980
Riegger, Wallingford b. Apr 29, 1885
Thomas, Charles Allen d. Mar 30, 1982
Almo, Georgia
Crews, Harry Eugene b. Jun 6, 1935
Americus, Georgia
Bell, Griffin Boyette b. Oct 31, 1918
Carter, Lillian d. Oct 30, 1983
Andersonville, Georgia
Pennington, John Selman b. 1924
Archery, Georgia
Stapleton, Ruth Carter b. Aug 7, 1929
Ashburn, Georgia
Dennison, George b. Sep 10, 1925
Athens, Georgia
Basinger, Kim b. Dec 8, 1953
Johnson, Hall b. Mar 12, 1888
Kottke, Leo b.
Long, Crawford Williamson
     d. Jun 16, 1878
McGarity, Lou (Roert Louis)
     b. Jul 22, 1917
Michael, Moina Belle d. May 10, 1944

Atlanta, Georgia
Adams, Brock(man) b. Jan 13, 1927
Allen, Ivan, Jr. b. Mar 15, 1911
Austin, John Paul d. Dec 1985
Bealer, Alex W(inkler III)
     d. Mar 17, 1980
Black, Frank J. d. Jan 29, 1968
Blackwell, Earl b. May 3, 1913
Boles, Paul Darcy d. May 4, 1984
Boorstin, Daniel J(oseph) b. Oct 1, 1914
Borden, Barry b. May 12, 1954
Candler, Asa Griggs d. Mar 12, 1929
Candler, Charles Howard b. Dec 2, 1878
Candler, Charles Howard d. Oct 1, 1957
Casey, Hugh Thomas d. Jul 3, 1951
Cleland, Max (Joseph Maxwell)
     b. Aug 24, 1942
Cobb, Ty(rus Raymond) d. Jul 17, 1961
Cook, Barbara b. Oct 25, 1927
Davis, James Curran d. Dec 28, 1981
Dickey, James b. Feb 2, 1923
Dobbs, Mattiwilda b. Jul 11, 1925
Felton, Rebecca Ann Latimer
     d. Jan 24, 1930
Frazier, Walt b. Mar 29, 1945
Free, World B b. Dec 9, 1953
Fuller, Hoyt William b. Sep 10, 1926
Fuller, Hoyt William d. May 11, 1981
Grady, Henry Woodfin b. May 24, 1850
Grady, Henry Woodfin d. Dec 23, 1889
Hardy, Oliver b. Jan 18, 1892
Harris, Joel Chandler d. Jul 3, 1908
Harwell, Ernie b. Jan 25, 1918
Henderson, Vivian Wilson d. Jan 25, 1976
Heywood, Eddie b. Dec 4, 1915
Higginbotham, "Jack" (Jay C)
     b. May 11, 1906
Howell, Clark d. Nov 14, 1936
Jones, Bobby (Robert Tyre)
     b. Mar 17, 1902
Jones, Bobby (Robert Tyre)
     d. Dec 18, 1971
Jordan, Vernon Eulion, Jr.
     b. Aug 15, 1935
Joyner, Wally (Wallace Keith)
     b. Jun 16, 1962
Kelley, DeForrest b. 1920
King, Alberta Christine Williams
     d. Jun 30, 1974
King, Martin Luther, Jr. b. Jan 15, 1929
King, Martin Luther, Sr. d. Nov 11, 1984
Knight, Gladys Maria b. May 28, 1944
Lee, Brenda b. Dec 11, 1944
Lipshutz, Robert Jerome b. Dec 27, 1921
Lundquist, Steve b. Feb 20, 1961
Lyon, Ben b. Feb 6, 1901
Maddox, Lester Garfield b. Sep 30, 1915
Major, Clarence b. Dec 31, 1936
McDonald, Larry (Lawrence Patton)
     b. Apr 1, 1935
McGill, Ralph Emerson d. Feb 3, 1969

Metcalfe, Ralph H b. May 30, 1910
Miller, James Clifford, III b. Jun 25, 1942
Millis, Walter b. Mar 16, 1899
Mitchell, Margaret b. Nov 8, 1900
Mitchell, Margaret d. Aug 16, 1949
Neal, Larry (Lawrence P) b. Sep 5, 1937
Parks, Bert b. Dec 30, 1914
Payne, Sidney d. Dec 18, 1976
Reed, Jerry b. Mar 20, 1937
Robinson, Wilbert d. Aug 8, 1934
Robitscher, Jonas Bondi, Jr.
　d. Mar 25, 1981
Roe, Tommy b. May 9, 1942
Russell, Nipsey b. Oct 13, 1924
South, Joe b. Feb 28, 1942
Stanton, Frank Lebby d. Jan 7, 1927
Stephens, Alexander Hamilton
　d. Mar 4, 1883
Talmadge, Eugene d. Dec 21, 1946
Terry, Bill (William Harold)
　b. Oct 30, 1898
Tracy, Lee b. Apr 4, 1898
White, Walter Francis b. Jul 1, 1893
Willingham, Calder Baynard, Jr.
　b. Dec 23, 1922
Wills, Garry b. May 22, 1934
Withers, Jane b. Apr 12, 1926
Woodruff, Robert Winship d. Mar 7, 1985

Attapulgis, Georgia
Williams, Hosea Lorenzo b. Jan 5, 1926

Augusta, Georgia
Billings, John Shaw d. Aug 25, 1975
Brown, James b. May 3, 1934
Gibbs, Terri b. Jun 15, 1954
Grant, Amy b. 1961
Johns, Jasper b. May 15, 1930
Meigs, Montgomery Cunningham
　b. May 3, 1816
Tobias, Channing Heggie b. Feb 1, 1882
Ward, John Montgomery d. Mar 4, 1925
Wheeler, Joseph b. Sep 10, 1836
Woodward, William E d. Sep 27, 1950
Yerby, Frank Garvin b. Sep 5, 1916

Bainbridge, Georgia
Griffin, Marvin (Samuel Marvin)
　b. Sep 4, 1907
Hopkins, Miriam b. Oct 18, 1902
Kirbo, Charles b. Mar 15, 1917
Stribling, Young (William Lawrence)
　b. Dec 26, 1904

Barstow, Georgia
Coleman, Lonnie William b. Aug 2, 1920
Crain, Jeanne b. May 25, 1925

Buckhead, Georgia
Casey, Hugh Thomas b. Oct 14, 1913

Buena Vista, Georgia
Gibson, Josh(ua) b. Dec 21, 1911

Burke County, Georgia
Bowie, James b. 1796
Hall, Lyman d. Oct 19, 1790

Cairo, Georgia
Robinson, Jackie (John Roosevelt)
　b. Jan 31, 1919

Canton, Georgia
Hannah, John Allen b. Apr 4, 1951
Smith, Marie D b.

Cedartown, Georgia
Holloway, Sterling b. Jan 4, 1905
Sanders, Doug(las) b. Jul 24, 1937

Cherokee County, Georgia
Rusk, Dean (David Dean) b. Feb 9, 1909

Clarksdale, Georgia
Stevens, Ray b. Jan 24, 1939

Clayton, Georgia
Bowling, Roger d. Dec 25, 1982

Cleveland, Georgia
Roberts, Xavier b. Oct 31, 1955

Cogdell, Georgia
Davis, Ossie b. Dec 18, 1917

College Hill, Georgia
Walton, George d. Feb 2, 1804

Columbus, Georgia
Johnson, Nunnally b. Dec 5, 1897
Knight, John S, III b. Apr 3, 1945
McCullers, Carson Smith b. Feb 19, 1917
Rainey, "Ma" (Gertrude) b. Apr 26, 1886
Rainey, "Ma" (Gertrude) d. Dec 22, 1939
Saunders, William Laurence
　b. Nov 1, 1856
Woodruff, Robert Winship b. Dec 6, 1889

Commerce, Georgia
Chandler, "Spud" (Spurgeon Ferdinand)
　b. Sep 12, 1909

Cordele, Georgia
Williams, Joe b. Dec 12, 1918

Culloden, Georgia
Blalock, Alfred b. Apr 5, 1899

Cumberland Island, Georgia
Lee, Henry d. Mar 25, 1818

Cumming, Georgia
Samples, "Junior" (Alvin) d. Nov 13, 1983

Curryville, Georgia
Hayes, Roland b. Jun 3, 1887

Cuthbert, Georgia
Henderson, Fletcher Hamilton
　b. Dec 18, 1897
Holmes, Larry b. Nov 3, 1949

Dacula, Georgia
Hinton, William Arthur b. Aug 31, 1908

Dales Mill, Georgia
Nichols, Anne b. Nov 26, 1891

Danielsville, Georgia
Long, Crawford Williamson
　b. Nov 1, 1815

Dawson, Georgia
Redding, Otis b. Sep 9, 1941
Washington, Walter Edward
　b. Apr 15, 1915

Demorest, Georgia
Mize, Johnny (John Robert) b. Jan 7, 1913

Duluth, Georgia
Rogers, George b. Dec 8, 1958
Dunsmuir, Georgia
Muller, Harold P b. Jun 12, 1901
Eastman, Georgia
Stuckey, Williamson d. Jan 7, 1977
Eatonton, Georgia
Harris, Joel Chandler b. Dec 9, 1848
Lamar, Lucius Q C b. Sep 17, 1825
Walker, Alice b. Feb 9, 1944
Elbert County, Georgia
Lamar, Joseph Rucker b. Oct 14, 1857
Fitzgerald, Georgia
Abram, Morris Berthold b. Jun 19, 1918
Forsyth, Georgia
Talmadge, Eugene b. Sep 23, 1884
Fort Benning, Georgia
Gramm, (William) Phil(ip) b. Jul 8, 1942
Franklin, Georgia
Davis, James Curran b. May 17, 1895
Frogtown, Georgia
Sherrill, Robert Glenn b. Dec 24, 1925
Gainesville, Georgia
Cameron, Rod d. Dec 21, 1983
Lance, (Thomas) Bert(ram) b. Jun 3, 1931
Longstreet, James d. Jan 2, 1904
Good Hope, Georgia
Michael, Moina Belle b. Aug 15, 1869
Griffin, Georgia
Andrews, Edward b. Oct 9, 1915
Drewry, John Eldridge b. Jun 4, 1902
Gault, Willie b. Sep 5, 1960
Holliday, "Doc" (John Henry) b. 1851
Kiker, Douglas b. Jan 7, 1930
Tyus, Wyomia b. Aug 29, 1945
Hopewell, Georgia
Broyhill, Joel Thomas b. Nov 4, 1919
Hoschton, Georgia
Murphy, (John) Reg(inald) b. Jan 7, 1934
Inman, Georgia
Burch, Robert Joseph b. Jun 26, 1925
Irwinton, Georgia
Carswell, George Harrold b. Dec 22, 1919
Knoxville, Georgia
Pemberton, John Stith b. Jul 8, 1831
Lafayette, Georgia
Bean, Andy b. Mar 13, 1953
Dodd, Ed(ward) Benton b. Nov 7, 1902
LaGrange, Georgia
Austin, John Paul b. Feb 14, 1915
Lagrange, Georgia
Callaway, Howard Hollis b. Apr 2, 1927
LaGrange, Georgia
Jarriel, Tom (Thomas Edwin)
b. Dec 29, 1934
Lawrenceville, Georgia
Charles, Ezzard b. Jul 7, 1921
Leesburg, Georgia
Hamilton, Roy b. Apr 16, 1929
Lithia Springs, Georgia
Suggs, Louise b. Sep 7, 1923

Macon, Georgia
Allman, Duane (Howard Duane)
d. Oct 29, 1971
Douglas, Melvyn b. Apr 5, 1901
Langley, Jane Pickens b.
Lanier, Sidney b. Feb 3, 1842
Little Richard b. Dec 25, 1935
Moore, Roy W b. Feb 27, 1891
Pate, Jerry b. Sep 16, 1953
Pinchback, Pinckney Benton Stewart
b. May 10, 1837
Stallings, Laurence b. Nov 25, 1894
Stribling, Young (William Lawrence)
d. Oct 2, 1933
Manchester, Georgia
Woods, Stuart b. Jan 9, 1938
Marietta, Georgia
Carmichael, James Vinson d. Nov 28, 1972
Clay, Lucius du Bignon b. Apr 23, 1897
McAdoo, William Gibbs b. Oct 31, 1863
Walker, Danton MacIntyre b. Jul 26, 1899
McRue, Georgia
Folsom, Marion Bayard b. Nov 23, 1894
Milledgeville, Georgia
O'Connor, Flannery d. Aug 3, 1964
Vinson, Carl b. Nov 18, 1883
Vinson, Carl d. Jun 1, 1981
Monroe, Georgia
Greer, Michael b. Sep 19, 1917
Van Brocklin, Norm(an Mack)
d. May 2, 1983
Montgomery, Georgia
Smith, Frances Scott Fitzgerald Lanahan
d. Jun 18, 1986
Moreland, Georgia
Caldwell, Erskine Preston b. Dec 17, 1903
Moultrie, Georgia
Melton, James b. Jan 2, 1904
Mount Berry, Georgia
Berry, Martha McChesney d. Feb 27, 1942
Narrows, Georgia
Cobb, Ty(rus Raymond) b. Dec 18, 1886
Nelson, Georgia
Akins, Claude b. May 25, 1918
Newman, Georgia
Upshaw, William David b. Oct 15, 1866
Norcross, Georgia
Dean, "Man Mountain" d. May 29, 1953
Oak Grove, Georgia
Johnston, Richard Malcolm b. Mar 8, 1822
Peach County, Georgia
Johnson, Pete b. Mar 2, 1954
Perry, Georgia
Hodges, Courtney b. Jan 5, 1887
Nunn, Sam(uel Augustus, Jr.)
b. Sep 8, 1938
Pike County, Georgia
Futrelle, Jacques b. Apr 9, 1875
Plains, Georgia
Carter, Amy b. Oct 19, 1967
Carter, Billy b. Mar 29, 1937

Carter, Jimmy (James Earl, Jr.)
b. Oct 1, 1924
Carter, Rosalynn Eleanor Smith
b. Aug 18, 1927
Preston, Georgia
George, Walter Franklin b. Jan 29, 1878
Richmond, Georgia
Carter, Lillian b. Aug 15, 1898
Rome, Georgia
Berry, Martha McChesney b. 1866
Towers, John Henry b. Jan 30, 1885
York, Rudy (Rudolph Preston)
d. Feb 5, 1970
Saint Simons Island, Georgia
Brown, Jim (James Nathaniel)
b. Feb 17, 1936
Sandersville, Georgia
Muhammad, Elijah b. Oct 10, 1897
Savannah, Georgia
Aiken, Conrad Potter b. Aug 5, 1889
Aiken, Conrad Potter d. Aug 17, 1973
Coburn, Charles Douville b. Jun 19, 1877
Coleman, Lonnie William d. Aug 13, 1982
Curb, Mike (Michael Charles)
b. Dec 24, 1944
Dent, "Bucky" (Russell Earl)
b. Nov 25, 1951
Fremont, John Charles b. Jan 21, 1813
Green, Anne b. Nov 11, 1899
Greene, Nathanael d. Jun 19, 1786
Gwinnett, Button d. May 19, 1777
Jaffee, Allan b. Mar 13, 1921
Jessup, Richard b. Jan 1, 1925
Kanter, Hal b. Dec 18, 1918
Keach, Stacy, Jr. b. Jun 2, 1941
Low, Juliette Gordon b. Oct 31, 1860
Low, Juliette Gordon d. Jan 18, 1927
Mercer, Johnny b. Nov 18, 1909
Morehouse, Ward b. Nov 24, 1899
O'Connor, Flannery b. Mar 25, 1925
Oliver, Joe (Joseph) d. Apr 8, 1938
Pulaski, Kazimierz d. Oct 11, 1779
Quinn, Sally b. Jul 1, 1941
Smith, Merriman b. Feb 10, 1913
Stacy, Hollis b. Mar 16, 1954
Wilson, Ellen Axson b. May 15, 1860
Young, "Trummy" (James Osborne)
b. Jan 12, 1912
Sea Island, Georgia
Coffin, Howard Earle d. Nov 21, 1937
Smyrna, Georgia
Carmichael, James Vinson b. Oct 2, 1910
Sparta, Georgia
Jackson, "Hurricane" (Thomas)
b. Aug 9, 1931
Stockbridge, Georgia
King, Martin Luther, Sr. b. Dec 19, 1899
Telfair County, Georgia
Talmadge, Herman Eugene b. Aug 9, 1913

Thomaston, Georgia
Holloman, "Bobo" (Alva Lee)
b. Mar 27, 1924
Thomasville, Georgia
Woodward, Joanne Gignilliat
b. Feb 27, 1930
Thomson, Georgia
Watson, Thomas Edward b. Sep 5, 1856
Tifton, Georgia
Hoffman, Robert C b. 1899
Upson County, Georgia
Gordon, John Brown b. Feb 6, 1832
Valdosta, Georgia
Bealer, Alex W(inkler III) b. Mar 6, 1921
Lomax, Louis b. Aug 6, 1922
Wilson, Demond b. Oct 13, 1946
Vidalia, Georgia
Blount, Mel(vin Cornell) b. Apr 10, 1948
McIntyre, James Talmadge, Jr.
b. Dec 17, 1940
Vienna, Georgia
Busbee, George Dekle b. Aug 7, 1927
George, Walter Franklin d. Aug 4, 1957
Powell, Jody (Joseph Lester)
b. Sep 30, 1943
Sherman, Vincent b. Jul 16, 1906
Villa Rica, Georgia
Candler, Asa Griggs b. Dec 30, 1851
Dorsey, Thomas Andrew b. Jul 1, 1900
Walker, Frederick E b. Sep 24, 1910
Vineville, Georgia
Lamar, Lucius Q C d. Jan 23, 1893
Warm Springs, Georgia
Roosevelt, Franklin Delano
d. Apr 12, 1945
Warrenton, Georgia
Bushnell, David d. 1824
Washington, Georgia
Toombs, Robert Augustus d. Dec 15, 1885
Waycross, Georgia
Miller, Caroline b. Aug 26, 1903
Roberts, Pernell b. May 18, 1930
Wilkes County, Georgia
Stephens, Alexander Hamilton
b. Feb 11, 1812
Toombs, Robert Augustus b. Jul 2, 1810
Winder, Georgia
Russell, Richard Brevard, Jr.
b. Nov 2, 1897
Wrightsville, Georgia
Walker, Herschel b. Mar 3, 1962

HAWAII

Elliman, Yvonne b. Dec 29, 1953
Honolulu, Hawaii
Bingham, Hiram b. Nov 19, 1875
Carter, "Chip" (James Earl, III)
b. Apr 12, 1950
Cartwright, Alexander Joy, Jr.
d. Jul 12, 1892

Darling, Ron(ald Maurice, Jr.)
b. Aug 19, 1960
Dole, Sanford Ballard b. Apr 23, 1844
Dreier, Alex b. Jun 26, 1916
Dvorak, Ann d. Dec 10, 1979
Fernandez, Sid (Charles Sidney)
b. Oct 12, 1962
Field, Kate d. May 19, 1896
Fong, Hiram b. Oct 1, 1907
Gulick, Luther Halsey b. Dec 4, 1865
Hoppe, Arthur Watterson b. Apr 23, 1925
Inouye, Daniel Ken b. Sep 7, 1924
Kahanamoku, Duke b. Aug 24, 1890
Kahanamoku, Duke d. Jan 22, 1968
Kaiser, Henry John d. Aug 24, 1967
Liliuokalani, Lydia Kamekeha
b. Sep 2, 1838
Midler, Bette b. Dec 1, 1945
Ory, "Kid" (Edward) d. Jan 23, 1973
Patterson, William Allan b. Oct 1, 1899
Rhee, Syngman d. Jul 19, 1965
Tregaskis, Richard William
d. Aug 15, 1973

Kailua, Hawaii
Kamehameha I d. May 5, 1819

Kakaako, Hawaii
Ho, Don b. Aug 13, 1930

Kauai Island, Hawaii
Kenney, Douglas C d. Aug 27, 1980
Matsunaga, Spark Masayuki b. Oct 8, 1916

Kealakekua, Hawaii
Onizuka, Ellison b. Jun 24, 1946

Kealakeua, Hawaii
Cook, James, Captain d. Feb 14, 1779

Kipahulu, Hawaii
Lindbergh, Charles Augustus
d. Aug 26, 1974

Kohala, Hawaii
Kamehameha I b. 1758

Lihue, Hawaii
Hulme, Kathryn Cavarly d. Aug 25, 1981

Mauai, Hawaii
Loo, Richard b. 1903

Maui, Hawaii
Ankers, Evelyn d. Aug 29, 1985
Dole, James d. May 14, 1958

Molokai, Hawaii
Damien, Father d. Apr 15, 1889

Paia, Hawaii
Mink, Patsy Takemoto b. Dec 6, 1927

IDAHO

Annis, Idaho
Fisher, Vardis b. Mar 31, 1895

Auburn, Idaho
Boles, Paul Darcy b. Mar 5, 1919

Bear Lake, Idaho
Borglum, Gutzon b. Mar 25, 1867

Boise, Idaho
Agee, William McReynolds b. Jan 5, 1938
Church, Frank b. Jul 25, 1924
Mathison, Richard Randolph
b. Oct 20, 1919
Owen, (John) Reginald d. Nov 5, 1972
Wells, Edward b. Aug 26, 1910
Wood, Robert Dennis b. Apr 17, 1925

Brownsburg, Idaho
Campbell, Donald Guy b. Jun 27, 1922

Buhl, Idaho
Reynolds, Marjorie b. Aug 12, 1921

Coeur d'Alene, Idaho
Boyington, "Pappy" (Gregory)
b. Dec 4, 1912

Evansville, Idaho
Catlett, "Big Sid" (Sidney) b. Jan 17, 1910

Gooding, Idaho
Cary, Frank Taylor b. Dec 14, 1920

Hailey, Idaho
Pound, Ezra Loomis b. Oct 30, 1885

Harpster, Idaho
Conklin, Gladys Plemon b. May 30, 1903

Idaho Falls, Idaho
Kornman, Mary b. 1917

Jerome, Idaho
Fisher, Vardis d. Jul 9, 1968

Ketchum, Idaho
Hemingway, Ernest Miller d. Jul 2, 1961

Lava Hot Springs, Idaho
Bell, Terrel Howard b. Nov 11, 1921

Malad, Idaho
Johnson, Sonia b. Feb 27, 1936

Mill Valley, Idaho
Hemingway, Mariel b. Nov 21, 1961

Moscow, Idaho
Brink, Carol Ryrie b. Dec 28, 1895

Nampa, Idaho
Symms, Steven Douglas b. Apr 23, 1938

Payette, Idaho
Killebrew, Harmon Clayton
b. Jun 29, 1936
McClure, James A b. Dec 27, 1924

Pocatello, Idaho
Bucher, Lloyd Mark b. Sep 1, 1927
Dickson, Gloria b. Aug 13, 1916

Stanley, Idaho
Blakeley, Ronee b. 1946

Twin Falls, Idaho
Deiss, Joseph Jay b. Jan 25, 1915
Pike, Gary b.

Wallace, Idaho
Turner, "Lana" (Julia Jean Mildred
Frances) b. Feb 8, 1920

Whitney, Idaho
Benson, Ezra Taft b. Sep 3, 1899

ILLINOIS

Courtright, Jim (Timothy Isaiah) b. 1845
Dubs, Adolph b. Aug 4, 1920

Ernst, Kenneth b. 1918
Guiteau, Charles Julius b. 1844
Ode, Robert C b. Dec 10, 1915
Runkle, Janice d. Jul 26, 1981

Acton, Illinois
Main, Marjorie b. Feb 24, 1890

Aledo, Illinois
Lee, Doris Emrick b. Feb 1, 1905

Alton, Illinois
Davis, Miles Dewey b. May 25, 1926
Long, Stephen H d. Sep 4, 1864
Lovejoy, Elijah P d. Nov 7, 1837
Ray, James Earl b. Mar 10, 1928

Arcola, Illinois
Gruelle, Johnny (John Barton)
 b. Dec 24, 1880

Argo, Illinois
Kluszewski, Ted (Theodore Bernard)
 b. Sep 10, 1924

Arlington Heights, Illinois
Wille, Lois Jean b. Sep 19, 1932

Auburn, Illinois
Leonard, "Dutch" (Emil John)
 b. Mar 25, 1909
Magill, Hugh Stewart b. Dec 5, 1868
Magill, Hugh Stewart d. Oct 2, 1958

Aurora, Illinois
Fonda, Shirlee b. 1931
Mansfield, Arabella d. Aug 2, 1911
Parrington, Vernon L(ouis) b. Aug 3, 1871
White, James Laurie d. Jul 7, 1939

Barry, Illinois
Dell, Floyd b. Jun 28, 1887

Batavia, Illinois
Anderson, Ken(neth Allan)
 b. Feb 15, 1949
Issel, Dan b. Oct 25, 1948

Beardstown, Illinois
Norvo, "Red" (Kenneth) b. Mar 31, 1908

Belleville, Illinois
Dixon, Alan John b. Jul 7, 1927
Goalby, Bob b. Mar 14, 1931
Groom, Bob (Robert) b. Sep 12, 1884
Groom, Bob (Robert) d. Feb 19, 1948
Hesse, Don b. Feb 20, 1918

Belvedere, Illinois
Charboneau, Joe (Joseph) b. Jun 17, 1955

Berwyn, Illinois
Watt, Richard Martin b. Nov 10, 1930

Bloomingdale, Illinois
Lillie, Gordon William b. Feb 14, 1860

Bloomington, Illinois
Anderson, George Everett b. Aug 20, 1869
Crothers, Rachel b. Dec 12, 1878
Davis, David d. Jun 26, 1886
Davisson, Clinton Joseph b. Oct 22, 1881
Goudy, Frederic William b. Mar 8, 1865
Hubbard, Elbert Green b. Jun 19, 1856
Mowrer, Edgar Ansel b. Mar 8, 1892
Mowrer, Paul Scott b. Jul 14, 1887

Radbourn, "Old Hoss" (Charles Gardner)
 d. Feb 5, 1897
Robinson, James Harvey b. Jun 29, 1863
Rockwell, George Lincoln b. Mar 9, 1918
Smith, (Robert) Sidney b. Feb 13, 1877
Stevenson, McLean b. Nov 14, 1929
Welch, William Henry b. Apr 8, 1850

Blue Island, Illinois
McCord, Andrew King b. Feb 11, 1904

Braidwood, Illinois
Mitchell, John b. Feb 4, 1870

Brocton, Illinois
Gard, Wayne b. Jun 21, 1899

Byron, Illinois
Spalding, Albert Goodwill b. Sep 2, 1850

Cairo, Illinois
Hart, George Overbury b. May 10, 1868
Ingram, Rex b. Oct 20, 1895
Strode, Hudson b. Oct 31, 1893

Camp Point, Illinois
Nevins, Allan b. May 20, 1890

Canton, Illinois
Duryea, Charles Edgar b. Dec 15, 1862
Mertz, Barbara Louise Gross
 b. Sep 29, 1927

Carbondale, Illinois
Ayres, Agnes b. Sep 4, 1898
Moore, Harry Thornton d. Apr 11, 1981
Trumbauer, Frank(ie) b. May 30, 1901

Carlinville, Illinois
Austin, Mary Hunter b. Sep 9, 1868
Mack, Peter b. Nov 1, 1916

Carlyle, Illinois
Dean, William Frishe b. Aug 1, 1899

Carrollton, Illinois
Allen, Karen b. Oct 5, 1951

Carthage, Illinois
Smith, Joseph d. Jun 27, 1844

Cary, Illinois
Schnering, Otto d. Jan 19, 1953

Cedarville, Illinois
Addams, Jane b. Sep 6, 1860

Centralia, Illinois
Brady, James Scott b. Aug 29, 1940
Madeira, Jean b. Nov 14, 1918

Champaign, Illinois
Bailar, Benjamin Franklin b. Apr 21, 1934
Coleman, John b. Nov 15, 1935
Randall, James Garfield d. Feb 20, 1953
Tobin, James b. Mar 5, 1918
Will, George F b. May 4, 1941
Zuppke, Robert C d. Dec 22, 1957

Chandlerville, Illinois
Lucas, Scott Wike b. Feb 19, 1892

Charleston, Illinois
Lawrence, Mildred Elwood
 b. Nov 10, 1907

Chester, Illinois
Segar, Elzie Crisler b. Dec 8, 1894

Chicago, Illinois
Aalberg, John O b. Apr 3, 1897
Abbott, Grace d. Jun 19, 1939
Abramovitz, Max b. May 23, 1908
Adams, Franklin P(ierce) b. Nov 15, 1881
Addams, Jane d. May 21, 1935
Adelman, Kenneth Lee b. Jun 9, 1946
Adler, David d. Sep 27, 1949
Agar, John b. Jan 31, 1921
Ager, Milton b. Oct 6, 1893
Aguirre, Mark b. Dec 10, 1959
Albright, Ivan Le Lorraine
    b. Feb 20, 1897
Albright, Malvin Marr b. Feb 20, 1897
Alinsky, Saul David b. Jan 30, 1909
Alley, Norman William b. Jan 22, 1895
Allison, Samuel King b. Nov 13, 1900
Ammons, "Jug" (Eugene) b. Apr 14, 1925
Ammons, "Jug" (Eugene) d. Aug 6, 1974
Ammons, Albert C b. 1907
Ammons, Albert C d. Dec 2, 1949
Amsterdam, Morey b. Dec 14, 1914
Anderson, Robert Orville b. Apr 13, 1917
Anson, "Cap" (Adrian Constantine)
    d. Apr 14, 1922
Anthony, Michael b. Jun 20, 1955
Ardrey, Robert b. Oct 16, 1908
Armstrong, Charles B d. Mar 25, 1985
Armstrong, Lil(lian Hardin)
    d. Aug 27, 1971
Armstrong, Otis b. Nov 11, 1950
Arnstein, Bobbie d. Jan 1975
Arvey, Jacob Meyer b. Nov 3, 1895
Arvey, Jacob Meyer d. Aug 25, 1977
Atwater, Edith b. Apr 22, 1911
Auel, Jean Marie b. Feb 18, 1936
Avery, Sewell d. Oct 31, 1960
Axelson, Kenneth Strong b. Jul 31, 1922
Ayer, Harriet Hubbard b. Jun 27, 1849
Bacon, Frank d. Nov 19, 1922
Bain, Barbara b. Sep 13, 1932
Balaban, Barney b. Jun 8, 1887
Baldwin, Adam b. 1962
Barnes, Edward Larrabee b. Apr 22, 1915
Barnes, Margaret Ayer b. Apr 8, 1886
Barnett, Claude A d. Aug 2, 1967
Barrie, Barbara b. May 23, 1931
Barrow, Keith E b. Sep 27, 1954
Barrow, Keith E d. Oct 22, 1983
Barrows, Marjorie (Ruth) b. 1902
Bartlett, Charles Leffingwell
    b. Aug 14, 1921
Baskin, Burton b. 1913
Beals, Jennifer b. Dec 19, 1963
Beck, John b. Jan 28, 1946
Beck, Marilyn (Mohr) b. Dec 17, 1928
Behn, Noel b. Jan 6, 1928
Bellamy, Ralph b. Jun 17, 1904
Belushi, Jim (James) b. Jun 15, 1954

Belushi, John b. Jan 24, 1949
Bennett, Harve b. Aug 17, 1930
Bensley, Russ b. Jun 12, 1930
Berenger, Tom (Thomas) b. May 31, 1950
Bergen, Edgar John b. Feb 16, 1903
Berkow, Ira Harvey b. Jan 7, 1940
Berman, Shelley (Sheldon Leonard)
    b. Feb 3, 1926
Bernstein, Sid(ney Ralph) b. Jan 29, 1907
Berry, Jim b. Jan 16, 1932
Bilandic, Michael Anthony b. Feb 13, 1923
Blackburn, "Jack" (Charles Henry)
    d. Apr 24, 1942
Bledsoe, Tempestt Kenieth b. 1973
Bloch, Robert Albert b. Apr 5, 1917
Block, Joseph Leopold b. Oct 6, 1902
Bloomfield, Mike (Michael) b. Jul 28, 1944
Boettiger, John b. Mar 25, 1900
Bohrod, Aaron b. Nov 21, 1907
Bondi, Beulah b. May 3, 1892
Borglum, Gutzon d. Mar 6, 1941
Bosley, Tom b. Oct 1, 1927
Bracey, John Henry, Jr. b. Jul 17, 1941
Brach, Emil J d. Oct 29, 1947
Breger, Dave b. 1908
Bresler, Jerry b. May 29, 1912
Brickman, Morrie b. Jul 24, 1917
Briggs, Fred b. May 31, 1932
Broonzy, "Big Bill" d. Aug 14, 1958
Brosten, Harve b. May 15, 1943
Brown, Eddy b. 1895
Brown, Oscar, Jr. b. Oct 10, 1926
Browning, Alice Crolley b. Nov 5, 1907
Browning, Alice Crolley d. Oct 15, 1985
Brunis, George d. Nov 19, 1974
Burck, Jacob d. May 11, 1982
Burr, Henry d. Apr 6, 1941
Burroughs, Edgar Rice b. Sep 1, 1875
Butkus, Dick (Richard J) b. Dec 9, 1942
Butler, Michael b. Nov 26, 1926
Butler, Paul b. Jun 23, 1892
Byrne, Jane Margaret Burke
    b. May 24, 1934
Cabrini, Saint Frances Xavier
    d. Dec 22, 1917
Calmer, Ned b. Jul 16, 1907
Canby, Vincent b. Jul 27, 1924
Capone, Teresa d. Nov 29, 1952
Caputo, Philip Joseph b. Jan 10, 1941
Carmichael, John P d. Jun 6, 1986
Carpenter, John Alden d. Apr 26, 1951
Carr, Allan b. May 27, 1941
Carter, Dorothy Sharp b. Mar 22, 1921
Caspary, Vera b. Nov 13, 1904
Catlett, "Big Sid" (Sidney)
    d. Mar 25, 1951
Cavarretta, Phil(ip Joseph) b. Jul 19, 1916
Cernan, Eugene Andrew b. Mar 14, 1934
Cetera, Peter b. Sep 13, 1944
Chalmers, William James b. Jul 10, 1852
Chalmers, William James d. Dec 10, 1938

Frost, Edwin Brant d. May 14, 1935
Fuller, Henry Blake b. Jan 9, 1857
Fuller, Henry Blake d. Jul 29, 1929
Gaedel, Eddie (Edward Carl)
   b. Jun 8, 1925
Gaedel, Eddie (Edward Carl)
   d. Jun 18, 1961
Gale, Zona d. Dec 27, 1938
Ganz, Rudolph d. Aug 2, 1972
Gardner, George d. Jul 8, 1954
Garrett, Ray, Jr. b. Aug 11, 1920
Gaynor, Mitzi b. Sep 4, 1931
Geis, Bernard b. Aug 30, 1909
Gelbart, Larry b. Feb 25, 1928
Gelber, Jack b. Apr 12, 1932
Gerson, Noel Bertram b. Nov 6, 1914
Geyer, Georgie Anne b. Apr 2, 1935
Gibbs, Marla Bradley b. Jun 14, 1931
Gobel, George Leslie b. May 20, 1919
Godowsky, Leopold, II b. 1901
Goldberg, Arthur Joseph b. Aug 8, 1908
Goldberg, Bertrand b. Jul 17, 1913
Goldman, James b. Jun 30, 1927
Goldman, William b. Aug 12, 1931
Golonka, Arlene b. Jan 23, 1936
Golub, Leon Albert b. Jan 23, 1922
Goodman, Benny (Benjamin David)
   b. May 30, 1909
Goodman, Steve(n Benjamin)
   b. Jul 25, 1948
Gorey, Edward St. John b. Feb 22, 1925
Gorton, Slade b. Jan 8, 1928
Gottschalk, Robert b. Mar 12, 1918
Graham, Evarts Ambrose b. Mar 19, 1883
Graham, Virginia b. Jul 4, 1912
Gray, Dolores b. Jun 7, 1924
Grebey, Ray b. 1927
Green, Rickey b. Aug 18, 1954
Greene, Shecky b. Apr 8, 1926
Gross, Michael b. Jun 21, 1947
Groth, John August b. Feb 26, 1908
Grubert, Carl Alfred b. Sep 10, 1911
Gunther, John b. Aug 3, 1910
Hagen, Jean b. Aug 3, 1923
Halas, George Stanley b. Feb 2, 1895
Halas, George Stanley d. Oct 31, 1983
Hale, George Ellery b. Jun 29, 1868
Halper, Albert b. Aug 3, 1904
Hambro, Leonid b. Jun 26, 1920
Hancock, Herbie (Herbert Jeffrey)
   b. Apr 12, 1940
Hannah, Daryl b.
Hansberry, Lorraine b. May 19, 1930
Hanson, Kitty b.
Hapgood, Norman b. Mar 28, 1868
Harlan, John Marshall b. May 20, 1899
Harnick, Sheldon Mayer b. Apr 30, 1924
Harper, William Rainey d. Jan 10, 1906
Harridge, Will(iam) b. Oct 16, 1881
Hathaway, Donny b. Oct 1, 1945
Haworth, Mary Robbins b. Jan 31, 1931

Healy, George Peter Alexander
   d. Jun 24, 1894
Hefner, Christie (Christine Ann)
   b. Nov 8, 1952
Hefner, Hugh Marston b. Apr 9, 1926
Henderson, Rickey Henley b. Dec 25, 1958
Henner, Marilu b. Apr 6, 1953
Herblock b. Oct 13, 1909
Hersh, Seymour b. Apr 8, 1937
Hess, Sol d. Dec 31, 1941
Hinton, William Augustus b. Dec 15, 1883
Hoffman, Julius Jennings b. Jul 7, 1895
Hoffman, Julius Jennings d. Jul 1, 1983
Hoffman, Paul Gray b. Apr 26, 1891
Hogarth, Burne b. Nov 25, 1911
Holmes, Burton b. Jan 8, 1870
Hornsby, Rogers d. Jan 5, 1963
Howard, Joseph Edgar d. May 19, 1961
Howell, Albert S d. Jan 3, 1951
Howlin' Wolf d. Jan 10, 1976
Hutton, Ina Ray b. Mar 3, 1916
Hynek, J(oseph) Allen b. May 1, 1910
Irvin, Robert W d. Dec 1, 1980
Jackson, George b. Sep 23, 1941
Jacobs, Walter L b. Jun 15, 1896
Jaeger, Andrea b. Jun 4, 1965
Jagan, Janet b. Oct 20, 1920
Jahoda, Gloria b. Oct 6, 1926
Jakes, John b. Mar 31, 1932
James, Joni b. Sep 22, 1930
Jefferson, Blind Lemon d. 1930
Jensen, Mike (Michael C) b. Nov 1, 1934
Johanson, Donald Carl b. Jun 28, 1943
Johnson, "Chic" (Harold Ogden)
   b. Mar 5, 1891
Johnson, Lynn-Holly b. 1959
Jones, Jo(nathan) b. Oct 7, 1911
Jones, Quincy Delight b. Mar 14, 1933
Jones, Rickie Lee b. Nov 8, 1954
Kaplan, Henry b. Apr 24, 1918
Kath, Terry b. Jan 31, 1946
Kemper, James S(cott) d. Sep 17, 1981
Keniston, Kenneth b. Jan 6, 1930
Kennedy, Madge b. 1892
Keppard, Freddie d. Jul 15, 1933
Kerner, Otto b. Aug 15, 1908
Kerner, Otto d. May 9, 1976
Khan, Chaka b. Mar 23, 1953
Kiley, Richard b. Mar 31, 1922
Kilgallen, Dorothy b. Jul 3, 1913
Kimball, William Wallace d. 1904
Kline, Otis Adelbert b. 1891
Kohut, Heinz d. Oct 8, 1981
Korman, Harvey Herschel b. Feb 15, 1927
Kraft, James Lewis d. Feb 16, 1953
Krieghoff, Cornelius d. Mar 9, 1872
Kroc, Ray(mond) Albert b. Oct 5, 1902
Krupa, Gene b. Jan 15, 1909
Kupcinet, Irv b. Jul 31, 1912
Lahey, Edwin A(loysius) b. Jan 11, 1902
Laine, Frankie b. Mar 30, 1913

Landis, Jessie Royce b. Nov 25, 1904
Landis, John David b. Aug 3, 1950
Landis, Kenesaw Mountain
　d. Nov 25, 1944
Lansing, Sherry Lee b. Jul 31, 1944
Lardner, Ring Wilmer, Jr.
　b. Aug 19, 1915
LaRocque, Rod b. Nov 29, 1898
Lawler, Richard Harold b. Aug 12, 1895
Lawler, Richard Harold d. Jul 24, 1982
Lawson, Donald Elmer b. May 20, 1917
Lawson, Victor Fremont b. Sep 9, 1850
Layden, Elmer d. Jun 30, 1973
Leiber, Fritz b. Dec 25, 1910
Leonard, Jack E b. Apr 24, 1911
Lester, Jerry b. 1910
Levi, Edward Hirsch b. Jun 26, 1911
Levin, Meyer b. Oct 8, 1905
Lewis, Janet b. Aug 17, 1899
Lewis, Jordan David b. Aug 9, 1937
Lewis, Ramsey Emanuel, Jr.
　b. May 27, 1935
Lichty, George b. May 16, 1905
Lincoln, Abbey b. Aug 6, 1930
Lindstrom, Fred(erick Charles)
　b. Nov 21, 1905
Lindstrom, Fred(erick Charles)
　d. Oct 4, 1981
Lipman, Clara b. Dec 6, 1889
Loeb, Richard A b. 1907
Lofgren, Nils b. Jun 21, 1951
Long, Richard b. Dec 17, 1927
Loughname, Lee b. Oct 21, 1946
Lowinsky, Edward Elias d. Oct 11, 1985
Luboff, Norman b. Apr 14, 1917
Lubovitch, Lar b.
Lunt, Alfred d. Aug 2, 1977
Lurie, Alison b. Sep 3, 1926
Luzinski, Greg(ory Michael)
　b. Nov 22, 1950
Lyman, Abe b. Aug 4, 1897
Lynn, Fred(ric Michael) b. Feb 3, 1952
Lynn, Janet b. Apr 6, 1953
MacCameron, Robert L b. Jan 14, 1866
Mahoney, Jock b. Feb 7, 1919
Mainbocher b. Oct 24, 1890
Malone, Dorothy b. Jan 30, 1925
Maltby, Richard E b. Jun 26, 1914
Mamet, David b. Nov 30, 1947
Manatt, Charles Taylor b. Jun 9, 1936
Manetti, Larry b.
Manzarek, Ray b. Feb 12, 1935
Mark, Norman (Barry) b. Sep 6, 1939
Markus, Robert b. Jan 30, 1934
Marsala, Joe b. Jan 5, 1907
Marsala, Marty b. Apr 2, 1909
Marshal, Alan d. Jul 9, 1961
Marshall, William b. Oct 12, 1917
Martin, David Stone b. Jun 13, 1913
Matheson, Scott Milne b. Jan 9, 1929
Mayer, Oscar Ferdinand d. Mar 11, 1955

Mayer, Oscar Gottfried b. Mar 10, 1888
Mayer, Oscar Gottfried b. Mar 16, 1914
Mayfield, Curtis b. Jun 3, 1942
Mayo, Charles Horace d. May 26, 1939
Mazel, Judy b. 1944
McCormach, Mark Hume b. Nov 6, 1930
McCormick, Cyrus Hall d. May 13, 1884
McCormick, Cyrus Hall b. Sep 22, 1890
McCormick, Joseph Medill
　b. May 16, 1877
McCormick, Robert Rutherford
　b. Jul 30, 1880
McDivitt, Jim (James Alton)
　b. Jun 10, 1929
McGivern, William Peter b. Dec 6, 1922
McGuinn, Roger b. Jul 13, 1942
McLain, Denny (Dennis Dale)
　b. Mar 29, 1944
McNair, Barbara b. Mar 4, 1937
McNally, Andrew, III b. Aug 17, 1909
McNellis, Maggi b. Jun 1, 1917
McPartland, Jimmy (James Duigald)
　b. Mar 15, 1907
Mead, George Herbert d. Apr 26, 1931
Metcalfe, Ralph H d. Oct 10, 1978
Meyer, Ray(mond Joseph) b. Dec 18, 1913
Mezzrow, "Mezz" (Milton) b. Nov 9, 1899
Middleton, Ray b. Feb 8, 1907
Mies van der Rohe, Ludwig
　d. Aug 18, 1969
Miles, Josephine b. Jun 11, 1911
Miller, Perry Gilbert Eddy b. Feb 25, 1905
Millikan, Clark Blanchard b. Aug 23, 1903
Mills, Donna b. Dec 11, 1943
Minnelli, Vincente b. Feb 28, 1913
Mitchell, Joan b. Feb 12, 1926
Moholy-Nagy, Laszlo d. Nov 24, 1946
Monroe, Harriet b. Dec 23, 1860
Moore, Clayton b. Sep 14, 1914
Moore, Stanford b. Sep 4, 1913
Moran, Polly b. Jun 28, 1883
Morgan, Helen Riggins d. Oct 9, 1941
Motley, Willard Francis b. Jul 14, 1912
Muczynski, Robert b. Mar 19, 1929
Muhammad, Elijah d. Feb 25, 1975
Mull, Martin b. Aug 18, 1943
Murphy, Jimmy (James Edward)
　b. Nov 20, 1891
Nebel, "Long" John b. Jun 11, 1911
Nelson, "Baby Face" (George)
　b. Dec 6, 1908
Nelson, "Battling" d. Feb 7, 1954
Ness, Eliot b. Apr 19, 1903
Netsch, Walter Andrew, Jr.
　b. Feb 23, 1920
Newhart, Bob (George Robert)
　b. Sep 5, 1929
Nielsen, Arthur C b. Sep 5, 1897
Nielsen, Arthur C d. Jun 1, 1980
Norris, Frank(lin) b. Mar 5, 1870
Novak, Kim (Marilyn) b. Feb 18, 1933

O'Connor, Donald b. Aug 28, 1925
O'Day, Anita b. Dec 18, 1919
O'Horgan, Tom b. May 3, 1926
O'Neil, Roger b. Apr 17, 1945
Oboler, Arch b. Dec 6, 1909
Packard, Elizabeth Parsons Ware
  d. Jul 25, 1897
Palevsky, Max b. Jul 24, 1924
Paley, William Samuel b. Sep 28, 1901
Palmer, Potter d. May 4, 1902
Panama, Norman b. Apr 21, 1914
Pankow, James b. Aug 20, 1947
Parazaider, Walter b. Mar 14, 1945
Parker, George Safford d. Apr 19, 1937
Patinkin, Mandy b. Nov 30, 1952
Patterson, Alicia b. Oct 15, 1909
Patterson, Eleanor Medill b. Nov 7, 1884
Patterson, Joseph Medill b. Jan 6, 1879
Paxton, Tom (Thomas R) b. Oct 31, 1937
Peattie, Donald Culross b. Jun 21, 1898
Pereira, William Leonard b. Apr 25, 1909
Perls, Frederick Salomon d. Mar 14, 1970
Perry, Walt b. 1945
Petrillo, James Caesar b. Mar 16, 1892
Petrillo, James Caesar d. Oct 23, 1984
Phillips, Irna d. Dec 22, 1973
Piccard, Jeannette Ridlon b. Jan 5, 1895
Pierrot, George Francis b. Jan 11, 1898
Pinkerton, Allan d. Jul 1, 1884
Pletcher, "Stew" (Stuart) b. Feb 21, 1907
Pollard, Fritz (Frederick D)
  b. Jan 27, 1894
Poole, Ernest b. Jan 23, 1880
Price, Florence Beatrice Smith
  d. Jun 3, 1953
Pritikin, Nathan b. Aug 29, 1915
Pritzker, Abram Nicholas b. Jan 6, 1896
Pritzker, Abram Nicholas d. Feb 9, 1986
Provensen, Alice Rose Twitchell
  b. Aug 14, 1918
Provensen, Martin b. Jul 10, 1916
Pullman, George Mortimer d. Oct 19, 1897
Purdy, Ken(neth) William b. Apr 28, 1913
Rader, Doug(las L) b. Jul 30, 1944
Radford, Arthur William b. Feb 27, 1896
Randolph, Georgiana Ann b. Jun 5, 1908
Raphael, Frederic Michael b. Aug 14, 1931
Rawls, Lou(is Allen) b. Dec 1, 1936
Reed, John Shedd b. Jun 9, 1917
Reed, John Shepard b. Feb 7, 1939
Reed, Myrtle b. Sep 27, 1874
Reed, Myrtle d. Aug 17, 1911
Reed, Robert b. Oct 19, 1932
Reiffel, Leonard b. Sep 30, 1927
Reuben, David b. Jul 29, 1933
Rice, Craig b. Jun 5, 1908
Richardson, Lee b. Sep 11, 1926
Richman, Charles b. Jan 12, 1870
Rifkin, Jeremy b. 1945
Rikhoff, Jean b. May 28, 1928
Riperton, Minnie b. Nov 8, 1948

Ritchard, Cyril d. Dec 18, 1977
Robards, Jason, Jr. b. Jul 22, 1922
Robinson, John Alexander b. Jul 25, 1935
Roebuck, Alvah Curtis d. Jun 19, 1948
Roos, Frank John, Jr. b. Jan 10, 1903
Root, John Wellborn b. Jul 14, 1887
Rose, Helen Bronberg b.
Rosenwald, Julius d. Jan 6, 1932
Ross, Barney d. Jan 18, 1967
Rostenkowski, Daniel David b. Jan 2, 1928
Roszak, Theodore b. 1933
Royko, Mike b. Sep 19, 1932
Rumsfeld, Donald b. Jul 9, 1932
Rusher, William Allen b. Jul 19, 1923
Russell, Gail b. Sep 23, 1924
Ryan, Robert (Bushnell) b. Nov 11, 1913
Saint John, Howard b. Oct 9, 1905
Saint John, Robert b. Mar 9, 1902
Sajak, Pat b. 1947
Salt, Waldo b. Oct 18, 1914
Samuels, Ernest b. May 19, 1903
Sands, Tommy b. Aug 27, 1937
Saperstein, Abraham d. Mar 15, 1966
Sarett, Lew R b. May 16, 1888
Schaefer, "Germany" (Herman A)
  b. Feb 4, 1878
Schalk, Ray(mond William)
  d. May 19, 1970
Schnering, Otto b. Oct 9, 1891
Scholl, William M d. Mar 30, 1968
Schoneberg, Sheldon Clyde b. Dec 3, 1926
Schreiber, Avery b. Apr 9, 1935
Seraphine, Danny (Daniel) b. Aug 28, 1948
Seymour, Dan b. Feb 22, 1915
Shawn, William b. Aug 31, 1907
Sheekman, Arthur b. Feb 5, 1901
Sheil, Bernard James, Archbishop
  b. Feb 18, 1888
Sheldon, Sidney b. Feb 11, 1917
Shepherd, Jean Parker b. Jul 26, 1929
Sherman, Allan b. Nov 30, 1924
Shirer, William L(awrence) b. Feb 23, 1904
Shoemaker, Vaughn Richard
  b. Aug 11, 1902
Shotwell, Louisa R b. 1902
Shriver, Maria Owings b. Nov 6, 1955
Sidaris, Andy b. Feb 20, 1932
Sills, Milton b. Jan 10, 1882
Sisco, Joseph John b. Oct 31, 1919
Siskel, Eugene Karl b. Jan 26, 1946
Skinner, Cornelia Otis b. May 30, 1901
Slick, Grace Wing b. Oct 30, 1943
Smith, Clarence d. Mar 14, 1929
Smith, Patti b. Dec 31, 1946
Snodgress, Carrie b. Oct 27, 1946
Sobieski, Carol b. Mar 16, 1939
Solomon, Hannah Greenebaum
  d. Dec 7, 1942
Sosnik, Harry b. Jul 13, 1906
Soul, David b. Aug 28, 1946
Spalding, Albert b. Aug 15, 1888

Spanier, "Muggsy" (Francis Joseph)
b. Nov 9, 1906
Stahl, Ben(jamin Albert) b. Sep 7, 1910
Starrett, Vincent (Charles Vincent
Emerson) d. Jan 4, 1974
Stein, James R b. Jan 9, 1950
Stettinius, Edward R, Jr. b. Oct 22, 1900
Stevens, John Paul b. Apr 20, 1920
Stevenson, Adlai Ewing d. Jun 14, 1914
Stevenson, Adlai Ewing, III
b. Oct 10, 1930
Stevenson, Janet b. Feb 4, 1913
Stingley, Darryl b. Sep 18, 1951
Stock, Frederick A d. Oct 20, 1942
Stone, W Clement b. May 4, 1902
Sturges, Preston b. Aug 29, 1898
Sukman, Harry b. Dec 2, 1912
Sullivan, Louis Henri d. Apr 14, 1924
Sunday, Billy (William Ashley)
d. Nov 6, 1935
Svensson, Robert b. Aug 27, 1907
Swanson, Carl A d. Oct 9, 1949
Swanson, Gloria May Josephine
b. Mar 27, 1899
Sweet, Blanche b. Jun 18, 1896
Swift, Gustavus Franklin d. Mar 29, 1903
T, Mr. b. May 21, 1952
Tabbert, William b. Oct 5, 1921
Targ, William b. Mar 4, 1907
Taurog, Norman b. Feb 23, 1899
Taylor, Henry Junior b. Sep 2, 1902
Taylor, June b. 1918
Taylor, Samuel (Albert) b. Jun 13, 1912
Teichmann, Howard Miles b. Jan 22, 1916
Teschemacher, Frank d. Feb 29, 1932
Thinnes, Roy b. Apr 6, 1936
Thomas, Bill b. Oct 13, 1921
Thomas, Isiah b. Apr 30, 1961
Thomas, Theodore d. Jan 4, 1905
Thompson, James Robert b. May 8, 1936
Tietjens, Eunice b. Jul 29, 1884
Tillich, Paul Johannes d. Oct 22, 1965
Tillis, James b. 1957
Tillstrom, Burr b. Oct 13, 1917
Torme, Mel(vin Howard) b. Sep 13, 1925
Touchy, Roger b. 1898
Touchy, Roger d. Dec 17, 1959
Townsend, Willard Saxby d. Feb 3, 1957
Tozzi, Giorgio b. Jan 8, 1923
Tristano, Leonard Joseph b. Mar 19, 1919
Trout, "Dizzy" (Paul Howard)
d. Feb 28, 1972
Tureck, Rosalyn b. Dec 14, 1914
Turner, Stansfield b. Dec 1, 1923
Tuthill, Harry J b. 1886
Utley, (Clifton) Garrick b. Nov 19, 1939
Valerio, James Robert b. Dec 2, 1938
Van Dellen, Theodore Robert
b. Aug 15, 1911
Van Peebles, Melvin b. Aug 21, 1932
VanAlstyne, Egbert Anson b. Mar 5, 1882

VanAlstyne, Egbert Anson d. Jul 9, 1951
Veeck, Bill (William Louis) b. Feb 9, 1914
Veeck, Bill (William Louis) d. Jan 2, 1986
Volner, Jill Wine b. May 5, 1943
Vonnegut, Mark b. May 11, 1947
Wakefield, Dick (Richard Cummings)
b. May 6, 1921
Walgreen, Charles Rudolph
d. Dec 11, 1939
Walgreen, Charles Rudolph, Jr.
b. Mar 4, 1906
Wallace, Chris b. Oct 12, 1947
Wallace, Irving b. Mar 19, 1916
Wallenstein, Alfred Franz b. Oct 7, 1898
Wallis, Hal Brent b. Sep 14, 1899
Wanamaker, Sam b. Jun 14, 1919
Ward, Lynd b. Jun 26, 1905
Warner, Rawleigh, Jr. b. Feb 13, 1921
Washburn, Charles b. 1890
Washington, Harold b. Apr 15, 1922
Watson, James Dewey b. Apr 6, 1928
Weissmuller, Johnny b. Jun 2, 1904
Welch, Raquel b. Sep 5, 1942
Wexler, Haskell b. 1926
Whiting, George b. Aug 16, 1884
Willard, Frank Henry b. Sep 21, 1893
Williams, Billy b. Oct 12, 1972
Williams, Robin b. Jul 21, 1952
Wirtz, Arthur M b. Jan 23, 1901
Wirtz, Arthur M d. Jul 21, 1983
Woolley, Catherine (Jane Thayer)
b. Aug 11, 1904
Wrigley, Philip Knight b. Dec 5, 1894
Wrigley, William b. Jan 21, 1933
Yablonky, Ben b. Aug 26, 1911
Yancey, Jimmy (James Edward) b. 1894
Yancey, Jimmy (James Edward)
d. Sep 17, 1951
Yordan, Philip b. 1913
Young, Clara Kimball b. Sep 1890
Young, Lyman b.
Young, Robert George b. Feb 22, 1907
Young, Victor b. Aug 8, 1900
Zabach, Florian b. Aug 15, 1921
Ziegfeld, Flo(renz) b. Mar 21, 1867
Ziff, William B b. Aug 1, 1898
Zmed, Adrian b. Mar 14, 1954

Chicago Heights, Illinois
Saberhagen, Bret William b. Apr 13, 1964

Christian County, Illinois
Sheean, (James) Vincent b. Dec 5, 1899

Christopher, Illinois
Collins, Doug b. Jul 28, 1951
Rayburn, Gene b. Dec 22, 1917

Cicero, Illinois
Marcinkus, Paul C b. Jan 15, 1922

Clay City, Illinois
Doherty, Robert Ernest b. Jan 22, 1885

Danville, Illinois
Bratkowski, Zeke (Edmund R)
b. Oct 20, 1931
Morgan, Helen Riggins b. Aug 2, 1900
Short, Bobby (Robert Waltrip)
b. Sep 15, 1926
Van Dyke, Jerry b. Jul 27, 1931
Wainwright, James b. Mar 5, 1938

Decatur, Illinois
Dressen, Charlie (Charles W)
b. Sep 20, 1898
Duffy, James E b. Apr 2, 1926
Felton, Rebecca Ann Latimer
b. Jun 10, 1835

DeKalb, Illinois
Hale, Barbara b. Apr 18, 1922

Dekalb, Illinois
Wirtz, William Willard b. Mar 14, 1912

Dixon, Illinois
Bestor, Arthur Eugene b. May 19, 1879

Downers Grove, Illinois
Dewar, James A d. Jun 30, 1985
Milnes, Sherrill Eustace b. Jan 10, 1935
Waters, "Muddy" d. Apr 30, 1983

Earlville, Illinois
Crisler, "Fritz" (Herbert Orin)
b. Jan 12, 1899

East St. Louis, Illinois
Bauer, Hank (Henry Albert)
b. Jul 31, 1922
Connors, Jimmy (James Scott)
b. Sep 2, 1952

Effingham, Illinois
McNaughton, F(oye) F(isk)
d. Dec 29, 1981

El Paso, Illinois
Sheen, Fulton John, Bishop
b. May 8, 1895

Elgin, Illinois
Boxleitner, Bruce b. May 12, 1951
Oldfield, Brian b. Jun 1, 1945
Shales, Tom (Thomas William)
b. Nov 3, 1948

Elmhurst, Illinois
Debs, Eugene Victor d. Oct 20, 1926
Sandburg, Helga b. Nov 24, 1918

Elmwood, Illinois
Taft, Lorado b. Apr 29, 1860

Evanston, Illinois
Barrows, Marjorie (Ruth) d. Mar 29, 1983
Britt, Steuart Henderson d. Mar 15, 1979
Christopher, William b. Oct 20,
Cryer, David b. Mar 8, 1936
Dart, Justin Whitlock b. Aug 7, 1907
Dawes, Charles Gates d. Apr 23, 1951
Downes, Olin (Edwin Olin)
b. Jan 27, 1886
Ed, Carl Frank Ludwig d. Oct 10, 1959
Garrett, Ray, Jr. d. Feb 3, 1980
Hammond, Laurens b. Jan 11, 1895

Harnwell, Gaylord Probasco
b. Sep 29, 1903
Harridge, Will(iam) d. Apr 9, 1971
Harris, Barbara b. 1935
Hart, Jim W b. Apr 29, 1944
Heston, Charlton b. Oct 4, 1922
Holabird, William d. Jul 19, 1923
Johnson, Charles Richard b. Apr 23, 1948
Kerr, Walter Francis b. Jul 8, 1913
Long, Scott b. Feb 24, 1917
MacDougall, Curtis Daniel
d. Nov 10, 1985
Mahin, John Lee b. 1902
Marquis, Albert Nelson d. Dec 21, 1943
May, Robert Lewis d. Aug 11, 1976
McGovern, Elizabeth b. 1961
McMurtrie, Douglas C d. Sep 29, 1944
Murray, Bill b. Sep 21, 1950
Naber, John b. Jan 20, 1956
Pearson, Drew b. Dec 13, 1897
Poole, William Frederick d. Mar 1, 1894
Wilson, Gahan b. Feb 18, 1930
Zipprodt, Patricia b. Feb 25, 1925

Evansville, Illinois
Ueberroth, Peter Victor b. Sep 2, 1937

Evergreen Park, Illinois
Feulner, Edwin John, Jr. b. Aug 12, 1941
Jackson, Mahalia d. Jan 27, 1972

Fairfield, Illinois
Borah, William E b. Jun 29, 1865

Fort Sheridan, Illinois
Kunz, George b. Jul 5, 1947
Shepard, Sam b. Nov 5, 1943

Fox River Grove, Illinois
Nelson, "Baby Face" (George)
d. Nov 27, 1934

Freeport, Illinois
Parsons, Louella Oettinger b. Aug 6, 1881
Thayer, Tiffany Ellsworth b. Mar 1, 1902

Fullersburg, Illinois
Fuller, Loie b. Jan 22, 1862

Galena, Illinois
Gilbertson, Mildred Geiger b. Jun 9, 1908
McNeill, Don(ald Thomas) b. Dec 3, 1907
Rawlins, John A b. Feb 13, 1831
Schwatka, Frederik b. Sep 29, 1849

Galesburg, Illinois
Block, John Rusling b. Feb 15, 1935
Davis, Loyal b. Jan 17, 1896
Ferris, George Washington Gale
b. Feb 14, 1859
Sandburg, Carl August b. Jan 6, 1878
Sundburg, Jim (James Howard)
b. May 18, 1951

Galva, Illinois
Kirby, Rollin b. Sep 4, 1876

Genesco, Illinois
Calkins, Earnest Elmo b. Mar 25, 1868

Lincoln, Illinois
Maxwell, William b. Aug 16, 1908
Lisle, Illinois
Morton, Joy d. May 9, 1934
Livingston City, Illinois
Townsend, Francis Everett b. Jan 13, 1867
Macoupin County, Illinois
Goodnight, Charles b. Mar 5, 1836
Marion, Illinois
Turner, Roscoe Wilson b. Jun 13, 1905
Mattoon, Illinois
Chamberlin, Thomas Chrowder
    b. Sep 25, 1843
Daringer, Helen Fern b. 1892
Harris, Patricia Roberts b. May 31, 1924
Maywood, Illinois
Brewer, Jim b. Dec 3, 1951
McLeansboro, Illinois
Smith, H(arry) Allen b. Dec 19, 1907
Melrose Park, Illinois
Lawrence, Carol b. Sep 5, 1935
Melvin, Illinois
Arends, Leslie Cornelius b. Sep 27, 1895
Mendota, Illinois
Hokinson, Helen b. 1899
Milan, Illinois
Frisco, Joe b. 1890
Minooka, Illinois
Barry, Leonora Marie Kearney
    d. Jul 15, 1930
Moline, Illinois
Bendix, Vincent b. Aug 12, 1882
Berry, Ken b. Nov 3, 1933
Deere, John d. May 17, 1886
Ed, Carl Frank Ludwig b. Jul 16, 1890
Monmouth, Illinois
Earp, Wyatt Berry Stapp b. Mar 19, 1848
Eigenmann, Rosa Smith b. Oct 7, 1858
Morrison, Illinois
Adams, Frank Ramsay b. Jul 7, 1883
Millikan, Robert Andrews b. Mar 22, 1868
Morton, Illinois
Lilienthal, David Eli b. Jul 8, 1899
Murphysboro, Illinois
Logan, John Alexander b. Feb 9, 1826
Nashville, Illinois
Blackmun, Harry Andrew b. Nov 12, 1908
Nauvoo, Illinois
Young, Ann Eliza Webb b. Sep 13, 1844
New Athens, Illinois
Herzog, "Whitey" (Dorrel Norman Elvert)
    b. Nov 9, 1931
New Salem, Illinois
Rutledge, Ann b. 1816
Rutledge, Ann d. Aug 25, 1835
Normal, Illinois
Hovey, Richard b. May 4, 1864
North Chicago, Illinois
Davis, Benjamin Oliver d. Nov 26, 1970
Northville, Illinois
Hess, Sol b. Oct 14, 1872

O'Fallon, Illinois
Holden, William b. Apr 17, 1918
Oak Brook, Illinois
Butler, Paul d. Jun 24, 1981
Oak Park, Illinois
Bach, Richard David b. Jun 23, 1936
Cotsworth, Staats b. Feb 17, 1908
DeSylva, "Buddy" (George Gard)
    d. Jul 11, 1950
Enright, Elizabeth b. Sep 17, 1909
Fearing, Kenneth Flexner b. Jul 28, 1902
Giancana, Salvatore (Sam) d. Jun 19, 1974
Greeley, Andrew Moran b. Feb 5, 1928
Haydon, Julie b. Jun 10, 1910
Hemingway, Ernest Miller b. Jul 21, 1899
Hemingway, Leicester b. Apr 1915
Humphrey, Doris b. Oct 17, 1895
Ilg, Frances Lillian b. Oct 11, 1902
Kerwin, Joseph Peter b. Feb 19, 1932
Nettleton, Lois June b. Aug 16, 1931
Rogers, Carl Ransom b. Jan 8, 1902
Tough, Dave b. Apr 26, 1908
White, Betty b. Jan 17, 1917
Wright, John Lloyd b. Dec 12, 1892
Wright, Lloyd (Frank Lloyd, Jr.)
    b. Mar 31, 1890
Oglesby, Illinois
Bottomley, Jim (James Leroy)
    b. Apr 23, 1900
Orangeville, Illinois
Young, Art(hur Henry) b. Jan 14, 1866
Ottawa, Illinois
McCulley, Johnston b. Feb 2, 1883
Paris, Illinois
Gordon, Thomas b. Mar 11, 1918
Pratt, Lawrence Arthur b. Dec 20, 1907
Switzer, Carl b. Aug 8, 1926
Zeckendorf, William b. Jun 30, 1905
Park Ridge, Illinois
Black, Karen b. Jul 1, 1942
Carpenter, John Alden b. Feb 28, 1876
Hartnett, "Gabby" (Charles Leo)
    d. Dec 20, 1972
Santee, David b. Jul 22, 1957
Pekin, Illinois
Dey, Susan Hallock b. Dec 10, 1952
Dirksen, Everett McKinley b. Jan 4, 1896
Peoria, Illinois
Correll, Charles J b. Feb 2, 1890
Fogelberg, Dan(iel Grayling)
    b. Aug 13, 1951
Friedan, Betty Naomi Goldstein
    b. Feb 4, 1921
Lord, James Lawrence b. Jun 20, 1915
McGee, Fibber b. Nov 16, 1896
McGee, Molly b. Apr 15, 1897
Michel, Robert H(enry) b. Mar 2, 1923
Pryor, Richard Franklin Lennox Thomas
    b. Dec 1, 1940
Stiers, David Ogden b. Oct 31, 1942

Thompson, Marshall b. Nov 27, 1926
Whiting, Richard Armstrong
  b. Nov 12, 1891
Peru, Illinois
Confrey, "Zez" (Edward E)
  b. Apr 3, 1895
Powell, Maud b. Aug 22, 1868
Pleasant Mound, Illinois
Pahlmann, William b. Dec 12, 1906
Princeton, Illinois
Fox, Virgil Keel b. May 3, 1912
Quincy, Illinois
Astor, Mary b. May 3, 1906
Stout, William Bushnell b. Mar 16, 1880
Vollbracht, Michaele J b. Nov 17, 1947
Ramsey, Illinois
Williams, Tex b. Aug 23, 1917
Roanoke, Illinois
Gray, Glen b. Jun 7, 1906
Robin's Nest, Illinois
Chase, Philander d. Sep 20, 1852
Robinson, Illinois
Jones, James b. Nov 6, 1921
Rochester, Illinois
Persinger, Louis b. Feb 11, 1888
Rock Falls, Illinois
Shepard, Odell b. Jul 22, 1884
Rock Island, Illinois
Albert, Eddie b. Apr 22, 1908
Almond, Gabriel Abraham b. Jan 12, 1911
Hauberg, John Henry b. Jun 24, 1916
Haver, June b. Jun 10, 1926
Hunt, Frazier b. Dec 1, 1885
McGinnity, Joe (Joseph Jerome)
  b. Mar 19, 1871
Snively, William Daniel, Jr. b. Feb 9, 1911
Weyerhaeuser, Frederick Edward
  b. Jan 16, 1895
Rock River, Illinois
Keokuk b. 1780
Rockford, Illinois
Abruzzo, Ben(jamine Lou) b. Jun 9, 1930
Anderson, John Bayard b. Feb 15, 1922
Brand, Stewart b. Dec 14, 1938
Breasted, James Henry b. Aug 27, 1865
Garst, Roswell b. 1898
George, Bill (William) d. Sep 30, 1982
Johnson, Martin Elmer b. Oct 9, 1884
Kuter, Laurence S(herman)
  b. May 28, 1905
Roseville, Illinois
Hoyt, Palmer (Edwin Palmer)
  b. Mar 10, 1897
Rushville, Illinois
Scripps, Edward Wyllis b. Jun 18, 1854
Sauk Village, Illinois
Black Hawk b. 1767
Savanna, Illinois
King, Wayne b. Feb 16, 1901
Waymack, W(illiam) W(esley)
  b. Oct 18, 1888

Sharpsburg, Illinois
Neihardt, John Gneisenau b. Jan 8, 1881
Shawneetown, Illinois
Cassidy, Claudia b. 1900
Sidell, Illinois
Beers, Victor Gilbert b. May 6, 1928
Springfield, Illinois
Barrow, Ed(ward Grant) b. May 10, 1868
Christoff, Steve b. Jan 23, 1958
Christy, June b. Nov 20, 1925
East, John Porter b. May 5, 1931
Eifert, Virginia Snider b. Jan 23, 1911
Howard, Jane Temple b. May 4, 1935
Leonard, "Dutch" (Emil John)
  d. Apr 17, 1983
Lincoln, Mary Todd d. Jul 16, 1882
Lincoln, Robert Todd b. Aug 1, 1843
Lindsay, (Nicholas) Vachel
  b. Nov 10, 1879
Lindsay, (Nicholas) Vachel d. Dec 5, 1931
May, Marjorie Merriweather
  b. Mar 15, 1887
Nicholson, Seth Barnes b. Nov 12, 1891
Post, Charles William b. Oct 26, 1854
Post, Marjorie Merriweather
  b. Mar 15, 1887
Rosenwald, Julius b. Aug 12, 1862
Smart, Jack Scott d. Jan 15, 1960
Stateville, Illinois
Loeb, Richard A d. Jan 1936
Sterling, Illinois
Flory, Paul John b. Jun 19, 1910
Streator, Illinois
Jamieson, Bob (Robert John)
  b. Feb 1, 1943
Mulford, Clarence Edward b. Feb 3, 1883
Summun, Illinois
Burnette, Smiley (Lester Alvin)
  b. Mar 18, 1911
Sumner, Illinois
Montgomery, Ruth Shick b. Jun 11, 1912
Tampico, Illinois
Reagan, Ronald Wilson b. Feb 6, 1911
Tinley Park, Illinois
Bettenhausen, Tony (Melvin E)
  b. Sep 12, 1916
Tiskilwa, Illinois
Giles, Warren Crandall b. May 28, 1896
Troy Grove, Illinois
Hickok, "Wild Bill" (James Butler)
  b. May 27, 1837
Turner Junction, Illinois
Gates, John Warne b. May 8, 1855
Union City, Illinois
Derringer, Rick b. 1947
Urbana, Illinois
Caudill, Rebecca d. Oct 2, 1985
Ebert, Roger Joseph b. Jun 18, 1942
Shannon, Fred Albert d. Feb 14, 1963

Vandalia, Illinois
Hunt, H(aroldson) L(afayette)
b. Feb 17, 1889
Walnut, Illinois
Marquis, Don Robert Perry
b. Jul 29, 1878
Washburn, Illinois
Duryea, J(ames) Frank b. Oct 8, 1869
Watseka, Illinois
Bacon, Henry b. Nov 28, 1866
Waukegan, Illinois
Benny, Jack b. Feb 14, 1894
Bradbury, Ray Douglas b. Aug 22, 1920
Graham, Otto Everett b. Dec 6, 1921
Wheaton, Illinois
Gary, Elbert H b. Oct 8, 1846
Kendrick, Pearl Luella b. Aug 24, 1890
McCormick, Robert Rutherford
d. Apr 1, 1955
Reber, Grote b. Dec 22, 1911
Wilder, Brooks b. Oct 4, 1928
Will County, Illinois
Van Horne, William Cornelius, Sir
b. Feb 3, 1843
Winnetka, Illinois
Elting, Victor, Jr. b. Aug 12, 1905
Hudson, Rock b. Nov 17, 1925
Milford, Penny (Penelope) b. 1949
Porter, Fairfield b. Jun 10, 1907
Winstanley Park, Illinois
Dean, Henry Trendley b. Aug 25, 1893
Woodstock, Illinois
Gould, Chester d. May 11, 1985
Zion, Illinois
Coleman, Gary b. Feb 8, 1968
Connelly, "One-Eyed" (James Leo)
d. Dec 20, 1953
Nype, Russell b. Apr 26, 1924

INDIANA

Baniszewski, Gertrude Wright b. 1929
West, Jessamyn b. Jul 18, 1902
Albany, Indiana
McCormick, Myron b. Feb 8, 1908
Algiers, Indiana
Capehart, Homer Earl b. Jun 6, 1897
Allen County, Indiana
Appleseed, Johnny d. Mar 11, 1847
Anderson, Indiana
Erskine, Carl Daniel b. Dec 13, 1926
Harroun, Ray d. Jan 19, 1968
Mattingly, Mack Francis b. Jan 7, 1931
Ryan, T(om) K b. Jun 6, 1926
Angola, Indiana
Hershey, Lewis Blaine d. 1977
Auburn, Indiana
Cuppy, Will(iam Jacob) b. Aug 23, 1884
Aurora, Indiana
Bechtel, Stephen Davison b. Sep 24, 1900
Davis, Elmer Holmes b. Jan 13, 1890

Bedford, Indiana
Coleman, James Samuel b. May 12, 1926
Guthrie, A(lfred) B(ertram), Jr.
b. Jan 13, 1901
Jenner, William Ezra d. Mar 9, 1985
Bippus, Indiana
Schenkel, Chris(topher Eugene)
b. Aug 21, 1924
Bloomington, Indiana
Carmichael, Hoagy (Hoagland Howard)
b. Nov 22, 1899
Kinsey, Alfred Charles d. Aug 25, 1956
Lockridge, Ross Franklin, Jr.
b. Apr 25, 1914
McCracken, Branch d. Jun 4, 1970
Roth, David Lee b. Oct 10, 1955
Boonville, Indiana
Denny, Ludwell b. Nov 18, 1894
Bourbon, Indiana
Phillips, Marjorie Acker b. Oct 25, 1894
Brazil, Indiana
Hoffa, Jimmy (James Riddle)
b. Feb 14, 1913
Redenbacher, Orville b. 1907
Brook, Indiana
Arthur, Joseph Charles d. Apr 30, 1942
Brookline, Indiana
Van Camp, Gilbert C b. Dec 25, 1817
Brookville, Indiana
Ade, George d. May 16, 1944
Wallace, Lewis b. Apr 10, 1827
Byesville, Indiana
Brown, Mordecai Peter Centennial
b. Oct 19, 1876
Clark County, Indiana
Girdler, Tom Mercer b. May 19, 1877
Clearspring, Indiana
Price, Byron b. Mar 25, 1891
Columbia City, Indiana
Douglas, Lloyd Cassel b. Aug 27, 1877
Columbus, Indiana
Cooper, Kent b. Mar 22, 1880
Covington, Indiana
Savage, Eugene Francis b. Mar 29, 1883
Crawfordsville, Indiana
DeParis, Wilbur b. Sep 20, 1900
Gerard, Dave b. Jun 18, 1909
Holman, Bill b. 1903
Lambert, Eleanor b.
Thompson, Oscar b. Aug 10, 1887
Wallace, Lewis d. Feb 15, 1905
Dale, Indiana
Henderson, Florence b. Feb 14, 1934
Dana, Indiana
Pyle, Ernie (Ernest Taylor) b. Aug 3, 1900
Danville, Indiana
Thompson, Sam(uel Luther)
b. Mar 5, 1860
Deacon's Mills, Indiana
Bennett, Richard b. May 21, 1873

Decater, Indiana
Fetzer, John Earl b. Mar 25, 1901
Decatur, Indiana
Lowes, John Livingston b. Dec 20, 1867
Smith, David b. Mar 9, 1906
Teague, Walter Dorwin b. Dec 18, 1883
Demotte, Indiana
Halleck, Charles Abraham b. Aug 22, 1900
East Chicago, Indiana
Palmer, Betsy b. Nov 1, 1926
Reedy, George Edward b. Aug 5, 1917
Reynolds, Frank b. Nov 29, 1923
Elwood, Indiana
Canary, David b. 1938
Willkie, Wendell Lewis b. Feb 18, 1892
Evansville, Indiana
Cook, Joe b. 1890
Dresser, Louise b. Oct 5, 1882
Garrigue, Jean b. Dec 8, 1914
Glass, Ron b. Jul 10, 1945
Griese, Bob (Robert Allen) b. Feb 3, 1945
Johnston, Annie Fellows b. May 15, 1863
Mattingly, Don(ald Arthur)
b. Apr 20, 1961
Miller, Marilyn d. Apr 7, 1936
Nolan, Jeannette Covert b. Mar 31, 1896
Rose, Fred b. Aug 24, 1897
Fairmount, Indiana
Ward, Mary Jane b. Aug 27, 1905
Fort Wayne, Indiana
Blass, Bill b. Jun 22, 1922
Foley, "Red" (Clyde Julian)
d. Sep 19, 1968
Lombard, Carole b. Oct 6, 1909
Long, Shelley b. Aug 23, 1950
Macy, Kyle Robert b. Apr 9, 1957
Masursky, Harold b. Dec 23, 1923
Nathan, George Jean b. Feb 14, 1882
Nelson, William Rockhill b. Mar 7, 1841
Scherer, Ray(mond Lewis) b. Jun 7, 1919
Scott, Ken b. Nov 6, 1918
Shaw, Wilbur d. Oct 30, 1954
York, Dick b. Sep 4, 1928
Frankfort, Indiana
Geer, Will b. Mar 9, 1902
Sharp, Zerna A d. Jun 17, 1981
Franklin, Indiana
McNutt, Paul Vories b. Jul 18, 1891
Mueller, Reuben Herbert d. Jul 5, 1982
Pease, James b. Jan 9, 1916
French Lick, Indiana
Bird, Larry Joe b. Dec 7, 1956
Gary, Indiana
Adderley, "Cannonball" (Julian Edwin)
d. Aug 8, 1975
Benjamin, Adam, Jr. b. Aug 6, 1935
Borman, Frank b. Mar 14, 1928
Bostock, Lyman Wesley d. Sep 24, 1978
Cordtz, Dan b. May 1, 1927
Defauw, Desire d. Jul 25, 1960

Jackson, Jackie (Sigmund Esco)
b. May 4, 1951
Jackson, Janet b. May 16, 1966
Jackson, Jermaine La Jaune
b. Dec 11, 1954
Jackson, Marlon David b. Mar 12, 1957
Jackson, Michael Joseph b. Aug 29, 1958
Jackson, Randy (Steven Randall)
b. Oct 29, 1961
Jackson, Tito (Toriano Adaryll)
b. Oct 15, 1953
Karras, Alex(ander G) b. Jul 15, 1935
Kittle, Ron(ald Dale) b. Jan 5, 1958
Malden, Karl b. Mar 22, 1913
Marshall, William b. Aug 19, 1924
McCracken, James b. Dec 16, 1926
Samuelson, Paul Anthony b. May 15, 1915
Williams, Deniece b. Jun 3, 1951
Zale, Tony b. May 29, 1913
Gas City, Indiana
Francis, Thomas, Jr. b. Jul 15, 1900
Georgetown, Indiana
Minton, Sherman b. Oct 20, 1890
Goodland, Indiana
Condon, Eddie b. Nov 16, 1905
Goshen, Indiana
Hawks, Howard Winchester
b. May 30, 1896
Maclaughlin, Don d. May 28, 1986
Greencastle, Indiana
Thomas, Elmer b. Sep 8, 1876
Greenfield, Indiana
Riley, James Whitcomb b. Oct 7, 1849
Hamilton County, Indiana
Bowers, Claude Gernade b. Nov 20, 1878
Hammond, Indiana
Crawford, William Hulfish
b. Mar 18, 1913
Power, Jules b. Oct 19, 1921
Rosand, Aaron b. Mar 15, 1927
Harlam, Indiana
Reichelderfer, Francis Wylton
b. Aug 6, 1895
Henryville, Indiana
Sanders, "Colonel" (Harland David)
b. Sep 9, 1890
Hillisburg, Indiana
Sharp, Zerna A b. Aug 12, 1889
Holland, Indiana
Buse, Don b. Aug 10, 1950
Huntington, Indiana
Link, Edwin Albert b. Jul 26, 1904
Indianapolis, Indiana
Anderson, Margaret Carolyn
b. Nov 24, 1886
Anderson, Philip Warren b. Dec 13, 1923
Beard, Mary Ritter b. Aug 5, 1876
Bettenhausen, Tony (Melvin E) d. 1961
Beveridge, Albert Jeremiah
d. Apr 27, 1927
Blue, Monte b. Jan 11, 1890

Bolton, Sarah Tittle Barrett
d. Aug 4, 1893
Budenz, Louis Francis b. Jul 17, 1891
Capehart, Homer Earl d. Sep 3, 1979
Charleston, Oscar McKinley
b. Oct 12, 1896
Dauss, George August b. Sep 22, 1889
Dillinger, John Herbert b. Jun 28, 1902
Duesenberg, August S d. Jan 18, 1955
Evans, Charles, Jr. b. Jul 18, 1893
Fairbanks, Charles Warren d. Jun 4, 1918
Farmer, Frances d. Aug 1, 1970
Finch, Rick (Richard) b. Jan 25, 1954
Flanner, Janet b. Mar 13, 1892
Glossop, Peter b. Jun 6, 1928
Grauman, Sid(ney Patrick)
b. Mar 17, 1879
Graves, Michael b. Jul 9, 1934
Graydon, James Weir b. Jan 18, 1848
Harger, Rolla d. Aug 8, 1983
Harrison, Benjamin d. Mar 13, 1901
Hendricks, Thomas Andrews
d. Nov 25, 1885
Honeywell, Mark Charles d. Sep 13, 1964
Hubbard, Kin (Frank McKinney)
d. Dec 26, 1930
Hulman, Tony (Anton), Jr.
d. Oct 27, 1977
Johnson, "J J" (James Louis)
b. Jan 22, 1924
Judy, Steven b. 1957
Klein, Chuck (Charles Herbert)
b. Oct 7, 1905
Klein, Chuck (Charles Herbert)
d. Mar 28, 1958
Letterman, David b. Apr 12, 1947
Lilly, Eli b. Apr 1, 1885
Lilly, Eli d. Jan 24, 1977
Lugar, Richard Green b. Apr 4, 1932
Major, Charles b. 1856
McGinnis, George b. Aug 12, 1950
McQueen, Steve (Terence Stephen)
b. Mar 24, 1930
Montgomery, Wes b. Mar 6, 1925
Montgomery, Wes d. Jun 15, 1968
Muller, Hermann Joseph d. Apr 5, 1967
Nolan, Jeannette Covert d. Oct 12, 1974
Omlie, Phoebe Jane Fairgrave
d. Jul 17, 1975
Owings, Nathaniel Alexander
b. Feb 5, 1903
Paige, Robert (John Arthur)
b. Dec 2, 1910
Pauley, (Margaret) Jane b. Oct 31, 1950
Pauley, Edwin Wendell b. Jan 7, 1903
Quayle, (James) Dan(forth) b. Feb 4, 1947
Randall, James Garfield b. Jun 24, 1881
Reisner, George Andrew b. Nov 5, 1867
Riley, James Whitcomb d. Jul 22, 1916
Ruckelshaus, William Doyle
b. Jul 24, 1934

Shirley, George Irving b. Apr 18, 1934
Sissle, Noble b. Jul 10, 1889
Smith, Walter Bedell b. Oct 5, 1895
Stevens, Ted (Theodore Fulton)
b. Nov 18, 1923
Tarkington, Booth b. Jul 29, 1869
Tarkington, Booth d. May 16, 1946
Turner, Roscoe Wilson d. 1970
Van Arsdale, Dick (Richard Albert)
b. Feb 22, 1943
Van Arsdale, Tom (Thomas)
b. Feb 22, 1943
Van Camp, Gilbert C d. Apr 4, 1900
Von Tilzer, Albert b. Mar 29, 1878
Von Zell, Harry b. Jul 11, 1906
Vonnegut, Kurt, Jr. b. Nov 11, 1922
Wakefield, Dan b. May 21, 1932
Webb, Clifton b. Nov 19, 1891
Weber, Dick b. Dec 23, 1929

Indianola, Indiana
King, Albert b. Apr 25, 1923

Jasper, Indiana
Schroeder, William b. Feb 14, 1932

Jeffersonville, Indiana
Roland, Duane b. Dec 3, 1952

Kent, Indiana
Wiley, Harvey Washington b. Oct 18, 1844

Kentland, Indiana
Ade, George b. Feb 9, 1866

Knightstown, Indiana
Beard, Charles Austin b. Nov 27, 1874
Elliott, George Paul b. Jun 16, 1918

Kokomo, Indiana
Hillis, Margaret b. Oct 1, 1921
Martin, Strother b. Mar 26, 1919

Lafayette, Indiana
DeRegniers, Beatrice Schenk
b. Aug 16, 1914
Fazenda, Louise b. Jun 17, 1899
Friend, Bob (Robert Bartmess)
b. Nov 24, 1930
Halleck, Charles Abraham d. Mar 3, 1986
Hannagan, Steve (Stephen Jerome)
b. Apr 4, 1899
Lambert, Ward L d. Jan 20, 1958
McIlhenny, Walter S d. Jun 23, 1985
Rogers, Bruce b. May 14, 1870

LaPorte, Indiana
Scholl, William M b. Jun 22, 1882

Lawrenceburg, Indiana
Eads, James Buchanan b. May 23, 1820
Skidmore, Louis b. Apr 8, 1897

Lebanon, Indiana
Saunders, Allen b. Mar 24, 1899

Liberty, Indiana
Burnside, Ambrose Everett
b. May 23, 1824
Miller, Joaquin, pseud. b. Sep 8, 1837

Linton, Indiana
Harris, Phil b. Jun 24, 1906

Lizion, Indiana
Davis, Adelle b. Feb 25, 1904
Logansport, Indiana
Hinkle, Paul b. Dec 19, 1899
Landis, Frederick b. Jan 17, 1912
Lowell, Indiana
Worley, Jo Anne b. Sep 6, 1937
Lynn, Indiana
Jones, Reverend Jim (James)
b. May 31, 1931
Macy, Indiana
Lane, Lola b. May 21, 1906
Madison, Indiana
Philips, David Graham b. Oct 31, 1867
Marenjo, Indiana
Jenner, William Ezra b. Jul 21, 1908
Marion, Indiana
Davis, Jim (James Robert) b. Jul 28, 1945
Dean, James b. Feb 8, 1931
Jones, Phil(ip Howard) b. Apr 27, 1937
Murphy, Charles b. Apr 10, 1907
Van Devanter, Willis b. Apr 17, 1859
Martinsville, Indiana
Wooden, John Robert b. Oct 14, 1910
Mentone, Indiana
Bell, Lawrence Dale b. Apr 5, 1894
Michigan City, Indiana
Baxter, Anne b. May 7, 1923
Hatcher, Richard Gordon b. Jul 10, 1933
Judy, Steven d. Mar 9, 1981
Larsen, Don(ald James) b. Aug 7, 1929
Millville, Indiana
Wright, Wilbur b. Apr 16, 1867
Mishawaka, Indiana
Brademas, John b. Mar 2, 1927
McKenney, Ruth b. Nov 18, 1911
Mitchell, Indiana
Bass, Sam b. Jul 21, 1851
Grissom, Virgil Ivan b. Apr 3, 1926
Monrovia, Indiana
McCracken, Branch b. Jun 9, 1908
Montezuma, Indiana
Allport, Gordon William b. Nov 11, 1897
Montgomery County, Indiana
Goodpasture, Ernest William
b. Oct 17, 1886
Mooresville, Indiana
Rusie, Amos William b. May 31, 1871
Morocco, Indiana
Rice, "Sam" (Edgar Charles)
b. Feb 20, 1892
Mount Vernon, Indiana
Monroe, Marion b. Feb 4, 1898
Muncie, Indiana
Ball, Edmund B d. Mar 8, 1925
Ball, Frank d. Mar 19, 1943
Cohen, Benjamin Victor b. Sep 23, 1894
Haines, Robert Terrel b. Feb 3, 1870
Kimbrough, Emily b. Oct 23, 1899

Munster, Indiana
Lema, Tony (Anthony David)
d. Jul 24, 1966
Nappanee, Indiana
Neher, Fred b. Sep 29, 1903
New Albany, Indiana
Herman, Billy (William Jennings)
b. Jul 7, 1909
Lynd, Robert Staughton b. Sep 26, 1892
Minton, Sherman d. Apr 9, 1965
Zoeller, "Fuzzy" (Frank Urban)
b. Nov 11, 1951
New Castle, Indiana
Indiana, Robert b. Sep 13, 1928
Newcastle, Indiana
Crane, Richard O b. Jun 6, 1918
Noble County, Indiana
Butz, Earl Lauer b. Jul 3, 1909
Noblesville, Indiana
Norell, Norman b. Apr 20, 1900
Roudebush, Richard Lowell
b. Jan 18, 1918
Stout, Rex Todhunter b. Dec 1, 1886
North Manchester, Indiana
Marshall, Thomas Riley b. Mar 14, 1854
Oakland City, Indiana
Roush, Edd J (Eddie) b. May 8, 1893
Peru, Indiana
Olsen, Ole b. Nov 6, 1892
Porter, Cole b. Jun 9, 1892
Schram, Emil b. Nov 23, 1893
Plainfield, Indiana
Tucker, Forrest Meredith b. Feb 2, 1919
Plymouth, Indiana
Walburn, Raymond b. Sep 9, 1887
Portland, Indiana
Ames, Leon b. Jan 20, 1903
Tharp, Twyla b. Jul 1, 1941
Princeton, Indiana
Hodges, Gil(bert Raymond) b. Apr 4, 1924
Ray, Indiana
McNaughton, F(oye) F(isk)
b. May 15, 1890
Rensselaer, Indiana
Harmon, Tom (Thomas D)
b. Sep 28, 1919
Richmond, Indiana
Ackerman, Carl William b. Jan 16, 1890
Burchenal, Elizabeth b. 1876
Ewbank, "Weeb" (Wilbur) b. May 6, 1907
Foster, Norman b. Dec 13, 1903
Purcell, Sarah b. Oct 8, 1948
Rorem, Ned b. Oct 23, 1923
Rochester, Indiana
Bowen, Otis Ray b. Feb 26, 1918
Rockville, Indiana
Britton, Edgar Clay b. Sep 25, 1891
Rosedale, Indiana
Cox, Herald Rea b. Feb 28, 1907

Saint Meinrad, Indiana
Schnellenberger, Howard Leslie
  b. Mar 13, 1934
Salem, Indiana
Hay, John Milton b. Oct 8, 1838
Sandcut, Indiana
Trout, "Dizzy" (Paul Howard)
  b. Jun 29, 1915
Saulsbury, Indiana
Hughes, Irene Finger b.
Seymour, Indiana
Mellencamp, John "Cougar"
  b. Oct 7, 1951
Shelbyville, Indiana
Major, Charles d. Feb 13, 1913
Shaw, Wilbur b. Oct 31, 1902
South Bend, Indiana
Bromfield, John b. Jun 11, 1922
Butterworth, Charles b. Jul 26, 1897
Coveleski, Stanley Anthony
  d. Mar 20, 1984
Everett, Chad b. Jun 11, 1937
Haynes, Lloyd (Samuel Lloyd)
  b. Oct 19, 1935
Keogan, George d. Feb 17, 1943
Messick, Dale b. 1906
Patrick, Van d. Sep 29, 1974
Pollack, Sydney b. Jul 1, 1934
Rexroth, Kenneth b. Dec 22, 1905
Rickey, George Warren b. Jun 6, 1907
Seaton, George b. Apr 17, 1911
Stein, Jules Caesar b. Apr 26, 1896
Studebaker, Clement d. Nov 27, 1901
Warren, Michael b. Mar 5, 1946
South Raub, Indiana
McCutcheon, John Tinney b. May 6, 1870
Spencer, Indiana
Moody, William Vaughn b. Jul 8, 1869
Spencer County, Indiana
Hanks, Nancy d. 1818
Stendal, Indiana
Hartke, Vance b. May 31, 1919
Steuben City, Indiana
Hershey, Lewis Blaine b. Sep 12, 1893
Sullivan, Indiana
Hays, Will Harrison b. Nov 5, 1879
Hays, Will Harrison d. Mar 7, 1954
Tabriz, Indiana
Gregorian, Vartan b. Apr 7, 1935
Terre Haute, Indiana
Bayh, Birch Evans, Jr. b. Jan 22, 1928
Brown, Mordecai Peter Centennial
  d. Feb 14, 1948
Carey, Max George b. Jan 11, 1890
Cox, John Rogers b. Mar 24, 1915
Crothers, "Scatman" (Benjamin Sherman)
  b. May 23, 1910
Debs, Eugene Victor b. Nov 5, 1855
Dreiser, Theodore b. Aug 27, 1871
Dreyfus, Hubert L b. Oct 15, 1929
Farmer, Philip Jose b. Jan 26, 1918

Gallagher, Richard b. Jul 28, 1891
Hulman, Tony (Anton), Jr.
  b. Feb 11, 1901
John, Tommy (Thomas Edward, Jr.)
  b. May 22, 1943
Thomas, Kurt b. Mar 29, 1956
Thornhill, Claude b. Aug 10, 1908
Treaty, Indiana
Howe, Edgar Watson b. May 3, 1853
Union City, Indiana
Noffsinger, James P(hilip) b. May 30, 1925
Valparaiso, Indiana
Arvin, Newton b. Aug 23, 1900
Veray, Indiana
Eggleston, Edward b. Dec 10, 1837
Vevey, Indiana
Maynard, Ken b. Jul 21, 1895
Vincennes, Indiana
Gimbel, Bernard Feustman
  b. Apr 10, 1885
Jones, Buck b. Dec 4, 1891
Skelton, "Red" (Richard) b. Jul 18, 1913
Wabash, Indiana
Honeywell, Mark Charles b. Dec 29, 1874
Wabash County, Indiana
Porter, Gene Stratton b. Aug 17, 1868
Walkerton, Indiana
Urey, Harold Clayton b. May 29, 1893
Wawaka, Indiana
Frick, Ford Christopher b. Dec 19, 1894
West Lafayette, Indiana
Jones, Anissa b. 1958
Whitley County, Indiana
Adams, Andy b. May 3, 1859
Whitney, Indiana
Frickie, Janie b. Dec 18, 1950
Williamsburg, Indiana
Chase, William Merritt b. Nov 1, 1849
Winchester, Indiana
Wise, Robert b. Sep 10, 1914
Yorktown, Indiana
Barker, Cliff b. Jan 15, 1921

IOWA

Holdren, Judd Clifton b. Oct 16, 1915
Adair, Iowa
Anderson, Eugenie Moore b. May 26, 1909
Adair County, Iowa
Wallace, Henry Agard b. Oct 7, 1888
Albia, Iowa
Clark, Charles Badger b. Jan 1, 1883
Algona, Iowa
Cowles, Gardner b. Jan 31, 1903
Cowles, John, Sr. b. Dec 14, 1898
Alton, Iowa
Schuller, Robert Harold b. Sep 16, 1926

Ames, Iowa
Kirby, Robert Emory b. Nov 8, 1918
Schickele, Peter b. Jul 17, 1935
Sunday, Billy (William Ashley)
   b. Nov 18, 1862
Anamosa, Iowa
Wood, Grant b. Feb 13, 1892
Avoco, Iowa
Beymer, Richard (George Richard)
   b. Feb 21, 1939
Blockton, Iowa
Hickenlooper, Bourke B b. Jul 21, 1896
Bloomfield, Iowa
Sheaffer, Walter A b. Jan 27, 1867
Boone, Iowa
Eisenhower, Mamie Geneva Doud
   b. Nov 14, 1896
Bryant, Iowa
Schrum, Marion Margaret b. Feb 1, 1924
Burlington, Iowa
Carothers, Wallace Hume b. Apr 27, 1896
Duke, Wayne b. Nov 9, 1928
Frawley, William b. Feb 26, 1893
Kent, Jack (John Wellington)
   b. Mar 10, 1920
Mansfield, Arabella b. May 23, 1846
Marshall, Robert J b. Aug 26, 1918
Noyce, Robert Norton b. Dec 12, 1927
Burnside, Iowa
Mollenhoff, Clark Raymond
   b. Apr 16, 1921
Carroll, Iowa
Garst, Roswell d. Nov 5, 1977
Cascade, Iowa
Faber, "Red" (Urban Charles)
   b. Sep 6, 1888
Cedar Falls, Iowa
Aldrich, Bess Streeter b. Feb 17, 1881
Cassill, R(onald) V(erlin) b. May 17, 1919
Jepsen, Roger William b. Dec 23, 1928
Cedar Rapids, Iowa
Boddicker, Mike (Michael James)
   b. Aug 23, 1957
Conrad, Paul Francis b. Jun 27, 1924
DeFore, Don b. Aug 25, 1917
Driscoll, Bobby b. Mar 3, 1936
Engle, Paul b. Oct 12, 1908
Fitch, Bill (William C) b. May 19, 1934
Hershfield, Harry b. Oct 13, 1885
Ruml, Beardsley b. Nov 5, 1894
Shedd, Charlie W b. Aug 8, 1915
Threlkeld, Richard D b. Nov 30, 1937
Van Vechten, Carl b. Jun 17, 1880
Centreville, Iowa
Estes, Simon Lamont b. Feb 2, 1938
Charles City, Iowa
Coover, Robert b. Feb 4, 1932
Clarinda, Iowa
Maxwell, Marilyn b. Aug 3, 1921
Miller, Glenn b. Mar 1, 1904

CLarinoa, Iowa
Shambaugh, Jessie Field d. Jan 15, 1971
Clear Lake, Iowa
Big Bopper, The d. Feb 3, 1959
Holly, "Buddy" (Charles Hardin)
   d. Feb 3, 1959
Valens, Richie d. Feb 3, 1959
Clinton, Iowa
Childs, Marquis William b. Mar 17, 1903
Russell, Lillian b. Dec 4, 1861
Colfax, Iowa
Hall, James Norman b. Apr 22, 1887
Columbus Junction, Iowa
Wilcox, Francis (Orlando) b. Apr 9, 1908
Corning, Iowa
Carson, Johnny b. Oct 23, 1925
Council Bluffs, Iowa
Beer, Thomas b. Nov 22, 1889
Bloomer, Amelia Jenks d. Dec 30, 1894
Brown, Samuel W, Jr. b. Jul 27, 1943
Chandler, Don b. Sep 9, 1934
DeForest, Lee b. Aug 26, 1873
Dodge, Grenville Mellen d. Jan 3, 1916
Langdon, Harry b. Jun 15, 1884
McCain, John Sidney, Jr. b. Jan 17, 1911
Pusey, Nathan Marsh b. Apr 4, 1907
Cresco, Iowa
Borlaug, Norman Ernest b. Mar 25, 1914
Chamberlain, Samuel b. Oct 28, 1895
Izac, Edouard Victor M b. Dec 18, 1891
Creston, Iowa
Cunningham, R Walter b. Mar 16, 1932
Cumming, Iowa
Harkin, Thomas R b. Nov 19, 1939
Dakota City, Iowa
Reasoner, Harry b. Apr 17, 1923
Davenport, Iowa
Beiderbecke, "Bix" (Leon Bismark)
   b. Mar 10, 1903
Craig, Roger Timothy b. Jul 10, 1960
Ficke, Arthur Davidson b. Nov 10, 1883
Glaspell, Susan Keating b. Jul 1, 1882
Layden, Elmer b. May 4, 1903
Margolin, Stuart b. Jan 31, 1940
Pendleton, Nat b. Aug 9, 1899
Willard, John Wesley b. Jun 23, 1907
Delaware County, Iowa
Merriam, Frank Finley b. Dec 22, 1865
Denison, Iowa
Garrison, Jim C b. Nov 20, 1921
Reed, Donna b. Jan 27, 1921
Des Moines, Iowa
Ball, George Wildman b. Dec 21, 1909
Bartkowski, Steve(n Joseph)
   b. Nov 12, 1952
Burton, Michael b. Jul 3, 1947
Collins, Stephen b. Oct 1, 1947
Darling, Jay Norwood d. Feb 12, 1962
Farrell, Carolyn b. 1936
Halston b. Apr 23, 1932
Jensen, Virginia Allen b. Sep 21, 1927

Kellems, Vivien b. Jun 7, 1896
Leachman, Cloris b. Apr 30, 1925
Marciano, Rocky d. Aug 31, 1969
McCree, Wade Hampton, Jr.
    b. Jul 3, 1920
Nelson, Harriet b. Jul 18, 1912
Omlie, Phoebe Jane Fairgrave
    b. Nov 21, 1902
Ray, Robert D b. Sep 26, 1928
Rense, Paige b. 1934
Schick, Jacob b. Sep 16, 1877
Thompson, Sada Carolyn b. Sep 27, 1929
Waymack, W(illiam) W(esley)
    d. Nov 5, 1960
Doon, Iowa
Manfred, Frederick Feikema b. Jan 6, 1912
Dubuque, Iowa
Bissell, Richard b. Jun 27, 1913
Bissell, Richard d. May 4, 1977
Keenan, Frank b. Apr 8, 1858
Lindsay, Margaret b. Sep 19, 1910
Rabe, David William b. Mar 10, 1940
Emmetsburg, Iowa
Bliven, Bruce b. Jul 27, 1889
Gould, Beatrice Blackmar b. 1898
Everly, Iowa
Paul, Lester Warner b. Dec 17, 1899
Fort Dodge, Iowa
Arkoff, Samuel Z b. Jun 12, 1918
Heggen, Thomas Orls, Jr. b. Dec 23, 1919
Fort Madison, Iowa
Boley, Forrest Irving b. Nov 27, 1925
O'Keefe, Dennis b. Mar 28, 1910
Greenfield, Iowa
Sidey, Hugh Swanson b. Sep 3, 1927
Hampton, Iowa
Leahy, William Daniel b. May 6, 1875
Hawarden, Iowa
Emerson, Hope b. Oct 29, 1898
Suckow, Ruth b. Aug 6, 1892
Hawthorne, Iowa
Cessna, Clyde Vernon b. Dec 5, 1879
Humboldt, Iowa
Baker, Laura Nelson b. Jan 7, 1911
Independence, Iowa
Yarnell, Harry E b. Oct 18, 1875
Indianola, Iowa
Lane, Priscilla b. Jun 12, 1917
Lane, Rosemary b. Apr 4, 1914
Iowa City, Iowa
Baker, Gladys Elizabeth b. Jul 22, 1908
Fischer, Irwin b. Jul 5, 1903
Guthrie, Janet b. Mar 7, 1938
Johnson, Nicholas b. Sep 23, 1934
Wood, Grant d. Feb 12, 1942
Jefferson, Iowa
Gallup, George Horace b. Nov 18, 1901
Keokuk, Iowa
Black Hawk d. Oct 3, 1838
Maxwell, Elsa b. May 24, 1883
Nagel, Conrad b. Mar 16, 1897

Keokuk County, Iowa
Mott, Frank Luther b. Apr 4, 1886
Keosauqua, Iowa
Strong, Philip Duffield b. 1899
Lake Mills, Iowa
Stegner, Wallace Earle b. Feb 18, 1909
Lakota, Iowa
Griese, Arnold b. Apr 13, 1921
LaPorrete City, Iowa
Allison, Fran(ces) b. Nov 20, 1924
Le Mars, Iowa
Harnack, Curtis Arthur b. Jun 27, 1927
Starzl, Thomas b. Mar 11, 1926
Luana, Iowa
Gould, Charles Bruce b. Jul 28, 1898
Lucas, Iowa
Lewis, John Llewellyn b. Feb 12, 1880
Macksburg, Iowa
Martin, Glenn Luther b. Jan 17, 1886
Mapleton, Iowa
Wood, Gar(field A) b. Dec 4, 1880
Marengo, Iowa
Whitehill, Clarence Eugene b. Nov 5, 1871
Marquette, Iowa
Goltz, Gene b. Apr 30, 1930
Marshalltown, Iowa
Anson, "Cap" (Adrian Constantine)
    b. Apr 17, 1851
Hurt, Mary Beth Supinger b. Sep 26,
Seberg, Jean b. Nov 13, 1938
Mason City, Iowa
Ar Buthnot, May Hill b. Aug 27, 1884
Willson, Meredith b. May 18, 1902
Maurice, Iowa
Keough, Donald Raymond b. Sep 4, 1926
McGregor, Iowa
Ringling, Charles b. Dec 2, 1863
Meridian, Iowa
Law, Vernon Sanders b. Mar 12, 1930
Montour, Iowa
Miller, Merle b. May 17, 1919
Mount Pleasant, Iowa
Van Allen, James Alfred b. Sep 7, 1914
Nashua, Iowa
Taylor, Kent b. May 11, 1907
Neola, Iowa
Felton, Harold W b. Apr 1, 1902
Lafferty, Raphael Aloysius b. Nov 7, 1914
Nevada, Iowa
Patterson, Neva b. Feb 10, 1922
New Hartford, Iowa
Grassley, Charles Ernest b. Sep 17, 1933
Newton, Iowa
Maytag, Elmer Henry b. Sep 18, 1883
Murray, Charles Alan b. Jan 8, 1943
Sattler, Helen Roney b. Mar 2, 1921
Orient, Iowa
Vance, Clarence Arthur b. Mar 4, 1891
Oskaloosa, Iowa
Bell, Steve (Stephen Scott) b. Dec 9, 1935
Conklin, Chester b. Jan 11, 1888

Ottumma, Iowa
Cone, Russell Glenn b. Mar 22, 1896
Ottumwa, Iowa
Loeser, Katinka b. Jul 2, 1913
Williams, Roy Lee b. Mar 22, 1915
Paris, Iowa
Clark, Richard Clarence b. Sep 14, 1929
Parkersburg, Iowa
Fenton, Carroll Lane b. Feb 12, 1900
Pella, Iowa
Earp, Morgan b. Apr 24, 1851
Perry, Iowa
Hamlin, Vincent T b. 1900
Pleasantville, Iowa
McKay, Scott b. May 28, 1915
Primghar, Iowa
Welch, Joseph Nye b. Oct 22, 1890
Randalia, Iowa
Oakes, Randi b. 1952
Red Oak, Iowa
Hunt, Jack Reed b. May 17, 1918
Logan, John b. Jan 23, 1923
Rock Valley, Iowa
Bell, Herbert A b. 1890
Scout County, Iowa
Cody, "Buffalo Bill" (William Frederick)
b. Feb 26, 1846
Shenandoah, Iowa
Shambaugh, Jessie Field b. Jun 26, 1881
Sioux City, Iowa
Bancroft, Dave (David James)
b. Apr 20, 1892
Carey, MacDonald (Edward Macdonald)
b. Mar 15, 1914
Herbst, Josephine Frey b. Mar 5, 1897
Hopkins, Harry Lloyd b. Aug 17, 1890
Landers, Ann b. Jul 4, 1918
Mathers, Jerry b. Jun 2, 1948
Means, Marianne Hansen b. Jun 13, 1934
Melcher, John b. Sep 6, 1924
Moore, Constance b. Jan 18, 1922
Van Buren, Abigail b. Jul 4, 1918
Storm Lake, Iowa
Dailey, Janet b. May 21, 1944
Stuart, Iowa
Peers, William Raymond b. Jun 14, 1914
Thompson, Iowa
Klemesrud, Judy Lee b. 1939
Traer, Iowa
Wilson, Margaret b. Jan 16, 1882
Van Meter, Iowa
Feller, Bob (Robert William Andrew)
b. Nov 3, 1918
Wall Lake, Iowa
Williams, Andy b. Dec 3, 1930
Waterloo, Iowa
Adams, Julie b. Oct 17, 1926
Becker, Carl Lotus b. Sep 7, 1873
Budd, Ralph b. Aug 20, 1879
Funston, George Keith b. Oct 12, 1910
Hoover, Lou Henry b. Mar 29, 1875

Webster City, Iowa
Eberle, Mary Abastenia St. Leger
b. Apr 6, 1878
Kantor, Mackinlay b. Feb 4, 1904
West Branch, Iowa
Hoover, Herbert Clark b. Aug 10, 1874
Wilton Junction, Iowa
Giesler, Jerry (Harold Lee) b. 1890
Winterset, Iowa
Clarke, Fred Clifford b. Oct 3, 1872
Smith, Courtney Craig b. Dec 20, 1916
Wayne, John b. May 26, 1907

KANSAS

Bickerdyke, Mary Ann Ball
d. Nov 8, 1901
Rockne, Knute Kenneth d. Mar 31, 1931
Willard, Jess b. Dec 29, 1881
Abilene, Kansas
Eisenhower, Milton Stover b. Sep 15, 1899
Engle, Joe Henry b. Aug 26, 1932
Alamena, Kansas
Sebelius, Keith George b. Sep 10, 1916
Alton, Kansas
Stover, Russell b. May 6, 1888
Atchison, Kansas
Earhart, Amelia Mary b. Jul 24, 1898
Howe, Edgar Watson d. Oct 3, 1937
Atlanta, Kansas
Cunningham, Glenn Clarence
b. Aug 4, 1909
Baldwin, Kansas
Liston, Emil d. Oct 26, 1949
Baxter Springs, Kansas
Harman, Jeanne Perkins b. Jul 27, 1919
Bucyrus, Kansas
Price, Garrett b. 1896
Burlingame, Kansas
Sutherland, Earl Wilbur, Jr.
b. Nov 19, 1915
Burton, Kansas
Stone, Milburn b. Jul 5, 1904
Bushton, Kansas
Huebner, Clarence R b. Nov 24, 1888
Caldwell, Kansas
Emerson, Gladys Anderson b. Jul 1, 1903
Centralia, Kansas
Riggins, John b. Aug 4, 1949
Chanute, Kansas
Johnson, Osa Helen Leighty
b. Mar 14, 1894
Chapman, Kansas
Poor, Henry Varnum b. Sep 30, 1888
Cherryvale, Kansas
Brooks, Louise b. Nov 14, 1906
Vance, Vivian b. Jul 26, 1912
Claflin, Kansas
Hickel, Walter Joseph b. Aug 18, 1919
Coffee City, Kansas
Windsor, Claire b. Apr 14, 1897

Coffeyville, Kansas
Dalton, Gratton d. Oct 5, 1892
Dalton, Robert d. Oct 5, 1892
Colby, Kansas
Ramey, Samuel Edward b. Mar 28, 1942
Columbus, Kansas
Terris, Norma b. 1904
Council Grove, Kansas
Rhodes, John Jacob b. Sep 18, 1916
Decatur County, Kansas
Harger, Rolla b. Jan 14, 1890
Dodge City, Kansas
Hopper, Dennis b. May 17, 1936
King, James Ambros b. May 22, 1925
Dunavant, Kansas
Curry, John Steuart b. Nov 14, 1897
El Dorado, Kansas
Brodie, Steve b. Nov 25, 1919
Fulton, Maude b. May 14, 1881
Walker, Mort b. Sep 3, 1923
Elk Falls, Kansas
Crandall, Prudence d. 1889
Elwood, Kansas
Moran, George b. 1882
Emporia, Kansas
Smith, Dean Edwards b. Feb 28, 1931
White, William Allen b. Feb 10, 1868
White, William Allen d. Jan 29, 1944
White, William Lindsay b. Jun 17, 1900
White, William Lindsay d. Jul 26, 1973
Fairview, Kansas
Rogers, Bernard William b. Jul 16, 1921
Falun, Kansas
Johnson, U(ral) Alexis b. Oct 17, 1908
Fintana, Kansas
Hibbs, Ben b. Jul 23, 1901
Fort Riley, Kansas
Beard, Dita Davis b. Nov 27, 1918
Fort Scott, Kansas
Canaday, John (Edwin John)
b. Feb 1, 1907
Clifford, Clark McAdams b. Dec 25, 1906
Johnson, Hugh S b. Aug 5, 1882
McCollum, Elmer Verner b. Mar 3, 1879
Parks, Gordon Alexander Buchanan
b. Oct 30, 1912
Franklin County, Kansas
Keokuk d. Jun 1848
Fredonia, Kansas
Lamb, Lawrence Edward b. Oct 13, 1926
Garden City, Kansas
Zorn, Jim (John Eldon) b. Sep 24, 1947
Garnett, Kansas
Capper, Arthur b. Jul 14, 1865
Masters, Edgar Lee b. Aug 23, 1869
Girard, Kansas
Haldeman-Julius, Emanuel d. Jul 31, 1951
Goessel, Kansas
Knight, Shirley b. Jul 5, 1937

Greenville, Kansas
Henson, Jim (James Maury)
b. Sep 24, 1936
Grenola, Kansas
Friganza, Trixie b. Nov 29, 1870
Halstead, Kansas
Rupp, Adolph F b. Sep 2, 1901
Harper, Kansas
Wedman, Scott Dean b. Jul 29, 1952
Hillsboro, Kansas
Klassen, Elmer Theodore b. Nov 6, 1908
Humboldt, Kansas
Johnson, Walter Perry b. Nov 6, 1887
Hutchinson, Kansas
Stafford, William Edgar b. Jan 17, 1914
Independence, Kansas
Inge, William b. May 3, 1913
Junction City, Kansas
Horner, Bob (James Robert)
b. Aug 6, 1957
Kitchell, Iva b. Mar 31, 1908
Pennell, Joseph Stanley b. Jul 4, 1908
Kansas City, Kansas
Allen, Lucius Oliver, Jr. b. Sep 26, 1947
Carr, Harold Noflet b. Mar 14, 1921
Downs, William Randall, Jr.
b. Aug 17, 1914
Lietzke, Bruce b. Jul 18, 1951
Parker, Charlie (Charles Christopher)
b. Aug 29, 1920
Thackrey, Russell I b. Dec 6, 1904
Treas, Terri b. Jul 19, 1959
Vaughan, Bill (William Edward)
d. Feb 26, 1977
Waggoner, Lyle b. Apr 13, 1935
Kirwin, Kansas
Hatch, Carl A b. Nov 27, 1889
La Cygne, Kansas
Clapper, Raymond Lewis b. Apr 30, 1892
Lawrence, Kansas
Adams, Alvan Leigh b. Jul 29, 1954
Allen, Forest Clare d. Sep 16, 1974
Beaumont, Hugh b. Feb 16, 1909
Fisher, Dorothy Frances Canfield
b. Feb 17, 1879
Houk, Ralph George b. Aug 9, 1919
Naismith, James A d. Nov 28, 1939
Taylor, Lucy Hobbs d. Oct 3, 1910
Wright, Henry b. Jul 2, 1878
Leavenworth, Kansas
Eddy, Sherwood b. Jan 11, 1871
Harvey, Frederick Henry d. Feb 9, 1901
Kelly, "Machine Gun" (George R)
d. Jul 18, 1954
Moran, "Bugs" (George C)
d. Feb 25, 1957
Nation, Carry A(melia Moore)
d. Jun 9, 1911
Pemberton, Brock b. Dec 14, 1885
Leawood, Kansas
Hall, Joyce Clyde d. Oct 29, 1982

Manhattan, Kansas
Runyon, Damon (Alfred Damon)
b. Oct 4, 1884
Marysville, Kansas
McClure, Michael b. Oct 20, 1932
Medicine Lodge, Kansas
Beals, Carleton b. Nov 13, 1893
Muscotah, Kansas
Roberts, Roy Allison b. Nov 25, 1887
Tinker, Joe (Joseph Bert) b. Jul 27, 1880
Newton, Kansas
Barker, Herman d. Sep 19, 1927
Unruh, Jesse Marvin b. Sep 30, 1922
Norcatur, Kansas
Fitzgerald, Pegeen b. Nov 24, 1910
Norton, Kansas
Sebelius, Keith George d. Sep 5, 1982
Oakley, Kansas
Haggerty, Sandra Clark b. Jul 26, 1939
Olathe, Kansas
Parks, Larry b. Dec 3, 1914
Rogers, "Buddy" (Charles)
b. Aug 13, 1904
Osage City, Kansas
Batchelor, Clarence Daniel b. Apr 1, 1888
Ottawa, Kansas
Hart, Gary Warren b. Nov 28, 1936
Paola, Kansas
Dickey, Lynn (Clifford Lynn)
b. Oct 19, 1949
Parsons, Kansas
Clayton, Buck b. Nov 12, 1911
Pitts, Zasu (Eliza Susan) b. Jan 3, 1900
Ryan, T(ubal) Claude b. Jan 3, 1898
Piqua, Kansas
Keaton, "Buster" (Joseph Francis)
b. Oct 4, 1896
Pittsburg, Kansas
Myers, Russell b. Oct 9, 1938
Rago, Kansas
Cessna, Clyde Vernon d. Nov 20, 1954
Rosedale, Kansas
McSpaden, Byron b. May 21, 1908
Russell, Kansas
Dole, Bob (Robert Joseph) b. Jul 22, 1923
Specter, Arlen b. Feb 12, 1930
Saint Francis, Kansas
Evans, Ronald Ellwin b. Nov 10, 1933
Salina, Kansas
Braniff, Thomas Elmer b. Dec 6, 1883
Craven, Thomas b. Jan 6, 1889
Mauch, Gene William b. Nov 18, 1925
Scranton, Kansas
Wakeman, Frederic b. Dec 26, 1909
Sedan, Kansas
Kelly, Emmett b. Dec 9, 1898
Sedgewick, Kansas
Stauffer, Charles Albert b. Mar 23, 1880
Severy, Kansas
Campbell, Walter Stanley b. Aug 15, 1887

Smith Center, Kansas
Arbuckle, "Fatty" (Roscoe Conkling)
b. Mar 24, 1887
Cromwell, Nolan b. Jan 30, 1955
Sterling, Kansas
Fleeson, Doris b. May 20, 1901
Stockdale, Kansas
Paddleford, Clementine Haskin
b. Sep 27, 1900
Sublette, Kansas
Christiansen, Jack b. Dec 20, 1928
Topeka, Kansas
Bolinger, Dwight Lemerton
b. Aug 18, 1907
Brooks, Gwendolyn b. Jun 7, 1917
Capper, Arthur d. Dec 19, 1951
Curtis, Charles b. Jan 25, 1860
Douglas, Aaron b. 1899
Kassebaum, Nancy Landon b. Jul 29, 1932
Kilmer, Billy (William O) b. Sep 5, 1939
Menninger, Karl Augustus b. Jul 23, 1893
Menninger, William C b. Oct 15, 1899
Menninger, William C d. Sep 6, 1966
Thompson, Bradbury James
b. Mar 25, 1911
Wilson, Lyle Campbell b. Aug 2, 1899
Wamego, Kansas
Chrysler, Walter Percy b. Apr 2, 1875
Wichita, Kansas
Alley, Kirstie b. Jan 12, 1955
Ballard, Robert Duane b. Jun 30, 1942
Beech, Walter Herschel d. Nov 29, 1950
Browder, Earl Russell b. May 20, 1891
Chapin, Dwight Lee b. Dec 2, 1940
Kenton, Stan(ley Newcomb)
b. Feb 19, 1912
Lehrer, Jim (James Charles)
b. May 19, 1934
McDaniel, Hattie b. Jun 10, 1895
Mears, Rick Ravon b. Dec 3, 1951
Rudd, Hughes Day b. Sep 14, 1921
Ryun, Jim (James Ronald)
b. Apr 29, 1947
Sayers, Gale Eugene b. May 30, 1940
Swayze, John Cameron, Sr. b. Apr 4, 1906
Woodard, Lynette b. 1959
Winfield, Kansas
Clarke, Fred Clifford d. Aug 14, 1960
McCarty, Mary b. 1923
Pallette, Eugene b. Jul 8, 1889

KENTUCKY

Everleigh, Ada b. 1876
Everleigh, Minna b. 1878
Moore, Bert C b. Mar 3, 1935
Skaggs, Ricky b. 1954
Ashland, Kentucky
McCoy, Clyde b. Dec 29, 1903
Reeves, George b. Apr 6, 1914

Augusta, Kentucky
Walker, Stuart Armstrong b. Mar 4, 1880
Bagdad, Kentucky
Collins, Martha Layne Hall b. Dec 7, 1936
Bardstown, Kentucky
Fitch, John d. Jul 12, 1798
Beargrass, Kentucky
Johnson, Richard Mentor b. Oct 17, 1781
Bluelick, Kentucky
Foley, "Red" (Clyde Julian)
   b. Jun 17, 1910
Bourbon County, Kentucky
Corwin, Thomas b. 1794
Bowling Green, Kentucky
Hines, Duncan b. Mar 26, 1880
Hines, Duncan d. Mar 15, 1959
Milburn, Frank Pierce b. Dec 12, 1868
Boyle County, Kentucky
Harlan, John Marshall b. Jun 1, 1833
Brooksville, Kentucky
Galloway, Don b. Jul 27, 1937
Brownie, Kentucky
Everly, Don b. Feb 1, 1937
Everly, Phil b. Jan 19, 1939
Bryant Station, Kentucky
Rogers, James Gamble b. Mar 3, 1867
Burgin, Kentucky
McDonald, Marie b. 1923
Burton Fork, Kentucky
Kazee, Buell H(ilton) b. Aug 29, 1900
Butcher Hollow, Kentucky
Lynn, Loretta Webb b. Apr 14, 1935
Campbellsville, Kentucky
Young, Margaret Ann Buckner
   b. Mar 20, 1922
Catawba, Kentucky
Regan, Theodore M, Jr. b. Jul 5, 1897
Cayce, Kentucky
Jones, "Casey" (John Luther)
   b. Mar 14, 1864
Christian County, Kentucky
Davis, Jefferson b. Jun 3, 1808
Stevenson, Adlai Ewing b. Oct 23, 1835
Clay City, Kentucky
Jackson, "Aunt" Molly b. 1880
Corbin, Kentucky
Lake, Arthur b. Apr 17, 1905
Corydon, Kentucky
Chandler, "Happy" (Albert Benjamin)
   b. Jul 14, 1898
Covington, Kentucky
Burman, Ben Lucien b. Dec 12, 1895
Camnitz, Howie (Samuel Howard)
   b. Aug 22, 1881
Duveneck, Frank b. Oct 9, 1848
Kirby, Durward b. Aug 24, 1912
Merkel, Una b. Dec 10, 1903
Peabody, Eddie d. Nov 7, 1970
Young, James Webb b. Jan 20, 1886
Ziegler, Ron(ald Louis) b. May 12, 1939

Cynthiana, Kentucky
Hall, Joe Beasman b. Nov 30, 1928
Danville, Kentucky
Duncan, Todd b. Feb 12, 1903
McCormick, Robert K b. Aug 11, 1911
McDowell, Ephraim d. Jun 25, 1830
Depoy, Kentucky
Oates, Warren b. Jul 5, 1928
Dixon, Kentucky
Rice, Cale Young b. Dec 7, 1872
Dry Ridge, Kentucky
Davis, Skeeter b. Dec 30, 1931
Eddyville, Kentucky
Fulks, Joe (Joseph E) d. Mar 21, 1976
Ekron, Kentucky
Reese, "Pee Wee" (Harold Henry)
   b. Jul 23, 1919
Elton, Kentucky
Rudolph, Paul Marvin b. Oct 23, 1918
Florence, Kentucky
Cauthen, Steve b. May 1, 1960
Fort Knox, Kentucky
Barker, Len (Leonard Harold, II)
   b. Jul 7, 1955
Frankfort, Kentucky
Crittenden, John Jordan d. Jul 26, 1863
Fall, Albert Bacon b. Nov 26, 1861
Johnson, Richard Mentor d. Nov 19, 1850
Polk, Willis Jefferson b. 1867
Franklin County, Kentucky
Blair, Montgomery b. May 10, 1813
Frogtown, Kentucky
Atchison, David R b. Aug 11, 1807
Fulton, Kentucky
Rascoe, Burton b. Oct 22, 1892
Garfield, Kentucky
Cramer, Polly b. Oct 14, 1903
Garrard County, Kentucky
Nation, Carry A(melia Moore)
   b. Nov 25, 1846
Glasgow, Kentucky
Goodman, Julian B b. May 1, 1922
Krock, Arthur b. Nov 16, 1886
Sawyer, Diane K b. Dec 22, 1945
Vaughn, Billy b. Apr 12, 1919
Glensboro, Kentucky
Townsend, William H(enry)
   b. May 31, 1890
Graves County, Kentucky
Barkley, Alben William b. Nov 24, 1877
Grayson County, Kentucky
Dargan, Olive Tilford b. 1869
Guthrie, Kentucky
Warren, Robert Penn b. Apr 24, 1905
Hardin County, Kentucky
Lincoln, Abraham b. Feb 12, 1809
Hardingburg, Kentucky
Beard, Ralph b. Dec 1, 1927
Harlan, Kentucky
Cheshire, Maxine b. Apr 5, 1930

Hart County, Kentucky
Buckner, Simon B b. Apr 1, 1823
Hartford, Kentucky
Bland, Richard Parks b. Aug 19, 1835
Curran, Charles Courtney b. Feb 13, 1861
Earp, Virgil W b. Jul 18, 1843
Hazard, Kentucky
Moore, William H b. May 8, 1916
Hazel, Kentucky
DeShannon, Jackie b. Aug 21, 1944
Henderson, Kentucky
Kimmel, Husband Edward b. Feb 26, 1882
Robinson, Francis Arthur b. Apr 28, 1910
Henderson County, Kentucky
Jones, "Grandpa" (Louis Marshall)
b. Oct 20, 1913
Henry County, Kentucky
Berry, Wendell b. Aug 5, 1934
Hopkinsville, Kentucky
Cayce, Edgar b. Mar 18, 1877
Jenkins, Kentucky
Bach, Bert Coates b. Dec 14, 1936
Kenton County, Kentucky
Carlisle, John Griffin b. Sep 5, 1835
La Grange, Kentucky
Griffith, D(avid Lewelyn) W(ark)
b. Jan 22, 1875
Lancaster County, Kentucky
Sims, James Marion b. Jan 25, 1813
Latonia, Kentucky
Allen, Robert Sharon b. Jul 14, 1900
Lawrenceburg, Kentucky
Clark, "Champ" (James Beauchamp)
b. Mar 7, 1850
Lebanon, Kentucky
Simms, Phil(ip) b. Nov 3, 1955
Lexington, Kentucky
Allen, James Lane b. Dec 21, 1849
Blair, Francis Preston b. Feb 10, 1821
Blanding, Sarah Gibson b. Nov 22, 1898
Breckinridge, John d. Dec 14, 1806
Breckinridge, John Cabell b. Jan 21, 1821
Breckinridge, John Cabell d. May 17, 1875
Breckinridge, Sophonisba Preston
b. Apr 1, 1866
Brown, John Young, Jr. b. 1933
Brown, William Wells b. 1815
Carter, Caroline Louise Dudley
b. Jun 10, 1862
Carter, Mrs. Leslie b. Jun 10, 1862
Cavanagh, Jerry (Jerome Patrick)
d. Nov 27, 1979
Compton, Joyce b. Jan 27, 1907
Cowley, Joe (Joesph Alan)
b. Aug 15, 1958
Hardwick, Elizabeth b. Jul 27, 1916
Jones, Benjamin Allyn d. Jun 13, 1961
Lincoln, Mary Todd b. Dec 13, 1818
McCann, Les b. Sep 23, 1935
Morgan, Thomas H b. Sep 25, 1866
Niles, John Jacob d. Mar 1, 1980

Rupp, Adolph F d. Dec 10, 1977
Schultze, Carl Edward b. May 25, 1866
Townsend, William H(enry)
d. Jul 25, 1964
Lincoln County, Kentucky
Sublette, William L b. 1799
Lincoln Ridge, Kentucky
Young, Whitney Moore, Jr.
b. Jul 31, 1921
Louisa, Kentucky
Vinson, Frederick Moore b. Jan 22, 1890
Louisville, Kentucky
Ali, Muhammad b. Jan 17, 1942
Anderson, Robert b. Jun 14, 1805
Beatty, Ned b. Jul 6, 1937
Bibb, Leon b. 1935
Bohannon, Judy (Judith Layton) b. Jun 30,
Bond, Sudie b. Jul 13, 1928
Brandeis, Louis Dembitz b. Nov 13, 1856
Brown, John Mason b. Jul 3, 1900
Browning, Tod b. Jul 12, 1882
Bubbles, John b. Feb 19, 1902
Buttrick, George Arthur d. Jan 23, 1980
Camnitz, Howie (Samuel Howard)
d. Mar 2, 1960
Cawein, Madison Julius b. Mar 23, 1865
Cawein, Madison Julius d. Dec 7, 1914
Clark, George Rogers d. Feb 13, 1818
Conrad, William b. Sep 27, 1920
Dunne, Irene Marie b. Dec 20, 1904
Flexner, Abraham b. Nov 13, 1866
Fox, Fontaine Talbot, Jr. b. Mar 3, 1884
Gilbert, Billy b. Sep 12, 1894
Goldman, Edwin Franko b. Jan 1, 1878
Griffith, Darrell Steven b. Jun 16, 1958
Halleck, Henry d. Jan 9, 1872
Hampton, Lionel b. Apr 20, 1914
Hopkins, Telma Louise b. Oct 28, 1948
Hornung, Paul Vernon b. Dec 23, 1935
Hull, Henry b. Oct 3, 1890
Humes, Helen b. Jun 23, 1913
Jones, Jonah b. Dec 31, 1909
Kelly, William d. Feb 11, 1888
Lewis, Meade Anderson Lux
b. Sep 5, 1905
Marcosson, Isaac Frederick
b. Sep 13, 1876
Martin, John b. Jun 2, 1893
Mature, Victor b. Jan 29, 1916
Meagher, Mary T b. Oct 27, 1964
Morton, Rogers Clark Ballard
b. Sep 19, 1914
Morton, Thruston Ballard b. Aug 19, 1907
Morton, Thruston Ballard d. Aug 14, 1982
Nichols, Bobby (Robert) b. Apr 14, 1936
Niles, John Jacob b. Apr 28, 1892
Norman, Marsha Williams b. Sep 21, 1947
Page, Greg b. 1958
Parks, Floyd Lavinius b. Feb 9, 1896
Patrick, John b. May 17, 1905
Pendleton, Clarence b. Nov 10, 1930

Quantrill, William Clarke d. Jun 6, 1865
Ragland, "Rags" (John Lee Morgan
    Beauregard) b. Aug 23, 1906
Reynolds, Richard S. d. Jul 29, 1955
Rice, Alice Caldwell Hegan
    d. Feb 10, 1942
Rice, Cale Young d. Jan 23, 1943
Robins, Elizabeth b. 1865
Sample, Paul Starrett b. Sep 14, 1896
Schroeder, William d. Aug 6, 1986
Stromberg, Hunt b. Jul 12, 1894
Sullivan, Danny b. 1950
Sutton, Carol d. Feb 19, 1985
Thompson, Hunter S(tockton)
    b. Jul 18, 1939
Towne, Charles Hanson b. Feb 2, 1877
Travers, Mary b. Nov 7, 1937
Underwood, Oscar Wilder b. May 6, 1862
Unseld, Wes(ley) b. Mar 14, 1946
Washington, "Buck" (Ford Lee)
    b. Oct 16, 1903
Wells, Linton b. Apr 1, 1893

Lynch, Kentucky
Kreps, Juanita Morris b. Jan 11, 1921

Madison County, Kentucky
Carson, "Kit" (Christopher)
    b. Dec 24, 1809
Clay, Cassius Marcellus b. Oct 19, 1810
Clay, Cassius Marcellus d. Jul 22, 1903

Magoffin County, Kentucky
Flynt, Larry Claxton b. Nov 1, 1942

Marshall County, Kentucky
Fulks, Joe (Joseph E) b. Oct 26, 1921

Mason County, Kentucky
Bean, Roy b. 1825

Mayfield, Kentucky
Holifield, Chet b. Dec 3, 1903

Maysville, Kentucky
Brown, Kelly (Elford Cornelious Kelly
    Kingman) b. Sep 24, 1928
Clooney, Rosemary b. May 23, 1928
Markey, Lucille (Parker) Wright
    b. Dec 14, 1896
Reed, Stanley Forman b. Dec 31, 1884

Meade County, Kentucky
Wrather, William Embry b. Jan 20, 1883

Mount Kisco, Kentucky
Davis, Rebecca Blaine Harding
    d. Sep 29, 1910

Munfordville, Kentucky
Buckner, Simon, Jr. b. Jul 18, 1886

Murray, Kentucky
Brooks, Cleanth b. Oct 16, 1906
Graham, Gene b. Aug 26, 1924

Newport, Kentucky
Bolton, Sarah Tittle Barrett
    b. Dec 18, 1814
Cowens, Dave (David William)
    b. Oct 25, 1948

Lurton, Horace Harmon b. Feb 26, 1844
Thompson, John Taliaferro
    b. Dec 31, 1860

Nicholasville, Kentucky
Phillips, Lena Madesin b. Sep 15, 1881

Olive Hill, Kentucky
Hall, Tom T b. May 25, 1936

Owensboro, Kentucky
Ewell, Tom b. Apr 29, 1909
Ford, Wendell Hampton b. Sep 8, 1924
Hagan, Cliff(ord Oldham) b. Dec 9, 1931
Waltrip, Darrell (Lee) b. Feb 5, 1947

Owingsville, Kentucky
Hood, John Bell b. Jun 1, 1831
Visscher, William Lightfoot
    b. Nov 25, 1842

Packard, Kentucky
Neal, Patricia b. Jan 20, 1926

Paducah, Kentucky
Cobb, Irvin Shrewsbury b. Jun 23, 1876
Matlock, "Matty" (Julian Clifton)
    b. Apr 27, 1909
McKinney, Bill (William) b. 1894
Randolph, "Boots" (Homer Louis, III) b.
Scopes, John Thomas b. Aug 3, 1900

Paintsville, Kentucky
Gayle, Crystal b. Jan 9, 1951

Pascagoula, Kentucky
Taylor, Margaret Smith d. Aug 18, 1852

Pebworth, Kentucky
Combs, Earle Bryan b. May 14, 1899

Perryville, Kentucky
Roberts, Elizabeth Madox b. 1886

Pewee Valley, Kentucky
Johnston, Annie Fellows d. Oct 5, 1931

Poor Fork, Kentucky
Caudill, Rebecca b. Feb 2, 1899

Prestonsburg, Kentucky
Allen, Jack b. Jun 18, 1914

Providence, Kentucky
Benjamin, Curtis G b. Jul 13, 1901

Rosewood, Kentucky
Travis, Merle b. Nov 29, 1917

Russellville, Kentucky
Crittendon, Thomas L b. May 15, 1819

Scott County, Kentucky
Thomas, Charles Allen b. Feb 15, 1900

Sharpsburg, Kentucky
Allen, Henry Tureman b. Apr 13, 1859

Shelbyville, Kentucky
Rice, Alice Caldwell Hegan
    b. Jan 11, 1870
Sanders, "Colonel" (Harland David)
    d. Dec 16, 1980

Somerset, Kentucky
Cooper, John Sherman b. Aug 23, 1901

Southgate, Kentucky
Bunning, Jim (James Paul David)
    b. Oct 23, 1931

Stoney Pointe, Kentucky
Fox, John W, Jr. b. Dec 16, 1863

Marksville, Louisiana
Edwards, Edwin Washington
  b. Aug 7, 1927
Stuart, Ruth McEnery b. May 21, 1849
McCall, Louisiana
Foster, "Pops" (George Murphy)
  b. May 19, 1892
Metaire, Louisiana
Gennaro, Peter b. 1924
Monroe, Louisiana
Delaney, Joe Alton d. Jun 29, 1983
McGee, Frank b. Sep 12, 1921
Russell, Bill (William Felton)
  b. Feb 12, 1934
Montegut, Louisiana
Ellender, Allen Joseph b. Sep 24, 1890
Mooringsport, Louisiana
Ledbetter, Huddie b. 1885
Natchitoches, Louisiana
Croce, Jim d. Sep 20, 1973
Johnson, Marques Kevin b. Feb 8, 1956
New Iberia, Louisiana
Johnson, "Bunk" (William Geary)
  d. Jul 7, 1949
New Orleans, Louisiana
Allen, "Red" (Henry James, Jr.)
  b. Jan 7, 1908
Armstrong, Anne Legendre
  b. Dec 27, 1927
Armstrong, Louis Daniel b. Jul 4, 1900
Ball, Edward d. Jun 24, 1981
Bares, Basile b. 1845
Bares, Basile d. 1902
Basso, Hamilton Joseph b. Sep 5, 1904
Beauregard, Pierre Gustav Toutant de
  d. Feb 20, 1893
Bechet, Sidney b. May 14, 1897
Bigard, Albany Barney Leon
  b. Mar 3, 1906
Bilbo, Theodore Gilmore d. Aug 21, 1947
Bolden, "Buddy" (Charles) b. 1868
Bolden, "Buddy" (Charles) d. Nov 4, 1931
Boswell, Connee b. Dec 3, 1912
Boswell, Martha b. 1905
Boswell, Vet (Helvetia) b. 1911
Bradford, Roark d. Nov 13, 1948
Brunis, George b. Feb 6, 1902
Burke, Paul b. Jul 21, 1926
Byrd, Henry d. Jan 30, 1980
Cable, George Washington b. Oct 12, 1844
Campbell, William Edward March
  d. May 15, 1954
Capote, Truman b. Sep 30, 1924
Carlisle, Kitty b. Sep 3, 1915
Carter, Hodding (William Hodding, III)
  b. Apr 7, 1935
Catledge, Turner d. Apr 27, 1983
Clairborne, William Charles
  d. Nov 23, 1817
Collins, Joseph L b. May 1, 1896
Collins, Lee b. Oct 17, 1901

Cushman, Pauline b. Jun 10, 1833
Davis, Jefferson d. Dec 6, 1889
Dinwiddie, John Ekin d. Sep 11, 1959
Dix, Dorothy, pseud. d. Dec 16, 1951
Dodds, "Baby" (Warren) b. Dec 24, 1898
Dodds, Johnny b. Apr 12, 1892
Domino, "Fats" (Antoine) b. Feb 26, 1928
Douvillier, Suzanne Theodore Vaillande
  d. Aug 30, 1826
Edeson, Robert b. 1868
Elliott, Robert B d. Aug 9, 1884
Fiske, Minnie Maddern b. Dec 19, 1865
Fountain, Pete(r Dewey) b. Jul 3, 1930
Gottschalk, Louis Moreau b. May 8, 1829
Grau, Shirley Ann b. Jul 8, 1929
Gumbel, Bryant Charles b. Sep 29, 1948
Healy, Mary b. Apr 14, 1918
Hebert, F(elix) Edward b. Oct 12, 1901
Hebert, F(elix) Edward d. Dec 29, 1979
Hellman, Lillian b. Jun 20, 1905
Herriman, George b. Aug 22, 1880
Higgins, Andrew J d. Aug 1, 1952
Hirt, Al b. Nov 7, 1922
Hood, John Bell d. Aug 30, 1879
Hunter, Jeffrey b. Nov 23, 1926
Jackson, Mahalia b. Oct 26, 1911
Johnson, "Bunk" (William Geary)
  b. Dec 27, 1879
Johnson, "Dink" (Oliver) b. Oct 28, 1892
Johnston, Frances Benjamin
  d. May 16, 1952
Joy, Leatrice b. Nov 7, 1893
Kane, Harnett T(homas) b. Nov 8, 1910
Kane, Harnett T(homas) d. Sep 4, 1984
Keppard, Freddie b. Feb 15, 1899
Keyes, Frances Parkinson d. Jul 3, 1970
Kiam, Victor Kermit, II b. Dec 7, 1926
King, Grace Elizabeth b. 1852
King, Grace Elizabeth d. Jan 12, 1932
Lamour, Dorothy b. Dec 10, 1914
Landrieu, "Moon" (Maurice Edwin)
  b. Jul 23, 1930
Larroquette, John b. Nov 25, 1947
Latrobe, Benjamin Henry d. Sep 3, 1820
Lea, Fanny Heaslip b. Oct 30, 1884
Leonard, Elmore John, Jr. b. Oct 11, 1925
Leslie, Miriam Florence Folline b. 1836
Manone, "Wingy" (Joseph)
  b. Feb 13, 1904
Mansfield, Jayne d. Jun 29, 1967
Marsalis, Wynton b. Oct 18, 1961
Menken, Adah Isaacs b. Jun 15, 1835
Monroe, Bill (William Blanc, Jr.)
  b. Jul 17, 1920
Morial, Ernest Nathan b. Oct 9, 1929
Morphy, Paul Charles b. Jun 22, 1837
Morphy, Paul Charles d. Jul 10, 1884
Nelson, Ed(win Stafford) b. Dec 21, 1928
Newton, Huey P b. Feb 17, 1942
Neyland, Robert Reese d. Mar 28, 1962
Niblo, Fred d. Nov 11, 1948

Bath, Maine
Jackson, John Adams b. Nov 5, 1825
Zorach, William d. Nov 15, 1967
Biddeford, Maine
Baker, Carlos Heard b. May 5, 1909
Bowie, Norman Ernest b. Jun 6, 1942
Blue Hill, Maine
Brace, Gerald Warner d. Jul 20, 1978
Chase, Mary Ellen b. Feb 24, 1887
Brunswick, Maine
Coffin, Robert Peter Tristram
b. Mar 18, 1892
Rockwell, "Doc" (George L)
d. Mar 3, 1978
Calais, Maine
Copeland, Charles Townsend
b. Apr 27, 1860
Camden, Maine
Fishback, Margaret d. Sep 25, 1985
Hilsberg, Alexander d. Aug 10, 1961
Cape Elizabeth, Maine
Ford, John b. Feb 1, 1895
Corinna, Maine
Patten, Gilbert b. Oct 25, 1866
Cornish, Maine
Clifford, Nathan d. Jul 25, 1881
Cranberry Isles, Maine
Liebow, Averill A(braham)
d. May 31, 1978
Damariscotta, Maine
Winslow, Ola Elizabeth d. Sep 27, 1977
Dexter, Maine
Brewster, Owen b. Feb 22, 1888
East Machias, Maine
Bates, Arlo b. Dec 16, 1850
East Oreland, Maine
Clark, Walter van Tilburg b. Aug 3, 1909
Ellsworth, Maine
Hartley, Marsden d. Sep 2, 1943
Lord, Phillips H d. Oct 19, 1975
Whitney, John Hay b. Aug 17, 1904
Falmouth, Maine
Cunningham, Mary Elizabeth
b. Sep 1, 1951
Farmington, Maine
Greenwood, Chester b. Dec 4, 1858
Greenwood, Chester d. Jul 5, 1937
Nordica, Lillian b. May 12, 1859
Gardiner, Maine
Richards, Laura Elizabeth Howe
d. Jan 14, 1943
Wilson, Dorothy Clarke b. May 9, 1904
Gorham, Maine
Guptill, Arthur Leighton b. Mar 19, 1891
Huntington, Henry S, Jr. b. 1882
White, Ellen Gould Harmon
b. Nov 26, 1827
Great Falls, Maine
Hall, Edwin Herbert b. Nov 7, 1855
Greenwood, Maine
Bean, L(eon) L(eonwood) b. 1872

Hampden, Maine
Dix, Dorothea Lynde b. Apr 4, 1802
Hampton Beach, Maine
Farnum, Dustin Lancy b. 1870
Hancock, Maine
Monteux, Pierre d. Jul 1, 1964
Harborside, Maine
Nearing, Scott d. Aug 24, 1983
Hatton, Maine
George, Gladys b. Sep 13, 1904
Haven, Maine
Powell, John Wesley d. Sep 23, 1902
Head Tide, Maine
Robinson, Edwin Arlington
b. Dec 22, 1869
Hog Island, Maine
Todd, Mabel Loomis d. Oct 14, 1932
Howland, Maine
Spencer, Percy Le Baron b. Jul 9, 1894
Kennebunk, Maine
Little, Charles Coffin b. Jul 25, 1799
Roberts, Kenneth b. Dec 8, 1885
Wood, Sarah Sayward Barrell Keating
d. Jan 6, 1855
Kennebunkport, Maine
Roberts, Kenneth d. Jul 21, 1957
Kittery, Maine
Whipple, William b. Jan 14, 1730
Kittery Point, Maine
White, Helen Magill d. Oct 28, 1944
Leeds, Maine
Howard, Oliver Otis b. Nov 8, 1830
Lewiston, Maine
Hartley, Marsden b. Jan 4, 1877
Longley, James Bernard b. Apr 22, 1924
Longley, James Bernard d. Aug 16, 1980
Livermore Falls, Maine
Bogan, Louise b. Aug 11, 1897
Lovell, Maine
Johnson, Eastman b. Jul 29, 1824
Manchester, Maine
Smith, Samantha b. Jun 29, 1972
Mercer, Maine
Munsey, Frank Andrew b. Aug 21, 1854
Newcastle, Maine
Fitch, Aubrey d. May 22, 1976
Nobleboro, Maine
Coatsworth, Elizabeth Jane
d. Aug 31, 1986
Norridgewock, Maine
Clarke, Rebecca Sophia b. Feb 22, 1833
Clarke, Rebecca Sophia d. Aug 10, 1906
North Brooklin, Maine
White, E(lwyn) B(rooks) d. Oct 1, 1985
Orland, Maine
Ginn, Edwin b. Feb 14, 1838
Orrington, Maine
Pierce, Edward Allen b. Aug 31, 1874
Oxford County, Maine
Kimball, William Wallace b. Mar 22, 1828

Paris, Maine
Deering, William b. Apr 25, 1826
Paris Hill, Maine
Hamlin, Hannibal b. Aug 27, 1809
Porter, Maine
Porter, Bernard H b. Feb 14, 1911
Portland, Maine
Ames, Louise Bates b. Oct 29, 1908
Babb, Howard Selden b. May 14, 1924
Bartholomew, Reginald b. Feb 17, 1936
Baxter, James Phinney, III
b. Feb 15, 1893
Bentley, Alvin Morell b. Aug 30, 1918
Casey, Edward Pearce b. Jun 18, 1864
Curtis, Cyrus Hermann Kotszchmar
b. Jun 18, 1850
Davis, Owen b. Jan 29, 1874
Fessenden, William Pitt d. Sep 8, 1869
Ford, Phil b. 1902
Gallant, Roy Arthur b. Apr 17, 1924
Gerber, John b. 1907
Gurney, Edward John b. Jan 12, 1914
King, Stephen Edwin b. Sep 21, 1947
Lavin, Linda b. Oct 15, 1939
Longfellow, Henry Wadsworth
b. Feb 27, 1807
Mulford, Clarence Edward
d. May 10, 1956
Parton, Sara Payson Willis b. Jul 9, 1811
Sharmat, Marjorie Weinman
b. Nov 12, 1928
Thaxter, Phyllis b. Nov 20, 1920
Willis, Nathaniel Parker b. Jan 20, 1806
Wilson, Hazel Hutchins b. Apr 8, 1898
Prouts Neck, Maine
Homer, Winslow d. Sep 29, 1910
Rockland, Maine
Elliott, Gertrude b. 1874
Elliott, Maxine b. Feb 5, 1873
Millay, Edna St. Vincent b. Feb 22, 1892
Piston, Walter b. Jan 20, 1894
Rockport, Maine
Luboshutz, Pierre d. Apr 18, 1971
Rumford, Maine
Muskie, Edmund Sixtus b. Mar 28, 1914
Saco, Maine
Brannan, Samuel b. Mar 2, 1819
Sangerville, Maine
Maxim, Hiram Stevens, Sir b. Feb 5, 1840
Scarboro, Maine
King, Rufus b. Mar 24, 1755
Searreport, Maine
Peirce, Waldo d. Mar 8, 1970
Shirley, Maine
Nye, Edgar Wilson (Bill) b. Aug 25, 1850
Skowhegan, Maine
Dolbier, Maurice b. May 5, 1912
Smith, Margaret Chase b. Dec 14, 1897
Somerset County, Maine
Coffin, Charles Albert b. Dec 1844

South Berwick, Maine
Jewett, Sarah Orne b. Sep 3, 1849
Jewett, Sarah Orne d. Jun 24, 1909
South Casco, Maine
Gulick, Luther Halsey d. Aug 13, 1918
South Paris, Maine
Shaw, Reta b. Sep 13, 1912
South Windham, Maine
Donnell, Jeff (Jean Marie) b. Jul 10, 1921
Strong, Maine
Allen, Elizabeth Ann Chase Akers
b. Oct 9, 1832
Thomaston, Maine
Knox, Henry d. Oct 25, 1806
Vienna, Maine
Bradley, Milton b. Nov 8, 1836
Waterford, Maine
Ward, Artemus, pseud. b. Apr 26, 1834
Waterville, Maine
Cody, Lew b. Feb 22, 1887
Lovejoy, Clarence Earle b. Jun 26, 1894
Mitchell, George John b. Aug 20, 1933
Webster, Maine
Simmons, Franklin b. Jan 11, 1839
West Gardiner, Maine
Stevens, John Frank b. Apr 25, 1853
West Pembroke, Maine
Best, Charles Herbert b. Feb 27, 1899
Bridges, Styles b. Sep 9, 1898
West Southport, Maine
Tenggren, Gustaf Adolf d. Apr 6, 1970
Westbrook, Maine
McCann, Harrison King b. 1880
Windham, Maine
Andrew, John Albion b. May 31, 1818
Wiscasset, Maine
Johnson, James Weldon d. Jun 26, 1938
York, Maine
Wood, Sarah Sayward Barrell Keating
b. Oct 1, 1759
York Harbor, Maine
DeRochemont, Louis d. Dec 23, 1978

MARYLAND

Bowie, Walter (Wat) b. 1837
Cooper, Miriam b. 1894
Reed, Peter Hugh b. 1892
Rodgers, John b. 1773
Abingdon, Maryland
Paca, William b. Oct 31, 1740
Paca, William d. Oct 13, 1799
Anacosta Heights, Maryland
Douglass, Frederick d. Feb 20, 1895
Annapolis, Maryland
Bowie, Walter (Wat) d. 1864
Cain, James Mallahan b. Jul 1, 1892
Carroll, Charles b. Sep 19, 1737
Cates, Clifton Bledsoe d. Jun 6, 1970
Green, Constance Windsor McLaughlin
d. Dec 5, 1975

Johnson, Reverdy b. May 21, 1796
Johnson, Reverdy d. Feb 10, 1876
Meyer, Debbie (Deborah) b. Aug 14, 1952
Peale, Raphael b. Feb 17, 1774
Pinkney, William b. Mar 17, 1764
Smith, Thorne b. 1892
Terrell, Mary Church d. Jul 24, 1954

Anne Arundel, Maryland
Hopkins, Johns b. May 19, 1795

Baltimore, Maryland
Adler, Larry (Lawrence Cecil)
  b. Feb 10, 1914
Agle, Nan Hayden b. Apr 13, 1905
Agnew, Spiro Theodore b. Nov 9, 1918
Albright, William Foxwell d. Sep 19, 1971
Armstrong, Bess (Elizabeth Key)
  b. Dec 11, 1953
Astin, John Allen b. Mar 30, 1930
Atkinson, William Walker b. Dec 5, 1862
Baldwin, Hanson Weightman
  b. Mar 22, 1903
Bamberger, Louis b. May 15, 1855
Banneker, Benjamin d. Oct 9, 1806
Bateman, Kate Josephine b. Oct 7, 1842
Beach, Sylvia b. 1887
Blake, Eubie (James Hubert)
  b. Feb 7, 1883
Blalock, Alfred d. Sep 15, 1964
Boehm, Edward M b. Aug 21, 1913
Bonaparte, Elizabeth Patterson
  b. Feb 6, 1785
Bonsal, Stephen b. Mar 29, 1865
Braly, Malcolm d. Apr 7, 1980
Breeskin, Adelyn Dohme b. Jul 19, 1896
Brooks, William Keith d. Nov 12, 1908
Bruce, David Kirkpatrick Estes
  b. Feb 12, 1898
Burns, William John b. Oct 19, 1861
Burt, Maxwell Struthers b. Oct 18, 1882
Bushman, Francis X(avier) b. Jan 10, 1883
Calvert, Catherine b. 1891
Carroll, Charles d. Nov 14, 1832
Carroll, John d. Dec 3, 1815
Chaney, Norman b. Jan 18, 1918
Chaney, Norman d. May 30, 1936
Chaplin, George b. 1950
Chase, Charley b. Oct 20, 1893
Chase, Samuel d. Jun 19, 1811
Childs, George William b. May 12, 1829
Clark, Peggy b. Sep 30, 1915
Cleveland, Frances Folsom d. Oct 29, 1947
Coburn, D(onald) L(ee) b. Aug 4, 1938
Conreid, Hans b. Apr 1, 1915
Corcoran, William Wilson b. Dec 27, 1798
Crosby, Joan Carew b. Feb 14, 1933
Danforth, David Charles d. Sep 19, 1970
Darling, Erik b. Sep 25, 1933
Davis, John Staige d. Dec 23, 1946
Decker, Alonzo G b. Jan 16, 1884
DosPassos, John d. Sep 28, 1970
Dunnock, Mildred b. Jan 25, 1906

Eisenhower, Milton Stover d. May 2, 1985
Elkin, Benjamin b. Aug 10, 1911
Fenton, Thomas Trail b. Apr 8, 1930
Ford, Paul b. Nov 2, 1901
Fox, "Nellie" (Jacob Nelson)
  d. Dec 1, 1975
Frazier, Edward Franklin b. Sep 24, 1897
Gans, Joe d. Aug 16, 1910
Gervasi, Frank b. Feb 5, 1908
Gibbons, James, Cardinal b. Jul 23, 1834
Gibbons, James, Cardinal d. Mar 24, 1921
Glanzman, Louis S b. Feb 8, 1922
Glass, Philip b. Jan 31, 1937
Goddard, Calvin Hooker b. Oct 30, 1891
Goddard, Robert Hutchings
  d. Aug 10, 1945
Goldman, Richard Franko d. Jan 19, 1980
Gottfried, Brian b. Jan 27, 1952
Graham, Donald Edward b. Apr 22, 1945
Gray, Gordon b. May 30, 1909
Harris, Emily Schwartz b. Feb 11, 1947
Hasselhof, David b. Jul 17, 1952
Hill, Calvin b. Jan 2, 1947
Hirschmann, Ira Arthur b. Jul 7, 1906
Hiss, Alger b. Nov 11, 1904
Holiday, Billie b. Apr 7, 1915
Holt, Henry b. Jan 3, 1840
Hopkins, Johns d. Dec 24, 1873
Howell, William H(enry) b. Feb 20, 1860
Hughes, Sarah Tilghman b. Aug 2, 1896
Johnson, Gerald White d. Mar 23, 1980
Johnston, Richard Malcolm
  d. Sep 23, 1898
Jones, Eli Stanley b. Jan 1, 1884
Kaline, Al(bert William) b. Dec 19, 1934
Kelley, Joe (Joseph James)
  d. Aug 14, 1943
Kennedy, John Pendleton b. Oct 25, 1795
Key, Francis Scott d. Jan 11, 1843
Kirby, John b. Dec 31, 1908
Krauss, Ruth Ida b. 1911
Lazear, Jesse William b. May 2, 1866
Lert, Ernst d. Jan 30, 1955
Lincoln, Victoria Endicott d. May 9, 1981
Lord, Walter b. Oct 8, 1917
Louis, Morris b. Nov 28, 1912
Lovejoy, Arthur Oncken d. Dec 30, 1962
Mackin, Catherine Patricia
  b. Aug 28, 1939
Mandel, Marvin b. Apr 19, 1920
Marquard, "Rube" (Richard William)
  d. Jun 1, 1980
Marshall, Thurgood b. Jul 2, 1908
Martin, Glenn Luther d. Dec 4, 1955
Mayehoff, Eddie b. Jul 7, 1914
McNeil, Claudia Mae b. Aug 13, 1917
Mencken, H(enry) L(ouis) b. Sep 12, 1880
Mencken, H(enry) L(ouis) d. Jan 29, 1956
Mergenthaler, Ottmar d. Oct 28, 1899
Middendorf, John William b. Sep 22, 1924
Mikulski, Barbara Ann b. Jul 20, 1938

Chesapeake Bay, Maryland
Wiley, George A d. Aug 8, 1973
Chestertown, Maryland
Peale, James b. 1749
Chevy Chase, Maryland
Abbe, Cleveland d. Oct 28, 1916
Hays, Brooks d. Oct 11, 1981
O'Hara, Mary d. Oct 15, 1980
Ward, Paul W d. Nov 24, 1976
Wright, Louis Booker d. Feb 26, 1984
Clear Springs, Maryland
Bobst, Elmer Holmes b. Dec 16, 1884
College Park, Maryland
Bias, Len d. Jun 19, 1986
Cumberland, Maryland
Avirett, John Williams, II b. May 13, 1902
Ord, Edward Otho Cresap b. Oct 18, 1818
Walsh, James Edward b. Apr 30, 1891
Dorchester, Maryland
Tubman, Harriet Ross b. 1826
Easton, Maryland
Girdler, Tom Mercer d. Feb 4, 1965
Lawrie, Lee d. Jan 23, 1961
Morton, Rogers Clark Ballard
d. Apr 19, 1979
Rouse, James Wilson b. Apr 26, 1914
Ellicott City, Maryland
Davis, Meyer b. Jan 10, 1895
Elliot's Mills, Maryland
Banneker, Benjamin b. Nov 9, 1731
Emmitsburg, Maryland
Seton, Elizabeth Ann Bayley, Saint
d. Jan 4, 1821
Fort Washington, Maryland
Cushman, Robert Everton, Jr.
d. Jan 2, 1985
Frederick, Maryland
Fritchie, Barbara b. 1766
Mathias, Charles McCurdy, Jr.
b. Jul 24, 1922
McCardell, Claire b. May 24, 1905
Wheeler, Earle G d. Dec 18, 1975
Frederick County, Maryland
Lee, Thomas Sim d. Nov 9, 1819
Schley, Winfield Scott b. Oct 9, 1839
Seiss, Joseph Augustus b. Mar 18, 1823
Garrett Park, Maryland
Leaf, Munro (Wilbur Munro)
d. Dec 21, 1976
Georgetown, Maryland
Wallop, Douglass (John Douglass, III)
d. Apr 1, 1985
Glen Burnie, Maryland
Eberly, Bob d. Nov 17, 1981
Glen Echo, Maryland
Barton, Clara Harlowe d. Apr 12, 1912
Glencoe, Maryland
Perky, Henry D d. Jun 29, 1906
Hagerstown, Maryland
Feld, Irvin b. May 9, 1918

Hamilton, Maryland
Leaf, Munro (Wilbur Munro)
b. Dec 4, 1905
Hartford City, Maryland
Booth, John Wilkes b. Aug 26, 1838
Havre de Grace, Maryland
Ripkin, Cal(vin Edwin, Jr.)
b. Aug 24, 1960
Tydings, Millard Evelyn b. Apr 6, 1890
Tydings, Millard Evelyn d. Feb 9, 1961
Hughesville, Maryland
Turner, Thomas Wyatt b. Apr 16, 1877
Huntsville, Maryland
Hunt, George Wylie Paul b. Nov 1, 1859
Hyattsville, Maryland
Bias, Len b. Nov 18, 1963
Cain, James Mallahan d. Oct 27, 1977
Kingston Hall, Maryland
Carroll, Anna Ella b. Aug 29, 1815
Laurel, Maryland
Jacobs, Al(bert T) d. Feb 13, 1985
Lonaconing, Maryland
Grove, "Lefty" (Robert Moses)
b. Mar 6, 1900
Lutherville, Maryland
Crowther, Bosley (Francis Bosley)
b. Jul 13, 1905
Cummins, George David d. Jun 25, 1876
Manchester, Maryland
Flutie, Doug(las Richard) b. Oct 23, 1962
Marlboro, Maryland
Patterson, Eleanor Medill d. Jul 24, 1948
Mount Savage, Maryland
Allen, Larry b. Oct 19, 1908
New Market, Maryland
Garnet, Henry Highland b. Dec 23, 1815
North East, Maryland
Read, George b. Sep 18, 1733
Oxon Hill, Maryland
Hanson, John d. Nov 22, 1783
Prince George County, Maryland
L'Enfant, Pierre Charles d. Jun 14, 1825
Surratt, John Harrison b. 1844
Prince George's County, Maryland
Lee, Thomas Sim b. Oct 29, 1745
Riverdale, Maryland
Abbot, Charles Greeley d. Dec 17, 1973
Rockville, Maryland
Bullard, Dexter Means d. Oct 5, 1981
Curtis, (James) Mike (Michael)
b. Mar 27, 1943
Monroney, Mike (Aimer Stillwell)
d. Feb 13, 1980
Nessen, Ron(ald Harold) b. May 25, 1934
Roland Park, Maryland
Baldwin, William, Jr. b. May 30, 1903
Rossmoor, Maryland
Rice, "Sam" (Edgar Charles)
d. Oct 13, 1974
Rowland Park, Maryland
Baldwin, Billy b. May 30, 1904

Saint Marys, Maryland
Hammett, (Samuel) Dashiell
b. May 27, 1894
Saint Michaels, Maryland
Baines, Harold Douglass b. Mar 15, 1959
Salisbury, Maryland
Sarbanes, Paul Spyros b. Feb 3, 1933
Woodcock, Amos Walter Wright
b. Oct 29, 1883
Woodcock, Amos Walter Wright
d. Jan 17, 1964
Sandy Springs, Maryland
Acheson, Dean Gooderham
d. Oct 12, 1971
Silver Spring, Maryland
Blair, Montgomery d. Jul 27, 1883
Carson, Rachel Louise d. Apr 14, 1964
Craig, Elizabeth May d. Jul 15, 1975
Goldfinger, Nathaniel d. Jul 22, 1976
Hart, Frances Noyes b. Aug 10, 1890
Hazam, Lou(is J) d. Sep 6, 1983
Jones, Mary Harris d. Nov 30, 1930
Porter, Katherine Anne d. Sep 18, 1980
Seiler, James, W d. Jan 2, 1983
Shulsky, Sam d. Apr 21, 1982
Silver Springs, Maryland
Pollard, Fritz (Frederick D)
d. May 11, 1986
Sinepuxent, Maryland
Decatur, Stephen b. Jan 5, 1779
Snow Hill, Maryland
Johnson, "Judy" (William Julius)
b. Oct 26, 1899
Stevenson, Maryland
Ponselle, Rosa d. May 25, 1981
Still Pond, Maryland
Hepbron, George b. Aug 27, 1863
Sudlersville, Maryland
Foxx, Jimmy (James Emory)
b. Oct 22, 1907
Sykesville, Maryland
Kanner, Leo d. Apr 3, 1981
Tacoma Park, Maryland
Kuhn, Bowie Kent b. Oct 28, 1926
Takoma Park, Maryland
Miller, Ray(mond Roger) b. Apr 30, 1945
Towson, Maryland
Decker, Alonzo G d. Mar 18, 1956
Mackin, Catherine Patricia
d. Nov 20, 1982
Trappe, Maryland
Baker, Frank (John Franklin)
b. Mar 13, 1886
Baker, Frank (John Franklin)
d. Jun 28, 1963
Tuckahoe, Maryland
Douglass, Frederick b. Feb 14, 1817
Union Bridge, Maryland
Rinehart, William H b. Sep 13, 1825
Upper Marlboro, Maryland
Carroll, John b. Jan 8, 1735

Walkerville, Maryland
Winebrenner, John b. Mar 25, 1797
Waterloo, Maryland
Surratt, Mary Eugenia Jenkins
b. May 1820
Waverly, Maryland
Reese, Lizette Woodworth b. Jan 9, 1856
Westminster, Maryland
Shriver, (Robert) Sargent b. Nov 9, 1915
White Hall, Maryland
Black, Samuel Duncan b. Aug 2, 1883

MASSACHUSETTS

Manship, Paul d. Jan 31, 1966
Sacco, Nicola d. Aug 23, 1927
Sampson, Deborah b. Dec 17, 1760
Secord, Laura Ingersoll b. 1775
Wortman, Denys d. Sep 20, 1958
Abingdon, Massachusetts
Sullivan, John L(awrence) d. Feb 2, 1918
Acton, Massachusetts
Brown, James b. May 19, 1800
Adams, Massachusetts
Anthony, Susan Brownell b. Feb 15, 1820
Allston, Massachusetts
Duffy, Hugh d. Oct 19, 1954
Amesbury, Massachusetts
Bartlett, Josiah b. Nov 21, 1729
Amherst, Massachusetts
Baker, Ray Stannard d. Jul 12, 1946
Dickinson, Emily Elizabeth
b. Dec 10, 1830
Dickinson, Emily Elizabeth
d. May 15, 1886
Garis, Howard Roger d. Nov 5, 1962
Jackson, Helen Maria Hunt Fiske
b. Oct 18, 1831
Symington, (William) Stuart
b. Jun 26, 1901
Andover, Massachusetts
Bradstreet, Anne d. Sep 16, 1672
Burns, John Horne b. Oct 7, 1916
Otis, James d. May 23, 1783
Phelps, Elizabeth Stuart b. Aug 13, 1815
Pierce, Jane Means d. Dec 2, 1863
Arlington, Massachusetts
Agassiz, Elizabeth Cabot Cary
d. Jun 27, 1902
Creeley, Robert White b. May 21, 1926
Trowbridge, John Townsend
d. Feb 12, 1916
Whitaker, Rogers E(rnest) M(alcolm)
b. Jan 15, 1899
Wilson, Samuel b. Sep 16, 1766
Ashfield, Massachusetts
DeMille, Cecil B(lount) b. Aug 12, 1881
Hall, Granville Stanley b. Feb 1, 1844
Attleboro, Massachusetts
Berberian, Cathy b. Jul 4, 1928
Bowen, Roger b. May 25, 1932

Conniff, Ray b. Nov 6, 1916
Manchester, William Raymond
  b. Apr 4, 1922
Rounseville, Robert Field b. Mar 25, 1914
Auburndale, Massachusetts
Clark, Sydney b. Aug 18, 1890
Barnstable, Massachusetts
Kittredge, G(eorge) L(yman)
  d. Jul 23, 1941
Warren, Mercy Otis b. Sep 14, 1728
Barre, Massachusetts
Riis, Jacob August d. May 26, 1914
Barrington, Massachusetts
DuBois, W(illiam) E(dward) B(urghardt)
  b. Feb 23, 1868
Lynes, Joseph Russell, Jr. b. Dec 2, 1910
Bedford, Massachusetts
Haney, Carol b. Dec 24, 1924
Belchertown, Massachusetts
Bartlett, Francis Alonzo b. Nov 13, 1882
Belmont, Massachusetts
Bush, Vannevar d. Jun 28, 1974
Howard, Cordelia d. Aug 10, 1941
Lanman, Charles Rockwell d. Feb 20, 1941
Piston, Walter d. Nov 12, 1976
Walker, Henry Oliver d. Jan 14, 1929
Zacharias, Jerrold R(einarch)
  d. Jul 16, 1986
Beverly, Massachusetts
Barnet, Will b. May 25, 1911
Brown, Frank Arthur, Jr. b. Aug 30, 1908
Carpenter, Bobby b. Jul 13, 1963
Larcom, Lucy b. Mar 5, 1824
Lodge, Henry Cabot, Jr. d. Feb 27, 1985
Whitney, Richard b. Aug 1, 1888
Wylie, Philip Gordon b. May 12, 1902
Billerica, Massachusetts
Peabody, Elizabeth Palmer
  b. May 16, 1804
Blackstone, Massachusetts
Tappan, Eva March b. Dec 26, 1854
Boston, Massachusetts
Adamowski, Timothee d. Apr 18, 1943
Adams, Brooks d. Feb 13, 1927
Adams, Charles Francis, Jr.
  b. May 27, 1835
Adams, Charles Francis, Sr.
  b. Aug 18, 1807
Adams, Charles Francis, Sr.
  d. Nov 21, 1886
Adams, Henry Brooks b. Feb 16, 1838
Adams, Samuel b. Sep 27, 1722
Adams, Samuel d. Oct 2, 1803
Agassiz, Elizabeth Cabot Cary
  b. Dec 5, 1822
Alcott, Amos Bronson d. Mar 4, 1888
Alcott, Louisa May d. Mar 6, 1888
Aldrich, Richard Stoddard
  b. Aug 17, 1902
Aldrich, Thomas Bailey d. Mar 19, 1907
Alexander, Jane b. Oct 28, 1939

Allen, Frederick Lewis b. Jul 5, 1890
Ames, Ed(mund Dantes) b. Jul 9, 1927
Andrew, John Albion d. Oct 30, 1867
Arnot, Robert Burns b. Feb 23, 1948
Attucks, Crispus d. Mar 5, 1770
Bailey, Charles Waldo, II b. Apr 28, 1929
Ballou, Maturin Murray b. Apr 14, 1820
Barber, Bernard b. Jan 29, 1918
Barnes, Joanna b. Nov 15, 1934
Barrasso, Tom (Thomas) b. Mar 31, 1965
Barron, Clarence Walker b. Jul 2, 1855
Barth, Roland Sawyer b. May 18, 1937
Bates, Arlo d. Aug 24, 1918
Benchley, Nathaniel Goddard
  d. Dec 14, 1981
Benirschke, Rolf Joachim b. Feb 7, 1955
Berle, Adolf Augustus, Jr. b. Jan 29, 1895
Bickford, Charles Ambrose d. Nov 9, 1967
Bigelow, Erastus Brigham d. Dec 6, 1879
Bigelow, Henry Bryant b. Oct 3, 1879
Biggs, Edward George Power
  d. Mar 10, 1977
Bishop, Elizabeth d. Oct 6, 1979
Bitzer, George William b. Apr 21, 1872
Blanchard, Thomas d. Apr 16, 1864
Bolger, Ray b. Jan 10, 1904
Bookspan, Martin b. Jul 30, 1926
Borg, Veda Ann b. Jan 15, 1915
Borofsky, Jonathan b. 1942
Bowditch, Nathaniel d. Mar 16, 1838
Bowdoin, James b. Aug 7, 1726
Bowdoin, James d. Nov 6, 1790
Bradford, Gamaliel b. Oct 9, 1863
Bradlee, Ben(jamin Crowninshield)
  b. Aug 26, 1921
Braff, Ruby b. Mar 16, 1927
Braithwaite, William Stanley Beaumont
  b. Dec 6, 1878
Bridgman, Laura Dewey d. May 24, 1889
Brooks, Phillips b. Dec 13, 1835
Brooks, Phillips d. Jan 23, 1893
Brown, Alice d. Jun 21, 1948
Brown, Walter Augustine d. Sep 7, 1964
Brown, William Hill b. Dec 1, 1765
Bulfinch, Charles b. Aug 8, 1763
Bulfinch, Charles d. Apr 15, 1844
Bulfinch, Thomas d. May 27, 1867
Bundy, McGeorge b. Mar 30, 1919
Burchard, John Ely d. Dec 25, 1975
Burgess, Gelett (Frank Gelett)
  b. Jan 30, 1866
Butterfield, Lyman Henry d. Apr 25, 1982
Byrd, Richard Evelyn d. Mar 11, 1957
Cabot, Susan b. Jul 6, 1927
Carlisle, Mary b. Feb 3, 1912
Carney, Harry Howell b. Apr 1, 1910
Cass, Peggy b. May 21, 1925
Chadwick, George Whitefield
  d. Apr 7, 1931
Channing, Walter d. Jul 27, 1876
Chickering, Jonas d. Dec 8, 1853

Ciardi, John Anthony b. Jun 24, 1916
Clapp, Patricia b. Jun 9, 1912
Cole, Maria b. Aug 1, 1920
Collins, Eddie (Edward Trowbridge, Sr.)
   d. Mar 25, 1951
Collins, Gary b. Aug 30, 1983
Colonna, Jerry b. Sep 17, 1905
Colson, Charles Wendell b. Oct 16, 1931
Connolly, James B b. 1868
Converse, Frederick Shepherd
   d. Jun 8, 1940
Converse, Marquis M d. Feb 9, 1931
Conway, Gary b. 1938
Coolidge, Charles Allerton b. Nov 30, 1858
Cooper, Joseph D b. May 25, 1917
Copeland, George b. 1882
Copley, John Singleton b. Jul 3, 1733
Corning, Erastus, III d. May 28, 1983
Corwin, Norman b. May 3, 1910
Costa, Don b. Jun 10, 1925
Cotton, John d. Dec 23, 1652
Cowl, Jane b. Dec 14, 1884
Crabtree, Lotta d. Sep 25, 1924
Crafts, James Mason b. Mar 8, 1839
Cram, Ralph Adams d. Sep 22, 1942
Craven, Frank b. 1878
Crosby, Harry b. 1898
Crosby, Norm(an Lawrence)
   b. Sep 15, 1927
Curley, James Michael b. Nov 20, 1874
Curley, James Michael d. Nov 12, 1958
Curtis, Charles Gordon b. Apr 20, 1860
Cushing, Richard James, Cardinal
   b. Aug 24, 1895
Cushing, Richard James, Cardinal
   d. Nov 2, 1970
Cushman, Charlotte Saunders
   b. Jul 23, 1816
Cushman, Charlotte Saunders
   d. Feb 17, 1876
Dahlberg, Edward b. Jul 22, 1900
Dallin, Cyrus d. Nov 14, 1944
Dawes, William b. Apr 6, 1745
Dawes, William d. Feb 25, 1799
Dewing, Thomas Wilmer b. May 4, 1851
Dole, James b. Sep 27, 1877
Downes, Edward Olin Davenport
   b. Aug 12, 1911
Durant, William Crapo b. Dec 8, 1861
Eliot, Charles William b. Mar 20, 1834
Elkins, Stanley Maurice b. Apr 29, 1925
Elliott, Bob b. Mar 26, 1923
Elliott, Robert B b. Aug 11, 1842
Emerson, Ralph Waldo b. May 25, 1803
Eruzione, Mike b. Oct 25, 1954
Evans, Charles b. Nov 13, 1850
Everett, Edward d. Jan 15, 1865
Farb, Peter d. Apr 8, 1980
Farmer, Fannie Merritt b. Mar 23, 1857
Farmer, Fannie Merritt d. Jan 15, 1915
Farnum, William b. Jul 4, 1876

Fellows, Edith b. May 20, 1923
Fiedler, Arthur b. Dec 17, 1894
Field, Betty b. Feb 8, 1918
Fields, James T d. Apr 24, 1881
Filene, Lincoln b. Apr 5, 1865
Fitts, Dudley b. Apr 28, 1903
Fitzgerald, Albert J d. May 1, 1982
Fitzgerald, John Francis b. Feb 11, 1863
Fitzgerald, John Francis d. Oct 2, 1950
Fleming, Williamina Paton Stevens
   d. May 21, 1911
Foley, Martha b. 1897
Foote, Arthur William d. Apr 8, 1937
Francis, Arlene b. Oct 20, 1908
Francis, James Bicheno d. Sep 18, 1892
Franklin, Benjamin b. Jan 17, 1706
Frazier, Brenda Diana Dudd
   d. May 3, 1982
Frederick, Pauline b. Aug 12, 1885
Frost, Robert Lee d. Jan 29, 1963
Gallen, Hugh J d. Dec 29, 1982
Garrigue, Jean d. Dec 27, 1972
Geschwind, Norman d. Jan 4, 1984
Giamatti, A(ngelo) Bartlett b. Apr 4, 1938
Gibran, Kahlil George b. Nov 29, 1922
Gilbert, A(lfred) C(arleton) d. Jan 24, 1961
Goodwin, Nat C b. 1857
Goodwin, Richard N(aradhof)
   b. Dec 7, 1931
Gray, Horace b. Mar 24, 1828
Greenough, Horatio b. Sep 6, 1805
Grew, Joseph Clark b. May 27, 1880
Griffis, Stanton b. May 2, 1887
Gropius, Walter Adolf d. Jul 5, 1969
Gross, Courtlandt Sherrington
   b. Nov 21, 1904
Gross, Robert Ellsworth b. May 11, 1897
Guber, Peter (Howard Peter)
   b. Mar 1, 1942
Guiney, Louise b. 1861
Gunn, Hartford Nelson, Jr. d. Jan 2, 1986
Hale, Edward Everett b. Apr 3, 1822
Hale, Lucretia Peabody b. Sep 2, 1820
Hale, Lucretia Peabody d. Jun 12, 1900
Hale, Nancy b. May 6, 1908
Haley, Jack b. Aug 10, 1900
Hawes, Harriet Ann Boyd b. Oct 11, 1871
Hawthorne, Julian b. Jun 22, 1846
Hayes, Roland d. Dec 31, 1976
Healy, George Peter Alexander
   b. Jul 15, 1813
Henderson, Lawrence Joseph
   d. Feb 10, 1942
Hentoff, Nat(han Irving) b. Jun 10, 1925
Herne, Chrystal Katharine d. Sep 19, 1950
Hewes, Henry b. Apr 9, 1917
Hicks, Louise Day b. Oct 16, 1923
Hightower, Florence Josephine Cole
   b. Jun 9, 1916
Hightower, Florence Josephine Cole
   d. Mar 6, 1981

Hitchcock, Henry Russell b. Jun 3, 1903
Holmes, Oliver Wendell d. Oct 7, 1894
Holmes, Oliver Wendell, Jr.
    b. Mar 8, 1841
Holt, John Caldwell d. Sep 14, 1985
Homer, Sidney b. Dec 9, 1864
Homer, Winslow b. Feb 24, 1836
Hooper, William b. Jun 17, 1742
Horner, Matina Souretis b. Jul 28, 1939
Howe, Mark De Wolfe b. May 22, 1906
Howe, Quincy b. Aug 17, 1900
Howe, Samuel Gridley b. Nov 10, 1802
Howe, Samuel Gridley d. Jan 9, 1876
Howland, Beth b. May 28, 1941
Hunsaker, Jerome Clarke d. Sep 10, 1984
Hutchinson, Thomas b. Sep 9, 1711
Hynes, John B d. Jan 6, 1970
Johnson, Howard Brennan b. Aug 23, 1932
Johnson, Howard Deering b. 1896
Jones, Buck d. Nov 30, 1942
Kahn, Madeline Gail b. Sep 29, 1942
Kalmus, Natalie Mabelle Dunfee
    d. Nov 15, 1965
Keaney, Frank b. Jun 5, 1886
Keith, Ian b. Feb 27, 1899
Kelly, "King" (Michael Joseph)
    d. Nov 8, 1894
Kemelman, Harry b. Nov 24, 1908
Kennedy, Caroline Bouvier
    b. Nov 27, 1957
Kennedy, Joseph Patrick, III
    b. Sep 24, 1952
Kennedy, Joseph Patrick, Sr.
    b. Sep 6, 1888
Kennedy, Rose Fitzgerald b. Jul 22, 1890
Kern, Harold G d. Feb 10, 1976
Keyworth, George Albert b. Nov 30, 1939
Kirstein, George G b. Dec 10, 1909
Kittredge, G(eorge) L(yman)
    b. Feb 28, 1860
Knox, Frank b. Jan 1, 1874
Knox, Henry b. Jul 25, 1750
Koussevitzky, Serge Alexandrovich
    d. Jun 4, 1951
Kozol, Jonathan b. Sep 5, 1936
Lahey, Frank Howard d. Jun 27, 1953
Langer, Walter C b. Feb 9, 1899
Larcom, Lucy d. Apr 17, 1893
Larsen, Roy Edward b. Apr 20, 1899
Leland, Timothy b. Sep 24, 1937
Lemmon, Jack (John Uhler, III)
    b. Feb 8, 1925
Lemoyne, W(illiam) J b. Apr 29, 1831
Levine, Jack b. Jan 3, 1915
Levine, Joseph Edward b. Sep 9, 1905
Lewis, Boyd de Wolf b. Aug 18, 1905
Lincoln, Mary Johnson Bailey
    d. Dec 2, 1921
Livermore, Mary Ashton Rice
    b. Dec 19, 1820
Lodge, Henry Cabot b. May 12, 1850

Lodge, Henry Cabot d. Nov 9, 1924
Loudon, Dorothy b. Sep 17, 1933
Lowell, Abbott Lawrence b. Dec 13, 1856
Lowell, Abbott Lawrence d. Jan 6, 1943
Lowell, Francis Cabot d. Aug 10, 1817
Lowell, Percival b. Mar 13, 1855
Lowell, Robert Trail Spence, Jr.
    b. Mar 1, 1917
Mackendrick, Alexander b. 1912
MacLeish, Archibald d. Apr 20, 1982
Maginnis, Charles Donagh d. Feb 15, 1955
Marca-Relli, Conrad b. Jun 5, 1913
Mason, Francis van Wyck b. Nov 11, 1901
Mather, Cotton b. Feb 12, 1663
Mather, Cotton d. Feb 13, 1728
Mather, Increase d. Aug 23, 1723
McAuliffe, Christa (Sharon Christa
    Corrigan) b. Sep 2, 1948
McCandless, Bruce, II b. Jun 8, 1937
McCarthy, Tommy (Thomas Francis
    Michael) d. Aug 5, 1922
McCobb, Paul b. 1917
McCormack, John William
    b. Dec 21, 1891
McCullough, Paul d. Mar 25, 1936
McHugh, Jimmy (James) b. Jul 10, 1894
Meader, Vaughn b. 1936
Medeiros, Humberto, Cardinal
    d. Sep 17, 1983
Mifflin, George Harrison b. May 1, 1845
Mollenhauer, Emil d. Dec 10, 1927
Mondello, "Toots" (Nuncio) b. 1912
Morgan, Jane b. 1920
Morison, Samuel Eliot b. Jul 9, 1887
Morison, Samuel Eliot d. May 15, 1976
Murray, John d. Sep 3, 1815
Mydans, Carl M b. May 20, 1907
Newman, Barry Foster b. Nov 7, 1938
Nimoy, Leonard b. Mar 26, 1931
Normand, Mabel b. Nov 10, 1894
Norton, Elliott b. May 17, 1903
O'Connor, Edwin Greene d. Mar 23, 1968
O'Donnell, Kenneth d. Sep 9, 1977
O'Neill, Eugene Gladstone
    d. Nov 27, 1953
Orkin, Ruth b. Sep 3, 1921
Osgood, Frances Sargent Locke
    b. Jun 18, 1811
Oteri, Joseph Santo b. Nov 7, 1930
Paine, Robert Treat b. Mar 11, 1731
Paine, Robert Treat d. May 12, 1814
Paley, Barbara Cushing b. Jul 5, 1915
Park, Maud May Wood b. Jan 25, 1871
Parker, George Swinnerton d. Sep 26, 1952
Parkman, Francis b. Sep 16, 1823
Parkman, Francis d. Nov 8, 1893
Patton, George Smith, III b. Dec 24, 1923
Pearce, Charles S b. Oct 13, 1851
Perkins, Frances b. Apr 10, 1882
Perry, Ralph Barton d. Jan 22, 1957
Phillips, Wendell b. Nov 29, 1811

Phillips, Wendell d. Feb 2, 1884
Pickering, Edward Charles b. Jul 19, 1846
Pickering, William Henry b. Feb 15, 1858
Pincus, Gregory d. Aug 22, 1967
Plath, Sylvia b. Oct 27, 1932
Poe, Edgar Allan b. Jan 19, 1809
Prendergast, Maurice Brazil b. Oct 1861
Prescott, William Hickling d. Jan 28, 1859
Prouty, Jed b. Apr 6, 1879
Remick, Lee b. Dec 14, 1935
Revere, Paul b. Jan 1, 1735
Revere, Paul d. May 10, 1818
Rey, Hans Augustus d. Aug 26, 1977
Rhinelander, John Bassett b. Jun 18, 1933
Richards, Laura Elizabeth Howe
    b. Feb 27, 1850
Richardson, Elliot Lee b. Jul 20, 1920
Rimmer, William d. Aug 20, 1879
Ring, Blanche b. Apr 24, 1872
Robbins, Frank b. Sep 9, 1917
Robinson, Henry Morton b. Sep 7, 1898
Rockwell, Willard F b. Mar 31, 1888
Rodzinski, Artur d. Nov 27, 1958
Roman, Ruth b. Dec 23, 1924
Rosen, Sidney b. Jun 5, 1916
Ross, Harold d. Dec 6, 1957
Roth, Frank b. Feb 22, 1936
Roth, Lillian b. Dec 13, 1910
Rudd, Paul Ryan b. May 5, 1940
Rudman, Warren Bruce b. May 18, 1930
Salinas (y Serrano), Pedro d. Dec 4, 1951
Savage, Henry Wilson d. Nov 29, 1927
Sawyer, Ruth b. Aug 5, 1880
Scott, Austin W d. Apr 9, 1981
Scourby, Alexander d. Feb 22, 1985
Seaga, Edward Phillip George
    b. May 28, 1930
Sears, Eleonora Randolph b. Sep 28, 1881
Sears, Richard Dudley b. Oct 26, 1861
Sears, Richard Dudley d. Apr 8, 1943
Sewall, Samuel d. Jan 1, 1730
Sharaff, Irene b. 1910
Shaw, Mary b. Jan 25, 1854
Shaw, Robert Gould b. Oct 10, 1837
Sheehan, William Edward, Jr. b. May 1925
Silk, Dave b. Jan 1, 1958
Silverstein, Elliot b. 1927
Sims, William Sowden d. Sep 25, 1936
Sissman, L(ouis) E(dward) d. Mar 10, 1976
Smith, Samuel Francis b. Oct 21, 1808
Smith, Samuel Francis d. Nov 16, 1895
Spottswood, Stephen Gill b. Jul 18, 1897
Stitt, "Sonny" (Edward) b. Feb 2, 1924
Stoopnagle, Lemuel Q, Colonel
    d. May 29, 1950
Stuart, Gilbert Charles d. Jul 9, 1828
Sullivan, John L(awrence) b. Oct 15, 1858
Sullivan, Louis Henri b. Sep 3, 1856
Sullivan, Tom b. Mar 27, 1947
Summer, Donna b. Dec 31, 1948
Sumner, Charles b. Jan 6, 1811

Sumner, Edwin V b. Jan 30, 1797
Taylor, James Vernon b. Mar 12, 1948
Taylor, Livingston b. Nov 21, 1950
Taylor, Phoebe Atwood d. Jan 9, 1976
Thayer, Abbott Handerson
    b. Aug 12, 1849
Thomas, Isaiah b. Jan 30, 1750
Thompson, Randall d. Jul 9, 1984
Train, Arthur Cheney b. Sep 6, 1875
Tufts, Sonny b. Jul 16, 1911
Tyler, Steve b. Mar 26, 1948
Ullman, James Ramsey d. Jun 20, 1971
Vanzetti, Bartolomeo d. Aug 23, 1927
Vendler, Helen Hennessy b. Apr 30, 1933
Villard, Helen Francis Garrison b. 1844
Walker, Henry Oliver b. May 14, 1843
Walsh, Michael Patrick b. Feb 28, 1912
Walsh, Michael Patrick d. Apr 23, 1982
Walters, Barbara b. Sep 25, 1931
Warner, Roger Sherman, Jr.
    b. Jun 12, 1907
Wein, George Theodore b. Oct 3, 1925
Wharton, Clifton Reginald, Jr.
    b. Sep 13, 1926
Wheatley, Phillis d. Dec 5, 1784
Wheeler, Roger Milton b. Feb 27, 1926
White, Kevin Hagan b. Sep 25, 1929
White, Paul Dudley d. Oct 31, 1973
White, Theodore Harold b. May 6, 1915
Wilmerding, John b. Apr 28, 1938
Winchester, Oliver Fisher b. Nov 30, 1810
Winthrop, John d. Mar 26, 1649
Wiseman, Frederick b. Jan 1, 1930
Wolf, Peter b. Mar 7, 1946
Wolff, Mary Evaline d. Jul 25, 1964
Wood, Leonard d. Aug 7, 1927
Woody, Regina Llewellyn Jones
    b. Jan 4, 1894
Wright, George d. Aug 31, 1937
Wright, John Joseph b. Jul 18, 1909
Yale, Elihu b. Apr 5, 1649
Yankelovich, Daniel b. 1924
Yawkey, Thomas Austin d. Jul 9, 1976
Ziolkowski, Korczak b. Sep 6, 1908

Boxford, Massachusetts
Sherrill, Henry Knox d. May 12, 1980

Bradford, Massachusetts
Snell, George Davis b. Dec 19, 1903

Braintree, Massachusetts
Adams, John b. Oct 30, 1735
Adams, John Quincy b. Jul 11, 1767
Hancock, John b. Jan 12, 1737
Thayer, Sylvanus, General b. Jun 9, 1785
Thayer, Sylvanus, General d. Sep 7, 1872

Bridgewater, Massachusetts
Cochrane, Mickey (Gordon Stanley)
    b. Apr 6, 1903
Fiske, Jamie b. Nov 26, 1981
Garry, Charles R b. Mar 17, 1909

Brighton, Massachusetts
Hebner, Richie (Richard Joseph)
   b. Nov 26, 1947
Hoyt, Lawrence W b. 1901
Brimfield, Massachusetts
Guthrie, Samuel b. 1782
Brinfield, Massachusetts
Fairbanks, Thaddeus b. Jan 17, 1796
Brockton, Massachusetts
Davis, Al(len) b. Jul 4, 1929
Dunham, "Sonny" (Elmer Lewis) b. 1914
Higgins, George V b. Nov 13, 1939
Kaminsky, Max b. Sep 7, 1908
Marciano, Rocky b. Sep 1, 1924
Wind, Herbert Warren b. Aug 11, 1916
Brookfield, Massachusetts
Holmes, Mary Jane Hawes b. Apr 5, 1825
Brookline, Massachusetts
Adams, Hannah d. Dec 15, 1831
Boutwell, George Sewell b. Jan 23, 1818
Brewster, Owen d. Dec 25, 1961
Cabot, Richard C b. May 21, 1868
Cobb, Stanley b. Dec 10, 1887
Dukakis, Michael Stanley b. Nov 3, 1933
Fiedler, Arthur d. Jul 10, 1979
Fowlie, Wallace b. Nov 8, 1908
Kennedy, Edward Moore b. Feb 22, 1932
Kennedy, John Fitzgerald b. May 29, 1917
Kennedy, Robert Francis b. Nov 20, 1925
Kitson, Theo Alice Ruggles b. 1871
Lehr, Lew d. Mar 6, 1950
Lowell, Amy b. Feb 9, 1874
Lowell, Amy d. Feb 9, 1925
Mason, Daniel Gregory b. Nov 20, 1873
Mather, Stephen Tyng d. Jan 22, 1930
McBurney, Charles d. Nov 7, 1913
Mirkin, Gabe b. Jun 18, 1935
Monteux, Claude b. Oct 15, 1920
Olmsted, Frederick Law d. Aug 28, 1903
Rhodes, James Ford d. Jan 22, 1927
Richardson, Henry Hobson
   d. Apr 27, 1886
Shriver, Eunice Mary Kennedy b. 1921
Susskind, David Howard b. Dec 19, 1920
Wallace, Mike (Myron Leon)
   b. May 9, 1918
Wellman, William Augustus
   b. Feb 29, 1896
Williams, Ben Ames d. Feb 4, 1953
Buckland, Massachusetts
Lyon, Mary b. Feb 28, 1797
Burlington, Massachusetts
Loeb, William d. Sep 13, 1981
Cambridge, Massachusetts
Agassiz, Louis (Jean Louis Radolphe)
   d. Dec 12, 1873
Allen, Fred b. May 31, 1894
Allport, Gordon William d. Oct 9, 1967
Anderson, Leroy b. Jun 29, 1908
Babbitt, Irving d. Jul 15, 1933
Balch, Emily G d. Jan 9, 1961

Barbour, Walworth b. Jun 4, 1908
Bartlett, John d. Dec 3, 1905
Bhumibol, Adulyadej b. Dec 5, 1927
Bickford, Charles Ambrose b. Jan 1, 1889
Bridgman, Percy Williams b. Apr 21, 1882
Buck, Paul Herman d. Dec 23, 1978
Cabot, John Moors b. Dec 11, 1901
Cannon, Annie Jump d. Apr 13, 1941
Capp, Al d. Nov 5, 1979
Chao, Yuen Ren d. Feb 24, 1982
Clarkson, John Gibson b. Jul 1, 1861
Clarkson, John Gibson d. Feb 4, 1909
Cobb, Stanley d. Feb 18, 1968
Cori, Carl Ferdinand d. Oct 20, 1984
Cummings, E(dward) E(stlin)
   b. Oct 14, 1894
Curtin, Jane Therese b. Sep 6, 1947
Dana, Richard Henry, Jr. b. Aug 1, 1815
Denny-Brown, Derek Ernest
   d. Apr 20, 1981
Deutsch, Helene R d. Mar 29, 1982
Dodge, Bertha S b. Mar 23, 1902
Duchin, Eddie b. Apr 1, 1909
Eliot, Martha May d. Feb 1978
Fuller, Margaret b. May 23, 1810
Glaser, Paul Michael b. Mar 25, 1942
Glueck, Sheldon (Sol Sheldon)
   d. Mar 10, 1980
Gray, Asa d. Jan 30, 1888
Hall, Edwin Herbert d. Nov 20, 1938
Hanfmann, George Maxim Anossov
   d. Mar 13, 1986
Hathaway, William Dodd b. Feb 21, 1924
Hayman, Richard Warren Joseph
   b. Mar 27, 1920
Higginson, Thomas Wentworth
   b. Dec 22, 1823
Hodges, Johnny b. Jul 25, 1906
Holmes, Oliver Wendell b. Aug 29, 1809
Hooton, Earnest Albert d. May 3, 1954
Howe, Mark De Wolfe d. Feb 28, 1967
Hyams, Joe (Joseph) b. Jun 6, 1923
James, Henry d. Dec 18, 1882
Jones, Howard Mumford d. May 12, 1980
Keefe, Tim(othy John) b. Jan 1, 1857
Keefe, Tim(othy John) d. Apr 23, 1933
Kelley, Joe (Joseph James) b. Dec 9, 1871
Kidder, Alfred Vincent d. Jun 11, 1963
Kistiakowsky, George Bogdan
   d. Dec 7, 1982
Kuznets, Simon d. Jul 8, 1985
Langdell, Christopher Columbus
   d. Jul 6, 1906
Langford, Sam d. Jan 12, 1956
Longfellow, Henry Wadsworth
   d. Mar 24, 1882
Lowell, James Russell b. Feb 22, 1819
Lowell, James Russell d. Aug 12, 1891
Marshall, Laurence d. Nov 5, 1980
Miller, Perry Gilbert Eddy d. Dec 9, 1963
Munroe, Charles Edward b. May 24, 1849

Norton, Charles Eliot b. Nov 16, 1827
Norton, Charles Eliot d. Oct 21, 1908
O'Neill, "Tip" (Thomas Philip)
  b. Dec 9, 1912
Peirce, Charles Sanders b. Sep 10, 1839
Pickering, Edward Charles d. Feb 3, 1919
Pound, Roscoe d. Jul 1, 1964
Regan, Donald Thomas b. Dec 21, 1918
Rosenberg, Jakob d. Apr 7, 1980
Royce, Josiah b. Sep 14, 1916
Sands, Dorothy b. Mar 5, 1893
Sheldon, William Herbert d. Sep 16, 1977
Skinner, Otis b. Jun 28, 1858
Story, Joseph d. Sep 10, 1845
Taussig, Helen Brooke b. May 24, 1898
Todd, Mabel Loomis b. Nov 10, 1856
Van Vleck, John Hasbrouck
  d. Nov 28, 1980
Waterston, Sam(uel Atkinson)
  b. Nov 15, 1940
Whitehead, Alfred North d. Dec 30, 1947
Wood, Wilbur Forrester b. Oct 22, 1941
Wright, John Joseph d. Aug 10, 1979

Cambridgeport, Massachusetts
Allston, Washington d. Jul 9, 1843

Canton, Massachusetts
Hinton, William Augustus d. Aug 8, 1959

Cape Cod, Massachusetts
Bitter, Francis d. Jul 26, 1967
Crawford, Jack (John Shea)
  d. Jan 19, 1973
Crosby, Enoch b. 1750
Dickinson, Edwin W d. Dec 2, 1978
Seymour, Charles d. Aug 11, 1963

Carmel, Massachusetts
Cone, Fairfax Mastick d. Jun 20, 1977

Centerville, Massachusetts
Gildersleeve, Virginia Crocheron
  d. Jul 7, 1965

Chappaquiddick, Massachusetts
Kopechne, Mary Jo d. Jul 19, 1969

Charleston, Massachusetts
O'Callahan, Jack b. Jul 24, 1957

Charlestown, Massachusetts
Ball, Thomas b. Jun 3, 1819
Harvard, John d. Sep 14, 1638
Morse, Samuel Finley Breese
  b. Apr 27, 1791
Warren, Joseph d. Jun 17, 1775

Charlton, Massachusetts
Morton, William Thomas Green
  b. Aug 9, 1819

Chatham, Massachusetts
Clay, Lucius du Bignon d. Apr 16, 1978
Hackett, Bobby (Robert Leo)
  d. Jun 7, 1976

Chatham Harbor, Massachusetts
Squanto d. 1622

Chelmsford, Massachusetts
Dalton, John Call b. Feb 2, 1825

Chelsea, Massachusetts
Brown, William Wells d. Nov 6, 1884
Corea, "Chick" (Armando) b. Jun 12, 1941
DeRochemont, Louis b. Jan 13, 1899
Elliot, Win (Irwin) b. May 7, 1915
Hoskins, Allen Clayton b. Aug 9, 1920
Kalmus, Herbert Thomas b. Nov 9, 1881

Cheshire, Massachusetts
Smith, Horace b. Oct 28, 1808

Chestnut Hill, Massachusetts
Buckmaster, Henrietta, pseud.
  d. Apr 26, 1983
Eddy, Mary Baker Morse d. Dec 3, 1910
Roosevelt, Alice Lee b. Jul 29, 1861
Saltonstall, Leverett b. Sep 1, 1892

Chicopee Falls, Massachusetts
Bellamy, Edward b. Mar 26, 1850
Bellamy, Edward d. May 22, 1898

Cliftondale, Massachusetts
Marston, William Moulton b. Mar 9, 1893

Clinton, Massachusetts
Brown, Clarence b. May 10, 1890
Moorehead, Agnes b. Dec 6, 1906
Schanberg, Sydney H b. Jan 17, 1934

Concord, Massachusetts
Bigelow, Henry Bryant d. Dec 11, 1967
Emerson, Ralph Waldo d. Apr 27, 1882
Greeley, Dana McLean d. Jun 13, 1986
Morse, Philip McCord d. Sep 5, 1985
Prescott, Samuel b. Aug 19, 1751
Thoreau, Henry David b. Jul 12, 1817
Thoreau, Henry David d. May 6, 1862
Weeks, Sinclair d. Jan 27, 1972

Conway, Massachusetts
Chesbro, "Happy Jack" (John Dwight)
  d. Nov 6, 1931
Field, Marshall b. Aug 18, 1834
Whitney, William Collins b. Jul 5, 1841

Cummington, Massachusetts
Bryant, William Cullen b. Nov 3, 1794

Cutty Hunk, Massachusetts
Cuffe, Paul b. Jan 17, 1759

Danvers, Massachusetts
Dodge, Grenville Mellen b. Apr 12, 1831
Kelsey, Alice Geer b. Sep 21, 1896

Dedham, Massachusetts
D'Amboise, Jacques b. Jul 28, 1934
McCormack, John William
  d. Nov 22, 1980
Nickerson, Albert L b. Jan 17, 1911

Dorchester, Massachusetts
Channing, Edward b. Jun 15, 1856
Conant, James Bryant b. Mar 26, 1893
Eliot, Martha May b. Apr 7, 1891
Everett, Edward b. Apr 11, 1794
Hassam, Childe b. Oct 17, 1859
Herne, Chrystal Katharine b. Jun 17, 1882
Mather, Increase b. Jun 21, 1639
Motley, John L b. Apr 15, 1814
Stone, Lucy d. Oct 18, 1893

Dover, Massachusetts
Saltonstall, Leverett d. Jun 17, 1979
Dracut, Massachusetts
Corey, Wendell b. Mar 20, 1914
Dunstable, Massachusetts
Richards, Ellen Henrietta Swallow
  b. Dec 3, 1842
Duxbury, Massachusetts
Alden, John d. Sep 12, 1687
Alden, Priscilla Mullens d. 1680
Standish, Miles d. Oct 3, 1656
East Boston, Massachusetts
Walker, Hiram b. Jul 4, 1816
East Brookfield, Massachusetts
Mack, Connie b. Dec 22, 1862
Thurber, Charles b. Jan 2, 1803
East Northfield, Massachusetts
Moody, Dwight Lyman b. Feb 5, 1837
Easton, Massachusetts
Ames, Oakes b. Jan 10, 1804
Ames, Oakes d. May 8, 1873
Edgartown, Massachusetts
Hough, Henry Beetle d. Jun 6, 1985
Egypt, Massachusetts
McCall, Thomas Lawson b. Mar 22, 1913
Essex County, Massachusetts
Choate, Rufus b. Oct 1, 1799
Everett, Massachusetts
Bush, Vannevar b. Mar 11, 1890
Fairhaven, Massachusetts
Jenney, William LeBaron b. Sep 25, 1832
Fall River, Massachusetts
Borden, Lizzie Andrew b. Jul 19, 1860
Borden, Lizzie Andrew d. Jun 1, 1927
Dean, Morton b. Aug 22, 1935
Lincoln, Victoria Endicott b. Oct 23, 1904
Falmouth, Massachusetts
Bates, Katherine Lee b. Aug 12, 1859
Boyd, William Clouser d. Feb 19, 1983
Harris, William Bliss d. Jun 22, 1981
Feeding Hills, Massachusetts
Sullivan, Anne b. Apr 14, 1866
Framingham, Massachusetts
Parkhurst, Charles Henry b. Apr 17, 1842
Traynor, "Pie" (Harold Joseph)
  b. Nov 11, 1899
Franklin, Massachusetts
Mann, Horace b. May 4, 1796
Gardner, Massachusetts
Cady, (Walter) Harrison b. 1877
Gloucester, Massachusetts
Anthony, Edward d. Aug 16, 1971
Barbour, Walworth d. Jul 21, 1982
Beaux, Cecelia d. Sep 17, 1942
Clark, Bennett Champ d. Jul 13, 1954
Coon, Carleton Stevens d. Jun 3, 1981
Fiske, John d. Jul 4, 1901
Hobbs, Leland Stanford b. Feb 24, 1892
Kroll, Leon d. Oct 25, 1974
Lane, "Fitz Hugh" (Nathaniel Rogers)
  b. Dec 19, 1804

Poirier, Richard b. Sep 9, 1925
Wengenroth, Stow d. Jan 22, 1978
Granville Centre, Massachusetts
Scott, Austin d. Aug 16, 1922
Greenfield, Massachusetts
Benjamin, Asher b. Jun 15, 1773
Eddy, Clarence b. Jun 23, 1851
Niebuhr, Helmut Richard d. Jul 5, 1962
Ripley, George b. Oct 3, 1802
Taylor, Charles Alonzo b. Jan 20, 1864
Groton, Massachusetts
Peabody, Endicott d. Nov 17, 1944
Hadley, Massachusetts
Hooker, Joseph b. Nov 13, 1814
Smith, Sophia d. Jun 12, 1870
Hampden, Massachusetts
Burgess, Thornton Waldo d. Jun 7, 1965
Hatfield, Massachusetts
Smith, Sophia b. Aug 27, 1796
Haverhill, Massachusetts
Appleton, Daniel b. Dec 10, 1785
Appleton, William Henry b. Jan 27, 1814
Cline, Maggie b. Jan 1, 1857
Crockett, James Underwood b. Oct 9, 1915
Fontaine, Frank b. Apr 19, 1920
Lahey, Frank Howard b. Jun 1, 1880
Whittier, John Greenleaf b. Dec 17, 1807
Hingham, Massachusetts
Brett, Jan Churchill b. Dec 1, 1949
Dwiggins, William Addison
  d. Dec 25, 1956
Stoddard, Richard Henry b. Jul 12, 1825
Holyoke, Massachusetts
Breck, John Henry b. Jun 5, 1877
Cox, Gardner b. Jan 22, 1906
Holmes, John Clennon b. Mar 12, 1926
Moffett, Anthony Toby b. Aug 18, 1944
Viereck, George Sylvester d. Mar 18, 1962
Hopkinton, Massachusetts
Brown, Walter Augustine b. Feb 10, 1905
Shays, Daniel b. 1747
Hudson, Massachusetts
Coolidge, William David b. Oct 23, 1873
Robinson, Wilbert b. Jun 2, 1864
Wheeler, Burton Kendall b. Feb 27, 1882
Hyannis, Massachusetts
Biddle, Francis Beverley d. Oct 4, 1968
Field, Betty b. Sep 13, 1973
Jones, Thomas Hudson d. Nov 4, 1969
Knaths, Karl (Otto Karl) d. Mar 9, 1971
Taber, Gladys Bagg d. Mar 11, 1980
Waksman, Selman Abraham
  d. Aug 16, 1973
Walker, Danton MacIntyre d. Aug 8, 1960
Welch, Joseph Nye d. Oct 6, 1960
Hyannis Port, Massachusetts
Kennedy, Joseph Patrick, Sr.
  d. Nov 18, 1969
Ipswich Hamlet, Massachusetts
Cutler, Manasseh d. Jul 28, 1823

Medford, Massachusetts
Adams, Edwin b. Feb 3, 1834
Adams, Hannah b. Oct 2, 1755
Brooks, Maria Gowen b. 1794
Child, Lydia Maria b. Feb 11, 1802
Larkin, Oliver Waterman b. Aug 17, 1896
Marshall, Laurence b. 1889
Ripley, William Zebina b. Oct 13, 1867
Melrose, Massachusetts
Atkinson, (Justin) Brooks b. Nov 28, 1894
Farrar, Geraldine b. Feb 28, 1882
Livermore, Mary Ashton Rice
   d. May 23, 1905
Speare, Elizabeth George b. Nov 21, 1908
Middleboro, Massachusetts
Tom Thumb, General d. Jul 15, 1883
Milton, Massachusetts
Bush, George Herbert Walker
   b. Jun 12, 1924
Fuller, "Bucky" (Richard Buckminster)
   b. Feb 12, 1895
Nahant, Massachusetts
Amory, Cleveland b. Sep 2, 1917
Johnson, Walter (Thomas Walter)
   b. Jun 27, 1915
Lodge, Henry Cabot, Jr. b. Jul 5, 1902
Nantucket, Massachusetts
Baldwin, Billy d. Nov 25, 1983
Baldwin, William, Jr. d. Nov 25, 1983
Fawcett, George d. Jun 6, 1939
Irving, Isabel d. Sep 1, 1944
Mitchell, Maria b. Aug 1, 1818
Mott, Lucretia Coffin b. Jan 3, 1793
Sarg, Tony (Anthony Frederick)
   d. Mar 7, 1942
Strong, Austin d. Sep 17, 1952
Thayer, Tiffany Ellsworth d. Aug 23, 1959
Natick, Massachusetts
Alger, Horatio d. Jul 18, 1899
Connolly, Thomas Henry d. Apr 28, 1961
Coolidge, Dane b. Mar 24, 1873
Needham, Massachusetts
Wyeth, N(ewell) C(onvers) b. Oct 22, 1882
New Bedford, Massachusetts
Green, Hetty b. Nov 21, 1834
Hough, Henry Beetle b. Nov 8, 1896
Paine, Albert Bigelow b. Jul 10, 1861
Ryder, Albert Pinkham b. Mar 19, 1847
Stone, Ezra (Chaim) b. Dec 2, 1917
Wexler, Norman b. Aug 16, 1926
Newbury, Massachusetts
Parker, Thomas d. Apr 24, 1677
Newburyport, Massachusetts
Andrews, Jane b. Dec 1, 1833
Andrews, Jane d. Jul 15, 1887
Cushing, Caleb d. Jan 2, 1879
Garrison, William Lloyd b. Dec 12, 1805
Greely, Adolphus Washington
   b. Mar 27, 1844
Lowell, Francis Cabot b. Apr 7, 1775
Lowell, John b. Jun 17, 1743

Marquand, John Phillips d. Jul 16, 1960
Parton, James d. Oct 17, 1891
Perkins, Jacob b. Jul 9, 1766
Thornton, Matthew d. Jun 24, 1803
Welchman, Gordon d. Oct 8, 1985
Whitefield, George d. Sep 30, 1770
Newton, Massachusetts
Benchley, Nathaniel Goddard
   b. Nov 13, 1915
Bulfinch, Thomas b. Jul 15, 1796
Converse, Frederick Shepherd
   b. Jan 5, 1871
Curtis, John Duffield, II b. Mar 9, 1948
Gardner, Isabella b. Sep 7, 1915
Gardner, Mary Sewall b. Feb 5, 1871
Goodman, Ellen Holtz b. Apr 11, 1941
Hull, Josephine b. 1884
Kimball, Fiske b. Dec 8, 1888
Morse, Robert Alan b. May 18, 1931
Sexton, Anne Harvey b. Nov 9, 1928
Sherman, Roger b. Apr 19, 1721
Spencer, Percy Le Baron d. Sep 7, 1970
Wightman, Hazel Virginia Hotchkiss
   d. Dec 5, 1974
Newton Centre, Massachusetts
Albright, Tenley Emma b. Jul 18, 1935
Burton, Virginia Lee b. Aug 30, 1909
Daddario, Emilio Quincy b. Sep 24, 1918
Wilkins, Ernest Hatch b. Sep 14, 1880
Newton Highlands, Massachusetts
Ovington, Mary White d. Jul 15, 1951
Preston, Robert b. Jun 8, 1918
Newtonville, Massachusetts
Gray, Elisha d. Jan 21, 1901
Lewin, Kurt d. Feb 12, 1947
Nonquitt, Massachusetts
Sheridan, Philip Henry d. Aug 5, 1888
North Adams, Massachusetts
Chesbro, "Happy Jack" (John Dwight)
   b. Jun 5, 1874
Durant, Will(iam James) b. Nov 5, 1885
Sibley, Hiram b. Feb 6, 1807
North Andover, Massachusetts
Houghton, Henry Oscar d. Aug 25, 1895
North Attleboro, Massachusetts
Martin, Joseph William, Jr.
   b. Nov 3, 1884
North Easton, Massachusetts
Ames, Blanche d. Mar 1, 1969
Craig, Jim (James) b. May 31, 1957
North Scituate, Massachusetts
Lowes, John Livingston d. Aug 15, 1945
Northampton, Massachusetts
Arvin, Newton d. Mar 21, 1963
Chase, Mary Ellen d. Jul 28, 1973
Coolidge, (John) Calvin d. Jan 5, 1933
Dwight, Timothy b. May 14, 1752
Foley, Martha d. Sep 5, 1977
Graham, Sylvester W d. Sep 11, 1851
Koffka, Kurt d. Nov 22, 1941
Larkin, Oliver Waterman d. Dec 17, 1971

Northbridge, Massachusetts
Thibault, Conrad b. Nov 13, 1908
Northfield, Massachusetts
Moody, Dwight Lyman d. Dec 22, 1899
Northhampton, Massachusetts
Coolidge, Grace Anne Goodhue
  d. Jul 8, 1957
Onset Bay, Massachusetts
Farrell, Charles b. Aug 9, 1901
Orleans, Massachusetts
Mortimer, Charles Greenough
  d. Dec 25, 1978
Osterville, Massachusetts
Cronin, Joe (Joseph Edward)
  d. Sep 7, 1984
Hughes, Charles Evans d. Aug 27, 1948
Otis, Massachusetts
Sokolsky, George E d. Dec 13, 1962
Oxford, Massachusetts
Barton, Clara Harlowe b. Dec 25, 1821
Peabody, Massachusetts
Lyons, James b. 1926
Peabody, George b. Feb 18, 1795
Poole, William Frederick b. Dec 24, 1821
Welch, John Francis, Jr. b. Nov 19, 1935
Pelham, Massachusetts
Foster, Abigail Kelley b. Jan 15, 1810
Pittsfield, Massachusetts
Graves, Nancy Stevenson b. Dec 23, 1940
Mercer, Mabel d. Apr 21, 1984
Piccolo, Brian b. Oct 21, 1943
Schachte, Henry Miner b. Jan 12, 1913
Thompson, J(ames) Walter b. Oct 28, 1847
Winship, Elizabeth b. May 17, 1921
Plainfield, Massachusetts
Warner, Charles Dudley b. Sep 12, 1829
Plymouth, Massachusetts
Bartlett, John b. Jun 14, 1820
Bradford, William d. May 9, 1657
Brewster, William d. Apr 10, 1644
Carver, John d. Apr 5, 1621
Chase, Richard Volney d. Aug 26, 1962
Gannett, Deborah Sampson
  b. Dec 17, 1760
Gray, Glen d. Aug 23, 1963
Jackson, Charles Thomas b. Jun 21, 1805
Wakefield, Ruth G d. 1977
Princeton, Massachusetts
Savage, Edward b. Nov 26, 1761
Savage, Edward d. Jul 6, 1817
Provincetown, Massachusetts
Kemp, (Harry) Hibbard d. Aug 6, 1960
MacMillan, Donald Baxter
  b. Nov 10, 1874
MacMillan, Donald Baxter d. Sep 7, 1970
Tworkov, Jack d. Sep 4, 1982
Queen Annes County, Massachusetts
Peale, Charles Willson b. Apr 15, 1741
Quincy, Massachusetts
Adams, Abigail Smith d. Oct 28, 1818
Adams, Brooks b. Jun 24, 1848

Adams, John d. Jul 4, 1826
Andre, Carl b. Sep 16, 1935
Baker, Elbert Hall, II b. Jul 18, 1910
Cheever, John b. May 27, 1912
Dana, Bill b. Oct 5, 1924
Hancock, John d. Oct 8, 1793
Priscilla of Boston b. Dec 14, 1916
Randolph, Massachusetts
Freeman, Mary E Wilkins b. Oct 31, 1852
Reading, Massachusetts
DeMar, Clarence d. Jun 11, 1958
Park, Maud May Wood d. May 8, 1955
Revere, Massachusetts
Alger, Horatio b. Jan 13, 1832
Conigliaro, Tony (Anthony Richard)
  b. Jan 7, 1945
Macy, Bill b. May 18, 1922
Rockport, Massachusetts
Birnie, William Alfred Hart
  d. Sep 19, 1979
Kieran, John Francis d. Dec 10, 1981
Roxbury, Massachusetts
Abbott, Lyman b. Dec 18, 1835
Corson, Juliet b. Jan 14, 1841
Currier, Nathaniel b. Mar 27, 1813
Eliot, John d. May 20, 1690
Gibson, Charles Dana b. Sep 14, 1867
Hale, Edward Everett d. Jun 10, 1909
Langley, Samuel Pierpont b. Aug 22, 1834
Lowell, John d. May 6, 1802
McBurney, Charles b. Feb 17, 1845
O'Callahan, Joseph Timothy
  b. May 14, 1905
Warren, Joseph b. Jun 11, 1741
White, Paul Dudley b. Jun 6, 1886
Salem, Massachusetts
Atwood, Francis Clarke b. May 7, 1893
Benson, Frank Weston b. Mar 24, 1862
Benson, Frank Weston d. Nov 14, 1951
Bowditch, Nathaniel b. Mar 26, 1773
Bowker, R(ichard) R(ogers) b. Sep 4, 1848
Douglas, Paul Howard b. Mar 26, 1892
Fenollosa, Ernest Francisco
  b. Feb 18, 1853
Filene, Edward Albert b. Sep 3, 1860
Foote, Arthur William b. Mar 5, 1853
Gifford, Walter Sherman b. Jan 10, 1885
Glover, John b. Nov 5, 1753
Hawthorne, Nathaniel b. Jul 4, 1804
Heller, Goldie b.
Page, Charles Grafton b. Jan 25, 1812
Parker, George Swinnerton
  b. Dec 12, 1866
Peabody, Endicott b. May 30, 1857
Peirce, Benjamin b. Apr 4, 1809
Poulter, Thomas Charles b. Mar 3, 1897
Prescott, William Hickling b. May 4, 1796
Putnam, Israel b. Jan 7, 1718
Rogers, John b. Oct 30, 1829
Story, William Wetmore b. Feb 12, 1819

Very, Jones b. Aug 28, 1813
Very, Jones d. May 8, 1880
Salisbury, Massachusetts
Cushing, Caleb b. Jan 17, 1800
Sandwich, Massachusetts
Burgess, Thornton Waldo b. Jan 14, 1874
Swift, Gustavus Franklin b. Jun 24, 1839
Scituate, Massachusetts
Woodworth, Samuel b. Jan 13, 1784
Sharon, Massachusetts
Davis, Arthur Vining b. May 30, 1867
Gannett, Deborah Sampson
    d. Apr 29, 1827
Sheffield, Massachusetts
Barnard, Frederick Augustus Porter
    b. May 5, 1809
Shelburne Falls, Massachusetts
Gregory, Horace Victor d. Mar 11, 1982
Zaturenska, Marya d. Jan 19, 1982
Shrewsbury, Massachusetts
Earle, Ralph b. May 11, 1751
Snoquaimie, Massachusetts
Raines, Ella b. Aug 6, 1921
Somerville, Massachusetts
Armstrong, Harry b. Jul 22, 1879
Carle, Richard b. Jul 7, 1876
Greenough, Horatio d. Dec 18, 1852
Hadley, Henry Kimball b. Dec 20, 1871
Hovhaness, Alan b. Mar 8, 1911
Jackson, Charles Thomas d. Aug 28, 1880
South Attleboro, Massachusetts
Lincoln, Mary Johnson Bailey
    b. Jul 8, 1844
South Boston, Massachusetts
McCarthy, Tommy (Thomas Francis
    Michael) b. Jul 24, 1864
South Duxbury, Massachusetts
Davenport, Fanny Lily Gypsy
    d. Sep 26, 1898
South Hadley, Massachusetts
Mead, George Herbert b. Feb 27, 1863
South Lee, Massachusetts
Brown, Henry Billings b. Mar 2, 1836
South Weymouth, Massachusetts
Carsey, Marcia b. Nov 21, 1944
South Williamston, Massachusetts
Vanderbilt, William Henry d. Apr 14, 1981
Spencer, Massachusetts
Howe, Elias b. Jul 9, 1819
Springfield, Massachusetts
Abrams, Creighton Williams
    b. Sep 15, 1914
Appleseed, Johnny b. Sep 26, 1774
Beach, Alfred Ely b. Sep 1, 1826
Benjamin, Asher d. Jul 26, 1845
Birnie, William Alfred Hart
    b. Aug 4, 1910
Blackmur, Richard Palmer b. Jan 21, 1904
Bowles, Chester Bliss b. Apr 5, 1901
Bowles, Samuel, II b. Feb 9, 1826
Bowles, Samuel, II d. Jan 16, 1878

Bradley, Milton d. May 30, 1911
Breck, John Henry d. Feb 16, 1965
Buoniconti, Nick b. Dec 15, 1940
Ellis, Harry Bearse b. Dec 9, 1921
Gage, Harlow W b. Feb 6, 1911
Garand, John Cantius d. Feb 16, 1974
Gorman, Herbert Sherman b. Jan 1, 1893
Gravel, Mike b. May 13, 1930
Leary, Timothy Francis b. Oct 22, 1920
MacArthur, Arthur b. Jun 2, 1845
Maranville, "Rabbit" (Walter James
    Vincent) b. Nov 11, 1891
Merriam, Charles d. Jul 9, 1887
Morello, Joseph A b. Jul 17, 1928
O'Brien, Larry (Lawrence Francis)
    b. Jul 7, 1917
Powell, Eleanor b. Nov 21, 1912
Russell, Kurt (Von Vogel)
    b. Mar 17, 1951
Sanderson, Julia b. Aug 22, 1887
Sanderson, Julia d. Jan 27, 1975
Seuss, Doctor, pseud. b. Mar 2, 1904
Shore, Eddie d. Mar 16, 1985
Sterling, Massachusetts
Butterick, Ebenezer b. May 29, 1826
Stockbridge, Massachusetts
Bowker, R(ichard) R(ogers)
    d. Nov 12, 1933
Field, Cyrus West b. Nov 30, 1819
French, Daniel Chester d. Oct 7, 1931
Hopkins, Mark b. Feb 4, 1802
Niebuhr, Reinhold d. Jun 1, 1971
Rockwell, Norman d. Nov 8, 1978
Sedgwick, Catherine Maria
    b. Dec 28, 1789
Stoneham, Massachusetts
Lewis, Clarence Irving b. Apr 12, 1883
Sturbridge, Massachusetts
Marcy, William Learned b. Dec 12, 1786
Sutton, Massachusetts
Blanchard, Thomas b. Jun 24, 1788
Swampscott, Massachusetts
Hegan, Jim (James Edward)
    d. Jun 17, 1984
Thomson, Elihu d. Mar 13, 1937
Taunton, Massachusetts
Foster, William Zebulon b. Feb 25, 1881
O'Connor, Basil b. Jan 8, 1892
Tyngsboro, Massachusetts
Dole, Charles Minot b. Apr 18, 1899
Tyringham, Massachusetts
Howard, Sidney Coe d. Aug 23, 1939
Vineyard Haven, Massachusetts
Cornell, Katharine d. Jun 9, 1974
Haydn, Hiram Collins d. Dec 2, 1973
Wakefield, Massachusetts
Beebe, Lucius Morris b. Dec 9, 1902
Coon, Carleton Stevens b. Jun 23, 1904
Dellinger, David T (Dave)
    b. Aug 22, 1915
Grattan, Clinton Hartley b. Oct 19, 1902

Horovitz, Israel b. Mar 31, 1939
Little, Royal b. Mar 1, 1896
Volpe, John Anthony b. Dec 8, 1908
Wales, Massachusetts
Wales, Salem Howe b. Oct 4, 1825
Walpole Prison, Massachusetts
DeSalvo, Albert d. Dec 27, 1973
Waltham, Massachusetts
Bailey, F(rancis) Lee b. Jun 10, 1933
Howe, Clarence Decatur b. Jan 15, 1886
Warren, Austin b. Jul 4, 1899
Wilson, Kenneth Geddes b. Jun 8, 1936
Ware, Massachusetts
Cummings, "Candy" (William Arthur)
b. Oct 17, 1848
Landes, Bertha Ethel b. Oct 19, 1868
Packard, Elizabeth Parsons Ware
b. Dec 28, 1816
Watertown, Massachusetts
Briggs, Ellis Ormsbee b. Dec 1, 1899
Hosmer, Harriet Goodhue b. Oct 9, 1830
Hosmer, Harriet Goodhue d. Feb 21, 1908
Pratt, Charles b. Oct 2, 1830
Waverly, Massachusetts
Copeland, Charles Townsend
d. Jul 24, 1952
Wayland, Massachusetts
Child, Lydia Maria d. Oct 22, 1880
Webster, Massachusetts
Warnke, Paul Culliton b. Jan 31, 1920
Wellesley, Massachusetts
Baldwin, Roger Nash b. Jan 21, 1884
Bates, Katherine Lee d. Mar 28, 1929
Kronenberger, Louis d. Apr 30, 1980
Squier, Billy b. May 12, 1950
Wellfleet, Massachusetts
Crowell, Luther Childs d. Sep 16, 1903
West Barnstable, Massachusetts
Otis, James b. Feb 5, 1725
West Boylston, Massachusetts
Bigelow, Erastus Brigham b. Apr 2, 1814
West Brookfield, Massachusetts
Merriam, Charles b. 1806
Stone, Lucy b. Aug 13, 1818
West Dennis, Massachusetts
Crowell, Luther Childs b. Sep 7, 1840
West Newton, Massachusetts
Jewett, Henry d. Jun 24, 1930
Perkins, Osgood (James Ridley Osgood)
b. May 16, 1892
Weeks, Sinclair b. Jun 15, 1893
West Roxbury, Massachusetts
Sedgwick, Catherine Maria d. Jul 31, 1867
West Springfield, Massachusetts
Day, Benjamin Henry b. Apr 10, 1810
Durocher, Leo Ernest b. Jul 27, 1906
Westboro, Massachusetts
Forbes, Esther b. Jun 28, 1894
Whitney, Eli b. Dec 8, 1765

Westfield, Massachusetts
Andrews, James Frederick b. Oct 8, 1936
Taylor, Edward d. 1729
Westford, Massachusetts
Bradley, Pat(ricia Ellen) b. Mar 24, 1951
Westminster, Massachusetts
Miles, Nelson A b. Aug 8, 1839
Weston, Massachusetts
Ashbrook, Joseph d. Aug 4, 1980
Sexton, Anne Harvey d. Oct 4, 1974
Westport, Massachusetts
Cuffe, Paul d. Sep 9, 1817
Weymouth, Massachusetts
Adams, Abigail Smith b. Nov 11, 1744
Whitman, Massachusetts
Spellman, Francis Joseph b. May 4, 1889
Wianno, Massachusetts
Kroger, Bernard Henry d. Jul 21, 1938
Underwood, John Thomas d. Jul 2, 1937
Williamstown, Massachusetts
Baxter, James Phinney, III d. Jun 17, 1975
Hopkins, Mark d. Jun 17, 1887
Perry, Bliss b. Nov 25, 1860
Winchendon, Massachusetts
Bowker, Albert Hosmer b. Sep 8, 1919
Winchester, Massachusetts
Welch, Robert Henry Winborne, Jr.
d. Jan 6, 1984
Winthrop, Massachusetts
Whorf, Richard b. Jun 4, 1906
Wollaston, Massachusetts
DeWolfe, Billy b. Feb 18, 1907
Gordon, Ruth b. Oct 30, 1896
Woods Hole, Massachusetts
Baird, Spencer Fullerton d. Aug 19, 1887
Worcester, Massachusetts
Bancroft, George b. Oct 3, 1800
Behrman, S(amuel) N(athaniel)
b. Jun 9, 1893
Bemis, Samuel Flagg b. Oct 20, 1891
Benchley, Robert Charles b. Sep 15; 1889
Bishop, Elizabeth b. Feb 8, 1911
Burkett, Jesse Cail d. May 27, 1953
Fidrych, Mark b. Aug 14, 1954
Forbes, Esther d. Aug 12, 1967
Foster, Abigail Kelley d. Jan 14, 1887
Fuller, Samuel b. Aug 12, 1911
Gibbs, Georgia b. Aug 26, 1926
Goddard, Robert Hutchings b. Oct 5, 1882
Hackett, Charles b. Nov 4, 1889
Hamilton, Billy (William Robert)
d. Dec 16, 1940
Harrison, Wallace Kirkman
b. Sep 28, 1895
Hoffman, Abbie (Abbott) b. Nov 30, 1936
Julian, "Doggie" (Alvin T) d. Jul 28, 1967
Kunitz, Stanley Jasspon b. Jul 29, 1905
Mekka, Eddie b. Jun 14, 1952
O'Callahan, Joseph Timothy
d. Mar 18, 1964
Olson, Charles b. Dec 27, 1910

Price, Irving L b. Sep 21, 1884
Shannon, William Vincent b. Aug 24, 1927
Stone, Lewis b. Nov 15, 1879
Thomas, Isaiah d. Apr 4, 1831
Thompson, Edward Herbert
  b. Sep 28, 1856
Wesson, Daniel Baird b. May 25, 1825
Worchester, Massachusetts
Dixon, Roland Burrage b. Nov 6, 1875
Earle, Alice Morse b. Apr 27, 1851
Hayes, John Michael b. May 11, 1919
Tappan, Eva March d. Jan 29, 1930
Worthington, Massachusetts
Stankiewicz, Richard Peter
  d. Mar 27, 1983

MICHIGAN

Crippen, Hawley Harvey b. 1862
Adrian, Michigan
Geddes, Norman Bel b. Apr 27, 1893
Albion, Michigan
Fisher, Mary Frances Kennedy
  b. Jul 3, 1908
Ann Arbor, Michigan
Angell, James Burrill d. Apr 1, 1916
Bennett, Harry Herbert b. Jan 17, 1892
Crisler, "Fritz" (Herbert Orin)
  d. Aug 19, 1982
Curtis, Heber Doust d. Jan 9, 1942
Cuyler, "Kiki" (Hazen Shirley)
  d. Feb 11, 1950
Denikin, Anton Ivanovich d. Aug 8, 1947
Green, Constance Windsor McLaughlin
  b. Aug 21, 1897
Hayden, Robert Earl d. Feb 25, 1980
Hewlett, William b. May 20, 1913
Landes, Bertha Ethel d. Nov 29, 1943
Leach, Rick (Richard Max)
  b. May 4, 1957
McIntyre, Frank J d. Jun 8, 1949
Monaghan, Tom b. Mar 25, 1937
Pop, Iggy b. 1947
Saarinen, Eero d. Sep 1, 1961
Seger, Bob b. May 6, 1945
Vickers, Martha b. May 28, 1925
Yost, Fielding Harris d. Aug 20, 1946
Atwood, Michigan
Beach, Rex Ellingwood b. Dec 1, 1877
Battle Creek, Michigan
Barron, Clarence Walker d. Oct 2, 1928
Dett, Robert Nathaniel d. Oct 2, 1943
Hutton, Betty b. Feb 26, 1921
Kellogg, John Harvey b. Feb 26, 1852
Kellogg, John Harvey d. Jan 16, 1943
Kellogg, Will Keith b. Apr 7, 1860
Kellogg, Will Keith d. Oct 6, 1951
Martin, Dick b. Jan 30, 1923
Oliver, Sy (Melvin James) b. Dec 17, 1910
Sheehan, Joseph Green b. May 27, 1918
Truth, Sojourner d. Nov 26, 1883

Bay City, Michigan
Billington, Ray Allen b. Sep 28, 1903
Madonna b. Aug 16, 1959
Belding, Michigan
Ford, Kathleen DuRoss b. Feb 11, 1940
Benton Harbor, Michigan
Johnson, Arte b. Jan 20, 1934
Berkley, Michigan
Goldsmith, Fred Ernest d. Mar 28, 1939
Berlin, Michigan
Cole, Edward Nicholas b. Sep 17, 1909
Birmingham, Michigan
Young, Sheila b. Oct 14, 1950
Bloomfield Hills, Michigan
Coughlin, Father (Charles Edward)
  d. Oct 27, 1979
Gordon, Lou d. May 24, 1977
Polk, Ralph Lane d. Feb 9, 1984
Runkle, Janice b. 1953
Saarinen, Eliel d. Jul 1, 1950
Boyne City, Michigan
Tebbel, John William b. Nov 16, 1912
Brooklyn, Michigan
Ingels, Marty b. Mar 9, 1936
Calumet, Michigan
Smith, Paul Joseph b. Oct 30, 1906
Capac, Michigan
Tucker, Preston Thomas b. Sep 21, 1903
Cass City, Michigan
MacPhail, Larry (Leland Stanford, Sr.)
  b. Feb 3, 1890
Central Lake, Michigan
Hathaway, Starke R b. Aug 22, 1903
Cheboygan, Michigan
Ford, Benson d. Jul 27, 1978
Humphrey, George Magoffin
  b. Mar 8, 1890
Chinook, Michigan
Maney, Richard b. Jun 11, 1892
Coldwater, Michigan
McDevitt, Ruth b. Sep 13, 1895
Dearborn, Michigan
Ford, Henry d. Apr 7, 1947
James, Art b. Oct 15,
Dearborn Township, Michigan
Ford, Henry b. Jul 30, 1863
Deerfield, Michigan
Thomas, Danny b. Jan 6, 1914
Detroit, Michigan
Adams, Jack (John James) d. May 1, 1968
Algren, Nelson b. Mar 28, 1909
Allen, Byron b. Apr 22, 1961
Allen, George b. Apr 29, 1922
Ally, Carl Joseph b. Mar 31, 1924
Altobelli, Joe (Joseph Salvatore)
  b. May 26, 1932
Atterbury, Grosvenor b. Jul 7, 1869
Bailey, James Anthony b. Jul 4, 1847
Ballard, Florence b. Jun 30, 1943
Ballard, Florence d. Feb 22, 1976
Ballard, Hank b. Nov 18, 1936

Levine, Philip b. Jan 10, 1928
Liggett, Louis Kroh b. Apr 4, 1875
Lindbergh, Charles Augustus
  b. Feb 4, 1902
Lipscomb, Eugene b. Nov 9, 1931
Lyons, Sophie Levy d. May 8, 1924
McCoy, Charles d. Apr 18, 1940
McCrory, Milton b. Feb 7, 1962
McHale, John Joseph b. Sep 21, 1921
McKechnie, Donna b. 1943
McMahon, Ed(ward Lee) b. Mar 6, 1923
Melchers, Gari b. Aug 11, 1860
Milner, Martin Sam b. Dec 28, 1931
Mitchell, Guy b. Feb 22, 1927
Mitchell, John Newton b. Sep 15, 1913
Mitchelson, Marvin M(orris)
  b. May 7, 1928
Moeller, Philip d. Nov 23, 1958
Morgan, Harry b. Apr 10, 1915
Moriarty, Michael b. Apr 5, 1942
Morton, Joy b. Sep 27, 1855
Muhammad, Wallace D b. Oct 30, 1933
Murphy, Frank d. Jul 17, 1949
Nederlander, James Morton
  b. Mar 21, 1922
Newberry, John Stoughton d. Jan 2, 1887
Newhouser, Harold (Hal) b. Nov 20, 1921
Nicholas, Denise b. Jul 12, 1944
Nugent, Ted b. 1949
Paciorek, Tom (Thomas Marian)
  b. Nov 2, 1946
Parker, Ray, Jr. b. May 1, 1954
Payne, Freda b. Sep 19, 1945
Payton, Lawrence b. 1930
Peete, Calvin b. Jul 18, 1943
Peppard, George b. Oct 1, 1928
Pierrot, George Francis d. Feb 16, 1980
Polk, Ralph Lane b. Jul 21, 1911
Quatro, Suzi b. Jun 3, 1950
Quine, Richard b. Nov 12, 1920
Radner, Gilda b. Jun 28, 1946
Redhead, Hugh McCulloch d. 1975
Reese, Della b. Jul 6, 1932
Reeves, Martha b. Jul 18, 1941
Reulbach, Ed(ward Marvin) b. Dec 4, 1882
Reuther, Roy d. Jan 10, 1968
Richard, Gabriel d. Sep 13, 1832
Robinson, "Smokey" (William, Jr.)
  b. Feb 19, 1940
Robinson, "Sugar" Ray b. May 3, 1920
Rockwell b. Mar 15, 1964
Rompollo, Dominic b. Jan 24, 1935
Roney, William Chapoton, Jr.
  b. Dec 19, 1924
Ross, Diana b. Mar 26, 1944
Roundfield, Dan(ny T) b. May 26, 1953
Ryder, Mitch b. Feb 26, 1945
Sachs, Eddy (Edward Julius)
  b. May 28, 1917
Satovsky, Abraham b. Oct 15, 1907
Schenck, Joe (Joseph T) d. Jun 28, 1930

Schlussel, Mark Edward b. Dec 14, 1940
Schwartz, Alan Earl b. Dec 21, 1925
Selleck, Tom b. Jan 29, 1945
Shapero, Nate S b. Sep 17, 1892
Silliphant, Stirling Dale b. Jan 16, 1918
Sillman, Leonard b. May 9, 1908
Sissman, L(ouis) E(dward) b. Jan 1, 1928
Skerritt, Tom (Thomas Roy)
  b. Aug 25, 1933
Slovik, Eddie (Edward Donald) b. 1920
Smith, Horton d. Oct 15, 1963
Smith, Margaret b. Feb 27, 1939
Souther, J(ohn) D(avid) b.
Stein, Herbert b. Aug 27, 1916
Stevens, Roger L b. Mar 12, 1910
Stritch, Elaine b. Feb 2, 1928
Stroh, Peter W b. Dec 18, 1927
Stubbs, Levi b.
Sturtzel, Jane Levington b. Jun 22, 1903
Tallent, Garry Wayne b. Oct 27, 1949
Talman, William b. Feb 4, 1915
Tanana, Frank Daryl b. Jul 3, 1953
Thomas, Marlo b. Nov 21, 1938
Thompson, Sam(uel Luther)
  d. Nov 7, 1922
Tomlin, "Lily" (Mary Jean) b. Sep 1, 1939
Trumbull, John d. May 11, 1831
Vanbiesbrouck, John b. Sep 4, 1963
Vesco, Robert Lee b. Dec 4, 1935
VonTilzer, Harry b. Jul 8, 1872
Wagner, Robert John, Jr. b. Feb 10, 1930
Wakefield, Dick (Richard Cummings)
  d. Aug 26, 1985
Walker, Hiram d. Jan 12, 1899
Washington, Dinah d. Dec 14, 1963
Welch, Bob (Robert Lynn) b. Nov 3, 1956
Wells, Mary b. May 13, 1943
Whiting, Margaret b. Jul 22, 1924
Williams, G Mennen b. Feb 23, 1911
Wilson, Jackie b. Jun 9, 1932
Wolfgang, Myra K d. Apr 12, 1976
Yamasaki, Minoru d. Feb 6, 1986
Yawkey, Thomas Austin b. Feb 21, 1903

Duluth, Michigan
Crystal, Lester M b. Sep 13, 1934

East Lansing, Michigan
Fairchild, David Grandison b. Apr 7, 1869
Smith, A(rthur) J(ames) M(arshall)
  d. Nov 21, 1980

East Tawas, Michigan
Clark, Marion L d. Sep 4, 1977

Eaton Rapids, Michigan
Curtice, Harlow Herbert b. Aug 15, 1893

Edmore, Michigan
Blough, Glenn Orlando b. Sep 5, 1907

Evart, Michigan
Voelker, Paul Frederick b. Sep 30, 1875

Farmington, Michigan
Dawber, Pam b. Oct 18, 1951

Fenton, Michigan
Lyons, Dorothy (Marawee) b. Dec 4, 1907

Lansing, Michigan
Baker, Ray Stannard b. Apr 17, 1870
Chapin, Roy Dikeman b. Feb 23, 1880
Davis, Rennie b. May 23, 1941
Johnson, Earvin b. Aug 14, 1959
Lapeer, Michigan
DeAngeli, Marguerite b. Mar 14, 1889
Lauriam, Michigan
Gipp, George b. Feb 18, 1895
Laurium, Michigan
Ross, Percy b. 1916
Lowell, Michigan
Graham, Ernest Robert b. Aug 22, 1866
Ludington, Michigan
Johnson, Walter (Thomas Walter)
    d. Jun 14, 1985
Marquette, Jacques, Pere d. May 18, 1675
McDole, Carol b. Dec 20, 1936
Mackinac Island, Michigan
Day, William Rufus d. Jul 9, 1923
Madison, Michigan
LaFollete, Philip Fox d. Aug 18, 1965
Marquette, Michigan
Humes, Harold Louis b. Jan 31, 1900
Kidder, Alfred Vincent b. Oct 29, 1885
Marshall, Michigan
Bellairs, John b. Jan 17, 1938
Mendon, Michigan
Estes, E(lliott) M(arantette) b. Jan 7, 1916
Midland, Michigan
Jarvik, Robert Koffler b. May 11, 1946
Monroe, Michigan
Brinkley, Christie b. Feb 2, 1953
Cantrick, Robert b. Dec 8, 1917
Custer, Elizabeth Bacon b. Apr 8, 1842
Sneider, Vernon John b. Oct 6, 1916
Sneider, Vernon John d. May 1, 1981
Mount Clemens, Michigan
Smith, Christopher Columbus
    d. Sep 9, 1939
Mount Pleasant, Michigan
Pohl, Dan(ny Joe) b. Apr 1, 1955
Muskegon, Michigan
Bakker, Jim (James Orsen) b. Jan 2, 1939
Curtis, Heber Doust b. Jun 27, 1872
Morrall, Earl E b. May 17, 1934
Nelson, Don(ald Arvid) b. May 15, 1940
Stanton, Frank b. Mar 20, 1908
New Era, Michigan
Aardema, Verna Norberg b. Jun 6, 1911
Niles, Michigan
Dodge, Horace Elgin b. May 17, 1868
Dodge, John Francis b. Oct 25, 1864
Lardner, Ring(gold Wilmer)
    b. Mar 3, 1885
North Dorr, Michigan
Bieber, Owen Frederick b. Dec 28, 1929
Norwood, Michigan
Darling, Jay Norwood b. Oct 21, 1876

Oscoda, Michigan
Abbott, Jack (Rufus Jack Henry)
    b. Jan 21, 1944
Owosso, Michigan
Bentley, Alvin Morell d. Apr 10, 1969
Curwood, James Oliver b. Jun 12, 1878
Curwood, James Oliver d. Aug 13, 1927
Dewey, Thomas Edmund b. Mar 24, 1902
Oxford, Michigan
Beemer, Brace d. Mar 1, 1965
Pellston, Michigan
Reuther, Walter Philip d. May 10, 1970
Petoskey, Michigan
Catton, Bruce b. Oct 9, 1899
Mischakoff, Mischa d. Feb 1, 1981
Pinckney, Michigan
Swarthout, Glendon Fred b. Apr 8, 1918
Pinconning, Michigan
Summerfield, Arthur Ellsworth
    b. Mar 17, 1899
Plymouth, Michigan
Hulce, Thomas b. Dec 6, 1953
Kirk, Russell b. Oct 19, 1918
Pontiac, Michigan
Gibson, Kirk Harold b. May 28, 1957
Hagopian, Louis Thomas b. Jun 1, 1925
Jones, Thad(deus Joseph) b. Mar 28, 1923
McCafferty, Don d. Jul 28, 1974
Thomas, Pinklon b. 1957
Port Huron, Michigan
Kalmbach, Herbert Warren
    b. Oct 19, 1921
Moore, Colleen b. Aug 19, 1902
Sanborn, Pitts b. Oct 19, 1878
Portland, Michigan
Kelland, Clarence Budington
    b. Jul 11, 1881
Redford, Michigan
Kiel, Richard b.
Rochester, Michigan
Kresge, Stanley Sebastian d. Jun 30, 1985
Romulus, Michigan
Lau, Charlie (Charles Richard)
    b. Apr 12, 1933
Royal Oak, Michigan
Breech, Ernest Robert d. Jul 3, 1978
Dawkins, Peter M b. 1941
George, Christopher b. Feb 25, 1929
Gordon, John F d. Jan 6, 1978
Hayden, Tom (Thomas Emmett)
    b. Dec 11, 1939
Muncey, Bill (William) b. Nov 12, 1928
Saginaw, Michigan
Armstrong, Robert b. Nov 20, 1896
Avery, Sewell b. Nov 4, 1874
Begle, Edward G(riffith) b. Nov 27, 1914
Jones, Howard Mumford b. Apr 16, 1892
Lavigne, "Kid" (George) b. Dec 6, 1869
McCoy, Tim(othy John Fitzgerald)
    b. Apr 10, 1891
Roethke, Theodore b. May 25, 1908

Tucker, Lem(uel) b. May 26, 1938
Wonder, Stevie b. May 13, 1951
Saint Clair, Michigan
Smith, Christopher Columbus
    b. May 20, 1861
Saint Ignace, Michigan
Fitch, Aubrey b. Jan 11, 1884
Saint John's, Michigan
Burnett, Leo b. Oct 21, 1891
Saint Joseph, Michigan
Chessman, Caryl Whittier b. May 27, 1921
South Haven, Michigan
Ludwig, Daniel Keith b. Jun 24, 1897
Spring Lake, Michigan
McCay, Winsor b. Sep 26, 1869
Sturgis, Michigan
Mesta, Perle Skirvin b. Oct 12, 1891
Three Oaks, Michigan
Donner, Frederic Garrett b. 1902
Three Rivers, Michigan
Collingwood, Charles Cummings
    b. Jun 4, 1917
Traverse City, Michigan
Hagen, Walter Charles d. Oct 5, 1969
Miller, Max b. Feb 9, 1899
Milliken, William G(rawn)
    b. Mar 26, 1922
Power, Eugene Barnum b. Jun 4, 1905
Wayne, David b. Jan 30, 1914
Union City, Michigan
Hubbard, Orville Liscum b. Apr 2, 1903
Odlum, Floyd Bostwick b. Mar 30, 1892
Vulcan, Michigan
Armstrong, Charlotte b. May 2, 1905
Washtenaw County, Michigan
Arnow, Harriette Louisa Simpson
    d. Mar 22, 1986
Waterloo, Michigan
Kearns, Jack b. Aug 17, 1882
West Branch, Michigan
Howell, Albert S b. Apr 17, 1879
White Lake, Michigan
Adams, Frank Ramsay d. Oct 8, 1963
Wyandotte, Michigan
Majors, Lee b. Apr 23, 1940
Ypsilanti, Michigan
Bugas, John Stephen d. Dec 2, 1982
Pitkin, Walter Boughton b. Feb 6, 1878
Tucker, Preston Thomas d. Jan 7, 1956
Zeeland, Michigan
DeKruif, Paul Henry b. Mar 2, 1890

MINNESOTA

Bok, Hannes Vajn b. Jul 2, 1914
Charmoli, Tony b.
Culligan, Emmett J b. 1893
Drew, Richard G b. 1899
Kronhausen, Phyllis Carmen
    b. Jan 26, 1929
Moran, "Bugs" (George C) b. 1893

Rader, Dotson b. 1942
Younger, Bob (Robert) d. 1889
Younger, Jim (James) d. 1902
Aitkin, Minnesota
William, Warren b. Dec 2, 1895
Albany, Minnesota
Rausch, James Stevens b. Sep 4, 1928
Albert Lea, Minnesota
Carlson, Richard b. Apr 29, 1912
Ross, Marion b. Oct 25, 1928
Alexandria, Minnesota
Hanson, Duane Elwood b. Jan 17, 1925
Anoka, Minnesota
Keillor, Garrison (Gary Edward)
    b. Aug 7, 1942
Atwater, Minnesota
Anderson, Vernon Ellsworth
    b. Jun 15, 1908
Aurora, Minnesota
Paulucci, Jeno Francisco b. Jul 7, 1918
Austin, Minnesota
Eberhart, Richard b. Apr 5, 1904
Bemidji, Minnesota
Russell, Jane b. Jun 21, 1921
Brainerd, Minnesota
Bender, "Chief" (Charles Albert)
    b. May 5, 1884
Donovan, Hedley Williams
    b. May 24, 1914
Breckenridge, Minnesota
Hodgson, Richa?d Sargeant
    b. Oct 18, 1924
Carson Lake, Minnesota
Perpich, Rudy George b. Jun 27, 1928
Ceylon, Minnesota
Mondale, Walter Frederick b. Jan 5, 1928
Cloquet, Minnesota
Lange, Jessica b. Apr 20, 1949
Powers, Anne b. May 7, 1913
Dafur, Minnesota
Stoutenburg, Adrien Pearl b. Dec 1, 1916
Dawson, Minnesota
Hodgson, James Day b. Dec 3, 1915
Duluth, Minnesota
Dempster, Carol b. 1901
Rubloff, Arthur b. Jun 25, 1902
Elmer, Minnesota
Gruber, Frank b. Feb 2, 1904
Eveleth, Minnesota
Pavelich, Mark b. Feb 28, 1958
Fergus Falls, Minnesota
Albertson, Frank b. Feb 2, 1909
Sterrett, Cliff b. Dec 12, 1883
Graceville, Minnesota
Conway, Jack b. Jul 17, 1887
Grand Rapids, Minnesota
Baker, Bill (William Robert)
    b. Nov 29, 1956
Garland, Judy b. Jun 10, 1922
Granite Falls, Minnesota
Volstead, Andrew J d. Jan 20, 1947

Grants, Minnesota
Todd, Mike (Michael) d. Mar 22, 1958
Halstad, Minnesota
Henderson, "Skitch" (Cedric)
b. Jan 27, 1918
Hawley, Minnesota
Hauge, Gabriel b. Mar 7, 1914
Hibbing, Minnesota
Bugliosi, Vincent T b. Aug 18, 1934
Dylan, Bob b. May 24, 1941
Maris, Roger Eugene b. Sep 10, 1934
Humboldt, Minnesota
Briggs, Austin Eugene b. Sep 8, 1908
Iron, Minnesota
Hall, Gus b. Oct 8, 1910
Keewatin, Minnesota
Cappeletti, "Duke" (Gino) b. Mar 26, 1934
Kenyon, Minnesota
Volstead, Andrew J b. Oct 31, 1860
LeSueur, Minnesota
Mayo, William James b. Jun 29, 1861
Litchfield, Minnesota
Sondergaard, Gale b. Feb 15, 1899
Lutsen, Minnesota
Nelson, Cindy b. Aug 19, 1955
Luverne, Minnesota
Wiggins, J(ames) R(ussell) b. Dec 4, 1903
Madison, Minnesota
Bly, Robert Elwood b. Dec 23, 1926
Mahnomen, Minnesota
Guyon, Joe b. Nov 26, 1892
Maine, Minnesota
Douglas, William Orville b. Oct 16, 1898
Mankato, Minnesota
Bate, Walter Jackson b. May 23, 1918
Colfax, Schuyler d. Jan 13, 1885
Marshall, Minnesota
Burchard, John Ely b. Dec 8, 1898
Minneapoils, Minnesota
Bayne, Beverly Pearl b. Nov 22, 1894
Minneapolis, Minnesota
Andrews, LaVerne b. Jul 6, 1915
Andrews, Maxine b. Jan 3, 1918
Andrews, Patti (Patricia) b. Feb 16, 1920
Arness, James b. May 26, 1923
Ayres, Lew b. Dec 28, 1908
Bakke, Allan Paul b. Feb 4, 1940
Beach, Joseph Warren d. Aug 13, 1957
Bell, James Ford d. May 7, 1961
Benton, William b. Apr 1, 1900
Berg, Patty (Patricia Jane) b. Feb 13, 1918
Berrigan, Philip Francis b. Oct 5, 1923
Berryman, John d. Jan 7, 1972
Blumenfeld, Isadore b. 1901
Brinig, Myron b. Dec 22, 1900
Britz, Jerilyn b. Jan 1, 1943
Brousse, Amy Elizabeth Thorpe b. 1910
Brown, Charlie d. Dec 5, 1983
Bruce, Virginia b. Sep 29, 1910
Chorzempa, Daniel Walter b. Dec 7, 1944
Christiansen, Olaf b. 1901

Chute, Beatrice Joy b. Jan 3, 1913
Chute, Marchette Gaylord b. Aug 16, 1909
Cowles, John, Sr. d. Feb 25, 1983
Crosby, Sumner McKnight b. Jul 29, 1909
Dahl, Arlene b. Aug 11, 1927
Doar, John b. Dec 3, 1921
Donnelly, Ignatius d. Jan 1, 1901
Engstrom, Elmer William b. Aug 25, 1901
Fraser, Donald Mackay b. Feb 20, 1924
Frawley, Dennis b. Jul 12, 1942
Freeman, Orville Lothrop b. May 9, 1918
Getty, J(ean) Paul b. Dec 15, 1892
Gilliam, Terry b. Nov 22, 1940
Gillman, Sidney b. 1911
Graves, Peter b. Mar 18, 1926
Hathaway, Starke R d. Jul 4, 1984
Heffelfinger, "Pudge" (William Walter)
b. Dec 20, 1867
Hill, George Roy b. Dec 20, 1922
Lamb, Gil b. Jun 14, 1906
Larson, Reed David b. Jul 30, 1956
Laughlin, Tom b. 1938
Leadon, Bernie b. Jul 19, 1947
Levin, Harry Tuchman b. Jul 18, 1912
Lewis, Meade Anderson Lux
d. Jun 7, 1964
Lord, Mary Pillsbury b. Nov 14, 1904
MacGregor, Clark b. Jul 12, 1922
Masterton, Bill (William) d. Jan 15, 1968
Meeker, Ralph b. Nov 21, 1920
Motley, Arthur Harrison b. Aug 22, 1900
Norstad, Lauris b. Mar 24, 1907
Parks, Gordon, Jr. b. 1935
Pegler, Westbrook b. Aug 2, 1894
Piccard, Jean Felix d. Jan 28, 1963
Piccard, Jeannette Ridlon d. May 17, 1981
Pillsbury, Charles Alfred d. Sep 17, 1899
Pillsbury, John Sargent b. Dec 6, 1878
Pillsbury, John Sargent d. Oct 18, 1901
Pillsbury, Philip Winston b. Apr 16, 1903
Pillsbury, Philip Winston d. Jun 14, 1984
Prince b. Jun 7, 1958
Ramsey, Mike (Michael Allen)
b. Dec 3, 1960
Saint Cyr, Lillian b. Jun 3, 1917
Salisbury, Harrison Evans b. Nov 14, 1908
Schulz, Charles Monroe b. Nov 26, 1922
Schumann, Walter d. Aug 21, 1958
Seaton, Frederick Andrew d. Jan 17, 1974
Simms, Hilda b. Apr 15, 1920
Stoll, George b. May 7, 1905
Sturtzel, Howard Allison b. Jun 25, 1894
Todd, Mike (Michael) b. Jun 2, 1907
Tyler, Anne b. Oct 25, 1941
Vessey, John William, Jr. b. Jun 29, 1922
Walter, Cyril b. Sep 16, 1915
Wilkinson, "Bud" (Charles)
b. Apr 23, 1916
Youngdahl, Luther W b. May 29, 1896

Minnesota City, Minnesota
Firestone, Idabelle Smith b. Nov 10, 1874

Minnesota Lakes, Minnesota
Keogan, George b. Mar 8, 1890
Moorhead, Minnesota
Comstock, Ada Louise b. Dec 11, 1876
Magnuson, Warren Grant b. Apr 12, 1905
Powers, Dudley b. Jun 25, 1911
Nashwauk, Minnesota
Gilruth, Robert Rowe b. Oct 8, 1913
New Ulm, Minnesota
Gag, Wanda b. May 11, 1893
Hedren, "Tippi" (Natalie Kay)
b. Jan 19, 1935
Ulric, Lenore b. Jul 21, 1894
Northfield, Minnesota
Chase, Sylvia b. Feb 23, 1938
Roelvaag, O(le) E(dvart) d. Nov 5, 1931
Rolvaag, Karl b. Jul 18, 1913
Rolvaag, Ole Edvart d. Nov 5, 1931
Odin Township, Minnesota
Laingen, (Lowell) Bruce b. Aug 6, 1922
Olivia, Minnesota
Winsor, Kathleen b. Oct 16, 1916
Owatonna, Minnesota
Marshall, E G (Edda Gunnar)
b. Jun 18, 1910
Pipestone, Minnesota
Petersen, Donald Eugene b. Sep 4, 1926
Steen, Roger b. Nov 13, 1949
Renville, Minnesota
Faralla, Dana (Dorothy W)
b. Aug 4, 1909
Rochester, Minnesota
Connolly, Mike d. Nov 19, 1966
Culver, John C b. Aug 8, 1932
Dow, Herbert Henry d. Oct 15, 1930
Harrah, Bill (William Fisk)
d. Jun 30, 1978
Mayo, Charles Horace b. Jul 19, 1865
Mayo, William James d. Jul 28, 1939
Moorehead, Agnes d. Apr 20, 1974
O'Malley, Walter Francis d. Aug 9, 1979
Roseau, Minnesota
Bergland, Bob (Robert Selmer)
b. Jul 22, 1928
Broten, Neal Lamoy b. Nov 29, 1959
Saint Cloud, Minnesota
Durenberger, David Ferdinand
b. Aug 19, 1934
Marty, Martin d. Sep 19, 1896
Shaughnessy, Clark Daniel b. Mar 6, 1892
Young, Gig b. Nov 4, 1913
Saint Paul, Minnesota
Abel, Walter Charles b. Jun 6, 1898
Anderson, Loni b. Aug 5, 1946
Anderson, Rich b. Aug 1, 1947
Anderson, Wendell Richard b. Feb 1, 1933
Ashley, Merrill b. 1950
Boyle, Kay b. Feb 19, 1903
Brooks, Herb(ert Paul) b. Aug 5, 1937
Burger, Warren Earl b. Sep 17, 1907
Calvin, Melvin b. Apr 8, 1911

Charney, Nicolas Herman b. May 11, 1941
Colby, William Egan b. Jan 4, 1920
Cushman, Robert Everton, Jr.
b. Dec 24, 1914
Davis, Joan b. Jun 29, 1907
Decter, Midge b. Jul 25, 1927
Demarest, William b. Feb 27, 1892
Dix, Richard b. Jul 18, 1894
Farrell, Mike b. Feb 6, 1939
Fawcett, Wilford Hamilton, Jr.
b. Aug 1, 1909
Fitzgerald, F(rancis) Scott (Key)
b. Sep 24, 1896
Gates, Larry b. Sep 24, 1915
Gibbons, Tom b. Mar 22, 1891
Gibbons, Tom d. Nov 19, 1960
Goffstein, Marilyn b. Dec 20, 1940
Greaza, Walter N b. Jan 1, 1897
Hill, James Jerome d. May 29, 1916
Janaszak, Steve b. Jan 7, 1957
Kellogg, Frank Billings d. Dec 21, 1937
Lee, Pinky b. 1916
Lilly, John C b. Jan 6, 1915
Manship, Paul b. Dec 25, 1885
Martin, Homer Dodge d. Feb 12, 1897
McClanahan, Rob b. Jan 9, 1958
Miller, Carl S d. Apr 20, 1986
Millett, Kate b. Sep 14, 1934
Morris, Jack (John Scott) b. May 16, 1956
Mueller, Reuben Herbert b. Jun 2, 1897
Neiman, LeRoy b. Jun 8, 1926
Ohman, Jack b. 1960
Oppenheim, James b. May 24, 1882
Paulson, Donald Lowell b. Sep 14, 1912
Ross, David b. Jun 17, 1922
Shulman, Max b. Mar 14, 1919
Solomon, Izler b. Jan 11, 1910
Stratton, William R b. Jun 6, 1934
Swanberg, William Andrew
b. Nov 23, 1907
Wallace, DeWitt b. Nov 12, 1889
Weyerhaeuser, Frederick Edward
d. Oct 18, 1945
Winfield, Dave (David Mark)
b. Oct 3, 1951
Yurka, Blanche b. Jun 19, 1887
Saratoga, Minnesota
Del Ray, Lester Ramon Alvarez
b. Jun 2, 1915
Sauk Centre, Minnesota
Lewis, Sinclair b. Feb 7, 1885
Shakopee, Minnesota
Stans, Maurice Hubert b. Mar 22, 1908
Stewartville, Minnesota
Sears, Richard Warren b. Dec 7, 1863
Still Water, Minnesota
Sullivan, C(harles) Gardner
b. Sep 18, 1886
Sunrise, Minnesota
Widmark, Richard b. Dec 26, 1914

Sunrise City, Minnesota
Lowden, Frank O(rren) b. Jan 26, 1861
Virginia, Minnesota
Berrigan, Daniel J b. May 9, 1921
Walker, Minnesota
Hemingway, Mary Welsh b. Apr 5, 1908
Warroad, Minnesota
Christian, Dave b. May 12, 1959
Waterville, Minnesota
Dehn, Adolf Arthur b. Nov 22, 1895
Watkins, Minnesota
McCarthy, Eugene Joseph b. Mar 29, 1916
Waverly, Minnesota
Humphrey, Hubert Horatio, Jr.
　d. Jan 13, 1978
West St. Paul, Minnesota
Stassen, Harold Edward b. Apr 13, 1907
Willow River, Minnesota
Nevers, Ernie (Ernest A) b. Jun 11, 1903
Winona, Minnesota
Fraser, James Earle b. Nov 4, 1876
Worthington, Minnesota
Davis, Mary L b. Mar 21, 1935
Zumbrota, Minnesota
Beck, C(harles) C(larence) b. Jun 8, 1910

MISSISSIPPI

Gaines, Steve d. Oct 20, 1977
Hamer, Fannie Lou Townsend b. 1917
Larue, Frederick Chaney b. 1928
Van Zant, Ronnie (Ronald)
　d. Oct 20, 1977
Williams, Milan b. 1947
Aberdeen, Mississippi
Bush, Guy Terrell b. Aug 23, 1901
Revels, Hiram R d. Mar 4, 1901
Ackerman, Mississippi
Catledge, Turner b. Mar 17, 1901
Alligator, Mississippi
Coe, Frederick H b. Dec 23, 1914
Arkabutla, Mississippi
Jones, James Earl b. Jan 17, 1931
Bay St. Louis, Mississippi
Barthe, Richmond b. Jan 28, 1901
Benoit, Mississippi
Moore, Archie b. Dec 13, 1916
Betonia, Mississippi
James, "Skip" (Nehemiah) b. Jun 9, 1902
Biloxi, Mississippi
Haise, Fred W b. Nov 14, 1933
Roberts, Eric b. 1956
Stewart, Alexander Peter d. Aug 30, 1908
Toole, John Kennedy d. Mar 26, 1969
Brandon, Mississippi
Wilson, Louis Hugh b. Feb 11, 1920
Chicasaw County, Mississippi
Gentry, Bobbie b. Jul 27, 1942
Clarksdale, Mississippi
Bennett, Lerone, Jr. b. Oct 17, 1928
Hooker, John Lee b. Aug 22, 1917

Smith, Bessie d. Sep 26, 1937
Turner, Ike b. Nov 5, 1931
Cleveland, Mississippi
Manning, Archie (Elisha Archie, III)
　b. May 19, 1949
Speakes, Larry Melvin b. Sep 13, 1939
Coldwater, Mississippi
Malone, Dumas b. Jan 10, 1892
Collins, Mississippi
Andrews, Dana b. Jan 1, 1909
McRaney, Gerald b. Aug 19, 1948
Columbia, Mississippi
Payton, Walter b. Jul 25, 1954
Columbus, Mississippi
Armstrong, Henry b. Dec 12, 1912
Barber, "Red" (Walter Lanier)
　b. Feb 17, 1908
Meriwether, Lee b. Dec 25, 1862
Williams, "Tennessee" (Thomas Lanier)
　b. Mar 26, 1911
Como, Mississippi
Young, Stark b. Oct 11, 1881
Corinth, Mississippi
Meadows, Earle b. Jun 29, 1913
Osborne, John Franklin b. Mar 15, 1907
Decatur, Mississippi
Evers, Charles b. Sep 11, 1923
Evers, Medgar Wiley b. Jul 2, 1926
Doddsville, Mississippi
Eastland, James Oliver b. Nov 28, 1904
Dumas, Mississippi
Wildmon, Donald Ellis b. Jan 18, 1938
Ellisville, Mississippi
Myer, "Buddy" (Charles Solomon)
　b. Mar 16, 1904
Enterprise, Mississippi
Harding, Chester b. Dec 31, 1866
Fayette, Mississippi
Truly, Richard H b. Nov 12, 1937
Friars Point, Mississippi
Twitty, Conway b. Sep 1, 1933
Fulton, Mississippi
Lunceford, Jimmy (James Melvin)
　b. Jun 6, 1902
Goodman, Mississippi
Lomax, John Avery b. Sep 23, 1867
Greenville, Mississippi
Lomax, John Avery d. Jan 26, 1948
White, Frank, Jr. b. Sep 4, 1950
Greenwood, Mississippi
Eastland, James Oliver d. Feb 19, 1986
Grenada, Mississippi
Hurt, Mississippi John d. Nov 2, 1966
Winter, William Forrest b. Feb 21, 1923
Hattiesburg, Mississippi
Hodges, Eddie (Samuel Edward)
　b. Mar 5, 1947
Hazelhurst, Mississippi
Ford, Ruth Elizabeth b. Jul 7, 1915
Hermanville, Mississippi
Bodenheim, Maxwell b. May 23, 1893

Holly Springs, Mississippi
Crump, Edward Hull b. 1874
McDowell, Katharine Sherwood Bonner
b. Feb 26, 1849
McDowell, Katharine Sherwood Bonner
d. Jul 22, 1883
Hot Coffee, Mississippi
Stevens, Stella b. Oct 1, 1938
Itta Bena, Mississippi
Berry, Marion Shepilov, Jr. b. Mar 6, 1936
King, B B (Riley B.) b. Sep 16, 1925
Iuka, Mississippi
Merrill, Henry Tindall b. 1894
Jackson, Mississippi
Engel, Lehman (Aaron Lehman)
b. Sep 12, 1910
Evers, Medgar Wiley d. Jun 12, 1963
Henderson, Jimmy b. May 20, 1954
Henley, Beth b. May 8, 1952
McNeil, Freeman b. Apr 22, 1959
Morris, Willie b. Nov 29, 1934
Pittman, Robert W b. Dec 28, 1953
Welty, Eudora b. Apr 13, 1909
Kemper County, Mississippi
Stennis, John Cornelius b. Aug 3, 1901
Kosciusko, Mississippi
Meredith, James Howard b. Jun 25, 1933
Winfrey, Ophra b. 1954
Laurel, Mississippi
Boston, Ralph b. May 9, 1939
Calhoun, Lee Q b. Feb 23, 1933
Price, Leontyne b. Feb 10, 1927
Long Beach, Mississippi
Boggs, Hale (Thomas Hale)
b. Feb 15, 1914
Louisville, Mississippi
Clark, Thomas Dionysius b. Jul 14, 1903
Macon, Mississippi
Williams, Ben Ames b. Mar 7, 1889
Marks, Mississippi
Smith, Frederick Wallace b. Aug 11, 1944
McCombs, Mississippi
Diddley, Bo b. Dec 30, 1928
Medford, Mississippi
Theroux, Paul Edward b. Apr 10, 1941
Meridian, Mississippi
Bandy, Moe b. 1944
Childress, Alvin b. 1908
Ethridge, Mark Foster b. Apr 22, 1896
Ladd, Diane b. Nov 29, 1932
Lancaster, Bruce Morgan b. Oct 5, 1923
Rodgers, Jimmie C b. Sep 8, 1897
Ruffin, Jimmy b. May 7, 1939
Mound Bayou, Mississippi
Hamer, Fannie Lou Townsend
d. Mar 1977
Natchez, Mississippi
Gilley, Mickey Leroy b. Mar 9, 1936
Wright, Richard b. Sep 4, 1908
New Albany, Mississippi
Faulkner, William b. Sep 25, 1897

Okalona, Mississippi
Raspberry, William b. Oct 12, 1935
Olive, Mississippi
Perkins, (Walter) Ray b. Dec 6, 1941
Oxford, Mississippi
Faulkner, William d. Jul 6, 1962
Pascagoula, Mississippi
Buffet, Jimmy b. Dec 25, 1946
Miller, William Mosley b. Jul 20, 1909
Pontotoc, Mississippi
Cochran, Thad b. Dec 7, 1937
Poplarville, Mississippi
Bilbo, Theodore Gilmore b. Oct 13, 1877
Ripley, Mississippi
Falkner, Murry Charles b. Jun 26, 1899
Rolling Fork, Mississippi
Waters, "Muddy" b. Apr 4, 1915
Scott, Mississippi
Broonzy, "Big Bill" b. Jun 26, 1893
Shannon, Mississippi
Bush, Guy Terrell d. Jun 1985
Silver City, Mississippi
Haywood, Spencer b. Apr 21, 1950
Sledge, Mississippi
Pride, Charley b. Mar 18, 1938
Starkville, Mississippi
Bell, "Cool Papa" (James Thomas)
b. May 17, 1903
Sunflower, Mississippi
Claiborne, Craig b. Sep 4, 1920
Teoc, Mississippi
Hurt, Mississippi John b. Mar 8, 1892
Tupelo, Mississippi
Presley, Elvis (Elvis Aaron) b. Jan 8, 1935
Wynette, Tammy b. May 4, 1942
Vaughan, Mississippi
Jones, "Casey" (John Luther)
d. Apr 30, 1900
Vicksburg, Mississippi
Thornell, Jack Randolph b. Aug 29, 1939
Weathersby, Mississippi
Torrance, Jack b. Jun 20, 1913
West Point, Mississippi
Harlan, Louis R b. Jul 13, 1922
Howlin' Wolf b. Jun 10, 1910
Woodville, Mississippi
Still, William Grant b. May 11, 1895
Young, Lester Willis b. Aug 27, 1909

MISSOURI

Bothwell, Jean d. Mar 2, 1977
Kauffman, Ewing Marion b. Sep 21, 1916
Pontiac d. Apr 20, 1769
Smedley, Agnes b. 1894
Anderson, Missouri
Corben, Richard Vance b. Oct 1, 1940
Atherton, Missouri
Cooper, Morton Cecil b. Mar 4, 1914

Aurora, Missouri
Barker, "Doc" (Arthur) b. 1899
Barker, Fred b. 1902
Barker, Herman b. 1894
Barker, Lloyd b. 1896
Bonne Terre, Missouri
Williams, Patrick b. Apr 23, 1939
Boonville, Missouri
Ashley, William Henry d. Mar 26, 1838
Hitch, Charles Johnston b. Jan 9, 1910
Bowling Green, Missouri
Clark, Bennett Champ b. Jan 8, 1890
Butler, Missouri
Heinlein, Robert Anson b. Jul 7, 1907
Cainsville, Missouri
Booth, George b. Jun 28, 1926
Cameron, Missouri
Gillis, Don b. Jun 17, 1912
Cape Girardeau, Missouri
Hecht, Chic b. Nov 30, 1928
Carthage, Missouri
Hubbell, Carl Owen b. Jun 22, 1903
Neville, Kris Ottman b. May 9, 1925
Perkins, (Richard) Marlin b. Mar 28, 1905
Perkins, Marlin (Richard Marlin)
    b. Mar 28, 1902
Starr, Belle Shirley b. Feb 5, 1848
Caruthersville, Missouri
Oliver, James A(rthur) b. Jan 1, 1914
Cass County, Missouri
Dalton, Emmett b. 1871
Dalton, Gratton b. 1862
Dalton, Robert b. 1867
Dalton, William b. 1873
Centerville, Missouri
James, Jesse Woodson b. Sep 5, 1847
Charleston, Missouri
Danforth, William H b. Sep 10, 1870
Rollins, Kenny b. Sep 14, 1923
Chillicothe, Missouri
Grant, Harry Johnston b. Sep 15, 1881
Clark, Missouri
Bradley, Omar Nelson b. Feb 12, 1893
Clay County, Missouri
James, Frank b. 1843
Clayton, Missouri
Franciscus, James Grover b. Jan 31, 1934
Clever, Missouri
Mandan, Robert b. Feb 2,
Columbia, Missouri
Froman, Jane d. Apr 22, 1980
Neihardt, John Gneisenau d. Nov 3, 1973
Rickey, Branch (Wesley Branch)
    d. Dec 9, 1965
Wiener, Norbert b. Nov 26, 1894
Concordia, Missouri
Kuhlman, Kathryn b. 1910
Creve Coeur, Missouri
Mueller, "Heinie" (Clarence Franklin)
    b. Sep 16, 1899

Crystal City, Missouri
Bradley, Bill (William Warren)
    b. Jul 28, 1943
Dearborn, Missouri
Boyd, William Clouser b. Mar 4, 1903
Deepwater, Missouri
Swarthout, Gladys b. Dec 25, 1904
DeSoto, Missouri
Mueller, "Heinie" (Clarence Franklin)
    d. Jan 23, 1974
Diamond, Missouri
Miller, Paul b. Sep 28, 1906
Diamond Grove, Missouri
Carver, George Washington b. Jan 5, 1864
Dundee, Missouri
Colter, John d. Nov 1813
Easton, Missouri
Iba, Henry P b. Aug 6, 1904
Edgerton, Missouri
Davis, Jim b. Aug 26, 1916
Elkton, Missouri
Rand, Sally b. Jan 2, 1904
Eve, Missouri
Ghostley, Alice (Allyce) b. Aug 14, 1926
Farmington, Missouri
Asbury, Herbert b. Sep 1, 1891
McBride, Lloyd b. Mar 8, 1916
Fayette, Missouri
McManaway, James b. Aug 24, 1899
Flat River, Missouri
Husky, Ferlin b. Dec 3, 1927
Florida, Missouri
Twain, Mark, pseud. b. Nov 30, 1835
Frederick, Missouri
Foreman, "Chuck" (Walter Eugene)
    b. Oct 26, 1950
Fulton, Missouri
Britt, Steuart Henderson b. Jun 17, 1907
Galbreath, Tony (Anthony)
    b. Jan 29, 1954
Stephens, Helen b. Feb 3, 1918
Galena, Missouri
Johnson, Don b. Dec 15, 1950
Glasgow, Missouri
Davis, "Wild Bill" (William Strethen)
    b. Nov 24, 1918
Vaughan, Harry Hawkins b. Nov 26, 1893
Gower, Missouri
Atchison, David R d. Jun 26, 1886
Grant City, Missouri
Winslow, Ola Elizabeth b. 1885
Greenridge, Missouri
White, Pearl b. Mar 4, 1889
Hamilton, Missouri
Penney, J(ames) C(ash) b. Sep 16, 1875
Wheat, Zack (Zachariah Davis)
    b. May 23, 1888
Hannibal, Missouri
Beckley, Jake (Jacob Peter) b. Aug 4, 1867
Edwards, Cliff b. Jul 14, 1895

Ulreich, Nura Woodson b. Dec 1899
Waller, "Fats" (Thomas Wright)
  d. Dec 15, 1943
Warren, Charles b. Apr 26, 1927
Watson, Tom (Sturges) b. Sep 4, 1949
Welch, Ken b. Feb 4, 1926
Whitney, Mrs. Cornelius b. Dec 24, 1925
Wood, Joseph b. Oct 25, 1889
Wood, Robert Elkington b. Jun 13, 1879
Kennett, Missouri
  Lasswell, Fred b. 1916
Keytesville, Missouri
  Hubbard, Cal (Robert Calvin)
    b. Oct 11, 1900
  Taylor, Maxwell Davenport
    b. Aug 26, 1901
Kirksville, Missouri
  Page, Geraldine b. Nov 22, 1924
  Still, Andrew Taylor d. Dec 12, 1917
Kirkwood, Missouri
  Johnson, Josephine Winslow
    b. Jan 20, 1910
Lafayette County, Missouri
  Creel, George b. Dec 1, 1876
Lamar, Missouri
  Truman, Harry S b. May 8, 1884
Lancaster, Missouri
  Hughes, Rupert b. Jan 31, 1872
Laredo, Missouri
  Tolson, Clyde Anderson b. May 22, 1900
Lebanon, Missouri
  Breech, Ernest Robert b. Feb 24, 1897
  Wilson, Lanford b. Apr 13, 1937
Lee's Summitt, Missouri
  Younger, Bob (Robert) b. 1853
  Younger, Jim (James) b. 1850
Liberty, Missouri
  Boyer, Ken(ton Lloyd) b. May 20, 1931
Linn City, Missouri
  Pershing, John J(oseph) b. Sep 13, 1860
Mansfield, Missouri
  Wilder, Laura Elizabeth Ingalls
    d. Jan 10, 1957
Marshall, Missouri
  Holloway, Emory b. Mar 16, 1885
Marshfield, Missouri
  Haymes, Joe b. 1908
  Hubble, Edwin Powell b. Nov 20, 1889
  McDowell, Frank b. Jan 30, 1911
Maryville, Missouri
  Caldwell, Sarah b. Mar 6, 1924
  Carnegie, Dale b. Nov 24, 1888
  Overman, Lynne b. Sep 19, 1887
Memphis, Missouri
  Horn, Tom b. 1860
Mill Spring, Missouri
  Macfadden, Bernarr Adolphus
    b. Aug 16, 1868
Millgrove, Missouri
  Masters, Kelly R b. Jun 16, 1897

Moberly, Missouri
  Conroy, Jack (John Wesley)
    b. Dec 5, 1899
Morrisville, Missouri
  Stewart, Wynn b. Jun 7, 1934
Nashville, Missouri
  Shapley, Harlow T b. Nov 2, 1885
Neosho, Missouri
  Benton, Thomas Hart b. Apr 15, 1889
Nevada, Missouri
  DeBernardi, Forrest S b. Mar 3, 1899
  Huston, John b. Aug 5, 1906
Nixa, Missouri
  Owen, "Mickey" (Arnold Malcolm)
    b. Apr 4, 1916
Palmyra, Missouri
  Darwell, Jane b. Oct 15, 1880
Paris, Missouri
  McBride, Mary Margaret b. Nov 16, 1899
Parnell, Missouri
  Jones, Benjamin Allyn b. Dec 31, 1882
Pierce City, Missouri
  Griffiths, Martha Wright b. Jan 29, 1912
Plattsburg, Missouri
  Barnhart, Clarence Lewis b. Dec 30, 1900
  McIntyre, Oscar Odd b. Feb 18, 1884
Princeton, Missouri
  Calamity Jane b. 1852
Ray County, Missouri
  Anderson, William d. Oct 1864
Raytown, Missouri
  Allison, Bob (William Robert)
    b. Jul 11, 1934
Rich Hill, Missouri
  Craig, Cleo F b. Apr 6, 1895
Richmond Heights, Missouri
  Sisler, George Harold d. Mar 26, 1973
Saint Charles, Missouri
  DuSable, Jean Baptiste d. Aug 28, 1818
Saint Charles County, Missouri
  Boone, Daniel d. Sep 26, 1820
Saint Joseph, Missouri
  Baird, Irwin Lewis b. Mar 11, 1925
  Craig, Malin b. Aug 5, 1875
  Cronkite, Walter Leland, Jr.
    b. Nov 4, 1916
  Davis, Frederick C(lyde) b. Jun 2, 1902
  Garrett, Betty b. May 23, 1919
  Harman, Fred b. Feb 9, 1902
  Hawkins, "Bean" (Coleman)
    b. Nov 21, 1904
  Hite, Shere b. Nov 2, 1942
  James, Jesse Woodson d. Apr 3, 1882
  Lockridge, Richard b. Sep 26, 1898
  Pryor, Arthur W b. Sep 22, 1870
  Ross, Nellie Taylor b. Nov 29, 1876
  Webb, James H(enry) b. Feb 9, 1946
  Wyman, Jane b. Jan 4, 1914
Saint Louis, Missouri
  Aiken, Howard Hathaway d. Mar 14, 1973
  Akins, Virgil b. Mar 10, 1928

Angelou, Maya Marguerita b. Apr 4, 1928
Baker, "Shorty" (Harold) b. May 26, 1914
Baker, Josephine b. Jun 3, 1906
Barrett, Stan b. 1944
Beaumont, William d. Apr 25, 1853
Benson, Sally b. Sep 3, 1900
Berra, "Yogi" (Lawrence Peter)
  b. May 12, 1925
Blair, Francis Preston d. Jul 8, 1875
Blair, Linda Denise b. Jan 22, 1959
Blake, Eugene Carson b. Nov 7, 1906
Blow, Susan Elizabeth b. Jun 7, 1843
Bottomley, Jim (James Leroy)
  d. Dec 11, 1959
Boyer, Ken(ton Lloyd) d. Sep 7, 1982
Broadhurst, Kent b. Feb 4, 1940
Bumbry, Grace Ann Jaeckel
  b. Jan 4, 1937
Burroughs, William S(eward)
  b. Feb 5, 1914
Busch, August Anheuser, Jr.
  b. Mar 28, 1899
Campbell, E Simms b. Jan 2, 1906
Carnovsky, Morris b. Sep 5, 1897
Carter, Don(ald Jones) b. Jul 29, 1926
Cervantes, Alfonso Juan b. Aug 27, 1929
Cervantes, Alfonso Juan d. Jun 23, 1983
Chopin, Kate b. Feb 8, 1851
Chopin, Kate d. Aug 22, 1904
Churchill, Winston b. 1871
Clark, William d. Sep 1, 1838
Clay, William Lacy b. Apr 30, 1931
Cody, John Patrick b. Dec 24, 1907
Converse, Frank b. May 22, 1938
Convy, Bert b. Jul 23, 1934
Conzelman, Jimmy (James Gleason)
  b. Mar 6, 1898
Conzelman, Jimmy (James Gleason)
  d. Jul 31, 1970
Cori, Gerty Theresa d. Oct 26, 1957
Cornell, Douglas B b. 1907
Danforth, John Claggett b. Sep 5, 1936
Danforth, William H d. Dec 24, 1952
Darcy, Tom b. Jun 7, 1916
Dauss, George August d. Jul 27, 1963
Davis, Billy, Jr. b. Jun 26, 1940
Davis, Dwight Filley b. Jul 5, 1879
Davis, Phil b. Mar 4, 1906
DeWitt, William Orville, Sr.
  b. Aug 3, 1902
DeYoung, Michel Harry b. Oct 1, 1849
Dooley, Thomas Anthony b. Jan 17, 1927
Dotson, Bob b. Oct 3, 1946
Eagleton, Thomas Francis b. Sep 4, 1929
Eames, Charles b. Jun 17, 1907
Eames, Charles d. Aug 21, 1978
Edgell, George Harold b. Mar 4, 1887
Edwards, Harry (Jr.) b. Nov 22, 1942
Eliot, T(homas) S(tearns) b. Sep 26, 1888
Erlanger, Joseph d. Dec 5, 1965
Evans, Walker b. Nov 3, 1903

Falk, Lee Harrison b. 1915
Farmer, Don b. Sep 27, 1938
Faylen, Frank b. 1907
Felker, Clay S b. Oct 2, 1928
Field, Eugene b. Sep 2, 1850
Field, Kate b. Oct 1, 1838
Fishbein, Morris b. Jul 22, 1889
Fitzpatrick, Daniel R d. May 18, 1969
Foxx, Redd b. Dec 9, 1922
Froman, Jane b. Nov 10, 1907
Galvin, "Pud" (James Francis)
  b. Dec 25, 1856
Garagiola, Joe (Joseph Henry)
  b. Feb 12, 1926
Gellhorn, Martha Ellis b. 1908
Goodman, George Jerome Waldo
  b. Aug 10, 1930
Grable, Betty b. Dec 18, 1916
Grant, Julia Dent b. Jan 26, 1826
Gray, Louis Patrick b. Jul 18, 1916
Gregory, Dick b. Oct 12, 1932
Grimm, Charlie (Charles John)
  b. Aug 28, 1899
Guenther, Charles John b. Apr 29, 1920
Guerin, Jules b. 1866
Guillaume, Robert b. Nov 30, 1937
Gunn, Moses b. Oct 2, 1929
Hahn, Emily b. Jan 14, 1905
Harkness, Rebekah West b. Apr 17, 1915
Harrington, Michael (Edward Michael)
  b. Feb 24, 1928
Hillenkoetter, Roscoe H(enry)
  b. May 8, 1897
Hirschfeld, Al(bert) b. Jun 21, 1903
Hotchner, Aaron Edward b. Jun 28, 1920
Howard, Elston Gene b. Feb 23, 1929
Ittner, William Butts b. Sep 4, 1864
Ittner, William Butts d. Jan 26, 1936
Johnson, (Byron) Ban(croft)
  d. Mar 18, 1931
Johnston, Johnny b. Dec 1, 1915
Jones, Clara Araminta Stanton
  b. May 14, 1913
Jones, Joseph John (Joe) b. Apr 7, 1909
Kearny, Stephen Watts d. Oct 31, 1848
Kline, Kevin b. Oct 24, 1947
Kohlmeier, Louis Martin, Jr.
  b. Feb 17, 1926
Kohn, William Roth b. Aug 23, 1931
Kuh, Katherine b. Jul 15, 1904
Kurland, Bob b. Dec 23, 1924
La Fontaine, Pat b. Feb 22, 1965
LaPlante, Laura b. Nov 1, 1904
Link, Theodore Carl d. Feb 14, 1923
Lynch, David b. 1930
Macauley, Ed b. Mar 22, 1928
MacNutt, Francis, Father b. Apr 22, 1925
Mallinckrodt, Edward b. Jan 21, 1845
Mallinckrodt, Edward d. Feb 1, 1928
Marlowe, Marion b. Mar 7, 1930

Martin, William McChesney, Jr.
b. Dec 17, 1906
Mason, Marsha b. Apr 3, 1942
May, Morton David b. 1914
May, Morton David d. Apr 13, 1983
Mayo, Virginia b. Nov 30, 1920
McCulloch, Robert P b. 1912
McDonald, Michael b.
McDonnell, James Smith d. Aug 22, 1980
McFee, Henry Lee b. Apr 14, 1886
McHenry, Donald Franchot
b. Oct 13, 1938
McKenzie, "Red" (William)
b. Oct 14, 1907
McKinley, Chuck (Charles Robert)
b. Jan 5, 1941
McManus, George b. Jan 23, 1884
Meriwether, Lee d. Mar 12, 1966
Merrick, David b. Nov 27, 1912
Moore, Marianne Craig b. Nov 15, 1887
More, Paul Elmer b. Dec 12, 1864
Nolan, Kathy (Kathleen) b. Sep 27, 1933
Patrick, Lynn d. Jan 26, 1980
Perkins, (Richard) Marlin d. Jun 14, 1986
Perkins, Marlin (Richard Marlin)
d. Jun 14, 1986
Perkoff, Stuart Z b. Jul 29, 1930
Pike, Jim b.
Price, Sterling d. Sep 29, 1867
Price, Vincent b. May 27, 1911
Pulitzer, Joseph, II d. Mar 30, 1955
Pulitzer, Ralph b. Jun 11, 1879
Queeny, Edgar Monsanto b. Sep 29, 1897
Queeny, Edgar Monsanto d. Jul 7, 1968
Rankin, Judy Torluemke b. Feb 18, 1945
Redhead, Hugh McCulloch b. Jul 18, 1920
Reid, Wallace Eugene b. Apr 15, 1891
Reiser, Pete (Harold Patrick)
b. Mar 17, 1919
Roberts, Doris b. Nov 4, 1930
Rombauer, Irma von Starkloff
b. Oct 30, 1877
Rombauer, Irma von Starkloff
d. Oct 14, 1962
Rosenbloom, Georgia b. 1926
Russell, "Pee Wee" (Charles Ellsworth)
b. Mar 27, 1906
Russell, Charles Marion b. Mar 19, 1864
Schlafly, Phyllis Stewart b. Aug 15, 1924
Scott, Dred d. Sep 17, 1858
Sherwood, Roberta b. Jul 1, 1912
Sims, Billy Ray b. Sep 18, 1955
Smith, Robert Lee b. Sep 18, 1928
Spinks, Leon b. Jul 11, 1953
Spinks, Michael b. Jul 29, 1956
Stilwell, Richard Dale b. May 6, 1942
Stoessel, Albert b. Oct 11, 1894
Stone, Chuck (Charles Sumner)
b. Jul 21, 1924
Sutton, Carol b. Jun 29, 1933
Swope, Gerard b. Dec 1, 1872

Swope, Herbert Bayard b. Jan 5, 1882
Teasdale, Sara b. Aug 8, 1884
Telva, Marion b. Sep 26, 1897
Terris, Susan b. May 6, 1937
Thomas, Betty b. Jul 27, 1948
Thompson, Kay b. Nov 9, 1913
Thum, Marcella b.
Tjader, Cal(len Radcliffe, Jr.)
b. Jul 16, 1925
Traubel, Helen b. Jun 20, 1899
Tucker, Orrin b. Feb 17, 1911
Tuthill, Harry J d. Jan 25, 1957
Vaughan, Bill (William Edward)
b. Oct 8, 1915
Ward, Fannie b. Nov 23, 1872
Warrick, Ruth b. Jun 29, 1915
Weathers, Felicia b. Aug 13, 1937
Weaver, Earl Sidney b. Aug 14, 1930
Webster, William Hedgcock
b. Mar 6, 1924
White, "Jo Jo" (Joseph) b. Nov 16, 1946
Wilkins, Roy b. Aug 30, 1901
Williams, Dick (Richard Hirschfield)
b. May 7, 1928
Wilson, Helen Dolan b. 1907
Winslow, Kellen Boswell b. Nov 5, 1957
Winters, Shelley b. Aug 18, 1922
Wolfson, Louis Elwood b. Jan 28, 1912
Wyman, Thomas Hunt b. Nov 30, 1929

Sedalia, Missouri
Oakie, Jack b. Nov 12, 1903
Shannon, Fred Albert b. Feb 12, 1893
Wheat, Zack (Zachariah Davis)
d. Mar 11, 1972

Sikeston, Missouri
Adams, John Hanly b. Nov 2, 1918

Somerset County, Missouri
Chase, Samuel b. Apr 17, 1741

Speed, Missouri
Corum, Martene Windsor b. Jul 20, 1895

Spickard, Missouri
Browning, Norma Lee b. Nov 24, 1914

Springfield, Missouri
Barker, "Ma" (Arizona Donnie Clark)
b. 1872
Genovese, Vito d. Feb 14, 1969
Hammond, Bray b. Nov 20, 1886
James, Marquis b. Sep 29, 1891
Johnson, Virginia E b. Feb 11, 1925
Lovelace, William Randolph, II
b. Dec 30, 1907
O'Neill, Rose Cecil d. Apr 6, 1944
Smith, Horton b. May 22, 1908
Stroud, Robert Franklin d. Nov 21, 1963
Turner, Kathleen b. Jun 19, 1954

Steelville, Missouri
Upchurch, John Jorden d. Jan 18, 1887

Stockton, Missouri
Liston, Emil b. Aug 21, 1890

Stringtown, Missouri
Griffith, Clark Calvin b. Nov 20, 1869

Ely, Nebraska
Nixon, Patricia (Thelma Catherine Patricia Ryan) b. Mar 16, 1912
Falls City, Nebraska
Erwin, "Pee Wee" (George) b. May 30, 1913
Filley, Nebraska
Taylor, Robert b. Aug 5, 1911
Fort Lisa, Nebraska
Sacagawea d. Dec 2, 1812
Fremont, Nebraska
Armstrong, William L b. Mar 16, 1937
Edgerton, Harold Eugene b. Apr 6, 1903
Friend, Nebraska
Strong, Anna Louise b. Nov 24, 1885
Gibbon, Nebraska
Cavett, Dick (Richard Alva) b. Nov 19, 1936
Cherrington, Ben Mark b. Nov 1, 1885
Grand Island, Nebraska
Abbott, Edith b. Sep 26, 1876
Abbott, Edith d. Jul 28, 1957
Abbott, Grace b. Nov 17, 1878
Baird, Bil (William Britton) b. Aug 15, 1904
Fonda, Henry Jaynes b. May 16, 1905
Reynolds, Bobby (Robert) b. 1930
Hastings, Nebraska
Dennis, Sandy b. Apr 27, 1937
Hefti, Neal Paul b. Oct 29, 1922
Warren, Gerald Lee b. Aug 17, 1930
Hebron, Nebraska
Darby, Ken b. May 13, 1909
Roper, Elmo Burns, Jr. b. Jul 31, 1900
Laurel, Nebraska
Coburn, James b. Aug 31, 1928
Lincoln, Nebraska
Aldrich, Bess Streeter d. Aug 3, 1954
Eiseley, Loren Corey b. Sep 3, 1907
Gann, Ernest Kellogg b. Oct 13, 1910
Kerrey, Bob (Joseph Robert) b. Aug 27, 1943
Lasch, Robert b. Mar 26, 1907
MacRae, Gordon d. Jan 24, 1986
McGee, Gale William b. Mar 17, 1915
Moores, Dick (Richard Arnold) b. Dec 12, 1909
Pound, Louise b. Jun 30, 1872
Pound, Louise d. Jun 17, 1958
Pound, Roscoe b. Oct 27, 1870
Ryan, Leo Joseph b. May 5, 1925
Sorensen, Ted (Theodore Chaikin) b. May 8, 1928
Starkweather, Charles b. 1940
Weidman, Charles b. Jul 22, 1901
Wilson, Don(ald Harlow) b. Sep 1, 1900
Yorty, Sam(uel William) b. Oct 1, 1909
Lincoln County, Nebraska
Graham, William Alexander b. Sep 5, 1804
Loup City, Nebraska
Moeller Michael E b. 1950

McCook, Nebraska
Norris, George William d. Sep 3, 1944
Naponee, Nebraska
Janssen, David b. Mar 27, 1931
Nebraska City, Nebraska
Hayward, Leland b. Sep 13, 1902
O'Neill, Nebraska
Dowling, Dan(iel Blair) b. Nov 16, 1906
Leahy, Frank b. Aug 27, 1908
Omaha, Nebraska
Addy, Wesley b. Aug 4, 1913
Astaire, Adele b. Sep 10, 1898
Astaire, Fred b. May 10, 1899
Baer, Max b. Feb 11, 1909
Baldrige, Malcolm (Howard Malcolm, Jr.) b. Oct 4, 1922
Berlin, Richard E b. Jan 18, 1894
Boggs, Wade Anthony b. Jun 15, 1958
Brando, Marlon b. Apr 3, 1924
Clark, Robert Edward b. May 14, 1922
Clift, Montgomery b. Oct 17, 1920
Creighton, Edward d. Nov 5, 1874
Denenberg, Herbert S b. Nov 20, 1929
Door, Rheta Childe b. Nov 2, 1866
Doyle, David Fitzgerald b. Dec 1, 1929
Ford, Gerald Rudolph b. Jul 14, 1913
Gibson, Bob (Robert) b. Nov 9, 1935
Kalber, Floyd b. Dec 23, 1924
Klein, Lawrence Robert b. Sep 14, 1920
Kurtz, Swoosie b. Sep 6, 1944
Laird, Melvin Robert b. Sep 1, 1922
Malcolm X b. May 19, 1925
McGuire, Dorothy b. Jun 14, 1918
Nolte, Nick b. Feb 8, 1942
Prescott, Ken b. Dec 28, 1948
Stephenson, "Skip" (Charles Frederick) b. 1948
Stoltzman, Richard Leslie b. Jul 12, 1942
Swenson, Inga b. Dec 29, 1932
Waybill, Fee b. Sep 17, 1950
Wedemeyer, Albert Coady b. Jul 9, 1897
Williams, Paul Hamilton b. Sep 19, 1940
Williams, Roger b. Oct 1, 1926
Wilson, Julie b. 1924
Woode, William Henri b. Sep 25, 1909
Zorinsky, Edward b. Nov 11, 1928
Osceola, Nebraska
Hathaway, Stanley Knapp b. Jul 19, 1924
Papillion, Nebraska
Curti, Merle Eugene b. Sep 15, 1897
Pender, Nebraska
Pate, Maurice b. Oct 14, 1894
Peru, Nebraska
Brownell, Herbert, Jr. b. Feb 20, 1904
Brownwell, Samuel Miller b. Apr 3, 1900
Conkle, Ellsworth Prouty b. Jul 10, 1899
Platte Center, Nebraska
Gruenther, Alfred Maximillian b. Mar 3, 1899
Platte County, Nebraska
Keogh, James b. Oct 29, 1916

Plattsmouth, Nebraska
Falter, John b. Feb 28, 1910
Rising City, Nebraska
Hillegass, C K b. 1918
Saint Paul, Nebraska
Alexander, Grover Cleveland
d. Nov 4, 1950
Scotts Bluff, Nebraska
Meisner, Randy b. Mar 8, 1946
Shelby, Nebraska
Miller, Arjay Ray b. Mar 4, 1916
Sheridan County, Nebraska
Sandoz, Mari b. 1900
Staplehurst, Nebraska
Gray, Coleen b. Oct 23, 1922
Sterling, Nebraska
Borland, Hal b. May 14, 1900
Table Rock, Nebraska
Lyman, William Roy b. Nov 30, 1898
Tememah, Nebraska
Gibson, "Hoot" (Edmund Richard)
b. Aug 6, 1892
Tilden, Nebraska
Ashburn, Don Richie b. Mar 19, 1927
Hubbard, L(afayette) Ron(ald)
b. Mar 13, 1911
Unadilla, Nebraska
Davis, Clyde Brion b. May 22, 1894
Wahoo, Nebraska ·
Anderson, C(larence) W(illiam)
b. Apr 12, 1891
Crawford, Sam(uel Earl) b. Apr 18, 1880
Hanson, Howard Harold b. Oct 28, 1896
Zanuck, Darryl Francis b. Sep 5, 1902
Waverly, Nebraska
Carlson, William Hugh b. Sep 5, 1898
Winside, Nebraska
Bothwell, Jean b.
York, Nebraska
Cordes, Eugene Harold b. Apr 7, 1936
Niblo, Fred b. Jan 6, 1874

NEVADA

Candelaria, Nevada
Casey, James E b. Mar 29, 1888
Carson City, Nevada
Litton, Charles d. Nov 14, 1972
Esmeralda County, Nevada
Wovoka b. 1856
Garfield, Nevada
Alexander, Ben (Nicholas Benton)
b. May 26, 1911
Goldfield, Nevada
Earp, Virgil W d. 1905
Henderson, Nevada
Charles, Lee b.
Las Vegas, Nevada
Bergen, Edgar John d. Sep 30, 1978
Dalton, Abby b. Aug 15, 1935
Fields, Totie d. Aug 2, 1978

Henry, Pat d. Feb 18, 1982
James, Harry d. Jul 5, 1983
Johnson, "Chic" (Harold Ogden)
d. Feb 1962
Kim, Duk Koo d. Nov 13, 1982
Kramer, Jack b. Aug 1, 1921
Liberace, George J d. Oct 16, 1983
Liston, "Sonny" (Charles) d. Jan 5, 1971
Lombard, Carole d. Jan 16, 1942
Louis, Joe d. Apr 12, 1981
Manone, "Wingy" (Joseph) d. Jul 9, 1982
Morgan, Russ d. Aug 7, 1969
Nichols, "Red" (Ernest Loring)
d. Jun 28, 1965
Podgwiski, Jeff b. 1954
Talmadge, Norma d. Dec 24, 1957
Teagarden, Charles d. Dec 10, 1984
Walker, Joseph d. Aug 1, 1985
Minden, Nevada
Stacton, David Derek b. Apr 25, 1925
Reno, Nevada
Clark, Walter van Tilburg d. Nov 10, 1971
Cord, E(rret) L(obban) d. Jan 2, 1974
Dean, "Dizzy" (Jay Hanna)
d. Jul 17, 1974
Irving, Jules d. Jul 28, 1979
Laxalt, Paul b. Aug 2, 1922
Lear, William Powell d. May 14, 1978
Purviance, Edna b. 1894
Zimbalist, Efrem d. Feb 22, 1985
Schurz, Nevada
Wovoka d. Oct 1932
Sherburne, Nevada
Matteson, Tompkins Harrison
d. Feb 2, 1884
Virginia City, Nevada
Cavanaugh, Hobart b. 1887
Wonder, Nevada
Adams, Eve Bertrand b. Sep 10, 1908

NEW HAMPSHIRE

Alton, New Hampshire
Savage, Henry Wilson b. Mar 21, 1859
Amherst, New Hampshire
Greeley, Horace b. Feb 3, 1811
Appledore, New Hampshire
Thaxter, Celia d. Aug 26, 1894
Ashland, New Hampshire
Whipple, George H b. Aug 28, 1879
Bedford, New Hampshire
Worcester, Joseph Emerson
b. Aug 24, 1784
Berlin, New Hampshire
Tupper, Earl Silas b. Jul 28, 1907
Boscawen, New Hampshire
Dix, John Adams b. Jul 24, 1798
Fessenden, William Pitt b. Oct 16, 1806
Bow, New Hampshire
Eddy, Mary Baker Morse b. Jul 16, 1821
Wheeler, Elmer P b. Feb 23, 1916

Bristol, New Hampshire
Pattee, Fred Lewis b. Mar 22, 1863
Bussum, New Hampshire
Wittop, Freddy b. Jul 26,
Charlestown, New Hampshire
Broderick, James Joseph b. Mar 7, 1927
Chesterfield, New Hampshire
Stone, Harlan Fiske b. Oct 11, 1872
Chocorua, New Hampshire
James, William d. Aug 26, 1910
Claremont, New Hampshire
Cochran, Barbara Ann b. Jan 4, 1951
Colby, Carroll Burleigh b. Sep 7, 1904
Concord, New Hampshire
Bridges, Styles d. Nov 26, 1961
Flynn, Elizabeth Gurley b. Aug 7, 1890
Morrison, Theodore b. Nov 4, 1901
Pierce, Franklin d. Oct 8, 1869
Cornish, New Hampshire
Chase, Philander b. Dec 14, 1775
Chase, Salmon Portland b. Jan 13, 1808
MacKaye, Percy Wallace d. Aug 31, 1956
Saint Gaudens, Augustus d. Aug 3, 1907
Deerfield, New Hampshire
Butler, Benjamin Franklin b. Nov 5, 1818
East Derry, New Hampshire
Shepard, Alan Bartlett, Jr.
   b. Nov 18, 1923
Enfield, New Hampshire
Koehler, Wolfgang d. Jun 11, 1967
Kohler, Wolfgang d. Jun 11, 1967
Exeter, New Hampshire
Cass, Lewis b. Oct 9, 1782
French, Daniel Chester b. Apr 20, 1850
Hicks, Granville b. Sep 9, 1901
Irving, John b. Mar 2, 1942
Perry, Bliss d. Feb 13, 1954
Farmington, New Hampshire
Wilson, Henry b. Feb 16, 1812
Fitzwilliam, New Hampshire
Drinker, Philip d. Oct 19, 1972
Franconia, New Hampshire
Gilman, Lawrence d. Sep 8, 1939
Franklin, New Hampshire
Damon, Ralph Shepard b. Jul 6, 1897
Gilford, New Hampshire
Rolfe, "Red" (Robert Abial) d. Jul 8, 1969
Gilmantown, New Hampshire
Mudgett, Herman Webster b.
Goffstown, New Hampshire
Gerould, Gordon Hall b. Oct 4, 1877
Hampton, New Hampshire
Pierce, Jane Means b. Mar 12, 1806
Hampton Falls, New Hampshire
Brown, Alice b. Dec 5, 1856
Cram, Ralph Adams b. Dec 16, 1863
Whittier, John Greenleaf d. Sep 7, 1892
Hanover, New Hampshire
Bridgman, Laura Dewey b. Dec 21, 1829
Conant, James Bryant d. Feb 11, 1978
Fairchild, Louis W d. Oct 16, 1981

Ford, Corey d. Jul 27, 1969
Sloan, John d. Sep 8, 1951
Sperry, Armstrong W d. Apr 28, 1976
Stefansson, Vihjalmur d. Aug 26, 1962
Stewart, Potter d. Dec 7, 1985
Wheelock, Eleazar d. Apr 24, 1779
Young, Charles Augustus b. Dec 15, 1834
Henniker, New Hampshire
Beach, Mrs. H H A b. Sep 5, 1867
Hillsboro, New Hampshire
Keith, Benjamin F b. 1846
Pierce, Franklin b. Nov 23, 1804
Hinsdale, New Hampshire
Dana, Charles Anderson b. Aug 8, 1819
Hopkinton, New Hampshire
Long, Stephen H b. Dec 30, 1784
Jaffrey, New Hampshire
Laughlin, James Laurence d. Nov 28, 1933
Keene, New Hampshire
Dutton, E(dward) P(ayson) b. Jan 4, 1831
Ellis, Carleton b. Sep 20, 1876
Laconia, New Hampshire
May, Mortimer b. Dec 20, 1892
Lakeport, New Hampshire
Chase, Richard Volney b. Oct 12, 1914
Littleton, New Hampshire
Porter, Eleanor H b. Dec 19, 1868
Londonderry, New Hampshire
Stark, John b. Aug 28, 1728
Lyme, New Hampshire
Converse, Marquis M b. Oct 23, 1861
Madison, New Hampshire
Hocking, William Ernest d. Jun 12, 1966
Manchester, New Hampshire
Blood, Ernest B b. Oct 4, 1872
Coxe, Louis Osborne b. 1918
Custin, Mildred b. 1906
Flanagan, Mike (Michael Kendall)
   b. Dec 16, 1951
Loeb, William b. Dec 26, 1905
Metalious, Grace de Repentigny
   b. Sep 8, 1924
O'Neil, James F(rancis) b. Jun 13, 1898
Revson, Charles Haskell b. Oct 11, 1906
Stark, John d. May 8, 1822
Mason Village, New Hampshire
Chickering, Jonas b. Apr 5, 1798
Meredith, New Hampshire
Montana, Bob d. Jan 4, 1975
Milton, New Hampshire
Jones, Robert Edmond b. Dec 12, 1887
Jones, Robert Edmond d. Nov 26, 1954
Monadnock, New Hampshire
Thayer, Abbott Handerson
   d. May 29, 1921
Nashua, New Hampshire
Gorman, Leon Arthur b. Dec 20, 1934
Thurber, Charles d. Nov 7, 1886
Welch, Mickey (Michael Francis)
   d. Jul 30, 1941

New Boston, New Hampshire
Langdell, Christopher Columbus
b. May 22, 1826
Newburg, New Hampshire
Hay, John Milton d. Jul 1, 1905
Newington, New Hampshire
Archibald, Joe (Joseph Stopford)
b. Sep 2, 1898
Newport, New Hampshire
Edgell, George Harold d. Jun 29, 1954
Hale, Sarah Josepha b. Oct 24, 1788
North Conway, New Hampshire
Cummings, E(dward) E(stlin)
d. Sep 3, 1962
McNair, Malcolm Perrine d. Sep 9, 1985
Shea, John b. Apr 14, 1949
North Stratford, New Hampshire
Goodman, Paul d. Aug 2, 1972
Penacook, New Hampshire
Rolfe, "Red" (Robert Abial)
b. Oct 11, 1908
Peterborough, New Hampshire
Rock, John d. Dec 4, 1984
Plainfield, New Hampshire
Parrish, Maxfield d. Mar 30, 1966
Plymouth, New Hampshire
Hawthorne, Nathaniel d. May 19, 1864
Portsmouth, New Hampshire
Aldrich, Thomas Bailey b. Nov 11, 1836
Astor, Brooke Marshall b.
Blalock, Jane b. Sep 19, 1945
Bonerz, Peter b. Aug 6, 1938
Boylston, Helen Dore b. Apr 4, 1895
Farragut, David Glasgow d. Aug 14, 1870
Fields, James T b. Dec 31, 1817
King, Ernest Joseph d. Jun 25, 1956
Langdon, John b. Jun 26, 1741
Langdon, John d. Sep 18, 1819
Nicholas, Nicholas John, Jr.
b. Sep 3, 1939
Rush, Tom b. Feb 8, 1941
Thaxter, Celia b. Jun 29, 1835
Whipple, William d. Nov 28, 1785
Randolph, New Hampshire
Bridgman, Percy Williams d. Aug 20, 1961
Rochester, New Hampshire
Carroll, Gladys Hasty b. Jun 26, 1904
Larouche, Lyndon H, Jr. b. Sep 8, 1922
Rumney, New Hampshire
Clifford, Nathan b. Aug 18, 1803
Salisbury, New Hampshire
Webster, Daniel b. Jan 18, 1782
Sandwich, New Hampshire
Rains, Claude d. May 30, 1967
Somersworth, New Hampshire
Chase, Stuart b. Mar 8, 1888
Sullivan, John b. Feb 17, 1740
Sutton, New Hampshire
Pillsbury, John Sargent b. Jul 29, 1828
Walpole, New Hampshire
Howland, Alfred Cornelius b. Feb 12, 1838

Warner, New Hampshire
Pillsbury, Charles Alfred b. Dec 3, 1842
White Mountains, New Hampshire
Brown, Dean d. Jul 10, 1973
Wilton, New Hampshire
Abbot, Charles Greeley b. May 31, 1872
Smith, William French b. Aug 26, 1917
Winchester, New Hampshire
Wood, Leonard b. Oct 9, 1860
Wolfeboro, New Hampshire
Marriott, John Willard d. Aug 13, 1985

NEW JERSEY

Adams, Cliff b. Oct 8, 1952
DiMuro, Lou b. 1932
Edwards, Jonathan d. Mar 22, 1758
Giroux, Robert b. Apr 8, 1914
Muses, Charles Arthur b. Apr 28, 1919
Nichols, Anne d. Sep 15, 1966
Sullivan, Kathryn D b. 1951
Allendale, New Jersey
Fairfax, Beatrice, pseud. d. Nov 28, 1945
Matheson, Richard Burton b. Feb 20, 1926
Allenhurst, New Jersey
Fields, Dorothy b. Jul 15, 1905
Alliance, New Jersey
Seldes, George Henry b. Nov 16, 1890
Seldes, Gilbert Vivian b. Jan 3, 1893
Alpine, New Jersey
Fokker, Anthony Herman Gerard
d. Dec 23, 1939
Lamb, Harold Albert b. Sep 1, 1892
Ancochs, New Jersey
Woolman, John b. Oct 19, 1720
Arlington, New Jersey
Scott, Adrian b. Feb 6, 1912
Asbury Park, New Jersey
Abbott, "Bud" (William A) b. Oct 2, 1900
Chase, Edna Woolman b. Mar 14, 1877
Atlantic City, New Jersey
Brady, "Diamond Jim" (James Buchanan)
d. Apr 13, 1917
Forrest, Helen b. Apr 12, 1918
Gimbel, Richard b. Jul 26, 1898
Gray, Barry b. Jul 2, 1916
Kaprow, Allan b. Aug 23, 1927
Lawrence, Jacob b. Sep 7, 1917
Lloyd, John Henry d. Mar 19, 1965
Luden, William H d. May 8, 1949
Lurton, Horace Harmon d. Apr 1914
Smathers, George Armistead
b. Nov 14, 1913
Thomas, R(ex) David b. Jul 2, 1932
Throckmorton, Cleon b. Oct 8, 1897
Wright, Harry (William Henry)
d. Oct 3, 1895
Avon, New Jersey
Howard, Bronson Crocker d. Aug 4, 1908

Bayonne, New Jersey
Dee, Sandra b. Apr 23, 1942
Donovan, Raymond James
   b. Aug 31, 1930
Kahn, Herman b. Feb 15, 1922
Keith, Brian b. Nov 14, 1921
Stein, Mark b. Mar 11, 1947
Belle Meade, New Jersey
Van Dusen, Henry Pitney d. Feb 13, 1975
Belleville, New Jersey
DeVito, Tommy b. Jun 19, 1935
Gardella, Kay b. 1923
Goodrich, Frances b. 1891
Belmar, New Jersey
Dunn, Alan b. Aug 11, 1900
Held, John, Jr. d. Mar 2, 1958
McMurtrie, Douglas C b. Jul 20, 1888
Moisseiff, Leon Solomon d. Sep 3, 1943
Belvidere, New Jersey
Schelling, Ernest Henry b. Jul 26, 1876
Bergen County, New Jersey
Smith, Allison b. 1970
Bergen Heights, New Jersey
Magonigle, Harold Van Buren
   b. Oct 17, 1867
Bernardsville, New Jersey
Welles, Sumner d. Sep 24, 1961
Beverley, New Jersey
Merritt, Abraham b. Jan 20, 1884
Boonton, New Jersey
Douglas, Helen Mary Gahagan
   b. Nov 25, 1900
Bordentown, New Jersey
Waugh, Frederick Judd b. Sep 13, 1861
Bound Brook, New Jersey
Bohay, Heidi b.
Sinclair, Upton Beall d. Nov 25, 1968
Talmadge, Thomas de Witt b. Jan 7, 1832
Trefflich, Henry Herbert Frederick
   d. Jul 7, 1978
Bridgeton, New Jersey
Goslin, "Goose" (Leon Allen)
   d. May 15, 1971
Bunnvale, New Jersey
Decker, Mary b. Aug 4, 1958
Burlington, New Jersey
Bard, John b. Feb 1, 1716
Cooper, James Fenimore b. Sep 15, 1789
Lawrence, James b. Oct 1, 1781
Caldwell, New Jersey
Cleveland, (Stephen) Grover
   b. Mar 18, 1837
Thornhill, Claude d. Jul 1, 1965
Camden, New Jersey
Ayer, Francis Wayland d. Mar 5, 1923
Cassidy, Joanna b. Aug 2, 1984
Cavanna, Betty (Elizabeth Allen)
   b. Jun 24, 1909
Dash, Samuel b. Feb 27, 1925
Pennington, Ann b. 1893
Renaldo, Duncan b. Apr 23, 1904

Sterban, Richard b. Apr 24, 1943
Unruh, Howard B b. 1921
Valeriani, Richard Gerard b. Aug 29, 1932
Whitman, Walt(er) d. Mar 26, 1892
Wilson, Henry Braid b. Feb 23, 1861
Cape May, New Jersey
O'Hara, Mary b. Jul 10, 1885
Volcker, Paul Adolph b. Sep 5, 1927
Carlstadt, New Jersey
Cuneo, Ernest b. May 27, 1905
Carteret, New Jersey
Medwick, Joe (Joseph Michael)
   b. Nov 4, 1911
Chatham, New Jersey
Day, Chon b. Apr 6, 1907
Ward, (Aaron) Montgomery
   b. Feb 17, 1843
Ward, (Aaron) Montgomery
   b. Feb 17, 1843
Cliffside Park, New Jersey
Blair, Betsy b. Dec 11, 1923
Dunninger, Joseph d. Mar 9, 1975
Lesnevich, Gus b. Feb 22, 1915
Lesnevich, Gus d. Feb 28, 1964
Clinton, New Jersey
Case, Anna b. 1889
Collingswood, New Jersey
Allen, Richard Vincent b. Jan 1, 1936
Coytesville, New Jersey
Price, George b. Jun 9, 1901
Van Fleet, James Alward b. Mar 19, 1892
Deal, New Jersey
Scialfa, Patty b. Jul 29, 1956
Dover, New Jersey
Kennedy, X J, pseud. b. Aug 21, 1929
East Orange, New Jersey
Aymar, Gordon Christian b. Jul 24, 1893
Blish, James Benjamin b. May 23, 1921
Brouthers, "Dan" (Dennis Joseph)
   d. Aug 3, 1932
Clapp, Margaret Antoinette
   b. Apr 11, 1910
Cole, "Cozy" (William Randolph)
   b. Oct 17, 1909
Dundee, Johnny d. Apr 22, 1965
Hillyer, Robert b. Jun 3, 1895
MacRae, Gordon b. Mar 12, 1921
Maddox, Elliott b. Dec 21, 1948
Warwick, Dionne b. Dec 12, 1941
Edison, New Jersey
Stevens, Robert Ten Broeck
   d. Jan 30, 1983
Elberon, New Jersey
Ferrer, Mel(chor Gaston) b. Aug 25, 1917
Garfield, James Abram d. Sep 19, 1881
Eldridge Park, New Jersey
Gilpin, Charles Sidney d. May 6, 1930
Elizabeth, New Jersey
Barry, Rick (Richard Francis, III)
   b. Mar 28, 1944
Blume, Judy Sussman b. Feb 12, 1938

Irvington, New Jersey
Mueller, Christian F d. Jan 7, 1926
Island Heights, New Jersey
Peto, John Frederick d. Nov 23, 1907
Jefferson, New Jersey
Durand, Asher Brown b. Aug 21, 1796
Durand, Asher Brown d. Sep 17, 1886
Jersey City, New Jersey
Allen, Elizabeth b. Jan 25, 1934
Bishop, Jim (James Alonzo)
    b. Nov 21, 1907
Brown, George b. Jan 5, 1949
Buttenheim, Edgar Joseph b. Oct 16, 1882
Catlin, George d. Dec 23, 1872
Conte, Richard b. Mar 24, 1914
Duffy, Edmund b. Mar 1, 1899
Flannery, Susan b. Jul 31, 1943
Hague, Frank b. Jan 17, 1876
Hague, Frank d. Jan 1, 1956
Heatherton, Ray b. Jun 1, 1910
James, Dennis b. Aug 24, 1917
James, Philip b. May 17, 1890
Kilian, Victor b. Mar 6, 1898
Krumgold, Joseph b. Apr 9, 1908
Macfadden, Bernarr Adolphus
    d. Oct 12, 1955
Marshall, Frank James d. Nov 9, 1944
McCoo, Marilyn b. Sep 3, 1943
McMahon, Jim (James Robert)
    b. Aug 21, 1959
Mickens, "Spike" (Robert) b.
Murphy, Warren b. Sep 13, 1933
Murray, Kathryn Hazel b. Sep 15, 1906
Nelson, Ozzie (Oswald George)
    b. Mar 20, 1906
Newman, Phyllis b. Mar 19, 1935
Nugent, Nelle b. Mar 24, 1939
Okun, Arthur Melvin b. Nov 28, 1928
Quidor, John d. Dec 13, 1881
Rovere, Richard Halworth b. May 5, 1915
Secunda, (Holland) Arthur
    b. Nov 12, 1927
Sheed, Frank (Francis Joseph)
    d. Nov 20, 1981
Sinatra, Frank, Jr. (Francis Albert)
    b. Jan 10, 1944
Sinatra, Nancy b. Jun 8, 1940
Smith, Claydes b. Sep 6, 1948
Sonneck, Oscar George Theodore
    b. Oct 6, 1873
Talmadge, Norma b. May 26, 1897
Thomas, Dennis b. Feb 9, 1951
Thompson, Vivian Laubach b. 1911
Warner, Malcolm-Jamal b. Aug 18, 1970
Washburn, Charles d. 1972
Wilson, "Flip" (Clerow) b. Dec 8, 1933
Juliustown, New Jersey
Lippincott, Joshua Ballinger
    b. Mar 18, 1813
Kearney, New Jersey
Mottola, Anthony b. Apr 18, 1918

Kearny, New Jersey
Dejongh, Peter d. Jul 5, 1983
Keyport, New Jersey
Hall, Juanita d. Feb 28, 1968
Kingston, New Jersey
Hewes, Joseph b. Jan 23, 1730
Lakewood, New Jersey
Confrey, "Zez" (Edward E)
    d. Nov 22, 1971
Lamberton, New Jersey
Pike, Zebulon Montgomery b. Feb 5, 1779
Lincoln Park, New Jersey
Kiick, Jim (James F) b. Aug 9, 1946
Linden, New Jersey
Grier, "Rosey" (Roosevelt) b. Jul 14, 1932
Livingston, New Jersey
Biondi, Frank J, Jr, b. Jan 9, 1945
Galento, Tony (Anthony) d. Jul 22, 1979
Guarnieri, Johnny (John A) d. Jan 7, 1985
Jensen, Alfred Julio d. Apr 4, 1981
Turnbull, Agnes Sligh d. Jan 31, 1982
Long Beach, New Jersey
Anderson, Richard Norman
    b. Aug 8, 1926
Barry, Daniel b. Jul 11, 1923
Long Branch, New Jersey
Clayton, Bessie d. Jul 16, 1948
Frank, Waldo b. Aug 25, 1889
Greer, "Sonny" (William Alexander)
    b. Dec 13, 1903
Hobart, Garret Augustus b. Jun 3, 1844
Howard, Tom d. Feb 27, 1955
Mailer, Norman b. Jan 31, 1923
Pratt, Fletcher d. Jun 10, 1956
Siegel, Stanley E b. May 7, 1928
Long Island, New Jersey
LaFeuer, Minard d. Sep 26, 1854
Madison, New Jersey
McGraw, Donald Cushing
    b. May 21, 1897
Newcombe, Don(ald) b. Jun 14, 1926
Mahwah, New Jersey
Guy-Blanche, Alice d. 1968
Mendham, New Jersey
Doubleday, Abner d. Jan 26, 1893
Merchantville, New Jersey
Walcott, "Jersey Joe" b. Jan 31, 1914
Metuchen, New Jersey
Ciardi, John Anthony d. Apr 1, 1986
Copperfield, David b. 1956
Fisher, Clara d. Nov 12, 1898
Freeman, Mary E Wilkins d. Mar 13, 1930
Middletown Point, New Jersey
Bartlett, John Sherren d. Aug 23, 1863
Monmouth County, New Jersey
Freneau, Philip Morin d. Dec 18, 1832
Montclair, New Jersey
Aldrin, Edwin E(ugene), Jr.
    b. Jan 20, 1930
Ball, Thomas d. 1911
Brown, George Scratchley b. Aug 17, 1918

Cole, Charles Woolsey b. Feb 8, 1907
Funk, Isaac Kauffman d. Apr 4, 1912
Funk, Wilfred John d. Jun 1, 1965
Hartford, George Ludlum d. Sep 23, 1957
Hayden, Sterling b. Mar 26, 1916
Keene, Laura d. Nov 4, 1873
Kirsten, Dorothy b. Jul 6, 1917
Kreskin b. Jan 12, 1935
Liquori, Marty (Martin A) b. Sep 11, 1949
Melcher, Frederic Gershon d. Mar 9, 1963
Mennen, William Gerhard d. Feb 17, 1968
Sullivan, A(loysius) M(ichael)
    d. Jun 10, 1980
Wesson, David d. May 22, 1934

Moorestown, New Jersey
Paul, Alice b. Jan 11, 1885
Paul, Alice d. Jul 9, 1977

Morris Plains, New Jersey
Quinlan, Karen Ann d. Jun 11, 1985

Morris Town, New Jersey
Harrison, Anna Tuthill Symmes
    b. Jul 25, 1775

Morristown, New Jersey
Cook, Phil d. Sep 18, 1958
Dalrymple, Jean b. Sep 2, 1910
Fillmore, Caroline Carmichael McIntosh
    b. Oct 21, 1813
Griswold, A Whitney b. Oct 27, 1906
Jones, Joseph John (Joe) d. Apr 9, 1963
LaFeuer, Minard b. Aug 10, 1798
Lebowitz, Fran(ces Ann) b. Oct 27, 1950
Lowry, Judith Ives b. Jul 27, 1890
Messer, Alfred A b. Oct 29, 1922
Scott, Tony b. Jun 17, 1921
Vail, Alfred Lewis b. Sep 25, 1807
Vail, Alfred Lewis d. Jan 18, 1859

Mount Holly, New Jersey
Harris, Franco b. Mar 7, 1950
Wilson, Jackie d. Jan 21, 1984

Mountain Lakes, New Jersey
Hinrichs, Gustav d. Mar 26, 1942

Mountainside, New Jersey
Campbell, John W d. Jul 11, 1971

Neptune, New Jersey
DeVito, Danny Michael b. Nov 27, 1944
Guerin, Jules d. Jun 13, 1946
Lyon, "Southside" Johnny b. Dec 4, 1948
Nicholson, Jack b. Apr 22, 1937
Schweickart, Russell L b. Oct 25, 1935

New Brunswick, New Jersey
Baskin, Leonard b. Aug 15, 1922
Cole, Jack b. Apr 27, 1914
Dickson, Earle Ensign d. Sep 21, 1961
Gilman, Dorothy b. Jun 25, 1923
Johnson, James Price b. Feb 1, 1891
Kilmer, Joyce (Alfred Joyce)
    b. Dec 6, 1886
Osterwald, Bibi (Margaret Virginia)
    b. Feb 3, 1920
Pass, Joe b. Jan 13, 1929
Scott, Austin W b. 1885

Theismann, Joe (Joseph Robert)
    b. Sep 9, 1949
Vanderbilt, William Henry b. May 8, 1821
Veronis, John James b. Mar 6, 1928
Wasserburg, Gerald Joseph
    b. Mar 25, 1927

Newark, New Jersey
Adams, Harriet Stratemeyer
    b. Dec 11, 1892
Addonizio, Hugh Joseph b. Jan 31, 1914
Amos, John b. Dec 27, 1942
Blacque, Taurean b. May 10, 1946
Blaine, Vivian b. Nov 21, 1924
Bouton, Jim (James Alan) b. Mar 8, 1939
Brennan, William Joseph b. Apr 25, 1906
Burr, Aaron b. Feb 6, 1756
Campbell, John W b. Jun 8, 1910
Cerone, Rick (Richard Aldo)
    b. May 19, 1954
Coles, Joanna b. Aug 11, 1944
Crane, Stephen b. Nov 1, 1871
DePalma, Brian Russell b. Sep 11, 1940
Ditmars, Raymond Lee b. Jun 20, 1876
Douglas, Amanda Minnie d. Jul 18, 1918
Fairchild, John Burr b. Mar 6, 1927
Fiedler, Leslie Aaron b. Mar 8, 1917
Forsythe, Albert E d. May 7, 1986
Francis, Connie b. Dec 12, 1938
Gaynor, Gloria b. Sep 7, 1949
Ginsberg, Allen b. Jun 3, 1926
Gusberg, Saul Bernard b. Aug 3, 1913
Hagler, Marvelous Marvin
    b. May 23, 1952
Hamilton, Billy (William Robert)
    b. Feb 16, 1866
Hepbron, George d. Apr 30, 1946
Holland, John Philip d. Aug 12, 1914
Holmes, Taylor b. 1878
Houston, "Cissy" (Emily Drinkard) b. 1932
Houston, Whitney b. Aug 9, 1963
Hughes, Emmet John b. Dec 26, 1920
Jones, Leroi b. Oct 7, 1934
Kearny, Stephen Watts b. Aug 30, 1794
Kilgore, Al b. Dec 19, 1983
Lasser, Jacob Kay b. Oct 7, 1896
Lawrence, Josephine b. 1897
Lewis, Jerry b. Mar 16, 1926
Lindsey, Mort b. Mar 21, 1923
Lowenstein, Allard Kenneth
    b. Jan 16, 1929
Lucas, Nick b. Aug 22, 1897
Massi, Nick b. Sep 19, 1935
McDougall, Walt(er) b. Feb 10, 1858
Meier, Richard Alan b. Oct 12, 1934
Mennen, William Gerhard b. Dec 20, 1884
Moore, Jack b. Oct 23, 1933
Mott, Charles Stewart b. Jun 2, 1875
Nehemiah, Renaldo b. Mar 24, 1959
Northrop, John Knudsen b. Nov 10, 1895
Pangborn, Franklin b. Jan 23, 1893
Pearson, Drew b. Jan 12, 1951

Ritz, Harry b. 1906
Rodino, Peter Wallace, Jr. b. Jun 7, 1909
Roth, Philip Milton b. Mar 19, 1933
Saint Denis, Ruth b. Jan 20, 1877
Saint, Eva Marie b. Jul 4, 1924
Schary, Dore b. Aug 31, 1905
Scheuer, Philip K(latz) b. Mar 24, 1902
Schneider, Richard Coy b. May 29, 1913
Schultz, Dutch d. Oct 24, 1935
Simeone, Harry b. May 9, 1911
Simon, Paul b. Nov 5, 1942
Stevens, Morton b. Jan 30, 1929
Stoneham, Horace b. 1904
Stratemeyer, Edward L d. May 10, 1930
Terhune, Albert Payson b. Dec 21, 1872
Tough, Dave d. Dec 6, 1948
Valli, Frankie b. May 3, 1937
Vaughan, Sarah b. Mar 27, 1924
Viorst, Judith (Stahl) b. Feb 2, 1931
Warden, Jack b. Sep 18, 1920
Westheimer, Irvin Ferdinand
     b. Sep 19, 1879
Weston, Edward F b. Oct 24, 1879

Newbold, New Jersey
Baxter, Frank Condie b. May 4, 1896

Newport, New Jersey
Hall, Juanita b. Nov 6, 1901

Newton, New Jersey
Bradley, Will b. Jul 12, 1912
Trotta, Maurice S d. Jul 11, 1976
Wright, Henry d. Jul 9, 1936

North Arlington, New Jersey
Eilshemius, Louis Michel b. Feb 4, 1864

North Bergen, New Jersey
Braddock, James J d. 1974
Leonetti, Tommy b. Sep 10, 1929

Nutley, New Jersey
Blake, Robert b. Sep 18, 1938
Bunner, Henry Cuyler d. May 11, 1896
Goodrich, Lloyd b. Jul 10, 1897

Oakland, New Jersey
Evans, Madge (Margherita)
     d. Apr 26, 1981
McKeon, Doug b. Jun 10, 1966

Ocean City, New Jersey
Andes, "Keith" (John Charles)
     b. Jul 12, 1920
Foster, Preston b. Aug 24, 1900
Talese, Gay b. Feb 7, 1932

Oradell, New Jersey
Riddle, Nelson b. Jun 1, 1921

Orange, New Jersey
Caulfield, Joan b. Jun 1, 1922
Feeney, "Chub" (Charles Stoneham)
     b. Aug 31, 1921
Fisher, Gail b. Aug 18, 1935
Galento, Tony (Anthony) b. Mar 10, 1909
Harbison, John Harris b. Dec 20, 1938
Hartford, John Augustine b. Feb 10, 1872
Hicks, Beatrice Alice b. Jan 2, 1919
Jeritza, Maria d. Jul 10, 1982

Mason, Lowell d. Aug 11, 1872
McClellan, George Brinton d. Oct 29, 1885
Olcott, Henry Steel b. Aug 2, 1832
Scheider, Roy Richard b. Oct 11, 1935
Smith, Tony b. 1912
Stetson, John Batterson b. May 5, 1830
Tomkins, Calvin b. Dec 17, 1925
Wiley, William Bradford b. Nov 17, 1910

Palisades, New Jersey
Bennett, Joan b. Feb 27, 1910

Paramus, New Jersey
Conroy, Frank d. Feb 4, 1964
Zayak, Elaine b. Apr 12, 1965

Passaic, New Jersey
Fagen, Donald b. Jan 10, 1948
Perkins, Millie b. May 12, 1940
Piscopo, Joe (Joseph Charles)
     b. Jun 17, 1951
Pollard, Michael J b. May 30, 1939
Swit, Loretta b. Nov 4, 1937
Zaentz, Saul b.

Paterson, New Jersey
Baker, Samm Sinclair b. Jul 29, 1909
Costello, Lou b. Mar 6, 1908
Einhorn, Eddie (Edward Martin)
     b. Jan 3, 1936
Hobart, Garret Augustus d. Nov 21, 1899
Kahn, Alfred Edward b. Oct 17, 1917
Kleinfield, "Sonny" (Nathan Richard)
     b. Aug 12, 1950
Lautenberg, Frank R b. Jan 23, 1924
Perranoski, Ron(ald Peter) b. Apr 1, 1936
Rochberg, George b. Jul 5, 1918
Simon, William E(dward) b. Nov 27, 1927
Sumner, William Graham b. Oct 30, 1840
Wheeler, Bert b. Apr 7, 1895

Penns Grove, New Jersey
Forsythe, John b. Jan 29, 1918
Foster, Paul b. Oct 15, 1931

Perth Amboy, New Jersey
Dunlap, William b. Feb 11, 1766
Franz, Arthur b. Feb 29, 1920
Margolius, Sidney Senier b. May 3, 1911

Phalanx, New Jersey
Woollcott, Alexander Humphreys
     b. Jan 19, 1887

Plainfield, New Jersey
Allen, John d. Mar 8, 1892
Brooks, Van Wyck b. Feb 16, 1886
Cox, Archibald b. May 17, 1912
DeGraff, Robert F(air) b. Jun 9, 1895
Dwiggins, Don b. Nov 15, 1913
Evans, Bill (William John)
     b. Aug 16, 1929
Gilbreth, Frank Bunker, Jr.
     b. Mar 17, 1911
Kirk, Phyllis b. Sep 18, 1930
Leonard, William Ellery b. Jan 25, 1876
Thompson, Edward Herbert
     d. May 11, 1935

Spring Lake, New Jersey
Boller, Paul F, Jr. b. Dec 31, 1916
Chesebrough, Robert Augustus
  d. Sep 8, 1933
Hartford, George Huntington
  d. Aug 29, 1917

Summit, New Jersey
Fleming, Peter b. Jan 21, 1955
Jackson, Charles Reginald b. Apr 6, 1903
Streep, Meryl (Mary Louise)
  b. Jun 22, 1949

Syracuse, New Jersey
Ross, Lillian b. Jun 8, 1927

Teaneck, New Jersey
Erwin, "Pee Wee" (George)
  d. Jun 20, 1981
Hare, James Henry d. Jun 24, 1946
McBride, Patricia b. Aug 23, 1942
Messmer, Otto d. Oct 28, 1983
Nelson, Rick (Eric Hilliard)
  b. May 8, 1940
Paul, Frank Rudolph d. Jun 29, 1963

Tenafly, New Jersey
Gore, Lesley b. May 2, 1946

Toms River, New Jersey
Messersmith, Andy (John Alexander)
  b. Aug 6, 1945

Trenton, New Jersey
Antheil, George b. Jul 8, 1900
Boehm, Edward M d. Jan 29, 1969
Bronson, Betty (Elizabeth Ada)
  b. Nov 17, 1906
Cristofer, Michael b. Jan 22, 1945
Crooks, Richard Alexander
  b. Jun 26, 1900
Dix, Dorothea Lynde d. Jul 17, 1887
Donnelly, Ruth b. May 17, 1896
Hauptmann, Bruno Richard
  d. Apr 3, 1936
Kovacs, Ernie b. Jan 23, 1919
Lawrence, Margaret b. Aug 2, 1889
Linowitz, Sol b. Dec 7, 1913
Pitcher, Molly b. Oct 13, 1750
Roebling, Washington Augustus
  d. Jul 21, 1926
Scalia, Antonin b. Mar 11, 1936
Shange, Ntozake b. Oct 18, 1948
Taylor, Peter b. Jan 8, 1917
Thompson, Frank, Jr. b. Jul 26, 1918

Union City, New Jersey
Messmer, Otto b. 1892

Union Hill, New Jersey
Cousins, Norman b. Jun 24, 1912
Lee, Lila b. Jul 25, 1902
Monty, Gloria b. Aug 12, 1921

Upper Montclair, New Jersey
Ives, Herbert Eugene d. Nov 13, 1953

Verona, New Jersey
Dana, Margaret b.

Weehawken, New Jersey
Bitter, Francis b. Jul 22, 1902
Hamilton, Alexander d. Jul 11, 1804
Rogers, Mary Cecilia d. Jul 25, 1841
Schwarz, Gerard b. Aug 19, 1947

West Bend, New Jersey
Parker, Dorothy Rothschild
  b. Aug 22, 1893

West End, New Jersey
Guggenheim, Harry Frank
  b. Aug 23, 1890

West Hoboken, New Jersey
DiDonato, Pietro b. Apr 3, 1911

West Long Beach, New Jersey
Pryor, Arthur W d. Jun 18, 1942

West New York, New Jersey
Hendl, Walter b. Jan 12, 1917

West Orange, New Jersey
Chapin, James Ormsbee b. Jul 9, 1887
Davis, Alexander Jackson d. Jan 14, 1892
Edison, Thomas Alva d. Oct 18, 1931
Herridge, Robert T b. 1918
Stagg, Amos Alonzo b. Aug 16, 1862

Westfield, New Jersey
Addams, Charles Samuel b. Jan 7, 1912
Apgar, Virginia b. Jul 7, 1909
Schifter, Peter Mark b. 1950

Whippany, New Jersey
North, Sterling d. Dec 21, 1974

Wildwood, New Jersey
Corle, Edwin b. May 7, 1906

Woodbine, New Jersey
Pincus, Gregory b. Apr 9, 1903

Woodstown, New Jersey
Shinn, Everett b. Nov 7, 1876

NEW MEXICO

Garrett, Pat(rick Floyd) d. Feb 29, 1908
McKerrow, Amanda b. Nov 7, 1964

Alamogordo, New Mexico
Clayton, Jan(e Byral) b. Aug 26, 1925
Condon, Edward b. Mar 2, 1902
Lord, Pauline d. Oct 11, 1950

Albuquerque, New Mexico
Abruzzo, Ben(jamine Lou) d. Feb 11, 1985
Anderson, Clint(on Presba)
  d. Nov 11, 1975
Crichton, Robert b. Jan 29, 1925
Cushman, Austin Thomas b. 1901
Domenici, Pete V(ichi) b. May 7, 1932
Fergusson, Francis b. Feb 21, 1904
Fergusson, Harvey b. Jan 28, 1890
Hatch, Carl A d. Sep 15, 1963
Jones, Preston St. Vrain b. Apr 7, 1936
LaFarge, Oliver d. Aug 2, 1963
Lange, Hans d. Aug 13, 1960
Lott, Ronnie (Ronald Mandel)
  b. May 8, 1959
Masters, John d. May 6, 1983
Olsen, Ole d. Jan 26, 1963

Smith, Madolyn Story b. 1957
Summerville, "Slim" (George J)
  b. Jul 10, 1896
Unser, Al b. May 29, 1939
Unser, Bobby b. Feb 20, 1924
Austin, New Mexico
Madden, John b. Apr 10, 1936
Carlsbad, New Mexico
Cabot, Bruce b. Apr 20, 1904
Clovis, New Mexico
Ruffin, Clovis b.
Deming, New Mexico
Brown, Nacio Herb b. Feb 22, 1896
Fort Sumner, New Mexico
Billy the Kid d. Jul 15, 1881
Greenville, New Mexico
Weaver, Thomas b. May 1, 1929
Jacona, New Mexico
Owings, Nathaniel Alexander
  d. Jun 13, 1984
Madrid, New Mexico
Marsh, Mae b. Nov 19, 1895
Melrose, New Mexico
Hanna, William Denby b. Jul 14, 1910
Moriarty, New Mexico
Anaya, Toney b. Apr 29, 1941
Mountain Park, New Mexico
Mauldin, Bill (William Henry)
  b. Oct 29, 1921
Roswell, New Mexico
Denver, John b. Dec 31, 1943
Hurd, Peter b. Feb 22, 1904
Hurd, Peter d. Jul 9, 1984
Moore, Demi b. Nov 11,
San Antonio, New Mexico
Hilton, Conrad Nicholson b. Dec 25, 1887
Santa Fe, New Mexico
Austin, Mary Hunter d. Aug 13, 1934
Bynner, Harold Witter d. Jun 1, 1968
Gilpin, Laura d. Nov 30, 1979
Hodge, Frederick Webb d. Sep 28, 1956
Hurley, Patrick Jay d. Jul 30, 1963
Kapp, Joe (Joseph) b. Mar 19, 1938
Lamy, Jean Baptist d. Feb 13, 1888
O'Keeffe, Georgia d. Mar 6, 1986
Seton, Ernest Thompson d. Oct 23, 1946
Young, James Webb d. Mar 1973
Santa Rita, New Mexico
Kiner, Ralph McPherran b. Oct 27, 1922
Schmitt, Harrison Hagan b. Jul 3, 1935
Santa Rosa, New Mexico
Lomax, Louis d. Jul 1970
Tularosa, New Mexico
Ortega, Katherine Davalos b. Jul 16, 1934
Stanley, Kim b. Feb 11, 1925

NEW YORK

Agron, Salvador b. 1944
Baker, Rick b. 1950
Bethune, Thomas Greene d. 1908

Bliss, Robert Woods d. Apr 19, 1962
Bloomingdale, Samuel d. May 10, 1968
Blotta, Anthony d. Sep 11, 1971
Bok, Hannes Vajn d. Apr 11, 1964
Chwast, Seymour b. Aug 18, 1931
Czolgosz, Leon F d. Oct 29, 1901
Downing, Andrew Jackson d. Jul 28, 1852
Ferguson, Elsie b. Aug 19, 1885
Fishbein, Harry J d. Feb 19, 1976
Genaro, Frankie b. Aug 26, 1901
Goodwin, Nat C d. Jan 31, 1919
Halsted, William Stewart b. Sep 23, 1852
Hastings, Thomas b. Mar 11, 1860
Kennedy, Moorehead Cowell, Jr.
  b. Nov 5, 1930
Lasser, Louise b. 1940
Lindbergh, Jon Morrow b. Aug 16, 1932
Mandelbaum, Fredericka b. 1818
Netanyahu, Yonatan b. 1946
Plummer, Amanda b. Mar 23, 1957
Steel, Danielle b. Aug 1948
Stevens, Emily A b. 1882
Taylor, Lucy Hobbs b. Mar 14, 1833
Tekakwitha, Kateri b. 1656
Tunis, Edwin Burdett b. Dec 8, 1897
Vedder, Elihu b. Feb 26, 1836
Wexley, John b. 1907
Young, Marian d. Dec 9, 1973
Adams, New York
Clarke, Bruce Cooper b. Apr 29, 1901
Morton, Julius Sterling b. Apr 22, 1832
Adams Center, New York
Dewey, Melvil b. Dec 10, 1851
Afton, New York
Hayes, Carlton Joseph Huntley
  b. May 16, 1882
Hayes, Carlton Joseph Huntley
  d. Sep 3, 1964
Albany, New York
Ackerman, Harry S b. Nov 17, 1912
Alexander, William d. Jan 15, 1783
Alston, Theodosia Burr b. 1783
Baker, Kathy b. Mar 20, 1961
Clinton, DeWitt d. Feb 11, 1828
Conkling, Roscoe b. Oct 30, 1829
Corning, Erastus d. Apr 9, 1872
Corning, Erastus, III b. Oct 7, 1909
DeMoss, Arthur S b. Oct 26, 1925
Devane, William b. Sep 5, 1937
Diamond, "Legs" (Jack) d. Dec 18, 1931
Elliott, Charles Loring d. Aug 25, 1868
Evers, John Joseph d. Mar 28, 1947
Fort, Charles Hoy b. 1874
Funk, Casimir d. Nov 19, 1967
Groves, Leslie Richard b. Aug 17, 1896
Hand, Learned b. Jan 27, 1872
Harte, (Francis Bret) b. Aug 25, 1836
Henry, Joseph b. Dec 17, 1797
James, Henry b. Jun 3, 1811
Kennedy, William b. Jan 16, 1928
Lewis, Edmonia b. Jul 4, 1845

Livingston, Philip b. Jan 15, 1716
Loeb, William b. Oct 9, 1866
Martin, Homer Dodge b. Nov 28, 1836
McCartan, Edward b. Aug 16, 1879
Palmer, Erastus Dow
    d. 1904
Pritikin, Nathan
    d. Feb 21, 1985
Rooney, Andy (Andrew Aitken)
    b. Jan 14, 1919
Schuyler, Phillip John b. Nov 20, 1773
Schuyler, Phillip John d. Nov 18, 1804
Sheridan, Philip Henry b. Mar 6, 1831
Simons, Howard b. Jun 3, 1928
Slobodkin, Louis b. Feb 19, 1903
Smith, David d. May 23, 1965
Smith, Theobald b. Jul 31, 1859
Tompkins, Angel b. Dec 20, 1943
Van Buren, Hannah Hoes d. Feb 5, 1819
Van Heusen, John b. Apr 14, 1869
Van Rensselaer, Stephen d. Jan 26, 1839
Winter, Alice Vivian Ames
    b. Nov 28, 1865
Woolley, Monty (Edgar Montillion)
    d. May 6, 1962
Yunich, David Lawrence b. May 21, 1917
Albany County, New York
Palmer, Potter b. May 20, 1826
Schoolcraft, Henry Rowe b. Mar 28, 1793
Allegheny, New York
Taylor, Paul b. Jul 29, 1930
Altmar, New York
Avery, Milton (Clark) b. Mar 7, 1893
Amenia Union, New York
Holabird, William b. Sep 11, 1854
Amityville, New York
Barrymore, Maurice d. Mar 26, 1905
Mayhew, Richard b. Apr 3, 1934
Munson, Gorham B(ert) b. May 26, 1896
Nash, George Frederick d. Dec 31, 1944
Amsterdam, New York
Douglas, Kirk b. Dec 9, 1916
Angola, New York
Carrier, Willis H b. Nov 26, 1876
Annandale, New York
Crittendon, Thomas L d. Oct 23, 1893
Arden, New York
Harriman, E(dward) Roland (Noel)
    d. Feb 16, 1978
Armonk, New York
London, George d. Mar 24, 1985
Astoria, New York
Brooke, Hillary b. Sep 8, 1914
Gallatin, Albert (Abraham Alfonse Albert)
    d. Aug 12, 1849
Gardner, Ed(ward Francis) b. Jun 29, 1905
Kelly, Jack b. 1927
Kenny, Nick b. Feb 3, 1895
Merman, Ethel b. Jan 16, 1909
Montez, Lola d. Jan 17, 1861

Oerter, Al(fred A) b. Sep 19, 1936
Walken, Christopher b. Mar 31, 1943
Auburn, New York
Burroughs, William Seward
    b. Jan 28, 1855
Hitchcock, Raymond b. 1865
Holland, Jerome Heartwell b. Jan 9, 1916
Miller, Olive Thorne b. Jun 25, 1831
Seward, William Henry d. Oct 10, 1872
Tubman, Harriet Ross d. Mar 10, 1913
Austerlitz, New York
Millay, Edna St. Vincent d. Oct 19, 1950
Babylon, New York
Dangerfield, Rodney b. Nov 22, 1921
Kobbe, Gustav d. Jul 27, 1918
Bainbridge, New York
Smith, Jedediah Strong b. Jan 6, 1799
Baldwin, New York
Demme, Jonathan b. 1944
Ballston Spa, New York
Doubleday, Abner b. Jun 26, 1819
Marcy, William Learned d. Jul 4, 1857
Batavia, New York
Brisbane, Albert b. Aug 2, 1809
Gardner, John Champlin, Jr.
    b. Jul 21, 1933
Bay Shore, New York
Faversham, William Alfred
    d. Apr 7, 1940
Kilgour, Joseph d. Apr 21, 1933
Markey, Enid d. Nov 15, 1981
Profaci, Joe (Joseph) d. Jun 6, 1962
Bayonne, New York
Langella, Frank b. Jan 1, 1940
Bayside, New York
Villella, Edward Joseph b. Oct 1, 1932
Beacon, New York
Baekeland, Leo Hendrick d. Feb 23, 1944
Forrestal, James Vincent b. Feb 15, 1892
Lavalle, Paul b. Sep 6, 1908
Montgomery, Robert Henry
    b. May 21, 1904
Phelps, "Digger" (Richard) b. Jul 4, 1941
Bedford, New York
Adair, Frank E(arl) d. Dec 31, 1981
Jay, John d. May 17, 1829
Oenslager, Donald Mitchell
    d. Jun 21, 1975
Wilder, Clinton d. Feb 14, 1986
Bedford Hills, New York
Frankel, Charles d. May 10, 1979
Hughes, Barnard b. Jul 16, 1915
Beekman, New York
Lossing, Benson John b. Feb 12, 1813
Bensonhurst, New York
Stone, Dorothy b. 1905
Berne, New York
Bradley, Joseph P b. Mar 14, 1813
Binghamton, New York
Casey, Dan(iel Maurice) b. Oct 2, 1965
Garis, Howard Roger b. Apr 25, 1873

Herbert, Hugh b. Aug 10, 1887
Hutton, Jim b. May 31, 1938
Link, Edwin Albert d. Sep 7, 1981
Luciano, Ron(ald Michael) b. Jun 28, 1937
Sharkey, Jack (Joseph Paul) b. Oct 6, 1902
Bloomingdale, New York
Renwick, James b. Nov 1, 1818
Blue Point, New York
Booth, Ballington d. Oct 5, 1940
Boonville, New York
Edmonds, Walter Dumaux b. Jul 15, 1903
Brentwood, New York
Gordon, Kitty d. May 26, 1974
Brewster, New York
Branigan, Laura b. Jul 3, 1957
Briarcliff, New York
Clark, Barrett H d. Aug 5, 1953
Bridgehampton, New York
Fascell, Dante Bruno b. Mar 9, 1917
Bridgewater, New York
Babcock, Stephen Moulton b. Oct 22, 1843
Bristol, New York
Gannett, Frank Ernest b. Sep 15, 1876
Brockport, New York
Holmes, Mary Jane Hawes d. Oct 6, 1907
Brocton, New York
Pullman, George Mortimer b. Mar 3, 1831
Bronx, New York
Archibald, Nate (Nathaniel)
    b. Apr 18, 1948
Armstrong, Harry d. Feb 28, 1951
Bernbach, William b. Aug 13, 1911
Bichler, Joyce b. Jan 19, 1954
Bird, Junius Bouton d. Apr 2, 1982
Bishop, Joey b. Feb 3, 1918
Cara, Irene b. Mar 18, 1959
Chapman, Ceil (Cecilia Mitchell)
    d. Jul 13, 1979
Chomsky, Marvin b. May 23, 1929
DeVita, Vincent Theodore, Jr.
    b. Mar 7, 1935
Di Mucci, Dion b. Jul 18, 1939
Donovan, Art b. Jun 5, 1925
Drexler, Rosalyn b. Nov 25, 1926
Epstein, Alvin b. May 24, 1925
Fielding, Temple Hornaday b. Oct 8, 1913
Flynn, Edward Joseph b. Sep 22, 1891
Fort, Charles Hoy d. May 3, 1932
Frehley, Ace b. Apr 27, 1951
Galella, Ron b. Jan 10, 1931
Gaudio, Bob b. Nov 17, 1942
Halberstam, Michael Joseph
    b. Aug 9, 1932
Husing, Ted b. Nov 27, 1901
Joel, Billy (William Martin)
    b. May 9, 1949
King, Evelyn b. Jul 1, 1960
Kirshner, Don b. Apr 17, 1934
Landesberg, Steve b. Nov 23,
Leigh, Carolyn b. Apr 21, 1926
Levin, Ira b. Aug 27, 1929

Linden, Hal b. Mar 20, 1931
Lopez, Priscilla b. Feb 26, 1948
Markham, "Pigmeat" (Dewey M)
    d. Dec 13, 1981
Martell, Vincent b. Nov 11, 1945
Messing, Shep b. Oct 9, 1949
Moriarty, Cathy b. Nov 29, 1960
Mulligan, Richard b. Nov 13, 1932
Munn, Frank b. 1894
Nyro, Laura b. Oct 18, 1947
Ojeda, Eddie b. Aug 5, 1954
Payne, Sidney b. Oct 11, 1930
Richman, Charles d. Dec 1, 1940
Rosen, Sheldon b. Aug 26, 1943
Rosenberg, Steven A b. Aug 2, 1940
Savage, Augusta Christine d. Mar 26, 1962
Savo, Jimmy b. 1896
Schultz, Dutch b. Aug 6, 1900
Scully, Vince(nt Edward) b. Nov 29, 1927
Sellecca, Connie b. May 25, 1955
Simpson, Valerie b. Aug 26, 1948
Sovern, Michael I(ra) b. Dec 1, 1931
Vale, Jerry b. Jul 8, 1932
Weidenbaum, Murray Lew b. Feb 10, 1927
Whiting, George d. Dec 18, 1943

Bronxville, New York
Brown, Henry Billings d. Sep 4, 1913
Butcher, Willard C(arlisle) b. Oct 25, 1926
Carmer, Carl Lamson d. Sep 11, 1976
Coslow, Sam d. Apr 2, 1982
Dixon, Mort d. Mar 23, 1956
Fickett, Mary b. May 23,
Fosdick, Harry Emerson d. Oct 5, 1969
Frick, Ford Christopher d. Apr 8, 1978
Hagerty, James Campbell d. Apr 11, 1981
Hagerty, James Campbell d. Apr 11, 1981
Keller, Arthur C d. Aug 25, 1983
Mann, Paul d. Sep 24, 1985
Rounds, David b. Oct 9, 1930
Shively, George Jenks d. Apr 11, 1980

Brookhaven, New York
Floyd, William b. Dec 17, 1734

Brooklyn, New York
Adams, James Truslow b. Oct 18, 1878
Adams, Joey b. Jan 6, 1911
Adams, Leonie Fuller b. Dec 9, 1899
Albert, Stephen Joel b. Feb 6, 1941
Allen, Woody b. Dec 1, 1935
Alzado, Lyle Martin b. Apr 3, 1949
Anderson, Warner b. Mar 10, 1911
Andrews, Tige b. Mar 19, 1920
Aptheker, Herbert b. Jul 31, 1915
Auerbach, "Red" (Arnold Jacob)
    b. Sep 20, 1917
Baillie, Hugh b. Oct 23, 1890
Baio, Scott Vincent b. Sep 22, 1961
Balaban, Emanuel b. Jan 27, 1895
Balin, Ina b. Nov 12, 1937
Balukas, Jean b. Jun 28, 1959
Bannerman, Francis d. Nov 26, 1918
Barnet, Sylvan M, Jr. b. Dec 11, 1926

Baron, Samuel b. Apr 27, 1925
Barr, George b. Nov 11, 1907
Beebe, William (Charles William)
　b. Jul 29, 1877
Beecher, Henry Ward d. Mar 8, 1887
Benarde, Melvin Albert b. Jun 15, 1923
Benatar, Pat b. Jan 10, 1952
Bennett, William John b. Jul 31, 1943
Berger, Melvin H b. Aug 23, 1927
Bergman, Alan b. Sep 11, 1925
Bergman, Marilyn Keith b. Nov 10, 1929
Berlinger, Warren b. Aug 31, 1937
Berndt, Walter b. Nov 22, 1899
Berrill, Jack b. 1924
Birdseye, Clarence Frank b. Dec 9, 1886
Black, Walter J b. May 12, 1893
Black, William b. 1904
Blackwell, Mr. (Richard) b.
Blake, Eubie (James Hubert)
　d. Feb 12, 1983
Bleiberg, Robert Marvin b. Jun 21, 1924
Bloom, Julius b. Sep 23, 1912
Bloom, Mickey (Milton) b. Aug 26, 1906
Bloomgarden, Kermit b. Dec 15, 1904
Boehm, Helen Francesca Stefanie Franzolin
　b. 1922
Bogart, Neil b. Feb 3, 1943
Bologna, Joseph b. 1938
Boole, Ella Alexander d. Mar 13, 1952
Borch, Fred J b. Apr 28, 1910
Brady, James b. Nov 15, 1928
Brady, Scott b. Sep 13, 1924
Brasher, Rex b. Jul 31, 1869
Breese, Edmund b. Jun 18, 1871
Brenner, Barbara Johnes b. Jun 26, 1925
Brett, Ken(neth Alvin) b. Sep 18, 1948
Brisebois, Danielle b. Jun 28, 1969
Brock, Alice May b. Feb 28, 1941
Brody, Jane Ellen b. May 5, 1941
Brook, Alexander b. Jul 14, 1898
Brooks, James L b. May 9, 1940
Broun, (Matthew) Heywood (Campbell)
　b. Dec 7, 1888
Brown, Roger b. May 22, 1942
Brownmiller, Susan b. Feb 15, 1935
Budd, Julie b. 1944
Bunny, John d. Apr 26, 1915
Bunting, Mary Ingraham b. Jul 10, 1910
Burchenal, Elizabeth d. Nov 21, 1956
Buzzell, Eddie b. Nov 13, 1907
Bynner, Harold Witter b. Aug 10, 1881
Cahill, Marie b. Dec 20, 1870
Califano, Joseph Anthony, Jr.
　b. May 15, 1931
Callas, Charlie b. Dec 20,
Capone, Al(phonse) b. Jan 17, 1899
Carey, Hugh Leo b. Apr 11, 1919
Carleton, Will d. Dec 18, 1912
Carlisle, Kevin b. Dec 24, 1935
Celler, Emanuel b. May 6, 1888
Chaikin, Joseph b. Sep 16, 1935

Chamberlin, William Henry
　b. Feb 17, 1897
Chambers, Robert W b. May 26, 1865
Chandler, Jeff b. Dec 15, 1918
Charlip, Remy b. Jan 10, 1929
Chisholm, Shirley Anita St. Hill
　b. Nov 30, 1924
Clayton, Lou b. 1887
Cleland, Thomas Maitland
　b. Aug 18, 1880
Clinton, Larry b. Aug 17, 1909
Cohen, "Mickey" (Meyer) b. 1913
Cohn, Al b. Nov 24, 1925
Colombo, Joseph Anthony b. Jun 16, 1923
Commoner, Barry b. May 28, 1917
Cooney, Barbara b. Aug 6, 1916
Cooney, Gerry (Gerald Arthur)
　b. Aug 24, 1956
Coots, J Fred b. May 2, 1897
Copland, Aaron b. Nov 14, 1900
Cortissoz, Royal b. Feb 10, 1869
Cox, Richard Joseph b. Aug 21, 1929
Criss, Peter b. Dec 20, 1947
Crosby, Percy b. Dec 8, 1930
Cunningham, Billy (William)
　b. Jun 3, 1943
D'Amato, Alfonse Marcello b. Aug 1, 1937
Dale, Alan b. Jul 9, 1926
Daly, Arnold b. Oct 4, 1875
Damon, Stuart b. Feb 5, 1937
Damone, Vic b. Jun 12, 1928
Daniels, William b. Mar 31, 1927
Dannay, Frederic b. Oct 20, 1905
Darken, Lawrence Stamper b. Sep 18, 1909
Davis, Clive Jay b. Apr 4, 1932
Davis, Tommy (Thomas Herman, Jr.)
　b. Mar 21, 1939
DellaFemina, Jerry b. Jul 22, 1936
DeLuise, Dom b. Aug 1, 1933
Denoff, Sam b. Jul 1, 1928
DeVries, William Castle b. Dec 19, 1943
Diamond, Neil b. Jan 24, 1941
Dibbs, Eddie (Edward George)
　b. Feb 23, 1951
Dillon, Leo b. Mar 2, 1933
Donaldson, Walter b. Feb 15, 1893
Donleavy, James Patrick b. Apr 23, 1926
Dorfman, Dan b. Oct 24, 1932
Doubleday, Frank Nelson b. Jan 8, 1862
Doubleday, Nelson b. Jun 16, 1889
Douglas, Donald Willis b. Apr 6, 1892
Dow, Charles Henry d. Dec 4, 1902
Drake, Stanley b. Nov 9, 1921
Dreyfuss, Richard Stephan b. Oct 29, 1947
DuBois, Guy Pene b. Jan 4, 1884
Dugan, Alan b. Feb 12, 1923
DuMont, Allen Balcom b. Jan 29, 1901
Economaki, Chris(topher Constantine)
　b. Oct 15, 1920
Edelman, Herb b. Nov 5, 1933
Edwards, Vince b. Jul 7, 1928

Eliot, George Fielding b. Jun 22, 1894
Ellin, Stanley b. Oct 6, 1916
Erickson, Eric b. 1890
Fadiman, Clifton Paul b. May 15, 1904
Farentino, James b. Feb 24, 1938
Farina, Richard b. 1936
Fass, Bob b. Jun 29, 1943
Faust, Lotta b. Feb 8, 1880
Feld, Eliot b. Jul 5, 1942
Ferrigno, Lou b. Nov 9, 1952
Fields, Shep b. Sep 12, 1910
Fierstein, Harvey Forbes b. Jun 6, 1954
Firbank, Louis b. Mar 2, 1942
Fischetti, John b. Sep 27, 1916
Fisher, Harrison b. Jul 27, 1875
Fitzsimmons, James E b. Jul 23, 1874
Flagg, Ernest b. Feb 6, 1857
Ford, Paul Leicester b. Mar 23, 1865
Foster, Phil b. Mar 29, 1914
Fox, Margaret d. Mar 8, 1893
Fox, Sonny b. Jun 17, 1925
Frazetta, Frank b. Feb 9, 1928
Freidberg, Jerry b. 1938
Friedman, Milton b. Jul 31, 1912
Frye, David b. 1934
Funk, Wilfred John b. Mar 20, 1883
Funt, Allen b. Sep 16, 1914
Gallagher, Helen b. Jul 19, 1926
Garment, Leonard b. May 11, 1924
Garraty, John Arthur b. Jul 4, 1920
Geffen, David b. Feb 21, 1943
Gelmis, Joseph Stephen b. Sep 28, 1935
Gershwin, George b. Sep 26, 1898
Gerulaitis, Vitas b. Jul 26, 1954
Giardello, Joey b. Jul 16, 1930
Gibbs, Terry b. Oct 13, 1924
Ginzburg, Ralph b. Oct 28, 1929
Gleason, Jackie b. Feb 26, 1916
Goethals, George Washington
   b. Jun 29, 1858
Gordon, Sid(ney) b. Aug 13, 1917
Gosset, Lou(is, Jr.) b. May 27, 1936
Gould, Elliott b. Aug 29, 1938
Green, Anna Katharine b. Nov 11, 1846
Green, Gerald b. Apr 8, 1922
Greenspun, Hank (Herman Milton)
   b. Aug 27, 1909
Griffiths, John Willis d. Mar 30, 1882
Grogan, Emmett b. Nov 28, 1942
Grossman, Lawrence K b. Jun 21, 1931
Guccione, Bob (Robert Charles Joseph
   Edward Sabatini) b. Dec 17, 1930
Gunnison, Foster b. Jun 9, 1896
Gurie, Sigrid b. May 18, 1911
Guthrie, Arlo b. Jul 10, 1947
Guttenberg, Steve b. Aug 24, 1958
Habberton, John b. Feb 24, 1842
Habib, Philip Charles b. Feb 25, 1920
Hadden, Briton b. Feb 18, 1898
Hadden, Briton d. Feb 27, 1929
Hamill, "Pete" (William) b. Jun 24, 1935

Handlin, Oscar b. Mar 29, 1915
Hartford, George Ludlum b. Nov 7, 1864
Havens, Richie b. Jan 21, 1941
Heller, Joseph b. May 1, 1923
Hill, Morton A(nthony) b. Jul 13, 1917
Hirschorn, Joel b. Mar 13, 1943
Hofsiss, Jack Bernard b. Sep 28, 1950
Holmes, Tommy (Thomas Francis)
   b. Mar 29, 1917
Holtzman, Elizabeth b. Aug 11, 1941
Horne, Lena Calhoun b. Jun 30, 1917
Howard, "Curly" (Jerry) b. 1906
Howard, Moe b. Jun 19, 1897
Howe, Elias d. Oct 3, 1867
Hoyt, Waite Charles b. Sep 9, 1899
Hugel, Max b. 1925
Hughan, Jessie Wallace b. Dec 25, 1876
Hutchins, Robert Maynard b. Jan 17, 1899
Jagel, Frederick b. Jun 10, 1897
Janeway, Elizabeth b. Oct 7, 1913
Janifer, Laurence b. Mar 17, 1933
Jeffreys, Garland b. 1944
Johnson, William d. Aug 4, 1834
Jordon, Michael Jeffery b. Feb 17, 1963
Josephson, Matthew b. Feb 15, 1899
Kahane, Meir David b. Aug 1, 1932
Kahn, Roger b. Oct 31, 1927
Kalmanoff, Martin b. May 24, 1920
Kaltenborn, H(ans) V(on) d. Jun 14, 1965
Kamp, Irene Kittle b. Oct 28, 1910
Kaplan, Gabe (Gabriel) b. Mar 31, 1945
Katims, Milton b. 1909
Kazin, Alfred b. Jun 5, 1915
Keeler, "Wee Willie" (William Henry)
   b. Mar 13, 1872
Keeler, "Wee Willie" (William Henry)
   d. Jan 1, 1923
Keitel, Harvey b. 1941
Kelly, "Patsy" (Sarah Veronica Rose)
   b. Jan 12, 1910
Kelly, Stephen Eugene b. May 13, 1919
Kelman, Charles David b. May 23, 1930
Keogh, Eugene James b. Aug 30, 1907
Kidd, Michael b. Aug 12, 1919
King, Carole b. Feb 9, 1941
King, Larry b. Nov 19, 1933
Klein, Anne b. Aug 3, 1923
Kolodin, Irving b. Feb 22, 1908
Koop, Charles Everett b. Oct 14, 1916
Kooper, Al b. Feb 5, 1944
Kopell, Bernie (Bernard Morton)
   b. Jun 21, 1933
Koufax, Sandy (Sanford) b. Dec 30, 1935
Krantz, Hazel Newman b. Jan 29, 1920
Krasner, Lee b. Oct 27, 1908
Krassner, Paul b. Apr 9, 1932
Kushner, Harold Samuel b. Apr 3, 1935
Laidler, Harry Wellington b. Feb 18, 1884
Lake, Veronica b. Nov 15, 1919
Lamm, Robert b. Oct 13, 1944
Lane, Abbe b. Dec 14, 1932

Langmuir, Irving b. Jan 31, 1881
LaRose, Rose b. 1913
Lasker, Joe b. Jun 26, 1919
Layden, Frank (Francis Patrick)
   b. Jan 5, 1932
Lazarus, Mell b. May 3, 1927
Lee, Manfred B(ennington) b. Jan 11, 1905
Lee, Will b. Aug 6, 1908
Leigh, Mitch b. Jan 30, 1928
Levine, David b. Dec 20, 1926
Levitt, Arthur, Jr. b. Feb 3, 1931
Levitt, William Jaird b. Feb 11, 1907
Lewis, (Myrtle) Tillie b. Jul 13, 1901
Lewis, Emmanuel b. Mar 9, 1971
Lewis, Robert Alvin b. 1918
Lieberman, Nancy b. Jul 1, 1958
Lindauer, Lois L b. Feb 6, 1934
Linder, Harold Francis b. Sep 13, 1900
Linn, Bambi b. Apr 26, 1926
Loughery, Kevin Michael b. Mar 28, 1940
Luckman, Sid(ney) b. Nov 21, 1916
Lynch, Joe d. Aug 1, 1965
MacMonnies, Fred W b. Sep 28, 1863
Maltz, Albert b. Oct 8, 1908
Manilow, Barry b. Jun 17, 1946
Manner, Harold b. Jul 31, 1925
Maslow, Abraham b. Apr 1, 1908
Maynard, Robert Clyve b. Jun 17, 1937
Mazursky, Paul b. Apr 25, 1930
Mazzilli, Lee Louis b. Mar 25, 1955
McCloskey, John b. Mar 10, 1810
McGinnity, Joe (Joseph Jerome)
   d. Nov 14, 1929
McGovern, Terry (John Terrence)
   d. Feb 26, 1918
Milano, Alyssa b. Dec 19, 1972
Mills, Stephanie b. Mar 22, 1957
Moe, Doug(las Edwin) b. Sep 21, 1938
Mollenhauer, Emil b. Aug 4, 1855
Money, Eddie b. 1949
Moore, Mary Tyler b. Dec 29, 1936
Mortimer, Charles Greenough
   b. Jul 26, 1900
Moss, Arnold b. Jan 28, 1911
Moss, Geoffrey b. Jun 30, 1938
Moss, Jerry (Jerome Sheldon) b. 1935
Mostel, Zero (Samuel Joel)
   b. Feb 28, 1915
Murphy, Patrick Vincent b. May 12, 1920
Neway, Patricia b. Sep 30, 1919
Nidetch, Jean b. Oct 12, 1923
O'Brien, John J b. Nov 4, 1888
O'Donnell, Emmett b. Sep 15, 1906
Ovington, Mary White b. Apr 11, 1865
Owens, Rochelle b. Apr 2, 1936
Palmer, Frances Flora Bond
   d. Aug 20, 1876
Papp, Joseph b. Jun 22, 1921
Paterno, Joseph V (Joe) b. Dec 21, 1926
Peabody, Josephine Preston
   b. May 30, 1874

Pepitone, Joe (Joseph Anthony)
   b. Oct 9, 1940
Perelman, S(idney) J(oseph) b. Feb 1, 1904
Perlman, Rhea b. Mar 31, 1946
Petrocelli, Rico (Americo Peter)
   b. Jun 27, 1943
Pierce, Frederick S b. 1934
Podhoretz, Norman b. Jan 16, 1930
Polykoff, Shirley b.
Powell, Earl d. Aug 1, 1966
Presley, Priscilla Ann Beaulieu
   b. May 24, 1946
Rabbitt, Eddie (Edward Thomas)
   b. Nov 27, 1941
Randisi, Robert Joseph b. Aug 24, 1951
Redman, Ben Ray b. Feb 21, 1896
Regan, Phil b. May 28, 1906
Rich, Adam b. Oct 12, 1968
Richards, Stanley b. Apr 23, 1918
Ridge, Lola d. May 19, 1941
Rodgers, Christopher Raymond Perry
   b. Nov 14, 1819
Rooney, John (James) b. Nov 29, 1903
Rooney, Mickey b. Sep 23, 1920
Ross, Herbert David b. May 13, 1927
Rostow, Eugene Victor b. Aug 25, 1913
Roth, Mark Stephan b. Apr 10, 1951
Rubicam, Raymond b. Jun 16, 1892
Rubin, Theodore Isaac b. Apr 11, 1923
Ruchlis, Hy(man) b. Apr 6, 1913
Russell, "Honey" (John) b. May 31, 1903
Sann, Paul b. Mar 7, 1914
Sarris, Andrew b. Oct 31, 1928
Sauter, Eddie (Edward Ernest)
   b. Dec 2, 1914
Saxon, John b. Aug 5, 1935
Schaap, Dick (Richard J) b. Sep 27, 1934
Schenck, Joe (Joseph T) b. 1892
Schisgal, Murray b. Nov 25, 1926
Schlein, Miriam b. Jun 6, 1926
Schnabel, Julian b. Oct 26, 1951
Schwartz, Arthur b. Nov 25, 1900
Schwartz, Delmore b. Dec 8, 1913
Scourby, Alexander b. Nov 13, 1913
Sedaka, Neil b. Mar 13, 1939
Segal, Erich Wolf b. Jun 16, 1937
Sendak, Maurice Bernard b. Jun 10, 1928
Sessions, Roger Huntington
   b. Dec 28, 1896
Severn, William Irving b. May 11, 1914
Shaw, Irwin b. Feb 27, 1913
Shear, Murray Jacob b. Nov 7, 1899
Sherrill, Henry Knox b. Nov 6, 1890
Shimkin, Leon b. Apr 7, 1907
Shulman, Irving b. May 21, 1913
Shuttlesworth, Dorothy Edwards b. 1907
Siegel, "Bugsy" (Benjamin)
   b. Feb 28, 1906
Sills, Beverly b. May 25, 1929
Silvers, Phil b. May 11, 1911
Sinclair, Jo, pseud. b. Jul 1, 1913

Slesar, Henry b. Jun 12, 1927
Sliwa, Curtis b. Mar 26, 1954
Slote, Alfred b. Sep 11, 1926
Smith, Betty b. Dec 15, 1904
Spear, Sammy b. 1910
Sperry, Elmer Ambrose d. Jun 10, 1930
Spillane, Mickey (Frank Morrison)
    b. Mar 9, 1918
Spivak, Lawrence b. Jun 11, 1900
Squibb, Edward Robinson d. Oct 25, 1900
Stanwyck, Barbara b. Jul 16, 1907
Stevens, Connie b. Aug 8, 1938
Stewart, Anita b. Feb 17, 1896
Stuart, Lyle b. Aug 11, 1922
Talmadge, Constance b. Apr 19, 1900
Tashman, Lilyan b. Oct 23, 1899
Tavoulareas, William Peter b. Nov 9, 1919
Tayback, Vic b. Jan 6, 1929
Terry, Walter b. May 14, 1913
Thalberg, Irving Grant b. May 30, 1899
Thomas, Franklin Augustine
    b. May 27, 1934
Tierney, Gene b. Nov 11, 1920
Torre, Joe (Joseph Paul) b. Jul 18, 1940
Tucker, Richard b. Aug 28, 1913
Turkus, Burton B b. 1902
Twelvetrees, Helen b. Dec 25, 1908
Ubell, Earl b. Jun 21, 1926
Unger, Irwin b. May 2, 1927
Vaccaro, Brenda b. Nov 18, 1939
Vairo, Lou b. 1945
Van Patten, Vince(nt) b. Oct 17, 1957
Waller, Fred(erick) b. Mar 10, 1886
Walter, Jessica b. Jan 31, 1944
Waterman, Lewis Edson d. May 1, 1901
Weil, Sanford I b. Mar 6, 1933
Weintraub, Jerry b. Sep 26, 1937
Welch, Mickey (Michael Francis)
    b. Jul 4, 1859
Werblin, "Sonny" (David Abraham)
    b. Mar 17, 1910
Werrenrath, Reinald b. Aug 7, 1883
Wesson, David b. Jan 14, 1861
West, Mae b. Aug 17, 1892
Westley, Helen b. Mar 28, 1879
Wheeler, Joseph d. Jan 25, 1906
Whitaker, Lou(is Rodman)
    b. May 12, 1957
Wilkens, Lenny (Leonard Randolph)
    b. Oct 28, 1937
Wolf, "Manny" (Emanuel L)
    b. Mar 27, 1927
Wolfman Jack b. Jan 21, 1938

Broome County, New York
Allen, John b. Nov 4, 1810

Buffalo, New York
Allen, Arthur Augustus b. Dec 28, 1885
Arlen, Harold b. Feb 15, 1905
Banning, Margaret Culkin b. Mar 18, 1891
Barrett, John L d. May 1, 1984
Bell, Lawrence Dale d. Oct 20, 1956

Bennett, Michael b. Apr 8, 1943
Bernhardt, Melvin b. Feb 26,
Blake, Amanda b. Feb 20, 1931
Boyd, Malcolm b. Jun 8, 1923
Brisbane, Arthur b. Dec 12, 1864
Cleveland, Frances Folsom b. Jul 21, 1864
Coatsworth, Elizabeth Jane
    b. May 31, 1893
Collins, James Joseph (Jimmy)
    d. Mar 6, 1943
Curtiss, Glenn Hammond d. Jul 23, 1930
DeMarco, Tony b. 1898
Donovan, Robert John b. Aug 21, 1912
Donovan, William Joseph b. Jan 1, 1883
Fargo, William George d. Aug 3, 1881
Fillmore, Millard d. Mar 8, 1874
Fosdick, Harry Emerson b. May 24, 1878
Fosdick, Raymond Blaine b. Jun 9, 1883
Gibson, Edward George b. Nov 8, 1936
Green, Anna Katharine d. Apr 11, 1935
Gurney, A(lbert) R(amsdell), Jr.
    b. Nov 1, 1930
Heller, Walter Wolfgang b. Aug 27, 1915
Henderson, Ray b. Dec 1, 1896
Herman, "Babe" (Floyd Caves)
    b. Jun 26, 1903
Hofstadter, Richard b. Aug 6, 1916
Horgan, Paul b. Aug 1, 1903
Hormel, George Albert b. Dec 4, 1860
Hudson, Joseph Lowthian, Jr.
    b. Jul 4, 1931
James, Rick b. Feb 1, 1952
Johnson, Beverly b. Oct 13, 1951
Jones, Thomas Hudson b. Jul 24, 1892
Kellogg, Howard b. Mar 26, 1881
Knudsen, Semon Emil b. Oct 2, 1912
Kuhn, Maggie (Margaret E)
    b. Aug 3, 1905
Lanier, Bob (Robert Jerry, Jr.)
    b. Sep 10, 1948
Lowery, Robert O b. Apr 20, 1916
Luhan, Mabel Dodge b. Feb 26, 1879
Mann, Carol Ann b. Feb 3, 1941
Marchand, Nancy b. Jun 19, 1928
McCarthy, Joe (Joseph Vincent)
    d. Jan 13, 1978
McKinley, William d. Sep 14, 1901
Miller, William E d. Jun 24, 1983
Miner, Worthington C b. Nov 13, 1900
Morgana, Nina b. 1895
Mullavey, Greg b. Sep 10, 1939
O'Brian, Jack b. Aug 16, 1914
Olcott, Chauncey (Chancellor)
    b. Jul 21, 1860
Pennario, Leonard b. Jul 9, 1924
Pratt, Fletcher b. Apr 25, 1897
Reinhardt, Ad(olph Frederick)
    b. Dec 24, 1913
Rich, Irene b. Oct 13, 1897
Ronan, William J b. Nov 8, 1912
Rothenberg, Susan b. Jan 20, 1945

Russell, Mark b. Aug 23, 1932
Shawn, Dick b. Dec 1, 1929
Shire, David b. Jul 3, 1937
Smith, Bob b. Nov 27, 1917
Spahn, Warren Edward b. Apr 23, 1921
Speicher, Eugene Edward b. Apr 5, 1883
Stephen, John b. 1912
Stoneman, George d. Sep 5, 1894
Stoopnagle, Lemuel Q, Colonel
  b. Oct 4, 1897
Swados, Elizabeth A (Liz) b. Feb 5, 1951
Swados, Harvey b. Oct 28, 1920
Tanner, Marion b. Mar 6, 1891
Washington, Grover, Jr. b. Dec 12, 1943
White, Jesse b. Jan 3, 1919
Williams, Curtis b. Dec 11, 1962
Williams, Jay b. May 31, 1914
Witherspoon, Herbert b. Jul 21, 1873
Yates, Elizabeth b. Dec 6, 1905

Busti, New York
Stoneman, George b. Aug 8, 1822

Cairo, New York
Weed, Thurlow b. Nov 15, 1797

Callicoon Depot, New York
Cook, Frederick Albert b. Jun 10, 1865

Campbell, New York
Watson, Thomas John, Sr. b. Feb 17, 1874

Campgaw, New York
Wyatt, Jane b. Aug 13, 1912

Canajoharie, New York
Kaiser, Henry John b. May 9, 1882

Canandaigua, New York
Dove, Arthur Garfield b. Aug 2, 1880
Eastman, Max Forrester b. Jan 4, 1883
Willys, John North b. Oct 25, 1873

Canton, New York
Remington, Frederic b. Oct 4, 1861
White, James Laurie b. Dec 7, 1847

Carthage, New York
Carpenter, John b. Jan 16, 1948

Catskill, New York
Cole, Thomas d. Feb 11, 1848
Marshall, S(amuel) L(yman) A(twood)
  b. Jul 18, 1900

Central Bridge, New York
Westinghouse, George b. Oct 6, 1846

Central Islip, New York
Curtis, Charles Gordon d. Mar 10, 1953
Madden, Donald d. Jan 22, 1983

Chappaqua, New York
Kahn, Herman d. Jul 7, 1983
Manville, Tommy (Thomas Franklin, Jr.)
  d. Oct 8, 1967
Pierson, Frank R(omer) b. May 12, 1925

Charlotte, New York
Henry, Charlotte b. Mar 3, 1913

Chittenango, New York
Baum, (Lyman) Frank b. May 15, 1856

Churchville, New York
Willard, Frances E b. Sep 28, 1839

Clarkon, New York
Selden, George Baldwin b. Sep 14, 1846

Claverack, New York
Lamont, Thomas William b. Sep 30, 1870

Clayton, New York
Bohlen, Charles Eustis b. Aug 30, 1904

Clermont, New York
Livingston, Robert R d. Feb 26, 1813

Clinton, New York
Root, Elihu b. Feb 15, 1845

Clinton Hollows, New York
Cook, Joe d. May 16, 1959

Cohoes, New York
Strout, Richard Lee b. Mar 14, 1898

Cold Spring, New York
Maury, Antonia Caetana De Paiua Pereira
  b. Mar 21, 1866

Cold Spring Harbor, New York
Abramson, Harold A(lexander)
  d. Sep 29, 1980

Colesville, New York
Palmer, Alice Elvira Freeman
  b. Feb 21, 1855

College Park, New York
Nakian, Reuben b. Aug 10, 1897

Columbia County, New York
Livingston, Edward b. May 26, 1764

Coney Island, New York
Carter, Jack b. Jun 24, 1923

Connery Pond, New York
Simmons, Calvin d. Aug 21, 1982

Cooperstown, New York
Beadle, Erastus Flavel d. Dec 18, 1894
Cooper, James Fenimore d. Sep 14, 1851
Potter, Henry Codman d. Jul 21, 1908

Corning, New York
Eddy, Duane b. Apr 26, 1938
Houghton, Amory b. Jul 27, 1899
Sanger, Margaret b. Sep 14, 1883
Tully, Alice b. Oct 11, 1902

Cornwall, New York
Roe, Edward Payson d. Jul 19, 1888

Cornwall-on-Hudson, New York
Barnes, Djuna b. Jun 12, 1892

Corona, New York
Bleyer, Archie b. Jun 12, 1909

Cortland, New York
Carmer, Carl Lamson b. Oct 16, 1893
Dillon, William A b. Nov 6, 1877
Silverman, Sime b. May 18, 1873
Sperry, Elmer Ambrose b. Oct 12, 1860
Swing, Raymond Gram b. Mar 25, 1887

Crestwood, New York
Schmemann, Alexander d. Dec 13, 1983

Croton, New York
Blinn, Holbrook d. Jun 24, 1928

Croton-on-Hudson, New York
Biddle, George d. Nov 6, 1973
Sands, Dorothy d. Sep 11, 1980
Strauss, Peter b. Feb 20, 1947

Cutchoque, New York
Moore, Douglas b. Aug 10, 1893
Decatur, New York
Waterman, Lewis Edson b. Nov 20, 1837
Delaware County, New York
Wheeler, Candace Thurber
  b. Mar 24, 1827
Delhi, New York
Vandercook, John Womack d. Jan 6, 1963
Dobbs Ferry, New York
Conklin, Peggy (Margaret Eleanor)
  b. Nov 2, 1912
Fix, Paul b. Mar 13, 1902
Maury, Antonia Caetana De Paiua Pereira
  d. Jan 8, 1952
Poe, James b. Oct 4, 1921
Sheeler, Charles d. May 7, 1965
Villard, Helen Francis Garrison d. 1928
Villard, Henry d. Nov 12, 1900
Wilson, Edward Arthur d. Oct 2, 1970
Dover Plains, New York
Lossing, Benson John d. Jun 3, 1891
Dresden, New York
Ingersoll, Robert Green b. Aug 11, 1833
Dunkirk, New York
Adams, Samuel Hopkins b. Jan 26, 1871
East Aurora, New York
Price, Irving L d. Nov 23, 1976
East Durham, New York
Dearie, Blossom b. Apr 28, 1926
East Hampton, New York
Bernstein, Felicia Montealegre
  d. Jun 16, 1978
Bronowski, Jacob d. Aug 22, 1974
Dooley, Rae (Rachel Rice) d. Jan 28, 1984
Hassam, Childe d. Aug 27, 1935
Lardner, Ring(gold Wilmer)
  d. Sep 25, 1933
Pollock, Jackson d. Aug 11, 1956
East Harlem, New York
Pacino, Al(fredo James) b. Apr 25, 1940
East Islip, New York
Kibbee, Guy d. May 24, 1956
Eaton, New York
Judson, Emily Chubbock b. Aug 22, 1817
Elizabethtown, New York
Blakelock, Ralph Albert d. Aug 9, 1919
Fisk, James Brown d. Aug 10, 1981
Elmhurst, New York
Casey, William Joseph b. Mar 13, 1913
Pastor, Tony (Antonio) d. Aug 26, 1908
Ryder, Albert Pinkham d. Mar 28, 1917
Elmira, New York
Eglevsky, Andre d. Dec 4, 1977
Fitch, (William) Clyde b. May 2, 1865
Friendly, Edwin Samson b. Jun 15, 1884
Griffes, Charles Tomlinson b. Sep 7, 1884
Griffes, Charles Tomlinson d. Apr 8, 1920
Lawes, Lewis Edward b. Sep 13, 1883
Roach, Hal b. Jan 14, 1892

Elmsford, New York
Shrady, Henry M d. Apr 12, 1922
Turnesa, Jim b. Dec 9, 1914
Turnesa, Jim d. Aug 27, 1971
Endicott, New York
Hart, John(ny Lewis) b. Feb 18, 1931
Euphrates, New York
Simmons, Zalmon G b. Sep 10, 1828
Far Rockaway, New York
Dehnert, Henry d. Apr 20, 1979
Gordon, Mary Catherine b. Dec 8, 1949
Ochs, Phil(ip David) d. Apr 9, 1976
Wheelock, John Hall b. Sep 9, 1886
Ferndale, New York
Fields, Freddie b. Jul 12, 1923
Fire Island, New York
Fuller, Margaret d. Jul 19, 1850
Floral Park, New York
Cord, Alex b. Aug 3, 1931
Ludlam, Charles b. Apr 12, 1943
Florida, New York
Seward, William Henry b. May 16, 1801
Flower Hill, New York
Slezak, Walter d. Apr 21, 1983
Flushing, New York
Bessell, Ted b. May 20, 1935
Carr, Martin b. Jan 20, 1932
Gilman, Lawrence b. Jul 5, 1878
Heckler, Margaret Mary b. Jun 21, 1931
Mayer, "Sandy" (Alex) b. Apr 5, 1952
Moog, Robert b. May 23, 1934
Mumford, Lewis b. Oct 19, 1895
Outcault, Richard Felton d. Sep 25, 1928
Rentzel, Lance b. Oct 14, 1943
Scorsese, Martin b. Nov 17, 1942
Walker, Robert Miller b. Dec 10, 1908
Williams, John Towner b. Feb 8, 1932
Forest Hills, New York
Arledge, Roone Pinckney b. Jul 8, 1931
Garfunkel, Art(hur) b. Oct 13, 1942
Karan, Donna Faske b. Oct 2, 1948
Landon, Michael b. Oct 31, 1937
Marquis, Don Robert Perry
  d. Dec 29, 1937
Sullivan, Anne d. Oct 20, 1936
Forestville, New York
Abbott, George Francis b. Jun 25, 1887
Fort Hamilton, New York
Benet, William Rose b. Feb 2, 1886
Franklinville, New York
Conway, Shirl b. Jun 13, 1916
Fredericksburg, New York
Kent, James b. Jul 31, 1763
Ludington, Sybil b. Apr 5, 1761
Fredonia, New York
Webster, Jean b. Jul 24, 1876
Garden City, New York
Hooker, Joseph d. Oct 31, 1879
Savalas, "Telly" (Aristoteles)
  b. Jan 21, 1923

Gardenville, New York
Burchfield, Charles d. Jan 10, 1967
Gardiner's Island, New York
Tyler, Julia Gardiner b. May 4, 1820
Garrison, New York
Fish, Hamilton d. Sep 6, 1893
Fish, Hamilton, III b. Dec 7, 1888
Lawes, Lewis Edward d. Apr 23, 1947
Upjohn, Richard d. Aug 17, 1878
Gasport, New York
Hull, Warren b. Jan 17, 1903
Geneva, New York
Fitzgerald, Robert Stuart b. Oct 12, 1910
Miller, Elizabeth Smith d. May 22, 1911
Gerry, New York
Schofield, John McAllister b. Sep 29, 1831
Glen Cove, New York
LeBoutillier, John b. May 26, 1953
Pierce, Samuel Riley, Jr. b. Sep 8, 1922
Pynchon, Thomas b. May 8, 1937
Tcherkassky, Marianna Alexsavena
  b. Oct 28, 1952
Woolworth, Frank Winfield d. Apr 8, 1919
Glens Falls, New York
Hughes, Charles Evans b. Apr 11, 1862
Reulbach, Ed(ward Marvin)
  d. Jul 17, 1961
Gloversville, New York
Beach, Joseph Warren b. Jan 14, 1880
Berger, Samuel David b. Dec 6, 1911
Coons, Albert Hewett b. Jun 28, 1912
Haughton, Billy b. Nov 2, 1923
Schine, G(erard) David b. Sep 11, 1927
Widdemer, Margaret d. Jul 31, 1978
Goshen, New York
Smith, Willie b. Nov 23, 1897
Grand Island, New York
Arias, Jimmy b. Aug 16, 1964
Grassy Point, New York
Farley, James A(loysius) b. May 30, 1888
Great Neck, New York
Brian, Donald d. Dec 22, 1948
Bruce, Carol b. Nov 15, 1919
Chrysler, Walter Percy d. Aug 18, 1940
Goddard, Paulette b. Jun 3, 1911
Meighan, Thomas d. Jul 8, 1936
Weber, Max d. Oct 4, 1961
Greece, New York
Bonstelle, Jessie b. Nov 18, 1871
Greenport, New York
Ford, "Senator" (Ed) d. 1970
Moore, Douglas d. Jul 25, 1969
Greenville, New York
Drake, Edwin Laurentine b. Mar 29, 1819
Greenwich, New York
Moses, "Grandma" (Anna Mary
  Robertson) b. Aug 7, 1860
Greenwich Village, New York
Vicious, Sid d. Feb 2, 1979

Groveland, New York
Cheney, John Vance b. Dec 29, 1848
Wadsworth, James Jeremiah (Jerry)
  b. Jun 12, 1905
Hamburg, New York
Hunt, E(verette) Howard b. Oct 9, 1918
Hamilton, New York
Judson, Emily Chubbock d. Jun 1, 1854
Neal, Larry (Lawrence P) d. Jan 6, 1981
Hammondsport, New York
Curtiss, Glenn Hammond b. May 21, 1878
Hampstead, New York
Harriman, Edward H b. Feb 25, 1848
Hampton, New York
Miller, Elizabeth Smith b. Sep 20, 1822
Harlem, New York
Berg, Gertrude b. Oct 3, 1899
Caesar, Adolph b. 1934
Jordan, June Meyer b. Jul 9, 1936
Rangel, Charles Bernard b. Jun 11, 1930
Harrison, New York
Coghlan, Rose d. Apr 2, 1932
Kiepura, Jan d. Aug 15, 1966
Hartsdale, New York
Booth, Evangeline Cory d. Jul 17, 1950
Hartwick, New York
Bissell, Melville Reuben b. Sep 25, 1843
Butterfield, Roger Place d. Jan 31, 1981
Hastings, New York
Draper, John William d. Jan 4, 1882
Hastings-on-Hudson, New York
Hine, Lewis Wickes d. Nov 3, 1940
Hauppauge, New York
Brokenshire, Norman d. May 4, 1965
Haverstraw, New York
Heindorf, Ray b. Aug 25, 1908
Hewitt, Abram Stevens b. Jul 31, 1822
Hawthorne, New York
Lathrop, Rose Hawthorne d. Jul 9, 1926
Hempstead, New York
Earle, Alice Morse d. Feb 16, 1911
Hempstead Township, New York
Hicks, Elias b. Mar 19, 1748
Henderson, New York
Burnham, Daniel H b. Sep 4, 1846
Charles, Glen b.
Crittenton, Charles Nelson b. Feb 20, 1833
Peck, George Wilbur b. Sep 28, 1840
Henrietta, New York
Blackwell, Antoinette Louisa Brown
  b. 1825
Herkimer, New York
Alpert, Hollis b. Sep 24, 1916
Ambers, Lou b. Nov 8, 1913
Herkimer, Nicholas b. Nov 10, 1728
Hicksville, New York
Kupchak, Mitch(ell) b. May 24, 1954
Highland, New York
Hunter, Glenn b. 1897

Lackawanna, New York
Jaworski, Ron(ald Vincent)
  b. Mar 23, 1951
Lake George, New York
Eggleston, Edward d. Sep 4, 1902
Irish, Edward Simmons (Ned)
  b. May 6, 1905
Owen, Robert Dale d. Jun 24, 1877
Lake Placid, New York
Collins, Ted d. May 27, 1964
Wood, Craig Ralph b. Nov 18, 1901
Lancaster, New York
Thompson, Dorothy b. Jul 9, 1894
Lansingburgh, New York
Kelly, "King" (Michael Joseph)
  b. Dec 31, 1857
Larchmont, New York
Dillon, Matt b. 1964
Drew, Louisa Lane d. Aug 31, 1897
Schaefer, Rudolph Jay b. Jul 9, 1900
Lawrence, New York
Auchincloss, Louis b. Sep 27, 1917
Cott, Nate d. Oct 5, 1973
Leroy, New York
Costanza, "Midge" (Margaret)
  b. Nov 28, 1928
Lew Beach, New York
Lazare, Kaplan d. Feb 12, 1986
Liberty, New York
Lasky, Victor b. Jan 7, 1918
Lima, New York
Keating, Kenneth B b. May 18, 1900
Raymond, Henry Jarvis b. Jan 24, 1820
Lindenhurst, New York
Barry, Jack b. Mar 20, 1918
Little Britain, New York
Clinton, DeWitt b. Mar 2, 1769
Clinton, George b. Jul 26, 1739
Little Falls, New York
Gerstenberg, Richard Charles
  b. Dec 24, 1909
Herkimer, Nicholas d. Aug 19, 1777
Riccardo, John Joseph b. Jul 2, 1924
Livingston, New York
Woolsey, Janette b. Dec 11, 1904
Lockport, New York
Hobart, Alice Tisdale Nourse
  b. Jan 28, 1882
Marsh, Othniel Charles b. Oct 29, 1831
Miller, William E b. Mar 22, 1914
Oates, Joyce Carol b. Jun 16, 1938
Raskob, John J b. Mar 19, 1879
Locust Grove, New York
Bailey, Florence Augusta Merriam
  b. Aug 8, 1863
Locust Valley, New York
Lovett, Robert A(bercrombie)
  d. May 7, 1986
Lomontville, New York
Rounds, David d. Dec 9, 1983

Long Beach, New York
Atlas, Charles d. Dec 23, 1972
Rhodes, Samuel b. Feb 13, 1941
Long Island, New York
Atterbury, Grosvenor d. Oct 18, 1956
Bloom, Eric b. Dec 1, 1944
Bouchard, Joe b. Nov 9, 1948
Brannigan, Bill b. Jan 12, 1936
Colden, Cadwallader d. Sep 28, 1776
Cooke, Donald b. 1955
Coolidge, Charles Allerton d. Apr 1, 1936
Crystal, Billy (William) b. Mar 14, 1947
DeFrank, Vincent b. Jun 18, 1915
Downey, Rick b. Aug 29, 1953
Gomez, Thomas b. Jul 10, 1905
Hale, Nathan d. Sep 22, 1776
Hillman, Sidney d. Jul 10, 1946
Hutchinson, Anne d. Aug 1643
Kaufman, Sue b. Aug 7, 1926
Lanier, Allen b. Jun 25, 1946
Longworth, Alice Roosevelt
  b. Feb 12, 1884
Macchio, Ralph George, Jr.
  b. Nov 4, 1962
Mantle, (Robert) Burns d. Feb 29, 1948
Moore, Victor d. Jul 23, 1962
Rea, Gardner d. Dec 27, 1966
Roeser, Donald b. Nov 12, 1947
Straight, Beatrice Whitney b. Aug 2, 1918
Tartikoff, Brandon b. Jan 13, 1949
Taylor, Cecil Percival b. Mar 15, 1933
Vought, Chance Milton d. Jul 25, 1930
Whittemore, Arthur Austin
  d. Oct 23, 1984
Williams, "Cootie" (Charles Melvin)
  d. Sep 15, 1985
Yon, Pietro Alessandro d. Nov 22, 1943
York, David b. 1929
Lowville, New York
Arthur, Joseph Charles b. Jan 11, 1850
Lucerne, New York
Allyson, June b. Oct 7, 1917
Lynbrook, New York
Keeshan, Bob b. Jun 27, 1927
Lyndonville, New York
Butterfield, Lyman Henry b. Aug 8, 1909
Butterfield, Roger Place b. Jul 29, 1907
Madison Barracks, New York
Clark, Mark Wayne b. May 1, 1896
Malba, New York
Frankenheimer, John b. Feb 19, 1930
Malone, New York
Wheeler, William Alrnon b. Jun 30, 1819
Wheeler, William Alrnon d. Jun 4, 1887
Mamaroneck, New York
Kirstein, George G d. Apr 3, 1986
Sheehy, Gail Henion b. Nov 27, 1937
Skouras, Spyros Panagiotes
  d. Aug 16, 1971
Wood, James Rushmore b. Sep 14, 1816

Manhasset, New York
Benzell, Mimi (Miriam Ruth)
  d. Dec 23, 1970
Buck, Gene d. Feb 24, 1957
Cordier, Andrew Wellington
  d. Jul 11, 1975
Gropper, William d. Jan 6, 1977
Grumman, Leroy Randle d. Oct 4, 1982
Musial, Joe d. Jun 6, 1977
Treacher, Arthur d. Dec 14, 1975
White, Josh(ua Daniel) d. Sep 5, 1969
Whitney, John Hay d. Feb 8, 1982

Manhattan, New York
Armstrong, Hamilton Fish d. Apr 24, 1973
Bogert, Tim b. Aug 27, 1944
Buchalter, "Lepke" (Louis) b. 1897
Casablancas, John(ny) b. Dec 12, 1942
Chapman, Gilbert Whipple
  d. Dec 16, 1979
Elisofon, Eliot b. Apr 17, 1911
Field, Michael b. Feb 21, 1915
Stuyvesant, Peter (Petrus) d. Feb 1672

Marlboro, New York
Goudy, Frederic William d. May 11, 1947

Martinsburg, New York
Hunt, Walter b. Jul 29, 1796

Massapequa, New York
Gambino, Don Carlo d. Oct 15, 1976
Snider, Dee (Daniel Dee) b. Mar 15, 1955

Mechanicville, New York
Eberly, Bob b. Jul 24, 1916

Menands, New York
Deukmejian, George, Jr. (Courken)
  b. Jun 6, 1928

Middleburgh, New York
Brayman, Harold b. Mar 10, 1900

Mill Neck, New York
DeGraff, Robert F(air) d. Nov 1, 1981

Millertown, New York
Collins, Eddie (Edward Trowbridge, Sr.)
  b. May 2, 1887

Mineola, New York
Barton, James d. Feb 19, 1962
Bruce, Lenny b. Oct 13, 1925
Damon, Ralph Shepard d. Jan 4, 1956
Ford, Paul d. Apr 12, 1976
Forman, James Douglas b. Nov 12, 1932
Sawchuk, Terry (Terrance Gordon)
  d. May 31, 1970
Studds, Gerry E b. May 12, 1937

Mineville, New York
Kelly, Walter C b. Oct 29, 1873

Minoa, New York
Costello, Larry b. Jul 2, 1931

Monticello, New York
Lapchick, Joseph Bohomiel
  d. Aug 10, 1970

Morris, New York
Daniels, Draper b. Aug 12, 1913

Morrisania, New York
Morris, Gouverneur b. Jan 31, 1752
Morris, Gouverneur d. Nov 6, 1816
Morris, Lewis b. Apr 8, 1726
Morris, Lewis d. Jan 22, 1796

Mount Kisco, New York
Balchen, Bernt d. Oct 17, 1973
Blyth, Ann Marie b. Aug 16, 1928
Burger, Carl Victor d. Dec 30, 1967
Cerf, Bennett Alfred d. Aug 27, 1971
Crowther, Bosley (Francis Bosley)
  d. Mar 7, 1981
Davis, Richard Harding d. Apr 11, 1916
Jenner, Bruce b. Oct 28, 1949
MacLeod, Gavin b. Feb 28, 1930
Rinkoff, Barbara Jean d. Feb 18, 1975
Schneider, John b. Apr 8, 1954
Wallace, DeWitt d. Mar 30, 1981
Wallace, Lila Bell Acheson d. May 8, 1984

Mount McGregor, New York
Grant, Ulysses S(impson) d. Jul 23, 1885

Mount Morris, New York
Powell, John Wesley b. Mar 24, 1834

Mount Vernon, New York
Bailey, James Anthony d. 1906
Becker, Stephen David b. Mar 31, 1927
Branca, Ralph Theodore Joseph
  b. Jan 6, 1926
Buchwald, Art(hur) b. Oct 20, 1925
Carney, Art b. Nov 4, 1918
Clark, Dick (Richard Wagstaff)
  b. Nov 30, 1929
Harris, Mark b. Nov 19, 1922
Hess, Victor Francis d. Dec 17, 1964
Marks, Johnny (John David)
  b. Nov 10, 1909
Shabazz, Attallah b. 1959
Thomopoulos, Anthony Denis
  b. Feb 7, 1938
White, E(lwyn) B(rooks) b. Jul 11, 1899
Williams, Gus b. Oct 10, 1953

Neponsit, New York
Levenson, Sam(uel) d. Aug 27, 1980

New Egypt, New York
Dancer, Stanley b. Jul 25, 1927

New Lebanon, New York
Tilden, Samuel Jones b. Feb 9, 1814

New Rochelle, New York
Agar, Herbert Sebastian b. Sep 29, 1897
Baldwin, Faith b. Oct 1, 1893
Branley, Franklyn Mansfield
  b. Jun 5, 1915
Castle, Irene Foote b. Apr 7, 1893
Catt, Carrie Chapman d. Mar 9, 1947
Chew, Peter b. Apr 5, 1924
Crean, Robert d. May 6, 1974
Denver, Bob b. Jan 9, 1935
Foy, Eddie, Jr. b. Feb 4, 1905
Hamilton, Roy d. Jul 20, 1969
Lantz, Walter b. Apr 27, 1900

Leyendecker, Joseph Christian
  d. Jul 25, 1951
McCartan, Edward d. Sep 20, 1947
McGraw, John Joseph d. Feb 25, 1934
McLean, Don b. Oct 2, 1945
Opper, Frederick Burr d. Aug 28, 1937
Raymond, Alex(ander Gillespie)
  b. Oct 2, 1909
Richardson, Scovel d. Mar 30, 1982
Rothstein, Arthur d. Nov 11, 1985
Roundtree, Richard b. Sep 7, 1942
Sangster, Margaret Elizabeth
  b. Feb 22, 1838
Sherwood, Robert Emmet b. Apr 4, 1896
Tower, Joan Peabody b. Sep 6, 1938
Wank, Roland A d. Apr 22, 1970
Weir, Robert W b. Jun 18, 1803
West, James Edward d. May 15, 1948

New Windsor, New York
Roe, Edward Payson b. Mar 7, 1838

New York, New York
Abbe, Cleveland b. Dec 3, 1838
Abbey, Henry Eugene d. Oct 17, 1896
Abbott, Lyman d. Oct 22, 1922
Abdul-Jabbar, Kareem b. Apr 16, 1947
Abplanalp, Robert H b. 1923
Abrahams, Doris Cole b. Jan 29, 1925
Abrams, Harry Nathan d. Nov 25, 1979
Abramson, Harold A(lexander)
  b. Nov 27, 1899
Abzug, Bella Savitsky b. Jul 24, 1920
Ace, Goodman d. Mar 25, 1982
Ace, Jane Sherwood d. Nov 11, 1974
Acheson, Edward Goodrich d. Jul 6, 1931
Ackerman, Carl William d. Oct 9, 1970
Adams, Brooke b. Feb 8, 1949
Adams, Don b. Apr 19, 1927
Adams, Franklin P(ierce) d. Mar 23, 1960
Adams, Herbert Samuel d. May 21, 1945
Adams, Mason b. Feb 26, 1919
Addison, Adele b. Jul 24, 1925
Adler, "Buddy" (Maurice) b. Jun 22, 1909
Adler, Felix d. Apr 24, 1933
Adler, Irving b. 1913
Adler, Jacob Pavlovitch d. Apr 1, 1926
Adler, Julius Ochs d. Oct 3, 1955
Adler, Luther (Lutha) b. May 4, 1903
Adler, Mortimer Jerome b. Dec 28, 1902
Adler, Richard b. Aug 3, 1921
Adler, Stella b. Feb 10, 1902
Agee, James Rufus d. May 16, 1955
Agostini, Peter b. Feb 13, 1913
Agron, Salvador d. Apr 22, 1986
Aitken, Hugh b. Sep 7, 1924
Aitken, Robert d. Jan 3, 1949
Albrand, Martha, pseud. d. Jun 24, 1981
Alda, Alan b. Jan 28, 1936
Alda, Robert b. Feb 26, 1914
Alden, Henry M d. Oct 7, 1919
Aldrich, Nelson Wilmarth d. Apr 16, 1915

Aldrich, Winthrop Williams
  d. Feb 25, 1974
Aldridge, Ira Frederick b. 1805
Aleichem, Shalom, pseud. d. May 13, 1916
Alexander, Clifford L, Jr. b. Sep 21, 1933
Alexander, Denise b. Nov 11, 1945
Alexander, Shana b. Oct 6, 1925
Alexander, William b. 1726
Alfred, William b. Aug 16, 1922
Allen, "Red" (Henry James, Jr.)
  d. Apr 17, 1967
Allen, Fred d. Mar 17, 1956
Allen, Frederick Lewis d. Feb 13, 1954
Allen, Irwin b. Jun 12, 1916
Allen, Nancy b. Jun 24, 1949
Allen, Steve (Stephen Valentine Patrick
  William) b. Dec 26, 1921
Allen, Viola Emily d. May 9, 1948
Allen, Vivian Beaumont d. Oct 10, 1962
Althouse, Paul Shearer d. Feb 6, 1954
Altman, Benjamin b. Jul 12, 1840
Altman, Benjamin d. Oct 7, 1913
Alvardo, Trini(dad) b. 1967
Amato, Pasquale d. Aug 12, 1942
Amen, Irving b. Jul 25, 1918
Amerasinghe, Hamilton Shirley
  d. Dec 4, 1980
Anastasia, Albert d. Oct 29, 1957
Anderson, Carl David b. Sep 3, 1905
Anderson, Dorothy Hansine
  d. Mar 3, 1963
Anderson, Elizabeth Milbank
  b. Dec 20, 1850
Anderson, Elizabeth Milbank
  d. Feb 22, 1921
Anderson, John Murray d. Jan 30, 1954
Anderson, Robert Woodruff
  b. Apr 28, 1917
Angell, Roger b. Sep 19, 1920
Angoff, Charles d. May 3, 1979
Anhalt, Edward b. Mar 28, 1914
Anievas, Augustin b. Nov 6, 1934
Anson, Jay b. 1924
Anspach, Susan b. Nov 23, 1939
Antheil, George d. Feb 12, 1959
Anthony, Edward b. Aug 4, 1895
Anthony, John J(ason) b. Sep 1, 1898
Anthony, Joseph b. Apr 9, 1897
Apgar, Virginia d. Aug 7, 1974
Appleton, Daniel d. Mar 27, 1849
Appleton, William Henry d. Oct 19, 1899
Aranason, H Harvard d. May 28, 1986
Arbus, Diane b. Mar 14, 1923
Arbus, Diane d. Jul 26, 1971
Archerd, Army (Armand) b. Jan 13, 1919
Archipenko, Alexander Porfirievich
  d. Feb 25, 1964
Arden, Elizabeth d. Oct 18, 1966
Arendt, Hannah d. Dec 4, 1975
Argentinita d. Sep 24, 1945
Arieti, Silvano d. Aug 7, 1981

Arkin, Alan Wolf b. Mar 26, 1934
Arlen, Harold d. Apr 23, 1986
Arlen, Michael d. Jun 25, 1956
Armour, Norman d. Sep 27, 1982
Armstrong, Edwin Howard
  b. Dec 18, 1891
Armstrong, Edwin Howard d. Feb 1, 1954
Armstrong, Hamilton Fish b. Apr 7, 1893
Armstrong, Louis Daniel d. Jul 6, 1971
Arno, Peter b. Jan 8, 1904
Arnold, Danny b. Jan 23, 1925
Arnold, Edward b. Feb 18, 1890
Arquette, Rosanna b. Aug 10, 1959
Arroyo, Martina b. Feb 2, 1940
Arthur, Beatrice b. May 13, 1926
Arthur, Chester Alan d. Nov 18, 1886
Arthur, Ellen Lewis Herndon
  d. Jan 12, 1880
Arthur, Jean b. Oct 17, 1908
Asbury, Herbert d. Feb 24, 1963
Ascoli, Max d. Jan 1, 1978
Assante, Armand b. Oct 4, 1949
Astor, John Jacob d. Mar 29, 1848
Astor, William Vincent b. Nov 15, 1891
Astor, William Vincent d. Feb 3, 1959
Astor, William Waldorf Astor, Viscount
  b. Mar 31, 1848
Auberjonois, Rene Murat b. Jun 1, 1940
Audubon, John James d. Jan 27, 1851
August, Jan b. 1912
August, Jan d. Jan 18, 1976
Auletta, Robert b. Mar 5, 1940
Austin, Patti b. Aug 10, 1948
Avallone, Michael Angelo, Jr.
  b. Oct 27, 1924
Avedon, Richard b. May 15, 1923
Avery, Milton (Clark) d. Jan 3, 1965
Axelrod, George b. Jun 9, 1922
Axthelm, Pete(r Macrae) b. Aug 27, 1943
Ayer, Harriet Hubbard d. Nov 23, 1903
Babbitt, Benjamin Talbot d. Oct 20, 1889
Bacall, Lauren b. Sep 16, 1924
Baccaloni, Salvatore d. Dec 31, 1969
Bach, Barbara b. Aug 27, 1947
Bacharach, Bert(ram Mark)
  d. Sep 15, 1983
Bache, Harold Leopold b. Jun 17, 1894
Bache, Harold Leopold d. Mar 14, 1968
Bache, Jules Sermon b. Nov 9, 1861
Bacon, Henry d. Feb 16, 1924
Baer, "Bugs" (Arthur) d. May 17, 1969
Baez, Joan b. Jan 9, 1941
Bailey, Mildred d. Dec 12, 1951
Baird, Cora Eisenberg b. Jan 26, 1912
Baird, Cora Eisenberg d. Dec 7, 1967
Baker, "Shorty" (Harold) d. Nov 8, 1966
Baker, Belle b. 1895
Baker, Sara Josephine d. Feb 22, 1945
Balanchine, George d. Apr 30, 1983
Bald, Kenneth b. 1920
Baldwin, James Arthur b. Aug 2, 1924

Ballantine, Ian b. Feb 15, 1916
Balsam, Martin Henry b. Nov 4, 1919
Bancroft, Anne b. Sep 17, 1931
Bangs, Lester d. Apr 30, 1982
Bankhead, Tallulah Brockman
  d. Dec 12, 1968
Banner, James Morril, Jr. b. May 3, 1935
Banning, Kendall b. Sep 20, 1879
Banton, Travis b. 1874
Barber, Samuel d. Jan 23, 1981
Barbera, Joseph Roland b. Mar 24, 1911
Barker, Lex (Alexander Crichlow, Jr.)
  d. Apr 11, 1973
Barnard, Chester Irving d. Jun 7, 1961
Barnard, Frederick Augustus Porter
  d. Apr 27, 1889
Barnard, George Grey d. Apr 24, 1938
Barnes, Djuna d. Jun 18, 1982
Barnet, Charlie (Charles Daly)
  b. Oct 26, 1913
Barrett, Rona b. Oct 8, 1936
Barrett, William Edmund b. Nov 16, 1900
Barry, Gene b. Jun 4, 1922
Barry, Jack d. May 2, 1984
Barry, Philip d. Dec 3, 1949
Barrymore, Diana b. Mar 3, 1921
Barrymore, Diana d. Jan 25, 1960
Barthelmess, Richard b. May 9, 1895
Bartlett, Robert Abram d. Apr 28, 1946
Bartok, Bela d. Sep 29, 1945
Barton, Bruce d. Jul 5, 1967
Baruch, Bernard Mannes d. Jun 20, 1965
Bass, Saul b. May 8, 1920
Bates, William Horatio b. 1860
Bavier, Frances b. Jan 14, 1905
Baxter, Anne d. Dec 12, 1985
Bayes, Nora d. Mar 19, 1928
Baziotes, William d. Jun 5, 1963
Beach, Alfred Ely d. Jan 1, 1896
Beach, Mrs. H H A d. Dec 27, 1944
Beard, George Miller d. Jan 23, 1883
Beard, James Andrews d. Jan 23, 1985
Beard, Peter Hill b. Jan 22, 1938
Beatty, Alfred Chester, Sir b. Feb 7, 1815
Beck, Julian b. May 31, 1925
Beck, Julian d. Sep 14, 1985
Beck, Martin d. Nov 16, 1940
Beckman, Johnny b. Oct 22, 1895
Beckmann, Max d. Dec 12, 1950
Bedelia, Bonnie b. Mar 25, 1948
Beer, Thomas d. Apr 18, 1940
Beery, Noah, Jr. b. Aug 10, 1916
Begelman, David b. Aug 26, 1921
Behrman, S(amuel) N(athaniel)
  d. Aug 9, 1973
Beiderbecke, "Bix" (Leon Bismark)
  d. Aug 7, 1931
Beilenson, Edna Rudolph b. Jun 16, 1909
Beilenson, Edna Rudolph d. Feb 28, 1981
Belafonte, Harry (Harold George, Jr.)
  b. Mar 1, 1927

Belafonte-Harper, Shari b. Sep 22, 1954
Belasco, David d. May 14, 1931
Belinsky, "Bo" (Robert) b. Dec 7, 1936
Bell, Daniel b. May 10, 1919
Bell, Herbert A d. Jan 31, 1970
Bellanca, Giuseppe Mario d. Dec 26, 1960
Bellison, Simeon d. May 4, 1953
Bellows, George Wesley d. Jan 8, 1925
Bellwood, Pamela b. Jun 26, 1946
Belmont, August d. Nov 24, 1890
Belmont, August, Jr. b. Feb 18, 1853
Belmont, Eleanor Robson d. Oct 24, 1979
Bemelmans, Ludwig d. Oct 1, 1962
Benaderet, Bea b. Apr 4, 1906
Benchley, Peter Bradford b. May 8, 1940
Benchley, Robert Charles d. Nov 21, 1945
Bendick, Jeanne b. Feb 25, 1919
Bendix, Vincent d. Mar 27, 1945
Bendix, William b. Jan 14, 1906
Benedict, Ruth Fulton b. Jun 5, 1887
Benedict, Ruth Fulton d. Sep 17, 1948
Benet, Stephen Vincent d. Mar 13, 1943
Benet, William Rose d. May 4, 1950
Benjamin, Richard b. May 22, 1938
Bennett, Constance Campbell
    b. Oct 22, 1905
Bennett, James Gordon d. Jun 1, 1872
Bennett, James Gordon, Jr.
    b. May 10, 1841
Bennett, Robert Russell d. Aug 18, 1981
Bennett, Tony b. Aug 3, 1926
Benton, William d. Mar 18, 1973
Bercovici, Konrad d. Dec 27, 1961
Berenson, Marisa b. Feb 15, 1948
Berg, Gertrude d. Sep 14, 1966
Berg, Paul b. Jun 30, 1926
Berger, Arthur b. May 15, 1912
Berger, Marilyn b. Aug 23, 1935
Berger, Meyer b. Sep 1, 1898
Berger, Meyer d. Feb 8, 1959
Berger, Terry b. Aug 11, 1933
Bergh, Henry b. Aug 29, 1811
Bergh, Henry d. Mar 12, 1888
Bergman, Jules Verne b. Mar 21, 1929
Bergmann, Carl d. Aug 16, 1876
Berigan, "Bunny" (Rowland Bernart)
    d. Jun 2, 1942
Berkowitz, Bob b. May 15, 1950
Berle, Adolf Augustus, Jr. d. Feb 17, 1971
Berle, Milton b. Jul 12, 1908
Berlenbach, Paul b. Feb 18, 1901
Berlitz, Charles L Frambach
    b. Nov 22, 1913
Berman, Emile Zola b. Nov 2, 1903
Berman, Emile Zola d. Jul 3, 1981
Bernardi, Hershel b. Oct 30, 1923
Bernbach, William d. Oct 1, 1982
Bernhard, Lucian d. May 29, 1972
Bernie, Ben b. May 30, 1891
Bernstein, Alice Frankau b. Dec 22, 1880
Bernstein, Alice Frankau d. Sep 7, 1955

Bernstein, Elmer b. Apr 4, 1922
Bernstein, Theodore Menline
    b. Nov 17, 1904
Bernstein, Theodore Menline
    d. Jun 27, 1979
Bessie, Alvah b. Jun 4, 1904
Bestor, Arthur Eugene d. Feb 3, 1944
Betancourt, Romulo d. Sep 28, 1981
Bettis, Valerie d. Sep 26, 1982
Biaggi, Mario b. Oct 26, 1917
Bianco, Margery Williams d. Sep 4, 1944
Biberman, Herbert d. Jun 30, 1971
Bierstadt, Albert d. Feb 18, 1902
Bikoff, James L b. May 26, 1940
Billingsley, Sherman d. Oct 4, 1966
Billy the Kid b. Nov 23, 1859
Bingham, Jonathan Brewster d. Jul 3, 1986
Birch, Stephen b. Mar 24, 1872
Birdseye, Clarence Frank d. Oct 7, 1956
Bitter, Karl Theodore Francis
    d. Apr 10, 1915
Black, William d. Mar 7, 1983
Blackmer, Sidney Alderman d. Oct 5, 1973
Blackton, Jay S b. Mar 25, 1909
Blackwell, Betsy Talbot b. 1905
Blaikie, William b. May 24, 1843
Blaikie, William d. Dec 6, 1904
Blakelock, Ralph Albert b. Oct 15, 1847
Blashfield, Edwin Howland
    b. Dec 15, 1848
Blatchford, Samuel b. Mar 9, 1820
Blatty, William Peter b. Jan 7, 1928
Block, Joseph Leopold d. Nov 17, 1976
Blondell, Joan b. Aug 30, 1912
Bloom, Murray Teigh b. May 19, 1916
Bloomgarden, Kermit d. Sep 20, 1976
Bloomingdale, Alfred S b. Apr 15, 1916
Bloomingdale, Joseph Bernard
    b. Dec 22, 1842
Bloomingdale, Joseph Bernard
    d. Nov 21, 1904
Bloomingdale, Samuel b. Jun 17, 1873
Blousteín, Edward J b. Jan 20, 1925
Blow, Susan Elizabeth d. Mar 26, 1916
Blumenfeld, Isadore d. 1981
Bly, Nellie, pseud. d. Jan 27, 1922
Boas, Franz d. Dec 21, 1942
Bobst, Elmer Holmes d. Aug 2, 1978
Bodanzky, Artur d. Nov 23, 1939
Bodenheim, Maxwell d. Feb 6, 1954
Boettiger, John d. Oct 31, 1950
Bofill, Angela b. 1955
Bogan, Louise d. Feb 4, 1970
Bogart, Humphrey de Forest
    b. Dec 25, 1899
Boland, Mary d. Jun 23, 1965
Bolotowsky, Ilya d. Nov 21, 1981
Bolton, Isabel d. Apr 13, 1975
Bond, Sudie d. Nov 10, 1984
Bonfanti, Marie d. Jan 25, 1921
Boni, Albert b. Oct 21, 1892

Booth, "Albie" (Albert James, Jr.)
d. Mar 1, 1959
Booth, Edwin Thomas d. Jun 7, 1893
Booth, Shirley b. Aug 30, 1907
Bordoni, Irene d. Mar 19, 1953
Bori, Lucrezia d. May 14, 1960
Boswell, Connee d. Oct 11, 1976
Boucicault, Dion d. Sep 18, 1890
Boudin, Kathy (Katherine)
b. May 13, 1942
Bourgholtzer, Frank b. Oct 26, 1919
Bourke-White, Margaret b. Jun 14, 1904
Bow, Clara Gordon b. Aug 25, 1905
Bowen, Billy d. Sep 27, 1982
Bowers, Claude Gernade d. Jan 21, 1958
Bowes, "Major" (Edward) d. Jun 13, 1946
Bowles, Jane Sydney b. Feb 22, 1917
Bowles, Paul b. Dec 30, 1910
Boyle, Harold Vincent d. Apr 1, 1974
Bracken, Eddie (Edward Vincent)
b. Feb 7, 1920
Braddock, James J b. Dec 6, 1905
Bradley, Omar Nelson d. Apr 8, 1981
Brady, "Diamond Jim" (James Buchanan)
b. Aug 12, 1856
Brady, Alice b. Nov 2, 1893
Brady, Alice d. Oct 28, 1939
Brady, Mathew B d. Jan 15, 1896
Brady, William Aloysius d. Jan 6, 1950
Brailowsky, Alexander d. Apr 25, 1976
Branner, Martin Michael b. Dec 28, 1888
Braslau, Sophie b. Aug 16, 1892
Braslau, Sophie d. Dec 22, 1935
Braun, Karl Ferdinand d. Apr 20, 1918
Bray, Charles William, III b. Oct 24, 1933
Breasted, James Henry d. Dec 2, 1933
Breese, Edmund d. Apr 6, 1936
Brennan, Peter Joseph b. May 24, 1918
Breuer, Marcel Lajos d. Jul 1, 1981
Brian, David b. Aug 5, 1914
Brice, Fanny b. Oct 29, 1891
Bricktop d. Jan 31, 1984
Brigati, Eddie b. Oct 22, 1946
Briggs, Clare b. Jan 3, 1930
Brill, Abraham Arden d. Mar 2, 1948
Brisbane, Arthur d. Dec 25, 1936
Brisson, Frederick d. Oct 8, 1984
Britton, Barbara d. Jan 18, 1980
Broadbent, Eleanor b. Nov 1, 1878
Broadbent, Eleanor d. Feb 3, 1934
Broderick, Matthew b. Aug 21, 1962
Bronk, Detlev Wulf b. Aug 13, 1897
Bronk, Detlev Wulf d. Nov 17, 1975
Brooks, Donald Marc b. Jan 10, 1928
Brooks, Geraldine b. Oct 29, 1925
Brooks, Mel b. Jun 28, 1928
Brothers, Joyce Diane Bauer
b. Oct 20, 1928
Broun, (Matthew) Heywood (Campbell)
d. Dec 18, 1939
Broun, Heywood Hale b. Mar 10, 1918

Brown, Harold b. Sep 19, 1927
Brown, John Mason d. Mar 16, 1969
Brown, Kenneth H b. Mar 9, 1936
Brown, Lew d. Feb 5, 1958
Brown, Margaret Wise b. May 23, 1910
Brown, Michael S b. Apr 13, 1941
Brown, Tom (Thomas Edward)
b. Jan 6, 1913
Browne, Dik b. Aug 11, 1917
Browne, Leslie b. Jun 29, 1957
Brownlee, John d. Jan 10, 1969
Brownscombe, Jennie Augusta
d. Aug 5, 1936
Bruce, Ailsa Mellon d. Aug 25, 1969
Bruner, Jerome Seymour b. Oct 1, 1915
Brustein, Robert Sanford b. Apr 21, 1927
Bryant, William Cullen d. Jun 12, 1878
Brynner, Yul d. Oct 10, 1985
Buckley, Charles Anthony b. Jun 23, 1890
Buckley, Charles Anthony d. Jan 22, 1967
Buckley, Emerson b. Apr 14, 1916
Buckley, James Lane b. Mar 9, 1923
Buckley, William F(rank), Jr.
b. Nov 24, 1925
Buechner, Frederick b. Jul 11, 1926
Bullard, Robert Lee d. Sep 11, 1947
Bunche, Ralph Johnson d. Dec 9, 1971
Bunny, John b. Sep 21, 1863
Burke, Johnny d. Feb 25, 1964
Burman, Ben Lucien d. Nov 12, 1984
Burns, David b. Jun 22, 1902
Burns, George b. Jan 20, 1896
Burnshaw, Stanley b. Jun 20, 1906
Burr, Aaron d. Sep 14, 1836
Burrows, Abe (Abram S) b. Dec 18, 1910
Burrows, Abe (Abram S) d. May 17, 1985
Burtin, Will d. Jan 18, 1972
Bushkin, Joe (Joseph) b. Nov 6, 1916
Bushmiller, Ernie (Ernest Paul)
b. Aug 23, 1905
Busoni, Rafaello d. Mar 17, 1962
Butler, Nicholas Murray d. Dec 4, 1947
Buttons, Red b. Feb 5, 1919
Byrne, Brendan b. Dec 28, 1908
Byrnes, Edd b. Jul 30, 1933
Byrnes, Eugene F b. 1889
Caan, James b. Mar 26, 1939
Cadmus, Paul b. Dec 17, 1904
Cady, (Walter) Harrison d. Dec 9, 1970
Caesar, Irving b. Jul 4, 1895
Cagle, "Red" (Christian Keener)
d. Dec 23, 1942
Cagney, James (James Francis, Jr.)
b. Jul 17, 1899
Cagney, Jeanne b. Mar 25, 1919
Cahan, Abraham d. Aug 31, 1951
Cahill, Marie d. Aug 23, 1933
Cahn, Sammy b. Jun 18, 1913
Caidin, Martin b. Sep 14, 1927
Calder, Alexander d. Nov 11, 1976
Calderone, Mary Steichen b. Jul 1, 1904

Calhern, Louis b. Feb 19, 1895
Calisher, Hortense b. Dec 20, 1911
Callas, Maria b. Dec 3, 1923
Cambridge, Godfrey b. Feb 26, 1933
Cameron, Roderick W b. Nov 15, 1913
Camp, Walter Chauncey d. Mar 14, 1925
Campanella, Joseph Mario b. Nov 21, 1927
Campo, John(ny) b. 1938
Canaday, John (Edwin John)
    d. Jul 19, 1985
Canfield, Cass b. Apr 26, 1897
Canfield, Cass d. Mar 27, 1986
Cannon, Jimmy (James J) b. Apr 10, 1909
Cannon, Jimmy (James J) d. Dec 5, 1973
Cannon, Poppy d. Apr 2, 1975
Cantor, Eddie b. Jan 31, 1892
Cantwell, Robert Emmett d. Dec 8, 1978
Canzoneri, Tony d. Dec 9, 1959
Caples, John b. May 1, 1900
Cardozo, Benjamin Nathan
    b. May 24, 1870
Carey, Ernestine Muller Gilbreth
    b. Apr 5, 1908
Carey, Harry b. Jan 16, 1878
Carlin, George Dennis b. May 12, 1937
Carlino, Lewis John b. Jan 1, 1932
Carlos, John b. Jun 5, 1945
Carlson, Chester d. Sep 19, 1968
Carnegie, Dale d. Nov 1, 1955
Carnegie, Hattie d. Feb 22, 1956
Carney, Harry Howell d. Oct 8, 1974
Carradine, John Richmond b. Feb 5, 1906
Carrier, Willis H d. Oct 7, 1950
Carroll, Diahann b. Jul 17, 1935
Carroll, Jim b. Aug 1, 1951
Carroll, Nancy b. Nov 19, 1906
Carroll, Nancy d. Aug 6, 1965
Carroll, Vinnette (Justine) b. Mar 11, 1922
Carson, Mindy b. Jul 16, 1926
Carter, Benny (Bennett Lester)
    b. Aug 8, 1907
Carter, Elliott Cook, Jr. b. Dec 11, 1908
Cartwright, Alexander Joy, Jr.
    b. Apr 17, 1820
Cary, Alice d. Feb 12, 1871
Cary, Phoebe d. Jul 31, 1871
Case, Anna d. Jan 7, 1984
Cassavetes, John b. Dec 9, 1929
Cassidy, David Bruce b. Apr 12, 1950
Cassidy, Jack b. Mar 5, 1927
Cassirer, Ernst d. Apr 13, 1945
Castellano, Richard b. Sep 4, 1934
Castellon, Frederico d. Sep 27, 1971
Castle, William b. Apr 24, 1914
Caston, Saul b. Aug 22, 1901
Cates, Phoebe b. 1964
Cather, Willa Sibert d. Apr 24, 1947
Cavallaro, Carmen b. May 6, 1913
Cawthorn, Joseph b. Mar 29, 1868
Cerf, Bennett Alfred b. May 25, 1898
Cesnola, Luigi Palma di d. Nov 20, 1904

Chadwick, Henry d. Apr 20, 1908
Chaikin, Sol Chick b. Jan 9, 1918
Chamberlin, Lee b. Feb 14, 1938
Champion, Gower d. Aug 25, 1980
Channing, Stockard b. Feb 13, 1944
Chapin, Harry Foster b. Dec 7, 1942
Chapin, Schuyler Garrison b. Feb 13, 1923
Chaplin, Saul b. Feb 19, 1912
Chapman, Ceil (Cecilia Mitchell)
    b. Feb 19, 1912
Chapman, Frank Michler d. Nov 15, 1945
Chartoff, Robert b. Aug 26, 1933
Chase, "Chevy" (Cornelius Crane)
    b. Oct 8, 1943
Chase, Ilka b. Apr 8, 1905
Chase, Lucia d. Jan 9, 1986
Chase, Salmon Portland d. May 7, 1873
Chasins, Abram b. Aug 17, 1903
Chatterton, Ruth b. Dec 24, 1893
Chayefsky, "Paddy" (Sidney)
    b. Jan 29, 1923
Chayefsky, "Paddy" (Sidney)
    d. Aug 1, 1981
Cherniavsky, Josef d. Nov 3, 1959
Chernov, Viktor Mikhailovich
    d. Apr 15, 1952
Chodorov, Edward b. Apr 17, 1904
Chodorov, Jerome b. Aug 10, 1911
Christian, Charlie (Charles) d. Mar 2, 1942
Christy, Howard Chandler d. Mar 4, 1952
Churchill, Jennie Jerome b. 1850
Cimino, Michael b. 1943
Clark, Bobby d. Feb 12, 1960
Clark, Dane b. Feb 18, 1913
Clark, John Bates d. Mar 21, 1938
Clark, Marguerite d. Sep 25, 1940
Clark, Tom (Thomas Campbell)
    d. Jun 1977
Clarke, Gilmore David b. Jul 12, 1892
Clarke, Shirley b. Oct 2, 1927
Classen, Willie d. Nov 28, 1979
Clayburgh, Jill b. Apr 30, 1944
Cleveland, James Harlan b. Jan 19, 1918
Clift, Montgomery d. Jul 23, 1966
Clinchy, Everett Ross b. Dec 16, 1896
Clurman, Harold Edgar b. Sep 18, 1901
Clurman, Harold Edgar d. Sep 9, 1980
Coates, Robert Myron d. Feb 8, 1973
Cobb, Irvin Shrewsbury d. Mar 10, 1944
Cobb, Lee J (Leo Jacob) b. Dec 9, 1911
Cobb, Vicki b. Aug 19, 1938
Cobb, Will D d. Jan 20, 1930
Coburn, Charles Douville d. Aug 30, 1961
Coco, James b. Mar 21, 1929
Coffin, Henry Sloane b. Jan 5, 1877
Coffin, William Sloan b. Jun 1, 1924
Cohan, George M(ichael) d. Nov 5, 1942
Cohan, Josephine b. Jul 12, 1916
Cohen, Alexander H b. Jul 24, 1920
Cohn, Roy Marcus b. Feb 20, 1927

Colavito, Rocky (Rocco Domenico)
   b. Aug 10, 1933
Cole, Kenneth Reese b. Jan 27, 1938
Coleman, Cy b. Jun 14, 1929
Colfax, Schuyler b. Mar 23, 1823
Colgate, William d. Mar 25, 1857
Collier, Constance d. Apr 25, 1955
Collier, William, Sr. b. Nov 12, 1866
Collingwood, Charles Cummings
   d. Oct 3, 1985
Collins, Ted b. Oct 12, 1899
Collyer, "Bud" (Clayton) b. Jun 18, 1908
Colum, Padraic d. Jan 12, 1972
Comden, Betty b. May 3, 1915
Compton, Betty d. Jul 12, 1944
Conaway, Jeff b. Oct 5, 1950
Condon, Eddie d. Aug 3, 1973
Condon, Richard Thomas b. Mar 18, 1915
Conkling, Roscoe d. Apr 18, 1888
Connelly, Marc(us Cook) d. Dec 21, 1980
Conniff, Frank d. May 25, 1971
Connors, "Chuck" (Kevin Joseph)
   b. Apr 10, 1921
Conover, Harry d. Jul 21, 1965
Conrad, Con b. Jun 18, 1891
Conrad, Michael b. Oct 16, 1927
Conroy, Frank b. Jan 15, 1936
Considine, Bob (Robert Bernard)
   d. Sep 25, 1975
Cook, Will Marion d. Jul 19, 1944
Cooke, Terence James b. Mar 1, 1921
Cooke, Terence James d. Oct 6, 1983
Cooper, Emil d. Nov 19, 1960
Cooper, Lester Irving b. Jan 20, 1919
Cooper, Lester Irving d. Jun 6, 1985
Cooper, Peter b. Feb 12, 1791
Cooper, Peter d. Apr 4, 1883
Coote, Robert d. Nov 25, 1982
Coots, J Fred d. Apr 8, 1985
Copeland, Jo b. 1899
Copeland, Jo d. Mar 20, 1982
Coplon, Judith b. 1921
Coppola, Carmine b. Jun 11, 1910
Corbett, James John d. Feb 18, 1933
Corcos, Lucille b. Sep 21, 1908
Corey, Irwin b. Jul 29, 1912
Corey, Jeff b. Aug 10, 1914
Corigliano, John b. Feb 16, 1938
Cornell, Don b. Apr 21, 1919
Corsaro, Frank b. Dec 22, 1925
Corso, Gregory b. Mar 26, 1930
Corson, Juliet b. Jun 18, 1897
Cortez, Ricardo d. May 28, 1977
Cortissoz, Royal d. Oct 17, 1948
Corum, Martene Windsor d. Dec 16, 1958
Coslow, Sam b. Dec 27, 1905
Cossart, Ernest d. Jan 21, 1951
Costa, Don d. Jan 19, 1983
Costain, Thomas B d. Oct 8, 1965
Costello, Frank d. Feb 1, 1973
Costello, Helene b. Jun 21, 1903

Cott, Ted d. Jun 13, 1973
Cousy, Bob (Robert Joseph)
   b. Aug 9, 1928
Covici, Pascal d. Oct 14, 1964
Cowan, Jerome b. Oct 6, 1897
Cowen, Joshua Lionel b. Aug 25, 1880
Cowen, Joshua Lionel d. Sep 8, 1965
Cowles, Fleur Fenton b. Feb 13, 1910
Cowles, Gardner d. Jul 8, 1985
Crabtree, Lotta b. Nov 7, 1847
Crane, Nathalia Clara Ruth
   b. Aug 11, 1913
Crapsey, Adelaide b. Sep 9, 1878
Crawford, Joan d. May 13, 1977
Crawford, Thomas b. Mar 22, 1813
Creston, Paul b. Oct 10, 1906
Crews, Laura Hope d. Nov 13, 1942
Crist, Judith Klein b. May 22, 1922
Crohn, Burrill Bernard b. Jun 13, 1884
Croker, "Boss" (Richard) d. Apr 29, 1922
Croly, Herbert David b. Jan 23, 1869
Croly, Jane Cunningham d. Dec 23, 1901
Crosby, Floyd Delafield b. Dec 12, 1899
Crosby, Harry d. Dec 10, 1929
Crosby, James Morris d. Apr 10, 1986
Crosby, John b. Jul 12, 1926
Crosby, Percy d. Dec 8, 1964
Cross, Milton John b. Apr 16, 1897
Cross, Milton John d. Jan 3, 1975
Crouse, Lindsay Ann b. May 12, 1948
Crouse, Russel d. Apr 3, 1966
Crowninshield, Francis Welch
   d. Dec 28, 1947
Crummell, Alexander b. Mar 1819
Cukor, George Dewey b. Jul 7, 1899
Cullen, Countee b. May 30, 1903
Cullen, Countee d. Jan 10, 1946
Cuppy, Will(iam Jacob) d. Sep 19, 1949
Curran, Charles Courtney d. Nov 9, 1942
Curran, Joseph Edwin b. Mar 1, 1906
Currie, Barton Wood b. Mar 8, 1878
Currier, Nathaniel d. Nov 20, 1888
Curtis, Alan d. Feb 1, 1953
Curtis, Tony b. Jun 3, 1925
Custer, Elizabeth Bacon d. Apr 4, 1933
Dabney, Virginius d. Jun 2, 1894
Dailey, Dan b. Dec 14, 1915
Dailey, Irene b. Sep 12, 1920
Dale, Chester b. May 3, 1882
Dale, Chester d. Dec 16, 1962
Daley, Arthur b. Jul 31, 1904
Daley, Arthur d. Jan 3, 1974
Dall, John b. 1918
Daly, Arnold d. Jan 12, 1927
Daly, Marcus d. Nov 12, 1900
Damrosch, Frank Heino d. Oct 22, 1937
Damrosch, Leopold d. Feb 15, 1885
Damrosch, Walter Johannes
   d. Dec 22, 1950
Danelli, Dino b. Jul 23, 1945
Danielian, Leon b. Oct 31, 1920

Dante, Nicholas b. Nov 22, 1941
Danton, Ray(mond) b. Sep 19, 1931
Danza, Tony b. Apr 21, 1951
DaPonte, Lorenzo d. Aug 17, 1838
Darin, Bobby b. May 14, 1936
Darion, Joseph b. Jan 30, 1917
Darnton, Robert Choate b. May 10, 1939
Darrow, Henry b. Sep 15, 1933
Darvas, Lili d. Jul 22, 1974
Davenport, Harry George Bryant
   b. Jan 19, 1886
Davenport, Homer Calvin d. May 2, 1912
Davenport, Marcia b. Jun 9, 1903
David, Hal b. May 25, 1921
David, Mack b. Jul 5, 1912
Davidson, Jo b. Mar 30, 1883
Davies, Marion b. Jan 3, 1897
Davis, "Tobe" (Coller) d. Dec 25, 1962
Davis, Alexander Jackson b. Jul 24, 1803
Davis, Hal Charles d. Jan 1, 1978
Davis, John Williams d. Mar 24, 1955
Davis, Meyer d. Apr 5, 1976
Davis, Owen d. Oct 13, 1956
Davis, Sammy, Jr. b. Dec 8, 1925
Davis, Stuart d. Jun 24, 1964
Day, Benjamin Henry d. Dec 21, 1889
Day, Clarence Shepard, Jr.
   b. Nov 18, 1874
Day, Clarence Shepard, Jr.
   d. Dec 28, 1935
Day, Dennis b. May 21, 1917
Day, Dorothy b. Nov 8, 1897
Day, Dorothy d. Nov 29, 1980
Day, Joseph Paul b. Sep 22, 1873
Day, Joseph Paul d. Apr 10, 1944
De Vorzon, Barry b. Jul 31, 1934
Dean, "Man Mountain" b. Jun 30, 1889
DeBeck, Billy d. Nov 11, 1942
DeCamp, L(yon) Sprague b. Nov 27, 1907
DeCordoba, Pedro b. Sep 28, 1881
DeCordova, Frederick Timmins
   b. Oct 27, 1910
Dehn, Adolf Arthur d. May 19, 1968
Dehner, John Forkum b. Nov 23, 1915
Dehnert, Henry b. Apr 5, 1898
Dekker, Albert b. Dec 20, 1905
DeKooning, Elaine Marie Catherine Fried
   b. Mar 12, 1920
Delacorte, George Thomas, Jr.
   b. Jun 20, 1894
Delany, Samuel Ray, Jr. b. Apr 1, 1942
Dello Joio, Norman Joseph
   b. Jan 24, 1913
Delmar, Vina Croter b. Jan 29, 1905
DeLong, George Washington
   b. Aug 22, 1844
DeLuca, Giuseppe d. Aug 27, 1950
DeMille, Agnes George b. Sep 18, 1905
Dempsey, Jack (William Harrison)
   d. May 31, 1983
DeNiro, Robert b. Aug 17, 1943

Dennis, Patrick, pseud. d. Nov 6, 1976
Densen-Gerber, Judianne b. Nov 13, 1934
DePaolis, Alessio d. Mar 9, 1964
DeParis, Wilbur d. Jan 1973
Depew, Chauncey M d. Apr 5, 1928
DeRivera, Jose d. Mar 21, 1985
DeSapio, Carmine Gerard b. Dec 10, 1908
DeSeversky, Alexander Procofieff
   d. Aug 24, 1974
Desmond, Paul Breitenfeld
   d. May 30, 1977
DeSylva, "Buddy" (George Gard)
   b. Jan 27, 1896
Deutsch, Babette b. Sep 22, 1895
Deutsch, Babette d. Nov 13, 1982
Deutsch, Helen b. Mar 21, 1906
DeValera, Eamon b. Oct 14, 1882
DeVinne, Theodore Low d. Feb 16, 1914
DeVoto, Bernard Augustine
   d. Nov 13, 1955
Dewey, John d. Jun 1, 1952
DeWilde, Brandon b. Apr 9, 1942
Dewing, Thomas Wilmer d. Nov 5, 1938
Dietz, Howard M b. Sep 8, 1896
Dietz, Howard M d. Jul 30, 1983
Digges, Dudley d. Oct 24, 1947
Dirks, Rudolph d. Apr 20, 1968
DiSalle, Michael Vincent b. Jan 6, 1908
Ditmars, Raymond Lee d. May 12, 1942
Dix, John Adams d. Apr 21, 1879
Dixon, Dean b. Jan 10, 1915
Dixon, Ivan b. Apr 6, 1931
Dixon, Jean d. Feb 12, 1981
Dixon, Mort b. Mar 20, 1892
Dockstader, Lew d. 1924
Doctorow, E(dgar) L(aurence)
   b. Jan 6, 1931
Dodge, Grace Hoadley b. May 21, 1856
Dodge, Grace Hoadley d. Dec 27, 1914
Dodge, John Francis d. Jan 4, 1920
Dodge, Mary Elizabeth Mapes
   b. Jan 26, 1831
Dohnanyi, Erno von d. 1960
Dolly, Rosie d. Feb 1, 1970
Donahue, Troy b. Jan 27, 1937
Donahue, Woolworth b. Jan 9, 1913
Donehue, Vincent J d. Jan 17, 1966
Donghia, Angelo R d. Apr 10, 1985
Donnelly, Ruth d. Nov 17, 1982
Donohue, Jack b. Nov 3, 1912
Dooley, Thomas Anthony d. Jan 18, 1961
Dorne, Albert b. Feb 7, 1904
Dorne, Albert d. Dec 15, 1965
Dorsey, Jimmy (James) d. Jun 12, 1957
Doubrovska, Felia d. Sep 18, 1981
Douglas, Amanda Minnie b. Jul 14, 1837
Douglas, Helen Mary Gahagan
   d. Jun 28, 1980
Douglas, Jack b. 1908
Douglas, Melvyn d. Aug 4, 1981
Douglas, Michael Kirk b. Sep 25, 1944

Farrar, John Chipman d. Nov 6, 1974
Farrar, Margaret Petherbridge
  b. Mar 23, 1897
Farrar, Margaret Petherbridge
  d. Jun 11, 1984
Farrell, Glenda d. May 1, 1971
Farrell, James Thomas d. Aug 22, 1979
Fast, Howard b. Nov 11, 1914
Faust, Lotta d. Jan 25, 1910
Faye, Alice b. May 5, 1915
Faye, Joey b. Jul 12, 1910
Fearing, Kenneth Flexner d. Jun 26, 1961
Feiffer, Jules Ralph b. Jan 26, 1929
Feininger, Lyonel b. Jul 17, 1871
Feis, Herbert b. Jun 7, 1893
Feldman, Alvin Lindbergh b. Dec 14, 1927
Feldshuh, Tovah b. Dec 27, 1952
Feldstein, Martin Stuart b. Nov 25, 1939
Fellig, Arthur d. Dec 26, 1968
Fenten, D X b. Jan 3, 1932
Fenwick, Millicent Hammond
  b. Feb 25, 1910
Ferber, Edna d. Apr 16, 1968
Ferrante, Arthur b. Sep 7, 1921
Feuer, Cy b. Jan 15, 1911
Feuermann, Emanuel d. May 25, 1942
Feynman, Richard Phillips
  b. May 11, 1918
Field, Cyrus West d. Jul 12, 1892
Field, Marshall d. Jan 16, 1906
Field, Marshall, III d. Nov 8, 1956
Field, Marshall, IV b. Jun 15, 1916
Field, Rachel Lyman b. Sep 19, 1894
Fielding, Lewis J b. Oct 2, 1909
Fields, Dorothy d. Mar 28, 1974
Fields, Joseph b. Feb 21, 1895
Fields, Lew Maurice b. Jan 1, 1867
Fine, Sidney Albert b. Sep 18, 1915
Fine, Sylvia b. Aug 29, 1893
Fineman, Irving b. Apr 9, 1893
Finletter, Thomas Knight d. Apr 24, 1980
Fischl, Eric b. Mar 9, 1948
Fish, Hamilton b. Aug 3, 1808
Fisher, "Bud" (Harry Conway)
  d. Sep 7, 1954
Fisher, Fred d. Jan 14, 1942
Fisher, Ham(mond Edward)
  d. Dec 27, 1955
Fisher, Harrison d. Jan 19, 1934
Fisher, Harry b. Feb 6, 1882
Fisher, Harry d. Dec 29, 1967
Fisher, Irving d. Apr 29, 1947
Fisk, Jim (James) d. Jan 7, 1872
Fitzgerald, Ed(ward) d. Mar 22, 1982
Fixx, James Fuller b. Apr 23, 1932
Flagg, Ernest d. Apr 10, 1947
Flagg, James Montgomery
  d. May 27, 1960
Flannagan, John Bernard d. Jan 6, 1942
Flanner, Janet d. Jan 7, 1978
Fleischer, Nat(haniel S) d. Jun 25, 1972

Fleishmann, Raoul H(erbert)
  d. May 11, 1969
Foat, Ginny b. Jun 21, 1941
Fogarty, Anne d. Jan 15, 1980
Folger, Henry Clay b. Jun 18, 1857
Fonda, Jane b. Dec 21, 1937
Fonda, Peter b. Feb 23, 1939
Forbes, Bertie Charles d. May 6, 1954
Forbes, Malcolm Stevenson
  b. Aug 19, 1919
Forbes, Ralph d. Mar 31, 1951
Ford, "Whitey" (Edward Charles)
  b. Oct 21, 1928
Ford, Corey b. Apr 29, 1902
Ford, Eileen b. Mar 25, 1922
Ford, Paul Leicester d. May 8, 1902
Foster, Joseph C d. Nov 10, 1971
Foster, Stephen Collins d. Jul 13, 1864
Fox, Charles b. Oct 30, 1940
Foy, Eddie b. Mar 9, 1856
Franciosa, Anthony b. Oct 25, 1928
Francis, Kay d. Aug 26, 1968
Frank, Jerome David b. May 30, 1909
Frankel, Charles b. Dec 13, 1917
Frankel, Emily b.
Frankenthaler, Helen b. Dec 12, 1928
Franklin, Irene b. Jun 13, 1876
Fredericks, Carlton b. Oct 23, 1910
Freed, Bert b. Nov 3, 1919
Freer, Charles Lang d. Sep 25, 1919
Fremont, John Charles d. Jul 13, 1890
French, Jay Jay b. Jul 20, 1954
French, Marilyn b. Nov 21, 1929
Freneau, Philip Morin b. Jan 2, 1752
Frick, Henry Clay d. Dec 2, 1919
Fried, Gerald b. Feb 13, 1928
Friedman, Bruce Jay b. Apr 26, 1930
Friedman, Herbert b. Jun 21, 1916
Friedman, Max b. Jul 12, 1889
Friedman, Max d. Jan 1, 1986
Friendly, Ed b. Apr 8, 1922
Friendly, Fred W b. Oct 30, 1915
Frisch, Frankie (Frank Francis)
  b. Sep 9, 1898
Frohman, Daniel d. Dec 26, 1940
Fuchs, Daniel b. Jun 25, 1909
Fuchs, Joseph b. Apr 26, 1900
Fuld, Stanley H b. Aug 23, 1903
Fulton, Robert d. Feb 24, 1815
Furness, Betty (Elizabeth Mary)
  b. Jan 3, 1916
Futter, Ellen Victoria b. Sep 21, 1949
Gabel, Martin d. May 22, 1986
Gaddis, William b. 1922
Gag, Wanda d. Jun 27, 1946
Galamian, Ivan d. Apr 14, 1981
Gallatin, Albert Eugene d. Jun 15, 1952
Gallico, Paul William b. Jul 26, 1897
Gallo, Fortune d. Mar 28, 1970
Gambling, John A b. 1930
Gannett, Ruth b. Aug 12, 1923

Geographic Index

Grauer, Ben(jamin Franklin)
   b. Jun 2, 1908
Grauer, Ben(jamin Franklin)
   d. May 31, 1977
Graziano, Rocky b. Jun 7, 1922
Greaza, Walter N d. Jun 1, 1973
Greb, Harry (Edward Henry)
   d. Oct 22, 1926
Green, Abel b. Jun 3, 1900
Green, Abel d. May 10, 1973
Green, Adolph b. Dec 2, 1915
Green, Hetty d. Jul 3, 1916
Green, Johnny (John W) b. Oct 10, 1908
Green, Mitzi b. Oct 22, 1920
Greenberg, Hank (Henry Benjamin)
   b. Jan 1, 1911
Greene, Belle da Costa d. May 10, 1950
Greenfield, Jeff b. Jun 10, 1943
Greenglass, David b. 1922
Greenspan, Alan b. Mar 6, 1926
Greenspan, Martin b. May 8, 1912
Greer, "Sonny" (William Alexander)
   d. Mar 23, 1982
Greer, Michael d. 1976
Gregg, Peter b. May 4, 1940
Gregory, Bettina Louise b. Jun 4, 1946
Gregory, James b. Dec 23, 1911
Gretchaninov, Aleksandr Tikhonovich
   d. Jan 3, 1956
Gribble, Harry Wagstaff Graham
   d. Jan 28, 1981
Griffis, Stanton d. Aug 29, 1974
Griffith, Melanie b. Aug 9, 1957
Griffiths, John Willis b. Oct 6, 1809
Grist, Reri b. 1934
Grofe, Ferde b. Mar 27, 1892
Groh, David Lawrence b. May 21, 1939
Gropper, William b. Dec 3, 1897
Gross, Milt b. Mar 4, 1895
Gruenberg, Sidonie Matsner
   d. Mar 11, 1974
Guardino, Harry b. Dec 23, 1925
Guare, John b. Feb 5, 1938
Guarnieri, Johnny (John A)
   b. Mar 23, 1917
Guggenheim, Peggy Marguerite
   b. Aug 26, 1898
Guggenheimer, Minnie b. Oct 22, 1882
Guggenheimer, Minnie d. May 23, 1966
Gunther, John d. May 29, 1970
Gunzberg, Nicolas de, Baron
   d. Feb 20, 1981
Guthrie, Woody (Woodrow Wilson)
   d. Oct 4, 1967
Gwynne, Fred b. Jul 10, 1926
Haber, Joyce b. Dec 28, 1932
Hackett, Albert b. Feb 16, 1900
Hackett, Buddy b. Aug 31, 1924
Hackett, Charles d. Jan 1, 1942
Hackett, Joan b. Mar 1, 1934
Hackett, Raymond b. Jul 15, 1902

Hadley, Henry Kimball d. Sep 6, 1937
Haenigsen, Harry William b. Jul 14, 1902
Hagedorn, Hermann b. Jul 18, 1882
Hagen, Walter Charles b. Dec 21, 1892
Haggart, Bob b. Mar 13, 1914
Haines, Robert Terrel d. May 6, 1943
Halberstam, David b. Apr 10, 1934
Hall, Huntz (Henry) b. 1920
Halop, Billy b. 1920
Halpert, Edith Gregor d. Oct 6, 1970
Halsman, Philippe d. Jun 25, 1979
Halsted, Anna Eleanor Roosevelt
   b. May 3, 1906
Halsted, Anna Eleanor Roosevelt
   d. Dec 1, 1975
Hamilton, Alice b. Feb 27, 1869
Hamilton, Nancy d. Feb 18, 1985
Hamlin, Talbot Faulkner b. Jun 16, 1889
Hamlisch, Marvin b. Jun 2, 1944
Hammer, Armand b. May 21, 1898
Hammerstein, Oscar d. Aug 1, 1919
Hammerstein, Oscar, II b. Jul 12, 1895
Hammett, (Samuel) Dashiell
   d. Jan 10, 1961
Hammond, John Henry, Jr.
   b. Dec 15, 1910
Hampden, Walter b. Jun 30, 1879
Hampton, Hope d. Jan 2, 1982
Hand, Learned d. Aug 18, 1961
Handy, W(illiam) C(hristopher)
   d. Mar 29, 1958
Hanks, Nancy d. Jan 7, 1983
Hansberry, Lorraine d. Jan 2, 1965
Harbach, Otto Abels d. Jan 24, 1963
Harburg, E(dgar) Y(ipsel) b. Apr 8, 1896
Hardwicke, Cedric Webster, Sir
   d. Aug 6, 1964
Harkness, Anna M Richardson
   d. Mar 27, 1926
Harkness, Rebekah West d. Jun 17, 1982
Harnett, William Michael d. Oct 29, 1892
Harper, Fletcher d. May 29, 1877
Harper, James d. Mar 27, 1869
Harper, John d. Apr 22, 1875
Harper, Joseph Wesley d. Feb 14, 1870
Harrell, Lynn Morris b. Jan 30, 1944
Harriman, E(dward) Roland (Noel)
   b. Dec 24, 1895
Harriman, W(illiam) Averell
   b. Nov 15, 1891
Harrington, Pat b. Aug 13, 1929
Harris, Jed d. Nov 1979
Harris, Leonard b. Sep 27, 1929
Harris, Sam Henry b. Feb 3, 1872
Harris, Sam Henry d. Jul 3, 1941
Harrison, Mary Scott Lord Dimmick
   d. Jan 5, 1948
Harrison, Wallace Kirkman d. Dec 2, 1981
Hart, Jeffrey b. Feb 24, 1930
Hart, Lorenz Milton b. May 2, 1895
Hart, Lorenz Milton d. Nov 22, 1943

Hart, Mickey b.
Hart, Moss b. Oct 24, 1904
Hartford, Huntington b. Apr 18, 1911
Hartford, John Augustine d. Sep 20, 1951
Hartford, John Cowan b. Dec 30, 1937
Hartley, Mariette b. Jun 21, 1940
Hatfield, Hurd b. Dec 7, 1918
Hathaway, Donny d. Jan 13, 1979
Hauge, Gabriel d. Jul 24, 1981
Hauk, Minnie b. Nov 16, 1851
Hauptman, Herbert Aaron b. Feb 14, 1917
Hawes, Elisabeth d. Sep 6, 1971
Hawkins, "Bean" (Coleman)
    d. May 19, 1969
Hayes, Patrick J b. Nov 20, 1867
Hayton, Lennie (Leonard George)
    b. Feb 13, 1908
Hayward, Susan b. Jun 30, 1919
Hayworth, Rita b. Oct 17, 1918
Healy, Katherine b. 1969
Hearst, David W b. Dec 2, 1916
Hearst, Millicent Willson b. Jul 16, 1882
Hearst, Millicent Willson d. Dec 6, 1974
Hearst, Randolph Apperson b. Dec 2, 1915
Hearst, William Randolph, Jr.
    b. Jan 27, 1908
Heatter, Gabriel b. Sep 17, 1890
Hecht, Anthony Evan b. Jan 16, 1923
Hecht, Ben b. Feb 28, 1893
Hecht, Ben d. Apr 18, 1964
Hecht, George Joseph b. Nov 1, 1895
Hecht, George Joseph d. Apr 23, 1980
Hecht, Harold b. Jun 1, 1907
Heggen, Thomas Orls, Jr. d. May 19, 1949
Heiden, Konrad d. Jul 18, 1966
Heiser, Victor George d. Feb 27, 1972
Heisman, John William d. Oct 3, 1936
Helburn, Theresa b. Jan 12, 1887
Helck, Peter (Clarence Peter)
    b. Jun 17, 1893
Held, Al b. Oct 12, 1928
Held, Anna d. Aug 12, 1918
Hellerman, Fred b. May 13, 1927
Hellinger, Mark b. Mar 21, 1903
Helmsley, Harry Brakmann b. Mar 4, 1909
Henderson, Fletcher Hamilton
    d. Dec 29, 1952
Hendrick, Burton Jesse d. Mar 23, 1949
Henri, Robert d. Jul 12, 1929
Henry, Buck b. Dec 9, 1930
Henry, Edward Lamson d. May 9, 1919
Henry, O, pseud. d. Jun 5, 1910
Henson, Matthew Alexander
    d. Mar 9, 1955
Herbert, Victor d. May 27, 1924
Herbst, Josephine Frey d. Jan 28, 1969
Herford, Oliver d. Jul 5, 1935
Herman, George b. Jan 14, 1920
Herman, Jerry b. Jul 10, 1933
Herrick, Elinore M b. Jun 15, 1895
Herrmann, Bernard b. Jun 29, 1911

Hershey, Lenore b. Mar 20, 1920
Hershfield, Harry d. Dec 15, 1974
Herzog, Arthur, Jr. b. 1901
Heschel, Abraham Joshua d. Dec 23, 1972
Hesse, Eva d. May 29, 1970
Higginbotham, "Jack" (Jay C)
    d. May 26, 1973
Highet, Gilbert Arthur d. Jan 20, 1978
Hill, "Chippie" (Bertha) d. May 7, 1950
Hill, Herbert b. Jan 24, 1924
Hill, Morton A(nthony) d. Nov 4, 1985
Hillenkoetter, Roscoe H(enry)
    d. Jun 18, 1982
Hilliard, Robert Cochran b. May 28, 1857
Hilliard, Robert Cochran d. Jun 6, 1927
Hines, Gregory Oliver b. Feb 14, 1946
Hirsch, Joseph d. Sep 21, 1981
Hirsch, Judd b. Mar 15, 1935
Hobart, Rose b. May 1, 1906
Hobson, Laura Zametkin b. Jun 19, 1900
Hobson, Laura Zametkin d. Feb 28, 1986
Hodges, Johnny d. May 11, 1970
Hoe, Richard March b. Sep 12, 1812
Hoff, Sydney b. Sep 4, 1912
Hoffer, Eric b. Jul 25, 1902
Hoffman, Al d. Jul 21, 1960
Hoffman, Anna Marie Lederer Rosenberg
    d. May 9, 1983
Hoffman, Charles Fenno b. Feb 7, 1806
Hoffman, Irwin b. Nov 26, 1924
Hoffman, Malvina b. Jun 15, 1887
Hoffman, Malvina d. Jul 10, 1966
Hoffman, Paul Gray d. Oct 8, 1974
Hofmann, Hans d. Feb 17, 1966
Hofstadter, Richard d. Oct 24, 1970
Hofstadter, Robert b. Feb 5, 1915
Hoge, James Fulton, Jr. b. Dec 25, 1936
Hogrogian, Nonny b. May 7, 1932
Holiday, Billie b. Jul 17, 1959
Hollander, John b. Oct 28, 1929
Holliday, Judy b. Jun 21, 1922
Holliday, Judy d. Jun 7, 1965
Hollister, Paul Merrick b. 1890
Holm, Celeste b. Apr 29, 1919
Holman, Eugene d. Aug 12, 1962
Holman, Nat b. Oct 18, 1896
Holmes, John Haynes d. Apr 3, 1964
Holt, John Caldwell b. Apr 14, 1923
Holzer, Harold b. Feb 5, 1949
Holzman, William b. Aug 10, 1920
Hook, Sidney b. Dec 20, 1902
Hooker, Brian b. Nov 2, 1880
Hoover, Herbert Clark d. Oct 20, 1964
Hoover, Lou Henry d. Jan 7, 1944
Hopkins, Arthur d. Mar 22, 1950
Hopkins, Harry Lloyd d. Jan 29, 1946
Hopkins, Miriam d. Oct 9, 1972
Hoppe, Willie (William F) b. Oct 11, 1887
Hopper, De Wolfe (William De Wolfe)
    b. Mar 30, 1858
Hopper, DeWolf b. Mar 30, 1858

Hopper, Edward d. May 15, 1967
Hopper, Grace Brewster Murray
  b. Dec 9, 1906
Hopper, William b. Jan 26, 1915
Horan, James David b. Jul 27, 1914
Horan, James David d. Oct 13, 1981
Horn, Paul Joseph b. Mar 17, 1930
Horney, Karen Danielson d. Dec 4, 1952
Horowitz, David Joel b. Jan 10, 1939
Horst, Louis d. Jan 23, 1964
Horton, Edward Everett b. Mar 18, 1886
Hottelet, Richard C(urt) b. Sep 22, 1917
House, Edward Mandell d. Mar 28, 1938
Hoving, Thomas Pearsall Field
  b. Jan 15, 1931
Howard, "Shemp" (Samuel)
  b. Mar 17, 1900
Howard, Elston Gene d. Dec 14, 1980
Howard, Eugene d. Aug 1, 1965
Howard, Joseph Edgar b. Feb 12, 1878
Howard, Roy Wilson d. Nov 20, 1964
Howard, Willie d. Jan 14, 1949
Howe, Irving b. Jun 11, 1920
Howe, Julia Ward b. May 27, 1819
Howe, Quincy d. Feb 17, 1977
Howells, William Dean d. May 10, 1920
Hubley, Season b. May 14, 1951
Huggins, Miller James d. Sep 25, 1929
Hughes, Langston (James Langston)
  d. May 22, 1967
Hull, Josephine d. Mar 12, 1957
Huneker, James Gibbons d. Feb 9, 1921
Hunt, Walter d. Jun 8, 1859
Hunter, Alberta d. Oct 17, 1984
Hunter, Evan b. Oct 15, 1926
Hunter, Glenn d. Dec 30, 1945
Hunter, Tab b. Jul 11, 1931
Huntington, Daniel b. Oct 14, 1816
Hurok, Sol d. Mar 5, 1974
Hurst, Fannie d. Feb 23, 1968
Hutton, Barbara b. Nov 14, 1912
Hutton, Edward F b. 1877
Huxtable, Ada Louise b. 1921
Ian, Janis b. May 7, 1950
Igoe, "Hype" (Herbert A) d. Feb 11, 1954
Ingersoll, Robert Green d. Jul 21, 1899
Inman, Henry d. Jan 17, 1846
Irving, Clifford Michael b. Nov 5, 1930
Irving, Jules b. Apr 13, 1925
Irving, Washington b. Apr 3, 1783
Irwin, May d. Oct 22, 1938
Irwin, Will d. Feb 24, 1948
Isham, Samuel b. May 12, 1855
Istomin, Eugene George b. Nov 26, 1925
Ives, Charles Edward d. May 11, 1954
Ives, James Merritt b. Mar 5, 1824
Jackson, Charles Reginald d. Sep 21, 1968
Jackson, William Henry d. Jun 30, 1942
Jacobs, Michael S b. Mar 10, 1880
Jacobs, Michael S d. Jan 25, 1953
Jacoby, Oswald b. Dec 8, 1902

Jaffe, Rona b. Jun 12, 1932
Jaffe, Sam b. Mar 8, 1893
James, Henry b. Apr 15, 1843
James, William b. Jan 11, 1842
Janeway, Eliot b. Jan 1, 1913
Janis, Conrad b. Feb 11, 1928
Janney, Russell Dixon d. Jul 14, 1963
Janssen, Herbert d. Jun 3, 1965
Janssen, Werner b. Jun 1, 1899
Jason, Rick b. May 21, 1926
Jastrow, Robert b. Sep 7, 1925
Javits, Jacob Koppel b. May 18, 1904
Jay, John b. Dec 12, 1745
Jenkins, Allen b. Apr 9, 1900
Jenkins, Carol Elizabeth Heiss
  b. Jan 20, 1940
Jergens, Adele b. 1922
Jessel, George Albert b. Apr 3, 1898
Jessup, Philip Caryl b. Jan 5, 1897
Johnson, Charlie (Charles Wright)
  d. Dec 13, 1959
Johnson, Crockett b. Oct 20, 1906
Johnson, Eastman d. Apr 5, 1906
Johnson, Hall d. Apr 30, 1970
Johnson, Howard Deering d. Jun 20, 1972
Johnson, James Price d. Nov 17, 1955
Johnson, Osa Helen Leighty d. Jan 7, 1953
Jones, Jo(nathan) d. Sep 3, 1985
Jong, Erica b. Mar 26, 1942
Jonsson, John Erik b. Sep 6, 1901
Joplin, Scott d. Apr 4, 1917
Jordan, Elizabeth Garver d. Feb 24, 1947
Jordan, Richard b. Jul 19, 1938
Jorgensen, Christine b. May 30, 1926
Joseph, Richard b. Apr 24, 1910
Joyce, Peggy Hopkins d. Jun 12, 1957
Juch, Emma d. Mar 6, 1939
Juilliard, Augustus D d. Apr 25, 1919
Jumel, Eliza d. Jul 16, 1865
Kaempffert, Waldemar (Bernhard)
  b. Sep 23, 1877
Kaempffert, Waldemar (Bernhard)
  d. Nov 27, 1956
Kahn, Ben d. Feb 5, 1976
Kahn, Louis I d. Mar 17, 1974
Kahn, Otto Hermann d. Mar 29, 1934
Kalb, Bernard b. Feb 5, 1932
Kalb, Marvin Leonard b. Jun 9, 1930
Kalish, Max d. Mar 18, 1945
Kalmar, Bert b. Feb 16, 1884
Kamali, Norma b. Jun 27, 1945
Kaminska, Ida d. May 21, 1980
Kampelman, Max M b. Nov 7, 1920
Kane, Helen b. Aug 4, 1908
Kane, Henry b. 1918
Kane, Joseph Nathan b. Jan 23, 1899
Kannon, Jackie d. Feb 1, 1974
Kantrowitz, Adrian b. Oct 4, 1918
Kapell, William b. Sep 20, 1922
Kaplan, Mordecai d. Nov 8, 1983
Kaplow, Herbert E b. Feb 2, 1927

Kardiner, Abram b. Aug 17, 1891
Karfiol, Bernard d. Aug 16, 1952
Karle, Jerome b. Jun 18, 1918
Karp, Lila b. Jun 7, 1933
Karpin, Fred Leon b. Mar 17, 1913
Kashdan, Isaac b. Nov 19, 1905
Kasper, Herbert b. Dec 12, 1926
Kauffer, Edward McKnight
    d. Oct 22, 1954
Kauffmann, Stanley Jules b. Apr 24, 1916
Kaufman, Andy b. Jan 17, 1949
Kaufman, Boris d. Jun 24, 1980
Kaufman, George S(imon) d. Jun 2, 1961
Kaufman, Irving R b. Jun 24, 1910
Kaufman, Joseph William b. Mar 27, 1899
Kaufman, Murray b. Feb 14, 1922
Kaufman, Sue d. Jun 25, 1977
Kaye, Danny b. Jan 18, 1913
Kaye, Nora b. 1920
Kaye, Stubby b. Nov 11, 1918
Kazan, Lainie b. May 16, 1940
Kean, Thomas Howard b. Apr 21, 1935
Keating, Kenneth B d. May 5, 1975
Keene, Thomas Wallace b. Oct 26, 1840
Keith, Ian d. Mar 26, 1960
Keith, Minor Cooper b. Jan 19, 1848
Keller, Arthur C b. Aug 18, 1901
Kelley, Edgar Stillman d. Nov 12, 1944
Kelly, "Shipwreck" (Alvin A)
    d. Oct 11, 1952
Kelly, Paul b. Aug 9, 1899
Kelly, Stephen Eugene d. Apr 6, 1978
Kennedy, George b. Feb 18, 1925
Kennedy, Joan Bennett b. Sep 5, 1936
Kennedy, Tom b. 1884
Kensett, John Frederick d. Dec 14, 1872
Kent, James d. Dec 12, 1847
Kerensky, Alexander Fedorovitch
    d. Jun 11, 1970
Kern, Jerome David b. Jan 17, 1885
Kern, Jerome David d. Nov 11, 1945
Kerr, John b. Nov 15, 1931
Kerr, Orpheus C b. Dec 13, 1836
Kertesz, Andre d. Sep 27, 1985
Kesselring, Joseph b. Jun 21, 1902
Ketchel, Stanley d. Oct 15, 1910
Kheel, Theodore Woodrow b. May 9, 1914
Kiam, Omar d. Mar 28, 1954
Kibbee, Robert Joseph b. Aug 19, 1920
Kibbee, Robert Joseph d. Jun 16, 1982
Kieran, John Francis b. Aug 2, 1892
Kilgallen, Dorothy d. Nov 8, 1965
Kilgore, Al d. Aug 15, 1983
King, Alan b. Dec 26, 1927
King, Alexander d. Nov 16, 1965
King, Charles b. Oct 31, 1894
King, Dennis d. May 21, 1971
King, Thomas Starr b. Dec 17, 1824
Kingsbury-Smith, Joseph b. Feb 20, 1908
Kingsley, Sidney b. Oct 18, 1906
Kirby, Jack b. Aug 28, 1917

Kirby, Rollin d. May 8, 1952
Kirk, Alan Goodrich d. Oct 15, 1963
Kirkland, Caroline Matilda Stansbury
    b. Jan 11, 1801
Kirkland, Caroline Matilda Stansbury
    d. Apr 6, 1864
Klein, Anne d. Mar 19, 1974
Klein, Calvin b. Nov 19, 1942
Klein, Robert b. Feb 8, 1942
Kline, Franz Joseph d. May 13, 1962
Kline, Nathan Schellenberg
    d. Feb 11, 1983
Kline, Otis Adelbert d. Oct 24, 1946
Klopfer, Donald Simon b. Jan 23, 1902
Klopfer, Donald Simon d. May 30, 1986
Knerr, H(arold) H d. Jul 8, 1949
Knopf, Alfred Abraham b. Sep 12, 1892
Kobbe, Gustav b. Mar 4, 1857
Kober, Arthur d. Jun 12, 1975
Koch, Ed(ward Irwin) b. Dec 12, 1924
Koch, John d. Apr 19, 1978
Kohler, Kaufmann d. Jan 28, 1926
Kollmar, Richard d. Jan 7, 1971
Komroff, Manuel b. Sep 7, 1890
Koo, V(i) K(yuin) Wellington
    d. Nov 14, 1985
Kopit, Arthur L b. May 10, 1937
Koren, Edward Benjamin b. Dec 13, 1935
Kotzky, Alex Sylvester b. Sep 11, 1923
Kramer, Stanley E b. Sep 29, 1913
Krantz, Judith b. Jan 9, 1928
Krasna, Norman b. Nov 7, 1909
Krasner, Lee d. Jun 19, 1984
Kredel, Fritz d. Jun 10, 1973
Kreisler, Fritz d. Jan 29, 1962
Krementz, Jill b. Feb 19, 1940
Kress, Samuel Henry d. Sep 22, 1955
Kreymborg, Alfred b. Dec 10, 1883
Kristol, Irving b. Jan 22, 1920
Kroll, Leon b. Dec 6, 1884
Kronold, Selma d. Oct 9, 1920
Kubrick, Stanley b. Jul 26, 1928
Kuhn, Walt b. Oct 27, 1880
Kunstler, William Moses b. Jul 7, 1919
Kurnitz, Harry b. Jan 5, 1909
Kurt, Melanie d. Mar 11, 1941
Kurzweil, Ray(mond) b. Feb 12, 1948
L'Engle, Madeleine b. Nov 28, 1918
La Bara, Fidel b. Sep 29, 1905
La Motta, Jake (Jacob) b. Jul 10, 1921
Lachaise, Gaston d. Oct 18, 1935
Ladnier, Tommy d. Jun 4, 1939
LaFarge, Christopher b. Dec 10, 1897
LaFarge, John b. Mar 31, 1835
LaFarge, Oliver b. Dec 19, 1901
LaGuardia, Fiorello Henry
    b. Dec 11, 1882
LaGuardia, Fiorello Henry d. Sep 20, 1947
Lahr, Bert b. Aug 13, 1895
Lahr, Bert d. Dec 4, 1967
Laidler, Harry Wellington d. Jul 14, 1970

Lampert, Zohra b. May 13, 1936
Lancaster, Burt(on Stephen)
  b. Nov 2, 1913
Landau, Ely A b. Jan 20, 1920
Landau, Martin b. Jun 30, 1933
Landers, Harry b. 1921
Lane, Burton b. Feb 2, 1912
Lane, Mark b. Feb 24, 1927
Lane, Stewart F b. May 3, 1951
Lang, Daniel b. May 30, 1915
Lang, Daniel d. Nov 17, 1981
Lang, Eddie d. Mar 26, 1933
Langer, Lawrence d. Dec 26, 1962
Langer, Suzanne K b. Dec 20, 1895
Langner, Nola b. Sep 24, 1930
Lanza, Anthony Joseph b. Mar 8, 1884
Lanza, Anthony Joseph d. Mar 23, 1964
LaRosa, Julius b. Jan 2, 1930
LaRue, Jack b. May 3, 1902
Lasker, Albert Davis d. May 30, 1952
Lasker, Edward d. Mar 23, 1981
Lasker, Emanuel d. Jan 11, 1941
Lasky, Jesse Louis, Jr. b. Sep 19, 1910
Lasser, Jacob Kay d. May 11, 1954
Lauder, Estee b. Jul 1, 1908
Lauder, Joseph H b. 1910
Lauder, Joseph H d. Jan 15, 1983
Lauren, Ralph b. Oct 14, 1939
Laurents, Arthur b. Jul 14, 1918
Laurie, Joe, Jr. b. 1892
Laurie, Joe, Jr. d. Apr 29, 1954
Lawrence, Gertrude d. Sep 6, 1952
Lawrence, Jack b. Apr 7, 1912
Lawrence, Josephine d. Feb 22, 1978
Lawrence, Robert b. Mar 18, 1912
Lawrence, Steve b. Jul 8, 1935
Lawrence, William Beach b. Oct 23, 1800
Lawrence, William Beach d. Mar 26, 1881
Lawrenson, Helen Brown d. Apr 5, 1982
Lawson, John Howard b. Sep 25, 1895
Lawson, Robert b. Oct 4, 1892
Lazarus, Emma b. Jul 22, 1849
Lazarus, Emma d. Nov 19, 1887
Lea, Fanny Heaslip d. Jan 13, 1955
Lear, Evelyn b. Jan 18, 1931
Ledbetter, Huddie d. Dec 6, 1949
Lederer, William Julius b. Mar 31, 1912
Lee, Canada b. May 3, 1907
Lee, Canada d. May 9, 1952
Lee, Gary Earl b. Feb 4, 1943
Lee, Stan b. Dec 28, 1922
Lee, Will d. Dec 7, 1982
Leech, Margaret Kernochan
  d. Feb 24, 1974
Lehman, Adele Lewisohn b. May 17, 1882
Lehman, Herbert Henry b. Mar 28, 1878
Lehman, Herbert Henry d. Dec 5, 1963
Lehrer, Tom (Thomas Andrew)
  b. Apr 9, 1928
Leibman, Ron b. Oct 11, 1938
Leibowitz, Samuel Simon d. Jan 11, 1978

Leigh, Carolyn d. Nov 19, 1983
Lembeck, Harvey b. Apr 15, 1923
Lemoyne, W(illiam) J d. Nov 6, 1905
Lengyel, Emil d. Feb 12, 1985
Lennon, John Winston d. Dec 8, 1980
Lenya, Lotte d. Nov 27, 1981
Leonard, Benny b. Apr 7, 1896
Leonard, Benny d. Apr 18, 1947
Leonard, Bill (William Augustus, II)
  b. Apr 9, 1916
Leonard, Eddie d. Jul 29, 1941
Leonard, Jack E d. May 9, 1973
Leonard, Sheldon b. Feb 22, 1907
Lerman, Leo b. May 23, 1914
Lerner, Alan Jay b. Aug 31, 1918
Lerner, Alan Jay d. Jun 14, 1986
Lescaze, William b. Mar 27, 1896
Lescaze, William d. Feb 9, 1969
Leslie, Frank, pseud. d. Jan 10, 1880
Levene, Sam b. Aug 28, 1907
Levene, Sam d. Dec 29, 1980
Levenson, Sam(uel) b. Dec 28, 1911
Leventhal, Albert Rice b. Oct 30, 1907
Leventhal, Albert Rice d. Jan 4, 1976
Levi, Julian Edwin b. Jun 20, 1900
Levi, Julian Edwin d. Feb 28, 1982
Levitt, Arthur, Jr. d. May 6, 1980
Levy, Florence b. Aug 13, 1870
Levy, Florence d. Nov 15, 1947
Levy, Julien b. Jan 22, 1906
Levy, Uriah Phillips d. Mar 22, 1862
Lewis, Anthony b. Mar 27, 1927
Lewis, Francis d. Dec 30, 1802
Lewis, Joe E b. Jan 12, 1902
Lewis, Joe E d. Jun 4, 1971
Lewis, Oscar b. Dec 25, 1914
Lewis, Oscar d. Dec 16, 1970
Lewis, Robert Q b. Apr 5, 1921
Lewis, Shari b. Jan 17, 1934
Lewis, Ted d. Aug 25, 1971
Lewisohn, Adolph d. Aug 17, 1938
Lewyt, Alexander Milton b. Dec 31, 1903
Ley, Willy d. Jun 24, 1969
Lhevinne, Josef d. Dec 2, 1944
Lichtenstein, Roy b. Oct 27, 1923
Liddy, G(eorge) Gordon b. Nov 30, 1930
Lidz, Theodore b. Apr 1, 1910
Lieber, Franz d. Oct 2, 1872
Liebes, Dorothy Katherine Wright
  d. Sep 20, 1972
Liebling, Abbot Joseph b. Oct 18, 1904
Liebling, Abbot Joseph d. Dec 28, 1963
Liebling, Estelle b. Apr 21, 1884
Liebling, Estelle d. Sep 25, 1970
Liebman, Max d. Jul 21, 1981
Liebmann, Philip b. Feb 19, 1915
Light, Enoch Henry d. Jul 31, 1978
Lightner, Theodore b. Nov 22, 1981
Lilienthal, David Eli d. Jan 14, 1981
Linder, Harold Francis d. Jun 22, 1981
Lindner, Richard d. Apr 16, 1978

Marcantonio, Vito Anthony
   b. Dec 10, 1902
Marcantonio, Vito Anthony
   d. Aug 9, 1954
Marcosson, Isaac Frederick
   d. Mar 14, 1961
Margolin, Janet b. Jul 25, 1943
Marinaro, Ed b. Mar 3, 1950
Mario, Queena d. May 28, 1951
Markel, Lester b. Jan 9, 1894
Markel, Lester d. Oct 23, 1977
Marks, Charles b. Sep 6, 1882
Marks, Johnny (John David)
   d. Sep 3, 1985
Marley, John b. Oct 17, 1916
Marlowe, Hugh d. May 2, 1982
Marlowe, Julia d. Nov 12, 1950
Marlowe, Sylvia b. Sep 26, 1908
Marlowe, Sylvia d. Dec 10, 1981
Marshall, Frank James b. Aug 10, 1877
Marshall, Garry Kent b. Nov 13, 1934
Marshall, Penny b. Oct 15, 1945
Martin, Jared b. Dec 21, 1943
Martin, John b. Dec 3, 1931
Martin, Riccardo d. Aug 11, 1952
Martinelli, Giovanni d. Feb 2, 1969
Martinson, Joseph Bertram b. Jul 24, 1911
Marvin, Lee b. Feb 19, 1924
Marx, "Chico" (Leonard) b. Mar 22, 1891
Marx, "Groucho" (Julius) b. Oct 2, 1890
Marx, "Gummo" (Milton) b. 1894
Marx, "Harpo" (Arthur) b. Nov 23, 1893
Marx, "Zeppo" (Herbert) b. Feb 25, 1901
Masterson, "Bat" (William Barclay)
   d. Oct 25, 1921
Masur, Harold Q b. Jan 29, 1909
Matthau, Walter b. Nov 1, 1920
Maurel, Victor d. Oct 22, 1923
Maurer, Alfred Henry b. 1868
Maxwell, Elsa d. Nov 1, 1963
Maxwell, Vera Huppe b. Apr 22, 1903
Maybeck, Bernard Ralph b. Feb 7, 1862
Mayer, Albert b. Dec 29, 1897
Mayer, Albert d. Oct 14, 1981
Mayer, Arthur Loeb d. Apr 14, 1981
Mayer, Edward Newton, Jr.
   d. Dec 1, 1975
Mayer, Gene (Eugene) b. Apr 11, 1956
Mayer, Martin Prager b. Jan 14, 1928
Mayes, Herbert Raymond b. Aug 11, 1900
McAdie, Alexander George b. Aug 4, 1863
McAvoy, May b. Sep 18, 1901
McCann, Elizabeth (Liz) b. 1932
McCardell, Claire d. Mar 22, 1958
McCarten, John d. Sep 26, 1974
McCarthy, Clem d. Jun 4, 1962
McCarthy, J(oseph) P(riestley)
   b. Mar 22, 1934
McCartney, Linda b. Sep 24, 1942
McCloskey, John d. Oct 10, 1885
McClure, Samuel Sidney d. Mar 21, 1949

McCord, David Thompson Watson
   b. Nov 15, 1897
McCormack, Patty b. Aug 21, 1945
McCormick, Anne (Elizabeth) O'Hare
   d. May 29, 1954
McCormick, Myron d. Jul 30, 1962
McCormick, Robert K d. Sep 4, 1985
McCracken, Joan d. Nov 1, 1961
McDougall, Alexander d. Jun 9, 1786
McFadden, Mary Josephine b. Oct 1, 1938
McGee, Frank d. Apr 17, 1975
McGill, William James b. Feb 27, 1922
McGinley, Phyllis d. Feb 22, 1978
McGinniss, Joe b. Dec 9, 1942
McGiver, John b. Nov 5, 1913
McGoohan, Patrick b. Mar 19, 1928
McGuire, Al b. Sep 7, 1928
McIntyre, James Francis b. Jun 25, 1886
McKean, Michael b. Oct 17, 1947
McKeen, John Elmer b. Jun 4, 1903
McKenzie, "Red" (William) d. Feb 7, 1948
McLane, James Woods b. Aug 19, 1839
McLean, John Milton b. Oct 24, 1909
McManus, Sean b. Feb 16, 1955
McMaster, John Bach b. Jun 29, 1852
McNamee, Graham d. May 9, 1942
McNutt, Paul Vories d. Mar 24, 1955
McPhatter, Clyde d. Jun 13, 1972
McRae, Carmen b. Apr 8, 1922
McWilliams, Carey d. Jun 27, 1980
Mead, Margaret d. Nov 15, 1978
Meany, George b. Aug 16, 1894
Meara, Anne b. Sep 20, 1924
Medford, Kay b. Sep 14, 1920
Medford, Kay d. Apr 10, 1980
Medina, Harold Raymond b. Feb 16, 1888
Meisner, Sanford b. Aug 31, 1905
Melanie b. Feb 3, 1948
Melnick, Daniel b. Apr 21, 1932
Melton, James d. Apr 21, 1961
Melville, Herman b. Aug 1, 1819
Melville, Herman d. Sep 28, 1891
Mendl, Lady Elsie de Wolfe
   b. Dec 20, 1865
Menken, Helen b. Dec 12, 1901
Menken, Helen d. Mar 27, 1966
Mennin, Peter d. Jun 17, 1983
Menuhin, Yehudi b. Apr 22, 1916
Meredith, Scott b. Nov 24, 1923
Merman, Ethel d. Feb 15, 1984
Merriam, Clinton Hart b. Feb 5, 1855
Merrill, Dina b. Dec 9, 1925
Merrill, James b. Mar 3, 1926
Merrill, Robert b. Jun 4, 1919
Merwin, W(illiam) S(tanley)
   b. Sep 30, 1927
Meyer, Nicholas b. Dec 24, 1945
Meyers, Ari(adne) b. 1970
Michener, James A(lbert) b. Feb 3, 1907
Midgeley, Thomas d. Nov 2, 1944
Mielziner, Jo d. Mar 15, 1976

Nichols, Ruth Rowland b. Feb 23, 1901
Nichols, Ruth Rowland d. Sep 25, 1960
Nielsen, Alice d. Mar 8, 1943
Nolte, Henry R, Jr. b. Mar 3, 1924
Norell, Norman d. Oct 25, 1972
Norris, Christopher b. Oct 7, 1953
Norton, Jack b. 1889
Nugent, Edward b. Feb 7, 1904
Nugent, Elliott d. Aug 9, 1980
Nunn, Harold F b. Feb 25, 1915
Nyad, Diana b. Aug 22, 1949
O'Brien, Edmond b. Sep 10, 1915
O'Connell, Arthur b. Mar 29, 1908
O'Connell, Hugh b. Aug 4, 1898
O'Connor, Carroll b. Aug 2, 1924
O'Connor, Una d. Feb 4, 1959
O'Dwyer, William d. Nov 24, 1964
O'Malley, Walter Francis b. Oct 9, 1903
O'Neil, James F(rancis) d. Jul 28, 1981
O'Neill, Eugene Gladstone b. Oct 16, 1888
O'Sheel, Shaemas b. Sep 19, 1886
O'Sullivan, Timothy H b. 1840
Oakland, Simon b. Aug 28, 1922
Oates, John b. Apr 7, 1949
Ohrbach, Nathan d. Nov 19, 1972
Okun, Milton b. Dec 23, 1923
Olderman, Murray b. Mar 27, 1922
Olds, Irving S d. Mar 4, 1963
Oliver, Edith b. Aug 11, 1913
Oliver, James A(rthur) d. Dec 2, 1981
Onassis, Christina b. Dec 11, 1950
Opatashu, David b. Jan 30, 1918
Oppenheim, James d. Aug 4, 1932
Oppenheimer, Frank F b. Aug 14, 1912
Oppenheimer, J(ulius) Robert
  b. Apr 22, 1904
Orbach Jerry b. Oct 20, 1935
Orkin, Ruth d. Jan 16, 1985
Orlando, Tony b. Apr 3, 1944
Ornitz, Samuel b. Nov 15, 1890
Ortega, Santos b. 1899
Osgood, Charles b. Jan 8, 1933
Osgood, Frances Sargent Locke
  d. May 12, 1850
Oursler, (Charles) Fulton d. May 24, 1952
Paddleford, Clementine Haskin
  d. Nov 13, 1967
Paderewski, Ignace Jan d. Jun 29, 1941
Padover, Saul Kussiel d. Feb 22, 1981
Page, "Hot Lips" (Oran Thaddeus)
  d. Nov 5, 1954
Paine, Thomas d. Jun 8, 1809
Pakula, Alan Jay b. Apr 7, 1928
Paley, Barbara Cushing d. Jul 6, 1978
Palmer, Jim (James Alvin) b. Oct 15, 1945
Paltrow, Bruce b. Nov 26, 1943
Papi, Genarro d. Nov 29, 1941
Pappas, Ike b. Apr 16, 1933
Parker, Charlie (Charles Christopher)
  d. Mar 12, 1955
Parker, Dorothy Rothschild d. Jun 7, 1967

Parnis, Mollie b. Mar 18, 1905
Parsons, Betty Pierson b. Jan 31, 1900
Parton, Sara Payson Willis d. Oct 10, 1872
Pascal, Gabriel d. Jul 6, 1954
Pastor, Tony (Antonio) b. May 28, 1837
Pate, Maurice d. Jan 19, 1965
Paterson, Basil Alexander b. Apr 27, 1926
Patrick, Lee b. Nov 22, 1906
Patterson, Alicia d. Jul 2, 1963
Patterson, Joseph Medill d. May 26, 1946
Payne, John Howard b. Jun 9, 1791
Payson, Joan Whitney b. Feb 5, 1903
Payson, Joan Whitney d. Oct 4, 1975
Pearce, Alice b. Oct 16, 1913
Pearl, Jack b. Oct 29, 1895
Pearl, Jack d. Dec 25, 1982
Pearlroth, Norbert d. Apr 14, 1983
Pease, James d. Apr 26, 1967
Pecora, Ferdinand d. Dec 7, 1971
Peerce, Jan b. Jun 3, 1904
Peerce, Jan d. Dec 15, 1984
Pell, Claiborne b. Nov 22, 1918
Pelletier, Wilfred d. Apr 9, 1982
Pemberton, Brock d. Mar 11, 1950
Penney, J(ames) C(ash) d. Feb 12, 1971
Pennington, Ann d. Nov 4, 1971
Pennock, Herb(ert Jefferis) d. Jan 30, 1948
Perahia, Murray b. Apr 19, 1947
Perelman, S(idney) J(oseph)
  d. Oct 17, 1979
Perkins, Anthony b. Apr 14, 1932
Perkins, Frances d. May 14, 1965
Perkins, Maxwell Evarts b. Sep 20, 1884
Perry, Antoinette d. Jun 28, 1946
Perry, Eleanor Bayer d. Mar 14, 1981
Perry, Frank b. 1930
Perry, Matthew Calbraith, Commodore
  d. Mar 4, 1858
Persinger, Louis d. Dec 31, 1966
Pescow, Donna b. Mar 24, 1954
Peters, Brandon d. Feb 27, 1956
Peters, Brock b. Jul 27, 1927
Peters, Roberta b. May 4, 1930
Peterson, Virgilia b. May 16, 1904
Peterson, Virgilia d. Dec 24, 1966
Petrocelli, Anthony d. Mar 2, 1974
Phelan, John Joseph b. May 17, 1931
Philips, David Graham d. Jan 24, 1911
Phillips, Kevin Price b. Nov 30, 1940
Phyfe, Duncan d. Aug 16, 1854
Piastro, Mishel d. Apr 10, 1970
Piccolo, Brian d. Jun 16, 1970
Picon, Molly b. Feb 28, 1898
Pierce, Edward Allen d. Dec 16, 1974
Pinchot, Gifford d. Oct 4, 1946
Pious, Minerva d. 1979
Platt, Harry (Henry Barstow) b.
Pleshette, Suzanne b. Jan 31, 1937
Plimpton, Francis Taylor Pearson
  b. Dec 7, 1900
Plimpton, George b. Mar 18, 1927

Rinkoff, Barbara Jean b. Jan 25, 1923
Ripley, Elmer Horton d. Apr 29, 1982
Ripley, George d. Jul 4, 1880
Ripley, Robert Leroy d. May 27, 1949
Ripley, William Zebina d. Aug 16, 1941
Ritt, Martin b. Mar 2, 1920
Ritter, Thelma b. Feb 14, 1905
Ritter, Thelma d. Feb 5, 1969
Rivera, Geraldo b. Jul 4, 1943
Rivers, Joan b. Jun 8, 1933
Rivers, Johnny b. Nov 7, 1942
Rivers, Larry b. Aug 17, 1923
Rivers, Thomas Milton d. May 12, 1962
Rizzuto, Phil(lip Francis) b. Sep 25, 1918
Robbins, Harold b. May 21, 1916
Robbins, Jerome b. Oct 11, 1918
Roberts, Tony (David Anthony)
   b. Oct 22, 1939
Robertson, Charles Sammis b. 1904
Robinson, Bill d. Nov 25, 1949
Robinson, Claude Everett d. Aug 7, 1961
Robinson, Edwin Arlington d. Apr 6, 1935
Robinson, Francis Arthur d. 1980
Robinson, Henry Morton d. Jan 13, 1961
Robinson, James Harvey d. Feb 16, 1936
Robinson, Jay b. Apr 14, 1930
Robitscher, Jonas Bondi, Jr.
   b. Oct 28, 1920
Roche, John P b. May 7, 1923
Rockefeller, Abby Aldrich d. Apr 15, 1948
Rockefeller, David b. Jun 12, 1915
Rockefeller, John D(avison), III
   b. Mar 21, 1906
Rockefeller, John D(avison), IV
   b. Jun 18, 1937
Rockefeller, Laurance Spelman
   b. May 26, 1910
Rockefeller, Mary French b. May 1, 1910
Rockefeller, Nelson A(ldrich)
   d. Jan 26, 1979
Rockefeller, Winthrop b. May 1, 1912
Rockwell, Norman b. Feb 3, 1894
Rodale, Jerome Irving b. Aug 16, 1898
Rodale, Jerome Irving d. Jun 7, 1971
Rodgers, Jimmie C d. May 26, 1933
Rodgers, Mary b. Jan 11, 1931
Rodgers, Nile b. Sep 19, 1952
Rodgers, Richard b. Jul 28, 1902
Rodgers, Richard d. Dec 30, 1979
Rodman, Selden b. Feb 19, 1909
Roebling, John Augustus d. Jul 22, 1869
Rogers, Will, Jr. b. Oct 12, 1912
Rollin, Betty b. Jan 3, 1936
Rollini, Adrian b. Jun 28, 1904
Rollins, "Sonny" (Theodore Walter)
   b. Sep 7, 1930
Romano, Umberto d. Sep 27, 1982
Romberg, Sigmund d. Nov 9, 1951
Romero, Cesar b. Feb 15, 1907
Romero, George A b. 1940
Romney, Seymour Leonard b. Jun 8, 1917

Rooney, Pat b. Jul 4, 1880
Rooney, Pat d. Sep 9, 1962
Roosevelt, Alice Lee d. Feb 14, 1884
Roosevelt, Eleanor b. Oct 11, 1884
Roosevelt, Eleanor d. Nov 7, 1962
Roosevelt, Elliot b. Sep 23, 1910
Roosevelt, James b. Dec 23, 1907
Roosevelt, John Aspinal d. Apr 27, 1981
Roosevelt, Theodore b. Oct 27, 1858
Root, Elihu d. Feb 7, 1937
Rose, Billy b. Sep 6, 1899
Rose-Marie b. Aug 15,
Rosenberg, Anna Marie d. May 9, 1983
Rosenberg, Ethel Greenglass
   b. Sep 28, 1915
Rosenberg, Julius b. May 12, 1918
Rosenberg, Sharon b. Dec 14, 1942
Rosenbloom, Maxie b. Sep 6, 1906
Rosenfeld, Henry J b. May 17, 1911
Rosenfeld, Henry J d. Feb 5, 1986
Rosenfeld, Paul b. May 4, 1890
Rosenfeld, Paul d. Jul 21, 1946
Rosenstein, Nettie d. Mar 13, 1980
Rosenstock, Joseph d. Oct 17, 1985
Rosenthal, Benjamin Stanley
   b. Jun 8, 1923
Rosenthal, Ida Cohen d. Mar 28, 1973
Rosenthal, Jean b. Mar 16, 1912
Rosenthal, Jean d. May 1, 1969
Rosenthal, Moriz d. Sep 3, 1946
Roskolenko, Harry b. Sep 21, 1907
Roskolenko, Harry d. Jul 17, 1980
Ross, Barney b. Dec 23, 1907
Ross, David b. 1891
Ross, David d. Nov 12, 1975
Ross, Ishbel d. Sep 21, 1975
Ross, Ruth N b.
Rossant, James Stephan b. Aug 17, 1928
Rossen, Robert b. Mar 16, 1908
Rossen, Robert d. Feb 18, 1966
Rossi, Peter Henry b. Dec 27, 1921
Rossner, Judith b. Mar 1, 1935
Rostow, Walt Whitman b. Oct 7, 1916
Roszak, Theodore d. Sep 3, 1981
Roth, Lillian d. May 12, 1980
Rothenberg, Jerome b. Dec 11, 1931
Rothier, Leon d. Dec 6, 1951
Rothko, Mark d. Feb 25, 1970
Rothstein, Arnold b. 1882
Rothstein, Arthur b. Jul 17, 1915
Rounseville, Robert Field d. Aug 6, 1974
Rous, Peyton d. Feb 16, 1970
Roxon, Lillian d. Aug 9, 1973
Royle, Selena b. 1904
Rubin, Benny b. 1899
Rubinstein, Helena d. Apr 1, 1965
Ruby, Harry b. Jan 27, 1895
Rudkin, Margaret Fogarty b. Sep 14, 1897
Rukeyser, Louis Richard b. Jan 30, 1933
Rukeyser, Merryle Stanley, Jr.
   b. Apr 15, 1931

Rukeyser, Muriel b. Dec 15, 1913
Rukeyser, Muriel d. Feb 12, 1980
Rukeyser, William Simon b. Jun 8, 1939
Runyon, Damon (Alfred Damon)
d. Dec 10, 1946
Rush, Richard b. 1931
Rushing, Jimmy d. Jun 8, 1972
Rutgers, Henry b. Oct 7, 1745
Rutgers, Henry d. Feb 17, 1830
Ruth, "Babe" (George Herman)
d. Aug 16, 1948
Ryan, Cornelius John d. Nov 23, 1974
Ryan, Robert (Bushnell) d. Jul 11, 1973
Ryan, Sylvester James b. Sep 10, 1896
Ryan, Sylvester James d. Apr 10, 1981
Ryan, Thomas Fortune d. Nov 23, 1928
Ryder, Alfred b. Jan 5, 1919
Ryskind, Morrie b. Oct 20, 1895
Saarinen, Aline Bernstein b. Mar 25, 1914
Saarinen, Aline Bernstein d. Jul 13, 1972
Sachs, Samuel, II b. Nov 30, 1935
Sackler, Howard Oliver b. Dec 19, 1927
Safire, William L b. Dec 17, 1929
Sagan, Carl Edward b. Nov 9, 1934
Sage, Margaret Olivia d. Nov 4, 1918
Sage, Russell d. Nov 4, 1906
Sager, Carole Bayer b. Mar 8, 1947
Saint John, Howard d. Mar 13, 1974
Saks, Gene b. Nov 8, 1921
Salant, Richard S b. Apr 14, 1914
Salinger, J(erome) D(avid) b. Jan 19, 1919
Salk, Jonas Edward b. Oct 28, 1914
Salk, Lee b. Dec 27, 1926
Salmi, Albert b. 1928
Samaroff, Olga d. May 17, 1948
Samstag, Nicholas b. Dec 25, 1903
Samuel, Maurice d. May 4, 1972
Sanborn, Pitts d. Mar 7, 1941
Sanders, Lawrence b. 1920
Sandoz, Mari d. Mar 10, 1966
Sands, Diana Patricia b. Aug 22, 1934
Sands, Diana Patricia d. Sep 21, 1973
Sanford, Isabel Gwendolyn
b. Aug 29, 1933
Sapir, Richard b. Jul 27, 1936
Sarandon, Susan Abigail b. Oct 4, 1946
Sardi, Vincent, Jr. b. Jul 23, 1915
Sardi, Vincent, Sr. d. Nov 19, 1969
Sarnoff, David d. Dec 12, 1971
Sarnoff, Dorothy b. May 25, 1919
Sarnoff, Robert W b. Jul 2, 1918
Saxon, Charles David b. Nov 13, 1920
Schacht, Al(exander) b. Nov 11, 1892
Schaefer, Rudolph Jay d. Sep 2, 1982
Schakne, Robert b. Aug 19, 1926
Schary, Dore d. Jul 7, 1980
Schayes, Dolph b. May 19, 1928
Schecter, Jerrold b. Nov 27, 1932
Scheer, Robert b. Apr 4, 1936
Scheff, Frizi d. Apr 8, 1954
Schell, Orville H b. May 20, 1940

Schelling, Ernest Henry d. Dec 8, 1939
Scherman, Harry d. Nov 12, 1969
Scherman, Thomas K b. Feb 12, 1917
Scherman, Thomas K d. May 14, 1979
Schick, Bela d. Dec 6, 1967
Schick, Jacob d. Jul 3, 1937
Schiff, Dorothy b. Mar 11, 1903
Schildkraut, Joseph d. Jan 21, 1964
Schillinger, Joseph d. Mar 23, 1943
Schipa, Tito d. Dec 16, 1965
Schippers, Thomas d. Dec 16, 1977
Schlesinger, Frank b. May 11, 1871
Schlesinger, James Rodney b. Feb 15, 1929
Schley, Winfield Scott d. Oct 2, 1909
Schoen-Rene, Anna d. Nov 13, 1942
Schoenbach, Sol Israel b. Mar 15, 1915
Schoenbrun, David b. Mar 15, 1915
Schoenfeld, Gerald b. 1924
Schonberg, Harold C b. Nov 29, 1915
Schoonmaker, Frank Musselman
d. Jan 11, 1976
Schorr, Daniel b. Aug 31, 1916
Schulberg, Budd Wilson b. Mar 27, 1914
Schulberg, Stuart d. Jun 28, 1979
Schuller, Gunther b. Nov 22, 1925
Schultze, Carl Edward d. Jan 18, 1939
Schumacher, Joel b. 1942
Schuman, William Howard b. Aug 4, 1910
Schumann, Elisabeth d. Apr 23, 1952
Schumann, Walter b. Oct 8, 1913
Schurz, Carl d. May 14, 1906
Schwab, Charles Michael d. Sep 18, 1939
Schwartz, Delmore d. Jul 11, 1966
Scott, Hazel Dorothy d. Oct 2, 1981
Scott, Norman b. Nov 30, 1928
Scott, Norman d. Sep 22, 1968
Scott, Raymond b. Sep 10, 1909
Scribner, Charles b. Feb 21, 1821
Sebastian, John b. Mar 17, 1944
Secunda, Sholom d. Jun 13, 1974
Sedran, Barney b. Jan 28, 1891
Sedran, Barney d. Jan 14, 1969
Seeger, Alan b. Jun 22, 1888
Seeger, Pete(r) b. May 3, 1919
Seeley, Blossom d. Apr 17, 1974
Segal, George b. Nov 26, 1924
Segal, George b. Feb 13, 1934
Seidl, Anton d. Mar 28, 1898
Selby, Hubert, Jr. b. Jul 23, 1928
Seldes, Gilbert Vivian d. Sep 29, 1970
Seldes, Marian b. Aug 23, 1928
Selznick, Irene b. Apr 2, 1910
Sembrich, Marcella d. Jan 11, 1935
Serkin, Peter A b. Jul 24, 1947
Serpico, Frank (Francisco Vincent)
b. Apr 14, 1936
Seton, Anya Chase b. 1916
Seton, Elizabeth Ann Bayley, Saint
b. Aug 28, 1774
Seymour, Anne Eckert b. Sep 11, 1909
Seymour, Dan b. Jun 28, 1914

Seymour, Dan d. Jul 27, 1982
Shahn, Ben(jamin) d. Mar 14, 1969
Shalit, Gene b. 1932
Shanker, Albert b. Sep 14, 1928
Shapiro, Stanley b. Jul 16, 1925
Shattuck, Roger Whitney b. Aug 20, 1923
Shaw, Albert d. Jun 25, 1947
Shaw, Artie b. May 23, 1910
Shaw, Mary d. May 18, 1929
Shawn, Wallace b. Nov 12, 1943
Shea, William Alfred b. Jun 21, 1907
Shean, Al d. Aug 12, 1949
Sheedy, Ally b. 1963
Sheen, Charlie b. Sep 3, 1965
Sheen, Fulton John, Bishop
   d. Dec 10, 1979
Sheppard, Eugenia Benbow
   d. Nov 11, 1984
Sherman, Richard Morton b. Jun 12, 1928
Sherman, William Tecumseh
   d. Feb 14, 1891
Sherwood, Robert Emmet d. Nov 14, 1955
Shields, Brooke b. May 31, 1965
Shinn, Everett d. May 1, 1953
Shirley, Anne b. Apr 17, 1918
Shor, "Toots" (Bernard) d. Jan 24, 1977
Shotwell, James Thomson d. Jul 15, 1965
Shrady, Henry M b. Oct 24, 1871
Shubert, Jacob J d. Dec 26, 1963
Shubert, Lee d. Dec 25, 1953
Shultz, George Pratt b. Dec 13, 1920
Shumlin, Herman Elliott d. Jun 14, 1979
Shutta, Ethel b. Dec 1, 1896
Sickles, Daniel Edgar b. Oct 20, 1825
Sickles, Daniel Edgar d. May 3, 1914
Sidney, George b. Oct 4, 1916
Sidney, Sylvia b. Aug 8, 1910
Siegel, Larry b. Oct 29, 1925
Siegmeister, Elie b. Jan 15, 1909
Sillman, Leonard d. Jan 23, 1982
Silverberg, Robert b.
Silverman, Fred b. Sep 13, 1937
Silverstein, Alvin b. Dec 30, 1933
Simon, (Marvin) Neil b. Jul 4, 1927
Simon, Abbey b. Jan 8, 1922
Simon, Carly b. Jun 25, 1945
Simon, Richard Leo b. Mar 6, 1899
Simpson, Adele Smithline b. Dec 8, 1903
Sims, "Zoot" (John Haley)
   d. Mar 23, 1985
Sims, James Marion d. Nov 13, 1883
Singer, Burns James Hyman
   b. Apr 29, 1928
Singleton, "Zutty" (Arthur James)
   d. Jul 14, 1975
Singleton, Ken(neth Wayne)
   b. Jun 10, 1947
Skinner, Cornelia Otis d. Jul 9, 1979
Skinner, Otis d. Jan 4, 1942
Skipworth, Alison d. Jul 5, 1952
Skolsky, Sidney b. May 5, 1905

Skulnik, Menasha d. Jun 4, 1970
Sloan, Alfred Pritchard, Jr.
   d. Feb 17, 1966
Sloan, Michael b. Oct 14, 1946
Sloane, Eric b. Feb 27, 1910
Sloane, Eric d. Mar 6, 1985
Sloane, Everett b. Oct 1, 1909
Sloane, John b. Apr 20, 1883
Slotnick, Daniel Leonid b. Nov 12, 1931
Smith, Alfred Emanuel b. Dec 30, 1873
Smith, Alfred Emanuel d. Oct 4, 1944
Smith, Dennis b. Sep 9, 1940
Smith, Gerrit d. Dec 28, 1874
Smith, Joe b. Feb 17, 1884
Smith, Joe d. Dec 2, 1937
Smith, Kent b. Mar 19, 1907
Smith, Pete b. Sep 4, 1892
Smith, Tony d. Dec 26, 1980
Smith, Willie d. Apr 18, 1973
Smothers, Dick (Richard) b. Nov 20, 1938
Smothers, Tommy (Thomas Bolyn, III)
   b. Feb 2, 1937
Snow, Carmel White d. May 7, 1961
Snow, Phoebe Laub b. Jul 17, 1952
Sobell, Morton b. Apr 11, 1917
Sockman, Ralph W d. Aug 29, 1970
Sodero, Cesare d. Dec 16, 1947
Soglow, Otto b. Dec 23, 1900
Soglow, Otto d. Apr 3, 1975
Sommers, Ben b. Dec 1, 1906
Sommers, Ben d. Apr 30, 1985
Sondheim, Stephen Joshua b. Mar 22, 1930
Sonneck, Oscar George Theodore
   d. Oct 30, 1928
Sontag, Susan b. Jan 28, 1933
Soria, Dario d. Mar 28, 1980
Sorvino, Paul b. 1939
Sothern, Edward Hugh d. 1933
Sour, Robert B(andler) b. Oct 31, 1905
Sour, Robert B(andler) d. Mar 6, 1985
Soyer, Isaac d. Jul 8, 1981
Soyer, Moses d. Sep 2, 1974
Spaeth, Sigmund Gottfried
   d. Nov 12, 1965
Spalding, Albert d. May 26, 1953
Speaks, Oley b. Aug 27, 1948
Spector, Phil(lip Harvey) b. Dec 25, 1940
Spellman, Francis Joseph d. Dec 2, 1967
Spewack, Samuel d. Oct 14, 1971
Spigelgass, Leonard b. Nov 26, 1908
Spingarn, Joel Elias b. May 17, 1875
Spingarn, Joel Elias d. Jul 26, 1939
Sprague, Frank Julian d. Oct 25, 1934
Stallone, Sylvester (Michael Sylvester)
   b. Jul 6, 1946
Stander, Lionel b. Jan 11, 1909
Stang, Arnold b. Sep 28, 1925
Stanton, Elizabeth Cady d. Oct 26, 1902
Stanton, Henry Brewster d. Jan 14, 1887
Stapleton, Jean b. Jan 19, 1923
Stark, "Koo" (Kathleen) b. 1957

Stark, Abe b. Sep 28, 1894
Stark, Abe d. Jul 3, 1972
Statler, Ellsworth Milton d. Apr 16, 1928
Steig, William b. Nov 14, 1907
Stein, Aaron Marc b. Nov 15, 1906
Stein, Aaron Marc d. Aug 29, 1985
Stein, Clarence S d. Feb 7, 1975
Stein, Joseph b. May 30, 1912
Steinbeck, John Ernst d. Dec 20, 1968
Steinberg, William (Hans Wilhelm)
   d. May 16, 1978
Steinitz, Wilhelm d. Aug 12, 1900
Steinman, David Barnard b. Jun 11, 1886
Steinman, David Barnard d. Aug 22, 1960
Steinway, Henry Engelhard
   d. Nov 30, 1896
Stella, Joseph d. Nov 5, 1946
Sterling, Jan b. Apr 3, 1923
Stern, Bert b. Oct 3, 1929
Stern, Carl (Leonard) b. Aug 7, 1937
Stern, Leonard Norman b. Mar 28, 1938
Stern, Max d. May 20, 1982
Stern, Richard Gustave b. Feb 25, 1928
Stern, Stewart b. Mar 22, 1922
Stevens, Emily A d. Jan 2, 1928
Stevens, Rise b. Jun 11, 1913
Stevens, Shane b. Oct 8, 1941
Stewart, Alexander Turney
   d. Apr 10, 1876
Stewart, Andrew b. Feb 8, 1938
Stewart, Michael b. Aug 1, 1929
Stewart, Paul b. Mar 13, 1908
Stieglitz, Alfred d. Jul 13, 1946
Stiller, Jerry b. Jun 8, 1926
Stillman, Irwin Maxwell b. Sep 11, 1895
Stimson, Henry Lewis (Harry)
   b. Sep 21, 1867
Stockton, Dick b. Feb 18, 1951
Stoessel, Albert d. May 12, 1943
Stone, Carol b. 1916
Stone, Edward Durell d. Aug 6, 1978
Stone, Louis b. 1910
Stone, Louis d. Mar 16, 1985
Stone, Melville Elijah d. Feb 15, 1929
Stone, Paula b. Jan 20, 1916
Stone, Richard Bernard (Dick)
   b. Sep 22, 1928
Stone, Robert Anthony b. Aug 21, 1937
Stone, Sidney d. Feb 12, 1986
Storch, Larry b. Jan 8, 1923
Strand, Paul b. Oct 16, 1890
Strasberg, Lee d. Feb 17, 1982
Strasberg, Susan Elizabeth b. May 22, 1938
Strassman, Marcia b. Apr 28, 1948
Straus, Jack Isidor b. Jan 13, 1900
Straus, Jack Isidor d. Sep 19, 1985
Straus, Nathan d. Jan 11, 1931
Straus, Oscar d. May 3, 1926
Straus, Roger W(illiams), Jr.
   b. Jan 3, 1917
Strauss, Robert b. Nov 8, 1913

Strauss, Robert d. Feb 20, 1974
Stravinsky, Igor Fedorovich d. Apr 6, 1971
Stravinsky, Vera de Bossett
   d. Sep 17, 1982
Strayhorn, Billy (William) d. May 31, 1967
Streeter, Edward b. Aug 1, 1891
Streeter, Edward d. Mar 31, 1976
Streisand, Barbra Joan b. Apr 24, 1942
Strouse, Charles b. Jun 7, 1928
Strudwick, Shepperd d. Jan 15, 1983
Struss, Karl b. Nov 30, 1886
Struther, Jan, pseud. d. Jul 20, 1953
Stuart, Mel b. Sep 2, 1928
Stulberg, Louis d. Dec 14, 1977
Sturges, Preston d. Aug 6, 1959
Sullivan, Barry b. Aug 12, 1912
Sullivan, Ed(ward Vincent) b. Sep 28, 1902
Sullivan, Ed(ward Vincent) d. Oct 13, 1974
Sullivan, Francis Loftus d. Nov 19, 1956
Sullivan, Susan b. Nov 18, 1944
Sullivan, Walter Seager, Jr. b. Jan 12, 1918
Sulzberger, Arthur Hays b. Sep 12, 1891
Sulzberger, Arthur Hays d. Dec 11, 1968
Sulzberger, Arthur Ochs b. Feb 5, 1926
Sulzberger, C(yrus) L(eon) b. Oct 27, 1912
Susann, Jacqueline d. Sep 21, 1974
Sutton, Horace (Ashley) b. May 17, 1919
Swanson, Gloria May Josephine
   d. Apr 4, 1983
Swayne, Noah d. Jun 8, 1884
Sweet, Blanche d. Sep 6, 1986
Swift, Kay b. Apr 19, 1905
Swinburne, Laurence b. Jul 2, 1924
Swope, Gerard d. Nov 20, 1957
Sylbert, Richard b. Apr 16, 1928
Taft, Robert A(lphonso) d. Jul 31, 1953
Taggard, Genevieve d. Nov 8, 1948
Talbot, Nita b. Aug 8, 1930
Tamiris, Helen b. Apr 24, 1902
Tamiris, Helen d. Aug 25, 1966
Tannenbaum, Frank d. Jun 1, 1969
Tanner, Marion d. Oct 30, 1985
Tarnower, Herman b. Mar 18, 1910
Tashman, Lilyan d. Mar 21, 1934
Tatum, Edward Lawrie d. Nov 5, 1975
Taubman, Howard (Hyman Howard)
   b. Jul 4, 1907
Taylor, (Joseph) Deems b. Dec 22, 1885
Taylor, (Joseph) Deems d. Jul 3, 1966
Taylor, Henry Junior d. Feb 26, 1984
Taylor, Laurette b. Apr 1, 1887
Taylor, Laurette d. Dec 7, 1946
Taylor, Sydney Brenner b. 1904
Teasdale, Sara d. Jan 28, 1933
Tebelak, John Michael d. Apr 2, 1985
Teilhard de Chardin, Pierre
   d. Apr 10, 1955
Terkel, Studs (Louis) b. May 16, 1912
Terry, Paul H d. Oct 25, 1971
Terry, Walter d. Oct 4, 1982
Tesla, Nikola d. Jan 7, 1943

Thant, U d. Nov 25, 1974
Thomas, Dylan Marlais d. Nov 9, 1953
Thomas, Edith Matilda d. Sep 13, 1925
Thomas, Piri b. Sep 30, 1928
Thomas, Richard Earl b. Jun 13, 1951
Thompson, J(ames) Walter d. Oct 16, 1928
Thompson, Oscar d. Jul 2, 1945
Thompson, Randall b. Apr 12, 1899
Thon, William b. Aug 8, 1906
Thorndike, Lynn d. Dec 28, 1965
Thurber, James Grover d. Nov 2, 1961
Tibbett, Lawrence Mervil d. Jul 15, 1960
Tieri, Frank d. Mar 29, 1981
Tiffany, Louis Comfort b. Feb 18, 1848
Tiffany, Louis Comfort d. Jan 17, 1933
Tiny Tim b. Apr 12, 1922
Tobias, Andrew b. Apr 20, 1947
Tobias, Channing Heggie d. Nov 5, 1961
Tobias, George b. 1905
Todman, Bill (William Selden)
    b. Jul 31, 1916
Todman, Bill (William Selden) d. 1979
Toffenetti, Dario Louis d. Jan 16, 1962
Toffler, Alvin b. Oct 4, 1928
Toller, Ernst d. May 22, 1939
Tone, Franchot d. Sep 18, 1968
Torrence, Ernest d. May 15, 1933
Torrence, Ridgley (Frederick Rridgley)
    d. Dec 25, 1950
Toscanini, Arturo d. Jan 16, 1957
Tourel, Jennie d. Nov 23, 1973
Towne, Charles Hanson d. Feb 28, 1949
Townsend, George Alfred d. Apr 15, 1914
Train, Arthur Cheney d. Dec 22, 1945
Traphagen, Ethel Leigh b. Oct 10, 1882
Traphagen, Ethel Leigh d. Apr 29, 1963
Traube, Shepard d. Jul 23, 1983
Treat, Lawrence b. Dec 21, 1903
Trevor, Claire b. Mar 8, 1909
Trilling, Diana Rubin b. Jul 21, 1905
Trilling, Lionel b. Jul 4, 1905
Trilling, Lionel d. Nov 5, 1975
Tripp, Paul b. Feb 20, 1916
Trippe, Juan Terry d. Apr 3, 1981
Trotta, Maurice S b. Aug 15, 1907
Troyanos, Tatiana b. Sep 12, 1938
Trudeau, Edward Livingston
    b. Oct 5, 1848
Trudeau, Garry (Garretson Beckman)
    b. 1948
Trumbull, John d. Nov 10, 1843
Trump, Donald John b. 1946
Tuchman, Barbara Wertheim
    b. Jan 30, 1912
Tucker, Sophie d. Feb 9, 1966
Tunney, "Gene" (James Joseph)
    b. May 25, 1898
Tunney, John Varick b. Jun 26, 1934
Turkus, Burton B d. Nov 22, 1982
Tweed, "Boss" (William Marcy)
    b. Apr 3, 1823

Tweed, "Boss" (William Marcy)
    d. Apr 12, 1878
Tyler, Parker d. Jul 24, 1974
Typhoid Mary d. Nov 11, 1938
Tyson, Cicely b. Dec 19, 1939
Uggams, Leslie b. May 25, 1943
Uhnak, Dorothy b. 1933
Ullman, James Ramsey b. Nov 24, 1907
Ullstein, Hermann d. Nov 23, 1943
Untermeyer, Louis b. Oct 1, 1885
Upson, Ralph Hazlett b. Jun 21, 1888
Urban, Joseph Maria d. Jul 10, 1933
Uris, Harold David b. May 26, 1905
Urrutia Lleo, Manuel d. Jul 5, 1981
Valachi, Joe (Joseph M) b. Sep 22, 1904
Valentino, Francesco b. Jan 6, 1907
Valentino, Rudolph d. Aug 23, 1926
Van Ark, Joan b. Jun 16, 1946
Van Cortlandt, Oloff Stevenszen
    d. Apr 5, 1684
Van Cortlandt, Stephanus b. May 7, 1643
Van Cortlandt, Stephanus d. Nov 25, 1700
Van Dine, S S, pseud. d. Apr 11, 1939
Van Doren, Charles Lincoln
    b. Feb 12, 1926
Van Loon, Hendrik Willem
    d. Mar 10, 1944
Van Paassen, Pierre d. Jan 8, 1968
Van Patten, Joyce b. Mar 9, 1934
Van Rensselaer, Stephen b. Nov 1, 1764
Van Slyke, Helen Lenore Vogt
    d. Jul 3, 1979
Van Vechten, Carl d. Dec 21, 1964
Van Zandt, Marie b. Oct 8, 1861
Van, Bobby b. Dec 6, 1935
Vanderbilt, Amy d. Dec 27, 1974
Vanderbilt, Cornelius d. Jan 4, 1877
Vanderbilt, Cornelius d. Sep 12, 1899
Vanderbilt, Cornelius, Jr. b. Apr 30, 1898
Vanderbilt, Gloria Morgan b. Feb 20, 1924
Vanderbilt, William Henry d. Dec 8, 1885
Vanderbilt, William Henry
    b. Nov 24, 1902
Vanderbilt, William Kissam
    b. Dec 12, 1849
Vandross, Luther b. Apr 20, 1951
Varese, Edgar d. Nov 6, 1965
Vaughn, Robert b. Nov 22, 1932
Vaux, Calvert d. Nov 19, 1895
Vernon, Jackie b. 1928
Vickrey, Robert b. Aug 20, 1926
Viereck, Peter Robert Edwin
    b. Aug 5, 1916
Vigoda, Abe b. Feb 24, 1921
Villard, Oswald d. Oct 1, 1949
Viscardi, Henry, Jr b. May 10, 1912
Vishinskii, Andrei Yanuarevich
    d. Nov 22, 1954
Volkov, Vladislav d. Jun 30, 1971
VonHoffman, Nicholas b. Oct 16, 1929
VonTilzer, Harry d. Jan 10, 1946

Vought, Chance Milton b. Feb 26, 1890
Wagner, Robert d. May 4, 1953
Wagner, Robert Ferdinand, Jr.
  b. Apr 20, 1910
Wain, Bea b. Apr 30, 1917
Walburn, Raymond d. Jul 26, 1969
Wald, Jerry (Jerome Irving)
  b. Sep 16, 1911
Walden, Robert b. Sep 25, 1943
Walker, Edyth d. Feb 19, 1950
Walker, Jimmie (James Carter)
  b. Jun 25, 1948
Walker, Jimmy (James John)
  b. Jun 19, 1881
Walker, Jimmy (James John)
  d. Nov 18, 1946
Walker, Sarah Breedlove d. May 25, 1919
Wallace, Ed(ward Tatum) d. Oct 10, 1976
Wallach, Eli b. Dec 7, 1915
Wallack, James William d. Dec 25, 1864
Wallenstein, Alfred Franz d. Mar 8, 1983
Waller, "Fats" (Thomas Wright)
  b. May 21, 1904
Wallop, Malcom b. Feb 27, 1933
Walsh, Raoul b. Mar 11, 1887
Walter, Cyril d. Aug 18, 1968
Walters, Vernon Anthony b. Jan 3, 1917
Wanger, Walter d. Nov 18, 1968
Warburg, Felix Moritz d. Oct 20, 1937
Warburg, Frederick Marcus
  b. Oct 14, 1897
Ward, Fannie d. Jan 27, 1952
Warfield, David d. Jun 27, 1951
Warner, Susan Bogert b. Jul 11, 1819
Warren, Harry b. Dec 24, 1893
Warren, Leonard b. Apr 21, 1911
Warren, Leonard d. Mar 4, 1960
Warren, Lesley Ann b. Aug 16, 1946
Washington, "Buck" (Ford Lee)
  d. Jan 31, 1955
Watson, Thomas John, Sr. d. Jun 19, 1956
Watt, Douglas (Benjamin) b. Jan 20, 1914
Wattenberg, Ben J b. Aug 26, 1933
Watts, Richard, Jr. d. Jan 2, 1981
Wayland, Francis b. Mar 11, 1796
Weaver, Sigourney b. 1949
Webb, William Seward b. Jan 31, 1851
Weber, Joseph M b. Aug 11, 1867
Webster, Jean d. Jun 11, 1916
Webster, Margaret b. Mar 15, 1905
Webster, Paul Francois b. Dec 20, 1907
Wechsler, David d. May 1981
Wechsler, James Arthur b. Oct 31, 1915
Wechsler, James Arthur d. Sep 11, 1983
Weed, Thurlow b. Nov 22, 1882
Weidman, Charles d. Jul 15, 1975
Weidman, Jerome b. Apr 4, 1913
Weill, Claudia b. 1947
Weill, Kurt d. Apr 3, 1950
Weinberg, Chester b. Sep 23, 1930
Weinberg, Chester d. Apr 24, 1985

Weir, Robert W d. May 1, 1889
Welch, Herbert b. Nov 7, 1862
Welch, Herbert d. Apr 4, 1969
Weld, Tuesday (Susan Kerr)
  b. Aug 27, 1943
Weller, Michael b. Sep 27, 1942
Welles, Sumner b. Oct 14, 1892
Wellman, Walter d. Jan 31, 1934
Wells, Horace d. Jan 24, 1848
Wengenroth, Stow b. Jul 25, 1906
Wenner, Jann b. Jan 7, 1947
Wenrich, Percy d. Mar 17, 1952
West, Nathanael, pseud. b. Oct 17, 1903
Westinghouse, George d. Mar 12, 1914
Westlake, Donald E(dwin) b. Jul 12, 1933
Whalen, Grover b. Jun 2, 1886
Whalen, Grover d. Apr 20, 1962
Wharton, Edith b. Jan 24, 1862
Wheeler, Bert d. Jan 18, 1968
Wheeler, Candace Thurber d. Aug 5, 1923
Wheelock, John Hall d. Mar 22, 1978
Whitaker, Rogers E(rnest) M(alcolm)
  d. May 11, 1981
White, Richard Grant b. May 23, 1821
White, Richard Grant d. Apr 8, 1885
White, Stanford b. Nov 9, 1853
White, Stanford d. Jun 25, 1906
White, Theodore Harold d. May 15, 1986
White, Walter Francis d. Mar 21, 1955
Whitehead, Edwin C b. Jun 1, 1919
Whitehill, Clarence Eugene
  d. Dec 19, 1932
Whitman, Marina VonNeumann
  b. Mar 6, 1936
Whitney, C(ornelius) V(anderbilt)
  b. Feb 20, 1899
Whitney, Gertrude Vanderbilt b. 1877
Whitney, Gertrude Vanderbilt
  d. Apr 18, 1942
Whitney, Harry Payne b. Apr 29, 1872
Whitney, Harry Payne d. Oct 26, 1930
Whitney, William Collins d. Feb 2, 1904
Wilbur, Richard Purdy b. Mar 1, 1921
Wilde, Cornel b. Oct 13, 1918
Wilkes, Charles b. Apr 3, 1798
Wilkins, Roy d. Sep 8, 1981
Wilkinson, J(ohn) Burke b. Aug 24, 1913
Willard, Frances E d. Feb 18, 1898
Wille, Frank b. Feb 27, 1931
Williams, "Tennessee" (Thomas Lanier)
  d. Feb 25, 1983
Williams, Bert (Egbert Austin)
  d. Mar 4, 1922
Williams, Billy Dee b. Apr 6, 1937
Williams, Clarence, III b. Aug 21, 1939
Williams, Garth Montgomery
  b. Apr 16, 1912
Williams, Gus b. Jul 19, 1847
Williams, Vanessa b. Mar 18, 1963
Willig, George b. Jun 11, 1949
Willkie, Wendell Lewis d. Oct 8, 1944

Wilson, Al d. Apr 25, 1951
Wilson, Charles Edward b. Nov 18, 1886
Wilson, Henry Braid d. Jan 30, 1954
Wilson, Malcolm b. Feb 26, 1914
Wilson, Mitchell b. Jul 17, 1913
Wilson, Theodore b. Dec 10, 1943
Winchell, Paul b. Dec 21, 1922
Winchell, Walter b. Apr 7, 1897
Windom, William b. Sep 28, 1923
Winkler, Henry Franklin b. Oct 30, 1945
Winkler, Irwin b. May 28, 1931
Winograd, Arthur b. Apr 22, 1920
Winston, Harry b. Mar 1, 1896
Winston, Harry d. Dec 1978
Wise, Stephen Samuel d. Apr 19, 1949
Wise, William H b. Jul 21, 1923
Witherspoon, Herbert d. May 10, 1935
Witmark, Isidore b. Jun 15, 1869
Witmark, Isidore d. Apr 9, 1941
Witt, Paul Junger b. Mar 20, 1943
Wodehouse, P(elham) G(renville)
    d. Feb 14, 1975
Wolfert, Ira b. Nov 1, 1908
Wolheim, Louis b. Mar 23, 1880
Wolper, David Lloyd b. Jan 11, 1928
Wood, James Rushmore d. May 4, 1882
Wood, Peggy b. Feb 9, 1892
Woodbridge, Frederick James Eugene
    d. Jun 1, 1940
Woodworth, Samuel d. Dec 9, 1842
Woollcott, Alexander Humphreys
    d. Jan 23, 1943
Woolley, Monty (Edgar Montillion)
    b. Aug 17, 1888
Woolman, John d. Oct 7, 1772
Wouk, Herman b. May 27, 1915
Wragge, Sidney b. Mar 10, 1908
Wright, George b. Jan 28, 1847
Wright, James Arlington d. Mar 25, 1980
Wright, Russel d. Dec 22, 1976
Wright, Teresa b. Oct 27, 1918
Wrightsman, Charles Bierer
    d. May 27, 1986
Wurf, Jerry (Jerome) b. May 18, 1919
Wycherley, Margaret d. Jun 6, 1966
Wylie, Elinor Hoyt d. Dec 16, 1928
Wynn, Keenan b. Jul 27, 1916
Yablans, Frank b. Aug 27, 1935
Yale, Linus d. Dec 25, 1868
Yalow, Rosalyn Sussman b. Jul 19, 1921
Yarrow, Peter b. May 31, 1938
Youmans, Vincent b. Sep 27, 1898
Young, Burt b. Apr 30, 1940
Young, Gig d. Oct 19, 1978
Young, Lester Willis d. Mar 15, 1959
Young, Mahonri M d. Nov 2, 1957
Young, Roland d. Jun 5, 1953
Young, Stark d. Jan 6, 1963
Yurka, Blanche d. Jun 6, 1974
Zadora, Pia b. 1955
Zeckendorf, William d. Oct 1, 1976

Zemlinsky, Alexander von d. Mar 16, 1942
Zenatello, Giovanni d. Feb 11, 1949
Zenger, John Peter d. Jul 28, 1746
Zevin, B(enjamin) D(avid)
    b. May 16, 1901
Ziegler, Edward d. Oct 25, 1947
Ziff, William B d. Dec 20, 1953
Zim, Herbert Spencer b. Jul 12, 1909
Zimbalist, Efrem, Jr. b. Nov 30, 1923
Zindel, Paul b. May 15, 1936
Zinn, Howard b. Aug 24, 1922
Zirato, Bruno d. Nov 28, 1972
Zolotow, Maurice b. Nov 23, 1913
Zuckerman, Ben d. Aug 9, 1979
Zukofsky, Louis b. Jan 23, 1904
Zwerling, Israel b. Jun 12, 1917

Newburgh, New York
Belknap, William Worth b. Sep 22, 1829
Colombo, Joseph Anthony
    d. May 23, 1978
Downing, Andrew Jackson b. Oct 30, 1815
Ferraro, Geraldine Anne b. Aug 26, 1935
Hart, William Surrey b. Dec 6, 1872
Inness, George b. May 1, 1825
Kelly, Ellsworth b. May 31, 1923
Leech, Margaret Kernochan
    b. Nov 7, 1893

Newton, New York
Harper, Fletcher b. Jan 31, 1806
Harper, James b. Apr 13, 1795
Harper, John b. Jan 22, 1797
Harper, Joseph Wesley b. Dec 25, 1801

Niagara Falls, New York
Collins, James Joseph (Jimmy)
    b. Jan 16, 1873
Frum, Barbara b. Sep 8, 1937
Hall, Charles Martin d. Dec 27, 1914
Maglie, Sal(vatore Anthony)
    b. Apr 26, 1917
Masselos, William b. 1920
Quinn, Jane Bryant b. Feb 5, 1939
Tone, Franchot b. Feb 27, 1905
Vanity b.

Nichols, New York
Prince, William b. Jan 26, 1913

Norfolk, New York
Rogers, William Pierce b. Jun 23, 1913

North Creek, New York
Durant, Thomas Clark d. Oct 5, 1885

North Salem, New York
Mills, Darius Ogden b. Sep 25, 1825

North Tarrytown, New York
Hays, Lee d. Aug 26, 1981

North Tonawanda, New York
Rand, James Henry b. Nov 18, 1886

Northport, New York
Beard, Myron Gould d. Dec 25, 1974
LuPone, Patti b. Apr 21, 1949

Norwich, New York
Borden, Gail b. Nov 9, 1801

Port Jefferson, New York
 Berndt, Walter d. Aug 13, 1979
 Haworth, Leland John d. Mar 5, 1979
 Zukofsky, Louis d. May 12, 1978
Port Jervis, New York
 Harris, "Bucky" (Stanley Raymond)
  b. Nov 8, 1896
Port Washington, New York
 Alexander, Hattie Elizabeth
  d. Jun 24, 1968
 Gunn, Hartford Nelson, Jr.
  b. Dec 24, 1926
Potsdam, New York
 Kellogg, Frank Billings b. Dec 22, 1856
Poughkeepsie, New York
 Baker, Sara Josephine b. Nov 15, 1873
 Butts, Alfred Mosher b. Apr 13, 1899
 Cott, Ted b. Jan 1, 1917
 Denning, Richard b. Mar 27, 1914
 Jordy, William H(enry) b. Aug 31, 1917
 Lipmann, Fritz Albert d. Jul 24, 1986
 Morgenthau, Henry, Jr. d. Feb 6, 1967
 Rattner, Abraham b. Jul 8, 1895
 Rovere, Richard Halworth
  d. Nov 23, 1979
 Vassar, Matthew d. Jun 23, 1868
Princeton, New York
 Stockton, Richard d. Feb 28, 1781
Purchase, New York
 Knopf, Alfred Abraham d. Aug 11, 1984
 Lehman, Adele Lewisohn d. Aug 11, 1965
 Tarnower, Herman d. Mar 10, 1980
Putnam County, New York
 Crosby, Fanny (Frances Jane)
  b. Mar 24, 1820
Queens, New York
 Deren, Maya d. Oct 13, 1961
 Field, Ron b. 1934
 Jackson, "Hurricane" (Thomas)
  d. Feb 14, 1982
 King, Warren Thomas b. Jan 3, 1916
 Lauper, Cyndi (Cynthia) b. Jun 20, 1953
 Peters, Bernadette b. Feb 28, 1948
 Simmons, Gene b. Aug 25, 1949
 Stanley, Paul b. Jan 20, 1949
 Taylor, Sydney Brenner d. Feb 12, 1978
Queens County, New York
 Cuomo, Mario Matthew b. Jun 15, 1932
Quogue, New York
 Scribner, Charles, Jr. b. Jul 13, 1921
Raquette Lake, New York
 Huntington, Collis Potter d. Aug 13, 1900
Redwood, New York
 Ryan, Tommy b. Mar 31, 1870
Remsen, New York
 Steuben, Friedrich Wilhelm Ludolf Gerhard
  Augustin, Baron d. Nov 28, 1794
 VonSteuben, Friedrich Wilhelm
  d. Nov 28, 1794
Rensselaer, New York
 Singer, Isaac Merrit b. Oct 27, 1811

Rensselaerville, New York
 Farnham, Eliza Wood Burhans
  b. Nov 17, 1815
Rhinebeck, New York
 Bachman, John b. Feb 4, 1790
 Hickok, Lorena A d. May 3, 1968
 Livingston, Edward d. May 23, 1836
 Morton, Levi Parsons d. May 16, 1920
Richford, New York
 Rockefeller, John D(avison) b. Jul 8, 1839
Richmond Hill, New York
 Barr, Amelia Edith Huddleston
  d. Mar 10, 1919
 Gould, Morton b. Dec 10, 1913
Richmondville, New York
 France, Harry Clinton b. Jul 17, 1890
Ripley, New York
 Ely, Richard Theodore b. Apr 13, 1854
 Goodrich, Benjamin Franklin
  b. Nov 4, 1841
Riverdale, New York
 Joy, Leatrice d. May 13, 1985
 Willys, John North d. Aug 26, 1935
Riverhead, New York
 Brooks, Geraldine d. Jun 19, 1977
 Pike, Otis b. Aug 31, 1921
Rochester, New York
 Adler, Elmer b. Jul 22, 1884
 Alden, Isabella Macdonald b. Nov 3, 1841
 Anthony, Susan Brownell d. Mar 13, 1906
 Antonelli, John(ny August)
  b. Apr 12, 1930
 Ashbery, John Lawrence b. Jul 28, 1927
 Barry, Philip b. Jun 18, 1896
 Bausch, Edward b. Sep 26, 1854
 Bausch, Edward d. Jul 30, 1944
 Bausch, John Jacob d. Feb 14, 1925
 Brooks, Louise d. Aug 8, 1985
 Brown, Marcia b. Jul 13, 1918
 Calloway, Cab(ell) b. Dec 25, 1907
 Courtney, Clint(on Dawson)
  d. Jun 16, 1975
 Diamond, David b. Jul 9, 1915
 Duel, Peter b. 1940
 Eastman, George d. Mar 14, 1932
 Finlay, Virgil b. 1914
 Folsom, Marion Bayard d. Sep 28, 1976
 Forster, Robert b. Jul 13, 1942
 Fullerton, (Charles) Gordon
  b. Oct 11, 1936
 Gannett, Frank Ernest d. Sep 3, 1957
 Gannett, Lewis Stiles b. Oct 3, 1891
 Gorkin, Jess b. Oct 23, 1913
 Hanson, Howard Harold d. Feb 26, 1981
 Haviland, Virginia b. May 21, 1911
 Kanin, Garson b. Nov 24, 1912
 Kirstein, Lincoln Edward b. May 4, 1907
 Klem, Bill (William Joseph)
  b. Feb 22, 1874
 Lamb, Harold Albert d. Apr 9, 1962
 Lincoln, Elmo b. 1899

Quezon (y Molina), Manuel Luis
d. Aug 1, 1944
Schaefer, "Germany" (Herman A)
d. May 16, 1919
Saratoga, New York
Sullivan, Frank b. Sep 22, 1892
Sullivan, Frank d. Feb 19, 1976
Saratoga County, New York
Scott, Clarence b. 1848
Scott, Edward Irvin b. 1846
Saratoga Springs, New York
Brackett, Charles b. Nov 26, 1892
Graham, William Alexander
d. Aug 11, 1875
Humphrey, Elliott S b. 1889
Martin, John d. May 19, 1985
Saugerties, New York
Fisher, Irving b. Feb 27, 1867
Wortman, Denys b. May 1, 1887
Sauquoit, New York
Gray, Asa b. Nov 18, 1810
Scarsdale, New York
Folsom, Frank M d. Jan 22, 1970
Harrar, J(acob) George d. Apr 18, 1982
Tompkins, Daniel D b. Jun 21, 1774
Van Heusen, John d. Dec 18, 1931
Wilson, Charles Edward d. Jan 3, 1972
Schenectady, New York
Alexanderson, Ernst Frederik Werner
d. May 14, 1975
Ball, John Dudley, Jr. b. Jul 8, 1911
Blodgett, Katherine Burr b. Jan 10, 1898
Blodgett, Katherine Burr d. Dec 10, 1979
Blum, Stella b. Oct 19, 1916
Coolidge, William David d. Feb 3, 1975
Davis, Ann Bradford b. May 3, 1926
Garroway, Dave (David Cunningham)
b. Jul 13, 1913
Langmuir, Irving d. Aug 17, 1957
Mackerras, Charles, Sir (Alan Charles
MacLaurin) b. Nov 17, 1925
Ponselle, Carmela b. Jun 7, 1892
Potter, Henry Codman b. Jun 25, 1834
Rourke, "Mickey" (Philip Andre) b. 1956
Steinmetz, Charles Proteus d. Oct 26, 1923
Taylor, Graham b. May 2, 1851
Tudor, John Thomas b. Feb 2, 1954
Schuyler Falls, New York
Bridges, Calvin Blackman b. Jan 11, 1889
Scipio, New York
Elliott, Charles Loring b. Oct 12, 1812
Scotia, New York
Doherty, Robert Ernest d. Oct 19, 1950
Seneca Falls, New York
Blatch, Harriot Eaton Stanton
b. Jan 20, 1856
Dickinson, Edwin W b. Oct 11, 1891
Giusti, Dave (David John, Jr.)
b. Nov 27, 1939

Setauket, New York
Mount, William Sidney b. Nov 26, 1807
Mount, William Sidney d. Nov 19, 1868
Shady, New York
Cowell, Henry Dixon d. Dec 10, 1965
Sharon Springs, New York
Delmonico, Lorenzo d. Sep 3, 1881
Shelter Island, New York
Hickenlooper, Bourke B d. Sep 4, 1971
Sidney, New York
Carlson, Evans Fordyce b. Feb 26, 1896
Silver Creek, New York
Ehmke, Howard Jonathan b. Apr 24, 1894
Sinclairville, New York
Tugwell, Rexford Guy b. Jul 10, 1891
Sing Sing, New York
Buchalter, "Lepke" (Louis) d. Mar 4, 1944
Fish, Albert d. Jan 16, 1936
Rosenberg, Ethel Greenglass
d. Jun 19, 1953
Rosenberg, Julius d. Jun 19, 1953
Skaneateles, New York
Danforth, William d. Apr 16, 1941
Smithtown, New York
Dean, Laura b. May 27, 1963
Sneden's Landing, New York
McClintic, Guthrie d. Oct 29, 1961
South Nyack, New York
Breger, Dave d. Jan 16, 1970
Southampton, New York
Barthelmess, Richard d. Aug 17, 1963
Cox, Edward Finch b. Oct 2, 1946
James, Philip b. Nov 1, 1975
Jones, James d. May 9, 1977
McIntyre, James d. Aug 18, 1937
Mellon, Andrew William d. Aug 26, 1937
Merrill, Charles Edward d. Oct 6, 1956
Onassis, Jacqueline Lee Bouvier Kennedy
b. Jul 28, 1929
Paton, Richard d. Feb 27, 1984
Porter, Fairfield d. Sep 18, 1975
Thayer, Mary Van Rensselaer b. 1903
Yastrzemski, Carl Michael
b. Aug 22, 1939
Southold, New York
Parsons, Betty Pierson d. Jul 23, 1982
Sparta, New York
Shays, Daniel d. Sep 29, 1825
Springville, New York
Warner, "Pop" (Glenn Scobey)
b. Apr 5, 1871
Stamford, New York
Judson, Edward Zane Carroll
b. Mar 20, 1823
Judson, Edward Zane Carroll
d. Jul 16, 1886
Stanfordville, New York
Cagney, James (James Francis, Jr.)
d. Mar 30, 1986
Star Lake, New York
Young, Marian b. Nov 21, 1908

Funicello, Annette b. Oct 22, 1942
Inman, Henry b. Oct 28, 1801
O'Neal, Ron b. Sep 1, 1937
Sherman, James Schoolcraft
  b. Oct 24, 1855
Sherman, James Schoolcraft
  d. Oct 30, 1912
Smith, Gerrit b. Mar 6, 1797
Sokolsky, George E b. Sep 5, 1893
Valatie, New York
O'Hanlon, Virginia d. 1971
Valhalla, New York
Criss, Charlie (Charles W) b. Nov 6, 1949
Haughton, Billy d. Jul 15, 1986
Vernon, New York
Mahan, Asa b. Nov 9, 1799
Vestal, New York
Locke, David Ross b. Sep 20, 1833
Wallkill, New York
Knorr, Nathan Homer d. Jun 15, 1977
Wappingers Falls, New York
Mulhall, Jack b. Oct 7, 1894
Warren County, New York
Brady, Mathew B b. 1823
Warrensburg, New York
Bennett, Floyd b. Oct 25, 1890
Washington Heights, New York
Lyman, Frankie b. Sep 30, 1942
Waterford, New York
Lindsay, Howard b. Mar 29, 1889
Waldron, Charles D b. Dec 23, 1875
Waterloo, New York
Rogers, Randolph b. Jul 6, 1825
Watertown, New York
Dulles, Allen Welsh b. Apr 7, 1893
Dulles, Eleanor Lansing b. Jun 1, 1895
Gary, John b. Nov 29, 1932
Lansing, Robert b. Oct 17, 1864
Mantle, (Robert) Burns b. Dec 1873
Smith, Chard Powers b. Nov 1, 1894
Yost, Charles Woodruff b. Nov 6, 1907
Waterville, New York
Eastman, George b. Jul 12, 1854
Fuess, Claude Moore b. Jan 12, 1885
Watervliet, New York
Lee, Ann d. Sep 8, 1784
Stanford, Leland (Amasa Leland)
  b. Mar 9, 1824
Wellsville, New York
Hayes, "Gabby" (George Francis)
  b. May 7, 1885
Hill, Grace Livingstone b. Apr 16, 1865
York, Edward Palmer b. 1865
West Fulton, New York
McGiver, John d. Sep 9, 1975
West Hills, New York
Whitman, Walt(er) b. May 31, 1819
West Island, New York
Dana, Charles Anderson d. Oct 17, 1879
West Islip, New York
Moses, Robert d. Jul 29, 1981

West Point, New York
Eisenhower, David b. Apr 1, 1947
Mahan, Alfred Thayer b. Sep 27, 1840
Scott, Winfield d. May 29, 1866
Vidal, "Gore" (Eugene Luther)
  b. Oct 3, 1925
Weir, John F(erguson) b. Aug 28, 1841
Weir, Julian Alden b. Aug 30, 1852
West Shokun, New York
McBride, Mary Margaret d. Apr 7, 1976
West Sparta, New York
McNair, Malcolm Perrine b. Oct 6, 1894
Westbury, New York
Haden, Pat(rick Capper) b. Jan 23, 1953
Hutton, Edward F d. Jul 11, 1962
McKeon, Nancy b. Apr 4, 1966
McKeon, Philip b. Nov 11, 1964
Westchester, New York
Beller, Kathleen b. Feb 10, 1956
Cornell, Ezra b. Jan 11, 1807
Farr, Felicia b. Oct 4, 1932
Lucci, Susan b. Dec 23,
MacGraw, Ali b. Apr 1, 1938
Westchester County, New York
Goldmark, Peter Carl d. Dec 7, 1977
Rockefeller, John D(avison), III
  d. Jul 10, 1978
Worden, John Lorimer b. Mar 12, 1818
Westernville, New York
Floyd, William d. Aug 4, 1821
Halleck, Henry b. Jan 16, 1815
Westhampton, New York
Steiger, Rod b. Apr 14, 1925
Westmoreland, New York
Appleby, John Francis b. May 23, 1840
Babbitt, Benjamin Talbot b. 1809
Westwood, New York
Kelton, Pert d. Oct 30, 1968
White Plains, New York
Bacheller, Irving d. Feb 24, 1950
Dannay, Frederic d. Sep 3, 1982
Davenport, Eva d. Sep 26, 1932
Duryea, Dan b. Jan 23, 1907
Frank, Waldo d. Jan 9, 1967
Grainger, Percy Aldridge d. Feb 20, 1961
Kissinger, Nancy Maginnes b. 1934
Kuhn, Walt d. Jul 13, 1949
Mabley, "Moms" (Jackie) d. May 23, 1975
Marx, Louis d. Feb 5, 1982
Oxnam, G(arfield) Bromley
  d. Mar 12, 1963
Plotnik, Arthur b. Aug 1, 1937
Rose, Leonard d. Nov 16, 1984
Schocken, Theodore d. Mar 20, 1975
Slavitt, David R b. Mar 23, 1935
Stafford, Jean d. Mar 26, 1979
Stuart, Ruth McEnery d. May 6, 1917
Waite, Ralph b. Jun 22, 1928
Whitmore, James Allen b. Oct 1, 1921
Whitehall, New York
Donehue, Vincent J b. Sep 22, 1922

Clarkton, North Carolina
Owen, Guy, Jr. b. Feb 24, 1925
Clayton, North Carolina
Dodd, William Edward b. Oct 21, 1869
Concord, North Carolina
Cannon, James W d. Dec 19, 1921
Deep Gap, North Carolina
Watson, "Doc" (Arthel) b. Mar 2, 1923
Denton, North Carolina
Lanier, Hal (Harold Clifton) b. Jul 4, 1942
Durham, North Carolina
Craig, Roger Lee b. Feb 17, 1931
Davis, Burke b. Jul 24, 1913
Duke, James Buchanan b. Dec 23, 1856
Markham, "Pigmeat" (Dewey M)
b. Apr 18, 1904
McDougall, William d. Nov 28, 1938
McPhatter, Clyde b. Nov 15, 1933
Sullivan, John d. Jan 23, 1795
Wiggins, Archibald Lee Manning
b. Apr 9, 1891
Williams, Mary Lou d. May 28, 1981
Edenton, North Carolina
Iredell, James d. Oct 2, 1799
Tucker, Mary Bradham d. May 26, 1984
Wilson, James d. Aug 21, 1798
Fayetteville, North Carolina
Caswell, Richard d. Nov 10, 1789
Revels, Hiram R b. Sep 1822
Rose, Augustus Steele b. Jul 14, 1907
Stapleton, Ruth Carter d. Sep 26, 1983
Flat Rock, North Carolina
Sandburg, Carl August d. Jul 22, 1967
Fletcher, North Carolina
Stroup, Thomas Bradley b. Dec 21, 1903
Flint Hill, North Carolina
Scruggs, Earl b. Jan 6, 1924
Fort Bragg, North Carolina
Floyd, Raymond b. Sep 14, 1942
Franklin County, North Carolina
Upchurch, John Jorden b. Mar 26, 1820
Franklinton, North Carolina
Bibby, Henry b. Nov 24, 1949
Fulton Davie County, North Carolina
Hanes, Pleasant H b. Oct 16, 1845
Gastonia, North Carolina
Bryson, Wally Carter b. Jul 18, 1949
Sowell, Thomas b. Jul 30, 1930
Goldsboro, North Carolina
Jeffreys, Anne b. Jan 26, 1923
Roberts, Gene (Eugene Leslie, Jr.)
b. Jun 15, 1932
Granville City, North Carolina
Webb, James Edwin b. Oct 7, 1906
Greensboro, North Carolina
Craddock, "Crash" (Billy) b. Jun 16, 1940
DeButts, John Dulany b. Apr 10, 1915
Evans, Vince(nt Tobias) b. Jun 14, 1955
Ferrell, Wes(ley Cheek) b. Feb 2, 1908
Henry, O, pseud. b. Sep 11, 1862
Hudson, Lou b. Jul 11, 1944

McAdoo, Bob (Robert) b. Sep 25, 1951
Murrow, Edward R(oscoe) b. Apr 25, 1908
Greenville, North Carolina
East, John Porter d. Jun 29, 1986
Taylor, Billy (William Edward)
b. Jul 24, 1921
Guilford County, North Carolina
Madison, Dolly Payne Todd
b. May 20, 1768
Hamlet, North Carolina
Coltrane, "Trane" (John William)
b. Sep 26, 1926
Wicker, Tom (Thomas Grey)
b. Jun 18, 1926
Happy Valley, North Carolina
Messick, Henry Hicks b. Aug 14, 1922
Henderson, North Carolina
King, Ben E b. Sep 28, 1938
Hendersonville, North Carolina
Price, Byron d. Aug 6, 1981
Hertford, North Carolina
Hunter, "Catfish" (James Augustus)
b. Apr 18, 1946
Hertford County, North Carolina
Gatling, Richard Jordan b. Sep 12, 1818
High Point, North Carolina
Appling, Luke (Lucius Benjamin)
b. Apr 2, 1907
Hillsboro, North Carolina
Benton, Thomas Hart b. Mar 14, 1782
Hooper, William d. Oct 14, 1790
Rhine, J(oseph) B(anks) d. Feb 20, 1980
Strudwick, Shepperd b. Sep 22, 1907
Huntersville, North Carolina
Wilhelm, Hoyt (James Hoyt)
b. Jul 26, 1923
Ingle Hollow, North Carolina
Johnson, Junior b. 1931
Jackson County, North Carolina
Brinkley, John Romulus b. Jul 8, 1885
Keyser, North Carolina
Vollmer, Lula b. 1898
Kinston, North Carolina
Snepp, Frank Warren, III b. May 3, 1943
Laurinburg, North Carolina
Sanford, Terry b. Aug 20, 1917
Level Cross, North Carolina
Petty, Richard b. Jul 2, 1938
Lillington, North Carolina
Green, Paul Eliot b. Mar 17, 1894
Morgan, Robert Burren b. Oct 5, 1925
Lincolnton, North Carolina
Guion, Connie Myers b. Aug 9, 1882
Lynn, North Carolina
Lanier, Sidney d. Sep 7, 1881
Marion, North Carolina
Loden, Barbara Ann b. Jul 8, 1937
Mars Hill, North Carolina
Martin, Graham Anderson b. Sep 22, 1912

Mecklenburg County, North Carolina
Cannon, James W b. Apr 25, 1852
Polk, James K(nox) b. Nov 2, 1795
Mocksville, North Carolina
Gibbs, Joe Jackson b. Nov 25, 1940
Moncure, North Carolina
Ethridge, Mark Foster d. Apr 5, 1981
Monroe, North Carolina
Helms, Jesse Alexander, Jr.
b. Oct 18, 1921
Mooresville, North Carolina
Washam, Wisner McCamey b. Sep 8, 1931
Morganton, North Carolina
Ervin, Sam(uel James, Jr.) b. Sep 27, 1896
Mount Airy, North Carolina
Chang and Eng d. Jan 17, 1874
Dean, Alfred Lovill b. Aug 24, 1916
Fargo, Donna b. Nov 10, 1949
Griffith, Andy (Andrew) b. Jun 1, 1926
New Bern, North Carolina
Bellamy, Walt b. Jul 24, 1939
Bradham, Caleb D b.
New Garden, North Carolina
Cannon, Joseph Gurney b. May 7, 1836
Coffin, Levi b. Oct 28, 1798
North Wilkesboro, North Carolina
Byrd, Robert Carlyle b. Jan 15, 1918
Ocracoke Island, North Carolina
Blackbeard d. Nov 22, 1718
Orange County, North Carolina
Duke, Benjamin Newton b. Apr 27, 1855
Pennert, North Carolina
McEachin, James Elton b. May 20, 1930
Plymouth, North Carolina
Daly, Augustin b. Jul 20, 1838
Raleigh, North Carolina
Barfield, Velma d. Nov 2, 1984
Coffin, Robert Peter Tristram
d. Oct 29, 1956
Commons, John Rogers d. May 11, 1945
Daniels, Jonathan Worth b. Apr 26, 1902
Dixon, Thomas d. Apr 3, 1946
Johnson, Andrew b. Dec 29, 1808
Johnson, Jack (John Arthur)
d. Jun 10, 1946
Owen, Guy, Jr. d. Jul 23, 1981
Royster, Vermont Connecticut
b. Apr 30, 1914
Sloan, Samuel d. Jul 19, 1884
Smith, Kate (Kathryn Elizabeth)
d. Jun 17, 1986
Richmond County, North Carolina
Morrison, Cameron b. Oct 5, 1869
Riverton, North Carolina
Johnson, Gerald White b. Aug 6, 1890
Roanoke Rapids, North Carolina
Grizzard, George b. Apr 1, 1928
Robinsville, North Carolina
Milsap, Ronnie b. Jan 16, 1944

Rockingham, North Carolina
Ford, Russ(ell William) d. Jan 24, 1960
Williams, Charles b. Nov 18, 1954
Rocky Mount, North Carolina
Boyce, Westray Battle b. Aug 1901
Ford, Phil Jackson b. Feb 9, 1956
Horne, Josh L d. Mar 15, 1974
Hyman, Earle b. Oct 11, 1926
Kyser, "Kay" (James Kern)
b. Jun 18, 1906
Leonard, "Buck" (Walter Fenner)
b. Sep 8, 1907
Monk, Thelonius Sphere b. Oct 10, 1920
Roxboro, North Carolina
Slaughter, Enos Bradsher b. Apr 27, 1916
Salisbury, North Carolina
Blackmer, Sidney Alderman
b. Jul 13, 1896
Dole, Elizabeth Hanford b. Jul 20, 1936
Evans, Mike (Michael Jonas)
b. Nov 3, 1949
Koontz, (Annie) Elizabeth Duncan
b. Jun 3, 1919
Sallsburg, North Carolina
Junior, E J (Ester James, III)
b. Dec 8, 1959
Sampson County, North Carolina
King, William Rufus de Vane
b. Apr 7, 1786
Seaboard, North Carolina
Goode, Wilson (Willie Wilson)
b. Aug 19, 1938
Shelby, North Carolina
Dixon, Thomas b. Jan 11, 1865
Thompson, David O'Neil b. Jul 13, 1954
Smithfield, North Carolina
Gardner, Ava b. Dec 24, 1922
Southern Pines, North Carolina
Irwin, Wallace d. Feb 14, 1959
Stevens, John Frank d. Jun 2, 1943
Tryon, North Carolina
Banning, Margaret Culkin d. Jan 4, 1982
Heyward, (Edwin) DuBose d. Jun 16, 1940
Lockridge, Richard d. Jun 19, 1982
Simone, Nina b. Feb 21, 1933
Unaka, North Carolina
Jenkins, Ray Howard b. Mar 18, 1897
Waco, North Carolina
Patterson, Floyd b. Jan 4, 1935
Wadesboro, North Carolina
Bennett, Hugh Hammond b. Apr 15, 1881
Wake County, North Carolina
Trout, Robert b. Oct 15, 1908
Wake Forest, North Carolina
Crittenden, Christopher b. Dec 1, 1902
Sales, Soupy b. Jan 8, 1930
Warrenton, North Carolina
Bragg, Braxton b. Mar 22, 1817
Washington, North Carolina
Wilkins, Dominique b. Jan 12, 1960

Waynesville, North Carolina
Ferguson, Homer Lenoir b. Mar 6, 1873
Whitakers, North Carolina
Horne, Josh L b. Dec 21, 1887
Wilkes County, North Carolina
Broyhill, James E b. 1892
Williamsburg, North Carolina
Penn, John d. Sep 14, 1788
Williamston, North Carolina
Perry, Gaylord Jackson b. Sep 15, 1938
Wilmington, North Carolina
Brinkley, David McClure b. Jul 10, 1920
Daniels, Charlie b. Oct 28, 1936
Gabriel, Roman, Jr. b. Aug 5, 1940
Jurgenson, "Sonny" (Christian Adolph, III)
   b. Aug 23, 1934
Kuralt, Charles Bishop b. Sep 10, 1934
Ruark, Robert Chester b. Dec 29, 1915
Wilson, North Carolina
Walsh, Thomas James d. Mar 2, 1933
Winston-Salem, North Carolina
Caston, Saul d. Jul 28, 1970
Cosell, Howard b. Mar 25, 1920
Ervin, Sam(uel James, Jr.) d. Apr 23, 1985
Grayson, Kathryn b. Feb 9, 1923
Grier, Pamela Suzette b. May 26, 1949
Hanes, Pleasant H d. Jun 9, 1925
Yanceyville, North Carolina
Fels, Samuel Simeon b. Feb 16, 1860
Zebulon, North Carolina
Daniel, Clifton, Jr. b. Sep 19, 1912

NORTH DAKOTA

Devils Lake, North Dakota
Frelich, Phyllis b. 1944
Dickinson, North Dakota
Stickney, Dorothy b. Jun 21, 1900
Fargo, North Dakota
Andrews, Mark N b. May 19, 1926
Edlund, Richard b. Dec 6, 1940
Emery, Anne b. Sep 1, 1907
Flannagan, John Bernard b. Apr 7, 1895
Gass, William H b. Jul 30, 1924
Grand Forks, North Dakota
Anderson, Lynn b. Sep 26, 1947
Rosenquist, James Albert b. Nov 29, 1933
Grandin, North Dakota
Still, Clyfford b. Oct 30, 1904
Granville, North Dakota
Hills, Lee b. May 28, 1906
Hanaford, North Dakota
Roy, Mike (Michael) b. Jul 18, 1912
Jamestown, North Dakota
L'Amour, Louis Dearborn b. 1908
Lee, Peggy b. May 20, 1920
Kulm, North Dakota
Dickinson, Angie b. Sep 30, 1931
Mandan, North Dakota
Haider, Michael Lawrence b. Oct 1, 1904

Manning, North Dakota
Ruder, Melvin b. Jan 19, 1915
Munich, North Dakota
Burdick, Quentin Northrop
   b. Jun 19, 1908
Scranton, North Dakota
Christopher, Warren Miner
   b. Oct 27, 1925
Sims, North Dakota
Jacobson, Leon Orris b. Dec 16, 1911
Souris, North Dakota
Tucker, Tommy b. May 18, 1908
Strasburg, North Dakota
Welk, Lawrence b. Mar 11, 1903
Valley City, North Dakota
Sothern, Ann b. Jan 22, 1909
Velva, North Dakota
Sevareid, (Arnold) Eric b. Nov 26, 1912

OHIO

Brant, Joseph b. 1742
Claflin, Tennessee Celeste b. 1846
Dellenbaugh, Frederick Samuel
   b. Sep 13, 1853
Mills, John d. Dec 8, 1967
Mullin, Willard b. 1902
Pontiac b. 1720
Purdy, James b. Jul 17, 1923
Smith, Joe b. Jun 1902
St. James, Lyn b. Mar 13, 1947
Ada, Ohio
May, Rollo b. Apr 21, 1909
Akron, Ohio
Abbey, Henry Eugene b. Jun 27, 1846
Albright, Lola Jean b. Jul 20, 1924
Backe, John David b. Jul 5, 1932
Battles, Cliff(ord Franklin) b. May 1, 1910
Bliss, Ray C(harles) b. Dec 16, 1907
Bliss, Ray C(harles) d. Aug 6, 1981
Cook, Marlow Webster b. Jul 27, 1926
Crawford, Cheryl b. Sep 24, 1902
Csonka, Larry Richard b. Dec 25, 1946
Dean, John Wesley b. Oct 14, 1938
Dokes, Michael b. Aug 10, 1958
Downs, Hugh b. Feb 14, 1921
Firestone, Harvey Samuel, Jr.
   d. Jun 1, 1973
Firestone, Idabelle Smith d. Jul 7, 1954
Gordon, John F b. May 15, 1900
Haney, Paul Prichard b. Jul 20, 1928
Hynde, Chrissie (Christine Elaine)
   b. Sep 7, 1951
Ingram, James b. Feb 16, 1956
Jenkins, Hayes Alan b. Mar 23, 1933
Jepson, Helen b. Nov 25, 1906
Keener, Jefferson Ward d. Jan 2, 1981
Knight, John Shively d. Jun 16, 1981
Mario, Queena b. Aug 21, 1896
Monroe, Vaughan b. Oct 7, 1911
Munson, Thurman Lee b. Jun 7, 1947

Parseghian, Ara Raoul b. May 10, 1923
Resnik, Judy (Judith) b. Apr 5, 1949
Saint Clair, James Draper b. Apr 14, 1920
Seiberling, Frank Augustus
    d. Aug 11, 1955
Smith, Robert Holbrook d. Nov 6, 1950
Sweet, Rachel b. 1966
Thurmond, Nate b. Jul 25, 1941
Tucker, Sterling b. Dec 21, 1923
Alliance, Ohio
Dawson, Len (Leonard Ray)
    b. Jun 20, 1935
King, Perry b. Apr 30, 1948
Turkle, Brinton Cassaday b. Aug 15, 1915
Ashland, Ohio
Roseboro, John H b. May 13, 1933
Ashtabula, Ohio
Burchfield, Charles b. Apr 9, 1893
Novello, Don b. Jan 1, 1943
Smeal, Eleanor Marie Cutri
    b. Jul 30, 1939
Athens, Ohio
Lin, Maya Ying b. 1960
Avondale, Ohio
Clark, Marguerite b. Feb 22, 1887
Bannock, Ohio
Hays, Wayne Levere b. Jun 13, 1911
Barberton, Ohio
Schembechler, "Bo" (Glenn Edward)
    b. Apr 1, 1929
Barnesville, Ohio
Gray, Elisha b. Aug 2, 1835
Jones, Sam(uel Pond) b. Jul 26, 1892
Jones, Sam(uel Pond) d. Jul 6, 1966
Bedford, Ohio
Flick, Elmer Harrison b. Jan 11, 1876
Flick, Elmer Harrison d. Jan 9, 1971
Willard, Archibald MacNeal
    b. Aug 22, 1836
Bellaire, Ohio
Watt, George Willard b. Jan 8, 1911
Bellefontaine, Ohio
Flora, James Royer b. Jan 25, 1914
Fritchey, Clayton b. 1905
Hubbard, Kin (Frank McKinney)
    b. Sep 1, 1868
Kiplinger, W(illard) M(onroe)
    b. Jan 8, 1891
Berea, Ohio
McElroy, Neil Hosler b. Oct 30, 1904
Moley, Raymond b. Sep 27, 1886
Beverly, Ohio
Adair, Frank E(arl) b. Apr 9, 1887
Blaine, Ohio
Niekro, Phil(ip Henry) b. Apr 1, 1939
Blooming Grove, Ohio
Harding, Warren G(amaliel)
    b. Nov 2, 1865
Boardman, Ohio
Barger, Floyd b. Oct 26, 1906
Kosar, Bernie b. Nov 25, 1963

Bowersville, Ohio
Peale, Norman Vincent b. May 31, 1898
Brown County, Ohio
Marquis, Albert Nelson b. Jan 12, 1854
Cadiz, Ohio
Dewey, Charles Schuveldt b. Nov 10, 1882
Gable, Clark b. Feb 1, 1901
Cambridge, Ohio
Boyd, William (Bill) b. Jun 5, 1898
Eyen, Tom b. Aug 14, 1941
Glenn, John Herschel, Jr. b. Jul 18, 1921
Canal Dover, Ohio
Quantrill, William Clarke b. Jul 31, 1837
Canal Winchester, Ohio
Speaks, Oley b. Jun 28, 1874
Canton, Ohio
Cordier, Andrew Wellington
    b. Mar 3, 1901
Craft, Christine b. 1945
Dierdorf, Dan(iel Lee) b. Jun 29, 1949
Garner, Peggy Ann b. Feb 3, 1931
Juilliard, Augustus D b. Apr 19, 1836
Light, Enoch Henry b. Aug 18, 1907
McKinley, Ida Saxton b. Jun 8, 1847
McKinley, Ida Saxton d. May 26, 1907
Munson, Thurman Lee d. Aug 2, 1979
Paar, Jack b. May 1, 1918
Page, Alan Cedric b. Aug 7, 1945
Peters, Jean b. Oct 15, 1926
Scali, John Alfred b. Apr 27, 1918
Carroll County, Ohio
Jeffries, James Jackson b. Apr 15, 1875
Vail, Theodore Newton b. Jul 16, 1845
Cedarville, Ohio
Parker, Eleanor b. Jun 26, 1922
Chagrin Falls, Ohio
Kitaj, R(onald) B(rooks) b. Oct 29, 1932
Chatham, Ohio
Thomas, Edith Matilda b. Aug 12, 1854
Chili, Ohio
Crile, George Washington b. Nov 11, 1864
Chillicothe, Ohio
Bennett, John b. May 17, 1865
Dun, Robert Graham b. 1826
Finley, Martha b. Apr 26, 1828
Hayes, Lucy Webb b. Aug 28, 1831
Savage, Robert Heath b. Nov 24, 1929
Wilson, Nancy b. Feb 20, 1937
Cincinnati, Ohio
Altrock, Nick (Nicholas) b. Sep 15, 1876
Arcaro, Eddie (George Edward)
    b. Feb 19, 1916
Balin, Marty b. Jan 30, 1943
Bara, Theda b. Jul 20, 1890
Beard, Daniel Carter b. Jun 21, 1850
Beavers, Louise b. Mar 8, 1902
Berger, Thomas Louis b. Jul 20, 1924
Bowman, Lee (Lucien Lee, Sr.)
    b. Dec 28, 1914

Brosnan, Jim (James Patrick)
    b. Oct 24, 1929
Brown, "Sonny" (William) b. 1928
Burton, Phillip b. Jun 1, 1926
Carruthers, George E b. Oct 1, 1940
Cary, Alice b. Apr 26, 1820
Cary, Phoebe b. Sep 4, 1824
Condit, Carl Wilbur b. Sep 29, 1914
Connolly, Walter b. Apr 8, 1887
Crosley, Powel, Jr. b. Sep 18, 1886
Crosley, Powel, Jr. d. Mar 28, 1961
Dane, Maxwell b. Jun 7, 1906
Daubert, Jake (Jacob Ellsworth)
    d. Oct 9, 1924
Day, Doris b. Apr 3, 1924
DeWitt, William Orville, Sr.
    d. Mar 3, 1982
Dine, Jim b. Jun 16, 1935
Drew, Elizabeth Brenner b. Nov 16, 1935
Duncanson, Robert Scott b. 1817
Durham, Leon b. Jul 31, 1957
Duveneck, Frank d. Jan 3, 1919
Eckstein, Gustav b. Oct 26, 1890
Eckstein, Gustav d. Sep 23, 1981
Engelman, Wilfred d. Feb 12, 1978
Ewing, "Buck" (William) d. Oct 20, 1906
Farrell, Suzanne b. Aug 16, 1945
Fleischmann, Charles Louis
    d. Dec 10, 1897
Fries, Charles W b. Sep 30, 1928
Gamble, James Norris b. Aug 9, 1836
Giles, Warren Crandall d. Feb 7, 1979
Gilligan, John Joyce b. Mar 22, 1921
Glueck, Nelson b. Jun 4, 1900
Glueck, Nelson d. Feb 12, 1971
Henize, Karl Gordon b. Sep 17, 1926
Henri, Robert b. Jun 25, 1865
Holman, Libby b. May 23, 1906
Horchow, S(amuel) Roger b. Jul 3, 1928
Hoyt, Waite Charles d. Aug 25, 1984
Huggins, Miller James b. Mar 27, 1879
Koch, Kenneth b. Feb 27, 1925
Kroger, Bernard Henry b. Jan 24, 1860
Kronenberger, Louis b. Dec 9, 1904
Levine, James b. Jun 23, 1943
Maddox, Garry Lee b. Sep 1, 1949
Manning, Irene b. Jul 17, 1918
Manson, Charles b. Nov 11, 1934
McElroy, Neil Hosler d. Nov 30, 1972
Miller, William Ernest d. Apr 12, 1976
Morgan, Arthur b. Jun 20, 1878
Ochs, Adolph Simon b. Mar 12, 1858
Oester, Ron(ald John) b. May 5, 1956
Pettit, William Thomas b. Apr 23, 1931
Potthast, Edward Henry b. Jun 10, 1857
Power, Tyrone b. May 5, 1914
Resor, Stanley Burnett b. Apr 30, 1879
Reynolds, Jack (John Sumner)
    b. Nov 22, 1947
Rhodes, Hari b. Apr 10, 1932
Richman, Harry b. Aug 10, 1895

Rixey, Eppa d. Feb 28, 1963
Rogers, Roy b. Nov 5, 1912
Rose, Pete(r Edward) b. Apr 14, 1941
Rubin, Jerry b. Jul 14, 1938
Sauer, William George b. Jul 18, 1915
Sawyer, Charles b. Feb 10, 1887
Schott, Marge (Margaret) b. Aug 18, 1928
Segal, Henry d. Jul 18, 1985
Spielberg, Steven b. Dec 18, 1947
Staubach, Roger Thomas b. Feb 5, 1942
Stemrick, Greg(ory Earl, Sr.)
    b. Oct 25, 1951
Stix, Nathan b. 1899
Stratemeyer, George E b. Nov 24, 1890
Strauss, Joseph Baermann b. Jan 9, 1870
Taft, Charles Phelps d. Jun 24, 1983
Taft, Helen Herron b. Jun 2, 1861
Taft, Robert A(lphonso) b. Sep 8, 1889
Taft, Robert Alphonso, Jr. b. Feb 26, 1917
Taft, William Howard b. Sep 15, 1857
Tahse, Martin b. Apr 24, 1930
Tekulve, Kent(on Charles) b. Mar 5, 1947
Townsend, Willard Saxby b. Dec 4, 1895
Trabert, Tony (Marion Anthony)
    b. Sep 16, 1930
Turner, Ted (Robert Edward, III)
    b. Nov 19, 1938
Twachtman, John H b. 1853
Vera-Ellen b. Feb 16, 1926
Wald, Lillian D b. Mar 10, 1867
Weber, Adam b. 1854
Wesselmann, Tom b. Feb 23, 1931
Westheimer, Irvin Ferdinand
    d. Dec 29, 1980
Wise, Isaac Mayer d. Mar 26, 1900
Wright, Frances (Fanny) d. Dec 13, 1852
Wurlitzer, Rudolph d. Jan 14, 1914
Zimmer, Don(ald William) b. Jan 17, 1931

Circleville, Ohio
Lewis, Ted b. Jun 9, 1892

Clarington, Ohio
Yost, Joseph Warren b. Jun 15, 1847

Clayton, Ohio
Haines, Jesse Joseph b. Jul 22, 1893

Cleveland, Ohio
Abdul, Raoul b. Nov 7, 1929
Allen, Leslie b. Mar 12, 1957
Ar Buthnot, May Hill d. Oct 2, 1969
Ault, George Christian b. Oct 11, 1891
Babin, Victor d. Mar 1, 1972
Backus, Jim (James Gilmore)
    b. Feb 25, 1913
Baker, Julius b. Sep 23, 1915
Ball, Ernest b. Jul 22, 1878
Ballard, Kaye b. Nov 20, 1926
Bampton, Rose Elizabeth b. Nov 28, 1909
Bee, Clair Francis d. May 20, 1983
Beutel, Bill (William Charles)
    b. Dec 12, 1930
Bolton, Frances Payne b. Mar 29, 1885
Bourjaily, Vance b. Sep 17, 1922

Brooks, William Keith b. Mar 25, 1848
Buckmaster, Henrietta, pseud. b. 1909
Cable, Mary b. Jan 24, 1920
Carmen, Eric b. Aug 11, 1949
Celeste, Richard F b. Nov 11, 1937
Chesnutt, Charles Waddell b. Jun 20, 1858
Chesnutt, Charles Waddell
   d. Nov 15, 1932
Cline, Genevieve Rose d. Oct 25, 1959
Cover, Franklin b. Nov 20, 1928
Crile, George Washington d. Jan 7, 1943
Croft, Arthur C b. May 26, 1890
Cushing, Harvey Williams b. Apr 8, 1869
Dandridge, Dorothy b. Nov 9, 1922
DaSilva, Howard b. May 4, 1909
Davis, Ernie (Ernest R) d. May 18, 1963
Dee, Ruby b. Oct 27, 1924
DeFreeze, Donald David b. Nov 16, 1943
Delahanty, Edward James b. Oct 31, 1867
Dietz, David b. Oct 6, 1897
Dietz, David d. Dec 9, 1984
Dillard, Harrison b. Jul 8, 1923
Donahue, Phil(ip John) b. Dec 21, 1935
Donaldson, Stephen Reeder
   b. May 13, 1947
Draper, Dorothy Tuckerman
   d. Mar 10, 1969
Dullea, Keir b. May 30, 1936
Eldjarn, Kristjan d. Sep 13, 1982
Ellison, Harlan Jay b. May 27, 1934
Fennell, Frederick b. Jul 2, 1914
Fish, Robert Lloyd b. Aug 21, 1912
Frank, Gerold b. 1907
Frey, Jim (James Gottfried)
   b. May 26, 1931
Garcia, Mike (Edward Miguel)
   d. Jan 13, 1986
Gilles, D(onald) B(ruce) b. Aug 30, 1947
Glaser, Donald Arthur b. Sep 21, 1926
Gold, Herbert b. Mar 9, 1924
Gordone, Charles b. Oct 12, 1925
Grey, Joel b. Apr 11, 1932
Hamilton, Margaret b. Sep 12, 1902
Harkness, Edward Stephen b. Jan 22, 1874
Hatcher, Mickey (Michael Vaughn, Jr.)
   b. Mar 15, 1955
Haydn, Hiram Collins b. Nov 3, 1907
Heisman, John William b. Oct 23, 1869
Henkle, Henrietta b. 1909
Hocking, William Ernest b. Aug 1, 1873
Holbrook, Hal (Harold Rowe, Jr.)
   b. Feb 17, 1925
Hopkins, Arthur b. Oct 4, 1878
Hopwood, Avery b. May 28, 1882
Humphrey, George Magoffin
   d. Jan 20, 1970
Hunter, Ross b. May 6, 1924
Hyatt, Joel b. May 6, 1950
Johnson, Phillip Cortelyou b. Jul 8, 1906
Joyce, Elaine b. Dec 19, 1945
Kane, Carol b. Jun 18, 1952

Kennedy, Edward Ridgway
   d. Jun 18, 1975
Kenney, Douglas C b. Dec 10, 1947
King, Don(ald) b. Dec 6, 1932
Kovel, Terry Horvitz b. Oct 27, 1928
Krol, John, Cardinal b. Oct 26, 1910
Kucinich, Dennis John b. Oct 8, 1946
Lausche, Frank John b. Nov 14, 1895
Lawrence, Jerome b. Jul 14, 1915
Lovell, Jim (James A, Jr.)
   b. Mar 25, 1928
Lynn, James Thomas b. Feb 27, 1927
Malcolm, Andrew H(ogarth)
   b. Jun 22, 1943
Mancini, Henry b. Apr 16, 1924
Marquard, "Rube" (Richard William)
   b. Oct 9, 1889
Marshall, Ken b. 1954
Martin, Freddy b. Dec 9, 1906
Masters, William Howell b. Dec 27, 1915
McCafferty, Don b. Mar 12, 1921
McPherson, Sarah Freedman b. 1894
Meredith, Burgess b. Nov 16, 1909
Metzenbaum, Howard M(orton)
   b. Jun 4, 1917
Mitchell, William Leroy b. Jul 2, 1912
Morris, Greg b. Sep 26, 1934
Ness, Eliot d. May 7, 1957
Newman, Paul b. Jan 26, 1925
Noll, Chuck (Charles H) b. Jan 5, 1932
Norton, Andre, pseud. b. Feb 17, 1912
Noyes, Blanche Wilcox b. Jun 23, 1900
O'Neill, Steve (Stephen Francis)
   d. Jan 26, 1962
Perry, Eleanor Bayer b. 1915
Presser, Jackie b. Aug 6, 1926
Priesand, Sally Jane b. Jun 27, 1946
Rhodes, James Ford b. May 1, 1848
Rich, Lee b.
Rockefeller, John D(avison), Jr.
   b. Jan 29, 1874
Rourke, Constance Mayfield
   b. Nov 14, 1885
Ruffing, "Red" (Charles Herbert)
   d. Feb 17, 1986
Sanders, Marlene b. Jan 10, 1931
Schaefer, Jack Warner b. Nov 19, 1907
Shapp, Milton J b. Jun 25, 1912
Shera, Jesse Hauk d. Mar 8, 1982
Siegel, Jerry b. Oct 17, 1914
Sill, Edward Rowland d. Feb 27, 1887
Silver, Abba Hillel d. Nov 28, 1963
Stevens, Mark b. Dec 13, 1922
Stokes, Carl Burton b. Jun 21, 1927
Stouffer, Vernon B b. Aug 22, 1901
Szell, George d. Jul 30, 1970
Tidyman, Ernest b. Jan 1, 1928
Toure, Ahmed Sekou d. Mar 26, 1984
Vanik, Charles Albert b. Apr 7, 1913
Vanocur, Sander b. Jan 8, 1928
Voinovich, George Victor b. Jul 15, 1936

Votipka, Thelma b. Dec 20, 1898
Walsh, Joe (Joseph Fidler)
   b. Nov 20, 1947
Walsh, Stella d. Dec 4, 1980
Walter, Eugene b. Nov 27, 1874
Ward, Robert Eugene b. Sep 13, 1917
Wasserman, Lew(is Robert)
   b. Mar 15, 1913
Weston, Jack b. Aug 21, 1915
Wick, Charles Z b. Oct 12, 1917
Wilbur, Cornelia Burwell b. Aug 26, 1908
Willard, Archibald MacNeal
   d. Oct 11, 1918
Williams, Edward Porter b. May 10, 1843
Winger, Debra b. May 17, 1955
Winpisinger, William Wayne
   b. Dec 10, 1924

CLeveland, Ohio
Woolsey, Sarah Chauncey b. Jan 29, 1835

Cleveland Heights, Ohio
Hyland, Diana b. Jan 25, 1936

Clifton, Ohio
Funk, Isaac Kauffman b. Sep 10, 1839
Hayes, "Woody" (Wayne Woodrow)
   b. Feb 14, 1913

Clinton, Ohio
Emmett, Daniel Decatur b. Oct 29, 1815

Coalton, Ohio
Jones, Isham b. Jan 31, 1894

Columbus, Ohio
Baxter, Warner b. Mar 29, 1891
Bellows, George Wesley b. Aug 12, 1882
Bricker, John William d. Mar 22, 1986
Bromfield, Louis Brucker d. Mar 18, 1956
Buck, Paul Herman b. Sep 25, 1899
Carr, Joseph F b. Oct 22, 1880
Cole, "Cozy" (William Randolph)
   d. Jan 29, 1981
Coulter, Ernest Kent b. Nov 14, 1871
D'Angelo, Beverly b. 1952
Eisele, Donn Fulton b. Jun 23, 1930
Firestone, Harvey Samuel b. Dec 20, 1868
Frings, "Ketti" b. Feb 28, 1915
Goodman, Dody b. Oct 28, 1929
Gowdy, Hank (Henry Morgan)
   b. Aug 24, 1889
Gowdy, Hank (Henry Morgan)
   d. Aug 1, 1966
Greene, Bob (Robert Bernard, Jr.)
   b. Mar 10, 1947
Griffin, Archie b. Aug 21, 1954
Heckart, Eileen b. Mar 29, 1919
Howard, Frank Oliver b. Aug 8, 1936
Janis, Elsie b. Mar 16, 1889
Kauff, Benny (Benjamin Michael)
   d. Nov 17, 1961
LeMay, Curtis Emerson b. Nov 15, 1906
Licavoli, Thomas d. Sep 16, 1973
McDowell, Irvin b. Oct 15, 1818
McKenney, Ruth d. Jun 25, 1972
Mitchell, Grant b. Jun 17, 1875

Nicklaus, Jack b. Jan 21, 1940
Poston, Tom b. Oct 17, 1927
Rickenbacker, Eddie (Edward Vernon)
   b. Oct 8, 1890
Ryder, James Arthur b. Jul 28, 1913
Schlesinger, Arthur Meier, Jr.
   b. Oct 15, 1917
Sheppard, Eugenia Benbow b. 1910
Sheppard, Sam(uel) d. Apr 6, 1970
Smith, Roger Bonham b. Jul 12, 1925
Stewart, Donald Ogden b. Nov 30, 1894
Thurber, James Grover b. Dec 8, 1894
Thurston, Howard b. Jul 20, 1869

Columbus Grove, Ohio
Jagger, Dean b. Nov 7, 1903

Conneaut, Ohio
Berry, "Chu" (Leon)
   d. Oct 31, 1941

Coshocton, Ohio
Brenley, Bob (Robert Earl)
   b. Feb 25, 1954
Green, William b. Mar 3, 1873
Green, William d. Nov 21, 1952

Crestline, Ohio
Morgan, Marabel b. Jun 25, 1937

Cuyahoga County, Ohio
Garfield, James Abram b. Nov 19, 1831

Dalton, Ohio
Harkness, Anna M Richardson
   b. Oct 25, 1837

Darke County, Ohio
Oakley, Annie b. Aug 13, 1860

Dayton, Ohio
Babbitt, Irving b. Aug 2, 1865
Barney, Natalie Clifford b. Oct 31, 1876
Battelle, Phyllis Marie b. Jan 4, 1922
Bombeck, Erma Louise b. Feb 21, 1927
Bryan, William Jennings d. Jul 26, 1925
Clemens, Roger (William Roger)
   b. Aug 4, 1962
Cook, Greg(ory Lynn) b. Nov 20, 1946
Cox, James Middleton, Jr. b. Jun 27, 1903
Cox, James Middleton, Sr. d. Jul 15, 1957
Crook, George b. Sep 23, 1829
Daniels, Frank b. 1860
Dickman, Joseph Theodore b. Oct 6, 1857
Dunbar, Paul Laurence b. Jun 27, 1872
Dunbar, Paul Laurence d. Feb 9, 1906
Faust, Gerry (Gerard Anthony, Jr.)
   b. May 21, 1935
Gish, Dorothy b. Mar 11, 1898
Guisewite, Cathy Lee b. Sep 5, 1950
Haines, Jesse Joseph d. Aug 5, 1978
Jump, Gordon b. Apr 1, 1927
Kettering, Charles Franklin
   d. Nov 25, 1958
Knebel, Fletcher b. Oct 1, 1911
Maier, Henry W b. Dec 7, 1918
Mead, George Houk b. Nov 5, 1877
Mead, George Houk d. Jan 1, 1963
Moses, Edwin b. Aug 31, 1955

Sandy, Gary b. Dec 25, 1946
Schmidt, Mike (Michael Jack)
　b. Sep 27, 1949
Sheen, Martin b. Aug 3, 1940
Strayhorn, Billy (William) b. Nov 29, 1915
Watson, Thomas John, Jr. b. Jan 8, 1914
Winters, Jonathan b. Nov 11, 1925
Wright, Orville b. Aug 19, 1871
Wright, Orville d. Jan 30, 1948
Wright, Wilbur d. May 30, 1912

Deerfield, Ohio
Laughlin, James Laurence b. Apr 2, 1850

Defiance, Ohio
Davison, William b. Jan 5, 1906
Duerk, Alene B b. Mar 29, 1920
Miller, Don b.

Delaware, Ohio
Hayes, Rutherford B(irchard)
　b. Oct 4, 1822
Rodgers, Bob (Robert Leroy)
　b. Aug 16, 1938

Delaware County, Ohio
Rosecrans, William Starke b. Sep 6, 1819

Dover, Ohio
Nugent, Elliott b. Sep 20, 1899
White, Stan(ley Ray) b. Oct 24, 1949

Dover Centre, Ohio
Miner, Jack (John Thomas)
　b. Apr 10, 1865

East Liverpool, Ohio
Blythe, David Gilmour b. May 9, 1815
Blythe, David Gilmour d. May 15, 1865
Floyd, "Pretty Boy" (Charles Arthur)
　d. Oct 22, 1934
Thompson, Josiah b. Jan 17, 1935

Euclid, Ohio
Adamle, Mike (Michael David)
　b. Oct 4, 1949

Fairview Park, Ohio
Cousineau, Tom b. May 16, 1957

Findlay, Ohio
Crouse, Russel b. Feb 20, 1893
Guyer, Tennyson b. Nov 29, 1913
Miller, Marilyn b. Sep 1, 1898
Ricketts, Howard T b. 1871

Franklin, Ohio
Evans, Bergen Baldwin b. Sep 19, 1904
Schenck, Robert Cumming b. Oct 4, 1809

Fremont, Ohio
Hayes, Lucy Webb d. Jun 25, 1889
Hayes, Rutherford B(irchard)
　d. Jan 17, 1893

Galloway, Ohio
Power, Donald Clinton d. Mar 11, 1979

Gambier, Ohio
Ransom, John Crowe d. Jul 5, 1974

Gano, Ohio
Howard, Roy Wilson b. Jan 1, 1883

Garfield Heights, Ohio
Wambsganss, Bill (William Adolph)
　b. Mar 19, 1894

Garrettsville, Ohio
Crane, Hart b. Jul 21, 1899

Geneva, Ohio
Olds, Ranson E(li) b. Jun 3, 1864

Gilmore, Ohio
Young, "Cy" (Denton True)
　b. Mar 29, 1867

Glendale, Ohio
McCulley, Johnston d. Nov 23, 1958
Procter, William Cooper b. Aug 25, 1862

Glenville, Ohio
Williams, Edward Porter d. May 4, 1903

Grand River, Ohio
Shula, Don Francis b. Jan 4, 1930

Green Creek, Ohio
McPherson, James Birdseye
　b. Nov 14, 1828

Greenfield, Ohio
Hull, John Edwin b. May 26, 1895
Paycheck, Johnny b. May 31, 1941

Greensburg, Ohio
Ball, Edmund B b. Oct 21, 1855
Ball, Frank b. Nov 24, 1857

Greenville, Ohio
Norris, Paul b. Apr 26, 1914
Oakley, Annie d. Nov 2, 1926

Hamilton, Ohio
DeLeeuw, Adele Louise b. Aug 12, 1899
Hurst, Fannie b. Oct 19, 1889
Liebman, Joshua Loth b. Apr 7, 1907
McCloskey, Robert b. Sep 15, 1914
Richter, Charles Francis b. Apr 26, 1900

Hancock County, Ohio
Campbell, William Wallace
　b. Apr 11, 1862

Highland County, Ohio
Beveridge, Albert Jeremiah b. Oct 6, 1862

Hillsboro, Ohio
Caniff, Milt(on Arthur) b. Feb 28, 1907

Hiram, Ohio
Garfield, Lucretia Rudolph
　b. Apr 19, 1832

Hoaglands, Ohio
Ewing, "Buck" (William) b. Oct 27, 1859

Holgate, Ohio
Brown, Joe Evan b. Jul 28, 1892

Hollansburg, Ohio
Commons, John Rogers b. Oct 13, 1862

Homer, Ohio
Woodhull, Victoria Claflin b. Sep 23, 1838

Ironton, Ohio
Rea, Gardner b. Aug 12, 1892
Stuart, Jesse Hilton d. Feb 17, 1984

Jackson, Ohio
Rhodes, James Allen b. Sep 13, 1909

Jacksonburg, Ohio
Cox, James Middleton, Sr.
　b. Mar 31, 1870

Jeffersonville, Ohio
Kirk, Grayson Louis b. Oct 12, 1903

Johnston, Ohio
Ashbrook, John Milan b. Sep 21, 1928
Kinsman, Ohio
Darrow, Clarence Seward b. Apr 18, 1857
Knox County, Ohio
Bickerdyke, Mary Ann Ball
    b. Jul 19, 1817
Lakewood, Ohio
Graebner, Clark b. Nov 4, 1943
Kaye, Sammy b. Mar 13, 1913
Schullian, Dorothy May b. May 19, 1906
Stouffer, Vernon B d. Jul 26, 1974
Wambsganss, Bill (William Adolph)
    d. Dec 8, 1985
Lancaster, Ohio
Outcault, Richard Felton b. Jan 14, 1863
Sherman, William Tecumseh
    b. Feb 8, 1820
Lebanon, Ohio
Hesseman, Howard b. Feb 27, 1940
Wright, Russel b. Apr 3, 1904
Licking Co., Ohio
Creighton, Edward b. Aug 31, 1820
Lima, Ohio
Diller, Phyllis b. Jul 17, 1917
Jardine, Al(lan) b. Sep 3, 1942
Jones, Weyman b. Feb 6, 1928
O'Connell, Helen b. May 23, 1921
Lithopolis, Ohio
Wagnalls, Adam Willis b. Sep 24, 1843
Liverpool, Ohio
Quad, M, pseud. b. Feb 15, 1842
Logan, Ohio
Harrigan, Edward b. Jul 27, 1844
Lorain, Ohio
Brasselle, Keefe b. Feb 7, 1923
Dohanos, Stevan b. May 18, 1907
Freedman, Gerald b. Jun 25, 1927
Hanley, William b. Oct 22, 1931
King, Ernest Joseph b. Nov 23, 1878
Morrison, Toni b. Feb 18, 1931
Overmyer, Robert F b. Jul 14, 1936
Ward, Paul W b. Oct 9, 1905
Lorraine County, Ohio
Leonard, "Dutch" (Hubert Benjamin)
    b. Jul 26, 1892
Loudonville, Ohio
Kettering, Charles Franklin
    b. Aug 29, 1876
Lyndhurst, Ohio
Bolton, Frances Payne d. Mar 9, 1977
Madison, Ohio
Opper, Frederick Burr b. Jan 2, 1857
Madison County, Ohio
Bricker, John William b. Sep 6, 1893
Byers, William Newton b. Feb 22, 1831
Magnolia, Ohio
Abel, I(orwith) W(ilbur) b. Aug 11, 1908
Manchester, Ohio
Sisler, George Harold b. Mar 24, 1893

Manhattan, Ohio
Lawton, Henry Ware b. Mar 17, 1843
Mansfield, Ohio
Bromfield, Louis Brucker b. Dec 27, 1896
Mantua, Ohio
Lambert, Jack (John Harold)
    b. Jul 8, 1952
Skinner, Halcyon b. Mar 6, 1824
Skinner, Halcyon d. Nov 28, 1900
Marietta, Ohio
Bosworth, Hobart van Zandt
    b. Aug 11, 1867
Cisler, Walker Lee b. Oct 8, 1897
Dawes, Charles Gates b. Aug 27, 1865
Maxon, Lou Russell b. Jul 28, 1900
Marion, Ohio
Harding, Florence Kling De Wolfe
    b. Aug 15, 1860
Harding, Florence Kling De Wolfe
    d. Nov 21, 1924
Thomas, Norman Mattoon
    b. Nov 20, 1884
Martins Ferry, Ohio
Groza, Alex b. Oct 7, 1926
Havlicek, John b. Apr 8, 1940
Howells, William Dean b. Mar 1, 1837
Peterson, Clarence b. Jul 14, 1904
Wright, James Arlington b. Dec 13, 1927
Martinsville, Ohio
Dwiggins, William Addison
    b. Jun 19, 1880
Massillon, Ohio
Coxey, Jacob Sechler d. May 18, 1951
Henrich, Tommy (Thomas David)
    b. Feb 20, 1913
Stuhldreher, Harry A b. Oct 14, 1901
Weiskopf, Tom Daniel b. Nov 9, 1942
Maumee, Ohio
Saunders, Allen d. Jan 28, 1985
Scott, Austin b. Aug 10, 1848
Mechanicsburg, Ohio
Saxbe, William Bart b. Jun 25, 1916
Meigs County, Ohio
Bierce, Ambrose Gwinett b. Jun 24, 1842
Mentor, Ohio
Wellman, Walter b. Nov 3, 1858
Middletown, Ohio
Butterfield, Billy b. Jan 14, 1917
Clevenger, Shobal Vail b. Oct 22, 1812
Lucas, Jerry b. Mar 30, 1940
Milan, Ohio
Edison, Thomas Alva b. Feb 11, 1847
Millville, Ohio
Landis, Kenesaw Mountain
    b. Nov 20, 1866
Minerva, Ohio
Wilson, Charles Erwin b. Jul 18, 1890
Mingo Junction, Ohio
Wilson, Harry E b. Aug 6, 1902
Montgomery, Ohio
Bobbs, William Conrad b. Jan 25, 1861

Montpelier, Ohio
Siple, Paul Allman b. Dec 18, 1908
Morgan County, Ohio
Christy, Howard Chandler b. Jan 10, 1873
Mount Holmes, Ohio
Perky, Henry D b. Dec 7, 1843
Mount Vernon, Ohio
Lynde, Paul Edward b. Jun 13, 1926
Sockman, Ralph W b. Oct 1, 1889
Murray City, Ohio
Carlson, "Doc" (Harold Clifford)
   b. Jul 4, 1894
New Carlisle, Ohio
Funston, Frederick b. Nov 9, 1865
New Concord, Ohio
Harper, William Rainey b. Jul 26, 1846
New Knoxville, Ohio
Wierwille, Victor Paul b. Dec 31, 1916
New Lisbon, Ohio
Hanna, Mark (Marcus Alonzo)
   b. Sep 24, 1837
New Rumley, Ohio
Custer, George Armstrong b. Dec 5, 1839
New Salem, Ohio
Peters, Frederick Emerson b. 1885
Newark, Ohio
Ashbrook, John Milan d. Apr 24, 1982
Niles, Ohio
McKinley, William b. Jan 29, 1843
Patchen, Kenneth b. Dec 13, 1911
North Bend, Ohio
Harrison, Anna Tuthill Symmes
   d. Feb 25, 1864
Harrison, Benjamin b. Aug 20, 1833
Northfield, Ohio
Eaton, Cyrus Stephen d. May 9, 1979
Norwalk, Ohio
Brown, Paul b. Jul 9, 1908
Grove, "Lefty" (Robert Moses)
   d. May 22, 1975
Johnson, (Byron) Ban(croft) b. Jan 8, 1864
Trendle, George Washington b. Jul 4, 1884
Norwood, Ohio
Chakiris, George b. Sep 16, 1934
Rule, Janice b. Aug 15, 1931
Oberlin, Ohio
Finney, Charles Grandison
   d. Aug 16, 1875
Oldtown, Ohio
Tecumseh b. Mar 1768
Orrville, Ohio
Knight, Bobby (Robert Montgomery)
   b. Oct 25, 1940
Sedelmaier, Joe (John Josef)
   b. May 31, 1933
Oxford, Ohio
Alston, Walter Emmons d. Oct 1, 1984
Harrison, Caroline Lavinia Scott
   b. Oct 1, 1832
Shera, Jesse Hauk b. Dec 8, 1903

Pagetown, Ohio
Fillmore, Myrtle Page b. Aug 6, 1845
Paine Station, Ohio
Power, Donald Clinton b. Dec 25, 1899
Painesville, Ohio
Harrar, J(acob) George b. Dec 2, 1906
Ladd, George Trumbull b. Jan 19, 1842
Parma, Ohio
Boiardi, Hector d. Jun 21, 1985
Peoli, Ohio
Young, "Cy" (Denton True)
   d. Nov 4, 1955
Pigeon Run, Ohio
Fairless, Benjamin F b. May 3, 1890
Piqua, Ohio
Mills, Donald b. Apr 29, 1915
Mills, Harry b. Aug 19, 1913
Mills, Herbert b. Apr 2, 1912
Plain City, Ohio
Barlow, Howard b. May 1, 1892
Point Pleasant, Ohio
Grant, Ulysses S(impson) b. Apr 27, 1822
Pomeroy, Ohio
Kauff, Benny (Benjamin Michael)
   b. Jan 5, 1890
Port Clinton, Ohio
Sowerby, Leo d. Jul 7, 1968
Ravenna, Ohio
Blum, Stella d. Jul 31, 1985
Day, William Rufus b. Apr 17, 1849
Rittman, Ohio
Strawser, Neil Edward b. Aug 16, 1927
Rockford, Ohio
Wilson, Earl b. May 3, 1907
Rocky River, Ohio
Steinbrenner, George Michael, III
   b. Jul 4, 1930
Saint Henry, Ohio
Post, Wally (Walter Charles)
   d. Jan 7, 1982
Saint Wendelin, Ohio
Post, Wally (Walter Charles)
   b. Jul 9, 1929
Salem, Ohio
Bryan, William Jennings b. Mar 19, 1860
Sandusky, Ohio
Cooke, Jay b. Aug 10, 1821
Frohman, Charles b. Jun 17, 1860
Frohman, Daniel b. Aug 22, 1851
Norris, George William b. Jul 11, 1861
Sandy Springs, Ohio
Wittenmyer, Annie Turner
   b. Aug 26, 1827
Sebring, Ohio
Woods, Rose Mary b. Dec 26, 1917
Shandon, Ohio
Shaw, Albert b. Jul 23, 1857
Shoshone, Ohio
Jennings, Talbot b. 1895
South Dayton, Ohio
Bergey, Bill b. Feb 9, 1945

Springfield, Ohio
Abbott, Berenice b. Jul 17, 1898
Boyer, Harold R b. Feb 25, 1899
Burnett, W(illiam) R(iley) b. Nov 25, 1899
Clark, Bobby b. Jun 16, 1888
Embry, Wayne b. Mar 26, 1937
Gish, Lillian Diana b. Oct 14, 1896
Lenski, Lois b. Oct 14, 1893
McCullough, Paul b. 1883
Renick, Marion Lewis b. Mar 9, 1905

Steubenville, Ohio
Fingers, Rollie (Roland Glen)
  b. Aug 25, 1946
Hunter, Dard b. Nov 29, 1883
Jimmy the Greek b. Sep 9, 1919
Martin, Dean b. Jun 17, 1917
Mosel, Tad b. May 1, 1922
Scarne, John b. Mar 4, 1903
Stanton, Edwin McMasters
  b. Dec 19, 1814

Stewartsville, Ohio
Jones, "Toothpick" (Samuel)
  b. Dec 14, 1925

Stockdale, Ohio
Rickey, Branch (Wesley Branch)
  b. Dec 20, 1881

Sugar Ridge, Ohio
Evans, Bob (Robert L) b. Mar 30, 1918

Tallmadge, Ohio
Bacon, Delia Salter b. Feb 2, 1811

Tappan, Ohio
Akeley, Mary Lee Jobe b. Jan 29, 1878

Thompson, Ohio
Hall, Charles Martin b. Dec 6, 1863

Tiffin, Ohio
Quinn, John b. Apr 24, 1870

Toledo, Ohio
Arquette, Cliff b. Dec 28, 1905
Ashley, Thomas William Ludlow
  b. Jan 11, 1923
Brady, Pat (Robert Patrick)
  b. Dec 31, 1914
Bresnaham, Roger Phillip b. Jun 11, 1879
Bresnaham, Roger Phillip d. Dec 4, 1944
Brewer, Theresa b. May 7, 1931
Cooke, Janet b. 1954
Cromwell, John b. Dec 23, 1887
Cummings, "Candy" (William Arthur)
  d. May 17, 1924
Dederich, Charles Edwin b. Mar 22, 1913
Farr, Jamie b. Jul 1, 1934
Gallo, Frank b. Jan 13, 1933
Gemmill, Henry b. Jun 11, 1917
Goldner, Orville b. May 18, 1906
Gordon, Steve b. 1940
Harsch, Joseph Close b. May 25, 1905
Joss, "Addie" (Adrian) d. Apr 14, 1911
Koch, John b. Aug 16, 1909
Kruger, Otto b. Sep 6, 1885
LaRose, Rose d. Jul 27, 1972

Leyland, Jim (James Richard)
  b. Dec 15, 1944
Locke, David Ross d. Feb 15, 1888
Loper, Don b. 1906
Owens, Michael Joseph d. Dec 27, 1923
Rider-Kelsey, Corinne d. Jul 10, 1947
Scholz, Tom b. Mar 10, 1947
Shriner, Herb b. May 29, 1918
Steinem, Gloria b. Mar 25, 1935
Tatum, Art(hur) b. Oct 13, 1910

Troy, Ohio
Lanston, Tolbert b. Feb 3, 1844

Tuppers Plains, Ohio
Ritchey, George Willis b. Dec 31, 1864

Unionville Center, Ohio
Fairbanks, Charles Warren
  b. May 11, 1852

Urbana, Ohio
Eichelberger, Robert Lawrence
  b. Mar 9, 1886
Whitlock, Brand b. Mar 4, 1869

Van Wert, Ohio
Boole, Ella Alexander b. Jul 26, 1858
Kemper, James S(cott) b. Nov 18, 1886

Venice, Ohio
Alston, Walter Emmons b. Dec 1, 1911

Waite Hill, Ohio
Allen, Florence Ellinwood d. Sep 12, 1966

Wapakoneta, Ohio
Armstrong, Neil Alden b. Aug 5, 1930

Warren, Ohio
Bach, Catherine b. Mar 1, 1954
Biggers, Earl Derr b. Aug 26, 1884
Browner, Ross b. Mar 22, 1954
Cline, Genevieve Rose b. Jul 27, 1878
Cox, Kenyon b. Oct 27, 1856
Gradishar, Randy Charles b. Mar 3, 1952
Lynd, Helen Merrell d. Jan 30, 1982
Warfield, Paul Dryden b. Nov 28, 1942

Washington Court House, Ohio
Schlicter, Art(hur E) b. Apr 25, 1960

Wauseon, Ohio
Oldfield, Barney (Berna Eli)
  b. Jan 29, 1878

Wayne, Ohio
Chance, (Wilmer) Dean b. Jun 1, 1941

Waynesville, Ohio
Evans, John b. Mar 9, 1814

West Milton, Ohio
Coffin, Howard Earle b. Sep 6, 1873

Western Star, Ohio
Seiberling, Frank Augustus b. Oct 6, 1859

Willoughby, Ohio
Conway, "Tim" (Thomas Daniel)
  b. Dec 13, 1933
Sherwin, Henry Alden d. Jun 26, 1916

Wilmington, Ohio
Janney, Russell Dixon b. Apr 14, 1885

Winona, Ohio
Binns, Joseph Patterson b. Jun 28, 1905

Woodington, Ohio
Thomas, Lowell Jackson b. Apr 6, 1892
Wooster, Ohio
Compton, Arthur Holly b. Sep 10, 1892
Compton, Karl Taylor b. Sep 14, 1887
Compton, Wilson Martindale
b. Oct 15, 1890
Nimmons, George Croll b. Jul 8, 1865
Xenia, Ohio
Chenoweth, Dean b. 1934
Grapewin, Charley (Charles)
b. Dec 20, 1875
Hyslop, James Hervey b. Aug 18, 1854
Morgan, Arthur d. Nov 12, 1975
Reid, Whitelaw b. Oct 27, 1837
Santmyer, Helen Hooven b. Nov 25, 1895
Santmyer, Helen Hooven d. Feb 21, 1986
Torrence, Ridgley (Frederick Rridgley)
b. 1875
Yellow Springs, Ohio
Furay, Richie b. May 9, 1944
Hamilton, Virginia b. Mar 13, 1936
Mann, Horace d. Aug 2, 1859
Youngstown, Ohio
Bell, "Kool" (Robert) b. Oct 8, 1950
Bell, Ronald b. Nov 1, 1951
Bilon, Michael Patrick b. 1947
Bilon, Michael Patrick d. Jan 27, 1983
Christopher, Jordan b. 1941
DeBartolo, Edward J, Jr. b. Nov 6, 1946
Flynn, Joe (Joseph Anthony)
b. Nov 8, 1925
Kemp, (Harry) Hibbard b. Dec 15, 1883
Laeri, J(ohn) Howard b. Mar 22, 1906
Laffer, Arthur Betz b. Aug 14, 1940
Mancini, Ray b. Mar 4, 1961
McGovern, Maureen Therese
b. Jul 27, 1949
Wells, Mary b. 1928
Zanesville, Ohio
Basehart, Richard b. Aug 31, 1914
Gilbert, Cass b. Nov 24, 1859
Grey, Zane b. Jan 31, 1875
Hendricks, Thomas Andrews
b. Sep 7, 1819
Jackson, Margaret E b. Sep 2, 1928
Untermeyer, Jean Starr b. Mar 13, 1886

OKLAHOMA

Cody, Iron Eyes b. Apr 3, 1915
Hall, Joseph M b. 1950
Hurley, Patrick Jay b. Jan 8, 1883
Kupke, Frederick Lee b. 1948
Owen, Steve (Stephen Joseph)
b. Apr 21, 1898
Ada, Oklahoma
Edwards, Douglas b. Jul 14, 1917
Kerr, Robert Samuel b. Sep 11, 1896
Roberts, Oral b. Jan 24, 1918

Akins, Oklahoma
Floyd, "Pretty Boy" (Charles Arthur)
b. 1904
Anadarko, Oklahoma
Bosin, Blackbear b. Jun 5, 1921
Ardmore, Oklahoma
Gastineau, Mark (Marcus D)
b. Nov 20, 1956
Hinckley, John Warnock, Jr.
b. May 29, 1955
Barnsdale, Oklahoma
Bryant, Anita b. Mar 25, 1940
Beggs, Oklahoma
Rowan, Dan b. Jul 2, 1922
Blaine City, Oklahoma
Chisholm, Jesse d. Mar 4, 1868
Boise City, Oklahoma
Miles, Vera b. Aug 23, 1930
Briartown, Oklahoma
Starr, Belle Shirley d. Feb 3, 1889
Broken Arrow, Oklahoma
O'Brien, George d. Sep 4, 1985
Broken Bow, Oklahoma
Brecheen, Harry David b. Oct 14, 1914
Checotah, Oklahoma
Lucas, Jim Griffing b. Jun 22, 1914
Chicasha, Oklahoma
Moody, Orville b. Dec 9, 1933
Chickasha, Oklahoma
Little, Cleavon Jake b. Jun 1, 1939
Claremore, Oklahoma
Riggs, Lynn b. Aug 31, 1899
Clarence, Oklahoma
Page, Patti b. Nov 8, 1927
Comanche, Oklahoma
Dark, Alvin Ralph b. Jan 7, 1923
Doughtery, Oklahoma
Starr, Kay b. Jul 21, 1924
Duncan, Oklahoma
Axton, Hoyt Wayne b. Mar 25, 1938
Howard, Ron b. Mar 1, 1954
Kirkpatrick, Jeane Duane Jordan
b. Nov 19, 1926
Earlsboro, Oklahoma
McFarland, Ernest William b. Oct 9, 1894
Stargell, Willie (Wilver Dornel)
b. Mar 4, 1941
El Reno, Oklahoma
Rhodes, Erik b. Feb 10, 1906
Elk City, Oklahoma
Webb, Jim b. Aug 15, 1946
Enid, Oklahoma
Billingsley, Sherman b. Mar 10, 1900
Burch, Dean b. Dec 20, 1927
Farrell, Glenda b. Jun 30, 1904
Garriott, Owen b. Nov 22, 1930
Wellman, Paul Iselin b. Oct 14, 1898
Erick, Oklahoma
Wooley, Sheb b. Apr 10, 1921
Eufaula, Oklahoma
Selmon, Lee Roy b. Oct 20, 1954

Fairfax, Oklahoma
Tallchief, Maria b. Jan 24, 1925
Fort Sill, Oklahoma
Geronimo d. Feb 17, 1909
Harris, William b. Jan 22, 1945
Quanah d. Feb 23, 1911
Fort Towson, Oklahoma
Reed, Ed b. Dec 13, 1907
Gore, Oklahoma
Owens, Steve b. Dec 9, 1947
Guthrie, Oklahoma
Covey, Cyclone b. May 21, 1922
Guyman, Oklahoma
Welch, Larry Dean b. Jun 9, 1934
Harrah, Oklahoma
Waner, Lloyd James b. Mar 16, 1906
Waner, Paul Glee b. Apr 16, 1903
Haworth, Oklahoma
Bolt, Tommy (Thomas) b. Mar 31, 1918
Healdton, Oklahoma
McClanahan, (Eddi-)Rue b. Feb 21,
Hickory, Oklahoma
Mosley, Oswald Ernald, Sir
 b. Dec 12, 1896
Mosley, Zack Terrell b. Dec 12, 1906
Hobart, Oklahoma
Wayne, Paula b. Nov 3, 1937
Holdenville, Oklahoma
Gulager, Clu b. Nov 16, 1928
Pickens, T(homas) Boone, (Jr.)
 b. May 22, 1928
Hugo, Oklahoma
Cleaver, William Joseph (Bill)
 b. Mar 20, 1920
Ling, James J b. 1922
Moyers, Bill (William Don) b. Jun 5, 1934
Kingfisher, Oklahoma
Blanding, Don b. Nov 7, 1894
Walton, Sam Moore b. Mar 29, 1918
Lawton, Oklahoma
Russell, Leon b. Apr 2, 1941
Leedey, Oklahoma
Hood, Darla Jean b. Nov 4, 1931
Lincoln County, Oklahoma
Harris, Roy Ellsworth b. Feb 12, 1898
Loyal, Oklahoma
Brazle, Al(pha Eugene) b. Oct 19, 1914
Mannford, Oklahoma
Hazelwood, Lee b. Jul 9, 1929
Marshall, Oklahoma
Beebe, Burdetta Faye b. Feb 4, 1920
McAlester, Oklahoma
Albert, Carl Bert b. May 10, 1908
Berryman, John b. Oct 25, 1914
Martin, "Pepper" (John Leonard Roosevelt)
 d. Mar 5, 1965
Muskogee, Oklahoma
Askew, Reubin O'Donovan b. Sep 11, 1928
Jones, James Robert b. May 5, 1939
Lewis, Ed d. Sep 7, 1966

Newkirk, Oklahoma
Fisher, Carl b. Nov 21, 1911
Norman, Oklahoma
Cobb, Jerrie b. Mar 5, 1931
Garner, James b. Apr 7, 1928
Okemah, Oklahoma
Guthrie, Woody (Woodrow Wilson)
 b. Jul 14, 1912
Pogue, William R(eid) b. Jan 23, 1930
Oklahoma City, Oklahoma
Allbritton, Louise b. Jul 3, 1920
Avery, R Stanton b. 1907
Bee, Molly b. Aug 18, 1939
Bench, Johnny Lee b. Dec 7, 1947
Bernstein, Jay b. Jun 7, 1937
Boone, Ron b. Sep 6, 1946
Brough, Louise Althea b. Mar 11, 1923
Cale, J J b. Dec 5, 1938
Chaney, Lon, Jr. (Creighton)
 b. Feb 10, 1905
Cochran, Eddie b. Oct 3, 1938
Cosgrove, Gordon Dean b. Mar 2, 1934
Ellison, Ralph Waldo b. Mar 1, 1914
Francis, Kay b. Jan 13, 1903
Frederickson, H Gray b. Jul 21, 1937
Goldman, Sylvan N d. Nov 25, 1984
Hall, David b. Oct 20, 1930
Hampton, James b. Jul 9, 1936
Hudson, Rochelle b. Mar 6, 1915
Jarman, John d. Jan 15, 1982
Kilpatrick, James J(ackson) b. Nov 1, 1920
Mesta, Perle Skirvin d. Mar 16, 1975
Monroney, Mike (Aimer Stillwell)
 b. Mar 2, 1902
Murcer, Bobby Ray b. May 20, 1946
O'Grady, Sean b. Feb 10, 1959
Pike, James Albert b. Feb 14, 1913
Robertson, Dale b. Jul 14, 1923
Rogell, Albert S b. Aug 21, 1901
Rushing, Jimmy b. Aug 26, 1903
Shackelford, Ted b. Jun 23, 1946
Silkwood, Karen d. Nov 13, 1974
Tiffin, Pamela Kimberley b. Oct 13, 1942
Waner, Lloyd James d. Jul 22, 1982
Wyler, Gretchen b. Feb 16, 1932
Okmulgee, Oklahoma
Pettiford, Oscar b. Sep 30, 1922
Oologah, Oklahoma
Rogers, Will(iam Penn Adair)
 b. Sep 5, 1879
Park Hill, Oklahoma
Travis, Merle d. Oct 20, 1983
Pawhuska, Oklahoma
Johnson, Ben b. Jun 13, 1918
Pawnee, Oklahoma
Gould, Chester b. Nov 20, 1900
Lillie, Gordon William d. Feb 3, 1942
Wrightsman, Charles Bierer
 b. Jun 13, 1895

Pendleton, Oregon
Kingman, Dave (David Arthur)
   b. Dec 21, 1948
Lappe, Francis Moore b. Feb 10, 1944
Steele, Bob b. Jan 23, 1906

Portland, Oregon
Barlow, Howard d. Jan 31, 1972
Bates, Blanche Lyon b. Aug 25, 1873
Beard, James Andrews b. May 5, 1903
Bloch, Ernest d. Jul 15, 1959
Braly, Malcolm b. Jul 16, 1925
Coffin, Charles Albert d. Nov 9, 1926
Cook, Donald b. Sep 26, 1901
Cunningham, Imogen b. Apr 12, 1883
Diebenkorn, Richard b. Apr 22, 1922
Dolby, Ray Milton b. Jan 18, 1933
Gaddis, Thomas (Eugene) d. Oct 10, 1984
Gallen, Hugh J b. Jul 30, 1924
Ghormley, Robert Lee b. Oct 15, 1883
Hemingway, Margaux b. Feb 1955
Holbrook, Stewart Hall d. Sep 3, 1964
Johnson, "Dink" (Oliver) d. Nov 29, 1954
Knight, Phil(ip H) b. Feb 24, 1938
Lampman, Evelyn Sibley d. Jun 13, 1980
Leahy, Frank d. Jun 21, 1973
Lolich, Mickey (Michael Stephen)
   b. Sep 12, 1940
Lomax, Neil Vincent b. Feb 17, 1959
McCall, Thomas Lawson d. Jan 8, 1983
Mitchell, Chad (William Chad bourne)
   b. Dec 5, 1936
Morse, Wayne Lyman d. Jul 22, 1974
Munson, Ona b. Jun 16, 1906
Murphy, Dale Bryan b. Mar 12, 1956
Musburger, Brent Woody b. May 26, 1939
Packwood, Bob (Robert William)
   b. Sep 11, 1932
Pauling, Linus Carl b. Feb 28, 1901
Poling, Daniel A b. Nov 30, 1884
Powell, Jane b. Apr 1, 1928
Robinson, Claude Everett b. Mar 22, 1900
Schroeder, Patricia Scott b. Jul 30, 1940
Schwatka, Frederik d. Nov 2, 1892
Scott, Gordon b. Aug 3, 1927
Shannon, Willie b. 1952
Simon, Norton b. Feb 5, 1907
Struthers, Sally Anne b. Jul 28, 1948
U'Ren, William Simon d. Mar 8, 1949
Yeon, John b. 1910

Roseburg, Oregon
Kennerly, David Hume b. Mar 9, 1947

Salem, Oregon
Gilbert, A(lfred) C(arleton)
   b. Feb 15, 1884
Gill, Amory Tingle b. May 1, 1901
McNary, Charles Linza b. Jun 12, 1874

Seaside, Oregon
Lunceford, Jimmy (James Melvin)
   d. Jul 13, 1947
Pennell, Joseph Stanley d. Sep 26, 1963

Silverton, Oregon
Davenport, Homer Calvin b. Mar 8, 1867
Toledo, Oregon
Osborne, Leone Neal b. Sep 25, 1914
Turner, Oregon
Cromwell, Dean Bartlett b. Sep 20, 1879
Yoncalla, Oregon
Davis, Harold Lenoir b. Oct 18, 1896

PENNSYLVANIA

Armstrong, Thomas M b. 1836
Fuisz, Robert E b. Oct 15, 1934
Heiser, Victor George b. Feb 5, 1873
Long, John Luther b. Jan 1, 1861
Metrinko, Michael John b. Nov 11, 1946
Royer, William Blackburn, Jr.
   b. Oct 21, 1931
Twelvetrees, Helen d. Feb 14, 1958
Aliquippa, Pennsylvania
Dorsett, Tony (Anthony Drew)
   b. Apr 7, 1954
Maneloveg, Herbert Donald
   b. Jan 25, 1925
Maravich, Pete b. Jun 28, 1948
Allegheny, Pennsylvania
Cassatt, Mary b. May 22, 1844
Deland, Margaret Wade b. Feb 23, 1857
Fields, Stanley b. 1880
Jackson, Anne b. Sep 3, 1926
Rinehart, Frederick Roberts b. 1903
Skelly, Hal b. 1891
Stein, Gertrude b. Feb 3, 1874
Allentown, Pennsylvania
Iacocca, Lee (Lido Anthony)
   b. Oct 15, 1924
Jarrett, Keith b. May 8, 1945
Voorhees, Donald b. Jul 26, 1903
Altoona, Pennsylvania
Anslinger, Harry Jacob b. May 20, 1892
Blair, Janet b. Apr 23, 1921
Piper, H(enry) Beam b. 1904
Winter, Paul Theodore b. Aug 31, 1939
Ambler, Pennsylvania
Creed, Linda d. Apr 10, 1986
Ashley, Pennsylvania
McGowan, William George
   b. Dec 10, 1927
Atlantic, Pennsylvania
Anderson, Maxwell b. Dec 15, 1888
Attleboro, Pennsylvania
Hicks, Edward b. Apr 4, 1780
Avondale, Pennsylvania
Sullivan, Mark b. Sep 10, 1874
Sullivan, Mark d. Aug 13, 1952
Bald Mount, Pennsylvania
Kresge, Sebastian Spering b. Jul 31, 1867
Barto, Pennsylvania
Bertoia, Harry d. Nov 6, 1978
Bath, Pennsylvania
Christopher, Matthew F b. Aug 16, 1917

Beaver Falls, Pennsylvania
Creach, "Papa" (John) b. May 17, 1917
Loeffler, Kenneth D b. Apr 14, 1902
Midgeley, Thomas b. May 18, 1889
Namath, Joe (Joseph William)
 b. May 31, 1943
Walton, Joe (Joseph Frank)
 b. Dec 15, 1935

Bedford, Pennsylvania
Bradley, David Henry, Jr. b. Sep 7, 1950
Mayo, Katherine d. Oct 9, 1940

Bellefonte, Pennsylvania
Barnard, George Grey b. May 24, 1863
Curtin, Andrew Gregg. Apr 28, 1817
Curtin, Andrew Gregg d. Oct 7, 1894
Mills, John b. Feb 11, 1889
Ward, John Montgomery b. Mar 3, 1860

Bellvernon, Pennsylvania
Bosson, Barbara b. Nov 1,

Belsano, Pennsylvania
Cowley, Malcolm b. Aug 24, 1898

Bentleyville, Pennsylvania
Anthony, Ray b. Jan 20, 1922

Bethany, Pennsylvania
Wilmot, David b. Jan 20, 1814

Bethlehem, Pennsylvania
Benet, Stephen Vincent b. Jul 22, 1898
Doolittle, Hilda b. Sep 10, 1886
Drake, Edwin Laurentine d. Nov 8, 1880
Fry, Franklin Clark b. Aug 30, 1900
Gipson, Lawrence Henry d. Sep 26, 1971
Holloway, Emory d. Jul 30, 1977
Kirkland, Gelsey b. Dec 29, 1952
Knorr, Nathan Homer b. Apr 23, 1905

Birchrunville, Pennsylvania
Martin, Pete (Thornton) d. Oct 13, 1980

Blair County, Pennsylvania
Ickes, Harold LeClair b. Mar 15, 1874

Bloomsburg, Pennsylvania
Magee, Harry L b. Apr 31, 1901
Magee, Harry L d. Oct 9, 1972

Blue Ridge Summit, Pennsylvania
Simpson, Wallis Warfield b. Jun 19, 1896

Boalsburg, Pennsylvania
Darken, Lawrence Stamper d. Jun 7, 1978

Boothwyn, Pennsylvania
Johnson, "Billy White Shoes" (William
 Arthur) b. Jan 21, 1952

Boyertown, Pennsylvania
Spaatz, Carl Andrew b. Jun 28, 1891

Braddock, Pennsylvania
Corey, William Ellis b. May 4, 1866
Knight, Billy (William R) b. Jun 9, 1952

Bradford, Pennsylvania
Horne, Marilyn b. Jan 16, 1934
Waddell, "Rube" (George Edward)
 b. Oct 13, 1876

Brownsville, Pennsylvania
Kirk, Lisa b. Feb 25, 1925

Bryn Mawr, Pennsylvania
Berwind, Charles G d. Nov 9, 1972
Bok, Derek Curtis b. Mar 22, 1930
Hart, Philip Aloysius b. Dec 10, 1912
Jordan, Kathy (Kathryn) b. Dec 3, 1957
Knerr, H(arold) H b. 1883
MacLeish, Rod(erick) b. Jan 15, 1926
Mansfield, Jayne b. Apr 19, 1932

Bucks Country, Pennsylvania
Pearl, Leslie b.

Bucks County, Pennsylvania
Brown, Jacob Jennings b. May 9, 1775
Morgan, Daniel b. 1736

Buena Vista Spring, Pennsylvania
Allen, Henry Tureman d. Aug 30, 1930

Butler, Pennsylvania
Aaron, Chester Norman b. May 9, 1923

California, Pennsylvania
Liuzzo, Viola b. 1925

Canonsburg, Pennsylvania
Como, Perry (Pierino Roland)
 b. May 18, 1912
Price, Gwilym Alexander b. Jun 20, 1895
Vinton, Bobby (Stanley Robert)
 b. Apr 16, 1935

Carlisle, Pennsylvania
Bakeless, John Edwin b. Dec 30, 1894
Pitcher, Molly d. Jan 22, 1832

Carnegie, Pennsylvania
Ditka, Mike b. Oct 18, 1939
Wagner, "Honus" (John Peter)
 b. Feb 24, 1874
Wagner, "Honus" (John Peter)
 d. Dec 6, 1955

Cecil, Pennsylvania
Gossett, D(aniel) Bruce b. Nov 9, 1941

Chadds Ford, Pennsylvania
Wyeth, Andrew b. Jul 12, 1917
Wyeth, N(ewell) C(onvers) d. Oct 19, 1945

Charleroi, Pennsylvania
Bellisario, Donald P b. Aug 8,

Charming Forge, Pennsylvania
Stiegel, Henry William d. Jan 10, 1785

Cheltenham, Pennsylvania
Cooke, Samuel d. May 22, 1965

Cherry Valley, Pennsylvania
Page, Joe (Joseph Francis) b. Oct 28, 1917

Cherryville, Pennsylvania
Kress, Samuel Henry b. Jul 23, 1863

Chester, Pennsylvania
Dale, Clamma Churita b. Jul 4, 1948
North, Alex b. Dec 4, 1910
Porter, David Dixon b. Jun 8, 1813
Pyne, Joe b. 1925
Waters, Ethel b. Oct 31, 1900

Chester County, Pennsylvania
Cox, Harvey Gallagher, Jr.
 b. May 19, 1929
McKim, Charles Follen b. Aug 24, 1847
Sloan, Samuel b. 1815

Clairton, Pennsylvania
Brown, Larry b. Sep 19, 1947
Clarksville, Pennsylvania
Yablonski, Joseph d. Jan 5, 1969
Cochrane's Mill, Pennsylvania
Bly, Nellie, pseud. b. May 5, 1867
Coloraine, Pennsylvania
Latzo, Pete b. Aug 1, 1902
Colver, Pennsylvania
Hartack, Billy (William, Jr.)
  b. Dec 9, 1932
Connellsville, Pennsylvania
Lujack, John(ny) b. Jan 4, 1925
Porter, Edwin b. Apr 21, 1870
Corner Ketch, Pennsylvania
Read, Thomas Buchanan b. Mar 12, 1822
Coulterville, Pennsylvania
Rooney, Art(hur Joseph) b. Jan 27, 1901
Cresson, Pennsylvania
Peary, Robert Edwin b. May 6, 1856
Cumberland County, Pennsylvania
Grier, Robert Cooper b. Mar 5, 1794
Dallastown, Pennsylvania
Mitchell, Cameron b. Nov 4, 1918
Darby, Pennsylvania
Scott, Thomas d. May 21, 1881
Dauphin City, Pennsylvania
Hershey, Milton Snavely b. Sep 13, 1857
Devon, Pennsylvania
Duane, William d. Mar 7, 1935
Donora, Pennsylvania
Musial, Stan(ley Frank) b. Nov 21, 1920
Doylestown, Pennsylvania
Burpee, David d. Jun 24, 1980
Hammerstein, Oscar, II d. Aug 23, 1960
Mercer, Henry Chapman b. Jun 24, 1856
Mercer, Henry Chapman d. Mar 9, 1930
Wexley, John d. Feb 4, 1985
Whiteman, Paul d. Dec 29, 1967
Widdemer, Margaret b. Sep 30, 1897
DuBois, Pennsylvania
Lyle, "Sparky" (Albert Walter)
  b. Jul 22, 1944
Dunmore, Pennsylvania
Chylak, Nester d. Feb 17, 1982
Duquesne, Pennsylvania
Hines, "Fatha" (Earl Kenneth)
  b. Dec 28, 1905
Skurzynski, Gloria b. Jul 6, 1930
East Norriton, Pennsylvania
Hastie, William Henry d. Apr 14, 1976
East Pittsburgh, Pennsylvania
Wambaugh, Joseph Aloysius, Jr.
  b. Jan 22, 1937
Easton, Pennsylvania
Cattell, James McKeen b. May 25, 1860
Crater, Joseph Force b. 1889
Powers, John Robert b. Sep 14, 1896
Taylor, George d. Feb 22, 1781
Economy, Pennsylvania
Rapp, George d. Aug 7, 1847

Edgeworth, Pennsylvania
Nevin, Ethelbert Woodbridge
  b. Nov 25, 1862
Ehrenfeld, Pennsylvania
Bronson, Charles b. Oct 3, 1922
Elizabethtown, Pennsylvania
Baldwin, Matthias William
  b. Dec 10, 1795
Ellwood City, Pennsylvania
Wilson, "Hack" (Lewis Robert)
  b. Apr 26, 1900
Erie, Pennsylvania
Anuszkiewicz, Richard Joseph
  b. May 23, 1930
Biletnikoff, Fred(erick) b. Feb 23, 1943
Burleigh, Harry Thacker b. Dec 2, 1866
Mennin, Peter b. May 17, 1923
Olds, Irving S b. Jan 22, 1887
Spencer, William b. Jun 1, 1922
Wayne, Anthony d. Dec 15, 1796
Erie County, Pennsylvania
Tarbell, Ida Minerva b. Nov 5, 1857
Factoryville, Pennsylvania
Mathewson, Christy (Christopher)
  b. Aug 12, 1880
Forksville, Pennsylvania
Grange, "Red" (Harold Edward)
  b. Jun 13, 1903
Fort Duquesne, Pennsylvania
Braddock, Edward d. Jul 13, 1755
Fort Loudon, Pennsylvania
Scott, Thomas b. Dec 28, 1823
Franklin, Pennsylvania
Marchibroda, Ted (Theodore Joseph)
  b. Mar 15, 1931
Franklin County, Pennsylvania
Corbin, Margaret Cochran b. Nov 12, 1751
Gallitzen, Pennsylvania
Frederick, Pauline b. Feb 13, 1908
Germantown, Pennsylvania
Alcott, Louisa May b. Nov 29, 1832
Coleman, William T b. Jul 7, 1920
Gibson, Henry b. Sep 21, 1935
Rittenhouse, David b. Apr 5, 1732
Taylor, Frederick Winslow
  b. Mar 20, 1856
Vandyke, Henry Jackson, Jr.
  b. Nov 10, 1852
Wister, Owen b. Jul 14, 1860
Gettysburg, Pennsylvania
Plank, Eddie (Edward Stewart)
  b. Aug 31, 1875
Plank, Eddie (Edward Stewart)
  d. Feb 24, 1926
Singmaster, Elsie d. Sep 30, 1958
Studebaker, John Mohler b. Oct 10, 1833
Gladwyne, Pennsylvania
Arnold, Henry Harley b. Jun 25, 1886
Grampian, Pennsylvania
Waln, Nora b. Jun 4, 1895

Loretto, Pennsylvania
Gallitzin, Demetrius Augustine
d. May 6, 1840
Lykens, Pennsylvania
Moffett, Ken(neth Elwood) b. Sep 11, 1931
Mahonoy Plains, Pennsylvania
Dorsey, Tommy (Thomas Francis)
b. Nov 19, 1905
Malvern, Pennsylvania
Westhead, Paul b. Feb 21, 1939
Manayunk, Pennsylvania
Johnson, Harold b. Aug 9, 1928
Marple, Pennsylvania
Bartram, John b. Mar 23, 1699
McDonald, Pennsylvania
Welch, Mitzie b. Jul 25,
McKeesport, Pennsylvania
Connelly, Marc(us Cook) b. Dec 13, 1890
Janis, Byron b. Mar 24, 1928
MacMahon, Aline b. May 3, 1899
Michals, Duane Steven b. Feb 18, 1932
Parrish, Lance Michael b. Jun 15, 1956
Warhol, Andy b. Aug 6, 1927
Wilson, Richard b. Dec 25, 1915
Meadville, Pennsylvania
Barnaby, Ralph S b. Jan 21, 1893
Kirkus, Virginia b. Dec 7, 1893
Mercersburg, Pennsylvania
Buchanan, James b. Apr 23, 1791
Merion, Pennsylvania
Currie, Barton Wood d. May 7, 1962
Merion Square, Pennsylvania
Neel, Alice Hartley b. Jan 28, 1900
Meyersdale, Pennsylvania
Thomas, John Charles b. Sep 6, 1891
Milford, Pennsylvania
Joslyn, Allyn Morgan b. Jul 21, 1905
Peirce, Charles Sanders d. Apr 19, 1914
Minooka, Pennsylvania
O'Neill, Steve (Stephen Francis)
b. Jul 6, 1891
Mix Run, Pennsylvania
Mix, Tom b. Jan 6, 1880
Monessen, Pennsylvania
Thebom, Blanche b. Sep 19, 1919
Monongahela, Pennsylvania
Montana, Joe (Joseph C, Jr.)
b. Jun 11, 1956
Mooresburg, Pennsylvania
Sholes, Christopher Latham
b. Feb 14, 1819
Mornsville, Pennsylvania
Clymer, George d. Jan 24, 1813
Morris Run, Pennsylvania
Nearing, Scott b. Aug 6, 1883
Mount Carmel, Pennsylvania
Trohan, Walter b. Jul 4, 1903
Mountainhome, Pennsylvania
Kresge, Sebastian Spering d. Oct 18, 1966

Nanticoke, Pennsylvania
Adams, Nick b. Jul 10, 1931
Gray, Peter J b. Mar 6, 1917
Narbeth, Pennsylvania
Harshaw, Margaret b. May 12, 1912
Nemacolin, Pennsylvania
Trumka, Richard Louis b. Jul 24, 1949
New Alexandria, Pennsylvania
Turnbull, Agnes Sligh b. Oct 14, 1888
New Britain, Pennsylvania
Door, Rheta Childe d. Aug 8, 1948
New Castle, Pennsylvania
Sterling, Robert b. Nov 13, 1917
Tanner, Chuck (Charles William, Jr.)
b. Jul 4, 1929
New Hope, Pennsylvania
Morris, Chester d. Sep 11, 1970
Savitch, Jessica Beth d. Oct 23, 1983
New Providence, Pennsylvania
Muhlenberg, Heinrich Melchior
d. Oct 7, 1786
New Salem, Pennsylvania
Davis, Ernie (Ernest R) b. Dec 14, 1939
Newton, Pennsylvania
Blanding, Sarah Gibson d. Mar 3, 1985
Burns, Eveline Mabel d. Sep 2, 1985
Kotsching, Walter Maria d. Jun 23, 1985
Newtown, Pennsylvania
Hicks, Edward d. Aug 23, 1849
Hunt, Frazier d. Dec 24, 1967
Jessup, Philip Caryl d. Jan 31, 1986
Norristown, Pennsylvania
Fisher, Jules b. Nov 12, 1937
Lasorda, Tom (Thomas Charles)
b. Sep 22, 1927
Schweiker, Richard Schultz b. Jun 1, 1926
Northumberland, Pennsylvania
Priestley, Joseph d. Feb 6, 1804
Walker, Robert James b. Jul 23, 1801
Ogortz, Pennsylvania
Cooke, Jay d. Feb 18, 1905
Oil City, Pennsylvania
Smalley, David Bruce b. Jul 10, 1949
Old Forge, Pennsylvania
Jones, Allan b. Oct 14, 1907
Plishka, Paul Peter b. Aug 28, 1941
Olyphant, Pennsylvania
Chylak, Nester b. May 11, 1922
Osceola Mills, Pennsylvania
Liveright, Horace Brisbin b. Dec 10, 1886
Ottsville, Pennsylvania
Darrow, Charles Bruce d. Aug 29, 1967
Paxton, Pennsylvania
Pickens, Andrew b. Sep 19, 1739
Pen Argyl, Pennsylvania
Ray, Aldo b. Sep 25, 1926
Penn Valley, Pennsylvania
Hibbs, Ben d. Mar 29, 1975
Pennsburg, Pennsylvania
Buchman, Frank Nathan Daniel
b. Jun 4, 1878

Philadelphia, Pennsylvania

Abbey, Edwin Austin b. Apr 1, 1852
Adams, Edwin d. Oct 25, 1877
Adler, Cyrus d. Apr 7, 1940
Agronsky, Martin Zama b. Jan 12, 1915
Alexander, Lloyd Chudley b. Jan 30, 1924
Allen, Richard b. Feb 14, 1760
Allen, Richard d. Mar 26, 1831
Amram, David Werner, III
     b. Nov 17, 1930
Anderson, Marian b. Feb 17, 1902
Arizin, Paul b. Apr 9, 1928
Ashbrook, Joseph b. Apr 4, 1918
Auslander, Joseph b. Oct 11, 1897
Avalon, Frankie b. Sep 18, 1940
Babbitt, Milton Byron b. May 10, 1916
Bacharach, Bert(ram Mark)
     b. Mar 10, 1898
Backus, John b. Dec 3, 1924
Bacon, Kevin b.
Baer, "Bugs" (Arthur) b. 1886
Bainbridge, William d. Jul 27, 1833
Baker, Phil b. Aug 24, 1896
Balderston, John Lloyd b. Oct 22, 1889
Baldwin, Matthias William d. Sep 7, 1866
Bancroft, George b. Sep 30, 1882
Barnum, P(hineas) T(aylor) d. Apr 7, 1891
Barris, Chuck b. Jun 2, 1929
Barry, John d. Sep 13, 1803
Barrymore, Ethel Mae Blythe
     b. Aug 15, 1879
Barrymore, Georgina Emma Drew
     b. Jul 11, 1854
Barrymore, John b. Feb 15, 1882
Barrymore, Lionel Blythe b. Apr 28, 1878
Barthelme, Donald b. Apr 7, 1931
Barton, George b. Jan 22, 1866
Bartram, William d. Jul 22, 1823
Baugh, Albert Croll b. Feb 26, 1891
Baugh, Albert Croll d. Mar 21, 1981
Beaux, Cecelia b. 1863
Bell, James Ford b. Aug 16, 1879
Bender, "Chief" (Charles Albert)
     d. May 22, 1954
Bettger, Lyle b. Feb 13, 1915
Biberman, Herbert b. Mar 4, 1900
Biddle, Anthony b. Dec 17, 1896
Biddle, George b. Jan 24, 1885
Biddle, Nicholas b. Jan 8, 1786
Biddle, Nicholas d. Feb 27, 1844
Black, Frank J. b. Nov 28, 1896
Blitzstein, Marc b. Mar 2, 1905
Bluford, Guion Stewart, Jr.
     b. Nov 22, 1942
Boland, Mary b. Jan 28, 1880
Bonsall, Joe b. May 18, 1948
Bova, Ben(jamin William) b. Nov 8, 1932
Boyle, Peter b. Oct 18, 1935
Braceland, Francis J(ames) b. Jul 22, 1900
Bradley, Ed b. Jun 22, 1941
Breen, Joseph Ignatius b. Oct 4, 1890

Brendel, El(mer) b. Mar 25, 1890
Brenner, David b. Feb 4, 1945
Bricklin, Malcolm N b. Mar 9, 1939
Broderick, Helen b. Aug 11, 1891
Brooks, Richard b. May 18, 1912
Brown, Charles Brockden b. Jan 17, 1771
Brown, Charles Brockden d. Feb 22, 1810
Bullins, Ed b. Jul 25, 1935
Bullitt, William C b. Jan 25, 1891
Burns, David d. Mar 12, 1971
Burpee, David b. Apr 5, 1893
Cahill, William Thomas b. Jun 25, 1912
Calder, Alexander b. Jul 22, 1898
Callan, Michael b. Nov 22, 1935
Cappelletti, John Raymond b. Aug 9, 1952
Carothers, Wallace Hume d. Apr 29, 1937
Chamberlain, Wilt(ton Norman)
     b. Aug 21, 1936
Chambers, Whittaker b. Apr 1, 1901
Charles, Suzette b. 1963
Charleston, Oscar McKinley
     d. Oct 5, 1954
Childs, George William d. Feb 3, 1894
Chomsky, Noam b. Dec 7, 1928
Christopher, Dennis b. Dec 2, 1955
Churchill, May (Beatrice Desmond)
     d. 1929
Clark, Joseph Sill b. Oct 21, 1901
Clarke, Stanley Marvin b. Jun 31, 1951
Clayton, Bessie b. 1885
Cleghorn, Sarah Norcliffe d. Apr 4, 1959
Clymer, George b. Mar 16, 1739
Cobb, Will D b. Jul 6, 1876
Coca, Imogene Fernandez y
     b. Nov 19, 1908
Cohn, Arthur b. Nov 6, 1910
Columbo, Russ b. Jan 4, 1908
Conrad, Charles, Jr. b. Jun 2, 1930
Cosby, Bill b. Jul 12, 1937
Covington, Warren b. Aug 7, 1921
Cramp, Charles Henry b. May 9, 1828
Cramp, Charles Henry d. Jun 6, 1913
Crawford, Broderick b. Dec 9, 1911
Cregar, Laird (Samuel) b. Jul 28, 1916
Creighton, Thomas H(awk)
     b. May 19, 1904
Cret, Paul P(hilippe) d. Sep 8, 1945
Croce, Jim b. Jan 10, 1943
Crumb, Robert b. Aug 30, 1943
DaCosta, Morton b. Mar 7, 1914
Dahlgren, John Adolph b. Nov 13, 1809
Dallas, George Mifflin b. Jul 10, 1792
Dallas, George Mifflin d. Dec 31, 1864
Daly, Thomas Augustine b. May 28, 1871
Daly, Thomas Augustine d. Oct 4, 1948
Danner, Blythe Katharine b. Feb 3, 1943
Darley, Felix Octavius Carr
     b. Jun 23, 1822
Darren, James b. Jun 8, 1936
Davis, Richard Harding b. Apr 18, 1864
Davis, Stuart b. Dec 7, 1894

Davis, William Morris b. Feb 12, 1850
Davison, Bruce b.
DeKnight, Jimmy b. Oct 26,
DelRuth, Roy b. Oct 18, 1895
Diamond, "Legs" (Jack) b. 1896
Divine, Father Major Jealous
    d. Sep 10, 1965
Doggett, Bill b. Feb 6, 1916
Donnelly, Ignatius b. Nov 3, 1831
Douglas, Paul b. Nov 4, 1907
Drew, John b. Nov 13, 1853
Drexel, Anthony J b. Sep 13, 1806
Drexel, Francis Martin d. Jun 5, 1863
Druckman, Jacob Raphael b. Jun 26, 1928
Duane, William b. Feb 17, 1872
Dundee, Angelo Mirena, Jr.
    b. Aug 30, 1921
Duryea, Charles Edgar d. Sep 28, 1938
Eakins, Thomas b. Jul 25, 1844
Eakins, Thomas d. Jun 25, 1916
Ehmke, Howard Jonathan d. Mar 17, 1959
Ehrlich, Paul b. May 29, 1932
Eiseley, Loren Corey d. Jul 9, 1977
Eklund, Carl Robert d. Nov 4, 1962
Elliott, "Jumbo" (James Francis)
    b. Aug 8, 1915
Ellsler, Effie b. Sep 17, 1854
Elman, Ziggy b. May 26, 1914
Ennis, Del(mer) b. Jun 8, 1925
Erhard, Werner b. Sep 5, 1935
Eustis, Dorothy Leib Harrison Wood
    b. May 30, 1886
Evans, Hiram W b. Oct 3, 1941
Evans, Orrin C d. Aug 7, 1971
Fabian b. Feb 6, 1943
Falana, Lola b. Sep 11, 1943
Fauset, Jessie Redmon b. 1884
Fell, Norman b. Mar 24, 1925
Fels, Samuel Simeon d. Jun 23, 1950
Fields, W C b. Jan 29, 1880
Fine, Larry b. 1911
Finletter, Thomas Knight b. Nov 11, 1893
Fischer, Louis b. Feb 29, 1896
Fisher, Eddie (Edwin Jack)
    b. Aug 10, 1928
Forbes, John d. Mar 11, 1759
Forrest, Edwin b. Mar 9, 1806
Forrest, Edwin d. Dec 12, 1872
Franklin, Benjamin d. Apr 17, 1790
Frost, Arthur Burdett b. Jan 17, 1851
Fuller, Charles b. Mar 5, 1939
Gabel, Martin b. Jun 19, 1912
Galamison, Milton Arthur b. Jan 25, 1923
Galanos, James b. Sep 20, 1924
Gallaudet, Thomas Hopkins
    b. Dec 10, 1787
Gans, Joe b. Nov 25, 1874
Gates, Thomas Sovereign, Jr.
    b. Apr 10, 1906
Gates, Thomas Sovereign, Jr.
    d. Mar 25, 1983

Gaynor, Janet b. Oct 6, 1906
George, Henry, Sr. b. Sep 2, 1839
Gere, Richard b. Aug 29, 1949
Getz, Stan b. Feb 2, 1927
Giannini, Dusolina b. Dec 19, 1902
Giannini, Vittorio b. Oct 19, 1903
Gibbs, William Francis b. Aug 24, 1886
Gibson, Walter B(rown) b. Sep 12, 1897
Glackens, William James b. Mar 13, 1870
Godey, Louis Antoine d. Nov 29, 1878
Gola, Thomas Joseph b. Jan 13, 1933
Gold, Harry d. Aug 28, 1972
Goldstein, Israel b. Jun 18, 1896
Golson, Benny b. Jan 25, 1929
Goren, Charles Henry b. Mar 4, 1901
Gottlieb, Eddie (Edward) d. Dec 7, 1979
Graham, Ronny b. Aug 26, 1919
Grant, Gogi b. Sep 20, 1924
Gratz, Rebecca b. Mar 4, 1781
Greco, Buddy (Armando) b. Aug 14, 1926
Greenwood, Charlotte b. Jun 25, 1893
Grier, Robert Cooper d. Sep 25, 1870
Grimke, Charlotte Lottie Forten
    b. Aug 17, 1837
Guarrera, Frank b. Dec 3, 1923
Guggenheim, Daniel b. 1856
Guggenheim, Solomon Robert
    b. Feb 2, 1861
Haig, Alexander Meigs, Jr. b. Dec 2, 1924
Haldeman-Julius, Emanuel b. Jul 30, 1889
Hale, Clara McBride b. Apr 1, 1905
Hamel, Veronica b. Nov 20, 1945
Hamilton, Andrew d. Aug 4, 1741
Harney, Benjamin Robertson
    d. Mar 1, 1938
Harris, Willard Palmer (Bill)
    b. Oct 28, 1916
Haupt, Herman b. Mar 26, 1817
Hemsley, Sherman b. Feb 1, 1938
Hergesheimer, Joseph b. Feb 15, 1880
Hesselius, John b. 1728
Hewes, Joseph d. Nov 10, 1779
Hill, George Washington b. Oct 22, 1884
Hirsch, Joseph b. Apr 25, 1910
Holm, John Cecil b. Nov 4, 1904
Holmes, John Haynes b. Nov 9, 1879
Hopkinson, Francis b. Sep 21, 1737
Hopkinson, Francis d. May 9, 1791
Hull, Isaac d. Dec 13, 1843
Humphries, Rolfe (George Rolfe)
    b. Nov 20, 1894
Huneker, James Gibbons b. Jan 31, 1860
Huntington, Henry Edwards
    d. May 23, 1927
Huntington, Henry S, Jr. d. Feb 16, 1981
Innaurato, Albert b. Jun 2, 1948
Ives, Frederic Eugene d. May 27, 1937
Ives, Herbert Eugene b. Jul 31, 1882
Jackson, Chevalier d. Aug 16, 1958
Jaggar, Thomas Augustus b. Jan 24, 1871
James, "Skip" (Nehemiah) d. Oct 3, 1969

Penner, Joe d. Jan 10, 1941
Perret, Gene b. Apr 3, 1937
Persichetti, Vincent b. Jun 6, 1915
Peto, John Frederick b. May 21, 1854
Pitlik, Noam b. Nov 4, 1932
Pitz, Henry Clarence b. Jun 16, 1895
Pitz, Henry Clarence d. Nov 26, 1975
Poling, Daniel A d. Feb 7, 1968
Powdermaker, Hortense b. Dec 24, 1896
Presser, Theodore d. Oct 27, 1925
Prosky, Robert b. Dec 13, 1930
Pully, B S d. Jan 6, 1972
Quillan, Eddie b. Mar 31, 1907
Quinn, Arthur Hobson b. 1875
Quinn, Edmond T b. Dec 20, 1868
Randall, Samuel J b. Oct 10, 1828
Rapp, Danny b. 1941
Ray, Man b. Aug 27, 1890
Reed, Henry Hope b. Jul 11, 1808
Repplier, Agnes b. Apr 1, 1858
Repplier, Agnes d. Dec 15, 1950
Richards, William Trost b. Nov 14, 1838
Rittenhouse, David d. Jun 26, 1796
Rivlin, Alice Mitchell b. Mar 4, 1931
Rizzo, Frank L b. Oct 23, 1920
Roberts, Robin Evan b. Sep 30, 1926
Robeson, Paul Leroy d. Jan 23, 1976
Rodgers, John d. Aug 10, 1838
Rosenbach, Abraham Simon Wolf
    b. Jul 22, 1876
Rosenbach, Abraham Simon Wolf
    d. Jul 1, 1952
Rosenfeld, Alvin Hirsch b. Apr 28, 1938
Ross, Betsy (Elizabeth Griscom)
    b. Jan 1, 1752
Ross, Betsy (Elizabeth Griscom)
    d. Jan 30, 1836
Rush, Benjamin b. Dec 24, 1745
Rush, Benjamin d. Apr 19, 1813
Rush, William b. Jul 5, 1756
Rush, William d. Jan 17, 1833
Rydell, Bobby b. Apr 26, 1942
Salomon, Haym d. Jan 6, 1785
Sample, Bill b. Dec 2, 1935
Sartain, John d. Oct 25, 1897
Schlessinger, David b. Mar 3, 1955
Segal, Vivienne b. Apr 19, 1897
Seidelman, Susan b. Dec 11, 1952
Seiss, Joseph Augustus d. Jun 20, 1904
Sellinger, Frank (Francis John)
    b. Jul 8, 1914
Sembello, Michael b. 1956
Sheeler, Charles b. Jul 16, 1883
Shippen, Margaret b. 1760
Shor, "Toots" (Bernard) b. May 6, 1905
Singleton, Penny b. Sep 15, 1908
Sledge, Debbie b. Jul 9, 1954
Sledge, Joni b. Sep 13, 1956
Sledge, Kathy b. Jan 6, 1959
Sledge, Kim b. Aug 21, 1957
Smith, Willi Donnell b. Feb 29, 1948

Soyer, David b. Feb 24, 1923
Spaeth, Sigmund Gottfried b. Apr 10, 1885
Stankiewicz, Richard Peter b. Oct 18, 1922
Stevenson, Parker b. Jun 4, 1951
Stockton, Frank (Francis Richard)
    b. Apr 5, 1834
Stone, I(sidor) F(einstein) b. Dec 24, 1907
Sully, Thomas d. Nov 5, 1872
Susann, Jacqueline b. Aug 20, 1921
Tassell, Gustave b. Feb 4, 1926
Taylor, Frederick Winslow
    d. Mar 21, 1915
Terrell, Tammi b. 1946
Terry, Luther Leonidas d. Mar 29, 1985
Thayer, George Chapman, Jr.
    b. Sep 18, 1933
Thomas, Martha Carey d. Dec 2, 1935
Thompson, Ruth Plumly b. Jul 27, 1891
Tilden, Bill (William Tatem, Jr.)
    b. Feb 10, 1893
Toomey, Bill (William) b. Jan 10, 1939
Trumbauer, Horace b. Dec 28, 1869
Trumbauer, Horace d. Sep 18, 1938
Tyne, George b. Aug 6, 1917
Van Dusen, Henry Pitney b. Dec 11, 1897
Ventura, Charlie b. Dec 2, 1916
Walcott, Mary Morris Vaux
    b. Jul 31, 1860
Walker, Nancy b. May 10, 1921
Walter, Thomas Ustick b. Sep 4, 1804
Walter, Thomas Ustick d. Oct 30, 1887
Walters, "Bucky" (William Henry)
    b. Apr 19, 1910
Wanamaker, John b. Jul 11, 1838
Wanamaker, John d. Dec 12, 1922
Wanamaker, Rodman b. 1863
Weir, Walter b. Mar 27, 1909
Wharton, Joseph b. Mar 3, 1826
Whitaker, Jack (John Francis)
    b. May 18, 1924
Widener, George D b. Mar 11, 1889
Widener, George D d. Dec 8, 1971
Wiggin, Kate Douglas b. Sep 28, 1856
Wilson, Alexander d. Aug 23, 1813
Wilson, Dolores b. 1929
Winner, Joseph Eastburn b. 1837
Winner, Joseph Eastburn d. 1918
Wolfington, Iggie b. Oct 14, 1920
Wood, Samuel Grosvenor b. Jul 10, 1884
Wrigley, William, Jr. b. Sep 3, 1861
Wummer, John b. 1899
Wynn, Ed b. Nov 9, 1886
Young, Jimmy b. 1949
Zimmerman, Paul b. Oct 23, 1932

Pine Grove, Pennsylvania
Richter, Conrad Michael b. Nov 13, 1890

Pinetown, Pennsylvania
Studebaker, Clement b. Mar 12, 1831

Pitcairn, Pennsylvania
Weems, Ted (Wilfred Theodore) b. 1900

Pittsburgh, Pennsylvania

Allen, Hervey (William Hervey)
b. Dec 8, 1889
Andersen, Eric b. Feb 14, 1943
Atherton, Alfred LeRoy, Jr.
b. Nov 22, 1921
Bazell, Robert b. Aug 21, 1946
Baziotes, William b. Jun 11, 1912
Bell, "Buddy" (David Gus)
b. Aug 27, 1951
Benson, George b. Mar 22, 1943
Berman, Pandro Samuel b. Mar 28, 1905
Betz, Carl b. Mar 9, 1920
Blakey, Art b. Oct 11, 1919
Blumenthal, Monica David
d. Mar 16, 1981
Bork, Robert Heron b. Mar 1, 1927
Boyer, Herbert Wayne b. Jul 10, 1936
Bruce, Ailsa Mellon b. Jun 28, 1901
Burke, Kenneth b. May 5, 1897
Caliguiri, Richard b. Oct 20, 1931
Carroll, Earl b. Sep 16, 1893
Commager, Henry Steele b. Oct 25, 1902
Conrad, Frank b. May 4, 1874
Cooper, Chuck (Charles H) d. Feb 5, 1984
Costello, Dolores b. Sep 17, 1905
Costello, Maurice b. 1877
Crawford, John Edmund b. Jan 21, 1904
Cullen, Bill (William Lawrence)
b. Feb 18, 1920
Davidson, John b. Dec 13, 1941
Davis, Hal Charles b. Feb 27, 1914
Delahanty, Thomas K b. 1935
Dillard, Annie Doak b. Apr 30, 1945
Doak, Bill (William Leopold)
b. Jan 28, 1891
Duse, Eleanora d. Apr 23, 1924
Eckstine, Billy b. Jul 8, 1914
Edel, Leon (Joseph Leon) b. Sep 9, 1907
Eldridge, Roy b. Jan 29, 1911
Feingold, Benjamin Franklin
b. Jun 15, 1900
Feldon, Barbara b. Mar 12, 1941
Ferris, George Washington Gale
d. Nov 22, 1896
Fiedler, Jean(nette Feldman) b.
Fink, Mike b. 1720
Fisher, Max Martin b. Jul 15, 1908
Flaherty, Joe b. Jun 21, 1940
Foerster, Norman b. Apr 14, 1887
Fogarty, Anne b. Feb 2, 1926
Foster, Stephen Collins b. Jul 4, 1826
Galvin, "Pud" (James Francis)
d. Mar 7, 1902
Gam, Rita Elenore b. Apr 2, 1928
Garner, Erroll b. Jun 15, 1921
Gibson, Josh(ua) d. Jan 20, 1947
Glenn, Scott b. 1939
Goldblum, Jeff b. Oct 22, 1952

Gorshin, Frank John b. Apr 5, 1934
Graham, Martha b. May 11, 1893
Greb, Harry (Edward Henry)
b. Jun 6, 1894
Grodin, Charles b. Apr 21, 1935
Hatch, Orrin Grant b. Mar 22, 1934
Heinz, (Henry) John, (III) b. Oct 23, 1938
Heinz, Henry John b. Oct 11, 1844
Heinz, Henry John d. May 14, 1919
Hench, Philip Showalter b. Feb 28, 1896
Hodiak, John b. Apr 16, 1914
Holland, William Jacob d. Dec 13, 1932
Irwin, James Benson b. Mar 17, 1930
Jamal, Ahmad b. Jul 7, 1930
Jeffers, (John) Robinson b. Jan 10, 1887
Kane, John d. Aug 10, 1934
Kaufman, George S(imon) b. Nov 16, 1889
Keaton, Michael b. Sep 9, 1951
Kelly, Gene b. Aug 23, 1912
Kelly, William b. Aug 21, 1811
Kennedy, Adrienne b. Sep 13, 1931
Laughlin, James, IV b. Oct 30, 1914
Levant, Oscar b. Dec 27, 1906
Lipscomb, Eugene d. May 10, 1963
Lucas, Maurice b. Feb 18, 1952
Marino, Dan(iel Constantine, Jr.)
b. Sep 15, 1961
Martin, Kiel b. Jul 26, 1945
May, Billy (E William) b. Nov 10, 1916
McCann, Alfred Watterson b. Jan 7, 1879
McCord, Andrew King d. Dec 17, 1974
McDonald, David John b. Nov 22, 1902
McDowell, Sam(uel Edward)
b. Sep 21, 1942
Meighan, Thomas b. Apr 9, 1879
Mellon, Andrew William b. Mar 24, 1855
Mellon, Paul b. Jun 11, 1907
Mellon, Richard King b. Jun 19, 1899
Mellon, Richard King d. Jun 3, 1970
Mellon, William Larimer, Jr. b. 1910
Menjou, Adolphe Jean b. Feb 8, 1890
Morris, "Mercury" (Eugene)
b. Jan 5, 1947
Muller-Munk, Peter d. Mar 12, 1967
O'Hair, Madalyn Murray b. Apr 13, 1919
Oakley, Don b. Nov 3, 1927
Poli, Robert E b. Feb 27, 1936
Powell, William b. Jul 29, 1892
Presser, Theodore b. Jul 3, 1848
Putch, William Henry b. Apr 22, 1924
Reed, Betty Jane b. Aug 6, 1921
Reinhart, Charles S b. May 16, 1844
Rigby, Harry b. Feb 21, 1925
Rinehart, Mary Roberts b. Aug 12, 1876
Rinehart, Stanley Marshall, Jr.
b. Aug 18, 1897
Robin, Leo b. Apr 6, 1895
Rockwell, Willard F d. Oct 16, 1978
Russell, Charles Taze b. Feb 16, 1852
Russell, Lillian d. Jun 6, 1922
Saperton, David b. 1890

Saudek, Robert b. Apr 11, 1911
Schmidt, Joe (Joseph Paul) b. Jan 18, 1932
Schmitt, Gladys b. May 31, 1909
Schmitt, Gladys d. Oct 3, 1972
Schoyer, (B) Preston b. Jun 13, 1912
Sellars, Peter b. 1958
Selznick, David O(liver) b. May 10, 1902
Shiras, George, Jr. b. Jan 26, 1832
Shiras, George, Jr. d. Sep 2, 1924
Smith, Ethel b. Nov 22, 1910
Solomon, Neil b. Feb 27, 1932
Stevens, Kaye (Catherine) b. Jul 21, 1935
Stotz, Charles Morse b. Aug 1, 1898
Stuhldreher, Harry A d. Jan 22, 1965
Sublette, William L d. Jul 23, 1845
Sullivan, Maxine b. May 13, 1911
Talbot, Lyle b. Feb 8, 1902
Tanner, Henry Ossawa b. Jun 21, 1859
Thaw, Harry Kendall b. Feb 1, 1871
Thomson, Meldrim, Jr. b. Mar 8, 1912
Thornburgh, Richard Lewis b. Jul 16, 1932
Toomey, Regis b. Aug 13, 1902
Traynor, "Pie" (Harold Joseph)
    d. Mar 16, 1972
Unitas, Johnny (John Constantine)
    b. May 7, 1933
Wallace, Bobby (Roderick John)
    b. Nov 4, 1874
Weaver, Fritz William b. Jan 19, 1926
Widdoes, James b. Nov 15, 1953
Wild, Earl b. Nov 26, 1915
Williams, Mary Lou b. May 8, 1910
Wright, Syretta b.
Yablonski, Joseph b. 1910
Yardley, Jonathan b. Oct 27, 1939

Pittston, Pennsylvania
Jennings, Hugh(ey Ambrose)
    b. Apr 2, 1870
MacArthur, John Donald b. Mar 6, 1897

Plainfield, Pennsylvania
Penn, Irving b. Jun 16, 1917

Plains, Pennsylvania
Walsh, Ed(ward Augustin)
    b. May 14, 1881

Pleasantville, Pennsylvania
Palmer, Frederick b. Jan 29, 1873

Pottstown, Pennsylvania
Hall, Daryl b. Oct 11, 1948
Landis, Walter Savage b. Jul 5, 1881

Pottsville, Pennsylvania
Bergen, John Joseph b. Aug 7, 1896
Golden, Clinton Strong b. Nov 16, 1886
O'Hara, John Henry b. Jan 31, 1905
Richter, Conrad Michael d. Oct 30, 1968

Quakertown, Pennsylvania
Crosby, Alexander L d. Jan 31, 1980

Quartzside, Pennsylvania
Rapp, Danny d. Apr 4, 1983

Radnor, Pennsylvania
Pleasants, Henry b. May 23, 1884

Reading, Pennsylvania
Althouse, Paul Shearer b. Dec 2, 1889
Baird, Spencer Fullerton b. Feb 3, 1823
Boone, Daniel b. Nov 2, 1734
Constantine, Michael b. May 22, 1927
Dwyer, Florence Price b. Jul 4, 1902
Eichhorn, Lisa b. 1952
Julian, "Doggie" (Alvin T) b. Apr 5, 1901
Kerr, Clark b. May 17, 1911
Smith, Martin Cruz b. Nov 3, 1942
Sousa, John Philip d. Mar 6, 1932
Stevens, Wallace b. Oct 2, 1879
Weiss, Theodore (Russell) b. Dec 16, 1916

Reinerton, Pennsylvania
Brown, Les(ter Raymond) b. Mar 12, 1912

Richboro, Pennsylvania
Peale, Rembrandt b. Feb 22, 1778

Richlandtown, Pennsylvania
Bloor, "Mother" Ella Reeve
    d. Aug 10, 1951

Ridgeway, Pennsylvania
Mayo, Katherine b. Jan 24, 1867

Ridley Park, Pennsylvania
Morton, John b. 1724
Morton, John d. 1777
Rigby, Bob b. Jul 3, 1951

Riegelsville, Pennsylvania
Adamic, Louis d. Sep 4, 1951

Riverside, Pennsylvania
Blough, Roger Miles b. Jan 19, 1904

Rose Valley, Pennsylvania
Stephens, Alice Barber d. Jul 13, 1932

Rosemont, Pennsylvania
Lattimore, Richmond Alexander
    d. Feb 26, 1984

Saint Davids, Pennsylvania
Helms, Richard McGarrah
    b. Mar 30, 1913

Saint Thomas, Pennsylvania
Fox, "Nellie" (Jacob Nelson)
    b. Dec 25, 1927

Saltzburg, Pennsylvania
McIlwain, Charles Howard
    b. Mar 15, 1871

Saxonburg, Pennsylvania
Roebling, Washington Augustus
    b. May 26, 1837

Saylorsburg, Pennsylvania
Gibbons, Floyd Phillips d. Sep 24, 1939

Schuylkill, Pennsylvania
Singmaster, Elsie b. Aug 29, 1897

Scottdale, Pennsylvania
Goldenson, Leonard Harry b. Dec 7, 1905

Scranton, Pennsylvania
Biden, Joseph Robinette, Jr.
    b. Nov 20, 1942
Carlucci, Frank Charles, III
    b. Oct 18, 1930
Chait, Lawrence G b. Jun 27, 1917
Crowley, Jim (James) d. Jan 15, 1986
Crowley, Pat b. Sep 17, 1929

Waynesburg, Pennsylvania
George, Bill (William) b. Oct 27, 1930
Goucher, John Franklin b. Jun 7, 1845
West Brownsville, Pennsylvania
Blaine, James Gillespie b. Jan 31, 1830
West Chester, Pennsylvania
Barber, Samuel b. Mar 9, 1910
Jarvis, Anna d. Nov 24, 1948
Matlack, Jon(athan Trumpbour)
  b. Jan 19, 1950
Pippin, Horace b. Feb 22, 1888
Rustin, Bayard b. Mar 17, 1910
Whyte, William Hollingsworth
  b. Oct 1, 1917
West Middlesex, Pennsylvania
Landon, Alf(red Mossman) b. Sep 9, 1887
West Overton, Pennsylvania
Frick, Henry Clay b. Dec 19, 1849
White Marsh, Pennsylvania
Evans, Rowland, Jr. b. Apr 28, 1921
Whitehall, Pennsylvania
McBride, Lloyd d. Nov 6, 1983
Wilkes-Barre, Pennsylvania
Catlin, George b. Jul 26, 1796
Fisher, Ham(mond Edward)
  b. Sep 24, 1900
Jones, Candy b. Dec 31, 1925
Kline, Franz Joseph b. May 23, 1919
Mankiewicz, Joseph Lee b. Feb 11, 1909
O'Neill, Rose Cecil b. Jun 25, 1874
Stark, Harold Raynsford b. Nov 12, 1880
Teicher, Louis b. Aug 24, 1924
Whalen, Michael b. Jun 30, 1902
Winterhalter, Hugo b. Aug 15, 1909
Wilkinsburg, Pennsylvania
McKechnie, Bill (William Boyd)
  b. Aug 7, 1887
Robinson, M(aurice) R(ichard)
  b. Dec 24, 1895
Snodgrass, W(illiam) D(eWitt)
  b. Jan 5, 1926
Williamsburg, Pennsylvania
Schwab, Charles Michael b. Feb 18, 1862
Williamsport, Pennsylvania
Humes, James Calhoun b. Oct 31, 1934
Luks, George Benjamin b. Aug 13, 1867
Willow Hill, Pennsylvania
McCurdy, Ed b. Jan 11, 1919
Windber, Pennsylvania
Bonfanti, Jim Alexander b. Dec 17, 1948
Wyalusing, Pennsylvania
Stern, Philip Van Doren b. Sep 10, 1900
Wyncote, Pennsylvania
Curtis, Cyrus Hermann Kotszchmar
  d. Jun 7, 1933
Jackson, Reggie (Reginald Martinez)
  b. May 18, 1946
York, Pennsylvania
Devers, Jacob Loucks b. Sep 8, 1887
Hoffman, Robert C d. Jul 18, 1985
Hunt, Lois b. Nov 26, 1925

Lefever, Ernest Warren b. Nov 12, 1919
Smith, James d. Jul 11, 1806
Woltman, Frederick Enos b. Mar 16, 1905
Youngstown, Pennsylvania
Palmer, Arnold Daniel b. Sep 10, 1929
Youngwood, Pennsylvania
Blanda, George Frederick b. Sep 17, 1927

RHODE ISLAND

Holm, John Cecil d. Oct 24, 1981
Bristol, Rhode Island
Burnside, Ambrose Everett d. Sep 13, 1881
Cranston, Rhode Island
Aldrich, Robert b. Aug 9, 1918
Sullivan, William Healy b. Oct 12, 1922
Foster, Rhode Island
Aldrich, Nelson Wilmarth b. Nov 6, 1841
Hopkinton, Rhode Island
Crandall, Prudence b. 1803
Lime Rock, Rhode Island
Lewis, Ida d. Oct 24, 1911
Newport, Rhode Island
Blatchford, Samuel d. Jul 7, 1893
Channing, Walter b. Apr 15, 1786
Channing, William Ellery b. Apr 7, 1780
Clarke, John d. Apr 28, 1676
Ellery, William b. Dec 22, 1727
Ellery, William d. Feb 15, 1820
Howe, Julia Ward d. Oct 17, 1910
Hunt, Richard Morris d. Jul 31, 1896
Ince, Thomas H(arper) b. Nov 6, 1882
Ingersoll, Stuart H d. Jan 29, 1983
Johnson, Van b. Aug 28, 1916
Kennedy, John Pendleton d. Aug 18, 1870
King, Clarence b. Jan 6, 1842
Knight, Frances Gladys b. Jul 22, 1905
Lewis, Ida b. Feb 25, 1842
Little, (William) Lawson, Jr.
  b. Jun 23, 1910
Mills, Ogden Livingston b. Aug 23, 1884
Moore, Clement Clarke d. Jul 10, 1863
Perry, Matthew Calbraith, Commodore
  b. Apr 10, 1794
Richards, William Trost d. 1905
Stephens, Ann Sophia d. Aug 20, 1886
Vanderbilt, Harold Stirling d. Jul 4, 1970
Woolsey, Sarah Chauncey d. Apr 9, 1905
Yarnell, Harry E d. Jul 7, 1959
North Kingstown, Rhode Island
Stuart, Gilbert Charles b. Dec 3, 1755
Wister, Owen d. Jul 21, 1938
North Providence, Rhode Island
DiGregorio, Ernie b. Jan 15, 1951
Pawtucket, Rhode Island
Corcoran, Thomas Gardiner
  b. Dec 29, 1900
Hartman, David Downs b. May 19, 1935
Hood, Raymond Matthewson
  b. Mar 29, 1881
Levine, Irving R b. Aug 26, 1922

Berkeley County, South Carolina
Marion, Francis b. 1732
Marion, Francis d. Feb 27, 1795
Rivers, L(ucius) Mendel b. Sep 28, 1905
Bishopville, South Carolina
Blanchard, "Doc" (Felix Anthony)
    b. Dec 11, 1924
Blacksburg, South Carolina
Killian, James Rhyne, Jr. b. Jul 24, 1904
Brandon Mills, South Carolina
Jackson, Joe (Joseph Jefferson)
    b. Jul 16, 1888
Cades, South Carolina
McNair, Robert Evander b. Dec 14, 1923
Calhoun Mills, South Carolina
Calhoun, John Caldwell b. Mar 18, 1782
Camden, South Carolina
Baruch, Bernard Mannes b. Aug 19, 1870
Benton, Brook b. Sep 19, 1931
Doby, Larry (Lawrence Eugene)
    b. Dec 13, 1924
Kalb, Johann de d. Aug 19, 1780
Kirkland, Lane (Joseph Lane)
    b. Mar 12, 1922
Charleston, South Carolina
Bennett, John d. Dec 28, 1956
Byrnes, James Francis b. May 2, 1879
Clark, Mark Wayne d. Apr 17, 1984
Cohen, Octavus Roy b. Jun 26, 1891
Craft, Ellen d. 1897
Daniel, Beth b. Oct 14, 1958
Dillon, George d. May 9, 1968
Freed, Arthur b. Sep 9, 1894
Gadsen, James b. May 15, 1788
Gadsen, James d. Dec 26, 1858
Gorrie, John b. Oct 3, 1803
Hampton, Wade b. Mar 28, 1818
Henry, Edward Lamson b. Jan 12, 1841
Heyward, (Edwin) DuBose
    b. Aug 31, 1885
Hill, "Chippie" (Bertha) b. 1905
Hollings, Ernest Frederick b. Jan 1, 1922
Houghton, Amory d. Feb 21, 1981
Hutton, Lauren (Mary Laurence)
    b. Nov 17, 1944
Johnson, William b. Dec 27, 1771
Just, Ernest Everett b. Aug 14, 1883
Laurens, Henry b. Mar 26, 1724
Laurens, Henry d. Dec 8, 1792
Middleton, Arthur b. Jun 26, 1742
Mills, Robert b. Aug 12, 1781
Moultrie, William b. Dec 4, 1730
Moultrie, William d. Sep 27, 1805
Pinckney, Charles Cotesworth
    b. Feb 25, 1746
Pinckney, Charles Cotesworth
    d. Aug 16, 1825
Poinsett, Joel Roberts b. Mar 2, 1779
Pulitzer, Joseph d. Oct 29, 1911
Rutledge, Edward b. Nov 23, 1749
Rutledge, Edward d. Jan 23, 1800

Rutledge, John b. Sep 1739
Rutledge, John d. Jul 18, 1800
Shaw, Robert Gould d. Jul 18, 1863
Simms, William Gilmore b. Apr 17, 1806
Simms, William Gilmore d. Jun 11, 1870
Stanton, Frank Lebby b. Feb 22, 1857
Timrod, Henry b. Dec 8, 1828
Cheraw, South Carolina
Gillespie, "Dizzy" (John Birks)
    b. Oct 21, 1917
Columbia, South Carolina
Anderson, Bill b. Nov 1, 1937
Baldwin, James Mark b. Jan 12, 1861
Bernardin, Joseph Louis, Cardinal
    b. Apr 2, 1928
Brawley, Benjamin Griffith
    b. Apr 22, 1882
Butler, Matthew Calbraith d. Apr 14, 1909
Byrnes, James Francis d. Apr 9, 1972
Donen, Stanley b. Apr 13, 1924
Gillis, Don d. Jan 10, 1978
Hampton, Wade d. Apr 11, 1902
Higbe, Kirby (Walter Kirby)
    b. Apr 8, 1915
Hoyt, Lamarr (Dewey Lamarr)
    b. Jan 1, 1955
MacLane, Barton b. Dec 25, 1900
Martin, Jerry Lindsey b. May 11, 1949
Reed, Susan b. 1927
Swearingen, John Eldred b. Sep 7, 1918
Timrod, Henry d. Oct 6, 1867
Turner, Glenn Wesley b. 1925
Converse, South Carolina
Boyd, Julian Parks b. Nov 3, 1903
Conway, South Carolina
Jenrette, John Wilson, Jr. b. May 19, 1936
Coosaw, South Carolina
Craig, Elizabeth May b. Dec 24, 1889
Cottageville, South Carolina
Ackerman, Bettye b. Feb 28, 1928
Easley, South Carolina
Baker, Bobby (Robert Gene)
    b. Nov 12, 1928
Edgefield, South Carolina
Thurmond, (James) Strom b. Dec 5, 1902
Edgefield District, South Carolina
Longstreet, James b. Jan 8, 1821
Fairfield, South Carolina
Ashford, Nickolas b. May 4, 1942
Florence, South Carolina
Jordan, Taft b. Feb 15, 1915
Purvis, Melvin d. Feb 29, 1960
Fort Moultrie, South Carolina
Osceola Nickanochee d. Jan 30, 1838
Fountain Inn, South Carolina
Bates, "Peg Leg" (Clayton)
    b. Nov 10, 1907
Georgetown, South Carolina
Rainey, Joseph Hayne b. Jun 21, 1832
Rainey, Joseph Hayne d. Aug 2, 1887

Woodruff, South Carolina
Harrelson, Ken(neth Smith) b. Sep 4, 1941
Yemassee, South Carolina
Blair, Frank b. May 30, 1915

SOUTH DAKOTA

Aberdeen, South Dakota
Hansen, Joseph b. Jul 19, 1923
Jones, David Charles b. Jul 9, 1921
Avon, South Dakota
Justus, Roy Braxton b. May 16, 1901
McGovern, George Stanley b. Jul 19, 1922
Bridgewater, South Dakota
Anderson, "Sparky" (George Lee)
    b. Feb 22, 1934
Canton, South Dakota
Lawrence, Ernest Orlando b. Aug 8, 1901
Tuve, Merle Antony b. Jun 27, 1901
Centerville, South Dakota
Anderson, Clint(on Presba)
    b. Oct 23, 1895
De Smet, South Dakota
Lane, Rose Wilder b. Dec 5, 1887
Deadwood, South Dakota
Hickok, "Wild Bill" (James Butler)
    d. Aug 2, 1876
Lambert, Ward L b. May 28, 1888
Provine, Dorothy Michele b. Jan 20, 1937
Eureka, South Dakota
Neuharth, Allen Harold b. Mar 22, 1924
Flandreau, South Dakota
Amdahl, Gene M(yron) b. Nov 16, 1922
Fort Yates, South Dakota
Grass, John d. May 10, 1918
Geddes, South Dakota
Exon, J(ohn) James, Jr. b. Aug 9, 1921
Grand River, South Dakota
Grass, John b. 1837
Sitting Bull b. 1831
Sitting Bull d. Dec 15, 1890
Groton, South Dakota
Sande, Earl b. 1898
Hot Springs, South Dakota
Thomas, Jess b. Apr 8, 1927
Howard, South Dakota
Hawley, Cameron b. Sep 19, 1905
Humboldt, South Dakota
Mundt, Karl Earl b. Jun 3, 1900
Pressler, Larry b. Mar 29, 1942
Huron, South Dakota
Humphrey, Muriel Fay Buck
    b. Feb 20, 1912
Ladd, Cheryl b. Jul 2, 1952
Sale, Charles Partlow b. 1885
Tiede, Tom Robert b. Feb 24, 1937
Joe Creek, South Dakota
Howe, Oscar b. May 13, 1915
Kennebec, South Dakota
Abdnor, James S b. Feb 13, 1923

Kimball, South Dakota
Ochsner, (Edward William) Alton
    b. May 4, 1896
Little Big Horn, South Dakota
Custer, George Armstrong d. Jun 25, 1876
Martin, South Dakota
Deloria, Vine, Jr. b. Mar 26, 1933
Mitchell, South Dakota
Owens, Gary b. May 10, 1935
Parade, South Dakota
Van Brocklin, Norm(an Mack)
    b. Mar 15, 1926
Pine Ridge, South Dakota
Means, Russell Charles b. Nov 10, 1940
Red Cloud, Chief d. 1909
Rapid Creek, South Dakota
Crazy Horse b. 1842
Rowena, South Dakota
Van Doren, Mamie b. Feb 6, 1933
Seneca, South Dakota
Evelyn, Judith b. 1913
Sioux Falls, South Dakota
Foss, Joseph Jacob b. Apr 17, 1915
Sisseton, South Dakota
Robbie, Joe (Joseph) b. Jul 7, 1916
Spearfish, South Dakota
Schoonmaker, Frank Musselman
    b. Aug 20, 1905
Sturgis, South Dakota
Ziolkowski, Korczak d. Oct 20, 1982
Terry, South Dakota
Calamity Jane d. Aug 1, 1903
Vermillion, South Dakota
Whittemore, Arthur Austin
    b. Oct 23, 1916
Viborg, South Dakota
Hansen, Alvin Harvey b. Aug 23, 1887
Virgil, South Dakota
Cleaver, Vera Allen b. Jan 6, 1919
Wallace, South Dakota
Humphrey, Hubert Horatio, Jr.
    b. May 27, 1911
Webster, South Dakota
Brokaw, Tom (Thomas John)
    b. Feb 6, 1940
Floren, Myron b. Nov 5, 1919
Woods, South Dakota
Abourezk, James George b. Feb 24, 1931

TENNESSEE

Allison, Clay b. 1840
Chisholm, Jesse b. 1806
Kelly, "Machine Gun" (George R) b. 1897
Moore, Grace b. Dec 1, 1901
Sanders, Bill (William Willard) b. 1933
Adamsville, Tennessee
Pusser, Buford d. Aug 21, 1974
Alcoa, Tennessee
Swann, Lynn Curtis b. Mar 7, 1952

Ashland, Tennessee
Bannister, Constance Gibbs
b. Feb 11, 1919
Bakerville, Tennessee
Anderson, William Robert b. Jun 17, 1921
Caraway, Hattie Wyatt b. Feb 1, 1878
Bells, Tennessee
Martindale, Wink (Winston Conrad)
b. Dec 4, 1934
Bethesda, Tennessee
Morgan, William Wilson b. Jan 3, 1906
Bristol, Tennessee
Ford, "Tennessee Ernie" (Ernest J)
b. Feb 13, 1919
Henderson, Vivian Wilson b. Feb 10, 1923
Reynolds, Richard S. b. Aug 5, 1881
Brownsville, Tennessee
Halliburton, Richard b. Jan 9, 1900
Smitherman, Geneva b. Dec 10, 1940
Camden, Tennessee
Cline, Patsy d. Mar 5, 1963
Campbellsville, Tennessee
Davidson, Donald Grady b. Aug 18, 1893
Carter Station, Tennessee
Johnson, Andrew d. Jul 31, 1875
Centerville, Tennessee
Pearl, Minnie b. Oct 25, 1912
Chapel Hill, Tennessee
Forrest, Nathan Bedford b. Jul 13, 1821
Charlotte, Tennessee
Robertson, Oscar b. Nov 24, 1938
Chattanooga, Tennessee
Adler, Julius Ochs b. Dec 3, 1892
Blanton, Jimmy b. 1918
Brock, Bill (William Emerson)
b. Nov 23, 1930
Hampton, Robert Edward b. Sep 21, 1922
Ochs, Adolph S, II b. Apr 14, 1885
Ochs, Adolph Simon d. Apr 8, 1935
Reed, Ishmael b. Feb 22, 1938
Smith, Bessie b. Apr 15, 1894
Clarksville, Tennessee
Scott, Evelyn b. Jan 17, 1893
Clinton, Tennessee
Stribling, Thomas Sigismund
b. Mar 4, 1881
Columbia, Tennessee
Doreset, Marion b. Dec 14, 1872
Covington, Tennessee
Hayes, Isaac b. Aug 20, 1942
Dayton, Tennessee
Hodges, Russ b. 1909
Del Rio, Tennessee
Guffey, Burnett b. May 26, 1905
Fayetteville, Tennessee
Dempsey, Rick (John Rikard)
b. Sep 13, 1949
Giles County, Tennessee
Davis, Sam(uel) d. Nov 27, 1863

Gordonsville, Tennessee
Bridges, Tommy (Thomas Jefferson Davis)
b. Dec 28, 1906
Grand Junction, Tennessee
Hearns, Thomas (Tommy) b. Oct 18, 1958
Grandview, Tennessee
Dickson, Earle Ensign b. Oct 10, 1892
Granville, Tennessee
Gore, Albert Arnold b. Dec 26, 1907
Greene City, Tennessee
Crockett, Davy (David) b. Aug 17, 1786
Greenville, Tennessee
Johnson, Eliza McCardle d. Jan 15, 1876
Halls, Tennessee
Middlecoff, Cary b. Jan 6, 1921
Hardeman County, Tennessee
Chisum, John Simpson b. Aug 15, 1824
Hardin County, Tennessee
Blanton, (Leonard) Ray b. Apr 10, 1930
Harriman, Tennessee
Lee, Dixie b. Nov 4, 1911
Henderson, Tennessee
Arnold, Eddy b. May 15, 1918
Hendersonville, Tennessee
Stewart, Wynn d. Jul 17, 1985
Huntsville, Tennessee
Baker, Howard Henry, Jr. b. Nov 15, 1925
Iron City, Tennessee
Montgomery, Melba b. Oct 14, 1938
Jackson, Tennessee
Crook, William Grant b. Sep 13, 1917
Dancy, John b. Aug 5, 1936
Jones, "Too Tall" (Edward Lee)
b. Feb 23, 1951
Jones, Christopher b. Aug 18, 1941
Perkins, Carl b. Apr 9, 1932
Ragan, David b. Aug 26, 1925
Sheppard, T G b. Jul 20, 1944
Johnson City, Tennessee
Hickman, Herman Michael, Jr.
b. Oct 1, 1911
Marshall, (Sarah) Catherine Wood
b. Sep 27, 1914
Marshall, Catherine b. Sep 27, 1915
Miller, William Ernest b. Feb 3, 1908
Knoxville, Tennessee
Agee, James Rufus b. Nov 27, 1909
Bergen, Polly b. Jul 14, 1930
Costa, Mary b. Apr 5, 1930
Cullum, John b. Mar 2, 1930
Farragut, David Glasgow b. Jul 5, 1801
Giovanni, Nikki b. Jun 7, 1943
Hastie, William Henry b. Nov 17, 1904
Jenkins, Ray Howard d. Dec 26, 1980
Keith, David b. 1954
Krutch, Joseph Wood b. Nov 25, 1893
Richberg, Donald R(andall) b. Jul 10, 1881
Whitehead, Don(ald Ford) d. Jan 12, 1981
Lauderdale City, Tennessee
Bradford, Roark b. Aug 21, 1896

Leesburg, Tennessee
Johnson, Eliza McCardle b. Oct 4, 1810
Lexington, Tennessee
Taylor, Sam b. Jul 12, 1916
Lookout Mountain, Tennessee
Carter, John Garnet d. Jul 21, 1954
Ross, John b. Oct 2, 1790
Tanner, (Leonard) Roscoe, (III)
  b. Oct 15, 1951
Loudon County, Tennessee
Sequoya b. 1770
Luttrell, Tennessee
Atkins, Chet (Chester B) b. Jun 20, 1924
Lynchburg, Tennessee
Early, Jubal Anderson d. Mar 2, 1894
Madisonville, Tennessee
Carter, Carlene b. 1957
Kefauver, Estes b. Jul 26, 1903
Maryville, Tennessee
Burger, Carl Victor b. Jun 18, 1888
Maynardsville, Tennessee
Acuff, Roy b. Sep 15, 1903
McMinnville, Tennessee
Snow, Dorothea Johnston b. Apr 7, 1909
West, Dottie b. Oct 11, 1932
Memphis, Tennessee
Ace, Johnny b. Jun 9, 1929
Allen, Deborah b. Sep 30, 1953
Armstrong, Lil(lian Hardin) b. Feb 3, 1902
Beck, Michael b. Feb 4, 1949
Bridgewater, Dee Dee b. May 27, 1950
Busse, Henry d. Apr 23, 1955
Butler, John b. Sep 29, 1920
Cash, Roseanne b. May 24, 1955
Chilton, Alex b. Dec 28, 1950
Cole, Olivia b. Nov 26, 1942
Crawford, James Strickland b. Jan 4, 1910
Crump, Edward Hull d. Oct 16, 1954
Cunningham, Bill b. Jan 23, 1950
Dunn, Mignon b.
Fidler, Jimmy (James M) b. 1900
Forrest, Nathan Bedford d. Oct 29, 1877
Fortas, Abe b. Jun 19, 1910
Franklin, Aretha b. Mar 25, 1942
Hamilton, George b. Aug 12, 1939
Hooks, Benjamin Lawson b. Jan 31, 1925
Humphrey, Claude B b. Jun 29, 1944
Hunter, "Ivory" Joe d. Nov 8, 1974
Hunter, Alberta b. Apr 1, 1897
Jones, "Gorilla" (William)
  b. May 12, 1906
Jones, Charles A, Jr. b. Jul 1, 1940
King, Martin Luther, Jr. d. Apr 4, 1968
Lanson, "Snooky" b. Mar 27, 1919
Little, Edward Herman d. Jul 12, 1981
Madlock, Bill (William Jr.)
  b. Jan 12, 1951
Needham, Hal b. Mar 6, 1931
Pinkwater, Daniel Manus b. Nov 15, 1941
Presley, Elvis (Elvis Aaron)
  d. Aug 16, 1977

Sasser, Jim (James Ralph) b. Sep 30, 1936
Shepherd, Cybill b. Feb 18, 1950
Stevens, Andrew b. Jun 10, 1955
Stiffel, Theodopholous b. 1899
Terrell, Mary Church b. Sep 23, 1863
Morristown, Tennessee
Wagner, Jane b. Feb 2, 1935
Murfreesboro, Tennessee
Lytle, Andrew Nelson b. Dec 26, 1902
Murfree, Mary Noailles b. Jan 24, 1850
Murfree, Mary Noailles d. Jul 31, 1922
Polk, Sarah Childress b. Sep 4, 1803
Rice, Grantland, (Henry Grantland)
  b. Nov 1, 1880
Nashville, Tennessee
Allman, Duane (Howard Duane)
  b. Nov 20, 1946
Allman, Gregg (Gregory Lenoir)
  b. Dec 7, 1947
Andrews, Frank M(axwell) b. Feb 3, 1884
Armstrong, Charles B b. Jul 22, 1923
Bond, Julian b. Jan 14, 1940
Bontemps, Arna Wendell d. Jun 4, 1973
Bridges, Tommy (Thomas Jefferson Davis)
  d. Apr 19, 1968
Carter, "Mother" Maybelle
  d. Oct 23, 1978
Caulkins, Tracy b. Jan 11, 1963
Coolidge, Rita b. May 1, 1945
Davidson, Donald Grady d. Apr 25, 1968
Dixon, Paul Rand b. Sep 29, 1913
Douglas, Aaron d. Feb 2, 1979
Frizzell, "Lefty" (William Orville)
  d. Jul 27, 1975
Fulton, Richard Harmon b. Jan 27, 1927
Gilliam, Jim (James William)
  b. Oct 17, 1928
Grooms, "Red" (Charles Roger)
  b. Jun 2, 1937
Howar, Barbara b. Sep 27, 1934
Jackson, Andrew d. Jun 8, 1845
Jackson, Rachel Donelson Robards
  d. Dec 22, 1828
Jarman, Claude, Jr. b. Sep 27, 1934
Jarrell, Randall b. May 6, 1914
Jones, Madison Percy, Jr. b. Mar 21, 1925
Lewis, Meriwether d. Oct 11, 1809
MacPhail, Lee (Leland Stanford, Jr.)
  b. Oct 25, 1917
Meek, Samuel Williams b. Sep 22, 1895
Meriwether, W(ilhelm) Delano
  b. Apr 23, 1943
Nielsen, Alice b. Jun 7, 1876
Polk, James K(nox) d. Jun 15, 1849
Polk, Sarah Childress d. Aug 14, 1891
Richardson, Scovel b. Feb 4, 1912
Ritter, "Tex" (Woodward Maurice)
  d. Jan 2, 1974
Robbins, Marty d. Dec 8, 1982
Robison, Paula Judith b. Jun 8, 1941
Rose, Fred d. Dec 1, 1954

Tate, Allen (John Orley) d. Feb 9, 1979
Tubb, Ernie (Ernest) d. Sep 6, 1984
Walker, William b. May 8, 1824
Wells, Kitty b. Aug 30, 1919
York, Sergeant (Alvin Cullum)
   d. Dec 2, 1964
Newport, Tennessee
Stokely, Alfred Jehu b. Mar 26, 1916
Nutbush, Tennessee
Turner, Tina b. Nov 26, 1938
Oak Ridge, Tennessee
Anderson, Elda Emma d. Apr 17, 1961
Overton County, Tennessee
Flatt, Lester Raymond b. Jun 28, 1914
Pall Mall, Tennessee
York, Sergeant (Alvin Cullum)
   b. Dec 13, 1887
Pegram, Tennessee
McCoy, Horace b. Apr 14, 1897
Pickett County, Tennessee
Hull, Cordell b. Oct 2, 1871
Pulaski, Tennessee
Beech, Walter Herschel b. Jan 30, 1891
Ransom, John Crowe b. Apr 30, 1888
Ravenscraft, Tennessee
Rowan, Carl Thomas b. Aug 11, 1925
Roane County, Tennessee
Rayburn, Sam(uel Taliaferro)
   b. Jan 6, 1882
Robbins, Tennessee
Barton, Bruce b. Aug 5, 1886
Robertson County, Tennessee
Jones, Jesse Holman b. Apr 5, 1874
Rogersville, Tennessee
Stewart, Alexander Peter b. Oct 2, 1821
Saint Bethelem, Tennessee
Rudolph, Wilma Glodean b. Jun 23, 1940
Sevierville, Tennessee
Parton, Dolly Rebecca b. Jan 19, 1946
Sewanee, Tennessee
Smith, Edmund Kirby d. Mar 8, 1893
Shelbyville, Tennessee
Locke, Sondra b. May 28, 1947
Shiloh, Tennessee
Johnston, Albert S d. Apr 6, 1862
Soddy, Tennessee
McGill, Ralph Emerson b. Feb 5, 1898
Spring City, Tennessee
Handy, Thomas Troy b. Mar 11, 1892
Stewart's Creek, Tennessee
Davis, Sam(uel) b. Oct 6, 1844
Stony Creek, Tennessee
Curtis, Jackie b. Feb 19, 1947
Summer County, Tennessee
Neal, James Foster b. Sep 7, 1929
Sweetwater, Tennessee
Carter, John Garnet b. Feb 9, 1883
Tiptonville, Tennessee
Cates, Clifton Bledsoe b. Aug 31, 1884
Winchester, Tennessee
Shore, Dinah b. Mar 1, 1917

Wolcottville, Tennessee
Kercheval, Ken b. Jul 15, 1935
Woodstock, Tennessee
Dix, Dorothy, pseud. b. Nov 18, 1870

TEXAS

Cacers, Ernest d. Jan 10, 1971
Church, George W b. 1887
Davis, (Thomas) Cullen b. 1933
Goodnight, Charles d. Dec 12, 1929
Hall, Jerry b. 1957
Miller, Nolan b. 1935
Patrick, Van b. 1916
Quanah b. 1845
Abbott, Texas
Nelson, Willie b. Apr 30, 1933
Abilene, Texas
Crane, Roy(ston Campbell)
   b. Nov 22, 1901
Sharman, Bill (William Walton)
   b. May 25, 1926
Williams, Mason b. Aug 24, 1938
Alba, Texas
Payne, Leon b. Jun 15, 1917
Alvarado, Texas
Southern, Terry b. May 1, 1924
Alvin, Texas
Ferguson, Joe Carlton, Jr. b. Apr 23, 1950
Amarillo, Texas
Britain, Radie b. Mar 17, 1903
Charisse, Cyd b. Mar 8, 1923
Jones, Carolyn b. Apr 28, 1933
Sargent, Ben b. Nov 26, 1948
Anson, Texas
Riley, Jeannie C b. Oct 19, 1945
Arlington, Texas
DiMuro, Lou d. Jun 6, 1982
Athens, Texas
Justice, William Wayne b. Feb 25, 1920
Murchison, Clint(on Williams) b. 1895
Murchison, Clint(on Williams)
   d. Jun 20, 1969
Richardson, Sid b. Apr 25, 1891
Austin, Texas
Ames, Jessie Daniel d. Feb 21, 1972
Austin, Stephen Fuller d. Dec 27, 1836
Baylor, Don Edward b. Jun 28, 1949
Byrd, Richard Evelyn b. Aug 13, 1860
Coleman, Dabney b. Jan 3, 1932
Crenshaw, Ben Daniel b. Jan 11, 1952
Dobie, J(ames) Frank d. Sep 18, 1964
Faulk, John Henry b. Aug 21, 1913
Ferguson, Miriam Amanda b. Jun 25, 1961
Grattan, Clinton Hartley d. Jun 25, 1980
Henderson, "Hollywood" (Thomas)
   b. Mar 1, 1953
Horton, Johnny d. Nov 5, 1960
Kenty, Hilmer b. Jul 30, 1955
Key, Valdimer Orlando, Jr.
   b. Mar 13, 1908

Lomax, Alan b. Jan 15, 1915
Schieffer, Bob b. Feb 25, 1937
Scott, Zachary b. Feb 24, 1914
Scott, Zachary d. Oct 3, 1965
Watt, George Willard d. Mar 29, 1980
Webb, Walter Prescott d. Mar 8, 1963
Wehrwein, Austin Carl b. Jan 12, 1916
Whitman, Charles Joseph d. Aug 1966
Wilson, Teddy (Theodore) b. Nov 24, 1912

Ballinger, Texas
Guion, David Wendel Fentress
    b. Dec 15, 1892

Beaumont, Texas
Crippen, Robert Laurel b. Sep 11, 1937
Davis, Walter b. Jan 5, 1931
Hofheinz, Roy Mark b. Apr 10, 1912
Robinson, Frank b. Aug 31, 1935
Vinson, Helen b. Sep 17, 1907
Winter, Edgar Holand b. Dec 28, 1946
Winter, Johnny (John Dawson, III)
    b. Feb 23, 1944
Zernial, Gus Edward b. Jun 27, 1923

Bell County, Texas
Ferguson, Miriam Amanda b. Jun 13, 1875

Big Spring, Texas
Buckley, Betty b. Jul 3, 1947

Blessing, Texas
Heffelfinger, "Pudge" (William Walter)
    d. Apr 2, 1954

Bloomington, Texas
Storm, Gale b. Apr 5, 1922

Blossom Prairie, Texas
Garner, John Nance b. Nov 22, 1868

Bonham, Texas
Morgan, Joe (Joseph Leonard)
    b. Sep 19, 1943
Rayburn, Sam(uel Taliaferro)
    d. Nov 16, 1961

Borden, Texas
Borden, Gail d. Jan 11, 1874

Borger, Texas
Anderson, Donny b. May 16, 1943

Bowie, Texas
Blocker, Dan b. 1927

Brenham, Texas
Cooper, Cecil b. Dec 20, 1949

Brownsville, Texas
Kristofferson, Kris b. Jun 22, 1937

Bryan, Texas
Ellerbee, Linda b. Aug 15, 1944

Calvert, Texas
Bradley, Tom (Thomas) b. Dec 29, 1917
McCrary, "Tex" (John Reagan) b. 1910

Celeste, Texas
Harrell, Mack b. Oct 8, 1909
Stratton, Monty Franklin Pierce
    b. May 21, 1912

Centerville, Texas
Hopkins, "Lightnin'" (Sam)
    b. Mar 15, 1912

Chandler, Texas
Yarborough, Ralph Webster b. Jun 8, 1903

Cherino, Texas
Miller, Ann b. Apr 12, 1923

Cisco, Texas
Crofts, Dash b. 1940

Clarksville, Texas
Gibbons, Euell b. Sep 8, 1911
Smith, Tommie b. Jun 5, 1944

Coleman, Texas
Birdwell, Russell Juarez b. Oct 17, 1903

Colorado, Texas
Dies, Martin, Jr. b. Nov 5, 1900

Commerce, Texas
Chennault, Claire Lee b. Sep 6, 1890

Corpus Christi, Texas
Berry, Raymond Emmett b. Feb 27, 1933
Borglum, James Lincoln Delamothe
    d. Jan 27, 1986
Browning, Edmond Lee b. Mar 11, 1929
Cottam, Clarence d. Mar 30, 1974
Donath, Helen b. 1940
Farenthold, Frances T b. Oct 2, 1926
Fawcett, Farrah Leni b. Feb 2, 1947
King, Richard d. Apr 14, 1885
Kleberg, Robert Justus, Jr.
    b. Mar 29, 1896
Mullin, Willard d. Dec 21, 1978

Corsicana, Texas
Frizzell, "Lefty" (William Orville)
    b. Mar 31, 1928

Crafton, Texas
Carter, Amon Giles b. Dec 11, 1880

Crisp, Texas
Tubb, Ernie (Ernest) b. Feb 9, 1914

Cross Plains, Texas
Howard, Robert Ervin d. Jun 12, 1936

Dallas, Texas
Banks, Ernie (Ernest) b. Jan 31, 1931
Benson, Robby b. Jan 21, 1957
Bond, Tommy b. Sep 16, 1927
Bond, Ward d. Nov 5, 1960
Christian, Charlie (Charles) b. 1919
Clark, (William) Ramsey b. Dec 18, 1927
Clark, Tom (Thomas Campbell)
    b. Sep 23, 1899
Connolly, Maureen d. Jun 21, 1969
Corn, Ira George, Jr. d. Apr 28, 1982
Daniels, "Bebe" (Virginia) b. Jan 14, 1901
Darnell, Linda b. Oct 16, 1921
Elder, Lee b. Jul 14, 1934
English, Doug (Lowell Douglas)
    b. Aug 25, 1953
Estridge, Philip D d. Aug 2, 1985
Evans, Clifford b. Jun 13, 1920
Fairchild, Morgan b. Feb 3, 1950
Giuffre, James Peter b. Apr 26, 1921
Gramatky, Hardie b. Apr 12, 1907
Granatelli, Anthony Joseph
    b. Mar 18, 1923
Griffin, John Howard b. Jun 16, 1920

Guion, David Wendel Fentress
  d. Oct 17, 1981
Halaby, Najeeb Elias b. Nov 19, 1915
Harrell, Mack d. Jan 29, 1960
Hughes, Sarah Tilghman d. Apr 23, 1985
Hunt, H(aroldson) L(afayette)
  d. Nov 29, 1974
Hunt, Lamar b. Aug 2, 1932
Jackson, Maynard Holbrook, Jr.
  b. Mar 23, 1938
Jacoby, Oswald d. Jun 27, 1984
Jefferson, John Larry b. Feb 3, 1956
Jones, Preston St. Vrain d. Sep 19, 1979
Keeler, William d. Jul 12, 1981
Kennedy, John Fitzgerald d. Nov 22, 1963
Lay, Herman Warden d. Dec 6, 1982
Lopez, Trini(dad, III) b. May 15, 1937
Lunn, Janet b. Dec 28, 1928
Mangrum, Lloyd b. Aug 1, 1914
Marcus, Stanley b. Apr 20, 1906
Martin, Harvey b. Nov 16, 1950
McKinley, Chuck (Charles Robert)
  d. Aug 11, 1986
Meat Loaf b. Sep 27, 1947
Miller, Steve b. Oct 5, 1943
O'Shea, Michael d. Dec 1973
Oswald, Lee Harvey d. Nov 24, 1963
Page, "Hot Lips" (Oran Thaddeus)
  b. Jan 27, 1908
Pons, Lily d. Feb 13, 1976
Rote, Kyle, Jr. b. Dec 25, 1950
Ruby, Jack d. Jan 3, 1967
Scaggs, "Boz" (William Royce)
  b. Jun 8, 1944
Scales, DeWayne Jay b. Dec 28, 1958
Seale, Bobby G b. Oct 20, 1936
Spelling, Aaron b. Apr 22, 1925
Stills, Stephen b. Jan 3, 1945
Stone, Sly b. Mar 15, 1944
Tabbert, William d. Oct 20, 1974
Tate, Sharon b. 1943
Trevino, Lee Buck b. Dec 1, 1939
Walker, Ewell Doak, Jr. b. Jan 1, 1927
Walls, Everson Collins b. Dec 28, 1959

Dawson, Texas
Comer, Anjanette b. Aug 7, 1942

Dekalb, Texas
Nelson, Rick (Eric Hilliard)
  d. Dec 31, 1985

DeLeon, Texas
White, William Smith b. Feb 5, 1907

Denison, Texas
Eisenhower, Dwight David b. Oct 14, 1890
Hillerman, John Benedict b. Dec 20, 1932

Denton, Texas
Conley, Eugene d. Dec 18, 1981
George, Phyllis b. Jun 25, 1949
O'Neill, Cherry Boone b. Jul 7, 1954
Sheridan, Ann b. Feb 21, 1915

Dublin, Texas
Hogan, Ben (William Benjamin)
  b. Aug 13, 1912
El Dorado, Texas
Hunt, Nelson Bunker b. Feb 22, 1926
El Paso, Texas
Bingaman, Jeff b. Oct 3, 1943
Carr, Vikki b. Jul 19, 1941
Cornell, Lydia b. 1957
Donaldson, Sam(uel Andrew)
  b. Mar 11, 1934
Fall, Albert Bacon d. Nov 30, 1944
Farah, Robert Norman b. Aug 5, 1952
Kibbee, Guy b. Mar 6, 1882
Knickerbocker, Suzy b. 1919
Lea, Tom b. Jul 11, 1907
Marshall, S(amuel) L(yman) A(twood)
  d. Dec 17, 1977
Mayer, Norman D b. Mar 31, 1916
Mott, Ruth Rawlings b. Oct 18, 1901
O'Connor, Sandra Day b. Mar 26, 1930
Ochs, Phil(ip David) b. Dec 19, 1940
Rechy, John Franklin b. Mar 10, 1934
Reynolds, Debbie (Marie Frances)
  b. Apr 1, 1932
Roddenberry, Gene (Eugene Wesley)
  b. Aug 19, 1921
Ryan, Irene Noblette b. Oct 17, 1903
Valachi, Joe (Joseph M) d. Apr 3, 1971
Watson, Jack Hearn, Jr. b. Oct 24, 1938
Ennis, Texas
Banner, Bob b. Aug 15, 1921
Fabens, Texas
Shoemaker, Willie (William Lee)
  b. Aug 19, 1931
Fannin County, Texas
Boyd, Bill b. 1911
Field Creek, Texas
Eaker, Ira Clarence b. Apr 13, 1896
Floresville, Texas
Connally, John Bowden, Jr.
  b. Feb 27, 1917
Valdez, Abelardo Lopez b. Aug 31, 1942
Fort Brown, Texas
Sykes, George d. Feb 8, 1880
Fort Hood, Texas
Stockman, David Allen b. Nov 10, 1946
Fort Sam Houston, Texas
Harding, Ann b. Aug 17, 1904
Fort Worth, Texas
Beneke, Tex b. Feb 12, 1914
Capshaw, Kate b.
Castle, Vernon d. Feb 15, 1918
Chapman, Mark David b. May 10, 1955
Chouteau, Yvonne b. 1929
Coleman, Ornette b. Mar 19, 1930
Courtright, Jim (Timothy Isaiah)
  d. Feb 8, 1887
Curry, Donald b. 1961
Griffin, John Howard d. Sep 9, 1980
Hagman, Larry b. Sep 21, 1931

Haynie, Sandra b. Jun 4, 1943
Heloise b. May 4, 1919
Highsmith, Patricia b. Jan 12, 1921
Hunnicutt, Gayle b. Feb 6, 1943
Hyer, Martha b. Aug 10, 1924
Manners, Dorothy b.
McFarland, "Spanky" (George Emmett)
    b. Oct 2, 1928
McKinley, Ray b. Jun 18, 1910
Merrifield, R(obert) Bruce b. Jul 5, 1921
Miller, Roger Dean b. Jan 2, 1936
Nelson, Byron (John Byron, Jr.)
    b. Feb 4, 1912
Parker, Fess b. Aug 16, 1927
Reed, Rex b. Oct 2, 1939
Smith, Liz (Mary Elizabeth)
    b. Feb 2, 1923
Thompson, Thomas b. Oct 3, 1933
Whelchel, Lisa b. May 29, 1963
Wills, Bob d. May 13, 1975
Wright, James C(laud), Jr. b. Dec 22, 1922

Fredericksburg, Texas
Nimitz, Chester William b. Feb 24, 1885

Gainesville, Texas
Austin, Gene b. Jun 24, 1900
Buck, Frank b. Mar 17, 1884
Franken, Rose b. Dec 28, 1898

Galveston, Texas
Bragg, Braxton d. Sep 27, 1876
Didrikson, "Babe" (Mildred)
    d. Sep 27, 1956
Helmond, Katherine b. Jun 5, 1933
Johnson, Jack (John Arthur)
    b. Mar 31, 1878
Perrine, Valerie b. Sep 3, 1943
Phillips, Esther b. Dec 23, 1935
Vidor, King Wallis b. Feb 8, 1894
White, Barry b. Sep 12, 1944

Gatesville, Texas
Weaver, Mike (Michael Dwayne)
    b. Jun 4, 1952

Gilmer, Texas
Henley, Don b. Jul 22, 1947

Golden Acres, Texas
Viguerie, Richard A(rt) b. Sep 23, 1933

Goose Creek, Texas
Busey, Gary b. 1944

Grand Prairie, Texas
Hamilton, Floyd (Garland) d. Jun 26, 1984

Grand Saline, Texas
Post, Wiley b. Nov 22, 1900

Granger, Texas
Danforth, David Charles b. Mar 7, 1890

Greenville, Texas
Boles, John b. Oct 18, 1895
Neyland, Robert Reese b. Feb 17, 1892
Stratton, Monty Franklin Pierce
    d. Sep 29, 1982

Groesbeck, Texas
Baker, Joe Don b. Feb 12, 1936

Hamlin, Texas
Strauss, Robert b. Oct 19, 1918

Harlingen, Texas
Haley, Bill (William John Clifford, Jr.)
    d. Feb 9, 1981

Haskell, Texas
Thornton, Charles Bates b. Jul 22, 1913

Henderson, Texas
Delaney, Joe Alton b. Oct 30, 1958
White, Mark Wells, Jr. b. Mar 17, 1940

Hereford, Texas
Ely, Ron b. Jun 21, 1938
Mitchell, Edgar Dean b. Sep 17, 1930

Hillsboro, Texas
Johnson, Rafer Lewis b. Aug 18, 1935

Hot Wells, Texas
Kay, Mary b.

Houston, Texas
Abercrombie, James Smither
    d. Jan 7, 1975
Abercrombie, Josephine b. 1926
Ace, Johnny d. Dec 25, 1954
Allen, Debbie b. Jan 16, 1950
Alworth, Lance Dwight b. Aug 3, 1940
Baker, James Addison, III b. Apr 28, 1930
Bankhead, Dan(iel Robert) d. May 2, 1976
Barry, Donald b. Jul 11, 1912
Bell, Ricky Lynn b. Apr 8, 1955
Bettis, Valerie b. Dec 20, 1919
Blyden, Larry b. Jun 23, 1925
Branch, Cliff(ord) b. Aug 1, 1948
Browles, William Dodson, Jr.
    b. Oct 8, 1944
Buck, Frank d. Mar 25, 1950
Chase, William Curtis d. Aug 21, 1986
Christian, Mary Blount b. Feb 20, 1933
Cobb, Arnett Cleophus b. Aug 10, 1918
Cooley, Denton Arthur b. Aug 22, 1920
Costa, Victor Charles b. Dec 17, 1935
Crosby, Kathryn b. Nov 25, 1933
Crowell, Rodney b. Aug 7, 1950
David b. Sep 21, 1971
David d. Feb 22, 1984
Demaret, Jimmy (James Newton B)
    b. May 10, 1910
Demaret, Jimmy (James Newton B)
    d. Dec 28, 1983
Drury, Allen Stuart b. Sep 2, 1918
Duncan, Charles William, Jr.
    b. Sep 9, 1926
Duvall, Shelley b. Jul 7, 1949
Flood, Curt(is Charles) b. Jan 18, 1938
Foxworth, Robert b. Nov 1, 1941
Foyt, A(nthony) J(oseph, Jr.)
    b. Jan 16, 1935
Gaines, Lee b. Apr 21, 1914
Gerber, John d. Jan 28, 1981
Gimbel, Sophie Haas b. 1898
Guerard, Albert Joseph b. Nov 2, 1914
Hampton, Hope b. 1901
Hartman, Lisa b.

Hayes, Lester b. Jan 22, 1955
Healy, Ted b. Oct 1, 1896
Hofheinz, Roy Mark d. Nov 21, 1982
Hopkins, "Lightnin'" (Sam)
    d. Jan 30, 1982
House, Edward Mandell b. Jul 26, 1858
Hughes, Howard Robard b. Dec 24, 1905
Hughes, Howard Robard d. Apr 5, 1976
Jones, Jesse Holman d. Jun 1, 1956
Jordan, Barbara C b. Feb 21, 1936
Kleberg, Robert Justus, Jr. d. Oct 13, 1974
Leonetti, Tommy d. Sep 15, 1979
Little Esther b. Dec 23, 1935
Lombardo, Guy Albert d. Nov 5, 1977
MacDonald, Jeanette d. Jan 14, 1965
MacRae, Meredith b. May 30, 1944
Mandrell, Barbara Ann b. Dec 25, 1948
Maris, Roger Eugene d. Dec 14, 1985
McNeil, Neil Venable b. Oct 24, 1927
Mecom, John Whitfield d. Oct 12, 1981
Nash, Johnny b. Aug 19, 1940
Nesmith, Mike b. Dec 30, 1942
Preston, Billy (William Everett)
    b. Sep 9, 1946
Pruitt, Greg(ory Donald) b. Aug 18, 1951
Quaid, Dennis b. Apr 9, 1954
Quaid, Randy b. May 11, 1950
Renfro, Mel(vin Lacy) b. Dec 30, 1941
Rogers, Kenny (Kenneth Ray)
    b. Aug 21, 1938
Singletary, Mike (Michael) b. Oct 9, 1958
Smith, Jaclyn b. Oct 26, 1948
Sophie b.
Swayze, Patrick b. Aug 18, 1955
Thomas, B(illy) J(oe) b. Aug 7, 1942
Tower, John Goodwin b. Sep 29, 1925
Valenti, Jack Joseph b. Sep 5, 1921
Vidor, Florence b. Jul 23, 1895
Vinson, "Cleanhead" (Eddie)
    b. Dec 18, 1917
Whitmire, Kathy b. Aug 15, 1946
Williams, Delvin b. Apr 17, 1951

Hubbard City, Texas
Speaker, Tris(tram E) b. Apr 4, 1888

Hughes Springs, Texas
Patman, (John Williams) Wright
    b. Aug 6, 1893

Huntsville, Texas
Abercrombie, James Smither b. Jul 7,
Brooks, Charlie, Jr. d. Dec 7, 1982
Forrest, Steve b. Sep 29, 1925
Houston, Sam(uel) d. Jul 26, 1863
Lovett, Robert A(bercrombie)
    b. Sep 14, 1895

Indian Creek, Texas
Porter, Katherine Anne b. May 15, 1894

Jacksonville, Texas
Dexter, Al b. May 4, 1902

Jefferson, Texas
Benefield, Barry b. 1887

Johnson City, Texas
Johnson, Lyndon Baines d. Jan 22, 1973

Justiceburg, Texas
Cash, Norm(an Dalton) b. Nov 10, 1934

Karnack, Texas
Johnson, "Lady Bird" (Claudia Alta
    Taylor) b. Dec 22, 1912

Kaufman, Texas
Parker, "Buddy" (Raymond)
    d. Mar 22, 1982

Kemp, Texas
Parker, "Buddy" (Raymond)
    b. Dec 16, 1913

Kilgore, Texas
Matson, Randy (James Randel)
    b. Mar 5, 1945

Killeen, Texas
Hobby, Oveta Culp b. Jan 19, 1905

Kingston, Texas
Murphy, Audie b. Jun 20, 1924

Kingsville, Texas
Denton, Steve b. Sep 5, 1956

Kirbyville, Texas
Hunter, "Ivory" Joe b. 1911

La Porte, Texas
Edmonds, Emma E d. Sep 5, 1898

Lake Lewisville, Texas
Dexter, Al d. Jan 28, 1984

Lake Whitney, Texas
Speaker, Tris(tram E) d. Dec 8, 1958

Lakeland Air Force Base, Texas
Twining, Nathan F(arragut)
    d. Mar 29, 1982

Lampasas, Texas
Walker, Stanley b. Oct 21, 1898
Walker, Stanley d. Nov 25, 1962

Lanesville, Texas
Mosely, Mark DeWayne b. Mar 12, 1948

Langtry, Texas
Bean, Roy d. Mar 16, 1903

Liberty, Texas
Mecom, John Whitfield b. Jan 13, 1911

Limestone County, Texas
Wills, Bob b. Mar 6, 1906

Linden, Texas
Buford, Don(ald Alvin) b. Feb 2, 1937
Walker, "T-Bone" (Aaron)
    b. May 28, 1910

Littlefield, Texas
Jennings, Waylon b. Jun 15, 1937
Jones, Tom b. Feb 17, 1928

Live Oak County, Texas
Dobie, J(ames) Frank b. Sep 26, 1888

Lockney, Texas
Ewing, William Maurice b. May 12, 1906
Templeton, Garry Lewis b. Mar 24, 1956

Longview, Texas
LeTourneau, Robert Gilmour
    d. Jun 1, 1969

Lubbock, Texas
Davis, Mac b. Jan 21, 1942
Ely, Joe b. 1947
Hipple, Eric Ellsworth b. Sep 16, 1957
Holly, "Buddy" (Charles Hardin)
b. Sep 7, 1936
Leland, "Mickey" (George Thomas)
b. Nov 27, 1944
McClinton, Delbert b. 1940
Richardson, Micheal Ray b. Apr 11, 1955
Lufkin, Texas
Dies, Martin, Jr. d. Nov 14, 1972
Houston, Ken(neth Ray) b. Nov 12, 1944
Mansfield, Texas
Morse, Ella Mae b. Sep 12, 1924
Marshall, Texas
Farmer, James b. Jan 12, 1920
Foreman, George b. Jan 10, 1949
Howard, Susan b. Jan 28, 1943
Tittle, Y(elberton) A(braham)
b. Oct 24, 1926
Mason County, Texas
Stevenson, Coke Robert b. Mar 20, 1888
McLennan County, Texas
Connally, Tom (Thomas Terry)
b. Aug 19, 1877
Mexia, Texas
Baxter, Les b. Mar 14, 1922
Midland, Texas
Love, Bessie b. Sep 10, 1898
Massey, D Curtis b. May 3, 1910
Minden, Texas
Arnold, Oren b. Jul 20, 1900
Minerva, Texas
Smith, Cyrus Rowlett b. Sep 9, 1899
Mission, Texas
Bentsen, Lloyd Millard, Jr.
b. Feb 11, 1921
Landry, Tom (Thomas Wade)
b. Sep 11, 1924
Monahans, Texas
Whitworth, Kathy (Kathrynne Ann)
b. Sep 27, 1939
Mount Calm, Texas
Graves, William Sidney b. Mar 27, 1865
Mount Vernon, Texas
Meredith, Don (Joseph Donald)
b. Apr 10, 1938
Muleshoe, Texas
Horsley, Lee b. May 15, 1955
Munday, Texas
Cousins, Margaret b. Jan 26, 1905
Murval, Texas
Ritter, "Tex" (Woodward Maurice)
b. Jan 12, 1907
Nacogdoches, Texas
Baker, Charlotte b. Aug 31, 1910
Navasota, Texas
Tex, Joe d. Aug 13, 1982
Needville, Texas
Jackson, Earnest b. Dec 18, 1959

Normangee, Texas
Roloff, Lester d. Nov 2, 1982
Oakwood, Texas
Colbert, Lester Lum b. Jun 13, 1905
Odessa, Texas
Gatlin, Larry Wayne b. May 2, 1949
Orange, Texas
Baker, Bonnie b. Apr 1, 1917
Phillips, "Bum" (Oail Andrew)
b. Sep 29, 1923
Smith, "Bubba" (Charles Aaron)
b. Feb 28, 1945
Palestine, Texas
Ames, Jessie Daniel b. Nov 2, 1883
Bradley, Bill (William) b. Jan 24, 1947
Pampa, Texas
Russell, Charles Taze d. Oct 31, 1916
Panola County, Texas
Webb, Walter Prescott b. Apr 3, 1888
Paris, Texas
Johnson, Mordecai Wyatt b. Jan 12, 1890
Pasadena, Texas
Millar, Jeff(rey) Lynn b. Jul 10, 1942
Pearland, Texas
Givens, Edward Galen d. Jun 6, 1967
Peaster, Texas
Howard, Robert Ervin b. Jan 22, 1906
Perryville, Texas
Price, Ray b. Jan 12, 1926
Petralia, Texas
Hadley, Reed b. 1911
Plainview, Texas
Dean, Jimmy b. Aug 10, 1928
Polk County, Texas
Foreman, Percy b. Jun 21, 1902
Port Arthur, Texas
Didrikson, "Babe" (Mildred)
b. Jun 26, 1912
Joplin, Janis b. Jan 19, 1943
Keyes, Evelyn Louise b. Nov 20, 1919
Rauschenberg, Robert b. Oct 22, 1925
Quitman, Texas
Spacek, "Sissy" (Mary Elizabeth)
b. Dec 25, 1949
Refugio, Texas
Ryan, Nolan (Lynn Nolan)
b. Jan 31, 1947
Rhonesboro, Texas
Inman, Bobby Ray b. Apr 4, 1931
Richland Springs, Texas
Wood, Woodrow Johnson b. Sep 29, 1918
Robstown, Texas
Upshaw, Gene (Eugene) b. Aug 15, 1945
Rockland, Texas
Dorsey, Bob Rawls b. Aug 27, 1912
Rockport, Texas
Cacers, Ernest b. Nov 22, 1911
Wood, John Howland, Jr. b. Mar 31, 1916
Rogers, Texas
Ailey, Alvin b. Jan 5, 1931
Tex, Joe b. Aug 8, 1933

Round Rock, Texas
Bass, Sam d. Jul 21, 1878
Rowena, Texas
Parker, Bonnie b. Oct 1, 1910
Sabinal, Texas
Rodriguez, Johnny b. Dec 10, 1951
Sabine Pass, Texas
Big Bopper, The b. Oct 24, 1930
Salado, Texas
Carpenter, Liz (Elizabeth Sutherland)
b. Sep 1, 1920
San Angelo, Texas
Allen, Jay Presson b. Mar 3, 1922
Boles, John d. Feb 27, 1969
Holman, Eugene b. May 2, 1895
Kemp, Steve(n F) b. Aug 7, 1954
Logan, Daniel b. Oct 14, 1936
Stevenson, Coke Robert d. Jun 28, 1975
San Antonio, Texas
Alessandro, Victor Nicholas
d. Nov 27, 1976
Bates, Florence b. Apr 15, 1888
Brinkley, John Romulus d. May 26, 1942
Burnett, Carol b. Apr 26, 1936
Cisneros, Henry Gabriel b. Jun 11, 1947
Crawford, Joan b. Mar 23, 1908
Cross, Christopher b. May 3, 1951
Davis, Harold Lenoir d. Oct 31, 1960
Eberle, Irmengarde b. Nov 11, 1898
Fain, Ferris Roy b. Mar 29, 1922
Freeman, Al, Jr. b. Mar 21, 1934
Gompers, Samuel d. Dec 13, 1924
Grogan, Steve b. Jul 24, 1958
Handy, Thomas Troy d. Apr 14, 1982
Heloise d. Dec 28, 1977
Hodges, Courtney d. Jan 16, 1966
Kent, Jack (John Wellington)
d. Oct 18, 1985
Lewenthal, Raymond b. Aug 29, 1926
Maverick, Maury b. Oct 23, 1895
Maverick, Maury d. Jun 7, 1954
Maverick, Samuel Augustus d. Sep 2, 1870
Medill, Joseph d. Mar 16, 1899
Parker, Suzy b. Oct 28, 1933
Patch, Alexander M(c Carrell)
d. Nov 21, 1945
Payne, Leon d. Sep 11, 1969
Prentiss, Paula b. Mar 4, 1939
Rote, Kyle b. Oct 27, 1928
Samaroff, Olga b. Aug 8, 1882
Scott, David Randolph b. Jun 6, 1932
Simms, Ginny (Virginia E)
b. May 25, 1916
Simpson, William Hood d. Aug 15, 1980
Stokowski, Olga Smaroff b. Aug 8, 1882
Waddell, "Rube" (George Edward)
d. Apr 1, 1914
Wainwright, Jonathan Mayhew
d. Sep 2, 1953
White, Ed(ward Higgins, II)
b. Nov 14, 1930

Wood, John Howland, Jr. d. May 29, 1979
Youngs, Ross Middlebrook d. Oct 22, 1927
San Benito, Texas
Fender, Freddy b. Jun 4, 1937
San Marcos, Texas
George, Lynda Day b. Dec 11, 1946
San Saba, Texas
Jones, Tommy Lee b. Sep 15, 1946
Stewart, Thomas b. Aug 19, 1928
Santa Anna, Texas
Layne, Bobby (Robert Lawrence)
b. Dec 19, 1926
Saratoga, Texas
Jones, George b. Sep 12, 1931
Seagoville, Texas
Wills, Chill b. Jul 18, 1903
Sealy, Texas
Dickerson, Eric Demetric b. Sep 2, 1960
Seminole, Texas
Tucker, Tanya b. Oct 10, 1958
Sherman, Texas
Owens, "Buck" (Alvis E, Jr.)
b. Aug 12, 1929
Shiner, Texas
Youngs, Ross Middlebrook
b. Apr 10, 1897
Sindey, Texas
Seals, Jim (James) b. 1942
Snyder, Texas
Boothe, Powers b. Jun 1, 1949
Stonewall, Texas
Johnson, Lyndon Baines b. Aug 27, 1908
Taylor, Texas
Avery, "Tex" (Frederick Bean)
b. Feb 26, 1908
Taylortown, Texas
Allen, Duane b. Apr 29, 1943
Telice, Texas
Barrow, Clyde b. Mar 24, 1909
Temple, Texas
Baugh, Sammy (Samuel Adrian)
b. Mar 17, 1914
Greene, Joe (Joseph) b. Sep 24, 1946
Torn, Rip b. Feb 6, 1931
Texarkana, Texas
Griffith, Corinne b. Nov 24, 1896
Hargis, Billy James b. Aug 3, 1925
Joplin, Scott b. Nov 24, 1868
Logan, Josh(ua Lockwood) b. Oct 5, 1908
Mathews, Eddie (Edwin Lee, Jr.)
b. Oct 13, 1931
Perot, (Henry) Ross b. Jun 27, 1930
Texas City, Texas
Lee, Johnny b. 1947
The Alamo, Texas
Bowie, James d. Mar 6, 1836
Crockett, Davy (David) d. Mar 6, 1836
Tioga, Texas
Autry, Gene (Orvon Gene)
b. Sep 29, 1907

Geographic Index

Trinity, Texas
  Goyen, William b. Apr 24, 1915
  Matson, Oliver G b. May 1, 1930
Tuxedo, Texas
  Davis, Kingsley b. Aug 20, 1908
Tyler, Texas
  Campbell, Earl Christian b. Mar 29, 1955
  Duncan, Sandy b. Feb 20, 1946
  Horton, Johnny b. Apr 30, 1927
  Wilson, "Dooley" (Arthur) b. Apr 3, 1894
Uvalde, Texas
  Briscoe, Dolph b. Apr 23, 1923
  Evans, Dale b. Oct 31, 1912
  Garner, John Nance d. Nov 7, 1967
Vernon, Texas
  Teagarden, Charles b. Jul 19, 1913
  Teagarden, Jack (Weldon John)
    b. Aug 20, 1905
Waco, Texas
  Alessandro, Victor Nicholas
    b. Nov 27, 1915
  Brann, William Cowper d. Apr 2, 1898
  Brazelton, T(homas) Berry
    b. May 10, 1918
  Eichelberger, Dave b. Sep 3, 1943
  Evans, Heloise Cruse b. Apr 15, 1951
  Guinan, "Texas" (Mary Louise Cecilia)
    b. 1889
  Jaworski, Leon b. Sep 19, 1905
  Malick, Terence (Terry) b. Nov 30, 1943
  Martin, Steve b. 1945
  Rogers, Bill (William Charles)
    b. Sep 10, 1951
  Rowe, "Schoolboy" (Lynwood Thomas)
    b. Jan 11, 1912
  Thompson, Hank b. Sep 3, 1925
  Wilson, Robert M b. Oct 4, 1944
Waxahachie, Texas
  Benton, Robert Douglass b. Sep 29, 1932
  Richards, Paul Rapier b. Nov 21, 1908
  Richards, Paul Rapier d. May 4, 1986
Weatherford, Texas
  Martin, Mary b. Dec 1, 1914
  Simpson, William Hood b. May 19, 1888
Wharton, Texas
  Foote, Horton (Albert Horton, Jr.)
    b. Mar 14, 1917
  Rather, Dan b. Oct 31, 1931
Wheeler, Texas
  Bean, Alan L b. Mar 15, 1932
Wichita Falls, Texas
  Grant, Bruce b. Apr 17, 1893
  McMurtry, Larry Jeff b. Jun 3, 1936
  Singer, Jane Sherrod b. May 26, 1917
  Tune, Tommy (Thomas James)
    b. Feb 28, 1939
Wimberley, Texas
  Jaworski, Leon d. Dec 9, 1982
Wink, Texas
  Orbison, Roy b. Apr 23, 1936

Winters, Texas
  Hornsby, Rogers b. Apr 27, 1896
Wortham, Texas
  Jefferson, Blind Lemon b. 1897

UTAH

Beaver, Utah
  Farnsworth, Philo Taylor b. Aug 19, 1906
Charlotte, Utah
  Grenfell, Wilfred Thomason, Sir
    d. Oct 9, 1940
Circleville, Utah
  Cassidy, Butch b. Apr 6, 1867
Coalville, Utah
  Geary, Anthony b. May 29, 1948
Huntsville, Utah
  McKay, David O b. Sep 8, 1873
Kimberley, Utah
  Priest, Ivy (Maude) Baker b. Sep 7, 1905
Logan, Utah
  Eccles, Marriner Stoddard b. Sep 9, 1890
  Gilbert, John b. Jul 10, 1897
  Olsen, Merlin b. Sep 15, 1940
  Swenson, May b. May 28, 1919
Magna, Utah
  Jarvis, Howard Arnold b. Sep 22, 1902
Marriott, Utah
  Marriott, John Willard b. Sep 17, 1900
Marysvale, Utah
  Windsor, Marie b. Dec 11, 1924
Midway, Utah
  Watkins, Arthur V(ivian) b. Dec 18, 1886
Murray, Utah
  Allred, Rulon Clark d. May 10, 1977
Ogden, Utah
  Ashby, Hal b. 1936
  Borglum, Solon Hannibal b. Dec 22, 1868
  Brodie, Fawn McKay b. Sep 15, 1915
  Browning, John Moses b. Jan 21, 1855
  Bushnell, Nolan Kay b. Feb 5, 1943
  Dawn, Hazel b. Mar 23, 1898
  DeVoto, Bernard Augustine
    b. Jan 11, 1897
  Janney, Leon b. Apr 1, 1917
  Nichols, "Red" (Ernest Loring)
    b. May 8, 1905
  Osmond, Donny (Donald Clark)
    b. Dec 9, 1958
  Osmond, Marie (Olive Marive)
    b. Oct 13, 1959
  Richards, Richard b. May 14, 1932
  Stevens, S(tanley) S(mith) b. Nov 4, 1906
Orem, Utah
  Watkins, Arthur V(ivian) d. Sep 1, 1973
Paradise, Utah
  Bickmore, Lee Smith b. Jun 5, 1908
Point of Mountain, Utah
  Gilmore, Gary Mark d. Jan 18, 1977
Price, Utah
  Westwood, Jean Miles b. Nov 22, 1923

East Dover, Vermont
Adams, Sherman Llewellyn b. Jan 8, 1899
Fairfield, Vermont
Arthur, Chester Alan b. Oct 5, 1829
Halifax, Vermont
Otis, Elisha Graves b. Aug 3, 1811
Hardwick, Vermont
Fixx, James Fuller d. Jul 20, 1984
Hartford, Vermont
Lord, Phillips H b. Jul 13, 1902
Wells, Horace b. Jan 21, 1815
Highgate, Vermont
Austin, Warren R(obinson)
b. Nov 12, 1877
Holland, Vermont
Tabor, Horace Austin Warner
b. Nov 26, 1830
Island Pond, Vermont
Vallee, Rudy (Herbert Prior)
b. Jul 28, 1901
Logan, Vermont
Romney, Lenore la Fount b.
Ludlow, Vermont
Fuller, Ida b. Sep 6, 1875
Manchester, Vermont
Keylor, Arthur W d. Aug 17, 1981
Middlebury, Vermont
Hewitt, Henry Kent d. Sep 15, 1972
Montpelier, Vermont
Aiken, George David d. Nov 19, 1984
Dewey, George b. Dec 26, 1837
Howe, Edmund Perry b. Dec 14, 1896
Leahy, Patrick Joseph b. Mar 31, 1940
Mount Tabor, Vermont
Alden, Henry M b. Nov 11, 1836
Newburg, Vermont
Porter, William Trotter b. Dec 24, 1809
Newport, Vermont
Holbrook, Stewart Hall b. Aug 22, 1893
North Bennington, Vermont
Jackson, Shirley d. Aug 8, 1965
North Hartland, Vermont
Williard, Daniel b. Jan 28, 1961
Norwich, Vermont
Sample, Paul Starrett d. Feb 26, 1974
Peacham, Vermont
Harvey, George Brinton M
b. Feb 16, 1864
Plymouth, Vermont
Coolidge, (John) Calvin b. Jul 4, 1872
Poultney, Vermont
Perry, Ralph Barton b. Jul 3, 1876
Richmond, Vermont
Edmunds, George Franklin b. Feb 1, 1828
LeTourneau, Robert Gilmour
b. Nov 30, 1888
Rock Pointe, Vermont
Hopkins, John Henry d. Jan 9, 1868

Rutland, Vermont
Burke, James Edward b. Feb 28, 1925
Deere, John b. Feb 7, 1804
Stafford, Robert Theodore b. Aug 8, 1913
Saint Albans, Vermont
Sherry, Louis b. 1856
Saint Johnsbury, Vermont
Fairbanks, Thaddeus d. Apr 12, 1886
Smith, Robert Holbrook b. Aug 8, 1879
Salisbury, Vermont
Davenport, Thomas d. Jul 6, 1851
Sharon, Vermont
Smith, Joseph b. Dec 23, 1805
Shoreham, Vermont
Morton, Levi Parsons b. May 16, 1824
Springfield, Vermont
Flanders, Ralph Edward d. Feb 19, 1970
Springville, Vermont
Dallin, Cyrus b. Nov 22, 1861
Stanstead, Vermont
Lee, Jason b. Jun 23, 1803
Lee, Jason d. Mar 12, 1845
Stockbridge, Vermont
Brownson, Orestes Augustus
b. Sep 16, 1803
Strafford, Vermont
Morrill, Justin Smith b. Apr 14, 1810
Sutton, Vermont
Houghton, Henry Oscar b. Apr 30, 1823
Thetford, Vermont
Hammond, Bray d. Jul 20, 1968
Wells, Henry b. Dec 12, 1805
Vergennes, Vermont
Magonigle, Harold Van Buren
d. Aug 29, 1935
West Concord, Vermont
Adams, Herbert Samuel b. Jan 28, 1858
Weybridge, Vermont
James, Edwin b. Aug 27, 1797
Whitingham, Vermont
Young, Brigham b. Jun 1, 1801
Williamstown, Vermont
Davenport, Thomas b. Jul 19, 1802
Williston, Vermont
Chittenden, Thomas d. Aug 25, 1797
Windham, Vermont
Goodeve, Grant b. 1952
Woodstock, Vermont
Albright, Ivan Le Lorraine
d. Nov 18, 1983
Powers, Hiram b. Jul 29, 1805

VIRGINIA

Beckwourth, James Pierson
b. Apr 26, 1798
Booth, John Wilkes d. Apr 26, 1865
Pocahontas b. 1595
Price, Sterling b. Sep 11, 1809
Randolph, Mary b. Aug 9, 1762
Robertson, Pat (Marion) b. 1930

Rochester, Nathaniel b. Feb 21, 1752
Walker, Joseph Reddeford b. Dec 13, 1798
Albemarle County, Virginia
Lewis, Meriwether b. Aug 18, 1774
Alexandria, Virginia
Arnold, Thurman Wesley d. Nov 7, 1969
Bane, Frank B d. Jan 23, 1983
Barr, Stringfellow d. Feb 3, 1982
Fawcett, George b. Aug 25, 1861
Greene, Belle da Costa b. Dec 13, 1883
Guyer, Tennyson d. Apr 12, 1981
Hansen, Alvin Harvey d. Jun 6, 1975
Mearns, David Chambers d. May 21, 1981
Phillips, MacKenzie (Laura MacKenzie)
   b. Nov 10, 1959
Russell, "Pee Wee" (Charles Ellsworth)
   d. Feb 15, 1969
Schmitt, Bernadotte Everly
   d. Mar 22, 1969
Schultze, Charles Louis b. Dec 12, 1924
Scott, Willard Herman, Jr. b. May 7, 1934
Smith, Howard Worth d. Oct 3, 1976
Smith, Merriman d. Apr 13, 1970
Stone, Thomas d. Oct 5, 1787
VonBraun, Wernher d. Jun 1977
Altavista, Virginia
Futrell, Mary Hatwood b. May 24, 1940
Amelia County, Virginia
Tabb, John B b. Mar 22, 1845
Amherst County, Virginia
Becknell, William b. 1796
Appalachia, Virginia
Castle, Peggie b. Dec 22, 1927
Arlington, Virginia
Elliot, Cass b. Feb 19, 1943
Lisagor, Peter Irvin d. Dec 10, 1976
Overstreet, Bonaro Wilkinson
   d. Sep 10, 1985
Rickover, Hyman George d. Jul 8, 1986
Rockwell, George Lincoln d. Aug 25, 1967
Siple, Paul Allman d. Nov 25, 1968
Arno, Virginia
Horton, Willie (William Wattison)
   b. Oct 18, 1942
Auburn, Virginia
Scobee, Dick (Francis Richard)
   b. May 19, 1939
Augusta County, Virginia
Bingham, George Caleb b. Mar 20, 1811
Breckinridge, John b. Dec 2, 1760
Austinville, Virginia
Austin, Stephen Fuller b. Nov 3, 1793
Bassett, Virginia
Bassett, John D b. 1866
Bassett, John D d. Feb 26, 1965
Berkeley County, Virginia
Zane, Ebenezer b. Oct 7, 1747
Bermuda Hundred, Virginia
Rolfe, John d. 1622
Bluefield, Virginia
Dudley, William b. Dec 24, 1921

Brandy Station, Virginia
Strauss, Lewis Lichtenstein d. Jan 21, 1974
Broad Run, Virginia
Smith, Howard Worth b. Feb 2, 1883
Buena Vista, Virginia
Jennings, Gary b. Sep 20, 1928
Buffalo, Virginia
Harvey, William Hope b. Aug 16, 1851
Burlington, Virginia
Angell, James Rowland b. May 8, 1869
Caroline County, Virginia
Clark, William b. Aug 1, 1770
Penn, John b. May 17, 1741
Cawsons, Virginia
Randolph, John b. Jun 2, 1773
Chantilly, Virginia
Lee, Richard Henry d. Jun 19, 1794
Charles City, Virginia
Harrison, Benjamin b. 1726
Harrison, Benjamin d. Apr 24, 1791
Harrison, William Henry b. Feb 9, 1773
Jefferson, Martha Wayles Skelton
   b. Oct 19, 1748
Tyler, John b. Mar 29, 1790
Charlotte County, Virginia
Henry, Patrick d. Jun 6, 1799
Charlottesville, Virginia
Arlen, Richard b. Sep 1, 1899
Clark, George Rogers b. Nov 19, 1752
Cooper, Miriam d. Apr 12, 1976
Davisson, Clinton Joseph d. Feb 1, 1958
Field, Marshall, V b. May 13, 1941
Jensen, Jackie (Jack Eugene)
   d. Jul 14, 1982
Keyes, Frances Parkinson b. Jul 21, 1885
Lowe, Rob(ert Hepler) b. Mar 17, 1964
MacDonald-Wright, Stanton b. Jul 8, 1890
McGuffey, William Holmes
   d. May 4, 1873
Palmer, Frederick d. Sep 2, 1958
Richberg, Donald R(andall)
   d. Nov 27, 1960
Rives, Amelie Louise d. Jun 15, 1945
Van Dine, S S, pseud. b. Oct 15, 1888
Vandegrift, Alexander Archer
   b. Mar 13, 1887
Christianburg, Virginia
King, Henry b. Jan 24, 1896
Chuckatuck, Virginia
Byrd, Charlie (Charles Lee)
   b. Sep 16, 1925
Churchland, Virginia
Ellis, Perry Edwin b. Mar 3, 1940
Colonial Heights, Virginia
Kempton, James Murray, Jr.
   d. Nov 26, 1971
Crystal City, Virginia
Ryskind, Morrie d. Aug 24, 1985
Culpeper, Virginia
Hill, Ambrose Powell b. Nov 9, 1825
Rixey, Eppa b. May 3, 1891

Danville, Virginia
Reeves, Rosser b. Sep 10, 1910
Dennisville, Virginia
Terhune, Mary Virginia b. Dec 31, 1831
Dunfries, Virginia
Lee, Henry b. Jan 29, 1756
Edgemont, Virginia
Mosby, John Singleton b. Dec 6, 1833
Elizabeth City, Virginia
McAdie, Alexander George d. Nov 1, 1943
Wythe, George b. 1726
Emporia, Virginia
Dalton, John Nichols b. Jul 11, 1931
Fairfax, Virginia
Wallington, Jimmy (James S.)
   d. Dec 22, 1972
Fairfax County, Virginia
Mason, George b. 1725
Underwood, Oscar Wilder d. Jan 25, 1929
Falls Church, Virginia
Ahern, Thomas Leo, Jr. b. 1932
Caraway, Hattie Wyatt d. Dec 21, 1950
Christie, John Walter d. Jan 11, 1944
Flexner, Abraham d. Sep 21, 1959
Falmouth, Virginia
Conway, Moncure Daniel b. Mar 17, 1832
Farmville, Virginia
Walton, George b. 1741
Fauquier County, Virginia
Eastman, Mary Henderson b. 1818
Floyd County, Virginia
Evans, Robley Dunglison b. Aug 18, 1846
Fort Belvoir, Virginia
Vaughan, Harry Hawkins d. May 20, 1981
Fort Meyer, Virginia
Selfridge, Thomas Etholen d. Sep 17, 1908
Fort Monroe, Virginia
Ridgway, Matthew Bunker b. Mar 3, 1895
Franklin, Virginia
Darden, Colgate Whitehead
   b. Feb 11, 1897
Franklin County, Virginia
Early, Jubal Anderson b. Nov 3, 1816
Washington, Booker T(aliafero)
   b. Apr 5, 1856
Frederick, Virginia
Arthur, Ellen Lewis Herndon
   b. Aug 30, 1837
Frederick County, Virginia
Swayne, Noah b. Dec 7, 1804
Fredericksburg, Virginia
Dinkeloo, John Gerard d. Jun 15, 1981
Disney, Doris Miles d. Mar 8, 1976
Maury, Matthew Fontaine b. Jan 14, 1806
Scott, Hugh D, Jr. b. Nov 11, 1900
Galax, Virginia
Dodd, Robert Lee (Bobby) b. Oct 11, 1908
Georgetown, Virginia
Southworth, Emma Dorothy Eliza Nevitte
   d. Jun 30, 1899

Germantown, Virginia
Marshall, John b. Sep 24, 1755
Gloucester, Virginia
Bacon, Nathaniel d. Oct 1676
Gloucester County, Virginia
Dabney, Virginius b. Feb 15, 1835
Reed, Walter b. Sep 13, 1851
Greenbackville, Virginia
Carter, Katherine Jones b. Feb 25, 1905
Greenville, Virginia
Smith, Kate (Kathryn Elizabeth)
   b. May 1, 1909
Greenwood, Virginia
Astor, Nancy Witcher (Langhorne) Astor,
   Viscountess b. May 19, 1879
Guinea Station, Virginia
Jackson, "Stonewall" (Thomas Jonathan)
   d. May 10, 1863
Gunston Hall, Virginia
Mason, George d. Oct 7, 1792
Hampton, Virginia
Carmines, Al b. Jul 25, 1937
Hanover County, Virginia
Clay, Henry b. Apr 12, 1777
Henry, Patrick b. May 29, 1736
Nelson, Thomas, Jr. d. Jan 4, 1789
Page, Thomas Nelson b. Apr 23, 1853
Page, Thomas Nelson d. Nov 1, 1922
Sumter, Thomas b. Aug 14, 1734
Harrisonburg, Virginia
Sampson, Ralph b. Jul 7, 1960
Hopewell, Virginia
Joanis, John W b. Jun 13, 1918
Hot Springs, Virginia
Snead, Sam(uel Jackson) b. May 27, 1912
Inman, Virginia
Whitehead, Don(ald Ford) b. Apr 8, 1908
Jerusalem, Virginia
Turner, Nat d. Nov 11, 1831
Jonesville, Virginia
Still, Andrew Taylor b. Aug 6, 1828
Lexington, Virginia
Armstrong, William Howard
   b. Sep 14, 1914
Barkley, Alben William d. Apr 30, 1956
Blair, Clay, Jr. b. May 1, 1925
Houston, Sam(uel) b. Mar 2, 1793
Lee, Robert E(dward) d. Oct 12, 1870
Maury, Matthew Fontaine d. Feb 1, 1873
Twombly, Cy b. Apr 25, 1928
Loudoun County, Virginia
Baker, Russell Wayne b. Aug 14, 1925
Lovingston, Virginia
Ryan, Thomas Fortune b. Oct 17, 1851
Lynchburg, Virginia
Falwell, Jerry b. Aug 11, 1933
Freeman, Douglas S b. May 16, 1886
Glass, Carter b. Jan 4, 1858
Maces Spring, Virginia
Carter, June b. Jun 23, 1929

Martinsburg, Virginia
Boyd, Belle (Isabellle) b. May 8, 1843
Mason County, Virginia
Owens, Michael Joseph b. Jan 1, 1859
McLean, Virginia
O'Donnell, Emmett d. Dec 26, 1971
Meaherrin, Virginia
Clark, Roy Linwood b. Apr 15, 1933
Millwood, Virginia
Randolph, Edmund Jennings
  d. Sep 12, 1813
Monongahela County, Virginia
Gregg, William b. Feb 2, 1800
Monticello, Virginia
Jefferson, Maria b. 1778
Jefferson, Maria d. Apr 1804
Jefferson, Martha b. Sep 27, 1772
Jefferson, Martha Wayles Skelton
  d. Sep 6, 1782
Jefferson, Thomas d. Jul 4, 1826
Montpelier, Virginia
Madison, Dolly Payne Todd
  d. Jul 12, 1849
Madison, James d. Jun 28, 1836
Mount Vernon, Virginia
Washington, George d. Dec 14, 1799
Washington, Martha Dandridge Curtis
  d. 1802
New Canton, Virginia
Woodson, Carter Godwin b. Dec 19, 1875
New Kent County, Virginia
Tyler, Letitia Christian b. Nov 12, 1790
Washington, Martha Dandridge Curtis
  b. Jun 2, 1732
New Market, Virginia
Sevier, John b. Sep 23, 1745
Newington, Virginia
Braxton, Carter b. Sep 10, 1736
Newport News, Virginia
Bailey, Pearl Mae b. Mar 28, 1918
Dobyns, Lloyd Allen, Jr. b. Mar 12, 1936
Fitzgerald, Ella b. Apr 25, 1918
Granger, Lester b. Sep 16, 1896
Lewis, Robert Alvin d. Jun 18, 1983
Patton, Edward L b. 1917
Rees, Ennis b. Mar 17, 1925
Styron, William Clark, Jr. b. Jun 11, 1925
Nickelsville, Virginia
Carter, "Mother" Maybelle
  b. May 10, 1909
Norfolk, Virginia
Bowser, Betty Ann b. 1944
Carr, Elizabeth Jordan b. Dec 28, 1981
Cleghorn, Sarah Norcliffe b. Feb 4, 1876
Clemons, Clarence b. Jan 11, 1942
Darden, Colgate Whitehead d. Jun 9, 1981
Davis, John Staige b. Jan 15, 1872
Eaton, Mary b. 1901
Joyce, Peggy Hopkins b. 1893
Maynor, Dorothy b. Sep 3, 1910
Mitscher, Marc A d. Feb 3, 1947

Newton, Wayne b. Apr 3, 1942
Pickett, George Edward d. Jul 30, 1875
Reid, Tim b. Dec 19, 1944
Smith, Keely b. Mar 9, 1932
Strange, Curtis b. Jan 30, 1955
Sullavan, Margaret b. May 16, 1896
Zolotow, Charlotte Shapiro b. Jun 26, 1915
Oak Hill, Virginia
Monroe, Elizabeth Kortright
  d. Sep 23, 1830
Orange County, Virginia
Scott, Randolph b. Jan 23, 1903
Taylor, Zachary b. Nov 24, 1784
Patrick County, Virginia
Stuart, "Jeb" (James Ewell Brown)
  b. Feb 6, 1833
Petersburg, Virginia
Cotten, Joseph b. May 15, 1905
Hill, Ambrose Powell d. Apr 2, 1865
Leach, Will (Wilford Carson)
  b. Aug 26, 1934
Malone, Moses Eugene b. Mar 23, 1955
Myers, Jerome b. Mar 20, 1867
Scott, Winfield b. Jun 13, 1786
Phoebus, Virginia
Kraft, Chris(topher Columbus, Jr.)
  b. Feb 28, 1924
Pittsylvania, Virginia
Hodges, Luther Hartwell b. Mar 9, 1898
Pittsylvania County, Virginia
Jackson, Rachel Donelson Robards
  b. Jun 15, 1767
Port Conway, Virginia
Madison, James b. Mar 16, 1751
Portsmouth, Virginia
Andrews, V(irginia) C b. Jun 6, 1924
Carter, Jack (John William) b. Jul 3, 1947
Garvin, Clifton Canter, Jr.
  b. Dec 22, 1921
Garwood, Robert Russell b. Dec 22, 1946
Jones, Matilda Sissieretta Joyner
  b. Jan 5, 1869
Lavelle, Rita Marie b. Sep 8, 1947
Murray, Mae b. Apr 10, 1889
Pound, Virginia
Powers, Francis Gary b. Aug 17, 1929
Powhatan County, Virginia
Ashley, William Henry b. Mar 26, 1778
Prince Edward, Virginia
Johnston, Joseph Eggleston b. Feb 3, 1807
Reedville, Virginia
Haynie, Hugh b. Feb 6, 1927
Reston, Virginia
Ward, Lynd d. Jun 28, 1985
Richard, Virginia
LaMarr, Barbara b. Jul 28, 1896
Richmond, Virginia
Ashe, Arthur b. Jul 10, 1943
Beatty, Warren b. Mar 30, 1937
Braxton, Carter d. Oct 10, 1797
Bridger, James b. Mar 11, 1804

Brisbane, Albert d. May 1, 1890
Brown, Charles Lee b. Aug 23, 1921
Cabell, James Branch b. Apr 14, 1879
Cabell, James Branch d. May 5, 1958
Dalton, John Nichols d. Jul 30, 1986
Dandridge, Bob (Robert L)
  b. Nov 15, 1947
Ezekiel, Moses Jacob b. Oct 28, 1844
Francisco, Peter d. 1831
Freeman, Douglas S d. Jun 13, 1953
Gilpin, Charles Sidney b. Nov 20, 1878
Glasgow, Ellen Anderson Gholson
  b. Apr 22, 1874
Glasgow, Ellen Anderson Gholson
  d. Nov 21, 1945
Gosden, Freeman Fisher b. May 5, 1899
Gravely, Samuel L b. Jun 4, 1922
Leonard, Eddie b. Oct 18, 1875
Lukeman, Henry A b. 1871
MacLaine, Shirley b. Apr 23, 1934
Mays, David John b. Nov 22, 1896
Mays, David John d. Feb 17, 1971
Munch, Charles d. Nov 6, 1968
Ogg, Oscar b. Dec 13, 1908
Pickett, George Edward b. Jan 25, 1825
Rives, Amelie Louise b. Aug 23, 1863
Robinson, Bill b. May 25, 1878
Robinson, Max C b. May 1, 1939
Stuart, "Jeb" (James Ewell Brown)
  d. May 12, 1864
Tarkenton, Fran(cis Asbury)
  b. Feb 3, 1940
Tyler, John d. Jan 18, 1862
Tyler, Julia Gardiner d. Jul 10, 1889
Van Lew, Elizabeth b. Oct 17, 1818
Van Lew, Elizabeth d. Sep 25, 1900
Wadkins, Lanny b. Dec 5, 1949
Wilder, Robert Ingersoll b. Jan 25, 1901
Wolfe, Tom (Thomas Kennerly, Jr.)
  b. Mar 2, 1931
Wythe, George d. Jun 8, 1806

Richmond County, Virginia
Lee, Francis Lightfoot d. Jan 11, 1797

Roanoke, Virginia
Anthony, Earl b. 1941
Bari, Lynn b. Dec 18, 1913
Everleigh, Ada d. Jan 3, 1960
Murphy, Audie b. Jun 1, 1971
Payne, John b. May 23, 1912
Randolph, John d. May 24, 1833

Roanoke Island, Virginia
Dare, Virginia b. Aug 18, 1587

Rockbridge County, Virginia
McCormick, Cyrus Hall b. Feb 15, 1809
McDowell, Ephraim b. Nov 11, 1771

Rockingham, Virginia
Conger, Clement Ellis b. Oct 15, 1912

Rockymount, Virginia
Derby, Jane (Jeanette Barr)
  b. May 17, 1895

Round Hill, Virginia
Dodd, William Edward d. Feb 9, 1940

Schuyler, Virginia
Hamner, Earl Henry, Jr. b. Jul 10, 1923

Shadwell, Virginia
Jefferson, Thomas b. Apr 13, 1743

Smithfield, Virginia
Bane, Frank B b. 1894

Southampton County, Virginia
Mahone, William b. Dec 1, 1826
Scott, Dred b. 1795
Thomas, George Henry b. Jul 31, 1816
Turner, Nat b. Oct 2, 1800

Spotsylvania, Virginia
Asbury, Francis d. Mar 31, 1816
Sedgwick, John d. May 9, 1864

Stateburg, Virginia
Sumter, Thomas d. Jun 1, 1832

Staunton, Virginia
Colter, John b. 1775
Haines, William b. Jan 1, 1900
Wilson, Woodrow (Thomas Woodrow)
  b. Dec 28, 1856

Strasburg, Virginia
Schmitt, Bernadotte Everly
  b. May 19, 1886

Stratford, Virginia
Lee, Richard Henry b. Jan 20, 1732
Lee, Robert E(dward) b. Jan 19, 1807

Suffolk, Virginia
Barr, Stringfellow b. Jan 15, 1897
Powell, Lewis Franklin, Jr. b. Sep 19, 1907

Sussex County, Virginia
Clairborne, William Charles b. 1775

Tappahannock, Virginia
Ritchie, Thomas b. Nov 5, 1778

Tidewater, Virginia
Ball, Edward b. Mar 21, 1888

Virginia Beach, Virginia
Cayce, Edgar d. Jan 3, 1945
Coors, Adolph d. Jun 5, 1919
Dixon, Robert Ellington d. Oct 21, 1981
Newton, Juice b. Feb 18, 1952

Warwick, Virginia
Ferguson, Homer Lenoir d. Mar 14, 1952

Westmoreland, Virginia
Lee, Francis Lightfoot b. Oct 14, 1734
Monroe, James b. Apr 28, 1758
Washington, George b. Feb 22, 1732

Wheeling, Virginia
Zane, Ebenezer d. 1811

Williamsburg, Virginia
Aldrich, Richard Stoddard
  d. Mar 31, 1986
Blair, James d. Apr 18, 1743
Randolph, Edmund Jennings
  b. Aug 10, 1753
Randolph, Peyton b. Sep 1721
Randolph, Peyton d. Oct 22, 1775
Warrington, Lewis b. Nov 3, 1782

Winchester, Virginia
Byrd, Harry Flood, Jr. b. Dec 20, 1914
Byrd, Richard Evelyn b. Oct 25, 1888
Cather, Willa Sibert b. Dec 7, 1873
Cline, Patsy b. Sep 8, 1932
Cooke, John Esten b. Nov 3, 1830
Denver, James William b. Oct 23, 1817
Fairfax, Thomas d. Nov 12, 1671
Holt, Jack (Charles John) b. May 31, 1888
LLoyd, Robin b. Oct 14, 1950
Morgan, Daniel d. Jul 6, 1802
Wise, Virginia
Dale, Carroll W b. Apr 24, 1938
Scott, George Campbell b. Oct 18, 1927
Wytheville, Virginia
Wilson, Edith Bolling Galt b. Oct 15, 1872
Yorktown, Virginia
Nelson, Thomas, Jr. b. Dec 26, 1738

WASHINGTON

Powell, Lawrence Clark b. Sep 3, 1906
Aberdeen, Washington
Motherwell, Robert Burns b. Jan 24, 1915
Simmons, Pat(rick) b. Jan 23, 1950
Bainbridge Isle, Washington
Roethke, Theodore d. Aug 1, 1963
Bellevue, Washington
Bauer, Eddie d. Apr 18, 1986
Patton, Edward L d. Mar 5, 1982
Wells, Edward d. Jul 1, 1986
Bellingham, Washington
Kendall, John Walker b. Mar 19, 1929
Bremerton, Washington
Duff, Howard b. Nov 24, 1917
Camas, Washington
Rodgers, Jimmie F b. Sep 18, 1933
Cashmere, Washington
Uhlman, Wes(ley Carl) b. Mar 13, 1935
Centralia, Washington
Cunningham, Merce b. Apr 16, 1919
Clayton, Washington
Carson, Robert b. Oct 6, 1909
Colfax, Washington
Canutt, Yakima (Enos Edward)
b. Nov 29, 1895
Colville, Washington
Joseph, Chief d. Sep 21, 1904
Darrington, Washington
Barker, Bob (Robert William)
b. Dec 12, 1923
Everett, Washington
Averill, Earl (Howard Earl)
d. Aug 16, 1983
Jackson, Henry Martin b. May 31, 1912
Jackson, Henry Martin d. Sep 1, 1983
Loggins, Kenny (Kenneth Clarke)
b. Jan 7, 1948
Fairmont, Washington
Knowles, John b. Sep 16, 1926

Fort Walla Walla, Washington
Whitman, Marcus d. Nov 29, 1847
Kelso, Washington
Hall, Josef Washington b. Feb 27, 1894
Kent, Washington
Anthony, Earl b. Apr 27, 1938
Kirkland, Washington
Carner, Joanne Gunderson b. Mar 4, 1939
Little Falls, Washington
Cantwell, Robert Emmett b. Jan 31, 1908
Olympia, Washington
Anderson, Douglas Dorland b. Jun 1, 1936
Strouse, Norman H b. Nov 4, 1906
Orcas Island, Washington
Bauer, Eddie b. Oct 19, 1899
Pasco, Washington
Chenoweth, Dean d. Jul 31, 1982
Port Angeles, Washington
Elway, John Albert b. Jun 28, 1960
Port Ludlow, Washington
Binns, Archie Fred b. Jul 30, 1899
Renton, Washington
Stigler, George Joseph b. Jan 17, 1911
Republic, Washington
Conley, Renie b. Jul 31, 1919
Seattle, Washington
Allen, William McPherson d. Oct 29, 1985
Anderson, Daryl b. Jul 1, 1951
Boeing, William Edward d. Sep 28, 1956
Bolcom, William Elden b. May 26, 1938
Brand, Max, pseud. b. May 29, 1892
Brown, Bobby (Robert William)
b. Oct 25, 1924
Carlson, Chester b. Feb 8, 1906
Casey, James E d. Jun 6, 1983
Channing, Carol b. Jan 31, 1923
Collins, Judy (Judith) b. May 1, 1939
Coryell, Don(ald David) b. Oct 17, 1924
Cummings, Constance b. May 15, 1910
Dean, Gordon Evans b. Dec 28, 1905
Engle, Eloise Katherine b. Apr 12, 1923
Evans, Daniel Jackson b. Oct 16, 1925
Farmer, Frances b. Sep 19, 1914
Faust, Frederick Schiller b. May 29, 1892
Francis, Russ(ell Ross) b. Apr 3, 1953
Garfinkle, Louis b. Feb 11, 1928
Goodman, Steve(n Benjamin)
d. Sep 20, 1984
Gordon, Richard Francis, Jr.
b. Oct 5, 1929
Greenfield, Meg b. Dec 27, 1930
Hanauer, "Chip" (Lee Edward)
b. Jul 1, 1954
Havoc, June b. Nov 8, 1916
Hendrix, Jimi (James Marshall)
b. Nov 27, 1942
Hills, Roderick M b. Mar 9, 1931
Hutchinson, Fred(erick Charles)
b. Aug 12, 1919
Joffrey, Robert b. Dec 24, 1930

Julesberg, Elizabeth Rider Montgomery
d. Feb 19, 1985
Ketcham, Hank (Henry King)
b. Mar 14, 1920
Lee, Gypsy Rose b. Feb 9, 1914
Livingstone, Mary b. Jun 22, 1908
Madison, Helene d. Nov 25, 1970
McCarthy, Kevin b. Feb 15, 1914
McCarthy, Mary b. Jun 21, 1912
McClintic, Guthrie b. Aug 6, 1893
McNamara, Margaret Craig
b. Aug 22, 1915
Nelson, Gene b. Mar 24, 1920
Reinking, Ann b. Nov 10, 1949
Robinson, Earl Hawley b. Jul 2, 1910
Ross, Lanny b. Jan 19, 1906
Rusie, Amos William d. Dec 6, 1942
Stroud, Robert Franklin b. 1890
Terry, Megan b. Jul 22, 1932
Venuti, Joe (Giuseppe) d. Aug 14, 1978
Voit, Willard D b. Nov 8, 1910
Winsten, Archer b. Sep 18, 1904
Wright, Martha b. Mar 23, 1926
Wurdemann, Audrey May b. Jan 1, 1911
Yamasaki, Minoru b. Dec 1, 1912

Snohmish, Washington
Averill, Earl (Howard Earl)
b. May 21, 1902

South Bend, Washington
Paulsen, Pat b. Jul 6, 1927

Spokane, Washington
Cowles, William Hutchinson, Jr.
d. Aug 12, 1971
Crosby, Bob (George Robert)
b. Aug 23, 1913
Danelo, Joe (Joseph Peter) b. Sep 2, 1953
Dodd, Mrs. John Bruce (Sonora Louise
Smart) d. Mar 22, 1978
Fontaine, Frank d. Aug 4, 1978
Horstmann, Dorothy Millicent
b. Jul 2, 1911
Jones, Chuck b. Sep 21, 1912
Kaiser, Edgar Fosburgh b. Jul 29, 1908
Kelley, Kitty b. Apr 4, 1942
Lesser, Sol b. Feb 17, 1890
McGavin, Darren b. May 7, 1922
McIntire, John b. Jun 27, 1907
Munsel, Patrice b. May 14, 1925
Peters, Susan b. Jul 3, 1921
Sandberg, Ryne Dee b. Sep 18, 1959
Sneva, Tom (Thomas Edsol)
b. Jun 1, 1948

Sprague, Washington
Folsom, Frank M b. May 14, 1894

Tacoma, Washington
Brautigan, Richard b. Jan 30, 1933
Cannon, Dyan b. Jan 4, 1938
Carlson, Edward Elmer b. Jun 4, 1911
Cey, Ron(ald Charles) b. Feb 15, 1948
Cone, Molly Lamken b. Oct 3, 1918

Crosby, "Bing" (Harry Lillis)
b. May 2, 1904
Donahue, Elinor b. Apr 19, 1937
Ehrlichman, John Daniel b. Mar 20, 1925
Herbert, Frank Patrick b. Oct 8, 1920
Paige, Janis b. Sep 16, 1923
Ray, Dixy Lee b. Sep 3, 1914

Tekoa, Washington
Bailey, Mildred b. Feb 27, 1907

Vancouver, Washington
Bell, Arthur Donald b. Jul 17, 1920
Yeend, Frances b. Jan 28, 1918

Waitsburg, Washington
Taggard, Genevieve b. Nov 28, 1894

Walla Walla, Washington
Cordiner, Ralph Jarron b. Mar 20, 1900
Morgan, Edward P b. Jun 23, 1910
Rush, Kenneth b. Jan 17, 1910
Wainwright, Jonathan Mayhew
b. Aug 23, 1883
West, Adam b. Sep 29, 1938

Wallowa Valley, Washington
Joseph, Chief b. 1840

Yakima, Washington
Mahre, Phil(lip) b. May 10, 1957
Mahre, Steve(n) b. May 10, 1957

WEST VIRGINIA

Williams, "Hank" (Hiram) d. Jan 1, 1953
Beckley, West Virginia
Sarandon, Chris b. Jul 24, 1942
Bluefield, West Virginia
Knight, John Shivley b. Oct 26, 1894
Steward, Emanuel b. Jul 7, 1944
Weatherford, Teddy b. Oct 11, 1903
Bolt, West Virginia
Dickens, "Little" Jimmy b. Dec 19, 1925
Buckhannon, West Virginia
Latham, Jean Lee b. Apr 19, 1902
Cabin Creek, West Virginia
West, Jerry b. May 28, 1938
Charles Town, West Virginia
Brown, John d. Dec 2, 1859
Charleston, West Virginia
Ferrell, Conchata Galen b. Mar 28, 1943
Gilliam, Joe b. Dec 29, 1950
Miller, Arnold Ray d. Jul 12, 1985
Moore, Sara Jane b. Feb 15, 1930
Price, Roger b. Mar 6, 1920
Strauss, Lewis Lichtenstein b. Jan 31, 1896
Clarksburg, West Virginia
Anthony, Tony b. Oct 16, 1937
Curtin, Phyllis Smith b. Dec 3, 1927
Davis, John Williams b. Apr 13, 1873
Jackson, "Stonewall" (Thomas Jonathan)
b. Jan 21, 1824
Vance, Cyrus Roberts b. Mar 27, 1917
Edna Gas, West Virginia
Huff, Sam (Robert Lee) b. Oct 4, 1934

Bear Creek, Wisconsin
Nieman, Lucius William b. Dec 13, 1857
Beaver Dam, Wisconsin
Hatfield, Bobby b. Aug 10, 1940
Beloit, Wisconsin
Andrews, Roy Chapman b. Jan 26, 1884
Bloomer, Wisconsin
Treptow, Martin A b. 1894
Burlington, Wisconsin
Garvey, Ed(ward Robert) b. Apr 18, 1940
Cambria, Wisconsin
Rowlands, Gena b. Jun 19, 1936
Cashon, Wisconsin
King, Frank b. Apr 9, 1883
Cazenovia, Wisconsin
Duren, Ryne (Rinold George)
    b. Feb 22, 1929
Clear Lake, Wisconsin
Grimes, Burleigh Arland b. Aug 18, 1893
Grimes, Burleigh Arland d. Dec 10, 1985
Clemansville, Wisconsin
Hooton, Earnest Albert b. Nov 20, 1887
Columbus, Wisconsin
Stare, Fredrick John b. Apr 11, 1910
Cumberland, Wisconsin
Wolff, Mary Evaline b. May 24, 1887
Delafield, Wisconsin
Cushing, William Barker b. Nov 4, 1842
Farber, Edward Rolke d. Jan 22, 1982
Durand, Wisconsin
Parkhurst, Helen b. Mar 7, 1887
Eagle River, Wisconsin
Comiskey, Charlie (Charles Albert)
    d. Oct 26, 1931
East Troy, Wisconsin
Hickok, Lorena A b. 1892
Eau Claire, Wisconsin
Knaths, Karl (Otto Karl) b. Oct 21, 1891
Edgerton, Wisconsin
North, Sterling b. Nov 4, 1906
Elkhorn, Wisconsin
Wrigley, Philip Knight d. Apr 12, 1977
Fairchild, Wisconsin
Landis, Carole b. Jan 1, 1919
Fond du Lac, Wisconsin
Brauer, Jerald Carl b. Sep 16, 1921
Doheny, Edward Lawrence
    b. Aug 10, 1856
Gillette, King Camp b. Jan 5, 1855
MacDougall, Curtis Daniel b. Feb 11, 1903
Wise, Winifred E b.
Genessee Depot, Wisconsin
Fontanne, Lynn d. Jul 30, 1983
Grafton, Wisconsin
Rienow, Robert b. Dec 4, 1909
Grand Chute, Wisconsin
McCarthy, Joe (Joseph Raymond)
    b. Nov 14, 1908

Green Bay, Wisconsin
Lambeau, "Curly" (Earl L) b. Apr 9, 1898
Smith, "Red" (Walter Wellesley)
    b. Sep 25, 1905
Green Lake, Wisconsin
Anderson, Elda Emma b. Apr 5, 1899
Hilbert, Wisconsin
Berigan, "Bunny" (Rowland Bernart)
    b. Nov 2, 1909
Hillsboro, Wisconsin
Mitscher, Marc A b. Jan 26, 1887
Hortonville, Wisconsin
Nye, Gerald Prentice b. Dec 19, 1892
Jamesville, Wisconsin
Comstock, John Henry b. Aug 24, 1849
Janesville, Wisconsin
Bond, Carrie Jacobs b. Aug 11, 1862
Jefferson County, Wisconsin
Witte, Edwin Emil b. Jan 4, 1887
Johnstown, Wisconsin
Wilcox, Ella Wheeler b. Nov 5, 1850
Jonesville, Wisconsin
Adamany, David Walter b. Sep 23, 1936
Juneau, Wisconsin
Joss, "Addie" (Adrian) b. Apr 12, 1880
Kenosha, Wisconsin
Ameche, Don b. May 31, 1908
Ameche, Jim b. 1915
McIntyre, James b. Aug 8, 1857
Molinaro, Al b. Jun 24, 1919
Newell, Edward Theodore b. Jan 15, 1886
Simmons, Zalmon G d. Feb 11, 1910
Travanti, Daniel J(ohn) b. Mar 7, 1940
Welles, Orson (George Orson)
    b. May 6, 1915
Kewaskum, Wisconsin
Wescott, Glenway b. Apr 11, 1901
Kilbourne, Wisconsin
Boyd, Belle (Isabelle) d. Jun 11, 1900
La Crosse, Wisconsin
Losey, Joseph b. Jan 14, 1909
Lucey, Patrick Joseph b. Mar 21, 1918
Michel, F Curtis b. Jun 5, 1934
Ray, Nicholas b. Aug 7, 1911
Starch, Daniel b. Mar 8, 1883
Sterling, Ford b. Nov 3, 1880
Toland, John Willard b. Jun 29, 1912
Lake Geneva, Wisconsin
Maytag, Elmer Henry d. Jul 20, 1940
Lancaster, Wisconsin
U'Ren, William Simon b. Jan 10, 1859
Lodi, Wisconsin
Wopat, Tom b. Sep 9, 1951
Madison, Wisconsin
Allyn, Stanley Charles b. Jul 20, 1891
Anderson, Carl Thomas b. Feb 14, 1865
Anderson, Carl Thomas d. Nov 4, 1948
Babcock, Stephen Moulton d. Jul 2, 1931
Bardeen, John b. May 23, 1908
Cole, Michael b. Jul 3, 1945
Crowley, Leo T d. Apr 15, 1972

Monroe, Wisconsin
Twining, Nathan F(arragut)
b. Oct 11, 1897

Montello, Wisconsin
Pratt, Gerald Hillary b. Dec 15, 1903

Neenah, Wisconsin
Shattuck, Arthur b. Apr 19, 1881

New Richmond, Wisconsin
McNally, John Victor b. Nov 27, 1904

Oak Creek, Wisconsin
Matuszak, John b. Oct 25, 1950

Osceola, Wisconsin
Stickley, Gustav b. Mar 9, 1858

Oshkosh, Wisconsin
Hine, Lewis Wickes b. Sep 26, 1874
Owen, Tobias Chant b. Mar 20, 1936
Tabor, Elizabeth Bonduel McCourt Doe
b. 1854

Pardeeville, Wisconsin
Smith, Gerald Lyman Kenneth
b. Feb 27, 1898

Pepin, Wisconsin
Wilder, Laura Elizabeth Ingalls
b. Feb 7, 1867

Plainfield, Wisconsin
Gein, Ed b. 1906

Platteville, Wisconsin
Gasser, Herbert Spencer b. Jul 5, 1888
Luce, Charles (Franklin) b. Sep 29, 1917

Portage, Wisconsin
Gale, Zona b. Aug 26, 1874
Turner, Frederick Jackson b. Nov 14, 1861

Prairie Chien, Wisconsin
Cannon, Walter Bradford b. Oct 19, 1871

Prentice, Wisconsin
Morgan, Dennis b. Dec 10, 1920

Primrose, Wisconsin
LaFollette, Robert Marion b. Jun 14, 1855

Racine, Wisconsin
Chones, Jim b. Oct 30, 1949
Corby, Ellen b. Jun 3, 1913
Horlick, Alexander James b. Oct 3, 1873
Johnson, Herbert Fisk b. Nov 15, 1899
Johnson, Herbert Fisk d. Dec 13, 1978
March, Fredric b. Aug 31, 1897

Reedsburgh, Wisconsin
Briggs, Clare b. Aug 5, 1875

Rhinelander, Wisconsin
Wasserman, Dale b. Nov 2, 1917

Rice Lake, Wisconsin
Olsen, Harold G b. May 12, 1895

Richland Center, Wisconsin
Wright, Frank Lloyd b. Jun 8, 1869

Ripon, Wisconsin
Catt, Carrie Chapman b. Jan 9, 1859
Maltby, Richard E, Jr. b. Oct 6, 1937
Selfridge, Harry Gordon b. Jan 11, 1858

River Falls, Wisconsin
Knowles, Warren Perley b. Aug 19, 1908

Sauk City, Wisconsin
Derleth, August b. Feb 24, 1909
Schorer, Mark b. May 17, 1908

Sheboygan, Wisconsin
Mason, Jackie b. 1931

Shorewood, Wisconsin
Chapelle, Dickey b. Mar 14, 1918

Shullsberg, Wisconsin
Parker, George Safford b. Nov 1, 1863

Shullsburg, Wisconsin
Holland, Leland James b. 1928

Sparta, Wisconsin
Kelley, Edgar Stillman b. Apr 14, 1857
Nestingen, Ivan Arnold b. Sep 23, 1921
Slayton, Donald Kent b. Mar 1, 1924

Sun Prairie, Wisconsin
O'Keeffe, Georgia b. Nov 15, 1887

Superior, Wisconsin
Bancroft, Dave (David James)
d. Oct 9, 1972
Fitzpatrick, Daniel R b. Mar 5, 1891
Grant, "Bud" (Harold Peter)
b. May 20, 1927

Thorp, Wisconsin
North, Andy b. Mar 9, 1950

Tomahawk, Wisconsin
Webster, Mike (Michael Lewis)
b. Mar 18, 1952

Tomanawk, Wisconsin
Eklund, Carl Robert b. Jan 27, 1909

Two Rivers, Wisconsin
Walsh, Thomas James b. Jun 12, 1859

Valders, Wisconsin
Veblen, Thorstein Bunde b. Jul 30, 1857

Viola, Wisconsin
Nye, Russel Blaine b. Feb 17, 1913

Watertown, Wisconsin
Davies, Joseph Edward b. Nov 29, 1876
Lasker, Mary Woodward b. Nov 30, 1900

Waukesha, Wisconsin
Bullard, Dexter Means b. Aug 14, 1898
Paul, Les b. Jun 9, 1916
Sears, Richard Warren d. Sep 28, 1914

Waupun, Wisconsin
Smith, Oliver b. Feb 13, 1918

Wausau, Wisconsin
Hirsch, "Crazylegs" (Elroy)
b. Jun 17, 1923

Wauwatosa, Wisconsin
Dickerson, Nancy Hanschman
b. Jan 19, 1930

West Allis, Wisconsin
Liberace b. May 16, 1919

West Salem, Wisconsin
Garland, Hamlin b. Sep 14, 1860

Wisconsin Rapids, Wisconsin
Daly, James b. Oct 23, 1918

WYOMING

Carbon, Wyoming
Hobbs, Leonard Sinclair b. Dec 20, 1896
Casper, Wyoming
Browning, Tom (Thomas Leo)
  b. Apr 28, 1960
Burford, Anne McGill Gorsuch
  b. Apr 21, 1942
Cheyenne, Wyoming
Horn, Tom d. Nov 20, 1903
Kerr, Andrew b. Oct 7, 1878
Cody, Wyoming
Pollock, Jackson b. Jan 28, 1912
Green River, Wyoming
Gowdy, Curt b. Jul 31, 1919
Jackson, Wyoming
Burt, Maxwell Struthers d. Aug 28, 1954
Laramie, Wyoming
Arnold, Thurman Wesley b. Jun 2, 1891
Lusk, Wyoming
Watt, James Gaius b. Jan 31, 1938
McDowell, Wyoming
Saunders, Stuart T b. Jul 16, 1909
Rock Springs, Wyoming
Bugas, John Stephen b. Apr 26, 1908
Dowler, Boyd b. Oct 18, 1937
Zenith, Wyoming
Hansen, Clifford Peter b. Oct 16, 1912

ALBERTA

Wray, Fay b. Sep 10, 1907
Calgary, Alberta
Aberhart, William d. May 23, 1943
Birney, Earle (Alfred Earle)
  b. May 13, 1904
Cameron, Rod b. Dec 7, 1912
Gadsby, Bill (William Alexander)
  b. Aug 8, 1927
Goodman, Martin Wise b. Jan 15, 1935
Kromm, Bobby (Robert) b. Jun 8, 1928
Lougheed, Peter b. Jul 26, 1928
Taylor, Kenneth Douglas b. Oct 5, 1934
Thompson, Cecil d. Feb 9, 1981
Edmonton, Alberta
Bucyk, John Paul b. May 12, 1935
Dickson, Gordon Rupert b. Nov 1, 1923
Fox, Michael J b. Jun 9, 1961
Hiller, Arthur b. Nov 22, 1923
McLuhan, (Herbert) Marshall
  b. Jul 21, 1911
Messier, Mark Douglas b. Jan 18, 1961
Miller, Carl S b. Jul 23, 1912
Peeters, Pete(r) b. Aug 1, 1957
Raskin, A(braham) H(enry)
  b. Apr 26, 1911
Unger, Garry Douglas b. Dec 7, 1947
High Prairie, Alberta
Lysiak, Tom (Thomas James)
  b. Apr 22, 1953

High River, Alberta
Clark, Joe (Charles Joseph) b. Jun 5, 1939
Sather, Glen Cameron b. Sep 2, 1943
Lacombe, Alberta
Michener, Roland b. Apr 19, 1900
Lethbridge, Alberta
Redpath, James b. Jun 8, 1908
MacLeon, Alberta
Cowdry, Edmund Vincent b. Jul 18, 1888
McLeod, Alberta
Mitchell, Joni b. Nov 7, 1943
Medicine Hat, Alberta
Gerussi, Bruno b. 1928
Provost, Alberta
Ullman, Norm(an Victor Alexander)
  b. Dec 26, 1935
Spruce Grove, Alberta
Fuhr, Grant b. Sep 28, 1962
Wainwright, Alberta
Seymour, Lynn b. Mar 8, 1939
Whitford, Alberta
Kurelek, William b. Mar 3, 1927

BRITISH COLUMBIA

Cranbrook, British Columbia
Yzerman, Steve b. May 9, 1965
Grand Forks, British Columbia
Dmytryk, Edward b. Sep 4, 1908
Kelowng, British Columbia
Bennett, William b. Apr 14, 1932
Mission City, British Columbia
Holmes, Anna Marie b. Apr 17, 1943
Monk, Allan James b. Aug 19, 1942
New Westminster, British Columbia
Burr, Raymond William Stacey
  b. May 21, 1917
Fox, Terry (Terrance Stanley)
  d. Jun 28, 1981
Nonaimo, British Columbia
Collishaw, Raymond b. Nov 22, 1893
North Vancouver, British Columbia
George, Chief Dan b. Jun 24, 1899
Penticton, British Columbia
Smith, Alexis b. Jun 8, 1921
Sandon, British Columbia
Thompson, Cecil b. May 31, 1905
Vancouver, British Columbia
Adams, Bryan b. Nov 5, 1959
Anderson, Glenn Chris b. Oct 2, 1960
Burns, Tommy d. May 10, 1955
DeCarlo, Yvonne b. Sep 1, 1924
Doohan, James Montgomery
  b. Mar 3, 1920
Ferguson, John Bowie b. Sep 5, 1938
Flynn, Errol d. Oct 14, 1959
George, Chief Dan d. Sep 23, 1981
Guinan, "Texas" (Mary Louise Cecilia)
  d. Nov 5, 1933
Harris, Lauren d. Jan 29, 1970
Hartley, Fred Lloyd b. Jan 16, 1917

Hayakawa, S(amuel) I(chiye)
b. Jul 18, 1906
Hines, Mimi b. Jul 17, 1933
Newell, Pete b. Aug 13, 1913
Parkins, Barbara b. May 22, 1942
Peter, Laurence Johnston b. Sep 16, 1919
Qualen, John Mandt b. Dec 8, 1899
Reno, Mike b. Jan 8, 1955
Stratten, Dorothy b. Feb 28, 1960
Trudeau, Margaret Joan Sinclair
b. Sep 10, 1948
Woodsworth, James Shaver
d. Mar 21, 1942

Victoria, British Columbia
Bosustow, Stephen b. Nov 6, 1911
Cabot, Sebastian d. Aug 23, 1977
Carr, Emily b. Dec 12, 1871
Carr, Emily d. Mar 2, 1945
Douglas, James, Sir d. Aug 2, 1877
Ireland, John b. Jan 30, 1915
McClung, Nellie Letitia Mooney
d. Sep 1, 1951
Patrick, Lester B d. Jun 1, 1960
Patrick, Lynn b. Feb 3, 1912
Tunnard, Christopher b. Jul 7, 1910
Tyson, Ian b. Sep 25, 1933

MANITOBA

Arnes, Manitoba
Stefansson, Vihjalmur b. Nov 3, 1879
Beausejour, Manitoba
Schreyer, Edward Richard b. Dec 21, 1935
Brandon, Manitoba
Broda, "Turk" (Walter) b. May 15, 1914
Bronfman, Samuel b. Mar 4, 1891
Ford, Russ(ell William) b. Apr 25, 1883
Woods, Donald b. Dec 2, 1904
Carman, Manitoba
Carson, Jack b. Oct 27, 1910
Emerson, Manitoba
Sweet, John Howard b. Mar 21, 1907
Flin Flon, Manitoba
Clarke, Bobby (Robert Earl)
b. Aug 13, 1949
Fort Gary, Manitoba
Henning, Doug(las James) b. May 3, 1947
Hamiota, Manitoba
Creighton, Fred(erick) b. Jul 14, 1933
Neepawa, Manitoba
Laurence, Margaret Jean b. Jul 18, 1926
Saint Boniface, Manitoba
Cariou, Len (Leonard) b. Sep 30, 1939
Goring, "Butch" (Robert Thomas)
b. Oct 22, 1949
Riel, Louis David b. Oct 23, 1844
Roy, Gabrielle b. Mar 22, 1909
Virden, Manitoba
Wallace, Lila Bell Acheson
b. Dec 25, 1889

Winkler, Manitoba
Sirluck, Ernest b. Apr 25, 1918
Winnipeg, Manitoba
Adelman, Sybil b. Mar 15, 1942
Armstrong, Jack Lawrence b. 1911
Bachman, Randy b. Sep 27, 1943
Bolt, Carol b. Aug 25, 1941
Brand, Oscar b. Feb 7, 1920
Cameron, Eleanor Francis b. Mar 23, 1912
Cummings, Burton b. Dec 31, 1947
Durbin, Deanna b. Dec 4, 1921
Fox, Terry (Terrance Stanley)
b. Jul 28, 1958
Hall, Monty b. Aug 25, 1924
MacKenzie, Gisele b. Jan 10, 1927
Masterton, Bill (William) b. Aug 16, 1938
Murray, Troy b. Jul 31, 1962
Nelsova, Zara b. Dec 24, 1924
Saidenberg, Daniel b. Nov 12, 1906
Sawchuk, Terry (Terrance Gordon)
b. Dec 28, 1929
Steinberg, David b. Aug 9, 1942
Stemkowski, Pete(r David)
b. Aug 25, 1943

NEW BRUNSWICK

Edmonds, Emma E b. Dec 1841
Bath, New Brunswick
Fox, Kate b. 1839
Fox, Margaret b. Oct 7, 1833
Campobello, New Brunswick
Roosevelt, Franklin Delano, Jr.
b. Aug 17, 1914
Douglas, New Brunswick
Roberts, Charles George Douglas, Sir
b. Jan 10, 1860
Drummond, New Brunswick
Turcotte, Ron b. Jul 22, 1941
Frederickton, New Brunswick
Carman, (William) Bliss b. Apr 15, 1861
Hopewell, New Brunswick
Bennett, Richard Bedford b. Jul 3, 1870
Saint Andrew's, New Brunswick
Walcott, Mary Morris Vaux
d. Aug 22, 1940
Saint Andrews, New Brunswick
Bannister, Edward Mitchell b. 1833
Saint John, New Brunswick
Medill, Joseph b. Apr 6, 1823
Pidgeon, Walter b. Sep 23, 1898
Sutherland, Donald b. Jul 17, 1934
Sheffiel, New Brunswick
Burpee, W(ashington) Atlee b. Apr 5, 1858
Woodstock, New Brunswick
Hatfield, Richard b. Apr 9, 1931

NEWFOUNDLAND

Clinton, Henry, Sir b. 1738
Brigus, Newfoundland
Bartlett, Robert Abram b. Aug 15, 1875

Grand Falls, Newfoundland
Pinsent, Gordon Edward b. Jul 12, 1930
Saint John's, Newfoundland
Anderson, John Murray b. Sep 20, 1886
Brian, Donald b. Feb 17, 1875
Western Bay, Newfoundland
Pratt, Edwin John b. Feb 4, 1883
Whitbourne, Newfoundland
Peckford, Alfred b. Aug 27, 1942

NORTHWEST TERRITORIES

Yellowknife, Northwest Territories
Kidder, Margot b. Oct 17, 1948

NOVA SCOTIA

Howe, Joseph d. Jun 1, 1873
Montor, Henry b. 1906
Baddeck, Nova Scotia
Bell, Alexander Graham d. Aug 2, 1922
Grosvenor, Gilbert Hovey d. Feb 4, 1966
Cape Breton, Nova Scotia
MacLennan, Hugh b. Mar 20, 1907
Grand Pre, Nova Scotia
Borden, Robert Laird, Sir b. Jun 26, 1854
Halifax, Nova Scotia
Choate, Rufus d. Jul 15, 1859
Cunard, Samuel, Sir b. Nov 15, 1787
Foster, Hal (Harold Rudolf)
b. Aug 16, 1892
Howe, Joseph b. Dec 13, 1804
Huggins, Charles Brenton b. Sep 22, 1901
Keeler, Ruby b. Aug 25, 1909
McColough, C(harles) Peter
b. Aug 1, 1922
Prescott, Samuel d. 1777
Thompson, John S D b. Nov 10, 1844
Williams, J(ames) R(obert)
b. Aug 18, 1888
Kings County, Nova Scotia
Fuller, Alfred Carl b. Jan 13, 1885
Liverpool, Nova Scotia
Snow, Hank b. May 9, 1914
New Albany, Nova Scotia
Whitman, Alden b. Oct 27, 1913
Port Hilford, Nova Scotia
Carter, Wilf b. Dec 12, 1904
Pugwash, Nova Scotia
Eaton, Cyrus Stephen b. Dec 27, 1883
Shelbourne, Nova Scotia
Larson, John Augustus b. Dec 11, 1892
Somerset, Nova Scotia
Robinson, Boardman b. Sep 6, 1876
Springhill, Nova Scotia
Murray, Anne b. Jun 20, 1945
Sydney, Nova Scotia
Buchanan, John b. Apr 22, 1931
Wallace, Nova Scotia
Newcomb, Simon b. Mar 12, 1835

Weymouth, Nova Scotia
Langford, Sam b. Mar 4, 1886
Wilmont Township, Nova Scotia
Slocum, Joshua b. Feb 20, 1844
Windsor, Nova Scotia
Haliburton, Thomas Chandler b. 1796
Yarmouth, Nova Scotia
Kenney, George Churchill b. Aug 6, 1889

ONTARIO

Silverheels, Jay b. May 26, 1922
Alliston, Ontario
Banting, Frederick Grant, Sir
b. Nov 17, 1891
Almonte, Ontario
Naismith, James A b. Nov 6, 1861
Anderson, Ontario
Meighen, Arthur b. Jun 16, 1874
Ayr, Ontario
Kilgour, Joseph b. 1863
Bancroft, Ontario
Watson, Bryan Joseph b. Nov 14, 1942
Belleville, Ontario
Dow, Herbert Henry b. Feb 26, 1866
Mowat, Farley McGill b. May 12, 1921
Berlin, Ontario
King, William Lyon Mackenzie
b. Dec 17, 1874
Bondhead, Ontario
Osler, William, Sir b. Jul 12, 1849
Bracebridge, Ontario
Crozier, Roger Allan b. Mar 16, 1942
Brampton, Ontario
Tawley, Howard b. Nov 21, 1934
Brantford, Ontario
Cook, William b. Oct 9, 1896
Costain, Thomas B b. May 8, 1885
Gretzky, Wayne b. Jan 26, 1961
Harris, Lauren b. Oct 23, 1885
Hillier, James b. Aug 22, 1915
Callander, Ontario
Dionne Sisters b. May 28, 1934
Dionne, Annette b. May 28, 1934
Dionne, Cecile b. May 28, 1934
Dionne, Emilie b. May 28, 1934
Dionne, Marie b. May 28, 1934
Dionne, Yvonne b. May 28, 1934
Callender, Ontario
Barber, Bill (William Charles)
b. Jul 11, 1952
Canoe Lake, Ontario
Thomson, Tom d. Jul 8, 1917
Carleton Place, Ontario
Brown, A Roy b. 1893
Chatham, Ontario
Couzens, James Joseph, Jr.
b. Aug 26, 1876
Jenkins, Ferguson Arthur b. Dec 13, 1943
La Marsh, Judy Verlyn b. Dec 20, 1924

LaMarsh, Judy (Julia Verlyn)
b. Dec 20, 1924
Tyson, Sylvia Fricker b. Sep 19, 1940
Chatsworth, Ontario
McClung, Nellie Letitia Mooney
b. Oct 20, 1873
Chippawa, Ontario
Secord, Laura Ingersoll d. Oct 17, 1868
Claremont, Ontario
Thomson, Tom b. 1877
Cobalt, Ontario
Drummond, William Henry d. Apr 6, 1907
Cobourg, Ontario
Dressler, Marie b. Nov 9, 1869
Cochrane, Ontario
Horton, Tim (Miles Gilbert)
b. Jan 12, 1930
Dresden, Ontario
Henson, Josiah d. May 15, 1883
Drummondsville, Ontario
Dett, Robert Nathaniel b. Oct 11, 1882
Dublin, Ontario
Crawford, Jack (John Shea)
b. Oct 26, 1916
Falconbridge, Ontario
McCourt, Dale Allen b. Jan 26, 1957
Fort Erie, Ontario
Delahanty, Edward James d. Jul 2, 1903
Fort William, Ontario
Adams, Jack (John James) b. Jun 14, 1895
Delvecchio, Alex b. Dec 4, 1931
Gravenhurst, Ontario
Bethune, Norman b. Mar 3, 1890
Grey County, Ontario
Diefenbaker, John George b. Sep 18, 1895
Guelph, Ontario
Hill, James Jerome b. Sep 16, 1838
Johnson, Edward b. Aug 22, 1881
Johnson, Edward d. Apr 20, 1959
McCrae, John b. Nov 30, 1872
Sparks, Ned b. 1883
Hamilton, Ontario
Augustyn, Frank Joseph b. Jan 27, 1953
Beatty, Robert b. Oct 9, 1909
Cooke, Jack Kent b. Sep 25, 1912
Coughlin, Father (Charles Edward)
b. Oct 25, 1891
Dupuy, Diane b. 1948
Howell, Harry (Henry Vernon)
b. Dec 28, 1932
Kain, Karen Alexandria b. Mar 28, 1951
Lawrence, Florence b. Jan 2, 1886
Quinn, Pat (John Brian Patrick)
b. Jan 29, 1943
Short, Martin b. Mar 26, 1950
Hamilton Lake, Ontario
Cranston, Toller b. 1949
Hanover, Ontario
Burns, Tommy b. Jun 17, 1881
Hespeler, Ontario
Woods, Paul William b. Apr 12, 1955

Hibbard Township, Ontario
Aberhart, William b. Dec 30, 1878
Ingersoll, Ontario
McPherson, Aimee Semple b. Oct 9, 1890
Iona Station, Ontario
Galbraith, John Kenneth b. Oct 15, 1908
Islington, Ontario
Dryden, Ken(neth Wayne) b. Aug 8, 1947
Kapuskasing, Ontario
Cameron, James b. Aug 16, 1954
Kingsmere, Ontario
King, William Lyon Mackenzie
d. Jul 22, 1950
Kingston, Ontario
Cherry, Don(ald Stewart) b. Feb 5, 1934
Cook, William d. May 5, 1986
Law, Andrew Bonar b. Sep 16, 1858
Roy, Ross b. Jul 22, 1898
Kingsville, Ontario
Miner, Jack (John Thomas) d. 1944
Kirkland Lake, Ontario
Thicke, Alan b. 1948
Kitchener, Ontario
Beaupre, Don(ald William) b. Sep 19, 1961
Maloney, Dave (David Wilfred)
b. Jul 31, 1956
Meeker, Howie (Howard William)
b. Nov 4, 1924
Millar, Margaret Ellis b. Feb 5, 1915
Sittler, Darryl Glen b. Sep 18, 1950
Kleinburg, Ontario
Jackson, A(lexander) Y(oung)
d. Apr 6, 1974
Lethbridge, Ontario
Bain, Conrad Stafford b. Feb 4, 1923
Levack, Ontario
Taylor, Dave (David Andrew)
b. Dec 4, 1955
Lindsay, Ontario
Maloney, Don(ald) b. Sep 5, 1958
Linwood, Ontario
Sterling, John Ewart Wallace
b. Aug 6, 1906
London, Ontario
Boyd, Liona Maria b. 1949
Cronyn, Hume b. Jul 18, 1911
Diamond, Selma b. 1921
Lockhart, Gene (Eugene) b. Jul 18, 1891
Lombardo, Carmen b. Jul 16, 1903
Lombardo, Guy Albert b. Jun 19, 1902
Morgan, Russell H b. Oct 9, 1911
Nelligan, Kate (Patricia Colleen)
b. Mar 16, 1951
Saunders, Charles E b. Feb 2, 1867
Warner, Jack Leonard b. Aug 2, 1892
Maple, Ontario
Beaverbrook, William Maxwell Aitken,
Baron b. May 25, 1879
Mimico, Ontario
MacMillan, Ernest Campbell, Sir
b. Aug 18, 1893

Skead, Ontario
Armstrong, George Edward b. Jul 6, 1930
Spadina, Ontario
Baldwin, Robert d. Dec 9, 1858
Stevensville, Ontario
Kraft, James Lewis b. Dec 11, 1874
Stouffville, Ontario
Brown, A Roy d. Mar 9, 1944
Stratford, Ontario
Erdman, Paul E b. May 19, 1932
Paterson, Tom b. Jun 20, 1920
Patterson, Tom (Harry Thomas)
  b. Jun 11, 1920
Strathroy, Ontario
Chadwick, Cassie L b. 1859
Knox, Alexander b. Jan 16, 1907
Shotwell, James Thomson b. Aug 6, 1874
Sudbury, Ontario
Arbour, Al(ger) b. Nov 1, 1932
Carlyle, Randy b. Apr 19, 1954
Duguay, Ron(ald) b. Jul 6, 1957
Foligno, Mike (Michael Anthony)
  b. Jan 29, 1959
Giacomin, Eddie (Edward) b. Jun 6, 1939
Trebek, Alex b. Jul 22, 1940
Terrace Bay, Ontario
Simmer, Charlie (Charles Robert)
  b. Mar 20, 1954
Thamesville, Ontario
Davies, Robertson b. Aug 28, 1913
Tecumseh d. Oct 5, 1813
Thunder Bay, Ontario
McEwen, Terence Alexander (Terry)
  b. Apr 13, 1929
Timmins, Ontario
Mahovlich, Frank (Francis William)
  b. Jan 10, 1938
Mahovlich, Pete(r Joseph) b. Oct 10, 1946
Stern, Sandor b. Jul 13, 1936
Toronto, Ontario
Ancerl, Karel d. Jul 3, 1973
Anglin, Margaret Mary d. Jan 7, 1958
Baldwin, Robert b. May 12, 1804
Barbour, John b. Apr 24,
Best, Charles Herbert d. Mar 31, 1978
Bochner, Hart b. Dec 3, 1956
Bochner, Lloyd b. Jul 29, 1924
Booth, George Gough b. Sep 24, 1864
Broda, "Turk" (Walter) d. Oct 17, 1972
Bruhn, Erik Belton Evers d. Apr 1, 1986
Callaghan, Morley Edward b. 1903
Carmichael, Franklin d. Oct 24, 1945
Chapin, James Ormsbee d. Jul 12, 1975
Chuvalo, George b. Sep 12, 1937
Clark, Barrett H b. Aug 26, 1890
Colicos, John b. Dec 10, 1928
Colville, Alex (David Alexander)
  b. Aug 24, 1920
Conacher, Charles, Sr. b. Dec 20, 1910
Conacher, Charles, Sr. d. Dec 30, 1967
Coulter, John William d. Dec 1980

DeLaRoche, Mazo b. Jan 15, 1885
DeLaRoche, Mazo d. Jul 12, 1961
Dempster, Arhur J b. 1886
Denison, George Taylor b. Aug 31, 1839
Denison, George Taylor d. Jun 6, 1925
Doherty, Brian b. Feb 3, 1906
Dwan, Allan b. Apr 3, 1885
Faith, Percy b. Apr 7, 1908
Fowler, Mark Stephen b. Oct 6, 1941
Furie, Sidney J b. Feb 28, 1933
Goldman, Emma d. May 14, 1940
Goodman, Martin Wise d. Dec 20, 1981
Gould, Glenn Herbert b. Sep 25, 1932
Gould, Glenn Herbert d. Oct 4, 1982
Gowans, Alan b. Nov 30, 1923
Harsh, George d. Jan 25, 1980
Hawerchuk, Dale b. Apr 4, 1963
Hayden, Melissa b. Apr 25, 1928
Herbert, John, pseud. b. Oct 13, 1926
Hewitt, Foster (William Foster)
  b. Nov 21, 1903
Hewitt, Foster (William Foster)
  d. Apr 21, 1985
Hill, Dan b. Jun 3, 1954
Huston, Walter b. Apr 6, 1884
Hutt, William Ian Dewitt b. May 2, 1920
Imlach, "Punch" (George) b. Mar 15, 1918
Ironside, Henry Allan b. Oct 14, 1876
Jacobi, Lou b. Dec 28, 1913
Jennings, Peter Charles b. Jul 29, 1938
Jewison, Norman b. Jul 21, 1926
Johnston, Frank H b. Jun 19, 1888
Kamen, Martin David b. Aug 27, 1913
La Marsh, Judy Verlyn d. Oct 27, 1980
LaMarsh, Judy (Julia Verlyn)
  d. Oct 27, 1980
Leacock, Stephen Butler d. Mar 28, 1944
Lee, Geddy b. Jul 29, 1953
Levy, Leonard Williams b. Apr 9, 1923
Lillie, Beatrice b. May 29, 1898
MacDonald, J(ames) E(dward) H(ervey)
  d. Nov 26, 1932
Mackenzie, Alexander d. Apr 17, 1892
Mackenzie, William Lyon d. Aug 28, 1861
Makepeace, Chris b. 1964
Mann, Paul b. Dec 20, 1915
Massey, Raymond Hart b. Aug 30, 1896
Massey, Vincent b. Feb 20, 1887
McLuhan, (Herbert) Marshall
  d. Dec 31, 1980
Meighen, Arthur d. Aug 5, 1960
Michaels, Lorne b. Nov 17,
Milne, David Brown d. Dec 26, 1953
Montgomery, Lucy Maud d. Apr 24, 1942
Moodie, Susanna d. Apr 8, 1885
Morris, Clara b. Mar 17, 1848
Neel, (Louis) Boyd d. Sep 30, 1981
Palmer, Daniel David b. Mar 7, 1845
Park, Brad (Douglas Bradford)
  b. Jul 6, 1948
Pearson, Lester Bowles b. Apr 23, 1897

Grand Mere, Quebec
McLerie, Allyn Ann b. Dec 1, 1926
Hull, Quebec
Larocque, Michel Raymond b. Apr 6, 1952
Potvin, Denis Charles b. Oct 29, 1953
Ile Perrot, Quebec
Lalonde, Marc b. Jul 26, 1929
La Salle, Quebec
Lemaire, Jacques Gerald b. Sep 7, 1945
Lac St. Jean, Quebec
Ratelle, (Joseph Gilbert Yvon) Jean
b. Oct 3, 1940
Lac-la-Tortue, Quebec
Pronovost, Marcel (Rene Marcel)
b. Jun 15, 1930
Lachine, Quebec
Bellow, Saul b. Jun 10, 1915
Levis, Quebec
Frechette, Louis-Honore b. Nov 16, 1839
Marbleton, Quebec
Tanguay, Eva b. Aug 1, 1878
Matapedia, Quebec
Hill, George Washington d. Sep 13, 1946
Montebello, Quebec
Papineau, Louis-Joseph d. Sep 25, 1871
Montreal, Quebec
Abel, Elie b. Oct 17, 1920
Aitken, Max (John William Maxwell)
b. Feb 15, 1910
Almond, Paul b. Apr 26, 1931
Berne, Eric Lennard b. May 10, 1910
Berry, Bob (Robert Victor)
b. Nov 29, 1943
Black, Conrad b. Aug 25, 1944
Blue, Ben b. Sep 12, 1901
Bossy, Mike (Michael) b. Jan 22, 1957
Bourassa, Henri b. Sep 1, 1868
Bourassa, Henri d. Aug 31, 1952
Bourassa, Robert b. Jul 14, 1933
Bourque, Ray(mond Jean) b. Dec 28, 1960
Bowman, Scotty (William Scott)
b. Sep 18, 1933
Bronfman, Edgar Miles b. Jun 20, 1929
Bronfman, Samuel d. Jul 10, 1971
Buchan, John, Sir d. Feb 11, 1940
Bujold, Genevieve b. Jul 1, 1942
Campbell, Clarence Sutherland
d. Jun 24, 1984
Cohen, Leonard b. Sep 21, 1934
D'Orsay, Fifi b. Apr 16, 1904
Demers, Jacques b. Aug 25, 1944
Dewhurst, Colleen b. Jun 3, 1926
Dionne, Marie d. Feb 27, 1970
Duluth, Daniel d. Feb 27, 1710
Dumas, Jean Baptiste Andre
b. Jun 4, 1925
Fonyo, Steve (Stephen, Jr.) b. Jun 29, 1965
Forrester, Maureen b. Jul 25, 1931
Forsyth, Rosemary b. Jul 6, 1944
Frechette, Louis-Honore d. May 31, 1908
Gallant, Mavis b. Aug 11, 1922

Geoffrion, Bernie (Bernard)
b. Feb 14, 1931
Gilbert, Rod(rique Gabriel) b. Jul 1, 1941
Glassco, John Stinson b. Dec 15, 1909
Glassco, John Stinson d. Jan 29, 1981
Guston, Philip b. Jun 27, 1913
Howe, Clarence Decatur d. Dec 31, 1960
Iberville, Pierre Le Moyne, sieur d'
b. Jul 20, 1661
Jackson, A(lexander) Y(oung)
b. Oct 3, 1882
Johnson, Pierre Marc b. Jul 5, 1946
Jutra, Claude b. Mar 11, 1930
Karpis, Alvin b. 1908
LaFontaine, Louis H, Sir d. Feb 26, 1864
Lemieux, Mario b. Oct 5, 1965
Lesage, Jean b. Jun 10, 1912
Leveille, Normand b. Jan 10, 1963
Lismer, Arthur d. Mar 23, 1969
London, George b. May 30, 1920
MacDermot, Galt b. Dec 19, 1928
MacNeil, Robert Breckenridge Ware
b. Jan 19, 1931
Martin, Richard Lionel b. Jul 26, 1951
Martineau, Jean b. Oct 6, 1895
McGill, James d. Dec 19, 1813
Molson, John d. Jan 11, 1836
Morrice, James Wilson b. Aug 10, 1865
Papineau, Louis-Joseph b. Oct 7, 1786
Parent, Bernie (Bernard Marcel)
b. Apr 3, 1945
Pelletier, Wilfred b. Jun 20, 1896
Peterson, Oscar (Emmauel)
b. Aug 15, 1925
Pollack, Sam b. Dec 15, 1925
Quilico, Louis b. Jan 14, 1929
Richard, Henri (Joseph Henri)
b. Feb 29, 1936
Richard, Maurice (Joseph Henri Maurice)
b. Aug 4, 1921
Richler, Mordecai b. Jan 27, 1931
Riopelle, Jean-Paul b. 1923
Ruddy, Al(bert Stotland) b. Mar 28, 1934
Ryan, Claude b. Jan 26, 1925
Sahl, Mort (Lyon) b. May 11, 1927
Savard, Serge A b. Jan 22, 1946
Scaasi, Arnold b. May 8, 1931
Scherman, Harry b. Feb 1, 1887
Selye, "Hans" (Hugo Bruno)
d. Oct 16, 1982
Shatner, William b. Mar 22, 1931
Shearer, Norma b. Aug 10, 1904
Smith, A(rthur) J(ames) M(arshall)
b. Nov 8, 1902
Thompson, David d. Feb 10, 1857
Torrey, Bill (William Arthur)
b. Jun 23, 1934
Tourel, Jennie b. Jun 18, 1910
Tremblay, Michel b. Jun 25, 1942
Trudeau, Pierre Elliott b. Oct 18, 1919
Vannelli, Gino b. Jun 16, 1952

Gillies, Clark b. Apr 7, 1954
Nielsen, Leslie b. Feb 11, 1926
Pocklington, Peter H b. Nov 18, 1941
Riel, Louis David d. Nov 16, 1885
Vernon, John b. Feb 24, 1932
Saskatoon, Saskatchewan
Bentley, Max (Maxwell Herbert Lloyd)
    d. Jan 19, 1984
Howe, Gordie (Gordon) b. Mar 31, 1928
Magnuson, Keith Arlen b. Apr 27, 1947
Mahoney, James P. b. Dec 7, 1927
Val Marie, Saskatchewan
Trottier, Bryan John b. Jul 17, 1956
Waldheim, Saskatchewan
Schultz, Dave (David William)
    b. Oct 14, 1949
Weyburn, Saskatchewan
Mitchell, William Ormond b. Mar 13, 1914
Williams, "Tiger" (David James)
    b. Feb 3, 1954

YUKON TERRITORY

Whitehorse, Yukon Territory
Berton, Pierre b. Jul 12, 1920

AFGHANISTAN

Kabul, Afghanistan
Mohammed Zahir Shah b. Oct 30, 1914

AFRICA

Boubangui, Africa
Bokassa I (Jean Bedel)
    b. Feb 21, 1921 3Al

ALBANIA

Kerce, Albania
Mili, Gjon b. Nov 28, 1904
Tirana, Albania
Hoxha, Enver d. Apr 11, 1985

ALBERTA

Lleshi, Haxhi b. 1913
Tirana, Alberta
Shehu, Mehmet b. Jan 10, 1913
Shehu, Mehmet d. Dec 17, 1981

ALGERIA

Leclerc, Jacques-Philippe d. Nov 28, 1947
Algiers, Algeria
Boumedienne, Houari d. Dec 27, 1978
Darlan, Jean Francois d. Dec 24, 1942
Durr, Francoise b. Dec 25, 1942
Bone, Algeria
Juin, Alphonse b. Dec 16, 1888
Clauzel, Algeria
Boumedienne, Houari b. Aug 23, 1932

Marnia, Algeria
Ben Bella, Ahmed b. Dec 1916
Mostaganem, Algeria
Borel d'Hauterive, Petrus d. Jul 14, 1859
Oran, Algeria
Saint Laurent, Yves Mathieu
    b. Aug 1, 1936
Orleansville, Algeria
Robert, Paul b. Oct 9, 1910
Taher, Algeria
Abbas, Ferhat b. Oct 24, 1899

ALGIERS

Mondovi, Algiers
Camus, Albert b. Nov 7, 1913
Mustapha, Algiers
Vieuxtemps, Henri d. Jun 6, 1881

AMERICAN SAMOA

Tutuwila, American Samoa
Thompson, Jack b. May 19, 1956 3An

ANNAM

Quang Bihn, Annam
Ngo dinh Diem b. 1901 3An

ANTIGUA ISLAND

Beatty, Morgan d. Jul 4, 1975

ARABIA

Mecca, Arabia
Abu Bakr b. 573 3Ar
Mansur, (Abu Jafar Ibn Muhammad), Al
    d. Oct 775 3Ar
Medina, Arabia
Ayesha b. 614 3Ar
Omar I d. 644 3Ar

ARGENTINA

DeVicenzo, Roberto b. Apr 14, 1923
Frondizi, Arturo b. Sep 28, 1908
Hunt, Martita b. Jan 30, 1900
Maradona, Diego b. Oct 30, 1960
Thyssen, Fritz d. Feb 8, 1951
Alta Gracia, Argentina
Falla, Manuel de d. Nov 14, 1946
Argentina, Argentina
Sabatini, Gabriela b. May 16, 1970
Buenos Aires, Argentina
Aramburu, Pedro Eugenio
    b. May 21, 1903
Argentinita b. Mar 25, 1905
Barenboim, Daniel b. Nov 15, 1942
Bioy-Casares, Adolfo b. Sep 15, 1914
Bonavena, Oscar b. Sep 25, 1942
Borges, Jorge Luis b. Aug 24, 1899

Bordertown, Australia
Hawke, Bob (Robert James Lee)
b. Dec 9, 1929
Brisbane, Australia
Cilento, Diane b. Oct 5, 1933
Gould, Shane b. Sep 4, 1956
Kingsford-Smith, Charles Edward b. 1897
Turnbull, Wendy b. Nov 26, 1952
Canberra, Australia
Curtin, John d. Jul 5, 1945
Canterbury, Australia
Southall, Ivan Francis b. Jun 8, 1921
Casterton, Australia
Matheson, Murray b. Jul 1, 1912
Creswick, Australia
Curtin, John b. Jan 8, 1885
Deans Marsh, Australia
Lawrence, Marjorie Florence
b. Feb 17, 1909
Fremantle, Australia
Hasluck, Paul Meernaa, Sir b. Apr 1, 1905
Geelong, Australia
Brownlee, John b. Jan 7, 1901
Geraldton, Australia
Stow, (Julian) Randolph b. Nov 28, 1935
Hobart, Australia
Warner, Denis Ashton b. Dec 12, 1917
Hunter Valley, Australia
White, Patrick Victor Martindale
b. May 28, 1912
Jeparit, Australia
Menzies, Robert Gordon, Sir
b. Dec 20, 1894
Kalgoorlie, Australia
Marsh, Graham B b. Jan 14, 1944
Kiama, Australia
Orry-Kelly b. Dec 31, 1897
Kingsway, Australia
Emerson, Roy b. Nov 3, 1936
Lismore, Australia
Wrightson, Patricia b. Jun 19, 1921
Melbourne, Australia
Austral, Florence Wilson b. Apr 26, 1894
Bridges, Harry Renton b. Jul 29, 1901
Browne, Coral Edith b. Jul 23, 1913
Bruce, David, Sir b. May 29, 1855
Burnet, MacFarlane (Frank MacFarlane)
d. Aug 31, 1985
Caldicott, Helen Broinowski
b. Aug 7, 1938
Caldwell, Zoe b. Sep 14, 1933
Clarke, Ron b. Feb 21, 1937
Cowen, Zelman, Sir b. Oct 7, 1919
Davison, Frank Dalby b. Jun 23, 1893
Davison, Frank Dalby d. May 24, 1970
Eccles, John Carew, Sir b. Jan 27, 1903
Evans, Mark b.
Fleming, Ian b. Sep 10, 1888
Fraser, John Malcolm b. Mar 21, 1930
Gorton, John Grey b. Sep 9, 1911
Grainger, Percy Aldridge b. Jul 8, 1882

Greer, Germaine b. Jan 29, 1939
Hicks, Peggy Glanville- b. Dec 29, 1912
Jones, Alan b. Feb 11, 1946
Kelly, Ned (Edward) d. Nov 11, 1880
Landy, John b. Apr 12, 1930
Melba, Dame Nellie b. May 19, 1859
Menzies, Robert Gordon, Sir
d. May 14, 1978
Moorehead, Alan b. Jul 22, 1910
Murdoch, Rupert (Keith Rupert)
b. Mar 11, 1931
Norman, Greg b. Feb 10, 1955
Reddy, Helen b. Oct 25, 1942
Richardson, Henry Handel, pseud.
b. Jan 3, 1870
Robson, May b. Apr 19, 1858
Rudd, Phil(lip) b. May 19, 1946
Sang, Samantha b. Aug 5, 1953
Tuckwell, Barry Emmanuel b. Mar 5, 1931
Villiers, Alan John b. Sep 23, 1903
West, Morris Langlo b. Apr 26, 1916
Whitlam, Edward Gough b. Jul 11, 1916
Williams, John b. Apr 24, 1941
Williamson, David b. Feb 24, 1942
Mont Albert, Australia
Sedgman, Frank (Francis Arthur)
b. Oct 29, 1927
Mount Bryan, Australia
Wilkins, George Hubert, Sir
b. Oct 31, 1888
Mount Gambier, Australia
Helpmann, Robert Murray, Sir
b. Apr 9, 1909
Mount Victoria, Australia
Childe, Vere Gordon d. Sep 19, 1957
New South Wales, Australia
Brinsmead, Hesba Fay b. Mar 15, 1922
Paddington, Australia
Carruthers, John(ny) b. Jul 5, 1929
Perth, Australia
Cowan, Peter Wilkinshaw b. Nov 4, 1914
Port Philip Bay, Australia
Holt, Harold Edward d. Dec 17, 1967
Queensland, Australia
Laver, Rod(ney George) b. Aug 9, 1938
Travers, P(amela) L(yndon) b. 1906
Southport, Australia
Kellerman, Annette d. Oct 30, 1975
Sydney, Australia
Austral, Florence Wilson d. May 15, 1968
Benjamin, Arthur b. Sep 18, 1893
Bonynge, Richard b. Sep 29, 1930
Brown, Bryan b. 1950
Brown, Carter, pseud. d. May 5, 1985
Browne, Walter Shawn b. Jan 10, 1949
Caldwell, John Charles b. Dec 8, 1928
Cantrell, Lana b. Aug 7, 1943
Childe, Vere Gordon b. Apr 14, 1892
Courtneidge, Cicely, Dame b. Apr 1, 1893
Crampton, Bruce Sidney b. Sep 28, 1935
Cuthbert, Betty b. Apr 20, 1938

Dent, Phil b. Feb 14, 1950
Errol, Leon b. Jul 3, 1881
Farrow, John Villiers b. Feb 10, 1906
Ferrier, Jim (James B) b. Feb 24, 1915
Fifield, Elaine b. Oct 28, 1930
Franklin, Miles, pseud. d. Sep 19, 1954
Holt, Harold Edward b. Aug 5, 1908
Hughes, Robert Studley Forrest
    b. Jul 28, 1938
Jacobs, Joseph b. Aug 29, 1854
Kellerman, Annette b. Jul 6, 1888
Marshal, Alan b. Jan 29, 1909
McKern, Leo b. Mar 16, 1920
Melba, Dame Nellie d. Feb 23, 1931
Murray, Gilbert (George Gilbert Aime)
    b. Jan 2, 1866
Newcombe, John b. May 23, 1944
Pollard, Jack b. Jul 31, 1926
Rafferty, "Chips" d. May 27, 1971
Ritchard, Cyril b. Dec 1, 1897
Rosewall, Ken b. Nov 2, 1934
Sheed, Frank (Francis Joseph)
    b. Mar 20, 1897
Shorrock, Glenn b. Jun 30, 1944
Springfield, Rick (Richard)
    b. Aug 23, 1949
Stead, Christina Ellen d. Mar 31, 1983
Stephenson, Jan b. Dec 22, 1951
Sutherland, Joan b. Nov 7, 1929
Taylor, Rod(ney) b. Jan 11, 1930
Weir, Peter b. Aug 8, 1944
Syndey, Australia
Stead, Christina Ellen b. Jul 17, 1902
Talbingo, Australia
Franklin, Miles, pseud. b. Oct 14, 1879
Tenterfield, Australia
Allen, Peter Woolnough b. Feb 10, 1944
Toowong, Australia
Dart, Raymond Arthur b. Feb 4, 1893
Toowoomba, Australia
Kenny, Sister Elizabeth d. Nov 30, 1952
Victoria, Australia
Burnet, MacFarlane (Frank MacFarlane)
    b. Sep 3, 1899
Jewett, Henry b. Jun 4, 1862
Powell, Gordon G b. Jan 22, 1911
Shute, Nevil d. Jan 12, 1960
Victoria Park, Australia
Porter, Hal b. Feb 16, 1911
Warrialda, Australia
Kenny, Sister Elizabeth b. Sep 20, 1886
Wellington, Australia
McCullough, Colleen b. Jun 1, 1937
Windsor, Australia
Graham, David B b. May 23, 1946

AUSTRIA

Bonaparte, Francois Charles Joseph d. 1832
Golacinski, Alan Bruce b. Jun 4, 1950
Goldberger, Joseph b. Jul 16, 1874

Gross, Chaim b. Mar 17, 1904
Hilbert, Egon b. 1899
Kirchschlager, Rudolf b. Mar 20, 1915
Kokoschka, Oskar b. Mar 1, 1886
Liebow, Averill A(braham)
    b. Mar 31, 1911
Reich, Wilhelm b. Mar 24, 1897
Root, Jack b. May 26, 1876
Stangl, Franz Paul b. 1908
Tannenbaum, Frank b. Mar 1893
Augsburg, Austria
Mozart, (Johann Georg) Leopold b. 1719
Ausfelden, Austria
Bruckner, Anton b. Sep 4, 1824
Bad Ischl, Austria
Lehar, Franz d. Oct 24, 1948
Straus, Oskar d. Jan 11, 1954
Baden, Austria
Hanslick, Eduard d. Aug 6, 1904
Reinhardt, Max b. Sep 9, 1873
Bielitz, Austria
Kurz, Selma b. Nov 15, 1875
Branau, Austria
Hitler, Adolf b. Apr 20, 1889
Brody, Austria
Kober, Arthur b. Aug 25, 1900
Brunn, Austria
Edelmann, Otto b. Feb 5, 1917
Jerger, Alfred b. Jun 9, 1889
Jeritza, Maria b. Oct 6, 1887
Korngold, Erich Wolfgang
    b. May 29, 1897
Schauffler, Robert Haven b. Apr 8, 1879
Budzanow, Austria
Strasberg, Lee b. Nov 17, 1901
Czernowitz, Austria
Jagendorf, Moritz b. Aug 24, 1888
Paur, Emil b. Aug 29, 1855
Dornbirn, Austria
Drexel, Francis Martin b. Apr 7, 1792
Edlach, Austria
Schalk, Franz d. Sep 2, 1931
Graz, Austria
Bohm, Karl b. Aug 28, 1894
Franz Ferdinand b. Dec 18, 1863
Klien, Walter b. Nov 27, 1928
Rosbaud, Hans b. Jul 22, 1895
Scaria, Emil b. Aug 18, 1838
Schuch, Ernst von b. Nov 23, 1846
Schwarzenegger, Arnold b. Jul 30, 1947
Stolz, Robert b. Aug 25, 1886
Haag, Austria
Bayer, Herbert b. Apr 5, 1900
Henndorf, Austria
Mayr, Richard b. Nov 18, 1877
Innsbruck, Austria
Keyserling, Hermann Alexander
    d. Apr 26, 1946
Rahner, Karl d. Mar 30, 1984
Schuschnigg, Kurt von d. Nov 18, 1977

Jaroslau, Austria
  Spiegel, Sam b. Nov 11, 1904
Judenburg, Austria
  Kotsching, Walter Maria b. Apr 9, 1901
Kalusz, Austria
  Schuster, Max Lincoln b. Mar 2, 1897
Kanczuga, Austria
  Brill, Abraham Arden b. Oct 12, 1874
Kierling, Austria
  Kafka, Franz d. Jun 3, 1924
Kleinarl, Austria
  Proell, Annemarie b. Mar 27, 1953
Klekotow, Austria
  Kanner, Leo b. Jun 13, 1894
Lake Wolfgang, Austria
  Jannings, Emil d. Jan 3, 1950
Laxenberg, Austria
  Rudolf of Hapsburg b. 1858
Lemberg, Austria
  Ewen, David b. Dec 6, 1907
  Ewen, Frederic b. Oct 11, 1899
  Goldhaber, Maurice b. Apr 18, 1911
  Muni, Paul b. Sep 22, 1895
  Sacher-Masoch, Leopold von
    b. Jan 27, 1836
Linz, Austria
  Tauber, Richard b. May 16, 1892
  Woss, Kurt b. May 2, 1914
Lipnik, Austria
  Schnabel, Artur b. Apr 17, 1882
Mariagru, Austria
  Krafft-Ebing, Richard von d. Dec 22, 1902
Mayerling, Austria
  Rudolf of Hapsburg d. Jan 30, 1889
Mittersill, Austria
  Webern, Anton von d. Sep 15, 1945
Moaswald, Austria
  Klammer, Franz b. 1952
Prague, Austria
  Cori, Carl Ferdinand b. Dec 5, 1896
  Cori, Gerty Theresa b. Aug 15, 1896
Rohrau, Austria
  Haydn, Franz Joseph b. Mar 31, 1732
Ruttka, Austria
  Hertz, John Daniel b. Apr 10, 1879
Rymahow, Austria
  Rabi, Isidor Isaac b. Jul 29, 1898
Saint Georgen, Austria
  Materna, Amalia b. Jul 10, 1844
Saint Leonhard, Austria
  Hofer, Andreas b. Nov 22, 1767
Saint Poelten, Austria
  Demus, Joreg b. Dec 2, 1928
Salzburg, Austria
  Berger, Helmut b. May 29, 1944
  Bohm, Karl d. Aug 14, 1981
  Doppler, Christian Johann b. Nov 30, 1803
  Hill, Virginia d. Mar 25, 1966
  Karajan, Herbert von b. Apr 5, 1908
  Lorenz, Max d. Jan 11, 1975
  Mozart, (Johann Georg) Leopold d. 1787

Mozart, Wolfgang Amadeus
    b. Jan 27, 1756
Paracelsus, Philippus Aureolus
    d. Sep 24, 1541
Paumgartner, Bernhard d. Jul 27, 1971
Pfitzner, Hans d. May 22, 1949
Stanislau, Austria
  Burns, Arthur F b. Apr 27, 1904
Straubing, Austria
  Schikaneder, Johann Emanuel
    b. Sep 1, 1748
Tarnopal, Austria
  Mazurki, Mike b. Dec 25, 1909
Texing, Austria
  Dollfuss, Engelbert b. Oct 4, 1892
Tirol, Austria
  Bemelmans, Ludwig b. Apr 27, 1898
Traunblick, Austria
  Wesendonck, Mathilde Luckemeyer b. 1828
Turas, Austria
  Mach, Ernst b. Feb 18, 1838
Unter St. Veit, Austria
  Mottl, Felix b. Aug 24, 1856
Valdi Sole, Austria
  Toffenetti, Dario Louis b. Jan 20, 1889
Vienna, Austria
  Adler, Alfred b. Feb 7, 1870
  Adler, Kurt Herbert b. Apr 2, 1905
  Andersen, Lale d. Aug 29, 1972
  Auden, W(ystan) H(ugh) d. Sep 28, 1973
  Barylli, Walter b. 1921
  Baum, Vicki b. Jan 24, 1888
  Beethoven, Ludwig van d. Mar 26, 1827
  Berg, Alban b. Feb 9, 1885
  Berg, Alban d. Dec 24, 1935
  Berger, Senta b. May 13, 1941
  Bergner, Elisabeth b. Aug 22, 1900
  Bernays, Edward L b. Nov 22, 1891
  Berry, Walter b. Apr 8, 1929
  Bettelheim, Bruno b. Aug 28, 1903
  Bey, Turhan b. Mar 30, 1920
  Bikel, Theodore Meir b. May 2, 1924
  Bing, Rudolf(Franz Josef), Sir
    b. Jan 9, 1902
  Bitter, Karl Theodore Francis
    b. Dec 6, 1867
  Bluhdorn, Charles G b. Sep 20, 1926
  Bodanzky, Artur b. Dec 16, 1887
  Bondi, Hermann, Sir b. Nov 1, 1919
  Bononcini, Giovanni Battista b. Jul 9, 1747
  Brahms, Johannes d. Apr 3, 1897
  Brown, Vanessa b. Mar 24, 1928
  Bruckner, Anton d. Oct 11, 1896
  Buber, Martin b. Feb 8, 1878
  Carnegie, Hattie b. 1889
  Cebotari, Maria d. Jun 9, 1949
  Christians, Mady b. Jan 19, 1900
  Cortez, Ricardo b. Sep 19, 1899
  Czerny, Karl b. Feb 20, 1791
  Czerny, Karl d. Jul 15, 1857
  Dantine, Helmut b. Oct 7, 1917

Dichter, Ernest b. Aug 14, 1907
Ditters, Karl b. Nov 2, 1739
Djerassi, Carl b. Oct 29, 1923
Doktor, Paul Karl b. 1919
Drucker, Peter b. Nov 9, 1909
Ehrlich, Bettina Bauer b. Mar 19, 1903
Fall, Bernard B b. Nov 11, 1926
Felsenstein, Walter b. May 30, 1901
Fleischer, Max b. Jul 19, 1883
Flesch, Rudolf b. May 8, 1911
Frank, Johann Peter d. Apr 24, 1821
Frankfurter, Felix b. Nov 15, 1882
Frankl, Viktor E b. Mar 26, 1905
Freud, Anna b. Dec 3, 1895
Fried, Alfred Hermann b. Nov 11, 1864
Fried, Alfred Hermann d. May 6, 1921
Frisch, Karl von b. Nov 20, 1886
Gernreich, Rudi b. Aug 8, 1922
Gluck, Christoph Wilibald d. Nov 15, 1787
Goldmark, Karl d. Jan 2, 1915
Goldsand, Robert b. 1922
Graf, Herbert b. Apr 10, 1903
Gregor, Arthur b. Nov 18, 1923
Grillparzer, Franz b. Jan 15, 1791
Grillparzer, Franz d. Jan 21, 1872
Grossinger, Jennie b. Jun 16, 1892
Gruen, Victor b. Jul 18, 1903
Gruen, Victor d. Feb 16, 1980
Gruenberg, Sidonie Matsner
    b. Jun 10, 1881
Gueden, Hilde b. Sep 15, 1917
Guiterman, Arthur b. Nov 20, 1871
Harris, Jed b. Feb 25, 1900
Haydn, Franz Joseph d. May 31, 1809
Hayek, Friedrich August von
    b. May 8, 1899
Herzl, Theodor d. Jul 3, 1904
Hilbert, Egon d. Jan 18, 1968
Hofmannsthal, Hugo Hoffmann
    b. Feb 1, 1874
Hofmannsthal, Hugo Hoffmann
    d. Jul 15, 1929
Homolka, Oscar b. Aug 12, 1903
Hubay, Jeno d. Mar 12, 1937
Hummel, Lisl b.
Hunndertwasser, Friedrich b. Dec 15, 1928
Illich, Ivan b. Sep 4, 1926
Jacobsson, Ulla d. Aug 22, 1982
Jerger, Alfred d. Nov 18, 1976
Jessner, Irene b. 1909
Jonas, Franz b. Oct 4, 1899
Jonas, Franz d. Apr 24, 1974
Juch, Emma b. Jul 4, 1863
Jurgens, Curt d. Jun 18, 1982
Kasznar, Kurt b. Aug 13, 1913
Kienzl, Wilhelm d. Oct 3, 1941
King, Alexander b. Nov 13, 1900
Kleiber, Erich b. Aug 5, 1890
Klein, Melanie b. Mar 30, 1882
Klimt, Gustav b. Jul 4, 1862
Klimt, Gustav d. Feb 6, 1918

Kohut, Heinz b. May 3, 1913
Kollek, Teddy (Theodore) b. May 27, 1911
Konetzne, Anni b. Feb 12, 1902
Konetzne, Anni d. Jun 9, 1968
Konetzni, Hilde b. Mar 21, 1905
Kraus, Felix von b. Oct 3, 1870
Krauss, Clemens b. Mar 31, 1893
Krauss, Gabrielle b. Mar 24, 1842
Krauss, Werner d. Oct 20, 1959
Kreisler, Fritz b. Feb 2, 1875
Krenek, Ernst b. Aug 23, 1900
Krips, Josef b. Apr 8, 1902
Kuerti, Anton b. 1938
Kunz, Erich b. May 20, 1909
Kurt, Melanie b. Jan 8, 1880
Kurz, Selma d. May 10, 1933
Lamarr, Hedy b. Sep 11, 1913
Landsteiner, Karl b. Jul 14, 1868
Lang, Fritz b. Dec 5, 1890
Lauda, Niki (Nikolaus-Andreas)
    b. Feb 22, 1949
Leinsdorf, Erich b. Feb 4, 1912
Lenya, Lotte b. Oct 18, 1900
Lert, Ernst b. May 12, 1883
Liebman, Max b. Aug 5, 1902
Lind, Jakov b. Feb 10, 1927
Lindtberg, Leopold b. Jun 1, 1902
List, Emanuel b. Mar 22, 1891
List, Emanuel d. Jun 21, 1967
Loewe, Frederick b. Jun 10, 1904
Losch, Tilly b. Nov 15, 1902
Low, George M(ichael) b. Jun 10, 1926
Lucca, Pauline b. Apr 25, 1841
Lucca, Pauline d. Feb 28, 1908
Mahler, Fritz b. Jul 16, 1901
Mahler, Gustav d. May 18, 1911
Maria Theresa b. May 13, 1717
Marie Antoinette b. Nov 2, 1755
Mark, Herman F b. May 3, 1895
Materna, Amalia d. Jan 18, 1918
Maximilian b. Jul 6, 1832
Mayr, Richard d. Dec 1, 1935
Meitner, Lise b. Nov 7, 1878
Metastasio, Pietro d. Apr 12, 1782
Metternich-Winneburg, Clemens
    d. Jun 11, 1859
Mildenburg, Anna von b. Nov 29, 1872
Mildenburg, Anna von d. Jan 27, 1947
Mindszenty, Jozsef, Cardinal
    d. Jun 6, 1975
Morini, Erica b. May 26, 1906
Morton, Frederic b. Oct 5, 1924
Mosenthal, Salomon Hermann von
    d. Feb 17, 1877
Mozart, Wolfgang Amadeus
    d. Dec 5, 1791
Neumann, Angelo b. Aug 18, 1838
Neumann, Robert Gerhard b. Jan 2, 1916
Neurath, Otto b. Dec 10, 1882
Neutra, Richard Joseph b. Apr 8, 1892
Ohrbach, Nathan b. Aug 31, 1885

Pabst, Georg Wilhelm d. May 29, 1967
Padover, Saul Kussiel b. Apr 13, 1905
Patzak, Julius b. Apr 9, 1898
Paul, Frank Rudolph b. 1884
Paumgartner, Bernhard b. Nov 14, 1887
Piaget, Jean d. Sep 16, 1980
Piccaver, Alfred d. Sep 23, 1958
Placzek, Adolf K(urt) b. Mar 9, 1913
Praeger, Frederick A b. Sep 16, 1915
Preminger, Otto Ludwig b. Dec 5, 1906
Prohaska, Felix b. May 16, 1912
Rainer, Luise b. Jan 12, 1912
Reik, Theodor b. May 12, 1888
Reznicek, Emil von b. May 4, 1860
Rohatyn, Felix George b. May 29, 1928
Roller, Alfred b. Feb 10, 1864
Roller, Alfred d. Jun 21, 1935
Rosenstein, Nettie b. Sep 26, 1893
Rudel, Julius b. Mar 6, 1921
Rysanek, Leonie b. Nov 12, 1926
Salieri, Antonio d. May 7, 1825
Sauer, Emil von d. Apr 29, 1942
Schalk, Franz b. May 27, 1863
Scheff, Frizi b. Aug 30, 1879
Schell, Maria Margarethe b. Jan 5, 1926
Schell, Maximilian b. Dec 8, 1930
Schikaneder, Johann Emanuel
    d. Sep 21, 1812
Schildkraut, Joseph b. Mar 22, 1896
Schlamme, Martha b. 1930
Schmedes, Erik d. Mar 23, 1931
Schneider, "Romy" b. Sep 23, 1938
Schneiderhan, Walther b. 1901
Schnitzler, Arthur b. May 15, 1862
Schnitzler, Arthur d. Oct 21, 1931
Schoenberg, Arnold b. Sep 13, 1874
Schroedinger, Erwin b. Aug 12, 1887
Schubert, Franz Peter b. Jan 31, 1797
Schubert, Franz Peter d. Nov 19, 1828
Segal, Lore Groszmann b. Mar 8, 1928
Selye, "Hans" (Hugo Bruno)
    b. Jan 26, 1907
Slezak, Walter b. May 3, 1902
Steiner, Max b. May 10, 1888
Stiedry, Fritz b. Oct 11, 1883
Straus, Oskar b. Apr 6, 1870
Strauss, Johann, Jr. b. Oct 25, 1825
Strauss, Johann, Jr. d. Jun 3, 1899
Strauss, Johann, Sr. b. Mar 14, 1804
Strauss, Johann, Sr. d. Sep 25, 1849
Toch, Ernst b. Dec 7, 1887
Trapp, Maria Augusta von b. Jan 26, 1905
Unger, Caroline b. Oct 28, 1803
Urban, Joseph Maria b. May 26, 1872
Vivaldi, Antonio d. Jul 27, 1741
VonDoderer, Heimito d. Dec 23, 1966
VonSternberg, Josef b. May 29, 1894
VonStroheim, Erich b. Sep 22, 1885
Walbrook, Anton b. Nov 19, 1900
Wallmann, Margherita b. Jun 22, 1904
Webern, Anton von b. Dec 3, 1883

Wechsberg, Joseph d. Apr 10, 1983
Wellek, Rene b. Aug 22, 1903
Wellesz, Egon b. Oct 21, 1885
Werner, Oskar b. Nov 13, 1922
Wilder, "Billy" (Samuel) b. Jun 22, 1906
Winkelmann, Hermann d. Jan 18, 1912
Wittgenstein, Ludwig b. Apr 26, 1889
Wolf, Hugo d. Feb 22, 1903
Zemlinsky, Alexander von b. Oct 4, 1872
Zinnemann, Fred b. Apr 25, 1907
Zweig, Stefan b. Nov 28, 1881

Villach, Austria
Backhaus, Wilhelm d. Jul 5, 1969
Vindobona, Austria
Marcus Aurelius Antoninus
    d. Mar 17, 180
Waizenkircen, Austria
Kienzl, Wilhelm b. Jan 17, 1857
Waldstein, Austria
Hess, Victor Francis b. Jun 24, 1883
Wiener Neustadt, Austria
Porsche, Ferdinand b. Sep 19, 1909
Wiener Nevstadt, Austria
Schreiber, Hermann Otto Ludwig
    b. May 4, 1920
Wiener-Neustadt, Austria
Machlup, Fritz b. Dec 15, 1902
Windischgraez, Austria
Wolf, Hugo b. Mar 13, 1860
Wisenberg, Austria
Brendel, Alfred b. Jan 5, 1931
Witfowitz, Austria
Ludwig, Leopold b. Jan 12, 1908
Woerdern, Austria
Waldheim, Kurt b. Dec 21, 1918
Worthersee, Austria
Kraus, Ernst d. Sep 6, 1941
Zara, Austria
Weingartner, Felix b. Jun 2, 1863
Zloczew, Austria
Fellig, Arthur b. Jul 12, 1899

AUSTRIA-HUNGARY

Roth, Henry b. Feb 8, 1906
Budapest, Austria-Hungary
Szabolcsi, Bence b. Aug 2, 1899
Hermannstadt, Austria-Hungary
Oberlith, Hermann Jules
    b. Jun 25, 1894
Mikulinsty, Austria-Hungary
Golden, Harry Lewis b. May 6, 1903
Prague, Austria-Hungary
Kelsen, Hans b. Oct 11, 1881
Smiljan, Austria-Hungary
Tesla, Nikola b. Jul 10, 1856

AUSTRO-HUNGARY

Bosnia, Austro-Hungary
Princip, Gavrilo b. 1895

BABYLON

Alexander the Great d. Jun 13, 323

BAHAMAS

Lockhart, Calvin b. 1936
Merrill, John Putnam d. Apr 4, 1984
Pindling, Lynden Oscar b. 1930
Freeport, Bahamas
Rand, James Henry d. Jun 3, 1968
Nassau, Bahamas
Eads, James Buchanan d. Mar 8, 1887
Forsythe, Albert E b. 1898
Thompson, Mychal b. Jan 30, 1955
New Providence Island, Bahamas
Williams, Bert (Egbert Austin) b. 1876

BANGLADESH

Chittagong, Bangladesh
Rahman, Ziaur d. May 30, 1981

BARBADOS

Adams, "Tom" (John Michael Geoffrey
   Maningham) b. Sep 24, 1931
Barrow, Ruth Nita, Dame
   b. Nov 15, 1916
Locke, William John b. Mar 20, 1863
Scott, Arleigh Winston b. Mar 27, 1900
Ward, Deighton Harcourt Lisle, Sir
   b. May 16, 1909
Bridgetown, Barbados
Adams, "Tom" (John Michael Geoffrey
   Maningham) d. Mar 12, 1985
Eastman, Max Forrester d. Mar 25, 1969
Messel, Oliver d. Jul 14, 1978
Saint Lucy, Barbados
Barrow, Errol Walton b. Jan 21, 1920

BAVARIA

Hartmann, Franz b. Nov 22, 1838
Brand, Bavaria
Reger, Max b. Mar 19, 1873
Dispeck, Bavaria
Einhorn, David b. Nov 10, 1809
Erlangen, Bavaria
Kraus, Ernst b. Jun 8, 1863
Essingen, Bavaria
Nicolay, John George b. Feb 26, 1832
Gunzburg, Bavaria
Mengele, Josef b. Mar 16, 1911
Huttendorf, Bavaria
Kalb, Johann de b. Jun 29, 1721
Kempten, Bavaria
Hartmann, Franz d. Aug 7, 1912
Lake Starnberg, Bavaria
Ludwig II d. 1886
Massing, Bavaria
Hummel, Berta b. 1909

Munich, Bavaria
Ockham, William of d. 1349
Oberhausen, Bavaria
LaTour D'Auvergne, Theophile de
   d. Jun 27, 1800
Schloss, Bavaria
Schott, Anton b. Jun 24, 1846
Speyer, Bavaria
Villard, Henry b. Apr 10, 1835
Tegernsee, Bavaria
Acton, John Emerich Edward Dalberg-
   Acton, Baron d. Jul 19, 1902
Wunsiedel, Bavaria
Richter, Jean Paul F b. Mar 21, 1763

BAY OF BISCAY

Howard, Leslie d. Jun 2, 1943 3Be

BELGIUM

Hulme, Thomas Ernest d. Sep 28, 1917
Picard, Edmond d. Feb 19, 1924
Antwerp, Belgium
Brouwer, Adriaen C d. Jan 1638
Bull, John d. Mar 12, 1622
Cleve, Joos van d. 1540
Cluytens, Andre b. Mar 26, 1905
Dyck, Anthony van b. 1599
Hals, Frans b. 1580
Heem, Jan Davidsz de d. 1684
Jordaens, Jacob b. May 19, 1593
Jordaens, Jacob d. Oct 18, 1678
Mabuse, Jan de d. 1533
Rubens, Peter Paul, Sir d. May 30, 1640
Schneider, Nina b. Jan 29, 1913
Teniers, David, the Younger
   b. Dec 14, 1610
Tyndale, William d. Oct 6, 1536
Van Dyck, Anthony, Sir b. Mar 22, 1599
Ath, Belgium
Hennepin, Louis b. Apr 7, 1640
Bruges, Belgium
Brangwyn, Frank, Sir b. May 13, 1867
Memling, Hans d. Aug 11, 1494
Brussels, Belgium
Albert b. Jun 6, 1934
Albert I b. Apr 8, 1875
Barzin, Leon Eugene b. Nov 27, 1900
Baudouin, Albert Charles b. Sep 7, 1930
Bordet, Jules Jean Baptiste Vincent
   d. Apr 6, 1961
Boulanger, Georges Ernest Jean Marie
   d. 1891
Brel, Jacques b. Apr 8, 1929
Bruegel, Pieter, (The Elder) d. Sep 5, 1569
Brughel, Jan b. 1568
Carlota b. 1840
Claiborne, Liz (Elisabeth) b. Mar 31, 1929
Claude, Albert d. May 20, 1983
Cortazar, Julio b. Aug 26, 1914
Culliford, "Peyo" (Pierre) b. Jun 25, 1928

Danco, Suzanne b. Jan 22, 1911
David, Jacques Louis d. Dec 29, 1825
Decoster, Charles Theodore
   d. May 7, 1879
Furstenberg, Diane Halfin von
   b. Dec 31, 1946
Ghelderode, Michel de d. Apr 1, 1962
Hepburn, Audrey b. May 4, 1929
Leopold II b. Apr 9, 1835
Leopold III b. Nov 3, 1901
Leopold III d. Sep 25, 1983
Levi-Strauss, Claude b. Nov 28, 1908
Magritte, Rene d. Aug 8, 1967
Monro, Harold Edward b. Mar 14, 1879
North, John Ringling d. Jun 4, 1985
Orley, Bernard van b. 1491
Orley, Bernard van d. Jan 6, 1542
Picard, Edmond b. Dec 15, 1836
Piccard, Jacques b. Jul 28, 1922
Puccini, Giacomo d. Nov 29, 1924
Ruhlmann, Francois b. Jan 11, 1868
Spaak, Fernand Paul Jules d. Jul 1981
Spaak, Paul-Henri d. Jul 31, 1972
Teniers, David, the Younger
   d. Apr 25, 1690
Van Hamel, Martine b. Nov 16, 1945
Van Itallie, Jean-Claude b. May 23, 1936
Van Vooren, Monique b. Mar 17, 1933
Varda, Agnes b. May 30, 1928
Vesalius, Andreas b. Dec 31, 1514
Weyden, Rogier van der d. Jun 16, 1464
Weygand, Maxime b. Jan 21, 1867
Yourcenar, Marguerite, pseud.
   b. Jun 8, 1913
Ysaye, Eugene d. May 13, 1931

Deinze, Belgium
Biebuyck, Daniel Prosper b. Oct 1, 1925

Dinant Meuse, Belgium
Sax, Adolphe b. Nov 6, 1814

Dinant-sur-Meuse, Belgium
Sax, Charles Joseph b. Feb 1, 1791

Elsene, Belgium
Ghelderode, Michel de b. Apr 3, 1898

Etterbeck, Belgium
Regine b. Dec 26, 1929

Forest, Belgium
Spaak, Fernand Paul Jules b. Aug 8, 1923

Ghent, Belgium
Baekeland, Leo Hendrick b. Nov 14, 1863
Defauw, Desire b. Sep 5, 1885
Gorr, Rita b. Feb 18, 1926
John of Gaunt b. Mar 1340
Louys, Pierre b. Dec 10, 1870
Maeterlinck, Maurice b. Aug 29, 1862

Laeken, Belgium
Leopold II d. Dec 17, 1909

Lichtervelde, Belgium
Van Depoele, Charles Joseph
   b. Apr 27, 1846

Liege, Belgium
Browning, John Moses d. Nov 26, 1926
Corneille b. 1922
Franck, Cesar Auguste b. Dec 10, 1822
Gretry, Andre Ernest Modeste
   b. Feb 9, 1741
Simenon, Georges b. Feb 13, 1903
Ysaye, Eugene b. Jul 16, 1858

Lierre, Belgium
Eyskens, Gaston b. Apr 1, 1905

Liverchies, Belgium
Reinhardt, Django (Jean Baptiste)
   b. Jan 23, 1910

Louvain, Belgium
Elzevir, Louis b. 1540
Massys, Quentin b. 1466

Namur, Belgium
Albert I d. Feb 17, 1934
Michaux, Henri b. May 24, 1899

Ostend, Belgium
Ensor, James b. Apr 13, 1860
Ensor, James d. Nov 19, 1949

Oudenaarde, Belgium
Brouwer, Adriaen C b. 1606

Schaerbeck, Belgium
Spaak, Paul-Henri b. Jan 25, 1899

Seligenstadt, Belgium
Memling, Hans b. 1430

Soighies, Belgium
Bordet, Jules Jean Baptiste Vincent
   b. Jun 13, 1870

Tournai, Belgium
Weyden, Rogier van der b. 1399

Traumeries, Belgium
Maison, Rene b. Nov 24, 1895

Tremeloo, Belgium
Damien, Father b. Jan 3, 1840

Uccle, Belgium
Folon, Jean-Michel b. Mar 1, 1934

Utrecht, Belgium
Heem, Jan Davidsz de b. 1606

Vergnies, Belgium
Gossec, Francois Joseph b. Jan 17, 1734

Verviers, Belgium
Vieuxtemps, Henri b. Feb 20, 1820

Wavre, Belgium
Deckers, Jeanine d. Mar 31, 1985

Wondelgem, Belgium
Sarton, May b. May 3, 1912

Zolder, Belgium
Villeneuve, Gilles d. May 8, 1982

Zwijndrecht, Belgium
Tindemans, Leo(nard) b. Apr 16, 1922

BELORUSSIA

Kosciuszko, Thaddeus b. Feb 12, 1746

BERING ISLAND

Bering, Vitus Jonassen
d. Dec 19, 1741

BERMUDA

Harmsworth, Harold Sidney
d. Nov 26, 1940
Mason, Francis van Wyck
d. Aug 28, 1978
Hamilton, Bermuda
Payne, Robert (Pierre Stephen Robert)
d. Feb 18, 1983
Rattigan, Terence Mervyn d. Nov 30, 1977
Rothermere, Harold Sidney Harmsworth
d. Nov 26, 1940

BITHYNIA

Osman I b. 1259

BOHEMIA

Aussig, Bohemia
Mengs, Anton Raphael b. 1728
Brunn, Bohemia
Mendel, Gregor Johann
d. Jan 6, 1884
Dux, Bohemia
Casanova (de Seingalt), Giovanni Giacomo
d. Jun 4, 1798
Ivancice, Bohemia
Mucha, Alphonse Marie b. 1860
Kamenitz, Bohemia
Novak, Vitezslav b. Dec 5, 1870
Leitmoritz, Bohemia
Muller, Maria b. Jan 29, 1898
Maffersdorf, Bohemia
Porsche, Ferdinand b. Sep 3, 1875
Neuhof, Bohemia
Ditters, Karl d. Dec 24, 1799
Prague, Bohemia
Cermak, Anton Joseph
b. May 9, 1873
Friml, Rudolf b. Dec 7, 1879
Werfel, Franz b. Sep 10, 1890
Raudnitz, Bohemia
Pabst, Georg Wilhelm
b. Aug 27, 1885
Steingrub, Bohemia
Wise, Isaac Mayer b. Mar 29, 1819

BOLIVIA

Coboja, Bolivia
Ovando Candia, Alfredo b. Apr 6, 1918
Cochabamba, Bolivia
Laredo, Jaime b. Jun 7, 1941
Patino, Simon Iturri b. Jun 1, 1862

La Paz, Bolivia
Ovando Candia, Alfredo d. Jan 24, 1982
Siles Zuazo, Hernan b. Mar 19, 1914
Santa Cruz, Bolivia
Banzer-Suarez, Hugo b. Jul 10, 1926

BOTSWANA

Gaborone, Botswana
Khama, Seretse M d. Jul 13, 1980
Serowe, Botswana
Head, Bessie d. Apr 17, 1986
Khama, Seretse M b. Jul 1, 1921

BRAZIL

Bahia, Brazil
Amado, Jorge b. Aug 10, 1912
Bertioga, Brazil
Mengele, Josef d. Feb 7, 1979
Brasilia, Brazil
Halliday, Richard d. Mar 3, 1973
Piquet, Nelson b. Aug 17, 1952
Diamantina, Brazil
Kubitschek (de Oliveira), Juscelino
b. Sep 12, 1902
Fortaleza, Brazil
Castello Branco, Humberto b. Sep 20, 1900
Mato Grosso, Brazil
Tors, Ivan d. Jun 4, 1983
Natal, Brazil
Parisot, Aldo b. 1920
Niteroi, Brazil
Mendes, Sergio b. Feb 11, 1941
Petropolis, Brazil
Zweig, Stefan d. Feb 22, 1942
Recife, Brazil
Bandeira, Manuel (Filho Manuel)
b. Apr 19, 1886
Rio de Janeiro, Brazil
Bandeira, Manuel (Filho Manuel)
d. Oct 13, 1968
Caetano, Marcello d. Oct 26, 1980
Cavalcanti, Alberto b. Feb 6, 1897
Costa e Silva, Arthur da d. Dec 17, 1969
Cunha, Euclides da d. Aug 15, 1909
Figueiredo, Joao Baptista de Oliveira
b. Jan 15, 1918
Gottschalk, Louis Moreau d. Dec 18, 1869
Kubitschek (de Oliveira), Juscelino
d. Aug 22, 1976
Lispector, Clarice d. Dec 9, 1977
Rio De Janeiro, Brazil
Moraes, Vinicius de d. 1980
Rio de Janeiro, Brazil
Niemeyer, Oscar b. Dec 15, 1907
O'Neill, Jennifer b. Feb 20, 1949
Pedro II b. Dec 2, 1825
Ponzi, Charles d. Jan 15, 1949
Purim, Flora b. Mar 6, 1942
Sayao, Bidu b. May 11, 1902
Vargas, Getulio Dornelles d. Aug 24, 1954

Villa-Lobos, Heitor b. Mar 5, 1887
Villa-Lobos, Heitor d. Nov 17, 1959
Rio de Janiero, Brazil
Nascimento, Milton b. 1942
Rio Grande, Brazil
Geisel, Ernesto b. Aug 3, 1907
Santa Rita, Brazil
Cunha, Euclides da b. Jan 20, 1866
Sao Bento, Brazil
Sarney, Jose b. Apr 30, 1930
Sao Borja, Brazil
Goulart, Joao b. Mar 1, 1918
Vargas, Getulio Dornelles b. 1883
Sao Paulo, Brazil
Almeida, Laurindo b. Sep 2, 1917
Bueno, Maria Ester Audion
  b. Oct 11, 1939
Castaneda, Carlos b. Dec 25, 1931
Fittipaldi, Emerson b. 1946
Jofre, Eder b. Mar 26, 1936
Novaes, Guiomar b. Feb 28, 1895
Novaes, Guiomar d. Mar 7, 1979
Taquari, Brazil
Costa e Silva, Arthur da b. Oct 3, 1902
Tres Coracoes, Brazil
Pele b. Oct 23, 1940
Umbuzeiro, Brazil
Assis Chateaubriand, Francisco de
  b. Apr 10, 1891

BRITISH GUIANA (EAST)

Jagan, Cheddi b. Mar 22, 1918

BRITISH WEST AFRICA

Nkrumah, Kwame b. Sep 21, 1909

BRITISH WEST INDIES

Dominica, British West Indies
Wilcoxon, Henry b. Sep 8, 1905
Nevis, British West Indies
Crosse, Rupert d. Mar 5, 1973
Saint Kitts, British West Indies
Douglas, Robert L b. Nov 4, 1884

BULGARIA

Dimitrov, Georgi b. Jun 18, 1882
Traikov, Georgi b. 1898
Zhivkov, Todor b. Sep 7, 1911
Borissova, Bulgaria
Welitsch, Ljuba b. Jul 10, 1913
Gabrovo, Bulgaria
Christo b. Jun 13, 1935
Plovdiv, Bulgaria
Tokatyan, Armand b. Feb 12, 1899
Roustchouk, Bulgaria
Arlen, Michael b. Nov 16, 1895
Ruschuk, Bulgaria
Canetti, Elias b. Jul 25, 1905

Sofia, Bulgaria
Christoff, Boris b. May 18, 1918
Dimitrov, Georgi d. Feb 7, 1949
Weissenberg, Alexis Sigismund
  b. Jul 26, 1929
Varna, Bulgaria
Zwicky, Fritz b. Feb 14, 1898
Velimgrad, Bulgaria
Ghiaurov, Nicolai b. Sep 13, 1929

BURMA

Akyab, Burma
Saki, pseud. b. Dec 18, 1870
Namkham, Burma
Seagrave, Gordon Stifler d. Mar 28, 1965
Pantanaw, Burma
Thant, U b. Jan 22, 1909
Rangoon, Burma
Annabella b. Oct 31, 1965
Seagrave, Gordon Stifler b. 1897
Townsend, Peter Wooldridge
  b. Nov 22, 1914

CAMBODIA

Pran, Dith b. 1943
Preyveng, Cambodia
Nol, Lon b. Nov 13, 1913

CAMEROON

Mbalmayo, Cameroon
Biyidi, Alexandre b. Jun 30, 1932

CANADA

Irving, Laurence Sidney d. May 29, 1914
Morrison, Cameron d. Aug 20, 1953
Augusta, Canada
Heck, Barbara Ruckle d. Aug 17, 1804
Cobourg, Canada
Duffy, Francis Patrick b. May 2, 1871

CANARY ISLANDS

Teneriffe, Canary Islands
Saunders, William Laurence
  d. Jun 25, 1931

CAPPADOCIA

Caesarea, Cappadocia
Basil (the Great), Saint b. 330

CAPRI

Tiberius Julius Caesar Augustus
  d. 37 AD

CEYLON

Colombo, Ceylon
Amerasinghe, Hamilton Shirley
b. Mar 18, 1913
Waldock, (Claud) Humphrey Meredith, Sir
b. Aug 13, 1904
Dullewa, Ceylon
Gopallawa, William b. Sep 16, 1897
Panadura, Ceylon
Rogers, Rosemary b. Dec 7, 1933

CHAD

Tombalbaye, Nagarta Francois
d. Apr 13, 1975

CHANNEL ISLANDS

Glyn, Elinor Sutherland
b. Oct 17, 1864

CHILE

Chillan, Chile
O'Higgins, Bernardo b. Aug 20, 1778
Vinay, Ramon b. Aug 31, 1912
Coquimbo, Chile
Albright, William Foxwell b. May 24, 1891
Kuortane, Chile
Aalto, Alvar Henrik (Hugo)
b. Feb 3, 1898
Parral, Chile
Neruda, Pablo b. Jul 12, 1904
Santiago, Chile
Alessandri, Jorge b. May 19, 1896
Alessandri, Jorge d. Sep 1, 1986
Allende, Salvador d. Sep 11, 1973
DeCuevas, Marquis b. May 26, 1885
Frei, Eduardo (Montalva Eduardo)
b. Jan 16, 1911
Frei, Eduardo (Montalva Eduardo)
d. Jan 22, 1982
Matta, Roberto Sebastian Antonio
Echaurren b. Nov 11, 1911
Neruda, Pablo d. Sep 23, 1973
Zanelli, Renato d. Mar 25, 1935
Temuco, Chile
Letelier, Orlando b. Apr 13, 1932
Valparaiso, Chile
Allende, Salvador b. Jul 26, 1908
Ankers, Evelyn b. Aug 17, 1918
Pinochet Ugarte, Augusto b. Nov 25, 1915
Zanelli, Renato b. Apr 1, 1892
Vicuna, Chile
Mistral, Gabriela b. Apr 7, 1899

CHINA

Bethune, Norman d. Nov 12, 1939
Chang Tso-Lin d. Jun 4, 1928

Liddell, Eric b. 1902
Wang Hung-Wen b. 1937
Amoy, China
Brattain, Walter Houser
b. Feb 10, 1902
Canton, China
Luke, Keye b. Jun 18, 1904
Pei, I(eoh) M(ing) b. Apr 26, 1917
Changchow, China
Lin, Yutang b. Oct 10, 1895
Chekiang, China
Pao, Y(ue) K(ong), Sir b. 1918
Chitai, China
Nowicki, Matthew b. 1910
Chucheng, China
Chiang, Ching b. 1913
Chungking, China
Bodard, Lucien Albert b. Jan 3, 1914
Fenghua, China
Chiang Kai-Shek b. Oct 31, 1886
Fengtien, China
Chang Tso-Lin b. 1873
Foochow, China
Beard, Myron Gould b. Nov 13, 1896
Hailar, China
Ussachevsky, Vladimir b. Oct 21, 1911
Henan Province, China
Zhao Ziyang b. 1919
Hofei, China
Yang, Chen Ning b. Sep 22, 1922
Hong Kong, China
Anders, William Alison
b. Oct 17, 1933
Kwan, Nancy Kashen b. May 19, 1939
Lee, Bruce d. Jul 30, 1973
Lin, Yutang d. Mar 26, 1976
Lorring, Joan b. 1931
Hupeh, China
Wang Shih-chieh b. Mar 10, 1891
Kueiyang, China
Ts'ai, Lun b. 50
Kuikiang, China
Bowra, Maurice, Sir b. Apr 8, 1898
Kuling, China
Peake, Mervyn Laurence b. Jul 9, 1911
Kung-Hsien, China
Tu, Fu b. 712
Kwangtung, China
Howe, James Wong b. Aug 28, 1899
Laichowfu, China
Glass, Hiram Bentley b. Jan 17, 1906
Lu, China
Confucius b. Aug 27, 551 BC
Nanking, China
Owen, Lewis James b. Apr 2, 1925
Paotingfu, China
Lattimore, Richmond Alexander
b. May 6, 1906
Peking, China
Ch'ien Lung b. Sep 25, 1711
Ch'ien Lung d. Feb 7, 1799

Chennault, Anna Chan b. Jun 23, 1925
Chiang, Yee d. Oct 17, 1977
Chu Te d. Aug 6, 1976
Cockburn, Claud(Francis Claud)
   b. Apr 12, 1904
Han, Suyin b. Sep 12, 1917
Lyle, Katie Letcher b. May 12, 1938
Mao Tse-Tung d. Sep 9, 1976
Robertson, Don b. Dec 5, 1922
Strong, Anna Louise d. Mar 29, 1970
Sun Yat-Sen, Chingling Soong, Madame
   d. May 29, 1981
Tz'u Hsi b. 1835
Zao-Wou-Ki b. 1921

Shaeshan, China
Mao Tse-Tung b. Dec 26, 1893

Shan-Yin, China
Lu, Yu b. 1125

Shanghai, China
DiSuvero, Mark b. Sep 18, 1933
Koo, V(i) K(yuin) Wellington b. 1887
Lee, Tsung-Dao b. Nov 24, 1926
Mabee, Carleton (Fred Carleton)
   b. Dec 25, 1914
Sun Yat-Sen, Chingling Soong, Madame
   b. 1890
Tsai, Gerald, Jr. b. Mar 10, 1928
Wang, An b. Feb 7, 1920
Young, Terence b. Jun 20, 1915

Shantung, China
Kang, Sheng b. 1899
Luce, Henry Robinson b. Apr 3, 1898

Shaohsing, China
Chou En-Lai b. 1898

Szechwan, China
Chu Te b. Dec 18, 1886
Li Po b. 701

T'an-Chou, China
Tu, Fu d. 777

Tientsin, China
Chao, Yuen Ren b. Nov 3, 1892

Tsingtao, China
Mifune, Toshiro b. Apr 1, 1920
Wilhelm, Hellmut b. Dec 10, 1905

Ungkung, China
Lin, Piao (Yu-Yung) b. 1908

Weihsien, China
Liddell, Eric d. Feb 21, 1945

Wu Chang, China
Meadows, Audrey b. 1924
Meadows, Jayne Cotter b. Sep 27, 1926

Wu-Chou, China
Tao-chi b. 1630

CILICIA

Selinus, Cilicia
Trajan d. 117

COLOMBIA

Aracatacca, Colombia
Garcia-Marquez, Gabriel b. Mar 6, 1928
Bogota, Colombia
Lleras Restrepo, Carlos b. Apr 12, 1908
Turbay Ayala, Julio Cesar b. Jun 18, 1916
Caucasia, Colombia
Chermayeff, Serge b. Oct 8, 1900
Medellin, Colombia
Botero (Angulo), Fernando
   b. Apr 19, 1932
Pasto, Colombia
Sucre, Antonio J de d. Jun 4, 1830
Santa Marta, Colombia
Bolivar, Simon d. Dec 17, 1830
Tunja, Colombia
Rojas Pinilla, Gustavo b. Mar 12, 1900

COMOROS

Corte, Comoros
Bonaparte, Joseph b. Jan 7, 1768

CONGO

Tshombe, Moise b. Nov 10, 1919
Boma, Congo
Kasavubu, Joseph d. Mar 24, 1969
Elisabethville, Congo
Lumumba, Patrice Emergy d. Jan 18, 1961
Oualua, Congo
Lumumba, Patrice Emergy b. Jul 2, 1925
Stanley Falls, Congo
Emin Pasha d. 1892

CORSICA

Bonaparte, Jerome b. Nov 15, 1784

COSTA RICA

Cartago, Costa Rica
Carazo (Odio), Rodrigo b. Dec 27, 1926
San Jose, Costa Rica
Oduber, Daniel b. Aug 25, 1921

CRETE

Kazantzakis, Nikos b. Dec 2, 1883
Iraklion, Crete
Elytis, Odysseus b. Nov 2, 1911

CROATIA

Stepinac, Alojzije, Cardinal
   b. May 8, 1898
Agram, Croatia
Mallinger, Mathilde b. Feb 17, 1847
Belgisc, Croatia
Ternina, Milka b. Dec 19, 1863

Zagreb, Croatia
Ternina, Milka d. May 18, 1941

CUBA

Banes, Cuba
Batista y Zaldivar, Fulgencio
b. Jan 16, 1901
Biran, Cuba
Castro, Raul b. Jun 3, 1931
Camaguey, Cuba
Gavilan, Kid b. Jan 6, 1926
Perez, Tony (Atanasio Rigal)
b. May 14, 1942
Cardones, Cuba
Adolfo b. Feb 15, 1933
Cienfuegos, Cuba
Dihigo, Martin d. May 20, 1971
Dlicias, Cuba
Stevenson, Teofilo b. Mar 23, 1952
Dos Rios, Cuba
Marti, Jose d. May 19, 1895
Havana, Cuba
Alonso, Alicia b. Dec 21, 1921
Anderson, Bonnie Marie b. Oct 22, 1955
Barker, Bernard L b. 1917
Bolet, Jorge b. Nov 15, 1914
Canseco, Jose b. Jul 2, 1964
Capablanca, Jose Raoul b. 1888
Cassidy, Harold Gomes b. Oct 17, 1906
Dihigo, Martin b. May 24, 1905
Estevez (de Galvez), Luis b. Dec 5, 1930
Goizueta, Roberto Crispulo
b. Nov 18, 1931
Goytisolo, Fermin b. Dec 31, 1951
Kane, Elisha Kent d. Feb 16, 1857
Lateiner, Jacob b. May 31, 1928
Luque, Dolf (Adolfo) b. Aug 4, 1890
Luque, Dolf (Adolfo) d. Jul 3, 1957
Marti, Jose b. Jan 28, 1853
Melis, Jose b. Feb 27, 1920
Mercader, Ramon d. Oct 18, 1978
Mitchell, Millard b. 1900
Ord, Edward Otho Cresap d. Jul 22, 1883
Ponce de Leon, Juan d. 1521
Roa (y Garcia), Raul b. Apr 18, 1907
Roa (y Garcia), Raul d. Jul 6, 1982
Salazar, Alberto b. Aug 7, 1958
Tiant, Luis Clemente b. Nov 23, 1940
Las Villas, Cuba
Suarez, Xavier Louis b. May 21, 1949
Mayari, Cuba
Castro (Ruz), Fidel b. Aug 13, 1926
Pinar del Rio, Cuba
Oliva, Tony (Antonio Pedro, Jr.)
b. Jul 20, 1940
Pueblo Nuevo, Cuba
Campaneris, Bert (Dagoberto Blanco)
b. Mar 9, 1942
Quemados, Cuba
Lazear, Jesse William d. Sep 25, 1900

Santa Clara, Cuba
Cuellar, Mike (Miguel Santana)
b. May 8, 1937
Machado y Morales, Gerardo
b. Sep 29, 1871
Santiago, Cuba
Arnaz, Desi b. Mar 2, 1917
Santiago de Las Vegas, Cuba
Calvino, Italo b. Oct 15, 1923
Yaguajay, Cuba
Urrutia Lleo, Manuel b. Dec 8, 1901

CYPRUS

Makarios III, Archbishop b. Aug 13, 1913
Zeno of Citium b. 334 BC
Larnaca, Cyprus
Yepremian, Garo (Garabed S)
b. Jun 2, 1944
Limassol, Cyprus
Cacoyannis, Michael b. Jun 11, 1922
Grivas, George Theodorus d. Jan 27, 1974
Kyprianou, Spyros b. Oct 28, 1932
Nicosia, Cyprus
Davies, Rodger Paul d. Aug 19, 1974
Makarios III, Archbishop d. Aug 2, 1977
Trikomo, Cyprus
Grivas, George Theodorus b. Mar 23, 1898

CZECHOSLOVAKIA

Hammer, Jan b. Apr 17, 1948
Beneschau, Czechoslovakia
Suk, Josef d. May 29, 1935
Bratislava, Czechoslovakia
Husak, Gustav b. Jan 10, 1913
Laban, Rudolf von b. Dec 15, 1879
Stastny, Anton b. Aug 9, 1959
Stastny, Marian b. Jan 8, 1953
Stastny, Peter b. Sep 18, 1956
Brno, Czechoslovakia
Kundera, Milan b. Apr 1, 1929
Schulz, George J b. Apr 29, 1925
Bruenn, Czechoslovakia
Godel, Kurt b. Apr 28, 1906
Budejovice, Czechoslovakia
Destinn, Emmy d. Jan 28, 1930
Bychory, Czechoslovakia
Kubelik, Rafael b. Jun 29, 1914
Caslav, Czechoslovakia
Forman, Milos b. Feb 18, 1932
Dedidocz, Czechoslovakia
Gottwald, Klement b. Nov 23, 1896
Eger, Czechoslovakia
Serkin, Rudolph b. Mar 28, 1903
Horznatin, Czechoslovakia
Svoboda, Ludvik b. Nov 25, 1895
Husinec, Czechoslovakia
Hus, Jan b. 1369
Ivancice, Czechoslovakia
Weisgall, Hugo David b. Oct 13, 1912

Jablonec, Czechoslovakia
Adler, Peter Herman b. Dec 2, 1899
Karlsbad, Czechoslovakia
Allers, Franz b. Aug 6, 1905
Komarno, Czechoslovakia
Reitman, Ivan b. 1946
Kozlany, Czechoslovakia
Benes, Eduard b. May 28, 1884
Lidice, Czechoslovakia
Heydrich, Reinhard d. Jun 4, 1942
Lieben, Czechoslovakia
Schumann-Heink, Ernestine Rossler
b. Jun 15, 1861
Lipnice, Czechoslovakia
Hasek, Jaroslav d. Jan 3, 1923
Michle, Czechoslovakia
Kubelik, Jan b. Jul 5, 1880
Moravia, Czechoslovakia
Kohoutek, Lubos b. 1935
Masaryk, Tomas Garrigue b. Mar 7, 1850
Mournies, Czechoslovakia
Venizelos, Eleutherios b. Aug 23, 1864
Napajedla, Czechoslovakia
Firkusny, Rudolf b. Feb 11, 1912
Ostrava, Czechoslovakia
Cernik, Oldrich b. Oct 27, 1921
Lendl, Ivan b. Mar 7, 1960
Reisz, Karel b. Jul 21, 1926
Wechsberg, Joseph b. Aug 29, 1907
Pilsen, Czechoslovakia
Trnks, Jiri b. Feb 24, 1912
Policka, Czechoslovakia
Martinu, Bohuslav b. Dec 8, 1890
Prague, Czechoslovakia
Baum, Kurt b. Mar 15, 1908
Brod, Max b. May 27, 1884
Destinn, Emmy b. Feb 26, 1878
Deutsch, Karl Wolfgang b. Jul 12, 1912
Hanslick, Eduard b. Sep 11, 1825
Hasek, Jaroslav b. Apr 24, 1883
Havel, Vaclav b. Oct 5, 1936
Janacek, Leos d. Aug 12, 1928
Kafka, Franz b. Jul 2, 1883
Klima, Ivan b. Sep 14, 1931
Kubelik, Jan d. Dec 5, 1940
Kylian, Jiri b. Mar 21, 1945
Lederer, Francis b. Nov 6, 1906
Lom, Herbert b. 1917
Ludikar, Pavel b. Mar 3, 1882
Mandlikova, Hana b. Feb 19, 1963
Masaryk, Jan Garrigue b. Sep 14, 1886
Masaryk, Jan Garrigue d. Mar 10, 1948
Moscheles, Ignaz b. May 30, 1794
Mucha, Alphonse Marie d. 1938
Mucha, Jiri b. Mar 12, 1915
Navratilova, Martina b. Oct 10, 1956
Nemec, Jan b. Jul 2, 1936
Neumann, Angelo d. Dec 20, 1910
Novotna, Jarmila b. Sep 23, 1907
Novotny, Antonin b. Dec 10, 1904
Novotny, Antonin d. Jan 28, 1975

Pollack, Egon b. May 3, 1879
Pollack, Egon d. Jun 14, 1933
Princip, Gavrilo d. Apr 30, 1918
Ralston, Vera b. Jul 12, 1919
Rilke, Rainer Maria b. Dec 4, 1876
Seifert, Jaroslav b. Sep 23, 1901
Seifert, Jaroslav d. Jan 10, 1986
Smetana, Bedrich d. May 12, 1884
Steinitz, Wilhelm b. May 17, 1836
Susskind, Walter b. May 1, 1913
Svoboda, Ludvik d. 1979
Swoboda, Henry b. 1897
Trnks, Jiri d. Dec 30, 1969
Wallerstein, Lothar b. Nov 6, 1882
Weinberger, Jaromir b. Jan 8, 1896
Prossnitz, Czechoslovakia
Husserl, Edmund b. Apr 8, 1859
Sazova, Czechoslovakia
Voskovec, George b. Jun 19, 1905
Skutec, Czechoslovakia
Novak, Vitezslav d. Jul 18, 1949
Sokolce, Czechoslovakia
Mikita, Stan(ley) b. May 20, 1940
Stannern, Czechoslovakia
Seyss-Inquart, Artur von b. Jul 2, 1892
Tucapy, Czechoslovakia
Ancerl, Karel b. Apr 11, 1908
Uhrovec, Czechoslovakia
Dubcek, Alexander b. Nov 27, 1921
Usti, Czechoslovakia
Benes, Eduard d. Sep 3, 1948
Uzhored, Czechoslovakia
Geray, Steven b. Nov 10, 1904
Zlin, Czechoslovakia
Stoppard, Tom b. Jul 3, 1937

DAHOMEY (NORTH)

Kerekou, Mathieu b. Sep 2, 1933

DALMATIA

Ragusa, Dalmatia
Boscovich, Ruggiero Giuseppe b. 1711

DARIEN

Balboa, Vasco Nunez de d. 1517

DENMARK

Christian IV b. Apr 12, 1577
Jantzen, Carl b. 1883
Roswaenge, Helge d. Aug 1972
Scheidemann, Philipp d. 1939
Aarhus, Denmark
Winding, Kai Chresten b. May 18, 1922

San Pedro, Dominican Republic
Guerrero, Pedro b. Jun 2, 1956
San Pedro de Macoris, Dominican Republic
Andujar, Joaquim b. Dec 21, 1952
Carty, Rico (Ricardo Adolfo Jacobo)
   b. Sep 1, 1939
Santiago, Dominican Republic
Jorge Blanco, Salvador b. Jul 5, 1926
Santo Domingo, Dominican Republic
DeLaRenta, Oscar b. Jul 22, 1932
Guzman, Antonio d. Jul 4, 1982
Villa Bisono, Dominican Republic
Balaguer, Joaquin b. Sep 1, 1907

DUTCH EAST INDIES

Batavia, Dutch East Indies
Tromp, Solco Walle b. Mar 9, 1909 3Ea

ECUADOR

Segura, "Pancho" (Francisco)
   b. Jun 20, 1921
Guachanama, Ecuador
Roldos Aguilera, Jamie d. May 24, 1981
Guayaquil, Ecuador
Ashton, Frederick William, Sir
   b. Sep 17, 1906
Nast, Thomas d. Dec 7, 1902
Roldos Aguilera, Jamie b. Nov 5, 1940
Huigra, Ecuador
Dickey, Herbert Spencer d. Oct 28, 1948
Quito, Ecuador
Velasco Ibarra, Jose Maria
   b. Mar 19, 1893
Velasco Ibarra, Jose Maria
   d. Mar 30, 1979

EGYPT

Antony, Marc d. 30 BC
Lucian d. 200
Lyot, Bernard Ferdinand d. Apr 2, 1952
Moses b. 1392 BC?
Naguib, Mohammed d. Aug 28, 1984
Pompey the Great d. 48 BC
Alexandria, Egypt
Arius b. 256
Arius d. 336
Claudian b. 365
Cleopatra VII d. Aug 30, 30 BC
Cleopatra VII b. 69 BC
Cyril of Alexandria, Saint b. 376
Cyril of Alexandria, Saint d. Jun 27, 444
Desses, Jean b. Aug 6, 1904
Ghorbal, Ashraf A. b. May 1925
Hess, Rudolf (Walter Richard Rudolf)
   b. Apr 26, 1894
Magnani, Anna b. Mar 7, 1909
Marinetti, Filippo Tommaso
   b. Dec 22, 1876

Moussa, Ibrahim b. Sep 30, 1946
Origen Adamantius b. 185
Pilou, Jeannette b.
Ptolemy b. 150
Sharif, Omar b. Oct 10, 1932
Ungaretti, Giuseppe b. Feb 10, 1887
Beni Mor, Egypt
Nasser, Gamal Abdel b. Jan 15, 1918
Cairo, Egypt
Ballou, Maturin Murray d. Mar 27, 1895
Cramm, Gottfried von, Baron
   d. Nov 8, 1976
Dolby, Thomas b. Oct 14, 1958
Farouk I b. Feb 11, 1920
Forester, Cecil Scott b. Aug 27, 1899
Hussein, Taha d. Oct 28, 1973
Idris I d. May 25, 1983
Kalthoum, Um d. Feb 3, 1975
Kleber, Jean Baptiste d. Jun 14, 1800
Lang, Harold d. Nov 16, 1970
Maimonides, Moses d. Dec 13, 1204
Martin, Kingsley d. Feb 16, 1969
Mohieddin, Faud d. Jun 5, 1984
Nasser, Gamal Abdel d. Sep 28, 1970
Opie, Peter Mason b. Nov 25, 1918
Pagett, Nicola b. Jun 15, 1945
Pahlevi, Mohammed Riza d. Jul 27, 1980
Reisner, George Andrew d. Jun 6, 1942
Sadat, Anwar el d. Oct 6, 1981
Sadat, Jihan Raouf b. Aug 1934
VonBulow, Hans Guido d. Feb 12, 1894
Fayoum, Egypt
Mortada, Saad b. Jul 1923
Ityai el Barud, Egypt
Nowicki, Matthew d. Aug 31, 1950
Kafr-El Meselha, Egypt
Mubarak, (Muhamed) Hosni
   b. May 4, 1928
Maghagha, Egypt
Hussein, Taha b. Nov 14, 1889
Memphis, Egypt
Anthony, Saint b. 251
Mount Kolzim, Egypt
Anthony, Saint d. 350
Oasis, Egypt
Nestorius d. 451
Talah Maonufiya, Egypt
Sadat, Anwar el b. Dec 25, 1918
Tamay-al-Zahirah, Egypt
Kalthoum, Um b. 1898

EL SALVADOR

Ahuchapan, El Salvador
Magana, Alvaro (Alfredo) b. Oct 8, 1925
Chalatenango, El Salvador
Romero, Carlos Humberto b. 1924
Ciudad Barrios, El Salvador
Romero y Galdamez, Oscar Arnulfo
   b. Aug 15, 1917

San Salvador, El Salvador
Duarte, Jose Napoleon b. Nov 23, 1926
Romero y Galdamez, Oscar Arnulfo
    d. Mar 24, 1980
Santa Tecla, El Salvador
D'Aubuisson, Roberto b. 1944

ENGLAND

Adams, William b. 1564
Alcott, John b. 1931
Alden, John b. 1599
Anne of Cleves d. 1557
Baffin, William b. 1584
Bangor, Edward Henry Harold Ward,
    Viscount b. Nov 5, 1905
Banks, Tony b. Mar 27, 1950
Beacham, Stephanie b. Feb 28, 1947
Blake, Quentin b. Dec 16, 1932
Bowes, Walter b. 1882
Brooke, James, Sir d. Jun 11, 1868
Bullock, Alain Louis Charles
    b. Dec 13, 1914
Caedmon, Saint b. 650
Caedmon, Saint d. 680
Calvert, Louis d. Jul 2, 1923
Camp, Hamilton b. Oct 30, 1934
Carey, Henry b. 1687
Carritt, David Graham (Hugh David
    Graham) b. Apr 15, 1927
Cartland, Barbara Hamilton b. Jul 9, 1901
Christie, James b. 1730
Clarkson, Ewan b. Jan 23, 1929
Crankshaw, Edward d. Nov 29, 1984
Crispin, Edmund, pseud. d. Sep 15, 1978
Daly, John b. 1937
Davis, Spencer b. Jul 17, 1942
Doulton, Henry, Sir b. 1820
Dulac, Edmund d. May 25, 1953
Emanuel, David b. 1953
Ferguson, Sarah Margaret b. Oct 1959
Finch, Jon b. 1941
Fisher, Clara b. Apr 14, 1811
Fleming, Joan Margaret d. Nov 15, 1980
Flinders, Matthew d. Jul 19, 1814
Gabriel, Peter b. May 13, 1950
Gage, Thomas d. Apr 2, 1787
Godkin, Edwin Lawrence d. May 21, 1902
Godolphin, Sidney b. Jun 15, 1645
Gorman, Leroy b.
Graham, Stephen b. 1884
Hackett, Steve b. Feb 12, 1950
Hart-Davis, Rupert (Charles Rupert)
    b. Aug 28, 1907
Hunter, Ian d. Sep 24, 1975
Huskisson, William d. Sep 15, 1830
Lang, Harold b. 1923
Lawrence, T(homas) E(dward)
    d. May 19, 1935
Leach, Robin b. 1942
Little Tich b. 1868
Lucile b. 1864

MacCorkindale, Simon b. Feb 12, 1953
Martin, James, Sir d. Jan 5, 1981
Mason, Charles b. 1730
McVie, John b. Nov 26, 1946
Morgan, Frederick b. Feb 5, 1894
Nicoll, (John Ramsay) Allardyce
    d. Apr 17, 1976
Oldfield, Maurice, Sir d. Mar 10, 1981
Pears, Charles d. Jan 1958
Phillips, Mark Anthony Peter
    b. Sep 22, 1948
Plimsoll, Samuel b. Feb 10, 1824
Plomer, William Charles Franklyn
    d. Sep 21, 1973
Price, Nancy (Lillian Nancy Bache)
    d. Mar 31, 1970
Pudney, John Sleigh d. Nov 10, 1977
Ransome, Arthur Mitchell d. Jun 3, 1967
Rickword, Edgell (John Edgell)
    d. Mar 15, 1982
Rutherford, Michael b. Oct 2, 1950
Ryle, Gilbert b. Aug 19, 1900
Sandys, Edwin Sir b. Dec 9, 1561
Stanley, Frederick Arthur, Earl of Derby
    b. Jan 15, 1841
Stanley, Frederick Arthur, Earl of Derby
    d. Jun 14, 1908
Staunton, Howard d. Jun 22, 1874
Tomlinson, Jill d. 1976
Toms, Carl b. May 29, 1927
Tuffin, Sally b.
Waite, John b. Jul 4, 1955
Wallis, Barnes Neville, Sir d. Oct 30, 1979
Walsingham, Francis, Sir b. 1530
Walsingham, Francis, Sir d. Apr 6, 1590
Warham, William b. 1450
Warham, William d. Aug 22, 1532
Welchman, Gordon b. 1906
Welland, Colin b. Jul 4, 1934
Williams, Billy b. 1929
Wolfe, Digby b. Jun 4, 1932
Yale, Elihu d. Jul 8, 1721
Abbotswood, England
Ferguson, Harry George d. Oct 25, 1960
Abingdon, England
Richardson, Dorothy Miller
    b. May 17, 1873
Acton, England
Fraser, Bruce Austin, Sir b. Feb 5, 1888
Adderbury, England
Kennedy, Margaret d. Jul 31, 1967
Addlestone, England
Knight, Charles d. Mar 9, 1873
Adleburgh, England
Fawcett, Dame Millicent Garrett b. 1847
Aisenby, England
Bateman, Mary b. 1768
Albury, England
Oughtred, William d. Jun 30, 1660
Aldborough, England
Crabbe, George b. Dec 24, 1754

Aldeburgh, England
Anderson, Elizabeth Garrett b. 1836
Britten, (Edward) Benjamin d. Dec 4, 1976
Pears, Peter, Sir d. Apr 3, 1986

Aldershot, England
Auchinleck, Claude, Sir b. Jun 21, 1884
Yates, Peter b. Jul 24, 1929

Alford, England
Hutchinson, Anne b. 1591

Aller, England
Cudworth, Ralph b. 1617

Alnwick, England
Cobden-Sanderson, Thomas James
    b. Dec 2, 1840

Alton, England
Gaskell, Elizabeth Cleghorn
    d. Nov 12, 1865
Murray, John b. Dec 10, 1741
Prime, Geoffrey Arthur b. 1938

Alvediston, England
Eden, Anthony d. Jan 14, 1977

Alverstoke, England
Melford, Austin (Alfred Austin)
    b. Aug 24, 1884

Amersham, England
Rice, Tim(othy Miles Bindon)
    b. Nov 10, 1944
Schoeffler, Paul d. Nov 21, 1977

Amesbury, England
Lodge, Oliver Joseph, Sir d. Aug 22, 1940

Ampney, England
Vaughan Williams, Ralph b. Oct 12, 1872

Annitsford, England
Brannigan, Owen b. 1909

Arnold, England
Bonington, Richard Parkes b. Oct 25, 1802

Arundel, England
Geeson, Judy b. Sep 10, 1948

Ascot Priory, England
Pusey, Edward Bouverie d. Sep 14, 1882

Ashburton, England
Smith, "Stevie" (Florence Margaret)
    d. Mar 7, 1971

Ashby, England
Harris, Rosemary b. Sep 19, 1930

Ashford, England
Austin, Alfred d. Jun 2, 1913
Forsyth, Frederick b. Aug 25, 1938
Weil, Simone d. Aug 24, 1943

Ashley, England
Bowdler, Thomas b. Jul 11, 1754

Ashridge, England
Davis, Andrew Frank b. Feb 4, 1944

Ashstead, England
MacDonald, George d. Sep 18, 1905

Aslacton, England
Cranmer, Thomas b. Jul 2, 1489

Ast Pey, England
Baldwin of Bewdley, Stanley Baldwin, Earl
    d. Dec 14, 1947

Atherston, England
Lawson, Leigh b. Jul 21, 1945

Austerfield, England
Bradford, William b. 1590

Axminster, England
Buckland, William b. Mar 12, 1784

Ayot St. Lawrence, England
Shaw, George Bernard d. Nov 2, 1950

Badminton, England
Raglan, Fitzroy James Henry Somerset,
    Baron b. Sep 30, 1788

Bakewell, England
Oldfield, Maurice, Sir b. Nov 6, 1915

Banbury, England
Hodgkin, Alan Lloyd b. Feb 5, 1914

Bannavem Taberniae, England
Patrick, Saint b. 385

Bardsey, England
Congreve, William b. Jan 24, 1670

Barnack, England
Kingsley, Henry b. Jan 2, 1830

Barnet, England
Byng, Julian Hedworth George, Viscount
    b. Sep 11, 1862
White, Chris(topher Taylor)
    b. Mar 7, 1943

Barnsley, England
Arden, John b. Oct 26, 1930
Scargill, Arthur b. Jan 11, 938

Barnstaple, England
Gay, John b. 1685

Barnt Green, England
Leighton, Margaret b. Feb 26, 1922

Barton-on-Humber, England
Treece, Henry d. Jun 10, 1966

Basingstake, England
Warton, Thomas b. Jan 9, 1728

Bath, England
Beckford, William d. May 2, 1844
Butler, Joseph d. Jun 16, 1752
D'Arcy, Martin Cyril b. Jun 15, 1888
Ewing, Julianna Horatia d. May 13, 1885
Haskell, Arnold Lionel d. Nov 14, 1980
Malthus, Thomas Robert d. Dec 23, 1834
Monk, Mary d. 1715
Parry, William Edward, Sir
    b. Dec 19, 1790
Saintsbury, George Edward Bateman
    d. Jan 28, 1933
Speke, John Hanning d. Sep 18, 1864

Batley, England
Palmer, Robert b. Jan 19, 1949

Battersea, England
Bolingbroke, Henry St. John, Viscount
    d. Dec 12, 1751

Batton, England
Ford, Wallace b. Feb 12, 1899

Beaconsfield, England
Burke, Edmund d. Jul 9, 1797
Machen, Arthur d. Dec 15, 1947

Read, Piers Paul b. Mar 7, 1941
Waller, Edmund d. Oct 21, 1687
Beckenham, England
Blyton, Carey b. Mar 14, 1932
Frampton, Peter b. Apr 22, 1950
Richardson, Dorothy Miller
  d. Jun 17, 1957
Beckington, England
Daniel, Samuel d. Oct 14, 1619
Bedford, England
Barker, Ronnie b. Sep 25, 1929
Huddleston, (Ernest Urban) Trevor
  b. Jun 15, 1913
Lavis, Gilson b. Jun 27, 1951
Bedfordshire, England
Young, Paul b. 1956
Berkeley, England
Jenner, Edward b. May 17, 1749
Jenner, Edward d. Jan 26, 1823
Berkhampstead, England
Cowper, William b. Nov 15, 1731
Greene, Graham b. Oct 2, 1904
Hordern, Michael b. Oct 3, 1911
Berkshire, England
Benson, Edward Frederic b. Jul 24, 1867
Chambers, Edmund Kerchever, Sir
  b. Mar 16, 1866
Dangerfield, George Bubb b. Oct 28, 1904
Masefield, John d. May 12, 1967
Newbery, John b. 1713
Berkswell, England
Brett, Jeremy b. Nov 3, 1935
Beverley, England
Fisher, John b. 1469
Bewdley, England
Baldwin of Bewdley, Stanley Baldwin, Earl
  b. Aug 3, 1867
Bexhill, England
Baird, John Logie d. Jun 14, 1946
Wilson, Angus b. Aug 11, 1913
Bexhill-on-Sea, England
Andrews, Michael Alford b. Jun 14, 1939
Bexley Heath, England
Boy George b. Jun 14, 1961
Bicester, England
Rose, George Walter b. Feb 19, 1920
Bingley, England
Hoyle, Fred b. Jun 24, 1915
Birchington, England
Rossetti, Dante Gabriel d. Apr 9, 1882
Birkdale, England
Taylor, A(lan) J(ohn) P(ercivale)
  b. Mar 25, 1906
Birkenhead, England
Brooke, L Leslie b. Sep 24, 1862
Birmingham, England
Allen, Walter Ernest b. Feb 23, 1911
Baker, Kenny b. Aug 24, 1934
Balcon, Michael Elias, Sir b. May 19, 1896
Bernard, Sam b. 1863
Burne-Jones, Edward b. Aug 23, 1833

Cadbury, George Adrian Hayhurst, Sir
  b. Apr 15, 1929
Cooper, Melville b. Oct 15, 1896
Cottrell, Alan Howard b. Jul 17, 1919
Curry, John Anthony b. Sep 9, 1949
Edgar, David b. Feb 26, 1948
Field, Sid(ney Arthur) b. Apr 1, 1904
Franks, Oliver Shewell, Sir
  b. Feb 16, 1905
Galton, Francis, Sir b. Feb 16, 1822
Guest, Edgar A(lbert) b. Aug 20, 1881
Hill, Thomas b. Sep 11, 1829
Holden, Fay b. Sep 26, 1895
Lynne, Jeff b. Dec 30, 1947
McVie, Christine Perfect b. Jul 12, 1943
Newman, John Henry, Cardinal
  d. Aug 11, 1890
Onions, Charles Talbut b. Sep 10, 1873
Osbourne, "Ozzie" (John) b. Dec 3, 1949
Palmer, Carl b. Mar 20, 1951
Powell, Enoch (John Enoch)
  b. Jun 16, 1912
Quayle, Anna b. Oct 6, 1936
Shorthouse, Joseph Henry b. Sep 9, 1834
Tynan, Kenneth Peacock b. Apr 2, 1927
Walters, Julie b. 1950
Watts, Pete b. May 13, 1947
Winwood, Steve (Stevie) b. May 12, 1948
Wood, Chris b. Jun 24, 1944
Wood, Chris d. Jul 12, 1983
Bishop's Stortford, England
Rhodes, Cecil John b. Jul 5, 1853
Bishopsbourne, England
Conrad, Joseph d. Aug 3, 1924
Hooker, Richard d. Nov 2, 1600
Bishopstoke, England
Sewall, Samuel b. Mar 28, 1652
Black Hills, England
Allard, Sydney d. Apr 12, 1966
Blackburn, England
McShane, Ian b. Sep 29, 1942
Morley, John b. Dec 24, 1838
Blackheath, England
Dane, Clemence, pseud. b. 1888
Blackpool, England
Anderson, Ian b. Aug 10, 1947
Nash, Graham b. Feb 2, 1942
Bletchingley, England
Stacey, Thomas Charles Gerard
  b. Jan 11, 1930
Blockley, England
Hicks, Ursula Kathleen Webb
  d. Jul 16, 1985
Bodmin, England
McNeile, Herman Cyril b. Sep 28, 1888
Bolton, England
Catherall, Arthur b. Jun 2, 1906
Cole, Thomas b. Feb 1, 1801
Gibbs, Anthony b. Mar 9, 1902
Leverhulme, William Hesketh Lever,
  Viscount b. 1851

Moran, Edward b. Aug 19, 1829
Moran, Thomas b. Jan 22, 1837
Boston, England
Jennings, Elizabeth b. Jul 18, 1926
Bourne, England
Worth, Charles Frederick b. Oct 13, 1825
Bourne End, England
Lehmann, John Frederick b. Jun 2, 1907
Bournemouth, England
Bailey, Donald Coleman, Sir
    d. May 5, 1985
Blunt, Anthony Frederick b. Sep 26, 1907
Brock, Tony b. Mar 31, 1954
Croft-Cooke, Rupert d. 1979
Geneen, Harold Sydney b. Jun 11, 1910
Hall, Radclyffe b. 1886
Keble, John d. Mar 27, 1866
Lake, Greg(ory) b. Nov 10, 1948
Nethersole, Olga d. Jan 9, 1951
Parry, Charles Hubert Hastings, Sir
    b. Feb 27, 1848
Russell, George William d. Jul 17, 1935
Shelley, Mary Wollstonecraft
    d. Feb 1, 1851
Tolkien, J(ohn) R(onald) R(euel)
    d. Sep 2, 1973
Wade, Virginia b. Jul 10, 1945
Bourton Abbots, England
Edgeworth, Maria b. Jan 1, 1767
Boxbourne, England
Henrit, Robert b. May 2, 1946
Boxhill, England
Meredith, George d. May 18, 1909
Brackenburg, England
Walpole, Hugh Seymour, Sir
    d. Jun 1, 1941
Bradfield, England
Fitzgerald, Edward b. Mar 31, 1809
Bradford, England
Appleton, Edward Victor, Sir
    b. Sep 6, 1892
Dee, Kiki b. Mar 6, 1947
Delius, Frederick b. Jan 29, 1862
Feather, Victor b. Apr 10, 1908
Firth, Peter b. Oct 27, 1953
Fletcher, Bramwell b. Feb 20, 1906
Hockney, David b. Jul 9, 1937
Irving, Henry, Sir d. Oct 13, 1905
Mawson, Douglas, Sir b. May 5, 1882
Priestley, J B (John Boynton)
    b. Sep 13, 1894
Rennie, Michael b. Aug 29, 1909
Rothenstein, William, Sir b. Jan 29, 1872
Bradgate, England
Grey, Jane, Lady b. Oct 1537
Bradpole, England
Forster, William Edward b. 1818
Bramhall, England
Hiller, Wendy b. Aug 15, 1912

Bray, England
Boulting, John b. Nov 21, 1913
Boulting, Roy b. Nov 21, 1913
Bremerton, England
Herbert, George d. Mar 9, 1633
Bridport, England
Urquhart, Brian Edward b. Feb 28, 1919
Brighouse, England
Booth, Ballington b. Jul 28, 1859
Brighton, England
Armour, Norman b. Oct 4, 1887
Astor, William Waldorf Astor, Viscount
    d. Jan 18, 1919
Beardsley, Aubrey Vincent
    b. Aug 21, 1872
Bridge, Frank b. Feb 26, 1879
Carpenter, Edward b. Aug 29, 1844
Clayton, Jack b. 1921
Crowley, Aleister (Edward Alexander)
    d. Dec 1, 1947
Garfield, Leon b. Jul 14, 1921
Garnett, David b. Mar 9, 1892
Gill, Eric b. Feb 22, 1882
Hilton, Daisy b. Feb 5, 1908
Hilton, Violet b. Feb 5, 1908
Hughes, Thomas d. Mar 22, 1896
Lindsay, David d. Jun 6, 1945
Lockhart, (Robert Hamilton) Bruce, (Sir)
    d. Feb 27, 1970
Maugham, Robin (Robert Cecil Romer)
    d. Mar 13, 1981
Noble, Ray b. 1908
Ovett, Steve b. Aug 9, 1955
Parker, Cecil d. Apr 21, 1971
Parnell, Charles Stewart d. Oct 6, 1891
Rawlinson, Herbert b. 1883
Robins, Elizabeth d. May 8, 1952
Robson, Flora McKenzie, Dame
    d. Jul 7, 1984
Simpson, Cedric Keith b. Jul 20, 1907
Spencer, Herbert d. Dec 8, 1903
Surtees, Robert Smith d. Mar 16, 1864
Treacher, Arthur b. Jul 2, 1894
Bristol, England
Bedells, Phyllis b. Aug 9, 1893
Blackbeard b. 1680
Blackwell, Elizabeth b. Feb 3, 1821
Bright, Richard b. Sep 28, 1789
Cartwright, Veronica b. 1950
Chatterton, Thomas b. Nov 20, 1752
Chatterton, Thomas d. Aug 25, 1770
Coleridge, Hartley b. Sep 19, 1796
Cousins, Robin b. 1957
Dinwiddie, Robert d. Jul 27, 1770
Dirac, Paul A M b. Aug 8, 1902
Donald, Peter b. 1918
Durie, Jo b. Jun 27, 1960
Friese-Greene, William Edward
    b. Sep 7, 1855
Fry, Christopher b. Dec 18, 1907
Godwin, Edward William b. 1833

Grant, Cary b. Jan 18, 1904
Hill, Archibald Vivian b. Sep 26, 1886
Household, Geoffrey b. Nov 30, 1900
Lane, Allen, Sir b. Sep 21, 1902
Lawrence, Thomas, Sir b. May 4, 1769
Nichols, Beverly b. Sep 9, 1899
Nichols, Peter b. Jul 31, 1927
Redgrave, Michael Scudamore, Sir
    b. Mar 20, 1908
Rosenberg, Issac b. 1890
Satherly, Arthur Edward b. Oct 19, 1889
Savage, Richard d. Aug 1, 1743
Sisson, Charles Hubert b. Apr 22, 1914
Slim, William Joseph b. Aug 6, 1891
Southey, Robert b. Aug 12, 1774
Stephens, Robert b. Jul 14, 1931
Symonds, John Addington b. Oct 5, 1840
Trollope, Frances b. Mar 10, 1780
Brixton, England
Morrison of Lambeth, Herbert Stanley
    Morrison, Baron b. Jan 3, 1888
Brixton Prison, England
MacSwiney, Terence d. Oct 24, 1920
Broadheath, England
Elgar, Edward William, Sir b. Jun 2, 1857
Broadlands, England
Palmerston, Henry John Temple, Viscount
    b. Oct 20, 1784
Broadstairs, England
Heath, Edward Richard George
    b. Jul 9, 1916
Johnson, Lionel Pigot b. Mar 15, 1867
Monro, Harold Edward d. Mar 16, 1932
Vyvyan, Jennifer Brigit b. Mar 13, 1925
Broadstone, England
Wallace, Alfred Russell d. Nov 7, 1913
Broadway, England
Anderson, Mary Antoinette
    d. May 29, 1940
Brockenhurst, England
Gilbert, Cass d. May 17, 1934
Brockley, England
Jones, David b. Nov 1, 1895
Brockmoor, England
Carder, Frederick b. 1863
Bromham, England
Moore, Thomas d. Feb 25, 1852
Bromley, England
Chadwick, William Owen b. May 20, 1916
Craik, Dinah Maria Mulock
    d. Oct 12, 1887
Gillott, Jacky b. Sep 24, 1939
Wells, H(erbert) G(eorge) b. Sep 21, 1866
Brompton, England
Hutchinson, Thomas d. Jun 3, 1780
Bromsgrove, England
Austin, Herbert b. May 23, 1941
Hill, Geoffrey b. Jun 18, 1932
Housman, Laurence b. Jul 18, 1865
Bromwich, England
Plant, Robert Anthony b. Aug 20, 1948

Broseley, England
Baddeley, Hermione Clinton
    b. Nov 13, 1906
Brozbourne, England
Bolton, Guy Reginald b. Nov 23, 1884
Buckinghamshire, England
Crispin, Edmund, pseud. b. Oct 2, 1921
Keyes, Roger d. Dec 26, 1945
McPartland, Margaret Marian
    b. Mar 20, 1918
Spencer, Stanley, Sir d. Dec 14, 1959
Ullman, Tracey b. Dec 30, 1959
Wright, Almroth Edward, Sir
    d. Apr 30, 1947
Bucklers Hard, England
Burnford, Sheila (Philip Cochrane Every)
    d. Apr 20, 1984
Bulwell, England
Cousins, Frank b. Sep 8, 1904
Burcot, England
Peake, Mervyn Laurence d. Nov 17, 1968
Burg, England
Charnley, John, Sir b. Aug 29, 1911
Burnham Thorpe, England
Nelson, Horatio Nelson, Viscount
    b. Sep 29, 1758
Burnley, England
McKellen, Ian Murray b. May 25, 1939
O'Malley, J Pat b. Mar 15, 1904
Burslem, England
Hollowood, Albert Bernard b. Jun 3, 1910
Wedgwood, Josiah b. Jul 12, 1730
Burton-on-Trent, England
Jackson, Joe b. Aug 11, 1955
Mercer, Mabel b. Jan 1900
Burwash, England
Kipling, Rudyard d. Jan 18, 1936
Bury, England
Lamburn, Richmal Crompton
    b. Nov 15, 1890
Bury St. Edmunds, England
Hall, Peter Reginald Frederick, Sir
    b. Nov 22, 1930
Hoskins, Bob b. Oct 26, 1942
Lofts, Norah Robinson d. Sep 10, 1983
Ouida, pseud. b. Jan 1, 1839
Bushey, England
LeBon, Simon b. Oct 27, 1958
Ridgeley, Andrew b. Jan 26, 1963
Caerleon, England
Machen, Arthur b. Mar 3, 1863
Cambridge, England
Abercrombie, Michael d. May 28, 1979
Adams, Douglas Noel b. Mar 11, 1952
Adams, John Couch d. Jan 21, 1892
Attenborough, Richard Samuel, Sir
    b. Aug 29, 1923
Barker, Ernest, Sir d. Feb 11, 1960
Barrett, "Syd" (Roger Keith) b. Jan 1946
Bateson, Gregory b. May 9, 1904
Brogan, Denis William, Sir d. Jan 5, 1974

Chadwick, James, Sir d. Jul 24, 1974
Cockcroft, John Douglas, Sir
  d. Sep 18, 1967
Cockerell, Christopher b. Jun 1910
Cole, George Douglas Howard
  b. Sep 25, 1889
Dale, Henry Hallett d. Aug 23, 1968
Daye, Stephen d. Dec 22, 1668
Eddington, Arthur Stanley, Sir
  d. Nov 22, 1944
Frazer, James George, Sir d. May 7, 1941
Gibbons, Orlando b. 1583
Gilmour, David b. Mar 6, 1947
Gray, Thomas d. Jul 30, 1771
Hopkins, Fredrick, Sir d. May 16, 1947
Housman, A(lfred) E(dward)
  d. Apr 30, 1936
Keynes, John Maynard, Baron
  b. Jun 5, 1883
Leavis, F(rank) R(aymond) b. Jul 14, 1895
Leavis, F(rank) R(aymond)
  d. Apr 14, 1978
Macaulay, Rose b. Aug 1, 1881
MacMillan, Daniel d. Jun 27, 1857
Maxwell, James Clerk d. Nov 5, 1879
Meitner, Lise d. Oct 28, 1968
Moore, George Edward d. Oct 24, 1958
Muir, Edwin d. Jan 3, 1959
Newton-John, Olivia b. Sep 26, 1948
Peel, Ronald Francis (Edward Waite)
  d. Sep 21, 1985
Prior, Matthew d. Sep 18, 1721
Ramsey, Arthur Michael b. Nov 14, 1904
Richards, Ivor Armstrong d. Sep 7, 1979
Rutherford, Ernest, Baron d. Oct 19, 1937
Ryle, Martin, Sir d. Oct 14, 1984
Searle, Ronald William Fordham
  b. Mar 3, 1920
Sidgwick, Henry d. Aug 28, 1900
Taylor, Jeremy b. Aug 1613
Thomson, George Paget b. May 3, 1892
Thomson, George Paget d. Sep 10, 1975
Trevelyan, George Macaulay
  d. Jul 21, 1962
Wittgenstein, Ludwig d. Apr 29, 1951

Canford Magna, England
Hibberd, Andrew Stuart b. Oct 5, 1893

Canterbury, England
A'Becket, Thomas d. Dec 29, 1170
Anselm, Saint d. 1109
Bloom, Harry d. Jul 28, 1981
Fleming, Ian Lancaster d. Aug 12, 1964
Gibbons, Orlando d. Jun 5, 1625
Grahame, Margot b. Feb 20, 1911
Johnson, Hewlett d. Oct 22, 1966
Laker, Freddie (Frederick Alfred)
  b. Aug 6, 1922
Linacre, Thomas b. 1460
Marlowe, Christopher b. Feb 6, 1564
Milner, Alfred d. May 13, 1925
Parton, James b. Feb 9, 1822

Powell, Michael b. Sep 30, 1905
Westmore, Perc(ival) b. Oct 29, 1904
Carlisle, England
Bragg, Melvyn b. Oct 6, 1939
Fraser, George MacDonald b. Apr 2, 1925
Carnarvon, England
Edward II b. 1284
Carnkie, England
Thomas, D(onald) M(ichael)
  b. Jan 27, 1935
Castletownshend, England
Coghill, Nevill Henry Kendall Aylmer
  b. Apr 19, 1899
Chadderton, England
McDougall, William b. Jun 22, 1871
Chalfont, England
Rutherford, Margaret d. May 22, 1972
Chard, England
Pissaro, Lucien d. Jul 10, 1944
Charlton, England
Bessemer, Henry, Sir b. Jan 19, 1813
DeLaMare, Walter b. Apr 25, 1873
Petrie, (William Matthew) Flinders, Sir
  b. Jun 3, 1853
Chatham, England
Jenner, William, Sir b. 1815
Rhodes, Zandra b. Sep 11, 1940
Chelmsford, England
Bloom, Ursula b. 1893
Strutt, Joseph b. Oct 27, 1749
Chelsea, England
Burney, Charles d. Apr 12, 1814
Chirol, Valentine, Sir d. Oct 22, 1929
Gaskell, Elizabeth Cleghorn
  b. Sep 29, 1810
Hayward, John Davy d. Sep 17, 1965
Cheltenham, England
Bradley, Andrew Cecil b. Mar 26, 1851
Cossart, Ernest b. Sep 24, 1876
Harris, Arthur Travers, Sir
  b. Apr 13, 1892
Harwood, Vanessa Clare b. 1947
Holst, Gustav b. Sep 21, 1874
Jones, Brian b. Feb 26, 1943
Page, Frederick Handley, Sir b. 1885
Richardson, Ralph David, Sir
  b. Dec 19, 1902
Cherryburn, England
Bewick, Thomas b. Aug 12, 1753
Chertsey, England
Cowley, Abraham d. Jul 28, 1667
Chesham, England
Bevan, Aneurin d. Jul 6, 1960
Cheshire, England
Abercrombie, Lascelles b. Jan 9, 1881
Barnes, Ernest William b. Apr 1, 1874
Carroll, Lewis, pseud. b. Jan 27, 1832
Cartwright, Angela b. Sep 9, 1952
Davies, Leslie Purnell b. Oct 20, 1914
Holmes, Rupert b. Feb 24, 1947

Craike, England
Inge, William Ralph b. Jun 6, 1860
Cranbrook, England
Dobell, Sydney Thompson b. Apr 5, 1824
Nicolson, Harold George, Sir
  d. May 1, 1968
Cranleigh, England
Swinnerton, Frank Arthur d. Nov 6, 1982
Cranley, England
Lemon, Mark d. May 23, 1870
Crawley, England
Blunt, Wilfrid Scawen b. Aug 14, 1840
Crowborough, England
Doyle, Arthur Conan, Sir d. Jul 7, 1930
Crowthorne, England
Dyson, Freeman John b. Dec 15, 1923
Croyden, England
Dawson, Bertrand Edward b. Mar 9, 1864
Fry, Charles Burgess b. 1872
Croydon, England
Ashcroft, Peggy, Dame (Edith Margaret
  Emily) b. Dec 22, 1907
Atwill, Lionel b. Mar 1, 1885
Booth, Hubert Cecil d. Jan 14, 1955
Castle, John b. Jan 14, 1940
Dean, Basil b. Sep 27, 1888
Holbrooke, Josef b. Jul 5, 1878
Lean, David b. Mar 25, 1908
Cuckfield, England
Kingsley, Henry d. May 24, 1876
Cullompton, England
Dashwood, Elizabeth Monica
  d. Dec 2, 1943
Cumberland, England
Bragg, William Henry, Sir b. Jul 2, 1862
Dalton, John b. Sep 6, 1766
Marlowe, Julia b. Aug 17, 1866
Dartford, England
Jagger, Mick (Michael Philip)
  b. Jul 26, 1943
Richard, Keith b. Dec 18, 1943
Trevithick, Richard d. Apr 22, 1833
Dartmouth, England
Kempson, Rachel b. May 28, 1910
Newcomen, Thomas b. Feb 24, 1663
Dean Prior, England
Herrick, Robert d. Oct 1674
Dedham, England
Munnings, Alfred James, Sir
  d. Jul 17, 1959
Denby, England
Flamsteed, John b. Aug 19, 1646
Denham, England
Redgrave, Michael Scudamore, Sir
  d. Mar 21, 1985
Denton, England
Darwin, Bernard Richard Meirion
  d. Oct 18, 1961
Deptford, England
Marlowe, Christopher d. May 30, 1593

Derby, England
Conroy, Frank b. Oct 14, 1890
Cotton, John b. Dec 4, 1584
Dexter, John b. Aug 2, 1925
Hobson, John Atkinson b. Jul 6, 1858
Spencer, Herbert b. Apr 27, 1820
Spry, Constance b. Dec 5, 1886
Derbyshire, England
Bates, Alan Arthur b. Feb 17, 1934
Booth, Catherine Mumford b. 1829
Carter, William b. 1830
Caulfield, Maxwell b. 1959
Richardson, Samuel b. Jul 31, 1689
Uttley, Alice Jane Taylor b. Dec 17, 1884
Wood, John b. 1930
Dereham, England
Aldiss, Brian Wilson b. Aug 18, 1925
Cowper, William d. Apr 25, 1800
Deritend, England
Cox, David b. Apr 29, 1783
Dernhall, England
Lee, Charles b. 1731
Devenport, England
Burgess, Guy Francis de Moncy b. 1911
Devon, England
Mallowan, Max Edgar Lucien, Sir
  d. Aug 19, 1978
Devonport, England
Scott, Robert Falcon b. Jun 6, 1868
Devonshire, England
Carlile, Richard b. 1790
Chambers, Edmund Kerchever, Sir
  d. Jan 21, 1954
Coleridge, Samuel Taylor b. Oct 21, 1772
Cook, Peter b. Nov 17, 1937
Drake, Francis, Sir b. 1540
Kingsley, Charles b. Jun 12, 1819
Mallock, William Hurrell b. 1849
Marlborough, John Churchill, Duke
  b. 1650
Partridge, Eric Honeywood d. Jun 1, 1979
Plath, Sylvia d. Feb 11, 1963
Raleigh, Walter, Sir b. 1552
Widgery, John Passmore, Baron
  b. Jul 24, 1911
Donnington, England
Flinders, Matthew b. Mar 16, 1774
Dorcaster, England
Frobisher, Martin b. 1535
Dorchester, England
Evans, Maurice b. Jun 3, 1901
Hardy, Thomas d. Jan 11, 1928
Powys, Llewelyn b. Aug 13, 1884
Dorking, England
Bennett, Richard Bedford d. Jun 26, 1947
Olivier, Laurence Kerr Olivier, Sir
  b. May 22, 1907
Stopes, Marie Charlotte Carmichael
  d. Oct 2, 1958

Hilliard, Nicholas b. 1537
Phillpotts, Eden d. Dec 29, 1960
Rhys, Jean d. May 14, 1979
Simcoe, John Graves d. Oct 26, 1806

Exning, England
Day, James Wentworth b. Apr 21, 1899

Eyam, England
Seward, Anna b. Dec 12, 1747

Failsworth, England
Fuller, Roy Broadbent b. Feb 11, 1912

Fairfield, England
Price, Alan b. Apr 19, 1942

Fairford, England
Keble, John b. Apr 25, 1792

Fallodon, England
Grey, Charles b. Mar 13, 1764

Fareham, England
Cremer, William Randal, Sir
    b. Mar 18, 1838

Faringdon, England
Barea, Arturo d. Dec 24, 1957

Farnham, England
Cobbett, William b. Mar 19, 1762
Pears, Peter, Sir b. Jun 22, 1910
Toplady, Augustus Montague
    b. Nov 4, 1740

Farnworth, England
Finlay, Frank b. Aug 6, 1926

Felixstowe, England
Addams, Dawn b. Sep 21, 1930
Hinde, Thomas b. Mar 26, 1926
Mills, John, Sir b. Feb 22, 1908

Fentonwoon, England
Wallis, Samuel b. Apr 23, 1728

Fieldhead, England
Priestley, Joseph b. Mar 13, 1733

Firle, England
Gage, Thomas b. 1721

Fishbourne, England
Horrocks, Brian Gwynne, Sir
    d. Jan 6, 1985

Fisher's Hill, England
Balfour, Arthur James Balfour, Earl
    d. Mar 19, 1930

Fockbury, England
Housman, A(lfred) E(dward)
    b. Mar 26, 1859

Folkestone, England
Coppard, A(lfred) E(dgar) b. Jan 4, 1878
Gordon, Kitty b. Apr 22, 1878
Harris, Augustus, Sir d. Jun 22, 1896
Harvey, William b. Apr 1, 1578

Fonthill, England
Beckford, William b. Sep 29, 1759

Fordingbridge, England
John, Augustus Edwin d. Oct 31, 1961

Forest Rowe, England
Freshfield, Douglas William d. Feb 9, 1934

Fotheringay Castle, England
Mary, Queen of Scots d. Feb 8, 1587
Richard III b. Oct 2, 1452

Fowey, England
Hewish, Antony b. May 11, 1924
Quiller-Couch, Arthur Thomas, Sir
    d. May 12, 1944

Fulmer, England
York, Michael b. Mar 27, 1942

Fulneck, England
Latrobe, Benjamin Henry b. May 1, 1764

Furnham, England
Bondfield, Margaret Grace b. 1873

Gainsborough, England
Mackinder, Halford John, Sir
    b. Feb 15, 1861
Thorndike, Sybil, Dame b. Oct 24, 1882

Gatcomb Park, England
Ricardo, David d. Sep 11, 1823

Gateshead, England
Bewick, Thomas d. Nov 8, 1828

Gerrards Cross, England
Currie, Finlay d. May 9, 1968
More, Kenneth Gilbert b. Sep 20, 1914
Reed, Austin Leonard d. May 5, 1954
Robinson, Joan Mary Gale Thomas
    b. 1910

Gillingham, England
Tizard, Henry Thomas, Sir
    b. Aug 23, 1885

Glanton, England
Trevor-Roper, Hugh Redwald
    b. Jan 15, 1914

Glastonbury, England
Aldridge, Michael b. Sep 9, 1920
Irving, Henry, Sir b. Feb 6, 1838

Glos, England
Hyde-White, Wilfrid b. May 12, 1903

Glossop, England
Lowry, Lawrence Stephen d. Feb 23, 1976

Gloucester, England
Brent, Margaret b. 1600
Gwinnett, Button b. 1735
Henley, William Ernest b. Aug 23, 1849
Horlick, William b. Feb 23, 1846
Mitford, Jessica b. Sep 11, 1917
Tyndale, William b. 1484
Webb, Beatrice Potter b. Jan 22, 1858
Wheatstone, Charles, Sir b. Feb 6, 1802
Whitefield, George b. Dec 27, 1714

Godalming, England
Huxley, Aldous Leonard b. Jul 26, 1894

Godshill, England
Dickens, Charles John Huffam
    d. Jun 9, 1870

Goodmayes, England
Holm, Ian b. Sep 12, 1931

Goodnestone, England
James, Montague Rhodes b. Aug 1, 1862

Goole, England
Empson, William, Sir b. Sep 27, 1906

Goring, England
Bolton, Guy Reginald d. Sep 5, 1979
Dodd, Charles Harold d. Sep 22, 1973

Hartford, England
Todd, Ann b. Jan 24, 1909
Hartlepool, England
Smythe, Reginald b. 1917
Haslemere, England
Galton, Francis, Sir d. Jan 17, 1911
Phillips, Robin b. Feb 28, 1942
Tennyson, Alfred, Lord d. Oct 6, 1892
Hassocho, England
Hamilton, Patrick b. Mar 17, 1904
Hastings, England
Blackwell, Elizabeth d. May 31, 1910
Grey Owl, pseud. b. Sep 1888
Harold II d. Oct 15, 1066
Kaye-Smith, Sheila b. Feb 4, 1887
Parker, Cecil b. Sep 3, 1898
Richardson, Henry Handel, pseud.
    d. Mar 20, 1946
Russell, Edward Frederick Langley, Baron
    of Liverpool d. Apr 8, 1981
Hatfield, England
Blunstone, Colin b. Jun 24, 1945
Brain, Dennis d. Sep 1, 1957
Salisbury, Robert Arthur Talbot, 3rd
    Marquess b. Feb 3, 1830
Salisbury, Robert Arthur Talbot, 3rd
    Marquess d. Aug 1903
Hawarden, England
Gladstone, William Ewart d. May 19, 1898
Hawick, England
Blyth, Chay b. 1940
Haworth, England
Bronte, Charlotte d. Mar 31, 1855
Bronte, Emily Jane d. Dec 19, 1848
Hayes, England
Pitt, William b. May 28, 1759
Pitt, William d. May 11, 1778
Hayling Island, England
Gray, Simon James Holliday
    b. Oct 21, 1936
Hazelmere, England
Ramsay, William, Sir d. Jul 23, 1916
Heacham, England
Goodall, John Strickland b. Jun 7, 1908
Headingley, England
Austin, Alfred b. May 30, 1835
Heanor, England
Howitt, William b. Dec 18, 1792
Heathfield, England
Watt, James d. Aug 19, 1819
Heavitree, England
Hooker, Richard b. Mar 1554
Hebburn, England
Holmes, Arthur b. Jan 14, 1890
Heddington, England
Lewis, C(live) S(taples) d. Nov 22, 1963
Helensburgh, England
Cronin, A(rchibald) J(oseph)
    b. Jul 19, 1896
Helpstone, England
Clare, John b. Jul 13, 1793

Helston, England
Fitzsimmons, Bob (Robert Prometheus)
    b. Jun 4, 1862
Page, Jimmy (James Patrick)
    b. Jan 9, 1944
Hemel Hempstead, England
Evans, Arthur John, Sir b. Jul 8, 1851
Hendon, England
Fisher, James Maxwell McConnell
    d. Sep 25, 1970
Shirley-Smith, Hubert b. Oct 13, 1901
Hendre, England
Rolls, Charles Stewart b. Aug 27, 1877
Henley, England
Cooper, Gladys, Dame d. Nov 17, 1971
Frederic, Harold d. Oct 19, 1898
Henley-on-Thames, England
Blish, James Benjamin d. Jul 30, 1975
Goudge, Elizabeth d. Apr 1, 1984
Hereford, England
Allen, Verden b. May 26, 1944
Garrick, David b. Feb 19, 1717
Gwyn, Nell (Eleanor) b. Feb 2, 1650
Honeyman-Scott, James (Jimmy)
    b. Nov 4, 1956
Lane, Edward William b. Sep 17, 1801
Oz, Frank b. May 24, 1944
Ralphs, Mick b. Mar 31, 1948
Reid, Beryl b. Jun 17, 1920
Hertfordshire, England
Burton, Richard Francis, Sir
    b. Mar 19, 1821
Elizabeth, the Queen Mother
    b. Aug 4, 1900
Martin, Kingsley b. Jul 28, 1897
Palmerston, Henry John Temple, Viscount
    d. Oct 18, 1865
Taylor, Mick b. Jan 17, 1948
Heversham, England
Bibby, Thomas Geoffrey b. Oct 14, 1917
Hexham, England
Fielding, Gabriel, pseud. b. Mar 25, 1916
Gibson, Wildred Wilson b. Oct 2, 1878
High Wycombe, England
Shrimpton, Jean Rosemary b. Nov 6, 1942
Trethowan, Ian b. Oct 20, 1922
Uttley, Alice Jane Taylor d. May 7, 1976
Higher Walter, England
Ferrier, Kathleen b. Apr 22, 1912
Highgate, England
Bacon, Francis, Sir d. Apr 9, 1626
Betjeman, John, Sir b. Aug 28, 1906
Lear, Edward b. May 12, 1812
Hillingdon, England
Seymour, Jane b. Feb 15, 1951
Hintlesham, England
Ellis, Havelock(Henry Havelock)
    d. Jul 8, 1939
Hitchin, England
Chapman, George b. 1560

Hogsthorpe, England
Addison, Christopher, Viscount
b. Jun 19, 1869
Holbeach, England
Angell, (Ralph) Norman, Sir
b. Dec 26, 1874
Holborn, England
Taylor, Jane b. Sep 26, 1783
Holdenby, England
Hatton, Christopher, Sir b. 1540
Hollingbourne, England
Colgate, William b. Jan 25, 1783
Hollow Park, England
Bell, Charles d. Apr 28, 1842
Holmbury St. Marg, England
Catto, Thomas Sivewright, Baron
d. Aug 23, 1959
Hore, England
Bruce Lockhart, Robert Hamilton, Sir
d. Feb 27, 1970
Horncastle, England
Sully, Thomas b. Jun 8, 1783
Hornsey, England
Keene, Charles Samuel b. Aug 10, 1823
Horsehay, England
Peters, Ellis, pseud. b. Sep 28, 1913
Horsforth, England
Knowles, Patric b. Nov 11, 1911
Horsham, England
Innes, Hammond, pseud. b. Jul 15, 1913
Horsley, England
Somes, Michael b. Sep 28, 1917
Horwich, England
Fleming, Joan Margaret b. Mar 27, 1908
Houghton, England
Walpole, Robert b. Aug 26, 1676
Walpole, Robert d. Mar 18, 1745
Hove, England
Arditi, Luigi d. May 1, 1903
Best, Edna b. Mar 3, 1900
Frankau, Gilbert d. Nov 4, 1952
Fraser, Ian b. Aug 23, 1933
Hoylake, England
Dempsey, Miles Christopher, Sir
b. Dec 15, 1896
Huddersfield, England
Mason, James Neville b. May 15, 1909
Wilson, Harold (James Harold, Sir)
b. Mar 11, 1916
Hull, England
Carmichael, Ian b. Jun 18, 1920
Courtenay, Tom b. Feb 25, 1937
Duveen, Joseph, Sir b. Oct 14, 1869
Gaunt, William b. Jul 5, 1900
Kendall, Kay b. 1926
Larkin, Philip d. Dec 2, 1985
Leginska b. Apr 13, 1880
Rank, J(oseph) Arthur b. Dec 23, 1888
Smith, "Stevie" (Florence Margaret)
b. 1903

Hungerford, England
Strachey, (Giles) Lytton d. Jan 21, 1932
Huntingdon, England
Cromwell, Oliver b. Apr 25, 1599
Hurstmonceaux, England
Mildmay, Audrey b. Dec 19, 1900
Hurstpierpoint, England
Scofield, Paul b. Jan 21, 1922
Huyton, England
Harrison, Rex (Reginald Carey)
b. Mar 5, 1908
Hythe, England
Clark, Kenneth McKenzie, Sir
d. May 21, 1983
Igatestone, England
Miles, Sarah b. Dec 31, 1943
Ilford, England
Levertov, Denise b. Oct 24, 1923
Smith, Maggie b. Dec 28, 1934
Illogan, England
Trevithick, Richard b. Apr 13, 1771
Ilsington, England
Ford, John b. 1586
Ince, England
Jones, Robert Trent b. Jun 20, 1906
Inglewood, England
Ireland, John b. Aug 13, 1879
Inverness-Shire, England
Baring, Maurice d. Dec 14, 1945
Ipsden, England
Reade, Charles b. Jun 8, 1814
Ipswich, England
Hendry, Ian b. 1931
Lapotaire, Jane b. Dec 26, 1944
Leslie, Frank, pseud. b. Mar 21, 1821
Nunn, Trevor Robert b. Jan 14, 1940
Wolsey, Thomas, Cardinal b. 1475
Isington, England
Montgomery of Alamein, Bernard Law
Montgomery, Viscount d. Mar 25, 1976
Isle of Wight, England
Noyes, Alfred d. Jun 28, 1958
Victoria d. Jan 22, 1901
Isleworth, England
Haliburton, Thomas Chandler
d. Aug 27, 1865
Islington, England
Pinero, Arthur Wing, Sir b. May 25, 1855
Watts, Charlie (Charles Robert)
b. Jun 2, 1941
Islip, England
Buckland, William d. Aug 14, 1856
Ispwich, England
Pritchett, V(ictor) S(awdon), Sir
b. Dec 16, 1900
Jarrow, England
Bede the Venerable d. 735
Jersey, England
Butlin, William Heygate Edmund, Sir
d. Jun 12, 1980

Jordans, England
Speke, John Hanning b. May 4, 1827

Jordanthorpe, England
Chantrey, Francis Legatt, Sir
　b. Apr 7, 1781

Kedleston Hall, England
Curzon of Kedleston, George Nathaniel
　Curzon, Marquis b. Jan 11, 1859

Keighley, England
Bottomley, Gordon b. Feb 20, 1874

Kendal, England
Eddington, Arthur Stanley, Sir
　b. Dec 28, 1882
Romney, George d. Nov 15, 1802
Walker, Adam b. 1766

Kensington, England
Anne d. Aug 1, 1714
Boyce, William d. Feb 7, 1779
Browne, "Phiz" (Hablot Knight)
　b. Jun 15, 1815
Chesterton, Gilbert Keith b. May 29, 1874
Macaulay, Thomas Babington Macaulay,
　Baron d. Dec 28, 1859
Newton, Isaac, Sir d. Mar 20, 1727
Tree, Herbert Beerbohm b. Dec 17, 1853

Kent, England
Bates, H(erbert) E(rnest) d. Jan 29, 1974
Blackwood, Algernon b. 1869
Boult, Adrian Cedric, Sir d. Feb 23, 1983
Box, John b. Jan 27, 1920
Bush, Kate b. Jul 30, 1958
Bushell, Anthony b. May 19, 1904
Doughty, Charles Montagu d. Jan 30, 1926
Dowding, Hugh C T, Baron
　d. Feb 15, 1970
Dowson, Ernest Christopher
　b. Aug 2, 1867
Elliott, Gertrude d. Dec 24, 1950
Evans, Edith Mary Booth, Dame
　d. Oct 14, 1976
Fuchs, Vivian Ernest, Sir b. Feb 11, 1908
Howard, Trevor Wallace b. Sep 29, 1916
Lovelace, Richard b. 1618
Morgan, Charles Langbridge
　b. Jan 22, 1894
Sackville-West, Victoria Mary
　d. Jun 2, 1962
Sassoon, Siegfried b. Sep 8, 1886
Sidney, Philip, Sir b. Nov 30, 1554
Terry, Ellen Alicia, Dame d. Jul 21, 1928
Wyatt, Thomas, Sir b. 1503

Keswick, England
Southey, Robert d. Mar 21, 1843

Kibworth, England
Knox, Ronald Arbuthnott b. Feb 17, 1888

Kidderminster, England
Hamer, Robert b. Mar 31, 1911
Hill, Rowland, Sir b. Dec 3, 1795

Kilburn, England
Drinkwater, John d. Mar 25, 1937
Hore-Belisha, Leslie, Baron b. Sep 7, 1893

Kimbolton, England
Catherine of Aragon d. Jan 7, 1536

King's Cliffe, England
Law, William b. 1686
Law, William d. 1761

King's Norton, England
Aherne, Brian de Lacy b. May 2, 1902

Kings Bench, England
Smart, Christopher d. May 21, 1771

Kingston, England
Galsworthy, John b. Aug 14, 1867
Muybridge, Eadweard b. Apr 9, 1830
Muybridge, Eadweard d. May 8, 1904
Sherriff, Robert Cedric b. Jun 6, 1896

Kingston-on-Thames, England
Gale, Richard Nelson, Sir d. Jul 29, 1982

Kingston-upon-Hull, England
Johnson, Amy b. 1903

Kingston-upon-Thames, England
Plomley, Roy b. Jan 20, 1914

Kinver, England
Price, Nancy (Lillian Nancy Bache)
　b. Feb 3, 1880

Kipling, England
Baltimore, George Calvert, Baron b. 1580

Kirbymoorside, England
Read, Herbert, Sir b. Dec 4, 1893

Knightsbridge, England
Bax, Clifford b. Jul 12, 1886

Knole Castle, England
Sackville-West, Victoria Mary
　b. Mar 9, 1892

Knutsford, England
Charnley, John, Sir d. Aug 12, 1982

Lacock Abbey, England
Talbot, William Henry Fox
　b. Feb 11, 1800
Talbot, William Henry Fox
　d. Sep 17, 1877

Ladywell, England
Fabian, Robert Honey b. Jan 31, 1901

Laleham, England
Arnold, Matthew b. Dec 24, 1822

Lancashire, England
Anderson, Jon b. Oct 25, 1944
Bentley, Eric b. Sep 14, 1916
Fuller-Maitland, John Alexander
　d. Mar 30, 1936
Glubb, John Bagot, Sir b. Apr 16, 1897
Hilton, James b. Sep 9, 1900
Horn, Alfred Aloysius, pseud. b. 1854
Jeans, James Hopwood, Sir
　b. Sep 11, 1877
Koppel, Ted (Edward James) b. 1940
Peel, Robert, Sir b. Feb 5, 1788
Quayle, Anthony b. Sep 7, 1913
Romney, George b. Dec 15, 1734
Shaw, Robert b. Aug 9, 1927
Standish, Miles b. 1584

Lancaster, England
Austin, John Langshaw b. Mar 26, 1911
Barr, Amelia Edith Huddleston
  b. Mar 29, 1831
Binyon, Laurence b. Aug 10, 1869
Brophy, John b. Nov 6, 1883

Landon, England
Hollyer, Samuel b. Feb 24, 1826

Laneast, England
Adams, John Couch b. Jun 5, 1819

Langham, England
Marryat, Frederick d. Aug 9, 1848

Langley, England
Pudney, John Sleigh b. Jan 19, 1909

Langport, England
Bagehot, Walter b. Feb 3, 1826
Bagehot, Walter d. Mar 24, 1877

Launceston, England
Causley, Charles Stanley b. Aug 24, 1917

Leamington, England
Crowley, Aleister (Edward Alexander)
  b. Oct 12, 1875
Enright, Dennis Joseph b. Mar 11, 1920
Spilsbury, Bernard Henry, Sir b. 1877

Leatherhead, England
Howatch, Susan b. Jul 14, 1940
Wheeler, Mortimer (Robert Eric Mortimer)
  d. Jul 22, 1976

Ledbury, England
Masefield, John b. Jun 1, 1878

Leeds, England
Ableman, Paul b. Jun 13, 1927
Armitage, Kenneth b. Jul 18, 1916
Burton, Montague Maurice, Sir
  d. Sep 21, 1952
Dunlop, Frank b. Feb 15, 1927
Harewood, George Henry Hubert Lascelles,
  Earl b. Feb 7, 1923
Johnson, Raynor C(arey) b. Apr 5, 1901
Marks, Simon b. Jul 9, 1888
McDowell, Malcolm b. Jun 13, 1943
Mott, Nevill Francis, Sir b. Sep 30, 1905
Ransome, Arthur Mitchell b. Jan 18, 1884
Scholes, Percy Alfred b. Jul 1877
Winwood, Estelle b. Jan 24, 1883

Leeds Castle, England
Fairfax, Thomas b. Jan 17, 1612

Leicester, England
Chapman, Graham b. Jan 8, 1941
Dyer-Bennet, Richard b. Oct 6, 1913
Ewing, Alfred Cyril b. May 11, 1899
Fox, George b. Jul 1624
Macaulay, Thomas Babington Macaulay,
  Baron b. Oct 25, 1800
Merrick, Joseph Carey b. 1862
Orton, Joe (John Kingsley) b. 1933
Palmer, Frances Flora Bond
  b. Jun 26, 1812
Richard II d. 1400
Richard III d. Aug 22, 1485

Snow, C(harles) P(ercy), Sir
  b. Oct 15, 1905
Wilson, Colin Henry b. Jun 26, 1931
Wolsey, Thomas, Cardinal d. Nov 29, 1530

Leicestershire, England
Croly, Jane Cunningham b. Dec 19, 1829

Leigh-on-Sea, England
Lloyd, John b. Aug 27, 1954

Lew-Trenchard, England
Baring-Gould, Sabine d. Jan 2, 1924

Lewes, England
Iredell, James b. Oct 5, 1751
Woolf, Virginia (Adeline Virginia Stephen)
  d. Mar 28, 1941

Lewisham, England
Baker, "Ginger" (Peter) b. Aug 19, 1940
Cooper, Gladys, Dame b. Dec 18, 1888
Lanchester, Elsa b. Oct 28, 1902

Leytonstone, England
Drinkwater, John b. Jun 1, 1882

Lichfield, England
Seward, Anna d. Mar 25, 1809

Lincoln, England
Astor, Nancy Witcher (Langhorne) Astor,
  Viscountess d. May 2, 1964
Coates, Edith b. May 31, 1908
Heywood, Thomas b. 1574
Marriner, Neville b. Apr 15, 1924
Wesley, John b. Jun 28, 1703

Lincolnshire, England
Molson, John b. 1764

Lindfield, England
Cochran, C(harles) B(lake) b. Sep 25, 1872

Lindley, England
Burton, Robert b. Feb 8, 1577

Liphook, England
Webb, Beatrice Potter d. Apr 30, 1943
Webb, Sidney James d. Oct 13, 1947

Liskeard, England
Nesbitt, Cathleen Mary b. Nov 24, 1889

Litchfield, England
Johnson, Samuel b. Sep 18, 1709

Little Barford, England
Rowe, Nicholas b. Jun 20, 1674

Little Hampton, England
Parry, Charles Hubert Hastings, Sir
  d. Oct 7, 1918

Littlehampton, England
Holloway, Stanley d. Jan 30, 1982

Liverpool, England
Arnold, Matthew d. Apr 15, 1888
Bainbridge, Beryl b. Nov 21, 1933
Banks, Leslie b. Jun 9, 1890
Bell, Tom b. 1932
Best, Peter b. 1941
Boulding, Kenneth Ewart b. Jan 18, 1910
Catlin, George Edward Gordon, Sir
  b. Jul 29, 1896
Crane, Walter b. Aug 15, 1845
D'Alvarez, Marguerite b. 1886
Draper, John William b. May 5, 1811

Duranty, Walter b. May 25, 1884
Epstein, Brian b. Sep 19, 1934
Fenton, Leslie b. Mar 12, 1902
Franklin, Frederic b. Jun 13, 1914
Gladstone, William Ewart b. Dec 29, 1809
Goossens, Leon Jean b. Jun 12, 1897
Gregson, John b. Mar 15, 1919
Harrison, George b. Feb 25, 1943
Hemans, Felicia Dorothea Browne
    b. Sep 25, 1793
Kletzki, Paul d. Mar 5, 1973
Laver, James b. Mar 14, 1899
LeGallienne, Richard b. Jan 20, 1866
Lennon, John Winston b. Oct 9, 1940
Lennon, Julian (John Charles Julian)
    b. Apr 8, 1963
Lloyd, (John) Selwyn Brooke
    b. Jul 28, 1904
Lowry, Malcolm (Clarence Malcolm)
    b. Jul 28, 1909
Madden, Owen Victor b. Jun 1892
Marsden, Gerry b. Sep 24, 1942
McCartney, Paul (James Paul)
    b. Jun 18, 1942
Monsarrat, Nicholas John Turney
    b. Mar 22, 1910
Morris, Robert b. Jan 31, 1734
Nevada, Emma d. Jun 20, 1940
Newman, Ernest b. Nov 30, 1868
Petrie, Charles Alexander, Sir
    b. Sep 28, 1895
Rimmer, William b. Feb 20, 1816
Runcie, Robert Alexander K
    b. Oct 21, 1921
Russell, Annie b. Jan 12, 1864
Russell, Edward Frederick Langley, Baron
    of Liverpool b. Apr 10, 1895
Scala, Gia b. Mar 3, 1934
Shaffer, Anthony b. May 15, 1926
Shaffer, Peter Levin b. May 15, 1926
Smith, Geoff b. 1954
Sothern, Edward Askew b. Apr 1, 1826
Starr, Ringo b. Jul 7, 1940
Stubbs, George b. 1724
Tait, Arthur Fitzwilliam b. Aug 5, 1819
Thomas, Brandon b. Dec 25, 1856
Tushingham, Rita b. Mar 14, 1942
Watkins, Ernest Shilston b. Jun 18, 1902
Whitty, May, Dame b. Jun 19, 1865

Lodsworth, England

Ward, Barbara Mary d. May 31, 1981

London, England

A'Becket, Thomas b. Dec 21, 1118
A'Beckett, Gilbert Abbott b. Feb 17, 1811
Abbey, Edwin Austin d. Aug 1, 1911
Abercrombie, Lascelles d. Oct 27, 1938
Abrahams, Harold d. Jan 14, 1978
Abrams, Harry Nathan b. Dec 8, 1904
Ackland, Joss b. Feb 29, 1928
Adam, James d. Oct 20, 1794
Adam, Robert d. Mar 3, 1792

Adams, Louisa Catherine b. Feb 12, 1775
Addams, Dawn d. May 7, 1985
Addinsell, Richard d. Nov 15, 1977
Addison, Joseph d. Jun 17, 1719
Agate, James Evershed d. Jun 6, 1947
Aguilar, Grace b. Jun 2, 1816
Aitken, Max (John William Maxwell)
    d. Apr 30, 1985
Albert, Prince d. Dec 13, 1861
Alice (Mary Victoria Augusta Pauline)
    d. Jan 3, 1981
Allard, Sydney b. Jul 1910
Allen of Hurtwood, Lady b. May 10, 1897
Allenby, Edmund Hynman Allenby,
    Viscount d. May 14, 1936
Allingham, Margery b. May 20, 1904
Alvarez, Alfred b. Aug 5, 1929
Ambler, Eric b. Jun 28, 1909
Amery, Julian (Harold Julian)
    b. Mar 27, 1919
Amies, Hardy b. Jul 17, 1909
Amis, Kingsley William b. Apr 16, 1922
Anderson, Michael b. Jan 30, 1920
Anderson, Michael, Jr. b. Aug 6, 1943
Andre, John b. 1751
Andrew b. Feb 19, 1960
Andrews, Anthony b. Jan 12, 1948
Anne b. Feb 6, 1665
Anne b. Aug 15, 1950
Annis, Francesca b. May 14, 1944
Ant, Adam b. Nov 3, 1954
Anthony, Evelyn, pseud. b. Jul 3, 1928
Ardizzone, Edward Jeffrey Irving
    d. Nov 8, 1979
Arliss, George b. Apr 10, 1868
Arliss, George d. Feb 5, 1946
Armstrong-Jones, Antony Charles Robert
    b. Mar 7, 1930
Arne, Thomas Augustine b. Mar 12, 1710
Arne, Thomas Augustine d. Mar 5, 1778
Arnold, Benedict d. Jun 14, 1801
Arnold, Edwin d. Mar 24, 1904
Asch, Sholem d. Jul 10, 1957
Asher, Peter b. Jun 22, 1944
Ashman, Matthew b.
Asquith, Anthony b. Nov 9, 1902
Asquith, Anthony d. Feb 20, 1968
Asquith, Emma Alice Margot
    d. Jul 28, 1945
Attenborough, David Frederick
    b. May 8, 1926
Attlee, Clement Richard Attlee, Earl
    b. Jan 3, 1883
Attlee, Clement Richard Attlee, Earl
    d. Oct 8, 1967
Auger, Brian b. Jul 18, 1939
Ayckbourn, Alan b. Apr 12, 1939
Ayer, Alfred Jules b. Oct 29, 1910
Aylward, Gladys b. 1902
Babbage, Charles b. Oct 18, 1871
Bach, Johann Christian d. Jan 1, 1782

Boothby, Robert John Graham, Lord
d. Jul 16, 1986
Boswell, James d. May 19, 1795
Bowen, Elizabeth Dorothea Cole
d. Feb 22, 1973
Bowie, David b. Jan 8, 1947
Boyce, William b. 1710
Boyle, Robert d. Dec 30, 1691
Bracken, Brendan Rendall, Viscount
d. Aug 8, 1958
Bradley, Andrew Cecil d. Sep 2, 1935
Bragg, William Henry, Sir
d. Mar 12, 1942
Bragg, William Lawrence, Sir
d. Jul 1, 1971
Braid, James d. Nov 27, 1950
Brain, Aubrey b. Jul 12, 1893
Brain, Aubrey d. Sep 21, 1955
Brain, Dennis b. May 17, 1921
Brandt, Bill (William) b. 1904
Brandt, Bill (William) d. Dec 20, 1983
Bream, Julian b. Jul 15, 1933
Brewer, Ebenezer b. May 2, 1810
Bricusse, Leslie b. Jan 29, 1931
Bridge, Frank d. Jan 11, 1941
Brook, Clive (Clifford) b. Jun 1, 1887
Brook, Clive (Clifford) d. Nov 18, 1974
Brook, Peter b. Mar 21, 1925
Brooke, L Leslie d. May 1, 1940
Brophy, Brigid b. Jun 12, 1929
Brown, Carter, pseud. b. Aug 1, 1923
Brown, George Alfred b. Sep 2, 1914
Brown, Georgia b. Oct 21, 1933
Brown, Lancelot d. Feb 6, 1783
Brown, Pamela b. Jul 8, 1917
Brown, Pamela d. Sep 18, 1975
Brown, Peter b. 1940
Brown, Robert d. Jun 10, 1858
Browning, Oscar b. Jan 17, 1837
Browning, Robert b. May 7, 1812
Bruce, David, Sir d. Nov 27, 1931
Brummell, "Beau" (George Bryan)
b. Jun 7, 1778
Brunel, Isambard Kingdom
d. Sep 15, 1859
Buchanan, Jack d. Oct 20, 1957
Bull, Peter b. Mar 21, 1912
Bull, Peter d. May 20, 1984
Bunyan, John d. Aug 31, 1688
Burgoyne, John d. Jun 4, 1792
Burke, Thomas b. Nov 1886
Burke, Thomas d. Sep 22, 1945
Burne-Jones, Edward d. Jun 17, 1898
Burney, Fanny (Frances) d. Jan 6, 1840
Burns, Eveline Mabel b. Mar 16, 1900
Burt, Cyril Lodowic, Sir b. Mar 23, 1883
Burt, Cyril Lodowic, Sir d. Oct 10, 1971
Burton, Isabel Arundel b. 1831
Busch, Fritz d. Sep 14, 1951
Bush, Alan b. Dec 22, 1900
Butler, Samuel d. Sep 25, 1680

Butler, Samuel d. Jun 18, 1902
Butterfield, William b. 1814
Byrd, William b. 1542
Byrd, William d. Jul 4, 1623
Byron, George Gordon Noel Byron, Baron
b. Jan 22, 1788
Cabot, Sebastian b. Jul 6, 1918
Cadogan, Alexander George Montague, Sir
d. Jul 9, 1968
Caine, Michael b. Mar 14, 1933
Calder, Nigel David Ritchie
b. Dec 2, 1931
Calder-Marshall, Anna Lucia
b. Jan 11, 1947
Calvert, Phyllis b. Feb 18, 1915
Campbell, Mrs. Patrick b. Feb 9, 1865
Campion, Thomas b. Feb 12, 1567
Campion, Thomas d. Mar 1, 1620
Canning, George b. Apr 11, 1770
Canning, George d. Aug 8, 1827
Cape, Herbert Jonathan b. Nov 15, 1879
Cape, Herbert Jonathan d. Feb 10, 1960
Cardus, Neville, Sir d. Feb 28, 1975
Carey, Henry d. Oct 4, 1743
Carlile, Richard d. 1843
Carlyle, Thomas d. Feb 4, 1881
Caro, Anthony b. Mar 8, 1924
Carrington, Peter Alexander Rupert, Baron
b. Jun 6, 1919
Carritt, David Graham (Hugh David
Graham) d. Aug 3, 1982
Carte, Richard d'Oyly b. May 3, 1844
Carte, Richard d'Oyly d. Apr 3, 1901
Casaubon, Isaac d. Jul 1, 1614
Casement, Roger David d. Aug 3, 1916
Caslon, William d. Jan 23, 1766
Cavendish, Henry d. Mar 10, 1810
Cavendish, William, Duke of Newcastle
d. Dec 25, 1676
Cecil, Edgar Algernon Robert
b. Sep 14, 1864
Chalk, Oscar Roy b. Jun 7, 1907
Chamberlain, Joseph b. Jul 8, 1836
Chambers, Paul, Sir b. Apr 2, 1904
Chambers, William, Sir d. Mar 8, 1796
Chandos, Oliver Lyttelton b. Mar 15, 1893
Chantrey, Francis Legatt, Sir
d. Nov 25, 1841
Chaplin, Charlie b. Apr 16, 1889
Chapman, George d. May 12, 1634
Chapple, Stanley b. Oct 29, 1900
Charles b. Nov 14, 1948
Charoux, Siegfried d. Apr 26, 1967
Chatfield, Alfred E Montacute, Baron
d. Nov 15, 1967
Chaucer, Geoffrey b. 1340
Chaucer, Geoffrey d. Oct 25, 1400
Chermayeff, Ivan b. Jun 6, 1932
Chesebrough, Robert Augustus
b. Jan 9, 1837

Day, Thomas d. Sep 28, 1789
Day-Lewis, Cecil d. May 22, 1972
Daye, Stephen b. 1594
Dean, Basil d. Apr 22, 1978
Dee, John b. 1527
Defoe, Daniel b. Apr 26, 1661
Defoe, Daniel d. Apr 26, 1731
DeHavilland, Geoffrey d. May 21, 1965
Deighton, Len (Leonard Cyril)
  b. Feb 18, 1929
Dekker, Thomas b. 1572
Dekker, Thomas d. 1632
Delderfield, Ronald Frederick
  b. Feb 12, 1912
DelMar, Norman Rene b. Jul 31, 1919
Deloney, Thomas b. 1543
DeManio, Jack b. Jan 26, 1914
Dent, Edward Joseph d. Aug 22, 1957
Deutsch, Adolph b. Oct 20, 1897
Dibdin, Thomas Frognall d. Nov 18, 1847
Dickens, Monica Enid b. May 10, 1915
Difford, Chris b. Apr 11, 1954
Disraeli, Benjamin b. Dec 21, 1804
Disraeli, Benjamin d. Apr 19, 1881
Diver, Jenny d. Mar 18, 1740
Donat, Robert d. Jun 9, 1958
Donne, John b. 1573
Donne, John d. Mar 31, 1631
Douglas-Home, Alexander Frederick
  b. Jul 2, 1903
Douglas-Home, Charles d. Oct 29, 1985
Dowell, Anthony b. Feb 16, 1943
Dowland, John d. Apr 7, 1626
Down, Lesley-Anne b. Mar 17, 1954
Dowson, Ernest Christopher
  d. Feb 23, 1900
Doyle, Richard b. Sep 1824
Doyle, Richard d. Dec 11, 1883
Drayton, Michael d. Dec 23, 1631
Drew, Louisa Lane b. Jan 10, 1820
Dryden, John d. May 1, 1700
Duff, Mary Ann Dyke b. 1794
DuMaurier, Daphne b. May 13, 1907
DuMaurier, George Louis P B
  d. Oct 8, 1896
DuMaurier, Gerald Hubert, Sir
  b. Mar 26, 1873
DuMaurier, Gerald Hubert, Sir
  d. Apr 11, 1934
Dunn, Michael d. Aug 29, 1973
Dunne, John William d. Aug 24, 1949
Dunsany, Edward J M Plunkett, Baron
  b. Jul 24, 1878
DuPont, Clifford Walter b. Dec 6, 1905
Duveen, Joseph, Sir d. May 25, 1939
Dyck, Anthony van d. 1641
Dyer, Edward, Sir d. May 1607
Eaton, Shirley b. 1936
Eden, Dorothy d. Mar 4, 1982
Eden, Nicholas b. Oct 3, 1930
Eden, Nicholas d. Aug 17, 1985

Edward b. Mar 10, 1964
Edward IV d. 1483
Edward the Black Prince d. 1376
Edward V d. 1483
Edward VI d. 1553
Edward VII b. 1841
Edward VII d. 1910
Elgar, Edward William, Sir
  d. Feb 23, 1934
Eliot, George, pseud. d. Dec 22, 1880
Eliot, T(homas) S(tearns) d. Jan 4, 1965
Elizabeth II b. Apr 21, 1926
Ellington, Edward d. Jun 13, 1967
Elliot, Cass d. Jul 29, 1974
Elliott, Denholm b. May 31, 1922
Ellis, Robin b. 1944
Ellis, Ruth d. Jul 13, 1955
Empson, William, Sir d. Apr 15, 1984
Engels, Friedrich d. Aug 5, 1895
Entwistle, John b. Sep 10, 1944
Epstein, Brian d. Aug 27, 1967
Epstein, Jacob, Sir b. Aug 9, 1880
Epstein, Jacob, Sir d. Aug 9, 1959
Esmond, Jill b. Jan 26, 1908
Evans, Edith Mary Booth, Dame
  b. Feb 8, 1888
Evans, Edward Ratcliffe Garth Russell
  b. Oct 28, 1880
Evins, David b.
Faithfull, Marianne b. Dec 29, 1946
Farjeon, Eleanor b. Feb 13, 1881
Farquhar, George d. Apr 29, 1707
Faversham, William Alfred
  b. Feb 12, 1868
Feather, Leonard Geoffrey b. Sep 13, 1914
Feather, Victor d. Jul 28, 1976
Feldman, Marty b. Jul 8, 1934
Fenollosa, Ernest Francisco
  d. Sep 21, 1908
Ferrier, Kathleen d. Oct 8, 1953
Ferris, Barbara Gillian b. Oct 3, 1940
Field, Virginia (Margaret Cynthia St. John)
  b. Nov 14, 1917
Finch, Peter b. Sep 28, 1916
Firbank, Ronald b. Jan 17, 1886
Fisher, Herbert Albert Laurens
  b. Mar 21, 1865
Fisher, Herbert Albert Laurens
  d. Apr 18, 1940
Fisher, John d. Jun 22, 1535
Fisher, Terence b. 1904
Flanders, Michael b. Mar 1, 1922
Flaxman, John d. Dec 7, 1826
Fleming, Alexander, Sir d. Mar 11, 1955
Fleming, Ian d. Jan 1, 1969
Fleming, Ian Lancaster b. May 28, 1908
Fleming, John Ambrose d. Apr 19, 1945
Fletcher, John d. Aug 1625
Flint, William Russell, Sir d. Dec 27, 1969
Florey, Howard Walter d. Feb 21, 1968
Fontanne, Lynn b. Dec 6, 1887

Forbes, Bryan b. Jul 22, 1926
Forbes, Ralph b. Sep 30, 1896
Forbes-Robertson, Johnston, Sir b. 1853
Forster, E(dward) M(organ) b. Jan 1, 1879
Forster, William Edward d. 1886
Foscolo, (Niccolo) Ugo d. Sep 10, 1827
Fowler, Henry Watson d. Dec 27, 1933
Fox, Charles James b. Jan 24, 1749
Fox, Edward b. Apr 13, 1937
Fox, James b. May 19, 1939
Foyle, Christina b. Jan 30, 1911
Foyle, Gilbert Samuel b. Mar 9, 1886
Foyle, William Alfred b. Mar 4, 1885
Franca, Celia b. Jun 25, 1921
Francis, Freddie b. 1917
Frankau, Gilbert b. Apr 21, 1884
Frankau, Pamela b. Jan 8, 1908
Fraser, Antonia Pakenham, Lady
   b. Aug 27, 1932
Fraser, Bruce Austin, Sir d. Feb 12, 1981
Frayn, Michael b. Sep 8, 1933
Frederick Louis d. Mar 20, 1751
Freeling, Nicolas b. Mar 3, 1927
Freeman, R(ichard) Austin
   b. Apr 11, 1862
Freud, Anna d. Oct 8, 1982
Freud, Sigmund d. Sep 23, 1939
Friese-Greene, William Edward d. 1921
Fry, Charles Burgess d. Sep 7, 1956
Fry, Roger Eliot b. Dec 14, 1866
Fry, Roger Eliot d. Sep 9, 1934
Fuller-Maitland, John Alexander
   b. Apr 7, 1856
Fuseli, Henry d. Apr 16, 1825
Gabor, Dennis d. Feb 9, 1979
Gainsborough, Thomas d. 1788
Gale, Richard Nelson, Sir b. Jul 25, 1896
Garcia, Manuel Patricio Rodriguez, II
   d. Jul 1, 1906
Garland, Judy d. Jun 22, 1969
Garnett, Richard d. Apr 13, 1906
Garrick, David d. Jan 20, 1779
Garvey, Marcus Moziah d. Jun 10, 1940
Gaunt, William d. May 24, 1980
Gay, John d. Dec 4, 1732
Genn, Leo b. Aug 9, 1905
Genn, Leo d. Jan 26, 1978
George Edward Alexander Edmund
   b. Dec 20, 1902
George II d. Oct 25, 1760
George III b. Jun 4, 1738
George IV b. Aug 12, 1762
George V b. 1865
George V d. Jan 20, 1936
George, Susan b. Jul 26, 1950
Gerhardi, William Alexander
   d. Jul 5, 1977
Gibbons, Grinling d. Aug 3, 1721
Gibbons, Stella Dorethea b. Jan 5, 1902
Gibbs, James d. Aug 5, 1754

Gielgud, (Arthur) John, Sir
   b. Apr 14, 1904
Gieseking, Walter Wilhelm d. Oct 26, 1956
Gilbert, William Schwenck, Sir
   b. Nov 18, 1836
Gilder, Nick b. Nov 7, 1951
Gilliatt, Penelope Ann Douglas
   b. Mar 25, 1932
Gillray, James b. 1757
Gillray, James d. Jun 1, 1815
Gilmore, Eddy Lanier King d. Oct 6, 1967
Gingold, Hermione Ferdinanda
   b. Dec 9, 1897
Girtin, Thomas d. Nov 9, 1802
Glaisher, James b. Apr 7, 1809
Glass, David Victor b. Jan 2, 1911
Glover, Julian b. Mar 27, 1935
Glyn, Elinor Sutherland d. Sep 23, 1943
Godolphin, Sidney d. Sep 15, 1712
Godwin, Mary Wollstonecraft
   b. Apr 27, 1759
Godwin, Mary Wollstonecraft
   d. Sep 10, 1797
Godwin, William d. Apr 7, 1836
Goldie, Grace Wyndham d. Jun 3, 1986
Goldin, Horace d. Aug 22, 1939
Goldsmith, Oliver d. Apr 4, 1774
Gollancz, Victor, Sir b. Apr 9, 1893
Gollancz, Victor, Sir d. Feb 8, 1967
Gompers, Samuel b. Jan 27, 1850
Gonne, Maud MacBride b. 1866
Goodall, Jane b. Apr 3, 1934
Goossens, Eugene, Sir b. May 26, 1893
Goossens, Eugene, Sir d. Jun 13, 1962
Gordon-Walker of Leyton, Patrick
   Chrestien Gordon-Walker, Baron
   d. Dec 2, 1980
Gore, Charles d. Jan 17, 1932
Gorgas, William Crawford d. Jul 3, 1920
Gosse, Edmund William, Sir
   b. Sep 21, 1849
Gottschalk, Ferdinand b. 1869
Gottschalk, Ferdinand d. Oct 10, 1944
Goulding, Edmund b. Mar 20, 1891
Gowers, Ernest Arthur, Sir b. Jun 2, 1880
Graham, Sheilah b. Sep 1908
Granger, Stewart b. May 6, 1913
Grant, Michael b. Nov 21, 1914
Granville-Barker, Harley b. Nov 25, 1877
Graves, Peter b. Oct 21, 1911
Graves, Robert Ranke b. Jul 26, 1895
Gray, Nicholas Stuart d. Mar 17, 1981
Gray, Thomas b. Dec 26, 1716
Green, Martyn b. Apr 22, 1899
Greenaway, Kate (Catherine)
   b. Mar 17, 1846
Greenwood, Joan b. Mar 4, 1921
Grenfell, Joyce Irene b. Feb 10, 1910
Grenfell, Joyce Irene d. Nov 30, 1979
Grew, Nehemiah d. Mar 25, 1712
Grey of Fallodon, Edward b. Apr 25, 1862

Grey, Jane, Lady d. Feb 12, 1554
Griffith, Hugh Emrys d. May 14, 1980
Grosvenor, Gerald Cavendish
  b. Dec 22, 1951
Grove, George, Sir d. May 18, 1900
Groves, Charles, Sir b. Mar 10, 1915
Guinness, Alec, Sir b. Apr 2, 1914
Gwyn, Nell (Eleanor) d. Nov 13, 1687
Haggard, Henry Rider, Sir
  d. May 14, 1925
Hakluyt, Richard d. Nov 23, 1616
Hall, Radclyffe d. Oct 7, 1943
Halley, Edmund b. Oct 29, 1656
Hamer, Robert d. Dec 4, 1963
Hamilton, Ian Standish Monteith, Sir
  d. Oct 12, 1947
Hampden, John b. 1594
Hampshire, Susan b. May 12, 1942
Handel, George Frederick d. Apr 14, 1759
Hansom, Joseph Aloysius d. Jun 29, 1882
Hare, James Henry b. Oct 3, 1856
Harris, Arthur Travers, Sir d. Apr 5, 1984
Harris, Sydney J(ustin) b. Sep 14, 1917
Harrison, Frederic b. Oct 18, 1831
Harrison, Noel b. Jan 29, 1936
Harte, (Francis Bret) d. May 5, 1902
Hartley, Leslie Poles d. Dec 13, 1972
Hartnell, Norman Bishop, Sir
  b. Jun 12, 1901
Harvard, John b. Nov 26, 1607
Harvey, Anthony b. Jun 3, 1931
Harvey, Frederick Henry b. 1835
Harvey, Laurence d. Nov 25, 1973
Haskell, Arnold Lionel b. Jul 19, 1903
Hathaway, Sibyl Collings d. Jul 14, 1974
Hatton, Christopher, Sir d. Nov 20, 1591
Hawkins, Jack b. Sep 14, 1910
Hawkins, Jack d. Jul 18, 1973
Haydn, Richard b. 1905
Hayes, Alfred b. 1911
Hayward, John Davy b. Feb 2, 1905
Hazlitt, William d. Sep 18, 1830
Head, Edmund Walker, Sir
  d. Jan 28, 1868
Heard, Gerald (Henry FitzGerald)
  b. Oct 6, 1889
Heath, Ted b. 1902
Helmore, Tom b. Jan 4, 1912
Henderson, Arthur d. Aug 28, 1968
Hendrix, Jimi (James Marshall)
  d. Sep 18, 1970
Henry of Wales b. Sep 15, 1984
Herbert, Alan Patrick, Sir b. Sep 24, 1890
Herbert, Alan Patrick, Sir d. Nov 11, 1971
Herrick, Robert b. Aug 24, 1591
Heseltine, Phillip Arnold b. Oct 30, 1894
Heseltine, Phillip Arnold d. Dec 17, 1930
Hess, Myra b. Feb 25, 1890
Heyer, Georgette b. Dec 16, 1902
Heyer, Georgette d. Jul 4, 1974
Heywood, Thomas d. Aug 1641

Hibbert, Eleanor Alice Burford b. 1906
Hill, Graham (Norman Graham)
  b. Feb 15, 1929
Hill, Graham (Norman Graham)
  d. Nov 30, 1975
Hinshelwood, Cyril, Sir b. Jun 19, 1897
Hinshelwood, Cyril, Sir d. Oct 9, 1967
Hitchcock, Alfred Joseph, Sir
  b. Aug 13, 1899
Hoare, Samuel John Gurney, Sir
  d. May 7, 1959
Hobson, John Atkinson d. Apr 1, 1940
Hogarth, William b. Nov 10, 1697
Hogarth, William d. Oct 26, 1764
Hogg, Ima d. Aug 19, 1975
Holbein, Hans, the Younger d. 1543
Holbrooke, Josef d. Aug 5, 1958
Holloway, Stanley b. Oct 1, 1890
Holmes, Arthur d. Sep 20, 1965
Holst, Gustav d. May 25, 1934
Honeyman-Scott, James (Jimmy)
  d. Jun 16, 1982
Hood, Thomas b. May 23, 1799
Hood, Thomas d. May 3, 1845
Hooke, Robert d. Mar 3, 1705
Hope, Anthony b. Feb 7, 1863
Hoppner, John b. Apr 4, 1758
Horenstein, Jascha d. Apr 2, 1973
Hough, John b. Nov 21, 1941
Howard, Leslie b. Apr 3, 1893
Howe, William, Viscount b. Aug 10, 1729
Howes, Sally Ann b. Jul 20, 1934
Hoyle, Edmond d. Aug 29, 1769
Hudson, William Henry d. Aug 18, 1922
Hughes, Arthur b. 1832
Hulbert, Jack d. Mar 25, 1978
Humphreys, Christmas (Travers Christmas)
  b. Feb 15, 1901
Humphreys, Christmas (Travers Christmas)
  d. Apr 13, 1983
Hunt, (William) Holman b. Apr 2, 1827
Hunt, (William) Holman d. Sep 7, 1910
Hunt, Martita d. Jun 13, 1969
Hunter, John d. Oct 16, 1793
Hussey, Christopher Edward Clive
  b. Oct 21, 1899
Hussey, Christopher Edward Clive
  d. Mar 20, 1970
Huxley, Andrew Fielding b. Nov 22, 1917
Huxley, Elspeth Josceline Grant
  b. Jul 23, 1907
Huxley, Julian Sorell, Sir b. Jun 22, 1887
Huxley, Julian Sorell, Sir d. Feb 14, 1975
Insull, Samuel b. Nov 11, 1859
Ireland, Jill b. Apr 24, 1936
Ironside, William E d. Sep 22, 1959
Irving, Laurence Sidney b. Dec 21, 1871
Irwin, Margaret b. 1889
Isaacs, Alick d. Jan 26, 1967
Jackson, John Hughlings d. Oct 7, 1911
Jacobi, Derek b. Oct 22, 1938

Jacobi, Mary Putnam b. Aug 31, 1842
Jacobs, William Wymark b. 1863
Jacobs, William Wymark d. Sep 1, 1943
James II b. Oct 14, 1633
James, George Payne Rainsford
  b. Aug 9, 1799
James, Henry d. Feb 28, 1916
Jay, Peter b. Feb 7, 1937
Jeffries, Lionel Charles b. 1926
John of Gaunt d. Feb 3, 1399
Johnson, Lionel Pigot d. Oct 4, 1902
Johnson, Pamela Hansford
  b. May 29, 1912
Johnson, Pamela Hansford d. Jun 18, 1981
Johnson, Samuel d. Dec 13, 1784
Jones, Brian d. Jul 3, 1969
Jones, David d. Oct 28, 1974
Jones, Inigo b. Jul 15, 1573
Jones, Inigo d. Jun 21, 1652
Jones, Kenny b. Sep 16, 1948
Karloff, Boris b. Nov 23, 1887
Karsavina, Tamara d. May 26, 1978
Kean, Edmund b. Mar 17, 1787
Keats, John b. Oct 31, 1795
Keefe, Barrie Colin b. Oct 31, 1945
Keene, Charles Samuel d. Jan 4, 1891
Keene, Laura b. Jul 20, 1820
Kemble, Charles d. Nov 12, 1854
Kemble, Fanny (Frances Anne)
  b. Nov 27, 1809
Kemble, Fanny (Frances Anne)
  d. Jan 15, 1893
Kendal, William Hunter b. Dec 16, 1843
Kendall, Kay d. Sep 6, 1959
Kennedy, Margaret b. Apr 23, 1896
Kerr, Graham b. Jan 22, 1934
Keynes, John Maynard, Baron
  d. Apr 21, 1946
Kidd, (Captain) William d. May 23, 1701
Kilbracken, John Raymond Godley
  b. Oct 17, 1920
Killanin, Michael Morris, Lord
  b. Jul 30, 1914
Killigrew, Thomas b. Feb 7, 1612
Killigrew, Thomas d. May 19, 1683
King, Charles d. Jan 11, 1944
Kinglake, Alexander William
  d. Jan 2, 1891
Klein, Melanie d. Sep 22, 1960
Kneller, Godfrey, Sir d. Nov 7, 1723
Knox, E(dmund) G(eorge) V(alpy)
  d. Jan 2, 1971
Knox, Ronald Arbuthnott d. Aug 24, 1957
Koestler, Arthur d. Mar 3, 1983
Kops, Bernard b. Nov 28, 1926
Korda, Alexander, Sir d. Jan 23, 1956
Korda, Michael Vincent b. Oct 8, 1933
Korner, Alexis d. Jan 1, 1984
Kray, Reggie (Reginald) b. Oct 24, 1933
Kray, Ronnie (Ronald) b. Oct 24, 1933
Kyd, Thomas b. Nov 6, 1558

Kyd, Thomas d. 1594
Laban, Rudolf von d. Jul 1, 1958
LaBern, Arthur Joseph b. Feb 28, 1909
Lakatos, Imre d. Feb 2, 1974
Lamb, Caroline Ponsonby, Lady
  d. Jan 24, 1828
Lamb, Charles b. Feb 10, 1775
Lamb, Mary Ann b. 1764
Lamb, Mary Ann d. May 20, 1847
Lambert, Constant b. 1905
Lambert, Constant d. Aug 21, 1951
Lambert, J(ack) W(alter) b. Apr 21, 1917
Lancaster, Osbert, Sir b. Aug 4, 1908
Landseer, Charles b. 1799
Landseer, Edwin Henry, Sir
  b. Mar 7, 1802
Landseer, Edwin Henry, Sir d. Oct 1, 1873
Lang, William Cosmo Gordon, Baron
  d. Dec 5, 1945
Langland, William d. 1400
Lansbury, Angela Brigid b. Oct 16, 1925
Laski, Harold Joseph d. Mar 24, 1950
Laud, William d. Jan 10, 1645
Laver, James d. Jun 3, 1975
Law, Andrew Bonar d. Oct 30, 1923
Lawford, Peter b. Sep 7, 1923
Lawrence, Gertrude b. Jul 4, 1901
Lawrence, Thomas, Sir d. Jan 7, 1830
Leakey, Louis Seymour Bazett
  d. Oct 1, 1972
Leakey, Mary Douglas b. Feb 6, 1913
Lecky, William Edward Hartpole d. 1903
Lee, Bernard b. Jan 10, 1908
Lee, Bernard d. Jan 16, 1981
Lee, Christopher b. May 27, 1922
Lee, Sidney, Sir b. Dec 5, 1859
Lee, Sidney, Sir d. Mar 3, 1926
Lee-Hamilton, Eugene Jacob b. Jan 6, 1845
Leech, John b. Aug 29, 1817
Leech, John d. Oct 29, 1864
LeGallienne, Eva b. Jan 11, 1899
Lehand, "Missy" (Marguerite Alice)
  d. Jul 31, 1944
Lehmann, Rosamond Nina b. Feb 3, 1901
Leigh, Vivien d. Jul 7, 1967
Leighton, Clare Veronica Hope
  b. Apr 12, 1900
Lemon, Mark b. Nov 30, 1809
Leoni, Franco d. Feb 8, 1949
Leppard, Raymond John b. Aug 11, 1927
Leverson, Ada b. 1865
Leverson, Ada d. 1936
Lewis, Matthew Gregory b. Jul 9, 1775
Lewis, Ted b. Oct 24, 1894
Lewis, Ted d. Oct 20, 1970
Lewis, Wyndham d. Mar 7, 1957
Liddell Hart, Basil Henry b. Oct 31, 1895
Linacre, Thomas d. Oct 20, 1524
Lindsay, David b. Mar 3, 1878
Linton, William James b. Dec 7, 1812
Litolff, Henri Charles b. Feb 6, 1818

Little Tich d. Feb 10, 1928
Little, "Little Jack" b. May 28, 1900
Littlewood, Joan b. 1916
Litvinoff, Emanuel b. Jun 30, 1915
Llewelyn-Davies, Richard d. Oct 26, 1981
Lloyd, Marie b. Feb 12, 1870
Lloyd, Marie d. Oct 7, 1922
Loder, John b. Jan 3, 1898
Losey, Joseph d. Jul 22, 1984
Louis Phillippe d. Aug 26, 1850
Love, Bessie d. Apr 27, 1986
Lovelace, Richard d. 1658
Low, David, Sir d. Sep 11, 1963
Lubbock, Percy b. Jun 4, 1879
Lunn, Arnold Henry Moore, Sir
   d. Jun 2, 1974
Lupino, Ida b. Feb 4, 1918
Lupino, Stanley b. Jun 17, 1896
Lupino, Stanley d. Jun 10, 1942
Lutyens, Edwin Landseer, Sir
   b. Mar 29, 1869
Lutyens, Edwin Landseer, Sir
   d. Jan 1, 1944
Lyell, Charles, Sir d. Feb 22, 1875
Lyly, John d. 1606
Lytton, Edward George Earle Lytton
   Bulwer-Lytton, 1st Baron Lytton
   b. May 15, 1803
Lytton, Edward Robert Bulwer-Lytton,
   Earl b. Nov 8, 1831
Lytton, Henry Alfred, Sir b. Jan 3, 1867
Lytton, Henry Alfred, Sir d. Aug 15, 1936
Macaulay, Rose d. Oct 30, 1958
Macfarren, George Alexander, Sir
   b. Mar 2, 1813
Macfarren, George Alexander, Sir
   d. Oct 31, 1887
MacGrath, Leueen b. Jul 3, 1914
Mackay, John William d. Jul 20, 1902
Mackenzie, Alexander, Sir d. Apr 28, 1935
Mackinder, Halford John, Sir
   d. Mar 6, 1947
Maclean, Donald Duart b. May 25, 1913
MacLeod, Iain Norman d. Jul 20, 1970
MacMillan, Harold b. Feb 10, 1894
MacNeice, Louis (Frederick Louis)
   d. Sep 3, 1963
MacRae, Sheila b. Sep 24, 1923
Magee, Patrick d. Aug 14, 1982
Malcolm, George b. Feb 28, 1917
Mallowan, Max Edgar Lucien, Sir
   b. May 6, 1904
Malone, Edmund d. May 25, 1812
Malory, Thomas, Sir d. Mar 12, 1471
Manners, Charles b. Dec 27, 1857
Mannheim, Karl d. Jan 9, 1947
Manning, Henry Edward d. Jan 14, 1892
Manning, Maria d. Nov 13, 1849
Manns, Augustus, Sir d. Mar 2, 1907
Manson, Patrick d. Apr 9, 1922
Mapleson, James Henry b. May 4, 1830

Mapleson, James Henry d. Nov 14, 1901
Marchesi, Mathilde de Castrone
   d. Nov 17, 1913
Margaret of Anjou d. Apr 25, 1482
Marie Alexandra Victoria b. 1875
Marina d. Aug 27, 1968

Markievicz, Constance Georgine, Countess
   b. Feb 4, 1868
Markova, Alicia b. Dec 1, 1910
Marks, Simon d. Dec 8, 1964
Marlowe, Derek b. May 21, 1938
Marryat, Frederick b. Jul 10, 1792
Marsh, Jean b. Jul 1, 1934
Marshall, Herbert b. May 23, 1890
Marston, John d. Jun 25, 1634
Marvell, Andrew d. Aug 18, 1678
Marx, Karl Heinrich d. Mar 14, 1883
Mary d. Mar 24, 1953
Mason, Pamela Helen b. Mar 10, 1922
Massey, Daniel Raymond b. Oct 10, 1933
Massey, Vincent d. Dec 30, 1967
Massinger, Philip d. Mar 1640
Maude, Cyril b. Apr 24, 1882
Maugham, Robin (Robert Cecil Romer)
   b. May 17, 1916
McClintock, Francis Leopold, Sir
   d. Nov 17, 1907
McCullin, Donald b. Oct 9, 1935
McDowall, Roddy (Roderick Andrew)
   b. Sep 17, 1928
McFee, William b. Jun 15, 1881
McKenna, Virginia b. Jun 7, 1931
McWhirter, A(lan) Ross b. Aug 12, 1925
McWhirter, A(lan) Ross d. Nov 27, 1975
McWhirter, Norris Dewar b. Aug 12, 1925
Medina, Patricia b. Jul 19, 1920
Medtner, Nicholas d. Nov 13, 1951
Melachrino, George d. Jun 18, 1965
Menuhin, Hephzibah d. Jan 1, 1981
Merchant, Vivien d. Oct 3, 1982
Merrick, Joseph Carey d. 1889
Messel, Oliver b. Jan 13, 1905
Meynell, Alice b. 1847
Meynell, Alice d. Nov 27, 1922
Middleton, Thomas b. Apr 18, 1570
Mildmay, Audrey d. May 31, 1953
Mill, James d. Jun 23, 1836
Mill, John Stuart b. May 20, 1806
Millais, John Everett, Sir d. Aug 13, 1896
Miller, Henry John b. Feb 1, 1860
Miller, Joe d. 1738
Miller, Jonathan b. Jul 21, 1934
Mills, Hayley b. Apr 18, 1946
Mills, Juliet b. Nov 21, 1941
Milne, A(lan) A(lexander) b. Jan 18, 1882
Milne, Christopher Robin b. Aug 21, 1920
Milton, John b. Dec 9, 1608
Milton, John d. Nov 8, 1674
Mitford, Nancy Freeman b. Nov 28, 1904

Petty, William, Sir d. Dec 16, 1687
Pevsner, Nikolaus Bernhard Leon, Sir
    d. Aug 18, 1983
Philidor, Francois Andre Danican
    d. Aug 24, 1795
Pickering, William b. Apr 2, 1796
Pickering, William d. Apr 27, 1854
Pinero, Arthur Wing, Sir d. Nov 23, 1934
Pinter, Harold b. Oct 10, 1930
Pitman, James (Isaac James)
    b. Aug 14, 1901
Pitt, Percy b. Jan 4, 1870
Pitt, Percy d. Nov 23, 1932
Plomley, Roy d. May 29, 1985
Pool, David de Sola b. 1885
Pope, Alexander b. May 21, 1688
Porter, Eric b. Apr 8, 1928
Potter, Beatrix (Helen Beatrix)
    b. Jul 6, 1866
Potter, Stephen b. Feb 1, 1900
Potter, Stephen d. Dec 2, 1969
Potts, Nadia b. Apr 20, 1948
Powell, Anthony Dymoke b. Dec 21, 1905
Power, Tyrone (Frederick Tyrone Edmond)
    b. 1869
Pritchard, John Michael b. Feb 5, 1921
Psalmanazar, George d. May 3, 1763
Purcell, Henry b. 1658
Quant, Mary b. Feb 11, 1934
Queensberry, William Douglas, Duke
    b. 1724
Quennell, Peter Courtney b. Mar 9, 1905
Radcliffe, Ann b. Jul 9, 1764
Radcliffe, Ann d. Feb 7, 1823
Raffles, Thomas Stamford, Sir
    d. Jul 5, 1826
Raine, William MacLeod b. Jun 22, 1871
Rains, Claude b. Nov 9, 1889
Raleigh, Walter Alexander, Sir
    b. Sep 5, 1861
Raleigh, Walter, Sir d. Oct 29, 1618
Rambert, Dame Marie d. Jun 12, 1982
Ramsbotham, Peter, Sir b. Oct 8, 1919
Rattigan, Terence Mervyn b. Jun 10, 1911
Rayner, Claire Berenice b. Jan 22, 1931
Reade, Charles d. Apr 11, 1884
Redgrave, Corin b. Jul 16, 1939
Redgrave, Lynn b. Mar 8, 1943
Redgrave, Vanessa b. Jan 30, 1937
Reed, Carol, Sir b. Dec 30, 1906
Reed, Carol, Sir d. Apr 25, 1976
Reed, Oliver (Robert Oliver)
    b. Feb 13, 1938
Reid Dick, William, Sir d. Oct 1, 1961
Reid, Kate (Daphne Kate) b. Nov 4, 1930
Reid, Whitelaw d. Dec 15, 1912
Renault, Mary, pseud. b. Sep 4, 1905
Reynolds, Joshua, Sir d. Feb 23, 1792
Ricardo, David b. Apr 19, 1772
Richardson, Ralph David, Sir
    d. Oct 10, 1983

Richardson, Samuel d. Jul 4, 1761
Riley, Bridget b. Apr 24, 1931
Risdon, Elizabeth b. Apr 26, 1888
Robey, George, Sir b. Sep 20, 1869
Robins, Denise Naomi b. Feb 1, 1897
Robins, Denise Naomi d. May 1, 1985
Rogers, Samuel b. Jul 30, 1763
Rogers, Samuel d. Dec 18, 1855
Roget, Peter Mark b. Jan 18, 1779
Rohmer, Sax, pseud. b. Feb 15, 1883
Rohmer, Sax, pseud. d. Jun 1, 1959
Ronald, Landon, Sir b. Jun 7, 1873
Ronald, Landon, Sir d. Aug 14, 1938
Roose-Evans, James b. Nov 11, 1927
Root, Alan b. 1936
Rose, David b. Jun 15, 1910
Rosebery, Archibald Philip Primrose, Earl
    b. May 7, 1847
Ross, Ronald, Sir d. Sep 16, 1932
Rossetti, Christina Georgina
    b. Dec 5, 1830
Rossetti, Christina Georgina
    d. Dec 29, 1894
Rossetti, Dante Gabriel b. May 12, 1828
Rossetti, Gabriele Pasquale Giuseppe
    d. Apr 24, 1854
Rossetti, William Michael b. Sep 25, 1829
Rotha, Paul b. Jun 3, 1907
Rothermere, Esmond Cecil Harmsworth,
    Viscount b. May 29, 1898
Rothermere, Esmond Cecil Harmsworth,
    Viscount d. Jul 12, 1978
Rothschild, Edmund Leopold de
    b. Jan 16, 1916
Rothschild, Lionel Nathan Rothschild,
    Baron b. Nov 22, 1808
Rothwell, Walter Henry b. Sep 22, 1872
Rowe, Nicholas d. Dec 6, 1718
Rowlandson, Thomas b. Jul 1756
Rowlandson, Thomas d. Apr 22, 1827
Ruark, Robert Chester d. Jul 1, 1965
Ruskin, John b. Feb 8, 1819
Russell, Anna b. Dec 27, 1911
Russell, Henry b. Nov 14, 1871
Russell, Henry d. Oct 11, 1937
Russell, John, Lord b. Aug 18, 1792
Russell, Sydney Gordon, Sir
    b. May 20, 1892
Rutherford, Margaret b. May 11, 1892
Said bin Taimusr b. Aug 13, 1910
Said bin Taimusr d. Oct 19, 1972
Sandow, Eugene d. Oct 14, 1925
Sansom, William b. Jan 18, 1912
Sansom, William d. Apr 20, 1976
Saperstein, Abraham b. Jul 4, 1903
Sargent, John Singer d. Apr 15, 1925
Sargent, Malcolm, Sir d. Oct 3, 1967
Sartain, John b. Oct 24, 1808
Sassoon, Vidal b. Jan 17, 1928
Schlesinger, John Richard b. Feb 16, 1926
Schneider, Alan d. May 3, 1984

Schonfield, Hugh b. May 17, 1901
Scott, Paul Mark b. Mar 25, 1920
Scott, Paul Mark d. Mar 1, 1978
Seaman, Owen, Sir b. Sep 18, 1861
Seaman, Owen, Sir d. Feb 2, 1936
Sears, Heather b. Sep 28, 1935
Selden, John d. Nov 30, 1654
Selfridge, Harry Gordon d. May 8, 1947
Sellers, Peter Richard Henry
    d. Jul 24, 1980
Serraillier, Ian Lucien b. Sep 24, 1912
Seton-Watson, Hugh (George Hugh
    Nicholas) b. Feb 15, 1916
Shadwell, Thomas d. Nov 20, 1692
Shaftesbury, Anthony Ashley Cooper, Earl
    b. Feb 26, 1671
Shanks, Michael (James Michael)
    b. Apr 12, 1927
Shearing, George Albert b. Aug 13, 1919
Sheed, Wilfrid John Joseph
    b. Dec 27, 1930
Sheinwold, Alfred b. Jan 26, 1912
Shelley, Carole b. Aug 16, 1939
Shelley, Mary Wollstonecraft
    b. Aug 30, 1797
Shepard, Ernest Howard b. Dec 10, 1879
Sheppard, Jack d. 1724
Sheraton, Thomas d. Oct 22, 1806
Sheridan, Clare Consuelo b. Sep 9, 1885
Sheridan, Richard Brinsley d. Jul 7, 1816
Shirley, James b. 1596
Shirley, James d. Oct 29, 1666
Shockley, William (Bradford)
    b. Feb 13, 1910
Shorthouse, Joseph Henry d. Mar 4, 1903
Siddons, Sarah Kemble d. Jun 8, 1831
Siemens, William, Sir d. Nov 18, 1883
Silkin, Jon b. 1930
Sim, Alastair d. Aug 19, 1976
Simmons, Jean b. Jan 31, 1929
Simpson, James Young, Sir
    d. May 6, 1870
Sitwell, Edith, Dame d. Dec 9, 1964
Sitwell, Osbert, Sir b. Dec 6, 1892
Skipworth, Alison b. Jul 25, 1870
Slim, William Joseph d. Dec 14, 1970
Smith Sydney d. Feb 22, 1845
Smith, C Aubrey b. Jul 21, 1863
Smith, John d. Jun 21, 1631
Snow, C(harles) P(ercy), Sir d. Jul 1, 1980
Soane, John, Sir d. Jan 20, 1837
Solomon b. Aug 9, 1902
Sothern, Edward Askew d. Jan 20, 1881
Speer, Albert d. Sep 1, 1981
Speight, Johnny b. Jun 2, 1921
Spender, Stephen b. Feb 28, 1909
Spenser, Edmund b. 1552
Spilsbury, Bernard Henry, Sir
    d. Dec 17, 1947
Spooner, William Archibald
    b. Jul 22, 1844

Spy, pseud. b. Nov 21, 1851
Spy, pseud. d. May 15, 1922
Squire, Chris b. Mar 4, 1948
Stamp, Terence b. Jul 22, 1940
Standing, Guy b. Sep 1, 1873
Stanley, Henry Morton, Sir
    d. May 10, 1904
Steel, Anthony b. May 21, 1920
Steele, Tommy b. Dec 17, 1936
Stephen, Leslie, Sir b. Nov 28, 1832
Stephens, James d. Dec 26, 1950
Sterne, Laurence d. Mar 18, 1768
Stevens, Cat b. Jul 21, 1948
Stevenson, Adlai Ewing, Jr.
    d. Jul 14, 1965
Stevenson, Robert b. 1905
Stewart, Donald Ogden d. Aug 2, 1980
Stocker, Wally b. Mar 17, 1954
Stokes, Donald Gresham Stokes, Baron
    b. Mar 22, 1914
Stokowski, Leopold b. Apr 18, 1882
Stokowski, Leopold d. Sep 13, 1977
Strachey, (Giles) Lytton b. Mar 1, 1880
Struther, Jan, pseud. b. Jun 6, 1901
Strutt, Joseph d. Oct 16, 1802
Stuckgold, Grete Schmeidt b. Jul 6, 1895
Styne, Jule (Julius Kerwin Stein)
    b. Dec 31, 1905
Sullivan, Arthur Seymour, Sir
    b. May 14, 1842
Sullivan, Arthur Seymour, Sir
    d. Nov 22, 1900
Sullivan, Francis Loftus b. Jan 6, 1903
Summerskill, Edith Clara, Baroness
    b. Apr 19, 1901
Summerskill, Edith Clara, Baroness
    d. Feb 4, 1980
Supervia, Conchita d. Mar 30, 1936
Sutherland, Graham Vivian
    b. Aug 24, 1903
Sutherland, Graham Vivian
    d. Feb 17, 1980
Swinburne, Algernon Charles
    b. Apr 5, 1837
Swinburne, Algernon Charles
    d. Apr 10, 1909
Symons, Julian Gustave b. May 30, 1912
Syms, Sylvia b. 1934
Tandy, Jessica b. Jun 7, 1909
Tate, Nahum d. Aug 12, 1715
Tauber, Richard d. Jan 8, 1948
Taylor, Ann b. Jun 30, 1782
Taylor, Elizabeth Rosemond
    b. Feb 27, 1932
Tempest, Marie b. Jul 15, 1864
Tempest, Marie d. Oct 15, 1942
Tennant, Veronica b. Jan 15, 1946
Tenniel, John, Sir b. Feb 28, 1820
Tenniel, John, Sir d. Feb 25, 1914
Terry-Thomas b. Jul 14, 1911
Teyte, Maggie, Dame d. May 27, 1976

Thackeray, William Makepeace
  d. Dec 24, 1863
Thomas, Brandon d. Jun 19, 1914
Thomas, Edward b. Mar 3, 1878
Thomas, Lowell Jackson, Jr.
  b. Oct 6, 1923
Thompson, Daley (Francis Daley)
  b. Jul 30, 1958
Thompson, David b. Apr 30, 1770
Thompson, Francis Joseph
  d. Nov 13, 1907
Thomson of Fleet, Roy Herbert Thomson,
  Baron d. Aug 4, 1976
Thomson, James d. Jun 3, 1882
Thorndike, Sybil, Dame d. Jun 6, 1976
Thorpe, Jeremy (John Jeremy)
  b. Apr 29, 1929
Tidyman, Ernest d. Jul 14, 1984
Tilbrook, Glenn b. Aug 31, 1957
Tiomkin, Dimitri d. Nov 11, 1979
Tippett, Michael Kemp, Sir b. Jan 2, 1905
Tomlinson, Henry Major b. 1873
Tomlinson, Henry Major d. Feb 5, 1958
Toplady, Augustus Montague
  d. Aug 11, 1778
Townshend, Peter Dennis Blandford
  b. May 19, 1945
Toye, Geoffrey d. Jun 11, 1942
Toynbee, Arnold Joseph b. Apr 14, 1889
Travers, Ben b. Nov 12, 1886
Travers, Ben d. Dec 18, 1980
Tree, Herbert Beerbohm d. Jul 2, 1917
Trelawny, Edward John b. Nov 13, 1792
Tremayne, Les b. Apr 16, 1913
Trench, Richard Chenevix d. Mar 28, 1886
Trenchard, Hugh Montague, First Viscount
  d. Feb 10, 1956
Trollope, Anthony b. Apr 24, 1815
Trollope, Anthony d. Dec 6, 1882
Trower, Robin b. Mar 9, 1945
Tudor, Antony b. Apr 4, 1908
Turner, Joseph Mallord William
  b. Apr 23, 1775
Turner, Joseph Mallord William
  d. Dec 19, 1851
Tussaud, (Marie Gresholtz), Madame
  d. Apr 15, 1850
Twiggy b. Sep 19, 1949
Tylor, Edward Bennett, Sir b. Oct 2, 1832
Underwood, John Thomas b. Apr 12, 1857
Unsworth, Geoffrey b. 1914
Unwin, Stanley, Sir b. Dec 19, 1884
Unwin, Stanley, Sir d. Oct 13, 1968
Ure, Mary d. Apr 3, 1975
Ustinov, Peter Alexander b. Apr 16, 1921
Utley, Freda b. Jan 23, 1898
Van Druten, John William b. Jun 1, 1901
Vanderbilt, Alfred G b. Sep 22, 1912
Vandercook, John Womack
  b. Apr 22, 1902
Vaughan Williams, Ralph d. Aug 26, 1958

Vaux, Calvert b. Dec 20, 1824
Velde, Willem van de d. 1707
Vestris, Lucia Elizabeth b. 1787
Vestris, Lucia Elizabeth d. Aug 8, 1856
Victoria b. May 24, 1819
Viotti, Giovanni Battista d. Mar 3, 1824
Vyvyan, Jennifer Brigit d. Apr 5, 1974
Wakeman, Rick b. May 18, 1949
Waley, Arthur David b. Aug 19, 1889
Wallack, James William b. Aug 24, 1795
Wallis, Samuel d. Jan 21, 1795
Walpole, Horace b. Sep 24, 1717
Walpole, Horace d. Mar 2, 1797
Ward, Rachel b. 1957
Ward, Simon b. Oct 19, 1941
Watts, George Frederic b. 1817
Watts, George Frederic d. 1904
Waugh, Alec (Alexander Raban)
  b. Jul 8, 1898
Waugh, Evelyn Arthur St. John
  b. Oct 28, 1903
Webb, Sidney James b. Jul 13, 1859
Webber, Andrew Lloyd b. Mar 22, 1948
Weber, Carl Maria von d. Jun 5, 1826
Webster, Ben(jamin) b. Jun 2, 1864
Webster, John b. 1580
Webster, Margaret d. Nov 13, 1972
Wells, H(erbert) G(eorge) d. Aug 13, 1946
Wesker, Arnold b. May 24, 1932
Wesley, John d. Mar 3, 1791
West, Benjamin d. Mar 11, 1820
West, Dame Rebecca, pseud.
  d. Mar 15, 1983
Wheeler, Hugh b. 1912
Whistler, James Abbott McNeill
  d. Jul 17, 1903
White, Antonia b. Mar 31, 1899
White, Antonia d. Apr 10, 1980
Whitlock, Albert b. 1915
Whymper, Edward b. Apr 27, 1840
Widgery, John Passmore, Baron
  d. Jul 25, 1981
Wigg, George (Edward Cecil)
  d. Aug 11, 1983
Wilcox, Herbert d. May 15, 1977
Wilde, Kim b. Nov 18, 1960
Wilkes, John b. Oct 17, 1727
Wilkes, John d. Mar 2, 1797
William of Wales b. Jun 21, 1982
Williams, Darnell b. Mar 3,
Williams, Jay d. Jul 12, 1978
Williams, Roger b. 1603
Williams, Shirley b. Jul 27, 1930
Wintle, Justin Beecham b. May 24, 1949
Wisdom, Norman b. Feb 4, 1925
Wise, Thomas J d. May 13, 1937
Wiseman, Nicholas Patrick Stephen
  d. Feb 15, 1865
Woffington, Margaret d. Mar 28, 1760
Wolfenden, John Frederick, Sir
  d. Jan 18, 1985

Wolfit, Donald, Sir d. Feb 17, 1968
Wood, Henry Joseph, Sir b. Mar 3, 1869
Wood, Henry Joseph, Sir d. Aug 19, 1944
Wood, Ron(ald) b. Jun 1, 1947
Woodville, Richard Caton d. 1855
Woolf, Leonard Sidney b. Nov 25, 1880
Woolf, Virginia (Adeline Virginia Stephen)
　　b. Jan 25, 1882
Woolley, Charles Leonard, Sir
　　b. Apr 17, 1880
Woolley, Charles Leonard, Sir
　　d. Feb 20, 1960
Wren, Christopher, Sir d. Feb 25, 1723
Wycherley, Margaret b. 1881
Wyman, Bill (William George)
　　b. Oct 24, 1941
Wynter, Dana b. Jun 8, 1932
Wynyard, Diana b. Jan 16, 1906
Wynyard, Diana d. May 13, 1964
York, Susannah b. Jan 9, 1941
Young, Roland b. Nov 11, 1887
Youngman, Henny b. 1905
Zaleski, August d. Apr 7, 1972
Zangwill, Israel b. Feb 14, 1864
Zangwill, Israel d. Aug 1, 1926

Long Sutton, England
Piccaver, Alfred b. Feb 15, 1884

Longworth, England
Blackmore, Richard Doddridge
　　b. Jun 7, 1825
Fell, John b. Jun 23, 1625

Loose, England
Rootes, William Edward Rootes, Baron
　　b. Jun 14, 1917

Loughton, England
Barker, George Granville b. Feb 26, 1913

Lowestoft, England
Britten, (Edward) Benjamin
　　b. Nov 22, 1913
Maurice, Frederick Denison
　　b. Aug 29, 1805
Nash, Thomas b. 1567

Luton, England
Hailey, Arthur b. Apr 5, 1920

Lye, England
Hardwicke, Cedric Webster, Sir
　　b. Feb 19, 1893

Lymington, England
Patmore, Coventry Kersey Dighton
　　d. Nov 26, 1896

Maidenhead, England
Brown, Tina b. Nov 21, 1953
Comstock, Elizabeth L b. Oct 30, 1815
Lofting, Hugh b. Jan 14, 1886

Maidstone, England
Hazlitt, William b. Apr 10, 1778

Malden, England
Gates, Horatio b. Jul 26, 1728

Maldon, England
Foyle, William Alfred d. Jul 4, 1963

Malmesbury, England
Hobbes, Thomas b. Apr 5, 1588

Malton, England
Read, Herbert, Sir d. Jun 12, 1968

Malvern, England
Conquest, Robert b. Jul 15, 1917
Faber, Geoffrey Cust, Sir b. Aug 23, 1889

Mancetter, England
Grew, Nehemiah b. 1641

Manchester, England
Agate, James Evershed b. Sep 9, 1877
Ainsworth, W(illiam) H(arrison)
　　b. Feb 4, 1805
Alcock, John William, Sir b. 1892
Bailey, Alice A(nne La Trobe-Bateman)
　　b. 1880
Bolt, Robert b. Aug 15, 1924
Bradley, Henry b. Dec 3, 1845
Burgess, Anthony b. Feb 25, 1917
Burnett, Frances Eliza Hodgson
　　b. Nov 24, 1849
Caldwell, Taylor (Janet Miriam Taylor)
　　b. Sep 7, 1900
Calvert, Louis b. 1859
Cardus, Neville, Sir b. Apr 2, 1889
Chadwick, James, Sir b. Oct 22, 1891
Connolly, Thomas Henry b. Dec 31, 1870
Cooke, (Alfred) Alistair b. Nov 20, 1908
Coulouris, George b. Oct 1, 1903
Dalton, John d. Jul 27, 1844
Davies, Peter Maxwell b. Sep 8, 1934
Donat, Robert b. Mar 18, 1905
Evans, Harold Matthew b. Jun 28, 1927
Gibb, Andy b. Mar 5, 1958
Gibb, Barry b. Sep 1, 1946
Gibb, Maurice b. Dec 22, 1949
Gibb, Robin b. Dec 22, 1949
Glass, Montague (Marsden) b. Jul 23, 1877
Graham, Winston Mawdesley
　　b. Jun 30, 1910
Halle, Charles, Sir d. Oct 25, 1895
Hampson, Frank b. Dec 21, 1918
Harvey, Frank Laird b. Aug 11, 1912
Johnson, Hewlett b. Jan 25, 1874
Jones, Davy (David) b. Dec 30, 1946
Laski, Harold Joseph b. Jun 30, 1893
Lee, Ann b. Feb 29, 1736
Lloyd George of Dwyfor, David Lloyd
　　George, Earl b. Jan 7, 1863
Lowry, Lawrence Stephen b. Nov 1, 1887
Malibran, Maria Felicita d. Sep 23, 1836
Mayall, John Brumwell b. Nov 29, 1933
Merchant, Vivien b. Jul 22, 1929
Mosley, Leonard b. 1913
Noone, Peter b. Nov 5, 1947
Pankhurst, (Estelle) Sylvia b. May 5, 1882
Pankhurst, Christabel, Dame b. 1880
Pankhurst, Emmeline Goulden
　　b. Jul 14, 1858
Thomson, Elihu b. Mar 29, 1853
Warner, David b. Jul 29, 1941

Wild, Jack b. Sep 30, 1952
Wood, Guy B b. Jul 24, 1912
Zucco, George b. Jan 11, 1886
Mangrove, England
Bonaparte, Louis Lucien b. 1813
Mansfield, England
Dodsley, Robert b. 1703
Marfield, England
Hooker, Thomas b. 1586
Margate, England
Deller, Alfred George b. May 31, 1912
Kelly, Michael d. Oct 9, 1826
Mayfield, England
Glubb, John Bagot, Sir d. Mar 17, 1986
Melbourne, England
Cook, Thomas b. Nov 22, 1808
Melton Mowbray, England
Markham, Beryl b. Oct 26, 1902
Merton, England
Bateson, William d. Feb 8, 1926
Beardsley, Aubrey Vincent
d. Mar 16, 1898
Fitzgerald, Edward d. Jun 14, 1883
Ford, Ford Madox b. Dec 17, 1873
Mexboro, England
Haigh, Kenneth b. Mar 25, 1931
Middlesbrough, England
Easton, Florence Gertrude b. Oct 25, 1884
Hornung, Ernest William b. Jun 7, 1866
Middlesex, England
Leon, Henry Cecil b. Sep 19, 1902
Middleton, England
Karloff, Boris d. Feb 2, 1969
Midhurst, England
Faber, Geoffrey Cust, Sir d. Mar 31, 1961
Gowers, Ernest Arthur, Sir
d. Apr 16, 1966
Shepard, Ernest Howard d. Mar 24, 1976
Mileham, England
Coke, Edward, Sir b. Feb 1, 1552
Milnthorpe, England
Holme, Constance b. 1881
Milston, England
Addison, Joseph b. May 1, 1672
Minehead, England
Clarke, Arthur C(harles) b. Dec 16, 1917
Missenden, England
Austin, Herbert b. Nov 8, 1866
Robinson, Robert d. Feb 8, 1975
Mobberley, England
Mallory, George Leigh b. Jun 18, 1886
Montgomery, England
Herbert, George b. Apr 3, 1593
Morley, England
Bedford, Brian b. Feb 16, 1935
Oxford and Asquith, Henry Herbert
Asquith, Earl b. Sep 12, 1852
Mortlake, England
Dee, John d. Dec 1608
Morton Village, England
Cook, James, Captain b. Oct 28, 1728

Muswell Hill, England
Davies, Dave (David) b. Feb 3, 1947
Davies, Ray(mond Douglas)
b. Jun 21, 1944
Mytholmroyd, England
Hughes, Ted b. Aug 17, 1930
Nailsworth, England
Dobell, Sydney Thompson d. Aug 22, 1874
Nantwich, England
Beatty, David Beatty, Earl b. 1871
Nelson, England
Hicks, Tony (Anthony) b. Dec 16, 1943
Nettlebed, England
Johnson, Celia, Dame d. Apr 25, 1982
New Windsor, England
Dors, Diana d. May 4, 1984
Newark, England
Hounsfield, Godfrey Newbold
b. Aug 28, 1919
John, King of England d. Oct 29, 1216
Kell, Reginald George b. 1918
Wolfit, Donald, Sir b. Apr 20, 1902
Newbury, England
Adams, Richard b. May 9, 1920
Newcastle, England
Brannigan, Owen d. May 9, 1973
Brittain, Vera Mary b. 1896
Hudson, Joseph Lowthian b. Oct 17, 1846
Newcastle-on-Tyne, England
Surtees, Robert Smith b. May 17, 1805
Newcastle-upon-Tyne, England
Catto, Thomas Sivewright, Baron
b. Mar 15, 1879
Travers, Bill b. Jan 3, 1922
Newington Butts, England
Middleton, Thomas d. Jul 4, 1627
Newport, England
Goring, Marius b. May 23, 1912
Norfolk, England
Boycott, Charles Cunningham
b. Mar 12, 1832
Burney, Fanny (Frances) b. Jun 13, 1752
Cavell, Edith b. 1865
Chapman, (Anthony) Colin (Bruce)
d. Dec 16, 1982
Cooper, Astley Paston, Sir
b. Aug 23, 1768
Greene, Richard b. Jun 1, 1985
Haggard, Henry Rider, Sir b. Jun 22, 1856
Murry, John Middleton d. May 13, 1957
Shadwell, Thomas b. 1642
Norham, England
Whitechurch, Victor Lorenzo
b. Mar 12, 1868
North Devon, England
Chichester, Francis Charles, Sir
b. Sep 17, 1901
North Hamptonshire, England
Dryden, John b. Aug 9, 1631
North Shields, England
Young, Alan (Angus) b. Nov 19, 1919

North Wiltshire, England
Jeffries, Richard b. Nov 6, 1848
Northam, England
Taylor, John Henry b. Mar 19, 1871
Taylor, John Henry d. Feb 10, 1963
Northampton, England
Arnold, Malcolm, Sir b. Oct 21, 1921
Bradstreet, Anne b. 1612
Carne, Judy b. Apr 27, 1939
Clare, John d. May 20, 1864
Crick, Francis Harry Compton
b. Jun 8, 1916
Douglas, Sholto (William Sholto)
d. Oct 29, 1969
Northamptonshire, England
Henry William Frederick Albert
d. Jun 9, 1974
Northumberland, England
Bunting, Basil b. 1900
Grey, Charles d. 1845
Northumbria, England
Bede the Venerable b. May 26, 673
Norton, England
Bairnsfather, Bruce d. Sep 29, 1959
Norton Park, England
Woodhull, Victoria Claflin d. Jun 10, 1927
Norwich, England
Ashford, Daisy d. Jan 15, 1972
Bullard, Edward Crisp, Sir b. Sep 21, 1907
Castle, Vernon b. May 2, 1887
Cotman, John S b. Aug 16, 1782
Crome, John b. Dec 22, 1768
Crome, John d. Apr 22, 1821
Gambling, John Bradley b. Apr 9, 1897
George, Graham Elias b. Apr 11, 1912
Sewell, Anna d. Apr 25, 1878
Norwood, England
Colvin, Sidney, Sir b. Jun 18, 1845
Nottingham, England
Dean, Christopher b. 1959
Hogwood, Christopher b. Sep 10, 1941
Torvill, Jane b. 1958
Nottinghamshire, England
Allenby, Edmund Hynman Allenby,
Viscount b. Apr 23, 1861
Arkwright, Richard, Sir d. Aug 3, 1792
Booth, William b. Apr 10, 1829
Brewster, William b. 1566
Butler, Samuel b. Dec 4, 1835
Cartwright, Edmund b. Apr 24, 1743
Carver, John b. 1576
Jayston, Michael b. Oct 29, 1936
Sillitoe, Alan b. Mar 4, 1928
Oakham, England
Oates, Titus b. 1649
Oare, England
Bottomley, Gordon d. Aug 25, 1948
Oates, England
Locke, John d. Oct 28, 1704
Odiham, England
Chamberlain, Neville d. Nov 9, 1940

Oldham, England
Brown, Louise Joy b. Jul 25, 1978
Turner, Eva b. Mar 10, 1892
Olton, England
Kendal, Felicity b. Sep 25, 1946
Ongar, England
Taylor, Jane d. Apr 12, 1824
Oswestry, England
Croft, Michael b. Mar 8, 1922
Owen, Wilfred b. Mar 18, 1893
Pym, Barbara Mary Crampton
b. Jun 2, 1913
Otterbourne, England
Yonge, Charlotte Mary b. Aug 11, 1823
Oulton, England
Bentley, Richard b. Jan 27, 1662
Borrow, George Henry d. Jul 26, 1881
Oxenhope, England
Butterfield, Herbert, Sir b. Oct 7, 1900
Oxford, England
Addinsell, Richard b. Jan 13, 1904
Angel, Heather b. Feb 9, 1909
Aubrey, John d. Jun 1697
Austin, John Langshaw d. Feb 8, 1960
Berkeley, George d. Jan 14, 1753
Beveridge, William Henry, Lord
d. Mar 16, 1963
Blackwell, Basil Henry, Sir
b. May 29, 1889
Bowra, Maurice, Sir d. Jul 4, 1971
Bradley, Henry d. May 23, 1923
Burton, Robert d. Jan 25, 1640
Busia, Kofi A d. Aug 28, 1978
Cary, Joyce (Arthur Joyce Lunel)
d. Mar 29, 1957
Coghill, Nevill Henry Kendall Aylmer
d. Nov 6, 1980
Cole, George Douglas Howard
d. Jan 14, 1959
Cranmer, Thomas d. Mar 21, 1556
Davenant, William, Sir b. Feb 1606
Douglas, Sholto (William Sholto)
b. Dec 23, 1893
DuPre, Jacqueline b. Jan 26, 1945
Edward the Confessor b. 1002
Garrod, Hethcote William d. Dec 25, 1960
Green, John Richard b. Dec 12, 1837
Haldane, J(ohn) B(urdon) S(anderson)
b. Nov 5, 1892
Haldane, John Scott d. Mar 14, 1936
Howes, Frank Stewart b. Apr 2, 1891
James, P(hyllis) D(orothy) b. Aug 3, 1920
John, King of England b. Dec 24, 1167
Krebs, Hans Adolf, Sir d. Nov 22, 1981
Latimer, Hugh d. Oct 16, 1555
Mathieson, Muir d. Aug 2, 1975
Mattingley, Garrett d. Dec 18, 1962
Murray, James Augustus Henry, Sir
d. Jul 26, 1915
Neurath, Otto d. Dec 22, 1945
Onions, Charles Talbut d. Jan 8, 1965

Osler, William, Sir d. Dec 29, 1919
Pater, Walter Horatio d. Jul 30, 1894
Raleigh, Walter Alexander, Sir
  d. May 18, 1922
Richard I b. Sep 8, 1157
Rothenstein, William, Sir d. Feb 14, 1945
Ryle, Martin, Sir b. Sep 27, 1918
Sayers, Dorothy Leigh b. 1893
Shirley, Ralph b. Dec 30, 1865
Shirley, Ralph d. Dec 29, 1946
Smedley, Agnes d. May 6, 1950
Steptoe, Patrick Christopher b. Jun 9, 1913
Swinton, Ernest Dunlop, Sir
  d. Jan 15, 1951
Tizard, Henry Thomas, Sir d. Oct 9, 1959
Toynbee, Philip (Theodore Philip)
  b. Jun 25, 1916
Warton, Thomas d. May 21, 1790
Waterhouse, Ellis Kirkham, Sir
  d. Sep 7, 1985
Wellesz, Egon d. Nov 9, 1974

Oxfordshire, England
Hailwood, Mike (Stanley Michael Bailey)
  b. Apr 4, 1940
Pym, Barbara Mary Crampton
  d. Jan 11, 1980

Oxton, England
Scott, Cyril (Meir) b. Sep 27, 1879

Paddington, England
Walker, Emery, Sir b. Apr 2, 1851

Paignton, England
Barker, Sue b. Apr 19, 1956

Painswick, England
Lohman, Ann Trow b. 1812

Pangbourne, England
Grahame, Kenneth d. Jul 6, 1932

Parbrook, England
Brown, Christy d. Sep 6, 1981

Peebleshire, England
Asquith, Emma Alice Margot
  b. Feb 2, 1864

Pelynt, England
Grigson, Geoffrey Edward Harvey
  b. Mar 2, 1902

Penkhull, England
Lodge, Oliver Joseph, Sir b. Jun 12, 1851

Penn, England
Soames, (Arthur) Christopher (John)
  b. Oct 12, 1920

Pentonville, England
Crippen, Hawley Harvey d. Nov 23, 1910

Pentonville Prison, England
Evans, Timothy d. Mar 9, 1950

Peterborough, England
Coghlan, Rose b. Mar 18, 1851
Royce, Frederick Henry, Sir
  b. Mar 27, 1863

Petersfield, England
Campbell, Clifford, Sir b. Jun 28, 1892
Horder, Thomas Jeeves d. Aug 13, 1955

Whitehead, (Walter) Edward
  d. Apr 16, 1978
Williams, Ursula Moray b. Apr 19, 1911

Petersham, England
Ashford, Daisy b. 1881
Vancouver, George d. Jun 10, 1798

Pimlico, England
Fenn, George Manville b. Jan 3, 1831

Pinner, England
John, Elton b. Mar 25, 1947

Plaistow, England
Essex, David b. Jul 23, 1947

Plymouth, England
Bligh, William, Captain b. Sep 9, 1754
Chichester, Francis Charles, Sir
  d. Aug 26, 1972
Dobson, Henry Austin b. Jan 18, 1840
Eastlake, Charles Lock b. Nov 17, 1793
Foot, Michael b. Jul 23, 1913
Francis, Trevor b. Apr 19, 1954
Frobisher, Martin d. Nov 22, 1594
Greene, Richard b. Aug 25, 1918
Hawkins, John, Sir b. 1532
Hodge, Frederick Webb b. Jan 5, 1864
Moffat, Donald b. Dec 26, 1930
Sinden, Donald b. Oct 9, 1923
Singer, Burns James Hyman
  d. Sep 8, 1964
Toye, Clive Roy b. Nov 23, 1932

Plympton, England
Reynolds, Joshua, Sir b. Jul 16, 1723

Pontefract, England
Pears, Charles b. Sep 9, 1870

Poole, England
LeCarre, John, pseud. b. Oct 19, 1931

Porlock Weir, England
Gregson, John d. Jan 8, 1975

Portsmouth, England
Besant, Walter, Sir b. Aug 14, 1836
Brunel, Isambard Kingdom b. Apr 9, 1806
Callaghan, James (Leonard James)
  b. Mar 27, 1912
Dickens, Charles John Huffam
  b. Feb 7, 1812
Manning, Olivia b. 1915
Meredith, George b. Feb 2, 1828

Prescott, England
Kemble, John Philip b. Feb 1, 1757

Preston, England
Arkwright, Richard, Sir b. Dec 23, 1732
Service, Robert William b. Jan 16, 1874
Thompson, Francis Joseph b. Dec 18, 1859

Prestwich, England
Sturgeon, William d. Dec 4, 1850

Pulborough, England
McNeile, Herman Cyril d. Aug 14, 1937

Pusey, England
Pusey, Edward Bouverie b. Mar 22, 1800

Salford, England
Clarke, Allan b. Apr 15, 1942
Delaney, Shelagh b. 1939
Finney, Albert b. May 9, 1936
Joule, James Prescott b. Dec 24, 1818
Powell, Robert b. Jun 1, 1944
Salisbury, England
Crawford, Michael Patrick b. Jan 19, 1942
Creasey, John d. Jun 9, 1973
Fawcett, Henry b. Aug 26, 1833
Gascoyne, David Emery b. Oct 10, 1916
Hitchcock, Tommy (Thomas, Jr.)
     d. Apr 19, 1944
John of Salisbury b. 1120
Massinger, Philip b. 1583
Saltash, England
Lympany, Moura b. Aug 18, 1916
Saltdean, England
Robey, George, Sir d. Nov 29, 1954
Salvington, England
Selden, John b. Dec 10, 1584
Sandbach, England
Richards, Ivor Armstrong b. Feb 26, 1893
Sanderstead, England
Bondfield, Margaret Grace d. Jun 16, 1953
Sandridge, England
Davis, John b. 1550
Sandringham, England
Alexandra Caroline Mary Charlotte
     d. Nov 20, 1925
Diana, Princess of Wales b. Jul 1, 1961
George VI b. Dec 14, 1895
George VI d. Feb 6, 1952
Henry William Frederick Albert
     b. Mar 31, 1900
Olaf V b. Jul 2, 1903
Sandwich, England
Greenstreet, Sydney Hughes
     b. Dec 27, 1879
Sawrey, England
Potter, Beatrix (Helen Beatrix)
     d. Dec 22, 1943
Scarborough, England
Bronte, Anne d. May 26, 1849
Laughton, Charles b. Jul 1, 1899
Sitwell, Edith, Dame b. 1887
Sitwell, Sacheverell, Sir b. Nov 15, 1897
Scunthorpe, England
Jacklin, Anthony b. Jul 7, 1944
Plowright, Joan b. Oct 28, 1929
Seaford, England
Lopokova, Lydia Vasilievna d. Jun 8, 1981
Seaham Harbour, England
Buttrick, George Arthur b. Mar 23, 1892
Semley, England
Morley, Robert b. May 26, 1908
Sevenoaks, England
Gribble, Harry Wagstaff Graham
     b. Mar 27, 1896
MacDonald, Malcolm John d. Jan 11, 1981

Shackhill, England
Wilcock, John b. 1927
Shadwell, England
Pater, Walter Horatio b. Aug 5, 1839
Shaftesbury, England
Canute d. Nov 12, 1035
Newton, Robert b. Jun 1, 1905
Upjohn, Richard b. Jan 22, 1802
Shaftsbury, England
Horder, Thomas Jeeves b. Jan 7, 1871
Sharpham Park, England
Fielding, Henry b. Apr 22, 1707
Sheffield, England
Allen, Rick b. Nov 1, 1963
Blackton, James Stuart b. Jan 5, 1875
Bradbury, Malcolm b. Sep 7, 1932
Carrack, Paul b. Apr 1951
Clark, Steve b. Apr 23, 1960
Cocker, "Joe" (Robert John)
     b. May 20, 1944
Coe, Sebastian Newbold b. Sep 29, 1956
Drabble, Margaret b. Jun 5, 1939
Elliott, Joe b. Aug 1, 1959
Herford, Oliver b. Dec 1, 1863
Lismer, Arthur b. Jun 27, 1885
Savage, Rick b. Dec 2, 1960
Shanks, Michael (James Michael)
     d. Jan 13, 1984
Siddal, Elizabeth Eleanor b. 1834
Varley, F(rederick) H(orseman)
     b. Jan 2, 1881
Wright, Harry (William Henry)
     b. Jan 10, 1835
Shelford, England
Davenport, Nigel b. May 23, 1928
Shepperton, England
Boorman, John b. Jan 18, 1933
Sherbourne, England
Wyatt, Thomas, Sir d. Oct 11, 1542
Sherringham, England
Hamilton, Patrick d. Sep 23, 1962
Shipbourne, England
Smart, Christopher b. Apr 22, 1722
Shipdham, England
Lofts, Norah Robinson b. Aug 27, 1904
Shipley, England
Richardson, Tony b. Jun 5, 1929
Shireborn, England
Bradley, James b. Mar 1693
Shirley, England
Powys, John Cowper b. Oct 8, 1872
Powys, Theodore Francis b. Dec 20, 1875
Shoreham, England
Sayer, "Leo" (Gerald) b. May 21, 1948
Shortlands, England
Swann, Michael Meredith, Sir
     b. Mar 1, 1920
Shrewsbury, England
Burney, Charles b. Apr 7, 1726
Darwin, Charles Robert b. Feb 12, 1809
Dyer, Charles b. Jul 17, 1928

Stoke-on-Trent, England
Craik, Dinah Maria Mulock
b. Apr 20, 1826
Leek, Sybil b. Feb 22, 1917
Tomlinson, Charles b. 1927
Wain, John Barrington b. Mar 14, 1925

Stratford, England
Hopkins, Gerard Manley b. Jun 28, 1844
Phillips, Adelaide b. 1833

Stratford-on-Avon, England
Priestley, J B (John Boynton)
d. Aug 14, 1984
Shakespeare, William b. Apr 23, 1564
Shakespeare, William d. Apr 23, 1616
Trevelyan, George Macaulay
b. Feb 16, 1876

Streatham, England
Bax, Arnold Edward Trevor, Sir
b. Nov 8, 1883
Dyce, William d. Feb 14, 1864
Maxim, Hiram Stevens, Sir
d. Nov 24, 1916

Streatley, England
Binyon, Laurence d. Mar 10, 1942

Sturmer, England
Rampling, Charlotte b. Feb 5, 1946

Sturminster, England
Powys, Theodore Francis d. Nov 27, 1953

Styal, England
Waite, Terry (Terence Hardy)
b. May 31, 1939

Styche, England
Clive, Robert b. Sep 29, 1725

Sudbury, England
Blunden, Edmund Charles d. Jan 20, 1974
Gainsborough, Thomas b. May 14, 1727
Perkin, William Henry, Sir d. Jul 14, 1907

Suffolk, England
Bacon, Nathaniel b. Jan 2, 1647
Cavendish, Thomas b. 1555
Doughty, Charles Montagu
b. Aug 19, 1843
Lowe, Nick b. Mar 25, 1949
Moodie, Susanna b. Dec 6, 1803
Munnings, Alfred James, Sir
b. Oct 8, 1878
Neill, A(lexander) S(utherland)
d. Sep 24, 1973
Winthrop, John b. Jan 12, 1588

Sunderland, England
Daiches, David b. Sep 2, 1912
Stewart, David b. Sep 19, 1952
Stewart, Mary (Florence Elinor)
b. Sep 17, 1916

Sunderstead, England
Muggeridge, Malcolm b. Mar 24, 1903

Surbiton, England
Cooper, Giles (Stannus) d. Dec 2, 1966

Surrey, England
Alden, Priscilla Mullens b. 1604
Angell, (Ralph) Norman, Sir
d. Oct 7, 1967
Ayres, Ruby Mildred d. Nov 14, 1955
Beaverbrook, William Maxwell Aitken,
Baron d. Jun 9, 1964
Beck, Jeff b. Jun 24, 1944
Campbell, Donald Malcolm
b. Mar 23, 1921
Cox, Constance b. Oct 25, 1915
Creasey, John b. Sep 17, 1908
Cushing, Peter b. May 26, 1913
Denny, Reginald Leigh d. Jun 16, 1967
Ellis, Havelock(Henry Havelock)
b. Feb 2, 1859
Ertz, Susan b. 1894
Faraday, Michael b. Sep 22, 1791
Field, Sid(ney Arthur) d. Feb 3, 1950
Getty, J(ean) Paul d. Jun 6, 1976
Gibbon, Edward b. Apr 27, 1737
Gibson, Wildred Wilson d. May 26, 1962
Hampson, Frank d. Jul 8, 1985
Idol, Billy b. Nov 30, 1955
Malthus, Thomas Robert b. Feb 17, 1766
Moore, George Edward b. Nov 4, 1873
Ockham, William of b. 1290
Tedder, Arthur William Tedder, Baron
d. Jun 3, 1967
Walton, Tony b. Oct 24, 1934
Wodehouse, P(elham) G(renville)
b. Oct 15, 1881

Sussex, England
Agar, Herbert Sebastian d. Nov 24, 1980
Barnes, Ernest William d. Nov 29, 1953
Bouche, Rene Robert d. Jul 3, 1963
Cobden, Richard b. Jun 3, 1804
Dashwood, Elizabeth Monica
b. Jun 9, 1890
Douglas, Alfred Bruce, Lord
d. Mar 20, 1945
Dunhill, Alfred Henry d. Jul 8, 1971
Fox, George d. Jan 13, 1691
Godden, Rumer, pseud. b. Dec 10, 1907
Godfrey, Isadore d. Sep 12, 1977
Homolka, Oscar d. Jan 27, 1978
Lowry, Malcolm (Clarence Malcolm)
d. Jun 1957
McLaren, Bruce Leslie d. Jun 2, 1970
Sheridan, Clare Consuelo d. May 31, 1970

Sutton, England
Crisp, Quentin, pseud. b. Dec 25, 1908
Knight, George Wilson b. Sep 19, 1897

Swaffham, England
Carter, Howard b. 1873

Swindon, England
Dors, Diana b. Oct 23, 1931
Wolfenden, John Frederick, Sir
b. Jun 26, 1906

Wallasey, England
Christiansen, Arthur b. Jul 27, 1904
Crichton, Charles b. Aug 6, 1910
Lewis, Saunders b. Oct 15, 1893
Stapledon, Olaf (Wiliam Olaf)
    b. May 10, 1886

Wallingford, England
Christie, Agatha Mary Clarissa Miller,
    Dame d. Jan 12, 1976
Inge, William Ralph d. Feb 26, 1954
Rotha, Paul d. Mar 7, 1984

Wallsend, England
Sting b. Oct 2, 1951

Walmer, England
Bridges, Robert Seymour b. Oct 23, 1844
Lister, Joseph d. Feb 10, 1912

Walsall, England
Jerome, Jerome Klapka b. May 2, 1859

Waltham Cross, England
Ballard, Russ(ell) b. Oct 31, 1947

Walton-on-Thames, England
Andrews, Julie b. Oct 1, 1935

Wandsworth, England
Joyce, William d. Jan 5, 1946

Wantage, England
Alfred the Great b. 849
Butler, Joseph b. May 18, 1692

Wardington, England
Marston, John b. 1575

Warfield Dale, England
Boulting, John d. Jun 19, 1985

Warwickshire, England
Bentley, John b. Dec 2, 1916
Congreve, Richard b. Sep 14, 1818
Drayton, Michael b. 1563
Eliot, George, pseud. b. Nov 22, 1819
Farnol, Jeffery b. Feb 10, 1878
Hailwood, Mike (Stanley Michael Bailey)
    d. Mar 23, 1981
Landor, Walter Savage b. Jan 30, 1775

Washington, England
Ireland, John d. Jun 12, 1962

Watford, England
Grillo, John b. Nov 29, 1942
Moore, Gerald b. Jul 30, 1899

Watthamstow, England
Morris, William b. Mar 24, 1834

Wavertree, England
Birrell, Augustine b. Jan 19, 1850

Weald, England
Lyly, John b. 1554

Weald of Kent, England
Caxton, William b. Aug 13, 1422

Weedon, England
Carroll, Leo G b. Oct 18, 1892

Wellington, England
Benson, Arthur Christopher
    b. Apr 24, 1862
Tylor, Edward Bennett, Sir d. Jan 2, 1917

Wells, England
Garrod, Hethcote William b. Jan 21, 1878
Goudge, Elizabeth b. Apr 24, 1900
Pearson, Cyril Arthur, Sir b. Feb 24, 1866

Welwyn, England
Gibbon, Lewis Grassic, pseud.
    d. Feb 21, 1935
Young, Edward d. Apr 5, 1765

Welwyn Garden, England
Purdom, Edmund b. Dec 19, 1926

Wembley, England
Churchill, Diana Josephine
    b. Aug 21, 1913
Moon, Keith b. Aug 23, 1946

West Brighton, England
Browne, "Phiz" (Hablot Knight)
    d. Jul 8, 1882

West Bronwich, England
Carroll, Madeleine b. Feb 26, 1909

West Cobham, England
Addison, John b. Mar 16, 1920

West Hartlepool, England
Mackenzie, Compton (Edward Montague,
    Sir) b. Jan 17, 1883

West Horsley, England
Ogilvy, David Mackenzie b. Jun 23, 1911

West Liss, England
Opie, Peter Mason d. Feb 5, 1982

West Malvern, England
Roget, Peter Mark d. Sep 12, 1869

West Milton, England
Allsop, Kenneth d. May 23, 1973

West Wickham, England
Carew, Thomas b. 1595

Westbury, England
Bartlett, Vernon b. Apr 30, 1894

Westcliff, England
Biggs, Edward George Power
    b. Mar 29, 1906

Westerham, England
Wolfe, James b. Jan 2, 1727

Westhorpe, England
Clarke, John b. Oct 8, 1609

Westminster, England
Caxton, William d. 1491
Clark, Colin Grant b. Nov 2, 1905
Edward I b. 1239
Edward V b. 1470
Hickey, William b. 1749
Jonson, Ben(jamin) b. Jun 11, 1572
Jonson, Ben(jamin) d. Apr 6, 1637
Pitt, William b. Nov 15, 1708
Purcell, Henry d. Nov 21, 1695
Skelton, John d. Jun 21, 1529
Spenser, Edmund d. Jan 13, 1599

Westmoreland, England
Staunton, Howard b. 1810

Weston-Super-Mare, England
Blackmore, Ritchie b. Apr 14, 1945
Cleese, John b. Oct 27, 1939

Weston-under-Penyard, England
Whiffen, Marcus b. Mar 4, 1916
Weybridge, England
Bisset, Jacqueline Fraser b. Sep 13, 1944
Davis, Colin b. Sep 25, 1927
Deeping, (George) Warwick
d. Apr 20, 1950
Hughes, Richard Arthur Warren
b. Apr 19, 1900
Weymouth, England
Henty, George Alfred d. Nov 16, 1902
Peacock, Thomas Love b. Oct 18, 1785
Wheathampstead, England
Owen, (John) Reginald b. Aug 5, 1887
Whitby, England
Bateson, William b. Aug 8, 1861
Jameson, Margaret Storm b. 1891
Whitchurch, England
Denning, Alfred Thompson
b. Jan 23, 1899
Soane, John, Sir b. Sep 10, 1753
Whitechapel, England
Mankowitz, Wolf b. Nov 7, 1924
Whitefield, England
Smith, "Dodie" (Dorothy Gladys) b. 1896
Whitstable, England
Horn, Alfred Aloysius, pseud.
d. Jun 26, 1927
Whittington, England
Sturgeon, William b. May 22, 1783
Whittlesea, England
Hartley, Leslie Poles b. Dec 30, 1895
Whitton, England
Lovesey, Peter Harmer b. Sep 10, 1936
Wickham, England
Warton, Joseph d. Feb 23, 1800
Widford, England
Eliot, John b. Aug 5, 1604
Wigan, England
Belmont, Eleanor Robson b. Dec 13, 1879
Willoughby, England
Smith, John b. Jan 1580
Wilts, England
Parker, Thomas b. Jun 8, 1595
Wiltshire, England
Balchin, Nigel Marlin b. Dec 3, 1908
Beaton, Cecil Walter Hardy, Sir
d. Jan 18, 1980
Clarendon, Edward Hyde, Earl
b. Feb 18, 1609
Morris, Desmond b. Jan 24, 1928
Sassoon, Siegfried d. Sep 1, 1967
Wren, Christopher, Sir b. Oct 20, 1632
Wimbledon, England
Gardiner, Reginald b. Feb 27, 1903
Gore, Charles b. Jan 22, 1853
Pullein-Thompson, Diana b.
Wimborne Minister, England
LeFleming, Christopher Kaye
b. Feb 26, 1908

Winborne, England
Prior, Matthew b. Jul 21, 1664
Winchcomb, England
Parrington, Vernon L(ouis) d. Jun 16, 1929
Winchester, England
Austen, Jane d. Jul 18, 1817
Cazenove, Christopher b. Dec 17, 1945
Grundy, Hugh b. Mar 6, 1945
Irving, Robert Augustine b. Aug 28, 1913
Justice, James Robertson d. Jul 2, 1975
Owsley, Frank Lawrence d. Oct 21, 1956
Rank, J(oseph) Arthur d. Mar 29, 1972
Toye, Francis b. Jan 27, 1883
Toye, Geoffrey b. Feb 17, 1889
Walton, Izaak d. Dec 15, 1683
Windsor, England
Alice (Mary Victoria Augusta Pauline)
b. Feb 25, 1883
Bonham, John Henry d. Sep 25, 1980
Collier, Constance b. Jan 22, 1878
Edward III b. 1312
George III d. Jan 29, 1820
George IV d. Jun 25, 1830
Hartnell, Norman Bishop, Sir
d. Jun 8, 1979
Knight, Charles b. 1791
Marlborough, John Churchill, Duke
d. Jun 16, 1722
Mountbatten of Burma, Louis Mountbatten,
Earl b. Jun 25, 1900
Spry, Constance d. Jan 3, 1960
Thompson, John S D d. Dec 2, 1894
Williams, Simon b. Jun 16, 1946
Winestead, England
Marvell, Andrew b. Mar 31, 1621
Winsford, England
Bevin, Ernest b. Mar 9, 1881
Witham, England
Sayers, Dorothy Leigh d. Dec 17, 1957
Wittersham, England
Symons, Arthur d. Jan 22, 1945
Woking, England
Bentley, Walter Owen d. Aug 13, 1971
Henley, William Ernest d. Jul 1, 1903
Ogilvy, Ian b. Sep 30, 1943
Wolverhampton, England
Chappell, William b. Sep 27, 1908
Noyes, Alfred b. Sep 16, 1880
Teyte, Maggie, Dame b. Apr 17, 1888
Wood Green, England
Swinnerton, Frank Arthur b. Aug 12, 1884
Woodbridge, England
Eno, Brian b. May 15, 1948
Woodbury, England
LeFleming, Christopher Kaye
d. Jun 19, 1985
Woodford, England
Crankshaw, Edward b. Jan 3, 1909
Patmore, Coventry Kersey Dighton
b. Jul 23, 1823
Smith Sydney b. Jun 6, 1771

Woodley, England
Barker, Ernest, Sir b. Sep 23, 1874

Woodstock, England
Churchill, Randolph Henry Spencer, Lord
b. Feb 13, 1849
Churchill, Winston Leonard Spencer, Sir
b. Nov 30, 1874
Edward the Black Prince b. 1330

Woolsthorpe, England
Newton, Isaac, Sir b. Dec 25, 1642

Woolwich, England
Gordon, Charles George b. Jan 28, 1833

Worcester, England
Brett, Simon Anthony Lee b. Oct 28, 1945
Mason, Dave b. May 10, 1946
Nuffield, William Richard Morris, Viscount
b. Oct 10, 1877

Worcestershire, England
Butler, Samuel b. Feb 14, 1612
Caton-Thompson, Gertrude
d. Apr 18, 1985
Garnett, Eve C R b.
Huskisson, William b. Mar 11, 1770

Worchester, England
Morris, William Richard b. Oct 10, 1877
Sherwood, Mary Martha d. Sep 22, 1851

Worksop, England
Boothroyd, John Basil b. Mar 4, 1910
Pleasence, Donald b. Oct 5, 1919

Wormington Orange, England
Ismay, Hastings Lionel, Baron
d. Dec 17, 1965

Worthing, England
Coates, Edith d. Jan 7, 1983
Gordon-Walker of Leyton, Patrick
Chrestien Gordon-Walker, Baron
b. Apr 7, 1907
Gray, Cecil d. Sep 9, 1951
Hudson, Joseph Lowthian d. Jul 15, 1912
Jeffries, Richard d. Aug 14, 1887
Lane, Edward William d. Aug 10, 1876

Wotton, England
Evelyn, John b. Oct 31, 1620
Evelyn, John d. Feb 27, 1706

Wotton-under-Edge, England
Biddle, John b. 1615

Wylam, England
Stephenson, George b. Jun 9, 1781

Wynd's Point, England
Lind, Jenny (Johanna Maria)
d. Nov 2, 1887

Yarmouth, England
Kell, Vernon, Sir b. 1873
Nash, Thomas d. 1601
Sewell, Anna b. Mar 30, 1820

Yattendon, England
Dempsey, Miles Christopher, Sir
d. Jun 6, 1969

York, England
Auden, W(ystan) H(ugh) b. Feb 21, 1907
Baker, Janet Abbott, Dame
b. Aug 21, 1933
Barry, John b. Nov 3, 1933
Cockcroft, John Douglas, Sir
b. May 27, 1897
Dench, Judith Olivia b. Dec 12, 1934
Fawkes, Guy b. 1570
Flaxman, John b. Jul 6, 1755
Halifax, Edward Frederick Lindley
d. Dec 23, 1959
Hansom, Joseph Aloysius b. Oct 26, 1803
Harrison, Peter b. Jun 14, 1716
Toynbee, Arnold Joseph d. Oct 22, 1975
Turpin, Dick (Richard) d. Apr 10, 1739
Ward, Barbara Mary b. May 23, 1914

Yorkshire, England
Allsop, Kenneth b. Jan 29, 1920
Bailey, Donald Coleman, Sir
b. Sep 5, 1901
Bishop, Isabella Lucy Bird b. 1832
Braine, John b. Apr 13, 1922
Carson, Jeannie b. May 28, 1929
Cayley, George, Sir b. Dec 27, 1773
Cayley, George, Sir d. Dec 15, 1857
Chippendale, Thomas b. Jun 5, 1718
Crapper, Thomas b. 1837
Davie, Donald b. Jul 17, 1922
Henry I b. 1068
Jackson, John Hughlings b. Apr 4, 1835
McCormick, Anne (Elizabeth) O'Hare
b. 1881
McLaughlin, John b. Jan 4, 1942
Moore, Henry b. Jul 30, 1898
Peel, Ronald Francis (Edward Waite)
b. Aug 22, 1912
Rigg, Diana b. Jul 20, 1938
Ryle, Gilbert d. Oct 6, 1976
Sidgwick, Henry b. May 31, 1838
Skelton, Robin b. Oct 12, 1925
Stephenson, James b. 1888
Wigglesworth, Michael b. Oct 18, 1631
Wilson, Peter Cecil b. Mar 8, 1913

Youlbury, England
Evans, Arthur John, Sir d. Jul 11, 1941

ESTONIA

Revel, Estonia
Koehler, Wolfgang b. Jan 21, 1887

ETHIOPIA

Addis Ababa, Ethiopia
Haile Selassie I d. Aug 27, 1975
Pankhurst, (Estelle) Sylvia d. Sep 27, 1960

Wollamo, Ethiopia
Mengistu, Haile Mariam b. 1937

FIJI

Suva, Fiji
Cakobau, Ratu George, Sir b. Nov 6, 1912

FINLAND

Hameenkyro, Finland
Sillanpaa, Frans E b. Sep 16, 1888
Helsingfors, Finland
Westermarck, Edward Alexander
b. Nov 20, 1862
Helsinki, Finland
Aalto, Alvar Henrik (Hugo)
d. May 11, 1976
Andreyev, Leonid Nikolayevich
d. Sep 12, 1919
Borg, Kim b. Aug 7, 1919
Granit, Ragnar Arthur b. Oct 30, 1900
Kekkonen, Urho Kaleva d. Aug 31, 1986
Kurri, Jarri b. May 18, 1960
Nurmi, Paavo d. Oct 2, 1973
Ritola, Ville d. Apr 24, 1982
Sillanpaa, Frans E d. Jun 3, 1964
Stiller, Mauritz b. Jul 17, 1883
Tanner, Valno Alfred b. Mar 12, 1881
Tanner, Valno Alfred d. Apr 19, 1966
Waltari, Mika b. Sep 19, 1908
Waltari, Mika d. Aug 26, 1979
Hiitola, Finland
Talvela, Martti Olavi b. Feb 4, 1935
Jarvenpaa, Finland
Sibelius, Jean d. Sep 20, 1957
Kuopio, Finland
Kolehmainen, Hannes b. Dec 9, 1889
Kyrkslatt, Finland
Saarinen, Eero b. Aug 20, 1910
Lapinlahti, Finland
Westermarck, Edward Alexander
d. Sep 3, 1939
Louhissaari, Finland
Mannerheim, Carl Gustav Emil, Baron
b. Jun 4, 1867
Peraseinajoki, Finland
Ritola, Ville b. Jan 18, 1896
Rantasalmi, Finland
Saarinen, Eliel b. Aug 28, 1873
Sveaborg, Finland
Belinsky, Vissarion b. May 30, 1811
Tavastehus, Finland
Sibelius, Jean b. Dec 8, 1865
Turkie, Finland
Chorell, Walentin b. Apr 4, 1912
Turku, Finland
Koivisto, Mauno Henrik b. Nov 25, 1923
Nurmi, Paavo b. Jun 13, 1897

FLANDERS

Jansen, Cornelis d. 1638
Renescure, Flanders
Comines, Philippe de b. 1445 3Fl

FRANCE

Alcott, John d. Jul 28, 1986
Ben Barka, Mehdi d. 1965
Brunhoff, Jean de b. 1899
Cartier, Pierre C b. 1878
Clayderman, Richard b. Dec 28, 1953
Dumont d'Urville, Jules Sebastian Cesar
b. May 23, 1790
Dunoyer de Segonzac, Andre
b. Jul 6, 1884
Henry I d. Dec 1, 1135
Lai, Francis b. 1933
Lattre de Tassigny, Jean de b. Feb 2, 1889
Owen, Wilfred d. Nov 4, 1918
Richthofen, Manfred von, Baron
d. Apr 21, 1918
Saint-Exupery, Antoine (Jean Baptiste
Marie Roger) de d. Jul 31, 1944
Sforza, Ludovico d. 1508
Sully, Maximilien de Bethune, Duc b. 1560
Sully, Maximilien de Bethune, Duc d. 1641
Trauner, Alexander b. 1906
Abloville, France
Marmontel, Jean Francois d. Dec 31, 1799
Agen, France
Scaliger, Joseph Justus b. Aug 4, 1540
Aix, France
Peiresc, Nicholas-Claude Fabri de
d. Jun 24, 1637
Aix-en-Provence, France
Cezanne, Paul b. Jan 19, 1839
Cezanne, Paul d. Oct 22, 1906
Guilbert, Yvette d. Feb 2, 1944
Milhaud, Darius b. Sep 4, 1892
Tournefort, Joseph Pitton de
b. Jun 3, 1656
Ungaro, Emanuel Matteotti
b. Feb 13, 1933
Aix-la-Chapelle, France
Burke, John d. Mar 27, 1848
Ajaccio, France
Napoleon I b. Aug 15, 1769
Albi, France
Toulouse-Lautrec (Monfa), (Henri Marie
Raymond de) b. Nov 24, 1864
Alencon, France
Therese of Lisieux b. 1873
Alsace, France
Dreyfus, Alfred b. Oct 9, 1859
Henner, Jean Jacques b. 1829
Ambert, France
Chabrier, (Alexis) Emmanuel
b. Jan 18, 1841
Amboise, France
Leonardo da Vinci d. May 2, 1519
Amiens, France
Benko, Paul Charles b. Jul 15, 1928
Bourget, Paul (Charles Joseph)
b. Sep 2, 1852

Sansom, Odette Marie Celine
  b. Apr 28, 1912
Verne, Jules d. Mar 24, 1905
Angers, France
Bazin, Andre b. Apr 18, 1918
Bazin, Rene b. Dec 26, 1853
Chevreul, Michel b. Aug 31, 1786
Souzay, Gerard b. Dec 8, 1920
Angouleme, France
Coulomb, Charles Augustin de
  b. Jun 14, 1736
Marguerite d'Angouleme b. Apr 11, 1492
Ravaillac, Francois b. 1578
Annecy, France
Sue, Eugene Joseph Marie d. Aug 3, 1875
Annoux, France
Davout, Louis Nicholas b. May 10, 1770
Antibes, France
Audiberti, Jacques b. Mar 25, 1899
Markevitch, Igor d. Mar 7, 1983
Stael, Nicolas de d. Mar 22, 1955
Walter, Marie Therese d. 1977
Aquitaine, France
Eleanor of Aquitaine b. 1122
Arcis-sur-Aube, France
Danton, Georges Jacques b. Oct 28, 1759
Argentan, France
Comines, Philippe de d. 1511
Leger, Fernand b. Feb 4, 1881
Argenteuil, France
Braque, Georges b. May 13, 1882
Arras, France
Robespierre, Maximilien Francois de
  b. May 6, 1758
Thomas, Edward d. Apr 9, 1917
Aubagne, France
Pagnol, Marcel Paul b. Apr 18, 1895
Auteuil, France
Home, Daniel Douglas d. Jun 21, 1886
Auvergne, France
Estaing, Charles Henri Hector, Comte d'
  b. Nov 28, 1729
Teilhard de Chardin, Pierre
  b. May 1, 1881
Auvers, France
Daubigny, Charles Francois
  d. Feb 19, 1878
Van Gogh, Vincent Willem d. Jul 29, 1890
Avignon, France
Bolitho, William d. Jun 2, 1930
Boulle, Pierre Francois Marie-Louis
  b. Feb 20, 1912
Eckhart, Johannes d. 1327
Messiaen, Olivier b. Dec 10, 1908
Mill, John Stuart d. May 8, 1873
Avranches, France
Ponty, Jean-Luc b. Sep 29, 1942
Babizon, France
Bodmer, Karl d. Oct 30, 1893
Baisyin Brabant, France
Godfrey of Bouillon b. 1058

Balaruc les Bains, France
Montgolfier, Joseph Michel
  d. Jun 26, 1810
Bandol, France
Kastler, Alfred d. Jan 7, 1984
Lumiere, Louis Jean d. Jun 6, 1948
Banyuls sur Mer, France
Maillol, Aristide b. Dec 8, 1861
Maillol, Aristide d. Oct 5, 1944
Bar-le-Duc, France
Poincare, Raymond b. Aug 20, 1860
Barbizon, France
Millet, Jean Francois d. Jan 20, 1875
Rousseau, (Pierre Etienne) Theodore
  d. Dec 22, 1867
Barcelonayye, France
Reynaud, Paul b. Oct 15, 1878
Barr, France
Grasse, Count Francois Joseph Paul de
  b. Sep 13, 1722
Barritz, France
Borotra, Jean Robert b. Aug 13, 1898
Basel, France
Froben, Johann d. Oct 1527
Bassens, France
Bandello, Matteo d. 1561
Bassillac, France
Bonnet, Georges b. Jul 23, 1889
Bayonne, France
Cassin, Rene b. Oct 5, 1887
Laffite, Jean b. Aug 29, 1780
Bazentin, France
Lamarck, Jean Baptiste Pierre
  b. Aug 1, 1744
Bealieu, France
Bennett, James Gordon, Jr.
  d. May 14, 1918
Beaugency, France
Charles, Jacques-Alexandre-Cesar
  b. Nov 12, 1746
Beaugensier, France
Peiresc, Nicholas-Claude Fabri de
  b. Dec 1, 1580
Beaumont-en-Auge, France
Laplace, Pierre Simon, Marquis de
  b. Mar 28, 1749
Beaumont-Hamel, France
Saki, pseud. d. Nov 13, 1916
Beaune, France
Copeau, Jacques d. Oct 20, 1949
Beauvais, France
Givenchy, Hubert de b. Feb 21, 1927
Beigles, France
Dache, Lilly b. 1904
Bellac, France
Giraudoux, Jean b. Oct 29, 1882
Bellay, France
Brillat-Savarin, Jean Anthelme
  b. Apr 1, 1755
Belleme, France
Martin du Gard, Roger d. Aug 22, 1958

Cajarc, France
Sagan, Francoise, pseud. b. Jun 21, 1935
Calais, France
Breton, Jules Adolphe b. 1827
Brown, Ford Maddox b. 1821
Debreu, Gerard b. Jul 4, 1921
Varesi, Felice b. 1813
Cambo-les-Bains, France
Bidault, Georges d. Jan 27, 1983
Cambrai, France
Bleriot, Louis b. Jul 1, 1872
Fenelon, Francois de Salignac
   d. Jan 7, 1715
Cannes, France
DeCuevas, Marquis d. Feb 22, 1961
Merimee, Prosper d. Sep 23, 1870
Monod, Jacques d. May 31, 1976
Philipe, Gerard b. Dec 4, 1922
Pons, Lily b. Apr 12, 1904
Rachel d. Jan 3, 1858
Tocqueville, Alexis, Comte de
   d. Apr 16, 1859
Van Zandt, Marie d. Dec 31, 1919
Whitlock, Brand d. May 24, 1934
Cantal, France
Pompidou, Georges Jean Raymond
   b. Jul 5, 1911
Carcassonne, France
Cayatte, Andre b. Feb 3, 1909
Carhaix, France
LaTour D'Auvergne, Theophile de
   b. Nov 23, 1743
Carlot, France
Bayle, Pierre b. Nov 18, 1647
Cartignie, France
Maurey, Pierre b. Jul 5, 1928
Castelnov, France
Brousse, Amy Elizabeth Thorpe d. 1963
Castelsarrasen, France
Cadillac, Antoine d. Oct 15, 1730
Castres, France
Jaures, Jean Leon b. Sep 3, 1859
Peyrefitte, Roger b. Aug 17, 1907
Cauchy a la Tour, France
Petain, Henri Philippe b. Apr 24, 1856
Cauderan, France
Olaf, Pierre b. Jul 14, 1928
Cavaillon, France
Castil-Blaze, Francois-Joseph
   b. Dec 1, 1784
Chaillot, France
Barras, Paul Francois Jean Nicolas, Comte
   de d. Jan 29, 1829
Challans, France
Auriol, Jacqueline Douet b. Nov 5, 1917
Chalon-sur-Saone, France
Abelard, Pierre d. Apr 21, 1142
Chalons-sur-Marne, France
Fitch, (William) Clyde d. Sep 4, 1909
Chalons-sur-Mayenne, France
Renard, Jules b. Feb 22, 1864

Chaluz, France
Richard I d. Apr 6, 1199
Chamagne, France
Lorrain, Claude Gellee b. 1600
Chambourcy, France
Derain, Andre d. Sep 10, 1954
Champrosay, France
Daudet, Alphonse Marie Leon
   d. Dec 16, 1897
Chamrosay, France
Goncourt, Edmond Louis Antoine Huot
   d. Jul 16, 1896
Chanteloup, France
Cartier-Bresson, Henri b. Aug 22, 1908
Chantilly, France
Prevost d'Exiles, Antoine Francois, Abbe
   d. Nov 23, 1763
Chappes, France
Camus, Marcel b. Apr 21, 1912
Charenton, France
Delacroix, (Ferdinand Victor) Eugene
   b. Apr 26, 1798
Eluard, Paul d. Nov 18, 1952
Sade, Marquis (Donatien Alphonse
   Francoise) de d. Dec 2, 1814
Charlesville, France
Rimbaud, (Jean Nicolas) Arthur
   b. Oct 20, 1854
Charmes-sur-Moselle, France
Barres, Maurice b. Sep 22, 1862
Chateau Bourbon, France
Rode, Jacques Pierre Joseph
   d. Nov 25, 1830
Chateau de Malrome, France
Toulouse-Lautrec (Monfa), (Henri Marie
   Raymond de) d. Sep 9, 1901
Chateau Thierry, France
LaFontaine, Jean de b. Jul 8, 1621
Treptow, Martin A d. Jul 28, 1918
Chateauroux, France
Boussac, Marcel b. Apr 17, 1889
Depardieu, Gerard b. Dec 27, 1948
Chatelden, France
Laval, Pierre b. Jun 28, 1883
Chatellerault, France
Chinard, Gilbert b. Oct 17, 1881
Chatou, France
Derain, Andre b. Jun 10, 1880
Chavaniac, France
Lafayette, Marie Joseph Paul, Marquis
   b. Sep 6, 1757
Chaville, France
Schwob, Marcel b. Aug 23, 1867
Soupault, Philippe b. Aug 2, 1897
Chenevelles, France
Tiffeau, Jacques Emile b. Oct 11, 1927
Cherbourg, France
Barthes, Roland b. Nov 12, 1915
Marais, Jean b. Dec 11, 1913
Nicolet, Jean b. 1598
Roosevelt, Theodore, Jr. d. Jul 12, 1944

Chevry Cossigny, France
Pathe, Charles b. Dec 25, 1863
Chimay, France
Froissart, Jean d. 1410
Chinon, France
Rabelais, Francois b. 1494
Choisy le Roi, France
Rouget de Lisle, Claude Joseph
d. Jun 20, 1836
Ciboure, France
Ravel, Maurice Joseph b. Mar 7, 1875
Clairvaux, France
Bernard of Clairvaux, Saint
d. Aug 20, 1153
Clamecy, France
Rolland, Romain b. Jan 29, 1866
Clermont, France
Apollinaris Sidonius, Gaius Sollius d. 487
Pascal, Blaise b. Jun 19, 1623
Cluny, France
Prudhon, Pierre b. Apr 4, 1758
Cognac, France
Monnet, Jean (Omer Gabriel)
b. Nov 9, 1888
Collioure, France
Machado, Antonio d. Feb 22, 1939
Collonges, France
Bocuse, Paul b. Feb 11, 1926
Colmar, France
Bartholdi, Auguste (Frederic Auguste)
b. Apr 2, 1834
Jean, Grand Duke of Luxembourg
b. Jan 5, 1921
Colombey les deux Eglises, France
DeGaulle, Charles Andre Joseph Marie
d. Nov 9, 1970
Compiegne, France
Lenglen, Suzanne b. May 24, 1899
Conde, France
DesPres, Josquin d. Aug 27, 1521
Conde sur l'Escaut, France
DesPres, Josquin b. 1445
Corbeil, France
Dauphin, Claude Le Grand Maria Eugene
b. Aug 19, 1903
Cormeilles en Parisis, France
Daguerre, Louis Jacques Mande
b. Nov 18, 1787
Coupvray, France
Braille, Louis b. Jan 4, 1809
Courbevoie, France
Arletty b. May 15, 1898
Celine, Louis-Ferdinand b. May 27, 1894
Craon, France
Volney, (Constantin) Francois Chasseboeuf
b. Feb 3, 1757
Cravant, France
Gilson, Etienne Henry d. Sep 19, 1978
Creteil, France
Barzun, Jacques Martin b. Nov 30, 1907
Gleizes, Albert L b. 1881

Croisset, France
Flaubert, Gustave d. May 8, 1880
Crozon, France
Jouvet, Louis b. Dec 24, 1887
Cuiseaux, France
Vuillard, (Jean) Edouard b. Nov 11, 1868
Dax, France
Utrillo, Maurice d. Nov 5, 1955
Deauville, France
Boudin, Eugene Louis d. Aug 8, 1898
Ford, Ford Madox d. Jun 26, 1939
Decazevelle, France
Calve, Emma b. Aug 15, 1858
Deusto, France
Cassou, Jean b. Jul 9, 1879
Dieppe, France
John, Gwendolyn Mary d. 1939
Dieuze, France
Charpentier, Gustave b. Jun 25, 1860
Digne, France
David-Neel, Alexandra d. Sep 8, 1969
Dijon, France
Bossuet, Jacques Benigne b. Sep 27, 1627
Eiffel, Alexandre Gustave b. Dec 15, 1832
Giraud, Henri Honore d. Mar 11, 1949
Guillemin, Roger b. Jan 11, 1924
Rameau, Jean-Philippe b. Sep 25, 1683
Sluter, Claus d. 1406
Dinan, France
Du Guesclin, Bertrand b. 1320
Dole, France
Douvillier, Suzanne Theodore Vaillande
b. Sep 28, 1778
Pasteur, Louis b. Dec 27, 1822
Domont, France
Houdry, Eugene Jules b. Apr 18, 1892
Domremy, France
Joan of Arc b. Jan 6, 1412
Dormans, France
Ledoux, Claude Nicolas b. Mar 21, 1736
Draguignan, France
Thill, Georges d. Oct 17, 1984
Drancy, France
Jacob, Max d. Mar 5, 1944
Draveil, France
Annaud, Jean-Jacques b. Jan 10, 1943
Dreux, France
Philidor, Francois Andre Danican
b. Sep 7, 1726
Drucat-Plessiel, France
Lesueur, Jean-Francois b. Feb 15, 1760
Dunkirk, France
Bart, Jean b. Oct 21, 1651
Elbeuf, France
Maurois, Andre b. Jul 26, 1885
Epinal, France
Beroff, Michel b. 1950
Durkheim, Emile b. Apr 15, 1858
Ermenonville, France
Rousseau, Jean Jacques d. Jul 2, 1778

Ermont, France
Printemps, Yvonne b. Jul 25, 1898
Etaples, France
Tanner, Henry Ossawa d. May 25, 1937
Eymet, France
Lemoyne, Jean-Baptiste b. Apr 3, 1751
Falaise, France
William the Conquerer b. 1027
Fauquembergue, France
Monsigny, Pierre-Alexandre
b. Oct 17, 1729
Figeac, France
Boyer, Charles b. Aug 28, 1899
Champollion, Jean Francois
b. Dec 23, 1790
Fontainebleau, France
Decamps, Alexandre Gabriel
d. Aug 22, 1860
Mansfield, Katherine d. Jan 9, 1923
Pasdeloup, Jules Etienne d. Aug 13, 1887
Reinhardt, Django (Jean Baptiste)
d. May 16, 1953
Fontaines-les-Dijon, France
Bernard of Clairvaux, Saint b. 1090
Fontenay, France
Bonnard, Pierre b. Oct 30, 1867
Forcalquier, France
Dufy, Raoul d. Mar 23, 1953
Fort-de-Joux, France
Toussaint l'Ouverture, Pierre Dominique
d. Apr 7, 1803
Fox-Amphoux, France
Barras, Paul Francois Jean Nicolas, Comte
de b. Jun 30, 1755
Foyles Lyon, France
Achard, Marcel b. Jul 5, 1900
Fumay, France
Plancon, Pol-Henri b. Jun 12, 1854
Gan, France
Mathieu, Noel Jean b. May 3, 1916
Gascony, France
Coste, Dieudonne b. Nov 4, 1893
Generac, France
Salignac, Eustase Thomas b. Mar 29, 1867
Giens, France
Leger, Alexis St. Leger (Marie-Rene Alexis
St. Leger) d. Sep 20, 1975
Gif-sur-Yvette, France
Leger, Fernand d. Aug 17, 1955
Giverny, France
Monet, Claude d. Dec 5, 1926
Givet, France
Mehul, Etienne Nicolas b. Jun 22, 1763
Granville, France
Dior, Christian b. Jan 21, 1905
Grasse, France
Fragonard, Jean Honore b. Apr 5, 1732
Fragonard, Jean Honore d. Aug 22, 1806
Journet, Marcel b. Jul 25, 1870
Lanvin, Jeanne b. 1867

Grenoble, France
Agrippa, Heinrich Cornelius
d. Feb 18, 1535
Arnoux, Rene Alexandre b. Jul 4, 1948
Fantin-Latour, (Ignace) Henri
b. Jan 14, 1836
Stendhal b. Jan 23, 1783
Grez-sur-Loing, France
Delius, Frederick d. Jun 10, 1934
Guebwiller, France
Kastler, Alfred b. May 3, 1902
Guingamp, France
Renault, Gilbert (Leon Etienne Theodore)
d. Jul 30, 1984
Guise, France
Desmoulins, Camille b. Mar 2, 1760
Hazebrouck, France
Maeght, Aime b. Apr 27, 1906
Hendaye, France
Loti, Pierre, pseud. d. Jun 10, 1923
Herrlingen, France
Rommel, Erwin Johannes Eugin
d. Jul 18, 1944
Hesdin, France
Prevost d'Exiles, Antoine Francois, Abbe
b. Apr 1, 1697
Honfleur, France
Boudin, Eugene Louis b. Jul 12, 1824
Satie, Erik b. May 17, 1866
Ile Bourbon, France
Bourdonnais, Louis Charles de la b. 1795
Jarcy, France
Boieldieu, Francois Adrien d. Oct 8, 1834
Jarnac, France
Mitterrand, Francois Maurice
b. Oct 26, 1916
Joigny, France
Ayme, Marcel b. Mar 28, 1902
Jouy, France
Jouy, Victor (Joseph-Etienne) de b. 1764
Juan les Pins, France
Elliott, Maxine d. Mar 5, 1940
Hopwood, Avery d. Jul 1, 1928
Kerlouanec, France
Laennec, Rene Theophile Hyacinthe
d. Aug 13, 1826
L'Isle Sorgue, France
Char, Rene (Emile) b. Jun 14, 1907
L'Isle-Adam, France
Breuil, Henri Abbe d. Aug 14, 1961
La Baslide-Fortumiere, France
Murat, Joachim b. Mar 25, 1767
La Baule, France
Vuillard, (Jean) Edouard d. Jun 21, 1940
La Chanaie, France
Lesseps, Ferdinand Marie de
d. Dec 7, 1894
La Chapelle-d'Angillon, France
Alain-Fournier, pseud. b. Oct 3, 1886
La Cote, France
Berlioz, Louis Hector b. Dec 11, 1803

La Fleche, France
Charlevoix, Pierre Francis Xavier de
d. Feb 1, 1761
La Haye, France
Descartes, Rene b. Mar 31, 1596
Laferte-Milon, France
Racine, Jean Baptiste b. Dec 1639
Lancieux, France
Service, Robert William d. Sep 11, 1958
Langres, France
Diderot, Denis b. Oct 5, 1713
Languedoc, France
Du Guesclin, Bertrand d. Jul 13, 1380
Psalmanazar, George b. 1679
Laon, France
Marquette, Jacques, Pere b. Jun 1, 1637
LaRochelle, France
DeVries, David Pieterson b. 1592
Fromentin, Eugene b. Oct 24, 1820
Fromentin, Eugene d. Aug 27, 1876
Laroche, Guy b. 1923
Laval, France
Jarry, Alfred b. Oct 8, 1873
Pare, Ambroise b. 1510
Rousseau, Henri b. May 21, 1844
Le Cateau, France
Matisse, Henri b. Dec 31, 1869
Le Croisic, France
Becquerel, Antoine Henri d. Aug 25, 1908
Le Havre, France
Coty, Rene b. Mar 20, 1882
Dubuffet, Jean b. Jul 31, 1901
Dufy, Raoul b. Jun 3, 1877
Honegger, Arthur b. Mar 10, 1892
Scudery, Madeleine de b. 1607
Le Mans, France
Francaix, Jean b. May 23, 1912
Le Pecq, France
Tati, Jacques b. Oct 9, 1908
Le Vesinet, France
Alain, pseud. d. Jun 2, 1951
LeCannet, France
Anderson, Margaret Carolyn
d. Oct 18, 1973
Bonnard, Pierre d. Jan 23, 1947
Lempdes, France
Lamy, Jean Baptist b. Oct 14, 1814
Lens, France
Carpentier, Georges b. Jan 12, 1894
LePuy, France
Wagner, Roger b. Jan 16, 1914
Les Laumets, France
Cadillac, Antoine b. Mar 5, 1658
Les Ternes, France
Herold, Louis Joseph Ferdinand
d. Jan 19, 1833
Lethor, France
Brodovitch, Alexey d. Apr 15, 1971
Levandou, France
Reyer, (Louis) Ernest (Etienne)
d. Jan 15, 1909

Leyden, France
Scaliger, Joseph Justus d. Jan 21, 1609
Libourne, France
Atget, Eugene (Jean-Eugene-Auguste)
b. 1855
Lille, France
Adoree, Renee b. Sep 30, 1898
DeGaulle, Charles Andre Joseph Marie
b. Nov 22, 1890
Duvivier, Julien b. Oct 8, 1896
Lalo, Edouard Victor Antoine
b. Jan 27, 1823
Monnoyer, Jean-Baptiste b. 1636
Limay, France
Chausson, Ernest d. Jun 10, 1899
Limoges, France
Renoir, (Pierre) Auguste b. Feb 25, 1841
Lisieux, France
Therese of Lisieux d. Sep 30, 1897
Loches, France
Vigny, Alfred Victor, Comte de
b. Mar 27, 1797
Lodeve, France
Auric, Georges b. Feb 15, 1899
Loiret, France
Becquerel, Antoine-Cesar b. Mar 7, 1788
Lons le Saulnier, France
Rouget de Lisle, Claude Joseph
b. May 10, 1760
Lorette, France
Prost, Alain Marie Pascal b. Feb 24, 1955
Lorient, France
Masse, Victor b. Mar 7, 1822
Lorraine, France
Margaret of Anjou b. Mar 23, 1430
Louey, France
Duclos, Jacques b. Oct 2, 1896
Lourdes, France
Bernadette of Lourdes b. Jan 7, 1844
Lumeville, France
Brandel, Fernand Paul b. Aug 24, 1902
Lunel, France
Feuillade, Louis b. Feb 19, 1873
Luneville, France
LaTour, George Dumesnil de
d. Jan 30, 1652
Lyon, France
Grolier, Jean b. 1479
Lyons, France
Ampere, Andre Marie b. Jan 22, 1775
Apollinaris Sidonius, Gaius Sollius b. 430
Bonaventure, Saint d. Jul 15, 1274
Borel d'Hauterive, Petrus b. Jun 28, 1809
Chevallier, Gabriel b. May 1895
Cochet, Henri b. Dec 14, 1901
Cret, Paul P(hilippe) b. Oct 23, 1876
Estienne, Henri d. 1598
Farrere, Claude, pseud. b. Apr 27, 1876
Gieseking, Walter Wilhelm b. Nov 5, 1895
Herriot, Edouard d. Mar 26, 1957
Jarre, Maurice b. Sep 13, 1924

Jussieu, Bernard de b. Aug 17, 1699
Lassale, Jean b. Dec 14, 1847
Lumiere, Auguste Marie Louis
   d. Apr 10, 1954
Martinon, Jean b. Jan 10, 1910
Meissonier, Jean Louis Ernest
   b. Feb 21, 1815
Puvis de Chavannes, Pierre Cecile
   b. Dec 14, 1824
Radisson, Pierre Espirit b. 1636
Recamier, (Jeanne Francoise) Julie(tte)
   Adelaide, Madame b. 1777
Saint-Exupery, Antoine (Jean Baptiste
   Marie Roger) de b. Jun 29, 1900
Widor, Charles Marie Jean Albert
   b. Feb 24, 1844

Macon, France
Lamartine, Alphonse Marie Louis de Prat
   de b. Oct 21, 1790

Magny Cours, France
Laffite, Jacques Henry Sabin
   b. Nov 21, 1943

Maillane, France
Mistral, Frederic b. Sep 8, 1830
Mistral, Frederic d. Mar 25, 1914

Maisons-Lafitte, France
Cocteau, Jean b. Jul 5, 1889

Malmaison, France
Josephine d. May 29, 1814

Manosque, France
Giono, Jean b. Mar 30, 1895
Giono, Jean d. Oct 9, 1970

Mans-en-Baroeul, France
Butor, Michel b. Sep 14, 1926

Mantauban, France
Friedel, Charles d. Apr 20, 1899

Marly, France
Mansart, Jules Hardouin d. May 11, 1708

Marseilles, France
Artaud, Antonin b. Sep 4, 1896
Baudo, Serge b. Jul 16, 1927
Bejart, Maurice b. Jan 1, 1927
Brian, Marcel b. Nov 21, 1895
Casadesus, Gaby Lhote b. Aug 9, 1901
Crespin, Regine b. Mar 23, 1927
Daumier, Honore b. Feb 26, 1808
Fernandel b. May 8, 1903
Francescatti, Zino Rene b. Aug 9, 1902
Jourdan, Louis b. Jun 19, 1920
Maurel, Victor b. Jun 17, 1848
Muratore, Lucien b. Aug 29, 1876
Nuyen, France b. Jul 31, 1939
Ozanam, Frederic d. Sep 8, 1853
Petipa, Marius b. Mar 11, 1822
Petri, Angelo b. Sep 5, 1883
Phillips, Lena Madesin d. May 21, 1955
Rampal, Jean-Pierre b. Jul 1, 1922
Rebuffat, Gaston Louis Simon
   b. May 7, 1921
Revel, Jean Francois b. Jan 19, 1924

Reyer, (Louis) Ernest (Etienne)
   b. Dec 1, 1823
Rimbaud, (Jean Nicolas) Arthur
   d. Nov 10, 1891
Rostand, Edmond Alexis b. Apr 1, 1868
Simon, Simone b. Apr 23, 1913
Thiers, Adolphe b. Apr 15, 1797

Maubeuge, France
Mabuse, Jan de b. 1478

Melun, France
Bonheur, Rosa (Marie Rosalie) d. 1899

Menerbes, France
Cameron, Roderick W d. Sep 18, 1985

Menton, France
Erickson, Eric d. Jan 24, 1983
LeGallienne, Richard d. Sep 14, 1947
Yeats, William Butler d. Jan 28, 1939

Mentone, France
Green, John Richard d. Mar 7, 1883

Merey, France
Quesnay, Francois b. Jun 4, 1694

Metz, France
Curel, Francois de b. Jun 10, 1854
Lemnitz, Tiana b. Oct 26, 1897
Pierne, Gabriel b. Aug 16, 1863
Schuman, Robert d. Sep 4, 1963
Thomas, (Charles Louis) Ambroise
   b. Aug 5, 1811
Verlaine, Paul Marie b. Mar 30, 1844

Meudon, France
Celine, Louis-Ferdinand d. Jul 4, 1961
DuPre, Marcel d. May 30, 1971
Rodin, Auguste (Francois Auguste Rene)
   d. Nov 17, 1917

Millan, France
Calve, Emma d. Jan 6, 1942

Millemont, France
Dufresne, Charles b. 1876

Mont-Dore, France
Maison, Rene d. Jul 15, 1962

Mont-Saint-Pere, France
L'Hermitte, Leon Augustin b. 1844

Montagne, France
Alain, pseud. b. Mar 3, 1868

Montargis, France
Boussac, Marcel d. Mar 31, 1980

Montauban, France
Ingres, Jean Auguste Dominique
   b. Aug 29, 1780

Montaud, France
Massenet, Jules Emile Frederic
   b. May 12, 1842

Montbard, France
Buffon, Georges Louis Leclerc
   b. Sep 7, 1707

Montbeliard, France
Cuvier, Georges, Baron b. Aug 23, 1769

Montbrison, France
Boulez, Pierre b. Mar 26, 1925

Montigny-le-Roi, France
Flammarion, Camille b. Feb 25, 1842

Nogent-sur-Marne, France
Sablon, Jean Georges b. Mar 25, 1909
Nohant, France
Sand, George, pseud. d. Jun 8, 1876
Noisy, France
Delannoy, Jean b. Jan 12, 1908
Nolay, France
Carnot, Lazare Nicolas b. May 13, 1753
Normandy, France
Breton, Andre b. Feb 18, 1896
Douglas, Keith Castellain d. Jun 1944
Guizot, Francois Pierre d. 1874
Maupassant, Guy de (Henri Rene Albert
Guy de) b. Aug 5, 1850
Millet, Jean Francois b. Oct 4, 1814
Montfort, Simon de b. 1208
Signoret, Simone Henrietta Charlotte
d. Sep 30, 1985
Noyelles Godault, France
Thorez, Maurice b. Apr 28, 1900
Noyon, France
Calvin, John b. Jul 10, 1509
Oloron St. Marie, France
Singher, Martial b. Aug 14, 1904
Opio, France
Popov, Dusko d. Aug 21, 1981
Ornans, France
Courbet, Gustave b. Jun 10, 1819
Vernier, Pierre b. Aug 19, 1580
Vernier, Pierre d. Sep 14, 1637
Orne, France
Mollet, Guy b. Dec 31, 1905
Pallet, France
Abelard, Pierre b. 1079
Pamiers, France
Faure, Gabriel Urbain b. May 12, 1845
Paris, France
Achard, Marcel d. Sep 4, 1974
Adam, Adolphe Charles b. Jul 24, 1803
Adam, Adolphe Charles d. May 3, 1856
Adamov, Arthur d. Mar 16, 1970
Adjani, Isabelle b. Jun 27, 1955
Aga Khan, Sadruddin, Prince
b. Jan 17, 1932
Aimee, Anouk b. Apr 27, 1934
Alembert, Jean le Rond d'
b. Nov 16, 1717
Alembert, Jean le Rond d' d. Oct 29, 1783
Alexander of Hales d. 1245
Allegret, Yves b. Oct 13, 1907
Annabella b. Jul 14, 1912
Apollinaire, Guillaume d. Nov 10, 1918
Aragon, Louis Marie Antoine Alfred
b. Oct 3, 1897
Aragon, Louis Marie Antoine Alfred
d. Dec 24, 1982
Artaud, Antonin d. Mar 4, 1948
Atget, Eugene (Jean-Eugene-Auguste)
d. Aug 1927
Attwood, William b. Jul 14, 1919

Auber, Daniel Francois Esprit
d. May 12, 1871
Audiard, Michel b. May 15, 1920
Audiard, Michel d. Jul 28, 1985
Audiberti, Jacques d. Jul 10, 1965
Aumont, Jean-Pierre b. Jan 5, 1909
Auric, Georges d. Jul 23, 1983
Auriol, Vincent d. Jan 1, 1966
Ayme, Marcel d. Oct 14, 1967
Aznavour, Charles b. May 22, 1924
Babeuf, Francois Noel d. Apr 27, 1797
Baker, Josephine d. Apr 12, 1975
Baldwin, James Mark d. Nov 8, 1934
Balmain, Pierre Alexandre d. Jun 29, 1982
Baltard, Victor b. 1805
Balthus b. Feb 29, 1908
Balzac, Honore de d. Aug 18, 1850
Barbier, Jules b. Mar 8, 1825
Barbier, Jules d. Jan 16, 1901
Bardot, Brigitte b. Sep 28, 1934
Barney, Natalie Clifford d. Feb 2, 1972
Barres, Maurice d. Dec 4, 1923
Barthes, Roland d. Mar 25, 1980
Bartholdi, Auguste (Frederic Auguste)
d. Oct 4, 1904
Baudelaire, Charles Pierre b. Apr 9, 1821
Baudelaire, Charles Pierre d. Aug 31, 1867
Bazin, Andre d. Nov 11, 1958
Beach, Sylvia d. Oct 6, 1962
Beaumarchais, Pierre Augustin Caron de
b. Jan 24, 1732
Beaumarchais, Pierre Augustin Caron de
d. May 18, 1799
Beauvoir, Simone de b. Jan 9, 1908
Beauvoir, Simone de d. Apr 14, 1986
Bechet, Sidney d. May 14, 1959
Becker, Jacques b. Sep 15, 1906
Becker, Jacques d. 1960
Becquerel, Antoine Henri b. Dec 15, 1852
Becquerel, Antoine-Cesar d. Jan 18, 1878
Belbenoit, Rene Lucien b. 1889
Benjamin, Judah Philip d. May 8, 1884
Beranger, Pierre Jean de b. Aug 19, 1780
Berdyayev, Nikolay A d. Mar 4, 1948
Bergson, Henri Louis b. Oct 18, 1859
Bergson, Henri Louis d. Jan 3, 1941
Berlioz, Louis Hector d. Mar 8, 1869
Bernanos, Georges b. May 5, 1888
Bernanos, Georges d. Jul 5, 1948
Bernard, Claude d. Feb 10, 1878
Bernhardt, Sarah b. Oct 23, 1844
Bernhardt, Sarah d. Mar 26, 1923
Bertillon, Alphonse b. Apr 24, 1853
Bertillon, Alphonse d. Feb 13, 1914
Bichat, Marie Francois Xavier
d. Jul 22, 1802
Biddle, Francis Beverley b. May 9, 1886
Binet, Alfred d. Oct 8, 1911
Bizet, Georges (Alexandre Cesar Leopold)
b. Oct 25, 1838
Bjornson, Bjornstjerne d. Apr 26, 1910

Bleriot, Louis d. Aug 2, 1936
Blum, Leon b. Apr 9, 1872
Boileau(-Despreaux), Nicolas
  b. Nov 1, 1636
Bonaparte, Francois Charles Joseph b. 1811
Bonaparte, Jerome d. Jun 24, 1860
Bonnet, Georges d. Jun 4, 1973
Bonneville, Benjamin b. Apr 14, 1796
Borduas, Paul-Emile d. Feb 22, 1960
Bossuet, Jacques Benigne d. Apr 12, 1704
Boucher, Francois b. Sep 29, 1703
Boucher, Francois d. May 30, 1770
Bougainville, Louis Antoine de
  b. Nov 12, 1729
Boulanger, Nadia Juliette b. Sep 16, 1887
Boulanger, Nadia Juliette d. Oct 22, 1979
Boulle, Charles Andre b. Nov 11, 1642
Boulle, Charles Andre d. Feb 29, 1732
Bourget, Paul (Charles Joseph)
  d. Dec 25, 1935
Brancusi, Constantin d. Mar 16, 1957
Brandel, Fernand Paul d. Nov 28, 1985
Braque, Georges d. Aug 31, 1963
Breton, Andre d. Sep 28, 1966
Briand, Aristide d. Mar 7, 1932
Brieux, Eugene b. Jan 19, 1858
Briggs, Austin Eugene d. Oct 13, 1973
Brillat-Savarin, Jean Anthelme
  d. Feb 2, 1826
Brugnon, Jacques b. May 11, 1895
Brugnon, Jacques d. Mar 20, 1978
Brunhoff, Laurent de b. Aug 30, 1925
Buffet, Bernard b. Jul 10, 1928
Buffon, Georges Louis Leclerc
  d. Apr 16, 1788
Bunin, Ivan Alekseevich d. Nov 8, 1953
Callas, Maria d. Sep 16, 1977
Calvet, Corinne b. Apr 30, 1925
Campanella, Tommaso d. May 21, 1639
Camus, Marcel d. Jan 13, 1982
Carne, Marcel b. Aug 18, 1909
Carol, Martine b. May 16, 1920
Caron, Leslie Clare Margaret
  b. Jul 1, 1931
Carpentier, Georges d. Oct 27, 1975
Casadesus, Jean b. Jul 7, 1927
Casadesus, Robert b. Apr 7, 1899
Casadesus, Robert d. Sep 19, 1972
Cassatt, Mary d. Jun 14, 1926
Cassin, Rene d. Feb 20, 1976
Cassini, Oleg Lolewski d. Apr 11, 1913
Castil-Blaze, Francois-Joseph
  d. Dec 11, 1857
Cavalcanti, Alberto d. Aug 23, 1982
Chaban-Delmas, Jacques b. Mar 7, 1915
Chabrier, (Alexis) Emmanuel
  d. Sep 13, 1894
Chabrol, Claude b. Jun 24, 1930
Chalgrin, Francois b. 1739
Chaliapin, Feodor Ivanovitch
  d. Apr 12, 1938

Chaminade, Cecile b. Aug 8, 1861
Champollion, Jean Francois
  d. Mar 4, 1832
Chanel, "Coco" (Gabrielle) d. Jan 10, 1971
Chanute, Octave b. Feb 18, 1832
Chapman, Christian Addison
  b. Sep 19, 1921
Charcot, Jean Martin b. Nov 29, 1825
Chardin, Jean Baptiste Simeon
  b. Nov 2, 1699
Chardin, Jean Baptiste Simeon
  d. Dec 6, 1779
Chardonnet, Louis Marie d. Mar 12, 1924
Charles, Jacques-Alexandre-Cesar
  d. Apr 7, 1823
Charpentier, Gustave d. Feb 18, 1956
Charpentier, Marc-Antoine b. 1634
Charpentier, Marc-Antoine d. Feb 24, 1704
Charron, Pierre b. 1541
Charron, Pierre d. Nov 16, 1603
Chateaubriand, Francois Rene de
  d. Jul 4, 1848
Chausson, Ernest b. Jun 21, 1855
Chautemps, Camille b. Feb 1, 1885
Chauvire, Yvette b. Apr 22, 1917
Cherubini, Maria Luigi d. Mar 15, 1842
Chevalier, Maurice Auguste
  b. Sep 12, 1888
Chevalier, Maurice Auguste d. Jan 1, 1972
Chevreul, Michel d. Apr 9, 1889
Chirac, Jacques Rene b. Nov 29, 1932
Chopin, Frederic Francois d. Oct 17, 1849
Chretien, Henri b. Feb 1, 1879
Christian-Jaque b. Sep 4, 1904
Cigna, Gina b. Mar 6, 1900
Citroen, Andre Gustave b. Feb 5, 1878
Clair, Rene b. Nov 11, 1898
Clary, Robert b. Mar 1, 1926
Claude, Georges b. Sep 24, 1870
Claudel, Paul Louis Charles
  d. Feb 23, 1955
Clemenceau, Georges Eugene Benjamin
  d. Nov 24, 1929
Cloete, Stuart b. Jul 23, 1897
Clouet, Francois d. 1572
Clouet, Jean d. 1540
Clouzot, Henri-George d. Jan 12, 1977
Cluytens, Andre b. Jun 3, 1967
Cocteau, Jean d. Oct 12, 1963
Colbert, Claudette b. Sep 13, 1905
Colette, pseud. d. Aug 3, 1954
Colonne, Edouard d. Mar 28, 1910
Comte, Auguste d. Sep 5, 1857
Constant de Rebeque, (Henri) Benjamin
  d. Dec 8, 1830
Copeau, Jacques b. 1878
Coppee, Francois Edouard Joachim
  b. Jan 26, 1842
Coppee, Francois Edouard Joachim
  d. May 23, 1908

Corday d'Armount, (Marie Anne) Charlotte
d. Jul 17, 1793
Corneille, Pierre d. Oct 1, 1684
Corot, Jean Baptiste Camille
b. Jul 16, 1796
Corot, Jean Baptiste Camille
d. Feb 22, 1875
Cortazar, Julio d. Feb 12, 1985
Coubertin, Pierre de, Baron b. Jan 1, 1862
Coulomb, Charles Augustin de
d. Aug 23, 1806
Couperin, Francois b. Nov 10, 1668
Couperin, Francois d. Sep 12, 1733
Cournand, Andre Frederic b. Sep 24, 1895
Cremieux, Isaac-Adolphe d. Feb 10, 1880
Crowninshield, Francis Welch
b. Jun 24, 1872
Curel, Francois de d. Apr 25, 1928
Curie, Eve b. Dec 6, 1904
Curie, Pierre b. May 15, 1859
Curie, Pierre d. Apr 19, 1906
Cuvier, Georges, Baron d. May 13, 1832
Daguerre, Louis Jacques Mande
d. Jul 12, 1851
Daladier, Edouard d. Oct 10, 1970
Daly, Augustin d. Jun 7, 1899
Daniloff, Nicholas b. Dec 30, 1934
Danton, Georges Jacques d. Apr 5, 1794
Darcel, Denise b. Sep 8, 1925
Dassault, Marcel b. Jan 22, 1892
Dassault, Marcel d. Apr 18, 1986
Daubigny, Charles Francois
b. Feb 15, 1817
Dauphin, Claude Le Grand Maria Eugene
d. Nov 17, 1978
David, Jacques Louis b. Aug 30, 1748
Davout, Louis Nicholas d. Jun 1, 1823
Debost, Michel H b. 1934
Debray, Regis (Jules Regis) b. Sep 2, 1940
Debre, Michel Jean Pierre b. Jan 15, 1912
DeBroca, Philippe Claude Alex
b. Mar 15, 1933
Debussy, Claude Achille d. Mar 25, 1918
Decamps, Alexandre Gabriel
b. Mar 3, 1803
Degas, (Hilaire Germain) Edgar
b. Jul 19, 1834
Degas, (Hilaire Germain) Edgar
d. Sep 27, 1917
Dejean, Alain d. Oct 25, 1981
Delacroix, (Ferdinand Victor) Eugene
d. Aug 13, 1863
Delaunay, Robert b. Apr 12, 1885
Delaunay-Terk, Sonia d. Dec 5, 1979
Delibes, Leo b. Feb 21, 1836
Delibes, Leo d. Jan 16, 1891
DeMontebello, Guy-Philippe
b. May 16, 1936
Deneuve, Catherine b. Oct 22, 1943
Deshayes, Catherine d. Feb 22, 1680
DeSica, Vittorio d. Nov 13, 1974

Desmoulins, Camille d. Apr 5, 1794
Desormiere, Roger d. Oct 25, 1963
Destouches, Louis-Ferdinand
b. May 27, 1894
Destouches, Louis-Ferdinand d. Jul 4, 1961
Dewaere, Patrick d. Jul 16, 1982
Diaz, Porfirio d. Jul 2, 1915
Diderot, Denis d. Jul 30, 1784
Diesel, Rudolf Christian Karl
b. Mar 18, 1858
Dolin, Anton, Sir d. Nov 25, 1983
Doriot, Georges Frederic b. Sep 24, 1899
Dorleac, Francoise b. Mar 21, 1942
Drake, Betsy b. Sep 11, 1923
Dubuffet, Jean d. May 12, 1985
Duclos, Jacques d. Apr 25, 1975
Duhamel, Georges b. Jun 30, 1884
Dukas, Paul Abraham b. Oct 1, 1865
Dukas, Paul Abraham d. May 17, 1935
Dumas, Alexandre b. Jul 27, 1824
Dumas, Alexandre d. Nov 27, 1895
DuMaurier, George Louis P B
b. Mar 6, 1834
DuPont de Nemours, Pierre Samuel
b. Sep 14, 1739
DuPont, Eleuthere Irenee b. Jun 24, 1771
DuPrez, Gilbert b. Dec 6, 1806
Durkheim, Emile d. Nov 15, 1917
Duveyrier, Anne Honore b. Nov 13, 1787
Duveyrier, Anne Honore d. Nov 1865
Duvivier, Julien d. Oct 29, 1967
Edward VIII d. May 18, 1972
Enesco, Georges d. May 4, 1955
Ernst, Max d. Apr 1, 1976
Estaing, Charles Henri Hector, Comte d'
d. Apr 28, 1794
Estienne, Henri b. 1531
Fabius, Laurent b. Aug 20, 1946
Farrere, Claude, pseud. d. Jun 21, 1957
Fath, Jacques d. Nov 13, 1954
Faure, Elie d. Oct 31, 1937
Faure, Gabriel Urbain d. Nov 4, 1924
Feininger, Andreas Bernhard Lyonel
b. Dec 27, 1906
Fenelon, Fania b. Sep 2, 1918
Fenelon, Fania d. Dec 20, 1983
Fernandel d. Feb 26, 1971
Feuillade, Louis d. 1925
Feuillet, Octave d. Dec 29, 1890
Feydeau, Georges b. Dec 8, 1862
Filene, Edward Albert d. Sep 26, 1937
Foch, Ferdinand d. Mar 20, 1929
Fonck, Rene d. Jun 18, 1953
Forain, Jean-Louis d. 1931
Foucault, Michel d. Jun 25, 1984
Fourier, Francois Marie Charles
d. Oct 8, 1837
Fournier, Pierre b. Jun 24, 1906
France, Anatole, pseud. b. Apr 16, 1844
Franck, Cesar Auguste d. Nov 8, 1890
Francois, Samson d. Sep 22, 1970

Khodasevich, Vladislav d. Jun 14, 1939
Korner, Alexis b. Apr 19, 1928
Krauss, Gabrielle d. Jan 6, 1906
Kreuger, Ivar d. Mar 12, 1932
Kroeber, Alfred Louis d. Oct 5, 1960
L'Enfant, Pierre Charles b. Aug 2, 1754
L'Hermitte, Leon Augustin d. 1925
La Tour du Pin, Patrice de
  b. Mar 16, 1911
La Tour du Pin, Patrice de
  d. Oct 28, 1975
Laboulage, Edouard Rose b. Jan 18, 1811
Laboulage, Edouard Rose d. May 25, 1883
LaBruyere, Jean de b. Aug 16, 1645
Lacan, Jacques Marie Emile
  b. Apr 13, 1901
Lacan, Jacques Marie Emile
  d. Sep 9, 1981
Lachaise, Gaston b. Mar 19, 1882
Laclos, (Pierre) Choderlos de
  b. Oct 19, 1741
Lacoste, (Jean-) Rene b. Jul 2, 1905
Lafayette, Marie Joseph Paul, Marquis
  d. May 20, 1834
LaFontaine, Jean de d. Apr 13, 1695
Laforgue, Jules d. Aug 20, 1887
Lalique, Rene d. May 9, 1945
Lalo, Edouard Victor Antoine
  d. Apr 22, 1892
Lamarck, Jean Baptiste Pierre
  d. Dec 18, 1829
Lamartine, Alphonse Marie Louis de Prat
  de d. Mar 1, 1869
Lamoureux, Charles d. Dec 21, 1899
Lancret, Nicolas b. Jan 22, 1690
Lancret, Nicolas d. Sep 14, 1743
Lanvin, Jeanne d. Jul 6, 1946
Laparra, Raoul d. Apr 4, 1943
Lapidus, Ted b. Jun 23, 1929
Laplace, Pierre Simon, Marquis de
  d. Mar 5, 1827
Largo Caballero, Francisco
  d. Mar 23, 1946
LaRochefoucauld, Francois, Duc de
  b. Sep 15, 1613
LaRochefoucauld, Francois, Duc de
  d. Mar 16, 1680
Larousse, Pierre Athanase d. Jan 3, 1875
Lartique, Jacques-Henri b. Jun 13, 1894
Lassale, Jean d. Sep 7, 1909
Laurencin, Marie b. 1885
Laurencin, Marie d. 1956
Lautreamont, Comte de, pseud.
  d. Nov 24, 1870
Lavoisier, Antoine Laurent
  b. Aug 13, 1743
Lavoisier, Antoine Laurent d. May 8, 1794
Layard, Austin Henry, Sir b. Mar 5, 1817
Leaud, Jean-Pierre b. May 5, 1944
Leboyer, Frederick b. 1918
Ledoux, Claude Nicolas d. Nov 19, 1806

Legrand, Michel Jean b. Feb 24, 1932
Leibowitz, Rene d. Aug 28, 1972
Lelong, Lucien b. Oct 11, 1889
Lelong, Lucien d. May 11, 1958
LeLouch, Claude b. Oct 30, 1937
Lemoyne, Jean-Baptiste d. Dec 30, 1796
Lenclos, Ninon de b. 1620
Lenclos, Ninon de d. 1705
Lenglen, Suzanne d. Jul 4, 1938
LeNotre, Andre b. Mar 12, 1613
LeNotre, Andre d. Sep 15, 1700
LeRoux, Gaston b. May 6, 1868
Leroux, Xavier d. Feb 2, 1919
Lesueur, Jean-Francois d. Oct 6, 1837
Levasseur, Nicolas Prosper d. Dec 7, 1871
LeVerrier, Urbain Jean Joseph
  d. Sep 25, 1877
Levy-Bruhl, Lucien b. Apr 10, 1857
Levy-Bruhl, Lucien d. Mar 13, 1939
Litolff, Henri Charles d. Aug 6, 1891
Litvinne, Felia d. Oct 12, 1936
Loewy, Raymond Fernand b. Nov 5, 1893
Lombard, Alain b. Oct 4, 1940
Lombard, Peter d. 1160
Longet, Claudine Georgette
  b. Jan 29, 1942
Louis Phillippe b. Oct 6, 1773
Louis, Jean b. Oct 5, 1907
Louys, Pierre d. Jun 4, 1925
Lubin, Germaine b. Feb 1, 1890
Lully, Jean-Baptiste d. Mar 22, 1687
Lyot, Bernard Ferdinand b. Feb 27, 1897
Lytton, Edward Robert Bulwer-Lytton,
  Earl d. Nov 24, 1891
Ma, Yo-Yo b. Oct 7, 1955
Maazel, Lorin b. Mar 5, 1930
Maginot, Andre b. Feb 17, 1877
Maginot, Andre d. Jan 7, 1932
Malherbe, Francois de d. Oct 16, 1628
Malibran, Maria Felicita b. Mar 24, 1808
Mallarme, Stephane b. Mar 18, 1842
Malraux, Andre b. Nov 3, 1901
Malraux, Andre d. Nov 23, 1976
Manet, Edouard b. Jan 23, 1832
Manet, Edouard d. Apr 30, 1883
Mansart, Francois b. Jan 23, 1598
Mansart, Francois d. Sep 23, 1666
Mansart, Jules Hardouin b. Apr 1645
Marcel, Gabriel Honore b. Dec 7, 1889
Marcel, Gabriel Honore d. Oct 9, 1973
Marchesi, Salvatore d. Feb 20, 1908
Marcoux, Vanni d. Oct 22, 1962
Marie Antoinette d. Oct 16, 1793
Marisol (Escobar) b. May 22, 1930
Maritain, Jacques b. Nov 18, 1882
Marivaux, Pierre Carlet de b. Feb 4, 1688
Marivaux, Pierre Carlet de
  d. Feb 12, 1763
Marquet, Albert d. 1947
Marsh, Reginald b. Mar 14, 1898
Martin du Gard, Roger b. Mar 23, 1881

Martinon, Jean d. Mar 1, 1976
Masse, Victor d. Jul 5, 1884
Massenet, Jules Emile Frederic
   d. Aug 13, 1912
Mathieu, Noel Jean d. Sep 22, 1984
Maugham, William Somerset
   b. Jan 25, 1874
Maupassant, Guy de (Henri Rene Albert
   Guy de) d. Jul 6, 1893
Mauriac, Francois d. Sep 1, 1970
Maurois, Andre d. Oct 9, 1967
Mayer, Jean b. Feb 19, 1920
Mead, William Rutherford d. Jun 20, 1928
Mehul, Etienne Nicolas d. Oct 18, 1817
Meissonier, Jean Louis Ernest
   d. Jan 31, 1891
Melies, Georges b. Dec 8, 1861
Melies, Georges d. Jan 21, 1938
Melville, Jean-Pierre b. Oct 20, 1917
Melville, Jean-Pierre d. Aug 2, 1973
Mendes-France, Pierre b. Jan 11, 1907
Mendes-France, Pierre d. Oct 18, 1982
Menken, Adah Isaacs d. Aug 10, 1868
Merejkowski, Dmitri Sergeyevich
   d. Dec 9, 1941
Merimee, Prosper b. Sep 28, 1803
Messager, Andre Charles Prosper
   d. Feb 24, 1929
Metzinger, Jean d. Nov 3, 1956
Meyerbeer, Giacomo d. May 2, 1864
Mezzrow, "Mezz" (Milton) d. Aug 5, 1972
Michaux, Henri d. Oct 17, 1984
Mielziner, Jo b. Mar 19, 1901
Mirabeau, Honore Gabriel Riquetti
   d. Apr 2, 1791
Mistral, Gabriela d. Jan 10, 1957
Modigliani, Amedeo d. Jan 25, 1920
Moliere, pseud. b. Jan 15, 1622
Moliere, pseud. d. Feb 17, 1673
Mollet, Guy d. Oct 3, 1975
Monet, Claude b. Nov 14, 1840
Monod, Jacques b. Feb 9, 1910
Monsigny, Pierre-Alexandre
   d. Jan 14, 1817
Monteilhet, Hubert b. 1928
Montesquieu, Charles Louis de
   d. Feb 10, 1755
Monteux, Pierre b. Apr 4, 1875
Montez, Maria d. Sep 7, 1951
Moreau, Gustave b. Apr 6, 1826
Moreau, Gustave d. Apr 18, 1898
Moreau, Jeanne b. Jan 23, 1928
Morisot, Berthe d. Mar 2, 1895
Morrison, Jim (James Douglas)
   d. Jul 3, 1971
Moszkowski, Moritz d. Mar 4, 1925
Muratore, Lucien d. Jul 16, 1954
Musset, Alfred de b. Dec 11, 1810
Musset, Alfred de d. May 2, 1857
Napoleon III b. Apr 20, 1808
Negrin, Juan d. Nov 14, 1956

Nerval, Gerard de b. May 22, 1808
Nerval, Gerard de d. Jan 25, 1855
Ney, Michel de la Moskova, Prince
   d. Dec 7, 1815
Nicot, Jean d. May 5, 1600
Nin, Anais b. Feb 21, 1903
Nougues, Jean d. Aug 28, 1932
Nourrit, Adolphe b. Mar 3, 1802
Nuitter, Charles Louis b. Apr 24, 1828
Nuitter, Charles Louis d. Feb 24, 1899
Offenbach, Jacques d. Oct 4, 1880
Onassis, Aristotle Socrates d. Mar 15, 1975
Paer, Ferdinando d. May 3, 1839
Pagnol, Marcel Paul d. Apr 18, 1974
Palmer, Alice Elvira Freeman
   d. Dec 6, 1902
Pare, Ambroise d. Dec 22, 1590
Pareto, Vilfredo b. Aug 15, 1848
Pascal, Blaise d. Aug 19, 1662
Pasdeloup, Jules Etienne b. Sep 15, 1819
Patachou b. 1918
Pater, Jean-Baptiste d. 1736
Patou, Jean d. Mar 1936
Patti, Carlotta d. Jun 27, 1889
Pedro II d. Dec 5, 1891
Peret, Benjamin d. 1959
Perrault, Charles b. Jan 12, 1628
Perrault, Charles d. May 16, 1703
Perrin, Emile Cesare d. Oct 8, 1885
Pevsner, Antoine d. Apr 12, 1962
Peyre, Henri Maurice b. Feb 21, 1901
Philipe, Gerard d. Nov 27, 1959
Piaf, Edith b. Dec 1915
Piaf, Edith d. Oct 11, 1963
Picabia, Francis b. Jan 22, 1879
Picabia, Francis d. Nov 30, 1953
Picasso, Paloma b. Apr 19, 1949
Pickford, Jack d. Jan 3, 1933
Pictet, Raoul-Pierre d. Jul 27, 1929
Pinel, Philippe d. Oct 26, 1826
Pissaro, Lucien b. Feb 20, 1863
Pissarro, Camille Jacob d. Nov 13, 1903
Plancon, Pol-Henri d. Aug 11, 1914
Planquette, Jean(-Robert) b. Jul 31, 1848
Planquette, Jean(-Robert) d. Jan 28, 1903
Poincare, Jules Henri d. Jul 17, 1912
Poincare, Raymond d. Oct 15, 1934
Poiret, Paul b. Apr 20, 1879
Poiret, Paul d. Apr 30, 1944
Polanski, Roman b. Aug 18, 1933
Pompadour, Jeanne Antoinette Poisson
   b. Dec 29, 1721
Pompidou, Georges Jean Raymond
   d. Apr 2, 1974
Poulenc, Francis b. Jan 7, 1899
Poulenc, Francis d. Jan 30, 1963
Presle, Micheline b. Aug 22, 1922
Prevost, Marcel b. May 1, 1862
Primaticcio, Francesco d. Sep 1570
Prin, Alice d. Mar 23, 1953
Printemps, Yvonne d. Jan 18, 1977

Proudhon, Pierre Joseph d. Jan 16, 1865
Proust, Marcel b. Jul 10, 1871
Proust, Marcel d. Nov 18, 1922
Prudhon, Pierre d. Feb 16, 1823
Puvis de Chavannes, Pierre Cecile
    d. Oct 10, 1898
Rabaud, Henri b. Nov 10, 1873
Rabaud, Henri d. Sep 11, 1949
Rabelais, Francois d. 1553
Racine, Jean Baptiste d. Apr 26, 1699
Raimu d. Sep 20, 1946
Rameau, Jean-Philippe d. Sep 12, 1764
Ravel, Maurice Joseph d. Dec 28, 1937
Ray, Man d. Nov 18, 1976
Rebuffat, Gaston Louis Simon
    d. May 31, 1985
Recamier, (Jeanne Francoise) Julie(tte)
    Adelaide, Madame d. 1849
Redon, Odilon d. Jul 6, 1916
Renan, (Joseph) Ernest d. Oct 2, 1892
Renard, Jules d. May 22, 1910
Renaud, Maurice d. Oct 16, 1933
Renault, Fernand b. 1865
Renault, Louis b. 1877
Renault, Louis d. Oct 24, 1944
Renault, Marcel b. 1872
Renoir, Jean b. Sep 15, 1894
Ricci, Nina d. Nov 29, 1970
Richelieu, Armand Jean du Plessis,
    Cardinal b. Sep 9, 1585
Richelieu, Armand Jean du Plessis,
    Cardinal d. Dec 4, 1642
Robert, Hubert b. 1733
Robert, Hubert d. 1808
Robespierre, Maximilien Francois de
    d. Jul 28, 1794
Rodin, Auguste (Francois Auguste Rene)
    b. Nov 12, 1840
Roland de la Porte, Henri-Horace b. 1724
Roland de la Porte, Henri-Horace d. 1793
Romains, Jules d. Aug 14, 1972
Rosa, Carl d. Apr 30, 1889
Rosay, Francoise b. Apr 19, 1891
Rosay, Francoise d. Mar 28, 1974
Rosenthal, Manuel b. 1904
Rostand, Edmond Alexis d. Dec 2, 1918
Rothschild, Guy Edouard Alphonse Paul
    de, Baron b. May 21, 1909
Rouault, Georges b. May 27, 1871
Rouault, Georges d. Feb 13, 1958
Rousseau, (Pierre Etienne) Theodore
    b. Apr 15, 1812
Rousseau, Henri d. Sep 2, 1910
Roze, Marie b. Mar 2, 1846
Roze, Marie d. Jun 21, 1926
Rubirosa, Porfirio d. Jul 5, 1965
Rudhyar, Dane b. Mar 23, 1895
Ruhlmann, Francois d. Jun 8, 1948
Sacchini, Antonio d. Oct 6, 1786
Sade, Marquis (Donatien Alphonse
    Francoise) de b. Jun 2, 1740

Saint Georges, Jules b. Nov 7, 1801
Saint Georges, Jules d. Dec 23, 1875
Saint-Saens, (Charles) Camille
    b. Oct 9, 1835
Saint-Simon, Claude-Henri de Rouvroy
    b. Oct 17, 1760
Saint-Simon, Claude-Henri de Rouvroy
    d. May 19, 1825
Sainte-Beuve, Charles Augustin
    d. Oct 13, 1869
Salignac, Eustase Thomas d. 1945
Sananikone, Phoui d. Dec 4, 1983
Sand, George, pseud. b. Sep 1, 1804
Sanda, Dominique b. 1948
Sanderson, Sybil d. May 15, 1903
Sardou, Victorien b. Sep 7, 1831
Sardou, Victorien d. Nov 8, 1908
Sarkis, Elias d. Jun 27, 1985
Sartre, Jean-Paul b. Jun 21, 1905
Sartre, Jean-Paul d. Apr 15, 1980
Satie, Erik d. Jul 1, 1925
Sax, Adolphe d. Feb 4, 1894
Sax, Charles Joseph d. Apr 26, 1865
Sbriglia, Giovanni d. Feb 20, 1916
Schiaparelli, (Elsa) d. Nov 14, 1973
Schneider, "Romy" d. May 29, 1982
Schneider, Maria b. Mar 27, 1952
Schumann, Maurice b. Apr 10, 1911
Schwob, Marcel d. Feb 26, 1905
Scudery, Madeleine de d. Jun 2, 1701
Seberg, Jean d. Aug 31, 1979
Servan-Schreiber, Jean-Claude
    b. Apr 11, 1918
Seurat, Georges Pierre b. Dec 2, 1859
Seurat, Georges Pierre d. Mar 29, 1891
Severini, Gino d. Feb 29, 1966
Signac, Paul b. Nov 11, 1863
Signac, Paul d. Aug 15, 1935
Simpson, Wallis Warfield d. Apr 24, 1986
Sisley, Alfred b. Oct 30, 1839
Smithson, James b. 1765
Sor, Fernando d. Jul 8, 1839
Soutine, Chaim d. Aug 9, 1943
Spectorsky, Auguste Compte
    b. Aug 13, 1910
Stael-Holstein, Anne Louise Germaine
    (Necker), Baroness b. Apr 22, 1766
Stael-Holstein, Anne Louise Germaine
    (Necker), Baroness d. Jul 13, 1817
Stendhal d. Mar 23, 1842
Stoltz, Rosine b. Feb 13, 1815
Stoltz, Rosine d. Jul 28, 1903
Strakosch, Maurice d. Oct 9, 1887
Sue, Eugene Joseph Marie b. Jan 20, 1804
Sully-Prudhomme, Rene Francois Armand
    b. Mar 16, 1839
Sully-Prudhomme, Rene Francois Armand
    d. Sep 7, 1907
Svetlova, Marina b. May 3, 1922
Tabouis, Genevieve d. Sep 22, 1985
Tailleferre, Germaine d. Nov 7, 1983

Taine, Hippolyte Adolphe d. Mar 9, 1893
Talleyrand-Perigord, Charles Maurice de
  b. Feb 13, 1754
Talleyrand-Perigord, Charles Maurice de
  d. May 17, 1838
Tanguy, Yves b. Jan 5, 1900
Tati, Jacques d. Nov 5, 1982
Tcherepnin, Nicholas (Nicolai)
  d. Jun 26, 1945
Thill, Georges b. Dec 14, 1897
Thomas, (Charles Louis) Ambroise
  d. Feb 12, 1896
Toklas, Alice B(abette) d. Mar 7, 1967
Tournefort, Joseph Pitton de
  d. Nov 28, 1708
Trigere, Pauline b. Nov 4, 1912
Truffaut, Francois b. Feb 6, 1932
Tzara, Tristan d. Dec 24, 1963
Utrillo, Maurice b. Dec 25, 1883
Vadim, Roger b. Jan 26, 1928
Valadon, Suzanne d. 1938
Valente, Caterina b. Jan 14, 1931
Valery, Paul Ambroise d. Jul 20, 1945
Vanderbilt, William Kissam d. Jul 22, 1920
Varese, Edgar b. Dec 22, 1883
Venizelos, Eleutherios d. Mar 18, 1936
Verlaine, Paul Marie d. Jan 8, 1896
Vertes, Marcel d. Oct 31, 1961
Veyron-Lacroix, Robert b. 1922
Viardot-Garcia, Pauline b. Jul 18, 1821
Viardot-Garcia, Pauline d. May 18, 1910
Vigny, Alfred Victor, Comte de
  d. Sep 17, 1863
Vigo, Jean b. Apr 26, 1905
Vigo, Jean d. Oct 5, 1934
Villechaize, Herve Jean Pierre
  b. Apr 23, 1943
Villon, Francois b. 1431
Villon, Francois d. 1463
Vincent de Paul, Saint d. Sep 27, 1660
Viollet le Duc, Eugene Emmanuel
  b. Jan 27, 1814
Vlaminck, Maurice de b. Apr 4, 1876
Vlaminck, Maurice de d. Oct 11, 1958
Volney, (Constantin) Francois Chasseboeuf
  d. Apr 25, 1820
Voltaire(, Francois Marie Arouet de)
  b. Nov 21, 1694
Voltaire(, Francois Marie Arouet de)
  d. May 30, 1778
VonStroheim, Erich d. May 12, 1957
Vreeland, Diana b. 1903
Vynnychenko, Volodymyr d. 1951
Wallace, Horace Binney d. Dec 16, 1852
Weicker, Lowell Palmer, Jr.
  b. May 16, 1931
Weil, Simone b. Feb 3, 1909
Werth, Alexander d. Mar 5, 1969
Weygand, Maxime d. Jan 28, 1965
Wharton, Edith d. Aug 11, 1937
Wheatstone, Charles, Sir d. Oct 19, 1875

White, Pearl d. Aug 4, 1938
Widor, Charles Marie Jean Albert
  d. Mar 12, 1937
Wilde, Oscar Fingal O'Flahertie Wills
  d. Nov 30, 1900
Wilson, Peter Cecil d. Jun 3, 1984
Wolff, Albert Louis b. Jan 19, 1884
Wolff, Albert Louis d. Feb 1970
Wolsky, Albert b. Nov 24, 1930
Worth, Charles Frederick d. Mar 10, 1895
Wright, Richard d. Nov 28, 1960
Zadkine, Ossip d. Nov 25, 1967
Zola, Emile Edouard Charles
  b. Apr 2, 1840
Zola, Emile Edouard Charles
  d. Sep 29, 1902

Passy, France
  Bretonneau, Pierre Fidele d. Feb 18, 1862
  DuPrez, Gilbert d. Sep 23, 1896
  Gossec, Francois Joseph d. Feb 16, 1829
  Piccini, Nicola d. May 7, 1800
  Rossini, Gioacchino Antonio
    d. Nov 13, 1868

Pau, France
  Campbell, Mrs. Patrick d. Apr 9, 1940
  Courreges, Andre b. Mar 9, 1923

Pau-St. Maur, France
  Tailleferre, Germaine b. Apr 19, 1892

Perigord, France
  Fenelon, Francois de Salignac
    b. Aug 6, 1651

Perigueux, France
  Bloy, Leon Marie b. Jul 11, 1846

Perpignan, France
  Leblanc, Maurice d. Nov 6, 1941

Picardy, France
  Lafarge, Marie b. 1816

Ploujean, France
  Pierne, Gabriel d. Jul 17, 1937

Poissy, France
  Louis IX b. Apr 25, 1215

Poitiers, France
  Foucault, Michel b. Oct 15, 1926

Polenc, France
  Trintignant, Jean-Louis Xavier
    b. Dec 11, 1930

Pont Chateau, France
  Demy, Jacques b. Jun 5, 1931

Pont-aux-Dames, France
  Coquelin, Benoit Constant d. Jan 27, 1909

Pouy, France
  Vincent de Paul, Saint b. Apr 24, 1581

Prades, France
  Merton, Thomas b. Jan 31, 1915

Puteaux, France
  Bellini, Vincenzo d. Sep 23, 1835

Puys, France
  Dumas, Alexandre d. Dec 5, 1870

Quimper, France
Jacob, Max b. Jul 11, 1876
Laennec, Rene Theophile Hyacinthe
    b. Feb 17, 1781
Rambouillet, France
Monnet, Jean (Omer Gabriel)
    d. Mar 16, 1979
Reims, France
Colbert, Jean Baptiste b. Aug 29, 1619
Couve de Murville, (Jacques) Maurice
    b. Jan 24, 1907
Entremont, Phillippe b. Jun 7, 1934
Forain, Jean-Louis b. 1852
Hore-Belisha, Leslie, Baron
    d. Feb 16, 1957
Rennes, France
Boulanger, Georges Ernest Jean Marie
    b. 1837
Revel, France
Auriol, Vincent b. Aug 25, 1884
Rheims, France
Rothier, Leon b. Dec 26, 1874
Ribemont, France
Condorcet, Marie-Jean-Antoine
    b. Sep 17, 1743
Rivesaltes, France
Joffre, Joseph Jacques Cesaire
    b. Jan 12, 1852
Riviera, France
Blasco-Ibanez, Vicente d. 1928
Rochefort, France
Champlain, Samuel de b. Jul 3, 1567
Loti, Pierre, pseud. b. Jan 14, 1850
Roquebrune, France
LeCorbusier d. Aug 27, 1965
Roubaix, France
Delerue, Georges b. Mar 12, 1925
Rouen, France
Boieldieu, Francois Adrien b. Dec 16, 1775
Bridgman, Frederic Arthur d. Jan 13, 1927
Clarendon, Edward Hyde, Earl
    d. Dec 9, 1674
Corneille, Pierre b. Jun 6, 1606
DuPre, Marcel b. May 3, 1886
Edward IV b. Apr 28, 1442
Flaubert, Gustave b. Dec 12, 1821
Gericault, Jean Louis Andre Theodore
    b. Sep 26, 1791
Joan of Arc d. May 30, 1431
LaSalle, Robert Cavelier, Sieur de b. 1643
Perrin, Emile Cesare b. Jan 19, 1814
William the Conquerer d. 1087
Royan, France
Roussel, Albert d. Aug 23, 1937
Rueil-Malmaison, France
Feydeau, Georges d. Jun 6, 1921
Ruget, France
Blanqui, Louis Auguste b. Feb 1, 1805
Saarlouis, France
Ney, Michel de la Moskova, Prince
    b. Jan 10, 1769

Saint Beat, France
Gallieni, Joseph Simon b. 1849
Saint Cloud, France
Belloc, Hilaire (Joseph Hilaire Pierre)
    b. Jul 27, 1870
Claude, Georges d. May 23, 1960
Killy, Jean-Claude b. Aug 30, 1943
Saint Denis, France
Eluard, Paul b. Dec 14, 1895
Saint Foy, France
Faure, Elie b. Apr 4, 1873
Saint Georges sur Cher, France
Bretonneau, Pierre Fidele b. Apr 3, 1778
Saint Germain, France
Debussy, Claude Achille b. Aug 22, 1862
Duluth, Daniel b. 1636
Mendes, Catulle (Abraham Catulle)
    d. Feb 8, 1909
Thiers, Adolphe d. Sep 3, 1877
Saint Germain en Laye, France
Jouy, Victor (Joseph-Etienne) de
    d. Sep 4, 1846
Saint Jean de Luz, France
Gissing, George Robert d. Dec 28, 1903
Hornung, Ernest William d. Mar 22, 1921
Saint Jean de Maurienne, France
Balmain, Pierre Alexandre
    b. May 18, 1914
Saint Just, France
Hauy, Rene Just b. Feb 28, 1743
Saint Leonard, France
Gay-Lussac, Joseph Louis b. Dec 6, 1778
Saint Leons, France
Fabre, Jean Henri b. Dec 22, 1823
Saint Lo, France
Feuillet, Octave b. Jul 11, 1821
LeVerrier, Urbain Jean Joseph
    b. May 11, 1811
Saint Malo, France
Cartier, Jacques b. Dec 31, 1491
Cartier, Jacques d. Sep 1, 1557
Clive, Colin b. Jan 20, 1900
Saint Omer, France
Blondin, Jean Francois Gravelet
    b. Feb 28, 1824
Saint Paul de Vence, France
Chagall, Marc d. Mar 28, 1985
Maeght, Aime d. Sep 5, 1981
Saint Prive, France
Harpignies, Henri d. 1916
Saint Quentin, France
Charlevoix, Pierre Francis Xavier de
    b. Oct 29, 1682
Saint Remy, France
Nostradamus b. Dec 14, 1503
Saint Saturnin, France
Corday d'Armount, (Marie Anne) Charlotte
    b. Jul 27, 1768
Saint Sauveur, France
Colette, pseud. b. Jan 28, 1873

Saint-Aignan, France
Paul-Boncour, Joseph b. Aug 4, 1873
Saint-Andre, France
Pinel, Philippe b. Apr 20, 1745
Werner, Pierre b. Dec 29, 1913
Saint-Brice, France
Dubos, Rene Jules b. Feb 20, 1901
Saint-Brieuc, France
Dewaere, Patrick b. Jan 26, 1947
Saint-Denis, France
Barre, Raymond b. Apr 12, 1924
Saint-Germain, France
Louis XIV b. Sep 16, 1638
Saint-Germain-en-Laye, France
James II d. Sep 16, 1701
Saint-Julien, France
Bernard, Claude b. Jul 12, 1813
Saint-Malo, France
Chateaubriand, Francois Rene de
b. Sep 4, 1768
Saint-Ouen, France
Manessier, Alfred b. Dec 5, 1911
Saint-Paul-de-Vence, France
Lurcat, Jean Marie d. Jan 6, 1966
Saint-Quentin, France
Babeuf, Francois Noel b. Nov 25, 1760
Sainte Andre de Cubzac, France
Cousteau, Jacques Yves b. Jun 11, 1910
Sainte Marie Mines, France
Slovik, Eddie (Edward Donald)
d. Jan 31, 1945
Sainte-Foyles, France
Carrel, Alexis b. Jun 28, 1873
Saintes, France
Guillotin, Joseph Ignace b. May 28, 1738
Richard, Gabriel b. Oct 15, 1767
Salon, France
Nostradamus d. Jul 2, 1566
Sarcelles, France
Crevecoeur, Michel-Guillaume Jean de
d. Nov 12, 1813
Sarzeau, France
Lesage, Alain Rene b. May 8, 1668
Saumur, France
Chanel, "Coco" (Gabrielle)
b. Aug 19, 1882
Savenay, France
Delano, Jane Arminda d. Apr 15, 1919
Saxony, France
Saxe, Maurice b. 1696
Seceaux, France
Delon, Alain b. Nov 8, 1935
Sedan, France
Noah, Yannick b. May 16, 1960
Selancourt, France
Peugeot, Rodolphe b. Apr 2, 1902
Sens, France
Camus, Albert d. Jan 4, 1960
Serigran, France
Fabre, Jean Henri d. Oct 11, 1915

Seringes, France
Kilmer, Joyce (Alfred Joyce)
d. Jul 30, 1918
Sermano, France
Falconetti, Renee Maria b. 1892
Serrieres, France
Montgolfier, Jacques Etienne
d. Aug 2, 1799
Sete, France
Brassens, Georges b. Oct 22, 1921
Brassens, Georges d. Oct 30, 1981
Valery, Paul Ambroise b. Oct 30, 1871
Seyne-sur-Mer, France
Dufresne, Charles d. 1938
Strasbourg, France
Arp, Hans b. Sep 16, 1887
Baldung(-Grien), Hans d. 1545
Dore, Gustave (Paul Gustave)
b. Jan 6, 1832
Friedel, Charles b. Mar 12, 1832
Kleber, Jean Baptiste b. Mar 9, 1753
Marceau, Marcel b. Mar 22, 1923
Munch, Charles b. Sep 26, 1891
Ungerer, Tomi (Jean Thomas)
b. Nov 28, 1931
Suresnes, France
Zog I d. Apr 9, 1961
Sury-en-Vaux, France
Aldington, Richard d. Jul 27, 1962
Tarbes, France
Foch, Ferdinand b. Oct 2, 1851
Gautier, Theophile (Pierre Jules Theophile)
b. Aug 31, 1811
Thoirette, France
Bichat, Marie Francois Xavier
b. Nov 11, 1771
Thonon, France
Bordeaux, Henry b. Jan 29, 1870
Thorey, France
Lyautey, Louis Hubert Gonzalve
d. Jul 27, 1934
Thumeries, France
Malle, Louis b. Oct 30, 1932
Toucy, France
Larousse, Pierre Athanase b. Oct 23, 1817
Toulon, France
Becaud, Gilbert b. Oct 24, 1927
Capucine b. Jan 6, 1935
Cousteau, Philippe b. Dec 30, 1940
Raimu b. Dec 17, 1883
Toulose, France
Bernard, Andrew Milroy b.
Toulouse, France
Aries, Philippe d. Feb 8, 1984
Dausset, Jean (Baptiste Gabriel Joachim)
b. Oct 19, 1916
Dulac, Edmund b. Oct 22, 1882
Gailhard, Pierre b. Aug 1, 1848
Leotard, Jules b. 1830
Maritain, Jacques d. Feb 12, 1973

Touraine, France
Ronsard, Pierre de d. Dec 26, 1585
Tourcoing, France
Lefebvre, Marcel Francois b. Nov 29, 1905
Roussel, Albert b. Apr 5, 1869
Tournay, France
Jammes, Francis b. Dec 2, 1868
Tournus, France
Greuze, Jean-Baptiste b. Aug 21, 1725
Tours, France
Balzac, Honore de b. May 20, 1799
Clouet, Francois b. 1510
Fouquet, Jean b. 1420
Fouquet, Jean d. 1480
France, Anatole, pseud. d. Oct 12, 1924
Treguier, France
Renan, (Joseph) Ernest b. Jan 27, 1823
Treport, France
Paray, Paul b. May 24, 1886
Troyes, France
Coue, Emile b. Feb 26, 1857
Girardon, Francois b. Mar 17, 1628
Herriot, Edouard b. Jul 5, 1872
Rashi b. 1040
Rashi d. Jul 13, 1105
Ussat, France
Lafarge, Marie d. 1852
Valence, France
Curie, Marie d. Jul 4, 1934
Valenciennes, France
Froissart, Jean b. 1338
Harpignies, Henri b. 1819
Levasseur, Rosalie b. Oct 8, 1749
Pater, Jean-Baptiste b. 1695
Watteau, Jean Antoine b. Oct 10, 1684
Valmondois, France
Daumier, Honore d. Feb 11, 1879
Duhamel, Georges d. Apr 13, 1966
Valvins, France
Mallarme, Stephane d. Sep 9, 1898
Vancluse, France
Daladier, Edouard b. Jun 18, 1884
Vannes, France
Renault, Gilbert (Leon Etienne Theodore)
b. Aug 6, 1904
Resnais, Alain b. Jun 3, 1922
Velay, France
Romains, Jules b. Aug 26, 1885
Vence, France
Craig, Gordon (Edward Henry Gordon)
d. Jul 30, 1966
Galli-Marie, Marie Celestine
d. Sep 22, 1905
Lawrence, D(avid) H(erbert)
d. Mar 2, 1930
Vendome, France
Rochambeau, Jean Baptiste Donatien de
Vimeur, Comte b. Jul 1, 1725
Vendomois, France
Ronsard, Pierre de b. Sep 11, 1524

Verdun, France
Marc, Franz d. Mar 4, 1916
Vernevil, France
Tocqueville, Alexis, Comte de
b. Jul 29, 1805
Versailles, France
Audran, Stephane b. 1939
Blum, Leon d. Mar 30, 1950
Ducis, Jean Francois b. Aug 22, 1733
Ducis, Jean Francois d. Mar 31, 1816
Genet, Edmond Charles Edouard b. 1763
Goldoni, Carlo d. Jan 6, 1793
Houdon, Jean Antoine b. Mar 20, 1741
Kreutzer, Rodolphe b. Nov 16, 1766
LaBruyere, Jean de d. May 10, 1696
Lesseps, Ferdinand Marie de
b. Nov 19, 1805
Louis XV b. Feb 15, 1710
Louis XVI b. Aug 23, 1754
Mendl, Lady Elsie de Wolfe
d. Jul 12, 1950
Mitford, Nancy Freeman d. Jun 30, 1973
Pompadour, Jeanne Antoinette Poisson
d. Apr 15, 1764
Quesnay, Francois d. Dec 16, 1774
Vesinet, France
Barrault, Jean-Louis b. Sep 8, 1910
Vesoul, France
Gerome, Jean Leon b. 1824
Vezelay, France
Rolland, Romain d. Dec 30, 1944
Vianne, France
Prevost, Marcel d. Apr 8, 1941
Vic sur Seille, France
LaTour, George Dumesnil de b. 1593
Vichy, France
Desormiere, Roger b. Sep 13, 1898
Vidalon les Annonay, France
Montgolfier, Jacques Etienne
b. Jan 7, 1745
Montgolfier, Joseph Michel
b. Aug 26, 1740
Ville d'Avray, France
Gobineau, Joseph Arthur, Comte de
b. Jul 14, 1816
Villemomble, France
Petit, Roland b. Jan 13, 1924
Villenluve, France
Claudel, Paul Louis Charles
b. Aug 6, 1868
Villers, France
Poussin, Nicolas b. Jun 1594
Villers-Cotterets, France
Dumas, Alexandre b. Jul 24, 1802
Vincennes, France
Fath, Jacques b. Sep 12, 1912
Mata Hari d. Oct 15, 1917
Mazarin, Jules, Cardinal d. Mar 9, 1661
Vittel, France
Journet, Marcel d. Sep 5, 1933

Vouziers, France
Taine, Hippolyte Adolphe b. Apr 21, 1828
Waziers, France
Pretre, Georges b. Aug 14, 1924
Wimereux, France
McCrae, John d. Jan 28, 1918
Yvelines, France
Strand, Paul d. Mar 31, 1976

FRENCH GUIANA

Kouroussa, French Guiana
Laye, Camara b. Jan 1, 1928

FRENCH INDOCHINA

Thieu, Nguyen Van b. Apr 5, 1923

FRENCH WEST INDIES

Guadeloupe, French West Indies
Leger, Alexis St. Leger (Marie-Rene Alexis St. Leger) b. May 31, 1887

GABON

Franceville, Gabon
Bongo, El Hadj Omar b. Dec 30, 1935
Lambarene, Gabon
Schweitzer, Albert d. Sep 4, 1965

GALICIA

Buczacz, Galicia
Agnon, S(hmuel) Y(osef) b. 1888

GAUL

Mantua, Gaul
Virgil b. Oct 15, 70 BC

GERMANY

Alexandra Feodorovna b. 1872
Barbie, Klaus b. 1914
Coors, Adolph b. 1847
Dean, John Gunther b. Feb 24, 1926
Dehmel, Richard b. Nov 18, 1868
Deterding, Henri Wilhelm August, Sir d. 1939
Faust, Frederick Schiller d. May 12, 1944
Fraenkel, Heinrich b. Sep 28, 1897
Geiger, Hans (Johannes Wilhelm) b. Sep 30, 1882
George I d. Jun 12, 1727
Gruber, Franz b. 1787
Hochhuth, Rolf b. Apr 1, 1931
Howard, Willie b. 1886
Kalisch, Paul d. Jan 17, 1946
Levasseur, Rosalie d. May 6, 1826
Levi, Hermann d. May 13, 1900
Nestle, Henri b. 1814

Perls, Frederick Salomon b. 1894
Phillips, Irna b. Jul 1, 1901
Rindt, Jochen b. Apr 18, 1942
Ritter, Karl b. Aug 17, 1779
Sack, Erna b. 1903
Szabo, Violette Bushell d. Jan 26, 1945
Tennenbaum, Silvia b. Mar 10, 1928
Wankel, Felix b. Aug 13, 1902
Westheimer, Ruth b. 1929
Zenger, John Peter b. 1697
Zeppelin, Ferdinand von, Count b. Jul 8, 1838
Aachen, Germany
Domgraf-Fassbaender, Willi b. Feb 19, 1897
Lambsdorff, Otto b. Dec 20, 1926
Mies van der Rohe, Ludwig b. Mar 27, 1886
Saerchinger, Cesar Victor Charles b. Oct 23, 1889
Aiz-la-Chapelle, Germany
Blech, Leo b. Apr 21, 1871
Allenskin, Germany
Mendelsohn, Eric b. Mar 21, 1887
Alsace-Lorraine, Germany
Bloch, Raymond A b. Aug 3, 1902
Alsenz, Germany
Frick, Wilhelm b. Mar 3, 1877
Altona, Germany
Bulow, Bernhard H M b. May 3, 1849
Alzei, Germany
Belmont, August b. Dec 8, 1816
Alzey, Germany
Adler, Felix b. Aug 13, 1851
Amberg, Germany
Switzer, Katherine Virginia b. Jan 5, 1947
Anklam, Germany
Gadski, Johanna b. Jun 15, 1872
Annemasse, Germany
Windgassen, Wolfgang Friedrich Hermann b. Jun 26, 1914
Apenrade, Germany
Reuter, Ernst b. Jul 29, 1889
Aplerbeck, Germany
Canaris, Wilhelm b. Jan 1, 1887
Aschaffenburg, Germany
Kirchner, Ernst Ludwig b. May 6, 1880
Aschersleben, Germany
Rundstedt, Karl Rudolf Gerd von b. Dec 12, 1875
Au, Germany
Vogl, Heinrich b. Jan 15, 1845
Auchsensheim, Germany
Egk, Werner b. May 17, 1901
Augsburg, Germany
Brecht, Bertolt Eugene Friedrich b. Feb 10, 1898
Holbein, Hans, the Younger b. 1497
Messerschmitt, Willy (Wilhelm) b. Jun 26, 1898
Olczewska, Maria b. Aug 12, 1892

Aurich, Germany
Eucken, Rudolf Christoph b. 1846
Babenhausen, Germany
Jochum, Eugen b. Nov 2, 1902
Bad Nauheim, Germany
Kesselring, Albert d. Jul 16, 1960
Bad Worishofen, Germany
Fassbinder, Rainer Werner
b. May 31, 1946
Baden-Baden, Germany
Jensen, Adolph d. Jan 23, 1879
Koch, Robert d. May 28, 1910
Lohse, Otto d. May 5, 1925
Mesmer, Franz Anton b. May 23, 1734
Badenweiler, Germany
Chekhov, Anton Pavlovich d. Jul 2, 1904
Crane, Stephen d. Jun 5, 1900
Baldenheim, Germany
Nessler, Victor E b. Jan 28, 1841
Bamberg, Germany
Wassermann, August von b. Feb 21, 1866
Barenstadt, Germany
Kallen, Horace M b. Aug 11, 1882
Barmen, Germany
Engels, Friedrich b. Sep 28, 1820
Bavaria, Germany
Gimbel, Adam b. 1815
Mayer, Oscar Ferdinand b. Mar 29, 1859
Bayreuth, Germany
Liszt, Franz (Ferencz) d. Jul 31, 1886
Richter, Hans d. Dec 5, 1916
Richter, Jean Paul F d. Nov 14, 1825
Wagner, Cosima Liszt d. Apr 1, 1930
Wagner, Siegfried (Helferich)
d. Aug 4, 1930
Wagner, Wieland Adolf Gottfried
b. Jan 5, 1917
Wagner, Wolfgang b. Aug 30, 1919
Beerfelden, Germany
Fuchs, Klaus Emil Julius b. 1912
Bergedorf, Germany
Hasse, Johann Adolph b. Mar 25, 1699
Berlin, Germany
Adam, Ken b. Feb 5, 1921
Agricola, Georgius d. Sep 22, 1566
Bach, Wilhelm Friedemann d. Jul 1784
Barth, Heinrich d. Dec 25, 1865
Bernstein, Eduard b. Jan 6, 1850
Blumenthal, W Michael b. Jan 3, 1926
Bomhard, Moritz b. Jun 19, 1912
Boschwitz, Rudy b. 1930
Brandes, Georg Morris Cohen
d. Feb 19, 1927
Brasch, Rudolph b. Nov 6, 1912
Brauchitsch, Heinrich Alfred
b. Oct 4, 1881
Braun, Eva d. Apr 30, 1945
Buchholz, Horst b. Dec 4, 1933
Busoni, Ferruccio Benvenuto
d. Jul 27, 1924
Busoni, Rafaello b. Feb 1, 1900

Chain, Ernest Boris, Sir b. Jun 19, 1906
Cornell, Katharine b. Feb 16, 1898
Dean, Patrick Henry, Sir b. Mar 16, 1909
Delbruck, Max b. Sep 4, 1906
DeWohl, Louis b. Jan 24, 1903
Diamand, Peter b. Jun 8, 1913
Dietrich, Marlene b. Dec 27, 1901
Doenitz, Karl C b. Sep 16, 1891
Dohnanyi, Christoph von b. Oct 8, 1929
Ebert, Carl (Anton Charles)
b. Feb 20, 1887
Ehricke, Krafft Arnold b. Mar 24, 1917
Eysenck, Hans Jurgen b. Mar 14, 1916
Faas, Horst b. Apr 28, 1933
Fallada, Hans, pseud. d. Feb 6, 1947
Feld, Fritz b. Oct 15, 1900
Fichte, Johann Gottlieb d. Jan 27, 1814
Fischer-Dieskau, Dietrich
b. May 28, 1925 3Ge
Foerster, Friedrich Wilhelm b. Jun 2, 1869
Fontane, Theodor d. Sep 20, 1898
Forssmann, Werner Theodor Otto
b. Aug 29, 1904
Foss, Lukas b. Aug 15, 1922
Frederick III d. Jun 15, 1888
Frederick the Great b. Jan 24, 1712
Frederick the Great d. Aug 17, 1786
Frederick William I b. Aug 15, 1688
Furtwangler, Wilhelm b. Jan 25, 1886
Gadski, Johanna d. Feb 22, 1932
Gay, Peter Jack b. Jun 20, 1923
Gebert, Ernst b. 1901
Geiger, Hans (Johannes Wilhelm)
d. Sep 24, 1945
Genthe, Arnold b. Jan 8, 1869
Gidal, Sonia b. Sep 23, 1922
Glinka, Mikhail Ivanovich d. Feb 15, 1857
Goebbels, Joseph (Paul Joseph)
d. May 3, 1945
Graham, Bill b. Jan 8, 1931
Grimm, Jakob Ludwig Karl
d. Sep 20, 1863
Grimm, Wilhelm Karl d. Dec 16, 1859
Grisi, Giulia d. Nov 29, 1869
Gropius, Walter Adolf b. May 18, 1883
Grosz, George Ehrenfried b. Jul 26, 1893
Hamburger, Michael b. 1924
Hammerstein, Oscar b. May 8, 1846
Harlan, Veit b. Sep 22, 1899
Hegel, Georg Wilhelm Friedrich
d. Nov 14, 1831
Heyse, Paul Johann b. Mar 15, 1830
Hitler, Adolf d. Apr 30, 1945
Hoffmann, Ernst Theodor Amadeus
d. Jun 25, 1822
Humboldt, Alexander, Freiherr von
b. Sep 14, 1769
Humboldt, Alexander, Freiherr von
d. May 6, 1859
Joachim, Joseph d. Aug 15, 1907
Kalisch, Paul b. Nov 6, 1855

Kipnis, Igor b. Sep 27, 1930
Kirchhoff, Gustav Robert d. Oct 17, 1887
Klarsfeld, Beate b. Feb 13, 1931
Klose, Margarete b. Aug 6, 1905
Koffka, Kurt b. Mar 18, 1886
Kronhausen, Eberhard Wilhelm
  b. Sep 12, 1915
Kruger, Hardy (Eberhard) b. Apr 12, 1928
Lehmann, Lilli d. May 17, 1929
Lehmann-Haupt, Hellmut E b. Oct 4, 1903
Lehmbruck, Wilhelm d. Mar 25, 1919
Leider, Frida b. Apr 18, 1888
Leitner, Ferdinand b. Mar 4, 1912
Levitin, Sonia b. Aug 18, 1934
Lewisohn, Ludwig b. May 30, 1882
Ley, Willy b. Oct 2, 1906
Lieber, Franz b. Mar 18, 1800
Liebknecht, Karl b. 1871
Lortzing, Gustav Albert b. Oct 23, 1801
Lortzing, Gustav Albert d. Jan 21, 1851
Lovejoy, Arthur Oncken b. Oct 10, 1873
Lubitsch, Ernst b. Jan 28, 1892
Ludwig, Christa b. Mar 16, 1924
Luxemburg, Rosa d. Jan 15, 1919
Mallinger, Mathilde d. Apr 19, 1920
Mansfield, Richard b. May 24, 1854
Marcuse, Herbert b. Jul 19, 1898
Marek, Kurt W b. Jan 20, 1915
Mason, John Brown b. Jul 13, 1904
Max, Peter b. Oct 19, 1937
Meyerbeer, Giacomo b. Sep 5, 1791
Milder-Hauptmann, Pauline Anna
  d. May 29, 1838
Muller, Johannes Peter d. Apr 28, 1858
Muller-Munk, Peter b. Jun 25, 1904
Nichols, Mike b. Nov 6, 1931
Nicolai, Carl Otto d. May 11, 1849
Niemann, Albert d. Jan 13, 1917
Pepusch, Johann Christoph (John) b. 1667
Politz, Alfred b. 1902
Previn, Andre b. Apr 6, 1929
Prey, Hermann b. Jul 11, 1929
Rakosi, Carl b. Nov 6, 1903
Ranke, Leopold von d. May 23, 1886
Rathenau, Walter b. 1867
Rathenau, Walter d. Jun 24, 1922
Reiss, Albert b. Feb 22, 1870
Reznicek, Emil von d. Aug 2, 1945
Richter, Hans b. 1888
Riefenstahl, Leni (Helene Bertha Amalie)
  b. Aug 22, 1902
Ritter, Karl d. Sep 28, 1859
Rosenberg, Jakob b. Sep 5, 1893
Sachs, Nelly b. Oct 12, 1891
Sachse, Leopold b. Jan 5, 1880
Salomon, Charlotte b. 1917
Sarti, Giuseppe d. Jul 28, 1802
Scherchen, Hermann b. Jun 21, 1891
Schillings, Max von d. Jul 23, 1933
Schleiermacher, Friedrich Ernst Daniel
  d. Feb 12, 1834

Schmidt-Isserstedt, Hans b. May 5, 1900
Schnabel, Karl Ulrich b. Aug 6, 1909
Scholem, Gershom Gerhard b. Dec 5, 1897
Schreker, Franz d. Mar 21, 1934
Schutzendorf, Gustav d. Apr 27, 1937
Siemens, (Ernst) Werner von
  d. Dec 6, 1892
Simmel, Georg b. Mar 1, 1858
Skorpen, Liespel Moak b. Jul 1, 1935
Sommer, Elke b. Nov 5, 1940
Sonnenfeldt, Helmut b. Sep 13, 1926
Spitta, Philipp (Julius August Philipp)
  d. Apr 13, 1894
Stresemann, Gustav b. May 10, 1878
Stresemann, Gustav d. Oct 3, 1929
Sudermann, Hermann d. Nov 21, 1928
Taylor, Bayard d. Dec 19, 1878
Treitschke, Heinrich Gotthard von
  d. Apr 28, 1896
Veidt, Conrad b. Jan 22, 1893
Virchow, Rudolf d. Sep 5, 1905
Von Eckardt, Wolf b. Mar 6, 1918
Wagner-Regeny, Rudolf b. Sep 18, 1969
Walter, Bruno b. Sep 15, 1876
Wassermann, August von d. Mar 15, 1925
Wegener, Alfred b. Nov 1, 1880
Weitz, John b. May 25, 1923
Wilhelm II b. Jan 27, 1859
Zorina, Vera b. Jan 2, 1917
Zuppke, Robert C b. Jul 12, 1879
Berlinchen, Germany
  Lasker, Emanuel b. Dec 24, 1868
Bernau, Germany
  Thoma, Hans b. 1839
Berneck, Germany
  Christaller, Walter b. Apr 21, 1893
Bielefeld, Germany
  Murnau, Friedrich W b. Dec 28, 1899
Blankenburg, Germany
  Frederika Louise b. Apr 18, 1917
  Spengler, Oswald b. May 29, 1880
Blankenese, Germany
  Dehmel, Richard d. Feb 8, 1920
Blasewitz, Germany
  Scaria, Emil d. Jul 22, 1886
Bochum, Germany
  Fritzsche, Hans b. Apr 21, 1900
Bonn, Germany
  Beethoven, Ludwig van b. Dec 16, 1770
Bottrop, Germany
  Albers, Josef b. Mar 19, 1888
Brandenburg, Germany
  Schleicher, Kurt von b. 1882
  Schmeling, Max(imilian) b. Sep 28, 1905
Braubach, Germany
  Schlusnus, Heinrich b. Aug 6, 1888
Breisach, Germany
  Schongauer, Martin d. Feb 2, 1491
Bremen, Germany
  Carstens, Karl Walter b. Dec 14, 1914
  Quidde, Ludwig b. Mar 23, 1858

Timken, Henry b. Aug 16, 1831
Uhde, Hermann b. Jul 20, 1914
Witte, Erich b. Mar 19, 1911

Breslau, Germany
Bonhoeffer, Dietrich b. Feb 4, 1906
Born, Max b. Dec 11, 1882
Gellhorn, Peter b. Oct 24, 1912
Klemperer, Otto b. May 14, 1885
Lassalle, Ferdinand b. Apr 11, 1825
Leitzel, Lillian b. 1892
Ludwig, Emil b. Jan 25, 1881
Marcus, Frank b. Jun 30, 1928
Meyerowitz, Jan b. Apr 23, 1913
Moszkowski, Moritz b. Aug 23, 1854
Prang, Louis b. Mar 12, 1824
Richthofen, Manfred von, Baron
   b. May 2, 1892
Schleiermacher, Friedrich Ernst Daniel
   b. Nov 21, 1768
Steinmetz, Charles Proteus b. Apr 9, 1865
Von Wangenheim, Chris b. 1942

Brieg, Germany
Masur, Kurt b. Jul 18, 1927

Brunswick, Germany
Gauss, Karl Friedrich b. Apr 30, 1777
Huch, Ricarda (Octavia) b. Jul 18, 1864
Lessing, Gotthold Ephraim
   d. Feb 15, 1781
Spohr, Louis Ludwig b. Apr 5, 1784
Winkelmann, Hermann b. Mar 8, 1849

Budesheim, Germany
George, Stefan Anton b. Dec 12, 1868

Burberg, Germany
Domagk, Gerhard d. Apr 24, 1964

Buttelstedt, Germany
Fasch, Johann Friedrich b. Apr 15, 1688

Calw, Germany
Hesse, Hermann b. Jul 2, 1877

Cassel, Germany
Mosenthal, Salomon Hermann von
   b. Jan 14, 1821
Spohr, Louis Ludwig d. Oct 22, 1859

Charlottenburg, Germany
Bedford, Sybille b. 1911
Helmholtz, Herman Ludwig Ferdinand von
   d. Sep 8, 1894
Mommsen, Theodor d. Nov 1, 1903

Chemnitz, Germany
Heym, Stefan b. Apr 10, 1913
May, Karl Friedrich b. Feb 25, 1842

Cleves, Germany
Anne of Cleves b. 1515

Coblenz, Germany
Kahn, Gus b. Nov 6, 1886
Metternich-Winneburg, Clemens
   b. May 15, 1773
Schoen-Rene, Anna b. Jan 12, 1864
Sontag, Henriette b. Jan 3, 1806

Coburg, Germany
Morgenthau, Hans Joachim
   b. Feb 17, 1904
Schroder-Devrient, Wilhelmine
   d. Jan 26, 1860

Colmar, Germany
Schongauer, Martin b. 1450

Cologne, Germany
Adenauer, Konrad b. Jan 5, 1876
Agrippa, Heinrich Cornelius
   b. Sep 14, 1486
Albertus Magnus, Saint d. Nov 15, 1280
Bruch, Max b. Jan 6, 1838
Burtin, Will b. Jan 27, 1908
Duns Scotus, John d. Nov 8, 1308
Eichenberg, Fritz b. Oct 24, 1901
Ernst, Jimmy b. Jun 24, 1920
Ernst, Max b. Apr 2, 1891
Etzioni, Amitai Werner b. Jan 4, 1929
Fisher, Fred b. Sep 30, 1875
Janssen, Herbert b. Sep 22, 1895
Jhabvala, Ruth Prawer b. May 7, 1927
Klemperer, Werner b. Mar 22, 1920
Offenbach, Jacques b. Jun 20, 1819
Otto, Nikolaus August d. Jan 26, 1891
Schurz, Carl b. Mar 2, 1829
Schutzendorf, Gustav b. 1883
Steinberg, William (Hans Wilhelm)
   b. Aug 1, 1899
Stiegel, Henry William b. May 13, 1729
Teschemacher, Marguerite b. Mar 3, 1903
Wallraff, Gunter b. 1942

Constance, Germany
Hus, Jan d. Jul 6, 1415
Wingler, Hans Maria b. Jan 5, 1920

Cusa, Germany
Nicholas of Cusa b. 1401

Danzig, Germany
Fahrenheit, Gabriel Daniel
   b. May 14, 1686
Grass, Gunter Wilhelm b. Oct 16, 1927
Rosovsky, Henry b. Sep 1, 1927
Schopenhauer, Arthur b. Jan 22, 1788

Darmstadt, Germany
Flotow, Friedrich von, Baron
   d. Jan 24, 1883
Koth, Erika b. Sep 15, 1927
Liebig, Justus von b. May 12, 1803
Muck, Karl b. Oct 22, 1859
Schmid, Eduard b. Oct 5, 1890

Dessau, Germany
Weill, Kurt b. Mar 2, 1900

Dinklage, Germany
Romberg, Bernhard b. Nov 11, 1767

Dornum, Germany
Shean, Al b. May 12, 1868

Dortmund, Germany
Weber, Carl b. Aug 7, 1925

Dresden, Germany
Augustus II b. May 12, 1670
Friedrich, Caspar David d. May 7, 1840

Hamilton, Edith b. Aug 12, 1867
Kastner, Erich b. Feb 23, 1899
Koch, Ilse b. 1907
Kollwitz, Kathe Schmidt d. Apr 22, 1945
Lohse, Otto b. Sep 21, 1859
Schlegel, Friedrich von (Karl Wilhelm
    Friedrich von) d. Jan 12, 1829
Schnorr, Ludwig, von Carolsfeld
    d. Jul 21, 1865
Schoeffler, Paul b. Sep 15, 1897
Schuch, Ernst von d. May 10, 1914
Schutz, Heinrich d. Nov 6, 1672
Siodmark, Curt b. Aug 10, 1902
Tichatschek, Joseph d. Jan 18, 1886
Treitschke, Heinrich Gotthard von
    b. Sep 15, 1834
Viertel, Peter b. Nov 16, 1920
VonBulow, Hans Guido b. Jan 8, 1830

Duisburg, Germany
Mercator, Gerhardus d. Dec 2, 1594

Dulich, Germany
Stock, Frederick A b. Nov 11, 1872

Duren, Germany
Schillings, Max von b. Apr 19, 1868

Dusseldorf, Germany
Alvary, Max b. May 3, 1856
Bierstadt, Albert b. Jan 7, 1830
Heine, Heinrich b. Dec 13, 1797
Kautner, Helmut b. Mar 25, 1908
Laubenthal, Rudolf b. Mar 10, 1886
Lorenz, Max b. May 17, 1901
Wenders, Wim b. 1945

Ebersbach, Germany
Bergmann, Carl b. Apr 11, 1821

Ebingen, Germany
Kiesinger, Kurt Georg b. Apr 6, 1904

Egern, Germany
Slezak, Leo d. Jun 1, 1946

Ehrenbrehstein, Germany
Brentano, Clemens Maria b. Sep 8, 1778

Einbech, Germany
Muhlenberg, Heinrich Melchior
    b. Sep 6, 1711

Eisenach, Germany
Bach, Johann Sebastian b. Mar 21, 1685
Schirmer, Gustave d. Aug 6, 1893

Eisleben, Germany
Agricola, Georgius b. Apr 20, 1494
Luther, Martin b. Nov 10, 1483

Elberfeld, Germany
Jaegers, Albert b. Mar 28, 1868
Knappertsbusch, Hans b. Mar 12, 1888
Stein, Horst b. May 28, 1928

Elbingerode, Germany
Ernst, Paul b. Mar 7, 1866

Emden, Germany
Peterson, Wolfgang b. Mar 14, 1941

Ems, Germany
Parry, William Edward, Sir d. Jul 8, 1855

Endenick, Germany
Schumann, Robert Alexander
    d. Jul 29, 1856

Enkhausen, Germany
Lubke, Heinrich b. Oct 11, 1894

Erasbach, Germany
Gluck, Christoph Wilibald b. Jul 2, 1714

Erfurt, Germany
Gehlen, Reinhard b. Apr 3, 1902
Weber, Max b. Apr 21, 1864

Erlangen, Germany
Ohm, Georg Simon b. Mar 16, 1787

Erxleben, Germany
Niemann, Albert b. Jan 15, 1831

Essen, Germany
Baedeker, Karl b. Nov 3, 1801
Krupp von Bohlen und Halbach, Bertha
    b. 1886
Krupp von Bohlen und Halbach, Bertha
    d. Sep 21, 1957
Krupp, Alfred b. Apr 26, 1812
Thomas, Theodore b. Oct 11, 1835

Eutin, Germany
Weber, Carl Maria von b. Nov 18, 1786

Flossenburg, Germany
Canaris, Wilhelm d. Apr 9, 1945

Frankfort, Germany
Huch, Ricarda (Octavia) d. Nov 17, 1947

Frankfurt, Germany
Aguilar, Grace d. Sep 16, 1847
Debus, Kurt Heinrich b. Nov 29, 1908
Elsheimer, Adam b. Mar 18, 1578
Erikson, Erik Homburger b. Jun 15, 1902
Francois, Samson b. May 18, 1924
Frank, Anne b. Jun 12, 1929
Fromm, Erich b. Mar 23, 1900
Goethe, Johann Wolfgang von
    b. Aug 28, 1749
Hahn, Otto b. Mar 8, 1879
Hertz, Alfred b. Jul 15, 1872
Kleist, Heinrich von b. Oct 18, 1777
Marchesi, Mathilde de Castrone
    b. Mar 24, 1821
Ophuls, Marcel b. Nov 1, 1927
Rothschild, Mayer Amschel
    b. Feb 23, 1743
Rothschild, Nathan Meyer b. Sep 16, 1777
Rudolf, Max b. Jun 15, 1902
Schiff, Jacob Henry b. 1847
Schopenhauer, Arthur d. Sep 20, 1860
Schumann, Clara Josephine Wieck
    d. May 20, 1896
Steffani, Agostino d. Feb 12, 1728
Udet, Ernst b. Apr 26, 1896

Frankfurt am Main, Germany
Loewi, Otto b. Jun 3, 1873

Freiburg, Germany
Bender, Hans b. Feb 5, 1907
Lasker, Albert Davis b. May 1, 1880
Rahner, Karl b. Mar 5, 1904

Freiburg im Breisqua, Germany
Husserl, Edmund d. Apr 27, 1938
Freudenstadt, Germany
Kollsman, Paul b. Feb 22, 1900
Friedenau, Germany
Bruch, Max d. Oct 2, 1920
Friedrichsruh, Germany
Bismarck, Otto Edward Leopold von
    d. Jul 30, 1898
Fuerth, Germany
Erhard, Ludwig b. Feb 4, 1897
Kissinger, Henry Alfred b. May 27, 1923
Kohler, Kaufmann b. May 10, 1843
Fulda, Germany
Braun, Karl Ferdinand b. Jun 6, 1850
Fulnek, Germany
Konwitschny, Franz b. Aug 14, 1901
Garding, Germany
Mommsen, Theodor b. Nov 30, 1817
Gera, Germany
Dix, Otto b. Dec 2, 1891
Frankel, Max b. Apr 3, 1930
Gernrode, Germany
Mohs, Friedrich b. Jan 29, 1773
Gestungshausen, Germany
Krauss, Werner b. 1884
Giebichenstein, Germany
Reichardt, Johann Friedrich
    d. Jun 27, 1814
Giessen, Germany
Dornberger, Walter Robert b. Sep 6, 1895
Levi, Hermann b. Nov 7, 1839
Milner, Alfred b. Mar 23, 1854
Goettingen, Germany
Blumenbach, Johann Friedrich
    d. Jan 22, 1840
Bunsen, Robert Wilhelm Eberhard
    b. Mar 31, 1811
Gauss, Karl Friedrich d. Feb 23, 1855
Hagen, Uta Thyra b. Jun 12, 1919
Planck, Max Karl Ernst Ludwig
    d. Oct 4, 1947
Goslar, Germany
Steinberg, Sigfrid Henry b. Aug 3, 1899
Gotha, Germany
Blumenbach, Johann Friedrich
    b. May 11, 1752
Gottingen, Germany
Vogel, Hans-Jochen b. Feb 3, 1926
Greifswald, Germany
Friedrich, Caspar David b. Sep 5, 1774
Greiz, Germany
Aroldingen, Karin von b. Jul 9, 1941
Gross-Tabarz, Germany
Alvary, Max d. Nov 7, 1898
Guben, Germany
Pieck, Wilhelm b. Jan 3, 1876
Gumund, Germany
Leutze, Emanuel b. May 24, 1816
Gustrow, Germany
Barlach, Ernst Heinrich d. Jan 24, 1938

Gutersloh, Germany
Henze, Hans Werner b. Jul 1, 1926
Hachtel, Germany
Mergenthaler, Ottmar b. May 11, 1854
Hagen, Germany
Halle, Charles, Sir b. Apr 11, 1819
Halle, Germany
Grunewald, Matthias d. 1528
Handel, George Frederick b. Feb 23, 1685
Heydrich, Reinhard b. Mar 9, 1904
Kappel, Gertrude b. Sep 1, 1893
Novalis b. May 2, 1772
Roux, Wilhelm d. Sep 15, 1924
Hamburg, Germany
Bach, Carl Philipp Emanuel
    d. Dec 15, 1788
Barth, Heinrich b. Feb 16, 1821
Brahms, Johannes b. May 7, 1833
Claudius, Matthias d. Jan 21, 1815
Enoch, Kurt b. Nov 22, 1895
Franck, James b. Aug 26, 1882
Hertz, Heinrich Rudolph b. Feb 22, 1857
Hesse, Eva b. Jan 11, 1936
Horney, Karen Danielson b. Sep 16, 1885
Kaempfert, Bert b. Oct 16, 1923
Keiser, Reinhard d. Sep 12, 1739
Klafsky, Katharina d. Sep 22, 1896
Klopstock, Friedrich Gottlieb
    d. Mar 14, 1803
Lagerfeld, Karl b. Sep 10, 1938
Lewisohn, Adolph b. 1849
Liliencron, (Friedrich Adolf Axel) Detlev
    von d. Jul 22, 1909
Lindner, Richard b. Nov 11, 1901
Mendelssohn, Felix b. Feb 3, 1809
Mengers, Sue b. Sep 2, 1938
Moltmann, Jurgen b. Apr 8, 1926
Neuendorff, Adolf b. Jun 13, 1843
Rey, Hans Augustus b. Sep 16, 1898
Romberg, Bernhard d. Aug 13, 1841
Rosa, Carl b. Mar 21, 1842
Rumann, Sig(fried) b. 1884
Sauer, Emil von b. Oct 8, 1862
Schmidt, Helmut Heinrich Waldemar
    b. Dec 23, 1918
Schroder-Devrient, Wilhelmine
    b. Dec 6, 1804
Springer, Axel Caesar b. May 2, 1912
Telemann, Georg Philipp d. Jun 25, 1767
Trefflich, Henry Herbert Frederick
    b. Jan 9, 1908
Warburg, Felix Moritz b. Jan 14, 1871
Warburg, James Paul b. Aug 18, 1896
Hamelin, Germany
Grese, Irma d. Dec 13, 1945
Hammelburg, Germany
Froben, Johann b. 1460
Hanau, Germany
Grimm, Jakob Ludwig Karl b. Jan 4, 1785
Grimm, Wilhelm Karl b. Feb 24, 1786
Hindemith, Paul b. Nov 16, 1895

Hannover, Germany
Arendt, Hannah b. Oct 14, 1906
Berliner, Emile b. May 20, 1851
Frederick Louis b. Jan 20, 1707
Herschel, William b. Nov 15, 1738
Husch, Gerhard b. Feb 2, 1901
Leibniz, Gottfried Wilhelm von
    d. Nov 14, 1716
Marschner, Heinrich d. Dec 14, 1861
Munchhausen, Hierony mus Karl Friedrich
    von, Baron b. May 11, 1720
Schlegel, Friedrich von (Karl Wilhelm
    Friedrich von) b. Mar 10, 1772
Wedekind, Frank b. Jul 24, 1864

Hanover, Germany
Busch, Wilhelm b. Apr 15, 1832
Panofsky, Erwin b. Mar 30, 1892

Hegenrath, Germany
Urlus, Jacques b. Jan 9, 1867

Heidelberg, Germany
Astor, John Jacob b. Jul 17, 1763
Bunsen, Robert Wilhelm Eberhard
    d. Aug 16, 1899
Burnham, Daniel H d. Jun 1, 1912
Ebert, Friedrich b. Feb 4, 1871
Gray, Hanna b. Oct 25, 1930
Patton, George Smith, Jr. d. Dec 21, 1945

Heppenheim, Germany
Antes, Horst b. Oct 28, 1936

Herrenburg, Germany
Andrae, Johann Valentin b. Aug 7, 1586

Hesse-Nasseau, Germany
Wagner, Robert b. Jun 8, 1877

Hildesheim, Germany
Krebs, Hans Adolf, Sir b. Aug 25, 1900

Hochheim, Germany
Eckhart, Johannes b. 1260

Hof, Germany
Boehm, Eric Hartzell b. Jul 15, 1918

Hohensaliza, Germany
Edwards, Gus b. Aug 18, 1879

Holstein, Germany
Barlach, Ernst Heinrich b. Jan 2, 1870

Holzhausen, Germany
Otto, Nikolaus August b. Jun 10, 1832

Ingolstadt, Germany
Hartmann, Rudolph b. Oct 11, 1900

Iptingen, Germany
Rapp, George b. Nov 1, 1757

Jena, Germany
Bernhard, Prince b. Jun 29, 1911
Eucken, Rudolf Christoph d. 1926
Roux, Wilhelm b. Jun 9, 1850

Juterbog, Germany
Kempff, (Wilhelm) Walter Friedrich
    b. Nov 25, 1895

Kamenz, Germany
Hauptmann, Bruno Richard
    b. Nov 26, 1900
Lessing, Gotthold Ephraim b. Jan 22, 1729

Kandern, Germany
Sutter, John Augustus b. Feb 15, 1803

Karlsruhe, Germany
Benz, Karl Friedrich b. Nov 26, 1844
Hofer, Karl b. 1878
Keilberth, Joseph b. Apr 19, 1908
Thoma, Hans d. 1924
Weinman, Adolph A b. Dec 11, 1870

Kassel, Germany
Reuter, Paul Julius Von b. 1816
Wunderlich, Fritz b. Sep 26, 1930

Kattaivitz, Germany
Mayer, Maria Goeppert b. Jun 28, 1906

Kaysersberg, Germany
Schweitzer, Albert b. Jan 14, 1875

Kempen, Germany
Lasker, Edward b. Dec 3, 1885
Thomas a Kempis b. 1380

Kempten, Germany
Mayr, Ernst Walter b. Jul 5, 1904

Kheitlingen, Germany
Eulenspiegel, Till b. 1290

Kiel, Germany
Liliencron, (Friedrich Adolf Axel) Detlev
    von b. Jun 3, 1844
Malina, Judith b. Jun 4, 1926
Planck, Max Karl Ernst Ludwig
    b. Apr 23, 1858
Wincelberg, Shimon b. Sep 26, 1924

Klein Glattbach, Germany
Neurath, Constantin Freiherr von
    b. Feb 2, 1873

Klotzche, Germany
Gjellerup, Karl Adolf d. Oct 11, 1919

Knittlingen, Germany
Faust, Johann b. 1480

Koblenz, Germany
Baedeker, Karl d. Oct 4, 1859
Giscard d'Estaing, Valery b. Feb 2, 1926
Laue, Max Theodor Felix von
    b. Oct 9, 1879

Koenigsbutte, Germany
Waxman, Franz b. Dec 24, 1906

Kongetvied, Germany
Seefried, Irmgard Maria Theresia
    b. Oct 9, 1919

Konigsberg, Germany
Hoffmann, Ernst Theodor Amadeus
    b. Jan 24, 1776
Jensen, Adolph b. Jan 12, 1837
Kant, Immanuel b. Apr 22, 1724
Kant, Immanuel d. Feb 12, 1804
Kollwitz, Kathe Schmidt b. Jul 8, 1867
Nicolai, Carl Otto b. Jun 9, 1810
Reichardt, Johann Friedrich
    b. Nov 25, 1752
Sandow, Eugene b. 1867

Konigsee, Germany
Schirmer, Gustave b. Sep 19, 1829

Kostritz, Germany
Schutz, Heinrich b. Oct 8, 1585

Krefeld, Germany
Beuys, Joseph b. May 12, 1921
Kreuzberg, Germany
Praetorius, Michael b. Feb 15, 1571
Kronach, Germany
Cranach, Lucas b. Oct 4, 1472
Kustrin, Germany
Tirpitz, Alfred von b. 1849
Lagow, Germany
Domagk, Gerhard b. Oct 30, 1895
Lamstedt, Germany
Spreckels, Claus b. Jul 9, 1828
Landau, Germany
Nast, Thomas b. Sep 27, 1840
Landshut, Germany
Feuerbach, Ludwig Andreas
b. Jul 28, 1804
Langenschwalbach, Germany
Busch, Adolphus d. Oct 10, 1913
Lauffen, Germany
Holderlin, Johann C F b. Feb 20, 1770
Lauingen, Germany
Albertus Magnus, Saint b. 1193
Laupheim, Germany
Laemmle, Carl, Sr. b. Jan 17, 1867
Leipzig, Germany
Bach, Johann Christian b. Sep 3, 1735
Bach, Johann Sebastian d. Jul 28, 1750
Backhaus, Wilhelm b. Mar 26, 1884
Beckmann, Max b. Feb 12, 1884
Bettmann, Otto Ludwig b. Oct 15, 1903
Fendler, Edvard b. Jan 22, 1902
Hartung, Hans b. Sep 21, 1904
Hempel, Frieda b. Jun 26, 1885
Hiller, Johann Adam d. Jun 16, 1804
Leibniz, Gottfried Wilhelm von
b. Jul 1, 1646
Mendelssohn, Felix d. Nov 4, 1847
Mobius, August Ferdinand d. Sep 26, 1868
Moscheles, Ignaz d. Mar 10, 1870
Nikisch, Arthur d. Jan 23, 1922
Ostwald, Wilhelm d. Apr 4, 1932
Pevsner, Nikolaus Bernhard Leon, Sir
b. Jan 30, 1902
Reger, Max d. May 11, 1916
Schumann, Clara Josephine Wieck
b. Sep 13, 1819
Ulbricht, Walter b. Jun 30, 1893
Wagner, Richard b. Mar 22, 1813
Lengfurt, Germany
Kahles, Charles William b. Jan 12, 1878
Lenthe, Germany
Siemens, (Ernst) Werner von
b. Dec 13, 1816
Siemens, William, Sir b. Apr 4, 1823
Lippe, Germany
Duesenberg, Frederick S b. Dec 6, 1876
Lippstadt, Germany
Niemoller, (Friedrich Gustav Emil) Martin
b. Jan 14, 1892

Loschwitz, Germany
Auer, Leopold d. Jul 15, 1930
Louenburg, Germany
Sapir, Edward b. Jan 26, 1884
Lubbenau, Germany
Gerhardt, Paul(us) d. May 27, 1676
Lubeck, Germany
Buxtehude, Dietrich d. May 9, 1707
Eulenspiegel, Till d. 1350
Kneller, Godfrey, Sir b. Aug 8, 1646
Mann, Heinrich Ludwig b. Mar 27, 1871
Mann, Thomas b. Jun 6, 1875
Ludwigshafen, Germany
Dieterle, William b. Jul 15, 1893
Kohl, Helmut Michael b. Apr 3, 1930
Luebeck, Germany
Brandt, Willy b. Dec 18, 1913
Luneburg, Germany
Himmler, Heinrich d. May 23, 1945
Lutzen, Germany
Gustavus Adolphus d. Nov 16, 1632
Magdeburg, Germany
Busse, Henry b. May 19, 1894
Kaiser, Georg b. Nov 25, 1878
Telemann, Georg Philipp b. Mar 14, 1681
Mainz, Germany
Busch, Adolphus b. Jul 10, 1839
Cornelius, Peter b. Dec 24, 1824
Cornelius, Peter d. Oct 26, 1874
Gutenberg, Johannes b. Feb 23, 1400
Hallstein, Walter b. Nov 17, 1901
Weyerhaeuser, Frederick b. Nov 21, 1834
Mannheim, Germany
Borkh, Inge b. May 26, 1921
Casewit, Curtis b. Mar 21, 1922
Cramer, Johann Baptist b. 1771
Kahn, Otto Hermann b. Feb 21, 1867
Klebe, Giselher b. Jun 28, 1925
Kotzebue, August Friedrich Ferdinand von
d. Mar 23, 1819
Krafft-Ebing, Richard von b. Aug 14, 1840
Mayer, Robert b. Jun 5, 1879
Morgenthau, Henry b. Apr 26, 1856
Speer, Albert b. Mar 19, 1905
Marbach, Germany
Schiller, Friedrich von (Johann Christoph
Friedrich von) b. Nov 10, 1759
Marburg, Germany
Behring, Emil Adolph von
d. Mar 31, 1917
Marienthal, Germany
Froebel, Friedrich Wilhelm August
d. Jun 21, 1852
Marktyl am Inn, Germany
Ratzinger, Joseph, Cardinal
b. Apr 16, 1927
Mechtshausen, Germany
Busch, Wilhelm d. Jan 9, 1908
Mecklenburg, Germany
Hinrichs, Gustav b. Dec 10, 1850

Meersburg, Germany
Mesmer, Franz Anton d. Mar 5, 1815
Meidereich, Germany
Lehmbruck, Wilhelm b. Jan 4, 1881
Meissen, Germany
Hahnemann, (Christian Friedrich) Samuel
b. Apr 10, 1755
Merseberg, Germany
Schumann, Elisabeth b. Jun 13, 1885
Merseburg, Germany
Tennstedt, Klaus b. Jun 6, 1926
Messkirch, Germany
Heidegger, Martin b. Sep 26, 1889
Heidegger, Martin d. May 26, 1976
Metzingen, Germany
Schonbein, Christian Friedrich
b. Oct 18, 1799
Speidel, Hans b. Oct 28, 1897
Minden, Germany
Boas, Franz b. Jul 9, 1858
Wiese, Kurt b. Apr 22, 1887
Modrath, Germany
Stockhausen, Karlheinz b. Aug 28, 1928
Mohrungen, Germany
Herder, Johann G von b. Aug 25, 1744
Montabour, Germany
Leyendecker, Joseph Christian
b. Mar 23, 1874
Muhlhausen, Germany
Loeffler, Charles Martin Tornov
b. Jan 30, 1861
Roebling, John Augustus b. Jun 12, 1806
Mulhouse, Germany
Wyler, William b. Jul 1, 1902
Munich, Germany
Aulaire, Edgar Parin d' b. Sep 30, 1898
Baader, Andreas b. 1943
Badura-Skoda, Paul b. Jan 15, 1927
Decoster, Charles Theodore
b. Aug 20, 1827
Einstein, Alfred b. Dec 30, 1880
Feuchtwanger, Lion b. Jul 7, 1884
Fischer, Anton Otto b. Feb 23, 1882
Fraunhofer, Joseph von d. Jun 7, 1826
Gidal, Tim b. May 18, 1909
Hanfstaengl, Ernst Franz Sedgwick
b. Feb 11, 1887
Haushofer, Karl b. Aug 27, 1869
Heiden, Konrad b. Aug 7, 1901
Herzog, Werner b. 1942
Heyse, Paul Johann d. 1914
Himmler, Heinrich b. Nov 7, 1900
Hoesslin, Franz von b. Dec 31, 1885
Jurgens, Curt b. Dec 12, 1915
Knote, Heinrich b. Nov 26, 1870
Kraus, Felix von d. Oct 30, 1937
Lassus, Orlandus de d. Jun 14, 1594
Liebig, Justus von d. Apr 18, 1873
Ludendorff, Erich Friedrich Wilhelm
d. Dec 20, 1937
Mach, Ernst d. Feb 19, 1916

Mann, Erika b. 1905
Mann, Klaus b. Nov 18, 1906
Meggendorfer, Lothar b. Nov 6, 1847
Meggendorfer, Lothar d. 1925
Mottl, Felix d. Jul 2, 1911
Murphy, Rosemary b. Jan 13, 1927
Nachbaur, Franz d. Mar 21, 1902
Ohm, Georg Simon d. Jul 7, 1854
Orff, Carl b. Jul 10, 1895
Penzias, Arno Allan b. Apr 26, 1933
Quidde, Ludwig d. Mar 5, 1941
Roentgen, Wilhelm Konrad
d. Feb 10, 1923
Sawallisch, Wolfgang b. Aug 26, 1923
Schindler, Alexander (Monroe)
b. Oct 4, 1925
Schnorr, Ludwig, von Carolsfeld
b. Jul 2, 1836
Senefelder, Aloys d. Feb 26, 1834
Spengler, Oswald d. May 8, 1936
Strauss, Franz Josef b. Sep 6, 1915
Strauss, Richard b. Jun 11, 1864
Trampler, Walter b. Aug 25, 1915
Van Rooy, Anton d. Nov 28, 1932
Viereck, George Sylvester b. Dec 31, 1884
Vogl, Heinrich d. Apr 21, 1900
Weber, Max d. Jun 14, 1920
Wedekind, Frank d. Mar 9, 1918
Wertham, Fredric b. 1895
Wolff, Fritz b. Oct 28, 1894
Murnau, Germany
Loeb, James d. May 28, 1933
Nackenheim, Germany
Zuckmayer, Carl b. Dec 27, 1896
Nassau, Germany
Altgeld, John Peter b. Dec 30, 1847
Neu-Ruppin, Germany
Fontane, Theodor b. Dec 30, 1819
Neubuckow, Germany
Schliemann, Heinrich b. Jan 6, 1822
Neudeck, Germany
Hindenburg, Paul von d. Aug 2, 1934
Neusess, Germany
Ruckert, Friedrich d. Jan 31, 1866
Neuss, Germany
Frings, Joseph Richard b. Feb 6, 1887
Neustadt, Germany
Howard, Eugene b. 1881
Neustrelitz, Germany
Humperdinck, Engelbert d. Sep 27, 1921
Niederbreitenbach, Germany
Ley, Robert b. Feb 15, 1890
Niederpoyritz, Germany
Kempe, Rudolf b. Jun 14, 1910
Nolde, Germany
Nolde, Emil b. Aug 7, 1867
Nowawes, Germany
Weiss, Peter b. Nov 8, 1916
Nuremberg, Germany
Durer, Albrecht b. May 21, 1471
Durer, Albrecht d. Apr 6, 1528

Frank, Hans d. Oct 16, 1946
Frick, Wilhelm d. Oct 16, 1946
Goering, Hermann Wilhelm
    d. Oct 15, 1946
Hechinger, Fred Michael b. Jul 7, 1920
Hopf, Hans b. Aug 2, 1916
Jahn, Helmut b. Jan 1, 1940
Keitel, Wilhelm d. Oct 16, 1946
Ley, Robert d. Oct 25, 1945
Modl, Martha b. Mar 22, 1912
Pachelbel, Johann b. Sep 1, 1653
Pachelbel, Johann d. Mar 3, 1706
Ribbentrop, Joachim von d. Oct 16, 1946
Rosenberg, Alfred d. Oct 16, 1946
Seyss-Inquart, Artur von d. Oct 16, 1946
Stoss, Veit b. 1445
Stoss, Veit d. 1533
Streicher, Julius d. Oct 16, 1946
Wassermann, Jakob b. Mar 10, 1873
Watts, Andre b. Jun 20, 1946
Nurnberg, Germany
Sachs, Hans b. Nov 5, 1494
Obersalzbrunn, Germany
Hauptmann, Gerhart b. Nov 15, 1862
Oberweissbach, Germany
Froebel, Friedrich Wilhelm August
    b. Apr 21, 1782
Offenbach-am-Main, Germany
Hotter, Hans b. Jan 19, 1909
Oldenburg, Germany
Jaspers, Karl b. Feb 23, 1883
Meinhof, Ulrike Marie b. 1934
Osnabruck, Germany
Remarque, Erich Maria b. Jun 22, 1898
Otterberg, Germany
Straus, Isidor b. Feb 6, 1845
Straus, Nathan b. Jan 31, 1848
Straus, Oscar b. Dec 23, 1850
Paehl bei Weilheim, Germany
Haushofer, Karl d. Mar 13, 1946
Parchim, Germany
Moltke, Helmuth Karl Bernhard von
    b. 1800
Perlberg, Germany
Lehmann, Lotte b. Feb 27, 1888
Planitz, Germany
Frobe, Gert b. Feb 25, 1912
Plauen, Germany
Richter, Karl b. Oct 15, 1926
Pomerania, Germany
Virchow, Rudolf b. Oct 31, 1821
Posen, Germany
Damrosch, Leopold b. Oct 22, 1832
Palmer, Lilli b. May 24, 1914
Potsdam, Germany
Frederick III b. 1831
Frederick William I d. May 31, 1740
Haeckel, Ernst Heinrich b. Feb 15, 1834
Helmholtz, Herman Ludwig Ferdinand von
    b. Aug 31, 1821
Humboldt, Wilhelm von b. Jun 22, 1767

Pressburg, Germany
Hummel, Johann Nepomuk
    b. Nov 14, 1778
Quedlinburg, Germany
Klopstock, Friedrich Gottlieb
    b. Jul 2, 1724
Radebeul, Germany
May, Karl Friedrich d. Mar 30, 1912
Rammenau, Germany
Fichte, Johann Gottlieb b. May 19, 1762
Rastenburg, Germany
Stauffenberg, Claus (Schenk Graf) Von
    d. Jul 20, 1944
Rechenberg, Germany
Feuerbach, Ludwig Andreas
    d. Sep 13, 1872
Regensburg, Germany
Kepler, Johannes d. Nov 15, 1630
Reideburg, Germany
Genscher, Hans-Dietrich b. Mar 21, 1927
Reinfeld, Germany
Claudius, Matthias b. Aug 15, 1740
Resitza, Germany
Meier-Graefe, Julius b. Jun 10, 1867
Rhaunen, Germany
Kahn, Albert b. Mar 21, 1869
Rheydt, Germany
Goebbels, Joseph (Paul Joseph)
    b. Oct 29, 1897
Rixdorf, Germany
Lawrie, Lee b. Oct 16, 1877
Rodalben, Germany
Frank, Johann Peter b. Mar 14, 1745
Rosenau, Germany
Albert, Prince b. Aug 26, 1819
Rosenheim, Germany
Goering, Hermann Wilhelm
    b. Jan 12, 1893
Rostock, Germany
Albrand, Martha, pseud. b. Sep 8, 1914
Blucher, Gebhard Leberecht von
    b. Dec 16, 1742
Grotius, Hugo d. Aug 28, 1645
Reichmann, Theodor b. Mar 15, 1848
Rottach-Egern, Germany
Patzak, Julius d. Jan 26, 1974
Rottluff, Germany
Schmidt-Rottluf, Karl b. Dec 1, 1884
Rottweil, Germany
Witz, Konrad b. 1400
Saarbrucken, Germany
Benary-Isbert, Margot b. Dec 2, 1899
Ophuls, Max b. May 6, 1902
Schroder, Gerhard b. Sep 11, 1910
Saint Georgen, Germany
Ernst, Paul d. May 13, 1933
Samotschin, Germany
Toller, Ernst b. Dec 1, 1893
Sauersberg, Germany
Schonbein, Christian Friedrich
    d. Aug 29, 1868

Saxony, Germany
Gerhardt, Paul(us) b. Mar 12, 1607
Pabst, Frederick b. Mar 28, 1836
Schlesian, Germany
Blucher, Gebhard Leberecht von
d. Sep 12, 1819
Ehrlich, Paul Ralph b. Feb 12, 1854
Schloss Tegel, Germany
Humboldt, Wilhelm von d. Apr 8, 1835
Schoenwald, Germany
Brach, Emil J b. 1859
Schoneck, Germany
Wurlitzer, Rudolph b. Jan 31, 1831
Schonhausen, Germany
Bismarck, Otto Edward Leopold von
b. Apr 1, 1815
Schreiberlau, Germany
Hauptmann, Gerhart d. Jun 6, 1946
Schulpforte, Germany
Mobius, August Ferdinand
b. Nov 17, 1790
Schwarzenburg, Germany
Rethberg, Elizabeth b. Sep 22, 1894
Schweinfurt, Germany
Ruckert, Friedrich b. May 16, 1788
Siegburg, Germany
Humperdinck, Engelbert b. Sep 1, 1854
Siegen, Germany
Busch, Fritz b. Mar 13, 1890
Site, Germany
Hoesslin, Franz von d. Sep 28, 1946
Solingen, Germany
Eichmann, Adolf (Otto Adolf)
b. Mar 19, 1906
Scheel, Walter b. Jul 8, 1919
Speyer, Germany
Haas, Karl b. May 15,
Starzeddal, Germany
Tillich, Paul Johannes b. Aug 20, 1886
Stettin, Germany
Catherine the Great b. Apr 21, 1729
Manns, Augustus, Sir b. Mar 12, 1825
Pannenberg, Wolfhart Ulrich
b. Oct 2, 1928
Strassburg, Germany
Bethe, Hans Albrecht b. Jul 2, 1906
Gottfried von Strassburg b. 1170
Heger, Robert b. Aug 19, 1886
Nessler, Victor E d. May 28, 1890
Simmel, Georg d. Sep 26, 1918
Straubing, Germany
Fraunhofer, Joseph von b. Mar 6, 1787
Strelno, Germany
Michelson, Albert Abraham
b. Dec 19, 1852
Stuttgart, Germany
Andrae, Johann Valentin d. Jan 27, 1654
Baader, Andreas d. Oct 18, 1977
Baumeister, Willi b. Jan 22, 1889
Bernhard, Lucian b. Mar 15, 1883
Daimler, Gottlieb d. Mar 6, 1900

Frank, Bruno b. Jun 13, 1887
Frick, Gottlob b. 1906
Hauff, Wilhelm b. Nov 29, 1802
Hauff, Wilhelm d. Nov 18, 1827
Hegel, Georg Wilhelm Friedrich
b. Aug 27, 1770
Jaeger, Gustav b.
Lowinsky, Edward Elias b. Jan 12, 1908
Meinhof, Ulrike Marie d. May 9, 1976
Muck, Karl d. Mar 3, 1940
Munchinger, Karl b. May 29, 1915
Schott, Anton d. Jan 6, 1913
Weizsacker, Richard Freiherr von
b. Apr 15, 1920
Suessen, Germany
Bausch, John Jacob b. Jul 25, 1830
Swabia, Germany
Rommel, Erwin Johannes Eugin
b. Nov 15, 1891
Tegernsee, Germany
Teschemacher, Marguerite d. May 19, 1959
Teuchern, Germany
Keiser, Reinhard b. Jan 9, 1674
Teutendorf, Germany
Flotow, Friedrich von, Baron
b. Apr 26, 1812
Tiefenbru, Germany
Gall, Franz Joseph b. Mar 9, 1758
Tingleff, Germany
Schacht, Hjalmar Horace Greeley
b. Jan 22, 1877
Treves, Germany
Marx, Karl Heinrich b. May 5, 1818
Tubingen, Germany
Blumenthal, Monica David b. Sep 1, 1930
Hauser, Gayelord b. May 17, 1895
Holderlin, Johann C F d. Jul 7, 1843
Ulm, Germany
Einstein, Albert b. Mar 14, 1879
Neff, Hildegarde b. Dec 28, 1925
Upper Franconia, Germany
Stauffenberg, Claus (Schenk Graf) Von
b. Nov 15, 1907
Vetschau, Germany
Hellmann, Richard b. 1876
Wandsbek, Germany
Bern, Paul b. Dec 3, 1889
Wannsee, Germany
Kleist, Heinrich von d. Nov 21, 1811
Wasseralfingen, Germany
Jooss, Kurt b. Jan 12, 1901
Wechold, Germany
Spitta, Philipp (Julius August Philipp)
b. Dec 27, 1841
Weckseldorf, Germany
Tichatschek, Joseph b. Jul 11, 1807
Weil der Stadt, Germany
Kepler, Johannes b. Dec 27, 1571
Weiler Giessen, Germany
Nachbaur, Franz b. Mar 25, 1835

Weimar, Germany
Bach, Carl Philipp Emanuel
   b. Mar 8, 1714
Bach, Wilhelm Friedemann b. 1710
Cranach, Lucas d. Oct 16, 1553
Goethe, Johann Wolfgang von
   d. Mar 22, 1832
Herder, Johann G von d. Dec 18, 1803
Hummel, Johann Nepomuk
   d. Oct 17, 1837
Kotzebue, August Friedrich Ferdinand von
   b. May 3, 1761
Nietzsche, Friedrich Wilhelm
   d. Aug 25, 1900
Schiller, Friedrich von (Johann Christoph
   Friedrich von) d. May 9, 1805

Weissenburg, Germany
Hofmann, Hans b. Mar 21, 1880

Weissenfels, Germany
Novalis d. Mar 25, 1801

Wenings, Germany
Kaufman, Henry b. 1927

Werl, Germany
Papen, Franz von b. Oct 29, 1879

Wesel, Germany
Minuit, Peter b. 1580
Ribbentrop, Joachim von b. Apr 30, 1893

Westphalia, Germany
Pemberton, John Clifford d. Jan 31, 1795
VonFurstenberg, Betsy b. Aug 16, 1932

Wiebelskirchen, Germany
Honecker, Erich b. Aug 25, 1912

Wiefelstede, Germany
Bultmann, Rudolf b. Aug 20, 1884

Wiehe, Germany
Ranke, Leopold von b. Dec 21, 1795

Wiesbaden, Germany
Daubeny, Peter Lauderdale, Sir
   b. Apr 1921
Schlondorff, Volker b. Mar 31, 1939
Signoret, Simone Henrietta Charlotte
   b. Mar 25, 1921
Villard, Oswald b. Mar 13, 1872

Wildhause, Germany
Zwingli, Huldreich b. Jan 1, 1484

Wimpfen, Germany
Link, Theodore Carl b. Mar 17, 1850

Wirsitz, Germany
VonBraun, Wernher b. Mar 23, 1912

Wolfenbuttel, Germany
Praetorius, Michael d. Feb 15, 1621

Wolfshagen, Germany
Steinway, Henry Engelhard
   b. Feb 15, 1797

Worms, Germany
Staudinger, Hermann b. Mar 23, 1881

Wuppertal, Germany
Carnap, Rudolf b. May 18, 1891

Wurttemberg, Germany
Daimler, Gottlieb b. Mar 17, 1834
Schelling, Friedrich Wilhelm Joseph von
   b. 1775

Wurttenberg, Germany
Mueller, Christian F b. Jun 23, 1839

Wurzburg, Germany
Grunewald, Matthias b. 1470
Heisenberg, Werner Karl b. Dec 5, 1901
Lehmann, Lilli b. Nov 24, 1848

Zerbst, Germany
Fasch, Johann Friedrich d. Dec 5, 1758

Zittau, Germany
Marschner, Heinrich b. Aug 16, 1795

Zwickau, Germany
Schocken, Theodore b. Oct 8, 1914
Schumann, Robert Alexander
   b. Jun 8, 1810

GERMANY (EAST)

Potzsch, Anett b. 1961
Reed, Dean d. Jun 17, 1986

Berlin, Germany (East)
Brecht, Bertolt Eugene Friedrich
   d. Aug 14, 1956
Felsenstein, Walter d. Oct 8, 1975
Pieck, Wilhelm d. Sep 7, 1960
Ulbricht, Walter d. Aug 1, 1973
Zweig, Arnold d. Nov 26, 1968

Koenigstein, Germany (East)
Christaller, Walter d. Mar 9, 1969

Plauen, Germany (East)
Ender, Kornelia b. Oct 25, 1958

Possneck, Germany (East)
Matthes, Roland b. Nov 17, 1950

GERMANY (WEST)

Knote, Heinrich d. Jan 15, 1953
Willis, Bruce b. Mar 19, 1955

Aachen, Germany (West)
Karman, Theodore Todor Von
   d. May 7, 1963

Bad Brueckenau, Germany (West)
Anderson, Max (Maxie Leroy)
   d. Jun 27, 1983

Bad Honnef, Germany (West)
Speidel, Hans d. Nov 28, 1984

Bad Reichenhall, Germany (West)
Goldmann, Nahum d. Aug 29, 1982

Baden-Baden, Germany (West)
Olczewska, Maria d. May 17, 1969

Bayreuth, Germany (West)
Muller, Maria d. Mar 13, 1958
Tietjen, Heinz d. Nov 1, 1967

Berlin, Germany (West)
Blech, Leo d. Aug 24, 1958
Braun, Otto d. Aug 15, 1974
Grosz, George Ehrenfried d. Jul 6, 1959
Hempel, Frieda d. Oct 7, 1955

Hofer, Karl d. Apr 3, 1955
Katona, George d. Jun 18, 1981
Kinski, Nastassja b. Jan 24, 1960
Klose, Margarete d. Dec 14, 1968
Laue, Max Theodor Felix von
    d. Apr 24, 1960
Leider, Frida d. Jun 4, 1975
Reuter, Ernst d. Sep 29, 1953
Springer, Axel Caesar d. Sep 22, 1985
Stolz, Robert d. Jun 27, 1975

Bonn, Germany (West)
Brauer, Max Julius Friedrich
    d. Feb 1, 1973
Erhard, Ludwig d. May 7, 1977
Lubke, Heinrich d. Apr 6, 1972

Braunschweig, Germany (West)
Brand, Jack b. Aug 4, 1953

Bremen, Germany (West)
Focke, Heinrich d. Feb 25, 1979

Cologne, Germany (West)
Boll, Heinrich b. Dec 21, 1917
Frings, Joseph Richard d. Dec 17, 1978
Fritzsche, Hans d. Sep 27, 1953
Massine, Leonide Fedorovich
    d. Mar 16, 1979

Dresden, Germany (West)
Paulus, Friedrich von d. Feb 1, 1957

Dusseldorf, Germany (West)
Beuys, Joseph d. Jan 23, 1986
Funk, Walther d. May 31, 1960
Stangl, Franz Paul d. Jun 28, 1971

Eberstein, Germany (West)
Furtwangler, Wilhelm d. Nov 30, 1954

Enzweihingen, Germany (West)
Neurath, Constantin Freiherr von
    d. Aug 14, 1956

Essen, Germany (West)
Bohlem, Arndt von d. May 13, 1986

Frankfurt, Germany (West)
Blakely, Susan b. Sep 7, 1948
Hindemith, Paul d. Dec 28, 1963
Schlusnus, Heinrich d. Jun 19, 1952

Freiberg im Breisgau, Germany (West)
Staudinger, Hermann d. Sep 9, 1965

Freiburg, Germany (West)
Kazantzakis, Nikos d. Oct 26, 1957

Friedrichshafen, Germany (West)
Eckener, Hugo d. Aug 14, 1954

Fussen, Germany (West)
Guderian, Heinz Wilhelm d. May 15, 1954

Garmisch, Germany (West)
Strauss, Richard d. Sep 8, 1949

Gavmisch, Germany (West)
Brundage, Avery d. May 8, 1975

Goettingen, Germany (West)
Born, Max d. Jan 5, 1970
Hahn, Otto d. Jul 28, 1968

Gunzberg, Germany (West)
Kelly, Petra Karin b. Nov 29, 1947

Hamburg, Germany (West)
Debus, Sigurd Friedrich d. Apr 16, 1981
Doenitz, Karl C d. Dec 24, 1980
Dornberger, Walter Robert d. Jun 1980
Marek, Kurt W d. Apr 12, 1972
Ophuls, Max d. Mar 26, 1957
Schmidt-Isserstedt, Hans d. May 28, 1973

Hanover, Germany (West)
Rundstedt, Karl Rudolf Gerd von
    d. Feb 24, 1953

Heidelberg, Germany (West)
Browne, Jackson b. Oct 9, 1950
Depailler, Patrick d. Aug 1, 1980
Wunderlich, Fritz d. Sep 17, 1966

Heidenheim, Germany (West)
Bauersfeld, Walther d. Oct 28, 1959

Heilbronn, Germany (West)
Jooss, Kurt d. May 22, 1979

Herzogenaurach, Germany (West)
Dassler, Adolf d. Sep 18, 1978

Hochheim, Germany (West)
Clark, James d. Apr 7, 1968

Hurtgenwald, Germany (West)
Boll, Heinrich d. Jul 16, 1985

Inning, Germany (West)
Egk, Werner d. Jul 10, 1983

Karl-Marx-Stadt, Germany (West)
Witt, Katarina b. Dec 1965

Kassel, Germany (West)
Arndt, Adolf d. Feb 13, 1974

Kiel, Germany (West)
Raeder, Erich d. Nov 6, 1960

Lake Starnberg, Germany (West)
Gehlen, Reinhard d. Jun 8, 1979

Landstuhl, Germany (West)
Burton, LeVar(dis Robert Martyn, Jr.)
    b. Feb 16, 1957

Liemen, Germany (West)
Becker, Boris b. Nov 22, 1967

Luneberg, Germany (West)
Ludwig, Leopold d. 1979

Marburg, Germany (West)
Bultmann, Rudolf d. Jul 30, 1976
Werner, Oskar d. Oct 23, 1984

Munich, Germany (West)
Bazna, Elyesa d. 1970
Beaumont, Hugh d. May 14, 1982
Berger, David d. Sep 5, 1972
Blab, Uwe Konstantine b. Mar 26, 1962
Board, Lillian d. Dec 26, 1970
Dagover, Lil (Marta Maria Liletta)
    d. Jan 30, 1980
Fassbinder, Rainer Werner d. Jun 10, 1982
Friedman, Ze'ev d. Sep 5, 1972
Frisch, Karl von d. Jun 12, 1982
Gimbel, Richard d. May 27, 1970
Goering, Emmy Sonnemann d. Jun 8, 1973
Guardini, Romano d. Oct 1, 1968
Gutfreund, Yosef d. Sep 5, 1972
Halfin, Eliezer d. Sep 5, 1972

Hanfstaengl, Ernst Franz Sedgwick
  d. Nov 6, 1975
Hanika, Sylvia b. Nov 30, 1959
Heisenberg, Werner Karl d. Feb 1, 1976
Kappel, Gertrude d. Apr 1971
Keilberth, Joseph d. Jul 7, 1968
Kimball, Fiske d. Aug 14, 1955
Knappertsbusch, Hans d. Oct 25, 1965
Lowery, "Nick" (Gerald Lowery)
  b. May 27, 1956
Mainbocher d. Dec 27, 1976
Messerschmitt, Willy (Wilhelm)
  d. Sep 15, 1978
Orff, Carl d. Mar 29, 1982
Richter, Karl d. Feb 16, 1981
Romano, Joseph d. Sep 5, 1972
Schacht, Hjalmar Horace Greeley
  d. Jun 4, 1970
Shapira, Amitzur d. Sep 5, 1972
Shorr, Kehat d. Sep 5, 1972
Slavin, Mark d. Sep 5, 1972
Spitzer, Andre d. Sep 5, 1972
Springer, Ya'acov d. Sep 5, 1972
Wagner, Wieland Adolf Gottfried
  d. Oct 16, 1966
Walbrook, Anton d. Aug 9, 1967
Weinberg, Moshe d. Sep 5, 1972
Wolff, Fritz d. Jan 18, 1957

Ottobrunn, Germany (West)
  Dieterle, William d. Dec 9, 1972

Reit im Winkl, Germany (West)
  Mittermaier, Rosi b. Aug 5, 1950

Rhondorf, Germany (West)
  Adenauer, Konrad d. Apr 19, 1967

Schopfheim, Germany (West)
  Forssmann, Werner Theodor Otto
    d. Jun 1, 1979

Starnberg, Germany (West)
  Marcuse, Herbert d. Jul 29, 1979

Stuttgart, Germany (West)
  Baumeister, Willi d. Aug 31, 1955
  Hallstein, Walter d. Mar 29, 1982
  Porsche, Ferdinand d. Jan 30, 1951
  Schilling, Peter b. Jan 28, 1956

Weisbaden, Germany (West)
  Vandeweghe, "Kiki" (Ernest Maurice)
    b. Aug 1, 1958

West Berlin, Germany (West)
  Schmidt-Rottluf, Karl d. Aug 9, 1976

Wiesbaden, Germany (West)
  McEnroe, John Patrick, Jr.
    b. Feb 16, 1959
  Niemoller, (Friedrich Gustav Emil) Martin
    d. Mar 6, 1984

Wuppertal, Germany (West)
  Neutra, Richard Joseph d. Apr 16, 1970

GHANA

Quaison-Sackey, Alex(ander)
  b. Aug 9, 1924
Accra, Ghana
  DuBois, W(illiam) E(dward) B(urghardt)
    d. Aug 27, 1963
  Rawlings, Jerry John b. Jun 22, 1947
Gwollu, Ghana
  Limann, Hilla b. Dec 12, 1934

GIBRALTAR

Clinton, Henry, Sir d. Dec 23, 1795

GREECE

Sappho b. 612 BC
Abdera, Greece
  Democritus b. 460 BC
  Protagoras b. 490 BC?
Argos, Greece
  Polycletus the Elder b.
Athens, Greece
  Bachauer, Gina b. May 21, 1913
  Bachauer, Gina d. Aug 22, 1976
  Balopoulos, Michael d. Mar 3, 1978
  Constantine XII b. Jun 2, 1940
  Costa-Gavras(, Henri) b. 1933
  Desses, Jean d. Aug 2, 1970
  Doxiadis, Constantinos Apostolos
    d. Jun 28, 1975
  Marina b. Dec 13, 1906
  Mercouri, "Melina" (Maria Amalia)
    b. Oct 18, 1925
  Metaxas, John(Ioannis) d. Jan 29, 1941
  Mitropoulos, Dimitri b. Feb 18, 1896
  Moscona, Nicola b. Sep 23, 1907
  Niarchos, Stavros Spyros b. Jul 3, 1909
  Paul I b. Dec 14, 1901
  Paxinou, Katina d. Feb 22, 1973
  Pericles d. 429 ?BC
  Phidias b. 500 BC
  Plato d. 347 BC
  Plato b. 427 BC
  Saud (Ibn Abdul Aziz al Saud)
    d. Feb 23, 1969
  Seferiades, Giorgos Styljanou
    d. Sep 20, 1971
  Sevitzky, Fabien d. Feb 2, 1967
  Socrates d. 399 ?BC
  Socrates b. 470 BC?
  Sophocles d. 406 ?BC
  Thucydides b. 460 BC
  Tsatsos, Constantinos b. Jul 1, 1899
  Xenophon b. 434 BC
Attica, Greece
  Demosthenes b. 384 BC
Calavria, Greece
  Demosthenes d. Oct 322 BC
Cephalonia, Greece
  Metaxas, John(Ioannis) b. Apr 12, 1871

Chaeronea, Greece
Plutarch b. 46
Plutarch d. 120
Chalcidice, Greece
Aristotle b. 384 BC
Chiliomondion, Greece
Papas, Irene b. Sep 3, 1926
Chios, Greece
Papandreou, Andreas George
b. Feb 5, 1919
Colonus, Greece
Sophocles b. 496 BC?
Comi, Greece
Papanicolaou, George Nicholas
b. May 13, 1883
Corfu, Greece
Philip, Prince b. Jun 10, 1921
Cyrene, Greece
Callimachus b. 305 BC
Eratosthenes b. 275 BC?
Eleochorian, Greece
Papadopoulos, George b. 1919
Eleusis, Greece
Aeschylus b. 524 BC?
Ionian Islands, Greece
Hearn, Lafcadio b. Jun 27, 1850
Kastoria, Greece
Samaras, Lucas b. Sep 14, 1936
Lefcohorion, Greece
Bardis, Panos Demetrios b. Sep 24, 1924
Missolonghi, Greece
Byron, George Gordon Noel Byron, Baron
d. Apr 19, 1824
Orchomenus, Greece
Hesiod d.
Patrae, Greece
Andrew, Saint d. 70 ?AD
Patras, Greece
Papandreou, George b. Feb 13, 1888
Pella, Greece
Euripides d. 406 ?BC
Pergamum, Greece
Galen b. 129
Phrygia, Greece
Alcibiades d. 404 ?BC
Piraeus, Greece
Paxinou, Katina b. Dec 17, 1900
White, T(erence) H(anbury)
d. Jan 17, 1964
Prote, Greece
Karamanlis, Constantine b. Feb 23, 1907
Pylos, Greece
Spyropoulos, Jannis b. Mar 12, 1912
Salamis, Greece
Euripides b. Sep 23, 480 BC?
Salonica, Greece
Abravanel, Maurice b. Jan 6, 1903
Salonika, Greece
Aldredge, Theoni A(thanasiou Vashlioti)
b. Aug 22, 1932

Samos, Greece
Epicurus b. 342 BC
Pythagoras b. 582 BC
Scyros, Greece
Brooke, Rupert Chawner d. Apr 23, 1915
Skourokhori, Greece
Skouras, Spyros Panagiotes
b. Mar 28, 1893
Stenimochos, Greece
Doxiadis, Constantinos Apostolos
b. May 14, 1913
Thaos, Greece
Polygnotus b.
Thebes, Greece
Pindar b. Sep 4, 518 BC?
Thermopylae, Greece
Leonidas I d. 480 BC
Tripolis, Greece
Stavropoulos, George Peter b. Jan 22, 1920
Vassilikon, Greece
Athenagoras I b. Mar 25, 1886
Volos, Greece
Chirico, Giorgio de b. Jul 10, 1888
Vangelis b. Mar 29, 1943
Zante, Greece
Foscolo, (Niccolo) Ugo b. 1778
Vesalius, Andreas d. Oct 15, 1564

GREENLAND

Rasmussen, Knud Johan Victor
b. Jun 7, 1879
Wegener, Alfred d. Nov 1930

GRENADA

Saint George's, Grenada
Bishop, Maurice d. Oct 19, 1983

GUAM

Agana, Guam
Calvo, Paul McDonald b. Jul 25, 1934
Canham, Erwin Dain d. Jan 3, 1982

GUATEMALA

Cochran, Steve d. Jun 15, 1965
Sarg, Tony (Anthony Frederick)
b. Apr 24, 1882
Guatemala City, Guatemala
Asturias, Miguel Angel b. Oct 19, 1899
Hendricks, Ted (Theodore Paul)
b. Nov 1, 1947
Jensen, Alfred Julio b. Dec 11, 1903
Mejia Victores, Oscar Humberto
b. Dec 9, 1930
Merida, Carlos b. Dec 2, 1891
Huehuetenango, Guatemala
Rios Montt, Jose Efrain b. Jun 16, 1926

GUINEA

Dessalines, Jean J b. 1758
Conakry, Guinea
Nkrumah, Kwame d. Apr 27, 1972

GUINEA-BISSEAU

Bissau, Guinea-Bisseau
Cabral, Luis de Almeida b. 1931

GUYANA

Demerara, Guyana
Chung, Arthur b. Jan 10, 1918
Georgetown, Guyana
Burnham, Forbes (Linden Forbes Sampson)
d. Aug 6, 1985
Jonestown, Guyana
Jones, Reverend Jim (James)
d. Nov 18, 1978
Ryan, Leo Joseph d. Nov 19, 1978
Kitty, Guyana
Burnham, Forbes (Linden Forbes Sampson)
b. Feb 20, 1923

HAITI

Audubon, John James b. Apr 26, 1785
Christophe, Henri d.
Dessalines, Jean J d. Oct 17, 1806
Cape Francois, Haiti
Toussaint l'Ouverture, Pierre Dominique
b. 1743
Port-au-Prince, Haiti
Duvalier, Francois b. Apr 14, 1907
Duvalier, Francois d. Apr 21, 1971
Duvalier, Jean-Claude b. Jul 3, 1951
Kostelanetz, Andre d. Jan 13, 1980

HOLLAND

Rotterdam, Holland
Bayle, Pierre d. Dec 28, 1706

HUNGARY

Alvary, Lorenzo b. Feb 20, 1909
Dobozy, Imre b. Oct 30, 1917
Gabor, Jolie b. Sep 29, 1896
Kilenyi, Edward, Sr. b. Jan 25, 1884
Mindszenty, Jozsef, Cardinal
b. Mar 29, 1892
Pascal, Gabriel b. Jun 4, 1894
Austria, Hungary
Beck, Martin b. Jul 30, 1867
Bacsbarsod, Hungary
Moholy-Nagy, Laszlo b. Jul 20, 1895
Balatonszarszo, Hungary
Jozsef, Attila d. Dec 3, 1937
Bolgar, Hungary
Schick, Bela b. Jul 16, 1877

Bolho, Hungary
Losonczi, Pal b. Sep 18, 1919
Brasso, Hungary
Brassai b. Sep 9, 1899
Budapest, Hungary
Anda, Geza b. Nov 19, 1921
Biro, Val b. Oct 6, 1921
Cafritz, Gwen b. 1912
Capa, Cornell b. Apr 19, 1918
Capa, Robert b. 1913
Curtiz, Michael b. Dec 24, 1898
Darvas, Lili b. Apr 10, 1906
DeErdely, Francis (Ferenc) b. May 3, 1904
Dolly, Jenny b. Oct 25, 1892
Dolly, Rosie b. Oct 25, 1892
Dorati, Antal b. Apr 9, 1906
Eggerth, Marta b. Apr 17, 1916
Esslin, Martin Julius b. Jun 8, 1918
Fabri, Zoltan b. Oct 15, 1917
Ferencsik, Janos b. Jan 18, 1907
Ferencsik, Janos d. Jun 12, 1984
Fleischmann, Charles Louis b. Nov 3, 1834
Fricsay, Ferenc b. Aug 9, 1914
Gabor, Dennis b. Jun 5, 1900
Gabor, Eva b. Feb 11, 1921
Gabor, Magda b. Jul 10, 1917
Gabor, Zsa Zsa (Sari) b. Feb 6, 1919
Gero, Erno b. Aug 17, 1898
Gero, Erno d. Mar 12, 1980
Goldmark, Peter Carl b. Dec 2, 1906
Herzl, Theodor b. May 2, 1860
Hevesy, George de b. Aug 1, 1885
Hoffman, Anna Marie Lederer Rosenberg
b. Jun 19, 1902
Houdini, Harry b. Mar 24, 1874
Hubay, Jeno b. Sep 14, 1858
Ivogun, Maria b. Nov 11, 1891
Jozsef, Attila b. Apr 11, 1905
Karfiol, Bernard b. May 6, 1886
Karman, Theodore Todor Von
b. May 11, 1881
Katona, George b. Nov 6, 1901
Kertesz, Andre b. Jul 2, 1894
Kertesz, Istvan b. Aug 29, 1929
Kodaly, Zoltan d. Mar 6, 1967
Koestler, Arthur b. Sep 5, 1905
Kraus, Lili b. Mar 4, 1908
Lengyel, Emil b. Apr 26, 1895
Lukas, Paul b. May 26, 1894
Magyar, Gabriel b. Dec 5, 1914
Mannheim, Karl b. Mar 27, 1893
Massey, Ilona b. Jun 16, 1910
Molnar, Ferenc b. 1878
Nyiregyhazi, Ervin b. Jan 19, 1903
Ormandy, Eugene b. Nov 18, 1899
Penner, Joe b. Nov 11, 1904
Polya, George b. Dec 13, 1887
Reiner, Fritz b. Dec 10, 1888
Rosenberg, Anna Marie b. Jul 19, 1900
Rozsa, Miklos b. Apr 18, 1907
Sakall, S Z b. Feb 2, 1884

Sebastian, George b. Aug 17, 1903
Seidl, Anton b. May 7, 1850
Solti, Georg, Sir b. Oct 21, 1912
Stader, Maria b. 1915
Starker, Janos b. Jul 5, 1924
Szabo, Gabor b. Mar 8, 1936
Szabo, Gabor d. Feb 26, 1982
Szabolcsi, Bence d. Jan 21, 1973
Szasz, Thomas Stephen b. Apr 15, 1920
Szell, George b. Jun 7, 1897
Szenkar, Eugen b. Apr 9, 1891
Szent-Gyorgyi, Albert von b. Sep 16, 1893
Szigeti, Joseph b. Sep 2, 1892
Szilard, Leo b. Feb 11, 1898
Teller, Edward b. Jan 15, 1908
Tors, Ivan b. Jun 12, 1916
Varga, Laszlo b. 1924
Von Karman, Theodore b. May 11, 1881
Von Neumann, John b. Dec 28, 1903
Wank, Roland A b. Oct 2, 1898
Weiss, Ted b. Sep 17, 1927
Wise, Stephen Samuel b. Mar 17, 1874
Cegled, Hungary
Pal, George b. Feb 1, 1908
Csuro, Hungary
Farago, Ladislas b. Sep 21, 1906
Czeged, Hungary
Zsigmond, Vilmos b. Jun 16, 1930
Debrecen, Hungary
Halasz, Laszlo b. Jun 6, 1905
Lakatos, Imre b. Nov 9, 1922
Fiume, Hungary
Kadar, Janos b. May 22, 1912
Heves, Hungary
Remenyi, Eduard b. Jul 17, 1830
Idvor, Hungary
Pupin, Michael Idvorsky b. Oct 4, 1858
Kaposvar, Hungary
Nagy, Imre b. 1896
Kassa, Hungary
Andrassy, Gyula, Count b. Mar 3, 1823
Kecskemet, Hungary
Bartok, Eva b. Jun 18, 1926
Kodaly, Zoltan b. Dec 16, 1882
Kenderes, Hungary
Horthy de Nagybanya, Nicholas
    b. Jun 18, 1868
Keszthely, Hungary
Goldmark, Karl b. May 18, 1830
Kisstee, Hungary
Joachim, Joseph b. Jun 28, 1831
Lebenyi Szent, Hungary
Nikisch, Arthur b. Oct 12, 1855
Leva, Hungary
Fodor, Eugene b. Oct 5, 1905
Lugos, Hungary
Devereux, George b. Sep 13, 1908
Lugosi, Bela b. Oct 20, 1882
Mako, Hungary
Pulitzer, Joseph b. Apr 10, 1847

Marosvasarhely, Hungary
Laszlo, Magda b. 1919
Monok, Hungary
Kossuth, Lajos b. Sep 19, 1802
Moson, Hungary
Flesch, Karl b. Oct 9, 1873
Nagykanizsa, Hungary
Romberg, Sigmund b. Jul 29, 1887
Nagyrodog, Hungary
Banky, Vilma b. Jan 9, 1903
Nagyszentmiklos, Hungary
Bartok, Bela b. May 25, 1881
Nagyvarad, Hungary
Schorr, Friedrich b. Sep 2, 1888
Pecs, Hungary
Breuer, Marcel Lajos b. May 22, 1902
Vasarely, Victor b. 1908
Presburg, Hungary
Dohnanyi, Erno von b. Jul 27, 1877
Raab, Hungary
Richter, Hans b. Apr 4, 1843
Raiding, Hungary
Liszt, Franz (Ferencz) b. Oct 22, 1811
Riese, Hungary
Zukor, Adolph b. Jan 7, 1873
Romorn, Hungary
Lehar, Franz b. Apr 30, 1870
Rosenberg, Hungary
Lorre, Peter b. Jun 26, 1904
Saint Johann, Hungary
Klafsky, Katharina b. Sep 19, 1855
Sarkad, Hungary
Konya, Sandor b. Sep 23, 1923
Szeged, Hungary
Pogany, Willy b. Aug 24, 1882
Sziget, Hungary
Gassner, John Waldhorn b. Jan 30, 1903
Tarna-Ors, Hungary
Orczy, Emmuska, Baroness b. Sep 23, 1865
Temesvar, Hungary
Bromberg, J. Edward b. Dec 25, 1903
Matzenauer, Margaret b. Jun 1, 1881
Turkeve, Hungary
Korda, Alexander, Sir b. Sep 16, 1893
Ujpest, Hungary
Vertes, Marcel b. Aug 10, 1895
Vac, Hungary
Jancso, Miklos b. Sep 27, 1922
Vesprem, Hungary
Auer, Leopold b. Jun 7, 1845
Volosca, Hungary
Andrassy, Gyula, Count d. Feb 18, 1890

ICELAND

Andrews, Frank M(axwell) d. May 3, 1943
Charcot, Jean Baptiste Etienne Auguste
    d. Sep 16, 1936
Ericson, Leif b. 975
Hermannsson, Steingrimur b. Jun 22, 1928

Reykjavik, Iceland
Finnbogadottir, Vigdis b. Apr 15, 1930
Laxness, Halldor Kiljan b. Apr 23, 1902
Tomasson, Helgi b. Oct 8, 1942
Thingvalla, Iceland
Benediktsson, Bjarni d. Jul 10, 1970
Tjorn, Iceland
Eldjarn, Kristjan b. Dec 6, 1916

INDIA

Adamson, George b. 1906
Bairnsfather, Bruce b. Jul 1888
Shankar, Uday b. 1901
Wingate, Orde Charles b. 1903
Adyar, India
Olcott, Henry Steel d. Feb 17, 1907
Agra, India
Babur d. Dec 26, 1530
Ahmaddnagar, India
Milligan, "Spike" (Terence Alan)
b. Apr 16, 1918
Allahabad, India
Gandhi, Indira Priyadarshini Nehru
b. Nov 19, 1917
Nehru, Jawaharlal b. Nov 14, 1889
Nehru, Jawaharlal d. May 27, 1964
Pandit, Vijaya Lakshmi (Nehru)
b. Aug 18, 1900
Almora, India
Ross, Ronald, Sir b. May 13, 1857
Ambala, India
Philby, Kim (Harold Adrian Russell)
b. 1912
Assam, India
Wingate, Orde Charles d. Mar 24, 1944
Attock Serai, India
Butler of Saffron Walden, Richard Austen,
Baron b. Dec 9, 1902
Bangalore, India
Anderson, Lindsay Gordon
b. Apr 17, 1923
Cowdrey, (Michael) Colin b. Dec 24, 1932
Bareilly, India
Jones, Eli Stanley d. Jan 26, 1973
Benares, India
Brooke, James, Sir b. Apr 29, 1803
Shankar, Ravi b. Apr 7, 1920

Bengal, India
Ghose, Sri Chinmoy Kumar
b. Aug 27, 1931
Rahman, Mujibur, Sheik b. 1920
Bhadeli, India
Desai, Morarji Ranchodji b. Feb 29, 1896
Bhubaneswar, India
Haldane, J(ohn) B(urdon) S(anderson)
d. Dec 1, 1964
Bihar, India
Prasad, Rajendra b. Dec 3, 1884
Bogra, India
Rahman, Ziaur b. Jan 19, 1936
Bombay, India
Gandhi, Rajiv Ratna b. Aug 20, 1944
Khambatta, Persis b. Oct 2, 1950
Kipling, Rudyard b. Dec 30, 1865
Mehta, Zubin b. Apr 29, 1936
Prowse, Juliet b. Sep 25, 1936
Spence, Basil, Sir b. Aug 13, 1907
White, T(erence) H(anbury)
b. May 29, 1906
Buxar, India
Prasad, Ananda Shiva b. Jan 1, 1928
Calcutta, India
Chaudhuri, Haridas b. May 24, 1913
Dibdin, Thomas Frognall b. 1776
Dragonette, Jessica b. Feb 14, 1910
Masters, John b. Oct 26, 1914
Murray, Margaret Alice b. Jul 13, 1863
Ray, Satyajit b. May 2, 1921
Shankar, Uday d. Sep 26, 1977
Tagore, Rabindranath, Sir b. May 6, 1861
Tawney, Richard Henry b. Nov 30, 1880
Thackeray, William Makepeace
b. Jul 18, 1811
Weatherford, Teddy d. Apr 25, 1945
Cawnpore, India
Roberts, Frederick b. 1832
Chukua, India
Christie, Julie b. Apr 14, 1940
Cochin, India
DaGama, Vasco d. Dec 24, 1524
Dacca, India
Khan, Fazlur Rahman b. Apr 3, 1929
Darjeeling, India
Durrell, Lawrence George b. Feb 27, 1912
Leigh, Vivien b. Nov 5, 1913
Tenzing, Norgay d. May 10, 1986
Delhi, India
Ahmed, Fakhruddin Ali b. May 13, 1905
Ali, Ahmed b. Jul 1, 1908
Dohad, India
Aurangzeb b. Oct 24, 1618
Fort Agra, India
Barrymore, Maurice b. 1847
Gagoda, India
Bhave, Acharya Vinoba b. Sep 11, 1895
Ghazipore, India
Cornwallis, Charles, Marquis
d. Oct 5, 1805

Quazin, Iran
Rajai, Mohammed Ali b. 1933
Teheran, Iran
Beheshti, Mohammad, Ayatollah
   d. Jun 28, 1981
Ghotbzadeh, Sadegh d. Sep 15, 1982
Hoveyda, Amir Abbas d. Apr 7, 1979
Mossadegh, Mohammad d. Mar 5, 1967
Pahlevi, Farah Diba b. Oct 14, 1938
Rajai, Mohammed Ali d. Aug 30, 1981
Tehran, Iran
Nicolson, Harold George, Sir
   b. Nov 21, 1886

IRAQ

Al Kufa, Iraq
Ali d. 661
Baghdad, Iraq
Bell, Gertrude Margaret d. Jul 11, 1926
Faisal II b. May 2, 1935
Kassem, Abdul Karim b. Nov 21, 1914
Kassem, Abdul Karim d. Feb 9, 1963
Tikrit, Iraq
Bakr, Ahmad Hasan al b. 1914
Hussain al Takriti, Saddam
   b. Apr 28, 1937
Hussein, Saddam b. May 2, 1935

IRELAND

Berkeley, George b. Mar 12, 1685
Blood, Thomas b. 1618
Chain, Ernest Boris, Sir d. Sep 14, 1979
Chesney, Francis Rawdon b. Mar 16, 1789
Colden, Cadwallader b. Feb 7, 1688
Conway, Thomas b. Feb 27, 1735
Craig, May b. 1889
Friel, Brian b. Jan 9, 1929
Howard, Tom b. 1886
Robinson, Lennox (Esme Stuart Lennox)
   b. Oct 4, 1886
Shields, James b. May 10, 1810
Stern, James b. Dec 26, 1907
Taylor, William Desmond b. Apr 26, 1877
Thornton, Matthew b. 1714
Annaghdown, Ireland
Brendan of Clonfert, Saint d. 577
Ardglass, Ireland
Hunter, Thomas b. Oct 19, 1831
Athlone, Ireland
McCormack, John b. Jun 14, 1884
O'Connor, Thomas Power b. Oct 5, 1848
Avondale, Ireland
Parnell, Charles Stewart b. 1846
Ballaghaderin, Ireland
O'Doherty, Brian b. 1934
Ballintogher, Ireland
Day-Lewis, Cecil b. Apr 27, 1904
Ballyjamesduff, Ireland
Daly, Marcus b. Dec 5, 1841

Ballylongford, Ireland
Kitchener, Horatio Herbert
   b. Jun 14, 1850
Ballyshannon, Ireland
Allingham, William b. Mar 19, 1824
Gallagher, Rory b. Mar 2, 1949
Beau Park, Ireland
Garrett, Eileen Jeanette Lyttle
   b. Mar 17, 1893
Blessington, Ireland
DeValois, Ninette b. Jun 6, 1898
Bohola, Ireland
O'Dwyer, Paul b. Jun 29, 1907
O'Dwyer, William b. Jul 11, 1890
Boyle, Ireland
O'Sullivan, Maureen b. May 17, 1911
Bray, Ireland
Moyes, Patricia b. Jan 19, 1923
Cahir, Ireland
Dempsey, John Noel b. Jan 3, 1915
Cahirsiveen, Ireland
O'Connell, Daniel b. Aug 6, 1775
Callan, Ireland
Cudahy, Michael b. Dec 7, 1841
Hoban, James b. 1762
Carlingford, Ireland
McGee, Thomas D'Arcy b. Apr 13, 1825
Castlebar, Ireland
Haughey, Charles James b. Sep 16, 1925
Chapelizod, Ireland
Northcliffe, Alfred Charles William
   Harmsworth, Viscount b. Jul 15, 1865
Clomnel, Ireland
Sterne, Laurence b. Nov 24, 1713
Clonakilty, Ireland
Croker, "Boss" (Richard) b. Nov 23, 1841
Clontarf, Ireland
Brian Boru d. Apr 23, 1014
Cloughjordan, Ireland
MacDonagh, Thomas b. 1878
Coleraine, Ireland
Blair, William Richards b. Nov 7, 1874
Connemara, Ireland
O'Toole, Peter Seamus b. Aug 2, 1933
Coole Park, Ireland
Gregory, Isabella Augusta Persse, Lady
   d. May 22, 1932
Cork, Ireland
Barry, Tom d. Jul 2, 1980
Bax, Arnold Edward Trevor, Sir
   d. Oct 3, 1953
Cockburn, Claud(Francis Claud)
   d. Dec 15, 1981
Jones, Mary Harris b. May 1, 1830
Knowles, James Sheridan b. May 12, 1784
MacLiammoir, Michael b. Oct 25, 1899
MacSwiney, Terence b. 1879
O'Connor, Frank, pseud. b. 1903
O'Faolain, Sean b. Feb 22, 1900
Wilcox, Herbert b. Apr 19, 1891

County Armagh, Ireland
Russell, George William b. Apr 10, 1867
County Cavan, Ireland
Fitzpatrick, Thomas b. 1799
County Clare, Ireland
Tobin, Daniel Joseph b. Apr 1875
County Cork, Ireland
Collins, Michael b. 1890
Harnett, William Michael b. Aug 10, 1848
Mulhare, Edward b. 1923
Summersby, Kay b. 1908
County Galway, Ireland
O'Flaherty, Liam b. Aug 28, 1896
County Kerry, Ireland
West, Dame Rebecca, pseud.
b. Dec 25, 1892
County Kildare, Ireland
Keane, Mary Nesta b. Jul 4, 1904
County Kilkenny, Ireland
O'Neill, James b. Oct 14, 1847
County Limerick, Ireland
Heck, Barbara Ruckle b. 1734
County Mayo, Ireland
Moore, George Augustus b. Feb 24, 1852
Redman, Joyce b. 1918
County Meath, Ireland
Brosnan, Pierce b. May 16, 1953
Moore, Tom b. 1885
County Monaghan, Ireland
Kavanagh, Patrick b. 1905
Dublin, Ireland
Adams, Tony (Anthony Patrick)
b. Feb 15, 1953
Allgood, Sara b. Oct 31, 1883
Andrews, Eamonn b. Dec 19, 1922
Bacon, Francis b. Oct 28, 1910
Barnardo, Thomas John b. Jul 4, 1845
Beckett, Samuel Barclay b. Apr 13, 1906
Behan, Brendan b. Feb 9, 1923
Behan, Brendan d. Mar 20, 1964
Boucicault, Dion b. Dec 26, 1820
Bowen, Elizabeth Dorothea Cole
b. Jun 7, 1899
Brambell, Wilfrid b. Mar 22, 1912
Brent, George b. Mar 15, 1904
Briscoe, Robert b. Sep 25, 1894
Brown, Christy b. Jun 5, 1932
Burke, Edmund b. Jan 12, 1729
Carson, Edward Henry b. 1854
Castlereagh, Robert Stewart, Viscount
b. 1769
Childers, (Robert) Erskine d. Nov 24, 1922
Clarke, Austin b. May 9, 1896
Clarke, Harry b. Mar 17, 1890
Coghlan, Eamonn b. 1953
Collinge, Patricia b. Sep 20, 1894
Cooper, Giles (Stannus) b. Aug 9, 1918
Cosgrave, Liam b. Apr 30, 1920
Cosgrave, William Thomas b. Jun 6, 1880
Cosgrave, William Thomas
d. Nov 16, 1965

Costello, John Aloysius b. Jun 20, 1891
Costello, John Aloysius d. Jan 5, 1976
Craig, May d. Feb 9, 1972
Crofts, Freeman Willis b. Jun 1879
Cunningham, Andrew Browne, Viscount
b. Jan 7, 1883
Davitt, Michael d. May 31, 1906
Desmond, William b. May 21, 1878
DeValera, Eamon d. Aug 30, 1975
Digges, Dudley b. Jun 9, 1880
Dowland, John b. Jan 1563
Dunsany, Edward J M Plunkett, Baron
d. Oct 25, 1957
Emmet, Robert b. Sep 20, 1178
Emmet, Robert b. Sep 20, 1803
Field, John b. Jul 26, 1782
Fitzgerald, Barry b. Mar 10, 1888
Fitzgerald, Barry d. Jan 4, 1961
FitzGerald, Garret b. Feb 9, 1926
Fitzgerald, Geraldine b. Nov 24, 1914
Fitzgibbon, (Robert Louis) Constantine
d. Mar 23, 1983
Geldof, Bob b. Oct 5, 1954
Geminiani, Francesco d. Dec 17, 1762
Gogarty, Oliver St. John b. Aug 17, 1878
Hemans, Felicia Dorothea Browne
d. May 16, 1835
Herbert, Victor b. Feb 1, 1859
Hicks, Ursula Kathleen Webb
b. Feb 17, 1896
Hopkins, Gerard Manley d. Jun 8, 1889
Hopkins, John Henry b. Jan 30, 1792
Hoult, Norah b. Sep 20, 1898
Joyce, James Augustus Aloysius
b. Feb 2, 1882
Kavanagh, Patrick d. Nov 30, 1967
Kelly, Michael b. Dec 25, 1762
Laffan, William Mackay b. Jan 22, 1848
Laird, Rick b.
Lardner, Dionysius b. Apr 3, 1793
Lecky, William Edward Hartpole
b. Mar 26, 1838
Leonard, Hugh, pseud. b. Nov 9, 1926
Llewellyn, Richard d. Nov 30, 1983
Lynott, Phil(ip) b. Aug 20, 1951
MacDonagh, Thomas d. May 3, 1916
Mackay, John William b. Nov 28, 1831
MacLiammoir, Michael d. Mar 6, 1978
Malone, Edmund b. Oct 4, 1741
Manners, Charles d. May 3, 1935
Markievicz, Constance Georgine, Countess
d. Jul 15, 1927
McCormack, John d. Sep 16, 1945
Monk, Mary b. 1677
Moore, Thomas b. May 28, 1779
Morton, (Henry) Digby b. Nov 27, 1906
Murdoch, Iris (Jean Iris) b. Jul 15, 1919
O'Brien, Conor Cruise b. Nov 3, 1917
O'Casey, Sean b. Mar 30, 1880
O'Connor, Frank, pseud. d. Mar 10, 1966
O'Donnell, Peador d. May 13, 1986

O'Flaherty, Liam d. Sep 7, 1984
O'Keeffe, John b. Jun 24, 1747
O'Shea, Milo b. Jun 2, 1926
Pearse, Padraic (Patrick Henry)
    b. Nov 10, 1879
Pearse, Padraic (Patrick Henry)
    d. May 3, 1916
Pilkington, Francis M b. Jun 16, 1907
Ridge, Lola b. Dec 12, 1873
Robinson, Lennox (Esme Stuart Lennox)
    d. Oct 14, 1958
Roche, Kevin (Eammon Kevin)
    b. Jun 14, 1922
Ryan, Cornelius John b. Jun 5, 1920
Saint Gaudens, Augustus b. Mar 1, 1848
Savage, John b. Dec 13, 1828
Shaw, George Bernard b. Jul 26, 1856
Sheridan, Richard Brinsley b. Oct 30, 1751
Snow, Carmel White b. Aug 21, 1887
Steele, Richard, Sir b. Mar 1672
Stephens, James b. 1882
Stoker, Bram b. 1847
Swift, Jonathan b. Nov 30, 1667
Swift, Jonathan d. Oct 19, 1745
Synge, John Millington b. Apr 16, 1871
Synge, John Millington d. Mar 24, 1909
Tate, Nahum b. 1652
Todd, Richard b. Jun 11, 1919
Trench, Richard Chenevix b. Sep 5, 1807
Ussher, James b. Jan 4, 1581
Weldon, John d. Feb 4, 1963
Wellington, Arthur Wellesley, Duke
    b. May 1, 1769
Wibberley, Leonard Patrick O'Connor
    b. Apr 9, 1915
Wilde, Oscar Fingal O'Flahertie Wills
    b. Oct 16, 1856
Woffington, Margaret b. Oct 18, 1714
Yeats, William Butler b. Jun 13, 1865

Dun Laoghaire, Ireland
Casement, Roger David b. Sep 1, 1864

Dundalk, Ireland
McClintock, Francis Leopold, Sir
    b. Jul 8, 1819

Edgeworthstown, Ireland
Edgeworth, Maria d. May 22, 1849

Elm Hall, Tipperary, Ireland
Burke, John b. 1787

Ennis, Ireland
Smithson, Harriet Constance
    b. Mar 18, 1800

Faughart, Ireland
Brigid of Kildare b. 453

Fermanagh, Ireland
Alanbrooke, Alan Francis Brooke, 1st
    Viscount b. Jul 23, 1883

Galway, Ireland
Clodagh b. Oct 8, 1937
Harris, Frank b. Feb 14, 1856

Hiskenstwown, Ireland
Weldon, John b. Sep 6, 1890

Keady, Ireland
Makem, Tommy b. 1932

Kearney, Ireland
Barry, Leonora Marie Kearney
    b. Aug 13, 1849

Kildare, Ireland
Brigid of Kildare d. 523

Kilkee, Ireland
Shackleton, Ernest Henry, Sir
    b. Feb 15, 1874

Kilkenny, Ireland
Hackett, Francis b. Jan 21, 1883

Killiney, Ireland
Starkie, Walter Fitzwilliam b. Aug 9, 1894

Kilmoganny, Ireland
Lavery, John, Sir d. Jan 10, 1941

Langford, Ireland
Colum, Padraic b. Dec 8, 1881

Lenister, Ireland
Columban, Saint b. 543

Limerick, Ireland
Harris, Richard b. Oct 1, 1930
Montez, Lola b. 1818
Rehan, Ada b. Apr 22, 1860

Liscannor, Ireland
Holland, John Philip b. Feb 24, 1841

Lisdoonvarna, Ireland
Gardner, George b. Mar 17, 1877

Lismore Castle, Ireland
Boyle, Robert b. Jan 25, 1627

Listowel, Ireland
Keane, John B b. Jul 21, 1928

Meenmore County, Ireland
O'Donnell, Peador b. Feb 22, 1893

Milltown, Ireland
O'Hara, Maureen b. Aug 17, 1921

Miltown-Malbay, Ireland
Hillery, Patrick John b. May 2, 1923

Mitchelstown, Ireland
Trevor, William b. May 24, 1928

Mohill, Ireland
Drummond, William Henry
    b. Apr 13, 1854

Monagham, Ireland
Bury, John Bagnell b. Oct 16, 1861

Moville, Ireland
Montgomery of Alamein, Bernard Law
    Montgomery, Viscount b. Nov 17, 1887

Mullaghmore, Ireland
Mountbatten of Burma, Louis Mountbatten,
    Earl d. Aug 27, 1979

Newbliss, Ireland
Guthrie, Tyrone d. May 15, 1971

Orrery, Ireland
Burke, William b. 1792

Pallas, Ireland
Goldsmith, Oliver b. Nov 10, 1728

Portadown, Ireland
Donlevy, Brian b. Feb 9, 1899

Queenstown, Ireland
Grace, William Russell b. May 10, 1832

Cecchetti, Enrico b. 1850
Corey, Lewis b. Oct 13, 1894
Correggio, Antonio Allegri da
  b. Aug 30, 1494
Gioconda, Lisa Gherardini b. 1479
Monte, Toti dal d. Jan 26, 1975
Moravia, Alberto, pseud. b. Nov 28, 1907
Parmenides b. 515 BC
Pierodella Francesca b. 1420
Pierodella Francesca d. Oct 12, 1492
Pope, Generoso b. 1927
Rindt, Jochen d. Sep 5, 1970
Rossellini, Isabella b. Jun 18, 1952
Segantini, Giovanni b. 1858
Severini, Gino b. 1883
Zangara, Joseph (Guiseppe) b. 1900

Acerra, Italy
Esposito, Joseph b. Apr 28, 1872

Acri, Italy
Atlas, Charles b. Oct 30, 1894

Adria, Italy
Previtali, Fernando b. Feb 16, 1907

Agardo, Italy
Mohs, Friedrich d. Sep 29, 1839

Alassio, Italy
D'Alvarez, Marguerite d. Oct 18, 1953

Albano Laziale, Italy
Traglia, Luigi, Cardinal b. Apr 3, 1896

Albisola, Italy
Julius II, Pope b. 1443

Altamura, Italy
Mercadante, Saverio b. Sep 1795

Ancona, Italy
Belluschi, Pietro b. Aug 18, 1899
Corelli, Franco b. Apr 8, 1923
Lisi, Virna b. Sep 8, 1937

Andria, Italy
Farinelli b. Jan 24, 1705

Angri, Italy
Sommer, Frederick b. Sep 7, 1905

Antium, Italy
Caligula b. Aug 31, 12

Anzi, Italy
Celebrezze, Anthony Joseph b. Sep 4, 1910

Aosta, Italy
Anselm, Saint b. 1033

Apulia, Italy
Sacco, Nicola b. Apr 22, 1891

Aquapendente, Italy
Fabricius, Hieronymus ab Aquapendente
  b. 1537

Aquila, Italy
Bernardine of Siena, Saint d. 1444

Aquinum, Italy
Juvenal (Decimus Junius Juvenalis) b. 60

Arcetri, Italy
Galileo d. Jan 8, 1642

Arezzo, Italy
Aretino, Pietro b. Apr 20, 1492
Petrarch, Francesco b. Jul 20, 1304

Redi, Francesco b. Feb 18, 1626
Vasari, Giorgio b. Jul 30, 1511

Arolo, Italy
Sheean, (James) Vincent d. Mar 15, 1975

Arona, Italy
Banks, Monty (Montague) d. Jan 7, 1950

Arpino, Italy
Cicero, Marcus Tullius b. Jan 3, 106 BC

Arqua, Italy
Petrarch, Francesco d. Jul 19, 1374

Assisi, Italy
Clare, Saint b. 1194
Clare, Saint d. 1253
Francis of Assisi, Saint b. 1182
Lazzari, Virgilio b. Apr 20, 1887

Asti, Italy
Alfieri, Vittorio b. Jan 16, 1749

Aucona, Italy
Adonis, Joe d. Nov 26, 1971

Aversa, Italy
Cimarosa, Domenico b. Dec 17, 1749
Jommelli, Niccolo b. Sep 10, 1714

Avignon, Italy
Martini, Simone d. 1344

Bagni di Lucca, Italy
Crawford, Francis Marion b. Aug 2, 1854

Bagnoregio, Italy
Bonaventure, Saint b. 1221

Baige, Italy
Agrippina d. 59

Bari, Italy
Albanese, Licia b. Jul 22, 1913
Castagna, Bruna b. Oct 15, 1908
Piccini, Nicola b. Jan 16, 1725

Basletta, Italy
Giulini, Carlo Maria b. May 9, 1914

Bassano del Grappo, Italy
Gobbi, Tito b. Oct 24, 1915

Bellagio, Italy
Marinetti, Filippo Tommaso
  d. Dec 2, 1944
Wagner, Cosima Liszt b. Dec 25, 1837

Belluno, Italy
John Paul I, Pope b. Oct 17, 1912
Powell, Cecil Frank d. Aug 9, 1969

Bergamo, Italy
Bonatti, Walter b. Jun 22, 1930
Donizetti, Gaetano b. Nov 29, 1797
Donizetti, Gaetano d. Apr 8, 1848
Locatelli, Pietro b. Sep 3, 1693
Natta, Giulio d. May 2, 1979

Bissone, Italy
Borromini, Francesco b. Sep 25, 1559

Bitonto, Italy
Logroscino, Nicola b. Oct 1698
Majorano, Gaetano b. Apr 12, 1710
Traetta, Tommaso b. Mar 30, 1727

Bobbia, Italy
Columban, Saint d. 615

Bogni di Lucca, Italy
Lee-Hamilton, Eugene Jacob
d. Sep 7, 1907

Bologna, Italy
Bacchelli, Riccardo b. Apr 19, 1891
Bernacchi, Antonio Maria b. Jun 23, 1685
Bernacchi, Antonio Maria d. Mar 13, 1756
Brazzi, Rossano b. Sep 18, 1916
Carducci, Giosue d. Feb 16, 1907
Carracci, Annibale b. Nov 3, 1560
Carracci, Lodovico b. Apr 21, 1555
Carracci, Lodovico d. Nov 13, 1619
Colbran, Isabella d. Oct 7, 1845
Cuzzoni, Francesca d. 1770
Deller, Alfred George d. Jul 16, 1979
Domenichino, Il b. Oct 21, 1581
Farinelli d. Jul 15, 1782
Gregory XIII, Pope b. Jan 1, 1502
Guercino d. 1666
Marconi, Guglielmo b. Apr 25, 1874
Maserati, Ernesto d. Dec 2, 1975
Masina, Giuletta b. Mar 22, 1921
Moninari-Pradelli, Francesco b. Jul 4, 1911
Morandi, Giorgio b. Jul 20, 1890
Morandi, Giorgio d. Jun 18, 1964
Naudin, Emilio d. May 5, 1890
Pasolini, Pier Paolo b. Mar 5, 1922
Primaticcio, Francesco b. 1503
Reni, Guido b. Nov 4, 1575
Reni, Guido d. Aug 18, 1642
Respighi, Ottorino b. Jul 9, 1879

Bonito, Italy
Ferragamo, Salvatore b. Jun 1898

Bordighera, Italy
Amicis, Edmond de d. Mar 12, 1908

Bracigliano, Italy
Romano, Umberto b. Feb 26, 1906

Brescia, Italy
Marcello, Benedetto d. 1739

Bressanone, Italy
Messner, Reinhold b. Sep 17, 1944

Brundisium, Italy
Virgil d. Sep 21, 19 BC

Brunello, Italy
Ghiringhelli, Antonio b. 1903

Burano, Italy
Galuppi, Baldassare b. Oct 18, 1706

Busseto, Italy
Strepponi, Giuseppina d. Nov 15, 1897

Cadigliano, Italy
Menotti, Gian Carlo b. Jul 7, 1911

Calabria, Italy
Zirato, Bruno b. Sep 27, 1884

Camerino, Italy
Betti, Ugo b. Feb 4, 1892

Campania, Italy
Lucilius b. 180
Sulla, Lucius C d. 78 BC

Campobasso, Italy
Giovannitti, Arturo b. Jan 7, 1884

Canelli, Italy
Sardi, Vincent, Sr. b. Dec 23, 1885

Caprese, Italy
Michelangelo b. Mar 6, 1475

Capri, Italy
Douglas, Norman d. Feb 9, 1952
Fields, Gracie d. Sep 27, 1979
Harlan, Veit d. Apr 13, 1964

Caravaggio, Italy
Caravaggio, Michelangelo da
b. Sep 8, 1569

Carpena di Forli, Italy
Mussolini, Rachele Guidi d. Oct 30, 1979

Carrara, Italy
Chinaglia, Giorgio b. Jan 24, 1947

Casale, Italy
Sobrero, Ascanio b. Oct 12, 1812

Casalecchio, Italy
Stracciari, Riccardo b. Jun 26, 1875

Casalmaggiore, Italy
Parmigiano d. Aug 24, 1540

Casarsa de Delicia, Italy
Jacuzzi, Candido b. 1903

Casatico, Italy
Castiglione, Baldassare, Conte
b. Dec 3, 1478

Casene, Italy
Banks, Monty (Montague) b. 1897

Castagno, Italy
Castagno, Andrea del b. 1423

Castel Gandolfo, Italy
Lazzari, Virgilio d. Oct 4, 1953
Paul VI, Pope d. Aug 6, 1978
Tieri, Frank b. 1904

Castelfranco, Italy
Steffani, Agostino b. Jul 25, 1654

Castellammare, Italy
Pliny the Elder d. Aug 24, 79

Castellaneta, Italy
Valentino, Rudolph b. May 6, 1895

Castellina, Italy
Kautner, Helmut d. Apr 20, 1980

Castelnuovo Scrivia, Italy
Bandello, Matteo b. 1485

Castelvecchio, Italy
Pascoli, Giovanni d. Apr 6, 1912

Castelvetrano, Italy
Gentile, Giovanni b. May 30, 1875

Celano, Italy
Corsi, Jacopo b. 1560

Ceneda, Italy
DaPonte, Lorenzo b. Mar 10, 1749

Cento, Italy
Guercino b. 1591

Certaldo, Italy
Boccaccio, Giovanni d. Dec 21, 1375

Cesena, Italy
Bonci, Alessandro b. Feb 10, 1870

Cesenatico, Italy
Hazan, Marcella Maddalena
b. Apr 15, 1924

Chiaravalle, Italy
    Montessori, Maria b. Aug 31, 1870
Chieti, Italy
    Galiani, Ferdinando b. Dec 2, 1728
Collebaccaro, Italy
    Battistini, Mattia d. Nov 7, 1928
Como, Italy
    Christ-Janer, Albert d. Dec 12, 1973
    Lamperti, Francesco d. May 1, 1892
    Pasta, Giuditta Negri d. Apr 1, 1865
    Pliny the Elder b. 23
    Pliny the Younger b. 62
    Tagliabue, Carlo b. Jan 13, 1898
    Volta, Alessandro b. Feb 18, 1745
Concesio, Italy
    Paul VI, Pope b. Sep 26, 1897
Consentia, Italy
    Alaric I d. 410
Corteno, Italy
    Golgi, Camillo b. Jul 7, 1843
Cortona, Italy
    Signorelli, Luca b. 1441
    Signorelli, Luca d. Oct 16, 1523
Cosenza, Italy
    Costello, Frank b. Jan 26, 1891
Crema, Italy
    Cavalli, Francesco b. Feb 14, 1602
    Gazzaniga, Giuseppe d. Feb 1, 1818
Cremona, Italy
    Amati, Nicolo (Nicolaus) d. Apr 12, 1684
    Amati, Nicolo (Nicolaus) b. Dec 3, 1956
    Guarnieri, Giuseppe Antonio
        b. Jun 8, 1683
    Monteverdi, Claudio b. May 15, 1567
    Stradivari, Antonio b. 1644
    Stradivari, Antonio d. Dec 17, 1737
Crescentino, Italy
    Arditi, Luigi b. Jul 22, 1822
    Cossotto, Fiorenza b. Apr 22, 1935
Crevalcore, Italy
    Malpighi, Marcello b. Mar 10, 1626
Cuneo, Italy
    Einaudi, Luigi b. Mar 24, 1874
    Pavese, Cesare b. Sep 9, 1908
Desenzano, Italy
    Angela Merici, Saint b. 1474
Domenico, Italy
    Bocklin, Arnold d. Jan 16, 1901
Dovia, Italy
    Mussolini, Benito b. Jul 29, 1883
Empoli, Italy
    Busoni, Ferruccio Benvenuto
        b. Apr 1, 1866
Fabriano, Italy
    Gentile da Fabriano b. 1370
    Pacchierotti, Gaspare b. May 1740
Faenza, Italy
    Nenni, Pietro b. Feb 9, 1891
    Sarti, Giuseppe b. Dec 1, 1729
    Tamburini, Antonio b. Mar 28, 1800

Ferrar, Italy
    Balbo, Italo b. Jun 6, 1896
Ferrara, Italy
    Antonioni, Michelangelo b. Sep 29, 1912
    Ariosto, Ludovico d. Jul 6, 1533
    Ascoli, Max b. Jun 25, 1898
    Frescobaldi, Girolamo b. 1583
    Gatti-Casazza, Giulio d. Sep 2, 1940
    Pisis, Filippo de b. 1896
    Roberti, Ercole b. 1450
    Savonarola, Girolamo b. Sep 21, 1452
    Tura, Cosme b. 1430
    Tura, Cosme d. 1495
Filottrano, Italy
    Carestini, Giovanni b. 1705
    Carestini, Giovanni d. 1760
Fiumetto, Italy
    Ferragamo, Salvatore d. Aug 7, 1960
Florence, Italy
    Agostino di Duccio b. 1418
    Agostino di Duccio d. 1481
    Alfieri, Vittorio d. Oct 8, 1803
    Bartolommeo, Fra d. Oct 31, 1517
    Bechi, Gino b. 1913
    Benelli, Giovanni, Cardinal d. Oct 26, 1982
    Boccaccio, Giovanni b. 1313
    Bonaparte, Joseph d. Jul 28, 1844
    Botticelli, Sandro b. 1444
    Botticelli, Sandro d. May 17, 1510
    Browning, Elizabeth Barrett
        d. Jun 30, 1861
    Brunelleschi, Filippo b. 1377
    Brunelleschi, Filippo d. Apr 16, 1446
    Caccini, Giulio d. Dec 10, 1618
    Campana, Dino d. Mar 11, 1932
    Castagno, Andrea del d. Aug 19, 1457
    Castelnuovo-Tedesco, Mario b. Apr 3, 1895
    Catherine de Medici b. Apr 13, 1519
    Cavalieri, Lina d. Feb 8, 1944
    Cecchi, Emilio b. 1884
    Cellini, Benvenuto b. Nov 1, 1500
    Cellini, Benvenuto d. Feb 14, 1571
    Cherubini, Maria Luigi b. Sep 14, 1760
    Cimabue, Giovanni b. 1240
    Cimabue, Giovanni d. 1302
    Clement VII b. 1475
    Collodi, Carlo, pseud. d. Oct 26, 1890
    Corsi, Jacopo d. 1604
    Dallapiccola, Luigi d. Feb 19, 1975
    Dante Alighieri b. May 27, 1265
    Davies, Arthur Bowen d. Oct 24, 1928
    DellaRobbia, Andrea b. 1435
    DellaRobbia, Giovanni b. 1469
    DellaRobbia, Luca b. 1400
    DellaRobbia, Luca d. Feb 23, 1482
    DelMonaco, Mario b. Jul 27, 1915
    DiSant'Angelo, Giorgio b. May 5, 1936
    Dolci, Carlo b. May 25, 1616
    Dolci, Carlo d. Jan 17, 1686
    Donatello b. 1386
    Donatello d. Dec 13, 1466

Draper, Paul b. Oct 25, 1909
Fallaci, Oriana b. Jun 29, 1930
Freccia, Massimo b. Sep 19, 1906
Gentile, Giovanni d. Apr 15, 1944
Ghiberti, Lorenzo b. 1378
Ghiberti, Lorenzo d. Dec 1, 1455
Ghirlandaio, Domenico b. 1449
Ghirlandaio, Domenico d. Jan 11, 1494
Giotto di Bondone d. Jan 8, 1337
Giusti, Giuseppe d. 1850
Gozzoli, Benozzo b. 1420
Gucci, Aldo b. May 26, 1909
Gucci, Maurizio b. 1948
Gui, Vittorio d. Oct 16, 1975
Guicciardini, Francesco b. Mar 6, 1483
Guicciardini, Francesco d. May 1540
Hoe, Richard March d. Jun 7, 1886
John, John Pico b. Mar 14, 1906
Landor, Walter Savage d. Sep 17, 1864
Leland, Charles Godfrey d. Mar 20, 1903
Lippi, Filippo (Lippo), Fra d. Oct 9, 1469
Lully, Jean-Baptiste b. Nov 28, 1632
Machiavelli, Niccolo b. May 3, 1469
Machiavelli, Niccolo d. Jun 22, 1527
Marie de Medicis b. 1573
Medici, Cosimo de b. Sep 27, 1389
Medici, Cosimo de d. Aug 1, 1464
Medici, Lorenzo de b. Jan 1, 1449
Medici, Lorenzo de d. Apr 8, 1492
Nightingale, Florence b. May 15, 1820
Papini, Giovanni b. Jan 9, 1881
Papini, Giovanni d. Jul 8, 1956
Parker, Theodore d. May 10, 1860
Patti, Carlotta b. Oct 30, 1835
Peretti, Elsa b. May 1, 1940
Peri, Jacopo d. Aug 12, 1633
Pico della Mirandola, Giovanni d. 1494
Pollaiuolo, Antonio b. 1431
Pontormo, Jacopo da d. Dec 1556
Powers, Hiram d. Jun 27, 1873
Pulci, Luigi b. Aug 15, 1432
Pyle, Howard d. Nov 9, 1911
Rinuccini, Ottavio b. Jan 20, 1562
Rinuccini, Ottavio d. Mar 28, 1621
Ruffo, Titta d. Jul 6, 1953
Sacchini, Antonio b. Jun 14, 1730
Sansovino, Jacopo b. 1486
Sargent, John Singer b. Jan 12, 1856
Sarto, Andrea del b. Jul 16, 1486
Sarto, Andrea del d. Sep 29, 1531
Savonarola, Girolamo d. May 23, 1498
Scherchen, Hermann d. Jun 12, 1966
Tetrazzini, Luisa b. Jun 29, 1874
Torricelli, Evangelista d. Oct 25, 1647
Toye, Francis d. Oct 31, 1964
Trollope, Frances d. Oct 6, 1863
Uccello, Paolo b. 1396
Uccello, Paolo d. Dec 10, 1475
Unger, Caroline d. Mar 23, 1877
Vasari, Giorgio d. Jun 27, 1574
Verrocchio, Andrea del b. 1435

Vespucci, Amerigo b. Mar 9, 1451
Zeffirelli, Franco b. Feb 12, 1923
Foggia, Italy
Giordano, Umberto b. Aug 27, 1867
Fondi, Italy
DeSantis, Giuseppe b. Feb 11, 1917
Fontana Liri, Italy
Mastroianni, Marcello b. Sep 28, 1924
Forli, Italy
Simionato, Guilietta b. May 12, 1916
Formia, Italy
Cicero, Marcus Tullius d. 43 BC
Fossannova, Italy
Aquinas, Thomas, Saint d. Mar 7, 1274
Fratta Polesine, Italy
Matteotti, Giacomo b. 1885
Frattamaggiore, Italy
Durante, Francesco b. Mar 31, 1684
Frosinone, Italy
Graziani, Rodolfo b. Aug 11, 1882
Fusignano, Italy
Corelli, Arcangelo b. Feb 17, 1653
Genoa, Italy
Alberti, Leon Battista b. Feb 14, 1404
Bortoluzzi, Paolo b. May 17, 1938
Cabot, John b. Jun 24, 1450
Catherine of Genoa, Saint b. 1447
Catherine of Genoa, Saint d. Sep 14, 1510
Columbus, Christopher b. 1451
Erede, Alberto b. Nov 8, 1909
Gassman, Vittorio b. Sep 1, 1922
Germi, Pietro b. Sep 14, 1904
Magnasco, Alessandro Lissandrino b. 1667
Magnasco, Alessandro Lissandrino
    d. Mar 12, 1749
Mazzini, Giuseppe b. Jun 22, 1805
Montale, Eugenio b. Oct 12, 1896
O'Connell, Daniel d. May 15, 1847
Paganini, Niccolo b. Oct 27, 1782
Romani, Felice b. Jan 31, 1788
Smithson, James d. Jun 29, 1829
Stradella, Alessandro d. Feb 28, 1682
Taddei, Giuseppe b. Jun 26, 1916
Togliatti, Palmiro b. Mar 26, 1893
Gissi, Italy
Gaspari, Remo b. 1921
Gorizia, Italy
Music, Antonio Zoran b. 1909
Rubbia, Carlo b. 1934
Imperia, Italy
Natta, Giulio b. Feb 26, 1903
Isola Carturo, Italy
Mantegna, Andrea b. 1431
Istria, Italy
Tartini, Giuseppe b. Apr 8, 1692
Ivrea, Italy
Olivetti, Adriano b. Apr 11, 1901
Jesi, Italy
Pergolesi, Giovanni Battista b. Jan 4, 1710
Sabatini, Rafael b. Apr 29, 1875

La Ragnaia, Italy
Swarthout, Gladys d. Jul 6, 1969
Lake Garda, Italy
Breeskin, Adelyn Dohme d. Jul 24, 1986
Lanuvium, Italy
Antoninus Pius b. Sep 19, 86
Larino, Italy
Lualdi, Adriano b. Mar 22, 1887
Le Roncole, Italy
Verdi, Giuseppe b. Oct 10, 1813
Lecce, Italy
Schipa, Tito b. Jan 2, 1889
Lecco, Italy
Venuti, Joe (Giuseppe) b. 1899
Leghorn, Italy
Burns, John Horne d. Aug 10, 1953
Mascagni, Pietro b. Dec 7, 1863
Modigliani, Amedeo b. Jul 12, 1884
Montefiore, Moses Haim, Sir
   b. Oct 24, 1784
Legnano, Italy
Salieri, Antonio b. Aug 18, 1750
Livorno, Italy
Ciano (di Cortellazzo), Conte Galeazzo
   b. Mar 8, 1903
Lodi, Italy
Guadagni, Gaetano b. 1725
Strepponi, Giuseppina b. Sep 18, 1815
Loreto, Italy
Crashaw, Richard d. Aug 21, 1649
Lotto, Lorenzo d. Sep 1, 1556
Lucca, Italy
Boccherini, Luigi b. Feb 19, 1743
Catalani, Alfredo b. Jun 19, 1854
Geminiani, Francesco b. Feb 5, 1687
Gherardi, Gherardo b. Jul 1, 1921
Puccini, Giacomo b. Dec 22, 1858
Sforza, Carlo b. Sep 25, 1872
Volpi, Alfredo b. 1895
Lugano, Italy
Rosbaud, Hans d. Dec 30, 1962
Lugo di Romagna, Italy
Pratella, Francesco Balilla b. Feb 1, 1880
Luino, Italy
Luini, Bernardino b. 1480
Luzzara, Italy
Donati, Danilo b.
Maglie, Italy
Moro, Aldo b. Sep 23, 1916
Majolati, Italy
Spontini, Gasparo b. Nov 14, 1774
Spontini, Gasparo d. Jan 24, 1851
Malnate, Italy
Lucioni, Luigi b. Nov 4, 1900
Mantua, Italy
Crichton, James d. Jul 3, 1582
Hofer, Andreas d. Feb 20, 1810
Mantegna, Andrea d. Sep 13, 1506
Marradi, Italy
Campana, Dino b. Aug 20, 1885

Massa di Carrera, Italy
Bernardine of Siena, Saint b. 1380
Mestre, Italy
DelMonaco, Mario d. Oct 16, 1982
Milan, Italy
Abbado, Claudio b. Jun 26, 1933
Ambrose, Saint d. Apr 4, 397
Annigoni, Pietro b. Jun 7, 1910
Barbaja, Domenica b. 1778
Barzini, Luigi Giorgio, Jr. b. Dec 21, 1908
Beccaria, Cesare b. Mar 15, 1738
Beccaria, Cesare d. Nov 28, 1794
Boito, Arrigo d. Jun 10, 1918
Bonfanti, Marie b. 1847
Borromeo, Charles, Saint d. Nov 3, 1584
Bugatti, Ettore b. Sep 15, 1881
Catalani, Alfredo d. Aug 7, 1893
Ceccato, Aldo b. Feb 18, 1934
Cortesa, Valentina b. Jan 1, 1925
Craxi, "Bettino" (Benedetto)
   b. Feb 24, 1934
Fabi, Teo b. 1954
Fracci, Carla b. Aug 20, 1936
Galli-Curci, Amelita b. Nov 18, 1882
Giordano, Umberto d. Nov 12, 1948
Grisi, Guilia b. Jul 28, 1811
Gucci, Rodolfo d. May 15, 1983
Janigro, Antonio b. Jan 21, 1918
Leoni, Franco b. Oct 24, 1864
Manzoni, Alessandro (Antonio)
   b. Mar 7, 1785
Manzoni, Alessandro (Antonio)
   d. Apr 28, 1873
Marinuzzi, Gino d. Aug 17, 1945
Mitropoulos, Dimitri d. Nov 2, 1960
Montale, Eugenio d. Sep 12, 1981
Mussolini, Benito d. Apr 28, 1945
Ozanam, Frederic b. Apr 23, 1813
Panizza, Ettore d. Nov 29, 1967
Pasero, Tancredi d. Feb 17, 1983
Pertile, Aureliano d. Jan 11, 1952
Petacci, Clara d. Apr 29, 1945
Piave, Francesco Maria d. Mar 5, 1876
Pirelli, Alberto b. Jul 28, 1882
Pisis, Filippo de d. Apr 2, 1956
Ponchielli, Amilcare d. Jan 16, 1886
Ponti, Carlo b. Dec 11, 1913
Ponti, Gio(vanni) b. Nov 18, 1891
Ponti, Gio(vanni) d. Sep 15, 1979
Sammarco, Mario b. Jan 24, 1930
Schiaparelli, Giovanni d. Jul 4, 1910
Siepi, Cesare b. Feb 10, 1923
Sironi, Mario d. Aug 13, 1961
Sonzogno, Edoardo b. Apr 21, 1836
Sonzogno, Edoardo d. Mar 14, 1920
Stabile, Mariano d. Jan 11, 1968
Stolz, Teresa d. Aug 23, 1902
Tetrazzini, Luisa d. Apr 28, 1940
Valentino b. May 11, 1932
Varesi, Felice d. Mar 13, 1889

Verdi, Giuseppe d. Jan 27, 1901
Visconti, Luchino b. Nov 2, 1906
Modena, Italy
Bononcini, Giovanni Battista
b. Jul 18, 1670
Ferrari, Enzo b. Feb 20, 1898
Freni, Mirella b. 1936
Pavarotti, Luciano b. Oct 12, 1935
Pico della Mirandola, Giovanni b. 1463
Mondovi, Italy
Giolitti, Giovanni b. 1842
Moneglia, Italy
Romani, Felice d. Jan 28, 1865
Monselice, Italy
Campagnolo, Gitullio d. Feb 1982
Monsummano, Italy
Giusti, Giuseppe b. May 12, 1809
Montand, Yves b. Oct 13, 1921
Montagnana, Italy
Martinelli, Giovanni b. Oct 22, 1885
Pertile, Aureliano b. Nov 9, 1885
Sitwell, Osbert, Sir d. May 4, 1969
Monte Cassino, Italy
Benedict, Saint d. Mar 21, 547
Monte Nero, Italy
Smollett, Tobias George d. Sep 17, 1771
Monte Sansavino, Italy
Sansovino, Andrea b. 1460
Montecatini, Italy
Dior, Christian d. Oct 24, 1957
Leoncavallo, Ruggiero d. Aug 9, 1919
Montecelli, Italy
Bronzino II b. Nov 17, 1503
Montemarano, Italy
Adonis, Joe b. Nov 22, 1902
Monterone, Italy
Velluti, Giovanni Battista b. Jan 28, 1780
Montferrato, Italy
Badoglio, Pietro b. Sep 28, 1871
Montona Trieste, Italy
Andretti, Mario Gabriel b. Feb 28, 1940
Montorio, Italy
Greco, Jose b. Dec 23, 1918
Monza, Italy
Ascari, Alberto d. May 27, 1955
Bacchelli, Riccardo d. Oct 8, 1985
Bellincioni, Gemma b. Aug 17, 1864
Peterson, Ronnie d. Sep 11, 1978
Tagliabue, Carlo d. Apr 5, 1978
Morimondo, Italy
Lattuada, Felice b. Feb 5, 1882
Morra Irpino, Italy
DeSanctis, Francesco b. Mar 28, 1817
Munra Lucano, Italy
Stella, Joseph b. Jun 13, 1880
Mureno, Italy
Piave, Francesco Maria b. May 18, 1810
Naples, Italy
Abarbanel, Judah d. 1535
Acton, John Emerich Edward Dalberg-
Acton, Baron b. Jan 10, 1834

Amato, Pasquale b. Mar 21, 1878
Autori, Franco b. Nov 29, 1903
Bellincioni, Gemma b. Apr 23, 1950
Bernini, Giovanni Lorenzo b. Dec 7, 1598
Caniglia, Maria b. May 5, 1905
Caruso, Enrico b. Feb 25, 1873
Caruso, Enrico d. Aug 2, 1921
Cipullo, Aldo Massimo Fabrizio
b. Nov 18, 1938
Corbett, Young, III b. May 27, 1905
Crescentini, Girolamo d. Apr 24, 1846
Croce, Benedetto d. Nov 20, 1952
DeSanctis, Francesco d. Dec 19, 1883
Domenichino, Il d. Apr 6, 1641
Durante, Francesco d. Aug 13, 1755
Galiani, Ferdinando d. Oct 30, 1787
Gardenia, Vincent b. Jan 7, 1922
Gesualdo, Carlo b. 1560
Gesualdo, Carlo d. Sep 8, 1613
Giordano, Luca b. 1632
Heiskell, Andrew b. Sep 13, 1915
Jommelli, Niccolo d. Aug 25, 1774
Lablache, Luigi b. Dec 6, 1794
Lablache, Luigi d. Jan 23, 1858
Lardner, Dionysius d. Apr 29, 1859
Lebrun, Rico (Frederico) b. Dec 10, 1900
Leo, Leonardo d. Oct 31, 1744
Leoncavallo, Ruggiero b. Mar 8, 1858
Leopardi, Giacomo d. Jun 14, 1837
Luciano, "Lucky" (Charles)
d. Jan 26, 1962
Majorano, Gaetano d. Jan 31, 1783
Marterie, Ralph b. Dec 24, 1914
Mercadante, Saverio d. Dec 17, 1870
Merola, Gaetano b. Jan 4, 1881
Mugnone, Leopoldo b. Sep 29, 1858
Mugnone, Leopoldo d. Dec 22, 1941
Muti, Riccardo b. Jul 28, 1941
Nicolini b. Apr 1673
Nicolini d. Jan 1, 1732
Nobile, Umberto b. Jan 21, 1885
Nourrit, Adolphe d. Mar 8, 1839
Paisiello, Giovanni d. Jun 5, 1816
Papi, Genarro b. Dec 21, 1886
Porpora, Niccolo b. Aug 19, 1686
Porpora, Niccolo d. Feb 1766
Pucci, Emilio Marchese di Barsento
b. Nov 20, 1914
Quasimodo, Salvatore d. Jun 14, 1968
Ribera, Jusepe (Jose) de d. Sep 2, 1652
Rosa, Salvator b. Jul 1615
Sbriglia, Giovanni b. Jun 23, 1832
Scarlatti, Alessandro d. Nov 24, 1725
Scarlatti, Domenico Girolamo
b. Oct 26, 1685
Scarlatti, Domenico Girolamo
d. Jul 23, 1757
Schliemann, Heinrich d. Dec 26, 1890
Scotti, Antonio b. Jan 25, 1866
Scotti, Antonio d. Feb 26, 1936

Shaftesbury, Anthony Ashley Cooper, Earl
   d. Feb 15, 1713
Sodero, Cesare b. Aug 2, 1886
Stignani, Ebe b. Jul 10, 1907
Stradella, Alessandro b. 1642
Victor Emmanuel III b. 1869
Zingarelli, Nicola Antonio b. Apr 4, 1752
Nicosia, Italy
Pecora, Ferdinand b. Jan 6, 1882
Nola, Italy
Augustus d. Aug 19, 14 BC
Bruno, Giordano b. 1548
Norcia, Italy
Benedict, Saint b. 480
Novara, Italy
Lombard, Peter b. 1100
Oneglia, Italy
Amicis, Edmond de b. Oct 21, 1846
Oniglia, Italy
Berio, Luciano b. Oct 24, 1925
Ortona, Italy
Tosti, Francesco Paola b. Apr 7, 1846
Orvieto, Italy
Mancinelli, Luigi b. Feb 5, 1848
Ostia, Italy
Pasolini, Pier Paolo d. Nov 2, 1975
Paderno, Italy
Ponchielli, Amilcare b. Aug 31, 1834
Padua, Italy
Anthony of Padua, Saint d. 1231
Berlinguer, Enrico d. Jun 11, 1984
Boito, Arrigo b. Feb 24, 1842
Gozzi, Gaspare d. Dec 27, 1786
Guadagni, Gaetano d. Nov 1792
Pacchierotti, Gasparo d. Oct 28, 1821
Palladio, Andrea b. Nov 30, 1508
Pulci, Luigi d. Nov 1484
Tartini, Giuseppe d. Feb 26, 1770
Palermo, Italy
Capra, Frank b. May 18, 1897
Legler, Henry Eduard b. Jun 22, 1861
Orlando, Vittorio Emanuele
   b. May 19, 1860
Rose, Vincent b. Jun 13, 1880
Palestrina, Italy
Palestrina, Giovanni b. Dec 27, 1525
Palmero, Italy
Cagliostro, Alessandro, Conte di
   b. Jun 2, 1743
Palmi, Italy
Cilea, Francesco b. Jul 26, 1866
Pamigliano, Italy
Leone, Giovanni b. Nov 3, 1908
Parma, Italy
Bertolucci, Bernardo b. Mar 16, 1940
Cuzzoni, Francesca b. 1700
Naudin, Emilio b. Oct 23, 1823
Paer, Ferdinando b. Jun 1, 1771
Parmigiano b. Jan 11, 1503
Pizzetti, Ildebrando b. Sep 20, 1880
Toscanini, Arturo b. Mar 25, 1867

Pasaro, Italy
Alberghetti, Anna Maria b. May 15, 1936
Passagno, Italy
Canova, Antonio b. Nov 1, 1757
Patavium, Italy
Livy d. 17 AD
Livy b. 59 BC
Pavia, Italy
Golgi, Camillo d. Jan 21, 1926
Muzio, Claudia b. Feb 7, 1889
Spallanzani, Lazzaro d. Feb 11, 1799
Perugia, Italy
Buitoni, Giovanni b. Nov 6, 1891
Lancetti, Pino b. 1932
Perugino b. 1445
Perugino d. 1523
Pinturicchio b. 1454
Pesaro, Italy
Rossini, Gioacchino Antonio
   b. Feb 29, 1792
Tebaldi, Renata b. Feb 1, 1922
Zandonai, Riccardo d. Jun 5, 1944
Pescara, Italy
D'Annunzio, Gabriele b. Mar 12, 1863
DiSalle, Michael Vincent d. Sep 15, 1981
Pescasseroli, Italy
Croce, Benedetto b. Feb 25, 1866
Pescia, Italy
Pacini, Giovanni d. Dec 6, 1867
Pescina, Italy
Mazarin, Jules, Cardinal b. Jul 14, 1602
Silone, Ignazio b. May 1, 1900
Piacenza, Italy
Armani, Giorgio b. 1936
Boiardi, Hector b. 1897
Pannini, Giovanni Paolo b. 1691
Pian di Carpine, Italy
Carpini, Giovanni de Piano b. 1180
Piancaldoli, Italy
Torricelli, Evangelista b. Oct 15, 1608
Pico, Italy
Landolfi, Tommaso b. Aug 9, 1908
Pinerolo, Italy
Tajo, Italo b. Apr 15, 1915
Pisa, Italy
Arieti, Silvano b. Jun 28, 1914
Eastlake, Charles Lock d. Dec 24, 1865
Galileo b. Feb 15, 1564
Mazzini, Giuseppe d. Mar 10, 1872
Pisano, Andrea b. 1290
Pisano, Antonio b. 1395
Pontecorvo, Gillo (Gilberto)
   b. Nov 19, 1919
Redi, Francesco d. Mar 1, 1698
Ruffo, Titta b. Jun 9, 1877
Pistoia, Italy
Benelli, Giovanni, Cardinal
   b. May 21, 1921
Pistoria, Italy
Gozzoli, Benozzo d. Oct 4, 1497
Marini, Marino b. Feb 27, 1901

Pizzo, Italy
Murat, Joachim d. Oct 13, 1815
Pola, Italy
Hills, Argentina b. 1922
Valli, Alida b. May 31, 1921
Polesine, Italy
Bergonzi, Carlo b. Jul 13, 1924
Pontedera, Italy
Gronchi, Giovanni b. Sep 10, 1887
Pontormo, Italy
Pontormo, Jacopo da b. 1494
Porzivncola, Italy
Francis of Assisi, Saint d. Oct 3, 1226
Posilipo, Italy
Barbaja, Domenica d. Oct 16, 1841
Potenza, Italy
Colombo, Emilio b. Apr 11, 1920
Pozzuoli, Italy
Pergolesi, Giovanni Battista
d. Mar 16, 1736
Pracchia, Italy
Jackson, John Adams d. Aug 30, 1879
Prado, Italy
Malaparte, Curzio b. Jun 9, 1898
Prato, Italy
Lippi, Filippo (Lippo), Fra b. 1406
Preve di Cadore, Italy
Titian b. 1477
Racconigi, Italy
Umberto II b. Sep 15, 1904
Rapallo, Italy
Beerbohm, Max (Sir Henry Maximilian)
d. May 20, 1956
Gish, Dorothy d. Jun 4, 1968
Ravenna, Italy
Dante Alighieri d. Sep 14, 1321
Pratella, Francesco Balilla d. May 18, 1955
Reate, Italy
Vespasian b. 8 BC
Recanati, Italy
Gigli, Beniamino b. Mar 20, 1890
Leopardi, Giacomo b. Jun 29, 1798
Reggio, Italy
Ariosto, Ludovico b. Sep 8, 1474
Reggio Emilia, Italy
Boiardo, Matteo Maria d. 1494
Tagliavini, Ferruccio b. Aug 14, 1913
Rimini, Italy
Cipriani, Amilcare b. 1845
Fellini, Federico b. Jan 20, 1920
Riva, Italy
Schuschnigg, Kurt von b. Dec 14, 1897
Rivarola, Italy
Cesnola, Luigi Palma di b. Jul 29, 1832
Rocca d'Arona, Italy
Borromeo, Charles, Saint b. Oct 2, 1538
Roccasecca, Italy
Aquinas, Thomas, Saint b. 1225
Gazzelloni, Severino b. Jan 5, 1919

Romano, Italy
Rubini, Giovanni-Battista b. Apr 7, 1794
Rubini, Giovanni-Battista d. Mar 2, 1854
Rome, Italy
Alberti, Leon Battista d. Apr 25, 1472
Alfonso XIII d. Feb 28, 1941
Allegri, Gregorio b. 1582
Allegri, Gregorio d. Feb 17, 1652
Amfiteatrof, Daniele d. Jul 7, 1983
Andreotti, Giulio b. Jan 14, 1919
Angelico, Fra d. Mar 18, 1455
Apollinaire, Guillaume b. Aug 26, 1880
Auer, Mischa d. Mar 5, 1967
Augustus b. Sep 23, 63 BC
Baccaloni, Salvatore b. Apr 14, 1900
Balla, Giacomo d. Mar 1, 1958
Barzini, Luigi Giorgio, Jr. d. Mar 30, 1984
Battistini, Mattia b. Feb 27, 1856
Berberian, Cathy d. Mar 6, 1983
Berman, Eugene d. Dec 14, 1972
Bernini, Giovanni Lorenzo
d. Nov 28, 1680
Betti, Ugo d. Jun 9, 1953
Borgia, Cesare b. 1475
Borgia, Lucrezia b. Apr 18, 1480
Borromini, Francesco d. Aug 3, 1677
Browning, Oscar d. Oct 6, 1923
Brumidi, Constantino b. Jul 26, 1805
Bruno, Giordano d. Feb 17, 1600
Buitoni, Giovanni d. Jan 13, 1979
Bulow, Bernhard H M d. Oct 28, 1929
Bury, John Bagnell d. Jun 1, 1927
Caccini, Giulio b. 1546
Cagliostro, Alessandro, Conte di
d. Aug 26, 1795
Caligula d. Jan 24, 41
Camerini, Mario b. Feb 6, 1895
Caniglia, Maria d. Apr 15, 1979
Cannizzaro, Stanislao d. May 10, 1910
Carracci, Annibale d. Jul 15, 1609
Catherine of Sienna d. Apr 29, 1380
Cecchi, Emilio d. 1966
Cecelia, Saint d. 230
Chirico, Giorgio de d. Nov 20, 1978
Claudius I d. Oct 13, 54 AD
Clement VII d. Sep 25, 1534
Clementi, Muzio b. 1752
Collins, Mike (Michael) b. Oct 31, 1930
Corelli, Arcangelo d. Jan 8, 1713
Dana, Richard Henry, Jr. d. Jan 6, 1882
Deledda, Grazia d. Aug 16, 1936
DeLuca, Giuseppe b. Dec 29, 1876
DePaolis, Alessio b. Apr 5, 1893
Elsheimer, Adam d. Dec 1610
Eustachio, Bartolomeo d. Aug 1574
Fabrizi, Aldo b. 1905
Farouk I d. Mar 18, 1965
Fermi, Enrico b. Sep 29, 1901
Feti, Domenico b. 1589
Firbank, Ronald d. May 21, 1926
Frescobaldi, Girolamo d. Mar 2, 1644

Gabrielli, Catarina b. Nov 12, 1730
Gabrielli, Catarina d. Apr 1796
Gentile da Fabriano d. 1427
Gerard, Francois b. May 4, 1770
Germi, Pietro d. Dec 5, 1974
Gigli, Beniamino d. Nov 30, 1957
Gobbi, Tito d. May 5, 1984
Grassi, Giovanni Battista d. May 4, 1925
Graziani, Rodolfo d. Jan 11, 1955
Gregory the Great b. 540
Gronchi, Giovanni d. Oct 17, 1978
Gui, Vittorio b. Sep 14, 1885
Howitt, Mary d. Jan 30, 1888
Ignatius of Loyola, Saint d. Jul 31, 1556
John XXIII, Pope d. Jun 3, 1963
Jones, R William b. Oct 5, 1906
Josephus, Flavius d. 101
Juan Carlos I b. Jan 5, 1938
Julius Caesar d. Mar 15, 44 BC
Julius Caesar b. Jul 12, 100 BC
Keats, John d. Feb 23, 1821
Landolfi, Tommaso d. Jul 7, 1979
Lanza, Mario d. Oct 7, 1959
Lauri-Volpi, Giacoma b. Dec 11, 1894
Lewis, Edmonia d. 1911
Lewis, Sinclair d. Jan 10, 1951
Loren, Sophia b. Sep 20, 1934
Lorrain, Claude Gellee d. Nov 21, 1682
Lucan d. Jun 30, 65
Magnani, Anna d. Sep 26, 1973
Malaparte, Curzio d. Jul 19, 1957
Malpighi, Marcello d. Nov 30, 1694
Mancinelli, Luigi d. Feb 2, 1921
Mangano, Silvana b. Apr 21, 1930
Marconi, Guglielmo d. Jul 20, 1937
Marcus Aurelius Antoninus b. Apr 20, 121
Mario, Giovanni Matteo d. Dec 11, 1883
Martinelli, Elsa b. Aug 3, 1933
Masaccio d. 1428
Mascagni, Pietro d. Aug 2, 1945
Mengs, Anton Raphael d. 1779
Metastasio, Pietro b. Jan 3, 1698
Michelangelo d. Feb 18, 1564
Modigliani, Franco b. Jun 18, 1918
Monicelli, Mario b. May 15, 1915
Morgan, J(ohn) P(ierpont) d. Mar 31, 1913
Moro, Aldo d. May 9, 1978
Muzio, Claudia d. May 24, 1936
Nenni, Pietro d. Jan 1, 1980
Nervi, Pier Luigi d. Jan 9, 1979
Nobile, Umberto d. Jul 29, 1978
Orlando, Vittorio Emanuele d. Dec 1, 1952
Ottaviani, Alfredo, Cardinal
    b. Oct 29, 1890
Palestrina, Giovanni d. Feb 2, 1594
Pannini, Giovanni Paolo d. 1765
Paul, Saint d. 64
Pei, Mario Andrew b. Feb 16, 1901
Pella, Giuseppe b. Apr 18, 1902
Pella, Giuseppe d. May 31, 1981
Peri, Jacopo b. Aug 20, 1561

Persiani, Fanny b. Oct 4, 1812
Petri, Elio b. Jan 29, 1929
Petri, Elio d. Nov 10, 1982
Pinza, Ezio b. May 18, 1892
Pirandello, Fausto d. Nov 30, 1975
Pirandello, Luigi d. Dec 10, 1936
Piranesi, Giovanni Battista d. Nov 1, 1778
Pisano, Antonio d. 1455
Pius XII, Pope b. Mar 2, 1876
Pius XII, Pope d. Oct 9, 1958
Pizzetti, Ildebrando d. Feb 13, 1968
Plautus, Titus Maccius d. 184 BC
Pollaiuolo, Antonio d. 1498
Poussin, Nicolas d. Nov 19, 1665
Praz, Mario b. Sep 6, 1896
Praz, Mario d. Mar 23, 1982
Raphael d. Apr 6, 1520
Respighi, Ottorino d. Apr 18, 1936
Rinehart, William H d. Oct 28, 1874
Rogers, Randolph d. Jan 15, 1892
Rosa, Salvator d. Mar 15, 1673
Rossellini, Renzo b. Feb 2, 1908
Rossellini, Roberto b. May 8, 1906
Rossellini, Roberto d. Jun 3, 1977
Santayana, George d. Sep 26, 1952
Scalchi, Sofia d. Aug 22, 1922
Schiaparelli, (Elsa) b. Sep 10, 1890
Segni, Antonio d. Dec 1, 1972
Seper, Franjo d. Dec 31, 1981
Serafin, Tullio d. Feb 2, 1968
Sforza, Carlo d. Sep 4, 1952
Simmons, Franklin d. Dec 8, 1913
Simonetta b. 1922
Soria, Dario b. May 21, 1912
Stracciari, Riccardo d. Oct 10, 1955
Stuart, Charles Edward Louis Philip
    b. Dec 31, 1720
Stuart, Charles Edward Louis Philip
    d. Jan 31, 1788
Stuarti, Enzo b. Mar 3, 1925
Symonds, John Addington d. Apr 19, 1893
Tasso, Torquato d. Apr 25, 1595
Tchelitchew, Pavel d. Jul 31, 1957
Tiberius Julius Caesar Augustus b. 42 BC
Titus b. 40
Tomasi di Lampedusa, Guiseppe
    d. Jul 26, 1957
Tosti, Francesco Paola d. Dec 6, 1916
Traglia, Luigi, Cardinal d. Nov 22, 1978
Valletti, Cesare b. Dec 18, 1922
Vignola, Giacomo da d. Jul 7, 1573
Visconti, Luchino d. Mar 17, 1976
Vitale, Milly b. Jul 16, 1938
Vitti, Monica b. Nov 3, 1931
Wertmuller, Lina von Eigg
    b. Aug 14, 1928
Zampa, Luigi b. Jan 2, 1905

Rosiglino, Italy
    Genovese, Vito b. Nov 27, 1879

Rottanova, Italy
    Serafin, Tullio b. Dec 8, 1878

Trier, Italy
Ambrose, Saint b. 340
Trieste, Italy
Barbieri, Fedora b. Jun 4, 1920
Burton, Richard Francis, Sir
  d. Oct 20, 1890
Cleva, Fausto b. May 17, 1902
DeSabata, Victor b. Apr 10, 1892
Fouche, Joseph d. 1820
Henreid, Paul b. Jan 10, 1908
Tropea, Italy
Anastasia, Albert b. Sep 26, 1902
Vallone, Raf(faele) b. Feb 17, 1918
Tunis, Italy
Cardinale, Claudia b. Apr 15, 1938
Turin, Italy
Agnelli, Giovanni b. Mar 12, 1921
Avogadro, Amedeo, Conte di Quaregna
  b. Jun 9, 1776
Avogadro, Amedeo, Conte di Quaregna
  d. Jul 9, 1856
Balla, Giacomo b. Jul 18, 1871
Bich, Marcel b. Jul 29, 1914
Brosio, Manilo Giovanni b. Jul 10, 1897
Brosio, Manilo Giovanni d. Mar 14, 1980
Cavour, Camillo Benso di b. Aug 10, 1810
Cavour, Camillo Benso di d. Jun 6, 1861
Gobineau, Joseph Arthur, Comte de
  d. Oct 13, 1882
Huxley, Laura Archera b.
Kossuth, Lajos d. Mar 20, 1894
Lagrange, Joseph-Louis b. 1736
Lombroso, Cesare d. Oct 19, 1909
Marcoux, Vanni b. Jun 12, 1877
Marot, Clement d. Sep 10, 1544
Pasero, Tancredi b. Jan 11, 1893
Pavese, Cesare d. Aug 1950
Pellico, Silvio d. Jan 31, 1854
Ricci, Nina b. 1883
Rocca, Lodovico b. Nov 29, 1895
Scalchi, Sofia b. Nov 29, 1850
Sobrero, Ascanio d. May 26, 1888
Soleri, Paolo b. Jun 21, 1919
Tamagno, Francesco b. Dec 28, 1850
Valdengo, Giuseppe b. May 24, 1920
Victor Emmanuel II b. Mar 14, 1820
Yon, Pietro Alessandro b. Aug 8, 1886
Tuscany, Italy
Collodi, Carlo, pseud. b. Nov 24, 1826
Fanfani, Amintore b. Feb 6, 1908
Tusculum, Italy
Cato, Marcus Porcius Censorius b. 234 BC
Udine, Italy
Gatti-Casazza, Giulio b. Feb 3, 1869
Urbania, Italy
Crescentini, Girolamo b. Feb 2, 1762
Urbino, Italy
Bramante, Donata d'Agnolo b. 1444
Raphael b. 1483
Val di Castello, Italy
Carducci, Giosue b. Jul 27, 1835

Val di Greve, Italy
Verrazano, Giovanni da b. 1485
Vallombrosa, Italy
Story, William Wetmore d. Oct 7, 1895
Varese, Italy
Tamagno, Francesco d. Aug 31, 1905
Vasto, Italy
Rossetti, Gabriele Pasquale Giuseppe
  b. Feb 28, 1783
Vatican City, Italy
John Paul I, Pope d. Sep 28, 1978
Ottaviani, Alfredo, Cardinal
  d. Aug 3, 1979
Velletri, Italy
Leroux, Xavier b. Oct 11, 1863
Venice, Italy
Abarbanel, Isaac Ben Jehudah d. 1508
Aherne, Brian de Lacy d. Feb 10, 1986
Albinoni, Tommaso b. 1671
Albinoni, Tommaso d. 1750
Alda, Frances d. Sep 18, 1952
Aretino, Pietro d. Oct 21, 1556
Bellini, Gentile b. 1429
Bellini, Gentile d. Feb 23, 1507
Bellini, Giovanni b. 1430
Bellini, Giovanni d. Nov 29, 1516
Bellotto, Bernardo b. Jan 30, 1720
Bordoni, Faustina d. Nov 4, 1781
Browning, Robert d. Dec 12, 1889
Cabot, Sebastian b. 1476
Canaletto, Antonio b. Oct 18, 1697
Canaletto, Antonio d. Apr 20, 1768
Canova, Antonio d. Oct 13, 1822
Cardin, Pierre b. Jul 7, 1922
Carriera, Rosalba b. 1675
Carriera, Rosalba d. 1757
Casanova (de Seingalt), Giovanni Giacomo
  b. Apr 2, 1725
Cavalli, Francesco d. Jan 14, 1676
Cimarosa, Domenico d. Jan 11, 1801
Corvo, Baron, pseud. d. Oct 26, 1913
Crivelli, Carlo b. 1435
Diaghilev, Sergei Pavlovich
  d. Aug 19, 1929
DiCamerino, Roberta b. Dec 8, 1920
Doppler, Christian Johann d. Mar 17, 1853
Feti, Domenico d. 1623
Gabrieli, Giovanni b. 1557
Gabrieli, Giovanni d. Aug 12, 1612
Galuppi, Baldassare d. Jan 3, 1785
Giorgione, Il b. 1477
Goldoni, Carlo b. Feb 25, 1707
Gozzi, Gaspare b. Dec 4, 1713
Guardi, Francesco b. Oct 5, 1712
Guardi, Francesco d. Jan 1, 1793
Guggenheim, Peggy Marguerite
  d. Dec 23, 1979
Hasse, Johann Adolph d. Dec 16, 1783
James, George Payne Rainsford
  d. May 9, 1860
Landi, Elissa b. Dec 6, 1904

Lombroso, Cesare b. Nov 6, 1836
Lotto, Lorenzo b. 1480
Malipiero, Gian Francesco b. Mar 18, 1882
Mantovani, Annunzio b. Nov 5, 1905
Manutius, Aldus d. Feb 3, 1515
Manuzio, Aldo b. 1449
Manuzio, Aldo d. 1515
Marcello, Benedetto b. 1686
Marco Polo b. 1254
Marco Polo d. Jan 9, 1324
Monteverdi, Claudio d. Nov 29, 1643
Nono, Luigi b. Jan 29, 1924
Piranesi, Giovanni Battista b. Oct 4, 1720
Polacco, Giorgio b. Apr 12, 1875
Pound, Ezra Loomis d. Nov 1, 1972
Tiepolo, Giambattista (Giovanni Battista)
    b. Mar 5, 1696
Tintoretto b. 1518
Tintoretto d. May 31, 1594
Titian d. Aug 27, 1576
Traetta, Tommaso d. Apr 6, 1779
Verrocchio, Andrea del d. Oct 7, 1488
Vivaldi, Antonio b. Mar 4, 1675
Wagner, Richard d. Feb 13, 1883
Wolf-Ferrari, Ermanno b. Jan 12, 1876
Wolf-Ferrari, Ermanno d. Jan 21, 1948
Zeno, Apostolo b. Dec 11, 1668
Zeno, Apostolo d. Nov 11, 1750
Verazza, Italy
Cilea, Francesco d. Nov 20, 1950
Vercelli, Italy
Viotti, Giovanni Battista b. May 23, 1753
Verona, Italy
Catullus, Gaius Valerius b. 84 BC
Dalla Rizza, Gilda b. Oct 12, 1892
Fracastoro, Gerolamo b. 1478
Fracastoro, Gerolamo d. Aug 8, 1553
Gazzaniga, Giuseppe b. 1743
Guardini, Romano b. Feb 17, 1885
Martini, Nino b. Aug 8, 1905
Montemezzi, Italo d. May 15, 1952
Rossi, Gaetano b. 1780
Rossi, Gaetano d. Jan 27, 1855
Veronese, Paolo b. 1528
Zenatello, Giovanni b. Feb 22, 1876
Vespignamo, Italy
Giotto di Bondone b. 1266
Viareggio, Italy
Marini, Marino d. Aug 6, 1980
Ouida, pseud. d. Jan 25, 1908
Shelley, Percy Bysshe d. Jul 8, 1822
Zita b. 1892
Vicchio, Italy
Angelico, Fra b. 1387
Vicenza, Italy
Barolini, Antonio b. May 29, 1910
Fogazzaro, Antonio b. Mar 25, 1842
Fogazzaro, Antonio d. Mar 7, 1911
Rumor, Mariano b. Jun 16, 1915
Vigasio, Italy
Montemezzi, Italo b. Aug 4, 1875

Vigerano, Italy
Duse, Eleanora b. 1859
Vignola, Italy
Muratori, Ludovico b. Oct 21, 1672
Vignola, Giacomo da b. Oct 1, 1507
Villafalletto, Italy
Vanzetti, Bartolomeo b. Jun 11, 1888
Vinci, Italy
Leonardo da Vinci b. Apr 15, 1452
Viterbo, Italy
Cavalieri, Lina b. Dec 25, 1874
Vitterba, Italy
Bonci, Alessandro d. Aug 8, 1940
Vittoriale, Italy
D'Annunzio, Gabriele d. Mar 1, 1938
Voghera, Italy
Garavani, Valentino b. 1932
Vogliera, Italy
Montana, "Bull" (Louis) b. May 16, 1887
Volaterrae, Italy
Persius b. Dec 4, 34

IVORY COAST

Houphouet-Boigny, Felix b. Oct 18, 1905

JAMAICA

Barrett, William, Sir b. Feb 10, 1844
Crockett, James Underwood
    d. Jul 11, 1979
Hochoy, Solomon, Sir b. Apr 20, 1905
Holland, William Jacob b. Aug 16, 1848
Pickering, William Henry d. Jan 16, 1938
Raffles, Thomas Stamford, Sir
    b. Jul 5, 1781
Shearer, Taddeus Errington (Ted)
    b. Nov 1, 1919
Stevenson, Edward A b. Nov 9, 1907
Irish Town, Jamaica
Bustamante, William Alexander
    d. Aug 6, 1977
Kingston, Jamaica
Coward, Noel Pierce, Sir d. Mar 26, 1973
Ewing, Patrick Aloysius b. May 5, 1962
Glasspole, Florizel Augustus
    b. Sep 25, 1909
Manley, Michael Norman b. Dec 10, 1923
Marley, Bob (Robert Nesta)
    b. Feb 5, 1945
Parsons, Charles Algernin, Sir
    d. Feb 11, 1931
Silvera, Frank b. Jul 24, 1914
Simpson, Louis b. Mar 27, 1923
Montego Bay, Jamaica
Rose, Billy d. Feb 10, 1966
Ocho Rios, Jamaica
Hench, Philip Showalter d. Mar 30, 1965
Port Antonio, Jamaica
Russwurm, John Brown b. Oct 1, 1799

Saint Ann's Bay, Jamaica
Garvey, Marcus Moziah b. Aug 17, 1887
Spanishtown, Jamaica
Jones, Grace b. May 19, 1952
Westmoreland, Jamaica
Tosh, Peter b. Oct 9, 1944

JAPAN

Adams, William d. 1620
Fukuda, Takeo b. Jan 14, 1905
Hasegawa, Kazuo b. Feb 29, 1908
Korin, Ogata b. 1658
Takada, Kenzo b. Feb 28, 1940
Abiko, Japan
Aoki, Isao b. Aug 31, 1942
Aichi Prefecture, Japan
Ichikawa, Fusae b. 1893
Anjo City, Japan
Iwama, Kazuo b. Feb 7, 1919
Chiba, Japan
Hayakawa, Sessue (Kintaro)
b. Jun 10, 1886
Choshu Province, Japan
Ito, Hirobumi b. Sep 2, 1841
Edo, Japan
Harunobu, Suzuki b. 1718
Harunobu, Suzuki d. 1770
Eichizen Province, Japan
Chikamatsu, Monzaemon b. 1653
Fukuoka, Japan
Principal, Victoria b. Jan 3, 1944
Hayama, Japan
Yoshihito d. Dec 25, 1926
Holdaido, Japan
Umeki, Miyoshi b. Apr 3, 1929
Hoten, Japan
Ozawa, Seiji b. Sep 1, 1935
Ichikawa, Japan
Nagai, Sokichi d. Apr 30, 1959
Iwata Gun, Japan
Honda, Soichiro b. Nov 17, 1906
Kanazawa, Japan
Suzuki, Daisetz Teitaro b. Oct 18, 1870
Kashiwara, Japan
Fuchida, Mitsuo d. May 30, 1976
Kinan, Japan
Onoda, Hiroo b. 1922
Kinjo, Japan
Toyoda, Eiji b. Sep 12, 1913
Kochi, Japan
Yamashita, Tomoyuki b. 1888
Kyoto, Japan
Mizoguchi, Kenji d. Aug 24, 1956
Mori, Hanae b. Jan 8, 1926
Mutsuhito b. 1852
Oshima, Nagrsa b. Mar 31, 1932
Yukawa, Hideki d. Sep 8, 1981
Matsuyama, Japan
Masaoka, Tsunenori b. Oct 14, 1867

Mie, Japan
Kinugasa, Teinousuke b. 1898
Nagaoka, Japan
Yamamoto, Isoroku b. Apr 4, 1884
Nagasaki, Japan
Hartmann, Sadakichi b. Oct 8, 1869
Nagoya, Japan
Morita, Akio b. Jan 26, 1921
Nara, Japan
Calhern, Louis d. May 12, 1956
Niigata, Japan
Hashimoto, Ken b. Jun 16, 1931
Oisi, Japan
Yoshida, Shigeru d. Oct 20, 1967
Okayama, Japan
Kuniyoshi, Yasuo b. Sep 1, 1893
Okinawa, Japan
Buckner, Simon, Jr. d. Jun 18, 1945
Okubo, Japan
Hearn, Lafcadio d. Sep 26, 1904
Osaka, Japan
Basho d. Nov 28, 1694
Kawabata, Yasunari b. Jun 11, 1899
Tange, Kenzo b. Sep 4, 1913
Tabuse, Japan
Sato, Eisaku b. Mar 27, 1901
Takasaki, Japan
Nakasone, Yasuhiro b. May 27, 1918
Tokushima-Ken, Japan
Miki, Takeo b. Mar 17, 1907
Tokyo, Japan
Abe, Isao b. 1865
Abe, Isao d. Feb 10, 1949
Akihito, (Togusama) b. Dec 23, 1933
DeHavilland, Olivia b. Jul 1, 1916
Endo, Shusaku b. Mar 27, 1923
Farrington, Elizabeth Pruett (Mary)
b. May 30, 1898
Fontaine, Joan b. Oct 22, 1917
Franklin, Pamela b. Feb 4, 1950
Hayakawa, Sessue (Kintaro)
d. Nov 23, 1974
Hirohito b. Apr 29, 1901
Horikoshi, Jiro d. Jan 11, 1982
Ichikawa, Fusae d. Feb 11, 1981
Iwama, Kazuo d. Aug 24, 1982
Kurosawa, Akira b. Mar 23, 1910
Kurusu, Saburo d. Apr 7, 1954
Landis, James McCauley b. Sep 25, 1899
Masaoka, Tsunenori d. Sep 19, 1902
Mishima, Yukio, pseud. b. Jan 14, 1925
Mishima, Yukio, pseud. d. Nov 25, 1970
Mizoguchi, Kenji b. May 16, 1898
Nagai, Sokichi b. Dec 3, 1879
Naruse, Mikio b. Aug 20, 1905
Naruse, Mikio d. 1969
Nomura, Kichisaburo d. May 8, 1964
Oh, Sadaharu b. May 5, 1940
Ohira, Masayoshi d. Jun 11, 1980
Okada, Kenzo d. Jul 25, 1982
Ono, Yoko b. Feb 18, 1933

Ozaki, Koyo, pseud. b. Oct 1, 1868
Ozaki, Koyo, pseud. d. Oct 30, 1903
Poons, Lawrence (Larry) b. Oct 1, 1937
Saito, Yoshishige b. May 4, 1904
Sato, Eisaku d. Jun 3, 1975
Sorge, Richard d. 1944
Suzuki, Daisetz Teitaro d. Jul 12, 1966
Tabei, Junko b. 1940
Teshigahara, Hiroshi b. 1927
Tojo, Hideki (Eiki) b. 1884
Tojo, Hideki (Eiki) d. Dec 23, 1948
Ullmann, Liv Johanne b. Dec 16, 1939
Yoshida, Shigeru b. Sep 22, 1878
Yoshihito b. Aug 31, 1879
Yukawa, Hideki b. Jan 23, 1907

Toyohama, Japan
Ohira, Masayoshi b. Mar 12, 1910

Ueno, Iga, Japan
Basho b. 1644

Wakayama-Ken, Japan
Nomura, Kichisaburo b. Dec 1877

Wasa Village, Japan
Matsushita, Konosuke b. Nov 27, 1894

Yedo, Japan
Hokusai b. 1760

Yokohama, Japan
Crowe, Colin Tradescant, Sir
    b. Sep 7, 1913
Kurusu, Saburo b. 1888
Okada, Kenzo b. Sep 28, 1902
Whitney, Phyllis Ayame b. Sep 9, 1903

Zusni, Japan
Kawabata, Yasunari d. Apr 16, 1972

JAVA

Semarang, Java
Norden, Carl Lukas b. Apr 23, 1880

JORDAN

Jaabari, Mohammed Ali, Sheik b. 1900
Amman, Jordan
Hussein (Ibn Talal) b. Nov 14, 1935
Shukairy, Ahmed d. Feb 26, 1980
Moab, Jordan
Moses d. 1272 ?BC

JUDEA

Bethlehem, Judea
Jerome, Saint d. 420

KASHMIR

Soura, Kashmir
Abdullah, Sheik Mohammad
    b. Dec 5, 1905

KENYA

Kenyatta, Jomo (Johnstone)
    b. Oct 20, 1891
Snow, Don b. Jan 13, 1957
Kaptagunyo, Kenya
Keino, Kip (Hezekiah Kipchoge)
    b. Jan 17, 1940
Kuriengwo, Kenya
Moi, Daniel b. Sep 1924
Lake Victoria, Kenya
Mboya, Tom (Thomas Joseph)
    b. Aug 15, 1930
Mombasa, Kenya
Kenyatta, Jomo (Johnstone)
    d. Aug 22, 1978
Nairobi, Kenya
Hannagan, Steve (Stephen Jerome)
    d. Feb 5, 1953
Leakey, Richard E b. Dec 19, 1944
Markham, Beryl d. Aug 3, 1986
Mboya, Tom (Thomas Joseph)
    d. Jul 5, 1969
Parks, Gordon, Jr. d. Apr 3, 1979
Root, Joan b. 1936
Nyeri, Kenya
Baden-Powell, Robert Stephenson Smyth
    Baden-Powell, Baron d. Jan 8, 1941
Shaba, Kenya
Adamson, Joy Friederike Victoria Gessner
    d. Jan 3, 1980

KOREA

Cheju, Korea
Park, Choong-Hoon b. Jan 19, 1919
Hayi-do, Korea
Kim Dae Jung b. Jan 6, 1924
Hwanghai, Korea
Rhee, Syngman b. Mar 26, 1875
Kangwon Province, Korea
Ch'oe Kyu Ha b. Jul 16, 1919
Mangyongdae, Korea
Kim, Il Sung b. Apr 15, 1912
Pyongyang, Korea
Park, Tongsun b. Mar 16, 1935
Sosan Gun, Korea
Park, Chung Hee b. Sep 30, 1917

KOREA (SOUTH)

Seoul, Korea (South)
Park, Chung Hee d. Oct 26, 1979

KUWAIT

Saud (Ibn Abdul Aziz al Saud)
    b. Jan 15, 1902

LAOS

Sananikone, Phoui b. Sep 6, 1903
Luang Prabang, Laos
Souvanna, Phouma b. Oct 7, 1901
Vientiane, Laos
Souvanna, Phouma d. Jan 10, 1984

LATVIA

Riga, Latvia
Kremer, Gidon b. Feb 27, 1947
Moisseiff, Leon Solomon b. Nov 10, 1872

LEBANON

Bechari, Lebanon
Gibran, Kahlil b. Apr 10, 1883
Beirut, Lebanon
Gemayel, Bashir d. Sep 14, 1982
Husseini, Haj Amin d. Jul 4, 1974
Jumblatt, Kamal Fouad d. Mar 16, 1977
Kerr, Malcolm (Hooper) b. Oct 8, 1931
Kerr, Malcolm (Hooper) d. Jan 18, 1984
Meloy, Francis Edward, Jr.
  d. Jun 16, 1976
Philby, Harold St. John Bridger
  d. Sep 30, 1960
Salam, Saeb b. 1905
Bikfaya, Lebanon
Gemayel, Amin b. 1942
Gemayel, Bashir b. Nov 10, 1947
Bitirram, Lebanon
Malik, Charles Habib b. Feb 11, 1906
Marjayoun, Lebanon
Haddad, Saad b. 1937
Haddad, Saad d. Jan 14, 1984
Mukhtara, Lebanon
Jumblatt, Kamal Fouad b. Jan 6, 1917
Shibaniyah, Lebanon
Sarkis, Elias b. Jul 20, 1924

LIBERIA

Russwurm, John Brown d. Jun 17, 1851
Bensonville, Liberia
Tolbert, William Richard, Jr.
  b. May 13, 1913
Harper, Liberia
Tubman, William Vacanarat Shadrach
  b. Nov 29, 1895
Tubman, William Vacanarat Shadrach
  d. Jul 23, 1971
Monrovia, Liberia
Garnet, Henry Highland d. Feb 13, 1882
Tolbert, William Richard, Jr.
  d. Apr 12, 1980
Monrovia Bay, Liberia
Scripps, Edward Wyllis d. Mar 12, 1926
Tuzon, Liberia
Doe, Samuel Kanyon b. May 6, 1951

Virginia, Liberia
Brooks, Angie Elizabeth b. Aug 24, 1928

LIBYA

Romano, Joseph b. 1940
Jaghbub, Libya
Idris I b. Mar 13, 1890
Misurata, Libya
Khadafy, Moammar b. 1942
Tobruk, Libya
Balbo, Italo d. Jun 28, 1940
Tripoli, Libya
Podesta, Rossana b. Jun 20, 1934

LIECHTENSTEIN

Brunhart, Hans b. Mar 28, 1945
Franz Josef II b. Aug 16, 1906

LITHUANIA

Bryant, Lane b. Dec 1, 1879
Burton, Montague Maurice, Sir
  b. Aug 15, 1885
Hoffenstein, Samuel Goodman
  b. Oct 8, 1890
Lipchitz, Jacques b. Aug 22, 1891
Silver, Abba Hillel b. Jan 28, 1893
Washkansky, Louis b. 1913
Eurburg, Lithuania
Zorach, William b. Feb 28, 1887
Janiskis, Lithuania
Harvey, Laurence b. Oct 1, 1928
Kaunas, Lithuania
Arens, Moshe b. Dec 27, 1925
Goldman, Emma b. Jun 27, 1869
Shahn, Ben(jamin) b. Sep 12, 1898
Sateiniai, Lithuania
Milosz, Czeslaw b. Jun 30, 1911
Swenziany, Lithuania
Kaplan, Mordecai b. Jun 11, 1881
Vilna, Lithuania
Romanoff, Mike b. 1890
Vilnius, Lithuania
Berenson, Bernard b. Jun 26, 1865
Wilno, Lithuania
Gary, Romain b. May 8, 1914
Zagare, Lithuania
Hillman, Sidney b. Mar 23, 1887

LUCANIA

Venosa, Lucania
Horace b. Dec 8, 65 BC

LUXEMBOURG

Claude, Albert b. Aug 23, 1898
Schuman, Robert b. Jun 29, 1886
Steichen, Edward Jean b. Mar 27, 1879
Thorn, Gaston b. Sep 3, 1928

Guadalajara, Mexico
Barragan, Luis b. 1902
Janney, Leon d. Oct 28, 1980
Jurado, Katy b. Jan 16, 1927
Lopez-Portillo y Rojas, Jose
    b. May 26, 1850
Royle, Selena d. Apr 23, 1983
Guanajuato, Mexico
Hidalgo y Costilla, Miguel b. May 8, 1753
Martin, Fletcher d. May 30, 1979
Rivera, Diego b. Dec 8, 1886
Hermosillo, Mexico
Barrios, Francisco Javier b. Jun 10, 1953
Barrios, Francisco Javier d. Apr 9, 1982
Hondo, Mexico
Fernandez, Emilio b. 1904
Itzancanal, Mexico
Cuauhtemoc d. Feb 26, 1525
Jalapa, Mexico
Santa Anna, Antonio Lopez de b. 1794
Jiquilpan, Mexico
Cardenas, Lazaro b. May 21, 1895
Juarez, Mexico
McQueen, Steve (Terence Stephen)
    d. Nov 7, 1980
Roland, Gilbert b. Dec 11, 1905
Las Mochis, Mexico
Higuera, Teddy (Teodoro Valenzuela)
    b. Nov 9, 1958
Logos de Morena, Mexico
Azuela, Mariano b. Jan 1, 1873
Mexico City, Mexico
Aleman, Miguel d. May 14, 1983
Alicia, Ana b. Dec 12, 1957
Armendariz, Pedro b. May 9, 1912
Azuela, Mariano d. Mar 1, 1952
Bunuel, Luis d. Jul 29, 1983
Calles, Plutarco d. Oct 19, 1945
Campora, Hector Jose d. Dec 19, 1980
Cantinflas b. Aug 12, 1911
Cardenas, Lazaro d. Oct 19, 1970
Chase, Ilka d. Feb 15, 1978
Chavez, Carlos b. Jun 13, 1899
Chavez, Carlos d. Aug 2, 1978
Covarrubias, Miguel b. Feb 4, 1904
Covarrubias, Miguel d. Feb 6, 1957
Diaz Ordaz, Gustavo d. Jul 15, 1979
Echeverria Alvarez, Louis b. Jan 17, 1922
Feldman, Marty d. Dec 2, 1982
Fernandez, Emilio d. Aug 6, 1986
Fuentes, Carlos b. Nov 11, 1928
Gurie, Sigrid b. Aug 14, 1969
Juarez, Benito Pablo d. Jul 18, 1872
Krauss, Clemens d. May 16, 1954
Kuiper, Gerard Peter d. Dec 24, 1973
Lopez Mateos, Adolfo d. Sep 22, 1969
Lopez Portillo, Jose b. Jul 16, 1920
Lopez-Portillo y Rojas, Jose
    d. May 22, 1923
Margo b. May 10, 1918
Moats, Alice-Leone b. Mar 12, 1911

Montalban, Ricardo b. Nov 25, 1920
Motley, Willard Francis d. Mar 5, 1965
Novi, Carlo b. Aug 7, 1949
Orozco, Jose Clemente d. Sep 7, 1949
Paz, Octavio b. Mar 31, 1914
Reyes, Alfonso d. Dec 27, 1959
Ricketts, Howard T d. May 3, 1910
Rivera, Diego d. Nov 25, 1957
Santa Anna, Antonio Lopez de
    d. Jun 20, 1876
Sontag, Henriette d. Jun 17, 1854
Traven, B, pseud. d. Mar 27, 1969
Trotsky, Leon d. Aug 21, 1940
Monterrey, Mexico
Kiam, Omar b. 1894
Reyes, Alfonso b. May 17, 1889
Nochistlan, Mexico
Alvarado, Pedro de d. 1541
Oaxaca, Mexico
Diaz, Porfirio b. Sep 15, 1830
Juarez, Benito Pablo b. Mar 21, 1806
Parral Chihuaha, Mexico
Villa, "Pancho" (Francisco) d. Jul 23, 1923
Puebla, Mexico
Diaz Ordaz, Gustavo b. Mar 12, 1911
Puerto Vallarta, Mexico
Allbritton, Louise d. Feb 16, 1979
Pryor, Roger d. Jan 31, 1974
Queretaro, Mexico
Maximilian d. Jun 19, 1867
Sanchez, Salvador d. Aug 12, 1982
Rio Grande, Mexico
Villa, "Pancho" (Francisco) b. Jun 5, 1878
Saltillo, Mexico
Brent, Romney b. Jan 26, 1902
San Angel, Mexico
Obregon, Alvaro d. Jul 17, 1928
San Luis Potosi, Mexico
Velez, Lupe b. Jul 18, 1908
San Miguel de Allende, Mexico
Cassady, Neal d. Feb 4, 1968
Santiago de Tianquistenco, Mexico
Sanchez, Salvador b. Feb 5, 1959
Sayula, Mexico
Aleman, Miguel b. Sep 29, 1903
Tamaulipas, Mexico
Sequoya d. 1843
Tampico, Mexico
Christian, Linda b. Nov 13, 1923
Taxco, Mexico
Alarcon y Mendoza, Juan Ruiz de b. 1580
Tenochtitlan, Mexico
Cuauhtemoc b. 1495
Montezuma I b. 1390
Montezuma I d. 1464
Montezuma II b. 1480
Montezuma II d. Jun 1520
Tlaxcalantongo, Mexico
Carranza, Venustiano d. May 21, 1920
Valladolid, Mexico
Iturbide, Augustin de b. Sep 27, 1783

Vera Cruz, Mexico
Avila, Bobby (Roberto Francisco Gonzalez)
b. Apr 2, 1924
Zapotlan, Mexico
Orozco, Jose Clemente b. Nov 23, 1883

MONACO

Gallico, Paul William d. Jul 15, 1976
Rainier III, Prince b. May 31, 1923
Schreker, Franz b. Mar 23, 1878
Monaco-Ville, Monaco
Stephanie, Princess b. Feb 1, 1965
Monte Carlo, Monaco
Albert b. Mar 14, 1958
Beatty, Alfred Chester, Sir d. Jan 20, 1968
Berry, James Gomer d. Feb 6, 1968
Carol, Martine d. Feb 6, 1967
Caroline, Princess b. Jan 23, 1957
Darvi, Bella d. Sep 10, 1971
Dongen, Kees van d. May 28, 1968
Kelly, Grace Patricia d. Sep 14, 1982
Langtry, Lillie d. Feb 12, 1929
Loewy, Raymond Fernand d. Jul 14, 1986
Molyneux, Edward H d. Mar 23, 1974
Olcott, Chauncey (Chancellor)
d. Mar 18, 1932
Paray, Paul d. Oct 10, 1979
Pathe, Charles d. Dec 25, 1957
Rossellini, Renzo d. May 14, 1982

MONTANA

Monte Carlo, Montana
Chaminade, Cecile d. Apr 18, 1944

MORAVIA

Brunn, Moravia
Maretzek, Max b. Jun 28, 1821
Freiberg, Moravia
Freud, Sigmund b. May 6, 1856
Koprivnice, Moravia
Zatopek, Emil b. Sep 19, 1922
Mistek, Moravia
Paur, Emil d. Jun 7, 1932
Schonberg, Moravia
Slezak, Leo b. Aug 18, 1875
Trest, Moravia
Schumpeter, Joseph Alois b. Feb 8, 1883
Unersky, Moravia
Comenius, Johann Amos b. Mar 28, 1592

MOROCCO

Agadir, Morocco
Blyden, Larry d. Jun 6, 1975

Algiers, Morocco
Saint-Saens, (Charles) Camille
d. Dec 16, 1921
Fez, Morocco
Ibn Batutah d. 1378
Marrakech, Morocco
Auchinleck, Claude, Sir d. Mar 23, 1981
Meknes, Morocco
Jobert, Michel b. Sep 11, 1921
Melilla, Morocco
Arrabal (Teran), Fernando
b. Aug 11, 1932
Rabat, Morocco
Mohammed V d. Feb 26, 1961
Tangiers, Morocco
Ibn Batutah b. 1304
Lukas, Paul d. Aug 15, 1971
Tietjen, Heinz b. Jun 24, 1881
Toledano, Ralph de b. Aug 17, 1916

MOZAMBIQUE

Chilembene, Mozambique
Machel, Samora Moises b. Sep 29, 1933

NAISSUS

Constantine I b. 280

NAMIBIA

Hippo, Namibia
Augustine, Saint d. 430
Madavros, Namibia
Apuleius, Lucius b. 125

NEPAL

Mallory, George Leigh d. Jun 8, 1924
Bharatpur, Nepal
Mahendra, Bir Bikram Shah Dev
d. Jan 31, 1972
Kathmandu, Nepal
Birendra Bir Bikram, Shah Dev
b. Dec 28, 1945
Mahendra, Bir Bikram Shah Dev
b. Jun 11, 1920
Tami, Nepal
Tenzing, Norgay b. 1914

NETHERLANDS

Agt, Andries Antonius Maria van
b. Feb 2, 1931
Clouet, Jean b. 1485
Fabritius, Carel b. 1622
Hobbema, Meindert b. Oct 31, 1638
Hobbema, Meindert d. Dec 7, 1709
Pavlova, Anna d. Jan 23, 1931
Rembrandt (Harmenszoon van Rijn)
d. Oct 4, 1669
Tromp, Solco Walle d. Mar 17, 1983

Aarnhem, Netherlands
Lorentz, Hendrick Antoon b. Jul 18, 1853
Acquoi, Netherlands
Jansen, Cornelis b. 1585
Agnietenberg, Netherlands
Thomas a Kempis d. Jul 25, 1471
Amersfoort, Netherlands
Mondrian, Piet(er Cornelis) b. Mar 7, 1872
Amsterdam, Netherlands
Appel, Karel Christian b. Apr 25, 1921
Berlage, Hendrik Petrus b. 1856
Comenius, Johann Amos d. Nov 15, 1670
Cruyff, Johan b. Apr 25, 1947
Den Uyl, Joor b. 1919
DeVries, Hugo d. May 21, 1935
DeWaart, Edo b. Jun 1, 1941
Euwe, Max (Machgielis) b. May 20, 1901
Euwe, Max (Machgielis) d. Nov 26, 1981
Haitink, Bernard b. Mar 4, 1929
Kalf, Willem d. 1693
Kondrashin, Kiril Petrovich
  d. Mar 7, 1981
Krieghoff, Cornelius b. 1815
Oistrakh, David Fyodorovich
  d. Oct 24, 1974
Ruysdael, Jacob van d. Mar 14, 1682
Spinoza, Baruch (Benedictus de)
  b. Nov 24, 1632
Sweelinck, Jan Pieterszoon b. 1562
Sweelinck, Jan Pieterszoon d. Oct 16, 1621
Ten Boom, Corrie b. Apr 15, 1892
Verwoerd, Hendrik F b. Sep 8, 1901
Anna Paulowna, Netherlands
Schenk, Ard b. Sep 19, 1944
Apeldoorn, Netherlands
DeJong, Petrus b. Apr 13, 1915
Arnheim, Netherlands
Beinum, Eduard van b. Sep 3, 1900
Sidney, Philip, Sir d. Oct 17, 1586
Beers, Netherlands
DeQuay, Jan E d. Jul 4, 1985
Blija, Netherlands
DeJong, David Cornel b. Jun 9, 1905
Breda, Netherlands
Parker, Thomas Andrew b. 1910
Breukelen, Netherlands
Hauer, Rutger b. Jan 23, 1944
Copenhagen, Netherlands
Nelson, "Battling" b. Jun 5, 1882
Cote-Saint-Andre, Netherlands
Jongkind, Johan Barthold d. Feb 9, 1891
De Steeg, Netherlands
Couperius, Louis (Marie Anne)
  d. Jul 16, 1923
Delfshaven, Netherlands
Dongen, Kees van b. Jan 26, 1877
Delft, Netherlands
Fabritius, Carel d. Oct 12, 1654
Grotius, Hugo b. Apr 10, 1583
Leeuwenhoek, Anton van b. Oct 24, 1632
Vermeer, Jan b. Oct 30, 1632

Deventer, Netherlands
Groote, Gerhard b. 1340
Ter Borch, Gerard d. Dec 8, 1681
Doorn, Netherlands
Wilhelm II d. Jun 4, 1941
Dordrecht, Netherlands
Cuyp, Aelbert b. 1620
Cuyp, Aelbert d. Nov 1691
Dronrijp, Netherlands
Alma-Tadema, Lawrence, Sir
  b. Jan 8, 1836
Druten, Netherlands
Kolvenback, Peter-Hans b. 1928
Exeter, Netherlands
Ladd, William b. May 10, 1778
Goreum, Netherlands
Van Paassen, Pierre b. Feb 7, 1895
Graveland, Netherlands
Koopmans, Tjalling (Charles)
  b. Aug 28, 1910
Groningen, Netherlands
Bernoulli, David b. Feb 8, 1700
Israels, Josef b. 1824
Kamerlingh Onnes, Heike b. Sep 21, 1853
Haarlem, Netherlands
Coster, Laurens Janszoon b. 1410
DeHartog, Jan b. Apr 22, 1914
DeVries, Hugo b. Feb 16, 1848
Meer, Jan van der b. 1628
Ostade, Adriaen van b. Dec 10, 1610
Ostade, Adriaen van d. May 2, 1685
Ruysdael, Jacob van b. 1628
Van Niel, Cornelius B(ernardus)
  b. Nov 4, 1897
Verspronk, Johannes b. 1597
Verspronk, Johannes d. 1662
Visser T Hooft, Willem Adolf
  b. Sep 20, 1900
Harencarspel, Netherlands
Kuiper, Gerard Peter b. Dec 7, 1905
Hertogenbosch, Netherlands
Bosch, Hieronymus b. 1450
Het Loo, Netherlands
Wilhelmina d. Nov 28, 1962
Hilversum, Netherlands
Escher, Maurits Cornelis d. 1972
Hoorn, Netherlands
Bok, Bart J(an) b. Apr 28, 1906
Coen, Jan Pieterszoon b. 1587
Lattrop, Netherlands
Jongkind, Johan Barthold b. Jun 3, 1819
Leeuwarden, Netherlands
Mata Hari b. Aug 7, 1876
Leiden, Netherlands
Arminius, Jacobus d. Oct 19, 1609
Dou, Gerard b. Apr 7, 1613
Dou, Gerard d. Feb 1675
Elzevir, Louis d. Feb 4, 1617
Foch, Nina b. Apr 20, 1924
Goyen, Jan Josephszoon van b. 1596
Kolff, Willem Johan b. Feb 14, 1911

Lucasvan Leyden b. 1494
Lucasvan Leyden d. 1533
Rembrandt (Harmenszoon van Rijn)
    b. Jul 15, 1607
Steen, Jan b. 1626
Steen, Jan d. Feb 3, 1679
Leyden, Netherlands
Velde, Willem van de b. 1633
Maastricht, Netherlands
Debye, Peter Joseph William
    b. Mar 24, 1884
Maeseyck, Netherlands
Van Eyck, Jan b. 1371
Mons, Netherlands
Lassus, Orlandus de b. 1532
Naarden, Netherlands
Martin, Frank d. Nov 21, 1974
Nijerk, Netherlands
Nouwen, Henri J M b. Jan 24, 1932
Nijmegen, Netherlands
Grol, Lini Richards b. Oct 7, 1913
Ivens, Joris b. Nov 18, 1898
Van Halen, Alex b. May 8, 1955
Van Halen, Eddie (Edward)
    b. Jan 26, 1957
Noordwijk, Netherlands
Montessori, Maria d. May 6, 1952
Oudewater, Netherlands
Arminius, Jacobus b. Oct 10, 1560
Portsmouth, Netherlands
Ladd, William d. Apr 9, 1841
Roermond, Netherlands
Cuypers, Petrus Josephus Hubertus b. 1827
Rotterdam, Netherlands
Ameling, Elly b. Feb 8, 1938
Brico, Antonia b. Jun 26, 1902
DeKooning, Willem b. Apr 24, 1904
Erasmus, Desiderius b. Oct 27, 1469
Gibbons, Grinling b. Apr 4, 1648
Hooch, Pieter de b. Dec 20, 1629
Kalf, Willem b. 1619
Kindler, Hans b. Jan 8, 1893
Lubbers, Ruud (Rudolphus Franciscus
    Maria) b. May 7, 1939
Luns, Joseph Marie Antoine Hubert
    b. Aug 28, 1911
Monmouth, James Scott, Duke
    b. Apr 9, 1649
Stove, Betty b. Jun 24, 1945
Van Loon, Hendrik Willem
    b. Jan 14, 1882
Van Rooy, Anton b. Jan 1, 1870
Vlieger, Simon Jacobsz de b. 1600
S'Hertogenbosch, Netherlands
DeQuay, Jan E b. 1901
Scherpenzeel, Netherlands
Stuyvesant, Peter (Petrus) b. 1610
Soestdijk, Netherlands
Beatrix b. Jan 31, 1938
Christina b. Feb 18, 1947
Irene b. Aug 5, 1939

Steins, Netherlands
Dykstra, John b. Apr 16, 1898
Terschelling, Netherlands
Barents, Willem b.
The Hague, Netherlands
Berlage, Hendrik Petrus d. 1934
Couperius, Louis (Marie Anne)
    b. Jun 10, 1863
Fahrenheit, Gabriel Daniel d. Sep 16, 1736
Gallitzin, Demetrius Augustine
    b. Dec 22, 1770
Goyen, Jan Josephszoon van d. 1656
Huygens, Christian b. Apr 14, 1629
Juliana b. Apr 30, 1909
Spinoza, Baruch (Benedictus de)
    d. Feb 20, 1677
Waldock, (Claud) Humphrey Meredith, Sir
    d. Aug 15, 1981
Wilhelmina b. Aug 31, 1880
William III b. 1650
Utrecht, Netherlands
Kristel, Sylvia b. Sep 28, 1952
Mengelberg, Willem (Josef Willem)
    b. Mar 28, 1871
Weesp, Netherlands
Vlieger, Simon Jacobsz de d. 1653
Wierum, Netherlands
Dejong, Meindert b. Mar 4, 1906
Wijk, Netherlands
Van Cortlandt, Oloff Stevenszen b. 1600
Zeist, Netherlands
Blyleven, Bert (Rikalbert) b. Apr 6, 1951
Zwolle, Netherlands
Ter Borch, Gerard b. 1617

NEW CALEDONIA

Leiden, New Caledonia
Einthoven, Willem d. Sep 28, 1927

NEW GUIANA

Demerara, New Guiana
Douglas, James, Sir b. Aug 15, 1803

NEW SOUTH WALES

Bateman, Henry Mayo
b. Feb 15, 1887

NEW ZEALAND

Bolitho, Henry Hector b. May 28, 1897
Garnett, Gale b. Jul 17, 1942
Russell, Franklin Alexander b. Oct 9, 1926
Auckland, New Zealand
Birley, Oswald Hornby Joseph, Sir
b. Mar 31, 1880
Duggan, Maurice Noel b. Nov 25, 1922
Hillary, Edmund Percival, Sir
b. Jul 20, 1919
Lewis, Chris b. Mar 9, 1957
McLaren, Bruce Leslie b. Aug 30, 1937
Muldoon, Robert David, Sir
b. Sep 25, 1921
Walpole, Hugh Seymour, Sir
b. Mar 13, 1884
Canterbury, New Zealand
Eden, Dorothy b. Apr 3, 1912
Christchurch, New Zealand
Alda, Frances b. May 31, 1883
Denny-Brown, Derek Ernest
b. Jun 1, 1901
Marsh, Dame Ngaio b. Apr 23, 1899
Marsh, Dame Ngaio d. Feb 18, 1982
Dunedin, New Zealand
Low, David, Sir b. Apr 7, 1891
Gisborne, New Zealand
Partridge, Eric Honeywood b. Feb 6, 1894
Te Kanawa, Kiri, Dame b. Mar 6, 1947
Levin, New Zealand
Silk, George b. Nov 17, 1916
Opunake, New Zealand
Snell, Peter George b. Dec 17, 1938
Otahuhu, New Zealand
Lange, David Russell b. Aug 4, 1942
Pahiatua, New Zealand
Holyoake, Keith Jacka, Sir
b. Feb 11, 1904

Rotu Rua, New Zealand
Ironside, Henry Allan d. Jan 15, 1951
Spring Grove, New Zealand
Rutherford, Ernest, Baron b. Aug 30, 1871
Stratford, New Zealand
Ashton-Warner, Sylvia Constance
b. Dec 17, 1908
Tasmania, New Zealand
Flynn, Errol b. Jun 20, 1909
Tauranga, New Zealand
Ashton-Warner, Sylvia Constance
d. Apr 28, 1984
Wellington, New Zealand
Holyoake, Keith Jacka, Sir d. Dec 8, 1983
Mansfield, Katherine b. Oct 14, 1888
Revill, Clive Selsby b. Apr 18, 1930

NICARAGUA

Dario, Nicaragua
Pastora (Gomez), Eden b. Jan 22, 1937
Jinotepe, Nicaragua
Cruz, Arturo b. Dec 18, 1923
La Libertad, Nicaragua
Ortega, Saavedra, Daniel b. Nov 11, 1945
Leon, Nicaragua
Somoza Debayle, Anastasio b. Dec 5, 1925
Managua, Nicaragua
Arguello, Alexis b. Apr 12, 1952
Carrera, Barbara b. 1945
Jagger, Bianca Teresa b. 1943
Somoza, Anastasio d. Sep 29, 1956
San Marcos, Nicaragua
Somoza, Anastasio b. Feb 1, 1896

NIGERIA

Olatunji, Michael Babatunde b.
Sade b. Jan 16, 1960
Abeokuta, Nigeria
Soyinka, Wole (Akinwande Oluwole)
b. Jul 13, 1934
Abeokuto, Nigeria
Obasanjo, Olusegun b. May 5, 1937
Bauchi, Nigeria
Balewa, Abubakar b. Dec 12, 1912
Fandou, Nigeria
Kountche, Seyni b. 1931
Ilesha, Nigeria
Aluko, Timothy Mofolorunso
b. Jun 14, 1918
Lagos, Nigeria
Balewa, Abubakar d. Jan 15, 1966
Olajuwon, Akeem Abdul Ajibola
b. Jan 23, 1963
Ochuga, Nigeria
Crowther, Samuel Adjai b. 1808
Ogidi, Nigeria
Achebe, Chinua b. Nov 16, 1930
Okenla, Nigeria
Delano, Isaac O b. Nov 4, 1904

Ostenso, Martha b. Sep 17, 1900
Rider-Kelsey, Corinne b. Feb 24, 1877
Borge, Norway
Amundsen, Roald Engelbregt
b. Jul 16, 1872
Christiania, Norway
Evinrude, Ole b. Apr 19, 1877
Ibsen, Henrik d. May 23, 1906
Nansen, Fridtjof b. Oct 10, 1861
Drammen, Norway
Lie, Jonas (Laurite Idemil) b. Nov 6, 1833
Fetsund, Norway
Stenerud, Jan b. Nov 26, 1943
Fredriksten, Norway
Charles XII d. Dec 11, 1718
Fryesdal, Norway
Quisling, Vidkun b. Jul 18, 1887
Golaa, Norway
Evans, Edward Ratcliffe Garth Russell
d. Aug 20, 1957
Helgeland, Norway
Rolvaag, Ole Edvart b. Apr 22, 1876
Sverdrup, Otto b. Jan 1, 1855
Horten, Norway
Norena, Eide b. Apr 26, 1884
Ronne, Finn b. Dec 20, 1899
Kongsberg, Norway
Aulaire, Ingri Mortenson d'
b. Dec 27, 1904
Sinding, Christian b. Jan 11, 1856
Kvikne, Norway
Bjornson, Bjornstjerne b. Dec 8, 1832
Larvik, Norway
Heyerdahl, Thor b. Oct 6, 1914
Loyten, Norway
Munch, Edvard b. Dec 12, 1863
Lysaker, Norway
Nansen, Fridtjof d. May 30, 1930
Lysoe, Norway
Bull, Ole Bornemann d. Aug 17, 1880
Meraker, Norway
Ingstad, Helge b. Dec 30, 1899
Notteroy, Norway
Bratteli, Trygve Martin b. Jan 11, 1910
Orkesdalsoren, Norway
Bojer, Johan b. Mar 6, 1872
Oslo, Norway
Andresen, Ivar b. Jul 17, 1896
Brundtland, Gro Harlem b. Apr 20, 1939
Bull, Odd b. Jun 28, 1907
Dobrowen, Issai d. Dec 9, 1953
Flagstad, Kirsten b. Jul 12, 1895
Flagstad, Kirsten d. Dec 7, 1962
Frisch, Ragnar b. Mar 2, 1895
Frisch, Ragnar d. Jan 31, 1973
Haakon VII d. Sep 21, 1957
Lie, Jonas (Laurite Idemil) d. Jul 5, 1908
Munch, Edvard d. Jan 23, 1944
Sinding, Christian d. Dec 3, 1941
Sverdrup, Otto d. Nov 26, 1930
Waitz, Grete b. Oct 1, 1953

Roelvaag, Norway
Roelvaag, O(le) E(dvart) b. Apr 22, 1876
Skien, Norway
Ibsen, Henrik b. Mar 20, 1828
Stange, Norway
Nordli, Odvar b. Nov 3, 1927
Tveit Topdal, Norway
Balchen, Bernt b. Oct 23, 1899
Voss, Norway
Rockne, Knute Kenneth b. Mar 4, 1888

NOVA SCOTIA

Abeokuta, Nova Scotia
Tutuola, Amos b. Jun 1920
Lagos, Nova Scotia
Young, Whitney Moore, Jr.
d. Mar 11, 1971

NYASALAND

Kasungu, Nyasaland
Banda, Hastings Kamuzu b. 1906

OUTER HEBRIDES ISLANDS

Lewis, Outer Hebrides Islands
Mackenzie, Alexander, Sir b. 1755

PAKISTAN

Karachi, Pakistan
Bhutto, Benazir b. Jun 21, 1953
Jinnah, Mohammed Ali b. Dec 25, 1876
Jinnah, Mohammed Ali d. Sep 11, 1948
Withers, Googie b. Mar 12, 1917
Karnal, Pakistan
Khan, Liaquat Ali b. Oct 1, 1895
Lahore, Pakistan
Ahmad, Mirza Ghulam Hazat
d. May 26, 1908
Faiz, Faiz Ahmad d. Nov 20, 1984
Larkana, Pakistan
Bhutto, Zulfikar Ali b. Jan 5, 1928
Peshawar, Pakistan
Yahya Khan, Agha Muhammad
b. Feb 4, 1917
Qadian, Pakistan
Ahmad, Mirza Ghulam Hazat
b. Feb 13, 1835
Rawalpindi, Pakistan
Khan, Liaquat Ali d. Oct 16, 1951
Rawalpirdi, Pakistan
Bhutto, Zulfikar Ali d. Apr 4, 1979
Rehana, Pakistan
Ayub Khan, Mohammad b. May 14, 1907
Umarkot, Pakistan
Akbar b. 1542

PALESTINE

Eusebius of Caesarea b. 264
Acre, Palestine
Shukairy, Ahmed b. 1908
Afula, Palestine
Dayan, Assaf b. 1945
Akka, Palestine
Baha'u'llah d. May 29, 1892
Degania, Palestine
Dayan, Moshe b. May 20, 1915
Haifa, Palestine
Abdu'l-Baha d. Nov 28, 1921
Bakshi, Ralph b. Oct 26, 1938
Bar-Ilian, David Jacob b. Feb 7, 1930
Gitlis, Ivry b. 1927
Safdie, Moshe b. Jul 14, 1938
Jerusalem, Palestine
Arafat, Yasir b. 1929
Ben-Yehuda, Eliezer d. Dec 16, 1922
Godfrey of Bouillon d. Jul 18, 1100
Husseini, Haj Amin b. 1893
Navon, Yitzhak b. Apr 19, 1921
Oz, Amos b. May 4, 1939
Persoff, Nehemiah b. Aug 14, 1920
Petrie, (William Matthew) Flinders, Sir
d. Jul 28, 1942
Rabin, Yitzhak b. Mar 1, 1922
Sirhan, Sirhan Bishara b. Mar 19, 1944
Szold, Henrietta d. Feb 13, 1945
Kafr Malal, Palestine
Sharon, Ariel b. 1928
Lydda, Palestine
Habash, George b. 1925
Rishon Letzion, Palestine
Agam, Yaacov b. May 11, 1928
Tel Aviv, Palestine
Bialik, Chaim Nachman d. Jul 4, 1934
Bufman, Zev b. Oct 11, 1930
Dinitz, Simcha b. Jun 23, 1930
Geller, Uri b. Dec 20, 1946
Ginott, Haim b. Aug 5, 1922
Perlman, Itzhak b. Aug 31, 1945
Tchernichovski, Saul Gutmanovich
d. Oct 14, 1943
Topol, Chaim b. Sep 9, 1935
Weizman, Ezer b. 1924
Tulkarm City, Palestine
Abu Salma, pseud. b. 1906

PANAMA

Torrijos Herrera, Omar d. Jul 31, 1981
Chorillo, Panama
Duran, Roberto b. Jun 16, 1951
Colon, Panama
Anderson, Sherwood d. Mar 8, 1941
Gatun, Panama
Carew, Rod(ney Cline) b. Oct 1, 1945

Panama City, Panama
Blades, Ruben b. Jul 16, 1948
Pincay, Laffit, Jr. b. Dec 29, 1946
Quintero, Jose b. Oct 15, 1924
Portobelo, Panama
Drake, Francis, Sir d. Jan 28, 1596
Laing, David d. Oct 18, 1878
Santiago, Panama
Torrijos Herrera, Omar b. Feb 13, 1929

PANAMA CANAL ZONE

Clark, Kenneth Bancroft
b. Jul 24, 1914

PERSIA

Hafiz, Shams-al-Din Muhammad
b. 1320
Mani d. 276
Hamaden, Persia
Avicenna (Ibn Sina) d. Jun 1037
Kesh, Persia
Tamerlane b. 1336
Khurasan, Persia
Nadir, Shah b. 1688
Rey, Persia
Harun-Al-Rashid b. 764
Shiraz, Persia
Saadi d. 1291
Teheran, Persia
Abdu'l-Baha b. May 23, 1844
Hoveyda, Amir Abbas
b. Feb 18, 1919
Pahlevi, Mohammed Riza
b. Oct 26, 1919

PERU

Arequipa, Peru
Monroe, Harriet d. Sep 26, 1936
Vargas, Alberto b. Feb 9, 1895
Huaras, Peru
Julesberg, Elizabeth Rider Montgomery
b. Jul 12, 1902
Ichocan, Peru
Sumac, Yma b. Sep 10, 1928
Lima, Peru
Belaunde-Terry, Fernando b. Oct 17, 1912
Garcia Perez, Alan b. May 23, 1949
Haya de la Torre, Victor Raul
d. Aug 2, 1979
Monk, Meredith b. Nov 20, 1942
Morales Bermudez, Francisco
b. Oct 4, 1921
O'Higgins, Bernardo d. Oct 24, 1842
Perez de Cuellar, Javier b. Jan 19, 1920
Pizarro, Francisco d. Jun 26, 1541
Velasco Alvarado, Juan d. Dec 24, 1977
Piura, Peru
Velasco Alvarado, Juan b. Jun 16, 1910

Tinta, Peru
Tupac Amaru b. 1742
Trujillo, Peru
Haya de la Torre, Victor Raul
b. Feb 22, 1895

PHILIPPINES

Garcia, Carlos P b. Nov 4, 1896
Lawton, Henry Ware d. Dec 19, 1899
Magellan, Ferdinand d. Apr 27, 1521
Marcos, Ferdinand Edralin b. Sep 11, 1917
Tjader, Cal(len Radcliffe, Jr.)
d. May 5, 1982
Baler, Philippines
Quezon (y Molina), Manuel Luis
b. Aug 19, 1878
Calamba, Philippines
Rizal, Jose b. 1861
Cavite, Philippines
Aguinaldo, Emilio b. Mar 22, 1869
Cebu, Philippines
Osmena, Sergio b. Sep 9, 1878
Concepcion, Philippines
Aquino, Benigno Simeon, Jr.
b. Nov 27, 1932
Iba, Philippines
Magsaysay, Ramon b. Aug 31, 1907
Lubao, Philippines
Macapagal, Diosdado Pangan
b. Sep 28, 1910
Luzon, Philippines
Yamashita, Tomoyuki d. Feb 23, 1946
Manila, Philippines
Aguinaldo, Emilio d. Feb 6, 1964
Aquino, Benigno Simeon, Jr.
d. Aug 21, 1983
Garcia, Carlos P d. Jun 14, 1971
Graves, Harold Nathan b. Jan 20, 1915
Osmena, Sergio d. Oct 19, 1961
Raines, Cristina b. Feb 28, 1953
Rizal, Jose d. 1896
Romulo, Carlos Pena b. Apr 14, 1899
Romulo, Carlos Pena d. Dec 15, 1985
Trinidad, Francisco Flores Corky, Jr.
b. May 26, 1939
Tacloban, Philippines
Marcos, Imelda Romualdez b. 1931
Tarlac, Philippines
Aquino, Corazon Cojuangco
b. Jan 25, 1933

POLAND

Ben-Elissar, Eliahu b. 1932
Biba b.
Bronowski, Jacob b. Jan 18, 1908
Burck, Jacob b. Jan 10, 1904
Drachler, Norman b. May 20, 1912
Dzerzhinsky, Felix Edmundovich b. 1877
Goldin, Horace b. Dec 17, 1873
Kolbe, Maximilian b. 1894

Lowe, Edwin S b. 1910
Mattus, Reuben b. 1914
Pearlroth, Norbert b. May 1893
Tramiel, Jack b. 1929
Warner, Albert b. Jul 23, 1884
Akopy, Poland
Ba'al Shem Tov, Israel b. 1700
Auschwitz, Poland
Kolbe, Maximilian d. Aug 14, 1941
Salomon, Charlotte d. 1943
Bemberg, Poland
Rosenthal, Moriz b. Dec 18, 1862
Biala, Poland
Tworkov, Jack b. 1900
Bialystok, Poland
Kaufman, Boris b. Aug 24, 1906
Raisa, Rosa b. May 30, 1893
Zamenhof, Ludwik Lazar b. Dec 15, 1859
Breslau, Poland
Anderssen, Adolf (Karl Ernst Adolf)
b. Aug 6, 1818
Anderssen, Adolf (Karl Ernst Adolf)
d. Mar 9, 1878
Cohn, Ferdinand Julius b. Jan 24, 1828
Cohn, Ferdinand Julius d. Jun 25, 1898
Brest-Litovsk, Poland
Begin, Menachem b. Aug 16, 1913
Dubinsky, David b. Feb 22, 1892
Buczacz, Poland
Wiesenthal, Simon b. Dec 31, 1908
Bunzlau, Poland
Kutuzov, Mikhail Ilarionovich
d. Apr 16, 1813
Chudnov, Poland
Masserman, Jules H(oman)
b. Mar 10, 1905
Cracow, Poland
Rubinstein, Helena b. 1870
Czestochowa, Poland
Huberman, Bronislaw b. Dec 19, 1882
Debica, Poland
Penderecki, Krzysztof b. Nov 23, 1933
Frauenburg, Poland
Copernicus, Nicolaus d. May 24, 1543
Garnek, Poland
DeReszke, Edouard d. May 25, 1917
Gradek, Poland
Martin, Ross b. Mar 22, 1920
Grodno, Poland
Cohen, Myron b. Jul 1, 1902
Inowroclaw, Poland
Glemp, Jozef, Cardinal b. Dec 18, 1929
Janowa, Poland
Negri, Pola b. Dec 31, 1894
Jarotschin, Poland
Schwarzkopf, Elisabeth b. Dec 9, 1915
Katowice Voivodship, Poland
Babiuch, Edward b. Dec 28, 1927
Kobiele Wielkie, Poland
Reymont, Wladyslaw Stanislaw
b. May 1867

Hilsberg, Alexander b. Apr 24, 1900
Infeld, Leopold d. Jan 16, 1968
Kaper, Bronislau b. Feb 5, 1902
Korjus, Miliza b. 1912
Korzybski, Alfred Habdank b. Jul 3, 1879
Landowska, Wanda b. Jul 5, 1877
Leibowitz, Rene b. Feb 17, 1913
Malcuzynski, Witold b. Aug 10, 1914
Mandelshtam, Osip Emilyevich
 b. Jan 15, 1891
Michalowski, Kazimierz d. Jan 1, 1981
Moniuszko, Stanislaus d. Jun 4, 1872
Peretz, Isaac Loeb d. Apr 3, 1915
Potok, Anna Maximilian Apfelbaum
 b. Jun 4, 1904
Rambert, Dame Marie b. Feb 20, 1888
Rapacki, Adam d. Oct 10, 1970
Reymont, Wladyslaw Stanislaw
 d. Dec 5, 1925
Skulnik, Menasha b. May 15, 1898
Spychalski, Marian d. Jun 7, 1980
Strasfogel, Ignace b. Jul 17, 1909
Szeryng, Henryk b. Sep 22, 1921
Topolski, Feliks b. Aug 14, 1907
Weintal, Edward b. Mar 21, 1901
Wyszynski, Stefan d. May 28, 1981

Wierzchownia, Poland
Walsh, Stella b. Apr 3, 1911

Wilno, Poland
Pilsudski, Jozef b. Dec 5, 1867
Schally, Andrew Victor b. Nov 30, 1926

Winiary, Poland
Pulaski, Kazimierz b. Mar 4, 1747

Wisnewo, Poland
Goldmann, Nahum b. Jul 10, 1895

Wisniewczyk, Poland
Sembrich, Marcella b. Feb 18, 1858

Wloclawek, Poland
Reichstein, Tadeus b. Jul 20, 1897

Wolozyn, Poland
Peres, Shimon b. Aug 16, 1923

Wrocanka, Poland
Kania, Stanislaw b. Mar 8, 1927

Yanow, Poland
Adler, Polly b. Apr 16, 1900

Zaborze, Poland
Eckert, Horst b. Mar 11, 1931

Zamosc, Poland
Luxemburg, Rosa b. 1870

Zamoszcz, Poland
Peretz, Isaac Loeb b. May 18, 1851

Zarnowiec, Poland
Barlow, Joel d. Dec 24, 1812

Zdunska-Wola, Poland
Roberts, Harold Selig b. Mar 14, 1911

Zelazowa Wola, Poland
Chopin, Frederic Francois b. Feb 22, 1810

PONTUS

Amasia, Pontus
Strabo b. 63 BC?

PORTUGAL

Cabrillo, Juan Rodriguez b. 1520
Salazar, Antonio de Oliveira
 b. Apr 28, 1889
Alcains, Portugal
Eanes, Antonio Ramalho b. Jan 25, 1935
Alverca, Portugal
Cousteau, Philippe d. Jun 28, 1979
Estoril, Portugal
Horthy de Nagybanya, Nicholas
 d. Mar 9, 1957
Lupescu, Magda (Elena) d. Jun 29, 1977
Lisbon, Portugal
Abarbanel, Isaac Ben Jehudah b. 1437
Abarbanel, Judah b. 1460
Alekhine, Alexander d. Mar 24, 1946
Anthony of Padua, Saint b. 1195
Caetano, Marcello b. Aug 17, 1906
Camoes, Luis de b. 1524
Camoes, Luis de d. 1580
Fielding, Henry d. Oct 8, 1754
Gulbenkian, Calouste S d. Oct 20, 1955
Pedro I b. Oct 12, 1798
Pedro I d. Sep 24, 1834
Salazar, Antonio de Oliveira
 d. Jul 27, 1970
Thomaz, Americo b. Nov 19, 1894
Thompson, Dorothy d. Jan 31, 1961
Madeira, Portugal
Mowrer, Edgar Ansel d. Mar 2, 1977
Marco Canavezes, Portugal
Miranda, Carmen b. Feb 9, 1909
Porto, Portugal
Henry the Navigator b. Mar 4, 1394
Sabrosa, Portugal
Magellan, Ferdinand b. 1480
Sagres, Portugal
Henry the Navigator d. Nov 13, 1460
Setubal, Portugal
Campbell, Roy d. Apr 22, 1957
Sines, Portugal
DaGama, Vasco b. 1460

PRUSSIA

George II b. Nov 10, 1683
Zweig, Arnold b. Nov 10, 1887

Salisbury, Rhodesia
  Brutus, Dennis Vincent b. Nov 28, 1924
  DuPont, Clifford Walter d. Jun 28, 1978
Seluwke, Rhodesia
  Smith, Ian Douglas b. Apr 8, 1919
Umtali, Rhodesia
  Muzorewa, Abel Tendekai b. Apr 14, 1925

ROMANIA

  Gutfreund, Yosef b. 1931
  Leibowitz, Samuel Simon b. Aug 14, 1893
  Shorr, Kehat b. 1919
  Spitzer, Andre b. 1945
  Zuckerman, Ben b. Jul 29, 1890
Barlad, Romania
  Gheorghiu-Dej, Gheorghe b. Nov 8, 1901
Bender, Romania
  Leonidoff, Leon b. Jan 2, 1895
Botosani, Romania
  Covici, Pascal b. Nov 4, 1885
Botosoni, Romania
  Eminescu, Mihail b. Dec 20, 1849
Braila, Romania
  Bercovici, Konrad b. Jun 22, 1882
  Xenakis, Iannis b. May 29, 1922
Bucharest, Romania
  Ciulei, Liviu b. Jul 7, 1923
  Coanda, Henri Marie b. Jun 6, 1885
  Comissiona, Sergiu b. Jun 16, 1928
  Eliade, Mircea b. Mar 9, 1907
  Eminescu, Mihail d. Jun 15, 1889
  Gluck, Alma b. May 11, 1884
  Houseman, John b. Sep 22, 1902
  Lipatti, Dinu b. Mar 19, 1917
  Maurer, Ion Gheorghe b. Sep 23, 1902
  Nastase, Ilie b. Jul 19, 1946
  Pauker, Ana b. 1894
  Pauker, Ana d. Jun 1960
  Robinson, Edward G b. Dec 12, 1893
  Serban, Andrei George b. Jun 21, 1943
  Spewack, Bella Cohen b. Mar 25, 1899
  Theodorescu, Ion N b. May 20, 1880
  Theodorescu, Ion N d. Jul 14, 1967
Campeni, Romania
  Trifa, Valerian b. Jun 28, 1914
Cimpia-Turzii, Romania
  Ruzici, Virginia b. Jan 31, 1955
Cordaremi, Romania
  Enesco, Georges b. Aug 7, 1881
Craiova, Romania
  Negulesco, Jean b. Feb 29, 1900
Czernowitz, Romania
  Ursuleac, Viorica b. Mar 26, 1899
Galati, Romania
  Cotrubas, Ileana b. Jun 9, 1939
  Lupu, Radu b. Nov 30, 1945
  Rubin, Reuven b. Nov 13, 1893
Kishinev, Romania
  Bein, Albert b. May 18, 1902

Lespede, Romania
  Wechsler, David b. Jan 12, 1896
Macin, Romania
  Samuel, Maurice b. Feb 8, 1895
Moinesti, Romania
  Tzara, Tristan b. Apr 4, 1896
Nieder-Rehbach, Romania
  Berger, Victor L b. Feb 28, 1860
Onesti, Romania
  Comaneci, Nadia b. Nov 12, 1961
Pestisanigorj, Romania
  Brancusi, Constantin b. Feb 21, 1876
Pitesti, Romania
  Antonescu, Ion b. Jun 15, 1882
Regen, Romania
  Wagner-Regeny, Rudolf b. Aug 28, 1903
Rimnicu-Sarat, Romania
  Steinberg, Saul b. Jun 15, 1914
Satu Mare, Romania
  Fried, Miriam b. Sep 9, 1946
Scornicesti-Olt, Romania
  Ceausescu, Nicolae b. Jan 26, 1918
Silagy, Romania
  Pasternak, Joe (Joseph Vincent)
    b. Sep 19, 1901
Sinaia, Romania
  Carol II b. 1893
Slatina, Romania
  Ionesco, Eugene b. Nov 26, 1912
Tirgu Neamt, Romania
  Simionescu, Mariana b. Nov 21, 1956
Tomi, Romania
  Ovid d. 17 AD
Unghani, Romania
  Diamond, I(sidore) A L b. Jun 27, 1920
Verbilao, Romania
  Culbertson, Ely b. Jul 22, 1891

RUSSIA

  Adler, Jacob Pavlovitch b. 1855
  Alekhine, Alexander b. Nov 1, 1892
  Alexander III b. 1845
  Alexander III d. 1894
  Berger, Raoul b. Jan 4, 1901
  Bickerman, Elias Joseph b. Jul 1, 1897
  Blume, Peter b. Oct 27, 1906
  Brodovitch, Alexey b. 1898
  Cherniavsky, Josef b. Mar 31, 1895
  Cournos, John b. Mar 6, 1881
  Gordon, Vera b. Jun 11, 1886
  Gruenberg, Louis b. Aug 3, 1884
  Hirshhorn, Joseph b. Aug 11, 1899
  Kahn, Ben b. 1887
  Kapitsa, Pyotr b. Jun 26, 1894
  Krylov, Ivan Andreyevich d. 1844
  Leokum, Arkady b. 1916
  Meyerhoff, Joseph b. Apr 8, 1899
  Nevelson, Louise Berliawsky b. 1900
  Oldenbourg, Zoe b. Mar 31, 1916
  Posell, Elsa Z b.

Rabin, Yehuda L b. 1917
Rasputin, Grigori Efimovich
  d. Dec 31, 1916
Semenenko, Serge b. 1930
Shevchenko, Taras d. Mar 10, 1861
Stolypin, Piotr Arkadevich b. 1862
Swerling, Jo b. May 18, 1897
Tchelitchew, Pavel b. Sep 21, 1898
Tucker, Sophie b. Jan 13, 1884
Werboff, Michael Alexander b. 1896
Werth, Alexander b. Feb 4, 1901
Alexandria, Russia
Secunda, Sholom b. Aug 23, 1894
Almazny, Russia
Zhukov, Georgi Alexandrovich
  b. Apr 23, 1908
Astapovo, Russia
Tolstoy, Leo Nikolayevich d. Nov 20, 1910
Bachmut, Russia
Spewack, Samuel b. Sep 16, 1899
Bagdadi, Russia
Mayakovsky, Vladimir b. Jul 19, 1893
Baku, Russia
Carter, Boake b. Sep 28, 1898
Landau, Lev Davidovich b. Jan 22, 1908
Sorge, Richard b. 1895
Tamiroff, Akim b. Oct 29, 1901
Berdichev, Russia
Conrad, Joseph b. Dec 3, 1857
Bialystok, Russia
Litvinov, Maxim b. Jul 17, 1871
Sabin, Albert Bruce b. Aug 26, 1906
Weber, Max b. Apr 18, 1881
Bolshaya Tes, Russia
Chernenko, Konstantin Ustinovich
  b. Sep 24, 1911
Borodino, Russia
Bagration, Petr Ivanovich d. Sep 24, 1812
Brailov, Russia
Galili, Israel b. May 1911
Malko, Nicolai b. May 4, 1888
Brest-Litovsk, Russia
Auerbach-Levy, William b. Feb 14, 1889
Briansk, Russia
Gabo, Naum Pevsner b. Aug 5, 1890
Chernigov, Russia
Baker, Rachel b. Mar 1, 1904
Chisinau, Russia
Milestone, Lewis b. Sep 30, 1895
Daugavpils, Russia
Rothko, Mark b. Sep 25, 1903
Denisovka, Russia
Lomonosov, Mikhail b. Nov 8, 1711
Diyalora, Russia
Ilyushin, Sergei Vladimirovich
  b. Mar 31, 1894
Efremov, Russia
Ivanov, Konstantin Konstantinovich
  b. May 21, 1907

Ekaterinoslav, Russia
Blavatsky, Helena Petrovna b. Jul 30, 1831
Piatigorsky, Gregor b. Apr 17, 1903
Elets, Russia
Khrennikov, Tikhon Nikolaevich
  b. Jun 10, 1913
Elisavetgrad, Russia
Gardner, Samuel b. Aug 25, 1891
Petroff, Ossip b. Nov 15, 1807
Trotsky, Leon b. Nov 8, 1879
Zinoviev, Grigori Evseevich b. Sep 1883
Elizabethgrad, Russia
Podoloff, Maurice b. Aug 18, 1890
Evpatoria, Russia
Vronsky, Vitya b.
Gatchina, Russia
Ippolitov-Ivanov, Mikhail Mikhailovich
  b. Nov 9, 1859
Georgia, Russia
Beria, Lavrenti Pavlovich b. Mar 29, 1899
Glukhov, Russia
Shklovsky, Iosif Samvilovitch
  b. Jul 1, 1916
Golodaevka, Russia
Grechko, Andrei Antonovick
  b. Oct 17, 1903
Gorky, Russia
Bulganin, Nikolai Aleksandrovich
  b. Jun 11, 1895
Gorokhovo, Russia
Leskov, Nikolai b. Feb 4, 1831
Gradizhsk, Russia
Delaunay-Terk, Sonia b. Nov 14, 1885
Greshnevo, Russia
Nekrasov, Nikolay Alexeyevich
  b. Dec 10, 1821
Grodak, Russia
Gorin, Igor b. Oct 26, 1908
Grodno, Russia
Lansky, Meyer b. Jul 4, 1902
Weizmann, Chaim b. Nov 27, 1874
Gurzuf, Russia
Petipa, Marius d. Jun 2, 1910
Irkutsk, Russia
Romm, Mikhail b. Jan 24, 1901
Ivanovka, Russia
Metchnikoff, Elie b. May 15, 1845
Kabany, Russia
Kaganovich, Lazar M b. Nov 22, 1893
Kalius, Russia
Shenker, Morris Abraham b. Jan 10, 1907
Kamenetz, Russia
Tracy, Arthur b. Jun 25, 1903
Kamenskoye, Russia
Brezhnev, Leonid Ilyich b. Dec 19, 1906
Karevo, Russia
Mussorgsky, Modest Petrovich
  b. Mar 21, 1839

Karlovka, Russia
Lysenko, Trofim Denisovich
b. Sep 29, 1898
Podgorny, Nikolai Viktorovich
b. Feb 18, 1903
Kazan, Russia
Chaliapin, Feodor Ivanovitch
b. Feb 13, 1873
Dali, Gala b. 1893
Vishnevsky, Alexander Alexandrovich
b. May 24, 1906
Zabolotskii, Nikolai Alekseevich
b. May 7, 1903
Keatz, Russia
Piastro, Mishel b. Sep 1892
Kharkov, Russia
Artsybashev, Mikhail Petrovich
b. Oct 18, 1878
Artzybasheff, Boris Mikhailovich
b. May 25, 1899
Cassandre, A(dolphe) M(ouron)
b. Jan 24, 1909
Kuznets, Simon b. Apr 30, 1901
Malik, Yakov Alexandrovich
b. Feb 11, 1906
Schillinger, Joseph b. Sep 1, 1895
Struve, Otto b. Aug 12, 1897
Kherson, Russia
Cooper, Emil b. Dec 20, 1877
Kulish, Mykola b. 1892
Rubinstein, Anton Gregorovitch
b. Nov 28, 1829
Sharett, Moshe b. Oct 3, 1894
Vynnychenko, Volodymyr b. 1880
Kiev, Russia
Archipenko, Alexander Porfirievich
b. May 30, 1887
Aronson, Boris b. Oct 15, 1900
Berdyayev, Nikolay A b. Mar 19, 1874
Brailowsky, Alexander b. Feb 16, 1896
Bulgakov, Mikhail b. 1891
Deren, Maya b. Apr 29, 1917
Ehrenburg, Ilya Grigoryevich
b. Jan 27, 1891
Gliere, Reinhold Moritzovich
b. Jan 11, 1875
Gottlieb, Eddie (Edward) b. Sep 15, 1898
Horenstein, Jascha b. May 6, 1899
Horowitz, Vladimir b. Oct 1, 1904
Kistiakowsky, George Bogdan
b. Nov 18, 1900
Liberman, Alexander b. Sep 4, 1912
Lifar, Serge b. Apr 2, 1905
Litvak, Anatole b. May 21, 1902
Malevich, Kasimir Severinovich
b. Feb 26, 1878
Markevitch, Igor b. Jul 27, 1912
Meir, Golda b. May 3, 1898
Miles, Jackie b. 1913
Moiseyev, Igor Alexandrovich
b. Jan 21, 1906

Nijinsky, Vaslav b. Feb 28, 1890
Sikorsky, Igor Ivanovich b. May 25, 1889
Stolypin, Piotr Arkadevich d. Sep 14, 1911
Tarsis, Valery Yakovlevich b. Sep 23, 1906
Valentina b. May 1, 1904
Youskevitch, Igor b. Mar 13, 1912
Zaturenska, Marya b. Sep 12, 1902
Kinishev, Russia
Friedman, William b. Sep 24, 1891
Kirov District, Russia
Molotov, Viacheslav Mikhailovich
b. Mar 9, 1890
Kishinev, Russia
Cebotari, Maria b. Feb 10, 1910
Kislovodsk, Russia
Adamov, Arthur b. Aug 23, 1908
Kizlar, Russia
Bagration, Petr Ivanovich b. 1765
Kobiankari, Russia
Papashvily, George b. Aug 23, 1898
Konno, Russia
Keyserling, Hermann Alexander
b. Jul 20, 1880
Konstantinovo, Russia
Esenin, Sergei Aleksandrovich
b. Feb 21, 1895
Kostroma, Russia
Gerasimov, Innokentii Petrovich
b. Dec 22, 1905
Kovna, Russia
Sackheim, Maxwell Byron b. Sep 25, 1890
Krasnoyarsk, Russia
Rebikov, Vladimir Ivanovich
b. May 31, 1866
Kronstadt, Russia
Bellinghausen, Fabian Gottlieb von
d. Jan 25, 1852
Kruzhilin, Russia
Sholokhov, Mikhail Aleksandrovich
b. May 24, 1905
Kuibyshev, Russia
Ustinov, Dmitri Fedorovich
b. Oct 30, 1908
Kursk, Russia
Khrushchev, Nikita Sergeyevich
b. Apr 17, 1894
Ladeino, Russia
Konev, Ivan S b. Dec 27, 1897
Latvia, Russia
Nimzowitsch, Aron b. 1886
Leningrad, Russia
Botvinnik, Mikhail Moiseevich
b. Aug 17, 1911
Chekhov, Michael b. Aug 28, 1891
Geva, Tamara b. 1908
Obraztsova, Elena b. Jul 7, 1939
Rudenko, Lyudmila b. Jul 27, 1904
Libau, Russia
Sterne, Maurice b. Jul 13, 1878
Luzhky, Russia
Ben-Yehuda, Eliezer b. Jan 7, 1858

Mikhailovka, Russia
Tchernichovski, Saul Gutmanovich
b. Jan 3, 1875

Minsk, Russia
Angoff, Charles b. Apr 22, 1902
Hoffman, Al b. Sep 25, 1902
Lerner, Max b. Dec 20, 1902
Mayer, L(ouis) B(urt) b. Jul 4, 1885
Nabokov, Nicolas b. Apr 4, 1903
Nijinska, Bronislava b. Jan 8, 1891
Rosenthal, Ida Cohen b. Jan 9, 1886
Sarnoff, David b. Feb 27, 1891
Taishoff, Sol Joseph b. Oct 8, 1904

Mir, Russia
Shazar, Zalman b. Nov 24, 1889

Mirgorod, Russia
Gogol, Nikolai Vasilievich b. Mar 21, 1809

Mitava, Russia
Rojankovsky, Feodor Stepanovich
b. Dec 24, 1891

Morintsy, Russia
Shevchenko, Taras b. Mar 9, 1814

Moscow, Russia
Aksakov, Sergei Timofeyevich
d. Apr 30, 1859
Alexander II b. 1818
Babin, Victor b. Dec 12, 1908
Baclanova, Olga b. Aug 19, 1899
Bellison, Simeon b. Dec 4, 1883
Bely, Andrey, pseud. b. Oct 14, 1880
Bukharin, Nikolai Ivanovich b. 1888
Dostoyevsky, Fyodor Mikhailovich
b. Nov 11, 1821
Field, John d. Jan 11, 1837
Godunov, Boris Fedorovich b. 1551
Gogol, Nikolai Vasilievich d. Mar 4, 1852
Goldovsky, Boris b. Jun 7, 1908
Gretchaninov, Aleksandr Tikhonovich
b. Oct 25, 1864
Kandinsky, Wassily b. Dec 4, 1866
Karrar, Paul b. Apr 21, 1889
Khodasevich, Vladislav b. May 29, 1886
Kondrashin, Kiril Petrovich
b. Feb 21, 1914
Kropotkin, Peter Alekseyevich, Prince
b. Nov 26, 1842
Krylov, Ivan Andreyevich b. Feb 14, 1768
Leontovich, Eugenie b. Mar 21, 1900
Lermontov, Mikhail (Michael Jurevich)
b. Oct 15, 1814
Lhevinne, Josef b. Dec 3, 1874
Lhevinne, Rosina L b. Mar 29, 1880
Lichine, Alexis b. Dec 3, 1913
Massine, Leonide Fedorovich
b. Aug 9, 1896
Medtner, Nicholas b. Dec 24, 1880
Mikhalkov, Sergei Vladimirovich
b. Mar 12, 1913
Ostrovsky, Aleksandr b. Apr 12, 1823
Ostrovsky, Aleksandr d. May 28, 1886

Pasternak, Boris Leonidovich
b. Feb 11, 1890
Peter the Great b. May 30, 1672
Pfitzner, Hans b. May 5, 1869
Prigogine, Ilya b. Jan 25, 1917
Pushkin, Aleksandr Sergeyevich
b. Jun 6, 1799
Scriabin, Alexander Nicholaevich
b. Jan 6, 1872
Scriabin, Alexander Nicholaevich
d. Apr 27, 1915
Soloviev, Sergei Mikhailovich
b. May 5, 1820
Stanislavsky, Konstantin Sergeyevich
b. Jan 17, 1863
Tsvetayeva, Marina Ivanovna
b. Sep 26, 1892
Uspenskii, Petr D b. 1878
Vassilenko, Sergei b. Mar 30, 1872
Wieniawski, Henri d. Apr 2, 1880

Mourom, Russia
Zworykin, Vladimir K(osma)
b. Jul 30, 1889

Nagutskaia, Russia
Andropov, Yuri Vladimirovich
b. Jun 15, 1914

Narovchat, Russia
Kuprin, Aleksandr Ivanovich b. Aug 1870

Nikolaevski-Samarskom, Russia
Tolstoy, Alexey Nikolaevich
b. Dec 20, 1882

Nikopol, Russia
Goodman, Al(fred) b. Aug 12, 1890

Nizhni-Novgorod, Russia
Balakirev, Mili Alekseyevich b. Jan 2, 1837
Diaghilev, Sergei Pavlovich
b. Mar 19, 1872
Dobrowen, Issai b. Feb 27, 1893
Gorky, Maxim, pseud. b. Mar 14, 1868

Novospaskoi, Russia
Glinka, Mikhail Ivanovich b. Jun 1, 1804

Odessa, Russia
Akhmatova, Anna, pseud. b. Jun 11, 1888
Babel, Isaac Emmanuelovich b. 1894
Brackman, Robert b. Sep 25, 1898
Brown, Lew b. Dec 10, 1893
Gilels, Emil Grigorevich b. Oct 19, 1916
Halpert, Edith Gregor b. Apr 25, 1900
Jabotinsky, Vladimir Evgenevich
b. Oct 18, 1880
Kaminska, Ida b. Sep 4, 1899
Katayev, Valentin b. Jan 28, 1897
Lapidus, Morris b. Nov 25, 1902
Luboshutz, Pierre b. Jun 22, 1894
Malinovsky, Rodion Y b. Nov 23, 1898
Milstein, Nathan b. Dec 31, 1904
Moiseiwitsch, Benno b. Feb 22, 1890
Oistrakh, David Fyodorovich
b. Oct 23, 1908
Pious, Minerva b. 1909
Reilly, Sidney George b. 1874

Seidel, Toscha b. Nov 17, 1899
Spanel, Abram N b. May 15, 1901
Spitalny, Phil b. Nov 7, 1890
Spivakovsky, Tossy b. Feb 4, 1907
Vishinskii, Andrei Yanuarevich
   b. Dec 10, 1883

Oesel, Russia
Bellinghausen, Fabian Gottlieb von
   b. Aug 30, 1779
Kahn, Louis I b. Feb 2, 1901

Olshani, Russia
Goldberg, Ben Zion b. Jan 9, 1894

Oneg, Russia
Rachmaninoff, Sergei Vasilyevich
   b. Apr 1, 1873

Oranienbaum, Russia
Stravinsky, Igor Fedorovich
   b. Jun 17, 1882

Orel, Russia
Andreyev, Leonid Nikolayevich
   b. Jun 18, 1871
Pevsner, Antoine b. Jan 18, 1886
Turgenev, Ivan Sergeevich b. Nov 9, 1818

Orenburg, Russia
Malenkov, Georgi Maximilianovich
   b. Jan 8, 1901

Penza, Russia
Pudovkin, Vsevolod b. Feb 6, 1893

Pereyaslavl, Russia
Aleichem, Shalom, pseud. b. Feb 18, 1859

Peterhof, Russia
Danilova, Alexandra b. Jan 20, 1904
Rubinstein, Anton Gregorovitch
   d. Nov 20, 1894

Petrograd, Russia
Ratoff, Gregory b. Apr 20, 1893
Savitt, Jan b. Sep 4, 1913

Pogar, Russia
Hurok, Sol b. Apr 9, 1888

Polotsk, Russia
Antin, Mary b. 1881

Priluki, Russia
Waksman, Selman Abraham b. Jul 2, 1888

Proskurov, Russia
Durant, Ariel (Ida Ariel Ethel Kaufman)
   b. May 10, 1898
Mischakoff, Mischa b. Apr 3, 1895

Pskov, Russia
Duke, Vernon b. Oct 10, 1903

Pyatigorsk, Russia
Lermontov, Mikhail (Michael Jurevich)
   d. Jul 27, 1841

Radomisl, Russia
Potofsky, Jacob Samuel b. Nov 16, 1894

Rady, Russia
Bialik, Chaim Nachman b. Jan 9, 1873

Reval, Russia
Kohler, Wolfgang b. Jan 21, 1887
Rosenberg, Alfred b. Jan 12, 1893

Riga, Russia
Berlin, Isaiah, Sir b. Jun 6, 1909
Eisenstein, Sergei Mikhailovich
   b. Jan 23, 1898
Halsman, Philippe b. May 2, 1906
Hillquit, Morris b. Aug 1, 1869
Jadlowker, Hermann b. Jul 5, 1879
Ostwald, Wilhelm b. Sep 2, 1853

Rostov, Russia
Alajalov, Constantin b. Nov 18, 1900
Zimbalist, Efrem b. Apr 9, 1889

Rostov-on-Don, Russia
Lev, Ray b. May 8, 1912
Lichine, David b. Oct 25, 1910

Rovno, Russia
Loeb, Sophia Irene Simon b. Jul 4, 1876

Rumni, Russia
Carr, Alexander b. 1878

Ryazan, Russia
Pavlov, Ivan Petrovich b. Sep 14, 1849

Rybinsk, Russia
Schenck, Joseph M b. Dec 25, 1878
Schenck, Nicholas Michael
   b. Nov 14, 1881

Saint Petersburg, Russia
Abel, Rudolf Ivanovich b. 1902
Alexander II d. Mar 13, 1881
Amfiteatrof, Daniele b. Oct 29, 1901
Andrew, Prince of Russia b. 1897
Auer, Mischa b. Nov 17, 1905
Balakirev, Mili Alekseyevich
   d. May 28, 1910
Balanchine, George b. Jan 9, 1904
Belinsky, Vissarion d. May 26, 1848
Berman, Eugene b. Nov 4, 1899
Blok, Aleksandr Aleksandrovich
   b. Nov 28, 1880
Bolotowsky, Ilya b. Jul 1, 1907
Borodin, Alexander Profirevich
   b. Nov 11, 1833
Borodin, Alexander Profirevich
   d. Feb 7, 1887
Cantor, Georg b. 1845
Chukovsky, Korney Ivanovich
   b. Mar 31, 1882
Coates, Albert b. Apr 23, 1882
Conway, Tom b. Sep 15, 1904
Dargomijsky, Alexander d. Jan 17, 1869
Dostoyevsky, Fyodor Mikhailovich
   d. Feb 9, 1881
Doubrovska, Felia b. 1896
Du Chaillu, Paul Belloni d. Apr 20, 1903
Erte b. Nov 23, 1892
Faberge, Peter Carl (Karl Gustavovich)
   b. May 30, 1846
Fokine, Michel b. Apr 26, 1880
Gabrilowitsch, Ossip b. Jan 26, 1878
Gerhardi, William Alexander
   b. Nov 21, 1895
Glazunov, Alexander Constantinovich
   b. Aug 10, 1865

Goncharov, Ivan A d. Sep 1891
Guitry, Sacha b. Feb 21, 1885
Hanfmann, George Maxim Anossov
  b. Nov 20, 1911
Janson, Horst Woldemar b. Oct 4, 1913
Jolson, Al b. May 26, 1886
Kabalevsky, Dmitri Borisovich
  b. Dec 30, 1904
Keyserlingk, Robert Wendelin
  b. Nov 2, 1905
Kostelanetz, Andre b. Dec 22, 1901
Kosygin, Aleksei Nikolaevich
  b. Feb 20, 1904
Kurtz, Efrem b. Nov 7, 1900
Kutuzov, Mikhail Ilarionovich
  b. Sep 5, 1745
Leskov, Nikolai d. Feb 21, 1895
Litvinne, Felia b. Oct 11, 1860
Lomonosov, Mikhail d. Apr 4, 1765
Lopokova, Lydia Vasilievna
  b. Oct 21, 1892
Martin y Soler, Vicente d. Jan 30, 1806
Mendeleev, Dmitri d. Feb 2, 1907
Merejkowski, Dmitri Sergeyevich
  b. Aug 14, 1865
Mravinsky, Eugene b. 1903
Mussorgsky, Modest Petrovich
  d. Mar 28, 1881
Nabokov, Vladimir b. Apr 23, 1899
Napravnik, Eduard d. Nov 23, 1916
Nekrasov, Nikolay Alexeyevich
  d. Jul 27, 1877
Pavlova, Anna b. Jan 31, 1885
Peter the Great d. Jan 28, 1725
Petroff, Ossip d. Mar 14, 1878
Pushkin, Aleksandr Sergeyevich
  d. Feb 10, 1837
Rand, Ayn b. Feb 2, 1905
Rimsky-Korsakov, Nikolai Andreevich
  d. Jun 21, 1908
Rosing, Vladimir b. Jan 23, 1890
Sanders, George b. Jul 3, 1906
Shostakovich, Dmitri Dmitryevich
  b. Sep 25, 1906
Slonimsky, Nicolas b. Apr 27, 1894
Smallens, Alexander b. Jan 1, 1889
Stael, Nicolas de b. 1914
Stravinsky, Vera de Bossett
  b. Dec 25, 1888
Tchaikovsky, Peter Ilyich d. Nov 6, 1893
Tcherepnin, Alexander b. Jan 20, 1899
Tcherepnin, Nicholas (Nicolai)
  b. May 14, 1873
Tiomkin, Dimitri b. May 10, 1899
Tukhachevski, Mikhail N b. 1893
Ulanova, Galina b. Jan 10, 1910
Vishniac, Roman b. Aug 19, 1897
Witte, Sergei d. Mar 12, 1915

Sakhalin, Russia
Brynner, Yul b. Jul 11, 1920

Sarativ, Russia
Mandelstam, Nadezhda Yakovlevna
  b. Oct 31, 1899
Saratov, Russia
Fedin, Konstantin b. Feb 27, 1892
Sedikov, Russia
Schwartz, Maurice b. Jun 18, 1890
Serebryanye Prudy, Russia
Chuikov, Vasili Ivanovitch b. Feb 12, 1900
Sevastopol, Russia
Papanin, Ivan D b. Nov 26, 1894
Raglan, Fitzroy James Henry Somerset,
  Baron d. Jun 28, 1855
Shakhovskol, Russia
Suslov, Mikhail Andreevich
  b. Nov 21, 1902
Siberia, Russia
DeLong, George Washington
  d. Oct 30, 1881
Slobodkina, Esphyr b. 1909
Simbirsk, Russia
Goncharov, Ivan A b. Jun 1812
Kerensky, Alexander Fedorovitch
  b. Apr 22, 1881
Lenin, Nikolai b. Apr 9, 1870
Smilovich, Russia
Soutine, Chaim b. 1894
Sofilovka, Russia
Kuznetsov, Vasili Vasilievich
  b. Feb 13, 1901
Sontsovka, Russia
Prokofiev, Sergei Sergeevich
  b. Apr 23, 1891
Sosnitsa, Russia
Dovzhenko, Alexander b. Sep 12, 1894
Starchevicvhi, Russia
Bleeker, Sonia b. Nov 28, 1909
Starye Gromyky, Russia
Gromyko, Andrei Andreevich
  b. Jul 5, 1909
Stelkovka, Russia
Zhukov, Georgi Konstantinovich
  b. Dec 2, 1896
Sukovoly, Russia
Yezierska, Anzia b. 1885
Sverdlovsk, Russia
Gerasimov, Sergei Appolinarievich
  b. May 21, 1906
Tallinn, Russia
Valtman, Edmund Siegfried
  b. May 31, 1914
Talnoye, Russia
Elman, Mischa b. Jan 21, 1891
Tambov, Russia
Plekhanov, Georgi Valentinovich
  b. Nov 26, 1857
Soyer, Isaac b. Apr 20, 1907
Soyer, Moses b. Dec 25, 1899
Soyer, Raphael b. Dec 25, 1899
Teganrog, Russia
Chekhov, Anton Pavlovich b. Jan 17, 1860

Temun, Russia
Berlin, Irving b. May 11, 1888
Tiflis, Russia
DeSeversky, Alexander Procofieff
b. Jun 7, 1894
Galitzine, Princess Irene b.
Kalatozov, Mikhail b. Dec 23, 1903
Khachaturian, Aram b. Jun 6, 1903
Mamoulian, Rouben b. Oct 8, 1897
Nemirovich-Danchenko, Vladimir I
b. Dec 23, 1858
Pressman, David b. Oct 10, 1913
Stalin, Joseph b. Dec 21, 1879
Witte, Sergei b. 1849
Tikhvin, Russia
Rimsky-Korsakov, Nikolai Andreevich
b. Mar 18, 1844
Timoshovka, Russia
Szymanowski, Karol b. Oct 6, 1882
Tobolsk, Russia
Mendeleev, Dmitri b. Feb 7, 1834
Rasputin, Grigori Efimovich b. 1871
Tokmak, Russia
Grade, Lew, Sir b. Dec 25, 1906
Tsarskoe Selo, Russia
Nicholas II b. May 18, 1868
Obolensky, Serge b. Oct 3, 1890
Tula, Russia
Dargomijsky, Alexander b. Feb 14, 1813
Ouspenskaya, Maria b. Jul 29, 1876
Turkistan, Russia
Kornilov, Lavr Georgyevich
b. Jul 18, 1870
Tver, Russia
Bakunin, Mikhail Aleksandrovich
b. May 18, 1814
Ufa, Russia
Aksakov, Sergei Timofeyevich
b. Sep 20, 1791
Ukraine, Russia
Cooke, Samuel b. Dec 29, 1898
Field, Stanley b. May 20, 1911
Freeman, Joseph b. Oct 7, 1897
Maltsev, Victor Fyodorovich
b. Jun 12, 1917
Ukrainka, Lesia b. 1871
Voroshilov, Kliment Efremovich
b. Feb 3, 1881
Upper Troitsa, Russia
Kalinin, Mikhail b. Nov 20, 1875
Urlow, Russia
Lipinski, Karl d. Dec 16, 1861
Urmanka, Russia
Timoshenko, Semen Konstantinovich
b. Feb 19, 1895
Uslian, Russia
Lyons, Eugene b. Jul 1, 1898
Verkhneye, Russia
Titov, Gherman Stepanovich (Herman)
b. Sep 11, 1935

Vetluga, Russia
Rozanov, Vasili b. 1856
Vilna, Russia
Berkman, Alexander b. Nov 21, 1870
Cahan, Abraham b. Jul 7, 1860
Cui, Cesar Antonovich b. Jan 18, 1835
Gest, Morris b. Jan 7, 1881
Heifetz, Jascha b. Feb 2, 1901
Reisenberg, Nadia b. Jul 14, 1904
Schneider, Alexander b. Oct 21, 1908
Vitebsk, Russia
Chagall, Marc b. Jul 7, 1887
Chotzinoff, Samuel b. Jul 4, 1889
Vologda, Russia
Shalamov, Varlam Tikhonovich
b. Jun 18, 1907
Volotchok, Russia
Sevitzky, Fabien b. Sep 30, 1893
Voronezh, Russia
Bunin, Ivan Alekseevich b. Oct 10, 1870
Votiwsk, Russia
Tchaikovsky, Peter Ilyich b. May 7, 1840
Vyshni Volochek, Russia
Furtseva, Ekaterina Alexeyevna
b. Dec 7, 1910
Koussevitzky, Serge Alexandrovich
b. Jul 26, 1874
Wilma, Russia
Godowsky, Leopold b. Feb 13, 1870
Yalta, Russia
Lewton, Val Ivan b. May 7, 1904
Nazimova, Alla b. Jun 4, 1879
Yasnaya Polyana, Russia
Tolstoy, Leo Nikolayevich b. Aug 28, 1828
Yekaterinburg, Russia
Alexandrov, Grigori b. Feb 23, 1903
Zabludora, Russia
Lazare, Kaplan b. Jul 17, 1883
Zhitomir, Russia
Kipnis, Alexander b. Feb 1, 1891
Korolenko, Vladimir Galaktionovich
b. 1853
Richter, Sviatoslav Theofilovich b. 1915
Zuzela, Russia
Wyszynski, Stefan b. Aug 3, 1901

RUSSIA-POLAND

Hirshfield, Morris b. Apr 10, 1872

RWANDA

Mount Mikeno, Rwanda
Akeley, Carl Ethan d. Nov 17, 1926
Virunga Mountains, Rwanda
Fossey, Dian d. Dec 27, 1985

SAMOA

Vailima, Samoa
Stevenson, Robert Louis Balfour
d. Nov 13, 1894

SARDINIA

Cagliara, Sardinia
Pavan, Marisa b. Jun 19, 1932
Nvoro, Sardinia
Deledda, Grazia b. Sep 27, 1875
Sassari, Sardinia
Cossiga, Francesco b. Jul 26, 1928

SAUDI ARABIA

Ibn-Saud d. Nov 9, 1953
Mecca, Saudi Arabia
Abdullah Ibn Hussein b. 1882
Riyadh, Saudi Arabia
Fahd ibn Abdul Aziz b. 1922
Faisal (Ibn Abdul-Aziz al Saud)
d. Mar 25, 1975
Khalid Ibn Abdul Aziz Al-Saud
b. 1913

SAXONY

Rocken, Saxony
Nietzsche, Friedrich Wilhelm
b. Oct 15, 1844

SCOTLAND

Byrne, David b. May 14, 1952
Darling, Frank Fraser, Sir b. Jun 23, 1903
Dowie, John Alexander b. May 25, 1847
Dunlop, John Boyd b. Feb 5, 1840
George Edward Alexander Edmund
d. Aug 25, 1942
Gray, Nicholas Stuart b. Oct 23, 1922
Hamilton, Andrew b. 1676
Hardie, James Keir b. 1856
Home, Daniel Douglas b. Mar 20, 1833
Inness, George d. Aug 3, 1894
McAdam, John Loudoun d. Nov 26, 1836
Park, Mungo b. Sep 10, 1771
Rafferty, Gerry b. 1945
Ross, Ishbel b. 1897
Thomson, James b. Nov 23, 1834
White, Michael Simon b. Jan 16, 1936
Abbotsford, Scotland
Scott, Walter, Sir d. Sep 21, 1832
Aberdeen, Scotland
Adler, Alfred d. May 28, 1937
Cruickshank, Andrew John
b. Dec 25, 1907
Donald, James b. May 18, 1917
Douglas, Norman b. Dec 8, 1868
Dyce, William b. Sep 19, 1806
Forbes, Bertie Charles b. May 14, 1880
Garden, Mary b. Feb 20, 1874
Garden, Mary d. Jan 4, 1967
Gibbs, James b. Dec 23, 1682
Keith, William b. 1839
Lennox, Annie b. Dec 25, 1954

Aberdeenshire, Scotland
Lang, William Cosmo Gordon, Baron
b. Oct 31, 1864
Manson, Patrick, Sir b. Oct 3, 1844
Aberfeldy, Scotland
Crisp, Donald b. Apr 18, 1880
Airdrie, Scotland
Bannen, Ian b. Jun 29, 1928
Annan, Scotland
Irving, Edward b. Aug 4, 1792
Anstruther, Scotland
Bruce Lockhart, Robert Hamilton, Sir
b. Sep 2, 1887
Arbroth, Scotland
Buick, David Dunbar b. Sep 17, 1854
Arbuthnott, Scotland
Gibbon, Lewis Grassic, pseud.
b. Feb 13, 1901
Aylsbury, Scotland
Ross, James Clark, Sir d. Sep 21, 1862
Ayrshire, Scotland
Burns, Robert b. Jan 25, 1759
Dent, Alan Holmes b. Jan 7, 1905
Kelvin, William Thomson, Baron
d. Dec 17, 1907
McAdam, John Loudoun b. Sep 21, 1756
Ballater, Scotland
Geddes, Patrick, Sir b. Oct 2, 1854
Balquhidder, Scotland
MacGregor, Robert d. Dec 28, 1734
Balsarroch, Scotland
Ross, James Clark, Sir b. Apr 15, 1800
Banchor, Scotland
Lang, Andrew d. Jul 20, 1912
Bathgate, Scotland
Simpson, James Young, Sir b. Jun 7, 1811
Bellshill, Scotland
Easton, Sheena b. Apr 27, 1959
Bladenock, Scotland
McArthur, John b. May 13, 1823
Blairgowrie, Scotland
Clyde, Andy b. Mar 18, 1892
Borthwick, Scotland
Robertson, William b. Sep 19, 1721
Braemar, Scotland
Waller, Gordon b. Jun 4, 1945
Brechin, Scotland
Boyd-Orr, John Boyd Orr, Baron
d. Jun 25, 1971
Orr, John Boyd d. Jun 25, 1971
Watson-Watt, Robert Alexander, Sir
b. Apr 13, 1892
Buchanan, Scotland
MacGregor, Robert b. Mar 7, 1671
Cardross, Scotland
Robert I d. Jun 1329
Clydebank, Scotland
Reston, James Barrett b. Nov 3, 1909
Coatbridge, Scotland
Marshall, Peter b. May 27, 1902

Cults, Scotland
Wilkie, David b. Nov 18, 1785
Dalquhurn, Scotland
Smollett, Tobias George b. Mar 1721
Deerness, Scotland
Muir, Edwin b. May 15, 1887
Doune, Scotland
Neilson, William A b. Mar 29, 1869
Dumfroes, Scotland
Burns, Robert d. Jan 21, 1796
Dunbar, Scotland
Muir, John b. Jul 21, 1838
Dunbartonshire, Scotland
Stewart, Jackie (John Young)
b. Jun 11, 1939
Dundee, Scotland
Bannerman, Francis b. Mar 24, 1851
Fleming, Williamina Paton Stevens
b. May 15, 1857
Fyffe, Will b. 1885
Mackenzie, William Lyon b. Mar 12, 1795
Spence, Lewis (James Lewis Thomas
Chalmers) b. Nov 25, 1874
Wright, Frances (Fanny) b. Sep 6, 1795
Dunfermline, Scotland
Carnegie, Andrew b. Nov 25, 1835
Forbes, John b. 1710
James I b. Jul 1394
Shearer, Moira b. Jan 17, 1926
Dunglass, Scotland
Hall, James, Sir b. Jan 17, 1761
Dunkeld, Scotland
Mackenzie, Alexander b. Jan 28, 1822
Duns, Scotland
Duns Scotus, John b. 1266
Dunure, Scotland
Curry, Peggy Simson b. Dec 30, 1912
East Lothian, Scotland
Balfour, Arthur James Balfour, Earl
b. Jul 25, 1848
Ecclefechan, Scotland
Carlyle, Thomas b. Dec 4, 1795
Edinburgh, Scotland
Adam, James b. Jul 21, 1730
Alison, Archibald b. 1757
Alison, Archibald b. May 17, 1839
Appleton, Edward Victor, Sir
d. Apr 21, 1965
Aytoun, William Edmonstoune
b. Jun 21, 1813
Bannerman, Helen b. 1863
Bannerman, Helen d. Oct 13, 1946
Barnetson, William Denholm, Lord
b. Mar 21, 1917
Bell, Alexander Graham b. Mar 3, 1847
Bell, Charles b. Nov 1774
Bell, Joseph b. 1837
Bishop, Isabella Lucy Bird d. 1904
Black, Joseph d. Nov 10, 1799
Blair, James b. 1655

Boothby, Robert John Graham, Lord
b. 1900
Boswell, James b. Oct 18, 1740
Bridie, James, pseud. d. Jan 29, 1951
Burke, William d. Jan 28, 1829
Charleson, Ian b. Aug 11, 1949
Connery, Sean b. Aug 25, 1930
Currie, Finlay b. Jan 20, 1878
DeQuincey, Thomas d. Dec 8, 1859
Dott, Gerard b.
Doyle, Arthur Conan, Sir b. May 22, 1859
Dyce. Alexander b. Jun 30, 1798
Faulkner, Eric b. Oct 21, 1955
Flint, William Russell, Sir b. Apr 4, 1880
Ged, William b. 1690
Grahame, Kenneth b. Mar 8, 1859
Grant, James b. Aug 1, 1822
Grant, James d. May 5, 1887
Gray, Cecil b. May 19, 1895
Haig, Douglas b. 1861
Haldane, John Scott b. May 3, 1860
Hall, James, Sir d. Jun 23, 1832
Hamilton, William, Sir d. May 6, 1856
Horsbrugh, Florence b. 1889
Horsbrugh, Florence d. Dec 6, 1969
Hume, David b. Apr 26, 1711
Hume, David d. Aug 25, 1776
Hurst, George b. May 20, 1926
Hutton, James b. Jun 3, 1726
Inescort, Frieda b. Jun 29, 1901
James I b. Jun 19, 1566
James II b. 1430
Jeffrey, Lord Francis b. 1773
Knox, John d. Nov 24, 1572
Laing, David b. Apr 20, 1793
Lehmann-Haupt, Christopher
b. Jun 14, 1934
Longmuir, Alan b. Jun 20, 1950
Longmuir, Derek b. Mar 19, 1955
MacDiarmid, Hugh, pseud. d. Sep 9, 1978
Mackenzie, Alexander, Sir b. Aug 22, 1847
Mackenzie, Compton (Edward Montague,
Sir) d. Nov 30, 1972
Mackenzie, Henry b. Aug 26, 1745
Mackenzie, Henry d. Jan 14, 1831
Maxwell, James Clerk b. Nov 13, 1831
McKeown, Leslie b. Nov 12, 1955
Mitchison, Naomi Haldane b. Nov 1, 1897
Musgrave, Thea b. May 27, 1928
Raeburn, Henry, Sir d. Jul 8, 1823
Ramsay, Allan b. 1713
Reith, John Charles Walsham
d. Jun 16, 1971
Robertson, William d. Jun 11, 1793
Sanderson, Ivan Terence b. Jan 30, 1911
Scott, Walter, Sir b. Aug 15, 1771
Sim, Alastair b. Oct 9, 1900
Smith, Adam d. Jul 17, 1790
Spark, Muriel Sarah b. Feb 1, 1918
Spence, Lewis (James Lewis Thomas
Chalmers) d. Mar 3, 1955

Huntley, Scotland
MacDonald, George b. Dec 10, 1824
Inverness, Scotland
Mackay, John Alexander b. May 17, 1889
Phyfe, Duncan b. 1768
Tey, Josephine, pseud. b. 1897
Watson-Watt, Robert Alexander, Sir
d. Dec 5, 1973
Ironside, Scotland
Ironside, William E b. May 6, 1880
Irvine, Scotland
Galt, John b. May 2, 1779
Islay, Scotland
McDougall, Alexander b. 1732
Isle of Lewis, Scotland
Smith, Iain Crichton b. Jan 1, 1928
Jedburgh, Scotland
Brewster, David, Sir b. Dec 11, 1781
Keith, Scotland
Bennett, James Gordon b. 1795
Kilmacolm, Scotland
Smith, Hedrick Laurence b. Jul 9, 1933
Kilmany, Scotland
Clark, James b. Mar 4, 1936
Kilmarnock, Scotland
Leiper, Robert Thomson b. Apr 17, 1881
Smith, Alexander b. Dec 31, 1830
Kilmaurs, Scotland
Boyd-Orr, John Boyd Orr, Baron
b. Sep 23, 1880
Orr, John Boyd b. Sep 23, 1880
Kinlochleven, Scotland
MacGregor, Ian b. Sep 21, 1912
Kinnordy, Scotland
Lyell, Charles, Sir b. Nov 14, 1797
Kirkcaldy, Scotland
Adam, Robert b. Jul 3, 1728
Smith, Adam b. Jun 5, 1723
Wilson, Bertha b. Sep 18, 1923
Kirkcudbright, Scotland
Jones, John Paul b. Jul 6, 1747
Kirriemuir, Scotland
Barrie, James Matthew, Sir b. May 9, 1860
Niven, (James) David Graham
b. Mar 1, 1910
Lanarkshire, Scotland
Livingstone, David b. Mar 19, 1813
Murray, Philip b. May 25, 1886
Langholm, Scotland
MacDiarmid, Hugh, pseud.
b. Aug 11, 1892
Largo, Scotland
Selkirk, Alexander b. 1676
Lemahagow, Scotland
Cairncross, Alexander Kirkland, Sir
b. Feb 11, 1911
Lenarkshire, Scotland
Lauder, Harry MacLennan, Sir
d. Feb 25, 1950
Lethington, Scotland
Maitland, John b. May 24, 1616

Linlithgow, Scotland
Mary, Queen of Scots b. Dec 1542
Little Duchrae, Scotland
Crockett, S(amuel) R(utherford)
b. Sep 24, 1860
Lochfield, Scotland
Fleming, Alexander, Sir b. Aug 6, 1881
Long Calderwood, Scotland
Hunter, John b. Feb 13, 1728
Lossiemouth, Scotland
MacDonald, James Ramsay
b. Oct 12, 1866
MacDonald, Malcolm John
b. Aug 17, 1901
Montrose, Scotland
Brown, Robert b. Dec 21, 1773
Morayshire, Scotland
Smith, Donald Alexander b. Aug 6, 1820
Mulnain, Scotland
Mackenzie, Alexander, Sir d. Mar 11, 1820
Musselburgh, Scotland
Oliphant, Margaret b. Apr 4, 1828
Nairn, Scotland
Rose, Murray b. Jan 6, 1939
Northwater Bridge, Scotland
Mill, James b. Apr 6, 1773
Paisley, Scotland
Conti, Tom (Thomas Antonio)
b. Nov 22, 1941
Sharp, William b. Sep 12, 1855
Wilson, Alexander b. Jul 6, 1766
Peebles, Scotland
Chambers, Robert b. Jul 10, 1802
Perth, Scotland
Buchan, John, Sir b. Aug 26, 1875
James I d. Feb 20, 1437
Perthshire, Scotland
Braddock, Edward b. 1695
Dewar, John b. 1806
Portobello, Scotland
Lauder, Harry MacLennan, Sir
b. Aug 4, 1870
Renfrew, Scotland
Davies, Hunter b. Jan 7, 1936
Dickie, Murray b. 1924
Roxborough, Scotland
Gregory, Isabella Augusta Persse, Lady
b. Mar 15, 1852
Roxburgh Castle, Scotland
James II d. 1460
Ruthven, Scotland
Macpherson, James b. Oct 27, 1736
Macpherson, James d. Feb 17, 1796
Saint Andrews, Scotland
Chambers, Robert d. Mar 17, 1871
Fyffe, Will d. Dec 14, 1947
Sauchieburn, Scotland
James III d. 1488
Scone, Scotland
Douglas, David b. 1798

Selkirk, Scotland
Lang, Andrew b. Mar 31, 1844
Shotts, Scotland
MacBeth, George Mann b. Jan 19, 1932
Stirling, Scotland
James III b. 1451
Mathieson, Muir b. Jan 24, 1911
McLaren, Norman b. Apr 11, 1914
Tedder, Arthur William Tedder, Baron
b. Jul 11, 1890
Stockbridge, Scotland
Raeburn, Henry, Sir b. Mar 4, 1756
Stonehaven, Scotland
Reith, John Charles Walsham
b. Jul 20, 1889
Stromness, Scotland
Brown, George Mackay b. Oct 17, 1921
Thurso, Scotland
Saint Clair, Arthur b. Mar 23, 1736
Tillypronie, Scotland
Astor, Gavin d. Jun 28, 1984
Upper Corrie, Scotland
MacMillan, Daniel b. Sep 13, 1813
Wardie, Scotland
Smith, Alexander d. Jan 5, 1867
West Calder, Scotland
Kane, John b. Aug 19, 1860
Wigtown, Scotland
Justice, James Robertson b. Jun 15, 1905
Yarrow, Scotland
Hogg, James d. Nov 21, 1835

SENEGAL

Wheatley, Phillis b. 1753
Dakar, Senegal
Laye, Camara d. Feb 4, 1980
Joal, Senegal
Senghor, Leopold Sedar b. Oct 9, 1906

SICILY

Archimedes b. 287 BC?
Sharp, William d. Dec 12, 1905
Agriegento, Sicily
Pirandello, Luigi b. Jun 28, 1867
Catania, Sicily
Bellini, Vincenzo b. Nov 3, 1801
Pacini, Giovanni b. Feb 17, 1796
Verga, Giovanni d. Jan 27, 1922
Messina, Sicily
Antonello da Messina b. 1430
Palermo, Sicily
Armetta, Henry b. Jul 4, 1888
Logroscino, Nicola d. 1765
Marchesi, Salvatore b. Jan 15, 1822
Sammarco, Mario b. Dec 13, 1868
Stabile, Mariano b. May 12, 1888

Syracuse, Sicily
Damocles b. 370 BC?
Dionysius the Elder d. 367 BC
Theocritus b. 310 BC

SIERRA LEONE

Stevens, Siaka Probyn b. Aug 24, 1905
Freetown, Sierra Leone
Berri, Nabih b. 1938

SIKKIM

Gangtok, Sikkim
Namgyal, Palden Thondup
b. May 22, 1923

SILESIA

Karwin, Silesia
Kentner, Louis Philip b. Jul 19, 1905
Neisse, Silesia
Eichendorff, Joseph Karl Benedict
d. Nov 26, 1857
Troppau, Silesia
Adamson, Joy Friederike Victoria Gessner
b. Jan 20, 1910

SINGAPORE

Ishak, Yusof bin d. Nov 23, 1970
Martinson, Joseph Bertram d. Oct 30, 1970
Sheares, Benjamin Henry b. Aug 12, 1907
Sheares, Benjamin Henry d. May 12, 1981

SOMALIA

Iman b. 1955

SOUTH AFRICA

Biko, Steven d. Sep 12, 1977
Bloom, Harry b. 1913
Cornelius, Henry b. Aug 18, 1913
Head, Bessie b. Jul 6, 1937
Krige, Alice b. 1955
Muller, Hilgard d. Jul 10, 1985
Pahlevi, Riza b. 1877
Verwoerd, Hendrik F d. Sep 6, 1966
Beaufort West, South Africa
Barnard, Christiaan Neethling
b. Oct 8, 1922
Bloemfontein, South Africa
Tolkien, J(ohn) R(onald) R(euel)
b. Jan 3, 1892
Bonnievale, South Africa
Breytenbach, Breyten b. Sep 16, 1939
Cape Province, South Africa
Ballinger, Margaret (Violet Margaret
Livingstone) d. Feb 7, 1980

Cape Town, South Africa
Little, Sally b. Oct 21, 1951
Vorster, Balthazar Johannes (John)
   d. Sep 10, 1983

Capetown, South Africa
Bolitho, William b. 1890
Butlin, William Heygate Edmund, Sir
   b. Sep 29, 1899
Cannon, Poppy b. 1907
Chaplin, Sydney Dryden b. Mar 17, 1885
Cloete, Stuart d. Mar 19, 1976
Coates, Albert d. Dec 11, 1953
Diederichs, Nicholaas d. Aug 21, 1978
Divine, Arthur Durham b. Jul 27, 1904
Eban, Abba b. Feb 2, 1915
Hunter, Ian b. Jun 13, 1900
Kellaway, Cecil b. Aug 22, 1893
Malan, Daniel F d. Feb 7, 1959
Oliphant, Laurence b. 1829
Renault, Mary, pseud. d. Dec 13, 1983
Rhodes, Cecil John d. Mar 26, 1902
Seed, Jenny b. May 18, 1930
Smuts, Jan Christian b. May 24, 1870
Washkansky, Louis d. Dec 21, 1967

Capetwon, South Africa
Blaiberg, Philip d. Aug 17, 1969

Colesberg, South Africa
Kruger, Paul (Stephanus Johannes Paulus)
   b. Oct 10, 1825

Durban, South Africa
Campbell, Roy b. Oct 2, 1901
Curren, Kevin b. Mar 2, 1958
Cusack, Cyril b. Nov 26, 1910
Langley, Noel b. Dec 25, 1911

Elliotdale, South Africa
Woods, Donald b. Dec 15, 1933

Germiston, Transvaal, South Africa
Locke, Bobbie b. Nov 20, 1917

Graaff Reinet, South Africa
Pretorius, Marthinus Wessel b. 1819

Groutville, South Africa
Luthuli, Albert John d. Jul 21, 1967

Honigfontein, South Africa
Botha, Louis b. Sep 27, 1862

Irene, South Africa
Smuts, Jan Christian d. Sep 11, 1950

Jamestown, South Africa
Vorster, Balthazar Johannes (John)
   b. Dec 13, 1915

Johannesburg, South Africa
Dalrymple, Ian (Murray) b. Aug 26, 1903
Daly, John Charles, Jr. b. Feb 20, 1914
Hayward, Louis b. Mar 19, 1909
Player, Gary Jim b. Nov 1, 1935
Rathbone, Basil b. Jun 13, 1892
Revson, Peter Jeffrey d. Mar 22, 1974
Suzman, Janet b. Feb 9, 1939

Kalk Bay, South Africa
Ardrey, Robert d. Jan 14, 1980

Kimberley, South Africa
Oppenheimer, Harry Frederick
   b. Oct 28, 1908

Klerksdrop, South Africa
Tutu, Desmond Mpilo b. Oct 7, 1931

Kutama, South Africa
Mugabe, Robert Gabriel b. Feb 21, 1924

Middleburg, South Africa
Fugard, Athol Harold b. Jun 11, 1932

Natal, South Africa
Paton, Alan Stewart b. Jan 11, 1903

Orange Free State, South Africa
Diederichs, Nicholaas b. Nov 17, 1904

Paul Roux, South Africa
Botha, Pieter Willem b. Jan 12, 1916

Philioppis, South Africa
Van Der Post, Laurens b. Dec 13, 1906

Pietersburg, South Africa
Plomer, William Charles Franklyn
   b. Dec 10, 1903

Ponogola, South Africa
Kriek, Johann b. Apr 5, 1958

Potchefstroom, South Africa
Muller, Hilgard b. May 4, 1914
Pretorius, Marthinus Wessel
   d. May 19, 1901

Pretoria, South Africa
Biko, Steven b. 1947
Botha, Louis d. Aug 27, 1919
Johns, Glynis b. Oct 5, 1923
Sloane, Dennis b. Jan 9, 1930
Theiler, Max b. Jan 30, 1899

Prospect Township, South Africa
Makeba, Miriam b. Mar 4, 1932

Riebeck, South Africa
Malan, Daniel F b. May 22, 1874

Rustenberg, South Africa
Cranko, John b. Aug 15, 1927

Rustenburg, South Africa
Botha, Roelof Pik b. Apr 27, 1932

Springs, South Africa
Gordimer, Nadine b. Nov 20, 1923

Transkei, South Africa
Mandela, Winnie b. 1936

Umtata, South Africa
Mandela, Nelson Rolihlahla
   b. Jul 18, 1918

Uniondale, South Africa
Blaiberg, Philip b. May 24, 1909

Witbank, South Africa
Masekela, Hugh Ramapolo b. Apr 4, 1939

SOUTH POLE

Scott, Robert Falcon d. Mar 27, 1912

SOUTH WALES

Swansea, South Wales
Heseltine, Michael Ray Dibdin
b. Mar 21, 1933

SPAIN

Barea, Arturo b. Sep 20, 1897
Cabeza de Vaca, Alvar Nunez b. 1490
Cabeza de Vaca, Alvar Nunez d. 1557
Charles V d. Sep 21, 1558
Columbus, Christopher d. May 20, 1506
Hadrian b. Jan 24, 76
Landa, Diego de b. 1524
Negrin, Juan b. 1892
Torquemada, Tomas de b. 1420
Urtain, Jose Manuel Ibar b. May 14, 1943
Alcala, Spain
Catherine of Aragon b. Dec 16, 1485
Cervantes (Saavedra), Miguel(de)
b. Sep 29, 1547
Alcolea de Cinca, Spain
Sender, Ramon Jose b. Feb 3, 1902
Almeria, Spain
Castellon, Frederico b. Sep 14, 1914
Altea, Spain
Lewis, Dominic Bevan Wyndham
d. Nov 23, 1969
Aragon, Spain
Goya y Lucientes, Francisco Jose de
b. Mar 30, 1746
Pertegaz, Manuel b.
Avila, Spain
John of the Cross, Saint b. Jun 24, 1542
Theresa, Saint b. 1515
Badajoz, Spain
Alvarado, Pedro de b. 1486
Barcarrota, Spain
DeSoto, Hernando b. 1500
Barcelona, Spain
Angeles, Victoria de los b. Nov 1, 1923
Caballe, Montserrat b. Apr 12, 1933
Carreras, Jose b. Dec 5, 1946
Clave, Antoni b. Apr 5, 1913
Cugat, Xavier b. Jan 1, 1900
Espriu, Salvador d. Feb 22, 1985
Falkenburg, Jinx (Eugenia Lincoln)
b. Jan 21, 1919
Hidalgo, Elvira de b. 1882
Larrocha, Alicia de b. May 23, 1923
Miro, Joan b. Apr 20, 1893
Samaranch, Juan Antonio b. Jul 17, 1920
Sert, Jose Luis b. Jul 1, 1902
Sert, Jose Luis d. Mar 15, 1983
Sor, Fernando b. Feb 13, 1778
Supervia, Conchita b. Dec 8, 1899
Bilbao, Spain
Lopez Bravo, Gregorio d. Feb 19, 1985
Unamuno (y Jugo), Miguel de
b. Sep 29, 1864

Bilbilis, Spain
Martial b. 43
Martial d. 104
Burgos, Spain
Cid, El b. 1040
Cadiz, Spain
Falla, Manuel de b. Nov 23, 1876
Meade, George Gordon b. Dec 31, 1815
Miranda, Francisco de d. Jul 14, 1816
Murillo, Bartolome Esteban d. Apr 3, 1682
Calagurris, Spain
Quintilian Marcus Fabius b. 35
Calahorra, Spain
Lopez de Ayala, Pero d. 1407
Calanda, Spain
Bunuel, Luis b. Feb 22, 1900
Cambo, Spain
Albeniz, Isaac Manuel Francisco
d. Jun 16, 1909
Canary Islands, Spain
Perez Galdos, Benito b. May 10, 1843
Carrion, Spain
Santillana, Inigo Lopez de Mendoza
b. Aug 19, 1398
Castelldefels, Spain
Sanders, George d. Apr 25, 1972
Catalonia, Spain
Espriu, Salvador b. 1913
Cebreros, Spain
Suarez Gonzales, Adolfo b. Sep 25, 1932
Comprodon, Spain
Albeniz, Isaac Manuel Francisco
b. May 29, 1860
Cordoba, Spain
Seneca, Lucius Annaeus, the Younger b. 4
Cordova, Spain
Averroes b. 1126
Gongora y Argote, Don Luis de
b. Jun 11, 1561
Gongora y Argote, Don Luis de
d. May 24, 1627
Lucan b. Jun 3, 39
Maimonides, Moses b. Mar 30, 1135
Manolete b. 1917
El Ferrol, Spain
Franco, Francisco b. Dec 4, 1892
Figueras, Spain
Dali, Salvador b. May 11, 1904
Fuente Vaqueros, Spain
Garcia Lorca, Federico b. Jun 5, 1899
Garcia Lorca, Federico d. Aug 19, 1936
Fuentes de Cantos, Spain
Zurbaran, Francisco b. Nov 7, 1598
Gallarta, Spain
Ibarruri, Dolores b. Dec 9, 1895
Gerona, Spain
Dali, Gala d. Jun 10, 1982
Granada, Spain
Eugenie b. 1826
Fortuny b. 1871
Orantes, Manuel b. Feb 6, 1949

Guadalajara, Spain
Amalrik, Andrei Alekseyevich
   d. Nov 11, 1980
DeCreeft, Jose b. Nov 27, 1884
Santillana, Inigo Lopez de Mendoza
   d. Mar 25, 1458
Guadalmina, Spain
Batista y Zaldivar, Fulgencio
   d. Aug 6, 1973
Guadix, Spain
Alarcon, Pedro Antonio de
   b. Mar 10, 1833
Guetaria, Spain
Balenciaga, Cristobal b. Jan 21, 1895
Huesca, Spain
Saura Carlos (Atares Carlos)
   b. Jan 4, 1932
Ibiza, Spain
Sackler, Howard Oliver d. Oct 13, 1982
Italica, Spain
Trajan b. 53
Jativa, Spain
Alexander VI b. Jan 1, 1431
Ribera, Jusepe (Jose) de b. Feb 17, 1590
Javea, Spain
Balenciaga, Cristobal d. Mar 23, 1972
Jerez Caballeros, Spain
Balboa, Vasco Nunez de b. 1475
La Coruna, Spain
Menendez Pidal, Ramon b. Mar 13, 1869
Lacoruna, Spain
Madariaga (y Rojo), Salvador de
   b. Jul 23, 1886
LaCoruna, Spain
Rey, Fernando b. Sep 20, 1917
Leon, Spain
Ponce de Leon, Juan b. Apr 8, 1460
Lerida, Spain
Granados, Enrique b. Jul 27, 1867
Linares, Spain
Manolete d. Aug 28, 1947
Segovia, Andres b. Feb 18, 1894
Lorca, Spain
Yepes, Narciso b. Nov 14, 1927
Loyola, Spain
Ignatius of Loyola, Saint b. 1491
Macharaviaya, Spain
Galvez, Bernardo de b. Jul 23, 1746
Madrid, Spain
Abruzzi, Luigi Amedeo b. 1873
Alarcon y Mendoza, Juan Ruiz de
   d. Aug 4, 1639
Alarcon, Pedro Antonio de d. Jul 20, 1891
Aleixandre, Vicente d. Dec 14, 1984
Asturias, Miguel Angel d. Jun 9, 1974
Benavente y Martinez, Jacinto
   b. Aug 12, 1866
Benavente y Martinez, Jacinto
   d. Jul 14, 1954
Berganza, Teresa b. Mar 16, 1935
Blanc, (Jean Joseph Charles) Louis b. 1811

Boccherini, Luigi d. May 28, 1805
Calderon de la Barca, Pedro
   b. Jan 17, 1600
Calderon de la Barca, Pedro
   d. May 25, 1681
Calvo Sotelo (y Bustelo), Leopoldo
   b. Apr 14, 1926
Candela, Felix (Outerino Felix)
   b. Jan 27, 1910
Castillo, Antonio Canovas del b. 1908
Cervantes (Saavedra), Miguel(de)
   d. Apr 23, 1616
Charriere, Henri d. Jul 29, 1973
Cienfuegos, Nicasio Alvarez de b. 1761
Colbran, Isabella b. Feb 2, 1785
Crosby, "Bing" (Harry Lillis)
   d. Oct 14, 1977
Domingo, Placido b. Jan 21, 1941
Dominguin, Luis Miguel b. Dec 9, 1926
Echegaray, Jose b. Apr 19, 1831
Echegaray, Jose d. Sep 15, 1916
Franco, Francisco d. Nov 20, 1975
Frederika Louise d. Feb 6, 1981
Garcia, Manuel Patricio Rodriguez, II
   b. Mar 17, 1805
Gris, Juan b. Mar 13, 1887
Hamen y Leon, Juan van der b. 1596
Hamen y Leon, Juan van der d. 1631
Iglesias, Julio b. Sep 23, 1943
Isabella II b. Oct 10, 1830
Lope de Vega b. 1562
Lope de Vega d. 1635
Lopez Bravo, Gregorio b. Dec 19, 1923
Machado, Manuel d. 1947
Martinez, Sierra Gregorio b. May 6, 1881
Martinez, Sierra Gregorio d. Oct 1, 1947
Menendez Pidal, Ramon d. Nov 14, 1968
Montoya, Carlos b. Dec 13, 1903
Ortega y Gasset, Jose b. May 9, 1883
Ortega y Gasset, Jose d. Oct 18, 1955
Patti, Adelina Juana Maria
   b. Feb 19, 1843
Perez Galdos, Benito d. Jan 4, 1920
Power, Tyrone d. Nov 15, 1958
Rojas Zorrilla, Francisco de d. 1648
Salinas (y Serrano), Pedro b. Nov 27, 1891
Santayana, George b. Dec 16, 1863
Starkie, Walter Fitzwilliam d. Nov 2, 1976
Vega (Carpio), Lope (Felix) de
   b. Nov 25, 1562
Vega (Carpio), Lope (Felix) de
   d. Aug 27, 1635
Velazquez, Diego Rodriguez de Silva
   d. Aug 6, 1660
Waln, Nora d. Sep 27, 1964
Zurbaran, Francisco d. Aug 27, 1664

Madrigal, Spain
Isabella I b. Apr 22, 1451

Madrigalejo, Spain
Ferdinand V d. Jan 23, 1516

Majorca, Spain
Emerson, Faye Margaret d. Mar 9, 1983
Graves, Robert Ranke d. Dec 7, 1985
Malaga, Spain
Baker, Stanley, Sir d. Jun 28, 1976
Bowles, Jane Sydney d. May 4, 1973
Guillen, Jorge d. Feb 6, 1984
Picasso, Pablo b. Oct 25, 1881
Medellin, Spain
Cortez, Hernando b. 1485
Medina del Campo, Spain
Isabella I d. Nov 26, 1504
Monguer, Spain
Jimenez, Juan Ramon b. Dec 23, 1881
Nino, Pedro Alonzo b. 1468
Moraira, Spain
Himes, Chester Bomar d. Nov 12, 1984
Murcia, Spain
Charo b. Jan 15, 1951
Nijar, Spain
Asencio, Diego Cortes b. Jul 15, 1931
Palma de Majorca, Spain
Fielding, Temple Hornaday
d. May 18, 1983
Miro, Joan d. Dec 25, 1983
Palma del Rio, Spain
Cordobes, El b. May 4, 1936
Pamplona, Spain
Francis Xavier, Saint b. 1506
Sarasate, Pablo de b. Mar 10, 1844
Pedrena, Spain
Ballesteros, Seve(riano) b. Apr 9, 1957
Penuela, Spain
John of the Cross, Saint d. Dec 14, 1591
Polanco, Spain
Pereda, Jose Marie de b. Feb 6, 1933
Puerto del Pico, Spain
Verrazano, Giovanni da d. Nov 1528
Reus, Spain
Gaudi y Cornet, Antonio b. Jun 25, 1852
Salamanca, Spain
Coronado, Francisco Vasquez de
b. Feb 25, 1510
Unamuno (y Jugo), Miguel de
d. Dec 31, 1936
San Sebastian, Spain
Chillida, Eduard b. Jan 10, 1924
Jorda, Enrique b. Mar 24, 1911
Zabaleta, Nicanor b. Jan 7, 1907
Santander, Spain
Pereda, Jose Marie de d. Mar 1, 1906
Sequals, Spain
Carnera, Primo b. Oct 26, 1906
Carnera, Primo d. Jun 29, 1967
Seville, Spain
Aleixandre, Vicente b. Apr 26, 1898
Garcia, Manuel del Popolo Vincente, I
b. Jan 22, 1775
Gonzalez Marquez, Felipe b. Mar 5, 1942
Machado, Antonio b. Jul 26, 1875
Machado, Manuel b. 1874

Mercer, Beryl b. Aug 13, 1882
Murillo, Bartolome Esteban b. Jan 1, 1618
Velazquez, Diego Rodriguez de Silva
b. Jun 6, 1599
Vespucci, Amerigo d. Feb 22, 1512
Wiseman, Nicholas Patrick Stephen
b. Aug 2, 1802
Sos, Spain
Ferdinand V b. Mar 10, 1452
Talavera, Spain
Rojas, Fernando de d. Apr 1541
Toledo, Spain
Caro, Joseph b. 1488
Castiglione, Baldassare, Conte
d. Feb 2, 1529
Greco, El d. Apr 6, 1614
Rojas Zorrilla, Francisco de b. 1607
Rojas, Fernando de b. 1475
Torremolinos, Spain
Karpis, Alvin d. Aug 12, 1979
Trujilo, Spain
Pizarro, Francisco b. 1470
Tudela, Spain
Benjamin of Tudela b. 1130
Valencia, Spain
Blasco-Ibanez, Vicente b. 1867
Bori, Lucrezia b. Dec 24, 1888
Cid, El d. Jul 10, 1099
Iturbi, Jose b. Nov 28, 1895
Martin y Soler, Vicente b. Jan 18, 1754
Valladolid, Spain
Guillen, Jorge b. Jan 18, 1893
Vendrell, Spain
Casals, Pablo (Pau Carlos Salvador)
b. Dec 29, 1876
Victoria, Spain
Lopez de Ayala, Pero b. 1332
Vigo, Spain
Norwich, Alfred Duff Cooper, Viscount
d. Jan 1, 1954
Villanueva de Sixena, Spain
Servetus, Michael b. Sep 29, 1511
Zaragoza, Spain
Lorengar, Pilar b. Jan 16, 1933

SRI LANKA

Colombo, Sri Lanka
Gopallawa, William d. Jan 30, 1981
Senanayake, Dudley d. Apr 12, 1973

ST. LUCIA

Linlithgow, St. Lucia
James V b. 1512

ST. MARTIN ISLAND

St. Martin Island, St. Martin Island
Spiegel, Sam d. Dec 31, 1985

STRAIT OF MALACCA

Davis, John d. Dec 29, 1605

SUDAN

Gogrial, Sudan
Bol, Manute b.
Khartoum, Sudan
Gordon, Charles George d. Jan 26, 1885
Naguib, Mohammed b. Feb 20, 1901
Omdurman, Sudan
Mahdi, Mohammed Ahmed
d. Jun 22, 1885
Wad Nubawi, Sudan
Nimeiry, Gaafar Mohammed al
b. Jan 1, 1930

SURINAM

Matzeliger, Jan Ernest b. 1852
Paramaribo, Surinam
Ferrier, Henry Eliza b. May 12, 1910
Sedny, Jules b. Sep 28, 1922

SWAZILAND

Sobhuza II b. Jul 22, 1899
Mbabane, Swaziland
Sobhuza II d. Aug 21, 1982

SWEDEN

Grove, Frederick Philip b. Feb 14, 1872
Hill, Joe, pseud. b. Oct 7, 1879
Tenggren, Gustaf Adolf b. Nov 3, 1896
Wallenberg, Raoul Gustav b. Aug 4, 1912
Algutsboda, Sweden
Moberg, Vihelm b. Aug 20, 1898
Backebo, Sweden
Broneer, Oscar Theodore b. Dec 28, 1894
Bosjokloster, Sweden
Rosenberg, Hilding b. Jun 21, 1892
Brunnby, Sweden
Jarring, Gunnar V b. Oct 12, 1907
Christiania, Sweden
Aurell, Tage b. Mar 2, 1895
Falun, Sweden
Larsson, Carl (Olof) d. Jan 22, 1919
Thorborg, Kerstin d. Apr 12, 1970
Folkarna, Sweden
Karlfeldt, Erik Axel b. Jul 20, 1864
Fredensborg, Sweden
Stacton, David Derek d. Jan 20, 1968
Gothenburg, Sweden
Chambers, William, Sir b. 1723
Hasselblad, Victor d. Aug 6, 1978
Jacobsson, Ulla b. May 23, 1929
Johansson, Ingemar b. Sep 22, 1932
Wahloo, Per b. Aug 5, 1926
Grenna, Sweden
Andree, Salomon August b. Oct 18, 1854

Gustafs, Sweden
Myrdal, Karl Gunnar b. Dec 6, 1898
Hagby, Sweden
Larsen-Todsen, Nanny b. Aug 2, 1884
Hedemora, Sweden
Thorborg, Kerstin b. May 19, 1896
Helsingborg, Sweden
Gustaf Adolf VI d. Sep 15, 1973
Huddinge, Sweden
Erlander, Tage Fritiof d. Jun 21, 1985
Jamshog, Sweden
Martinson, Harry Edmund b. May 6, 1905
Jonkoping, Sweden
Hammarskjold, Dag b. Jul 29, 1905
Josesjo, Sweden
Stenmark, Ingemar b. Mar 18, 1956
Kalmar, Sweden
Kreuger, Ivar b. Mar 2, 1880
Karlskrona, Sweden
Swanson, Carl A b. May 1, 1876
Karlstad, Sweden
Hagegard, Hakan b. Nov 25, 1945
Lagga, Sweden
Milles, Carl b. Jun 23, 1875
Lidingo, Sweden
Britt, May b. Mar 22, 1933
Ljungberg, Gota d. Jun 28, 1955
Lidkoping, Sweden
Anderson, Mary b. Aug 27, 1872
Limhamn, Sweden
Troell, Jan b. Jul 23, 1931
Linkoping, Sweden
Theorell, (Axel) Hugh Teodor
b. Jul 6, 1903
Logdo, Sweden
Angstrom, Anders Jonas b. Aug 13, 1814
Lulea, Sweden
Adams, Maud b. Feb 12, 1945
Lund, Sweden
VonSydow, Max Carl Adolf
b. Apr 10, 1929
Malmo, Sweden
Asther, Nils b. Jan 17, 1901
Ehrling, Sixten b. Apr 3, 1918
Ekberg, Anita b. Sep 29, 1931
Ralf, Torsten b. Jan 2, 1901
Wahloo, Per d. Jun 22, 1975
Widerberg, Bo b. Jun 8, 1930
Mansrog, Sweden
Aurell, Tage d. Feb 20, 1976
Marbacka, Sweden
Lagerlof, Selma Ottiliana Lovisa
b. Nov 20, 1858
Lagerlof, Selma Ottiliana Lovisa
d. Mar 16, 1940
Moheda, Sweden
Nykvist, Sven Vilhem b. Dec 3, 1922
Mora, Sweden
Zorn, Anders Leonhard b. 1860

Timra, Sweden
Dahlin, Kjell b. Feb 2, 1963
Uddevalla, Sweden
Wenner-Gren, Axel b. Jun 5, 1881
Umea, Sweden
Oland, Warner b. Oct 3, 1880
Uppsala, Sweden
Alexanderson, Ernst Frederik Werner
b. Jan 25, 1878
Angstrom, Anders Jonas d. Jun 21, 1874
Arrhenius, Svante August b. Feb 19, 1859
Bergman, Ingmar b. Jul 14, 1918
Celsius, Anders b. Nov 27, 1701
Lindfors, Viveca b. Dec 29, 1920
Linnaeus, Carolus d. Jan 10, 1778
Myrdal, Alva Reimer b. Jan 31, 1902
Varmland, Sweden
Ericsson, John b. Jul 31, 1803
Vastby, Sweden
Falldin, Thorbjorn Nils Olof
b. Apr 24, 1926
Vasteras, Sweden
Svanholm, Set b. Sep 2, 1904
Zetterling, Mai Elisabeth b. May 24, 1925
Vaversunda, Sweden
Berzelius, Jons Jacob, Baron
b. Aug 29, 1779
Vaxholm, Sweden
Gripe, Maria b. Jul 25, 1923
Vaxjo, Sweden
Lagerkvist, Par b. May 23, 1891
Willander, Mats b. Aug 22, 1964
Vimmerby, Sweden
Lindgren, Astrid b. Nov 14, 1907
West Karup, Sweden
Nilsson, Birgit b. May 17, 1918
Wexio, Sweden
Nilsson, Christine b. Aug 20, 1843
Ystad, Sweden
Nilsson, Anna Q(uerentia) b. Mar 30, 1888

SWITZERLAND

Brunhoff, Jean de d. Oct 16, 1937
Chevrolet, Louis Joseph b. Dec 25, 1878
Corena, Fernando d. Nov 26, 1984
Kruger, Paul (Stephanus Johannes Paulus)
d. Jul 14, 1904
LeCorbusier b. Oct 6, 1887
Muller, Bobby (Robert) b. Jul 27, 1945
Necker, Jacques d. Apr 4, 1804
Norena, Eide d. Nov 19, 1968
Aargau, Switzerland
Pestalozzi, Johann Heinrich
d. Feb 17, 1827
Adelbosen, Switzerland
King, Francis Henry b. Mar 4, 1923
Aldenbogen, Switzerland
Sabatini, Rafael b. Feb 13, 1950

Ascona, Switzerland
Kaiser, Georg d. Jun 5, 1945
Ludwig, Emil d. Sep 17, 1948
Axenstein, Switzerland
Schnabel, Artur d. Aug 15, 1951
Basel, Switzerland
Arp, Hans d. Jun 7, 1966
Barth, Karl b. May 10, 1886
Barth, Karl d. Dec 9, 1966
Bernoulli, David d. Mar 17, 1782
Bocklin, Arnold b. Oct 16, 1827
Burckhardt, Carl Jacob b. Sep 10, 1891
Erasmus, Desiderius d. Jul 12, 1536
Euler, Leonhard b. Apr 15, 1707
Fricsay, Ferenc d. Feb 20, 1963
Haug, Hans b. Jul 27, 1900
Jaspers, Karl d. Feb 26, 1969
Jung, Carl Gustav b. Jul 26, 1875
Keller, Marthe b. 1946
Piccard, Auguste b. Jan 28, 1884
Piccard, Jean Felix b. Jan 28, 1884
Sacher, Paul b. Apr 28, 1906
Witz, Konrad d. 1447
Bern, Switzerland
Andress, Ursula b. Mar 19, 1936
Bakunin, Mikhail Aleksandrovich
d. Jul 13, 1876
Gold, Harry b. 1910
Klee, Paul b. Dec 18, 1879
Tarsis, Valery Yakovlevich d. Mar 3, 1983
Tussaud, (Marie Gresholtz), Madame
b. Dec 7, 1760
Wyss, Johann David b. 1743
Boudry Neuch, Switzerland
Marat, Jean Paul b. 1743
Brunnen, Switzerland
Schoech, Othmar b. Sep 1, 1886
Burgdorf, Switzerland
DellaCasa, Lisa b. Feb 1, 1919
Celigny, Switzerland
Pareto, Vilfredo d. Aug 19, 1923
Chateau D'Oex, Switzerland
Niven, (James) David Graham
d. Jul 29, 1983
Chene-Bourg, Switzerland
Lipatti, Dinu d. Dec 2, 1950
Chur, Switzerland
Giacometti, Alberto d. Jan 11, 1966
Corre, Switzerland
Clarke, Harry d. 1931
Davos, Switzerland
Kirchner, Ernst Ludwig d. Jun 15, 1938
Powys, Llewelyn d. Dec 2, 1939
Shaw, Irwin d. May 16, 1984
Taeuber-Arp, Sophie b. Jan 19, 1889
Einsiedelin, Switzerland
Paracelsus, Philippus Aureolus
b. Nov 10, 1493
Eysins, Switzerland
Snow, Edgar Parks d. Feb 15, 1972

Feuerthalen, Switzerland
  Sutermeister, Heinrich b. Aug 12, 1910
Geneva, Switzerland
  Abernethy, Robert Gordon b. Nov 5, 1927
  Aga Khan IV b. Dec 13, 1936
  Ansermet, Ernest Alexandre
    d. Feb 20, 1969
  Best, Edna d. Sep 18, 1974
  Bloch, Ernest b. Jul 24, 1880
  Borges, Jorge Luis d. Jun 14, 1986
  Burton, Kate (Katherine) b. Sep 10, 1957
  Burton, Richard d. Aug 5, 1984
  Calvin, John d. May 27, 1564
  Casaubon, Isaac b. Feb 8, 1559
  Corena, Fernando b. Dec 22, 1923
  Coubertin, Pierre de, Baron d. Sep 1, 1937
  Davy, Humphrey, Sir d. May 29, 1829
  Dillon, (Clarence) Douglas
    b. Aug 21, 1909
  Dunant, Jean Henri b. May 8, 1828
  Fournier, Pierre d. Jan 8, 1986
  Gallatin, Albert (Abraham Alfonse Albert)
    b. Jan 29, 1761
  Ginastera, Alberto d. Jun 25, 1983
  Giroud, Francoise b. Sep 21, 1916
  Graf, Herbert d. Apr 1973
  Kreutzer, Rodolphe d. Jan 6, 1831
  Krips, Josef d. Oct 12, 1974
  Liotard, Jean-Etienne b. 1702
  Liotard, Jean-Etienne d. 1789
  Ludlow, Fitz Hugh d. Sep 12, 1870
  Martin, Frank b. Sep 15, 1890
  Milhaud, Darius d. Jun 22, 1974
  Necker, Jacques b. Sep 30, 1732
  Pictet, Raoul-Pierre b. Apr 4, 1846
  Plante, Jacques (Joseph Jacques Omer)
    d. Feb 27, 1986
  Rousseau, Jean Jacques b. Jun 28, 1712
  Rubinstein, Arthur d. Dec 20, 1982
  Servetus, Michael d. Oct 27, 1553
  Silone, Ignazio d. 1978
  Umberto II d. Mar 18, 1983
  Visser T Hooft, Willem Adolf
    d. Jul 4, 1985
Glion, Switzerland
  Cronin, A(rchibald) J(oseph)
    d. Jan 6, 1981
Greifensee, Switzerland
  Bodmer, Johann Jakob b. Jul 19, 1698
Heiden, Switzerland
  Dunant, Jean Henri d. Oct 30, 1910
Herisau, Switzerland
  Rorschach, Hermann d. Apr 2, 1922
Hirzel, Switzerland
  Spyri, Johanna Heuser b. Jun 12, 1827
Kappel, Switzerland
  Zwingli, Huldreich d. Oct 10, 1531
Kilchberg, Switzerland
  Keller, Gottfried d. Jul 16, 1890
Konolfingen, Switzerland
  Durrenmatt, Friedrich b. Jan 5, 1921

Kreuzlingen, Switzerland
  Binswanger, Ludwig b. Apr 13, 1881
Lake Constance, Switzerland
  Flick, Friedrich d. Jul 20, 1972
Langenthal, Switzerland
  Holliger, Heinz b. May 21, 1939
Langnau, Switzerland
  Guggenheim, Meyer b. Feb 1, 1828
Lausanne, Switzerland
  Constant de Rebeque, (Henri) Benjamin
    b. Oct 25, 1767
  Flesch, Karl d. Nov 15, 1944
  Furstenberg, Egon von b. Jun 29, 1946
  Kemble, John Philip d. Feb 26, 1823
  Mannerheim, Carl Gustav Emil, Baron
    d. Jan 27, 1951
  Mason, James Neville d. Jul 27, 1984
  May, Edna d. Jan 1, 1948
  Piccard, Auguste d. Mar 1, 1962
  Szymanowski, Karol d. Mar 29, 1937
  Tappy, Eric b. May 19, 1931
  Viollet le Duc, Eugene Emmanuel
    d. Sep 17, 1879
Liestal, Switzerland
  Martinu, Bohuslav d. Aug 28, 1959
  Spitteler, Karl Friedrich Georg
    b. Apr 24, 1845
Locarno, Switzerland
  George, Stefan Anton d. Dec 4, 1933
  Madariaga (y Rojo), Salvador de
    d. Dec 14, 1978
  Remarque, Erich Maria d. Sep 25, 1970
  Richter, Hans d. Feb 1, 1976
Locle, Switzerland
  Tschirky, Oscar b. Sep 28, 1866
Lucerne, Switzerland
  DeWohl, Louis d. Jun 2, 1961
  Ducloux, Walter b. Apr 17, 1913
  Scribner, Charles d. Aug 26, 1871
  Spitteler, Karl Friedrich Georg
    d. Dec 28, 1924
  Szigeti, Joseph d. Feb 20, 1973
Magliasco, Switzerland
  Onegin, Sigrid d. Jun 16, 1943
Marbach, Switzerland
  Reichmann, Theodor d. May 22, 1903
Marengo, Switzerland
  Delmonico, Lorenzo b. Mar 13, 1813
Montagnola, Switzerland
  Hesse, Hermann d. Aug 9, 1962
Montreux, Switzerland
  Kokoschka, Oskar d. Feb 22, 1980
  Nabokov, Vladimir d. Jul 2, 1977
Motier, Switzerland
  Agassiz, Louis (Jean Louis Radolphe)
    b. May 28, 1807
Mumpf, Switzerland
  Rachel b. Feb 28, 1820
Muralto, Switzerland
  Fromm, Erich d. Mar 18, 1980
  Klee, Paul d. Jun 29, 1940

Muzot, Switzerland
  Rilke, Rainer Maria d. Dec 29, 1926
Nant Corsier, Switzerland
  Huberman, Bronislaw d. Jun 16, 1947
Neuchatel, Switzerland
  Bovet, Daniele b. Mar 23, 1907
  Nicolet, Aurele b. 1926
  Piaget, Jean b. Aug 9, 1896
Payerne, Switzerland
  Chessex, Jacques b. Mar 1, 1934
Riesbach, Switzerland
  Bodmer, Karl b. Feb 6, 1809
Rolle, Switzerland
  Bouquet, Henry b. 1719
Rorschach, Switzerland
  Jannings, Emil b. Jul 26, 1886
Saint Gallen, Switzerland
  Maag, Peter b. 1919
Saint Moritz, Switzerland
  Kreuger, Kurt b. Jul 23, 1917
Schaffhausen, Switzerland
  Ammann, Othmar Hermann
    b. Mar 26, 1876
Schwyz, Switzerland
  Marty, Martin b. Jan 12, 1834
Solothurn, Switzerland
  Kosciuszko, Thaddeus d. Nov 15, 1817
  Ratoff, Gregory d. Dec 14, 1960
Stampa, Switzerland
  Giacometti, Alberto b. Oct 10, 1901
Stiebschen, Switzerland
  Wagner, Siegfried (Helferich)
    b. Jan 6, 1869
Sursee, Switzerland
  Kung, Hans b. Mar 19, 1928
Triebschen, Switzerland
  Hauk, Minnie d. Feb 6, 1929
Tschingel, Switzerland
  Gallup, George Horace d. Jul 26, 1984
Uznach, Switzerland
  Hofmann, Albert b. Feb 27, 1933
Versoix, Switzerland
  Aga Khan III d. Jul 11, 1957
Vevey, Switzerland
  Ansermet, Ernest Alexandre
    b. Nov 11, 1883
  Baclanova, Olga d. Sep 6, 1974
  Chaplin, Charlie d. Dec 25, 1977
  Courbet, Gustave d. Dec 31, 1877
  Scholes, Percy Alfred d. Aug 2, 1958
  Sienkiewicz, Henryk d. Nov 15, 1916
Vinzel, Switzerland
  Burckhardt, Carl Jacob d. Mar 3, 1974
Visp, Switzerland
  Zuckmayer, Carl d. Jan 18, 1977
Vulpera, Switzerland
  Schmid, Eduard d. Aug 31, 1966
Winterthur, Switzerland
  Weingartner, Felix d. May 7, 1942
Zofingen, Switzerland
  VonDaeniken, Erich b. Apr 14, 1935

Zug, Switzerland
  Dornier, Claude d. Dec 5, 1969
Zuort, Switzerland
  Mengelberg, Willem (Josef Willem)
    d. Mar 22, 1951
Zurich, Switzerland
  Anda, Geza d. Jun 13, 1976
  Bloch, Felix b. Oct 23, 1905
  Bloch, Felix d. Sep 10, 1983
  Bodmer, Johann Jakob d. Jan 2, 1783
  Brunner, Emil d. Apr 6, 1966
  Doolittle, Hilda d. Sep 27, 1961
  Dubin, Al b. Jun 10, 1891
  Frisch, Max b. May 15, 1911
  Fuseli, Henry b. Feb 7, 1741
  Ganz, Rudolph b. Feb 24, 1877
  Joyce, James Augustus Aloysius
    d. Jan 13, 1941
  Jung, Carl Gustav d. Jun 6, 1961
  Karrar, Paul d. Jun 18, 1971
  Keller, Gottfried b. Jul 19, 1819
  Kempe, Rudolf d. May 11, 1976
  Kleiber, Erich d. Jan 27, 1956
  Klemperer, Otto d. Jul 6, 1973
  Kubler-Ross, Elisabeth b. Jul 8, 1926
  Lavater, Johann Casper b. Nov 15, 1741
  Lavater, Johann Casper d. Jan 2, 1801
  Liebermann, Rolf b. Sep 14, 1910
  Mann, Erika d. Aug 27, 1969
  Mann, Thomas d. Aug 12, 1955
  Norden, Carl Lukas d. Jun 15, 1965
  Pestalozzi, Johann Heinrich
    b. Jan 12, 1746
  Rickenbacker, Eddie (Edward Vernon)
    d. Jul 23, 1973
  Rorschach, Hermann b. Nov 8, 1884
  Schoech, Othmar d. Mar 8, 1957
  Spyri, Johanna Heuser d. Jul 7, 1901
  Stiedry, Fritz d. Aug 9, 1968
  Taeuber-Arp, Sophie d. Jan 13, 1943
  Varviso, Silvio b. Feb 26, 1924
  Vollenweider, Andreas b. 1953

SYRIA

Alep, Syria
  Carzou, Jean b. Jan 1, 1907
Emesa, Syria
  Heliogabalus b. 204
Germanicia, Syria
  Nestorius b. 389
Jazzini, Syria
  Haggar, Joseph M b. 1892
Qardaha, Syria
  Assad, Hafez al b. Oct 6, 1930
Samosato, Syria
  Lucian b. 125

TAHITI

Papeete, Tahiti
  Hall, James Norman d. Jul 6, 1951

TAIWAN

Taipei, Taiwan
Aylward, Gladys d. Jan 3, 1970
Chiang Kai-Shek d. Apr 5, 1975
Wang Shih-chieh d. Apr 1981

TANGANYIKA

Butiama, Tanganyika
Nyerere, Julius Kambarage
b. Mar 1922

TASMANIA

Hobart, Tasmania
Oberon, Merle b. Feb 19, 1911

THAILAND

Bangkok, Thailand
Merton, Thomas d. Dec 10, 1968
Osborne, Adam b. Mar 6, 1939
Meklong, Thailand
Chang and Eng b. May 11, 1811
Tak, Thailand
Kittikachorn, Thanom b. Aug 11, 1911

TIBET

Chhija Nangso, Tibet
Dalai Lama, the 14th Incarnate
b. Jul 6, 1935

TRANSYLVANIA

Sighet, Transylvania
Wiesel, Elie(zer) b. Sep 30, 1928

TRINIDAD

Clarke, Ellis Emmanuel
b. Dec 28, 1917
Guy, Rosa Cuthbert b. Sep 1, 1928
Holder, Geoffrey b. Sep 1, 1930
Julian, Hubert Fauntleroy b. 1897
Mallory, Stephen R b. 1812
Ocean, Billy b. Jan 21, 1950
Selvon, Samuel Dirkson b. May 20, 1923
Port of Spain, Trinidad
Scott, Hazel Dorothy b. Jun 11, 1920
Williams, Eric Eustace b. Sep 25, 1911
Williams, Eric Eustace d. Mar 29, 1981

TUNISIA

Monastir, Tunisia
Bourguiba, Habib Ben Ali b. Aug 3, 1903
Tunis, Tunisia
Louis IX d. Aug 25, 1270
Morrice, James Wilson d. Jan 23, 1924
Payne, John Howard d. Apr 9, 1852

TURKEY

Gulbenkian, Calouste S b. 1869
Alasehir, Turkey
Evren, Kenan b. 1918
Ankara, Turkey
Inonu, Ismet d. Dec 25, 1973
Antioch, Turkey
Adams, Walter Sydney b. Dec 20, 1876
Apana, Turkey
Enver Pasha b. Nov 23, 1881
Bukhara, Turkey
Enver Pasha d. Aug 4, 1922
Constantinople, Turkey
Chenier, Marie-Andre de b. Oct 30, 1762
Grosvenor, Gilbert Hovey b. Oct 28, 1875
Kazan, Elia b. Sep 7, 1909
Milder-Hauptmann, Pauline Anna
b. Dec 13, 1785
Rossi-Lemeni, Nicola b. Nov 6, 1920
Schildkraut, Rudolph b. 1865
Farghana, Turkey
Babur b. Feb 14, 1483
Islamkoy, Turkey
Demirel, Suleyman b. Oct 6, 1924
Istanbul, Turkey
Athenagoras I d. Jul 6, 1972
Cornfeld, Bernard b. Aug 17, 1927
Ecevit, Bulent b. May 28, 1925
Ertegun, Ahmet b. Jul 31, 1923
Lange, Hans b. Feb 14, 1884
Riklis, Mishulam b. Dec 2, 1924
Sunay, Cevdet d. May 22, 1982
Malatya, Turkey
Ozal, Turgut b. 1927
Malatya Hekinhan, Turkey
Agca, Mehmet Ali b. 1958
Marash, Turkey
Bagdikian, Ben Haig b. Jun 30, 1920
Phanar, Turkey
Zaharoff, Basil, Sir b. 1850
Salonika, Turkey
Ataturk, Kemal b. 1880
Smyrna, Turkey
Brewer, David Josiah b. Jun 20, 1837
Nikolaidi, Elena b. Jun 13, 1909
Onassis, Aristotle Socrates b. Jan 15, 1906
Trabzon, Turkey
Sunay, Cevdet b. Feb 10, 1900

U.S.S.R.

Dzerzhinsky, Felix Edmundovich d. 1926
Halfin, Eliezer b. 1948
Haywood, "Big Bill" (William Dudley)
d. May 18, 1928
Kharlamov, Valeri d. 1981
Kogan, Leonid Borisovich d. Dec 17, 1982
Kornilov, Lavr Georgyevich
d. Apr 13, 1918

Kropotkin, Peter Alekseyevich, Prince
d. Feb 8, 1921
Kubasov, Valery Nikolaevich
b. Jan 7, 1935
Lonsdale, Gordon Arnold b. 1922
Lysenko, Trofim Denisovich
d. Nov 20, 1976
Press, Tamara b. May 10, 1937
Rodnina, Irina b. 1949
Saneev, Viktor b. Oct 3, 1945
Shukshin, Vasilii Makarovich b. 1929
Slavin, Mark b. 1954
Tretyak, Vladislav b. Apr 25, 1952
Vysotsky, Vladimir Semyonovich b. 1938
Amavir, U.S.S.R.
Avakian, George b. Mar 15, 1919
Baku, U.S.S.R.
Kasparov, Garry Kimovich
b. Apr 13, 1963
Rostropovich, Mstislav Leopoldovich
b. Aug 12, 1927
Bar, U.S.S.R.
Timerman, Jacobo b. Jan 6, 1923
Barnaul, U.S.S.R.
Streich, Rita b. Dec 18, 1920
Bessarabia, U.S.S.R.
Bertini, Gary b. May 1, 1927
Byelozerka, U.S.S.R.
Bondarchuk, Sergei b. Sep 25, 1922
Dnepropetrovsk, U.S.S.R.
Kogan, Leonid Borisovich b. Oct 14, 1924
Dubrowna, U.S.S.R.
Zeitlin, Zvi b. Feb 21, 1923
Dzhizak, U.S.S.R.
Rashidov, Sharaf Rashidovich
b. Nov 6, 1917
Ekaterinburg, U.S.S.R.
Alexandra Feodorovna d. Jul 16, 1918
Nicholas II d. Jul 16, 1918
Romanov, Anastasia d. Jul 16, 1918
Estonia, U.S.S.R.
Schmemann, Alexander b. 1921
Gorki, U.S.S.R.
Ashkenazy, Vladimir Davidovich
b. Jul 6, 1937
Lenin, Nikolai d. Jan 21, 1924
Gorlovka, U.S.S.R.
Shevchenko, Arkady Nikolayevich
b. Oct 11, 1930
Grodno, U.S.S.R.
Korbut, Olga b. May 16, 1955
Grozny, U.S.S.R.
Turischeva, Ludmila b. Oct 7, 1952
Gzhatsk, U.S.S.R.
Gagarin, Yuri Alexseyevich b. Mar 9, 1934
Irkutsk, U.S.S.R.
Nureyev, Rudolf b. Mar 17, 1938
Kalzan, U.S.S.R.
Arbuzov, Aleksandr d. Jan 22, 1968
Kharkov, U.S.S.R.
Schneider, Alan b. Dec 12, 1917

Kiev, U.S.S.R.
Kuznetsov, Anatoli b. Aug 18, 1929
Podgorny, Nikolai Viktorovich
d. Jan 11, 1983
Kislovodsk, U.S.S.R.
Solzhenitsyn, Aleksandr Isayevich
b. Dec 11, 1918
Krasnaya Gorka, U.S.S.R.
Dobrynin, Anatoly Fedorovich
b. Nov 16, 1919
Kreminiecz, U.S.S.R.
Stern, Isaac b. Jul 21, 1920
Kuntsevo, U.S.S.R.
Andropov, Yuri Vladimirovich
d. Feb 9, 1984
Leningrad, U.S.S.R.
Berman, Lazar b. Feb 26, 1930
Brodsky, Joseph Alexandrovich
b. May 24, 1940
Esenin, Sergei Aleksandrovich
d. Dec 28, 1925
Ginzburg, Aleksandr Ilich b. 1936
Kuprin, Aleksandr Ivanovich
d. Oct 25, 1938
Makarova, Natalia b. Nov 21, 1940
Malevich, Kasimir Severinovich
d. May 15, 1935
Pavlov, Ivan Petrovich d. Feb 27, 1936
Plekhanov, Georgi Valentinovich
d. May 30, 1918
Protopopov, Oleg Alekseevich
b. Jul 16, 1932
Rudenko, Lyudmila d. Mar 2, 1986
Shafran, Daniel b. Feb 13, 1923
Spassky, Boris Vasilyevich b. Jan 30, 1937
Szewinska, Irena b. May 24, 1946
Vishnevskaya, Galina (Pavlovna)
b. Oct 25, 1926
Listvyanka, U.S.S.R.
Leonov, Alexei Arkhipovich
b. May 30, 1934
Mamati, U.S.S.R.
Shevardnadze, Eduard Amvrosiyevich
b. Jan 25, 1928
Melitopol, U.S.S.R.
Chukrai, Grigori b. 1921
Moscow, U.S.S.R.
Abel, Rudolf Ivanovich d. Nov 15, 1971
Akhmatova, Anna, pseud. d. Mar 5, 1966
Alexandrov, Grigori d. Dec 19, 1983
Amalrik, Andrei Alekseyevich
b. May 12, 1938
Arbatov, Georgi b. May 19, 1923
Bely, Andrey, pseud. d. Jan 8, 1934
Brezhnev, Leonid Ilyich d. Nov 10, 1982
Bukovsky, Vladimir b. Dec 30, 1942
Bulgakov, Mikhail d. 1940
Bulganin, Nikolai Aleksandrovich
d. Feb 24, 1975
Burgess, Guy Francis de Moncy d. 1963

Chernenko, Konstantin Ustinovich
 d. Mar 10, 1985
Chuikov, Vasili Ivanovitch
 d. Mar 18, 1982
Chukovsky, Korney Ivanovich
 d. Oct 28, 1969
Eglevsky, Andre b. Dec 21, 1917
Ehrenburg, Ilya Grigoryevich
 d. Aug 31, 1967
Eisenstein, Sergei Mikhailovich
 d. Feb 10, 1948
Fedin, Konstantin d. Jul 15, 1977
Flynn, Elizabeth Gurley d. Sep 5, 1964
Foster, William Zebulon d. Sep 1, 1961
Furtseva, Ekaterina Alexeyevna
 d. Oct 25, 1974
Gagarin, Yuri Alexseyevich
 d. Mar 27, 1968
Gerasimov, Innokentii Petrovich
 d. Mar 30, 1985
Gerasimov, Sergei Appolinarievich
 d. Nov 28, 1985
Gilels, Emil Grigorevich d. Oct 14, 1985
Gliere, Reinhold Moritzovich
 d. Jun 23, 1956
Gorbatov, Aleksandr Vassil'evich
 d. Dec 7, 1973
Gorky, Maxim, pseud. d. Jun 18, 1936
Grechko, Andrei Antonovick
 d. Apr 26, 1976
Ilyushin, Sergei Vladimirovich
 d. Feb 9, 1977
Ippolitov-Ivanov, Mikhail Mikhailovich
 d. Jan 26, 1935
Kalatozov, Mikhail d. Mar 28, 1973
Kalinin, Mikhail d. Jun 3, 1946
Kapitsa, Pyotr d. Apr 8, 1984
Khachaturian, Aram d. May 1, 1978
Khaikin, Boris d. May 11, 1978
Kharitonov, Yevgeni d. Jun 29, 1981
Khrushchev, Nikita Sergeyevich
 d. Sep 11, 1971
Khrushchev, Nina Petrovna
 d. Aug 8, 1984
Konev, Ivan S d. May 21, 1973
Korinetz, Yuri b. Jan 14, 1923
Kosygin, Aleksei Nikolaevich
 d. Dec 19, 1980
Landau, Lev Davidovich d. Apr 2, 1968
Litvinov, Maxim d. Dec 31, 1951
Lonsdale, Gordon Arnold d. Oct 9, 1970
Maclean, Donald Duart d. Mar 6, 1983
Malik, Yakov Alexandrovich
 d. Feb 11, 1980
Malinovsky, Rodion Y d. Mar 13, 1967
Mandelstam, Nadezhda Yakovlevna
 d. Dec 29, 1980
Mayakovsky, Vladimir d. Aug 14, 1930
Mikoyan, Artem I d. Dec 9, 1970
Mintz, Shlomo b. Oct 30, 1957

Nemirovich-Danchenko, Vladimir I
 d. Apr 25, 1943
Papanin, Ivan D d. Jan 30, 1980
Pasternak, Boris Leonidovich
 d. May 29, 1960
Petrosian, Tigran Vartanovich
 d. Aug 13, 1984
Plisetskaya, Maya Mikhailovna
 b. Nov 20, 1925
Popov, Oleg Konstantinovich
 b. Aug 3, 1930
Prokofiev, Sergei Sergeevich
 d. Mar 5, 1953
Rokossovsky, Konstantin d. Aug 3, 1968
Romm, Mikhail d. Nov 1, 1971
Rozhdestvensky, Gennadi Nikolaevich
 b. 1931
Rubin, Vitalii b. Sep 14, 1923
Sakharov, Andrei Dmitrievich
 b. May 21, 1921
Shalamov, Varlam Tikhonovich
 d. Jan 17, 1982
Shchedrin, Rodion Konstantinovich
 b. Dec 16, 1932
Shklovsky, Iosif Samvilovitch
 d. Mar 3, 1985
Shostakovich, Dmitri Dmitryevich
 d. Aug 9, 1975
Shukshin, Vasilii Makarovich
 d. Oct 2, 1974
Sinyavsky, Andrei b. Oct 8, 1925
Smyslov, Vasili Vasil'evich b. Mar 23, 1921
Stalin, Joseph d. Mar 5, 1953
Stalina, Svetlana Alliluyeva
 b. Feb 28, 1926
Stanislavsky, Konstantin Sergeyevich
 d. Aug 7, 1938
Suslov, Mikhail Andreevich
 d. Jan 26, 1982
Timoshenko, Semen Konstantinovich
 d. Mar 31, 1970
Tolstoy, Alexey Nikolaevich
 d. Feb 22, 1945
Trifonov, Yuri Valentinovich
 b. Aug 28, 1925
Trifonov, Yuri Valentinovich
 d. Mar 21, 1981
Vassilenko, Sergei d. Mar 11, 1956
Voroshilov, Kliment Efremovich
 d. Dec 2, 1968
Vysotsky, Vladimir Semyonovich
 d. Jul 25, 1980
Wallenberg, Raoul Gustav d. Jul 17, 1947
Zabolotskii, Nikolai Alekseevich
 d. Oct 14, 1958
Zhukov, Georgi Konstantinovich
 d. Jun 18, 1974
Zinoviev, Grigori Evseevich
 d. Aug 25, 1936

Odessa, U.S.S.R.
Dobrovolsky, Georgi b. 1928
Oistrakh, Igor Davidovich b. Apr 27, 1931
Petrograd, U.S.S.R.
Blok, Aleksandr Aleksandrovich
d. Sep 7, 1921
Petrovichi, U.S.S.R.
Asimov, Isaac b. Jan 2, 1920
Polatava, U.S.S.R.
Korolenko, Vladimir Galaktionovich
d. 1921
Privolnoye, U.S.S.R.
Gorbachev, Mikhail S b. Mar 2, 1931
Riga, U.S.S.R.
Baryshnikov, Mikhail b. Jan 28, 1948
D'Albert, Eugene d. Mar 3, 1932
Pudovkin, Vsevolod d. Jun 30, 1953
Tal, Mikhail Nekhemyevich b. 1936
Saint Petersburg, U.S.S.R.
Cui, Cesar Antonovich d. Mar 24, 1918
Sakhalin, U.S.S.R.
Godunov, Alexander (Boris Alexander)
b. Nov 28, 1949
Shorshely, U.S.S.R.
Nikolayev, Andrian G b. Sep 5, 1929
Siberia, U.S.S.R.
Babel, Isaac Emmanuelovich d. 1941
Kulish, Mykola d. 1942
Snovsk, U.S.S.R.
Olitski, Jules b. Mar 27, 1922
Tbilisi, U.S.S.R.
Petrosian, Tigran Vartanovich
b. Jun 17, 1929
Tiflis, U.S.S.R.
Medvedev, Zhores Aleksandrovich
b. Nov 14, 1925
Ter-Arutunian, Rouben b. Jul 24, 1920
Ukraine, U.S.S.R.
Shcharansky, Anatoly Borisovich
b. Jan 20, 1948
Ulyanousk, U.S.S.R.
Protopopov, Ludmilla Evgenievna
Belousova b. Nov 22, 1935
Ventsy Zarja, U.S.S.R.
Gorbatko, Viktor Vasiliyevich
b. Dec 3, 1934
Veshenskaya, U.S.S.R.
Sholokhov, Mikhail Aleksandrovich
d. Feb 21, 1984
Vilno, U.S.S.R.
Panov, Valery b. Mar 12, 1938
Vladivostok, U.S.S.R.
Mandelshtam, Osip Emilyevich
d. Dec 28, 1938
Voronezh, U.S.S.R.
Feoktistov, Konstantin Petrovich
b. Feb 7, 1926
Yalta, U.S.S.R.
Rebikov, Vladimir Ivanovich
d. Dec 1, 1920

Yelabuga, U.S.S.R.
Tsvetayeva, Marina Ivanovna
d. Aug 31, 1941
Zima, U.S.S.R.
Evtushenko, Evgeniy Alexandrovich
b. Jul 18, 1933
Zlatoust, U.S.S.R.
Karpov, Anatoly Yevgenyevich
b. May 23, 1951

UGANDA

Akokoro, Uganda
Obote, Milton (Apollo Milton) b. 1924
Entebbe, Uganda
Netanyahu, Yonatan d. Jul 3, 1976
Koboko, Uganda
Amin, Idi b. 1925

UKRAINE

Chechelnik, Ukraine
Lispector, Clarice b. Dec 10, 1925

UPPER VOLTA

Dianra Tougan, Upper Volta
Lamizana, Sangoule b. 1916

URUGUAY

Montevideo, Uruguay
Frasconi, Antonio b. Apr 28, 1919
Laforgue, Jules b. Aug 16, 1860
Lautreamont, Comte de, pseud.
b. Apr 4, 1846
Salto, Uruguay
Quiroga, Horacio b. Dec 31, 1878

VENEZUELA

Carlos b. 1947
Acarigua, Venezuela
Herrera Campins, Luis b. May 4, 1925
Angostura, Venezuela
Perry, Oliver Hazard, Admiral
d. Aug 23, 1819
Caracas, Venezuela
Bolivar, Simon b. Jul 24, 1783
Gagn, Reynaldo b. Aug 9, 1875
Gallegos, Romulo b. Aug 2, 1884
Gallegos, Romulo d. Apr 4, 1969
Miranda, Francisco de b. 1750
Perez de la Cova, Carlos b. Apr 27, 1904
Cumana, Venezuela
Sucre, Antonio J de b. 1795
Guatire, Venezuela
Betancourt, Romulo b. Feb 22, 1908
Maracaibo, Venezuela
Aparicio, Luis Ernesto b. Apr 29, 1934

Ocumare del Tuy, Venezuela
Guillen, Ozzie (Oswaldo Jose)
b. Jan 20, 1964
Tachira, Venezuela
Perez Jimenez, Marcos b. Apr 25, 1914

VIETNAM

Fall, Bernard B d. Feb 21, 1967
Le Duc Tho b. Oct 14, 1911
Chulai, Vietnam
Chapelle, Dickey d. Nov 4, 1965
Da Lat, Vietnam
Pisier, Marie-France b. May 1946
Hanoi, Vietnam
Capa, Robert d. May 25, 1954
Le Duan d. Jul 10, 1986
Thang, Ton Duc d. Mar 30, 1980
Ton-duc-thong d. 1980
Xuan Thuy b. Sep 2, 1912
Kim Lien, Vietnam
Ho Chi Minh b. May 19, 1890
Long Xuyen Province, Vietnam
Thang, Ton Duc b. Aug 20, 1888
My Tho, Vietnam
Duong Van Minh b. Feb 19, 1916
Quang Nam, Vietnam
Pham van Dong b. Mar 1, 1906
Quang Tri Province, Vietnam
Le Duan b. 1907
Quangblin, Vietnam
Giap, Vo Nguyen b. Sep 1, 1912
Saigon, Vietnam
Dumurq, Charles b. 1944
Ut, Huynh Cong b. Mar 29, 1951
Son Tay, Vietnam
Ky, Nguyen Cao b. Sep 8, 1930

VIETNAM (NORTH)

Hanoi, Vietnam (North)
Ho Chi Minh d. Sep 3, 1969

VIRGIN ISLANDS

Griffith, Emile Alphonse b. Feb 3, 1938
Innis, Roy b. Jun 6, 1934
Frederiksted, Virgin Islands
Irvin, Rea d. May 28, 1972
Saint Croix, Virgin Islands
Spectorsky, Auguste Compte
d. Jan 17, 1972

WALES

Arundel, Honor Morfydd b. Aug 15, 1919
Dalton, Timothy b. 1944
Flanders, Michael d. Apr 14, 1975
Jones, Glyn b. Feb 28, 1905
Powys, John Cowper d. Jun 17, 1963
Russell, Bertrand Arthur William
d. Feb 2, 1970

Abergavenny, Wales
Pym, Francis Leslie b. Feb 13, 1922
Abersychan, Wales
Jenkins, Roy Harris b. Nov 11, 1920
Aberystwyth, Wales
Rees, Roger b. May 5, 1944
Anglesey, Wales
Griffith, Hugh Emrys b. May 30, 1912
Barry, Wales
Livesey, Roger b. Jun 25, 1906
Bettws, Wales
Phillips, Sian b. May 14, 1934
Blackwood, Wales
Jones, Gwynn b. May 24, 1907
Price, Margaret Berenice b. Apr 13, 1941
Brecknock, Wales
Kemble, Charles b. Nov 25, 1775
Patti, Adelina Juana Maria
d. Sep 27, 1919
Brecon, Wales
Siddons, Sarah Kemble b. Jul 5, 1755
Caenarvon, Wales
Leonowens, Anna Harriette Crawford
b. Nov 5, 1834
Cardiff, Wales
Abse, Dannie b. Sep 22, 1923
Bassey, Shirley b. Jan 8, 1937
Cudlipp, Hugh b. Aug 28, 1913
Edmunds, Dave b. Apr 15, 1944
Follett, Ken(neth Martin) b. Jun 5, 1949
Lewis, Saunders d. Sep 1, 1985
Novello, Ivor b. Jan 15, 1893
O'Shea, Tessie b. Mar 13, 1918
Ready, William Bernard b. Sep 16, 1914
Templeton, Alec b. Jul 4, 1910
Thomas, Craig D b. Nov 24, 1942
Thomas, Gwyn d. Apr 13, 1981
Thomas, James William Tudor
d. Jan 23, 1976
Thomas, Ronald Stuart b. 1913
Carmarthen, Wales
Steele, Richard, Sir d. Sep 1, 1729
Colwyn Bay, Wales
Jones, Terry b. Feb 1, 1942
Denbigh, Wales
Stanley, Henry Morton, Sir
b. Jan 31, 1841
Glamorgan, Wales
Baker, Stanley, Sir b. Feb 28, 1928
Gwenn, Edmund b. Sep 26, 1875
Haverfordwest, Wales
John, Gwendolyn Mary b. 1876
Henfynw, Wales
David, Saint b. 495
Llandaff, Wales
Dahl, Roald b. Sep 13, 1916
Lewis, Francis b. Mar 21, 1713
Llanelly, Wales
Roberts, Rachel b. Sep 20, 1927
Swann, Donald Ibrahim b. 1923

Llansantfraed, Wales
Vaughan, Henry b. Apr 17, 1622
Llanystumdwy, Wales
Lloyd George of Dwyfor, David Lloyd
George, Earl d. Mar 26, 1945
Merioneth, Wales
Hughes, Richard Arthur Warren
d. Apr 28, 1976
Merthyr Tydfil, Wales
Ashley, Laura Mountney b. Sep 7, 1925
Berry, James Gomer b. May 7, 1883
Milford Haven, Wales
Symons, Arthur b. Feb 28, 1865
Mostyn, Wales
Williams, Emlyn (George Emlyn)
b. Nov 26, 1905
Mynyw, Wales
David, Saint d. 589
Neath, Wales
Gwilym, Mike b. Mar 5, 1949
Milland, Ray(mond Alton) b. Jan 3, 1908
Newport, Wales
Baxter, Keith b. Apr 29, 1935
Newtown, Wales
Owen, Robert b. May 14, 1771
Owen, Robert d. Nov 17, 1858
Pontnewynydd, Wales
Jones, Gwyneth b. Nov 7, 1936
Pontrhydfen, Wales
Burton, Richard b. Nov 10, 1925
Pontypridd, Wales
Evans, Geraint Llewellyn, Sir
b. Feb 16, 1922
Jones, Tom b. Jun 7, 1940
Port Talbot, Wales
Hopkins, Anthony b. Dec 31, 1937
Howe, (Richard Edward) Geoffrey, Sir
b. Dec 20, 1926
Porth, Wales
Thomas, Gwyn b. Jul 6, 1913
Portmadoc, Wales
Lawrence, T(homas) E(dward)
b. Aug 15, 1888
Prestatyn, Wales
Cummins, Peggy b. Dec 18, 1926
Rhyl, Wales
Ellis, Ruth b. 1927
Saint David's, Wales
Llewellyn, Richard b. Dec 8, 1906
Swansea, Wales
Connolly, Sybil b. Jan 24, 1921
Grove, William Robert, Sir b. Jul 11, 1811
Secombe, Harry b. Sep 8, 1921
Thomas, Dylan Marlais b. Oct 27, 1914
Tyler, Bonnie b. Jun 8, 1953
Taylorstown, Wales
Christopher, Sybil Williams Burton b. 1928
Tenby, Wales
Francis, Dick b. Oct 31, 1920
John, Augustus Edwin b. Jan 4, 1878

Tredegar, Wales
Bevan, Aneurin b. Nov 15, 1897
Kinnock, Neil Gordon b. Mar 28, 1942
Ystradgynlais, Wales
Hopkin, Mary b. May 3, 1950

WEST INDIES

Stephenson, Henry b. Apr 16, 1871
Grenada, West Indies
Gairy, Eric M, Sir b. 1922
Roseau, West Indies
Rhys, Jean b. Aug 24, 1894
Saint Lucia, West Indies
Lewis, Allen Montgomery, Sir
b. Oct 26, 1909

YUGOSLAVIA

Bijedic, Dzemal d. Jan 18, 1977
Elazar, David b. 1925
Popov, Dusko b. 1912
Vlasic, Joseph b. 1904
Belgrade, Yugoslavia
Andric, Ivo d. Mar 13, 1975
Dedijer, Vladimir b. Feb 2, 1914
Konwitschny, Franz d. Jul 27, 1962
Pogorelich, Ivo b. 1959
Simic, Charles b. May 9, 1938
Drnis, Yugoslavia
Planinc, Milka b. 1924
Grebenac, Yugoslavia
Popa, Vasko b. Jul 29, 1922
Ivanjica, Yugoslavia
Mihajlovic, Draza b. 1893
Kolasin, Yugoslavia
Djilas, Milovan b. 1911
Krasic, Yugoslavia
Stepinac, Alojzije, Cardinal
d. Feb 10, 1960
Kumrovec, Yugoslavia
Tito b. May 25, 1892
Ljublijana, Yugoslavia
Tito d. May 4, 1980
Maribor, Yugoslavia
Jausovec, Mima b. Jul 20, 1956
Mostar, Yugoslavia
Bijedic, Dzemal b. Apr 12, 1917
Osijek, Yugoslavia
Seper, Franjo b. Oct 2, 1905
Pancevo, Yugoslavia
Mihajlov, Mihajlo b. Sep 26, 1934
Pisino, Yugoslavia
Dallapiccola, Luigi b. Feb 3, 1904
Sarajevo, Yugoslavia
Franz Ferdinand d. Jun 28, 1914
Skopje, Yugoslavia
Teresa, Mother b. Aug 27, 1910
Slavonski-Brod, Yugoslavia
Slavenska, Mia b. Feb 20, 1916

Split, Yugoslavia
  Rodzinski, Artur b. Jan 2, 1894
Subotica, Yugoslavia
  Simon, John Ivan b. May 12, 1925
Travnik, Yugoslavia
  Andric, Ivo b. Oct 10, 1892
  Jurinac, Sena b. Oct 24, 1921
Trnjani, Yugoslavia
  Rothmuller, Marko A b. Dec 31, 1908
Veskueb, Yugoslavia
  Wolff, Helen b. Jul 27, 1906
Zagreb, Yugoslavia
  Milanov, Zinka Kunc b. May 17, 1906

ZAMBIA

Ilala, Zambia
  Livingstone, David d. May 1, 1873
Lubwa, Zambia
  Kaunda, Kenneth David
    b. Apr 28, 1924

ZIMBABWE

  Price, Nick b. Jan 28, 1957

Occupation Index

ABOLITIONIST

Blackwell, Antoinette Louisa Brown
Brown, John
Channing, William Ellery
Clay, Cassius Marcellus
Coffin, Levi
Comstock, Elizabeth L
Craft, Ellen
Crandall, Prudence
Foster, Abigail Kelley
Garnet, Henry Highland
Garrison, William Lloyd
Larcom, Lucy
Lovejoy, Elijah P
Phillips, Wendell
Russwurm, John Brown
Stevens, Thaddeus
Truth, Sojourner
Tubman, Harriet Ross
Wilberforce, William

ACTING TEACHER

Strasberg, Lee

ACTIVIST

Day, Dorothy

ACTOR

Aames, Willie
Abel, Walter Charles
Abraham, F Murray
Ackland, Joss
Adams, Don
Adams, Edwin
Adams, Mason
Adams, Nick
Addy, Wesley
Adler, Jacob Pavlovitch
Adler, Larry (Lawrence Cecil)
Adler, Luther (Lutha)
Agar, John
Aherne, Brian de Lacy
Akins, Claude

Albert, Eddie
Albert, Edward
Albertson, Frank
Albertson, Jack
Alda, Alan
Alda, Robert
Aldridge, Ira Frederick
Aldridge, Michael
Alexander, Ben (Nicholas Benton)
Allen, Rex E, Sr.
Allen, Steve (Stephen Valentine Patrick
  William)
Allen, Woody
Ameche, Don
Ameche, Jim
Ames, Ed(mund Dantes)
Ames, Leon
Amos, John
Amsterdam, Morey
Anderson, Daryl
Anderson, Eddie
Anderson, Gilbert M
Anderson, Harry
Anderson, Michael, Jr.
Anderson, Richard Norman
Anderson, Warner
Andes, "Keith" John Charles
Andrews, Anthony
Andrews, Dana
Andrews, Edward
Andrews, Harry
Andrews, Tige
Anglim, Philip
Anthony, Tony
Archerd, Army (Armand)
Arkin, Alan Wolf
Arlen, Richard
Arliss, George
Armendariz, Pedro
Armetta, Henry
Armstrong, R G
Armstrong, Robert
Arnaz, Desi
Arnaz, Desi(derio Alberto, IV), Jr.
Arness, James
Arnold, Edward

Arquette, Cliff
Artaud, Antonin
Asner, Ed(ward)
Assante, Armand
Astaire, Fred
Asther, Nils
Astin, John Allen
Astin, Mackenzie Alexander
Atherton, William
Atkins, Christopher
Attenborough, Richard Samuel, Sir
Atwill, Lionel
Auberjonois, Rene Murat
Auer, Mischa
Aumont, Jean-Pierre
Austin, Gene
Autry, Gene (Orvon Gene)
Avalon, Frankie
Axton, Hoyt Wayne
Aykroyd, Dan(iel Edward)
Ayres, Lew
Aznavour, Charles
Baby Leroy
Backus, Jim (James Gilmore)
Bacon, Frank
Bacon, Kevin
Baer, Max
Baer, Max, Jr.
Bailey, Raymond
Bain, Conrad Stafford
Baio, Scott Vincent
Baker, Joe Don
Baker, Kenny
Baker, Kenny (Kenneth Lawrence)
Baker, Stanley, Sir
Bakewell, William
Baldwin, Adam
Balsam, Martin Henry
Bancroft, George
Banks, Leslie
Banks, Monty (Montague)
Bannen, Ian
Bannon, Jim
Barker, Lex (Alexander Crichlow, Jr.)
Barker, Ronnie
Barrault, Jean-Louis
Barry, Donald
Barry, Gene
Barrymore, John
Barrymore, John Blythe Drew, Jr.
Barrymore, Lionel Blythe
Barrymore, Maurice
Barthelmess, Richard
Bartholomew, Freddie (Frederick Llewellyn)
Barton, James
Basehart, Richard
Bass, Alfie (Alfred)
Bates, Alan Arthur
Baxter, Keith
Baxter, Warner
Beal, John

Bean, Orson
Beard, Matthew, Jr.
Beatty, Ned
Beatty, Robert
Beatty, Warren
Beaumont, Hugh
Beck, John
Beck, Julian
Beck, Michael
Bedford, Brian
Beemer, Brace
Beery, Noah
Beery, Noah, Jr.
Beery, Wallace
Begley, Ed(ward James)
Begley, Ed, Jr.
Belafonte, Harry (Harold George, Jr.)
Bell, Tom
Bellamy, Ralph
Belmondo, Jean-Paul
Belushi, Jim (James)
Belushi, John
Bendix, William
Benedict, Dirk
Benjamin, Richard
Bennett, Richard
Benson, Robby
Bentley, John
Beradino, John
Berenger, Tom (Thomas)
Beresford, Harry
Berger, Helmut
Bergerac, Jacques
Berle, Milton
Berliner, Ron
Berlinger, Warren
Berman, Shelley (Sheldon Leonard)
Bernard, Sam
Bernardi, Hershel
Berry, Ken
Bessell, Ted
Betterton, Thomas
Bettger, Lyle
Betz, Carl
Bey, Turhan
Beymer, Richard (George Richard)
Bickford, Charles Ambrose
Bikel, Theodore Meir
Bill, Tony
Bilon, Michael Patrick
Birney, David Edwin
Bixby, Bill
Blackmer, Sidney Alderman
Blacque, Taurean
Blake, Robert
Blakely, Colin
Blanc, Mel(vin Jerome)
Bledsoe, Jules
Blinn, Holbrook
Blocker, Dan
Blore, Eric

Blue, Monte
Blyden, Larry
Bochner, Hart
Bochner, Lloyd
Bogarde, Dirk
Bogart, Humphrey de Forest
Boles, John
Bolger, Ray
Bologna, Joseph
Bond, Tommy
Bond, Ward
Bondarchuk, Sergei
Bonerz, Peter
Bonner, Frank
Bono, "Sonny" Salvatore Phillip
Boone, "Pat" Charles Eugene
Boone, Richard
Booth, Edwin Thomas
Booth, John Wilkes
Booth, Junius Brutus
Boothe, Powers
Borgnine, Ernest
Bosley, Tom
Bostwick, Barry
Bosworth, Hobart van Zandt
Bottoms, Joseph
Bottoms, Sam
Bottoms, Timothy
Bowen, Roger
Bowie, David
Bowman, Lee (Lucien Lee, Sr.)
Boxleitner, Bruce
Boyd, Stephen
Boyd, William (Bill)
Boyer, Charles
Boyle, Peter
Bracken, Eddie (Edward Vincent)
Brady, Pat (Robert Patrick)
Brady, Scott
Brady, William Aloysius
Brambell, Wilfrid
Brand, Neville
Brando, Marlon
Brannigan, Owen
Brasselle, Keefe
Brazzi, Rossano
Breese, Edmund
Brendel, El(mer)
Breneman, Tom
Brennan, Walter Andrew
Brent, George
Brent, Romney
Brett, Jeremy
Brian, David
Brian, Donald
Bridges, "Beau" Lloyd Vernet, III
Bridges, Jeff
Bridges, Lloyd (Lloyd Vernet II)
Bridges, Todd
Broadhurst, Kent
Broderick, James Joseph

Broderick, Matthew
Brodie, Steve
Brolin, James
Bromberg, J. Edward
Bromfield, John
Bronson, Charles
Brook, Clive (Clifford)
Brooks, Albert
Brooks, Foster Murrell
Brooks, James L
Brooks, Mel
Brosnan, Pierce
Broun, Heywood Hale
Brown, Bryan
Brown, Jim (James Nathaniel)
Brown, Joe Evan
Brown, Johnny Mack
Brown, Kelly (Elford Cornelious Kelly Kingman)
Brown, Oscar, Jr.
Brown, Tom (Thomas Edward)
Bruce, Nigel
Brynner, Yul
Buchanan, Edgar
Buchanan, Jack
Buchholz, Horst
Bull, Peter
Bunny, John
Buono, Victor (Charles Victor)
Burbage, James
Burbage, Richard
Burghoff, Gary
Burke, Paul
Burnette, Smiley (Lester Alvin)
Burns, Bob
Burns, David
Burns, George
Burr, Raymond William Stacey
Burton, LeVar(dis Robert Martyn, Jr.)
Burton, Richard
Busey, Gary
Bushell, Anthony
Bushman, Francis X(avier)
Butkus, Dick (Richard J)
Butterworth, Charles
Buttons, Red
Buttram, Pat
Buzzell, Eddie
Byrnes, Edd
Caan, James
Cabot, Bruce
Cabot, Sebastian
Caesar, Adolph
Caesar, Sid
Cagney, James (James Francis, Jr.)
Caine, Michael
Calhern, Louis
Calhoun, Rory
Callan, Michael
Callas, Charlie
Calvert, Louis

Cambridge, Godfrey
Cameron, Kirk
Cameron, Rod
Camp, Hamilton
Campanella, Joseph Mario
Campbell, Douglas
Canary, David
Candy, John
Cantinflas
Canutt, Yakima (Enos Edward)
Carey, Harry
Carey, MacDonald (Edward Macdonald)
Carey, Phil(ip)
Cariou, Len (Leonard)
Carle, Richard
Carlson, Richard
Carmichael, Ian
Carney, Art
Carney, Don
Carnovsky, Morris
Carr, Alexander
Carradine, David
Carradine, John Richmond
Carradine, Keith Ian
Carradine, Robert Reed
Carrillo, Leo
Carroll, Leo G
Carson, Jack
Cassavetes, John
Cassidy, David Bruce
Cassidy, Jack
Cassidy, Shaun Paul
Castellano, Richard
Castle, John
Catlett, Walter
Caulfield, Maxwell
Cavanaugh, Hobart
Cawthorn, Joseph
Cazenove, Christopher
Chaikin, Joseph
Chakiris, George
Chamberlain, Richard
Chamberlin, Lee
Chandler, Jeff
Chaney, Lon (Alonso)
Chaney, Lon, Jr. (Creighton)
Chaney, Norman
Chaplin, Charlie
Chaplin, Sydney Dryden
Chapman, Graham
Charleson, Ian
Charlip, Remy
Chase, "Chevy" Cornelius Crane
Chevalier, Maurice Auguste
Childress, Alvin
Christopher, Dennis
Christopher, Jordan
Christopher, William
Cibber, Colley
Ciulei, Liviu
Clark, Barrett H

Clark, Dane
Clark, Fred
Clary, Robert
Clayton, Herbert
Clayton, Lou
Cleese, John
Clift, Montgomery
Clive, Colin
Clyde, Andy
Cobb, Joe
Cobb, Lee J (Leo Jacob)
Coburn, Charles Douville
Coburn, James
Cochran, Steve
Coco, James
Cody, Iron Eyes
Cohan, George M(ichael)
Cohen, Alexander H
Colasanto, Nicholas
Cole, Dennis
Cole, George
Cole, Michael
Cole, Nat "King" Nathaniel Adams
Coleman, Dabney
Coleman, Gary
Colicos, John
Collier, William, Sr.
Collins, Gary
Collins, Ray
Collins, Stephen
Colman, Ronald
Columbo, Russ
Conaway, Jeff
Condon, Jackie
Connelly, Christopher
Connery, Sean
Connolly, Walter
Connors, "Chuck" Kevin Joseph
Connors, Mike
Conrad, Michael
Conrad, Robert
Conrad, William
Conreid, Hans
Conroy, Frank
Considine, Tim
Constantine, Eddie
Constantine, Michael
Conte, Richard
Conti, Tom (Thomas Antonio)
Converse, Frank
Convy, Bert
Conway, "Tim" Thomas Daniel
Conway, Gary
Conway, Jack
Conway, Tom
Coogan, Jackie (Jack Leslie)
Cook, Donald
Cook, Elisha, Jr.
Cook, Joe
Cook, Peter
Cooper, "Gary" Frank James

Cooper, Jackie (John, Jr.)
Cooper, Melville
Coote, Robert
Coquelin, Benoit Constant
Cord, Alex
Corey, Irwin
Corey, Jeff
Corey, Wendell
Corrigan, Douglas
Corsaro, Frank
Cort, Bud
Cortez, Ricardo
Cosby, Bill
Cossart, Ernest
Costello, Lou
Costello, Maurice
Cotsworth, Staats
Cotten, Joseph
Coulouris, George
Courtenay, Tom
Cover, Franklin
Cowan, Jerome
Coward, Noel Pierce, Sir
Cox, Wally (Wallace Maynard)
Crabbe, "Buster" Larry
Crane, Bob
Crane, Richard O
Craven, Frank
Crawford, Broderick
Crawford, Michael Patrick
Cregar, Laird (Samuel)
Crenna, Richard
Crisp, Donald
Cristofer, Michael
Cromwell, John
Cronyn, Hume
Crosby, "Bing" Harry Lillis
Cross, Ben (Bernard)
Crothers, "Scatman" (Benjamin Sherman
Cruickshank, Andrew John
Cruise, Tom
Cryer, David
Crystal, Billy (William)
Cullum, John
Culp, Robert
Cummings, Bob (Robert Orville)
Currie, Finlay
Curtis, Alan
Curtis, Ken
Curtis, Tony
Cusack, Cyril
Cushing, Peter
DaCosta, Morton
Dailey, Dan
Dale, Jim
Dall, John
Dalton, Charles
Dalton, Timothy
Daly, Arnold
Daly, James
Damon, Stuart

Damone, Vic
Dana, Bill
Danforth, William
Daniell, Henry
Daniels, Frank
Daniels, Jeff
Daniels, Mickey
Daniels, William
Danson, Ted (Edward Bridge, III)
Dantine, Helmut
Danton, Ray(mond)
Danza, Tony
Darin, Bobby
Darren, James
Darro, Frankie
Darrow, Henry
DaSilva, Howard
Dauphin, Claude Le Grand Maria Eugene
Davenport, Harry George Bryant
Davenport, Nigel
Davidson, John
Davis, Brad
Davis, Clifton
Davis, Jim
Davis, Mac
Davis, Ossie
Davis, Sammy, Jr.
Davison, Bruce
Dawson, Richard
Day, Dennis
Dayan, Assaf
Deacon, Richard
Dean, Basil
Dean, James
DeCordoba, Pedro
DeFore, Don
Dehner, John Forkum
Dekker, Albert
Dell, Gabriel
Delmar, Kenny
Delon, Alain
DeLuise, Dom
DeMarco, Tony
Demarest, William
DeNiro, Robert
Denning, Richard
Denny, Reginald Leigh
Denver, Bob
Denver, John
Depardieu, Gerard
Derek, John
Dern, Bruce MacLeish
DeSica, Vittorio
Desmond, Johnny
Desmond, William
Devane, William
Devine, Andy
DeVito, Danny Michael
Dewaere, Patrick
DeWilde, Brandon
DeWolfe, Billy

DeYoung, Cliff
Diamond, Neil
Digges, Dudley
Dillman, Bradford
Dillon, Matt
Dix, Richard
Dixon, Ivan
Dobson, Kevin
Donahue, Troy
Donald, James
Donald, Peter
Donat, Robert
Donlevy, Brian
Donohue, Jack
Doohan, James Montgomery
Douglas, Kirk
Douglas, Melvyn
Douglas, Michael Kirk
Douglas, Paul
Dourif, Brad
Dow, Tony
Dowling, Eddie (Edward)
Downs, Johnny
Doyle, David Fitzgerald
Drake, Tom
Drew, John
Dreyfuss, Richard Stephan
Driscoll, Bobby
Drury, James
Dryer, Fred (John Frederick)
Duel, Peter
Duff, Howard
Duffy, Patrick
Dukes, David
Dullea, Keir
Dumke, Ralph
Duncan, Augustin
Duncan, Todd
Dunn, James Howard
Dunn, Michael
Durning, Charles
Duryea, Dan
Duvall, Robert Selden
Dyer, Charles
Eastwood, Clint
Ebsen, Buddy
Eddy, Nelson
Edelman, Herb
Edeson, Robert
Edwards, Alan
Edwards, Cliff
Edwards, Vince
Egan, Richard
Elam, Jack
Elizondo, Hector
Elliott, Denholm
Elliott, Sam
Ellis, Robin
Eltinge, Julian
Ely, Ron
Erickson, Leif

Errol, Leon
Erwin, Stuart
Essex, David
Estevez, Emilio
Estrada, Erik (Henry Enrique)
Evans, Bob (Robert)
Evans, Maurice
Evans, Mike (Michael Jonas)
Everett, Chad
Evers, Jason
Evigan, Greg(ory Ralph)
Ewell, Tom
Fabian
Fabrizi, Aldo
Fairbanks, Douglas
Fairbanks, Douglas, Jr.
Falk, Peter
Farentino, James
Farnsworth, Richard
Farnum, Dustin Lancy
Farnum, William
Farr, Jamie
Farrell, Charles
Farrell, Mike
Fassbinder, Rainer Werner
Faversham, William Alfred
Fawcett, George
Faye, Joey
Faylen, Frank
Feld, Fritz
Feldman, Marty
Fell, Norman
Felsenstein, Walter
Fenton, Leslie
Fernandel
Fernandez, Emilio
Ferrer, Jose Vicente
Ferrer, Mel(chor Gaston)
Ferrigno, Lou
Fetchit, Stepin
Fields, Stanley
Fields, W C
Fierstein, Harvey Forbes
Finch, Jon
Finch, Peter
Fine, Larry
Finlay, Frank
Finney, Albert
Firth, Peter
Fitzgerald, Barry
Fix, Paul
Flaherty, Joe
Flanders, Michael
Fleming, Ian
Fletcher, Bramwell
Flippen, Jay C
Flynn, Errol
Flynn, Joe (Joseph Anthony)
Flynn, Sean
Fonda, Henry Jaynes
Fonda, Peter

Foran, Dick John Nicholas
Forbes, Ralph
Forbes-Robertson, Johnston, Sir
Ford, Glenn
Ford, Harrison
Ford, Paul
Ford, Steven Meigs
Ford, Wallace
Forrest, Edwin
Forrest, Steve
Forster, Robert
Forsythe, John
Foster, Norman
Foster, Phil
Foster, Preston
Fox, Edward
Fox, James
Fox, Michael J
Foxworth, Robert
Foxx, Redd
Foy, Eddie
Foy, Eddie, Jr.
Franciosa, Anthony
Franciscus, James Grover
Franz, Arthur
Franz, Eduard
Frawley, William
Freed, Bert
Freeman, Al, Jr.
Frisco, Joe
Frobe, Gert
Fugard, Athol Harold
Fuller, Robert
Fyffe, Will
Gabel, Martin
Gabin, Jean
Gable, Clark
Gail, Max(well Trowbridge, Jr.)
Gallagher, Richard
Galloway, Don
Gardenia, Vincent
Gardiner, Reginald
Garfield, John
Garfunkel, Art(hur)
Gargan, William
Garner, James
Garrett, Leif
Garrick, David
Gassman, Vittorio
Gates, Larry
Gautier, Dick
Gavin, John
Gaxton, William
Gazzara, Ben (Biago Anthony)
Geary, Anthony
Geer, Will
Geldof, Bob
Genn, Leo
George, Chief Dan
George, Christopher
Gerard, Gil

Geray, Steven
Gere, Richard
Gerussi, Bruno
Giannini, Giancarlo
Gibson, "Hoot" Edmund Richard
Gibson, Henry
Gibson, Mel
Gielgud, (Arthur) John, Sir
Gilbert, Billy
Gilbert, John
Gilford, Jack
Gillette, William Hooker
Gilpin, Charles Sidney
Glaser, Paul Michael
Glass, Ron
Gleason, Jackie
Gleason, James
Glenn, Scott
Glover, Danny
Glover, Julian
Godfrey, Arthur Michael
Goldblum, Jeff
Gomez, Thomas
Goodeve, Grant
Goodwin, Bill
Goodwin, Nat C
Gorcey, Leo
Gordon, C Henry
Gordon, Gale
Gordone, Charles
Gorin, Igor
Goring, Marius
Gorshin, Frank John
Gortner, (Hugh) Marjoe (Ross)
Gosset, Lou(is, Jr.)
Gottschalk, Ferdinand
Gould, Elliott
Goulet, Robert
Grady, Don
Granger, Farley
Granger, Stewart
Grant, Cary
Grant, Kirby
Grapewin, Charley (Charles)
Graves, Peter
Graves, Peter
Graziano, Rocky
Greaza, Walter N
Green, Abel
Green, Martyn
Greene, Lorne
Greene, Richard
Greene, Shecky
Greenstreet, Sydney Hughes
Gregory, James
Gregson, John
Grey, Joel
Grier, "Rosey" Roosevelt
Griffith, Andy (Andrew)
Griffith, D(avid Lewelyn) W(ark)
Griffith, Hugh Emrys

Grillo, John
Grizzard, George
Grodin, Charles
Groh, David Lawrence
Gross, Michael
Guardino, Harry
Guillaume, Robert
Guinness, Alec, Sir
Guitry, Sacha
Gulager, Clu
Gunn, Moses
Guttenberg, Steve
Gwenn, Edmund
Gwilym, Mike
Gwynne, Fred
Hackett, Albert
Hackett, Raymond
Hackman, Gene (Eugene Alden)
Hadley, Reed
Haggerty, Dan
Hagman, Larry
Haid, Charles
Haigh, Kenneth
Haines, Robert Terrel
Haines, William
Hale, Alan
Hale, Alan, Jr.
Haley, Jack
Hall, Huntz (Henry)
Halop, Billy
Hamer, Rusty
Hamill, Mark
Hamilton, George
Hamilton, Neil
Hamilton, Patrick
Hamlin, Harry
Hampden, Walter
Hampton, James
Hanks, Tom
Hardwicke, Cedric Webster, Sir
Harmon, Mark
Harrigan, Edward
Harrington, Pat
Harris, Jonathan
Harris, Richard
Harrison, Gregory
Harrison, Noel
Harrison, Rex (Reginald Carey)
Hart, William Surrey
Hartman, David Downs
Hartman, Paul
Harvey, Frank Laird
Harvey, Laurence
Hasegawa, Kazuo
Hasselhof, David
Hatch, Richard Lawrence
Hatfield, Hurd
Hauer, Rutger
Hawkins, Jack
Hayakawa, Sessue (Kintaro)
Hayden, Russell

Hayden, Sterling
Haydn, Richard
Hayes, "Gabby" George Francis
Hayes, Peter Lind
Haynes, Lloyd (Samuel Lloyd)
Hays, Robert
Hayward, Louis
Healy, Ted
Heard, John
Heatherton, Ray
Hedison, David (Albert David, Jr.)
Heflin, Van Emmett Evan
Heggie, O P
Hegyes, Robert
Helm, Levon
Helmore, Tom
Helpmann, Robert Murray, Sir
Hemmings, David Leslie Edward
Hemsley, Sherman
Hendry, Ian
Henreid, Paul
Henry, Buck
Herbert, Hugh
Herrmann, Edward
Hersholt, Jean
Hesseman, Howard
Heston, Charlton
Hewitt, Martin
Hexum, Jon-Erik
Hickman, Darryl
Hickman, Dwayne
Hill, Arthur
Hill, Howard
Hillerman, John Benedict
Hilliard, Robert Cochran
Hines, Gregory Oliver
Hingle, Pat (Martin Patterson)
Hirsch, Judd
Hitchcock, Raymond
Hodges, Eddie (Samuel Edward)
Hodiak, John
Hoffman, Dustin
Holbrook, Hal (Harold Rowe, Jr.)
Holden, William
Holder, Geoffrey
Holdren, Judd Clifton
Holliman, Earl
Holloway, Stanley
Holloway, Sterling
Holm, Ian
Holm, John Cecil
Holmes, Taylor
Holt, Jack (Charles John)
Holt, Tim
Holtz, Lou
Homolka, Oscar
Hooks, Robert
Hope, Bob (Leslie Townes)
Hopkins, Anthony
Hopkins, Bo
Hopper, De Wolfe (William De Wolfe)

Hopper, Dennis
Hopper, DeWolf
Hopper, William
Hordern, Michael
Horsley, Lee
Horton, Edward Everett
Horton, Robert
Hoskins, Allen Clayton
Hoskins, Bob
Houseman, John
Howard, Clint
Howard, Eddy
Howard, Eugene
Howard, Ken(neth Joseph Jr.)
Howard, Leslie
Howard, Ron
Howard, Tom
Howard, Trevor Wallace
Hudson, Rock
Hughes, Barnard
Hulce, Thomas
Hull, Henry
Hull, Warren
Hunnicutt, Arthur
Hunter, Glenn
Hunter, Ian
Hunter, Jeffrey
Hunter, Tab
Hurt, John
Hurt, William
Huston, John
Huston, Walter
Hutchins, Bobby
Hutchins, Will
Hutton, Jim
Hutton, Robert
Hutton, Timothy James
Hyde-White, Wilfrid
Hyman, Earle
Idle, Eric
Ingels, Marty
Ingram, Rex
Ireland, John
Irons, Jeremy
Irving, Henry, Sir
Irving, Jules
Irving, Laurence Sidney
Ives, Burl
Jackson, Gordon
Jackson, Michael Joseph
Jacobi, Derek
Jacobi, Lou
Jaeckel, Richard
Jaffe, Sam
Jagger, Dean
Jameson, House
Janis, Conrad
Janney, Leon
Jannings, Emil
Janssen, David
Jarman, Claude, Jr.

Jason, Rick
Jayston, Michael
Jefferson, Joseph
Jefferson, Thomas
Jeffries, James Jackson
Jeffries, Lionel Charles
Jenkins, Allen
Jessel, George Albert
Jewett, Henry
Johnson, "Chic" Harold Ogden
Johnson, Arte
Johnson, Ben
Johnson, Don
Johnson, Richard
Johnson, Van
Johnston, Johnny
Jones, Allan
Jones, Barry
Jones, Buck
Jones, Christopher
Jones, Davy (David)
Jones, Dean
Jones, Henry
Jones, James Earl
Jones, Preston St. Vrain
Jones, Terry
Jones, Tommy Lee
Jordan, Bobby
Jordan, Richard
Jory, Victor
Joslyn, Allyn Morgan
Jourdan, Louis
Jouvet, Louis
Julia, Raul
Jump, Gordon
Jurgens, Curt
Justice, James Robertson
Kamen, Milt
Kanaly, Steve(n Francis)
Kaplan, Gabe (Gabriel)
Karloff, Boris
Karras, Alex(ander G)
Kasznar, Kurt
Katt, William
Kaufman, Andy
Kaye, Danny
Kaye, Stubby
Keach, Stacy, Jr.
Kean, Edmund
Keaton, "Buster" Joseph Francis
Keaton, Michael
Keel, Howard
Keenan, Frank
Keene, Thomas Wallace
Keitel, Harvey
Keith, Brian
Keith, David
Keith, Ian
Kellaway, Cecil
Kelley, DeForrest
Kellin, Mike

Kelly, Gene
Kelly, Jack
Kelly, Paul
Kelly, Walter C
Kemble, Charles
Kemble, John Philip
Kendal, William Hunter
Kennedy, Arthur
Kennedy, Edgar
Kennedy, George
Kennedy, Tom
Kenney, Douglas C
Kercheval, Ken
Kerr, John
Kert, Larry (Frederick Lawrence)
Kerwin, Lance
Kibbee, Guy
Kiel, Richard
Kilbride, Percy
Kiley, Richard
Kilgour, Joseph
Kilian, Victor
King, Charles
King, Dennis
King, Perry
King, Walter Woolf
Kingsley, Ben
Kirby, Durward
Klein, Robert
Klemperer, Werner
Kline, Kevin
Klugman, Jack
Knight, Ted
Knotts, Don
Knowles, Patric
Knox, Alexander
Kohler, Fred
Kopell, Bernie (Bernard Morton)
Kovacs, Ernie
Kramm, Joseph
Krauss, Werner
Kreuger, Kurt
Kristofferson, Kris
Kruger, Hardy (Eberhard)
Kruger, Otto
Ladd, Alan
Lahr, Bert
Lake, Arthur
Lamas, Fernando
Lamas, Lorenzo
Lamb, Gil
Lancaster, Burt(on Stephen)
Landau, Martin
Landers, Harry
Landesberg, Steve
Landon, Michael
Lang, Harold
Langdon, Harry
Lange, Ted
Langella, Frank
Lansing, Robert

Lanza, Mario
LaRocque, Rod
Larroquette, John
LaRue, Jack
Laughlin, Tom
Laughton, Charles
Laurel, Stan
Law, John Philip
Lawford, Peter
Lawrence, Steve
Lawson, Leigh
Leaud, Jean-Pierre
Lederer, Francis
Lee, Bernard
Lee, Bruce
Lee, Canada
Lee, Christopher
Lee, Will
Lehr, Lew
Leibman, Ron
Lembeck, Harvey
Lemmon, Jack (John Uhler, III)
Lemoyne, W(illiam) J
Leonard, Eddie
Leonard, Sheldon
Lester, Mark
Levene, Sam
Lewis, Ed
Lewis, Emmanuel
Lewis, Joe E
Lincoln, Elmo
Linden, Hal
Lindsay, Howard
Linville, Larry Lavon
Liston, "Sonny" Charles
Lithgow, John Arthur
Little, Cleavon Jake
Livesey, Roger
Livingston, Barry
Livingston, Stanley
Lloyd, Christopher
Lloyd, Harold
Lockhart, Calvin
Lockhart, Gene (Eugene)
Lockwood, Gary
Loder, John
Lom, Herbert
Long, Richard
Loo, Richard
Lord, Jack
Lord, Phillips H
Lorre, Peter
Lovejoy, Frank
Lowe, Edmund Dante
Lowe, Rob(ert Hepler)
Ludlam, Charles
Lugosi, Bela
Lukas, Paul
Luke, Keye
Lund, Art(hur Earl, Jr.)
Lund, John

Lundigan, William
Lunt, Alfred
Lupino, Stanley
Lupus, Peter
Lydon, James (Jimmy)
Lynde, Paul Edward
Lyon, Ben
Lytell, Bert
Lytton, Henry Alfred, Sir
MacArthur, Charles
MacArthur, James
Macchio, Ralph George, Jr.
MacCorkindale, Simon
MacLane, Barton
Maclaughlin, Don
MacLeod, Gavin
MacLiammoir, Michael
MacMurray, Fred(erick Martin)
MacNee, Patrick
MacRae, Gordon
Macready, George
Macy, Bill
Madden, Donald
Madison, Guy
Magee, Patrick
Maharis, George
Mahoney, Jock
Majors, Lee
Makepeace, Chris
Malden, Karl
Mandan, Robert
Manetti, Larry
Mann, Paul
Mansfield, Richard
Marais, Jean
Marceau, Marcel
March, Fredric
March, Hal
Marciano, Rocky
Margolin, Stuart
Marinaro, Ed
Markham, Monte
Marks, Charles
Marley, John
Marlowe, Hugh
Marshal, Alan
Marshall, E G (Edda Gunnar)
Marshall, Herbert
Marshall, Ken
Marshall, Peter
Marshall, Tully
Marshall, William
Marshall, William
Martin, Dean
Martin, Dean Paul (Dino, Jr.)
Martin, Jared
Martin, John
Martin, Kiel
Martin, Ross
Martin, Steve
Martin, Strother

Martino, Al
Marvin, Lee
Mason, James Neville
Massey, Daniel Raymond
Massey, Raymond Hart
Mastroianni, Marcello
Mathers, Jerry
Matheson, Murray
Matheson, Tim
Matthau, Walter
Mature, Victor
Maude, Cyril
Mayehoff, Eddie
Maynard, Ken
Mazurki, Mike
McCallister, Lon
McCallum, David
McCarthy, Kevin
McClure, Doug
McCord, Kent
McCormick, Myron
McCowen, Alec (Alexander Duncan)
McCoy, Charles
McCoy, Tim(othy John Fitzgerald)
McCrea, Joel
McCullough, Paul
McDowall, Roddy (Roderick Andrew)
McDowell, Malcolm
McEachin, James Elton
McFarland, "Spanky" George Emmett
McGavin, Darren
McGee, Fibber
McGinnis, Scott
McGiver, John
McGoohan, Patrick
McGuire, "Biff" William J
McHugh, Frank (Francis Curray)
McIntire, John
McIntyre, Frank J
McIntyre, James
McKay, Scott
McKean, Michael
McKellen, Ian Murray
McKeon, Doug
McKeon, Philip
McKern, Leo
McLaglen, Victor
McMahon, Horace
McNichol, Jimmy (James Vincent)
McQueen, Steve (Terence Stephen)
McRaney, Gerald
McShane, Ian
Meader, Vaughn
Meat Loaf
Meek, Donald
Meeker, Ralph
Meighan, Thomas
Meisner, Sanford
Mekka, Eddie
Melachrino, George
Melford, Austin (Alfred Austin)

Menjou, Adolphe Jean
Meredith, Burgess
Merivale, Philip
Merrill, Gary Franklin
Michell, Keith
Middleton, Ray
Mifune, Toshiro
Miles, Nelson A
Milhaud, Darius
Milland, Ray(mond Alton)
Miller, Barry
Miller, Henry John
Miller, Jason
Miller, Joe
Miller, Jonathan
Mills, John, Sir
Milner, Martin Sam
Mineo, Sal
Mitchell, Cameron
Mitchell, Grant
Mitchell, Guy
Mitchell, Millard
Mitchell, Thomas
Mitchum, Robert (Robert Charles Duran)
Mix, Tom
Moffat, Donald
Moliere, pseud.
Molinaro, Al
Montalban, Ricardo
Montana, "Bull" Louis
Montand, Yves
Montgomery, George
Montgomery, Robert Henry
Moody, Ron
Moore, Clayton
Moore, Dick(ie)
Moore, Dudley Stuart John
Moore, Roger George
Moore, Tom
Moore, Victor
Moran, George
More, Kenneth Gilbert
Morgan, Dennis
Morgan, Frank
Morgan, Harry
Morgan, Ralph
Morgan, Terence
Moriarty, Michael
Morita, "Pat" Noriyuki
Morley, Robert
Morris, Chester
Morris, Greg
Morris, Howard
Morris, Wayne
Morrow, Vic
Morse, Barry
Morse, Robert Alan
Moss, Arnold
Most, Donny
Mostel, Zero (Samuel Joel)
Mowbray, Alan

Mulhall, Jack
Mulhare, Edward
Mull, Martin
Mullavey, Greg
Mulligan, Richard
Muni, Paul
Munshin, Jules
Murphy, Audie
Murphy, Ben(jamin Edward)
Murphy, George Lloyd
Murray, Bill
Murray, Don(ald Patrick)
Murray, Ken
Nabors, Jim (James Thurston)
Nader, George
Nader, Michael
Nagel, Conrad
Naish, J(oseph) Carrol
Namath, Joe (Joseph William)
Nardini, Tom
Nash, George Frederick
Naughton, David
Nelson, Barry
Nelson, David
Nelson, Ed(win Stafford)
Nelson, Gene
Nelson, Ozzie (Oswald George)
Nelson, Rick (Eric Hilliard)
Nero, Franco
Neville, John
Newley, Anthony
Newman, Barry Foster
Newman, Paul
Newton, Robert
Ney, Richard
Nicholson, Jack
Nielsen, Leslie
Nimoy, Leonard
Niven, (James) David Graham
Nolan, Lloyd
Nolte, Nick
Norris, Chuck (Carlos Ray)
North, Jay
Norton, Jack
Norworth, Jack
Novarro, Ramon
Novello, Don
Novello, Ivor
Nugent, Edward
Nugent, Elliott
Nye, Louis
Nype, Russell
O'Brian, Hugh
O'Brien, Edmond
O'Brien, George
O'Brien, Pat (William Joseph Patrick)
O'Connell, Arthur
O'Connell, Hugh
O'Connor, Carroll
O'Connor, Donald
O'Herlihy, Dan

O'Keefe, Dennis
O'Keefe, Walter
O'Malley, J Pat
O'Neal, Patrick
O'Neal, Ron
O'Neal, Ryan
O'Neill, James
O'Shea, Michael
O'Shea, Milo
O'Toole, Peter Seamus
Oakie, Jack
Oakland, Simon
Oates, Warren
Ober, Philip
Ogilvy, Ian
Olaf, Pierre
Oland, Warner
Olcott, Chauncey (Chancellor)
Olivier, Laurence Kerr Olivier, Sir
Ontkean, Michael
Opatashu, David
Orbach Jerry
Ortega, Santos
Osmond, Donny (Donald Clark)
Osmond, Ken
Overman, Lynne
Owen, (John) Reginald
Owens, Gary
Pacino, Al(fredo James)
Paige, Robert (John Arthur)
Palance, Jack
Palillo, Ron
Palin, Michael
Pallette, Eugene
Palmer, Peter
Pangborn, Franklin
Paris, Jerry
Parker, Cecil
Parker, Fess
Parker, Jameson
Parks, Bert
Parks, Larry
Parks, Michael
Passarella, Art
Pastor, Tony (Antonio)
Pavarotti, Luciano
Payne, John
Payne, John Howard
Peary, Harold
Peck, Gregory
Pendleton, Nat
Penn, Sean
Peppard, George
Perkins, Anthony
Perkins, Osgood (James Ridley Osgood)
Persoff, Nehemiah
Peters, Brandon
Peters, Brock
Peterson, Paul
Philipe, Gerard
Phillips, Robin

Pickens, Slim
Pickford, Jack
Pidgeon, Walter
Pinero, Miguel
Pinsent, Gordon Edward
Piscopo, Joe (Joseph Charles)
Pleasence, Donald
Pleshette, John
Plummer, Christopher (Arthur Christopher)
Poitier, Sidney
Pollard, Michael J
Porter, Eric
Portman, Eric
Poston, Tom
Powell, Dick
Powell, Robert
Powell, William
Power, Tyrone
Power, Tyrone (Frederick Tyrone Edmond)
Prescott, Ken
Presley, Elvis (Elvis Aaron)
Presnell, Harve
Pressman, David
Preston, Robert
Price, Dennis
Price, Vincent
Prince, William
Prinze, Freddie
Prosky, Robert
Prouty, Jed
Pryor, Nicholas
Pryor, Richard Franklin Lennox Thomas
Pryor, Roger
Pully, B S
Purdom, Edmund
Pyle, Denver
Quaid, Dennis
Quaid, Randy
Qualen, John Mandt
Quayle, Anthony
Quillan, Eddie
Quine, Richard
Quinn, Anthony Rudolph Oaxaca
Rafferty, "Chipscq
Raft, George
Ragland, "Rags" John Lee Morgan
  Beauregard
Raimu
Rains, Claude
Rambo, Dack
Randall, Tony
Rankin, Arthur
Rathbone, Basil
Ratoff, Gregory
Rawlinson, Herbert
Ray, Aldo
Ray, Charles
Rayburn, Gene
Raymond, Gene
Reardon, John
Redford, Robert

Redgrave, Corin
Redgrave, Michael Scudamore, Sir
Reed, Alan
Reed, Jerry
Reed, Oliver (Robert Oliver)
Reed, Robert
Reems, Harry
Rees, Roger
Reese, Mason
Reeve, Christopher
Reeves, George
Reeves, Steve
Regan, Phil
Reid, Elliott
Reid, Tim
Reid, Wallace Eugene
Reilly, Charles Nelson
Reiner, Carl
Reiner, Rob(ert)
Renaldo, Duncan
Rennie, Michael
Revill, Clive Selsby
Rey, Alejandro
Rey, Fernando
Reynolds, Burt
Reynolds, William
Rhodes, Erik
Rhodes, Hari
Rice, Thomas Dartmouth
Rich, Adam
Richardson, Lee
Richardson, Ralph David, Sir
Richman, Charles
Rippy, Rodney Allen
Ritchard, Cyril
Ritter, "Tex" Woodward Maurice
Ritter, Blake
Ritter, John(athan Southworth)
Robards, Jason
Robards, Jason, Jr.
Roberts, Eric
Roberts, Pernell
Roberts, Tony (David Anthony)
Robertson, "Robbie" Jaime
Robertson, Cliff
Robertson, Dale
Robeson, Paul Leroy
Robey, George, Sir
Robinson, Bill
Robinson, Edward G
Robinson, Jay
Rogers, "Buddy" Charles
Rogers, Roy
Rogers, Wayne
Rogers, Will(iam Penn Adair)
Rogers, Will, Jr.
Roland, Gilbert
Rollins, Howard Ellsworth, Jr.
Romero, Cesar
Rooney, Mickey
Rooney, Pat

Rose, George Walter
Rosenbloom, Maxie
Ross, Barney
Rounds, David
Roundtree, Richard
Rounseville, Robert Field
Rourke, "Mickey" Philip Andre
Rubinstein, John
Rudd, Paul Ryan
Ruggles, Charles
Rumann, Sig(fried)
Russell, Kurt (Von Vogel)
Russell, Nipsey
Ryan, Robert (Bushnell)
Ryder, Alfred
Sabu
Saint Jacques, Raymond
Saint John, Howard
Sakall, S Z
Sale, Charles Partlow
Salmi, Albert
Sand, Paul
Sanders, George
Sanders, Richard Kinard
Sandy, Gary
Sarandon, Chris
Sargent, Dick
Sarrazin, Michael
Savage, John
Savalas, "Telly" Aristoteles
Savo, Jimmy
Saxon, John
Scarpelli, Glenn
Scheider, Roy Richard
Schell, Maximilian
Schikaneder, Johann Emanuel
Schildkraut, Joseph
Schildkraut, Rudolph
Schneider, John
Schreiber, Avery
Schroder, Ricky
Schwartz, Maurice
Schwarzenegger, Arnold
Scofield, Paul
Scott, George Campbell
Scott, Gordon
Scott, Randolph
Scott, Zachary
Scourby, Alexander
Sebring, Jay
Secombe, Harry
Segal, George
Selby, David
Selleck, Tom
Sellers, Peter Richard Henry
Serrault, Michel
Seymour, Dan
Shackelford, Ted
Sharif, Omar
Shatner, William
Shaw, Robert

Shawn, Dick
Shawn, Wallace
Shea, John
Shean, Al
Sheen, Charlie
Sheen, Martin
Shepherd, Jean Parker
Sherman, Bobby
Sherman, Lowell
Short, Martin
Shukshin, Vasilii Makarovich
Sikking, James B
Sillman, Leonard
Sills, Milton
Silvera, Frank
Silverheels, Jay
Simon, Paul
Simpson, O(renthal) J(ames)
Sinatra, Frank (Francis Albert)
Sinden, Donald
Skelly, Hal
Skelton, "Red" Richard
Skerritt, Tom (Thomas Roy)
Skinner, Otis
Skulnik, Menasha
Slezak, Walter
Sloane, Everett
Smart, Jack Scott
Smith, C Aubrey
Smith, Kent
Smith, Loring
Smith, Rex
Smith, Roger
Soo, Jack
Sorvino, Paul
Soul, David
Soule, Olan
Spano, Joe
Sparks, Ned
Springfield, Rick (Richard)
Stack, Robert
Stacy, James
Stallone, Sylvester (Michael Sylvester)
Stamp, Terence
Stander, Lionel
Stanislavsky, Konstantin Sergeyevich
Steel, Anthony
Steele, Eob
Steele, Tommy
Steiger, Rod
Stephen, John
Stephens, Robert
Stephenson, Henry
Stephenson, James
Sterling, Ford
Sterling, Robert
Stevens, Andrew
Stevens, Mark
Stevens, Onslow
Stevenson, McLean
Stevenson, Parker

Stewart, Donald Ogden
Stewart, Jimmy (James Maitland)
Stewart, Paul
Stiers, David Ogden
Stiller, Jerry
Sting
Stockwell, Dean
Stockwell, Guy
Stone, Fred
Stone, Harold J
Stone, Lewis
Stone, Milburn
Stoopnagle, Lemuel Q, Colonel
Storch, Larry
Strasberg, Lee
Strauss, Peter
Strauss, Robert
Strode, Woody
Strudwick, Shepperd
Sullivan, Barry
Sullivan, Francis Loftus
Sullivan, Tom
Sutherland, Donald
Sutton, John
Swayze, Patrick
Switzer, Carl
T, Mr.
Tabbert, William
Tabori, Kristoffer
Talbot, Lyle
Talman, William
Tamblyn, Russ
Tamiroff, Akim
Tayback, Vic
Taylor, Kent
Taylor, Robert
Taylor, Rod(ney)
Terry-Thomas
Thayer, Tiffany Ellsworth
Thespis
Thicke, Alan
Thinnes, Roy
Thomas, Billy
Thomas, Brandon
Thomas, Danny
Thomas, Henry
Thomas, Philip Michael
Thomas, Richard Earl
Thompson, Marshall
Thomson, Gordon
Tobias, George
Todd, Richard
Toler, Sidney
Tone, Franchot
Toomey, Regis
Topol, Chaim
Torn, Rip
Torrence, Ernest
Tracy, Lee
Tracy, Spencer
Travanti, Daniel J(ohn)

Travers, Bill
Travolta, John
Treacher, Arthur
Tree, Herbert Beerbohm
Tremayne, Les
Trintignant, Jean-Louis Xavier
Tripp, Paul
Troup, Bobby (Robert William)
Truex, Ernest
Tryon, Thomas
Tucker, Forrest Meredith
Tucker, Richard
Tufts, Sonny
Tully, Tom
Tyne, George
Uecker, Bob (Robert George)
Urich, Robert
Ustinov, Peter Alexander
Valentino, Rudolph
Vallee, Rudy (Herbert Prior)
Vallone, Raf(faele)
Van Cleef, Lee
Van Dyke, Dick
Van Dyke, Jerry
Van Patten, Dick
Van Patten, Vince(nt)
Van Peebles, Melvin
Van, Bobby
Vaughn, Robert
Veidt, Conrad
Vereen, Ben
Vernon, John
Vigoda, Abe
Villechaize, Herve Jean Pierre
Vincent, Jan-Michael
Visscher, William Lightfoot
Vogel, Mitch
Voight, Jon
Von Zell, Harry
VonStroheim, Erich
VonSydow, Max Carl Adolf
Voskovec, George
Vysotsky, Vladimir Semyonovich
Waggoner, Lyle
Wagner, Jack Peter
Wagner, Robert John, Jr.
Wainwright, James
Waite, Ralph
Wakely, Jimmy
Walbrook, Anton
Walburn, Raymond
Walden, Robert
Waldron, Charles D
Walken, Christopher
Walker, Clint
Walker, Jimmie (James Carter)
Walker, Robert
Wallach, Eli
Wallack, James William
Wallington, Jimmy (James S.)
Walmsley, Jon

Walsh, Raoul
Walston, Ray
Walthall, Henry B
Wanamaker, Sam
Ward, Burt
Ward, Douglas Turner
Ward, Simon
Warden, Jack
Warfield, David
Warner, David
Warner, Malcolm-Jamal
Warren, Michael
Warwick, Robert
Waterston, Sam(uel Atkinson)
Waxman, Al
Wayne, David
Wayne, John
Wayne, Patrick
Weaver, "Doodles" Winstead Sheffield
    Glendening Dixon
Weaver, Dennis
Weaver, Fritz William
Webb, Clifton
Webster, Ben(jamin)
Weissmuller, Johnny
Weitz, Bruce Peter
Welch, Joseph Nye
Weldon, John
Welland, Colin
Welles, Orson (George Orson)
Wendt, George
Werner, Oskar
West, Adam
Weston, Jack
Whalen, Michael
Whitaker, Johnny
White, George
White, Jesse
Whiting, Leonard
Whitman, Stuart
Whitmore, James Allen
Whorf, Richard
Widdoes, James
Widmark, Richard
Wilcox, Larry Dee
Wilcoxon, Henry
Wild, Jack
Wilde, Cornel
Wilder, Gene
Wilding, Michael
Willard, Jess
William, Warren
Williams, Anson
Williams, Barry
Williams, Bert (Egbert Austin)
Williams, Billy Dee
Williams, Clarence, III
Williams, Darnell
Williams, Emlyn (George Emlyn)
Williams, Gus
Williams, Robin

Williams, Samm-Art
Williams, Simon
Williams, Treat
Williamson, Nicol
Willig, George
Willis, Bruce
Wills, Chill
Wilson, "Dooley" Arthur
Wilson, "Flip" Clerow
Wilson, Demond
Wilson, Theodore
Winchell, Paul
Windom, William
Winfield, Paul Edward
Winkler, Henry Franklin
Winninger, Charles
Winter, Edward
Winters, Jonathan
Wisdom, Norman
Wiseman, Joseph
Wolfington, Iggie
Wolfit, Donald, Sir
Wolheim, Louis
Wood, John
Woods, Donald
Woods, James
Wooley, Sheb
Woolley, Monty (Edgar Montillion)
Woolsey, Robert
Wopat, Tom
Wynn, Keenan
Yarnell, Bruce
York, Dick
York, Michael
Young, Alan (Angus)
Young, Burt
Young, Gig
Young, Robert George
Young, Roland
Young, Stephen
Yung, Victor Sen
Zerbe, Anthony
Zimbalist, Efrem, Jr.
Zmed, Adrian
Zucco, George

ACTRESS

Aadland, Beverly
Ace, Jane Sherwood
Ackerman, Bettye
Adams, Brooke
Adams, Edie
Adams, Julie
Adams, Maud
Adams, Maude
Addams, Dawn
Adjani, Isabelle
Adler, Stella
Adoree, Renee
Agutter, Jenny
Aimee, Anouk

Alberghetti, Anna Maria
Albright, Lola Jean
Alexander, Denise
Alexander, Jane
Alexander, Katherine
Alicia, Ana
Allan, Elizabeth
Allbritton, Louise
Allen, Debbie
Allen, Elizabeth
Allen, Karen
Allen, Nancy
Allen, Viola Emily
Alley, Kirstie
Allgood, Sara
Allison, Fran(ces)
Allyson, June
Alvardo, Trini(dad)
Anders, Merry
Anderson, Judith, Dame
Anderson, Loni
Anderson, Mary Antoinette
Anderson, Melissa Sue
Andersson, Bibi
Andersson, Harriet
Andress, Ursula
Andrews, Julie
Angel, Heather
Angeli, Pier
Angelou, Maya Marguerita
Anglin, Margaret Mary
Ankers, Evelyn
Ann-Margret
Annabella
Annis, Francesca
Anspach, Susan
Anton, Susan
Archer, Anne
Arden, Eve
Arletty
Armstrong, Bess (Elizabeth Key)
Arnaz, Lucie Desiree
Arquette, Rosanna
Arthur, Beatrice
Arthur, Jean
Ashcroft, Peggy, Dame (Edith Margaret
  Emily)
Ashley, Elizabeth
Astor, Mary
Atwater, Edith
Audran, Stephane
Avedon, Doe
Ayres, Agnes
Bacall, Lauren
Bach, Barbara
Bach, Catherine
Baclanova, Olga
Baddeley, Angela (Madeleine Angela
  Clinton)
Baddeley, Hermione Clinton
Bailey, Pearl Mae

Bain, Barbara
Bainter, Fay Okell
Baker, Belle
Baker, Blanche
Baker, Carroll
Baker, Diane
Balin, Ina
Ball, Lucille
Ballard, Kaye
Bancroft, Anne
Bankhead, Tallulah Brockman
Banky, Vilma
Bara, Theda
Barbeau, Adrienne
Bardot, Brigitte
Bari, Lynn
Barnes, "Binniecq
Barnes, Joanna
Barrie, Barbara
Barrie, Mona
Barrie, Wendy
Barrymore, Diana
Barrymore, Drew
Barrymore, Elaine Jacobs
Barrymore, Ethel Mae Blythe
Barrymore, Georgina Emma Drew
Bartok, Eva
Basinger, Kim
Bateman, Justine
Bateman, Kate Josephine
Bates, Blanche Lyon
Bates, Florence
Bavier, Frances
Baxley Barbara
Baxter, Anne
Baxter-Birney, Meredith
Bayes, Nora
Bayne, Beverly Pearl
Beacham, Stephanie
Beals, Jennifer
Beavers, Louise
Bedelia, Bonnie
Beecher, Janet
Belafonte-Harper, Shari
Beller, Kathleen
Bellwood, Pamela
Belmont, Eleanor Robson
Benaderet, Bea
Benet, Brenda
Bennett, Constance Campbell
Bennett, Joan
Benton, Barbie
Benzell, Mimi (Miriam Ruth)
Berenson, Marisa
Berg, Gertrude
Bergen, Candice
Bergen, Polly
Berger, Senta
Bergman, Ingrid
Bergner, Elisabeth
Bernhardt, Sarah

Bernstein, Felicia Montealegre
Bertinelli, Valerie
Best, Edna
Bettis, Valerie
Billingsley, Barbara
Bishop, Julie
Bisset, Jacqueline Fraser
Black, Karen
Black, Shirley Temple
Blackman, Honor
Blaine, Vivian
Blair, Betsy
Blair, Janet
Blair, June
Blair, Linda Denise
Blake, Amanda
Blakeley, Ronee
Blakely, Susan
Blane, Sally
Bledsoe, Tempestt Kenieth
Blondell, Joan
Bloom, Claire
Blyth, Ann Marie
Blythe, Betty
Bohannon, Judy (Judith Layton)
Bohay, Heidi
Boland, Mary
Bond, Sudie
Bondi, Beulah
Bonet, Lisa
Bonstelle, Jessie
Booth, Shirley
Bordoni, Irene
Borg, Veda Ann
Bosson, Barbara
Boswell, Connee
Bow, Clara Gordon
Boyd, Belle (Isabellle)
Brady, Alice
Brennan, Eileen Regina
Brent, Evelyn
Brewer, Theresa
Brice, Fanny
Bridgewater, Dee Dee
Brinkley, Christie
Brisebois, Danielle
Britt, May
Brittany, Morgan
Britton, Barbara
Broderick, Helen
Bron, Eleanor
Bronson, Betty (Elizabeth Ada)
Brooke, Hillary
Brooks, Geraldine
Brooks, Louise
Brown, Blair
Brown, Georgia
Brown, Pamela
Brown, Pamela Beatrice
Brown, Vanessa
Browne, Coral Edith

Crews, Laura Hope
Cristal, Linda
Crosby, Cathy Lee
Crosby, Kathryn
Crosby, Mary Frances
Crosman, Henrietta
Crouse, Lindsay Ann
Crowley, Pat
Cummings, Constance
Cummings, Quinn
Cummins, Peggy
Curtin, Jane Therese
Curtis, Jamie Lee
Cushman, Charlotte Saunders
Cushman, Pauline
D'Angelo, Beverly
D'Orsay, Fifi
Dagmar
Dagover, Lil (Marta Maria Liletta)
Dahl, Arlene
Dailey, Irene
Dalton, Abby
Daly, Tyne (Ellen Tyne)
Damita, Lily
Dandridge, Dorothy
Daniels, "Bebe" (Virginia
Danner, Blythe Katharine
Darby, Kim
Darcel, Denise
Darnell, Linda
Darrieux, Danielle
Darvas, Lili
Darvi, Bella
Darwell, Jane
Davenport, Eva
Davenport, Fanny Lily Gypsy
Davies, Marion
Davis, Ann Bradford
Davis, Bette (Ruth Elizabeth)
Davis, Joan
Davis, Judy
Davis, Patti
Dawber, Pam
Dawn, Hazel
Day, Doris
Day, Laraine
Dean, Laura
DeCamp, Rosemary
DeCarlo, Yvonne
Dee, Frances
Dee, Ruby
Dee, Sandra
DeHaven, Gloria
DeHavilland, Olivia
DelRio, Dolores
DeMornay, Rebecca
Dempster, Carol
Dench, Judith Olivia
Deneuve, Catherine
Dennis, Sandy
Derek, Bo

Dern, Laura Elizabeth
Dewhurst, Colleen
DeWitt, Joyce
Dey, Susan Hallock
Diamond, Selma
Dickinson, Angie
Dickson, Gloria
Dietrich, Marlene
Diller, Phyllis
Dillon, Melinda
Dixon, Jean
Donahue, Elinor
Donnell, Jeff (Jean Marie)
Donnelly, Ruth
Dooley, Rae (Rachel Rice)
Dorleac, Francoise
Dors, Diana
Douglas, Donna
Down, Lesley-Anne
Drake, Betsy
Draper, Ruth
Dresser, Louise
Dressler, Marie
Drew, Louisa Lane
Dru, Joanne
Duff, Mary Ann Dyke
Duke, Patty (Anna Marie)
Dumont, Margaret
Dunaway, Faye (Dorothy Faye)
Duncan, Sandy
Dunne, Dominique
Dunne, Irene Marie
Dunnock, Mildred
Dupree, Minnie
Durbin, Deanna
Duse, Eleanora
Dussault, Nancy
Duvall, Shelley
Dvorak, Ann
Eagels, Jeanne
Eaton, Mary
Eaton, Shirley
Eden, Barbara Jean
Eggar, Samantha
Eggerth, Marta
Eichhorn, Lisa
Ekberg, Anita
Ekland, Britt
Eldridge, Florence
Elliott, Gertrude
Elliott, Maxine
Ellsler, Effie
Emerson, Faye Margaret
Emerson, Hope
Engel, Georgia Bright
Esmond, Jill
Evans, Dale
Evans, Edith Mary Booth, Dame
Evans, Linda
Evans, Madge (Margherita)
Evelyn, Judith

Fabares, Shelley (Michelle Marie)
Fabray, Nanette
Fairchild, Morgan
Faithfull, Marianne
Falana, Lola
Falconetti, Renee Maria
Falkenburg, Jinx (Eugenia Lincoln)
Farmer, Frances
Farr, Felicia
Farrell, Glenda
Farrow, Mia Villiers
Faust, Lotta
Fawcett, Farrah Leni
Faye, Alice
Fazenda, Louise
Feldon, Barbara
Feldshuh, Tovah
Fellows, Edith
Felton, Verna
Ferguson, Elsie
Ferrell, Conchata Galen
Ferris, Barbara Gillian
Fickett, Mary
Field, Betty
Field, Kate
Field, Sally Margaret
Field, Virginia (Margaret Cynthia St. John)
Fisher, Carrie Frances
Fisher, Clara
Fisher, Gail
Fiske, Minnie Maddern
Fitzgerald, Geraldine
Flagg, Fannie (Frances Carlton)
Flannery, Susan
Fleming, Erin
Fleming, Rhonda
Fletcher, Louise
Foch, Nina
Fonda, Jane
Fontaine, Joan
Fontanne, Lynn
Ford, Ruth Elizabeth
Forsyth, Rosemary
Foster, "Jodie" Alicia Christian
Foster, Susanna
Francis, Anne
Francis, Arlene
Francis, Genie
Francis, Kay
Franklin, Bonnie Gail
Franklin, Irene
Franklin, Pamela
Frederick, Pauline
Frelich, Phyllis
Friganza, Trixie
Froman, Jane
Fulton, Maude
Funicello, Annette
Furness, Betty (Elizabeth Mary)
Fyodorova, Victoria
Gabor, Eva

Gabor, Magda
Gabor, Zsa Zsa (Sari)
Gallagher, Helen
Gam, Rita Elenore
Garbo, Greta
Gardner, Ava
Garland, Beverly
Garland, Judy
Garner, Peggy Ann
Garnett, Gale
Garr, Teri
Garrett, Betty
Garson, Greer
Garver, Kathy
Gaynor, Janet
Geddes, Barbara Bel
Geeson, Judy
George, Gladys
George, Grace
George, Lynda Day
George, Susan
Gersten, Berta
Ghostley, Alice (Allyce)
Gibbs, Marla Bradley
Gilbert, Melissa
Gilmore, Virginia
Gilstrap, Suzy
Gingold, Hermione Ferdinanda
Girardot, Annie
Gish, Dorothy
Gish, Lillian Diana
Gleason, Lucille
Gless, Sharon
Goddard, Paulette
Goldberg, Whoopi
Golonka, Arlene
Goodfriend, Lynda
Goodman, Dody
Gordon, Kitty
Gordon, Ruth
Gordon, Vera
Grable, Betty
Grahame, Gloria
Grahame, Margot
Grant, Lee
Granville, Bonita
Grassle, Karen Gene
Gray, Coleen
Gray, Dolores
Gray, Linda
Grayson, Kathryn
Green, Mitzi
Greenwood, Charlotte
Greenwood, Joan
Greer, Jane
Grenfell, Joyce Irene
Grey, Virginia
Grier, Pamela Suzette
Griffith, Corinne
Griffith, Melanie
Grimes, Tammy Lee

Guinan, "Texas" Mary Louise Cecilia
Gurie, Sigrid
Gustafson, Karin
Gwyn, Nell (Eleanor)
Hack, Shelley
Hackett, Joan
Hagen, Jean
Hagen, Uta Thyra
Hale, Barbara
Hall, Juanita
Halop, Florence
Hamel, Veronica
Hamilton, Margaret
Hamilton, Nancy
Hampshire, Susan
Hampton, Hope
Hannah, Daryl
Hansen, Patti (Patricia Evina)
Harding, Ann
Harlow, Jean
Harper, Tess
Harper, Valerie
Harris, Barbara
Harris, Julie
Harris, Rosemary
Harrison, Jenilee
Hartley, Mariette
Hartman, Lisa
Hasso, Signe Eleonora Cecilia
Haver, June
Havoc, June
Hawn, Goldie Jean
Haydon, Julie
Hayes, Helen
Hayward, Brooke
Hayward, Susan
Hayworth, Rita
Healy, Katherine
Healy, Mary
Heatherton, Joey
Heckart, Eileen
Hedren, "Tippi" Natalie Kay
Held, Anna
Helmond, Katherine
Hemingway, Margaux
Hemingway, Mariel
Henderson, Florence
Henie, Sonja
Henner, Marilu
Henning, Linda Kaye
Henry, Charlotte
Henry, Martha
Hensley, Pamela Gail
Hepburn, Audrey
Hepburn, Katharine Houghton
Herlie, Eileen
Herne, Chrystal Katharine
Hershey, Barbara
Hill, Virginia
Hiller, Wendy
Hobart, Rose

Hobson, Valerie Babette
Hoffa, Portland
Holden, Fay
Holliday, Jennifer Yvette
Holliday, Judy
Holliday, Polly Dean
Holm, Celeste
Holm, Eleanor
Holman, Libby
Hood, Darla Jean
Hopkins, Miriam
Hopkins, Telma Louise
Hopper, Hedda
Horne, Lena Calhoun
Houghton, Katharine
Howard, Cordelia
Howard, Susan
Howes, Sally Ann
Howland, Beth
Hubley, Season
Hudson, Rochelle
Hull, Josephine
Hunnicutt, Gayle
Hunt, Linda
Hunt, Lois
Hunt, Martita
Hunter, Kim
Huppert, Isabelle
Hurt, Mary Beth Supinger
Hussey, Olivia
Hussey, Ruth Carol
Huston, Anjelica
Hutton, Betty
Hutton, Lauren (Mary Laurence)
Hyer, Martha
Hyland, Diana
Iman
Inescort, Frieda
Ireland, Jill
Irving, Isabel
Irwin, May
Jackson, Anne
Jackson, Glenda
Jackson, Janet
Jackson, Kate
Jacobsson, Ulla
Jagger, Bianca Teresa
Janis, Elsie
Jeanmaire, Renee Marcelle
Jeffreys, Anne
Jens, Salome
Jergens, Adele
Jillian, Ann
Johns, Glynis
Johnson, Celia, Dame
Johnson, Lynn-Holly
Jones, Anissa
Jones, Carolyn
Jones, Grace
Jones, Jennifer
Jones, Shirley

Joy, Leatrice
Joyce, Alice
Joyce, Elaine
Joyce, Peggy Hopkins
Jurado, Katy
Kahn, Madeline Gail
Kallen, Kitty
Kaminska, Ida
Kane, Carol
Kane, Helen
Kaprisky, Valerie
Kavner, Julie Deborah
Kay, Dianne
Keaton, Diane
Keeler, Ruby
Keene, Laura
Keller, Marthe
Kellerman, Annette
Kellerman, Sally
Kelly, Grace Patricia
Kelly, Nancy
Kelsey, Linda
Kelton, Pert
Kemble, Fanny (Frances Anne)
Kempson, Rachel
Kendal, Felicity
Kendal, Madge
Kendall, Kay
Kennedy, Jayne
Kennedy, Madge
Kerr, Deborah Jane
Keyes, Evelyn Louise
Khambatta, Persis
Kidder, Margot
King, Cammie
King, Morganna
King, Yolanda Denise
Kinski, Nastassja
Kirk, Phyllis
Knight, Shirley
Kohner, Susan
Kornman, Mary
Krige, Alice
Kristel, Sylvia
Kulp, Nancy
Kurtz, Swoosie
Kwan, Nancy Kashen
Ladd, Cheryl
Ladd, Diane
Lahti, Christine
Laine, Cleo
Lake, Veronica
LaMarr, Barbara
Lamarr, Hedy
Lamour, Dorothy
Lampert, Zohra
Lanchester, Elsa
Landers, Audrey
Landers, Judy
Landi, Elissa
Landis, Carole

Landis, Jessie Royce
Lane, Abbe
Lane, Lola
Lane, Priscilla
Lane, Rosemary
Lange, Hope Elise Ross
Lange, Jessica
Langford, Frances
Langtry, Lillie
Lansbury, Angela Brigid
Lansing, Joi
LaPlante, Laura
Lapotaire, Jane
Lasser, Louise
Laurie, Piper
Lavin, Linda
Lawrence, Florence
Lawrence, Gertrude
Lawrence, Margaret
Lawrence, Vicki
Leachman, Cloris
Learned, Michael
Lecouvreur, Adrienne
Lee, Dixie
Lee, Lila
Lee, Michele
Lee, Peggy
LeGallienne, Eva
Leigh, Janet
Leigh, Vivien
Leighton, Margaret
Lenska, Rula
Lenya, Lotte
Lenz, Kay
Leontovich, Eugenie
Leslie, Joan
Light, Judith
Lillie, Beatrice
Lincoln, Abbey
Lindfors, Viveca
Lindley, Audra
Lindsay, Margaret
Lipman, Clara
Lipton, Peggy
Lisi, Virna
Locke, Sondra
Lockhart, June
Locklear, Heather
Lockwood, Margaret Mary
Loden, Barbara Ann
Loftus, Cissie
Logan, Ella
Lollobrigida, Gina
Lombard, Carole
London, Julie
Long, Shelley
Longet, Claudine Georgette
Lopez, Priscilla
Lord, Marjorie
Lord, Pauline
Loren, Sophia

Loring, Gloria Jean
Lorne, Marion
Lorring, Joan
Loudon, Dorothy
Louise, Anita
Louise, Tina
Love, Bessie
Lovelace, Linda
Lowry, Judith Ives
Loy, Myrna
Lucci, Susan
Lulu
Lupino, Ida
LuPone, Patti
Lynley, Carol
Lynn, Diana
MacDonald, Jeanette
MacGrath, Leueen
MacGraw, Ali
MacKenzie, Gisele
MacLaine, Shirley
MacMahon, Aline
MacRae, Meredith
MacRae, Sheila
Madonna
Magnani, Anna
Main, Marjorie
Malina, Judith
Malone, Dorothy
Malone, Nancy
Mangano, Silvana
Mann, Erika
Manning, Irene
Mansfield, Jayne
Marchand, Nancy
Margo
Margolin, Janet
Markey, Enid
Marlowe, Julia
Marlowe, Marion
Marsh, Jean
Marsh, Mae
Marshall, Brenda
Marshall, Penny
Martin, Mary
Martin, Millicent
Martin, Pamela Sue
Martinelli, Elsa
Marvin, Michelle Triola
Masina, Giuletta
Mason, Marsha
Mason, Pamela Helen
Massey, Anna
Massey, Ilona
Maxwell, Marilyn
May, Edna
May, Elaine
Mayo, Virginia
McArdle, Andrea
McAvoy, May
McCambridge, Mercedes

McCarty, Mary
McCashin, Constance Broman
McClanahan, (Eddi-)Rue
McCoo, Marilyn
McCormack, Patty
McCracken, Joan
McDaniel, Hattie
McDevitt, Ruth
McDonald, Marie
McDonough, Mary Elizabeth
McGee, Molly
McGovern, Elizabeth
McGuire, Dorothy
McKechnie, Donna
McKenna, Siobhan
McKenna, Virginia
McKeon, Nancy
McLerie, Allyn Ann
McNeil, Claudia Mae
McNichol, Kristy
McQueen, "Butterfly" Thelma
Meadows, Audrey
Meadows, Jayne Cotter
Meara, Anne
Medford, Kay
Medina, Patricia
Menken, Adah Isaacs
Menken, Helen
Mercer, Beryl
Merchant, Vivien
Mercouri, "Melina" Maria Amalia
Meriwether, Lee
Merkel, Una
Merman, Ethel
Merrill, Dina
Meyers, Ari(adne)
Midler, Bette
Milano, Alyssa
Miles, Sarah
Miles, Sylvia
Miles, Vera
Milford, Penny (Penelope)
Miller, Ann
Miller, Cheryl
Miller, Marilyn
Mills, Donna
Mills, Hayley
Mills, Juliet
Mills, Stephanie
Mimieux, Yvette Carmen M
Minnelli, Liza
Miranda, Carmen
Mirren, Helen
Mitchell, Margaret Julia
Mobley, Mary Ann
Modjeska, Helena
Monroe, Marilyn
Montez, Maria
Montgomery, Elizabeth
Moore, Colleen
Moore, Constance

Provine, Dorothy Michele
Prowse, Juliet
Purl, Linda
Purviance, Edna
Quayle, Anna
Quinlan, Kathleen
Rachel
Radner, Gilda
Rae, Charlotte
Raffin, Deborah
Rainer, Luise
Raines, Cristina
Raines, Ella
Ralston, Esther
Ralston, Vera
Rambeau, Marjorie
Rampling, Charlotte
Rashad, Phylicia
Ratzenberger, John
Redgrave, Lynn
Redgrave, Vanessa
Redman, Joyce
Reed, Donna
Reese, Della
Rehan, Ada
Reid, Beryl
Reid, Kate (Daphne Kate)
Remick, Lee
Revere, Anne
Reynolds, Debbie (Marie Frances)
Reynolds, Marjorie
Rice-Davies, Mandy
Rich, Irene
Richardson, Susan
Rigg, Diana
Ring, Blanche
Ringwald, Molly
Risdon, Elizabeth
Ritter, Thelma
Roberts, Doris
Roberts, Rachel
Robson, Flora McKenzie, Dame
Robson, May
Rogers, Ginger
Roker, Roxie
Roland, Ruth
Rolle, Esther
Roman, Ruth
Rosay, Francoise
Ross, Diana
Ross, Katharine
Ross, Marion
Rossellini, Isabella
Rowlands, Gena
Royle, Selena
Rubens, Alma
Rule, Janice
Rush, Barbara
Russell, Annie
Russell, Gail
Russell, Jane

Russell, Lillian
Russell, Rosalind
Rutherford, Ann
Rutherford, Margaret
Ryan, Irene Noblette
Ryan, Peggy (Margaret O'Rene)
Saint James, Susan
Saint John, Betta
Saint John, Jill
Saint, Eva Marie
Salt, Jennifer
Sanda, Dominique
Sanderson, Julia
Sands, Diana Patricia
Sands, Dorothy
Sanford, Isabel Gwendolyn
Sarandon, Susan Abigail
Sarnoff, Dorothy
Saunders, Lori
Scala, Gia
Schafer, Natalie
Schell, Maria Margarethe
Schlamme, Martha
Schneider, "Romycq
Schneider, Maria
Scott, Lizabeth
Scott, Martha Ellen
Scott, Pippa (Phillippa)
Sears, Heather
Seberg, Jean
Seeley, Blossom
Segal, Vivienne
Seldes, Marian
Sellecca, Connie
Seymour, Anne Eckert
Seymour, Jane
Shabazz, Attallah
Shaver, Helen
Shaw, Mary
Shaw, Reta
Shearer, Moira
Shearer, Norma
Sheedy, Ally
Shelley, Carole
Shepherd, Cybill
Sheridan, Ann
Shields, Brooke
Shire, Talia Rose Coppola
Shirley, Anne
Shore, Dinah
Shutta, Ethel
Siddons, Sarah Kemble
Sidney, Sylvia
Signoret, Simone Henrietta Charlotte
Simmons, Jean
Simms, Hilda
Simms, Lu Ann
Simon, Simone
Sinclair, Madge
Singleton, Penny
Skinner, Cornelia Otis

Skipworth, Alison
Slezak, Erika
Smith, Alexis
Smith, Allison
Smith, Jaclyn
Smith, Madolyn Story
Smith, Maggie
Smith, Samantha
Smithers, Jan
Smithson, Harriet Constance
Snodgress, Carrie
Somers, Brett
Somers, Suzanne
Sommer, Elke
Sondergaard, Gale
Sothern, Ann
Spacek, "Sissy" Mary Elizabeth
Stanley, Kim
Stanwyck, Barbara
Stapleton, Jean
Stapleton, Maureen
Stark, "Koo" Kathleen
Steenburgen, Mary
Sterling, Jan
Stevens, Connie
Stevens, Emily A
Stevens, Inger
Stevens, K T
Stevens, Kaye (Catherine)
Stevens, Stella
Stewart, Anita
Stickney, Dorothy
Stone, Dorothy
Storm, Gale
Straight, Beatrice Whitney
Strasberg, Susan Elizabeth
Strassman, Marcia
Stratten, Dorothy
Streep, Meryl (Mary Louise)
Streisand, Barbra Joan
Stritch, Elaine
Struthers, Sally Anne
Sullavan, Margaret
Sullivan, Susan
Susann, Jacqueline
Suzman, Janet
Suzuki, Pat (Chiyoko)
Swanson, Gloria May Josephine
Sweet, Blanche
Swenson, Inga
Swit, Loretta
Syms, Sylvia
Talbot, Nita
Talmadge, Constance
Talmadge, Norma
Tandy, Jessica
Tanguay, Eva
Tashman, Lilyan
Tate, Sharon
Taylor, Elizabeth Rosemond
Taylor, Estelle

Taylor, Laurette
Tempest, Marie
Templeton, Fay
Terris, Norma
Terry, Ellen Alicia, Dame
Thaxter, Phyllis
Thomas, Betty
Thomas, Marlo
Thompson, Sada Carolyn
Thorndike, Sybil, Dame
Thulin, Ingrid
Tiegs, Cheryl
Tierney, Gene
Tiffin, Pamela Kimberley
Tilton, Charlene
Todd, Ann
Todd, Thelma
Tomlin, "Lily" Mary Jean
Tompkins, Angel
Toren, Marta
Totter, Audrey
Trask, Diana
Treas, Terri
Trevor, Claire
Turner, "Lana" Julia Jean Mildred
    Frances
Turner, Claramae
Turner, Kathleen
Tushingham, Rita
Tuttle, Lurene
Twelvetrees, Helen
Tyrrell, Susan
Tyson, Cicely
Tyzack, Margaret
Uggams, Leslie
Ullman, Tracey
Ullmann, Liv Johanne
Ulric, Lenore
Umeki, Miyoshi
Ure, Mary
Vaccaro, Brenda
Valentine, Karen
Valli, Alida
Van Ark, Joan
Van Devere, Trish
Van Doren, Mamie
Van Fleet, Jo
Van Patten, Joyce
Van Vooren, Monique
Vance, Vivian
Vanderbilt, Gloria Morgan
Vanity
VanKamp, Merete
Varsi, Diane
Velez, Lupe
Venuta, Benay
Vera-Ellen
Verdon, Gwen (Gwyneth Evelyn)
Verdugo, Elena
Vickers, Martha
Vidor, Florence

Vinson, Helen
Vitale, Milly
Vitti, Monica
Vohs, (Elinor) Joan
VonFurstenberg, Betsy
Wagner, Lindsay
Walker, Nancy
Walley, Deborah
Wallis, Shani
Walter, Jessica
Walters, Julie
Walters, Laurie
Ward, Fannie
Ward, Rachel
Warren, Lesley Ann
Warrick, Ruth
Waters, Ethel
Wayne, Paula
Weaver, Sigourney
Weber, Lois
Webster, Margaret
Welch, Raquel
Weld, Tuesday (Susan Kerr)
Weldon, Joan
West, Mae
Westley, Helen
Whelchel, Lisa
White, Betty
White, Pearl
Whitelaw, Billie
Whitty, May, Dame
Widdoes, Kathleen
Williams, Cindy
Williams, Esther
Wilson, Julie
Wilson, Marie (Katherine Elizabeth)
Windsor, Claire
Windsor, Marie
Winfrey, Ophra
Winger, Debra
Winters, Shelley
Winwood, Estelle
Withers, Googie
Withers, Jane
Woffington, Margaret
Wong, Anna May (Lu Tsong)
Wood, Natalie
Wood, Peggy
Woodward, Joanne Gignilliat
Worley, Jo Anne
Worth, Irene
Wray, Fay
Wright, Martha
Wright, Teresa
Wyatt, Jane
Wycherley, Margaret
Wyler, Gretchen
Wyman, Jane
Wynter, Dana
Wynyard, Diana
York, Susannah

Yothers, Tina
Young, Clara Kimball
Young, Loretta Gretchen
Yurka, Blanche
Zadora, Pia
Zetterling, Mai Elisabeth
Zimbalist, Stephanie
Zorina, Vera

ADMIRAL

Anson, George, Baron
Beatty, David Beatty, Earl
Blake, Robert
Buchanan, Pat
Canaris, Wilhelm
Carney, Robert Bostwick
Chatfield, Alfred E Montacute, Baron
Codrington, Edward, Sir
Dennison, Robert Lee
Doenitz, Karl C
Doria, Andrea
Drake, Francis, Sir
Duerk, Alene B
Ellsberg, Edward
Evans, Edward Ratcliffe Garth Russell
Fisher, John Arbuthnot
Fraser, Bruce Austin, Sir
Grasse, Count Francois Joseph Paul de
Gravely, Samuel L
Halsey, William Frederick
Horthy de Nagybanya, Nicholas
Howe, Richard
Jellicoe, John
Kimmel, Husband Edward
King, Ernest Joseph
Mahan, Alfred Thayer
McCain, John Sidney, Jr.
Nomura, Kichisaburo
Parry, William Edward, Sir
Radford, Arthur William
Rodney, George Brydges
Sandwich, Edward Montagu, Earl
Spruance, Raymond Ames
Tirpitz, Alfred von
Togo, Heihachiro
Towers, John Henry
Vernon, Edward, Sir
Worden, John Lorimer
Zumwalt, Elmo Russell, Jr.

ADVENTURER

Blood, Thomas
Blyth, Chay
Bowles, William Augustus
Casanova (de Seingalt), Giovanni Giacomo
Chichester, Francis Charles, Sir
Crichton, James
Horn, Alfred Aloysius, pseud.
Judson, Edward Zane Carroll
Perkins, Marlin (Richard Marlin)

Ridgeway, Rick
Scott, Walter
Selkirk, Alexander
Slocum, Joshua
Thorne, Jim
Trelawny, Edward John
Uemura, Naomi
Villiers, Alan John
Walker, William

ADVERTISING EXECUTIVE

Ally, Carl Joseph
Ayer, Francis Wayland
Barton, Bruce
Bates, Ted (Theodore Lewis)
Bernbach, William
Burnett, Leo
Calkins, Earnest Elmo
Caples, John
Chait, Lawrence G
Cone, Fairfax Mastick
Dane, Maxwell
Daniels, Draper
DellaFemina, Jerry
Duffy, Ben (Bernard Cornelius)
Elting, Victor, Jr.
Fitz-Gibbon, Bernice Bowles
Green, Paula
Hagopian, Louis Thomas
Heller, Goldie
Hollister, Paul Merrick
Johnson, Arno Hollock
Lasker, Albert Davis
Liebmann, Philip
Maneloveg, Herbert Donald
Maxon, Lou Russell
May, Robert Lewis
Mayer, Edward Newton, Jr.
McCann, Harrison King
Meek, Samuel Williams
Ogilvy, David Mackenzie
Philbrick, Herbert Arthur
Polykoff, Shirley
Procter, Barbara Gardner
Redhead, Hugh McCulloch
Reeves, Rosser
Regan, Theodore M, Jr.
Resor, Stanley Burnett
Roth, Richard Lynn
Roy, Ross
Rubicam, Raymond
Sackheim, Maxwell Byron
Samstag, Nicholas
Savage, Robert Heath
Schachte, Henry Miner
Seymour, Dan
Strouse, Norman H
Svensson, Robert
Thompson, J(ames) Walter
Weir, Walter

Wells, Mary
Young, James Webb

ADVICE COLUMNIST

Landers, Ann
Van Buren, Abigail

AERONAUTICAL ENGINEER

Cierva, Juan de la
DeSeversky, Alexander Procofieff
Eckener, Hugo
Gilruth, Robert Rowe
Grumman, Leroy Randle
Horikoshi, Jiro
Hunsaker, Jerome Clarke
Johnson, Clarence Leonard
Kollsman, Paul
Martin, James Slattin, Jr.
Shute, Nevil
Sikorsky, Igor Ivanovich
Sopwith, Thomas O M
Upson, Ralph Hazlett
Von Karman, Theodore
Vought, Chance Milton

AGENT

Mengers, Sue
Weintraub, Jerry

AGRICULTURALIST

Borlaug, Norman Ernest

AGRICULTURIST

Garst, Roswell
Saunders, William

AIR FORCE OFFICER

Armstrong, Jack Lawrence
Bader, Douglas Robert Steuart, Sir
Cooke, Christopher M
Davis, Benjamin Oliver, Jr.
Dowding, Hugh C T, Baron
Gibson, Guy
LeMay, Curtis Emerson
Norstad, Lauris
Twining, Nathan F(arragut)

AIR MARSHAL

Bishop, Billy (William Avery)
Ellington, Edward

AIRCRAFT DESIGNER

Beard, Myron Gould
Fokker, Anthony Herman Gerard
Hobbs, Leonard Sinclair

Ilyushin, Sergei Vladimirovich
Junkers, Hugo
Messerschmitt, Willy (Wilhelm)
Mitchell, Reginald Joseph
Zeppelin, Ferdinand von, Count

AIRCRAFT MANUFACTURER

Allen, William McPherson
Beech, Walter Herschel
Bell, Lawrence Dale
Bellanca, Giuseppe Mario
Boullioun, E(rnest) H(erman, Jr.)
Cessna, Clyde Vernon
Curtiss, Glenn Hammond
Dassault, Marcel
DeHavilland, Geoffrey
Dornier, Claude
Douglas, Donald Willis
Gross, Robert Ellsworth
Martin, Glenn Luther
McDonnell, James Smith
Northrop, John Knudsen
Page, Frederick Handley, Sir
Piper, William Thomas
Ryan, T(ubal) Claude

AIRLINE EXECUTIVE

Borman, Frank
Braniff, Thomas Elmer
Damon, Ralph Shepard
Feldman, Alvin Lindbergh
Gross, Courtlandt Sherrington
Halaby, Najeeb Elias
Kerkorian, Kirk
Laker, Freddie (Frederick Alfred)
Patterson, William Allan
Rabin, Yehuda L
Smith, Cyrus Rowlett
Solomon, Samuel Joseph
Trippe, Juan Terry

AIRPLANE MANUFACTURER

Boeing, William Edward

ALLEGED EXTORTIONIST

Lewis, James W

ANARCHIST

Bakunin, Mikhail Aleksandrovich
Berkman, Alexander
Cohn-Bendit, Daniel
Goldman, Emma
Proudhon, Pierre Joseph

ANESTHETIST

Apgar, Virginia

ANIMAL DEALER

Buck, Frank
Trefflich, Henry Herbert Frederick

ANIMAL EXPERT

Adamson, George
Adamson, Joy Friederike Victoria Gessner

ANIMAL TRAINER

Humphrey, Elliott S
Weatherwax, Rudd B

ANTHROPOLOGIST

Barnett, Steve
Bateson, Gregory
Beals, Ralph Leon
Benedict, Ruth Fulton
Biebuyck, Daniel Prosper
Bird, Junius Bouton
Boas, Franz
Brinton, Daniel Garrison
Bunzel, Ruth L
Castaneda, Carlos
Cobb, William Montague
Coon, Carleton Stevens
Dart, Raymond Arthur
Devereux, George
Dixon, Roland Burrage
Du Chaillu, Paul Belloni
Edmonson, Munro Sterling
Eiseley, Loren Corey
Frazer, James George, Sir
Geertz, Clifford
Goodall, Jane
Heyerdahl, Thor
Hodge, Frederick Webb
Hooton, Earnest Albert
Hurston, Zora Neale
Johanson, Donald Carl
Kroeber, Alfred Louis
LaFarge, Oliver
Leakey, Louis Seymour Bazett
Leakey, Mary Douglas
Leakey, Richard E
Levi-Strauss, Claude
Levy-Bruhl, Lucien
Lewis, Oscar
Linton, Ralph
Malinowski, Bronislaw
Mead, Margaret
Montagu, Ashley Montague Francis
Powdermaker, Hortense
Powell, John Wesley
Sapir, Edward
Turnbull, Collin M(acmillan)
Tylor, Edward Bennett, Sir
Weaver, Thomas
Westermarck, Edward Alexander

ANTI-FEMINIST

Morgan, Marabel
Schlafly, Phyllis Stewart

ANTIQUARIAN

Aubrey, John
Kovel, Ralph Mallory
Kovel, Terry Horvitz
Laing, David

APACHE CHIEF

Cochise

ARCHAEOLOGIST

Albright, William Foxwell
Anderson, Douglas Dorland
Bell, Gertrude Margaret
Bibby, Thomas Geoffrey
Bordes, Francois
Breasted, James Henry
Breuil, Henri Abbe
Broneer, Oscar Theodore
Carter, Howard
Caton-Thompson, Gertrude
Cesnola, Luigi Palma di
Childe, Vere Gordon
Collingwood, Robin George
Evans, Arthur John, Sir
Evans, Clifford
Glueck, Nelson
Gorman, Chester
Hanfmann, George Maxim Anossov
Hawes, Harriet Ann Boyd
Herbert, George Edward Stanhope
    Molyneux
Kidder, Alfred Vincent
Layard, Austin Henry, Sir
Mallowan, Max Edgar Lucien, Sir
Mercer, Henry Chapman
Michalowski, Kazimierz
Murray, Margaret Alice
Nuttall, Zelia Maria
Peiresc, Nicholas-Claude Fabri de
Petrie, (William Matthew) Flinders, Sir
Reisner, George Andrew
Schliemann, Heinrich
Sukenik, Eliazer Lipa
Thompson, Edward Herbert
Wheeler, Mortimer (Robert Eric Mortimer)
Wood, J Turtle
Woolley, Charles Leonard, Sir
Yadin, Yigael

ARCHER

Hill, Howard

ARCHITECT

Aalto, Alvar Henrik (Hugo)
Abramovitz, Max
Adam, James
Adam, Robert
Adler, David
Alberti, Leon Battista
Allen of Hurtwood, Lady
Altdorfer, Albrecht
Asplund, Erik Gunnar
Atterbury, Grosvenor
Bacon, Henry
Baltard, Victor
Barnes, Edward Larrabee
Barragan, Luis
Bartolommeo, Fra
Bayer, Herbert
Bellini, Giovanni
Belluschi, Pietro
Benjamin, Asher
Berlage, Hendrik Petrus
Bernini, Giovanni Lorenzo
Born, Ernest Alexander
Borromini, Francesco
Bramante, Donata d'Agnolo
Breuer, Marcel Lajos
Brown, Lancelot
Brunelleschi, Filippo
Bulfinch, Charles
Burlington, Richard Boyle, Earl
Burnham, Daniel H
Butterfield, William
Butts, Alfred Mosher
Candela, Felix (Outerino Felix)
Casey, Edward Pearce
Chalgrin, Francois
Chambers, William, Sir
Clarke, Gilmore David
Coolidge, Charles Allerton
Cosimo, Piero di
Costa, Lucio
Cram, Ralph Adams
Cramp, Charles Henry
Creighton, Thomas H(awk)
Cret, Paul P(hilippe)
Cuypers, Petrus Josephus Hubertus
Davis, Alexander Jackson
Dinkeloo, John Gerard
Dinwiddie, John Ekin
Dolci, Danilo
Douglass, Lathrop
Downing, Andrew Jackson
Doxiadis, Constantinos Apostolos
Farrand, Beatrix Jones
Fitch, James Marston
Flagg, Ernest
Frisch, Max

Fuller, "Bucky" Richard Buckminster
Gabriel, Ange-Jacques
Gardner, Jean Louis Charles
Gaudi y Cornet, Antonio
Gibberd, Frederick
Gibbs, James
Gibbs, William Francis
Gilbert, Cass
Giorgio, Francesco di
Giotto di Bondone
Godwin, Edward William
Goldberg, Bertrand
Goodhue, Bertram G
Graham, Ernest Robert
Graves, Michael
Griffiths, John Willis
Gropius, Walter Adolf
Gruen, Victor
Grunewald, Matthias
Gunnison, Foster
Harris, Harwell Hamilton
Harrison, Peter
Harrison, Wallace Kirkman
Hastings, Thomas
Hoban, James
Holabird, William
Holbein, Hans, the Elder
Hood, Raymond Matthewson
Humphreys, Joshua
Hunt, Richard Morris
Hussey, Christopher Edward Clive
Hutton, Addison
Ittner, William Butts
Jacobsen, Arne
Jahn, Helmut
Jenney, William LeBaron
Johnson, Phillip Cortelyou
Jones, Edward Vason
Jones, Inigo
Jones, Robert Trent
Kahn, Albert
Kahn, Louis I
Kesselring, Joseph
Khan, Fazlur Rahman
Kimball, Fiske
Kopit, Arthur L
L'Enfant, Pierre Charles
LaFarge, Christopher
LaFeuer, Minard
Lapidus, Morris
Latrobe, Benjamin Henry
LeCorbusier
Ledoux, Claude Nicolas
LeNotre, Andre
Lescaze, William
Link, Theodore Carl
Llewelyn-Davies, Richard
Luckman, Charles
Lutyens, Edwin Landseer, Sir
Maginnis, Charles Donagh
Magonigle, Harold Van Buren

Maher, George Washington
Mansart, Francois
Mansart, Jules Hardouin
Maybeck, Bernard Ralph
Mayer, Albert
McArthur, John
McKim, Charles Follen
Mead, William Rutherford
Medary, Milton B
Meier, Richard Alan
Mellor, Walter
Mendelsohn, Eric
Mies van der Rohe, Ludwig
Milburn, Frank Pierce
Mills, Robert
Mizner, Addison
Morgan, Julia
Mould, Jacob Wrey
Mullett, Alfred Bult
Mullgardt, Louis Christian
Mumford, Lewis
Murchison, Kenneth MacKenzie
Nash, John
Neff, Wallace
Nelson, George H.
Nervi, Pier Luigi
Netsch, Walter Andrew, Jr.
Neutra, Richard Joseph
Nichols, Anne
Niemeyer, Oscar
Nimmons, George Croll
Nowicki, Matthew
Obata, Gyo
Olmsted, Frederick Law
Orr, Douglas William
Owings, Nathaniel Alexander
Palladio, Andrea
Patrick, John
Paxton, Joseph, Sir
Pei, I(eoh) M(ing)
Pelli, Cesar
Pereira, William Leonard
Perrault, Claude
Pevsner, Nikolaus Bernhard Leon, Sir
Pisano, Andrea
Pisano, Giovanni
Polk, Willis Jefferson
Ponti, Gio(vanni)
Pope, John Russell
Portman, John Calvin
Primaticcio, Francesco
Raphael
Renwick, James
Repton, Humphry
Richardson, Henry Hobson
Roche, Kevin (Eammon Kevin)
Rodia, Simon
Rodilla, Simon
Rogers, Isaiah
Rogers, James Gamble
Root, John Wellborn

Rossant, James Stephan
Rossetti, Gino (Louis A)
Rudolph, Paul Marvin
Saarinen, Eero
Saarinen, Eliel
Safdie, Moshe
Sert, Jose Luis
Sherman, Frank Dempster
Skidmore, Louis
Sloan, Samuel
Soane, John, Sir
Soleri, Paolo
Sostratus
Speer, Albert
Spence, Basil, Sir
Spychalski, Marian
Stein, Clarence S
Steinberg, Saul
Stirling, James
Stone, Edward Durell
Stotz, Charles Morse
Stuart, James
Sullivan, Louis Henri
Tallmadge, Thomas Eddy
Tange, Kenzo
Taylor, Samuel (Albert)
Trumbauer, Horace
Tunnard, Christopher
Upjohn, Richard
Utzon, Joern
Vasari, Giorgio
Vaux, Calvert
Vignola, Giacomo da
Viollet le Duc, Eugene Emmanuel
Vitruvius
Vreeland, Thomas Reed, Jr.
Walker, Ralph Thomas
Walter, Thomas Ustick
Wank, Roland A
White, Stanford
Williams, Paul R(evere)
Wren, Christopher, Sir
Wright, Frank Lloyd
Wright, Henry
Wright, John Lloyd
Wright, Lloyd (Frank Lloyd, Jr.)
Wurster, William
Yamasaki, Minoru
Yeon, John
York, Edward Palmer
Yost, Joseph Warren

ARMY OFFICER

Abrams, Creighton Williams
Alexander, William
Arnold, Benedict
Bennett, John Charles
Bonneville, Benjamin
Bouquet, Henry
Browning, Frederick A(rthur) M(ontague),
  Sir

Burnside, Ambrose Everett
Calley, William Laws
Carpenter, William S, Jr.
Caswell, Richard
Chase, William Curtis
Chu Te
Clay, Lucius du Bignon
Collins, Joseph L
Conway, Thomas
Costa e Silva, Arthur da
Custer, George Armstrong
Davison, Frederic Ellis
Dean, William Frishe
Dempsey, Miles Christopher, Sir
Devers, Jacob Loucks
Doolittle, James Harold
Dreyfus, Alfred
Eaker, Ira Clarence
Eichelberger, Robert Lawrence
Forbes, John
Gage, Thomas
Gavin, James Maurice
Goethals, George Washington
Goodpaster, Andrew Jackson
Gowon, Yakubu
Graves, William Sidney
Greely, Adolphus Washington
Groves, Leslie Richard
Gruenther, Alfred Maximillian
Haddad, Saad
Handy, Thomas Troy
Harding, Chester
Harmon, Ernest N
Havelock, Henry
Henderson, Oran K
Hershey, Lewis Blaine
Horrocks, Brian Gwynne, Sir
Houston, Sam(uel)
Howard, Oliver Otis
Huebner, Clarence R
Ironside, William E
Kehoe, Vincent Jeffre-Roux
Lattre de Tassigny, Jean de
Lemnitzer, Lyman Louis
MacArthur, Arthur
MacArthur, Douglas
Marcus, David
McAuliffe, Anthony Clement
McDowell, Irvin
Medina, Ernest L
Meigs, Montgomery Cunningham
Merrill, Frank Dow
Milne, George
Morgan, Frederick
Muenchhausen, Friedrich Ernst von
Napier, Charles
Napier, Robert Cornelis
Netanyahu, Yonatan
Ord, Edward Otho Cresap
Patton, George Smith, III
Patton, George Smith, Jr.

Pershing, John J(oseph)
Pike, Zebulon Montgomery
Rawlins, John A
Roberts, Frederick
Rosecrans, William Starke
Scobie, Ronald Mackenzie
Sedgwick, John
Shrapnel, Henry
Simpson, William Hood
Stauffenberg, Claus (Schenk Graf) Von
Sumner, Edwin V
Timoshenko, Semen Konstantinovich
Van Rensselaer, Stephen
VonSteuben, Friedrich Wilhelm
Wright, Horatio Governeur

ART COLLECTOR

Altman, Benjamin
Beatty, Alfred Chester, Sir
Dale, Chester
Duveen, Joseph, Sir
Guggenheim, Peggy Marguerite
Gulbenkian, Calouste S
Halpert, Edith Gregor
Hirshhorn, Joseph
Lehman, Adele Lewisohn
Maeght, Aime
Molyneux, Edward H
Quinn, John
Soane, John, Sir
Tate, Henry, Sir

ART CRITIC

Apollinaire, Guillaume
Bell, Clive
Berenson, Bernard
Berger, John
Canaday, John (Edwin John)
Cheney, Sheldon Warren
Coates, Robert Myron
Craven, Thomas
DeKooning, Elaine Marie Catherine Fried
Elytis, Odysseus
Frankfurter, Alfred Moritz
Fry, Roger Eliot
Genauer, Emily
Hughes, Robert Studley Forrest
Meier-Graefe, Julius
Read, Herbert, Sir
Rodman, Selden
Rossetti, William Michael
Ruskin, John
Saarinen, Aline Bernstein
Sitwell, Sacheverell, Sir
Soby, James Thrall

ART DIRECTOR

Adam, Ken
Aymar, Gordon Christian

De Cuir, John
Levy, Florence
Parsons, Betty Pierson
Sylbert, Richard
Trauner, Alexander

ART HISTORIAN

Andrews, Wayne
Aranason, H Harvard
Barr, Alfred Hamilton, Jr.
Blunt, Anthony Frederick
Carritt, David Graham (Hugh David Graham)
Clark, Kenneth McKenzie, Sir
Crosby, Sumner McKnight
Faure, Elie
Fenollosa, Ernest Francisco
Hoving, Thomas Pearsall Field
Huisman, Philippe
Levy, Julien
Panofsky, Erwin
Pevsner, Nikolaus Bernhard Leon, Sir
Rosenberg, Jakob
Waterhouse, Ellis Kirkham, Sir

ART PATRON

Burlington, Richard Boyle, Earl
Hartford, Huntington
Kahn, Otto Hermann
Martinson, Joseph Bertram
Phillips, Marjorie Acker
Rockefeller, Abby Aldrich
Whitney, Gertrude Vanderbilt

ARTIST

Abbey, Edwin Austin
Agam, Yaacov
Alajalov, Constantin
Albers, Josef
Albright, Ivan Le Lorraine
Albright, Malvin Marr
Alfieri, Vittorio
Allston, Washington
Alma-Tadema, Lawrence, Sir
Altdorfer, Albrecht
Amen, Irving
Ames, Blanche
Angelico, Fra
Annigoni, Pietro
Antes, Horst
Antonello da Messina
Anuszkiewicz, Richard Joseph
Apelles
Appel, Karel Christian
Archipenko, Alexander Porfirievich
Arisman, Marshall
Audubon, John James
Auerbach-Levy, William
Ault, George Christian

Chase, William Merritt
Chermayeff, Ivan
Chicago, Judy
Chillida, Eduard
Chirico, Giorgio de
Christ-Janer, Albert
Christo
Christy, Howard Chandler
Church, Frederick Edwin
Cimabue, Giovanni
Clave, Antoni
Cleve, Joos van
Clouet, Francois
Clouet, Jean
Colby, Carroll Burleigh
Cole, Thomas
Colonna di Castiglione, Adele
Colville, Alex (David Alexander)
Constable, John
Cooper, Samuel
Copley, John Singleton
Corben, Richard Vance
Corinth, Lovis
Corneille
Cornelius, Peter von
Cornell, Joseph
Corot, Jean Baptiste Camille
Correggio, Antonio Allegri da
Cosimo, Piero di
Cotman, John S
Cotsworth, Staats
Courbet, Gustave
Covarrubias, Miguel
Cox, David
Cox, Gardner
Cox, John Rogers
Cox, Kenyon
Cranach, Lucas
Crane, Walter
Crivelli, Carlo
Crome, John
Cropsey, Jasper Francis
Cruikshank, George
Cuneo, Terence Tenison
Curran, Charles Courtney
Curry, John Steuart
Cuyp, Aelbert
Daguerre, Louis Jacques Mande
Dali, Salvador
Daubigny, Charles Francois
Daumier, Honore
David, Gerard
David, Jacques Louis
Davies, Arthur Bowen
Davis, Stuart
Decamps, Alexandre Gabriel
DeErdely, Francis (Ferenc)
Degas, (Hilaire Germain) Edgar
Dehn, Adolf Arthur
DeKooning, Elaine Marie Catherine Fried
DeKooning, Willem

Delacroix, (Ferdinand Victor) Eugene
Delaroche, Hippolyte
Delaunay, Robert
Delaunay-Terk, Sonia
Dellenbaugh, Frederick Samuel
Demuth, Charles
Derain, Andre
DeRivera, Jose
Dewing, Thomas Wilmer
Diaz de la Pena, Narciso Virgilio
Dickinson, Edwin W
Diebenkorn, Richard
Dine, Jim
Dix, Otto
Dodd, Mrs. John Bruce (Sonora Louise
   Smart)
Doesburg, Theo van
Dohanos, Stevan
Dolci, Carlo
Domenichino, Il
Donatello
Dongen, Kees van
Dore, Gustave (Paul Gustave)
Dou, Gerard
Douglas, Aaron
Doulton, Henry, Sir
Dove, Arthur Garfield
Doyle, Richard
DuBay, William Bryan
DuBois, Guy Pene
Dubuffet, Jean
Duccio di Buoninsegna
Duchamp, Marcel
Dufresne, Charles
Dufy, Raoul
Dulac, Edmund
DuMaurier, George Louis P B
Duncanson, Robert Scott
Dunlap, William
Dunn, Alan
Dunoyer de Segonzac, Andre
Durand, Asher Brown
Durer, Albrecht
Durrie, George Henry
Duveneck, Frank
Dyce, William
Dyck, Anthony van
Eakins, Thomas
Earle, Ralph
Eastlake, Charles Lock
Eberle, Mary Abastenia St. Leger
Ehrlich, Bettina Bauer
Eilshemius, Louis Michel
Elisofon, Eliot
Elliott, Charles Loring
Elsheimer, Adam
Enright, Elizabeth
Ensor, James
Ernst, Jimmy
Ernst, Max
Escher, Maurits Cornelis

Evergood, Philip Howard
Fabritius, Carel
Fantin-Latour, (Ignace) Henri
Feininger, Lyonel
Fernandez-Muro, Jose Antonio
Feti, Domenico
Feuerbach, Anselm
Fini, Leonor
Fischl, Eric
Flagg, James Montgomery
Flaxman, John
Flint, William Russell, Sir
Folon, Jean-Michel
Forain, Jean-Louis
Fouquet, Jean
Fragonard, Jean Honore
Francis, Sam
Frankenthaler, Helen
Frasconi, Antonio
Frazetta, Frank
Freud, Lucian
Friedrich, Caspar David
Friesz, Othon
Fry, Roger Eliot
Fuertes, Louis Agassiz
Fuller, George
Fuseli, Henry
Gainsborough, Thomas
Gallatin, Albert Eugene
Gallo, Frank
Gauguin, Paul (Eugene Henri Paul)
Gaulli, Giovanni Battista
Gaunt, William
Gentile da Fabriano
Gentileschi, Orazio
George, Don
George, Jean Craighead
Gerard, Francois
Gericault, Jean Louis Andre Theodore
Gerome, Jean Leon
Ghiberti, Lorenzo
Ghirlandaio, Domenico
Gibran, Kahlil
Gibran, Kahlil George
Gilot, Francoise
Giordano, Luca
Giorgio, Francesco di
Giorgione, Il
Giotto di Bondone
Giovanni di Paulo
Girtin, Thomas
Glackens, William James
Glanzman, Louis S
Gleizes, Albert L
Goes, Hugo van der
Golden, William
Golub, Leon Albert
Goodall, John Strickland
Gorky, Arshile
Gorman, Rudolph Carl
Gottlieb, Adolph

Goya y Lucientes, Francisco Jose de
Goyen, Jan Josephszoon van
Gozzoli, Benozzo
Graves, Morris Cole
Graves, Nancy Stevenson
Greco, El
Greuze, Jean-Baptiste
Gris, Juan
Grooms, "Red" Charles Roger
Gropper, William
Gross, Chaim
Grosz, George Ehrenfried
Groth, John August
Grunewald, Matthias
Guardi, Francesco
Guercino
Guerin, Jules
Guston, Philip
Hals, Frans
Hamen y Leon, Juan van der
Haring, Keith
Harnett, William Michael
Harpignies, Henri
Harris, Lauren
Hart, George Overbury
Hartley, Marsden
Hartung, Hans
Harunobu, Suzuki
Hassam, Childe
Healy, George Peter Alexander
Heem, Jan Davidsz de
Helck, Peter (Clarence Peter)
Held, Al
Heller, Goldie
Henner, Jean Jacques
Henri, Robert
Henry, Edward Lamson
Hesse, Eva
Hesselius, John
Hicks, Edward
Hildebrand, Adolf von
Hill, Thomas
Hilliard, Nicholas
Hiroshige, Ando
Hirsch, Joseph
Hirschfeld, Al(bert)
Hirshfield, Morris
Hoban, Russell
Hobbema, Meindert
Hockney, David
Hodler, Ferdinand
Hofer, Karl
Hofmann, Hans
Hogarth, William
Holbein, Hans, the Elder
Holbein, Hans, the Younger
Homer, Winslow
Hooch, Pieter de
Hopper, Edward
Hoppner, John
Howe, Oscar

Howland, Alfred Cornelius
Hughes, Arthur
Hummel, Berta
Hunndertwasser, Friedrich
Hunt, (William) Holman
Hunt, William Morris
Huntington, Daniel
Hurd, Peter
Indiana, Robert
Ingres, Jean Auguste Dominique
Inman, Henry
Inness, George
Ironside, Christopher
Irvin, Rea
Irving, Edith
Isham, Samuel
Israels, Josef
Ives, James Merritt
Jackson, A(lexander) Y(oung)
Jackson, William Henry
Jacob, Max
Jamison, Philip Duane, Jr.
Jarvis, John Wesley
Jenkins, Paul
Jenney, Neil
Jensen, Alfred Julio
John, Augustus Edwin
John, Gwendolyn Mary
Johns, Jasper
Johnson, Cletus Merlin
Johnson, Eastman
Johnson, Joshua
Johnston, Frank H
Jones, David
Jones, Joseph John (Joe)
Jongkind, Johan Barthold
Jordaens, Jacob
Kahlo, Frida
Kalf, Willem
Kandinsky, Wassily
Kane, John
Kano, Motonobu
Kaprow, Allan
Karfiol, Bernard
Kauffmann, Angelica
Keene, Charles Samuel
Keith, William
Kelly, Ellsworth
Kensett, John Frederick
Kent, Rockwell
Kirchner, Ernst Ludwig
Kitaj, R(onald) B(rooks)
Klee, Paul
Klimt, Gustav
Kline, Franz Joseph
Knaths, Karl (Otto Karl)
Kneller, Godfrey, Sir
Koch, John
Kohn, William Roth
Kokoschka, Oskar
Kollwitz, Kathe Schmidt

Korin, Ogata
Krasner, Lee
Kredel, Fritz
Krieghoff, Cornelius
Kroll, Leon
Kuhn, Walt
Kuniyoshi, Yasuo
Kupka, Frank
Kurelek, William
L'Hermitte, Leon Augustin
LaFarge, John
Lancret, Nicolas
Landseer, Charles
Landseer, Edwin Henry, Sir
Lane, "Fitz Hugh" Nathaniel Rogers
Larsson, Carl (Olof)
Lartique, Jacques-Henri
Lasker, Joe
LaTour, George Dumesnil de
Laurencin, Marie
Lavery, John, Sir
Lawrence, Jacob
Lawrence, Thomas, Sir
Lawrie, Lee
Lea, Tom
Lear, Edward
Lebrun, Rico (Frederico)
LeClear, Thomas
Lee, Doris Emrick
Leger, Fernand
Leonardo da Vinci
Leutze, Emanuel
Levi, Julian Edwin
Levine, David
Levine, Jack
Lewis, Edmonia
Lewis, Wyndham
Lewisohn, Ludwig
LeWitt, Sol
Leyendecker, Joseph Christian
Liberman, Alexander
Lichtenstein, Roy
Lindner, Richard
Linton, William James
Lionni, Leo
Liotard, Jean-Etienne
Lippi, Filippino
Lippi, Filippo (Lippo), Fra
Lismer, Arthur
Lord, Jack
Lorenzetti, Ambrogio
Lorjou, Bernard Joseph Pierre
Lorrain, Claude Gellee
Losch, Tilly
Lotto, Lorenzo
Louis, Morris
Lowry, Lawrence Stephen
Lucasvan Leyden
Lucioni, Luigi
Luini, Bernardino
Luke, Keye

Pippin, Horace
Pirandello, Fausto
Pisano, Antonio
Pisis, Filippo de
Pissaro, Lucien
Pissarro, Camille Jacob
Pollaiuolo, Antonio
Pollock, Jackson
Polygnotus
Pontormo, Jacopo da
Poons, Lawrence (Larry)
Poor, Henry Varnum
Porter, Fairfield
Potthast, Edward Henry
Poussin, Nicolas
Powell, William Henry
Prendergast, Maurice Brazil
Prestopino, George
Primaticcio, Francesco
Prudhon, Pierre
Puvis de Chavannes, Pierre Cecile
Quidor, John
Quinteros, Adolfo
Raeburn, Henry, Sir
Raffaelinodel Garbo
Ramsay, Allan
Rand, Ellen Gertrude Emmet
Raphael
Rattner, Abraham
Rauschenberg, Robert
Ray, Man
Read, Thomas Buchanan
Redon, Odilon
Reinhardt, Ad(olph Frederick)
Reinhart, Charles S
Rembrandt (Harmenszoon van Rijn)
Remington, Frederic
Reni, Guido
Renoir, (Pierre) Auguste
Repin, Ilya Yefimovich
Reynolds, Joshua, Sir
Ribera, Jusepe (Jose) de
Richards, William Trost
Riley, Bridget
Riopelle, Jean-Paul
Rivera, Diego
Rivers, Larry
Robert, Hubert
Roberti, Ercole
Robinson, Boardman
Rojankovsky, Feodor Stepanovich
Roland de la Porte, Henri-Horace
Rollins, Carl Purington
Romano, Umberto
Romney, George
Rosa, Salvator
Rosenquist, James Albert
Rossetti, Dante Gabriel
Roth, Frank
Rothenberg, Susan
Rothenstein, William, Sir

Rothko, Mark
Rouault, Georges
Rousseau, (Pierre Etienne) Theodore
Rousseau, Henri
Rubens, Peter Paul, Sir
Rubin, Reuven
Ruysdael, Jacob van
Ryder, Albert Pinkham
Saito, Yoshishige
Salomon, Charlotte
Samaras, Lucas
Sample, Paul Starrett
Sansovino, Andrea
Sansovino, Jacopo
Sargent, John Singer
Sarto, Andrea del
Sassetta
Savage, Edward
Savage, Eugene Francis
Schmidt-Rottluf, Karl
Schnabel, Julian
Schoneberg, Sheldon Clyde
Schongauer, Martin
Scorel, Jan van
Searle, Ronald William Fordham
Secunda, (Holland) Arthur
Segantini, Giovanni
Serra, Richard Anthony
Seurat, Georges Pierre
Severini, Gino
Shahn, Ben(jamin)
Shearer, Taddeus Errington (Ted)
Sheeler, Charles
Sheets, Millard Owen
Shepard, Ernest Howard
Sheridan, Clare Consuelo
Shinn, Everett
Siddal, Elizabeth Eleanor
Signac, Paul
Signorelli, Luca
Siqueiros, David A
Sironi, Mario
Sisley, Alfred
Sloan, John
Sloane, Eric
Sommer, Frederick
Soutine, Chaim
Soyer, Isaac
Soyer, Moses
Soyer, Raphael
Speicher, Eugene Edward
Spencer, Stanley, Sir
Spier, Peter Edward
Spode, Josiah
Spry, Constance
Spyropoulos, Jannis
Stael, Nicolas de
Stahl, Ben(jamin Albert)
Stankiewicz, Richard Peter
Steen, Jan
Steichen, Edward Jean

Steinberg, Saul
Stella, Frank Philip
Stella, Joseph
Stephens, Alice Barber
Sterne, Maurice
Still, Clyfford
Stravinsky, Vera de Bossett
Stuart, Gilbert Charles
Stuart, James
Stubbs, George
Sully, Thomas
Sutherland, Graham Vivian
Szyk, Arthur
Taeuber-Arp, Sophie
Tait, Arthur Fitzwilliam
Tamayo, Rufino
Tanguy, Yves
Tanner, Henry Ossawa
Tao-chi
Taubes, Frederic
Tchelitchew, Pavel
Teniers, David, the Younger
Tenniel, John, Sir
Ter Borch, Gerard
Terbrugghen, Hendrick
Thayer, Abbott Handerson
Thiebaud, Wayne Morton
Thoma, Hans
Thomson, Tom
Thon, William
Tiepolo, Giambattista (Giovanni Battista)
Tiepolo, Giovanni Domenico
Tiffany, Louis Comfort
Tintoretto
Titian
Topolski, Feliks
Toulouse-Lautrec (Monfa), (Henri Marie
    Raymond de)
Trumbull, John
Tryon, Dwight William
Tura, Cosme
Turner, Joseph Mallord William
Twachtman, John H
Twombly, Cy
Tworkov, Jack
Uccello, Paolo
Utamaro, Kitagawa
Utrillo, Maurice
Valadon, Suzanne
Valdes-Leal, Juan de
Valerio, James Robert
Van Dyck, Anthony, Sir
Van Eyck, Hubert
Van Eyck, Jan
Van Gogh, Vincent Willem
Vanderbilt, Gloria Morgan
Vanderlyn, John
Vargas, Alberto
Varley, F(rederick) H(orseman)
Vasarely, Victor
Vasari, Giorgio

Vedder, Elihu
Velazquez, Antonio Gonzalez
Velazquez, Diego Rodriguez de Silva
Velde, Willem van de
Vereshchagin, Vasil
Vermeer, Jan
Veronese, Paolo
Verrocchio, Andrea del
Verspronk, Johannes
Vertes, Marcel
Vickrey, Robert
Vigee-Lebrun, Marie Anne Elisabeth
Vlaminck, Maurice de
Vlieger, Simon Jacobsz de
Vollbracht, Michaele J
Volpi, Alfredo
Vonnoh, Robert W
Vos, Cornelis de
Vos, Martin de
Vouet, Simon
Vuillard, (Jean) Edouard
Walcott, Mary Morris Vaux
Walker, Henry Oliver
Walker, Mickey
Walton, William Turner
Ward, Lynd
Warhol, Andy
Watteau, Jean Antoine
Watts, George Frederic
Waugh, Frederick Judd
Weber, Max
Wedgwood, Josiah
Wedgwood, Thomas
Weir, John F(erguson)
Weir, Julian Alden
Weir, Robert W
Werboff. Michael Alexander
Wesselmann, Tom
West, Benjamin
Weyden, Rogier van der
Whistler, James Abbott McNeill
Whymper, Edward
Wilkie, David
Willard, Archibald MacNeal
Williams, Kit
Wilson, Edward Arthur
Witz, Konrad
Wood, Grant
Woodville, Richard Caton
Wyeth, Andrew
Wyeth, Henriette
Wyeth, Jamie (James Browning)
Wyeth, N(ewell) C(onvers)
Zadkine, Ossip
Zao-Wou-Ki
Zorach, William
Zorn, Anders Leonhard
Zurbaran, Francisco

ARTISTS

Eight, The
Group of Seven

ASSASSIN

Booth, John Wilkes
Corday d'Armount, (Marie Anne) Charlotte
Czolgosz, Leon F
Mercader, Ramon
Oswald, Lee Harvey
Princip, Gavrilo
Ravaillac, Francois
Ray, James Earl
Sirhan, Sirhan Bishara
Weiss, Carl Austin
Zangara, Joseph (Guiseppe)

ASTROLOGER

Dee, John
Dixon, Jeane Pinckert
Dunninger, Joseph
Leek, Sybil
Nostradamus
Omarr, Sydney
Righter, Carroll

ASTRONAUT

Aldrin, Edwin E(ugene), Jr.
Anders, William Alison
Armstrong, Neil Alden
Bean, Alan L
Bluford, Guion Stewart, Jr.
Borman, Frank
Brand, Vance DeVoe
Carpenter, Scott (Malcolm Scott)
Carr, Gerald Paul
Cernan, Eugene Andrew
Chaffee, Roger Bruce
Collins, Mike (Michael)
Conrad, Charles, Jr.
Cooper, (Leroy) Gordon, Jr.
Crippen, Robert Laurel
Cunningham, R Walter
Duke, Charles Moss, Jr.
Eisele, Donn Fulton
Engle, Joe Henry
Evans, Ronald Ellwin
Fullerton, (Charles) Gordon
Garneau, Marc
Garriott, Owen
Gibson, Edward George
Givens, Edward Galen
Glenn, John Herschel, Jr.
Gordon, Richard Francis, Jr.
Grissom, Virgil Ivan
Haise, Fred W
Henize, Karl Gordon
Irwin, James Benson

Jarvis, Gregory
Kerwin, Joseph Peter
Lousma, Jack
Lovell, Jim (James A, Jr.)
McCandless, Bruce, II
McDivitt, Jim (James Alton)
McNair, Ronald
Michel, F Curtis
Mitchell, Edgar Dean
Onizuka, Ellison
Overmyer, Robert F
Pogue, William R(eid)
Resnik, Judy (Judith)
Ride, Sally K
Roosa, Stuart
Schirra, Wally (Walter Marty, Jr.)
Schmitt, Harrison Hagan
Schweickart, Russell L
Scobee, Dick (Francis Richard)
Scott, David Randolph
Seddon, Rhea
Shepard, Alan Bartlett, Jr.
Slayton, Donald Kent
Smith, Michael John
Stafford, Thomas P(atten)
Sullivan, Kathryn D
Swigert, Jack (John Leonard, Jr.)
Truly, Richard H
White, Ed(ward Higgins, II)
Worden, Alfred Merrill
Young, John Watts

ASTRONOMER

Abell, George O(gden)
Adams, John Couch
Adams, Walter Sydney
Anaximander
Angstrom, Anders Jonas
Argelander, Friedrich Wilhelm August
Ashbrook, Joseph
Bok, Bart J(an)
Bowditch, Nathaniel
Bradley, James
Brahe, Tyge
Campbell, William Wallace
Cannon, Annie Jump
Celsius, Anders
Copernicus, Nicolaus
Curtis, Heber Doust
Dixon, Jeremiah
Douglass, Andrew Ellicott
Drake, Frank Donald
Eddington, Arthur Stanley, Sir
Flammarion, Camille
Flamsteed, John
Fleming, Williamina Paton Stevens
Frost, Edwin Brant
Galileo
Gill, Jocelyn Ruth
Hale, George Ellery
Halley, Edmund

Henize, Karl Gordon
Herschel, John Frederick William, Sir
Herschel, William
Hipparchus
Horrocks, Jeremiah
Hoyle, Fred
Hubble, Edwin Powell
Huygens, Christian
Hynek, J(oseph) Allen
Jastrow, Robert
Jeans, James Hopwood, Sir
Kepler, Johannes
Kohoutek, Lubos
Kuiper, Gerard Peter
Lagrange, Joseph-Louis
Langley, Samuel Pierpont
Laplace, Pierre Simon, Marquis de
LeVerrier, Urbain Jean Joseph
Lowell, Percival
Lyot, Bernard Ferdinand
Mason, Charles
Maury, Antonia Caetana De Paiua Pereira
Mitchell, Maria
Morgan, William Wilson
Newcomb, Simon
Nicholson, Seth Barnes
Omar Khayyam
Peirce, Benjamin
Pickering, Edward Charles
Pickering, William Henry
Ptolemy
Ritchey, George Willis
Rittenhouse, David
Ryle, Martin, Sir
Sagan, Carl Edward
Schlesinger, Frank
Shapley, Harlow T
Shklovsky, Iosif Samvilovitch
Struve, Otto
Walker, Adam
Young, Charles Augustus
Zwicky, Fritz

ATHEIST

O'Hair, Madalyn Murray

ATHLETIC DIRECTOR

Bryant, "Bear" Paul William
Duke, Wayne
Elliott, "Jumbo" James Francis

ATTEMPTED ASSASSIN

Agca, Mehmet Ali
Bremer, Arthur Herman
Collazo, Oscar
Fromme, Lynette Alice
Hinckley, John Warnock, Jr.
Moore, Sara Jane
Torresola, Griselio

AUCTIONEER

Sotheby, John
Sotheby, Samuel Leigh

AUTHOR

Aardema, Verna Norberg
Aaron, Chester Norman
Abbas, Khwaja Ahmad
Abbott, Edith
Abbott, Jack (Rufus Jack Henry)
Abdul, Raoul
Abelard, Pierre
Abell, George O(gden)
Abercrombie, Lascelles
Aberle, John Wayne
Ableman, Paul
Abse, Dannie
Achebe, Chinua
Ackerman, Forest J
Adam, Juliette Lamber
Adamic, Louis
Adamov, Arthur
Adams, Abigail Smith
Adams, Andy
Adams, Charles Francis, Sr.
Adams, Douglas Noel
Adams, Frank Ramsay
Adams, Hannah
Adams, Henry Brooks
Adams, James Truslow
Adams, Joey
Adams, John Hanly
Adams, Leonie Fuller
Adams, Richard
Adams, Samuel Hopkins
Adamson, Joy Friederike Victoria Gessner
Adler, Alfred
Adler, Felix
Adler, Irving
Adler, Mortimer Jerome
Adler, Richard
Aesop
Agar, Herbert Sebastian
Agassiz, Louis (Jean Louis Radolphe)
Agate, James Evershed
Agee, James Rufus
Agee, Philip
Agnon, S(hmuel) Y(osef)
Agrippa, Heinrich Cornelius
Aguilar, Grace
Aiken, Joan Delano
Ainsworth, W(illiam) H(arrison)
Akhmatova, Anna, pseud.
Aksakov, Sergei Timofeyevich
Alain-Fournier, pseud.
Alarcon, Pedro Antonio de

Albee, Edward Franklin, III
Alberti, Leon Battista
Albrand, Martha, pseud.
Alcott, Louisa May
Alden, Henry M
Alden, Isabella Macdonald
Aldington, Richard
Aldiss, Brian Wilson
Aldrich, Bess Streeter
Aldrich, Richard Stoddard
Aldrich, Thomas Bailey
Aleichem, Shalom, pseud.
Alexander, Lloyd Chudley
Alexander, Shana
Alger, Horatio
Algren, Nelson
Ali, Ahmed
Alice (Mary Victoria Augusta Pauline)
Allen of Hurtwood, Lady
Allen, Hervey (William Hervey)
Allen, Jack
Allen, James Lane
Allen, Jay Presson
Allen, Robert Sharon
Allen, Steve (Stephen Valentine Patrick
   William)
Allen, Walter Ernest
Allingham, Margery
Allsop, Kenneth
Almond, Gabriel Abraham
Alsop, Joseph Wright, Jr.
Alsop, Stewart Johonnot Oliver
Aluko, Timothy Mofolorunso
Alvarez, Walter Clement
Amado, Jorge
Amalrik, Andrei Alekseyevich
Ambler, Eric
Amery, Julian (Harold Julian)
Amicis, Edmond de
Amis, Kingsley William
Amory, Cleveland
Anand, Mulk Raj
Andersen, Hans Christian
Anderson, Maxwell
Anderson, Peggy
Anderson, Sherwood
Anderson, Vernon Ellsworth
Andrews, James Frederick
Andrews, Mary Raymond Shipman
Andrews, Michael Alford
Andrews, V(irginia) C
Andrews, Wayne
Andreyev, Leonid Nikolayevich
Andric, Ivo
Andrzejewski, Jerzy
Angell, (Ralph) Norman, Sir
Angell, Roger
Angelou, Maya Marguerita
Angoff, Charles
Anson, Jay
Anson, Robert Sam

Anthony, Earl
Anthony, Edward
Anthony, Evelyn, pseud.
Antin, Mary
Apollinaire, Guillaume
Aptheker, Herbert
Apuleius, Lucius
Ar Buthnot, May Hill
Archer, Jeffrey Howard
Archibald, Joe (Joseph Stopford)
Ardizzone, Edward Jeffrey Irving
Ardrey, Robert
Arendt, Hannah
Aretino, Pietro
Aries, Philippe
Arieti, Silvano
Aristophanes
Aristotle
Arlen, Michael
Armour, Richard Willard
Armstrong, Charlotte
Armstrong, Garner Ted
Arnold, Edwin
Arnold, Matthew
Arnow, Harriette Louisa Simpson
Arp, Hans
Arrabal (Teran), Fernando
Artsybashev, Mikhail Petrovich
Artzybasheff, Boris Mikhailovich
Arundel, Honor Morfydd
Asbury, Herbert
Asch, Sholem
Ascoli, Max
Ashbery, John Lawrence
Ashford, Daisy
Ashley, Merrill
Ashmore, Harry Scott
Ashton-Warner, Sylvia Constance
Asimov, Isaac
Asquith, Emma Alice Margot
Asturias, Miguel Angel
Atherton, Gertrude Franklin
Attenborough, David Frederick
Attlee, Clement Richard Attlee, Earl
Atwood, Margaret Eleanor
Aubrey, John
Auchincloss, Louis
Audiberti, Jacques
Audubon, John James
Auel, Jean Marie
Auerbach-Levy, William
Aumont, Jean-Pierre
Aurell, Tage
Auslander, Joseph
Austen, Jane
Austin, Alfred
Austin, Mary Hunter
Avallone, Michael Angelo, Jr.
Ayer, Alfred Jules
Ayme, Marcel
Ayres, Ruby Mildred

Bellamy, Edward
Belli, Melvin Mouron
Belloc, Hilaire (Joseph Hilaire Pierre)
Bellow, Saul
Bemelmans, Ludwig
Benarde, Melvin Albert
Benary-Isbert, Margot
Benchley, Nathaniel Goddard
Benchley, Peter Bradford
Benchley, Robert Charles
Bendick, Jeanne
Benedict, Ruth Fulton
Benedictus, David
Benefield, Barry
Benet, Stephen Vincent
Benet, William Rose
Benjamin of Tudela
Benjamin, Asher
Bennett, Arnold
Bennett, Hal
Bennett, James Gordon, Jr.
Bennett, John
Bennett, Lerone, Jr.
Benson, Arthur Christopher
Benson, Edward Frederic
Benson, Sally
Bentham, Jeremy
Bentley, Edmund Clerihew
Bentley, Eric
Bentley, Richard
Benton, Robert Douglass
Bercovici, Konrad
Berenson, Bernard
Beresford, Harry
Berger, John
Berger, Melvin H
Berger, Meyer
Berger, Raoul
Berger, Terry
Berger, Thomas Louis
Bergson, Henri Louis
Berkeley, George
Berkow, Ira Harvey
Berkowitz, Bernard
Berlin, Isaiah, Sir
Berlitz, Charles L Frambach
Bernanos, Georges
Berne, Eric Lennard
Bernstein, Carl
Bernstein, Leonard
Berrigan, Philip Francis
Berryman, John
Berton, Pierre
Besant, Annie Wood
Besant, Walter, Sir
Bessie, Alvah
Bettelheim, Bruno
Bialik, Chaim Nachman
Bichler, Joyce
Biddle, George
Biebuyck, Daniel Prosper

Bierce, Ambrose Gwinett
Biggers, Earl Derr
Billings, Josh, pseud.
Binns, Archie Fred
Bioy-Casares, Adolfo
Birmingham, Stephen
Birney, Earle (Alfred Earle)
Birrell, Augustine
Bishop, Isabella Lucy Bird
Bishop, Jim (James Alonzo)
Biyidi, Alexandre
Blackmore, Richard Doddridge
Blackstone, William, Sir
Blackwell, Earl
Blackwell, Elizabeth
Blackwood, Algernon
Blaikie, William
Blair, Clay, Jr.
Blanc, (Jean Joseph Charles) Louis
Blanding, Don
Blasco-Ibanez, Vicente
Blassingale, Wyatt Rainey
Blatty, William Peter
Blish, James Benjamin
Blitzstein, Marc
Bliven, Bruce
Blixen, Karen Christentze, Baroness
Bloch, Robert Albert
Blofeld, John
Blok, Aleksandr Aleksandrovich
Bloom, Harry
Bloom, Murray Teigh
Bloom, Ursula
Blough, Glenn Orlando
Blount, Charles
Bloustein, Edward J
Bloy, Leon Marie
Blume, Judy Sussman
Blyth, Chay
Blyton, Carey
Blyton, Enid Mary
Boccaccio, Giovanni
Bodard, Lucien Albert
Bode, Carl
Bodenheim, Maxwell
Bodsworth, Charles Frederick
Boehm, Eric Hartzell
Boettiger, John
Bogarde, Dirk
Bogart, Leo
Boileau(-Despreaux), Nicolas
Bojer, Johan
Bok, Edward William
Bok, Hannes Vajn
Boles, Paul Darcy
Boley, Forrest Irving
Bolingbroke, Henry St. John, Viscount
Bolinger, Dwight Lemerton
Bolitho, Henry Hector
Bolitho, William
Boll, Heinrich

Brownson, Orestes Augustus
Bruce Lockhart, Robert Hamilton, Sir
Bruce, Lenny
Brunhoff, Laurent de
Brunner, Emil
Bruno, Giordano
Brustein, Robert Sanford
Brzezinski, Zbigniew Kazimierz
Buber, Martin
Buchan, John, Sir
Buchwald, Art(hur)
Buck, Paul Herman
Buck, Pearl S(ydenstricker)
Buckley, James Lane
Buckley, William F(rank), Jr.
Buckmaster, Henrietta, pseud.
Budge, Ernest Alfred
Buechner, Frederick
Buffon, Georges Louis Leclerc
Bugliosi, Vincent T
Bulfinch, Thomas
Bulgakov, Mikhail
Bull, Peter
Bullins, Ed
Bullitt, William C
Bullock, Alain Louis Charles
Bunin, Ivan Alekseevich
Bunner, Henry Cuyler
Bunyan, John
Bunzel, Ruth L
Burch, Robert Joseph
Burchard, John Ely
Burdick, Eugene Leonard
Burger, Carl Victor
Burgess, Anthony
Burgess, Gelett (Frank Gelett)
Burgess, Thornton Waldo
Burke, Edmund
Burke, John
Burke, Kenneth
Burke, Thomas
Burman, Ben Lucien
Burnett, Frances Eliza Hodgson
Burnett, W(illiam) R(iley)
Burnett, Whit
Burney, Fanny (Frances)
Burnford, Sheila (Philip Cochrane Every)
Burns, George
Burns, John Horne
Burnshaw, Stanley
Burroughs, Edgar Rice
Burroughs, John
Burroughs, William S(eward)
Burt, Maxwell Struthers
Burton, Isabel Arundel
Burton, Richard Francis, Sir
Burton, Robert
Buscaglia, Leo (Felice Leonardo)
Bush-Brown, Albert
Butler, Samuel
Butor, Michel

Butterfield, Herbert, Sir
Buttrick, George Arthur
Bynner, Harold Witter
Cabell, James Branch
Cable, George Washington
Cable, Mary
Caen, Herb
Cage, John Milton, Jr.
Cahan, Abraham
Caidin, Martin
Cain, James Mallahan
Caine, Hall, Sir
Cairncross, Alexander Kirkland, Sir
Calder, Nigel David Ritchie
Calder, Peter Ritchie
Caldicott, Helen Broinowski
Caldwell, Erskine Preston
Caldwell, Taylor (Janet Miriam Taylor)
Calisher, Hortense
Callaghan, Morley Edward
Calvino, Italo
Cameron, Eleanor Francis
Cameron, Roderick W
Camoes, Luis de
Camp, Walter Chauncey
Campanella, Tommaso
Campbell, Donald Guy
Campbell, John W
Campbell, Roy
Campbell, Walter Stanley
Campbell, William Edward March
Camus, Albert
Canaday, John (Edwin John)
Canetti, Elias
Canfield, Francis X(avier)
Cantacuzene, Princess
Cantwell, Robert Emmett
Capek, Karel
Caples, John
Capote, Truman
Caputo, Philip Joseph
Cardus, Neville, Sir
Carey, Ernestine Muller Gilbreth
Carlson, William Hugh
Carman, (William) Bliss
Carmer, Carl Lamson
Carnegie, Dale
Carpenter, Edward
Carr, Emily
Carr, John Dickson
Carroll, Anna Ella
Carroll, Gladys Hasty
Carroll, Lewis, pseud.
Carson, Rachel Louise
Carson, Robert
Carter, Ernestine Marie
Cartland, Barbara Hamilton
Cary, Alice
Cary, Joyce (Arthur Joyce Lunel)
Casanova, (de Seingalt), Giovanni Giacomo
Casewit, Curtis

Casey, William Joseph
Caspary, Vera
Cassady, Neal
Cassidy, Harold Gomes
Cassill, R(onald) V(erlin)
Cassou, Jean
Castaneda, Carlos
Castil-Blaze, Francois-Joseph
Cater, Douglass
Cather, Willa Sibert
Catherall, Arthur
Caton-Thompson, Gertrude
Catton, Bruce
Causley, Charles Stanley
Cavendish, William, Duke of Newcastle
Caxton, William
Cecil, Edgar Algernon Robert
Celine, Louis-Ferdinand
Chamberlain, Samuel
Chamberlin, William Henry
Chambers, Robert
Chambers, Robert W
Chandler, Jeff
Chandler, Raymond Thornton
Chaplin, Charlie
Charlevoix, Pierre Francis Xavier de
Charlip, Remy
Charriere, Henri
Charteris, Leslie
Chase, Chris
Chase, Ilka
Chase, Mary Coyle
Chase, Stuart
Chateaubriand, Francois Rene de
Chatterton, Ruth
Chaudhuri, Haridas
Cheever, John
Chekhov, Anton Pavlovich
Chenier, Marie-Andre de
Chennault, Anna Chan
Chermayeff, Serge
Chesney, Marion
Chesnutt, Charles Waddell
Chessex, Jacques
Chessman, Caryl Whittier
Chesterfield, Philip Dormer, Earl
Chevallier, Gabriel
Chew, Peter
Cheyney, Peter (Reginald E)
Chiang, Yee
Chidsey, Donald Barr
Child, Julia McWilliams
Child, Lydia Maria
Childers, (Robert) Erskine
Childs, Marquis William
Chipperfield, Joseph Eugene
Chirol, Valentine, Sir
Chisholm, Shirley Anita St. Hill
Chodorov, Edward
Chopin, Kate
Chretien de Troyes

Christ-Janer, Albert
Christie, Agatha Mary Clarissa Miller,
  Dame
Churchill, Winston
Churchill, Winston Leonard Spencer, Sir
Chute, Beatrice Joy
Chute, Marchette Gaylord
Ciardi, John Anthony
Cibber, Colley
Claiborne, Craig
Clair, Rene
Clark, Barrett H
Clark, John Bates
Clark, Kenneth McKenzie, Sir
Clark, Marion L
Clark, Sydney
Clark, Thomas Dionysius
Clark, Walter van Tilburg
Clarke, Arthur C(harles)
Clarke, John Henrik
Clarkson, Ewan
Claudel, Paul Louis Charles
Clausewitz, Karl von
Clavell, James Dumaresq
Cleaver, Eldridge
Cleaver, William Joseph (Bill)
Cleghorn, Sarah Norcliffe
Cleland, John
Cloete, Stuart
Clurman, Harold Edgar
Coates, Robert Myron
Cobb, Irvin Shrewsbury
Cobbett, William
Cobleigh, Ira Underwood
Cocteau, Jean
Coffin, Robert Peter Tristram
Coffin, William Sloan
Coghill, Nevill Henry Kendall Aylmer
Cohen, Daniel
Cohen, Joan Lebold
Cohen, Leonard
Cohen, Octavus Roy
Cohen, Wilbur Joseph
Coit, Margaret Louise
Colby, Carroll Burleigh
Colden, Cadwallader
Cole, George Douglas Howard
Coleman, Lonnie William
Coleridge, Mary Elizabeth
Coleridge, Samuel Taylor
Colette, pseud.
Collier, John
Collier, Peter
Collins, Larry
Collins, Wilkie (William)
Collodi, Carlo, pseud.
Colum, Padraic
Comenius, Johann Amos
Comfort, Alexander
Compton-Burnett, Ivy, Dame
Comstock, Anthony

Comte, Auguste
Conant, James Bryant
Condit, Carl Wilbur
Condon, Richard Thomas
Connell, Evan S, Jr.
Connolly, Cyril Vernon
Connolly, James B
Conquest, Robert
Conrad, Joseph
Conrad, Paul Francis
Conroy, Frank
Conroy, Jack (John Wesley)
Constant de Rebeque, (Henri) Benjamin
Conway, Moncure Daniel
Conze, Edward
Cook, Peter
Cooke, John Esten
Cooke, Rose Terry
Coolidge, Dane
Coon, Carleton Stevens
Cooper, James Fenimore
Cooper, Lester Irving
Coover, Robert
Coppard, A(lfred) E(dgar)
Cordes, Eugene Harold
Corelli, Marie, pseud.
Corey, Lewis
Corle, Edwin
Corman, Roger William
Corson, Juliet
Cortazar, Julio
Cortissoz, Royal
Corvo, Baron, pseud.
Corwin, Norman
Coryell, John Russell
Costain, Thomas B
Costello, Chris
Couperius, Louis (Marie Anne)
Cournos, John
Cousteau, Jacques Yves
Covey, Cyclone
Covington, Warren
Cowan, Peter Wilkinshaw
Cowley, Malcolm
Cox, Palmer
Coxe, George Harmon
Cozzens, James Gould
Craik, Dinah Maria Mulock
Crane, Nathalia Clara Ruth
Crane, Stephen
Crankshaw, Edward
Craven, Thomas
Crawford, Christina
Crawford, Francis Marion
Crawford, John Edmund
Creasey, John
Creel, George
Creeley, Robert White
Creighton, Thomas H(awk)
Crevecoeur, Michel-Guillaume Jean de
Crews, Harry Eugene

Crichton, (John) Michael
Crichton, Robert
Crile, George Washington
Crisp, Quentin, pseud.
Crispin, Edmund, pseud.
Crockett, James Underwood
Crockett, S(amuel) R(utherford)
Croft-Cooke, Rupert
Crofts, Freeman Willis
Cromie, Robert Allen
Cronin, A(rchibald) J(oseph)
Cronyn, Hume
Crosby, Alexander L
Crossman, Richard Howard Stafford
Crowley, Aleister (Edward Alexander)
Crozier, Eric
Culliford, "Peyo" Pierre
Cummings, E(dward) E(stlin)
Cuneo, Ernest
Cunha, Euclides da
Cunninghame, Graham Robert Boutine
Curie, Eve
Curry, Peggy Simson
Curtis, George William
Curwood, James Oliver
Custer, Elizabeth Bacon
D'Annunzio, Gabriele
D'Arcy, Martin Cyril
D'Israeli, Isaac
Dabney, Virginius
Dahl, Roald
Dahlberg, Edward
Daiches, David
Dailey, Janet
Daly, Maureen Patricia
Dampier, William
Dana, Bill
Dana, Charles Anderson
Dana, Richard Henry, Jr.
Dane, Clemence, pseud.
Dangerfield, George Bubb
Daniel, Samuel
Daniels, Jonathan Worth
Daniloff, Nicholas
Dannay, Frederic
Dargan, Olive Tilford
Darley, Felix Octavius Carr
Darling, Frank Fraser, Sir
Darnton, Robert Choate
Darrow, Whitney, Jr.
Darwin, Charles Robert
Dashwood, Elizabeth Monica
Daudet, Alphonse Marie Leon
Daudet, Leon
Davenport, Marcia
David, Elizabeth
David-Neel, Alexandra
Davie, Donald
Davies, Hunter
Davies, Leslie Purnell
Davies, Robertson

Dunbar, Helen Flanders
Dunbar, Paul Laurence
Duncan, David Douglas
Duncan, Robert
Dunlap, William
Dunne, Finley Peter
Dunne, John Gregory
Dunsany, Edward J M Plunkett, Baron
Durant, Ariel (Ida Ariel Ethel Kaufman)
Durant, Will(iam James)
Duranty, Walter
Duras, Marguerite, pseud.
Durrell, Lawrence George
Durrenmatt, Friedrich
Dwight, Timothy
Dyer, Charles
Dyer, Wayne
Earle, Alice Morse
Eastlake, William
Eastman, Mary Henderson
Eastman, Max Forrester
Eberhart, Mignon Good
Eberhart, Richard
Eberle, Irmengarde
Eckstein, Gustav
Eddy, Sherwood
Edel, Leon (Joseph Leon)
Eden, Dorothy
Edgell, George Harold
Edmonds, Walter Dumaux
Edwards, Harry (Jr.)
Edwards, Jonathan
Eggleston, Edward
Ehrenburg, Ilya Grigoryevich
Eichelberger, Robert Lawrence
Eilshemius, Louis Michel
Eisenhower, David
Eisenhower, John Sheldon Doud
Eisenhower, Julie Nixon
Eisenstaedt, Alfred
Elegant, Robert Sampson
Eliot, George, pseud.
Elkin, Stanley Lawrence
Ellin, Stanley
Elliott, George Paul
Elliott, Osborn
Ellison, Harlan Jay
Ellison, Ralph Waldo
Ellsberg, Daniel
Ellsberg, Edward
Eluard, Paul
Emanuel, James A
Emanuelli, Enrico
Emery, Anne
Endo, Shusaku
Engel, Lehman (Aaron Lehman)
Engle, Eloise Katherine
Engle, Paul
Enright, Dennis Joseph
Enright, Elizabeth
Ephron, Nora

Epstein, Alvin
Epstein, Edward Jay
Erasmus, Desiderius
Erdman, Paul E
Ernst, Jimmy
Ernst, Paul
Erskine, John
Ertz, Susan
Espriu, Salvador
Esslin, Martin Julius
Etchison, Dennis (William Dennis)
Eucken, Rudolf Christoph
Evans, Bergen Baldwin
Evans, Charles, Jr.
Evans, Clifford
Evans, Harold Matthew
Evelyn, John
Ewen, David
Ewen, Frederic
Ewing, Alfred Cyril
Eysenck, Hans Jurgen
Faber, Geoffrey Cust, Sir
Fabre, Jean Henri
Fadiman, Clifton Paul
Fairbank, Janet Ayer
Fairfax, Beatrice, pseud.
Falk, Lee Harrison
Falkner, Murry Charles
Fall, Bernard B
Fallada, Hans, pseud.
Falls, Joe
Farago, Ladislas
Farb, Peter
Farina, Richard
Farjeon, Eleanor
Farley, Walter
Farmer, Philip Jose
Farnol, Jeffery
Farrar, John Chipman
Farrell, James Thomas
Farrere, Claude, pseud.
Farrow, John Villiers
Fassbinder, Rainer Werner
Fast, Howard
Faulkner, William
Fauset, Jessie Redmon
Faust, Frederick Schiller
Fearing, Kenneth Flexner
Fedin, Konstantin
Feiffer, Jules Ralph
Feingold, Benjamin Franklin
Feininger, Andreas Bernhard Lyonel
Feis, Herbert
Fell, John
Felton, Harold W
Fenelon, Fania
Fenelon, Francois de Salignac
Fenn, George Manville
Fenton, Carroll Lane
Ferber, Edna
Fergusson, Francis

Fuller, Roy Broadbent
Fuller-Maitland, John Alexander
Furstenberg, Diane Halfin von
Furstenberg, Egon von
Fuseli, Henry
Futrelle, Jacques
Gaddis, Thomas (Eugene)
Gaddis, William
Gaines, Ernest J
Galbraith, John Kenneth
Gale, Zona
Galen
Galiani, Ferdinando
Gallant, Mavis
Gallatin, Albert Eugene
Gallegos, Romulo
Gallico, Paul William
Galsworthy, John
Galt, John
Gann, Ernest Kellogg
Garcia-Marquez, Gabriel
Gardner, Erle Stanley
Gardner, John Champlin, Jr.
Garfield, Brian Wynne
Garfield, Leon
Garis, Howard Roger
Garland, Hamlin
Garnett, David
Garnett, Richard
Garraty, John Arthur
Garrett, George Palmer, Jr.
Garrison, William Lloyd
Garrod, Hethcote William
Gary, Romain
Gaskell, Elizabeth Cleghorn
Gass, William H
Gassner, John Waldhorn
Gault, William Campbell
Gaunt, William
Gautier, Theophile (Pierre Jules Theophile)
Gavin, James Maurice
Gay, Peter Jack
Geertz, Clifford
Gehlen, Reinhard
Gelb, Arthur
Gelb, Barbara Stone
Gelber, Jack
Gellhorn, Martha Ellis
Gellis, Roberta Leah Jacobs
Gelmis, Joseph Stephen
Genauer, Emily
Genet, Jean
George, Don
George, Henry, Sr.
George, Jean Craighead
George, Phyllis
Gerhardi, William Alexander
Gerould, Gordon Hall
Gerson, Noel Bertram
Geyer, Georgie Anne
Ghose, Sri Chinmoy Kumar

Gibberd, Frederick
Gibbon, Lewis Grassic, pseud.
Gibbons, Euell
Gibbons, Stella Dorethea
Gibbs, Anthony
Gibran, Kahlil George
Gibson, Henry
Gibson, Walter B(rown)
Gidal, Sonia
Gide, Andre Paul Guillaume
Gilbertson, Mildred Geiger
Gilbreth, Frank Bunker, Jr.
Gilder, George
Gilfond, Henry
Gill, Brendan
Gill, Eric
Gillott, Jacky
Gilman, Dorothy
Gilot, Francoise
Gilpin, Laura
Gingrich, Arnold
Ginott, Haim
Giono, Jean
Giovanni, Nikki
Giraudoux, Jean
Gissing, George Robert
Giusti, Giuseppe
Gjellerup, Karl Adolf
Gladstone, William Ewart
Glasgow, Ellen Anderson Gholson
Glaspell, Susan Keating
Glass, Montague (Marsden)
Glassco, John Stinson
Glazer, Nathan
Glubb, John Bagot, Sir
Glyn, Elinor Sutherland
Gobineau, Joseph Arthur, Comte de
Godden, Rumer, pseud.
Godwin, Mary Wollstonecraft
Godwin, William
Goethe, Johann Wolfgang von
Goffstein, Marilyn
Gogarty, Oliver St. John
Gogol, Nikolai Vasilievich
Gold, Herbert
Gold, Michael
Golden, Harry Lewis
Golding, William Gerald
Goldman, Eric F
Goldman, James
Goldman, William
Goldner, Orville
Goldsmith, Oliver
Goldwater, Barry Morris
Gombrowicz, Witold
Goncharov, Ivan A
Goncourt, Edmond Louis Antoine Huot
Goncourt, Jules Alfred Huot de
Goodman, George Jerome Waldo
Goodman, Mitchell
Goodman, Paul

Hardwick, Elizabeth
Hardy, Thomas
Harlan, Louis R
Harman, Jeanne Perkins
Harnack, Curtis Arthur
Harrington, Michael (Edward Michael)
Harris, Frank
Harris, Joel Chandler
Harris, Leonard
Harris, Mark
Harris, William Bliss
Harrison, Frederic
Hart, Frances Noyes
Hart, Jeffrey
Hart, Moss
Hart, William Surrey
Hart-Davis, Rupert (Charles Rupert)
Harte, (Francis Bret)
Hartley, Leslie Poles
Hartmann, Franz
Hartmann, Sadakichi
Harvey, Frank Laird
Harwell, Ernie
Hasek, Jaroslav
Hathaway, Sibyl Collings
Hathaway, Starke R
Hauff, Wilhelm
Hauptmann, Gerhart
Hawes, Elisabeth
Hawkes, John Clendennin Burne, Jr.
Hawley, Cameron
Hawthorne, Nathaniel
Hay, John Milton
Hayakawa, S(amuel) I(chiye)
Hayden, Sterling
Haydn, Hiram Collins
Hayek, Friedrich August von
Hayes, Alfred
Hayes, Peter Lind
Hays, Brooks
Hayward, Brooke
Hazan, Marcella Maddalena
Hazlitt, William
Head, Bessie
Heard, Gerald (Henry FitzGerald)
Hearn, Lafcadio
Hearst, Patty (Patricia Campbell)
Hechinger, Fred Michael
Hecht, Ben
Heckscher, August
Heffer, Eric Samuel
Heggen, Thomas Orls, Jr.
Heidegger, Martin
Heiden, Konrad
Heidenstam, Carl Gustaf Verner von
Heimlich, Henry J
Heinlein, Robert Anson
Heiser, Victor George
Heller, Joseph
Hellman, Lillian
Heloise

Hemingway, Ernest Miller
Hemingway, Leicester
Hemingway, Mary Welsh
Hemphill, Paul
Henderson, Lawrence Joseph
Henkle, Henrietta
Henley, William Ernest
Henry, Buck
Henry, O, pseud.
Herbert, Alan Patrick, Sir
Herbert, Frank Patrick
Herbert, George
Herbst, Josephine Frey
Herford, Oliver
Hergesheimer, Joseph
Herlihy, James Leo
Herrick, Robert
Herridge, Robert T
Herriot, James, pseud.
Hersey, John Richard
Hertzberg, Arthur
Herzen, Aleksandr
Hesburgh, Theodore Martin
Heseltine, Phillip Arnold
Hesse, Hermann
Hewitt, Foster (William Foster)
Heyer, Georgette
Heym, Stefan
Heyse, Paul Johann
Heyward, (Edwin) DuBose
Hibbert, Eleanor Alice Burford
Hickok, Lorena A
Hicks, Granville
Higgins, George V
Higginson, Thomas Wentworth
Highet, Gilbert Arthur
Highsmith, Patricia
Hill, Grace Livingstone
Hillerman, Tony
Hillyer, Robert
Hilton, James
Himes, Chester Bomar
Hinde, Thomas
Hines, Duncan
Hinton, S(usan) E(loise)
Hite, Shere
Hoban, Russell
Hobart, Alice Tisdale Nourse
Hobbes, Thomas
Hobson, Laura Zametkin
Hochhuth, Rolf
Hodgson, Richard Sargeant
Hoff, Sydney
Hoffer, Eric
Hoffman, Abbie (Abbott)
Hoffman, Al
Hoffmann, Ernst Theodor Amadeus
Hogg, James
Hoke, Henry Reed
Holbrook, Stewart Hall
Hollander, John

Occupation Index

Jessup, Richard
Jewett, Sarah Orne
Jhabvala, Ruth Prawer
John of Salisbury
Johnson, Arno Hollock
Johnson, Charles Richard
Johnson, Crockett
Johnson, James Ralph
Johnson, James Weldon
Johnson, Josephine Winslow
Johnson, Martin Elmer
Johnson, Pamela Hansford
Johnson, Phillip Cortelyou
Johnson, Raynor C(arey)
Johnston, Richard Malcolm
Jones, David
Jones, Glyn
Jones, Gwynn
Jones, Howard Mumford
Jones, James
Jones, Madison Percy, Jr.
Jones, Weyman
Jong, Erica
Jordan, Elizabeth Garver
Jordan, June Meyer
Joseph, Helen
Josephson, Matthew
Joyce, James Augustus Aloysius
Judson, Emily Chubbock
Kael, Pauline
Kaempffert, Waldemar (Bernhard)
Kafka, Franz
Kahn, Roger
Kalb, Bernard
Kamp, Irene Kittle
Kane, Harnett T(homas)
Kane, Henry
Kanin, Garson
Kanner, Leo
Kantor, Mackinlay
Kaplan, Mordecai
Karp, Lila
Kassorla, Irene Chamie
Kastner, Erich
Katayev, Valentin
Kaufman, Bel
Kaufman, Sue
Kawabata, Yasunari
Kaye, Mary Margaret Mollie
Kaye-Smith, Sheila
Kazantzakis, Nikos
Keane, John B
Keane, Mary Nesta
Kearns, Doris H
Keble, John
Keeshan, Bob
Kelland, Clarence Budington
Keller, Gottfried
Keller, Helen Adams
Kelley, Kitty
Kelsen, Hans

Kelsey, Alice Geer
Kemble, Fanny (Frances Anne)
Kemelman, Harry
Kemp, (Harry) Hibbard
Kempton, James Murray, Jr.
Kempton, Jean Goldschmidt
Kennedy, John Pendleton
Kennedy, Margaret
Kennedy, William
Kennedy, X J, pseud.
Kent, Rockwell
Kerouac, Jack
Kerr, (Bridget) Jean Collins
Kerr, Jean
Kerr, Malcolm (Hooper)
Kerr, Orpheus C
Kerr, Walter Francis
Kesey, Ken
Key, Theodore
Key, Valdimer Orlando, Jr.
Keyes, Frances Parkinson
Keys, Ancel Benjamin
Kicknosway, Faye
Kiely, Benedict
Kienzle, William X(avier)
Kieran, John Francis
Kierkegaard, Soren Aabye
Kiker, Douglas
Kilbracken, John Raymond Godley
Kimbrough, Emily
King, Alexander
King, Francis Henry
King, Grace Elizabeth
King, Stephen Edwin
King, Thomas Starr
Kinglake, Alexander William
Kingsley, Charles
Kingsley, Henry
Kingston, Maxine Hong
Kintner, Robert Edmonds
Kipling, Rudyard
Kirk, Ruth Kratz
Kirkland, Caroline Matilda Stansbury
Kirkus, Virginia
Kirkwood, James
Kittredge, G(eorge) L(yman)
Klein, Melanie
Kleinfield, "Sonny" Nathan Richard
Kleist, Heinrich von
Klima, Ivan
Kline, Otis Adelbert
Knebel, Fletcher
Knight, Charles
Knight, George Wilson
Knight, John S, III
Knowles, James Sheridan
Knowles, John
Knox, Ronald Arbuthnott
Kobbe, Gustav
Kober, Arthur
Koch, Kenneth

Koehler, Wolfgang
Koestler, Arthur
Kohl, Herbert R
Kokoschka, Oskar
Kollek, Teddy (Theodore)
Komroff, Manuel
Kops, Bernard
Koren, Edward Benjamin
Korinetz, Yuri
Korolenko, Vladimir Galaktionovich
Kosinski, Jerzy Nikodem
Kotzebue, August Friedrich Ferdinand von
Kovel, Ralph Mallory
Kovel, Terry Horvitz
Kovic, Ron
Kozol, Jonathan
Kraft, Joseph
Krantz, Hazel Newman
Krantz, Judith
Krassner, Paul
Krauss, Ruth Ida
Krementz, Jill
Krishnamurti, Jiddu
Kristol, Irving
Kroeber, Alfred Louis
Kroeber, Theodora Kracaw
Kronenberger, Louis
Krumgold, Joseph
Krutch, Joseph Wood
Krylov, Ivan Andreyevich
Kubler-Ross, Elisabeth
Kumin, Maxine Winokur
Kundera, Milan
Kung, Hans
Kunitz, Stanley Jasspon
Kuprin, Aleksandr Ivanovich
Kurtz, Katherine
Kushner, Harold Samuel
Kuznetsov, Anatoli
Kyne, Peter Bernard
L'Amour, Louis Dearborn
L'Engle, Madeleine
LaBern, Arthur Joseph
Laboulage, Edouard Rose
LaBruyere, Jean de
Lacey, Robert
Laclos, (Pierre) Choderlos de
LaFarge, Christopher
LaFarge, John
LaFarge, Oliver
LaFeuer, Minard
Lafferty, Raphael Aloysius
LaFontaine, Jean de
Laforgue, Jules
Lagerkvist, Par
Lagerlof, Selma Ottiliana Lovisa
Lahr, John
Laidler, Harry Wellington
Laing, R(onald) D(avid)
Lamantia, Philip
LaMarsh, Judy (Julia Verlyn)

Lamb, Caroline Ponsonby, Lady
Lamb, Charles
Lamb, Harold Albert
Lamb, Mary Ann
Lamburn, Richmal Crompton
Landolfi, Tommaso
Landor, Walter Savage
Lane, Edward William
Lane, Rose Wilder
Lang, Andrew
Lang, Daniel
Langland, William
Langner, Nola
Lappe, Francis Moore
Lardner, Dionysius
Lardner, Ring(gold Wilmer)
Larkin, Oliver Waterman
Larkin, Philip
LaRochefoucauld, Francois, Duc de
Larsson, Carl (Olof)
Lasker, Edward
Lasky, Jesse Louis, Jr.
Lasky, Victor
Latham, Jean Lee
Lattimore, Owen
Lauda, Niki (Nikolaus-Andreas)
Laurel, Alicia Bay
Laurence, Margaret Jean
Laurents, Arthur
Lavater, Johann Casper
Laver, James
Law, William
Lawrence, D(avid) H(erbert)
Lawrence, Jack
Lawrence, Jerome
Lawrence, Josephine
Lawrence, Mildred Elwood
Lawrence, T(homas) E(dward)
Lawrenson, Helen Brown
Lawson, Robert
Laxness, Halldor Kiljan
Laye, Camara
Lea, Fanny Heaslip
Lea, Homer
Lea, Tom
Least Heat Moon, William, pseud.
Leavis, F(rank) R(aymond)
Leblanc, Maurice
Lebowitz, Fran(ces Ann)
Leboyer, Frederick
LeCarre, John, pseud.
Lecky, William Edward Hartpole
Lederer, William Julius
Lee, Charles
Lee, Harper (Nelle Harper)
Lee, Manfred B(ennington)
Leech, Margaret Kernochan
Leek, Sybil
LeGallienne, Eva
Legler, Henry Eduard
LeGuin, Ursula Kroeber

Lehmann, John Frederick
Lehmann, Rosamond Nina
Lehmann-Haupt, Hellmut E
Leiber, Fritz
Leighton, Clare Veronica Hope
Leland, Charles Godfrey
Lenin, Nikolai
Lenski, Lois
Leokum, Arkady
Leon, Henry Cecil
Leonard, Elmore John, Jr.
Leonard, John
Leopold, Nathan Freudenthal
Lerman, Leo
Lermontov, Mikhail (Michael Jurevich)
Lerner, Max
LeRoux, Gaston
Lesage, Alain Rene
Leskov, Nikolai
Leslie, Eliza
Leslie, Miriam Florence Folline
Lessing, Doris May
Lessing, Gotthold Ephraim
Leverson, Ada
Levin, Ira
Levin, Meyer
Levine, Albert Norman
Levine, David
Levine, Philip
Levy, Julien
Lewis, Boyd de Wolf
Lewis, C(live) S(taples)
Lewis, Dominic Bevan Wyndham
Lewis, Janet
Lewis, Matthew Gregory
Lewis, Oscar
Lewis, Shari
Lewis, Sinclair
Lewis, Wyndham
Lewisohn, Ludwig
Ley, Willy
Lichine, Alexis
Liddell Hart, Basil Henry
Lie, Jonas (Laurite Idemil)
Liebow, Averill A(braham)
Lifshin, Lyn
Liliencron, (Friedrich Adolf Axel) Detlev
    von
Lilienthal, Otto
Lilly, Doris
Lilly, John C
Lin, Yutang
Linacre, Thomas
Lincoln, George A
Lincoln, Joseph Crosby
Lincoln, Mary Johnson Bailey
Lincoln, Victoria Endicott
Lind, Jakov
Lindbergh, Anne Spencer Morrow
Lindgren, Astrid
Lindsay, (Nicholas) Vachel

Lindsay, David
Linnaeus, Carolus
Linton, William James
Lippmann, Walter
Lispector, Clarice
Little, (Flora) Jean
Littledale, Freya Lota
Litvinoff, Emanuel
Llewellyn, Richard
Locke, William John
Lockhart, (Robert Hamilton) Bruce, (Sir)
Lockridge, Frances Louise
Lockridge, Richard
Lockridge, Ross Franklin, Jr.
Loeb, Gerald Martin
Loeser, Katinka
Lofting, Hugh
Lofts, Norah Robinson
Lomax, Louis
London, Jack (John Griffith)
Long, John Luther
Longus
Longworth, Alice Roosevelt
Loos, Anita
Lopez de Ayala, Pero
Lopez-Portillo y Rojas, Jose
Lord, Phillips H
Lord, Walter
Lortz, Richard
Lossing, Benson John
Loti, Pierre, pseud.
Louys, Pierre
Lovecraft, H(oward) P(hillips)
Lovejoy, Clarence Earle
Lovelace, Linda
Lovesey, Peter Harmer
Lowenfels, Walter
Lowndes, Marie Adelaide Belloc
Lowndes, Robert A(ugustine) W(ard)
Lowry, Malcolm (Clarence Malcolm)
Lucan
Lucas, Jerry
Luce, Clare Boothe
Lucian
Luciano, Ron(ald Michael)
Ludlow, Fitz Hugh
Ludlum, Robert
Ludwig, Emil
Luhan, Mabel Dodge
Lukas, J Anthony
Lummis, Charles Fletcher
Lurie, Alison
Lyle, Katie Letcher
Lyly, John
Lynd, Helen Merrell
Lynes, Joseph Russell, Jr.
Lyons, Dorothy (Marawee)
Lyons, Enid Muriel
Lyons, Eugene
Lyons, James
Lytle, Andrew Nelson

Lytton, Edward George Earle Lytton
  Bulwer-Lytton, 1st Baron Lytton
Maas, Peter
Mabee, Carleton (Fred Carleton)
MacDiarmid, Hugh, pseud.
MacDonald, George
MacDonald, John Dann
MacDonald, Ross, pseud.
Macfadden, Bernarr Adolphus
Machado, Antonio
Machado, Manuel
Machen, Arthur
Machiavelli, Niccolo
Machlup, Fritz
MacInnes, Helen
Mackay, John Alexander
MacKellar, William
Mackenzie, Alexander, Sir
Mackenzie, Compton (Edward Montague,
  Sir)
Mackenzie, Henry
MacLean, Alistair
MacLennan, Hugh
Macpherson, James
Madariaga (y Rojo), Salvador de
Maestro, Giulio
Magnante, Charles
Mailer, Norman
Major, Charles
Major, Clarence
Malamud, Bernard
Malaparte, Curzio
Malcolm, Andrew H(ogarth)
Malherbe, Francois de
Mallock, William Hurrell
Mallowan, Max Edgar Lucien, Sir
Malone, Dumas
Malone, Edmund
Malory, Thomas, Sir
Malraux, Andre
Maltz, Albert
Manchester, William Raymond
Mandelstam, Nadezhda Yakovlevna
Manfred, Frederick Feikema
Mankowitz, Wolf
Mann, Erika
Mann, Heinrich Ludwig
Mann, Klaus
Mann, Thomas
Mannes, Marya
Manning, Irene
Manning, Olivia
Mansfield, Katherine
Manzoni, Alessandro (Antonio)
Mao Tse-Tung
Marchetti, Victor L
Marco Polo
Marcum, John Arthur
Marcus Aurelius Antoninus
Marek, Kurt W
Margolius, Sidney Senier

Marguerite d'Angouleme
Marie Alexandra Victoria
Marivaux, Pierre Carlet de
Marks, Percy
Marlowe, Derek
Marmontel, Jean Francois
Marquand, John Phillips
Marryat, Frederick
Marsh, Dame Ngaio
Marshall, (Sarah) Catherine Wood
Marshall, Catherine
Marston, John
Martin du Gard, Roger
Martin, Judith
Martin, Robert Bernard
Marvell, Andrew
Masefield, John
Mason, Daniel Gregory
Mason, John Brown
Massey, Gerald
Massinger, Philip
Masters, John
Masters, Kelly R
Masur, Harold Q
Mather, Cotton
Matheson, Richard Burton
Mathison, Richard Randolph
Matisse, Henri
Matthiessen, Francis Otto
Maugham, Robin (Robert Cecil Romer)
Maugham, William Somerset
Maupassant, Guy de (Henri Rene Albert
  Guy de)
Mauriac, Francois
Maurois, Andre
Maxwell, William
May, Karl Friedrich
Mayer, Edward Newton, Jr.
Mayer, Martin Prager
Mayo, Katherine
Mazel, Judy
McAdie, Alexander George
McCall, Dorothy Lawson
McCann, Alfred Watterson
McCarthy, Justin Huntly
McCarthy, Mary
McCloskey, Robert
McClung, Nellie Letitia Mooney
McCoy, Horace
McCullers, Carson Smith
McCulley, Johnston
McCullough, Colleen
McDowell, Katharine Sherwood Bonner
McFee, William
McGinley, Phyllis
McGinniss, Joe
McGivern, William Peter
McGuffey, William Holmes
McHale, Tom
McIntyre, John Thomas
McKelway, St. Clair

McKenney, Ruth
McLuhan, (Herbert) Marshall
McMullen, Mary, pseud.
McMurtry, Larry Jeff
McNair, Malcolm Perrine
McNeile, Herman Cyril
McWhirter, A(lan) Ross
McWhirter, Norris Dewar
McWilliams, Carey
Mead, Margaret
Mears, Walter R(obert)
Mehta, Ved Parkash
Meier-Graefe, Julius
Melville, Herman
Mendes, Catulle (Abraham Catulle)
Meredith, George
Merejkowski, Dmitri Sergeyevich
Merimee, Prosper
Meriwether, Lee
Merriam, Clinton Hart
Merrill, James
Merritt, Abraham
Merton, Thomas
Mertz, Barbara Louise Gross
Messer, Alfred A
Messner, Reinhold
Metalious, Grace de Repentigny
Meyer, Nicholas
Michener, James A(lbert)
Mihajlov, Mihajlo
Mikhalkov, Sergei Vladimirovich
Miles, Nelson A
Millar, Margaret Ellis
Millay, Edna St. Vincent
Miller, Alice Duer
Miller, Caroline
Miller, Henry
Miller, Jonathan
Miller, Max
Miller, Merle
Miller, Olive Beaupre
Milligan, "Spike" Terence Alan
Millis, Walter
Milne, A(lan) A(lexander)
Milne, Christopher Robin
Milosz, Czeslaw
Mishima, Yukio, pseud.
Mitchell, Margaret
Mitchell, Silas Weir
Mitchell, William Ormond
Mitchison, Naomi Haldane
Mitford, Jessica
Mitford, Nancy Freeman
Moats, Alice-Leone
Moberg, Vihelm
Molloy, John T
Molnar, Ferenc
Monaghan, (James) Jay, (IV)
Moncreiffe, Jain (Rupert Jain)
Mondale, Joan Adams
Monk, Maria

Monro, Harold Edward
Monsarrat, Nicholas John Turney
Montagu, Mary Wortley, Lady
Monteilhet, Hubert
Monteleone, Thomas F(rancis)
Montgomery, Lucy Maud
Moodie, Susanna
Moore, Brian
Moore, George Augustus
Moore, Harry Thornton
Moore, Jack
Moorehead, Alan
Moraes, Vinicius de
Moravia, Alberto, pseud.
More, Thomas, Sir
Morgan, Charles Langbridge
Morgan, Edwin George
Morgan, Marabel
Morley, Christopher Darlington
Morris, Clara
Morris, William
Morris, Willie
Morris, Wright Marion
Morrison, Theodore
Morrison, Toni
Mortimer, John Clifford
Morton, Frederic
Mosenthal, Salomon Hermann von
Mosley, Leonard
Motley, Willard Francis
Mott, Frank Luther
Mottley, John
Mowat, Farley McGill
Moyes, Patricia
Mucha, Jiri
Muggeridge, Malcolm
Muir, Edwin
Muir, John
Mulford, Clarence Edward
Mumford, Lewis
Munsey, Frank Andrew
Munson, Gorham B(ert)
Murasaki, Shikibu, Lady
Murdoch, Iris (Jean Iris)
Murfree, Mary Noailles
Murphy, Warren
Murray, Charles Alan
Murray, Gilbert (George Gilbert Aime)
Murry, John Middleton
Muses, Charles Arthur
Musset, Alfred de
Myerson, Bess
Myrdal, Jan
Nabokov, Vladimir
Nader, Ralph
Nagai, Sokichi
Naipaul, V(idiahar) S(urajprasad)
Naisbitt, John
Nash, N Richard
Nash, Ogden Frederick
Nash, Thomas

Pennell, Joseph Stanley
Percy, Charles Harting
Percy, Walker
Pereda, Jose Marie de
Perelman, S(idney) J(oseph)
Peret, Benjamin
Peretz, Isaac Loeb
Perez Galdos, Benito
Perls, Frederick Salomon
Perrault, Charles
Perry, Bliss
Perry, Eleanor Bayer
Perry, Ralph Barton
Pestalozzi, Johann Heinrich
Peter, Laurence Johnston
Peterkin, Julia Mood
Peters, Ellis, pseud.
Petronius, Gaius
Peyre, Henri Maurice
Peyrefitte, Roger
Phaedrus
Philbrick, Herbert Arthur
Philby, Harold St. John Bridger
Philips, David Graham
Phillips, Wendell
Picabia, Francis
Picard, Edmond
Picard, Raymond
Pierrot, George Francis
Pike, James Albert
Pinkwater, Daniel Manus
Piper, H(enry) Beam
Pirandello, Luigi
Pitkin, Walter Boughton
Pitrone, Jean M
Pitt, William
Pitz, Henry Clarence
Plain, Belva
Plath, Sylvia
Plato
Pleasants, Henry
Plimpton, George
Pliny the Elder
Plomer, William Charles Franklyn
Plotnik, Arthur
Poe, Edgar Allan
Pohl, Frederik
Poincare, Raymond
Politi, Leo
Pollard, Jack
Pollock, Channing
Pollock, Jackson
Polykoff, Shirley
Pontoppidan, Henrik
Poole, Ernest
Popov, Dusko
Porsche, Ferdinand
Porter, Bernard H
Porter, Eleanor H
Porter, Gene Stratton
Porter, Hal

Porter, Katherine Anne
Porter, Sylvia Field
Porter, William Trotter
Portis, Charles
Posell, Elsa Z
Post, Elizabeth Lindley
Post, Emily Price
Potok, Chaim
Potter, Beatrix (Helen Beatrix)
Potter, Stephen
Powdermaker, Hortense
Powell, Anthony Dymoke
Powell, Gordon G
Powell, Lawrence Clark
Powers, Anne
Powers, James Farl
Powys, John Cowper
Powys, Llewelyn
Powys, Theodore Francis
Prather, Richard Scott
Pratt, Fletcher
Pratt, Gerald Hillary
Prevost d'Exiles, Antoine Francois, Abbe
Prevost, Marcel
Priestley, J B (John Boynton)
Pritchett, V(ictor) S(awdon), Sir
Prokosch, Frederic
Proust, Marcel
Pudney, John Sleigh
Pulci, Luigi
Purdy, James
Purdy, Susan Gold
Pusey, Edward Bouverie
Pusey, Merlo John
Pushkin, Aleksandr Sergeyevich
Puzo, Mario
Pyle, Howard
Pym, Barbara Mary Crampton
Pynchon, Thomas
Quasimodo, Salvatore
Queen, Ellery, pseud.
Quiller-Couch, Arthur Thomas, Sir
Quinn, Anthony Rudolph Oaxaca
Quiroga, Horacio
Raab, Selwyn
Radcliffe, Ann
Rader, Dotson
Rafferty, Max(well Lewis, Jr.)
Ragan, David
Raine, William MacLeod
Rajneesh, Bhagwan Shree
Rakosi, Carl
Rama Rau, Santha
Rand, Ayn
Randall, James Garfield
Randhawa, Mohinder Singh
Randi, James
Randisi, Robert Joseph
Randolph, Georgiana Ann
Randolph, Mary
Ranke, Leopold von

Ransom, John Crowe
Ransome, Arthur Mitchell
Raphael, Frederic Michael
Raphaelson, Samson
Rather, Dan
Rawlings, Marjorie Kinnan
Rayner, Claire Berenice
Read, Piers Paul
Reade, Charles
Rebuffat, Gaston Louis Simon
Rechy, John Franklin
Redford, Robert
Redgrave, Michael Scudamore, Sir
Redi, Francesco
Reed, Ishmael
Reed, Myrtle
Reed, Peter Hugh
Reems, Harry
Reik, Theodor
Reiner, Carl
Remarque, Erich Maria
Renan, (Joseph) Ernest
Renard, Jules
Renault, Mary, pseud.
Reuben, David
Revel, Jean Francois
Reymont, Wladyslaw Stanislaw
Rhodes, Hari
Rhys, Jean
Ricardo, David
Rice, Alice Caldwell Hegan
Rice, Anne
Rice, Cale Young
Rice, Craig
Richards, Laura Elizabeth Howe
Richards, Stanley
Richardson, Dorothy Miller
Richardson, Henry Handel, pseud.
Richardson, Jack
Richardson, S(tanley) D(ennis)
Richardson, Samuel
Richberg, Donald R(andall)
Richler, Mordecai
Richter, Conrad Michael
Richter, Jean Paul F
Rico, Don(ato)
Rifkin, Jeremy
Rinehart, Mary Roberts
Ringer, Robert J
Ripley, Robert Leroy
Ritchie, Jean
Rivers, Joan
Rives, Amelie Louise
Roa (y Garcia), Raul
Roark, Garland
Robbe-Grillet, Alain
Robbins, Harold
Robert, Paul
Roberts, Charles George Douglas, Sir
Roberts, Elizabeth Madox
Roberts, Harold Selig

Roberts, Kenneth
Robertson, Don
Robertson, William
Robins, Denise Naomi
Robins, Elizabeth
Robinson, Henry Morton
Robinson, Joan Mary Gale Thomas
Robinson, Lennox (Esme Stuart Lennox)
Robinson, Paul Minnich
Robitscher, Jonas Bondi, Jr.
Roche, John P
Rockwell, "Doc" George L
Rodale, Jerome Irving
Rodgers, Mary
Roe, Edward Payson
Roelvaag, O(le) E(dvart)
Roessner, Elmer
Roethke, Theodore
Rogers, Rosemary
Rogers, Samuel
Rogers, Thomas
Rohmer, Eric, pseud.
Rohmer, Sax, pseud.
Rojas, Fernando de
Rolland, Romain
Rollin, Betty
Rolvaag, Ole Edvart
Romains, Jules
Rombauer, Irma von Starkloff
Rooney, Andy (Andrew Aitken)
Roos, Frank John, Jr.
Roose-Evans, James
Rosenberg, Sharon
Rosenfeld, Alvin Hirsch
Rosenthal, Abraham Michael
Roskolenko, Harry
Ross, Ishbel
Ross, Lillian
Rossner, Judith
Rosten, Leo Calvin
Roszak, Theodore
Roth, Henry
Roth, Philip Milton
Rotha, Paul
Roueche, Berton
Rourke, Constance Mayfield
Rousseau, Jean Jacques
Rovere, Richard Halworth
Roy, Gabrielle
Roy, Mike (Michael)
Royce, Josiah
Royko, Mike
Rozanov, Vasili
Ruark, Robert Chester
Rubin, Jerry
Rubin, Theodore Isaac
Rubin, Vitalii
Rubinstein, Arthur
Rubinstein, S(amuel) Leonard
Rudhyar, Dane
Rukeyser, Louis Richard

Runyon, Damon (Alfred Damon)
Rushmore, Robert
Ruskin, John
Russell, Edward Frederick Langley, Baron
  of Liverpool
Russell, Franklin Alexander
Russell, Sydney Gordon, Sir
Saarinen, Aline Bernstein
Sabatini, Rafael
Sabato, Ernesto
Sacher-Masoch, Leopold von
Sackville-West, Edward Charles
Sackville-West, Victoria Mary
Sade, Marquis (Donatien Alphonse
  Francoise) de
Saerchinger, Cesar Victor Charles
Safire, William L
Sagan, Francoise, pseud.
Saint Georges, Jules
Saint Johns, Adela Rogers
Saint-Exupery, Antoine (Jean Baptiste
  Marie Roger) de
Saintsbury, George Edward Bateman
Saki, pseud.
Salinger, J(erome) D(avid)
Salk, Lee
Samstag, Nicholas
Samuel, Maurice
Samuels, Ernest
Sanborn, Pitts
Sancho, Ignatius
Sand, George, pseud.
Sandburg, Carl August
Sanders, Ed Parish
Sanders, Lawrence
Sanderson, Ivan Terence
Sandoz, Mari
Sangster, Margaret Elizabeth
Sansom, William
Santayana, George
Santmyer, Helen Hooven
Sapir, Edward
Sapir, Richard
Sarasin, Jean Francois
Sarcey, Francisque
Sargeant, Winthrop
Sargent, Ben
Sarnoff, Dorothy
Saroyan, William
Sarris, Andrew
Sarton, May
Sartre, Jean-Paul
Sassoon, Siegfried
Sayers, Dorothy Leigh
Schaefer, Jack Warner
Schecter, Jerrold
Schell, Orville H
Scherman, Harry
Schickel, Richard
Schiller, Friedrich von (Johann Christoph
  Friedrich von)

Schlafly, Phyllis Stewart
Schlesinger, Arthur Meier, Jr.
Schmid, Eduard
Schmitt, Gladys
Scholem, Gershom Gerhard
Scholes, Percy Alfred
Schonfield, Hugh
Schoonmaker, Frank Musselman
Schopenhauer, Arthur
Schorer, Mark
Schoyer, (B) Preston
Schreiber, Hermann Otto Ludwig
Schroedinger, Erwin
Schulberg, Budd Wilson
Schuller, Robert Harold
Schumann, Maurice
Schwartz, Delmore
Schwarzenegger, Arnold
Schwob, Marcel
Scott, Austin W
Scott, Cyril (Meir)
Scott, Duncan Campbell
Scott, Evelyn
Scott, Paul Mark
Scott, Walter, Sir
Scudery, Madeleine de
Seagrave, Gordon Stifler
Seale, Bobby G
Searle, Ronald William Fordham
Sedgwick, Anne Douglas
Sedgwick, Catherine Maria
Seed, Jenny
Seferiades, Giorgos Styljanou
Segal, Erich Wolf
Segal, Lore Groszmann
Selby, Hubert, Jr.
Seldes, Gilbert Vivian
Selvon, Samuel Dirkson
Sendak, Maurice Bernard
Sender, Ramon Jose
Serling, Rod
Service, Robert William
Seton, Anya Chase
Seton, Ernest Thompson
Seuss, Doctor, pseud.
Severn, William Irving
Sewell, Anna
Sforza, Carlo
Shaffer, Anthony
Shalamov, Varlam Tikhonovich
Shands, Alfred Rives, Jr.
Shannon, William Vincent
Sharp, Margery
Sharp, William
Shattuck, Roger Whitney
Shaw, Irwin
Shaw, Robert
Shedd, Charlie W
Sheean, (James) Vincent
Sheed, Frank (Francis Joseph)
Sheed, Wilfrid John Joseph

Sheehan, Joseph Green
Sheehy, Gail Henion
Sheen, Fulton John, Bishop
Sheinwold, Alfred
Sheldon, Sidney
Shelley, Mary Wollstonecraft
Shepard, Odell
Shepard, Sam
Shepherd, Jean Parker
Sheridan, Clare Consuelo
Sherriff, Robert Cedric
Sherrill, Robert Glenn
Sherwood, Robert Emmet
Shirer, William L(awrence)
Shively, George Jenks
Shockley, William (Bradford)
Sholokhov, Mikhail Aleksandrovich
Shorthouse, Joseph Henry
Shukshin, Vasilii Makarovich
Shulman, Irving
Shulman, Morton
Shute, Nevil
Sidey, Hugh Swanson
Sidgwick, Henry
Siegel, Stanley E
Sienkiewicz, Henryk
Sillanpaa, Frans E
Sillitoe, Alan
Sillman, Leonard
Silone, Ignazio
Silverberg, Robert
Simenon, Georges
Simmons, Richard
Simms, William Gilmore
Simon, Claude
Simonetta
Simpson, Cedric Keith
Simpson, Louis
Sinclair, Jo, pseud.
Sinclair, Upton Beall
Singer, Isaac Bashevis
Singer, Jane Sherrod
Singmaster, Elsie
Sinyavsky, Andrei
Siodmark, Curt
Sitwell, Edith, Dame
Sitwell, Osbert, Sir
Sitwell, Sacheverell, Sir
Sjowall, Maj
Skinner, B(urrhus) F(rederic)
Skinner, Cornelia Otis
Skurzynski, Gloria
Slaughter, Frank G
Slavitt, David R
Slobodkin, Louis
Slobodkina, Esphyr
Slocum, Joshua
Smart, Christopher
Smedley, Agnes
Smith, "Dodie" Dorothy Gladys
Smith, Betty

Smith, Chard Powers
Smith, Dennis
Smith, Goldwin
Smith, H(arry) Allen
Smith, Kenneth Danforth
Smith, Lillian
Smith, Margaret
Smith, Marie D
Smith, Martin Cruz
Smith, Thorne
Smitherman, Geneva
Smollett, Tobias George
Sneider, Vernon John
Snepp, Frank Warren, III
Snow, C(harles) P(ercy), Sir
Sobol, Louis
Soby, James Thrall
Sokolsky, George E
Solomon
Solotaroff, Theodore
Solzhenitsyn, Aleksandr Isayevich
Sontag, Susan
Soupault, Philippe
Southern, Terry
Southey, Robert
Southworth, Emma Dorothy Eliza Nevitte
Soyinka, Wole (Akinwande Oluwole)
Spaeth, Sigmund Gottfried
Spargo, John
Spark, Muriel Sarah
Sparks, Fred
Speare, Elizabeth George
Spectorsky, Auguste Compte
Spencer, William
Spender, Stephen
Sperry, Armstrong W
Spier, Peter Edward
Spillane, Mickey (Frank Morrison)
Spingarn, Joel Elias
Spitta, Philipp (Julius August Philipp)
Spitteler, Karl Friedrich Georg
Spock, Benjamin McLane
Spry, Constance
Spyri, Johanna Heuser
Stacey, Thomas Charles Gerard
Stacton, David Derek
Stael-Holstein, Anne Louise Germaine
    (Necker), Baroness
Stafford, Jean
Stafford, William Edgar
Stalina, Svetlana Alliluyeva
Stallings, Laurence
Stanton, Frank
Stapledon, Olaf (Wiliam Olaf)
Starrett, Vincent (Charles Vincent
    Emerson)
Staudinger, Hermann
Stead, Christina Ellen
Stedman, Edmund Clarence
Steel, Danielle
Steel, Flora Annie Webster

Stegner, Wallace Earle
Steig, William
Stein, Aaron Marc
Stein, Gertrude
Steinbeck, John Ernst
Steinberg, David
Stendhal
Stephen, Leslie, Sir
Stephens, Ann Sophia
Stephens, James
Stephens, John Lloyd
Stern, James
Stern, Philip Van Doren
Stern, Richard Gustave
Sterne, Laurence
Stevens, Shane
Stevens, Wallace
Stevenson, Janet
Stevenson, Robert Louis Balfour
Stewart, Donald Ogden
Stewart, John Innes Mackintosh
Stewart, Mary (Florence Elinor)
Stockton, Frank (Francis Richard)
Stoker, Bram
Stokes, Doris
Stone, Chuck (Charles Sumner)
Stone, I(sidor) F(einstein)
Stone, Irving
Stone, Robert Anthony
Stoppard, Tom
Storey, David Malcolm
Story, William Wetmore
Stotz, Charles Morse
Stout, Rex Todhunter
Stowe, Harriet (Elizabeth) Beecher
Strasberg, Susan Elizabeth
Strauss, Lewis Lichtenstein
Streeter, Edward
Stribling, Thomas Sigismund
Strindberg, August (Johan August)
Strode, Hudson
Strong, Austin
Strong, Philip Duffield
Stroup, Thomas Bradley
Struther, Jan, pseud.
Strutt, Joseph
Stuart, Jesse Hilton
Stuart, Ruth McEnery
Sturgeon, Theodore Hamilton
Styron, William Clark, Jr.
Suckow, Ruth
Sue, Eugene Joseph Marie
Suhl, Yuri
Sullivan, A(loysius) M(ichael)
Sullivan, Arthur Seymour, Sir
Sumner, Charles
Sunshine, Linda
Surtees, Robert Smith
Susann, Jacqueline
Sutton, Horace (Ashley)
Suzuki, Daisetz Teitaro

Swados, Elizabeth A (Liz)
Swados, Harvey
Swanberg, William Andrew
Swarthout, Glendon Fred
Swift, Jonathan
Swinburne, Laurence
Swinnerton, Frank Arthur
Symons, Arthur
Symons, Julian Gustave
Synge, John Millington
Taber, Gladys Bagg
Talese, Gay
Talmadge, Thomas de Witt
Tarbell, Ida Minerva
Tarkington, Booth
Tarnower, Herman
Tarsis, Valery Yakovlevich
Tasso, Torquato
Tatum, Edward Lawrie
Taubman, Howard (Hyman Howard)
Tawney, Richard Henry
Taylor, A(lan) J(ohn) P(ercivale)
Taylor, Bayard
Taylor, Peter
Taylor, Phoebe Atwood
Teale, Edwin Way
Teasdale, Sara
Tebbel, John William
Tedder, Arthur William Tedder, Baron
Teller, Edward
Ten Boom, Corrie
Tennenbaum, Silvia
Terhune, Albert Payson
Terhune, Mary Virginia
Terkel, Studs (Louis)
Terrell, Mary Church
Terry, Walter
Tey, Josephine, pseud.
Thackeray, William Makepeace
Thayer, Ernest
Thayer, George Chapman, Jr.
Thayer, Mary Van Rensselaer
Thayer, Tiffany Ellsworth
Theresa, Saint
Theroux, Paul Edward
Thomas a Kempis
Thomas, Caitlin Macnamara
Thomas, Craig D
Thomas, D(onald) M(ichael)
Thomas, Dylan Marlais
Thomas, Edward
Thomas, Gwyn
Thomas, Joyce Carol
Thomas, Lowell Jackson
Thomas, Lowell Jackson, Jr.
Thomas, Norman Mattoon
Thomas, Piri
Thompson, Edward Herbert
Thompson, Ernest (Richard Ernest)
Thompson, Josiah
Thompson, Kay

Thompson, Oscar
Thompson, Ruth Plumly
Thompson, Thomas
Thoreau, Henry David
Thorne, Jim
Thurber, James Grover
Thurman, Howard
Tidyman, Ernest
Tietjens, Eunice
Timerman, Jacobo
Tobias, Andrew
Tocqueville, Alexis, Comte de
Todd, Mabel Loomis
Toffler, Alvin
Toland, John Willard
Toledano, Ralph de
Tolkien, J(ohn) R(onald) R(euel)
Tolstoy, Alexey Nikolaevich
Tolstoy, Leo Nikolayevich
Tomasi di Lampedusa, Guiseppe
Tomkins, Calvin
Tomlinson, Henry Major
Toole, John Kennedy
Toomer, Jean
Tourneur, Cyril
Tovey, Donald Francis, Sir
Townsend, George Alfred
Townsend, Peter Wooldridge
Townsend, William H(enry)
Toye, Francis
Toynbee, Philip (Theodore Philip)
Train, Arthur Cheney
Trapp, Maria Augusta von
Traven, B, pseud.
Travers, Ben
Travers, Mary
Travers, P(amela) L(yndon)
Treat, Lawrence
Treece, Henry
Tregaskis, Richard William
Trevelyan, George Macaulay
Trevor, William
Trifonov, Yuri Valentinovich
Trillin, Calvin Marshall
Trilling, Diana Rubin
Trilling, Lionel
Tripp, Paul
Trollope, Anthony
Trollope, Frances
Tromp, Solco Walle
Trotsky, Leon
Trotta, Maurice S
Trowbridge, John Townsend
Trudeau, Margaret Joan Sinclair
Truman, Margaret (Mary Margaret)
Trumbo, Dalton
Trumbull, Charles Gallaudet
Tryon, Thomas
Tucci, Toni
Tucker, Larry
Tugwell, Rexford Guy

Turgenev, Ivan Sergeevich
Turnbull, Agnes Sligh
Turner, Morrie
Tutuola, Amos
Twain, Mark, pseud.
Tweedale, Violet Chambers
Twitchell, Paul
Tyler, Anne
Tynan, Kenneth Peacock
Tyndall, John
Tzara, Tristan
Uhnak, Dorothy
Ullman, James Ramsey
Unamuno (y Jugo), Miguel de
Undset, Sigrid
Untermeyer, Jean Starr
Untermeyer, Louis
Unwin, Stanley, Sir
Updike, John Hoyer
Upshaw, William David
Uris, Leon Marcus
Uspenskii, Petr D
Utley, Freda
Van Der Post, Laurens
Van Dine, S S, pseud.
Van Doren, Dorothy Graffe
Van Doren, Mark
Van Paassen, Pierre
Van Slyke, Helen Lenore Vogt
Van Vechten, Carl
Van Vooren, Monique
Vance, Louis Joseph
Vanderbilt, Amy
Vandercook, John Womack
Varese, Edgar
Vasari, Giorgio
Vaughan, Agnes Carr
Vaughan, Bill (William Edward)
Vaughan, Henry
Verga, Giovanni
Verissimo, Erico Lopes
Verne, Jules
Verrill, Alpheus Hyatt
Very, Jones
Vidal, "Gore" Eugene Luther
Viereck, George Sylvester
Viertel, Peter
Vigny, Alfred Victor, Comte de
Villiers, Alan John
Viorst, Judith (Stahl)
Voelker, John Donaldson
Voelker, Paul Frederick
Volney, (Constantin) Francois Chasseboeuf
Voltaire(, Francois Marie Arouet de)
Von Eckardt, Wolf
VonDaeniken, Erich
VonDoderer, Heimito
Vonnegut, Kurt, Jr.
Vonnegut, Mark
Vynnychenko, Volodymyr
Wahloo, Per

Wain, John Barrington
Wakefield, Dan
Wakeman, Frederic
Waley, Arthur David
Walford, Roy L(ee, Jr.)
Walker, Alice
Walker, Harold Blake
Wallace, Amy
Wallace, Edgar
Wallace, Horace Binney
Wallace, Irving
Wallace, Lewis
Wallant, Edward Lewis
Wallechinsky, David
Wallop, Douglass (John Douglass, III)
Wallraff, Gunter
Walpole, Horace
Walpole, Hugh Seymour, Sir
Waltari, Mika
Walton, Izaak
Wambaugh, Joseph Aloysius, Jr.
Ward, Barbara Mary
Ward, Mary Jane
Warhol, Andy
Warner, Charles Dudley
Warner, Denis Ashton
Warner, Susan Bogert
Warner, Sylvia Townsend
Warren, Austin
Warren, Robert Penn
Warton, Joseph
Warton, Thomas
Washington, Booker T(aliafero)
Wassermann, Jakob
Watkins, Ernest Shilston
Watt, Richard Martin
Wattenberg, Ben J
Waugh, Alec (Alexander Raban)
Waugh, Auberon
Waugh, Evelyn Arthur St. John
Wayman, Dorothy
Weaver, Thomas
Webb, Jack Randolph
Webb, James H(enry)
Webb, Walter Prescott
Weber, Max
Weber, Max
Webster, Donald Blake
Webster, Jean
Webster, Noah
Wechsberg, Joseph
Wechsler, James Arthur
Wedekind, Frank
Weidman, Jerome
Weingarten, Violet
Weir, John F(erguson)
Wellek, Rene
Welles, Sumner
Wellman, Paul Iselin
Wells, Carolyn
Wells, H(erbert) G(eorge)

Welty, Eudora
Werfel, Franz
Wertham, Fredric
Wescott, Glenway
West, Dame Rebecca, pseud.
West, Jessamyn
West, Morris Langlo
West, Nathanael, pseud.
Westlake, Donald E(dwin)
Wharton, Edith
Whiffen, Marcus
Whistler, James Abbott McNeill
Whitaker, Rogers E(rnest) M(alcolm)
White, Antonia
White, E(lwyn) B(rooks)
White, Patrick Victor Martindale
White, Richard Grant
White, Stewart Edward
White, T(erence) H(anbury)
White, Theodore Harold
White, Walter Francis
White, William Allen
Whitechurch, Victor Lorenzo
Whiting, George
Whitlock, Brand
Whitman, Alden
Whitney, Mrs. Cornelius
Whitney, Phyllis Ayame
Whyte, William Hollingsworth
Wibberley, Leonard Patrick O'Connor
Wicker, Tom (Thomas Grey)
Widdemer, Margaret
Wiese, Kurt
Wiesel, Elie(zer)
Wiesenthal, Simon
Wigg, George (Edward Cecil)
Wilbur, Richard Purdy
Wilcock, John
Wilde, Oscar Fingal O'Flahertie Wills
Wilder, "Billy" Samuel
Wilder, Laura Elizabeth Ingalls
Wilder, Robert Ingersoll
Wilder, Thornton Niven
Wildmon, Donald Ellis
Wilkinson, J(ohn) Burke
Wille, Lois Jean
Williams, "Tennessee" Thomas Lanier
Williams, Ben Ames
Williams, Eric Eustace
Williams, Hosea Lorenzo
Williams, Kit
Williams, Mason
Williams, William Carlos
Wills, Garry
Wilmerding, John
Wilson, Angus
Wilson, Colin Henry
Wilson, Dorothy Clarke
Wilson, Edmund
Wilson, Erica
Wilson, Gahan

Wilson, Margaret
Wilson, Mitchell
Wilson, Sloan
Wimsatt, William Kurtz, Jr.
Wind, Herbert Warren
Wingler, Hans Maria
Winship, Elizabeth
Winslow, Ola Elizabeth
Winsor, Kathleen
Winter, Alice Vivian Ames
Winterich, John Tracy
Wintle, Justin Beecham
Winwar, Frances (Francesca Vinciguerra)
Wise, Stephen Samuel
Wise, William H
Wister, Owen
Wodehouse, P(elham) G(renville)
Wolfe, Thomas Clayton
Wolfe, Tom (Thomas Kennerly, Jr.)
Wood, Guy B
Wood, Mrs. Henry
Wood, Peggy
Wood, Sarah Sayward Barrell Keating
Woodhull, Victoria Claflin
Woodiwiss, Kathleen E
Woodruff, Judy Carline
Woodruff, Maurice
Woods, Donald
Woods, Stuart
Woodson, Carter Godwin
Woodward, William E
Woodworth, Samuel
Woolf, Leonard Sidney
Woolf, Virginia (Adeline Virginia Stephen)
Woollcott, Alexander Humphreys
Woolley, Catherine (Jane Thayer)
Woolsey, Janette
Woolsey, Sarah Chauncey
Wouk, Herman
Wright, Frances (Fanny)
Wright, Harold Bell
Wright, Richard
Wrightson, Patricia
Wycliffe, John
Wylie, Elinor Hoyt
Wylie, Philip Gordon
Wyss, Johann David
Wyss, Johann Rudolf
Yarrow, Peter
Yellen, Jack
Yerby, Frank Garvin
Yezierska, Anzia
Yonge, Charlotte Mary
Young, Andrew
Young, Ann Eliza Webb
Young, Art(hur Henry)
Young, Edward
Young, Stark
Yourcenar, Marguerite, pseud.
Zangwill, Israel
Zim, Herbert Spencer

Zimmerman, Paul
Zindel, Paul
Zola, Emile Edouard Charles
Zolotow, Maurice
Zukofsky, Louis
Zweig, Arnold
Zweig, Stefan

AUTHORS

Coles, Manning, pseud.
Lathen, Emma, joint pseud.
Richthofen Family

AUTO EXECUTIVE

Agnelli, Giovanni
Allard, Sydney
Bennett, Harry Herbert
Chapin, Roy Dikeman
Cole, Edward Nicholas
Cord, E(rret) L(obban)
Curtice, Harlow Herbert
DeLorean, John Zachary
Estes, E(lliott) M(arantette)
Ferrari, Enzo
Ford, Benson
Ford, Edsel Bryant
Ford, Edsel Bryant, II
Ford, William Clay
Gerstenberg, Richard Charles
Gordon, John F
Hoffman, Paul Gray
Honda, Soichiro
Iacocca, Lee (Lido Anthony)
Mitchell, William Leroy
Murphy, Thomas Aquinas
Nolte, Henry R, Jr.
Petersen, Donald Eugene
Peugeot, Rodolphe
Riccardo, John Joseph
Smith, Roger Bonham
Stokes, Donald Gresham Stokes, Baron
Townsend, Lynn Alfred
Toyoda, Eiji

AUTO MANUFACTURER

Austin, Herbert
Bentley, Walter Owen
Benz, Karl Friedrich
Bugatti, Ettore
Buick, David Dunbar
Chapman, (Anthony) Colin (Bruce)
Chevrolet, Gaston
Chrysler, Walter Percy
Citroen, Andre Gustave
Daimler, Gottlieb
Dodge, Horace Elgin
Dodge, John Francis
Duesenberg, August S
Duesenberg, Frederick S

Durant, William Crapo
Ford, Henry
Ford, Henry, II
Knudsen, Semon Emil
Leland, Henry Martyn
Maserati, Ernesto
McLaren, Bruce Leslie
Nuffield, William Richard Morris, Viscount
Opel, Wilhelm von
Porsche, Ferdinand
Porsche, Ferdinand
Renault, Fernand
Renault, Louis
Renault, Marcel
Rolls, Charles Stewart
Royce, Frederick Henry, Sir
Studebaker, John Mohler
Tucker, Preston Thomas

AUTO RACER

Allison, Bobby (Robert Arthur)
Andretti, Mario Gabriel
Arnoux, Rene Alexandre
Ascari, Alberto
Baker, "Buddy" Elzie Wylie, Jr.
Bettenhausen, Tony (Melvin E)
Bondurant, Bob (Robert L)
Bonnier, Joe (Joachim)
Brabham, Jack (John Arthur)
Breedlove, (Norman) Craig
Campbell, Donald Malcolm
Campbell, Malcolm, Sir
Chevrolet, Louis Joseph
Clark, James
Depailler, Patrick
DePalma, Ralph
Fabi, Teo
Fangio, Juan Manuel
Fittipaldi, Emerson
Foyt, A(nthony) J(oseph, Jr.)
Garlits, Don
Granatelli, Anthony Joseph
Gregg, Peter
Gurney, Dan
Guthrie, Janet
Hailwood, Mike (Stanley Michael Bailey)
Harroun, Ray
Hill, Graham (Norman Graham)
Hunt, James
Johnson, Junior
Jones, Alan
Jones, Parnelli (Rufus Parnell)
Laffite, Jacques Henry Sabin
Lauda, Niki (Nikolaus-Andreas)
Maserati, Ernesto
McCluskey, Roger
McLaren, Bruce Leslie
Mears, Rick Ravon
Moss, Stirling Crauford
Muldowney, Shirley
Nuvolari, Tazio Giorgio

Oldfield, Barney (Berna Eli)
Ongais, Danny
Parsons, Benny
Pearson, David
Penske, Roger
Peterson, Ronnie
Petty, Richard
Piquet, Nelson
Prost, Alain Marie Pascal
Rahal, Bobby
Reutemann, Carlos
Reventlow, Lance
Revson, Peter Jeffrey
Rindt, Jochen
Roberts, Edward Glenn
Rosberg, Keke
Sachs, Eddy (Edward Julius)
Shaw, Wilbur
Sneva, Tom (Thomas Edsol)
St. James, Lyn
Stewart, Jackie (John Young)
Sullivan, Danny
Surtees, John
Unser, Al
Unser, Al, Jr.
Unser, Bobby
Villeneuve, Gilles
Waltrip, Darrell (Lee)
Ward, Rodger
Watson, John
Yarborough, Cale (William Caleb)
Yarbrough, Lee Roy

AVIATOR

Abruzzo, Ben(jamine Lou)
Alcock, John William, Sir
Andrews, Frank M(axwell)
Balchen, Bernt
Bennett, Floyd
Bleriot, Louis
Castle, Frederick W
Castle, Vernon
Chanute, Octave
Chennault, Claire Lee
Corrigan, Douglas
Coste, Dieudonne
Doolittle, James Harold
Eaker, Ira Clarence
Fonck, Rene
Fuchida, Mitsuo
Harsh, George
Hughes, Howard Robard
Immelmann, Max
Julian, Hubert Fauntleroy
Kelly, Colin Purdie
Kerkorian, Kirk
Kingsford-Smith, Charles Edward
Kuter, Laurence S(herman)
Lindbergh, Charles Augustus
Link, Edwin Albert
Nungesser, Charles

Post, Wiley
Richthofen, Manfred von, Baron
Rickenbacker, Eddie (Edward Vernon)
Saint-Exupery, Antoine (Jean Baptiste
   Marie Roger) de
Turner, Roscoe Wilson
Udet, Ernst
Wright, Orville
Wright, Wilbur

AVIATRIX

Auriol, Jacqueline Douet
Cochran, Jacqueline
Earhart, Amelia Mary
Elder, Ruth
Johnson, Amy
Markham, Beryl
Nichols, Ruth Rowland
Noyes, Blanche Wilcox
Omlie, Phoebe Jane Fairgrave
Quimby, Harriet

BACTERIOLOGIST

Cox, Herald Rea
DeKruif, Paul Henry
Fleming, Alexander, Sir
Isaacs, Alick
Pasteur, Louis
Welch, William Henry
Wright, Almroth Edward, Sir

BALLERINA

Alonso, Alicia
Aroldingen, Karin von
Ashley, Merrill
Bedells, Phyllis
Bonfanti, Marie
Browne, Leslie
Chase, Lucia
Danilova, Alexandra
Doubrovska, Felia
Farrell, Suzanne
Fedorova, Alexandra
Fifield, Elaine
Fonteyn, Margot, Dame
Fracci, Carla
Franca, Celia
Gregory, Cynthia Kathleen
Hayden, Melissa
Healy, Katherine
Kain, Karen Alexandria
Karsavina, Tamara
Kaye, Nora
Kent, Allegra
Kirkland, Gelsey
Kistler, Darci
Lander, Toni
Lopokova, Lydia Vasilievna
Makarova, Natalia

Markova, Alicia
McBride, Patricia
McKerrow, Amanda
Miller, Linda Kay
Nijinska, Bronislava
Pavlova, Anna
Plisetskaya, Maya Mikhailovna
Potts, Nadia
Rambert, Dame Marie
Seymour, Lynn
Svetlova, Marina
Tcherkassky, Marianna Alexsavena
Tennant, Veronica
Ulanova, Galina
Van Hamel, Martine
Verdy, Violette
Watts, Heather (Linda Heather)
Wilde, Patricia

BALLET DANCER

Andersen, Ib Steen
Augustyn, Frank Joseph
Baryshnikov, Mikhail
Blair, David
Bortoluzzi, Paolo
Bruhn, Erik Belton Evers
D'Amboise, Jacques
Eglevsky, Andre
Godunov, Alexander (Boris Alexander)
Grigorovich, Yuri Nikolaevich
Helpmann, Robert Murray, Sir
Lifar, Serge
Linn, Bambi
Nureyev, Rudolf
Panov, Valery
Reagan, Ronald Prescott
Taglioni, Maria
Tomasson, Helgi
Villella, Edward Joseph
Youskevitch, Igor

BALLET PROMOTER

DeCuevas, Marquis
Diaghilev, Sergei Pavlovich
Kirstein, Lincoln Edward

BALLOONIST

Abruzzo, Ben(jamine Lou)
Anderson, Max (Maxie Leroy)
Blanchard, Francois
Glaisher, James
Lunardi, Vincenzo
Montgolfier, Jacques Etienne
Montgolfier, Joseph Michel
Nadar, pseud.
Piccard, Jeannette Ridlon
Santos-Dumont, Alberto

BAND LEADER

Alpert, Herb
Anthony, Ray
Armstrong, Louis Daniel
Arnaz, Desi
August, Jan
Barnet, Charlie (Charles Daly)
Basie, "Count" (William James, Jr.
Baxter, Les
Beneke, Tex
Berigan, "Bunny" Rowland Bernart
Bloch, Raymond A
Bradley, Will
Brown, Les(ter Raymond)
Calloway, Cab(ell)
Cavallaro, Carmen
Clinton, Larry
Cole, Nat "King" Nathaniel Adams
Condon, Eddie
Conniff, Ray
Crosby, Bob (George Robert)
Cugat, Xavier
Dorsey, Jimmy (James)
Dorsey, Tommy (Thomas Francis)
Duchin, Eddie
Duchin, Peter
Eberly, Bob
Eldridge, David Roy
Ellington, "Duke" Edward Kennedy
Ellington, Mercer
Fields, Shep
Garber, Jan
Goldman, Edwin Franko
Goodman, Benny (Benjamin David)
Gray, Glen
Hampton, Lionel
Hawkins, Erskine Ramsey
Heath, Ted
Heidt, Horace Murray
Henderson, Fletcher Hamilton
Herman, Woody (Woodrow Charles)
Howard, Eddy
Hutton, Ina Ray
James, Harry
Jones, "Spike" Lindsay Armstrong
Jones, Isham
Kaye, Sammy
Kenton, Stan(ley Newcomb)
King, Wayne
Krupa, Gene
Kyser, "Kay" James Kern
Lanin, Lester
Lewis, Ted
Little, "Little Jackcq
Lombardo, Guy Albert
Lopez, Vincent
Lyman, Abe
Martin, Freddy
May, Billy (E William)
McKinley, Ray
McPartland, Jimmy (James Duigald)

Melis, Jose
Mendes, Sergio
Miller, Glenn
Monroe, Vaughan
Nelson, Ozzie (Oswald George)
Noble, Ray
Oliver, Joe (Joseph)
Pastor, Tony
Powell, Teddy
Rey, Alvino
Savitt, Jan
Scott, Raymond
Severinsen, "Doc" Carl H
Spear, Sammy
Spitalny, Phil
Spivak, Charlie
Teagarden, Jack (Weldon John)
Thompson, Hank
Thornhill, Claude
Tucker, Orrin
Tucker, Tommy
Waring, Fred Malcolm
Weems, Ted (Wilfred Theodore)
Welk, Lawrence
Williams, "Hank" Hiram
Williams, Tex
Willson, Meredith
Winterhalter, Hugo

BANKER

Aldrich, Winthrop Williams
Bagehot, Walter
Belmont, August, Jr.
Biddle, Nicholas
Butcher, Willard C(arlisle)
Clausen, A(lden) W(inship)
Cooke, Jay
Dale, Chester
Dean, Gordon Evans
Dillon, (Clarence) Douglas
Dodge, Joseph Morrell
Drexel, Anthony J
Drexel, Francis Martin
Funk, Walther
Giannini, Amadeo Peter
Griffis, Stanton
Hauge, Gabriel
Hayman, Richard
Hutton, Edward F
Junot, Philippe
Kahn, Otto Hermann
Kelly, Orie R
Lance, (Thomas) Bert(ram)
Le Poer Trench, (William Francis) Brinsley
Levitt, Arthur, Jr.
Linder, Harold Francis
Loeb, James
McNamara, Robert S(trange)
McNeill, Robert Edward, Jr.
Rebozo, "Bebe" Charles Gregory
Renault, Gilbert (Leon Etienne Theodore)

Robertson, Charles Sammis
Rochester, Nathaniel
Rockefeller, David
Rohatyn, Felix George
Roosevelt, John Aspinal
Rothschild, Edmond, Baron
Rothschild, Edmund Leopold de
Rothschild, Guy Edouard Alphonse Paul
 de, Baron
Rothschild, Leopold David
Rothschild, Lionel Nathan Rothschild,
 Baron
Rothschild, Nathan Meyer
Snyder, John Wesley
Wallenberg, Marcus
Warburg, Felix Moritz
Warburg, Frederick Marcus
Wille, Frank
Wilson, Malcolm
Wriston, Walter Bigelow

BASEBALL COACH

Hegan, Jim (James Edward)
Kluszewski, Ted (Theodore Bernard)
Lau, Charlie (Charles Richard)
Lowrey, "Peanuts" Harry Lee
Richardson, Bobby (Robert Clinton)
Sain, Johnny (John Franklin)
Schacht, Al(exander)

BASEBALL EXECUTIVE

Autry, Gene (Orvon Gene)
Barrow, Ed(ward Grant)
Briggs, Walter Owen, Jr.
Brown, Bobby (Robert William)
Bulkeley, Morgan
Busch, August Anheuser, Jr.
Cashen, Frank
Comiskey, Charlie (Charles Albert)
Cronin, Joe (Joseph Edward)
Crosley, Powel, Jr.
DeWitt, William Orville, Sr.
Doubleday, Nelson
Ebbets, Charles H
Einhorn, Eddie (Edward Martin)
Feeney, "Chub" Charles Stoneham
Fetzer, John Earl
Finley, Charlie (Charles Oscar)
Frick, Ford Christopher
Galbreath, John Wilmer
Giamatti, A(ngelo) Bartlett
Giles, Warren Crandall
Grebey, Ray
Green, Dallas (George Dallas, Jr.)
Griffith, Clark Calvin
Harrelson, Ken(neth Smith)
Harridge, Will(iam)
Johnson, (Byron) Ban(croft)
Kauffman, Ewing Marion
Kroc, Ray(mond) Albert

Kuhn, Bowie Kent
Landis, Kenesaw Mountain
MacPhail, Larry (Leland Stanford, Sr.)
MacPhail, Lee (Leland Stanford, Jr.)
McHale, John Joseph
Miller, Marvin Julian
Monaghan, Tom
O'Malley, Walter Francis
Paul, Gabe (Gabriel)
Payson, Joan Whitney
Rosen, Al(bert Leonard)
Schott, Marge (Margaret)
Steinbrenner, George Michael, III
Stoneham, Horace
Topping, Dan(iel Reid)
Ueberroth, Peter Victor
Veeck, Bill (William Louis)
Webb, Del(bert Eugene)
Weiss, George Martin
Williams, Edward Bennett
Wrigley, Philip Knight
Yawkey, Thomas Austin

BASEBALL MANAGER

Alston, Walter Emmons
Altobelli, Joe (Joseph Salvatore)
Anderson, "Sparky" George Lee
Anson, "Cap" Adrian Constantine
Bamberger, George Irvin
Bauer, Hank (Henry Albert)
Berra, "Yogi" Lawrence Peter
Chance, Frank Leroy
Charleston, Oscar McKinley
Clarke, Fred Clifford
Cochrane, Mickey (Gordon Stanley)
Collins, Eddie (Edward Trowbridge, Sr.)
Corrales, Pat(rick)
Cox, Bobby (Robert Joe)
Craig, Roger Lee
Crandall, Del(mar Wesley)
Dark, Alvin Ralph
Dressen, Charlie (Charles W)
Durocher, Leo Ernest
Felske, John Frederick
Frisch, Frankie (Frank Francis)
Gordon, Joe (Joseph Lowell)
Green, Dallas (George Dallas, Jr.)
Grimm, Charlie (Charles John)
Harris, "Bucky" Stanley Raymond
Hartnett, "Gabby" Charles Leo
Herzog, "Whitey" Dorrel Norman Elvert
Hornsby, Rogers
Houk, Ralph George
Howser, Dick (Richard Dalton)
Huggins, Miller James
Hutchinson, Fred(erick Charles)
Jennings, Hugh(ey Ambrose)
Johnson, Dave (David Allen)
Johnson, Walter Perry
Kling, John Gradwohl
Lanier, Hal (Harold Clifton)

LaRussa, Tony (Anthony, Jr.)
Lasorda, Tom (Thomas Charles)
Lemon, Bob (Robert Granville)
Leyland, Jim (James Richard)
Mack, Connie
Martin, "Billy" Alfred Manuel
Mauch, Gene William
McCarthy, Joe (Joseph Vincent)
McGraw, John Joseph
McKechnie, Bill (William Boyd)
McNamara, John Francis
Miller, Ray(mond Roger)
Moore, Jackie Spencer
O'Neill, Steve (Stephen Francis)
Ott, Mel(vin Thomas)
Piniella, Lou(is Victor)
Rader, Doug(las L)
Richards, Paul Rapier
Rickey, Branch (Wesley Branch)
Robinson, Frank
Robinson, Wilbert
Rodgers, Bob (Robert Leroy)
Rolfe, "Red" Robert Abial
Schoendienst, "Red" Albert Fred
Stengel, "Casey" Charles Dillon
Tanner, Chuck (Charles William, Jr.)
Tebbetts, "Birdie" George Robert
Terry, Bill (William Harold)
Torre, Joe (Joseph Paul)
Traynor, "Pie" Harold Joseph
Valentine, Bobby (Robert John)
Weaver, Earl Sidney
Williams, Dick (Richard Hirschfield)
Williams, Jimy (James Francis)
Williams, Ted (Theodore Samuel)
Wright, Harry (William Henry)
Zimmer, Don(ald William)

BASEBALL PLAYER

Aaron, Hank (Henry Louis)
Aikens, Willie Mays
Ainge, Dan(iel Rae)
Alexander, Grover Cleveland
Allen, Richie (Richard Anthony)
Allison, Bob (William Robert)
Alou, Felipe Rojas
Alou, Jesus Maria Rojas
Alou, Matty (Mateo Rojas)
Altrock, Nick (Nicholas)
Andujar, Joaquim
Anson, "Cap" Adrian Constantine
Antonelli, John(ny August)
Aparicio, Luis Ernesto
Appling, Luke (Lucius Benjamin)
Ashburn, Don Richie
Averill, Earl (Howard Earl)
Avila, Bobby (Roberto Francisco Gonzalez)
Baines, Harold Douglass
Baker, Frank (John Franklin)
Bancroft, Dave (David James)
Bankhead, Dan(iel Robert)

Banks, Ernie (Ernest)
Barfield, Jesse Lee
Barker, Len (Leonard Harold, II)
Barrios, Francisco Javier
Bauer, Hank (Henry Albert)
Baylor, Don Edward
Beckley, Jake (Jacob Peter)
Belinsky, "Bo" Robert
Bell, "Buddy" David Gus
Bell, "Cool Papa" James Thomas
Bench, Johnny Lee
Bender, "Chief" Charles Albert
Beradino, John
Berra, "Yogi" Lawrence Peter
Blue, Vida Rochelle
Blyleven, Bert (Rikalbert)
Boddicker, Mike (Michael James)
Boggs, Wade Anthony
Bonds, Bobby Lee
Bostock, Lyman Wesley
Bottomley, Jim (James Leroy)
Boudreau, Lou(is)
Bouton, Jim (James Alan)
Bowa, Larry (Lawrence Robert)
Boyer, Ken(ton Lloyd)
Branca, Ralph Theodore Joseph
Brazle, Al(pha Eugene)
Brecheen, Harry David
Brenley, Bob (Robert Earl)
Bresnaham, Roger Phillip
Brett, George Howard
Brett, Ken(neth Alvin)
Bridges, Tommy (Thomas Jefferson Davis)
Briles, Nelson Kelley
Brissie, Lou (Leland Victor, Jr.)
Brock, Lou(is Clark)
Brosnan, Jim (James Patrick)
Brouthers, "Dan" Dennis Joseph
Brown, Bobby (Robert William)
Brown, Mordecai Peter Centennial
Browning, Tom (Thomas Leo)
Buckner, Bill (William Joseph)
Buford, Don(ald Alvin)
Bunning, Jim (James Paul David)
Burdette, Lew (Selva Lewis, Jr.)
Burgess, "Smoky" Forrest Harrill
Burkett, Jesse Cail
Bush, Guy Terrell
Camilli, Dolph (Adolph Louis)
Camnitz, Howie (Samuel Howard)
Campanella, Roy
Campaneris, Bert (Dagoberto Blanco)
Canseco, Jose
Carew, Rod(ney Cline)
Carey, Max George
Carlton, Steve(n Norman)
Carter, Gary Edmund
Carty, Rico (Ricardo Adolfo Jacobo)
Casey, Dan(iel Maurice)
Casey, Hugh Thomas
Cash, Norm(an Dalton)

Cavarretta, Phil(ip Joseph)
Cedeno, Cesar
Cepeda, Orlando
Cerone, Rick (Richard Aldo)
Cey, Ron(ald Charles)
Chance, (Wilmer) Dean
Chance, Frank Leroy
Chandler, "Spud" Spurgeon Ferdinand
Charboneau, Joe (Joseph)
Charleston, Oscar McKinley
Chesbro, "Happy Jack" John Dwight
Cicotte, Eddie (Edward V)
Clark, Jack Anthony
Clarke, Fred Clifford
Clarkson, John Gibson
Clemens, Roger (William Roger)
Clemente, Roberto Walker
Cobb, Ty(rus Raymond)
Cochrane, Mickey (Gordon Stanley)
Colavito, Rocky (Rocco Domenico)
Coleman, Vince(nt Maurice)
Collins, Eddie (Edward Trowbridge, Sr.)
Collins, James Joseph (Jimmy)
Combs, Earle Bryan
Comiskey, Charlie (Charles Albert)
Conigliaro, Tony (Anthony Richard)
Connor, Roger
Cooper, Cecil
Cooper, Morton Cecil
Courtney, Clint(on Dawson)
Coveleski, Harry Frank
Coveleski, Stanley Anthony
Cowley, Joe (Joesph Alan)
Crandall, Del(mar Wesley)
Crawford, Sam(uel Earl)
Cronin, Joe (Joseph Edward)
Cuellar, Mike (Miguel Santana)
Cummings, "Candy" William Arthur
Curtis, John Duffield, II
Cuyler, "Kiki" Hazen Shirley
Danforth, David Charles
Dark, Alvin Ralph
Darling, Ron(ald Maurice, Jr.)
Daubert, Jake (Jacob Ellsworth)
Dauss, George August
Davis, Tommy (Thomas Herman, Jr.)
Davis, Willie (William Henry)
Dawson, Andre Nolan
Dean, "Daffy" Paul Dee
Dean, "Dizzy" Jay Hanna
Dean, Alfred Lovill
Deer, Rob(ert George)
Delahanty, Edward James
Dempsey, Rick (John Rikard)
Denny, John Allen
Dent, "Bucky" Russell Earl
Dickey, Bill (William Malcolm)
Dihigo, Martin
DiMaggio, Dom(inic Paul)
DiMaggio, Joe (Joseph Paul)
DiMaggio, Vince(nt Paul)

Doak, Bill (William Leopold)
Doby, Larry (Lawrence Eugene)
Doerr, Bobby (Robert Pershing)
Dropo, Walt
Drysdale, Don(ald Scott)
Duffy, Hugh
Duren, Ryne (Rinold George)
Durham, Leon
Durocher, Leo Ernest
Ehmke, Howard Jonathan
Ellis, Dock Phillip, Jr.
Ennis, Del(mer)
Erskine, Carl Daniel
Evers, John Joseph
Ewing, "Buck" William
Faber, "Red" Urban Charles
Face, Roy (Elroy Leon)
Fain, Ferris Roy
Feigner, Eddie (Edward)
Feller, Bob (Robert William Andrew)
Fernandez, Sid (Charles Sidney)
Ferrell, Wes(ley Cheek)
Fidrych, Mark
Fingers, Rollie (Roland Glen)
Fisk, Carlton Ernest
Flanagan, Mike (Michael Kendall)
Flick, Elmer Harrison
Flood, Curt(is Charles)
Ford, "Whitey" Edward Charles
Ford, Russ(ell William)
Forsch, Bob (Robert Herbert)
Forsch, Ken(neth Roth)
Foster, George Arthur
Fox, "Nellie" Jacob Nelson
Foxx, Jimmy (James Emory)
Freehan, Bill (William Ashley)
Frey, Jim (James Gottfried)
Friend, Bob (Robert Bartmess)
Frisch, Frankie (Frank Francis)
Furillo, Carl Anthony
Gaedel, Eddie (Edward Carl)
Galvin, "Pud" James Francis
Garagiola, Joe (Joseph Henry)
Garcia, Damaso Domingo
Garcia, Mike (Edward Miguel)
Garrett, Michael Lockett
Garvey, Steve Patrick
Gehrig, Lou (Henry Louis)
Gehringer, Charlie (Charles Leonard)
Gibson, Bob (Robert)
Gibson, Josh(ua)
Gibson, Kirk Harold
Gilliam, Jim (James William)
Giusti, Dave (David John, Jr.)
Glasscock, Jack (John Wesley)
Goldsmith, Fred Ernest
Gomez, "Lefty" Vernon Louis
Gooden, Dwight Eugene
Gordon, Joe (Joseph Lowell)
Gordon, Sid(ney)
Goslin, "Goose" Leon Allen

Gossage, "Goose" Richard Michael
Gowdy, Hank (Henry Morgan)
Gray, Peter J
Greenberg, Hank (Henry Benjamin)
Griffith, Clark Calvin
Grimes, Burleigh Arland
Grimm, Charlie (Charles John)
Groat, Dick (Richard Morrow)
Groom, Bob (Robert)
Grove, "Lefty" Robert Moses
Guerrero, Pedro
Guidry, Ron(ald Ames)
Guillen, Ozzie (Oswaldo Jose)
Gwynn, Tony (Anthony Keith)
Hafey, "Chick" Charles James
Haines, Jesse Joseph
Hamilton, Billy (William Robert)
Harrelson, Ken(neth Smith)
Harris, "Bucky" Stanley Raymond
Hartnett, "Gabby" Charles Leo
Hatcher, Mickey (Michael Vaughn, Jr.)
Hebner, Richie (Richard Joseph)
Hegan, Jim (James Edward)
Heilmann, Harry Edwin
Henderson, Rickey Henley
Henrich, Tommy (Thomas David)
Herman, "Babe" Floyd Caves
Herman, Billy (William Jennings)
Hernandez, Keith
Hernandez, Willie (Guillermo Villaneuva)
Higbe, Kirby (Walter Kirby)
Higuera, Teddy (Teodoro Valenzuela)
Hiller, John Frederick
Hodges, Gil(bert Raymond)
Holloman, "Bobo" Alva Lee
Holmes, Tommy (Thomas Francis)
Hooper, Harry Bartholomew
Horner, Bob (James Robert)
Hornsby, Rogers
Horton, Willie (William Wattison)
Houk, Ralph George
Howard, Elston Gene
Howard, Frank Oliver
Howser, Dick (Richard Dalton)
Hoyt, Lamarr (Dewey Lamarr)
Hoyt, Waite Charles
Hubbell, Carl Owen
Huggins, Miller James
Hunter, "Catfish" James Augustus
Hutchinson, Fred(erick Charles)
Irvin, Monte (Monford Merrill)
Jackson, "Bo" Vincent Edward
Jackson, Joe (Joseph Jefferson)
Jackson, Reggie (Reginald Martinez)
Jackson, Travis Calvin
Jay, Joseph Richard (Joey)
Jenkins, Ferguson Arthur
Jennings, Hugh(ey Ambrose)
Jensen, Jackie (Jack Eugene)
John, Tommy (Thomas Edward, Jr.)
Johnson, "Judy" William Julius

Johnson, Alex(ander)
Johnson, Dave (David Allen)
Johnson, Walter Perry
Johnstone, Jay (John William, Jr.)
Jones, "Toothpick" Samuel
Jones, Randy (Randall Leo)
Jones, Sam(uel Pond)
Joss, "Addie" Adrian
Joyner, Wally (Wallace Keith)
Kaline, Al(bert William)
Kauff, Benny (Benjamin Michael)
Keefe, Tim(othy John)
Keeler, "Wee Willie" William Henry
Kell, George Clyde
Kelley, Joe (Joseph James)
Kelly, "King" Michael Joseph
Kelly, George Lange
Kemp, Steve(n F)
Killebrew, Harmon Clayton
Kiner, Ralph McPherran
Kingman, Dave (David Arthur)
Kittle, Ron(ald Dale)
Klein, Chuck (Charles Herbert)
Kling, John Gradwohl
Kluszewski, Ted (Theodore Bernard)
Koufax, Sandy (Sanford)
Kubek, Tony (Anthony Christopher)
Lajoie, Nap(oleon)
Landreaux, Ken(neth Francis)
Lanier, Hal (Harold Clifton)
Larsen, Don(ald James)
Lary, Frank Strong
Lasorda, Tom (Thomas Charles)
Lau, Charlie (Charles Richard)
Law, Vernon Sanders
Lazzeri, Tony (Anthony Michael)
Le Flore, Ron(ald)
Leach, Rick (Richard Max)
Lemon, Bob (Robert Granville)
Leonard, "Buck" Walter Fenner
Leonard, "Dutch" Emil John
Leonard, "Dutch" Hubert Benjamin
Lindstrom, Fred(erick Charles)
Lloyd, John Henry
Lolich, Mickey (Michael Stephen)
Lombardi, Ernie (Ernesto Natali)
Lonborg, Jim (James Reynold)
Lopat, Ed(mund Walter)
Lopes, Davey (David Earl)
Lopez, Al(fonso Ramon)
Lowrey, "Peanuts" Harry Lee
Luque, Dolf (Adolfo)
Luzinski, Greg(ory Michael)
Lyle, "Sparky" Albert Walter
Lynn, Fred(ric Michael)
Lyons, Ted (Theodore Amar)
Maddox, Elliott
Maddox, Garry Lee
Madlock, Bill (William Jr.)
Maglie, Sal(vatore Anthony)
Mantle, Mickey Charles

Manush, "Heinie" Henry Emmett
Maranville, "Rabbit" Walter James
  Vincent
Marichal, Juan Antonio Sanchez
Marion, "Slats" Martin Whiteford
Maris, Roger Eugene
Marquard, "Rube" Richard William
Martin, "Billy" Alfred Manuel
Martin, "Pepper" John Leonard Roosevelt
Martin, Jerry Lindsey
Mathews, Eddie (Edwin Lee, Jr.)
Mathewson, Christy (Christopher)
Matlack, Jon(athan Trumpbour)
Mattingly, Don(ald Arthur)
Mauch, Gene William
Mays, Willie Howard, Jr.
Mazeroski, Bill (William Stanley)
Mazzilli, Lee Louis
McAuliffe, Dick (Richard John)
McCarthy, Tommy (Thomas Francis
  Michael)
McCovey, Willie Lee
McDougald, Gil(bert James)
McDowell, Sam(uel Edward)
McGee, Willie Dean
McGinnity, Joe (Joseph Jerome)
McGraw, "Tug" Frank Edwin
McGraw, John Joseph
McHale, John Joseph
McKechnie, Bill (William Boyd)
McLain, Denny (Dennis Dale)
McNally, Dave (David Arthur)
Medwick, Joe (Joseph Michael)
Messersmith, Andy (John Alexander)
Mize, Johnny (John Robert)
Morgan, Joe (Joseph Leonard)
Morris, Jack (John Scott)
Mueller, "Heinie" Clarence Franklin
Munson, Thurman Lee
Murcer, Bobby Ray
Murphy, Dale Bryan
Murphy, John Joseph
Murray, Eddie Clarence
Musial, Stan(ley Frank)
Myer, "Buddy" Charles Solomon
Nettles, Graig
Newcombe, Don(ald)
Newhouser, Harold (Hal)
Newsom, "Bobo" Louis Norman
Nichols, "Kid" Charles Augustus
Niekro, Phil(ip Henry)
O'Neill, Steve (Stephen Francis)
O'Rourke, Jim (James Henry)
Oester, Ron(ald John)
Oh, Sadaharu
Oliva, Tony (Antonio Pedro, Jr.)
Ott, Mel(vin Thomas)
Owen, "Mickey" Arnold Malcolm
Paciorek, Tom (Thomas Marian)
Page, Joe (Joseph Francis)
Paige, "Satchel" Leroy Robert

Palmer, Jim (James Alvin)
Parrish, Lance Michael
Pennock, Herb(ert Jefferis)
Pepitone, Joe (Joseph Anthony)
Perez, Tony (Atanasio Rigal)
Perranoski, Ron(ald Peter)
Perry, Gaylord Jackson
Petrocelli, Rico (Americo Peter)
Piniella, Lou(is Victor)
Plank, Eddie (Edward Stewart)
Podres, Johnny (John Joseph)
Porter, Darrell Ray
Post, Wally (Walter Charles)
Quisenberry, Dan(iel Raymond)
Radbourn, "Old Hoss" Charles Gardner
Rader, Doug(las L)
Raines, Tim(othy)
Randolph, Willie (William Larry, Jr.)
Reese, "Pee Wee" Harold Henry
Reiser, Pete (Harold Patrick)
Reulbach, Ed(ward Marvin)
Rhodes, "Dusty" James Lamar
Rice, "Sam" Edgar Charles
Rice, Jim (James Edgar)
Richard, J(ames) R(odney)
Richards, Paul Rapier
Richardson, Bobby (Robert Clinton)
Rickey, Branch (Wesley Branch)
Righetti, Dave (David Allan)
Ripkin, Cal(vin Edwin, Jr.)
Rixey, Eppa
Rizzuto, Phil(lip Francis)
Roberts, Robin Evan
Robinson, Brooks Calbert, Jr.
Robinson, Frank
Robinson, Jackie (John Roosevelt)
Robinson, Wilbert
Rolfe, "Red" Robert Abial
Rose, Pete(r Edward)
Roseboro, John H
Rosen, Al(bert Leonard)
Roush, Edd J (Eddie)
Rowe, "Schoolboy" Lynwood Thomas
Rozema, Dave (David Scott)
Ruffing, "Red" Charles Herbert
Rusie, Amos William
Ruth, "Babe" George Herman
Ryan, Nolan (Lynn Nolan)
Saberhagen, Bret William
Sain, Johnny (John Franklin)
Sandberg, Ryne Dee
Sanguillen, Manny (Manuel DeJesus)
Saucier, Kevin Andrew
Sawatski, Carl Ernest
Schacht, Al(exander)
Schaefer, "Germany" Herman A
Schalk, Ray(mond William)
Schmidt, Mike (Michael Jack)
Schoendienst, "Red" Albert Fred
Score, Herb(ert Jude)
Scott, Mike (Michael Warren)

Seaver, Tom (George Thomas)
Sewell, Joe (Joseph Wheeler)
Sherry, Larry (Lawrence)
Simmons, Al(oysius Harry)
Singleton, Ken(neth Wayne)
Sisler, George Harold
Slaughter, Enos Bradsher
Smalley, Roy Frederick, III
Smith, Ozzie (Osborne Earl)
Snider, "Duke" Edwin Donald
Soto, Mario Melvin
Spahn, Warren Edward
Spalding, Albert Goodwill
Speaker, Tris(tram E)
Stargell, Willie (Wilver Dornel)
Staub, "Rusty" Daniel Joseph
Stengel, "Casey" Charles Dillon
Stieb, Dave (David Andrew)
Stone, George
Stratton, Monty Franklin Pierce
Strawberry, Darryl Eugene
Sunday, Billy (William Ashley)
Sundburg, Jim (James Howard)
Sutcliffe, Rick (Richard Lee)
Sutter, (Howard) Bruce
Sutton, Don(ald Howard)
Tanana, Frank Daryl
Tebbetts, "Birdie" George Robert
Tekulve, Kent(on Charles)
Templeton, Garry Lewis
Terry, Bill (William Harold)
Thompson, Sam(uel Luther)
Thomson, Bobby (Robert Brown)
Thorpe, Jim (James Francis)
Tiant, Luis Clemente
Tinker, Joe (Joseph Bert)
Torre, Joe (Joseph Paul)
Trammell, Alan Stuart
Traynor, "Pie" Harold Joseph
Trout, "Dizzy" Paul Howard
Tudor, John Thomas
Uecker, Bob (Robert George)
Valenzuela, Fernando
Vance, Clarence Arthur
Vander Meer, Johnny (John Samuel)
Vaughn, Joseph Floyd
Waddell, "Rube" George Edward
Wagner, "Honus" John Peter
Wakefield, Dick (Richard Cummings)
Walker, Frederick E
Wallace, Bobby (Roderick John)
Walsh, Ed(ward Augustin)
Walters, "Bucky" William Henry
Wambsganss, Bill (William Adolph)
Waner, Lloyd James
Waner, Paul Glee
Ward, John Montgomery
Warneke, Lon(nie)
Weaver, Earl Sidney
Welch, Bob (Robert Lynn)
Welch, Mickey (Michael Francis)

Wheat, Zack (Zachariah Davis)
Whitaker, Lou(is Rodman)
White, Frank, Jr.
White, James Laurie
Wilhelm, Hoyt (James Hoyt)
Williams, Billy Leo
Williams, Dick (Richard Hirschfield)
Williams, Ted (Theodore Samuel)
Wills, Maury (Maurice Morning)
Wilson, "Hack" Lewis Robert
Wilson, Willie James
Winfield, Dave (David Mark)
Witt, Mike (Michael Arthur)
Wood, Joseph
Wood, Wilbur Forrester
Wright, George
Wynn, Early
Yastrzemski, Carl Michael
Yeager, Steve (Stephen Wayne)
York, Rudy (Rudolph Preston)
Young, "Cy" Denton True
Youngs, Ross Middlebrook
Yount, Robin R
Zernial, Gus Edward
Zimmer, Don(ald William)

BASEBALL UMPIRE

Ashford, Emmett Littleton
Chylak, Nester
Conlan, "Jocko" John Bertrand
Connolly, Thomas Henry
DiMuro, Lou
Evans, Billy (William George)
Hubbard, Cal (Robert Calvin)
Klem, Bill (William Joseph)
Luciano, Ron(ald Michael)
Passarella, Art
Warneke, Lon(nie)

BASKETBALL COACH

Allen, Forest Clare
Auerbach, "Red" Arnold Jacob
Bee, Clair Francis
Blood, Ernest B
Brown, Hubie (Hubert Jude)
Brown, Larry
Cann, Howard Goodsell
Carlson, "Doc" Harold Clifford
Carnevale, Ben (Bernard L)
Costello, Larry
Crum, Denny Edwin
Dehnert, Henry
Douglas, Robert L
Fisher, Harry
Fitch, Bill (William C)
Fitzsimmons, "Cotton" Lowell
Gill, Amory Tingle
Gottlieb, Eddie (Edward)
Hagan, Cliff(ord Oldham)
Hall, Joe Beasman

Hannum, Alex(ander Murray)
Hinkle, Paul
Holman, Nat
Holzman, William
Iba, Henry P
Jones, KC
Julian, "Doggie" Alvin T
Keaney, Frank
Keogan, George
Knight, Bobby (Robert Montgomery)
Lambert, Ward L
Lapchick, Joseph Bohomiel
Layden, Frank (Francis Patrick)
Liston, Emil
Loeffler, Kenneth D
Loughery, Kevin Michael
Macauley, Ed
McCracken, Branch
McGuire, Al
Meyer, Ray(mond Joseph)
Motta, John Richard
Nelson, Don(ald Arvid)
Newell, Pete
Olsen, Harold G
Phelps, "Digger" Richard
Reed, Willis
Ripley, Elmer Horton
Rupp, Adolph F
Russell, "Honey" John
Russell, Bill (William Felton)
Saperstein, Abraham
Schayes, Dolph
Sharman, Bill (William Walton)
Silas, Paul
Smith, Dean Edwards
Valvano, Jim
West, Jerry
Westhead, Paul
Wilkens, Lenny (Leonard Randolph)
Wooden, John Robert

BASKETBALL EXECUTIVE

Brown, Walter Augustine
Buss, Jerry Hatten
DeBusschere, Dave (David Albert)
Douglas, Robert L
Embry, Wayne
Gottlieb, Eddie (Edward)
Irish, Edward Simmons (Ned)
Jones, R William
Kennedy, Walter
O'Brien, John J
O'Brien, Larry (Lawrence Francis)
Podoloff, Maurice

BASKETBALL PLAYER

Abdul-Jabbar, Kareem
Adams, Alvan Leigh
Aguirre, Mark
Ainge, Dan(iel Rae)

Allen, Lucius Oliver, Jr.
Archibald, Nate (Nathaniel)
Arizin, Paul
Awtrey, Dennis
Barker, Cliff
Barkley, Charles Wade
Barnes, Marvin
Barry, Rick (Richard Francis, III)
Baylor, Elgin
Beard, Ralph
Beckman, Johnny
Bellamy, Walt
Bias, Len
Bibby, Henry
Bing, Dave (David)
Bird, Larry Joe
Birdsong, Otis Lee
Blab, Uwe Konstantine
Bol, Manute
Boone, Ron
Borgmann, "Benny" Bernhard
Bradley, Bill (William Warren)
Brewer, Jim
Brown, "Rooky" William
Brown, Roger
Buse, Don
Cann, Howard Goodsell
Carr, Austin George
Carroll, Joe Barry
Cartwright, Bill (James William)
Chamberlain, Wilt(ton Norman)
Chenier, Phil(ip)
Chones, Jim
Collins, Doug
Cooper, Chuck (Charles H)
Cousy, Bob (Robert Joseph)
Cowens, Dave (David William)
Criss, Charlie (Charles W)
Cummings, Terry (Robert Terrell)
Cunningham, Billy (William)
Dandridge, Bob (Robert L)
Dantley, Adrian Delano
Davies, Bob (Robert Edris)
Dawkins, Darryl
DeBernardi, Forrest S
DeBusschere, Dave (David Albert)
Dehnert, Henry
DiGregorio, Ernie
Drew, John E
Embry, Wayne
Erving, Julius Winfield
Ewing, Patrick Aloysius
Fisher, Harry
Ford, Phil Jackson
Frazier, Walt
Free, World B
Friedman, Max
Fulks, Joe (Joseph E)
Gervin, George
Gianelli, John
Gilmore, Artis

Gola, Thomas Joseph
Goodrich, Gail Charles
Green, Rickey
Greer, Hal (Harold Everett)
Griffith, Darrell Steven
Groza, Alex
Hagan, Cliff(ord Oldham)
Havlicek, John
Hayes, Elvin Ernest
Haywood, Spencer
Heinsohn, Tommy
Holman, Nat
Hudson, Lou
Issel, Dan
Johnson, Dennis W
Johnson, Earvin
Johnson, Eddie
Johnson, Evelyn
Johnson, Marques Kevin
Jordon, Michael Jeffery
Kelser, Greg(ory)
Knight, Billy (William R)
Kupchak, Mitch(ell)
Kurland, Bob
Lambert, Ward L
Lanier, Bob (Robert Jerry, Jr.)
Lapchick, Joseph Bohomiel
Lee, Keith Deywane
Lemon, "Meadowlark" Meadow George,
  III
Lieberman, Nancy
Lloyd, Lewis Kevin
Lucas, Jerry
Lucas, Maurice
Luisetti, Angelo Enrico
Macauley, Ed
Macy, Kyle Robert
Malone, Moses Eugene
Maravich, Pete
McAdoo, Bob (Robert)
McBride, Floyd Mickey
McCracken, Branch
McGinnis, George
Moe, Doug(las Edwin)
Moncrief, Sidney
Monroe, Earl
Mullin, Chris(topher Paul)
Murphy, Calvin
Murphy, Charles
Nance, Larry Donnell
O'Brien, John J
Olajuwon, Akeem Abdul Ajibola
Pettit, Bob
Reed, Willis
Richardson, Micheal Ray
Ripley, Elmer Horton
Robertson, Oscar
Rollins, Kenny
Roundfield, Dan(ny T)
Rupp, Adolph F
Russell, "Honey" John

Russell, Bill (William Felton)
Sampson, Ralph
Scales, DeWayne Jay
Schayes, Dolph
Sedran, Barney
Sharman, Bill (William Walton)
Sikma, Jack Wayne
Silas, Paul
Thomas, Isiah
Thompson, David O'Neil
Thompson, Mychal
Thurmond, Nate
Tisdale, Wayman Lawrence
Tomjanovich, Rudy (Rudolph)
Toney, Andrew
Tripucka, Kelly (Patrick Kelly)
Unseld, Wes(ley)
Van Arsdale, Dick (Richard Albert)
Van Arsdale, Tom (Thomas)
Vandeweghe, "Kiki" Ernest Maurice
Walton, Bill
Wedman, Scott Dean
West, Jerry
Westphal, Paul Douglas
White, "Jo Jo" Joseph
Wilkens, Lenny (Leonard Randolph)
Wilkes, Jamaal
Wilkins, Dominique
Williams, Gus
Woodard, Lynette
Wooden, John Robert

BASKETBALL REFEREE

Hepbron, George

BASKETBALL TEAM

Harlem Globetrotters

BEAUTY CONTEST WINNER

Charles, Suzette
Williams, Vanessa

BEVERAGE MANUFACTURER

Goizueta, Roberto Crispulo
Morgan, Al(fred Y)

BIBLICAL CHARACTER

Aaron
Abel
Abraham
Adam
Amos
Andrew, Saint
Barabbas
Bartholomew, Saint
Bathsheba
Cain

Daniel
Deborah
Delilah
Elijah
Esau
Esther
Eve
Goliath
Hannah
Herod the Great
Isaac
Jacob (Israel)
James the Greater, Saint
James the Less, Saint
Job
John the Baptist
Jonah
Joseph
Joseph of Arimathea
Joseph, Saint
Joshua
Judah
Judas Iscariot
Jude, Saint
Judith
Lazarus
Leah
Lot
Luke, Saint
Mark, Saint
Mary Magdalene
Matthew, Saint
Methuseleh
Michael, the Archangel
Miriam
Moses
Nehemiah
Nicodemus
Noah
Paul, Saint
Peter, Saint
Philip, Saint
Rachel
Rebecca
Ruth
Salome
Samson
Samuel
Sarah
Shadrach
Simeon
Simon, Saint
Thomas, Saint

BIBLIOGRAPHER

Bartlett, John Russell
Evans, Charles
Greg, Walter Wilson, Sir
McMurtrie, Douglas C
Wise, Thomas J

BILLIARDS PLAYER

Balukas, Jean
Davis, Joe
Hoppe, Willie (William F)
Masconi, Willie
Minnesota Fats
Mosconi, Willie (William Joseph)
Pelkey, Edward

BIOCHEMIST

Asimov, Isaac
Berg, Paul
Boyer, Herbert Wayne
Chain, Ernest Boris, Sir
Coleman, Lester L
Cori, Carl Ferdinand
Cori, Gerty Theresa
Dam, (Carl Peter) Henrik
Doisy, Edward Adelbert
Emerson, Gladys Anderson
Funk, Casimir
Henderson, Lawrence Joseph
Hopkins, Fredrick, Sir
Kamen, Martin David
Kendall, Edward C(alvin)
Krebs, Hans Adolf, Sir
Lipmann, Fritz Albert
Merrifield, R(obert) Bruce
Monod, Jacques
Moore, Stanford
Schally, Andrew Victor
Shear, Murray Jacob
Szent-Gyorgyi, Albert von
Tatum, Edward Lawrie
Theorell, (Axel) Hugh Teodor
Von Euler, Ulf
Watson, James Dewey

BIOGRAPHER

Beer, Thomas
Boswell, James
Cecil, Edward Christian David Gascoyne
Coffin, Robert Peter Tristram
Day, Clarence Shepard, Jr.
Drinkwater, John
Hendrick, Burton Jesse
Hubbard, Elbert Green
Newman, Ernest
Nicolay, John George
Partridge, Bellamy
Plutarch
Rowse, Alfred Leslie
Steegmuller, Francis
Strachey, (Giles) Lytton
Suetonius
Van Doren, Carl Clinton
Walton, Izaak

BIOLOGIST

Abercrombie, Michael
Bateson, William
Bronk, Detlev Wulf
Brown, Frank Arthur, Jr.
Carrel, Alexis
Carson, Rachel Louise
Comfort, Alexander
Commoner, Barry
Cottam, Clarence
Crick, Francis Harry Compton
Ehrlich, Paul
Ehrlich, Paul Ralph
Geddes, Patrick, Sir
Glass, Hiram Bentley
Huxley, Julian Sorell, Sir
Huxley, Thomas Henry
Just, Ernest Everett
Kendrick, Pearl Luella
Manner, Harold
Mayr, Ernst Walter
Medvedev, Zhores Aleksandrovich
Metchnikoff, Elie
Sabin, Albert Bruce
Sagan, Carl Edward
Sanger, Frederick
Sperry, Roger Woolcott
Van Niel, Cornelius B(ernardus)
Vishniac, Roman

BOAT RACER

Campbell, Donald Malcolm
Campbell, Malcolm, Sir
Chenoweth, Dean
Crawford, Jim
Hanauer, "Chip" Lee Edward
Muncey, Bill (William)
Wood, Gar(field A)

BODYBUILDER

Atlas, Charles
LaLanne, Jack
Schwarzenegger, Arnold

BOOKSELLER

Dodsley, Robert
Foyle, Christina
Foyle, Gilbert Samuel
Foyle, William Alfred
Rosenbach, Abraham Simon Wolf

BOTANIST

Arthur, Joseph Charles
Bartram, John
Bartram, William
Brown, Robert
Camerarius, Rudolf Jakob

Carver, George Washington
Chase, Mary Agnes
Cohn, Ferdinand Julius
Colden, Cadwallader
Cowles, Henry Chandler
DeVries, Hugo
Dioscorides, Pedacius
Douglas, David
Fairchild, David Grandison
Gray, Asa
Harrar, J(acob) George
Hoffer, George Nissley
Jussieu, Bernard de
Linnaeus, Carolus
Mendel, Gregor Johann

BOWLER

Anthony, Earl
Burton, Nelson, Jr.
Carter, Don(ald Jones)
Day, Ned (Edward Gately)
Garms, Shirley Rudolph
Hardwick, Billy
Ladewig, Marion
Roth, Mark Stephan
Varipapa, Andy
Weber, Dick

BOXER

Akins, Virgil
Ali, Muhammad
Ambers, Lou
Angott, Sammy (Samuel Engotti)
Apostoli, Fred B
Arguello, Alexis
Armstrong, Henry
Baer, Max
Berlenbach, Paul
Blackburn, "Jack" Charles Henry
Bonavena, Oscar
Braddock, James J
Burns, Tommy
Canzoneri, Tony
Carnera, Primo
Carpentier, Georges
Carruthers, John(ny)
Carter, "Hurricane" Rubin
Carter, Jimmy (James W)
Chaplin, George
Charles, Ezzard
Chuvalo, George
Classen, Willie
Cooney, Gerry (Gerald Arthur)
Corbett, James John
Corbett, Young, III
Curry, Donald
Danza, Tony
Davis, Perscell
Delaney, Jack
Dempsey, Jack (William Harrison)

Dokes, Michael
Dundee, Johnny
Duran, Roberto
Escobar, Sixto
Firpo, Luis Angel
Fitzsimmons, Bob (Robert Prometheus)
Foreman, George
Frazier, Joe
Galento, Tony (Anthony)
Gans, Joe
Gardner, George
Gavilan, Kid
Genaro, Frankie
Giardello, Joey
Gibbons, Tom
Graziano, Rocky
Greb, Harry (Edward Henry)
Griffith, Emile Alphonse
Hagler, Marvelous Marvin
Hearns, Thomas (Tommy)
Holmes, Larry
Hunter, Bobby Lee
Jackson, "Hurricane" Thomas
Jeffries, James Jackson
Jofre, Eder
Johansson, Ingemar
Johnson, Harold
Johnson, Jack (John Arthur)
Jones, "Gorilla" William
Jones, "Too Tall" Edward Lee
Jordan, Don
Kenty, Hilmer
Ketchel, Stanley
Kim, Duk Koo
Knoetze, Kallie (Nikolaas)
La Bara, Fidel
La Motta, Jake (Jacob)
Laguna, Ismael
Langford, Sam
Latzo, Pete
Lavigne, "Kid" George
Lee, Canada
Leonard, "Sugar" Ray
Leonard, Benny
Lesnevich, Gus
Levinsky, Battling
Lewis, Ted
Liston, "Sonny" Charles
Loughran, Tommy
Louis, Joe
Lynch, Benny
Lynch, Joe
Mancini, Ray
Marciano, Rocky
Mathis, Buster
McCoy, Charles
McCrory, Milton
McGovern, Terry (John Terrence)
McLarnin, Jimmy
Moore, Archie
Nelson, Battling

Norton, Ken(neth Howard)
O'Grady, Sean
Page, Greg
Patterson, Floyd
Pep, Willie
Podgwiski, Jeff
Quarry, Jerry
Robinson, "Sugar" Ray
Root, Jack
Rosenbloom, Maxie
Ross, Barney
Ryan, Tommy
Sanchez, Salvador
Schmeling, Max(imilian)
Shannon, Willie
Sharkey, Jack (Joseph Paul)
Shavers, Ernie
Spinks, Leon
Spinks, Michael
Stevenson, Teofilo
Stribling, Young (William Lawrence)
Sullivan, John L(awrence)
Thomas, Pinklon
Tillis, James
Tunney, "Gene" James Joseph
Urtain, Jose Manuel Ibar
Walcott, Jersey Joe
Walker, Mickey
Weaver, Mike (Michael Dwayne)
Willard, Jess
Young, Jimmy
Zale, Tony

BOXING PROMOTER

Jacobs, Michael S
Kearns, Jack
King, Don(ald)
Smith, Harold

BOXING TRAINER

Blackburn, "Jack" Charles Henry
Brown, Drew
Dundee, Angelo Mirena, Jr.
Steward, Emanuel

BREWER

Busch, August Anheuser, Jr.
Coors, Adolph
Coors, Joseph
Labatt, John K
Miller, Frederic
Molson, John
Pabst, Frederick
Schaefer, Frederick M E
Schaefer, Rudolph Jay
Sellinger, Frank (Francis John)

Stroh, Bernard
Stroh, Peter W
Vassar, Matthew

BREWERY EXECUTIVE

Coors, William K (Bill)

BRIDGE PLAYER

Corn, Ira George, Jr.
Culbertson, Ely
Fishbein, Harry J
Gerber, John
Goren, Charles Henry
Jacoby, Oswald
Lightner, Theodore
Sheinwold, Alfred

BROADCAST JOURNALIST

Abel, Elie
Adamle, Mike (Michael David)
Agronsky, Martin Zama
Anderson, Bonnie Marie
Bazell, Robert
Bell, Steve (Stephen Scott)
Benton, Nelson (Joseph Nelson, Jr.)
Berger, Marilyn
Bergman, Jules Verne
Berkowitz, Bob
Beutel, Bill (William Charles)
Blair, Frank
Bourgholtzer, Frank
Bowser, Betty Ann
Bradley, Ed
Briggs, Fred
Brinkley, David McClure
Brokaw, Tom (Thomas John)
Broun, Heywood Hale
Carter, Hodding (William Hodding, III)
Chancellor, John William
Chase, Sylvia
Chung, Connie (Constance Yu-Hwa)
Collingwood, Charles Cummings
Compton, Ann
Cordtz, Dan
Craft, Christine
Cronkite, Walter Leland, Jr.
Dancy, John
Day, Robin
Dean, Morton
DeManio, Jack
DeVarona, Donna
Dickerson, Nancy Hanschman
Dietz, David
Dobyns, Lloyd Allen, Jr.
Donaldson, Sam(uel Andrew)
Dotson, Bob
Downs, William Randall, Jr.
Economaki, Chris(topher Constantine)
Ellerbee, Linda

Farmer, Don
Frederick, Pauline
Frum, Barbara
Grauer, Ben(jamin Franklin)
Gumbel, Bryant Charles
Hart, John
Hartz, James Leroy
Harvey, Paul
Herman, George
Huntley, Chet (Chester Robert)
Jaffe, Sam(uel Anderson)
Jamieson, Bob (Robert John)
Jarriel, Tom (Thomas Edwin)
Jensen, Mike (Michael C)
Jones, Phil(ip Howard)
Kalb, Marvin Leonard
Kalber, Floyd
Kaltenborn, H(ans) V(on)
Kiker, Douglas
Koppel, Ted (Edward James)
Kuralt, Charles Bishop
Kurtis, Bill Horton (William)
Lehrer, Jim (James Charles)
Levine, Irving R
Lewis, Fulton, Jr.
LLoyd, Robin
Lunden, Joan
Mackin, Catherine Patricia
MacNeil, Robert Breckenridge Ware
Margolies, Marjorie Sue
Martin, John
McCormick, Robert K
McGee, Frank
McLaughlin, Marya
Monroe, Bill (William Blanc, Jr.)
Mudd, Roger Harrison
Murrow, Edward R(oscoe)
Newman, Edwin Harold
O'Neil, Roger
Osgood, Charles
Pappas, Ike
Pauley, (Margaret) Jane
Pierpoint, Robert Charles
Quint, Bert
Rather, Dan
Reasoner, Harry
Reynolds, Frank
Robinson, Max C
Rollin, Betty
Rowan, Ford
Rudd, Hughes Day
Rukeyser, Louis Richard
Safer, Morley
Sanders, Marlene
Savitch, Jessica Beth
Sawyer, Diane K
Scherer, Ray(mond Lewis)
Schieffer, Bob
Schorr, Daniel
Sevareid, (Arnold) Eric
Shriver, Maria Owings

Smith, Howard K(ingsbury)
Snyder, Tom
Stahl, Lesley Rene
Stern, Carl (Leonard)
Strawser, Neil Edward
Streithorst, Tom
Sullivan, Kathleen
Swing, Raymond Gram
Threlkeld, Richard D
Trotta, Liz (Elizabeth)
Trout, Robert
Ubell, Earl
Valeriani, Richard Gerard
Vandercook, John Womack
Vanocur, Sander
Wallace, Chris
Wallace, Mike (Myron Leon)
Walters, Barbara
Woodruff, Judy Carline

BROADCASTER

Bowes, "Major" Edward
Conrad, Frank
Cooke, (Alfred) Alistair
Gardella, Kay
Garland, Ailsa
Gemmell, Alan
Gerussi, Bruno
Harwell, Ernie
Hewitt, Foster (William Foster)
Hibberd, Andrew Stuart
Howe, Quincy
Ironside, Henry Allan
Liebman, Joshua Loth
Mark, Norman (Barry)
McNamee, Graham
Robertson, Pat (Marion)
Simpson, Jim

BROADCASTING EXECUTIVE

Dimmock, Peter
Duffy, James E
Goodman, Julian B
Grossman, Lawrence K
Koplovitz, Kay Smith
Leonard, Bill (William Augustus, II)
McManus, Sean
Newhouse, Donald E
Salant, Richard S
Seiler, James, W
Trethowan, Ian
Tucker, Lem(uel)

BULLFIGHTER

Cordobes, El
Dominguin, Luis Miguel
Manolete

BUSINESS EXECUTIVE

Allen, Ivan, Jr.
Amdahl, Gene M(yron)
Amos, Wally
Andrus, Cecil D(ale)
Ashley, Laura Mountney
Atkins, Chet (Chester B)
Aubrey, James Thomas, Jr.
Austin, John Paul
Ayer, Harriet Hubbard
Ball, Edward
Bamberger, Julian Maas
Barnard, Chester Irving
Barnett, Claude A
Barnett, Marvin Robert
Bartlett, Francis Alonzo
Bechtel, Stephen Davison
Bell, James Ford
Benn, Anthony
Bernstein, Sid(ney Ralph)
Bickmore, Lee Smith
Billingsley, Sherman
Birch, Stephen
Bissell, Anna
Black, Conrad
Black, William
Boehm, Helen Francesca Stefanie Franzolir
Bogart, Neil
Bugas, John Stephen
Buitoni, Giovanni
Burke, James Edward
Callaway, Howard Hollis
Candler, Charles Howard
Carmichael, James Vinson
Casablancas, John(ny)
Casey, James E
Chalk, Oscar Roy
Chandler, Colby H
Chapman, Gilbert Whipple
Cisler, Walker Lee
Coffin, Charles Albert
Cole, Kenneth Reese
Cooke, Jack Kent
Cooper, Wilhelmina Behmenburg
Cornell, Ezra
Cosgrove, Gordon Dean
Cowles, John, Sr.
Craig, Cleo F
Crosby, James Morris
Cunningham, Harry Blair
Cunningham, Mary Elizabeth
Cushman, Austin Thomas
Custin, Mildred
Daly, Marcus
Danforth, William H

Dart, Justin Whitlock
Davis, "Tobe" Coller
Davison, Ian Frederic Hay
DeButts, John Dulany
Deterding, Henri Wilhelm August, Sir
DeVos, Richard Martin
Diebold, Alfred John
Dole, Charles Minot
Doriot, Georges Frederic
DuPont, Pierre Samuel, III
Edmiston, Mark Morton
Engstrom, Elmer William
Erteszek, Jan
Farah, Robert Norman
Ferragamo, Salvatore
Fey, Thomas Hossler
Fields, Debbi (Debra Jane Sivyer)
Flagler, Henry Morrison
Ford, Eileen
Foster, Joseph C
Gage, Harlow W
Gelb, Lawrence
Genet, Arthur Samuel
Gerber, Daniel Frank
Gilbert, A(lfred) C(arleton)
Goldman, Eric W
Gorman, Leon Arthur
Grant, Cary
Gucci, Maurizio
Haas, Walter A(braham), Jr.
Haas, Walter A(braham), Sr.
Haider, Michael Lawrence
Hall, Donald Joyce
Hall, Joyce Clyde
Hartley, Fred Lloyd
Hefner, Christie (Christine Ann)
Herrick, Elinore M
Hertz, John Daniel
Hicks, Beatrice Alice
Hillenkoetter, Roscoe H(enry)
Hirschmann, Ira Arthur
Hofheinz, Roy Mark
Houghton, Amory
Hoving, Walter
Hoyt, Lawrence W
Hulman, Tony (Anton), Jr.
Hunt, Nelson Bunker
Inatome, Rick
Iwama, Kazuo
Iwasaki, Yataro
Jacobs, Walter L
Jones, Candy
Jonsson, John Erik
Kapor, Mitchell
Keker, Samuel J
Keough, Donald Raymond
Kiam, Victor Kermit, II
Kingsborough Donald
Knight, Phil(ip H)
Knowles, Warren Perley
Knox, Rose Markward

Kohler, William R
Kresge, Stanley Sebastian
Lay, Herman Warden
LeTourneau, Robert Gilmour
Lewis, (Myrtle) Tillie
Lewyt, Alexander Milton
Lichine, Alexis
Ling, James J
Little, Edward Herman
Little, Royal
Loew, Arthur M
Luce, Charles (Franklin)
Ludwig, Daniel Keith
MacGregor, Ian
Magee, Harry L
Marshall, Laurence
Martinson, Joseph Bertram
McColough, C(harles) Peter
McCone, John A
McCord, Andrew King
McElroy, Neil Hosler
McGowan, William George
McIlhenny, Walter S
McKeen, John Elmer
McNerney, Walter James
Mead, George Houk
Mellon, Paul
Meredith, Scott
Merrill, Charles Edward
Miller, Arjay Ray
Moore, George Stevens
Moore, Roy W
Murphy, Patrick Vincent
Neuharth, Allen Harold
Nicholas, Nicholas John, Jr.
Nidetch, Jean
Noyce, Robert Norton
Opel, John Roberts
Packard, David
Palmer, Potter
Paulucci, Jeno Francisco
Penske, Roger
Peters, Jon
Phelan, John Joseph
Pitman, James (Isaac James)
Platt, Harry (Henry Barstow)
Pocklington, Peter H
Politz, Alfred
Pomerantz, Fred P
Post, Marjorie Merriweather
Power, Donald Clinton
Powers, John Robert
Price, Gwilym Alexander
Queeny, Edgar Monsanto
Rand, James Henry
Regine
Rockefeller, Laurance Spelman
Rockefeller, Rodman C
Rootes, William Edward Rootes, Baron
Ross, Percy
Rudkin, Margaret Fogarty

BUSINESSMAN

Duke, James Buchanan
Dykstra, John
Eisele, Donn Fulton
Ertegun, Ahmet
Estridge, Philip D
Fargo, William George
Feld, Irvin
Fels, Samuel Simeon
Ferris, George Washington Gale
Fetzer, John Earl
Feulner, Edwin John, Jr.
Finley, Charlie (Charles Oscar)
Fitzgerald, John Francis
Folsom, Frank M
Freer, Charles Lang
French, Robert T
Funston, George Keith
Gaines, Clarence F
Gary, Elbert H
Gates, Thomas Sovereign, Jr.
Geneen, Harold Sydney
Getty, Gordon Peter
Goulding, Phil G
Grace, William Russell
Graebner, Clark
Granatelli, Anthony Joseph
Grosvenor, Gerald Cavendish
Gruenther, Alfred Maximillian
Hanna, Mark (Marcus Alonzo)
Harkness, Edward Stephen
Harmsworth, Harold Sidney
Harrah, Bill (William Fisk)
Harriman, Edward H
Hartford, George Huntington
Hartford, George Ludlum
Hartford, John Augustine
Hauberg, John Henry
Helmsley, Harry Brakmann
Hewlett, William
Hoffman, Robert C
Hoover, William K
Horchow, S(amuel) Roger
Howell, Albert S
Hudson, Joseph Lowthian
Hudson, Joseph Lowthian, Jr.
Hugel, Max
Hyatt, Joel
Ilitch, Mike
Inman, Bobby Ray
Jacuzzi, Candido
Johnson, Herbert Fisk
Jones, Arthur A
Kauffman, Ewing Marion
Kellogg, Will Keith
Kerby, William Frederick
Khashoggi, Adnan
Knott, Walter
Kroger, Bernard Henry
Lamont, Thomas William
Landon, Alf(red Mossman)
Lazar, Irving Paul

Lazarus, Charles P
Libby, Arthur
Libby, Charles
Litton, Charles
Loeb, William
Lowe, Edwin S
Mackay, John William
Martin, John C
Mather, Stephen Tyng
Mathers, Jerry
McCormach, Mark Hume
McDivitt, Jim (James Alton)
Mills, Darius Ogden
Molloy, John T
Monaghan, Tom
Monro, Harold Edward
Morita, Akio
Neiman, Abraham
Nielsen, Arthur C
Noyes, David
Obolensky, Serge
Olivetti, Adriano
Park, Tongsun
Parker, George Swinnerton
Pate, Maurice
Perot, (Henry) Ross
Peterson, Clarence
Post, Charles William
Raskob, John J
Rathbone, Monroe Jackson
Reagan, Michael
Robbins, Irvine
Roberts, Xavier
Rock, Arthur
Romney, George Wilcken
Roper, Elmo Burns, Jr.
Rosenbloom, Carroll D
Rubell, Steve
Russell, Donald Joseph
Saunders, Stuart T
Schine, G(erard) David
Schirra, Wally (Walter Marty, Jr.)
Schlessinger, David
Schram, Emil
Scott, Clarence
Scott, Edward Irvin
Seiberling, Frank Augustus
Selfridge, Harry Gordon
Shapero, Nate S
Sheaffer, Walter A
Sibley, Hiram
Siegel, Morris J
Soria, Dario
Spalding, Albert Goodwill
Spanel, Abram N
Stafford, Thomas P(atten)
Starch, Daniel
Stiffel, Theodopholous
Stokely, James
Stokely, John
Stone, Louis

Stone, W Clement
Stouffer, Vernon B
Stuckey, Williamson
Swanson, Carl A
Tanny, Vic
Thomas, Samuel Bath
Thornton, Charles Bates
Tunney, "Gene" James Joseph
Turner, Ted (Robert Edward, III)
Ueberroth, Peter Victor
Vail, Theodore Newton
Vanderbilt, Harold Stirling
Vanderbilt, William Kissam
Villard, Henry
Viscardi, Henry, Jr
Von Bulow, Claus
Walgreen, Charles Rudolph, Jr.
Walter, James Willis
Walters, Henry
Warburg, James Paul
Washkansky, Louis
Webb, Del(bert Eugene)
Welch, Thomas B
Wells, Henry
Werblin, "Sonny" David Abraham
Westheimer, Irvin Ferdinand
Whitney, C(ornelius) V(anderbilt)
Whitney, Harry Payne
Whitney, William Collins
Wiggins, Archibald Lee Manning
Wilder, Brooks
Wolfson, Erwin Service
Wrigley, Philip Knight

CABINETMAKER

Chippendale, Thomas
Hepplewhite, George
Hitchcock, Lambert
Phyfe, Duncan

CALL GIRL

Keeler, Christine
Rice-Davies, Mandy

CANCER VICTIM

Bichler, Joyce
Fonyo, Steve (Stephen, Jr.)
Fox, Terry (Terrance Stanley)
Green, Chad

CANDY MANUFACTURER

Brach, Emil J
Cadbury, John
Clark, David L
Heath, Lawrence S
Hershey, Milton Snavely
Luden, William H
Mars, Forrest

Nestle, Henri
Reese, Harry B
Schnering, Otto
Stover, Russell
Whitman, Stephen F

CARTOONIST

Addams, Charles Samuel
Anderson, Carl Thomas
Archibald, Joe (Joseph Stopford)
Arno, Peter
Arriola, Gus
Avery, "Tex" Frederick Bean
Baer, "Bugs" Arthur
Bairnsfather, Bruce
Baker, George
Bakshi, Ralph
Bald, Kenneth
Barbera, Joseph Roland
Barks, Carl
Barry, Daniel
Batchelor, Clarence Daniel
Bateman, Henry Mayo
Beck, C(harles) C(larence)
Berndt, Walter
Berrill, Jack
Berry, Jim
Berryman, Clifford Kennedy
Bode, Vaughn
Booth, George
Branner, Martin Michael
Breger, Dave
Brickman, Morrie
Briggs, Clare
Browne, Dik
Burck, Jacob
Burroughs, Edgar Rice
Bushmiller, Ernie (Ernest Paul)
Byrnes, Eugene F
Cady, (Walter) Harrison
Calkins, Dick
Campbell, E Simms
Caniff, Milt(on Arthur)
Capp, Al
Carlson, Wally (Wallace A)
Clampett, Bob (Robert)
Conrad, Paul Francis
Covarrubias, Miguel
Crane, Roy(ston Campbell)
Crawford, William Hulfish
Crosby, Percy
Crumb, Robert
Culliford, "Peyo" Pierre
Darcy, Tom
Darling, Jay Norwood
Darrow, Whitney, Jr.
Davenport, Homer Calvin
Davis, Jim (James Robert)
Davis, Phil
Day, Chon
DeBeck, Billy

Deighton, Len (Leonard Cyril)
Deitch, Kim
Dirks, Rudolph
Disney, Walt(er Elias)
Dodd, Ed(ward) Benton
Dorgan, Thomas Aloysius
Dowling, Dan(iel Blair)
Drake, Stanley
Duffy, Edmund
Dunn, Alan
Ed, Carl Frank Ludwig
Edson, Gus
Ernst, Kenneth
Falk, Lee Harrison
Feiffer, Jules Ralph
Feininger, Lyonel
Fischetti, John
Fisher, "Bud" Harry Conway
Fisher, Ham(mond Edward)
Fitzpatrick, Daniel R
Fleischer, Max
Foster, Hal (Harold Rudolf)
Fox, Fontaine Talbot, Jr.
Fradon, Dana
Frazetta, Frank
Freyse, William
Gerard, Dave
Gilliam, Terry
Gillray, James
Goldberg, Rube (Reuben Lucius)
Goscinny, Rene
Gould, Chester
Graham, Alex
Gray, Gilda
Gross, Milt
Gruelle, Johnny (John Barton)
Guisewite, Cathy Lee
Haenigsen, Harry William
Hamilton, William
Hamlin, Vincent T
Hampson, Frank
Hanna, William Denby
Harman, Fred
Harman, Hugh
Hart, John(ny Lewis)
Hatlo, Jimmy
Haynie, Hugh
Held, John, Jr.
Herblock
Herriman, George
Hershfield, Harry
Hess, Sol
Hesse, Don
Hirschfeld, Al(bert)
Hogarth, Burne
Hokinson, Helen
Holman, Bill
Igoe, "Hype" Herbert A
Illingworth, Leslie Gilbert
Irvin, Rea
Iwerks, Ub(be)

Jaffee, Allan
Johnson, Crockett
Jones, Chuck
Justus, Roy Braxton
Kahles, Charles William
Keane, Bil
Kelly, Walt
Kent, Jack (John Wellington)
Ketcham, Hank (Henry King)
Key, Theodore
Kilgore, Al
King, Frank
King, Warren Thomas
Kirby, Jack
Kirby, Rollin
Kling, Ken
Knerr, H(arold) H
Kotzky, Alex Sylvester
Lancaster, Osbert, Sir
Lantz, Walter
Lasswell, Fred
Lazarus, Mell
Lee, Stan
Leech, John
Lichty, George
Links, Marty
Long, Scott
Low, David, Sir
MacNelly, Jeff(rey Kenneth)
Marston, William Moulton
Mauldin, Bill (William Henry)
McCay, Winsor
McDougall, Walt(er)
McLaren, Norman
McManus, George
McWilliams, Alden
Meggendorfer, Lothar
Messick, Dale
Messmer, Otto
Mikkelsen, Henning Dahl
Millar, Jeff(rey) Lynn
Montana, Bob
Moore, Don W
Moores, Dick (Richard Arnold)
Mosley, Zack Terrell
Moss, Geoffrey
Mullin, Willard
Murphy, Jimmy (James Edward)
Musial, Joe
Myers, Russell
Nast, Thomas
Naylor, Bob
Neher, Fred
Norris, Paul
Nowlan, Phil
O'Brien, Willis Harold
Ohman, Jack
Olderman, Murray
Oliphant, Patrick Bruce
Opper, Frederick Burr
Outcault, Richard Felton

Overgard, Bill
Parker, Brant (Julian)
Partch, Virgil Franklin, II
Plumb, Charles
Price, Garrett
Price, George
Raymond, Alex(ander Gillespie)
Raymond, James C
Rea, Gardner
Reed, Ed
Ripley, Robert Leroy
Robbins, Frank
Roberge, Frank
Rockwell, "Doc" George L
Rose, Carl
Rowlandson, Thomas
Ryan, T(om) K
Sanders, Bill (William Willard)
Sargent, Ben
Saunders, Allen
Saxon, Charles David
Schultze, Carl Edward
Schulz, Charles Monroe
Segar, Elzie Crisler
Shearer, Taddeus Errington (Ted)
Shoemaker, Vaughn Richard
Shuster, Joe
Siegel, Jerry
Smith, (Robert) Sidney
Smythe, Reginald
Soglow, Otto
Spy, pseud.
Steinberg, Saul
Sterrett, Cliff
Swinnerton, James Guilford
Terry, Paul H
Thurber, James Grover
Trinidad, Francisco Flores Corky, Jr.
Trudeau, Garry (Garretson Beckman)
Turner, Morrie
Tuthill, Harry J
Valtman, Edmund Siegfried
Walker, Mort
Weber, Robert Maxwell
Webster, H(arold) T(ucker)
Westover, Russell
Willard, Frank Henry
Williams, J(ames) R(obert)
Wilson, Gahan
Wingert, Dick
Wortman, Denys
Yates, Bill
Young, "Chic" Murat Bernard
Young, Art(hur Henry)
Young, Lyman

CATALOGER

Sotheby, John
Sotheby, Samuel Leigh

CELEBRITY FRIEND

Exner, Judith Campbell
Fairfax, Sally (Sarah Cary)
Hemings, Sally
Leverson, Ada
Rutherfurd, Lucy Page Mercer
Wesendonck, Mathilde Luckemeyer
Wilson, Helen Dolan

CELEBRITY RELATIVE

Abercrombie, Josephine
Alston, Theodosia Burr
Arthur, Ellen Lewis Herndon
Astaire, Adele
Auchincloss, Hugh D
Ayesha
Barrymore, Diana
Barrymore, Drew
Barrymore, John Blythe Drew, Jr.
Bohlem, Arndt von
Bonaparte, Elizabeth Patterson
Bonaparte, Joseph
Bonaparte, Louis Lucien
Bonaparte, Lucien
Bonaparte, Maria Letizis
Bono, Chastity
Boone, Rebecca B
Borghese, Maria Paolina
Braun, Eva
Bush, Barbara Pierce
Cagney, Jeanne
Calpurnia
Capone, Teresa
Carter, "Chip" James Earl, III
Carter, Amy
Carter, Billy
Carter, Jack (John William)
Carter, Jeff (Donnel Jeffrey)
Carter, Lillian
Cash, Roseanne
Casiraghi, Stefano
Castro, Raul
Chaplin, Sydney
Churchill, Clementine Ogilvy (Hozier)
    Spencer, Baroness
Churchill, Jennie Jerome
Churchill, Randolph
Churchill, Sarah
Clairmont, Claire
Cole, Maria
Cox, Edward Finch
Crane, Cheryl
Crosby, Mary Frances
Crosby, Nathaniel
Curtis, Jamie Lee
Darnley, Henry Stuart, Lord
Davis, Loyal
Davis, Patti
Djugashvili, Ekaterina
Eisenhower, Julie Nixon

Fabiola, Queen of Belgium
Fatima
Fillmore, Caroline Carmichael McIntosh
Fitzgerald, Zelda
Flynn, Sean
Fonda, Shirlee
Ford, Anne McDonnell
Ford, Charlotte
Ford, Christina
Ford, Eleanor Clay
Ford, Jack (John Gardner)
Ford, Kathleen DuRoss
Ford, Mary Litogot
Ford, Michael Gerald
Ford, Steven Meigs
Ford, Susan Elizabeth
Freud, Martha Bernays
Gable, John Clark
Gabor, Jolie
Gandhi, Sanjay
Goering, Emmy Sonnemann
Hanks, Nancy
Harrison, Mary Scott Lord Dimmick
Hart, Jane Briggs
Hathaway, Anne
Hearst, Catherine
Hefner, Christie (Christine Ann)
Hugo, Adele
Humphrey, Muriel Fay Buck
Jagger, Jade
Jefferson, Maria
Jefferson, Martha
Jefferson, Martha Wayles Skelton
Johnson, Evelyn
Johnson, Luci Baines
Johnson, Lynda Bird
Jumel, Eliza
Junot, Philippe
Kelly, John Brenden
Kelly, John Brenden, Jr.
Kennedy, Caroline Bouvier
Kennedy, David Anthony
Kennedy, Ethel Skakel
Kennedy, Joan Bennett
Kennedy, John Fitzgerald, Jr.
Kennedy, Joseph Patrick, III
Kennedy, Joseph Patrick, Jr.
Kennedy, Rose Fitzgerald
Khan, Princess Yasmin
Khrushchev, Nina Petrovna
King, Alberta Christine Williams
King, Coretta Scott
Kissinger, Nancy Maginnes
Krupp von Bohlen und Halbach, Bertha
Lawford, Pat(ricia Kennedy)
Lawrence, Frieda
Lincoln, Robert Todd
Lindbergh, Charles Augustus
Lindstrom, Pia
Linkletter, Jack
Longworth, Alice Roosevelt

Luft, Lorna
Marcos, Imelda Romualdez
Mariamne the Hasmonaean
Marie Louise
Marlborough, Sarah (Jennings) Churchill, Duchess
McGovern, Eleanor Stegeberg
Mitchell, Martha Elizabeth Beall
Mondale, Joan Adams
Mountbatten, Edwina
Mussolini, Rachele Guidi
Mussolini, Rosa Maltoni
Nixon, Patricia (Thelma Catherine Patricia Ryan)
Nixon, Tricia
O'Dwyer, Sloan Simpson
Octavia
Onassis, Jacqueline Lee Bouvier Kennedy
Ormsby Gore, Julian
Oswald, Marina Nikolaevna
Pahlevi, Riza Cyrus
Phillips, Mark Anthony Peter
Picasso, Paloma
Pike, Diana Kennedy
Pompeia
Presley, Lisa Marie
Presley, Priscilla Ann Beaulieu
Pulitzer, Roxanne
Radziwill, (Caroline) Lee Bouvier,
Raleigh, Elizabeth Throckmorton
Reagan, Maureen
Reagan, Michael
Reagan, Ronald Prescott
Redford, Lola Van Wagenen
Rockefeller, "Bobo" Barbara
Rockefeller, "Happy" Margaretta Large
Rockefeller, Michael Clark
Rockefeller, Sharon Lee
Romanov, Anastasia
Romney, Lenore la Fount
Roosevelt, Alice Lee
Roosevelt, Anna Hall
Roosevelt, Kermit
Roosevelt, Quentin
Roosevelt, Sara Delano
Roosevelt, Theodore, Jr.
Roxana
Sadat, Jihan Raouf
Shabazz, Attallah
Shippen, Margaret
Shriver, Eunice Mary Kennedy
Shriver, Maria Owings
Simpson, Wallis Warfield
Sinatra, Barbara Marx Spencer
Sinatra, Christina
Sinatra, Frank, Jr. (Francis Albert)
Sinatra, Nancy
Smith, Frances Scott Fitzgerald Lanahan
Stalina, Svetlana Alliluyeva
Stapleton, Ruth Carter
Stephanie, Princess

Stuart, Charles Edward Louis Philip
Truman, Margaret (Mary Margaret)
Van Buren, Hannah Hoes
Villa, Luz Corral de
Wagner, Cosima Liszt
Wallace, Cornelia Folsom
Warren, Lavinia
Washington, Lawrence
Whistler, Anna Matilda McNeill

CHEF

Appert, Francois Nicolas
Beard, James Andrews
Beck, Simone (Simca)
Bocuse, Paul
Boiardi, Hector
Brillat-Savarin, Jean Anthelme
Child, Julia McWilliams
Escoffier, Georges Auguste
Farmer, Fannie Merritt
Kerr, Graham
Roy, Mike (Michael)
Sherry, Louis

CHEMICAL MANUFACTURER

Wellcome, Henry, Sir

CHEMIST

Alder, Kurt
Arbuzov, Aleksandr
Arrhenius, Svante August
Baekeland, Leo Hendrick
Barton, Derek Harold Richard
Berthollet, Claude Louis, Comte
Berzelius, Jons Jacob, Baron
Black, Joseph
Bottger, Johann Friedrich
Boussingault, Jean
Bovet, Daniele
Britton, Edgar Clay
Bunsen, Robert Wilhelm Eberhard
Calvin, Melvin
Cannizzaro, Stanislao
Carothers, Wallace Hume
Carver, George Washington
Cassidy, Harold Gomes
Cavendish, Henry
Chardonnet, Louis Marie
Chesebrough, Robert Augustus
Chevreul, Michel
Claude, Georges
Conant, James Bryant
Crafts, James Mason
Crookes, William, Sir
Curie, Marie
Curie, Pierre
Darken, Lawrence Stamper
Djerassi, Carl
Domagk, Gerhard

Doreset, Marion
Dow, Herbert Henry
Ellis, Carleton
Fischer, Emil
Flory, Paul John
Frey, Charles N
Friedel, Charles
Gay-Lussac, Joseph Louis
Geist, Jacob
Giauque, William F(rancis)
Gilbert, Joseph Henry, Sir
Graham, Thomas
Hall, James, Sir
Hevesy, George de
Hofmann, Albert
Ingold, Christopher
Karrar, Paul
Kistiakowsky, George Bogdan
Landis, Walter Savage
Lavoisier, Antoine Laurent
Libby, Willard Frank
Liebig, Justus von
Macintosh, Charles
Mark, Herman F
McCollum, Elmer Verner
McLaughlin, John J
Mendeleev, Dmitri
Midgeley, Thomas
Munroe, Charles Edward
Natta, Giulio
Oersted, Hans Christian
Ostwald, Wilhelm
Pasteur, Louis
Pauling, Linus Carl
Perkin, William Henry, Sir
Pictet, Raoul-Pierre
Priestley, Joseph
Prigogine, Ilya
Reichstein, Tadeus
Richards, Ellen Henrietta Swallow
Robinson, Robert
Scheele, Karl Wilhelm
Schonbein, Christian Friedrich
Seaborg, Glenn Theodore
Silliman, Benjamin
Sobrero, Ascanio
Staudinger, Hermann
Urey, Harold Clayton
Watt, George Willard
Weizmann, Chaim
Welsbach, Carl Auer von, Baron
Wesson, David
Wiley, Harvey Washington
Willard, John Wesley
Wohler, Friedrich

CHESS PLAYER

Alekhine, Alexander
Anderssen, Adolf (Karl Ernst Adolf)
Benko, Paul Charles
Botvinnik, Mikhail Moiseevich

Bourdonnais, Louis Charles de la
Bronstein, David
Browne, Walter Shawn
Capablanca, Jose Raoul
Euwe, Max (Machgielis)
Fischer, Bobby (Robert James)
Karpov, Anatoly Yevgenyevich
Kashdan, Isaac
Kasparov, Garry Kimovich
Korchnoi, Viktor
Lasker, Edward
Lasker, Emanuel
Marshall, Frank James
Meyer, Eugene Brown
Morphy, Paul Charles
Nimzowitsch, Aron
Petrosian, Tigran Vartanovich
Philidor, Francois Andre Danican
Reshevsky, Samuel
Rudenko, Lyudmila
Smyslov, Vasili Vasil'evich
Spassky, Boris Vasilyevich
Staunton, Howard
Steinitz, Wilhelm
Tal, Mikhail Nekhemyevich

CHILD ACTORS

Our Gang

CHILDREN'S AUTHOR

Adams, Harriet Stratemeyer
Agle, Nan Hayden
Alexander, Sue
Anderson, C(larence) W(illiam)
Andrews, Jane
Anglund, Joan Walsh
Armstrong, William Howard
Arnold, Oren
Aulaire, Edgar Parin d'
Aulaire, Ingri Mortenson d'
Baker, Rachel
Bannerman, Helen
Bealer, Alex W(inkler III)
Beebe, Burdetta Faye
Behn, Harry
Best, Oswald Herbert
Bianco, Margery Williams
Blake, Quentin
Bleeker, Sonia
Bothwell, Jean
Brett, Jan Churchill
Brown, Margaret Wise
Brunhoff, Jean de
Burton, Virginia Lee
Byars, Betsy
Carter, Dorothy Sharp
Carter, Katherine Jones
Caudill, Rebecca
Cavanna, Betty (Elizabeth Allen)
Chaffin, Lillie Dorton

Chase, Mary Ellen
Christian, Mary Blount
Christopher, Matthew F
Chukovsky, Korney Ivanovich
Clapp, Patricia
Clarke, Rebecca Sophia
Cleaver, Vera Allen
Coatsworth, Elizabeth Jane
Cobb, Vicki
Coles, Joanna
Colonius, Lillian
Cone, Molly Lamken
Conklin, Gladys Plemon
Cooke, David Coxe
Coombs, Charles Ira
Cooney, Barbara
Corbett, Scott (Winfield Scott)
Cousins, Margaret
Coy, Harold
Craig, Helen
Crouch, Marcus
Dalgleish, Alice
Daringer, Helen Fern
Davis, Burke
Davis, Mary L
DeAngeli, Marguérite
Dejong, Meindert
DeLeeuw, Adele Louise
DeRegniers, Beatrice Schenk
Dodge, Bertha S
Douglas, Amanda Minnie
Dwiggins, Don
Eckert, Horst
Edgeworth, Maria
Eifert, Virginia Snider
Elkin, Benjamin
Ellison, Virginia Howell
Elting, Mary Letha
Estes, Eleanor Ruth Rosenfeld
Ets, Marie Hall
Ewing, Julianna Horatia
Faralla, Dana (Dorothy W)
Farrow, George Edward
Fenten, D X
Fiedler, Jean(nette Feldman)
Field, Rachel Lyman
Gag, Wanda
Gallant, Roy Arthur
Gannett, Ruth
Garnett, Eve C R
Grahame, Kenneth
Gramatky, Hardie
Gray, Nicholas Stuart
Greenaway, Kate (Catherine)
Grimm, Jakob Ludwig Karl
Grimm, Wilhelm Karl
Havighurst, Walter Edwin
Haviland, Virginia
Hawthorne, Julian
Henty, George Alfred
Hightower, Florence Josephine Cole

Howitt, Mary
Johnston, Annie Fellows
Julesberg, Elizabeth Rider Montgomery
Kent, Jack (John Wellington)
Lampman, Evelyn Sibley
Lawson, Donald Elmer
Levitin, Sonia
Lothrop, Harriet Mulford Stone
Lunn, Janet
Mason, Francis van Wyck
McDole, Carol
Miller, Olive Thorne
Nesbit, Edith
Osborne, Leone Neal
Phelps, Elizabeth Stuart
Phillpotts, Eden
Pilkington, Francis M
Pringle, Laurence
Provensen, Alice Rose Twitchell
Provensen, Martin
Pullein-Thompson, Diana
Raskin, Ellen
Reed, Betty Jane
Rees, Ennis
Renick, Marion Lewis
Rikhoff, Jean
Rinkoff, Barbara Jean
Rosen, Sidney
Ruchlis, Hy(man)
Russell, Solveig Paulson
Saint John, Robert
Sandburg, Helga
Sanderlin, George William
Sattler, Helen Roney
Sawyer, Ruth
Schlein, Miriam
Schneider, Herman
Schneider, Nina
Serraillier, Ian Lucien
Sharmat, Marjorie Weinman
Sherwood, Mary Martha
Shippen, Katherine Binney
Shotwell, Louisa R
Shuttlesworth, Dorothy Edwards
Silverstein, Alvin
Simon, Norma Feldstein
Skorpen, Liespel Moak
Slote, Alfred
Smith, William Jay
Snow, Dorothea Johnston
Sorensen, Virginia
Southall, Ivan Francis
Sperry, Armstrong W
Stewart, George Rippey
Stoutenburg, Adrien Pearl
Stratemeyer, Edward L
Sturtzel, Howard Allison
Sturtzel, Jane Levington
Sutton, Margaret Beebe
Tappan, Eva March
Taylor, Ann

Taylor, Sydney Brenner
Terris, Susan
Tharp, Louise Hall
Thompson, George Selden
Thompson, Vivian Laubach
Thum, Marcella
Tomlinson, Jill
Trevino, Elizabeth Borton de
Tunis, Edwin Burdett
Udry, Janice May
Ungerer, Tomi (Jean Thomas)
Unkelbach, Kurt
Uttley, Alice Jane Taylor
VanAllsburg, Chris
Wiggin, Kate Douglas
Williams, Jay
Williams, Ursula Moray
Wilson, Hazel Hutchins
Wise, Winifred E
Woody, Regina Llewellyn Jones
Yates, Elizabeth
Young, Margaret Ann Buckner
Zolotow, Charlotte Shapiro

CHOREOGRAPHER

Ailey, Alvin
Ashton, Frederick William, Sir
Balanchine, George
Baryshnikov, Mikhail
Bejart, Maurice
Bennett, Michael
Berkeley, Busby
Bettis, Valerie
Butler, John
Carlisle, Kevin
Champion, Gower
Charmoli, Tony
Cole, Jack
Cranko, John
Cunningham, Merce
Danielian, Leon
Danilova, Alexandra
Dean, Laura
DeValois, Ninette
Dolin, Anton, Sir
Dolly, Jenny
Dolly, Rosie
Dunham, Katherine
Faison, George
Falco, Louis
Field, Ron
Flatt, Ernest O
Fosse, Bob
Franca, Celia
Frankel, Emily
Gennaro, Peter
Geva, Tamara
Graham, Martha
Greco, Jose
Haney, Carol
Joffrey, Robert

Jooss, Kurt
Kidd, Michael
Kylian, Jiri
Laban, Rudolf von
Lavroky, Leonid
Lichine, David
Limon, Jose Arcadio
Loring, Eugene
Lubovitch, Lar
Markert, Russell
Martins, Peter
Massine, Leonide Fedorovich
Mitchell, Arthur
Moiseyev, Igor Alexandrovich
Monk, Meredith
Nijinska, Bronislava
Nikolais, Alwin
Petipa, Marius
Petit, Roland
Piro, Frank
Prescott, Ken
Robbins, Jerome
Saddler, Donald
Saint Denis, Ruth
Svetlova, Marina
Tamiris, Helen
Taylor, June
Taylor, Paul
Tharp, Twyla
Tudor, Antony
Tune, Tommy (Thomas James)
Villella, Edward Joseph
Wilde, Patricia

CIRCUS OWNER

Bailey, James Anthony
Barnum, P(hineas) T(aylor)
Lillie, Gordon William
North, John Ringling
Ringling, Albert C
Ringling, Alfred T
Ringling, Charles
Ringling, John
Ringling, Otto

CIRCUS PERFORMER

Adoree, Renee
Leitzel, Lillian
Leotard, Jules
Tom Thumb, General
Wallenda, Karl
Zacchini, Edmondo

CIVIL RIGHTS ACTIVIST

Anthony, Earl
Brown, H(ubert) Rap
Chavis, Ben
Douglas, Emmitt
Evers, Charles

Evers, Medgar Wiley
Hamer, Fannie Lou Townsend
Lewis, John Robert
Liuzzo, Viola
Means, Russell Charles
Meredith, James Howard
Robeson, Paul Leroy
Rustin, Bayard
Wilkins, Roy

CIVIL RIGHTS LEADER

Abernathy, Ralph David
Abram, Morris Berthold
Bond, Julian
Carmichael, Stokely
Clements, George Harold
Farmer, James
Galamison, Milton Arthur
Haynes, George Edward
Hooks, Benjamin Lawson
Houston, Charles Hamilton
Innis, Roy
Jackson, Jesse Louis
Jordan, Vernon Eulion, Jr.
King, Martin Luther, Jr.
Lowery, Joseph E
McKissick, Floyd Bixler
Mitchell, Clarence M
Parks, Rosa Lee
Shuttlesworth, Fred Lee
Tucker, Sterling
Turner, Thomas Wyatt
White, Walter Francis
Wiley, George A
Williams, Hosea Lorenzo
Young, Whitney Moore, Jr.

CLERGYMAN

Abernathy, Ralph David
Alger, Horatio
Alison, Archibald
Andrae, Johann Valentin
Backus, Isaac
Bakker, Jim (James Orsen)
Baring-Gould, Sabine
Barnes, Ernest William
Beecher, Henry Ward
Bentley, Richard
Blair, James
Blake, Eugene Carson
Bosley, Harold A
Boyd, Malcolm
Brawley, Benjamin Griffith
Brewer, Ebenezer
Buckland, William
Buechner, Frederick
Buttrick, George Arthur
Captein, Jacques Eliza Jean
Cartwright, Edmund
Channing, William Ellery

CLOWN

COLONIAL FIGURE

COLONIAL LEADER

Head, Edmund Walker, Sir
Hutchinson, Thomas
Mason, George
Minuit, Peter
Otis, James
Raffles, Thomas Stamford, Sir
Standish, Miles
Stuyvesant, Peter (Petrus)
Taylor, George
Winslow, Edward
Wolcott, Roger
Yale, Elihu

COLONIZER

Austin, Stephen Fuller
Baltimore, George Calvert, Baron
Cuffe, Paul
DeVries, David Pieterson
Oglethorpe, James Edward
Penn, William
Smith, John

COMA VICTIM

Quinlan, Karen Ann
Von Bulow, "Sunny" Martha Sharp
   Crawford

COMEDIAN

Abbott, "Bud" William A
Adams, Don
Adams, Joey
Allen, Byron
Allen, Fred
Amsterdam, Morey
Arbuckle, "Fatty" Roscoe Conkling
Aykroyd, Dan(iel Edward)
Baker, Phil
Barbour, John
Barker, Ronnie
Bean, Orson
Belushi, John
Benny, Jack
Bergen, Edgar John
Berle, Milton
Berman, Shelley (Sheldon Leonard)
Bernie, Ben
Bishop, Joey
Blue, Ben
Borge, Victor
Brendel, El(mer)
Brenner, David
Brooks, Albert
Brooks, Foster Murrell
Brown, Joe Evan
Bruce, Lenny
Buchanan, Jack
Burns, George
Burns, Jack
Buttons, Red

Byner, John
Caesar, Sid
Callas, Charlie
Cambridge, Godfrey
Candy, John
Cantinflas
Cantor, Eddie
Carlin, George Dennis
Carter, Jack
Chaplin, Sydney Dryden
Chase, "Chevy" Cornelius Crane
Chase, Charley
Clark, Bobby
Clyde, Andy
Cody, Lew
Cohen, Myron
Colonna, Jerry
Conklin, Chester
Conway, "Tim" Thomas Daniel
Cook, Phil
Corey, Irwin
Correll, Charles J
Cosby, Bill
Costello, Lou
Cox, Wally (Wallace Maynard)
Crosby, Norm(an Lawrence)
Crystal, Billy (William)
Curtis, Alan
Dana, Bill
Dangerfield, Rodney
Davis, Michael
DeLuise, Dom
DeRita, Joe
Douglas, Jack
Durante, Jimmy (James Francis)
Efron, Marshall
Elliott, Bob
Erwin, Stuart
Faye, Joey
Field, Sid(ney Arthur)
Fields, Lew Maurice
Fine, Larry
Fontaine, Frank
Ford, "Senator" Ed
Ford, Phil
Foster, Phil
Foxx, Redd
Frye, David
Gardner, Ed(ward Francis)
Gleason, Jackie
Gobel, George Leslie
Gorshin, Frank John
Gosden, Freeman Fisher
Goulding, Ray
Greene, Shecky
Gregory, Dick
Hackett, Buddy
Handelman, Stanley Myron
Hardy, Oliver
Harris, Phil
Henry, Pat

COMEDIENNE

Allen, Gracie Ethel Cecil Rosaline
Baddeley, Hermione Clinton
Ball, Lucille
Ballard, Kaye
Berberian, Cathy
Burnett, Carol
Buzzi, Ruth Ann
Canova, Judy
Carne, Judy
Carroll, Pat(ricia Ann Angela Bridgit)
Carson, Jeannie
Coca, Imogene Fernandez y
Curtin, Jane Therese
Davis, Joan
Diller, Phyllis
Fields, Gracie
Fields, Totie
Flagg, Fannie (Frances Carlton)
Hartman, Grace
Hines, Mimi
Kelly, "Patsy" Sarah Veronica Rose
Lanchester, Elsa
Lillie, Beatrice
Livingstone, Mary
Mabley, "Moms" Jackie
Meara, Anne
Miles, Sylvia
Moran, Polly
O'Shea, Tessie
Pearl, Minnie
Radner, Gilda
Raye, Martha
Rivera, Chita
Rivers, Joan
Rose-Marie
Russell, Anna
Talbot, Nita
Talmadge, Constance
Tomlin, "Lily" Mary Jean

COMEDY TEAM

Abbott and Costello
Cheech and Chong
Marx Brothers, The
McKenzie Brothers, The
Monty Python's Flying Circus
Ritz Brothers
Three Stooges, The
Wayne and Shuster
Weber and Fields

COMIC STRIP ARTIST

Gray, Harold

COMMUNIST LEADER

Beria, Lavrenti Pavlovich
Braun, Otto
Brezhnev, Leonid Ilyich
Browder, Earl Russell
Bukharin, Nikolai Ivanovich
Castro (Ruz), Fidel
Dimitrov, Georgi
Dubcek, Alexander
Duclos, Jacques
Gheorghiu-Dej, Gheorghe
Gottwald, Klement
Ho Chi Minh
Kadar, Janos
Kaganovich, Lazar M
Kamenev, Lev Borisovich
Kaminsky, Grigorii Naumovich
Kang, Sheng
Khrushchev, Nikita Sergeyevich
Kosygin, Aleksei Nikolaevich
Kun, Bela
Lenin, Nikolai
Liebknecht, Karl
Liu Shao-Ch'i
Mao Tse-Tung
Radek, Karl
Svoboda, Ludvik
Togliatti, Palmiro
Trotsky, Leon
Ulbricht, Walter
Wang Hung-Wen
Zhdanov, Andrei Alexandrovich

COMPOSER

Addinsell, Richard
Addison, John
Adler, Larry (Lawrence Cecil)
Adler, Richard
Ager, Milton
Aitken, Hugh
Albeniz, Isaac Manuel Francisco
Albert, Stephen Joel
Albinoni, Tommaso
Allegri, Gregorio
Almeida, Laurindo
Amfiteatrof, Daniele
Andersen, Eric
Anderson, "Cat" William Alonzo
Anderson, Leroy
Animuccia, Giovanni
Antheil, George
Armstrong, Harry
Arne, Thomas Augustine
Arnold, Malcolm, Sir
Auric, Georges
Babbitt, Milton Byron
Bach, Carl Philipp Emanuel
Bach, Johann Christian
Bach, Johann Sebastian
Bach, Wilhelm Friedemann
Bacharach, Burt
Baker, Phil
Balakirev, Mili Alekseyevich
Ball, Ernest

Bantock, Granville, Sir
Barber, Samuel
Barnes, Billy
Barry, John
Bart, Lionel
Bartok, Bela
Bax, Arnold Edward Trevor, Sir
Beach, Mrs. H H A
Beethoven, Ludwig van
Bennett, Robert Russell
Berg, Alban
Berger, Arthur
Berio, Luciano
Berlin, Irving
Berlioz, Louis Hector
Bernstein, Elmer
Bernstein, Leonard
Bertini, Gary
Bizet, Georges (Alexandre Cesar Leopold)
Black, Frank J.
Blake, Eubie (James Hubert)
Blech, Leo
Bliss, Arthur, Sir
Blitzstein, Marc
Bloch, Ernest
Bloom, Mickey (Milton)
Blyton, Carey
Boccherini, Luigi
Bock, Jerry (Jerrold Lewis)
Boieldieu, Francois Adrien
Boito, Arrigo
Bolcom, William Elden
Bond, Carrie Jacobs
Bond, Victoria
Bononcini, Giovanni Battista
Borodin, Alexander Profirevich
Boulanger, Nadia Juliette
Boulez, Pierre
Bowles, Paul
Boyce, William
Brahms, Johannes
Bresler, Jerry
Bricusse, Leslie
Bridge, Frank
Britain, Radie
Britten, (Edward) Benjamin
Brown, "Sonny" William
Brown, Lawrence
Brown, Oscar, Jr.
Bruch, Max
Bruckner, Anton
Bull, John
Bull, Ole Bornemann
Burke, Johnny
Bush, Alan
Busoni, Ferruccio Benvenuto
Buxtehude, Dietrich
Byrd, Henry
Byrd, William
Caccini, Giulio
Cadman, Charles Wakefield

Cage, John Milton, Jr.
Carey, Henry
Carle, Frankie
Carmines, Al
Carpenter, John Alden
Carter, Elliott Cook, Jr.
Casadesus, Robert
Casals, Pablo (Pau Carlos Salvador)
Castelnuovo-Tedesco, Mario
Catalani, Alfredo
Cavalli, Francesco
Chabrier, (Alexis) Emmanuel
Chadwick, George Whitefield
Chaminade, Cecile
Chaplin, Charlie
Charles, Ray
Charpentier, Gustave
Charpentier, Marc-Antoine
Chasins, Abram
Chausson, Ernest
Chavez, Carlos
Cherniavsky, Josef
Cherubini, Maria Luigi
Chopin, Frederic Francois
Chorzempa, Daniel Walter
Cilea, Francesco
Cimarosa, Domenico
Clarke, Jeremiah
Clarke, Stanley Marvin
Clementi, Muzio
Coates, Albert
Cohn, Al
Cohn, Arthur
Coleridge-Taylor, Samuel
Confrey, "Zez" Edward E
Conrad, Con
Conti, Bill
Converse, Frederick Shepherd
Cook, Will Marion
Coots, J Fred
Copland, Aaron
Coppola, Carmine
Corelli, Arcangelo
Corigliano, John
Cornelius, Peter
Coslow, Sam
Couperin, Francois
Coward, Noel Pierce, Sir
Cowell, Henry Dixon
Cramer, Johann Baptist
Creston, Paul
Crispin, Edmund, pseud.
Cui, Cesar Antonovich
Czerny, Karl
D'Albert, Eugene
Dallapiccola, Luigi
Damrosch, Walter Johannes
Dankworth, John Philip William
Darby, Ken
Dargomijsky, Alexander
David, Mack

Davies, Peter Maxwell
Davis, Clifton
Davis, Miles Dewey
De Vorzon, Barry
Dean, Laura
Debussy, Claude Achille
DeKnight, Jimmy
DeKoven, (Henry Louis) Reginald
Delerue, Georges
Delibes, Leo
Delius, Frederick
Dello Joio, Norman Joseph
DeLugg, Milton
DeSabata, Victor
DesPres, Josquin
Dett, Robert Nathaniel
Deutsch, Adolph
Diamond, David
Diemer, Emma Lou
Ditters, Karl
Dohnanyi, Erno von
Dorati, Antal
Dorsey, Thomas Andrew
Dowland, John
Druckman, Jacob Raphael
Dukas, Paul Abraham
Duke, Vernon
DuPre, Marcel
DuPrez, Gilbert
Durante, Francesco
Dvorak, Anton
Edwards, Sherman
Egk, Werner
Elgar, Edward William, Sir
Ellington, "Duke" Edward Kennedy
Enesco, Georges
Erwin, "Pee Wee" George
Evans, Bill (William John)
Evans, Ray
Falla, Manuel de
Fasch, Johann Friedrich
Faure, Gabriel Urbain
Feather, Leonard Geoffrey
Fendler, Edvard
Ferrante, Arthur
Field, John
Firestone, Idabelle Smith
Fischer, Irwin
Fisher, Fred
Fletcher, Grant
Flotow, Friedrich von, Baron
Floyd, Carlisle
Fogelberg, Dan(iel Grayling)
Foote, Arthur William
Foss, Lukas
Foster, Stephen Collins
Fox, Charles
Francaix, Jean
Franck, Cesar Auguste
Fraser, Ian
Frescobaldi, Girolamo

Fried, Gerald
Friml, Rudolf
Gabrieli, Giovanni
Gagn, Reynaldo
Gaines, Lee
Galuppi, Baldassare
Ganz, Rudolph
Garcia, Manuel del Popolo Vincente, I
Garner, Erroll
Gaubert, Philippe
Gazzaniga, Giuseppe
Geminiani, Francesco
George, Don
Gershwin, George
Gesualdo, Carlo
Giannini, Vittorio
Gibbons, Orlando
Gibbs, Terry
Gillis, Don
Ginastera, Alberto
Giordano, Umberto
Glass, Philip
Glazunov, Alexander Constantinovich
Gliere, Reinhold Moritzovich
Glinka, Mikhail Ivanovich
Godard, Benjamin L P
Goldman, Edwin Franko
Goldman, Richard Franko
Goldmark, Karl
Goldsmith, Jerry
Goodman, Al(fred)
Goossens, Eugene, Sir
Gorin, Igor
Gossec, Francois Joseph
Gottschalk, Louis Moreau
Gould, Glenn Herbert
Gould, Morton
Gounod, Charles Francois
Gozzi, Gaspare
Graham, Ronny
Grainger, Percy Aldridge
Granados, Enrique
Gray, Cecil
Green, Adolph
Green, Johnny (John W)
Gretchaninov, Aleksandr Tikhonovich
Gretry, Andre Ernest Modeste
Grieg, Edvard Hagerup
Griffes, Charles Tomlinson
Grofe, Ferde
Groves, Charles, Sir
Gruenberg, Louis
Guion, David Wendel Fentress
Hadley, Henry Kimball
Haggart, Bob
Hallstrom, Ivar
Hamlisch, Marvin
Hancock, Herbie (Herbert Jeffrey)
Handel, George Frederick
Handy, W(illiam) C(hristopher)
Hanson, Howard Harold

Harbison, John Harris
Harburg, E(dgar) Y(ipsel)
Harkness, Rebekah West
Harney, Benjamin Robertson
Harris, Roy Ellsworth
Hasse, Johann Adolph
Hasso, Signe Eleonora Cecilia
Haydn, Franz Joseph
Hayes, Peter Lind
Hayton, Lennie (Leonard George)
Hefti, Neal Paul
Heger, Robert
Heindorf, Ray
Hendl, Walter
Henze, Hans Werner
Herbert, Victor
Herold, Louis Joseph Ferdinand
Herrmann, Bernard
Heseltine, Phillip Arnold
Heywood, Eddie
Hiller, Johann Adam
Hindemith, Paul
Hoffman, Al
Holbrooke, Josef
Holst, Gustav
Homer, Sidney
Honegger, Arthur
Horenstein, Jascha
Hovhaness, Alan
Hubay, Jeno
Hummel, Johann Nepomuk
Humperdinck, Engelbert
Ibert, Jacques
Indy, Paul (Marie Theodore Vincent d')
Inghelbrecht, Desire
Ippolitov-Ivanov, Mikhail Mikhailovich
Ireland, John
Iturbi, Jose
Ives, Charles Edward
Jacobs, Al(bert T)
James, Philip
Janacek, Leos
Janssen, Werner
Jarre, Maurice
Jarrett, Keith
Jenkins, Gordon
Jensen, Adolph
Johnson, Hall
Jolas, Betsy
Jommelli, Niccolo
Jones, Quincy Delight
Joplin, Scott
Kabalevsky, Dmitri Borisovich
Kalmanoff, Martin
Kander, John
Kaper, Bronislau
Kay, Hershy
Keiser, Reinhard
Kelley, Edgar Stillman
Kempff, (Wilhelm) Walter Friedrich
Kern, Jerome David

Key, Francis Scott
Khachaturian, Aram
Khrennikov, Tikhon Nikolaevich
Kienzl, Wilhelm
Kilenyi, Edward, Sr.
Klebe, Giselher
Klemperer, Otto
Klenau, Paul von
Knopfler, Mark
Kodaly, Zoltan
Kolb, Barbara Anne
Korngold, Erich Wolfgang
Koussevitzky, Serge Alexandrovich
Krenek, Ernst
Kreutzer, Rodolphe
Kubelik, Rafael
Lai, Francis
Lalo, Edouard Victor Antoine
Lambert, Constant
Lane, Burton
Laparra, Raoul
Lassus, Orlandus de
Laszlo, Miklos
Lavalle, Paul
Lawrence, Elliot
Lawrence, Jack
LeFleming, Christopher Kaye
Legrand, Michel Jean
Lehar, Franz
Leibowitz, Rene
Leigh, Mitch
Lemoyne, Jean-Baptiste
Leo, Leonardo
Leoni, Franco
Leroux, Xavier
Lesueur, Jean-Francois
Levant, Oscar
Lewis, Ramsey Emanuel, Jr.
Liebermann, Rolf
Lindsey, Mort
Lipinski, Karl
Liszt, Franz (Ferencz)
Litolff, Henri Charles
Locatelli, Pietro
Loeffler, Charles Martin Tornov
Loesser, Frank
Loewe, Frederick
Logroscino, Nicola
Lortzing, Gustav Albert
Luboff, Norman
Luboshutz, Pierre
Lully, Jean-Baptiste
Lutoslawski, Witold
MacDermot, Galt
MacDowell, Edward Alexander
Macfarren, George Alexander, Sir
Mackenzie, Alexander, Sir
Mackerras, Charles, Sir (Alan Charles MacLaurin)
Magnante, Charles
Mahler, Gustav

Malipiero, Gian Francesco
Maltby, Richard E
Mancinelli, Luigi
Mancini, Henry
Mangione, Chuck (Charles Frank)
Mannes, Leopold Damrosch
Marcello, Benedetto
Marinuzzi, Gino
Marks, Johnny (John David)
Marley, Bob (Robert Nesta)
Marschner, Heinrich
Marterie, Ralph
Martin y Soler, Vicente
Martin, Frank
Martinon, Jean
Martinu, Bohuslav
Mascagni, Pietro
Mason, Daniel Gregory
Mascn, Lowell
Masse, Victor
Massenet, Jules Emile Frederic
McCoy, Van
McDonald, Harl
McPartland, Margaret Marian
Medtner, Nicholas
Mehul, Etienne Nicolas
Mendelssohn, Felix
Mennin, Peter
Menotti, Gian Carlo
Mercadante, Saverio
Messager, Andre Charles Prosper
Messiaen, Olivier
Meyer, Joseph
Milhaud, Darius
Mills, Irving
Mitropoulos, Dimitri
Moniuszko, Stanislaus
Monk, Thelonius Sphere
Monsigny, Pierre-Alexandre
Montemezzi, Italo
Monteverdi, Claudio
Morgan, Russ
Morton, "Jelly Roll" Joseph Ferdinand
Moscheles, Ignaz
Moszkowski, Moritz
Mozart, (Johann Georg) Leopold
Mozart, Wolfgang Amadeus
Muczynski, Robert
Musgrave, Thea
Mussorgsky, Modest Petrovich
Nabokov, Nicolas
Napravnik, Eduard
Nathan, Robert
Nessler, Victor E
Nevin, Ethelbert Woodbridge
Newman, Alfred
Nichols, Beverly
Nicolai, Carl Otto
Nielsen, Carl August
Nikolais, Alwin
Niles, John Jacob

Nolan, Bob
North, Alex
Nougues, Jean
Novak, Vitezslav
Novello, Ivor
O'Horgan, Tom
Offenbach, Jacques
Ogdon, John Andrew Howard
Okun, Milton
Olcott, Chauncey (Chancellor)
Oliver, Sy (Melvin James)
Orff, Carl
Pachelbel, Johann
Pacini, Giovanni
Paer, Ferdinando
Paganini, Niccolo
Paisiello, Giovanni
Palestrina, Giovanni
Parry, Charles Hubert Hastings, Sir
Partch, Harry
Paumgartner, Bernhard
Penderecki, Krzysztof
Pennario, Leonard
Pepusch, Johann Christoph (John)
Pergolesi, Giovanni Battista
Peri, Jacopo
Persichetti, Vincent
Pfitzner, Hans
Philidor, Francois Andre Danican
Piccini, Nicola
Pierne, Gabriel
Piston, Walter
Pizzetti, Ildebrando
Planquette, Jean(-Robert)
Pleasants, Henry
Ponchielli, Amilcare
Ponty, Jean-Luc
Porpora, Niccolo
Porter, Cole
Porter, Quincy
Poulenc, Francis
Praetorius, Michael
Pratella, Francesco Balilla
Previn, Andre
Price, Florence Beatrice Smith
Prokofiev, Sergei Sergeevich
Pryor, Arthur W
Purcell, Henry
Rabaud, Henri
Rachmaninoff, Sergei Vasilyevich
Rameau, Jean-Philippe
Ravel, Maurice Joseph
Rebikov, Vladimir Ivanovich
Reger, Max
Reich, Steve
Reichardt, Johann Friedrich
Reinhardt, Django (Jean Baptiste)
Remenyi, Eduard
Respighi, Ottorino
Reyer, (Louis) Ernest (Etienne)
Reznicek, Emil von

Riddle, Nelson
Riegger, Wallingford
Rimsky-Korsakov, Nikolai Andreevich
Robinson, Earl Hawley
Rochberg, George
Rodgers, Mary
Rodgers, Richard
Rollins, "Sonny" Theodore Walter
Romberg, Bernhard
Romberg, Sigmund
Rome, Harold Jacob
Rorem, Ned
Rose, Vincent
Ross, Lanny
Rousseau, Jean Jacques
Roussel, Albert
Rozsa, Miklos
Rubinstein, Anton Gregorovitch
Ruggles, Carl
Sablon, Jean Georges
Sacchini, Antonio
Sachs, Hans
Saint-Saens, (Charles) Camille
Sainte-Marie, "Buffy" Beverly
Salieri, Antonio
Sarasate, Pablo de
Sarti, Giuseppe
Satie, Erik
Sauter, Eddie (Edward Ernest)
Scarlatti, Alessandro
Scarlatti, Domenico Girolamo
Schelling, Ernest Henry
Schickele, Peter
Schifrin, Lalo Claudio
Schillinger, Joseph
Schillings, Max von
Schoech, Othmar
Schoenberg, Arnold
Schreker, Franz
Schubert, Franz Peter
Schuller, Gunther
Schuman, William Howard
Schumann, Robert Alexander
Schumann, Walter
Schutz, Heinrich
Schwartz, Stephen L
Schwarz, Gerard
Scott, Cyril (Meir)
Scott, Raymond
Scott, Tony
Scriabin, Alexander Nicholaevich
Sessions, Roger Huntington
Shankar, Ravi
Shchedrin, Rodion Konstantinovich
Sherman, Richard Morton
Shire, David
Shostakovich, Dmitri Dmitryevich
Sibelius, Jean
Siegmeister, Elie
Simeone, Harry
Sinding, Christian

Skrowaczewski, Stanislaw
Slonimsky, Nicolas
Smetana, Bedrich
Smith, Paul Joseph
Snider, Dee (Daniel Dee)
Sondheim, Stephen Joshua
Sor, Fernando
Sousa, John Philip
Sowerby, Leo
Speaks, Oley
Spohr, Louis Ludwig
Spontini, Gasparo
Steffani, Agostino
Steiner, Max
Stevens, Morton
Stewart, "Slam" Leroy
Still, William Grant
Stockhausen, Karlheinz
Stolz, Robert
Straus, Oskar
Strauss, Johann, Jr.
Strauss, Johann, Sr.
Strauss, Richard
Stravinsky, Igor Fedorovich
Strouse, Charles
Suk, Josef
Sukman, Harry
Sullivan, Arthur Seymour, Sir
Sullivan, Tom
Svetlanov, Evgeni Fyodorovich
Swados, Elizabeth A (Liz)
Swann, Donald Ibrahim
Sweelinck, Jan Pieterszoon
Szymanowski, Karol
Tailleferre, Germaine
Taktakishvili, Otar Vasilevich
Tallis, Thomas
Tartini, Giuseppe
Taylor, (Joseph) Deems
Tchaikovsky, Peter Ilyich
Tcherepnin, Alexander
Tcherepnin, Nicholas (Nicolai)
Teicher, Louis
Theodorakis, Mikis
Thompson, Randall
Thomson, Virgil Garnett
Thornhill, Claude
Tiomkin, Dimitri
Tippett, Michael Kemp, Sir
Toch, Ernst
Tortelier, Paul
Tosti, Francesco Paola
Tovey, Donald Francis, Sir
Tower, Joan Peabody
Traetta, Tommaso
Travers, Mary
Trumbauer, Frank(ie)
Ussachevsky, Vladimir
Van Peebles, Melvin
VanAlstyne, Egbert Anson
Vangelis

Varese, Edgar
Vassilenko, Sergei
Vaughan Williams, Ralph
Vieuxtemps, Henri
Villa-Lobos, Heitor
Viotti, Giovanni Battista
Vivaldi, Antonio
Von Tilzer, Albert
Wagner, Richard
Wagner, Siegfried (Helferich)
Wagner-Regeny, Rudolf
Waller, "Fats" Thomas Wright
Walter, Cyril
Ward, Robert Eugene
Watt, Douglas (Benjamin)
Waxman, Franz
Webb, Jim
Webber, Andrew Lloyd
Weber, Carl Maria von
Webern, Anton von
Weill, Kurt
Weinberger, Jaromir
Weingartner, Felix
Weisgall, Hugo David
Welch, Ken
Welch, Mitzie
Wenrich, Percy
Whiting, Richard Armstrong
Widor, Charles Marie Jean Albert
Wieniawski, Henri
Wild, Earl
Wilder, Alec (Alexander Lafayette Chew)
Williams, John Towner
Williams, Mary Lou
Williams, Mason
Williams, Patrick
Willson, Meredith
Wilson, John N
Wilson, Sandy (Alexander Galbraith)
Winner, Joseph Eastburn
Wolf, Hugo
Wolf-Ferrari, Ermanno
Wood, Guy B
Wood, Henry Joseph, Sir
Wood, Woodrow Johnson
Xenakis, Iannis
Yarrow, Peter
Yon, Pietro Alessandro
Youmans, Vincent
Young, Victor
Ysaye, Eugene
Zandonai, Riccardo
Zemlinsky, Alexander von
Zimbalist, Efrem, Jr.
Zingarelli, Nicola Antonio
Zwilich, Ellen Taaffe

COMPOSERS

Les Six

COMPUTER EXECUTIVE

Bushnell, Nolan Kay
Osborne, Adam
Wozniak, Steven

COMPUTER SCIENTIST

Backus, John

CONDUCTOR

Abbado, Claudio
Abravanel, Maurice
Adler, Kurt Herbert
Adler, Peter Herman
Alessandro, Victor Nicholas
Allers, Franz
Amfiteatrof, Daniele
Amram, David Werner, III
Ancerl, Karel
Anderson, Leroy
Anello, John David
Ansermet, Ernest Alexandre
Arditi, Luigi
Autori, Franco
Bacharach, Burt
Balaban, Emanuel
Bantock, Granville, Sir
Barbirolli, John, Sir
Barenboim, Daniel
Barlow, Howard
Barzin, Leon Eugene
Baudo, Serge
Beecham, Thomas, Sir
Beinum, Eduard van
Bergmann, Carl
Berio, Luciano
Bernstein, Elmer
Bernstein, Leonard
Bertini, Gary
Blackton, Jay S
Blech, Leo
Bloch, Alexander
Bloch, Raymond A
Bodanzky, Artur
Bohm, Karl
Bomhard, Moritz
Bond, Victoria
Bonynge, Richard
Boulanger, Nadia Juliette
Boulez, Pierre
Boult, Adrian Cedric, Sir
Brico, Antonia
Bruch, Max
Buckley, Emerson
Buketoff, Igor
Burgin, Richard
Busch, Fritz
Bush, Alan
Caldwell, Sarah
Casals, Pablo (Pau Carlos Salvador)

Caston, Saul
Ceccato, Aldo
Celibidache, Sergiu
Chapple, Stanley
Chavez, Carlos
Cherniavsky, Josef
Christiansen, Olaf
Cleva, Fausto
Cluytens, Andre
Coates, Albert
Cohn, Arthur
Colonne, Edouard
Comissiona, Sergiu
Condie, Richard P
Cooper, Emil
Coppola, Carmine
Costa, Don
Craft, Robert
Crosby, John
Dalvit, Lewis David, Jr.
Damrosch, Leopold
Damrosch, Walter Johannes
Dankworth, John Philip William
Darby, Ken
Davis, Andrew Frank
Davis, Colin
Davis, Meyer
Defauw, Desire
DeFrank, Vincent
Delerue, Georges
DelMar, Norman Rene
DeLugg, Milton
DeSabata, Victor
Desormiere, Roger
DeWaart, Edo
Dixon, Dean
Dobrowen, Issai
Dohnanyi, Christoph von
Dohnanyi, Erno von
Dorati, Antal
Downes, Edward Olin Davenport
Dragon, Carmen
Ducloux, Walter
Ehrling, Sixten
Elgar, Edward William, Sir
Engel, Lehman (Aaron Lehman)
Erede, Alberto
Faith, Percy
Fendler, Edvard
Fennell, Frederick
Ferencsik, Janos
Fiedler, Arthur
Fischer, Irwin
Fistoulari, Anatole
Fletcher, Grant
Foss, Lukas
Fox, Charles
Fraser, Ian
Freccia, Massimo
Fricsay, Ferenc
Furtwangler, Wilhelm

Gabrilowitsch, Ossip
Gagn, Reynaldo
Ganz, Rudolph
Gaubert, Philippe
Gebert, Ernst
George, Graham Elias
Gibbs, Terry
Giulini, Carlo Maria
Godfrey, Isadore
Goldovsky, Boris
Golschmann, Vladimir
Goodman, Al(fred)
Goossens, Eugene, Sir
Green, Johnny (John W)
Grevillius, Nils
Gui, Vittorio
Haitink, Bernard
Halasz, Laszlo
Halle, Charles, Sir
Hanson, Howard Harold
Harrison, Guy Fraser
Hasselmans, Louis
Hayton, Lennie (Leonard George)
Heger, Robert
Heindorf, Ray
Henderson, "Skitch" Cedric
Hendl, Walter
Herbert, Victor
Hermann, Bernard
Hertz, Alfred
Hillis, Margaret
Hilsberg, Alexander
Hinrichs, Gustav
Hoesslin, Franz von
Hoffman, Irwin
Hogwood, Christopher
Horenstein, Jascha
Hurst, George
Inghelbrecht, Desire
Irving, Robert Augustine
Iturbi, Jose
Ivanov, Konstantin Konstantinovich
James, Philip
Janigro, Antonio
Janssen, Werner
Jenkins, Gordon
Jenkins, Newell
Jochum, Eugen
Jorda, Enrique
Kalmanoff, Martin
Karajan, Herbert von
Katims, Milton
Keilberth, Joseph
Kempe, Rudolf
Kertesz, Istvan
Khaikin, Boris
Kindler, Hans
Kleiber, Erich
Klemperer, Otto
Klenau, Paul von
Kletzki, Paul

Knappertsbusch, Hans
Kondrashin, Kiril Petrovich
Konwitschny, Franz
Kostelanetz, Andre
Koussevitzky, Serge Alexandrovich
Krauss, Clemens
Krips, Josef
Kubelik, Rafael
Kurtz, Efrem
Lamoureux, Charles
Lange, Hans
Lavalle, Paul
Lawrence, Elliot
Lawrence, Robert
Leginska
Legrand, Michel Jean
Leibowitz, Rene
Leinsdorf, Erich
Leitner, Ferdinand
Lemoyne, Jean-Baptiste
Leppard, Raymond John
Lert, Ernst
Levi, Hermann
Levine, James
Lewenthal, Raymond
Lewis, Henry Jay
Lindsey, Mort
Lohse, Otto
Lombard, Alain
Luboff, Norman
Ludwig, Leopold
Maag, Peter
Maazel, Lorin
Mackerras, Charles, Sir (Alan Charles
   MacLaurin)
MacMillan, Ernest Campbell, Sir
Mahler, Fritz
Mahler, Gustav
Malko, Nicolai
Maltby, Richard E
Mancinelli, Luigi
Mannes, David
Manns, Augustus, Sir
Mantovani, Annunzio
Marinuzzi, Gino
Markevitch, Igor
Marriner, Neville
Marterie, Ralph
Martineau, Jean
Martinon, Jean
Masur, Kurt
Mathieson, Muir
Matthews, Denis
McArthur, Edwin Douglas
Mehta, Zubin
Melachrino, George
Mendelssohn, Felix
Mengelberg, Willem (Josef Willem)
Merola, Gaetano
Messager, Andre Charles Prosper
Miller, Mitch(ell William)

Mitropoulos, Dimitri
Mollenhauer, Emil
Moninari-Pradelli, Francesco
Monteux, Claude
Monteux, Pierre
Morgan, Russ
Mottl, Felix
Mravinsky, Eugene
Muck, Karl
Mugnone, Leopoldo
Munch, Charles
Munchinger, Karl
Musgrave, Thea
Muti, Riccardo
Napravnik, Eduard
Neel, (Louis) Boyd
Neuendorff, Adolf
Newman, Alfred
Nikisch, Arthur
North, Alex
Ormandy, Eugene
Ozawa, Seiji
Panizza, Ettore
Papi, Genarro
Paray, Paul
Pasdeloup, Jules Etienne
Paur, Emil
Pelletier, Wilfred
Perahia, Murray
Perlea, Jonel
Persinger, Louis
Piastro, Mishel
Pitt, Percy
Polacco, Giorgio
Pollack, Egon
Pretre, Georges
Previn, Andre
Previtali, Fernando
Pritchard, John Michael
Prohaska, Felix
Puente, Tito
Queler, Eve Rabin
Rabaud, Henri
Rachmaninoff, Sergei Vasilyevich
Reichardt, Johann Friedrich
Reiner, Fritz
Richter, Hans
Richter, Karl
Rodzinski, Artur
Ronald, Landon, Sir
Rosbaud, Hans
Rose, Vincent
Rosenstock, Joseph
Rosenthal, Manuel
Rothwell, Walter Henry
Rozhdestvensky, Gennadi Nikolaevich
Rudel, Julius
Rudolf, Max
Ruhlmann, Francois
Sacher, Paul
Saerchinger, Cesar Victor Charles

Saidenberg, Daniel
Salieri, Antonio
Sargent, Malcolm, Sir
Sawallisch, Wolfgang
Schalk, Franz
Schelling, Ernest Henry
Scherchen, Hermann
Scherman, Thomas K
Schillings, Max von
Schippers, Thomas
Schmidt-Isserstedt, Hans
Schoech, Othmar
Schuch, Ernst von
Schuller, Gunther
Schumann, Walter
Sebastian, George
Secunda, Sholom
Seidl, Anton
Serafin, Tullio
Sevitzky, Fabien
Shaw, Robert Lawson
Shostakovich, Maksim
Siegmeister, Elie
Simmons, Calvin
Sissle, Noble
Skrowaczewski, Stanislaw
Slatkin, Leonard
Slonimsky, Nicolas
Smallens, Alexander
Smetana, Bedrich
Sodero, Cesare
Solomon, Izler
Solti, Georg, Sir
Sosnik, Harry
Sousa, John Philip
Spohr, Louis Ludwig
Stein, Horst
Steinberg, William (Hans Wilhelm)
Steiner, Max
Stevens, Morton
Stiedry, Fritz
Stock, Frederick A
Stoessel, Albert
Stokowski, Leopold
Strasfogel, Ignace
Strauss, Johann, Jr.
Strauss, Johann, Sr.
Strauss, Richard
Sukman, Harry
Susskind, Walter
Svetlanov, Evgeni Fyodorovich
Swoboda, Henry
Szell, George
Szenkar, Eugen
Tennstedt, Klaus
Thomas, Michael Tilson
Thomas, Theodore
Tietjen, Heinz
Toscanini, Arturo
Toye, Geoffrey
Trumbauer, Frank(ie)

Varviso, Silvio
VonBulow, Hans Guido
Voorhees, Donald
Wagner, Siegfried (Helferich)
Wallenstein, Alfred Franz
Walter, Bruno
Waxman, Franz
Weber, Adam
Weingartner, Felix
Werrenrath, Reinald
Whiteman, Paul
Williams, John Towner
Wilson, John N
Winograd, Arthur
Woldike, Mogens
Wolff, Albert Louis
Wood, Henry Joseph, Sir
Woss, Kurt
Young, Victor
Zemlinsky, Alexander von

CONGRESSMAN

Barton, Bruce
Broyhill, Joel Thomas
Cain, Richard H
Cannon, Joseph Gurney
Clay, William Lacy
Corning, Erastus
Crane, Philip Miller
Crump, Edward Hull
Dawson, William L
DePriest, Oscar Stanton
Dies, Martin, Jr.
Fish, Hamilton, III
Guyer, Tennyson
Hayakawa, S(amuel) I(chiye)
Holifield, Chet
Jones, James Robert
Kemp, Jack French
LeBoutillier, John
Lindbergh, Charles Augustus
Mathias, Bob (Robert Bruce)
Maverick, Maury
McCloskey, Paul Norton, Jr.
McCormack, John William
Meskill, Thomas J
Michel, Robert H(enry)
Morgan, Daniel
Murphy, John Michael
Murtha, John Patrick
Myers, Michael O
Powell, Adam Clayton, Jr.
Rangel, Charles Bernard
Rayburn, Sam(uel Taliaferro)
Raymond, Henry Jarvis
Rooney, John (James)
Smith, Howard Worth
Swigert, Jack (John Leonard, Jr.)
Thompson, Frank, Jr.
Tiernan, Robert Owens
Udall, Mo(rris King)

Ullman, Al(bert Conrad)
Vanik, Charles Albert
Vinson, Carl
Volstead, Andrew J
Wiggins, Charles Edward
Wright, James C(laud), Jr.

CONGRESSWOMAN

Burke, Yvonne Brathwaite Watson
Chisholm, Shirley Anita St. Hill
Douglas, Helen Mary Gahagan
Dwyer, Florence Price

CONQUEROR

Alvarado, Pedro de
Cortez, Hernando
Genghis Khan
Guzman, Nuno Beltran de
Lopez de Legaspi, Miguel
Mahmud of Ghazni
Pizarro, Francisco
Tamerlane

CONSORT

Albert, Prince
Alexandra Caroline Mary Charlotte
Anne of Bohemia
Anne of Cleves
Bernhard, Prince
Boleyn, Anne
Catherine de Medici
Catherine of Aragon
Catherine of Valois
Charlotte Sophia
Cooke, Hope
Eleanor of Aquitaine
Elizabeth, the Queen Mother
Ferguson, Sarah Margaret
Frederika Louise
Howard, Catherine
Maintenon, Francoise d'Aubigne, Marquise
Margaret of Anjou
Marie Antoinette
Marie de Medicis
Marina
Mary
Nagako, Empress
Noor, Queen
Parr, Catherine
Philip, Prince
Seymour, Jane
Silvia
Theodora

CONSPIRATOR

Surratt, John Harrison
Surratt, Mary Eugenia Jenkins

CONTINENTAL CONGRESSMAN

Braxton, Carter
Harrison, Benjamin
Hart, John
Lee, Francis Lightfoot
Lee, Thomas Sim
Lewis, Francis
Livingston, Philip
Lowell, John
Lynch, Thomas, Jr.
Middleton, Arthur
Morris, Lewis
Morton, John
Paca, William
Penn, John
Randolph, Peyton
Read, George
Ross, George
Stockton, Richard
Thornton, Matthew
Whipple, William

COOK

Typhoid Mary

CORPORATION EXECUTIVE

Agee, William McReynolds
Anderson, Robert Orville
Anderson, Roy A(rnold)
Anderson, William Robert
Ash, Roy Lawrence
Axelson, Kenneth Strong
Bechtel, Steve (Stephen Davison, Jr.)
Berlin, Richard E
Bloomingdale, Alfred S
Bluhdorn, Charles G
Blumenthal, W Michael
Bobst, Elmer Holmes
Bricklin, Malcolm N
Cordiner, Ralph Jarron
Cunningham, R Walter
Fisher, Max Martin
Fisk, James Brown
Gottschalk, Robert
Jobs, Steven Paul
Keener, Jefferson Ward
Kirby, Robert Emory
Lauder, Joseph H
Love, George Hutchinson
Mahoney, David Joseph, Jr.
Mortimer, Charles Greenough
Olds, Irving S
Pfeiffer, Jane Cahill
Pickens, T(homas) Boone, (Jr.)
Stern, Leonard Norman
Stern, Max
Swearingen, John Eldred
Welch, John Francis, Jr.
Wrigley, William

COSMETICS EXECUTIVE

Arden, Elizabeth
Bergerac, Michel C
Bishop, Hazel
Factor, Max
Kay, Mary
Lauder, Estee
Quant, Mary
Revson, Charles Haskell
Rubinstein, Helena
Turner, Glenn Wesley
Westmore, Perc(ival)

COSMONAUT

Beregovoy, Georgi
Dobrovolsky, Georgi
Dzhanibekov, Vladimir Alexandrovich
Feoktistov, Konstantin Petrovich
Gagarin, Yuri Alexseyevich
Gorbatko, Viktor Vasiliyevich
Khrunov, Evgeny
Komarov, Vladimir
Kubasov, Valery Nikolaevich
Leonov, Alexei Arkhipovich
Nikolayev, Andrian G
Popovich, Pavel Romanovich
Rukavishnikov, Nikolai Nikolayevich
Savitskaya, Svetlana Y
Tereshkova-Nikolaeva, Valentina
Titov, Gherman Stepanovich (Herman)
Volkov, Vladislav

COURTESAN

Duplessis, Marie
Lais
Lenclos, Ninon de
Phryne

COURTIER

Beaumarchais, Pierre Augustin Caron de
Bellman, Carl Michael
Castiglione, Baldassare, Conte
Damocles
Devereaux, Robert
Montaigne, Michel Eyquem de
Raleigh, Walter, Sir
Sidney, Philip, Sir
Tyrrell, James, Sir

CRIMINAL

Apache Kid
Barfield, Velma
Barker, "Doc" Arthur
Barker, "Ma" Arizona Donnie Clark
Barker, Fred
Barker, Herman
Barker, Lloyd

Biggs, Ronald Arthur
Blumenfeld, Isadore
Carlisle, William
Cartouche, Louis Dominique
Chadwick, Cassie L
Chapman, Eddie (Edward Arnold)
Chessman, Caryl Whittier
Churchill, May (Beatrice Desmond)
Cooper, D B
Cutpurse, Moll
Dalton, William
DeSalvo, Albert
Deshayes, Catherine
Diamond, "Legs" Jack
Dillinger, John Herbert
Diver, Jenny
Escobedo, Danny
Esposito, Joseph
Floyd, "Pretty Boy" Charles Arthur
Harsh, George
Hill, Virginia
Holliday, "Doc" John Henry
Jackson, George
Jones, W D
Jukes, Margaret
Karpis, Alvin
Kelly, "Machine Gun" George R
Licavoli, Peter Joseph, Sr.
Licavoli, Thomas
Lohman, Ann Trow
Luciano, "Lucky" Charles
Lyons, Sophie Levy
Madden, Owen Victor
Mandelbaum, Fredericka
Miranda, Ernesto
Murphy, Jack R
Nelson, "Baby Face" George
Owen, Richard Lee, II
Parker, Bonnie
Peters, Frederick Emerson
Ponzi, Charles
Profaci, Joe (Joseph)
Sheppard, Jack
Shinburn, Mark
Stavisky, Serge Alexandre
Stroud, Robert Franklin
Sutton, Willie (William Francis)
Tieri, Frank
Turpin, Dick (Richard)
Valachi, Joe (Joseph M)
Weil, Joseph R

CRIMINALS

Scottsboro Boys
Younger Brothers, The

CRIMINOLOGIST

Bertillon, Alphonse
Glueck, Sheldon (Sol Sheldon)
Goddard, Calvin Hooker

Lawes, Lewis Edward
Lombroso, Cesare

CRITIC

Abercrombie, Lascelles
Aiken, Conrad Potter
Aldiss, Brian Wilson
Allen, Walter Ernest
Allsop, Kenneth
Alvarez, Alfred
Anderson, Lindsay Gordon
Arnold, Matthew
Austin, Alfred
Babbitt, Irving
Bangs, Lester
Barnes, Clive Alexander
Bax, Clifford
Bayle, Pierre
Bazin, Andre
Beach, Joseph Warren
Beerbohm, Max (Sir Henry Maximilian)
Bennett, Arnold
Bentley, Richard
Binyon, Laurence
Birney, Earle (Alfred Earle)
Blackmur, Richard Palmer
Blackwell, Mr. (Richard)
Blunden, Edmund Charles
Bodmer, Johann Jakob
Bogan, Louise
Boileau(-Despreaux), Nicolas
Bourget, Paul (Charles Joseph)
Bowra, Maurice, Sir
Bradley, Andrew Cecil
Braithwaite, William Stanley Beaumont
Breen, Joseph Ignatius
Brooks, Cleanth
Brown, John Mason
Callimachus
Campion, Thomas
Canby, Henry Seidel
Canby, Vincent
Carducci, Giosue
Carlyle, Thomas
Cassidy, Claudia
Cassou, Jean
Cecchi, Emilio
Cecil, Edward Christian David Gascoyne
Chamberlin, William Henry
Chambers, Edmund Kerchever, Sir
Chesterton, Gilbert Keith
Clark, Barrett H
Coleridge, Samuel Taylor
Colvin, Sidney, Sir
Croce, Benedetto
Dahlberg, Edward
Davidson, Donald Grady
Dent, Alan Holmes
DeSanctis, Francesco
DeVoto, Bernard Augustine
Dickey, James

Dobell, Sydney Thompson
Downes, Olin (Edwin Olin)
DuBois, Guy Pene
Dyce. Alexander
Einstein, Alfred
Eliot, T(homas) S(tearns)
Empson, William, Sir
Ernst, Paul
Fadiman, Clifton Paul
Faure, Elie
Fletcher, John Gould
France, Anatole, pseud.
Frankenstein, Alfred Victor
Frawley, Dennis
Fuller, Hoyt William
Fuller, Margaret
Gannett, Lewis Stiles
Gaunt, William
Gautier, Theophile (Pierre Jules Theophile)
Gide, Andre Paul Guillaume
Gilliatt, Penelope Ann Douglas
Gissing, George Robert
Gordon, Caroline
Gould, Jack
Granville-Barker, Harley
Harewood, George Henry Hubert Lascelles,
    Earl
Harris, Leonard
Heine, Heinrich
Herder, Johann G von
Highet, Gilbert Arthur
Howe, Irving
Huneker, James Gibbons
Huxley, Aldous Leonard
Huxtable, Ada Louise
Johnson, Pamela Hansford
Johnson, Samuel
Kauffmann, Stanley Jules
Kazin, Alfred
Khodasevich, Vladislav
Krasna, Norman
Lahr, John
Lambert, J(ack) W(alter)
Laver, James
Lawrence, Robert
Levin, Bernard
Lewis, Saunders
Lowell, Amy
Lyons, James
MacDonald, Dwight
Meres, Francis
Merimee, Prosper
Millar, Jeff(rey) Lynn
Miller, Perry Gilbert Eddy
Molloy, John T
Montale, Eugenio
More, Paul Elmer
Muir, Edwin
Nachman, Gerald Weil
Nathan, George Jean
North, Sterling

Cecchetti, Enrico
Chace, Marian
Chakiris, George
Champion, Gower
Champion, Marge Celeste
Chappell, William
Charisse, Cyd
Charlip, Remy
Chauvire, Yvette
Checker, Chubby
Chouteau, Yvonne
Cranko, John
Cunningham, Merce
Dailey, Dan
Danielian, Leon
Davis, Sammy, Jr.
DeLavallade, Carmen
DeMarco, Tony
DeMille, Agnes George
Dolin, Anton, Sir
Dolly, Jenny
Dolly, Rosie
Donohue, Jack
Douvillier, Suzanne Theodore Vaillande
Dowell, Anthony
Draper, Paul
Duncan, Isadora
Dunham, Katherine
Ebsen, Buddy
Falana, Lola
Falco, Louis
Feld, Eliot
Fokine, Michel
Foy, Eddie, Jr.
Frankel, Emily
Franklin, Bonnie Gail
Franklin, Frederic
Fuller, Loie
Gaynor, Mitzi
Geva, Tamara
Goodman, Dody
Graham, Martha
Greco, Jose
Grey, Joel
Grimes, Tammy Lee
Haney, Carol
Hartman, Grace
Harwood, Vanessa Clare
Heatherton, Joey
Hightower, Rosella
Hines, Gregory Oliver
Holmes, Anna Marie
Holmes, David
Horst, Louis
Hulbert, Jack
Humphrey, Doris
Jahan, Marine
Jamison, Judith
Jeanmaire, Renee Marcelle
Joyce, Elaine
Keeler, Ruby

Kelly, Gene
Kitchell, Iva
Kylian, Jiri
Lawrence, Carol
Lee, Michele
Limon, Jose Arcadio
Loring, Eugene
Losch, Tilly
Lubovitch, Lar
MacLaine, Shirley
Martins, Peter
Massine, Leonide Fedorovich
Mata Hari
McKechnie, Donna
Miller, Ann
Miranda, Carmen
Mitchell, Arthur
Montez, Lola
Murray, Arthur
Murray, Kathryn Hazel
Murray, Mae
Nelson, Gene
Newmar, Julie
Nijinsky, Vaslav
O'Connor, Donald
Petipa, Marius
Petit, Roland
Piro, Frank
Powell, Eleanor
Premice, Josephine
Prescott, Ken
Provine, Dorothy Michele
Prowse, Juliet
Ragozina, Galina
Rand, Sally
Reinking, Ann
Rivera, Chita
Robinson, Bill
Rogers, Ginger
Saint Denis, Ruth
Schaufuss, Peter
Shankar, Uday
Shawn, Ted (Edwin Meyers)
Shearer, Moira
Slavenska, Mia
Somes, Michael
Tallchief, Maria
Tamiris, Helen
Taylor, June
Taylor, Paul
Tharp, Twyla
Toumanova, Tamara
Van, Bobby
Vera-Ellen
Verdon, Gwen (Gwyneth Evelyn)
Vereen, Ben
Warren, Lesley Ann
Weidman, Charles
Zorina, Vera

DANDY

Brummell, "Beau" George Bryan

DENTIST

Allen, John
Angle, Edward Hartley
Blaiberg, Philip
Clark, Barney Bailey
Dean, Henry Trendley
Holliday, "Doc" (John Henry
Morton, William Thomas Green
Taylor, Lucy Hobbs
Welch, Thomas B
Wells, Horace

DESIGNER

Adam, Ken
Aldredge, Theoni A(thanasiou Vashlioti)
Alter, Hobie (Hobart, Jr.)
Aronson, Boris
Ashley, Laura Mountney
Baker, Rick
Baldwin, Billy
Baldwin, William, Jr.
Banton, Travis
Beall, Lester Thomas
Beaton, Cecil Walter Hardy, Sir
Berman, Eugene
Bernstein, Alice Frankau
Bertoia, Harry
Biba
Bodoni, Giambattista
Bogner, Willi
Bosin, Blackbear
Boulle, Charles Andre
Breuer, Marcel Lajos
Brodovitch, Alexey
Burtin, Will
Capezio, Salvatore
Carfagno, Edward
Castel, Frederic
Chermayeff, Ivan
Chwast, Seymour
Clark, Peggy
Clodagh
Conley, Renie
Craig, Gordon (Edward Henry Gordon)
Cranach, Lucas
Delaunay-Terk, Sonia
DiCamerino, Roberta
Donati, Danilo
Donghia, Angelo R
Draddy, Vincent de Paul
Dreyfuss, Henry
Eames, Charles
Evins, David
Famolare, Joseph P
Fisher, Avery
Fisher, Jules

Ford, Charlotte
Fox, Uffa
Frizon, Maud
Geddes, Norman Bel
Geddes, Patrick, Sir
Godwin, Edward William
Gucci, Aldo
Hermes, Thierry
Hicks, David Nightingale
Hood, Frederick Emmart
Ironside, Christopher
Jaeger, Gustav
Jean Louis
John, John Pico
Jones, Robert Edmond
Kahn, Ben
Lane, Kenneth Jay
Lelong, Lucien
Lenox, Walter S
Levine, Beth
Levine, Herbert
Lexcen, Ben
Liebes, Dorothy Katherine Wright
Lionni, Leo
Loewy, Raymond Fernand
Lubalin, Herbert Frederick
Lucile
Lustig, Alvin
MacLiammoir, Michael
Max, Peter
McCobb, Paul
Messel, Oliver
Mielziner, Jo
Moholy-Nagy, Laszlo
Mori, Hanae
Morton, (Henry) Digby
Muller-Munk, Peter
Nash, Paul
Nelson, George H.
Nichols, Dale
Noguchi, Isamu
Oenslager, Donald Mitchell
Peretti, Elsa
Picasso, Paloma
Piech, Paul Peter
Potok, Anna Maximilian Apfelbaum
Pucci, Emilio Marchese di Barsento
Pulitzer, Lilly
Rand, Paul
Rhodes, Zandra
Ricci, Nina
Roebling, John Augustus
Rogers, Bruce
Roller, Alfred
Rosenstein, Nettie
Rosenthal, Jean
Russell, Sydney Gordon, Sir
Scott, Ken
Sharaff, Irene
Sheraton, Thomas
Smith, Oliver

Steinman, David Barnard
Sylbert, Paul
Tassell, Gustave
Teague, Walter Dorwin
Ter-Arutunian, Rouben
Thomas, Bill
Thompson, Bradbury James
Throckmorton, Cleon
Tiffany, Louis Comfort
Toms, Carl
Trnks, Jiri
Turkle, Brinton Cassaday
Urban, Joseph Maria
Van Heusen, John
Vanderbilt, Gloria Morgan
Vera
Victor, Sally Josephs
Wagner, Robin
Walton, Tony
Wheeler, Candace Thurber
White, Miles
Willis, Mary
Wittop, Freddy
Wolsky, Albert
Wragge, Sidney
Wright, Russel
Zipprodt, Patricia

DETECTIVE

Burns, William John
Fabian, Robert Honey
Pinkerton, Allan

DIARIST

Brant, Alice Dayrell
Frank, Anne
Pepys, Samuel

DIPLOMAT

Aga Khan, Sadruddin, Prince
Agar, Herbert Sebastian
Ali, Ahmed
Alphand, Herve
Amerasinghe, Hamilton Shirley
Anderson, Eugenie Moore
Anderson, George Everett
Angell, James Burrill
Annenberg, Walter Hubert
Armour, Norman
Asencio, Diego Cortes
Asturias, Miguel Angel
Attwood, William
Bancroft, George
Barbour, Walworth
Baring, Maurice
Barlow, Joel
Bartholomew, Reginald
Ben-Elissar, Eliahu
Bentley, Alvin Morell

Berger, Samuel David
Berle, Adolf Augustus, Jr.
Bernadotte, Folke, Count
Black, Shirley Temple
Bliss, Robert Woods
Bodley, Thomas, Sir
Bohlen, Charles Eustis
Bowers, Claude Gernade
Bowles, Chester Bliss
Braden, Spruille
Briggs, Ellis Ormsbee
Brooks, Angie Elizabeth
Brosio, Manilo Giovanni
Bruce Lockhart, Robert Hamilton, Sir
Bruce, David Kirkpatrick Estes
Bryce, James Bryce, Viscount
Bunker, Ellsworth
Burckhardt, Carl Jacob
Cabot, John Moors
Cadogan, William
Carlucci, Frank Charles, III
Casement, Roger David
Castiglione, Baldassare, Conte
Ch'oe Kyu Ha
Chapman, Christian Addison
Clarke, Ellis Emmanuel
Claudel, Paul Louis Charles
Coeur, Jacques
Cole, Charles Woolsey
Comines, Philippe de
Conant, James Bryant
Cooper, John Sherman
Cordier, Andrew Wellington
Crowe, Colin Tradescant, Sir
Cruz, Arturo
Cushing, Caleb
Davies, Joseph Edward
Davies, Rodger Paul
Dean, John Gunther
Dean, Patrick Henry, Sir
Dillon, (Clarence) Douglas
Dinitz, Simcha
Dobrynin, Anatoly Fedorovich
Dubs, Adolph
Duke, Angier Biddle
Dulles, Allen Welsh
Dulles, Eleanor Lansing
Dyer, Edward, Sir
Eban, Abba
Eisenhower, John Sheldon Doud
Finletter, Thomas Knight
Galbraith, John Kenneth
Gary, Romain
Gavin, John
Genscher, Hans-Dietrich
Ghorbal, Ashraf A.
Giraudoux, Jean
Gopallawa, William
Graves, Harold Nathan
Gromyko, Andrei Andreevich
Habib, Philip Charles

Hallstein, Walter
Harlech, William David Ormsby-Gore,
  Baron
Harvey, George Brinton M
Herter, Christian Archibald
Hoare, Samuel John Gurney, Sir
House, Edward Mandell
Hurley, Patrick Jay
Irving, Washington
Jarring, Gunnar V
Jay, Peter
Jessup, Philip Caryl
Jobert, Michel
Johnson, Reverdy
Johnson, U(ral) Alexis
Kampelman, Max M
Kennan, George Frost
Kennedy, Joseph Patrick, Sr.
Kirk, Alan Goodrich
Kirkpatrick, Jeane Duane Jordan
Kneip, Richard
Kurusu, Saburo
Kuznetsov, Vasili Vasilievich
Laingen, (Lowell) Bruce
Lancaster, Bruce Morgan
Leger, Alexis St. Leger (Marie-Rene Alexis
  St. Leger)
Lesseps, Ferdinand Marie de
Letelier, Orlando
Lie, Trygve Halvdan
Linowitz, Sol
Livingston, Robert R
Lockhart, (Robert Hamilton) Bruce, (Sir)
Lodge, Henry Cabot, Jr.
Lopez Bravo, Gregorio
Lord, Mary Pillsbury
Luns, Joseph Marie Antoine Hubert
Lytton, Edward Robert Bulwer-Lytton,
  Earl
MacDonald, Malcolm John
Malik, Yakov Alexandrovich
Maltsev, Victor Fyodorovich
Martin, Graham Anderson
Massey, Vincent
Maurer, Ion Gheorghe
McCloskey, Robert James
McCloy, John Jay
McGee, Gale William
Mein, J Gordon
Meloy, Francis Edward, Jr.
Mesta, Perle Skirvin
Middendorf, John William
Mitchell, Clarence M
Moncreiffe, Jain (Rupert Jain)
Monnet, Jean (Omer Gabriel)
Morgenthau, Henry
Morris, Gouverneur
Morrow, Dwight Whitney
Mortada, Saad
Motley, John L
Moynihan, Daniel Patrick

Myrdal, Alva Reimer
Neruda, Pablo
Neumann, Robert Gerhard
Nguyen thi Binh, Madame
Nicot, Jean
Noel-Baker, Philip John
O'Brien, Conor Cruise
O'Dwyer, William
Page, Thomas Nelson
Pandit, Vijaya Lakshmi (Nehru)
Papen, Franz von
Patino, Simon Iturri
Perez de la Cova, Carlos
Pinkney, William
Plimpton, Francis Taylor Pearson
Prior, Matthew
Quaison-Sackey, Alex(ander)
Ramsbotham, Peter, Sir
Reid, Whitelaw
Richelieu, Louis Francois Armand de
Roa (y Garcia), Raul
Rohde, Ruth Bryan Owen
Rosecrans, William Starke
Rowan, Carl Thomas
Rubirosa, Porfirio
Saxbe, William Bart
Scali, John Alfred
Scheel, Walter
Schurman, Jacob Gould
Seferiades, Giorgos Styljanou
Service, John Stewart
Shannon, William Vincent
Shevardnadze, Eduard Amvrosiyevich
Shevchenko, Arkady Nikolayevich
Shotwell, James Thomson
Spaak, Fernand Paul Jules
Stephens, John Lloyd
Stevenson, Adlai Ewing, Jr.
Straus, Oscar
Sullivan, Mark
Taylor, Henry Junior
Taylor, Kenneth Douglas
Tomlinson, Frank
Toon, Malcolm
Urquhart, Brian Edward
Vishinskii, Andrei Yanuarevich
Volpe, John Anthony
Wallenberg, Raoul Gustav
Walters, Vernon Anthony
Wang Shih-chieh
Welles, Sumner
Whitlock, Brand
Whitney, John Hay
Wiggins, J(ames) R(ussell)
Williams, G Mennen
Woodcock, Leonard Freel
Yost, Charles Woodruff
Young, Owen

DIRECTOR

Abbott, George Francis
Abrahams, Jim
Achard, Marcel
Ackerman, Robert Allan
Adler, Luther (Lutha)
Alda, Alan
Aldrich, Robert
Aldridge, Michael
Alexandrov, Grigori
Allegret, Yves
Allen, Irwin
Altman, Robert B
Anderson, John Murray
Anderson, Lindsay Gordon
Anderson, Michael
Anger, Kenneth
Annaud, Jean-Jacques
Antonioni, Michelangelo
Arbuckle, "Fatty" Roscoe Conkling
Arkin, Alan Wolf
Artaud, Antonin
Arzner, Dorothy
Ashby, Hal
Asquith, Anthony
Astin, John Allen
Attenborough, Richard Samuel, Sir
Audiard, Michel
Averback, Hy
Ayckbourn, Alan
Ayres, Lew
Baer, Max, Jr.
Baldwin, James Arthur
Banks, Leslie
Banks, Monty (Montague)
Banner, Bob
Barrault, Jean-Louis
Baryshnikov, Mikhail
Bass, Saul
Beatty, Roger
Beatty, Warren
Becker, Jacques
Benedictus, David
Benton, Robert Douglass
Bergman, Ingmar
Berkeley, Busby
Bern, Paul
Bernhardt, Melvin
Bertolucci, Bernardo
Bestor, Arthur Eugene
Biberman, Herbert
Bill, Tony
Bogdanovich, Peter
Bondarchuk, Sergei
Bonerz, Peter
Bonstelle, Jessie
Boorman, John
Borzage, Frank
Boulting, John
Bracken, Eddie (Edward Vincent)
Brent, Romney

Bresson, Robert
Bridges, James
Brook, Peter
Brooks, James L
Brooks, Mel
Brooks, Richard
Brosten, Harve
Brown, Clarence
Browning, Tod
Bunuel, Luis
Burrows, James
Butler, Robert
Buzzell, Eddie
Caan, James
Cacoyannis, Michael
Caldwell, Sarah
Camerini, Mario
Cameron, James
Camus, Marcel
Capra, Frank
Cariou, Len (Leonard)
Carlisle, Kevin
Carne, Marcel
Carpenter, John
Carr, Martin
Cassavetes, John
Castle, William
Cates, Joseph
Cavalcanti, Alberto
Cayatte, Andre
Chabrol, Claude
Chaikin, Joseph
Chekhov, Michael
Chodorov, Edward
Chodorov, Jerome
Chomsky, Marvin
Christian-Jaque
Chukrai, Grigori
Cimino, Michael
Ciulei, Liviu
Clark, Barrett H
Clarke, Shirley
Clayton, Herbert
Clayton, Jack
Clement, Rene
Clouzot, Henri-George
Clurman, Harold Edgar
Cocteau, Jean
Collier, William, Sr.
Comencini, Luigi
Conrad, William
Conway, Jack
Coppola, Francis Ford
Corman, Roger William
Cornelius, Henry
Corsaro, Frank
Corwin, Norman
Costa-Gavras(, Henri)
Craig, Gordon (Edward Henry Gordon)
Craven, Frank
Crichton, (John) Michael

Crichton, Charles
Croft, Michael
Cromwell, John
Cronyn, Hume
Crothers, Rachel
Cukor, George Dewey
Curtis, Heber Doust
Curtiz, Michael
DaCosta, Morton
Dalrymple, Jean
DaSilva, Howard
Dassin, Jules
Daubeny, Peter Lauderdale, Sir
Dean, Basil
DeCordova, Frederick Timmins
Delannoy, Jean
DelRuth, Roy
DeMille, Cecil B(lount)
Demme, Jonathan
Demy, Jacques
DePalma, Brian Russell
DeSantis, Giuseppe
DeSica, Vittorio
Dexter, John
Dieterle, William
Dmytryk, Edward
Donati, Pino
Donehue, Vincent J
Donen, Stanley
Donohue, Jack
Dovzhenko, Alexander
Dreyer, Carl Theodore
Dunlop, Frank
Duvivier, Julien
Dwan, Allan
Dyer, Charles
Eastwood, Clint
Ebert, Carl (Anton Charles)
Edwards, Blake
Eisenstein, Sergei Mikhailovich
Erman, John
Evans, Jerry
Eyen, Tom
Fabri, Zoltan
Faison, George
Farrow, John Villiers
Fassbinder, Rainer Werner
Feldman, Marty
Fellini, Federico
Felsenstein, Walter
Fenton, Leslie
Fernald, John Bailey
Ferrer, Jose Vicente
Feuer, Cy
Feuillade, Louis
Field, Ron
Fields, Joseph
Finney, Albert
Fisher, Terence
Flaherty, Robert Joseph
Fleming, Victor

Forbes, Bryan
Ford, Alexander
Ford, John
Foreman, Carl
Forman, Milos
Fosse, Bob
Foster, Norman
Francis, Freddie
Frankenheimer, John
Freedman, Gerald
Freleng, Friz
Friedkin, William
Fugard, Athol Harold
Fuller, Samuel
Furie, Sidney J
Furman, Roger
Gabel, Martin
Gance, Abel
Garrett, Lila
Gassman, Vittorio
Gentele, Goeran
Gerasimov, Sergei Appolinarievich
Germi, Pietro
Ghiringhelli, Antonio
Gielgud, (Arthur) John, Sir
Godard, Jean Luc
Goldovsky, Boris
Gordon, Steve
Gordone, Charles
Goulding, Edmund
Graf, Herbert
Greenspan, Bud
Gribble, Harry Wagstaff Graham
Griffith, D(avid Lewelyn) W(ark)
Grodin, Charles
Guitry, Sacha
Gunn, Moses
Guthrie, Tyrone
Guy-Blanche, Alice
Hackford, Taylor
Haley, Jack, Jr. (John J.)
Hall, Peter Reginald Frederick, Sir
Hamer, Robert
Hamilton, Guy
Hancock, John D
Harlan, Veit
Hart, Moss
Harvey, Anthony
Harvey, Frank Laird
Hathaway, Henry
Hawks, Howard Winchester
Haydn, Richard
Hemion, Dwight
Henreid, Paul
Herbert, John, pseud.
Herzog, Werner
Hilbert, Egon
Hill, George Roy
Hiller, Arthur
Hitchcock, Alfred Joseph, Sir
Hofsiss, Jack Bernard

Hopkins, Arthur
Hopper, Dennis
Hough, John
Houseman, John
Howard, Ron
Huston, John
Hutt, William Ian Dewitt
Ince, Thomas H(arper)
Irving, Jules
Ivens, Joris
Ivory, James
Jancso, Miklos
Jewison, Norman
Johnson, Nunnally
Jones, Terry
Jutra, Claude
Kalatozov, Mikhail
Kanin, Garson
Kanter, Hal
Kasdan, Lawrence Edward
Kautner, Helmut
Kazan, Elia
King, Henry
Kinugasa, Teinousuke
Kramer, Stanley E
Kubrick, Stanley
Kurosawa, Akira
Lamas, Fernando
Landis, John David
Landon, Michael
Lang, Fritz
Laughlin, Tom
Lawrence, Bill
Leach, Will (Wilford Carson)
Lean, David
Lee, Will
LeLouch, Claude
Leontovich, Eugenie
Leroy, Mervyn
Lester, Richard
Liebman, Max
Lindtberg, Leopold
Littlewood, Joan
Litvak, Anatole
Lloyd, Frank
Logan, Josh(ua Lockwood)
Losey, Joseph
Lubitsch, Ernst
Lucas, George
Lumet, Sidney
MacArthur, Charles
Mackendrick, Alexander
MacLiammoir, Michael
Malick, Terence (Terry)
Malle, Louis
Mamoulian, Rouben
Mankiewicz, Joseph Lee
Mann, Paul
Manulis, Martin
Margolin, Stuart
Marker, Chris

May, Elaine
Mazursky, Paul
McCarey, Leo
McEwen, Terence Alexander (Terry)
McKellen, Ian Murray
Meisner, Sanford
Melford, Austin (Alfred Austin)
Melies, Georges
Melville, Jean-Pierre
Menzel, Jiri
Meyer, Nicholas
Meyer, Russ
Milestone, Lewis
Milland, Ray(mond Alton)
Miller, Jonathan
Milligan, "Spike" (Terence Alan
Minnelli, Vincente
Mirisch, Walter Mortimer
Mizoguchi, Kenji
Monicelli, Mario
Montgomery, Robert Henry
Morris, Howard
Moss, Arnold
Murnau, Friedrich W
Needham, Hal
Negulesco, Jean
Nemec, Jan
Neville, John
Newman, Paul
Niblo, Fred
Nichols, Mike
Nicholson, Jack
Nugent, Elliott
Nunn, Trevor Robert
O'Horgan, Tom
Olivier, Laurence Kerr Olivier, Sir
Ophuls, Marcel
Ophuls, Max
Oshima, Nagrsa
Pabst, Georg Wilhelm
Pakula, Alan Jay
Pal, George
Paltrow, Bruce
Panama, Norman
Papp, Joseph
Paris, Jerry
Parker, Alan William
Parks, Gordon Alexander Buchanan
Parks, Gordon, Jr.
Pasolini, Pier Paolo
Paterson, Tom
Peckinpah, (David) Sam(uel)
Pemberton, Brock
Penn, Arthur Heller
Perry, Antoinette
Perry, Frank
Peterson, Wolfgang
Petri, Elio
Philipe, Gerard
Phillips, Robin
Pierson, Frank R(omer)

Pitlik, Noam
Poitier, Sidney
Polanski, Roman
Pollack, Sydney
Pontecorvo, Gillo (Gilberto)
Porter, Edwin
Powell, Michael
Preminger, Otto Ludwig
Prescott, Ken
Prince, Hal (Harold Smith)
Pudovkin, Vsevolod
Putch, William Henry
Quayle, Anthony
Quine, Richard
Quintero, Jose
Rambert, Dame Marie
Ratoff, Gregory
Ray, Nicholas
Ray, Satyajit
Redford, Robert
Reed, Carol, Sir
Reilly, Charles Nelson
Reiner, Rob(ert)
Reinhardt, Max
Reisz, Karel
Reitman, Ivan
Renoir, Jean
Resnais, Alain
Rey, Alejandro
Richardson, Tony
Riefenstahl, Leni (Helene Bertha Amalie)
Ritchard, Cyril
Ritt, Martin
Rivers, Joan
Roach, Hal
Rogell, Albert S
Rohmer, Eric, pseud.
Romm, Mikhail
Roose-Evans, James
Ross, David
Ross, David
Ross, Herbert David
Rossellini, Roberto
Rossen, Robert
Rush, Richard
Russell, Ken
Ryder, Alfred
Sachse, Leopold
Saks, Gene
Sandrich, Jay
Sands, Dorothy
Saura Carlos (Atares Carlos)
Schifter, Peter Mark
Schlesinger, John Richard
Schlondorff, Volker
Schneider, Alan
Schrader, Paul Joseph
Schwartz, Maurice
Scorsese, Martin
Seaton, George
Sedelmaier, Joe (John Josef)

Seidelman, Susan
Sellars, Peter
Sennett, Mack
Serban, Andrei George
Sherman, Lowell
Sherman, Vincent
Shukshin, Vasilii Makarovich
Shumlin, Herman Elliott
Sidaris, Andy
Sidney, George
Silverstein, Elliot
Sim, Alastair
Siodmark, Curt
Sirk, Douglas
Sjoberg, Alf
Sjostrom, Victor
Soria, Dario
Spielberg, Steven
Stallone, Sylvester (Michael Sylvester)
Stanislavsky, Konstantin Sergeyevich
Stein, Meridee
Stern, Sandor
Stevens, George
Stevens, Leslie
Stevenson, Robert
Stiller, Mauritz
Stone, Ezra (Chaim)
Stuart, Mel
Sturges, Preston
Svanholm, Set
Swados, Elizabeth A (Liz)
Syberberg, Hans Jurgen
Sylbert, Paul
Tati, Jacques
Taurog, Norman
Taylor, William Desmond
Tebelak, John Michael
Teshigahara, Hiroshi
Torre-Nilsson, Leopoldo
Tors, Ivan
Traube, Shepard
Travers, Bill
Troell, Jan
Truffaut, Francois
Tune, Tommy (Thomas James)
Tyne, George
Vadim, Roger
Van Dyke, W(oodbridge) S(trong)
Varda, Agnes
Verdy, Violette
Vidor, King Wallis
Vigo, Jean
Visconti, Luchino
VonSternberg, Josef
VonStroheim, Erich
Voskovec, George
Wagner, Jane
Wagner, Wieland Adolf Gottfried
Wajda, Andrzej
Walker, Stuart Armstrong
Wallerstein, Lothar

Walsh, Raoul
Walston, Ray
Walters, Charles
Wanamaker, Sam
Waxman, Al
Wayne, John
Webb, Jack Randolph
Weber, Carl
Weber, Lois
Webster, Margaret
Weill, Claudia
Weir, Peter
Welles, Orson (George Orson)
Wellman, William Augustus
Wenders, Wim
Wertmuller, Lina von Eigg
Wexler, Haskell
Whale, James
White, George
Whorf, Richard
Widerberg, Bo
Wilde, Cornel
Wilder, "Billy" Samuel
Wilson, Richard
Wise, Robert
Witt, Paul Junger
Wolfe, Digby
Wood, Samuel Grosvenor
Wyler, William
Yates, Peter
Young, Terence
Zampa, Luigi
Zeffirelli, Franco
Zetterling, Mai Elisabeth
Zieff, Howard
Zinnemann, Fred

DISC JOCKEY

Kaufman, Murray

DISSIDENT

Amalrik, Andrei Alekseyevich
Sakharov, Andrei Dmitrievich

DISTILLER

Beam, James B
Bronfman, Edgar Miles
Bronfman, Samuel
Seagram, Joseph Edward Frowde
Seagram, Joseph William
Walker, Hiram

DOCTOR

Palmer, William

DRAMA CRITIC

Agate, James Evershed
Atkinson, (Justin) Brooks
Bentley, Eric
Chapman, John (Arthur)
Cheney, Sheldon Warren
Gibbs, Woolcott
Gill, Brendan
Glover, William H
Gottfried, Martin
Hewes, Henry
Hobson, Harold
Kalem, Ted
Kerr, Walter Francis
Krutch, Joseph Wood
Mantle, (Robert) Burns
Morrison, Hobe
Nicoll, (John Ramsay) Allardyce
Norton, Elliott
Oliver, Edith
Simon, John Ivan
Stallings, Laurence
Tynan, Kenneth Peacock
Watts, Richard, Jr.

DRAMATIST

A'Beckett, Gilbert Abbott
Abbott, George Francis
Ableman, Paul
Achard, Marcel
Adamov, Arthur
Addison, Joseph
Ade, George
Aeschylus
Akins, Zoe
Alarcon y Mendoza, Juan Ruiz de
Albee, Edward Franklin, III
Alfieri, Vittorio
Alfred, William
Ambrose, David Edwin
Anderson, Maxwell
Anderson, Robert Woodruff
Andreyev, Leonid Nikolayevich
Anouilh, Jean Marie Lucienpierre
Arden, John
Aretino, Pietro
Aristophanes
Arrabal (Teran), Fernando
Artsybashev, Mikhail Petrovich
Asch, Sholem
Auden, W(ystan) H(ugh)
Auletta, Robert
Axelrod, George
Ayckbourn, Alan
Babel, Isaac Emmanuelovich
Bagnold, Enid
Balderston, John Lloyd
Baldwin, James Arthur
Balzac, Honore de
Barlach, Ernst Heinrich

Barnes, Margaret Ayer
Barrie, James Matthew, Sir
Barry, Philip
Bart, Lionel
Bax, Clifford
Beaumarchais, Pierre Augustin Caron de
Beaumont, Francis
Beck, Julian
Beckett, Samuel Barclay
Behan, Brendan
Behn, Aphra
Behrman, S(amuel) N(athaniel)
Bein, Albert
Belasco, David
Benavente y Martinez, Jacinto
Benedictus, David
Betti, Ugo
Bissell, Richard
Bolt, Carol
Bolton, Guy Reginald
Bond, Edward
Bonham, Frank
Bottomley, Gordon
Bradford, Roark
Brecht, Bertolt Eugene Friedrich
Brent, Romney
Brentano, Clemens Maria
Bridie, James, pseud.
Brieux, Eugene
Broadhurst, Kent
Brown, Kenneth H
Bulgakov, Mikhail
Bullins, Ed
Burgoyne, John
Burrows, Abe (Abram S)
Calderon de la Barca, Pedro
Carlino, Lewis John
Cartland, Barbara Hamilton
Cervantes (Saavedra), Miguel(de)
Chapman, George
Chase, Mary Coyle
Chayefsky, "Paddy" Sidney
Chekhov, Anton Pavlovich
Chikamatsu, Monzaemon
Chodorov, Jerome
Chorell, Walentin
Christie, Agatha Mary Clarissa Miller, Dame
Churchill, Caryl
Cibber, Colley
Claus, Hugo
Cleland, John
Coburn, D(onald) L(ee)
Cohan, George M(ichael)
Collier, William, Sr.
Colum, Padraic
Congreve, William
Conkle, Ellsworth Prouty
Connelly, Marc(us Cook)
Cook, Michael
Cooper, Giles (Stannus)

Copeau, Jacques
Coppee, Francois Edouard Joachim
Corneille, Pierre
Coulter, John William
Coward, Noel Pierce, Sir
Cowl, Jane
Cox, Constance
Craven, Frank
Crean, Robert
Cristofer, Michael
Crothers, Rachel
Cueva de Garoza, Juan de la
Curel, Francois de
Curtis, Jackie
Daly, Augustin
Daniel, Samuel
Dante, Nicholas
Davenant, William, Sir
Davis, Ossie
Davis, Owen
Dekker, Thomas
Delaney, Shelagh
Delderfield, Ronald Frederick
Dell, Floyd
Dickens, Charles John Huffam
Dodsley, Robert
Doherty, Brian
Donleavy, James Patrick
Dowling, Eddie (Edward)
Dryden, John
Ducis, Jean Francois
Dumas, Alexandre
Dumas, Alexandre
Duveyrier, Anne Honore
Echegaray, Jose
Edgar, David
Epstein, Philip G
Espriu, Salvador
Euripides
Eyen, Tom
Farquhar, George
Feuchtwanger, Lion
Feuillet, Octave
Feydeau, Georges
Field, Rachel Lyman
Fielding, Henry
Fierstein, Harvey Forbes
Fitch, (William) Clyde
Fletcher, John
Ford, John
Foster, Paul
Franken, Rose
Friel, Brian
Frings, Ketti
Fry, Christopher
Fugard, Athol Harold
Fuller, Charles
Fulton, Maude
Galsworthy, John
Garcia Lorca, Federico
Gay, John

Gelber, Jack
Genet, Jean
Genet, Louis Rene Fernandat
Ghelderode, Michel de
Gibson, Wildred Wilson
Gibson, William
Gielgud, Val Henry
Gilbert, William Schwenck, Sir
Gilles, D(onald) B(ruce)
Gillette, William Hooker
Gilroy, Frank D
Giraudoux, Jean
Glaspell, Susan Keating
Glass, Montague (Marsden)
Godden, Rumer, pseud.
Goethe, Johann Wolfgang von
Golden, John
Goldman, James
Goldoni, Carlo
Goldsmith, Oliver
Gordon, Ruth
Gordone, Charles
Gorky, Maxim, pseud.
Granville-Barker, Harley
Gray, Simon James Holliday
Green, Adolph
Green, Paul Eliot
Gregory, Isabella Augusta Persse, Lady
Gribble, Harry Wagstaff Graham
Grillo, John
Grillparzer, Franz
Guare, John
Guitry, Sacha
Gurney, A(lbert) R(amsdell), Jr.
Hamilton, Patrick
Hampton, Christopher James
Hanley, William
Hansberry, Lorraine
Hare, David
Harrigan, Edward
Hart, Moss
Havel, Vaclav
Hayes, Alfred
Hecht, Ben
Heggen, Thomas Orls, Jr.
Heller, Joseph
Hellman, Lillian
Henley, Beth
Herbert, John, pseud.
Heywood, Thomas
Hochhuth, Rolf
Hofmannsthal, Hugo Hoffmann
Holm, John Cecil
Hooker, Brian
Hopwood, Avery
Horovitz, Israel
Housman, Laurence
Howard, Bronson Crocker
Howard, Sidney Coe
Hughes, Richard Arthur Warren
Hugo, Victor Marie

Ibsen, Henrik
Inge, William
Innaurato, Albert
Ionesco, Eugene
Isherwood, Christopher William
Jarry, Alfred
Jeffers, (John) Robinson
Jellicoe, Ann
Jennings, Talbot
Jones, Leroi
Jones, Preston St. Vrain
Jones, Tom
Jonson, Ben(jamin)
Jouy, Victor (Joseph-Etienne) de
Kaiser, Georg
Kaufman, George S(imon)
Keefe, Barrie Colin
Kelly, George Edward
Kennedy, Adrienne
Kerr, Jean
Kesselring, Joseph
Kharitonov, Yevgeni
Killigrew, Thomas
Kingsley, Sidney
Kleist, Heinrich von
Kopit, Arthur L
Kramm, Joseph
Krasna, Norman
Kreymborg, Alfred
Kulish, Mykola
Kurnitz, Harry
Kyd, Thomas
Lagerkvist, Par
Langer, Lawrence
LaPlace, Pierre-Antoine de
Laszlo, Miklos
Laurents, Arthur
Lawrence, Jerome
Lawson, John Howard
Laxness, Halldor Kiljan
Lea, Fanny Heaslip
Leblanc, Maurice
Lemon, Mark
Leonard, Hugh, pseud.
Lerner, Alan Jay
Lesage, Alain Rene
Lewis, Saunders
Lewis, Sinclair
Lindsay, Howard
Livius Andronicus
Llewellyn, Richard
Long, John Luther
Loos, Anita
Lope de Vega
Lortz, Richard
Lowell, Robert Trail Spence, Jr.
Luce, Clare Boothe
Ludlam, Charles
Lupino, Stanley
MacArthur, Charles
Machado, Manuel

MacKaye, Percy Wallace
Maeterlinck, Maurice
Mamet, David
Marcel, Gabriel Honore
Marcus, Frank
Marlowe, Christopher
Marmontel, Jean Francois
Marquis, Don Robert Perry
Martinez, Sierra Gregorio
Masefield, John
Masters, Edgar Lee
Maugham, William Somerset
Mayakovsky, Vladimir
McClure, Michael
McIntyre, John Thomas
McNally, Terrence
Mercer, David
Metastasio, Pietro
Middleton, Thomas
Miller, Arthur
Miller, Jason
Moeller, Philip
Moliere, pseud.
Molnar, Ferenc
Monteleone, Thomas F(rancis)
Moody, William Vaughn
Morley, Robert
Mosel, Tad
Mosenthal, Salomon Hermann von
Nash, Thomas
Neal, Larry (Lawrence P)
Nemirovich-Danchenko, Vladimir I
Nichols, Anne
Nichols, Beverly
Nichols, Peter
Norman, Marsha Williams
Novello, Ivor
Nugent, Elliott
O'Casey, Sean
O'Keeffe, John
O'Neill, Eugene Gladstone
Oboler, Arch
Odets, Clifford
Orton, Joe (John Kingsley)
Osborne, John James
Oursler, (Charles) Fulton
Owens, Rochelle
Pagnol, Marcel Paul
Patrick, John
Payne, John Howard
Peabody, Josephine Preston
Peele, George
Pinero, Arthur Wing, Sir
Pinero, Miguel
Pinter, Harold
Pirandello, Luigi
Plautus, Titus Maccius
Plomley, Roy
Pollock, Channing
Prevost, Marcel
Priestley, J B (John Boynton)

Pudney, John Sleigh
Rabe, David William
Racine, Jean Baptiste
Ranke, Leopold von
Rattigan, Terence Mervyn
Reade, Charles
Resnik, Muriel
Rice, Elmer
Richards, Stanley
Richardson, Jack
Riggs, Lynn
Rinehart, Mary Roberts
Robinson, Lennox (Esme Stuart Lennox)
Rojas Zorrilla, Francisco de
Rolland, Romain
Rosen, Sheldon
Rostand, Edmond Alexis
Russell, George William
Ryskind, Morrie
Sabatini, Rafael
Sachs, Hans
Sackler, Howard Oliver
Saroyan, William
Sartre, Jean-Paul
Savage, John
Schisgal, Murray
Schnitzler, Arthur
Schwartz, Stephen L
Segal, Erich Wolf
Seneca, Lucius Annaeus, the Younger
Shadwell, Thomas
Shaffer, Peter Levin
Shakespeare, William
Shange, Ntozake
Shaw, George Bernard
Shaw, Irwin
Shaw, Robert
Shawn, Wallace
Sheridan, Richard Brinsley
Sherriff, Robert Cedric
Sherwood, Robert Emmet
Shirley, James
Simon, (Marvin) Neil
Slade, Bernard, pseud.
Smith, "Dodie" Dorothy Gladys
Sophocles
Spewack, Bella Cohen
Spewack, Samuel
Spigelgass, Leonard
Steele, Richard, Sir
Stein, Joseph
Stewart, Michael
Storey, David Malcolm
Strindberg, August (Johan August)
Sudermann, Hermann
Swerling, Jo
Swinburne, Algernon Charles
Synge, John Millington
Tarkington, Booth
Taylor, Charles Alonzo
Taylor, Samuel (Albert)

Tebelak, John Michael
Teichmann, Howard Miles
Terence
Terry, Megan
Thespis
Thomas, Brandon
Toller, Ernst
Torrence, Ridgley (Frederick Rridgley)
Totheroh, Dan
Travers, Ben
Treece, Henry
Tremblay, Michel
Trevor, William
Ustinov, Peter Alexander
Van Druten, John William
Van Itallie, Jean-Claude
Van Peebles, Melvin
Vega (Carpio), Lope (Felix) de
Vidal, "Gore" Eugene Luther
Vigny, Alfred Victor, Comte de
Vollmer, Lula
Voskovec, George
Walter, Eugene
Ward, Douglas Turner
Warren, Mercy Otis
Washburn, Charles
Wasserman, Dale
Webster, John
Weiss, Peter
Weldon, John
Weller, Michael
Werfel, Franz
Wesker, Arnold
Wexley, John
Wilde, Oscar Fingal O'Flahertie Wills
Wilder, Thornton Niven
Williams, "Tennessee" Thomas Lanier
Williams, Emlyn (George Emlyn)
Williams, Samm-Art
Williams, William Carlos
Willingham, Calder Baynard, Jr.
Wilson, Lanford
Wilson, Robert M
Wilson, Sandy (Alexander Galbraith)
Wouk, Herman
Yeats, William Butler
Zangwill, Israel
Zindel, Paul
Zuckmayer, Carl
Zweig, Arnold

ECCENTRIC

Collyer, Homer Lusk
Collyer, Langley
Connelly, "One-Eyed" James Leo
Kelly, "Shipwreck" Alvin A
Manville, Tommy (Thomas Franklin, Jr.)

ECONOMIST

Agar, Herbert Sebastian
Alphand, Herve
Bagehot, Walter
Beveridge, William Henry, Lord
Bohm von Bawerk, Eugene
Booz, Paul E
Boulding, Kenneth Ewart
Brimmer, Andrew Felton
Bruning, Heinrich
Burns, Arthur F
Burns, Eveline Mabel
Cairncross, Alexander Kirkland, Sir
Carazo (Odio), Rodrigo
Chase, Stuart
Clark, Colin Grant
Clark, John Bates
Cobden, Richard
Cobleigh, Ira Underwood
Commons, John Rogers
Compton, Wilson Martindale
Debreu, Gerard
Douglas, Paul Howard
Dunlop, John Thomas
DuPont de Nemours, Pierre Samuel
Eccles, Marriner Stoddard
Ellsberg, Daniel
Ely, Richard Theodore
Erdman, Paul E
Erhard, Ludwig
Fanfani, Amintore
Fawcett, Henry
Feis, Herbert
Feldstein, Martin Stuart
Fisher, Irving
Friedman, Milton
Frisch, Ragnar
Galbraith, John Kenneth
Galiani, Ferdinando
George, Henry, Sr.
Gilder, George
Gramm, (William) Phil(ip)
Greenspan, Alan
Gresham, Thomas
Hambleton, Hugh George
Harriman, John Walter
Harvey, William Hope
Hauge, Gabriel
Hayek, Friedrich August von
Heller, Walter Wolfgang
Henderson, Leon
Henderson, Vivian Wilson
Hicks, Ursula Kathleen Webb
Hobson, John Atkinson
Hollowood, Albert Bernard
Howe, Clarence Decatur
Janeway, Eliot
Jay, Peter
Johnson, Arno Hollock
Katona, George
Kaufman, Henry

Kesselring, Albert
Keynes, John Maynard, Baron
Klein, Lawrence Robert
Koopmans, Tjalling (Charles)
Kuznets, Simon
Laffer, Arthur Betz
Laidler, Harry Wellington
Lalonde, Marc
Laughlin, James Laurence
Leacock, Stephen Butler
Livingston, J(oseph) A(rnold)
Machlup, Fritz
Malthus, Thomas Robert
McNair, Malcolm Perrine
Mill, John Stuart
Modigliani, Franco
Monnet, Jean (Omer Gabriel)
Okun, Arthur Melvin
Pareto, Vilfredo
Pella, Giuseppe
Penner, Rudolph Gerhard
Petty, William, Sir
Quesnay, Francois
Ricardo, David
Ripley, William Zebina
Rosovsky, Henry
Rostow, Eugene Victor
Samuelson, Paul Anthony
Schultze, Charles Louis
Schuman, Robert
Schumpeter, Joseph Alois
Shanks, Michael (James Michael)
Smith, Adam
Sowell, Thomas
Stein, Herbert
Stigler, George Joseph
Sumner, William Graham
Tawney, Richard Henry
Tobin, James
Veblen, Thorstein Bunde
Ward, Barbara Mary
Weidenbaum, Murray Lew
Whitman, Marina VonNeumann
Witte, Edwin Emil
Wojnilower, Albert M

EDITOR

A'Beckett, Gilbert Abbott
Abbott, Lyman
Abercrombie, Michael
Abernethy, Robert Gordon
Ackerman, Forest J
Adamic, Louis
Adams, John Hanly
Ainsworth, W(illiam) H(arrison)
Alden, Henry M
Aldiss, Brian Wilson
Aldrich, Thomas Bailey
Allingham, William
Alpert, Hollis
Anderson, Margaret Carolyn

Andrews, James Frederick
Angell, Roger
Angoff, Charles
Anthony, Joseph
Arbatov, Georgi
Arias, Roberto Emilio
Armstrong, Charles B
Armstrong, Hamilton Fish
Arnold, Oren
Ascoli, Max
Ashbrook, Joseph
Ashmore, Harry Scott
Bagehot, Walter
Bakeless, John Edwin
Ballou, Maturin Murray
Barger, Floyd
Barnes, Clive Alexander
Barrett, Edward Ware
Barron, Clarence Walker
Barrows, Marjorie (Ruth)
Beck, Marilyn (Mohr)
Beers, Victor Gilbert
Behrens, Earl Charles
Bemis, Samuel Flagg
Bennett, Lerone, Jr.
Benton, Thomas Hart
Berman, Morton
Bernstein, Sid(ney Ralph)
Billings, John Shaw
Birnie, William Alfred Hart
Blackwell, Betsy Talbot
Blair, Clay, Jr.
Bleeker, Sonia
Bleiberg, Robert Marvin
Bliven, Bruce
Bok, Edward William
Booth, George Gough
Bova, Ben(jamin William)
Bowdler, Thomas
Bowker, R(ichard) R(ogers)
Boyd, Julian Parks
Braceland, Francis J(ames)
Braden, Anne
Bradlee, Ben(jamin Crowninshield)
Brady, James
Brandon, Henry Oscar
Brann, William Cowper
Brooks, Walter R(ollin)
Browles, William Dodson, Jr.
Brown, Charles Brockden
Brown, Helen Gurley
Brown, Tina
Browning, Alice Crolley
Brownson, Orestes Augustus
Bryant, William Cullen
Buckley, William F(rank), Jr.
Bukharin, Nikolai Ivanovich
Burnett, Whit
Byers, William Newton
Byrd, Harry Flood, Jr.
Cable, Mary

Cahan, Abraham
Callahan, Daniel
Campbell, John W
Canby, Henry Seidel
Canfield, Francis X(avier)
Cantwell, Robert Emmett
Capper, Arthur
Carter, Hodding (William Hodding, III)
Cater, Douglass
Catledge, Turner
Cattell, James McKeen
Chambers, Whittaker
Chandler, Otis
Chase, Edna Woolman
Christiansen, Arthur
Claiborne, Craig
Colby, Anita
Colvin, Sidney, Sir
Cousins, Norman
Covici, Pascal
Cowles, Fleur Fenton
Crowninshield, Francis Welch
Currie, Barton Wood
Curtis, George William
Dabney, Virginius
Dana, Charles Anderson
Daniel, Dan(iel)
Dannay, Frederic
Davies, Hunter
Dawson, Geoffrey (George Geoffrey)
Day, Dorothy
Day-Lewis, Cecil
Dell, Floyd
Dellinger, David T (Dave)
Dennison, George
Diderot, Denis
Dillon, George
Doctorow, E(dgar) L(aurence)
Dodge, Mary Elizabeth Mapes
Douglas-Home, Charles
Dreiser, Theodore
DuBay, William Bryan
Duhamel, Georges
Dunne, Finley Peter
Duyckinck, Evert Augustus
Einstein, Alfred
Elliott, Osborn
Evans, Harold Matthew
Ewen, David
Fadiman, Clifton Paul
Fanning, Katherine
Farb, Peter
Farrar, Margaret Petherbridge
Fell, John
Fenn, George Manville
Fischetti, John
Fishbein, Morris
Fodor, Eugene
Foley, Martha
Forbes, Malcolm Stevenson
Fortune, Timothy Thomas

Frankfurter, Alfred Moritz
Fuller, Hoyt William
Geis, Bernard
Gemmill, Henry
Gingrich, Arnold
Giroux, Robert
Golden, Harry Lewis
Goodman, George Jerome Waldo
Gorkin, Jess
Gould, Beatrice Blackmar
Gould, Charles Bruce
Greeley, Horace
Green, Abel
Greenfield, Meg
Grosvenor, Melville Bell
Grove, Frederick Philip
Hackett, Francis
Hapgood, Norman
Harris, William Bliss
Hart-Davis, Rupert (Charles Rupert)
Haydn, Hiram Collins
Hayward, John Davy
Hearst, William Randolph, Jr.
Hebert, F(elix) Edward
Hershey, Lenore
Herter, Christian Archibald
Hesse, Don
Hickey, Margaret A
Hicks, Ursula Kathleen Webb
Hoke, Henry Reed
Holinshed, Raphael
Hollowood, Albert Bernard
Holzer, Harold
Horne, Josh L
Hotchner, Aaron Edward
Howard, Anthony
Howe, Edgar Watson
Howe, Irving
Howe, Mark De Wolfe
Howe, Quincy
Howell, Clark
Howells, William Dean
Huxtable, Ada Louise
Irvin, Rea
Irvin, Robert W
Johnson, Lionel Pigot
Jones, Jenkin Lloyd
Jordan, Elizabeth Garver
Justus, Roy Braxton
Kaempffert, Waldemar (Bernhard)
Kaltenborn, H(ans) V(on)
Kamp, Irene Kittle
Kane, Joseph Nathan
Kashdan, Isaac
Kenney, Douglas C
Kimbrough, Emily
King, Alexander
King, Warren Thomas
Knox, E(dmund) G(eorge) V(alpy)
Korda, Michael Vincent
Krassner, Paul

Kristol, Irving
Kuh, Katherine
Kunitz, Stanley Jasspon
Laing, David
Lanman, Charles Rockwell
Lasch, Robert
Laughlin, James, IV
Lawrenson, Helen Brown
Lawson, Donald Elmer
Lawson, Victor Fremont
Lee, Stan
Leland, Charles Godfrey
Leland, Timothy
Leslie, Eliza
Lewis, Boyd de Wolf
Lewis, Wilmarth Sheldon
Liberman, Alexander
Lieber, Franz
Lin, Yutang
Linton, William James
Lippmann, Walter
Long, Scott
Lossing, Benson John
Lovejoy, Clarence Earle
Lowell, James Russell
Lowndes, Robert A(ugustine) W(ard)
Luce, Henry Robinson
Lynes, Joseph Russell, Jr.
Lyons, Eugene
Lytle, Andrew Nelson
MacBeth, George Mann
Markel, Lester
Martin, Kingsley
Maxwell, William
Mayes, Herbert Raymond
McCormick, Bernard
McGee, Thomas D'Arcy
McNaughton, F(oye) F(isk)
Mears, Walter R(obert)
Mencken, H(enry) L(ouis)
Monroe, Harriet
More, Paul Elmer
Morris, Willie
Motherwell, William
Muggeridge, Malcolm
Munson, Gorham B(ert)
Murray, James Augustus Henry, Sir
Nathan, George Jean
Navasky, Victor Saul
Neville, Kris Ottman
Newfield, Jack
Newquist, Roy
Nye, Gerald Prentice
Onassis, Jacqueline Lee Bouvier Kennedy
Opie, Peter Mason
Ornitz, Samuel
Orwell, Sonia
Osborne, John Franklin
Paddleford, Clementine Haskin
Parker, Daniel Francis
Patterson, Alicia

Peel, Ronald Francis (Edward Waite)
Perkins, Maxwell Evarts
Pierrot, George Francis
Plotnik, Arthur
Podhoretz, Norman
Pohl, Frederik
Potok, Chaim
Price, Byron
Pulitzer, Joseph
Pulitzer, Joseph, II
Pusey, Merlo John
Quennell, Peter Courtney
Ragan, David
Rascoe, Burton
Rashidov, Sharaf Rashidovich
Raymond, Henry Jarvis
Redman, Ben Ray
Rense, Paige
Rexroth, Kenneth
Rickword, Edgell (John Edgell)
Robinson, M(aurice) R(ichard)
Rodman, Selden
Roessner, Elmer
Rosenfeld, Alvin Hirsch
Rosenthal, Abraham Michael
Ross, Harold
Rovere, Richard Halworth
Ruder, Melvin
Rukeyser, William Simon
Russell, George William
Ryle, Gilbert
Saerchinger, Cesar Victor Charles
Saffir, Leonard
Sanders, Bill (William Willard)
Scheuer, Philip K(latz)
Schmitt, Bernadotte Everly
Schmitt, Gladys
Schwartz, Delmore
Seaman, Owen, Sir
Searle, Ronald William Fordham
Seldes, Gilbert Vivian
Shaw, Albert
Shawn, William
Shirley, Ralph
Shively, George Jenks
Smith, Gerald Lyman Kenneth
Sparks, Jared
Spectorsky, Auguste Compte
Spence, Lewis (James Lewis Thomas Chalmers)
Steinberg, Sigfrid Henry
Stephens, Ann Sophia
Stickley, Gustav
Stieglitz, Alfred
Stone, Lucy
Sutton, Carol
Swope, Herbert Bayard
Taggard, Genevieve
Taishoff, Sol Joseph
Talmadge, Thomas de Witt
Tarbell, Ida Minerva

Thomas, Edith Matilda
Thompson, Hunter S(tockton)
Towne, Charles Hanson
Trumbull, Charles Gallaudet
Untermeyer, Louis
Van Doren, Charles Lincoln
Viereck, George Sylvester
Wallace, Lila Bell Acheson
Waltari, Mika
Warner, Charles Dudley
Waymack, W(illiam) W(esley)
Weiss, Theodore (Russell)
White, William Allen
White, William Lindsay
Wilder, Joseph
Winterich, John Tracy
Woodhull, Victoria Claflin
Woodson, Carter Godwin

EDUCATOR

Aaron, Chester Norman
Abbott, Edith
Abel, Elie
Abelard, Pierre
Abercrombie, Michael
Aberle, John Wayne
Adler, Cyrus
Adler, Felix
Agassiz, Elizabeth Cabot Cary
Agassiz, Louis (Jean Louis Radolphe)
Aiken, Howard Hathaway
Alain, pseud.
Albers, Josef
Alcott, Amos Bronson
Alexander, Franz Gabriel
Alexander, Leo
Alfred, William
Allen, Jack
Almond, Gabriel Abraham
Anderson, Vernon Ellsworth
Andrews, Jane
Andrews, Wayne
Andrus, Ethel Percy
Armour, Richard Willard
Armstrong, Anne Legendre
Armstrong, William Howard
Arnold, Matthew
Arnold, Thomas
Ascoli, Max
Ashton-Warner, Sylvia Constance
Auden, W(ystan) H(ugh)
Auletta, Robert
Ayer, Alfred Jules
Aytoun, William Edmonstoune
Baker, Gladys Elizabeth
Baldwin, James Mark
Balla, Giacomo
Barber, Bernard
Barker, Ernest, Sir
Barnard, Frederick Augustus Porter
Barnard, Henry

Barnet, Sylvan M, Jr.
Barnet, Will
Barr, Stringfellow
Barraclough, Geoffrey
Barrett, Edward Ware
Barzun, Jacques Martin
Baskin, Wade
Bate, Walter Jackson
Bates, Katherine Lee
Baugh, Albert Croll
Baxter, Frank Condie
Baxter, James Phinney, III
Beard, Charles Austin
Begle, Edward G(riffith)
Bell, Arthur Donald
Bell, Daniel
Bell, Joseph
Beltrami, Eugenio
Benarde, Melvin Albert
Benedict, Ruth Fulton
Bentley, Eric
Benton, William
Berg, Paul
Berger, Raoul
Berry, Martha McChesney
Berry, Wendell
Bestor, Arthur Eugene
Bethune, Mary McLeod
Bettelheim, Bruno
Bickerman, Elias Joseph
Biebuyck, Daniel Prosper
Bigelow, Henry Bryant
Billington, Ray Allen
Bing, Rudolf (Franz Josef), Sir
Bitter, Francis
Blackmur, Richard Palmer
Blair, James
Blanding, Sarah Gibson
Blasingame, Francis James Levi
Bloch, Felix
Blough, Glenn Orlando
Bloustein, Edward J
Blow, Susan Elizabeth
Blumenthal, Monica David
Boas, Franz
Bode, Carl
Boerhaave, Herman
Bok, Derek Curtis
Boley, Forrest Irving
Bolinger, Dwight Lemerton
Boller, Paul F, Jr.
Bondurant, Bob (Robert L)
Bouchet, Edward Alexander
Boulding, Kenneth Ewart
Bowker, Albert Hosmer
Bowra, Maurice, Sir
Brace, Gerald Warner
Branley, Franklyn Mansfield
Brauer, Jerald Carl
Brawley, Benjamin Griffith
Brayman, Harold

Brewer, Ebenezer
Brewster, Kingman, Jr.
Brinton, Clarence Crane
Brown, Frank Arthur, Jr.
Browning, Alice Crolley
Brownwell, Samuel Miller
Brustein, Robert Sanford
Brutus, Dennis Vincent
Brzezinski, Zbigniew Kazimierz
Buck, Paul Herman
Buckland, William
Budenz, Louis Francis
Bullock, Alain Louis Charles
Bundy, McGeorge
Bunting, Mary Ingraham
Burns, Arthur F
Buscaglia, Leo (Felice Leonardo)
Butler, Nicholas Murray
Cairncross, Alexander Kirkland, Sir
Caldwell, John Charles
Calvin, Melvin
Camerarius, Rudolf Jakob
Canby, Henry Seidel
Canfield, Francis X(avier)
Canfield, James Hulme
Cantrick, Robert
Cardozo, Francis Louis
Carmer, Carl Lamson
Carnap, Rudolf
Carver, George Washington
Cash, Jim
Cassidy, Harold Gomes
Cater, Douglass
Catlin, George Edward Gordon, Sir
Cecil, Edward Christian David Gascoyne
Chain, Ernest Boris, Sir
Chase, Richard Volney
Chaudhuri, Haridas
Chavis, John
Cherrington, Ben Mark
Chiang, Yee
Chinard, Gilbert
Christ-Janer, Albert
Clapp, Margaret Antoinette
Clark, Kenneth Bancroft
Cobb, William Montague
Coghill, Nevill Henry Kendall Aylmer
Cohen, Wilbur Joseph
Cole, Charles Woolsey
Cole, George Douglas Howard
Comenius, Johann Amos
Commager, Henry Steele
Comstock, Ada Louise
Comstock, John Henry
Conant, James Bryant
Condit, Carl Wilbur
Conkle, Ellsworth Prouty
Cooley, Denton Arthur
Copeland, Charles Townsend
Cordes, Eugene Harold
Couperius, Louis (Marie Anne)

Cowles, Henry Chandler
Crandall, Prudence
Cret, Paul P(hilippe)
Crosby, Sumner McKnight
Cross, Wilbur
Cudworth, Ralph
Daiches, David
Daniloff, Nicholas
DaPonte, Lorenzo
Darden, Colgate Whitehead
Davidson, J Brownlee
DeErdely, Francis (Ferenc)
DeMott, Benjamin Haile
Dempster, Arhur J
Denenberg, Herbert S
DeSanctis, Francesco
DeVita, Vincent Theodore, Jr.
DeVries, Hugo
Dewey, John
Diemer, Emma Lou
Dinwiddie, John Ekin
Dixon, Roland Burrage
Dobie, J(ames) Frank
Dodd, William Edward
Dodds, Harold Willis
Dodge, Grace Hoadley
Doherty, Robert Ernest
Doriot, Georges Frederic
Drachler, Norman
Drewry, John Eldridge
Drinker, Philip
Duane, William
Ducloux, Walter
Dulles, Eleanor Lansing
Duncan, Todd
Duveneck, Frank
Dyson, Freeman John
Edmonson, Munro Sterling
Edwards, Harry (Jr.)
Eisenhower, Milton Stover
Eliot, Charles William
Elkins, Stanley Maurice
Epstein, Edward Jay
Erhard, Werner
Erskine, John
Etchison, Dennis (William Dennis)
Euwe, Max (Machgielis)
Evans, John
Ewen, Frederic
Ewing, William Maurice
Faiz, Faiz Ahmad
Farenthold, Frances T
Finley, John Huston
Finney, Charles Grandison
Fisher, Welthy (Blakesley Honsinger)
Fitts, Dudley
Flexner, Abraham
Flory, Paul John
Foerster, Friedrich Wilhelm
Foerster, Norman
Fowlie, Wallace

Francis, Thomas, Jr.
Franck, James
Frank, Jerome David
Frankenstein, Alfred Victor
Frazier, Edward Franklin
Freidberg, Jerry
Froebel, Friedrich Wilhelm August
Fuess, Claude Moore
Gaddis, Thomas (Eugene)
Gallegos, Romulo
Garraty, John Arthur
Garrett, George Palmer, Jr.
Gay, Peter Jack
Gerould, Gordon Hall
Geschwind, Norman
Giauque, William F(rancis)
Gildersleeve, Virginia Crocheron
Gilman, Daniel Coit
Gipson, Lawrence Henry
Godoy Alcayaga, Lucila
Goheen, Robert Francis
Goldstein, Joseph Leonard
Goodman, Paul
Goucher, John Franklin
Gould, Laurence McKinley
Gowans, Alan
Grant, Michael
Gray, Asa
Gray, Hanna
Greer, Germaine
Gregorian, Vartan
Gregory, Horace Victor
Grimes, Martha
Grimke, Charlotte Lottie Forten
Griswold, A Whitney
Gruenberg, Sidonie Matsner
Guerard, Albert Joseph
Gulick, Luther Halsey
Gusberg, Saul Bernard
Hale, George Ellery
Hall, Edwin Herbert
Hall, Granville Stanley
Handlin, Oscar
Hanfmann, George Maxim Anossov
Hansen, Alvin Harvey
Hanson, Howard Harold
Harbison, John Harris
Harnwell, Gaylord Probasco
Harper, William Rainey
Harris, Harwell Hamilton
Harris, Joseph Pratt
Hart, Jeffrey
Hastie, William Henry
Hayakawa, S(amuel) I(chiye)
Hayes, Carlton Joseph Huntley
Hazan, Marcella Maddalena
Henderson, Leon
Henderson, Vivian Wilson
Hesburgh, Theodore Martin
Highet, Gilbert Arthur
Hill, Rowland, Sir

Hillyer, Robert
Hitchcock, Henry Russell
Hocking, William Ernest
Hofstadter, Robert
Holland, William Jacob
Holloway, Emory
Holmes, Arthur
Holt, John Caldwell
Hopkins, Mark
Hopper, Grace Brewster Murray
Horner, Matina Souretis
Houssay, Bernardo Alberto
Howe, Harold, II
Howe, Samuel Gridley
Howes, Frank Stewart
Hunter, Thomas
Hussein, Taha
Hutchins, Robert Maynard
Huxley, Andrew Fielding
Ilg, Frances Lillian
Illich, Ivan
Ironside, Henry Allan
Jacobson, Leon Orris
Janson, Horst Woldemar
Jaspers, Karl
Johnson, Mordecai Wyatt
Johnson, Robert Willard
Johnson, Walter (Thomas Walter)
Jones, Gwynn
Jordy, William H(enry)
Kallen, Horace M
Karrar, Paul
Kaufman, Bel
Kearns, Doris H
Keble, John
Kelsen, Hans
Keniston, Kenneth
Kermode, (John) Frank
Kerr, Clark
Kerr, Malcolm (Hooper)
Kohl, Herbert R
Kohn, William Roth
Koontz, (Annie) Elizabeth Duncan
Kozol, Jonathan
Kraus, Lili
Kung, Hans
Laboulage, Edouard Rose
Landis, James McCauley
Langdell, Christopher Columbus
Langston, J William
Lanman, Charles Rockwell
Larkin, Oliver Waterman
Lattimore, Richmond Alexander
Laue, Max Theodor Felix von
Leacock, Stephen Butler
Leary, Timothy Francis
Lee, Sidney, Sir
Lefever, Ernest Warren
LeFleming, Christopher Kaye
Levi, Edward Hirsch
Levy, Leonard Williams

Lewis, Clarence Irving
Lidz, Theodore
Lieber, Franz
Lilly, John C
Lin, Yutang
Lincoln, Mary Johnson Bailey
Lipmann, Fritz Albert
Lowell, Abbott Lawrence
Lowes, John Livingston
Lowinsky, Edward Elias
Lynd, Helen Merrell
Lyon, Mary
MacDougall, Curtis Daniel
Mackay, John Alexander
Magill, Hugh Stewart
Mahan, Asa
Malik, Charles Habib
Malpighi, Marcello
Mann, Horace
Manner, Harold
Mannheim, Karl
Mark, Herman F
Martin, John
Martin, Robert Bernard
Mason, John Brown
Mathews, Forrest David
Matthiessen, Francis Otto
Mattingley, Garrett
Maurice, Frederick Denison
Mayr, Ernst Walter
McDougall, William
McGuffey, William Holmes
McIlwain, Charles Howard
McLuhan, (Herbert) Marshall
McNair, Malcolm Perrine
McNamara, Margaret Craig
Meiklejohn, Alexander
Mennin, Peter
Middleton, Christopher
Miles, Josephine
Millikan, Clark Blanchard
Milosz, Czeslaw
Moody, William Vaughn
Moore, Jack
Morgan, Arthur
Morrison, Philip
Mott, Frank Luther
Mundt, Karl Earl
Nagai, Sokichi
Natta, Giulio
Neill, A(lexander) S(utherland)
Neilson, William A
Neurath, Otto
Noffsinger, James P(hilip)
Norton, Charles Eliot
Nye, Russel Blaine
O'Callahan, Joseph Timothy
Olitski, Jules
Osler, William, Sir
Owen, Lewis James
Ozanam, Frederic

Padover, Saul Kussiel
Palmer, Alice Elvira Freeman
Palmer, Austin Norman
Panofsky, Erwin
Parkhurst, Helen
Parrington, Vernon L(ouis)
Pattee, Fred Lewis
Paul, Lester Warner
Peabody, Elizabeth Palmer
Peabody, Endicott
Pei, Mario Andrew
Perlea, Jonel
Perry, Bliss
Perry, Ralph Barton
Peter, Laurence Johnston
Petty, William, Sir
Peyre, Henri Maurice
Phelps, Robert Eugene
Phelps, William Lyon
Polya, George
Pound, Louise
Pound, Roscoe
Powell, Cecil Frank
Powell, Lawrence Clark
Prasad, Ananda Shiva
Pratt, Gerald Hillary
Pusey, Edward Bouverie
Pusey, Nathan Marsh
Quiller-Couch, Arthur Thomas, Sir
Rafferty, Max(well Lewis, Jr.)
Raikes, Robert
Raleigh, Walter Alexander, Sir
Ransom, John Crowe
Ready, William Bernard
Reed, Henry Hope
Reisner, George Andrew
Renard, Jules
Richard, Gabriel
Rienow, Robert
Riles, Wilson C
Ripley, William Zebina
Robinson, James Harvey
Rochberg, George
Roche, John P
Rogers, Fred McFeely
Romano, Umberto
Romney, Seymour Leonard
Ronan, William J
Roos, Frank John, Jr.
Rose, Leonard
Rosovsky, Henry
Ross, Roy G
Rossi, Peter Henry
Rubik, Erno
Rubin, Vitalii
Sadat, Jihan Raouf
Saintsbury, George Edward Bateman
Samuels, Ernest
Sanford, Terry
Santayana, George
Schioetz, Aksel

Schlesinger, Arthur Meier, Jr.
Schlesinger, Frank
Schmitt, Bernadotte Everly
Schneider, Richard Coy
Scholem, Gershom Gerhard
Schonfield, Hugh
Schorer, Mark
Schroedinger, Erwin
Schrum, Marion Margaret
Schulz, George J
Scott, Austin
Scott, Austin W
Sears, Robert Richardson
Seymour, Charles
Sforza, Carlo
Shambaugh, Jessie Field
Shannon, Fred Albert
Shattuck, Roger Whitney
Sheehan, Joseph Green
Shera, Jesse Hauk
Sherman, Frank Dempster
Shirley, James
Shklovsky, Iosif Samvilovitch
Shockley, William (Bradford)
Shulman, Irving
Sidgwick, Henry
Siegel, Stanley E
Sill, Edward Rowland
Silliman, Benjamin
Simon, Herbert Alexander
Sirluck, Ernest
Smith, Courtney Craig
Smith, Margaret
Smitherman, Geneva
Spingarn, Joel Elias
Spitta, Philipp (Julius August Philipp)
Spooner, William Archibald
Sproul, Robert Gordon
Stapledon, Olaf (Wiliam Olaf)
Stevens, S(tanley) S(mith)
Stewart, George Rippey
Strode, Hudson
Stroup, Thomas Bradley
Struve, Otto
Sumner, William Graham
Suzuki, Daisetz Teitaro
Swann, Michael Meredith, Sir
Szabolcsi, Bence
Szasz, Thomas Stephen
Tange, Kenzo
Tannenbaum, Frank
Tappan, Eva March
Tatum, Edward Lawrie
Tebbel, John William
Teller, Edward
Terrell, Mary Church
Thayer, Sylvanus, General
Thomas, Martha Carey
Thompson, Josiah
Thurman, Howard
Towle, Katherine Amelia

Trotta, Maurice S
Turner, Thomas Wyatt
Unger, Irwin
Van Dellen, Theodore Robert
Van Doren, Charles Lincoln
Van Dusen, Henry Pitney
Van Niel, Cornelius B(ernardus)
Vandyke, Henry Jackson, Jr.
Vendler, Helen Hennessy
Viereck, Peter Robert Edwin
Voelker, Paul Frederick
Walker, Robert Miller
Walsh, Michael Patrick
Washington, Booker T(aliafero)
Wayland, Francis
Weed, Steven Andrew
Weir, John F(erguson)
Weir, Robert W
Wellek, Rene
Westrup, J(ack) A(llan)
Wheelock, Eleazar
Whiffen, Marcus
White, Andrew Dickson
White, Helen Magill
Wigle, Ernest Douglas
Wilbur, Cornelia Burwell
Wilbur, Richard Purdy
Wiley, George A
Wilkins, Ernest Hatch
Willard, Emma Hart
Williams, Daniel Hale
Williams, Eric Eustace
Wimsatt, William Kurtz, Jr.
Winslow, Ola Elizabeth
Witherspoon, John
Wittgenstein, Ludwig
Wolff, Mary Evaline
Woodbridge, Frederick James Eugene
Wright, Louis Booker
Yablonky, Ben
Zim, Herbert Spencer
Zwerling, Israel

EGYPTOLOGIST

Budge, Ernest Alfred
Champollion, Jean Francois
Herbert, George Edward Stanhope
    Molyneux
Petrie, (William Matthew) Flinders, Sir

EMPEROR

Akbar
Caligula
Caracalla, Marcus Aurelius Antonius
Ch'ien Lung
Claudius I
Constantine I
Constantine V
Constantine VI
Constantine XI

Cuauhtemoc
Dessalines, Jean J
Diocletian
Ferdinand I
Frederick I
Frederick II
Frederick III
Gratian
Hadrian
Haile Selassie I
Heliogabalus
Hirohito
Iturbide, Augustin de
Jehangir
Joseph II
Julian (Flavius Claudius Julianus)
Kublai Khan
Mahmud of Ghazni
Marcus Aurelius Antoninus
Maximilian
Maximilian I
Maximilian II
Menelik II
Ming, T'ai-Tsu
Montezuma I
Montezuma II
Mutsuhito
Napoleon I
Napoleon III
Nero
Pedro I
Pedro II
Robert Guiscard
Rudolf II
Sigismond
Theodosius I
Tiberius Julius Caesar Augustus
Titus
Trajan
Vespasian

EMPRESS

Agrippina
Carlota
Eugenie
Josephine
Maria Theresa
Mumtaz Mahal
Pahlevi, Farah Diba
Zita

ENGINEER

Aalberg, John O
Alexanderson, Ernst Frederik Werner
Amdahl, Gene M(yron)
Ammann, Othmar Hermann
Armstrong, Edwin Howard

Bailey, Donald Coleman, Sir
Baird, John Logie
Baird, Spencer Fullerton
Barnaby, Ralph S
Bauersfeld, Walther
Beard, George Miller
Beatty, Alfred Chester, Sir
Bechtel, Stephen Davison
Bell, William Holden
Bessemer, Henry, Sir
Blackett, Patrick Maynard Stuart
Bleriot, Louis
Born, Max
Bosch, Carl
Boulton, Matthew
Bridgman, Percy Williams
Brindley, James
Brunel, Isambard Kingdom
Bugatti, Ettore
Bush, Vannevar
Cabot, Richard C
Campbell, Donald Fraser
Candela, Felix (Outerino Felix)
Cayley, George, Sir
Chadwick, James, Sir
Chanute, Octave
Christie, John Walter
Coanda, Henri Marie
Cobb, Stanley
Cockcroft, John Douglas, Sir
Cockerell, Christopher
Coffin, Howard Earle
Compton, Arthur Holly
Condon, Edward
Cone, Russell Glenn
Conrad, Frank
Cooke, William Fothergil, Sir
Cott, Nate
Crapper, Thomas
Dale, Henry Hallett
Dalen, Nils Gustaf
Davidson, J Brownlee
Dejongh, Peter
Diesel, Rudolf Christian Karl
Dinkeloo, John Gerard
Dodge, Grenville Mellen
Doherty, Robert Ernest
Dornberger, Walter Robert
Drew, Richard G
Drinker, Philip
DuMont, Allen Balcom
Eads, James Buchanan
Edgerton, Harold Eugene
Eiffel, Alexandre Gustave
Ellsberg, Edward
Ericsson, John
Feoktistov, Konstantin Petrovich
Florey, Howard Walter
Francis, James Bicheno
Fremont-Smith, Frank

Fulton, Robert
Gabor, Dennis
Garand, John Cantius
Gilbreth, Lillian Moller
Ginzburg, Charles Pauson
Goethals, George Washington
Goldmark, Peter Carl
Graydon, James Weir
Grunewald, Matthias
Hall, Charles Martin
Harding, Chester
Harroun, Ray
Haupt, Herman
Hench, Philip Showalter
Hess, Victor Francis
Hewlett, William
Hinshelwood, Cyril, Sir
Hinton, Christopher, Sir
Hinton, William Arthur
Humes, Harold Louis
Hunt, Jack Reed
Issigonis, Alec Arnold C, Sir
Jenner, William, Sir
Jenney, William LeBaron
Jones, "Casey" John Luther
Karman, Theodore Todor Von
Kellems, Vivien
Kettering, Charles Franklin
Koch, Robert
Kraft, Chris(topher Columbus, Jr.)
L'Enfant, Pierre Charles
Lake, Simon
Langmuir, Irving
Lanza, Anthony Joseph
Lawrence, Ernest Orlando
Lear, William Powell
Lesseps, Ferdinand Marie de
LeTourneau, Robert Gilmour
Lilienthal, Otto
Lippold, Richard
Long, Crawford Williamson
Maltsev, Victor Fyodorovich
Martin, James, Sir
McAdam, John Loudoun
McBurney, Charles
McLean, John Milton
Menninger, William C
Michelson, Albert Abraham
Mills, Robert
Moisseiff, Leon Solomon
Morgan, Arthur
Morgan, Thomas H
Muller, Hermann Joseph
Nervi, Pier Luigi
Norden, Carl Lukas
Otto, Nikolaus August
Paine, Thomas Otten
Patton, Edward L
Pincus, Gregory
Popov, Aleksandr Stepanovich
Redpath, James

Remsen, Ira
Ricketts, Howard T
Rillieux, Norbert
Rockwell, Willard F
Roebling, John Augustus
Roebling, Washington Augustus
Ross, Ronald, Sir
Rous, Peyton
Russo, Anthony J
Saunders, William Laurence
Schick, Bela
Shearer, Douglas
Shirley-Smith, Hubert
Siemens, William, Sir
Sims, James Marion
Sprague, Frank Julian
Steinman, David Barnard
Steinmetz, Charles Proteus
Stephenson, George
Stevens, John Frank
Stout, William Bushnell
Strauss, Joseph Baermann
Sutherland, Earl Wilbur, Jr.
Sydenham, Thomas
Szilard, Leo
Taylor, Frederick Winslow
Tesla, Nikola
Theiler, Max
Waksman, Selman Abraham
Wallace, Alfred Russell
Wallis, Barnes Neville, Sir
Wang, An
Wankel, Felix
Warner, Roger Sherman, Jr.
Watson-Watt, Robert Alexander, Sir
Watt, James
Wells, Edward
Wright, Horatio Governeur
Wright, John Lloyd
Zacharias, Jerrold R(einarch)
Zworykin, Vladimir K(osma)

ENGRAVER

Bewick, Thomas
Calvert, Edward
Cole, Timothy
Cousins, Samuel
Fragonard, Jean Honore
Gill, Eric
Granjon, Robert
Havell, Robert
Hogarth, William
Hokusai
Hollyer, Samuel
Piranesi, Giovanni Battista
Quinteros, Adolfo
Sartain, John
Schongauer, Martin

ENTERTAINER

Avalon, Frankie
Blondin, Jean Francois Gravelet
Carson, Johnny
Cavett, Dick (Richard Alva)
Clark, Dick (Richard Wagstaff)
Cody, "Buffalo Bill" William Frederick
Dockstader, Lew
Ferrare, Christina
Griffin, Merv(yn)
Hickok, "Wild Bill" James Butler
Hilton, Daisy
Hilton, Violet
Howard, Joseph Edgar
Keith, Benjamin F
Kreskin
LaRose, Rose
Lee, Gypsy Rose
Liberace
Little, Rich(ard Caruthers)
Lloyd, Marie
Lucas, Nick
McMahon, Ed(ward Lee)
Mills, Florence
Mistinguett
Morath, Max Edward
Nash, Clarence
Paar, Jack
Prin, Alice
Pyne, Joe
Saint Cyr, Lillian
Smith, Bob
Sothern, Edward Askew
Sothern, Edward Hugh
Standing, Guy
Stone, Carol
Tiny Tim
Williams, Wendy O(rlean)

ENTERTAINERS

Shields and Yarnell

ESSAYIST

Addison, Joseph
Alain, pseud.
Amicis, Edmond de
Baldwin, James Arthur
Baring-Gould, Sabine
Beerbohm, Max (Sir Henry Maximilian)
Benson, Edward Frederic
Cecchi, Emilio
Chambers, Edmund Kerchever, Sir
Chesterton, Gilbert Keith
Congreve, Richard
Cowley, Abraham
D'Israeli, Isaac
Day, Clarence Shepard, Jr.
Dobson, Henry Austin
Emerson, Ralph Waldo

Fisher, Dorothy Frances Canfield
Guiney, Louise
Holmes, Oliver Wendell
Kilmer, Joyce (Alfred Joyce)
Lamb, Charles
LeGallienne, Richard
Lowell, James Russell
Lubbock, Percy
Macaulay, Rose
Macaulay, Thomas Babington Macaulay, Baron
Mallarme, Stephane
Martin, Kingsley
Meynell, Alice
Montaigne, Michel Eyquem de
Papashvily, George
Powys, John Cowper
Powys, Llewelyn
Raleigh, Walter Alexander, Sir
Repplier, Agnes
Reyes, Alfonso
Schauffler, Robert Haven
Senghor, Leopold Sedar
Sissman, L(ouis) E(dward)
Smith Sydney
Smith, Alexander
Steele, Richard, Sir
Stevenson, Robert Louis Balfour
Swados, Harvey
Thompson, Francis Joseph
Thomson, James
Whitman, Sarah Helen Power
Whitman, Walt(er)
Whittier, John Greenleaf
Xenophon

ETHNOLOGIST

Fletcher, Alice Cunningham
Frisch, Karl von
Goodall, Jane

EVANGELIST

Armstrong, Garner Ted
Armstrong, Henry
Dowie, John Alexander
Evans, Dale
Gortner, (Hugh) Marjoe (Ross)
Graham, Billy (William Franklin)
Hargis, Billy James
Humbard, Rex
Ike, Reverend
Jones, "Prophet" James F
Kuhlman, Kathryn
McPherson, Aimee Semple
Moody, Dwight Lyman
Roberts, Oral
Robertson, Pat (Marion)
Schuller, Robert Harold
Sunday, Billy (William Ashley)

EXPLORER

Abruzzi, Luigi Amedeo
Akeley, Mary Lee Jobe
Allen, Henry Tureman
Amundsen, Roald Engelbregt
Andree, Salomon August
Andrews, Roy Chapman
Anza, Juan Bautista de
Bailey, Frederick Marshman
Balboa, Vasco Nunez de
Balchen, Bernt
Ballard, Robert Duane
Barents, Willem
Barth, Heinrich
Bartlett, Robert Abram
Beccaria, Cesare
Becknell, William
Beebe, William (Charles William)
Bellinghausen, Fabian Gottlieb von
Bingham, Hiram
Boas, Franz
Bodmer, Karl
Boyd, Louise Arner
Burton, Richard Francis, Sir
Byng, George Torrington, Viscount
Byrd, Richard Evelyn
Cabeza de Vaca, Alvar Nunez
Cabot, John
Cabot, Sebastian
Cabral, Pedro Alvarez
Cabrillo, Juan Rodriguez
Cadillac, Antoine
Caillie, Rene
Cartier, Jacques
Catlin, George
Champlain, Samuel de
Chancellor, Richard
Charcot, Jean Baptiste Etienne Auguste
Chesney, Francis Rawdon
Clark, William
Colter, John
Columbus, Christopher
Cook, Frederick Albert
Cook, James, Captain
Cordoba, Francisco Fernandez
Coronado, Francisco Vasquez de
Cruzen, Richard H
DaGama, Vasco
Dampier, William
David-Neel, Alexandra
Davis, John
DeLong, George Washington
DeSoto, Hernando
Dickey, Herbert Spencer
Duluth, Daniel
Eklund, Carl Robert
Ellsworth, Lincoln
Emin Pasha
Ericson, Leif
Estevanico
Ferraris, Galileo

Fitzpatrick, Thomas
Flinders, Matthew
Franklin, John
Fremont, John Charles
Freuchen, Peter
Freydis, Ericsdotter
Fuchs, Vivian Ernest, Sir
Galton, Francis, Sir
Gilbert, Humphrey, Sir
Gould, Laurence McKinley
Greely, Adolphus Washington
Gurdjieff, Georges Ivanovitch
Halliburton, Richard
Hearne, Samuel
Hennepin, Louis
Henson, Matthew Alexander
Heyerdahl, Thor
Hillary, Edmund Percival, Sir
Humboldt, Alexander, Freiherr von
Humphreys, Noel
Iberville, Pierre Le Moyne, sieur d'
James, Edwin
Johnson, Martin Elmer
Johnson, Osa Helen Leighty
Jolliet, Louis
Kane, Elisha Kent
Laing, Alexander Gordon
Lander, Richard Lemon
LaSalle, Robert Cavelier, Sieur de
Lewis, Meriwether
Livingstone, David
Long, Stephen H
Lummis, Charles Fletcher
Mackenzie, Alexander, Sir
MacMillan, Donald Baxter
Magellan, Ferdinand
Marquette, Jacques, Pere
Mawson, Douglas, Sir
McClintock, Francis Leopold, Sir
Nansen, Fridtjof
Nicolet, Jean
Nobile, Umberto
Ortega, Francisco de
Palmer, Nathaniel Brown
Papanin, Ivan D
Park, Mungo
Parry, William Edward, Sir
Peary, Robert Edwin
Philby, Harold St. John Bridger
Piccard, Jacques
Pike, Zebulon Montgomery
Ponce de Leon, Juan
Poulter, Thomas Charles
Przhevalsky, Nikolai Mikhailovich
Radisson, Pierre Espirit
Rasmussen, Knud Johan Victor
Roggeveen, Jacob
Ronne, Finn
Ross, James Clark, Sir
Schiaparelli, Giovanni
Schoolcraft, Henry Rowe

FARMER

FASHION DESIGNER

Mellinger, Frederick
Milgrim, Sally
Miller, Nolan
Molyneux, Edward H
Norell, Norman
Olga
Orry-Kelly
Parnis, Mollie
Patou, Jean
Pertegaz, Manuel
Petrocelli, Anthony
Picone, Evan
Pignatelli, Luciana, Princess
Poiret, Paul
Priscilla of Boston
Quant, Mary
Rentner, Maurice
Rompollo, Dominic
Rose, Helen Bronberg
Rosenfeld, Henry J
Ruffin, Clovis
Saint Laurent, Yves Mathieu
Scaasi, Arnold
Schiaparelli, (Elsa)
Shamask, Ronaldus
Shields, Alexander
Simonetta
Simpson, Adele Smithline
Smith, Willi Donnell
Sophie
Stavropoulos, George Peter
Stephanie, Princess
Takada, Kenzo
Tiffeau, Jacques Emile
Tinling, Ted
Traphagen, Ethel Leigh
Trigere, Pauline
Tuffin, Sally
Ungaro, Emanuel Matteotti
Valentina
Valentino
Vollbracht, Michaele J
Weinberg, Chester
Weitz, John
Worth, Charles Frederick
Zuckerman, Ben

FASHION EDITOR

Coburn, Julia
Green, Robert L
Gunzberg, Nicolas de, Baron
Kempner, Nan
Sheppard, Eugenia Benbow
Snow, Carmel White
Vreeland, Diana

FEMINIST

Atkinson, Ti-Grace
Baker, Sara Josephine
Blackwell, Antoinette Louisa Brown

Blatch, Harriot Eaton Stanton
Bloor, "Mother" Ella Reev
Brent, Margaret
Brownmiller, Susan
Catt, Carrie Chapman
Chicago, Judy
Child, Lydia Maria
Croly, Jane Cunningham
Davison, Emily Wilding
Door, Rheta Childe
Duniway, Abigail Jane Scott
Fawcett, Dame Millicent Garrett
Foat, Ginny
Friedan, Betty Naomi Goldstein
Godwin, Mary Wollstonecraft
Goldsmith, Judith Ann Becker
Hawes, Elisabeth
Ichikawa, Fusae
Johnson, Sonia
Kennedy, Florynce
Millett, Kate
Naidu, Sarojini
Phillips, Lena Madesin
Smeal, Eleanor Marie Cutri
Stanton, Elizabeth Cady
Steinem, Gloria
Stone, Lucy
Thomas, Martha Carey
Truth, Sojourner

FIELD MARSHAL

Badoglio, Pietro
Blucher, Gebhard Leberecht von
Gneisenau, August Neithardt von
Haig, Douglas
Kitchener, Horatio Herbert
Konev, Ivan S
Kutuzov, Mikhail Ilarionovich
Mannerheim, Carl Gustav Emil, Baron
Paulus, Friedrich von
Perignon, Dominique Catherine
Potemkin, Grigori Alexsandrovich
Raglan, Fitzroy James Henry Somerset,
    Baron
Schlieffen, Alfred, Graf von
Suvorov, Aleksandr V
Wavell, Archibald Percival Wavell, Earl

FIGURE SKATER

Albright, Tenley Emma
Allen, Lisa Marie
Babilonia, Tai Reina
Biellmann, Denise
Blumberg, Judy
Brooks, Lela
Cousins, Robin
Cranston, Toller
Curry, John Anthony
Dean, Christopher
Fleming, Peggy Gale

Fratianne, Linda
Gardner, Randy
Hamill, Dorothy
Hamilton, Scott
Henie, Sonja
Hoffmann, Jan
Jenkins, Hayes Alan
Johnson, Lynn-Holly
Lynn, Janet
Orser, Brian
Potzsch, Anett
Protopopov, Ludmilla Evgenievna
  Belousova
Protopopov, Oleg Alekseevich
Rodnina, Irina
Santee, David
Scott, Barbara Ann
Seibert, Michael
Thomas, Debi
Tickner, Charlie
Torvill, Jane
Witt, Katarina
Zaitsev, Alexsander
Zayak, Elaine

FILM EXECUTIVE

Ackerman, Harry S
Arkoff, Samuel Z
Balaban, Barney
Begelman, David
Diller, Barry Charles
Disney, Roy O
Goldenson, Leonard Harry
Gordy, Berry, Jr.
Laemmle, Carl, Sr.
Lansing, Sherry Lee
Lasky, Jesse L
Mayer, Arthur Loeb
Mayer, L(ouis) B(urt)
Melnick, Daniel
Oshima, Nagrsa
Rank, J(oseph) Arthur
Schenck, Joseph M
Schenck, Nicholas Michael
Simon, John Alan
Valenti, Jack Joseph
Warner, Albert
Warner, Harry Morris
Warner, Jack Leonard
Warner, Jack, Jr.
Warner, Sam(uel Louis)
Wasserman, Lew(is Robert)
Wolf, "Manny" Emanuel L
Zanuck, Darryl Francis
Zanuck, Richard Darryl
Zukor, Adolph

FILMMAKER

Abbas, Khwaja Ahmad
Abbott, L(enwood) B(allard)

Alcott, John
Bitzer, George William
Blackton, James Stuart
Box, John
Clampett, Bob (Robert)
Crosby, Floyd Delafield
DeBroca, Philippe Claude Alex
Deren, Maya
Elisofon, Eliot
Fraker, William A
Francis, Freddie
Gest, Morris
Guffey, Burnett
Howe, James Wong
Johnson, Martin Elmer
Kaufman, Boris
Lurie, Jane
Naruse, Mikio
Nykvist, Sven Vilhem
Pathe, Charles
Reems, Harry
Richter, Hans
Romero, George A
Root, Alan
Root, Joan
Rotha, Paul
Sedelmaier, Joe (John Josef)
Strand, Paul
Struss, Karl
Sullivan, C(harles) Gardner
Taylor, Ronnie
Trnks, Jiri
Unsworth, Geoffrey
Vanderbilt, Cornelius, Jr.
Waite, Ric
Wexler, Haskell
Williams, Billy
Willis, Gordon
Wiseman, Frederick
Zsigmond, Vilmos

FILMMAKERS

Hollywood Ten

FINANCIER

Astor, John Jacob
Astor, William Vincent
Astor, William Waldorf Astor, Viscount
Bache, Jules Sermon
Belmont, August
Bergen, John Joseph
Brady, "Diamond Jim" James Buchanan
Catto, Thomas Sivewright, Baron
Corcoran, William Wilson
Cornfeld, Bernard
Corning, Erastus
Dawkins, Peter M
Dow, Charles Henry
Drew, Daniel
Dreyfus, Jack Jonas

Dun, Robert Graham
Durant, Thomas Clark
Eaton, Cyrus Stephen
Estes, Billie Sol
Field, Cyrus West
Fisk, Jim (James)
Fitzgerald, A(rthur) Ernest
Gallatin, Albert (Abraham Alfonse Albert)
Gates, John Warne
Gould, Jay (Jason)
Granville, Joseph E(nsign)
Green, Hetty
Guggenheim, Daniel
Gulbenkian, Nubar Sarkis
Hammer, Armand
Harriman, E(dward) Roland (Noel)
Hartford, Huntington
Hirshhorn, Joseph
Hopkins, Johns
Insull, Samuel
Kennedy, Joseph Patrick, Sr.
Kreuger, Ivar
Laeri, J(ohn) Howard
Lasser, Jacob Kay
Loeb, Gerald Martin
March, Juan Alberto
Mellon, Andrew William
Morgan, J(ohn) P(ierpont)
Morris, Robert
Morse, Joseph
Murchison, Clint(on Williams)
Necker, Jacques
Odlum, Floyd Bostwick
Pierce, Edward Allen
Pritzker, Abram Nicholas
Reed, John Shepard
Riklis, Mishulam
Roney, William Chapoton, Jr.
Roosevelt, James
Rothschild, Mayer Amschel
Rubinstein, Serge
Ryan, Thomas Fortune
Sage, Russell
Schacht, Hjalmar Horace Greeley
Schultz, Harry D
Semenenko, Serge
Smith, Donald Alexander
Spear, Roger Elliot
Vanderbilt, Cornelius
Vanderbilt, Cornelius
Vanderbilt, William Henry
Vesco, Robert Lee
Zaharoff, Basil, Sir

FIREFIGHTER

Adair, "Red" Paul Neal

FIRST LADY

Adams, Abigail Smith
Adams, Louisa Catherine

Carter, Rosalynn Eleanor Smith
Cleveland, Frances Folsom
Coolidge, Grace Anne Goodhue
Eisenhower, Mamie Geneva Doud
Fillmore, Abigail Powers
Ford, Betty (Elizabeth Bloomer)
Garfield, Lucretia Rudolph
Grant, Julia Dent
Harding, Florence Kling De Wolfe
Harrison, Anna Tuthill Symmes
Harrison, Caroline Lavinia Scott
Hayes, Lucy Webb
Hoover, Lou Henry
Jackson, Rachel Donelson Robards
Johnson, "Lady Bird" Claudia Alta Taylor
Johnson, Eliza McCardle
Lincoln, Mary Todd
Madison, Dolly Payne Todd
McKinley, Ida Saxton
Monroe, Elizabeth Kortright
Pierce, Jane Means
Polk, Sarah Childress
Reagan, Nancy Davis
Roosevelt, Edith Kermit Carow
Roosevelt, Eleanor
Taft, Helen Herron
Taylor, Margaret Smith
Truman, Bess
Tyler, Julia Gardiner
Tyler, Letitia Christian
Washington, Martha Dandridge Curtis
Wilson, Edith Bolling Galt
Wilson, Ellen Axson

FOLKLORIST

Dobie, J(ames) Frank
Jacobs, Joseph
Jagendorf, Moritz
Lomax, Alan
Lomax, John Avery
Spence, Lewis (James Lewis Thomas
   Chalmers)

FOOTBALL COACH

Allen, George
Baugh, Sammy (Samuel Adrian)
Berry, Raymond Emmett
Blaik, "Red" Earl Henry
Blanchard, "Doc" Felix Anthony
Booth, "Albie" Albert James, Jr.
Brill, Marty (Martin)
Brown, Paul
Bryant, "Bear" Paul William
Burns, Jerry (Jerome Monahan)
Chamberlin, (B) Guy
Christiansen, Jack
Clark, "Dutch" Earl
Clark, Monte
Conzelman, Jimmy (James Gleason)
Coryell, Don(ald David)

Crisler, "Fritz" Herbert Orin
Devine, Dan(iel John)
Ditka, Mike
Dodd, Robert Lee (Bobby)
Ewbank, "Weeb" Wilbur
Fairbanks, Chuck (Charles Leo)
Faust, Gerry (Gerard Anthony, Jr.)
Flores, Tom (Thomas Raymond)
Gibbs, Joe Jackson
Gillman, Sidney
Grant, "Bud" Harold Peter
Halas, George Stanley
Hayes, "Woody" Wayne Woodrow
Heisman, John William
Holtz, Lou
Hornung, Paul Vernon
Jones, "Biff" Lawrence M
Kapp, Joe (Joseph)
Kerr, Andrew
Knox, Chuck (Charles Robert)
Lambeau, "Curly" Earl L
Landry, Tom (Thomas Wade)
Leahy, Frank
Little, Lou(is)
Lombardi, Vince(nt Thomas)
Marchibroda, Ted (Theodore Joseph)
McCafferty, Don
McKay, John H
Neyland, Robert Reese
Noll, Chuck (Charles H)
Owen, Steve (Stephen Joseph)
Parker, "Buddy" Raymond
Parseghian, Ara Raoul
Paterno, Joseph V (Joe)
Perkins, (Walter) Ray
Phillips, "Bum" Oail Andrew
Pollard, Fritz (Frederick D)
Robinson, Eddie
Robinson, John Alexander
Rockne, Knute Kenneth
Rogers, Darryl D
Ronzani, Gene
Royal, Darrell
Schembechler, "Bo" Glenn Edward
Schmidt, Joe (Joseph Paul)
Schnellenberger, Howard Leslie
Shaughnessy, Clark Daniel
Shula, Don Francis
Stagg, Amos Alonzo
Starr, Bart (Bryan B)
Switzer, Barry
Van Brocklin, Norm(an Mack)
Wade, Wallace
Walsh, Bill (William)
Walton, Joe (Joseph Frank)
Warner, "Pop" Glenn Scobey
Wilkinson, "Bud" Charles
Yost, Fielding Harris
Zuppke, Robert C

FOOTBALL EXECUTIVE

Allen, George
Camp, Walter Chauncey
Carr, Joseph F
Davis, Al(len)
DeBartolo, Edward J, Jr.
Ford, William Clay
Gordon, Richard Francis, Jr.
Hess, Leon
Hunt, Lamar
Mara, Wellington T
Murchison, Clint(on Williams, Jr.)
Robbie, Joe (Joseph)
Rooney, Art(hur Joseph)
Rosenbloom, Carroll D
Rosenbloom, Georgia
Rozelle, "Pete" Alvin Ray
Schramm, Tex(as Edward)
Williams, Edward Bennett

FOOTBALL PLAYER

Allen, Marcus
Alworth, Lance Dwight
Alzado, Lyle Martin
Anderson, Donny
Anderson, Ken(neth Allan)
Anderson, O(ttis) J(erome)
Armstrong, Otis
Bartkowski, Steve(n Joseph)
Battles, Cliff(ord Franklin)
Baugh, Sammy (Samuel Adrian)
Bell, Ricky Lynn
Benirschke, Rolf Joachim
Bergey, Bill
Berry, Raymond Emmett
Biletnikoff, Fred(erick)
Blanchard, "Doc" Felix Anthony
Blanda, George Frederick
Bleier, "Rocky" Robert Patrick
Blount, Mel(vin Cornell)
Booth, "Albie" Albert James, Jr.
Bradley, Bill (William)
Bradshaw, Terry Paxton
Branch, Cliff(ord)
Bratkowski, Zeke (Edmund R)
Brill, Marty (Martin)
Brodie, John Riley
Brown, Eddie Lee
Brown, Jim (James Nathaniel)
Brown, Johnny Mack
Brown, Larry
Brown, Ron(ald James)
Browner, Ross
Buoniconti, Nick
Butkus, Dick (Richard J)
Cagle, "Red" Christian Keener
Campbell, Earl Christian
Cappelletti, "Duke" Gino
Cappelletti, John Raymond
Carmichael, Harold

Carpenter, William S, Jr.
Carter, Anthony
Chamberlin, (B) Guy
Chandler, Don
Christiansen, Jack
Clark, "Dutch" Earl
Clark, Monte
Collinsworth, (Anthony) Chris
Cook, Greg(ory Lynn)
Cousineau, Tom
Craig, Roger Timothy
Cromwell, Nolan
Crowley, Jim (James)
Csonka, Larry Richard
Cunningham, Sam
Curtis, (James) Mike (Michael)
Curtis, Isaac
Dale, Carroll W
Danelo, Joe (Joseph Peter)
Danielson, Gary
Davis, Ernie (Ernest R)
Davis, Glenn
Davis, Willie (William Henry)
Dawson, Len (Leonard Ray)
Delaney, Joe Alton
Dickerson, Eric Demetric
Dickey, Lynn (Clifford Lynn)
Dierdorf, Dan(iel Lee)
Ditka, Mike
Donovan, Art
Dorsett, Tony (Anthony Drew)
Dowler, Boyd
Dryer, Fred (John Frederick)
Dudley, William
Eason, Tony (Charles Carroll, IV)
Elway, John Albert
English, Doug (Lowell Douglas)
Evans, Vince(nt Tobias)
Fears, Tom (Thomas Jesse)
Ferguson, Joe Carlton, Jr.
Ferragamo, Vince
Fletcher, Glenn Robert
Flutie, Doug(las Richard)
Foreman, "Chuck" Walter Eugene
Fortmann, Daniel John
Fouts, Dan(iel Francis)
Francis, Russ(ell Ross)
Francis, Wallace
Gabriel, Roman, Jr.
Galbreath, Tony (Anthony)
Garrett, Michael Lockett
Gastineau, Mark (Marcus D)
Gault, Willie
George, Bill (William)
Gifford, Frank (Francis Newton)
Gilliam, Joe
Gipp, George
Gossett, D(aniel) Bruce
Gradishar, Randy Charles
Graham, Otto Everett
Grange, "Red" Harold Edward

Greene, Joe (Joseph)
Grier, "Rosey" Roosevelt
Griese, Bob (Robert Allen)
Griffin, Archie
Grogan, Steve
Guyon, Joe
Haden, Pat(rick Capper)
Ham, Jack
Hannah, John Allen
Harmon, Tom (Thomas D)
Harris, Cliff(ord Allen)
Harris, Franco
Hart, Jim W
Hayes, Lester
Heffelfinger, "Pudge" William Walter
Heisman, John William
Henderson, "Hollywood" Thomas
Hendricks, Ted (Theodore Paul)
Hickman, Herman Michael, Jr.
Hill, Calvin
Hipple, Eric Ellsworth
Hirsch, "Crazylegs" Elroy
Hornung, Paul Vernon
Houston, Ken(neth Ray)
Hubbard, Cal (Robert Calvin)
Huff, Sam (Robert Lee)
Humphrey, Claude B
Humphries, Stefan
Jackson, "Bo" Vincent Edward
Jackson, Earnest
Jaworski, Ron(ald Vincent)
Jefferson, John Larry
Johnson, "Billy White Shoes" (William Arthur
Johnson, Pete
Jones, "Too Tall" Edward Lee
Jones, Bert(ram Hays)
Junior, E J (Ester James, III)
Jurgenson, "Sonny" Christian Adolph, III
Justice, "Choo Choo" Charles Ronald
Kapp, Joe (Joseph)
Karras, Alex(ander G)
Kemp, Jack French
Kennedy, Bill (William Patrick)
Kiick, Jim (James F)
Kilmer, Billy (William O)
Kosar, Bernie
Kunz, George
Lambeau, "Curly" Earl L
Lambert, Jack (John Harold)
Lamonica, Daryle Pat
Layden, Elmer
Layne, Bobby (Robert Lawrence)
Lipscomb, Eugene
Lomax, Neil Vincent
Lott, Ronnie (Ronald Mandel)
Lowery, "Nick" Gerald Lowery
Luckman, Sid(ney)
Lujack, John(ny)
Lyman, William Roy
Manning, Archie (Elisha Archie, III)

Marchetti, Gino
Marinaro, Ed
Marino, Dan(iel Constantine, Jr.)
Martin, Harvey
Matson, Oliver G
Matuszak, John
McElhenny, Hugh
McMahon, Jim (James Robert)
McNally, John Victor
McNeil, Freeman
Meredith, Don (Joseph Donald)
Miller, Don
Montana, Joe (Joseph C, Jr.)
Moon, Warren
Morrall, Earl E
Morris, "Mercury" Eugene
Morton, Craig
Mosely, Mark DeWayne
Muller, Harold P
Muncie, "Chuck" Henry Vance
Nagurski, "Bronko" Bronislaw
Namath, Joe (Joseph William)
Nehemiah, Renaldo
Nevers, Ernie (Ernest A)
Olsen, Merlin
Owens, Steve
Page, Alan Cedric
Pastorini, Dan
Payton, Walter
Pearson, Drew
Perry, William
Piccolo, Brian
Plunkett, Jim (James William, Jr.)
Pruitt, Greg(ory Donald)
Redfield, William
Reese, Don(ald Francis)
Renfro, Mel(vin Lacy)
Rentzel, Lance
Reynolds, Bobby (Robert)
Reynolds, Jack (John Sumner)
Riggins, John
Rockne, Knute Kenneth
Rogers, Don(ald Lavert)
Rogers, George
Ronzani, Gene
Rote, Kyle
Sayers, Gale Eugene
Schlicter, Art(hur E)
Schmidt, Joe (Joseph Paul)
Selmon, Lee Roy
Simms, Phil(ip)
Simpson, O(renthal) J(ames)
Sims, Billy Ray
Singletary, Mike (Michael)
Sipe, Brian Winfield
Smith, "Bubba" Charles Aaron
Stabler, Ken(neth Michael)
Stallworth, John Lee
Starr, Bart (Bryan B)
Staubach, Roger Thomas
Stemrick, Greg(ory Earl, Sr.)

Stenerud, Jan
Stingley, Darryl
Strong, Ken
Stuhldreher, Harry A
Swann, Lynn Curtis
Tarkenton, Fran(cis Asbury)
Tatum, Jack (John David)
Theismann, Joe (Joseph Robert)
Thompson, Jack
Thorpe, Jim (James Francis)
Tittle, Y(elberton) A(braham)
Todd, Richard
Unitas, Johnny (John Constantine)
Upshaw, Gene (Eugene)
Van Brocklin, Norm(an Mack)
Walker, Ewell Doak, Jr.
Walker, Herschel
Walker, Wesley Darcel
Walls, Everson Collins
Warfield, Paul Dryden
Warner, Curt
Waters, Charlie (Charles Tutan)
Webster, Mike (Michael Lewis)
White, Charles Raymond
White, Randy Lee
White, Stan(ley Ray)
Williams, Delvin
Williams, Doug(las Lee)
Wilson, Harry E
Winslow, Kellen Boswell
Wojciechowicz, Alexander
Yepremian, Garo (Garabed S)
Youngblood, (Herbert) Jack(son)
Zorn, Jim (John Eldon)

FOOTBALL PLAYERS

Four Horsemen of Notre Dame, The

FORMER DIPLOMAT

Sullivan, William Healy

FRONTIERSMAN

Beckwourth, James Pierson
Bridger, James
Carson, "Kit" Christopher
Cody, "Buffalo Bill" William Frederick
Crockett, Davy (David)
Fink, Mike
Hickok, "Wild Bill" James Butler
Lillie, Gordon William

FRONTIERSWOMAN

Calamity Jane
Oakley, Annie
Tabor, Elizabeth Bonduel McCourt Doe

FUR TRADER

Ashley, William Henry
Astor, John Jacob
Bridger, James
McGill, James
McLoughlin, John
Smith, Jedediah Strong

FURNITURE DESIGNER

Adam, Robert
Chippendale, Thomas
Hepplewhite, George
Hitchcock, Lambert
Phyfe, Duncan
Sheraton, Thomas

GAMBLER

Brummell, "Beau" George Bryan
Harrah, Bill (William Fisk)
Holliday, "Doc" John Henry
Nick the Greek
Rothstein, Arnold

GANGSTER

Capone, Al(phonse)
Colombo, Joseph Anthony
Giancana, Salvatore (Sam)
Hamilton, Floyd (Garland)
Kray, Reggie (Reginald)
Kray, Ronnie (Ronald)
Lucchese, Thomas
Moran, "Bugs" George C
Schultz, Dutch
Siegel, "Bugsy" Benjamin
Stompanato, Johnny
Touchy, Roger

GAS STATION ATTENDANT

Dummar, Melvin

GENERAL

Agrippa, Marcus Vipsanius
Aguinaldo, Emilio
Alanbrooke, Alan Francis Brooke, 1st
  Viscount
Alexander of Tunis, Harold Rupert Leofric
  George Alexander, Earl
Allon, Yigal
Amherst, Jeffrey
Belisarius
Belknap, William Worth
Ben-Gal, Avigdor
Bradley, Omar Nelson
Bragg, Braxton
Breckinridge, John Cabell
Brown, George Scratchley

Burgoyne, John
Butler, Benjamin Franklin
Cadogan, William
Calles, Plutarco
Cardigan, Earl
Cassius
Castle, Frederick W
Chapman, Leonard F, Jr.
Clark, Mark Wayne
Clarke, Bruce Cooper
Cornwallis, Charles, Marquis
Crassus, Marcus Lincinius
Crittendon, Thomas L
Cromwell, Oliver
Crook, George
Cunningham, Alan Gordon, Sir
Cushman, Robert Everton, Jr.
Denikin, Anton Ivanovich
Dodge, Grenville Mellen
Doubleday, Abner
Duong Van Minh
Elazar, David
Enver Pasha
Evren, Kenan
Fairfax, Thomas
Gale, Richard Nelson, Sir
Gallieni, Joseph Simon
Gamelin, Maurice Gustave
Gates, Horatio
Giraud, Henri Honore
Gorbatov, Aleksandr Vassil'evich
Gordon, Charles George
Gordon, John Brown
Greene, Nathanael
Haig, Alexander Meigs, Jr.
Hamilton, Ian Standish Monteith, Sir
Hampton, Wade
Herbert, Anthony B
Hindenburg, Paul von
Hodge, John Reed
Howe, William, Viscount
Iturbide, Augustin de
Jones, David Charles
Josephus, Flavius
Julius Caesar
Kalb, Johann de
Kenney, George Churchill
Kuter, Laurence S(herman)
Laclos, (Pierre) Choderlos de
Lafayette, Marie Joseph Paul, Marquis
Leclerc, Jacques-Philippe
Lee, Charles
Lee, Robert E(dward)
Leigh Guzman, Jorge Gustavo
Longstreet, James
Lucullus, Lucius Licinius
Ludendorff, Erich Friedrich Wilhelm
Lyon, Nathaniel
Marlborough, John Churchill, Duke
Marshall, George Catlett
Marshall, S(amuel) L(yman) A(twood)

McDougall, Alexander
Mitchell, Billy (William)
Montgomery, Richard
Morgan, Daniel
Moultrie, William
Neyland, Robert Reese
Nobile, Umberto
Park, Chung Hee
Pilsudski, Jozef
Pompey the Great
Pulaski, Kazimierz
Putnam, Israel
Ridgway, Matthew Bunker
Rochambeau, Jean Baptiste Donatien de
    Vimeur, Comte
Rokossovsky, Konstantin
Rommel, Erwin Johannes Eugin
Sadeh, Itzhak
Scipio Africanus, Publius Cornelius
Scipio, Publius Cornelius
Scott, Winfield
Smith, Walter Bedell
Spaatz, Carl Andrew
Stark, John
Stilwell, Joseph Warren
Stoneman, George
Stratemeyer, George E
Stuart, "Jeb" James Ewell Brown
Sulla, Lucius C
Sullivan, John
Sumter, Thomas
Swinton, Ernest Dunlop, Sir
Taylor, Maxwell Davenport
Tojo, Hideki (Eiki)
Toledo, Fernando Alvarez de
Torrijos Herrera, Omar
Van Fleet, James Alward
Vandegrift, Alexander Archer
Vandenberg, Hoyt Sanford
Vaughan, Harry Hawkins
Wadsworth, James Samuel
Wainwright, Jonathan Mayhew
Waller, Sir William
Wellington, Arthur Wellesley, Duke
Wilson, Louis Hugh
Wingate, Orde Charles
Wolfe, James
Wood, Leonard
Wrangel, Pietr Nikolayevich
Yamashita, Tomoyuki
Zhdanov, Andrei Alexandrovich

GENETICIST

Bridges, Calvin Blackman
Brown, Michael S
Jacob, Francois
Lysenko, Trofim Denisovich
McClintock, Barbara
Mendel, Gregor Johann
Tatum, Edward Lawrie
Wortman, Sterling

GEOGRAPHER

Christaller, Walter
Davis, William Morris
Freshfield, Douglas William
Gerasimov, Innokentii Petrovich
Grosvenor, Gilbert Hovey
Hakluyt, Richard
Mercator, Gerhardus
Peel, Ronald Francis (Edward Waite)
Przhevalsky, Nikolai Mikhailovich
Pytheas
Ritter, Karl
Ronne, Finn
Siple, Paul Allman
Strabo
Thompson, David

GEOLOGIST

Ballard, Robert Duane
Buckland, William
Chamberlin, Thomas Chrowder
Dana, James Dwight
Davis, William Morris
Fuchs, Vivian Ernest, Sir
Hall, James, Sir
Holmes, Arthur
Hutton, James
Jaggar, Thomas Augustus
King, Clarence
Lyell, Charles, Sir
Masursky, Harold
Mawson, Douglas, Sir
Menard, H William
Powell, John Wesley
Silliman, Benjamin
Tromp, Solco Walle
Tyrrell, Joseph Burr
Wegener, Alfred
Wrather, William Embry

GOLFER

Alcott, Amy
Aoki, Isao
Baker, Kathy
Ballesteros, Seve(riano)
Bean, Andy
Berg, Patty (Patricia Jane)
Blalock, Jane
Bolt, Tommy (Thomas)
Boros, Julius Nicholas
Boswell, Charles Albert
Bradley, Pat(ricia Ellen)
Braid, James
Britz, Jerilyn
Brophy, Catherine Mary
Caponi, Donna
Carner, Joanne Gunderson
Casper, Billy (William Earl)
Clampett, Bobby

Collett, Glenna
Crampton, Bruce Sidney
Crenshaw, Ben Daniel
Crosby, Nathaniel
Daniel, Beth
Demaret, Jimmy (James Newton B)
DeVicenzo, Roberto
Eichelberger, Dave
Elder, Lee
Espinosa, Al
Evans, Charles, Jr.
Ferrier, Jim (James B)
Floyd, Raymond
Ford, Doug
Geiberger, Al(len L)
Goalby, Bob
Graham, David B
Green, Hubie (Hubert)
Hagen, Walter Charles
Haynie, Sandra
Hill, Dave
Hogan, Ben (William Benjamin)
Irwin, Hale
Jacklin, Anthony
Jones, Bobby (Robert Tyre)
Lema, Tony (Anthony David)
Lietzke, Bruce
Little, (William) Lawson, Jr.
Little, Sally
Littler, Gene (Eugene Alex)
Locke, Bobbie
Lopez, Nancy
Mangrum, Lloyd
Mann, Carol Ann
Marsh, Graham B
McSpaden, Byron
Middlecoff, Cary
Miller, Johnny Laurence
Moody, Orville
Nelson, Byron (John Byron, Jr.)
Nelson, Larry Gene
Nichols, Bobby (Robert)
Nicklaus, Jack
Norman, Greg
North, Andy
Palmer, Arnold Daniel
Pate, Jerry
Peete, Calvin
Player, Gary Jim
Pohl, Dan(ny Joe)
Post, Sandra
Price, Nick
Rankin, Judy Torluemke
Rawls, Betsy (Elizabeth Earle)
Rodriguez, "Chi-Chi" Juan
Rogers, Bill (William Charles)
Sanders, Doug(las)
Sarazen, Gene
Smith, Horton
Snead, Sam(uel Jackson)
Stacy, Hollis

Stadler, Craig
Stephenson, Jan
Stockton, Dave (David)
Strange, Curtis
Suggs, Louise
Taylor, John Henry
Trevino, Lee Buck
Turnesa, Jim
Vare, Glenna Collett
Wadkins, Lanny
Wall, Art(hur Johnathan), Jr.
Watson, Tom (Sturges)
Weiskopf, Tom Daniel
Whitworth, Kathy (Kathrynne Ann)
Wood, Craig Ralph
Wright, Mickey
Zoeller, "Fuzzy" Frank Urban

GOVERNESS

Leonowens, Anna Harriette Crawford

GOVERNMENT OFFICIAL

Acheson, Dean Gooderham
Adams, Brock(man)
Adams, Eve Bertrand
Adelman, Kenneth Lee
Agee, Philip
Alexander, Clifford L, Jr.
Alexander, Donald Crichton
Allen, Richard Vincent
Amerasinghe, Hamilton Shirley
Andrus, Cecil D(ale)
Arens, Moshe
Armstrong, Anne Legendre
Askew, Reubin O'Donovan
Atherton, Alfred LeRoy, Jr.
Austin, Warren R(obinson)
Bailar, Benjamin Franklin
Baker, Bobby (Robert Gene)
Baker, James Addison, III
Balbo, Italo
Baldrige, Malcolm (Howard Malcolm, Jr.)
Ball, George Wildman
Ballantrae, Lord
Bane, Frank B
Barnard, Chester Irving
Barre, Raymond
Beesley, H(orace) Brent
Bell, Terrel Howard
Bennett, William John
Benson, Ezra Taft
Bergland, Bob (Robert Selmer)
Berri, Nabih
Bevin, Ernest
Biddle, Francis Beverley
Blatchford, Joseph Hoffer
Block, John Rusling
Blumenthal, W Michael
Bolger, William Frederick
Bondfield, Margaret Grace

Boorstin, Daniel J(oseph)
Boyce, Westray Battle
Bray, Charles William, III
Brennan, Peter Joseph
Bright, John
Brimmer, Andrew Felton
Brinegar, Claude Stout
Broadbent, Ed (John Edward)
Brown, George Alfred
Brown, Harold
Brown, Samuel W, Jr.
Brownell, Herbert, Jr.
Browning, James Louis
Brownwell, Samuel Miller
Buchan, John, Sir
Buchanan, Angela Marie
Bundy, William Putnam
Burch, Dean
Burford, Anne McGill Gorsuch
Butterfield, Alexander Porter
Butz, Earl Lauer
Byrne, Brendan
Byrnes, James Francis
Cabral, Luis de Almeida
Callaghan, James (Leonard James)
Callaway, Howard Hollis
Campbell, Clifford, Sir
Carlisle, John Griffin
Carlucci, Frank Charles, III
Carter, Hodding (William Hodding, III)
Chapin, Roy Dikeman
Chayes, Abram J
Christopher, Warren Miner
Civiletti, Benjamin R
Clark, (William) Ramsey
Clark, William P(atrick, Jr.)
Cleland, Max (Joseph Maxwell)
Clifford, Clark McAdams
Cline, Genevieve Rose
Cochrane, Edward Lull
Colby, William Egan
Colman, Norman Jay
Conger, Clement Ellis
Cooper, Joseph D
Costa Mendez, Nicanor
Costle, Douglas Michael
Daniels, Josephus
Darlan, Jean Francois
Davis, Dwight Filley
Davis, Edward Michael
Day, J(ames) Edward
Debray, Regis (Jules Regis)
Debus, Kurt Heinrich
Dewey, Charles Schuveldt
Dixon, Paul Rand
Dodge, Joseph Morrell
Dole, Elizabeth Hanford
Dominick, Peter Hoyt
Donovan, Raymond James
Drucker, Peter
Dulles, John Foster

Duncan, Charles William, Jr.
Eberstadt, Ferdinand
Eden, Nicholas
Edwards, James Burrows
Eizenstat, Stuart E
Eliot, Martha May
Evans, John
Fall, Albert Bacon
Field, Stanley
Finch, Robert Hutchison
Flemming, Arthur Sherwood
Fletcher, Arthur A
Folsom, Marion Bayard
Foreman, Carol Lee Tucker
Fortas, Abe
Fowler, Mark Stephen
Frankel, Charles
Franks, Oliver Shewell, Sir
Freeman, Orville Lothrop
Furtseva, Ekaterina Alexeyevna
Gairy, Eric M, Sir
Gardner, John William
Garrett, Ray, Jr.
Gaud, William Steen, Jr.
George, Walter Franklin
Gero, Erno
Ghotbzadeh, Sadegh
Golar, Simeon
Gray, Gordon
Gray, Louis Patrick
Grechko, Andrei Antonovick
Greenspan, Alan
Grolier, Jean
Hagerty, James Campbell
Haig, Alexander Meigs, Jr.
Hampton, Robert Edward
Hanks, Nancy
Harriman, W(illiam) Averell
Harris, Patricia Roberts
Heckler, Margaret Mary
Heller, Walter Wolfgang
Helms, Richard McGarrah
Heseltine, Michael Ray Dibdin
Hickel, Walter Joseph
Hill, Rowland, Sir
Hills, Carla Anderson
Hills, Roderick M
Hobby, Oveta Culp
Hodges, Luther Hartwell
Hodgson, James Day
Hoffman, Anna Marie Lederer Rosenberg
Holland, Jerome Heartwell
Hoover, J(ohn) Edgar
Houghton, Amory
Howe, (Richard Edward) Geoffrey, Sir
Hufstedler, Shirley (Ann) M(ount)
Hugel, Max
Inman, Bobby Ray
Izac, Edouard Victor M
James, Daniel, Jr.
Jaworski, Leon

Johnson, Hugh S
Johnson, Nicholas
Johnson, William, Sir
Jones, David Charles
Jones, Jesse Holman
Kalb, Bernard
Kania, Stanislaw
Katzenbach, Nicholas de Belleville
Kell, Vernon, Sir
Kelley, Clarence Marion
Kennedy, David M
Keyworth, George Albert
Kim, Il Sung
Kissinger, Henry Alfred
Klassen, Elmer Theodore
Klein, Herbert George
Kleindienst, Richard Gordon
Klutznick, Philip M
Knauer, Virginia Harrington Wright
Knight, Frances Gladys
Knox, Frank
Knox, Henry
Koop, Charles Everett
Kotsching, Walter Maria
Kraft, Chris(topher Columbus, Jr.)
Kreps, Juanita Morris
La Marsh, Judy Verlyn
LaFollette, Bronson Cutting
Laird, Melvin Robert
Lambsdorff, Otto
Lance, (Thomas) Bert(ram)
Landis, James McCauley
Landrieu, "Moon" Maurice Edwin
Lansing, Robert
Lavelle, Rita Marie
Le Duc Tho
Lehman, John Francis, Jr.
Levesque, Rene
Levi, Edward Hirsch
Levitt, Arthur, Jr.
Lewis, Allen Montgomery, Sir
Lewis, Drew (Andrew Lindsay, Jr.)
Lewis, Jordan David
Lin, Piao (Yu-Yung)
Lovelace, William Randolph, II
Lovett, Robert A(bercrombie)
Lucas, Scott Wike
Lyng, Richard E
Lynn, James Thomas
MacGregor, Clark
MacLeod, Iain Norman
Malenkov, Georgi Maximilianovich
Malraux, Andre
Marshall, George Catlett
Marshall, Ray
Martin, William McChesney, Jr.
Mather, Stephen Tyng
Mathews, Forrest David
McAdoo, William Gibbs
McCree, Wade Hampton, Jr.
McElroy, Neil Hosler

McFarlane, Robert Carl
McHenry, Donald Franchot
McIntyre, James Talmadge, Jr.
McNamara, Robert S(trange)
McNutt, Paul Vories
Meese, Edwin, III
Mellon, Andrew William
Michener, Roland
Miller, G(eorge) William
Miller, James Clifford, III
Miller, William Mosley
Mitchell, John Newton
Moffett, Ken(neth Elwood)
Moley, Raymond
Molotov, Viacheslav Mikhailovich
Morgenthau, Henry, Jr.
Morton, Julius Sterling
Morton, Rogers Clark Ballard
Moscone, George Richard
Mott, William Penn, Jr.
Muller, Hilgard
Myerson, Bess
Ness, Eliot
Nestingen, Ivan Arnold
Norton, Eleanor Holmes
Nott, John William Frederic
O'Donnell, Kenneth
Oldfield, Maurice, Sir
Ortega, Katherine Davalos
Paine, Thomas Otten
Palme, (Sven) Olof (Joachim)
Pate, Maurice
Pendleton, Clarence
Perkins, Frances
Perkins, Milo Randolph
Pierce, Samuel Riley, Jr.
Pindling, Lynden Oscar
Poinsett, Joel Roberts
Porritt, Arthur Espie, Sir
Price, Byron
Priest, Ivy (Maude) Baker
Profumo, John Dennis
Purvis, Melvin
Pym, Francis Leslie
Randall, Samuel J
Rapacki, Adam
Regan, Donald Thomas
Resor, Stanley Rogers
Rhinelander, John Bassett
Rhodes, Cecil John
Richardson, Elliot Lee
Rivers, L(ucius) Mendel
Rivlin, Alice Mitchell
Rockefeller, Mary French
Rogers, William Pierce
Rolvaag, Karl
Rosenberg, Anna Marie
Rostow, Walt Whitman
Rothschild, Lionel Nathan Rothschild,
    Baron
Roudebush, Richard Lowell

Rowe, James Henry, Jr.
Ruckelshaus, William Doyle
Rumsfeld, Donald
Ruppee, Loret Miller
Rush, Kenneth
Rusk, Dean (David Dean)
Sapir, Pinchas
Sawyer, Charles
Schlesinger, James Rodney
Schreyer, Edward Richard
Schweiker, Richard Schultz
Seaborg, Glenn Theodore
Seton-Watson, Hugh (George Hugh Nicholas)
Seward, William Henry
Shamir, Yitzhak
Shanks, Michael (James Michael)
Sharett, Moshe
Sharon, Ariel
Shultz, George Pratt
Simcoe, John Graves
Simon, William E(dward)
Sisco, Joseph John
Smathers, George Armistead
Smith, William French
Snepp, Frank Warren, III
Snyder, John Wesley
Soames, (Arthur) Christopher (John)
Sonnenfeldt, Helmut
Sorensen, Ted (Theodore Chaikin)
Sparkman, John Jackson
Speakes, Larry Melvin
Stanford, Leland (Amasa Leland)
Stans, Maurice Hubert
Steelman, John R
Stettinius, Edward R, Jr.
Stevens, Robert Ten Broeck
Stimson, Henry Lewis (Harry)
Stockman, David Allen
Stratton, William R
Strougal, Lubomir
Sullivan, Daniel P
Summerfield, Arthur Ellsworth
Thang, Ton Duc
Tolson, Clyde Anderson
Train, Russell Errol
Turner, Stansfield
Udall, Stewart Lee
Ustinov, Dmitri Fedorovich
Valdez, Abelardo Lopez
Valenti, Jack Joseph
Vance, Cyrus Roberts
Volcker, Paul Adolph
Wadsworth, James Jeremiah (Jerry)
Walker, Robert James
Warnke, Paul Culliton
Warren, Charles
Watson, Jack Hearn, Jr.
Watt, James Gaius
Weaver, Robert Clifton
Webster, William Hedgcock

Weeks, Sinclair
Weidenbaum, Murray Lew
Weinberger, Caspar Willard
Wheeler, Earle G
Wick, Charles Z
Wille, Frank
Wilson, Charles Erwin
Wirtz, William Willard
Woodcock, Amos Walter Wright
Wrather, William Embry
Yamani, Ahmad Zaki, Sheik

GOVERNOR

Andrew, John Albion
Chittenden, Thomas
Clairborne, William Charles
Dempsey, John Noel
Denver, James William
Faubus, Orval Eugene
Ferguson, Miriam Amanda
Ferrier, Henry Eliza
Gilligan, John Joyce
Graham, William Alexander
Grasso, Ella
Hathaway, Stanley Knapp
Hochoy, Solomon, Sir
Kerner, Otto
Kirk, Claude Roy, Jr.
Lee, Henry
Long, Earl Kemp
Longley, James Bernard
Lubbock, Francis Richard
Lucey, Patrick Joseph
Matheson, Scott Milne
McNair, Robert Evander
Moore, Arch Alfred, Jr.
Moultrie, William
Munoz Marin, Luis
Ogilvie, Richard Buell
Rhodes, James Allen
Romero Barcelo, Carlos
Ross, Nellie Taylor
Sanford, Terry
Shapp, Milton J
Stevenson, Coke Robert
Thompson, James Robert
Thomson, Meldrim, Jr.
Thornburgh, Richard Lewis
Vanderbilt, William Henry
Wallace, Lurleen Burns
Winter, William Forrest
Winthrop, John
Youngdahl, Luther W

GUARD

Wills, Frank

GYMNAST

Comaneci, Nadia
Korbut, Olga
Leitzel, Lillian
Retton, Mary Lou
Rigby, Cathy
Thomas, Kurt
Turischeva, Ludmila
Turnbow, Donna

HAIRSTYLIST

Alexandre
Kenneth
Leonard
Rock, Monti
Sassoon, Vidal
Sebring, Jay

HERO

Robin Hood

HEROES

Four Chaplains

HEROINE

Corbin, Margaret Cochran
Fritchie, Barbara
Gannett, Deborah Sampson
Joan of Arc
Laurie, Annie
Lewis, Ida
Ludington, Sybil
Pitcher, Molly
Secord, Laura Ingersoll

HISTORIAN

Acton, John Emerich Edward Dalberg-
    Acton, Baron
Adams, Brooks
Adams, Charles Francis, Jr.
Adams, Henry Brooks
Adams, James Truslow
Allen, Frederick Lewis
Amalrik, Andrei Alekseyevich
Amory, Cleveland
Andrews, Charles McLean
Aptheker, Herbert
Arendt, Hannah
Bancroft, George
Bartlett, John Russell
Barton, George
Barzun, Jacques Martin
Beard, Charles Austin
Beard, Mary Ritter
Becker, Carl Lotus
Bemis, Samuel Flagg

Bennett, Lerone, Jr.
Bettmann, Otto Ludwig
Beveridge, Albert Jeremiah
Bickerman, Elias Joseph
Billington, Ray Allen
Bowers, Claude Gernade
Boyd, Julian Parks
Brandel, Fernand Paul
Brandes, Georg Morris Cohen
Brauer, Jerald Carl
Breasted, James Henry
Brinton, Clarence Crane
Brown, Dee (Alexander)
Bryce, James Bryce, Viscount
Burchard, John Ely
Burckhardt, Carl Jacob
Bury, John Bagnell
Butterfield, Lyman Henry
Butterfield, Roger Place
Carlyle, Thomas
Cato, Marcus Porcius Censorius
Chadwick, William Owen
Channing, Edward
Chidsey, Donald Barr
Clapp, Margaret Antoinette
Clarendon, Edward Hyde, Earl
Clark, Abraham
Clark, Thomas Dionysius
Comines, Philippe de
Commager, Henry Steele
Commons, John Rogers
Cooke, John Esten
Crawford, Francis Marion
Crittenden, Christopher
Curti, Merle Eugene
Davidson, Donald Grady
Denison, George Taylor
Dionysius of Halicarnassus
Dodd, William Edward
Draper, John William
Durant, Will(iam James)
Dutton, Ralph Stawell
Dyce. Alexander
Earle, Alice Morse
Elkins, Stanley Maurice
Eusebius of Caesarea
Feis, Herbert
Fisher, Herbert Albert Laurens
Fiske, John
Ford, Paul Leicester
Frankel, Charles
Freeman, Douglas S
Fremont, John Charles
Gard, Wayne
Garraty, John Arthur
Gay, Peter Jack
Gibbon, Edward
Gilson, Etienne Henry
Gipson, Lawrence Henry
Goldman, Eric F
Green, Constance Windsor McLaughlin

Green, John Richard
Griswold, A Whitney
Grote, George
Guicciardini, Francesco
Guizot, Francois Pierre
Handlin, Oscar
Hayes, Carlton Joseph Huntley
Heiden, Konrad
Henderson, Robert W
Herodotus
Hitchcock, Henry Russell
Hofstadter, Richard
Horan, James David
Hrushevsky, Mykhailo
Hume, David
Irving, Washington
Jablonski, Henryk
Johnson, Walter (Thomas Walter)
Josephus, Flavius
Kane, Joseph Nathan
Kennan, George Frost
Kuykendall, Ralph Simpson
Lamartine, Alphonse Marie Louis de Prat de
Lecky, William Edward Hartpole
Leech, Margaret Kernochan
Lengyel, Emil
Levy, Leonard Williams
Livy
Lodge, Henry Cabot
Lopez de Ayala, Pero
Lord, Walter
Lovejoy, Arthur Oncken
Macaulay, Thomas Babington Macaulay, Baron
Mahan, Alfred Thayer
Mannheim, Karl
Mattingley, Garrett
McCarthy, Justin Huntly
McGee, Gale William
McMaster, John Bach
Menendez Pidal, Ramon
Meres, Francis
Merimee, Prosper
Mill, James
Miller, Perry Gilbert Eddy
Mommsen, Theodor
Monaghan, (James) Jay, (IV)
Morison, Samuel Eliot
Motley, John L
Muratori, Ludovico
Nevins, Allan
Owsley, Frank Lawrence
Padover, Saul Kussiel
Parkman, Francis
Parrington, Vernon L(ouis)
Parry, Charles Hubert Hastings, Sir
Pederson, Christiern
Petrie, Charles Alexander, Sir
Poole, William Frederick
Prescott, William Hickling

Quidde, Ludwig
Raleigh, Walter, Sir
Randall, James Garfield
Ranke, Leopold von
Renan, (Joseph) Ernest
Rhodes, James Ford
Robertson, William
Robinson, James Harvey
Roszak, Theodore
Russell, John, Lord
Schlesinger, Arthur Meier, Jr.
Schmitt, Bernadotte Everly
Schreiber, Hermann Otto Ludwig
Schullian, Dorothy May
Scott, Walter, Sir
Seymour, Charles
Shannon, Fred Albert
Shotwell, James Thomson
Snorri, Sturluson
Soloviev, Sergei Mikhailovich
Sonneck, Oscar George Theodore
Sparks, Jared
Spitta, Philipp (Julius August Philipp)
Starkie, Walter Fitzwilliam
Steinberg, Sigfrid Henry
Strabo
Strachey, (Giles) Lytton
Symonds, John Addington
Tacitus, Cornelius
Taylor, A(lan) J(ohn) P(ercivale)
Thierry, Augustin
Thiers, Adolphe
Thompson, Ruth Plumly
Thorndike, Lynn
Thou, Jacques Auguste de
Thucydides
Toland, John Willard
Toynbee, Arnold Joseph
Treitschke, Heinrich Gotthard von
Trevelyan, George Macaulay
Trevor-Roper, Hugh Redwald
Tuchman, Barbara Wertheim
Turner, Frederick Jackson
Unger, Irwin
Warren, Mercy Otis
Williams, Eric Eustace
Woodward, C(omer) Vann
Wroth, Lawrence Councelman
Xenophon
Zinn, Howard

HISTORICAL FIGURE

Rutledge, Ann

HOCKEY COACH

Adams, Jack (John James)
Arbour, Al(ger)
Berenson, "Red" Gordon Arthur
Berry, Bob (Robert Victor)
Bowman, Scotty (William Scott)

Brooks, Herb(ert Paul)
Cherry, Don(ald Stewart)
Creighton, Fred(erick)
Delvecchio, Alex
Demers, Jacques
Gadsby, Bill (William Alexander)
Imlach, "Punch" George
Kromm, Bobby (Robert)
Lindsay, Ted (Robert Blake Theodore)
Magnuson, Keith Arlen
Pronovost, Marcel (Rene Marcel)
Quinn, Pat (John Brian Patrick)
Vairo, Lou

HOCKEY EXECUTIVE

Buss, Jerry Hatten
Campbell, Clarence Sutherland
Clancy, "King" (Francis Michael)
Ferguson, John Bowie
Francis, Emile Percy
Ilitch, Mike
Imlach, "Punch" George
Nanne, Lou(is Vincent)
Patrick, Lester B
Patrick, Lynn
Pocklington, Peter H
Pollack, Sam
Sather, Glen Cameron
Smythe, Conn
Torrey, Bill (William Arthur)
Wirtz, Arthur M
Ziegler, John Augustus, Jr.

HOCKEY PLAYER

Abel, Sid(ney Gerald)
Adams, Jack (John James)
Anderson, Glenn Chris
Arbour, Al(ger)
Armstrong, George Edward
Baker, Bill (William Robert)
Barber, Bill (William Charles)
Barrasso, Tom (Thomas)
Beaupre, Don(ald William)
Beliveau, Jean Marc
Bellows, Brian
Bentley, Max (Maxwell Herbert Lloyd)
Berenson, "Red" Gordon Arthur
Berry, Bob (Robert Victor)
Boivin, Leo Joseph
Bossy, Mike (Michael)
Bourque, Ray(mond Jean)
Bowman, Scotty (William Scott)
Broda, "Turk" Walter
Broten, Neal Lamoy
Bucyk, John Paul
Carlyle, Randy
Carpenter, Bobby
Christian, Dave
Christoff, Steve
Clancy, "King" Francis Michael

Clark, Wendel
Clarke, Bobby (Robert Earl)
Coffey, Paul
Conacher, Charles, Sr.
Cook, William
Craig, Jim (James)
Crawford, Jack (John Shea)
Crozier, Roger Allan
Dahlin, Kjell
Delvecchio, Alex
Dionne, Marcel
Dryden, Ken(neth Wayne)
Duguay, Ron(ald)
Eruzione, Mike
Esposito, Phil(ip)
Esposito, Tony (Anthony James)
Federko, Bernie (Bernard Allan)
Ferguson, John Bowie
Foligno, Mike (Michael Anthony)
Francis, Emile Percy
Froese, Bob
Fuhr, Grant
Gadsby, Bill (William Alexander)
Gainey, Bob (Robert Michael)
Geoffrion, Bernie (Bernard)
Giacomin, Eddie (Edward)
Gilbert, Rod(rique Gabriel)
Gillies, Clark
Goring, "Butch" Robert Thomas
Goulet, Michel
Gretzky, Wayne
Hall, Glenn Henry
Hawerchuk, Dale
Hedberg, Anders
Horton, Tim (Miles Gilbert)
Houle, Rejean
Howe, Gordie (Gordon)
Howe, Mark Steven
Howe, Syd(ney Harris)
Howell, Harry (Henry Vernon)
Hull, Bobby (Robert Martin)
Janaszak, Steve
Johnson, Mark
Keon, Dave (David Michael)
Kerr, Tim
Kharlamov, Valeri
Kurri, Jarri
La Fontaine, Pat
Lach, Elmer James
Lafleur, Guy Damien
Larocque, Michel Raymond
Larson, Reed David
Lemaire, Jacques Gerald
Lemieux, Claude
Lemieux, Mario
Lessard, Mario
Leveille, Normand
Lindbergh, Pelle (Per-Eric)
Lindsay, Ted (Robert Blake Theodore)
Liut, Mike (Michael)
Lonsberry, Ross (David Ross)

Lumley, Harry
Lysiak, Tom (Thomas James)
Magnuson, Keith Arlen
Mahovlich, Frank (Francis William)
Mahovlich, Pete(r Joseph)
Maloney, Dave (David Wilfred)
Maloney, Don(ald)
Martin, "Pit" Hubert Jacques
Martin, Richard Lionel
Masterton, Bill (William)
McClanahan, Rob
McCourt, Dale Allen
Meeker, Howie (Howard William)
Messier, Mark Douglas
Mikita, Stan(ley)
Morrow, Ken
Murray, Troy
Nanne, Lou(is Vincent)
Nilsson, Kent
Nilsson, Ulf Gosta
Nystrom, Bob (Thor Robert)
O'Callahan, Jack
Ogrodnick, John Alexander
Orr, Bobby (Robert Gordon)
Parent, Bernie (Bernard Marcel)
Park, Brad (Douglas Bradford)
Patrick, Lynn
Pavelich, Mark
Peeters, Pete(r)
Perreault, Gilbert
Plante, Jacques (Joseph Jacques Omer)
Pollack, Sam
Potvin, Denis Charles
Pronovost, Marcel (Rene Marcel)
Quinn, Pat (John Brian Patrick)
Ramsey, Mike (Michael Allen)
Ratelle, (Joseph Gilbert Yvon) Jean
Richard, Henri (Joseph Henri)
Richard, Maurice (Joseph Henri Maurice)
Robinson, Larry (Laurence Clark)
Sanderson, Derek Michael
Sather, Glen Cameron
Savard, Denis
Savard, Serge A
Sawchuk, Terry (Terrance Gordon)
Schultz, Dave (David William)
Shore, Eddie
Shutt, Steve (Stephen John)
Silk, Dave
Simmer, Charlie (Charles Robert)
Sittler, Darryl Glen
Smith, Billy (William John)
St. Laurent, Andre
Stastny, Anton
Stastny, Marian
Stastny, Peter
Stemkowski, Pete(r David)
Suter, Gary
Taylor, Dave (David Andrew)
Thompson, Cecil
Tretyak, Vladislav

Trottier, Bryan John
Ullman, Norm(an Victor Alexander)
Unger, Garry Douglas
Vachon, Rogie (Rogatien Rosarie)
Vaive, Rick Claude
Vanbiesbrouck, John
Watson, Bryan Joseph
Williams, "Tiger" David James
Woods, Paul William
Worsley, "Gump" (Lorne John
Yzerman, Steve

HOME ECONOMIST

Cannon, Poppy

HORSE TRAINER

Calvert, "Sunshine" Melvin
Campo, John(ny)
Fitzsimmons, James E
Haughton, Billy
Markey, Lucille (Parker) Wright
Price, H(enry) Ryan

HORTICULTURIST

Burbank, Luther
Burpee, David
Burpee, W(ashington) Atlee
Crockett, James Underwood
Downing, Andrew Jackson

HOSTAGE IN IRAN

Ahern, Thomas Leo, Jr.
Barnes, Clair Cortland
Belk, William E
Blucker, Robert Olof
Cooke, Donald
Daugherty, William J
Engelmann, Robert A
Gallegos, William
German, Bruce W
Gillette, Duane
Golacinski, Alan Bruce
Graves, John Earl
Hall, Joseph M
Hermening, Kevin Jay
Hohman, Donald
Holland, Leland James
Howland, Michael
Jones, Charles A, Jr.
Kalp, Malcolm
Kennedy, Moorehead Cowell, Jr.
Keough, William Francis, Jr.
Kirtley, Steven William
Koob, Kathryn L
Kupke, Frederick Lee
Laingen, (Lowell) Bruce
Lauterbach, Steven
Lee, Gary Earl

Lewis, Paul Edward
Limbert, John William, Jr.
Lopez, James Michael (Jimmy)
McKeel, Johnny (John D, Jr.)
Metrinko, Michael John
Miele, Jerry J
Moeller Michael E
Moore, Bert C
Morefield, Richard H
Needham, Paul M, Jr.
Ode, Robert C
Persinger, Gregory A
Plotkin, Jerry
Queen, Richard I
Ragan, Regis
Roeder, David
Rosen, Barry
Royer, William Blackburn, Jr.
Schaefer, Thomas E
Scott, Charles Wesly
Sharer, Donald A
Sickmann, Rodney Virgil
Subic, Joseph, Jr.
Swift, Elizabeth Ann
Tomseth, Victor Lloyd
Ward, Phillip R

HOTEL EXECUTIVE

Binns, Joseph Patterson
Grossinger, Jennie
Hilton, Conrad Nicholson
Hilton, William Barron
Lewis, Rosa
Ritz, Cesar
Statler, Ellsworth Milton
Tschirky, Oscar

HUMANITARIAN

Bergh, Henry

HUMORIST

A'Beckett, Gilbert Abbott
Ace, Goodman
Adams, Franklin P(ierce)
Ade, George
Aleichem, Shalom, pseud.
Bemelmans, Ludwig
Benchley, Robert Charles
Buchwald, Art(hur)
Burrows, Abe (Abram S)
Chase, Ilka
Cobb, Irvin Shrewsbury
Cuppy, Will(iam Jacob)
Day, Clarence Shepard, Jr.
Dunne, Finley Peter
Ford, Corey
Frost, Arthur Burdett
Gilbert, William Schwenck, Sir
Hershfield, Harry

Hoffenstein, Samuel Goodman
Hubbard, Kin (Frank McKinney)
Irwin, Wallace
Jerome, Jerome Klapka
Kerr, (Bridget) Jean Collins
Lardner, Ring(gold Wilmer)
Leacock, Stephen Butler
Leaf, Munro (Wilbur Munro)
Levenson, Sam(uel)
Lewis, Dominic Bevan Wyndham
Nye, Edgar Wilson (Bill)
Papashvily, George
Peck, George Wilbur
Perelman, S(idney) J(oseph)
Petrarch, Francesco
Phillips, Harry Irving
Rabelais, Francois
Rogers, Will(iam Penn Adair)
Rogers, Will, Jr.
Shriner, Herb
Shulman, Max
Smith, H(arry) Allen
Streeter, Edward
Sullivan, Frank
Thurber, James Grover
Ward, Artemus, pseud.
Wells, Carolyn
White, E(lwyn) B(rooks)

HUNGER STRIKER

Devine, Michael
Doherty, Kieran
Hughes, Francis
Hurson, Martin
Lynch, Kevin
MacSwiney, Terence
McCreesh, Raymond
McDonnell, Joe (Joseph)
McIlwee, Thomas
O'Hara, Patrick
Sands, Bobby (Robert Gerard)

ILLUSTRATOR

Abbey, Edwin Austin
Alajalov, Constantin
Anglund, Joan Walsh
Ardizzone, Edward Jeffrey Irving
Arisman, Marshall
Artzybasheff, Boris Mikhailovich
Aulaire, Edgar Parin d'
Aulaire, Ingri Mortenson d'
Bacon, Peggy
Beall, Lester Thomas
Beardsley, Aubrey Vincent
Bemelmans, Ludwig
Bendick, Jeanne
Bennett, John
Bewick, Thomas
Biro, Val
Blake, Quentin

Blanding, Don
Bonestell, Chesley
Bouche, Rene Robert
Breger, Dave
Brett, Jan Churchill
Briggs, Austin Eugene
Brindle, Melbourne
Brinkley, Nell
Brooke, L Leslie
Browne, "Phiz" Hablot Knight
Brunhoff, Jean de
Brunhoff, Laurent de
Burger, Carl Victor
Burton, Virginia Lee
Busch, Wilhelm
Cady, (Walter) Harrison
Carle, Eric
Chwast, Seymour
Clarke, Harry
Clave, Antoni
Cleland, Thomas Maitland
Cooney, Barbara
Corcos, Lucille
Cox, Palmer
Craig, Helen
Crane, Walter
Cruikshank, George
Darley, Felix Octavius Carr
Dillon, Diane Claire Sorber
Dillon, Leo
Dohanos, Stevan
Dongen, Kees van
Dorne, Albert
Dwiggins, William Addison
Eckert, Horst
Eichenberg, Fritz
Falter, John
Fenton, Carroll Lane
Finlay, Virgil
Fischer, Anton Otto
Fisher, Harrison
Flora, James Royer
Folon, Jean-Michel
Fox, Fontaine Talbot, Jr.
Frost, Arthur Burdett
Funikawa, Gyo
Gag, Wanda
Garnett, Eve C R
Gibson, Charles Dana
Gilliam, Terry
Glanzman, Louis S
Glaser, Milton
Goodall, John Strickland
Gorey, Edward St. John
Gramatky, Hardie
Grant, Gordon
Greenaway, Kate (Catherine)
Grol, Lini Richards
Helck, Peter (Clarence Peter)
Held, John, Jr.
Herford, Oliver

Hoff, Sydney
Hogrogian, Nonny
Hughes, Arthur
Hummel, Lisl
Hurd, Peter
James, Will(iam)
Kauffer, Edward McKnight
Kingman, Dong M
Kredel, Fritz
Kupka, Frank
Kurelek, William
Lacroix, Georges
Lasker, Joe
Laurel, Alicia Bay
Lawson, Robert
Leaf, Munro (Wilbur Munro)
Leech, John
Leighton, Clare Veronica Hope
Lenski, Lois
Leslie, Frank, pseud.
Levine, David
Marsh, Reginald
Martin, David Stone
Meggendorfer, Lothar
Moss, Geoffrey
Nast, Thomas
O'Neill, Rose Cecil
Paul, Frank Rudolph
Peake, Mervyn Laurence
Pears, Charles
Peirce, Waldo
Pinkwater, Daniel Manus
Pogany, Willy
Politi, Leo
Potter, Beatrix (Helen Beatrix)
Price, Garrett
Provensen, Alice Rose Twitchell
Provensen, Martin
Purdy, Susan Gold
Pyle, Howard
Rackham, Arthur
Raskin, Ellen
Rey, Hans Augustus
Rico, Don(ato)
Robinson, Boardman
Rockwell, Norman
Rose, Carl
Sendak, Maurice Bernard
Seuss, Doctor, pseud.
Shepard, Ernest Howard
Slobodkin, Louis
Slobodkina, Esphyr
Sperry, Armstrong W
Stahl, Ben(jamin Albert)
Steig, William
Tenggren, Gustaf Adolf
Tenniel, John, Sir
Trnks, Jiri
Turkle, Brinton Cassaday
Ulreich, Nura Woodson
Ungerer, Tomi (Jean Thomas)

VanAllsburg, Chris
VonSchmidt, Harold
Wiese, Kurt
Williams, Garth Montgomery
Wilson, Edward Arthur
Wyeth, N(ewell) C(onvers)

IMPOSTER

Demara, Ferdinand Waldo, Jr.
Ireland, William Henry
Monmouth, James Scott, Duke
Orton, Arthur
Psalmanazar, George
Pugachev, Yemelyan I
Wilson, Sarah

IMPRESARIO

Cochran, C(harles) B(lake)
Dent, Edward Joseph
Fox, Carol
Frohman, Charles
Hammerstein, Oscar
Hurok, Sol
Mann, Joseph
Manners, Charles
Mapleson, James Henry
Maretzek, Max
Morley, Eric Douglas
Perrin, Emile Cesare
Rosa, Carl
Russell, Henry
Savage, Henry Wilson
Strakosch, Maurice

INDIAN

Osceola Nickanochee
Osceola, Joe Dan

INDIAN CHIEF

Black Hawk
Crazy Horse
Dull Knife
George, Chief Dan
Geronimo
Grass, John
Joseph, Chief
Keokuk
Manhiller, Wilma P
Pontiac
Powhatan
Quanah
Red Cloud, Chief
Ross, John
Sitting Bull
Tecumseh

INDIAN GUIDE

Sacagawea
Squanto

INDUSTRIALIST

Allard, Sydney
Baldwin, Matthias William
Bergen, John Joseph
Berwind, Charles G
Breech, Ernest Robert
Butler, Paul
Carnegie, Andrew
Chandos, Oliver Lyttelton
Corey, William Ellis
Cowen, Joshua Lionel
Deere, John
Duke, Benjamin Newton
DuPont, Eleuthere Irenee
Eastman, George
Ferguson, Harry George
Flick, Friedrich
Folger, Henry Clay
Frick, Henry Clay
Goodrich, Benjamin Franklin
Gregg, William
Guggenheim, Harry Frank
Guggenheim, Meyer
Hasselblad, Victor
Horlick, William
Hughes, Howard Robard
Kaiser, Edgar Fosburgh
Kaiser, Henry John
Keith, Minor Cooper
Kent, Arthur Atwater
Knudsen, William S
Krupp, Alfred
Lowell, Francis Cabot
Matsushita, Konosuke
McCarthy, Glenn Herbert
Michelin, Francois
Morris, William Richard
Mott, Charles Stewart
Oppenheimer, Harry Frederick
Palevsky, Max
Patino, Simon Iturri
Rathenau, Walter
Schwab, Charles Michael
Siemens, (Ernst) Werner von
Sloan, Alfred Pritchard, Jr.
Swope, Gerard
Thyssen, Fritz
Wenner-Gren, Axel
Willys, John North
Winchester, Oliver Fisher
Wolfson, Louis Elwood

INSURANCE COMPANY EXECUTIVE

Fisher, Carl

INSURANCE EXECUTIVE

DeMoss, Arthur S
Fischer, Carl
Gaston, Arthur George
Joanis, John W
Kemper, James S(cott)
MacArthur, John Donald

INTERIOR DECORATOR

Draper, Dorothy Tuckerman
Greer, Michael
Hicks, David Nightingale
Mendl, Lady Elsie de Wolfe
Pahlmann, William

INVENTOR

Abbott, Scott
Abplanalp, Robert H
Acheson, Edward Goodrich
Alexanderson, Ernst Frederik Werner
Allen, John
Appleby, John Francis
Arkwright, Richard, Sir
Armstrong, Edwin Howard
Atwood, Francis Clarke
Babbage, Charles
Babbitt, Benjamin Talbot
Baekeland, Leo Hendrick
Bailey, Donald Coleman, Sir
Banneker, Benjamin
Bauersfeld, Walther
Bausch, Edward
Bausch, John Jacob
Beach, Alfred Ely
Bell, Alexander Graham
Bell, Herbert A
Bendix, Vincent
Berliner, Emile
Bessemer, Henry, Sir
Bigelow, Erastus Brigham
Birdseye, Clarence Frank
Bissell, Melville Reuben
Bitter, Francis
Bjorn-Larsen, Knut
Blair, William Richards
Blanchard, Thomas
Booth, Hubert Cecil
Borden, Gail
Bowie, James
Bradham, Caleb D
Braestrup, Carl Bjorn
Bramah, Joseph
Browning, John Moses
Brunel, Isambard Kingdom
Budding, Edwin
Bunsen, Robert Wilhelm Eberhard
Burroughs, William Seward
Bushnell, David
Butterick, Ebenezer

Carlson, Chester
Carrier, Willis H
Cartwright, Edmund
Chardonnet, Louis Marie
Chretien, Henri
Christie, John Walter
Coanda, Henri Marie
Colt, Samuel
Cooke, William Fothergil, Sir
Coolidge, William David
Coster, Laurens Janszoon
Cowen, Joshua Lionel
Crosley, Powel, Jr.
Crowell, Luther Childs
Curtis, Charles Gordon
Curtiss, Glenn Hammond
Daguerre, Louis Jacques Mande
Dahl, Gary
Daimler, Gottlieb
Dalen, Nils Gustaf
Daniell, John Frederic
Darrow, Charles Bruce
Davenport, Thomas
DeForest, Lee
Dewar, James A
Dickson, Earle Ensign
Diesel, Rudolf Christian Karl
Dolby, Ray Milton
Dunlop, John Boyd
Dunne, John William
Duryea, Charles Edgar
Duryea, J(ames) Frank
Eastman, George
Edison, Thomas Alva
Ellis, Carleton
Epperson, Frank W
Evans, Oliver
Evinrude, Ole
Fairbanks, Thaddeus
Fairchild, Sherman Mills
Farber, Edward Rolke
Farnsworth, Philo Taylor
Ferris, George Washington Gale
Fessenden, Reginald Aubrey
Fitch, John
Focke, Heinrich
Friese-Greene, William Edward
Garand, John Cantius
Gatling, Richard Jordan
Ged, William
Gerber, Daniel Frank
Gernsback, Hugo
Gillette, King Camp
Godowsky, Leopold, II
Goldman, Sylvan N
Goldmark, Peter Carl
Goodwin, Hannibal Williston
Goodyear, Charles
Gorrie, John
Gougelman, Pierre
Gray, Elisha

Graydon, James Weir
Greenwood, Chester
Gutenberg, Johannes
Hammond, Laurens
Haney, Chris
Haney, John
Hansom, Joseph Aloysius
Henry, Joseph
Hoe, Richard March
Holland, John Philip
Honeywell, Mark Charles
Hotchkiss, Benjamin Berkeley
Houdry, Eugene Jules
Howe, Elias
Hunt, Walter
Ingersoll, Simon
Ives, Frederic Eugene
Ives, Herbert Eugene
Iwatani, Toro
Jacquard, Joseph Marie
Jacuzzi, Candido
Jarvik, Robert Koffler
Jones, Arthur A
Judson, Egbert Putnam
Kalmus, Herbert Thomas
Kalmus, Natalie Mabelle Dunfee
Keller, Arthur C
Kellogg, John Harvey
Kelly, William
Kurzweil, Ray(mond)
Kyriakides, Anastasios
Laennec, Rene Theophile Hyacinthe
Lake, Simon
Land, Edwin Herbert
Langley, Samuel Pierpont
Lanston, Tolbert
Latimer, Lewis Howard
Lewyt, Alexander Milton
Libby, Willard Frank
Lilienthal, Otto
Link, Edwin Albert
Loomis, Mahion
Lumiere, Auguste Marie Louis
Lumiere, Louis Jean
Lyot, Bernard Ferdinand
Macintosh, Charles
Mannes, Leopold Damrosch
Marconi, Guglielmo
Mason, John L
Mason, Max
Matzeliger, Jan Ernest
Maxim, Hiram Stevens, Sir
McCormick, Cyrus Hall
Mergenthaler, Ottmar
Midgeley, Thomas
Miller, Carl S
Montgolfier, Jacques Etienne
Montgolfier, Joseph Michel
Moog, Robert
Morse, Samuel Finley Breese
Newcomen, Thomas

Nobel, Alfred Bernhard
Norden, Carl Lukas
Olds, Ranson E(li)
Otis, Elisha Graves
Oughtred, William
Page, Charles Grafton
Parsons, Charles Algernin, Sir
Paul, Les
Pemberton, John Stith
Perkins, Jacob
Perky, Henry D
Piccard, Jacques
Pitman, Isaac
Pitney, Arthur
Porsche, Ferdinand
Pullman, George Mortimer
Pupin, Michael Idvorsky
Richter, Charles Francis
Saunders, William Laurence
Sax, Adolphe
Schick, Jacob
Schweppe, Jacob
Selden, George Baldwin
Senefelder, Aloys
Siemens, (Ernst) Werner von
Siemens, William, Sir
Singer, Isaac Merrit
Skinner, Halcyon
Smith, Horace
Smith, Robert Lee
Spanel, Abram N
Spencer, Percy Le Baron
Sperry, Elmer Ambrose
Stephenson, George
Stout, William Bushnell
Talbot, William Henry Fox
Taylor, Frederick Winslow
Tesla, Nikola
Thomas, Sidney Gilchrist
Thompson, John Taliaferro
Thomson, Elihu
Thurber, Charles
Timken, Henry
Trevithick, Richard
Ts'ai, Lun
Tupper, Earl Silas
Vail, Alfred Lewis
Van Depoele, Charles Joseph
Verrill, Alpheus Hyatt
Walker, Joseph
Waller, Fred(erick)
Wallis, Barnes Neville, Sir
Waring, Fred Malcolm
Waterman, Lewis Edson
Watt, James
Welsbach, Carl Auer von, Baron
Westinghouse, George
Wheatstone, Charles, Sir
Wheeler, Schuyler Skaats
Whitney, Eli
Wilson, Jerry

Woods, Granville T
Wright, Orville
Wright, Wilbur
Zwicky, Fritz

JAZZ MUSICIAN

Allen, "Red" Henry James, Jr.
Ammons, Albert C
Armstrong, Lil(lian Hardin)
Baker, "Shorty" Harold
Basie, "Count" William James, Jr.
Bechet, Sidney
Beiderbecke, "Bix" Leon Bismark
Berry, "Chu" Leon
Bigard, Albany Barney Leon
Blakey, Art
Blanton, Jimmy
Bolden, "Buddy" Charles
Braff, Ruby
Brubeck, Dave (David Warren)
Brunis, George
Bushkin, Joe (Joseph)
Busse, Henry
Butterfield, Billy
Byrd, Charlie (Charles Lee)
Byrd, Donald
Carney, Harry Howell
Carter, Benny (Bennett Lester)
Christian, Charlie (Charles)
Clayton, Buck
Cohn, Al
Coleman, Ornette
Coltrane, "Trane" John William
Condon, Eddie
Corea, "Chick" Armando
Covington, Glen
Crawford, James Strickland
Davie, Alan
Davis, Miles Dewey
Davison, William
DeFranco, Buddy
DeParis, Wilbur
Dodds, "Baby" Warren
Dodds, Johnny
Eldridge, Roy
Erwin, "Pee Wee" George
Farmer, Arthur Stewart
Ferguson, Maynard
Firbank, Louis
Foster, "Pops" George Murphy
Fountain, Pete(r Dewey)
Gillespie, "Dizzy" John Birks
Giuffre, James Peter
Golson, Benny
Granz, Norman
Grappelli, Stephane
Guarnieri, Johnny (John A)
Hackett, Bobby (Robert Leo)
Harris, Willard Palmer (Bill)
Hawkins, "Bean" Coleman

Haymes, Joe
Hill, "Chippie" Bertha
Hines, "Fatha" Earl Kenneth
Hirt, Al
Hodges, Johnny
Jackson, Milt(on)
Jacquet, Illinois
Jamal, Ahmad
Johnson, "Bunk" William Geary
Johnson, "Dink" Oliver
Johnson, "J J" James Louis
Johnson, Charlie (Charles Wright)
Johnson, James Price
Jones, Jo(nathan)
Kaminsky, Max
Keppard, Freddie
Konitz, Lee
Ladnier, Tommy
Lang, Eddie
Lawson, "Yank" John R
Lunceford, Jimmy (James Melvin)
Mangione, Chuck (Charles Frank)
Mann, Herbie
Manne, Shelly (Sheldon)
Manone, "Wingy" Joseph
Marsala, Marty
Mayall, John Brumwell
McCoy, Clyde
McGarity, Lou (Roert Louis)
McIntyre, Hal (Harold W)
McPartland, Jimmy (James Duigald)
Mezzrow, "Mezz" Milton
Mondello, "Toots" Nuncio
Morello, Joseph A
Morton, "Jelly Roll" Joseph Ferdinand
Moten, Bennie
Mulligan, Gerry (Gerald Joseph)
Murphy, "Turk" Melvin
Musso, Vido
Navarro, "Fats" Theodore
Noone, Jimmie
Norvo, "Red" Kenneth
Ory, "Kid" Edward
Page, "Hot Lips" Oran Thaddeus
Parker, Charlie (Charles Christopher)
Pepper, Art(hur Edward)
Peterson, Oscar (Emmauel)
Pettiford, Oscar
Pletcher, "Stew" Stuart
Powell, Earl
Redman, Don
Reinhardt, Django (Jean Baptiste)
Rich, "Buddy" Bernard
Roach, Max(well)
Rogers, "Shorty" Milton M
Rugolo, Pete
Rushing, Jimmy
Russell, "Pee Wee" Charles Ellsworth
Sauter, Eddie (Edward Ernest)
Scott, Hazel Dorothy
Silver, Horace Ward Martin Tavares

Sims, "Zoot" John Haley
Smith, Clarence
Smith, Joe
Spanier, "Muggsy" Francis Joseph
Stewart, "Slam" Leroy
Stitt, "Sonny" Edward
Strayhorn, Billy (William)
Tatum, Art(hur)
Taylor, Billy (William Edward)
Taylor, Sam
Teagarden, Charles
Teagarden, Jack (Weldon John)
Teschemacher, Frank
Tjader, Cal(len Radcliffe, Jr.)
Tough, Dave
Tristano, Leonard Joseph
Turner, Joe
Ventura, Charlie
Venuti, Joe (Giuseppe)
Vinson, "Cleanhead" Eddie
Waller, "Fats" Thomas Wright
Washington, "Buck" Ford Lee
Weatherford, Teddy
Webb, "Chick" William
Wiley, Lee
Williams, "Cootie" Charles Melvin
Wilson, Teddy (Theodore)
Winding, Kai Chresten
Yancey, Jimmy (James Edward)
Young, "Trummy" James Osborne
Young, Lester Willis

JEWELER

Bulgari, Constantine
Bulgari, Giorgio
Bulova, Joseph
Cartier, Claude
Cartier, Pierre C
Faberge, Peter Carl (Karl Gustavovich)
Lalique, Rene
Schlumberger, Jean
Tiffany, Charles Lewis
Winston, Harry

JEWELRY DESIGNER

Cipullo, Aldo Massimo Fabrizio

JOCKEY

Arcaro, Eddie (George Edward)
Atkinson, Ted
Cassidy, Marshall
Cauthen, Steve
Cordero, Angel Tomas
Dancer, Stanley
Hartack, Billy (William, Jr.)
Haughton, Billy
Longden, Johnny
Pincay, Laffit, Jr.
Rogers, Karen

Rubin, Barbara Jo
Sande, Earl
Shoemaker, Willie (William Lee)
Smith, Robyn Caroline
Turcotte, Ron

JOURNALIST

Abbas, Khwaja Ahmad
Abbott, Scott
Abernethy, Robert Gordon
Ackerman, Carl William
Adams, Franklin P(ierce)
Adams, Samuel Hopkins
Aldrich, Thomas Bailey
Allen, Frederick Lewis
Allen, Larry
Allen, Robert Sharon
Allsop, Kenneth
Alsop, Joseph Wright, Jr.
Alsop, Stewart Johonnot Oliver
Alvarez, Walter Clement
Ames, Louise Bates
Anderson, Jack Northman
Andrews, Bert
Angelou, Maya Marguerita
Anson, Robert Sam
Anthony, Joseph
Arcaro, Eddie (George Edward)
Archerd, Army (Armand)
Armstrong, Hamilton Fish
Assis Chateaubriand, Francisco de
Atkinson, (Justin) Brooks
Attwood, William
Auerbach-Levy, William
Axthelm, Pete(r Macrae)
Ayer, Harriet Hubbard
Bacharach, Bert(ram Mark)
Baer, "Bugs" Arthur
Bailey, H(enry) C(hristopher)
Baillie, Hugh
Baker, Russell Wayne
Baldwin, Hanson Weightman
Bandeira, Manuel (Filho Manuel)
Bangor, Edward Henry Harold Ward,
  Viscount
Barbanell, Maurice
Baring, Maurice
Barlow, Joel
Barnes, Clive Alexander
Barnes, Djuna
Barnetson, William Denholm, Lord
Barr, Amelia Edith Huddleston
Barrett, Rona
Bartlett, Charles Leffingwell
Battelle, Phyllis Marie
Baum, (Lyman) Frank
Beach, Alfred Ely
Beale, Betty
Beatty, Morgan
Beck, Marilyn (Mohr)
Beebe, Lucius Morris

Benchley, Peter Bradford
Benet, William Rose
Bentley, Edmund Clerihew
Berger, Meyer
Berkow, Ira Harvey
Bernstein, Carl
Bernstein, Theodore Menline
Berton, Pierre
Bierce, Ambrose Gwinett
Biossat, Bruce
Birnie, William Alfred Hart
Bishop, Jim (James Alonzo)
Black, Winifred Sweet
Bloom, Murray Teigh
Bly, Nellie, pseud.
Bodard, Lucien Albert
Bodsworth, Charles Frederick
Bolitho, William
Bolles, Don F
Bombeck, Erma Louise
Bonatti, Walter
Bonsal, Stephen
Bottel, Helen Alfea
Bowles, Samuel, II
Boyle, Harold Vincent
Bradlee, Ben(jamin Crowninshield)
Brand, Max, pseud.
Brann, William Cowper
Bratteli, Trygve Martin
Brayman, Harold
Breslin, Jimmy
Briand, Rena
Brisbane, Arthur
Brody, Jane Ellen
Broun, (Matthew) Heywood (Campbell)
Brown, David
Brown, Ned (Edward Gerald)
Brown, Tina
Browne, Walter Shawn
Browning, Norma Lee
Brunton, Paul
Buchanan, Patrick Joseph
Buchwald, Art(hur)
Buckmaster, Henrietta, pseud.
Bugbee, Emma
Bunner, Henry Cuyler
Burgess, Anthony
Burgess, Thornton Waldo
Burman, Ben Lucien
Burt, Richard
Butterfield, Roger Place
Byrd, Harry Flood, Jr.
Caen, Herb
Calder, Peter Ritchie
Caldwell, Erskine Preston
Calmer, Ned
Campbell, Donald Guy
Campbell, Roy
Canby, Vincent
Canham, Erwin Dain
Cannon, Jimmy (James J)

Cannon, Poppy
Capa, Cornell
Caputo, Philip Joseph
Carbine, Patricia Theresa
Carleton, Will
Carlile, Richard
Carmichael, John P
Carpenter, Leslie
Carpenter, Liz (Elizabeth Sutherland)
Carter, Ernestine Marie
Cassini, Igor Loiewski
Catledge, Turner
Catton, Bruce
Cerf, Bennett Alfred
Chadwick, Henry
Chamberlain, John Rensselear
Chambers, Whittaker
Chandler, Dorothy Buffum
Chapais, Thomas, Sir
Chataway, Christopher John
Chennault, Anna Chan
Chernov, Viktor Mikhailovich
Cheshire, Maxine
Chew, Peter
Childs, Marquis William
Chirol, Valentine, Sir
Christy, Marian
Claflin, Tennessee Celeste
Clapper, Raymond Lewis
Clark, Marion L
Clark, Michele
Clark, Robert Edward
Cobb, Irvin Shrewsbury
Cobbett, William
Cochran, Jacqueline
Cockburn, Alexander
Cockburn, Claud(Francis Claud)
Coleridge, Hartley
Collins, Larry
Conniff, Frank
Connolly, Mike
Connor, William Neil, Sir
Connors, Dorsey
Considine, Bob (Robert Bernard)
Constant de Rebeque, (Henri) Benjamin
Cony, Edward Roger
Cooke, (Alfred) Alistair
Cooke, Janet
Cooper, Kent
Cornell, Douglas B
Cortissoz, Royal
Corum, Martene Windsor
Costain, Thomas B
Craig, Elizabeth May
Cramer, Polly
Crane, Stephen
Crankshaw, Edward
Creel, George
Croly, Herbert David
Croly, Jane Cunningham
Cromie, Robert Allen

Cromley, Raymond Avolon
Crosby, Alexander L
Crosby, Joan Carew
Crosby, John Campbell
Crouse, Russel
Crowther, Bosley (Francis Bosley)
Cudlipp, Hugh
Curie, Eve
Currie, Barton Wood
Daley, Arthur
Daly, Thomas Augustine
Dana, Charles Anderson
Dana, Margaret
Daniel, Clifton, Jr.
Daniel, Dan(iel)
Daniels, Jonathan Worth
Daniels, Josephus
Daniloff, Nicholas
Darwin, Bernard Richard Meirion
Davis, "Tobe" Coller
Davis, Clyde Brion
Davis, Elmer Holmes
Davis, Rebecca Blaine Harding
Davis, Richard Harding
Decter, Midge
Denny, Ludwell
Dent, Alan Holmes
Desmoulins, Camille
DeVoto, Bernard Augustine
Didion, Joan
Divine, Arthur Durham
Dix, Dorothy, pseud.
Dolbier, Maurice
Donovan, Hedley Williams
Donovan, Robert John
Door, Rheta Childe
Dorfman, Dan
Dorgan, Thomas Aloysius
Dreifus, Claudia
Drew, Elizabeth Brenner
Drummond, Roscoe (James Roscoe)
Duranty, Walter
Durslag, Melvin
Dwyer, Cynthia
Ecevit, Bulent
Edel, Leon (Joseph Leon)
Eder, Shirley
Edwards, India
Edwards, Willard
Elegant, Robert Sampson
Elkin, Stanley Lawrence
Ellis, Harry Bearse
Emanuelli, Enrico
Evans, Heloise Cruse
Evans, Orrin C
Evans, Richard Louis
Evans, Rowland, Jr.
Evans, Walker
Fairfax, Beatrice, pseud.
Faiz, Faiz Ahmad
Falkenburg, Jinx (Eugenia Lincoln)

Falkner, Frank
Fall, Bernard B
Fallaci, Oriana
Falls, Joe
Fanning, Katherine
Farrell, James Thomas
Farrington, Elizabeth Pruett (Mary)
Faubus, Orval Eugene
Felker, Clay S
Fenton, Thomas Trail
Fidler, Jimmy (James M)
Field, Eugene
Field, Marshall
Fischer, John
Flanner, Janet
Fleeson, Doris
Foley, Martha
Foot, Michael
Forbes, Bertie Charles
Fowler, Gene
Fraenkel, Heinrich
France, Harry Clinton
Frankel, Max
Freeman, Douglas S
Freneau, Philip Morin
Frick, Ford Christopher
Friedan, Betty Naomi Goldstein
Friedman, Milton
Friendly, Alfred
Fritchey, Clayton
Gale, Zona
Gallico, Paul William
Gard, Wayne
Gardner, Hy
Gardner, Martin
Gelb, Arthur
Gellhorn, Martha Ellis
Genthe, Arnold
George, Henry, Jr.
Gerold, Karl
Gervasi, Frank
Geyer, Georgie Anne
Gibbons, Floyd Phillips
Gidal, Tim
Gilbreth, Frank Bunker, Jr.
Gillott, Jacky
Gilman, Lawrence
Gilmore, Eddy Lanier King
Ginzburg, Ralph
Giroud, Francoise
Gleason, Ralph Joseph
Glendenning, Raymond Carl
Godkin, Edwin Lawrence
Goldberg, Ben Zion
Goltz, Gene
Goodman, Ellen Holtz
Goodrich, Samuel Griswold
Gordimer, Nadine
Gordon, Lou
Goren, Charles Henry
Gorkin, Jess

Gorman, Herbert Sherman
Grady, Henry Woodfin
Graham, Fred Patterson
Graham, Gene
Graham, Sheilah
Grant, Bruce
Grant, Jane
Greeley, Horace
Greene, Bob (Robert Bernard, Jr.)
Greene, Ward
Greenfield, Meg
Gregory, Bettina Louise
Grimsby, Roger
Groth, John August
Guest, Edgar A(lbert)
Guiterman, Arthur
Gunther, John
Guthrie, A(lfred) B(ertram), Jr.
Haber, Joyce
Hagerty, James Campbell
Haggerty, Sandra Clark
Halberstam, David
Hale, Sarah Josepha
Haley, Alex Palmer
Hamill, "Pete" William
Haney, Paul Prichard
Hannagan, Steve (Stephen Jerome)
Hanson, Kitty
Hare, James Henry
Harman, Jeanne Perkins
Harris, Frank
Harris, Sydney J(ustin)
Harsch, Joseph Close
Harte, (Francis Bret)
Harvey, George Brinton M
Haskell, Arnold Lionel
Hearn, Lafcadio
Heatter, Gabriel
Heckscher, August
Hellinger, Mark
Helms, Jesse Alexander, Jr.
Heloise
Hemingway, Ernest Miller
Hemingway, Mary Welsh
Hendrick, Burton Jesse
Henkle, Henrietta
Henry, O, pseud.
Henry, William M
Hentoff, Nat(han Irving)
Hersey, John Richard
Hersh, Seymour
Herzl, Theodor
Hibbs, Ben
Hickok, Lorena A
Higgins, Marguerite
Holbrook, Stewart Hall
Hoppe, Arthur Watterson
Hopper, Hedda
Hottelet, Richard C(urt)
Hough, Henry Beetle
Hoult, Norah

Howar, Barbara
Howard, Jane Temple
Howard, Roy Wilson
Howard, Sidney Coe
Howe, Edmund Perry
Howe, Louis McHenry
Howell, Clark
Hubbard, Kin (Frank McKinney)
Hughes, Emmet John
Hughes, Irene Finger
Hughes, Langston (James Langston)
Huie, William Bradford
Hunt, Frazier
Hyams, Joe (Joseph)
Igoe, "Hype" Herbert A
Ingersoll, Ralph McAllister
Irwin, Wallace
Irwin, Will
Jacoby, Oswald
Jennings, Peter Charles
Jimmy the Greek
Johnson, Gerald White
Johnson, Lionel Pigot
Jones, Jenkin Lloyd
Joseph, Richard
Kahn, Roger
Kantor, Mackinlay
Kaplow, Herbert E
Karpin, Fred Leon
Karsh, Yousuf
Kaufman, George S(imon)
Kenny, Nick
Keogh, James
Kertesz, Andre
Keynes, John Maynard, Baron
Kieran, John Francis
Kilgallen, Dorothy
Kilgore, Bernard
Kilpatrick, James J(ackson)
Kingsbury-Smith, Joseph
Kiplinger, W(illard) M(onroe)
Kirk, Russell
Kleinfield, "Sonny" Nathan Richard
Klemesrud, Judy Lee
Knebel, Fletcher
Knickerbocker, Suzy
Knox, E(dmund) G(eorge) V(alpy)
Kofoed, Jack (John C)
Kohlmeier, Louis Martin, Jr.
Kraft, Joseph
Krassner, Paul
Krock, Arthur
Kupcinet, Irv
Lahey, Edwin A(loysius)
Lambert, Eleanor
Lardner, Ring(gold Wilmer)
Lasky, Victor
Lawrence, David
Lea, Tom
Lemon, Mark
Lerner, Max

Leslie, Frank, pseud.
Levin, Bernard
Lewis, Anthony
Liebling, Abbot Joseph
Lilly, Doris
Lincoln, G(eorge) Gould
Lindauer, Lois L
Lindstrom, Pia
Lippmann, Walter
Lisagor, Peter Irvin
Livermore, Mary Ashton Rice
Locke, David Ross
Locke, Richard Adams
Loeb, Sophia Irene Simon
Loeb, William
Lovejoy, Elijah P
Lucas, Jim Griffing
Luce, Clare Boothe
Luedtke, Kurt (Mamre)
Lyons, Leonard
MacDonald, Dwight
MacDougall, Curtis Daniel
MacLeish, Archibald
MacLeish, Rod(erick)
Maddox, Gaynor
Malcolm, Andrew H(ogarth)
Maney, Richard
Mankiewicz, Frank Fabian
Manners, Dorothy
Mannes, Marya
Marcosson, Isaac Frederick
Markus, Robert
Marquis, Don Robert Perry
Marshack, Megan
Marshall, S(amuel) L(yman) A(twood)
Martin, Judith
Martin, Pete (Thornton)
Mathieu, Noel Jean
Mathison, Richard Randolph
Maxwell, Elsa
McCarten, John
McCormick, Anne (Elizabeth) O'Hare
McCormick, Joseph Medill
McCrary, "Tex" John Reagan
McCutcheon, John Tinney
McGill, Ralph Emerson
McIntyre, Oscar Odd
McNeil, Neil Venable
Means, Marianne Hansen
Mears, Walter R(obert)
Medill, Joseph
Mehta, Ved Parkash
Meltzer, Bernard C
Messick, Henry Hicks
Millar, Jeff(rey) Lynn
Miller, Merle
Miller, Paul
Mitford, Jessica
Moats, Alice-Leone
Mollenhoff, Clark Raymond
Molloy, John T

Montgomery, Ruth Shick
Moorehead, Alan
Moravia, Alberto, pseud.
Morehouse, Ward
Morgan, Edward P
Morley, Christopher Darlington
Morley, John
Morris, Jan (James Humphrey)
Morton, Bruce Alexander
Morton, Julius Sterling
Mosley, Leonard
Mowrer, Edgar Ansel
Mowrer, Paul Scott
Moyers, Bill (William Don)
Mucha, Jiri
Muggeridge, Malcolm
Murphy, (John) Reg(inald)
Murray, Jim
Nachman, Gerald Weil
Nenni, Pietro
Nessen, Ron(ald Harold)
Nevins, Allan
North, Sterling
Novak, Robert
Noyes, David
O'Brian, Jack
O'Connor, Thomas Power
Oakley, Don
Older, Fremont
Olderman, Murray
Omarr, Sydney
Osborne, John Franklin
Oursler, (Charles) Fulton
Packard, Vance Oakley
Paddleford, Clementine Haskin
Palmer, Frederick
Paludan, Jacob (Stig Henning Jacob
   Puggard)
Panter-Downes, Mollie
Parker, Dorothy Rothschild
Parsons, Louella Oettinger
Parton, Sara Payson Willis
Patterson, Tom (Harry Thomas)
Paul, Elliot Harold
Payne, Sidney
Pearlroth, Norbert
Pearson, Drew
Peck, George Wilbur
Pegler, Westbrook
Pennington, John Selman
Pettit, William Thomas
Phelps, William Lyon
Philips, David Graham
Phillips, Harry Irving
Phillips, Kevin Price
Pierson, Frank R(omer)
Poe, Edgar Allan
Poole, Ernest
Porter, Sylvia Field
Post, Emily Price
Powell, Jody (Joseph Lester)

Prentice, George Denison
Prescott, Peter Sherwin
Proudhon, Pierre Joseph
Purdy, Ken(neth) William
Pyle, Ernie (Ernest Taylor)
Quad, M, pseud.
Quimby, Harriet
Quinn, Jane Bryant
Quinn, Sally
Raab, Selwyn
Randolph, Nancy, pseud.
Rascoe, Burton
Raskin, A(braham) H(enry)
Raspberry, William
Reed, Rex
Reedy, George Edward
Reid, Whitelaw
Reiffel, Leonard
Reston, James Barrett
Reuter, Paul Julius Von
Reynolds, Quentin
Rice, Grantland, (Henry Grantland)
Richman, Milton
Riesel, Victor
Riis, Jacob August
Ritchie, Thomas
Rivera, Geraldo
Roberts, Roy Allison
Rochefort, Henri
Romulo, Carlos Pena
Ross, Albion
Ross, Lillian
Ross, Ruth N
Rothermere, Harold Sidney Harmsworth
Rowan, Carl Thomas
Rowen, Hobart
Roxon, Lillian
Royall, Anne Newport
Royko, Mike
Runyon, Damon (Alfred Damon)
Russwurm, John Brown
Ryan, Claude
Ryan, Cornelius John
Ryskind, Morrie
Safire, William L
Saint John, Robert
Saint Johns, Adela Rogers
Salinger, Pierre Emil George
Salisbury, Harrison Evans
Samuel, Maurice
Sann, Paul
Savage, John
Scali, John Alfred
Schaap, Dick (Richard J)
Schakne, Robert
Schanberg, Sydney H
Schecter, Jerrold
Scheer, Robert
Schell, Orville H
Schiff, Dorothy
Schoenbrun, David

Schonberg, Harold C
Schulberg, Budd Wilson
Schwob, Marcel
Scripps, Robert Paine
Segal, Henry
Seldes, George Henry
Servan-Schreiber, Jean-Claude
Shales, Tom (Thomas William)
Shalit, Gene
Sheean, (James) Vincent
Sheehy, Gail Henion
Sheppard, Eugenia Benbow
Shirer, William L(awrence)
Sholes, Christopher Latham
Shulsky, Sam
Shuster, Alvin
Silk, George
Sinclair, Gordon
Skolsky, Sidney
Smedley, Agnes
Smith, "Red" Walter Wellesley
Smith, Hedrick Laurence
Smith, Liz (Mary Elizabeth)
Smith, Merriman
Snow, Edgar Parks
Sobol, Louis
Sokolsky, George E
Sorge, Richard
Spassky, Boris Vasilyevich
Spender, Stephen
Sperling, Godfrey, Jr.
Spewack, Bella Cohen
Stanley, Henry Morton, Sir
Stanton, Frank Lebby
Stare, Fredrick John
Stedman, Edmund Clarence
Steffens, Lincoln
Steinem, Gloria
Stone, Chuck (Charles Sumner)
Stone, I(sidor) F(einstein)
Stone, Marvin Lawrence
Stowe, Leland
Strong, Anna Louise
Strout, Richard Lee
Sullivan, Ed(ward Vincent)
Sullivan, Frank
Sullivan, Walter Seager, Jr.
Sulzberger, Arthur Hays
Sulzberger, C(yrus) L(eon)
Swayze, John Cameron, Sr.
Swope, Herbert Bayard
Taber, Gladys Bagg
Tabouis, Genevieve
Talese, Gay
Taubman, Howard (Hyman Howard)
Taylor, Henry Junior
TerHorst, Jerald Franklin
Terhune, Albert Payson
Terkel, Studs (Louis)
Thackrey, Russell I
Thayer, Mary Van Rensselaer

Thomas, Helen A
Thompson, Dorothy
Thompson, Hunter S(tockton)
Thomson of Fleet, Roy Herbert Thomson,
   Baron
Tiede, Tom Robert
Timerman, Jacobo
Tinney, Cal(vin Lawrence)
Toland, John Willard
Toledano, Ralph de
Townsend, George Alfred
Toye, Francis
Toynbee, Philip (Theodore Philip)
Trohan, Walter
Trowbridge, John Townsend
Twain, Mark, pseud.
Tyler, Gus
Utley, (Clifton) Garrick
Utley, Freda
Van Horne, Harriet
Van Loon, Hendrik Willem
Van Paassen, Pierre
Vanderbilt, Amy
Vanderbilt, Cornelius, Jr.
Vaughan, Bill (William Edward)
Villard, Henry
Villard, Oswald
Volkov, Leon
VonHoffman, Nicholas
Vonnegut, Kurt, Jr.
Wahloo, Per
Wales, Salem Howe
Walker, Danton MacIntyre
Walker, Harold Blake
Walker, Stanley
Wallace, Ed(ward Tatum)
Wallraff, Gunter
Waln, Nora
Ward, Artemus, pseud.
Ward, Paul W
Warner, Denis Ashton
Washburn, Charles
Wasson, R(obert) Gordon
Watson, Mark Skinner
Weaver, William
Wechsberg, Joseph
Wechsler, James Arthur
Weed, Thurlow
Wehrwein, Austin Carl
Weingarten, Violet
Weintal, Edward
Wellman, Paul Iselin
Wellman, Walter
Wells, Linton
Wenner, Jann
Werth, Alexander
West, Dame Rebecca, pseud.
White, William Allen
White, William Smith
Whitehead, Don(ald Ford)
Whitman, Alden

Whitman, Walt(er)
Wibberley, Leonard Patrick O'Connor
Wicker, Tom (Thomas Grey)
Wiesel, Elie(zer)
Wiggins, J(ames) R(ussell)
Wilder, Robert Ingersoll
Will, George F
Wille, Lois Jean
Williams, Ben Ames
Willis, Nathaniel Parker
Wilson, Earl
Wilson, Lyle Campbell
Winchell, Walter
Wind, Herbert Warren
Wolfe, Tom (Thomas Kennerly, Jr.)
Wolfert, Ira
Woltman, Frederick Enos
Woods, Donald
Woodward, Bob (Robert Upshur)
Woodworth, Samuel
Wright, Cobina
Yablonky, Ben
Yardley, Jonathan
Yarmon, Betty
Zenger, John Peter
Zhukov, Georgi Alexandrovich
Zola, Emile Edouard Charles

JUDGE

Adams, Annette Abbott
Allen, Florence Ellinwood
Allen, Macon B
Arndt, Adolf
Bentsen, Lloyd Millard, Jr.
Blackstone, William, Sir
Bork, Robert Heron
Carson, Edward Henry
Carswell, George Harrold
Cassin, Rene
Celebrezze, Anthony Joseph
Cline, Genevieve Rose
Cockrell, Ewing
Coke, Edward, Sir
Crater, Joseph Force
Cushing, Caleb
Denning, Alfred Thompson
Donlon, Mary Honor
Ellery, William
Ferguson, Homer
Feuerbach, Paul Johann Anseim
Fuld, Stanley H
Gesell, Gerhard Alden
Grotius, Hugo
Haliburton, Thomas Chandler
Hand, Learned
Hastie, William Henry
Haynsworth, Clement Furman, Jr.
Hoffman, Julius Jennings
Hopkins, Stephen
Hufstedler, Shirley (Ann) M(ount)
Hughes, Sarah Tilghman

Humphreys, Christmas (Travers Christmas)
Huntington, Samuel
Justice, William Wayne
Kaufman, Irving R
Kaufman, Joseph William
Kerner, Otto
Landis, Frederick
Landis, Kenesaw Mountain
Livingston, Edward
Lowell, John
Medina, Harold Raymond
Meskill, Thomas J
Miller, William Ernest
O'Dalaigh, Cearbhall
Orlando, Vittorio Emanuele
Pecora, Ferdinand
Richardson, Scovel
Russell, Edward Frederick Langley, Baron
   of Liverpool
Ryan, Sylvester James
Selden, John
Sewall, Samuel
Sirica, John Joseph
Thompson, John S D
Trumbull, John
Trumbull, Jonathan
Urrutia Lleo, Manuel
Vishinskii, Andrei Yanuarevich
Voelker, John Donaldson
Walton, George
Widgery, John Passmore, Baron
Williams, G Mennen
Williams, William
Wolcott, Oliver, Sr.
Wood, John Howland, Jr.
Wythe, George
Youngdahl, Luther W

KIDNAP VICTIM

Bronfman, Samuel
Hearst, Patty (Patricia Campbell)

KIDNAPPER

Hauptmann, Bruno Richard
Leopold, Nathan Freudenthal
Loeb, Richard A

KING

Cambyses II
Canute
Carl Gustaf XVI
Carol II
Charlemagne
Cheops
Christian IV
Christophe, Henri
Constantine XII
David
Duncan I

Edgar
Edmund, Saint
Edward I
Edward II
Edward III
Edward IV
Edward the Confessor
Edward V
Edward VI
Edward VII
Edward VIII
Edwy
Eric IX
Fahd ibn Abdul Aziz
Faisal II
Farouk I
Ferdinand V
Francis I
Frederick IX
Frederick the Great
Frederick William I
George I
George II
George II
George III
George IV
George V
George VI
Gustaf Adolf VI
Gustavus Adolphus
Hammurabi
Harold II
Hassan II
Hugh Capet
Hussein (Ibn Talal)
Ibn-Saud
Ikhnaton
John, King of England
Kalakaua, David
Kamehameha I
Leonidas I
Leopold II
Leopold III
Louis I
Louis IX
Louis Phillippe
Louis XIV
Louis XV
Louis XVI
Ludwig II
Manuel I
Matthias, Corvinus
Mausolus
Menes
Michael V
Mohammed V
Mongkut
Moshoeshoe II
Mutesa
Nadir, Shah
Nebuchadnezzar I

Norodom Sihanouk (Varman), Samdech
  Preah
Olaf V
Paul I
Peter II
Philip II
Philip II
Philip II
Philip V
Philip VI
Quabus bin Saud
Richard I
Richard II
Richard III
Robert I
Said bin Taimusr
Saladin Yusuf ibn Ayyub
Saud (Ibn Abdul Aziz al Saud)
Sennacherib
Sobhuza II
Solomon
Tutankhamen
Umberto II
William I
William III
William the Conquerer
Xerxes I
Zog I

LABOR UNION OFFICIAL

Abel, I(orwith) W(ilbur)
Anderson, Mary
Barry, Leonora Marie Kearney
Beck, David
Bevin, Ernest
Bieber, Owen Frederick
Boyle, Tony (William Anthony)
Bridges, Harry Renton
Brophy, John
Chaikin, Sol Chick
Chavez, Cesar
Church, Sam(uel Morgan, Jr.)
Cousins, Frank
Curran, Joseph Edwin
Davis, Hal Charles
Debs, Eugene Victor
Dubinsky, David
Feather, Victor
Fitzgerald, Albert J
Fitzsimmons, Frank
Foster, William Zebulon
Fraser, Douglas Andrew
Futrell, Mary Hatwood
Garvey, Ed(ward Robert)
Gillmore, Frank
Gleason, Thomas W

Golden, Clinton Strong
Goldfinger, Nathaniel
Gompers, Samuel
Green, William
Hardie, James Keir
Haywood, "Big Bill" William Dudley
Hill, Joe, pseud.
Hillman, Sidney
Hoffa, Jimmy (James Riddle)
Huerta, Dolores Hernandez
Jones, Mary Harris
Kirkland, Lane (Joseph Lane)
Lewis, John Llewellyn
McBride, Lloyd
McDonald, David John
Meany, George
Miller, Arnold Ray
Mitchell, John
Mooney, Tom (Thomas J)
Murray, Philip
Parkhurst, Michael Hus
Petrillo, James Caesar
Poli, Robert E
Potofsky, Jacob Samuel
Presser, Jackie
Quill, Mike (Michael J)
Randolph, Asa Philip
Reuther, Roy
Reuther, Walter Philip
Scanlon, Hugh Parr
Scargill, Arthur
Shanker, Albert
Tobin, Daniel Joseph
Townsend, Willard Saxby
Trumka, Richard Louis
Upchurch, John Jorden
Walesa, Lech
Williams, Roy Lee
Winpisinger, William Wayne
Wolfgang, Myra K
Woodcock, Leonard Freel
Wurf, Jerry (Jerome)
Yablonski, Joseph

LAWMAN

Bean, Roy
Courtright, Jim (Timothy Isaiah)
Earp, Morgan
Earp, Virgil W
Earp, Wyatt Berry Stapp
Garrett, Pat(rick Floyd)
Horn, Tom
Masterson, "Bat" (William Barclay
Pusser, Buford

LAWYER

Abourezk, James George
Abram, Morris Berthold
Abzug, Bella Savitsky
Adams, Brock(man)

Garvey, Ed(ward Robert)
Gaspari, Remo
Gaud, William Steen, Jr.
Gerry, Elbridge Thomas
Giesler, Jerry (Harold Lee)
Glass, Montague (Marsden)
Goodell, Charles Ellsworth
Goodwin, Richard N(aradhof)
Griffin, Bob (Robert Paul)
Griffiths, Martha Wright
Gurney, Edward John
Haggard, Henry Rider, Sir
Halleck, Charles Abraham
Hamilton, Andrew
Hastie, William Henry
Hatch, Carl A
Heyward, Thomas, Jr.
Hickey, William
Hills, Roderick M
Hirschorn, Joel
Hiss, Alger
Hoffman, Anna Marie Lederer Rosenberg
Holtzmann, Fanny E
Hooper, William
Hore-Belisha, Leslie, Baron
Hosmer, Craig (Chester Craig)
Houston, Charles Hamilton
Hoyle, Edmond
Humes, James Calhoun
Humphreys, Christmas (Travers Christmas)
Hurley, Patrick Jay
Hutchins, Robert Maynard
Hyatt, Joel
Ingersoll, Robert Green
Jaworski, Leon
Jenkins, Ray Howard
Jordan, Barbara C
Kagel, Sam
Kalmbach, Herbert Warren
Kampelman, Max M
Katzenbach, Nicholas de Belleville
Kaufman, Irving R
Kaufman, Joseph William
Keating, Kenneth B
Kelsen, Hans
Kennedy, Florynce
Kennedy, Robert Francis
Kent, James
Key, Francis Scott
Kheel, Theodore Woodrow
Kiesinger, Kurt Georg
Kirbo, Charles
Krishna Menon, V(engalil) K(rishnan)
Kuhn, Bowie Kent
Kunstler, William Moses
La Marsh, Judy Verlyn
LaGuardia, Fiorello Henry
Lane, Mark
Langdell, Christopher Columbus
Lansing, Robert
LaRussa, Tony (Anthony, Jr.)

Lausche, Frank John
Lawrence, William Beach
Laxalt, Paul
Leibowitz, Samuel Simon
Lie, Jonas (Laurite Idemil)
Lie, Trygve Halvdan
Lilienthal, David Eli
Lincoln, Robert Todd
Lindsay, John Vliet
Lipshutz, Robert Jerome
Lockwood, Belva Ann Bennett
Lowden, Frank O(rren)
Lowenstein, Allard Kenneth
Mankiewicz, Frank Fabian
Mansfield, Arabella
Mardian, Robert Charles
Marshall-Hall, Edward, Sir
Martin, Jennifer
Maverick, Maury
Mays, David John
McCloy, John Jay
McCormach, Mark Hume
McCormack, John William
McKissick, Floyd Bixler
Mikva, Abner Joseph
Mills, Ogden Livingston
Minow, Newton Norman
Mitchelson, Marvin M(orris)
Montagu, Ewen (Edward Samuel)
Moore, John Bassett
Morgenthau, Robert Morris
Morrison, Trudi Michelle
Mortimer, John Clifford
Nader, Ralph
Neal, James Foster
Nizer, Louis
Norton, Eleanor Holmes
O'Connor, Basil
O'Dwyer, Paul
O'Hair, Madalyn Murray
O'Malley, Walter Francis
Oteri, Joseph Santo
Ozanam, Frederic
Page, Alan Cedric
Patman, (John Williams) Wright
Paul, Alice
Phillips, Lena Madesin
Picard, Edmond
Pinchback, Pinckney Benton Stewart
Plimpton, Francis Taylor Pearson
Power, Donald Clinton
Procter, Bryan Walter
Quinn, John
Randolph, Edmund Jennings
Randolph, Peyton
Richberg, Donald R(andall)
Rivera, Geraldo
Roa (y Garcia), Raul
Robbie, Joe (Joseph)
Root, Elihu
Roper, Daniel C

Rostow, Eugene Victor
Rush, Kenneth
Saint Clair, James Draper
Satovsky, Abraham
Scherr, Max
Schlussel, Mark Edward
Schroder, Gerhard
Schwartz, Alan Earl
Sears, John Patrick
Segretti, Donald H
Shea, William Alfred
Shenker, Morris Abraham
Shriver, (Robert) Sargent
Smith, James
Sorensen, Ted (Theodore Chaikin)
Spaak, Paul-Henri
Stassen, Harold Edward
Stevenson, Adlai Ewing
Stevenson, Adlai Ewing, III
Stone, Thomas
Story, William Wetmore
Straus, Oscar
Taft, Charles Phelps
Terry, Alfred Howe
Thomas, Franklin Augustine
Thorn, Gaston
Tiernan, Robert Owens
Tilden, Samuel Jones
Townsend, William H(enry)
Train, Arthur Cheney
Trumka, Richard Louis
Turkus, Burton B
Uhlman, Wes(ley Carl)
Vance, Cyrus Roberts
Vargas, Getulio Dornelles
Volner, Jill Wine
Vorster, Balthazar Johannes (John)
Wagner, Robert Ferdinand, Jr.
Walinsky, Adam
Walsh, Thomas James
Warnke, Paul Culliton
Watkins, Arthur V(ivian)
Watkins, Ernest Shilston
Watson, Jack Hearn, Jr.
Webb, James Edwin
Webster, Daniel
Welch, Joseph Nye
Werner, Pierre
Wilder, Brooks
Wille, Frank
Williams, Harrison Arlington, Jr.
Wilson, John Johnston
Wirtz, William Willard
Woodcock, Amos Walter Wright
Yarborough, Ralph Webster
Young, Owen
Ziegler, John Augustus, Jr.

LECTURER

Ackerman, Forest J
Alexander, Shana

Angell, (Ralph) Norman, Sir
Aptheker, Herbert
Belli, Melvin Mouron
Blatch, Harriot Eaton Stanton
Bolitho, Henry Hector
Brown, John Mason
Carey, Ernestine Muller Gilbreth
Carleton, Will
Carnegie, Dale
Curtis, George William
Deloria, Vine, Jr.
Douglass, Frederick
Farnham, Eliza Wood Burhans
Fletcher, Alice Cunningham
Fowler, Orson Squire
France, Harry Clinton
Frost, Edwin Brant
Hall, Josef Washington
Janeway, Eliot
Keller, Helen Adams
Kimbrough, Emily
Leary, Timothy Francis
Lerner, Max
Lindsay, (Nicholas) Vachel
Livermore, Mary Ashton Rice
Norton, Elliott
Robbe-Grillet, Alain
Rogers, Will(iam Penn Adair)
Rogers, Will, Jr.
Smith, Chard Powers
Smith, Gerald Lyman Kenneth
Strode, Hudson
Tennenbaum, Silvia
Van Loon, Hendrik Willem
Ward, Artemus, pseud.
Westrup, J(ack) A(llan)
Young, Ann Eliza Webb

LEGENDARY FIGURE

Arthur, King
Helen of Troy
Hiawatha
Manco Capac
Robin Hood
Romulus
Tell, William (Wilhelm)

LEXICOGRAPHER

Barnhart, Clarence Lewis
Bartlett, John
Bradley, Henry
Evans, Bergen Baldwin
Fowler, Henry Watson
Gould, George Milbry
Johnson, Samuel
Larousse, Pierre Athanase
Partridge, Eric Honeywood
Robert, Paul
Roget, Peter Mark

Webster, Noah
Worcester, Joseph Emerson

LIBRARIAN

Canfield, James Hulme
Carlson, William Hugh
Cheney, John Vance
Dewey, Melvil
Dibdin, Thomas Frognall
Evans, Charles
Guenther, Charles John
Haviland, Virginia
Henderson, Robert W
Jones, Clara Araminta Stanton
Larkin, Philip
Legler, Henry Eduard
Mearns, David Chambers
Mumford, Lawrence Quincy
Placzek, Adolf K(urt)
Poole, William Frederick
Ready, William Bernard
Schenker, Tillie Abramson
Schullian, Dorothy May
Shera, Jesse Hauk
Sonneck, Oscar George Theodore
Wroth, Lawrence Councelman

LIBRARY ADMINISTRATOR

Greene, Belle da Costa
Gregorian, Vartan
Wright, Louis Booker

LIBRETTIST

Boito, Arrigo
DaPonte, Lorenzo
Duveyrier, Anne Honore
Harbach, Otto Abels
Hooker, Brian
Marmontel, Jean Francois
Metastasio, Pietro
Mosenthal, Salomon Hermann von
Nuitter, Charles Louis
Piave, Francesco Maria
Rice, Tim(othy Miles Bindon)
Rinuccini, Ottavio
Romani, Felice
Rossi, Gaetano
Saint Georges, Jules
Schikaneder, Johann Emanuel
Stein, Joseph
Wagner, Richard
Zeno, Apostolo

LINGUIST

Chomsky, Noam
Korzybski, Alfred Habdank
Menendez Pidal, Ramon
Zamenhof, Ludwik Lazar

LITERARY CRITIC

Arvin, Newton
Barthes, Roland
Brandes, Georg Morris Cohen
Burke, Kenneth
Chase, Richard Volney
Connolly, Cyril Vernon
Cowley, Malcolm
Frye, H(erman) Northrop
Kermode, (John) Frank
Kirkus, Virginia
Leavis, F(rank) R(aymond)
Lehmann-Haupt, Christopher
Levin, Harry Tuchman
Lubbock, Percy
Redman, Ben Ray
Richards, Ivor Armstrong
Trilling, Diana Rubin
Winwar, Frances (Francesca Vinciguerra)

LITHOGRAPHER

Currier, Nathaniel
Prang, Louis
Wengenroth, Stow

LUMBER EXECUTIVE

Weyerhaeuser, Frederick Edward

LYRICIST

Barnes, Billy
Bart, Lionel
Bergman, Alan
Bergman, Marilyn Keith
Bricusse, Leslie
Darion, Joseph
David, Hal
Deutsch, Helen
Edwards, Sherman
Fine, Sylvia
Gershwin, Ira
Hammerstein, Oscar, II
Harnick, Sheldon Mayer
Hart, Lorenz Milton
Jacobs, Al(bert T)
Lerner, Alan Jay
Marks, Johnny (John David)
Porter, Cole
Previn, Dory Langdon
Robin, Leo
Sherman, Richard Morton
Sondheim, Stephen Joshua
Sour, Robert B(andler)
Swann, Donald Ibrahim
Swift, Kay
Taupin, Bernie
Webster, Paul Francois
Wilson, Al

MADAM

Adler, Polly
Everleigh, Ada
Everleigh, Minna

MAGICIAN

Blackstone, Harry
Cagliostro, Alessandro, Conte di
Copperfield, David
Crowley, Aleister (Edward Alexander)
Dee, John
Dunninger, Joseph
Faust, Johann
Goldin, Horace
Henning, Doug(las James)
Houdin, Jean Eugene Robert
Houdini, Harry
Randi, James
Scarne, John
Thurston, Howard

MANAGER

Abbey, Henry Eugene
Albee, Edward Franklin
Aldrich, Richard Stoddard
Baylis, Lilian Mary
Beck, Martin
Bing, Rudolf (Franz Josef), Sir
Boycott, Charles Cunningham
Chapin, Schuyler Garrison
Coburn, Charles Douville
Dillingham, Charles Bancroft
Epstein, Brian
Evans, Maurice
Forbes-Robertson, Johnston, Sir
Frohman, Daniel
Gailhard, Pierre
Gatti-Casazza, Giulio
Hammerstein, Oscar
Harris, Sam Henry
Hartmann, Rudolph
Hilbert, Egon
Johnson, Edward
Juch, Emma
Kellogg, Clara Louise
Ludikar, Pavel
Miller, Henry John
Parker, Thomas Andrew
Pastor, Tony (Antonio)
Riordan, Bill
Robinson, Francis Arthur
Shubert, Jacob J
Tree, Herbert Beerbohm
Wallack, James William
Ziegler, Edward

MANUFACTURER

Allyn, Stanley Charles
Ames, Oakes
Babbitt, Benjamin Talbot
Ball, Edmund B
Ball, Frank
Bass, Henry
Bendix, Vincent
Bich, Marcel
Bigelow, Erastus Brigham
Boiardi, Hector
Boulton, Matthew
Boussac, Marcel
Bradley, Milton
Buitoni, Giovanni
Cadbury, George Adrian Hayhurst, Sir
Campagnolo, Gitullio
Campbell, Joseph
Candler, Asa Griggs
Carder, Frederick
Carter, William
Chalmers, William James
Chapin, Roy Dikeman
Chickering, Jonas
Coats, James
Colgate, William
Converse, Marquis M
Danforth, William H
Dassler, Adolf
Deering, William
Dewar, John
Dow, Herbert Henry
Durkee, Eugene R
Duryea, Charles Edgar
Evinrude, Ole
Farah, James
Farah, William
Farber, Simon W
Fender, Leo
Firestone, Harvey Samuel
Firestone, Harvey Samuel, Jr.
Fischer, Carl
Fischer, Herman G
Fleischmann, Charles Louis
Fleishmann, Raoul H(erbert)
Folger, James A
Fruehauf, Harvey Charles
Fuller, Alfred Carl
Gamble, James Norris
Gilbert, Alfred Carlton, Jr.
Girdler, Tom Mercer
Gucci, Guccio
Guerlain, Pierre Francois Pascal
Haggar, Joseph M
Hammer, Armand
Handler, Elliot
Handler, Ruth
Hanes, John Wesley
Hanes, Pleasant H
Heinz, Henry John
Hellmann, Richard

Occupation Index

Hires, Charles E
Honeywell, Mark Charles
Horlick, Alexander James
Hupp, Louis Gorham
Jantzen, Carl
Jergens, Andrew
Johnson, Samuel C
Kellems, Vivien
Kellogg, Howard
Kerr, Alexander H
Kimball, William Wallace
Kraft, James Lewis
Lear, William Powell
Lee, Henry D
Lenox, Walter S
Leverhulme, William Hesketh Lever,
  Viscount
Lilly, Eli
Mack, John M
Mallinckrodt, Edward
Marx, Louis
Matchabelli, Georges, Prince
Mattus, Reuben
May, Mortimer
Maytag, Elmer Henry
McCormick, Cyrus Hall
McCormick, Cyrus Hall
Michelin, Andre
Miller, Howard
Morton, Joy
Mueller, Christian F
Nunn, Harold F
Olivetti, Adriano
Otis, Elisha Graves
Owen, Robert
Owens, Michael Joseph
Parker, George Safford
Perky, Henry D
Pfizer, Charles
Phillips, Charles
Pillsbury, Charles Alfred
Pillsbury, John Sargent
Pillsbury, John Sargent
Pillsbury, Philip Winston
Pinkham, Lydia Estes
Pirelli, Alberto
Price, Irving L
Procter, Harley T
Procter, William Cooper
Redenbacher, Orville
Remington, Eliphalet
Reynolds, Richard S.
Rockwell, Willard F
Sax, Charles Joseph
Schwinn, Ignaz
Scranton, George Whitfield
Sherwin, Henry Alden
Shorthouse, Joseph Henry
Simmons, Zalmon G
Smith, Amanda W
Smith, Christopher Columbus

Smith, Horace
Smucker, Jerome
Sommers, Ben
Spreckels, Claus
Squibb, Edward Robinson
Steinway, Henry Engelhard
Stetson, John Batterson
Stiegel, Henry William
Strauss, Levi
Studebaker, Clement
Swift, Gustavus Franklin
Tappan, William J
Tate, Henry, Sir
Thomas, Samuel Bath
Thomas, Seth
Timken, Henry
Underwood, John Thomas
Upjohn, Lawrence Northcote
Vail, Alfred Lewis
Vickers, Edward
Wakefield, Ruth G
Wesson, Daniel Baird
Westinghouse, George
Weston, Edward F
Wharton, Joseph
Williams, Edward Porter
Wrigley, William, Jr.
Wurlitzer, Rudolph
Yale, Linus
Zeiss, Carl
Zellerbach, William Joseph
Zuckerman, Ben

MANUFACTURERS

Smith Brothers

MATHEMATICIAN

Aiken, Howard Hathaway
Alembert, Jean le Rond d'
Apollonius of Perga
Archimedes
Babbage, Charles
Banneker, Benjamin
Begle, Edward G(riffith)
Beltrami, Eugenio
Bernoulli, David
Bondi, Hermann, Sir
Boscovich, Ruggiero Giuseppe
Bowditch, Nathaniel
Bronowski, Jacob
Cantor, Georg
Carroll, Lewis, pseud.
Charles, Jacques-Alexandre-Cesar
Condorcet, Marie-Jean-Antoine
Dee, John
Descartes, Rene
Dirac, Paul A M
Doppler, Christian Johann
Euclid
Euler, Leonhard

Fermat, Pierre de
Galileo
Galois, Evariste
Gauss, Karl Friedrich
Gibbs, Josiah Willard
Godel, Kurt
Hopper, Grace Brewster Murray
Hypatia
Jeans, James Hopwood, Sir
Kelvin, William Thomson, Baron
Lagrange, Joseph-Louis
Laplace, Pierre Simon, Marquis de
Lehrer, Tom (Thomas Andrew)
Leibniz, Gottfried Wilhelm von
Mason, Max
Maxwell, James Clerk
Mobius, August Ferdinand
Muses, Charles Arthur
Newton, Isaac, Sir
Oughtred, William
Pascal, Blaise
Peirce, Benjamin
Picard, Charles Emile
Poincare, Jules Henri
Polya, George
Ptolemy
Pythagoras
Rittenhouse, David
Russell, Bertrand Arthur William
Saunderson, Nicholas
Vernier, Pierre
Von Neumann, John
Welchman, Gordon
Whitehead, Alfred North
Wiener, Norbert

MAYOR

Brauer, Max Julius Friedrich
Cermak, Anton Joseph
Farrell, Carolyn
Gibson, Kenneth Allen
Hatcher, Richard Gordon
Impellitteri, Vincent R
Jackson, Maynard Holbrook, Jr.
Maier, Henry W
Morial, Ernest Nathan
O'Dwyer, William
Reuter, Ernst
Uhlman, Wes(ley Carl)
Voinovich, George Victor
Wagner, Robert Ferdinand, Jr.
Walworth, William, Sir
Washington, Walter Edward
Whitington, Dick (Richard)

MEAT PACKER

Cudahy, Michael
Hormel, George Albert
Mayer, Oscar Ferdinand

Mayer, Oscar Gottfried
Mayer, Oscar Gottfried

MERCHANT

Altman, Benjamin
Bacardi, Don Facundo
Bamberger, Louis
Bannerman, Francis
Bauer, Eddie
Bloomingdale, Joseph Bernard
Bowdoin, James
Brookings, Robert Somers
Burton, Montague Maurice, Sir
Calas, Jean
Cannon, James W
Clymer, George
Coeur, Jacques
Cudahy, Michael
Eaton, Timothy
Ferkauf, Eugene
Field, Cyrus West
Field, Marshall
Filene, Edward Albert
Filene, Lincoln
Fugger, Jacob
Goldman, Sylvan N
Gorham, Jabez
Gucci, Guccio
Hartford, George Huntington
Hartford, George Ludlum
Hartford, John Augustine
Hewes, Joseph
Hills, Austin H
Hills, Reuben W
Hopkins, Stephen
Juilliard, Augustus D
Kimball, William Wallace
Kinney, George Romanta
Kresge, Sebastian Spering
Kress, Samuel Henry
Laurens, Henry
Lazare, Kaplan
Lee, Henry D
Lewis, Francis
Liggett, Louis Kroh
Lipton, Thomas Johnstone, Sir
Lorillard, Pierre
May, Morton David
Melrose, William
Mennen, William Gerhard
Ohrbach, Nathan
Peabody, George
Penney, J(ames) C(ash)
Rochester, Nathaniel
Roebuck, Alvah Curtis
Rosenthal, Ida Cohen
Rosenwald, Julius
Rylands, John
Sears, Richard Warren
Skaggs, M(arion) B
Stewart, Alexander Turney

Stix, Nathan
Straus, Isidor
Straus, Jack Isidor
Straus, Nathan
Twining, Thomas
Vassar, Matthew
Walgreen, Charles Rudolph
Wanamaker, John
Wanamaker, Rodman
Ward, (Aaron) Montgomery
Ward, (Aaron) Montgomery
Whalen, Grover
Williams, William
Woolworth, Frank Winfield
Yunich, David Lawrence

METEOROLOGIST

Abbe, Cleveland
Coleman, John
Glaisher, James
McAdie, Alexander George
Reichelderfer, Francis Wylton

MILITARY LEADER

Alcibiades
Ali Pasha
Allen, Ethan
Allen, Henry Tureman
Allenby, Edmund Hynman Allenby,
    Viscount
Anderson, Robert
Andrews, Frank M(axwell)
Arnold, Henry Harley
Auchinleck, Claude, Sir
Babur
Baden-Powell, Robert Stephenson Smyth
    Baden-Powell, Baron
Bagration, Petr Ivanovich
Barry, Tom
Batu Khan
Beauregard, Pierre Gustav Toutant de
Bliss, Tasker H
Bloch, Claude Charles
Borgia, Cesare
Botha, Louis
Braddock, Edward
Brauchitsch, Heinrich Alfred
Brown, Jacob Jennings
Buckner, Simon B
Buckner, Simon, Jr.
Buford, John
Bullard, Robert Lee
Cates, Clifton Bledsoe
Chang Tso-Lin
Chauncey, Isaac
Chuikov, Vasili Ivanovitch
Clausewitz, Karl von
Clinton, Henry, Sir
Craig, Malin
Cunningham, Andrew Browne, Viscount

Cushing, William Barker
Davis, Benjamin Oliver
Davout, Louis Nicholas
Dickman, Joseph Theodore
Dill, John Greer, Sir
Dixon, Robert Ellington
Douglas, Sholto (William Sholto)
Dozier, James Lee
Drum, Hugh A
Du Guesclin, Bertrand
Early, Jubal Anderson
Evans, Robley Dunglison
Farragut, David Glasgow
Foch, Ferdinand
Foote, Andrew Hull
Forrest, Nathan Bedford
Funston, Frederick
Glubb, John Bagot, Sir
Graziani, Rodolfo
Grivas, George Theodorus
Grubert, Carl Alfred
Guderian, Heinz Wilhelm
Halleck, Henry
Hannibal
Harris, Arthur Travers, Sir
Heaton, Leonard
Herkimer, Nicholas
Hill, Ambrose Powell
Hobbs, Leland Stanford
Hobson, Richmond Pearson
Hodges, Courtney
Hood, John Bell
Hooker, Joseph
Hopper, Grace Brewster Murray
Hull, Isaac
Hull, John Edwin
Hunyadi, Janos
Ingersoll, Stuart H
Ismay, Hastings Lionel, Baron
Jackson, "Stonewall" Thomas Jonathan
Joffre, Joseph Jacques Cesaire
Johnston, Albert S
Johnston, Joseph Eggleston
Kirk, Alan Goodrich
Knox, Henry
Kornilov, Lavr Georgyevich
Lawton, Henry Ware
Lincoln, George A
Littlejohn, Robert McGowan
Malinovsky, Rodion Y
Marion, Francis
McClellan, George Brinton
McPherson, James Birdseye
Meade, George Gordon
Mitscher, Marc A
Montcalm, Louis Joseph de
Montgomery of Alamein, Bernard Law
    Montgomery, Viscount
Morelos y Pavon, Jose M
Murat, Joachim
Ney, Michel de la Moskova, Prince

O'Donnell, Emmett
Parks, Floyd Lavinius
Patch, Alexander M(c Carrell)
Peers, William Raymond
Pelopidas
Pemberton, John Clifford
Petain, Henri Philippe
Pickens, Andrew
Pickett, George Edward
Porter, David Dixon
Power, Thomas
Price, Sterling
Rogers, Bernard William
Roosevelt, Theodore, Jr.
Rundstedt, Karl Rudolf Gerd von
Saint Clair, Arthur
Sampson, William T
Samsonov, Aleksandr Vasilievich
Saxe, Maurice
Schofield, John McAllister
Shafter, William Rufus
Shaw, Robert Gould
Sheridan, Philip Henry
Sherman, William Tecumseh
Sims, William Sowden
Smith, Holland McTeire
Speidel, Hans
Stewart, Alexander Peter
Stirling, Lord
Stulberg, Louis
Sykes, George
Tedder, Arthur William Tedder, Baron
Terry, Alfred Howe
Thayer, Sylvanus, General
Thomas, George Henry
Towle, Katherine Amelia
Trenchard, Hugh Montague, First Viscount
Tukhachevski, Mikhail N
Turenne, Henri D'Auvergne, Vicomte
Vessey, John William, Jr.
Wedemeyer, Albert Coady
Welch, Larry Dean
Westmoreland, William Childs
Weygand, Maxime
Wheeler, Joseph
Wolcott, Oliver, Sr.
Wyman, Willard Gordon
Yamamoto, Isoroku
Zhukov, Georgi Konstantinovich

MINERALOGIST

Agricola, Georgius
Friedel, Charles
Hauy, Rene Just
Mohs, Friedrich

MINISTER

Bachman, John
Blackwell, Antoinette Louisa Brown
Bunyan, John

Ford, Arthur A
Hooks, Benjamin Lawson
LaHaye, Tim
Ripley, George
Roloff, Lester

MISSIONARY

Aylward, Gladys
Boniface, Saint
Brant, Joseph
Columba, Saint
Crummell, Alexander
Damien, Father
Dooley, Thomas Anthony
Fisher, Welthy (Blakesley Honsinger)
Francis Xavier, Saint
Gall, Saint
Gallitzin, Demetrius Augustine
Grenfell, Wilfred Thomason, Sir
Jones, Eli Stanley
Lee, Jason
Liddell, Eric
Livingstone, David
Marquette, Jacques, Pere
Marty, Martin
Ricci, Matteo
Schweitzer, Albert
Teresa, Mother
Townsend, William Cameron
Whitman, Marcus

MISTRESS

DuBarry, Comtesse Jeanne Becu
Hamilton, Emma
Lupescu, Magda (Elena)
Morgan, Vicki
O'Murphy, Louise
Petacci, Clara
Pompadour, Jeanne Antoinette Poisson
Stoffels, Hendrickje

MODEL

Adams, Maud
Alexis, Kim
Andersen, Anna
Basinger, Kim
Berenson, Marisa
Bettina
Brinkley, Christie
Colby, Anita
Cooper, Wilhelmina Behmenburg
Dali, Gala
Dey, Susan Hallock
Duplessis, Marie
Fawcett, Farrah Leni
Ferrare, Christina
Fourment, Helena
Fyodorova, Victoria
Hack, Shelley

Hall, Jerry
Hamel, Veronica
Hansen, Patti (Patricia Evina)
Hemingway, Margaux
Hutton, Lauren (Mary Laurence)
Iman
Johnson, Beverly
Jones, Candy
Jones, Grace
MacGraw, Ali
Marshall, Esme
O'Neill, Jennifer
Oakes, Randi
Parker, Suzy
Peretti, Elsa
Peterson, Lorraine Collett
Raffin, Deborah
Rossellini, Isabella
Roventini, Johnny
Shepherd, Cybill
Shields, Brooke
Shrimpton, Jean Rosemary
Siddal, Elizabeth Eleanor
Stoffels, Hendrickje
Stratten, Dorothy
Tiegs, Cheryl
Tiffin, Pamela Kimberley
Tucker, Mary Bradham
Twiggy
Veruschka
Walter, Marie Therese
Ward, Rachel
Welch, Raquel

MONK

Lippi, Filippino

MOTORCYCLE RACER

Hailwood, Mike (Stanley Michael Bailey)

MOUNTAINEER

Freshfield, Douglas William
Goodwin, Daniel
Hillary, Edmund Percival, Sir
Mallory, George Leigh
Messner, Reinhold
Rebuffat, Gaston Louis Simon
Tabei, Junko
Tenzing, Norgay

MOVIE CRITIC

Alpert, Hollis
Crist, Judith Klein
Crowther, Bosley (Francis Bosley)
Ebert, Roger Joseph
Gelmis, Joseph Stephen
Greenspun, Roger
Kael, Pauline

Knight, Arthur
Maltin, Leonard
Reed, Rex
Schickel, Richard
Shalit, Gene
Simon, John Ivan
Winsten, Archer

MURDER VICTIM

Berger, David
Friedman, Ze'ev
Genovese, Kitty
Gutfreund, Yosef
Halfin, Eliezer
Rogers, Mary Cecilia
Romano, Joseph
Shapira, Amitzur
Shorr, Kehat
Slavin, Mark
Spitzer, Andre
Springer, Ya'acov
Weinberg, Moshe

MURDERER

Abbott, Jack (Rufus Jack Henry)
Agron, Salvador
Anastasia, Albert
Anderson, William
Atkins, Susan Denise
Baniszewski, Gertrude Wright
Bateman, Mary
Bathory, Elizabeth
Beadle, William
Berkowitz, David
Billington, John
Borden, Lizzie Andrew
Brooks, Charlie, Jr.
Brooks, David Owen
Bundy, Ted
Burke, William
Carlos
Chapman, Mark David
Charriere, Henri
Christie, John Reginald Halliday
Corona, Juan
Crippen, Hawley Harvey
Defeo, Ronald
Dillinger, John Herbert
Dominici, Gaston
Dumurq, Charles
Ellis, Ruth
Evans, Timothy
Fish, Albert
Ford, Bob (Robert Newton)
Franklin, Joseph Paul
Fugate, Caril Ann
Gacy, John Wayne, Jr.
Gein, Ed
Gilmore, Gary Mark
Graham, Barbara

Guiteau, Charles Julius
Hare, William
Harris, Jean Witt Struven
Hauptmann, Bruno Richard
Hickock, Richard Eugene
Horn, Tom
Jack the Ripper
Judd, Winnie Ruth McKinnell
Judy, Steven
Kray, Reggie (Reginald)
Kray, Ronnie (Ronald)
Lafarge, Marie
Landru, Henri Desire
Leopold, Nathan Freudenthal
Loeb, Richard A
Manning, Maria
Manson, Charles
Mudgett, Herman Webster
Noziere, Violette
Packer, Alfred G
Palmer, William
Ruby, Jack
Smith, Madeline Hamilton
Smith, Perry Edward
Snider, Paul
Speck, Richard Franklin
Spenkelink, John Arthur
Starkweather, Charles
Thaw, Harry Kendall
Todd, Sweeney
Unruh, Howard B
Whitman, Charles Joseph
Williams, Wayne Bertram
Zodiac Killer

MUSEUM DIRECTOR

Barr, Alfred Hamilton, Jr.
Blum, Stella
Breeskin, Adelyn Dohme
Brown, John Carter
Colvin, Sidney, Sir
DeMontebello, Guy-Philippe
Edgell, George Harold
Goldazher, Herbert
Kimball, Fiske
Sachs, Samuel, II
Smith, Kenneth Danforth
Waterhouse, Ellis Kirkham, Sir
Wolfenden, John Frederick, Sir

MUSIC CRITIC

Avakian, George
Bookspan, Martin
Chotzinoff, Samuel
Davenport, Marcia
DeKoven, (Henry Louis) Reginald
Feather, Leonard Geoffrey
Fuller-Maitland, John Alexander
Gilman, Lawrence
Haas, Karl

Hanslick, Eduard
Hentoff, Nat(han Irving)
Howes, Frank Stewart
Kolodin, Irving
Newman, Ernest
Pleasants, Henry
Sanborn, Pitts
Sargeant, Winthrop
Schonberg, Harold C
Smith, Cecil Michener
Taylor, (Joseph) Deems
Thompson, Oscar
Van Vechten, Carl

MUSIC DIRECTOR

Bloom, Julius
Chacksfield, Frank
Chaplin, Saul
Courboin, Charles
Diamand, Peter
Gellhorn, Peter
Harewood, George Henry Hubert Lascelles, Earl
Stoll, George
Zimbalist, Efrem
Zirato, Bruno

MUSIC EXECUTIVE

Boosey, Leslie Arthur
Hammond, John Henry, Jr.
Witmark, Isidore

MUSIC GROUP

ABBA
ABC
AC-DC
Ace
Adam and the Ants
Aerosmith
Air Supply
Alabama
Allman Brothers Band
Amboy Dukes, The
America
Ames Brothers, The
Andrews Sisters
Animals, The
April Wine
Argent
Ashford and Simpson
Asia
Association, The
Atlanta Rhythm Section
Average White Band
B-52's
Babys, The
Bachman-Turner Overdrive
Bad Company
Badfinger

Band, The
Bay City Rollers
Beach Boys, The
Beatles, The
Bee Gees, The
Bellamy Brothers, The
Big Brother and the Holding Company
Big Country
Black Oak Arkansas
Black Sabbath
Blind Faith
Blondie
Blood, Sweat and Tears
Blue Oyster Cult
Boney M.
Booker T and the MG's
Boomtown Rats
Boston
Boswell Sisters
Bow Wow Wow
Box Tops, The
Bread
Brewer and Shipley
Brothers Johnson, The
Buckinghams, The
Buffalo Springfield
Byrds, The
Captain and Tennille, The
Carpenters, The
Cars, The
Carter Family, The
Chad and Jeremy
Charlie Daniels Band, The
Cheap Trick
Chicago
Clara Ward and Her Gospel Singers
Clash, The
Climax Blues Band, The
Coasters
Commander Cody & His Lost Planet
    Airmen
Commodores, The
Country Joe and the Fish
Cowsills, The
Cream
Creedence Clearwater Revival
Critters
Crosby, Stills, Nash, & Young
Crusaders, The
Culture Club
Dave Clark Five
Dazz Band
DeBarge
Deep Purple
Def Leppard
Delaney and Bonnie
DeMarco Sisters
Devo
Dion and the Belmonts
Dire Straits
Doobie Brothers, The

Doors, The
Drifters, The
Duran Duran
E-Street Band
Eagles, The
Earth, Wind, and Fire
Electric Light Orchestra
Emerson, Lake, and Palmer
England Dan and John Ford Coley
English Beat
Eurythmics
Everly Brothers
Exile
Fifth Dimension
Fine Arts Quartet, The
Firefall
Fixx, The
Fleetwood Mac
Flock of Seagulls
Flying Burrito Brothers, The
Foghat
Foreigner
Four Freshmen, The
Four Lads, The
Four Seasons, The
Four Tops
Frijid Pink
Fugs, The
Gary Puckett and the Union Gap
Genesis
Gerry and the Pacemakers
Gladys Knight and the Pips
Go-Go's, The
Golden Earring
Graham Parker and the Rumour
Grand Funk Railroad
Grass Roots, The
Grateful Dead, The
Greg Kihn Band, The
Guess Who
Hall and Oates
Heart
Herman's Hermits
Hollies, The
Honeycombs, The
Honeydrippers, The
Hot Tuna
Hudson Brothers, The
Hues Corporation, The
Huey Lewis and the News
Human League
Humble Pie
Ian and Sylvia
Ike and Tina Turner
Incredible String Band, The
Ink Spots, The
INXS
Irish Rovers
Iron Butterfly
Iron Maiden
Isley Brothers

J Geils Band, The
Jackson Five, The
James Gang
Jan and Dean
Jay and the Americans
Jefferson Starship
Jethro Tull
Joan Jett and the Blackhearts
Journey
Judas Priest
Juilliard String Quartet, The
Junior Walker and the All Stars
K C and the Sunshine Band
King Crimson
King Sisters
Kingston Trio, The
Kinks, The
Kiss
Knack, The
Kool and the Gang
Kraftwerk
Led Zeppelin
Lettermen, The
Little Anthony and the Imperials
Little River Band, The
Loggins and Messina
Loverboy
Lovin' Spoonful
Lynyrd Skynard
Madness
Mahavishnu Orchestra, The
Mamas and the Papas, The
Manhattan Transfer
Marshall Tucker Band, The
Martha and the Vandellas
McGuire Sisters
Men at Work
Midnight Oil
Mills Brothers, The
Missing Persons
Mitch Ryder and the Detroit Wheels
Modern Jazz Quartet, The
Modernaires, The
Molly Hatchet
Monkees, The
Moody Blues
Motels, The
Mothers of Invention, The
Motley Crue
Mott (the Hoople)
Mr. Mister
Nazareth
Night Ranger
Nitty Gritty Dirt Band, The
O'Jays, The
Oak Ridge Boys, The
Osmonds, The
Outlaws, The
Pablo Cruise
Paul Revere and the Raiders
Peter and Gordon

Peter, Paul, and Mary
Phil Napoleon and Memphis Six
Pink Floyd
Plasmatics, The
Platters, The
Poco
Pointer Sisters, The
Police, The
Pretenders, The
Procol Harum
QuarterFlash
Queen
Quicksilver Messenger Service
Quiet Riot
Ramones, The
Rare Earth
Rascals, The
Raspberries, The
REO Speedwagon
Righteous Brothers, The
Ritchie Family, The
Rockets, The
Rockpile
Rolling Stones, The
Romantics, The
Roxy Music
Rush
Sam and Dave
Sam the Sham and the Pharaohs
Sandler and Young
Santana
Scorpions
Seals and Crofts
Sex Pistols
Sha Na Na
Shirelles, The
Simon and Garfunkel
Sister Sledge
Sly and the Family Stone
Smokey Robinson and the Miracles
Soft Cell
Sonny and Cher
Sons of the Pioneers
Souther-Hillman-Furay Band, The
Southside Johnny and the Asbury Jukes
Spandau Ballet
Spencer Davis Group, The
Squeeze
Starship
Statler Brothers
Steely Dan
Steppenwolf
Stray Cats
Styx
Supertramp
Supremes, The
Survivor
Sylvers, The
T. Rex
Talking Heads, The
Taste of Honey

Tears for Fears
Temptations, The
Ten CC
Thin Lizzy
Thirty-Eight Special
Thompson Twins
Three Dog Night
Tom Petty and the Heartbreakers
Toto
Traffic
Triumph
Tubes, The
Twisted Sister
U2
UB 40
UFO
Uriah Heep
Van Halen
Vanilla Fudge
Velvet Underground, The
Ventures, The
Village People, The
Vogues, The
Wang Chang
Weather Report
Weavers, The
Wham!
Who, The
Whodini
X
Yardbirds
Yes
Zombies, The
ZZ Top

MUSICIAN

Adamowski, Timothee
Adams, Bryan
Adams, Cliff
Adderley, "Cannonball" Julian Edwin
Adler, Larry (Lawrence Cecil)
Allen, Duane
Allen, Rick
Allen, Rick
Allen, Verden
Allman, Gregg (Gregory Lenoir)
Almeida, Laurindo
Alpert, Herb
Ammons, "Jug" Eugene
Amram, David Werner, III
Anderson, "Cat" William Alonzo
Anderson, Ian
Anderson, John
Anderson, Jon
Anderson, Rich
Andersson, Benny
Anievas, Augustin
Anthony, Michael
Argent, Rod(ney Terence)
Argerich, Martha
Armstrong, Louis Daniel

Arnold, Eddy
Arnot, Robert Burns
Arrau, Claudio
Ashkenasi, Shmuel
Ashkenazy, Vladimir Davidovich
Ashman, Matthew
Atkins, Chet (Chester B)
Auer, Leopold
Auger, Brian
August, Jan
Ayres, Lew
Bacharach, Burt
Bachauer, Gina
Bachman, Randy
Backhaus, Wilhelm
Badura-Skoda, Paul
Bailey, Philip
Baker, "Ginger" Peter
Baker, Chet
Baker, Julius
Ballard, Russ(ell)
Balsam, Artur
Banks, Tony
Bar-Ilian, David Jacob
Barbarossa, Dave
Barenboim, Daniel
Bares, Basile
Baron, Samuel
Barylli, Walter
Bauer, Harold
Beck, Jeff
Bell, "Kool" Robert
Bell, Ronald
Bellison, Simeon
Bender, Ariel
Benson, George
Benson, Renaldo
Bentley, John
Berger, Al
Berigan, "Bunny" Rowland Bernart
Berman, Lazar
Bernie, Ben
Bernstein, Leonard
Berry, Chuck (Charles Edward Anderson)
Best, Peter
Bethune, Thomas Greene
Bibb, Leon
Biggs, Edward George Power
Bishop, Elvin
Bittan, Roy
Black, Frank J.
Blackmore, Ritchie
Blanc, Mel(vin Jerome)
Bleyer, Archie
Bloch, Alexander
Bloom, Eric
Bloom, Mickey (Milton)
Bloomfield, Mike (Michael)
Blunstone, Colin
Bogert, Tim
Boggs, Tom (Thomas)

Bolan, Marc
Bolcom, William Elden
Bolet, Jorge
Bonfanti, Jim Alexander
Bonham, John Henry
Borden, Barry
Bouchard, Joe
Boult, Adrian Cedric, Sir
Boyd, Liona Maria
Bradley, Will
Brailowsky, Alexander
Brain, Aubrey
Brain, Dennis
Bream, Julian
Brendel, Alfred
Bridgetower, George Augustus
Brock, Tony
Broonzy, Big Bill
Brown, Eddy
Brown, George
Browning, John
Bruce, Jack
Brymer, Jack
Bryson, Wally Carter
Buckingham, Lindsey
Bull, Ole Bornemann
Busey, Gary
Byrd, Henry
Byrne, David
Cacers, Ernest
Campbell, Glen Travis
Campion, Thomas
Capaldi, Jim
Carlton, Larry Eugene
Carmen, Eric
Carpenter, Richard Lynn
Carrack, Paul
Casadesus, Gaby Lhote
Casadesus, Jean
Casadesus, Robert
Casady, Jack
Casals, Pablo (Pau Carlos Salvador)
Casey, H(arry) W(ayne)
Catlett, "Big Sid" Sidney
Cavaliere, Felix
Cetera, Peter
Charles, Ray
Chorzempa, Daniel Walter
Christopher, Jordan
Clark, Dave
Clark, Roy Linwood
Clark, Steve
Clarke, Stanley Marvin
Clayderman, Richard
Clemons, Clarence
Cliburn, Van (Harvey Lavan, Jr.)
Cobb, Arnett Cleophus
Cocker, "Joe" Robert John
Cole, "Cozy" William Randolph
Collins, Lee
Collins, Phil

Colonna, Jerry
Contino, Dick
Cooder, Ry(land Peter)
Cook, Will Marion
Cooke, Sam
Copeland, George
Corby, Mike
Corelli, Arcangelo
Corigliano, John
Cornish, Gene
Corsi, Jacopo
Cotten, Michael
Couperin, Francois
Covington, Warren
Cowell, Henry Dixon
Cramer, Floyd
Creach, "Papa" John
Criss, Peter
Crothers, "Scatman" Benjamin Sherman
Crowell, Rodney
Cummings, Burton
Cunningham, Bill
Curzon, Clifford Michael, Sir
Dale, Alan
Dallapiccola, Luigi
Damrosch, Frank Heino
Danelli, Dino
Daniels, Charlie
Darling, Erik
Daugherty, Pat
Davies, Dave (David)
Davies, Ray(mond Douglas)
Davis, "Wild Bill" William Strethen
Davis, Spencer
DeBarge, El(dra)
DeBarge, James
DeBarge, Mark
DeBarge, Randy
Debost, Michel H
Densmore, John
Derringer, Rick
Desmond, Paul Breitenfeld
DeVito, Tommy
Dichter, Mischa
Diddley, Bo
Diemer, Emma Lou
Difford, Chris
Ditters, Karl
Doggett, Bill
Dohnanyi, Erno von
Doktor, Paul Karl
Dolby, Thomas
Donahue, Sam Koontz
Donati, Pino
Donegan, Dorothy
Dorsey, Jimmy (James)
Dott, Gerard
Downey, Rick
Dragon, Daryl
Dryden, Spencer
Dunham, "Sonny" Elmer Lewis

DuPre, Jacqueline
DuPre, Marcel
Eddy, Duane
Edmunds, Dave
Eldridge, David Roy
Elgar, Edward William, Sir
Ellington, Mercer
Elman, Mischa
Elman, Ziggy
Ely, Joe
Emerson, Keith
Eno, Brian
Entremont, Phillippe
Entwistle, John
Evans, Hiram W
Evans, Mark
Everly, Don
Everly, Phil
Ewen, David
Fain, Sammy
Faulkner, Eric
Faure, Gabriel Urbain
Federici, Daniel Paul
Felder, Don(ald William)
Feliciano, Jose
Fenelon, Fania
Feuermann, Emanuel
Field, Michael
Finch, Rick (Richard)
Firkusny, Rudolf
Fizdale, Robert
Flatt, Lester Raymond
Fleetwood, Mick
Fleisher, Leon
Flesch, Karl
Floren, Myron
Fodor, Eugene Nicholas
Ford, Mary
Fournier, Pierre
Fox, Virgil Keel
Francaix, Jean
Francescatti, Zino Rene
Franck, Cesar Auguste
Francois, Samson
Freeman, "Bud" Lawrence
Frehley, Ace
French, Jay Jay
Frescobaldi, Girolamo
Frey, Glenn
Frickie, Janie
Fried, Miriam
Friml, Rudolf
Fuchs, Joseph
Furay, Richie
Gabrieli, Giovanni
Gabrilowitsch, Ossip
Gaines, Steve
Gallagher, Rory
Galway, James
Ganz, Rudolph
Garcia, Jerry (Jerome John)

Gardner, Samuel
Garner, Erroll
Gaubert, Philippe
Gaudio, Bob
Gazda, Ricky
Gazzelloni, Severino
Geldof, Bob
Gendron, Maurice
Getz, Stan
Giardini, Felice de
Gibb, Andy
Gibbons, Orlando
Gibbs, Terri
Gibson, Bob
Gieseking, Walter Wilhelm
Gilels, Emil Grigorevich
Gilley, Mickey Leroy
Gilmour, David
Gimpel, Jakob
Gitlis, Ivry
Glass, Philip
Glazer, David
Godowsky, Leopold
Gold, Arthur
Goldsand, Robert
Goodman, Benny (Benjamin David)
Goossens, Leon Jean
Gorman, Leroy
Gottschalk, Louis Moreau
Gould, Glenn Herbert
Gould, Morton
Goytisolo, Fermin
Graffman, Gary
Graham, Larry (Lawrence, Jr.)
Grainger, Percy Aldridge
Granados, Enrique
Grant, Earl
Greco, Buddy (Armando)
Green, Johnny (John W)
Greer, "Sonny" William Alexander
Grieg, Edvard Hagerup
Griffin, Dale
Gruber, Franz
Grundy, Hugh
Guion, David Wendel Fentress
Gulda, Friedrich
Guthrie, Woody (Woodrow Wilson)
Haas, Karl
Hackett, Steve
Hagar, Sammy
Haggart, Bob
Haley, Bill (William John Clifford, Jr.)
Hall, Daryl
Halle, Charles, Sir
Hambro, Leonid
Hamilton, Scott
Hamlisch, Marvin
Hammer, Jan
Handy, W(illiam) C(hristopher)
Hardin, Louis Thomas
Harrell, Lynn Morris

Ledbetter, Huddie
Lee, Geddy
Leginska
Lennon, John Winston
Lennon, Julian (John Charles Julian)
Leonardo da Vinci
Lesh, Phil
Lev, Ray
Levant, Oscar
Lewis, Jerry Lee
Lewis, John Aaron
Lewis, Meade Anderson Lux
Lewis, Ramsey Emanuel, Jr.
Lhevinne, Josef
Lhevinne, Rosina L
Liberace
Liberace, George J
Light, Enoch Henry
Lipatti, Dinu
Lipinski, Karl
List, Eugene
Litolff, Henri Charles
Loewe, Frederick
Lofgren, Nils
Loggins, Kenny (Kenneth Clarke)
Longmuir, Alan
Longmuir, Derek
Loughname, Lee
Love, Mike
Lowe, Jack Warren
Lowe, Nick
Luboshutz, Pierre
Lupu, Radu
Lympany, Moura
Lynne, Jeff
Lynott, Phil(ip)
Lyon, "Southside" Johnny
Ma, Yo-Yo
Mack, Ted
Magyar, Gabriel
Malcolm, George
Malcuzynski, Witold
Mandrell, Barbara Ann
Manion, Eddie
Mannes, David
Manzarek, Ray
Marley, Bob (Robert Nesta)
Marlowe, Sylvia
Marsala, Joe
Marsalis, Wynton
Marsden, Gerry
Martell, Vincent
Masekela, Hugh Ramapolo
Mason, Dave
Massey, D Curtis
Massi, Nick
Matlock, "Matty" Julian Clifton
May, Brian
McCann, Les
McCartney, Linda
McClary, Thomas

McCoy, Van
McDonald, Country Joe
McGuinn, Roger
McKeown, Leslie
McKernan, Ron
McKinley, Ray
McKinney, Bill (William)
McLaughlin, John
McVie, John
Meat Loaf
Medtner, Nicholas
Meisner, Randy
Mendelssohn, Felix
Mendes, Sergio
Mendoza, Mark
Menuhin, Hephzibah
Mercury, Freddie
Messiaen, Olivier
Michelangeli, Arturo Benedetti
Mickens, "Spike" Robert
Miller, Steve
Mills, Irving
Milstein, Nathan
Mingus, Charles
Mintz, Shlomo
Mischakoff, Mischa
Moiseiwitsch, Benno
Mollenhauer, Emil
Monk, Thelonius Sphere
Montenegro, Hugo
Monteux, Claude
Montgomery, Wes
Montoya, Carlos
Moon, Keith
Moore, Dudley Stuart John
Moore, Gerald
Morini, Erica
Morrow, Buddy
Moscheles, Ignaz
Moszkowski, Moritz
Mottola, Anthony
Mozart, (Johann Georg) Leopold
Muczynski, Robert
Nascimento, Milton
Nash, Graham
Navarra, Andre
Nelson, Willie
Nelsova, Zara
Nichols, "Red" Ernest Loring
Nicolet, Aurele
Noone, Peter
Novaes, Guiomar
Novi, Carlo
Nuitter, Charles Louis
Nyiregyhazi, Ervin
O'Hara, Mary
Odetta
Offenbach, Jacques
Ogdon, John Andrew Howard
Oistrakh, David Fyodorovich
Oistrakh, Igor Davidovich

Ojeda, Eddie
Olatunji, Michael Babatunde
Oliver, Joe (Joseph)
Ono, Yoko
Orange, Walter
Orbison, Roy
Owens, "Buck" Alvis E, Jr.
Page, Jimmy (James Patrick)
Palligrosi, Tony
Palmer, Carl
Palmer, Robert
Pankow, James
Parazaider, Walter
Parisot, Aldo
Parker, Ray, Jr.
Pass, Joe
Paul, Les
Paxton, Tom (Thomas R)
Peabody, Eddie
Pennario, Leonard
Pentifallo, Kenny
Pero, A J
Perry, Walt
Persinger, Louis
Petty, Tom
Piatigorsky, Gregor
Piston, Walter
Pogorelich, Ivo
Powell, Maud
Powell, Teddy
Powers, Dudley
Praetorius, Michael
Preston, Billy (William Everett)
Price, Ray
Price, Steve
Prima, Louis
Primrose, William
Prince
Prince, Prairie
Prokofiev, Sergei Sergeevich
Prokop, Eugen
Pryor, Arthur W
Rabin, Michael
Rachmaninoff, Sergei Vasilyevich
Ralphs, Mick
Rampal, Jean-Pierre
Randolph, "Boots" Homer Louis, III
Reisenberg, Nadia
Remenyi, Eduard
Respighi, Ottorino
Rey, Alvino
Reynolds, Ricky
Rhodes, Samuel
Ricci, Ruggiero
Rich, Charlie (Charles Allan)
Richard, Keith
Richman, Harry
Richter, Karl
Richter, Sviatoslav Theofilovich
Riddle, Nelson
Ridgeley, Andrew

Robertson, "Robbie" Jaime
Robison, Paula Judith
Rode, Jacques Pierre Joseph
Rodford, Jim (James)
Rodgers, Nile
Rodriguez, Johnny
Roeser, Donald
Roland, Duane
Rollini, Adrian
Rollins, "Sonny" Theodore Walter
Rosand, Aaron
Rose, David
Rose, Leonard
Rosen, Nathaniel
Rosenstock, Joseph
Rosenthal, Moriz
Rostropovich, Mstislav Leopoldovich
Roth, David Lee
Rubinstein, Anton Gregorovitch
Rudd, Phil(lip)
Rundgren, Todd
Rush, Billy
Rushen, Patrice
Russell, Charles Marion
Russell, Leon
Rutherford, Michael
Saidenberg, Daniel
Saint-Saens, (Charles) Camille
Samaroff, Olga
Sanders, Marty
Santana, Carlos (Devadip Carlos)
Sarasate, Pablo de
Sauer, Emil von
Savage, Rick
Scaggs, "Boz" William Royce
Scheja, Staffan
Schelling, Ernest Henry
Schickele, Peter
Schifrin, Lalo Claudio
Schillinger, Joseph
Schirmer, Gustave
Schmidt, Tim(othy B)
Schnabel, Artur
Schnabel, Karl Ulrich
Schneider, Alexander
Schneiderhan, Walther
Schoenbach, Sol Israel
Scholz, Tom
Schumann, Clara Josephine Wieck
Schumann, Henrietta
Schwarz, Gerard
Scott, Tony
Scriabin, Alexander Nicholaevich
Scruggs, Earl
Seger, Bob
Segovia, Andres
Seidel, Toscha
Sembello, Michael
Seraphine, Danny (Daniel)
Serkin, Peter A
Serkin, Rudolph

Severinsen, "Doc" Carl H
Shafran, Daniel
Shankar, Ravi
Shattuck, Arthur
Shaw, Artie
Shearing, George Albert
Sheila E
Sheppard, T G
Shields, Larry
Short, Bobby (Robert Waltrip)
Simmons, Gene
Simon, Abbey
Simone, Nina
Simpson, Valerie
Singleton, "Zutty" Arthur James
Skaggs, Ricky
Slenczynska, Ruth
Slonimsky, Nicolas
Smalley, David Bruce
Smetana, Bedrich
Smith, Claydes
Smith, Ethel
Smith, Jerome
Smith, Ronnie
Snow, Don
Solomon
Solti, Georg, Sir
Sonneck, Oscar George Theodore
Sor, Fernando
South, Joe
Soyer, David
Spaeth, Sigmund Gottfried
Spalding, Albert
Spivak, Charlie
Spivakovsky, Tossy
Spooner, Bill
Springfield, Rick (Richard)
Squier, Billy
Squire, Chris
Stanley, Paul
Starker, Janos
Starr, Ringo
Steen, Roger
Stein, Mark
Stevens, Ray
Stewart, David
Stills, Stephen
Sting
Stocker, Wally
Stokowski, Leopold
Stokowski, Olga Smaroff
Stoltzman, Richard Leslie
Stone, Sly
Suk, Josef
Swann, Donald Ibrahim
Sweelinck, Jan Pieterszoon
Szabo, Gabor
Szeryng, Henryk
Szigeti, Joseph
Tallent, Garry Wayne
Talley, Gary

Taylor, Cecil Percival
Taylor, Mick
Templeton, Alec
Thomas, Dennis
Thompson, Hank
Thomson, Virgil Garnett
Tilbrook, Glenn
Tiomkin, Dimitri
Toch, Ernst
Tork, Peter
Tortelier, Paul
Townshend, Peter Dennis Blandford
Trampler, Walter
Travis, Merle
Trotter, John Scott
Troup, Bobby (Robert William)
Trower, Robin
Tubb, Ernie (Ernest)
Tuckwell, Barry Emmanuel
Tureck, Rosalyn
Tyler, Steve
Ulmer, James
Ulvaeus, Bjorn
Van Halen, Alex
Van Halen, Eddie (Edward)
Van Zant, Ronnie (Ronald)
VanAlstyne, Egbert Anson
Vandross, Luther
Varga, Laszlo
Veyron-Lacroix, Robert
Vieuxtemps, Henri
Viotti, Giovanni Battista
Vivaldi, Antonio
Vollenweider, Andreas
VonBulow, Hans Guido
Vronsky, Vitya
Wagner, Roger
Wakeman, Rick
Walker, "T-Bone" Aaron
Wallenstein, Alfred Franz
Waller, Gordon
Walsh, Joe (Joseph Fidler)
Walter, Cyril
Washington, Grover, Jr.
Waters, Muddy
Watts, Andre
Watts, Charlie (Charles Robert)
Watts, Pete
Wein, George Theodore
Weinberg, Max M
Weir, Bob (Robert Hall)
Weissenberg, Alexis Sigismund
Welch, Bob
Welnick, Vince
Wenrich, Percy
West, Riff
Westrup, J(ack) A(llan)
Whittemore, Arthur Austin
Wild, Earl
Williams, Charles
Williams, Cliff

Williams, Curtis
Williams, John
Williams, Mary Lou
Williams, Mason
Williams, Milan
Williams, Roger
Wilson, "Dooley" Arthur
Wilson, Ann
Wilson, Dennis
Wilson, Nancy
Wilson, Wesley
Winter, Edgar Holand
Winter, Johnny (John Dawson, III)
Winter, Paul Theodore
Winwood, Steve (Stevie)
Wittgenstein, Paul
Wonder, Stevie
Wood, Chris
Wood, Ron(ald)
Wood, Stuart
Woode, William Henri
Wooley, Sheb
Wright, Gary
Wummer, John
Wyman, Bill (William George)
Yepes, Narcisco
Young, Angus
Young, Faron
Young, Malcolm
Young, Neil
Ysaye, Eugene
Zabach, Florian
Zabaleta, Nicanor
Zander, Robin
Zappa, Frank (Francis Vincent, Jr.)
Zeitlin, Zvi
Zingarelli, Nicola Antonio
Zuchermann, Pinchas

MUSICIANS

Couperin
Jerry Murad's Harmonicats

MUSICOLOGIST

Burney, Charles
Einstein, Alfred
Paumgartner, Bernhard
Scholes, Percy Alfred
Spitta, Philipp (Julius August Philipp)
Szabolcsi, Bence
Tovey, Donald Francis, Sir
Wellesz, Egon

MYSTIC

Blake, William
Boehme, Jakob
Cabell, Grete
Eckhart, Johannes
Fox, Kate

Fox, Margaret
Groote, Gerhard
Gurdjieff, Georges Ivanovitch
Hartmann, Franz
Irving, Edward
Juan, Don
Maskelyne, John Nevill
Suso, Heinrich
Swedenborg, Emanuel
Wovoka

NATURALIST

Akeley, Carl Ethan
Attenborough, David Frederick
Bachman, John
Bailey, Frederick Marshman
Bodsworth, Charles Frederick
Born, Max
Buffon, Georges Louis Leclerc
Burroughs, John
Cook, Frederick Albert
Coolidge, Dane
Cruzen, Richard H
Darwin, Charles Robert
DeLong, George Washington
Ditmars, Raymond Lee
Fisher, James Maxwell McConnell
Fitzpatrick, Thomas
Fossey, Dian
Gibbons, Euell
Grey Owl, pseud.
Holland, William Jacob
Holling, Holling C(lancy)
Hudson, William Henry
Kieran, John Francis
Lamarck, Jean Baptiste Pierre
Leeuwenhoek, Anton van
Long, Stephen H
Maeterlinck, Maurice
Merriam, Clinton Hart
Muir, John
Peattie, Donald Culross
Peiresc, Nicholas-Claude Fabri de
Porter, Gene Stratton
Redi, Francesco
Root, Alan
Root, Joan
Schoolcraft, Henry Rowe
Schwatka, Frederik
Seton, Ernest Thompson
Sublette, William L
Teale, Edwin Way
Walcott, Mary Morris Vaux
Walker, Joseph Reddeford
Wilkes, Charles
Wilson, Alexander

NAVAL OFFICER

Anderson, William Robert
Bainbridge, William

Barry, John
Bart, Jean
Bellinghausen, Fabian Gottlieb von
Bligh, William, Captain
Bucher, Lloyd Mark
Burke, Arleigh Albert
Chadwick, French Ensor
Dahlgren, John Adolph
Decatur, Stephen
Dewey, George
Estaing, Charles Henri Hector, Comte d'
Farrere, Claude, pseud.
Fitch, Aubrey
Fluckey, Eugene Bennett
Fuchida, Mitsuo
Garneau, Marc
Ghormley, Robert Lee
Goldsborough, Louis M
Goodman, Robert O, Jr.
Grenville, Richard
Grenville, Richard
Hawkins, John, Sir
Hewitt, Henry Kent
Jones, John Paul
Keyes, Roger
Langsdorff, Hans
Lawrence, James
Leahy, William Daniel
Levy, Uriah Phillips
Luckner, Felix von, Count
MacDonough, Thomas
Moorer, Thomas H(inman)
Mountbatten of Burma, Louis Mountbatten,
  Earl
Nelson, Horatio Nelson, Viscount
Nimitz, Chester William
Pepys, Samuel
Perry, Matthew Calbraith, Commodore
Perry, Oliver Hazard, Admiral
Rickover, Hyman George
Rodgers, Christopher Raymond Perry
Rodgers, John
Schley, Winfield Scott
Stark, Harold Raynsford
Warrington, Lewis
Wilson, Henry Braid
Yarnell, Harry E

NAVIGATOR

Adams, William
Baffin, William
Bering, Vitus Jonassen
Bermudez, Juan de
Bougainville, Louis Antoine de
Cabot, John
Cartier, Jacques
Cavendish, Thomas
Cook, James, Captain
DaGama, Vasco
Dias, Bartholomew
Drake, Francis, Sir

Dumont d'Urville, Jules Sebastian Cesar
Eric the Red
Ericson, Leif
Frobisher, Martin
Gilbert, Humphrey, Sir
Hudson, Henry
Magellan, Ferdinand
Nino, Pedro Alonzo
Pytheas
Raleigh, Walter, Sir
Roggeveen, Jacob
Verrazano, Giovanni da
Vespucci, Amerigo
Wallis, Samuel

NAZI LEADER

Barbie, Klaus
Bormann, Martin Ludwig
Collin, Frank
Frank, Hans
Frick, Wilhelm
Fritzsche, Hans
Funk, Walther
Goebbels, Joseph (Paul Joseph)
Haushofer, Karl
Hess, Rudolf (Walter Richard Rudolf)
Heydrich, Reinhard
Himmler, Heinrich
Hitler, Adolf
Kutschmann, Walter
Ley, Robert
Mengele, Josef
Papen, Franz von
Ribbentrop, Joachim von
Rohm, Ernst
Rosenberg, Alfred
Seyss-Inquart, Artur von
Speer, Albert

NAZI WAR CRIMINAL

Eichmann, Adolf (Otto Adolf)
Goering, Hermann Wilhelm
Grese, Irma
Keitel, Wilhelm
Koch, Ilse
Neurath, Constantin Freiherr von
Raeder, Erich
Stangl, Franz Paul
Streicher, Julius

NEUROLOGIST

Denny-Brown, Derek Ernest
Ferrier, David
Golgi, Camillo
Jackson, John Hughlings
Mitchell, Silas Weir
Rose, Augustus Steele

NEWSPAPER EDITOR

Bailey, Charles Waldo, II
Bartlett, John Sherren
Canham, Erwin Dain
Curtis, Charlotte Murray
DeYoung, Michel Harry
Hechinger, Fred Michael
Hoge, James Fulton, Jr.
Knight, John S, III
Maury, Reuben
Maynard, Robert Clyve
Nelson, William Rockhill
Roberts, Gene (Eugene Leslie, Jr.)
Royster, Vermont Connecticut
Simons, Howard
Watterson, Henry
Wilcock, John

NEWSPAPER EXECUTIVE

Adler, Julius Ochs
Friendly, Edwin Samson
Goodman, Martin Wise
Graham, Donald Edward
Graham, Katharine Meyer
Hearst, Randolph Apperson
Hearst, William Randolph, III
Jones, Richard Lloyd, Jr.
Noyes, Frank B
Ochs, Adolph S, II
Reid, Helen Rogers
Sulzberger, Arthur Ochs

NEWSPAPER PUBLISHER

Baker, Elbert Hall, II
Bennett, James Gordon
Brittain, Harry Ernest, Sir
Chandler, Norman
Chandler, Otis
Curtis, Cyrus Hermann Kotszchmar
Dryfoos, Orvil E
Field, Marshall, V
Flynn, F M
Gannett, Frank Ernest
Grant, Harry Johnston
Greenspun, Hank (Herman Milton)
Halsted, Anna Eleanor Roosevelt
Hearst, William Randolph
Hills, Lee
Hoyt, Palmer (Edwin Palmer)
Kern, Harold G
Knight, John Shivley
Knowland, William Fife
Laffan, William Mackay
Martin, Harold Eugene
McClure, Samuel Sidney
McCormick, Robert Rutherford
McLean, Robert
Newhouse, Samuel Irving
Nieman, Lucius William

Northcliffe, Alfred Charles William
    Harmsworth, Viscount
Ochs, Adolph Simon
Reid, Ogden Mills
Ridder, Bernard Herman
Rothermere, Esmond Cecil Harmsworth,
    Viscount
Scripps, Edward Wyllis
Seaton, Frederick Andrew
Stone, Melville Elijah
Walter, John

NEWSPAPERMAN

Boettiger, John

NOBLEMAN

Bothwell, James Hepburn
John of Gaunt
Pulaski, Kazimierz
Queensberry, John Sholto Douglas
Richard, Duke of York
Sforza, Ludovico
Tupac Amaru

NOBLEWOMAN

Borgia, Lucrezia
Francesca da Rimini
Gioconda, Lisa Gherardini

NUCLEAR TECHNICIAN

Silkwood, Karen

NUN

Deckers, Jeanine
Farrell, Carolyn
Heloise
Lathrop, Rose Hawthorne
Teresa, Mother
Veronica Giuliani, Saint
Wolff, Mary Evaline

NURSE

Barrow, Ruth Nita, Dame
Bickerdyke, Mary Ann Ball
Blake, Florence G
Breckinridge, Mary
Carter, Lillian
Cavell, Edith
Delano, Jane Arminda
Edmonds, Emma E
Galard, Genevieve
Gardner, Mary Sewall
Ileana
Kenny, Sister Elizabeth
Nightingale, Florence
Sanger, Margaret

NUTRITIONIST

Boyd-Orr, John Boyd Orr, Baron
Davis, Adelle
Emerson, Gladys Anderson
Fredericks, Carlton
Hauser, Gayelord
Lappe, Francis Moore
McCollum, Elmer Verner
Pritikin, Nathan
Stare, Fredrick John

OCEANOGRAPHER

Cousteau, Jacques Yves
Cousteau, Philippe
Lindbergh, Jon Morrow
Maury, Matthew Fontaine

OIL WELL TECHNICIAN

Adair, "Red" Paul Neal

OILMAN

Davis, (Thomas) Cullen
Davis, Marvin
Doheny, Edward Lawrence
Dorsey, Bob Rawls
Drake, Edwin Laurentine
Garvin, Clifton Canter, Jr.
Getty, J(ean) Paul
Gulbenkian, Calouste S
Hess, Leon
Holman, Eugene
Hunt, H(aroldson) L(afayette)
Keeler, William
Kerr, Robert Samuel
McCulloch, Robert P
Mecom, John Whitfield
Nickerson, Albert L
Pauley, Edwin Wendell
Pratt, Charles
Richardson, Sid
Rockefeller, John D(avison)
Tavoulareas, William Peter
Warner, Rawleigh, Jr.

OLYMPIC ATHLETE

Berger, David
Carr, Sabin
Coroebus
Davenport, Willie
Desjardins, Pete
Jenkins, Carol Elizabeth Heiss
King, "Micki" Maxine Joyce
Romano, Joseph

OLYMPIC OFFICIAL

Brundage, Avery
Coubertin, Pierre de, Baron
Kane, Robert Joseph
Kelly, John Brenden, Jr.
Killanin, Michael Morris, Lord
Samaranch, Juan Antonio

OPERA COMPOSER

Adam, Adolphe Charles
Arditi, Luigi
Auber, Daniel Francois Esprit
Bellini, Vincenzo
Benjamin, Arthur
Donizetti, Gaetano
Gluck, Christoph Wilibald
Halevy, Jacques Francois Fromental
Haug, Hans
Lattuada, Felice
Leoncavallo, Ruggiero
Lualdi, Adriano
Meyerbeer, Giacomo
Meyerowitz, Jan
Moore, Douglas
Nono, Luigi
Puccini, Giacomo
Rocca, Lodovico
Rosenberg, Hilding
Rossellini, Renzo
Rossini, Gioacchino Antonio
Stradella, Alessandro
Sutermeister, Heinrich
Telemann, Georg Philipp
Thomas, (Charles Louis) Ambroise
Verdi, Giuseppe
Wellesz, Egon

OPERA LIBRETTIST

Barbier, Jules

OPERA SINGER

Abdul, Raoul
Addison, Adele
Albanese, Licia
Alda, Frances
Althouse, Paul Shearer
Alvary, Lorenzo
Alvary, Max
Amara, Lucine
Amato, Pasquale
Ameling, Elly
Andresen, Ivar
Angeles, Victoria de los
Arroyo, Martina
Austral, Florence Wilson
Baccaloni, Salvatore
Baker, Janet Abbott, Dame
Bampton, Rose Elizabeth

Barbaja, Domenica
Barbieri, Fedora
Bastianini, Ettore
Battistini, Mattia
Baum, Kurt
Bechi, Gino
Bellincioni, Gemma
Benzell, Mimi (Miriam Ruth)
Berberian, Cathy
Berganza, Teresa
Bergonzi, Carlo
Bernacchi, Antonio Maria
Berry, Walter
Bible, Frances Lillian
Bjoerling, Jussi
Blegen, Judith Eyer
Bonci, Alessandro
Bonelli, Richard
Bordoni, Faustina
Borg, Kim
Bori, Lucrezia
Borkh, Inge
Branzell, Karin
Braslau, Sophie
Broadbent, Eleanor
Brownlee, John
Bumbry, Grace Ann Jaeckel
Caballe, Montserrat
Callas, Maria
Calve, Emma
Caniglia, Maria
Carestini, Giovanni
Carreras, Jose
Carte, Richard d'Oyly
Caruso, Enrico
Case, Anna
Castagna, Bruna
Cavalieri, Lina
Cebotari, Maria
Chaliapin, Feodor Ivanovitch
Christoff, Boris
Cigna, Gina
Colbran, Isabella
Conley, Eugene
Conner, Nadine
Cordon, Norman
Corelli, Franco
Corena, Fernando
Cossotto, Fiorenza
Costa, Mary
Cotrubas, Ileana
Cox, Jean
Crescentini, Girolamo
Crespin, Regine
Crooks, Richard Alexander
Cuzzoni, Francesca
D'Alvarez, Marguerite
Dalis, Irene
Dalla Rizza, Gilda
Dalmores, Charles
Danco, Suzanne

DellaCasa, Lisa
DellaChiesa, Vivian
Deller, Alfred George
DelMonaco, Mario
DeLuca, Giuseppe
DePaolis, Alessio
DeReszke, Edouard
DeReszke, Jean
Destinn, Emmy
Diaz, Justino
Dickie, Murray
DiStefano, Giuseppe
Dobbs, Mattiwilda
Domgraf-Fassbaender, Willi
Domingo, Placido
Donath, Helen
Dragonette, Jessica
Drake, Alfred
Dunn, Mignon
DuPrez, Gilbert
Eames, Emma Hayden
Easton, Florence Gertrude
Eda-Pierre, Christiane
Edelmann, Otto
Elias, Rosalind
Elvira, Pablo
Engelman, Wilfred
Estes, Simon Lamont
Evans, Geraint Llewellyn, Sir
Farinelli
Farrar, Geraldine
Farrell, Eileen
Ferrier, Kathleen
Fischer-Dieskau, Dietrich
Flagstad, Kirsten
Forrester, Maureen
Freni, Mirella
Frick, Gottlob
Fuchs, Marta
Gabrielli, Catarina
Gadski, Johanna
Gailhard, Pierre
Galli-Curci, Amelita
Galli-Marie, Marie Celestine
Gallo, Fortune
Garcia, Manuel del Popolo Vincente, I
Garcia, Manuel Patricio Rodriguez, II
Garden, Mary
Gedda, Nicolai
Ghiaurov, Nicolai
Giannini, Dusolina
Gigli, Beniamino
Glossop, Peter
Gluck, Alma
Gobbi, Tito
Gorr, Rita
Grisi, Guilia
Grist, Reri
Guadagni, Gaetano
Guarrera, Frank
Gueden, Hilde

Hackett, Charles
Hagegard, Hakan
Harper, Heather
Harrell, Mack
Harris, Augustus, Sir
Harshaw, Margaret
Hauk, Minnie
Hawkins, Osie Penman, Jr.
Hayes, Roland
Hempel, Frieda
Hicks, Peggy Glanville-
Hidalgo, Elvira de
Hines, Jerome
Homer, Louise
Hopf, Hans
Horne, Marilyn
Hotter, Hans
Howells, Anne Elizabeth
Husch, Gerhard
Ivogun, Maria
Jadlowker, Hermann
Jagel, Frederick
Janssen, Herbert
Jepson, Helen
Jerger, Alfred
Jeritza, Maria
Jessner, Irene
Jobin, Raoul
Johnson, Edward
Jones, Gwyneth
Journet, Marcel
Juch, Emma
Jurinac, Sena
Kalisch, Paul
Kappel, Gertrude
Kellogg, Clara Louise
Kelly, Michael
King, James Ambros
Kipnis, Alexander
Kirsten, Dorothy
Klafsky, Katharina
Klose, Margarete
Knote, Heinrich
Konetzne, Anni
Konetzni, Hilde
Konya, Sandor
Korjus, Miliza
Koth, Erika
Kraus, Ernst
Kraus, Felix von
Krauss, Gabrielle
Kronold, Selma
Kunz, Erich
Kurt, Melanie
Kurz, Selma
Lablache, Luigi
Lanza, Mario
Larsen-Todsen, Nanny
Lassale, Jean
Laszlo, Magda
Laubenthal, Rudolf

Lauri-Volpi, Giacoma
Lawrence, Marjorie Florence
Lazzari, Virgilio
Lear, Evelyn
Lehmann, Lilli
Lehmann, Lotte
Leider, Frida
Lemnitz, Tiana
Levasseur, Nicolas Prosper
Levasseur, Rosalie
Lind, Jenny (Johanna Maria)
Lipton, Martha
List, Emanuel
Litvinne, Felia
Ljungberg, Gota
London, George
Lorengar, Pilar
Lorenz, Max
Lubin, Germaine
Lucca, Pauline
Ludikar, Pavel
Ludwig, Christa
Madeira, Jean
Maison, Rene
Majorano, Gaetano
Malbin, Elaine
Malibran, Maria Felicita
Mallinger, Mathilde
Manners, Charles
Marchesi, Salvatore
Marcoux, Vanni
Mario, Giovanni Matteo
Mario, Queena
Martin, Riccardo
Martinelli, Giovanni
Martini, Nino
Materna, Amalia
Matzenauer, Margaret
Maurel, Victor
Mayr, Richard
McCormack, John
McCracken, James
Melba, Dame Nellie
Melchior, Lauritz
Melton, James
Merrill, Robert
Merriman, Nan
Mesple, Mady
Milanov, Zinka Kunc
Mildenburg, Anna von
Milder-Hauptmann, Pauline Anna
Mildmay, Audrey
Milnes, Sherrill Eustace
Modl, Martha
Moffo, Anna
Monk, Allan James
Monte, Toti dal
Morris, James Peppler
Moscona, Nicola
Muller, Maria
Muratore, Lucien

Occupation Index

Stuckgold, Grete Schmeidt
Supervia, Conchita
Sutherland, Joan
Svanholm, Set
Swarthout, Gladys
Taddei, Giuseppe
Tagliabue, Carlo
Tagliavini, Ferruccio
Tajo, Italo
Talvela, Martti Olavi
Tamagno, Francesco
Tamburini, Antonio
Tappy, Eric
Tauber, Richard
Te Kanawa, Kiri, Dame
Tebaldi, Renata
Telva, Marion
Ternina, Milka
Teschemacher, Marguerite
Tetrazzini, Luisa
Teyte, Maggie, Dame
Thebom, Blanche
Thill, Georges
Thomas, Jess
Thomas, John Charles
Thorborg, Kerstin
Tibbett, Lawrence Mervil
Tichatschek, Joseph
Tokatyan, Armand
Torrence, Ernest
Tourel, Jennie
Tozzi, Giorgio
Traubel, Helen
Troyanos, Tatiana
Tucci, Gabriella
Tucker, Richard
Turner, Claramae
Turner, Eva
Uhde, Hermann
Unger, Caroline
Uppman, Theodor
Urlus, Jacques
Ursuleac, Viorica
Valdengo, Giuseppe
Valente, Benita
Valentino, Francesco
Valleria, Alwina
Valletti, Cesare
Van Rooy, Anton
Van Zandt, Marie
Varesi, Felice
Varnay, Astrid
Velluti, Giovanni Battista
Verrett, Shirley
Vestris, Lucia Elizabeth
Viardot-Garcia, Pauline
Vickers, Jon
Vinay, Ramon
Vishnevskaya, Galina (Pavlovna)
Vogl, Heinrich
VonStade, Frederica

Votipka, Thelma
Vyvyan, Jennifer Brigit
Walker, Edyth
Weathers, Felicia
Weede, Robert
Welitsch, Ljuba
Whitehill, Clarence Eugene
Windgassen, Wolfgang Friedrich Hermann
Winkelmann, Hermann
Witherspoon, Herbert
Witte, Erich
Wolff, Fritz
Wunderlich, Fritz
Yeend, Frances
Zanelli, Renato
Zenatello, Giovanni
Zylis-Gara, Teresa

ORATOR

Antiphon of Rhamnus
Apuleius, Lucius
Bevan, Aneurin
Bossuet, Jacques Benigne
Burke, Edmund
Canning, George
Cicero, Marcus Tullius
Demosthenes
Grady, Henry Woodfin
Hyperides
Isocrates
Phillips, Wendell
Pliny the Younger
Quintilian Marcus Fabius
Tacitus, Cornelius

ORGANIST

Bach, Johann Christian
Bach, Johann Sebastian
Bach, Wilhelm Friedemann
Boyce, William
Bruckner, Anton
Bull, John
Burney, Charles
Buxtehude, Dietrich
Byrd, William
Courboin, Charles
Eddy, Clarence
Foote, Arthur William
Pachelbel, Johann
Sowerby, Leo
Tallis, Thomas
Yon, Pietro Alessandro

ORGANIZED CRIME FIGURE

Adonis, Joe
Anastasia, Albert
Bonanno, Joseph
Buchalter, "Lepke" Louis
Cohen, "Mickey" Meyer

Costello, Frank
Dio, Johnny
Gambino, Don Carlo
Genovese, Vito
Giacalone, Anthony
Lansky, Meyer

ORIENTALIST

Binyon, Laurence
Burton, Richard Francis, Sir
Lane, Edward William
Selden, John

ORNITHOLOGIST

Allen, Arthur Augustus
Audubon, John James
Bailey, Florence Augusta Merriam
Beebe, William (Charles William)
Brasher, Rex
Chapman, Frank Michler
Fuertes, Louis Agassiz
Hosking, Eric J
Miner, Jack (John Thomas)
Peterson, Roger Tory
Stroud, Robert Franklin

OUTLAW

Allison, Clay
Anderson, William
Barrow, Clyde
Bass, Sam
Billy the Kid
Cassidy, Butch
Dalton, Emmett
Dalton, Gratton
Dalton, Robert
Hart, Pearl
James, Frank
James, Jesse Woodson
Kelly, Ned (Edward)
MacGregor, Robert
Quantrill, William Clarke
Riley, James
Ringo, John(ny)
Starr, Belle Shirley
Sundance Kid, The
Younger, Bob (Robert)
Younger, Cole (Thomas Coleman)
Younger, Jim (James)

PALEONTOLOGIST

Brown, Barnum
Gould, Stephen Jay
Horner, Jack (John R)
Marsh, Othniel Charles
Teilhard de Chardin, Pierre

PAMPHLETEER

Carroll, Anna Ella
Lilburne, John
Seabury, Samuel

PANTOMIMIST

Marceau, Marcel

PATHOLOGIST

Fibiger, Johannes Andreas Grib
Gherardi, Gherardo
Goodpasture, Ernest William
Landsteiner, Karl
Smith, Theobald
Spilsbury, Bernard Henry, Sir
Virchow, Rudolf
Welch, William Henry
Whipple, George H

PATIENT

David

PATRIOT

Attucks, Crispus
Carroll, Charles
Foscolo, (Niccolo) Ugo
Garibaldi, Guiseppe
Giusti, Giuseppe
Gonne, Maud MacBride
Gwinnett, Button
Henry, Patrick
Hofer, Andreas
Hopkinson, Francis
Knox, Henry
Kossuth, Lajos
MacDonagh, Thomas
Marti, Jose
Pearse, Padraic (Patrick Henry)
Prescott, Samuel
Revere, Paul
Rizal, Jose
Rutledge, Edward
Salem, Peter
Salomon, Haym

PATRIOTS

Maccabees

PHILANTHROPIST

Abercrombie, James Smither
Allen, Vivian Beaumont
Anderson, Elizabeth Milbank
Astor, Brooke Marshall
Bache, Harold Leopold
Baldwin, Matthias William

Bamberger, Louis
Belmont, Eleanor Robson
Black, William
Bliss, Robert Woods
Brookings, Robert Somers
Bruce, Ailsa Mellon
Candler, Asa Griggs
Christie, James
Christie, John
Cooke, Jay
Cooper, Peter
Corcoran, William Wilson
Crittenton, Charles Nelson
Dedman, Robert H
Depew, Chauncey M
Dodge, Grace Hoadley
Drexel, Anthony J
Duke, Doris
Duke, James Buchanan
Dunant, Jean Henri
Eustis, Dorothy Leib Harrison Wood
Fairless, Benjamin F
Fels, Samuel Simeon
Field, Marshall, III
Finley, John Huston
Folsom, Frank M
Frick, Henry Clay
Fry, Elizabeth Gurney
Gary, Elbert H
Getty, Gordon Peter
Gifford, Walter Sherman
Girard, Stephen
Gonne, Maud MacBride
Gratz, Rebecca
Guggenheim, Daniel
Guggenheim, Meyer
Guggenheim, Solomon Robert
Guggenheimer, Minnie
Harkness, Anna M Richardson
Harkness, Edward Stephen
Harkness, Rebekah West
Harriman, Edward H
Hearst, Millicent Willson
Hogg, Ima
Hopkins, Johns
Huntington, Henry Edwards
Johnson, Herbert Fisk
Juilliard, Augustus D
Lamont, Thomas William
Lasker, Mary Woodward
Lathrop, Rose Hawthorne
Lehman, Adele Lewisohn
Lehman, Herbert Henry
Lewisohn, Adolph
Litton, Charles
Loeb, James
Mackay, John William
May, Marjorie Merriweather
Mayer, Robert
McGill, James
Mellon, Richard King

Mellon, William Larimer, Jr.
Mennen, William Gerhard
Meyerhoff, Joseph
Mills, Darius Ogden
Montefiore, Moses Haim, Sir
Montor, Henry
Morgan, J(ohn) P(ierpont), Jr.
Morris, William Richard
Mott, Ruth Rawlings
Mott, Stewart Rawlings
Neiman, Abraham
Nobel, Alfred Bernhard
Peabody, George
Pearson, Cyril Arthur, Sir
Perot, (Henry) Ross
Pestalozzi, Johann Heinrich
Post, Marjorie Merriweather
Pratt, Charles
Procter, William Cooper
Rockefeller, Abby Aldrich
Rockefeller, John D(avison), III
Rockefeller, John D(avison), Jr.
Rosenstein, Nettie
Rosenwald, Julius
Ross, Percy
Rutgers, Henry
Rylands, John
Sage, Margaret Olivia
Schiff, Jacob Henry
Sharp, Granville
Smith, Gerrit
Smith, Sophia
Spanel, Abram N
Stone, W Clement
Straus, Isidor
Straus, Nathan
Tanner, Marion
Tully, Alice
Uris, Harold David
Vanderbilt, Cornelius
Vanderbilt, William Henry
Walker, Sarah Breedlove
Warburg, Felix Moritz
Warburg, James Paul
Whitney, William Collins
Wrightsman, Charles Bierer
Yale, Elihu

PHILOSOPHER

Abarbanel, Judah
Adler, Mortimer Jerome
Alain, pseud.
Albertus Magnus, Saint
Alembert, Jean le Rond d'
Alexander of Hales
Anaxagoras
Anaximander
Anaximenes of Miletus
Andreas-Salome, Lou
Antisthenes
Aquinas, Thomas, Saint

Arendt, Hannah
Aristotle
Arnaud, Georges d'
Augustine, Saint
Austin, John Langshaw
Averroes
Avicenna (Ibn Sina)
Ayer, Alfred Jules
Bacon, Francis, Sir
Bacon, Roger
Bayle, Pierre
Bentham, Jeremy
Berdyayev, Nikolay A
Bergson, Henri Louis
Berkeley, George
Biddle, John
Boethius
Bosanquet, Bernard
Brewster, David, Sir
Bruno, Giordano
Buber, Martin
Buchner, Ludwig
Buddha
Butler, Joseph
Callahan, Daniel
Campanella, Tommaso
Camus, Albert
Cardano, Cirolamo
Carnap, Rudolf
Cassirer, Ernst
Cato, Marcus Porcius Uticensis
Cicero, Marcus Tullius
Collingwood, Robin George
Comte, Auguste
Condorcet, Marie-Jean-Antoine
Confucius
Congreve, Richard
Croce, Benedetto
Cudworth, Ralph
Democritus
Descartes, Rene
Dewey, John
Diderot, Denis
Diogenes
Draper, John William
Dunne, John William
Eberhard, Johann August
Eckhart, Johannes
Emerson, Ralph Waldo
Empedocles
Epictetus
Epicurus
Erasmus, Desiderius
Erigena, John Scotus
Eucken, Rudolf Christoph
Fanon, Frantz
Feuerbach, Ludwig Andreas
Fichte, Johann Gottlieb
Fiske, John
Foucault, Michel
Fourier, Francois Marie Charles

Frankel, Charles
Gentile, Giovanni
Ghazzali, Abu al-
Gilson, Etienne Henry
Gobineau, Joseph Arthur, Comte de
Grote, George
Guardini, Romano
Hamilton, William, Sir
Hegel, Georg Wilhelm Friedrich
Heidegger, Martin
Heraclitus of Ephesus
Hobbes, Thomas
Hoffer, Eric
Hook, Sidney
Hooke, Robert
Hulme, Thomas Ernest
Hume, David
Husserl, Edmund
Hutcheson, Francis
Hypatia
Hyslop, James Hervey
Iqbal, Mahomed
James, Henry
James, William
Jaspers, Karl
Kallen, Horace M
Kant, Immanuel
Keyserling, Hermann Alexander
Kierkegaard, Soren Aabye
Krishnamurti, Jiddu
LaBruyere, Jean de
Ladd, George Trumbull
Lakatos, Imre
Langer, Suzanne K
Lao-Tzu
Leibniz, Gottfried Wilhelm von
Levy-Bruhl, Lucien
Lewis, Clarence Irving
Locke, Alain Leroy
Locke, John
Lovejoy, Arthur Oncken
Machiavelli, Niccolo
Madariaga (y Rojo), Salvador de
Maeterlinck, Maurice
Maimonides, Moses
Marcel, Gabriel Honore
Marcus Aurelius Antoninus
Marcuse, Herbert
Maritain, Jacques
Marx, Karl Heinrich
Masaryk, Tomas Garrigue
Mencius
Mill, James
Mill, John Stuart
Montesquieu, Charles Louis de
Moore, George Edward
More, Paul Elmer
Newton, Isaac, Sir
Nietzsche, Friedrich Wilhelm
Ockham, William of
Origen Adamantius

Ortega y Gasset, Jose
Paine, Thomas
Parmenides
Peirce, Charles Sanders
Philo
Pico della Mirandola, Giovanni
Plato
Plekhanov, Georgi Valentinovich
Plotinus
Priestley, Joseph
Protagoras
Pythagoras
Rama, Swami
Renan, (Joseph) Ernest
Revel, Jean Francois
Romains, Jules
Rousseau, Jean Jacques
Royce, Josiah
Russell, Bertrand Arthur William
Ryle, Gilbert
Saint-Simon, Claude-Henri de Rouvroy
Santayana, George
Schelling, Friedrich Wilhelm Joseph von
Schleiermacher, Friedrich Ernst Daniel
Schopenhauer, Arthur
Schurman, Jacob Gould
Seneca, Lucius Annaeus, the Younger
Shaftesbury, Anthony Ashley Cooper, Earl
Simmel, Georg
Socrates
Spencer, Herbert
Spengler, Oswald
Spinoza, Baruch (Benedictus de)
Steiner, Rudolf
Suzuki, Daisetz Teitaro
Taine, Hippolyte Adolphe
Teilhard de Chardin, Pierre
Thales
Unamuno (y Jugo), Miguel de
Vico, Giovanni Battista
Voltaire(, Francois Marie Arouet de)
Watts, Alan Wilson
Weil, Simone
Westermarck, Edward Alexander
Whitehead, Alfred North
Wittgenstein, Ludwig
Wycliffe, John
Xenophanes
Zeno of Citium
Zeno of Elea

PHILOSOPHERS

Damon and Pythias

PHOTOGRAPHER

Abbott, Berenice
Adams, Ansel Easton
Albert, Edward
Arbus, Diane
Armstrong-Jones, Antony Charles Robert

Atget, Eugene (Jean-Eugene-Auguste)
Avedon, Richard
Bannister, Constance Gibbs
Beard, Peter Hill
Beaton, Cecil Walter Hardy, Sir
Bitzer, George William
Brady, Mathew B
Brandt, Bill (William)
Brassai
Broadhurst, Kent
Brown, Dean
Capa, Cornell
Capa, Robert
Cartier-Bresson, Henri
Chamberlain, Samuel
Cunningham, Imogen
Curtis, Edward Sheriff
Dahl-Wolfe, Louise
Elisofon, Eliot
Evans, Walker
Faas, Horst
Feininger, Andreas Bernhard Lyonel
Fellig, Arthur
Flynn, Sean
Friese-Greene, William Edward
Galella, Ron
Genthe, Arnold
Gilpin, Laura
Gordon, Seton
Griffin, John Howard
Halsman, Philippe
Hine, Lewis Wickes
Hurrell, George
Jackson, William Henry
Johnston, Frances Benjamin
Karsh, Yousuf
Kennerly, David Hume
Kertesz, Andre
Krementz, Jill
Lange, Dorothea Nutzhorn
Lartique, Jacques-Henri
Liberman, Alexander
Lichfield, Patrick (Thomas Patrick John
   Anson, Earl)
Lumiere, Auguste Marie Louis
Lumiere, Louis Jean
McCartney, Linda
McCullin, Donald
Michals, Duane Steven
Mili, Gjon
Moholy-Nagy, Laszlo
Muybridge, Eadweard
Mydans, Carl M
Nadar, pseud.
Newman, Arnold Abner
Nutting, Wallace
O'Sullivan, Timothy H
Orkin, Ruth
Parkinson, Norman
Parks, Gordon Alexander Buchanan
Penn, Irving

Power, Eugene Barnum
Powolny, Frank
Pran, Dith
Ray, Man
Rothstein, Arthur
Ryun, Jim (James Ronald)
Scavullo, Francesco
Sheeler, Charles
Silk, George
Sommer, Frederick
Steichen, Edward Jean
Stern, Bert
Stieglitz, Alfred
Strand, Paul
Talbot, William Henry Fox
Thornell, Jack Randolph
Van Der Zee, James
Von Wangenheim, Chris
Walker, Joseph
Wedgwood, Thomas
Weston, Edward

PHOTOJOURNALIST

Alexander, Denise
Alley, Norman William
Bergen, Candice
Bourke-White, Margaret
Chapelle, Dickey
Dejean, Alain
Duncan, David Douglas
Eisenstaedt, Alfred
Haney, Chris
Rebbot, Olivier
Rosenthal, Joe (Joseph J)
Ut, Huynh Cong

PHYSICAL FITNESS EXPERT

Atlas, Charles
LaLanne, Jack
Prudden, Bonnie

PHYSICIAN

Addison, Thomas
Alexander, Franz Gabriel
Alexander, Hattie Elizabeth
Alvarez, Walter Clement
Anderson, Dorothy Hansine
Anderson, Elizabeth Garrett
Appel, James Ziegler
Arnot, Robert Burns
Avicenna (Ibn Sina)
Baird, Spencer Fullerton
Baker, Sara Josephine
Baldwin, Horace
Bannister, Roger, Sir
Banting, Frederick Grant, Sir
Bard, John
Barry, James Miranda
Bartlett, Josiah

Bates, William Horatio
Beard, George Miller
Beaumont, William
Blackwell, Elizabeth
Blasingame, Francis James Levi
Boerhaave, Herman
Bond, George Foote
Bowen, Otis Ray
Boyd, William Clouser
Brazelton, T(homas) Berry
Bretonneau, Pierre Fidele
Bridgman, Percy Williams
Bright, Richard
Bruce, David, Sir
Brunier, Oscar
Cabot, Richard C
Caius, John
Calderone, Mary Steichen
Caldicott, Helen Broinowski
Carlson, "Doc" Harold Clifford
Carlson, Earl
Chadwick, James, Sir
Channing, Walter
Charcot, Jean Martin
Clevenger, Shobal Vail
Cobb, Stanley
Cockcroft, John Douglas, Sir
Compton, Arthur Holly
Crohn, Burrill Bernard
Cronin, A(rchibald) J(oseph)
Crook, William Grant
Culpeper, Nicholas
Dafoe, Allan Roy
Dale, Henry Hallett
Dawson, Bertrand Edward
Destouches, Louis-Ferdinand
DeVita, Vincent Theodore, Jr.
Dickey, Herbert Spencer
Dioscorides, Pedacius
Doyle, Arthur Conan, Sir
Drummond, William Henry
Eliot, Martha May
Emin Pasha
Enders, John Franklin
Evans, Herbert McLean
Falkner, Frank
Feingold, Benjamin Franklin
Fielding, Gabriel, pseud.
Fishbein, Morris
Florey, Howard Walter
Fracastoro, Gerolamo
Frank, Johann Peter
Fremont-Smith, Frank
Galen
Gall, Franz Joseph
Galvani, Luigi
Geschwind, Norman
Gesell, Arnold
Gilbert, William
Gogarty, Oliver St. John
Goldberger, Joseph

Goldstein, Joseph Leonard
Gorgas, William Crawford
Gorrie, John
Gougelman, Pierre
Gould, George Milbry
Gram, Hans Christian Joachim
Grenfell, Wilfred Thomason, Sir
Guillotin, Joseph Ignace
Guion, Connie Myers
Gulick, Luther Halsey
Gusberg, Saul Bernard
Guthrie, Samuel
Hahnemann, (Christian Friedrich) Samuel
Halberstam, Michael Joseph
Hall, Charles Martin
Hamilton, Alice
Hartmann, Franz
Harvey, William
Heaton, Leonard
Heimlich, Henry J
Heiser, Victor George
Hench, Philip Showalter
Hess, Victor Francis
Hinshelwood, Cyril, Sir
Hinton, William Augustus
Hippocrates
Horder, Thomas Jeeves
Horstmann, Dorothy Millicent
Humphreys, Noel
Ilg, Frances Lillian
Jackson, Charles Thomas
Jacobi, Mary Putnam
Jarvik, Robert Koffler
Jaspers, Karl
Jenner, Edward
Jenner, William, Sir
Kane, Elisha Kent
Kaplan, Henry
Kerwin, Joseph Peter
Kolff, Willem Johan
Lamaze, Fernand
Lamb, Lawrence Edward
Langmuir, Irving
Langston, J William
Lanza, Anthony Joseph
Laveran, Alphonse
Lazear, Jesse William
Leboyer, Frederick
Lee, Rebecca
Liebow, Averill A(braham)
Lilly, John C
Linacre, Thomas
Loewi, Otto
Lombroso, Cesare
Long, Crawford Williamson
Malpighi, Marcello
Manson, Patrick, Sir
Masters, William Howell
McBurney, Charles
McCrae, John
McLane, James Woods

McLean, John Milton
Mellon, William Larimer, Jr.
Menninger, William C
Meriwether, W(ilhelm) Delano
Mermer, Friedrich Anton
Merrill, John Putnam
Mesmer, Franz Anton
Michelson, Albert Abraham
Mirkin, Gabe
Montessori, Maria
Morgan, Russell H
Morgan, Thomas H
Mudd, Samuel Alexander
Muller, Hermann Joseph
Naismith, James A
Negrin, Juan
Niepce, Joseph Nicephore
Nostradamus
Orr, John Boyd
Osler, William, Sir
Palmer, Daniel David
Papanicolaou, George Nicholas
Paracelsus, Philippus Aureolus
Paton, Richard
Paul, Lester Warner
Paul, Oglesby
Perrault, Claude
Petty, William, Sir
Pincus, Gregory
Pinel, Philippe
Quesnay, Francois
Rabelais, Francois
Redi, Francesco
Reiffel, Leonard
Remsen, Ira
Ricketts, Howard T
Rivers, Thomas Milton
Rock, John
Roget, Peter Mark
Romney, Seymour Leonard
Ross, Ronald, Sir
Rous, Peyton
Rush, Benjamin
Salk, Jonas Edward
Sauer, William George
Schick, Bela
Schneider, Richard Coy
Scholl, William M
Servetus, Michael
Sheldon, William Herbert
Sheppard, Sam(uel)
Simpson, Cedric Keith
Simpson, James Young, Sir
Sims, James Marion
Smith, Asa
Smollett, Tobias George
Snively, William Daniel, Jr.
Spock, Benjamin McLane
Steptoe, Patrick Christopher
Still, Andrew Taylor
Stillman, Irwin Maxwell

Sue, Eugene Joseph Marie
Summerskill, Edith Clara, Baroness
Sutherland, Earl Wilbur, Jr.
Sydenham, Thomas
Szilard, Leo
Tarnower, Herman
Taussig, Helen Brooke
Terry, Luther Leonidas
Theiler, Max
Townsend, Francis Everett
Trudeau, Edward Livingston
Van Dellen, Theodore Robert
Waksman, Selman Abraham
Walford, Roy L(ee, Jr.)
Walker, Mary Edwards
Wallace, Alfred Russell
Warren, Joseph
Wassermann, August von
White, Paul Dudley
Whitman, Marcus
Wigglesworth, Michael
Wigle, Ernest Douglas
Wilbur, Cornelia Burwell
Williams, William Carlos
Wood, Leonard
Wright, Almroth Edward, Sir

PHYSICIST

Allison, Samuel King
Alvarez, Luis Walter
Anderson, Elda Emma
Anderson, Philip Warren
Angstrom, Anders Jonas
Appleton, Edward Victor, Sir
Argo, Dominique Francois Jean
Avogadro, Amedeo, Conte di Quaregna
Bardeen, John
Barrett, William, Sir
Becquerel, Antoine Henri
Becquerel, Antoine-Cesar
Bethe, Hans Albrecht
Black, Joseph
Blackett, Patrick Maynard Stuart
Blair, William Richards
Bloch, Felix
Blodgett, Katherine Burr
Bohr, Niels Henrik David
Boley, Forrest Irving
Boscovich, Ruggiero Giuseppe
Bragg, William Henry, Sir
Bragg, William Lawrence, Sir
Brattain, Walter Houser
Braun, Karl Ferdinand
Bullard, Edward Crisp, Sir
Carlson, Chester
Carruthers, George E
Cavendish, Henry
Chandrasekhar, Subrahmanyan
Charles, Jacques-Alexandre-Cesar
Cherwell, Frederick Alexander L
Claude, Georges

Cole, Kenneth Stewart
Compton, Karl Taylor
Condon, Edward
Coulomb, Charles Augustin de
Davisson, Clinton Joseph
Debye, Peter Joseph William
Dempster, Arhur J
Dirac, Paul A M
Doppler, Christian Johann
Duane, William
Dyson, Freeman John
Einstein, Albert
Euler, Leonhard
Fahrenheit, Gabriel Daniel
Fermi, Enrico
Feynman, Richard Phillips
Fisk, James Brown
Fleming, John Ambrose
Foucault, Jean Bernard
Fourier, Jean Baptiste
Franck, James
Fraunhofer, Joseph von
Friedman, Herbert
Fuchs, Klaus Emil Julius
Galvani, Luigi
Gay-Lussac, Joseph Louis
Geiger, Hans (Johannes Wilhelm)
Gell-Mann, Murray
Gibbs, Josiah Willard
Glaser, Donald Arthur
Goddard, Robert Hutchings
Goldhaber, Maurice
Gould, Gordon
Graves, Alvin Cushman
Green, Elmer Ellsworth
Greenspan, Martin
Grove, William Robert, Sir
Hahn, Otto
Hall, Edwin Herbert
Harnwell, Gaylord Probasco
Hauptman, Herbert Aaron
Haworth, Leland John
Heisenberg, Werner Karl
Helmholtz, Herman Ludwig Ferdinand von
Henry, Joseph
Hertz, Heinrich Rudolph
Hillier, James
Hofstadter, Robert
Huygens, Christian
Infeld, Leopold
Ives, Herbert Eugene
Johnson, Raynor C(arey)
Joliot(-Curie), (Jean) Frederic
Joliot-Curie, Irene
Joule, James Prescott
Kahn, Herman
Kamerlingh Onnes, Heike
Kapitsa, Pyotr
Karle, Jerome
Karman, Theodore Todor Von
Kastler, Alfred

Kelvin, William Thomson, Baron
Kirchhoff, Gustav Robert
Land, Edwin Herbert
Laue, Max Theodor Felix von
Lawrence, Ernest Orlando
Lee, Tsung-Dao
Lippmann, Gabriel
Lorentz, Hendrick Antoon
Mach, Ernst
Maiman, Theodore
Maxwell, James Clerk
Mayer, Maria Goeppert
Meitner, Lise
Millikan, Robert Andrews
Morrison, Philip
Morse, Philip McCord
Mott, Nevill Francis, Sir
Oersted, Hans Christian
Ohm, Georg Simon
Oppenheimer, Frank F
Oppenheimer, J(ulius) Robert
Owen, Tobias Chant
Pauling, Linus Carl
Penzias, Arno Allan
Piccard, Auguste
Planck, Max Karl Ernst Ludwig
Powell, Cecil Frank
Pupin, Michael Idvorsky
Raman, Venkata
Rubbia, Carlo
Rutherford, Ernest, Baron
Sakharov, Andrei Dmitrievich
Schroedinger, Erwin
Schulz, George J
Shockley, William (Bradford)
Siemens, William, Sir
Sturgeon, William
Teller, Edward
Thomson, George Paget
Tuve, Merle Antony
Tyndall, John
Van Allen, James Alfred
Van Vleck, John Hasbrouck
Volta, Alessandro
Weber, Wilhelm Eduard
Wilson, Kenneth Geddes
Yalow, Rosalyn Sussman
Yang, Chen Ning
Yukawa, Hideki
Zacharias, Jerrold R(einarch)
Zworykin, Vladimir K(osma)

PHYSIOLOGIST

Behring, Emil Adolph von
Bernard, Claude
Best, Charles Herbert
Blumenbach, Johann Friedrich
Cannon, Walter Bradford
Cournand, Andre Frederic
Dalton, John Call
Eckstein, Gustav

Edwards, Robert Geoffrey
Einthoven, Willem
Erlanger, Joseph
Gasser, Herbert Spencer
Granit, Ragnar Arthur
Guillemin, Roger
Haldane, John Scott
Helmholtz, Herman Ludwig Ferdinand von
Hill, Archibald Vivian
Hodgkin, Alan Lloyd
Houssay, Bernardo Alberto
Howell, William H(enry)
Jackson, Margaret E
Keys, Ancel Benjamin
Pavlov, Ivan Petrovich

PIANIST

Albeniz, Isaac Manuel Francisco
Anda, Geza
Babin, Victor
Benjamin, Arthur
Beroff, Michel
Blake, Eubie (James Hubert)
Borge, Victor
Brahms, Johannes
Brown, Lawrence
Busoni, Ferruccio Benvenuto
Carle, Frankie
Chasins, Abram
Chopin, Frederic Francois
Chotzinoff, Samuel
Clementi, Muzio
Cramer, Johann Baptist
Czerny, Karl
D'Albert, Eugene
Demus, Joreg
Duchin, Eddie
Duchin, Peter
Durante, Jimmy (James Francis)
Evans, Bill (William John)
Ferrante, Arthur
Field, John
Liszt, Franz (Ferencz)
MacDowell, Edward Alexander
Masselos, William
Menuhin, Jeremy
Menuhin, Yaltah
Nero, Peter
Paderewski, Ignace Jan
Perahia, Murray
Previn, Andre
Rubinstein, Arthur
Saperton, David
Sukman, Harry
Tcherepnin, Alexander
Teicher, Louis

PILOT

Beard, Myron Gould
Boyington, "Pappy" Gregory

Brown, A Roy
Cobb, Jerrie
Collishaw, Raymond
Forsythe, Albert E
Foss, Joseph Jacob
Hunt, Jack Reed
Lewis, Robert Alvin
Merrill, Henry Tindall
Powers, Francis Gary
Tibbets, Paul Warfield
Tiburzi, Bonni
Warner, Emily Howell
Yeager, Chuck (Charles Elwood)

PIONEER

Anderson, Elizabeth Garrett
Appleseed, Johnny
Boone, Daniel
Bozeman, John M
Brannan, Samuel
Chisholm, Jesse
Comstock, Henry Tompkins Paige
Daly, Marcus
DuSable, Jean Baptiste
Fowler, Lydia Folger
Starr, Belle Shirley
Sutter, John Augustus
Zane, Ebenezer

PIRATE

Blackbeard
Bonnet, Stede
Bonny, Anne
Gibbs, Charles
Kidd, (Captain) William
Laffite, Jean
Morgan, Henry, Sir

POET

Abarbanel, Judah
Abercrombie, Lascelles
Ableman, Paul
Abu Salma, pseud.
Addison, Joseph
Aeschylus
Agee, James Rufus
Aiken, Conrad Potter
Akhmatova, Anna, pseud.
Akins, Zoe
Aleixandre, Vicente
Allen, Elizabeth Ann Chase Akers
Allen, Hervey (William Hervey)
Allingham, William
Allston, Washington
Alvarez, Alfred
Anacreon
Andersen, Hans Christian
Anderson, Sherwood
Apollinaire, Guillaume

Aragon, Louis Marie Antoine Alfred
Aretino, Pietro
Ariosto, Ludovico
Arnold, Matthew
Arrabal (Teran), Fernando
Artaud, Antonin
Atwood, Margaret Eleanor
Auden, W(ystan) H(ugh)
Audiberti, Jacques
Auslander, Joseph
Austin, Alfred
Bandeira, Manuel (Filho Manuel)
Bandello, Matteo
Baring, Maurice
Barker, George Granville
Basho
Bates, Arlo
Bates, Katherine Lee
Baudelaire, Charles Pierre
Bax, Clifford
Bellman, Carl Michael
Bely, Andrey, pseud.
Benet, Stephen Vincent
Bennett, Arnold
Benson, Edward Frederic
Beranger, Pierre Jean de
Bernard, Andrew Milroy
Berrigan, Daniel J
Berry, Wendell
Berryman, John
Betjeman, John, Sir
Betti, Ugo
Bialik, Chaim Nachman
Binyon, Laurence
Birney, Earle (Alfred Earle)
Bishop, Elizabeth
Bjornson, Bjornstjerne
Blackmur, Richard Palmer
Blake, William
Blok, Aleksandr Aleksandrovich
Blunden, Edmund Charles
Blunt, Wilfrid Scawen
Bly, Robert Elwood
Bodenheim, Maxwell
Bodmer, Johann Jakob
Bogan, Louise
Boiardo, Matteo Maria
Boileau(-Despreaux), Nicolas
Bolton, Sarah Tittle Barrett
Borel d'Hauterive, Petrus
Bottomley, Gordon
Bradstreet, Anne
Braithwaite, William Stanley Beaumont
Branch, Anna Hempstead
Brassens, Georges
Brautigan, Richard
Brecht, Bertolt Eugene Friedrich
Brentano, Clemens Maria
Breton, Andre
Breytenbach, Breyten
Bridges, Robert Seymour

Brodsky, Joseph Alexandrovich
Bronte, Patrick Branwell
Brooke, Rupert Chawner
Brooks, Gwendolyn
Brooks, Maria Gowen
Brown, Christy
Brown, George Mackay
Browning, Elizabeth Barrett
Browning, Robert
Brutus, Dennis Vincent
Bryant, William Cullen
Bunner, Henry Cuyler
Bunting, Basil
Burns, Robert
Busch, Wilhelm
Butler, Samuel
Byron, George Gordon Noel Byron, Baron
Caedmon, Saint
Callimachus
Camoes, Luis de
Campana, Dino
Campanella, Tommaso
Campbell, Thomas
Campion, Thomas
Carducci, Giosue
Carew, Thomas
Carey, Henry
Carleton, Will
Carman, (William) Bliss
Carpenter, Edward
Carroll, Jim
Cary, Alice
Cary, Phoebe
Catullus, Gaius Valerius
Cawein, Madison Julius
Cervantes (Saavedra), Miguel(de)
Chao, Yuen Ren
Chapman, George
Char, Rene (Emile)
Chatterton, Thomas
Chaucer, Geoffrey
Cheney, John Vance
Chenier, Marie-Andre de
Chesterton, Gilbert Keith
Chretien de Troyes
Ciardi, John Anthony
Cienfuegos, Nicasio Alvarez de
Clare, John
Clark, Charles Badger
Clarke, Austin
Claudel, Paul Louis Charles
Claudian
Claudius, Matthias
Claus, Hugo
Coatsworth, Elizabeth Jane
Cocteau, Jean
Coffin, Robert Peter Tristram
Coleridge, Hartley
Coleridge, Mary Elizabeth
Coleridge, Samuel Taylor
Collins, William

Colum, Padraic
Cooke, Rose Terry
Coppard, A(lfred) E(dgar)
Coppee, Francois Edouard Joachim
Corbiere, Tristan
Corneille, Pierre
Corso, Gregory
Cowley, Abraham
Cowper, William
Coxe, Louis Osborne
Crabbe, George
Crane, Hart
Crane, Nathalia Clara Ruth
Crane, Stephen
Crapsey, Adelaide
Crashaw, Richard
Creeley, Robert White
Crosby, Harry
Cueva de Garoza, Juan de la
Cullen, Countee
Cummings, E(dward) E(stlin)
Cynewulf
Cyrano de Bergerac, Savinien de
D'Annunzio, Gabriele
Daly, Thomas Augustine
Daniel, Samuel
Dante Alighieri
DaPonte, Lorenzo
Dargan, Olive Tilford
Daryush, Elizabeth Bridges
Davenant, William, Sir
Davidson, Donald Grady
Davie, Alan
Day-Lewis, Cecil
Dehmel, Richard
DeLaMare, Walter
Deutsch, Babette
Dickey, James
Dickinson, Emily Elizabeth
Dobell, Sydney Thompson
Dobson, Henry Austin
Donne, John
Doolittle, Hilda
Doughty, Charles Montagu
Douglas, Alfred Bruce, Lord
Douglas, Keith Castellain
Dowson, Ernest Christopher
Drake, Joseph Rodman
Drayton, Michael
Drinkwater, John
Drummond, William Henry
Dryden, John
Ducis, Jean Francois
Duke, Vernon
Dunbar, Paul Laurence
Dunbar, William
Dwight, Timothy
Dyer, Edward, Sir
Eichendorff, Joseph Karl Benedict
Eliot, T(homas) S(tearns)
Elytis, Odysseus

Emerson, Ralph Waldo
Eminescu, Mihail
Empson, William, Sir
Esenin, Sergei Aleksandrovich
Espriu, Salvador
Euphorion
Eusden, Laurence
Everson, William Oliver
Evtushenko, Evgeniy Alexandrovich
Faiz, Faiz Ahmad
Faust, Frederick Schiller
Ferlinghetti, Lawrence
Ficke, Arthur Davidson
Field, Eugene
Field, Rachel Lyman
Fishback, Margaret
Fitzgerald, Edward
Fletcher, John Gould
Fogazzaro, Antonio
Ford, Ford Madox
Foscolo, (Niccolo) Ugo
France, Anatole, pseud.
Frechette, Louis-Honore
Freneau, Philip Morin
Froissart, Jean
Frost, Robert Lee
Garcia Lorca, Federico
Gardner, Isabella
Garrigue, Jean
Gascoyne, David Emery
Gautier, Theophile (Pierre Jules Theophile)
Gay, John
Genet, Louis Rene Fernandat
George, Stefan Anton
Gerhardt, Paul(us)
Ghose, Sri Chinmoy Kumar
Gibbons, Stella Dorethea
Gibran, Kahlil
Gibson, Wildred Wilson
Ginsberg, Allen
Ginzburg, Aleksandr Ilich
Giorno, John
Giovanni, Nikki
Giovannitti, Arturo
Godden, Rumer, pseud.
Godoy Alcayaga, Lucila
Goethe, Johann Wolfgang von
Goldsmith, Oliver
Gongora y Argote, Don Luis de
Gorbanevskaya, Natalya
Gottfried von Strassburg
Graham, William Sydney
Graves, Robert Ranke
Gray, Thomas
Gregor, Arthur
Grigson, Geoffrey Edward Harvey
Guest, Edgar A(lbert)
Guillen, Jorge
Guiney, Louise
Guiterman, Arthur
Gumilev, Nikolai

Gunn, Thom
Ha-Levi, Judah
Hafiz, Shams-al-Din Muhammad
Hagedorn, Hermann
Hall, Radclyffe
Halleck, Fritz-Greene
Hamburger, Michael
Hammon, Jupiter
Hansen, Joseph
Hardy, Thomas
Harper, Frances Ellen Watkins
Hauptmann, Gerhart
Hayden, Robert Earl
Hayes, Alfred
Hecht, Anthony Evan
Heidenstam, Carl Gustaf Verner von
Heine, Heinrich
Hemans, Felicia Dorothea Browne
Henley, William Ernest
Herder, Johann G von
Herrick, Robert
Hesiod
Hill, Geoffrey
Hillyer, Robert
Hoffenstein, Samuel Goodman
Hoffman, Charles Fenno
Hofmannsthal, Hugo Hoffmann
Holderlin, Johann C F
Holmes, Oliver Wendell
Hopkins, Gerard Manley
Hopkinson, Francis
Horace
Housman, A(lfred) E(dward)
Hovey, Richard
Huch, Ricarda (Octavia)
Hughes, Langston (James Langston)
Hughes, Ted
Humphries, Rolfe (George Rolfe)
Hunt, Leigh
Iqbal, Mahomed
Jacob, Max
Jarrell, Randall
Jarry, Alfred
Jeffers, (John) Robinson
Jimenez, Juan Ramon
John of the Cross, Saint
Jones, Leroi
Jonson, Ben(jamin)
Joyce, James Augustus Aloysius
Jozsef, Attila
Kafka, Franz
Karlfeldt, Erik Axel
Kastner, Erich
Kavanagh, Patrick
Keats, John
Kerouac, Jack
Kharitonov, Yevgeni
Khodasevich, Vladislav
Kilmer, Joyce (Alfred Joyce)
Kinnell, Galway
Kipling, Rudyard

Kleist, Heinrich von
Klopstock, Friedrich Gottlieb
Kreymborg, Alfred
Kunitz, Stanley Jasspon
La Tour du Pin, Patrice de
Laforgue, Jules
Lagerkvist, Par
Lamartine, Alphonse Marie Louis de Prat
  de
Lampman, Archibald
Landor, Walter Savage
Lang, Andrew
Lanier, Sidney
Larcom, Lucy
Larkin, Philip
Lattimore, Richmond Alexander
Laughlin, James, IV
Lautreamont, Comte de, pseud.
Lazarus, Emma
Lear, Edward
Lee-Hamilton, Eugene Jacob
LeGallienne, Richard
Leger, Alexis St. Leger (Marie-Rene Alexis
  St. Leger)
Leonard, William Ellery
Leopardi, Giacomo
Lermontov, Mikhail (Michael Jurevich)
Levertov, Denise
Levine, Philip
Lewis, Janet
Li Po
Liliencron, (Friedrich Adolf Axel) Detlev
  von
Lindbergh, Anne Spencer Morrow
Lindsay, (Nicholas) Vachel
Livius Andronicus
Logan, John
Longfellow, Henry Wadsworth
Lope de Vega
Louys, Pierre
Lovelace, Richard
Lowell, Amy
Lowell, Robert Trail Spence, Jr.
Lowry, Malcolm (Clarence Malcolm)
Lu, Yu
Lucan
Lucilius
Lucretius
Lytton, Edward George Earle Lytton
  Bulwer-Lytton, 1st Baron Lytton
Lytton, Edward Robert Bulwer-Lytton,
  Earl
Macaulay, Rose
MacBeth, George Mann
MacDonagh, Thomas
MacKaye, Percy Wallace
MacLeish, Archibald
MacNeice, Louis (Frederick Louis)
Maeterlinck, Maurice
Malherbe, Francois de
Mallarme, Stephane

Mandelshtam, Osip Emilyevich
Marinetti, Filippo Tommaso
Markham, Edwin
Marlowe, Christopher
Marot, Clement
Marquis, Don Robert Perry
Martial
Martinson, Harry Edmund
Marvell, Andrew
Marx, Anne Loewenstein
Masaoka, Tsunenori
Masefield, John
Masters, Edgar Lee
Mathieu, Noel Jean
Mayakovsky, Vladimir
McClure, Michael
McCord, David Thompson Watson
McCrae, John
McGinley, Phyllis
McKuen, Rod
Medici, Lorenzo de
Menken, Adah Isaacs
Meredith, George
Merton, Thomas
Merwin, W(illiam) S(tanley)
Metastasio, Pietro
Mew, Charlotte Mary
Meynell, Alice
Michaux, Henri
Michelangelo
Middleton, Christopher
Miles, Josephine
Millay, Edna St. Vincent
Miller, Joaquin, pseud.
Milton, John
Mistral, Frederic
Mistral, Gabriela
Monk, Mary
Monroe, Harriet
Montale, Eugenio
Moody, William Vaughn
Moore, Clement Clarke
Moore, Julia A Davis
Moore, Marianne Craig
Moore, Thomas
Morgan, Edwin George
Morike, Eduard Friedrich
Morris, William
Motherwell, William
Naidu, Sarojini
Neal, Larry (Lawrence P)
Nemerov, Howard
Neruda, Pablo
Nerval, Gerard de
Nietzsche, Friedrich Wilhelm
Novalis
Noyes, Alfred
Olson, Charles
Omar Khayyam
Oppenheim, James
Osgood, Frances Sargent Locke

Ovid
Owen, Wilfred
Owens, Rochelle
Parker, Dorothy Rothschild
Pascoli, Giovanni
Patchen, Kenneth
Patmore, Coventry Kersey Dighton
Paz, Octavio
Peabody, Josephine Preston
Pearse, Padraic (Patrick Henry)
Peele, George
Peret, Benjamin
Perkoff, Stuart Z
Perrault, Charles
Petrarch, Francesco
Pindar
Plath, Sylvia
Poe, Edgar Allan
Popa, Vasko
Pope, Alexander
Pound, Ezra Loomis
Powys, John Cowper
Pratt, Edwin John
Prior, Matthew
Procter, Bryan Walter
Prokosch, Frederic
Pulitzer, Ralph
Pushkin, Aleksandr Sergeyevich
Pye, Henry
Racine, Jean Baptiste
Randall, Dudley
Ransom, John Crowe
Ransome, Arthur Mitchell
Read, Herbert, Sir
Read, Thomas Buchanan
Reese, Lizette Woodworth
Rexroth, Kenneth
Rice, Cale Young
Rice, Grantland, (Henry Grantland)
Rich, Adrienne
Rickword, Edgell (John Edgell)
Ridge, Lola
Riding, Laura
Riley, James Whitcomb
Rilke, Rainer Maria
Rimbaud, (Jean Nicolas) Arthur
Rinuccini, Ottavio
Robinson, Edwin Arlington
Robinson, Henry Morton
Rodman, Selden
Ronsard, Pierre de
Rosenberg, Issac
Rossetti, Christina Georgina
Rossetti, Dante Gabriel
Rossetti, Gabriele Pasquale Giuseppe
Rothenberg, Jerome
Rowe, Nicholas
Ruckert, Friedrich
Rukeyser, Muriel
Russell, George William
Saadi

Sachs, Hans
Sachs, Nelly
Sackville-West, Victoria Mary
Salinas (y Serrano), Pedro
Sancho, Ignatius
Sandburg, Carl August
Santillana, Inigo Lopez de Mendoza
Sappho
Sardou, Victorien
Sarett, Lew R
Sarton, May
Sassoon, Siegfried
Savage, John
Savage, Richard
Schauffler, Robert Haven
Scott, Duncan Campbell
Scott, Walter, Sir
Seeger, Alan
Seifert, Jaroslav
Senghor, Leopold Sedar
Service, Robert William
Seward, Anna
Sexton, Anne Harvey
Shadwell, Thomas
Shakespeare, William
Shalamov, Varlam Tikhonovich
Shange, Ntozake
Shapiro, Karl Jay
Sharp, William
Shelley, Percy Bysshe
Sherman, Frank Dempster
Shevchenko, Taras
Shirley, James
Sidney, Philip, Sir
Sigourney, Lydia Howard
Silkin, Jon
Sill, Edward Rowland
Simic, Charles
Singer, Burns James Hyman
Sissman, L(ouis) E(dward)
Sisson, Charles Hubert
Sitwell, Edith, Dame
Sjowall, Maj
Skelton, John
Skelton, Robin
Smart, Christopher
Smith, "Stevie" Florence Margaret
Smith, A(rthur) J(ames) M(arshall)
Smith, Alexander
Smith, Iain Crichton
Smith, Patti
Smith, Samuel Francis
Snodgrass, W(illiam) D(eWitt)
Snyder, Gary Sherman
Sophocles
Soupault, Philippe
Southey, Robert
Spence, Lewis (James Lewis Thomas
    Chalmers)
Spenser, Edmund
Spitteler, Karl Friedrich Georg

Stanton, Frank Lebby
Stephens, James
Sterling, George
Stevens, Wallace
Stevenson, Robert Louis Balfour
Stoddard, Richard Henry
Stow, (Julian) Randolph
Strand, Mark
Stuart, Jesse Hilton
Sully-Prudhomme, Rene Francois Armand
Swenson, May
Swinburne, Algernon Charles
Symonds, John Addington
Symons, Arthur
Tabb, John B
Taggard, Genevieve
Tagore, Rabindranath, Sir
Tate, Allen (John Orley)
Tate, Nahum
Taylor, Ann
Taylor, Edward
Taylor, Jane
Tchernichovski, Saul Gutmanovich
Teasdale, Sara
Tennyson, Alfred, Lord
Terence
Thaxter, Celia
Theocritus
Theodorescu, Ion N
Thespis
Thomas, Edith Matilda
Thomas, Edward
Thomas, Ronald Stuart
Thompson, Francis Joseph
Thomson, James
Thomson, James
Tietjens, Eunice
Timrod, Henry
Toller, Ernst
Tomlinson, Charles
Toomer, Jean
Torrence, Ridgley (Frederick Rridgley)
Towne, Charles Hanson
Treece, Henry
Trench, Richard Chenevix
Trumbull, John
Tsvetayeva, Marina Ivanovna
Tu, Fu
Tyler, Parker
Tzara, Tristan
Ukrainka, Lesia
Ungaretti, Giuseppe
Valery, Paul Ambroise
Van Doren, Mark
Vandyke, Henry Jackson, Jr.
Vega (Carpio), Lope (Felix) de
Verlaine, Paul Marie
Viereck, Peter Robert Edwin
Vigny, Alfred Victor, Comte de
Villon, Francois
Viorst, Judith (Stahl)

Virgil
Visscher, William Lightfoot
Wagner, Richard
Wakoski, Diane
Wallace, Horace Binney
Waller, Edmund
Warren, Robert Penn
Warton, Joseph
Watts-Dunton, Theodore (Walter)
Weiss, Theodore (Russell)
Wellesley, Dorothy
Wesendonck, Mathilde Luckemeyer
Wheatley, Phillis
Wheelock, John Hall
Whitehead, William
Whitman, Sarah Helen Power
Whitman, Walt(er)
Whittier, John Greenleaf
Wigglesworth, Michael
Wilbur, Richard Purdy
Wilcox, Ella Wheeler
Wilde, Oscar Fingal O'Flahertie Wills
Williams, William Carlos
Wilson, Alexander
Wordsworth, William
Wright, James Arlington
Wurdemann, Audrey May
Wyatt, Thomas, Sir
Yeats, William Butler
Zabolotskii, Nikolai Alekseevich
Zaturenska, Marya
Zeno, Apostolo

POLICE OFFICER

Connor, "Bull" Theophilus Eugene
Delahanty, Thomas K
Egan, Eddie
Sample, Bill
Serpico, Frank (Francisco Vincent)
White, Dan(iel James)

POLITICAL ACTIVIST

Alinsky, Saul David
Baez, Joan
Berrigan, Daniel J
Berrigan, Elizabeth McAlister
Berrigan, Philip Francis
Biko, Steven
Breytenbach, Breyten
Bukovsky, Vladimir
Chomsky, Noam
Cleaver, Eldridge
Dellinger, David T (Dave)
Deloria, Vine, Jr.
DePugh, Robert Bolivar (William Robert Bolivar)
Devlin, Bernadette Josephine
Dohrn, Bernadine Rae
Ellsberg, Daniel
Farenthold, Frances T

Fonda, Jane
Froines, John Radford
Ginzburg, Aleksandr Ilich
Gitlow, Benjamin
Gregory, Dick
Groppi, James E
Hall, Gus
Harris, Joseph Pratt
Hatchett, John F
Hayden, Tom (Thomas Emmett)
Hoffman, Abbie (Abbott)
Hughan, Jessie Wallace
Joseph, Helen
Lewis, Saunders
Malcolm X
Mandela, Nelson Rolihlahla
Mandela, Winnie
Mayer, Norman D
McGuinness, Martin
Melville, Marjorie
Melville, Thomas
Mihajlov, Mihajlo
O'Donnell, Peador
Ochs, Phil(ip David)
Place, Francis
Rifkin, Jeremy
Rockwell, George Lincoln
Rubin, Jerry
Sacco, Nicola
Sasway, Benjamin H
Seale, Bobby G
Vanzetti, Bartolomeo
Welch, Robert Henry Winborne, Jr.

POLITICAL ACTIVISTS

Chicago Seven, The

POLITICAL LEADER

Abbas, Ferhat
Abdallah, Ahmed
Abdullah, Sheik Mohammad
Abe, Isao
Aberhart, William
Adams, "Tom" John Michael Geoffrey
    Maningham
Adams, John Quincy
Aguinaldo, Emilio
Ahidjo, Ahmadou
Ahmed, Fakhruddin Ali
Albert, Carl Bert
Albuquerque, Affonso de
Aleman, Miguel
Alessandri, Jorge
Alfonsin Foulkes, Raul Ricardo
Allende, Salvador
Amin, Idi
Andreotti, Giulio
Andropov, Yuri Vladimirovich
Antonescu, Ion
Antony, Marc

Aquino, Corazon Cojuangco
Arafat, Yasir
Aramburu, Pedro Eugenio
Arvey, Jacob Meyer
Assad, Hafez al
Astor, Nancy Witcher (Langhorne) Astor,
    Viscountess
Ataturk, Kemal
Attlee, Clement Richard Attlee, Earl
Auriol, Vincent
Ayub Khan, Mohammad
Babbitt, Bruce Edward
Babiuch, Edward
Bagaza, Jean-Baptiste
Bakr, Ahmad Hasan al
Balaguer, Joaquin
Balewa, Abubakar
Balopoulos, Michael
Banda, Hastings Kamuzu
Bandaranaike, Sirimavo
Bani-Sadr, Abolhassan
Banzer-Suarez, Hugo
Barrow, Errol Walton
Batista y Zaldivar, Fulgencio
Baunsgaard, Hilmar Tormod Ingolf
Beccaria, Cesare
Begin, Menachem
Beheshti, Mohammad, Ayatollah
Belaunde-Terry, Fernando
Ben Barka, Mehdi
Ben Bella, Ahmed
Ben-Gurion, David
Bennett, Richard Bedford
Benton, Thomas Hart
Berlinguer, Enrico
Betancur, Belisario
Bevan, Aneurin
Bhutto, Benazir
Bhutto, Zulfikar Ali
Bijedic, Dzemal
Bishop, Maurice
Bjornson, Bjornstjerne
Bliss, Ray C(harles)
Boeynants, Paul Vanden
Bokassa I (Jean Bedel)
Bonaparte, Francois Charles Joseph
Bongo, El Hadj Omar
Borden, Robert Laird, Sir
Botha, Louis
Botha, Pieter Willem
Botha, Roelof Pik
Brandt, Willy
Bratteli, Trygve Martin
Brooke, James, Sir
Brundtland, Gro Harlem
Bryan, William Jennings
Bulganin, Nikolai Aleksandrovich
Bulow, Bernhard H M
Burnham, Forbes (Linden Forbes Sampson)
Burr, Aaron
Burrenchobay, Dayendranath

Byng, Julian Hedworth George, Viscount
Caetano, Marcello
Campora, Hector Jose
Carranza, Venustiano
Castello Branco, Humberto
Castro, Raul
Cernik, Oldrich
Chaban-Delmas, Jacques
Chaka
Chautemps, Camille
Chernenko, Konstantin Ustinovich
Chiang, Ching
Cobden, Richard
Colombo, Emilio
Cossiga, Francesco
Couve de Murville, (Jacques) Maurice
Cowen, Zelman, Sir
Cox, James Middleton, Sr.
Craxi, "Bettino" (Benedetto
Curley, James Michael
Curtin, Andrew Gregg
Cyrankiewicz, Josef
Cyrus the Great
Daladier, Edouard
Davis, Jefferson
Debre, Michel Jean Pierre
DeGaulle, Charles Andre Joseph Marie
Demirel, Suleyman
DeQuay, Jan E
Desai, Morarji Ranchodji
Diaz, Porfirio
Diederichs, Nicholaas
Doe, Samuel Kanyon
Dollfuss, Engelbert
Dorman, Maurice
Douglas, James, Sir
Duarte, Jose Napoleon
Duplessis, Maurice le Noblet
Duvalier, Jean-Claude
Enver Pasha
Evren, Kenan
Fabius, Laurent
Fanfani, Amintore
Farley, James A(loysius)
FitzGerald, Garret
Flynn, Elizabeth Gurley
Foster, William Zebulon
Franco, Francisco
Franz Ferdinand
Fraser, John Malcolm
Frei, Eduardo (Montalva Eduardo)
Fritchey, Clayton
Frontenac, Louis de
Fukuda, Takeo
Gallegos, Romulo
Galtieri, Leopoldo Fortunato
Gandhi, Rajiv Ratna
Garcia Perez, Alan
Garvey, Marcus Moziah
Gasperi, Alcide de
Gemayel, Bashir

Glasspole, Florizel Augustus
Gomulka, Wladyslaw
Gonzalez Marquez, Felipe
Gorbachev, Mikhail S
Guzman, Antonio
Habash, George
Hammarskjold, Knut Hjalmar L
Harun-Al-Rashid
Hasluck, Paul Meernaa, Sir
Haughey, Charles James
Hawke, Bob (Robert James Lee)
Haya de la Torre, Victor Raul
Hermannsson, Steingrimur
Herzog, Chaim
Hillery, Patrick John
Holyoake, Keith Jacka, Sir
Hore-Belisha, Leslie, Baron
Horthy de Nagybanya, Nicholas
Hoveyda, Amir Abbas
Hoxha, Enver
Hussein, Saddam
Husseini, Haj Amin
Illia, Arturo Umberto
Jaruzelski, Wojciech Witold
Jawara, Alhaji Dawda Kairaba, Sir
Jayewardene, Junius Richard
Jenkins, Roy Harris
Jinnah, Mohammed Ali
Jorge Blanco, Salvador
Jumblatt, Kamal Fouad
Kalinin, Mikhail
Kekkonen, Urho Kaleva
Kerensky, Alexander Fedorovitch
Khadafy, Moammar
Khan, Liaquat Ali
Kohl, Helmut Michael
Konoye, Fumimaro, Prince
Lange, David Russell
Laval, Pierre
Le Duan
Limann, Hilla
Lubbers, Ruud (Rudolphus Franciscus
   Maria)
Lumumba, Patrice Emergy
Luthuli, Albert John
MacDonald, John Alexander
Machel, Samora Moises
Mackenzie, Alexander
MacMillan, Harold
Madrid Hurtado, Miguel de la
Magana, Alvaro (Alfredo)
Mansur, (Abu Jafar Ibn Muhammad), Al
Marcos, Ferdinand Edralin
Maurey, Pierre
Mboya, Tom (Thomas Joseph)
McEntee, Peter Donovan
Meighen, Arthur
Meir, Golda
Mejia Victores, Oscar Humberto
Mengistu, Haile Mariam
Metaxas, John(Ioannis)

Mitterrand, Francois Maurice
Mohieddin, Faud
Montfort, Simon de
Mossadegh, Mohammed
Mubarak, (Muhamed) Hosni
Mugabe, Robert Gabriel
Muldoon, Robert David, Sir
Mulroney, Brian (Martin Brian)
Mussolini, Benito
Naguib, Mohammed
Nehru, Jawaharlal
Newton, Huey P
Nkrumah, Kwame
Nol, Lon
O'Connell, Daniel
Obasanjo, Olusegun
Obote, Milton (Apollo Milton)
Ojukwu, Chukwuemeka Odumegwu
Orlando, Vittorio Emanuele
Ortega, Saavedra, Daniel
Osman I
Osmena, Sergio
Ovando Candia, Alfredo
Ozal, Turgut
Paisley, Ian Richard Kyle
Panchen Lama X
Papandreou, Andreas George
Papandreou, George
Papineau, Louis-Joseph
Park, Chung Hee
Parnell, Charles Stewart
Pastora (Gomez), Eden
Pauker, Ana
Pearson, Lester Bowles
Pendergast, Thomas J
Peres, Shimon
Peron, Eva Duarte
Peron, Isabel
Peron, Juan
Pham van Dong
Pieck, Wilhelm
Pilate, Pontius
Pinochet Ugarte, Augusto
Planinc, Milka
Pol Pot
Pollitt, Harry
Quezon (y Molina), Manuel Luis
Rabin, Yitzhak
Ramgoolam, Seewoosagur, Sir
Ratsirka, Didier
Rawlings, Jerry John
Rios Montt, Jose Efrain
Roldos Aguilera, Jamie
Rumor, Mariano
Sabah al-Ahmad al, Sheik
Saint Laurent, Louis Stephen
Salam, Saeb
Sananikone, Phoui
Santa Anna, Antonio Lopez de
Sarkis, Elias
Sarney, Jose

Sauve, Jeanne Mathilde Benoit
Savimbi, Jonas Malheiro
Scheidemann, Philipp
Schleicher, Kurt von
Schmidt, Helmut Heinrich Waldemar
Schuschnigg, Kurt von
Scott, Arleigh Winston
Shukairy, Ahmed
Siles Zuazo, Hernan
Slim, William Joseph
Smith, Alfred Emanuel
Souvanna, Phouma
Speransky, Mikhail
Stalin, Joseph
Stambuliski, Aleksandr
Stanley, Frederick Arthur, Earl of Derby
Stolypin, Piotr Arkadevich
Sui, Wen Ti
Sukarno, Achmed
Sulla, Lucius C
Sun Yat-Sen
Sun Yat-Sen, Chingling Soong, Madame
Sunay, Cevdet
Thatcher, Margaret Hilda Roberts
Thorpe, Jeremy (John Jeremy)
Tito
Tojo, Hideki (Eiki)
Torricelli, Evangelista
Toussaint l'Ouverture, Pierre Dominique
Trudeau, Pierre Elliott
Tshombe, Moise
Turbay Ayala, Julio Cesar
Turner, John Napier
Vargas, Getulio Dornelles
Veil, Simone Annie Jacob
Virchow, Rudolf
Wallace, Henry Agard
Walton, George
Ward, Deighton Harcourt Lisle, Sir
Weizsacker, Richard Freiherr von
Welles, Gideon
Westwood, Jean Miles
Wolcott, Oliver, Sr.
Young, Coleman A(lexander)
Yuan, Shih-Kai
Zhao Ziyang
Zinoviev, Grigori Evseevich

POLITICAL SCIENTIST

Barker, Ernest, Sir
Brogan, Denis William, Sir
Catlin, George Edward Gordon, Sir
Cleveland, James Harlan
Deutsch, Karl Wolfgang
Dodds, Harold Willis
Key, Valdimer Orlando, Jr.
Lieber, Franz
Moley, Raymond
Morgenthau, Hans Joachim
Parkinson, C(yril) Northcote
Rosten, Leo Calvin

Tugwell, Rexford Guy
Wilcox, Francis (Orlando)

POLITICIAN

Abdnor, James S
Abourezk, James George
Abzug, Bella Savitsky
Adams, Annette Abbott
Adams, Charles Francis, Sr.
Addison, Christopher, Viscount
Addonizio, Hugh Joseph
Adenauer, Konrad
Agnew, Spiro Theodore
Agt, Andries Antonius Maria van
Aiken, George David
Alioto, Joseph Lawrence
Allen, Ivan, Jr.
Altgeld, John Peter
Amery, Julian (Harold Julian)
Ames, Oakes
Anaya, Toney
Anderson, Clint(on Presba)
Anderson, Jack Zuinglius
Anderson, John Bayard
Anderson, Wendell Richard
Andrews, Mark N
Aquino, Benigno Simeon, Jr.
Archer, Jeffrey Howard
Arends, Leslie Cornelius
Arens, Moshe
Armstrong, William L
Ashbrook, John Milan
Ashley, Thomas William Ludlow
Ashley, William Henry
Askew, Reubin O'Donovan
Aspin, Leslie, Jr.
Atchison, David R
Badillo, Herman
Baker, Howard Henry, Jr.
Ballinger, Margaret (Violet Margaret
　Livingstone)
Bankhead, William Brockman
Barkley, Alben William
Barras, Paul Francois Jean Nicolas, Comte
　de
Bartlett, Vernon
Baucus, Max Sieben
Bayh, Birch Evans, Jr.
Beame, Abraham David
Benjamin, Adam, Jr.
Bennett, William
Bentley, Alvin Morell
Benton, William
Berry, Marion Shepilov, Jr.
Berryer, Pierre Antoine
Beveridge, Albert Jeremiah
Biaggi, Mario
Bidault, Georges
Biden, Joseph Robinette, Jr.
Bilandic, Michael Anthony
Bilbo, Theodore Gilmore

Bingaman, Jeff
Bingham, Jonathan Brewster
Blanchard, James J
Blanton, (Leonard) Ray
Blunt, Wilfrid Scawen
Boggs, Hale (Thomas Hale)
Boggs, Lindy
Bohm von Bawerk, Eugene
Bolton, Frances Payne
Bond, Julian
Bonnet, Georges
Boothby, Robert John Graham, Lord
Bosch, Juan
Bose, Subhas Chandra
Boulanger, Georges Ernest Jean Marie
Bourassa, Henri
Bourassa, Robert
Boutwell, George Sewell
Bowen, Otis Ray
Brademas, John
Bradley, Tom (Thomas)
Brewster, Owen
Bricker, John William
Brillat-Savarin, Jean Anthelme
Briscoe, Dolph
Brooke, Edward William
Brooks, Jack Bascom
Brown, Jerry (Edmund Gerald, Jr.)
Brown, John Young, Jr.
Brown, Pat (Edmund Gerald)
Brunhart, Hans
Brutus, Marcus Junius
Buchanan, John
Buckley, Charles Anthony
Buckley, James Lane
Buckner, Simon, Jr.
Bukharov, Alexandr Semyonovich
Bumpers, Dale Leon
Burdick, Quentin Northrop
Burton, Phillip
Busbee, George Dekle
Butler, Benjamin Franklin
Byrd, Richard Evelyn
Byrne, Jane Margaret Burke
Cahill, William Thomas
Cakobau, Ratu George, Sir
Caliguiri, Richard
Calvo Sotelo (y Bustelo), Leopoldo
Calvo, Paul McDonald
Campbell, Gordon Thomas
Cannon, Howard Walter
Capper, Arthur
Caraway, Hattie Wyatt
Carey, Hugh Leo
Carmichael, James Vinson
Carrington, Peter Alexander Rupert, Baron
Carson, Edward Henry
Case, Clifford Philip
Cassius
Castle, Barbara Anne Betts
Castlereagh, Robert Stewart, Viscount

Caswell, Richard
Cavanagh, Jerry (Jerome Patrick)
Celebrezze, Anthony Joseph
Celeste, Richard F
Celler, Emanuel
Cervantes, Alfonso Juan
Chandler, "Happy" Albert Benjamin
Chataway, Christopher John
Chirac, Jacques Rene
Church, Frank
Ciano (di Cortellazzo), Conte Galeazzo
Cisneros, Henry Gabriel
Clark, "Champ" James Beauchamp
Clark, Bennett Champ
Clark, Joe (Charles Joseph)
Clark, Richard Clarence
Clayton, John Middleton
Clinton, Bill (William Jefferson)
Clymer, George
Cochran, Thad
Cohen, William Sebastian
Colfax, Schuyler
Collins, Martha Layne Hall
Connally, John Bowden, Jr.
Connally, Tom (Thomas Terry)
Conyers, John, Jr.
Corcoran, Thomas Gardiner
Corning, Erastus, III
Costa e Silva, Arthur da
Couthon, Georges
Couzens, James Joseph, Jr.
Craig, William
Crane, Daniel B
Crittenden, John Jordan
Croker, "Boss" Richard
Crosland, Charles
Cruz, Arturo
Culver, John C
Cuomo, Mario Matthew
Curb, Mike (Michael Charles)
Curtis, Charles
D'Amato, Alfonse Marcello
D'Aubuisson, Roberto
Daddario, Emilio Quincy
Daley, Richard Joseph
Dalton, John Nichols
Danforth, John Claggett
Darden, Colgate Whitehead
Daudet, Leon
Davis, James Curran
Davis, John Williams
DeConcini, Dennis Webster
Dellums, Ronald
Den Uyl, Joor
Denton, Jeremiah Andrew, Jr.
DeSapio, Carmine Gerard
Deukmejian, George, Jr. (Courken)
Devine, Donald
Dewey, Thomas Edmund
Diggs, Charles Coles, Jr.
Dingell, John David, Jr.

Dirksen, Everett McKinley
DiSalle, Michael Vincent
Dixon, Alan John
Djilas, Milovan
Dodd, Christopher John
Dodd, Thomas Joseph
Dole, Bob (Robert Joseph)
Domenici, Pete V(ichi)
Dominick, Peter Hoyt
Donnelly, Ignatius
Douglas, Stephen Arnold
Douglas-Home, Alexander Frederick
Draco
Dukakis, Michael Stanley
DuPont, Pierre Samuel, IV
Durenberger, David Ferdinand
Dzerzhinsky, Felix Edmundovich
Eagleton, Thomas Francis
East, John Porter
Eastland, James Oliver
Eastwood, Clint
Ecevit, Bulent
Echeverria Alvarez, Louis
Edmunds, George Franklin
Edwards, Edwin Washington
Edwards, India
Eldjarn, Kristjan
Ellender, Allen Joseph
Elliott, Robert B
Engle, Clair
Erhard, Ludwig
Erlander, Tage Fritiof
Ervin, Sam(uel James, Jr.)
Evans, Daniel Jackson
Exon, J(ohn) James, Jr.
Fairbanks, Charles Warren
Farrington, Elizabeth Pruett (Mary)
Fascell, Dante Bruno
Fauntroy, Walter E
Feinstein, Dianne
Felton, Rebecca Ann Latimer
Fenwick, Millicent Hammond
Ferguson, Homer
Ferraro, Geraldine Anne
Ferre, Maurice Antonio
Fessenden, William Pitt
Fitzgerald, John Francis
Flood, Daniel J
Flynn, Edward Joseph
Foot, Michael
Fraser, Donald Mackay
Frondizi, Arturo
Fulbright, James William
Fulton, Richard Harmon
Gadsen, James
Galili, Israel
Gallen, Hugh J
Gandhi, Indira Priyadarshini Nehru
Garn, Jake (Edwin Jacob)
Garner, John Nance
Gaspari, Remo

Gayoom, Maumoon Abdul
Gemayel, Sheikh Pierre
George, Walter Franklin
Getty, Donald
Gierek, Edward
Giroud, Francoise
Giscard d'Estaing, Valery
Glenn, John Herschel, Jr.
Goldschmidt, Neil Edward
Goldwater, Barry Morris, Jr.
Goode, Wilson (Willie Wilson)
Gordon-Walker of Leyton, Patrick
   Chrestien Gordon-Walker, Baron
Gorton, Slade
Grace, William Russell
Graham, Bob (Daniel Robert)
Gramm, (William) Phil(ip)
Grassley, Charles Ernest
Griffin, Bob (Robert Paul)
Griffin, Marvin (Samuel Marvin)
Griffiths, Martha Wright
Gronchi, Giovanni
Gurney, Edward John
Hague, Frank
Hall, David
Halleck, Charles Abraham
Hamilton, Alexander
Hanna, Mark (Marcus Alonzo)
Harkin, Thomas R
Harrington, Michael (Edward Michael)
Hart, Gary Warren
Hatch, Carl A
Hatch, Orrin Grant
Hatfield, Mark Odom
Hatfield, Richard
Hathaway, William Dodd
Hawkins, Gus (Augustus Freeman)
Hawkins, Paula Fickes
Hayden, Carl Trumball
Haynie, Carol
Hays, Brooks
Hays, Wayne Levere
Heath, Edward Richard George
Hebert, F(elix) Edward
Hecht, Chic
Heinz, (Henry) John, (III)
Helms, Jesse Alexander, Jr.
Hendricks, Thomas Andrews
Hernandez-Colon, Rafael
Hewitt, Abram Stevens
Hicks, Louise Day
Hill, Lester
Hollings, Ernest Frederick
Holtzman, Elizabeth
Honecker, Erich
Hosmer, Craig (Chester Craig)
Houphouet-Boigny, Felix
Howe, Clarence Decatur
Howe, Joseph
Howell, Thomas Heflin
Hua, Kuo-Feng

Hubbard, Orville Liscum
Huddleston, Walter Darlington
Humphrey, Gordon John
Humphrey, Hubert Horatio, Jr.
Humphrey, Muriel Fay Buck
Hunt, George Wylie Paul
Hynes, John B
Ichikawa, Fusae
Ingersoll, Robert Green
Jaabari, Mohammed Ali, Sheik
Jackson, Henry Martin
Jagan, Cheddi
Jagan, Janet
Jarman, John
Jaroszewicz, Piotr
Jenner, William Ezra
Jenrette, John Wilson, Jr.
Johnson, Pierre Marc
Johnson, Richard Mentor
Johnston, J Bennett, Jr.
Jordan, Barbara C
Kassebaum, Nancy Landon
Kassem, Abdul Karim
Kean, Thomas Howard
Keating, Kenneth B
Kelly, Petra Karin
Kennedy, Edward Moore
Kennedy, John Pendleton
Kennedy, Joseph Patrick, III
Keogh, Eugene James
Kerrey, Bob (Joseph Robert)
Kerry, John F
Kiesinger, Kurt Georg
Kim Dae Jung
Kim, Young Sam
Kinnock, Neil Gordon
Kneip, Richard
Koch, Ed(ward Irwin)
Kollek, Teddy (Theodore)
Kubitschek (de Oliveira), Juscelino
Kucinich, Dennis John
Kuznetsov, Vasili Vasilievich
LaFollete, Philip Fox
LaFollette, Robert Marion
LaGuardia, Fiorello Henry
Lalonde, Marc
LaMarsh, Judy (Julia Verlyn)
Lamizana, Sangoule
Lamm, Richard D
Landes, Bertha Ethel
Landon, Alf(red Mossman)
Langdon, John
Larouche, Lyndon H, Jr.
Laurier, Wilfrid, Sir
Lausche, Frank John
Lautenberg, Frank R
Laxalt, Paul
Le Poer Trench, (William Francis) Brinsley
Leahy, Patrick Joseph
Lee, James
Lehman, Herbert Henry

Leland, "Mickey" George Thomas
Levin, Carl Milton
Lindsay, John Vliet
Lleshi, Haxhi
Lloyd, (John) Selwyn Brooke
Lodge, Henry Cabot, Jr.
Logan, John Alexander
Long, Earl Kemp
Long, Huey Pierce
Long, Russell Billiu
Lougheed, Peter
Lowden, Frank O(rren)
Ludendorff, Erich Friedrich Wilhelm
Lugar, Richard Green
Luns, Joseph Marie Antoine Hubert
Lyons, Enid Muriel
Macapagal, Diosdado Pangan
Mack, Peter
Mackinder, Halford John, Sir
Maddox, Lester Garfield
Maginot, Andre
Magnuson, Warren Grant
Mahone, William
Makarios III, Archbishop
Malan, Daniel F
Mallory, Stephen R
Manatt, Charles Taylor
Mandel, Marvin
Mann, Horace
Mansfield, Michael Joseph
Marat, Jean Paul
Marcantonio, Vito Anthony
Marshall, Thomas Riley
Martin, Joseph William, Jr.
McCall, Thomas Lawson
McCarthy, Eugene Joseph
McCarthy, Joe (Joseph Raymond)
McConnell, Mitch
McCormick, Joseph Medill
McDonald, Larry (Lawrence Patton)
McFarland, Ernest William
McGovern, George Stanley
McGuinness, Martin
Menzies, Robert Gordon, Sir
Mercouri, "Melina" Maria Amalia
Merriam, Frank Finley
Metcalfe, Ralph H
Miki, Takeo
Mikoyan, Anastas Ivanovich
Mikulski, Barbara Ann
Miller, William E
Mills, Ogden Livingston
Mills, Wilbur Daigh
Mink, Patsy Takemoto
Mitchel, John Purroy
Moffett, Anthony Toby
Mondale, Walter Frederick
Monroney, Mike (Aimer Stillwell)
Moro, Aldo
Morrill, Justin Smith
Morris, Newbold

Morrison, Cameron
Morse, Wayne Lyman
Morton, Levi Parsons
Morton, Thruston Ballard
Mosley, Oswald Ernald, Sir
Moss, Frank Edward
Moynihan, Daniel Patrick
Murat, Joachim
Murphy, George Lloyd
Muskie, Edmund Sixtus
Naidu, Sarojini
Negrin, Juan
Ngo dinh Nhu, Madame
Nickles, Donald Lee
Nkomo, Joshua
Novotny, Antonin
O'Dwyer, Paul
O'Neill, "Tip" Thomas Philip
Packwood, Bob (Robert William)
Pandit, Vijaya Lakshmi (Nehru)
Park, Choong-Hoon
Paterson, Basil Alexander
Paton, Alan Stewart
Peckfard, Alfred
Pell, Claiborne
Pepper, Claude Denson
Perez Jimenez, Marcos
Perez, Leander Henry
Perpich, Rudy George
Peterson, David
Pike, Otis
Pillsbury, John Sargent
Pinchback, Pinckney Benton Stewart
Pinchot, Gifford
Pitman, James (Isaac James)
Plimsoll, Samuel
Podgorny, Nikolai Viktorovich
Poulson, Norris
Powell, Enoch (John Enoch)
Prasad, Rajendra
Pretorius, Marthinus Wessel
Proxmire, William
Pryor, David Hampton
Purtell, William Arthur
Quayle, (James) Dan(forth)
Rainey, Joseph Hayne
Ram, Jagjivan
Rankin, Jeannette
Ray, Dixy Lee
Ray, Robert D
Reagan, Maureen
Revels, Hiram R
Reynaud, Paul
Rhodes, John Jacob
Ribicoff, Abraham Alexander
Riegle, Donald Wayne, Jr.
Rizzo, Frank L
Robb, Charles Spittal
Rockefeller, John D(avison), IV
Rockefeller, Nelson A(ldrich)
Rockefeller, Winthrop

Rodino, Peter Wallace, Jr.
Rodney, Caesar
Rohde, Ruth Bryan Owen
Romney, George Wilcken
Roosevelt, Elliot
Roosevelt, Franklin Delano, Jr.
Roper, Daniel C
Rosenthal, Benjamin Stanley
Rostenkowski, Daniel David
Roth, William Victor, Jr.
Rothermere, Esmond Cecil Harmsworth,
    Viscount
Rowling, Wallace Edward
Royo, Aristides
Russell, John, Lord
Russell, Richard Brevard, Jr.
Ryan, Leo Joseph
Salinger, Pierre Emil George
Saltonstall, Leverett
Santander, Francisco de Paula
Saragat, Giuseppe
Schaefer, William Donald
Schenck, Robert Cumming
Schlafly, Phyllis Stewart
Schmitt, Harrison Hagan
Schroder, Gerhard
Schroeder, Patricia Scott
Schumann, Maurice
Schurz, Carl
Scott, Hugh D, Jr.
Scranton, William Warren
Sebelius, Keith George
Shehu, Mehmet
Sheridan, Richard Brinsley
Sherman, James Schoolcraft
Shields, James
Simon, Paul
Smith, Ellison DuRant
Smith, Margaret Chase
Spaak, Paul-Henri
Spychalski, Marian
Stanford, Sally
Stassen, Harold Edward
Stennis, John Cornelius
Stevens, Siaka Probyn
Stevens, Thaddeus
Stevenson, Adlai Ewing
Stevenson, Adlai Ewing, III
Stevenson, Adlai Ewing, Jr.
Stevenson, Edward A
Stokes, Carl Burton
Stone, Richard Bernard (Dick)
Stoneman, George
Strauss, Franz Josef
Strauss, Lewis Lichtenstein
Strong, James Matthew
Stronge, (Charles) Norman (Lockhart), Sir
Studds, Gerry E
Suarez, Xavier Louis
Summerskill, Edith Clara, Baroness
Suslov, Mikhail Andreevich

Taft, Robert A(lphonso)
Taft, Robert Alphonso, Jr.
Talmadge, Eugene
Tawley, Howard
Thomas, Elmer
Thomaz, Americo
Thompson, John S D
Thorez, Maurice
Thorn, Gaston
Thurmond, (James) Strom
Tilden, Samuel Jones
Tompkins, Daniel D
Traikov, Georgi
Trible, Paul S, Jr.
Trujillo (Molina), Rafael Leonidas
Trumbull, Jonathan
Tsedenbal, Yumzahgin
Tsiranana, Philibert
Tsongas, Paul Efthemios
Tunney, John Varick
Tweed, "Boss" (William Marcy
Unruh, Jesse Marvin
Upshaw, William David
Van Cortlandt, Oloff Stevenszen
Van Cortlandt, Stephanus
Van Rensselaer, Stephen
Vandenberg, Arthur Hendrick
Vogel, Hans-Jochen
Voroshilov, Kliment Efremovich
Vorster, Balthazar Johannes (John)
Walker, Daniel
Walker, Jimmy (James John)
Wallace, George Corley
Walsh, Thomas James
Warner, John William
Washington, Harold
Watkins, Arthur V(ivian)
Watson, Thomas Edward
Weed, Thurlow
Weicker, Lowell Palmer, Jr.
Weiss, Ted
Weizman, Ezer
Werner, Pierre
Wheeler, William Alrnon
White, Kevin Hagan
White, Mark Wells, Jr.
Whitmire, Kathy
Wigg, George (Edward Cecil)
Williams, Eric Eustace
Williams, G Mennen
Williams, Harrison Arlington, Jr.
Williams, Shirley
Willkie, Wendell Lewis
Wilmot, David
Wilson, Henry
Wilson, Malcolm
Wilson, Pete
Woodsworth, James Shaver
Xuan Thuy
Yarborough, Ralph Webster
Yorty, Sam(uel William)

Young, Andrew J
Zablocki, Clement John
Zhivkov, Todor
Zhukov, Georgi Alexandrovich
Zorinsky, Edward

POLLSTER

Caddell, Pat(rick Hayward)
Crossley, Archibald Maddock
Gallup, George Horace
Harris, Louis
Robinson, Claude Everett

PRELATE

William of Waynflete

PREMIER

Nasser, Gamal Abdel

PRESIDENT

Armour, Jenner
Azikiwe, Nnamdi
Bignone, Reynaldo Benito Antonio
Boumedienne, Houari
Bourguiba, Habib Ben Ali
Buttigieg, Anton
Cardenas, Lazaro
Carstens, Karl Walter
Ceausescu, Nicolae
Chiang, Ching-Kuo
Chun Doo Hwan
Chung, Arthur
DeRoburt, Hammer
Diaz Ordaz, Gustavo
DuPont, Clifford Walter
Duvalier, Francois
Eanes, Antonio Ramalho
Ebert, Friedrich
Einaudi, Luigi
Eyadema, Gnassingbe
Faure, Felix
Figueiredo, Joao Baptista de Oliveira
Figueres Ferrer, Jose
Finnbogadottir, Vigdis
Garcia, Carlos P
Geisel, Ernesto
Gemayel, Amin
Goulart, Joao
Guevara Arze, Walter
Habre, Hissein
Habyarimana, Juvenal
Heinemann, Gustav Walter
Herrera Campins, Luis
Hindenburg, Paul von
Husak, Gustav
Hussain al Takriti, Saddam
Ishak, Yusof bin
Jonas, Franz

Juarez, Benito Pablo
Karamanlis, Constantine
Karmal, Babrak
Kasavubu, Joseph
Kaunda, Kenneth David
Kayibanda, Gregoire
Kenyatta, Jomo (Johnstone)
Kerekou, Mathieu
Khama, Seretse M
Kirchschlager, Rudolf
Koivisto, Mauno Henrik
Kountche, Seyni
Kyprianou, Spyros
Lebrun, Albert
Leone, Giovanni
Lleras Restrepo, Carlos
Lopez Mateos, Adolfo
Lopez Portillo, Jose
Losonczi, Pal
Lubke, Heinrich
Lucas Garcia, Fernando Romeo
Machado y Morales, Gerardo
Madero, Francisco Indalecio
Magsaysay, Ramon
Mannerheim, Carl Gustav Emil, Baron
Mobutu, Joseph-Desire
Moi, Daniel
Morales Bermudez, Francisco
Navon, Yitzhak
Ne Win, U
Ngo dinh Diem
Nimeiry, Gaafar Mohammed al
Nyerere, Julius Kambarage
Oduber, Daniel
Paz Garcia, Policarpo
Pereira, Aristides
Pertini, Alessandro
Pompidou, Georges Jean Raymond
Rahman, Mujibur, Sheik
Rahman, Ziaur
Rajai, Mohammed Ali
Reddy, N(eelam) Sanjiva
Rojas Pinilla, Gustavo
Romero, Carlos Humberto
Sadat, Anwar el
Segni, Antonio
Shagari, Alhaji Shehu Usman Aliyu
Shazar, Zalman
Sheares, Benjamin Henry
Somoza Debayle, Anastasio
Somoza, Anastasio
Souphanouvong, Prince
Stroessner, Alfredo
Suharto, General
Sun Yat-Sen
Tolbert, William Richard, Jr.
Tombalbaye, Nagarta Francois
Ton-duc-thong
Toure, Ahmed Sekou
Trare, Moussa
Tsatsos, Constantinos

Tubman, William Vacanarat Shadrach
Urrutia Lleo, Manuel
Velasco Alvarado, Juan
Velasco Ibarra, Jose Maria
Videla, Jorge Rafael
Yahya Khan, Agha Muhammad
Zia-ul-Haq, Mohammad

PRESIDENTIAL AIDE

Anderson, Jack Zuinglius
Baker, James Addison, III
Brady, James Scott
Cole, Kenneth Reese
Costanza, "Midge" Margaret
Hopkins, Harry Lloyd
Jordan, Hamilton (William Hamilton)
Kahn, Alfred Edward
McLaughlin, John J
Meese, Edwin, III
Nessen, Ron(ald Harold)
Nofziger, Lyn (Franklyn Curran)
Powell, Jody (Joseph Lester)
Rafshoon, Gerald Monroe
Sloan, Hugh W
Strauss, Robert
Vandenberg, Arthur Hendrick, Jr.
Warren, Gerald Lee

PRIEST

Bandello, Matteo
Berrigan, Daniel J
Canfield, Francis X(avier)
Coughlin, Father (Charles Edward)
D'Arcy, Martin Cyril
Duffy, Francis Patrick
Ezra
Flanagan, Edward Joseph, Father
Greeley, Andrew Moran
Groppi, James E
Hidalgo y Costilla, Miguel
Hill, Morton A(nthony)
Morelos y Pavon, Jose M
Nouwen, Henri J M
O'Callahan, Joseph Timothy
Richard, Gabriel
Schmemann, Alexander
Teilhard de Chardin, Pierre

PRIME MINISTER

Bakhtiar, Shahpur
Benediktsson, Bjarni
Busia, Kofi A
Bustamante, William Alexander
Chamberlain, Neville
Chung, Il-Kwon
Cosgrave, Liam
Costello, John Aloysius
Curtin, John
DeJong, Petrus

Diefenbaker, John George
Diouf, Abdou
Eshkol, Levi
Eyskens, Gaston
Falldin, Thorbjorn Nils Olof
Faulkner, Brian
Gorton, John Grey
Hasani, Ali Nasir Muhammad
Heath, Edward Richard George
Holt, Harold Edward
Jonathan, Leabua, Chief
Jorgensen, Anker Henrik
Khalil, Mustafa
King, William Lyon Mackenzie
Kittikachorn, Thanom
Krag, Jens Otto
Lee, Kuan Yew
Lynch, John
Manley, Michael Norman
Muzorewa, Abel Tendekai
Nakasone, Yasuhiro
Nordli, Odvar
North, Frederick North, Baron
Ohira, Masayoshi
Papadopoulos, George
Pitt, William
Rahman, Abdul, Prince
Rosebery, Archibald Philip Primrose, Earl
Sato, Eisaku
Seaga, Edward Phillip George
Sedny, Jules
Smith, Ian Douglas
Suarez Gonzales, Adolfo
Suzuki, Zenko
Tanaka, Kakuei
Tindemans, Leo(nard)
Verwoerd, Hendrik F
Whitlam, Edward Gough
Yoshida, Shigeru

PRINCE

Akihito, (Togusama)
Albert
Albert
Andrew
Andrew, Prince of Russia
Charles
Dracula
Edward
Edward the Black Prince
Faisal ibn Musaed
Frederick Louis
George Edward Alexander Edmund
Henry of Wales
Henry the Navigator
Henry William Frederick Albert
Louis Napoleon
Rudolf of Hapsburg
Souvanna, Phouma
William of Wales

PRINCESS

Alice (Mary Victoria Augusta Pauline)
Anne
Astrid
Caroline, Princess
Christina
Christina
Diana, Princess of Wales
Ileana
Irene
Irene
Jezebel
Kelly, Grace Patricia
Margaret
Pocahontas
Radziwill, (Caroline) Lee Bouvier,
Stephanie, Princess
Victoria Ingrid Alice Desiree

PRINTER

Baskerville, John
Beadle, Erastus Flavel
Bradshaw, George
Caxton, William
Cobden-Sanderson, Thomas James
Cuesta, Juan de la
Daye, Stephen
DeVinne, Theodore Low
Estienne, Henri
Froben, Johann
Fust, Johann
Hunter, Dard
Manutius, Aldus
Manuzio, Aldo
Plantin, Christophe
Raikes, Robert
Richard, Gabriel
Sholes, Christopher Latham
Updike, Daniel Berkeley
Walker, Emery, Sir
Zenger, John Peter

PRINTMAKER

Baldung(-Grien), Hans

PRISON WARDEN

Duffy, Clinton Truman

PRISONER

Little, Joan

PRODUCER

Abrahams, Doris Cole
Ackerman, Harry S
Adams, Tony (Anthony Patrick)
Adler, "Buddy" Maurice

Aldrich, Richard Stoddard
Aldrich, Robert
Allen, Irwin
Allen, Woody
Almond, Paul
Altman, Robert B
Ames, Ed(mund Dantes)
Anderson, Gerry
Andrews, Michael Alford
Arkoff, Samuel Z
Arnaz, Desi
Arnold, Danny
Asher, Peter
Attenborough, Richard Samuel, Sir
Averback, Hy
Ayres, Lew
Baer, Max, Jr.
Balcon, Michael Elias, Sir
Ball, Lucille
Banner, Bob
Barris, Chuck
Barry, Jack
Bass, Saul
Bayer, Wolfgang
Beatty, Warren
Behn, Noel
Belasco, David
Bellisario, Donald P
Bennett, Harve
Bensley, Russ
Bergman, Ingmar
Berman, Pandro Samuel
Bertinelli, Valerie
Biberman, Herbert
Bill, Tony
Blinn, Holbrook
Bloomgarden, Kermit
Bocho, Steven
Bogart, Neil
Bogdanovich, Peter
Bosustow, Stephen
Boulting, Roy
Brackett, Charles
Brady, William Aloysius
Brakhage, Stan
Brasselle, Keefe
Brisson, Frederick
Brooks, James L
Brooks, Mel
Brosten, Harve
Brown, David
Bruhn, Erik Belton Evers
Buck, Gene
Bufman, Zev
Bullins, Ed
Burrows, James
Cagney, James (James Francis, Jr.)
Cannell, Stephen J
Capra, Frank
Carlisle, Kevin
Carr, Allan

Carr, Martin
Carroll, Earl
Carsey, Marcia
Castle, William
Cates, Joseph
Chaplin, Saul
Charles, Glen
Charles, Lee
Charteris, Leslie
Chartoff, Robert
Chase, David
Chodorov, Edward
Clair, Rene
Clarke, Shirley
Clayton, Herbert
Codron, Michael
Coe, Frederick H
Cohan, George M(ichael)
Cohen, Alexander H
Collins, Ted
Conrad, William
Cook, Peter
Cooney, Joan Ganz
Cooper, Jackie (John, Jr.)
Corman, Gene
Corman, Roger William
Corsi, Jacopo
Corwin, Norman
Costello, Robert E
Cousteau, Philippe
Crawford, Cheryl
Crouse, Russel
Crozier, Eric
DaCosta, Morton
Daley, Robert H
Dalrymple, Ian (Murray)
Dalrymple, Jean
Daly, John
DaSilva, Howard
De Patie, David H
DeCordova, Frederick Timmins
DeLaurentiis, Dino
DeLaurentiis, Federico
DeMille, Cecil B(lount)
Denoff, Sam
DeRochemont, Louis
DeSylva, "Buddy" (George Gard
Dillingham, Charles Bancroft
Disney, Walt(er Elias)
Doherty, Brian
Douglas, Michael Kirk
Dowling, Eddie (Edward)
DuMaurier, Gerald Hubert, Sir
Duncan, Augustin
Edmunds, Dave
Edwards, Blake
Edwards, Ralph
Einstein, Bob
Elkins, Hillard
Eno, Brian
Evans, Bob (Robert)

Fairbanks, Douglas, Jr.
Feld, Irvin
Felsenstein, Walter
Ferrer, Jose Vicente
Feuer, Cy
Fields, Freddie
Fine, Sylvia
Fontana, Tom
Foreman, Carl
Foster, Norman
Fox, Carol
Frankovich, Mike J
Frederickson, H Gray
Freed, Arthur
Freeman, Seth
Freleng, Friz
Friendly, Ed
Friendly, Fred W
Fries, Charles W
Frohman, Charles
Fryer, Robert
Fuisz, Robert E
Funt, Allen
Gabel, Martin
Garrett, Lila
Geffen, David
Gelbart, Larry
Geller, Bruce
Gest, Morris
Gielgud, (Arthur) John, Sir
Gilbert, Bruce
Goldberg, Leonard
Golden, John
Goldie, Grace Wyndham
Goldner, Orville
Goldwyn, Samuel
Golenpaul, Dan
Goodson, Mark
Gordon, Max
Graham, Bill
Granville-Barker, Harley
Greenspan, Bud
Guber, Peter (Howard Peter)
Hackford, Taylor
Haley, Jack, Jr. (John J.)
Halliday, Richard
Harris, Jed
Hartmann, Rudolph
Hawkins, Jack
Hawks, Howard Winchester
Hayward, Leland
Hazam, Lou(is J)
Hecht, Harold
Helburn, Theresa
Helms, Chet
Hemion, Dwight
Herridge, Robert T
Holmes, Burton
Hopkins, Arthur
Hopper, DeWolf
Houseman, John

Hunter, Ross
Hutt, William Ian Dewitt
Ince, Thomas H(arper)
Irving, Jules
Janney, Russell Dixon
Kanter, Hal
Keillor, Garrison (Gary Edward)
Kollmar, Richard
Kooper, Al
Korda, Alexander, Sir
Kramer, Stanley E
Krofft, Marty
Krofft, Sid
Krumgold, Joseph
Ladd, Alan Walbridge, Jr.
Landau, Ely A
Lane, Stewart F
Langer, Lawrence
Laughlin, Tom
Lawrence, Bill
Lear, Norman Milton
Leonard, Sheldon
Leonidoff, Leon
Leroy, Mervyn
Lesser, Sol
Levine, Joseph Edward
Lewton, Val Ivan
Liebman, Max
Lindsay, Howard
Liveright, Horace Brisbin
Loew, Marcus
Lord, Jack
Lord, Phillips H
Lortel, Lucille
Ludden, Allen Ellsworth
Ludlam, Charles
Lupino, Stanley
Majors, Lee
Mankiewicz, Joseph Lee
Mann, Theodore
Manulis, Martin
Marsh, Dame Ngaio
Marshall, Garry Kent
Martin, Quinn
Massey, Raymond Hart
Mayer, L(ouis) B(urt)
McCann, Elizabeth (Liz)
McClintic, Guthrie
Melford, Austin (Alfred Austin)
Melies, Georges
Melnick, Daniel
Merrick, David
Michaels, Lorne
Miller, Gilbert Heron
Miner, Worthington C
Minsky, Abraham Bennett
Minsky, Harold
Mirisch, Walter Mortimer
Monty, Gloria
Moussa, Ibrahim
Muto, Anthony

Neagle, Anna, Dame
Nederlander, James Morton
Nemirovich-Danchenko, Vladimir I
Newman, Paul
Nicholson, Jack
Nugent, Elliott
Nugent, Nelle
Olivier, Laurence Kerr Olivier, Sir
Pagnol, Marcel Paul
Pal, George
Paltrow, Bruce
Panama, Norman
Papp, Joseph
Pascal, Gabriel
Pasternak, Joe (Joseph Vincent)
Pemberton, Brock
Peters, Jon
Pleasence, Donald
Ponti, Carlo
Powell, Michael
Power, Jules
Preminger, Otto Ludwig
Price, Nancy (Lillian Nancy Bache)
Prince, Hal (Harold Smith)
Ransohoff, Martin
Reinhardt, Max
Reitman, Ivan
Renaldo, Duncan
Richardson, Tony
Rigby, Harry
Robinson, "Smokey" William, Jr.
Roddenberry, Gene (Eugene Wesley)
Rogell, Albert S
Rohmer, Eric, pseud.
Rooney, Andy (Andrew Aitken)
Rose, Billy
Ross, David
Ross, David
Rossen, Robert
Ruddy, Al(bert Stotland)
Rush, Richard
Saint-Subber, Arnold
Schary, Dore
Schenck, Joseph M
Schikaneder, Johann Emanuel
Schneider, Bert
Schulberg, Stuart
Schwartz, Maurice
Schwary, Ronald L
Scott, Adrian
Seaton, George
Seidelman, Susan
Selznick, David O(liver)
Selznick, Irene
Sennett, Mack
Serling, Rod
Shapiro, Arnold
Shapiro, Stanley
Sherman, Harry R
Shubert, Jacob J
Shubert, Lee

Shumlin, Herman Elliott
Sidaris, Andy
Sidney, George
Silliphant, Stirling Dale
Sillman, Leonard
Sim, Alastair
Simpson, Donald C
Siodmark, Curt
Skouras, Spyros Panagiotes
Sloan, Michael
Smith, Oliver
Smith, Pete
Spector, Phil(lip Harvey)
Spelling, Aaron
Spiegel, Sam
Spivak, Lawrence
Stern, Leonard B
Stevens, George, Jr.
Stevens, Leslie
Stevens, Roger L
Stewart, Ellen
Stigwood, Robert C
Stone, Ezra (Chaim)
Stone, Paula
Stromberg, Hunt
Styne, Jule (Julius Kerwin Stein)
Susskind, David Howard
Tahse, Martin
Tanen, Ned
Taylor, Charles Alonzo
Terry, Paul H
Thalberg, Irving Grant
Thomas, Danny
Thomas, Lowell Jackson, Jr.
Tinker, Grant A
Todd, Mike (Michael)
Todman, Bill (William Selden)
Tors, Ivan
Traube, Shepard
Travers, Bill
Trendle, George Washington
Tripp, Paul
Tucker, Larry
Van Dyke, W(oodbridge) S(trong)
Wagner, Wieland Adolf Gottfried
Wagner, Wolfgang
Wald, Jerry (Jerome Irving)
Walker, Stuart Armstrong
Wallis, Hal Brent
Wallmann, Margherita
Wanger, Walter
Waxman, Al
Wein, George Theodore
Weintraub, Jerry
Weiskopf, Bob
Welles, Orson (George Orson)
White, George
White, Michael Simon
Whitehead, Robert
Whitney, C(ornelius) V(anderbilt)
Wilcox, Herbert

Wilcoxon, Henry
Wilde, Cornel
Wilder, "Billy" Samuel
Wilder, Clinton
Wilson, Richard
Wilson, Robert M
Winkler, Irwin
Wise, Robert
Witt, Paul Junger
Witte, Erich
Wolfe, Digby
Wolper, David Lloyd
Wyler, William
Yablans, Frank
Zaentz, Saul
Zanuck, Darryl Francis
Zanuck, Richard Darryl
Ziegfeld, Flo(renz)
Zukor, Adolph

PROPHET

Amos
Ezekiel
Hosea
Isaiah
Jeremiah
Meher Baba
Mercurius, Joannes
Zoroaster

PSYCHIATRIST

Abramson, Harold A(lexander)
Alexander, Leo
Berne, Eric Lennard
Binswanger, Ludwig
Blumenthal, Monica David
Braceland, Francis J(ames)
Brill, Abraham Arden
Bullard, Dexter Means
Densen-Gerber, Judianne
Dunbar, Helen Flanders
Fielding, Lewis J
Frank, Jerome David
Frankl, Viktor E
Jung, Carl Gustav
Klein, Melanie
Kline, Nathan Schellenberg
Krafft-Ebing, Richard von
Kubler-Ross, Elisabeth
Laing, R(onald) D(avid)
Larson, John Augustus
Lidz, Theodore
Masserman, Jules H(oman)
Menninger, Karl Augustus
Perls, Frederick Salomon
Radecki, Thomas
Reuben, David
Robitscher, Jonas Bondi, Jr.
Romano, John
Rorschach, Hermann

Szasz, Thomas Stephen
Wertham, Fredric
Westheimer, Ruth
Wilder, Joseph

PSYCHIC

Barbanell, Maurice
Brown, Rosemary
Cayce, Edgar
Garrett, Eileen Jeanette Lyttle
Geller, Uri
Home, Daniel Douglas
Hurkos, Peter
Kreskin
Roberts, Estelle
Stokes, Doris
Theresa, Saint

PSYCHOANALYST

Adler, Alfred
Arieti, Silvano
Berkowitz, Bernard
Deutsch, Helene R
Erikson, Erik Homburger
Fanon, Frantz
Frailberg, Selma
Freud, Anna
Freud, Sigmund
Fromm, Erich
Horney, Karen Danielson
Kardiner, Abram
Kohut, Heinz
Lacan, Jacques Marie Emile
Langer, Walter C
May, Rollo
Newman, Mildred
Reich, Wilhelm
Reik, Theodor
Rubin, Theodore Isaac

PSYCHOLOGIST

Allport, Gordon William
Ames, Louise Bates
Baldwin, James Mark
Bateson, Gregory
Bell, Arthur Donald
Bender, Hans
Bettelheim, Bruno
Binet, Alfred
Britt, Steuart Henderson
Brothers, Joyce Diane Bauer
Bruner, Jerome Seymour
Burt, Cyril Lodowic, Sir
Cattell, James McKeen
Clark, Kenneth Bancroft
Coue, Emile
Crawford, John Edmund
Dichter, Ernest
Dollard, John

Ellis, Havelock(Henry Havelock)
Ginott, Haim
Gordon, Thomas
Hathaway, Starke R
Haworth, Mary Robbins
James, William
Janov, Arthur
Jensen, Arthur Robert
Johnson, Virginia E
Jung, Carl Gustav
Kanner, Leo
Kassorla, Irene Chamie
Keniston, Kenneth
Koehler, Wolfgang
Koffka, Kurt
Kohler, Wolfgang
Kronhausen, Eberhard Wilhelm
Kronhausen, Phyllis Carmen
Ladd, George Trumbull
Ladd-Franklin, Christine
Lewin, Kurt
Marston, William Moulton
Maslow, Abraham
McDougall, William
Mead, George Herbert
Monroe, Marion
Myers, Garry Cleveland
Piaget, Jean
Rhine, J(oseph) B(anks)
Rogers, Carl Ransom
Salk, Lee
Sears, Robert Richardson
Sheehan, Joseph Green
Sheldon, William Herbert
Simon, Herbert Alexander
Skinner, B(urrhus) F(rederic)
Stevens, S(tanley) S(mith)
Watson, John Broadus
Wechsler, David
Wertheimer, Max

PUBLIC OFFICIAL

Adams, Sherman Llewellyn
Arbatov, Georgi
Bailey, Kay
Beard, Dita Davis
Blount, Winton Malcolm
Bonham Carter, (Helen) Violet
Briscoe, Robert
Clay, Cassius Marcellus
Craig, Malin
Creel, George
Crowley, Leo T
Duke, Robin (Anthony Hare)
Fong, Hiram
Forrestal, James Vincent
Furness, Betty (Elizabeth Mary)
Goldmann, Nahum
Gowers, Ernest Arthur, Sir
Granger, Lester
Henry, Edward Richard, Sir

Hill, Herbert
Hiss, Alger
Howard, Oliver Otis
Hume, David
Ickes, Harold LeClair
Kelley, Frank Joseph
Killian, James Rhyne, Jr.
Lilienthal, David Eli
Lipshutz, Robert Jerome
Lowery, Robert O
Lyautey, Louis Hubert Gonzalve
Maverick, Samuel Augustus
Milliken, William G(rawn)
Moses, Robert
Norris, George William
Paine, Robert Treat
Park, Maud May Wood
Reith, John Charles Walsham
Richards, Richard
Ronan, William J
Sevier, John
Shriver, (Robert) Sargent
Sickles, Daniel Edgar
Solomon, Neil
Stark, Abe
Tabor, Horace Austin Warner
Tekere, Edgar Zivanai
Tree, Marietta Endicott Peabody
Underwood, Oscar Wilder
Vandenberg, Arthur Hendrick, Jr.
Wales, Salem Howe
Wilcox, Francis (Orlando)
Ziegler, Ron(ald Louis)

PUBLIC RELATIONS EXECUTIVE

Baldrige, Letitia Katherine
Bernays, Edward L
Birdwell, Russell Juarez
DeVilleneuve, Justin
Garth, David
Lord, James Lawrence
Pappas, Irene

PUBLISHER

Abrams, Harry Nathan
Adler, Elmer
Aitken, Max (John William Maxwell)
Annenberg, Walter Hubert
Anthony, Edward
Appleton, Daniel
Appleton, William Henry
Armstrong, Charles B
Astor, Gavin
Attwood, William
Baedeker, Karl
Ballantine, Ian
Barron, Clarence Walker
Bartlett, John
Beach, Sylvia
Beadle, Erastus Flavel

Beaverbrook, William Maxwell Aitken, Baron
Beilenson, Edna Rudolph
Benjamin, Curtis G
Bennett, James Gordon, Jr.
Benton, William
Berry, James Gomer
Black, Walter J
Blackwell, Basil Henry, Sir
Blackwell, Earl
Bleiberg, Robert Marvin
Bobbs, William Conrad
Boehm, Eric Hartzell
Boni, Albert
Bowker, R(ichard) R(ogers)
Bracken, Brendan Rendall, Viscount
Bradley, Milton
Brady, James
Brand, Stewart
Brett, George Platt, Jr.
Brown, James
Burden, Carter (Shirley Carter, Jr.)
Buttenheim, Edgar Joseph
Canfield, Cass
Cape, Herbert Jonathan
Capper, Arthur
Carter, Amon Giles
Cerf, Bennett Alfred
Chambers, Robert
Charney, Nicolas Herman
Childs, George William
Conrad, Con
Covici, Pascal
Cowles, Gardner
Cowles, John, Sr.
Cowles, William Hutchinson, Jr.
Cox, James Middleton, Jr.
Croft, Arthur C
Crosby, Harry
Crowninshield, Francis Welch
Cuneo, Ernest
Day, Benjamin Henry
Day, James Wentworth
Debrett, John
DeGraff, Robert F(air)
Delacorte, George Thomas, Jr.
Dodsley, Robert
Doubleday, Frank Nelson
Doubleday, Nelson
Doubleday, Nelson
Dow, Charles Henry
Dutton, E(dward) P(ayson)
Economaki, Chris(topher Constantine)
Elzevir, Louis
Engel, Lyle Kenyon
Enoch, Kurt
Ethridge, Mark Foster
Ethridge, Mark Foster, Jr.
Faber, Geoffrey Cust, Sir
Fairchild, John Burr
Fairchild, Louis W

Farrar, John Chipman
Fawcett, Wilford Hamilton, Jr.
Ferril, Thomas Hornsby
Field, Marshall, III
Field, Marshall, IV
Fields, James T
Fischer, Carl
Fleischer, Nat(haniel S)
Fleishmann, Raoul H(erbert)
Flynt, Larry Claxton
Fodor, Eugene
Forbes, Malcolm Stevenson
Funk, Isaac Kauffman
Funk, Wilfred John
Garrett, Eileen Jeanette Lyttle
Geis, Bernard
Gernsback, Hugo
Ginn, Edwin
Ginzburg, Ralph
Giroux, Robert
Godey, Louis Antoine
Golden, Harry Lewis
Golenpaul, Dan
Gollancz, Victor, Sir
Griffin, Marvin (Samuel Marvin)
Grosvenor, Melville Bell
Guccione, Bob (Robert Charles Joseph
   Edward Sabatini)
Guggenheim, Harry Frank
Guptill, Arthur Leighton
Hadden, Briton
Haldeman-Julius, Emanuel
Harper, Fletcher
Harper, James
Harper, John
Harper, Joseph Wesley
Hart-Davis, Rupert (Charles Rupert)
Hearst, David W
Hearst, William Randolph, Jr.
Hecht, George Joseph
Hefner, Hugh Marston
Hefti, Neal Paul
Heiskell, Andrew
Henson, Lisa
Hillegass, C K
Hills, Argentina
Hines, Duncan
Hoffman, Rob
Holt, Henry
Horne, Josh L
Houghton, Henry Oscar
Hubbard, Elbert Green
Ingersoll, Ralph McAllister
Johnson, John Harold
Jovanovich, William Iliya
Kelly, Stephen Eugene
Kennedy, Edward Ridgway
Keylor, Arthur W
Keyserlingk, Robert Wendelin
Kiplinger, Austin Huntington
Kirshner, Don

Kirstein, George G
Klopfer, Donald Simon
Knight, Charles
Knopf, Alfred Abraham
Korda, Michael
Lane, Allen, Sir
Larsen, Roy Edward
Laughlin, James, IV
Lawson, Victor Fremont
Leslie, Miriam Florence Folline
Leventhal, Albert Rice
Lippincott, Joshua Ballinger
Little, Charles Coffin
Liveright, Horace Brisbin
Loeb, William
Luce, Henry Robinson
Macfadden, Bernarr Adolphus
MacMillan, Daniel
Macy, George
Manley, Joan A Daniels
Marquis, Albert Nelson
McCormick, Bernard
McGraw, Donald Cushing
McGraw, Harold Whittlesey, Sr.
McNally, Andrew, III
McNaughton, F(oye) F(isk)
McWhirter, A(lan) Ross
McWhirter, Norris Dewar
Melcher, Frederic Gershon
Merriam, Charles
Mifflin, George Harrison
Miles, Tichi Wilkerson
Motley, Arthur Harrison
Muir, Malcolm
Munsey, Frank Andrew
Murdoch, Rupert (Keith Rupert)
Nast, Conde
Neuharth, Allen Harold
Newbery, John
Newhouse, Donald E
O'Neil, James F(rancis)
Patterson, Alicia
Patterson, Eleanor Medill
Patterson, Joseph Medill
Pearson, Cyril Arthur, Sir
Pickering, William
Polk, Ralph Lane
Pope, Generoso
Praeger, Frederick A
Presser, Theodore
Pulitzer, "Peter" Herbert, Jr.
Pulitzer, Joseph
Pulitzer, Joseph, II
Pulitzer, Ralph
Ricordi, Giovanni
Rinehart, Frederick Roberts
Rinehart, Stanley Marshall, Jr.
Robinson, M(aurice) R(ichard)
Rodale, Jerome Irving
Rusher, William Allen
Saffir, Leonard

Scherman, Harry
Scherr, Max
Schiff, Dorothy
Schirmer, Gustave
Schocken, Theodore
Schuster, Max Lincoln
Scribner, Charles
Scribner, Charles, Jr.
Sheed, Frank (Francis Joseph)
Shimkin, Leon
Shirley, Ralph
Silverman, Sime
Simon, Richard Leo
Sonzogno, Edoardo
Springer, Axel Caesar
Stauffer, Charles Albert
Stewart, Andrew
Stickley, Gustav
Stone, Louis
Straus, Roger W(illiams), Jr.
Stuart, Lyle
Sweet, John Howard
Taishoff, Sol Joseph
Targ, William
Thomas, Isaiah
Ullstein, Hermann
Unwin, Stanley, Sir
Updike, Daniel Berkeley
Van Nostrand, David
Veronis, John James
Viguerie, Richard A(rt)
VonTilzer, Harry
Wagnalls, Adam Willis
Wallace, DeWitt
Wallace, Lila Bell Acheson
Wenner, Jann
White, William Lindsay
Whitney, John Hay
Wiley, William Bradford
Witmark, Isidore
Wolff, Helen
Woolf, Leonard Sidney
Zenger, John Peter
Zevin, B(enjamin) D(avid)
Ziff, William B

PUPPETEER

Baird, Bil (William Britton)
Baird, Cora Eisenberg
Dupuy, Diane
Henson, Jim (James Maury)
Krofft, Marty
Krofft, Sid
Oz, Frank
Sarg, Tony (Anthony Frederick)
Tillstrom, Burr

QUEEN

Anne
Artemisia

Beatrix
Christina
Cleopatra VII
Elizabeth I
Elizabeth II
Grey, Jane, Lady
Ingrid
Juliana
Liliuokalani, Lydia Kamekeha
Margrethe II
Marguerite d'Angouleme
Marie Alexandra Victoria
Mary I
Mary, Queen of Scots
Nefertiti
Sheba
Vashti
Victoria
Wilhelmina

QUINTUPLET

Dionne, Annette
Dionne, Cecile
Dionne, Emilie
Dionne, Marie
Dionne, Yvonne

QUINTUPLETS

Dionne Sisters
Kienast Family

RABBI

Brasch, Rudolph
Eilberg, Amy
Einhorn, David
Gamaliel the Elder
Ha-Levi, Judah
Hertzberg, Arthur
Heschel, Abraham Joshua
Kahane, Meir David
Kaplan, Mordecai
Korff, Baruch
Kushner, Harold Samuel
Maimonides, Moses
Pool, David de Sola
Priesand, Sally Jane
Schindler, Alexander (Monroe)
Silver, Abba Hillel

RADIO ACTOR

Cantor, Charles

RADIO COMMENTATOR

Banghart, Kenneth
Carter, Boake
Coughlin, Father (Charles Edward)
Davis, Elmer Holmes

Dreier, Alex
Eliot, George Fielding
Fidler, Jimmy (James M)
Hall, Josef Washington
Heatter, Gabriel
Kiernan, Walter
McBride, Mary Margaret
Sinclair, Gordon
Thomas, Lowell Jackson
Young, Marian

RADIO ENTERTAINER

McGee, Molly
Pearl, Jack

RADIO EXECUTIVE

Cott, Ted
Kintner, Robert Edmonds
Paley, William Samuel
Sarnoff, David
Sheehan, William Edward, Jr.

RADIO PERFORMER

Ace, Goodman
Ameche, Don
Ameche, Jim
Anthony, John J(ason)
Barrett, John L
Berle, Milton
Big Bopper, The
Block, Martin
Brokenshire, Norman
Cross, Milton John
Drake, Galen
Edwards, Douglas
Elliot, Win (Irwin)
Fadiman, Clifton Paul
Fennelly, Parker
Fenneman, George
Fitzgerald, Ed(ward)
Fitzgerald, Pegeen
Freed, Alan
Gambling, John A
Gambling, John Bradley
Gray, Barry
King, Larry
Lauck, Chester H
McCarthy, J(oseph) P(riestley)
McGee, Fibber
McNeill, Don(ald Thomas)
Nebel, "Long" Joh
Piscopo, Joe (Joseph Charles)
Plomley, Roy
Rayburn, Gene
Reber, Grote
Simms, Ginny (Virginia E)
Torin, Sid
Wilson, Don(ald Harlow)
Wolfman Jack

RADIO PERFORMERS

Tex and Jinx

RAILROAD EXECUTIVE

Budd, Ralph
Crocker, Charles
Durant, Thomas Clark
Gadsen, James
Hill, James Jerome
Huntington, Collis Potter
Huntington, Henry Edwards
Keith, Minor Cooper
Moore, William H
Newberry, John Stoughton
Scott, Thomas
Stanford, Leland (Amasa Leland)
Van Horne, William Cornelius, Sir
Vanderbilt, William Henry
Webb, William Seward
Williard, Daniel

RAILWAY EXECUTIVE

Reed, John Shedd

RANCHER

Abdnor, James S
Adams, Andy
Chisum, John Simpson
Goodnight, Charles
Kilbracken, John Raymond Godley
King, Richard
Kleberg, Robert Justus, Jr.
Maverick, Samuel Augustus

RAPE VICTIM

Little, Joan

REAL ESTATE EXECUTIVE

Davis, Arthur Vining
Day, Joseph Paul
Rebozo, "Bebe" Charles Gregory
Rouse, James Wilson
Rubloff, Arthur
Wirtz, Arthur M
Zeckendorf, William

REALTOR

Woods, Donald

REBEL

Childers, (Robert) Erskine

RECORD EXECUTIVE

Gordy, Berry, Jr.
Moss, Jerry (Jerome Sheldon)
Phillips, Sam
Satherly, Arthur Edward
Stein, Jules Caesar

REFORM LEADER

DuBois, W(illiam) E(dward) B(urghardt)

REFORMER

Adler, Felix
Ames, Jessie Daniel
Anthony, Susan Brownell
Barrow, Ruth Nita, Dame
Bates, Mary Elizabeth
Beers, Clifford Whittingham
Bergh, Henry
Bethune, Mary McLeod
Boole, Ella Alexander
Brown, Judie
Brown, William Wells
Caldicott, Helen Broinowski
Calvin, John
Carlile, Richard
Collins, Marva Deloise Nettles
Comstock, Anthony
Corrigan, Mairead
Coxey, Jacob Sechler
Cremer, William Randal, Sir
Davis, Rennie
Dix, Dorothea Lynde
Ely, Richard Theodore
Farnham, Eliza Wood Burhans
Forten, James
Fry, Elizabeth Gurney
George, Henry, Sr.
Graham, Sylvester W
Groote, Gerhard
Hamilton, Alice
Holmes, John Haynes
Hughes, Thomas
Huntington, Henry S, Jr.
Jarvis, Anna
Klarsfeld, Beate
Knox, John
Lightner, Candy
Livermore, Mary Ashton Rice
Loeb, Sophia Irene Simon
Miller, Elizabeth Smith
Montessori, Maria
Nightingale, Florence
Ovington, Mary White
Packard, Elizabeth Parsons Ware
Patrick, Ted
Senesh, Hannah
Silhouette, Etienne de
Solomon, Hannah Greenebaum
Stanton, Henry Brewster

Steffens, Lincoln
Taylor, Lucy Hobbs
Wauneka, Annie Dodge
Wildmon, Donald Ellis
Wiley, Harvey Washington
Wilkes, John
Williams, Betty Smith
Wright, Frances (Fanny)
Zwingli, Huldreich

RELIGIOUS FIGURE

Albertus Magnus, Saint
Angela Merici, Saint
Anthony of Padua, Saint
Apollinaris Sidonius, Gaius Sollius
Augustine, Saint
Benedict, Saint
Bernadette of Lourdes
Bernard of Cluny
Bernardine of Siena, Saint
Blaise, Saint
Bonaventure, Saint
Boniface, Saint
Brendan of Clonfert, Saint
Brigid of Kildare
Cabrini, Saint Frances Xavier
Carpini, Giovanni de Piano
Casimir, Saint
Catherine of Alexandria, Saint
Catherine of Genoa, Saint
Cecelia, Saint
Christopher, Saint
Clare, Saint
Columban, Saint
Cyril of Alexandria, Saint
Damian, Saint
David, Saint
Dominic, Saint
Elizabeth of Hungary, Saint
Galgani, Gemma
Genevieve, Saint
George, Saint
Gertrude the Great, Saint
Hildegard of Bingen, Saint
Hubert
Jerome, Saint
Kolbe, Maximilian
Mary, the Virgin Mother
Nanak
Origen Adamantius
Patrick, Saint
Pio da Pietrelcina, Father (Francisco Forglone)
Rasputin, Grigori Efimovich
Rita of Cascia, Saint
Tekakwitha, Kateri
Therese of Lisieux
Torquemada, Tomas de
Wolsey, Thomas, Cardinal

RELIGIOUS LEADER

A'Becket, Thomas
Aaron
Abbott, Lyman
Abdu'l-Baha
Abu Bakr
Adler, Cyrus
Aga Khan III
Aga Khan IV
Ahmad, Mirza Ghulam Hazat
Alexander VI
Ali
Allen, Richard
Allred, Rulon Clark
Ambrose, Saint
Anselm, Saint
Anthony, Saint
Asbury, Francis
Athenagoras I
Atkinson, William Walker
Augustine of Canterbury, Saint
Ba'al Shem Tov, Israel
Baha'u'llah
Basil (the Great), Saint
Benedictos I
Benelli, Giovanni, Cardinal
Benson, Ezra Taft
Bernard of Clairvaux, Saint
Bernardin, Joseph Louis, Cardinal
Blavatsky, Helena Petrovna
Boehme, Jakob
Booth, William
Borromeo, Charles, Saint
Brooks, Phillips
Browning, Edmond Lee
Buchman, Frank Nathan Daniel
Buddha
Bushnell, Horace
Carroll, John
Catherine of Sienna
Clement VII
Cody, John Patrick
Coggan, Frederick Donald
Comstock, Elizabeth L
Cooke, Terence James
Cotton, John
Cranmer, Thomas
Crowther, Samuel Adjai
Cummins, George David
Cushing, Richard James, Cardinal
Dalai Lama, the 14th Incarnate
Dearden, John Francis, Cardinal
Dharmapala, Anagarika
Divine, Father Major Jealous
Drexel, Mary Katherine
Eddy, Mary Baker Morse
Fillmore, Myrtle Page
Fleury, Andre Hercule de
Fox, George
Francis of Assisi, Saint
Frings, Joseph Richard

Gandhi, Mahatma
Gibbons, James, Cardinal
Glemp, Jozef, Cardinal
Goldstein, Israel
Gorton, Samuel
Greeley, Dana McLean
Gregory the Great
Gregory XIII, Pope
Guardini, Romano
Gumbleton, Thomas
Hayes, Patrick J
Heck, Barbara Ruckle
Hicks, Elias
Hines, John Elbridge
Hopkins, John Henry
Hubbard, L(afayette) Ron(ald)
Huddleston, (Ernest Urban) Trevor
Hus, Jan
Hutchinson, Anne
Hutton, Addison
Iakovos, Archbishop
Ignatius of Loyola, Saint
Inge, William Ralph
Jabotinsky, Vladimir Evgenevich
Jackson, Jesse Louis
Jesus Christ
John Paul I, Pope
John Paul II, Pope
John XXIII, Pope
Johnson, Hewlett
Jones, Bob
Jones, Reverend Jim (James)
Julius II, Pope
Julius III, Pope
Khomeini, Ayatollah Ruhollah
Kimball, Spencer Woolley
Knorr, Nathan Homer
Knox, John
Knox, Ronald Arbuthnott
Kolvenback, Peter-Hans
Krol, John, Cardinal
Lamy, Jean Baptist
Landa, Diego de
Langton, Stephen
Latimer, Hugh
Laud, William
Lee, Ann
Lefebvre, Marcel Francois
Liebman, Joshua Loth
Lonergan, Bernard J F
Luther, Martin
MacNutt, Francis, Father
Maharaj Ji
Mahavira
Mahdi, Mohammed Ahmed
Mahesh Yogi, Maharishi
Mahoney, James P.
Makarios III, Archbishop
Mani
Manning, Henry Edward
Marcinkus, Paul C

Marshall, Peter
Mazarin, Jules, Cardinal
McIntyre, James Francis
McKay, David O
Medeiros, Humberto, Cardinal
Meher Baba
Melanchthon, Philip Schwarzerd
Mindszenty, Jozsef, Cardinal
Mohammed
Moon, Sung Myung
Mueller, Reuben Herbert
Muhammad, Elijah
Muhammad, Wallace D
Muhlenberg, Heinrich Melchior
Murray, John
Nestorius
Nicholas of Cusa
Nicholas, Saint
O'Connor, John Joseph, Cardinal
Omar I
Ottaviani, Alfredo, Cardinal
Oxnam, G(arfield) Bromley
Panchen Lama X
Parker, Theodore
Paul VI, Pope
Piccard, Jeannette Ridlon
Pike, James Albert
Pius XII, Pope
Poling, Daniel A
Rajneesh, Bhagwan Shree
Ramakrishna, Sri
Ramsey, Arthur Michael
Rapp, George
Ratzinger, Joseph, Cardinal
Rausch, James Stevens
Romero y Galdamez, Oscar Arnulfo
Rosen, Moishe
Runcie, Robert Alexander K
Russell, Charles Taze
Savonarola, Girolamo
Seabury, Samuel
Seper, Franjo
Seton, Elizabeth Ann Bayley, Saint
Sharietmadari, Ayatollah Seyed
Sheen, Fulton John, Bishop
Sheil, Bernard James, Archbishop
Shipler, Guy Emery
Silver, Eliezer
Smith, Joseph
Smith, Joseph Fielding
Sockman, Ralph W
Spellman, Francis Joseph
Spottswood, Stephen Gill
Stepinac, Alojzije, Cardinal
Szoka, Edmund Casimir
Szold, Henrietta
Taft, Charles Phelps
Taylor, Jeremy
Tobias, Channing Heggie
Traglia, Luigi, Cardinal
Trifa, Valerian

Turner, Henry McNeal
Tutu, Desmond Mpilo
Urban II, Pope
Ussher, James
Vincent de Paul, Saint
Visser T Hooft, Willem Adolf
Walsh, James Edward
Warham, William
Weizmann, Chaim
Welch, Herbert
Wesley, John
White, Ellen Gould Harmon
Whitefield, George
Wierwille, Victor Paul
Wildmon, Donald Ellis
Wise, Isaac Mayer
Wise, Stephen Samuel
Wiseman, Nicholas Patrick Stephen
Witherspoon, John
Woolman, John
Wovoka
Wright, John Joseph
Wyszynski, Stefan
Young, Brigham
Zoroaster

RESTAURATEUR

Aoki, Hiroaki
Bergeron, Victor J
Bocuse, Paul
Bricktop
Brock, Alice May
Chen, Joyce Liao
Church, George W
Delmonico, Lorenzo
Evans, Bob (Robert L)
Handwerker, Nathan
Harvey, Frederick Henry
Johnson, Howard Brennan
Johnson, Howard Deering
Kroc, Ray(mond) Albert
Marriott, John Willard
Marriott, John Willard, Jr.
McDonald, Maurice James
McDonald, Richard
Moore, "Dinty" James H
Murphy, Patricia
Rempp, Adolph
Rice-Davies, Mandy
Ritz, Cesar
Romanoff, Mike
Sanders, "Colonel" Harland David
Sardi, Vincent, Jr.
Sardi, Vincent, Sr.
Sherry, Louis
Shor, "Toots" Bernard
Stouffer, Vernon B
Toffenetti, Dario Louis

RETAILER

Avery, Sewell
Bean, L(eon) L(eonwood)
Bloomingdale, Samuel
Bryant, Lane
Donahue, Woolworth
Gimbel, Adam
Gimbel, Bernard Feustman
Gimbel, Richard
Macy, R(owland) H(ussey)
Magnin, Grover Arnold
Marcus, Stanley
Marks, Simon
Reed, Austin Leonard
Wanamaker, John Rodman

REVOLUTIONARIES

Catonsville Nine
Irish Hunger Strikers
S(ymbionese) L(iberation) A(rmy)

REVOLUTIONARY

Adams, Samuel
Atwood, Angela
Baader, Andreas
Babeuf, Francois Noel
Bar Kokhba, Simon
Ben Bella, Ahmed
Bhave, Acharya Vinoba
Blanqui, Louis Auguste
Bolivar, Simon
Boudin, Kathy (Katherine)
Carnot, Hippolyte
Carnot, Lazare Nicolas
Christian, Fletcher
Cinque, Joseph
Cipriani, Amilcare
Collins, Michael
Condorcet, Marie-Jean-Antoine
Corday d'Armount, (Marie Anne) Charlotte
Danton, Georges Jacques
Davis, Angela Yvonne
Davitt, Michael
Dawes, William
DeFreeze, Donald David
Desmoulins, Camille
Devine, Michael
Doherty, Kieran
Emmet, Robert
Fouche, Joseph
Glendower, Owen
Glover, John
Guevara, Che Ernesto
Hale, Nathan
Hall, Camilla Christine
Hampton, Fred
Harris, Emily Schwartz
Harris, William
Henry, Patrick

Hereward the Wake
Hidalgo y Costilla, Miguel
Ho Chi Minh
Hughes, Francis
Hurson, Martin
Ibarruri, Dolores
Kirov, Sergei Mironovich
Kleber, Jean Baptiste
Litvinov, Maxim
Ludd, Ned
Lynch, Kevin
MacSwiney, Terence
Madero, Francisco Indalecio
Markievicz, Constance Georgine, Countess
Mazzini, Giuseppe
McCreesh, Raymond
McDonnell, Joe (Joseph)
McIlwee, Thomas
Meinhof, Ulrike Marie
Mirabeau, Honore Gabriel Riquetti
O'Hara, Patrick
Perry, Nancy Ling
Primo de Rivera, Jose A
Riel, Louis David
Robespierre, Maximilien Francois de
Rudd, Mark
San Martin, Jose de
Sanchez Manduley, Celia
Sands, Bobby (Robert Gerard)
Santander, Francisco de Paula
Soltysik, Patricia Michelle
Sucre, Antonio J de
Tone, Theobald Wolfe
Tonge, Israel
Tyler, Wat
Villa, "Pancho" Francisco
Wolfe, William Lawton
Zapata, Emiliano

ROCK MUSICIAN

Clapton, Eric

RULER

Abdullah Ibn Hussein
Achab
Alaric I
Albert I
Alexander I
Alexander II
Alexander III
Alexander the Great
Alexius Comnenus
Alfonso XIII
Alfred the Great
Antoninus Pius
Asoka the Great
Atahualpa
Attila
Augustus
Augustus II

Aurangzeb
Baudouin, Albert Charles
Bhumibol, Adulyadej
Birendra Bir Bikram, Shah Dev
Boadicea
Bonaparte, Jerome
Bonaparte, Joseph
Brian Boru
Charles I
Charles II
Charles II
Charles Martel
Charles V
Charles VII
Charles XII
Charlotte Aldegonde E M Wilhelmine
Croesus
Dalai Lama, the 14th Incarnate
Darius I
Demetrius I
Dionysius the Elder
Faisal (Ibn Abdul-Aziz al Saud)
Franz Josef II
Franz Joseph I
Godfrey of Bouillon
Haakon VII
Henry I
Henry II
Henry III
Henry IV
Henry V
Henry VI
Henry VII
Henry VIII
Herod Antipas
Herod the Great
Hitotsubashi
Hulagu Khan
Idris I
Isabella I
Isabella II
Ivan III
Ivan IV
James I
James I
James II
James II
James III
James IV
James V
Jean, Grand Duke of Luxembourg
John III, Sobieski
Joseph I
Juan Carlos I
Justinian I (Flavius Anicius Justinianus)
Khalid Ibn Abdul Aziz Al-Saud
Kropotkin, Peter Alekseyevich, Prince
Macbeth
Mahendra, Bir Bikram Shah Dev
Medici, Cosimo de
Medici, Francesco de

Medici, Lorenzo de
Mohammed Zahir Shah
Namgyal, Palden Thondup
Nebuchadnezzar II
Pahlevi, Mohammed Riza
Pahlevi, Riza
Pepin III
Rainier III, Prince
Rameses II
Suleiman I
Thani, Shiekh Khalifa Ben Hamad al
Tz'u Hsi
Victor Emmanuel II
Victor Emmanuel III
Vitellius, Aulus
Wilhelm II
Yoshihito

RUNNER

Benoit, Joan
Dixon, Rod
Fixx, James Fuller
Fonyo, Steve (Stephen, Jr.)
Fox, Terry (Terrance Stanley)
Gareau, Jacqueline
Pizzolato, Orlando
Rodgers, Bill (William Henry)
Ruiz, Rosie
Salazar, Alberto
Scott, Steve
Smith, Geoff
Snell, Peter George
Switzer, Katherine Virginia
Virgin, Craig
Waitz, Grete

SATIRIST

Freberg, Stan
Horace
Juvenal (Decimus Junius Juvenalis)
Mencken, H(enry) L(ouis)
Persius
Rabelais, Francois
Swift, Jonathan
Waugh, Evelyn Arthur St. John

SCHOLAR

Agrippa, Heinrich Cornelius
Alcuin
Bede the Venerable
Ben-Yehuda, Eliezer
Biddle, Nicholas
Bodley, Thomas, Sir
Bonaparte, Louis Lucien
Caro, Joseph
Casaubon, Isaac
Chukovsky, Korney Ivanovich
Coghill, Nevill Henry Kendall Aylmer
Crichton, James

Daiches, David
Elijah Ben Solomon
Erasmus, Desiderius
Eratosthenes
Estienne, Henri
Euphorion
Froben, Johann
Gamaliel the Elder
Garrod, Hethcote William
Genung, John Franklin
Goldmann, Nahum
Grotius, Hugo
Haden, Pat(rick Capper)
Hillel
Housman, A(lfred) E(dward)
James, Montague Rhodes
Lee, Sidney, Sir
Lewis, C(live) S(taples)
Lewis, Wilmarth Sheldon
Lowes, John Livingston
Mandelstam, Nadezhda Yakovlevna
Manutius, Aldus
Manuzio, Aldo
McManaway, James
Moore, Clement Clarke
Newell, Edward Theodore
Nicot, Jean
Pliny the Elder
Pound, Louise
Praz, Mario
Rashi
Rossetti, Gabriele Pasquale Giuseppe
Rowse, Alfred Leslie
Scaliger, Joseph Justus
Sequoya
Trench, Richard Chenevix
Wilhelm, Hellmut

SCIENTIST

Abbot, Charles Greeley
Agassiz, Elizabeth Cabot Cary
Agricola, Georgius
Alberti, Leon Battista
Ampere, Andre Marie
Anderson, Carl David
Ardrey, Robert
Babcock, Stephen Moulton
Bacon, Roger
Baird, Irwin Lewis
Baird, Spencer Fullerton
Beard, George Miller
Bekhterev, Vladimir Mikhailovich
Bennett, Hugh Hammond
Bichat, Marie Francois Xavier
Bishop, Hazel
Blackett, Patrick Maynard Stuart
Bonifacio, Jose
Boolootian, Richard Andrew
Bordet, Jules Jean Baptiste Vincent
Boyle, Robert
Braestrup, Carl Bjorn

Brewster, David, Sir
Bridgman, Percy Williams
Brunler, Oscar
Burnet, MacFarlane (Frank MacFarlane)
Cabot, Richard C
Cayley, George, Sir
Chadwick, James, Sir
Clarke, Arthur C(harles)
Claude, Albert
Cobb, Stanley
Cobb, Vicki
Cockcroft, John Douglas, Sir
Compton, Arthur Holly
Comstock, John Henry
Condon, Edward
Coons, Albert Hewett
Cottrell, Alan Howard
Cowdry, Edmund Vincent
Cutler, Manasseh
Dale, Henry Hallett
Dalton, John
Darling, Frank Fraser, Sir
Dausset, Jean (Baptiste Gabriel Joachim)
Davy, Humphrey, Sir
Delbruck, Max
Douglass, Andrew Ellicott
Drew, Charles Richard
Dubos, Rene Jules
Dumas, Jean Baptiste Andre
Eads, James Buchanan
Eccles, John Carew, Sir
Eigenmann, Rosa Smith
Eustachio, Bartolomeo
Ewing, William Maurice
Fabre, Jean Henri
Faraday, Michael
Ferraris, Galileo
Florey, Howard Walter
Francis, Thomas, Jr.
Franklin, Benjamin
Fremont-Smith, Frank
Gajdusek, D(aniel) Carleton
Galton, Francis, Sir
Garriott, Owen
Gerasimov, Innokentii Petrovich
Gibbs, Josiah Willard
Gilbert, William
Grew, Nehemiah
Haldane, J(ohn) B(urdon) S(anderson)
Hall, Charles Martin
Harger, Rolla
Hashimoto, Ken
Hench, Philip Showalter
Hess, Victor Francis
Hewish, Antony
Hinshelwood, Cyril, Sir
Hooke, Robert
Hounsfield, Godfrey Newbold
Humboldt, Alexander, Freiherr von
Hunter, William
Huxley, Andrew Fielding

Jackson, Charles Thomas
Jackson, Chevalier
Jacobson, Leon Orris
Jenner, William, Sir
Kaplan, Henry
Kendall, John Walker
Kinsey, Alfred Charles
Koch, Robert
Landau, Lev Davidovich
Langmuir, Irving
Lanza, Anthony Joseph
Lawrence, Ernest Orlando
Leiper, Robert Thomson
Leonardo da Vinci
Ley, Willy
Lodge, Oliver Joseph, Sir
Loewi, Otto
Logan, Daniel
Lomonosov, Mikhail
Long, Crawford Williamson
Low, George M(ichael)
Lumiere, Auguste Marie Louis
Lumiere, Louis Jean
Mayer, Jean
McBurney, Charles
McLean, John Milton
Menninger, William C
Michelson, Albert Abraham
Mikoyan, Artem I
Montagnier, Luc
Morgagni, Giovanni Battista
Morgan, Thomas H
Muller, Hermann Joseph
Muller, Johannes Peter
Nicholas of Cusa
Niepce, Joseph Nicephore
Noyce, Robert Norton
Oberlith, Hermann Jules
Piccard, Jean Felix
Pincus, Gregory
Rabi, Isidor Isaac
Ramsay, William, Sir
Remsen, Ira
Ricketts, Howard T
Rivers, Thomas Milton
Roentgen, Wilhelm Konrad
Ross, Ronald, Sir
Rous, Peyton
Roux, Wilhelm
Salk, Jonas Edward
Saunders, Charles E
Schiaparelli, Giovanni
Schick, Bela
Secchi, Pietro Angelo
Segre, Emilio
Selye, "Hans" Hugo Bruno
Shcharansky, Anatoly Borisovich
Sims, James Marion
Sisakyan, Norayr M
Sloane, Dennis
Slotnick, Daniel Leonid

Smithson, James
Snell, George Davis
Snow, C(harles) P(ercy), Sir
Solomon, Neil
Soustelle, Jacques
Spallanzani, Lazzaro
Stopes, Marie Charlotte Carmichael
Sutherland, Earl Wilbur, Jr.
Swedenborg, Emanuel
Sydenham, Thomas
Szilard, Leo
Theiler, Max
Thomas, Sidney Gilchrist
Thomson, Elihu
Tizard, Henry Thomas, Sir
Torricelli, Evangelista
Tournefort, Joseph Pitton de
Tsiolkovsky, Konstantin Eduardovich
Van Depoele, Charles Joseph
Vane, John Robert, Sir
Vesalius, Andreas
VonBraun, Wernher
Waksman, Selman Abraham
Wallace, Alfred Russell
Wasserburg, Gerald Joseph
Wasson, R(obert) Gordon
Watson-Watt, Robert Alexander, Sir
Wheatstone, Charles, Sir
Wheeler, Elmer P

SCREENWRITER

Allen, Jay Presson
Almond, Paul
Ambler, Eric
Ambrose, David Edwin
Anderson, Robert Woodruff
Anhalt, Edward
Audiard, Michel
Behrman, S(amuel) N(athaniel)
Bessie, Alvah
Biberman, Herbert
Bloch, Robert Albert
Brackett, Charles
Bridges, James
Briley, John Richard
Brooks, James L
Brooks, Richard
Cash, Jim
Caspary, Vera
Cooper, Lester Irving
Curtis, Jackie
Dahl, Roald
Dalrymple, Ian (Murray)
Dane, Clemence, pseud.
Deutsch, Helen
Diamond, I(sidore) A L
Eastman, Carol
Epps, Jack, Jr.
Epstein, Philip G
Fellini, Federico
Fields, Joseph

Foote, Horton (Albert Horton, Jr.)
Forbes, Bryan
Foreman, Carl
Fuller, Samuel
Goldman, William
Green, Paul Eliot
Hayes, John Michael
Hunter, Ian
Innaurato, Albert
Jennings, Talbot
Johnson, Nunnally
Kasdan, Lawrence Edward
Kautner, Helmut
Kenney, Douglas C
Kurnitz, Harry
Langley, Noel
Lardner, Ring Wilmer, Jr.
Lasky, Jesse Louis, Jr.
Luedtke, Kurt (Mamre)
Mahin, John Lee
Malick, Terence (Terry)
Maltz, Albert
Marion, Frances
Mathison, Melissa
Mercer, David
Perry, Eleanor Bayer
Pierson, Frank R(omer)
Poe, James
Raphael, Frederic Michael
Raphaelson, Samson
Renoir, Jean
Romero, George A
Salt, Waldo
Sargent, Alvin
Schary, Dore
Schlondorff, Volker
Scott, Adrian
Seaton, George
Sheekman, Arthur
Silliphant, Stirling Dale
Stern, Stewart
Sturges, Preston
Sullivan, C(harles) Gardner
Swerling, Jo
Syberberg, Hans Jurgen
Thomas, Dave
Tidyman, Ernest
Trumbo, Dalton
Varda, Agnes
Walter, Eugene
Ward, David S
Weber, Lois
Weller, Michael
Wells, George
Wexler, Norman
Young, Burt

SCULPTOR

Adams, Herbert Samuel
Agostini, Peter
Agostino di Duccio

Aitken, Robert
Albright, Malvin Marr
Andre, Carl
Armitage, Kenneth
Arp, Hans
Ball, Thomas
Barlach, Ernst Heinrich
Barnard, George Grey
Barthe, Richmond
Bartholdi, Auguste (Frederic Auguste)
Bartlett, Paul Wayland
Baskin, Leonard
Bernini, Giovanni Lorenzo
Bitter, Karl Theodore Francis
Boehm, Edward M
Bolotowsky, Ilya
Borglum, Gutzon
Borglum, James Lincoln Delamothe
Borglum, Solon Hannibal
Brancusi, Constantin
Brown, Henry Kirke
Brunelleschi, Filippo
Caro, Anthony
Carrier-Belleuse, Albert Ernest
Cellini, Benvenuto
Chares
Charoux, Siegfried
Clevenger, Shobal Vail
Crawford, Thomas
Dallin, Cyrus
Davidson, Jo
DeCreeft, Jose
DellaRobbia, Andrea
DellaRobbia, Giovanni
DellaRobbia, Luca
DeRivera, Jose
DiSuvero, Mark
Epstein, Jacob, Sir
Ezekiel, Moses Jacob
Farnham, Sally James
Flannagan, John Bernard
Fraser, James Earle
French, Daniel Chester
Gabo, Naum Pevsner
Giacometti, Alberto
Gibbons, Grinling
Gibran, Kahlil George
Gibson, John
Gill, Eric
Giorgio. Francesco di
Girardon, Francois
Greenough, Horatio
Hanson, Duane Elwood
Hepworth, Barbara
Hesse, Eva
Hoffman, Malvina
Holbein, Hans, the Elder
Hosmer, Harriet Goodhue
Houdon, Jean Antoine
Jackson, John Adams
Jaegers, Albert

Jones, Thomas Hudson
Kalish, Max
Kitson, Henry Hudson
Kitson, Theo Alice Ruggles
Lachaise, Gaston
Laessle, Albert
Lehmbruck, Wilhelm
Lipchitz, Jacques
Lippold, Richard
Lukeman, Henry A
Lysippus
MacMonnies, Fred W
Manship, Paul
Marini, Marino
Marisol (Escobar)
McCartan, Edward
Mestrovic, Ivan
Milles, Carl
Moore, Henry
Myron
Noguchi, Isamu
Oldenburg, Claes Thure
Palmer, Erastus Dow
Papashvily, George
Phidias
Pisano, Andrea
Pisano, Nicola
Polycletus the Elder
Powers, Hiram
Pratt, Bela Lyon
Praxiteles
Quercia, Jacopo della
Quinn, Edmond T
Reid Dick, William, Sir
Remington, Frederic
Rickey, George Warren
Rimmer, William
Rinehart, William H
Rodin, Auguste (Francois Auguste Rene)
Rogers, John
Rogers, Randolph
Roszak, Theodore
Rush, William
Saint Gaudens, Augustus
Savage, Augusta Christine
Savage, Eugene Francis
Schadow, (Johann) Gottfried
Scopas
Segal, George
Shrady, Henry M
Simmons, Franklin
Slobodkin, Louis
Sluter, Claus
Smith, David
Smith, Tony
Story, William Wetmore
Stoss, Veit
Taft, Lorado
Thorvaldsen, Albert Bertel
Tinguely, Jean
Ward, J(ohn) Q(uincy) A(dams)

Weinman, Adolph A
Westermann, H(orace) C(lifford)
Whitney, Gertrude Vanderbilt
Yamagughi, Paulo
Young, Mahonri M
Ziolkowski, Korczak
Zorach, William

SECRETARY

Arnstein, Bobbie
Gallagher, Mary Barelli
Howe, Louis McHenry
Kopechne, Mary Jo
Leclerc, Marie-Andree
Lehand, "Missy" Marguerite Alice
Marsh, Edward, Sir
Marshack, Megan
Pang, May
Ray, Elizabeth
Rutherfurd, Lucy Page Mercer
Summersby, Kay
Toklas, Alice B(abette)
Woods, Rose Mary

SENATOR

Bentsen, Lloyd Millard, Jr.
Borah, William E
Boren, David Lyle
Boschwitz, Rudy
Bradley, Bill (William Warren)
Bridges, Styles
Brock, Bill (William Emerson)
Byrd, Harry Flood, Jr.
Byrd, Robert Carlyle
Capehart, Homer Earl
Chafee, John Hubbard
Chiles, Lawton Mainor, Jr.
Choate, Rufus
Clark, Joseph Sill
Cook, Marlow Webster
Cotton, Norris
Cranston, Alan MacGregor
Depew, Chauncey M
Douglas, Paul Howard
Flanders, Ralph Edward
Ford, Wendell Hampton
Glass, Carter
Goldwater, Barry Morris
Goodell, Charles Ellsworth
Gore, Albert Arnold
Gravel, Mike
Hansen, Clifford Peter
Harris, Fred Roy
Hart, Philip Aloysius
Hartke, Vance
Hruska, Roman Lee
Inouye, Daniel Ken
Javits, Jacob Koppel
Jepsen, Roger William
Kasten, Robert W, Jr.

Kefauver, Estes
Kennedy, Robert Francis
Kerr, Robert Samuel
Knowland, William Fife
Lamar, Lucius Q C
Mathias, Charles McCurdy, Jr.
Matsunaga, Spark Masayuki
Mattingly, Mack Francis
McClellan, John Little
McClure, James A
McMahon, (James O') Brien
Melcher, John
Metcalf, Lee
Metzenbaum, Howard M(orton)
Mitchell, George John
Montoya, Joseph Manuel
Morgan, Robert Burren
Morris, Robert
Mundt, Karl Earl
Murkowski, Frank Hughes
Nunn, Sam(uel Augustus, Jr.)
Nye, Gerald Prentice
Pastore, John Orlando
Percy, Charles Harting
Pressler, Larry
Randolph, Jennings
Reynolds, Robert Rice
Rudman, Warren Bruce
Sarbanes, Paul Spyros
Sasser, Jim (James Ralph)
Simpson, Alan Kooi
Specter, Arlen
Stafford, Robert Theodore
Stevens, Ted (Theodore Fulton)
Symington, (William) Stuart
Symms, Steven Douglas
Talmadge, Herman Eugene
Tower, John Goodwin
Tydings, Millard Evelyn
Wagner, Robert
Wallop, Malcom
Wheeler, Burton Kendall

SHIPPING EXECUTIVE

Cramp, Charles Henry
Cunard, Samuel, Sir
Dollar, Robert
Ferguson, Homer Lenoir
Higgins, Andrew J
Luckenbach, Edgar Frederick, Jr.
Niarchos, Stavros Spyros
Onassis, Aristotle Socrates
Onassis, Christina
Pao, Y(ue) K(ong), Sir

SIAMESE TWINS

Chang and Eng

SINGER

Aadland, Beverly
Ace, Johnny
Acuff, Roy
Adams, Bryan
Adams, Edie
Alberghetti, Anna Maria
Allen, Deborah
Allen, Duane
Allen, Elizabeth
Allen, Peter Woolnough
Allen, Rex E, Sr.
Allman, Duane (Howard Duane)
Allman, Gregg (Gregory Lenoir)
Ames, Ed(mund Dantes)
Ames, Nancy
Andersen, Eric
Andersen, Lale
Anderson, Bill
Anderson, Ian
Anderson, Ivie
Anderson, John
Anderson, Jon
Anderson, Lynn
Anderson, Marian
Andersson, Benny
Andrews, Julie
Andrews, LaVerne
Andrews, Maxine
Andrews, Patti (Patricia)
Anka, Paul
Annabella
Ant, Adam
Anton, Susan
Appice, Carmine
Argent, Rod(ney Terence)
Armatrading, Joan
Arnaz, Desi
Arnaz, Lucie Desiree
Arnold, Eddy
Asher, Peter
Ashford, Nickolas
Astaire, Fred
Auger, Arleen
Austin, Patti
Autry, Gene (Orvon Gene)
Avalon, Frankie
Axton, Hoyt Wayne
Aznavour, Charles
Bachman, Randy
Baez, Joan
Bailey, Mildred
Bailey, Pearl Mae
Bailey, Philip
Baker, "Ginger" Peter
Baker, Bonnie
Baker, Josephine
Baker, Kenny (Kenneth Lawrence)
Balin, Marty
Ballard, Florence
Ballard, Hank

Ballard, Kaye
Ballard, Russ(ell)
Bandy, Moe
Barnes, Billy
Barrett, "Syd" Roger Keith
Barrow, Keith E
Bassey, Shirley
Bayes, Nora
Becaud, Gilbert
Bedelia, Bonnie
Bee, Molly
Belafonte, Harry (Harold George, Jr.)
Bell, "Kool" Robert
Benatar, Pat
Benedict, Dirk
Beneke, Tex
Bennett, Tony
Benson, George
Benson, Renaldo
Benton, Barbie
Benton, Brook
Bergen, Polly
Berger, Al
Bernardi, Hershel
Berry, Chuck (Charles Edward Anderson)
Berry, Jan
Berry, Ken
Bibb, Leon
Big Bopper, The
Bikel, Theodore Meir
Bishop, Stephen
Bittan, Roy
Black, David, Jay
Blades, Ruben
Blakeley, Ronee
Bledsoe, Jules
Bloom, Eric
Bloomfield, Mike (Michael)
Bofill, Angela
Bogert, Tim
Bonds, Gary U S
Bono, "Sonny" Salvatore Phillip
Bonoff, Karla
Bonsall, Joe
Boone, "Pat" Charles Eugene
Boone, Debby (Deborah Ann)
Boswell, Connee
Boswell, Martha
Boswell, Vet (Helvetia)
Bouchard, Joe
Bowen, Billy
Bowie, David
Boy George
Boyd, Bill
Bracken, Eddie (Edward Vincent)
Brady, Pat (Robert Patrick)
Brand, Oscar
Branigan, Laura
Brannigan, Owen
Brassens, Georges
Brewer, Theresa

Brian, Donald
Brice, Fanny
Bricktop
Bridgewater, Dee Dee
Brigati, Eddie
Brock, Tony
Broonzy, Big Bill
Brown, James
Brown, Jim Ed (James Edward)
Brown, Peter
Browne, Jackson
Bruce, Carol
Bryant, Anita
Bryson, Peabo (Robert Peabo)
Buckley, Tim
Budd, Julie
Buffet, Jimmy
Burdon, Eric
Burleigh, Harry Thacker
Burnett, Carol
Burns, George
Burr, Henry
Bush, Kate
Butala, Tony
Cagney, James (James Francis, Jr.)
Cale, J J
Calloway, Cab(ell)
Campbell, Glen Travis
Canova, Judy
Cantor, Eddie
Cantrell, Lana
Capaldi, Jim
Cara, Irene
Carawan, Guy
Cariou, Len (Leonard)
Carlisle, Belinda
Carlisle, Kitty
Carmen, Eric
Carnes, Kim
Carpenter, Karen Ann
Carpenter, Richard Lynn
Carr, Vikki
Carrack, Paul
Carradine, Keith Ian
Carroll, Diahann
Carroll, Jim
Carson, Jeannie
Carson, Mindy
Carter, "Mother" Maybell
Carter, Betty
Carter, Carlene
Carter, June
Carter, Lynda
Carter, Nell
Carter, Wilf
Casady, Jack
Casey, H(arry) W(ayne)
Cash, Johnny
Cash, Roseanne
Cassidy, David Bruce
Cassidy, Jack

Cassidy, Shaun Paul
Cavaliere, Felix
Cetera, Peter
Chapin, Harry Foster
Charles, Ray
Charo
Checker, Chubby
Cher
Chevalier, Maurice Auguste
Chilton, Alex
Christy, June
Churchill, Sarah
Clark, Dave
Clark, Petula
Clark, Roy Linwood
Clarke, Allan
Clemons, Clarence
Cline, Maggie
Cline, Patsy
Clooney, Rosemary
Coates, Edith
Cochran, Eddie
Cocker, "Joe" Robert John
Cohen, Leonard
Cole, Maria
Cole, Nat "King" Nathaniel Adams
Cole, Natalie (Stephanie Natalie Maria)
Cole, Tina
Collins, Dorothy
Collins, Judy (Judith)
Collins, Phil
Colter, Jessie
Columbo, Russ
Como, Perry (Pierino Roland)
Compton, Betty
Conway, Shirl
Cook, Barbara
Cooke, Sam
Coolidge, Rita
Cooper, Alice
Corby, Mike
Cornell, Don
Costello, Elvis
Covington, Warren
Craddock, "Crash" Billy
Cramer, Floyd
Creed, Linda
Criss, Peter
Croce, Jim
Crofts, Dash
Crosby, "Bing" Harry Lillis
Crosby, David
Cross, Christopher
Crothers, "Scatman" Benjamin Sherman
Cummings, Burton
Curtin, Phyllis Smith
D'Angelo, Beverly
Dale, Alan
Dale, Clamma Churita
Dale, Jim
Dalton, Abby

Dalton, Lacy J
Daltrey, Roger
Damone, Vic
Dandridge, Dorothy
Daniels, Billy
Darcel, Denise
Darin, Bobby
Darling, Erik
Darren, James
Davidson, John
Davies, Dave (David)
Davies, Ray(mond Douglas)
Davis, Billy, Jr.
Davis, Clifton
Davis, Janette
Davis, Mac
Davis, Sammy, Jr.
Davis, Skeeter
Davis, Spencer
Day, Dennis
Day, Doris
Dean, Jimmy
Deane, Sandy
Dearie, Blossom
DeBarge, Bunny
DeBarge, El(dra)
DeBarge, James
DeBarge, Mark
DeBarge, Randy
Deckers, Jeanine
Dee, Kiki
Dee, Sandra
Densmore, John
Denver, John
Derringer, Rick
DeShannon, Jackie
Desmond, Johnny
DeVito, Tommy
Dexter, Al
DeYoung, Dennis
Di Mucci, Dion
Diamond, Neil
Dickens, "Little" Jimmy
Dietrich, Marlene
Difford, Chris
Dinning, Max
Doggett, Bill
Dolby, Thomas
Dolenz, Mickey
Domino, "Fats" Antoine
Donovan
Dott, Gerard
Douglas, Helen Mary Gahagan
Douglas, Mike
Downey, Morton
Downey, Rick
Dryden, Spencer
Duncan, Todd
Durante, Jimmy (James Francis)
Dussault, Nancy
Dyer-Bennet, Richard

Dylan, Bob
Easton, Sheena
Eberle, Ray
Eberly, Bob
Eckstine, Billy
Eddy, Nelson
Edwards, Cliff
Edwards, Dennis
Edwards, Joan
Egan, Walter Lindsay
Eggerth, Marta
Elliman, Yvonne
Elliot, Cass
Elliott, Joe
Ely, Joe
Entwistle, John
Erickson, Leif
Essex, David
Etting, Ruth
Everly, Don
Everly, Phil
Fabian
Fagen, Donald
Fain, Sammy
Faithfull, Marianne
Fakir, Abdul
Falana, Lola
Faltskog, Agnetha
Fargo, Donna
Farina, Richard
Fass, Bob
Faulkner, Eric
Faye, Alice
Federici, Daniel Paul
Felder, Don(ald William)
Feliciano, Jose
Fellows, Edith
Fender, Freddy
Fenelon, Fania
Ferry, Bryan
Fisher, Eddie (Edwin Jack)
Fitzgerald, Ella
Flack, Roberta
Flatt, Lester Raymond
Fleetwood, Mick
Fogelberg, Dan(iel Grayling)
Foley, "Red" Clyde Julian
Fontaine, Frank
Ford, "Tennessee Ernie" Ernest J
Ford, Mary
Forrest, Helen
Foster, Susanna
Frampton, Peter
Franchi, Sergio
Francis, Connie
Franklin, Aretha
Franklin, Mel(vin)
Frazier, Dallas June
Frehley, Ace
Frey, Glenn
Frickie, Janie

Friganza, Trixie
Frizzell, "Lefty" William Orville
Froman, Jane
Funicello, Annette
Gabriel, Peter
Gaines, Lee
Garcia, Jerry (Jerome John)
Garfunkel, Art(hur)
Garland, Judy
Garnett, Gale
Garrett, Leif
Gary, John
Gates, David
Gatlin, Larry Wayne
Gaudio, Bob
Gaye, Marvin (Marvin Pentz)
Gayle, Crystal
Gaynor, Gloria
Gaynor, Mitzi
Geldof, Bob
Genevieve
Gentry, Bobbie
Gibb, Andy
Gibb, Barry
Gibb, Maurice
Gibb, Robin
Gibbs, Georgia
Gibbs, Terri
Gibson, Bob
Gilder, Nick
Gilmour, David
Godfrey, Arthur Michael
Gold, Andrew
Golden, William Lee
Goldsboro, Bobby
Gore, Lesley
Gorin, Igor
Gorme, Eydie
Goulet, Robert
Graham, Larry (Lawrence, Jr.)
Grant, Amy
Grant, Gogi
Greco, Buddy (Armando)
Greco, Juliette
Green, Al
Greenbaum, Norman
Greenwood, Lee
Grey, Joel
Grimes, Tammy Lee
Grundy, Hugh
Guilbert, Yvette
Guthrie, Arlo
Guthrie, Woody (Woodrow Wilson)
Hagar, Sammy
Haggard, Merle Ronald
Haines, Connie
Haley, Bill (William John Clifford, Jr.)
Hall, Daryl
Hall, Juanita
Hall, Tom T
Halliday, Johnny

Kiepura, Jan
Kiley, Richard
King, B B (Riley B.)
King, Ben E
King, Carole
King, Evelyn
King, Peggy
King, William
Kirk, Lisa
Kitt, Eartha Mae
Knight, Gladys Maria
Krause, Bernie (Bernard Leo)
Kreutzmann, Bill
Krieger, Robby
Kristofferson, Kris
LaBelle, Patti
Laine, Cleo
Laine, Frankie
Laird, Rick
Lake, Greg(ory)
Lamm, Robert
Lamour, Dorothy
Lane, Abbe
Lane, Lola
Lane, Priscilla
Lane, Rosemary
Langford, Frances
Langley, Jane Pickens
Lanier, Allen
Lansbury, Angela Brigid
Lanson, "Snookycq
LaPread, Ronald
LaRosa, Julius
Larson, Nicolette
Lattisaw, Stacy
Lauder, Harry MacLennan, Sir
Lauper, Cyndi (Cynthia)
Lavin, Linda
Lawrence, Carol
Lawrence, Steve
Lawrence, Vicki
Leadon, Bernie
LeBon, Simon
Ledbetter, Huddie
Lee, Brenda
Lee, Geddy
Lee, Johnny
Lee, Peggy
Lennon, Dianne
Lennon, Janet
Lennon, John Winston
Lennon, Julian (John Charles Julian)
Lennon, Kathy
Lennon, Peggy
Lennox, Annie
Lenya, Lotte
Leonetti, Tommy
Lesh, Phil
Lewis, Huey
Lewis, Jerry Lee
Liebling, Estelle

Lightfoot, Gordon Meredith
Lincoln, Abbey
Little Esther
Little Eva
Little Richard
Lofgren, Nils
Loggins, Kenny (Kenneth Clarke)
Lombardo, Carmen
London, Julie
Longet, Claudine Georgette
Longmuir, Alan
Longmuir, Derek
Lopez, Trini(dad, III)
Lor, Denise
Loring, Gloria Jean
Love, Mike
Lowe, Nick
Luft, Lorna
Lulu
Lyman, Frankie
Lynch, David
Lyngstad-Fredriksson, Annifrid
Lynn, Loretta Webb
Lynott, Phil(ip)
Lyon, "Southside" Johnny
Mabley, "Moms" Jackie
MacDonald, Jeanette
MacKenzie, Gisele
MacRae, Gordon
MacRae, Sheila
Madonna
Makeba, Miriam
Makem, Tommy
Manchester, Melissa Toni
Mandrell, Barbara Ann
Mangrum, Jim Dandy
Manilow, Barry
Manning, Irene
Manzarek, Ray
Marlowe, Marion
Marsden, Gerry
Martin, Dean
Martin, Mary
Martin, Millicent
Martin, Tony
Martino, Al
Marvin, Michelle Triola
Masiello, Alberta
Massey, D Curtis
Massi, Nick
Mathis, Johnny (John Royce)
May, Brian
Mayfield, Curtis
Maynor, Dorothy
McArdle, Andrea
McCabe, Mary O'Connell
McCann, Les
McCartney, Paul (James Paul)
McClary, Thomas
McClinton, Delbert
McCoo, Marilyn

McCracken, Joan
McCurdy, Ed
McDonald, Country Joe
McDonald, Michael
McGovern, Maureen Therese
McKenzie, "Red" William
McKeown, Leslie
McKernan, Ron
McKinley, Ray
McKuen, Rod
McLaughlin, John
McLean, Don
McNair, Barbara
McNichol, Jimmy (James Vincent)
McPhatter, Clyde
McRae, Carmen
McVie, Christine Perfect
Medley, Bill
Meisner, Randy
Melanie
Mellencamp, John Cougar
Mercer, Johnny
Mercer, Mabel
Mercury, Freddie
Merman, Ethel
Messina, Jim
Michael, George
Midler, Bette
Milano, Fred
Miller, Ann
Miller, Roger Dean
Miller, Steve
Mills, Donald
Mills, Harry
Mills, Herbert
Mills, John
Mills, Stephanie
Milsap, Ronnie
Mineo, Sal
Minnelli, Liza
Miranda, Carmen
Mitchell, Chad (William Chad bourne)
Mitchell, Guy
Mitchell, Joni
Mobley, Mary Ann
Money, Eddie
Monroe, Vaughan
Montana, Patsy
Montand, Yves
Montgomery, Melba
Moore, Grace
Moore, Melba
Moreno, Rita
Morgan, Dennis
Morgan, Helen Riggins
Morgan, Jane
Morgan, Jaye P
Morgana, Nina
Morrison, Jim (James Douglas)
Morrison, Van
Morse, Ella Mae

Muldaur, Maria
Munn, Frank
Munsel, Patrice
Murray, Anne
Nabors, Jim (James Thurston)
Nascimento, Milton
Nash, Graham
Nash, Johnny
Naughton, David
Nelson, Harriet
Nelson, Rick (Eric Hilliard)
Nelson, Willie
Nesmith, Mike
Newley, Anthony
Newman, Phyllis
Newman, Randy
Newton, Juice
Newton, Wayne
Newton-John, Olivia
Nicks, "Stevie" Stephanie
Niles, John Jacob
Nolan, Bob
Noone, Peter
Nugent, Ted
Nyro, Laura
O'Connell, Helen
O'Connor, Donald
O'Day, Anita
O'Hara, Mary
O'Shea, Tessie
O'Sullivan, Gilbert
Oates, John
Ocean, Billy
Ochs, Phil(ip David)
Odetta
Orange, Walter
Orbach Jerry
Orbison, Roy
Orlando, Tony
Osbourne, "Ozzie" John
Osbourne, Jeffrey
Osmond, Donny (Donald Clark)
Osmond, Marie (Olive Marive)
Owens, "Buck" Alvis E, Jr.
Page, Patti
Paige, Janis
Pallandt, Nina, Baroness van
Palmer, Peter
Palmer, Robert
Parker, Graham
Parker, Ray, Jr.
Parsons, Gram
Parton, Dolly Rebecca
Patachou
Patti, Carlotta
Paxton, Tom (Thomas R)
Paycheck, Johnny
Payne, Freda
Payton, Lawrence
Pearl, Leslie
Pendergrass, Teddy (Theodore D)

Perry, Steve
Peters, Bernadette
Peters, Brock
Peterson, Paul
Phillips, Esther
Phillips, John
Phillips, Michelle Gillam
Piaf, Edith
Pickett, Wilson
Pierce, Webb
Pike, Gary
Pike, Jim
Place, Mary Kay
Plant, Robert Anthony
Pointer, Anita
Pointer, Bonnie
Pointer, June
Pointer, Ruth
Pop, Iggy
Powell, Jane
Premice, Josephine
Presley, Elvis (Elvis Aaron)
Preston, Billy (William Everett)
Previn, Dory Langdon
Price, Alan
Price, Ray
Price, Steve
Pride, Charley
Prince
Printemps, Yvonne
Provine, Dorothy Michele
Prysock, Arthur
Purim, Flora
Quatro, Suzi
Quinn, Carmel
Rabbitt, Eddie (Edward Thomas)
Rafferty, Gerry
Rainey, "Ma" Gertrude
Raitt, Bonnie
Raitt, John Emmet
Rapp, Danny
Rawls, Lou(is Allen)
Ray, Johnnie (John Alvin)
Raye, Martha
Redding, Otis
Reddy, Helen
Reed, Dean
Reed, Jerry
Reed, Lou
Reed, Susan
Reese, Della
Reeves, Martha
Regan, Phil
Reno, Mike
Reynolds, Debbie (Marie Frances)
Rich, Charlie (Charles Allan)
Richard, Cliff
Richard, Keith
Richie, Lionel
Rider-Kelsey, Corinne
Riley, Jeannie C

Ring, Blanche
Riperton, Minnie
Ritchie, Jean
Ritter, "Tex" Woodward Maurice
Ritter, Blake
Rivera, Chita
Rivers, Johnny
Robbins, Marty
Robeson, Paul Leroy
Robinson, "Smokey" William, Jr.
Robinson, Earl Hawley
Rockwell
Rodgers, Jimmie C
Rodgers, Jimmie F
Roe, Tommy
Roeser, Donald
Rogers, Kenny (Kenneth Ray)
Rogers, Roy
Ronstadt, Linda
Rose, Fred
Rose-Marie
Ross, Diana
Ross, Lanny
Roth, David Lee
Roth, Lillian
Ruffin, Jimmy
Rundgren, Todd
Rush, Tom
Russell, Andy
Russell, Leon
Russell, Lillian
Rutherford, Michael
Rydell, Bobby
Ryder, Mitch
Sablon, Jean Georges
Sade
Sadler, Barry
Sager, Carole Bayer
Sainte-Marie, "Buffy" Beverly
Sanderson, Julia
Sands, Tommy
Sang, Samantha
Sarnoff, Dorothy
Sayer, "Leo" Gerald
Scaggs, "Boz" William Royce
Scarbury, Joey
Schenck, Joe (Joseph T)
Schilling, Peter
Schioetz, Aksel
Schlamme, Martha
Schmidt, Tim(othy B)
Schneider, John
Scholz, Tom
Scialfa, Patty
Seals, Jim (James)
Sebastian, John
Secombe, Harry
Sedaka, Neil
Seeger, Pete(r)
Seger, Bob
Sembello, Michael

Seville, David
Shea, George Beverly
Sheila E
Sheppard, T G
Sherman, Bobby
Sherwood, Roberta
Shore, Dinah
Shorrock, Glenn
Simmons, Gene
Simmons, Pat(rick)
Simms, Ginny (Virginia E)
Simon, Carly
Simon, Joe
Simon, Paul
Simone, Nina
Simpson, Valerie
Sinatra, Frank (Francis Albert)
Sinatra, Frank, Jr. (Francis Albert)
Sinatra, Nancy
Skaggs, Ricky
Sledge, Debbie
Sledge, Joni
Sledge, Kathy
Sledge, Kim
Slick, Grace Wing
Smith, Bessie
Smith, Cathy Evelyn
Smith, Kate (Kathryn Elizabeth)
Smith, Keely
Smith, Patti
Smith, Rex
Smith, Sammi
Smith, Willie
Smothers, Dick (Richard)
Smothers, Tommy (Thomas Bolyn, III)
Snider, Dee (Daniel Dee)
Snow, Don
Snow, Hank
Snow, Phoebe Laub
Sommers, Joanie
South, Joe
Souther, J(ohn) D(avid)
Springfield, Dusty
Springfield, Rick (Richard)
Springsteen, Bruce
Squier, Billy
Squire, Chris
Stafford, Jim
Stafford, Jo
Stanley, Paul
Starr, Kay
Starr, Ringo
Stein, Mark
Sterban, Richard
Stevens, Cat
Stevens, Connie
Stevens, Ray
Stewart, Al
Stewart, Rod(erick David)
Stewart, Wynn
Stills, Stephen

Sting
Stocker, Wally
Stone, Sly
Stookey, (Noel) Paul
Streisand, Barbra Joan
Stritch, Elaine
Stuarti, Enzo
Stubbs, Levi
Styles, Re
Sullivan, Maxine
Sullivan, Tom
Sumac, Yma
Summer, Donna
Suzuki, Pat (Chiyoko)
Sweet, Rachel
Tabbert, William
Taylor, J T (James)
Taylor, James Vernon
Taylor, Livingston
Teena Marie
Tennille, Toni
Terrell, Tammi
Tex, Joe
Thibault, Conrad
Thomas, B(illy) J(oe)
Thompson, Hank
Thompson, Kay
Thor
Thornton, Willie Mae
Tilbrook, Glenn
Tillis, Mel(vin)
Tork, Peter
Torme, Mel(vin Howard)
Torrence, Dean
Tosh, Peter
Tracy, Arthur
Trapp, Maria Augusta von
Trask, Diana
Travers, Mary
Travolta, John
Traynor, John Jay
Troup, Bobby (Robert William)
Tubb, Ernie (Ernest)
Tucker, Sophie
Tucker, Tanya
Tully, Alice
Turner, Ike
Turner, Joe
Turner, Tina
Twitty, Conway
Tyler, Bonnie
Tyler, Steve
Tyson, Ian
Tyson, Sylvia Fricker
Uggams, Leslie
Ullman, Tracey
Ulvaeus, Bjorn
Umeki, Miyoshi
Vale, Jerry
Valens, Richie
Valente, Caterina

Vallee, Rudy (Herbert Prior)
Valli, Frankie
Van Halen, Eddie (Edward)
Van Zant, Ronnie (Ronald)
Van, Bobby
Vance, Kenny
Vandross, Luther
Vanity
Vannelli, Gino
Vaughan, Sarah
Vaughn, Billy
Venuta, Benay
Vereen, Ben
Vicious, Sid
Vinton, Bobby (Stanley Robert)
Vysotsky, Vladimir Semyonovich
Wagner, Jack Peter
Wagoner, Porter
Wain, Bea
Waite, John
Wakely, Jimmy
Walker, "T-Bone" Aaron
Walker, Nancy
Waller, Gordon
Walsh, Joe (Joseph Fidler)
Warfield, William Caesar
Warnes, Jennifer
Warren, Leonard
Warwick, Dionne
Washington, Dinah
Waters, Muddy
Waters, Ethel
Watson, "Doc" Arthel
Watts, Charlie (Charles Robert)
Waybill, Fee
Weir, Bob (Robert Hall)
Wells, Kitty
Wells, Mary
Werrenrath, Reinald
West, Dottie
White, Barry
White, Chris(topher Taylor)
White, Josh(ua Daniel)
Whiting, George
Whiting, Margaret
Wilde, Kim
Williams, "Hank" Hiram
Williams, Andy
Williams, Anson
Williams, Billy
Williams, Deniece
Williams, Hank, Jr.
Williams, Joe
Williams, Milan
Williams, Paul Hamilton
Williams, Tex
Williamson, Robin
Wills, Bob
Wilson, Ann
Wilson, Brian Douglas
Wilson, Carl Dean

Wilson, Dennis
Wilson, Dolores
Wilson, Jackie
Wilson, Nancy
Wilson, Nancy
Wilson, Wesley
Winchester, Jesse (James Ridout)
Winter, Edgar Holand
Winter, Johnny (John Dawson, III)
Winwood, Steve (Stevie)
Withers, Bill
Wolf, Peter
Wonder, Stevie
Wood, Stuart
Wooley, Sheb
Worley, Jo Anne
Wright, Cobina
Wright, Martha
Wright, Syretta
Wrightson, Earl
Wynette, Tammy
Yankovic, "Weird Al" Alfred Matthew
Yarborough, Glenn
Yarrow, Peter
Young, Faron
Young, Paul
Young, Ralph
Zadora, Pia
Zander, Robin
Zappa, Frank (Francis Vincent, Jr.)
Zappa, Moon Unit

SKATER

Button, Dick (Richard Totten)

SKIER

Bogatja, Vinto
Chaffee, Suzy
Cochran, Barbara Ann
Fraser, Gretchen Kunigh
Greene, Nancy Catherine
Johnson, Bill (William D)
Killy, Jean-Claude
Kinmont, Jill
Klammer, Franz
Koch, Bill
Mahre, Phil(lip)
Mahre, Steve(n)
Mittermaier, Rosi
Nelson, Cindy
Proell, Annemarie
Sabich, "Spider" Vladimir
Schranz, Karl
Stenmark, Ingemar
Tokle, Torger
Wenzel, Hanni

SLAVE

Androcles
Cinque, Joseph
Craft, Ellen
Hemings, Sally
Henson, Josiah
Scott, Dred
Spartacus
Toussaint l'Ouverture, Pierre Dominique
Turner, Nat

SOCCER EXECUTIVE

Busby, Matthew, Sir
Ertegun, Ahmet
Toye, Clive Roy

SOCCER PLAYER

Best, George
Brand, Jack
Charlton, Robert
Chinaglia, Giorgio
Cruyff, Johan
Francis, Trevor
Maradona, Diego
Messing, Shep
Pele
Rigby, Bob
Rote, Kyle, Jr.

SOCIAL REFORMER

Abbott, Grace
Baden-Powell, Olave St. Claire, Lady
Balch, Emily G
Baldwin, Roger Nash
Barnardo, Thomas John
Barton, Clara Harlowe
Beecher, Henry Ward
Bellamy, Edward
Besant, Annie Wood
Besant, Walter, Sir
Bloomer, Amelia Jenks
Booth, Ballington
Booth, Catherine Mumford
Booth, Evangeline Cory
Booth, William
Breckinridge, Sophonisba Preston
Brisbane, Albert
Ceresole, Pierre
Coulter, Ernest Kent
Cox, Harvey Gallagher, Jr.
Dederich, Charles Edwin
Delany, Martin R
Dolci, Danilo
Fauntroy, Walter E
Fuller, Ida
Fuller, Margaret
Gerry, Elbridge Thomas
Glasser, Ira

Godiva, Lady
Hale, Clara McBride
Harris, LaDonna Crawford
Hill, Morton A(nthony)
Howe, Julia Ward
Howe, Samuel Gridley
Jacob, John Edward
Jarvis, Howard Arnold
Joyce, William
Kuhn, Maggie (Margaret E)
Ladd, William
Lockwood, Belva Ann Bennett
Lopez-Portillo y Rojas, Jose
Low, Juliette Gordon
Michael, Moina Belle
Moltke, Helmuth James, graf von
Mott, Lucretia Coffin
Nation, Carry A(melia Moore)
Noyes, John Humphrey
Owen, Robert
Owen, Robert Dale
Plimsoll, Samuel
Potter, Henry Codman
Ripley, George
Roosevelt, Eleanor
Sanger, Margaret
Sliwa, Curtis
Smith, Robert Holbrook
Stanton, Elizabeth Cady
Townsend, Francis Everett
Villard, Helen Francis Garrison
Wilkins, Roy
Willard, Frances E
Wittenmyer, Annie Turner

SOCIAL REFORMERS

Willmar 8

SOCIAL WORKER

Addams, Jane
Brace, Charles Loring
Wald, Lillian D
West, James Edward
York, David

SOCIALIST LEADER

Berger, Victor L
Bernstein, Eduard
Blanc, (Jean Joseph Charles) Louis
Debs, Eugene Victor
Engels, Friedrich
Gaitskell, Hugh Todd Naylor
Hillquit, Morris
Jablonski, Henryk
Jaures, Jean Leon
Largo Caballero, Francisco
Laski, Harold Joseph
Lassalle, Ferdinand
Luxemburg, Rosa

Marx, Karl Heinrich
Matteotti, Giacomo
Mollet, Guy
Nenni, Pietro
Nu, U Thakin
Thomas, Norman Mattoon
Webb, Sidney James

SOCIALITE

Alice (Mary Victoria Augusta Pauline)
Armstrong-Jones, Antony Charles Robert
Belmont, Alva Erskine Smith Vanderbilt
Cramm, Gottfried von, Baron
Duke, Doris
Ford, Charlotte
Frazier, Brenda Diana Dudd
Guggenheim, Peggy Marguerite
Hampton, Hope
Hutton, Barbara
Jagger, Bianca Teresa
Leverson, Ada
Longworth, Alice Roosevelt
Maxwell, Elsa
McLean, Evalyn Walsh
Norwich, Diana (Manners) Cooper,
  Viscountess
Paley, Barbara Cushing
Recamier, (Jeanne Francoise) Julie(tte)
  Adelaide, Madame
Tanner, Marion
Trudeau, Margaret Joan Sinclair
Von Bulow, "Sunny" Martha Sharp
  Crawford

SOCIOLOGIST

Adamic, Louis
Bardis, Panos Demetrios
Bell, Daniel
Bogart, Leo
Chiang Mei-Ling
Coleman, James Samuel
Davis, Kingsley
Duffey, Joseph Daniel
Durkheim, Emile
Edwards, Harry (Jr.)
Etzioni, Amitai Werner
Fine, Sidney Albert
Frazier, Edward Franklin
Geddes, Patrick, Sir
Glass, David Victor
Greeley, Andrew Moran
Karp, Lila
Lynd, Helen Merrell
Lynd, Robert Staughton
Mannheim, Karl
Murray, Charles Alan
Myrdal, Alva Reimer
Myrdal, Karl Gunnar
Nearing, Scott
Simmel, Georg

Sumner, William Graham
Taylor, Graham
Ward, Lester Frank
Webb, Beatrice Potter
Weber, Max
Yankelovich, Daniel

SOLDIER

Antony, Marc
Bairnsfather, Bruce
Bayard, Pierre du Terrail
Blair, Francis Preston
Boulanger, Georges Ernest Jean Marie
Bowie, James
Brant, Joseph
Brock, Isaac, Sir
Butler, Matthew Calbraith
Carlson, Evans Fordyce
Carnot, Lazare Nicolas
Chesney, Francis Rawdon
Choiseul, Cesar, Comte Du Plessis-Praslin,
  duc de
Cid, El
Clark, George Rogers
Cleaveland, Moses
Clive, Robert
Cordoba, Francisco Fernandez
Coriolanus, Gaius
Cui, Cesar Antonovich
Cyrano de Bergerac, Savinien de
D'Annunzio, Gabriele
Davis, Sam(uel)
Dayan, Moshe
Delany, Martin R
Denison, George Taylor
Dix, John Adams
Douglas, Keith Castellain
Edmonds, Emma E
Farnese, Alessandro
Fastolf, John, Sir
Fawkes, Guy
Flipper, Henry Ossian
Francisco, Peter
Garibaldi, Guiseppe
Garwood, Robert Russell
Germain, George Sackville
Godfrey of Bouillon
Iberville, Pierre Le Moyne, sieur d'
Johnson, Henry
Juin, Alphonse
Kearny, Stephen Watts
Kenney, George Churchill
Kosciuszko, Thaddeus
Kovic, Ron
L'Enfant, Pierre Charles
Laing, Alexander Gordon
LaTour D'Auvergne, Theophile de
Lawrence, T(homas) E(dward)
Lea, Homer
Logan, John Alexander
Mihajlovic, Draza

Miles, Nelson A
Miller, Dorie
Miranda, Francisco de
Moltke, Helmuth Karl Bernhard von
Mosby, John Singleton
Munchhausen, Hierony mus Karl Friedrich
  von, Baron
Nelson, Thomas, Jr.
Nevski, Alexander, Saint
O'Higgins, Bernardo
Onoda, Hiroo
Publius Horatius Cocles
Quantrill, William Clarke
Renault, Gilbert (Leon Etienne Theodore)
Richelieu, Louis Francois Armand de
Rutgers, Henry
Sampson, Deborah
Sassoon, Siegfried
Schleicher, Kurt von
Selfridge, Thomas Etholen
Shays, Daniel
Sickles, Daniel Edgar
Sidney, Philip, Sir
Simcoe, John Graves
Slovik, Eddie (Edward Donald)
Smith, Asa
Smith, Edmund Kirby
Smuts, Jan Christian
Steuben, Friedrich Wilhelm Ludolf Gerhard
  Augustin, Baron
Treptow, Martin A
Voroshilov, Kliment Efremovich
Warren, Joseph
Wayne, Anthony
York, Sergeant (Alvin Cullum)
Zeppelin, Ferdinand von, Count

SONGWRITER

Adams, Frank Ramsay
Allen, Deborah
Allen, Peter Woolnough
Allen, Rex E, Sr.
Allen, Steve (Stephen Valentine Patrick
  William)
Anderson, Bill
Anka, Paul
Anthony, Ray
Arlen, Harold
Armatrading, Joan
Ashford, Nickolas
Auger, Brian
Austin, Gene
Axton, Hoyt Wayne
Balin, Marty
Barrett, "Syd" Roger Keith
Barrow, Keith E
Berry, Chuck (Charles Edward Anderson)
Bishop, Stephen
Blades, Ruben
Bofill, Angela
Bonds, Gary U S

Bowie, David
Bowling, Roger
Brel, Jacques
Brown, Lew
Brown, Nacio Herb
Browne, Jackson
Bryant, Felice
Buck, Gene
Buckley, Tim
Buffet, Jimmy
Burleigh, Harry Thacker
Bush, Kate
Byrd, William
Caesar, Irving
Cahn, Sammy
Cale, J J
Carawan, Guy
Carmichael, Hoagy (Hoagland Howard)
Carnes, Kim
Carpenter, Richard Lynn
Carter, "Mother" Maybelle
Carter, Carlene
Cash, Johnny
Chapin, Harry Foster
Charles, Ray
Clark, Roy Linwood
Cobb, Will D
Cochran, Eddie
Cohen, Leonard
Coleman, Cy
Comden, Betty
Cooper, Alice
Costello, Elvis
Cravens, Rupert Thomas
Creed, Linda
Croce, Jim
Crofts, Dash
Crosby, David
Cross, Christopher
Crowell, Rodney
Dale, Jim
Daniels, Charlie
Davis, Mac
Denver, John
DeShannon, Jackie
DeSylva, "Buddy" George Gard
Dexter, Al
Diamond, Neil
Dickens, "Little" Jimm y
Diddley, Bo
Dietz, Howard M
Dillon, William A
Dixon, Mort
Doggett, Bill
Donaldson, Walter
Donovan
Dragon, Daryl
Dubin, Al
Dylan, Bob
Ebb, Fred
Edwards, Gus

Edwards, Joan
Egan, Richard B
Egan, Walter Lindsay
Emmett, Daniel Decatur
Fagen, Donald
Fain, Sammy
Fargo, Donna
Farina, Richard
Felder, Don(ald William)
Fender, Freddy
Ferry, Bryan
Fields, Dorothy
Finch, Rick (Richard)
Firbank, Louis
Frampton, Peter
Franklin, Irene
Frazier, Dallas June
Freed, Alan
Freed, Arthur
Frey, Glenn
Gabriel, Peter
Gates, David
Gatlin, Larry Wayne
Gentry, Bobbie
Gibb, Andy
Gibb, Barry
Gibb, Maurice
Gibb, Robin
Goldsboro, Bobby
Goodman, Steve(n Benjamin)
Greco, Buddy (Armando)
Green, Al
Greenbaum, Norman
Greenfield, Howard
Greenwood, Lee
Hall, Tom T
Hamilton, Nancy
Hardin, Tim
Harrison, George
Hartford, John Cowan
Hartman, Dan
Hathaway, Donny
Hayes, Isaac
Hays, Lee
Hazelwood, Lee
Hellerman, Fred
Henderson, Ray
Herman, Jerry
Herzog, Arthur, Jr.
Higgins, Bertie (Elbert)
Hill, Joe, pseud.
Holly, "Buddy"   Charles Hardin
Holmes, Rupert
Howard, Eddy
Howard, Joseph Edgar
Howlin' Wolf
Hunter, "Ivory" Joe
Hunter, Alberta
Hynde, Chrissie (Christine Elaine)
Ian, Janis
Iglesias, Julio

Ingram, James
Jeffreys, Garland
Joel, Billy (William Martin)
John, Elton
Jones, Isham
Jones, Rickie Lee
Jones, Tom
Kahn, Gus
Kalmar, Bert
Kenny, Nick
Khan, Chaka
King, Carole
Krause, Bernie (Bernard Leo)
Kristofferson, Kris
Lehrer, Tom (Thomas Andrew)
Leigh, Carolyn
Lennon, John Winston
Lightfoot, Gordon Meredith
Loggins, Kenny (Kenneth Clarke)
Lombardo, Carmen
Maltby, Richard E, Jr.
Manchester, Melissa Toni
Manilow, Barry
Marks, Johnny (John David)
Massey, D Curtis
Mayfield, Curtis
McCartney, Paul (James Paul)
McDonald, Country Joecq
McDonald, Michael
McHugh, Jimmy (James)
McLean, Don
McVie, Christine Perfect
Mellencamp, John "Cougar
Mercer, Johnny
Messina, Jim
Miller, Roger Dean
Mitchell, Joni
Montgomery, Melba
Morrison, Van
Nascimento, Milton
Nesmith, Mike
New!~v, Anthony
Newman, Randy
Nicks, "Stevie" Stephanie
Nyro, Laura
Oates, John
Parker, Graham
Parker, Ray, Jr.
Parsons, Gram
Parton, Dolly Rebecca
Paxton, Tom (Thomas R)
Payne, Leon
Pearl, Leslie
Perkins, Carl
Pettiford, Oscar
Pickett, Wilson
Preston, Billy (William Everett)
Price, Alan
Prince
Rabbitt, Eddie (Edward Thomas)
Rafferty, Gerry

Raitt, Bonnie
Redding, Otis
Reddy, Helen
Reed, Jerry
Reed, Lou
Robertson, Don
Robinson, "Smokey" William, Jr.
Rodgers, Jimmie C
Rouget de Lisle, Claude Joseph
Ruby, Harry
Rush, Tom
Sager, Carole Bayer
Sanders, Marty
Schwartz, Arthur
Scruggs, Earl
Seals, Jim (James)
Sedaka, Neil
Seeger, Pete(r)
Simmons, Pat(rick)
Simon, Carly
Simon, Paul
Simone, Nina
Simpson, Valerie
Sissle, Noble
Smith, Bessie
Smith, Willie
South, Joe
Souther, J(ohn) D(avid)
Springsteen, Bruce
Stafford, Jim
Stevens, Cat
Stewart, Wynn
Stills, Stephen
Stookey, (Noel) Paul
Styne, Jule (Julius Kerwin Stein)
Swift, Kay
Taylor, James Vernon
Tillis, Mel(vin)
Torme, Mel(vin Howard)
Troup, Bobby (Robert William)
Tubb, Ernie (Ernest)
Turner, Ike
Twitty, Conway
Tyson, Ian
Tyson, Sylvia Fricker
Van Heusen, Jimmy (James)
Vannelli, Gino
VonTilzer, Harry
Vysotsky, Vladimir Semyonovich
Waite, John
Wakely, Jimmy
Walker, "T-Bone" Aaron
Walker, Jimmy (James John)
Warren, Harry
Welch, Ken
Welch, Mitzie
Williams, "Hank" Hiram
Williams, Billy
Williams, Paul Hamilton
Williams, Tex
Wilson, Brian Douglas

Winchester, Jesse (James Ridout)
Withers, Bill
Wonder, Stevie
Wright, Syretta
Yellen, Jack

SPECIAL EFFECTS TECHNICIAN

Edlund, Richard
Harryhausen, Ray
O'Brien, Willis Harold
Whitlock, Albert

SPEED SKATER

Enke, Karin
Heiden, Beth
Heiden, Eric
Jaffee, Irving
Mueller, Leah Poulos
Schenk, Ard
Young, Sheila

SPORTSCASTER

Abel, Sid(ney Gerald)
Allen, Mel
Barber, "Red" Walter Lanier
Barry, Rick (Richard Francis, III)
Brodie, John Riley
Button, Dick (Richard Totten)
Cherry, Don(ald Stewart)
Cosell, Howard
Dawson, Len (Leonard Ray)
Dean, "Dizzy" Jay Hanna
Drysdale, Don(ald Scott)
Flemming, Bill (William Norman)
Garagiola, Joe (Joseph Henry)
George, Phyllis
Gifford, Frank (Francis Newton)
Glickman, Marty
Gowdy, Curt
Harmon, Tom (Thomas D)
Hill, Jimmy (James William Thomas)
Hodges, Russ
Hull, Bobby (Robert Martin)
Husing, Ted
Jenner, Bruce
Jimmy the Greek
Jurgenson, "Sonny" Christian Adolph, III
Kaline, Al(bert William)
Kell, George Clyde
Kiner, Ralph McPherran
Koufax, Sandy (Sanford)
Kubek, Tony (Anthony Christopher)
Madden, John
McCarthy, Clem
McGuire, Al
McKay, Jim
Meeker, Howie (Howard William)
Meredith, Don (Joseph Donald)
Musburger, Brent Woody

Olsen, Merlin
Palmer, "Bud" John S
Parseghian, Ara Raoul
Patrick, Van
Rizzuto, Phil(lip Francis)
Robinson, Brooks Calbert, Jr.
Rote, Kyle
Schaap, Dick (Richard J)
Schenkel, Chris(topher Eugene)
Scully, Vince(nt Edward)
Stern, Bill (William)
Trabert, Tony (Marion Anthony)
Venturi, Ken(neth)
Vermeil, Dick (Richard Albert)
Whitaker, Jack (John Francis)
Wilkinson, "Bud" (Charles

SPORTSMAN

Arnot, Robert Burns
Blaikie, William
Cartwright, Alexander Joy, Jr.
Chichester, Francis Charles, Sir
Cooke, Jack Kent
Cowdrey, (Michael) Colin
Crauste, Michel
Doubleday, Abner
Fry, Charles Burgess
Hitchcock, Tommy (Thomas, Jr.)
Hoffman, Robert C
Hulman, Tony (Anton), Jr.
Jones, Benjamin Allyn
Kelly, John Brenden
Kleberg, Robert Justus, Jr.
Lunn, Arnold Henry Moore, Sir
Mahan, Larry
Murray, George
Newman, Paul
Sampson, Charles
Sandow, Eugene
Smith, Cecil
Spartacus
Turner, Ted (Robert Edward, III)
Vanderbilt, Alfred G
Whitney, Harry Payne
Whittingham, Charlie
Widener, George D
Zass, Aleksandr

SPORTSWOMAN

Didrikson, "Babe" Mildred
Sears, Eleonora Randolph

SPY

Abel, Rudolf Ivanovich
Andre, John
Bazna, Elyesa
Bell, William Holden
Bentley, Elizabeth Terrill
Birch, John

Blunt, Anthony Frederick
Bowie, Walter (Wat)
Boyce, Christopher John
Boyd, Belle (Isabellle)
Brousse, Amy Elizabeth Thorpe
Burgess, Guy Francis de Moncy
Canaris, Wilhelm
Carre, Mathilde
Chapman, Eddie (Edward Arnold)
Coplon, Judith
Crosby, Enoch
Cushman, Pauline
Eastern Jewel
Erickson, Eric
Fuchs, Klaus Emil Julius
Gehlen, Reinhard
Gold, Harry
Greenglass, David
Guillaume, Gunter
Hale, Nathan
Hambleton, Hugh George
Lee, Andrew Daulton
Lonsdale, Gordon Arnold
Maclean, Donald Duart
Mata Hari
Popov, Dusko
Prime, Geoffrey Arthur
Reilly, Sidney George
Sansom, Odette Marie Celine
Sobell, Morton
Sorge, Richard
Szabo, Violette Bushell
Van Lew, Elizabeth

STATESMAN

Adams, Samuel
Aga Khan III
Agrippa, Marcus Vipsanius
Alcibiades
Aldrich, Nelson Wilmarth
Allon, Yigal
Anderson, Clint(on Presba)
Andrassy, Gyula, Count
Andrew, John Albion
Anslinger, Harry Jacob
Antonelli, Giacomo
Arndt, Adolf
Austin, Warren R(obinson)
Bacon, Francis, Sir
Baldwin of Bewdley, Stanley Baldwin, Earl
Baldwin, Robert
Balfour, Arthur James Balfour, Earl
Baruch, Bernard Mannes
Beaverbrook, William Maxwell Aitken, Baron
Benes, Eduard
Benjamin, Judah Philip
Benn, Tony (Anthony Wedgwood)
Bentinck, William Henry Cavendish, Lord
Betancourt, Romulo
Biddle, Anthony

Hatton, Christopher, Sir
Hay, John Milton
Hays, Will Harrison
Heffer, Eric Samuel
Henderson, Arthur
Herbert, Alan Patrick, Sir
Herriot, Edouard
Hickenlooper, Bourke B
Hoffman, Paul Gray
Horsbrugh, Florence
Houston, Sam(uel)
Hrushevsky, Mykhailo
Hua, Kuo-Feng
Hull, Cordell
Humboldt, Wilhelm von
Humphrey, George Magoffin
Hunt, George Wylie Paul
Huskisson, William
Hyperides
Inonu, Ismet
Ito, Hirobumi
Johnson, Hiram W
Julius Caesar
Kanaris, Constantine
Kellogg, Frank Billings
King, Rufus
King, William Lyon Mackenzie
Koo, V(i) K(yuin) Wellington
Kossuth, Lajos
Krishna Menon, V(engalil) K(rishnan)
Kruger, Paul (Stephanus Johannes Paulus)
L'Hopital, Michel de
Lafayette, Marie Joseph Paul, Marquis
LaFontaine, Louis H, Sir
Laurens, Henry
Law, Andrew Bonar
Leblanc, Claude
Lee, Richard Henry
Leger, Jules
Lesage, Jean
Lilburne, John
Litvinov, Maxim
Livingston, Edward
Lloyd George of Dwyfor, David Lloyd
   George, Earl
Lodge, Henry Cabot
Lopez de Ayala, Pero
Macaulay, Thomas Babington Macaulay,
   Baron
MacDonald, James Ramsay
Mackenzie, William Lyon
Maitland, John
Malik, Charles Habib
Marcy, William Learned
Marlborough, John Churchill, Duke
Masaryk, Jan Garrigue
Masaryk, Tomas Garrigue
Mazarin, Jules, Cardinal
McGee, Thomas D'Arcy
McNary, Charles Linza
Mendes-France, Pierre

Metternich-Winneburg, Clemens
Milner, Alfred
Mirabeau, Honore Gabriel Riquetti
Moltke, Helmuth Karl Bernhard von
More, Thomas, Sir
Morgan, Henry, Sir
Morris, Gouverneur
Morrison of Lambeth, Herbert Stanley
   Morrison, Baron
Murphy, Robert Daniel
Nagy, Imre
Nansen, Fridtjof
Necker, Jacques
Nehru, Jawaharlal
Nicolson, Harold George, Sir
Nitti, Francesco Saverio
Norwich, Alfred Duff Cooper, Viscount
O'Higgins, Bernardo
Obregon, Alvaro
Oxford and Asquith, Henry Herbert
   Asquith, Earl
Paderewski, Ignace Jan
Palmerston, Henry John Temple, Viscount
Paul-Boncour, Joseph
Peel, Robert, Sir
Peres, Shimon
Perez de Cuellar, Javier
Pericles
Petain, Henri Philippe
Pilsudski, Jozef
Pinckney, Charles Cotesworth
Pitt, William
Pliny the Younger
Poincare, Raymond
Pompey the Great
Prado Ugarteche, Manuel
Queensberry, William Douglas, Duke
Rabin, Yitzhak
Randolph, Edmund Jennings
Randolph, John
Rhee, Syngman
Richelieu, Armand Jean du Plessis,
   Cardinal
Romulo, Carlos Pena
Root, Elihu
Salazar, Antonio de Oliveira
Salisbury, Robert Arthur Talbot, 3rd
   Marquess
San Martin, Jose de
Sandys, Duncan
Sandys, Edwin Sir
Schuman, Robert
Schuyler, Phillip John
Senanayake, Dudley
Seneca, Lucius Annaeus, the Younger
Sforza, Carlo
Shaftesbury, Anthony Ashley Cooper, Earl
Shastri, Lal Badahur
Sherman, Roger
Sidney, Philip, Sir
Smith, Donald Alexander

Smuts, Jan Christian
Soong, T V
Soustelle, Jacques
Southampton, Henry Wriothesley, Earl
Spruance, Raymond Ames
Stanton, Edwin McMasters
Stephens, Alexander Hamilton
Stresemann, Gustav
Sully, Maximilien de Bethune, Duc
Sun Yat-Sen
Sykes, Mark, Sir
Talleyrand-Perigord, Charles Maurice de
Tanner, Valno Alfred
Thant, U
Thiers, Adolphe
Thieu, Nguyen Van
Thou, Jacques Auguste de
Toombs, Robert Augustus
U'Ren, William Simon
Van De Velde, Emile
Venizelos, Eleutherios
Waldheim, Kurt
Waldock, (Claud) Humphrey Meredith, Sir
Waller, Sir William
Walpole, Robert
Walsingham, Francis, Sir
Walton, George
Webster, Daniel
Wellington, Arthur Wellesley, Duke
Wilson, Harold (James Harold, Sir)
Witte, Sergei
Wythe, George
Zaleski, August

STUDENT

Bakke, Allan Paul
Billings, Grace Bedell
Bridgman, Laura Dewey
Holdereid, Kristine
Lin, Maya Ying
O'Hanlon, Virginia
Smith, Samantha

STUNTMAN

Barrett, Stan
Canutt, Yakima (Enos Edward)
Goodwin, Daniel
Knievel, "Evel" Robert Craig
Needham, Hal
Willig, George

SUFFRAGETTE

Addams, Jane
Anthony, Susan Brownell
Belmont, Alva Erskine Smith Vanderbilt
Bugbee, Emma
Duniway, Abigail Jane Scott
Miller, Elizabeth Smith
Pankhurst, (Estelle) Sylvia

Pankhurst, Christabel, Dame
Pankhurst, Emmeline Goulden
Park, Maud May Wood
Stone, Lucy

SUFFRAGIST

Rankin, Jeannette

SUPREME COURT JUSTICE

Black, Hugo LaFayette
Blackmun, Harry Andrew
Blatchford, Samuel
Bradley, Joseph P
Brandeis, Louis Dembitz
Brennan, William Joseph
Brewer, David Josiah
Brown, Henry Billings
Burger, Warren Earl
Cardozo, Benjamin Nathan
Chase, Salmon Portland
Chase, Samuel
Clark, Tom (Thomas Campbell)
Clifford, Nathan
Davis, David
Day, William Rufus
Douglas, William Orville
Field, Stephen Johnson
Frankfurter, Felix
Goldberg, Arthur Joseph
Gray, Horace
Grier, Robert Cooper
Harlan, John Marshall
Harlan, John Marshall
Holmes, Oliver Wendell, Jr.
Hughes, Charles Evans
Iredell, James
Jackson, Robert Houghwout
Jay, John
Johnson, William
Lamar, Joseph Rucker
Lamar, Lucius Q C
Lurton, Horace Harmon
Marshall, John
Marshall, Thurgood
Minton, Sherman
Murphy, Frank
O'Connor, Sandra Day
Powell, Lewis Franklin, Jr.
Reed, Stanley Forman
Rehnquist, William Hubbs
Rutledge, John
Scalia, Antonin
Shiras, George, Jr.
Stevens, John Paul
Stewart, Potter
Stone, Harlan Fiske
Story, Joseph
Swayne, Noah
Taney, Roger Brooke
Van Devanter, Willis

Vinson, Frederick Moore
Waite, Morrison Remick
Warren, Earl
White, Byron Raymond
White, Edward Douglass
Wilson, Bertha
Wilson, James

SURGEON

Adair, Frank E(arl)
Agpaoa, Tony (Antonio)
Barnard, Christiaan Neethling
Bates, Mary Elizabeth
Bell, Charles
Bell, Joseph
Bethune, Norman
Billroth, Albert Christian Theodor
Blalock, Alfred
Brinkley, John Romulus
Carrel, Alexis
Charnley, John, Sir
Cooley, Denton Arthur
Cooper, Astley Paston, Sir
Crile, George Washington
Cushing, Harvey Williams
Davis, John Staige
Davis, Loyal
DeBakey, Michael Ellis
DeVries, William Castle
Fabricius, Hieronymus ab Aquapendente
Forssmann, Werner Theodor Otto
Graham, Evarts Ambrose
Halsted, William Stewart
Huggins, Charles Brenton
Hunter, John
Hunter, William
Kantrowitz, Adrian
Kellogg, John Harvey
Kelman, Charles David
Lahey, Frank Howard
Lawler, Richard Harold
Lister, Joseph
Mayo, Charles Horace
Mayo, William James
McDowell, Ephraim
McDowell, Frank
Merrill, John Putnam
Morton, Donald Lee
Ochsner, (Edward William) Alton
Paget, James, Sir
Pare, Ambroise
Parkinson, James
Paulson, Donald Lowell
Pratt, Gerald Hillary
Pratt, Lawrence Arthur
Reed, Walter
Rosenberg, Steven A
Seagrave, Gordon Stifler
Shands, Alfred Rives, Jr.
Slaughter, Frank G
Starzl, Thomas

Thomas, James William Tudor
Vishnevsky, Alexander Alexandrovich
Williams, Daniel Hale
Wood, James Rushmore

SURVEYOR

Dixon, Jeremiah
Mason, Charles

SWIMMER

Babashoff, Shirley
Belote, Melissa
Burton, Michael
Caulkins, Tracy
Chadwick, Florence
Cox, Lynne
Crabbe, "Buster" Larry
Curtis, Ann
DeVarona, Donna
Ederle, Gertrude Caroline
Ender, Kornelia
Fraser, Dawn
Goodell, Brian Stuart
Gould, Shane
Holm, Eleanor
Kahanamoku, Duke
Kellerman, Annette
Kolb, Claudia
Konno, Ford
Louganis, Greg(ory Efthimios)
Lundquist, Steve
Madison, Helene
Matthes, Roland
McCormick, Patricia Keller
Meagher, Mary T
Meyer, Debbie (Deborah)
Naber, John
Nyad, Diana
Rose, Murray
Schollander, Don(ald Arthur)
Spitz, Mark Andrew
Vassallo, Jesse
Weissmuller, Johnny
Williams, Esther
Woodhead, Cynthia

TALENT AGENT

Bernstein, Jay
Marx, "Gummo" Milton
Meiklejohn, William
Morris, William, Jr.

TEACHER

Auer, Leopold
Barton, Clara Harlowe
Boulanger, Nadia Juliette
Braille, Louis
Brown, Charlie

Burchenal, Elizabeth
Collins, Marva Deloise Nettles
Corson, Juliet
Delano, Jane Arminda
Fillmore, Abigail Powers
Flesch, Karl
Galamian, Ivan
Gallaudet, Thomas Hopkins
Garcia, Manuel Patricio Rodriguez, II
Hidalgo, Elvira de
Isocrates
Jagel, Frederick
Kinmont, Jill
Lamperti, Francesco
Lhevinne, Josef
Lhevinne, Rosina L
Marchesi, Mathilde de Castrone
McAuliffe, Christa (Sharon Christa Corrigan)
Naismith, James A
Ochsner, (Edward William) Alton
Porpora, Niccolo
Quinn, Arthur Hobson
Rama, Swami
Salignac, Eustase Thomas
Sbriglia, Giovanni
Schoen-Rene, Anna
Scopes, John Thomas
Shanker, Albert
Sharp, Zerna A
Sullivan, Anne
Thompson, Randall
Weber, Carl
Wilde, Patricia

TENNIS PLAYER

Allen, Leslie
Amaya, Victor
Arias, Jimmy
Ashe, Arthur
Austin, Tracy Ann
Barker, Sue
Bartkowicz, Peaches
Becker, Boris
Betz, Pauline
Borg, Bjorn
Borotra, Jean Robert
Brough, Louise Althea
Brugnon, Jacques
Budge, Don (John Donald)
Bueno, Maria Ester Audion
Casals, Rosemary
Clerc, Jose-Luis
Cochet, Henri
Connolly, Maureen
Connors, Jimmy (James Scott)
Court, Margaret
Cramm, Gottfried von, Baron
Curren, Kevin
Dent, Phil
Denton, Steve

Dibbs, Eddie (Edward George)
DuPont, Margaret Osborne
Durie, Jo
Durr, Francoise
Emerson, Roy
Evert, Chris(tine Marie)
Evert, Jeanne
Fibak, Wojtek
Fleming, Peter
Fromholtz, Dianne
Gerulaitis, Vitas
Gibson, Althea
Gonzales, "Pancho" Richard Alonzo
Goolagong, Evonne
Gottfried, Brian
Graebner, Clark
Hanika, Sylvia
Holladay, Terry Ann
Hu Na
Jacobs, Helen Hull
Jaeger, Andrea
Jausovec, Mima
Jordan, Kathy (Kathryn)
King, Billie Jean
Kramer, Jack
Krickstein, Aaron
Kriek, Johann
Lacoste, (Jean-) Rene
Lamb, Peter
Laver, Rod(ney George)
Lendl, Ivan
Lenglen, Suzanne
Lewis, Chris
Lloyd, John
Lutz, Bob (Robert Charles)
Mallory, Molla
Mandlikova, Hana
Marble, Alice
Mayer, "Sandy" Alex
Mayer, Gene (Eugene)
McEnroe, John Patrick, Jr.
McKinley, Chuck (Charles Robert)
Moody, Helen Wills
Moran, Gussie (Gertrude Augusta)
Nastase, Ilie
Navratilova, Martina
Newcombe, John
Noah, Yannick
Orantes, Manuel
Parker, Frank
Pasarell, Charlie
Ramirez, Raul
Richards, Rene
Riessen, Marty (Martin Clare)
Riggs, Bobby (Robert Larimore)
Rinaldi, Kathy
Rosewall, Ken
Ruzici, Virginia
Sabatini, Gabriela
Sears, Richard Dudley
Sedgman, Frank (Francis Arthur)

Segura, "Pancho" Francisco
Shriver, Pam(ela Howard)
Simionescu, Mariana
Smith, Stan(ley Roger)
Solomon, Harold Charles
Stevens, Greer
Stockton, Dick
Stove, Betty
Tanner, (Leonard) Roscoe, (III)
Teacher, Brian
Teltscher, Eliot
Tilden, Bill (William Tatem, Jr.)
Turnbull, Wendy
Van Patten, Vince(nt)
Vilas, Guillermo
Vines, Ellsworth
Wade, Virginia
Wightman, Hazel Virginia Hotchkiss
Willander, Mats

TENNIS PLAYERS

Four Musketeers, The

TERRORIST

Abu Daoud
Agca, Mehmet Ali
Baader, Andreas
Carlos
Curcio, Renato
Debus, Sigurd Friedrich
Khaalis, Hamaas Abdul
Meinhof, Ulrike Marie
Moretti, Mario
Okamoto, Kozo

TEST TUBE BABY

Brown, Louise Joy
Carr, Elizabeth Jordan

THEATER OWNER

Albee, Edward Franklin
Grauman, Sid(ney Patrick)
Loew, Marcus
Nederlander, James Morton
Schoenfeld, Gerald
Shubert, Lee

THEATRICAL PRODUCER

Carroll, Vinnette (Justine)

THEOLOGIAN

Abarbanel, Isaac Ben Jehudah
Abelard, Pierre
Agrippa, Heinrich Cornelius
Alcuin
Aquinas, Thomas, Saint

Arius
Arminius, Jacobus
Barth, Karl
Bede the Venerable
Berdyayev, Nikolay A
Berengar of Tours
Bonhoeffer, Dietrich
Brunner, Emil
Bultmann, Rudolf
Butler, Joseph
Calvin, John
Casaubon, Isaac
Charron, Pierre
Comenius, Johann Amos
Cox, Harvey Gallagher, Jr.
Dodd, Charles Harold
Duns Scotus, John
Edwards, Jonathan
Eliade, Mircea
Fenelon, Francois de Salignac
Geiger, Abraham
Gerhardt, Paul(us)
Glueck, Nelson
Grotius, Hugo
Hirsch, Samson Raphael
Hooker, Richard
Jansen, Cornelis
Kohler, Kaufmann
Kung, Hans
Lavater, Johann Casper
Lombard, Peter
Maurice, Frederick Denison
Moffatt, James
Newman, John Henry, Cardinal
Niebuhr, Helmut Richard
Niemoller, (Friedrich Gustav Emil) Martin
Pannenberg, Wolfhart Ulrich
Pascal, Blaise
Pederson, Christiern
Rahner, Karl
Rauschenbusch, Walter
Schleiermacher, Friedrich Ernst Daniel
Schmemann, Alexander
Seabury, Samuel
Servetus, Michael
Sherrill, Henry Knox
Soderblom, Nathan
Sterne, Laurence
Thomas a Kempis
Tillich, Paul Johannes
Watts, Isaac

TOBACCO EXECUTIVE

Dunhill, Alfred Henry
Hill, George Washington
Lorillard, Louis
Reynolds, Richard Joshua

TRACK ATHLETE

Abrahams, Harold
Ashford, Evelyn
Bannister, Roger, Sir
Bell, Earl
Blankers-Koen, Fanny
Board, Lillian
Boit, Mike
Boston, Ralph
Bragg, Donald
Brown, "Tarzan" Ellison
Calhoun, Lee Q
Carlos, John
Clarke, Ron
Coe, Sebastian Newbold
Coghlan, Eamonn
Cote, Gerard
Crockett, Ivory
Cunningham, Glenn Clarence
Cuthbert, Betty
Davis, Walter
Decker, Mary
DeMar, Clarence
Dillard, Harrison
Gault, Willie
Hagg, Gunder
Hightower, Stephanie
Huntley, Joni
Jenner, Bruce
Johnson, Rafer Lewis
Juantorena, Alberto
Keino, Kip (Hezekiah Kipchoge)
Kolehmainen, Hannes
Kozakiewicz, Wladyslaw
Landy, John
Larrieu, Francie
Lewis, Carl (Frederick Carlton)
Lewis, Carol
Liddell, Eric
Liquori, Marty (Martin A)
Manning, Madeline
Mathias, Bob (Robert Bruce)
Matson, Randy (James Randel)
McTear, Houston
Meadows, Earle
Moses, Edwin
Myricks, Larry
Nehemiah, Renaldo
Nurmi, Paavo
O'Brien, Parry
Oerter, Al(fred A)
Oldfield, Brian
Ovett, Steve
Owens, Jesse (James Cleveland)
Prefontaine, Steve Roland
Press, Tamara
Ritola, Ville
Rudolph, Wilma Glodean
Ryun, Jim (James Ronald)
Saneev, Viktor
Seagren, Bob (Robert Lloyd)

Sefton, William
Smith, Tommie
Stephens, Helen
Stones, Dwight
Szewinska, Irena
Thompson, Daley (Francis Daley)
Thorpe, Jim (James Francis)
Toomey, Bill (William)
Toomey, Mary Rand
Torrance, Jack
Tyus, Wyomia
Viren, Lasse
Walsh, Stella
Warmerdam, Cornelius
Wessinghage, Ellen
Wessinghage, Thomas
Young, Candy (Canzetta)
Zatopek, Emil

TRACK COACH

Cromwell, Dean Bartlett

TRAITOR

Arnold, Benedict
Axis Sally
Philby, Kim (Harold Adrian Russell)
Quisling, Vidkun
Rosenberg, Ethel Greenglass
Rosenberg, Julius
Tokyo Rose

TRANSLATOR

Aurell, Tage
Bodmer, Johann Jakob
Boethius
Bunin, Ivan Alekseevich
Burke, Kenneth
Day-Lewis, Cecil
Fitzgerald, Edward
Fitzgerald, Robert Stuart
Garnett, Constance
Gorbanevskaya, Natalya
Gregory, Horace Victor
Howitt, Mary
Khodasevich, Vladislav
Landolfi, Tommaso
Lattimore, Richmond Alexander
Lee-Hamilton, Eugene Jacob
Mallarme, Stephane
Manheim, Ralph
Moffatt, James
Murray, Gilbert (George Gilbert Aime)
Nerval, Gerard de
Orwell, Sonia
Pederson, Christiern
Prevost d'Exiles, Antoine Francois, Abbe
Smollett, Tobias George
Symonds, John Addington
Theodorescu, Ion N

Tyndale, William
Weaver, William

TRANSPLANT PATIENT

Blaiberg, Philip
Clark, Barney Bailey
Fiske, Jamie
Schroeder, William
Washkansky, Louis

TRANSSEXUAL

Jorgensen, Christine
Richards, Rene

TRAVELER

Benjamin of Tudela
Bishop, Isabella Lucy Bird
Blunt, Wilfrid Scawen
Burton, Isabel Arundel
Carpini, Giovanni de Piano
Charlevoix, Pierre Francis Xavier de
Clark, Sydney
Cunninghame, Graham Robert Boutine
Du Chaillu, Paul Belloni
Hickey, William
Ibn Batutah
Leo Africanus
Mandeville, John, Sir
Marco Polo
Miranda, Francisco de
Nordhoff, Charles Bernard
Pierrot, George Francis
Royall, Anne Newport
Stephens, John Lloyd
Taylor, Bayard

TV EXECUTIVE

Arledge, Roone Pinckney
Backe, John David
Biondi, Frank J, Jr,
Cott, Ted
Cox, Richard Joseph
Crystal, Lester M
De Passe, Suzanne
Goldenson, Leonard Harry
Grade, Lew, Sir
Grimes, J William
Gunn, Hartford Nelson, Jr.
Hagerty, James Campbell
Heyworth, James
Kintner, Robert Edmonds
Nugent, Patrick
Paley, William Samuel
Pierce, Frederick S
Pittman, Robert W
Rich, Lee
Rukeyser, Merryle Stanley, Jr.
Sarnoff, David

Saudek, Robert
Sheehan, William Edward, Jr.
Silverman, Fred
Stanton, Frank
Tartikoff, Brandon
Taylor, Arthur Robert
Thomopoulos, Anthony Denis
Tinker, Grant A
Wood, Robert Dennis
Wyman, Thomas Hunt

TV HOST

Bailey, Jack
Barris, Chuck
Barry, Jack
Carson, Johnny
Crane, Les
Daly, John Charles, Jr.
Dawson, Richard
Douglas, Mike
Griffin, Merv(yn)
Hall, Monty
Hartman, David Downs
James, Art
James, Dennis
LaMarsh, Judy (Julia Verlyn)
Leach, Robin
Ludden, Allen Ellsworth
Mack, Ted
Mark, Norman (Barry)
Marshall, Peter
Martindale, Wink (Winston Conrad)
Perkins, (Richard) Marlin
Rayburn, Gene
Sajak, Pat
Sullivan, Ed(ward Vincent)
Tarkenton, Fran(cis Asbury)
Trebek, Alex
Williams, Roy

TV PERSONALITY

Allen, Steve (Stephen Valentine Patrick
    William)
Amsberry, Bob
Andrews, Eamonn
Bakker, Jim (James Orsen)
Barker, Bob (Robert William)
Berle, Milton
Berton, Pierre
Blyden, Larry
Buckley, William F(rank), Jr.
Child, Julia McWilliams
Collyer, "Bud" Clayton
Cullen, Bill (William Lawrence)
Donahue, Phil(ip John)
Downs, Hugh
Dreier, Alex
Edwards, Douglas
Faulk, John Henry
Frost, David

Garroway, Dave (David Cunningham)
Gordon, Jackie
Gordon, Lou
Graham, Virginia
Healy, Mary
Jones, "Grandpa" Louis Marshall
Keeshan, Bob
Kerr, Graham
Kieran, John Francis
Kilgallen, Dorothy
King, Larry
Lescoulie, Jack
Letterman, David
Lewis, Robert Q
Linkletter, Art(hur Gordon)
McNellis, Maggi
Moore, Garry
Morgan, Henry
Olson, Johnny
Perkins, Marlin (Richard Marlin)
Purcell, Sarah
Rogers, Fred McFeely
Sales, Soupy
Scott, Willard Herman, Jr.
Shriner, Herb
Simmons, Richard
Smith, Robert Lee
Snyder, Tom
Spivak, Lawrence
Stephenson, "Skip" Charles Frederick
Stone, Sidney
Will, George F
Winfrey, Ophra
Woodhouse, Barbara Blackburn

TYPE DESIGNER

Arrighi, Ludovico degli
Baskerville, John
Bernhard, Lucian
Caslon, William
Cassandre, A(dolphe) M(ouron)
Cochin, Charles Nicholas
Dwiggins, William Addison
Garamond, Claude
Goudy, Frederic William
Granjon, Robert
McMurtrie, Douglas C
Ogg, Oscar
Walker, Emery, Sir
Zapf, Hermann

TYPOGRAPHER

Bodoni, Giambattista

UNIVERSITY ADMINISTRATOR

Adamany, David Walter
Angell, James Burrill
Angell, James Rowland
Bok, Derek Curtis

Brademas, John
Bush-Brown, Albert
Cordier, Andrew Wellington
Elliott, Osborn
Futter, Ellen Victoria
Giamatti, A(ngelo) Bartlett
Goheen, Robert Francis
Hitch, Charles Johnston
Kibbee, Robert Joseph
Kirk, Grayson Louis
McGill, William James
Schmidt, Benno Charles, Jr.
Sovern, Michael I(ra)
Sterling, John Ewart Wallace
Tedder, Arthur William Tedder, Baron
Wharton, Clifton Reginald, Jr.
White, Andrew Dickson

URBAN PLANNER

Douglass, Lathrop
Howard, Ebenezer, Sir
Levitt, William Jaird
Llewelyn-Davies, Richard
Mayer, Albert
Pereira, William Leonard
Pollock, Alex
Stein, Clarence S

US PRESIDENT

Adams, John
Arthur, Chester Alan
Buchanan, James
Carter, Jimmy (James Earl, Jr.)
Cleveland, (Stephen) Grover
Coolidge, (John) Calvin
Eisenhower, Dwight David
Fillmore, Millard
Ford, Gerald Rudolph
Garfield, James Abram
Grant, Ulysses S(impson)
Harding, Warren G(amaliel)
Harrison, Benjamin
Harrison, William Henry
Hayes, Rutherford B(irchard)
Hoover, Herbert Clark
Jackson, Andrew
Jefferson, Thomas
Johnson, Andrew
Johnson, Lyndon Baines
Kennedy, John Fitzgerald
Lincoln, Abraham
Madison, James
McKinley, William
Monroe, James
Nixon, Richard Milhous
Pierce, Franklin
Polk, James K(nox)
Reagan, Ronald Wilson
Roosevelt, Franklin Delano
Roosevelt, Theodore

Taft, William Howard
Taylor, Zachary
Truman, Harry S
Tyler, John
Van Buren, Martin
Washington, George
Wilson, Woodrow (Thomas Woodrow)

VENTRILOQUIST

Bergen, Edgar John
Lewis, Shari
Nelson, Jimmy
Senor Wences
Winchell, Paul

VETERANS' LEADER

Muller, Bobby (Robert)

VETERINARIAN

Herriot, James, pseud.
Runkle, Janice

VICE-PRESIDENT

Bush, George Herbert Walker
Clinton, George
Colfax, Schuyler
Dallas, George Mifflin
Gerry, Elbridge
Hobart, Garret Augustus
King, William Rufus de Vane
Ky, Nguyen Cao
Mondale, Walter Frederick

VINTNER

Gallo, Ernest
Gallo, Julio
Masson, Paul
Petri, Angelo
Rothschild, Philippe, Baron
Sebastiani, Samuele
Taylor, Walter

VIOLIN MAKER

Amati
Amati, Nicolo (Nicolaus)
Guarnieri, Giuseppe Antonio
Stradivari, Antonio

VIOLINIST

Albinoni, Tommaso
Boccherini, Luigi
Enesco, Georges
Geminiani, Francesco
Glenn, Carroll
Locatelli, Pietro

Loeffler, Charles Martin Tornov
Menuhin, Yehudi
Paganini, Niccolo
Perlman, Itzhak
Ponty, Jean-Luc
Spohr, Louis Ludwig
Stern, Isaac
Strauss, Johann, Jr.
Tartini, Giuseppe
Wieniawski, Henri
Zimbalist, Efrem
Zukerman, Pinchas

WATERGATE PARTICIPANT

Barker, Bernard L
Buzhardt, J(oseph) Fred, Jr.
Chapin, Dwight Lee
Colson, Charles Wendell
Dash, Samuel
Dean, John Wesley
Ehrlichman, John Daniel
Haldeman, H(arry) R(obert)
Hunt, E(verette) Howard
Kalmbach, Herbert Warren
Krogh, Egil, Jr.
Larue, Frederick Chaney
Liddy, G(eorge) Gordon
Magruder, Jeb Stuart
Mardian, Robert Charles
Martinez, Eugenio R
McCord, James Walter
Segretti, Donald H

WAX MODELER

Tussaud, (Marie Gresholtz), Madame

WRESTLER

Dean, Man Mountain
Gotch, Frank
Hogan, Hulk
Lewis, Ed
Londos, Jim
Zaharias, George
Zbyszko, Stanislaus

WRITER

Adelman, Sybil
Alda, Alan
Allen, Irwin
Allen, Woody
Astaire, Fred
Astin, John Allen
Aykroyd, Dan(iel Edward)
Ballard, Kaye
Barbour, John
Beatts, Anne
Beatty, Roger
Bellisario, Donald P

Bocho, Steven
Bologna, Joseph
Bricusse, Leslie
Brooks, Albert
Brosten, Harve
Brown, David
Cannell, Stephen J
Carr, Martin
Castiglione, Baldassare, Conte
Chapman, Graham
Charles, Glen
Charles, Lee
Chase, David
Cimino, Michael
Cleese, John
Costigan, James
Crosby, Fanny (Frances Jane)
De Passe, Suzanne
Debray, Regis (Jules Regis)
Denoff, Sam
Eckstein, George
Einstein, Bob
Epstein, Julius
Feldman, Marty
Flaherty, Joe
Fontana, Tom
Freeman, Seth
Fuisz, Robert E
Furia, John
Gance, Abel
Garfinkle, Louis
Garrett, Lila
Geller, Bruce
Grodin, Charles
Huston, John
Jones, Robert C
Jones, Terry
Kanter, Hal
Keillor, Garrison (Gary Edward)
Landon, Michael
Lathrop, Rose Hawthorne
Laughlin, Tom
Liebman, Max
Michaels, Lorne
Miranda, Francisco de
Murray, Bill
Nicholson, Jack
Novello, Don
Peppard, George
Perret, Gene
Phillips, Irna
Pinsent, Gordon Edward
Place, Mary Kay
Ruy Lopez de Segura
Sargent, Herb
Saura Carlos (Atares Carlos)
Schrader, Paul Joseph
Schumacher, Joel
Scorsese, Martin
Semple, Lorenzo, Jr.
Shapiro, Stanley

Shyer, Charles
Siegel, Larry
Silver, Franelle
Simmons, Richard Alan
Slesar, Henry
Sloan, Michael
Smith, Frances Scott Fitzgerald Lanahan
Sobieski, Carol
Speight, Johnny
Stein, James R
Stern, Leonard B
Stern, Sandor
Stevens, Jeremy
Stevens, Leslie
Stone, Peter
Strauss, Theodore
Stumpf, Richard J
Sullivan, Tom
Tarloff, Frank
Tertullian, Quintus Septimus Florens
Towne, Robert (Burton)
Wagner, Jane
Washam, Wisner McCamey
Waxman, Al
Weber, Carl
Weinberger, Edwin B
Weiskopf, Bob
Welch, Ken
Welch, Mitzie
Welland, Colin
Welles, Orson (George Orson)
Wheeler, Hugh
Williamson, David
Wincelberg, Shimon
Wolfe, Digby
Wynn, Tracy Keenan
Yordan, Philip

YOGI

Yogananda, Paramahansa

ZOOLOGIST

Agassiz, Louis (Jean Louis Radolphe)
Andrews, Roy Chapman
Bigelow, Henry Bryant
Brooks, William Keith
Cuvier, Georges, Baron
Durrell, Gerald Malcolm
Elton, Charles Sutherland
Frisch, Karl von
Grassi, Giovanni Battista
Haeckel, Ernst Heinrich
Minguy, Claude
Morris, Desmond
Oliver, James A(rthur)
Perkins, (Richard) Marlin
Ray, Dixy Lee
Sanderson, Ivan Terence
Schaudinn, Fritz Richard